THE
ALL ENGLAND
LAW REPORTS
1982

Volume 2

Editor
PETER HUTCHESSON LL M
Barrister, New Zealand

Assistant Editor
BROOK WATSON
of Lincoln's Inn, Barrister
and of the New South Wales Bar

Consulting Editor
WENDY SHOCKETT
of Gray's Inn, Barrister

London
BUTTERWORTHS

ENGLAND: Butterworth & Co (Publishers) Ltd
                88 Kingsway, London WC2B 6AB

AUSTRALIA: Butterworths Pty Ltd
                271–273 Lane Cove Road, North Ryde, NSW 2113
                Also at Melbourne, Brisbane, Adelaide and Perth

CANADA: Butterworth & Co (Canada) Ltd
                2265 Midland Avenue, Scarborough, Ont M1P 4S1

                Butterworth & Co (Western Canada) Ltd
                409 Granville Street, Ste 856, Vancouver, BC V6C 1T2

NEW ZEALAND: Butterworths of New Zealand Ltd
                33–35 Cumberland Place, Wellington

SINGAPORE: Butterworth & Co (Asia) Pte Ltd
                Crawford Post Office Box 770, Singapore 9119

SOUTH AFRICA: Butterworth & Co (South Africa) (Pty) Ltd
                152–154 Gale Street, Durban 4001

USA: Mason Publishing Co
                Finch Bldg, 366 Wacouta Street, St Paul, Minn 55101

                Butterworth (Legal Publishers) Inc
                160 Roy Street, Ste 300, Seattle, Wash 98109

                Butterworth (Legal Publishers) Inc
                381 Elliot Street, Newton, Upper Falls, Mass 02164

©

Butterworth & Co (Publishers) Ltd

1982

ISBN 0 406 85144 1

Typeset by CCC, printed and bound in Great Britain by William Clowes (Beccles) Limited, Beccles and London

House of Lords

The Lord High Chancellor: Lord Hailsham of St Marylebone

Lords of Appeal in Ordinary

Lord Diplock
Lord Fraser of Tullybelton
Lord Russell of Killowen
    (retired 27 June 1982)
Lord Keith of Kinkel

Lord Scarman
Lord Roskill
Lord Bridge of Harwich
Lord Brandon of Oakbrook
Lord Brightman

Court of Appeal

The Lord High Chancellor

The Lord Chief Justice of England: Lord Lane
(President of the Criminal Division)

The Master of the Rolls: Lord Denning
(President of the Civil Division)

The President of the Family Division: Sir John Lewis Arnold

The Vice-Chancellor: Sir Robert Edgar Megarry

Lords Justices of Appeal

Sir John Frederick Eustace Stephenson
Sir Frederick Horace Lawton
Sir Roger Fray Greenwood Ormrod
Sir George Stanley Waller
Sir James Roualeyn Hovell-Thurlow-
    Cumming-Bruce
Sir Edward Walter Eveleigh
Sir Sydney William Templeman
Sir John Francis Donaldson
Sir Desmond James Conrad Ackner

Sir Robin Horace Walford Dunn
Sir Peter Raymond Oliver
Sir Tasker Watkins VC
Sir Patrick McCarthy O'Connor
Sir William Hugh Griffiths
Sir Michael John Fox
Sir Michael Robert Emanuel Kerr
Sir John Douglas May
Sir Christopher John Slade

Chancery Division

The Lord High Chancellor

The Vice-Chancellor

Sir Peter Harry Batson Woodroffe Foster
Sir John Norman Keates Whitford
Sir Ernest Irvine Goulding
Sir Raymond Henry Walton
Sir Nicolas Christopher Henry Browne-
  Wilkinson
Sir John Evelyn Vinelott

Sir George Brian Hugh Dillon
Sir Martin Charles Nourse
Sir Douglas William Falconer
Sir Jean-Pierre Frank Eugene Warner
Sir Peter Leslie Gibson
Sir David Herbert Mervyn Davies

Queen's Bench Division

The Lord Chief Justice of England

Sir John Thompson
Sir Helenus Patrick Joseph Milmo
Sir Joseph Donaldson Cantley
Sir Hugh Eames Park
Sir Bernard Caulfield
Sir Hilary Gwynne Talbot
Sir William Lloyd Mars-Jones
Sir Ralph Kilner Brown
Sir Peter Henry Rowley Bristow
Sir Hugh Harry Valentine Forbes
Sir Neil Lawson
Sir David Powell Croom-Johnson
Sir John Raymond Phillips
  (died 2 August 1982)
Sir Leslie Kenneth Edward Boreham
Sir Alfred William Michael Davies
Sir John Dexter Stocker
Sir Kenneth George Illtyd Jones
Sir Haydn Tudor Evans
Sir Peter Richard Pain
Sir Kenneth Graham Jupp
Sir Robert Lionel Archibald Goff
Sir Stephen Brown
Sir Roger Jocelyn Parker
Sir Ralph Brian Gibson
Sir Walter Derek Thornley Hodgson
Sir James Peter Comyn

Sir Anthony John Leslie Lloyd
Sir Frederick Maurice Drake
Sir Brian Thomas Neill
Sir Michael John Mustill
Sir Barry Cross Sheen
Sir David Bruce McNeill
Sir Harry Kenneth Woolf
Sir Christopher James Saunders French
  (transferred from Family
  Division, 21 June 1982)
Sir Thomas Patrick Russell
Sir Peter Edlin Webster
Sir Thomas Henry Bingham
Sir Iain Derek Laing Glidewell
Sir Henry Albert Skinner
Sir Peter Murray Taylor
Sir Murray Stuart-Smith
Sir Christopher Stephen Thomas Jonathan
  Thayer Staughton
Sir Donald Henry Farquharson
Sir Anthony James Denys McCowan
Sir Iain Charles Robert McCullough
Sir Hamilton John Leonard
Sir Alexander Roy Asplan Beldam
Sir David Cozens-Hardy Hirst
Sir John Stewart Hobhouse
  (appointed 7 May 1982)

Family Division

The President of the Family Division

Sir John Brinsmead Latey
Sir Alfred Kenneth Hollings
Sir Charles Trevor Reeve
Sir Francis Brooks Purchas
Dame Rose Heilbron
Sir Brian Drex Bush
Sir Alfred John Balcombe
Sir John Kember Wood
Sir Ronald Gough Waterhouse
Sir John Gervase Kensington Sheldon

Sir Thomas Michael Eastham
Dame Margaret Myfanwy Wood Booth
Sir Christopher James Saunders French
  (transferred to Queen's
  Bench Division, 21 June 1982)
Sir Anthony Leslie Julian Lincoln
Dame Ann Elizabeth Oldfield Butler-Sloss
Sir Anthony Bruce Ewbank
Sir John Douglas Waite
  (appointed 21 June 1982)

CITATION

These reports are cited thus:

[1982] 2 All ER

REFERENCES

These reports contain references to the following major works of legal reference described in the manner indicated below.

Halsbury's Laws of England

The reference 35 Halsbury's Laws (3rd edn) 366, para 524, refers to paragraph 524 on page 366 of volume 35 of the third edition, and the reference 26 Halsbury's Laws (4th edn) para 577 refers to paragraph 577 on page 296 of volume 26 of the fourth edition of Halsbury's Laws of England.

Halsbury's Statutes of England

The reference 5 Halsbury's Statutes (3rd edn) 302 refers to page 302 of volume 5 of the third edition of Halsbury's Statutes of England.

The Digest

References are to the blue band replacement volumes and the green band reissue volumes of The Digest (formerly the English and Empire Digest), and to the continuation volumes.

The reference 48 Digest (Repl) 645, 6207 refers to case number 6207 on page 645 of Digest Blue Band Replacement Volume 48.

The reference 36(2) Digest (Reissue) 764, 1398 refers to case number 1398 on page 764 of Digest Green Band Reissue Volume 36(2).

The reference Digest (Cont Vol E) 640, 2392a refers to case number 2392a on page 640 of Digest Continuation Volume E.

Halsbury's Statutory Instruments

The reference 20 Halsbury's Statutory Instruments (4th reissue) 302 refers to page 302 of the fourth reissue of volume 20 of Halsbury's Statutory Instruments; references to subsequent reissues are similar.

CORRIGENDA

[1982] 1 All ER
p 531. **A-G of the Duchy of Lancaster v G E Overton (Farms) Ltd.** Solicitors for the respondents: *Bolton & Lowe* were agents for *Epton & Co*, Lincoln.
p 537. **Home Office v Harman.** Line *c* 5. For 'improvity' read 'improbity'

[1982] 2 All ER
p 98. **Cohen v Nessdale Ltd.** Counsel for the landlords should read '*David Neuberger*' instead of '*Paul de la Piquerie*'.
p 152. **Vervaeke v Smith (Messina and A-G intervening).** Lines *a* 4 and *a* 5 should read '. . . although I agree with them in seeing nothing offensive or unjust as between the parties in the doctrine of public policy propounded by the Belgian courts . . .'
pp 342, 348. **Emanuel v Emanuel.** On p 342 line *h* 3 and p 348 line *g* 1 for 'flaunt' read 'flout'.
p 610. **Re Signland Ltd.** Lines *a* 5 and *a* 6: these lines should refer to advertisement before *service* of the petition.
p 710. **Birkett v Hayes.** Line *c* 1 should read '. . . 2% from the date of service of the writ to the date of the trial . . .'
p 767. **Alexander v Immigration Appeal Tribunal.** Counsel for the appellant should read '*Michael Beloff QC* and *David Pannick*'.

Cases reported in volume 2

	Page
A-G v English [QBD and HL]	903
A-G, Raymond v [CA]	487
A-G's Reference (No 1 of 1981) [CA] ..	417
Alexander v Immigration Appeal Tribunal [HL]	766
Amari Plastics Ltd, Commission for Racial Equality v [CA]	499
Anderton, Hill v [HL]	963
ARC (an infant), ex p, R v Tottenham Juvenile Court [QBD]	321
Aspden (Inspector of Taxes) v Hildesley [ChD]	53
Baltic Mercantile and Shipping Exchange Ltd, Harakas v [CA]	701
Bernstein v Jackson [CA]	806
Berry v Warnett (Inspector of Taxes) [HL] ..	630
Bilton (Percy) Ltd v Greater London Council [HL]	623
Birkett v Hayes [CA]	710
Borg, Grant v [HL]	257
Bowley, Wills v [HL]	654
Boyesen, R v [HL]	161
British Rail Engineering Ltd, Garland v [CJEC and HL]	402
Bromley Park Garden Estates Ltd v Moss [CA]	890
Bunston v Rawlings [QBD]	697
Burrell (Inspector of Taxes), Conservative and Unionist Central Office v [CA]	1
Burrows (J) (Leeds) Ltd, Re [ChD] ..	882
C (a minor), Southwark London BC v [FamD]	636
C (minors) v Martin [FamD]	636
Campbell v Tameside Metropolitan BC [CA]	791
Campbell, ex p, R v Surrey Coroner [QBD] ..	545
Capital and Counties plc, International Military Services Ltd v [ChD]	20
Central Securities (Holdings) Bhd, Haron bin Mohd Zaid v [PC]	481
Chakki v United Yeast Co Ltd [EAT]	446
City of Birmingham DC, R v, ex p O [CA] ..	356
Cohen v Nessdale Ltd [CA]	97
Cole Bros Ltd v Phillips (Inspector of Taxes) [HL]	247
Commission for Racial Equality v Amari Plastics Ltd [CA]	499
Comr of Police of the Metropolis v Simeon [HL]	813
Comr of Police of the Metropolis, Hehir v [CA]	335
Conservative and Unionist Central Office v Burrell (Inspector of Taxes) [CA]	1
Cooke (E D & A D) Bourne (Farms) Ltd v Mellows [CA]	208
Court v Court [FamD]	531
Cousins, R v [CA]	115
Creehouse Ltd, Re [ChD]	422
Crewe v Social Security Comr [CA]	745
Cullen v Rogers [HL]	570
D (J), Re [ChD]	37
Daley, Re [HL]	974
Devlin v F (a juvenile) [QBD]	450
Donkersley, Leek v [ChD]	855
Drayton Commercial Investment Co Ltd, Stanton (Inspector of Taxes) v [HL]	942
Ealing London BC, Lambert v [CA]	394
Ellerine Bros (Pty) Ltd v Klinger [CA] ..	737
Emanuel v Emanuel [FamD]	342
EMI Records Ltd v Ian Cameron Wallace Ltd [ChD]	980
English, A-G v [QBD and HL]	903
Essex Area Health Authority, McKay v [CA]	771
F (a juvenile), Devlin v [QBD]	450
Farquharson, ex p, R v Horsham Justices [QBD and CA]	269
Fay v Fay [HL]	922
Firth (Inspector of Taxes), Johnson v [CA] ..	9
Firth (Inspector of Taxes), Wicks v [CA] ..	9
Forster v Outred & Co (a firm) [CA]	753
G (a minor) (wardship: costs), Re [CA] ..	32

	Page
Gaffney, ex p, R v Governor of Blundeston Prison [QBD]	492
Galley (Michael) Footwear Ltd (in liq) v Iaboni [QBD]	200
Garland v British Rail Engineering Ltd [CJEC and HL]	402
Ghosh, R v [CA]	689
Gilbert v Spoor [CA]	576
GKN Bolts and Nuts Ltd Sports and Social Club, Re [ChD]	855
Government of Italy, Zezza v [HL]	513
Governor of Blundeston Prison, R v, ex p Gaffney [QBD]	492
Grant v Borg [HL]	257
Greater London Council, Percy Bilton Ltd v [HL]	623
Greater London Council, Tate & Lyle Food and Distribution Ltd v [CA]	854
Hamilton, Shaw v [QBD]	718
Harakas v Baltic Mercantile and Shipping Exchange Ltd [CA]	701
Haron bin Mohd Zaid v Central Securities (Holdings) Bhd [PC]	481
Hayes, Birkett v [CA]	710
Hayman, Lincoln v [CA]	819
Hehir v Comr of Police of the Metropolis [CA]	335
Hemisphere Shipping Co Ltd, International Sea Tankers Inc v [CA]	437
Hildesley, Aspden (Inspector of Taxes) v [ChD]	53
Hill v Anderton [HL]	963
Hodge Finance Ltd, Leadbitter v [QBD] ..	167
Holden v White [CA]	328
Home Office, Williams v (No 2) [CA] ..	564
Horner v Horner [CA]	495
Horsham Justices, R v, ex p Farquharson [QBD and CA]	269
Iaboni, Michael Galley Footwear Ltd (in liq) v [QBD]	200
Ian Cameron Wallace Ltd, EMI Records Ltd v [ChD]	980
Immigration Appeal Tribunal, Alexander v [HL]	766
Immigration Offficer, R v, ex p Shah [QBD] ..	264
Indian Association of Alberta, ex p, R v Secretary of State for Foreign and Commonwealth Affairs [CA]	118
International Military Services Ltd v Capital and Counties plc [ChD]	20
International Sea Tankers Inc v Hemisphere Shipping Co Ltd [CA]	437
International Transport Workers' Federation, Universe Tankships Inc of Monrovia v [HL]	67
IRC v Metrolands (Property Finance) Ltd [HL]	557
IRC v Scottish and Newcastle Breweries Ltd [HL]	230
IRC v Trustees of Sir John Aird's Settlement [ChD]	929
ITC Film Distributors v Video Exchange Ltd [ChD]	241
Jackson, Bernstein v [CA]	806
Johnson v Firth (Inspector of Taxes) [CA] ..	9
Joshi, ex p, R v Tottenham Justices [QBD] ..	507
Kanwar, R v [CA]	528
Kelly v London Transport Executive [CA] ..	842
Keyser, ex p, Re Stern (a bankrupt) [CA] ..	600
Khan v Khan [CA]	60
Khawaja, ex p, R v Secretary of State for the Home Dept [CA]	523
Klinger, Ellerine Bros (Pty) Ltd v [CA] ..	737
Lambert v Ealing London BC [CA]	394
Law Society, Swain v [HL]	827
Leadbitter v Hodge Finance Ltd [QBD] ..	167
Leedale (Inspector of Taxes) v Lewis [CA] ..	644
Leek v Donkersley [ChD]	855
Lewis, Leedale (Inspector of Taxes) v [CA] ..	644

	Page
Lilley, Valentine v [QBD]	583
Lincoln v Hayman [CA]	819
Lines Bros Ltd, Re [CA]	183
London Transport Executive, Kelly v [CA]	842
Lyus v Prowsa Developments Ltd [ChD]	953
McKay v Essex Area Health Authority [CA]	771
McLoughlin v O'Brian [HL]	298
Marshall v Osmond [QBD]	610
Martin, C (minors) v [FamD]	636
Mears v Safecar Security Ltd [CA]	865
Mellows, E D & A D Cooke Bourne (Farms) Ltd v [CA]	208
Metrolands (Property Finance) Ltd, IRC v [HL]	557
Miller, R v [CA]	386
Moss, Bromley Park Garden Estates Ltd v [CA]	890
Murray, R v [CA]	225
Nessdale Ltd, Cohen v [CA]	97
Newton, Wallace v [QBD]	106
Norman, Parkin v [QBD]	583
Nottinghamshire CC v Q [FamD]	641
O, ex p, R v City of Birmingham DC [CA]	356
O'Brian, McLoughlin v [HL]	298
O'Malley v O'Malley [CA]	112
Osmond, Marshall v [QBD]	610
Outred & Co (a firm), Forster v [CA]	753
Parkin v Norman [QBD]	583
Parr, Warner Bros Records Inc v [ChD]	455
Peart v Stewart [CA]	369
Pepper (Inspector of Taxes), Toovey v [CA]	644
Peters, Whitter v [CA]	369
Phillips (Inspector of Taxes), Cole Bros Ltd v [HL]	247
Pigg, R v [CA]	591
Plymouth Justices, R v, ex p Rogers [QBD]	175
Pollard, RCA Corp v [ChD]	468
Practice Direction (Admiralty: directions: funds in court) [Adm Ct]	480
Practice Direction (Companies Court: applications in Long Vacation) [Companies Ct]	454
Practice Direction (Crown Office list: uncontested proceedings) [QBD]	704
Practice Direction (lump sum applications: costs) [FamD]	800
Prowsa Developments Ltd, Lyus v [ChD]	953
Q, Nottinghamshire CC v [FamD]	641
R v Boyesen [HL]	161
R v City of Birmingham DC, ex p O [CA]	356
R v Cousins [CA]	115
R v Ghosh [CA]	689
R v Governor of Blundeston Prison, ex p Gaffney [QBD]	492
R v Horsham Justices, ex p Farquharson [QBD and CA]	269
R v Immigration Officer, ex p Shah [QBD]	264
R v Kanwar [CA]	528
R v Miller [CA]	386
R v Murray [CA]	225
R v Pigg [CA]	591
R v Plymouth Justices, ex p Rogers [QBD]	175
R v Rose [CA]	536
—— [HL]	731
R v Secretary of State for Foreign and Commonwealth Affairs, ex p Indian Association of Alberta [CA]	118
R v Secretary of State for the Home Dept, ex p Khawaja [CA]	523
R v Surrey Coroner, ex p Campbell [QBD]	545
R v Tottenham Justices, ex p Joshi [QBD]	507
R v Tottenham Juvenile Court, ex p ARC (an infant) [QBD]	321
R v Tottenham Magistrates' Court, ex p Williams [QBD]	705
R v Varley [CA]	519
R v Welch [CA]	821
R v West Yorkshire Coroner, ex p Smith [QBD]	801
Rawlings, Bunston v [QBD]	697

	Page
Raymond v A-G [CA]	487
RCA Corp v Pollard [ChD]	468
Robinson v Robinson [CA]	699
Roche v Sherrington [ChD]	426
Rogers, Cullen v [HL]	570
Rogers, ex p, R v Plymouth Justices [QBD]	175
Rose, R v [CA]	536
—— [HL]	731
Royal Bank of Canada, United City Merchants (Investments) Ltd v [HL]	720
Safecar Security Ltd, Mears v [CA]	865
St Nicholas's, Baddesley Ensor, Re [Con Ct]	351
Scottish and Newcastle Breweries Ltd, IRC v [HL]	230
Secretary of State for Foreign and Commonwealth Affairs, R v, ex p Indian Association of Alberta [CA]	118
Secretary of State for the Home Dept, R v, ex p Khawaja [CA]	523
Shah, ex p, R v Immigration Officer [QBD]	264
Shaw v Hamilton [QBD]	718
Sherrington, Roche v [ChD]	426
Signland Ltd, Re [ChD]	609
Simeon, Comr of Police of the Metropolis v [HL]	813
Smith, ex p, R v West Yorkshire Coroner [QBD]	801
Smith (Messina and A-G intervening), Vervaeke v [HL]	144
Social Security Comr, Crewe v [CA]	745
Solicitors (taxation of costs), Re [ChD]	683
Southwark London BC v C (a minor) [FamD]	636
Spoor, Gilbert v [CA]	576
Stanton (Inspector of Taxes) v Drayton Commercial Investment Co Ltd [HL]	942
Stern (a bankrupt), Re, ex p Keyser [CA]	600
Stewart, Peart v [CA]	369
Surrey Coroner, R v, ex p Campbell [QBD]	545
Sutton Common, Wimborne, Re [ChD]	376
Swain v Law Society [HL]	827
Tameside Metropolitan BC, Campbell v [CA]	791
Tate & Lyle Food and Distribution Ltd v Greater London Council [CA]	854
Tillmire Common, Heslington, Re [ChD]	615
Toovey v Pepper (Inspector of Taxes) [CA]	644
Tottenham Justices, R v, ex p Joshi [QED]	507
Tottenham Juvenile Court, R v, ex p ARC (an infant) [QBD]	321
Tottenham Magistrates' Court, R v, ex p Williams [QBD]	705
Trustees of Sir John Aird's Settlement, IRC v [ChD]	929
Ullmann Ltd v The bankrupt [CA]	600
United City Merchants (Investments) Ltd v Royal Bank of Canada [HL]	720
United Yeast Co Ltd, Chakki v [EAT]	446
Universe Tankships Inc of Monrovia v International Transport Workers' Federation [HL]	67
Valentine v Lilley [QBD]	583
Varley, R v [CA]	519
Vervaeke v Smith (Messina and A-G intervening) [HL]	144
Video Exchange Ltd, ITC Film Distributors v [ChD]	241
Wallace v Newton [QBD]	106
Warner Bros Records Inc v Parr [ChD]	455
Warnett (Inspector of Taxes), Berry v [HL]	630
Welch, R v [CA]	821
Wenjiang, The [CA]	437
West Yorkshire Coroner, R v, ex p Smith [QBD]	801
White, Holden v [CA]	328
Whitter v Peters [CA]	369
Wicks v Firth (Inspector of Taxes) [CA]	9
Williams v Home Office (No 2) [CA]	564
Williams, ex p, R v Tottenham Magistrates' Court [QBD]	705
Wills v Bowley [HL]	654
Zezza v Government of Italy [HL]	513

Digest of cases reported in volume 2

ADMIRALTY – Summons for directions – Investment of funds in court
Practice Direction ..   ..   **Adm Ct**   **480**

AGRICULTURAL HOLDING – Termination of tenancy – Validity of claim for compensation
E D & A D Cooke Bourne (Farms) Ltd v Mellows   ..   ..   **CA**   **208**

ANIMAL – Horse – Unpredictable temperament – Liability for injuries
Wallace v Newton   ..   ..   **Park J**   **106**

ARBITRATION – Leave to appeal against award – Guidance for arbitrators
International Sea Tankers Inc v Hemisphere Shipping Co Ltd (The Wenjiang) ..   **CA**   **437**

——Stay of court proceedings – Matters agreed to be referred to arbitration
Ellerine Bros (Pty) Ltd v Klinger   ..   ..   **CA**   **737**

ARREST – Arrest without warrant – Grounds for arrest – Belief of constable
Wills v Bowley   ..   ..   **HL**   **654**

BANK – Letter of credit – Non-conforming documents – Seller acting in good faith – Duty of bank
United City Merchants (Investments) Ltd v Royal Bank of Canada   ..   ..   **HL**   **720**

BANKRUPTCY – Discharge – Relevance of conduct prior to bankruptcy
Re Stern (a bankrupt), ex p Keyser Ullmann Ltd v The bankrupt ..   ..   ..   **CA**   **600**

BUILDING CONTRACT – Delay in completion – Withdrawal of sub-contractor
Percy Bilton Ltd v Greater London Council   ..   ..   **HL**   **623**

CANADA – Treaty rights of Indians – Enforceability against United Kingdom government
R v Secretary of State for Foreign and Commonwealth Affairs, ex p Indian Association of Alberta   ..   ..   **CA**   **118**

CAPITAL GAINS TAX – Chargeable gains – Cost of acquisition of asset
Stanton (Inspector of Taxes) v Drayton Commercial Investment Co Ltd   ..   **HL**   **942**

——Gift in settlement – Transfer of fund to trustees
Berry v Warnett (Inspector of Taxes) ..   ..   **HL**   **630**

——Husband and wife – Transfer of interest in property on divorce
Aspden (Inspector of Taxes) v Hildesley   ..   ..   **Nourse J**   **53**

——Interest in settled property – Apportionment of gains to beneficiaries
Leedale (Inspector of Taxes) v Lewis ..   ..   **CA**   **644**

CARRIERS – Loss of goods – Liability of carrier – Carrier not negligent
Michael Galley Footwear Ltd (in liq) v Iaboni   ..   ..   ..   **Hodgson J**   **200**

CASE STATED – Limitation of time – Extension
Devlin v F (a juvenile)   ..   ..   **Woolf J**   **450**

CHILDREN AND YOUNG PERSONS – Care proceedings in juvenile court – Appeal by parents
Southwark London Borough Council v C (a minor) ..   ..   **DC**   **636**

——Place of safety order – Appeal
Nottinghamshire CC v Q ..   ..   **DC**   **641**

——Wardship proceedings by local authority
Re G (a minor) (wardship: costs)   ..   ..   **CA**   **32**

CLUB – Dissolution – Distribution of assets
Re GKN Bolts and Nuts Ltd Sports and Social Club ..   ..   ..   **Megarry V-C**   **855**

COMMONS – Confirmation of registration by commissioner – Evidence required
Re Sutton Common, Wimborne   ..   ..   **Walton J**   **376**

COMMONS – Registration – Amendment of register – Procedure
Re Tillmire Common, Heslington   ..   ..   Dillon J   615

COMMONWEALTH – Divisibility of Crown
R v Secretary of State for Foreign and Commonwealth Affairs, ex p
Association of Alberta   ..   ..   CA   118

COMPANIES COURT – Practice – Applications in Long Vacation
Practice Direction ..   ..   Companies Ct   454

COMPANY – Compulsory winding up – Advertisement of petition – Premature advertisement
Re Signland Ltd   ..   ..   Slade J   609

——Voluntary winding up – Distribution of assets – Debt in foreign currency
Re Lines Bros Ltd   ..   ..   CA   183

——Winding up – Proceedings against company
Re J Burrows (Leeds) Ltd   ..   ..   Ch D   882

CONFLICT OF LAWS – Foreign nullity decree – Recognition
Vervaeke v Smith (Messina and A-G intervening)   ..   ..   HL   144

CONSTITUTIONAL LAW – Divisibility of Crown – Proceedings against Crown
R v Secretary of State for Foreign and Commonwealth Affairs, ex p Indian
Association of Alberta   ..   ..   CA   118

——Visiting forces – Deserter – Evidence
R v Tottenham Magistrates' Court, ex p Williams   ..   ..   DC   705

CONTEMPT OF COURT – Committal – Breach of injunction – County court
Whitter v Peters   ..   ..   CA   369

——Publication concerning legal proceedings – Report of committal proceedings – Postponement
R v Horsham Justices, ex p Farquharson   ..   ..   DC and CA   269

——Publications concerning legal proceedings – Newspaper article on matter of public interest
A-G v English   ..   ..   QBD and HL   903

COPYRIGHT – Infringement – Bootlegging – Persons entitled to bring action
Warner Bros Records Inc v Parr ..   ..   Julian Jeffs QC   455
RCA Corp v Pollard   ..   ..   Vinelott J   468

CORONER – Inquest – Judicial review – Jursidiction – Verdict – Selection of jurors
R v Surrey Coroner, ex p Campbell   ..   ..   DC   545

——Inquest – Jurisdiction – Death occurring abroad
R v West Yorkshire Coroner, ex p Smith   ..   ..   DC   801

COSTS – Taxation – Order for costs on 'indemnity' basis – Solicitor and own client costs
EMI Records Ltd v Ian Cameron Wallace Ltd   ..   ..   Megarry V-C   980

COUNSEL – Counsel's fees – Legal aid – Instruction of leading counsel
Re Solicitors, Re Taxation of Costs   ..   ..   Megarry V-C   683

CRIMINAL EVIDENCE – Evidence against co-accused – Cross-examination
R v Varley   ..   ..   CA   519

CRIMINAL LAW – Arson – Actus reus
R v Miller   ..   ..   CA   386

——Costs – Magistrates' court – Determination
Bunston v Rawlings   ..   ..   DC   697

——Costs – Magistrates' court – Just and reasonable costs
R v Tottenham Justices, ex p Joshi   ..   ..   DC   507

——Director of Public Prosecutions – Aborting of private prosecution
Raymond v A-G   ..   ..   CA   487

CRIMINAL LAW – Handling stolen goods – Wife using stolen goods brought home by husband
R v Kanwar .. .. CA 528

——Loitering with intent – Abolition of offence – Effect of abolition
Comr of Police of the Metropolis v Simeon .. .. HL 813

——Perverting course of justice – Attempt – Tampering with blood sample
R v Murray .. .. CA 225

——Rape – Recklessness whether victim consented
R v Pigg .. .. CA 591

——Retirement of jury – Judge communicating with jury without consulting counsel
R v Rose .. .. CA 536

——Theft – Obtaining property by deception – Dishonesty
R v Ghosh .. .. CA 689

——Threat to kill – Defence – Lawful excuse
R v Cousins .. .. CA 115

——Trial – Material irregularity – Retrial
R v Rose .. .. CA 536; HL 731

CROWN – Divisibility – Crown in right of Canada – Proceedings against UK government
R v Secretary of State for Foreign and Commonwealth Affairs, ex p Indian
Association of Alberta .. .. CA 118

CROWN COURT – Procedure – Appeal against binding-over order
Shaw v Hamilton .. .. DC 718

CURRENCY CONTROL – Exchange control – Exchange contract – Effect of unenforceable
contract on related contract
United City Merchants (Investments) Ltd v Royal Bank of Canada .. .. HL 720

CUSTOMS AND EXCISE – Fraudulent importation of prohibited goods – Proof
A-G's Reference (No 1 of 1981) .. .. CA 417

DAMAGES – Personal injury – Deductions – Suplementary benefit
Lincoln v Hayman .. .. CA 819

——Personal injury – Interest – Pain, suffering and loss of amenities
Birkett v Hayes .. .. CA 710

——Personal injury – Nervous shock
McLoughlin v O'Brian .. .. HL 298

DEVELOPMENT LAND TAX – Disposal of interest in land – Time of disposal
IRC v Metrolands (Property Finance) Ltd .. .. HL 557

DISCOVERY – Privilege – Educational psychologist's reports on pupil
Campbell v Tameside Metropolitan Borough Council .. .. CA 791

——Privilege – Statements to police during investigation of complaint
Hehir v Comr of Police of the Metropolis .. .. CA 335

DISCRIMINATION – Discrimination against a woman – Employment
Garland v British Rail Engineering Ltd .. .. CJEC and HL 402

DIVORCE – Ancillary relief – Financial provision – Anton Piller order
Emanuel v Emanuel .. .. Wood J 342

——Decree absolute – Applcation for decree made out of time – Cohabitation after decree nisi
Court v Court .. .. Arnold P 531

——Financial provision – Disclosure – Setting aside order
Robinson v Robinson (note) .. .. CA 699

DIVORCE – Petition within three years of marriage – Exceptional hardship or exceptional depravity
Fay v Fay .. .. HL 922

DOCUMENT – Admissibility in evidence – Improperly obtained evidence
ITC Film Distributors v Video Exchange Ltd .. .. Warner J 241

DOMESTIC VIOLENCE – Injunction – County court's jurisdiction – Power of arrest
Horner v Horner .. .. CA 495

DRUGS – Unlawful possession – Visible and measurable particles
R v Boyesen .. .. HL 161

ECCLESIASTICAL LAW – Consistory court – Jurisdiction – Faculty for burial of non-parishioner
Re St Nicholas's, Baddesley Ensor .. .. Con Ct 351

ECONOMIC DURESS – Trade dispute
Universe Tankships Inc of Monrovia v International Transport Workers' Federation HL 67

EMPLOYMENT – Contract of service – Payment of sick pay
Means v Safecar Security Ltd .. .. CA 865

——Discrimination against a woman – Provision in relation to retirement
Garland v British Rail Engineering Ltd .. .. CJEC and HL 402

——Frustration of contract of employment by imprisonment
Chakki v United Yeast Co Ltd .. .. EAT 446

EQUITY – Undue influence – Presumption – Religious organisation
Roche v Sherrington .. .. Slade J 426

EUROPEAN COURT – Reference to European Court – Power of magistrates
R v Plymouth Justices, ex p Rogers .. .. DC 175

EVIDENCE – Document obtained improperly – Admissibility
ITC Film Distributors v Video Exchange Ltd .. .. Warner J 241

——Self-incrimination – Proceeds of cheque – Tracing order
Khan v Khan .. .. CA 60

EXCHANGE CONTROL – Effect of unenforceable contract on related contract
United City Merchants (Investments) Ltd v Royal Bank of Canada .. .. HL 720

EXTRADITION – Surrender – Conviction and sentence in contumacy
Zezza v Government of Italy .. .. HL 513

HOUSING – Homeless person – Intentional homelessness
Lambert v Ealing London Borough Council .. .. CA 394

HUSBAND AND WIFE – Injunction – Domestic violence – County court's jurisdiction
Horner v Horner .. .. CA 495

——Injunction – Exclusion from matrimonial home
O'Malley v O'Malley .. .. CA 112

IMMIGRATION – Leave to enter – Non-patrial – Duty to disclose facts
R v Secretary of State for the Home Dept, ex p Khawaja .. .. CA 523

——Leave to enter – Non-patrial – Student
Alexander v Immigration Appeal Tribunal .. .. HL 766

——Leave to enter – Refusal – Removal of immigrant
R v Immigration Officer, ex p Shah .. .. Woolf J 264

——Offence – Time limit for prosecution
Grant v Borg .. .. HL 257

INCOME TAX – Benefits derived by higher-paid employees – Scholarships for children
Wicks v Firth (Inspector of Taxes) .. .. CA 9

INCOME TAX – Capital allowances – Plant
IRC v Scottish and Newcastle Breweries Ltd   ..   ..   **HL**   230
Cole Bros Ltd v Phillips (Inspector of Taxes) ..   ..   **HL**   247

INJUNCTION – County court – Husband and wife – Harassment not involving violence
Horner v Horner   ..   ..   **CA**   495

——Exclusion from matrimonial home – County court jurisdiction
O'Malley v O'Malley   ..   ..   **CA**   112

INSURANCE – Law Society's indemnity insurance scheme – Commission received by Law Society
Swain v Law Society   ..   ..   **HL**   827

INTEREST – Damages – Personal injury – Pain, suffering and loss of amenities
Birkett v Hayes   ..   ..   **CA**   710

JUDGMENT – Final or interlocutory order – Test
Haron bin Mohd Zaid v Central Securities (Holdings) Bhd ..   ..   **PC**   481

JURY – Intimidating or threatening jury – Time limit to reach verdict
R v Rose   ..   ..   **CA**   536

——Majority verdict – Failure to state number of dissentients
R v Pigg   ..   ..   **CA**   591

LAND – Restrictive covenant – Conditions for discharge or satisfaction
Gilbert v Spoor   ..   ..   **CA**   576

LANDLORD AND TENANT – Business premises – Compensation for disturbance
International Military Services Ltd v Capital and Counties plc   ..   ..   **Slade J**   20

——Landlord's consent to assignment of lease – Consent not to be unreasonably withheld
Bromley Park Garden Estates Ltd v Moss   ..   ..   **CA**   890

LEGAL AID – Instruction of leading counsel – Duty of solicitor
Re Solicitors   ..   ..   **Megarry V-C**   683

——Unassisted party's costs – Judgment for less than amount paid into court
Kelly v London Transport Executive   ..   ..   **CA**   842

LIBEL AND SLANDER – Interlocutory injunction
Harakas v Baltic Mercantile and Shipping Exchange Ltd   ..   ..   **CA**   701

LIMITATION OF ACTION – Cause of action – Economic loss suffered in consequence of solicitor's negligent advice
Forster v Outred & Co (a firm)   ..   ..   **CA**   753

LOCAL GOVERNMENT – Documents – Inspection by councillor
R v City of Birmingham DC, ex p O   ..   ..   **CA**   356

MAGISTRATES – Laying of information – Requirements
Hill v Anderton   ..   ..   **HL**   963

——Offence triable summarily or on indictment – Date accused attaining age of 17
Re Daley   ..   ..   **DC**   321; **HL**   974

MASTER AND SERVANT – Contract of service – Frustration – Imprisonment
Chakki v United Yeast Co Ltd   ..   ..   **EAT**   446

MENTAL HEALTH – Patient's property – Execution of will
Re D (J)   ..   ..   **Megarry V-C**   37

NATIONAL INSURANCE – Unemployment benefit – Early retirement
Crewe v Social Security Comr   ..   ..   **CA**   745

NEGLIGENCE – Duty to take care – Driver of motor vehicle – Police officer in hot pursuit
Marshall v Osmond   ..   ..   **Milmo J**   610

NEGLIGENCE – Nervous shock – Persons to whom duty of care owed – Person told of but not seeing road accident

McLoughlin v O'Brian .. .. HL 298

——Wrongful entry into life – Whether reasonable cause of action

McKay v Essex Area Health Authority .. .. CA 771

NULLITY OF MARRIAGE – Recognition of foreign decree

Vervaeke v Smith (Messina and A-G intervening) .. .. HL 144

OCCUPIER'S LIABILITY – Visitor – Right of way

Holden v White .. .. CA 328

PLEADING – Leave to amend after trial

Williams v Home Office (No 2) .. .. CA 564

POLITICAL PARTY – Funds – Liability to tax

Conservative and Unionist Central Office v Burrell (Inspector of Taxes) .. CA 1

PRACTICE – Companies Court – Applications in Long Vacation

Practice Direction .. .. Companies Ct 454

——Family Division – Lump sum applications – Costs

Practice Direction .. .. Fam D 800

——Parties – Adding defendant – Date from which added defendant a party

Leadbitter v Hodge Finance Ltd .. .. Bush J 167

——Uncontested proceedings – Crown Office list

Practice Direction .. .. QBD 704

PUBLIC ORDER – Insulting behaviour – Homosexual advances to plain clothes police officer

Parkin v Norman .. .. DC 583

RACE RELATIONS – Non-discrimination notice – Appeal

Commission for Racial Equality v Amari Plastics Ltd .. .. .. CA 499

RESTRICTIVE COVENANT AFFECTING LAND – Discharge or modification – Conditions to be satisfied

Gilbert v Spoor .. .. CA 576

SALE OF LAND – Conditional contract – specific performance

Cohen v Nessdale Ltd .. .. CA 97

SENTENCE – Probation order – Day centre attendance

Cullen v Rogers .. .. HL 570

——Reduction – Period spent in custody – Concurrent sentences

R v Governor of Blundeston Prison, ex p Gaffney .. .. DC 492

——Release on licence – Revocation of licence – Appeal

R v Welch .. .. CA 821

SETTLEMENT – Contingent interest – Newspaper-Franco scheme

IRC v Trustees of Sir John Aird's Settlement .. .. Nourse J 929

SOLICITOR – Negligent advice – Accrual of cause of action

Forster v Outred & Co (a firm) .. .. CA 753

——Solicitor ceasing to act for party – Service of application

Re Creehouse Ltd .. .. Vinelott J 422

SPECIFIC PERFORMANCE – Sale of land – Conditional contract

Cohen v Nessdale Ltd .. .. CA 97

STATUTE – Penal statute – Double repeal – Effect

Comr of Police of the Metropolis v Simeon .. .. HL 813

TRADE DISPUTE – Economic duress – Recovery of money paid to welfare fund
Universe   Tankships   Inc   of   Monrovia   v   International   Transport
Workers' Federation   ..   ..   **HL**   **67**

TRIAL – Offence triable summa₁ly or on indictment – Date accused attaining age of 17
Re Daley   ..   ..   **DC**   **321; HL**   **974**

TRUST AND TRUSTEE – Constructive trust – Contract between vendor and purchaser
subject to plaintiff's contract with vendor
Lyus v Prowsa Developments Ltd   ..   ..   **Dillon J**   **953**

——Profit from trust – Commission – Professional indemnity insurance
Swain v Law Society   ..   ..   **HL**   **827**

UNDUE INFLUENCE – Religious organisation
Roche v Sherrington   ..   ..   **Slade J**   **426**

UNINCORPORATED ASSOCIATION – Political party – Funds
Conservative and Unionist Central Office v Burrell (Inspector of Taxes)   ..   **CA**   **1**

VISITING FORCES – Deserter – Evidence – Burden of proof
R v Tottenham Magistrates' Court, ex p Williams   ..   ..   **DC**   **705**

WARD OF COURT – Practice – Official Solicitor's costs
Re G (a minor) (wardship: costs)   ..   ..   **CA**   **32**

WRIT – Renewal – Failure to renew – Order for service after expiration of validity of writ
Bernstein v Jackson   ..   ..   **CA**   **806**

Conservative and Unionist Central Office v Burrell (Inspector of Taxes)

COURT OF APPEAL, CIVIL DIVISION
LAWTON, BRIGHTMAN AND FOX LJJ
9, 10, 11, 12, 13, 16, 17 NOVEMBER, 10 DECEMBER 1981

Unincorporated association – Requirements of an unincorporated association – Political party constituted by members of local constituency associations and both Houses of Parliament – Funds raised by party treasurers held by party's central office which provided administrative services to party – Expenditure of funds under control of party leader – Party leader providing link between members of party – Whether party an unincorporated association – Whether central office holding income from funds on behalf of an unincorporated association – Whether central office liable to corporation tax on income from funds – Income and Corporation Taxes Act 1970, s 526(5).

The Conservative Party was a political party made up of three elements, namely (i) the Parliamentary Party comprising those members of both Houses of Parliament who took the Conservative whip, (ii) the mass membership represented by the National Union of Conservative and Unionist Associations (the national union) comprising constituency associations, and (iii) the party headquarters known as the Central Office, which operated the party organisation and the party's research department. The party leader, who linked the three elements of the party together, was selected by a ballot of Conservative members of Parliament and presented for election to a party meeting consisting of the Parliamentary Party, Parliamentary candidates and the executive committee of the national union. Party treasurers appointed by the party leader and assisted by a board of finance were responsible for raising party funds. The moneys so raised were under the control of the Central Office and the party leader had power to direct how those moneys were to be spent. The Central Office was assessed to corporation tax on investment income and interest over a five-year period from 1972 to 1976 on the basis that it was an unincorporated association within s 526(5)[a] of the Income and Corporation Taxes Act 1970 and therefore fell within the meaning of 'company' in s 526(5). The Central Office appealed to the Special Commissioners against the assessment contending (i) that it was not an unincorporated association, (ii) that even if the national union could be said to be an unincorporated association the funds did not belong to the national union since they were administered by the Central Office, and (iii) that, in any event, the Conservative Party was an amorphous combination of various elements which lacked the characteristics of an unincorporated association and therefore if the funds were owned by the party the income arising therefrom was not assessable to corporation tax. The Crown accepted that the Central Office was not itself an unincorporated association but contended that the party was, and that the funds held by the Central Office belonged to the party. The Crown based its contention on the submission that the party was linked together both by the powers of the leader and by a contract between the members of the party arising in part out of the rules of the national union, in part out of the rules regulating the party meeting and selection of the leader, and in part out of the rules of the local constituency associations. The Crown further contended that the ownership of the party funds had to be in a body which had legal capacity to own property either as a trustee or as a beneficial

---

a   Section 526(5), so far as material, is set out at p 3 j to p 4 a, post

owner and that, since the moneys contributed to the party's funds were given for a
purpose and could not therefore have been given to a non-charitable trust, it followed *a*
that there had to be an unincorporated association which was to be treated as the owner
of the funds. The commissioners found that the funds held by the party treasurers for
the use of Central Office were held on behalf of the members of an unincorporated
association, which they identified as the Conservative Party, comprising all the members
of the local constituency associations together with the members of both Houses taking
the party whip, and accordingly upheld the assessments. The judge allowed an appeal by *b*
the Central Office. The Crown appealed.

Held – Since a 'company' within s 526(5) of the 1970 Act included any body corporate
or unincorporated association but not a partnership, it was clear that for the purposes of
the 1970 Act the word 'company' had a meaning extending beyond a body corporate but
not as far as a partnership, and it was to be inferred that 'unincorporated association' in *c*
the context meant two or more persons bound together for one or more common
purposes, not being business purposes, by mutual undertakings, each having mutual
duties and obligations, in an organisation which had rules which identified in whom
control of it and its funds rested and on what terms and which could be joined or left at
will. Since there were no mutual understandings between all the members of the *d*
Conservative Party, no mutual rights and obligations and no rules governing control,
which clearly lay in the leader of the party, and since no occasion could be identified
when any agreement was made bringing into existence any association, it followed that
the funds and the income therefrom held by the Central Office of the party were not held
on behalf of an unincorporated association. The appeal would accordingly be dismissed
(see p 4 *a* to *c f g j*, p 5 *f h j*, p 6 *d* to *h*, p 7 *a b* and p 8 *e f*, post).
     Per curiam. The treasurer of an organisation which receives and applies funds from *e*
multifarious sources for certain political purposes has authority to add to the mixed fund
money paid to him by contributors; and once that money has, with the authority of the
contributor, been mixed with other money the contributor's mandate becomes
irrevocable and he has no legal right to demand the return of his contribution. The
contributor has, however, a remedy against the recipient (ie the treasurer or the officials *f*
at whose direction the treasurer acts) to restrain or make good a misapplication of the
mixed fund except so far as it may appear on ordinary accounting principles that his own
contribution was spent before the threatened or actual misapplication (see p 6 *g h*, p 7 *g*
to *j* and p 8 *f*, post).
     Decision of Vinelott J [1980] 3 All ER 42 affirmed.

g

Notes
For what constitutes an unincorporated association, see 9 Halsbury's Laws (4th edn) para
1201.
     For the Income and Corporation Taxes Act 1970, s 526, see 33 Halsbury's Statutes (3rd
edn) 681.

h

Case referred to in judgments
Recher's Will Trusts, Re, National Westminster Bank Ltd v National Anti-Vivisection Society Ltd
     [1971] 3 All ER 401, [1972] Ch 526, [1971] 3 WLR 321, 8(1) Digest (Reissue) 297, 398.

Cases also cited   *j*
Bucks Constabulary Widows' and Orphans' Fund Friendly Society, Re, Thompson v Holdsworth
     [1978] 2 All ER 571, [1978] 1 WLR 641.
Caledonian Employees' Benevolent Society, Re 1928 SC 633.
Clarke v Dunraven (Earl), The Satanita [1897] AC 59, HL.
Forbes v Eden (1867) LR 1 Sc & Div 568.

a General Assembly of Free Church of Scotland v Lord Overtoun, Macalister v Young [1904] AC
  515, HL.
  Gillingham Bus Disaster Fund, Re, Bowman v Official Solicitor [1958] 2 All ER 749, [1959] Ch
  62, CA.
  Harington v Sendall [1903] 1 Ch 921.
  Leahy v Attorney General of New South Wales [1959] 2 All ER 300, [1959] AC 457, PC.
  Price, Re, Midland Bank Executor and Trustee Co Ltd v Harwood [1943] 2 All ER 505, [1943]
b   Ch 422.
  Rigby v Connol (1880) 14 Ch D 482, [1874–80] All ER Rep 592.
  Smith, Re, Johnson v Bright-Smith [1914] 1 Ch 937.
  Smith v Anderson (1880) 15 Ch D 247, [1874–80] All ER Rep 1121, CA.
  Thackrah, Re, Thackrah v Wilson [1939] 2 All ER 4.

c **Appeal**
  The Crown appealed against the decision of Vinelott J ([1980] 3 All ER 42, [1980] STC
  400) dated 2 April 1980 allowing an appeal by the Conservative and Unionist Central
  Office by way of case stated (set out at [1980] 3 All ER 44–52) by the Commissioners for
  the Special Purposes of the Income Tax Acts in respect of their decision confirming
  assessments to corporation tax made on the Central Office in respect of the years ending
d 31 March 1972 to 31 March 1976. The facts are set out in the judgment of Lawton LJ.

  John Knox QC and C H McCall for the Crown.
  Andrew Park QC and David Goldberg for the Central Office.

                                                                    Cur adv vult
e

  10 December. The following judgments were read.

  LAWTON LJ. This is an appeal by the Crown from an order of Vinelott J ([1980] 3 All
  ER 42, [1980] STC 400) made on 2 April 1980 whereby he adjudged on the hearing of
  an appeal by way of case stated from a decision of the Commissioners for the Special
f Purposes of the Income Tax Acts that such decision was erroneous and that assessments
  to corporation tax on the Conservative and Unionist Central Office for each of the five
  years ending on 31 March 1972 to 31 March 1976 be discharged. The Special
  Commissioners had decided that the Central Office was an unincorporated association
  and as such was chargeable to corporation tax on its profits under the provisions of
  ss 238(1) and 526(5) of the Income and Corporation Taxes Act 1970. Vinelott J adjudged
g that it was not such an association, so that corporation tax was not chargeable. It was
  agreed before us that the Central Office was nothing more than an administrative unit
  of the Conservative and Unionist Party (the party). No point has ever been taken by
  either side as to the name used for the purpose of the assessments. Both parties to this
  appeal asked the court to consider the legal nature of the party. If it is an unincorporated
h association, corporation tax has to be paid on the income identified in the Conservative
  and Unionist Party income and expenditure accounts for the relevant years as 'investment
  income and interest'. If it is not such an association, income tax will have to be paid on
  this income. We have not been concerned to decide who will have to pay income tax but
  we were told by counsel for the party that whatever income tax is payable will be paid
  out of the party's central funds. The reason why the party is contesting the assessments
j to corporation tax which have been made on it is that for the relevant years the rates at
  which corporation tax was charged were much higher than the rates for income tax.
      The charging section of the Income and Corporation Taxes Act 1970, s 238(1), starts
  with these words: 'Corporation tax shall be charged on profits of companies . . .' Section
  526 is an interpretation section. Subsection (5) defines 'company' as follows:

      '"company" means, subject to subsection (6) below [which has no relevance in this case], any body corporate or unincorporated association, but does not include a partnership, a local authority or a local authority association.'   *a*

It is against this statutory background that a meaning has to be given to the words 'unincorporated association'. It is sufficiently like a 'company' for it to be put in the charging section within the ambit of that word. The interpretation section makes it clear that the word 'company' has a meaning extending beyond a body corporate but not as far as a partnership or a local authority. I infer that by 'unincorporated association' in this context Parliament meant two or more persons bound together for one or more common purposes, not being business purposes, by mutual undertakings, each having mutual duties and obligations, in an organisation which has rules which identify in whom control of it and its funds rests and on what terms and which can be joined or left at will. The bond of union between the members of an unincorporated association has to be contractual. This was accepted by the Special Commissioners and was the basis of their conclusion. The point of law which arises is whether on the facts they found they could properly have come to the conclusion which they did. The facts are set out fully in the case ([1980] 3 All ER 42 at 44–52). For the purposes of this judgment I need do no more than refer to those which I consider to be relevant to the point of law.

b

c

Since membership of an unincorporated association is based on agreement between the members, a starting point for examining the legal nature of the party is to consider how anyone can join it. To this there is a short answer: no one can join the party directly. Membership can be obtained either through a local constituency association or through the parliamentary party. Members of local constituency associations, and such associations themselves, have no constitutional links with the parliamentary party although there are many political links. These local associations choose their own parliamentary candidates from a list of candidates approved by the party's standing advisory committee. If a candidate of their choice is elected a member of the House of Commons he becomes a member of the parliamentary party when he accepts the Conservative whip, which he will do on election but which he may refuse later, in which event he will no longer be a member of the parliamentary party. Once elected, members of the House of Commons become representative of the constituency for which they have been elected, not delegates of the local constituency associations which may have put them up as candidates. On the facts as found I can find nothing which links contractually and directly members of local constituency associations to Conservative members of the House of Commons representing their constituencies. The lack of a contractual link is even more clear in the case of peers who are members of the parliamentary party as long as they accept the Conservative whip in the House of Lords.

d

e

f

Counsel for the Crown did not suggest that there was any direct link. His submission was that all the different sections of the party are linked together through the national union and the party leader and that anyone joining a local constituency association (which is the only way in which a member of the public, not being a peer or a member of the House of Commons, can join the party) by that act impliedly accepts the linkage so that he becomes a member of an unincorporated association which is the party.

g

Anyone joining a local constituency association impliedly agrees to become linked to the national union. Between 1972 and 1975 the members of that body were local constituency associations. In 1975 the rules were changed so that anyone who subscribed annually to any registered constituency association became a member of the national union. Counsel for the party accepted that all who were members of the national union were members of an unincorporated body. But that still leaves a constitutional gap between the national union and the parliamentary party. The Special Commissioners were of the opinion that the gap was bridged by the rules which regulate the party meeting and the selection of the leader of the party. Without such a bridge having its foundations in contractual relationships there could not be, in my judgment, an unincorporated association. Peers, particularly Scottish representative peers, and Conservative members of the House of Commons would have no bonds of union with local constituency members.

h

j

The keystone of the bridge is said to be the party leader. In a booklet, entitled 'The
a Party Organisation', which was annexed to the case, the leader's position and functions
are described as follows:

'The Leader of the Party stands at the apex of the entire structure of the Party,
linking together the three elements of Parliamentary Party, National Union, and
Party Headquarters... the Leader heads both the Conservative Party in Parliament
b and the Conservative Party Organisation in the country, including the Party
Headquarters. He is elected in the first place by the Conservative Members of
Parliament in the House of Commons... The Leader elected by the Parliamentary
Party in the House of Commons is then presented for election to a special meeting
representing the Party as a whole. This meeting is organised by the National Union
and the Chief Whip jointly. Conservative Members of both Houses, Parliamentary
c Candidates and Members of the National Union Executive Committee covering all
sections of the Party are eligible to attend this meeting... The Leader of the Party
appoints the officers of the Party—the Chairman, Deputy Chairman, Vice-Chairmen
and Treasurers—who are directly responsible to him for the state of the Party
organisation throughout the country and the Party's finances. The Leader of the
Party also appoints the Chairman of the Conservative Research Department.'

d The procedure for electing the leader is contained in rules made in 1965. The case
does not state who made the rules. All that is clear is that neither the local constituency
associations nor the national union had any rule-making powers which enabled them to
direct the 'members of the House of Commons in receipt of the Conservative and
National Liberal Whips' to elect a leader. Nor are there any rule-making powers in these
bodies to change the mode of election. Whoever made the rules can change them. This
e must mean that somewhere in the party there is an unidentified rule-making body
which at any time can make fundamental changes affecting the organisation and
leadership of the party, including the destruction of the bridge which is said to exist
between the leader and the mass membership and over which the mass membership has
no control. In my judgment, however viable such a body may be as a political
movement, it lacks the characteristics of an unincorporated association for the purposes
f of the taxing statutes. There are no mutual understandings between all the members, no
mutual rights and obligations and no rules governing control where it clearly lies, which
is in the leader. It is no answer to say, as counsel for the Crown did, that on joining a local
constituency association members impliedly agree to accept what he called the
conventions of the party. Agreements which confer rights and impose obligations, as
membership of unincorporated associations do, must be reasonably certain because they
g may become justiciable and those creating unincorporated associations sometimes do.
No member of a local constituency association, basing his claim on contractual rights,
could ask the court to protect those rights in respect of the parliamentary party's election
of a leader who was 'presented for election as Party Leader to the Party Meeting
constituted as at present': see the 'Procedure for the Selection of the Leader of the
Conservative and Unionist Party' set out in the booklet to which I have referred.
h Another approach to the problem presented by this case is to ask when the
unincorporated association which is said to exist was formed. If, as was accepted by both
the Special Commissioners and the Crown, such an association is a creature of contract,
the agreement which brought it about must have been made on some identifiable
occasion or in some identifiable circumstances. I can find in the party's history as set out
in the case and the documents annexed thereto no such occasion or circumstances.
j According to the booklet to which I have already referred, the parliamentary party can
trace its origins back 'for several hundred years', certainly back to the second decade of
the reign of Charles II. The same booklet states that the local constituency associations
developed out of the registration societies which were formed after 1832 to carry out the
task of making sure that the names of supporters entitled to vote were included in the
register of electors. In 1867 it was decided to form a federation of local associations in

England and Wales. This was the beginning of the national union. In 1870 an important
event happened in the constitutional history of the party. Mr Disraeli founded the *a*
Conservative Central Office. Until 1911 the general control and direction of that office
was in the hands of the whips. In that year the first party chairman was appointed.
From its earliest days the Central Office collected funds for the party's use. At first these
funds were under the direct control of the leader; in modern times the party's honorary
treasurers have been responsible for the funds. There is now a board of finance whose
function it is to raise money for the central funds of the party. Since the financial year *b*
which ended on 31 March 1968 the party has published an income and expenditure
account of its central funds, together with a statement of the net cash and invested
reserves. It is these accounts which probably have attracted the attention of the
Revenue. The central funds are derived mainly from donations; but a substantial
proportion comes from contributions made by local constituency associations on a quota
basis. They are expected to meet their quotas but some associations do not do so. The *c*
Central Office administers the funds for party purposes but neither the national union
nor the local constituency associations have any right under any rule to a say in how the
funds are to be used. When I asked counsel for the Crown during the course of
argument when the Revenue suggested that the party had become an unincorporated
association he said that it had done so when the funds administered by the party's officers
through the Central Office had come to be recognised as the funds of the party rather *d*
than mere financial help given to the leader to be used by him for party purposes. In my
judgment, this would be no beginning of such an association. Further, I can find no
event in the history of the party which looks like a beginning of such an association. The
indications are that the separate bodies which make up the party co-operate with each
other for political purposes but maintain independent existences for organisation
purposes. *e*
   The Crown's main argument, however, was based on the proposition that the party's
unquestioned, valid control of funds could only be possible in law if it were an
unincorporated association. The officers of the party who receive donations, legacies and
constituency association quota subscriptions for party purposes could not hold them as
trustees since the law does not recognise trusts for non-charitable purposes. Clearly they
could not use the funds for their own purposes. The only form of holding which made *f*
legal sense, so it was submitted, was that they held the funds for the benefit of the
members of the party, being an unincorporated association, to be used by them for the
party's purposes. I reject this argument for three reasons: first, because I find this
working back kind of argument a most unsatisfactory way of establishing the existence
of an association which could only have come into existence as the result of an agreement
between two or more persons; second, because it disregards the history of the central *g*
funds; and, third, because it ignores what most people intend when they make donations
to central funds. I have had the benefit of reading in draft Brightman LJ's analysis of the
legal nature of a donation to Central Office central funds. I agree with what he will say.
   I would dismiss the appeal.

BRIGHTMAN LJ. The issue is whether or not the investment income of the *h*
Conservative Party Central Office funds during the relevant years was the income of an
unincorporated association. The Crown does not allege that the Central Office itself is
an unincorporated association. The assertion is that Central Office funds are held for
the purposes of an organisation known as the Conservative Party, or more fully as the
Conservative and Unionist Party, that such organisation has all the necessary requirements
for qualifying as an unincorporated association and that the Special Commissioners were *j*
justified in finding that it is such an association. The members of the association are said
to be (i) all the persons who are members of the local constituency associations (which
local associations are themselves unincorporated associations) and (ii) the members of
both Houses of Parliament who accept the Conservative Party whip. The contract which
is alleged to bind together the members of this unincorporated association known as the

Conservative Party is said to consist of the rules forming the constitution of the National
a Union of Conservative and Unionist Associations, the rules regulating 'party meetings' at
which the candidate chosen by the Parliamentary Conservative Party as leader of the
party is presented for election as party leader and the rules forming the respective
constitutions of the local constituency associations. I agree, for the reasons given by
Lawton LJ, that no such overall unincorporated association exists.

Before, however, that conclusion is accepted, I think that a critical observer is entitled
b to ask the question what, on that hypothesis, would be the legal relationship between a
contributor to Central Office funds and the recipient of the contribution so made.

Strictly speaking, this court does not have to answer that question; it has only to decide
the issue whether the Special Commissioners were entitled to find that the Conservative
Party is an unincorporated association. But, if no realistic legal explanation of the
relationship is forthcoming except the existence of an unincorporated association, one
c might justifiably begin to entertain doubts as to the credibility of the hypothesis on
which the question is asked. I will therefore attempt an answer.

If the Conservative Party is rightly described as an unincorporated association with an
identifiable membership bound together by identifiable rules, and Central Office funds
are funds of the Conservative Party, no problem arises. In that event, decided cases say
that the contribution takes effect in favour of the members of the unincorporated
d association known as the Conservative Party as an accretion to the funds which are the
subject matter of the contract which such members have made inter se: see, for example,
Re Recher's Will Trusts [1971] 3 All ER 401, [1972] Ch 526. If, however, the Conservative
Party is not an unincorporated association, that easy answer is not available.

I will consider the hypothesis by stages. No legal problem arises if a contributor (as I
will call him) hands to a friend (whom I will call the recipient) a sum of money to be
e applied by the recipient for political purposes indicated by the contributor, or to be
chosen at the discretion of the recipient. That would be a simple case of mandate or
agency. The recipient would have authority from the contributor to make use of the
money in the indicated way. So far as the money is used within the scope of the
mandate, the recipient discharges himself vis-à-vis the contributor. The contributor can
at any time demand the return of his money so far as not spent, unless the mandate is
f irrevocable, as it might be or become in certain circumstances. But once the money is
spent, the contributor can demand nothing back, only an account of the manner of
expenditure. No trust arises, except the fiduciary relationship inherent in the relationship
of principal and agent. If, however, the recipient were to apply the money for some
purpose outside the scope of the mandate, clearly the recipient would not be
discharged. The recipient could be restrained, like any other agent, from a threatened
g misapplication of the money entrusted to him, and like any other agent could be
required to replace any money misapplied.

The next stage is to suppose that the recipient is the treasurer of an organisation which
receives and applies funds from multifarious sources for certain political purposes. If the
contributor pays money to that treasurer, the treasurer has clear authority to add the
contribution to the mixed fund (as I will call it) that he holds. At that stage I think the
h mandate becomes irrevocable. That is to say, the contributor has no right to demand his
contribution back, once it has been mixed with other money under the authority of the
contributor. The contributor has no legal right to require the mixed fund to be
unscrambled for his benefit. This does not mean, however, that all contributors lose all
rights once their cheques are cashed, with the absurd result that the treasurer or other
officers can run off with the mixed fund with impunity. I have no doubt that any
j contributor has a remedy against the recipient (ie the treasurer, or the officials at whose
direction the treasurer acts) to restrain or make good a misapplication of the mixed fund
except so far as it may appear on ordinary accounting principles that the plaintiff's own
contribution was spent before the threatened or actual misapplication. In the latter
event the mandate given by the contributor will not have been breached. A complaining
contributor might encounter problems under the law of contract after a change of the

office holder to whom his mandate was originally given. Perhaps only the original recipient can be sued for the malpractices of his successors. It is not necessary to explore *a* such procedural intricacies.

So in the present case it seems to me that the status of a contribution to the Conservative Party central funds is this. The contributor draws a cheque (for example) in favour of, or hands it to, the treasurers. The treasurers are impliedly authorised by the contributor to present the cheque for encashment and to add the contribution to Central Office funds. Central Office funds are the subject matter of a mandate which permits them to *b* be used for the purposes of the Conservative Party as directed by the leader of the party. The contributor cannot demand his money back once it has been added to Central Office funds. He could object if Central Office funds were used or threatened to be used otherwise than in accordance with their declared purposes, unless it is correct to say, on ordinary accounting principles, that his contribution has already passed out of Central Office funds. *c*

This discussion of mandates, and complaining contributors, is all very remote and theoretical. No contributor to Central Office funds will view his contribution in this way, or contemplate even the remotest prospect of legal action on his part. He believes he is making an out and out contribution or gift to a political party. And so he is in practical terms. The only justification for embarking on a close analysis of the situation is the challenge, which was thrown down by counsel for the Crown in opening, to *d* suggest any legal framework which fits the undoubted fact that funds are held by the Central Office and are administered for the use and benefit of the Conservative Party, except the supposition that the Conservative Party is an unincorporated association.

I see no legal difficulty in the mandate theory. It is not necessary to invent an unincorporated association in order to explain the situation. The only problem which might arise in practice under the mandate theory would be the case of an attempted *e* bequest to Central Office funds, or to the treasurers thereof, or to the Conservative Party, since no agency could be set up at the moment of death between a testator and his chosen agent. A discussion of this problem is outside the scope of this appeal and, although I think that the answer is not difficult to find, I do not wish to prejudge it.

I would dismiss the appeal.
f

FOX LJ. I have had the benefit of reading the judgments that Lawton and Brightman LJJ have delivered and I agree with them.

Appeal dismissed. Leave to appeal to the House of Lords refused.

Solicitors: *Solicitor of Inland Revenue*; *Trower, Still & Keeling* (for the Central Office).

Edwina Epstein   Barrister.

a

Wicks v Firth (Inspector of Taxes)
Johnson v Firth (Inspector of Taxes)

COURT OF APPEAL, CIVIL DIVISION
LORD DENNING MR, OLIVER AND WATKINS LJJ
26, 27 OCTOBER, 13 NOVEMBER 1981

b

Income tax – Emoluments from office or employment – Benefits derived by directors and higher-paid employees from employment – Scholarship awarded to employee's child by employer – Whether award emolument from parent's employment – Income and Corporation Taxes Act 1970, s 375(1) – Finance Act 1976, ss 61(1), 72(3).

c In 1977 a large public company established an educational trust for the award of scholarships to children of employees of the company or of certain of its nominated subsidiaries for full-time study at university or comparable institutions. The award of the scholarships was at the discretion of the trustees. The taxpayer was a higher-paid employee of the company who was assessed to income tax in 1978–79 under Sch E on a scholarship awarded by the trustees to his son. The assessment was made under s 61(1)[a]
d of the Finance Act 1976 on the basis that as a person 'employed in ... higher-paid employment' there had 'by reason of his employment [been] provided for him, or ... members of his family ... [a] benefit'. The taxpayer appealed against the assessment, contending that s 375(1)[b] of the Income and Corporation Taxes Act 1970 which exempted 'income arising from a scholarship' applied in his case. The Crown contended that for the purpose of s 61 of the 1976 Act the charge was on the 'cash equivalent of a
e benefit', and that it was impossible to equate that with 'income arising from a scholarship' within s 375(1) of the 1970 Act, for, although the two might be the same in amount, they were different in character, and that, accordingly, s 375(1) could not confer exemption on a charge which arose under s 61. The Special Commissioners dismissed the taxpayer's appeal, holding that the charge under s 61 of the 1976 Act was on the cash equivalent of the benefit provided, which was to be treated as an emolument, and that
f a notional sum so treated was not 'income arising from a scholarship' within s 375(1) of the 1970 Act. The judge allowed an appeal by the taxpayer, holding that the scheme of assessing the cash equivalent of benefits under s 61 of the 1976 Act was aimed generally at benefits given not in cash but in kind, and was not intended to nullify or impair the unqualified exemption from tax conferred by s 375(1) of the 1970 Act on income arising from a scholarship, that exemption not being restricted to the scholarship holder. The
g Crown appealed.

Held – (1) On its true construction s 61 of the 1976 Act applied to benefits which an employee would not have received unless he had been an employee, the fact of employment being one of the causes of the benefit being provided although it did not need to have been the sole, or even the dominant, cause. It followed, therefore, that the
h scholarship had been provided for the taxpayer's son 'by reason of [the taxpayer's] employment' within s 61(1). In any event (per Lord Denning MR and Oliver LJ), since the scholarship had been provided by the employer, it was deemed by s 72(3)[c] of the 1976 Act to have been provided 'by reason of [the taxpayer's] employment' (see p 12 d to p 13 d and j to p 14 a, p 16 e f, p 17 d to j and p 18 j, post).

(2) (Lord Denning MR dissenting) On its true construction, and bearing in mind its

j

---

a   Section 61(1), so far as material, is set out at p 12 b c, post
b   Section 375(1) is set out at p 13 e, post
c   Section 72(3), so far as material, provides: '... all such provision as is mentioned in this Chapter which is made for an employee, or for members of his family or household, by his employer, are deemed to be paid to or made for him or them by reason of his employment ...'

legislative history, s 375 of the 1970 Act did not apply to exempt from income tax an
amount equal to the cash equivalent of the scholarship because (per Oliver LJ) it applied **a**
only to income 'arising from' a scholarship and it was inapt to describe a notional sum
measured by an amount equal to the cost to the provider as 'arising from' the scholarship
or because (per Watkins LJ) the benefit of the exemption was given only to the recipient
of the scholarship. It followed that the cash equivalent of the benefit provided was to be
treated as an emolument of the taxpayer, and the appeal would accordingly be allowed
(see p 15 *f* to p 16 *c*, p 18 *f*, p 19 *d* to *h* and p 20 *a b*, post).   **b**

Decision of Goulding J [1981] 1 All ER 506 reversed.

Notes
For the taxation of benefits received by reason of employment, see 23 Halsbury's Laws
(4th edn) paras 694–696.

For scholarship income, see ibid para 1077.   **c**

For the Income and Corporation Taxes Act 1970, s 375, see 33 Halsbury's Statutes (3rd
edn) 490.

For the Finance Act 1976, ss 61, 72, see 46 ibid 1672, 1687.

Cases referred to in judgments
Hochstrasser (Inspector of Taxes) v Mayes [1959] 3 All ER 817, [1960] AC 376, [1960] 2 **d**
WLR 63, 38 TC 673, HL; affg [1958] 3 All ER 285, [1959] Ch 22, [1958] 3 WLR 215,
38 TC 673, CA, 28(1) Digest (Reissue) 326, 1164.
Stedeford (Inspector of Taxes) v Beloe [1932] AC 388, 16 TC 505, HL, 28(1) Digest (Reissue)
324, 1158.

Cases also cited   **e**
Beynon (Inspector of Taxes) v Thorpe (1928) 14 TC 1.
Blakiston v Cooper (Surveyor of Taxes) [1909] AC 104, 5 TC 347, HL.
Brumby (Inspector of Taxes) v Milner [1976] 3 All ER 636, [1976] STC 534, HL.
C v C [1979] 1 All ER 556, [1980] Fam 23, CA.
Cunard's Trustees v IRC [1946] 1 All ER 159, 27 TC 122, CA.
Hughes (Inspector of Taxes) v Bank of New Zealand [1938] 1 All ER 778, [1938] AC 366, 21 **f**
TC 472, HL.
Lindus and Horton v IRC (1933) 17 TC 442.
Ormond Investment Co Ltd v Betts (Inspector of Taxes) [1928] AC 143, 13 TC 400, HL.
Turner (Surveyor of Taxes) v Cuxon (1888) 22 QBD 150, 2 TC 422, DC.

Appeal   **g**
The Crown appealed against the order of Goulding J dated 6 November 1980 ([1981] 1
All ER 506, [1981] STC 28) allowing appeals by the taxpayers, Malcom James Wicks and
Maurice Johnson, from a decision of the Commissioners for the Special Purposes of the
Income Tax Acts dismissing the taxpayers' appeals against assessments to income tax
under s 61(1) of the Finance Act 1976 in respect of scholarship awards paid to their
children by the trustees of an educational trust established by the taxpayers' employers. **h**
The facts are set out in the judgment of Lord Denning MR.

D C Potter QC and Robert Carnwath for the Crown.
F Heyworth Talbot QC and Graham Aaronson for the taxpayers.

Cur adv vult **j**

13 November. The following judgments were read.

LORD DENNING MR. ICI have established an educational trust. It is for the benefit
of the sons and daughters of their higher paid employees, that is those whose salary is
£7,500 a year upwards. ICI have paid into the trust fund about £1m a year. Out of it the

trustees have awarded scholarships for the sons and daughters at the universities. Their

a value ranges from £200 to £600 a year, or even more. The awards go to about 2,500 students a year.

Now it is quite clear that the students are not themselves liable for tax on these scholarships. But the Crown claims that their fathers are liable to tax. The Crown says that the amount of the scholarship is to be added to the father's income, and that he is to be taxed on it as if it was part of his emoluments. The Crown says that this follows

b because the scholarships are confined to students whose fathers are employed by ICI. These scholarships, says the Crown, are 'fringe benefits' which are to be treated, under modern legislation, as if they were part of the income of the employee himself.

Two cases have been brought before the courts to test the position.

Martin Wicks is a student at King's College, Cambridge. His father is in the agricultural division of ICI. His home is in Stockton-on-Tees. He is reading for an

c honours degree in natural sciences. He applied for a grant from the county of Cleveland, which is their local education authority. The county paid his tuition fees at the university. They also made him a grant of £409 towards his maintenance. They knew that that would not be sufficient for him to manage on. They thought that a student needed £1,100 for his maintenance. But they said that his parents ought to contribute £691 so as to bring his total maintenance up to £1,100.

d It was in those circumstances that Martin applied for one of the ICI scholarships. He was eligible for it because on his examination results he had obtained a place at the university, and his father was a higher paid employee of ICI. His salary was about £10,000 a year. The trustees awarded Martin a scholarship of £600 in all, made up of £400 basic award and £200 merit award.

It is that award which gives rise to this case. The Crown says that the £600 award is

e to be added to the father's salary and that tax is to be paid by the father on the total. In the assessment on the father, they inserted this addition: 'Benefit—I.C.I. Educational Trust £600.'

Christine Johnson is a student at the University of Newcastle. Her father is in the petro-chemicals division of ICI. Her home is in Middlesbrough. She is reading medicine, and has done exceptionally well. She too applied for a grant from the local education

f authority. They paid her tuition fees at the university. They made her a grant of £542 towards her maintenance, but they said that her parents ought to contribute £558 so as to bring her total maintenance up to £1,100. Christine applied for one of the ICI scholarships. The trustees awarded her £460. This was £260 as a basic award and £200 as a merit award. The Revenue assessed her father on his salary of about £10,000 a year, and added this item: 'I.C.I. Educational Trust £460.'

g So the problem is this. The Crown says that the father is liable to pay tax on the amount of the scholarship as if it were part of his own emoluments. They regard it as a 'fringe benefit' which has become taxable under s 61 of the Finance Act 1976.

Before 1976

Before 1976 each father was chargeable to tax under Sch E on the 'emoluments

h therefrom', that is the 'emoluments from' his employment. The word 'emolument' covers any advantage which can be turned to pecuniary account. The word 'therefrom' brings in the test of causation. In order that any pecuniary advantage can be taxable in the hands of the employee, the employment has to be the causa causans of the money being received. The payment must be made as a remuneration or reward for his services. It is not sufficient for the employment to be the causa sine qua non. Nor is it

j sufficient to say that the employee would not have received it unless he had been an employee. Thus, when ICI gave financial assistance to any of their employees who wanted to buy a house or to move house, the employee was held not liable to tax on the amount. The payment was a housing grant. It was not a reward or return for his services. So he was held not taxable on it: see *Hochstrasser (Inspector of Taxes) v Mayes* [1959] 3 All ER 817 esp at 822, 823–824, [1960] AC 376 esp at 389, 392, 38 TC 673 at 705–706, 708 per Lord Simonds and Lord Radcliffe.

The Finance Act 1976
   Thereafter many employers granted 'fringe benefits' to their employees. The *a* employers used them as a means of giving benefits to their employees free of tax. So much so that in 1976 Parliament enacted a comprehensive clause designed to make fringe benefits taxable in the hands of the recipients. They did so by s 61 of the Finance Act 1976, which is in these terms:

> '(1) . . . where in any year a person is employed in director's or higher-paid *b* employment and—(a) by reason of his employment there is provided for him, or for others being members of his family or household, any benefit to which this section applies; and (b) the cost of providing the benefit is not (apart from this section) chargeable to tax as his income, there is to be treated as emoluments of the employment, and accordingly chargeable to income tax under Schedule E, an amount equal to whatever is the cash equivalent of the benefit.
> (2) The benefits to which this section applies are accommodation (other than *c* living accomodation), entertainment, domestic or other services, and other benefits and facilities of whatsoever nature (whether or not similar to any of those mentioned above in this subsection) . . .'

I will take the important phrases in order.

d

'By reason of his employment'
   It seems to me that the words 'by reason of' are far wider than the word 'therefrom' in the 1970 Act. They are deliberately designed to close the gap in taxability which was left by the House of Lords in *Hochstrasser (Inspector of Taxes) v Mayes*. The words cover cases where the fact of employment is the causa sine qua non of the fringe benefits, that is *e* where the employee would not have received fringe benefits unless he had been an employee. The fact of employment must be one of the causes of the benefit being provided, but it need not be the sole cause, or even the dominant cause. It is sufficient if the employment was an operative cause, in the sense that it was a condition of the benefit being granted. In this case, the fact of the father being employed by ICI was a condition of the student being eligible for an award. There were other conditions also, *f* such as that the student had sufficient educational attainments and had a place at a university. But still, if the father's employment was one of the conditions, that is sufficient. If two students at a university were talking to one another, both of equal attainments in equal need, and the one asked the other, 'Why do you get this scholarship and not me?' he would say, 'Because my father is employed by ICI.' That is enough. The scholarship was provided for the son 'by reason of the father's employment'.

g

'The cash equivalent of the benefit'
   This section is designed to overcome the evasion of tax by giving 'fringe benefits'. These fringe benefits are often in kind and not in cash. They may be such as not to be able to be turned to pecuniary account. Nevertheless Parliament intends them to be *h* taxed. It does so by saying that tax is to be charged on 'an amount equal to whatever is the cash equivalent of the benefit'.
   But, if the fringe benefit is in cash and not in kind, then it seems to me that the tax is to be charged on the cash. There is no need to seek for a cash equivalent when the benefit is in cash. So the section should be interpreted as if it read: '. . . and accordingly chargeable to income tax under Sch E [on] the cash (when the benefit is in cash) or [on] *j* an amount equal to whatever is the cash equivalent of the benefit (when the benefit is in kind).' In short, when the benefit is paid in cash, the cash is itself to be treated as an emolument of the employment. So the 'emolument' here was the actual sum paid in cash to the son. It was paid 'by reason of' the father's employment. So prima facie it is chargeable by s 61 and is taxable as if it was part of the emoluments of the father.

'Provision made by his employer'

a   Even if I were wrong in thinking that these scholarships were awarded 'by reason of the employment' of the father, nevertheless the statute contains a 'deeming' provision. Section 72(3) says that when a fringe benefit is provided by his employer it is deemed to be 'by reason of his employment'.

In this case the provision of the scholarship was made by the educational trust. This in turn was provided with funds by ICI. Does that mean that the benefit is provided by
b   ICI? I think so. If this were not so, it would be an easy way for any employer to evade the tax. He could form a subsidiary company, provide it with funds with which to provide fringe benefits for his employees. To avoid such a result, we must hold that the benefit is provided by the persons 'at whose cost the provision is made'. That is, in this case, by ICI. So the benefit is in any event 'deemed' to be made 'by reason of [the father's] employment'.

c

Result of 1976 Act

If I were to stop at this point, I would hold that these scholarships were fringe benefits which were taxable in the hands of the employee, either as being emoluments 'by reason of his employment' or, alternatively, as being provision made 'by his employer', and so 'deemed' to be made for him by reason of his employment.
d   But now I come to the decisive question in this case. Are these scholarships exempt by reason of s 375 of the Income and Corporation Taxes Act 1970? It says, under the cross-heading 'Other exemptions':

'(1) Income arising from a scholarship held by a person receiving full-time instruction at a university, college, school or other educational establishment shall
e   be exempt from income tax, and no account shall be taken of any such income in computing the amount of income for income tax purposes.

(2) In this section "scholarship" includes an exhibition, bursary or any other similar educational endowment . . .'

Scholarships

Those words are very wide. They seem to me to cover these two cases exactly and to
f   exempt the fathers from tax. The Crown argues against it in two ways.

First, it refers to the words 'cash equivalent of the benefit' in s 61(1) of the Finance Act 1976. It says that the 'cash equivalent' is a notional sum and not income. This argument appealed to the commissioners, but it does not appeal to me. When the benefit is paid in cash, it is income. When the benefit is given in kind, it is still income to be assessed at a cash equivalent. Here it is paid in cash. It is 'income', and within the wide words of
g   s 375.

Second, it refers to the history of the section going back to 1920. It says that at that time the words only applied when the scholarship holder is himself the person to be taxed. Likewise they only applied in 1970. So even today the Crown says the words only apply when the scholarship holder is the person to be taxed.

I do not agree with this fall back on history. When Parliament in 1976 made fringe
h   benefits taxable, it made several express exceptions to it. It said nothing about scholarships because there was no need to do so. They were already exempt by the wide words of s 375.

In short, I would not myself limit the beneficial provision in s 375 by reference to history. These scholarships are the young people's own income. Parliament clearly intended that there should be no income tax paid on them. They are not the father's
j   income, and he should not be taxed on them.

Conclusion

Taking s 61 of the 1976 Act alone, I think that these scholarships were provided for members of the employee's household 'by reason of his employment', and that the amounts paid to the son and daughter are to be treated as emoluments of the

employee. The fathers would be chargeable to tax on them by s 61, except for the
general provision in s 375 of the 1970 Act. This gives a wide exemption for all *a*
scholarships. It frees scholarship moneys from tax, either in the hands of the scholarship
holder or in the hands of his father or anyone else. This is as it should be. It was the view
held by Goulding J. I agree with him. I would dismiss the appeal.

OLIVER LJ. We are here concerned with a taxing statute, and it is trite law that the
subject is not to be taxed save by clear words. That is, I think, a fortiori the case where *b*
it is sought to tax him on moneys which he has never personally received. Nevertheless,
that said, I find the wording of the sections on which the Crown relies, taken in the
context of the express legislative purpose which emerges clearly from the fasciculus of
sections of which they form part, to be too clear to permit of any different conclusion
from that reached by the Special Commissioners. The purpose of ss 60 to 72 of the
Finance Act 1976 was to bring into charge for tax purposes the pecuniary value of all *c*
kinds of benefits conferred by employers on their directors and senior managers which
do not directly form part of the emoluments of their employment but which, because
paid for by or at the instance of the employer, enable them to enjoy a standard of life
substantially higher than that which could be sustained if reliance had to be placed solely
on their own cash resources. That is quite clearly the purpose and it is not for this court
to question or to evaluate the social justification for the legislation. The legislature may *d*
have cast the net wider than it needed to and even wider than, objectively, it should have
done. It may seem a pity, at a time of grave educational economies, that any application
of legislative provision should have the result of impeding or discouraging a proper and
benevolent educational endeavour; but that cannot, in my judgment, justify the court in
adopting a construction of the statutory provisions at variance with what, with tolerable
clarity, these provisions expressly say.   *e*
    Lord Denning MR has already referred, in his judgment, to the words of the relevant
sections and I will not repeat them, beyond referring to what seem to me to be a number
of critical phrases on which the main part of the argument has focused. In the first place
this chapter of the 1976 Act and s 61 in particular are directed to sums of money or other
benefits which are provided 'by reason of his [ie the director's or employee's]
employment', a phrase which will have to be considered in the context of the second *f*
argument advanced by the taxpayer. Secondly, that which is to be brought into charge
is, in the words of s 61(1), 'to be treated as emoluments of the employment, and
accordingly chargeable to income tax under Schedule E'. In other words, as counsel for
the taxpayers submits, and this is common ground, it is or is to be treated as income, for
income tax is a tax on income.
    Thirdly, what is brought into charge is not the benefit which is received by the *g*
employee or the member of his family but 'an amount equal to whatever is the cash
equivalent of the benefit'; and s 63(1) and (2) contains a formula for arriving at the cash
equivalent. The amount brought into charge under s 61 is, by s 63(1), the amount equal
to 'the cost of the benefit, less so much (if any) of it as is made good by the employee to
those providing the benefit'. Section 63(2) defines the 'cost' of the benefit as 'the amount
of any expense incurred in or in connection with its provision, and . . . includes a proper *h*
proportion of any expense relating partly to the benefit and partly to other matters'. Just
to complete the references on this part of the case, the expression 'those providing the
benefit' in s 63(1) is a reference back to s 61(3) which provides that, for relevant purposes,
'the persons providing a benefit are those at whose cost the provision is made'.
    It will be necessary to come back to these sections in connection with the question
raised by the taxpayers whether the benefits claimed to be taxable here ever were *j*
provided 'by reason of' the taxpayers' employment, but I can leave them for the moment,
having indicated what seem to me to be the salient points, and turn to s 375 of the
Income and Corporation Taxes Act 1970.
    Again I need not set out the provisions of the section in extenso. It exempts from
income tax, and directs that there be excluded from computation for tax purposes,

'Income arising from a scholarship held by a person receiving full-time instruction' at
a one or other of the specified types of educational establishment.

   Counsel for the Crown's submissions raised the question whether in any event the
sums paid to the taxpayers' children in the two appeals before us could be said to be
'income' from a scholarship, since neither had any enforceable right to receive them nor,
in any real sense, were they annual payments. The proper analysis, he suggested, was
that the scholarships in this case were merely voluntary grants from time to time
b resolved to be distributed by the trustees in the same way as the retirement allowance
paid to the former headmaster of Bradfield College in *Stedeford (Inspector of Taxes) v Beloe*
[1932] AC 388, 16 TC 505. I think that there is a good deal to be said for this view of the
matter and the more so because, in sub-s (2) of s 375, there appears a definition which
seems to suggest that what the legislature was there contemplating was income from an
endowed scholarship. But counsel for the Crown is content to deal with the case on the
c footing that the scholarships actually paid do constitute 'income from a scholarship' and
it is unnecessary to decide the point since, either way, the submission of counsel for the
taxpayers remains unaffected. His submission is that whatever be the nature of the grant
made to the scholarship holder we are not concerned with that but with the notional cash
equivalent which is statutorily deemed to form part of the parents' emoluments. Since,
by definition, an emolument is income, the notional sum included in it is income and
d the question therefore is not: what is the nature of the scholarship? but: does that which
is the cash equivalent of the cost of provision of the scholarship and which is statutorily
deemed to be income constitute 'income arising from the scholarship held by the
taxpayer's child'?

   That is the short, indeed the only, question on this part of the case and counsel for the
taxpayers submits that it is susceptible of only one answer. It becomes part of the
e taxpayer's income because the benefit of the scholarship has been provided to the child.
That which triggers off the notional addition to the parent's emoluments is the receipt by
the child of the scholarship. Therefore, the submission is, it arises from the scholarship
and, since it is, ex concessis, income, it is 'income arising from a scholarship' and so
exempt from tax.

   The submission is an engagingly simple one but it is not one by which I find myself
f able to feel persuaded.

   In the first place, I find myself unable to read s 375 as affecting or exempting any
income other than that of the holder of the scholarship. Certainly the legislative history
appears, as counsel for the Crown suggests, to support such a construction. The section
dates back to the Finance Act 1920 and counsel for the Crown suggests that its purpose
was simply to put scholarships which conferred on the holder a vested right to receive
g annual amounts (and which might therefore have been considered to be the income of
the recipient for tax purposes) on the same footing as scholarships of the *Stedeford
(Inspector of Taxes) v Beloe* type, that is voluntary grants, which could not be so
considered. Quite clearly, it was not the purpose of the section to protect the income of
a scholarship fund itself from taxation, for that is the income out of which the scholarship
is paid and not income arising *from* the scholarship; and the legislature patently did not
h contemplate the income as being that of anyone other than the holder of the scholarship,
for the exemption from tax is not absolute. It applies only to income from a scholarship
held by a person with a particular qualification, namely that he is receiving *full-time*
instruction at some educational establishment. But in any event and even assuming that
the exemption were aptly expressed to cover the income of some person other than the
scholarship holder, I do not feel able to accept the submission of counsel for the taxpayers
j that the amount deemed to be included in the emoluments of the employee can properly
be described as income 'arising from' a scholarship. Accepting that that which triggers
off s 61 of the 1976 Act is the provision of the benefit in the form of a scholarship, it
seems to me to be wholly inappropriate to describe a notional sum measured by an
amount equal to the cost to the provider as 'arising from a scholarship held etc'. That is
a sum which, if it can be said to 'arise from' anything, arises simply from the

circumstances that a benefit of the type envisaged in s 61 has been provided for the child
or dependant of an employee, whether or not taxable in the hands of the child or *a*
dependant. The assumption is, of course, that the benefit will not indeed be taxable in
the hands of the dependant recipient. That is the rationale of the charging provisions.
Section 61(2) enumerates a number of specific non-taxable benefits, non-taxable, that is,
apart from the section, to which the section applies, but it goes on, in terms, to apply it
to 'other benefits and facilities of whatsoever nature (whether or not similar to any of
those mentioned above in this subsection)'. It then goes on to exclude certain benefits *b*
such as the use of motor cars, loans at reduced rates and options which are themselves
expressly made taxable by ss 64 to 68. It is beyond argument that this subsection applies
to a benefit of the type here in question and I do not consider that a rational construction
of s 375 can fairly be held to exclude its operation.
   For these reasons, therefore, I cannot agree with the learned judge's conclusion as
regards the interplay of ss 61 and 375.   *c*
   But that, of course, is not the end of the case, because s 61 brings into charge only those
benefits which are provided 'by reason of [the] employment'. The learned judge, because
of the view which he took of the ambit of s 375 of the Income and Corporation Taxes Act
1970, found it unnecessary to deal with this point. The Special Commissioners concluded
that, leaving aside the deeming provisions of s 72(3) to which I will come in a moment,
the scholarship was not provided by reason of the employment of the scholarship *d*
holder's parent even though the relationship to an employee of the company was the
essential sine qua non without which he could not have qualified for an award at all.
Junior counsel for the taxpayers has, with persistence and ability, sought to uphold that
decision both as a conclusion of fact which cannot be challenged in this court and as based
on a correct construction of the section. On an initial reading of the Special
Commissioners' reasons for decision, it appeared to me that they were at one point saying *e*
that although the employment of the father might be one reason for the award to the
child it was not the only reason and that, therefore, the benefit could not be said to have
been provided 'by reason of' that employment. If that is what they were saying, I cannot
think that they were right, for the section does not say 'by reason *only*' of the employment,
and, if the correct approach is to look for the events or circumstances which brought
about the award, the employment was clearly one of them. But junior counsel for the *f*
taxpayers submits that that was not in fact the commissioners' approach and he points to
the last sentence of para 9(10) of their decision which certainly affords support for his
contention. There the commissioners say this: 'We do not infer that ICI's purpose was to
remunerate its employees or to add an additional perquisite to their emoluments' (see
[1981] 1 All ER 506 at 513, [1981] STC 28 at 35).
   That, junior counsel for the taxpayers submits, reflects the correct approach. He has *g*
been good enough to refer the court to a number of authorities, but the point is perhaps
best encapsulated in Hochstrasser (*Inspector of Taxes*) v Mayes [1959] 3 All ER 817, [1960]
AC 376, 38 TC 673, where the question was as to the taxability of payments made by an
employer to employees in respect of losses sustained by them on the sales of their houses
when they were transferred by their employer to another part of the country. The
House of Lords held that these payments were not taxable under Sch E under the *h*
description of 'salaries, fees, wages, perquisites or profits whatsoever therefrom', the
'therefrom' meaning 'arising or accruing from an office or employment'. Viscount
Simonds postulated the issue as turning on whether the employment was the causa
causans or only the sine qua non of the benefit and pointed out that it was for the Crown
to demonstrate that the payment was a reward for the employee's services. The same
distinction had been made in the judgment of Jenkins LJ in the Court of Appeal, and *j*
junior counsel for the taxpayers points to the learned Lord Justice's equation of 'profits
of their employment' with 'remuneration accruing to them by reason of their
employment' (see [1958] 3 All ER 285 at 294, [1959] Ch 22 at 52, 38 TC 689 at 696).
Lord Radcliffe said ([1959] 3 All ER 817 at 823, [1960] AC 376 at 391, 38 TC 673 at 707):

   'The test to be applied is the same for all. It is contained in the statutory

requirement that the payment, if it is to be the subject of assessment, must arise
"from" the office or employment . . . For my part, I think that their meaning [that
is, the meaning of the words of the statute] is adequately conveyed by saying that,
while it is not sufficient to render a payment assessable that an employee would not
have received it unless he had been an employee, it is assessable if it has been paid
to him in return for acting as or being an employee . . . [He concluded that] the
circumstance that brought about his entitlement to the money was not any services
given by him but his personal embarrassment in having sold his house for a smaller
sum than he had given for it.'

The essence of the submission of junior counsel for the taxpayers is that the words 'by
reason of' in s 61 are merely a synonymous alternative for the word 'from' as construed
in that case and that they must be given the same meaning, so that the question to be
asked (and on which the commissioners, as a finding of fact, answered in the negative) is
simply: was the child's scholarship a remuneration or reward for the father's services?
He points out that the original charge to Sch E in the Income Tax Act 1842 was on
salaries etc 'accruing by reason of' an office or employment and that the fasciculus of
sections with which this appeal is concerned is headed 'Benefits derived by Company
Directors and others From their Employment'. Thus, the argument runs, unless it can
be said, and the question is one of fact for the commissioners, that the benefit under
consideration is provided, in effect, as part of the consideration for the rendering of the
employees' services, it is not a benefit arising from or provided by 'reason of' the
employment.
    Whilst I see the attraction of an argument which attributes to the legislature an
admirable consistency in the expression of its intention, I find myself unable to accept
the submissions of junior counsel for the taxpayers on this point. Accepting once more
that the subject is not to be taxed except by clear words, the words must, nevertheless, be
construed in the context of the provisions in which they appear and of the intention
patently discernible on the face of those provisions from the words used. As it seems to
me, the obvious intention of this legislation, presumably in an attempt to produce
fairness between taxpayers, is to impose tax on the value of those otherwise untaxed
advantages which the employee enjoys because he is employed, advantages which may
not even accrue to him directly but which, because of their receipt by a member of his
household, benefit him by relieving him of an expense which he might otherwise expect
to bear out of his own resources. These are, in many cases, by definition, benefits which
could not in any ordinary sense be attributed to a reward for the employee's services, for
instance the use of a car for the private purposes of a member of the employee's family
or an interest-free loan to one of his relatives, and to restrict the operation of the section
in the way suggested by junior counsel for the taxpayers would, in my judgment,
virtually deprive it of any operation at all in the case of benefits other than those provided
to the employee himself. Speaking only for myself I do not in the case of this legislation,
find the philosophical distinction between a causa causans and a causa sine qua non
helpful. I see no reason why a benefit 'derived' from the employment (to use the words
of the chapter title) necessarily has to be invested with an intention on the part of the
employer to remunerate the employee for the performance of his duties. One is directed
to see whether the benefit is provided by reason of the employment and in the context
of these provisions that, in my judgment, involves no more than asking the question,
'What is it that enables the person concerned to enjoy the benefit?' without the necessity
for too sophisticated an analysis of the operative reasons why that person may have been
prompted to apply for the benefit or to avail himself of it.
    For the reasons which the commissioners gave, however, the question is, I think,
academic in the instant case, because they found, and in my judgment rightly found,
that the benefit with which the appeal is concerned was provided by the employer so that
s 72(3) deems it to be provided by reason of the employment.
    Counsel for the taxpayers do not dispute that, although s 61(3) is introduced by the
words 'For the purposes of this section and sections 62 and 63 below', that subsection is

to be applied in determining whether, for the purposes of s 72(3), a given provision is
made 'by the employer'. The argument has centred on the question whether, having   **a**
regard to the fact that the scholarships concerned were provided by the trustees from
moneys already affected by an exhaustive trust, admittedly created by and at the expense
of the employer, the benefit (ie the scholarship) can be said to have been provided 'at the
cost of' the employer. The Special Commissioners thought that it was a wholly
inaccurate use of language to say that the scholarships were provided 'at the cost' of the
trustees. They said ([1981] 1 All ER 506 at 513, [1981] STC 28 at 35):   **b**

> 'Each year it cost ICI the sum which ICI contributed to the fund to provide the
> awards paid out of the fund in that year. To the extent to which what ICI paid into
> the fund in the year was in excess of the awards paid out, the cost was in part
> attributable to awards paid out in subsequent years. We see no reason to distinguish
> the income of the trust fund from the capital in identifying the source.'
>   **c**

I find myself unable to disagree with that analysis on the facts of this case. The summary
of accounts in the Special Commissioners' reasons shows that each year ICI paid to the
trustees sums to finance the awards (see [1981] 1 All ER 506 at 511, [1981] STC 28 at
33). It is true that at the end of each of the years 1977 and 1978 a surplus was carried
forward and that the funds were increased during those years by substantial amounts of
deposit interest, but these, after deducting income tax, were insufficient to cover the   **d**
administration expenses. In the year ended 30 September 1979 there was an excess of
net deposit interest over expenses. This appeal is concerned with scholarships awarded
in November 1978 and paid over the ensuing year and if one asks, therefore, the question
'Who paid the cost of the scholarships?' I think, as the Special Commissioners thought,
that there can, realistically, be only one answer. It is submitted, however, that at least
where the benefit is provided out of the income of an endowment, the cost of the   **e**
provision cannot be attributed to the settlor, for, the endowment having been irrevocably
devoted to trusts under which the settlor has no interest, the income never was his, so
that he has been deprived of nothing. That may be so and I would prefer to leave the
point until it arises. It is not this case.

In my judgment the Special Commissioners' decision was correct, and I would
therefore allow this appeal.   **f**

WATKINS LJ. This is, we are told, the first case to come before this court involving
consideration of the provisions of s 61 of the Finance Act 1976. The question for
determination is whether the taxpayers, employees of ICI, have received fringe benefits
on which they are liable to pay tax under Sch E for the year 1978–79, because their
children, whilst at university or college, have been awarded scholarships from the ICI   **g**
educational trust.

Although it has laudable purposes which are in the main to provide benefits for
educational charities and scholarships for educational instruction and it is conscientiously
and impeccably administered by the trustees, this is unfortunately a non-charitable
trust. In the few short years of its existence it has brought welcome financial relief to
many young students who exist on government grants. It is to be regretted, therefore,   **h**
that it has become a means by which, so the Crown contends, a taxable fringe benefit has
been put into the hands of a person who is either a director of or in the higher-paid
employment of ICI.

I have to acknowledge, however, albeit with reluctance, that without regard for the
moment to the provisions of s 375 of the Income and Corporation Taxes Act 1970 this
contention is, in my view, well founded. The effects of the provisions of s 61(1) and (2)   **j**
allow of no other conclusion than that by reason of his employment with ICI there has
been provided for members of each taxpayer's family a cash benefit which is to be treated
as an emolument of the taxpayer's employment and is accordingly liable to tax under
Sch E.

I have been greatly assisted in reaching this conclusion by the construction put on s 61
by Lord Denning MR, with which in every respect I entirely agree.

a　Therefore, I am left only with the problem of deciding whether (1) the children of the taxpayers can be said to receive an income from a scholarship and (2) if that be so, do the provisions of s 375(1) of the 1970 Act exempt the taxpayers from paying tax on the value of the scholarships although they are fringe benefits to them.

Section 375(1) and (2), under the cross-heading 'Other exemptions', provides:

b　'(1) Income arising from a scholarship held by a person receiving full-time instruction at a university, college, school or other educational establishment shall be exempt from income tax, and no account shall be taken of any such income in computing the amount of income for income tax purposes.

(2) In this section "scholarship" includes an exhibition, bursary or any other similar educational endowment.'

Counsel for the Crown submits that a voluntary payment from a discretionary trust, c　for instance, is not as a general rule deemed to be income. Thus, it is not chargeable to tax as though it were income in the hands of the recipient. But I did not understand him to say, at any rate with confidence, that scholarship moneys received by the taxpayers' children, if received regularly over a period of years, could not constitute an exception to what he called the general rule and become, therefore, income chargeable to tax.

The ICI trust, so it seems to me, provides for repetitive awards to one beneficiary of a d　scholarship over a number of years. As counsel for the taxpayers said, and I agree with him, the award was practically automatic once entitlement to it was first established. Furthermore, I see nothing in the provisions of s 375 which excludes from the term 'income arising from a scholarship' moneys which have come from a source which is not an endowment fund.

So I would be disposed to hold that the taxpayers' children received income arising e　from a scholarship on which they themselves would not, of course, because of the exempting provisions affecting scholarships pay tax.

This enables me to deal with the second and crucial question which cannot be answered without attention to the history of s 375. It was first enacted as s 28 of the Finance Act 1920, when fringe benefits and taxation of them were unheard of. At that time the provisions of s 28 could only conceivably be taken, in my view, having regard to the Act f　as a whole to give exemption from tax to the recipient of the scholarship income. The only benefit derived out of this by anyone else arose out of s 21 of the 1920 Act which made provision for a reduction of assessable income in respect of children in the calculation of whose income, if any, scholarship income was to be excluded. A similar provision now appears in s 10(5) of the 1970 Act.

Nothing occurred, so far as I know, during the 50 years between the 1920 Act and the g　1970 Act which serves to disturb the effect I have attributed to s 28. There is nothing in the 1970 Act which disturbs it. On the contrary, its layout, its division into parts and so forth, when compared with the 1920 Act serves to reinforce the conclusion that the benefit of s 28 was given to the recipient of the scholarship alone and goes to show that s 375 provides for a similar singular benefit of exemption from taxation.

Does the 1976 Act affect this view or in any other way prove that s 375 imposes itself h　on s 61?

I listened with an interest approaching awe to the arguments which revolved around the words 'cash equivalent of the benefit' used in s 61(1) as this equivalent in cash of a gift in kind was translated from income into a notional sum and back again in the course of an exhausting and I confess for me meaningless intellectual exercise which both parties seemed at times to contend assisted them.

i　When an inspector seeks to impose a tax on a fringe benefit he wants to know, if it was a gift in cash, the amount of it and, if it was a gift in kind, the cash value of it. There surely cannot be anything notional about the results of those two usually elementary exercises. Each of them is a sum of money capable of being regarded as income and if the circumstances warrant it income from a scholarship.

The submission of counsel for the Crown that, if it was intended that a fringe benefit in the form of a scholarship income should be exempt from the provisions of s 61, the

1976 Act would have expressly provided for it I find more appealing and to some extent persuasive.

But in the end, what must govern the answer to this second question is, comparing it with the 1920 Act, the construction of the 1970 Act. Section 375 lies squarely within that part in which there are set out a variety of exemptions from tax for the benefit exclusively of he who receives the material income. There is nothing within the provisions of s 375 which leads me to think that it is different in the extent of its beneficial effect from any of the sections which surround it. So I find that it is the recipient of the scholarship income alone who is exempt from tax.

Accordingly, although I derive no pleasure from saying so, I too would allow this appeal.

Appeal allowed. Leave to appeal to House of Lords granted.

Solicitors: *V O White* (for the taxpayers); *Solicitor of Inland Revenue.*

Edwina Epstein   Barrister.

International Military Services Ltd v Capital and Counties plc

CHANCERY DIVISION
SLADE J
7, 8, 10 DECEMBER 1981

Landlord and tenant – Business premises – Compensation for disturbance – Amount of compensation – Amount altered by amendment of statutory provision – Landlord serving notice to terminate tenancy before amendment coming into force – Landlord entitled to possession after amendment coming into force – Amount of compensation payable by landlord to tenant on quitting premises – Whether compensation payable according to statutory scale in force at date of landlord's notice or at date tenant quitting holding – Landlord and Tenant Act 1954, s 37(2) – Local Government, Planning and Land Act 1980, Sch 33, para 4(1) – Landlord and Tenant Act 1954 (Appropriate Multiplier) Regulations 1981.

Section 193 of and para 4(1)[d] of Sch 33 to the Local Government, Planning and Land Act 1980, which received the royal assent on 13 November 1980, amended s 37(2)(b)[b] of the Landlord and Tenant Act 1954 by altering the amount of compensation payable to a tenant under s 37(1)[c] of the 1954 Act on quitting business premises in circumstances in which s 37(2)(b) applied. The amount of compensation was altered from the rateable value of the premises to the rateable value increased by 'the appropriate multiplier' as prescribed by the Secretary of State by statutory instrument. On 17 December 1980 the landlords of business premises to which s 37(2)(b) applied served on the tenants a notice under s 25[d] of the 1954 Act terminating the tenancy on 24 June 1981. On 21 January 1981 the Secretary of State made the Landlord and Tenant Act 1954 (Appropriate Multiplier) Regulations 1981[e] which came into force on 25 March 1981. The regulations provided that the appropriate multiplier for the purposes of s 37(2)(b) was $2\frac{1}{4}$ times the rateable value of the premises. On 19 April 1981 the landlords acquired an indefeasible right to possession on 24 June 1981 and on the latter date the tenants quit. The question arose whether the compensation to which the tenants were entitled was limited to the

---

a   Paragraph 4(1) is set out at p 24 *g h*, post
b   Section 37(2) is set out at p 24 *d*, post
c   Section 37(1) is set out at p 24 *a b*, post
d   Section 25, so far as material, is set out at p 23 *b* to *d*, post
e   The 1981 regulations are set out at p 25 *g*, post

rateable value of the premises or was $2\frac{1}{4}$ times that value. The tenants issued an
a originating summons for the determination of that question. The landlords contended
that the amendment of s 37(2)(b) of the 1954 Act by para 4(1) of Sch 33 to the 1980 Act
was not effective until the 1981 regulations came into force on 25 March 1981 and
therefore was not applicable where the landlord served a s 25 notice terminating the
tenancy before that date.

b **Held** – The tenants were entitled to compensation amounting to $2\frac{1}{4}$ times the rateable
value, for the following reasons—
(1) Since under s 37(1) of the 1954 Act the only event which entitled the tenants to
compensation was the actual quitting of the premises, the amount of their entitlement
was to be assessed in accordance with the law as it stood at the date they quit the premises,
viz 24 June 1981, which was the date when the entitlement arose (see p 26 j, p 27 a b and
c p 30 f, post).
(2) The amendment of s 37(2)(b) made by para 4(1) of Sch 33 to the 1980 Act came into
full force and effect on the coming into force of the 1981 regulations on 25 March 1981,
ie before 24 June 1981 (see p 25 c to e, p 26 e f and p 30 f, post).
(3) Although the effect of applying s 37(2)(b) of the 1954 Act in its amended form and
in conjunction with the 1981 regulations but without regard to the date of service of the
d landlord's s 25 notice involved a degree of retrospective effect, in that the amount of
compensation which the landlords anticipated they would have to pay at the then going
rate when they served their s 25 notice was subsequently increased, nevertheless—
(a) the effect of the amendment was merely to increase the quantum of a prospective
right to compensation, which right the tenants already possessed before the amendment
came into force on 25 March 1981 (see p 28 h, p 29 c and p 30 f, post); Re 14 Grafton Street,
e London W 1 [1971] 2 All ER 1 distinguished;
(b) the landlords had not obtained an indefeasible right to possession before the
amendment came into force on 25 March 1981, but even if they had they would not
have been deprived of that right by the coming into force of the amendment (see p 28
h j, p 29 c and p 30 f, post); Re 14 Grafton Street, London W 1 [1971] 2 All ER 1
distinguished;
f (c) at the time they served their s 25 notice the landlords ought already to have been
put on notice by the passing of the 1980 Act that a new scale of compensation might be
introduced in the near future (see p 29 a and p 30 f, post);
(d) any expectation which the landlords had that they would only have to pay
compensation at the rate then current when they served their s 25 notice was at best a
vague and inchoate right which could be affected retrospectively without offending
g against the presumption against retrospectivity (see p 29 a b and p 30 f, post);
(e) the language of s 37 of the 1954 Act, as amended, was, in any event, plain and
unambiguous and drew no distinction between tenants who quit pursuant to a s 25
notice served before the coming into force of the 1981 regulations on 25 March 1981 and
those who quit pursuant to such a notice served after that date (see p 29 f to j and p 30
e f, post).

h **Notes**
For compensation for disturbance on quitting business premises and the amount of
compensation, see 27 Halsbury's Laws (4th edn) paras 518–519.
For the Landlord and Tenant Act 1954, ss 25, 37, see 18 Halsbury's Statutes (3rd edn)
559, 576.
For the Local Government, Planning and Land Act 1980, s 193, Sch 33, para 4, see
50(2) ibid 1385, 1421.

Cases referred to in judgment
*Grafton Street (14), London W 1, Re, De Havilland (Antiques) Ltd v Centrovincial Estates
(Mayfair) Ltd* [1971] 2 All ER 1, [1971] Ch 935, [1971] 2 WLR 159, 31(2) Digest
(Reissue) 939, 7705.

Lauri v Renad [1892] 3 Ch 402, CA, 44 Digest (Repl) 287, 1166.
Tate & Lyle Food and Distribution Ltd v Greater London Council [1981] 3 All ER 716, [1982] **a**
1 WLR 149.

Originating summons
By an originating summons dated 30 June 1981 the plaintiffs, International Military
Services Ltd, the former tenants of premises at St Andrew's House, 40 Broadway, London
SW1, sought as against the defendants, their former landlords, Capital and Counties plc **b**
(1) determination of the question whether under and by virtue of s 37 of the Landlord
and Tenant Act 1954, as amended by the Local Government, Planning and Land Act
1980, and in the events which happened, the plaintiffs became entitled on quitting the
premises on 24 June 1981 to recover from the defendants by way of compensation an
amount determined in accordance with the provisions of the 1954 Act as amended, (2)
if the answer to question (1) was in the affirmative, determination of the question **c**
whether the amount to which the plaintiffs became entitled on quitting the premises on
24 June 1981 was (a) £45,180 (the rateable value of the premises) or (b) £101,655 (2¼
times the rateable value, (3) payment of the amount determined in answer to question
(2), (4) interest pursuant to the Law Reform (Miscellaneous Provisions) Act 1934 on that
amount from 24 June 1981 to the date of judgment, (5) further or other relief, and (6)
costs. The facts are set out in the judgment. **d**

John Cherryman for the plaintiffs.
John Stuart Colyer QC and *Michael R King* for the defendants.

Cur adv vult
                                                                                    e
10 December. **SLADE J** read the following judgment: In this originating summons the
plaintiffs are International Military Services Ltd. The defendants are Capital and
Counties plc, formerly called Capital and Counties Property Company Ltd. They were
also formerly the plaintiffs' landlords in respect of certain premises in London.
   The Landlord and Tenant Act 1954 in certain circumstances gives a tenant the right
to receive compensation on leaving the premises. By a notice of 17 December 1980 **f**
served pursuant to s 25 of the 1954 Act, the defendants gave notice terminating the
plaintiffs' tenancy of the premises on 24 June 1981. It is common ground that the
plaintiffs quit the premises on 24 June 1981 and then became entitled to compensation. Effectively, the principal issue in the case now is whether such compensation falls
to be assessed in accordance with a statutory scale of compensation which was in force on
24 June 1981, as the plaintiffs assert, or in accordance with a scale which was in force on **g**
17 December 1980, as the defendants assert.
   By a lease of 13 May 1976 (the 1976 lease), made between the defendants of the one
part and Four Millbank Nominees Ltd of the other part, certain office premises
comprising the fourth floor at St Andrew's House, 40 Broadway, London SW1 were
demised by the defendants to Four Millbank Nominees Ltd for a term from 23 February
1976 to 25 March 1978 at a yearly rent of £32,000. By a deed of variation and **h**
supplemental lease (the 1977 deed) dated 18 April 1977, and made between the same
parties, the 1976 lease was varied so that it should thenceforth be construed as granting
a term from 26 February 1976 to 24 June 1981, instead of a term expiring on 25 March
1978. The defendants thereby demised office premises comprising the second floor
annexe and the third floor at St Andrew's House to Four Millbank Nominees Ltd from
7 February 1977 for the residue of the term of the 1976 lease as varied by the 1977 deed, **j**
at the additional yearly rent of £34,000. By an assignment dated 19 July 1978 Four
Millbank Nominees Ltd assigned the second, third and fourth floor premises to the
plaintiffs for all the residue of the term created by the 1976 lease and 1977 deed. I will
call these premises collectively 'the premises'.
   At all material times the rateable value of the premises has been £45,180. It is
common ground that the tenancy is one to which Part II of the 1954 Act applies.

At this point it will be convenient to summarise some of the history of the legislation relevant to the present case. Section 24(1) of the 1954 Act, as amended, provides: 'A tenancy to which this Part of this Act applies shall not come to an end unless terminated in accordance with the provisions of [Part II] of this Act . . .' It further confers on the tenant under such tenancy the right, subject to certain conditions, to apply to the court for a new tenancy (a) if the landlord has given notice under s 25 to terminate the tenancy or (b) if the tenant has made a request for a new tenancy in accordance with s 26. Section 25(1) confers on the landlord the right to terminate a tenancy to which Part II of the Act applies 'by a notice given to the tenant in the prescribed form specifying the date at which the tenancy is to come to an end', though this subsection has effect subject to later provisions in the Act. Section 25(2) provides:

'Subject to the provisions of the next following subsection, a notice under this section shall not have effect unless it is given not more than twelve nor less than six months before the date of termination specified therein.'

Section 25(5) provides;

'A notice under this section shall not have effect unless it requires the tenant, within two months after the giving of the notice, to notify the landlord in writing whether or not, at the date of termination, the tenant will be willing to give up possesssion of the property comprised in the tenancy.'

Section 25(6) requires a landlord's notice under the section to state whether he would oppose an application to the court under Part II of the Act for the grant of a new tenancy and, if so, to state on which grounds mentioned in s 30 he would do so.

Section 29 provides:

'(1) Subject to the provisions of this Act, on an application under subsection (1) of section twenty-four of this Act for a new tenancy the court shall make an order for the grant of a tenancy comprising such property, at such rent and on such other terms, as are hereinafter provided.

(2) Where such an application is made in consequence of a notice given by the landlord under section twenty-five of this Act, it shall not be entertained unless the tenant has duly notified the landlord that he will not be willing at the date of termination to give up possession of the property comprised in the tenancy.

(3) No application under subsection (1) of section twenty-four of this Act shall be entertained unless it is made not less than two nor more than four months after the giving of the landlord's notice under section twenty-five of this Act or, as the case may be, after the making of the tenant's request for a new tenancy.'

Section 30(1) begins with the following words:

'The grounds on which a landlord may oppose an application under subsection (1) of section twenty-four of this Act are such of the following grounds as may be stated in the landlord's notice under section twenty-five of this Act or, as the case may be, under subsection (6) of section twenty-six thereof, that is to say . . .'

There then follow seven paragraphs, of which I need only read para (g):

'subject as hereinafter provided, that on the termination of the current tenancy the landlord intends to occupy the holding for the purposes, or partly for the purposes, of a business to be carried on by him therein, or as his residence.'

Section 31(1) provides:

'If the landlord opposes an application under subsection (1) of section twenty-four of this Act on grounds on which he is entitled to oppose it in accordance with the last foregoing section and establishes any of those grounds to the satisfaction of the court, the court shall not make an order for the grant of a new tenancy.'

Section 37(1), in its amended form, provides:

'Where on the making of an application under section twenty-four of this Act the court is precluded (whether by subsection (1) or subsection (2) of section thirty-one of this Act) from making an order for the grant of a new tenancy by reason of any of the grounds specified in paragraphs (e), (f) and (g) of subsection (1) of section thirty of this Act and not of any grounds specified in any other paragraph of that subsection or where no other ground is specified in the landlord's notice under section 25 of this Act or, as the case may be, under section 26(6) thereof, than those specified in the said paragraphs (e), (f) and (g) and either no application under the said section 24 is made or such an application is withdrawn, then, subject to the provisions of this Act, the tenant shall be entitled on quitting the holding to recover from the landlord by way of compensation an amount determined in accordance with the following provisions of this section.'

The words in this subsection from 'or where' to 'is withdrawn' were inserted by s 11 of the Law of Property Act 1969 as from 1 January 1970. I pause to comment that no reliance has been placed by either side in the present case on the phrase 'subject to the provisions of this Act'. These words appear to refer to s 38 of and para 5 of Sch 9 to the 1954 Act, and possibly to other provisions. Section 37(2), up to 25 March 1981, when it was amended in circumstances which I will describe later, read:

'The said amount shall be as follows, that is to say,—(a) where the conditions specified in the next following subsection are satisfied it shall be twice the rateable value of the holding, (b) in any other case it shall be the rateable value of the holding.'

It is common ground that this is a para (b) case, because the conditions of s 37(3) are not satisfied.

Section 37(5)(a), so far as material, provides:

'For the purposes of subsection (2) of this section the rateable value of the holding shall be determined as follows:—(a) where in the valuation list in force at the date on which the landlord's notice under section twenty-five . . . is given a value is then shown as the annual value (as hereinafter defined) of the holding, the rateable value of the holding shall be taken to be that value . . .'

On 13 November 1980 the Local Government, Planning and Land Act 1980 received the royal assent. Part V (ss 28–47) amended the General Rate Act 1967 so as to abolish the statutory requirement for quinquennial revisions of rateable values. The legislature considered that this would or might necessitate certain changes to the provisions governing the appropriate multiplier for the purpose of s 37(2)(a) and (b) of the 1954 Act. Section 193 provided that the enactments specified in Sch 33 to the 1980 Act should have effect subject to the amendments specified in that schedule. Paragraph 4 of Sch 33, which was headed 'Landlord and Tenant Act 1954', reads as follows:

'(1) In subsection (2) of section 37 of the Landlord and Tenant Act 1954 (compensation where order for new tenancy precluded on certain grounds) the words "the product of the appropriate multiplier and" shall be inserted after the word "be" in paragraphs (a) and (b).

(2) The following subsections shall be added after subsection (7) of that section—

"(8) In subsection (2) of this section "the appropriate multiplier" means such multiplier as the Secretary of State may by order made by statutory instrument prescribe.

(9) A statutory instrument containing an order under subsection (8) of this section shall be subject to annulment in pursuance of a resolution of either House of Parliament.".'

In the absence of any further provision, the provisions of para 4 of Sch 33 would presumably have come into operation as soon as the 1980 Act received the royal assent. However, sub-s (5) of s 47, which was the last of the sections in Part V of the 1980 Act dealing with rates, made it clear that such was not the intention. Section 47(5) provided:

a   'The provisions of Schedule 33 to this Act which give the Secretary of State power by order to prescribe multipliers and which are specified in subsection (6)(a), (b) and (c) below shall not have effect until he exercises the power conferred by them.'

Section 47(6), so far as it is material, provided:

'The provisions of Schedule 33 mentioned in subsection (5) above are—(a) paragraph 4 . . .'

b   The wording of s 47(5) is not, perhaps, entirely happy. First, the use of the words 'which give the Secretary of State power by order to prescribe multipliers' are a little puzzling, since the provisions of Sch 33 specified in s 47(6) do much more than give the Secretary of State 'power by order to prescribe multipliers'. Second, it is not entirely clear what meaning is to be attached to the phrase 'until he exercises the power conferred by them' if, as in the event which happened in the present case, the Secretary of State makes c   an order prescribing multipliers, but declares by his order that it is not to come into operation until a later date. In my judgment, however, and I do not think there is really any substantial dispute about this, the only proper sense that can be given to s 47(5) is to construe it as meaning that the amendment to the various specified statutory provisions relating to multipliers, including s 37(2) of the 1954 Act, which are to be effected by Sch 33 are not to have effect until the date on which an exercise of the Secretary of State's d   power to prescribe multipliers is expressed by his order to have operative effect. Any other construction of s 47(5) could result in a twilight period between the making of a statutory instrument and the date on which the relevant regulations came into operation, during which there was no appropriate multiplier at all for the purpose of s 37(2) of the 1954 Act.

I now revert to the history of the present case. On 17 December 1980, that is more e   than a month after the 1980 Act received the royal assent, the defendants served a written notice of that date on the plaintiffs terminating their tenancy of the premises on 24 June 1981. The notice, as usual, required the tenants within two months after the giving of the notice to notify the landlords in writing whether or not they would be willing to give up possession of the premises on the specified date. It further stated that the defendants would oppose an application to the court under Part II of the Act for the grant of a new f   tenancy, on the ground that, on the termination of the current tenancy, the defendants intended to occupy the premises for the purposes of a business to be carried on by them in the premises, that is to say on the ground specified in s 30(1)(g) of the 1954 Act.

On 21 January 1981 the Secretary of State for the Environment, in exercise of the new powers conferred on him, made the Landlord and Tenant Act 1954 (Appropriate Multiplier) Regulations 1981, SI 1981/69. These provided:

g   '1. These regulations may be cited as the Landlord and Tenant Act 1954 (Appropriate Multiplier) Regulations 1981 and shall come into operation on 25th March 1981.

2. The appropriate multiplier for the purposes of paragraphs (a) and (b) of section 37(2) of the Landlord and Tenant Act 1954 shall be 2¼.'

h   These regulations were subject to annulment in pursuance of a resolution of either House of Parliament within forty days of 2 February 1981, which was the day on which the regulations were laid before Parliament (see para 4 of Sch 33 to the 1980 Act and s 5 of the Statutory Instruments Act 1946). The regulations never were annulled and so came into operation on 25 March 1981.

In the meantime, by a letter of 6 February 1981, the plaintiffs gave the defendants j   notice that they would not be willing to give up possession of the premises on the date specified in the defendants' s 25 notice. The plaintiffs, however, made no application to the court for a new tenancy. The last date on which it would have been open to them to do so would have been 18 April 1981. They let that date pass by, so that by 19 April the defendant landlords had acquired an indefeasible right to possession of the premises on the following 24 June 1981. By a letter of 16 April 1981 the defendants had claimed, first, that the plaintiffs were not entitled to any compensation at all under s 37 of the

1954 Act and, second, that, even if some compensation was payable, the scale of compensation should be ascertained by reference to the date on which the s 25 notice had *a* been given.

The plaintiffs duly quit the premises on 24 June 1981. In the light of the information as to the defendants' attitude which they had received, they issued an originating summons on 30 June 1981, in which they sought the following relief:

'(1) That it may be determined whether, under and by virtue of the provisions of *b* Section 37 of the Landlord and Tenant Act 1954 (as amended) and in the events which have happened, the Plaintiff became entitled on quitting the premises on the 24th June 1981 to recover from the Defendant by way of compensation an amount determined in accordance with the provisions of the said Act.

(2) If the answer to question (1) is in the affirmative, that it may be determined whether the said amount which the Plaintiff became entitled on quitting the premises on the 24th June 1981 to recover from the Defendant was: (a) £45,180 *c* (being the rateable value of the premises) or (b) £101,655 (being two and one quarter times such rateable value).

(3) Payment of the amount determined in answer to question (2) above.

(4) Interest pursuant to the Law Reform (Miscellaneous Provisions) Act 1934 on the said amount from the 24th June to the date of Judgment. *d*

(5) Further or other relief.

(6) Costs.'

To complete the history, by a letter of 2 October 1981 the defendants accepted that compensation is payable to the plaintiffs under the 1954 Act, and said that in the circumstances the only issue was one as to quantum.

I now turn to consider the nature and extent of the plaintiffs' right to compensation. *e* Very briefly, they contend that question 2 of the originating summons should be answered in the sense of alternative (b). The defendants claim that it should be answered in the sense of alternative (a).

The effect of the 1981 regulations, when read in conjunction with s 47(5) and (6)(a) of the 1980 Act, was in my judgment that as from 25 March 1981 both the regulations themselves and the amending provisions of para 4 of Sch 33 to the 1980 Act, relating to *f* multipliers, came into full force and effect. The consequences were as follows. First, s 37(2) of the 1954 Act thenceforth took effect in its amended form so as to read:

'The said amount shall be as follows, that is to say,—(a) where the conditions specified in the next following subsection are satisfied it shall be the product of the appropriate multiplier and twice the rateable value of the holding, (b) in any other case it shall be the product of the appropriate multiplier and the rateable value of the *g* holding.'

Second, as from 25 March 1981 the 'appropriate multiplier' for the purpose of these two paragraphs became 2¼.

According to the terms of s 37(1) of the 1954 Act, as amended, there are a number of conditions precedent (some of them alternative) which have to be fulfilled if a tenant is *h* to be entitled to compensation on quitting the holding. The relevant conditions which have been satisfied in the present case are the following: (1) the landlord has served on the tenant a notice under s 25; (2) the notice has specified no ground other than one of the grounds specified in para (*e*), (*f*) and (*g*) of s 30 of the 1954 Act; and (3) the tenant has made no application for a new tenancy.

Nevertheless, though conditions of the nature specified in s 37(1) have to be satisfied *j* before a tenant's right to compensation can arise, the only event which entitles the tenant to compensation is the actual quitting of the holding. If for any reason whatever he does not quit, he does not become entitled to compensation. The relevant wording of s 37(1) of the 1954 Act is:

'... then, subject to the provisions of this Act, the tenant shall be entitled on a quitting the holding to recover from the landlord by way of compensation an amount determined in accordance with the following provisions of this section.'

The word 'then', in my judgment, merely means 'in that event', that is to say if the earlier conditions specified in the subsection are fulfilled. The entitlement arises on the quitting of the holding (*and not before*). In my judgment, therefore, it is quite plain that the amount of the entitlement must be assessed in accordance with the law as it stands at the date of the quitting. I am not sure that this point is really in dispute.

b The argument of counsel on behalf of the defendants, if I have understood it correctly, in essence involves the submission that the amendments to s 37 of the 1954 Act, which were introduced by the combined effect of s 193 of and Sch 33, para 4, to the 1980 Act and of the 1981 regulations which altered the scale of compensation to which tenants quitting the premises were to be entitled should be read with some implied limitation to the effect that they were not to apply in respect of tenants who quit their premises

c following the service of a landlord's s 25 notice which had been served before 25 March 1981. The latter is, of course, the day when the 1981 regulations came into operation. Any other reading of the relevant statutory provisions would in his submission involve giving them retrospective effect. He submitted that it is to be presumed that a statute, or statutory instrument, of a substantive rather than a procedural nature is not to have

d retrospective effect; and that the 1980 Act and the 1981 regulations read together can only have retrospective effect, if a clear legislative intention of this nature has been demonstrated. Such intention, in his submission, has not been shown.

In support of his submissions, counsel for the defendants relied heavily on a decision of Brightman J in *Re 14 Grafton Street, London W 1* [1971] 2 All ER 1, [1971] Ch 935. The headnote to that case, omitting immaterial references to authorities at the end, reads as follows ([1971] Ch 935):

e 'On September 27, 1969, the landlords gave notice under section 25 of the Landlord and Tenant Act 1954 terminating a business tenancy of certain premises on April 1, 1970. The notice required the tenants to notify the landlords within two months whether they would give up possession or not; it also stated that any application for a new tenancy would be opposed by the landlords on the basis that

f the premises were to be reconstructed and that the tenants could not claim compensation unless an application was made to the court for a new tenancy. The tenants' intention to vacate the premises was communicated to the landlords by a letter dated October 13, 1969. On October 22, 1969, the Royal Assent was given to the Law of Property Act 1969 which came into force on January 1, 1970. Section 11 of that Act amended section 37(1) of the Act of 1954 with the effect that a tenant

g was entitled to compensation without having first applied to the court for a new tenancy. On February 11, 1970, the tenants inquired about compensation. The landlords denied liability. On the tenants' summons seeking compensation to be paid:—

Held, (1) that in order to be entitled to compensation for disturbance a tenant must, first, have served a counter notice on the landlord under section 29(2) of the

h Act of 1954, stating that he was unwilling to vacate the premises and secondly, under section 37(1) of the Act (before amendment), he must have applied to the court for a new tenancy; that a counter notice which expressed willingness to quit was irrevocable; and that, accordingly, after October 13, the tenants could not give a notice of unwillingness to quit and had lost their right to apply to the court and the landlords, in turn, had acquired an indefeasible right to obtain possession on

j April 1, 1970, without paying compensation.

(2) That on its true construction the amendment to section 37(1) of the Act of 1954, not being procedural, could not have retrospective effect so as to revive the tenants' right to compensation; and that, accordingly, the tenants were not entitled to compensation.'

I accept the submission of counsel for the defendants that this case is authority for the

proposition that the amendment to the law which was effected by the relevant statutory
provisions in the present case was substantive rather than procedural. This point has not *a*
been in dispute. Likewise, the case is authority for the proposition that enactments are
not to be construed so as to have a retrospective operation unless their language is such
as to require such a construction. Brightman J quoted with approval a number of
passages from judgments in earlier cases which established this principle. I need only
read one. In *Lauri v Renad* [1892] 3 Ch 402 at 420–421 Lindley LJ said:

> 'It certainly requires very clear and unmistakable language in a subsequent Act of *b*
> Parliament to revive or recreate an expired right. It is a fundamental rule of English
> law that no statute shall be construed so as to have a retrospective operation unless
> its language is such as plainly to require such a construction; and the same rule
> involves another and subordinate rule to the effect that a statute is not to be
> construed so as to have a greater retrospective operation than its language renders
> necessary.'   *c*

Brightman J pointed out that, in the events which had happened, the landlords on any
footing 'had an indefeasible right to recover possession on 1st April 1970, without the
payment of compensation . . .' (see [1971] 2 All ER 1 at 7, [1971] Ch 935 at 944). His
conclusion, on the retrospectivity point, is to be found summarised in the following
words ([1971] 2 All ER 1 at 9, [1971] Ch 935 at 947):   *d*

> 'Under the Act of 1954, by virtue of the unopposed notice served by the landlords,
> they had acquired the right before the commencement of the 1969 Act to future
> possession of business premises without compensation. If the 1969 Act is construed
> in such a way as to deprive them of that right, that Act would in my view be
> retrospective. Under the Act of 1954, by virtue of the notice served by the landlords,
> the tenants at one time had a contingent right to compensation, ie a right to *e*
> compensation contingent on the landlords successfully opposing an application
> made by the tenant for an order for the grant of a new tenancy. The tenants lost
> that right before the 1969 Act came into operation, by reason of their failure to take
> certain steps open to them. If the 1969 Act is construed in such a way as to revive
> that right, that Act would in my view be retrospective.'   *f*

Having then decided that the 1969 Act could not properly be described as procedural,
Brightman J concluded ([1971] 2 All ER 1 at 10, [1971] Ch 935 at 949):

> 'In the result I dismiss the application, on the ground that the 1969 Act did not
> deprive the landlords of their right to recover possession without payment of
> compensation and did not revive the tenants' lost right to compensation.'   *g*

I pause to comment that there is one obvious point of distinction between the facts of
the *14 Grafton Street* case and those of the present case. In the former case the effect of the
construction contended for by the tenants was to revive a right to compensation which,
before the relevant legislation, had been wholly lost. In the present case, there is no
question of any right of the tenants to compensation ever having been wholly lost. At
very most, what has happened is that the introduction of the new legislation increased *h*
the quantum of a prospective right which the tenants had at all relevant times. On the
facts of the present case, as counsel for the plaintiffs pointed out, the landlords did not,
on any footing, obtain an indefeasible right to possession of the premises until 19 April
1981, that is to say several weeks after the relevant statutory provisions came into
effect. On the present facts, therefore, the relevant statutory provisions, even if applied
according to their letter, will not have any retrospective effect at all in the strict sense. *j*
When they came into operation, even if they are construed in the manner for which the
plaintiffs contend, they operated as between the plaintiffs and the defendants merely for
the future and not for the past.

Counsel for the defendants suggested that they did at least deprive the defendants of
an inchoate right, in the sense that, as from the service of their s 25 notice, the defendants
could reasonably have expected that, if the plaintiff tenants made no application under

s 24, the defendant landlords would both be able to get possession on 24 June 1981 and
a only have to pay compensation according to the tariff in force on 17 December 1980. I
do not find this argument compelling. First, the s 25 notice was served after the 1980
Act had received the royal assent, so that anyone interested had been warned that a new
'appropriate multiplier' might be introduced in the near future. Second, counsel for the
defendants referred me to no authority in support of his proposition that the presumption
against retrospectivity applies in respect of such vague inchoate rights as those of the
b defendants as at 17 December 1980 on which he relies for this purpose.

I attach rather more weight to another of his points. He observed that, though on the
timetable of the present case the defendants had not yet acquired an indefeasible right to
possession by 25 March 1981, they could have done so, if their s 25 notice had been
served rather earlier; in this contingency, the defendants before 25 March 1981 might
have acquired an indefeasible right to recover possession at a date later than 25 March
c 1981. On this hypothetical timetable, the coming into operation of the 1981 regulations
would still not have deprived the defendants of an indefeasible right to possession, so that
the case would not even then have been on all fours with the *14 Grafton Street* case.
Nevertheless, the regulations would have altered the scale of compensation which the
defendants would have had to pay to the plaintiffs, as the price of this indefeasible right,
if and when the plaintiffs left the holding. As counsel for the defendants pointed out, the
d service of the landlord's s 25 notice is the first of the steps which begins the process of
determining the tenant's rights to compensation; when he serves it, he may be influenced
by, inter alia, consideration of the amount of the compensation which he may in due
course have to pay to the tenant on quitting. I therefore accept that, by analogy with the
14 Grafton Street case, the plaintiffs' construction of the relevant statutory provisions,
which makes no distinction between cases where landlords' s 25 notices have been served
e before 25 March 1981 and those where they have been served after that date, could be
said to involve a degree of retrospective effect in the hypothetical circumstances
postulated by counsel for the defendants. For this reason I also accept that they should
not be construed so as to have greater retrospective effect than the lanaguage renders
necessary.

Nevertheless, subject to the points arising on s 47(5) of the 1980 Act, with which I have
f already dealt, the language of the relevant statutory provisions seems to me plain and
unambiguous. When they are read together, ss 47 and 193 of the 1980 Act, para 4 of Sch
33 to that Act and the 1981 regulations in my judgment make it quite clear that as from
25 March 1981 the new amendments to paras (*a*) and (*b*) of s 37(2) of the 1954 Act are to
apply in the case of every tenant who thereafter quits a holding, provided only that the
other conditions of s 37(1) have been satisfied. It would have been easy for Parliament
g in the 1980 Act, or for the Secretary of State in the 1981 regulations, expressly to provide
that the amending provisions should not apply in cases where the landlord's s 25 notice
had been served before 25 March 1981. No such exception was made, and I can see no
sufficient grounds for implying one.

On the facts of the present case, the plaintiffs on quitting the premises on 24 June 1981
for the first time acquired the benefit of what Brightman J in the *14 Grafton Street* case
h [1971] 2 All ER 1 at 5, [1971] Ch 935 at 942 described as 'a debt created by statute, on
which the tenant may sue in other proceedings if necessary'. For the purposes of
ascertaining the amount of that debt one must, in my judgment, look at the provisions
of s 37 of the 1954 Act as they stood in their reamended form at 24 June 1981, when the
right arose. In this reamended form they were, in my judgment, unequivocal. When
they are so looked at, it is plain that the tenants' compensation falls to be calculated with
j the application of an appropriate multiplier of 2¼ to the rateable value of the holding.

This, I think, is really the end of the defendants' case, but in deference to the argument
of counsel for the defendants I should refer to one or two other points. He drew my
attention to a number of suggested capricious results or anomalies, which might follow
if the plaintiffs' construction of the relevant statutory provisions were correct. In
particular, he pointed out that the plaintiffs' construction involves taking the rateable
value of the premises as at 17 December 1980 but the 'appropriate multiplier' as at 24

June 1981, when the landlords' notice expired and the plaintiffs quit the premises. This, he submitted, means that like would not be related to like. He contended that one *a* would expect the provisions for an 'appropriate multiplier' to be prescribed so as to ensure that in any given case the relevant multiplier would be ascertained as at the same day as that which falls to be multiplied is ascertained.

I think that, so far as it goes, this comment is a fair one. On the other hand, in my judgment, it has to be accepted that the statutory purpose of the introduction of the new system of 'appropriate multipliers' was, as counsel for the plaintiffs submitted, to effect *b* from time to time a rough and ready uplift in the amount of the statutory compensation to be given to tenants under s 37 of the 1954 Act, in place of the automatic uplift that they would otherwise have enjoyed by virtue of the system of automatic quinquennial rating valuations, which was abolished by the 1980 Act. The introduction of a new 'appropriate multiplier' was, I think, bound to produce some anomalies, particularly in the early stages. Nor do the anomalies appear to me all to lie in one direction, when the *c* competing constructions are considered. If counsel for the defendants were right in submitting that the relevant statutory provisions have no application in any case where the landlord's s 25 notice has been served before 25 March 1981, this would mean that landlords who chose to serve a s 25 notice during the period between 21 January 1981 (when the 1981 regulations were made) and 25 March 1981 (when they came into effect) would escape the liability to pay compensation on the higher scale, even if the tenant quit *d* the premises long after 25 March 1981. It is hard to see any statutory purpose reflected in this result.

Counsel for the defendants did raise some other points, but I hope he will forgive me if I do not refer to all of them. For, once it is accepted that the relevant amendment of s 37(2) of the 1954 Act and the introduction of the new 'appropriate multiplier' came into full force and effect on 25 March 1981, as I think it must be accepted, it seems to me *e* inevitably to follow, on the clear wording of the section as amended, that the plaintiffs' rights fall to be determined in accordance with the tariff which represented the law when they quit the premises. The words of the subsection as amended are entirely apt to apply to the plaintiffs' situation on 24 June 1981, and the defendants, in my judgment, can point to no statutory provision which enables them to escape from their full effect.

In answer to the questions raised by paras 1 and 2 of the originating summons, I *f* therefore propose to answer question 1 in the affirmative sense and question 2 in the sense of alternative (b).

[The court then heard submissions from counsel with respect to interest.]

SLADE J. It is common ground that, on the basis of my judgment, the plaintiffs are *g* entitled to interest on the amount of £101,655 from 30 June 1981 to the date of judgment. The plaintiffs have not asked for interest in respect of the period from 24 to 30 June, I understand, because, although they had formally quit the premises on 24 June, they did continue to have certain use of the premises for certain purposes for the next six days.

The question arises as to the rate of interest which should be awarded to the plaintiffs *h* in the discretion of the court. In this context I have been assisted by a reference to the recent decision of Forbes J in *Tate & Lyle Food and Distribution Ltd v Greater London Council* [1981] 3 All ER 716, [1982] 1 WLR 149. The facts of that case were very different, but he made some pertinent observations as to matters of principle. In particular, he pointed out that there are considerable differences between personal injury cases and cases involving injury to business concerns. He said, for example ([1981] 3 All ER 716 at 722, *j* [1982] 1 WLR 149 at 154):

'. . . I do not think the modern law is that interest is awarded against the defendant as a punitive measure for having kept the plaintiff out of his money. I think the principle now recognised is that it is all part of the attempt to achieve restitutio in integrum. One looks, therefore, not at the profit which the defendant wrongfully a   made out of the money he withheld (this would indeed involve a scrutiny of the defendant's financial position) but at the cost to the plaintiff of being deprived of the money which he should have had. I feel satisfied that in commercial cases the interest is intended to reflect the rate at which the plaintiff would have had to borrow money to supply the place of that which was withheld. I am also satisfied that one should not look at any special position in which the plaintiff may have been; one should disregard, for instance, the fact that a particular plaintiff, because

b   of his personal situation, could only borrow money at a very high rate or, on the other hand, was able to borrow at specially favourable rates. The correct thing to do is to take the rate at which plaintiffs in general could borrow money. This does not, however, to my mind, mean that you exclude entirely all attributes of the plaintiff other than that he is a plaintiff. There is evidence here that large public companies of the size and prestige of these plaintiffs could expect to borrow at 1% over MLR,

c   while for smaller and less prestigious concerns the rate might be as high as 3% over MLR. I think it would always be right to look at the rate at which plaintiffs with the general attributes of the actual plaintiff in the case (though not, of course, with any special or peculiar attribute) could borrow money as a guide to the appropriate interest rate. If commercial rates are appropriate I would take 1% over MLR as the proper figure for interest in this case.'

d   This was the rate which, subject to certain qualifications, Forbes J awarded.

   Counsel for the plaintiffs has told me on instructions, and this has not been disputed, that the plaintiffs are a wholly-owned subsidiary of the Ministry of Defence but, nevertheless, run their business as a commercial business. There is, I think, no doubt at all that the defendant company similarly runs its business. This can, I think, fairly be described as a commercial dispute in which, on the basis of my judgment, the plaintiffs

e   have been kept out of the greater part of a debt which has been due to them since 24 June 1981. I say 'the greater part', because in October a payment was made by the defendants on account. In all the circumstances of the case, I think that commercial rates are appropriate to apply for the purpose of assessing the amount that should be paid to the plaintiffs. I think that, on the facts which I know, it is right to treat these particular plaintiffs as being plaintiffs of standing and prestige, who, with the benefit of these

f   attributes, would be able to borrow at a more favourable rate than smaller and less prestigious concerns. I am told that minimum lending rate ceased to have effect on 21 September 1981 and that from then on the equivalent rate has been the clearing bank base rate.

   In all the circumstances, following the guidance of the *Tate & Lyle* case, I propose to award the plaintiffs interest on the sum of £101,655 from 30 June 1981 to judgment at

g   the rate of 1% over minimum lending rate from 30 June to 21 September, and at 1% above the clearing bank base rate from 21 September onwards until judgment. Credit, however, is to be given to the defendants for the interest on the sum of £45,180 which has already been paid by them to the plaintiffs.

   I think that it may be desirable that there should be some further definition of the

h   clearing bank base rate for the purpose of the order which I am making. Subject to further submissions, I think a convenient way of dealing with this would be for the plaintiffs' counsel and the defendants' junior counsel to agree and sign a minute embodying these provisions in clear workable form.

Order accordingly.

21 December. Slade J refused an application by the defendants for a certificate under s 12 of the Administration of Justice Act 1969 to appeal direct to the House of Lords.

Solicitors: *Clifford-Turner* (for the plaintiffs); *Debenham & Co* (for the defendants).

Jacqueline Metcalfe   Barrister.

Re G (a minor) (wardship: costs)

COURT OF APPEAL, CIVIL DIVISION
ORMROD AND FOX LJJ
21, 29 JANUARY 1982

Ward of court – Practice – Official Solicitor's costs – Appointment of Official Solicitor as guardian ad litem – Payment of Official Solicitor's costs – Supreme Court Act 1981, s 51(1).

Child – Care – Local authority – Wardship proceedings by local authority – Appointment of Official Solicitor as guardian ad litem – Appointment by court or on application of party – Payment of Official Solicitor's costs – Supreme Court Act 1981, s 51(1).

Where a minor in care who is the subject of wardship proceedings initiated by the local authority is made a party to the proceedings and the Official Solicitor is appointed the minor's guardian ad litem in the proceedings, there is no rule that the Official Solicitor's costs must be paid by the local authority, since the appointment of the Official Solicitor is not a necessary step in the proceedings, as the minor is not a necessary party and is only made a defendant in order to enable the Official Solicitor to take part in the proceedings. Nor does the fact that the local authority and the Official Solicitor are both public bodies acting in the ward's interest in pursuance of their public duty require that there should be no order as to costs between them. Instead, the trial judge has an unfettered discretion under s 51(1)[a] of the Supreme Court Act 1981 to deal with the payment of the Official Solicitor's costs. In exercising that discretion the judge should have regard to (i) the fact that the Official Solicitor is funded out of central funds (and therefore the judge should feel free to invoke his assistance without being constrained by the effect on the costs of the parties) and (ii) the fact that the Official Solicitor, like other guardians ad litem, can only be appointed as such where he consents so to act and that he can make his consent conditional on his being given a full or partial indemnity as to his costs. However, where the judge of his own motion invokes the assistance of the Official Solicitor, he should have regard to the fact that the Official Solicitor will then rarely, if ever, have the protection of an indemnity and that it may in such circumstances be just to order that his costs be borne by either or both parties (ie the local authority or the parents). Similarly, where the Official Solicitor is appointed on the application of one or both parties it may be just to order that the whole or part of his costs be borne by the party who applied for his appointment. On the other hand, where the local authority has initiated the proceedings, the desirable course is for the authority and the Official Solicitor to agree between themselves how the Official Solicitor's costs are to be dealt with, and where the proceedings are between the parents, acting bona fide in the minor's interest, no order as to the Official Solicitor's costs need be made if it is thought appropriate not to do so (see p 35 d e g h and p 36 a to h, post).

Fraser v Thompson (1859) 4 De G & J 659, *Eady v Elsden* [1901] 2 KB 460, *Jackson v Jackson* [1908] P 308, *Timins v Timins* [1938] 4 All ER 180 and *Re P C (an infant)* [1961] 2 All ER 308 distinguished.

Notes

For the wardship jurisdiction in relation to a local authority's powers, see 24 Halsbury's Laws (4th edn) para 580.

For the parties to wardship proceedings, see ibid para 586.

---

a   Section 51(1), so far as material, provides: 'Subject to the provisions of this or any other Act and to rules of court, the costs of and incidental to all proceedings in the civil division of the Court of Appeal and in the High Court . . . shall be in the discretion of the court, and the court shall have full power to determine by whom and to what extent the costs are to be paid.'

a The Supreme Court Act 1981, s 51, which replaced s 50 of the Supreme Court of Judicature (Consolidation) Act 1925, came into force on 1 January 1982.

Cases referred to in judgment

Eady v Elsden [1901] 2 KB 460, CA, 28(2) Digest (Reissue) 903, 2157.
Emanuel v Kirk (1885) 24 SJ 258, 33 Digest (Repl) 703, 1623.
b F (a minor) (adoption: parental consent), Re [1982] 1 All ER 321, [1982] 1 WLR 102, CA.
Fraser v Thompson (1859) 4 De G & J 659, 45 ER 256, LC & LJJ, 28(2) Digest 903, 2152.
Harbin v Masterman [1896] 1 Ch 351, [1895–9] All ER Rep 695, CA, 8(1) Digest 381, 1071.
Jackson (orse Macfarlane) v Jackson [1908] P 308, 27(2) Digest (Reissue) 766, 6116.
P v P [1981] CA Bound Transcript 312.
c P C (an infant), Re [1961] 2 All ER 308, [1961] Ch 312, [1961] 2 WLR 710, 28(2) Digest (Reissue) 903, 2160.
R (P M) an infant, Re [1968] 1 All ER 691, [1968] 1 WLR 385, 28(2) Digest (Reissue) 921, 2296.
S (infants), Re [1967] 1 All ER 202, [1967] 1 WLR 396, 28(2) Digest (Reissue) 929, 2295.
Timins v Timins [1938] 4 All ER 180, 27(1) Digest (Reissue) 479, 3483.

d
Interlocutory appeal

In wardship proceedings under the Law Reform (Miscellaneous Provisions) Act 1949 and the Guardianship of Minors Acts 1971 and 1973 initiated by the London Borough of Lewisham as plaintiffs (the local authority) in respect of two minors in their care, seeking care and control of the minors with a view to bringing adoption proceedings, on the local e authority's application the minors were made parties to the proceedings and the Official Solicitor was appointed guardian ad litem to represent them in the proceedings and to assist the court, in particular by obtaining expert reports on the minors. On 17 February 1981 Hollings J ordered that the minors should continue to be wards of court and that they should be committed to the local authority's care and control. The Official Solicitor applied for payment of his costs of the proceedings by the local authority. Hollings J, on f 17 February, ordered that the local authority should pay one-half of the Official Solicitor's costs. The local authority appealed against that order. The facts are set out in the judgment of the court.

Anthony Scrivener QC and Anita M Ryan for the local authority.
Lionel Swift QC and Paul Collins for the Official Solicitor.
g
Cur adv vult

29 January. **ORMROD LJ** read the following judgment of the court: This is an appeal by leave of the judge from an order as to costs made by Hollings J in wardship proceedings h on 17 February 1981. By his order the plaintiffs, the London Borough of Lewisham, were directed to pay one half of the costs of the Official Solicitor, who was acting as guardian ad litem of the wards. The appeal is brought on a 'friendly' basis to determine an issue which has become, in recent years, a matter of considerable importance to local authorities and to the Official Solicitor, namely: what, if any, provision should be made for the Official Solicitor's costs, as guardian ad litem of the ward, in wardship proceedings, j initiated by a local authority in what they consider to be the interests of the child or children concerned?

The problem, which is a relatively novel one, arises from two recent developments. Since the transfer of wardship cases from the Chancery Division to the Family Division by the Administration of Justice Act 1970, s 1, the number of cases has risen very considerably, and this jurisdiction is being used increasingly by local authorities,

particularly in difficult cases, in preference to proceedings in magistrates' courts. At the
same time, a policy of strict control of public spending has been adopted by the a
government, involving the imposition of 'cash limits', which means that it has become
a matter of concern to all public bodies to watch their expenditure very carefully. It is,
therefore, no longer appropriate to approach the problem raised by this appeal by saying
that the costs will have to be borne by the public either way, so it matters little out of
which public pocket they are paid. It now matters very much to the individual pockets
concerned. The parties to the appeal have each filed evidence dealing with their b
respective financial problems, which indicate the scale of their expenditure in wardship
proceedings. Though not relevant to the issues in the appeal, this clearly demonstrates
the seriousness of the issues involved in it.

Parallel with these developments, a significant change of practice seems to have taken
place. It appears to have become something of a routine in these cases to make the
children parties to the proceedings and bring in the Official Solicitor as guardian ad litem c
at a very early stage. This must have considerably increased the work load of the Official
Solicitor and his necessary expenditure.

In two cases, *Re F (a minor) (adoption: parental consent)* [1982] 1 All ER 321, [1982] 1
WLR 102 and *P v P* [1981] CA Bound Transcript 312, this court drew attention to this
new practice and questioned its value in all cases. As a result, the President has issued a
practice direction (8 December 1981) ([1982] 1 All ER 319, [1982] 1 WLR 118) to the d
effect that orders of this kind should only be made where the judge or registrar considers
there is a special reason for bringing in the Official Solicitor. This direction, which is no
more than a return to the older practice, should reduce the costs and the burden on the
Official Solicitor, and so, largely, eliminate in the future the problem raised by this
appeal. However, there are, as we were informed at the bar, a considerable number of
other cases awaiting the decision in this case. e

Counsel on behalf of the appellant local authority contended, first, that in principle, in
cases in which both a local authority and the Official Solicitor are involved in wardship
proceedings, the costs are at the unfettered discretion of the trial judge, and there is no
general rule or presumption that the local authority should pay the Official Solicitor's
costs, second, that the judge did not properly exercise his discretion in that, as shown by
the transcript of the discussion on costs, he made his order simply on the basis of f
'splitting the difference', and, third, that where two public bodies are acting in pursuance
of their public duty in the interests of the ward there should normally be no order as to
costs between them.

Counsel for the Official Solicitor submitted that the opposite approach was the proper
one, namely that the Official Solicitor's costs should be paid by the local authority which
initiated the proceedings as plaintiff unless there are special reasons to the contrary. g

There is now no specific provision in the Rules of the Supreme Court relating to the
costs of the Official Solicitor as guardian ad litem since Ord 65, r 13 was rescinded in or
about 1961. The statute (the Supreme Court of Judicature (Consolidation) Act 1925,
s 50; now s 51 of the Supreme Court Act 1981) gives the trial judge an unfettered
discretion as to costs, subject to the rules of court. No fetter, imposed by the rules of
court, applies to the present case, because Ord 62, rr 3 and 6 have no application. Prima h
facie, therefore, the question of costs as between the local authority plaintiff and the
Official Solicitor are in the unrestricted discretion of the trial judge.

The judge, as appears from the transcript, did not have the benefit of the full argument
which we have had, thanks to the efforts of counsel on each side; indeed there was
scarcely any argument at all before him and he had no reason to appreciate the gravity
of the matter, and so did not apply his mind to the underlying considerations which were j
not brought to his attention. In these circumstances he could be said, without any
disrespect, to have disposed of this matter of costs on a judgment of Solomon basis, and
so not to have exercised his discretion judicially. His order is, therefore, open to review
by this court.

The submission of counsel for the Official Solicitor is that, on the authorities on which

he relies, there is an established practice of long standing that the Official Solicitor, when
a acting as guardian ad litem, gets his costs from the plaintiff in the first place, who may,
or may not, have a right over against the defendant or some other party to recover the
amount so paid to the Official Solicitor. The cases on which he relies are *Fraser v
Thompson* (1859) 4 De G & J 659, 45 ER 256 (assignees of a bankrupt seeking to set aside
a settlement in which an infant was a defendant), *Emanuel v Kirk* (1885) 24 SJ 258 (an
action for the price of jewellery), *Eady v Elsden* [1901] 2 KB 460 (an action in tort against
b an infant for setting fire to the plaintiff's house), *Jackson v Jackson* [1908] P 308 (a nullity
suit against a respondent of unsound mind), *Timins v Timins* [1938] 4 All ER 180 (a
divorce suit against a respondent of unsound mind) and *Re P C (an infant)* [1961] 2 All ER
308, [1961] Ch 312 (a wardship involving a girl respondent and a young man).

With the exception of the last case, *Re P C (an infant)*, which requires more detailed
examination, in all these cases the Official Solicitor was acting as guardian ad litem to an
c infant who was a defendant in ordinary litigation in which the infant had to be made a
defendant to enable the plaintiff to proceed with his action. 'The appointment of the
Official Solicitor was, therefore, a *sine qua non* to the proceedings going on and being
effectively disposed of': see per Buckley J in *Re P C (an infant)* [1961] 2 All ER 308 at 312,
[1961] Ch 312 at 318. In such cases a plaintiff is obliged by RSC Ord 80, r 6, to apply to
the court for the apointment of a guardian ad litem and may not proceed with his action
d until a guardian ad litem is appointed. No such provision applies to either wardship
proceedings or proceedings concerning children under the Matrimonial Causes Act
1973. The child is not a necessary party and the case can, and usually does, proceed
without making the child a party to the proceedings. These authorities, therefore, have
no application to the present case. The analogy sought to be drawn from them is,
therefore, misleading.

e *Re P C (an infant)*, however, was a wardship case but there the father was applying for
an injunction against his daughter, the ward, personally to restrain her from associating
with a young man. She was, therefore, a necessary party to the proceedings in the sense
that the plaintiff father could not obtain the relief he sought without making the ward
a party to the proceedings and, therefore, without the appointment of a guardian ad
litem. This case is, therefore, analogous to the other cases relied on by counsel for the
f Official Solicitor.

At one point in his argument counsel for the Official Solicitor observed that the
Official Solicitor was not a welfare agency, a statement which would have startled
generations of judges exercising the custodial jurisdiction, either in wardship or under
statute, who have always regarded the Official Solicitor as an indispensable last resort
when all other welfare agencies and services have, or are likely to fail. His assistance, but
g not as a mere guardian ad litem, has enabled the court to solve many intractable 'welfare'
problems.

Wardship proceedings are, in fact, the exact converse of the cases cited by counsel for
the Official Solicitor. The children are made defendants in order to give the Official
Solicitor the locus standi of a guardian ad litem which enables him to take part in the
proceedings. In the other class of case the Official Solicitor is made guardian ad litem as
h a necessary step in the plaintiff's action. In custody cases the Official Solicitor is much
more than a mere guardian ad litem. He is at once an amicus curiae, an independent
solicitor acting for the children, an investigator, an adviser and sometimes a supervisor.
Perhaps the nearest analogy is that of counsel to a tribunal of inquiry, a relatively new
office but a valuable one. This, however, is not a new role for the Official Solicitor, as is
borne out by *The Supreme Court Practice* 1982, vol 2, p 987, para 3452A where the
j following passage is to be found:

'The Official Solicitor is a servant of the Court and may at any time be called upon
by a Judge to carry out an investigation or to assist the Court to see that justice is
done between the parties (see *Re Harbin and Masterman* ([1896] 1 Ch 351 at 368, 371
[1895–9] All ER Rep 695 at 700, 701–702), per A. L. Smith, L.J., and per Rigby,

L.J.). He is appointed to act where, if this were not done, there would be a denial or miscarriage of justice.'   *a*

For these reasons the exercise of the trial judge's discretion in the present case is not controlled by the authorities relied on by counsel for the Official Solicitor, and there is no rule of practice in wardship and custody cases which requires the court to order a plaintiff in wardship proceedings to pay the Official Solicitor's costs, unless there are special reasons to the contrary. Conversely, there is no rule of practice in such cases that the parties should pay their own costs, unless there are special reasons to the contrary. The   *b* statute (the Supreme Court of Judicature (Consolidation) Act 1925, s 50; the Supreme Court Act 1981, s 51) gives the trial judge an unfettered discretion over costs.

All that this court can properly do is to direct attention to some of the considerations which trial judges should bear in mind in reaching their decisions as to costs, which of course, must always be reached in the light of all the circumstances of the individual case.

The first and most important of these considerations is that a judge, whenever he   *c* thinks it would be right to invoke the assistance of the Official Solicitor, should feel free to do so without being constrained by anxiety about the possible effect in relation to costs on one or other, or both of the other parties to the proceedings. It is one of the many valuable functions of the Official Solicitor to provide such assistance, and he is funded by central funds for this and other purposes. This consideration applies particularly where the Official Solicitor is appointed guardian ad litem on the judge's own motion (see the   *d* Matrimonial Causes Rules 1977, SI 1977/344, r 115). That does not, of course, mean that it will not be just in some cases to order one or other of the parties to bear the costs rather than the taxpayer.

In other cases the Official Solicitor is appointed on the application of one, or sometimes both, parties either to assist generally in the interests of the child or children, or for a particular purpose, eg as in this case, to obtain a psychiatric or other expert report on the   *e* child in compliance with the rule in Re S (infants) [1967] 1 All ER 202, [1967] 1 WLR 396, and Re R (P M) an infant [1968] 1 All ER 691, [1968] 1 WLR 385. In such cases it may be just to order the Official Solicitor's costs, or a proportion of them, to be borne by the party asking for his assistance.

The Official Solicitor, like all guardians ad litem, can only be appointed if he has consented to act. This enables him, where he thinks it right, to ask for a full, or partial,   *f* indemnity for his costs. This is some protection, but where the appointment is on the judge's own motion it will rarely, if ever, be applicable.

Where the proceedings are between the parents, both of whom are acting bona fide in the interests of the child, it is not uncommon to make no order as to the costs of the proceedings.

Where a local authority has initiated the proceedings there seems to be no reason to   *g* approach the question of costs in any special way. It is to be hoped that when public bodies are involved they will be able to agree between themselves how the Official Solicitor's costs should be dealt with. If not, the matter will have to be determined by the judge in the light of all the circumstances of the case.

In the present case the judge's order can probably be supported on the foregoing considerations, but this court is not in possession of all the facts and circumstances so that   *h* if either party wishes, it would be right to send the case back to the judge to reconsider his order.

If this judgment is less helpful than the parties hoped, as it almost certainly is, the reason lies in the terms of the statute, which places the discretion so unequivocally on the trial judge that it leaves little or no room for an appellate court to lay down principles or even guidelines.   *j*

Order accordingly.

Solicitors: *R A Joy*, Catford (for the local authority); *Official Solicitor*.

Bebe Chua   Barrister.

a

Re D (J)

CHANCERY DIVISION
SIR ROBERT MEGARRY V-C
22, 23, 27 JULY, 14 OCTOBER 1981

b   *Mental health – Patient's property – Execution of will – Appeal to judge – Power of judge on appeal from master of Court of Protection – Discretion – Exercise of discretion – Whether judge having unfettered discretion on appeal – Mental Health Act 1959, ss 100(4), 102(1)(c), 103(1)(dd).*

Mental health – Patient's property – Execution of will – Application to master – Power to make will – Exercise of power – Matters to be considered – Whether execution of will ought to be stayed pending appeal – Mental Health Act 1959, ss 100(4), 102(1)(c), 103(1)(dd).

c

Mental health – Patient's property – Execution of will – Costs of application – Taxation – Costs of successful applicant – Basis on which award of costs should be made.

d   Following the death of the patient's husband in 1956, one of her daughters, A, who was divorced, went to live with the patient in her house until 1972. The patient had four other children. In 1962 the patient, who knew A intended to remarry, made a will devising and bequeathing the house and its contents to A and bequeathing the residue of her estate to the five children in equal shares. In 1972 A remarried and went to live with her husband. Shortly afterwards, the patient, who was beginning to become senile, visited A and insisted on remaining with her. In 1973 the patient's house was sold for £13,500, thus adeeming A's legacy under the will. The patient purchased a smaller house, near A, out of the proceeds of sale, but never lived in the new house and continued living with A and her husband. There was some evidence that the patient knew the devise to A was no longer effective. The expense of maintaining the patient was borne by A and her husband until November 1978 when the Court of Protection, which had control of the patient's affairs and had appointed another daughter, R, to be the patient's receiver, authorised payment out of the patient's estate of £40 a week to A. In addition, A received the patient's pension and an attendance allowance, making a total of £82 a week received by A in respect of the patient. The patient's estate was worth about £50,000. In May 1979 A and R applied to the Court of Protection, under s 103(1)(dd)[a] of the Mental Health Act 1959, for the execution of a codicil to the 1962 will, specifically devising and bequeathing to A the patient's new house and contents, in place of the adeemed legacy of the old house and contents. The respondents to the application were the patient's other three children. The patient's new house was sold later in 1979 for £22,000. The application was heard by the deputy master of the Court of Protection, who ordered the execution of a will for the patient giving A a legacy of £10,000 and bequeathing the residue of the patient's estate to her five children in equal shares with gifts over to their children and a gift over of A's share of the residue to her husband if she predeceased the patient without leaving children. A and R appealed, seeking increased provision for A out of the patient's estate. It was common ground that the 1962 will remained effective, apart from the ademption of A's legacy, and that under it the five children would take the whole of the patient's estate in equal shares. The respondents conceded that A was entitled to a greater share of the estate than the other four children in recognition of her care of, and devotion to, the patient, but the extent of that share remained in issue. The basis on which any order for costs should be made was also considered by the court.

e

f

g

h

j

Held – (1) On an appeal under s 111(1)[b] of the 1959 Act to the judge from a decision of

---

a   Section 103(1), so far as material is set out at p 42 b to e, post
b   Section 111(1) provides: 'Subject to and in accordance with rules under this Part of this Act, an
(Continued on p 38)

the master or the deputy master of the Court of Protection in regard to a patient's property, the judge had a complete discretion to consider the matter at large, unfettered a by the decision of the master or deputy master, since s 100(4)^c conferred the complete jurisdiction and discretion to deal with a patient's property on the nominated judges and only some of that jurisdiction and discretion on the master or deputy master. The judge was therefore not restricted on an appeal to considering whether the master or deputy master had erred in principle (see p 45 f to j, post).

(2) Because s 102(1)(c)^d of the 1959 Act gave the judge power to make provision for b persons or purposes 'for whom or which the patient might be expected to provide if he were not mentally disordered', the judge, in exercising his discretion under s 103(1)(dd) to order execution of a will for a patient, had to seek to make such a will as the actual, not a hypothetical, patient, acting reasonably, would have been likely to make. Furthermore, the judge had to make such a will as the patient would have been likely to make during a notional lucid interval before he lost testamentary capacity and as if he c had his full mental capacity, memory and foresight, and on the basis also (a) that the patient would have recognised in the will in broad terms any claims on his bounty and (b) that he was being advised by a competent solicitor in making the will (see p 42 h to p 43 j, post); Re D M L [1965] 2 All ER 129 and Re W J G L [1965] 3 All ER 865 applied; dictum of Fox J in Re Davey (decd) [1980] 2 All ER at 348 considered.

(3) Applying those principles and having regard to the general requirement of fairness d and what was appropriate in all the circumstances, A ought to be given a legacy of £15,000 out of the patient's estate and the residue of the estate should be divided between the five children in equal shares. Moreover, the substitution clause in favour of A's husband should apply to her legacy as well as to her share of residue, since the husband had been involved with A in the patient's care. There would therefore be a direction that a will on those terms be executed and, to that extent, the appeal would be e allowed (see p 48 g to p 49 c and p 51 e, post).

(4) Although on a hearing at first instance the costs of all parties would normally be ordered to be paid out of the patient's estate on a common fund basis, that did not necessarily apply to an appeal, especially where the respondent had rejected the appellants' prior offer to settle the appeal on terms which in the event substantially accorded with the decision on appeal. In the circumstances the respondents would be ordered to pay f the appellants half their costs of the appeal on a party and party basis, and the appellants would be allowed the rest of their costs out of the estate on a common fund basis (see p 52 c to h, post); Re C E F D [1963] 1 All ER 685 distinguished.

Per curiam. (1) On an application for the execution of a will for a patient the court should be provided with reasonably detailed information about the patient's capital and income, the expenses of maintaining the patient, his nature when he was still of g testamentary capacity, and the financial and other circumstances of those claiming to benefit under the will (see p 49 d to f, post).

(2) Where there is general agreement on the terms of the will to be executed and the parties desire to avoid the expense of referring the case to the judge, the case can properly be disposed of by the master or deputy master of the Court of Protection. Where, however, the terms of the will to be executed are not agreed, the master or deputy master h should not accept jurisdiction in the matter without first stating the grounds on which he considers he has jurisdiction and ought to exercise it, namely whether it is the unreasonable expense of, or the delay of, a hearing before the judge. Furthermore, if the case comes before the master or deputy master in an atmosphere of compromise but no compromise is achieved, he ought then to consider whether he can properly hear the case

j

(Continued from p 37)

appeal shall lie to a nominated judge from any decision of the Master or Deputy Master of the Court of Protection or any officer of the Court of Protection nominated under subsection (3) of section one hundred of this Act.'

c   Section 100(4), so far as material, is set out at p 44 d to f, post
d   Section 102(1) is set out at p 42 a, post

a

as contested proceedings and, if he concludes that he can, he should briefly state his reasons for doing so (see p 50 *f* to *j* and p 51 *c*, post); *Practice Direction* [1970] 1 All ER 208 considered.

(3) Normally, where the master or deputy master determines an application for the execution of a statutory will by ordering the execution of such a will, the order should not be stayed pending an appeal and the will should be executed notwithstanding an appeal (see p 51 *c* to *e*, post).

b

(4) On an appeal from a decision of the master or deputy master there should be either a note of any oral evidence given before him or a statement that all the parties have concurred in dispensing with any such note (see p 46 *a b*, post).

Notes

c

For the power to order the execution of a statutory will for a person suffering from mental disorder, see 30 Halsbury's Laws (4th edn) para 1246.

For the Mental Health Act 1959, ss 100, 102, 103, 111, see 25 Halsbury's Statutes (3rd edn) 129, 131, 140.

Cases referred to in judgments

C E F D, Re [1963] 1 All ER 685, [1963] 1 WLR 329, Digest (Cont Vol A) 1126, *1536a*.

d

C M G, Re [1970] 2 All ER 740, [1970] Ch 574, [1970] 3 WLR 80, 12 Digest (Reissue) 137, *754*.

Cooper v Cooper (Parish, intervener; Williams, party cited) [1936] 2 All ER 542, [1936] WN 205, 27(2) Digest (Reissue) 720, *5589*.

D M L, Re [1965] 2 All ER 129, [1965] Ch 1133, [1965] 3 WLR 740, Digest (Cont Vol B) 526, *937a*.

e

Davey (decd), Re [1980] 3 All ER 342, [1981] 1 WLR 164.

Evans v Bartlam [1937] 2 All ER 646, [1937] AC 473, HL, 50 Digest (Repl) 401, *1113*.

W, Re [1970] 2 All ER 502, [1971] Ch 123, [1970] 3 WLR 87, Digest (Cont Vol C) 678, *723a*.

W J G L, Re [1965] 3 All ER 865, [1966] Ch 135, [1966] 2 WLR 233, Digest (Cont Vol B) 525, *710a*.

f

Appeal

By summons dated 24 May 1979 the appellants, A and R, daughters of D (the patient), whose affairs were under the control of the Court of Protection, applied under s 103(1)(*dd*) of the Mental Health Act 1959 for an order that R, the receiver of the patient's affairs, be directed in the name of and on behalf of the patient to execute a codicil to the patient's will in the terms of the draft codicil accompanying the application or in such other terms

g

as the court deemed fit. The respondents to the application were the patient's other children. On 9 April 1979 the deputy master of the Court of Protection ordered that the Official Solicitor be directed to execute a will bequeathing to A a legacy of £10,000 free of capital transfer tax and bequeathing the residue of the patient's estate, which had a net value of £50,000, equally between the patient's five children including A. The deputy master directed the Official Solicitor not to execute the will if an appeal was lodged. The

h

appellants appealed, asking that a further statutory will be ordered increasing the provision for A. The appeal and the subsequent argument on costs were heard in chambers but judgment was given by Sir Robert Megarry V-C in open court. The facts are set out in the judgment.

R W Ham for the appellants.

j

Gregory Hill for the respondents.

Peter Rawson for the patient.

Cur adv vult

27 July. **SIR ROBERT MEGARRY V-C** read the following judgment: This case concerns the making of a will for a patient under the Mental Health Act 1959. As a number of points both of principle and of procedure have arisen, I am delivering

judgment in open court; and this course has the support of all parties. As Ungoed-Thomas J pointed out in Re W [1970] 2 All ER 502 at 509, [1971] Ch 123 at 141, it is *a* important that the public should be kept informed of the principles on which the Court of Protection acts, and this is best secured by making public (with, of course, suitable safeguards of anonymity) any judgments which deal with matters of principle or, I would add, matters of procedure. This is none the less important where the jurisdiction in question is relatively novel, and reported authority is scanty. The power to make a will for a patient was conferred by the Administration of Justice Act 1969, s 17(1), and *b* counsel were not able to refer me to any reported case on this power save Re Davey (decd) [1980] 3 All ER 342, [1981] 1 WLR 164.

The patient in this case is a widow aged some 80 years. About eight years ago she began to show signs of senile dementia, and since then her condition has deteriorated. In April 1978 proceedings in the Court of Protection for the appointment of a receiver were commenced, and on 30 November 1978 one of her daughters, Mrs R, was appointed *c* receiver. It is perfectly plain that, as all parties accept, the patient is now incapable of making a valid will for herself, so that s 103(3)(b) of the Mental Health Act 1959 (as added by the Administration of Justice Act 1969, s 17(2)) is satisfied. On 31 August 1962 the patient made a will, and there is no suggestion that when she made it she lacked testamentary capacity. The patient's husband had died in 1956, and her immediate family consisted of a son and four daughters. All five are parties to these proceedings. *d* By her will the patient specifically devised her house with her household furniture and personal effects in it to one of her daughters, Mrs A, and left the rest of her property equally between her five children. I think that I should recount the circumstances existing when that will was made, and the events which occurred subsequently.

In 1955 the patient and her husband were living in Cornwall. Mrs A was married, but was separated from her husband and was working in Manchester. In about October *e* 1955 the patient wrote to Mrs A to say that her father, the patient's husband, was ill. Mrs A obtained leave from her job and went to her parents in Cornwall. The father was seriously ill, and died of cancer in April 1956. After the funeral Mrs A continued to live with the patient in Cornwall as she was very upset by her husband's death; and she left most business matters, including winding up the father's estate, to Mrs A. In September 1957 the house in Cornwall was sold, and for a few months the patient and Mrs A went *f* to live with Mrs W, another daughter of the patient's, and then in lodgings. Early in 1958 the patient and Mrs A moved into a house in Hampshire which the patient had bought. This is the house which the patient specifically devised to Mrs A. About three years before the will was made Mrs A's marriage ended in divorce. By this time she had met her present husband, who was separated from his wife, but intended to marry Mrs A when he was free; and in February 1972 this marriage occurred. When the patient *g* made her will in 1962, she knew of this relationship.

In about May 1972, soon after Mrs A had remarried and had left the patient's house, the patient came to stay with Mrs A. The visit was intended to last for only a month, but the patient refused to return to her house to live on her own, and insisted on remaining with Mrs A. This was about the time when the patient's signs of senile dementia began to manifest themselves. Next year, in April 1973, the patient's Hampshire house was *h* sold for £13,500; and that, of course, adeemed the specific devise to Mrs A. Out of the proceeds the patient bought a smaller house for £10,800. This new house (which I shall call 'no 5') was only a few doors away from the house in which Mrs A lived; I think it was next door but one. The idea was that the patient would live in no 5; but although at first she slept there for a few nights, she very soon had moved in to live with Mrs A and her husband, merely visiting no 5 for an hour or two during the day. The patient has lived *j* with Mrs A and her husband ever since. In July 1979 they bought a larger house, and the patient went with them. In October 1979, no 5 was sold, fetching some £22,200 net. Until the beginning of 1978, Mr and Mrs A had to bear most or all of the expense of maintaining the patient, as well as the burden of looking after her. Before her second marriage, I should say, Mrs A earned a good salary as a secretary. However, in November

1978 the Court of Protection authorised the payment of £40 per week out of the
a patient's estate to Mrs A. In addition, Mrs A is at present receiving the patient's pension
of £27·40 per week and a constant attendance allowance from the Department of Health
and Social Security of £14·75 per week, so that in all she receives about £82 a week in
respect of the patient.

The patient's estate is worth about £50,000, though this makes no allowance for the
costs of these proceedings. The proceedings were commenced by a summons dated 24
b May 1979, taken out by Mrs R, the receiver, and Mrs A, seeking a direction that a codicil
be executed specifically bequeathing to Mrs A the leasehold house no 5 and the household
furniture and personal effects therein. The object, of course, was to this extent to reverse
the effect of the ademption of the devise of the house in the 1962 will; and at this time
no 5 had not been sold. The summons was fixed to be heard on 17 July 1979, but it was
adjourned, and the parties concerned engaged in various discussions. Finally, the
c summons was restored to be heard on 9 April 1981, and it came before the deputy master
then. On that day the deputy master made an order for the Official Solicitor, who was
representing the patient, to execute a will in the terms of a draft initialled by him. The
substance of the will was that Mrs A was given a legacy of £10,000, and the rest of the
estate was to be divided equally between the patient's five children, with a substitution
clause for their children, and in the case of Mrs A a substitution clause for her present
d husband as regards the share of residue (but not the legacy) if she left no child living at
the patient's death.

At this stage a somewhat curious event occurred. On a date which I do not know the
deputy master orally directed the Official Solicitor not to execute the will if an appeal
against his order was lodged; and on 22 May this direction was confirmed in writing. At
that time the order had not been drawn up, so that no appeal could very well be
e lodged. However, on 27 May the order was entered, and on 29 May Mrs A and Mrs R
gave notice of appeal, stating that they would seek an increased provision to be made for
Mrs A. The respondents to the appeal are those who were respondents to the original
application, namely, the patient's other children, Mr D, Mrs W and Mrs B. I may say that
Mrs A and Mrs R were represented by Mr Ham, the respondents were represented by Mr
Hill, and the patient by Mr Rawson, instructed by the Official Solicitor. As matters
f stand, the 1962 will remains fully effective, apart from the ademption, and so if the
patient dies the five children will all take in equal shares. It was common ground before
me that Mrs A should take a greater part of the estate than the other four children, but
that subject to this the children should take in equal shares. The one real issue is thus
how much extra Mrs A ought to get.

There are three main contentions. The first is that the deputy master's order is right,
g so that Mrs A will get a legacy of £10,000 and an equal one-fifth share of residue with her
brother and sisters. This contention was supported by the respondents. Mrs A's primary
contention is that she should have a legacy of £22,000 (representing the price that no 5
fetched) and an equal one-fifth share of residue with her brother and sisters. Mrs A's
alternative contention is that she should have a legacy of £12,500 and a double share of
residue, so that in addition to the legacy she would receive one-third of residue and her
h brother and sisters one-sixth each. I shall leave the effect of these provisions until later,
though at this stage I should mention that the importance of a legacy to Mrs A is that if
some of the capital owned by the patient is hereafter consumed in providing for the
needs of the patient, thereby reducing the size of the residue, this would not alter the size
of the legacy unless, indeed, so much is consumed that no residue is left.

Before I can examine the rival contentions, I must consider the questions of principle
j and procedure that arose during the hearing. The main question, I think, is that of the
considerations which the court should have in mind when deciding what provisions to
insert in the will. Though the statutory guidance is exiguous, it seems possible to state
five principles or factors which should guide the court. At the outset I think that I should
cite the relevant statutory provisions. I begin with s 102(1) of the Mental Health Act
1959:

'The judge may, with respect to the property and affairs of a patient, do or secure
the doing of all such things as appear necessary or expedient—(a) for the *a*
maintenance or other benefit of the patient, (b) for the maintenance or other benefit
of members of the patient's family, (c) for making provision for other persons or
purposes for whom or which the patient might be expected to provide if he were
not mentally disordered, or (d) otherwise for administering the patient's affairs.'

Section 103(1) begins as follows: *b*

'Without prejudice to the generality of the foregoing section, the judge shall have
power to make such orders and give such directions and authorities as he thinks fit
for the purposes of that section, and in particular may for those purposes make
orders or give directions or authorities for . . .'

There then follows a long list of the transactions which the judge may authorise,
including the managing and dealing with the patient's property, the acquisition   *c*
of property in the patient's name, and making settlements and gifts of the patient's
property. At that point the Administration of Justice Act 1969 inserted a new paragraph,
para (*dd*), into the list: and this runs:

'the execution for the patient of a will making any provision (whether by way of
disposing of property or exercising a power or otherwise) which could be made by *d*
a will executed by the patient if he were not mentally disordered, so however that
in such cases as a nominated judge may direct the powers conferred by this
paragraph shall not be exercisable except by the Lord Chancellor or a nominated
judge.'

(I pause only to utter the warning that in this paragraph as reproduced in *Heywood and
Massey's Court of Protection Practice* (10th edn, 1978) p 310, the sense of the second limb *e*
of the paragraph is inverted by omitting the word 'except' from the last ten words.) The
list continues with a number of other matters such as carrying on a trade or business,
carrying out contracts and so on.

I should also mention s 103A, inserted by s 18 of the 1969 Act. This makes various
provisions as to the formalities of executing wills under the 1969 Act, and curtails the *f*
operation of such wills in relation to immovables outside England and Wales. It ends
with sub-s (5), which I think I should read:

'For the purposes of the application of the Inheritance (Family Provision) Act
1938 in relation to a will executed in accordance with subsection (1) of this section,
in section 1(7) of that Act (which relates to the deceased's reasons for disposing of his
estate in a particular way)—(a) any reference to the deceased's reasons for which *g*
anything is done or not done by his will shall be construed as a reference to the
reasons for which it is done or (as the case may be) not done by that will, and (b) any
reference to a statement in writing signed by the deceased shall be construed as
a reference to a statement in writing signed by the authorised person in accordance
with a direction given in that behalf by the judge.'

h
The first of the principles or factors which I think it is possible to discern is that it is to
be assumed that the patient is having a brief lucid interval at the time when the will is
made. The second is that during the lucid interval the patient has a full knowledge of the
past, and a full realisation that as soon as the will is executed he or she will relapse into
the actual mental state that previously existed, with the prognosis as it actually is. These
propositions emerge, I think, from the judgment of Cross J in *Re W J G L* [1965] 3 All ER *j*
865 at 871–872, [1966] Ch 135 at 144–145. In that case the judge was dealing with the
making of a settlement for the patient, not a will: but I cannot see that the distinction
matters. Paragraph (*dd*), dealing with wills, has been inserted immediately after para (d),
dealing with settlements and gifts, and both are governed by the same general statutory
provisions.

The third proposition is that it is the actual patient who has to be considered and not
a hypothetical patient. One is not concerned with the patient on the Clapham omnibus.
I say that because the will is being made by the court, and so by an impartial entity skilled
in the law, rather than the actual patient, whose views while still of a sound disposing
mind might be idiosyncratic and far from impartial. In *Re Davey (decd)* [1980] 3 All ER
342 at 348, [1981] 1 WLR 164 at 171 Fox J is reported as saying, in relation to a will made
by the Court of Protection, that the essential question was 'what if anything would be
reasonable provision in all the circumstances for the various contestants', and it could be
said that this indicates an objective approach made with the wisdom of the court rather
than the approach likely to be made by the patient if restored to full testamentary
capacity. I very much doubt if the judge meant to indicate this, and in any case I do not
think it is right. The whole approach of Cross J in *Re W J G L* [1965] 3 All ER 865, [1966]
Ch 135 was that of considering the particular patient, momentarily restored to full
mental capacity, as being the settlor. Further, in s 102(1)(c), the question is one of
making provision for persons or purposes 'for whom or which the patient might be
expected to provide if he were not mentally disordered'; and I think that this provision
governs the making of a will for the patient, and contemplates the particular patient: and
see *Re C M G* [1970] 2 All ER 740 at 741, [1970] Ch 574 at 575. Before losing testamentary
capacity the patient may have been a person with strong antipathies or deep affections for
particular persons or causes, or with vigorous religious or political views; and of course
the patient was then able to give effect to those views when making a will. I think that
the court must take the patient as he or she was before losing testamentary capacity. No
doubt allowance may be made for the passage of years since the patient was last of full
capacity, for sometimes strong feelings mellow into indifference, and even family feuds
evaporate. Furthermore, I do not think that the court should give effect to antipathies
or affections of the patient which are beyond reason. But subject to all due allowances,
I think that the court must seek to make the will which the actual patient, acting
reasonably, would have made if notionally restored to full mental capacity, memory and
foresight. If I may adapt Dr Johnson's words, used for another purpose, the court is to do
for the patient what the patient would fairly do for himself, if he could.

Fourth, I think that during the hypothetical lucid interval the patient is to be envisaged
as being advised by competent solicitors. The court will in fact be making the will, of
course, and the court should not make a will on the assumption that the terms of the will
are to be framed by someone who, for instance, knows nothing about lapse and
ademption. Furthermore, as the court will be surveying the past and the future, the
hypothetically lucid patient should be assumed to have a skilled solicitor to draw his or
her attention to matters which a testator should bear in mind. In *Re D M L* [1965] 2 All
ER 129 at 133, [1965] Ch 1133 at 1139, a case on a proposed purchase of an annuity in
order to save estate duty, Cross J put a lucid explanation of the proposal into the mouth
of a hypothetical legal adviser to the hypothetically lucid patient. In any case, I cannot
imagine that Parliament intended the court to match the sort of home-made will that
some testators make. I do not, of course, say that one must treat the patient as being
bound to accept the imaginary legal advice that is given to him: but the patient is to be
treated as doing what he does either because of the advice or in spite of it, and not
without having had it.

Fifth, in all normal cases the patient is to be envisaged as taking a broad brush to the
claims on his bounty, rather than an accountant's pen. There will be nothing like a
balance sheet or profit and loss account. There may be many to whom the patient feels
morally indebted; and some of that moral indebtedness may be readily expressible in
terms of money, and some of it may not. But when giving legacies or shares of residue
few testators are likely to reckon up in terms of cash the value of the hospitality and gifts
that he has received from his friends and relations, and then seek to make some form of
testamentary repayment, even if his estate is large enough for this. Instead, there is
likely to be some general recognition of outstanding kindnesses by some gift which in
quantum may bear very little relation to the cost or value of those kindnesses.

Now I certainly do not say that these principles or factors are either exhaustive or very precise, nor am I altogether convinced that the notional lucid interval is the best way of expressing what the court has to do. Indeed, Cross J more than once referred to the 'curious assumptions' that it involves. However, it has found its way into this branch of the law; in most ordinary cases I think it will suffice, and so I have adapted and, perhaps, expanded it. During the argument there was much discussion of the points that I have set out, but at the end of the day I think that counsel were substantially in agreement with what I have said. Yet before I approach the facts of the case with these matters in mind, I must consider a procedural point on which there was a sharp difference between counsel for the respondents on the one hand and counsel for the appellants and counsel for the patient on the other hand. This concerns the status of a decision of the master or deputy master of the Court of Protection when there is an appeal to the judge.

The point at issue is whether on such an appeal the decision of the master or deputy master is to be affirmed unless the judge considers that the master or deputy master has erred in principle, as counsel for the respondents contends, or whether the matter is at large, as counsel for the appellants and counsel for the patient submit. Put another way, where a discretion has to be exercised, is the discretion that of the master or deputy master or that of the judge? This requires some examination of the structure of jurisdiction in the Court of Protection.

By s 100(4) of the Mental Health Act 1959, the functions expressed to be conferred by Part VIII of the Act on 'the judge' are to be exercisable by the Lord Chancellor or by 'any nominated judge'. The Lord Chancellor rarely, if ever, exercises any contentious jurisdiction under the Act, and the nominated judges consist of all the judges of the Chancery Division. Wherever possible, I shall therefore omit further references to the Lord Chancellor and refer simply to 'the judge'. The subsection goes on to provide that the functions in question 'shall also be exercisable by the Master or Deputy Master of the Court of Protection', or by any officer nominated under sub-s (3), but 'in the case of the Master, Deputy Master or any such nominated officer, subject to any express provision to the contrary in this Part of this Act or any rules thereunder'; and then there is provision for further restrictions on the deputy master and any nominated officer. The subsection ends by providing that references in that Part of the Act to 'the judge' are to be construed accordingly. When one comes to paras (d) and (dd) of s 103(1), respectively dealing with the making of settlements and gifts and the execution of wills, there is in each case a provision that in such cases as a nominated judge may direct the powers conferred by the paragraph 'shall not be exercisable except by the Lord Chancellor or a nominated judge'. (Heywood and Massey p 310 makes another mistake, this time trivial, by substituting 'in' for the first 'by' in para (d).) In pursuance of these provisions, virtually identical directions were given by Danckwerts J for para (d) and by Ungoed-Thomas J for para (dd): see Practice Direction [1960] 3 All ER 447, [1960] 1 WLR 1253; Practice Direction [1970] 1 All ER 208, [1970] 1 WLR 259. In each case the direction was that the jurisdiction was not to be exercisable 'except by the Lord Chancellor or a nominated judge unless by reason of the amount involved or the general circumstances of the case unreasonable expense or delay would be caused'. (In the earlier direction, 'circumstances generally' appears in place of 'general circumstances'.)

The drafting falls short of perfection: the apposition of 'not' and 'except' in the Act is overtopped by the 'not', 'except' and 'unless' of the practice directions. I cannot remember finding even in a Finance Act any example of an exception on an exception from a negative. But at the end of the trail it is clear that the final result is that the judge has complete jurisdiction, though the master or deputy master may exercise it if the amount involved or the general circumstances of the case mean that unreasonable expense or delay would be caused by sending it to the judge. I am sorry to say that Heywood & Massey p 12 states the effect of the practice directions the wrong way round by omitting the word 'except'.

By comparison with the original jurisdiction, the provisions for appeals from the master to the judge are meagre. Section 111(1) of the Mental Health Act 1959 provides

that subject to and in accordance with rules under Part VIII of the Act an appeal lies to the
a judge from a decision of the master, deputy master or nominated officer. Rule 62 of the
Court of Protection Rules 1960, SI 1960/1146, simply provides that any person aggrieved
by an order or decision of the master (a term which includes the deputy master) may
within eight days from the entry of the order appeal to a nominated judge. There is
nothing to which I have been referred which states the basis on which such an appeal
lies. Rule 62(4) prohibits the filing of further evidence in support of an appeal or in
b opposition to it without the leave of the court, but that does not help much. Nor do
rr 30, 31, 32, or 33, providing for affidavit evidence, evidence that would be inadmissible
in a court of law, unsworn evidence, and the cross-examination of deponents.

In those circumstances counsel for the appellants relied on there being an analogy with
the Queen's Bench Division. There, an appeal lies from a master to a judge; and it has
been settled since *Evans v Bartlam* [1937] 2 All ER 646, [1937] AC 473 that in such cases
c the discretion is the discretion of the judge and not that of the master. The judge is
wholly unfettered by the master's exercise of his discretion, and on an appeal to the Court
of Appeal what has to be considered is the way in which the discretion was exercised by
the judge, not by the master (see [1937] 2 All ER 646 at 648–649, 652–653 [1937] AC
473 at 478, 484, per Lord Atkin and per Lord Wright).

The rule is clear: but what is the reason for it? Counsel were unable to explain what
d this was. However, I think that some assistance is to be obtained from *Cooper v Cooper*
[1936] WN 205, which both Lord Atkin and Lord Wright cited with approval. I shall
refer to the better report of the case in the All England Law Reports ([1936] 2 All ER
542). The case concerned a decision of Merriman P, reversing a decision of a registrar of
the Probate, Divorce and Admiralty Division in a discretionary matter; and the Court of
Appeal held that the substantive discretion was vested in the President rather than the
e registrar. As the rules stood, the masters in the King's Bench Division and the registrars
in the Probate, Divorce and Admiralty Division were in the same position. They were
both empowered to transact all such business, and exercise all such authority and
jurisdiction, as might be transacted or exercised by a judge at chambers, with a number
of specified exceptions. From this Lord Wright MR concluded that 'the powers of the
masters and registrars are the powers of the judge', so that what had to be considered was
f the discretion of the President and not that of the registrar (see [1936] 2 All ER 542 at
544).

It seems to me from the provisions of the Mental Health Act 1959 and the practice
directions that I have cited that the position as between the master or deputy master of
the Court of Protection and the nominated judges is similar. The complete jurisdiction
is that of the nominated judges; and although the master and deputy master are
g empowered to exercise some of it, though not all, that does not alter the fact that the
jurisdiction, and the discretion that goes with it, is the jurisdiction of the judges. This
view is, I think, reinforced by r 45. This directs the master to refer to the judge any
proceedings, or any question arising in any proceedings, 'which ought, by virtue of any
enactment or in the opinion of the Master, to be considered by the Judge'. The process
of passing a matter from a master to a judge without making any decision is, of course,
h a commonplace of the Chancery Division, where it is plain that the discretion is the
discretion of the judge. This contrasts with the Queen's Bench Division, where, at any
rate normally, the path from the master to the judge is only by way of appeal, after a
decision by the master. Under the 1959 Act the position of the master or deputy master
is thus even less promising than in the Queen's Bench Division for the contention that
the discretion is the master's discretion, and not that of the judge. In the result I hold
that counsel for the respondents is wrong and that counsel for the appellants and counsel
for the patient are right. The discretion is that of the judge, and he is in no way fettered
by any decision of the master or deputy master.

One other procedural matter that I should mention is that of the evidence. I have
before me the affidavits which were before the deputy master, together with a later
affidavit which, without opposition, I allowed to be used. (As I have mentioned, r 62(4)

provides that on an appeal no further evidence is to be filed in support of or in opposition to the appeal without the leave of the court.) However, I was told that before the deputy *a* master there had been some cross-examination of deponents; yet the papers sent with the appeal included no note of any of the oral evidence. From what I was told it does not seem that this omission is of any real consequence: but I think that on future appeals there ought either to be a note of any oral evidence or else a statement that all the parties have concurred in dispensing with any such note.

I can now at last return to the facts of the case. What disposition of the patient's estate *b* should now be made according to the principles or factors which I have stated and the general requirements of fairness and appropriateness for all concerned? The main claim of Mrs A to the larger share of the estate which it is conceded that she should have rests on the burden that she and her husband have discharged over the past nine years or so; for throughout that period the patient has lived with them nearly continuously. Until the middle of 1977 the patient went to stay with Mrs B from time to time (the extent is *c* in dispute) and with Mrs W for a few visits, but never with Mr D: she clearly has been living for nearly the whole time with Mr and Mrs A. Nobody should underestimate the effect that this must have on the daily life of Mr and Mrs A.

There are many factors that have to be taken into account. From the beginning of 1978, the period when the payments to Mrs A out of the estate, with the other payments, began to make some substantial recompense to Mrs A, the direct financial burden has *d* been removed. But Mrs A has been unable to go to work and so to earn what a skilled secretary can earn. Mr and Mrs A have also incurred the burden of increased mortgage payments resulting from moving to a larger house in 1979, though no details have been put forward, and in any case part of the payments go to increase the value of their capital asset. Their old house was sold for £22,600 and their new house cost £35,000. Mr and Mrs A also effected considerable improvements to no 5 while the patient owned it, and *e* also to her previous house; but no details of cost or value have been given, and I do not know to what extent, if any, these improvements resulted in a higher price being obtained by the patient for these houses.

Counsel for the appellants relied on certain other matters. But for going to live with the patient in 1955, Mrs A could have used her savings (which, on inquiry, I was told were then about £250) to buy a small cottage in the Manchester area, and this would by *f* now have greatly appreciated in value, in the way that investing the money (eg in equities) would not have done. But there is no real evidence that Mrs A ever seriously intended to do this, or took any steps towards it (her affidavit merely states that she had saved enough money to do it), and a mere possibility so remote in time can carry little weight. There was also some discussion about the ademption, and how far the patient realised that the sale of the Hampshire house had destroyed the gift to Mrs A without the *g* purchase of no 5 replacing it. Indeed, the primary claim of counsel for the appellants is that Mrs A should be given the equivalent of the net proceeds of sale as a legacy, thereby representing a notional continuance of the devise of the Hampshire house. The respondents contend that the devise was made in 1962 because Mrs A was then in the position of an unmarried daughter living with the patient, and the patient wished her to have a roof over her head. All this changed when Mrs A remarried in 1972, and so the *h* purpose of the devise went. Mrs A's reply is that before the patient began to lose her testamentary capacity she knew all about the relationship between Mrs A and Mr A, and their intention to marry, and neither before nor after the marriage did she do anything to revoke or disapprove the devise. Mrs B, indeed, said that the patient knew that the devise would lapse when the house was sold, and said that she was satisfied to know that this would be the case. But the whole question is beset with much uncertainty. *j*

The respondents also emphasise that from 1956 to 1971 the patient provided a home for Mrs A, though it is disputed how far Mrs A contributed towards the household costs. They also point to the payments, now some £82 a week or about £4,200 a year, that Mrs A has been receiving since the beginning of 1978, and urge that this is a substantial recompense. If £1,200 a year went to pay the additional mortgage a repayments, that would still leave the ample sum of £3,000 a year for maintaining the patient. There is also the position of the individual respondents to be considered. The patient certainly stayed with Mrs B for some weeks from time to time until an incident in 1977. I know virtually nothing of her financial position; her husband is in the RAF. Mr D is aged 57 years and has just been made redundant, with a redundancy payment of £9,000, a pension of £25 per week and small prospects of obtaining other employment. Mrs W owns her house but depends on her widow's pension, her savings

b of some £2,000 and a rates rebate to make ends meet.

It seems reasonably clear that both the patient's husband and the patient recognised the desirability of producing equality of benefit between their children, to be disturbed only for good reason. There is plainly good reason in the present case, as is accepted on all hands, but the question is how that good reason should be expressed in financial terms. Considering matters as they stand today, I think the patient would look at

c matters broadly, and with the emphasis on the more recent past rather than the more distant past. I doubt whether she would attach much weight to any benefit that Mrs A received from living in the patient's house between 1955 and 1972, even if Mrs A did not fully pay her way, for the patient was receiving the companionship and moral support from Mrs A that I think the patient needed. Nor do I think that the improvements that Mr and Mrs A effected to the patient's houses would loom large. What would rightly

d predominate would be the expenditure of care and devotion, and until 1978 money, which for the last eight or nine years Mrs A and her husband have provided for the patient. The advantage of having a settled home with a daughter, instead of living on her own, or being moved every few weeks or months from the house of one of her children to the house of another, or living in some old persons' home, is one which must stand very high, not only in its own right but also as showing the strength of filial

e affection and duty. I do not doubt that Mrs A has acted with devotion and kindliness, and not reluctantly or grudgingly. She has supplied what so many old people need and crave. I am, of course, making a number of assumptions about the patient, for I have very little evidence about her nature: but I do not think that in those circumstances it is wrong to assume that she follows the usual pattern. She is plainly not one of those sturdy individualists who demand independence and seclusion.

f It also seems to me that the future would loom large in the patient's thoughts, and that until mental or physical infirmity made it impossible for her to continue living with Mrs A, she would want to continue there. Her recognition for the past would therefore include an element of expectation for the future. She would realise (I am assuming, of course, that she has the advice of a skilled solicitor) that whereas at present her income is more than sufficient to pay the £40 a week that Mrs A is receiving from her estate, there

g is a very real risk of having to resort to capital if she has to go to a home or hospital and live there for some while. I pause there to say that I do not know what the income of the estate is; but all concerned accepted that the patient was being maintained out of income, and that the deputy master had erred in saying that there was at the present time the necessity for some resort to capital. It was also not known whether the national health service would reduce or obviate the need for payments, for nobody knows what type of

h assistance will be needed. But at the very least there is the possibility of the capital being to some extent needed for the patient in the future, with a consequent reduction in the amount distributable under the will.

In those circumstances, I think that the right approach is to give a substantial legacy to Mrs A, and subject to that to divide the residue equally between the five children. If the capital value of the estate is reduced, Mrs A will still get the legacy in full, but in common with her sisters and brother will suffer a reduction in the share of residue. In determining the amount of the legacy I cannot see much relevance in the amount received from the sale of no 5. The devise of the Hampshire house was made in 1962, much has happened since then, and there is at least some evidence that the patient knew and accepted that the devise was no longer effective. The substratum for providing for Mrs A consists of everything that she has done for the patient since the time when the devise was adeemed,

and I cannot see why the value of the house that replaced the house devised should be any
sort of measuring rod for what legacy Mrs A should receive. The provision of a house for *a*
Mrs A to live in became irrelevant when the patient in effect moved into Mr and Mrs A's
house, if not before. I would therefore discard the £22,200 which represents the net
proceeds of sale of no 5; I do not think that it provides any guidance for the present
purpose.

On day 2, counsel for the respondents very helpfully put in a table which showed the
benefits that each of the parties would receive on certain assumptions; and later in the *b*
day counsel for the appellants equally helpfully put in a further copy of the same
document with the addition of further assumptions and some percentages. The starting
point was the amount distributable. Counsel for the respondents' two assumptions were
that (a) £43,000 and (b) £38,000 would be distributable, thus taking the £50,000 and
allowing under (a) £7,000 for the costs of both hearings and the administration, and
allowing under (b) for a further £5,000 out of capital to be spent on the patient. Counsel *c*
for the appellants' assumption was that (c) £45,000 would be distributable, reducing
counsel for the respondents' £7,000 to £5,000. I have no real information about the
accuracy of these figures. I do not think that I should set out the tables in this judgment,
but I must indicate their thrust; and I think I can do this by contrasting the most
favourable and the least favourable of these figures, counsel for the appellants' £45,000
(the (c) figure) and counsel for the respondents' £38,000 (the (b) figure). I should add *d*
that if in the future it appears that the real figures will differ widely from these (for
example, if £10,000 is spent on the patient's welfare), an application for a new will can
be made.

I turn, then, to consider the contentions in relation to these figures. If, as the deputy
master decided, Mrs A's legacy were to be £10,000, then under (c) she would get £17,000
and the others £7,000 each, while under (b) the figures would be £15,600 and £5,600 *e*
respectively. This does not seem to me to be a sufficient recognition of the difference
between Mrs A and the others. If instead Mrs A's legacy were to be £22,000, in
accordance with counsel for the appellants' primary claim, then under (c) she would get
£26,600 and the others £4,600 each, while under (b) she would get £25,200 and the
others £3,200 each. This seems to me to favour Mrs A unduly at the expense of the other
children. She would take some 60% of the estate, or more, and they would merely get *f*
some 10% apiece. Counsel for the appellants' alternative submission of a legacy of
£12,500 and a double share of residue seems to me to be nearer the mark. This would
give Mrs A £21,000 under (b) and £23,333 under (c), as against £4,250 and £5,417 each
for the others, respectively. Though nearer the mark, I think it is still a little on the high
side for Mrs A and on the low side for the others; and I am doubtful about the suitability
of a double share as part of the means of recognising Mrs A's special position. *g*

In the end my conclusion is that Mrs A should be given a legacy of £15,000. The
result under (b) would be that she would get £19,600 in all and the others £4,600 each,
while under (c) she would get £21,000 and the other four £6,000 each. The figures of
£4,600 and £6,000 for the other four may be compared with the £7,600 and £9,000
that they would each get if Mrs A were to be given no legacy at all, and the estate were
to be divided equally between all five. These matters must inevitably be largely matters *h*
of impression after immersing oneself in the relevant facts and law, and I can only say
that it strikes me as being about right for Mrs A to receive a little over £20,000 in all and
for each of the others to receive a little over £5,000 in all, with the figures varying
upwards or downwards with the size of the estate. This represents giving about half the
estate to Mrs A and the other half to her sisters and brother. This seems to me to give
substantial recognition to the claims of all the children, as such, and at the same time to *j*
reflect Mrs A's special claims. I should make it clear that I am not for one moment saying
that I regard the market value of what Mrs A has done and is doing for the patient as
being £15,000. If the prospective estate were larger, she would have a strong claim to a
greater sum, and if it were smaller she would receive less. What has to be done is to

consider the proper distribution of what is available as between those who have any

a claim on it.

In general, the terms of the draft will directed to be executed by the deputy master's order seem to be satisfactory, with the substitution of £15,000 for the £10,000 and, of course, a change in the date of the order. But I think that the substitution clause whereby Mrs A's present husband is to take her share of residue if, being childless, she predeceases the patient, should not be confined to residue but should apply to the legacy

b as well. Indeed, it might be said that it should apply only to the legacy, for it is the legacy rather than the share of residue which is intended to recognise Mrs A's care of the patient, and the substitution clause was inserted, as the master said, because Mr A had been involved with Mrs A in that care. He refused to extend the substitution clause to the legacy because, he said, the legacy was intended solely for Mrs A. I do not follow this reasoning. I will, if desired, hear counsel on the point; but subject to that I shall direct

c that the substitution clause for Mr A is to apply to the legacy and the share of residue alike. The draft will as approved should also be revised so as to correct a spelling mistake and to remove a lack of uniformity in stating the addresses of the patient and Mrs A. Neither point matters much, but if the Court of Protection directs a will to be executed, that will ought to look well drafted.

It will be observed that there are many matters on which I have little or no

d information. I hope that in future cases, whether before the master or deputy master or the judge, more attention will be paid to setting out what may be called the hard facts of the case. Those who seek to have a will made for a patient should at least provide reasonably detailed information as to the size of the estate, the income, and the expenses of maintaining the patient. A person making a will, whether for himself or anyone else, ought to have a reasonable knowledge of what there is, and what there is likely to be, for

e disposal under the will. The financial and other circumstances of all those who claim to receive benefits under a will ought also to be made clear. Many a testator will discriminate between those who are well provided for and those who are needy. Some idea should also be given of the nature of the patient while still of testamentary capacity, even if only to state the negative of the patient being ordinary in every way and having no relevant prejudices or the like. But I need not go on. It will be apparent from this

f judgment that the evidence left something to be desired, and it can be seen what sort of deficiencies there were that might have been supplied. I forbore from directing further affidavits because of the delay, coupled with the fact that the patient is 80 and is or has recently been suffering from pneumonia, I was told. I may add that some exhibits to the affidavits were stitched into them. This is prohibited in the High Court (see RSC Ord 41, r 11(1)), and I understand that it is contrary to the practice in the Court of Protection.

g The reason for the rule is obvious. The exhibits should be detached and the affidavits re-stitched.

There are two other matters with which I should deal. One is the direction given by the deputy master to the Official Solicitor not to execute the will if an appeal was lodged. The order was made on 9 April and the direction was given orally at some time between 9 April and 22 May, when written confirmation of the direction was given. On

h 27 May the order was entered, and in it there was no mention of the direction which rendered it inoperative. The result is that there is a formal order of the Court of Protection requiring the Official Solicitor to do an act and yet the Official Solicitor is directed, by a direction that I have not seen, not to act on the order 'if an appeal was lodged'. Presumably this means 'until the time for appealing has elapsed, and thereafter indefinitely if an appeal is lodged in due time'. An appeal was entered on 29 May, and at some stage the Official Solicitor very properly issued a summons for directions as to the execution of the will. The deputy master heard this summons on 3 July, and adhered to his view that the will that he had directed should not be executed. The deputy master referred to his power under s 119(2) of the Mental Health Act 1959 to revoke or vary an order, and intimated that he was minded to revoke the order and then refer the matter to the judge under the Court of Protection Rules 1960, r 45. Not surprisingly, this proposal appealed to none of the parties, and after a short adjournment they felt *a* constrained to accept the direction not to proceed on the order pending the appeal, and then, if the case was not settled within the next week, to proceed on the order by way of appeal.

The deputy master's reasons for giving his direction were primarily because if the will was executed and the patient died before the appeal was heard this would not do justice to all the parties. He thought it unjust that Mrs A should be free to accept what the order *b* gave her and yet go to the judge and ask for more. He rejected the contention that it could be unjust to Mrs A if the will was not executed before the appeal was heard. He also thought that there was no urgency in the matter and that it was preferable not to tie the hands of the judge by allowing the will to be executed.

I find difficulty in following this reasoning. The deputy master had heard the case and made a decision; and obviously he must have thought that his decision did justice to all *c* parties. How, then, would it be unjust to anyone if the just will which he had directed to be made were to be brought into operation by the patient's death? Only if the will were unjust would injustice be caused. Further, I find it difficult to see the injustice in Mrs A seeking to obtain more than the master had ordered, just as I could see no injustice if the respondents had attempted to see that she got less. If it is thought just that she should get an extra £10,000, why is it just that she should be told that she is not to get *d* it if she seeks to obtain more and the patient dies before the appeal is heard? Nor do I see why the execution of the will should be thought to tie the hands of the judge, for he is free to direct the execution of another will.

That leads me to the second point. I have been told that recently there has been a considerable increase in the number of applications for wills to be made under the Act. I understand that since last September there have been some 90 applications, and that of *e* these very few have been or are likely to be referred to the judge. The great majority are dealt with by the master or deputy master under the practice direction. Some, like *Re Davey (decd)* [1980] 3 All ER 342, [1981] 1 WLR 164 (a striking case), are matters of urgency; there, the order and the will were made less than a week before the patient died. Most, I think, are cases where there is general agreement as to the terms of the will that is to be made, and it is naturally and very properly desired to avoid the expense of *f* referring the case to the judge. It seems to me entirely proper that such cases should be disposed of without reference to the judge. The master or deputy master must of course be satisfied that all whose claims ought to be considered are in agreement, and that there are no circumstances (such as a large estate or complex dispositions) which make it desirable to refer the case to the judge. In such cases the general circumstances of the case would normally result in a reference to the judge incurring unreasonable expense. *g*

Where, however, the terms of the will are not agreed, I think that the master or deputy master should address his mind to the question of jurisdiction, and should not hear the case without first deciding whether it is 'unreasonable expense' or 'delay' which enables him to hear it, and whether it is the 'amount involved' or 'the general circumstances of the case' which produce that result. Whichever it is, it seems desirable that the master or deputy master should state briefly the grounds on which he considers he has *h* jurisdiction and ought to exercise it. The practice direction is in terms of whether the unreasonable expense or delay 'would' be caused, and this suggests that the test is objective: but it would certainly be more convenient if it were to be made explicit that the test is subjective, as by inserting words such as 'in the opinion of the Master or Deputy Master' between 'would' and 'be caused'. Indeed, the wording of each of the practice directions might with advantage be reconsidered, and I propose to take steps to *j* this end. I shall also direct attention to the paucity of provisions in the rules for the conduct of appeals, not least in relation to the material to be put before the judge.

The relevance to the first point of what I have just said is that the case now before me has been the subject of various attempts at a settlement. I understand that when the deputy master decided the case on 9 April last, he gave some oral reasons, though not

until 20 July did he give the written reasons which are now before me. In those written
a reasons he observed that when the application came before him on 9 April 'it appeared
to be in an atmosphere of compromise', though counsel for the appellants asked him to
adjudicate; and this he proceeded to do. There is nothing to show the basis on which he
accepted jurisdiction in a contested case. As he said in relation to his direction that the
will be not executed, there seemed to be no urgency, so presumably his jurisdiction was
based on his view of unreasonable expense. If that is so, then it seems unfortunate that
b the expense of the full hearing before the deputy master should have produced an order
which could only be acted on if nobody appealed. It is not as if the case was so plain that
no appeal could possibly be justifiable, as events have shown. It would have been even
more unfortunate if the deputy master had carried out his suggestion of revoking his
order and referring the case to the judge, thus rendering the hearing before him
nugatory.
c   On this point it seems to me that if a case comes before the master or deputy master
'in an atmosphere of compromise', and no compromise is achieved, the master or deputy
master must consider whether he can properly hear the matter as contested proceedings.
If he concludes that he can and should, he should say so, and briefly state his reasons. If
he then determines the case, he should normally not halt the operation of the order that
he makes. There may, of course, be special circumstances where some sort of stay is
d proper and desirable, but I can see no such circumstances in the present case. It seems
undesirable that a stay should be imposed which could be regarded as discouraging an
appeal by one party and encouraging an appeal by other parties. In all normal cases of
making statutory wills, where the master or deputy master exercises the jurisdiction I
think that the order should be made and acted on, and any appeal left to take its course.
I have no doubt that in this case the deputy master acted with the best of intentions; but
e I also feel no doubt that he took the wrong course.
    In the result, I allow the appeal to the extent that I have indicated. I shall hear any
submissions that counsel may wish to make on the ambit of the substitution clause for
Mr A; and if any other submissions arise out of my judgment, I shall hear them also.

Appeal allowed ; order accordingly.

f
14 October. The court heard argument on costs.

R W Ham for the appellants.
Gregory Hill for the respondents.
Peter Rawson for the Official Solicitor.
g
SIR ROBERT MEGARRY V-C. I have to deal with the costs of the appeal to this
court from the decision of the deputy master. His order as to costs has been left
undisturbed by the parties.
    The costs of the Official Solicitor occasion no difficulty. He seeks to have his costs out
of the patient's estate on a solicitor and own client basis, and nobody has suggested that
h any other order should be made. I therefore make that order.
    The other costs are in dispute. On behalf of the successful appellants, counsel seeks an
order that their costs should be paid by the unsuccessful respondents on a party and party
basis, and that, so far as that does not discharge their costs, they should be entitled to the
balance out of the patient's estate on a common fund basis. On behalf of the unsuccessful
respondents, counsel resists that application, and says that the costs of the appellants and
j the respondents should be borne by the patient's estate on a common fund basis, in
accordance with *Re C E F D* [1963] 1 All ER 685, [1963] 1 WLR 329. On all hands it is
accepted that the matter is one for the discretion of the court.
    The main point of counsel for the appellants is based on an open offer and counter-
offer made respectively about 3½ weeks and 2½ weeks before the hearing before me
began. The respondents offered to agree that a legacy to Mrs A of £13,000 should be

inserted in the statutory will in place of the £10,000 ordered by the deputy master, and
the appellants made a counter-offer that they would agree a legacy of £15,000. Without *a*
knowledge of the offer and counter-offer, of course, I directed that the legacy should be
£15,000, the figure put forward by the appellants. On this footing it is contended that,
by resisting the appeal, the respondents did no better than they would have done if they
had accepted the counter-offer, and so they should bear the costs of the appellants in
prosecuting the appeal. The counter-offer wore at least some of the aspects of the
familiar 'sealed offer' in cases of the compulsory acquisition of land, and is plainly of *b*
considerable importance.

Counsel for the respondents relied strongly on Re C E F D [1963] 1 WLR 329, and in
this he was supported by counsel for the Official Solicitor. Despite the changes in the
Rules of the Supreme Court about costs made since that case was decided, the principle
applied there by Wilberforce J appears to be still applicable. That principle is that in a
normal case the costs of all parties to an application of this type (in that case it was for the *c*
making of a settlement rather than the making of a will) should be borne by the patient's
estate on a common fund basis, with the costs of the Official Solicitor on a solicitor and
own client basis. Thus far, the case gives counsel for the respondents much support.
However, I think that is is important to observe that so for as can be seen from the reports
of that case it was not an appeal from the master or deputy master to a nominated judge,
but was a hearing at first instance. I have looked at the report of Re C E F D in the All *d*
England Law Reports, and I can see nothing in either report which suggests that the
judge was hearing an appeal.

That seems to me to be a matter of some importance. If one accepts that in any fair
case of dispute those concerned have a reasonable expectation of having their costs, on a
common fund basis, paid out of the estate so far as the hearing at first instance is
concerned, it does not by any means necessarily follow that the same rule will apply on *e*
an appeal. The order of the deputy master in this case does indeed seem to be in accord
with Re C E F D, save that I am not at all sure that he was entitled to direct that the costs
of the present appellants and respondents should be paid out of the estate on the basis of
solicitor and own client instead of on a common fund basis. But the costs of the appeal
to this court, and of any possible further appeal, seem to me to rest on a different
footing. Counsel for the respondents, and also counsel for the Official Solicitor, stressed *f*
that many matters were explored before me which were of some general importance and
also of some degree of novelty, and concluded from this that it was proper for the estate
to bear the costs. Yet had the counter-offer been accepted, these costs would never have
been incurred. At the same time, I accept that the counter-offer was not made until 9 July
(late in the day, I understand), and that was little more than 2½ weeks before the hearing
of the appeal began. I must also bear in mind what the disposition of the residue of the *g*
estate is under the order that I have made.

I bear all these factors in mind, and also the other points that were put before me in
argument. I attach little weight, I may say, to the fact that the substitution clause was
extended by reason of my decision. Looking at the case as a whole, and taking a broad
sword to the costs involved, I think the right order to make is that the respondents should
bear half the appellants' costs on a party and party basis, that the appellants should be *h*
entitled to take the balance of their costs on a common fund basis out of the patient's
estate, and that I should make no order as to the respondents' costs. I have already dealt
with the costs of the Official Solicitor. I direct the taxation of all the costs ordered to be
paid in accordance with this order.

Order accordingly.

Solicitors: *Rowleys & Blewitts*, Manchester (for the appellants); *Woodford & Ackroyd*,
Southampton (for the respondents); *Official Solicitor*.

Azza M Abdallah   Barrister.

Aspden (Inspector of Taxes) v Hildesley

CHANCERY DIVISION
NOURSE J
27, 30 NOVEMBER 1981

b   *Capital gains tax – Disposal of assets – Husband and wife – Transfer of interest in property pursuant to consent order made on decree nisi of divorce – Transfer of husband's joint interest in property – Wife undertaking to authorise her personal representatives to pay to husband value of interest transferred in the event of her death within specified period – Whether disposal under a contract – Whether disposal under a conditional contract – Whether transfer of interest 'by way of security' – Finance Act 1965, s 22(4)(a)(6), Sch 7, para 17(2) – Finance Act 1971, Sch 10, para 10.*

The taxpayer and his wife separated in 1970, and in 1975 the taxpayer commenced divorce proceedings. Since 1964 the taxpayer and his wife had been the joint legal and beneficial owners of a property which had not at any material time been the main residence of either of them. On 12 February 1976, on the making of the decree nisi, it was ordered by consent of the taxpayer and his wife that the taxpayer should forthwith transfer his interest in the property to his wife and make certain periodical payments for a specified period. The wife undertook to give irrevocable authority to her personal representatives in the event of her dying before 10 December 1984 in the lifetime of the taxpayer to distribute from her estate a sum equal to one-half of the then equity in the property, and in the event of her disposing of the property prior to 10 December 1984 in the lifetime of the taxpayer to retain assets to enable her to carry out the first undertaking. Those terms were ordered to be filed and made a rule of court. The decree absolute was made during the financial year 1976–77. The taxpayer was assessed to capital gains tax for the year 1975–76 on the footing that he had made a disposal of his joint interest in the property. The General Commissioners allowed an appeal by the taxpayer against the assessment on the ground that, since the taxpayer had a contingent interest in the property until 1984, the transfer was a transfer by way of security within s 22(6)[a] of the Finance Act 1965 and accordingly was not to treated as involving any acquisition or disposal. The Crown appealed, contending that s 22(4)(a)[b] of the 1965 Act applied since the transfer was, by virtue of paras 17(2)[c] and 21(2)[d] of Sch 7 to the 1965 Act, a transaction between connected persons and the exemption provided by Sch 7, para 20 for disposals between husband and wife did not apply as the taxpayer and his wife were not living together. The Crown pointed out that it could be argued that the transfer had not taken place on the making of the order on 12 February 1976 but conditionally on the making of the decree absolute, with the result that the disposal would be treated by Sch 10, para 10[e] to the Finance Act 1971 as having taken place on the satisfaction of the condition.

Held – The appeal would be allowed for the following reasons—

(1) Although the transfer by the taxpayer of his interest in the property to his wife contained no element of gift, under the combined effect of s 22(4)(a) of and Sch 7, para

---

a   Section 22(6) is set out at p 59 *f*, post
b   Section 22(4), so far as is material, is set out at p 57 *h*, post
c   Paragraph 17(2) is set out at p 58 *a*, post
d   Paragraph 21(2) provides: 'A person is connected with an individual if that person is the individual's husband or wife, or is a relative, or the husband or wife of a relative, of the individual or of the individual's husband or wife.'
e   Paragraph 10 is set out at p 58 *e f*, post

17(2) to the 1965 Act the taxpayer was deemed to have disposed of his interest and his wife to have acquired it for a consideration equal to its market value (see p 57 *d e* and p 58 *b* to *d*, post); *Turner v Follett (Inspector of Taxes)* [1973] STC 148 applied.

(2) Since a consent order made before decree absolute was to be regarded as taking effect under a contract, and since the transfer of the taxpayer's interest to his wife was not made conditional on the making of the decree absolute but was to be made 'forthwith', the transfer was not made under a conditional contract to which Sch 10, para 10 to the 1971 Act applied. It followed that the transfer was a disposal which gave rise to a charge *b* to capital gains tax and which was made on the making of the consent order on 12 February 1976 (see p 58 *g* to *j* and p 59 *b*, post); *Re Shaw* [1918] P 47 followed; *de Lasala v de Lasala* [1979] 2 All ER 1146 and *Thwaite v Thwaite* [1981] 2 All ER 789 distinguished.

(3) After the transfer the taxpayer had no interest in the property since the wife's undertaking gave him only a contingent right to a sum of money and a breach of that undertaking would not have given him the right to set aside the transfer. The transfer *c* could not therefore be regarded as giving the taxpayer a contingent interest in the property. Furthermore, the transfer could not be regarded as a 'transfer of [an] interest . . . by way of security' within s 22(6) of the 1965 Act since, on its true construction, s 22(6) applied only to a conveyance or transfer of property to secure compliance with an obligation on the performance of which the property reverted to the transferor (see p 59 *e* to *j*, post).

Notes

For the time of disposal of assets under conditional contracts, see 5 Halsbury's Laws (4th edn) para 33.

For the transfer of assets by way of security, see ibid para 61.

For assets deemed to be transferred at market value, see ibid para 182.

For the Finance Act 1965, s 22, Sch 7, paras 17, 20, 21, see 34 Halsbury's Statutes (3rd edn) 877, 959, 961, 962.

For the Finance Act 1971, Sch 10, para 10, see 41 ibid 1534.

The Finance Act 1965, s 22(4) and (6) and Sch 7, paras 17(2), 20 and 21(2) and the Finance Act 1971, Sch 10, para 10 were replaced by the Capital Gains Tax Act 1979, *f* ss 19(3), 23(1), 62(2), 44, 63(2) and 27 respectively.

In relation to acquisitions and disposals on or after 10 March 1981, s 19(3) of the 1979 Act was repealed by the Finance Act 1981, Sch 19, Part VIII.

Cases referred to in judgment

de Lasala v de Lasala [1979] 2 All ER 1146, [1980] AC 546, [1979] 3 WLR 390, PC, Digest (Cont Vol E) 354, 708a.

Marren (Inspector of Taxes) v Ingles [1980] 3 All ER 95, [1980] 1 WLR 983, [1980] STC 500, HL.

Shaw, Re, Smith v Shaw [1918] P 47, CA, 28(1) Digest (Reissue) 291, 986.

Thwaite v Thwaite [1981] 2 All ER 789, [1981] 3 WLR 96, CA.

Turner v Follett (Inspector of Taxes) [1973] STC 148, CA, Digest (Cont Vol D) 474, 1451a.

Case stated

1. At a meeting of the Commissioners for the General Purposes of Income Tax for the division of St Martin-in-the-Fields held at the Law Society's Hall, Chancery Lane, in the City of Westminster on 15 February and 7 June 1979 Raymond James Hildesley (the taxpayer) appealed against an assessment to capital gains tax made on him for the year 1975–76 in the sum of £6,651.

2. The question for determination was whether on the transfer by the taxpayer of his half interest in the property known as 21 Westmoreland Terrace, Pimlico, Westminster, in the County of Greater London (the property) to his former wife Eileen Dolores Hildesley (Mrs Hildesley) there accrued to him a chargeable gain for the purposes of the capital gains tax legislation.

3. The taxpayer appeared in person. The Crown was represented by the inspector of
taxes.

4. It was proved or admitted as follows. (i) At all material times prior to 12 February
1976 the taxpayer owned the property jointly with Mrs Hildesley but the property was
not the residence of the taxpayer or Mrs Hildesley. The taxpayer had paid for the
property at the time of its purchase but had put it in the joint names of himself and Mrs
Hildesley at that time. (ii) The taxpayer and Mrs Hildesley had lived separate and apart
since January 1970. (iii) On 12 February 1976 Dunn J by consent of the taxpayer and
Mrs Hildesley made an order on making a decree nisi in proceedings before him between
the taxpayer and Mrs Hildesley that, inter alia, the taxpayer should transfer forthwith to
Mrs Hildesley all his interest both legal and equitable in the property. (iv) The order was
made on the undertakings by Mrs Hildesley, inter alia, (1) to give irrevocable authority
to her personal representatives that in the event of her dying before 10 December 1984
and predeceasing the taxpayer they would distribute from her estate a sum equal to one-
half of the then equity in the property calculated by deducting only the outstanding
mortgage and costs of sale or any equivalent money, chattel or real property to the
taxpayer, such payment to take priority over all other bequests or payments from her
estate, and (2) that in the event of her disposing of the property prior to 10 December
1984 and during the lifetime of the taxpayer she would retain assets in her estate
equivalent to one-half of the equity raised by such sale in order to enable her personal
representatives to carry out the irrevocable undertaking. Pursuant to the order the
taxpayer transferred to Mrs Hildesley his interest in the property. (v) The difference
between the value of the property at cost and at the time of transfer by the taxpayer of
his interest was £6,650, on one-half of which (£3,325) capital gains tax was assessed in
the sum of £997·50.

5. On behalf of the taxpayer it was contended: (a) that the transfer by him of his
interest in the property was part of a divorce settlement arrived at after many years of
negotiation; (b) that he had derived no capital sum or other gain from the transfer in
terms of either s 19(1) or s 22(10) of the Finance Act 1965; (c) that the transfer in fact
represented a loss to him; (d) that the transfer was by way of security within s 22(6) of the
1965 Act, Mrs Hildesley's answer in the divorce proceedings between them having
included a claim for secured provision; (e) that 'a gain' was not clearly defined in the 1965
Act but by a dictionary definition no gain had accrued to him; (f) that the order of
Dunn J should be construed as creating a charge on the property which was in fact
registrable although it had not been registered; (g) that until Mrs Hildesley disposed of
the property there was no capital gain.

6. On behalf of the Crown it was contended: (a) that, albeit under some element of
compulsion, the taxpayer had by the transfer of his interest in the property given away
his money; (b) that although there was no definition in the 1965 Act of 'chargeable gain'
there were various circumstances arising by statute giving rise to such a gain
notwithstanding the normal dictionary definition of the word; (c) that by virtue of
s 22(1) of the 1965 Act all forms of property were assets, the property was 'property' and
the taxpayer had disposed of his half share by gift to Mrs Hildesley in consideration of the
termination of their marriage and formed part of a contract on the change of relationship
thereby arising; (d) that s 22(4) of the 1965 Act deemed a gain in certain circumstances
and as the transaction in question was between connected persons it could not be at arm's
length and in consequence s 22(4) applied; (e) that the position would be the same even
if the transaction were not between husband and wife, and para 20(1) of Sch 7 to the 1965
Act did not apply because the husband and wife were not living together at the relevant
time; (f) that the 1965 Act had to be construed strictly and it had always been Revenue
practice to construe the words 'accruing to a person on the disposal of assets' in s 19(1) of
that as meaning that the gain was chargeable on the person making the disposal of the
asset over which he had title; (g) that nothing in Mrs Hildesley's answer indicated that
the transfer of the taxpayer's interest in the property was in the nature of 'security' within
s 22(6) of the 1965 Act as the transfer by the taxpayer was of an absolute right and did not

create a debtor and creditor situation; (h) that the assessment should be determined in
the sum of £3,325.   *a*

7. The commissioners found—

'that [the taxpayer] had a contingent interest in the Property until 1984 and that
accordingly the transfer by [the taxpayer] of his interest in the Property was by way
of security within the meaning of Section 22(6) of the Act and that it followed that the
transfer did not give rise to a charge to Capital Gains Tax.'
                                                                                          b
8. The Crown thereupon expressed dissatisfaction with the determination as being
erroneous in point of law and required the commissioners to state and sign a case for the
opinion of the High Court.

9. The question of law for the opinion of the court was whether on the facts as found the
commissioners were entitled to decide as they did.

                                                                                          c
C H McCall for the Crown.
The taxpayer appeared in person.

NOURSE J. The question in this case is whether capital gains tax was payable on a
transfer of a joint interest in property pursuant to a consent order made in 1976 on the
granting of a decree nisi for the dissolution of the taxpayer's marriage. The General   *d*
Commissioners for the St Martin-in-the-Fields division held that tax was not payable, and
the Crown now appeals to this court.

The taxpayer is Major Raymond James Hildesley. He was formerly married to Mrs
Eileen Dolores Hildesley. They separated in June 1970, and in 1975 the taxpayer
commenced divorce proceedings. Since 1964 the taxpayer and Mrs Hildesley had been the
joint legal and beneficial owners of 21 Westmoreland Terrace, Pimlico, but it was not at   *e*
any material time the only or main residence of either of them. On 12 February 1976
Dunn J, on the making of the decree nisi, ordered that certain terms be filed and made a
rule of court. Those terms took the form of cross-undertakings followed by a consent
order.

The convenient course is to refer first to paras 1, 2 and 3 of the consent order. Paragraph 1
ordered the taxpayer to transfer forthwith to Mrs Hildesley 'all his interest both legal and *f*
equitable' in 21 Westmoreland Terrace. Paragraph 2 ordered the taxpayer to make
periodical payments to Mrs Hildesley at the rate of £2,500 per annum payable monthly,
less tax, from decree absolute during a period which I need not specify. Paragraph 3
ordered that the foregoing financial provision was in satisfaction of all Mrs Hildesley's
claims for ancillary relief and against the taxpayer's estate.

The first undertaking was one by the taxpayer to effect in favour of Mrs Hildesley, and   *g*
to keep up, a policy on his life in an amount sufficient to discharge the mortgage on 21
Westmoreland Terrace in the event of his death during the period for which the periodical
payments were to be payable. There were then two undertakings by Mrs Hildesley. The
first was to give irrevocable authority to her personal representatives that in the event of
her dying before 10 December 1984 in the lifetime of the taxpayer they would distribute
from her estate a sum equal to one-half of the then equity in 21 Westmoreland Terrace,
calculated in a manner which I need not recite. The second was that in the event of her
disposing of the property prior to 10 December 1984 in the lifetime of the taxpayer she
would 'retain assets in her estate equivalent to one-half of the equity raised by such sale in
order to enable her personal representatives to carry out the first undertaking. It is on the
construction and effect of Dunn J's order and those terms that the claim for capital gains tax
depends.

The remaining facts can be shortly stated. Pursuant to the order the taxpayer transferred
to Mrs Hildesley all his interest, both legal and equitable, in 21 Westmoreland Terrace.
The decree was made absolute on some date during the financial year 1976–77, but that
fact was not one of those found by the commissioners and counsel for the Crown accepts
that he cannot rely on it for the purposes of this appeal. In due course the taxpayer was

assessed to capital gains tax for the year 1975–76 on the footing that he had made a disposal
a for capital gains tax purposes of his joint interest in 21 Westmoreland Terrace on the date
of the consent order, namely 12 February 1976. If the claim is a good one, it is agreed that
the chargeable gain on the property was £6,650, on half of which capital gains tax at the
rate of 30% amounts to £997·50.

Counsel for the Crown told me that this is the first occasion on which the court has had
to consider the impact of the capital gains tax legislation on dispositions made for giving
b effect to financial provision or property adjustment orders pursuant to ss 23 and 24 of the
Matrimonial Causes Act 1973. Such dispositions would normally be outside the capital
transfer tax legislation, which provides that dispositions for the maintenance of one's
family shall not be transfers of value for the purposes of that tax. But there are no
comparable provisions in the capital gains tax legislation. That is not so surprising as it
might seem. In very general terms, capital transfer tax is a tax on gifts inter vivos or on
c death but not on dispositions made for consideration or in pursuance of some obligation.
Capital gains tax, on the other hand, is a tax on disposals of assets, and it is in general
irrelevant whether they are made for consideration or pursuant to some obligation or by
way of gift.

That was made very clear by the decision of the Court of Appeal in *Turner v Follett*
(Inspector of Taxes) [1973] STC 148, where it was held that the effect of s 22(4)(*a*) of the
d Finance Act 1965 was that a disposal by way of gift must be deemed to have been a disposal
for a consideration equal to the market value of the asset and was liable to capital gains tax
accordingly. Although the Crown accepts that there was no gift by the taxpayer to Mrs
Hildesley, its claim in this case again depends primarily on s 22(4)(*a*). It claims that on 12
February 1976 the taxpayer disposed of his joint interest in 21 Westmoreland Terrace and,
for reasons which will appear, that it should be deemed to have been a disposal for a
e consideration equal to the market value of that interest.

I must now examine the 1965 Act and one provision of the Finance Act 1971 with some
care in order to see whether that claim is made out. Having referred to *Turner v Follett
(Inspector of Taxes)*, in which Russell LJ (at 151) traced the now familiar provisions of
ss 19(1) and 20(1), (3) and (4) of the 1965 Act, and commented on them in terms which I
respectfully adopt, I can start with s 22. Subsection (1) of that section defines assets in terms
f fully wide enough to embrace the taxpayer's joint interest in 21 Westmoreland Terrace.
Subsection (2)(*a*) provides that references to a disposal of an asset normally include
references to a part disposal of an asset. Subsection (2)(*b*) then tells you what a part disposal
is. Counsel for the Crown very properly drew my attention to the possibility of an
argument favourable to the taxpayer based on the proposition that a transaction whereby
he received Mrs Hildesley's two undertakings in exchange for the transfer of his interest
g constituted only a part disposal of the interest. Without going into detail it seems to me
that that argument could not succeed, it having been practically concluded against the
taxpayer by the view which the House of Lords clearly thought was correct in *Marren
(Inspector of Taxes) v Ingles* [1980] 3 All ER 95, [1980] STC 500.

Subsection (4) is in these terms:

h 'Subject to the provisions of this Part of this Act, a person's acquisition of an asset
and the disposal of it to him shall for the purposes of this Part of this Act be deemed
to be for a consideration equal to the market value of the asset—(*a*) where he acquires
the asset otherwise than by way of a bargain made at arm's length and in particular
where he acquires it by way of gift or by way of distribution from a company in
respect of shares in the company, or (*b*) where he acquires the asset wholly or partly for
a consideration that cannot be valued . . .'

I need not read any more for the purposes of this case. I need not read sub-s (5); and I will
come to sub-ss (6) and (7) later.

I must next refer to certain provisions in Sch 7 to the 1965 Act. First, para 17(1) provides
that that paragraph shall apply where a person acquires an asset and the person making the
disposal is connected with him. Sub-paragraph (2) is in these terms:

'Without prejudice to the generality of section 22(4) of this Act the person acquiring the asset and the person making the disposal shall be treated as parties to a transaction *a* otherwise than by way of a bargain made at arm's length.'

Paragraph 21(2) provides that a person is connected with an individual if that person is, inter alios, the individual's husband or wife.

Counsel for the Crown says, correctly, that if the disposal was made on 12 February 1976 the taxpayer and Mrs Hildesley were still then husband and wife, since a marriage subsists until dissolved by decree absolute. He therefore claims that they were connected persons *b* on the material date. On the other hand, it is not possible for the taxpayer to take advantage of the general exemption applying to disposals between husband and wife under para 20 of Sch 7, because that exemption applies only when they are living together. On one view that is a somewhat paradoxical state of affairs, but the material provisions are clear and there may well have been good reasons for them.

The result to which they lead, submits counsel for the Crown, is that under the *c* combined effect of s 22(4)(*a*) and para 17(2) the taxpayer must be deemed to have disposed of his interest and Mrs Hildesley to have acquired it for a consideration equal to its market value. Alternatively, he submits that the disposal and acquisition were made for a consideration which cannot be valued within s 22(4)(*b*), with the same result. I accept counsel for the Crown's submission as to the combined effect of s 22(4)(*a*) and para 17(2). It is unnecessary for me to decide, and I do not decide, whether the alternative claim under *d* s 22(4)(*b*) is also correct.

Counsel for the Crown accepts that the Crown's success in these proceedings depends on its being able to establish that the disposal took place on 12 February 1976 because otherwise there can have been no disposal during the year of assessment 1975–76. That involves a consideration of the Finance Act 1971, Sch 10, para 10, which is in these terms:

> '(1) Subject to section 45(5) of the Finance Act 1965 and sub-paragraph (2) below, where an asset is disposed of and acquired under a contract the time at which the disposal and acquisition is made is the time the contract is made (and not, if different, the time at which the asset is conveyed or transferred).
>
> (2) If the contract is conditional (and, in particular, if it is conditional on the exercise of an option) the time at which the disposal and acquisition is made is the time when *f* the condition is satisfied.'

Section 45(5) of the 1965 Act has no relevance to this case.

In the light of the provisions I have read counsel for the Crown has to show, first, that the order of 12 February 1976 was a contract and, second, that it was not conditional within para 10(2). As to the first of these matters counsel for the Crown referred me to the recent case in the Court of Appeal of *Thwaite v Thwaite* [1981] 2 All ER 789, [1981] 3 WLR 96, in *g* which it was held that where parties to matrimonial proceedings agreed terms, and by consent those terms were embodied in an order of the court, the legal effect of their agreement derived from the court's order and not from contract. However, it is clear that the consent order there in question had been made after decree absolute, and in the light of ss 23(5) and 24(3) of the Matrimonial Causes Act 1973 I do not think that either that case or *de Lasala v de Lasala* [1979] 2 All ER 1146, [1980] AC 546, a decision of the Privy Council *h* on which the Court of Appeal based itself, is to be taken as a decision on the effect of a consent order made before decree absolute. In such a case the matter would appear to rest on contract in accordance with the normal rule which was recognised by the Court of Appeal in *Thwaite v Thwaite*.

Moreover, in this case the order was not a full consent order but an order that the agreed terms 'be filed and made a Rule of Court'. That is a very familiar formula in the Family *j* Division. It seems clear from the decision of the Court of Appeal in *Re Shaw, Smith v Shaw* [1918] P 47, and in particular from the judgment of Warrington LJ (at 53–54), that the effect of an order in that form is that the obligation remains contractual.

In all the circumstances it seems to me to be clear that the consent order of 12 February 1976 was a contract within para 10 of Sch 10 to the Finance Act 1971. I must now consider whether the contract to transfer the taxpayer's joint interest in 21 Westmoreland Terrace

forthwith was an unconditional contract or was a conditional one within para 10(2). That
is a point which has troubled me. It seems to me that it might be possible to say that any
contract which was entered into in circumstances such as these was impliedly conditional
on the decree being made absolute. Counsel for the Crown saw the force of that as a
general point but said that in this particular case it could not be right. He pointed to the
contrast between the agreement to transfer the taxpayer's interest in the property forthwith
and the agreement that the periodical payments should start from decree absolute. He
submitted that in those circumstances it would have been impossible for the taxpayer to
have set aside the contract if the decree had not been made absolute. On consideration I
think that that submission is correct. I would have felt happier about acceding to it if I had
heard an argument to the contrary, but the taxpayer, who appears in person, understandably
did not advance one. His main point was that which is concluded against him by *Turner
v Follett (Inspector of Taxes)* [1973] STC 148.

Accordingly, unless there is any other objection, it seems to me that counsel for the
Crown has made out the Crown's claim based on a disposal on 12 February 1976. It
remains for me to consider the ground on which the commissioners decided the case in
favour of the taxpayer. They expressed themselves as follows:

> 'We the Commissioners found that [the taxpayer] had a contingent interest in the
> Property until 1984 and that accordingly the transfer by [the taxpayer] of his interest
> in the Property was by way of security within the meaning of Section 22(6) of the Act
> and that it followed that the transfer did not give rise to a charge to Capital Gains Tax.'

No further reasons were given for the decision.

As to that, it is clear, first, that the taxpayer did not have a contingent interest in the
property. After the disposal he had no interest in the property at all. He had, and he has,
a contingent right to a sum of money under Mrs Hildesley's undertaking, but that is a mere
chose in action conferring no interest in the property. Second, and irrespective of whether
that is right or wrong, it is impossible to say that the transfer of the taxpayer's interest was
by way of security within s 22(6) of the 1965 Act. Subsection (6) is in these terms:

> 'The conveyance or transfer by way of security of an asset or of an interest or right
> in or over it, or transfer of a subsisting interest or right by way of security in or over
> an asset (including a retransfer on redemption of the security), shall not be treated for
> the purposes of this Part of this Act as involving any acquisition or disposal of the
> asset.'

It is clear on a reading of that subsection and sub-s (7) together that the expression 'by
way of security' is used in its conventional legal sense. It is talking about a conveyance or
transfer of property to secure compliance with an obligation on performance of which the
property reverts to the transferor. That is not this case. The taxpayer made an out and out
transfer of his interest and a breach of Mrs Hildesley's undertaking would give him no
more than a right to payment of damages. It is therefore clear that the commissioners'
decision cannot be supported. I should add, in order that there may be no doubt about it,
that it is equally clear that the taxpayer's interest was not an interest in settled property for
the purposes of the capital gains tax legislation.

I should also emphasise that the decision in this case is not likely to apply to the normal
case of a dwelling house which was the only or main residence of the parties to the
marriage; as to that, see s 29 of the Finance Act 1965.

The taxpayer was good enough to express his appreciation for the very full and fair way
in which counsel for the Crown argued this case on behalf of the Crown. I would like to
add my own appreciation to his. The appeal must be allowed.

Appeal allowed. No order as to costs.

Solicitors: *Solicitor of Inland Revenue.*

Edwina Epstein   Barrister.

Khan v Khan and others

COURT OF APPEAL, CIVIL DIVISION
STEPHENSON, GRIFFITHS AND KERR LJJ
9, 16 NOVEMBER, 21 DECEMBER 1981

Evidence – Privilege – Incrimination of witness or spouse – Exception to rule against self-incrimination – Proceedings for recovery of property – Self-incrimination of theft in proceedings for recovery of property not protected – Tracing order requiring defendant to give details of whereabouts of proceeds of cheque and how they were applied – Defendant claiming that compliance with order would expose him to risk of criminal prosecution for both theft and forgery of cheque – Defendant claiming that exception to rule against self-incrimination not applying because of risk of prosecution for forgery – Whether defendant excused from complying with tracing order – Theft Act 1968, s 31(1).

The plaintiff gave blank signed cheques to the first defendant, allegedly for the purpose of paying the balance of the purchase price of a property which the plaintiff was acquiring and for incidental expenses. The first defendant made out one of the cheques for £40,000 payable to the second defendant, a company controlled by him. The proceeds of the cheque were paid into the second defendant's account at the third defendant, a bank. Subsequently all or part of the £40,000 was removed from the account and used for other purposes. The plaintiff brought an action against the defendants seeking the replacement of the £40,000, damages for breach of trust, disclosure of the whereabouts of the £40,000 and an account of how it had been applied. No defence to the action was served but the first defendant's solicitors alleged in a letter to the plaintiff's solicitors that the plaintiff had lent the £40,000 to the first defendant. The plaintiff obtained ex parte a tracing order requiring the first defendant personally and the second defendant by its directors to swear affidavits setting out full details of the facts and matters within their knowledge concerning the whereabouts and application of the £40,000. The defendants applied to have the order discharged or varied but the judge refused their application. The defendants appealed to the Court of Appeal, submitting that if they complied with the tracing order the first defendant would incriminate himself of offences under both the Theft Act 1968 and the Forgery Act 1913, and that the exception to the rule against self-incrimination contained in s 31(1)[a] of the 1968 Act (which provided that a person was not to be excused on the grounds of self-incrimination from complying with an order made in proceedings for the recovery of property) only applied 'in proceedings for an offence under [the 1968 Act]' and did not apply in the circumstances because the first defendant was also at risk of incriminating himself of an offence under the 1913 Act. The plaintiff conceded that his case necessarily involved an allegation of forgery, in that the first defendant by altering a blank cheque outside the scope of the authority given to him as agent had in law forged the cheque. On the defendants' appeal against the tracing order,

Held – The tracing order would be upheld and the appeal dismissed, for the following reasons—

(1) Assuming that compliance with the tracing order would expose the first defendant to, or materially increase, the risk of criminal proceedings against him, nevertheless the exception to the rule against self-incrimination contained in s 31(1) of the 1968 Act applied to the first defendant because the substance of any foreseeable criminal proceedings against him if he were required to comply with the tracing order and thereby incriminate himself would be a prosecution 'for an offence under [the 1968 Act]', within s 31(1), and even if an alternative charge of forgery were brought against him the proceedings for theft and forgery would in substance still be proceedings for

---

a   Section 31(1) is set out at p 63 *e f*, post

theft and therefore 'proceedings for an offence under [the 1968 Act]'. Similarly, the

a protection conferred on the first defendant by s 31(1)(b) preventing any statement or admission made by him in compliance of the tracing order from being admissible in evidence against him would apply even if an alternative charge of forgery were brought against him (see p 64 *h j*, p 65 *a c d h j*, p 66 *e f j* and p 67 *a*, post).

   (2) In any event, compliance with the tracing order would not expose the defendants to, or materially increase, the risk of criminal proceedings against them because the first

b defendant was already exposed to such a risk by the circumstances in which he had handed over the cheque for £40,000 to the second defendant and any disclosure regarding the subsequent disposal of the proceeds of the cheque could not materially add to that existing risk (see p 66 *a* to *c g* to *j* and p 67 *a*, post).

Notes

c For privilege from discovery on the ground of self-incrimination generally, see 13 Halsbury's Laws (4th edn) para 92, and for cases on the subject, see 22 Digest (Reissue) 433–436, 4310–4336.

   For the statutory exception to the rule against self-incrimination, see 11 Halsbury's Laws (4th edn) para 431.

   For the Theft Act 1968, s 31, see 8 Halsbury's Statutes (3rd edn) 802.

Cases referred to in judgments

R v Bateman (1845) 1 Cox CC 186, 15 Digest (Reissue) 1465, *12,972*.
Rank Film Distributors Ltd v Video Information Centre [1981] 2 All ER 76, [1981] 2 WLR 668, HL.
Reynolds, Re, ex p Reynolds (1882) 20 Ch D 294, CA, 22 Digest (Reissue) 434, *4315*.

Interlocutory appeals

The first and second defendants, Iqbal Ali Khan and Watford Tradelink Ltd, appealed against the order of Stuart Smith J dated 27 October 1981 that the first defendant personally and the second defendant by its directors make and serve on the solicitors for the plaintiff, Mohammed Krim Khan, affidavits setting out details within their knowledge of the whereabouts and application of the sum of £40,000, and of any assets acquired through use of that sum, paid on 14 August 1981 to the second defendant from the plaintiff's bank account, and against the order of Woolf J dated 3 November 1981 refusing to vary or discharge the tracing order. The grounds of the appeal were that compliance with the order might incriminate the first and second defendants or either of them of offences other than offences under the Theft Act 1968. The third defendant, Lloyds Bank Ltd, was not a party to the appeals. The facts are set out in the judgment of Stephenson LJ.

Richard Slowe for the first and second defendants.
John Higham for the plaintiff.

Cur adv vult

21 December. The following judgments were read.

STEPHENSON LJ. The first and second defendants, Mr Iqbal Ali Khan and Watford Tradelink Ltd, apply for leave to appeal against, in effect, one of two injunctions granted ex parte by Stuart Smith J on 27 October 1981 at the suit of the plaintiff, Dr Mohammed Krim Khan. On that date that judge granted what can be described as a tracing order and a Mareva injunction. The Mareva injunction is not now questioned before us. But Woolf J was asked to discharge or vary both parts of Stuart Smith J's order and it is his order of 3 November refusing to discharge or vary the tracing order against which the applicants want leave to appeal. We have granted them leave, which Woolf J refused, and heard the application as an appeal. The tracing order was in these terms:

'IT IS ORDERED that the First Defendant personally and the Second Defendant by
its Directors make and serve upon the Plaintiff's solicitors, Messrs. McKenna & Co. *a*
[and their address is given] forthwith and in any event within 48 hours from service
of the Order, Affidavits setting out full details of all facts and matters within their
knowledge and/or information concerning the whereabouts of and what has become
of the sum of £40,000 paid on or about 14th August, 1981 to the Second Defendant
from the bank account of the Plaintiff with the branch of National Westminster
Bank Limited at Stanhope Gate, 18A, Curzon Street, London W1 and/or any monies *b*
or assets purchased or acquired, whether directly or indirectly, through the use of
such sum or any part thereof and to exhibit thereto all documents within their
custody, possession or power relating to the whereabouts of and/or application of
such sum and/or such monies or assets'

and then there was liberty to apply.
The appellants want us to vary that injunction by adding the words: *c*

'save and unless and solely to the extent that compliance herewith might
incriminate the First and Second Defendants or either of them of offences other
than any which may be charged under the Theft Act 1968 or 1978.'

The injunction was obtained by the plaintiff, Dr Khan, to assist him in his action
against the first and second defendants and a third defendant, Lloyds Bank Ltd, who is *d*
not a party to this appeal, in recovering the sum of £40,000, which he claims to have paid
to the first defendant, Mr Khan, in the following manner. Last August the plaintiff gave
the first defendant three cheques drawn and signed by the plaintiff in blank on his
account with the National Westminster Bank. The first of them was to be used by the
first defendant to pay the balance of the purchase price of a leasehold property in Portsea
Place, London, on which the plaintiff had already paid a deposit of £20,000. The other *e*
two cheques were to be used to pay surveyors' fees and for furnishing the property. The
plaintiff wanted the property to live in on his frequent visits to this country from Saudi
Arabia, where he practises as a doctor of medicine. He had given the first defendant a
general power of attorney and hoped to find the purchase of his property completed. But
on his return to this country on 1 October 1981 the first defendant told him that that was
not so as he had paid the monies standing to the credit of the plaintiff's account to the *f*
second defendant, Watford Tradelink Ltd.
It is common ground that the first defendant had completed one of the plaintiff's
cheques by making it payable to the second defendant in the sum of £40,000; that the
first defendant was a director and controlling shareholder of the second defendant; that
the proceeds of the cheque were credited to the second defendant's account with the
third defendant, Lloyds Bank Ltd on 14 August, from which account these proceeds or *g*
part of them have been removed; that neither the cheque not its proceeds were used for
the purchase of the property or the other purposes connected with the purchase; and that
the first and second defendants have failed to account to the plaintiff for the proceeds, or
any part of the proceeds, of the cheque. So the plaintiff has had to complete the purchase
of the property with other monies.
No defence to the plaintiff's claim for declarations, replacement of the sum of £40,000, *h*
damages, an account and disclosure of the whereabouts and application of the £40,000
has yet been served. But on 22 October solicitors for the first defendant wrote to the
plaintiff's solicitors as follows:

'Dear Sir,
                    Dr. Mohammed Krim Khan
We refer to our telephone conversation of the 19th October when we informed *j*
you that we act for Mr. Iqbal Ali Khan and enquired from you whether you had
received instructions to issue any proceedings against our Client in connection with
a loan of approximately £39,000 made by your Client to our Client. We informed
you over the telephone that our instructions were that your Client of his own

a volition allowed our Client to borrow this money and had agreed that it should be paid back at the rate of £217 per month over a period of 15 years. Would you kindly note that we now act for Mr. Iqbal Khan and kindly advise us immediately any proceedings are contemplated.'

If the £40,000 was indeed lent to the first defendant by the plaintiff and not entrusted to him to purchase the property, there would be no objection to the first defendant or the b second defendant acting as they did with the cheque and no liability to account to the plaintiff for the proceeds of the cheque.

The second defendant's account with the third defendant shows a receipt of £40,000 on 14 August, two payments of £15,000 by cheques cashed by the first defendant on 21 August and 6 October and a payment by standing order of £217 on 15 October for the credit of the plaintiff's account with the National Westminster Bank.

c The law gives a party all permissible help in tracing property which is the subject of dispute by compelling disclosure, but it has also fixed its canon against self-incrimination. A party is not compelled to give discovery which will tend to criminate him or expose him to proceedings for a penalty: see *The Supreme Court Practice 1982*, vol 1, p 456, para 24/5/10. He has a right in any legal proceedings other than criminal proceedings to refuse to answer any question or produce any document or thing if to do d so would tend to expose him to proceedings for an offence or for the recovery of a penalty: see s 14(1) of the Civil Evidence Act 1968.

But Parliament has also recognised, in s 31 of the Theft Act 1968, the importance and difficulty of tracing stolen property and protecting the owners of property, including (since this year's decision of the House of Lords in *Rank Film Distributors Ltd v Video Information Centre* [1981] 2 All ER 76, [1981] 2 WLR 668) intellectual property as defined e in s 72 of the Supreme Court Act 1981. Section 31 of the 1968 Act provides, by sub-s (1):

'A person shall not be excused, by reason that to do so may incriminate that person or the wife or husband of that person of an offence under this Act—(a) from answering any question put to that person in proceedings for the recovery or administration of any property, for the execution of any trust or for an account of any property or dealings with property; or (b) from complying with any order made in any such proceedings; but no statement or admission made by a person in answering a question put or complying with an order made as aforesaid shall, in proceedings for an offence under this Act, be admissible in evidence against that person or (unless they married after the making of the statement or admission) against the wife or husband of that person.'

f The statute removes the excuse of tendency to incriminate but prevents the penal consequences of incrimination, only, however, within defined limits. (1) It is only in proceedings for the recovery or administration of any property, for the execution of any trust or for an account of any property or dealings with property that answers or compliance with an order are not excused. (2) It is only incrimination of an offence under the Theft Act which is no excuse. (3) It is only in proceedings for an offence under g the Theft Act that the penal consequences are averted by statements or admissions made in answering questions or complying with orders being made inadmissible in evidence.

It is now conceded by counsel for the first and second defendants (1) that the order under appeal was made in proceedings for the recovery of property (as defined in s 4(1) of the 1968 Act) and indeed for an account of property. But what he submits is (2) that compliance with the order in its present form may incriminate them of an offence other than under the Theft Act, namely an offence under the Forgery Act 1913, and (3) that proceedings may be taken against them for an offence under the latter Act and so their answers in compliance with the order may be admissible to incriminate them of forgery.

It is conceded by counsel for the plaintiff that on the plaintiff's case the first defendant has committed an offence of forgery in relation to the plaintiff's cheque as well as an offence of theft, for if a cheque, including a blank cheque, is given to a person with a

certain authority the agent is confined strictly within the limits of that authority, and if
he chooses to alter it the crime of forgery is committed: see *R v Bateman* (1845) 1 Cox CC
186 and the cases cited in *Archbold's Criminal Pleading, Evidence and Practice* (40th edn,
1979) p 1143, para 2149. It was forgery at common law, and forgery of a cheque if
committed with intent to defraud is an offence punishable with 14 years' imprisonment:
see s 2(2)(*a*) of the Forgery Act 1913.

Well then, says counsel for the defendants, if the first defendant and the second
defendant by him comply with the order, the police, who have interrogated the first
defendant for two hours but have not yet charged him with any offence, will take
proceedings, for theft most probably but probably also for forgery; for it is easier to prove
the intent to defraud required by s 2(2) of the Forgery Act 1913 than to prove the
intention of permanently depriving the plaintiff of his property required by s 1(1) of the
Theft Act 1968, and if the first defendant is not committed on a charge of forgery, a
count for forgery will be added to the indictment after committal under proviso (i) to
s 2(2) of the Administration of Justice (Miscellaneous Provisions) Act 1933, and whatever
this court or defending counsel may say, prosecuting counsel may ask the judge of the
Crown Court to admit his statement made in compliance with the order under appeal
and the judge may grant his request.

That horrifying forecast counsel for the defendants supports (1) by two draft affidavits
prepared by counsel on instructions (which are of course privileged), one setting out
what the first defendant would swear if the judge's tracing order stands and the other
what he could and would swear without incriminating himself if the order is varied, (2)
by counsel's opinion that the material appearing in the first affidavit but omitted from
the second could reveal 'surrounding circumstances tending to show that Mr Khan had
mens rea appropriate for theft, deception and/or forgery and accordingly in the
circumstances of the case he might incriminate himself of any of those offences'.

Now it might be thought difficult to say or see that if the £40,000 was lent by the
plaintiff to the first defendant, any statements he might make about what he did with
the borrowed money could incriminate him of any criminal offence. Or it might be
thought that his story of a loan was in all the circumstances as at present understood so
unlikely that no account of what he did with the money would materially increase the
likelihood of his being charged or convicted of stealing the money or forging the
cheque. And it is common ground that there must be a real risk of incrimination or a
material increase of an existing risk. I accept that once there is reasonable ground to
apprehend danger to the first defendant from being compelled to answer in compliance
with the order, great latitude should be allowed him in judging for himself of the effect
of doing so; but he is not the sole judge and the court cannot be satisfied with an
unsupported claim by the first defendant that compliance may tend to criminate him or
with the bare possibility of legal peril: see, for instance, the judgments of Jessel MR and
Cotton LJ in *Re Reynolds, ex p Reynolds* (1882) 20 Ch D 294. Here the first defendant's
claim is supported by counsel's opinion and I will assume that compliance with the order
would tend to expose him to the danger of criminal proceedings and conviction of some
criminal offence or materially increase that danger. The question then is: what
proceedings? Proceedings for what offence? What is the offence of which compliance
with the order may incriminate him if not excused by the court from complying?

I reply without doubt: proceedings under the Theft Act, for an offence under the Theft
Act; the reason why he is not to be excused is that to comply may incriminate him of an
offence under the Theft Act. There is really no doubt that if any criminal proceedings
are taken against him, they will be proceedings under the Theft Act. The only doubt is
whether those proceedings will at any stage include a charge under the Forgery Act.

In estimating the risk of the first defendant being prosecuted for forgery, I would place
it between the 'real and appreciable' risk of Mr Lee and Mrs Gomberg in *Rank Film
Distributors Ltd v Video Information Centre* [1981] 2 All ER 76, [1981] 2 WLR 668 being
prosecuted for conspiracy to defraud and the 'totally insubstantial' risk of their being

prosecuted for a breach of s 21 of the Copyright Act 1956. Let me assume then that that risk is not 'remote and fanciful' and cannot be disregarded. But it is fanciful to suppose that the first defendant, if prosecuted, will be prosecuted for forgery alone. What is possible is that he may be prosecuted for theft and forgery. But proceedings for theft and forgery would, in my judgment, still be proceedings for an offence under the Theft Act. It would be monstrous if the assistance given by s 31 to persons seeking to recover their stolen property could be defeated by the bare possibility of an alternative charge of an offence under some other Act, or at common law, being introduced into the criminal proceedings. And, although this court cannot control the discretion of a prosecutor or the Crown Court, I think it would be monstrous also if the prosecution were to resort to what Lord Wilberforce in *Rank Film Distributors Ltd v Video Information Centre* [1981] 2 All ER 76 at 80, [1981] 2 WLR 668 at 674 described as 'a contrived addition to other charges' for the purpose of defeating the protection given to a defendant by the section and introducing otherwise inadmissible evidence.

But if an attempt were made to introduce any statement made by the first defendant in compliance with this order into proceedings for theft and forgery, the court would have to consider the substance of the proceedings and the real reason why he has not been excused from compliance with the order, and then the proceedings will be seen to be in substance proceedings for an offence under the Theft Act and so he could not have been compelled to incriminate himself except for an offence under that Act. Accordingly, any such statement would not be admissible in evidence against him in the proceedings.

On that ground I would uphold the unamended order. It is not clear to me from the approved note that we have of Woolf J's judgment whether that is the ground on which he upheld Stuart Smith J's order unamended. What he said was:

'[Counsel for the defendants] says that protection is confined to proceedings under the Theft Act 1968 and that these proceedings may incriminate the defendant of other offences, for example forgery. Apart from the question of construction, I think it unlikely that there will be a charge of forgery. On the material before me I think it far more likely to give rise to charges under the Theft Act. Assuming these facts, is s 31 still available to the plaintiff? In my view although it is surprising that the Theft Act limits the protection to subsequent proceedings under the Theft Act, the section can be used where a defendant may incriminate himself with offences other than under the Theft Act. Parliament could easily have limited the section to instances where the defendant would otherwise "incriminate himself under this Act". I think that it would be unduly restrictive to apply s 31 as limited to matters where the incrimination was going to be of offences under the Theft Act ... I do not feel that [counsel for the defendants'] substantive argument is right on the construction point so I do not need to limit the order to except incrimination of offences other than under the Theft Act. This would defeat s 31 as it would be so often possible to find another offence outside the Theft Act, although the more obvious offence would be within the Act. Since [counsel for the defendants] concedes it is otherwise proper that the order should remain, I am of the view that the order should stand.'

I agree with the judge that 'it is unlikely that there will be a charge of forgery', but he does not seem to have had in mind a prosecution charging both theft and forgery. I agree also that it is 'often possible to find another offence outside the Theft Act', but I do not see how that stratagem could be prevented from defeating s 31 by construing the section in a way which ignores or contradicts the reference to 'an offence under this Act' where those words first occur in sub-s (1). In my opinion counsel for the defendants is plainly right in construing the subsection as restricting its operation to incrimination of offences under the Act as well as to proceedings under the Act. However, where (as here) the substance of any foreseeable proceedings is a prosecution under the Theft Act, s 31 applies and cannot be defeated.

There is, however, a shorter and simpler ground on which, in my judgment, the order can be affirmed without amendment. So far I have assumed that compliance with the *a* order would tend to expose the first defendant to the risk of criminal proceedings or would materially increase that risk. But I do not consider that the first defendant is entitled to the benefit of so unrealistic an assumption. He admits that he made out the plaintiff's cheque in favour of the second defendant in the sum of £40,000. If it was the first defendant's money, albeit on loan, there was nothing criminal in that, but if the plaintiff's version of the facts is true and all the cheques were to be used for the plaintiff's *b* purposes the first defendant had no authority to do what he did with the cheque and no belief that he had such authority. What he did reeks of dishonesty and could not have been done without an intent to defraud the plaintiff or to deprive him permanently of the proceeds of the cheque. He would already be exposed to the risk of criminal proceedings for theft and perhaps forgery, and what he may have to say about the subsequent disposal of the £40,000 adds nothing of substance to that existing risk. *c*

On that point I am in complete agreement with the judgment which Griffiths LJ is about to give and on that ground also I would dismiss the appeals of both defendants. We have not been asked to consider the second defendant's appeal separately, or what the position would be if the second defendant were to make an affidavit by its directors other than the first defendant. Both appeals must therefore fail together.

d

GRIFFITHS LJ. I will not repeat the agreed facts, which are fully set out in the judgment of Stephenson LJ. Either the first defendant stole £40,000 from the plaintiff and paid it into the account of his company, the second defendant, or, as the first defendant asserts through his solicitor, the plaintiff lent him the sum of £40,000. If the first defendant stole the money, he did so by means of one of the signed cheques with which he had been entrusted by the plaintiff, and was thus guilty of forgery. *e*

If criminal proceedings are brought against the first defendant I can have no doubt that the substantive charge will be that of theft of £40,000. It is possible, but I think extremely unlikely, that the prosecution may also include a count of forgery. If this is a case of theft, forgery is merely the technical means by which the first defendant achieved the theft. It is inconceivable that a judge would impose any additional sentence for the count of forgery to that which he imposed for the count of theft, and I can see no *f* useful purpose to be served by including the count of forgery in an indictment.

However, let me assume that the indictment is framed to include counts of theft and forgery. The counts would in any event stand or fall together and depend on whether the jury believed the plaintiff's account of the circumstances in which the money was taken from his bank account, in which case the first defendant is guilty of both theft and forgery, or whether the jury thought it might be a loan, in which case the defendant is *g* guilty of neither theft nor forgery.

For my part I am quite unable to see how the question of what happened to the money after it had been admittedly paid by the first defendant into his company's account has any bearing on his guilt of either theft or forgery. The guilt or innocence of the first defendant depends on the circumstances in which he paid the money to his company, the second defendants, and not on what happened to the money thereafter. *h*

For the purposes of assisting the plaintiff to trace the money, it is of the utmost importance that the first defendant should be required to swear an affidavit setting out what has become of it since it entered the account of his company. As the first defendant admits that he paid the £40,000 to the second defendant company, any information that he can give about the subsequent whereabouts or use of the money cannot add a pennyweight to the strength of the criminal case against him. Accordingly, in my *j* opinion to require him to swear the affidavit in the form ordered by the judge would not tend to incriminate him either in the sense of setting up a case against him or strengthening an already existing case.

For these reasons, and for those given by Stephenson LJ, I agree that these appeals should be dismissed.

STEPHENSON LJ. Kerr LJ has read, in draft, the judgments which have just been
a delivered, and he agrees with both of them.

Appeals of both defendants dismissed. Leave to appeal to House of Lords refused.

Solicitors: *Gasquet, Metcalf & Walton* (for the first and second defendants); *McKenna & Co*
(for the plaintiff).

b

April Weiss   Barrister.

Universe Tankships Inc of Monrovia v International Transport Workers' Federation

HOUSE OF LORDS

LORD DIPLOCK, LORD CROSS OF CHELSEA, LORD RUSSELL OF KILLOWEN, LORD SCARMAN AND LORD
BRANDON OF OAKBROOK

d 22, 23, 24 FEBRUARY, I APRIL 1982

*Trade dispute – Duress – Economic duress – Threat to black vessel unless payment made by
shipowners to international seafarers welfare fund on behalf of crew members – Whether money
recoverable by shipowners on basis of resulting trust or as money paid under duress – Whether
pressure legitimate so as to exclude restitutionary remedy in action for money had and received –*
*e Whether dispute as to payment to fund 'connected with terms and conditions of employment' –
Trade Union and Labour Relations Act 1974, ss 13(2), 29(1).*

A Liberian corporation owned a vessel sailing under a flag of convenience which was
under time charter to an oil company. In July 1978, when the vessel docked at Milford
Haven to discharge cargo, a representative of an international federation of trade unions
f (the ITF), whose policy was to black vessels sailing under flags of convenience unless the
owners of the vessel complied with ITF demands as to rates of pay and other terms of
employment of crew, handed the master a document setting out the conditions to be
fulfilled before the vessel could be issued with a certificate exempting it from the
blacking policy. These conditions required the shipowners to sign two collective
agreements with the ITF. Meanwhile the vessel was blacked by tugboat crews and
g thereby prevented from continuing its voyage until 29 July, when the shipowners
yielded to the demands of the ITF that they should sign the two agreements, pay the sum
of $US80,000 to the ITF pursuant to the agreements and enter into new contracts of
employment with each member of the vessel's crew incorporating the standard ITF
collective agreement. The blacking was then lifted. Of the sum of $80,000, $6,480
represented a payment required to be made under the agreements on behalf of the crew
h members to a welfare fund established under the auspices of the ITF to 'help provide
welfare, social and recreational facilities in ports around the world for seafarers of all
nations, especially those serving in flag-of-convenience ships . . .' After the vessel sailed
the shipowners demanded the return of, inter alia, the $6,480 paid as a contribution to
the welfare fund, on the grounds (i) that the payment was made on the trusts of the
welfare fund and that since those trusts were void because they were not exclusively
charitable the payment was held on a resulting trust in favour of the shipowners, and (ii)
alternatively, that it was recoverable from the ITF as money had and received by the ITF
to the shipowners' use, since it was exacted by subjecting the shipowners to economic
duress. The trial judge held that the shipowners were entitled to recover the sum of
$6,480 both on the basis of a resulting trust and as being money paid under duress, but
the Court of Appeal reversed his decision on the grounds that the money was

irrecoverable because the shipowners had no equitable interest in the money by virtue
of any resulting trust and that the ITF's acts concerned a 'trade dispute' within s 29(1)^d of   *a*
the Trade Union and Labour Relations Act 1974 since they were 'connected with . . .
terms and conditions of employment' in that the ultimate object of the ITF's campaign
against flag of convenience vessels was to stop the use of cheap labour on such vessels.
Since the ITF had acted 'in contemplation or furtherance of a trade dispute' in demanding
payment from the shipowners it was, so the Court of Appeal held, entitled under s 13(1)^b
of the 1974 Act to immunity from suit by the shipowners even if its demands amounted   *b*
to duress. The shipowners appealed to the House of Lords. The ITF conceded that the
payment to the welfare fund was induced by economic duress, but relied on the
immunity from action given by s 13 of the 1974 Act.

Held – (1) The rules of the welfare fund did not declare or impress the fund with any
trusts and the fund was merely a fund which the ITF had set apart from its other assets   *c*
and earmarked for a special purpose but which remained in law part of the general assets
of the ITF and available to be used for other purposes if the ITF so decided. The
contribution by the shipowners of $6,480 to the welfare fund was therefore not held
by the ITF on trust and no resulting trust could arise in favour of the shipowners (see p 75
b to *e*, p 79 *e f*, p 81 *d* to *f*, p 82 *h*, p 85 *j* to p 86 *c* and *h*, p 93 *d* to *g* and p 96 *g*, post).

    (2) (Lord Scarman and Lord Brandon dissenting) The dispute concerning the payment   *d*
to the fund was not 'connected with . . . terms and conditions of employment' of the
crew members' by the shipowners so as to constitute a trade dispute within s 29(1) of the
1974 Act and thereby qualify the ITF for immunity under s 13 thereof, because the
entitlement of the crew members to take advantage of any benefit that might be
provided out of the fund did not depend on the existence of a relationship of employee
and employer between the crew members and the shipowners, since the crew members   *e*
did not obtain any rights to benefit from the welfare fund as a result of the shipowners'
contributions to the fund. Furthermore, the fact that contributions to the ITF as a whole
might be said to benefit its members did not establish any connection between the ITF's
demand for a contribution and the terms and conditions of employment of the crew (see
p 77 *j* to p 78 *d*, p 79 *b* to *j*, p 82 *b c*, p 83 *a* to *d*, p 84 *g* to *j* and p 86 *b c*, post); dictum of
Lord Diplock in *NWL Ltd v Woods* [1979] 3 All ER at 622 explained; *BBC v Hearn* [1978]   *f*
1 All ER 111 considered.

    (3) (Lord Scarman and Lord Brandon dissenting) Accordingly, the shipowners'
contribution of $6,480 to the welfare fund was recoverable by the shipowners as money
had and received to their use, because public policy as indicated by the 1974 Act did not
require that the economic duress exerted by the ITF should be legitimised by depriving
the shipowners of their restitutional remedy by way of an action for money had and   *g*
received to regain money exacted by economic duress (see p 80 *j* to p 81 *d*, p 83 *d* and
p 86 *b c*, post).

    Per Lord Diplock, Lord Cross and Lord Russell. If a trade union makes two demands,
one of which is legitimate and the other of which is not, the existence of the legitimate
demand does not preclude the employer from recovering money paid under duress in
complying with the illegitimate demand (see p 78 *g h*, p 81 *h j* and p 86 *b c*, post).   *h*

Notes
For the legal liability of trade unions, see Supplement to 38 Halsbury's Laws (3rd edn)
para 677B.3.
    For money paid under duress, see 9 Halsbury's Laws (4th edn) para 297.
    For the Trade Union and Labour Relations Act 1974, s 13(1) (as substituted by the   *j*

---

a   Section 29(1), so far as material, is set out at p 95*a*, post
b   Section 13(1), so far as material, provides: 'An act done by a person in contemplation or furtherance
     of a trade dispute shall not be actionable in tort on the ground only—(*a*) that it induces another
     person to break a contract of employment . . .'

a Trade Union and Labour Relations (Amendment) Act 1976, s 3(2)), see 46 Halsbury's Statutes (3rd edn) 1941, and for s 29 of the 1974 Act, see 44 ibid 1779.

Cases referred to in opinions

Barton v Armstrong [1975] 2 All ER 465, [1976] AC 104, [1975] 2 WLR 1050, PC, Digest (Cont Vol D) 117, *486a.

b *BBC v Hearn* [1978] 1 All ER 111, [1977] 1 WLR 1004, CA, Digest (Cont Vol E) 610, 1444b.

Hadmor Productions Ltd v Hamilton [1982] 1 All ER 1042, [1982] 2 WLR 322, HL.

Maskell v Horner [1915] 3 KB 106, [1914–15] All ER Rep 595, CA, 12 Digest (Reissue) 688, 4960.

North Ocean Shipping Co Ltd v Hyundai Construction Co Ltd, The Atlantic Baron [1978] 3 All ER 1170, [1979] QB 705, Digest (Cont Vol E) 104, 673a.

c *NWL Ltd v Woods, NWL Ltd v Nelson* [1979] 3 All ER 614, [1979] 1 WLR 1294, HL, Digest (Cont Vol E) 612, 1457a.

Pao On v Lau Yiu [1979] 3 All ER 65, [1980] AC 614, [1979] 3 WLR 435, PC, Digest (Cont Vol E) 107, 1899a.

Siboen, The, and the Sibotre, Occidental Worldwide Investment Corp v Skibs A/S Avanti, Skibs A/S Glarona, Skibs A/S Navalis [1976] 1 Lloyd's Rep 293.

d *Star Sea Transport Corp v Slater, The Camilla M* [1979] 1 Lloyd's Rep 26, CA.

Thorne v Motor Trade Association [1937] 3 All ER 157, [1937] AC 797, HL, 45 Digest (Repl) 571, 1434.

Appeal

By a writ issued on 17 August 1978 as amended the plaintiffs, Universe Tankships Inc of
e Monrovia (the shipowners), a company incorporated under the laws of Liberia, and owners of the tankship Universe Sentinel, brought an action against the defendants, the International Transport Workers' Federation (the ITF) and Brian Laughton, the secretary of the Special Seafarers Section of the ITF seeking (1) the sum of $US80,000 as money had and received by the ITF on or about 28 July 1978 and paid by the shipowners under duress in relation to the Universe Sentinel, alternatively, damages, (2) a declaration that
f the agreements between the shipowners and the ITF dated 28 July 1978 (namely, the special agreement and the typescript agreement) were invalid, (3) a declaration that the trusts of the Seafarers International Welfare Protection and Assistance Fund were void and that the sum of $6,480 paid by the shipowners to the ITF on such trusts (and any moneys representing the same together with interests thereon) was held on resulting trusts for the shipowners, (4) a declaration that certain sums held by the ITF on behalf of
g the crew of the Universe Sentinel were by virtue of assignments executed by them held on trusts for the shipowners absolutely. At the trial 11 named members of the crew who had executed assignments in favour of the shipowners of such interest that they might have in the sum of $71,720 (part of the sum of $80,000) deposited by the shipowners with the ITF in respect of estimated back pay were added as defendants and interveners in the action so that they might challenge the validity of the assignments on the ground,
h inter alia, of duress and undue influence but their claims were settled by agreement and the proceedings against them stayed. The shipowners conceded that the Trade Union and Labour Relations Act 1974 was effective to deprive them of the right to recover any part of the $80,000 save the welfare fund portion of $6,480. On 2 April 1980 Parker J held (1) that the sum of $6,480 was recoverable by the shipowners both on the basis of a resulting trust and as money paid under duress, (2) that the typescript agreement was
j a collective agreement within s 30(1) of the 1974 Act and thus unenforceable under s 18, and (3) that the shipowners were entitled to payment over of the apportioned shares of the sum of $71,720, amounting to $24,576·78, attributable to those who executed assignments other than the interveners who had been released therefrom. The ITF appealed against the judgment of Parker J in so far as it was ordered that the sums of $6,480 and $24,256·78 were recoverable by the shipowners. On 10 July 1980 the Court

of Appeal (Megaw, Brightman and Watkins LJJ) allowed the appeal in part and varied the order of Parker J holding (1) that the sum of $6,480 was irrecoverable by the shipowners *a* because the shipowners had no equitable interest in the money by virtue of any resulting trust and that the dispute between the shipowners and the ITF in respect of the payments to the welfare fund was a trade dispute within s 29(1) of the 1974 Act so that s 131(1) of the 1974 Act applied, but (2) that the assignments were effective to transfer to the shipowners a due proportion of the sum of $71,720. The shipowners appealed to the House of Lords with leave of the Appeal Committee granted on 25 November 1980. *b* The facts are set out in the opinion of Lord Diplock.

Roger Buckley QC, John Chadwick QC and *Martin Keenan* for the shipowners.
Leonard H Hoffmann QC and *V V Veeder* for the ITF.

Their Lordships took time for consideration.   *c*

1 April. The following opinions were delivered.

LORD DIPLOCK. My Lords, the facts that gave rise to this action, brought by the appellants (the shipowners) as owners of the Liberian tankship Universe Sentinel against the respondent trade union (the ITF), present no novelty. They afford a typical example *d* of the application by the ITF and the affiliated national trade unions who are its members, of the policy of 'blacking' vessels sailing under what the ITF regards as 'flags of convenience' unless the owners of the vessel comply with the ITF's demands as to the rates of pay and other terms of employment of the crew and as to various other matters to which it will become necessary to advert in detail.

Other examples of the way in which the blacking of flag of convenience vessels is *e* carried out are to be found in the judgments in *Star Sea Transport Corp v Slater, The Camilla M* [1979] 1 Lloyd's Rep 26 and *NWL Ltd v Woods* [1979] 3 All ER 614, [1979] 1 WLR 1294, where the object sought to be achieved by the blacking policy and reasons why it does not always command the support of the crews of vessels to which it is applied are also discussed. Both of these, however, were cases in which an interlocutory injunction was sought by shipowners against trade union officials to restrain them from *f* committing the tort of inducing port workers to break their contracts of employment by preventing or refusing to assist in enabling the blacked vessel to leave port; and the only issue of law before the court was whether the defendants were likely to establish that they were entitled to immunity from suit in tort by virtue of s 13(1) of the Trade Union and Labour Relations Act 1974, an issue that was decided in favour of the trade union officials by this House in *NWL Ltd v Woods*. In those two cases it was necessary to identify *g* the nature of the demands that the ITF was making on the shipowner as the price for obtaining the lifting of the blacking, but it was not necessary to examine the means by which compliance with those demands would be effected if the shipowner found himself compelled to succumb to them.

What is novel in the instant case is that the action was brought after the shipowners did succumb and is not brought in tort, but is an action to recover from the ITF part of *h* the moneys paid by them to the ITF in order to have the blacking of their vessel lifted so as to enable it to leave the port of Milford Haven. Although a substantially larger sum was claimed in the courts below (with partial success), the only part of the shipowners' claim which is the subject of appeal to your Lordships' House, relates to a sum of $6,480 paid as a contribution to a so-called welfare fund administered by the ITF. This sum is sought to be recovered on one of two alternative grounds: the first is that it is the subject *j* of a resulting trust in favour of the shipowners, since the trusts on which it was received from them by the ITF were void; the second is that it is recoverable from the ITF as money had and received, since it was exacted by subjecting the shipowners to economic duress. To determine whether the shipowners can succeed on either of these grounds calls for a close consideration of the contemporary documents relating to the payment, and of the rules of the welfare fund.

My Lords, the judgment of Parker J in the Commercial Court and that of the Court of
a Appeal (Megaw, Brightman and Watkins LJJ), delivered by Megaw LJ, are reported
together (see [1980] 2 Lloyd's Rep 523). Both judgments set out the facts briefly and
contain lengthy quotations from the relevant documents; but, in view of the division of
opinion between your Lordships as to what ought to be the fate of this appeal, I see no
way of avoiding repetition of the greater part of such quotations here.

The shipowners are a Liberian company. The tankship which they owned, Universe
b Sentinel, was of 269,092 tons deadweight; the crew consisted in the main of Asians
employed at rates of pay substantially less than those on which the ITF insists, and which
are provided for in what it calls the ITF collective agreement. In July 1978 the Universe
Sentinel was on time charter to Texaco and arrived on 17 July at the Texaco terminal at
Milford Haven to discharge her cargo there. On her arrival the master was handed, by
a representative of the ITF, a copy of a standard form of document headed: 'Conditions
c to be fulfilled before flag-of-convenience vessels can be issued with ITF Blue
Certificates.' An ITF blue certificate, though this is nowhere spelt out in the documents,
is well understood by shipowners, charterers and shippers, and by the constituent trade
unions of the ITF, to exempt a vessel sailing under a flag of convenience from being
subject to the blacking policy of the ITF. These conditions refer to a special agreement
which it will be necessary to refer to in some detail, but the only extract from the
d conditions themselves which requires to be reproduced is para 3:

> 'The Special Agreement also covers the owners' contributions to the Seafarers'
> International Welfare, Protection and Assistance Fund. The contributions are
> US$162. per man per year. The Fund was set up to help provide welfare, social and
> recreational facilities in ports around the world for seafarers of all nations, especially
e > those serving in flag-of-convenience ships, and is administered by an international
> committee of representatives of ITF-affiliated unions.'

Parker J placed considerable reliance on these words in deciding what I shall refer to as
the trust point in the shipowners' favour, but, for reasons which will appear, I think that
he was wrong in doing so.

The Universe Sentinel finished discharging on 18 July, but because of being blacked
f by tugboat crews, she was prevented from sailing until 29 July, when the blacking was
lifted in consequence of a meeting held at the offices of the ITF in London on the
previous day between representatives of the shipowners and officials of the ITF at which
the shipowners yielded to the demands of the ITF that they should pay to the ITF the sum
of $80,000 and enter into two agreements with the ITF, namely one headed 'Special
Agreement' on a standard printed form and the second in typescript (the typescript
g agreement).

The special agreement, after setting out the parties, namely the shipowners, therein
called 'the Company', and the ITF, starts with recitals:

> 'WHEREAS: (1) the ITF is an independent trade union organisation comprising
> fully autonomous trade union organisations in transport and allied services
h > throughout the world and members of the Special Seafarers' Section of the ITF; (2)
> the Company is the registered owner/manager of the Ship described in Schedule 1
> hereto; (3) the ITF and the Company desire to regulate the conditions of employment
> of all seafarers (hereinafter individually called a "Seafarer") serving from time to
> time aboard the Ship . . .'

i I pause to say that recital 1 is not strictly accurate. Under its constitution membership
of the ITF is restricted to trade unions; there are no personal members; but in return for
what is called an entrance fee and annual membership fee to what it describes as the
Special Seafarers' Section (or department), the ITF does issue to seamen who are not
members of a national trade union affiliated to the ITF, a membership card which
entitles the holder to request assistance from any such affiliated trade union in whatever
country he may find himself in need of it.

Article 1 of the special agreement needs to be set out in full:

'The Company undertakes as follows: (a) to employ each Seafarer in accordance **a** with the terms of the current ITF Collective Agreement for World Wide trading (hereinafter called the ITF Collective Agreement) as amended from time to time in accordance with Article 5 below; (b) to incorporate the terms and conditions of the ITF Collective Agreement into the individual contract of employment of each seafarer and into the Ship's Articles and furnish copies of these documents to the ITF. Any seafarer enjoying terms and conditions which are, taken as a whole, **b** recognised by the ITF as more favourable to the seafarer, shall continue to enjoy such terms and conditions; (c) to pay on behalf of each Seafarer contributions and fees at the rates shown in Schedule 2 hereto to the Seafarers' International Welfare Protection and Assistance Fund and to the Special Seafarers' Section of the ITF. The contributions and fees shall be paid to the ITF annually and in advance; (d) to display aboard the Ship copies of the Special Agreement, the ITF Collective Agreement and **c** the ITF Blue Certificate to be issued under Article 2 hereof in a prominent place to which each Seafarer shall have access at all times; and (e) to grant to representatives of the ITF and of trade union organisations affiliated to the ITF free access to each Seafarer at all reasonable times whether or not aboard the Ship, whether the ship is in berth or not.'
d

Articles 2, 3 and 4 deal with the issue and withdrawal of the blue certificate; while art 5 entitles the ITF, on giving two months' notice, to change the rates of pay in the collective agreement and the rates of entrance and membership fees to the ITF Special Seafarers' Section and contributions to the welfare fund referred to in art 1(c) and set out in Sch 2. Schedule 2 itself is as follows:

e

'ITF SPECIAL SEAFARERS' SECTION		
Entrance fees	40 at US$15 per man	US$......
Membership fees	40 at US$30 per man per year	US$......
SEAFARERS' INTERNATIONAL WELFARE		
PROTECTION AND ASSISTANCE FUND	40 at US$162 per man per year	US$......
TOTAL		US$8280.—

f

The sum of US$......is equivalent to......
Received with thanks:
Brian Laughton
on behalf of the ITF'

Although the separate totals for the entrance and membership fees to the ITF Special Seafarers' Section are not filled in, simple arithmetic discloses that of the grand total of **g** $8,280, the sum of $6,480 is attributable to the contribution to Seafarers' International Welfare Protection and Assistance Fund (the welfare fund); and this is the sum that the shipowners seek to recover in their appeal to this House.

The collective agreement, which is referred to in art 1(b), contains provisions as to rates of wages and other terms and conditions of employment of a kind that are generally to be found in collective agreements negotiated between trade unions and employers. The **h** collective agreement, as such, is not a legally enforceable contract, because of s 18 of the Trade Union and Labour Relations Act 1974; but art 1(b) of the special agreement requires its terms and conditions to be incorporated in the individual contract of employment of each seaman, by whom it would be enforceable. New contracts incorporating, by reference, the collective agreement were, in fact, signed with most of the members of the crew on 29 July 1978, and the Universe Sentinel was permitted to sail **j** on that date.

Only one of the provisions of the collective agreement requires to be set out:

'All seafarers covered by this Agreement shall be either members of an appropriate national trade union affiliated to the ITF or, in the absence of any suitable organisation, members of the Special Seafarers' Section of the ITF in which case the

a   Company shall pay on behalf of each seafarer an Entrance Fee of US $15 and a Membership Fee of US $30 per annum, annually and in advance. The Company undertakes to notify any crew changes made in the ship, sending names, addresses, ranks and details of qualifications, together with the appropriate Entrance and Membership fees to the ITF as soon as possible after the crew changes are made. The Company acknowledges the right of the ITF to appoint a liaison representative from

b   among seafarers serving on board the vessel covered by this Agreement.'

It is to be noted that this is confined to entrance and membership fees to the Special Seafarers' Section of the ITF. By incorporating the provisions of the collective agreement in the contract of employment of the individual seaman, the shipowners assume no obligation whatever to the seaman to make any contribution to the welfare fund.

In addition to the demands by the ITF, which are dealt with in the special agreement,

c   shipowners, in order to obtain the lifting of the blacking, are required to pay, for distribution to each seaman concerned, the difference between the rates of pay provided for in the collective agreement and the lower rates which had been actually paid to the seaman since the date of his engagement on the vessel. It is mainly with this additional requirement that the typescript agreement is concerned. While its terms were highly relevant to that part of the shipowners' claim which is not the subject of their appeal to

d   this House, this makes it unnecessary to refer to any other provisions of the typescript agreement except those contained in the first paragraph:

'The ITF confirms receipt today of US$80,000 (Eighty thousand United States dollars) which is accepted by the ITF as to the one part of $8,280 for the Union Entrance Fees, Annual Subscriptions and Welfare Fund Contributions and as to the

e   other part of $71,720, as a discretionary trustee. The beneficiaries are the Master, Officers, Engineers and crew members on board on 28th July 1978.'

The sum of $71,720 referred to in this paragraph, was an estimate, which turned out to be inaccurate, of the difference between the actual and collective agreement rates of pay of each member of the crew of the Universe Sentinel during the period between the date of his engagement under ship's articles and 29 July 1978. The remaining paragraphs

f   of the typescript agreement deal with the machinery for ascertaining the detailed facts relating to each member of the crew, and for the adjustment of the sum paid or payable by the shipowners when those facts have been ascertained.

Lastly, I find it necessary to set out nearly all of what are described as the 'Rules for Seafarers' International Assistance Welfare and Protection Fund':

g   '1. The Fund shall be known as the Seafarers' International Assistance Welfare and Protection Fund. It is established under the auspices of the International Transport Workers' Federation.

2. The object of the Fund shall be the financing of any such work as may be sanctioned by the Executive Committee of the Federation for the purpose of promoting, advancing or protecting by any such means as the Executive Committee

h   in their absolute discretion may decide, the interests of seafarers generally or groups of seafarers, national or otherwise, or of assisting individual seafarers, or otherwise of serving seafarers' interests.

3. The income of the Fund shall consist of contributions received under agreements concluded on behalf of the Seafarers' Section of the Federation with shipping undertakings or shipowners, the income of investments mentioned in

j   clause 5 of these Rules, and such other monies as the Executive Committee of the Federation may from time to time determine.

4. The Fund shall be administered by the Fair Practices Committee elected by the Seafarers' and Dockers' Sections of the Federation, and the General Secretary of the Federation shall be responsible to that Committee for the day to day management of the Fund. The Fair Practices Committee may invite any person representing

such shipping undertakings and shipowners as shall have entered into agreements to contribute to the Fund to act as a consultant on the administration of the Fund; *a* provided that there should not at any time be more than one such consultant.

5. The General Secretary of the Federation shall receive all money paid to the Fund. Subject to the overriding authority of the Executive Committee under clause 2 of these rules, he shall spend such money in accordance with the directions of the Fair Practices Committee, provided that no money belonging to the Fund shall be spent otherwise than for the object of the Fund as defined in the said clause 2. The *b* General Secretary may invest, in accordance with the directions of the Fair Practices Committee, any money belonging to the Fund which, in the opinion of the Fair Practices Committee, is not required for immediate expenditure for the object of the Fund as defined as aforesaid.'

The references to the seafarers' section and the dockers' section appearing in these rules *c* are references to two of the industrial sections into which the membership of the ITF (consisting as it does of national trade unions of workers involved in all forms of transport) are divided. The powers of industrial sections are dealt with in r XIII of the constitution of the ITF. For present purposes, it is enough to say that the sections appear to be subject to the general control or tutelage of the executive board; and the only provision of r XIII that it is necessary to set out is para (1) under which, presumably, the *d* Seafarers' Assistance Welfare and Protection Fund was created:

'There shall be industrial sections, as defined in the Preamble of this Constitution, to deal with matters concerning individual branches of transport and allied activities. The Executive Board shall have authority to set up such further sections or special departments as deemed necessary to improve the services of the ITF to its affiliates or to deal efficiently with particular activities or problems, and may create *e* or provide for special funds in connection with such sections or departments. The Executive Board shall determine their terms of reference and generally be authorized to guide their activities.'

Very shortly after the Universe Sentinel had sailed, the shipowners, on 10 August 1978, demanded return of the $80,000 as money paid under duress and asserted that the *f* special agreement and the typescript agreement were void on that ground. Return of the money was refused by the ITF and later in 1978 some 27 members of the crew assigned to the shipowners their interest in the $71,720 estimated back pay of members of the crew from the date of their engagements referred to in para 1 of the typescript agreement. By the time the action came on for hearing before Parker J, some of these assignments had been withdrawn; but your Lordships are not now concerned with any *g* claim by the shipowners to recover any part of the $71,720, either by virtue of the assignments or as money paid under duress. The shipowners were held by Parker J, and by the Court of Appeal, to be entitled to recover an aliquot portion of that sum which was attributable to those assignments that were undisputed and there is no appeal to this House on that part of the case. The shipowners did not pursue, before Parker J, the claim that they had originally asserted to recover that part of the sum of $8,280 referred to in *h* para 1 of the typescript agreement that was attributable to entrance and membership fees of members of the crew to the ITF Special Seafarers' Section. So that is how it comes about that all that is in issue in the appeal to this House is the $6,480 paid as a contribution to the welfare fund.

Recovery of this sum, as I have already mentioned, is claimed on one or other of two alternative grounds, the first of which is that it is subject to a resulting trust in favour of *j* the shipowners, as donors, since it was paid by them to the ITF on trusts that were void, because their purposes were not exclusively charitable.

My Lords, there is a certain air of artificiality about treating the shipowners as donors of money for trust purposes, when the only object that they had in mind in paying any money to the ITF was to get the blacking of the Universe Sentinel lifted, and thereafter a   to get the money back from the ITF if they could; but for the purposes of determining what it is convenient to refer to as the trust point, one must treat the payment as having been 'voluntary' in the sense that the shipowners' consent to making it was not vitiated by duress, and one must ascertain the legal nature of the payment from the relevant documents, for no oral evidence was directed to the matter.

b   I have had the advantage of reading the speech to be delivered by my noble and learned friend Lord Russell, which deals fully with the trust point. I agree with his reasoning and with the conclusion that he reaches, that the money was not held by the ITF on any trust but was, in its legal nature, a contribution to the funds of the ITF which the ITF, by taking appropriate steps under its rules, could use for any purpose it thought fit.

c   The Court of Appeal reached the same conclusion. It is contrary to that of Parker J, who had based his opinion on the assumption that the money had been paid by the shipowners for the purposes of a trust, whose objects had been represented by the ITF to be those referred to in para 3 of the document handed to the master of the Universe Sentinel on 17 July 1978, which I have quoted above. Since the shipowners were not, at that time, aware of the rules of the welfare fund, there might have been a plausible argument in favour of the conclusion reached by Parker J if the evidence had established that, in making the payment of $6,480 on 28 July 1978, reliance had been placed by the

d   shipowners on the description of the welfare fund and its purposes set out in the document that had been handed to the master; but no mention of this document, or of any reliance on it by the shipowners, is to be found either in the pleadings or in the oral evidence of the master, or of the representatives of the shipowners who conducted the negotiations with the ITF that resulted in the payment. So the trust point depends on the other documents dealt with by Lord Russell, and there is nothing that I can usefully add

e   to what he will say about the legal effect of those.

My Lords, I turn to the second ground on which repayment of the $6,480 is claimed, which I will call the duress point. It is not disputed that the circumstances in which the ITF demanded that the shipowners should enter into the special agreement and the typescript agreement and should pay the moneys of which the latter documents acknowledge receipt amounted to economic duress on the shipowners; that is to say, it

f   is conceded that the financial consequences to the shipowners of the Universe Sentinel continuing to be rendered off hire under her time charter to Texaco, while the blacking continued, were so catastrophic as to amount to a coercion of the shipowners' will which vitiated their consent to those agreements and to the payments made by them to the ITF. This concession makes it unnecessary for your Lordships to use the instant appeal as the occasion for a general consideration of the developing law of economic duress as a

g   ground for treating contracts as voidable and obtaining restitution of money paid under economic duress as money had and received to the plaintiffs' use. That economic duress may constitute a ground for such redress was recognised, albeit obiter, by the Privy Council in *Pao On v Lau Yiu* [1979] 3 All ER 65, [1980] AC 614. The Board in that case referred with approval to two judgments at first instance in the Commercial Court which recognised that commercial pressure may constitute duress: one by Kerr J in *The*

h   *Siboen and the Sibotre, Occidental Worldwide Investment Corp v Skibs A/S Avanti* [1976] 1 Lloyd's Rep 293, the other by Mocatta J in *North Ocean Shipping Co Ltd v Hyundai Construction Co Ltd, The Atlantic Baron* [1978] 3 All ER 1170, [1979] QB 705, which traces the development of this branch of the law from its origin in the eighteenth and early nineteenth century cases.

j   It is, however, in my view crucial to the decision of the instant appeal to identify the rationale of this development of the common law. It is not that the party seeking to avoid the contract which he has entered into with another party, or to recover money that he has paid to another party in response to a demand, did not know the nature or the precise terms of the contract at the time when he entered into it or did not understand the purpose for which the payment was demanded. The rationale is that his apparent consent was induced by pressure exercised on him by that other party which the law does not regard as legitimate, with the consequence that the consent is treated in law as revocable unless approbated either expressly or by implication after the illegitimate *a* pressure has ceased to operate on his mind. It is a rationale similar to that which underlies the avoidability of contracts entered into and the recovery of money exacted under colour of office, or under undue influence or in consequence of threats of physical duress.

Commercial pressure, in some degree, exists wherever one party to a commercial transaction is in a stronger bargaining position than the other party. It is not, however, *b* in my view, necessary, nor would it be appropriate in the instant appeal, to enter into the general question of the kinds of circumstances, if any, in which commercial pressure, even though it amounts to a coercion of the will of a party in the weaker bargaining position, may be treated as legitimate and, accordingly, as not giving rise to any legal right of redress. In the instant appeal the economic duress complained of was exercised in the field of industrial relations to which very special considerations apply.   *c*

My Lords, so far as is relevant to this appeal, the policy of Parliament, ever since the Trade Disputes Act 1906 was passed to overrule a decision of this House, has been to legitimise acts done by employees, or by trade unions acting or purporting to act on their behalf, which would otherwise be unlawful wherever such acts are done in contemplation or furtherance of a dispute which is connected with the terms and conditions of employment of any employees. I can confine myself to the kind of acts and the *d* particular subject matter of the trade dispute that was involved in the instant case, and I use the expression 'legitimise' as meaning that the doer of the act is rendered immune from any liability to damages or any other remedy against him in a court of justice, at the suit of a person who has suffered loss or damage in consequence of the act; save only a remedy for breach of contract where the act is done in breach of a direct contract between the doer of the act and the person by whom the damage is sustained.   *e*

The statutory provisions in force when the events with which this appeal is concerned took place, and which point to the public policy to which effect ought to be given by your Lordships, are chiefly contained in ss 13, 14 and 29 of the Trade Union and Labour Relations Act 1974. The legislative history of these sections is referred to in the recent decision of this House in *Hadmor Productions Ltd v Hamilton* [1982] 1 All ER 1042, [1982] 2 WLR 322. In terms they are confined to bestowing immunity from liability in tort; *f* they do not deal with immunity in any other type of action. In the case of a trade union such immunity is extended by s 14 to virtually all torts; in the case of individuals, it is extended by s 13 to defined classes of torts (which would include the blacking of the Universe Sentinel) which are limited, not only in their nature, but also by the requirement that what would otherwise be the tortious act must be committed in contemplation or furtherance of a trade dispute as defined in s 29.   *g*

The use of economic duress to induce another person to part with property or money is not a tort per se; the form that the duress takes may, or may not, be tortious. The remedy to which economic duress gives rise is not an action for damages but an action for restitution of property or money exacted under such duress and the avoidance of any contract that had been induced by it; but where the particular form taken by the economic duress used is itself a tort, the restitutional remedy for money had and received *h* by the defendant to the plaintiff's use is one which the plaintiff is entitled to pursue as an alternative remedy to an action for damages in tort.

In extending into the field of industrial relations the common law concept of economic duress and the right to a restitutionary remedy for it which is currently in process of development by judicial decisions, this House would not, in my view, be exercising the restraint that is appropriate to such a process if it were so to develop the concept that, by *j* the simple expedient of 'waiving the tort', a restitutionary remedy for money had and received is made enforceable in cases in which Parliament has, over so long a period of years, manifested its preference for a public policy that a particular kind of tortious act should be legitimised in the sense that I am using that expression.

It is only in this indirect way that the provisions of the Trade Union and Labour

Relations Act 1974 are relevant to the duress point. The immunities from liability in
a tort provided by ss 13 and 14 are not directly applicable to the shipowners' cause of action
for money had and received. Nevertheless, these sections, together with the definitions
of trade dispute in s 29, afford an indication, which your Lordships should respect, of
where public policy requires that the line should be drawn between what kind of
commercial pressure by a trade union on an employer in the field of industrial relations
ought to be treated as legitimised despite the fact that the will of the employer is thereby
b coerced, and what kind of commercial pressure in that field does amount to economic
duress that entitles the employer victim to restitutionary remedies.

My Lords, the ITF does not suggest that the immunity from suit in most kinds of tort
conferred on trade unions by s 14 whether or not they are committed in contemplation
or furtherance of a trade dispute, points to a public policy that trade unions should be
immune from a restitutionary action for money had and received. Such a suggestion
c would not be sustainable. If Parliament had intended to give to trade unions, simply
because they are trade unions, a wider immunity from suit than that for which s 14
provides, it would have done so. What the ITF relies on is the immunity from actions
for particular kinds of tort given by s 13 to every person, whether a trade union or not.

To qualify for immunity under s 13, an act, which would otherwise be actionable in
tort, must be done in contemplation or in furtherance of a trade dispute; and for a
d dispute to qualify as a trade dispute within the meaning of s 29(1), it must be a dispute
which is connected with one or more of a number of subject matters, of which the only
one relied on by the ITF in this appeal is the 'terms and conditions of employment' of the
crew of the Universe Sentinel. The members of the crew themselves were not in dispute
with the shipowners about the terms and conditions of their own employment, but this,
for the reasons mentioned in *NWL Ltd v Woods*, is generally the case when the ITF
e intervenes in order to carry out its policy in respect of vessels sailing under flags of
convenience. Such disputes as did exist were disputes between the shipowners and the
ITF acting on its own behalf and not as representative of or agent for the members of the
crew collectively or individually. But these disputes would qualify as trade disputes
under the definition in s 29, so long as they were connected with the terms and
conditions of employment of the members of the crew of the Universe Sentinel, however
f unwelcome to those members the intervention of the ITF in their affairs might be.

My Lords, it was accepted by this House in *Hadmor Productions Ltd v Hamilton* [1982]
1 All ER 1042 at 1051, [1982] 2 WLR 322 at 331, which was decided after the judgment
of the Court of Appeal in the instant case, that 'terms and conditions of employment' is
a wide expression. As Lord Denning MR had put it in a passage in his judgment in *BBC
v Hearn* [1978] 1 All ER 111 at 116, [1977] 1 WLR 1004 at 1010, that was quoted with
g approval in the *Hadmor* case, the expression—

'may include not only the contractual terms and conditions but those terms
which are understood and applied by the parties in practice, or habitually, or by
common consent, without ever being incorporated into the contract.'

h A typical example of terms and conditions of employment that are not contractual
which, although far from being exhaustive, is relevant to this appeal is supplied by
provisions of a collective agreement which does not comply with the requirements of
s 18(1) of the Trade Union and Labour Relations Act 1974, and is accordingly conclusively
presumed not to be intended to be a legally enforceable contract. By definition a
'collective agreement' is an agreement or arrangement made by a trade union with an
j employer relating to one of the matters referred to in s 29(1), which include 'terms and
conditions of employment'. The ITF collective agreement falls within this particular
category. But wide as the expression 'terms and conditions of employment' is, it is
limited to terms which regulate the relationship between an employee and the person
for whom he works, ie his employer. It does not extend to terms which regulate a
relationship between an employer and some third party acting as principal and not as

agent for an employee and for which no provision is made in the terms under which the employee works for the employer.

'Connected with' also is a wide expression, but it, too, has its limits. In my view, it is not enough in order to create the necessary connection between a dispute relating to terms and conditions of employment of employees of a particular employer, and a demand made on that employer by a trade union acting on its own behalf and not on behalf of employees working for the employer, that the demand should be made at a time when the trade union is negotiating a collective agreement relating to the terms and conditions of employment of those employees, and the employer's yielding to that demand is made a condition precedent to the lifting of the blacking additional to the condition precedent that the employer should also agree to the terms of the collective agreement insisted on by the trade union. To take an extreme example, if a trade union were to demand as a condition precedent to lifting a blacking that the employer should make a contribution to a particular political party favoured by the union, or to a guerilla group in some foreign country, such a demand whenever it was made would not, in my opinion, have the necessary connection with any dispute about terms or conditions of employment in furtherance of which the blacking was imposed.

A preliminary observation appears to me to be called for as to the way in which the special agreement and the typescript agreement should be approached in dealing with the duress point. The court is not engaged in its normal task of construing an agreement in order to determine the common intention of the parties as expressed in the words that they have used. Ex hypothesi, and also ex concessis in the instant case, at the time that they entered into these agreements the will of the shipowners was coerced. They had no choice as to the words in which the agreements were expressed; these were dictated solely by the ITF. Recital 3 to the special agreement, which states the desire of the parties to regulate the terms and conditions of employment of the crew of the Universe Sentinel, is not to be regarded as any assent by the shipowners to the accuracy of the statement that everything that they were required by the special agreement to do was connected with the terms and conditions of employment of the crew, even if that would have been the true effect of the recital if the special agreement had not been executed under duress, a matter on which I share the doubts expressed by Lord Russell. The recital ought in my view to be wholly disregarded by a court which is called on to determine whether a particular requirement is connected with terms or conditions of employment of the crew or not. In the same way the court would disregard a recital insisted on by the ITF which said in terms that the special agreement was not induced by economic duress, or an express covenant by the shipowners that they would not claim back any money paid to the ITF pursuant to any term of it. Likewise the fact that the ITF chose to put a demand for a payment that was not connected with terms and conditions of employment in the same clause of the special agreement as a demand for payment that was so connected cannot, in my view, alter the nature of the demand. To place a demand that is not legitimate in juxtaposition to a demand that is legitimate and to describe the two demands as a package deal is not, in my view, capable of legitimising the otherwise illegitimate demand.

With these considerations in mind, I turn to the special agreement and typescript agreement, and in particular to art 1(a), (b), and (c) of the special agreement. The special agreement is made by the ITF as principal; it does not purport to be acting as agent for any member of the crew of the Universe Sentinel, and this is confirmed by the provision in para 1 of the typescript agreement that the excess back pay is to be held by the ITF, not as agent for the members of the crew, but as trustee. Paragraphs (a) and (b) of art 1 clearly relate to terms and conditions of employment of the crew of the Universe Sentinel. Paragraph (c), however, deals with two distinct subject matters: (1) the payment by the shipowners on behalf of members of the crew employed by them of those crew members' entrance and annual membership fees to the ITF Special Seafarers' Section, and (2) the payment by the shipowners of contributions to the welfare fund; such contributions also being expressed to be paid on behalf of each member of the crew.

a As respects the first category of payments, entrance and membership fees to the ITF Special Seafarers' Section, the payment of these fees by the shipowners on behalf of each member of the crew of the Universe Sentinel is made one of the terms and conditions of employment of such crew member by section 24 of the ITF collective agreement, and the crew member obtains, by virtue of his membership of the Special Seafarers' Section, benefits available to him on production of his membership card to which he would not otherwise be entitled. So the necessary connection with terms and conditions of

b employment is present as respects these payments; and the shipowners have advanced no contention to the contrary.

As respects the second category of payments, contributions to the welfare fund, to speak of these as being made 'on behalf' of any member of the crew is inaccurate. All that it means, if anything, in relation to these contributions is that the number of members of the crew is a factor in the calculation of the total payment to be made, and

c this is not a legally accurate meaning which the expression 'on behalf of' is capable of bearing. The shipowners are given no authority under the ITF collective agreement or otherwise by any member of the crew to make any such payment as his agent, nor is any duty owed directly by a crew member to the ITF to contribute to the welfare fund created by the special agreement, to which the only parties are the shipowners and the ITF. The crew member has no right to require the shipowners to make the payment or

d to withhold the payment and to account to him for it by paying it to the crew member himself or expending it for some other purpose on his behalf. Put colloquially as well as legally, the contribution to the welfare fund provided for in art 1(c) has nothing to do with him as a member of the crew; nor, with respect, do I see how the fact that art 1(d) incorporates a requirement that the special agreement as well as the collective agreement should be displayed on the Universe Sentinel so as to be open to inspection by members

e of the crew is capable of converting into a term or condition of their employment an obligation assumed by the shipowners to the ITF that lacks the legal characteristics of a term or condition of employment.

My Lords, as pointed out in the speech of Lord Russell, the contribution to the welfare fund was in law a contribution to the funds of the ITF which, by taking appropriate steps under its rules, it could use for any purpose it thought fit, consistent with its objects, even

f though that purpose was designed to benefit exclusively employees engaged in other forms of transport and had nothing to do with employees engaged in transport by sea. It may be a reasonable expectation that some part of the fund, at any rate, will continue to be used for the benefit of seamen, whether they are in or out of a job at the time they seek to avail themselves of the benefit, although the accounts suggest that such expectation would have been justified in relation only to a relatively minor part of the

g fund. But what I regard as fatal to the contention that the demand for contributions to the welfare fund was connected with terms and conditions of employment is that there is nothing whatever to suggest the entitlement of a member of the crew of the Universe Sentinel to take advantage of any benefits that might be provided for out of the fund would be in any way dependent on the existence or non-existence of a relationship of employee and employer between the crew member and the shipowners. The availability

h of such benefits, if any, as the welfare fund might provide, had nothing to do with the terms and conditions of the crew members' employment by the shipowners, and a demand for payment to a fund is not, in my view, 'connected with' the terms and conditions of employment of anyone at all; nor can such connection be created merely by accompanying the demand with another demand that is connected with a trade dispute.

j As Parker J put it ([1980] 2 Lloyd's Rep 523 at 532):

'... it is inherently unlikely that it [sc Parliament] can have intended to confer upon unions an unlimited power to extract money provided only that what may be called a trade dispute demand was made at the same time, and it is a clear principle of law that any derogation of the subject's rights under the law can only be achieved by express words or necessary implication. In the present case the demand was, in my judgment, paid under what amounts to duress.'

    The Court of Appeal would have taken the same view and upheld the judgment of Parker J on the duress point had they not felt that they were prevented from doing so by certain observations in the judgment of Roskill LJ in *BBC v Hearn* [1978] 1 All ER 111 at 120, [1977] 1 WLR 1044 at 1015, and of my own in my speech in *NWL Ltd v Woods* [1979] 3 All ER 614 at 622, [1979] 1 WLR 1294 at 1302. So far as it was stated by Roskill LJ in *BBC v Hearn* that the expression 'terms and conditions of employment' has a 'very wide meaning' I have already pointed out that there is nothing in the judgments in *BBC v Hearn*, or the reference to those judgments in *Hadmor Productions Ltd v Hamilton* [1982] 1 All ER 1042, [1982] 2 WLR 322, that throws any doubt on the correctness in law of the passage I have quoted from the judgment of Parker J. I must, however, take the blame for expressing myself in *NWL Ltd v Woods* in terms that could be understood as being inconsistent with that passage in Parker J's judgment in the instant case.

    All that was said in the speeches in this House in *NWL Ltd v Woods* was said in the context of an application for an interlocutory injunction against officials of the ITF to restrain them from blacking a vessel sailing under a flag of convenience. It was held in that case, overruling *The Camilla M* [1979] 1 Lloyd's Rep 26, that in order for a dispute to be connected with terms and conditions of employment of the crew engaged on a flag of convenience vessel, so as to attract the immunity from an action in tort conferred by s 13(1) of the Trade Union and Labour Relations Act 1974, it was not necessary that the improvement of the terms and conditions of employment of the particular seamen who composed that crew should be the predominant purpose of the blacking. It was sufficient that changes in terms and conditions of employment of the crew was a matter on which the officials of the ITF were insisting. In my own speech, after referring to the suggestion that the ultimate object of the ITF's campaign of blacking vessels sailing under flags of convenience unless their crews are engaged on the ITF standard articles at the ITF standard rates of wages was to drive flags of convenience (as they define them) off the seas, and saying that this would not prevent the immediate dispute from being a dispute connected with the terms and conditions of employment of the crew of the ship that was being blacked, I ended that paragraph of my speech ([1979] 3 All ER 614 at 622, [1979] 1 WLR 1294 at 1302) with the words cited by the Court of Appeal in the instant case:

> '... one of the main commercial attractions of registering vessels under flags of convenience is that it facilitates the use of cheap labour to man them. So even the ultimate object of ITF's campaign is connected with the terms and conditions of employment of seamen.'

    The Court of Appeal in the instant case treated these words as an expression of my opinion that any demand for money made by the ITF on a shipowner in the course of pursuing its ultimate objective of driving flags of convenience off the seas was, ipso facto, connected with terms and conditions of employment of seamen. It was certainly not my intention to suggest by those words that a demand, for instance, by the ITF that the owner of a flag of convenience vessel should pay to the union's funds £1m as the sole condition to be fulfilled in order that the blacking should be lifted would entitle the ITF's officers who were inducing the blacking to immunity from an action in tort by virtue of s 13(1). That such was not my intention is, I hope, apparent from later passages in my speech and certainly no support for it is to be found in either of the other speeches in the case.

    Section 13(1) was directly applicable to the remedy sought in *NWL Ltd v Woods*. In the instant case it is only indirectly relevant as an indication of what kind of demand for money public policy requires should be excluded from giving rise to a restitutionary remedy by way of an action for money had and received, notwithstanding that the money was exacted in circumstances that would otherwise have amounted to economic duress. As Parker J did, and as the Court of Appeal would have done had they not been misled by an incautious phrase in my own speech in *NWL Ltd v Woods*, I see nothing in the Trade Union and Labour Relations Act 1974 that indicates any parliamentary intention that public policy does so require; and for the reasons that I have already given, I would allow this appeal on the duress point.

In view of the difference of opinion between the members of this House on the duress point it may be appropriate that before departing from the subject I should state that my opinion that the demand for a contribution to the welfare fund is not legitimised so as to deprive the shipowners of a restitutionary remedy would not necessarily be different if a requirement that the shipowners should make such a contribution were incorporated in the ITF collective agreement. Sections 13 and 29 of the Trade Union and Labour Relations Act 1974 are not directly applicable to restitutional remedies; they are relevant only for such indications as they give of the public policy as to what kinds of demands ought to be regarded as legitimate in the field of industrial relations notwithstanding that compliance with them is induced by economic duress. The fact that the ITF had also insisted that a term as to the requirement of payment to the welfare fund should be inserted in the ITF collective agreement would not, in my opinion, affect the public policy under which it is excluded from being legitimised.

LORD CROSS OF CHELSEA. My Lords, the facts of this case have been stated by my noble and learned friend Lord Diplock. The appeal raises two points: the 'trust' point and the 'duress' point.

In common with all your Lordships I think that the decision of the Court of Appeal on the 'trust' point was right. The case for the shipowners on this point, as pleaded, was that the welfare fund is not part of the general assets of the ITF but is held on separate, albeit void, trusts and that accordingly any contributions made to it by third parties become held on resulting trusts for the contributors. In my opinion, the rules of the welfare fund do not impress it with any trusts. It is simply a fund which the ITF set apart from its other assets with a view to its use for specified purposes but which remains in law part of the general assets of the ITF and can be used if the ITF so decides for other purposes.

The 'duress' point raises the question whether the demand made by the ITF that the shipowners should make contributions to the welfare fund was a 'legitimate' demand in the sense that although compliance with it was enforced by pressure that amounted to duress the shipowners are, nevertheless, not entitled to recover the contributions as 'money had and received'. The fact that your Lordships do not agree on the answer to be given to this question, shows that it is a difficult one. Up to a point there was agreement between the parties. In the first place, it was common ground between them that, although none of the provisions of the Trade Union and Labour Relations Act 1974 have any direct application to this case, guidance as to where the line should be drawn in the field of industrial relations between 'legitimate' and 'illegitimate' demands by a trade union can be found in the provisions of the Act giving immunity from liability in tort for certain acts done in contemplation or furtherance of a trade dispute, and that the demand in this case would rank as legitimate if a refusal by the shipowners to comply with it would have given rise to a dispute between the shipowners and the ITF connected with the terms and conditions of employment of the crew of the Universe Sentinel. Second, it was common ground that if a trade union were to make two demands, one of which was legitimate and the other not, the existence of the legitimate demand would not preclude the employer from recovering money paid under duress in compliance with the illegitimate demand. If, to take an example suggested by Lord Diplock, the ITF had coupled its demand that the shipowners should increase the wages of the crew with a demand that they should contribute to a fund to assist the guerillas in El Salvador, and the shipowners had complied with both demands under duress, the fact that they could not recover the increase in wage payments would not preclude them from recovering the contributions to the guerilla fund. I would add, although on the facts of this case the point does not arise for decision, that I fully concur with the view expressed by my noble

and learned friend in the concluding paragraph of his speech that in the case supposed it
would have made no difference to the right of the shipowners to recover the payments *a*
to the guerilla fund that the ITF had insisted, as a condition of lifting the 'blacking' of the
vessel, that an undertaking by the shipowners to make the payments should be inserted
in the contracts of employment of each member of the crew and that the shipowners
had, under duress, entered into such undertakings with each member. A trade union
cannot turn a dispute which in reality has no connection with terms and conditions of
employment into a dispute connected with terms and conditions of employment by *b*
insisting that the employer inserts appropriate terms into the contracts of employment
into which he enters.

Then, was the demand that the shipowners should make contributions to the welfare
fund, a demand a refusal to comply with which would have involved a dispute between
the ITF and the shipowners connected with the terms and conditions of employment of
the crew of the Universe Sentinel? I would begin by observing that the fund is not *c*
properly described as a welfare fund at all. Rule 2 of the present rules says that the object
of the fund shall be—

> 'the financing of any such work as may be sanctioned by the Executive Committee
> of the Federation for the purpose of promoting, advancing or protecting by any
> such means as the Executive Committee in their absolute discretion may decide, the
> interests of seafarers generally or groups of seafarers, national or otherwise, or of *d*
> assisting individual seafarers, or otherwise of serving seafarers' interests.'

There is nothing to limit the expression 'work' to 'welfare' work. The fund could be
expended if the executive committee thought fit in the work of driving flags of
convenience from the seas. The accounts of the welfare fund for the years 1976, 1977
and 1978 were produced on discovery. Their effect is summarised in the following *e*
passage in the judgment of the Court of Appeal ([1980] 2 Lloyd's Rep 523 at 538):

> 'The accounts are headed "Seafarers International Assistance, Welfare and
> Protection Fund", but in fact the income account includes not only contributions to
> the Welfare Fund but also the contributions payable for crew membership of the
> Special Seafarers' Section. The latter contributions are relatively small, amounting
> in 1978 to under 8 per cent. of the total income. The total income of the Welfare *f*
> Fund in these years, in round figures, advanced from £1,700,000 in 1976 to
> £3,500,000 in 1978; expenditure on the welfare of seafarers progressed from
> £263,000 to £763,000; administration expenses grew from £220,000 to £613,000;
> the surplus income added to capital in each of these years went from £1,200,000 to
> £2,100,000, being an accumulation of no less than £5,700,000 in the three years.'

It appears from art 5 of the special agreement that the rates of contribution to the welfare *g*
fund are fixed by the ITF and may be increased by it from time to time at its
discretion. The ITF called no evidence to explain the position disclosed by these
accounts. The assets of the welfare fund, which at the end of 1978 were worth some
£7,870,000 net are, as a matter of law, the property of the ITF to use as it likes. No
doubt, it would be only in very exceptional circumstances that the ITF would apply any *h*
of those assets to purposes other than the purposes of the Seafarers' Section. But even if
one assumes that in practice the welfare fund will always be applied for the purposes set
out in rule 2, I cannot see how a contribution to the welfare fund differs in principle from
a contribution to the general funds of a seamen's union, nor did I understand counsel for
the ITF to contend that there was any difference. His reply to the point was to say: 'The
shipowners admit that they cannot recover the crew membership fees; what difference *j*
is there between them and the contributions to the welfare fund?' To my mind there is
a world of difference. By paying his membership fees and getting his membership card,
the member secures a right to certain benefits and services from the union. These are
analogous to the benefits obtained from a private health insurance scheme or a private
pension fund, and the fees paid are presumably calculated with some reference to the

expense of providing the benefits and services. If an employer defrays the expense of
obtaining such benefits for his employees, his payments are in substance additional
wages and the benefits obtained are properly described as 'fringe benefits' of the
employment. By contrast, the members of the crew do not obtain any rights to benefit
from the welfare fund as a result of the shipowners' contributions to it. Their chance of
receiving some benefit from the fund is just the same whether or not the shipowners
contribute to the fund or whether or not they remain in the employment of the
shipowners. All that one can say is that the contributions add to the resources of the
union. It might, I suppose, be argued that any increase in the wealth of a trade union
must be beneficial to its members. As a general proposition that might well be doubted;
but even if it were universally true, the fact would not establish any connection between
the demand and the terms and conditions of employment of the crew. I cannot bring
myself to think that even in this day and age a demand that an employer shall make
contributions to union funds at rates fixed from time to time by the union (for that, as
I see it, is all that this demand amounts to) is a demand which can be legitimately
enforced by duress. In fact, of course, the shipowners did not enter into any agreements
with the members of the crew to make the welfare contributions but, as I have already
indicated, I do not think that if they had entered into such agreements under duress that
circumstance would have precluded them from recovering the payments.

I agree with my noble and learned friends Lord Diplock and Lord Russell that the
appeal should be allowed.

LORD RUSSELL OF KILLOWEN. My Lords, this appeal is concerned with an
episode in a substantially worldwide battle between the International Transport Workers'
Federation (the ITF) and owners of vessels sailing under flags of convenience. The ITF is
an unincorporated trade union the members of which consist of other trade unions in
various countries and has its headquarters in London. The facts and the circumstances
leading to the payment to the ITF by the appellant owners of the large tankship Universe
Sentinel of the sum of $US6,480 presently in dispute have been outlined by my noble
and learned friend Lord Diplock and are also to be found in the report of the case at first
instance (Parker J) and in the Court of Appeal (Megaw, Brightman and Watkins LJJ)
([1980] 2 Lloyd's Rep 523). The size of the sum now claimed suggests that the owners'
appeal has the backing of other flag of convenience owners who may have paid or may
be required to pay similar sums in similar circumstances.

The owners' claim to repayment of the sum mentioned is based on two contentions.
The first contention is that the payment was made to the ITF as trustee to be held on
certain supposed trusts, that those trusts were not as such valid or enforceable, and that
consequently the sum was held by the ITF on trust for the owners under the principle of
a resulting trust. The second contention was that the payment was extorted by the ITF
by the application of illegitimate and irresistible pressure in that the vessel was taken out
of service as long as the ITF continued to procure (as the ITF would have done unless the
owners complied with the ITF demands including payment of, inter alia, this sum) that
tug service would not be available to enable the vessel to sail. Under this head the owners
claimed repayment as money had and received.

The first contention I will label the trust point; and the second contention I will label
the duress point. I deal first with the trust point which found favour with Parker J but
not with the Court of Appeal.

In order to procure the cessation of blacking of the vessel by the tugs the owners were
required by the ITF to qualify for a blue certificate. The first document was served by the
ITF on the captain of the vessel on 17 July 1978 and set out the conditions of such
qualification. These were, first, that the owners sign with the ITF a special agreement
undertaking to apply to the crew all sections of the ITF collective agreement which were
to cover the terms and conditions of employment of the crew. Second, in so far as any
member of the crew was not eligible to become a member of a union member of the ITF,
that he be enrolled in the ITF Special Seafarers' Section, which was set up by the seafarers'

union members of the ITF; such enrolment would entitle those enrolled to trade union representation although not a member of a member union, nor of course of the ITF the membership of which consisted of trade unions. These benefits of 'outside membership' were dependent on payment on their behalf of entrance and annual fees of $US15 per man and $US30 per man per annum. The collective contract of employment required such payments to be made by the owner employer. Third, it was noted that the special agreement—

'also covers the owners' contributions to the Seafarers International Welfare, Protection and Assistance Fund, [at] $162 per man per year. The Fund was set up to help provide welfare, social and recreational facilities in ports around the world for seafarers of all nations, especially those serving in flag-of-convenience ships, and is administered by an international committee of representatives of ITF-affiliated unions'.

It is, my Lords, important to note that the document last summarised is in no way relied on by the owners in the pleadings in support of the contention that the welfare fund was held on or intended to be held on trusts, as distinct from being a fund belonging to the ITF at its disposal from time to time as the constituent members pursuant to the contract contained in the constitution of the unincorporated ITF should decide.

On 28 July 1978 what is referred to as the special agreement was signed on behalf of the owners and the ITF. The owners undertook to employ each seafarer in accordance with the terms of the ITF collective agreement and to incorporate its terms into the individual contract of each seafarer; and (by art 1(c)—

'to pay on behalf of each seafarer contributions and fees at the rates shown in Schedule 2 hereto to the Seafarers' International Welfare Protection and Assistance Fund and to the Special Seafarers' Section of the ITF. The contributions and fees shall be paid to the ITF annually and in advance.'

The schedule described the payments to be made as:

'ITF SPECIAL SEAFARERS' SECTION
Entrance fees   40 at US$15 per man   US$......
Membership fees   40 at US$30 per man per year   US$......
SEAFARERS' INTERNATIONAL WELFARE
PROTECTION AND ASSISTANCE FUND   40 at US$162 per man per year   US$......'

This last head of contributions, as distinct from fees, amounted to $US6,480, the sum now in dispute. The owners paid the special agreement sums to the ITF. (It is suggested on behalf of the ITF, though this point relates to the duress point rather than to the trust point, that because the special agreement recited under recital 3 that 'the ITF and the [owners] desire to regulate the conditions of employment of all seafarers . . . serving from time to time aboard the Ship', that meant that the parties had laid it down that everything that was agreed in the body of the agreement was a condition of such employment, including the agreement to contribute to the welfare fund. I cannot accept that suggestion. There is ample in the body of the agreement within the scope of the recital without embracing the contributions which are markedly not within the collective agreement.)

On the same day the owners and the ITF signed what is referred to as the typescript agreement. The function of this was to estimate and provide for the total due to members of the crew applying the new rates since signing on. I need say no more on this save to note that it shows that the amount of the estimate and of the special agreement sums (including the fund contribution of $US6,480) were included in a sum of $US80,000 paid to the ITF and accepted as to the $US6,480 for welfare fund contributions.

Under the points of claim the owners alleged that 'under and by virtue of the special agreement' the sum of $US6,480 was paid by the owners 'upon the trusts of the Seafarers International Welfare Protection and Assistance Fund' and that 'the trusts of the Welfare Fund are declared by a document entitled "Rules for Seafarers International Assistance Welfare and Protection Fund which was adopted by the ITF in December 1958"'. Accordingly the trust point is squarely based on the allegation that the rules establish a trust fund to be held on trusts which however must in law be held to be ineffective. Those rules have been set out in the speech of my noble and learned friend Lord Diplock.

In connection with those rules it is convenient to note some points in the constitution of the ITF. Congress is the supreme authority meeting normally every three years with delegates from the constituent unions members of the ITF. Congress appoints members of the general council, which exercises functions delegated to it by congress and meets after each ordinary congress and when called on to do so by the executive board. Then there is the executive board which consists of 23 members elected by congress from among the members of the general council, plus the general secretary. This board, which was formally called the executive committee, is the governing body of the ITF. The constituent members of the ITF are divided into industrial sections of which one is the seafarers' section and another the dockers' section.

In 1952 the dockers' and seafarers' sections met in joint conference with a view to a campaign to deal with flag of convenience ship problems. It was agreed to establish a Seafarers' International Welfare Fund as part of the campaign, and that six individuals should be appointed to administer the fund, as I understand it to be known as the Fair Practices Committee and formerly styled the Boycott Committee. At the same conference 'Rules to govern the functioning of the Welfare Fund' were approved: these rules were replaced in December 1958. This replacement was the work of the executive committee (board) of the ITF and in their final form have already been set out. Parker J in concluding that here was an intended trust placed some reliance on the fact that the first draft of the 1958 rules contained a clause to say that the executive committee might alter the rules or add to them at any time, which did not appear in the rules as adopted; in my opinion any such reliance in construing the rules is unsound and at least arguably impermissible.

The accounts of the fund are summarised in the judgment of the Court of Appeal thus ([1980] 2 Lloyd's Rep 523 at 538):

'We have before us the accounts of the Welfare Fund for the years 1976, 1977 and 1978. The accounts are headed "Seafarers International Assistance, Welfare and Protection Fund", but in fact the income account includes not only contributions to the Welfare Fund but also the contributions payable for crew membership of the Special Seafarers' Section. The latter contributions are relatively small, amounting in 1978 to under 8 per cent of the total income. The total income of the Welfare Fund in these years, in round figures, advanced from £1,700,000 in 1976 to £3,500,000 in 1978; expenditure on the welfare of seafarers progressed from £263,000 to £763,000; administration expenses grew from £226,000 to £613,000; the surplus income added to capital in each of these years went from £1,200,000 to £2,100,000, being an accumulation of no less than £5,700,000 over the three years.'

I would however comment on that extract that what are referred to as 'contributions' payable for crew membership of the Special Seafarers' Section are more accurately described as 'fees'.

My Lords, it is commonplace for a trade union to have, in addition to its general funds, special funds. Indeed in the constitution of ITF special funds are envisaged: see rr IX(3) and XIII(1). Essentially the internal affairs of the union, including the use and destination of any funds of the union, are dependent not on the setting up of trust funds but on the contract between the members found in the constitution.

The points of claim, as I have already indicated, assert that the rules of the welfare fund declare trusts, and it is on that assertion that the trust point is based. In my opinion that is a false assertion: the fund is a fund of the ITF subject for the time being to an earmarking subject to the contractual arrangements between the members under the *a* constitution. The contribution of the owners to the ITF under this head is not a contribution to the ITF on trust, and is not in law different from a payment generally to the ITF. That view may well not assist the ITF in argument on the duress point, but in my opinion it suffices to deny the trust point to the owners.

I turn next to the second contention of the owners: the duress point. I have earlier in this speech in a parenthesis touched on this point by expressing my opinion that the *b* third recital in the special agreement cannot be regarded as establishing that the welfare fund contribution relates to the terms and conditions of employment of the crew. For the rest, on this point, I content myself with adopting the speech of my noble and learned friend Lord Diplock, and on that basis I would allow the appeal. I finally observe that that would have been the view of the four judges below had the Court of Appeal not, in my opinion, misconstrued a passage in a speech of my noble and learned friend Lord *c* Diplock in *NWL Ltd v Woods* [1979] 3 All ER 614 at 622, [1979] 1 WLR 1294 at 1302.

LORD SCARMAN. My Lords, the decisive question in this appeal is whether in any circumstances, and if in any in what circumstances, an employer who has paid money to a trade union under the compulsion of actual or threatened industrial action can recover the money as having been paid under duress.   *d*

My noble and learned friend Lord Diplock has stated the facts and outlined the history of the litigation. It is nevertheless necessary for me, as I am respectfully dissenting from his conclusion that the appeal should be allowed, to state briefly those facts on which I base my view that the appeal should be dismissed.

The original claim of the appellant shipowners (the owners) against the respondent trade union (the ITF) was for (i) a declaration that two agreements (the 'special agreement' *e* and the 'typescript agreement') are invalid, (ii) a declaration that the ITF hold on trust for the owners the sum of $US80,000 paid to the ITF by the owners pursuant to the special agreement, (iii) $80,000, a sum certain together with interest. There was also a claim for damages and for certain other declaratory relief. By the time the case reached your Lordships' House one issue alone remained, namely whether the ITF is liable to repay to *f* the owners the sum of $US6,480, being that part of the $80,000 which constituted a contribution which the owners were required to make to the Seafarers' International Welfare, Protection and Assistance Fund (the welfare fund) under the terms of the special agreement. Parker J held at first instance that the sum must be repaid. The Court of Appeal allowed the appeal of the ITF and held that it is irrecoverable.

The appellant owners put their case in two ways: (1) the trust point: the sum of $6,480 *g* was paid, it is submitted, on the trusts of the welfare fund, those trusts are void and of no effect, accordingly the sum is held on resulting trusts for the owners; (2) the duress point: the two agreements, it is submitted, were signed and the moneys paid under duress; accordingly the owners can recover the $6,480 as money had and received to their use.

I have had the advantage of reading the opinions of my noble and learned friends Lord Cross and Lord Russell on the trust point and I agree with them. There is, in my opinion, *h* no resulting trust. It follows that to recover the sum of $6,480 the owners must show a common law right to recover the sum as money paid under duress.

The facts follow a familiar pattern, although the relief and remedies sought are unusual in this area of litigation. Questions as to the validity of trusts are more frequently raised in the quiet waters of family settlements, gifts, and bequests to charity than on the turbulent seas navigated by the ITF. It is highly artificial to impute to these owners any *j* intention of gift or settlement. Their common law claim accurately reflects the true nature of their case; and it is, so far as I am aware, the first time that a shipowner has sought in the English courts to recover as money had and received a sum paid to a trade union to secure the release of his ship from a blacking procured by the trade union. The claim raises an important question as to the interrelation of the law of duress with the statutory immunities enjoyed under English law by persons acting in contemplation or furtherance of a trade dispute.

The owners, a company incorporated in Liberia, own and operate the tankship, the Universe Sentinel, 269,092 tons deadweight. The ship is registered in Liberia and sails under the Liberian flag. The ITF is an international federation of national trade unions which represent transport workers, including seamen, in many countries of the world. The ITF is a trade union for the purposes of the Trade Union and Labour Relations Act 1974, even though it has no individual members. It maintains, however, a Special Seafarers' Section in which seafarers who are not eligible for membership of an ITF affiliate union may be enrolled. The purpose of the Special Seafarers' Section is to provide trade union representation for crews of flag of convenience ships who have no national union which they can join.

The policy of the ITF towards ships which sail under what it regards as flags of convenience has been described by my noble and learned friend Lord Diplock in *NWL Ltd v Woods* [1979] 3 All ER 614 at 617, [1979] 1 WLR 1294 at 1297. It seeks to compel the owners of such ships to employ seamen on terms comparable to those contained in collective agreements negotiated by its affiliate unions for ships registered in Western Europe. To this end the ITF seeks to procure the 'blacking' of flag of convenience ships whose owners have not accepted ITF terms.

The Universe Sentinel was regarded by the ITF as sailing under a flag of convenience. On 17 July 1978 she docked at Milford Haven. By the afternoon of 18 July she was ready to sail. But she could not because she was 'blacked'. The ITF had procured those who were operating the tugs at Milford Haven to refuse, in breach of their contracts of employment, to make tugs available to assist the ship's departure from port.

The blacking of the ship followed on a presentation by an ITF representative to the master of the union's demands. These were contained in an ITF document entitled 'Conditions to be fulfilled before flag-of-convenience vessels can be issued with ITF Blue Certificates—effective from 1st September 1977'. A blue certificate is a notice that terms of employment on board ship comply with ITF requirements. The conditions included a requirement that the owner sign a 'special agreement' undertaking to apply all sections of the ITF collective agreement to all seafarers on board the ship; a requirement that any seafarers not eligible for membership of an ITF affiliate union must be enrolled in the ITF Special Seafarers' Section; a requirement that the owner pay each crew member's union entrance fee and annual subscriptions; and a requirement that the owner contribute annually to the welfare fund which was described as having been set up 'to help provide welfare, social and recreational facilities in ports around the world for seafarers of all nations, especially those serving in flag-of-convenience ships'. The document made it very clear that unless and until the owner signed the 'special agreement' incorporating these requirements, a printed draft of which the ITF provided for the owner to fill in the blanks and sign, and paid the moneys demanded, no blue certificate would be issued and the blacking would continue.

By 29 July the owners had complied with these demands and the ship was able to sail. The owners had on 28 July signed two agreements and paid by cheque to the order of the ITF the sum of $US80,000.

The first of the two agreements was the 'special agreement'. It recited that 'the ITF and the Company desire to regulate the conditions of employment of all seafarers . . . serving from time to time aboard the Ship' and included seven articles of agreement and two schedules. I need quote only art 1(c) and Sch 2:

> '**Article** 1 . . . (c) to pay on behalf of each Seafarer contributions and fees at the rates shown in Schedule 2 hereto to the Seafarers' International Welfare Protection and Assistance Fund and to the Special Seafarers' Section of the ITF. The contributions and fees shall be paid to the ITF annually and in advance . . .

'Schedule 2

ITF SPECIAL SEAFARERS' SECTION		
Entrance fees	40 at US$15 per man	US$.........
Membership fees	40 at US$30 per man per year	US$.........
SEAFARERS' INTERNATIONAL WELFARE		
PROTECTION AND ASSISTANCE FUND	40 at US$162 per man per year	US$.........
TOTAL		US$8280.—'

The $6,480 now claimed is the total of the contributions to the fund included in the $80,000 paid to the union.

The second agreement (the 'typescript agreement', so called to distinguish it from the printed draft of the special agreement) confirmed receipt of the $80,000 and included provisions for calculating the wages and other benefits due to crew members under the ITF collective agreement.

In his written case the owners have, in my view correctly, summarised the effect of these transactions as follows: (1) they yielded to the demands made on them as being the only means open to them of regaining the use of their ship; (2) the loss of use of their ship was to them so disastrous that they had no practical option but to submit; (3) the acts done by the ITF to deny them the use of their ship were, subject to any statutory immunity which the ITF might enjoy, tortious. In a sentence, they had no choice but to submit to the economic pressure applied by the prima facie unlawful acts of the union. The ITF, as I understand its case, do not challenge that such was the effect of what it did but deny that it acted unlawfully or that its pressure was illegitimate. It relies on the policy of the law granting statutory immunity from tortious liability to persons acting in contemplation or furtherance of a trade dispute: see s 13(1) of the Act as amended in 1976.

The issue between the parties is a narrow one. Was the dispute over the contributions to the welfare fund a trade dispute within the meaning of s 29 of the Act? The owners conceded that if it was, the moneys paid would be irrecoverable. The issue turns on analysis of what the parties agreed and on the proper construction of s 29 of the Act.

Before turning to this issue, it is necessary to state, albeit very briefly, my view as to the nature of the modern law of duress.

It is, I think, already established law that economic pressure can in law amount to duress; and that duress, if proved, not only renders voidable a transaction into which a person has entered under its compulsion but is actionable as a tort, if it causes damage or loss: see *Barton v Armstrong* [1975] 2 All ER 465, [1976] AC 104 and *Pao On v Lau Yiu* [1979] 3 All ER 65, [1980] AC 614. The authorities on which these two cases were based reveal two elements in the wrong of duress: (1) pressure amounting to compulsion of the will of the victim; and (2) the illegitimacy of the pressure exerted. There must be pressure, the practical effect of which is compulsion or the absence of choice. Compulsion is variously described in the authorities as coercion or the vitiation of consent. The classic case of duress is, however, not the lack of will to submit but the victim's intentional submission arising from the realisation that there is no other practical choice open to him. This is the thread of principle which links the early law of duress (threat to life or limb) with later developments when the law came also to recognise as duress first the threat to property and now the threat to a man's business or trade. The development is well traced in Goff and Jones *The Law of Restitution* (2nd edn, 1978) ch 9.

The absence of choice can be proved in various ways, e g by protest, by the absence of independent advice, or by a declaration of intention to go to law to recover the money paid or the property transferred: see *Maskell v Horner* [1915] 3 KB 106, [1914–15] All ER Rep 595. But none of these evidential matters goes to the essence of duress. The victim's silence will not assist the bully, if the lack of any practicable choice but to submit is proved. The present case is an excellent illustration. There was no protest at the time, but only a determination to do whatever was needed as rapidly as possible to release the ship. Yet nobody challenges the judge's finding that the owners acted under compulsion. He put it thus:

'It was a matter of the most urgent commercial necessity that the plaintiffs should regain the use of their vessel. They were advised that their prospects of obtaining an injunction were minimal, the vessel would not have been released unless the payment was made, and they sought recovery of the money with sufficient speed once the duress had terminated.'

The real issue in the appeal is, therefore, as to the second element in the wrong duress: was the pressure applied by the ITF in the circumstances of this case one which the law recognises as legitimate? For, as Lord Wilberforce and Lord Simon in *Barton v Armstrong* [1975] 2 All ER 465 at 476–477, [1976] AC 104 at 121 said: '. . . the pressure must be one of a kind which the law does not regard as legitimate.'

As Lord Wilberforce and Lord Simon remarked, in life, including life in commerce and finance, many acts are done 'under pressure, sometimes overwhelming pressure'; but they are not necessarily done under duress. That depends on whether the circumstances are such that the law regards the pressure as legitimate.

In determining what is legitimate two matters may have to be considered. The first is as to the nature of the pressure. In many cases this will be decisive, though not in every case. And so the second question may have to be considered, namely, the nature of the demand which the pressure is applied to support.

The origin of the doctrine of duress in threats to life or limb, or to property, suggests strongly that the law regards the threat of unlawful action as illegitimate, whatever the demand. Duress can, of course, exist even if the threat is one of lawful action; whether it does so depends on the nature of the demand. Blackmail is often a demand supported by a threat to do what is lawful, e g to report criminal conduct to the police. In many cases, therefore, 'what [one] has to justify is not the threat, but the demand . . .' (see *Thorne v Motor Trade Association* [1937] 3 All ER 157 at 160, [1937] AC 797 at 806 per Lord Atkin).

The present is a case in which the nature of the demand determines whether the pressure threatened or applied, i e the blacking, was lawful or unlawful. If it was unlawful, it is conceded that the owner acted under duress and can recover. If it was lawful, it is conceded that there was no duress and the sum sought by the owners is irrecoverable. The lawfulness or otherwise of the demand depends on whether it was an act done in contemplation or furtherance of a trade dispute. If it was, it would not be actionable in tort: s 13(1) of the Act. Although no question of tortious liability arises in this case and s 13(1) is not, therefore, directly in point, it is not possible, in my view, to say of acts which are protected by statute from suit in tort that they nevertheless can amount to duress. Parliament having enacted that such acts are not actionable in tort, it would be inconsistent with legislative policy to say that, when the remedy sought is not damages for tort but recovery of money paid, they become unlawful.

In order to determine whether the making of the demand was an act done in contemplation or furtherance of a trade dispute, it is necessary to refer to s 29 which sets out the statutory meaning of 'trade dispute'.

The issue therefore is reduced to the one question. Was the demand for contributions to the welfare fund connected with one or more of the matters specified in s 29 of the Act? It is common ground that unless the demand was connected with 'terms and conditions of employment' it was not within the section.

Parker J found it 'plain' that a dispute about payments to the ITF for the welfare fund would not be connected with any of the matters mentioned in s 29. The Court of Appeal would have have been disposed to take the same view, if they had not felt that they were precluded from doing so by the guidance given in *BBC v Hearn* [1978] 1 All ER 111 at 120, [1977] 1 WLR 1004 at 1015 by Roskill LJ and in *NWL Ltd v Woods* [1979] 3 All ER 614 at 622, [1979] 1 WLR 1294 at 1302 by Lord Diplock. While I am prepared to accept, for the reasons given by my noble and learned friend Lord Diplock, that the Court of Appeal misunderstood the guidance given in those two cases, it does not follow that the payments to the welfare fund were unconnected with the terms and conditions of employment of the crew members of the ship.

It is not necessary to spend time on the construction of s 29. It has been accepted since *BBC v Hearn* that 'terms and conditions of employment' is a phrase of wide meaning and *a* includes not only the rights and but also the customary benefits and reasonable expectations provided by reason of his employment to the employee by his employer. But it is said that in this case the employer's obligation was to the union, not to the employee. The argument may be summarised as follows: (1) the crew members are not obliged to make the contributions, which are an exaction by the ITF from the owners and not an undertaking by the owners to discharge an obligation owed by crew members *b* to their union; (2) unlike union entrance fees and annual subscriptions, they are not mentioned in the collective agreement; (3) they are not benefits made available by an employer expressly, impliedly, or by customary practice to his employee, but merely contributions exacted by a trade union from an employer to its funds; (4) if the contributions are of any benefit to seafarers on board the ship, the benefit is marginal, if not infinitesimal; (5) in so far as the fund is beneficial to anyone other than the union *c* whose fund it is, it benefits all seafarers without anything special or exclusive to those employed on the Universe Sentinel.

The demand that the special agreement be signed was one which certainly related to the terms and conditions of employment on board the ship. The parties were well aware that the special agreement was, as recited, intended to regulate the conditions of employment; and its terms were such that it clearly did specify the terms and conditions *d* on which crew members were to be employed. But did the demand for contributions to the welfare fund relate to their terms and conditions of employment? The question cannot be answered save by an examination of the circumstances in which it was made.

It is of some significance, though not in itself decisive, that the demand is to be found in the same set of documents as the other demands as to rates of pay and the payment of union fees which were indisputably connected with terms and conditions of *e* employment. However, it would be wrong (quite apart from any question of duress) to adopt towards the documents of agreement in this case the strict approach which the law requires in determining the true construction of a commercial contract. What calls for analysis and explanation is the nature of the demand. And this can only be understood by a commonsense approach, after considering such ancillary questions as whether the demand was made merely for the union's benefit or was made for the benefit, or on *f* behalf, of the workers whose terms and conditions of employment the union was admittedly seeking to regulate by the documents which contain the demand.

The demand was expressed to be made 'on behalf of each seafarer' on board ship. It was for contributions to a fund which, though not a trust fund, existed, as a matter of contract between the affiliate unions of the ITF, for the benefit of seafarers. There was no indication in the evidence that the ITF had any intention of scrapping the fund or *g* going back on its word to apply the payments in the manner and for the purpose stated in the special agreement. I have no doubt that its intentions in regard to the fund were as set out in the 'Blue Certificate Conditions' and the special agreement. There is certainly no evidence to the contrary; and it would be unjust to the point of cynicism to impute to the ITF any intention other than to use the fund for the purpose set forth in those conditions.

I turn, therefore, to the five points enumerated above. Do they constitute a case *h* against the view that the obligation accepted by the owners under the pressure of blacking their ship to contribute to the fund was related to the terms and conditions of employment on board the ship?

(1) *and* (2). The fact that there is no obligation on crew members to contribute to the fund proves nothing. The demand on the owners to contribute was made by the union *j* for the benefit of the crew and on their behalf and incorporated in the special agreement. Each seaman secured a written contract, the terms of which were 'the current ITF Collective Agreement, brought into force by the Special Agreement . . .' The owners were obliged to display aboard the ship copies of the special agreement, the ITF collective agreement and the blue certificate in a prominent place accessible to all

seamen. Bearing in mind the very wide meaning given by the law to terms and conditions of employment (see *BBC v Hearn*), I find it totally unreal to infer that because the seamen are themselves not obliged to contribute to the fund the obligation accepted by the owners to contribute 'on behalf of each seafarer' was not an obligation related to the conditions of employment. The owners have undertaken, albeit under pressure, to make payments on behalf of each seaman which could be of benefit to him; and the undertaking was recognised as a term of the total bargain between the union and the owners on the basis on which the seaman was to be employed. Further, it can be of no importance that the collective agreement makes no mention of the obligation, when it is incorporated in the special agreement which is not only mentioned in the seaman's contract but has to be published on board the ship.

Finally, could it be said, I ask, that the obligation to contribute 'on behalf of each seafarer' to the fund would not be a condition of employment if it had been mentioned in the ITF collective agreement? I suggest not. And, if it be capable of being a condition of employment, I would think its presence in the special agreement, of which each seaman had notice, would constitute sufficient notice to make its absence from the ITF collective agreement immaterial.

(3) to (5). It is a necessary part of the immediately preceding argument that payments to the union for the fund were made on behalf of crew members and were intended to be for their benefit. The fund is governed by rules which the ITF, if it acts in accordance with the rules, can amend. The objects of the fund, as defined by the rules, are very wide ('promoting ... by any such means as the Executive Committee in their absolute discretion may decide, the interests of seafarers': see r 2); and there is no legal principle to prevent the ITF, if it acts constitutionally, from winding up the fund and transferring its substantial cash assets to itself. But the fund does exist; it is used to provide amenities in many ports for seamen; there is no indication that the union has any present intention other than to maintain the fund in the interests of seafarers; and without contributions obtained from owners there would be no fund available for their welfare. I am not prepared, on the evidence, to find that the payment of contributions to the fund is not of benefit to seafarers in general, or to the crew members of this ship, even though I recognise that some may never benefit from it.

For these reasons I conclude that the demand for contributions related to the terms and conditions of employment on the ship, and, if it had been resisted by the owners, would have led to a trade dispute. Blacking the ship in support of the demand was, therefore, not actionable in tort. It was, accordingly, a legitimate exercise of pressure and did not constitute duress. The owners cannot recover the contributions. I would dismiss the appeal.

LORD BRANDON OF OAKBROOK. My Lords, this appeal arises out of the blacking at the port of Milford Haven in July 1978 of the tankship Universe Sentinel, which I shall call 'the ship'. The ship was owned by the respondent corporation, which I shall call 'the shipowning company'. The blacking, which took the form of a refusal by tugs' crews to give to the ship the assistance which she needed in order to leave the port, was instigated by the appellant federation, which I shall call 'the ITF', in the course of its long-continuing campaign against what it regards as 'flag of convenience' ships and their owners.

By 28 July 1978, as a result of the blacking, the ITF had compelled the shipowning company, as the price of putting an end to the severe financial loss caused to it by the detention of the ship, to comply with two demands presented to it by the ITF. The first demand was that the shipowning company should enter into two written agreements with the ITF relating to improvements in the pay and other terms and conditions of employment of those on board the ship. Those agreements have been called 'the special agreement' and 'the typescript agreement' respectively. Their effect was to oblige the shipowning company to substitute for the rates of pay and other terms and conditions of employment prescribed by the existing contracts of employment of those on board the ship the higher rates of pay and improved other terms and conditions of employment, approved by the ITF and laid down by it in what is known as the ITF collective agreement.

The second demand was that the shipowning company should pay forthwith to the ITF the sum of $US80,000. This sum was made up of three separate items: first, $US71,720, being an estimate of the back pay due to those on board the ship on the footing that the agreed higher rates of pay should be applied retrospectively; second, $US1,800 in respect of entrance and membership fees payable by those on board the ship to the Special Seafarers' Section of the ITF; and, third, $US6,480 paid by way of contributions to a fund of the ITF known as the Seafarers' International Welfare Protection and Assistance Fund, which I shall call 'the fund'.

Following compliance by the shipowning company with the two demands referred to above, the blacking of the ship was lifted, the necessary tug assistance became available and the ship, which had been detained in the port of Milford Haven for about ten days, left that port and resumed her interrupted voyage.

It had been the intention of the shipowning company all along, while acceding to the ITF's demands in order to obtain the release of the ship, to claim back later by legal proceedings the sum of $US80,000 which it had been compelled to pay. In accordance with that intention the shipowning company subsequently began an action against the ITF and one of its officers in the Commercial Court, claiming, inter alia, on various legal grounds repayment of the whole or part of the sum of $US80,000 which had been exacted from it.

The action was tried by Parker J and, either before or in the course of the trial, the matters in dispute between the shipowning company and the ITF were narrowed down to four questions of which only the first three are now material. These three questions were: (1) was the shipowning company entitled to recover back from the ITF the sum of $US6,480 which it had paid by way of contributions to the fund, on the ground that such sum was paid for the purposes of a void trust and was therefore held by the ITF on a resulting trust for the benefit of the shipowning company? (2) was the dispute between the shipowning company and the ITF, in so far as it related to the payment of the sum of $US6,480 by way of contributions by the shipowning company to the fund, a trade dispute within s 29(1) of the Trade Union and Labour Relations Act 1974? (3) if the answer to question (2) was in the negative, was the payment of the sum of $US6,480 induced by duress, and therefore recoverable as money had and received by the ITF to the use of the shipowning company?

Parker J answered all three questions in favour of the shipowning company: that is to say he gave an affirmative answer to question (1), a negative answer to question (2) and an affirmative answer to question (3).

The ITF appealed against the decision of Parker J to the Court of Appeal, consisting of Megaw, Brightman and Watkins LJJ. By the judgment of that court, which was delivered by Megaw LJ, the ITF's appeal was allowed. Question (1) was answered in the negative and question (2) in the affirmative, with the result that it was not necessary to answer question (3). The shipowning company now appeals, with the leave of the Appeal Committee, against the judgment of the Court of Appeal, seeking to have the judgment of Parker J in its favour restored.

It is necessary to state, by way of preliminary matter, that the parties, for the purposes of the ITF's present appeal to your Lordships' House, have agreed to treat as correct the following four propositions of law. First, that, if the sum of $US6,480 paid by the shipowning company to the ITF was paid for the purposes of a trust, such trust was not a charitable one, and the consequence of that is that the sum was held by the ITF on a resulting trust for the benefit of the shipowning company. Second, that severe economic pressure could amount to duress in law. Third, that, if the relevant economic pressure was applied in furtherance of a trade dispute within the meaning of s 29(1) of the 1974 Act, it would not constitute duress in law, and any sum exacted by such pressure would not be recoverable. But, fourth, that, if the relevant economic pressure was applied in furtherance of a dispute which was not a trade dispute within the meaning of s 29(1), any sum exacted as a result of such pressure would be recoverable as money had and received by the payee to the use of the payer. The effect of this last agreed proposition was to give an agreed affirmative answer to question (3).

My Lords, there can, I think, be no doubt about the correctness of the first and second of these four agreed propositions of law. With regard to the other two propositions, however, the fact that the parties were agreed about them has meant that your Lordships have not heard any argument either supporting or attacking the correctness of them. In these circumstances, while I think that your Lordships should accept, for the purposes of this appeal alone, that the last two propositions of law agreed between the parties are correct, it should be made quite clear that your Lordships are not necessarily, by doing so, giving the seal of your approval to those propositions.

I turn now to consider the only two questions now remaining in dispute, namely question (1) (the trust point) and question (2) (the duress point).

With regard to question (1), the administration of the fund was governed by a body of rules, six in number, which I shall call 'the fund rules'. The material terms of the fund rules are set out in the speech of my noble and learned friend Lord Diplock (see p 73 g to p 74 b, ante), and it is therefore not necessary that I should set them out in full again here. The view of the Court of Appeal about the effect of the fund rules can be summarised in this way. The fund had been set up by the executive board (then the executive committee) pursuant to its power to create or provide for special funds in connection with industrial sections or special departments. The executive committee had power to set up such a fund, either by way of trust or by way of contract between the affiliated unions. The language of the fund rules was capable of being interpreted in either way. To interpret them as creating a trust would, however, defeat the whole purpose for which the fund was set up, whereas to interpret them as creating a contract would give effect to such purpose. It is an established principle of construction that, where an instrument was capable of two interpretations, one of which would give effect to the purpose of the persons who drew it up, and the other of which would frustrate such purpose, to prefer the former interpretation to the latter. Parker J was, therefore, wrong to interpret the fund rules as purporting to create a trust which was void, and the right way to interpret them was as creating a contract between the affiliated unions which was valid (see [1980] 2 Lloyd's Rep 523 at 540–541).

I find myself in complete agreement with that analysis by the Court of Appeal of the effect of the fund rules, and it follows that I think that that court was right to answer question (1) in the negative.

It remains to consider question (2), namely whether the dispute between the shipowning company and the ITF, in so far as it related to the payment of $US6,480, by way of contributions to the fund, was a trade dispute within s 29(1) of the 1974 Act. In considering that question it is, in my view, essential to take two matters fully into account. Those matters are, first, so much of the terms of the special agreement and the typescript agreement as is relevant to the obligation of the shipowning company to make contributions to the fund, and secondly, the indication of the purposes of the fund contained in the fund rules.

The special agreement begins by setting out the names and addresses of the parties to it and indicating that the shipowning company will in the remainder of the agreement be referred to as 'the Company'. The agreement then continues as follows:

'WHEREAS: (1) the ITF is an independent trade union organisation comprising fully autonomous trade union organisations in transport and allied services throughout the world and members of the Special Seafarers' Section of the ITF; (2) the Company is the registered owner/manager of the Ship; described in Schedule 1 hereto; (3) the ITF and the Company desire to regulate the conditions of employment of all seafarers (hereinafter individually called a "Seafarer") serving from time to time aboard the Ship;

NOW IT IS AGREED:

Article 1: The Company undertakes as follows: (a) to employ each Seafarer in *a* accordance with the terms of the current ITF Collective Agreement for World Wide trading (hereinafter called the ITF Collective Agreement) as amended from time to time . . .; (b) to incorporate the terms and conditions of the ITF Collective Agreement into the individual contract of employment of each seafarer and into the Ship's Articles and furnish copies of these documents to the ITF. Any seafarer enjoying terms and conditions which are, taken as a whole, recognised by the ITF *b* as more favourable to the seafarer, shall continue to enjoy such terms and conditions; (c) to pay on behalf of each Seafarer contributions and fees at the rates shown in Schedule 2 hereto to the Seafarers' International Welfare Protection and Assistance Fund and to the Special Seafarers' Section of the ITF. The contributions and fees shall be paid to the ITF annually and in advance; (d) to display aboard the Ship copies of the Special Agreement, the ITF Collective Agreement and the ITF Blue Certificate *c* to be issued under Article 2 hereof in a prominent place to which each Seafarer shall have access at all times; and (e) to grant to representatives of the ITF and of trade union organisations affiliated to the ITF free access to each Seafarer at all reasonable times whether or not aboard the Ship, whether the Ship is in berth or not.

Article 2: the ITF undertakes, having received and approved the copies of the documents referred to in Article 1(b) above, and received the fees and contributions *d* payable under Article 1(c) above, to issue and each year to renew an ITF Blue Certificate . . . certifying that the Ship is covered by a Collective Agreement acceptable to the ITF . . .'

Following arts 1 and 2 quoted above there come four further articles numbered 3 to 7, the terms of which it is not necessary to set out. Then, on the second page of the agreement there appear two schedules, numbered 1 and 2 respectively. Schedule 1 *e* contains a description of the ship. Schedule 2 is in this form:

'ITF SPECIAL SEAFARERS' SECTION

Entrance fees	40 at US$15 per man	US$.........
Membership fees	40 at US$30 per man per year	US$.........
SEAFARERS' INTERNATIONAL WELFARE PROTECTION AND ASSISTANCE FUND	40 at US$162 per man per year	US$.........
TOTAL		US$8280.—'

Although the relevant sub-totals were left blank in Sch 2, it is apparent that the total of $US8,280 was made up of entrance and membership fees in respect of the Special Seafarers' Section of $US600 and $US1,200 respectively, and contributions to the fund of $US6,480.

The typescript agreement begins by setting out the names and addresses of the parties to it. It then continues with the following heading and first paragraph:

'IN RESPECT OF THE LIBERIAN FLAG TANKER "UNIVERSAL SENTINEL"

The ITF confirms receipt to-day of US$80,000 . . . which is accepted by the ITF as to the one part of $8,280 for the Union Entrance Fees, Annual Subscriptions and Welfare Fund Contributions, and as to the other part of $71,720 as a discretionary trustee. The beneficiaries are the Master, Officers, Engineers and crew members on board on 28th July 1978.'

Rule 2 of the fund rules provided:

'The object of the Fund shall be the financing of any such work as may be sanctioned by the Executive Committee of the Federation for the purpose of promoting, advancing or protecting by any such means as the Executive Committee in their absolute discretion may decide, the interests of seafarers generally or groups of seafarers, national or otherwise, or of assisting individual seafarers, or otherwise of serving seafarers' interests.'

Section 29(1) and (4) of the 1974 Act provide:

'(1) In this Act "trade dispute" means a dispute between employers and workers, or between workers and workers, which is connected with one or more of the following, that is to say—(a) terms and conditions of employment . . .
(4) A dispute to which a trade union . . . is a party shall be treated for the purposes of this Act as a dispute to which workers . . . are parties.'

The dispute in the present case, in so far as it related to the payment by the shipowning company of $US6,480 by way of contributions to the fund, was a dispute between an employer and a trade union. The effect of s 29(4) above is that the dispute concerned must be treated as a dispute between employers and workers for the purposes of s 29(1). It follows that the only issue to be determined in relation to question (2) is whether the dispute between the shipowning company and the ITF about the payment of those contributions was, to use the words of s 29(1)(a), connected with terms and conditions of employment.

It has been established by authority that the expression 'terms and conditions of employment', as used in s 29(1)(a) of the 1974 Act, is to be given the widest possible construction: see BBC v Hearn [1978] 1 All ER 111 at 116, 120, [1977] 1 WLR 1004 at 1010, 1015 per Lord Denning MR and Roskill LJ. The relevant observations of Lord Denning MR in that case were expressly approved by your Lordships' House in the recent case of Hadmor Productions Ltd v Hamilton [1982] 1 All ER 1042, [1982] 2 WLR 322 in a speech of Lord Diplock with which all the other four members of the Appellate Committee agreed. The effect of giving the expression concerned the very wide meaning which these authorities show that it should be given is that any arrangement which affects, directly or indirectly, the benefits which a worker enjoys in connection with his employment, can properly be treated as a condition of such worker's employment for the purposes of s 29(1)(a) of the 1974 Act, even though there is no reference to such arrangement, expressly or by incorporation, in the contract under which the worker is employed.

My Lords, it appears to me to be crystal clear that the parties themselves regarded the dispute, in so far as it related to the payment by the shipowning company of contributions to the fund, as being a dispute connected with the terms and conditions of employment of those on board the ship, both those on board her at the time and those contemplated as being on board her from time to time in the future. I say that for two reasons. The first reason is to be found in the terms of the special agreement. The recital numbered 3 in that agreement stated unequivocally that the purpose of the parties in entering into the agreement was to regulate the conditions of employment of all seafarers serving from time to time aboard the ship. It is, in my view, a necessary inference from this that the parties, in agreeing to the substantive provisions of the agreement contained in arts 1 to 7, were intending to give effect, directly or indirectly, to their previously recited purpose. The obligation of the shipowning company to make contributions to the fund was imposed by para (c) of art 1, which is sandwiched between other obligations of the shipowning company imposed by paras (a) and (b) of art 1 above and para (d) and (e) below. These five paragraphs of art 1 must, in my view, be regarded as a package of terms imposed by the ITF on the shipowning company for the benefit of those who were then, or would be later, employed on board the ship and, having regard to the stated purpose of the agreement, namely, the regulation of the conditions of employment of such persons, it must be inferred that the parties intended those paragraphs to form part of the process of giving effect to that purpose.

The second reason is to be found in the terms of the first paragraph of the typescript agreement, which I also set out earlier. Here again the whole tenor of the paragraph is only consistent with the conclusion of a package deal in which both the payment of the union entrance and membership fees on the one hand, and the payment of contributions to the fund on the other hand, are treated as having the same quality. It was conceded on behalf of the shipowning company that its obligation to pay union entrance and membership fees came within the expression 'terms and conditions of employment' as

used in s 29(1)(a) of the 1974 Act. If the concession was rightly made, as I consider that
it was, then it seems to me that it is impossible to treat as having a different quality the *a*
closely linked obligation of the shipowning company to pay contributions to the fund.

Two main arguments were, however, advanced on behalf of the shipowning company
in order to show that, whatever the parties themselves may have intended, the obligation
of the shipowning company to pay contributions to the fund did not come within the
expression 'terms and conditions of employment' as used in s 29(1)(a) of the 1974 Act.
The first argument was that the obligation was not contained in the then current ITF *b*
collective agreement and was not therefore incorporated into the individual contracts of
those on board the ship. The second argument was that there was nothing to show that
those on board the ship would ever receive any benefit from the contributions to the
fund made by the shipowning company.

With the greatest respect to those of your Lordships who think otherwise, I do not find
these arguments convincing. So far as the first argument is concerned, it seems to me *c*
that it is inconsistent with the established principle, to which I referred earlier, that the
expression 'terms and conditions of employment' as used in s 29(1)(a) of the 1974 Act,
should be given the widest possible meaning. So far as the second argument is concerned,
I accept that it cannot be established affirmatively that persons employed as seafarers on
board the ship, either in July 1978 or subsequently, have benefited, or will necessarily
benefit in the future, from the contributions made by the shipowning company to the *d*
fund. On the other hand, the fund has been established and maintained for the benefit
of such persons, and is funded solely by contributions from shipowners. In these
circumstances it seems to me that the existence of the fund, maintained by contributions
from the shipowning company here concerned and many other shipowners on whom
the same obligation to contribute has been imposed, should be regarded as constituting
at least a potential fringe benefit to workers on board the ship. *e*

On the footing, first, that the contributions to the fund can fairly be regarded as going
to maintain a potential fringe benefit for those on board the ship and, second, that the
fact that the shipowning company's obligation to make such contributions is not written
into either the ITF collective agreement or the individual contracts of those persons is not
of itself a reason for excluding such obligation from the expression 'terms and conditions
of employment' as used in s 29(1)(a) of the 1974 Act, I am of opinion that such obligation *f*
can and should be categorised by the court, as it was by necessary implication categorised
by the parties themselves, as a term or condition of employment of those on board the
ship within the meaning of that statutory provision.

My Lords, the effect of the views which I have expressed is that the shipowning
company fails both on the resultant trust point (question (1)) and on the duress point
(questions (2) and (3)). It follows that I would dismiss the appeal. *g*

Appeal allowed.

Solicitors: *Holman, Fenwick & Willan* (for the shipowners); *Clifford-Turner* (for the ITF).

Mary Rose Plummer   Barrister.

Cohen v Nessdale Ltd

COURT OF APPEAL, CIVIL DIVISION
CUMMING-BRUCE, DONALDSON LJJ AND SIR SEBAG SHAW
13 JANUARY 1982

Specific performance – Sale of land – Conditional contract – Waiver of conditions – Subject to contract – Parties negotiating sale and purchase of lease 'subject to contract' – Tenant breaking off negotiations in May – Parties reaching oral agreement in November – Letter from vendor confirming terms of oral agreement but stated to be subject to contract – Whether oral agreement in November subject to contract – Whether 'subject to contract' qualification of previous negotiations continuing and applying to oral agreement – Whether oral agreement the result of new negotiations or resumption of existing negotiations.

The tenant occupied a flat as a statutory tenant holding over on the expiry of a long lease. His landlords entered into negotiations with him for the sale of a long lease by offering, in March 1977, to sell a long lease of the flat to him for £20,000, 'subject to contract'. Negotiations ensued between the parties without agreement until May, when the tenant broke them off on discovering that the landlords had applied to the rent officer to increase the rent. In July and August the tenant wrote on other matters to the estate agents appointed by the landlords to collect the rent but suggesting that the question of the new lease be resolved. On 2 November the landlords wrote to the tenant referring to the negotiations and then suggesting further consideration of the sale and purchase of the leasehold interest. The letter was expressed to be 'without prejudice' but not 'subject to contract'. On 18 November the landlords and the tenant met and orally agreed the sale of a 99-year lease for £17,000. No reference was made to the agreement being subject to contract, and it was mutually understood that documentation would be completed by their respective solicitors by the end of the year. On the same day the landlords confirmed the agreement in writing, but 'subject to contract'. On 24 November the tenant confirmed the agreement in writing. The landlords later informed the tenant that they did not intend to proceed with the sale. The plaintiff brought an action against the landlords, seeking specific performance of the contract on the ground, inter alia, that the landlord's letter of 18 November was evidence of a final contract which had been agreed by the parties without being subject to contract and which the tenant had part performed by making the first payment of rent under the new lease. The judge dismissed the tenant's action, on the ground that the negotiations in November were not new negotiations and were still covered by the 'subject to contract' qualification which had applied to the earlier negotiations. The tenant appealed.

Held – A 'subject to contract' qualification, once introduced into negotiations, could only cease to apply to the negotiations if the parties expressly or by necessary implication agreed that it should be expunged. There had been no express agreement that the discussions in November 1977 were not to be subject to contract, nor could such an agreement necessarily be implied, because, in view of the facts that the tenant had broken off the discussions in May 1977 not over the terms of the lease but as a result of the landlords' attempt to raise the rent and that he thereafter continued to make overtures to the landlords through the estate agents, the meeting in November was not the commencement of new negotiations but merely the resumption of existing negotiations which had been interrupted and which continued on the basis that the previously existing 'subject to contract' qualification still applied. Furthermore, even if the parties had entered into new negotiations in November 1977, it was not necessarily to be implied that they had done so on a completely different basis from that on which they had hitherto conducted negotiations and that their negotiations were no longer to be subject to contract. Accordingly, the judge had been right to refuse the tenant specific performance because the landlord's letter of 18 November did not constitute a final contract. The tenant's appeal would therefore be dismissed (see p 104 *b* to *e* and p 105 *a* to *j*, post).

Sherbrooke v Dipple (1980) 41 P & CR 173 applied.
Decision of Kilner Brown J [1981] 3 All ER 118 affirmed.

Notes
For the sale of land 'subject to contract', see 9 Halsbury's Laws (4th edn) paras 232, 265, and for cases on the subject, see 12 Digest (Reissue) 105–112, 548–618.

Cases referred to in judgments
Sherbrooke v Dipple (1980) 41 P & CR 173, CA.
Tevanan v Norman Brett (Builders) Ltd (1972) 223 EG 1945.

Appeal
The plaintiff, Ronald Cohen (the tenant), appealed from the judgment of Kilner Brown J ([1981] 3 All ER 118) on 11 February 1981 dismissing his claim against the defendants, Nessdale Ltd (the landlords), for specific performance of an agreement made on 18 November 1977 to grant a lease to the plaintiff of flat 2, 11 Rutland Gate, Kensington, London SW7, for a term of 99 years. The facts are set out in the judgment of Cumming-Bruce LJ.

Robert Bailey-King for the tenant.
David Neuberger for the landlords.

CUMMING-BRUCE LJ. This appeal raises first, and, on the view which I have formed, raises only, one short point. The facts have been set out in the judgment of the judge below ([1981] 3 All ER 118) and in the circumstances it will not be necessary for me to elaborate very much on the facts which I am content to take from the findings of the judge.

The background of the matter is that at all material times the plaintiff tenant below (the appellant in this court) was statutory tenant of a flat in a building at 11 Rutland Gate, Kensington, holding from the defendant landlords below (the respondents in this court) a company called Nessdale Ltd. The history of the tenancy prior to the year 1976 included a protracted argument in which the tenant was alleging that the landlords had failed to observe their covenants for repair, which had led him to withhold his rent. The history includes the fact that the landlords, for practical purposes, consisted of two persons: someone called Sadleir and a person called Henderson, who had been charged by the company with responsibility for negotiations with tenants or prospective purchasers as to the terms of their leases or purchases.

The well-known firm of Goddard & Smith had instructions from the landlords to deal with tenants or prospective purchasers of leases on three matters, and three matters only: collection of rents; business arising out of the obligations of the landlords to observe their covenants; and third, in connection with the negotiation of long leases, such work as was requisite for the purpose of ascertaining the detail of apportionment of service charges between the landlords on the one hand and their several tenants on the other.

The first, and on my view of the appeal, the only question that arises on this appeal is whether the judge was right in holding that the discussion and agreement entered into and arrived at between the landlords on the one hand and the tenant on the other hand, on 18 November, was, by necessary implication, proceeding under the same umbrella as that which had covered earlier negotiations in the year, whereby those negotiations were all subject to contract.

For the purpose of deciding whether the judge was right in his conclusion about that,
a it is necessary to look in a little detail at the history between 15 March 1977 and 10 May
1977, which represented the first stage of negotiations between the parties connected
either with the negotiations of a long lease or, alternatively, terms for surrender by the
tenant of his interest in the premises. I say that was the first stage in the negotiations, but
it is right to refer to the fact, though it is not of importance, that in 1971 there had been
earlier discussions which had come to nothing.

b   So one comes to consider that history which conveniently can begin with a letter from
Mr Henderson, on behalf of the landlords, to the tenant, dated 15 March 1977:

'I refer to our meeting last year and wonder whether you have further considered
purchasing a leasehold interest of the above. We are prepared to sell a term of 99
years from 25/12/1968 for the sum of £20,000, subject to contract. The ground
c   rent will be £50 p.a. for the first 33 years doubling every 33 years thereafter. There
will be a service charge of £60 p.a. payable on account being 25% of the landlords
outgoings. Should this not be of interest to you we are prepared to pay you a sum
of monies for the surrender of your tenancy providing this takes place in the
relatively near future. I look forward to hearing from you in due course.'

d   So there is a proposal in which the interest proposed to be transferred is a term of 99
years. The consideration is offered at £20,000 together with the stated ground rent and
the proposed service charge, which, as the tenant later observed, called for clarification,
because it is offered as '£60 p.a. payable on account being 25% of the landlords
outgoings'. Therefore it did require some clarification in order to see the exact obligation
that was being undertaken over the years.

e   On 2 May the tenant replied, thanking Mr Henderson for his letter. He said:

'I have considered what you say and would point out the following; I assume that
the price you are quoting for approximately 90 years takes into account that I am a
sitting tenant, but nevertheless I am advised that £20,000 is rather on the high side
for this particular flat. However I would be prepared to consider, subject to contract,
f   a figure of £15,000 on the same conditions subject to clarification of the Service
Charge which I don't, at the moment, quite follow. Alternatively, bearing in mind
my own circumstances and what this would entail for me to vacate the property, I
would be prepared to consider subject to agreement a payment of £12,000 to
surrender my position here.'

g   So there, at the beginning of that correspondence, you have both the landlords'
representative, Mr Henderson, and the tenant both negotiating, expressly stating that
they are so doing, subject to contract.

Those negotiations continued. The landlords, on 3 May, in a letter with a label at the
bottom 'SUBJECT TO CONTRACT AND WITHOUT PREJUDICE', say: 'Having given the matter
some consideration, we would be prepared to proceed at a compromise figure of £18,500,
h   subject to contract . . .'

On 5 May the tenant came back, in a letter addressed to Mr Glover of the landlords,
saying:

'I don't really feel that £18,500 is a compromise and therefore I think that the
best course would be to proceed along the second alternative suggested in your letter
j   of March 15th [on] which I have made an offer.'

The next day Mr Glover answered, and said:

'If you do not feel that £18,500 . . . is a compromise figure, I do not think that it
is very likely that you will consider the maximum which we are able to pay by way

of compensation for vacant possession to be a compromise, as we certainly cannot reach anywhere near your figure. I would, however, advise you that if you were to *a* give vacant possession by the end of June, we would be able to pay to you compensation of £5,000 or if you were to complete the purchase of the long lease by that date, we would be prepared to make a small further reduction to £17,500, subject to contract.'

That letter has 'SUBJECT TO CONTRACT AND WITHOUT PREJUDICE' written at the bottom. *b*
The next material matter is that the tenant received notice of an application by the landlords to the rent registration offices for an increase in rent. That he felt was an action really quite inconsistent with the kind of negotiations that were proceeding. He was evidently very angry. It may be, I do not know, that the explanation was that Goddard & Smith, who were dealing with the rent matter, were a right hand not aware of what the left hand was doing. However, the tenant wrote to Mr Glover on 10 May: *c*

'Thank you for your letter of 6th May. In the meantime I have received notice from the Rent Registration Office upon your application for an increase in the rent. In these circumstances obviously there is nothing further we can do in the matter.'

d

That is the letter which was relied on below, and in this court, as bringing those negotiations subject to contract to a complete end, thus finally ending and interrupting that negotiation. It is against that background that the submission on behalf of the tenant is that what happened afterwards in November was not in any sense a continuation of negotiations, but that it was the opening of a new chapter which was not affected by what had gone before. *e*
It is necessary to note the further activities of the tenant in his correspondence with Goddard & Smith. Goddard & Smith were, of course, dealing with the application to the rent office for an increase in the statutory rent, and they were also responsible for dealing on behalf of the landlords with the controversy about the landlords' alleged failure to comply with, and observe, their covenants to repair. So it was that, on 7 July, the tenant wrote to the senior partner in Goddard & Smith, and in that letter, in the second *f* paragraph, he said:

'I would venture to put you in the picture about this flat . . . I am holding over as a Sitting Tenant from an original Lease which expired in 1969 and recently in May Messrs. Nessdale, the Landlords, wrote to me and asked me if I would like a new 99 year Lease or alternatively, would I like to be bought out by surrendering my *g* interest. We started some correspondence on the matter which did not finalise because in the middle of the correspondence I had notice from the Fair Rent Tribunal that an application had been made to increase the Rent. I was quite flabbergasted to find myself firstly in negotiation with my Landlord at his instigation and then he applies to have the Rent increased, whereas one would have expected that since he was in negotiation with me he would have written about this *h* and suggested something instead of carrying out the procedure in this extraordinary manner. As a result of this I terminated the negotiations.'

Then he dealt with his troubles about the failure of the landlord to comply with his covenants and he went on:

j

'I am trying to be reasonable about this matter and this is why I am writing to you because I am quite prepared now to have my premises done up completely if we can only get some sense out of Messrs. Nessdale and conclude a Lease at a proper price and not £20,000 being asked for a Sitting Tenant.'

He said that the rent people suggested that 'the correct price ought to be £10,000'. He

a then said:

> 'Bearing in mind all the above . . . matters perhaps you could try and see whether we can do something constructive on the lines suggested . . . Thanking you very much for your assistance, I await hearing from you.'

b The tenant was there hoping to use the good offices of Goddard & Smith, who I may say come very well out of this history, in order to get the landlords to take what the tenant thought to be a more realistic view of the appropriate consideration for the negotation of a long lease. Goddard & Smith acknowledged his letter.

Then, on 2 August, the tenant wrote another letter to Goddard & Smith, in which he said:

c > 'Now I have to do all these repairs and, as I have said before, I am quite prepared to have the porch roof repaired whilst my Builders are here but it is going to be very expensive if I have to have them in twice in relation to having the flat done up. I must now ask the Landlords to deal with this matter properly and I repeat that I am willing to pay £10,000 for the Lease, which is the correct price, and then to have the flat done up and all the repairs carried out. Can I now please have some action on this so that we can stop all this going backwards and forwards which is getting no

d > one anywhere.'

On 22 August the tenant, again to Goddard & Smith, mention the problem of the porch and said:

e > 'May I remind you that your Clients came to me to either take a Lease or to give up my Tenancy and, at the same time, went to the Fair Rents Tribunal to increase the rent . . . I want to get the builders in here in one go and I want to get this matter of the Lease resolved, together with the question of the rent.'

Goddard & Smith, on 25 August, answered and said:

f > 'We are forwarding a copy of your letter to our clients with whom you have been negotiating the terms for a new lease, in order that they may deal direct. Meanwhile we will proceed with arranging for remedial works . . . to the porch and balcony.'

Goddard & Smith did that, and wrote to Mr Sadleir of the landlords, enclosing a copy of the tenant's letter.

The next letter to which I may refer is Goddard & Smith to the tenant dated 25 October 1977. It referred to dealings with contractors and referred to a letter of 12

g October from the tenant addressed to Mr Ongley of Goddard and Smith. That letter is not in the bundle and we do not know what it said. I only refer to it because the last paragraph of that letter said:

> 'With regard to the other matters raised in your letter, we would respectfully point out that these are matters which are subject to discussion between yourself

h > and our clients, and we are therefore unable to comment.'

Thus, the stance of Goddard & Smith throughout, which was perfectly correct, was that they were not going to come in to the negotations for a new lease, which was why they had sent the tenant's earlier letter about the new lease and resumption, or beginning, of negotations straight on to the landlords.

So one comes to the crucial period of the history when at last the landlords responded

j to the approaches of the tenant made to them through the intermediary, Goddard & Smith. On 2 November 1977 Mr Henderson of the landlords wrote to the tenant:

> 'You may recall our earlier meeting concerning our proposals for the flat you occupy. Namely the possibility of you surrendering your tenancy in favour of a

capital sum, or in purchasing a leasehold interest. I would have thought it to be in _a_
your interest to take advantage of your position as a sitting tenant rather than
continue occupying on a somewhat negative basis as at present. If you would care
to communicate with me at the above I will be happy to discuss the matter
further. Accordingly I look forward to hearing from you in due course.'

That led to a vital meeting between Mr Henderson, for the landlords, and the tenant
to discuss the question of a new lease or surrender. About that meeting, the judge has _b_
made findings of fact. I quote from the judgment ([1981] 3 All ER 118 at 122):

'There is a conflict of evidence as to what was said at that meeting and I accept the
[tenant's] evidence and reject that given by Mr Henderson. The [tenant's] evidence
was to the effect that there was a general discussion trying to get the whole thing
settled. He acknowledged that rent for the year 1977 had not been paid because in
his opinion he was entitled to withhold this rent because the landlords had defaulted _c_
on their obligations and that the negotiations for sale of the lease had broken down
because the landlords were wholly unreasonable. Therefore, taking all these matters
into consideration a figure of £17,000 by way of premium was agreed. It was
further agreed that the maintenance charge should be £100 a year, being 25% of the
outgoings, and that ground rent should be £50 a year payable as from 1st January
next. The lease and contract were to be drawn up and completed by the end of the _d_
year. At the end of the discussion Mr Henderson said that he was so glad that
everything was agreed and they shook hands on it. Nothing was said at any time
about the decisions reached being subject to contract. I find as a fact that that is
what happened. I do not believe Mr Henderson when he gave evidence to the effect
that he made it plain that [the] whole discussion was subject to contract in the
accepted sense. The contemporary and subsequent documents indicate that he _e_
regarded the agreement as final and binding and he gave a very significant answer
when giving evidence as to his understanding of the words "subject to contract".
He said and I quote from the transcript, as well as relying on my note: "I understand
them to mean subject to the terms being reduced in an agreement which would be
finalised by the solicitors or in writing at a later date." On the afternoon of the same
day, 18th November, Mr Henderson sent a letter in the following terms: "Further _f_
to our discussion, I have pleasure in confirming the sale of the above to you for the
sum of £17,000 subject to contract. This is for a term of 99 years from 25th
December 1968 with a service charge of £100 per annum payable on account being
25% of the landlords' outgoings. The ground rent will be £50 per annum for the
first 33 years doubling every 33 thereafter. I have requested our solicitors Messrs.
Harold Stern and Company of 6 Holborn Viaduct ... to submit a draft contract to _g_
Messrs. Kood Kingdom Sompen [sic] attention Mr. J. M. Davies for their approval."
In fact [as the judge found] Mr Henderson wrote to Harold Stern & Co not on that
day but by letter dated 21st November. This began with the significant words, "I
have pleasure in advising that I have sold the above flat to the tenant, Mr. R. Cohen
subject to contract".'

In the letter of 18 November in which Mr Henderson began with the words 'Further _h_
to our discussion, I have pleasure in confirming the sale of the above to you for the sum
of £17,000 subject to contract', he added at the bottom of the letter in capital letters the
ditty 'SUBJECT TO CONTRACT & WITHOUT PREJUDICE'.
The judge summarised it in this way (at 125):

'Later the same day, 18th November, Mr Henderson confirmed the agreement in _j_
writing but introduced the words "subject to contract" in that confirmatory letter.'

So the facts are that in the conversation between Mr Henderson for the landlords and
the tenant on his own behalf, there was no express mention that the discussion or
agreement was subject to contract. It is against that background that this court has to
consider the correctness or otherwise of the judge's finding that, although there was no

a   express reference to that agreement being subject to contract, there was an implication
     to that effect because that discussion was still under the umbrella 'subject to contract',
     which had clearly been erected over the negotiations which had ended in May when the
     tenant had called the negotiations off.

     I do not think, for the purposes of the limited question with which I am dealing, that
     it is necessary for me to repeat or to recite any part of the judge's findings on the history
     after the letter of 18 November, save to say that the effect of those findings was that Mr
b   Sadleir, with great acuteness and indeed cunning, succeeded in keeping the tenant under
     the illusion that the landlords were intending to honour the agreement of 18 November
     entered into between Mr Henderson and the tenant, and, by a clever strategem of
     carefully avoiding answering the tenant's letters, they left him expecting and assuming,
     quite wrongly, that Mr Sadleir's standards of commercial conduct were such that, though
     it was taking a long time, the agreement was clearly going to be honoured, though there
c   seemed to be some delay about completing the documentation.

     The judge's findings make it plain that any reliance of the tenant on Mr Sadleir's
     standards of commercial behaviour was wholly mistaken, as it is perfectly clear from the
     histories recited by the judge that this was a careful strategem executed, as I say, with
     great shrewdness, but the tenant took far too long to awake to the vendors' methods of
     doing property business. In the event, finally on 7 September, when I suppose Mr Sadleir
d   decided that for his own reasons it was time to come out into the open, he called the
     whole deal off, and said that the landlords were not bound by any contract and therefore
     there was no point in proceeding any further. Not surprisingly, the tenant and his
     solicitors went into action in order to see whether the law could give them a remedy in
     order to surmount this manifest history of trickery.

     As it is a matter of real property law, in which the law has, necessarily, to be settled and
e   has reached a high degree of certainty, the tenant was, of course, in very considerable
     difficulty. Below and in this court, every argument that can possibly be put forward on
     the tenant's behalf has been put forward. For myself, I take the same view as the judge:
     if one could help the tenant by finding a legal remedy in order to frustrate the artifices
     of Mr Sadleir, clearly one would be eager to do so, but real property law has to attain a
     certain certainty and the question is whether, on the facts that I have summarised, it can
f   be shown that the judge was wrong in the implication that he found.

     The starting point, as counsel for the tenant recognises, is really the statement of the
     law recited in this court in *Sherbrooke v Dipple* (1980) 41 P & CR 173 and in particular the
     judgments in this court. Lord Denning MR said (at 176):

         'But there is this overwhelming point: Everything in the opening letter was
         "subject to contract." All the subsequent negotiations were subject to that
g   overriding initial condition. We were referred by [counsel for the plaintiffs] to a
         decision of Brightman J. in 1972. It is *Tevanan v Norman Brett (Builders) Ltd* (223 EG
         1945 at 1947). Brightman J. said that "parties could get rid of the qualification of
         'subject to contract' only if they both expressly agreed that it should be expunged or
         if such an agreement was to be necessarily implied".'

h   Lord Denning MR went on to deal with the application of that principle to the facts
     of the case before him.

     Templeman LJ quoted (41 P & CR 173 at 176) the whole of the passage to which Lord
     Denning MR had referred from the judgment of Brightman J, and I quote it:

         '. . . when parties started their negotiations under the umbrella of the "subject to
         contract" formula, or some similar expression of intention, it was really hopeless for
j   one side or the other to say that a contract came into existence because the parties
         became of one mind notwithstanding that no formal contracts had been
         exchanged. Where formal contracts were exchanged, it was true that the parties
         were inevitably of one mind at the moment before the exchange was made. But
         they were only of one mind on the footing that all the terms and conditions of the

sale and purchase had been settled between them, and even then the original
intention still remained intact that there should be no formal contract in existence   *a*
until the written contracts had been exchanged.'

Templeman LJ went on to say (41 P & CR 173 at 176):

> 'Mr Justice Brightman thought parties could get rid of the qualification of "subject
> to contract" only if they both expressly agreed that it should be expunged or if such
> an agreement was to be necessarily implied.'   *b*

I do not think that any assistance is to be derived from looking at the facts in *Sherbrooke
v Dipple* or in *Tevanan v Brett*. Brightman J neatly and accurately stated the question: in
such a situation, have the parties expressly agreed that subject to contract qualifications
should be expunged or should it necessarily be implied? In this court counsel for the
tenant has submitted (I hope that I do him justice when I try to summarise his   *c*
submission) that what happened in this case was this: there was an initial period of
negotiation which was clearly subject to contract, but that was terminated; as the tenant
himself said in his correspondence, he terminated that negotiation. I observe that it is
perfectly plain, and the tenant would accept, that he did not terminate that negotiation
because of any difficulty in continuing the negotiation having regard to the terms that
the parties were respectively putting forward for agreement. He terminated because he   *d*
was very angry at what he thought was really outrageous behaviour on the part of the
landlords: on the one hand trying to deal with him as a gentleman on the negotiation of
the long lease, and then behind his back going along to the rent people to raise his rent,
which he probably interpreted as an attempt to bring pressure on him to accede to the
negotiating offer then being put forward by the landlords. Whether he was right about
that is another matter, but that was the reason why he terminated the negotiations.
Counsel submits that that very context explains the fact that when the tenant terminated   *e*
the negotiation he intended to terminate it. It was his state of wrath about his view of
the conduct of the landlords that led him to break the whole thing off altogether, and,
having broken it off altogether, what began to happen in November 1978 was the
opening of a completely new chapter in the history and not a continuance of the earlier
negotiation. I hope that summarises the way in which counsel put it in this court.

There are, to my mind, and I say it with regret, very great difficulties about accepting   *f*
that approach. First, the parties to the transaction: on the one hand the landlords, who
were manifestly experienced, and indeed fly, commerical men, second, the tenant
himself, who described himself in his correspondence with a rather splendid though
faintly obscure title, as a consultant in commerce and the law. It was those two parties
who in May had been carefully covering their offers, their negotiations, with the
qualification 'subject to contract'. Indeed, the landlords seem commonly not only to   *g*
have put it in the text of the letter, but, in case the recipient cannot read, they also put it
in capital letters at the bottom.

How far do the facts support the submission that the termination was such a final
termination that it is a misunderstanding to think in terms of a resumption or
continuance of the negotiations begun in May? The difficulty is this: although the   *h*
tenant after May did not, until November, communicate directly to Mr Sadleir or Mr
Henderson, he did, in the correspondence to which I have referred, make a number of
requests to the landlords' agents, albeit agents with a limited scope of authority, to
encourage the landlords to reopen the negotiations. I have referred to the letters and I
have described how Goddard & Smith did pass correspondence on to Mr Sadleir. So, far
from the truth being that the tenant, like Achilles, got into his tent and stayed in it, he
got into his tent, but then he put out feelers through Goddard & Smith with a view to   *j*
resumption of negotiations.

It is against that background that one comes to the letter of 2 November 1977 written
by Mr Henderson, with the label 'WITHOUT PREJUDICE' at the bottom, when he used this
expression:

'You may recall our earlier meeting concerning our proposals for the flat you occupy . . . If you would care to communicate with me at the above I will be happy to discuss the matter further.'

In that letter Mr Henderson is inviting further discussion on the matter which had been the subject of the landlords' earlier proposals. To my mind it is very difficult, against that history of the transactions between the parties, to take the view that, when Mr Henderson and the tenant began their discussions on 18 November, they were not, by so doing, resuming the interrupted negotiations which had been interrupted for what I would call a collateral reason, namely the alleged misbehaviour of the landlords in going behind the tenant's back while they were negotiating and trying to get an uplift in rent. There is no question here of any express agreement to expunge the qualification involved in the words 'subject to contract'.

It is necessary, against this history, to imply that the parties on 18 November intended that, though they had previously always been negotiating subject to contract, they were on that day intending to enter into a firm contract in which all the essential terms had been agreed, so the solicitors would do nothing except put on the dots and fill in the gaps which could readily be filled in. I do not think so.

These parties must have realised, both of them, that in connection with this kind of real property transaction the normal procedure that both parties would expect was a procedure by which there would be no concluded contract until solicitors had settled the terms of the contract, signatures had been obtained from the parties and contracts exchanged. I can see no reason to suppose that, when the tenant and Mr Henderson met and had a discussion in which they managed to reach agreement on 18 November, it was a common intention that the parties would abandon the stance which they had hitherto taken up, a stance which may be described as the normal stance of experienced business people dealing with a property transaction, and had decided to take up a new position in which a firm and final contract without any qualification and without anything in writing was to be completed or made on 18 November in an oral discussion.

It would to my mind be perfectly reasonable to imply such a term, but the question for decision is not whether it is reasonable to imply the term but whether it is necessary to do so. Like the judge, I find myself constrained, reluctantly, to the view that, however badly these landlords, Nessdale Ltd, behaved (and, of course, they did behave badly), it is not possible to arrive at the conclusion that it is necessary to imply into the conversation of 18 November that the stance which had been a most important qualification accepted by both of them a few months before had been abandoned so that the qualification no longer applied. For those reasons, I would dismiss the appeal.

DONALDSON LJ. I share Cumming-Bruce LJ's regret that this appeal must be dismissed, but dismissed it must be. The effect of the 'subject to contract' qualification to the earlier negotiations was not in my judgment spent when agreement was reached between the parties on 18 November 1977. It follows that that agreement was, in law, provisional in nature and so unenforceable.

I, too, would dismiss the appeal.

SIR SEBAG SHAW. I agree that this appeal fails. I reach that conclusion with regret, particularly as, on the findings of fact of the judge, the conduct of this matter by those who acted for the landlords (I mean of course Mr Sadleir and Mr Henderson) reflects little credit on their integrity or on their sense of business propriety. However, the matter is concluded on the judge's findings, which are not subject to any challenge.

I would dismiss the appeal.

Appeal dismissed. Leave to appeal to the House of Lords refused.

Solicitors: *Coode, Kingdon, Somper & Co* (for the tenant); *Harold Stern & Co* (for the landlords).

a

Henrietta Steinberg   Barrister.

b

Wallace v Newton

QUEEN'S BENCH DIVISION
PARK J
18, 19, 20 NOVEMBER 1981

c

Animal – Horse – Horse having characteristics not normally found in other horses – Horse having unpredictable temperament – Horse becoming violent while being led by plaintiff onto trailer and crushing plaintiff's arm – Plaintiff bringing action against keeper of horse – Whether plaintiff required to prove that horse had vicious tendency to injure – Whether sufficient for plaintiff to prove merely that horse had characteristics not normally found in horses – Animals Act 1971, s 2(2).

d

The plaintiff was a groom employed by the defendant to look after several horses. One of the horses in the plaintiff's charge was known to have a nervous and unpredictable temperament. One day, while loading the horse onto a horse box trailer, it became violent and uncontrollable and leaped forward, crushing the plaintiff's arm against a breast bar. The plaintiff sued the defendant for damages for breach of duty under, inter alia, s 2(2)^a of the Animals Act 1971 contending (i) that the likelihood of damage was due to characteristics of the horse which were not normally found in horses, and (ii) that those characteristics were known to the defendant.

e

Held – On the true construction of s 2(2) of the 1971 Act the words 'characteristics of the animal which are not normally found in animals of the same species' were to be given their ordinary, natural meaning. The plaintiff therefore was not required to prove that the horse had a vicious tendency to injure people by attacking them, but merely that the horse had characteristics of a kind not normally found in horses. On the facts, the horse had characteristics not usually found in other horses in that it was unpredictable and unreliable in its behaviour, and, since those characteristics were known to the defendant at the material time, she was liable to the plaintiff for damages under the provisions of s 2(2) of the 1971 Act (see p 110 g to p 111 d, post).

f

g

Notes
For the liability of owners and keepers of animals, see 2 Halsbury's Laws (4th edn) paras 424–428, and for cases on the subject, see 2 Digest (Reissue) 375–388, 2114–2162.

For the Animals Act 1971, s 2, see 41 Halsbury's Statutes (3rd edn) 86.

h

Action
By a writ issued on 22 August 1979 the plaintiff, Elaine Joan Wallace, claimed damages for personal injuries against the defendant, Urcula Newton, for breach of statutory duty

j

---

a   Section 2(2), so far as material, provides: 'Where damage is caused by an animal which does not belong to a dangerous species, a keeper of the animal is liable for the damage . . . if—(a) the damage is of a kind which the animal, unless restrained, was likely to cause . . . and (b) the likelihood of the damage . . . was due to characteristics of the animal which are not normally found in animals of the same species . . . and (c) those characteristics were known to that keeper or were at any time known to a person who at that time had charge of the animal as that keeper's servant . . .'

under s 2(2) of the Animals Act 1971 when a horse owned by the defendant and being looked after by the plaintiff, became violent and uncontrollable and crushed the plaintiff's arm. In an amended statement of claim the plaintiff also alleged negligence against the defendant, her servants or agents. The facts are set out in the judgment.

J R L Posnansky for the plaintiff.
S D Robbins for the defendant.

PARK J. In this case the plaintiff claims damages for the serious injury to her right forearm sustained when, on 3 July 1977 in the course of her employment by the defendant as a groom, the arm was crushed against the breast bar of a trailer into which the plaintiff was loading a horse called Lord Justice. The plaintiff's case is that by virtue of s 2(2) of the Animals Act 1971 the defendant is liable to her for the injury and the consequential loss which she has suffered. She also says in the alternative that the injury and loss was caused by negligence on the part of the defendant, her servants or agents.

The plaintiff was born in June 1958. She started riding horses at the age of six, and throughout her life up to the time of this injury she had had considerable experience of horses. She had ridden horses at gymkhanas and in show jumping. She had frequently loaded and unloaded horses into horse boxes and horse box trailers. In 1976, when she was 17 to 18 years, she worked as a groom in Surrey doing this kind of work. In consequence she came to know a great deal about horses. She came to know that no two horses were alike, that their temperaments differed and that their behaviour could be unpredictable and that on occasions they might bolt.

In November 1976 she started work for the defendant as a groom at the defendant's stables at Church Farm, Melton Mowbray. There the defendant has a large farm, which is situated not far away from another farm belonging to her son. At Church Farm she has stables where she kept horses of all kinds: hunters, race horses, show jumpers and one-day and three-day eventers. There were approximately 14 of such horses at Church Farm and other horses of the defendant's were at stables at her son's farm. All her life the defendant has been concerned with horses of all descriptions, and, among other things, she has been and is a member of the Pony Club Horse Trials Committe and other such committees.

The plaintiff's duties were to groom, exercise and look after three or four horses at Church Farm. After she had been employed for a few months, that is in about February or March 1977, the plaintiff was told by Tom Read, the head man in charge of the defendant's horses, though he was in fact more concerned with the race horses, that she would be looking after a horse called Lord Justice and another one called Jet Set. Although the defendant had owned Lord Justice since 1974, when he was a five-year-old, the plaintiff had not seen him before this time, because he had been stabled at the other farm. Tom Read told the plaintiff that Lord Justice had been playing up and misbehaving, and he warned her to be careful. When Lord Justice did come under her care, the plaintiff found him to be nervous and unreliable, both when she was working on him in the stable and when leading him. 'He was', she said, 'all right one moment and then he would panic for no reason.' On a couple of occasions he ran back against his head collar and broke it. After that she tied him up loosely, so that if he pulled back nothing would be broken. Although the plaintiff rode all the other horses in her care, she did not ride Lord Justice as Tom Read told her she would not be able to do so.

Lord Justice and Jet Set had both been bought by the defendant for her daughter Nichola, who was 17 in January 1977, and was still at school in the summer of 1977. Nichola came home from school every weekend. It was her custom to ride either or both these horses at weekends. During the week they were ridden and had been ridden over the years by her elder sister, Carol, and her brother's girl friend, who later became his wife, Emma. Lord Justice had been trained as a show jumper and had been bought by the defendant for Nichola so that Nichola could take part in show jumping competitions.

At weekends in the summer of 1977 it frequently happened that the defendant's horse box and horse box trailer were needed to take Carol's horses wherever she wished to ride

and Nichola's horses to her destination. The family on such occasions decided among
themselves which sister was to have the horse box and which the horse box trailer. Thus   *a*
the plaintiff found herself accompanying Nichola to show jumping events with her two
horses. On every occasion except two the horse box was used. The plaintiff says that
although the horse box would take four horses, the partition was taken out on these
occasions to enable Lord Justice to have the space normally available for two horses.
Accordingly, the plaintiff experienced no difficulty, with Nichola's assistance, in loading   *b*
and unloading Lord Justice on and off the horse box.

One week before 3 July 1977 the plaintiff for the first time had experience of Lord
Justice and the horse box trailer. At their destination Nichola unloaded Jet Set and went
off to the show ring. She told the plaintiff to put on Lord Justice's bridle and saddle
inside the trailer. There is some dispute about this particular matter. Nichola says that
the saddle would have been put on at the start of the journey, as it would be impossible
to put it on in the trailer. The plaintiff says that she put the bridle on, but as she was   *c*
putting on the saddle Lord Justice reared about, lashed out and broke the back strap on
the bridle, which is the part of the equipment in the trailer used to secure the horse
during the journey. So violent was Lord Justice's conduct that the trailer rocked to and
fro. This movement attracted the attention of someone at the show, who came to the
plaintiff's assistance, and Lord Justice was brought under control. Eventually Nichola
returned. By then Lord Justice was quiet. The plaintiff told Nichola what had happened   *d*
and showed her the broken bridle. Nichola was annoyed and blamed the plaintiff for
Lord Justice's behaviour. Nichola says that she remembers nothing about this incident.
She made the observation that a bridle can break very easily and that the incident, to use
her words, 'was not really unusual'.

On their return to Church Farm the plaintiff told Tom Read what had happened. The
plaintiff says that Tom Read told the defendant and in consequence the decision was   *e*
made to alter the procedure when transporting Lord Justice and Jet Set in future. The
new procedure was that the bridle and the saddle would be put on Lord Justice in the
yard before he was loaded on to the horse box trailer. The defendant says that she was
never told about this incident; she never gave any instruction for the procedure to be
altered; she considered it dangerous for a horse to travel with its bridle on and she would
be very surprised, she said, if a completely different procedure were followed without her   *f*
knowledge. Both the defendant and Nichola say that Tom Read was not the kind of
person who would listen to a complaint of the type made by the plaintiff. Tom Read,
they say, who unhappily was not called as a witness by either side, would have told the
plaintiff to speak to the defendant; something which the plaintiff could very easily have
done.

On the following week the new procedure was followed at the yard. Lord Justice and
Jet Set were loaded into the trailer. The journey to the show was uneventful. Lord   *g*
Justice was to be ridden first at the show. He was unloaded without trouble. Nichola
rode him at the show, but apparently he did not do very well on the second round. He
was brought back to the trailer; he was to be loaded by the plaintiff leading him and by
Nichola bringing up the rear in order to clip the back strap into position and pull up the
ramp. The plaintiff says that in loading Lord Justice she held the reins in her right hand,
leading Lord Justice from her right. She was just in front of him. She was walking and   *h*
led him up the ramp to the left-hand compartment of the horse box trailer; she herself
was thus against the left-hand side of the trailer. Lord Justice walked up the trailer on to
the level part; he was either at the top of the ramp or a little way along in the trailer
when, without any warning, he leaped or lunged forward. The plaintiff decided to let go
of the bridle, duck under the breast bar and let Lord Justice come into the trailer. She
said, 'I let go, but I could not get out of the way. I ducked under the breast bar and Lord   *j*
Justice came at me as if I was not there. He came up behind me.' She said that after
ducking under the bar she was facing the horse at an angle; the horse's chest caught her
trailing arm and crushed it on the breast bar.

She was asked a number of questions about her knowledge of the behaviour of
horses. She agreed that on entering a horse box like this a horse is most likely to display

nervousness, and so it was wise for the groom to make sure that she kept out of the
way. She agreed too that she had to expect that Lord Justice might come into the trailer
a bit faster than usual. She had been told, and she knew from her own experience, that
the horse was nervous, 'but', said the plaintiff, 'a nervous horse would not go into the
trailer in the way in which Lord Justice did on this occasion'. She said that when a
nervous horse panics it does not run forward; it runs back and rears up. She said that a
nervous horse would not go into a trailer as Lord Justice did, and she described Lord
Justice as being dangerous and temperamental, but not vicious. The injuries to her right
arm indicate that the horse must have come against her arm, crushing it against the bar,
with some force. Immediately after the incident it was obvious to the plaintiff that her
arm was broken, and she said, 'The shape of the bar was on it.'

Nichola was assisting the loading of Lord Justice at the rear. Her description of what
happened was that when Lord Justice's backside came to the smaller area, by which she
meant the entry into this compartment of the trailer, he went in in his usual way. He
did not charge in. She heard a scream, and then she almost certainly put on the clip and
put up the ramp. She then went through the attendant's door at the rear of the trailer
and was surprised to find the plaintiff on the horse's side of the bar. Lord Justice was
standing there. The plaintiff was very distressed and in great pain. She was then taken
to Nottingham General Hospital.

As I have said, the plaintiff contends that the defendant is liable to pay damages by
virtue of s 2(2) of the Animals Act 1971. That means that the plaintiff has to establish,
among other things, that the injury which she suffered was due to Lord Justice's
characteristics which were characteristics not normally to be found in a horse. It was
necessary for me to hear, and I did hear, a good deal of evidence about Lord Justice's
characteristics. Mrs Pirah had owned Lord Justice for about 18 months between 1972
and 1974. Her husband is an international show jumper and horse dealer. Mrs Pirah
rode Lord Justice in show jumping competitions; she said she had no problems with the
horse. However, she found that Lord Justice was sensitive and nervous. He was being
trained for show jumping, but he was not really big enough to be a top international
show jumper. 'He was', she said, 'all right with quiet handling', by which she meant, to
use her words, 'you could get more out of him by not showing him the whip than by
aggression'. By her standards Lord Justice was not a dangerous horse. If he had been she
and her husband would not have sold him on; they would have put him in a sale and cut
their losses.

In 1974, Nichola then being 14, the defendant was looking for a horse that Nichola
would be able to ride in show jumping. She watched Mrs Pirah show jumping Lord
Justice. In July 1974 the defendant decided to buy him. Mrs Pirah says that she told the
defendant everything about the horse: that it was not a quiet gentle horse, but a horse
that was nervous. The point is made that Mrs Pirah thought it necessary to impart that
information to the defendant. The defendant says that Mrs Pirah told her that 'you had
to be careful when you rode Lord Justice, that it was a high class horse which had
potential'.

The defendant says that over the three years prior to the accident to the plaintiff, her
daughters and Emma had ridden him. In show jumping and eventing Lord Justice had
performed adequately, and Nichola had got him into the category of a grade C show
jumper. 'Lord Justice', she said, 'was not dangerous, but because he was a thoroughbred
he was more nervous than half breeds. At times he was difficult to mount, and he was
always slightly temperamental at the start of a three day event.' The defendant said that
while she had met difficult horses, by which she meant horses which were difficult to get
into trailers, she did not think she had ever met a dangerous horse, by which she meant
a horse that kicked a lot or bit people or constantly ran away with its rider. Both she and
Nichola had loaded and unloaded Lord Justice from the horse box and the horse box
trailer without difficulty on numerous occasions. At some time Nichola had taken Lord
Justice to a training establishment. The defendant said she would never have allowed
Nichola to go to such a place with a horse which she knew was dangerous.

Nichola Newton, who is now aged 21, like her mother is very experienced with horses,

although she gave up show jumping about three years ago. She said of Lord Justice that
the horse needed respecting. 'If you were good to him he was good to you, but you had
to be careful with him. A horse knows when you are scared of him. There was nothing
abnormal about him. He was special, but you have to be careful with all horses.'

Another witness, Mr Leyland, has over 40 years' experience of horses. He holds, and
has held, many high positions in the world of British show jumping. His business is the
training of horses and their riders for competitions. He has some recollection of Nichola
Newton and Lord Justice being brought by the defendant to his establishment for
training and thereafter of Nichola and the horse going to his establishment
unaccompanied by the defendant. Mr Leyland said of Lord Justice that he was a horse
which was absolutely safe to ride. He was essentially a competition horse and not at all
dangerous. He was, however, a sensitive horse and a responsive horse. I came to the
conclusion that the passage of time had somewhat blurred Mr Leyland's recollection of
Lord Justice, but I have no doubt whatever that he was honestly doing his best to recall
what he could about the horse's characteristics.

The plaintiff's sole witness was a Miss Bowring. She was a completely independent
witness. She had some years' experience as a groom. Like the plaintiff, she was employed
by the defendant as a groom between March and October 1977. She worked in the same
yard as the plaintiff, and in that way she came across Lord Justice and saw him daily.
Although she did not have much to do with him, she was able to observe his
behaviour. She described one incident with which she was personally concerned, when
for no reason at all when she was trying to put a saddle on Lord Justice the horse sat on
the floor. She did not know what to do about the matter and had to send for Tom
Read. Miss Bowring said, 'I would say he was a very nervous horse. You get the odd one
in a yard like that. He was different from the other horses.' Miss Bowring, although
plainly an intelligent young woman, appeared to have some difficulty in choosing the
rights words to describe the horse, and eventually she said, 'Well, it was a long time ago.
I cannot really remember much about him, but he does stand out in my mind as not
being normal, though I do not think he would set out on purpose to kick.'

I found each of the witnesses to whose evidence I have referred completely honest. I
think each one was trying to the best of her ability to tell me what she remembered and
believed to be true, but, for reliability, I have come to the conclusion that the plaintiff is
in a class of her own. I have no hesitation in accepting her evidence.

Under s 2(2)(a) of the Animals Act 1971 the plaintiff has to establish first that the
damage which she suffered was of a kind which Lord Justice was likely to cause, and on
this part of the case there is no dispute. Under s 2(2)(b) the plaintiff has to establish that
the likelihood of the damage was due to characteristics of Lord Justice which were not
normally found in horses. The question is whether the words 'characteristics which are
not normally found in horses' have to be interpreted as meaning that Lord Justice must
be shown to have had a vicious tendency to injure people by attacking them or whether
the words have to be given their ordinary natural meaning, that is that Lord Justice had
characteristics of a kind not usually found in horses. If the plaintiff has to establish that
her injuries were due to Lord Justice's vicious tendency to injure people, then her claim
would fail. He was not, as the plaintiff herself agreed, a vicious horse or a dangerous
horse in the way in which the defendant understood that word. On the other hand, if
she has to establish that her injuries were due to a characteristic of Lord Justice which was
unusual in a horse, then she would establish this limb of her case. I think this is the
meaning to be given to the words in s 2(2)(b).

On the evidence I am satisfied that, certainly during the period that the plaintiff had
Lord Justice in her charge, the horse was unpredictable and unreliable in his behaviour,
and in that way he was, as the plaintiff said, dangerous. The injury to her arm was due
to this characteristic, which is not normally found in a horse. So, in my judgment, the
plaintiff has established the second limb of her case.

Under s 2(2)(c) the plaintiff has to prove that these characteristics were known to the
defendant, as Lord Justice's keeper, or at any time known to a person who at that time

had charge of Lord Justice as the defendant's servant. I have no doubt at all that Tom Read well knew about Lord Justice's unpredictability and unreliability and because of that knowledge he very properly warned the plaintiff about the horse. The defendant says that she knew nothing of the incident a week before the plaintiff's accident and of the consequent change of procedure. I am sure that her evidence is honest, but she is, and has been since her husband's death in 1969, a very busy, active woman. She has a large farm, she has stables, she has horses of all kinds and many outside interests, particularly in the world of ponies and horses. The events with which this case is concerned happened over four years ago. Lord Justice was first put on the market for sale about three years ago and was eventually sold in 1979. I think the defendant has completely forgotten all that happened to the plaintiff in 1977. Indeed she has had no need to remember the plaintiff's troubles. I got the impression they made little mark on her mind at the time, and I very much doubt if she has thought about them since. To me it is inconceivable that Tom Read did not tell her everything about Lord Justice and in particular about the incident which occurred a week before the accident. I think that the defendant at the material time knew as much about the horse as Tom Read.

For these reasons I am satisfied that the defendant is liable to the plaintiff under the provisions of s 2(2) of the Act. Having come to that conclusion, it is not necessary for me to make any finding, nor do I make any finding, on the alternative ground that the plaintiff's injuries were caused by negligence on the part of the defendant, her servants or agents.

There is an allegation of contributory negligence. Throughout the case I found it very difficult to discover what it was that the plaintiff is supposed to have done wrong. I asked the defendant that question. All the defendant could say was that she thought the plaintiff might have got under the breast bar a little more quickly than she did. There is nothing in the allegation of contributory negligence, and I reject it.

[His Lordship then considered the medical evidence relating to the plaintiff's injuries and assessed damages in the sum of £10,000 for pain and suffering and loss of amenities and £3,000 for loss of future earnings.]

Judgment for the plaintiff.

Solicitors: *Cartwright, Cunningham, Haselgrove & Co*, Walthamstow (for the plaintiff); *Stevensons* (for the defendant).

K Mydeen Esq   Barrister.

O'Malley v O'Malley

COURT OF APPEAL, CIVIL DIVISION
ORMROD, FOX LJJ AND BALCOMBE J
8 DECEMBER 1981

Injunction – Exclusion of party from matrimonial home – County court – Jurisdiction – Equity jurisdiction – Application for injunction made after decree absolute but during pendency of proceedings for ancillary relief – Parties continuing to live in matrimonial home after decree absolute but wife living in extension to home without any amenities – Wife applying for injunction to exclude husband from home – Whether court having jurisdiction – Whether proper exercise of discretion to grant injunction if court having jurisdiction.

The marriage of the husband and wife was finally dissolved by decree absolute on 27 August 1981 but proceedings by the wife for ancillary relief under ss 23 and 24 of the Matrimonial Causes Act 1973 were still pending. The parties continued to live with three of the children of the marriage in the former matrimonial home, the wife living apart from the husband in an extension to the home which had no amenities and had a leaking roof. On 27 October 1981, when the ancillary proceedings were still pending, the wife applied in the county court under the court's inherent equitable jurisdiction for an injunction to exclude the husband from the home in order to enable her to live there on her own. She also applied for an injunction to restrain him from molesting her. On 12 November the judge made an order excluding the husband from the home. The husband appealed, contending that the judge had had no jurisdiction to make the order.

Held – Once a marriage was finally dissolved by decree absolute then, even though ancillary proceedings were pending, a county court had no jurisdiction to grant an ouster injunction. Such an order could only be made in the ancillary proceedings under the court's common law jurisdiction and then only if there were compelling reasons for making such an order. Since the wife was in the house as an independent adult, and not as a spouse, and had only the rights of any other independent adult licensee, there were no compelling reasons for granting her an ouster injunction against the husband. It followed that the judge had had no jurisdiction to grant the wife an injunction excluding the husband from the home; but, even if he had had jurisdiction, it would have been a wrong exercise of the jurisdiction to grant the injunction because it was not required for the protection of any property interests of the wife or for her personal protection. The appeal would accordingly be allowed (see p 113 *h j* and p 114 *a c* to *e*, post).

Montgomery v Montgomery [1964] 2 All ER 22 applied.

Per curiam. When a marriage is breaking down it is an abuse of the process of the court to use the invaluable power the court has to order one party to the marriage to leave the matrimonial home in order to improve the standing of the other party in relation to pending ancillary proceedings. There may, however, be cases where intervention by way of an ouster injunction is necessary to protect assets or to preserve the situation pending the decision in the ancillary proceedings, but such cases will be unusual (see p 113 *g h* and p 114 *b d e*, post).

Notes

For the inherent jurisdiction of county courts to grant injunctions, see 10 Halsbury's Laws (4th edn) paras 58–59.

For Matrimonial Causes Act 1973, ss 23, 24, see 43 Halsbury's Statutes (3rd edn) 564, 566.

Cases referred to in judgments

Brent v Brent [1974] 2 All ER 1211, [1975] Fam 1, [1974] 3 WLR 296, Digest (Cont Vol D) 434, 7555*b*.

Montgomery v Montgomery [1964] 2 All ER 22, [1965] P 46, [1964] 2 WLR 1036, 27(2)
a   Digest (Reissue) 936, 7555.

Interlocutory appeal

After the parties' marriage had been dissolved by decree absolute the wife, on 27 October
1981, applied in Maidstone County Court, under s 1(1) of the Domestic Violence and
Matrimonial Proceedings Act 1976, for an injunction to exclude the husband from the
b   former matrimonial home where the parties were still living. On 12 November 1981
Mr Recorder Balston made an order excluding the husband from the home. The
husband appealed submitting that as the wife's application had been made after the
pronouncement of the decree absolute the recorder had no jurisdiction to make the
order. The facts are set out in the judgment of Ormrod LJ.

c   *Roderic Wood* for the husband.
Christopher Morris-Coole for the wife.

ORMROD LJ. This is an appeal from an order which was made by Mr Recorder
Balston at the Maidstone County Court on 12 November 1981. The order which the
recorder made was what is now called an ouster injunction against the husband. Counsel,
d   who did not appear in the court below but is appearing in this court on behalf of the
husband, has taken a preliminary point as to jurisdiction.

The facts, very briefly, are that these parties have been married for a long time, I think
over 20 years. They have four children, of whom the youngest is 27. On 23 June 1981
the wife obtained a decree nisi against the husband in undefended proceedings on the
ground of his conduct, and that decree was made absolute on 27 August 1981. She and
e   her husband and three out of the four children are living in the former matrimonial
home, but the wife has been living in an extension to the house, which is said to be very
uncomfortable, having a leaking roof and no heating and no amenities generally. She
has had an application for ancillary relief under ss 23 and 24 of the Matrimonial Causes
Act 1973 on the file since June, but those proceedings unfortunately have not yet been
heard, and it is clearly a case in which they ought to be heard, and heard quickly. But on
f   27 October 1981 the wife filed an application for an injunction, seeking an order that the
husband should be ordered to leave the former matrimonial home in order to enable her
to live there on her own. There was also a claim for an injunction restraining the
husband from assaulting, molesting or otherwise interfering with her until further
order. It is in those circumstances that counsel for the husband takes the jurisdiction
point.

g   Before I deal with that, I think it is desirable to say that there appears to me to be a
fashion developing, which is relatively new, of parties applying for injunctions ousting
the other party to the marriage from the former matrimonial home at a late stage in
divorce proceedings and while the ancillary proceedings are pending. It is difficult to
avoid the inference that this is being done in order to set the scene for the ancillary
proceedings when they actually come to hearing. This is, I think I am right in saying, the
h   fourth of these cases that have been before this court this term, and it is an abuse of the
process of the court to use the invaluable power that the court has to cause one party to
the marriage to leave the matrimonial home when the situation is beginning to reach the
point when no one reasonably could be expected to put up with it as a sort of boost when
it comes to the ancillary relief proceedings. We have allowed at least three appeals on this
point already this term. This case is more extreme than most of them, because in this
j   case it is quite plain that the marriage had been finally dissolved by decree absolute
before the application for an injunction was made; and there is clear authority that at
that stage the court cannot intervene unless it can do so under its ordinary common law
jurisdiction.

The first case, which was a decision of my own, *Montgomery v Montgomery*, [1964] 2 All
ER 22, [1965] P 46, was a case of a wife after a decree of judicial separation seeking to turn
her husband out of a flat of which he was the sole tenant. In that case I held that there

was no jurisdiction to order him out, because the wife had no proprietary right in the premises. She could not rely on the inherent jurisdiction of the court to intervene to *a* protect the interests of minor children, she could not rely on the inherent jurisdiction of the court to protect her from interference pending proceedings; and now, as counsel for the husband points out, she cannot rely on the Matrimonial Homes Act 1967 either: see also *Brent v Brent* [1974] 2 All ER 1211, [1975] Fam 1. So, unless there is some compelling reason to make such an order in the ancillary proceedings, then I can see no basis for the jurisdiction to make the order which the recorder made in this case. But it *b* is not just a matter of jurisdiction, which is important enough. It is highly undesirable that this most useful procedure, useful in the stages of crisis when the marriage is breaking down, should be used or permitted to be used or attempted to be used to improve the standing of one or other party in relation to ancillary proceedings which are pending. There may be cases where some intervention is necessary to protect the assets or to preserve the situation pending the decision in the ancillary proceedings, but they *c* must be very unusual cases, and this is certainly not one of them.

One is very sorry for the wife; but, quite frankly, she is in the house now as an independent adult, and she has no more rights than any other independent adult licensee in that house. In those circumstance, the recorder (who was not, I hasten to say, referred to any of the authorities on the point), in my judgment, was wrong in law. But, assuming he had jurisdiction in the matter, which I do not think he had, I think he *d* wrongly exercised his discretion, because this was not a case in which it was necessary for the protection of any property interests, future or possible, contingent or actual, of the wife, or indeed for her personal protection.

In those circumstances, this appeal must be allowed.

FOX LJ. I agree.   *e*

BALCOMBE J. I agree. I would not wish to add anything on the jurisdictional point. I simply add that, in my judgment, the power to make an ouster order (as it is commonly called) is a very valuable weapon in the court's armoury, but it is not to be used except with care. I would respectfully agree with everything Ormrod LJ has said about the dangers of its abuse.

Appeal allowed.

Solicitors: *Argles & Court*, Maidstone (for the husband); *Gulland & Gulland*, Maidstone (for the wife).

Bebe Chua   Barrister.

R v Cousins

a

COURT OF APPEAL, CRIMINAL DIVISION
EVELEIGH LJ, MILMO AND DRAKE JJ
19 JANUARY, 9 FEBRUARY 1982

b *Criminal law – Threat to kill – Defence – Lawful excuse – Self-defence or prevention of crime – Whether threat to kill a lawful excuse only if defendant's life in immediate jeopardy – Whether threat to kill a lawful excuse if reasonably made to prevent crime or in self-defence – Direction to jury – Offences against the Person Act 1861, s 16.*

c Self-defence or the prevention of crime can amount to a lawful excuse to a charge of threatening to kill, contrary to s 16[a] of the Offences against the Person Act 1961, if it is reasonable in the circumstances to make the threat. Accordingly, whether a threat to kill is lawfully excusable does not depend on whether the life of the defendant was in immediate jeopardy when he made the threat (see p 117 d to f, post).

d Where a charge is brought under s 16 of the 1861 Act alleging a threat to kill, and there is evidence of facts which could give rise to the defence of lawful excuse, it is the duty of the judge to direct the jury regarding those facts, to remind them that the onus lies with the prosecution to prove the absence of lawful excuse, and then to leave it to the jury to decide whether the prosecution has discharged that onus of proof. If there is no evidence of any facts which could give rise to a lawful excuse, it is the duty of the judge to direct the jury accordingly (see p 117 g h, post).

Notes
e For the offence of threatening to kill, see 11 Halsbury's Laws (4th edn) para 1160, and for cases on the subject, see 15 Digest (Reissue) 1110–1111, 9328–9335.

For self-defence and the prevention of crime as defences to criminal charges, see 11 Halsbury's Laws (4th edn) para 1180, and for cases on the subject, see 15 Digest (Reissue) 1170–1171, 1189–1190, 9945–9957, 9964–9968, 10,196–10,207.

f For the Offences against the Person Act 1861, s 16 (as substituted by the Criminal Law Act 1977, Sch 12), see 47 Halsbury's Statutes (3rd edn) 179.

Case referred to in judgment
Reference under s 48A of the Criminal Appeal (Northern Ireland) Act 1968 (No 1 of 1975) [1976] 2 All ER 937, [1977] AC 105, [1976] 3 WLR 235, HL, 14(2) Digest (Reissue)
g 750, *4799.

Appeal
On 23 October 1981 in the Crown Court at Oxford before his Honour Judge Mynett QC and a jury the defendant, Robert William Cousins, was arraigned on an indictment containing, inter alia, a charge of threatening to kill Kelly Reed, contrary to s 16 of the *h* Offences against the Person Act 1861. He was found guilty of that offence and was sentenced to four months' imprisonment. The defendant appealed, by leave of the single judge, on the ground that the judge erred in withdrawing from the jury the issue whether, on the evidence, the defendant had a defence of lawful excuse. The facts are set out in the judgment of the court.

i *Guy Boney* (assigned by the Registrar of Criminal Appeals) for the defendant.
Robert Turner for the Crown.

Cur adv vult

---

a   Section 16 is set out at p 117 a, post

9 February. **MILMO J** read the following judgment of the court: On 22 October 1981 in the Crown Court at Oxford before his Honour Judge Mynett QC the defendant was   *a*
arraigned on an indictment containing four counts. Count 1 charged him with threatening on 29 April 1981 to kill one Kelly Reed, contrary to s 16 of the Offences against the Person Act 1861, as substituted by Sch 12 to the Criminal Law Act 1977. Count 2 charged him with having in his possession on the same day a firearm, namely a shotgun, without holding a firearm certificate. Count 3 charged him with having on the same day unlawfully shortened the barrels of the shotgun. Count 4 charged him   *b*
with, being a person sentenced to a term of two years' imprisonment before the expiration of five years from the date of his release on 27 October 1978, having a firearm and ammunition in his possession.

He pleaded not guilty to counts 1 and 2 and guilty to counts 3 and 4. On the following day he was convicted on count 1. Count 2 was not proceeded with. He was sentenced to six months' imprisonment on count 1 and to four months' imprisonment on counts   *c*
3 and 4, all to run concurrently, making a total of six months' imprisonment.

He now appeals by leave of the single judge against his conviction on count 1 and against sentence.

On 23 April 1981 William Reed, a notoriously violent man, was attacked and beaten up when leaving a public house where the defendant had been. There was no evidence that the defendant had anything to do with this assault as a result of which William Reed   *d*
was detained in hospital for a few days.

On the afternoon of 29 April 1981 the defendant, carrying a double-barrelled shotgun, came to the Reed home where he inquired as to the whereabouts of Kelly Reed, the son of Mr and Mrs William Reed. Mr Reed asked the defendant what he was going to do with the gun and, according to him, the reply was, 'I am coming after Kelly with a gun. When I see him I'm going to kill him. I'm going to blow his brains out, when I see   *e*
him.' Mrs Reed confirmed this evidence. She said that the defendant had pointed the gun at her husband's head and said: 'I am after your Kelly. I want to see Kelly because he is after me and I'm going to blow his head off.' Both Mr and Mrs Reed said that they believed the defendant intended to carry out the threat he had made and the defendant in cross-examination conceded that he meant them to do so. He said: 'I went to the Reeds to make a threat. I wanted to convey that threat to them, backing it up with a   *f*
gun. I wanted them to think that the gun was loaded. I intended Reed should believe the threat and that was to kill their son Kelly if he came anywhere near any of my family or me.' In re-examination he stated that what he meant by the foregoing statements was that he wanted William Reed to know that he had got a gun and that if Kelly Reed came near him that he (the defendant) knew how to use it. The defendant's version of what he had said to the Reeds was different from theirs. He said that what he had told the   *g*
Reeds was that if Kelly came after him, he would kill Kelly. In cross-examination Mrs Reed said: 'He [the defendant] did say he would blow Kelly's head off. "If he comes for me I'm going to blow his brains off".'

The defendant gave evidence denying that he had anything to do with the beating up of William Reed. He said that three days after the incident, three men whom he knew told him in a public house that he ought to watch out, because they had heard that there   *h*
was a contract out to shoot him. These men said that Kelly Reed and a cousin of his had put out a contract because they had heard that the defendant was the man who had beaten up William Reed. The defendant said that he had panicked. He had borrowed the gun from a nephew and had gone to the Reed house to give them warning of what he would do if he was attacked or his wife or children endangered. He admitted that at a later stage he had converted the weapon into a sawn-off shotgun which he intended to   *j*
use if attacked by Kelly Reed.

The offence charged in count 1 is under s 16 of the Offences against the Person Act 1861 which, until 1977, read as follows:

'Whosoever shall maliciously send, deliver, or utter, or directly or indirectly cause to be received, knowing the contents thereof, any letter or writing threatening to kill or murder any person, shall be guilty of a felony, and being convicted thereof a shall be liable, at the discretion of the court, to be kept in penal servitude for any term not exceeding ten years . . .'

By Sch 12 to the Criminal Law Act 1977, the following was substituted for s 16 of the 1861 Act:

b 'Threats to kill. A person who without lawful excuse makes to another a threat, intending that that other would fear it would be carried out, to kill that other or a third person shall be guilty of an offence and liable on conviction on indictment to imprisonment for a term not exceeding ten years.'

It was argued on behalf of the defendant that in making the threat to William Reed the defendant was both seeking to forestall an attack which he reasonably believed that Kelly Reed was planning to make on him, and also to prevent the commission of the crime which such an attack would have involved. Section 3 of the Criminal Law Act c 1967 was relied on, the relevant parts of which read as follows:

'(1) A person may use such force as is reasonable in the circumstances in the prevention of crime . . .
(2) Subsection (1) above shall replace the rules of the common law on the question when force used for a purpose mentioned in the subsection is justified by that d purpose.'

It is, of course, true that the charge against the defendant was not that he used force but that he threatened to use force. However, if force is permissible, something less, for example a threat, must also be permissible if it is reasonable in the circumstances. Moreover, in criminal proceedings the common law recognises that it is lawful for a person to use reasonable means for self-defence. Consequently it can amount to a lawful e excuse for a threat to kill if the threat is made for the prevention of crime or for self-defence, provided it is reasonable in the circumstances to make such a threat. What is reasonable in the circumstances is always a question for the jury, never a 'point of law' for the judge: see Reference under s 48A of the Criminal Appeal (Northern Ireland) Act 1968 (No 1 of 1975) [1976] 2 All ER 937 at 947, [1977] AC 105 at 137 per Lord Diplock.

As is pointed out in Smith and Hogan Criminal Law (4th edn, 1978) p 333:

f 'A threat to kill may, however, be excusable where actual killing would not. To cause fear of death might be reasonable to prevent crime or to arrest an offender whereas actually to kill would be quite unreasonable.'

It will be desirable in many cases to tell the jury this.

In order to obtain the conviction of the defendant under count 1, the onus lay on the g prosecution to establish (a) the making by the defendant to William Reed of a threat to kill Kelly Reed, (b) that the defendant made the threat intending that William Reed would fear that the threat would be carried out, and (c) that there was no lawful excuse for making the threat. Of these elements, (a) and (b) were pure questions of fact for the jury. As to (c), if there was evidence of facts which could give rise to a lawful excuse, it was the duty of the judge to direct the jury to these facts and having reminded them that h the onus lay with the prosecution to prove the absence of lawful excuse, to have left it to the jury to decide whether the existence of lawful excuse had been disposed of. On the other hand, if there was no evidence of any facts which would give rise to a lawful excuse, it was the duty of the judge to direct the jury accordingly.

One ground only is given for the appeal against conviction. It reads as follows:

i '. . . the learned judge erred in directing the jury that there could be no question of lawful excuse for the issue of the said warning threat because "the life of the defendant was not in immediate jeopardy" and that, accordingly, the Defendant was not entitled to use the threat of force in self-defence or in prevention of crime. The learned judge thereby wrongly withdrew from the jury the question which should have been for them to decide:—did the defendant act in reasonable self-defence/prevention of crime in issuing a deterrent threat.'

In the judgment of this court this criticism of the summing up is well founded. What the judge in fact did was to withdraw from the jury the issue whether the defendant had any lawful excuse for making to William Reed the threat alleged. Throughout the a summing up one finds that the judge is directing the jury that lawful excuse does not come into the matter at all. Indeed, after the jury had been out for close on two hours, they sent a note to the judge: 'Please clarify lawful excuse and unlawful excuse.' In answer to this request, the final words of the judge to the jury were:

'Well, let us forget, shall we, the unlawful excuse, because that is no excuse at all. We will deal with the lawful excuse. I am not going to attempt a comprehensive b definition because you will be considering purely this case, and my reply to your question is to be taken within the context of this case. First of all, if you are not satisfied that the threat, as alleged, has been proved, that is an end to the matter: the accused is entitled to be acquitted. If, on the other hand, the threat to kill has been proved and that it was intended that Mr Reed senior should take that threat seriously, in the actual words alleged, then the threat to kill is something which the c law does not allow in those circumstances. There would therefore be no lawful excuse for it, because at the time that the threat was issued the life of the defendant was not in immediate jeopardy. Now, does that help you?'

For the foregoing reason, this appeal against conviction must be allowed and the conviction on count 1 is quashed. d

This court can find no ground whatever for interfering with the concurrent sentences of four months on counts 3 and 4.

Appeal allowed.

Solicitors: *C S Hoad*, Kidlington (for the Crown). e

April Weiss   Barrister.

R v Secretary of State for Foreign and Commonwealth Affairs, ex parte Indian Association of Alberta and others f

COURT OF APPEAL, CIVIL DIVISION

LORD DENNING MR, KERR AND MAY LJJ

14, 15, 18, 19, 20, 28 JANUARY 1982 g

Crown – Divisibility – Proceedings against the Crown – Proceedings against the Crown in right of Canada – Whether proceedings against the Crown in right of Canada can be brought against the Crown in right of the United Kingdom – British North America Act 1867 – Statute of Westminster 1931, s 7.

h

Commonwealth – Colony or dominion – Governmental obligation – Whether United Kingdom government owing obligations to Canadian Indians.

Canada – Constitutional law – Treaty rights granted to Canadian Indians – Whether treaty rights enforceable against United Kingdom government.

j

By a royal proclamation on 7 October 1763 George III declared that there would be reserved for the Indian peoples of Canada such territory described therein which was not ceded to or purchased by the Crown, the territory concerned being substantial parts of the North American territories ceded to England by France under the Treaty of Paris 1763, but excluding Quebec and territory granted to the Hudson's Bay Company. By a

series of treaties made between 1693 and 1906, a number of Indian tribes ceded territory
a to the Crown in return for the reservation of land for their use and for hunting, trapping
and fishing rights.   By the British North America Act 1867 the United Kingdom
Parliament created the Dominion of Canada by setting up a federal government and a
Dominion parliament with its own legislative powers.   By s 9 of that Act the executive
government of, and authority over, Canada was 'to continue and be vested in the Queen'
and by s 91(24) the Dominion parliament was to have exclusive power to legislate 'for
b Indians, and lands reserved for the Indians'.   The 1867 Act continued to be the
constitution of Canada, alterable only by the United Kingdom Parliament, and subject to
amendments subsequently made by that Parliament.   The Dominion of Canada acquired,
largely by agreement and convention, increasing independence from the United
Kingdom over and above that given to it by the 1867 Act, until, by virtue of the Statute
of Westminster 1931, it attained complete independence subject to the provisions of s 7
c of the 1931 statute, which entrenched the constitution of Canada in Westminster by
providing that the United Kingdom Parliament had sole power to repeal, amend or alter,
inter alia, the British North America Act 1867.   In 1981 the government of Canada
sought the 'repatriation' of the Canadian constitution in the terms proposed by Sch B to
the Canada Bill, which was introduced into the United Kingdom Parliament.   The Bill
proposed, inter alia, the amendment of the British North America Act 1867 and the
d repeal of s 7(1) of the Statute of Westminster to provide for future constitutional changes
to be within the sole authority of the legislature of Canada.   Various Indian associations
in Canada opposed the Canada Bill, fearing that the special rights granted to Indians
under the royal proclamation of 1763 and the treaties made between 1693 and 1906
would be in danger of being reduced or extinguished if the Bill were passed.   Following
representations by the associations to the United Kingdom government, the Foreign and
e Commonwealth Office stated in a memorandum to the Foreign Affair Committee of the
House of Commons on 11 November 1980 that 'All relevant treaty obligations insofar as
they still subsisted became the responsibility of the Government of Canada with the
attainment of independence, at the latest with the Statute of Westminster 1931'.   The
Indian Association of Alberta together with other Indian associations in New Brunswick
and Nova Scotia applied to the Divisional Court of the Queen's Bench Division for
f declarations that the statement was wrong in law and that obligations entered into by the
Crown under various treaty and statutory provisions were owed to the Indian peoples by
Her Majesty in right of the United Kingdom government.   The application was
dismissed.   The applicants appealed, contending, inter alia, (1) that under the royal
proclamation of 1763 and the treaties, whether made before or after the 1867 Act, the
Crown assumed obligations to the Indian peoples in return for formal concessions of
g territory by the Indian peoples and those obligations still subsisted against the Crown in
right of the United Kingdom because they had never been transferred to the federal or
provincial governments of Canada, and (2) that having in law retained, by virtue of ss 55
to 57 the 1867 Act and s 7 of the Statute of Westminster, ultimate power to deny royal
assent to Canadian legislation the Crown, in right of the United Kingdom, had retained
a degree of sovereignty over the Canadian constitution which carried with it some
h obligation in the Crown in right of the United Kingdom to the Indian peoples of Canada
under the royal proclamation of 1763 and the treaties which would continue until
Canada's total independence was achieved by the Canada Bill.

Held – Such obligations under the royal proclamation of 1763 and under the Indian
treaties as had the force of law were owed by the Crown in right of Canada and not in
right of the United Kingdom, and accordingly the matters raised by the applicants were
justiciable in the courts of Canada and not those of the United Kingdom and the appeal
would therefore be dismissed because—
    (1) (Per Lord Denning MR) The Crown, although at one time single and indivisible
throughout the British Empire, had by constitutional usage and practice become separate
and divisible for each particular territory in which it was sovereign.   Accordingly, those

obligations which were previously binding on the Crown simpliciter were now to be
treated as divided and were to be applied and confined to the territory to which they *a*
related (see p 127 *j*, p 128 *c e f*, p 129 *a b j* and p 130 *a*, post); *R v Secretary of State for the
Home Dept, ex p Bhurosah* [1967] 3 All ER 831 and *Mellenger v New Brunswick Development
Corp* [1971] 2 All ER 593 followed.

(2) (Per Kerr LJ) It was settled law, that although the Queen was the personal sovereign
of the peoples inhabiting different territories within the British Commonwealth, all
rights and obligations of the Crown, other than those concerning the Queen in her *b*
personal capacity, could only arise in relation to a particular government within those
territories, since the situs of obligations owed by the Crown was to be found only in that
territory within the realm of the Crown where such obligations could be enforced
against a local administration. Independence or the degree to which a territory was
independent was wholly irrelevant to the issue of situs because the rights and obligations
of the Crown arose exclusively in right or respect of any government outside the bounds *c*
of the United Kingdom as soon as it could be seen that there was an established
government of the Crown in the overseas territory in question. A fortiori, on the grant
of a representative legislature to a dominion, the government thereof was to be regarded
as distinct from the United Kingdom government and rights and obligations of the
Crown within that dominion could only be enforced against the Crown in right of the
dominion. It followed that the effect of the 1867 Act and its successors was to transfer *d*
every aspect of legislative and executive power in relation to Canada's internal affairs to
Canada and that the situs of rights and obligations of the Crown in relation to the Indian
peoples of Canada was the Crown in right of Canada (see p 131 *a b e g*, p 132 *b f*, p 133 *e*,
p 134 *a b f g* and p 135 *a b g* to *j*, post); *Re Holmes* (1861) John & H 527, dicta of Earl
Loreburn LC in *A-G for Ontario v A-G for Canada* [1912] AC at 581, 584, of Viscount
· Haldane in *Bonanza Creek Gold Mining Co Ltd v R* [1916–17] All ER Rep at 1005, *A-G v* *e*
Great Southern and Western Rly Co of Ireland [1925] AC 754, *Federal Comr of Taxation v
Official Liquidator of E O Farley Ltd* (1940) 63 CLR 278 and *R v Secretary of State for the
Home Dept, ex p Bhurosah* [1967] 3 All ER 831 applied.

(3) (Per May LJ) Any rights or obligations of the Crown in right of the United
Kingdom devolved on the Crown in right of a particular territory as soon as that territory
attained self-government to a greater or lesser degree. Accordingly, all treaty or other *f*
obligations entered into with the Indian peoples of Canada by the Crown in right of the
United Kingdom had become the responsibility of the government of Canada with the
attainment of independence, or at the latest with the Statute of Westminster. Although
as a matter of construction of s 7 of the Statute of Westminster the Crown in right of the
United Kingdom retained limited sovereignty over the Dominion of Canada, that did
not mean that treaty or other obligations into which the Crown may have entered with *g*
the Indian peoples of Canada still enured against the Crown in right of the United
Kingdom. To the extent that those obligations still continued, they were owed by the
Crown in right of the Dominion of Canada or in right of a particular province of Canada
(see p 136 *d* to *g*, p 137 *d* to *f*, p 140 *d e*, p 141 *c j* to p 142 *d* and p 143 *a* to *d*, post); *Re
Holmes* (1861) 2 John & H 527, dicta of Lord Watson in *Liquidators of the Maritime Bank of
Canada v Receiver-General of New Brunswick* [1892] AC at 441–442, of Earl Loreburn LC *h*
in *A-G for Ontario v A-G for Canada* [1912] AC at 581 and *A-G v Great Southern and Western
Rly Co of Ireland* [1925] AC 754 applied.

Notes

For the unity and the divisibility of the Crown, see 6 Halsbury's Laws (4th edn) para 820.

For the Queen as Sovereign of her dominions, see ibid para 817. *j*

For the constitution of Canada and the amendment thereof, see ibid paras 836, 926–
930.

For the British North America Act 1867, ss 9, 55, 56, 57, 91, see 4 Halsbury's Statutes
(3rd edn) 188, 196, 197, 203.

For the Statute of Westminster 1931, s 7, see ibid 22.

Cases referred to in judgments

A-G v Great Southern and Western Rly Co of Ireland [1925] AC 754, CA, 8(2) Digest (Reissue) 862, 1054.

A-G for Ontario v A-G for Canada [1912] AC 571, PC, 8(2) Digest (Reissue) 685, 141.

Bonanza Creek Gold Mining Co Ltd v R [1916] 1 AC 566, [1916–17] All ER Rep 999, PC, 8(2) Digest (Reissue) 713, 277.

Calder v A-G of British Columbia (1973) DLR (3d) 145, 8(2) Digest (Reissue) 784, *1419.

Campbell v Hall (1774) 1 Cowp 204, [1558–1774] All ER Rep 252, 8(2) Digest (Reissue) 655, 9.

Faithorn v Territory of Papua (1938) 60 CLR 772.

Federal Comr of Taxation v Official Liquidator of E O Farley Ltd (1940) 63 CLR 278, 11 Digest (Reissue) 664, *10.

Hodge v R (1883) 9 App Cas 117, PC, 8(2) Digest (Reissue) 684, 132.

Holmes, Re (1861) 2 John & H 527, 70 ER 1167, 11 Digest (Reissue) 396, 372.

Maritime Bank of Canada (liquidators) v Receiver-General of New Brunswick [1892] AC 437, PC, 8(2) Digest (Reissue) 659, 23.

Mellenger v New Brunswick Development Corp [1971] 2 All ER 593, [1971] 1 WLR 604, CA, 8(2) Digest (Reissue) 665, 38.

New Windsor Corp v Mellor [1975] 3 All ER 44, [1975] Ch 380, [1975] 3 WLR 25, CA, Digest (Cont Vol D) 101, 1106.

R v Isaac (1975) 9 APR 175.

R v Polchies (2 December 1981, unreported).

R v Secretary of State for the Home Dept, ex p Bhurosah [1967] 3 All ER 831, [1968] 1 QB 266, [1967] 3 WLR 1259, CA, 2 Digest (Reissue) 197, 1147.

St Catherine's Milling and Lumber Co v R (1889) 14 App Cas 46, PC, 8(2) Digest (Reissue) 780, 477.

Theodore v Duncan [1919] AC 696, PC.

Williams v Howarth [1905] AC 551, PC, 8(2) Digest (Reissue) 684, 131.

Cases also cited

A-G for Australia v Colonial Sugar Refining Co Ltd [1914] AC 237, PC.

A-G for Canada v A-G for Ontario, A-G for Quebec v A-G for Ontario [1897] AC 199, PC.

A-G for Canada v A-G for Ontario, Re Employment and Social Insurance Act [1937] AC 355, PC.

A-G for Quebec v A-G for Canada [1921] 1 AC 401, PC.

Adams v Adams (A-G intervening) [1970] 3 All ER 572, [1971] P 188.

Baker Lake (Hamlet) v A-G for Canada (1979) 107 DLR (3d) 513.

Buck v A-G [1965] 1 All ER 882, [1965] Ch 745, CA.

Buttes Gas and Oil Co v Hammer (Nos 2 & 3), Occidental Petroleum Corp v Buttes Gas and Oil Co (Nos 1 & 2) [1981] 3 All ER 616, [1981] 3 WLR 797, HL.

Canada (Dominion) v Province of Ontario [1910] AC 637, PC.

Madzimbamuto v Lardner-Burke [1968] 3 All ER 561, [1969] 1 AC 645, PC.

Mutasa v A-G [1979] 3 All ER 257, [1980] QB 114.

Ontario Mining Co Ltd v Seybold [1903] AC 73, PC.

R v George [1966] SCR 267.

R v Sikyea (1964) 42 DLR (2d) 135.

Appeal

The applicants, the Indian Association of Alberta, the Union of New Brunswick Indians and the Union of Nova Scotia Indians, appealed with the leave of the Court of Appeal granted on 21 December 1981 against the decision of Woolf J, hearing the Crown Office List, on 9 December 1981 whereby he refused the applicants leave to apply for judicial review by way of declarations (i) that the decision of the respondent, the Secretary of State for Foreign and Commonwealth Affairs, that all relevant treaty obligations entered into by the Crown with the Indian peoples of Canada in so far as they still subsisted became the responsibility of the government of Canada with the attainment of independence, at the latest with the Statute of Westminster 1931, was wrong in law and (ii) that treaty and other obligations entered into by the Crown to the Indian peoples of Canada were still owed by Her Majesty in right of her government in the United Kingdom. The government of Canada appeared as intervener. The facts are set out in the judgment of Lord Denning MR.

Louis Blom-Cooper QC and *Richard Drabble* for the applicants.
Robert Alexander QC and *Simon D Brown* for the Secretary of State.
Andrew Morritt QC and *Peter Irvin* for the Canadian government.

Cur adv vult

28 January. The following judgments were read.

LORD DENNING MR.

1. *The Indian peoples come here*

Over 200 years ago, in the year 1763, the King of England made a royal proclamation under the Great Seal. In it he gave solemn assurances to the Indian peoples of Canada. These assurances have been honoured for the most part ever since. But now the Indian peoples feel that the assurances are in danger of being dishonoured. They are anxious about the Canada Bill which is now before the Parliament of the United Kingdom. Under it there is to be a new constitution for Canada. The Indian peoples distrust the promoters of the Bill. They feel that, if it is passed, their own special rights and freedoms will be in peril of being reduced or extinguished. They have not gone to the courts of Canada for redress. They have come to this court. They say that the assurances which were given 200 years ago, and repeated in treaties 100 years later, were binding on the Crown of the United Kingdom. So they come to the courts of this country to plead their case. They come in particular from Alberta, Nova Scotia and New Brunswick. But the other Indian peoples from the other provinces are watching closely too. They want to see what happens. Seeing that their claim is against the Crown in respect of the United Kingdom, they are entitled, I think, to come here to put their case. They ask this court to make a declaration 'that treaty or other obligations entered into by the Crown to the Indian peoples of Canada are still owed by Her Majesty in right of Her Government in the United Kingdom'.

This is disputed by the Department of State in the United Kingdom. When the matter was under consideration by the Foreign Affairs Committee of the House of Commons, the question was put to the Foreign and Commonwealth Office (Foreign Affairs Committee minutes of evidence (HC Papers (1979–80) no 362–xxi) p 63): 'Has the UK any treaty or other responsibilities to Indians in Canada?' The answer given by that office on 11 November 1980 was: 'No. All relevant treaty obligations insofar as they still subsisted became the responsibility of the Government of Canada with the attainment of independence, at the latest with the Statute of Westminster 1931.'

The Indian peoples dispute that answer. In order to challenge it, they have brought these proceedings for judicial review. They seek declarations (i) that the answer is wrong in law, (ii) 'that treaties or other obligations entered into by the Crown to the Indian peoples of Canada are still owed by Her Majesty in right of Her Government in the United Kingdom'.

In order to decide the case we have had to look into the constitutional law affecting the colonies of the United Kingdom, just as Lord Mansfield CJ did years ago. He had to consider this very royal proclamation of 1763. He did it in 1774 in the great case of *Campbell v Hall* (1774) 1 Cowp 204, [1558–1774] All ER Rep 252, which has been ever since a landmark in the law. So I will try to trace the history of the rights and freedoms of the aboriginal peoples of Canada.

2. Aboriginal rights and freedoms

The Indian peoples of Canada have been there from the beginning of time. So they are called the 'aboriginal peoples'. In the distant past there were many different tribes scattered across the vast territories of Canada. Each tribe had its own tract of land, mountain, river or lake. They got their food by hunting and fishing and their clothing by trapping for fur. So far as we know they did not till the land. They had their chiefs and headmen to regulate their simple society and to enforce their customs. I say 'to enforce their customs', because in early societies custom is the basis of law. Once a custom is established it gives rise to rights and obligations which the chiefs and headmen will enforce. These customary laws are not written down. They are handed down by tradition from one generation to another. Yet beyond doubt they are well established and have the force of law within the community.

In England we still have laws which are derived from customs from time immemorial. Such as rights of villagers to play on the green; or to graze their cattle on the common: see *New Windsor Corp v Mellor* [1975] 3 All ER 44, [1975] 1 Ch 380. These rights belong to members of the community and take priority over the ownership of the soil.

3. The coming of the English

To return to primitive societies, their solitude was disturbed by the coming of the English from across the seas. They came as explorers, like Captain Cook in 1774, or Captain Vancouver in 1792; or as traders, like the East India Company, or the Hudson's Bay Company; or as colonists, like those who sailed across the ocean to found Virginia and Massachusetts. Wherever the English came, they came as representatives of the Crown of England. They carried with them the rights of Englishmen. They were loyal to the Crown and acted with the direct authority of the Crown under royal charter. Thus in 1600 there was the charter of the East India Company. In 1606 the first charter of Virginia drawn by Sir Edward Coke. In 1629 the charter of Massachusetts Bay. In 1670 the charter of the Hudson's Bay Company. In 1681 Pennsylvania. And so on.

Our long experience of these matters taught us how to treat the indigenous peoples. As matter of public policy, it was of the first importance to pay great respect to their laws and customs, and never to interfere with them except when necessary in the interests of peace and good order. It was the responsibility of the Crown of England, and those representing the Crown, to see that the rights of the indigenous people were secured to them, and that they were not imposed on by the selfish or the thoughtless or the ruthless. Witness the impeachment of Warren Hastings in Westminster Hall for his conduct of affairs as Governor General of Bengal.

4. The unity of the Crown

In all these matters in the eighteenth and nineteenth centuries it was a settled doctrine of constitutional law that the Crown was one and indivisible. The colonies formed one realm with the United Kingdom, the whole being under the sovereignty of the Crown. The Crown had full powers to establish such executive, legislative and judicial arrangements as it thought fit. In exercising these powers, it was the obligation of the Crown (through its representatives on the spot) to take steps to ensure that the original inhabitants of the country were accorded their rights and privileges according to the customs coming down the centuries, except in so far as these conflicted with the peace and good order of the country or the proper settlement of it. This obligation is evidenced most strikingly in the case of Canada by the royal proclamation of 1763.

5. The royal proclamation of 1763

You will all recall the events which preceded this proclamation. In the year 1759 James Wolffe with his redcoats crept stealthily and silently by night up the St Lawrence River and scaled the Heights of Abraham. It was the turning-point in the Seven Years War between England and France. It was followed in 1763 by the Treaty of Paris, under which the French surrendered all the rights which they had previously held or acquired in Canada. England gained dominion over Quebec. Later in that very same year, on 7 October 1763, the Crown made this solemn proclamation:

> 'And whereas it is just and reasonable, and essential to our Interest, and the Security of our Colonies, that the several Nations or Tribes of Indians with whom We are connected, and who live under our Protection, should not be molested or disturbed in the Possession of such Parts of Our Dominions and Territories as, not having been ceded to or purchased by Us, are reserved to them, or any of them, as their Hunting Grounds.—We do therefore, with the Advice of our Privy Council, declare it to be our Royal Will and Pleasure . . .'

Then followed detailed assurances by which the Crown bound itself to reserve 'under our Sovereignty, Protection and Dominion, for the use of the said Indians, all the lands and territories' thereafter described.

The royal proclamation superseded earlier agreements for other territories. Thus in 1752 in Nova Scotia a treaty had been made with the Indians by which it was agreed:

> 'That all Transactions during the late War shall on both sides be buried in Oblivion with the Hatchet, And that the said Indians shall have all favour, Friendship & Protection shewn them from this His Majesty's Government.'

I cannot forbear from mentioning also that in 1794 in New Brunswick there was this delightful little treaty with the Micmacs:

> 'And the English King said to the Indian King "Henceforth you will teach your children to maintain peace and I give you this paper upon which are written many promises which will never be effaced." Then the Indian King, John Julian with his brother Francis Julian begged His Majesty to grant them a portion of land for their own use and for the future generations. His Majesty granted their request. A distance of six miles was granted from Little South West on both sides and six miles at North West on both sides of the rivers. Then His Majesty promised King John Julian and his brother Francis Julian "Henceforth I will provide for you and for the future generation so long as the sun rises and river flows."'

The effect of the royal proclamation

The royal proclamation of 1763 had great impact throughout Canada. It was regarded as of high constitutional importance. It was ranked by the Indian peoples as their Bill of Rights, equivalent to our own Bill of Rights in England 80 years before. It came under the close consideration of Lord Mansfield CJ himself in the great case of *Campbell v Hall* (1774) 1 Cowp 204, [1558–1774] All ER Rep 252. That case came from the island of Grenada in the West Indies which we conquered from the French during the war. It was one of the places to which the 1763 proclamation expressly applied. Lord Mansfield CJ emphasised that by it the King made an immediate and irrevocable grant to all who were or should become habitants. Lord Mansfield CJ took the opportunity to lay down five fundamental propositions, of which I would quote two 1 Cowp 204 at 208, 209, [1558–1774] All ER Rep 252 at 254:

> 'A country conquered by the British arms becomes a dominion of *the King in the right of his Crown*; and, therefore, necessarily subject to the Legislature, the Parliament of *Great Britain* . . . that the laws of a conquered country continue in force, until they are altered by the conqueror . . .'

To my mind the royal proclamation of 1763 was equivalent to an entrenched provision in the constitution of the colonies in North America. It was binding on the Crown 'so long as the sun rises and the river flows'. I find myself in agreement with what was said a few years ago in the Supreme Court of Canada in *Calder v A-G of British Columbia* (1973) 34 DLR (3d) 145 at 203, in a judgment in which Laskin J concurred with Hall J and said:

> 'This Proclamation was an Executive Order having the force and effect of an Act of Parliament and was described by Gwynne, J., . . . as the "Indian Bill of Rights"

'. . . Its force as a statute is analogous to the status of Magna Carta which has always been considered to be the law throughout the Empire. It was a law which followed the flag as England assumed jurisdiction over newly-discovered or acquired lands or territories . . . In respect of this Proclamation, it can be said that when other exploring nations were showing a ruthless disregard of native rights England adopted a remarkably enlightened attitude towards the Indians of North America. The Proclamation must be regarded as a fundamental document upon which any just determination of original rights rests.'

The 1763 proclamation governed the position of the Indian peoples for the next hundred years at least. It still governs their position throughout Canada, except in those cases when it has been supplemented or superseded by a treaty with the Indians. It still is the basis of the rights of the aboriginals in those provinces of Nova Scotia and New Brunswick. That is shown by the decision of the Supreme Court of Nova Scotia in *R v Isaac* (1975) 9 APR 175, and of the Provincial Court of New Brunswick in *R v Polchies* (2 December 1981, unreported).

But I must say that the proclamation is most difficult to apply so as to enable anyone to say what lands are reserved to the Indians and what are not. It contains general statements which are wanting in particularity. In this respect it is like other Bills of Rights. The details have to be worked out by the courts or in some other way. To this I will return.

6. The British North America Act 1867

This brings me to the British North America Act 1867. It proclaimed the union of the provinces of Ontario, Quebec, Nova Scotia and New Brunswick into one dominion under the name of Canada. It contained powers to admit other colonies later into the union. It was the result of consultation over many years before. It set up a federal government. It contained a written constitution which was to last for over 100 years and more. It declared in s 9 that the executive government and authority of and over Canada was 'to continue and be vested in the Queen'. That is, in the Crown of England. The Governor General was her representative. It set up a Dominion parliament with its own legislative powers. It refashioned the provincial governments with their own Lieutenant Governors and their own parliaments. It set out detailed provisions, in ss 91 and 92, distributing legislative powers between the Dominion parliament and the provincial legislatures. It delegated, by ss 12 and 65, executive authority in similar respects to the Governor General and Lieutenant Governors respectively. It provided for a judicature and it contained detailed provisions about revenue, debts, assets and taxation.

The effect on the Indians

How did this Act affect the Indians? Section 91(24) gave the Dominion parliament the exclusive power to legislate for 'Indians, and lands reserved for the Indians'. The 1867 Act contained nothing specific about the executive power, but I think it mirrored the legislative division so that the executive power in regard to the 'Indians, and lands reserved for the Indians' was vested in the Governor General of the Dominion, acting through his representative; and he in turn represented the Queen of England, that is the Crown, which, as I have said, was in our constitutional law at that time regarded as one and indivisible.

Save for that reference in s 91(24), the 1867 Act was silent on Indian affairs. Nothing was said about the title to property in the 'lands reserved for the Indians', nor to the revenues therefrom, nor to the rights and obligations of the Crown or the Indians thenceforward in regard thereto. But I have no doubt that all concerned regarded the royal proclamation of 1763 as still of binding force. It was an unwritten provision which went without saying. It was binding on the legislatures of the Dominion and the provinces just as if there had been included in the statute a sentence: 'The aboriginal peoples of Canada shall continue to have all their rights and freedoms as recognised by the royal proclamation of 1763.'

No power to alter the 1867 Act

There is this other important point. The 1867 Act could not be altered either by the Dominion parliament or by the provincial legislatures. There was no provision in the statute for any means of altering it. This was, no doubt, at the wish of the provinces. They did not want the Dominion parliament to alter it to their prejudice. If it was to be altered at all, it could only be done by the Parliament of the United Kingdom. This shows to my mind, quite conclusively, that the Crown of the United Kingdom was regarded at that time as still the Crown of the Dominion and of the provinces of Canada. It was all one Crown, single and indivisible. As Lord Haldane said in *Theodore v Duncan* [1919] AC 696 at 706: 'The Crown is one and indivisible throughout the Empire, and it acts in self-governing States on the initiative and advice of its own Ministers in those States.'

7. *The making of the treaties*

After the 1867 Act was passed, there were a series of important treaties made with the Indian peoples across the greater part of Canada affecting all the provinces. They follow the same pattern but suffice it to state as an example a treaty made in 1873 between 'The Queen of Great Britain and Ireland, by Her Commissioners' and 'The Saulteaux Tribe of the Ojibbeway Indians by their Chiefs'.

After describing a tract of land, the treaty goes on to provide that the tribe and all other Indians—

'do hereby cede, release, surrender and yield up to the Government of the Dominion of Canada for Her Majesty the Queen and Her successors forever, all their rights, titles and privileges whatsoever, to the lands . . . To have and to hold the same to Her Majesty the Queen, and Her successors forever.'

In return Her Majesty the Queen entered into several obligations to the Indians, of which I select some as illustrations:

'And Her Majesty the Queen hereby agrees and undertakes to lay aside reserves for farming lands, due respect being had to lands at present cultivated by the said Indians, and also to lay aside and reserve for the benefit of the said Indians, to be administered and dealt with for them by Her Majesty's Government of the Dominion of Canada, in such a manner as shall seem best, other reserves of land in the said territory hereby ceded . . . And further, Her Majesty agrees to maintain schools for instruction in such reserves hereby made as to Her Government of Her Dominion of Canada may seem advisable whenever the Indians of the reserve shall desire it . . . Her Majesty further agrees with Her said Indians that they, the said Indians, shall have right to pursue their avocations of hunting and fishing throughout the tract surrendered as hereinbefore described, subject to such regulations as may from time to time be made by Her Government of Her Dominion of Canada, and saving and excepting such tracts as may, from time to time, be required or taken up for settlement, mining, lumbering or other purposes by Her said Government of the Dominion of Canada, or by any of the subjects thereof duly authorized therefor by the said Government.'

Then follow the signatures from which you can get the charming scene:

'IN WITNESS WHEREOF, Her Majesty's said Commissioners and the said Indian Chiefs have hereunto subscribed and set their hands at the North-West Angle of the Lake of the Woods this day and year herein first above named.'

The effect of the treaties

That treaty gave rise to a most important case. It is *St Catherine's Milling and Lumber Co v R* (1889) 14 App Cas 46. The Dominion asserted that it had the right to the produce of the Indian lands. It granted a licence to a milling company to cut and carry away one million feet of timber. The Province of Ontario disputed it. The Privy Council decided in favour of the province. It was the province, and not the Dominion government

which was entitled to the revenues from the sale of timber. The Privy Council considered
a the rights of the various persons in the Indian lands. The judgment was given by Lord
Watson, who, being bred in Scots law, expressed himself in the concepts of Roman law.
He said that the Indian tribes had a 'personal and usufructuary right' in the lands reserved
to the Indians, by which he meant that they had a right to use and take the fruits and
products of these lands and to hunt and fish thereon. Underneath the Indian title, there
had been—

b
'all along vested in the Crown a substantial and paramount estate, underlying the
Indian title, which became a plenum dominium whenever that title was surrendered
or otherwise extinguished.'

(See 14 App Cas 46 at 55.)
By the treaty the Indians ceded and surrendered much of their lands to the Crown and
c in return the Crown undertook the obligations to the Indians specified in the treaty.
So the Crown by the treaty obtained a 'plenum dominium' in the lands. That 'plenum
dominium' was distributed between the Dominion and the province. By reason of s 109
of the 1867 Act the revenues from timber, mines and so forth belonged to the Province
of Ontario. But the administration of the lands was left to the Dominion. The
obligations under the treaty remained the obligations of the Crown.
d That judgment was given at a time when, in constitutional law, the Crown was single
and indivisible. In view of it, and later cases, I think that the Indian title (by which I
mean 'the personal and usufructuary right' of the Indians in respect of 'lands reserved to
the Indians') was a title superior to all others save in so far as the Indians themselves
surrendered or ceded it to the Crown. That title was guaranteed to them by the
Crown. Then by treaties which covered much of Canada the Indians did cede and
e surrender their right in some lands to the Crown and in return the Crown undertook to
fulfil the obligations set out in the treaties. Those treaty obligations were obligations of
the Crown, the single and indivisible Crown, which was at that time the Crown of the
United Kingdom.
Apart from the ceded lands, ceded under the treaties, there were Indian reserves, not
ceded to the Crown, in which the Indian peoples still retained their 'personal and
usufructuary right' to the fruits and produce of the lands and to hunt and fish thereon.

8. *The British North America Act 1930*
Similar treaties were made in 1876, 1877 and 1899 with the Indian tribes who were
living in what is now Alberta, with which we are here particularly concerned. The
Province of Alberta was formed in 1905 and joined the union. In 1929 an agreement
was made between the Dominion government and the provincial government of
Alberta. Similar agreements were made with the provinces of Manitoba, British
Columbia and Saskatchewan. The agreements were in every case 'subject to approval by
the Parliament of Canada and by the Legislature of the Province and also to confirmation
by the Parliament of the United Kingdom'.
In 1930, by the British North America Act 1930, the United Kingdom Parliament
g gave the force of law to those agreements. It recognised that Canada was bound 'to fulfil
its obligations under the treaties with the Indians of the Province' and that—

'the said Indians shall have the right, which the Province hereby assures to them,
of hunting, trapping and fishing game and fish for food at all seasons of the year on
all unoccupied Crown lands and on any other lands to which the said Indians may
have a right of access.'

This 1930 Act seems to me to recognise that the Crown had subsisting obligations to
the Indians under the treaties. That is why it was necessary to have the agreements
confirmed by the Parliament of the United Kingdom with the assent of the Queen.

The division of the Crown
Hitherto I have said that in constitutional law the Crown was single and indivisible.
But that law was changed in the first half of this century, not by statute, but by

constitutional usage and practice. The Crown became separate and divisible, according to the particular territory in which it was sovereign. This was recognised by the Imperial Conference of 1926 (Cmd 2768). It framed the historic definition of the status of Great Britain and the dominions as—

> 'autonomous Communities within the British Empire, equal in status, in no way subordinate one to another in any aspect of their domestic or external affairs, though united by a common allegiance to the Crown, and freely associated as members of the British Commonwealth of Nations.'

It was also agreed that—

> 'the Governor-General in a Dominion is the representative of the Crown holding in all essential respects the same position in relation to the administration of public affairs in a Dominion as is held by His Majesty the King in Great Britain and that he is not the representative or agent of His Majesty's Government in Great Britain or of any Department of that Government.'

(See Cmd 2768, pp 14, 16.)

Thenceforward the Crown was no longer single and indivisible. It was separate and divisible for each self-governing dominion or province or territory. Thus in 1968 it was held in this court that the Queen was the Queen of Mauritius, and the Crown in right of Mauritius could issue passports to its citizens: see *R v Secretary of State for the Home Dept, ex p Bhurosah* [1967] 3 All ER 831, [1968] 1 QB 266: and in 1971 it was held, again in this court, that the Queen was the Queen of the Province of New Brunswick, and that province was entitled to state immunity: see *Mellenger v New Brunswick Development Corp* [1971] 2 All ER 593, [1971] 1 WLR 604.

As a result of this important constitutional change, I am of opinion that those obligations which were previously binding on the Crown simpliciter are now to be treated as divided. They are to be applied to the dominion or province or territory to which they relate: and confined to it. Thus the obligations to which the Crown bound itself in the royal proclamation of 1763 are now to be confined to the territories to which they related and binding only on the Crown in respect of those territories; and the treaties by which the Crown bound itself in 1875 are to be confined to those territories and binding on the Crown only in respect of those territories. None of them is any longer binding on the Crown in respect of the United Kingdom.

9. The Statute of Westminster 1931

The Statute of Westminster 1931 gave considerable independence to the dominions. By s 4 it was enacted that no Act of Parliament of the United Kingdom was to extend to a dominion as part of the law of the dominion unless 'it is expressly declared in that Act that that Dominion has requested, and consented to, the enactment thereof'.

But, at the same time, there was an express limitation in s 7(1): 'Nothing in this Act shall be deemed to apply to the repeal, amendment or alteration of the British North America Acts, 1867 to 1930 . . .'

That provision shows that the Parliament of the United Kingdom has still the power to repeal, amend or alter the British North America Acts 1867 to 1930 and that the Dominion parliament has no such power. No doubt the Parliament of the United Kingdom would not exercise this power except at the request of the Dominion itself and the consent of the majority of the provinces. But still in point of law the power still rests in the Parliament of the United Kingdom to repeal, amend or alter the British North America Acts 1867 to 1930. To my mind this shows that, in strict constitutional law, the Dominion of Canada is not completely independent. It is still tied hand and foot by the British North America Acts 1867 to 1930. The Dominion itself cannot alter one jot or tittle of those Acts.

But the Crown, as I have said already, was separate and divisible.

10. The Crown Proceedings Act 1947

In order that proceedings should be brought against the Crown in this country, it is *a* necessary that the liability of the Crown should be a liability 'in respect of Her Majesty's Government in the United Kingdom': see s 40(2)(c) of the Crown Proceedings Act 1947.

Now, at the time when the Crown entered into the obligations under the 1763 proclamation or the treaties of the 1870s, the Crown was in constitutional law one and indivisible. Its obligations were obligations in respect of the government of the United Kingdom as well as in respect of Canada: see *Williams v Howarth* [1905] AC 551. But, now that the Crown is separate and divisible, I think that the obligations under the *b* proclamation and the treaties are obligations of the Crown in respect of Canada. They are not obligations of the Crown in respect of the United Kingdom. It is, therefore, not permissible for the Indian peoples to bring an action in this country to enforce these obligations. Their only recourse is in the courts of Canada.

11. *The Canada Bill 1982*

c   This brings me to the Canada Bill. It is designed to give complete independence to Canada. It is to be done by 'patriating' the constitution, to use a coined word. It is to be done by the Constitution Act 1982. No longer will the United Kingdom Parliament have any power to pass any law extending to Canada. No longer will it have power to repeal, amend or alter the British North America Acts 1867 to 1930. But the Dominion parliament will have power to do so. This is to be done by setting out a new constitution *d* for Canada to be enacted by the United Kingdom Parliament. This new constitution contains a charter of rights and freedoms. It specifically guarantees to the aboriginal peoples the rights and freedoms which I have discussed earlier. These are the relevant sections:

> '**25.** The guarantee in this Charter of certain rights and freedoms shall not be construed so as to abrogate or derogate from any aboriginal, treaty or other rights or freedoms that pertain to the aboriginal peoples of Canada, including (a) any rights or freedoms that have been recognized by the Royal Proclamation of October 7, 1763; and (b) any rights or freedoms that may be acquired by the aboriginal peoples of Canada by way of land claims settlement.'

> '**35.**—(1) The existing aboriginal and treaty rights of the aboriginal peoples of Canada are hereby recognized and affirmed.
> (2) In this Act, "aboriginal peoples of Canada" includes the Indian, Inuit and Métis peoples of Canada.'

It also provides for a constitutional conference to be called within one year. That conference is to consider—

> 'an item respecting constitutional matters that directly affect the aboriginal peoples of Canada, including the identification and definition of the rights of those peoples . . .'

(See s 37(2).)

Conclusion

It seems to me that the Canada Bill itself does all that can be done to protect the rights and freedoms of the aboriginal peoples of Canada. It entrenches them as part of the constitution, so that they cannot be diminished or reduced except by the prescribed procedure and by the prescribed majorities. In addition, it provides for a conference at the highest level to be held so as to settle exactly what their rights are. That is most important, for they are very ill-defined at the moment.

There is nothing, so far as I can see, to warrant any distrust by the Indians of the government of Canada. But, in case there should be, the discussion in this case will strengthen their hand so as to enable them to withstand any onslaught. They will be able to say that their rights and freedoms have been guaranteed to them by the Crown, originally by the Crown in respect of the United Kingdom, now by the Crown in respect of Canada, but, in any case, by the Crown. No parliament should do anything to lessen the worth of these guarantees. They should be honoured by the Crown in respect of

Canada 'so long as the sun rises and river flows'. That promise must never be broken. There is no case whatever for any declaration. I would dismiss the appeal accordingly. *a*

KERR LJ. In connection with the 'repatriation' of the Canadian constitution, a number of statements have been made on behalf of Her Majesty's government in Parliament to the effect that all treaty obligations entered into by the Crown with the Indian peoples of Canada became the responsibility of the government of Canada with the attainment of independence, at latest with the Statute of Westminster 1931. The repatriation of the *b* Canadian constitution is now proposed by means of the Canada Bill which is awaiting its second reading in the House of Commons. By ss 25 and 35 of the annexed Constitution Act 1982 the rights of the aboriginal peoples of Canada, including in particular of the Indian peoples, are expressly preserved. However, various Canadian Indian organisations, and perhaps all of them, are dissatisfied with the present situation. They contend that the government's conclusion as to the legal position is wrong. The applicants accordingly *c* seek a declaration by way of judicial review to the effect that this conclusion is wrong in law and that all 'treaty and other obligations entered into by the Crown to the Indian peoples of Canada are still owed by Her Majesty in right of Her Government in the United Kingdom'.

We are here only directly concerned with the Indian organisations in the provinces of Alberta, New Brunswick and Nova Scotia. But on the voluminous material placed before *d* us it is clear that the same considerations apply throughout Canada. Thus, the applicants rely on the royal proclamation of 1763 which purported to extend to the Indian peoples beyond those parts of eastern Canada, the Maritime Provinces and parts of Quebec, which had by then been opened up for settlement. They also rely on the pattern of the so-called 'treaties' concluded between the Crown and many Indian 'bands', which ultimately covered most of the territory of Canada, and to which most or all of the *e* remaining Indians subsequently adhered. They contend that under all of these, whether made before or after the British North America Act 1867 which set up the Dominion of Canada, as well as under the royal proclamation, the Crown assumed obligations to the Indians in return for formal concessions of territory by the Indians, and that these obligations still subsist and have never been transferred to Canada.

As to the subsistence of these rights, we have been referred to many legislative enactments and decisions of the courts in Canada in which the continuing binding effect of the proclamation and treaties has been recognised. Their binding effect has also been accepted before us by counsel on behalf of the Secretary of State and of the government of Canada as interveners in the proceedings, as well as in the Canada Bill mentioned above. However, the Indian peoples wish to achieve certain political objectives, viz a *g* greater degree of recognition, and the right of consultation on those aspects of the constitution of Canada resulting from its 'repatriation' which may affect them. This is the object of these proceedings and of the declarations which they seek.

However great may be one's sympathy with the grievances and aspirations of the Indian peoples of Canada, this court can only concern itself with the decision of justiciable *h* issues on the basis of law. The issue raised in the declarations which are sought, quite apart from any question whether this should be dealt with by any formal declaration, is in my view only justiciable as a matter of concession by the court, faced with the wish of the applicants to have it decided and of the respondents' non-objection to its decision. The reason is that the applicants are not asserting any breach of any of the obligations on the part of the Crown, and are a fortiori not asking for any relief or remedy in respect of *j* such obligations. Indeed, it has been virtually conceded by counsel on behalf of the applicants, rightly in my view, that no such relief or remedy could be obtained in our courts; and for the reasons explained hereafter this factor is in itself a crucial pointer to the decision. In effect, however, the parties are agreed that this court should determine the abstract and bare issue as to the situs of obligations which are ultimately owed by the Crown, whether in right or respect of the United Kingdom on the one hand or of the Dominion or provinces of Canada on the other. Since we have heard full argument on this issue over several days, whereas the position in this respect was different before

Woolf J who dismissed the application for other reasons, I think that we should express

a our views on this issue.

It is settled law that, although Her Majesty is the personal Sovereign of the peoples inhabiting many of the territories within the Commonwealth, all rights and obligations of the Crown, other than those concerning the Queen in her personal capacity, can only arise in relation to a particular government within those territories. The reason is that such rights and obligations can only be exercised and enforced, if at all, through some

b governmental emanation or representation of the Crown. Thus, the Crown Proceedings Act 1947 distinguishes between liabilities in respect of, and proceedings in right of, Her Majesty in the United Kingdom on the one hand and outside the United Kingdom on the other. In relation to the latter class, it is open to the Secretary of State under s 40(3) to issue a certificate which is conclusive for the purposes of that Act. This has not been done in the present case, though without prejudice to the Secretary of State's contention that

c the legal position of the Indian peoples of Canada has no connection with the Crown in right of the United Kingdom. It is accordingly necessary to examine the constitutional principles which determine the situs of the Crown's rights and obligations in this regard, but bearing in mind that, although the relevant agreements with the Indian peoples are known as 'treaties', they are not treaties in the sense of public international law. They were not treaties between sovereign states, so that no question of state succession arises.

d The principles which govern the situs of rights and obligations of the Crown are conveniently summarised in 6 Halsbury's Laws (4th edn) para 820, under the heading 'Unity and Divisibility of the Crown'. For present purposes it is sufficient to refer to two passages and to a number of authorities cited in support of these.

First, as there stated, it is clear that—

e 'on the grant of a representative legislature, and perhaps even as from the setting up of courts, legislative council and other such structures of government, Her Majesty's government in a colony is to be regarded as distinct from Her Majesty's government in the United Kingdom.'

Thus, in *R v Secretary of State for the Home Dept, ex p Bhurosah* [1967] 3 All ER 831, [1968]

f 1 QB 266 an issue arose as to passports issued in Mauritius, which was then a dependent British colony, on behalf of the Governor. The passports were issued 'in the name of Her Majesty' to persons who were British subjects and citizens of the United Kingdom and Colonies under s 1 of the British Nationality Act 1948. The issue was whether they were 'United Kingdom passports' within the Commonwealth Immigrants Act 1962. It was held that they were not, because, in effect, they had been issued in the name of Her Majesty in right of the government of Mauritius and not of the United Kingdom.

g This being the position in relation to a dependent colony, the government of a dominion is clearly in an a fortiori position, and neither of these forms of established government within the Commonwealth presents any constitutional problem for present purposes. In times long past there was such a problem, when many of the territories which are now within the Commonwealth had not yet been opened up for settlement, or even fully discovered, and there was no established government on behalf of the

h Crown. Thus, the royal charter of 1670, granting Rupert's Land to the Hudson's Bay Company, described the territory as 'one of our Plantacions or Colonyes in America' and conveyed it 'as of our Mannor of East Greenwich in our County of Kent in free and common Soccage'. This was clearly a Crown grant in right of the government here. Subsequently, as the overseas territories gradually came to be settled and colonised, there may have been an indeterminate and intermediate stage of constitutional development

i in many cases, when it was uncertain whether rights and obligations concerning the overseas territory arose in right or respect of the Crown here or of the emerging forms of local administration overseas. This may still have been the position at the time of the eighteenth century 'Maritime Treaties' and of the royal proclamation of 1763, although all these contain references to the then emerging colonial governments of what later became the eastern provinces of Canada and the eastern states of America. However, for the reasons explained hereafter, it is unnecessary to determine what was the resulting

situs of the rights and obligations of the Crown in these territories at that time, since the
subsequent constitutional development of Canada in my view puts the present issue   *a*
beyond doubt.

The second relevant principle stated in the same passage in Halsbury's Laws is that—

> 'the liabilities of the Crown in right of, or under the laws of, one of the Crown's
> territories can be satisfied only out of the revenues, and by the authority of the
> legislature, of that territory.'
>   *b*

In effect, the situs of obligations on the part of the Crown is to be found only in that
territory within the realm of the Crown where such obligations can be enforced against
a local administration. A nineteenth century illustration of this principle in relation to
Canada, which is interesting because the case was decided before the British North
America Act 1867, was *Re Holmes* (1861) 2 John & H 527, 70 ER 1167. This concerned
disputes arising out of certain lands vested in the Crown, in the then Province of Upper   *c*
Canada, in relation to which a petition of right was brought in the Court of Chancery
here. It was held by Page Wood V-C that, whether or not the Crown was a trustee of the
land, the situs of any resulting rights and obligations lay in Canada and that these were
only enforceable there. He said (2 John & H 527 at 543, 70 ER 1167 at 1174): '. . . as the
holder of Canadian land for the public purposes of Canada, the Queen should be
considered as present in Canada, and out of the jurisdiction of this Court.' In other   *d*
words, any resulting rights and obligations existed only in right or respect of the Crown
in what was then Upper Canada, and not in right or respect of what was then Great
Britain.

An even more important illustration for present purposes of the same principle is to
be found in the decision of the House of Lords in *A-G v Great Southern and Western Rly Co
of Ireland* [1925] AC 754, which has been followed in the Australian courts in relation to   *e*
similar problems as between Australia and Papua in *Faithorn v Territory of Papua* (1938)
60 CLR 772 and as between the rights of the Crown in respect of the Commonwealth of
Australia and the State of New South Wales in *Federal Comr of Taxation v Official Liquidator
of E O Farley Ltd* (1940) 63 CLR 278. The importance of this case for present purposes is
that it shows that there may be a devolution of rights and obligations of the Crown in
respect of the government of Great Britain to another government within the   *f*
Commonwealth without any express statutory or other transfer, but merely by virtue of
the creation of the new government and of the assignment to it of responsibilities which
relate to the rights and obligations in question. This was a point on which counsel for the
applicants strongly sought to rely in relation to the Crown obligations arising out of the
royal proclamation and the various Indian treaties, particularly those before 1867, which
he contended had never been formally transferred to the federal or provincial   *g*
governments in Canada.

The facts of that case were briefly as follows. By agreements made in 1917 and 1918
between the President of the Board of Trade in Britain, which were subsequently
transferred to the Minister of Transport, and a railway company in what was then
Southern Ireland, certain rights of compensation were conferred on the company in
consideration of the company taking up the rails and sleepers on portions of their line,   *h*
since these were required for public purposes in the war effort. Thereafter the Irish Free
State was created with—

> 'the same constitutional status in the Community of Nations known as the British
> Empire as the Dominion of Canada, the Commonwealth of Australia, the Dominion
> of New Zealand, and the Union of South Africa . . .'

and a provisional government was established. Then, by an Order in Council which   *j*
recited that a Ministry of Economic Affairs had been set up within the provisional
government, responsible for, inter alia, transport, including functions hitherto performed
by the Minister of Transport and the Board of Trade, the corresponding functions were
transferred to the provisional government together with (purportedly) 'any property,

a rights and liabilities' connected with those functions. The company thereupon brought a petition of right, contending that, notwithstanding those enactments, the responsibility for the obligations under the original agreement remained with the British government. The company's contention in relation to the purported transfer of liabilities under the Order in Council was that those had not been effectively transferred, either on the true construction of the order, or because the order was ultra vires and to that extent void. This contention failed.

b Although most of the speeches proceeded on the basis of the construction of the order, it is clear that in the view of the House the same result also followed from the mere devolution of governmental responsibility for the matters to which the obligations related. In particular, the following passage is worth citing from the speech of Viscount Haldane in which Lord Dunedin and Lord Carson concurred ([1925] AC 754 at 773–774):

c 'In the present case Parliament transferred the duty of producing the fund out of which the liability in question, when it accrued, should be met to the Irish Parliament. It thereby declared its intention not itself to provide the money required out of its own Consolidated Fund. It does not matter whether the liability was in terms transferred to the Irish Government. By its very character it would cease when it became operative to be a liability of the British Consolidated Fund and *d* become one of the Irish Legislature Central Fund, if they chose to so provide.'

This is a clear illustration, of the highest authority, of the second of the principles concerning the situs of Crown obligations to which I have referred. Its effect is that such obligations exist only in respect of that government within the realm of the Crown against which such obligations can be enforced.

e In the light of the foregoing principles, I return to the position in relation to all obligations assumed by the Crown under the royal proclamation and the various treaties with the Indian peoples of Canada. The treaties fall into two parts: the Maritime Treaties, which also covered what is now part of the Province of Quebec, and which were made before the British North America Act 1867, and the subsequent treaties numbered 1 to 11 which were thereafter made in relation to what became parts of the Prairie *f* Provinces, the North Western Territory and British Columbia. For this purpose it is unnecessary to review the historical and constitutional development in Canada, which has extended into the present century. It is also irrelevant to consider whether, as maintained by the applicants but denied on behalf of the Secretary of State and the government of Canada, the pre-1867 treaties were mere treaties of peace, or whether these also gave rise to Crown obligations concerning 'personal and usufructuary' rights of the Indian peoples, in particular in relation to hunting and fishing. I am content to *g* assume this in favour of the applicants for present purposes. Finally, it is irrelevant to consider whether any Crown obligations under these treaties arose in respect of the Crown in Great Britain or whether, as I am inclined to think, they would already have arisen in respect of the developing governments of the Maritime Provinces and Quebec. It is sufficient to turn directly to the British North America Act 1867.

h This Act created the Dominion of Canada, then constituted by the four provinces of Ontario, Quebec, Nova Scotia and New Brunswick. By s 146 it provided for the admission of Newfoundland, Prince Edward Island, British Columbia, Rupert's Land and the North Western Territory by Order in Council, as subsequently happened. It set up the structure of the Dominion and provincial legislatures and executive governments in Canada. The executive power was to remain vested in the Crown, to be exercised for the *i* Dominion by the Governor General appointed by the Sovereign, in certain cases in conjunction with the newly created Queen's Privy Council of Canada. Executive power within the provinces was vested in Lieutenant Governors to be appointed by the Governor General and responsible to him. A Consolidated Reserve Fund for Canada was created, and it was provided that the Dominion was to be liable for the debts and liabilities of each province.

This Act was subsequently extended by amendment and by other Acts until 1930 to the whole of the present territory of the Dominion and provinces of Canada.

The effect of the 1867 Act and its successors, up to the Statute of Westminster 1931, was accordingly to create an all-embracing federal governmental structure for Canada, which, subject to one point discussed hereafter, was wholly independent and autonomous in relation to all internal affairs. For present purposes only a few of its provisions require to be mentioned specifically. First, ss 91 and 92 conferred exclusive legislative powers on the Dominion and the provinces respectively in relation to the matters therein mentioned. By s 91(24), the Dominion government was invested with exclusive powers in relation to 'Indians, and lands reserved for the Indians'. Second, however, by s 109 all lands, mines, minerals and royalties belonging to the provinces were expressly declared to continue to belong to them.

Since the passing of this Act there have been numerous cases, many of which reached the Privy Council, concerning the respective rights and obligations as between the Dominion and the provinces. In the present context the most important ones arose out of the dichotomy between ss 91(24) and 109: whereas the Dominion government was vested with exclusive legislative power concerning the Indian peoples and the lands reserved for them, the lands themselves, and the usufructuary rights arising out of them, were vested in the provinces. The problem was that large parts of those lands were subsequently ceded by the Indians under the treaties nos 1 to 11 and accordingly accrued to the provinces. This dichotomy gave rise to a number of disputes, of which *St Catherine's Milling and Lumber Co v R* (1888) 14 App Cas 46 is the leading authority. The issue concerned the right to timber growing on land covered by the royal proclamation of 1763 and ceded on behalf of the Salteaux Tribe of Ojibbeway Indians under treaty no 3 of 1873, subject to certain privileges of hunting and fishing. It was held by the Privy Council that the Indian usufructuary rights were preserved and did not fall within s 109, but that this section, and the cession under the treaty, vested the whole of the beneficial interest in the land (including its timber etc) in the Province to the exclusion of the Dominion, notwithstanding the legislative power of the Dominion under s 91(24).

This decision was followed in many subsequent cases to which we were referred. It is unnecessary to discuss these further, other than to mention that I cannot accept that it follows from one sentence in the judgment of Lord Watson in the *St Catherine's* case 14 App Cas 46 at 60 that any right or obligation in relation to the Indian peoples remained vested in the Crown in respect of what was then Great Britain. On the contrary, subsequent decisions of the Privy Council have authoritatively established that the effect of the 1867 Act and of its successors was to transfer to Canada, as between the governments of the Dominion and of the provinces, every aspect of legislative and executive power in relation to Canada's internal affairs. Thus in *A-G for Ontario v A-G for Canada* [1912] AC 571 at 581, 584, Earl Loreburn LC said:

'It would be subversive of the entire scheme and policy of the Act to assume that any point of internal self-government was withheld from Canada . . . For whatever belongs to self-government in Canada belongs either to the Dominion or to the provinces, within the limits of the British North America Act.'

(I return to the reference to the limits under the Act hereafter.)

Similarly, in *Bonanza Creek Gold Mining Co Ltd v R* [1916] 1 AC 566 at 579, [1916–17] All ER Rep 999 at 1005 Viscount Haldane stated:

'It is to be observed that the British North America Act has made a distribution between the Dominion and the provinces which extends not only to legislative but to executive authority.'

We are here not concerned with the many difficult and complex problems concerning the distribution of power and responsibility as between the Dominion and the provinces, which have given rise to so much litigation. We are only concerned with the question

whether any of these still remain vested in the Crown in right or respect of the United
a Kingdom. On the basis of the principles discussed earlier in this judgment, and of the
British North America Act 1867 and its successors, there can in my view be no doubt that
the answer to this is in the negative. So far as rights and obligations in relation to the
Indian peoples of Canada are concerned, the entire devolution of these from the Crown
in right of what is now the United Kingdom to the Crown in right of the Dominion or
provinces of Canada, is further confirmed by numerous Canadian enactments, both
b federal and provincial, culminating in the consolidated Indian Act 1970. This derives its
ultimate constitutional authority under the Crown from s 91(24) of the 1867 Act, as
mentioned above, and deals comprehensively with all matters concerning the Indian
peoples. The devolution to Canada of all legislative and executive powers in this regard
is therefore complete.

It then only remains to deal with one further argument put forward by counsel on
c behalf of the applicants. This is that, by virtue of ss 55 to 57 of the British North America
Act 1867, the Crown, in right of what is now the United Kingdom, retained the ultimate
power over all legislation enacted by the Dominion of Canada. On this basis it is said that
the Crown in right of the United Kingdom also indirectly maintained ultimate power
over the enactments of the provincial legislatures, but it is unnecessary further to
consider the constitutional complexities in relation to this latter aspect apart from
d mentioning that the independence of the provinces under the Crown, in the same way
as that of the Dominion, was recognised by the Privy Council in *Liquidators of Maritime
Bank of Canada v Receiver-General of New Brunswick* [1892] AC 437. The argument,
however, is that Canada has never been, and still is not, wholly independent, since there
is an ultimate power to deny royal assent to Canadian legislation. The fact that it has
become an established constitutional convention not to invoke this ultimate power is
e said to be irrelevant, since this derives from convention and not from law. Further, the
fact that the entire independence and self-government of the Dominion of Canada in all
matters, both internal and external, was recognised or affirmed by the Statute of
Westminster 1931 is also said to be irrelevant, since s 7 of the 1931 Act expressly provides
that nothing in that Act—

> 'shall be deemed to apply to the repeal, amendment or alteration of the British
> North America Acts, 1867 to 1930, or any order, rule or regulation made
> thereunder.'

What is contended, in other words, is that Canada is still not wholly independent from
the Crown in right of the United Kingdom, and that its total independence will only be
achieved by the enactment of the Canada Bill, which has not yet taken place.

With respect, in my judgment, this argument is wholly fallacious. As shown by the
basic constitutional principles discussed at the beginning of this judgment, it is perfectly
clear that the question whether the situs of rights and obligations of the Crown is to be
found in right or respect of the United Kingdom, or of other governments within those
parts of the Commonwealth of which Her Majesty is the ultimate sovereign, has nothing
whatever to do with the question whether those governments are wholly independent
or not. The situs of such rights and obligations rests with the overseas governments
within the realm of the Crown, and not with the Crown in right or respect of the United
Kingdom, even though the powers of such governments fall a very long way below the
level of independence. Indeed, independence, or the degree of independence, is wholly
irrelevant to the issue, because it is clear that rights and obligations of the Crown will
arise exclusively in right or respect of any government outside the bounds of the United
Kingdom as soon as it can be seen that there is an established government of the Crown
in the overseas territory in question. In relation to Canada this had clearly happened by
1867.

It follows in my judgment that the declarations sought by the applicants have no
foundation in law, and that this appeal must be dismissed.

MAY LJ. The application in this case is for two declarations: first, that the decision of
the Secretary of State for Foreign and Commonwealth Affairs that all treaty obligations   *a*
entered into by the Crown with the Indian peoples of Canada became the responsibility
of the government of Canada with the attainment of independence, at the latest with the
Statute of Westminster 1931, is wrong in law; and, second, that treaty and other
obligations entered into by the Crown to the Indian peoples of Canada are still owed by
Her Majesty in right of her government in the United Kingdom.

There is no question that the decision is one that has been come to by the Secretary of   *b*
State for Foreign and Commonwealth Affairs and which has been communicated in the
various ways to which Lord Denning MR and Kerr LJ have referred. Indeed it is quite
clear that the decision is one on which the governments of both the United Kingdom and
Canada are agreed.

These applications therefore raise three specific questions. First, with what treaty or
other obligations are we concerned? Second, were these or any of them ever owed to the   *c*
persons with whom they were made by Her Majesty or the Crown in the right of the
United Kingdom? Third, are they or any of them still so owed?

Before seeking to answer these three questions, however, I think that it is first necessary
to consider and reach a clear understanding of the constitutional questions and law
involved. Whilst, like Lord Denning MR and Kerr LJ, I have every sympathy for the
interests of the Indian peoples of Canada and understand why they come to the courts of
England at this time when the Canada Bill is before the Parliament of the United
Kingdom, I also feel that there is at the root of their application and the arguments in
support of it a fundamental misunderstanding of the constitutional position.

Although at one time it was correct to describe the Crown as one and indivisible, with
the development of the Commonwealth this is no longer so. Although there is only one
person who is the Sovereign within the British Commonwealth, it is now a truism that
in matters of law and government the Queen of the United Kingdom, for example, is
entirely independent and distinct from the Queen of Canada. Further, the Crown is a
constitutional monarchy and thus when one speaks today, and as was frequently done in
the course of the argument on this application, of the Crown 'in right of Canada', or of
some other territory within the Commonwealth, this is only a short way of referring to
the Crown acting through and on the advice of her ministers in Canada or in that other
territory within the Commonwealth.

Another consequence of this process of evolution from a single undivided imperial
Crown, to which counsel for the applicants frequently but as I think erroneously referred
in the course of his submissions, to the multi-limbed Crown of the British Commonwealth
is that as different territories within the Commonwealth attained self-government to a
greater or less extent, acquired the right to legislate on some and ultimately all matters
within and affecting that territory, and thus to raise the finance to enable them to
manage their own affairs, so pro tanto did any rights or obligations of what had been the
Imperial Crown, that is to say the Crown in right of the United Kingdom, devolve on the
Crown in right of the particular territory concerned.

This divisibility of the Crown was recognised by the courts in this country at a
relatively early stage in the evolution from Empire to Commonwealth. In *Re Holmes*
(1861) 2 John & H 527, 70 ER 1167 the Court of Chancery was asked to entertain a
petition of right presented under the then recent Petitions of Right Act 1860 claiming
the restoration of certain lands taken for a canal by an Act of the provincial legislature of
Canada and vested in the Queen. This was before the British North America Act 1867
at a time when the then Province of Canada comprised the two provinces of what had
been Upper Canada and Lower Canada respectively. In fact three provincial Acts were
concerned: two of the provincial parliament of Upper Canada, before the merger, and
the third of the provincial parliament of the merged Province of Canada itself. In essence
the argument on behalf of the suppliants was that, although the land concerned was land
in Canada and the relevant statutes had been passed by the Canadian legislatures,
nevertheless the Queen in her person was within the United Kingdom and that
accordingly a petition of right under the new Act would lie. In rejecting that claim Page
Wood V-C said (2 John & H 527 at 543–544, 70 ER 1167 at 1174):

'Now it is said that the Queen is present here, and therefore amenable (by virtue of the recent Act) to the jurisdiction of this Court. But it would be at least as correct to say that, as the holder of Canadian land for the public purposes of Canada, the Queen should be considered as present in Canada, and out of the jurisdiction of this Court. This alone supplies a sufficient answer to the argument of the suppliants; and, without entering into a number of other questions which the case involves, it is enough to say that, when land in Canada is vested in the Queen, not by prerogative, but under an Act of the Provincial Legislature, for the purposes of the province, and subject to any future directions which may be given by the Provincial Legislature, I hold that, for the purpose of any claims to such land made under the provincial statutes, the Queen is not to be regarded as within the jurisdiction of this Court. I wish to rest my decision on the broadest ground, that it was not the object of the Petitions of Right Act, 1860, to transfer jurisdiction to this country from any colony in which an Act might be passed vesting lands in the Crown for the benefit of the colony; and upon that ground I allow the demurrer . . . I prefer to rest upon the higher ground that this land cannot be withdrawn from the control of the Canadian Legislature, and brought within the jurisdiction of this Court, merely on the technical argument that the Queen, in whom it is vested for Canadian purposes, is present in this country.'

That the duties and liabilities of the Crown in right of the United Kingdom in respect of another territory or its peoples within the Commonwealth should devolve in this way on the Crown in right of that territory as the latter attained its own legislature, and with that its own revenue and Consolidated Fund, was itself merely a natural consequence of that progress of self-government and ultimately independence. It necessarily followed from the political concept, convention or, in some cases, specific legislation which realised, accepted or enacted that Parliament in the United Kingdom would not thereafter interfere with or derogate from laws passed by the legislature in the self-governing territory on any subject which had in truth been left to its jurisdiction. To contemplate any other result would be to contemplate legislative and inter-governmental chaos.

On this point, however, I do not have to rest solely on political theory. There is in my judgment good support for it in the speeches of their Lordships' House in *A-G v Great Southern and Western Rly Co of Ireland* [1925] AC 754. By agreements made in 1917 and 1918 the President of the Board of Trade in the United Kingdom agreed that, if the Irish railway company took up the rails and sleepers on parts of their line and transferred them to the British government to enable them to construct certain other lines to help their transport of coal for local use during the 1914–18 war, then after the war the latter government would pay the railway company the cost of new rails and sleepers and of reconstructing their previous railway line. The company duly transferred the rails and sleepers to the government. Subsequently by legislation and an Order in Council the liabilities so incurred by the Board of Trade were transferred to the British Minister of Transport. There followed in 1922 two further Acts of the Parliament at Westminster creating the Irish Free State and an Order in Council transferring relevant functions from certain British ministers to Irish ones. The railway company claimed a declaration on a petition of right that notwithstanding those statutes and orders the liability of the British government under the 1917 and 1918 agreements still subsisted. The decision in the House of Lords that the liability had been transferred to and vested in the government of the Irish Free State rested principally on the proper construction and effect of the statutes and orders involved, but having so held that that was their result Viscount Cave LC continued (at 765–766):

'That this conclusion is in accordance, not only with the terms of the several Acts and Orders, but with the reason of the case, is (I think) plain. The Free State Government now holds the branch lines to which the rails and sleepers were transferred. That Government alone can sanction the replacement of the lines removed from the respondents' railway and can regulate the method of replacement and control the expense incurred. The lines when replaced will be for the benefit

of the surrounding population, and the betterment of the respondents' line (for
which under the terms of the Castlecomer Agreement the respondents are to make   *a*
an allowance) will proceed from that population. At the time when the Acts and
Orders were passed, it was plain that the administration of all the railways in
Southern Ireland would pass out of the jurisdiction and control of the British
Ministry of Transport and would become a function of the Free State; and it was
natural that the assets and future liabilities connected with that function should at
the same time be transferred to the Government of that State. I think that on the   *b*
true construction of the Acts and Orders this was their effect, and accordingly that
this appeal should succeed.'

Viscount Haldane, with whose speech Lord Carson concurred, having considered the
point of construction and then referred to three other cases concerning Newfoundland,
New Zealand and England respectively, said (at 773–774):
                                                                                        c
    'My Lords, I am of opinion that the judgments in these three cases illustrate a
    principle which is definitely recorded in our textbooks of constitutional law.
    However clear it may be that before the Revolution Settlement the Crown could be
    taken to contract personally, it is equally clear that since that Settlement its ordinary
    contracts only mean that it will pay out of funds which Parliament may or may not
    supply. In the present case Parliament transferred the duty of producing the fund   *c*
    out of which the liability in question, when it accrued, should be met to the Irish
    Parliament. It thereby declared its intention not itself to provide the money
    required out of its own Consolidated Fund. It does not matter whether the liability
    was in terms transferred to the Irish Government. By its very character it would
    cease when it became operative to be a liability of the British Consolidated Fund and
    become one of the Irish Legislature Central Fund, if they chose to so provide.'   *e*

Finally Lord Phillimore in his speech said (at 779–780):

    'So far then it is merely a departmental question whether a particular property is
    stated to be vested in one Minister or another. But when it becomes a question of
    a transfer from the Home Government to the Irish Free State or to any other
    Dominion, it is necessary to look into it somewhat more closely. The property of   *f*
    the Crown in the Dominion is held for the purposes of that Dominion. Its benefits
    accrue to the Dominion Exchequer, and liabilities in connection with it must be
    discharged out of the same Exchequer. His Majesty has separate Attorney-Generals
    to sue and be sued in respect of each Dominion . . . In these circumstances I am of
    opinion that no petition of right can be brought in the High Court of Justice of
    England which has for its object a judgment against the Crown which is to be   *g*
    satisfied out of the Exchequer of a Dominion, and that no judgment can be obtained
    on a petition of right so brought in respect of liabilities incident to the Ministry of
    a Dominion, because such liabilities are not to be satisfied out of the Exchequer of
    the United Kingdom.'

It was in these circumstances, and as a part of the evolutionary and devolutionary
process to which I have referred, that the British North America Act 1867 was passed.
I will myself refer to a few specific sections in a moment, but its general effect has been
described in two judgments of the Privy Council. In *Liquidators of the Maritime Bank of
Canada v Receiver-General of New Brunswick* [1892] AC 437 at 441–442, Lord Watson said:

    'The object of the Act was neither to weld the provinces into one, nor to
    subordinate provincial governments to a central authority, but to create a federal
    government in which they should all be represented, entrusted with the exclusive
    administration of affairs in which they had a common interest, each province
    retaining its independence and autonomy. That object was accomplished by
    distributing, between the Dominion and the provinces, all powers executive and
    legislative, and all public property and revenues which had previously belonged to

a the provinces; so that the Dominion Government should be vested with such of these powers, property, and revenues as were necessary for the due performance of its constitutional functions, and that the remainder should be retained by the provinces for the purposes of provincial government. But, in so far as regards those matters which, by sect. 92, are specially reserved for provincial legislation, the legislation of each province continues to be free from the control of the Dominion, and as supreme as it was before the passing of the Act. In *Hodge* v. *The Queen* ((1883)

b 9 App Cas 117 at 132), Lord Fitzgerald[1], delivering the opinion of this Board, said: "When the British North America Act enacted that there should be a legislature for Ontario, and that its legislative assembly should have exclusive authority to make laws for the province and for provincial purposes in relation to the matters enumerated in sect. 92, it conferred powers not in any sense to be exercised by delegation from or as agents of the Imperial Parliament, but authority as plenary

c and as ample within the limits prescribed by sect. 92 as the Imperial Parliament in the plenitude of its power possessed and could bestow. Within these limits of subjects and area the local legislature is supreme, and has the same authority as the Imperial Parliament, or the Parliament of the Dominion." The Act places the constitutions of all provinces within the Dominion on the same level; and what is true with respect to the legislature of Ontario has equal application to the legislature

d of New Brunswick.'

Secondly, in *A-G for Ontario v A-G for Canada* [1912] AC 571 at 581 Earl Loreburn LC said:

'In 1867 the desire of Canada for a definite Constitution embracing the entire Dominion was embodied in the British North America Act. Now, there can be no

e doubt that under this organic instrument the powers distributed between the Dominion on the one hand and the provinces on the other hand cover the whole area of self-government within the whole area of Canada. It would be subversive of the entire scheme and policy of the Act to assume that any point of internal self-government was withheld from Canada. Numerous points have arisen, and may hereafter arise, upon those provisions of the Act which draw the dividing line

f between what belongs to the Dominion or to the province respectively. An exhaustive enumeration being unattainable (so infinite are the subjects of possible legislation), general terms are necessarily used in describing what either is to have, and with the use of general terms comes the risk of some confusion, whenever a case arises in which it can be said that the power claimed falls within the description of what the Dominion is to have, and also within the description of what the province

g is to have. Such apparent overlapping is unavoidable, and the duty of a Court of law is to decide in each particular case on which side of the line it falls in view of the whole statute.'

For our present purposes it is sufficient to recall that s 3 of the 1867 Act enacted that the Queen by proclamation might constitute the three then provinces of Canada, Nova

h Scotia and New Brunswick into the Dominion of Canada. The Province of Canada, which had earlier been formed by the joinder of Upper and Lower Canada, became the two new provinces of Ontario and Quebec. The Act then created separate self-governing constitutions for the Dominion and each of the four provinces. Sections 91 and 92 laid down the classes of subject which were to be within the exclusive legislative powers of the Dominion parliament and provincial legislatures respectively. Among these, by

j s 91(24), the power to legislate in respect of 'Indians, and lands reserved for the Indians' was given to the Dominion parliament. By s 109 all lands, mines, minerals and royalties belonging to the three existing provinces were to continue to belong to the four provinces thereafter to form the Dominion, subject to any trusts existing in respect thereof and to

---

1 Sic. According to the report of *Hodge v R*, although Lord FitzGerald presided, the judgment of their Lordships was delivered by Sir Barnes Peacock (see 9 App Cas 117 at 121)

any interest other than that of the provinces in the same. The effect of this section was considered in *St Catherine's Milling and Lumber Co v R* (1888) 14 App Cas 46, in which the Privy Council held that lands ceded by Indians under treaties made with the Crown after federation became vested in the relevant province. Section 132 provided that the parliament and government of the Dominion should have all the necessary powers to enable it to perform the obligations of Canada or any province, as part of the British Empire, towards foreign countries arising under treaties between the Empire and such foreign countries. Finally, s 146 gave power to admit to the Dominion, inter alia, what was then Rupert's Land and the North Western Territory, which were each then vested in the Hudson's Bay Company under the latter's charter.

By the 1867 Act, therefore, the Dominion and the provinces acquired a substantial degree of self-government and their own treasuries. Between then and the Imperial Conferences of 1926 and 1930 the Dominion acquired, largely by agreement and convention, increasing independence over and above that given it by the 1867 Act from the United Kingdom and its Parliament until, by the Statute of Westminster 1931, it and the other Dominions referred to in that statute attained complete independence subject, in the case of Canada, to s 7, which, as it was put in argument, entrenched the constitution of Canada and its provinces in Westminster, subject to this, that such constitution can only be amended at the request and with the consent of the Dominion.

As a result of this process and on the authorities to which I have referred, I have no doubt that any treaty or other obligations which the Crown had entered into with the Indian peoples of Canada in right of the United Kingdom had become the responsibility of the government of Canada with the attainment of independence, at the latest with the Statute of Westminster 1931. I therefore think that this application must fail.

However, as counsel have dealt with the general facts and merits of this case, I shall do so shortly myself. As will finally appear, however, I do not think that it is the function of this court in all the circumstances to do so.

It is a matter of history, in so far as is material in this case, that the royal charter granting Rupert's Land to the Hudson's Bay Company was made in 1670. Thereafter, as a result of the Treaty of Utrecht 1713, Hudson Bay, Nova Scotia and Newfoundland passed to England and ultimately the rest of the territory claimed by France in North America was ceded to England in 1763 by the Treaty of Paris.

In that same year George III issued a proclamation with which I shall have to deal in a moment. However, prior to this and to the formal hostilities between Great Britain and France called the Seven Years War, a number of treaties were entered into between the local Indian communities and the English Crown or representatives of it. These are what have been described as the Maritime Treaties in this case and are the first class of documents under which it is alleged that the Indian peoples of Canada obtained rights against the English Crown. I do not agree. I think that if one looks at these treaties as they have been shown to us, they were merely articles of submission. The Indians concerned had been engaging in hostilities against the English Crown. By these treaties they agreed to cease to do so and in the main to trade and treat with the British rather than with the French. Only two of these treaties, namely those of 1752 and 1794, both with the Micmac Indians, could in any way be said to have granted anything to the Indians, but even then this was in such general terms that it is impossible to say to what, if anything, they relate in a context 200 years after they were made.

There was then the royal proclamation of 1763. It is agreed on both sides that this had and continues to have the effect at least of secondary legislation, if not of a statute. After setting up the four self-governing colonies of Quebec, East Florida, West Florida and Grenada, it reserved under the Crown's sovereignty, protection and dominion, for the use of the Indian inhabitants of such land, substantial parts of the territories recently ceded to England by France, but not including the four colonies I have mentioned, or lands within the limits of the territory earlier granted to the Hudson's Bay Company under its charter.

From some of the Canadian decisions which have been shown to us it seems that the Canadian courts have held that the provisions of the royal proclamation did and do

extend to the provinces of Nova Scotia and New Brunswick, subject to the terms of any
a cessions of land to the Crown by Indians in those provinces which have been made since
1763. From the arguments addressed to us I would respectfully agree with this view of
the Canadian courts. As I shall indicate, however, I do not think that it is competent for
this or any English court to pronounce definitively on the point and had I disagreed with
the Canadian judges I would not have thought it correct for me to say so.

Of the many Canadian cases we have seen, I think that it is sufficient for present
b purposes to refer to *R v Isaac* (1975) 9 APR 175, a decision of the Nova Scotia Supreme
Court, as an authority for the existence of an aboriginal or Canadian common law right
possessed by Indians to hunt and fish over their lands. Were it within my jurisdiction
now to do so, I would hold that this right was confirmed to the Indians by the
proclamation and, save to the extent where it has been extinguished by the cession of
Indian lands or a Dominion statute pursuant to s 91(24) of the British North America Act
c 1867, is still an Indian right over relevant land. This was the decision not only in *R v
Isaac* but also in a number of the other Canadian cases to which our attention was
directed.

It is a right which the Indians possess against the Crown, but for the reasons I have
given against the Crown in right of Canada and not in right of the United Kingdom.

I turn finally to the post-federation treaties, those which have been described in this
d case as the Prairie Treaties, and in particular to treaty no 6 of 1876, which is the one
relating to the Alberta Indians, whose association was the first of the applicants in these
proceedings.

I shall refer to the terms of the treaty shortly, but, in addition to the general reasons
which I have already given for my conclusion that any rights owed today by the Crown
to the Indian population of Canada are owed by the Crown in right of Canada, the history
e of Alberta, and for that matter Manitoba and Saskatchewan, is also relevant. The
territory of what is now the Province of Alberta was part of Rupert's Land, which was
granted to the Hudson's Bay Company by its charter of 1670. As such the Indians
occupying it were expressly excluded from the reservation of sovereignty in the
proclamation of 1763 to which I have referred. The Hudson's Bay Company surrendered
Rupert's Land to the Crown in November 1769 and by an Order in Council pursuant to
f s 146 of the British North America Act 1867 the Crown admitted Rupert's Land into the
Dominion the same year. At that stage Rupert's Land and the power to legislate for it
was given to the Dominion government. However, by the Alberta Act 1905, the
relevant part of Rupert's Land was established as the Province of Alberta and a system of
local self-government set up as in the other provinces. The land itself, however, still
remained vested in the Dominion. Nevertheless by the schedule to the British North
g America Act 1930 the land constituting Alberta was transferred from the Dominion to
the province, except for the lands included in the Indian Reserves, which, because of the
responsibility of the Dominion government for Indians and their lands, under s 91(24)
of the 1867 Act, remained vested in the Dominion.

Thus, at least in so far as Alberta itself was concerned, at the date of the treaty which
we have been asked to consider its land was vested in the Dominion. Then,
h understandably, when the lands constituting Alberta were vested in the province, so as
to put it in the same position as other provinces, that land which by the treaties had been
reserved to the Indians was still kept vested in the Dominion government, which had the
responsibility for these people.

Further, although treaty no 6 was expressed to have been made by Her Majesty the
Queen of Great Britain and Ireland with the Indians, it was nevertheless made by her
through commissioners, including the Lieutenant Governor of the relevant lands. In
addition the cession of lands by the Indians, in exchange for which the Crown granted
them certain rights and privileges, was to the government of the Dominion of Canada
for Her Majesty the Queen. Next, when the Crown in the treaty agreed to lay aside
reserves for the Indians, they were to be administered and dealt with for them by Her
Majesty's government of the Dominion of Canada.

On both the general and also these particular grounds, therefore, I think that the rights granted to the Alberta Indians by the relevant treaty were granted to them by the Crown in right of Canada and not by the Crown in right of the United Kingdom. $\quad$ **a**

In essence, the argument of counsel for the applicants was that, because at least some element of sovereignty over the Canadian constitution remained in Westminster, this necessarily carried with it at least some obligation in the Crown in the right of the United Kingdom to the Indian peoples of Canada under the royal proclamation of 1763 and the Prairie Treaties to which I have referred. As a matter of construction, clearly s 7 of the Statute of Westminster 1931 did retain a limited sovereignty of the Crown in right of the $\quad$ **b** United Kingdom over the Dominion. But, in my opinion, on both the general and particular considerations to which I have referred, I do not think that this in any way means that any treaty or other obligations into which the Crown may have entered with its Indian peoples of Canada still enure against the Crown in right of the United Kingdom. Quite clearly, to the extent that these still continue, and I think that it is clear that the Canadian courts have held that they do, they are owed by the Crown in right of $\quad$ **c** the Dominion or in right of the particular province.

As I have said earlier, the Crown is a constitutional monarchy, acting only on the advice of its relevant ministers. Two hundred years ago, in so far as North America was concerned, these were clearly the ministers of the United Kingdom government. Equally clearly, in 1982 and in the events which have occurred, notwithstanding s 7 of the 1931 statute, the relevant ministers on whose advice the Crown acts in relation to $\quad$ **d** Canada and its provinces are those of her government in the Dominion and those provinces.

In the course of his argument counsel for the applicants referred to s 7(1)(*b*) of the India Independence Act 1947, relating to India in Asia, and the corresponding provision in s 1(3) of the Burma Independence Act 1947. By these legislative provisions the Crown's suzerainty of the Indian states and the Karenni states respectively was to lapse on the $\quad$ **e** appointed day and with it, inter alia, all obligations of the Crown to these various states and their rulers at the same time. Counsel for the applicants argued that the absence of any similar provision in the British North America Act 1867, the Statute of Westminster 1931 or the present Canada Bill relating to the Crown's suzerainty of and obligations to the Indian peoples of Canada clearly meant that these were to continue and remain the responsibilities of the Crown in right of the United Kingdom. It is always dangerous to $\quad$ **f** argue from default in this way: circumstances vary so much from case to case and Parliamentary draftsmen in the nineteenth century may have adopted a very different approach from their successors in the twentieth century. In any event, if, for instance, one looks at s 6 and analagous sections (as to India) and s 320 (as to Burma) of the Government of India Act 1935, one can see that there were substantial formal relationships between the Crown in right of the United Kingdom and local rulers in $\quad$ **g** India and Burma which had to be set aside when those two countries obtained their independence. Further, this was obtained by these two countries once and for all by their respective Acts of 1947. Similar independence for Canada, and within her for the provinces, was not the result of one simple legislative act of the United Kingdom Parliament at Westminster, either in 1867 or 1931. It was a gradual process which, save for the entrenched constitution, had been effected by 1931. $\quad$ **h**

For these reasons, the comparative argument of counsel for the applicants relating to India and Burma is, in my opinion, of little, if any, force.

Finally, counsel on behalf of the Crown in right of the United Kingdom, in particular the Foreign and Commonwealth Office, and counsel on behalf of the Crown in right of Canada, each argue that the issues raised by these applications are outside the jurisdiction of the English courts, that they ought not to be considered by them, and that in any event $\quad$ **j** it is inappropriate to grant any declaration in this or any other similar application. With all respect to these arguments, I think that the last is dependent on our decision on the first two. If the issues raised in this case are within this court's jurisdiction, then I see no reason why we should not make an appropriate declaration on the application of one side or the other. On the other hand, if the issues raised are not within this court's

jurisdiction, then not only should we in truth not hear them but certainly we should
a make no declaration, in favour of either side.

On the authority of the decisions of this court in such cases as *Mellenger v New
Brunswick Development Corp* [1971] 2 All ER 593, [1971] 1 WLR 604, I do not think that
this court has any jurisdiction to consider the issues raised by this application, and not
merely no jurisdiction, but that it would be contrary to the comity existing between
independent nations were we to do so. The rights and obligations on which we have
b been asked to adjudicate are said to be enjoyed by and owed to citizens of Canada in
respect of land which is itself within the Dominion. Further, any enforcement of these
rights and obligations could ex hypothesi only be carried out within Canada and would
have to be subject to the relevant provisions of Canadian law. We have only heard the
arguments on the merits de bene esse and out of consideration of those who have
travelled 4,000 miles and further to hear their cause pleaded before us. We appreciate
c their anxieties; we have done all that we can relevant to this application to learn about
their history and understand the arguments put before us on their behalf.

In the end, however, I am quite satisfied both, on general constitutional grounds as
well as on the construction of the relevant instruments and the history of the relevant
provinces themselves, that any treaty or other obligations still owed by the Crown to the
Indian peoples of Canada are owed by the Crown in right of the Dominion of Canada and
d not in the right of the United Kingdom. If such obligations still exist, and, if they do,
their extent, is, in my opinion, not a matter for this court: it is a matter for the courts of
Canada.

I, too, would therefore refuse this application.

Application for judicial review refused; application for leave to appeal to the House of Lords
e *refused.*

11 March. The Appeal Committee of the House of Lords (Lord Diplock, Lord Fraser of
Tullybelton, Lord Russell of Killowen, Lord Scarman and Lord Bridge of Harwich) heard
a petition by the applicants for leave to appeal.

f *Louis Blom-Cooper QC* for the applicants.
Robert Alexander QC for the Secretary of State.
Andrew Morritt QC for the Canadian government.

LORD DIPLOCK. Their Lordships do not grant leave to appeal in this case. They
wish to make it clear that their refusal of leave is not based on any technical or procedural
g grounds, although it is not to be taken as their view that there is jurisdiction to entertain
an application for judicial review in such a case as this. Their refusal of leave is because
in their opinion, for the accumulated reasons given in the judgments of the Court of
Appeal, it simply is not arguable that any obligations of the Crown in respect of the
Indian peoples of Canada are still the responsibility of Her Majesty's government in the
United Kingdom. They are the responsibility of Her Majesty's government in Canada,
h and it is the Canadian courts and not the English courts that alone have jurisdiction to
determine what those obligations are.

Petition dismissed.

Solicitors: *Radcliffes & Co* (for the applicants); *Treasury Solicitor; Linklaters & Paines* (for
the Canadian government).

Diana Procter   Barrister.

Vervaeke v Smith (Messina and Attorney General intervening)

HOUSE OF LORDS

LORD HAILSHAM OF ST MARYLEBONE LC, LORD DIPLOCK, LORD SIMON OF GLAISDALE, LORD KEITH
OF KINKEL AND LORD BRANDON OF OAKBROOK

15, 16 FEBRUARY, 7 APRIL 1982

*Nullity – Recognition of foreign decree – Right to recognition – Marriage celebrated in England
– Decision of English court that marriage valid under English law – Decision based on petitioner's
consent to marriage – Foreign court subsequently granting decree of nullity on ground that
marriage a sham although consented to – That ground not raised in English proceedings – English
decision and foreign decree based on respective public policy which was contradictory – Whether
foreign decree entitled to recognition by English court.*

In 1954 the petitioner, who was born in Belgium and resided there until 1954, went
through a ceremony of marriage in London with the respondent, who was a domiciled
Englishman. On 12 March 1970 the petitioner went through another ceremony of
marriage in Italy with M who died that day leaving real property in England. If the
petitioner's marriage to M was valid she was entitled to a share in that property. By a
petition dated 29 May 1970 in the Family Division of the High Court, the petitioner
prayed for a declaration that her marriage to the respondent was null and void on the
ground that she had not consented to it because she was ignorant of the true nature of the
ceremony. A member of M's family intervened in the proceedings to contest the relief
sought. On 7 May 1971 Ormrod J[a] dismissed the petition on the ground that the
petitioner knew that the 1954 ceremony was a marriage ceremony and had consented to
it. On 6 December 1971 the petitioner, who had returned to Belgium in May 1970 and
been resident there for 18 months, began proceedings in a Belgian court seeking a
declaration that the 1954 marriage was a nullity ab initio on the alternative pleas that (i)
she had not consented to the marriage through ignorance of the true nature of the
ceremony or (ii) it was a mock marriage, or mere formality, not accompanied by the
parties' intention to cohabit, and was contracted solely to enable the petitioner to acquire
British nationality and avoid deportation from England. In the Belgian proceedings the
respondent admitted the second plea. The intervener again intervened to oppose the
relief sought, on the ground that the matter was res judicata by virtue of Ormrod J's
decision and that the validity of the 1954 marriage was governed by English law and
therefore the same conclusion would be reached in the Belgian court as had been reached
by Ormrod J. On 7 March 1972 the petitioner's appeal to the English Court of Appeal
from Ormrod J's decision was dismissed by consent. On 9 June 1972 the Belgian court
decreed that the 1954 marriage was void ab initio on the ground that, although the
parties had consented to it, it was a mock marriage not intended to constitute a lifelong
community between them and, as such, was invalid under Belgian law. The court
rejected the petitioner's plea of lack of consent to the marriage. The intervener appealed
to a Belgian appeal court, which on 27 April 1973 dismissed the appeal, holding that the
plea of lack of consent to the marriage was barred by the res judicata afforded by Ormrod
J's decision but that the plea of a mock marriage was not res judicata since it had not been
argued before Ormrod J. The court accordingly upheld the latter plea, thus rendering
the marriage invalid under Belgian law. By a petition in the High Court in England
dated 7 September 1973 the petitioner sought as against the respondent a declaration
under RSC Ord 15, r 16[b] that the Belgian decree was entitled to recognition in the

---

a   See *Messina v Smith* [1971] 2 All ER 1046

b   Rule 16 provides: 'No action or other proceeding shall be open to objection on the ground that a
    merely declaratory judgment or order is sought thereby, and the Court may make binding
    declarations of right whether or not any consequential relief is or could be claimed.'

English courts and by a further petition the petitioner applied under s 45(1)^c of the Matrimonial Causes Act 1973 for a declaration that her marriage to M was valid and subsisting at the date of his death. Members of M's family intervened in both petitions to oppose the relief claimed in them. On 8 May 1979 Waterhouse J dismissed both petitions and his decision was affirmed by the Court of Appeal. The petitioner appealed to the House of Lords.

Held – The appeal failed in limine and would be dismissed for the following reasons—

(1) The decision of Ormrod J that the English marriage was not rendered invalid on the ground of absence of consent was a decision on the point at issue in the Belgian courts, ie the question of the right to have the English marriage declared void, and therefore, since the matter in dispute in the Belgian proceedings had, prior to the date of the Belgian judgment, been the subject of a final and conclusive judgment by a court having jurisdiction (ie the English court), the issue was then res judicata and the Belgian judgment could not be recognised by the English courts, on the ground of cause of action estoppel. With respect to the petitioner's application under s 45 of the 1973 Act for a declaration that the Italian marriage was valid, although she only was debarred by Ormrod J's judgment by what was technically 'issue estoppel' rather than 'cause of action estoppel' from asserting in an English court that the English marriage was void, she was still precluded from relying on the Belgian judgment that the English marriage was invalid, since the validity of the English marriage went to the root of the question which she had to prove in order to establish the validity of the Italian marriage, ie that the Italian marriage was not contracted at a time when the English marriage was still subsisting (see p 151 j, p 152 g h, p 154 c to p 155 a and p 156 c d g to j, post); dictum of Wigram V-C in *Henderson v Henderson* [1843–60] All ER Rep 381–382 applied.

(2) Furthermore, the English rule as to the validity and consequences of a marriage applied by Ormrod J in his judgment was based on public policy, and since the Belgian judgment was the result of the application of a contradictory Belgian public policy to the same facts as were finally ascertained by Ormrod J, the court would, in the circumstances, decline to accord recognition to the Belgian judgment. Moreover, public policy precluded recognition having regard to the fact that the Belgian decree of nullity had been obtained only after, and because, the original and fraudulent basis of the petitioner's claim had been disposed of against her by the English court (see p 152 b to h, p 154 a to c, p 155 b h, p 156 f, p 158 d e, p 159 g h and p 160 b to d, post); *Henderson v Henderson* [1843–60] All ER Rep 378 applied.

Decision of the Court of Appeal [1981] 1 All ER 55 affirmed.

Notes

For recognition of foreign decrees of nullity of marriage, see 8 Halsbury's Laws (4th edn) paras 500–502, and for cases on the subject, see 11 Digest (Reissue) 557–560, 1232–1246.

For the Matrimonial Causes Act 1973, s 45, see 43 Halsbury's Statutes (3rd edn) 594.

Cases referred to in opinions

Berthiaume v Dastous [1930] AC 79, [1929] All ER Rep 111, PC, 11 Digest (Reissue) 514, 1031.

Brisbane City Council v A-G for Queensland [1978] 3 All ER 30, [1979] AC 411, [1978] 3 WLR 299, PC, Digest (Cont Vol E) 38, 154a.

Brodie v Brodie [1917] P 271, [1916–17] All ER Rep 237, 27(1) Digest (Reissue) 253, 1862.

Castrique v Imrie (1870) LR 4 HL 414, [1861–73] All ER Rep 508, HL, 11 Digest (Reissue) 611, 1550.

Corbett v Corbett (orse Ashley) [1970] 2 All ER 33, [1971] P 83, [1970] 2 WLR 1306, 27(1) Digest (Reissue) 29, 137.

---

c   Section 45(1), so far as material, provides: 'Any person who is a British subject, or whose right to be deemed a British subject depends wholly or in part . . . on the validity of any marriage, may, if he . . . claims any real or personal estate situate in England and Wales, apply by petition to the High Court for a decree declaring . . . that his own marriage was a valid marriage.'

Dalrymple v Dalrymple (1811) 2 Hag Con 54, 161 ER 665; *on appeal* (1814) 2 Hag Con 137n, 161 ER 693n, 22 Digest (Reissue) 684, 7294.

De Reneville v De Reneville [1948] 1 All ER 56, [1948] P 100, 11 Digest (Reissue) 542, 1182.

Fender v Mildmay [1937] 3 All ER 402, [1938] AC 1, HL, 12 Digest (Reissue) 325, 2352.

Formosa v Formosa [1962] 3 All ER 419, sub nom *Gray (orse Formosa) v Formosa* [1963] P 259, [1962] 3 WLR 1246, CA, 11 Digest (Reissue) 559, 1245.

Godard v Gray (1870) LR 6 QB 139, 11 Digest (Reissue) 608, 1535.

Hayward v Hayward [1961] 1 All ER 236, [1961] P 152, [1961] 2 WLR 993, 27(1) Digest (Reissue) 492, 3549.

Henderson v Henderson (1843) 3 Hare 100, [1843–60] All ER Rep 378, 67 ER 313, 21 Digest (Reissue) 56, 374.

Hoystead v Taxation Comr [1926] AC 155, [1925] All ER Rep 56, PC, 21 Digest (Reissue) 61, 388.

Indyka v Indyka [1967] 2 All ER 689, [1969] 1 AC 33, [1967] 3 WLR 510, HL, 11 Digest (Reissue) 551, 1224.

Kelly (orse Hyams) v Kelly (1932) 148 LT 143, 27(1) Digest (Reissue) 32, 150.

Kenward v Kenward [1950] 2 All ER 297, [1951] P 124, CA; *rvsg sub nom Way v Way* [1949] 2 All ER 959, [1950] P 71, 11 Digest (Reissue) 511, 1015.

Lepre v Lepre [1963] 2 All ER 49, [1965] P 52, [1963] 2 WLR 735, 11 Digest (Reissue) 558, 1238.

Macartney, Re, Macfarlane v Macartney [1921] 1 Ch 522, 11 Digest (Reissue) 581, 1356.

Mehta (orse Kohn) v Mehta [1945] 2 All ER 690, 11 Digest (Reissue) 502, 971.

Messina (formerly Smith orse Vervaeke) v Smith (Messina intervening) [1971] 2 All ER 1046, [1971] P 322, [1971] 3 WLR 118, 11 Digest (Reissue) 549, 1217.

Miles v Chilton (falsely calling herself Miles) (1849) 1 Rob Eccl 684, 163 ER 1178, 27(2) Digest (Reissue) 601, 4354.

Morgan v Morgan (orse Ransom) [1959] 1 All ER 539, [1959] P 92, [1959] 2 WLR 487, 27(1) Digest (Reissue) 329, 2389.

Silver (orse Kraft) v Silver [1955] 2 All ER 614, [1955] 1 WLR 728, 27(1) Digest (Reissue) 30, 141.

Szechter (orse Karsov) v Szechter [1970] 3 All ER 905, [1971] P 286, [1971] 2 WLR 170, 11 Digest (Reissue) 540, 1179.

Thoday v Thoday [1964] 1 All ER 341, [1964] P 181, [1964] 2 WLR 371, CA, 27(2) Digest (Reissue) 642, 4790.

Warrender v Warrender (1835) 2 Cl & Fin 488, 6 ER 1239, HL, 11 Digest (Reissue) 382, 364.

Yat Tung Investment Co Ltd v Dao Heng Bank Ltd [1975] AC 581, [1975] 2 WLR 690, PC, 21 Digest (Reissue) 60, 387.

Appeal

The petitioner, Marie Thérèse Rachelle Vervaeke, appealed with leave of the Court of Appeal against the decision of the Court of Appeal (Arnold P, Cumming-Bruce and Eveleigh LJJ) ([1981] 1 All ER 55, [1981] Fam 77) on 8 July 1980 dismissing an appeal by the appellant against the decision of Waterhouse J ([1981] 1 All ER 55, [1981] Fam 77) on 8 May 1979 dismissing two petitions dated 7 September 1973 and 20 April 1979 filed by the appellant whereby she sought recognition in England under RSC Ord 15, r 16 of a foreign decree of nullity in respect of her marriage in England on 11 August 1954 to one William George Smith and a declaration under s 45 of the Matrimonial Causes Act 1973 that her marriage to one Eugenio Messina on 12 March 1970 in San Remo, Italy was valid and subsisting on his death. William George Smith was the respondent to the first petition but took no further part in the proceedings after the service on him of the petition and he died on 2 August 1978. Salvatore Messina, replaced as from 30 August 1977 by Attilio Messina, and the Attorney General intervened in the proceedings and were the respondents to the appeal. The facts are set out in the opinion of Lord Hailsham LC.

Joseph Jackson QC and *Mathew Thorpe* QC for the appellant.
Ian Karsten for the respondent Messina.
Anthony Hollis QC and *Nicholas Wilson* for the Attorney General.

Their Lordships took time for consideration.

7 April. The following opinions were delivered.

LORD HAILSHAM OF ST MARYLEBONE LC. My Lords, the more I reflect about this appeal, the more convinced I become that on a correct analysis of the facts and issues the appellant's position is unsustainable. We have before us in effect two petitions. The first dated 7 September 1973 prays for a declaration that a decree of nullity obtained in Belgium in respect of a ceremony of marriage between her and William George Smith, the original respondent to the petition, but who has played no part in the proceedings beyond acknowledging service and giving notice that he did not desire to defend the proceedings, is entitled to be recognised in this country. This prayer for relief was formulated under RSC Ord 15, r 16. The second, amending the first, filed on 20 April 1979 pursuant to leave granted by order of Waterhouse J granted on 22 March 1979 as a result of his refusal to grant the first prayer, is founded on s 45 of the Matrimonial Causes Act 1973 and prays that the marriage celebrated in Italy on 12 March 1970 between the appellant and Eugenio Messina was a valid marriage still subsisting at the date of Eugenio Messina's death. To both these proceedings William George Smith was the original respondent, but, as I have indicated, has played no part in resisting either prayer, and has now, indeed, died. Both petitions are however resisted by two interveners (respondents to the appeal), namely (1) Salvatore Messina, who, after his death was replaced as from 30 August 1977 by Attilio Messina, both being the brothers of Eugenio Messina, and (2) the Attorney General, who intervenes pursuant to the order of Waterhouse J made 20 March 1979. The result of the appeal depends on the decision of your Lordships as to the validity of a ceremony of marriage performed in England on 11 August 1954 between the appellant and William George Smith, and this, in turn, depends on the recognition (or otherwise) by your Lordships of the above-mentioned Belgian nullity decree. The real bone of contention between the parties is, however, the right to succeed to the property in England of Eugenio Messina, which, at the time of his death, was considerable. The appellant has failed before Waterhouse J and the Court of Appeal (Arnold P, Cumming-Bruce and Eveleigh LJJ) (see [1981] 1 All ER 55, [1981] Fam 77) and now, by leave of the Court of Appeal, appeals to your Lordships' House.

The time has now come when I must rehearse the facts.

On 11 August 1954 at the register office in the district of Paddington the appellant, at that time a spinster, of Belgian nationality and Belgian domicile, went through a ceremony of marriage with William George Smith, a man of British nationality, according to his own account down and out in London, drinking, and out of work, and induced to take part in the ceremony in return for a bribe of £50 and a ticket to South Africa. At one time it was alleged that this marriage was bigamous since William George Smith had previously been married in the Far East to a Russian woman, Helen Josephine Gavrilkina, but it has since been determined that at the relevant date that marriage had been dissolved by a Nevada divorce which, under the rules of English law, was recognised as valid by the English courts: see *Messina (formerly Smith orse Vervaeke) v Smith (Messina intervening)* [1971] 2 All ER 1046, [1971] P 322.

Although valid in point of form the marriage with Smith was not in any sense an ordinary one. There was no intention to cohabit as man and wife. To quote from the judgment of Ormrod J in the previous proceedings in a part of the judgment that is not reported:

'This was a mere marriage of convenience between a man and a woman who were unknown to one another, for the sole purpose of enabling the woman to apply for

British nationality so that she could not be deported as a prostitute or an undesirable
alien.'

The expression 'marriage of convenience' in the above sentence is unfortunate. It is
obvious from the context that Ormrod J was not finding the marriage to be a 'marriage
of convenience' in the popular sense. But the marriage achieved its purpose. Again
quoting from the same judgment ([1971] P 323 at 328), the appellant—

> 'worked as a prostitute between 1954 and 1963 in various brothels in London run
> by the Messina organisation. During this period she accumulated over 100
> convictions for soliciting.'

By means of the marriage ceremony with Smith, the appellant had acquired the British
nationality she sought, a British passport and the legal right to reside in the United
Kingdom despite her 100 convictions.

In point of fact the appellant parted from Smith at the doors of the register office and
saw him only once or twice thereafter in connection with her application for British
nationality and for a British passport.

It is obvious that proceedings of this kind, described by Ormrod J as part of 'a horrible
and sordid story' can raise issues of public policy, as to which there can be more than one
possible answer. The first is given by Ormrod J in the passage immediately following
that which I have just quoted. According to Ormrod J (in a part of his judgment which
is not reported):

> 'Where a man and woman consent to marry one another in a formal ceremony
> conducted in accordance with the formalities required by law, knowing that it is a
> marriage ceremony it is immaterial that they do not intend to live together as man
> and wife. It is, of course, quite otherwise where one of the parties believes that the
> ceremony is something different, eg a formal betrothal ceremony as in *Kelly (orse
> Hymans) v Kelly* (1932) 148 LT 143 . . . or as in *Mehta (orse Kohn) v Mehta* [1945] 2 All
> ER 690, a ceremony of religious conversion. In such cases, the essence of marriage,
> the mutual exchange of consents accompanied by the formalities required by law,
> is missing, and such marriages are, therefore, void or perhaps voidable. On the
> other hand, if the parties exchange consents to marry with due formality, intending
> to acquire the status of married persons, it is immaterial that they intend the
> marriage to take effect in some limited way or that one or both of them may have
> been mistaken about, or unaware of, some of the incidents of the status which they
> have created. To hold otherwise would impair the effect of the whole system of law
> regulating marriages in this country, and gravely diminish the value of the system
> of registration of marriages on which so much depends in a modern community.
> Lord Merrivale P in *Kelly v Kelly* 148 LT 143 at 144 said: "In a country like ours,
> where the marriage status is of very great consequence and where the enforcement
> of the marriage laws is a matter of great public concern, it would be intolerable if
> the marriage law could be played with by people who thought fit to go to a register
> office and subsequently, after some change of mind, to affirm that it was not a
> marriage because they did not so regard it." See also the observations of Hodson J
> in *Way v Way* [1949] 2 All ER 959 at 963, [1950] P 71 at 79, approved by the Court
> of Appeal in same case sub nom *Kenward v Kenward* [1950] 2 All ER 297 at 302,
> [1951] P 124 at 133 and in *Silver (orse Kraft) v Silver* [1955] 2 All ER 614, [1955] 1
> WLR 728.'

There has been no serious dispute before your Lordships that the above statement is a
correct statement of English law. Nor, in the light of the quotation from Lord Merrivale
P above can it seriously be contested that the law as there enunciated is based on grounds
of public policy, at least as regards marriages in England between British subjects. I
would not wish to be thought to extend this doctrine into a statement of universal
application, but I have no doubt that it would extend to a marriage as here celebrated in

England between a British to a foreign national in circumstances where the ceremony was intended to achieve the status of British nationality in the foreign national by means of the marriage and the private arrangement between the parties was simply to limit their personal relationships to the achievement of the status of married person with a view to acquiring British nationality for the previously alien partner. In addition to the citation of authority by Ormrod J in the passage quoted above one might also refer to the decision in *Brodie v Brodie* [1917] P 271, [1916–17] All ER Rep 237. However, I regard the position as incontestable at least to the extent that I have stated above. The fact is that in the English law of marriage there is no room for mental reservations or private arrangements regarding the parties' personal relationships once it is established that the parties are free to marry one another, have consented to the achievement of the married state and observed the necessary formalities. If further authority is required for this proposition, I refer to the impressive array of citations in *Morgan v Morgan (orse Ransom)* [1959] 1 All ER 539, [1959] P 92.

Whilst all civilised nations deplore the transaction above described as morally indefensible, it by no means follows that the public policy of all civilised systems of jurisprudence agree that the consequence, viz that the marriage must stand as valid, is the correct result. In particular it is not the view adopted by those European countries which follow the tradition of the Code Napoléon or the Roman Curia in their civil codes, and in further particular we know from the present proceedings that it is not the view recognised in the Belgian courts. According to this alternative view such a marriage as is under discussion is so repugnant that, if validly brought to the attention of a court of competent jurisdiction, it will be declared void ab initio on the ground that what has been consented to is not a marriage. In this connection I quote in the translation afforded us the language used in relation to the impugned marriage in the present case of the Belgian Court of Appeal upholding the decree in the court of first instance to illustrate the point and to establish that it is, for Belgian law, itself a question of the public policy to be applied to the law of marriage:

'According to Section 146 Civil Law, there is no marriage when there is no consent. The consent being an essential condition and element of the marriage, the lack of consent has as consequence the absolute invalidity of that marriage. As the parties [sc the appellant and Smith] delusively indulged in a marriage ceremony without in fact really consenting to a marriage, they behaved against public policy. The disturbancy of public order, the protection of what belongs to the essence of a real marriage and of human dignity, exact that such a sham-marriage be declared invalid.'

For reasons which I will develop later, these two opposed quotations (from Ormrod J and from the Belgian Court of Appeal) lie really at the heart of the question to be answered by your Lordships' House.

But it is now time to return to the facts. While William George Smith was still alive and, if his marriage to the appellant was a valid marriage, whilst the marriage between him and the appellant was still subsisting, the appellant was married again, this time in Italy on 12 March 1970 to Eugenio Messina, one of the principals in the organisation which had been managing her activities as a prostitute. Again the formalities were valid by the lex loci celebrationis. The marriage was void if bigamous, but effective if the marriage with Smith is declared a nullity.

Events now took a dramatic turn. On the very day of his marriage to the appellant, at the very celebration party given in honour of their union, Eugenio Messina died, leaving the appellant, if she was married to him, a widow.

Eugenio did not die a poor man. He died possessed of two freehold houses and a long leasehold house in London, valued in 1970 at £100,000. This property forms the real subject of contention between the appellant and the two successive intervening brothers of Eugenio, Salvatore and Attilio. These took out letters of administration to Eugenio's English estate. The title to this estate depends on the validity or otherwise of the appellant's marriage to Eugenio and the validity or otherwise of the appellant's marriage to Eugenio depends in turn on the validity or otherwise of her then subsisting 'marriage' *a* to William George Smith.

The appellant soon took steps designed to achieve her purpose by impugning her marriage to Smith in the English courts. At first she obtained a decree nisi for nullity, but this was set aside by Ormrod J on 7 May 1971 in the Probate, Divorce, and Admiralty Division of the High Court of Justice in London. It is reported as *Messina (formerly Smith orse Vervaeke) v Smith (Messina intervening)* [1971] 2 All ER 1046, [1971] P 322, mainly on *b* the recognition of Smith's earlier divorce. It is, however, from the transcript of Ormrod J's judgment (more relevant for the present purpose) that I have been quoting hitherto.

Apart from the attack on the Smith marriage on the ground that it was bigamous (which has now disappeared) and a further plea of duress, which was not even then persisted in, the appellant's case before Ormrod J was found by him to be false and fraudulent, and must have been considered perjured, and her appeal from his decision *c* was subsequently and by her own consent dismissed with costs on 7 March 1972. In brief her case was that she did not at the time know that the ceremony at the Paddington register office on 11 August 1954 was a marriage at all. She told a detailed, circumstantial and to my mind wholly incredible story in support of her contention. She was not believed by Ormrod J who found:

'My conclusion, therefore, on this part of the case is that the petitioner did in fact know at the time of the ceremony on 11 August 1954 that it was a marriage ceremony, and that the purpose of it was to enable her to obtain British nationality and a British passport.'

In the event, therefore, the appellant's first set of proceedings ended for her in disaster.

At this stage, and before her English appeal had been finally dismissed by consent, the appellant had resort to the Belgian courts, and this time she succeeded. On 6 December 1971 the appellant applied to the Kortrijk County Court for a declaration of nullity of her marriage to Smith. The application was originally on two grounds. The first was a repetition of her bogus claim of misapprehension of the nature of the proceedings. This was rejected by the Belgian court as res judicata. But her second claim was based on the very facts found by Ormrod J, namely that the marriage to Smith was subject to the *g* private arrangement with regard to non-cohabitation undertaken solely for the purpose of acquiring British nationality and the application to these facts of the doctrine of Belgian law to which I have already referred. This time she succeeded, and the decision of the court of first instance at Kortrijk given on 9 June 1972 was upheld on appeal by the Court of Appeal at Ghent on the grounds which I have already quoted. The intervener, Salvatore Messina, then still alive and representing the Messina family, was a party to the proceedings. The basis of the decision of the Kortrijk court was to the effect that the marriage with Smith was 'sham' or 'feigned' as containing no real consent to leading together a real conjugal life, and is based on a number of texts, included in the papers before your Lordships, clearly showing that the doctrine was based on public policy or public order considerations, as was the decision of the Ghent Court of Appeal upholding the decree. Salvatore Messina had objected that the whole issue had been dealt with by Ormrod J and was therefore 'res judicata', in effect, as we should say, by reason of cause of action estoppel. But this plea was rejected by the Belgian Courts broadly on the ground that, whilst Ormrod J's judgment was conclusive on the facts of what I have called the false and fraudulent case placed before him, it was not decisive of the second issue. They came to this view on two grounds. In the first place, they thought (as I believe erroneously) that the point had not been before Ormrod J. Second, their decision was based on grounds of public policy, or ordre public. I quote first from the opinion of the Advocate-General in the translation afforded to us:

'If you were of opinion that the English judge did sentence about the nullity of the attacked marriage due to lack of real consent—*quod non*—in that case his

sentence should have no binding force for the Belgian judge because, for the reasons
a mentioned hereabove, the said decision should be *in opposition with the principles of
public policy which are at the root of the Belgian marriage institution.'* (Emphasis mine.)

I now quote from the judgment of the Kortrijk court, as translated, accepting this view
of the Advocate-General:

> 'Fictitious or feigned marriage exists when a man and a woman, declaring to the
b > Registrar that they want to marry, do not wish at all to form a community of life:
> it then concerns a marriage without the least consent, without the intention of
> forming a permanent association and without the will to live together as husband
> and wife. Such a marriage does not respond at all to the principles of the institution
> of marriage (DE PAGE, Part I, no 563); the participants wish to evade the legal
> consequences because they pursue a mark which is completely strange to the
c > institution itself of marriage; and, as Prof. Jean DABIN puts it accurately in a
> remarquable [sic] note published in the R.C.J.B. 1947, page 37 and following:
> "More than in any other matter of law, and more in particular because of its
> importance, the earnest and solemn stamp of the institution of marriage must
> prevail on the vague formal assertion of will. The real will is thus by right and in
> fact the essential condition for the permanency of the solemnized marriage; in the
d > negative the marriage is built upon nothing, because it is only a paper marriage."'

I have already cited the relevant quotation from the Ghent Court of Appeal.

It is thus that the instant proceedings in the English courts came into being. Armed
with her Belgian decree of nullity sustained by the Ghent court, the appellant entered the
English lists for the second time, praying as I have set out in the first paragraphs in this
e speech for a declaration under RSC Ord 15, r 16 regarding the recognition of the Belgian
decree and, when she failed on this, pursuing a claim under s 45 of the Matrimonial
Causes Act 1973 for a declaration in favour of the Italian marriage with Eugenio Messina
and its subsequent recognition in the courts of Italy (with the details of which I need not
weary your Lordships, since admittedly the whole case stands or falls with the answers
to the questions of the recognition of the Belgian decree and the validity or otherwise of
the Smith marriage).

A number of interesting and disputable questions were canvassed before Waterhouse
J and the Court of Appeal, but, in the event, it was clear enough that, if either the
judgment of Ormrod J of 1971 in fact concluded the matter against the appellant per
rem judicatam, or alternatively if the matter were concluded against the appellant by any
rule of English public policy, the appeal must fail in limine, since both public policy and
the doctrine of res judicata are exceptions to the rules governing the recognition of
f foreign judgments and in particular Belgian judgments whether at common law, under
the Foreign Judgments (Reciprocal Enforcement) Act 1933 or the Anglo-Belgian
Convention for the reciprocal enforcement of judgments of May 1934: see the Reciprocal
Enforcement of Foreign Judgments (Belgium) Order in Council 1936, SR & O 1936/1169,
Sch. To some extent the various points overlap. It will therefore suffice if I summarise
my opinion on them as follows.

g First, in my view the decision of Ormrod J was a decision on the very point at issue in
the Belgian courts. Having disposed of the bogus or fraudulent claim the passage I have
quoted shows that he went on to consider what in English law was the effect of the facts
which he had found and came to a conclusion on it. The only reason why the issue was
not canvassed more fully (it had obviously been referred to at the hearing) was that the
English law on the subject was so plain. I agree with Arnold P that the 'matter in dispute
in the proceedings in Kortrijk and Ghent . . . was the subject of Ormrod J's judgment,
namely the question of the right to have the marriage between the petitioner and the
respondent declared void' (see [1981] 1 All ER 55 at 90, [1981] Fam 77 at 126). It may
be argued that, so far as regards the prayer in the second petition under s 45 of the
Matrimonial Causes Act 1973, the estoppel per rem judicatam may have been in a sense
'issue estoppel' and not 'cause of action estoppel', but, if so, it was a point which 'went to

the root of the matter on the prior occasion' (see *Hoystead v Taxation Comr* [1926] AC 155 at 171, [1925] All ER Rep 56 at 64 per Lord Shaw cited with approval by Lord Wilberforce in *Yat Tung Investment Co Ltd v Dao Heng Bank Ltd* [1975] AC 581 at 590–591).

There is a second ground on which I would found my opinion. Contrary to the view of the Court of Appeal and Waterhouse J, although I agree with them in seeing nothing offensive or unjust as between the parties in the doctrine of public policy propounded by the Belgian courts, I am of the opinion that the law of England as propounded by Ormrod J in the passage I have quoted is a doctrine of public policy and so at least in the present case takes the case outside the rules for the recognition of foreign, and, in particular, Belgian, decrees, that is at least as regards a marriage celebrated in England between a British national and an alien for an extraneous purpose of the kind contemplated by the parties in the present case, viz using the marriage as a vehicle for conferring British nationality on the alien partner so as to save her from deportation after conviction for criminal offences.

Third and whatever the limits of *Henderson v Henderson* (1843) 3 Hare 100, [1843–60] All ER Rep 378 (which I regard as a sound rule in ordinary civil litigation) may ultimately turn out to be, I believe that it must apply to a case like the present, where the petitioner in the first proceedings not merely does not rely on the grounds then already in theory available to her, but deliberately conceals the real facts (on which she now relies) from the court in order to put forward a bogus case which is radically inconsistent with them. Counsel for the appellant had no difficulty in persuading me on the basis of numerous authorities which he cited that in the case of a marriage absolutely void as between e g Oedipus and Jocasta, or e g on the ground of bigamy, or, for instance, because the parties were members of the same sex, the inquisitorial nature of the jurisdiction in nullity would prevent the court from accepting as true facts which on grounds of estoppel or misconduct would otherwise be found false or apply any legal consequences other than those which would follow from the true facts; cf for example *Miles v Chilton* (*falsely calling herself Miles*) (1849) 1 Rob Eccl 684, 163 ER 1178, *Corbett v Corbett (orse Ashley)* [1970] 2 All ER 33, [1971] P 83, *Hayward v Hayward* [1961] 1 All ER 236, [1961] P 152. But the present proceedings depend on the recognition of a Belgian decree of nullity which was obtained only after, and because, the original and fraudulent basis of the claim had been disposed of against her, and after the English judge had discovered for himself the true facts inconsistent with her bogus case and stated them in an unmistakable form. I believe that to recognise such a decree so obtained does offend the conscience of the court to such an extent that public policy precludes recognition.

In my view, therefore, the appeal fails and must be dismissed, first on the ground of res judicata, second on the ground of public policy, and third, because in the circumstances of the present case the rule in *Henderson v Henderson*, which is both a rule of public policy and an application of the law of res judicata, should apply to the attempt by the appellant to claim recognition in these courts of the Belgian decree. Indeed, it is difficult not to invoke against the appellant's attempt to claim recognition for the Belgian decree in these proceedings after what had happened in the first proceedings before Ormrod J the condemnation pronounced by Lord Wilberforce in *Yat Tung Investment Co Ltd v Dao Heng Bank Ltd* [1975] AC 581 at 590 and repeated by him in *Brisbane City Council v A–G for Queensland* [1978] 3 All ER 30 at 36, [1979] AC 411 at 425.

In the result, my advice to the House is that the appeal must be dismissed.

LORD DIPLOCK. My Lords, the facts of this sordid case have been sufficiently stated by my noble and learned friend Lord Hailsham LC. They are very special and do not, in my opinion, provide a suitable occasion for any general consideration of English rules of conflict of laws applicable to nullity of marriage. They present what appears to me to be a plain case of estoppel per rem judicatam. The Court of Appeal so dealt with it and I limit my own consideration of the appeal to this ground. The relevant res judicata is the judgment in the High Court of Ormrod J of 7 May 1971 (the Ormrod judgment) dismissing the appellant's petition for a decree of nullity of her marriage to the defendant on 11 August 1954 (the English marriage); the relevant proceedings in which the estoppel operated are those brought by the appellant in the High Court before Waterhouse J by petitions of 7 September 1973 (the recognition proceedings) and 20 April 1979 (the s 45 proceedings).

That Ormrod J had jurisdiction to hear and determine the appellant's petition for a decree of nullity of the English marriage is beyond dispute: the marriage was celebrated in this country, the defendant was resident and domiciled here. Your Lordships are not concerned with whether the Ormrod judgment was right or not; on the question of estoppel per rem judicatam all that matters is that it was final. Nor do I think your Lordships are concerned with the proceedings brought by the appellant in Belgium in the District Court of Kortrijk or the Court of Appeal of Ghent (the Belgian proceedings) except for the purpose of identifying the judgment of the District Court of Kortrijk (the Belgian judgment) that was the subject of the recognition proceedings and the grounds on which the Belgian judgment was sought by the appellant and made. I see no reason in the instant case to enter into any consideration whether the jurisdiction of the Belgian courts to hear and determine the Belgian proceedings would be recognised under English rules of conflict of laws. The instant appeal can be disposed of by this House on the assumption in favour of the appellant that it would. Nor do I find it necessary to explore what the consequences might have been if the appellant had chosen to launch her first attack on the validity of the English marriage in a Belgian court. The crucial fact is that she elected to start proceedings in the High Court of England to obtain a decree of nullity of the English marriage.

The ground on which the appellant initially based her claim that the English marriage was void in the nullity proceedings that were disposed of by the Ormrod judgment was absence of consent to marriage: she alleged she did not know that she was taking part in a marriage ceremony. This allegation, supported as it had been by her perjured evidence when obtaining the decree nisi of nullity, was rejected by Ormrod J who, in the Ormrod judgment, found the true facts to be that the appellant knew at the time of the English marriage that it was a marriage ceremony in which she was taking part and that her purpose and that of the defendant in going through it was not with an intention of living together as man and wife but to enable her, by virtue of her status as the wife of a British national, to acquire British nationality and a British passport for herself.

The true facts being found, the Ormrod judgment goes on to consider whether the legal consequence of them was that the English marriage was void. This was a matter which in the exercise of the jurisdiction of the High Court in matrimonial matters it was his duty to determine, notwithstanding the fact that it was not the way in which her petition the appellant had put the case. That Ormrod J must have heard full argument about it is evident from the fact that in the passage in the judgment (cited by Lord Hailsham LC) which sets out his conclusion that a marriage entered into for some ulterior purpose with no intention on the party of either spouse to live together as husband and wife is nevertheless a valid marriage, the judge refers to a number of authorities in support of this conclusion.

In the Belgian proceedings the ground of nullity of the English marriage on which the appellant relied was once more absence of consent. The facts relied on were what had been found in the Ormrod judgment to have been the true facts in relation to that ceremony. The Belgian courts, applying Belgian domestic law under their own rules of conflict of laws, held that on grounds of Belgian public policy (ordre public) the consent to marriage that is requisite to its validity under art 146 of the Belgian Civil Code is vitiated by the absence of an intention of the parties to the marriage ceremony to live together as man and wife. The Belgian courts did not regard the question of nullity of the English marriage on the ground of absence of consent as having become res judicata (chose jugée) as a result of the Ormrod judgment. The Belgian judgment, ie that of the District Court of Kortrijk which had been upheld by the judgment of the Court of Appeal of Ghent, was that the English marriage was null and void ab initio.

What was sought by the appellant in the recognition proceedings was a declaration by the High Court of England that the Belgian judgment was entitled to be recognised under s 8(1) of the Foreign Judgments (Reciprocal Enforcement) Act 1933, that is to say 'recognised . . . as conclusive between the parties thereto in all proceedings founded on the same cause of action'.

My Lords, I do not find it necessary to determine whether a judgment affecting matrimonial status falls within s 8(1) of the 1933 Act, for, on the assumption that it does, the combined effect of ss 8(2)(b) and 4(1) is that the foreign judgment is not entitled to be recognised as conclusive if it would have been set aside on some ground specified in s 4(1), of which the relevant grounds are those specified in paras (b) and (a)(v).

Adapting the general language of para (b) to the facts of the instant case: the Belgian judgment may be set aside if the High Court is satisfied that the matter in dispute in the Belgian proceedings had previously to the date of the Belgian judgment been the subject of a final and conclusive judgment by a court having jurisdiction in the matter, viz the Ormrod judgment. The refusal of recognition of a foreign judgment under para (b) is discretionary whereas under para (a)(v) it is compulsory. The general wording of this paragraph similarly adapted is: the Belgian judgment must be refused recognition if its enforcement would be contrary to public policy in England.

My Lords, the Ormrod judgment, which was previous in date to the Belgian judgment, made it res judicata that the English marriage was not rendered invalid on the ground of absence of consent. So far as any subsequent claim that the English marriage was a nullity on that ground by a party to the High Court proceedings in which the Ormrod judgment was given, that party would be debarred from asserting it in any English court by what, since *Thoday v Thoday* [1964] 1 All ER 341, [1964] P 181, has come to be known as 'cause of action' estoppel; and such estoppel, as I pointed out in *Thoday v Thoday* [1964] 1 All ER 341 at 352, [1964] P 181 at 198, is itself an application of a rule of public policy allowed by the courts in England and expressed in the Latin maxim nemo debet bis vexari pro una et eadem causa. Yet this is precisely what the appellant was seeking to do in the recognition proceedings. She was seeking to obtain from the High Court in England a judgment the effect of which would be to declare that her cause of action for a decree of nullity based on absence of consent was well founded despite the existence of the final and conclusive Ormrod judgment to the contrary. So far as cause of action estoppel is concerned, the appellant's position is no stronger by reason of the intervening Belgian judgment than it would have been if she had commenced fresh proceedings in the High Court before Waterhouse J claiming a decree of nullity on the facts found by Ormrod J in the Ormrod judgment on which he had already held that the appellant was not entitled to a decree of nullity. Waterhouse J was, in my view, bound to dismiss the recognition proceedings on the ground of cause of action estoppel.

In the s 45 proceedings the appellant's cause of action was not technically the same as in the original proceedings before Ormrod J in 1971. In the s 45 proceedings she sought a declaration that her marriage in Italy to Eugenio Messina on 12 March 1970 was valid; and to obtain this she had to establish that it was not bigamous, ie that it was not contracted at a time when there still subsisted a valid marriage between her and the defendant Smith. For this purpose she relied on the Belgian judgment which had apparently been declared to be valid in Italy but with what consequences in Italian law we do not know, nor has any point been made of this in argument, either in the courts below or in your Lordships' House. As in the recognition proceedings the argument on behalf of the appellant has been directed to the effect to be given to the Belgian judgment in English law. As already mentioned, the facts on which the Belgian judgment was based were the identical facts that had been found by Ormrod J to be the true facts and formed the basis of the Ormrod judgment that the English marriage was valid. To establish her cause of action for a declaration that the Italian marriage was valid one of the conditions that she had to prove had been fulfilled was that the English marriage was void. This had been decided against her by the Ormrod judgment which was res judicata so that she was debarred by what is technically 'issue estoppel' rather than 'cause of action estoppel' from asserting in an English court that that condition was fulfilled.

Issue estoppel is also an application of the same rule of public policy followed by the courts in England, as applies to cause of action estoppel. So the s 45 proceedings must in my view suffer the same fate as the recognition proceedings.

Like the Court of Appeal, I regard the unusual facts of this case, when correctly analysed, as presenting a plain example of estoppel per rem judicatam which does not call for any greater citation of authority than that which I have already made. I would dismiss the appeal.

To avoid any possible future misunderstanding in a case which it seems possible may attract some academic comment, I should make it clear that my adoption of the economic course of confining myself to estoppel per rem judicatam should not be regarded as an expression of opinion that the reasoning of Lord Hailsham LC on either of the other two grounds on which he would dismiss the appeal is incorrect.

LORD SIMON OF GLAISDALE. My Lords, I have had the advantage of reading in draft the speeches just delivered by my noble and learned friends Lord Hailsham LC and Lord Diplock. I beg leave to take advantage of Lord Hailsham LC's factual narration and of Lord Diplock's nomenclature (the Ormrod judgment etc).

In the end the case comes down to considering the effect of the Belgian judgment in our private international law. It is true that the s 45 proceedings are concerned with the Italian marriage; but the validity of that marriage depends on the capacity of the appellant to contract it; this in turn depends on whether she was subsistently bound in matrimony by the English marriage; and the appellant relies on the Belgian judgment as effectively declaring to the English law of succession that she was not.

My noble and learned friend Lord Hailsham LC bases his judgment partly on res judicata arising from the Ormrod judgment; but he invokes also wider considerations of public policy which lead to a refusal to recognise the efficacy of the Belgian judgment. My noble and learned friend Lord Diplock, while agreeing with Lord Hailsham LC, puts the main weight of his argument on res judicata.

The application of the doctrine of res judicata may itself seem to be no more than an application of English public policy. But this is apt to be misleading in a case such as the instant. It is true that the doctrine of res judicata has two bases: first, that it is a hardship on an individual that he should be twice vexed with the same matter and, second, public policy (interest reipublicae ut sit finis litium). Nevertheless, the doctrine of res judicata consists of legal rules; and public policy, in the sense in which it arises in this appeal, denotes consideration of wider social interests which call for modification of a normal legal rule (in this case the conflict rule which normally leads to accord of recognition to the judgment of a foreign court of competent jurisdiction). That the distinction between the two aspects of the appeal, res judicata and public policy, is a real one can be seen by consideration that, even if there had been no English proceedings culminating in the Ormrod judgment, your Lordships might still be concerned with whether English public policy calls for refusal of recognition of the Belgian judgment and for affirmation of the validity of the English marriage.

Notwithstanding any predilection for a narrow rather than a wide ground of decision, I agree with my noble and learned friends on the issue of public policy as well as of res judicata.

Res judicata

The appellant relied on two matters in seeking from the Belgian court a decree of nullity in respect of the English marriage: (1) that she had been mistaken as to the nature of the formalities at the Paddington register office; (2) that, in accordance with the facts as found by Ormrod J, it was no marriage at all. As to (1) the Belgian court held that the Ormrod judgment constituted rem judicatam against the appellant; but not (2).

In coming to this decision the Belgian court was understandably unaware of the peculiar duty of a judge in English matrimonial proceedings. He does not exercise the role of a merely passive arbiter over adversary proceedings. Having a claim for nullity before him, based on an allegation of absence of consent, and having ascertained the true facts, Ormrod J, as a matrimonial judge, was bound to act as he did, namely consider whether the marriage was in the true circumstances null and void as alleged. That this is what he did appears from the following passage in part of the Ormrod judgment which is not reported:

> 'In one sense it was an unreal marriage in that it was never intended that the normal relationship of husband and wife should be established between Mr Smith and herself. But this cannot affect *the question which I have to determine, whether the marriage was, in law, a valid marriage.* Where a man and a woman consent to marry one another in a formal ceremony, conducted in accordance with the formalities required by law, knowing that it is a marriage ceremony, it is immaterial that they do not intend to live together as man and wife.' (My emphasis.)

Having addressed himself to this question, Ormrod J found the marriage to be valid, and dismissed the petition. I doubt whether he heard argument on the point; it is clear beyond argument. If he had found that the true facts rendered the marriage void he would (possibly ordering the petition to be amended appropriately) have pronounced a decree of nullity. The validity of the marriage on the true facts thereby passed, in English law, into rem judicatam. It was established as a fact, and could not be relitigated.

Two conflict rules are relevant to the decision of the Belgian court that the alleged invalidity of the English marriage by reason of its ulterior purpose and the common intention not to cohabit was not res judicata by Ormrod J. First, English courts never examine the judgment of a foreign court to see whether it has correctly applied its own or any relevant rule of foreign (even English) law: see *Godard v Gray* (1870) LR 6 QB 139; *Castrique v Imrie* (1870) LR 4 HL 414, [1861–73] All ER Rep 508. But, second, rules of adjectival (in contradistinction to substantive) law, including rules of evidence, fall for decision according to the lex fori (in the instant case, English law). Whether an estoppel per rem judicatam is substantive or adjective is not entirely clear (see e g *Dicey and Morris on the Conflict of Laws* (10th edn, 1980) vol 2, p 1190). My own view is that the estoppel per rem judicatam in question here is on principle a rule of adjectival, evidentiary law and that the balance of authority also favours this view. But I do not pause to undertake the considerable argument involved, in view of the fact that in my judgment the appeal also fails on the issue of public policy.

There is abundant authority that cause of action estoppel applies to foreign judgments, and on principle the same must be true of issue estoppel: see *Cheshire and North on Private International Law* (10th edn, 1979) pp 651–655, 658. Section 4(1)(b) of the Foreign Judgments (Reciprocal Enforcement) Act 1933, though dealing not with recognition but with setting aside a registered foreign judgment on the ground of res judicata, lends some weight to the authorities to which *Cheshire and North* refers.

Assuming, as I do, that English law applies, I agree with my noble and learned friend Lord Hailsham LC that the much quoted judgment of Wigram V-C in *Henderson v Henderson* (1843) 3 Hare 100 at 114–115, [1843–60] All ER Rep 378 at 381–382 would if necessary be applicable to the instant case:

> 'The plea of *res judicata* applies, except in special cases, not only to points upon which the court was actually required by the parties to form an opinion and pronounce a judgment, but to every point which properly belonged to the subject of litigation, and which the parties, exercising reasonable diligence, might have brought forward at the time.'

It seems to me that parties seeking to impugn a marriage should be expected to bring forward at the outset whatever they allege might invalidate it and not proceed from one alleged defect to another and from forum to forum. What Lord Shaw said in *Hoystead v Taxation Comr* [1926] AC 155 at 165–166, [1925] All ER Rep 56 at 62 is particularly pertinent in the instant case:

> 'Parties are not permitted to begin fresh litigations because of new views they may entertain of the law of the case, or new versions which they present as to what

should be a proper apprehension by the Court of the legal result ... If this were permitted litigation would have no end, except when legal ingenuity is exhausted. It is a principle of law that this cannot be permitted, and there is abundant authority reiterating that principle.'

Public policy

It is clear from the citations made by my noble and learned friend Lord Hailsham LC from the Belgian proceedings that the Belgian judgment was the result of application of Belgian public policy to the same facts as were finally ascertained by Ormrod J. That the English rule, which leads to a contrary result, is also based on public policy appears most clearly from *Brodie v Brodie* [1917] P 271, [1916–17] All ER Rep 237, though that case is only the culmination of a long line of authority. In *Brodie v Brodie* a wife, petitioning for restitution of conjugal rights, had been expecting to be delivered of a child of whom the respondent was the father. She pressed him to marry her; and he agreed to do so if, and only if, she would sign an agreement to separate after marriage. This she did; and a ceremony took place forthwith at a register office. It was held that the agreement not to cohabit was void as against public policy; and a decree of restitution of conjugal rights was pronounced. Such a decree is a judgment affirming the validity of the marriage in question.

English and Belgian law, both based clearly on respective public policy, being thus contradictory as to the validity and consequences of a marriage such as that instantly in issue, the question arises whether English law is bound to surrender its own concept of the public policy involved and defer to that of Belgian law as expressed in the Belgian judgment.

If your Lordships should hold that English public policy justifies refusal to accord binding recognition to the Belgian judgment, your Lordships are, in the light of *Brodie v Brodie*, acting within the principle stated by Lord Thankerton in *Fender v Mildmay* [1937] 3 All ER 402 at 414, [1938] AC 1 at 23:

'... the proper function of the courts in questions of public policy ... is to expound, and not to expand, such policy. That does not mean that they are precluded from applying an existing principle of public policy to a new set of circumstances, where such circumstances are clearly within the scope of the policy.'

Non-recognition of the Belgian judgment will, of course, involve a 'limping marriage'. This is a situation which our law will generally seek to avoid; and under an ideal system of conflict of laws it would not arise. But it is bound to happen in a juristically imperfect world where there is not universal agreement on such concepts as characterisation and the appropriate connecting factor. Its main evil, that a marriage valid in one country might be invalidated in another with which a party has some real and substantial connection, does not seem to arise here. Although in her petition in the s 45 proceedings the appellant claimed to be a British subject, it appears both in that petition and in the earlier one in the recognition proceedings that she is permanently resident in Belgium; she may, moreover, have double nationality, the Belgian court made no reference to English as her personal law.

There is abundant authority that an English court will decline to recognise or apply what would otherwise be the appropriate foreign rule of law when to do so would be against English public policy; although the court will be even slower to invoke public policy in the field of conflict of laws than when a purely municipal legal issue is involved. There is little authority for refusing, on the ground of public policy, to recognise an otherwise conclusive foreign judgment, no doubt because the conclusiveness of a judgment of a foreign court of competent jurisdiction is itself buttressed by the rule of public policy interest reipublicae ut sit finis litium, the 'commonwealth' in conflict of laws extending to the whole international community. Nevertheless, there is some judicial authority that the English court will in an appropriate case refuse on the ground of public policy to accord recognition to the judgment of a foreign court of competent jurisdiction (see *Re Macartney, Macfarlane v Macartney* [1921] 1 Ch 522; see also *Formosa v Formosa* [1962] 3 All ER 419, [1963] P 259, as explained in *Lepre v Lepre* [1963] 2 All ER 49 at 57–58, [1965] P 52 at 64–65); and the leading textbooks acknowledge this exception to the general recognition rules (see, e g *Dicey and Morris on the Conflict of Laws* (10th edn, 1980) p 1086, r 188, repeating a rule similarly expressed in earlier editions). Although an English court will exercise such a jurisdiction with extreme reserve, in my judgment the instant is a case where it should be invoked, for the following reasons:

(1) Quite apart from its having been legally adopted and its being consonant with our general law of contract (see *Dalrymple v Dalrymple* (1811) 2 Hag Con 54 at 105–106, 161 ER 665 at 683 per Sir William Scott), the English policy towards the sort of marriage in question here seems as soundly based, morally, socially and in reason, as the Belgian; and there appears to be no inherent reason why, giving every weight to the international spirit of the conflict of laws, we should surrender our own policy to that of any foreign society. The type of 'sham' marriage in question is not necessarily entered into for a nefarious purpose. Auden married the daughter of the great German novelist, Thomas Mann, in order to facilitate her escape from persecution in Nazi Germany; see also *Szechter (orse Karsov) v Szechter* [1970] 3 All ER 905, [1971] P 286.

(2) Although an English court will take cognisance of English public policy irrespective of plea, it hardly lies in the mouth of the appellant to invoke in her favour the maxim interest reipublicae ut sit finis litium. She started proceedings in England, entered an appeal to the English Court of Appeal, switched to the Belgian forum, and then returned to England in the recognition proceedings. And here she is as appellant in your Lordships' House.

(3) English proceedings (in which English public policy became relevant on the ascertainment of the true facts) were started by the appellant before ever she invoked the jurisdiction of the Belgian court to apply their own contradictory rule of public policy; and the Ormrod judgment expressing English public policy towards this marriage was, therefore, prior to the Belgian judgment expressing their contrary public policy.

(4) The characterisation of the defect in this marriage in the eyes of Belgian law is not altogether easy; nor, in consequence, is it easy to determine what is the proper choice of law to apply to it. It is understandable to invoke the personal law when the personality and the law are closely intermeshed in a juristic situation. Thus, capacity is the ability to perform an act with desired legal consequences; volition and law are therein converging forces towards a juristic resultant; so that it is plausible to invoke the personal law as the law which is relevant. Then, status is the condition of belonging to a class of society to which the law ascribes peculiar rights and obligations, capacities and incapacities; so that the choice of the personal law for a judgment as to status may be justified. Yet again, reality of consent to marry has been on such a basis referred to the personal law: see *Way v Way* [1949] 2 All ER 959 at 963, [1950] P 71 at 79 and on appeal sub nom *Kenward v Kenward* [1950] 2 All ER 297 at 302, [1951] P 124 at 133. But in the instant case there is no question (once the validity of the Nevada divorce had been disposed of) that both parties had full capacity to marry. Nor was it questionable (once the true facts had been ascertained) that they were entirely and unimpairedly ad idem; both understood that they were joining in a ceremony of marriage; both intended that it should confer on each the status of married person; neither intended that any further right or obligation should flow from this status (such as cohabitation or mutual maintenance). The only question is whether this constituted a marriage, as to which English and Belgian public policy, as expressed in their respective laws, have returned different answers. If the crucial distinction is between forms and ceremonies on the one hand and essential validity on the other, this was a matter of essential validity. If, as seems to me to be intelligible, questions of capacity and perhaps reality of consent are to be hived off and separately considered, this was a question of quintessential validity; and I can see no reason why the personal law should be invoked, particularly as the personal law of the parties differed and, moreover, each imported a different connecting factor (domicile and nationality respectively). I venture to propose two other possible choices of the law to adjudge this sort of quintessential validity: first, the lex loci celebrationis; and, second and to my

mind preferably, the law of the territory with which the marriage has the most real and
substantial connection.

The lex loci celebrationis has the authority of the frequently cited passage from the
opinion of Lord Brougham in *Warrender v Warrender* (1835) 2 Cl & Fin 488 at 530, 6 ER
1239 at 1254:

> '... the question always must be, Did the parties intend to contract marriage?
> And if they did that which in the place they were in is deemed a marriage, they
> cannot reasonably, or sensibly, or safely, be considered otherwise than as intending
> a marriage contract.'

And in *Berthiaume v Dastous* [1930] AC 79 at 83, [1929] All ER Rep 111 at 114 Viscount
Dunedin, delivering the judgment of the Privy Council, said (albeit going wider than the
issue, which related to formalities, demanded):

> 'If there is one question better settled than any other in international law, it is that
> as regards marriage—putting aside the question of capacity—locus regit actum. If
> a marriage is good by the laws of the country where it is effected, it is good all the
> world over ...'

The second test is the application to choice of law of the criterion which your Lordships
proposed in *Indyka v Indyka* [1967] 2 All ER 689, [1969] 1 AC 33 in considering
recognition of the jurisdiction of a foreign divorce court. This criterion of a real and
substantial connection seems to me to be useful and relevant in considering the choice of
law for testing, if not all questions of essential validity, at least the question of the sort of
quintessential validity in issue in this appeal, the question which law's public policy
should determine the validity of the marriage. The territorial law with which a marriage
has the most real and substantial connection will often be the law of the prospective
matrimonial home; this was the law favoured to govern all questions of essential validity
by *Cheshire*, and by Lord Greene MR (Somervell LJ concurring) in *De Reneville v De
Reneville* [1948] 1 All ER 56 at 61–62, [1948] P 100 at 114. The test of the most real and
substantial connection may obviate some of the objections to the test of the prospective
matrimonial home, eg that the latter gives no guidance where no matrimonial home is
clearly indicated or, as here, no cohabitation at all is proposed. Undoubtedly, in the
instant case, England was the territory with which the marriage had the most real and
substantial connection: the ceremony was in England, the 'husband' was of English
domicile and British nationality, the 'wife' was to assume British nationality and take
advantage of it, and she was to become permanently resident in England. There was
indeed no other territorial law with which the marriage had any real or substantial
connection.

If, as I think, our choice-of-law rule (whether Lord Brougham's or the extension of the
Indyka principle) indicates English law as determinant of the validity of this marriage, it
provides a potent reason for preferring the legally recognised English public policy and
thus for refusing recognition to the Belgian judgment based on a contrary public policy.

(5) The appellant intended by the marriage to, and did as a result of the marriage, take
advantage of English public law. I do not say that a party can by approbation convert a
void or non-existent into a valid marriage, or that anyone can be 'married by estoppel'.
Nor do I think that the appellant's career of criminal sexual prostitution or her perjury
are relevant factors. But her having taken advantage of English public law in
consequence of the marriage does seem to me to be a factor to be taken into account in
determining whether to prefer English public policy as to the validity of the marriage,
and thus refuse to accord binding force to the Belgian judgment.

(6) The real contest behind this appeal is as to succession to Eugenio Messina's estate
in England. This being immovable property it is governed by the lex situs, ie English
law. No doubt English law extends to its conflict rules. But the fact that the law of
primary reference is English seems to me to be a marginal consideration pointing in

favour of preferring the public policy expressed in English law to the exclusion of that expressed in the Belgian judgment.

The procedural point

Your Lordships did not find it necessary to hear argument on this point (the refusal of a declaration under RSC Ord 16, r 15 and direction of a petition under s 45). As to this, the judgment of a Court of Appeal particularly well qualified to pronounce stands for guidance.

I would dismiss the appeal.

LORD KEITH OF KINKEL. My Lords, I have had the benefit of reading in draft the speech delivered by my noble and learned friend Lord Diplock. I agree with it, and for the reasons which he gives I too would dismiss the appeal.

LORD BRANDON OF OAKBROOK. My Lords, I have had the advantage of reading in draft the speeches prepared by my noble and learned friends Lord Hailsham LC, Lord Diplock and Lord Simon. I agree that the appeal should be dismissed, first, on the ground of res judicata and, second, on the ground of public policy.

Appeal dismissed.

Solicitors: *Theodore Goddard & Co* (for the appellant); *Lieberman, Leigh & Co* (for the respondent Messina); *Treasury Solicitor.*

Mary Rose Plummer   Barrister.

R v Boyesen

HOUSE OF LORDS
LORD WILBERFORCE, LORD FRASER OF TULLYBELTON, LORD SCARMAN, LORD ROSKILL AND LORD BRIDGE OF HARWICH
10 MARCH, 22 APRIL 1982

Drugs – Dangerous drugs – Unlawful possession – Visible and measurable particles – Traces of dangerous drug – Relevance of quantity possessed –Test to be applied – Whether quantity must be usable for possession to be unlawful – Whether possession unlawful merely if quantity visible, tangible and measurable – Misuse of Drugs Act 1971, s 5(1)(2).

In order to obtain a conviction for the offence of being in possession of a controlled drug, contrary to s 5(2)[a] of the Misuse of Drugs Act 1971, it is not necessary for the prosecution to prove possession of a quantity of the drug that is usable but merely possession of any quantity, however minute, that is visible, tangible and measurable. Thus, 5 mg of cannabis resin is sufficient in size for possession of such a quantity to be unlawful under s 5(1) of the 1971 Act (see p 162 c and p 166 b to d and j to p 167 b, post).

    Keane v Gallacher 1980 JC 77 approved.

    R v Carver [1978] 3 All ER 60 overruled.

    Bocking v Roberts [1973] 3 All ER 962 explained.

    Where the quantity of a controlled drug in the custody or control of a person is so minute that his knowledge of it canot be proved, then his possession of it cannot be established (see p 162 c and p 166d to f and j to p 167b, post).

    Dictum of Lord Diplock, in *DPP v Brooks* [1974] 2 All ER at 842 explained.

Notes

For unlawful possession of a controlled drug, see 11 Halsbury's Laws (4th edn) para 1092.

    For the Misuse of Drugs Act 1971, s 5, see 41 Halsbury's Statutes (3rd edn) 884.

Cases referred to in opinions

Bocking v Roberts [1973] 3 All ER 962, [1974] QB 307, [1973] 3 WLR 465, DC, Digest (Cont Vol D) 645, 243bcfa.

DPP v Brooks [1974] 2 All ER 840, [1974] AC 862, [1974] 2 WLR 899, PC, Digest (Cont Vol D) 646, *291c.

Keane v Gallacher 1980 JC 77, 1980 SLT 144.

Police v Emirali [1976] 1 NZLR 286.

R v Carver [1978] 3 All ER 60, [1978] QB 472, [1978] 2 WLR 872, CA, Digest (Cont Vol E) 154, 9164a.

R v Worsell [1969] 2 All ER 1183, [1970] 1 WLR 111, CA, Digest (Cont Vol C) 670, 243bcc.

Searle v Randolph [1972] Crim LR 779, DC.

Warner v Metropolitan Police Comr [1968] 2 All ER 356, [1969] 2 AC 256, [1968] 2 WLR 1303, HL, Digest (Cont Vol C) 671, 243d.

Appeal

The Crown appealed with leave of the Appeal Committee of the House of Lords granted on 23 July 1981 against the decision of the Court of Appeal, Criminal Division (Shaw LJ, Wien and Bingham JJ) on 17 July 1980 allowing an appeal by the respondent, Peregrine

---

a   Section 5, so far as material, provides:

    '(1) Subject to any regulations under section 7 of this Act for the time being in force, it shall not be lawful for a person to have a controlled drug in his possession.

    (2) Subject to section 28 of this Act and to subsection (4) below, it is an offence for a person to have a controlled drug in his possession in contravention of subsection (1) above . . .'

Boyesen, against his conviction in the Crown Court at Cambridge on 24 January 1979 before his Honour Judge Wild and a jury on a charge of unlawful possession of a class B controlled drug, namely 5 mg of cannabis resin, contrary to s 5(1) and (2) of the Misuse of Drugs Act 1971. The facts are set out in the opinion of Lord Scarman.

Desmond Fennell QC and *John Farmer* for the Crown.
Barbara A Calvert QC and *Anthony Shaw* for the respondent.

Their Lordships took time for consideration.

22 April. The following opinions were delivered.

LORD WILBERFORCE. My Lords, I concur with Lord Scarman.

LORD FRASER OF TULLYBELTON. My Lords, I have had the advantage of reading in draft the speech of my noble and learned friend Lord Scarman. I agree with it, and, for the reasons explained by him, I would allow the appeal and restore the conviction.

LORD SCARMAN. My Lords, the certified point of law in this appeal is:

'Whether the offence of possession of a controlled drug contrary to section 5(2) of the Misuse of Drugs Act 1971 is only proved if the quantity of the drug detected is capable of use.'

Strictly, the point arises on s 5(1) which makes the possession unlawful. Section 5(2) merely creates the offence of a contravention of sub-s (1).

There is a difference of opinion on the point between the Court of Appeal in England and the High Court of Justiciary in Scotland. In the instant case the Court of Appeal followed an earlier decision of the court in which it was held that—

'if the evidence be that the quantity is so minute that it is not usable in any manner which the Misuse of Drugs Act 1971 was intended to prohibit, then a conviction for being in possession of the minute quantity of the drug would not be justified.'

(See *R v Carver* [1978] 3 All ER 60 at 63, [1978] QB 472 at 478.) The High Court of Justiciary, however, has held that 'It is the possession of the controlled drug which is made punishable by section 5(1) and (2) [of the Act], not its use or potential use', and has criticised the decision in *Carver*'s case as importing into s 5(1) a qualification to the term 'controlled drug' which is not to be found in the subsection, namely 'which is capable of being used': see *Keane v Gallacher* 1980 JC 77 at 81 (more fully reported 1980 SLT 144).

On 24 January 1979 the respondent was convicted at the Crown Court at Cambridge of unlawful possession, on 9 May 1978, of 5 mg of cannabis resin, a class B controlled drug. At the conclusion of the prosecution's case the trial judge overruled a defence submission that the prosecution must prove possession not merely of a quantity of the drug but of a quantity sufficient to be usable in any way which the Act was intended to prohibit. He was referred to the decision in *Carver*'s case, but ruled that if, which was the evidence for the Crown, the quantity could be seen, touched, and manipulated it was usable. When he came to sum up the case to the jury, he dealt with the defence that the quantity was too small to justify a conviction by giving this direction:

'All you need to be satisfied of in this case is that it could be seen, touched and manipulated and put into a cigarette. Therefore, in my direction to you it is capable of being possessed, and the only question is, "Was it possessed?" and the only argument advanced to meet the fact that it was . . . is that [the accused] says that he did not know that it was there.'

The Court of Appeal allowed the respondent's appeal against conviction. Its 'ratio decidendi is not absolutely clear. It seems to have been that the trial judge failed to leave to the jury the question whether the minute quantity, 5 mg, was capable of being used. But in criticising the prosecution and trial judge, the court went further: it criticised the prosecuting authority for bringing a case where the quantity was so minute and the judge for failing to accede to the defence submission 'that there was no usable quantity of cannabis resin in this case'. It would appear, therefore, that it was also the view of the court that the Crown had not established a case fit to go to the jury.

The facts and the statutory context within which the alleged offence falls to be considered are within a narrow compass. On 9 May 1978 police officers entered a house in Cambridge to execute a search warrant. They were looking for drugs. The respondent arrived at the house and was met by a police officer who searched him. He was found to be carrying a small metal tin in which was a tiny polythene bag containing traces of a brown substance. He was cautioned and arrested on suspicion of being in possession of a controlled drug. According to the police officer's evidence, he then answered some questions, including the following:

'Q. What is in the tin? A. I use it for my cannabis.
Q. Is that why the plastic bag has traces in it? A. Yes, that's all I've got left.'

The respondent denied this conversation, but the jury's verdict requires the House for the purpose of this appeal to accept that it took place.

Dr Fouweather, a forensic scientist, later examined the tin, the bag and the traces of brown substance. He found that the substance was cannabis resin, that it was visible to the eye and that it was a measurable quantity, namely 5 mg. He accepted a description that 1 mg would cover a pin-head. In cross-examination he was asked whether 1 mg of cannabis resin was a usable substance and answered Yes, adding that it was usable 'in the sense that you could pick it up and place it in a reefer cigarette and/or a pipe'. He refused to venture an opinion whether 1 mg would be of any value to anybody (the normal range for a reefer cigarette being said to be within 50 to 100 mg). Pressed further in cross-examination, he said he thought it was usable because it was 'tangible' and 'you can manipulate it'. He summed up his test of quantity and usability as being that of visibility and manipulation and was of the opinion that 5 mg met the test.

The statutory offence may be described as an absolute one in the sense that the prosecution establish it by proving possession without authority: see s 5(1) and (2) of the Act. Section 28 provides for certain defences which, if they are to succeed, the defendant must prove on a balance of probabilities. They do not arise for consideration in this appeal.

Possession is a deceptively simple concept. It denotes a physical control or custody of a thing plus knowledge that you have it in your custody or control. You may possess a thing without knowing or comprehending its nature; but you do not possess it unless you know you have it. I would adopt the description of possession given by Lord Wilberforce in *Warner v Metropolitan Police Comr* [1968] 2 All ER 356 at 393, [1969] 2 AC 256 at 310–311:

'The question to which an answer is required, and in the end a jury must answer it, is whether in the circumstances the accused should be held to have possession of the substance rather than mere control. In order to decide between these two, the jury should, in my opinion, be invited to consider all the circumstances—to use again the words of POLLOCK AND WRIGHT [*Possession in the Common Law* (1888) p 119]—the "modes or events" by which the custody commences and the legal incident in which it is held. By these I mean relating them to typical situations, that they must consider the manner and circumstances in which the substance, or something which contains it, has been received, what knowledge or means of knowledge or guilty knowledge as to the presence of the substance, or as to the nature of what has been received, the accused had at the time of receipt or thereafter up to the moment when he is found with it, his legal relation to the substance or package (including his right of access to it). On such matters as these (not exhaustively stated) they must make the decision whether, in addition to physical control, he has, or ought to have imputed to him the intention to possess, or knowledge that he does possess, what is in fact a prohibited substance. If he has this intention or knowledge, it is not additionally necessary that he should know the nature of the substance.'

There can be no doubt that the respondent had in his pocket a tin and bag in which there was a measurable quantity of a brown substance which on analysis proved to be cannabis resin, a class B controlled drug and he knew he had the tin, the bag and the traces of the brown substance (which on analysis were measured as 5 mg). The only question, therefore, is whether the quantity was too minute to be recognised by the law. It was present in the respondent's custody and control as a matter of fact; but was it sufficient in size for its possession to be unlawful under s 5(1) of the Misuse of Drugs Act 1971?

The case law reveals a division of judicial opinion as to the legal criterion for determining whether a person has in his possession a controlled drug. The question arose on a case stated in the Divisional Court in *Bocking v Roberts* [1973] 3 All ER 962, [1974] QB 307. Lord Widgery CJ, giving the majority judgment of the court, said ([1973] 3 All ER 962 at 964, [1974] QB 307 at 309):

'In my judgment it is quite clear that when dealing with a charge of possessing a dangerous drug without authority, the ordinary maxim of de minimis is not to be applied, in other words, if it is clearly established that the accused had a dangerous drug in his possession without authority, it is no answer for him to say: "Oh, but the quantity of the drug which I possessed was so small that the law should take no account of it". The doctrine of de minimis as such in my judgment does not apply, but on the other hand, since the offence is possessing a dangerous drug, it is quite clear that the prosecution have to prove that there was some of the drug in the possession of the accused to justify the charge, and the distinction which I think has to be drawn in cases of this kind is whether the quantity of the drug was enough to justify the conclusion that he was possessed of a quantity of the drug or whether on the other hand the traces were so slight that they really indicated no more than that at some previous time he had been in possession of the drug. It seems to me that that is the distinction that has to be drawn, although its application to individual cases is by no means easy.'

Lord Widgery CJ formulated no test such as the 'usable' test which the Court of Appeal later accepted. Directing his attention to the statutory formulation of the offence, ie having a drug in one's possession, he held that the question the law requires to be answered is whether the traces found were so slight as to amount to nothing other than an indication that the accused had been possessed of the drug at some previous time. Lord Widgery CJ was here emphasising the need for a practical approach; and he formulated a test which, whatever its limitation in logic, enables a jury or a bench of magistrates to make a commonsense judgment on the facts of a case without importing into the offence an element, ie 'usability', which is not mentioned in the statute creating it.

There was nothing in the ruling of Lord Widgery CJ in *Bocking's* case which conflicted with previous authority, though the origin of the 'usable' test can be detected in an earlier decision of the Court of Appeal, *R v Worsell* [1969] 2 All ER 1183, [1970] 1 WLR 111. The court in that case, of course, had under consideration the Dangerous Drugs Act 1965, but the point was the same. The accused was charged with possession of two or three tiny drops of heroin remaining in a tube. Delivering the judgment of the court, Salmon LJ said that the court had come to the clear conclusion that the tube was empty. 'There was nothing in reality in the tube.' The droplets were invisible, and could be neither measured nor poured out. The court was, therefore, applying the same test as that which later commended itself to Lord Widgery CJ in *Bocking's* case. But Salmon LJ, explaining the court's view that the tube was in reality empty, did say: 'Whatever it [ie the tube] contained, obviously it could not be used and could not be sold.'

Another relevant decision, also under the 1965 Act, is *Searle v Randolph* [1972] Crim LR 779, in which a defendant was convicted of being in possession of 3 mg of cannabis contained in a cigarette.

In *R v Carver* [1978] 3 All ER 60, [1978] QB 472 the Court of Appeal had to consider a case in which the quantities alleged as being in the accused's possession were an item of 20 μg and another item of 2 mg. The court expressly accepted the reasoning of Lord Widgery CJ in *Bocking's* case but went on to formulate a further test. Michael Davies J, delivering the judgment of the court, put it thus ([1978] 3 All ER 60 at 63, [1978] QB 472 at 477–478):

'However, this court is of the opinion that, whilst it would be inappropriate to rely on the ordinary maxim of de minimis, if the quantity of the drug found is so minute as in the light of common sense to amount to nothing or, even if that cannot in a particular case be said, if the evidence be that the quantity is so minute that it is not usable in any manner which the Misuse of Drugs Act 1971 was intended to prohibit, then a conviction for being in possession of the minute quantity of the drug would not be justified.'

In this passage, the court gave two rulings: (1) if the quantity is so minute as in the light of common sense to amount to nothing, there is no offence; but (2) even if the quantity does amount to something, no offence is established unless the drug is present in a quantity usable in some manner which the Act was intended to prohibit.

The Crown submits that the second ruling is wrong in law, and that the error is that the court imported the adjectival expression 'capable of being used in a manner prohibited by law' into s 5(1) of the Act. The language of the subsection, it is submitted, is such as to constitute a prohibition on possession without any qualification other than those to which express reference is made in sub-ss (1) and (2). There is no reference in either subsection to 'usability'.

This is a powerful submission. The respondent seeks to counter it in two ways. It is submitted, first, that it would be contrary to the intention of the Act to extend the prohibition on possession to a quantity which could not itself be the subject of misuse. The Act strikes at misuse of drugs: possession is unlawful only because it enables misuse to occur. Second, counsel for the respondent, in the course of her able argument, drew attention to a number of unreported cases in which the Court of Appeal has followed with approval the decision in *Carver's* case.

My Lords, I find myself entirely persuaded by the reasoning of the Lord Justice-Clerk (Wheatley) in *Keane v Gallacher* 1980 JC 77 at 81–82:

'The decision in *R. v. Carver* seems to entail the importation into section 5(1) of a qualification to the term "controlled drug", namely "which is capable of being used". If that be the case, it would add an additional onus on the prosecution to prove that fact. If Parliament had intended that such a qualification should be added it would have been simple to give express effect to it. The plain unqualified words of the subsection simply refer to a controlled drug and *ex facie* anything which is capable of being identified as a controlled drug is struck at by the subsection. It is the possession of the controlled drug which is made punishable by section 5(1) and (2), not its use or potential use. There is no ambiguity in the words used and no absurdity is produced. If it is argued that anything short of a "usable" amount of the controlled drug produces an absurdity in section 5(1), it is an argument which we cannot accept. The plain wording of that subsection makes "identification in an acceptable manner" and not "capable of being used" the test, and there does not appear to us to be any absurdity in that.'

If it be said that an 'identification' test is itself not expressly stated in the subsection, I would reply that it is implicit. Unless the thing possessed is shown by evidence to be a a controlled drug, there is no offence.

If I were disposed, which I am not, to add to the subsection by judicial interpretation words which are not there, I would not accept the words suggested, ie capable of being used in a manner prohibited by the Act. The uncertainty and imprecision of such a criterion of criminal responsibility would in themselves be mischievous. But, further, the view that possession is only serious enough, as a matter of legal policy, to rank as an b offence if the quantity possessed is itself capable of being misused is a highly dubious one. Small quantities can be accumulated. It is a perfectly sensible view that the possession of any quantity which is visible, tangible, measurable and 'capable of manipulation' (to borrow Dr Fouweather's term) is a serious matter to be prohibited if the law is to be effective against trafficking in dangerous drugs and their misuse. I find, therefore, no assistance in the policy argument addressed to the House. c

Accordingly, I have concluded that the 'usability' test is incorrect in law. The question is not usability but possession. Quantity is, however, of importance in two respects when one has to determine whether or not an accused person has a controlled drug in his possession. First, is the quantity sufficient to enable a court to find as a matter of fact that it amounts to something? If it is visible, tangible, and measurable, it is certainly something. The question is one of fact for the common sense of the tribunal. This was d the decision in *Bocking's* case [1973] 3 All ER 962, [1974] QB 307, and I believe Lord Widgery CJ's approach to the question was correct in law.

Second, quantity may be relevant to the issue of knowledge. Lord Diplock, delivering the judgment of the Privy Council in *DPP v Brooks* [1974] 2 All ER 840 at 842, [1974] AC 862 at 866, defined possession in the case of dangerous drugs as follows: e

'In the ordinary use of the word "possession", one has in one's possession whatever is, to one's own knowledge, physically in one's custody or under one's physical control.'

If the quantity in custody or control is minute, the question arises: was it so minute that it cannot be proved that the accused knew he had it? If knowledge cannot be proved, f possession would not be established. A good illustration of the relevance of quantity to knowledge is to be found in the New Zealand case, *Police v Emirali* [1976] 1 NZLR 286. In the present case, the question, however, does not arise. On the evidence which, after a correct direction on knowledge, the jury accepted the respondent knew that the traces of brown substance were there. He also knew, though this knowledge would only g become relevant if he had sought to establish a defence under s 28 of the Act, that the brown substance was cannabis.

Finally, I would make two comments on the criticisms levelled by the Court of Appeal at the prosecuting authority and the trial judge. In my opinion, they were not justified. The Chief Constable of Cambridge, who authorised the prosecution, was fully justified in doing so. He was correct in law and the reasons which led him to decide in favour of prosecution were not known to the Court of Appeal and were not that court's h business unless they amounted to an abuse of process, which was certainly not the fact in the present case. The trial judge certainly made his view of the law very plain in his exchanges with counsel for the defence; but there is no harm in that, even if he later be held to have been wrong. It would be a matter for serious criticism if he could be shown to have defied the ruling in *Carver's* case, which he was bound to follow. But he did no such thing: he put an interpretation on it which did not commend itself to the Court of j Appeal. In effect, I think he reached a correct conclusion; but that in itself would not excuse him, if he had in truth ignored the decision in *Carver's* case.

For these reasons I would allow the appeal and restore the conviction. The sentence, a fine of £25, and a contribution of £150 towards the costs of the prosecution are not before your Lordships' House. The appellant should have his costs here and below out of central funds.

LORD ROSKILL. My Lords, I have had the advantage of reading in draft the speech
a prepared by my noble and learned friend Lord Scarman, with which I agree. I too would
allow the appeal and restore the conviction.

LORD BRIDGE OF HARWICH. My Lords, I have had the advantage of reading in
advance the speech of my noble and learned friend Lord Scarman. I agree with it and for
the reasons he gives I too would allow the appeal.

b *Certified question answered in the negative, order of the Court of Appeal of 17 July 1980 reversed
and the conviction by the Crown Court at Cambridge on 24 January 1979 restored.*

Solicitors: *Sharpe, Pritchard & Co*, agents for *D C Beal*, Huntingdon (for the appellant);
Bindman & Partners, agents for *Peter Soar*, Cambridge (for the respondent).

Mary Rose Plummer   Barrister.

Leadbitter v Hodge Finance Ltd and others

QUEEN'S BENCH DIVISION AT NEWCASTLE UPON TYNE
d BUSH J
23, 26 JANUARY 1981

*Practice – Parties – Adding defendant – Amendment of writ – Date from which added defendant
becomes party to proceedings – Claim against proposed defendant more than three years from
date on which cause of action accrued – Plaintiff claiming cause not time-barred because limitation
period running from date he acquired knowledge of relevant facts – Procedure for determining
issue of date of plaintiff's knowledge – Whether issue of date of plaintiff's knowledge can be
determined on application in existing action to amend writ to add proposed defendant – Whether
plaintiff required to issue fresh writ against proposed defendant – Limitation Act 1939, s
2A(4)(b)(8).*

In September 1976 the plaintiff was severely injured when he lost control of his car while
driving in heavy rain and crashed into a lamp post. He was discharged from hospital in
November 1977 but was off work until about April 1978. In about May 1978 he
consulted solicitors, who inquired into the mechanical condition of the car but did not
inquire into the road conditions at the time of the accident. They advised the plaintiff
that he had no claim against any third party. Later the plaintiff consulted different
solicitors, who were advised by counsel in August 1979 to obtain the complete police
report of the accident. On 12 September, the plaintiff issued a writ claiming damages for
personal injuries against certain defendants, including the supplier and manufacturer of
the car. On 17 October the solicitors received the police report which indicated that the
road was flooded at the time of the accident and the solicitors for the first time considered
the possibility of a cause of action against the highway authority. There was further
delay while the solicitors ascertained the identity of the appropriate highway authority,
and then, on 2 September 1980, the plaintiff applied to the registrar for leave to amend
the writ by adding the highway authority as a defendant to the action and claiming
damages for negligence against it. The registrar adjourned the application to the
judge. The plaintiff served notice of the application on the highway authority. On the
hearing of the application in January 1981 the plaintiff submitted that the earliest date
of his knowledge of the condition of the road and the identity of the highway authority
was 17 October 1979 when his solicitors received the police report. He contended that
under s 2A(4)(b)[a] of the Limitation Act 1939 the relevant limitation period for the claim
against the highway authority was three years from that date, and accordingly his cause
of action against the highway authority was not time-barred at the date of the hearing of

a   Section 2A(4), so far as material, is set out at p 173 *c*, post the application. The highway authority submitted (i) that, where a plaintiff who was otherwise time-barred sought to add a defendant to an existing action on the ground that the limitation period under s 2A(4)(b) applied, the issue of the date on which he first acquired knowledge of the relevant facts could not be determined as a preliminary issue in the existing action, and the proper procedure was for the plaintiff to issue a fresh writ against the proposed defendant raising the issue of his knowledge of the relevant facts, and, if given leave to proceed with the second action, then to consolidate it with the existing action, and (ii) alternatively, that, since the first thing the plaintiff or his advisers should have done was to obtain a copy of the police report, he could reasonably have been expected to acquire knowledge of the facts giving rise to a cause of action against the proposed defendant earlier than three years before the hearing of the application to amend the writ and, since he was presumed by virtue of s 2A(8)[b] of the 1939 Act to have such knowledge, his claim against the highway authority was time-barred.

Held – For the purpose of applying the rule of practice that a defendant would not be added to an existing action if the claim against him was time-barred, the relevant date for considering whether the claim was time-barred was the date on which the application to amend the writ was heard. Thus, although a plaintiff who, in reliance on s 2A(4)(b) of the 1939 Act, alleged that his claim against a proposed defendant was brought within three years of the date on which he first acquired knowledge of the relevant facts could proceed by issuing a fresh writ against the proposed defendant raising the issue of the date of the plaintiff's knowledge, that was not the only method of proceeding: the issue of the date of the plaintiff's knowledge could alternatively be determined either as a preliminary issue in the existing action or as an issue in the trial of that action. Accordingly, the plaintiff was not time-barred on the ground that he had not issued a fresh writ against the highway authority within three years of the date of the accident, and it was open to the court to determine the issue of the date of the plaintiff's knowledge when determining his application to amend his writ. In all the circumstances, the plaintiff could not reasonably have been expected to have acquired knowledge of his cause of action against the highway authority before 31 July 1978, and that date was within the limitation period of three years prior to the hearing of his application to amend the writ. The plaintiff's claim against the highway authority was therefore not time-barred, and leave to amend the writ by adding the highway authority as defendant would be granted (see p 173 a to h and p 175 b to d, post).

Gawthrop v Bolton [1978] 3 All ER 615 and *Liff v Peasley* [1980] 1 All ER 623 applied.

Per curiam. If there is a risk that the three-year limitation period from the date of the plaintiff's knowledge will expire before leave to amend the writ is granted, either the application to amend should be heard ex parte and the added defendant be left to apply to set aside the amendment or the plaintiff should issue a new writ against the proposed defendant (see p 173 j, post).

Notes

For amendment of a writ in relation to the statutory bar of an action by time, see 28 Halsbury's Laws (4th edn) para 635, for amendment of a writ by change of parties, see ibid para 641, and for cases on amendment of writ by change of parties, see 32 Digest (Reissue) 725–728, 5254–5277.

For the Limitation Act 1939, s 2A (as inserted by the Limitation Act 1975, s 1), see 45 Halsbury's Statutes (3rd edn) 848.

As from 1 May 1981, s 2A of the 1939 Act was replaced by ss 11 and 14 of the Limitation Act 1980.

---

b   Section 2A(8) is set out at p 174 f to h, post

Cases referred to in judgment

a *Gawthrop v Bolton* [1978] 3 All ER 615, [1979] 1 WLR 268, Digest (Cont Vol E) 389,
     5273a.
Liff v Peasley [1980] 1 All ER 623, [1980] 1 WLR 781, CA.

Cases also cited

Birkett v James [1977] 2 All ER 801, [1978] AC 297, HL.
b *Buck v English Electric Co Ltd* [1978] 1 All ER 271, [1977] 1 WLR 806.
Chappell v Cooper [1980] 2 All ER 463, [1980] 1 WLR 958, CA.
Firman v Ellis [1978] 2 All ER 851, [1978] QB 886, CA.
Jones v G D Searle & Co Ltd [1978] 3 All ER 654, [1979] 1 WLR 101, CA.
Lucy v W T Henleys Telegraph Works Co Ltd [1969] 3 All ER 456, [1970] 1 QB 393, CA.
Marubeni Corp v Pearlstone Shipping Corp, The Puerto Acevedo [1978] 1 Lloyd's Rep 38, CA.
c *Miller v London Electrical Manufacturing Co Ltd* [1976] 2 Lloyd's Rep 284, CA.
Walkley v Precision Forgings Ltd [1979] 2 All ER 548, [1979] 1 WLR 606, HL.

Interlocutory application

By a writ dated 12 September 1979 the plaintiff, George Leadbitter, brought an action
against the first three defendants, Hodge Finance Ltd, Harry Wood Ltd and Reliant
d Motor Co Ltd, claiming damages for personal injuries sustained in an accident in
Newcastle upon Tyne on 26 September 1976 while he was driving a Reliant Robin motor
car. By a notice dated 6 August 1980 the plaintiff applied to the registrar in the
Newcastle upon Tyne District Registry for leave to amend the writ by adding as fourth
defendant the Newcastle City Council, being the highway authority responsible for the
road where the accident occurred. On 2 September 1980 that application was amended
e to join the Tyne and Wear County Council as the fourth defendant, it being the
appropriate highway authority. On 15 October 1980 the registrar ordered that the
application be adjourned to a High Court Judge. The application was heard in chambers
but judgment was given by Bush J in open court. The facts are set out in the judgment.

Roger Thorn for the plaintiff.
Robert Moore for the Tyne and Wear County Council.

Cur adv vult

26 January. **BUSH J** read the following judgment: The plaintiff, George Leadbitter,
makes his application to amend the writ of summons in this action which was filed on
f 12 September 1979, and he applies to amend it by joining the Tyne and Wear County
Council as fourth defendant. He relies on RSC Ord 15, r 6. He seeks to show that his
case against the proposed defendant is not barred by s 2A of the Limitation Act 1939, as
inserted by the Limitation Act 1975; alternatively he would have to show it would be
equitable to disapply the statute having regard to the provisions of s 2D as inserted by the
1975 Act.

g   The facts are that on 26 September 1976 the plaintiff was driving his three-wheeler
Reliant Robin motor car in heavy rain along the Scotswood Road (the A695) in Newcastle
upon Tyne. Near to the Crooked Billet public house, the plaintiff lost control of the
motor car and crashed into a lamp post. The plaintiff suffered severe personal injuries.
He was in the intensive care unit for three weeks and was eventually discharged from
hospital on 10 November 1976. He then attended as an out-patient until he was finally
h discharged on 10 November 1977. He then went back to work but it was too soon, and
he was off work until April 1978, having only been back about a month. In February
1979 he was off work with gall bladder trouble and the gall bladder was removed by
operation in July 1979. The plaintiff remembers nothing about the accident or its
cause. He made a short statement to that effect to the police on 6 October 1976. Though
it is by no means clear from the plaintiff's affidavit as to when he first consulted a solicitor

about his accident, one construction of paras 5 and 6 of his affidavit is that it was about   *a*
May 1978. Paragraphs 5 and 6 of that affidavit read as follows:

> 'Initial enquiries into the cause of this accident were prompted and focused by
> growing publicity about the instability of Reliant three-wheelers such as I was
> driving at the time of the accident. By a circular dated the 10th January 1977 . . .
> the Third Defendants [the manufacturers] advised the Second Defendants [the
> suppliers] of a defect in the steering column assembly of vehicles of this type within
> a range of chassis numbers including my particular vehicle, which required   *b*
> modification. By a further circular, the envelope of which was postmarked the 11th
> May 1978 . . . the Second Defendants advised me of this and its importance. [And
> then para 6 goes on:] I therefore instructed my previous solicitors to act on my
> behalf to make inquiries arising out of those circulars and the increasing number of
> similar accidents involving this type of vehicle. Amongst other matters they
> obtained the Police Examiner's Report (but not the full Police Report) and the   *c*
> opinion of a Consulting Motor Engineer. As a result of all these matters, my
> solicitors advised me by letter dated 11th July 1978 that an inquiry into the
> requirements of the modification for the steering column and therefore the
> possibility of a mechanical failure or defect in the van did not cause this accident and
> that therefore their legal advice was that: "there are no grounds on which you could
> establish liability for this accident against any Third Party." This was in respect of   *d*
> the steering assembly of the three-wheeler, the defects of which had been brought
> to my attention as set out above.'

No attempt has been made by either side to throw any light on what might be an
obfuscation of an important point as to the date of first instructing the solicitor. In any
event it is to be noted that the thrust of the inquiries was towards the mechanical   *e*
condition of the vehicle and not to the road conditions, though road conditions must
have been material when considering the behaviour of the vehicle so far as it was
known. An investigative BBC programme on the Reliant Robin caused the plaintiff to
go to other solicitors. They took counsel's opinion dated 31 August 1979 and counsel
suggested further inquiries directed to the roadworthiness of the vehicle and, most
important, suggested that the complete police report should be obtained. The writ was   *f*
issued on 12 September 1979 against three defendants, the finance company who
provided part of the means for the purchase of the vehicle were first defendants, the
suppliers were second defendants and the manufactureres were third defendants. About
the same time a statement of claim was delivered. On 17 October 1979 the complete
police report was received which contained a witness statement by a Mr Cork which said:
'At the time of the accident the rain was fairly heavy and there was a large puddle at the   *g*
Billet bus stop.' The sketch plan made by the attending police officer showed a pool of
water extending well into the road. It would have been on the plaintiff's nearside and in
his carriageway as he went in an easterly direction. In addition, the plaintiff, obviously
commenting on the police report, made a further statement in which he said:

> '. . . on the day of the accident it was raining quite heavily. Water was lying on
> the road. I cannot remember anything about the puddle near the accident, although   *h*
> I think there must have been one there, because I recall that I think the Fire Service
> had to be called to pump away the surface water round about the accident.'

In the accident report provided by the police the words 'Road flooded' appear.
Paragraph 8 of the plaintiff's affidavit then describes the state of mind of his legal advisers
at that time on receipt of that information and reads: *j*

> 'As a result of these pieces of information it then became material to attempt to
> discover whether this was merely a "puddle" in the road and in particular what the
> depth of the water was. Eventually permission was granted to my solicitors to
> interview and take a statement from the attending Police Officer, P.C. Graeme
> Stock, who stated "there was a pool of water at the scene of the accident which was
> 87' in length, 11½' wide and approximately 6' . . . maximum in depth. It was ankle

deep at the point where the car collided with the lamp post". [I assume that the reference to 6′ is in mistake for 6″.] This was the first we knew of the depth of the water and the real possibility of a cause of action against the Highway Authority.'

I am told and it seems both counsel accept that permission to interview the police officer would not have been granted until the statement of claim and defence had been delivered as between the defendants and that therefore he was interviewed as soon as practicable. There was some further delay in finding out precisely which was the highway authority concerned. An application to amend the writ and join the City of Newcastle upon Tyne as fourth defendant was made on 6 August 1980. This had to be amended on 2 September 1980 because the plaintiff's advisers were then told on 29 August 1980 that the highway authority concerned was in fact the Tyne and Wear County Council.

The first point taken by the proposed defendant is that the correct procedure is for the plaintiff to issue a fresh writ and in due course, if allowed to proceed with the action, consolidate it with the present action. There is clear authority for the proposition that a plaintiff will not be allowed to amend the writ to add a defendant outside the limitation period where, by so adding, any claim that that defendant might have to the protection of the Limitation Acts would be defeated.

In *Liff v Peasley* [1980] 1 All ER 623 at 631–632, [1980] 1 WLR 781 at 791 Stephenson LJ reviewed the authorities and said:

'There is no doubt about the practice long established before the 1975 Act. It is not to permit a person to be made a defendant in an existing action at a time when he could have relied on a statute of limitation as barring the plaintiff from bringing a fresh action against him. The reason for this practice, or rather the way in which this practice is justified or the legal basis on which it is rested, is, curiously more doubtful. There appear to be two alternative bases: (1) the action against the added defendant relates back to the date of the original writ, the plaintiff is deemed to have begun his action against the defendant when he began it against the original defendant, and so the defendant is deprived of his right to rely on the statute of limitations; (2) the action against the added defendant is begun at the date of the amendment joining him in the action, and so he can rely on the statute as barring the plaintiff from suing him. In most cases it will not matter which of the two possible dates is regarded as the date of the commencement of the action brought against the added defendant. If he applies to set aside the order joining him as co-defendant, he will succeed, either because he would be deprived of his right to rely on the statute if the earlier date were preferred or because he would be able to rely on the statute and defeat the plaintiff's claim if the later date were preferred. But in this case the added defendant has elected to plead the statute in answer to the plaintiff's claim before challenging the plaintiff's right to make him a defendant. Can he at that later stage allege that his joinder, though properly made in the first instance, is improper, only if he can successfully rely on the statute, because he was not sued until the later date, so that it would be pointless and unnecessary that he should be, or remain, a defendant? But if he cannot rely on the statute because he is deemed to have been sued from the earlier date, how can he then deny that he is, and remains a proper and necessary party to the action?'

Brandon LJ said ([1980] 1 All ER 623 at 639, [1980] 1 WLR 781 at 799):

'It is an established rule of practice that the court will not allow a person to be added as defendant to an existing action if the claim sought to be made against him is already statute-barred and he desires to rely on that circumstance as a defence to the claim. Alternatively, if the court has allowed such addition to be made ex parte in the first place, it will not, on objection then being taken by the person added, allow the addition to stand. I shall refer to that established rule of practice as "the rule of practice". There are two alternative bases on which the rule of practice can be justified. The first basis is that, if the addition were allowed, it would relate back so that the action would be deemed to have been begun as against the person added, not on the date of amendment, but on the date of the original writ; that the effect of such relation back would be to deprive the person added of an accrued defence to the claim on the ground that it was statute-barred; and that this would be unjust to that person. I shall refer to this first basis of the rule of practice as the "relation back" theory. The second and alternative basis for the rule is that, where a person is added as defendant in an existing action, the action is only deemed to have been begun as against him on the date of amendment of the writ; that the defence that the claim is statute-barred therefore remains available to him; and that, since such defence affords a complete answer to the claim, it would serve no useful purpose to allow the addition to be made. I shall refer to this second and alternative basis of the rule of practice as the "no useful purpose" theory.'

In that case as I understand it both Stephenson and Brandon LJJ rejected the 'relation back' theory in favour of the 'no useful purpose' approach. Brandon LJ set out the usual practice. He said ([1980] 1 All ER 623 at 639, [1980] 1 WLR 781 at 799–800):

'An application by a plaintiff for leave to add a person as defendant in an existing action is, or should ordinarily, be made ex parte under RSC Ord 15, r 6(2)(b). If the application is allowed, the writ must then be amended under r 8(1), and served on the person added under r 8(2) of the same order. If the person added as defendant, having had the amended writ served on him, objects to being added on the ground that the claim against him was already statute-barred before the writ was amended, the ordinary practice is for him to enter a conditional appearance under RSC Ord 12, r 7, and then to apply to set aside the amended writ and the service of it on him under Ord 12, r 8. Then, if he establishes that the claim against him was statute-barred before the writ was amended, he is entitled as of right, in accordance with the rule of practice, to the relief for which he has asked, unless the case is of the special kind covered by RSC Ord 20, r 5(3). Provided that the person added as defendant follows the ordinary practice described above, he gets the benefit of the rule of practice, and it is not material to consider which of the two alternative bases for that rule, that is to say the "relation back" theory on the one hand or the "no useful purpose" theory on the other, is the true one. In the present case, however, the solicitors acting for Mr Spinks did not follow the ordinary practice. Instead, after they had accepted service on him of the amended writ, they entered an unconditional appearance in the action on his behalf, and later, after accepting service of the amended statement of claim, they served a defence containing a plea that the claim against him was statute-barred.'

In fact the court decided that by entering an unconditional appearance to the writ the defendants in that case had not deprived themselves of the defence of the Limitation Act, if it were available to them. In the present case the application, could, I suppose, be regarded as ex parte on notice, and indeed the proposed defendant having had notice of the application has appeared and taken full part in the arguments and has filed an affidavit. There may be disadvantages to this approach relating to the time that it has taken for the matter in fact to come before me for determination of the issue, but I shall refer to that at a later stage. The plaintiff has by his affidavit sought to show a date later than three years after the accident as his date of knowledge within the meaning of the Limitation Act 1939 as amended. Further he has exhibited a proposed amended statement of claim. The application has been remitted to me by the registrar, and as I have indicated earlier is one for leave to amend the writ by adding a party. Now, in *The Supreme Court Practice 1979*, vol 1, p 351, para 20/5–8/18 there appears the following statement:

'It would seem that an amendment will not be allowed to add a defendant in an action for personal injuries or under the Fatal Accidents Acts where it is alleged that the action is brought against him three years from the plaintiff's date of knowledge which is later than the three years from the accrual of the cause of action under s. 2A or s. 2B of the Act. The proper course for the plaintiff to take is to issue a fresh writ founded on his contention that the accrual of his cause of action was from his date of knowledge, and the Court may then consolidate the two actions.'

There is no authority cited for this statement. It does not agree with the procedure outlined by Brandon LJ in *Liff*'s case to which I have already referred, and although it is a method of proceeding I do not think that it is true to say that this is the only way in which the matter can be dealt with. In fact the procedure adopted here by the plaintiff was the one suggested by Walton J in a case in the Chancery Division, *Gawthrop v Bolton* [1978] 3 All ER 615, [1979] 1 WLR 268.

If in fact it is plain and decided that the action is not statute-barred then I can see no objection to the court giving leave to amend the writ. Indeed that would have been consistent with the old practice. Where the difficulty now arises is that under s 2A(4) of the Limitation Act 1939 (as inserted by s 1 of the Limitation Act 1975) the primary limitation period is not three years from the date on which the cause of action accrued as was formerly the case, but is a period of 'three years from—(a) the date on which the cause of action accrued, or (b) the date (if later) of the plaintiff's knowledge'. In *Liff*'s case the court was not concerned with the knowledge point, it being clear and accepted that the action was time-barred. If the action is brought within three years of the plaintiff's knowledge as defined in s 2A then it cannot in law be described as time-barred, even though it is outside the three-year period since the cause of action arose. To say that the court will not add a defendant if such addition will defeat the right to rely on the Limitation Act 1939 as amended by the 1975 Act begs the question. The question is: what is the period of limitation that applies? How is the question to be determined? Is it to be determined as a preliminary issue or as an issue in the trial itself? There are difficulties attendant on both courses. If as a preliminary issue, then the issue may not be capable of as full an investigation as it would have at the date of the trial. The reason for this being in some cases that the facts on which the preliminary issue is to be decided may be inextricably commingled with facts giving rise to the substantive issue. If the issue is left to the trial itself then it may be that in investigating the state of knowledge of the plaintiff it would be necessary to refer to facts and documents which if the main action stood alone would be privileged and inadmissible. Further, if the relation back theory is correct then it does not really matter what the decision at the trial is because by the very act of granting leave it is said that the action against the defendant so joined then dates for limitation purposes from the date of issue of the writ. However this cannot in my view be so, for Parliament has stated in terms what the primary limitation period is. It is for this reason that I take the view that the effect of the Limitation Act 1975 (for it cannot be given practical force otherwise) is to make impossible an approach based on a relation back to the date of the original writ. For this reason I respectfully follow the views expressed by Stephenson and Brandon LJJ, and I take the view that for limitation purposes the relevant date is the date on which the writ is amended with leave. This approach is consistent, as was pointed out by Stephenson LJ in *Liff v Peasley* [1980] 1 All ER 623 at 634–635, [1980] 1 WLR 781 at 794–795, with RSC Ord 15, r 8 and CCR Ord 15, r 2.

A word of warning. If as in the present case the plaintiff is seeking to argue that his case is within the three-year period of knowledge and gives notice of the application then those who advise him must beware that the primary limitation period does *not* expire before the writ is amended.

The dates are such in the present case that this danger does not arise but one can imagine the sort of case where it would, for in the instant case through no fault of the plaintiff or the proposed defendant or their advisers the hearing of this application only comes before me some five months after it was made and some four months after the application was amended. If there is such a risk involved, then one of two courses would have to be adopted, either that suggested by Brandon LJ where the application itself is treated as ex parte and then the defendant is left to apply to set aside the amendment, or by the issue of a new writ, cumbersome though that procedure may be.

Now the plaintiff says that the earliest date of his knowledge was in October 1979 when his advisers received the police report and the date when P c Stock was interviewed and it was found the puddle, or whatever it was called, was six inches deep and ankle deep where the car collided with the lamp post. After that it took a further month to discover the correct highway authority. It is said the relevant date for the expiry of the limitation period would be October or November 1982. The proposed defendant says in its affidavit, by para 5:

> 'The plaintiff was advised by solicitors [throughout] . . . the plaintiff's memory of the accident being unclear it should have been the first and obvious move to obtain a copy of the full Police Report . . . When the plaintiff changed solicitors he should have asked for all reasonable enquiries to be conducted in order to ascertain how the accident happened . . . Again this would have necessitated the obtaining of a full Police Report . . . Although it is not clear because the plaintiff does not give dates, it looks as though there was a delay of something like a year between the plaintiff changing solicitors and those solicitors instructing counsel'

which might be relevant under s 2D but on the facts of this case is not relevant under s 2A.

Now, as I observed earlier, the plaintiff has not sought to clear up doubts as to the dates when he instructed solicitors and most importantly the date when he instructed those who first represented him. This information is important because the proposed defendant can rightly say that any solicitors in these circumstances would immediately obtain the full police report. Once that was obtained then further inquiries could have been made. Even if the witness, Mr Cork, could not have helped any more there was always the possibility of inquiries from the fire brigade. If the plaintiff's subsequent recollection is correct then he knew the fire brigade had been there.

Now, by s 2A(6) it is provided that references to a person's date of knowledge are references to the date on which he first had knowledge of the following facts, set out in paras (b) and (c) of s 2A(6):

> '(b) that that injury was attributable in whole or in part to the act or omission which is alleged to constitute negligence, nuisance, or breach of duty, and (c) the identity of the defendant'

and by s 2A(8) it is provided:

> 'For the purposes of the said sections a person's knowledge includes knowledge which he might reasonably have been expected to acquire—(a) from facts observable or ascertainable by him, or (b) from facts ascertainable by him with the help of medical or other appropriate expert advice which it is reasonable for him to seek,'

and then there is the proviso to that:

> 'but a person shall not be fixed under this subsection with knowledge of a fact ascertainable only with the help of expert advice so long as he has taken all reasonable steps to obtain (and, where appropriate, to act on) that advice.'

Now the plaintiff in fact knew that the injuries were attributable in whole or in part to the act or omission which is alleged to constitute negligence or breach of duty on the part of the defendant on 17 October 1979. I do not think that the interview with the police officer which established the approximate depth as six inches was more than additional evidence as to the nature of the flooding.

The plaintiff in fact knew of the identity of the proposed defendant as the highway authority on 29 August 1980. Either of these dates puts the plaintiff's action well within the limitation period contemplated by s 2A(4)(b). However s 2A(8) that I have read requires the court to take into account knowledge which the plaintiff might reasonably have been expected to acquire. The expert advice referred to in para (b) of course includes the advice of his solicitors, not as to law because that is excluded expressly by the statute, but as to the obtaining of evidence. However the facts concerned are *not* facts which are in my view ascertainable *only* with the help of expert advice, in the sense that any member of the public may obtain a police report and can make inquiries of the fire brigade or local residents and interview potential witnesses so that the plaintiff is fixed with any knowledge that his solicitors acting on his behalf ought to have acquired.

I must look then to see the date of knowledge which has to be assumed. In view of the uncertainties as to the evidence I mentioned earlier I have been much exercised in my mind whether to grant leave to amend (the plaintiff having shown a prima facie case for defeating any limitation period) and then leave the trial of the issues of the plaintiff's knowledge to the main trial itself. However both counsel are most anxious that I should come to a conclusion on the facts before me. I think it is open to me to take a broad approach and to say that, having regard to all the circumstances, including the nature of the plaintiff's injuries referred to in the full medical report before me, one would have expected that he could have gone to a solicitor or conducted inquiries on his own behalf, say by November 1977. However he was off work again after a month until April 1978, and I think one must take the later date and allow two months for solicitors to make the inquiries about the road and weather conditions that they should have made and did not. The notional date then when the plaintiff (and this includes his legal advisers) might reasonably have been expected to have acquired the relevant knowledge as to (i) the fact that the injury in whole or in part was due to the act or omission of a third party and (ii) the identity of that third party was 31 July 1978.

It follows the plaintiff's claim against the proposed defendant is not statute-barred and leave to amend the writ will be given accordingly. In view of this there is no need for me to consider the operation of s 2D of the Limitation Act.

Leave to amend granted.

Solicitors: *Dickinson, Dees*, Newcastle upon Tyne (for the plaintiff); *Crutes*, Middlesbrough (for the proposed defendant).

John M Collins Esq   Barrister.

R v Plymouth Justices, ex parte Rogers

QUEEN'S BENCH DIVISION
LORD LANE CJ AND WOOLF J
21, 22 JANUARY, 8 FEBRUARY 1982

European Economic Community – Reference to European Court – Referral by court of member state of question regarding validity of EEC enactment – Referral by magistrates' court – Power to make referral – Magistrates' court referring question of validity of EEC regulation at close of prosecution case on defence submission of no case to answer on ground EEC regulation invalid – Facts still in issue – Whether magistrates' court having power to make referral where issues of fact still to be determined – Whether desirable that referral be made by superior court – EEC Treaty, art 177.

The prosecutor laid a charge in a magistrates' court against the defendant that being the master of a fishing boat not registered in the United Kingdom he carried in the boat, in waters adjacent to the United Kingdom, a fishing net with a device attached to it which obstructed or diminished the net's mesh, contrary to both EEC and United Kingdom regulations. At the hearing the defendant admitted all the evidence adduced by the prosecution except for the evidence adduced that the device had obstructed or diminished the net. That issue of fact, therefore, remained to be resolved by the magistrates and the defendant was entitled to call evidence on it; in all the circumstances, however, it would have been perverse of the magistrates to find in favour of the defendant on the issue. At the close of the prosecution case the defendant submitted that there was no case to answer and that the charge should be dismissed because the EEC regulations and the United Kingdom regulations were both invalid under EEC law. The prosecutor disputed that contention. The defendant then submitted to the magistrates that certain questions regarding the effect of the regulations in EEC law should be referred to the Court of Justice of the European Communities for a preliminary ruling, pursuant to art 177[a] of the EEC Treaty, and that the proceedings should be adjourned to enable the referral to be made. The magistrates, purporting to act under art 177, decided to adjourn the proceedings to enable those questions to be referred to the European Court. The prosecutor applied for judicial review of the magistrates' decision, submitting that because there was an issue of fact (viz whether the device had obstructed or diminished the net) yet to be determined and that if it was determined in favour of the defendant the prosecution must fail and a referral to the European Court would be unnecessary, it could not be said that, at the stage the proceedings had reached, a decision on the questions to be referred was 'necessary to enable [the magistrates' court] to give judgment', within art 177, and therefore the magistrates did not have jurisdiction under art 177 to refer the questions to the European Court or to adjourn the proceedings for that purpose.

Held – The application would be dismissed for the following reasons—

(1) On a submission of no case to answer in a criminal trial the court, whether it was a magistrates' court or a higher tribunal, had jurisdiction under art 177 of the EEC Treaty to refer to the Court of Justice of the European Communities a question as to the validity of an EEC enactment if it considered a decision on the question was 'necessary' to enable it to give judgment, and that was so even if all the facts in the case had not been admitted or determined, since the word 'necessary' in art 177 was to be construed as conferring a wide discretion on the tribunal in question to refer relevant questions to the European Court, that interpretation of the power to refer being in accord with the approach to art 177 of the European Court and of English case law. Accordingly, if a magistrates' court took the view that a decision by the European Court on a relevant question was required in order to do justice, then, so long as the court did not misdirect itself or act unreasonably in deciding to make the referral, the Divisional Court would not interfere with the decision to refer (see p 180 g h and p 181 b to g, post); *Rheinmühlen-Düsseldorf v Einfuhr- und Vorratsstelle für Getreide und Futtermittel* Case 166/73 [1974] ECR 33, *Polydor Ltd and RSO Records v Harlequin Record Shops Ltd* [1980] 2 CMLR 413 and dictum of Lord Diplock in *R v Henn* [1980] 2 All ER at 196 applied; *H P Bulmer Ltd v J Bollinger SA* [1974] 2 All ER 1226 considered.

(2) It followed that even though there was an outstanding issue of fact at the time when the decision to refer was made, the magistrates' court had jurisdiction under art 177 to refer the questions to the European Court. Furthermore, although in an ordinary case it was highly undesirable, because of the expense of a referral to the European Court, for a magistrates' court to make a referral under art 177 until all the evidence in the case had been called and it was satisfied there could not be an acquittal on the facts, in all the circumstances the court had properly exercised its discretion to refer at the stage the proceedings had reached because only technically could it be said that there was an outstanding issue of fact to be resolved since it would have been perverse for the magistrates to find in favour of the defendant on the outstanding issue of whether the device had obstructed or diminished the net (see p 181 e and h to p 182 a and f, post).

Per curiam. Even after they have heard all the evidence magistrates should exercise considerable caution before referring a question to the European Court and generally should decide any question of EEC law themselves; then, if their decision is wrong, a higher court, which usually will be the more suitable forum to make the reference to the European Court because it is in a better position to assess the appropriateness of and to formulate the question to be referred, can make any necessary reference to the European Court (see p 182 c d, post).

---

a   Article 177 is set out at p 178 f g, post

Notes

a For the jurisdiction of the Court of Justice of the European Communities to give preliminary rulings on the validity and interpretation of EEC enactments, see Supplement to 39A Halsbury's Laws (3rd edn) para 32, and for cases on the subject, see 21 Digest (Reissue) 232–239, 1594–1624.

For the EEC Treaty, art 177, see 42A Halsbury's Statutes (3rd edn) 436.

b **Cases referred to in judgment**

H P Bulmer Ltd v J Bollinger SA [1974] 2 All ER 1226, [1974] Ch 401, [1974] 3 WLR 202, CA, 21 Digest (Reissue) 240, 1630.

Polydor Ltd and RSO Records v Harlequin Record Shops Ltd [1980] 2 CMLR 413, CA.

R v Henn Case 34/79 [1980] 2 All ER 166, [1980] 2 WLR 597, [1979] ECR 3795, CJEC and HL, 21 Digest (Reissue) 249, 1662.

c *Rheinmühlen-Düsseldorf v Einfuhr- und Vorratsstelle für Getreide und Futtermittel* Case 166/73 [1974] ECR 33, CJEC.

Application for judicial review

Lt-Cdr Anthony George Rogers RN applied, with the leave of Hodgson J granted on 19 October 1981, for judicial review of the decision of the Plymouth Magistrates' Court,
d made on 6 August 1981, to adjourn the hearing of an information laid by the applicant, on behalf of the Ministry of Agriculture, Fisheries and Food, against the respondent, M Hubert Bernard Louis Darthenay, charging him as the master of a fishing boat not registered in the United Kingdom with carrying in the boat a fishing net with a device attached to it, contrary to art 7 of EC Council Regulation 2527/80 and art 8 of the Fishing Nets (No 2) Order 1980, SI 1980/1994 (amended by SI 1981/906), so that certain questions
e relating to the interpretation of art 7 of the EC regulation could be referred to the Court of Justice of the European Communities for a preliminary ruling under art 177 of the EEC Treaty. The grounds on which the relief was sought were that (1) the justices erred in law in ordering that the questions relating to the interpretation of art 7 be referred to the European Court at the close of the prosecution case, (2) the justices failed to exercise their discretion to refer the questions according to law because (a) by art 177 of the EEC Treaty it was a condition precedent to the exercise of the justices' discretion that they should consider it necessary to obtain a decision of the European Court on the questions to enable them to reach their own conclusion in the case and (b) the justices failed to consider whether it was necessary to refer the questions and (3) if the justices did consider that it was necessary to refer the questions to the European Court they wrongly interpreted the word 'necessary' in art 177 of the EEC Treaty, alternatively they reached a conclusion as to the meaning of that word which no reasonable tribunal properly directing itself could have reached because (a) whichever way a decision on the questions referred was decided such decision would not have been conclusive of the case and (b) it was not possible to determine whether referral of the questions was necessary until all the facts of the case had been heard and a decision on them made, neither of which events had taken place at the time of the justices' order. The facts are set out in the judgment of the court.

Alan Moses for the applicant.
Patrick O'Connor for the respondent.

At the conclusion of the arguments, the court announced that, for reasons to be given later, the application would be dismissed, leave to appeal to the House of Lords would be refused but the court would be prepared to certify that a point of law of general public importance was involved in the case.

8 February.   **LORD LANE CJ** read the following judgment of the court: This is an application by Lt-Cdr Anthony George Rogers RN for judicial review in respect of the decision of the Plymouth Magistrates' Court on 6 August 1981 to adjourn the hearing of

the proceedings which were then before the court, so that certain questions could be referred to the Court of Justice of the European Communities for a preliminary ruling under art 177 of the EEC Treaty. The application raises the question as to when it is proper for a magistrates' court to refer questions as to the interpretation of the EEC Treaty to the Court of Justice of the European Communities.

The hearing which was adjourned by the Plymouth Magistrates' Court was into an information laid by the applicant on behalf of the Ministry of Agriculture, Fisheries and Food against M Hubert Bernard Louis Darthenay (the respondent). The charge was that on 5 August 1981, being master of a fishing boat not registered in the United Kingdom, namely Christine Marie, he did carry in the said boat in waters adjacent to the United Kingdom, and within British fishery limits, a trawl Danish seine or similar net having attached to it a device, namely a second piece of net, having the effect of obstructing or diminishing the mesh in contravention of art 7 of EC Council Regulation 2527/80, contrary to art 8 of the Fishing Nets (No 2) Order 1980, SI 1980/1994, as amended by the Fishing Nets (No 2) (Variation) (No 5) Order 1981, SI 1981/906, made in accordance with ss 3 and 11 of the Seafish (Conservation) Act 1967, as amended.

The respondent did not admit that the second piece of net necessarily had the effect of obstructing or diminishing the original net, but subject to this he admitted the evidence which was adduced on behalf of the prosecution to establish the commission of the offence. However, at the close of the prosecution case, the respondent contended that the charge should be dismissed because the regulations on which it was based were invalid as a matter of Community law. It was argued to the contrary by the prosecutor and it was then submitted on behalf of the respondent that certain questions which would resolve this dispute should be referred to the Court of Justice of the European Communities and the proceedings should be adjourned to enable this to be done. Although the prosecution argued to the contrary, the magistrates acceded to this submission.

There is no dispute that in the appropriate circumstances a magistrates' court has jurisdiction to refer questions to the European Court under art 177 of the EEC Treaty. That article provides:

'The Court of Justice shall have jurisdiction to give preliminary rulings concerning: (a) the interpretation of this Treaty; (b) the validity and interpretation of acts of the institutions of the Community; (c) the interpretation of the statutes of bodies established by an act of the Council, where those statutes so provide.

Where such a question is raised before any court or tribunal of a Member State, that court or tribunal may, if it considers that a decision on the question is necessary to enable it to give judgment, request the Court of Justice to give a ruling thereon.

Where any such question is raised in a case pending before a court or tribunal of a Member State, against whose decision there is no judicial remedy under national law, that court or tribunal shall bring the matter before the Court of Justice.'

The magistrates' court is a 'court or tribunal' falling within the second paragraph of the article which has a discretion to refer a question if it considers it 'necessary to enable it to give judgment'. The position of the magistrates' court is to be contrasted with that of a court against whose decision there is no judicial remedy who must refer such a matter to the European Court.

The questions the respondent proposed should be referred to the European Court arise out of the provisions of EC Council Regulation 2527/80 of 30 September 1980, which lays down technical measures for the conservation of fishery resources. Article 7 deals with the attachments to nets and provides:

'No device shall be used by means of which the mesh in any part of a fishing net is obstructed or otherwise effectively diminished. This provision does not exclude the use of the devices referred to in the detailed implementing rules to be adopted in accordance with the procedure laid down in Article 20.'

The detailed implementing rules have not as yet been adopted, and the respondent argues that until they are the article is of no effect because it is incomplete. Furthermore, the statutory instrument under which the charge is laid, namely the Fishing Nets (No 2) Order 1980, is invalid, because member states are no longer entitled independently to exercise any power of their own in the matter of fishery conservation, as this has been a matter for the Community since the expiration on 1 January 1979 of the transitional period laid down by art 102 of the Act of Accession.

It is not necessary to give any further indication of the nature of the respondent's contentions, because it was not argued that if it was proper for the Plymouth Magistrates' Court to refer questions to the European Court at the stage which they did, the questions proposed were inappropriate questions on which to seek the opinion of the European Court. The questions were: (a) whether art 7 of EC Council Regulation 2527/80 has any effect when no detailed implementing rules had been adopted? (b) if not, has a member state any competence to adopt a measure such as SI 1980/1994? (c) if art 7 does have some effect when no implementing rules have been adopted, has a member state any power to define the exceptions to the prohibition on net attachments in such a way as SI 1980/1994 does? (d) if the answer is No to questions (a), (b) and (c), what rights result for an EEC citizen prosecuted under a law such as SI 1980/1994?

The conflicting contentions of the parties were put with admirable clarity by counsel on behalf of the applicant and counsel on behalf of the respondent.

The argument of counsel for the applicant was confined to the wording of art 177 of the EEC Treaty. He submits that at the stage which the case had reached before the magistrates' court the justices had no jurisdiction to refer the questions to the Court of Justice. Before they can do so they must consider that a decision on the questions is necessary to enable them to give judgment. At the time they made the decision in this case they were not in a position to reach such a conclusion because there was still an issue as to fact to be resolved, this being that the respondent had not admitted that the second piece of net had the effect of obstructing or diminishing the original net. It was a matter on which he was entitled to call evidence and until he had been given an opportunity to do so and the justices had decided whether this had been proved, it could not be said whether it was necessary to have the opinion of the European Court or not. It was at that stage still possible that the magistrates would not be satisfied that the second piece of net had the effect alleged and if they were not, a reference would serve no purpose.

In support of his contentions counsel for the applicant relied strongly on the judgments of the Court of Appeal in *H P Bulmer Ltd v J Bollinger SA* [1974] 2 All ER 1226, [1974] 1 Ch 401. In that case Lord Denning MR and Stephenson LJ laid down guidance as to the practice to be adopted with regard to referring questions to the European Court. Lord Denning MR said ([1974] 2 All ER 1226 at 1234, [1974] 1 Ch 401 at 421):

'An English court can only refer the matter to the European Court "*if it considers* that a decision on the question is necessary to enable it to give judgment*". Note the words "if it considers". That is, "if the *English court* considers". On this point again the opinion of the English courts is final, just as it is on the matter of discretion. An English judge can say either "I consider it necessary", or "I do not consider it necessary". His discretion in that respect is final. Let me take the two in order. (i) If the English judge considers it *necessary* to refer the matter, no one can gainsay it save the Court of Appeal.'

Later Lord Denning MR said ([1974] 2 All ER 1226 at 1234–1235, [1974] 1 Ch 401 at 422–423):

'The English court has to consider whether "a decision on the question is *necessary* to enable it to give *judgment*". That means judgment in the very case which is before the court. The judge must have got to the stage when he says to himself: "This clause of the treaty is capable of two or more meanings. If it means *this*, I give judgment for the plaintiff. If it means *that*, I give judgment for the defendant." In short, the point must be such that, whichever way the point is decided, it is conclusive of the case. Nothing more remains but to give judgment . . . (iv) *Decide the facts first.* It is to be noticed, too, that the word is "necessary". This is much stronger than "desirable" or "convenient". There are some cases where the point, if decided one way, would shorten the trial greatly. But, if decided the other way, it would mean that the trial would have to go its full length. In such a case it might be "convenient" or "desirable" to take it as a preliminary point because it might save much time and expense. But it would not be "necessary" at that stage. When the facts were investigated, it might turn out to have been quite unnecessary. The case would be determined on another ground altogether. As a rule you cannot tell whether it is necessary to decide a point until all the facts are ascertained. So in general it is best to decide the facts first.'

While referring to the last passage we draw attention to the fact that Lord Denning MR prefaced his remark about 'it is best to decide the facts first' by the words 'in general'.

Stephenson LJ, with whose judgment Stamp LJ agreed, on this point said much the same as Lord Denning MR. He puts the matter in this way ([1974] 2 All ER 1226 at 1240, [1974] 1 Ch 401 at 429):

'It was argued for the appellants that a decision of question A might shorten proceedings and enable the judge to give judgment without going into evidence of passing-off or acquiescence. But art 177 does not provide for a court considering that a decision on the question is expedient or convenient or necessary to enable it to give judgment shortly, or more shortly, or more cheaply and conveniently, but necessary to enable it to give it—justly of course but with no other implication or qualification.'

Applying these judgments to the facts of the present case, counsel for the applicant submits that if the answer to the questions were in favour of the prosecution, that would not be the end of the case, it would still be necessary for the justices to give an opportunity to the respondent to deal with the issue which he did not admit. He concedes that if the answer was in favour of the respondent, that would be the end of the case, but this, he contends, is not sufficient.

Taking the argument of counsel for the applicant to its logical conclusion, it means that no court or tribunal can refer questions to the European Court under art 177 unless all the facts have been admitted or found on all the issues in the case. It must be a situation where, subject to argument as to the effect of the answers given by the European Court, it is in a position to give final judgment. In the case of a criminal trial this means that it has no jurisdiction to refer on a submission being made that there is no case to answer unless all the facts have been admitted. This involves giving an extremely narrow interpretation to the word 'necessary' in art 177.

Such an interpretation is not in accord with the general approach to art 177 adopted by the European Court. For example in the course of its judgment in *Rheinmühlen-Düsseldorf v Einfuhr- und Vorratsstelle für Getreide und Futtermittel* Case 166/73 [1974] ECR 33 at 38 it is stated:

'Article 177 is essential for the preservation of the Community character of the law established by the Treaty and has the object of ensuring that in all circumstances this law is the same in all States of the Community. Whilst it thus aims to avoid divergences in the interpretation of Community law which the national courts have to apply, it likewise tends to ensure this application by making available to the national judge a means of eliminating difficulties which may be occasioned by the requirement of giving Community law its full effect within the framework of the judicial systems of the Member States . . . This Article gives national courts the power and, where appropriate, imposes on them an obligation to refer a case for a preliminary ruling, as soon as the judge perceives either of his own motion or at the request of the parties that the litigation depends on a point referred to in the first paragraph of Article 177. It follows that national courts have the widest discretion in referring matters to the Court of Justice if they consider that a case pending before them raises questions involving interpretation, or consideration of the validity, of provisions of Community law, necessitating a decision on their part.'

Furthermore it is inconsistent with the approach adopted by the Court of Appeal in the later case of *Polydor Ltd and RSO Records v Harlequin Record Shops Ltd* [1980] 2 CMLR 413. In that case both Templeman and Ormrod LJJ gave a more generous interpretation to art 177. Templeman LJ, although he felt as an English judge that the plaintiffs had not disclosed a triable issue on the effect of the treaty, acknowledged (at 426) that 'it is the right of the plaintiffs to go to the European Court and to see whether that approach is to be upheld or whether it is to be overruled'. Templeman LJ took this view, although he had earlier stated with regard to Lord Denning MR's guidelines in the *Bollinger* case that counsel had 'referred to those guidelines which state that, generally speaking, a reference should not be made until the facts have been found and the reference should not be made at an interlocutory stage. With that, with great respect, I thoroughly agree.'

Ormrod LJ said (at 428): 'I would not, for my part, be inhibited by any nice questions of necessity, and would regard the word "necessary" as meaning "reasonably necessary" in ordinary English are not "unavoidable".'

Both counsel relied on Lord Diplock's speech in *R v Henn* [1980] 2 All ER 166 esp at 196, [1980] 2 WLR 597 esp at 635. Lord Diplock did not deal expressly with the issue before this court, but his speech does give some help to the respondent in that Lord Diplock treated the circuit judge as having a discretion to refer or not to refer a question to the European Court when the application was made as part of a motion to a circuit judge to quash a count in the indictment.

Having regard to these authorities, it is not right to say that the magistrates' court in this case had no jurisdiction to agree to refer questions to the European Court at the stage which the case which was then before them had reached. The validity of the regulations was the substantive issue before the court. As counsel for the respondent correctly pointed out, in a criminal case a defendant was entitled to have a decision whether there was a case to answer before he was called on to lead evidence in support of his defence. To rule on the submission, a decision on the questions of Community law raised by the respondent was necessary, since if the decision was in the respondent's favour he would be acquitted and if it was not, he would have to decide whether to contest further the one issue of fact which remained.

Although it is the decision of a magistrates' court which is under consideration, the test is no more stringent in the case of a magistrates' court than it is in the case of the High Court. If the justices take the view that a decision on the question is required in order to do justice, then, as long as they have not misdirected themselves in law or acted unreasonably, this court cannot interfere. Applying that approach, there is no material indicating that the Plymouth justices misdirected themselves in any way or acted unreasonably.

It is true that there was technically an issue of fact yet to be resolved. However, it is only just qualified as an issue. It is scarcely putting it too high to say that the magistrates would have been acting perversely had they found on it in favour of the respondent. Moreover, counsel for the respondent made it clear in the course of argument that he was prepared on behalf of his client to make the necessary admission. The situation was very similar to that in the *Polydor* case where Ormrod LJ described the remaining point as being 'sedulously preserved' and went on to say that the court should deal with the broad issue which was the matter on which the parties wanted a decision. On the special facts of the present case, it would be unreal to make any distinction between the position at the end of the prosecution's case and the position after the defence had had an opportunity to call such evidence as they wanted to put before the justices.

Counsel on behalf of the applicant did not advance an alternative argument suggesting that the justices, even if they had jurisdiction, had exercised their discretion improperly in deciding to refer. This is understandable on the facts of this case. We wish to add that in the ordinary case, it would be highly undesirable for the justices to decide to refer until all the evidence had been called and until they could be satisfied there was no question of the respondent being acquitted on the facts. In the normal way it is the obvious precaution to take to avoid the expense and delay of a reference to the European Court. It may involve the justices themselves taking a decision on the issue as to Community law without the advantage of the guidance of the European Court. However this should not be regarded as unfairly prejudicing the respondent, since his position would be exactly the same as in the case where the magistrates had to make a ruling on domestic law. In such a case it would only be after the conclusion of the hearing that the defendant could exercise his right to appeal or his right to apply to this court for judicial review.

It is for the same reason that in the ordinary way justices should exercise considerable caution before referring even after they have heard all the evidence. If they come to a wrong decision on Community law, a higher court can make the reference and frequently the higher court would be the more suitable forum to do so. The higher court is as a rule in a better position to assess whether any reference is desirable. On references the form of the question referred is of importance and the higher court will normally be in a better position to assess the appropriateness of the question and to assist in formulating it clearly. Leaving it to the higher court will often also avoid delay.

In *R v Henn* [1980] 2 All ER 166 at 196, [1980] 2 WLR 597 at 635 Lord Diplock said:

'Apart from this, however, in a criminal trial on indictment it can seldom be proper exercise of the presiding judge's discretion to seek a preliminary ruling before the facts of the alleged offence have been ascertained, with the result that the proceedings will be held up for nine months or more in order that at the end of the trial he may give to the jury an accurate instruction as to the relevant law, if the evidence turns out in the event to be as was anticipated at the time the reference was made, which may not always be the case. It is generally better, as the judge himself put it, that the question be decided by him in the first instance and reviewed hereafter if necessary through the hierarchy of the national courts.'

This applies with added force to trials before magistrates. The justices in the present case were however correct in judging it to be one of the exceptional cases where not only had they jurisdiction to refer but it was also proper for them so to do.

Application dismissed.

The court refused leave to appeal to the House of Lords but certified, under s 1(2) of the Administration of Justice Act 1960, that the following point of law of general public importance was involved in the decision: whether a magistrates' court was entitled to refer questions for the opinion of the Court of Justice of the European Communities under art 177 of the EEC Treaty at the close of the prosecution case on a submission of no case before the court had decided all the facts of the case.

Solicitors: *Solicitor to the Ministry of Agriculture, Fisheries and Food* (for the applicant); *Leo Abse & Cohen*, Cardiff (for the respondent).

Dilys Tausz   Barrister.

Re Lines Bros Ltd

COURT OF APPEAL, CIVIL DIVISION
LAWTON, BRIGHTMAN AND OLIVER LJJ
20, 21, 25, 26, 27, 28 JANUARY, 11 FEBRUARY 1982

Company – Voluntary winding up – Distribution of assets – Debt in foreign currency – Ascertainment of liability – Date – Whether sterling liability of debt to be ascertained at date of commencement of winding up or date of payment of dividends to creditors.

An international bank lent an English company 18·5m Swiss francs repayable in the same currency on 5 November 1971. The contract was governed by Swiss law. On 28 September 1971 the company went into creditors' voluntary liquidation. At that date the rate of exchange was 9·386 Swiss francs to the pound but thereafter sterling began to depreciate against the Swiss franc. The liquidators paid the provable debts in full by five dividends, the first on 10 November 1972 when the rate of exchange was 8·81 francs to the pound, and the last and final dividend on 20 June 1978 when the rate was 3·4725 Swiss francs to the pound. All dividends were paid in sterling, and in calculating the entitlement of the foreign currency creditors, including the bank, the liquidators converted all foreign currency debts into sterling at the rates of exchange prevailing on 28 September 1971, the date of the commencement of the winding up. As a result, in sterling terms, the bank lost £1·8m and received back in terms of Swiss francs less than 60% of its debt. After discharging provable debts in full the liquidators had a surplus of about £2m which they intended to distribute in satisfaction of other claims against the company for interest accruing after the liquidation had commenced. The bank was dissatisfied with the distribution and claimed that since its debt was a foreign debt it was owed foreign currency and not sterling, and that, if the bank was to be repaid its debt pari passu as required by s 302[a] of the Companies Act 1948, the liquidators were required to repay the actual foreign currency debt (or the proportion thereof being paid when each dividend was distributed) at the rate of exchange prevailing on the date of payment and not merely the notional sterling equivalent of the claim as at the date of the winding up. The bank thus claimed that it should have received back in full the 18·5m Swiss francs it had lent to the company. The liquidators applied to the court for directions as to the correct date for fixing the rate of exchange. The judge held that the bank's foreign currency debt was properly converted into sterling at the date of the winding up and that dividends paid thereafter to the bank were required to be the appropriate proportion of that sterling amount. The bank appealed.

Held – The appeal would be dismissed for the following reasons—

(1) Liquidation of a company, whether compulsory or voluntary, was a form of collective enforcement of liabilities in which like had to be compared with like if the property of the company was to be applied in satisfaction of its liabilities pari passu pursuant to s 302 of the 1948 Act. In order, therefore, for a proper comparison of liabilities to be made, the liquidator was required to convert claims in a foreign currency to sterling as at the date of the commencement of the winding up, since that was the date on which existing liabilities were to be valued and the date beyond which no further liabilities could accrue. The bank was, therefore, not entitled to be repaid its actual foreign currency debt converted at the exchange rate prevailing on the date when payment was made (see p 188 *j* to p 189 *g*, p 190 *a* and *d* to *g*, p 192 *c d*, p 194 *a* to *d* and *j* to p 195 *b*, p 196 *b c*, p 198 *a b h* and p 199 *g* to *j*, post); *Re Humber Ironworks and Shipbuilding Co, Warrant Finance Co's Case* (1869) LR 4 Ch App 643 and *Re Dynamics Corp of America* [1976] 2 All ER 669 followed; *Miliangos v George Frank (Textiles) Ltd* [1975] 3 All ER 801 considered; dictum of Lord Wilberforce in *Miliangos v George Frank (Textiles) Ltd* [1975] 3 All ER at 814 not followed.

---

a Section 302, so far as material, is set out at p 198 *b*, post

(2) (Per Brightman and Oliver LJJ) Similarly, the surplus of £2m available to the liquidators after discharging the provable debts was not available to discharge the shortfall suffered by the bank by reason of the fall in sterling against the Swiss franc between the date of winding up and the dates of payment of dividends, because it was implicit in the concept of pari passu that creditors, both in sterling and in foreign currency, should not be at risk because of, or be affected by, the vagaries of exchange rates. Thus the right of sterling creditors who were entitled to post-liquidation interest and who would be entitled to the £2m if it was not applied to the bank's shortfall should not be diminished by the adverse movements of exchange rates affecting the bank's claim (see p 195 j to p 196 c and p 199 g to j, post).

Per Brightman and Oliver LJJ. In the case of a wholly solvent liquidation, if a foreign currency creditor has been paid less than his full contractual currency debt it may well be the duty of the liquidator to make good the foreign currency creditor's shortfall before he pays anything to the shareholders (see p 195 h j and p 199 e f, post).

Per Brightman LJ. Creditors do not rank pari passu if the sterling creditors are required to underwrite the exchange rate of sterling for the benefit of foreign currency creditors (see p 191 j to p, p 192 a and p 196 a b, post).

Notes

For proof of claims in a foreign currency in the winding up of a company, see 7 Halsbury's Laws (4th edn) para 1267.

For proof of interest in case of insolvent company, see ibid para 1274.

For the Companies Act 1948, s 302, see 5 Halsbury's Statutes (3rd edn) 337.

Cases referred to in judgments

Albert Life Assurance Co, Re, Craig's Executors' Case (1870) LR 9 Eq 706.
Anglo-Baltic and Mediterranean Bank v Barber & Co [1924] 2 KB 410, [1924] All ER Rep 226, CA, 10 Digest (Reissue) 1170, 7284.
Ayerst (Inspector of Taxes) v C & K (Construction) Ltd [1975] 2 All ER 537, [1976] AC 167, [1975] 3 WLR 16, Digest (Cont Vol D) 492, 1664a.
British American Continental Bank Ltd, Goldzieher and Penso's Claim [1922] 2 Ch 575, CA, 35 Digest (Repl) 199, 83.
Craven v Blackpool Greyhound Stadium and Racecourse Ltd [1936] 3 All ER 513, CA, 10 Digest (Reissue) 1168, 7269.
Duncan (W W) & Co, Re [1905] 1 Ch 307, 10 Digest (Reissue) 1061, 6513.
Dynamics Corp of America, Re [1976] 2 All ER 669, [1976] 1 WLR 757, Digest (Cont Vol E) 432, 84a.
English Assurance Co, Re, Holdich's Case (1872) LR 14 Eq 72, 10 Digest (Reissue) 1265, 7972.
European Assurance Society, Re, Wallberg's Case (1872) 17 SJ 69, Marrack's European Assurance Reports 50, Reilly's European Arbitration (Lord Westbury's Decisions) 65.
House Property Investment Co Ltd, Re [1953] 2 All ER 1525, [1954] Ch 576, 10 Digest (Reissue) 1151, 7166.
Humber Ironworks and Shipbuilding Co, Re, Warrant Finance Co's Case (1869) LR 4 Ch App 643, LJJ; *rvsg* 20 LT 508, 10 Digest (Reissue) 1061, 6511.
Law Car and General Insurance Corp, Re [1913] 2 Ch 103, [1911–13] All ER Rep 1024, CA, 10 Digest (Reissue) 1266, 7980.
Miliangos v George Frank (Textiles) Ltd [1975] 3 All ER 801, [1976] AC 443, [1975] 3 WLR 758, HL, Digest (Cont Vol D) 691, 64c.
Northern Counties of England Fire Insurance Co, Re, Macfarlane's Claim (1880) 17 Ch D 337, 10 Digest (Reissue) 1265, 7976.
Parana Plantations Ltd, Re [1946] 2 All ER 214, CA, 12 Digest (Reissue) 569, 3966.
Smith, Knight & Co, Re, ex p Ashbury (1868) LR 5 Eq 223, 10 Digest (Reissue) 1153, 7178.

Cases also cited

Barclays Bank International Ltd v Levin Bros (Bradford) Ltd [1976] 3 All ER 900, [1977] QB 270.
Bower v Morris (1841) Cr & Ph 351, 41 ER 525, LC.
Bradberry, Re, National Provincial Bank v Bradberry, Re Fry, Tasker v Gulliford [1942] 2 All ER 629, [1943] Ch 35.
Browne and Wingrove, Re, ex p Ador [1891] 2 QB 574, CA.
Bwllfa and Merthyr Dare Steam Collieries (1891) *Ltd v Pontypridd Waterworks Co* [1903] AC 426, [1900–3] All Er Rep 600, HL.
Choice Investments Ltd v Jeromnimon [1981] 1 All ER 225, [1981] QB 149, CA.
Company, Re a [1915] 1 Ch 520, CA.
Dodds, Re, ex p Vaughan's Executors (1890) 25 QBD 529.
Elder's Trustee and Executor Co Ltd v Beneficial Finance Corp Ltd (1979) 21 SASR 216.
Halcyon the Great, The [1975] 1 All ER 882, [1975] 1 WLR 515.
Israel–British Bank Ltd, Re (19 December 1976) District Court, Tel Aviv-Jaffa; *affd* sub nom *Wallace Bros Commodities Ltd v Milo* (16 January 1979) Supreme Court of Israel.
Kloebe, Re, Krannreuther v Geiselbrecht (1884) 28 Ch D 175, [1881–5] All ER Rep 1120.
Mitchelson v Piper (1836) 8 Sim 64, 59 ER 26.
Pottinger, Re, ex p Stewart (1878) 8 Ch D 621.
Schorsch Meier GmbH v Hennin [1975] 1 All ER 152, [1975] QB 416, CA.
Simpson v Jones (Inspector of Taxes) [1968] 2 All ER 929, [1968] 1 WLR 1066.
Wilson v Paul (1836) 8 Sim 63, 59 ER 25.

Appeal

By a summons issued on 8 July 1980 Paul Frederick Martin Shewell and Michael Anthony Jordan, the joint liquidators of Lines Bros Ltd (the company), sought in the voluntary liquidation thereof the directions of the court, inter alia, as to (1) which of a number of dates was the correct date on which the principal amount of indebtedness of the company, being indebtedness payable in a currency other than sterling (the foreign currency debt), should for the purposes of the payment of dividends in respect of such foreign currency debt in the voluntary winding up of the company be converted into sterling, (2) whether the difference between a foreign currency debt converted into sterling as at the commencement of the winding up of the company on 28 September 1971, and such foreign currency debt converted into sterling at some later date, gave rise to a claim on the part of the creditor in respect of such foreign currency debt to participate further in the assets of the company and, if so, directions as to the date on which such conversion fell to be effected and the method of calculating such claim, (3) whether interest accruing down to the commencement of the winding up of the company on a foreign currency debt should for the purposes of the payment of dividends or other sums in respect of such interest in the voluntary winding up of the company be converted into sterling, (4) whether the difference between interest accruing down to the commencement of the winding up of the company on a foreign currency debt and converted into sterling as at such commencement, gave rise to a claim on the part of the creditor in respect of such interest to participate further in the assets of the company, and, if so, directions as to the date on which such conversion fell to be effected and the method of calculating such claim, (5) whether for the purposes of any conversion falling to be effected in respect of interest on a foreign currency debt accruing down to the commencement of the winding up of the company any distinction and, if so, what distinction, fell to be drawn between interest calculated or purportedly calculated at 5% per annum pursuant to s 66 of the Bankruptcy Act 1914 and interest to the extent that it exceeded such interest (the deferred interest). The respondent to the summons was Lloyds Bank International Ltd (formerly Lloyds Bank Europe Ltd) (the bank), a creditor of the company. On 15 April 1981 Slade J held (i) that for the purposes of the payment of dividends in the voluntary winding up of the company the debt of a foreign currency creditor fell to be converted into sterling as at the date of the commencement of the

voluntary winding up of the company, viz 28 September 1971, (ii) that the difference
between a foreign currency debt which had been converted into sterling as at 28
September 1971 and a foreign currency debt which had been converted subsequently
thereto did not give rise to a claim on the part of the creditor in respect of such foreign
currency debt to participate further in the assets of the company, (iii) that the interest
accruing, if any, down to 28 September 1971 on a foreign currency debt should, for the
purposes of the payment of dividends or other sums in respect of such interest in the
voluntary winding up of the company, be converted into sterling as at 28 September
1971, (iv) that the difference between interest accruing down to 28 September 1971 on
a foreign currency debt and converted into sterling as at 28 September 1971 and interest
converted into sterling on a date subsequent thereto did not give rise to a claim on the
part of the creditor in respect of such interest further to participate in the assets of the
company, and (v) that for the purposes of any conversion falling to be effected in respect
of interest on a foreign currency debt accruing down to 28 September 1971 no distinction
fell to be drawn between interest calculated at 5% per annum pursuant to s 66 of the
Bankruptcy Act 1914 (the statutory interest) and interest to the extent that it exceeded
such statutory interest and that any conversion must be effected as at 28 September
1971. The bank appealed. The facts are set out in the judgment of Lawton LJ.

William Stubbs QC and *Mary Arden* for the bank.
David Graham QC and *Robin Potts* for the liquidators.

Cur adv vult

11 February. The following judgments were read.

LAWTON LJ. The issue in this appeal is this: when a creditors' voluntary liquidation
carried on within the jurisdiction of the Supreme Court takes a long time and some of
the company's debts are in a foreign currency and claimed in that currency, should the
liquidator pay dividends in sterling at the rate of exchange prevailing at the date of the
resolution to wind up or at the rates prevailing when any payments are made? If, as in
this case, dividends are paid in sterling and that currency depreciates against the foreign
currency between the date of the winding up and the date of payment, the creditors in
the foreign currency on converting their sterling dividends into the foreign currency in
which the debts were incurred and the claims made, will get a smaller proportion of their
claims in that currency to what their claims bore to the other claims at the date of the
winding-up resolution.

The experienced joint liquidators of Lines Bros Ltd (the company) thought that the
rate of exchange was fixed at the date of the resolution to wind up the company, which
was 28 September 1971. From time to time thereafter they paid dividends to the
creditors in foreign currencies at the rate of exchange then prevailing. One of those
creditors was Lloyds Bank International Ltd (the bank). It had lent the company 18·5m
Swiss francs repayable in the same currency on 5 November 1971. It was admitted
before us that the proper law of the contract was Swiss. On 28 September 1971 the
pound was worth 9·836 Swiss francs. Thereafter sterling began to depreciate against the
Swiss franc. Four interim dividends were paid, the first on 10 November 1972 when the
rate of exchange was 8·81 Swiss francs to the pound. The second was paid on 2 January
1975 when the rate was 6·025; the third on 13 February 1976 when the rate was 5·17;
the fourth on August 1976 when the rate was 4·435 and a final dividend on 20 June 1978
when the rate was 3·4725. All the dividends were paid in sterling.

The liquidation had been fairly satisfactory for some of the creditors: the sterling
creditors had been paid the amount of their claims, but the creditors in foreign currencies
had been paid their claims in their sterling equivalents on 28 September 1971. After
paying these dividends the liquidators now have available about £2m which, after

deducting the expenses of the liquidation, they propose to distribute in part satisfaction of the post-liquidation date claims for interest arising under contract. The bank has such a claim.

The bank, however, is dissatisfied with this distribution. Had Swiss francs been bought with its sterling dividends on the dates when they were paid it would have received not 100% of its claim as the sterling creditors did but 58·776%. In sterling terms it had lost about £1·8m. The bank has not been the only loser. An English merchant bank which lent the company DM 1,183,533 has received in that currency 66·049% of its claim. An Italian bank, however, which lent 40m lire has received more or less the whole of its claim in that currency because it has depreciated at about the same rate as sterling against Swiss francs and Deutschmarks. The bank claimed that when the liquidators were ready to pay a dividend they should, before doing so, have worked out the proportions between the claims and have paid the bank either in Swiss francs or in sterling calculated at the prevailing rate which would then have bought in Swiss francs the fraction of the claims which they intended to pay. If, for example, they had intended to pay a dividend representing 10% of the total claims, they should have paid 10% of the bank's claim, that is, 1,850,000 Swiss francs, or its sterling equivalent at the date of payment.

The bank accepted in this court, and I assume it did so in its negotiations with the liquidators before proceedings started, that in paying dividends in the way they did the liquidators had followed a practice which had been recognised as correct in law from the 1860s onwards. The bank's argument was, and has been in this court, that the old practice has been invalidated by the decision of the House of Lords in *Miliangos v George Frank (Textiles) Ltd* [1975] 3 All ER 801, [1976] AC 443. Since that case, it was submitted, all liquidators, whether acting under a winding-up order of the court or a resolution to wind up should either pay dividends in the foreign currency in which the debt had been incurred or in the sterling equivalent at the date of payment. It was in these circumstances that the liquidators decided to ask the court for directions. They issued an originating summons on 8 July 1980. In it they asked the court to direct them as to which of a number of dates was the correct one for fixing the rate of exchange. This was because of obiter dicta in the speeches in the *Miliangos* case. The experienced counsel who appeared for both sides in this court accepted that there were only two possible dates, either the date of the winding up, which in the case of a compulsory winding up would be the date of the court's order and in the case of a voluntary winding up the date of the resolution, or at the close of business on the last practical day before making payment. After hearing argument for 11 days in February 1981, Slade J delivered a reserved judgment on 15 April 1981 whereby he adjudged that for the purposes of the payment of dividends in the liquidation under consideration the bank's foreign currency debt was properly converted into sterling as at the date of the commencement of the voluntary winding up, namely 28 September 1971. In deciding as he did he followed a judgment of Oliver J in *Re Dynamics Corp of America* [1976] 2 All ER 669, [1976] 1 WLR 757. The bank has appealed to this court against Slade J's judgment.

In the course of his submissions to this court, counsel for the bank on a number of occasions reminded us that justice should be done to his clients. Of course it should; but when rates of exchange fluctuate from day to day, sometimes from hour to hour, every variation means that someone gains and another loses. Had sterling appreciated against the Swiss franc, the sterling creditors would probably have made the same complaint as the bank has done. The practice which went unchallenged for over a hundred years had this advantage: after the creditors, including those in a foreign currency, had seen the statement of affairs prepared by the liquidators they knew what their financial prospects of getting anything out of the liquidation were and they could plan accordingly. If the *Miliangos* case has changed liquidation practice, the certainty of the past will be replaced by the uncertainty of the future. Administrative convenience, however, does not entitle us to disregard decisions of the House of Lords which are binding on us.

The solution to the problem before us lies, in my opinion, in the answers to these questions: first, what did the *Miliangos* case decide relevant to a liquidation; and, second, do the provisions of the Companies Act 1948 stop the application to liquidations of whatever the *Miliangos* case did decide? Both before Slade J and this court reference was made to many authorities. Most of them, in my opinion, were only of marginal, if any, help. I intend to rely on very few.

I start with the *Miliangos* case. The facts and the history leading up to the decision are so well known that I need not repeat them in this judgment. The House decided (Lord Simon dissenting) that the Swiss plaintiff could in an action brought in England ask for judgment in the currency of account which was Swiss francs. The House recognised, however, that there would have to be provision for converting the foreign currency into sterling if the judgment was to be enforced here. There was discussion as to what the conversion date should be. As Lord Fraser pointed out ([1975] 3 All ER 801 at 841, [1976] AC 443 at 501), theoretically it should be the date of actual payment of the debt. He went on to say that theory must yield to practical necessity to the extent that, if a judgment has to be enforced here, it must be converted before enforcement. All their Lordships, other than Lord Simon, agreed that the conversion date should be when the court authorised enforcement in terms of sterling.

Following this decision, as Lord Wilberforce had expected (see [1975] 3 All ER 801 at 814, [1976] AC 443 at 469), a practice direction was issued (see [1976] 1 All ER 669, [1976] 1 WLR 83) setting out the practice to be followed in relation to the making of claims and the enforcement of judgments expressed in a foreign currency. Paragraph 9 directed how judgments in a foreign currency were to be entered. The sum in foreign currency in which judgment had been ordered was to be set out followed by the words 'or the sterling equivalent at the time of payment'. Paragraph 11 dealt with the enforcement of a judgment debt in a foreign currency by the writ of fieri facias. The praecipe for the issue of the writ has to be indorsed with the amount of the sterling equivalent at the close of business on *the date nearest or most nearly preceding the date of the issue of the writ of fi fa*. Paragraph 12 deals with garnishee proceedings and provides for a sterling conversion date to be specified in the supporting affidavit. Other forms of enforcement are provided for in para 13 and once again provision is made for a sterling conversion. The inference which I draw from the *Miliangos* case itself and the amended practice of the court which the House of Lords anticipated would follow is that, if a judgment creditor who has a judgment for the payment of a sum in a foreign currency wants to enforce it by means of a form of execution under English law, there has to be a conversion into sterling before execution can start.

Counsel for the liquidators based their submissions on this inference. Counsel for the bank queried whether the practice direction accurately reflected the basic proposition established in the *Miliangos* case. He could see no reason why a judgment creditor for a debt in a foreign currency could not garnishee an account held in that currency. Nowadays many banks have accounts in foreign currencies. But even if the inference were right, it was, submitted counsel for the bank, irrelevant to his main submission because the *Miliangos* case had decided that a debt in a foreign currency was one recognised by English law. The bank had bargained to be paid in the currency of its choice and only in that currency. The liquidators had a statutory duty under the Companies Act 1948 to pay the debts of the company. Debts in a foreign currency were debts which the liquidators had to pay. If they could not, or would not, pay them in the foreign currency, they should pay them in the sterling equivalent at the date of payment. There was nothing in the Companies Act 1948 which excused the liquidators from paying foreign currency debts in this way.

Before considering the effect of the Companies Act 1948 on the issue in this appeal I must explain why I agree with counsel on both sides that some comments made by Lord Wilberforce and accepted as correct by Lord Cross in the *Miliangos* case should not be followed. When discussing the problem of a conversion date into sterling Lord Wilberforce said ([1975] 3 All ER 801 at 814, [1976] AC 443 at 469):

'So I would favour the payment date, in the sense I have mentioned. In the case of a company in liquidation, the corresponding date for conversion would be the date when the creditor's claim in terms of sterling is admitted by the liquidator.'

Lord Cross said that he agreed with Lord Wilberforce on this point (see [1975] 3 All ER 801 at 838, [1976] AC 443 at 498). Lord Wilberforce's comment was clearly obiter; but what he says obiter always calls for careful consideration. Counsel have satisfied me that a date based on a liquidator's admission of a claim would cause confusion since claims are made at different times and may not be admitted in the order in which they are received. He may have to make protracted inquiries about a claim before admitting it. Lord Wilberforce, however, must be understood to have rejected the winding-up date as a possible date and to have thought that some other date in the winding-up process, but not the date of payment of the dividend, was the correct conversion date. I have asked myself why one so learned in company law and practice, when thinking of enforcement, should seemingly have rejected the date of payment of a dividend. Counsel for the liquidators provided an answer in the way they put the liquidators' case. They submitted that liquidation, whether compulsory or voluntary, was a form of collective enforcement under the law. The liabilities could be in the form of judgment debts, present unpaid debts or likely future or contingent debts or claims. Once a winding-up order has been made by the courts creditors have to accept the collective enforcement procedure unless the court gives leave to enforce in some other way: see s 231 of the Companies Act 1948. In the case of a voluntary winding up a creditor need not join in. He can issue a writ and proceed to judgment; but a liquidator can apply to stay execution and, if he does so, the court will grant the application unless there are very exceptional reasons why it should not do so: see *Anglo-Baltic and Mediterranean Bank v Barber & Co* [1924] 2 KB 410, [1924] All ER Rep 226. A creditor in a voluntary winding up cannot claim in the liquidation and later issue a writ: see *Craven v Blackpool Greyhound Stadium and Racecourse Ltd* [1936] 3 All ER 513. Being a form of collective enforcement, the beginning of a winding up was in its legal nature the equivalent of the court giving leave to enforce a judgment; and just as a judgment in a foreign currency could not be enforced until it was converted into sterling so a liquidator could not apply the property of a company in satisfaction of its liabilities pari passu until he had put a value in sterling on any claims made in a foreign currency. The liquidator has to compare like with like and a Swiss franc cannot be compared with a pound until the sterling value is known. A convenient date for making the valuation is the date when the winding up starts since this is the date which, for over a hundred years before the *Miliangos* case, was accepted as the date beyond which no further liabilities could accrue. The assets realised 'should be applied equally and rateably in payment of the debts as they existed at the date of the winding up': see *Re Humber Ironworks and Shipbuilding Co, Warrant Finance Co's Case* (1869) LR 4 Ch App 643 at 646 per Selwyn LJ.

Counsel for the bank did not query this analysis. A valuation at some date, and the date of the beginning of the winding up might be a convenient one, for the purpose of finding out in what proportions the claims stood to one another probably was necessary; but once the proportions had been determined the liquidators in this case had a statutory duty under s 302 of the Companies Act 1948 to apply the property of the company in satisfaction of its liabilities pari passu. Any dividends had to be paid in the same proportions as the claims had stood to one another at the beginning of the liquidation. This, he submitted, was what pari passu meant in s 302. By notionally converting the bank's foreign currency claim into sterling as at 28 September 1971 and later paying dividends in the ratio to which the bank's notional sterling claim stood at the beginning of the liquidation to the other claims, all expressed in sterling even though some were foreign currency claims, that produced a result whereby the bank's debt, which was a Swiss franc debt, was not paid fully whereas all the truly sterling debts were. The liquidators could not be said to have paid the debts pari passu as they should have done.

At the end of the opening of counsel for the bank I thought his submission was right. Counsel for the liquidators, however, persuaded me that it ignores the juridical nature of liquidation and is fallacious. As I have already said, liquidation is a form of collective enforcement of liabilities under English law. Liabilities are what the court will enforce. It will not enforce judgments for debts in Swiss francs but their equivalents in sterling at the dates when leave to enforce is given. Liquidation affects the contractual relationship between debtor and creditor. When the liquidation starts, no further liabilities under contract become payable until such time as it is clear that the pre-liquidation liabilities have been satisfied in full: see *Re Humber Ironworks and Shipbuilding Co.* The beneficial interest in the company's assets is transferred to the liquidator. In *Ayerst (Inspector of Taxes) v C & K (Construction) Ltd* [1975] 2 All ER 537, [1976] AC 167 the House of Lords had to consider the legal effect of a winding-up order. Lord Diplock delivered the leading speech with which the other members of the Appeal Committee agreed. He pointed out that the making of a winding-up order brings into operation a statutory scheme for dealing with the assets of a company which is being wound up. It matters not whether the winding up is by order or pursuant to a resolution. The assets of the company when realised provide a fund which the liquidator administers in many respects, but not in all, as if he were managing a trust fund. Creditors' contractual rights to be paid by the company become under the statutory scheme a statutory right to a share in the trust fund. The size of this fund has to be ascertained as soon as possible because until it is ascertained it cannot be applied in satisfaction of the company's liabilities; and as like has to be compared with like, the valuation of the fund has to be in sterling. Ever since *Re Humber Ironworks and Shipbuilding Co* it has been the practice to value the fund as at the date of liquidation. I can see no reason why a different date should be fixed merely because one or more of the liabilities is stated in a foreign currency. It follows that such a foreign liability has to be valued at the rate of exchange when the valuation is made. Since the application of the fund in satisfaction of all the liabilities is a form of enforcement, in my judgment payments out of it by way of dividends should be in sterling just as judgment debts in foreign currencies are paid in sterling at the rate appropriate when leave to enforce is given.

I can see no reason for criticising the way in which the liquidators in this case performed their duties. I would dismiss the appeal.

BRIGHTMAN LJ. I agree with Lawton LJ that for the purpose of applying the company's property in satisfaction of its liabilities pari passu pursuant to s 302 of the 1948 Act, the foreign debts of the company, as existing at the date of liquidation, should be converted into sterling at the buying rate of the foreign currency at the date of the resolution to wind up. I deal separately with the position which arises in relation to the surplus assets of the company remaining after its indebtedness, so calculated, has been discharged in full.

It is common ground that the indebtedness of the company to the bank arose under a contract of which the proper law was Swiss, and under which the currency of account and of payment was Swiss francs.

As a result of the decision of the House of Lords in *Miliangos v George Frank (Textiles) Ltd* [1975] 3 All ER 801, [1976] AC 443, it is also common ground that, had the company defaulted on the debt prior to liquidation and been sued in England by the bank, the bank could have obtained a judgment against the company expressed in Swiss francs, and could have executed such judgment against the property of the company in a sum of sterling representing the judgment debt converted into sterling at the buying rate of Swiss francs at the date when execution was authorised by the court.

The principal question before us is the effect of this reinterpretation of the law on a foreign currency claim in the liquidation of a company.

We are concerned with a creditors' voluntary winding up. It would, however, be unrealistic to disregard the fact that the identical issue can arise in the liquidation of a prosperous company which has more than enough assets to answer its full contractual indebtedness. Further, there can be no reason for any distinction between a voluntary liquidation and a compulsory liquidation.

Much argument has revolved around the precise wording of s 302. This section applies to voluntary liquidations only: '. . . the property of a company shall, on its winding up, be applied in satisfaction of its liabilities pari passu . . .' Although there is no comparable section in the case of a compulsory liquidation, there is no doubt that the same principle applies.

The accounts of a liquidator can only be expressed in a single currency. They cannot be expressed partly in one currency and partly in another. It follows that whenever the liquidator or an officer of the company produces an account for the purposes of the liquidation, assuming that sterling is the currency of the liquidation, he will be bound to convert a foreign currency debt into sterling, as the currency of the account. Conversion is inevitable. The question is: at what date or dates is that conversion to be effected? The argument of the bank is that the conversion is to be recalculated from time to time. Its argument means that a debt of 18m Swiss francs shown in the statement of affairs (under s 235 or s 293) as £1·8m (if the exchange rate is 10 francs to the pound) will have to be shown a year later in the interim account under s 342 (Form 92) as £3·6m if the exchange rate has altered to 5 francs to the pound. If the total indebtedness of the company is estimated in such statement of affairs at £7·2m, and the estimated net realisations at £5·4m, the statement of affairs would indicate an estimated dividend of 75p in the pound. But, by the date of the first interim account, the estimated indebtedness would have risen to £9m, and the potential distribution would have fallen to 60p in the pound. Other figures could produce an exactly opposite result, namely an increase in the potential distributions. In the case of a foreign debt expressed in a currency which tends to appreciate against sterling, the sterling creditors would bear the risk of the depreciation in sterling. In the case of a foreign debt expressed in a depreciating currency (some currencies suffer repeated devaluations) the sterling creditors would stand to gain the greater the delay in making distributions.

I turn to consider the policy underlying the *Miliangos* decision. Lord Wilberforce observed ([1975] 3 All ER 801 at 811, [1976] AC 443 at 465):

'First, I do not for myself think it doubtful that, in a case such as the present, justice demands that the creditor should not suffer from fluctuations in the value of sterling . . .'

And again ([1975] 3 All ER 801 at 813, [1976] AC 443 at 468):

'It is for the courts, or for arbitrators, to work out a solution in each case best adapted to giving the injured plaintiff that amount in damages which will most fairly compensate him for the wrong which he has suffered.'

The policy behind the decision, as is apparent from that quotation and as recognised by counsel in argument before us, was that the foreign currency debtor should not be entitled to impose on the foreign currency creditor the risk of a fall in the value of sterling. Justice demands that the risk shall be borne by the debtor, who is the party in default. Hence the justice of the reinterpretation of the law, that the debtor in default is not to be excused from his contractual obligation by payment of anything less than the sterling equivalent of the money contractually due at the date of payment.

If this statement of the reasoning behind the *Miliangos* decision is correct, clearly it has no role to play in the distribution of the assets of an insolvent company. The sterling creditors are not in default vis-à-vis the foreign currency creditors. Therefore, there is no obvious reason why the risk of depreciation in the value of sterling pending distribution of the assets should be borne by the sterling creditors. The company is the wrongdoer towards both the sterling creditors and the foreign currency creditors. There is no particular reason, in the field of abstract justice, why the currency risk should be borne by one description of creditor rather than by another description of creditor when they are all directed to rank pari passu. They do not rank pari passu if the sterling creditors are required to underwrite the exchange rate of the pound for the benefit of the foreign currency creditors. The just course, as it seems to me, is to value the foreign debt once and for all at an appropriate date, and to keep to that rate of conversion throughout the liquidation until all debts have been paid in full. The loss and the benefit from changes in exchange rates will then lie where they fall. In terms of sterling, if that is the currency of the liquidation, the amount of the debts will be unaffected by movements on the foreign exchange market. In the case of a debt expressed in a depreciating currency the other creditors will stand to gain nothing from a protracted liquidation. In the case of a debt expressed in an appreciating currency, the liquidator will not be faced with the question whether expedited payment of such foreign debt, if that can be effected, might be to the advantage of sterling creditors. All the creditors will be treated alike. No recalculations will have to be made of the company's indebtedness, and no forecasts of distributions will need to be revised on account of exchange factors. The position will be stabilised and all creditors will be treated alike.

If a single conversion date has to be chosen, all parties are agreed that the only candidate in the present case is the date when the company was placed in liquidation, ie the date of the resolution to wind up. It seems to me that such a conclusion is consistent with early authority, to which I now turn, while a revaluation of a foreign currency debt from time to time would be inconsistent with the trend of authority.

In *Re Humber Ironworks and Shipbuilding Co, Warrant Finance Co's Case* (1869) LR 4 Ch App 643, the company, which was insolvent, was indebted to Warrant Finance Co in the sum of £25,000 carrying interest at 20% from a date which was subsequent to the winding-up order. Lord Romilly MR (see 20 LT 508) decided that Warrant Finance Co could prove for interest down to the date of the declaration of the dividend. This decision was reversed by the Court of Appeal in Chancery. Selwyn LJ said (LR 4 Ch App 643 at 646–647):

'I think the tree must lie as it falls; that it must be ascertained what are the debts *as they exist at the date of the winding-up*, and that all dividends in the case of an insolvent estate must be declared in respect of the debts so ascertained.'

Giffard LJ expressed the same view, both on the ground of convenience and on the ground of fairness. He said (LR 4 Ch App 643 at 647):

'. . . if we are to consider convenience, it is quite clear that, where an estate is insolvent, convenience is in favour of stopping all the computations *at the date of the winding-up* . . . I am of opinion that dividends ought to be paid on the debts as they stand at the date of the winding-up; for when the estate is insolvent this rule distributes the assets in the fairest way.'

This approach is echoed in a number of early cases, though not perhaps winning immediate acceptance. In *Re Albert Life Assurance Co, Craig's Executors' Case* (1870) LR 9 Eq 706 at 721 James V-C, in considering the case where a life assured by an insolvent company died after the date of liquidation, referred to the death 'as affording evidence of the value of the life at the time of taking in the claim'. But two years later, in *Re English Assurance Co, Holdich's Case* (1872) LR 14 Eq 72 at 80, Lord Romilly MR had 'no doubt *the day of the winding-up order* is the time at which *the value* of the policy or annuity is to be calculated'. The same view was forcefully expressed a little later in the same year by Lord Westbury sitting as statutory arbitrator in *Re European Assurance Society, Wallberg's Case* (1872) 17 SJ 69 at 70:

'. . . with regard to the time of the valuation of a policy or annuity, it is matter of surprise to me that any doubt should have been entertained. Doubts, however, have been entertained by different judges . . . But if you examine the subject, I think it will be admitted at once that there can be no doubt upon the question. The necessity for a valuation of these claims against the company arises from this fact, that all the property of the company is, under the winding-up order, handed over for equal distribution among its creditors. Of those creditors annuitants and holders of policies granted by the company are some, and the necessity of making an equal distribution of the assets of the insolvent company, renders necessary also a valuation of these claims. These are claims to arise, as in the case of annuities, from time to time, *in futuro*. In the case of policies they are contingent claims arising upon a contingent event, namely, the death of the person to whom the policy is granted. The Legislature has determined, and in all insolvencies the same rule applies, that in the course of the administration of the estate of an insolvent company these debts shall be valued; they must be valued; you could not withhold out of the assets of the company a large sum of money, and keep it invested, or in suspense, to answer the claims when they arise. You must have a present value put on these future claims, and that present value represents the sum for which the claimant, the holder of the claims, will be entitled to rank among the rest of the creditors. Now then, where does the necessity for this valuation arise? It arises immediately on the property of the company, the debtor, being directed to be equally distributed. But when is the property of the debtor company subjected to equal distribution among the creditors? At the date of the winding-up order. Then, and not until then, is the company divested of its property. In effect, the property is handed over to the official liquidator to be broken up and distributed in proportionate parts among the creditor claimants who are entitled. Well, then, it follows immediately that the valuation must be made when the necessity for a valuation arises. The necessity arises, as I have said, when the order to wind-up is made; and that, therefore, becomes necessarily *the date of the valuation.*'

We find the same in *Re W W Duncan & Co* [1905] 1 Ch 307 at 315 per Buckley J: 'Now what do you admit to proof for dividend in the winding-up of a company? *The amount of the debt at the commencement of the winding-up*', referring, I think, to the date of the order of the resolution. He repeated this in *Re Law Car and General Insurance Corp* [1913] 2 Ch 103 at 121–122:

> '. . . the fact that the life had dropped was admissible for the purpose of shewing what was *at the date of the winding-up* the just estimate of *the value* of the then contingent claim . . . For the purpose of proof under s 158 of the Companies Act, 1862 [now s 316 of the Companies Act 1948], there is to be ascertained the *value at the winding-up* of the contingent claim.'

In *Re British American Continental Bank Ltd, Goldzieher and Penso's Claim* [1922] 2 Ch 575 at 582–583 P O Lawrence J, whose decision was affirmed by the Court of Appeal, said:

> 'In a winding up, this Court has to ascertain all the liabilities of the company being wound up for the purposes of effecting the proper distribution of its assets amongst its creditors. A date has necessarily to be fixed on which all debts and other liabilities are to be treated as definitely ascertained, both for the purpose of placing all creditors on an equality and for the purpose of properly conducting the winding up of the affairs of the company. According to the rules and practice now prevailing, the date so fixed is *the date of the winding-up order.* One effect of fixing that date is to compel those creditors whose claims do not consist of debts or of liquidated demands ascertained and payable before that date to estimate and assess the amounts which they claim to be due to them on that date. Another effect of fixing that date is that when a claim is disputed this Court will decide the dispute as though it were being determined on the day when the winding-up order was made. Accordingly, in a case where a creditor has an unsatisfied claim against the company for damages for breach of contract, and the amount of those damages is in dispute, this Court will ascertain the correct amount as if it were sitting *on the day of the winding-up order* and were then trying an action for damages for the breach of that contract.'

Finally, in *Re Parana Plantations Ltd* [1946] 2 All ER 214 at 218–219, Lord Greene MR said: 'The proof must speak from the date of the winding up . . . and the right of the claimant was to put *a value up on his claim as at that date.'*

I have quoted at length from authorities on a proposition which is accepted as axiomatic in order to underline the point that the winding-up date is *the date of valuation* of liabilities. As an account can only be struck in a single currency, it must follow that the scheme of company liquidation requires that a foreign debt shall be converted into sterling (if sterling is the currency of the liquidation) as at the date of liquidation and at no other date.

A great deal of what I have ventured to say in this part of my judgment is inevitably mere repetition of what was said by Oliver J in the Chancery Division in *Re Dynamics Corp of America* [1976] 2 All ER 669, [1976] 1 WLR 757 when he was called on to decide, in effect, between date of liquidation and date of proof as the correct (single) date for conversion. A multiplicity of conversion dates, involved in the bank's argument before us, was raised, apparently, but not debated before him.

I am accordingly of the opinion that the liquidators' submission that a foreign currency debt should be proved or claimed according to its value as at the date on which the company was placed in liquidation, besides answering the justice of the case, is entirely in accordance with the general rule for the valuation in a winding up of the claims of creditors.

The bank sought to found an argument in favour of subsequent revaluations of a foreign currency debt on the principle found in such cases as *Craig's Executors' Case* (1870) LR 9 Eq 706, *Holdich's Case* (1872) LR 14 Eq 72 and *Re Northern Counties of England Fire Insurance Co, Macfarlane's Claim* (1880) 17 Ch D 337, in which it was held that a policy holder could revalue his contingent claim by reference to a relevant event, such as a death or a fire, taking place after the winding up had started. It also relies on *Re Parana Plantations Ltd*. In that case a company owed a pre-war debt in German marks. The company was wound up during the war. Shortly after the end of the war a distribution to creditors fell to be made. It was held that the right course was to value the debt according to the official rate of exchange of 40 marks to the pound which prevailed immediately after the end of the war.

In my opinion the argument based on these cases must be rejected. All are examples of a claim which was difficult or impossible to value accurately at the date of the winding up. So it was necessary to resort to subsequent events in order to enable a valuation to be made as at the date of the winding up. That problem does not arise in the instant case. A precise valuation can be made of the bank's debt as at the date of liquidation because the exchange rate at that date is precisely known. It is unnecessary and indeed erroneous to look at later exchange rates in order to assess the value of the debt at the date of liquidation.

Not only does the liquidators' submission accord with the justice of the case and with a long line of authority directed to the proper date of valuation of liabilities for the purposes of the liquidation, but it also accords with the principles of the *Miliangos* case. Outside the field of liquidation, if a creditor is owed a sum of money which the debtor will not pay, the creditor may sue in order, first, to establish the liability and, second, to establish the quantum of the liability. If the debtor continues in default, the creditor may proceed to execute his judgment against the property of the debtor. The *Miliangos* case establishes that if the debt is owed in a foreign currency, the creditor may in appropriate circumstances issue a writ to establish liability for the debt in that currency and he may recover judgment in that currency. He may then proceed to execution. The foreign currency debt will be converted into sterling at the latest practical date, namely when the creditor becomes entitled to issue execution. If the creditor petitions to wind up a company, or claims in a liquidation initiated by others, he is not engaged in proceedings to establish the company's liability or the quantum of the liability (although liability and quantum may be put in issue) but to enforce the liability. Indeed, he is precluded from initiating or supporting a winding-up petition if his status as a creditor is bona fide disputed by the company. The liquidation of an insolvent company is a process of collective enforcement of debts for the benefit of the general body of creditors. Although it is not a process of execution, because it is not for the benefit of a particular creditor, it is nevertheless akin to execution because its purpose is to enforce, on a pari passu basis, the payment of the admitted or proved debts of the company. When, therefore, a company goes into liquidation a process is initiated which, for all creditors, is similar to the process which is initiated, for one creditor, by execution. If the commencement of the process of execution is the correct date for the conversion of a foreign currency debt in the case of a defendant whose affairs are under his own control, it seems to me entirely consistent that the date of liquidation should be the due date for conversion in the case of a company whose affairs are committed to a liquidator.

The conclusion which I reach is in line with the decision in the *Dynamics* case, with the reasoning of which I respectfully agree.

We were much pressed in argument by the bank with the injustice which might arise, on the liquidators' submission, in the case of a wholly solvent company. Take a simple example. A company has English assets of £1m, and has borrowed 100,000 Swiss francs from a Swiss bank in Switzerland repayable on demand under a Swiss contract in the same currency. If the company for some reason declined to repay on demand, judgment could be recovered against it in Swiss francs in England, and could be executed against the assets in an equivalent sum of sterling converted as at the date when execution is authorised. Suppose, however, that the company goes into voluntary liquidation. Suppose that sterling is devalued by 10% before the liquidator can discharge the debt. The Swiss creditor, it is said, would on the liquidators' argument receive less than his due entitlement in Swiss francs, and the profit on the exchange caused by the company's default would enure for the benefit of the undeserving shareholders. Per contra, if sterling had been revalued upwards, it would (it is said) be open to the liquidator, like any other foreign currency debtor, to discharge the company's obligation in the currency of the contract. So, in the end, the foreign currency creditor will get the worst of both worlds; he will gain nothing if the exchange rate moves against the currency of the contract, and he will lose if it moves in favour of the currency of the contract.

This is not a problem with which we are directly concerned, and I wish to guard against expressing any concluded view on it. But when the problem arises for decision, it may be relevant to observe that the view has been repeatedly expressed in relation to interest that, once the provable debts have been satisfied in full, so that the company has in that sense a surplus of assets, the duty of the liquidator is to discharge the contractual indebtedness of the company in respect of such debts to the extent that the contractual indebtedness exceeds the provable indebtedness. 'As soon as it is ascertained that there is a surplus, the creditor whose debt carries interest is remitted to his rights under the contract': see *Re Humber Ironworks and Shipbuilding Co, Warrant Finance Co's Case* (1869) LR 4 Ch App 643 at 647 per Gifford LJ; see also Selwyn LJ to the same effect (at 645).

It is on that principle that a creditor may claim post-liquidation interest. He does this on the basis that obligations under the contract are not necessarily discharged despite the fact that all provable debts have been paid at 100p in the pound. It may well be the duty of the liquidator, in the case of a wholly solvent liquidation, if a foreign currency creditor has been paid less than his full contractual foreign currency debt, to make good the shortfall before he pays anything to the shareholders. I do not say that this is necessarily the solution to the problem posed, but I have not heard any convincing objection to that solution.

The only remaining question is this. There is in the instant case a surplus of some £2m after discharging provable debts in full. This surplus is available to discharge post-liquidation interest on the principles I have just stated. Is it also available, pro rata, to discharge the shortfall suffered by the bank if the sterling dividends it has received are converted into Swiss francs as at the respective dates of payment? I think not, for this reason. It is implicit in the concept of 'pari passu' that neither the sterling creditors nor the foreign currency creditors should be at risk because of, or should be affected by, the vagaries of exchange rates. There is no reason, if my judgment on the main point is correct, why sterling creditors who are entitled to recover post-liquidation interest should have that right diminished because of movements in exchange rates. As I have said before, the sterling creditors are not wrongdoers who ought to be left to shoulder the exchange rate risk. It is not for the sterling creditors to underwrite the foreign currency creditors and protect them against loss. I do not think, therefore, that a foreign currency creditor can base a claim on the depreciation in the cross rate between sterling and the foreign currency until the liquidator has assets in his hands which will otherwise go to the shareholders. At that stage, but not earlier, as it seems to me, it would be entirely just to allow the foreign currency creditor to recover the same amount as he would have been able to recover if no liquidation had ever taken place.

For the reasons which I have endeavoured to express, I would dismiss the appeal.

OLIVER LJ. I agree. This appeal raises, in relation to a creditors' voluntary winding up, similar problems to those raised in relation to a compulsory winding up in *Re Dynamics Corp of America* [1976] 2 All ER 669, [1976] 1 WLR 757. In the court below Slade J followed that decision and held that the debt of a foreign currency creditor fell to be converted into sterling at the rate of exchange prevailing at the date of the winding-up resolution. Counsel for one of the major foreign currency creditors, Lloyds Bank International Ltd (the bank), has forcefully contended that that decision was wrong and that the decision in the *Dynamics* case was also wrong and ought to be overruled. The *Dynamics* case was, of course, a decision of my own at first instance, and I have had to re-examine it with some care in the light of the powerful arguments which counsel for the bank has advanced. He contends, first (which is unanswerable), that *Miliangos v George Frank (Textiles) Ltd* [1975] 3 All ER 801, [1976] AC 443 in the House of Lords establishes beyond doubt that, apart from liquidation or bankruptcy, a foreign currency creditor is, as a matter of contract, owed foreign currency and not sterling and is entitled, if he elects to be paid in sterling or if the debtor chooses to pay in sterling, to receive that amount which is sufficient, at the date of payment (or the nearest date to payment which the practicalities of our legal procedures admit), to purchase the requisite amount of currency according to the exchange rate then prevailing. Second, he contends that there is nothing in the Companies Act 1948 or in the statutory scheme of distribution established by that Act, as interpreted by the courts, which has the effect of altering the creditors' contractual rights save to the extent, where there is a deficiency of assets available for payment, of scaling down those rights in the same way as every other creditor's rights fall to be scaled down. The creditor's entitlement remains an entitlement to receive the appropriate scaled down amount of foreign currency and accordingly the sterling equivalent of that scaled down amount has to be calculated, as nearly as the practicalities allow, at the date when payment is actually made. In the case of a voluntary winding up that will be the close of business on the day immediately preceding that on which the cheque is written. In a compulsory winding up, although this was not fully argued because it was unnecessary to do so in the instant case, it would probably be the date of the notice of dividend which leads to the authorisation of the cheque drawn on the Companies Liquidation Account.

These submissions effectively cover one of the dates propounded by the summons in the *Dynamics* case, although, according to my recollection of the argument in that case, this particular way of putting the matter was not argued by the dollar creditors, or not, at any rate, argued with any enthusiasm, attention being concentrated rather on the date of admission to proof which had been suggested obiter in the speeches of Lord Wilberforce and Lord Cross in the *Miliangos* case. For the reasons which I there gave I felt compelled to reject that as a practicable date for conversion and counsel for the bank does not quarrel with that rejection. Where he suggests that the *Dynamics* case was wrong was in the proposition that the scheme of pari passu distribution established by the Companies Act 1948 and the Bankruptcy Act 1914 compelled the conclusion that conversion had to take place at the date of winding up or, in the case of a compulsory liquidation, the date of the winding-up order.

I have to confess that his arguments have a logical cogency which has from time to time during the appeal severely shaken such confidence as I may have entertained in the correctness of the *Dynamics* decision. I hope that I do no injustice to the argument if I summarise it shortly as follows.

It proceeds in a series of steps. First, the result of the *Miliangos* case and of its subsequent applications is that a creditor of an English debtor whose debt is payable in foreign currency is a creditor for that amount of foreign currency. Second, if such a creditor seeks to recover his debt in England his claim is not for a sterling sum but for the very amount of foreign currency that he is owed. Third, if he actually seeks to enforce here a judgment expressed in foreign currency it will be practically necessary to effect a conversion into sterling in order that the law enforcement agencies shall know what sum it is that they have to raise out of the assets here. Such conversion is then made at the latest practicable date which is the date of the affidavit leading to execution. Finally, the extent to which the debt is satisfied by any interim or partial payment of sterling is to be ascertained by applying to it the rate of exchange prevailing at the date of payment.

These are the opening and underlying propositions of counsel for the bank. Applying them to the case where the debtor is a corporate debtor which is being wound up in England, he accepts that the amount for which the foreign currency creditor is entitled to prove is fixed once and for all at the date of the winding up. But, he argues, the winding up does not alter the creditor's underlying contractual right. True it is that if what he is then owed is $US1,000 that is all that he can claim in the liquidation (subject to the question of interest if there should prove to be a surplus). But he still proves for and is entitled to be paid $US1,000 and not the sterling equivalent of that sum. Thus against the total mass or fund of assets in the hands of the liquidator there are claims which, throughout, fall to be expressed in different currencies, so that the overall amount of the company's debts expressed as a sterling sum is necessarily, throughout the liquidation, a fluctuating amount consisting of £X (the sterling claims) + £Y (the foreign currency claims) where Y is a variable. Any difficulties to which this might, at first sight, seem to give rise are, counsel for the bank submits, more illusory than real. The liquidator collects and converts the assets in the ordinary way and counsel for the bank, I think, accepts that s 248 of the Companies Act 1948 practically involves, in a compulsory winding up at any rate, a conversion into sterling for the purpose of making payment into the Companies Liquidation Account at the Bank of England. When he comes to make a first distribution among the creditors, the liquidator knows how much he requires to retain and thus the actual sterling sum which he is able to distribute by way of dividend (let us call it Z). What he does not know at that moment is what is the value of Y. Having ascertained the value of Y at that date he is then able to calculate the percentage of the composite X + Y which is represented by Z, say, for the sake of example, 10%. He then pays to the creditors 10% of their respective debts converted, in the case of the foreign currency debts, at that date.

Similarly when he comes to pay any subsequent dividend, he will again have to ascertain the value of Y at, or immediately before, the payment date and divide the total amount of each dividend between the creditors on the basis of the sterling values as then calculated.

Thus, counsel for the bank submits, the debts will have been dealt with pari passu in the sense that each creditor will have received the same percentage of his debt, although if one takes the relative values of the debts at the date of winding up the foreign currency creditors will have participated in the funds available for distribution in a proportion greater or less (according to whether sterling depreciates or appreciates against the particular currency) than the proportion which their debts bear to the total value of all the debts.

The counter-argument advanced on behalf of the joint liquidators is, in brief, that the argument of counsel for the bank fails to distinguish between the enforcement of the foreign creditor's substantive rights when ascertained (with which the Miliangos case was directly concerned and to which the main thrust of the decision was directed) and the *a* quantification or ascertainment of those substantive rights in any given situation. It is axiomatic, as all the authorities show, that the date for the ascertainment of the company's liabilities in a winding up is the date of the winding up and the submission to proof of a foreign debt is part of the statutory scheme of collective enforcement and thus subject to the same universal rule for ascertainment and quantification as any other debt.

Both sides submit that the key section of the Act is s 302, which provides that 'Subject *b* to the provisions of this Act as to preferential payments, the property of a company shall, on its winding up, be applied in satisfaction of its liabilities pari passu . . .' A great deal of argument has been devoted on both sides to the meaning of the expression 'pari passu'. Counsel for the bank submits that the principles of application of the section must be the same as that of s 319(5) in relation to preferential claims, that section providing that if there are insufficient assets the debt shall 'abate in equal proportions'. *c* The joint liquidators argue, on the other hand, that what s 302 provides is that the *property* of the company shall be distributed pari passu, that is to say that it shall be divided between the creditors proportionately and on an equal footing, so that each receives the proportion of the divisible assets which the amount of his debt bears to the total amount of the proved liabilities. So long, of course, as one single date is provided for the ascertainment in a common currency of all liabilities, the result is exactly the *d* same in each case, but the latter construction is difficult to reconcile with more than one single date for calculation. Speaking for myself, I do not find it necessary to resolve this particular contest, although the approach of counsel for the bank appears on analysis to have, perhaps, a firmer grammatical foundation. The key word in this section appears to me to be the word 'liabilities' which counsel for the bank concedes have to be ascertained at the date of the winding up. The contest is not as to when they are to be *e* ascertained but as to how they are to be treated when they have been ascertained, counsel for the bank's point being that there is nothing in the statute which compels or even points to the conclusion that a debt ascertained at $US1,000 ceases to be a debt of $US1,000.

Now his argument has an engaging, indeed an almost unanswerable, logic about it if one once accepts his major premise, but it is here that I find myself unable to follow *f* him, for what, as it seems to me, he is seeking to do is to attribute to the Miliangos case a greater force than it has in fact. In effect what he seeks to do is to suggest that because the Miliangos case establishes that a creditor in foreign currency is owed foreign currency, it follows that the debtor is a debtor in foreign currency alone and cannot obtain his discharge by anything but a foreign currency payment. But this is to stand the Miliangos case on its head. What the Miliangos case is concerned with is not *g* how the debtor is to be compelled to pay in the currency of the debt but the measure of his liability in sterling when, ex hypothesi, he has not paid and is unwilling to pay in the currency of the debt.

Applying that to the case of a liquidation, in which the assets have to be distributed in discharge of the company's liabilities, one of the liquidator's tasks is to ascertain what 'the liabilities' are and it is not in dispute that 'the liabilities' are the liabilities as they exist at *h* the winding up.

Now the amount of a liability is to be measured by that which the person liable can be compelled, in the currency of the forum in which he is so compelled, to pay in order to discharge his obligation. Suppose, for the sake of example, that the price of gold at the date of winding up is £200 per ounce and the company's obligation is to deliver an ounce of gold or to pay a sum of £150. If one is asked to quantify the company's 'liability' at *j* that date, the answer must be £150, for that is the sum which would provide a discharge of the obligation. Similarly, as it seems to me, if the position be that the rate of exchange for the US dollar is two to the pound and a creditor for $1,000 issues a writ on the day of the winding up for that sum, the 'liability' of the debtor ascertained at that date is £500. If he pays £500 and the costs on the receipt of the writ the action could not, quite apart from the liquidation, properly proceed. It does not seem to me to be right, with respect, to assume, as counsel for the bank has to in order to found his argument, that because a creditor at the date of winding up is owed $1,000 the company's liability at that date is and remains $1,000. Its liability in the sense of what, at that date, it can be compelled or is entitled to pay is whatever sum in sterling will then discharge the debt; and the ascertainment of that liability does not appear to me to depend, except as a matter of instantaneous measurement, on the currency of the contract or the currency in which the creditor chooses to express his proof of debt.

Counsel for the bank, submits, and rightly submits, that the measurement of liability at the date of winding up produces curious and unfair results in the winding up of a solvent company in the absence of any express provision for making up any shortfall before distribution among the shareholders. It may, however, be added that his own solution may produce equally curious and unfair results if, for instance, sterling has appreciated against the currency of the contract between the date of the winding up and the date of distribution. But that may be merely to say that the statutory scheme of distribution does not produce wholly fair results in all circumstances. The principle was expressed thus by Lord Romilly MR in *Re Smith, Knight & Co, ex p Ashbury* (1868) LR 5 Eq 223 at 226:

'The Act of Parliament unquestionably says, that everybody shall be paid *pari passu*, but that means everybody after the winding-up has commenced ... It takes them exactly as it finds them, and divides the assets amongst the creditors, paying them their dividend on their debts as they then exist.'

That is the scheme of the statute and it does undoubtedly result in certain circumstances in the possibility of creditors getting less than their full contractual entitlement even in a fully solvent liquidation (see, for instance, *Re House Property and Investment Co Ltd* [1953] 2 All ER 1525, [1954] Ch 576). We are not, however, here concerned with a solvent company and the point must be left for decision when it arises. Certainly for my part I do not dissent from the proposition that the answer to the criticism of counsel for the bank may well be found in the way suggested in the judgment of Brightman LJ.

Counsel for the bank also submits that it can be deduced from the *Miliangos* decision that at least those two of their Lordships who dealt with the point rejected in terms the winding-up date as the date for conversion, although he does not seek to support the alternative date of admission of proof. This has, I think, to be accepted but equally both their Lordships clearly had in mind that there would be a single date for conversion and not, as counsel for the bank submits, a series of dates geared to the distribution of dividends.

Although, as I have said, I was much impressed by the logic of the submissions of counsel for the bank, I have, for the reasons which I have endeavoured to state and for the reasons stated in the judgments of Lawton and Brightman LJJ with which I respectfully concur, felt compelled to reject them. The second question raised by the summons before Slade J reflects the alternative submission of counsel for the bank, that the *Dynamics* case is to be distinguished from the instant case, because here the assets are sufficient to pay each creditor the full amount of his debt converted at the date of the winding up, and that the foreign currency creditors are entitled to be paid the full amount of their foreign currency debts converted at the date of payment before any payment of interest is made. For the reasons given by Slade J and by Brightman LJ, I feel equally unable to accept that alternative submission. The answers to the two questions in the sense indicated dictated, as Slade J held, the answers to the other questions raised by the summons with which this appeal is concerned. I have been persuaded that he answered those questions correctly and I therefore agree that the appeal should be dismissed.

Appeal dismissed. Leave to appeal to House of Lords granted.

Solicitors: *Cameron Markby* (for the bank); *Simmons & Simmons* (for the liquidators).

Mary Rose Plummer   Barrister.

Michael Galley Footwear Ltd (in liq) v Iaboni

QUEEN'S BENCH DIVISION
HODGSON J
19, 20 FEBRUARY, 11 MARCH 1981

Carriers – Loss or damage to goods – Determination of carrier's liability – Loss caused through circumstances which carrier could not avoid – Goods stolen from parked lorry – Carrier taking reasonable precautions to prevent theft but leaving lorry unguarded – Carrier not negligent but loss avoidable if diligence exercised – Whether carrier liable for loss of goods – Carriage of Goods by Road Act 1965, Sch, art 17(1)(2).

The defendant, who carried on business as a road haulier, was engaged by the plaintiffs' agents to carry a consignment of shoes from Milan in Italy to England. The defendant and an employee loaded the goods onto one of the defendant's lorries in Milan and then parked the lorry in an unguarded lorry park in order to have a meal. The only guarded lorry park in Milan was two hours' drive away and to have driven there would have required the defendant to breach EEC regulations relating to maximum continuous driving periods. When parking the lorry the defendant and his employee took all available precautions to secure it from theft. However, while they were away having a meal, thieves cut the alarm system on the lorry and stole it, complete with its consignment of shoes. The plaintiffs claimed damages against the defendant under art 17(1)[a] of the Convention on the Contract for the International Carriage of Goods by Road 1965 (CMR) as set out in the schedule to the Carriage of Goods by Road Act 1965, under which 'The carrier [was] liable for the total or partial loss of the goods . . . occurring between the time when he [took] over the goods and the time of delivery'. The defendant contended that art 17(2) relieved him of liability because the loss was caused 'through circumstances which the carrier could not avoid and the consequences of which he was unable to prevent'. The defendant submitted that under art 17(2) a carrier could avoid liability if he could show that he had exercised diligence and not been negligent.

Held – Since art 17 of CMR was concerned not with the question of fault but with clarifying in any given situation on which of two innocent parties the risk should fall, the standard of reasonable care and due diligence appropriate to the tort of negligence was irrelevant in deciding whether the carrier could have avoided the circumstances and prevented the consequences of the loss. What the carrier was obliged under art 17(2) to demonstrate in order to avoid the primary liability imposed on him by art 17(1) was that he could not have avoided the loss. Therefore, although the defendant had not been negligent in that he had exercised the diligence of a reasonably careful carrier, he was nevertheless liable to the plaintiffs under art 17(1) because he could have avoided the loss if, for example, he and his employee had taken turns to guard the lorry while the other was having a meal (see p 206 *h* to p 207 *a c* to *g* and p 208 *a*, post).

Notes

For the Convention on the Contract for the International Carriage of Goods by Road (CMR), see 5 Halsbury's Laws (4th Edn) paras 417–418.

For the Carriage of Goods by Road Act 1965, Sch, art 17, see 28 Halsbury's Statutes (3rd edn) 449.

Cases referred to in judgment

Anon (1966) 4 ETL 888, Bundesgerichtshof.
Anon (1975) 10 ETL 516, Bundesgerichtshof.

---

a   Article 17, so far as material, is set out at p 202 *j* to 203 *a*, post

Buchanan (James) & Co Ltd v Babco Forwarding and Shipping (UK) Ltd [1977] 3 All ER 1048,
    [1978] AC 141, [1977] 3 WLR 907, HL, Digest (Cont Vol E) 36, *1435*.
Camera & Cie Seine Rhone v Ets Clemessy et Sté Lesage & Cie (1975) 10 ETL 406.
Kühne & Nagel v Transports Internationaux Van Mieghem (1973) 9 ETL 330.
NV La Préservatrice v Well Transport (1979) 14 ETL 924.
NV Maatschappij van Assurantie v A J Koeneman en Zn, Internationale Tranporten NV (1965)
    1 ETL 137.
PVBA KC v PVBA Roeckens (1971) 7 ETL 1058.
SA Soffritti v Usines Balteau (1977) 12 ETL 881.
Thermo Engineers Ltd v Ferrymasters Ltd [1981] 1 All ER 1142, [1981] 1 WLR 1470.
*Zeilemakers Transportbedrijf v NV Transportverzekeringsmaatschappij van de Nederlanden
    van 1845* (1965) 1 ETL 305.

Action

By a writ issued on 15 December 1977 and amended and reamended on 6 December
1978 and 27 March 1980, the plaintiffs, Michael Galley Footwear Ltd (in liquidation),
claimed against the defendants, Dominic Iaboni (trading as Domia International), Domia
International Transport Ltd, Albini & Pitigliani SAS and W R Williams & Co (Freight)
Ltd, damages for breach of contract and/or duty and/or negligence in or about the
loading, handling, stowage, custody, care and discharge of the plaintiffs' cargo and the
carriage thereof by road from Verona in Italy to Leicester in England. The proceedings
were pursued only against the first defendant. The facts are set out in the judgment.

Nigel Wilkinson for the plaintiffs.
Nicholas Underhill for the first defendant.

Cur adv vult

11 March. **HODGSON J** read the following judgment: I am in this case concerned
with the Carriage of Goods by Road Act 1965, and with the Convention on the Contract
for the International Carriage of Goods by Road (CMR) set out in the schedule to that
Act. In particular, I have to construe art 17 of the convention.

The plaintiff company imports and distributes footwear in England. The first
defendant carries on business as a haulier. His business is based in England and he
specialises in carriage between Italy and England. In 1976 he owned two lorries, one of
which he drove himself. In December 1976 the other lorry was driven by his servant,
Mr Esposito. The plaintiff purchased a large quantity of shoes from vendors in Verona
on fob terms. The shoes had an eventful existence. When being transported through
France by other carriers the consignment was hijacked, but the majority of the goods
were recovered, 216 cartons being returned to the forwarding agents, Albini & Pitigliani
SAS, who appear on the pleadings as the third defendants. No claim is, however, now
prosecuted against them and the only effective defendant is Mr Iaboni.

The forwarding agents on behalf of the plaintiffs employed the first defendant to carry
the shoes from Milan to England. On the morning of 16 December 1976 Mr Iaboni was
south of Florence with one of his lorries and Mr Esposito was in Bologna with the
other. Sensibly, whenever possible, Mr Iaboni liked to drive in convoy with his other
lorry. He arranged to meet Mr Esposito in Milan.

During the morning, Mr Esposito drove from Bologna, a journey which took him
some 2½ hours. Mr Iaboni's journey from south of Florence lasted some four hours.
They met at the forwarding agent's in the early afternoon and loading of the shoes began
at about 2 o'clock in the afternoon. It is customary for drivers to remain on the premises
during loading and, although taking no physical part, to exercise general supervision.
The loading yard was open to the street so that anyone passing could have seen what sort
of goods were being loaded into any particular lorry. The loading and documentation
was finished at about 6 o'clock in the evening. According to Mr Iaboni's evidence, they

could have driven some 1½ to 2 hours without a meal and without thereby being in breach of the regulations, being EEC Council Regulation 543/69 on the harmonisation of certain social legislation relating to road transport, regulations which have been referred to somewhat inaccurately in this case as the 'tachograph regulations'.

Mr Iaboni intended driving some 100 kilometres that night. That would have been a journey exceeding two hours. At that time there was only one guarded parking place open in Milan. That was in the Via Stevenson in the north-east of the city. The forwarding agents were in the south. I am prepared to accept that at 6 o'clock in the evening it might easily have taken them over two hours to reach Via Stevenson. It would also have taken the lorries well out of their way. I heard detailed argument as to the effect and application of the relevant regulations and I accept that to drive to Via Stevenson would probably have involved Mr Iaboni and Mr Esposito in breaking them.

Mr Esposito was the driver of the lorry loaded with the shoes. The load was sheeted; the cab was curtained; the main control switch on the dashboard was anonymous, some four switches looking exactly alike. The lorry was fitted with an alarm system which is operated by a pendulum system on any movement of the lorry. If operated, it sounds continuously for 30 seconds and thereafter at three second intervals. To turn it off you have to have a key. The place where it is turned off is hidden in a recess by the driver's foot pedals. The wires operating the alarm system are under the lorry and can be pulled out and disconnected without setting off the alarm, but, of course, that could only be done by somebody who knew exactly where to look for them.

No criticism is made of the physical protection supplied for this lorry and it is not suggested that in 1976 there was any better alarm system available.

Thefts from motor lorries are, and were in 1976, prevalent in Italy. Milan is a town where the risk is great, though not, according to Mr Iaboni, as bad as Florence. The greatest risk areas are those near Customs and near the premises of forwarding agents. Shoes are among the most popular targets for thieves, as being products easily placed on the market.

Via Fantoli is a wide road in the vicinity of the forwarding agents, much used for parking lorries. On the road there is a bar/restaurant called the Atlantic. Mr Iaboni decided at about 6 o'clock that he and Mr Esposito would have a quick meal before starting their journey. They parked the two lorries in the Via Fantoli. The first lorry they parked very close to another lorry and the second they drove close to the rear of the first. They then took all the precautions available to them in respect of both lorries. They had no way of knowing when the stationary lorry behind which they parked would be driven away. They then repaired together to the Atlantic bar/restaurant. It was some 35 yards away from their vehicles; they could not see their lorries from where they were seated; had the alarm sounded they would have heard it.

Whilst they were having their meal, thieves tore the wiring from the alarm system and drove the lorry with the shoes on it away. When Mr Iaboni and Mr Esposito had finished their meal, they returned to find the lorry gone. The police were informed, but the consignment of shoes was never recovered. The plaintiffs now claim against Mr Iaboni under the provisions of the convention. If that claim succeeds, it is agreed that damages including interest of £9,012·25 should be awarded against the first defendant. The claim is made under art 17(1) of the convention. The defendant seeks to be relieved of his liability under the provisions of art 17(2).

Article 17(1) of the convention reads:

'The carrier shall be liable for the total or partial loss of the goods and for damage thereto occurring between the time when he takes over the goods and the time of delivery, as well as for any delay in delivery.'

That article clearly places the primary liability for the loss on the carrier. The relevant words of art 17(2) read as follows:

'The carrier shall however be relieved of liability if the loss, damage or delay was *a*   caused . . . through circumstances which the carrier could not avoid and the consequences of which he was unable to prevent.'

The carrier is also relieved of liability if the loss is caused by fault of the claimant or by inherent vice of the goods. Article 17(3) should also be referred to. It reads:

b   'The carrier shall not be relieved of liability by reason of the defective condition of the vehicle used by him in order to perform the carriage, or by reason of the wrongful act or neglect of the person from whom he may have hired the vehicle or of the agents or servants of the latter.'

Article 18(1) places the burden of proving that loss was due to one of the causes specified in art 17 on the carrier. In this case, therefore, Mr Iaboni is liable unless he can prove that the loss of the shoes was caused through circumstances which he could not avoid and the consequences of which he was unable to prevent. It is the meaning of those words in art *c*   17(2) which has been the subject of controversy in this case. There is no English authority which is directly relevant to this point of construction.

The argument advanced on behalf of the defendant is that these words place a duty on a carrier to show due diligence only and that if he establishes that he exercised reasonable care or, in other words, was not negligent he escapes liability. It is argued that, because *d*   any circumstances can logically be avoided, this takes away any weight from the word 'could'. A carrier whose lorry is involved in a road accident which, once embarked on its journey and being at that place at that time, could not by any action of its driver have been avoided could logically have been avoided by starting earlier or later or following a different route. This sort of argument leads, it is said, to a construction of what, on their face, seem to me clear words which is different from what seems to me to be their natural meaning.

e   It appears to me that art 17(3) is really conclusive against this reasoning. A carrier could have avoided the loss by hiring from, for instance, somebody else.

It is also submitted that the weight of authority points to a test of duty of care being imposed on a carrier by art 17(2) rather than any more strict duty, or more strict liability, I should say. It is clear that in the interests of harmonisation I am entitled to look at authorities from the jurisdictions of other countries who are signatories to the *f*   convention: see *James Buchanan & Co Ltd v Babco Forwarding and Shipping (UK) Ltd* [1977] 3 All ER 1048, [1978] AC 141. A number of such authorities have been brought to my attention by the diligence of counsel. I have, in most of them however, only the headnotes written in English. In so far as the facts appear from those headnotes, it seems to me that the decisions themselves accord with what I take to be the natural meaning of the words in the article, although it is true that some are, for reasons which on analysis *g*   seem to me to be perfectly understandable, cast in terms of duty of care.

Counsel for the defendant cited seven cases to me, the headnotes of which have been supplied to me in photocopies, but one of these authorities, *Camera & Cie Seine Rhone v Ets Clemessy & Sté Lesage & Cie* (1975) 10 ETL 406, does not seem to be a case on the convention.

h   *Zeilemakers Transportbedrijf v NV Transportverzekeringsmaatschappij van de Nederlanden van 1845* (1965) 1 ETL 305 is a Dutch case. I do not know what the facts of that case were as I have not been provided with a translation of the Dutch text, but the important part of the headnote reads:

'The carrier must however show that the extraneous force could not have been noticed or prevented by his employees exercising due care.'

The second case (once again, I only have the headnote) is a German case, heard in the Bundesgerichtshof ((1975) 10 ETL 516). The headnote reads:

'The carrier is relieved from liability when goods were damaged or lost by a traffic accident, which the driver of the motor vehicle could not avoid under the circumstances even with the greatest of care.'

SA Soffritti v Usines Balteau (1977) 12 ETL 881 is a case from Brussels. The headnote reads:

> 'A sudden braking movement and swerve to avoid a collision caused by a third-party's action does not exonerate the carrier where he has stowed the goods negligently.'

NV Maatschappij van Assurantie v A J Koeneman en Zn, Internationale Transporten NV (1965) 1 ETL 137 is from Rotterdam and the headnote reads:

> 'The carrier may rely on article 17/2 of the CMR Convention if it appears that the damage was the result of an extraneous factor, in this case by a reduction in the air pressure of a tyre, caused by a sharp object giving rise to heating and the burning of the tyre where the tyres were in good condition and had been checked both before and in the course of the journey.'

NV La Préservatrice v Well Transport (1979) 14 ETL 924 is a case from Antwerp, and that is a case where, in fact, a translation in English of the facts is provided. The headnote to that case reads:

> 'It is imprudent to leave a lorry loaded with cigarettes, unguarded in a parking lot in Italy especially when local circumstances point to such goods being particularly attractive to thieves. Where theft of the goods has been committed in such circumstances which could have been defeated by the presence of the driver, the carrier is not entitled to the benefit of exoneration of liability.'

And the facts of that case in so far as they seem to me to be important are set out in the judgment (14 ETL 924 at 931):

> 'Whereas, as regards the main issue, the First Court judiciously decided that the carrier was liable on the basis of Article 17 of the CMR: carriage had not yet been completed and the goods were not delivered to the consignee; the circumstances, owing to which the lorries had to wait in the parking area next to the Chiasso Customs Hall, do not play any part in the matter; it is apparent from the driver's statement that he went off to Turin on Saturday evening, leaving the lorry which was due to be cleared through Customs only on Monday; to leave the lorry unguarded was all the more imprudent since it is well known that an in-transit load of cigarettes constitutes a much-desired loot in Italy in view of the extensive smuggling of these goods that goes on to evade the high duties; there is nothing to show that the parking area is anything other than an ordinary waiting area, and there are no guards nor any signs that it may be considered as a safe stopping place; Whereas, therefore, it is unacceptable that the theft was a circumstance which the carrier could not avoid; and the presence of the driver would have defeated any attempt at theft . . .'

And, lastly of the cases cited to me by counsel for the defendant, another German case heard in the Bundesgerichtshof ((1966) 4 ETL 888), the headnote reads:

> 'The road haulier is liable for the theft of a load of cobalt from an unguarded lorry parked at the frontier during the night. Such a theft cannot be considered as being an unavoidable circumstance within the meaning of art 17 CMR.'

Two cases were cited to me by counsel for the plaintiffs. The headnote to *Kühne & Nagel v Transports Internationaux Van Mieghem* (1973) 9 ETL 330 reads:

> 'The carrier shall be liable for a burglary committed during carriage. Burglary does not come under the heading of "force majeure".'

And *PVBA KC v PVBA Roeckens* (1971) 7 ETL 1058 from Antwerp; the headnote reads:

a

'Sudden violent braking cannot be put forward as a ground for release from liability within the meaning of Article 17, 2 of the C.M.R. except insofar as the carrier can produce proper proof that violent braking was really necessary in the actual circumstances; in view, however, of the heavy traffic of the present day the said conditions must be such as to be regarded as quite abnormal and unforeseeable . . .'

b

I have also been referred to a helpful article written by Professor Roland Loewe 'Commentary on the Convention of 19 May 1956 on the Contract for the International Carriage of Goods by Road (CMR)' (1976) 11 ETL 311 at 362–364, and I read paragraphs 153 and 154 of that article:

c

'153. The concluding words of paragraph 2 constitute one of the many definitions of the concept of circumstances which cannot be avoided, which is very close to the concept of *force majeure*. It is of course well known that the definition of the concept of *force majeure* differs considerably, not only between different legal orders but even, in many cases, within one and the same legal order. It is essential, when applying the formulation used in CMR, to try not to be influenced by national

d

definitions of this kind or by the meaning which national courts or jurists attribute to them. A comparison of the CMR rule with national definitions of *force majeure* shows, first, that CMR does not mention the condition of unforeseeability, which is often required. It is indeed difficult to imagine many cases in which it would be possible to foresee particular circumstances (in time) but impossible to avoid them; but, in any event, the carrier could in such cases be relieved of liability. The

e

provision is often distorted by the introduction of ideas originating in certain legal systems which take into account only external circumstances or events. Such an interpretation is not in keeping with the text or the intention of the authors. This is confirmed *inter alia* by the existence of paragraph 3, which would be superfluous if a restrictive interpretation of this kind had been intended. The carrier may thus, in accordance with paragraph 2, be relieved of liability if he provides proof of circumstances which he could not avoid, and the consequences of which he was unable to prevent, even if the circumstances in question occurred within his enterprise. Some examples of such circumstances might be: a strike which the carrier could not have avoided even by making financial promises to his employees; or an unforeseen breakdown of a vehicle which is not due to a defect in its condition. A carrier might also claim relief from liability on grounds of a traffic

f

accident which was not caused by him or by any of the persons for whom he is responsible under article 3. He could not in general be relieved of liability for theft of the goods by a third party, unless the theft took place in circumstances so unusual that the carrier, even acting with the greatest possible diligence, could not have prevented it.

g

154. Some writers have come to a conclusion which is different from that set out above, and their line of reasoning has been as follows: the term *"force majeure"* was used in earlier versions of CIM; when CIM was revised in 1952, this term was replaced, in article 27, paragraph 2, by the formulation which now appears in CMR; these writers maintain that this amendment was not designed to change the substance of the provision, and that the same must be true in the case of CMR which—on this point as on many others—follows CIM. This argument is not convincing. In the first place, it is often difficult to ascertain the opinion of representatives who have drafted an international convention—and of course opinions may have been divided; but in any case their views could not have been contrary to the relatively clear wording of the convention itself, which has acquired the force of law as a result of its acceptance by national parliaments. It cannot be argued, by way of interpretation, that black should be white because that was what

the negotiators meant it to be. Even if this conclusion were (wrongly) accepted in the case of CIM, it could not affect another international agreement, which was negotiated by different persons and to which different States are parties. In the negotiations which led to the drafting of CMR, there was no statement by a delegation—let alone unanimous agreement—to the effect that the terms used in 17, paragraph 2, should exclude any circumstances occurring within the carrier's enterprise.'

The words in their natural and ordinary meaning seem to me to be clear and, although their construction was unnecessary to the decision of the actual case, they seem also to have appeared clear to Neill J in *Thermo Engineers Ltd v Ferrymasters Ltd* [1981] 1 All ER 1142 at 1149–1150, [1981] 1 WLR 1470 at 1478–1479. What Neill J said of this article in that judgment was this:

'Counsel for the defendants argued that the concluding words of para 2 mean that a carrier can escape liability if he proves that he used due diligence. Counsel for the plaintiffs, on the other hand, contended that the words were equivalent to a force majeure. He drew my attention in support of this contention to one of the four cases to which I referred earlier in general terms, *Kühne & Nagel v Transports Internationaux van Mieghem* (1974) 9 ETL 330, a decision of the Tribunal de commerce in Brussels. I have already said that I consider that the general effect of art 3 when considered in the light of the 1965 Act and CMR as a whole is to make the carrier by road responsible for the acts of sub-carriers. The damage here was caused by those responsible for loading the trailer onto the Orion. In my view these persons were plainly persons of whose services Ferrymasters were making use for the performance of the carriage. I am therefore satisfied that even if the standard envisaged by art 17, para 2 is one of due diligence, Ferrymasters would not be able to escape liability. I am inclined to the view, however, that the words "through circumstances which the carrier could not avoid" allow a more limited relief from liability than would have been the case if words such as "by the exercise of reasonable care" had been added. Both the English and the French texts show that the court is concerned to inquire: was the damage caused through circumstances which the carrier *could not* avoid? The words I have emphasised should be given their full meaning.'

I do not find it surprising that, in applying the words of this article to given fact situations, judgments sometimes speak in terms of breach of duty, sometimes in terms of force majeure. In the great majority of cases where a carrier fails to bring himself within art 17(2) it will be because he has failed to be as careful as he ought to have been. Equally, when he is able to escape liability it will frequently be because of circumstances which amount to force majeure. But I do not, myself, think that either of these concepts can or do assist in the construction of the plain words of art 17. There are examples in Professor Loewe's article which would fall within neither category but which plainly are controlled by the wording of art 17.

I do not think that the tests used in any given fact situation to decide whether a person has exercised reasonable care are helpful. I do not think that the negligence equations apply at all. In deciding whether a carrier could avoid circumstances or prevent consequences, the magnitude and likelihood of the risk, the gravity of the consequences and the cost and practicality of overcoming the risk are not, in my judgment, relevant. If he could have avoided the circumstance and prevented the consequence, then he will be liable although, judged by negligence standards, he was not behaving unreasonably in failing to overcome the risk. In my judgment, it avails a carrier nothing to show that he complied with common practice if he could, by taking precautions not required by common practice, have avoided the loss. What he has to show is that he could not have avoided the loss and I do not think that in any given fact situation it is difficult to decide whether he could have done so or not.

It seems to me that the articles are not concerned with fault, but are concerned to make clear where on any given set of facts the risk between innocent parties shall lie, and the party on whom the risk is made to fall should, by insurance, guard against the risk and recover the cost of the premium in his freight charges. The only gloss I would think must be placed on the words in the article is the perhaps obvious requirement that what the carrier could have done must be lawful.

I think that one of the examples given by Professor Loewe shows how comparatively simple it is to apply the ordinary meaning of the words to any fact situation. It is the example which is precisely relevant to this case which I have in mind. Had the facts been that the driver had remained with the lorry but had been overpowered by armed robbers, then no doubt in that fact situation the carrier would have been exonerated from liability.

Although the burden of proof is clearly on the carrier, it is convenient in considering where on the facts of this case the risk falls to look at what it is alleged Mr Iaboni could have done. I do not think I am simplifying the case when I say that there were only two things that the defendant could have done and did not do which would have prevented this loss. He could have driven across Milan to the secure park or he and Mr Esposito could have had their meals separately, leaving the other with the vehicles. One could have sat in the cab of the rear vehicle whilst the other had his meal. If they had done that, this theft would have been prevented.

I decide this case on the basis that Mr Iaboni could not have driven across Milan to the secure park without being in breach of the tachograph regulations. He could not, therefore, have lawfully prevented the loss in that way. It seems clear to me, however, that this loss could have been prevented by first one and then the other of these two men remaining with the vehicles until relieved by the other. Because that is something Mr Iaboni and Mr Esposito could have done and because doing it would have prevented the loss, he is unable in my judgment to avail himself of the provisions of art 17(2) and there must be judgment in this case for the plaintiffs against Mr Iaboni.

That is all that is necessary for the decision of this case, but two further matters call for brief attention. The case has been fully argued on the basis that a carrier can avail himself of art 17(2) by showing that he has not been negligent. The facts in this case are not, I think, really in issue and are, I hope, accurately set out in this judgment. It is not strictly necessary for me to make a finding whether the defendant was negligent or not: an appellate court will be in as good a position as I am. However, had it been necessary for me to make a finding as to negligence, I should have held that the defendant had established that he had exercised the skill of a reasonably careful carrier. Taking into account what I called the negligence equations earlier in this judgment and, in particular, the common practice in the carrying trade of having only the driver of a lorry with the vehicle, I do not think that Mr Iaboni was negligent in all the circumstances when he and Mr Esposito left these vehicles close to the bar/restaurant for little more than half an hour.

Finally, I must mention the actual insurance position so far as the parties to this case are concerned. I only do so because I have been told what the position is by counsel, and it and its rather strange result being agreed by counsel an argument based on it has been mounted by counsel for the defendant.

The plaintiff company insured the consignment of shoes. They have been indemnified by their insurers against the loss. Their insurers in reality bring by subrogation this action. The forwarding agents insured this consignment either on behalf of the vendors or against their possible liability to the vendors under Italian law, I do not know which. I am told that under Italian law an insurable interest is not a necessary requirement for an effective insurance. The vendors have been paid the full sale price of the shoes by the Italian insurers. Whether they still have a claim for the price against the plaintiffs I know not; so far, they have made no such claim. The unfortunate Mr Iaboni had no insurance cover. The result is that the plaintiffs, or perhaps eventually the vendors, will get a windfall because the Italian insurers and the defendant will both have paid.

I am quite satisfied that the insurance background of this case is of no concern to me whatsoever. As I said, I mention them only because of the argument, courageous but in my judgment wholly unfounded, which has been advanced on the defendant's behalf. In those circumstances, there must be judgment for the plaintiff against the first defendant for the sum I have mentioned in my judgment.

Judgment for the plaintiffs for £9,012·25.

Solicitors: *Clyde & Co* (for the plaintiffs); *Kenwright & Cox*, agents for *Kenneth Cooke & Co*, Walsall (for the first defendant).

K Mydeen Esq   Barrister.

E D & A D Cooke Bourne (Farms) Ltd v Mellows and another

COURT OF APPEAL, CIVIL DIVISION
CUMMING-BRUCE, TEMPLEMAN LJJ AND DAME ELIZABETH LANE
4, 5 NOVEMBER 1981

Agricultural holding – Termination of tenancy – Compensation – Notice of claim – Validity – Statement of claim not containing 'all necessary particulars' when filed – Whether arbitrator having power to allow amendment of statement of claim and particulars – Principles on which arbitrator should allow amendment – Agricultural Holdings Act 1948, Sch 6, para 6.

Following the termination of the tenancy of an agricultural holding, the tenants served notice on the landlords that they intended claiming, under s 47[a] of the Agricultural Holdings Act 1948, compensation of £75,000 for new improvements, namely a barn and a store shed. The parties agreed on the appointment of an arbitrator to settle the amount of compensation and in accordance with para 6[b] of Sch 6 to the 1948 Act the tenants served on the arbitrator within 28 days of his appointment a statement of case and particulars. The tenant's statement of case was defective in certain respects; in particular, although the statement of claim did not refer to s 13[c] of the 1948 Act, it made a claim for the value of the improvements as on a claim under s 13, even though a claim under s 13 could not arise, because as the landlords pointed out in their statement of case any claim under s 13 was misconceived and if the claim was instead made under s 47 the tenants had omitted to allege or give particulars of the landlords' consent to the erection of the buildings. The landlords' statement of claim went on to contend, on the basis that the tenants were claiming under s 47, that the compensation should not exceed £35,000. More than three months later the tenants submitted an amended statement of case to the arbitrator in which they conceded that they could not claim under s 13, stated that the claim was in fact being made under s 47, and set out particulars of the landlords' consent to the erection of the buildings. At a preliminary hearing of the arbitration the arbitrator refused the tenants leave to file their amended statement of claim, on the ground that he was prevented by authority from allowing a fundamental change to a statement of case. The tenants appealed to the county court, where the judge held that, although the amendment to the tenant's statement of case could be made without causing injustice to the landlords, the tenants had not submitted a valid statement of case in the first place within the required time because they had not included 'all necessary particulars' as required by para 6 of Sch 6 to the 1948 Act, and therefore there was

---

a   Section 47, so far as material, is set out at p 216 c, post
b   Paragraph 6 is set out at p 216 j to p 217 a, post
c   Section 13, so far as material, is set out at p 215 h to p 216 a, post

nothing to amend. The judge accordingly dismissed the tenants' appeal. The tenants appealed to the Court of Appeal.

Held – The appeal would be allowed for the following reasons—

(1) Having regard to the history of the agricultural holdings legislation and the fact that in contrast to previous legislation the 1948 Act provided, in para 6 of Sch 6, for the amendment of a party's statement of case or the particulars therein to be allowed after the 28-day period within which the statement of case was to be served if the arbitrator consented to the amendment, the arbitrator had been wrong to consider himself bound to refuse the tenants leave to amend their case because it introduced a fundamental change. An arbitrator was ordinarily required to give leave to amend if after the amendment the respondent would know sufficiently the particulars of the case he had to meet and if (per Templeman LJ) he would be no worse off than if the statement of case had been properly drafted when originally filed. As the judge had rightly decided, the amendment proposed by the tenants could be made without causing injustice to the landlords, and therefore the arbitrator ought to have given leave to amend (see p 217 *b* to *f*, p 218 *a* to *c* and *f* to *j*, p 219 *j* to p 220 *b e g*, p 221 *d e*, p 223 *g* to *j* and p 224 *c d f g*, post); *Church Comrs for England v Mathews* (1979) 251 EG 1074 distinguished.

(2) Similarly, the judge had been wrong to decide that the 28-day period was a mandatory and inflexible period within which a statement of case with 'all necessary particulars' had to be filed. The mere fact that para 6 of Sch 6 to the 1948 Act stated that amendment to the statement of case or particulars could be made after that period with the arbitrator's consent indicated that the legislation contemplated that the statement of case or particulars might be deficient when the case was first filed (see p 219 *b* to *d*, p 220 *c d f g*, p 221 *d e* and p 224 *c d g*, post); *Jones v Evans* [1923] 1 KB 12 and *Re O'Connor and Brewin's Arbitration* [1933] 1 KB 20 distinguished.

Notes

For arbitration in respect of an agricultural holding, see 1 Halsbury's Laws (4th edn) paras 1132–1135.

For the Agricultural Holdings Act 1948, ss 13, 47, Sch 6, para 6, see 1 Halsbury's Statutes (3rd edn) 700, 723, 761.

Cases referred to in judgments

Church Comrs for England v Mathews (1979) 251 EG 1074, Weston-super-Mare Cty Ct.
Gray v Lord Ashburton [1917] AC 26, [1916–17] All ER Rep 380, HL, 2 Digest (Reissue) 58, 265.
Jones v Evans [1923] 1 KB 12, CA, 2 Digest (Reissue) 88, 433.
O'Connor and Brewin's Arbitration, Re [1933] 1 KB 20, CA, 2 Digest (Reissue) 90, 442.
Spreckley v Leicestershire CC [1934] 1 KB 366, CA, 2 Digest (Reissue) 90, 443.

Appeal

E D & A D Cooke Bourne (Farms) Ltd, the tenants of an agricultural holding known as High Park and Low Park in the parishes of Aslackby and Laughton, Lincolnshire, appealed against the decision of his Honour Judge Kellock QC in the Spalding County Court on 18 September 1981 whereby on a special case stated by the arbitrator (E B Brown Esq) in an arbitration between the tenants and the landlords of the holding, A R Mellows and H C O'Neill, the judge held that the arbitrator should not accede to the tenants' application for leave to serve a supplemental statement of case. The facts are set out in the judgment of Cumming-Bruce LJ.

John Knox QC and *Vivian Chapman* for the tenants.
Anthony Cripps QC and *Patrick Darby* for the landlords.

CUMMING-BRUCE LJ. On 8 October 1975 the landlords, described as the executors of the late Mr E D Cooke, who had died in 1960, entered into a tenancy agreement with

the tenants described as E D & A D Cooke Bourne (Farms) Ltd whereby Bourne Farms   *a*
Ltd became, under the agreement, tenants of an agricultural holding described as High
Park and Low Park, to hold from 11 October 1975 on a yearly tenancy determined on 11
October in any given year, for a rent of £6,000.   There were elaborate but usual
covenants by the landlords and the tenants and the obligations of the landlords included
obligations for repair, and I refer in particular to cl 3 of Sch 2 to the agreement and cll 4
and 5 of those agreements.   By cl 6 of the agreement the landlords were under no
obligation to execute repairs or replacements or to insure buildings or fixtures which 'are   *b*
the property of the tenant'.   There was a special provision inserted which read as follows:

> 'It is hereby agreed between the parties that the following buildings erected on
> High Park Farm shall be regarded as Tenant's Fixtures:– The Ten Bay Dutch Barn,
> Workshops and glasshouses and the Grain and Potato Store with two fan tunnel
> equipment.   Also Brick and Asbestos Open Shed and Workshop at Brickpits off   *c*
> West Road, Bourne.'

Whatever effects that special provision may or may not have had it clearly had a
relevance to the obligations of the landlords to repair, since these buildings are to be
regarded as tenants' fixtures.   It may well be that in arriving at the rent which the tenants
were to pay during the period that they enjoyed the occupation of the land with its
buildings and fixtures that that rent may have been agreed between the parties by   *d*
reference to the provision in the special provision.

By the same agreement, when one comes to the rights of the parties on the
determination of the tenancy, the landlords accepted the obligation in cl 2:

> 'On termination of the tenancy to pay the Tenant compensation:– (a) for the
> unexhausted value of the improvements referred to in the Second and Third
> Schedules to the [Agricultural Holdings] Act, subject to and in accordance with the   *e*
> provisions of the Act, (b) for fixtures paid for on entry at a fair valuation and in
> respect of other fixtures subject to and in accordance with the provisions of the Act.'

The parties did address their minds to the question of compensation on the termination
of the tenancy, and agreed that the landlords should be under an obligation to pay for the
value of improvements referred to in the Schs 2 and 3 to the Act in accordance with the   *f*
provisions of the Act.

This agreement succeeded an earlier oral tenancy.   The background of the whole
matter was that Mr Cooke senior, the late E D Cooke who died in 1960, by his will
constituted trusts of the will and it emerged that there were disputes between the
beneficiaries which led to an action, *Re Cooke (decd)*, the title of which appears in the title
to the Tomlin order made on 18 November 1976.   The action was compromised on the
terms of the Tomlin order.

It is not necessary for me to refer at this juncture to other provisions of the agreement
which took its final form in the Tomlin order, save to remark that under those provisions
that come under the heading of 'The Final Distribution' and provide for the final
distribution from the trust fund as soon as practicable after the death of Mrs Cooke there
are careful provisions providing for the change in the voting rights in the company—

> 'in order to procure that Bourne Farms will surrender its tenancy of the land
> comprised in the Trust Fund without compensation being payable in respect
> thereof, save as provided in paragraph 12.2 hereof.'

Paragraph 12.2 of the Tomlin order provided:

> 'Tenant right and Compensation for tenants improvements and tenants fixtures
> shall be payable to Bourne Farms in accordance with the provisions of the
> Agricultural Holdings Act 1948 (or any re-enactment thereof) . . .'

Further provisions for final distribution provided:

> 'Andrew shall have the option of purchasing the land comprised in the Trust
> Fund at the value determined in accordance with paragraph 2 hereof.'

In para 2 the provisions for valuation had been set out, and the subsequent provisions dealt with the exercise of the option. I think it is unnecessary to refer further to the Tomlin order. That was made on 18 November 1976, that is to say just over a year after the commencement of the tenancy under the subsisting tenancy agreement.

In September 1978 Mrs Cooke died, which brought into practical operation the provisions for the final distribution following the death of Mrs Cooke, and the tenancy in accordance with those provisions was duly terminated by surrender on 28 March 1980.

On 3 April 1980 agents for the tenants served a notice under the Agricultural Holdings Act 1948 on the trustees of E D Cooke deceased and gave notice as follows:

'I HEREBY GIVE YOU NOTICE pursuant to Sect. 70 of the above Act of my intention to make against you certain claims arising out of the termination of the tenancy of the above holding or part thereof, the nature of which claims is set out in the Schedule hereto.'

THE SCHEDULE

Nature of Claim   Statutory provisions, Customs or
                                                   term of Agreement under which
                                                   the claim is made.'

Those are the headings. Under the nature of claim the endorsement was: 'Tenantright Fixtures of the above Farms £60,000. Tenantright of the above farms £15,000.' The statutory provisions: 'Agricultural Holdings Act 1948 (or any re-enactment there in of) As provided under clause 12.2 of the statement in the High Court of Justice Chancery Division', namely the Tomlin order.

That notice was addressed to the trustees of the deceased. It was followed by a second notice dated 22 May. That notice recited again that it was a notice pursuant to s 70 of the Agricultural Holdings Act 1948, and set out a different schedule. Under 'Nature of Claim' appeared the following words:

'Compensation for new Improvements, viz: the erection of a grain and potato store in the field Ordnance Survey Number 1 and the erection of a Dutch Barn in the field Ordnance Survey Number 42 the sum of £75,000.00.'

Further, under 'Nature of Claim': 'Compensation for Tenantright matters, viz: seeds sown and cultivations fallows and acts of husbandry performed on the holding at the expense of the Tenant.'

When one looks at what was indorsed under the heading 'Statutory Provisions . . .' etc, it reads:

'Section 47 of the above Act. Third Schedule or part I of the Fourth Schedule and Minute 12.2 of the Minute of Order of the High Court of Justice Chancery Division in the matter of the estate of Everitt Delanoix Cooke deceased and in the Matter of the Trusts of the Will of Everitt Delanoix Cooke deceased dated 29th November 1960 and in the Matter of the Judicial Trustees Act 1897 and in the Matter of the Trustee Act 1925 between Joy Delanoix Richardson and Robert Kevin Andrew Feltham (formerly Kevin Andrew Richardson) as Plaintiffs and Kate Elizabeth Cooke and Andrew Delanoix Cooke and Paul Delanoix Tointon as Defendants. Section 47 of the above Act and Part II of the Fourth Schedule and the above mentioned Minute of Order.'

On 2 July the arbitrator was appointed, and we are told that the practice was followed of serving documents thereafter on the arbitrator. Thus it came about that on 14 July in the same year a tenant's statement of case was served on the arbitrator. That statement of case reads as follows:

'Statement of Case for the Arbitrator with particulars on behalf of the Tenant.
1. The Tenant, a Limited Company, was formed on 10th May 1951 and from that date assumed the Tenancy of the Holding on a verbal agreement only.

2. On 8th October 1975 a written Tenancy Agreement was drawn up and remained in force until it was terminated by the provisions of an Order of the High Court of Justice, Chancery Division (Group A) given by Mr. Justice Templeman on 18th November 1976. The date of termination was 28th March 1980.

3. With one exception every provision of the aforementioned Order of the High Court has been discharged by mutual agreement between Landlord and Tenant.

4. Under Clause 12(2) of the High Court Order, the Tenant was to be paid for Tenantright and Compensation for Tenants Improvements and Tenants Fixtures in accordance with the provisions of the Agricultural Holdings Act 1948 (or any re-enactment thereof).

5. The Tenant claims Compensation in respect of Tenants Fixtures situate at High Park Farm, Aslackby as Scheduled in the Tenancy Agreement.

6. The Tenant claims the sum of £75,000 (SEVENTY FIVE THOUSAND POUNDS) being the value of the two buildings referred to in paragraph 5 above.

7. The Tenant will produce evidence in support of the sum claimed as compensation which fairly represents the value of the two buildings to an incoming tenant.

8. The Tenant reserves the right to be legally represented at the Arbitration Hearing if such representation should be considered necessary to support his case.

Particulars of Claim referred to above

Compensation for Tenants Fixtures viz:

The 120–ft. × 105–ft. steel framed and asbestos-clad corn and Potato Store Shed, together with the concrete apron surrounds £60,000

The 180–ft. × 30–ft. steel framed and corrugated-iron clad Dutch Barn   ..   ..   £15,000.'

On 28 July the landlords served on the arbitrator their statement of case. It was submitted on behalf of the landlords by their experienced agents, and I summarise it by saying that it began by reciting that the tenants had claimed under s 70 of the 1948 Act under a formal claim dated 3 April, which was attached to the landlord's statement of case. The landlords then pleaded their case in respect of tenants' fixtures, which would be a claim under s 13. The landlords' agents, Messrs Strutt & Parker, recited the provisions of s 13 and accurately pointed out that the provisions of s 13(2) had not been followed, and therefore the s 13 claim could not get off the ground. They appreciated and drew the attention of the arbitrator to the fact that the s 13 claim, based as it had to be on a notice by the landlords to purchase the buildings, could not arise on the determination of this tenancy in the circumstances that had happened. The landlords' case continued by referring to an alternative method of considering claims for tenantright fixtures, namely to regard them as tenants' improvements. They did not in that passage of the landlords' statement of case refer to the notice of 22 May. I know not the explanation and I do not think it matters. They did not refer to it, but they set out that in so far as there was an alternative claim for tenants' improvements the landlords claimed to defeat such claim because the tenants had not produced to them, the landlords' agents, 'any evidence that a written landlords' consent exists in connection with the improvements for which compensation is claimed'. They go on:

'We thus submit that any claim made by the Tenants in this matter, either for Tenantright Fixtures or alternatively as Tenants' Improvements is invalid: and that under the legal requirements of the Agricultural Holdings Act 1948 the Landlords are entitled to dismiss any claim for compensation.'

Then they went on in their statement of case: 'Assuming an unconditional landlords' consent, compensation for New Improvments must be assessed in accordance with Section 48 of the Act.' They recite part of that section, and then they plead a case on the merits, leading to the conclusion that if there were a legal enforceable claim under s 47 the amount of compensation would not exceed £35,000 as compared to the claim for

£75,000 which had been particularised in the tenants' statement of case. At that stage those were the statements of case which the respective parties served on the arbitrator.

On 14 October the tenants' agents submitted to the arbitrator a document entitled 'Supplemental statement of case', which reads as follows:

> '9. The tenant has read the Landlord's statement of case dated 28th July 1980.
>
> 10. The tenant accepts that no compensation is due under s. 13 of the Agricultural Holdings Act 1948.
>
> 11. The tenant's case is that compensation is due under s. 47 of the Agricultural Holdings Act 1948.
>
> 12. The landlord's written consent to the erection of the Corn and Potato Store Shed was given on 2nd March 1965.
>
> 13. The tenant will ask the arbitrator to infer that the landlord's written consent to the erection of the Dutch Barn was also given in that the said barn was erected with the assistance of a Government grant, a precondition of which grant is production of evidence of landlord's written consent to erection.'

On 23 November, we are told, the tenants wrote to the landlords giving them notice of their application for leave to amend. The arbitrator fixed a preliminary meeting to deal with the tenants' application for leave to amend, and fixed that meeting for 9 February 1981. When that hearing came on before the arbitrator the tenants sought leave, and if they were given leave to file their supplemental statement of case, leave to file a further amendment pleading that the tenants had quitted the holding, the subject matter of the claim for compensation. There was an amendment for which the landlords were seeking leave on the same basis, and it was agreed before the arbitrator and accepted by the arbitrator that if he gave leave to the tenants to file a supplemental statement of case the further amendment would follow and the landlords' amendment to their statement of case should also be allowed.

Those further amendments, therefore, gave rise to no issue, and the only issue before the arbitrator was whether he should give leave to file and serve the supplemental statement of case.

The arbitrator heard argument on that issue. He understood counsel for the landlords to make the following submissions:

> '19. The Landlord appeared by counsel who submitted: 1. The Tenant's statement of case of 14th July 1980 is the Statement of Claim and in paragraph 5 is restricted by reference to "Tenants fixtures" that is to say s. 13 of the 1948 Act. 2. Tenant's counsel has already admitted s. 13 is not a sustainable basis of claim in this case. 3. The claim for cultivations and acts of husbandry referred to in the Notice of Intention to Claim dated 22nd May 1980 was dropped before the claim was made and the claim, so far as the buildings are concerned, relates to tenants fixtures and hence a s.13 claim. 4. Once the buildings had been accepted by both parties as Tenant's Fixtures, no claim for compensation could be sustainable in respect of them under any other category than as Tenant's Fixtures. 5. To consent to the Tenant's request would give rise to injustice to the Landlords as they would then have to come again for a two to three day and then a one to two day hearing on two further separate matters. 6. Whilst the sixth paragraph of the Sixth Schedule to the 1948 Act gives an arbitrator power to consent to an amendment it follows that the arbitrator also has the power not to consent, there is nothing automatic about it, the arbitrator should decide what is just.'

The decision of the arbitrator, with his reasons, is set out in paras 20, 21 and 22 of his statement of case, which read as follows:

> '20. Although not referred to by Landlord's or Tenant's counsel my subsequent researches brought to light the case of *Church Comrs for England v Mathews* ((1979) 251 EG 1074) which seems to have followed previous precedents established in

County Court judgments which prevents fundamental changes to Statements of Case under the 1948 Act.

21. Having considered in detail the arguments put forward at the preliminary hearing and having read the legal research referred to and having done my own research I conclude that following precedent I could not accept the fundamental amendment to the Tenant's Statement of Case and accordingly my Decision in writing dated 20th February 1981 indicated that I would refuse my consent to the admission of the Tenant's first supplemental statement of case.

22. At the preliminary hearing counsel for both Landlords and tenant requested me to state in the form of a special case for the opinion of a County Court the following question of law arising in the course of the arbitration.'

On that reasoning the arbitrator refused leave to amend by filing the supplementary statement of case and the further amendment, therefore, fell with it.

The tenants asked for a case stated, for an opinion of the court. That case was stated, from which I have already quoted, and the matter came before the county court judge, who gave judgment and made an order on 23 September 1981 ordering that there be judgment in accordance with the copies delivered to the advocates, which does not reveal very much. That refers back, I suppose, to the note of judgment which the county court judge signed on 18 September 1981. In effect, the judge upheld the decision of the arbitrator, on different grounds, and gave leave to appeal.

With regard to the decision of the judge, he took the view, and I quote:

'In this case, subject to the fundamental point as to there being a valid statement of case to be amended, I have no doubt that the amendments or additions proposed could be effected without manifest or grave injustice. The landlords have had it well in mind from the beginning that these claims might be being made.'

But he decided the case and upheld the decision of the arbitrator on the ground that there was no valid statement of case. So there was nothing to amend. That is to say, on a scrutiny of the statement of case filed by the tenants, on the proper understanding of that statement of case there was no valid statement of case within the relevant legislation.

I now, therefore, turn, before examining the reasoning of the judge, to the scheme of the legislation, and I begin by referring to the Agricultural Holdings Act 1923, since it was in relation to the statutory scheme under that Act that two important decisions of this court were made. By the 1923 Act provision was made for compensation to the tenant for various kinds of loss, compensation for improvements on holdings, compensation for damage by gale, compensation for disturbance. Section 16 provided the procedure for settling any question or difference arising out of any claim by the tenant of a holding against a landlord, or for any sums claimed to be due to the tenant from the landlord for breach of contract. The provision which is relevant for consideration was s 16(2), which read:

'Any such claim as is mentioned in this section shall cease to be enforceable after the expiration of two months from the termination of the tenancy unless particulars thereof have been given by the landlord to the tenant or by the tenant to the landlord, as the case may be, before the expiration of that period . . .'

There is a provision for extension in the proviso under a certain contingency.

When one considers s 16(2), it is apparent that there was a statutory and mandatory period within which the claimant was under an obligation to give particulars of the claim, and there was no provision in sub-s (2) or elsewhere in that Act for any amendment or correction or addition to the particulars required by sub-s (2). Therefore, if the tenant failed to give particulars such as were in contemplation by the subsection he was for ever precluded from proceeding with his claim. That is the subsection which was under consideration in this court in 1933 and 1934. In *Re O'Connor and Brewin's Arbitration* [1933] 1 KB 20 the matter for consideration was whether sufficient particulars had been delivered pursuant to s 16(2), and the court decided that on the facts in that case no sufficient particulars had been delivered and, therefore, the claim was barred. Giving his judgment in that case, Slesser LJ referred (at 32) to a passage in the judgment of Warrington LJ in *Jones v Evans* [1923] 1 KB 12 at 20 where Warrington LJ said:

> 'It is in general sufficient if the document or the conversation which contains the particulars gives an indication to the landlord or the tenant, as the case may be, of the particular kind of claim which is going to be made in order that he may have an opportunity of himself examining the subject-matter and seeing what evidence he will have to adduce, or what information he will have to give the arbitrator.'

Slesser LJ, approving that passage in the judgment, considered the facts of the case before him, and decided that on those facts the landlord had not by the particulars given by the tenant been given the particulars to which he was entitled. Slesser LJ went on (at 33):

> 'Indeed I find great difficulty in seeing that he has really been given any particulars at all. It is required under the Act that the landlord shall receive notice of a claim, and that notice of a claim is to be made before the tenant had ended the tenancy. What is called "particulars" in this case appears to be no more than a notice of a claim given after the tenancy has come to an end.'

In the following year, in *Spreckley v Leicestershire CC* [1934] 1 KB 366, the court decided, reversing the decision of the county court judge–

> 'that no sufficient particulars had been delivered and, therefore, that the claim was barred, on the grounds: (1.) that the notice of November 23, 1931, was merely a notice that a claim would be made and not a rendering of particulars . . .'

So there again, the question was against the background of the statute which imposed on the claimant the obligation to particularise his claim sufficiently to enable the opposite party to appreciate the nature of the claim and to determine what evidence was required in order to meet it. The court decided on the facts that there were no particulars which would sufficiently arm the opposite party with the opportunity for understanding the nature of the claim and for appreciating the evidence that it would be necessary to give in order to meet it.

Those were the cases which gave guidance as to the kind of particularity which was appropriate to valid particulars complying with the statutory requirement laid down in s 16(2) of the 1923 Act.

I have referred to those cases because they evidently played a part, not only in the subsequent decision of *Church Comrs for England v Mathews* (1979) 251 EG 1074, but also in the reasoning of the judge when he was considering the instant case.

By contrast, I come to the scheme of legislation in the Agricultural Holdings Act 1948, which incorporates provisions that first appeared in the Agriculture Act 1947, to which it is unnecessary to make separate reference. In the 1948 Act, I refer first to two provisions for compensation.

By s 13 it was provided:

> '(1) Subject to the provisions of this section . . . (b) any building (other than one in respect of which the tenant is entitled to compensation under this Act or otherwise) erected by him on the holding . . . shall be removable by the tenant at any time during the continuance of the tenancy or before the expiration of two months from the termination of the tenancy, and shall remain his property so long as he may remove it by virtue of this subsection.
>
> (2) The right conferred by the foregoing subsection shall not be exercisable in relation to a fixture or building unless the tenant—(a) has paid all rent . . . and (b) has, at least one month before both the exercise of the right and the termination of the tenancy, given to the landlord notice in writing of his intention to remove the fixture or building.
>
> (3) If, before the expiration of the notice aforesaid, the landlord gives to the

tenant a counter-notice in writing electing to purchase a fixture or building comprised in the notice, subsection (1) of this section shall cease to apply to that fixture or building, but the landlord shall be liable to pay to the tenant the fair value thereof to an incoming tenant of the holding . . .'

It is to be observed that by virtue of that section it is provided that the tenant may give notice of the intention to remove fixtures or buildings, but if after such notice the landlord gives a counter-notice electing to purchase the fixture or building, then the landlord may purchase, but on such purchase shall be liable to pay a fair value thereof to an incoming tenant of the holding.

I turn next to s 47. By that section and the succeeding sections there is provision for compensation for new improvements and for other matters:

'(1) The tenant shall, subject to the provisions of this Act, be entitled on the termination of the tenancy, on quitting the holding, to obtain from his landlord compensation for a new improvement carried out by the tenant and for any such matter as is specified in Part II of the Fourth Schedule to this Act . . .'

subject to certain provisos which do not arise in the present case.

By s 48 the measure of compensation for long term new improvements was enacted, and I quote:

'The amount of any compensation under this Act for new improvement specified in the Third Schedule thereto shall be an amount equal to the increase attributable to the improvement in the value of the agricultural holding as a holding, having regard to the character and situation of the holding and the average requirements of tenants reasonably skilled in husbandry.'

That measure of compensation may be contrasted with the different measure of purchase price imposed on the landlord under s 13 if he elects to purchase.

I refer next to s 50, which provides that where the landlord has refused consent there is an alternative provision that the tenant may apply to the minister to override the landlord and grant a consent which binds the landlord.

By s 70 the Act sets out the scheme for the settlement of claims between landlord and tenant on termination of tenancy, and specifies that disputes should be settled by arbitration; it sets out the provisions relating to the appointment of an arbitrator and has an important and quite new provision in sub-s (2):

'No such claim as aforesaid shall be enforceable unless before the expiration of two months from the termination of the tenancy the claimant has served notice in writing on his landlord or tenant, as the case may be, of his intention to make the claim. A notice under this subsection shall specify the nature of the claim, and it shall be a sufficient specification thereof if the notice refers to the statutory provision, custom or term of an agreement under which the claim is made.'

It is to be observed that that imposes on the claimant the duty in pursuit of a claim which has not been settled to give a notice in writing of an intention to make the claim, and that notice is sufficient if it specifies the nature of the claim by specifying the statutory provision, custom or term of agreement under which the claim was made.

So, to use the language which has appeared in some of the judgments given in this court in relation to the 1923 Act Parliament, by s 70(2) has provided that the first stage in pursuing a disputed claim shall be to give a notice which specifies the class of claim as compared to the particulars of claim.

After such notice, the procedure is enacted in Sch 6. After appointment of the arbitrator, by para 6 of Sch 6:

'The parties to arbitration shall, within twenty-eight days from the appointment of the arbitrator, deliver to him a statement of their respective cases with all necessary particulars and—(a) no amendment or addition to the statement or particulars delivered shall be allowed after the expiration of the said twenty-eight days except with the consent of the arbitrator; (b) a party to the arbitration shall be confined at the hearing to the matters alleged in the statement and particulars delivered by him and any amendment thereof or addition thereto duly made.'

Thus, in contrast to the statutory procedure prescribed under s 16 of the 1923 Act, the 1948 Act prescribes a procedure materially different in two respects. It became a two-stage procedure instead of a one-stage procedure. The two stages were to be: a notice specifying the nature of the claim, followed by a statement of case pursuant to para 6 of Sch 6, which instead of stating particulars has to state all necessary particulars. Second, whereas under the 1923 Act the particulars served were final and did not provide for amendment or addition of any description, by para 6 of Sch 6 to the 1948 Act, whereas the statement of case had to state all necessary particulars as compared to all particulars, it provided that those particulars could be amended or added to provided that the arbitrator gave consent. By sub-para (b) to para 6 the party to the arbitration is confined at the hearing to matters alleged in the statement and particulars delivered by him and amendment thereof or addition thereto duly made.

It seems to me clear that the explanation of this important relaxation of the procedure enacted in 1923 was that Parliament had appreciated by 1947 that an arbitration under the Agricultural Holdings Act had characteristics arising from the subject matter which made the arbitration something importantly different from arbitrations under the Arbitration Acts or from proceedings at law. In particular, it was likely that a significant number of claimants would be small people, landlords or tenants of smallholdings who competent, no doubt, as farmers, were likely to be ill-versed in the delicacy of pleading for the purposes of a statutory arbitration. The draconian character or the draconian effect of s 16(2) of the 1923 Act was recognised by Parliament as being inappropriate to the kind of arbitration which was provided for in the Agricultural Holdings Acts. Against that background it is easy to understand how it was that Parliament, while imposing on the claimant a duty to file not only particulars, but more elaborately all necessary particulars within a stated time, decided that there should be room for amendment or addition to those particulars, provided that the arbitrator gave his consent to the amendment or addition. The scheme was completed by the provision under sub-para (b) of para 6 that at the arbitration the parties shall be confined to the statement and particulars delivered and any amendment or addition thereto duly made, that is to say with the consent of the arbitrator.

The relevance of the observations in the judgments in the cases to which I have referred, being cases under the 1923 Act, has to be very carefully considered in the light of the novelty of the statutory scheme under the 1948 Act, because those cases under the 1923 Act were concerned with s 16(2) of the 1923 Act, which made it mandatory on the claimant to complete his particulars without any opportunity for addition or amendment. The courts decided that in that legislation those particulars which alone were the particulars which fell for consideration at the arbitration must be such as would enable the opposite party to appreciate the nature of the claim, and to appreciate the evidence that he should produce in order to meet that claim.

For the purposes of the scheme in Sch 6, the guidance given in the judgments in the cases to which I refer remains, in my view, an entirely appropriate guidance provided that the arbitrator focuses his attention on the sufficiency of the particulars given by the claimant, not only in his original statement of case but also in the statement of case which has been amended or been the subject of addition on supplemental statements, leave to file which has been the subject of consent by the arbitrator.

It seems to me that it would be entirely misleading and quite wrong to apply the reasoning of this court in the two cases to which I have referred to the statement of case filed under Sch 6, rather than applying the reasoning of those judgments to a statement of case, together with such amendment or addition as an arbitrator thinks it right to consent to. The schemes of legislation are significantly different in the ways to which I have already referred. It is now a two-stage instead of a one-stage procedure; the second stage of that procedure does not impose on the claimant an obligation to get everything right the first time, but an obligation to do his best to get everything right, providing that he can get it right by amendment and addition to which the arbitrator gives his consent.

So I come in the light of the present statutory scheme to consider the judgment in this case. First I refer to the decision of the arbitrator. It is quite clear to me that the arbitrator took the view, expressed in his judgment, that he was precluded by authority from exercising his discretion because he took the view, in my view quite wrongly, that he had no power, in the light of the guidance given in the county court in *Church Comrs for England v Mathews* (1979) 251 EG 1074, to consent to the particulars. That view, which I think he clearly expressed, is based on a complete misunderstanding of the case to which he refers.

Church Comrs for England v Mathews is reported only in the Estates Gazette. What the case was concerned with was the sufficiency of a landlord's statement of case, for the purposes of para 6 of Sch 6 to the 1948 Act, and the point of the case was that the landlords had delivered a statement of case which they never sought to amend, and the county court judge decided that the purported statement of case hopelessly failed to comply with the statutory requirement of a statement of case with all necessary particulars. The statement of case there under consideration read as follows:

'If the arbitrator finds that the above notice was valid, he will be asked to give an award on the validity and/or quantum of 30 items of dilapidations to house, buildings, cottage and land still outstanding between valuers.'

The county court judge, and I would respectfully submit correctly, took the view that there was no particularity at all about the landlord's statement of case, and it therefore failed to comply with the provisions of para 6. That case is nihil ad rem to the issues in the instant case, and the arbitrator was wrong in thinking that it would assist him, because the point in the case was that the statement of case, without any application for amendment was hopelessly inadequate, and there was no conclusion that the county court judge could reach other than that which he did reach. The problem before the arbitrator was not the problem that faced the county court judge in *Church Comrs for England v Mathews*. It was a quite different problem. Faced with an imperfect statement of case, as the arbitrator undoubtedly was in the instant case, he had to ask himself: 'Ought I to permit it to be made clear by amendment or addition as drafted by the landlords' agent in the application to file a supplemental statement of case?' I find it impossible to see how in answering that question there is any reason for thinking that any assistance would be derived from the county court judge's judgment in *Church Comrs for England v Mathews*. But it is clear that the arbitrator thought that he was bound, as he said: 'Following precedent I could not accept the fundamental amendment to the tenants' statement of claim.' That was a misconception, because he was not bound at all by anything that appeared in the case that he was relying on.

So the matter came before the county court judge. It is to be observed that in his note of judgment the county court judge began by expressing his conclusion that he had no doubt that the amendments or additions proposed could be effected without manifest or grave injustice, although there had been apparently an argument to the contrary. On the facts, that finding of the judge was clearly right.

The judge then went on to consider another question, and he put it like this:

'The landlords allege that the amendments produce such a fundamental change of case that they should not be allowed even if the statement of case is valid in itself. I find this a difficult argument to accept as the tenants' statement of case is so vague in itself that a claim under s 13 or s 47 can be justified under it. This is the real difficulty in this case. The rules in Sch 6 to the 1948 Act lay down that "The parties . . . shall within twenty-eight days from the appointment of the arbitrator, deliver to him a statement of their respective cases with all necessary particulars. . ." The time limit is mandatory and inflexible. If this is not done the party is unable to produce any evidence in support of his case.'

Therein the judge was wrong. The time limit is not mandatory and inflexible, because the time limit in para 6 is a time limit of 28 days for the delivery of the statement with all necessary particulars, but there is provision for amendment or addition to a statement or particulars with the consent of the arbitrator. There is nothing mandatory or inflexible about the scheme of Sch 6. Indeed, as I understand it, the reason for the legislative change between the scheme in s 16(2) of the 1923 Act and the scheme in para 6 of Sch 6 to the 1948 Act was to introduce a flexibility that was absent from the 1923 Act. The object of the change was to enable the claimant to put his house in order. I quite understand that there could be, hypothetically, a filing of a purported statement of case which was so hopelessly at variance with the intention of a statement of case within para 6 that it could be said that there was nothing to amend. I think it is unnecessary to elaborate the kind of hypothetical situations that I have in mind. If the statement of case was merely frivolous or something of that sort it might well be held that there was nothing to amend. But that is not this case at all.

The notice dated 22 May 1980 gave notice of a claim for compensation for new improvements under s 47 of the 1948 Act. As the judge found, it superseded the first notice.

The trouble arose, of course, from the extraordinary muddled statement of case which the tenants' agents filed in purported compliance with the duty of the claimant to give all necessary particulars. It was an odd document. It used language that on its face would leave a respondent in profound obscurity as to what kind of case the claimant was really presenting. Paragraph 4 recited a provision of the Tomlin order. Paragraph 5 read: 'The Tenant claims Compensation in respect of Tenants Fixtures . . . as scheduled in the Tenancy Agreement.' Paragraph 6 claimed £75,000, 'being the value of the two buildings referred to. . .' If the draftsman thought he was presenting a claim under s 47 he would only have pleaded that measure of loss if he had completely failed to appreciate the measure of compensation provided for the purposes of a claim under s 47, because the measure of compensation under s 48 is not the value of the buildings.

There was a sufficient particularity of the physical subject matter of the claim because two buildings were sufficiently described and a figure was put against each of them in respect of their value. I do understand that as long as the opposite party was faced only with that document he could have been in great difficulty in deciding what was the case that he had to meet.

The statement of the landlords' case does indicate that the landlords' agent realised there was confusion, because they pleaded reasons for negativing the s 13 claim and then proceeded to plead an affirmative case in the event of the claim being eventually regarded as a s 47 claim, as had been foreshadowed in the notice of 22 May. But all those difficulties were swept away as soon as the supplementary statement of case was considered by the arbitrator or by the landlords' agents, because in the supplemental statement of case the tenants, by para 10, accepted that no compensation was due under s 13, pleaded that the case for compensation was under s 47, and pleaded that the landlords had given written consent for the erection of the corn and potato shed, and pleaded the facts relied on as leading to an inference of consent by the landlords to the erection of the Dutch barn. That was still imperfect and defective, because they still failed to plead that the tenants had quitted the holding. That was the subject matter of the further supplement, which everybody agreed should be allowed if the supplemental statement of case was consented to as an amendment or addition.

For my part, once the supplemental statement of case is scrutinised it clears up all the difficulties arising from the muddle of language and confused thinking in the statement of case originally filed; and faced with the statement of case, plus the supplemental statement of case, a respondent would have no difficulty in appreciating the nature of the landlords' case, the particulars that describe that case, and in mobilising his resources by way of evidence in order to meet it. When the two are read together, all the difficulties are swept away. If the amendment is allowed, the statement of case thus amended and added to, with the further addition to which I have referred, will comply completely with the prescribed requisite of pleading all the necessary particulars.

In this court I think it is unnecessary to dwell longer on the question of whether those amendments could have been consented to without injustice, because I find it quite impossible to apprehend any injustice or any difficulty confronting the landlords that could not adequately be dealt with by an adjournment, if any adjournment was necessary, and by costs if costs were thrown away. I say adjournment if any adjournment was necessary, because the appointment for the arbitrator in February was only an appointment for the purpose deciding a preliminary point, namely consent to the amendment, and as far as the information before this court goes no date for the arbitration on the merits was ever fixed.

So I come to the reasons relied on by the judge as the basis of his decision in upholding the determination of the arbitrator to refuse his consent. In my view, the error into which the judge fell is manifest on reading the last two pages of his note of judgment. He was misled by *Re O'Connor and Brewin's Arbitration* [1933] 1 KB 20 and *Jones v Evans* [1923] 1 KB 12 into thinking that faced with an application for leave to amend it was appropriate to look at the defective statement of case to decide whether it by itself afforded all necessary particulars, and on reaching that decision the judge evidently thought that he was precluded from giving leave to amend or that it would be wrong to give leave to amend. But that reasoning was based on a misapprehension of the scheme set out in the 1948 Act. This two-stage scheme, culminating in a statement of case which may be amended or added to with the consent of the arbitrator has this effect: on an application to amend ordinary considerations of justice and fairness make it appropriate to amend, if after amendment the respondent will know sufficiently the particulars of the case that he has to meet. In such a situation, leave to amend should ordinarily be granted. The consent should ordinarily be given. It is manifest that when Sch 6 expressly enacted the power to amend or add, Parliament contemplated that the statement of case first filed would be defective in some respect. Otherwise there would be no point in seeking leave to add necessary particulars. The mere fact of the absence of all necessary particulars in the original statement of case cannot itself be a ground for refusing consent to an attempt to remedy the deficiency.

As I understand it, if the notice given on 22 May is read with the statement of case, together with the amendments and additions sought to be made, all the requirements of Sch 6 to the 1948 Act would be amply satisfied. For those reasons I would, respectfully, reverse the judge's decision and state that the arbitrator was wrong in refusing his consent and that the judge was wrong in upholding his decision.

Two other points arise for mention. Counsel for the landlords drew the court's attention to the familiar case of *Gray v Lord Ashburton* [1917] AC 26, [1916–17] All ER Rep 380 which brought home the point that an arbitration under the Agricultural Holding Acts has characteristics which differentiate and distinguish it from an arbitration under the Arbitration Acts or an action at law. So that, as was held in that case in the House of Lords, the way in which the arbitrator under the Agricultural Holdings Act 1908 exercised his discretion in relation to costs was not bad because he did not follow the practice of the High Court in relation to the judicial exercise of discretion as to costs in the High Court. But, having said that, I am unable to discover in the guidance in the speeches in the House of Lords any assistance for the purpose of deciding the question before this court, which is whether the arbitrator and the county court judge were wrong in law in the decisions which they respectively reached.

Another point was raised by counsel for the landlords which turned on the effect of a special provision which was a provision of the tenancy agreement of 8 October 1975 in relation to the obligations of the landlords. That special provision stated:

'It is hereby agreed between the parties that the following buildings erected on High Park Farm shall be regarded as Tenant's Fixtures:—The Ten Bay Dutch Barn . . . Grain and Potato Store . . . Brick and Asbestos Open Shed . . .'

Counsel for the landlords' argument was that because those buildings had been the subject of that agreement that they should be regarded as tenants' fixtures that agreement in some way precluded the tenants from exercising his right to claim for new improvements. This is a very puzzling submission in the light of cl 2(1) of the tenancy agreement, which provided that:

'On the termination of the tenancy to pay to the Tenant compensation: (a) for the unexhausted value of the improvements referred to in the Second and Third Schedules to the Act, subject to and in accordance with the provisions of the Act, (b) for fixtures paid for an entry at a fair valuation and in respect of other fixtures subject to and in accordance with the provisions of the Act . . .'

In spite of counsel's argument I remain unable to follow how he could submit successfully that the special provision which I have recited could possibly have the effect of negativing or modifying or reducing any claim of the tenants for unexhausted value of the improvements without meeting the difficulty provided for by s 65 of the 1948 Act, which expressly provides that contracting out is not permitted. The grounds that he submitted suggesting a special agreement to the contrary seem to me difficult to sustain.

For those reasons, I would reverse the order of the county court judge, and I would move that consent to this amendment should have been given by the arbitrator because nothing in the facts recited in the case stated by the arbitrator could be consistent with any just determination of the application for leave to amend, save consent. There is, therefore, to my mind, no room for sending the case back to the arbitrator because the facts stated by the arbitrator point only to one correct legal conclusion, which is that consent should be given to the amendments sought. I would allow the appeal.

TEMPLEMAN LJ. I agree that there were no grounds on which consent to the additions and amendments to the statement of case sought by the tenants could properly have been withheld. But as the arbitrator and the judge in their different ways have gone sadly astray in construing and applying the relevant provisions of the Agricultural Holdings Act 1948, I will as shortly as possible endeavour to give my reasons.

On 22 May 1980 the tenants served on the landlords a notice that they were seeking under s 47 of the 1948 Act compensation for new improvements identified as the erection of a grain and potato store in Ordnance Survey no 1 and the erection of a Dutch Barn in Ordnance Survey no 42 on the holding known as High Park Farm and Low Park Farm, Aslackby, in the County of Lincoln, in the sum of £75,000. Nothing could be plainer or clearer. However, the tenants' statement of case which followed was defective. First, the statement of case dated 14 July 1980 did not refer either to s 13 or s 47 of the 1948 Act in express terms. So far as the landlords were concerned s 13 was out, because s 13 can only come into play if the landlords had elected to purchase the fixtures in question, and the landlords above all knew that they had not made any such election. Second, the statement of case gave the wrong measure of damages. but that did not affect the landlords who could prove and give evidence of the right measure of damages. Third, the statement of case did not specify the date of quitting. But it did give the date of termination of 28 March 1980, which was the same as the date of quitting, and it does not seem to me that the landlords were in any difficulty, as they presumably knew as much as the tenants; and the arbitrator waiting in the wings could always be enlightened by both of them. Fourth, and more important, the statement did not allege or give particulars of the landlords' consent which is a prerequisite to an entitlement to compensation under s 47. Therefore, if the landlords chose to challenge the tenants on the question of consent (and at that stage nobody knew whether they would or would not) and if, that consent being challenged, the tenants' statement of case was not amended, then clearly the tenants would be bound to fail in their application.

That this was all clear to the landlords appears from the landlords' own statement of case, dated 28 July 1980. First of all, they dealt with a possible claim under s 13, which in my view was an unnecessary elaboration, but understandable in view of the difficulties in the tenants' statement. Second, they dealt with the tenants' failure to allege and prove that the landlords' consent had been given for the purpose of s 47. They took the point, and the point being taken was good, so long as the tenants' statement of case remained unamended. Then, no doubt feeling the possibility that the tenants might wish to amend, no doubt feeling in their bones that there might be some possibility that the amendment might be allowed, the landlords' statement of case very efficiently and in great detail dealt with the merits of the application for compensation under s 47, ending with the conclusion that the compensation payable to the tenants could not exceed £35,000.

When the landlords' statement of case was received by the tenants, or when for some other reason the tenants woke up, they realised the defects in their original statement of case, and so they applied for additions and amendments. On 17 November 1980 the landlords received the tenants' supplemental case in which the tenants proposed to make additions and amendments to their statement of case which would repair all the defects which I have mentioned in their original statement of case. In particular, the tenants supplied the necessary particulars with regard to what they said was the landlords' consent given for the purposes of s 47. At that stage, the landlords had a choice. They could either go along to the arbitrator and say: 'We consent to your making the order which the tenants seek', or they could choose to oppose. They chose to oppose and that is the reason we are here today. I say that, not to blame them: it was a choice perfectly open to them and they took it.

The arbitrator on 21 February 1981 gave two reasons for refusing to consent to the tenants' application to repair the defects in their original statement of case. The first reason he gave was:

'After consideration of legal argument and accepting that the tenancy agreement clearly scheduled both buildings in question as tenants fixtures, I concluded that no claim for these items under s 47 of the Agricultural Holdings Act 1948 could possibly be sustained.'

In the first place, that conclusion as a matter of law on the construction of the tenancy agreement was quite wrong. In the second place the arbitrator was not being asked to construe the tenancy agreement or the claim; he was being asked to allow an amendment. Then the arbitrator stated that his researches had established 'County court judgments which prevent fundamental changes to statements of case under the 1948 Act'. There is no trace in the Act of any reference to fundamental changes, and one reason why the arbitrator may have gone wrong is that he entirely failed to set out and consider the perfectly simple words of para 6 of Sch 6 to the 1948 Act, which told him what he ought to be doing. The principle of 'no fundamental change' has as much relevance to this case as the principle of 'No Popery'. However, those were the reasons given by the arbitrator, and so the parties, not unnaturally, went along to the county court judge.

The county court judge was not impressed with the arbitrator's reasons, and in his judgment he considered what attitude the arbitrator should have taken. In the first place, and quite correctly, as Cumming-Bruce LJ has pointed out, he said:

'. . . I have no doubt that the amendments or additions proposed could be effected without manifest or grave injustice. The landlords have had it well in mind from the beginning that these claims might be being made.'

But then the judge proceeded so far as I can see without applying his mind to the exact works of para 6 of Sch 6 with which he ought to have been concerned. He began to point out defects in the original statement of claim. He said: '. . . I see that there is no reference to either s 47 or s 13 in it.' That is precisely why the tenants sought an amendment, and it is no answer to a request for an amendment to say that the original document was wrong and to knock out the amendment because of the defect in the earlier document. He said that the tenants' original statement of case would leave any landlord in a state of confusion; but, that was the object of the amendment. The object of the tenants' amendment was to remove the state of confusion and make everything clear to the landlords to whom, as I have said, it was already pretty clear in the first place. It cannot be right to refuse an amendment because an amendment is necessary.

In my judgment, one simply has to look at the words of para 6 of Sch 6 as amended by the Agriculture (Miscellaneous Provisions) Act 1963, s 20. Parliament has provided that a claimant shall deliver a statement of case with all necessary particulars within 28 days from the appointment of the arbitrator. Parliament has recognised that the draftsman of the statement of case may be fallible, whether he be farmer, bailiff, chartered surveyor, solicitor or counsel. Parliament in its wisdom has given the draftsman an opportunity to repent. He can repent at will within the 28 days, because the paragraph goes on:

> '... no amendment or addition to the statement of particulars delivered shall be allowed after the expiration of the said twenty-eight days except with the consent of the arbitrator ...'

So that if within that 28 days the draftsman has a rush of common sense to the head and realises that he has left out a necessary particular he can rapidly fill in the gap. Or if he has another rush of common sense and realises that he has got it wrong and that the statement needs amending he can do so. Parliament in its wisdom has realised that people do not necessarily come to their senses within a fixed limit of 28 days. So Parliament has given the draftsman another chance of repenting: after the 28 days he can amend with the consent of the arbitrator, and he can go along and say: 'I have made a mistake. I have left this out. I have put this wrongly. I have not given the necessary particulars, and now I want to do so.' If the arbitrator and the county court judge are right, it is open to them to say: 'Oh, how wicked you have been! Look what a mess you have made of it. We are not going to help you out of your difficulty.' That is not the object of the power given by that paragraph; that is not the object of requiring the consent of the arbitrator. The object is to enable the arbitrator to allow an amendment or an addition to be made, and the reason that his consent is required and can be refused is simply this, that he has to say to himself: 'What about the poor landlord? Is he going to be any worse off than he would have been if the amendment had been incorporated in the original statement of case?' It is no good the landlord saying: 'Oh, but if you allow this amendment the tenants might be able to get £35,000 out of me.' The £35,000 does not become payable because of the amendment. It becomes payable because the necessary conditions are satisfied, if they are satisfied, which Parliament has laid down for the payment of £35,000. But, of course, if the landlord is going to be in any worse position as a result of the amendment than he would have been if it had originally been in the statement of case, then the arbitrator may pause. If he finds that since the original statement of case by lapse of time or because the landlord has altered his position or for some other reason it would be unfair on the landlord to impose the amendment on him, then the arbitrator has power to refuse consent. But if the answer is, as it is in the present case, that the landlord is no worse off, then consent ought to be given to the amendment. Although there may be some difficulty in knocking sense into the Agricultural Holdings Act 1948, we have not yet got to the stage where arbitrators and county court judges can foist on the Act the kind of machinery that is more appropriate to the ages of Lord Eldon and the Circumlocution Office than it is to the twentieth century. The object and proper construction of para 6 of Sch 6 are quite clear and I hope that there will be no difficulty in the future. Amendments ought to be allowed as of course, unless the landlords have a strong case for saying that because the tenants got it wrong in the first place and because of actions taken thereafter or for various other reasons it would be unfair to allow the amendment; and the test as I have adumbrated it is whether the landlords are any worse off than they would have been if the statement of case had been properly drafted in the first instance.

That only leaves counsel for the landlords' point that all this is beating the air anyway, because the tenants cannot get their claim under s 47 off the ground, because of the addition of the special provisions of Sch 2 to the tenancy agreement.

That addition makes it quite clear that the Dutch barn and the grain and potato store are not to be taken into account when fixing the rent, because they are tenant's fixtures. They are not to pin on the landlords liability for repairing them because they are tenant's fixtures. It makes it quite clear that notwithstanding that this appears to be a new tenancy agreement, and notwithstanding that the Dutch barn and the grain and potato store have been there from the beginning, they were nevertheless in the tenants' part of the world instead of the landlords' part of the world. That means to my mind that there was recorded not only the facts as regards these two building but also maintenance of any claim which the tenants might have in respect of them either under s 13 or under s 47 or under any other section of the 1948 Act. The insertion of that special provision had advantages from the landlords' point of view and the tenants' point of view. It may be that it was unnecessary, because s 53 of the 1948 Act provides that the rights of a tenant with regard to improvements and compensation can be preserved from one tenancy through a succession of tenancies, but no doubt it was put in ex abundanti cautela. That this particular provision has to be wrenched by construction into an abandonment by the tenants of any rights they may have under s 47 seems to me quite unarguable; and, as Cumming-Bruce LJ has pointed out, it is not only unarguable, it is also probably illegal.

For those reasons I agree with Cumming-Bruce LJ.

DAME ELIZABETH LANE. I also agree, and would make only these comments. In the second paragraph of s 70(2) of the Agricultural Holdings Act 1948 there is a description, if not a definition, of what amounts to a sufficient specification, for the purposes of a notice of claim. But when it comes to para 6 of Sch 6 to the 1948 Act and the mandatory requirement of a statement of case with all necessary particulars, no guidance whatsoever is given as to what particulars are necessary, and there are no statutory prescribed forms such as are to be found, for example, in the Rent Acts, rules and regulations or in the Matrimonial Causes Rules.

So, a layman, seeking as he may under this Act to draft a statement of case, who is unlikely to have studied such authorities as those to which we have been referred or a report of this case or any helpful textbook, is left to guess what particulars are necessary.

Unless and until such forms are prescribed, in my view, whoever has drafted the statement of case, an arbitrator, exercising his discretion under this Act, should expect to be, and be, liberal in the exercise of the discretion to consent to amendments so long as such amendments will not cause injustice to the opposite party, as was the case here; and if there are any consequential costs, those can be ordered in the opposite party's favour.

I agree that this appeal should be allowed, and the order suggested made.

Appeal allowed. Leave to appeal to House of Lords refused.

Solicitors: *Andrews, Stanton & Ringrose*, Bourne (for the tenants); *Turner Peacock* (for the landlords).

Henrietta Steinberg   Barrister.

R v Murray

COURT OF APPEAL, CRIMINAL DIVISION
LORD LANE CJ, STEPHEN BROWN AND TAYLOR JJ
22 FEBRUARY 1982

Criminal law – Obstructing course of justice – Attempting to pervert course of justice – Attempt – Ingredients of offence – Accused tampering with blood sample provided by him under road traffic legislation – Accused subsequently submitting sample for analysis – Evidence of intention to pervert course of justice – Whether accused's conduct having tendency to pervert course of justice.

The appellant was stopped by the police while driving his car and asked to give a breath test. He refused and was taken to a police station where he agreed to give a specimen of blood. It was dealt with in the usual way under the Road Traffic Act 1972, ie one half of the specimen was retained by the police for analysis and the other half was handed to the appellant in a sealed container, so that he could, if he wished, have it analysed by an analyst of his own choice. The specimen kept by the police, when analysed, contained 157 mg of alcohol in 100 ml of blood. The appellant's analyst found only 47 mg of alcohol in 100 ml of blood in the specimen which the appellant gave him. He reported the fact to the appellant's solicitor, who in turn reported it to the relevant authority. Investigation ensued, as a result of which the appellant was charged with, and subsequently convicted of, attempting to pervert the course of justice by altering a specimen of blood and subsequently delivering it to an analyst, knowing that the resulting analysis was likely to be used in his defence in proceedings against him under the 1972 Act. He appealed against conviction, contending that since the acts complained of did not go beyond private action they could not amount to an 'attempt to pervert the course of justice'.

Held – (1) In order to prove the offence of attempting to pervert the course of justice it had to be shown not only that the accused intended to pervert the course of justice but also that what he had done, without more, had a tendency to produce that result; and, to establish that, it was not necessary to show that the tendency had in fact materialised: it was sufficient if there was evidence that the accused had done enough for there to be a risk, without further action by him, that injustice would result (see p 228 *g* to *j*, post); *R v Machin* [1980] 3 All ER 151 applied; *R v Vreones* [1891] 1 QB 360 and *R v Rowell* [1978] 1 All ER 665 considered.

(2) In the circumstances, the evidence showed not only that the appellant had intended to pervert the course of justice but also that what he done had, without more, had a tendency to produce that result, because once his analyst had analysed the specimen of blood and found that it contained a minimal quantity of alcohol it was a practical certainty that that information would be communicated either to the solicitor or to the prosecuting authority or to the police. It followed that the appellant had been rightly convicted and the appeal would accordingly be dismissed (see p 228 *j* to p 229 *b* and *g h*, post).

Notes

For perversion of the course of justice, see 11 Halsbury's Laws (4th edn) paras 955, 957, and for cases on the subject, see 15 Digest (Reissue) 975–977, 8423–8446.

For the Road Traffic Act 1972, see 42 Halsbury's Statutes (3rd edn) 1633.

Cases referred to in judgment

R v Bailey [1956] NI 15, CCA, 15 Digest (Reissue) 1090, *6994.
R v Britton [1973] RTR 502, CA, Digest (Cont Vol D) 878, 322fd.
R v Machin [1980] 3 All ER 151, [1980] 1 WLR 763, 71 Cr App R 166, CA.

R v Manley [1933] 1 KB 529, [1932] All ER Rep 565, CCA, 15 Digest (Reissue) 1088, 9194.

R v Rowell [1978] 1 All ER 665, [1978] 1 WLR 132, CA, Digest (Cont Vol E) 152, 8401a.

R v Thomas, R v Ferguson [1979] 1 All ER 577, [1979] QB 326, CA, [1979] 2 WLR 144, CA, Digest (Cont Vol E) 152, 8574a.

R v Vreones [1891] 1 QB 360, CCR, 15 Digest (Reissue) 974, 8412.

Cases also cited

R v Andrews [1973] 1 All ER 857, [1973] QB 422, CA.

R v Grimes [1968] 3 All ER 179.

R v Selvage [1982] 1 All ER 96, [1981] 3 WLR 811, CA.

R v Sharpe [1938] 1 All ER 48, CCA.

Appeal

On 20 July 1981 in the Crown Court at Leeds before his Honour Judge Beaumont and a jury, the appellant, Gordon Ellison Murray, was convicted of attempting to pervert the course of public justice by altering a blood sample supplied under the Road Traffic Act 1972 and by delivering the altered sample to the public analyst knowing that the resulting analysis was likely to be used in his defence in proceedings against him under s 6(1) of the 1972 Act, and sentenced to nine months' imprisonment. He appealed against conviction on a point of law certified by the trial judge and against sentence. The facts are set out in the judgment of the court.

H H Ognall QC and *R S Smith* for the appellant.

F J Müller QC and *Margaret Bickford-Smith* for the Crown.

LORD LANE CJ delivered the following judgment of the court: On 20 July 1981, in the Crown Court at Leeds before his Honour Judge Beaumont and a jury the appellant was convicted on a majority verdict of the jury of attempting to pervert the course of public justice and was sentenced to nine months' imprisonment. He now appeals against that conviction on a point of law, and despite the fact that it was a point of law, it was certified by the learned judge. The question posed is as follows:

> 'Whether the act of tampering with a blood sample provided to the Defendant under the relevant provisions of the Road Traffic Act 1972 and its subsequent submission for analysis to an analyst of the Defendant's choice, without more, albeit that both acts are accompanied by an intent to pervert the course of public justice, is capable as a matter of law of having a tendency to pervert the course of public justice.'

The facts of the case are these. The appellant was stopped by the police whilst driving his motor car. It was New Year's Eve, 31 December 1979. The appellant was asked to give a breath test and refused. He was taken to the police station and there he agreed to give a sample of blood. All the necessary procedure were carried out by the police. The specimen of blood was divided into two, half of which was retained by the police for analysis by their scientist, and the other half in the sealed container was handed to the appellant for him, if he wished, to have it analysed by his own analyst. He did so have it analysed by one of the gentlemen who was on the list of analysts which was handed to him by the police, who happened to be a man (Mr Davies) employed by the public analyst in Leeds. That half of the sample was found to contain only 47 mg of alcohol in 100 ml of blood, as against the prosecution sample which contained no less than 157 mg of alcohol in 100 ml of blood.

The prosecution case, which was plainly accepted by the jury as the verdict indicates, was that the vial into which the appellant's sample of blood was put had been duly labelled and initialled, either by the doctor or by the policeman. The vial in its turn had been put into a 'jiffy' envelope, sealed with sellotape and stamped across the margin of the sellotape with a constabulary stamp in order to prevent, if possible, the envelope being opened and tampered with. When closely examined, it was apparent that both the envelope and the sellotape and the seal on the septum of the vial and the septum itself (that is the rubber cap of the vial) had all been tampered with; the suggestion being, from those facts and from other facts about the amount of chemical preservative which was in the sample, that some of the initial sample had been withdrawn by way of a hypodermic syringe through the septum of the vial and in its place had been put in to the vial blood which was not contaminated by alcohol. Hence the vast disparity between the two samples. The prosecution submitted that on those facts it was open to the jury to come to the conclusion that this man was guilty of the offence as alleged.

There is no doubt that, although there was no evidence before the jury on this point, in due course information as to the low alcohol content of the appellant's sample had reached the prosecuting authority. We are told very properly by counsel for the appellant, although I repeat it was not part of the evidence in the case, that what happened was that Mr Davies the analyst, when he discovered this remarkably low percentage of alcohol, took steps to get in touch with the appellant's solicitor. The appellant's solicitor not surprisingly, as counsel for the appellant put it, in his turn got in touch with the prosecuting authority and investigations then started.

At the conclusion of the prosecution case, a submission was made to the learned judge that there was no evidence fit to go to the jury to substantiate this count. That is a submission which is repeated by counsel for the appellant in his attractive argument before this court today. The way he puts it is this. First of all, he submits that before conduct can be described as 'an attempt to pervert the course of public justice' it must go beyond mere private action. By that, he means that there must be proof of some steps taken by the appellant of the following possible different natures: firstly, by way of interference with possible witnesses; secondly, by tampering with documents or other exhibits or potential exhibits; thirdly, by the manufacture of false exhibits which are likely to become or may possibly become exhibits at the instance of the Crown (and he gives the example of the forging of a driving licence); or fourthly, by the deliberate provision or indication of misleading information known to be misleading, either at his subsequent trial or to a representative of the prosecution in advance of any trial, so as to make it possible that a decision will be made by the court or a discretion exercised by the prosecution on a false premise. He submits, and correctly so far as it has been possible to discover, that there is no reported instance of a conviction being recorded of this offence without the defendant in some way involving himself with the potential or possible prosecution of himself or another by conduct which may directly affect the prosecuting authority in its discretion of its witnesses, of its exhibits, or by interference with or subornation of possible defence witnesses, or the manufacture of false evidence and its introduction into the system of justice.

In order to make his point, counsel for the appellant has referred us to a number of cases, some of which it is necessary for us to refer to, and some of which are perhaps unnecessary to deal with except by way of mention out of deference to his arguments. The first and locus classicus of the offence is *R v Vreones* [1891] 1 QB 360, where the defendant tampered with a sample of wheat preparatory to a possible arbitration on the quality of the wheat which was the subject of a contract. Counsel for the appellant points out that there was nothing there which the defendant needed to do beyond what he did to introduce the bogus evidence into the system of justice, as he described it.

R v Rowell [1978] 1 All ER 665, [1978] 1 WLR 132 is a case which deserves perhaps closer attention. This involved a communication by the defendant to someone in authority of the bogus story, because he reported the matter to the police. That case in its turn (see [1978] 1 All ER 665 at 669–670, [1978] 1 WLR 132 at 136–137), deals with *R v Manley* [1933] 1 KB 529, [1932] All ER Rep 565, and *R v Bailey* [1956] NI 15, in each of which there were communications to the police. In *R v Manley* it was held that the making of false statements to the police might in appropriate circumstances be indictable as public mischief. In *R v Bailey*, the defendant made a false confession to the police

implicating two other men and himself in a murder. From *R v Rowell* itself there
emerges the sort of test which has to be applied to the facts in order to determine
whether this offence is made out. Ormrod LJ, delivering the judgment of the court, said
this ([1978] 1 All ER 665 at 671, [1978] 1 WLR 132 at 138):

> 'Consequently, all the appellant's acts, his two false statements to the police
> accusing the man, described but not identified by name, of robbery, the placing of
> the toy pistol in the bus, and the arranging that it should be found by Cronin, are
> all part of a course of conduct, between the dates alleged, which had a tendency and,
> as the jury must have found, was intended to pervert the course of justice.'

Finally, on this aspect of the case, the decision of *R v Machin* [1980] 3 All ER 151, 71
Cr App R 166 (and also in [1980] 1 WLR 763, a report which has the advantage of setting
out the terms of the indictment laid against Machin at the trial), the headnote to which
reads (71 Cr App R 166):

> 'The appellant made a written statement at a police station admitting certain
> motoring offences. He then went outside the station and, at his request, a friend
> punched him in the eye causing it to swell. The friend then agreed to give evidence
> that the police in the station had caused the injury. The appellant told other persons
> that the police had hit him and his wife lodged a formal complaint to that effect at
> another police station. The appellant then had a professional photograph taken of
> his eye injury but did not collect it. He was charged with attempting to pervert the
> course of public justice.'

Counsel for the appellant points out that here once again was a direct communication
to the police through the man's wife. But the passage which this court desires to read and
draw attention to is where Eveleigh LJ, delivering the judgment of this court, said
([1980] 3 All ER 151 at 153–154, [1980] 1 WLR 763 at 767):

> 'The particular acts or conduct in question may take many different forms
> including conduct that amounts in itself to some other criminal offence or attempt
> thereat in the strict sense of a inchoate offence. The gist of the offence is conduct
> which may lead and is intended to lead to a miscarriage of justice whether or not a
> miscarriage actually occurs. We therefore respectfully agree that the use of the
> word "attempt" in the present context is misleading as was said in *R v Rowell*. The
> word is convenient for use in the case where it cannot be proved that the course of
> justice was actually perverted but it does no more than describe a substantive
> offence which consists of conduct which has the tendency and is intended to pervert
> the course of justice. To do an act with the intention of perverting the course of
> justice is not of itself enough. The act must also have that tendency.'

So what the learned judge in the present case had to decide was whether there was
evidence which was fit to go before the jury, that first of all this man had the intention
to pervert the course of justice (which plainly he did), but, much more importantly,
whether there was evidence that what he did had a tendency to have that effect. In the
view of this court, there must be evidence that the man has done enough for there to be
a risk, without further action by him, that injustice will result. In other words, there
must be a possibility that what he has done 'without more' might lead to injustice. It
seems to us that he does not himself have to introduce the evidence into the process of
justice, as counsel for the appellant invites us to rule. It is sufficient that what he has
done 'without more' has a tendency to produce that result.

To establish a tendency or a possibility, you do not have to prove that the tendency or
possibility in fact materialised. If it did, and if there is evidence of that, then of course
that is powerful argument to show that there was a tendency; but it is not necessary. In
our view, in the present case there plainly was evidence of such a tendency or possibility,
because once the analyst (whether he was a private analyst or a public analyst) analysed
this sample of blood and found that it contained a minimal quantity of alcohol, (as in the

particular circumstances of this case) it was a practical certainty, let alone a possibility, that that information would be communicated either to the solicitor or to the prosecuting authority, or to the police as indeed happened.

Consequently, on that aspect of the matter alone, it seems to us that the learned judge was right in the conclusion which he reached.

Our attention has also been drawn to *R v Britton* [1973] RTR 502. The facts of that particular case are perhaps not of sufficient merit for us to have to read them, but there is a passage we wish to read. The judgment of the court, as delivered by Lord Widgery CJ, states (at 506–507):

> '[Counsel for the Crown], supporting the conviction, invites us to say that the offence is proved if there is some course upon which justice has embarked and the accused deliberately tampers with that course or interferes with it. I have not perhaps exactly recorded [counsel's] words, and he will forgive me if I do not do entire justice to the way he put it, but that was the substance of it. The emphasis of his argument, of course, is that there must be some course upon which justice has embarked before there can be any proper case of interference with that course. He submits that in the present case the course of justice is mapped out by the Road Safety Act 1967, the precise steps to be taken are there laid down, and once a police officer has reached the stage of setting that course of action in motion by requiring the provision of a specimen of breath for a breath test from a motorist, then, says [counsel], anything which the accused does thereafter which interferes with and upsets the due working out of the statutory course of action is within the scope of the offence which was charged here.'

That decision was cited with approval in *R v Thomas, R v Ferguson* [1979] 1 All ER 577 at 581, [1979] QB 326 at 331, and the passage, which we need not read, is to be found in the judgment of Bridge LJ, giving the judgment of the court.

It seems to us, although we do not base our decision on this particular argument, that there was interference (to use the word approved of in both those decisions) with the process of justice in the present case by the simple tampering with the sample, because having adulterated this sample, as the jury found that he did, the appellant was placed in this dilemma. If he chose to use the sample, then quite plainly the offence is committed. If he realised that by using the sample he was likely to get himself into deeper trouble and therefore had disqualified himself from using it, there again he had interfered with the process of law, because one of the processes in this particular type of offence is that the defendant should have the opportunity of having his own sample analysed and put before the court by way of an analysis and by way of defence.

As I say, we do not base our decision on that line of argument. Nevertheless, it seems to us that, on the strength of *R v Britton* [1973] RTR 502, the prosecution here had a second leg to their argument on which they could have relied had they wished. We base our decision on the earlier grounds which I have mentioned, and for those reasons this appeal will be dismissed so far as conviction is concerned.

[The court then went on to consider the appeal against sentence. It reduced the sentence from nine months' imprisonment to three months' imprisonment.]

Appeal against conviction dismissed. Appeal against sentence allowed in part.

Solicitors: *Ronald Teeman & Co*, Leeds (for the appellant); *M D Shaffner*, Wakefield (for the Crown).

April Weiss   Barrister.

Inland Revenue Commissioners v Scottish and Newcastle Breweries Ltd

HOUSE OF LORDS

LORD WILBERFORCE, LORD SALMON, LORD FRASER OF TULLYBELTON, LORD LOWRY AND LORD BRIDGE OF HARWICH

19, 20 OCTOBER 1981, 4 MARCH 1982

Income tax – Capital allowances – Plant – Apparatus used by taxpayer for purposes of business – Hotels – Whether electric light fittings, decor and murals for hotels and licensed premises plant – Finance Act 1971, s 41(1).

The taxpayers owned and managed a large number of hotels and licensed premises in Scotland and England. In 1972–73 they decided that to maintain or increase their turnover they ought to brighten and modernise the facilities offered to the public. They accordingly incurred expenditure on the provision of new electric light fittings, decor and murals, such as plaques, tapestries and pictures, for their premises in order to produce an 'atmosphere' which would be attractive to their customers. The taxpayers contended that the expenditure had been incurred on the provision of 'plant' for the purposes of their trade, and accordingly claimed a first-year allowance in respect of it under s 41[a] of the Finance Act 1971. The inspector of taxes disallowed the claim, but on appeal the Special Commissioners reversed the inspector's decision and upheld the taxpayers' claim. The Special Commissioners' decision was affirmed by the Court of Session. The Crown appealed to the House of Lords.

Held – The meaning to be given to the word 'plant' in s 41 of the 1971 Act was a question of law, for the courts to interpret having regard to the context in which it occurred, but there was no fixed definition of plant nor were there any detailed or exhaustive rules for application to any particular set of circumstances; a decision by commissioners that something was plant was a decision on a question of fact or degree which could not be upset as being erroneous in point of law unless the commissioners showed by some reason given or statement made that they had misunderstood or misapplied the law in some relevant particular. Where it was claimed that part of a taxpayer's premises was plant, the test to be applied was that something which became part of the premises, instead of merely embellishing them, was not plant except in the rare case where the premises were themselves plant. In relation to a hotel, the creation of the right atmosphere or setting to make the interior attractive to customers was a means to an end in the carrying on of such a trade, and was not a trade in itself or a separate part of the trade. Accordingly, the amenities and decoration were not the setting in which the taxpayers carried on their business, but the setting which they offered to their customers for them to resort to and enjoy. It followed that the expenditure incurred by the taxpayers on the electric light fittings, decor and murals qualified for relief as expenditure on the provision of 'plant' within s 41(1) of the 1971 Act. The appeal would be dismissed (see p 233 *e* to p 234 *a* and *h j*, p 237 *f* to *j*, p 238 *g* to *j*, p 239 *j* and p 240 *f g*, post).

Dicta of Lindley LJ in *Yarmouth v France* (1887) 19 QBD at 658 and of Lowry LCJ in *Schofield (Inspector of Taxes) v R & H Hall Ltd* [1975] STC at 360 applied.

J Lyons & Co Ltd v A-G [1944] 1 All ER 477, *Benson (Inspector of Taxes) v Yard Arm Club Ltd* [1979] 2 All ER 336 and *Hampton (Inspector of Taxes) v Fortes Autogrill Ltd* [1980] STC 80 distinguished.

---

a   Section 41, so far as material, is set out at p 234 *d*, post

Notes

For first-year allowances, see 23 Halsbury's Laws (4th edn) para 426.

For the meaning of plant, see ibid para 416, and for cases on the subject, see 28(1) Digest (Reissue) 214–216, 637–643.

For the Finance Act 1971, s 41, see 41 Halsbury's Statutes (3rd edn) 1459.

Cases referred to in opinions

Benson (Inspector of Taxes) v Yard Arm Club Ltd [1979] 2 All ER 336, [1979] 1 WLR 347, CA, Digest (Cont Vol E) 309, 1676e.

Brown (Inspector of Taxes) v Burnley Football and Athletic Co Ltd [1980] 3 All ER 244.

Cole Bros Ltd v Phillips (Inspector of Taxes) [1980] STC 518; varied [1981] STC 671, CA.

Cooke (Inspector of Taxes) v Beach Station Caravans Ltd [1974] 3 All ER 159, [1974] 1 WLR 1398, Digest (Cont Vol D) 456, 640a.

Dixon (Inspector of Taxes) v Fitch's Garage Ltd [1975] 3 All ER 455, [1976] 1 WLR 215, Digest (Cont Vol D) 493, 1676c.

Edwards (Inspector of Taxes) v Bairstow [1955] 3 All ER 48, [1956] AC 14, 28(1) Digest (Reissue) 566, 2089.

Hampton (Inspector of Taxes) v Fortes Autogrill Ltd [1980] STC 80.

IRC v Barclay Curle & Co Ltd [1969] 1 All ER 732, [1969] 1 WLR 675, HL, 28(1) Digest (Reissue) 465, 1676.

Jarrold (Inspector of Taxes) v John Good & Sons Ltd [1963] 1 All ER 141, [1963] 1 WLR 214, 28(1) Digest (Reissue) 215, 642.

Lyons (J) & Co Ltd v A-G [1944] 1 All ER 477, [1944] Ch 281, 17 Digest (Reissue) 542, 324.

Schofield (Inspector of Taxes) v R & H Hall Ltd [1975] STC 353, CA, Digest (Cont Vol D) 493, 1676d.

Yarmouth v France (1887) 19 QBD 647, DC, 20 Digest (Reissue) 515, 4005.

Appeal

The Crown appealed from an interlocutor of the First Division of the Court of Session as the Court of Exchequer in Scotland (the Lord President (Emslie), Lord Cameron and Lord Stott), dated 20 November 1980 ([1981] STC 50), refusing an appeal by the Crown by way of case stated (set out at [1981] STC 51–56) against a determination of the Commissioners for the Special Purposes of the Income Tax Acts, dated 28 November 1978, upholding a claim by Scottish and Newcastle Breweries Ltd (the taxpayer company) that expenditure incurred by them on the provision of decor, murals and electric light fittings for the purpose of producing an 'atmosphere' attractive to customers in their hotels and licensed premises was expenditure incurred on the provision of 'plant' within s 41 of the Finance Act 1971. The facts are set out in the opinion of Lord Lowry.

W D Prosser QC (Vice-Dean of Faculty), Robert Carnwath and A C Hamilton (of the Scottish Bar) for the Crown.

Lord McCluskey QC and J E Drummond Young (both of the Scottish Bar) for the taxpayer company.

Their Lordships took time for consideration.

4 March. The following opinions were delivered.

LORD WILBERFORCE. My Lords, the taxpayer company own and manage a large number of hotels and licensed premises in Scotland and England. In 1972–73 they decided that if they were to increase or even maintain their turnover they ought to brighten and modernise the facilities offered to the public. They therefore spent money on electrical rewiring and installation of new electric light fittings and of various categories of decor and murals, such as plaques, tapestries and pictures. In one hotel they set up two elaborate metal sculptures said to represent seagulls in flight. The question of law for us is whether all or part of this expenditure attracts a first-year capital allowance which would entitle them to deduct from their trading income the whole of the expenditure in the first year.

The Finance Act 1971 states as the condition for obtaining the allowance that the claimant must be carrying on a trade (as the taxpayer company undoubtedly were) and incur capital expenditure on the provision of machinery or plant for the purposes of the trade (see s 41). The question for decision, which both courts below have answered in the taxpayer company's favour, is whether the expenditure, undoubtedly capital expenditure, was on the provision of 'plant'.

Of the claimed items of expenditure the Special Commissioners disallowed that on electrical wiring and against that decision there is no appeal. The remaining items totalled some £105,000, of which about £44,000 was on decor and murals and the rest on electric light fittings. The case stated contains a detailed description and prices of the various items, but I do not think it is necessary to reproduce it, because both sides were agreed to treat them as falling within a broad category which can be described as decor and to have the question of law answered as regards the category as a whole. It is, however, necessary to draw attention to some of the findings of the commissioners as to the taxpayer company's business and the purpose for which the money was spent. These findings are as follows.

The taxpayer company's hotels and licensed premises are either purpose-built or acquired as a shell and completed according to their special requirements for lighting and decor. The taxpayer company consider on commercial principles what type of clientele they wish to attract and on that basis instruct architects and interior designers. They may make changes in interior design from time to time with a view to attracting a different class of customer. The type, design and layout of the lighting arrangements, particularly in the common living areas, are selected with the aims of producing the atmosphere appropriate to attract the type of customers sought. This is regarded by the taxpayer company as an important factor in the commercial success of their premises, a view supported by market research and which the commissioners said that they accepted. Examples were given, and accepted by the commissioners, of cases where this was proved by results. The same appears to be true of the decor and murals. Was, then, this expenditure incurred in the provision of plant?

The word 'plant' has frequently been used in fiscal and other legislation. It is one of a fairly large category of words as to which no statutory definition is provided ('trade', 'office', even 'income' are others), so that it is left to the court to interpret them. It naturally happens that as case follows case, and one extension leads to another, the meaning of the word gradually diverges from its natural or dictionary meaning. This is certainly true of 'plant'. No ordinary man, literate or semi-literate, would think that a horse, a swimming pool, movable partitions or even a dry dock was plant, yet each of these has been held to be so: so why not such equally improbable items as murals or tapestries or chandeliers? The courts have, over the years, provided themselves with some guidance in principle, starting with Lindley LJ in *Yarmouth v France* (1887) 19 QBD 647 at 658. Plant, he said—

'in its ordinary sense . . . includes whatever apparatus is used by a business man for carrying on his business—not his stock-in-trade which he buys or makes for sale; but all goods and chattels, fixed or moveable, live or dead, which he keeps for permanent employment in his business.'

Later cases have revealed that a permanent structure may be plant (see *IRC v Barclay Curle & Co Ltd* [1969] 1 All ER 732, [1969] 1 WLR 675) and argument has ranged over the question whether, to constitute plant, an item of property must fulfil an active role or whether a passive role will suffice, a distinction which led to some agreeable casuistry in relation to a swimming pool (see *Cooke (Inspector of Taxes) v Beach Station Caravans Ltd* [1974] 3 All ER 159, [1974] 1 WLR 1398). Perhaps the most useful discrimen, for

present purposes, where we are concerned with something done to premises, is to be
found in that of 'setting'; to provide a setting for the conduct of a trade or business is not
to provide plant: see *J Lyons & Co Ltd v A-G* [1944] 1 All ER 477, [1944] Ch 281,
concerning electric lamps, sockets and cords for lighting a tea shop. But this, too, is not
without difficulty. In the *Lyons* case itself Uthwatt J thought that different considerations
(so that they might qualify as apparatus) might apply to certain specific lamps because
they might 'be connected with the needs of the particular trade carried on upon the
premises' (see [1944] 1 All ER 477). In *Jarrold (Inspector of Taxes) v John Good & Sons Ltd*
[1963] 1 All ER 141, [1963] 1 WLR 214 some fixed but movable partitions though in a
sense 'setting' were thought capable of being also 'apparatus'. And in *Schofield (Inspector
of Taxes) v R & H Hall Ltd* [1975] STC 353, the same argument was applied to the external
walls of grain silos as well as to the connected machinery.

Another much used test word is 'functional'. This is useful as expanding the notion
of 'apparatus'; it was used by Lord Reid in *IRC v Barclay Curle & Co Ltd*. But this, too,
must be considered, in itself, as inconclusive. Functional for what? Does the item serve
a functional purpose in providing a setting? Or one for use in the trade?

It is easy, without excessive imagination, to devise perplexing cases. A false ceiling
designed to hide unsightly pipes is not plant, though the pipes themselves may be (see
Hampton (Inspector of Taxes) v Fortes Autogrill Ltd [1980] STC 80); is a tapestry hung on an
unsightly wall any different from a painted mural? And does it make a difference
whether there was a damp patch underneath? What limit can be placed on attractions,
interior or exterior, designed to make premises more pleasing, to the eye or other
sense? There is no universal formula which can solve these puzzles.

In the end each case must be resolved, in my opinion, by considering carefully the
nature of the particular trade being carried on, and the relation of the expenditure to the
promotion of the trade. I do not think that the courts should shrink, as a backstop, from
asking whether it can really be supposed that Parliament desired to encourage a particular
expenditure out of, in effect, taxpayers' money, and perhaps ultimately, in extreme cases,
to say that this is too much to stomach. It seems to me, on the commissioners' findings,
which are clear and emphatic, that the taxpayer company's trade includes, and is intended
to be furthered by, the provision of what may be called 'atmosphere' or 'ambience',
which (rightly or wrongly) they think may attract customers. Such intangibles may in
a very real and concrete sense be part of what the trader sets out, and spends money, to
achieve. A good example might be a private clinic or hospital, where quiet and seclusion
are provided, and charged for accordingly. One can well apply the 'setting' test to these
situations. The amenities and decoration in such a case as the present are not, by contrast
with the *Lyons* case, the setting in which the trader carries on his business, but the setting
which he offers to his customers for them to resort to and enjoy. That it is setting in the
latter and not the former sense for which the money was spent is proved beyond doubt
by the commissioners' findings.

I do not find it impossible to attribute to Parliament an intention to encourage by fiscal
inducement the improvement of hotel amenity. Like the commissioners one may feel
some doubt about individual items, for example the seagull sculptures at the Atlantic
Tower Hotel, Liverpool: decision cannot I think turn on whether they were movable or
fixed to the structure. But I would not differ from their hesitant conclusion that these
artifacts have to be grouped with the other more prosaic objects and can, no less but no
more artificially, be regarded as apparatus of the trade and so as plant.

The commissioners' examination of the facts was exceedingly careful and helpful, and
their decision was agreed in by all members of the Inner House. I am disposed to accept
the conclusion as correct and would dismiss the appeal.

LORD SALMON. My Lords, I entirely agree, for the reasons stated in the speeches of
my noble and learned friends Lord Wilberforce and Lord Lowry, that this appeal should
be dismissed.

LORD FRASER OF TULLYBELTON. My Lords, I have had the advantage of
reading in draft the speeches prepared by my noble and learned friends Lord Wilberforce
and Lord Lowry. I entirely agree with them and I do not consider that I can usefully add
anything to them. For the reasons stated in those speeches I would dismiss this appeal.

LORD LOWRY. My Lords, this is an appeal from an interlocutor of the Court of
Session refusing an appeal by way of case stated under s 56 of the Taxes Management Act
1970 taken by the Crown from a determination by the Commissioners for the Special
Purposes of the Income Tax Acts of an appeal by the taxpayer company against an
assessment to corporation tax for their accounting period from 1 May 1972 to 20 April
1973 in the sum of £11,040,000 (later adjusted without prejudice to £11,038,915).

The subject matter of the proceedings is a claim by the taxpayer company, whose trade
was to carry on hotels and public houses, that capital expenditure in the relevant
accounting period on electric light fittings, decor and 'murals' (a term I shall explain)
should be allowed as expenditure incurred on the provision of plant within the meaning
of s 41 of the Finance Act 1971 which, so far as relevant, provides:

'(1) Subject to the provisions of this Chapter, where—(a) a person carrying on a
trade incurs capital expenditure on the provision of machinery or plant for the
purposes of the trade, and (b) in consequence of his incurring the expenditure, the
machinery or plant belongs to him at some time during the chargeable period
related to the incurring of the expenditure, there shall be made to him for that
period an allowance (in this Chapter referred to as "a first-year allowance") which
shall be of an amount determined in accordance with section 42 below . . .'

The issue, as defined by the Crown, is 'whether expenditure incurred by a hotelier or
keeper of licensed premises on the provision of decor, murals and electric light fittings
for the purpose of producing an "atmosphere" attractive to customers is [such]
expenditure'.

The original appeal by the taxpayer company had extended to money spent on
installing electric wiring, but the commissioners decided this point against the taxpayer
company, who did not challenge that part of the determination and now accept it as
correct. The amount of capital expenditure finally in issue was £105,770, of which
£44,122 represented expenditure on various types of decor and murals, namely wall
decor, plaques, tapestries, murals, pictures and metal sculptures, and the balance consisted
of expenditure on electric light fittings. The question of law for the opinion of the court,
and now for consideration by your Lordships' House, is baldly stated in the case to be
'whether our decision except in so far as it relates to electrical wiring was correct'.

Appeals are of many different kinds, and it is important to understand and apply the
ground rules relevant to each type. For present purposes, my Lords, I might be permitted
to repeat in a slightly condensed form what I said on an earlier occasion in *Schofield*
(Inspector of Taxes) v R & H Hall Ltd [1975] STC 353 at 360, a case which was also
concerned with plant: (1) it is a question of law what meaning is to be given to the word
'plant', and it is for the courts to interpret its meaning, having regard to the context in
which it occurs; (2) the law does not supply a definition of plant or prescribe a detailed
or exhaustive set of rules for application to any particular set of circumstances, and there
are cases which, on the facts found, are capable of decision either way; (3) a decision in
such a case is a decision on a question of fact and degree and cannot be upset as being
erroneous in point of law unless the commissioners show by some reason they give or
statement they make in the case stated that they have misunderstood or misapplied the
law in some relevant particular; (4) the commissioners err in point of law when they
make a finding which there is no evidence to support; (5) the commissioners may also err
by reaching a conclusion which is inconsistent with the facts which they have found. I
would also refer to the classic statement of Lord Radcliffe in *Edwards (Inspector of Taxes)*
v Bairstow [1955] 3 All ER 48 at 58, [1956] AC 14 at 36.

An agreed statement of facts at para VIII (3) of the case stated included a detailed description of the decor (see [1981] STC 50 at 52–53). I mention three items:

> 'Wall Decor consists of general decorative items, such as: pictures, plaques, tapestries, plates, horse harnesses, stags heads, pewterware, brassware, copperware, swords, axes, bagpipes, pistols and deer skins. The afore mentioned items can be either screwed to the wall and easily removed or hung on the wall and movable ... Murals are fibre glass, leather or metal sculptured panels which are screwed to the wall. They are removable and often are removed for redecoration purposes or change of theme. All murals are specially designed to suit specific themes ... Two Metal Sculptures. One hangs from the ceiling to which it is bolted and is supported by steel rods. The other is a standing feature which is permanently fixed to the forecourt. The sculptures represent "Seagulls in Flight".'

The metal sculptures cost £5,450. They were the only items 'fixed but not easily removable'. The balance of the £44,122 spent on 'decor and murals' was accounted for by 'items fixed but easily removed' costing £35,820 and 'items not fixed but movable' costing £2,852.

Paragraph VIII (5) sets out additional facts which were found proved and which I now summarise briefly: the premises are purpose-built or leased as a shell; in either case the taxpayer company choose the fittings and decor likely to create an appropriate atmosphere to suit different types of clientele; changes of decor and lighting are made for commercial reasons and the success of the change can be demonstrated, as at the King James and Royal Scot hotels, the aim being to produce atmosphere to attract custom of the kind sought.

In working towards an answer to their problem, the commissioners started in time-honoured fashion by quoting the definition of plant given by Lindley LJ in Yarmouth v France (1887) 19 QBD 647 at 658. The fact that the learned Lord Justice was classifying vice in a horse as a defect in the condition of plant within the meaning of the Employers' Liability Act 1880 did not rob this judicial definition of its felicity and general usefulness or its authority, now of nearly a hundred years' standing. The commissioners then marched along a well-signposted road via J Lyons & Co Ltd v A-G [1944] 1 All ER 477, [1944] Ch 281, Jarrold (Inspector of Taxes) v John Good & Sons Ltd [1963] 1 All ER 141, [1963] 1 WLR 214, IRC v Barclay Curle & Co Ltd [1969] 1 All ER 732, [1969] 1 WLR 675 and Dixon (Inspector of Taxes) v Fitch's Garage Ltd [1975] 3 All ER 455 [1976] 1 WLR 215 to apply the principles extracted from those authorities to the facts of the case. The commissioners appreciated that the atmosphere point was the general touchstone, but they also considered all the items of alleged plant individually. In the result they found in the taxpayer company's favour on every item except the electrical wiring, about which they said ([1981] STC 50 at 55):

> 'We regard this as integral with the fabric of the building—as to which no question arises in the proceedings. We find that the electrical wiring is not plant and to this extent the Company's appeal fails.'

They considered that the other items were 'apparatus which (in the same way as the light fittings) serves a functional purpose in the Company's trade'. Therefore, they found them to be plant, and continued (at 55):

> 'We found more difficulty with the 2 metal sculptures of seagulls at the Atlantic Towers Hotel, Liverpool ... They are clearly part of the setting and we think it fair to describe them as structures but, as we interpret the authorities, neither of these factors taken alone disqualifies the sculptures from being plant. They are fixed but not easily removed and on balance (but not without doubt) we are of the view that they should not be regarded as part of the permanent structure of the hotel but they can be properly described as apparatus which in view of the nature of the Company's trade, functions as plant.'

My Lords, I have mentioned the detailed findings in order to set in clear perspective the reasoning of the commissioners and next I wish to look at the opinion of the learned *a* judges of the First Division, which are worthy of study for the clarity and cogency of their expression and in which the determination of the commissioners was upheld.

These judgments, when read in their entirety, strongly support the commissioners' determination but, because the point at issue before your Lordships is whether that determination was correct in point of law, I shall be content to cite a few passages, starting with the opinion of the Lord President ([1981] STC 50 at 58–59):   *b*

> 'In the present case it is not suggested that the articles held by the Special Commissioners to be plant fall to be regarded as part of the structure of the various premises. They are undoubtedly "apparatus" used by the company "for carrying on their business" and articles which they keep "for permanent employment" in their business. [The words in quotation marks constitute a reference back to *Yarmouth v France*.] ... one must bear in mind that "setting" and "plant" are not mutually *c* exclusive ... As I read the findings of the Special Commissioners they have recognised that the special feature of the trade in which the company is engaged is the marketing of the setting—including atmosphere—itself. All the articles of furniture in their premises—those conceded to be plant and the articles in dispute— play their intended part in creating the planned character and atmosphere of the *d* various settings, and all were selected carefully to play this part.'

Turning next to Lord Cameron's opinion, I have found the following observations particularly helpful (at 60–62):

> 'In my opinion the commissioners have not been shown to have misdirected themselves nor is the conclusion at which they arrived in any sense unreasonable. The problem which the commissioners were called on to solve was one concerned *e* with a "service industry": I think this factor is important, because the question of what is properly to be regarded as "plant" can only be answered in the context of the particular industry concerned and, possibly, in light also of the particular circumstances of the individual taxpayer's own trade ... I think that much difficulty is caused by seeking to place limitative interpretations on the simple word "plant": I do not think that the classic definition propounded in *Yarmouth v France* *f* suggests that it is a word which is other than of comprehensive meaning— "whatever apparatus is used by a businessman for carrying on his business"— whatever the business may be ... It is difficult to see that the provision of conditions of comfort or even luxury lies outside the legitimate operations of an hotel keeper or by consequence that he should not be entitled in his business to make use of articles designed to subserve that purpose ... To do this may, in one *g* sense of the word, no doubt be regarded as providing or enhancing the "setting" in which the services are themselves provided—but at the same time the "setting" (as opposed to the structure or place within which the businessman conducts his business) ... is something the use of which is itself one of the services which the hotel owner makes available to his customer ... I do not think that the fact that certain objects of furnishing or even of decorative quality alone can be characterised *h* as serving only an "amenity" purpose is in any way to be regarded as a prima facie ground for rejecting a claim to have expenditure on them held to be expenditure on "plant".'

Lord Stott, who concurred in the opinions of his brethren, said inter alia (at 63–64): *j*

> 'In the present case the fallacy in the Crown's contention, as it seems to me, comes from a failure to recognise the true character of a hotelier's trade ... The chair and table which provide for the bodily comfort of the guests, and the lighting and decor which provide for his visual or mental enjoyment, are alike material by the use of which the hotelier may provide the service which it is part of his function to

provide, and accordingly in my opinion may alike be held to fall within the definition of "plant" as the word has been construed in the relevant authorities.'

Counsel for the Crown contended in the course of a well-presented argument that the commissioners, and by necessary implication the judges of the First Division, had misunderstood and misapplied the relevant legal principles. As the foundation for this proposition he advanced the view (1) that the setting of a trade was synonymous with the premises or place *in* which the trade is carried on, in contrast to the apparatus, or plant, *with* which it is carried on, (2) that articles which were used merely to enhance or adorn the setting and thereby to create atmosphere could not in law be plant because they were not used, or meant to be used, in the activity carried on in the setting, and therefore (3) that the only articles which could qualify as plant were those used in the processes of the trade, such as chairs to sit on, plates to eat off and glasses to drink out of (which might in themselves be chosen partly for their aesthetic qualities).

Counsel further contended that the commissioners had misunderstood and misapplied the functional test by wrongly assuming that anything which *serves a functional purpose* in a trade must be plant used for carrying on that trade: this could not be so, because, for example, the premises here (and also the electrical wiring) performed a function, but this did not mean that they were plant. He also pressed your Lordships with the argument in terrorem that to accede to the taxpayer company's wide interpretation would open the gate into a large field with no definable limits.

Counsel for the taxpayer company had the easier task, but discharged it with no less skill. Generally, he supported the reasoning of the commissioners and the First Division, but he also relied on what Pearson LJ said in *Jarrold (Inspector of Taxes) v John Good & Sons Ltd* [1963] 1 All ER 141 at 149, [1963] 1 WLR 214 at 225 (which my noble and learned friend Lord Wilberforce described as the high-water mark for respondents in this type of case) to the effect that, where either of two views might have been taken, the one which the commissioners preferred must stand if there was evidence to support it and no error of principle. He also submitted that an artifact is prima facie more likely to be plant.

My Lords, the Crown's primary fallacy, in my opinion, was to identify 'setting' inevitably with 'premises' or 'place' by misapplying to this case the observations of the judges in *Jarrold* when facing the question whether the articles are part of the premises or setting in which the business is carried on or part of the plant with which it is carried on. This was in a case where the word 'setting' had no theatrical or artistic significance, as it would have in the phrase 'appropriate setting' meaning 'the right atmosphere'. And, even if one assumes that 'the setting' is the same thing as 'the premises', it is fallacious to say that articles used to adorn the setting thereby ceased to be apparatus used by the taxpayer company for carrying on their business.

It is, in my view, equally fallacious to deny that the creation of atmosphere is, for the purposes of his trade, an important function of the successful hotelier; in fact, this was admitted on behalf of the Crown before your Lordships. Now the creation of the right atmosphere is a means to an end in the carrying on of such a trade; it is not a trade in itself or a separate part of the trade. This objective can be achieved by a combination of things, a beautiful or unusual or historic building, attractive views, gardens, shrubberies and waterfalls, ornaments, the equipment used by the staff and the glasses, china, cutlery, table linen, and the tables and chairs used by the customers. Everything in this list, from the ornaments onwards, is apparatus used in the hotel business and the ornaments are used purely to create atmosphere. The mere fact that some of the ornaments are free-standing on the floor or on shelves or tables and that others are suspended from or affixed to walls or ceilings is quite beside the point. They are all part of the hotelier's plant as defined in *Yarmouth v France*. And, as my noble and learned friend Lord Salmon put it in the course of argument, one of the trade functions of a hotelier is to make the interior attractive to customers; why then should one deny that the items used for this purpose are plant?

Counsel for the Crown sought to persuade your Lordships that, because 'murals' affixed to the wall performed the same function (of enhancing the setting) as attractive wallpaper or mural paintings, they were not plant. By this fallacy he presented in reverse *a* the argument which he attributed to the commissioners: the walls and the electric wiring and the electric light fittings all perform an indispensable function, but only the fittings are plant. In the same way, the mural paintings and the wallpaper, when executed or applied, are part of the walls and not plant, whereas the 'murals', being apparatus, are plant. The fact that two different things perform the same function or role is not the point. One thing functions as part of the premises, the other as part of the *b* plant.

One speaks of the setting of a play. The producer creates this by the use of chattels or movables in the shape of theatrical properties or 'props', which affect the audience by conveying atmosphere across the footlights, as the 'props' (or plant) of the hotelier affect the customer. Your Lordships will also recall the apt illustration of counsel for the Crown of the furnishings and atmosphere to be found in a private nursing home or *c* clinic.

In support of the argument that the functional test had been misapplied, the Crown referred to a passage in the case stated ([1981] STC 50 at 55):

> 'In our view, and we so find, all the light fittings . . . are of such a design and are so laid out as to be properly regarded as apparatus *serving a functional purpose* in the Company's trade.'   *d*

But here one must stress not only the words I have emphasised but the word 'apparatus'. The Crown also tried to take advantage of the words attributed to counsel for the Crown by Lord Cameron in his opinion, when he said ([1981] STC 50 at 61):

> 'Counsel for the Crown in his elegantly propounded submissions urged the necessity of giving proper meaning to words which could be of "slippery" *e* interpretation: it was necessary to distinguish those objects which enhanced or embellished what he called "setting" from those which had a functional use for the purposes of the taxpayer's trade.'

In this passage 'functional' is used as the equivalent of something like 'directly practical'; chairs and china for use are being distinguished from ornaments, and Lord Cameron is *f* surely not falling into the error of saying that the electrical wiring (which is not plant) has no *functional* use. It is correct, as the Crown contends, that the setting, for example a beautiful house or garden, may attract custom and create atmosphere without being plant. That does not mean that a chattel or movables used (as part of the setting) to create atmosphere is *not* plant.

Having regard to the legal history of the word 'plant', there is no warrant for arbitrarily *g* confining its meaning as suggested by the Crown. One might as well say that the tools and jigs of a wartime factory were part of the plant but that the apparatus used to convey 'music while you work' to those employed was not.

My Lords, the length to which the Crown's argument must go illustrates its frailty. It is also an illusion to think that a more general interpretation of plant leads to unjustified exemptions. We do not lack examples of claims which are rejected by the *h* Special Commissioners or favourable decisions which are later reversed by the courts. Moreover, the test accepted in this case by the commissioners and affirmed by the Inner House draws a line which can be held without trouble: something which becomes part of the premises, instead of merely embellishing them, is not plant, except in the rare case where the premises are themselves plant, like the dry dock in *IRC v Barclay Curle & Co Ltd* or the grain silo in *Schofield (Inspector of Taxes) v R & H Hall Ltd*. And, in the last *j* resort, if after enduring nearly a century of *Yarmouth v France* Parliament decides that 'plant' must receive a statutory definition, something can no doubt be done to curb the 'excesses' of the Special Commissioners and the judiciary. My Lords, both sides recognised that most of the cases are illustrations rather than authorities, but I must mention some of those relied on by the Crown.

In *Brown (Inspector of Taxes) v Burnley Football and Athletic Co Ltd* [1980] 3 All ER 244 a new concrete stand was held not to be 'plant', since it was not part of the apparatus with which the club carried on its trade (although the seating affixed to the stand was agreed to be plant). Vinelott J adopted the conclusion of the Special Commissioners that 'the stand is not "plant" functioning, whether passively or actively, in the actual processes which constitute the trade'. But the Crown can get help from that case only by falsely assuming that the 'actual processes' which constitute the hotelier's trade are strictly confined to the serving of food and drink and providing accommodation in a limited sense.

In *Hampton (Inspector of Taxes) v Fortes Autogrill Ltd* [1980] STC 80 the taxpayers, who carried on the trade of public caterers, installed permanent false ceilings which both supported and concealed water pipes, ventilation trunking, electrical conduits and lighting apparatus. The General Commissioners allowed the claim that the ceilings were plant being 'part and parcel of the services which they supported and covered', but the court reversed this determination, holding that the ceilings were not necessary for the functioning of any apparatus used for the purposes of the company's trade and were not part of the means by which the trade was carried on. The Crown has relied on observations of Fox J who said (at 84):

> 'The covering provided by the false ceiling is not, it seems to me, part of the means by which the taxpayer company provides food and drink to its customers . . . It is merely a covering [for plant] in the form of a plaster ceiling. The fact that it covers the pipes and services does not, it seems to me, make it plant, any more than the fact that the pipes and services were placed behind a true ceiling or wall would make that ceiling or wall into plant . . . If a trader has an unsightly piece of plant and wishes to mask it by some covering, the fact that what is being masked is itself plant does not turn the masking (which itself performs no function in carrying on the operations of the trade) into plant. It is plant alone which attracts the allowances . . . No doubt it is, in a restaurant, desirable visually that pipes and services should be covered by a false ceiling if they are not inside the ordinary walls or ceilings. But that merely means that the place *in* which the trade is carried on is made more attractive: it does not establish that the false ceilings are means *by* which the trade is carried on.' (Fox J's emphasis.)

The Crown relied on the reference to 'the means by which the taxpayer company provides food and drink to its customers', but there was (quite apart from other considerations) no issue about the creation of atmosphere. They also pointed to the statements that the masking 'performs no function in carrying on the operations of the trade' and that 'the place *in* which the trade is carried on is made more attractive'.

My Lords, what the Crown's argument, based on *Forte*, disregards is what Fox J said (at 84–85):

> 'A permanent ceiling, true or false, is part of the premises in which the trade is carried on. The fact that plant is attached to it does not, in my view, make the ceiling plant. It is just a ceiling, and, as such, does not perform a function in carrying out the trade any more than the remainder of the premises do. Similarly, a wall of a building may provide support for plant but, it seems to me, is not thereby plant itself.'

In other words, the ceiling in *Forte* was part of the realty and therefore part of the premises *in* which the trade was carried on. The articles now in dispute were apparatus, some of which was suspended from or attached to the wall, and the apparatus was, as the commissioners found, plant used by the taxpayer company in their business.

Cooke (Inspector of Taxes) v Beach Station Caravans Ltd [1974] 3 All ER 159, [1974] 1 WLR 1398 was concerned with a swimming pool on a caravan site and, so far as it is relevant, causes much more difficulty for the Crown than for the taxpayer company.

In *Dixon (Inspector of Taxes) v Fitch's Garages Ltd* [1975] 3 All ER 455, [1976] 1 WLR

215 a canopy at a self-service petrol station was held not to be plant but merely part of the 'setting'. This case seems to me to have been capable of decision either way but involves no principle destructive of the commissioners' findings in the present case, because the word 'setting' was used synonymously with 'the place in which'.

Passing over *Cole Bros Ltd v Phillips (Inspector of Taxes)* [1980] STC 518; [1981] STC 671, CA, which illustrates no new principle, I come to *Benson (Inspector of Taxes) v Yard Arm Club Ltd* [1979] 2 All ER 336, [1979] 1 WLR 347, in which a ship, or floating hulk, used as a restaurant was held not to be plant. The Crown relied on the case because of the fact that the ship was used to create a 'shipboard feeling', in other words, a certain kind of atmosphere, among the patrons. But the distinction is that the ship, although a chattel, was the *place in which* the trade was carried on and was therefore the equivalent of the various premises in which the present taxpayer company carry on their trade and not of the apparatus used as an adjunct of the trade carried on in those premises. Thus the ship, with all its novelty and atmosphere, could no more be called plant than a restaurant consisting of an Elizabethan manor house, a thatched cottage, a barn or a converted windmill, although like all those buildings it could be embellished and adorned with 'plant' suitable to the surroundings and to the purposes of the trade. This is another way of saying that the site is not an adjunct to the carrying on of a business, although the setting can be; the good ship Hispaniola cannot bring the Crown safe to port.

The dry dock in *IRC v Barclay Curle & Co Ltd* [1969] 1 All ER 732, [1969] 1 WLR 675 was a structure as well as plant. Therefore the case does not directly help the taxpayer company because their premises are not plant. But the Crown also relies in vain on *Barclay Curle*. It appeared to say that the dry dock, although it was the setting, was also plant, whereas the hotel premises are the setting but are not plant; therefore articles used to adorn the hotel setting are *not* plant either, although they are 'goods and chattels, fixed or moveable ... which [the taxpayer company] keeps for permanent employment in [their] business' (see *Yarmouth v France* (1887) 19 QBD 647 at 658 per Lindley LJ). *Barclay Curle*, however, shows that a structure in which a trade is carried on *can* be plant *with* which it is carried on; it would therefore be strange indeed if articles used in a building 'for the purposes of the trade' could not also be plant within the meaning of s 41.

My Lords, for the reasons set out in this opinion, I would dismiss the appeal.

LORD BRIDGE OF HARWICH. My Lords, I have had the advantage of reading in advance the speeches of my noble and learned friends Lord Wilberforce and Lord Lowry. For the reasons they give I would also dismiss the appeal.

Appeal dismissed.

Solicitors: *Solicitor of Inland Revenue*; *Martin & Co*, agents for *Shepherd & Wedderburn WS* (for the taxpayer company).

Mary Rose Plummer   Barrister.

ITC Film Distributors v Video Exchange Ltd and others

CHANCERY DIVISION
WARNER J
7, 8, 9, 12 OCTOBER 1981

Document – Admissibility in evidence – Illegally or improperly obtained evidence – Copy of original document – Secondary evidence of contents of document – Document privileged from production – Party to litigation improperly obtaining documents brought into court by other party and copying them – Copies exhibited to affidavit by party improperly obtaining documents – Whether copies exhibited to affidavit admissible as relevant secondary evidence of original documents – Whether copies should be excluded in the interests of administration of justice to prevent documents brought into court being stolen or filched.

In a copyright action between the plaintiffs and a defendant, certain motions and cross-motions by the respective parties were being heard by the judge in open court on 31 July 1981. After the judge had risen, the defendant obtained by a trick documents belonging to the plaintiffs' solicitors and brought into court by them. When the defendant refused to return the documents the plaintiffs issued a notice of motion on 23 September seeking (i) an injunction restraining the defendant from making copies of the documents, (ii) delivery up forthwith of the documents and any copies of them in the defendant's possession, power, custody or control, and (iii) an injunction restraining the defendant from making use of the documents or copies of them. On 1 October the defendant swore an affidavit in the action to which he exhibited copies of some of the documents and during the hearing of the defendant's cross-motions the judge looked at some of the exhibits to the affidavit and some were also used in cross-examination of a witness. Although the defendant consented to the rest of the relief sought by the plaintiffs in their motion of 23 September, he refused to consent to being deprived of the use, for the purposes of the action, of the copy documents exhibited to his affidavit of 1 October. Accordingly, on 8 October, on the hearing of the plaintiffs' motion of 23 September, the judge ordered that the plaintiffs be granted the relief they sought provided that the defendant was to be entitled, pending further order, to use the copy documents exhibited to his affidavit for the purposes of the action. By further motion the plaintiffs sought to have the proviso deleted from the order of 8 October. The defendant opposed the motion, contending that the proviso should remain, under the general rule of evidence in civil proceedings that relevant evidence was not to be excluded even though it was obtained improperly or illegally and that if a document was privileged a copy of it might be given in evidence as secondary evidence even though the copy had been improperly obtained.

Held – The public interest in the ascertainment of the truth in litigation, which was the reason for the rule allowing secondary evidence of privileged documents to be adduced even though improperly obtained, was outweighed by the public interest in the proper administration of justice in regard to a litigant being able to bring his documents into court without fear that his opponent would filch them by stealth or a trick. Furthermore, for a party to litigation by stealth or a trick to take possession of documents in court belonging to the other side was probably a contempt of court which the court should not countenance by admitting the documents in evidence in the litigation. Accordingly, the defendant would not be permitted to use in evidence in the action the copy documents exhibited to his affidavit of 1 October, except for those which the judge had already looked at and which had already been used in evidence and could therefore not be excluded (see p 246 *b c* and *h j* and p 247 *b* to *d*, post).

Dictum of Waller LJ in *Riddick v Thames Board Mills Ltd* [1977] 3 All ER at 702 applied. *Calcraft v Guest* [1895–9] All ER Rep 346 considered.

Notes

For admissiblity of relevant evidence improperly obtained, see 17 Halsbury's Laws (4th edn) para 12.

For secondary evidence of documents generally, see ibid para 142.

Cases referred to in judgment

Ashburton (Lord) v Pape [1913] 2 Ch 469, [1911–13] All ER Rep 708, CA, 22 Digest (Reissue) 236, 2033.

Calcraft v Guest [1898] 1 QB 759, [1895–9] All ER Rep 346, CA, 22 Digest (Reissue) 236, 2032.

D v National Society for the Prevention of Cruelty to Children [1977] 1 All ER 589, [1978] AC 171, [1977] 2 WLR 201, HL; *rvsg* [1976] 2 All ER 993, [1978] AC 171, [1976] 3 WLR 124, CA, Digest (Cont Vol E) 185, 1301b.

Helliwell v Piggott-Sims [1980] FSR 356, CA.

R v Tompkins (1977) 67 Cr App R 181, CA.

Riddick v Thames Board Mills Ltd [1977] 3 All ER 677, [1977] QB 881, [1977] 3 WLR 63, CA, Digest (Cont Vol E) 180, 495b.

Motion

When motions in a copyright action brought by the plaintiffs, ITC Film Distributors Ltd, United Artists Corp and Warner Bros Inc, against, inter alios, Anthony Richard Malcolm Chappell, the second defendant, were being heard in court Mr Chappell, on 31 July 1981, improperly took certain documents from a box brought into court by the plaintiffs' solicitors and refused to return them. By a notice of motion dated 23 September 1981 the plaintiffs sought an order (1) that Mr Chappell be restrained from making copies or authorising or procuring others to make copies of any documents belonging to the plaintiffs which he had removed, (2) that he forthwith deliver up to the plaintiffs' solicitors all the documents he removed and all copies of such documents in his possession, power, custody or control, (3) that he forthwith take all necessary steps to procure the return of the documents and copies thereof, (4) that he forthwith disclose to the plaintiffs' solicitors the names and addresses of all persons, firms and companies to whom he had given or supplied such documents or copies thereof and all whom he knew or believed to have possession of them, and (5) that he be restrained from disclosing or making any use of the documents or copies thereof or any information contained in the documents or copies thereof. On 8 October Warner J sitting in camera ordered, inter alia, that Mr Chappell forthwith deliver up to the plaintiffs' solicitors all the documents removed by him without the plaintiffs' consent and all copies of such documents in his possession, power, custody or control, provided that Mr Chappell should be entitled, pending further order, to retain for use in the copyright action one set of the copy documents exhibited to an affidavit sworn by him in the action on 1 October 1981. On 9 October the plaintiffs moved the court to delete that proviso from the order of 8 October. Mr Chappell opposed the deletion. The facts are set out in the judgment.

Mark Platts-Mills for the plaintiffs
Mr Chappell appeared in person.

WARNER J. This case has come before me on motions and cross-motions in a copyright action. There are three plaintiffs in the action: ITC Film Distributors Ltd, which sues on its own behalf and on behalf of and as representing all other members of the Society of Film Distributors Ltd; United Artists Corp, which sues on its own behalf and on behalf of and as representing all other members of the Motion Picture Association of America Inc; and Warner Bros Inc. There are four defendants, the first of which is a company, Video Exchange Ltd, the second is Mr Anthony Richard Malcolm Chappell, and the third and fourth are individuals described in the writ as 'Hooper (a male)' and 'G. Holland (a male)'.

The Society of Film Distributors Ltd is a trade association of companies involved in the distribution in the United Kingdom of cinematograph feature films. The Motion Picture Association of America Inc is the trade association of the major film companies in the United States of America. Its members are involved both in the production of cinematograph feature films and in the worldwide distribution of such films, whether produced by them or by others. Warner Bros Inc is the owner of the copyright in films produced by that company.

Video Exchange Ltd was incorporated on 19 September 1979 with a share capital of £100 divided into 100 shares of £1 each. Of those shares, 90 are held by Mr Chappell, who is also the managing director of the company. The other 10 are held by Mr Richard Johnstone, whom Mr Chappell describes as his former partner. They fell out early in 1980. The business of Video Exchange Ltd included the management of a club providing, among other things, facilities for the exchange of video cassettes between its members and for the copying of video tapes for its members.

The plaintiffs are represented before me by counsel, who is instructed by Messrs Clifford-Turner. Mr Chappell appears in person. The other defendants are unrepresented, but Mr Chappell has conducted his case on the footing that Video Exchange Ltd is his alter ego.

The case first came before me on 27 July 1981. At that time there was one motion by the plaintiffs and there were two cross-motions by Mr Chappell. Those three motions were part of the sequel to an Anton Piller order which was made by Whitford J on 26 February 1981 on the application of the plaintiffs against the defendants, and which was served and executed at Video Exchange Ltd's premises in Bath on 2 March 1981. The plaintiffs' motion was against Video Exchange Ltd and Mr Chappell for them to be dealt with for their contempt of court in failing to comply with undertakings given on their behalf by counsel to Dillon J on 5 March 1981. Of Mr Chappell's cross-motions, one was against the plaintiffs and Mr Percy Arthur Browne for alleged contempt of court in various respects, Mr Browne being amongst other things one of the plaintiffs' witnesses on whose evidence the Anton Piller order had been obtained; and the other was for relief on the basis that the Anton Piller order had been improperly obtained, improperly served and improperly executed. At the end of last term the case was part-heard and was adjourned to 1 October.

During the vacation five fresh notices of motion were served, one by the plaintiffs and four by Mr Chappell. I have already dismissed Mr Chappell's four new motions for reasons which I indicated in each instance at the time. The plaintiffs' new motion arises out of an incident that occurred in this building on the afternoon of 31 July after I had risen.

The only facts that it is necessary for me to state about that incident are these. Messrs Clifford-Turner had in my court a number of boxes containing video cassettes and a box containing files that they did not need for immediate use. They employed a firm called Pegasus Couriers to remove those boxes from the court and to take them back to their offices. Pegasus Couriers sent one of their vanmen, Mr Michael McMahon, to do the job. What then happened was described to me in affidavits sworn by Mr McMahon and by Mr Chappell, and both of them were cross-examined on their affidavits. I need not go into their evidence in detail for this reason. The outcome of what happened was that, when Mr McMahon took away the box that had contained Messrs Clifford-Turner's files, it in fact contained some papers of Mr Chappell's; whilst Mr Chappell had got possession of Messrs Clifford-Turner's files that had been in the box. Mr McMahon's and Mr Chappell's accounts of how that came about tallied, except on one crucial point. On that point their evidence conflicted. Mr Chappell very properly conceded that if on that point I preferred Mr McMahon's evidence to his own, I must hold that he had obtained Messrs Clifford-Turner's files by a trick and not merely by accident. I then told Mr

Chappell that I did prefer Mr McMahon's evidence on that point, and I told him briefly why I did so. Thereupon, Mr Chappell consented to the plaintiffs being granted most of the relief sought in their notice of motion. That relief included, among other things, an injunction restraining Mr Chappell from making copies of any of the documents contained in the files in question, an order requiring him forthwith to deliver up to Messrs Clifford-Turner the originals and any copies of those documents still in his possession, power, custody or control, and an injunction restraining him from making any use of the documents or of any copies of them or of any information contained in them.

Mr Chappell's consent to that order being made was, however, subject to one qualification. Copies of some of the documents are among the exhibits to an affidavit sworn by Mr Chappell on 1 October 1981. Mr Chappell was not prepared to consent to his being deprived of the use, for the purposes of this action, of any exhibits to that affidavit. My order accordingly contained provisos entitling Mr Chappell, pending further order, to retain and to use, for the purposes of this action only, copies of documents exhibited to that affidavit.

I have now heard argument on, in effect, the question whether those provisos should stand, and this judgment is confined to that question.

Before I come to the law I should, I think, state these further facts. Mr Chappell's affidavit of 1 October 1981 is a long one and it has not yet been read in full, though small parts of it were read to me by Mr Chappell when I was considering some of his new motions, and others have been referred to by him on the hearing of the present motion. There are a hundred exhibits to that affidavit, some of which are and some of which are not copies of documents obtained by Mr Chappell from Messrs Clifford-Turner's files. Of those that are copies of documents from those files there are some that I have already looked at, either because I was referred to them in the course of the argument on Mr Chappell's new motions or because they were put to Mr Browne in cross-examination, Mr Browne's cross-examination having been, for his personal convenience and at counsel for the plaintiffs' request, taken earlier than it normally would have been. In so far, however, as I have looked at those exhibits I have, again at counsel for the plaintiffs' request, done so in camera so that their contents should not be made public before I decided the present question. Lastly I should mention that, of those exhibits, some are copies of documents, such as documents emanating from Video Exchange Ltd itself, that would not be privileged from disclosure on discovery in the action, whilst others are of documents that would be so privileged, for instance a joint opinion of counsel obtained by Messrs Clifford-Turner on behalf of the plaintiffs, correspondence between Messrs Clifford-Turner and the plaintiffs about the case, Messrs Clifford-Turner's attendance notes about it, and so forth.

I turn to the law.

Mr Chappell relies on the general rule that in civil, as distinct from criminal, proceedings the court has no power to exclude relevant evidence, even though that evidence has been unlawfully or improperly obtained; and on the cognate rule that, if the original of a document is privileged, secondary evidence of its contents, such as a copy of it, may if available be adduced. He relies in particular on *Calcraft v Guest* [1898] 1 QB 759, [1895–9] All ER Rep 346 and *Helliwell v Piggott-Sims* [1980] FSR 356.

Counsel for the plaintiffs puts his case in two ways.

First, he relies on *Lord Ashburton v Pape* [1913] 2 Ch 469, [1911–13] All ER Rep 708. He submits, and I agree, that that was not an isolated decision but is illustrative of a general rule that, where A has improperly obtained possession of a document belonging to B, the court will, at the suit of B, order A to return the document to B and to deliver up any copies of it that A has made, and will restrain A from making any use of any such copies or of the information contained in the document. In *Lord Ashburton v Pape* [1913] 2 Ch 469 at 473, [1911–13] All ER Rep 708 at 710 Cozens Hardy MR said:

'The rule of evidence as explained in *Calcraft v. Guest* ([1898] 1 QB 759, [1895–9] All ER Rep 346) merely amounts to this, that if a litigant wants to prove a particular document which by reason of privilege or some circumstance he cannot furnish by the production of the original, he may produce a copy as secondary evidence although that copy had been obtained by improper means, and even, it may be, by criminal means. The Court in such an action is not really trying the circumstances under which the document was produced. That is not an issue in the case and the Court simply says "Here is a copy of a document which cannot be produced; it may have been stolen, it may have been picked up in the street, it may have improperly got into the possession of the person who proposes to produce it, but that is not a matter which the Court in the trial of the action can go into". But that does not seem to me to have any bearing upon a case where the whole subject-matter of the action is the right to retain the originals or copies of certain documents which are privileged.'

Then Kennedy LJ said this ([1913] 2 Ch 469 at 474, [1911–13] All ER Rep 708 at 711):

'The only question is, and that is the difficulty my brother Neville felt, that it is also quite clear that if the ground for secondary evidence has been properly laid at the trial it is no objection to using that secondary evidence in the shape of a copy of a document that that copy ought not to have been obtained in the way that it has been. Neville J., there being here unquestionably legal proceedings in which the question of the production of an original or the use of a copy, being a copy which had been wrongfully obtained, may be material, has thought he ought to hold his hand. I agree that the better view seems to me to be that although it is true that the principle which is laid down in *Calcraft* v. *Guest* ([1898] 1 QB 759, [1895–9] All ER Rep 346) must be followed, yet, at the same time, if, before the occasion of the trial when a copy may be used, although a copy improperly obtained, the owner of the original can successfully promote proceedings against the person who has improperly obtained the copy to stop his using it, the owner is none the less entitled to protection, because, if the question had arisen in the course of a trial before such proceedings, the holder of the copy would not have been prevented from using it on account of the illegitimacy of its origin. If that is so, it decides this case.'

Swinfen Eady LJ put it this way [1913] 2 Ch 469 at 476–477, [1911–13] All ER Rep 708 at 712–713):

'Then objection was raised in the present case by reason of the fact that it is said that Pape, who now has copies of the letters, might wish to give them in evidence in certain bankruptcy proceedings, and although the original letters are privileged from production he has possession of the copies and could give them as secondary evidence of the contents of the letters, and, therefore, ought not to be ordered either to give them up or to be restrained from divulging their contents. There is here a confusion between the right to restrain a person from divulging confidential information and the right to give secondary evidence of documents where the originals are privileged from production, if the party has such secondary evidence in his possession. The cases are entirely separate and distinct. If a person were to steal a deed, nevertheless in any dispute to which it was relevant the original deed might be given in evidence by him at the trial. It would be no objection to the admissibility of the deed in evidence to say you ought not to have possession of it. His unlawful possession would not affect the admissibility of the deed in evidence if otherwise admissible. So again with regard to any copy he had. If he was unable to obtain or compel production of the original because it was privileged, if he had a copy in his possession it would be admissible as secondary evidence. The fact, however, that a document, whether original or copy, is admissible in evidence is no answer to the demand of the lawful owner for the delivery up of the document, and no answer to an application by the lawful owner of confidential information to restrain it from being published or copied.'

I have little doubt that if, on or before 1 October, the plaintiffs and Messrs Clifford-Turner (for it appears to me that some at least of the documents here in question probably belong to Messrs Clifford-Turner rather than to the plaintiffs) had issued a writ against Mr Chappell claiming relief on the lines of that granted in *Lord Ashburton v Pape*, and had on a motion in that action sought an order for such relief, they would have been held entitled to it. But there seem to me to be difficulties in the way of my granting the plaintiffs such relief on the basis of *Lord Ashburton v Pape* now.

I need not, however, discuss those difficulties because counsel for the plaintiffs has satisfied me that as regards, at all events, the exhibits to Mr Chappell's affidavit that I have not yet looked at, he is entitled to succeed on his alternative submission.

That submission is in a nutshell that, in the circumstances of this case, I must balance the public interest that the truth should be ascertained, which is the reason for the rule in *Calcraft v Guest* [1898] 1 QB 759, [1895–9] All ER Rep 346, against the public interest that litigants should be able to bring their documents into court without fear that they may be filched by their opponents, whether by stealth or by a trick, and then used by them in evidence. Counsel for the plaintiffs referred me in particular to *Riddick v Thames Board Mills Ltd* [1977] 3 All ER 677, [1977] 1 QB 881, where it was held that a document obtained on discovery in an action could not be used as the basis of a subsequent action. By the same token, said counsel for the plaintiffs, such a document could not be used in evidence in a subsequent action. This case is, counsel for the plaintiffs submitted, a fortiori because in *Riddick v Thames Board Mills Ltd* the document had been lawfully obtained in the first place. At the end of his judgment in that case, Waller LJ cites a passage from the speech of Lord Simon in *D v National Society for the Prevention of Cruelty to Children* [1977] 1 All ER 589 at 607, [1978] AC 171 at 233. What Waller LJ says is this ([1977] 3 All ER 677 at 702, [1977] 1 QB 881 at 911–912):

> 'In *D v National Society for the Prevention of Cruelty to Children* Lord Simon of Glaisdale sets out a number of examples of evidence which as a matter of public policy should be excluded from forensic scrutiny. He instances legal professional privilege, without prejudice communications and others and says: "... without attempting to be exhaustive I have tried to show that there is a continuum of relevant evidence which may be excluded from forensic scrutiny. This extends from that excluded in the interest of the forensic process itself as an instrument of justice (eg evidence of propensity to commit crime), through that excluded for such and also for cognate interests (eg legal professional privilege), through again that excluded in order to facilitate the avoidance of forensic contestation (eg 'without prejudice' communications) to evidence excluded because its adduction might imperil the security of that civil society which the administration of justice itself also subserves (eg sources of police information or state secrets)." I would add the present case to this number. The interests of the proper administration of justice require that there should be no disincentive to full and frank discovery.'

Counsel for the plaintiffs submits that I should in my turn add the present case to the list. I think that the interests of the proper administration of justice require that I should do so. I do not overlook that for a party to litigation to take possession by stealth or by a trick of documents belonging to the other side within the precincts of the court is probably contempt of court, so that there may be another sanction. But it seems to me that, if it is contempt of court, then the court should not countenance it by admitting such documents in evidence. Nor do I overlook the decision of the Court of Appeal in *R v Tompkins* (1967) 67 Cr App R 181. But that case proceeded on the footing that the document in question there had come into the possession of the prosecution fortuitously. The relevance of possible impropriety was not discussed.

Mr Chappell asked me to allow him to use the exhibits in question on two main grounds. The first was that the plaintiffs had themselves been guilty of misconduct in the way in which they had obtained Whitford J's order, in the way in which they had served and executed that order and in the way in which they had obtained evidence subsequently. Those are matters that I shall have to deal with when I come to the motions that were already before me last term. But, assuming for present purposes that there was misconduct on the part of the plaintiffs, the short answer to Mr Chappell's point is, I think, that two wrongs do not make a right. Mr Chappell's second ground was that, quite apart from those matters, the exhibits disclosed iniquity on the part of the plaintiffs of a kind that they should not be entitled to conceal. It seemed to me however that the examples of such iniquity given to me by Mr Chappell were not very convincing.

On the other hand, I do not think it possible for me now to exclude the documents that I have already looked at. Of course, it often happens that a judge is called on to look at a document in order to see whether it is admissible in evidence. If, having done so, he decides that it is not, he puts its contents out of his mind, even though that is not always an easy mental feat. But here the documents, although perhaps they have not been formally put in evidence, have in fact been used as evidence. It is quite impossible for me, for instance, to ignore the answers given by Mr Browne when such documents were put to him. I therefore think that the provisos in my order must stand as regards those documents. I draw comfort from the thought that counsel for the plaintiffs could have excluded them if he had opened the present motion on 1 October, instead of inviting me to deal first with Mr Chappell's new motions and then to hear Mr Browne's cross-examination. I do not wish, in saying that, to imply any criticism of counsel for the plaintiffs' conduct of the case, for which there were no doubt good reasons, but merely to indicate that a different course would have led to a different result.

Order accordingly.

Solicitors: *Clifford-Turner* (for the plaintiffs).

Azza M Abdallah   Barrister.

Cole Bros Ltd v Phillips (Inspector of Taxes)

HOUSE OF LORDS

LORD HAILSHAM OF ST MARYLEBONE LC, LORD WILBERFORCE, LORD EDMUND-DAVIES, LORD RUSSELL OF KILLOWEN AND LORD BRIDGE OF HARWICH

1, 2, 3, 4 FEBRUARY, 11 MARCH 1982

Income tax – Capital allowances – Plant – Single or separate items of plant – Electrical installation – Installation consisting of trunking, transformers, switchgear, switchboard and lighting system – Whether installation to be considered as single entity or separate items – Finance Act 1971, s 41.

A company which was a member of the same group as the taxpayer incurred expenditure of £945,600 on electrical equipment installed in a building in which a third member of the group carried on business as a department store. The installation consisted of trunking for a telephone system, emergency lighting and standby lighting systems, wiring to heating and ventilation equipment, to fire alarm and public address systems and to lifts, escalators and other apparatus, transformers and associated switchgear, a main electrical switchboard and a complete lighting installation including fittings, conduits, cables, trunking and riser cubicles. The taxpayer contended that the expenditure had been incurred on the provision of 'plant' for the purposes of the trade carried on and claimed a first-year allowance in respect of the installations under s 41[a] of the Finance Act 1971. (As a result of arrangements between members of the group it was not disputed that the taxpayer would be entitled to take advantage of any capital allowance available.) The inspector of taxes allowed part of the claim but disallowed the remainder.

_____

Section 41, so far as material, is set out at p 249 j, post

On appeal by the taxpayer, the Special Commissioners rejected a contention by the taxpayer that the installation should be considered as a single entity and concluded that, in view of the multiplicity of the elements in the installation and the differing purposes which they served, they should consider the individual items separately. On that basis the commissioners found that certain additional items also attracted a first-year allowance. Except in relation to certain other items, the Court of Appeal dismissed an appeal by the taxpayer. The taxpayer appealed to the House of Lords, contending that the Special Commissioners had been wrong in law not to look at the installation as a single entity.

Held – It was open to the commissioners as a tribunal of fact to decide that the multiplicity of elements in the taxpayer's installation and the differing purposes which those elements served entitled them not to look at the installation as a whole but to analyse its individual components having regard to the nature and function of each. Since the commissioners had rejected the 'single entity' approach not on the basis that such an approach was wrong in principle but as a result of their examination of the facts, the case was clearly one in the realm of fact and degree, and, in the absence of a clear and identifiable misdirection in point of law, the court was not entitled to differ from the commissioners. The appeal would accordingly be dismissed (see p 253 b c and f to j, p 254 b and j to p 255 e and g to j and p 256 c to j, post).

Jarrold (Inspector of Taxes) v John Good & Sons Ltd [1963] 1 All ER 141, *Cooke (Inspector of Taxes) v Beach Station Caravans Ltd* [1974] 3 All ER 159 and *Benson (Inspector of Taxes) v Yard Arm Club Ltd* [1979] 2 All ER 336 approved.

Dictum of Kitto J in *Imperial Chemical Industries of Australia and New Zealand Ltd v Federal Comr of Taxation* (1970) 120 CLR at 398–399 followed.

Per Lord Hailsham LC, Lord Edmund-Davies and Lord Bridge. The recent practice of stating a case for the opinion of the court in the form of a mingled series of propositions of mixed fact and law with the inconsequent addition that 'the question of law for the opinion of the court is whether on the facts found the decision was erroneous in point of law' is a bad practice which should be dropped (see p 252 g to p 253 a and p 255 j to p 256 a d e and j, post).

Notes

For first-year allowances, see 23 Halsbury's Laws (4th edn) para 426.

For the meaning of plant, see ibid para 416, and for cases on the subject, see s 28(1) Digest (Reissue) 214–216, 637–643.

For the Finance Act 1971, s 41, see 41 Halsbury's Statutes (3rd edn) 1459.

Cases referred to in opinions

Benson (Inspector of Taxes) v Yard Arm Club Ltd [1979] 2 All ER 336, [1979] 1 WLR 347, CA, Digest (Cont Vol E) 309, 1676e.

Bridge House (Reigate Hill) Ltd v Hinder (Inspector of Taxes) (1971) 47 TC 182, CA, Digest (Cont Vol D) 493, 1676a.

Cooke (Inspector of Taxes) v Beach Station Caravans Ltd [1974] 3 All ER 159, [1974] 1 WLR 1398, Digest (Cont Vol D) 456, 640a.

Dixon (Inspector of Taxes) v Fitch's Garage Ltd [1975] 3 All ER 455, [1976] 1 WLR 215, Digest (Cont Vol D) 493, 1676c.

Federal Comr of Taxation v Broken Hill Pty Co Ltd (1969) 120 CLR 240, Aust HC (Kitto J and Full Ct).

Federal Comr of Taxation v ICI (Australia) Ltd (1972) 127 CLR 529, Aust HC (Walsh J and Full Ct).

Hampton (Inspector of Taxes) v Fortes Autogrill Ltd [1981] STC 80.

Imperial Chemical Industries of Australia and New Zealand Ltd v Federal Comr of Taxation (1970) 120 CLR 396, Aust HC.

IRC v Barclay Curle & Co Ltd [1969] 1 All ER 732, [1969] 1 WLR 675, HL, 28(1) Digest (Reissue) 465, 1676.

IRC v Scottish and Newcastle Breweries Ltd [1981] STC 50, CS; affd [1982] 2 All ER 230, HL.

Jarrold (Inspector of Taxes) v John Good & Sons Ltd [1963] 1 All ER 141, [1963] 1 WLR 214,
   CA, 28(1) Digest (Reissue) 215, 642.
Lyons (J) & Co Ltd v A-G [1944] 1 All ER 477, [1944] Ch 281, 17 Digest (Reissue) 542, 324.
St John's School (Mountford and Knibbs) v Ward (Inspector of Taxes) [1974] STC 69; *affd* [1975]
   STC 7, CA, Digest (Cont Vol D) 493, 1676b.
Schofield (Inspector of Taxes) v R & H Hall Ltd [1975] STC 353, CA, Digest (Cont Vol D) 493,
   1676d.
Yarmouth v France (1887) 19 QBD 647, DC, 20 Digest (Reissue) 515, 4005.

Appeal

Cole Bros Ltd (the taxpayer company) appealed against the decision of the Court of Appeal
(Stephenson, Oliver LJJ and Sir David Cairns) ([1981] STC 671) affirming the decision of
Vinelott J ([1980] STC 518) dismissing the taxpayer company's appeal by way of case stated
(set out at [1980] STC 519–527) against the determination of the Commissioners for the
Special Purposes of the Income Tax Acts rejecting the taxpayer company's claim for capital
allowances in the year 1975–76 in respect of capital expenditure incurred in providing
electrical installations at a department store of the taxpayer company. The facts are set out
in the opinion of Lord Hailsham LC.

Barry Pinson QC and *John Gardiner* for the taxpayer company.
John Hobhouse QC and *Robert Carnwath* for the Crown.

Their Lordships took time for consideration.

11 March. The following opinions were delivered.

LORD HAILSHAM OF ST MARYLEBONE LC. My Lords, the question in this case
revolves round the entitlement of the taxpayer company to an initial capital allowance in
respect of the installation of various items of electrical equipment in a multiple store at the
Brent Cross Shopping Centre. The store was erected by John Lewis Properties Ltd and the
business there is carried on by John Lewis & Co Ltd, a member of the same group as John
Lewis Properties Ltd. The taxpayer company, Cole Bros Ltd, is also a member of this
group, and, as the result of arrangements between its members, it is not disputed that if
capital allowance is attracted by the items remaining in question the taxpayer company is
entitled to the advantage of it.

The items still involved in this appeal amount in value to a total of £453,218 out of a
total cost of £945,600. The individual items, presented in the form of an agreed document
to your Lordships, included lighting fittings, standard and specially designed, with their
conduits and cables, trunking, conduits and cables to socket fittings, restaurant lightings
and fittings, and sub-main cables and riser cubicles. In the light of what I am about to say
the precise details do not matter. The balance of the £945,600, ie £492,382, represents
items in the installation which now admittedly attract allowance. Some of these were
conceded by the Crown, some accepted by the Special Commissioners and an additional
portion representing switchgear allowed by the Court of Appeal, as to which last, there
being no cross-appeal on behalf of the Crown, there is no longer any question before your
Lordships' House.

Entitlement to the allowance is claimed under s 41(1)(a) of the Finance Act 1971, which,
so far as material, provides as follows:

> 'Subject to the provisions of this Chapter, where—(a) a person carrying on a trade
> incurs capital expenditure on the provision of machinery or plant for the purposes
> of the trade, and (b) in consequence of his incurring the expenditure, the machinery
> or plant belongs to him . . . during the chargeable period related to the incurring of
> the expenditure, there shall be made to him for that period an allowance (in this
> Chapter referred to as "a first-year allowance") which shall be of an amount
> determined in accordance with section 42 below . . .'

Neither the proviso to sub-s (1) nor the remaining subsections of s 41 are material to the determination of the instant appeal, and the sole bone of contention arising out of s 41(1)(a) which I have quoted above is whether or not the capital expenditure admittedly incurred in respect of the disputed items was incurred 'on the provision of . . . plant'. None of the items disputed were incurred on the provision of machinery and all were incurred for the purposes of the trade carried on at the premises in Brent Cross Shopping Centre.

In the course of the numerous authorities cited before us, including the Court of Appeal judgment in the instant case (see [1981] STC 671), it has been repeatedly stated that the expression 'plant', where it is used in s 41, is an ordinary English word to be interpreted, in the words of Buckley LJ, in *Benson (Inspector of Taxes) v Yard Arm Club Ltd* [1979] 2 All ER 336 at 339, [1979] 1 WLR 347 at 351—

> 'as a man who speaks English and understands English accurately but not pedantically would interpret it in [the] context, applying it to the particular subject-matter in question in the circumstances of the particular case.'

To this admirable precept Oliver LJ, in delivering the judgment of the Court of Appeal in the instant case, warily, and perhaps wearily, added the cautionary rider that 'the English speaker must, I think, be assumed to have studied the authorities' (see [1981] STC 671 at 682). These however, as he cautiously admitted in an earlier passage (at 676), cannot be pretended to be at all easy to reconcile, and, as he said in a still earlier passage (at 675): '. . . it is now beyond doubt that [the word "plant"] is used in the relevant section in an artificial and largely judge-made sense.' In this Oliver LJ was, perhaps unconsciously, only echoing the words of Mrs Piozzi in 1789 who first came across the word 'plant' in its present signification when applied to 'a large portion of ground in Southwark . . . destined to the purposes of extensive commerce', and added 'but the appellation of a plant gave me much disturbance from my inability to fathom the meaning of it' (Hester Lynch Piozzi *Observations and Reflections made in the Course of a Journey through France, Italy and Germany* (London, 1789) vol 1, pp 132–133).

From all this I think it may be inferred that the word 'plant' in the relevant sense, although admittedly not a term of art, and therefore part of the general English tongue, is not, in this sense, an ordinary word, but one of imprecise application, and, so far as I can see, has been applied to industrial and commercial equipment in a highly analogical and metaphorical sense, borrowed, unless I am mistaken, from the world of botany.

Since I find it myself helpful in analysing the various authorities beginning with the observations of Lindley LJ in *Yarmouth v France* (1887) 19 QBD 647 at 658, I think it worth while spending a moment's time in reflecting briefly on what the botanical analogy is.

In the field of botany 'plant' is used in three quite separate contexts. It can mean a vegetable organism synthesizing its nourishment from inorganic materials by the use of chlorophyll. In this sense an oak tree is a plant, whilst the Matterhorn is not. It can mean a vegetable organism with a soft stem. In this sense a bluebell is a plant, but an oak tree is not. Neither of these senses affords the analogy. But the word can mean a vegetable organism deliberately placed in an artificially prepared setting. A gardener can say, 'I am going to dig my flower beds in readiness for my plants' or 'I am going to buy some plants at my garden centre.' It is this sense which gives it its analogical meanings, eg in medicine ('an organ transplant'), in crime ('it was planted on me') or in industry, which is the sense we are now discussing, as the means by which a trade is carried on in an appropriately prepared setting. In each case the contrast is between the thing implanted, ie the plant, and the prepared setting into which it is placed (cf Oliver LJ in the instant case ([1981] STC 671 at 676–677), Pearson LJ in *Jarrold (Inspector of Taxes) v John Good & Sons Ltd* [1963] 1 All ER 141 at 149, [1963] 1 WLR 214 at 225, *IRC v Barclay Curle & Co Ltd* [1969] 1 All ER 732, [1969] 1 WLR 675, Megarry J in *Cooke (Inspector of Taxes) v Beach Station Caravans Ltd* [1974] 3 All ER 159, [1974] 1 WLR 1398), from which it has extended even to the horse in *Yarmouth v France* in the field of employer's liability. It also explains Uthwatt J's interpretation of this last authority in *J Lyons & Co Ltd v A-G* [1944]

1 All ER 477 at 479, [1944] Ch 281 at 287, where he cites *Yarmouth v France* as contrasting plant not merely with stock-in-trade as stated by Lindley LJ but with the place in which the business is carried on.

The last citation raises a question which has underlain much of the controversy in the present case and in the other authorities referred to. If 'plant' is to be contrasted with the place in which the business is carried on, the line must be drawn somewhere. This is a practical necessity in the case of capital allowances, since plant attracts one type of allowance, rated currently at 100%, whereas the building in which the plant is housed rates another, and lower rated, allowance, and the building in which the business of a retail shop such as that at Brent Cross is carried on is excluded from that type of allowance altogether. There must therefore be a criterion (or criteria) by which the courts define the frontier between the two. Thus arises the analysis of function in the authorities (cf the analysis of the function of the dry dock in *IRC v Barclay Curle & Co Ltd* [1969] 1 All ER 732 esp at 740–741, [1969] 1 WLR 675 esp at 679 by Lord Reid, which largely guided his decision when your Lordships' committee was split three to two). Counsel for the taxpayer company in the present case strove mightily to limit the relevance of function to 'building or structure' cases, like the dry dock in the *Barclay Curle* case or the swimming pool in the *Beach Station Caravans* case, or perhaps 'place only' cases where, he claimed, the functional test could not be satisfied. The basis of the argument was that if the equipment under discussion was established to be 'apparatus' no question as to function could arise. Unfortunately this contention appears to me to beg the question. If the plant is to be distinguished from the housing of the plant ('the place where the business is carried on' as distinct from the means by which it is to be carried on) it is necessary before it is possible to decide whether the disputed object is apparatus or not to look at it in order to see what it is and then consider what, in the context of the business actually being carried on, is its function. This proves to be a trap for the unwary, for in certain cases, notably that of a hotelier and restaurant proprietor, the very thing the trader is selling includes an 'ambience' or 'setting'. This is well illustrated by the decision in *IRC v Scottish and Newcastle Breweries Ltd* [1981] STC 50, since upheld in your Lordships' House (see [1982] 2 All ER 230), where the 'plant' included some ornamental seagulls and mural decorations. Similarly, in *Jarrold v John Good & Sons Ltd* [1963] 1 All ER 141 at 147, [1963] 1 WLR 214 at 222 Donovan LJ, following Pennycuick J, is recorded as saying: '... I agree with PENNYCUICK J., that "setting" and "plant" are not mutually exclusive conceptions. The same thing may be both', and in the *Barclay Curle* case [1969] 1 All ER 732 at 740, [1969] 1 WLR 675 at 679 Lord Reid said: 'Undoubtedly this concrete dry dock is a structure but is it also plant?' This result is to be contrasted with the Hispaniola restaurant case, *Benson v Yard Arm Club Ltd* [1979] 2 All ER 336, [1979] 1 WLR 347, where the hull of a floating restaurant was held not to be plant though it was expressly stated that had the floating restaurant not been engineless and moored, but fitted with engines and moving up and down the Thames, the result would have been different. The distinction can also be observed in *St John's School (Mountford and Knibbs) v Ward (Inspector of Taxes)* [1974] STC 69, where a free standing gymnasium and laboratory, including minor electrical apparatus valued at £240, was found not to be plant, when contrasted with *Jarrold v John Good & Sons Ltd*, where moving partitions in an office building were decided to be plant, and with the Northern Ireland case, *Schofield (Inspector of Taxes) v R & H Hall Ltd* [1975] STC 353, where grain silos were also so held. In the same line as the *St John's School* case were the so called 'false' ceilings in *Hampton (Inspector of Taxes) v Fortes Autogrill Ltd* [1981] STC 80 which were held not to be plant, whereas the fittings or apparatus they concealed were plant. If *Dixon (Inspector of Taxes) v Fitch's Garage Ltd* [1975] 3 All ER 455, [1976] 1 WLR 215 can stand in the light of the decision in the *Scottish and Newcastle Breweries* case, which may be doubted, this is another example of the same distinction, where the housing is to be distinguished from the plant which it houses.

Reference was also made to a number of Australian cases including *Imperial Chemical Industries of Australia and New Zealand Ltd v Federal Comr of Taxation* (1970) 120 CLR 396. Here the taxpayer company's counsel rightly stressed that caution is required since the statutory context in Australia differs from that in England, and Collins English Dictionary denotes a subsidiary meaning of 'plant' in the Australian usage which differs *a* from that in England. Speaking for myself, however, I find the use of this Australian decision of Kitto J (subsequently approved by the Full High Court in *Federal Comr of Taxation v ICI (Australia) Ltd* (1972) 127 CLR 529) and *Federal Comr of Taxation v Broken Hill Pty Co Ltd* (1968) 120 CLR 240 by Oliver LJ in the instant appeal ([1981] STC 671 at 676 and, inferentially, at 677–678) perfectly proper and convincing, based as it was partly on English authorities cited above. The first Australian *Imperial Chemical Industries* case *b* was of interest because it was the only recent case when an electrical installation per se had come up for consideration in the present context, and Kitto J had said that for himself—

> 'I see no difference for present purposes between these electricity reticulating agents and the water reticulating pipes which run throughout such a building [an office building]. It seems to me impossible to regard these elements in the *c* equipment of the building as "plant" any more than as "articles".'

(See 120 CLR 396 at 399.) To be just to the taxpayer company one must contrast this statement by Kitto J with the remark of Donovan LJ in *Jarrold v John Good & Sons Ltd* [1963] 1 All ER 141 at 147, [1963] 1 WLR 214 at 223:

> 'The heating installation of a building may be passive in the sense that it involves no moving machinery, but few would deny it the name of "plant". The same thing could no doubt be said of many air conditioning and water softening installations.'

Speaking for myself, I would find it very difficult to draw a significant distinction between the 'reticulation' of a heating installation and the reticulation of an electrical installation, but it is precisely at this point that I begin to wonder whether your Lordships are in truth being invited to decide a question of fact and degree (as to which there is no appeal from the commissioners) or a true question of law (as to which an appeal will lie). As Pearson LJ said in *Jarrold v John Good & Sons Ltd* [1963] 1 All ER 141 at 149, [1963] 1 WLR 214 at 225:

> '. . . the short question in this case is whether the partitioning is part of the *f* premises in which the business is carried on or part of the plant with which the business is carried on. *Either view could have been taken* . . . I think the commissioners have, in effect, preferred the second view, and it cannot be said that there was no evidence to support it, or that any error of principle was involved.' (My emphasis.)

The resolution of my doubt as to this is not rendered easier by the form in which the case has been stated by the commissioners, who, following recent, and to my mind not particularly admirable, practice, have stated their decision in the form of a mingled series of propositions of mixed fact and law, and then added somewhat inconsequently: 'The question of law for the opinion of the Court is whether, on the facts found, our decision was erroneous in point of law.' The scheme devised by Parliament was to limit appeals from the commissioners to questions of law only by providing that appeals should be by way of case stated, and it seems to me as a comparatively rare visitor to this field of jurisprudence that the commissioners do rather less than their duty to Parliament if, with the aid of counsel on both sides, particularly of counsel for the party demanding the case to be stated, they do not identify a definable point of law for the decision of the court, but leave the court to guess what is the precise point of law it is being asked to decide, and counsel for the appellant to be reduced to argue, as he was in the instant appeal, that, if the question was one of fact, the decision of fact upheld by the commissioners, Vinelott J and three members of the Court of Appeal was not one at which any properly directed set of commissioners could reasonably have arrived, and therefore, per se, a question of law. The whole form in which special cases have recently come to be stated, of which the present appeal only affords one example, seems to me to add force to the doubts expressed in his Hamlyn Lecture by Mr Hubert Monroe QC as to the value of the present four-tier system of appeal (*Intolerable Inquisition? Reflections on the Law of Tax* (1981) pp 82–83).

In my search for a definable question of law on which a decision of a court could be founded I was at first attracted by the argument for the taxpayer company, first presented to the commissioners and persisted in to the last, that the whole electrical installation, from the point where it was delivered by the Electricity Board at 11,000 volts to the point at which having been transformed to 240 volts and delivered in the form of light and power to various points in the store, 'should be looked at as a whole, not analysed into its component parts'. If this were a point of law, it was rejected by Vinelott J and by the Court of Appeal and it would therefore be open to review by your Lordships. The more this simplistic view was considered, however, the more clearly I came to realise that, whether or not I would have come to this conclusion had I been a commissioner (as to which I still feel some doubt), the commissioners, as a tribunal of fact, were entitled to decide, after analysing the evidence and visiting the factory, as they did decide in the circumstances of the particular case in para 18 of their decision ([1980] STC 518 at 525):

> 'We do not accept [counsel for the taxpayer's] contention that the entire electrical installation should be regarded as a single whole, and we reject his submissions (1) and (2). Notwithstanding the *Barclay, Curle* case, where Lord Reid and Lord Donovan set their faces against the "piecemeal" approach, and the *St John's School* case, where Templeman J, as he then was, said: "In my judgment, one looks at the whole . . .", we consider, after careful reflection, that the multiplicity of elements in the Brent Cross installation, and the differing purposes which they serve, make the present case distinguishable from the dry dock in *Barclay, Curle* and the laboratory and the gymnasium in *St John's School*, each of which, despite its component parts, was directed towards a single purpose. To adopt the approach advocated by [counsel] seems to us to be too sweeping, not only in the particular circumstances we have before us, but as a general approach.'

I am not myself happy about the phraseology of the last sentence if it was intended to convey that the 'single entity' submission could never be right in any case or that they were not free in law to reach a different conclusion. If it had been so intended I am inclined to think that it would have been a misdirection, but it seems to me that the decision in the particular circumstances which the commissioners had before them was one of fact and degree to be decided on evidence and inspection; and their finding is therefore a proposition which I do not feel able to contradict. In my view, to quote again from the judgment of Pearson LJ, 'Either view could have been taken'; in other words the question was one of fact. If, as Donovan LJ said in the short passage I have already cited, a heating apparatus can be regarded in the way for which the appellants contend, I do not see why, as a matter of principle, the same cannot be said of an entire electrical installation. But the commissioners have decided in the instant appeal that the multiplicity of components in the Brent Cross installation preclude this approach, and, if I am right, they were entitled to do so.

Once the 'single entity' submission is rejected, as I have felt it necessary to do, the plausibility of the taxpayer company's case as a proposition of law seems to me to melt into thin air. Once it is accepted that it was open to the commissioners to decide as a tribunal of fact that 'the multiplicity of elements in the Brent Cross installation, and the differing purposes which they serve' entitled the commissioners to reject the 'entire entity' submission and come to an analysis of its individual components having regard to the nature and function of each, it seems to me that we are clearly in the realm of fact and degree, and, in the absence of a clear and identifiable misdirection in point of law, I do not think it possible to differ from it, at least as to the items still in dispute after the decision of the Court of Appeal had disposed of the main switchboard in the taxpayer company's favour. The one submission on behalf of the taxpayer company on this part of the case to the effect that a distinction can be drawn between 'apparatus cases', 'building or structure cases' and 'place only' cases, except for the purposes of arguments directed towards fact and degree, appears to me, for the reasons I have said, to rest on a logical fallacy. I can therefore see no reason to find fault with the judgment of Oliver LJ or, in so far as it was affirmed, of Vinelott J and, in particular, I would wish to affirm my agreement with Oliver LJ ([1981] STC 671 at 682) in his evident reliance on the expository judgment of Buckley LJ in *Benson v Yard Arm Club Ltd* and on the passages in the judgments of Pearson LJ in *Jarrold v John Good & Sons Ltd* and of Megarry J in *Cooke v Beach Station Caravans Ltd* on which Oliver LJ also evidently placed reliance at several points.

In the event, I come to the conclusion, not without some wavering from time to time, that this appeal must be dismissed.

LORD WILBERFORCE. My Lords, in the appeal, recently heard by this House, in *IRC v Scottish and Newcastle Breweries Ltd* [1982] 2 All ER 230 Lord Lowry made a comprehensive review of the authorities relating to the meaning of 'plant' in the Finance Act 1971, s 41 and other statutes. He also stated, by reference to his preceding judgment in *Schofield (Inspector of Taxes) v R & H Hall Ltd* [1975] STC 353, the principles by which courts should be guided in reviewing decisions, whether particular items of property should be regarded as 'plant', of the General and Special Commissioners. That recent appeal was concerned with items of lighting and decor installed in the taxpayer's premises for the purpose of its trade. It was decided in the taxpayer's favour on the basis of clear and strong findings of fact by the Special Commissioners that (I summarise) the items in question were not merely the setting in which the trader carried on his business but represented or created something which he offered to his customers to resort to and enjoy.

We are here concerned with a different trade, that of a department store, and with different items. As the case was presented to the commissioners, these consisted of a large number of pieces of equipment, the total cost of which was £945,600. I group these for convenience under four heads: (i) trunking for the telephone system, emergency lighting and standby lighting systems, wiring to heating and ventilation equipment, to fire alarm and public address systems, to lifts and escalators and other apparatus; (ii) transformers and their associated switchgear; (iii) the main electrical switchboard; and (iv) the complete lighting installation, including fittings, some specially designed, their conduits and cables, trunking, riser cubicles etc.

The entirety of this equipment was ordered by the owner of the department store, John Lewis Properties Ltd, for installation in a large purpose built building at Brent Cross. It was provided under a separate contract from that relating to the building itself and on the basis of a specification and drawings prepared within the John Lewis group. For reasons which I need not develop, it is not disputed that such capital allowances as are available in respect of this installation may be claimed by the taxpayer company, Cole Bros Ltd.

The taxpayer company claimed that it was entitled to capital allowances in respect of expenditure on the provision of the totality of the equipment as being 'machinery or plant' provided 'for the purposes of ... trade'. In dealing with this claim the commissioners had to decide in the first place whether they should regard the expenditure as having been made in respect of one single entity or whether they should look separately at individual items or groups of items. They were strongly urged to adopt the single entity approach, but they did not agree to do so. Instead they decided that, in view of what they described as 'the multiplicity of elements in the Brent Cross installation, and the differing purposes which they serve', they should place these elements in suitable categories, and this they did. This decision was strongly attacked in the appeal and learned counsel were able to suggest a number of quite plausible arguments in favour of a single entity approach. These arguments fail however, in my opinion, for the fundamental reason that, whatever merits that approach may have, to reject it involves no error of law. The commissioners' decision to reject it, and instead to consider categories, or single items, was not, as I read it, based on any general proposition that a 'single entity' approach is, as a matter of principle, wrong; if it had been I should regard it critically. It was one based on their examination of the facts and on their personal inspection, and so was in the realm of pure fact. Indeed, if one asks what is the principle of law which they can be said to have violated, it is impossible to state it, unless by an assertion that no reasonable body of commissioners could have come to the conclusion which they reached. Such an assertion I should be most reluctant to accept if I were reviewing the commissioners' findings for the first time. After it has been reviewed, but without success, in two courts, reluctance becomes impossibility. The first and main line of the taxpayer company's argument, in my opinion, fails.

That being so, the taxpayer company is obliged to attack the commissioners' individual findings as regards individual items or categories. It is not wholly without ammunition. As regards the main electrical system, including conduits and cables and riser cubicles, it can point to the anomaly of regarding heating systems as plant, as it appears that the Crown is willing to accept, but not electrical systems. It can appeal to the fact that, although the commissioners refused to agree that the switchboard constitutes plant, the Court of Appeal reversed their decision; so it is said that this House should not hesitate to disagree with the commissioners on other items. There is some attraction in both of these arguments. As regards the switchboard there has been no appeal to this House. On the whole argument, however, the taxpayer company fails to satisfy me that the commissioners erred in law. As regards the main electrical system, there is no finding that it was in any way special to the taxpayer company's business, or anything more than the standard equipment of a commercial business. The commissioners were entitled on this point to derive support from the judgment of Kitto J in the High Court of Australia in *Imperial Chemical Industries of Australia and New Zealand Ltd v Federal Comr of Taxation* (1970) 120 CLR 396. Although that case was concerned with a different statute and, of course, with its own facts, the learned judge considered and relied on English authorities on the meaning of 'plant'. His judgment shows, at least, that the similar approach of the commissioners to the present case can be supported (at 398–399):

> 'The electrical wiring with its enclosing conduits, and the trunking, are also parts of the general equipment of the building, fixtures beyond question, and having no relevance to the activities of the appellant beyond the relevance they would have to any occupier's activities. Together with switchboards, sub-switchboards and junction boxes, they form the reticulation system for conveying throughout the building electric current which is drawn ordinarily from the Melbourne City Council's power supply mains . . . The construction of the building as a building of the general type to which it belongs would be incomplete without them, and their function does not go beyond making the building a suitable general setting for a wide range of possible activities.'

This is, of course, not a statement of law: it leaves the commissioners free to find the facts of the case before them otherwise. But there is no error in law if, as they did, they make similar findings; there was certainly evidence on which they could do so.

Some other individual findings were attacked, these relating to 'special lighting'. It is not appropriate for me to say whether I agree with them. They were near or on the borderline. But that is a common feature of cases about 'plant': see *Jarrold (Inspector of Taxes) v John Good & Sons Ltd* [1963] 1 All ER 141 at 149, [1963] 1 WLR 214 at 225 per Pearson LJ; the decision must be left to the commissioners.

For these reasons I hold that the appeal fails and must be dismissed.

LORD EDMUND-DAVIES. My Lords, I have had the great advantage of reading in draft the speech prepared by the Lord Chancellor and I too doubt that I should have decided this case in the same way in all respects as that which commended itself to the commissioners.

The regrettable absence from their stated case of specification of the point or points of law on which the views of an appellate court were sought has substantially increased my difficulty. For some time during the hearing of the appeal I was in doubt whether the commissioners had regarded themselves as *obliged* to adopt what for convenience was called the 'piecemeal' approach to the individual items constituting the electrical installation in the taxpayer company's Brent Cross premises. This doubt was in part generated by the statement in para 18 of their decision that adoption of the general or 'entire entity' approach '. . . seems to us to be too sweeping, *not only in the particular circumstances we have before us, but as a general approach*' (see [1980] STC 518 at 525; my emphasis).

If this meant that the commissioners felt compelled as a matter of law to reject the 'entire entity' approach, this would have run counter to some of the decided cases and would itself have constituted a question of law calling for careful consideration. But I was at length won over to the view that this was not so, and that the commissioners, while recognising that in some circumstances a general approach would be the proper one, had concluded that the type and nature of the taxpayer company's Brent Cross electrical installation called for the 'piecemeal' approach. And that conclusion, as I see it, was one of fact for the commissioners alone.

Having formed that view, for the reasons propounded in the speech of the Lord Chancellor, with which I am in respectful and complete agreement, it appeared to me that there existed no question of law calling for the decision of your Lordships, and that the appeal must accordingly be dismissed.

It is a conclusion which could well have been arrived at by others at an earlier stage of this protracted and doubtless expensive litigation had an attempt been made to identify the points of law considered to be involved. In fairness to the commissioners, it should be added that the formula they adopted in their case (viz 'The question of law for the opinion of the Court is whether, on the facts found, our decision was erroneous in point of law') has for some time crept into common usage in many branches of the law. But it is a bad formula, and it should be dropped.

I concur in the dismissal of the appeal.

LORD RUSSELL OF KILLOWEN. My Lords, I incline to the view that had I been the Special Commissioners I might well have come to the conclusion that electrical equipment remaining in this case in dispute was relevantly 'plant'. It was ordered and installed under a contract separate from the contract under which the building designed for use as a department store was erected. The equipment had as its purpose the lighting of the department store in the manner considered most appropriate for the use of the building in carrying on the trade therein of selling such goods as are commonly found on sale in a department store. The equipment was not integral structurally with the building.

However, the question in any case such as this is basically one of fact and degree for the Special Commissioners to decide. It is not for your Lordships' House to substitute its view unless an error of law is to be discerned as having been made by the Special Commissioners, applying well-known principles. In common with your Lordships, whose opinions I have been able to peruse in draft, I am unable to discern any error in law, and accordingly I also would dismiss this appeal.

LORD BRIDGE OF HARWICH. My Lords, I have had the advantage of reading in advance the speech of my noble and learned friend on the Woolsack. I entirely agree with it and for the reasons he gives I too would dismiss the appeal.

Appeal dismissed.

Solicitors: *Clifford-Turner* (for the taxpayer company); *Solicitor of Inland Revenue.*

Mary Rose Plummer   Barrister.

Grant v Borg

HOUSE OF LORDS

LORD DIPLOCK, LORD FRASER OF TULLYBELTON, LORD RUSSELL OF KILLOWEN, LORD SCARMAN AND LORD BRIDGE OF HARWICH

15 MARCH, 22 APRIL 1982

Immigration – Illegal entry and other offences – Time limit for prosecution – Continuing offences – Remaining in United Kingdom beyond time limited for leave – Immigrant applying for further leave to remain – Leave to remain expiring while application being considered – Immigrant refused further leave to remain and then making further application to Home Office – Application subsequently refused – Whether immigrant 'knowingly' committing offence when leave expiring or when further application refused – Immigration Act 1971, s 24(1)(b)(i).

On 8 November 1975 the appellant, a non-patrial, entered the United Kingdom as a visitor with leave to remain only until 8 May 1976. On 27 April 1976 the appellant applied to the immigration authorities for further leave to remain without any restriction on his obtaining employment. His original leave expired while that application was being considered. On 17 January 1977 his application for further leave was refused but he was told he could refer the matter to the Home Office if he gave notice of such intention within 14 days. On 31 January he applied for all conditions on his leave to remain in the United Kingdom to be revoked on the ground that he had married a woman who was settled in the United Kingdom. On 18 April 1977 that application was refused and on 26 May 1979 an information was preferred against him charging him with having, on a date between 19 April 1977 and 24 May 1979, 'knowingly' remained beyond the time limited by his leave, contrary to s 24(1)(b)(i)[a] of the Immigration Act 1971. At the hearing of the information the appellant contended that if an offence had been committed it had been committed when his original leave expired on 9 May 1976 and that therefore the information had not been preferred within three years from the date of the commission of the offence, as required by ss 24(3) and 28 of the 1971 Act. The magistrates convicted the appellant on the ground that his leave had been extended ex gratia by the Home Office to 18 April 1977 and that therefore the offence had not occurred until 19 April 1977, although it was later conceded by the respondent on appeal that the magistrates' finding was untenable. The appellant appealed to the Divisional Court, where the respondent submitted that, because the offence was 'knowingly' remaining beyond the time limited by the leave, the offence could not have been committed until the respondent had knowledge that his actions in fact contravened the law and that accordingly the offence could have been committed at any time up until all hope of obtaining further leave was extinguished on 18 April 1977 and could therefore have been committed within three years prior to the information being laid depending on when the appellant first knew that his leave had in fact expired. The Divisional Court accepted that argument and remitted the case to the magistrates to determine the date when the appellant first knew that his leave had expired. The appellant appealed to the House of Lords.

Held – The appeal would be allowed for the following reasons—

(1) Applying the principle that ignorance of the law was not a defence to a criminal charge, the offence of 'knowingly' remaining beyond the time limited for leave to enter, contrary to s 24(1)(b)(i) of the 1971 Act, was committed if the person overstaying his leave merely had knowledge of the facts material to the offence without having knowledge of the relevant law. Accordingly, if the appellant had believed up until all hope of obtaining further leave was extinguished on 18 April 1977 that his leave had not

---

a Section 24(1), so far as material, is set out at p 261 *b*, post

expired, that would have been merely a mistake of law on his part and would not have affected the fact that his leave had in fact expired on 9 May 1976 (see p 258 *j*, p 260 *c* to *g* and p 263 *b* to *d* and *h j*, post).

(2)　The offence under s 24(1)(*b*)(i) of the 1971 Act of knowingly remaining beyond the time limited by the leave, not being a continuing offence, could only be committed on the day after the leave expired and not thereafter.　Accordingly, the appellant had committed an offence under s 24(1)(*b*)(i) on 9 May 1976 and since an information had not been preferred against him within three years of that date the prosecution was time-barred (see p 258 *j*, p 260 *e* to *g* and p 263 *f* to *j*, post).

Notes
For illegal entry and similar offences, see 4 Halsbury's Laws (4th edn) para 1027.
　　For the Immigration Act 1971, ss 24, 28, see 41 Halsbury's Statutes (3rd edn) 43, 49.

Cases referred to in opinions
R v Immigration Appeal Tribunal, ex p Subramaniam [1976] 3 All ER 604, [1977] QB 190, [1976] 3 WLR 630, CA, 2 Digest (Reissue) 220, *1233*.
R v Tzanatos (17 March 1978, unreported), CA.
Secretary of State for Trade and Industry v Hart [1982] 1 All ER 817, [1982] 1 WLR 481, DC.
Singh (Gurdev) v R [1974] 1 All ER 26, [1973] 1 WLR 1444, DC, 2 Digest (Reissue) 224, *1243*.
Suthendran v Immigration Appeal Tribunal [1976] 3 All ER 611, [1977] AC 359, [1976] 3 WLR 725, HL, 2 Digest (Reissue) 221, *1234*.

Appeal
On 1 October 1979 in the Wells Street Magistrates' Court the justices of the Inner London Area acting in and for the petty sessional division of North Westminster heard an information laid by the respondent, Pc Mark Grant, that, on a date between 19 April 1977 and 24 May 1979 at a place unknown within the United Kingdom, the appellant, Mario Borg, being a person who was not a patrial and having leave to enter or remain in the United Kingdom only until 18 April 1977, knowingly remained beyond the time limited by the leave, contrary to s 24(1)(*b*)(i) of the Immigration Act 1971.　The appellant was found guilty and fined £50 and a recommendation of deportation was made.　On an appeal by way of case stated the Divisional Court of the Queen's Bench Division (Donaldson LJ and Forbes J) on 29 June 1981 ordered that the determination of the justices be set aside, the appeal allowed, the conviction quashed and the case remitted to the justices for rehearing.　The Divisional Court refused the appellant leave to appeal to the House of Lords but certified, under s 1(2) of the Administration of Justice Act 1960, that a point of law of general public importance was involved in the decision.　Pursuant to leave granted by the Appeal Committee of the House of Lords on 13 July 1981 the appellant appealed to the House of Lords against the order of the Divisional Court that the case be reheard by the justices.　The facts are set out in the opinion of Lord Russell.

Michael Beloff QC and *Owen Davies* for the appellant.
L K Lassman for the respondent.

Their Lordships took time for consideration.

22 April.　The following opinions were delivered.

LORD DIPLOCK.　My Lords, I have had the advantage of reading in draft the speech prepared by my noble and learned friend Lord Bridge.　I agree with it and with the order he has proposed.

LORD FRASER OF TULLYBELTON.　My Lords, I have had the advantage of reading in advance the speech prepared by my noble and learned friend Lord Bridge.　I agree with it and with the order he proposes.

LORD RUSSELL OF KILLOWEN. My Lords, the appellant is a non-patrial who entered this country on 8 November 1975 with leave to remain as a visitor until 8 May 1976 which had expired by 9 May 1976. He did not then leave and remained here until information was preferred against him on 26 May 1979 that he had committed an offence under s 24(1)(b)(i) of the Immigration Act 1971, which makes it an offence if a non-patrial 'having only limited leave to . . . remain . . . knowingly . . . remains beyond the time limited by the leave'.

Two points arise for special consideration. One is that the offence is not a continuing offence: on the first day of so remaining the offence is committed, which, if nothing more be said, would thus far have been 9 May 1976 (see *Singh (Gurdev) v R* [1974] 1 All ER 26, [1973] 1 WLR 1444). The other is that by virtue of ss 24(3) and 28 the information must be preferred not later than three years after the committing of the offence, which means that if nothing more be said the information was too late to be entertained by the magistrates.

The information charged the offence as having been committed on a date unknown between 19 April 1977 and 24 May 1979. The explanation for the selection of those dates, which if established as the correct bracket of time would mean that the information was preferred within the 3-year limitation, is to be found in the following facts.

On 27 April 1976 the appellant applied to the authorities for further leave to remain and without conditions against obtaining employment. While this application was being considered or processed his leave to remain had expired on 9 May. On 17 January 1977 his application was refused; but at the same time he was told that he could refer the matter to the Under-Secretary of State at the Home Office if he gave notice of such intention within 14 days. At the expiration of that period, on 31 January 1977, he applied for revocation of the occupational ban because he had married here. On 18 April 1977 this was refused.

The selection of 19 April 1977 as the first possible date of the offence was presumably because the prosecution thought either that in some sort his original leave to remain was extended until the last refusal on 18 April 1977 or that he would not be 'knowingly' remaining while he still had hope that his applications might be acceded to.

It would appear that in their dealings with the appellant's various approaches the authorities were making some extra-statutory attempts to mitigate the rigour of the law laid down by this House in the *Suthendran v Immigration Appeal Tribunal* [1976] 3 All ER 611, [1977] AC 359, the decision of the Appellate Committee having been announced at the conclusion of the hearing in July 1976. That attempt was pursued by the Immigration (Variation of Leave) Order 1976, SI 1976/1572, which, however, by its terms did not apply to the appellant. It was, rightly in my view, accepted by counsel for the respondent in this House that in law the only leave to remain under the Act expired by 9 May 1976.

The magistrates convicted the appellant, and at the request of the appellant stated a case for the consideration of the Divisional Court. The magistrates (in brief) expressed their opinion that the leave to remain had been 'ex gratia' extended by the Home Office to 18 April 1977, and that the spirit of the Immigration (Variation of Leave) Order 1976 had been adopted in favour of the appellant and his leave to remain had as a matter of fact been extended at the discretion of the Secretary of State for the Home Office. Thus, the 3-year limitation on proceedings did not apply.

The Divisional Court, while quashing the conviction, felt itself obliged to remit the matter to the magistrates for a rehearing so that they might determine on what date the appellant first 'knowingly' remained after his only leave to remain had expired on 9 May 1976, they not having decided on a date. The Divisional Court accepted that the only leave in law to remain expired then and that nothing that happened thereafter could be in law a leave to remain, and the contrary was not argued for the respondent in this House. In taking the course of remission, the Divisional Court acted on an obiter dictum in *R v Tzanatos* (17 March 1978, unreported), CA, which was not in my opinion justified. The Divisional Court certified that a point of law of general public importance was involved in its decision, viz:

'For the purpose of ascertaining when time begins to run under S. 28(1)(a) of the Immigration Act 1971 for bringing a prosecution under S. 24(1)(b)(ii)[1] of that Act is that offence committed: (1) On the day after limited leave expires and only on that day? or (2) On that day or any later day on which the Defendant is proved to have first known that his limited leave had expired?'

The Divisional Court refused leave to appeal to this House, which was granted by the Appeal Committee. The somewhat topsy-turvy situation was then displayed that the appellant was contending that the offence was knowingly committed on 9 May 1976, and the respondent prosecutor was contending that the offence was not knowingly committed until all hope was finally extinguished on 18 April 1977. The appellant gave no evidence before the magistrates, before whom the prosecutor was a police constable. I am not at all sure what would happen on a remission to the magistrates. I would suppose that the appellant would, if he gave evidence, say that he well knew that his leave expired but he remained in hope that it might be extended in effect retrospectively. That evidence would present a considerable problem in cross-examination.

But even if he thought that his leave had not expired that would have been but a mistake in law. It is, I suppose, conceivable that in some circumstances under some statute the requirement of 'knowingly' can only embrace a mistake of law. But in the instant case there is quite sufficient subject matter for the word without introducing a mistake in the law that follows from known facts. An immigrant unfamiliar with the language and perhaps illiterate may, by a misunderstanding of what he was told or what was written on his passport, genuinely think as a fact that he has leave to remain; I give this as a possible example of a case in which he would lack the knowledge in point of fact that he was remaining after the expiration of his leave. But, if it were the case of his thinking that that which was not in law leave was in law leave, that would be to show ignorance of the law and does not enable him to plead lack of knowledge.

In those circumstances it is, in my opinion, clear that in this case the only possible answer is that the offence was committed on 9 May 1976 and the prosecution was time-barred before the information was preferred. Accordingly, while retaining that part of the order of the Divisional Court which quashed the conviction, I would set aside that part which remitted the case to the magistrates.

In the circumstances, I do not think that the questions of law posed can usefully be answered in general terms. Indeed, such answer might be misleading.

Accordingly, I would allow the appeal to the extent indicated.

LORD SCARMAN. My Lords, I have had the advantage of reading a draft of the speech to be delivered by my noble and learned friend Lord Bridge. I agree with it. I would allow the appeal. I would answer the certified question in the way my noble and learned friend proposes.

LORD BRIDGE OF HARWICH. My Lords, this is an appeal by leave of your Lordships' House from a decision of the Queen's Bench Divisional Court (Donaldson LJ and Forbes J) quashing the appellant's conviction by the North Westminster Magistrates' Court of an offence under s 24(1)(b)(i) of the Immigration Act 1971 but remitting the case to that court for rehearing in the light of the Divisional Court's judgment.

The essential facts are conveniently summarised in the case stated by the justices as follows:

'(a) The appellant was not a "Patrial" and had no right of abode in the United Kingdom within the meaning of Section 2 of the Immigration Act 1971.

(b) The appellant had entered the United Kingdom on the 8th November 1975 as a visitor with limited leave to remain only until the 8th May 1976. On the 27th April 1976 he called at the Home Office seeking the grant of further leave to remain in the United Kingdom and take up employment. By letter dated the 17th January

---

[1] Sic. The provision referred to should be s 24(1)(b)(i)

1977 the Home Office informed the appellant of refusal of that leave but pointed out that he could have the matter referred to the Under-Secretary of State for the Home Office (Appeals Section) provided notice was given of that intention not later than 14 days after the date of that letter (the 17th January 1977).

(c) The appellant called at the Home Office on the 31st January 1966 and requested revocation of conditions on the basis of his marriage to a woman settled in the United Kingdom, and by letter dated the 18th April 1977 he was notified of the Immigration Department's refusal of this application.'

Section 24(1)(b)(i) of the Act, so far as material, provides:

'A person who is not patrial shall be guilty of an offence ... (b) if, having only a limited leave to enter or remain in the United Kingdom, he knowingly ... (i) remains beyond the time limited by the leave ...'

The decision of the Divisional Court in *Singh (Gurdev) v R* [1974] 1 All ER 26, [1973] 1 WLR 1444 establishes that the offence so created is not a continuing offence but a 'once and for all' offence committed on the day following the expiry of the immigrant's limited leave to remain. The correctness of this decision has not been challenged in any later case and was not questioned at any stage in the proceedings culminating in the present appeal. The time limit for prosecution, in certain circumstances which it is common ground were present in the instant case, is three years from the date of the commission of the offence. So far, then, the law is clear.

In 1976, however, at the time of the relevant events, there was great doubt as to the true construction and effect of s 14(1) of the Act which gives to a person 'who has a limited leave ... to ... remain in the United Kingdom' a right of appeal to an adjudicator against any refusal to vary it and provides that pending determination of such an appeal the appellant shall not be required to leave the United Kingdom. I need not go into detail. The full report of *R v Immigration Appeal Tribunal, ex p Subramaniam* [1976] 3 All ER 604, [1977] QB 190, including in particular the report of the argument of counsel for the Home Secretary (see [1977] QB 190 at 196–198), shows the diverse views reflected (1) in the practice of the Home Office and the appellate authorities under the Act up to 1976, (2) in the decision of the Divisional Court given in February 1976 and (3) in the decision of the Court of Appeal given in May 1976. The doubt was not finally resolved until the decision of this House in *Suthendran v Immigration Appeal Tribunal* [1976] 3 All ER 611, [1977] AC 359, which affirmed, by a majority, what I may perhaps respectfully call the rigorous and literalist view of s 14(1) first expressed by the Divisional Court in *Ex p Subramaniam*, sc that, if an application for extension of the period of a limited leave to remain was made during the currency of that leave, but, following some administrative delay, refused after the period the leave had expired, the applicant had no right of appeal to an adjudicator or to the consequential benefits accruing from such an appeal under s 14(1) of the Act. Although the speeches in this case were not delivered until 27 October 1976, the effect of the majority decision was announced at the conclusion of the argument on 28 July 1976 (see [1977] AC 359 at 363).

Following this decision, the Secretary of State, in order no doubt to alleviate the inevitable hardship which would in many cases flow from the strict construction of s 14(1) which had prevailed, exercised his power under the Act to provide by statutory instrument that, subject to certain exceptions, an applicant for extension of a limited leave to remain should enjoy an automatic extension of that leave until 28 days after the decision on the application, thus ensuring that he would not be deprived of his right of appeal under s 14(1) by administrative delay: see the Immigration (Variation of Leave) Order 1976, SI 1976/1572. The statutory instrument came into operation on 27 September 1976. It did not apply to a case such as that of the present appellant, whose limited leave to remain had expired before that date.

I have thought it right to explain this background at some length in order to account for the offer by the Home Office to the appellant on 17 January 1977 to have the matter referred to the Under-Secretary of State for the Home Office (Appeals Section). This was presumably an attempt to provide, outside the statutory machinery, for something roughly comparable to an appeal to an adjudicator under s 14(1), for the benefit of those excluded from the new rights conferred by the statutory instrument.

The information was laid against the appellant on 26 May 1979 and alleged that the offence under s 24(1)(b)(i) was committed between 19 April 1977 and 24 May 1979. The defence took the point that the prosecution was out of time: the offence had been committed on 9 May 1976. The prosecution, brought by the respondent constable, was not legally represented and hence could give the magistrates' court no assistance.

The justices held that 'on the facts the Appellant's leave to remain had been "ex gratia" extended to the 18th April 1977 as per Home Office letter'. This conclusion is manifestly untenable and no argument was addressed to the Divisional Court or to your Lordships' House in support of it.

It is clear from the judgment of Donaldson LJ that, apart from authority, he would simply have allowed the appeal on the ground that, applying the *Suthendran* principle, the offence was committed on 9 May 1976 and the prosecution was out of time. The respondent, however, now represented by counsel, took a new point. It was submitted, in view of the word 'knowingly' in the definition of the offence, that the offence could have been committed on any date after the appellant's limited leave in fact expired whenever the appellant first knew that his leave had expired. Counsel supported his submission on this point by reference to an unreported decision of the Court of Appeal, Criminal Division in *R v Tzanatos* on 17 March 1978. I am bound to say first, with respect, that it was wrong to allow this new point to be taken at all. It was not a point of pure law arising from facts found in the case stated. If the appellant's state of mind was relevant, it was for the prosecution to pursue the matter in evidence at the trial and obtain from the justices the appropriate findings of fact in the case stated. It is difficult to see how they could possibly have done so. But in any event it could not be right to send the case back to give the prosecution a second chance to prove the commission of an offence within the limitation period of three years before 26 May 1979.

In *R v Tzanatos* the appellant had been convicted on indictment of an offence under s 24(1)(b)(i) of the 1971 Act alleged in the relevant count to have been committed 'on a day between 30th September, 1976 and 18th February, 1977'. The appellant's limited leave to remain expired on 30 September 1976. He subsequently applied for an extension. This application was refused in February 1977 and it would appear that notice of the refusal was received by the appellant not later than 17 February 1977. The judgment of the court (Geoffrey Lane LJ, Thompson and Stephen Brown JJ) was delivered extempore by Geoffrey Lane LJ. No point was taken that the prosecution was out of time. The argument for the appellant, as summarised in the judgment, is difficult to follow. It was described by Geoffrey Lane LJ as a totally false point. However, counsel for the respondent in the present case relied on the following passage in the judgment:

'What the prosecution have to prove is that on the date laid in the indictment the defendant was in the position of knowingly remaining in this country beyond the time limited by that leave. In this particular case, the prosecution has succeeded in laying it accurately. They were not in a position precisely to pin-point the date on which this man became seised of the necessary knowledge. They laid it in fact correctly, and as it turns out, on the defendant's own evidence, the material date was 17 February 1977, which lay between the two dates selected by the prosecution for their indictment.'

It was submitted that, by necessary implication, this passage establishes two propositions. First, that the knowledge required to establish guilt of an offence under s 24(1)(b)(i) is not merely knowledge of the relevant facts which prove the commission of the offence but also knowledge in law that the offence has been committed. Second, that the date of the commission of the offence is not necessarily the day after the immigrant's limited leave to remain expires, but may be any later date when he is still remaining following expiry of his leave to remain and when he first becomes aware that he is guilty of an offence in so doing. It was on the basis of accepting these two propositions that the Divisional Court ordered the case to be remitted for rehearing. They certified that the following point of law of general public importance was involved in their decision:

'For the purpose of ascertaining when time begins to run under S. 28(1)(*a*) of the Immigration Act 1971 for bringing a prosecution under S. 24(1)(*b*)(ii)[1] of that Act is that offence committed: (1) On the day after limited leave expires and only on that day? or (2) On that day or any later day on which the Defendant is proved to have first known that his limited leave had expired?'

If the Court of appeal in *R v Tzanatos* intended to enunciate either of these propositions accepted by the Divisional Court, I must express my respectful but emphatic dissent from both.

First, the principle that ignorance of the law is no defence in crime is so fundamental that to construe the word 'knowingly' in a criminal statute as requiring not merely knowledge of the facts material to the offender's guilt, but also knowledge of the relevant law, would be revolutionary and, to my mind, wholly unacceptable. I reserve my opinion whether the courts might nevertheless be driven to that extremity if a statutory offence embodying a requirement of knowledge in the definition of the offence were of such a nature that it was impossible to envisage circumstances in which the facts necessary to establish the offender's guilt would not be known to him. But that is certainly not this case. It would be unusual, but by no means impossible, for an immigrant (as, for example, one who was wholly illiterate) to remain beyond the time in fact limited by his leave, but nevertheless to be honestly mistaken in believing that his leave had not expired. I should mention in this connection a reference made in the course of argument by counsel for the respondent to the decision of the Divisional Court (Ormrod LJ and Woolf J) in *Secretary of State for Trade and Industry v Hart* [1982] 1 All ER 817, [1982] 1 WLR 481 on 24 November 1981, which considered the mens rea required under the provisions of s 13(5) and (6) of the Companies Act 1976, which make it an offence for a person to act as auditor of a company at a time when he knows that he is disqualified for appointment to that office. As the only report of the case made available was that in The Times newspaper (see (1981) Times, 30 November) and your Lordships heard no argument on the statute, it would, it seems to me, be wholly inappropriate either to look to that case as establishing any proposition of law relevant to the present appeal or to make any comment on it.

Second, the logic of the decision in *Singh (Gurdev) v R* leads, to my mind, inexorably to the conclusion that an offence under s 24(1)(*b*)(i) of the 1971 Act can only be committed on the day after the limited leave expires, in just the same way as the offence of knowingly entering the United Kingdom without leave under s 24(1)(*a*) can only be committed on the day of entry. In either case, if the offence cannot be proved to have been committed on that day because the immigrant remained or entered in ignorance of some fact constituting a necessary element of the offence, his acquisition of knowledge of that fact on a later date, when he is still in the United Kingdom without leave, will not render him guilty of any offence on that later date.

It is right to add that these conclusions with respect to criminal liability under s 24 in no way affect the liability of the immigrant who remains beyond the time limited by his leave to deportation under s 3(5)(*a*) or the liability of the person who has entered without leave to removal as an 'illegal entrant' pursuant to s 4(2) and Sch 2.

My Lords, for these reasons I would allow the appeal, affirm that part of the order of the Divisional Court which quashed the appellant's conviction, but set aside that part which remitted the case to the justices for rehearing. I would answer the certified question to the effect that an offence under s 24(1)(*b*)(i) of the 1971 Act can be committed on the day after the limited leave expires and only on that day.

Appeal allowed. Certified question answered accordingly.

Solicitors: *Winstanley-Burgess* (for the appellant); *R E T Birch* (for the respondent).

Mary Rose Plummer   Barrister.

---

[1] Sic. The provision referred to should be s 24(1)(*b*)(i)

R v Immigration Officer, ex parte Shah

QUEEN'S BENCH DIVISION (CROWN OFFICE LIST)
WOOLF J
6 NOVEMBER, 2 DECEMBER 1981

Immigration – Leave to enter – Refusal of leave – Removal of immigrant – Direction to airline to remove immigrant – Validity – Locus standi of immigrant to challenge validity of direction – Direction to remove immigrant when his application to enter finally resolved – Whether direction valid if merely indicating immigrant might be required to be removed – Whether direction must indicate immediate requirement to remove immigrant – Immigration Act 1971, Sch 2, para 8(1)(b).

The applicant was an Indian and a citizen of the United Kingdom and Colonies who had been working in Kenya but was required to leave that country. His family had settled in England and in July 1981 he went to England with the intention of settling there, but arrived without the necessary entry voucher and on arrival was refused leave to enter. He was however allowed temporary admission pending consideration of his case but was notified that the immigration officer proposed under para 8(1)[a] of Sch 2 to the Immigration Act 1971 to give directions to an airline for his removal from the United Kingdom and was then given a copy of a direction, dated 6 July 1981, by the immigration officer to an airline, which was a printed common form direction, directing the airline to remove the applicant to India 'as soon as his application to enter the United Kingdom is finally resolved'. The applicant made representations to the Home Office but the department indicated that there appeared to be no grounds for allowing him to remain in the United Kingdom. Accordingly, on 10 August, the immigration officer amended the direction of 6 July by inserting in it the date and flight for the applicant's removal by the airline to India. The Home Office then decided to give further consideration to the applicant's case, so the immigration officer reamended the direction to the airline back to its original form. In September the Home Office finally decided to refuse the applicant permission to remain. On 23 September the immigration officer purported to give a further direction to the airline to remove the applicant to India on or after 25 September and asked for the flight on which it was proposed to remove him. However, by then more than two months had elapsed from the date on which the applicant was first refused leave to enter, and therefore under para 8(2) of Sch 2 to the 1971 Act the immigration officer had no power to give a further direction which, under para 10[b], should have been given by the Secretary of State in accordance with para 8(1)(c) of Sch 2, and should probably have directed removal of the applicant to Kenya. The applicant applied for an order of certiorari to quash the directions given to the airline on the grounds (i) that the direction of 6 July, both in its original form and after reamendment back to its original form, did not comply with the requirement in para 8(1)(b) of Sch 2 that a direction should require the airline to remove the immigrant in an aircraft 'indicated' in the direction and was no more than a notification of intention to give a direction at a later stage, and (ii) that the direction given on 23 September was invalid because it ought to have been given by the Secretary of State, in accordance with para 10, and not by the immigration officer. The Home Office submitted that as the directions were not addressed to the applicant he had no locus standi to challenge their validity. There was evidence that India might not be willing to accept the applicant.

Held – The application for certiorari would be granted for the following reasons—

(1) Directions given to an airline under para 8(1) of Sch 2 to the 1971 Act were not merely notifications to the airline of its obligations but were part of the machinery of the 1971 Act for removing an immigrant which could prejudice the immigrant, because,

---

a   Paragraph 8 is set out at p 267 *a* to *c*, post
b   Paragraph 10 is set out at p 267 *d* to *f*, post

provided a direction was valid, it empowered the immigration officer, under para 11^c of Sch 2, to place the immigrant to whom the direction related on board an aircraft for removal from the United Kingdom. An immigrant affected by a direction given under para 8(1) was therefore entitled, in appropriate circumstances, to challenge its validity. It followed that the applicant had the necessary locus standi to challenge the validity of the directions given to the airline for his removal (see p 267 *j* to p 268 *c*, post).

(2) A direction given by an immigration officer pursuant to para 8(1)(*b*) was only valid if it clearly indicated that the immigrant was then required to be removed by the airline. Although a valid direction might be derived from more than one document a direction was incomplete if it merely indicated that the immigrant might be required to be removed at a later date. It followed that the original direction given on 6 July was invalid because it only indicated that the airline might be required to remove the applicant when his application to remain was finally resolved, and, although if the amendment made on 10 August had stood it would have validated the original direction, since it had been reamended back to its original defective form it remained invalid. The direction given in September was likewise invalid (see p 268 *f* to *h* and p 269 *a b*, post).

(3) Furthermore, even though the applicant conceded he had no right to remain in the United Kingdom, it would, in all the circumstances, be a wrong exercise of the court's discretion to refuse him the relief sought because to do so would mean placing him on an aircraft pursuant to invalid directions and removing him to a country (India) which might not be prepared to receive him (see p 268 *j* to p 269 *b*, post).

Notes

For removal of person refused leave to enter, see 4 Halsbury's Laws (4th edn) para 1008.

For the Immigration Act 1971, Sch 2, paras 8, 10, 11, see 41 Halsbury's Statutes (4th edn) 64, 65.

Application for judicial review

Nitinchandra Somchand Shah applied, with the leave of Phillips J granted on 15 October 1981, for orders of prohibition and certiorari in respect of purported directions given by an immigration officer to an airline for the applicant's removal from the United Kingdom to India, pursuant to para 8(1) of Sch 2 to the Immigration Act 1971. The facts are set out in the judgment.

Malcolm Knott for the applicant.
David Latham for the respondent.

Cur adv vult

2 December. **WOOLF J** read the following judgment: Nitinchandra Somchand Shah seeks judicial review in respect of removal directions given by an immigration officer on 6 July and 23 September 1981. He obtained leave to make the application on 15 October 1981 from Phillips J. The unusual feature of the case is that it is conceded by Mr Shah that he has no legal right to remain in this country and that, if the Secretary of State had properly exercised his powers, he had power to remove him. He contends however that the directions which have been given for his removal are unlawful and of no effect. This has led to three issues being raised in argument before me. Firstly, is the applicant entitled to seek relief in respect of a direction which is given to an airline for his removal (the standing issue)? Secondly, the validity of the direction (the validity issue). Thirdly, assuming the direction was not properly given should the court in its discretion refuse to intervene if the airline raises no objection as to the form of the direction (the discretion issue)?

The facts giving rise to the application can be stated briefly. As in many of these cases, they indicate a situation which invites sympathy for the applicant. His parents are

---

c   Paragraph 11 is set out at p 267 *f*, post

Indian but he was born in Kenya on 7 April 1958. In addition to his parents there are five
sisters and one brother. All the sisters were born in Kenya, but the brother was born in
India after the family returned there from Kenya in 1964. While in India in June 1975
the father, as the family were citizens of the United Kingdom and Colonies, applied
under the special voucher scheme to come to the United Kingdom for settlement.

When the applicant became 18 a separate application had to be made by him in his
own right and this he made in July 1976. The applicant completed his studies in India
in August 1978. He was then unable to find work there and so he returned to Kenya
with a work permit for one year which expired on 9 June 1980. This permit was
extended until 5 July 1981 when he was required to leave Kenya.

In the meantime the remainder of the family had already arrived in England, partly
as the result of marriages that had taken place to persons settled in the United Kingdom
and partly under the special voucher scheme.

However, by the time the applicant was required to leave Kenya he had no voucher,
but, notwithstanding this, on 6 July 1981 he travelled from Kenya to London and on his
arrival, having been interviewed, he was refused leave to enter, the notice of refusal
reciting as the reason the fact that, although the applicant was a citizen of the United
Kingdom and Colonies holding a United Kingdom passport, he did not hold a special
voucher. The notice went on to state: 'I have given/propose to give directions for your
removal on a date and flight to be arranged.'

He was also given a copy of a direction to British Airways, also dated 6 July, given by
an immigration officer on a printed form the relevant part of which reads: 'I hereby
direct that the above-named person(s) be removed by you from the United Kingdom on
a/your United Kingdom to Bombay (place) (India) (country) scheduled service as soon as
(a) his/her application to enter the United Kingdom is finally resolved.' I do not need to
read the remainder of that document, but it is relevant to point out that the part of the
form which I have read was stamped on the document which indicates that, although as
far as I am aware no similar case has been before the courts, the directions under attack
are ones which have been given in a great many cases.

The reason that this form of direction was used is because, although the applicant had
been refused leave to enter, there were clearly features of the case which required
consideration by higher authority and, to give time, he was temporarily allowed
admission under the provision of the Immigration Act 1971 which enables this to be
done. The representations which the applicant made, and which were made on his
behalf, were unsuccessful, and on 21 September 1981 the Minister of State at the Home
Office wrote indicating that he could see no strong compassionate grounds for an exercise
of discretion and accordingly 'the proper course therefore is to remove him and we shall
now make fresh arrangements to do so.'

The direction to which I have already referred was amended on 10 August 1981 by
inserting a particular flight for the applicant's removal, namely, flight BA 003 to Bombay
on 13 August 1981. There was then a further amendment while the matter was being
considered by the Minister of State which reverted to the previous form.

The final document dealing with removal is a pro-forma letter dated 23 September
1981 to British Airways, which having recited the applicant's name, goes on to say:

> 'This passenger was refused leave to enter the United Kingdom on 6.7.81.
> Directions for his removal from the United Kingdom were given to you on 6.7.81.
> I enclose a copy of those directions for ease of reference. I am writing to advise you
> that the passenger may be removed after 25.9.81. (date). Will you now please tell
> me on what flight you propose to have him removed.'

That document is the second of the two directions which are the subject of this
application. The only other matter that I should mention is that in addition to bringing
these proceedings the applicant has also applied to the European Commission of Human
Rights complaining about his proposed removal.

The relevant statutory provisions are to be found mainly in Sch 2 of the Immigration
Act 1971. Paragraph 8 provides:

'(1) Where a person arriving in the United Kingdom is refused leave to enter, an immigration officer may, subject to sub-paragraph (2) below—(a) give the captain of the ship or aircraft in which he arrives directions requiring the captain to remove him from the United Kingdom in that ship or aircraft; or (b) give the owners or agents of that ship or aircraft directions requiring them to remove him from the United Kingdom in any ship or aircraft specified or indicated in the directions, being a ship or aircraft of which they are the owners or agents; or (c) give those owners or agents directions requiring them to make arrangements for his removal from the United Kingdom in any ship or aircraft specified or indicated in the directions to a country or territory so specified, being either—(i) a country of which he is a national or citizen; or (ii) a country or territory in which he has obtained a passport or other document of identity; or (iii) a country or territory in which he embarked for the United Kingdom; or (iv) a country or territory to which there is reason to believe that he will be admitted.

(2) No directions shall be given under this paragraph in respect of anyone after the expiration of two months beginning with the date on which he was refused leave to enter the United Kingdom.'

Paragraph 10 reads:

'(1) Where it appears to the Secretary of State either (a) that directions might be given in respect of a person under paragraph 8 or 9 above, but that it is not practicable for them to be given or that, if given, they would be ineffective; or (b) that directions might have been given in respect of a person under paragraph 8 above but that the time limited by paragraph 8(2) has passed; then the Secretary of State may give to the owners or agents of any ship or aircraft any such directions in respect of that person as are authorised by paragraphs 8(1)(c).

(2) Where the Secretary of State may give directions for a person's removal in accordance with sub-paragraph (1) above, he may instead give directions for his removal in accordance with arrangements to be made by the Secretary of State to any country or territory to which he could be removed under sub-paragraph (1).

(3) The costs of complying with any directions given under this paragraph shall be defrayed by the Secretary of State.'

Paragraph 11 reads:

'A person in respect of whom directions are given under any of paragraphs 8 to 10 above may be placed, under the authority of an immigration officer, on board any ship or aircraft in which he is to be removed in accordance with the directions.'

It is to be observed that before the two months' period expires it is the immigration officer who gives directions, and after two months' period it is the Secretary of State who gives the directions. Furthermore, the Secretary of State can only give the directions which are authorised by para 8(1)(c). The Secretary of State has also to bear the costs where he gives the directions, but it is the carrier who bears the cost where the immigration officer gives the directions. I will now deal in turn with the three issues.

The standing issue

Counsel on behalf of the Home Office argued that the directions which are sought to be attacked were not addressed to the applicant, but to British Airways who had raised no objection to their form. It was British Airways who would be affected, not the applicant, if the form of the direction was defective, the purpose of the direction being to notify British Airways as to their obligations and their entitlement, if any, to be paid for his removal. While I accept that the direction is of importance to British Airways, I do not accept its validity is not capable of being of importance to a person in the position of the applicant as well. The direction is not merely a means of notifying British Airways of their obligations but is a part, and an important part, of the machinery provided in the Immigration Act 1971 for removing persons who are refused leave to enter and unlawful immigrants.

Paragraph 11 of Sch 2 is a most important provision, since without it the immigration officer would not be able to place the immigrant on board a ship or aircraft. That authority is limited to a person in respect of whom directions are given who is to be removed in accordance with the direction. If these directions were to be quashed, then an immigration officer would be acting unlawfully in placing the applicant, without his consent, on board a ship or aircraft unless and until fresh valid directions are issued. It is to be remembered that, although the present applicant had no right of appeal in respect of the directions which were in issue, directions can give rights of appeal in different circumstances, as appears from ss 16 and 17 of the Act, and in such circumstances it is a requirement that a copy of the directions is served on the applicant notifying him of his rights of appeal. Although ss 16 and 17 are not of direct application, they do tend to confirm the importance of the directions vis-à-vis the person who is to be removed. The directions are capable of prejudicing him and it is therefore right that he should be able to challenge the directions in appropriate circumstances. I therefore regard the applicant as having the necessary locus standi to make this application.

The validity issue

Counsel on behalf of the applicant contends that the practice illustrated by the documents in this case reveals use of a device to enable immigration officers to give directions in a case where really the directions should be given by the Secretary of State. He contends that the document of 6 July and the later document in the same form cannot be a direction under para 8 since there is no ship or aircraft specified or indicated in the direction to comply with the wording of para 8(1)(*b*) and there is no request to British Airways to make arrangements, which is what is involved in para 8(1)(*c*). In the view of counsel for the applicant the so-called directions are no more than a notification of an intention to make directions at a later stage. Counsel for the Home Office, on the other hand, stresses that all that is required is that the aircraft shall be 'indicated in the directions'. He contends that, as long as within a reasonable time from the giving of the directions the aircraft is ascertained, that is sufficient. He submits that the language which is used reflects earlier Acts and that Sch 2 has to be construed in the situation which now exists of many many flights which makes it very difficult to specify a suitable flight a little time ahead.

While I agree with counsel for the Home Office that the use of the word 'indicated' does suggest some degree of latitude as to the framing of a direction, I am clearly of the view that the directions in the present case fall short of the minimum requirements of Sch 2. I would see no objection to a direction being given in more than one document, but before a direction is complete it must at least make it clear that the applicant is someone whom the airline is then required to remove. The form of the stamp indicates no more than the applicant is a person who may be required to be removed. The direction could be varied pursuant to s 32 of the Act and the first amendment made on 10 August 1981 would create a valid direction. This amendment was made before the expiry of the two months' period, and if the matter had ended there the direction would have been valid. It had however to be amended again and this amendment reintroduced the defect. It follows therefore that I regard the direction as being invalid, and, if there had been an application by British Airways to quash it, I have no doubt that the court would have granted relief.

That takes me to the final issue, *the discretion issue*. This issue is related to the first issue. Counsel for the Home Office urges me as a matter of discretion to refuse relief. He stresses the applicant has no right to remain in this country and that British Airways are prepared to remove him. He contends there can be no question of the applicant being prejudiced and that the provision that the applicant is seeking to rely on is one inserted not for the applicant's benefit but for the benefit of the airline.

In support of his argument counsel for the Home Office helpfully referred me to Wade *Administrative Law* (4th edn, 1977) pp 300, 347, 560. Notwithstanding the attractive way in which counsel for the Home Office puts his argument, I have no doubt that this is a case in which it would be quite wrong to seek to exercise my discretion to refuse relief. Were I to do so, the applicant would no doubt be placed on an aircraft, pursuant to what I consider to be invalid directions. The directions are for his removal to India, a country on the evidence before me which may not be prepared to accept him. The direction has been given by the immigration officer, whereas it should have been given by the Secretary of State. The direction purports to be given under para 8(1)(*b*), whereas the Secretary of State would only have power to give a direction under para 8(1)(*c*). It is true that the Secretary of State has undoubtedly power to make a direction but it may be that he could only give a direction for the removal of the applicant to Kenya. The Secretary of State might not be prepared to make a direction for removal to that country. So far as I am aware, no consideration has been given to the question of removal of the applicant to Kenya. In my view the applicant is entitled to have the present directions quashed and I would make an order of certiorari in respect thereof. There should not however be any need for any further relief.

Order of certiorari issued.

Solicitors: *Bindman & Partners* (for the applicant); *Treasury Solicitor.*

Sepala Munasinghe Esq   Barrister.

R v Horsham Justices, ex parte Farquharson and another

QUEEN'S BENCH DIVISION
FORBES AND GLIDEWELL JJ
9, 10, 11, 13 NOVEMBER 1981

COURT OF APPEAL, CIVIL DIVISION
LORD DENNING MR, SHAW AND ACKNER LJJ
7, 8, 9, 21 DECEMBER 1981

Committal – Proceedings – Newspaper report – Contempt of court – Order postponing publication – Risk of prejudice to administration of justice – Jurisdiction of magistrates hearing committal proceedings to order postponement of publication of proceedings – Whether breach of order a contempt of court – Criminal Justice Act 1967, s 3 – Contempt of Court Act 1981, ss 4(2), 6(b).

Contempt of court – Publications concerning legal proceedings – Postponement of publication – Committal proceedings – Jurisdiction of magistrates hearing committal proceedings to order postponement of publication of proceedings – Whether breach of order a contempt of court – Criminal Justice Act 1967, s 3 – Contempt of Court Act 1981, ss 4(2), 6(b).

Four men were charged with exporting firearms and ammunition, contrary to customs regulations restricting the export of such articles. The accused first appeared before magistrates on holding charges in May 1981. On 23 June one of the accused applied to the court under s 3(2)[a] of the Criminal Justice Act 1967 to have reporting restrictions lifted and that application was granted. On 13 August 'old style' committal proceedings (which required the examination and cross-examination of witnesses to see whether there was a prima facie case for trial) were formally commenced against the accused and adjourned until October. On 27 August the Contempt of Court Act 1981 came into force. Section 4(2)[b] of that Act provided that in legal proceedings held in public the court

---

a   Section 3(2) provides: 'A magistrates' court shall, on an application for the purpose made with reference to any committal proceedings by the defendant or one of the defendants, as the case may be, order that [the restrictions on reports of committal proceedings in] the foregoing subsection shall not apply to reports of those proceedings.'

b   Section 4, so far as material, is set out at p 275 *b d*, post

had power to order that the publication of any report of the proceedings be postponed for
such period as the court thought necessary where such an order was necessary to avoid
'a substantial risk of prejudice . . . in those proceedings, or in any other proceedings
pending or imminent'. On 16 October, when committal proceedings against the accused
were resumed, the accused applied for an order under s 4(2) of the 1981 Act prohibiting
publication of any report of the committal proceedings until the commencement of any
subsequent trial. The magistrates made the order sought. A reporter and the reporter's
newspaper and union applied to the High Court for an order of certiorari to quash the
magistrates' order on the ground that the magistrates had no jurisdiction to make an
order under s 4(2) of the 1981 Act when they had already made an order under s 3(2) of
the 1967 Act. The court rejected that argument but held that the order made under s
4(2) was too wide and ought to be reconsidered by the magistrates. The reporter and the
union appealed on the issue of the magistrates' jurisdiction, contending that since the
reporting of committal proceedings was governed by the particular provisions of s 3 of
the 1967 Act the general provisions in s 4(2) of the 1981 Act relating to publication of
reports in all 'legal proceedings held in public' did not, applying the principle generalia
specialibus non derogant, apply to committal proceedings.

Held – The fact that s 3 of the 1967 Act provided for the restricting of reporting in the
specific case of committal proceedings did not prevent the restrictions on reporting
generally which were contained in s 4(2) of the 1981 Act from also applying to committal
proceedings, since the two sections imposed restrictions in different situations and for
different purposes, namely (in the case of s 3 of the 1967 Act) where publication of
committal proceedings was prejudicial to the interests of the defendant and (in the case
of s 4(2) of the 1981 Act) where publication of proceedings, whether or not prejudicial
to the defendant, would be a contempt of court (eg because it would prejudice other
persons and other trials or because it would reveal the true identity where the judge
directed a pseudonym to be used or would reveal what took place in camera or at a trial
within a trial). Accordingly, the magistrates had jurisdiction under s 4(2) of the 1981 Act
to make a postponement order, but, on the facts, the order made by the magistrates was
too wide and would be quashed (see p 281 *j*, p 283 *g j*, p 286 *d* to *j*, p 287 *f* to *j*, p 288 *a
b e f*, p 289 *e* to *j*, p 290 *d e*, p 291 *e*, p 294 *c* to *f* and p 297 *c* to *g*, post).

Per curiam. In deciding under s 4(2) of the 1981 Act whether there is a substantial risk
of prejudice to the administration of justice 'in those proceedings' the only relevant risk
of prejudice to be considered is the risk of prejudice to the proceedings being heard at the
relevant time, which in the case of committal proceedings is the risk to the committal
proceedings themselves and not any subsequent trial. However, risk of prejudice to
other 'proceedings pending or imminent', which must also be taken into account under
s 4(2), includes risks to potential proceedings in the Crown Court (see p 283 *j*, p 290 *e* and
p 296 *j* to p 297 *b*, post).

Per Lord Denning MR. When an order postponing publication is made under s 4(2)
of the 1981 Act disregard of that order does not amount to contempt unless the
publication would also be a contempt at common law (see p 284 *b c* and p 287 *b*, post).

Per Shaw and Ackner LJJ. Section 4(1) of the 1981 Act creates a new head of contempt
of court and if a journalist reports proceedings that are the subject of a postponement
order under s 4(2) he is guilty of contempt of court regardless of whether the conduct
complained of would have amounted to contempt prior to the passing of the 1981 Act
(see p 290 *c d* and p 295 *g* to *j*, post).

Per Ackner LJ. Section 6(*b*)[c] of the 1981 Act does not prevent magistrates from
making an order the breach of which would render a journalist liable to contempt
proceedings in circumstances in which he could not have been so liable at common law
(see p 296 *e f*, post).

---

c   Section 6, so far as material, is set out at p 284 *h*, post

Notes

For contempt of court arising out of the reporting of criminal proceedings, see 9 Halsbury's Laws (4th edn) para 13 and 11 ibid para 139.

For the Criminal Justice Act 1967, s 3, see 21 Halsbury's Statutes (3rd edn) 368.

As from 6 July 1981, s 3 of the 1967 Act has been replaced by the Magistrates' Courts Act 1980, s 8.

Cases referred to in judgments

A-G v Leveller Magazine Ltd [1979] 1 All ER 745, [1979] AC 440, [1979] 2 WLR 247, HL, 16 Digest (Reissue) 53, *500*.

Blackpool Corp v Starr Estate Co Ltd [1922] 1 AC 27, [1921] All ER Rep 79, HL, 11 Digest (Reissue) 219, *708*

Curry v Walter (1976) 1 Bos & P 525, 126 ER 1046, 32 Digest (Reissue) 260, *2165*.

F (a minor), (publication of information), Re [1977] 1 All ER 114, [1977] Fam 58, [1976] 3 WLR 813, CA, 16 Digest (Reissue) 44, *430*.

Kimber v Press Association [1893] 1 QB 65, CA, 16 Digest (Reissue) 172, *1715*.

Lewis v Levy (1858) EB & E 537, 120 ER 610, 32 Digest (Reissue) 262, *2175*.

R v Armstrong [1951] 2 All ER 219, CCA, 14(2) Digest (Reissue) 787, *6713*.

R v Beaverbrook Newspapers Ltd, Associated Newspapers Ltd [1962] NI 15, 16 Digest (Reissue) 25, *244*.

R v Blackpool Justices, ex p Beaverbrook Newspapers Ltd [1972] 1 All ER 388, [1972] 1 WLR 95, 14(1) Digest (Reissue) 223, *1605*.

R v Border Television Ltd, ex p A-G, R v Newcastle Chronicle and Journal Ltd, ex p A-G (1978) 68 Cr App R 375, DC.

R v Bow Street Magistrate, ex p Kray [1968] 3 All ER 872, [1969] 1 QB 473, [1968] 3 WLR 1111, DC, 14(1) Digest (Reissue) 222, *1604*.

R v Clarke, ex p Crippen (1910) 103 LT 636, 16 Digest (Reissue) 9, *76*.

R v Clement (1821) 4 B & Ald 218, 106 ER 918, 16 Digest (Reissue) 7, *44*.

R v Duffy, ex p Nash [1960] 2 All ER 891, [1960] 2 QB 188, [1960] 3 WLR 320, DC, 16 Digest (Reissue) 41, *414*.

R v Evening News, ex p Hobbs [1925] 2 KB 158, DC, 16 Digest (Reissue) 21, *211*.

R v Gray (1865) 10 Cox CC 184.

R v Greater London Council, ex p Blackburn [1976] 3 All ER 184, [1976] 1 WLR 550, CA, Digest (Cont Vol E) 587, *183a*.

R v IRC, ex p National Federation of Self-Employed and Small Businesses Ltd [1981] 2 All ER 93, [1981] 2 WLR 722, HL; rvsg in part [1980] 2 All ER 378, [1980] 1 QB 407, [1980] 2 WLR 579, CA.

R v Parke [1903] 2 KB 432, [1900–3] All ER Rep 721, DC, 16 Digest (Reissue) 20, *206*.

R v Poulson (1974) Times, 2 January.

R v Russell, ex p Beaverbrook Newspapers Ltd [1968] 4 All ER 695, [1969] 1 QB 342, [1968] 3 WLR 999, DC, 14(1) Digest (Reissue) 222, *1603*.

R v Sanderson (1915) 31 TLR 447, CCA, 14 (2) Digest (Reissue) 503, *4124*.

R v Socialist Worker Printers and Publishers Ltd, ex p A-G [1975] 1 All ER 142, [1975] QB 637, [1974] 3 WLR 801, DC, 16 Digest (Reissue) 52, *496*.

R v Wright (1799) 8 TR 293, 101 ER 1396, 32 Digest (Reissue) 225, *1921*.

Scott v Scott [1913] AC 417, [1911–13] All ER Rep 1, HL, 16 Digest (Reissue) 42, *426*.

Seward v The Vera Cruz (1884) 10 App Cas 59, [1881–5] All ER Rep 216, HL, 1(1) Digest (Reissue) 38, *253*.

Wednesbury Corp v Ministry of Housing and Local Government [1965] 1 All ER 186, [1965] 1 WLR 261, CA, 18 Digest (Reissue) 157, *1280*.

Cases also cited

A-G v Butterworth [1962] 3 All ER 326, sub nom *Re A-G's Application* [1963] 1 QB 696, CA.

A-G v Times Newspapers Ltd [1973] 3 All ER 54, [1974] AC 273, HL.

Delbert-Evans v Davies and Watson [1945] 2 All ER 167, sub nom *R v Davies, ex p Delbert-Evans* [1945] KB 435, DC.

R v Chief Immigration Officer, Heathrow Airport, ex p Salamat Bibi [1976] 3 All ER 843,
   [1976] 1 WLR 979, CA.
R v Kray (1969) 53 Cr App R 412.
R v Newcastle upon Tyne Justices, ex p Vickers (1981) Times, 18 April.

Applications for judicial review

Ian William Farquharson, the National Union of Journalists and West Sussex County
Times Ltd applied by leave granted on 6 November 1981 to the Divisional Court of the
Queen's Bench Division for judicial review by way of an order of certiorari to quash an
order made by the Horsham magistrates under s 4(2) of the Contempt of Court Act 1981
prohibiting the publication of any report of the committal proceedings in a prosecution
brought by the Customs and Excise Commissioners against Sayeed Bukhari, Barry
Howson, Derek Moore and Peter Amos for exporting firearms and ammunition contrary
to s 56(2) of the Customs and Excise Act 1952 and the Export of Goods (Control) Order
1978, SI 1978/796. The magistrates' order prohibited the reporting of any part of the
committal proceedings until the commencement of any trial hearing. The grounds on
which the applicants applied for judicial review were (i) that the magistrates had no
jurisdiction to make an order under s 4(2) of the 1981 Act in committal proceedings
when reporting restrictions had already been lifted, (ii) that the magistrates had made the
order without evidence that the interests of justice would be prejudiced, (iii) that no
reasonable magistrates properly instructed could on the available evidence have reached
the conclusion that publication would prejudice the interests of justice, and (iv) that the
order was unnecessarily wide in its restriction of publication of reports of the
proceedings. The respondents to the applicants' motion were the magistrates, the
Commissioners of Customs and Excise and the defendants to the commissioners'
prosecution. The facts are set out in the judgment of Forbes J.

Andrew Nicol for Mr Farquharson and the National Union of Journalists.
Desmond Browne for West Sussex County Times Ltd.
Mordecai Levene for Mr Howson and Mr Amos.
Brian Leary QC and *Sibghatullah Kadri* for Mr Bukhari.
Simon D Brown for the Customs and Excise Commissioners.

Cur adv vult

13 November. The following judgments were read.

FORBES J. These are two motions arising out of the same proceedings and raising the
same points. We have heard them together. In the first, Mr Farquharson and the
National Union of Journalists, and in the second, the West Sussex County Times Ltd,
apply for orders of certiorari to bring up and quash a certain decision of the Horsham
justices.

The Horsham justices are sitting as examining justices in a case involving four
defendants charged with various offences. The charges are, as Glidewell J mentioned in
the last case, an offence of conspiracy to evade the Export of Goods (Control) Order 1978,
SI 1978/796 controlling the export of firearms and ammunition, and certain specific
offences of exporting firearms contrary to the provisions of that order. The prosecution
is in the hands of the Commissioners of Customs and Excise.

The accused first appeared before the Horsham justices on holding charges on 12 May
1981. There have been various appearances since then. On 23 June, at one of these
appearances, the solicitor acting for Mr Bukhari applied to the court under s 3 of the
Criminal Justice Act 1967 to have reporting restrictions lifted and that application was
acceded to. Subsequently, other charges were added. On 13 August the committal
proceedings formally started. They were 'old style' committal proceedings; that is,
proceedings to which s 1 of the Criminal Justice Act 1967 did not apply.

On 27 August the Contempt of Court Act 1981 came into force, and on the next appearance before the justices, on 16 October, counsel for two of the accused, Mr Howson and Mr Amos, applied to the justices for an order under s 4(2) of the new Act prohibiting publication of any report of the proceedings until the commencement of any subsequent trial. This application was supported by or on behalf of both the other defendants. It is this order which is now challenged by both applicants.

I should deal first with the question of locus. From *R v Russell, ex p Beaverbrook Newspapers Ltd* [1968] 3 All ER 695, [1969] 1 QB 342 it is clear that newspaper proprietors, editors and journalists are persons aggrieved so as to give them a locus to apply for certiorari in cases concerning s 3 of the 1967 Act because, on the ratio of that case, they or any of them run the risk of committing a contempt if they publish. They would also seem to have, according to that case, a locus to apply for mandamus because they have a specific legal right. I merely refer to the passage in Lord Parker CJ's judgment ([1968] 3 All ER 695 at 697, [1969] 1 QB 342 at 348).

I doubt very much whether the National Union of Journalists has any locus at all under either of those headings. However, as counsel was here both for Mr Farquharson, who clearly has such a locus, and for the National Union of Journalists, the point seems to me to be academic so far as this hearing is concerned. I mention this point solely for the reason that I do not want it to be thought that I accept in any way that the National Union of Journalists is entitled to be heard on an application of this kind in these circumstances.

There are three main grounds put forward for challenging the decision urged both by counsel for Mr Farquharson and counsel for West Sussex County Times Ltd. They are effectively: (1) that the justices had no jurisdiction to make the order under s 4(2) of the 1981 Act when they had already made an order under s 3(2) of the 1967 Act; (2) that there was inadequate material before the justices to enable them to make the order which they purported to make; and (3) that the order was wider in its terms than was necessary and was made for an indefinite time.

I should dispose of one point at the outset. It was said that a letter from the clerk to the justices indicated that the order was made for an unlimited time. We have an affidavit from the chairman of the justices which sets out the order made. It is in these terms: '. . . prohibiting the reporting of any part of the proceedings until the commencement of any trial hearing.' That is the only evidence we have of the terms of this order and it must be taken that that is the order appealed against. It is clear that any suggestion that it was unlimited in time is erroneous.

The argument on the first ground, that there was no jurisdiction to make an order under s 4(2) in the circumstances of this case, provoked an investigation into the reasons behind the passing of s 3 of the Criminal Justice Act 1967. We were referred to passages from speeches in the House of Lords in *A-G v Leveller Magazines Ltd* [1979] 1 All ER 745, [1979] AC 440, notably that of Lord Diplock ([1979] 1 All ER 745 at 749–750, [1979] AC 440 at 449–450):

'As a general rule the English system of administering justice does require that it be done in public: *Scott v Scott* [1913] AC 417, [1911–13] All ER Rep 1. If the way that courts behave cannot be hidden from the public ear and eye this provides a safeguard against judicial arbitrariness or idiosyncrasy and maintains the public confidence in the administration of justice. The application of this principle of open justice has two aspects: as respects proceedings in the court itself it requires that they should be held in open court to which the Press and public are admitted and that, in criminal cases at any rate, all evidence communicated to the court is communicated publicly. As respects the publication to a wider public of fair and accurate reports of proceedings that have taken place in court the principle requires that nothing should be done to discourage this. However, since the purpose of the general rule is to serve the ends of justice it may be necessary to depart from it where the nature or circumstances of the particular proceeding are such that the application of the general rule in its entirety would frustrate or render impracticable the administration of justice or would damage some other public interest for whose protection Parliament has made some statutory derogation from the rule.'

Of course, the public nature of the administration of justice and the right of the wider public to be informed by the press of what is taking place are matters of the greatest importance. But, as their Lordships point out in the *Leveller* case, sometimes in particular cases these matters must be subordinated to the interests of justice.

A typical case in my view is afforded by the provisions of s 3 of the 1967 Act. The wide public dissemination of the evidence given in committal proceedings may work to the prejudice of the defendants at the subsequent trial because the memory of what they have read may make it more difficult for a jury to try the case solely on the evidence before them. Most juries are robust enough to surmount this difficulty but the possibility of prejudice to the defence is there.

Weighing in the balance the importance of public dissemination of information with the importance of ensuring a fair trial, Parliament decided in s 3 of the 1967 Act that the scales moved against public dissemination and hence that section provided for a restriction on reporting of committal proceedings unless a defendant applied for that restriction to be lifted. As I read the section, once any defendant applies the justices have no discretion to refuse and, what is more, no reasons have to be given by the defendant who so applies.

It would be wholly wrong to suggest, and I think there was a suggestion of it during the course of the argument, that the justices had any duty to weigh the interests of public reporting against the interests of the defence or the interests of justice. Any such balancing of interests had already been done by Parliament in enacting that provision.

The cases, and I need not rehearse them, show two things. First, the interest which any co-accused might have in maintaining restriction on reporting was not a matter which justices could take into account. Indeed, as I have said, they appear to have no discretion to exercise in the matter at all.

Second, once the application and the inevitable order had been made, there was no possibility that that order could be recalled. Even cogent and respectable reasons for a change of heart by a defendant could not result in the revocation of the order. The justices simply have no power to revoke.

The first of these points has now been altered. The Criminal Justice (Amendment) Act 1981 provides for the insertion of a new sub-s (2A), after sub-s (2) in s 8 of the Magistrates' Courts Act 1980:

'Where in the case of two or more accused one of them objects to the making of an order under subsection (2) above, the court shall make the order if, and only if, it is satisfied after hearing the representations of the accused, that it is in the interests of justice to do so.'

That Act received the royal assent on 2 July 1981 and came into force on 2 October 1981. It had been preceded by the Magistrates' Courts Act 1980, which re-enacted in s 8, so far as I can see without alteration, the provisions of s 3 of the Criminal Justice Act 1967. As that later Act did not come into force until 6 July 1981, and these proceedings started before that date, it is the earlier Act which governs these proceedings.

To complete the statutory timetable, the Contempt of Court Act 1981 received the royal assent on 27 July 1981 and came into force on 27 August 1981.

From the dates of these enactments counsel for Mr Farquharson constructs this proposition: that in s 3 of the 1967 Act Parliament was dealing with a specific area, that of committal proceedings and the rules to be followed in reporting them; that those rules included the irrevocable nature to be attributed to a decision to lift reporting restrictions, and that although s 4(2) of the Contempt of Court Act 1981 provides a discretion to all courts to impose reporting restrictions it cannot be construed so as to upset the rules specifically laid down in the 1967 Act for committal proceedings.

This argument appears to be based on the principle generalia specialibus non derogant, as epitomised, for instance, in the speech of Lord Selborne LC in *Seward v The Vera Cruz* (1884) 10 App Cas 59 at 68, [1881–5] All ER Rep 216 at 220, and in the speech of Lord Haldane in *Blackpool Corp v Starr Estate Co Ltd* [1922] 1 AC 27 at 34, [1921] All ER Rep 79 at 82. The principle is so well known that I do not think I need go further than that.

I think this argument, founded as it is on the irrevocable nature of the decision to lift reporting restrictions, is based on a misapprehension of the effect of s 3 of the 1967 Act, of the position before the Contempt of Court Act 1981 came into force, and of the fundamental change in the law of contempt brought about by that Act.

Until that Act certain incidents during trials were well known to all journalists to be matters which should not be reported and they were not. I believe that was due, for the most part, to journalists' inherent sense of what was fair rather than the possibility of proceedings for contempt of court. That publication of those matters would be contempt, however, there is no doubt. Typical examples would be evidence given in a trial within a trial, pleas of guilty when other charges remained to be tried, and so on.

Section 4(1) of the Contempt of Court Act 1981 changed all that:

> 'Subject to this section a person is not guilty of contempt of court under the strict liability rule in respect of a fair and accurate report of legal proceedings held in public, published contemporaneously and in good faith.'

Thus, so long as it is fair, accurate, contemporaneous and bona fide it is not contempt, as I see it, to publish matters of this kind, publication of which might be clearly prejudicial to a fair trial.

Section 4(2), however, then reverses the process. That gives the court power to make orders not prohibiting but postponing publication of such matters. Subsection (2) reads:

> 'In any such proceedings the court may, where it appears to be necessary for avoiding a substantial risk of prejudice to the administration of justice in those proceedings, or in any other proceedings pending or imminent, order that the publication of any report of the proceedings, or any part of the proceedings, be postponed for such period as the court thinks necessary for that purpose.'

I should, I think, just look at the definition of 'court' and 'legal proceedings'. They are to be found in s 19: '"Court" includes any tribunal or body exercising the judicial power of the State, and "legal proceedings" shall be construed accordingly.'

Thus, if I may look at the matter historically, the position before the 1967 Act was, it seems to me, this: all proceedings in all courts were reportable, subject to (a) specific instances where the court was given power to exclude both public and press, (b) some specific instances where the court has power to order non-disclosure of names, and so on (the Children and Young Persons Act 1933, for example), and (c) the general law of contempt, namely that the publication of matter intended or likely to prejudice a fair trial or the conduct of the proceedings was a contempt of court.

There may have been a common law power to order in certain cases that publication of court proceedings should be postponed until the case was concluded (see, for instance *Scott v Scott* [1913] AC 417, [1911–13] All ER Rep 1, but such cases would have been exceptional).

In general, the courts had no power to make orders prohibiting publication of any part of the proceedings. The familiar instance of the trial within a trial, which I have mentioned, was not, and has not been usually, or ever, as far as I know, the subject of an order by the trial judge. Such evidence is not reported not because of any order of the court but because the journalist knows that it would be a contempt to do so.

There might be difficult cases where fair and accurate reports of one trial might still prejudice another trial still to be held. This particular difficulty arose during the trial of the then notorious John Poulson. It is worth referring to the passage in Miller *Contempt of Court* (1976) p 118:

> 'The trial of John Poulson provides a recent example of a case in which publicity was restrained. During his examination-in-chief Poulson had referred to his association with another man against whom separate proceedings in conjunction with Poulson himself were still outstanding. Waller, J., the presiding judge, is reported as having said: I do not see myself how the press can properly report this evidence without running the risk of being in contempt of this other trial. When

we are dealing with someone who is subject to another trial, things have been said here which might be highly prejudicial to that trial, and therefore must not be published.'

That, as I understand it, was not an order by the judge. It was a warning by the judge that if material of that kind was published it would in fact be highly prejudicial to a fair trial of the subsequent proceedings.

Before the 1967 Act came into force committal proceedings can have been in no different position. I have no doubt that a report of part of committal proceedings (for instance evidence about previous convictions), even though fair and accurate, might be contempt of court if in fact that part reported was intended or was likely to prejudice the fair trial which might or might not follow.

After 1967 there was a blanket ban on reporting any part of committal proceedings except those matters set out in s 3(4).

I do not believe that the lifting of restrictions under s 3(2) did away with the liability of journalists to proceedings for contempt if in fact they reported material likely to prejudice a fair trial. There is nothing in the trilogy of cases to which we have been referred (*R v Bow Street Magistrate, ex p Kray* [1968] 3 All ER 872, [1969] 1 QB 473; *R v Russell, ex p Beaverbrook Newspapers Ltd* [1968] 3 All ER 695, [1969] 1 QB 342; and *R v Blackpool Justices, ex p Beaverbrook Newspapers Ltd* [1972] 1 All ER 388, [1972] 1 WLR 95) which suggests that it did.

What s 3 did was to add a new statutory offence: to make it unlawful to publish any report at all of the proceedings (other, of course, than those matters set out in sub-s (4)) irrespective of whether a report was likely to prejudice a fair trial. A successful application under s 3(2) did no more than remove this additional and very wide prohibition on reporting and thus left the position exactly as it had been before the 1967 Act; namely, that reports of what I shall call 'prejudicial material' might still attract proceedings for contempt. Thus, although a decision to lift restrictions was irrevocable this was because the court simply had no power to make an order banning publication. It did not affect the law that publication of prejudicial material might still be contempt.

When we come to the Contempt of Court Act 1981, we are in a different world. Instead of the burden being on the reporter to see that what he reports is not material which may put him in contempt, it is now on the court to make an order banning publication of particular material and the reporter is safe to publish anything else that occurs in the trial so long as it is fair, accurate, contemporaneous and bona fide. The Contempt of Court Act 1981, by s 4, thus does away with the uncertainty for the journalist as to whether what he is reporting is likely to get him into trouble or not. In cases other than committals he now knows that he can report anything (even obviously prejudicial matter) so long as the report is fair, accurate, contemporaneous and bona fide, provided that there is no court order under s 4(2) to stop him. In committal cases he can report nothing save the matters referred to in s 8(4) of the Magistrates' Courts Act 1980 unless reporting restrictions have been lifted. So much is clear.

Is the position any different if reporting restrictions have been lifted? I can see no reason why it should be. It would, it seems to me, be very odd if Parliament, having taken away the uncertainty for the journalist in the reporting of legal proceedings and replaced it by a system which involved the court's consideration of whether particular circumstances demanded a specific order banning publication, should in committal proceedings alone, and then only in that small proportion of committal proceedings where reporting restrictions had been lifted, have put the journalist in a position which he did not enjoy before the 1981 Act of being able to report any matter however prejudicial without fear of contempt proceedings because that court alone was unable to restrain him from doing so.

I cannot see that any canon of construction requires us to hold that examining justices, simply because there exist certain earlier provisions dealing with a different situation, were not intended to exercise these general powers given to all the courts. It seems to me, therefore, that this argument fails. There is nothing, as I have said, in the trilogy of cases to suggest that the irrevocable nature of the decision to remove the special reporting restrictions imposed by s 3(1) of the 1967 Act operated to permit a publication which before 1967 would have been contemptuous, and thus the situation created by that Act cannot be one that cuts down the general application of the later statute.

Counsel for West Sussex County Times Ltd argues that the application with which we are dealing was one made by co-defendants and that as the position of co-defendants was specifically dealt with by Parliament in the Criminal Justice (Amendment) Act 1981, an Act passed but 25 days before the Contempt of Court Act 1981, the latter Act must be read as if it excluded the right of co-defendants to apply for an order under s 4(2).

This argument suffers from the same defect as the earlier argument. The Criminal Justice (Amendment) Act 1981 is only dealing with the blanket ban on publication of all the committal proceedings, the special ban imposed by the 1967 Act.

Suppose Parliament had never passed the Contempt of Court Act 1981 at all. What would have been the position about the reporting of committal proceedings after the coming into force of the Criminal Justice (Amendment) Act 1981? The answer is that if the co-defendants were successful in opposing the lifting of restrictions the special ban under the 1967 Act would remain. If they were unsuccessful it would merely mean that the reporting of unprejudicial matter could continue but that proceedings for contempt might be instituted in respect of any report which might prejudice a fair trial.

The uncertainty of that situation from the journalist's point of view has now been removed and the justices in my view can make an order in appropriate cases under s 4(2). Of course, an order can only be made if it appears to the justices to be necessary to avoid the type of prejudice specified in the subsection.

If a defendant has asked for reporting restrictions to be lifted this seems a fairly good indication that, as far as he is concerned, there could be no prejudice to his fair trial by allowing reports to be published. To that extent it may be more difficult for him to convince justices of such prejudice if he makes a subsequent application under the Contempt of Court Act 1981.

Similarly, if, under the Criminal Justice (Amendment) Act 1981, justices have already been through the process of deciding whether, as between two or more defendants, the interests of justice do or do not require the ban on reporting to remain, something new might well be required before they felt that the possibility of prejudice required the reimposition of any particular ban under s 4 of the Contempt of Court Act 1981.

I turn from the argument based on the principle generalia specialibus non derogant to a different argument used by counsel for West Sussex County Times Ltd. This depends on the use of the word 'proceedings' in s 4. In so far as there ever was an argument that that section did not apply to committal proceedings at all, that it seems to me, can be disposed of very shortly by quick reference to s 4(3), which clearly envisages that the term 'proceedings' includes 'committal proceedings'.

The argument of counsel for West Sussex County Times Ltd was more subtle than that, however. If I have grasped it at all, it goes like this. The prejudice to which justices must have regard is prejudice in 'those proceedings or any other proceedings pending or imminent'. The term 'those proceedings' cannot mean proceedings from arrest to verdict, ie both committal and Crown Court trial, because if that were so the justices having power to ban publication of 'the proceedings' could do so in relation to the whole proceedings including the Crown Court part. This must be absurd. Ergo, argues counsel, 'those proceedings' must refer only to the committal proceedings.

If this is so, the argument goes on, then the only prejudice which the justices can look at is the prejudice to the committal proceedings. The complaint here is not that these were prejudiced but one of prejudice to the subsequent trial. Nor, says counsel for West Sussex County Times Ltd, can it be said that the justices have power to ban publication because of possible prejudice to the potential trial, because those proceedings are neither pending nor imminent.

Asked for an explanation of the distinction between 'pending' and 'imminent' counsel for West Sussex County Times Ltd was unable to produce one. They must, he said, mean the same thing.

I think the answer to the first part of his argument is to be found in the Act itself. I have already referred to the definition of 'legal proceedings'. The term must have the same meaning throughout the Act. For the purposes of s 2, Sch 1, which I need not read in full, divides 'legal proceedings' in a fashion clearly intended to be exhaustive into three categories: criminal proceedings, appellate proceedings and other proceedings. So far as criminal proceedings are concerned these are said for our purposes to be active from arrest to the conclusion of any trial in the Crown Court.

The term 'proceedings' in s 4(2), therefore, is, in my view, meant to include as one set of proceedings both the committal proceedings and any subsequent Crown Court proceedings.

Section 4(2), of course, is intended to cater for all proceedings in every conceivable kind of court. It is thus drawn in very wide terms. If the section does give justices power to ban publication of the proceedings in the Crown Court they would obviously be exceeding the bounds of reasonableness as understood in *Wednesbury Corp v Ministry of Housing and Local Government* [1965] 1 All ER 186, [1965] 1 WLR 261 if they did so. Reasonable justices would confine their order to their own part of the proceedings. They can, however, look to the possible mischief affecting the Crown Court trial because that is possible prejudice to the Crown Court part of 'those proceedings'.

I think this disposes of this argument; but if I am wrong the argument, it seems to me, fails on its second limb. If 'those proceedings' in s 4(2) means only the committal proceedings, and, as it is conceded, there can be no prejudice to those proceedings, are the potential proceedings in the Crown Court 'other proceedings pending or imminent'? The meaning of these two terms is well known in the law of contempt. In *R v Parke* [1903] 2 KB 432, [1900–3] All ER Rep 721 it was held that a trial at assizes was 'pending' after the defendant's arrest but before he was actually committed for trial to the assizes. Similarly, in *R v Clarke, ex p Crippen* (1910) 103 LT 636 it was held that a criminal case was pending at any time after a person had been arrested and was in custody.

Criminal proceedings are 'imminent' if it must be obvious that a suspect is about to be arrested. The authority for that is the Northern Ireland case of *R v Beaverbrook Newspapers Ltd, Associated Newspapers Ltd* [1962] NI 15. I have been unable to obtain a copy of that report and I take my knowledge of it from Miller *Contempt of Court* (1976) p 77.

What appears to have happened is that a Daily Express reporter, knowing full well that a gentleman called McGladdery was under constant surveillance, with police officers guarding the front and rear of his house, nevertheless went in with a camera and took a series of photographs which were published. McGladdery was arrested the following day and charged with murder. The Northern Ireland court had no difficulty in coming to the conclusion that proceedings were imminent having regard to the reporter's knowledge of what was going on.

Parliament, in using the expression 'pending or imminent' in s 4(2), and the same expression is used in s 11 of the Administration of Justice Act 1960, must be taken to have realised its legal significance. Hence I have no doubt that a potential trial at the Crown Court of the defendant presently before the examining justices is a matter which is pending during committal proceedings.

I therefore reject the argument that examining justices, once they have lifted restrictions under s 3(2) of the 1967 Act (now s 8(2) of the Magistrates' Courts Act 1980), have no jurisdiction to make an order under s 4(2) of the Contempt of Court Act 1981. For the reasons given I think they have such jurisdiction and this ground of objection to their order therefore fails.

The second ground, that there was not sufficient material before the justices to enable them to exercise their discretion is not, as I understand it, now pursued.

A late affidavit from the solicitor for Mr Howson and Mr Amos, who actually made the application to the justices in June, shows that the reason advanced was that there was certain sensitive matter disclosed in some of the prosecution evidence which if published might prejudice the defendants. Because of this possible prejudice this court made an order under s 4(2) earlier this week prohibiting publication of this material in the form disclosed to this court in that affidavit. But this part of the objection is no longer live on this ground.

The content of the affidavit remains however a matter of importance when considering the third ground. This ground is that the order made by the justices was too wide both in ambit and in time. The latter complaint arose from a misunderstanding of the terms of the order. No criticism can be made of the order on that score now.

That the order was too wide seems to me, however, quite apparent. I have to say, in sympathy with the justices, that this was a wholly new statutory provision and they had no argument or assistance as to what they should do about it. But it seems to me that any court considering whether to make an order under s 4(2) is bound to satisfy itself that the order is no wider than necessary to secure the desired end; namely, the prevention of prejudice to the administration of justice.

It may be that on the material we have before us, which is the same material as was before the justices, all that was necessary, and all that reasonable justices properly directing themselves could have considered was necessary, was an order preventing publication of the evidence relating to what I have called the sensitive material referred to in the affidavit.

It is not our task to substitute our view of what would have been a proper order for that of the justices but it is clear that these justices never addressed themselves at all to the question whether a more restricted order than the one they had made would nevertheless suffice to prevent prejudice. They have my sympathy, but undoubtedly they erred in failing to turn their minds to this point and the case should go back to them so that they may decide on the appropriate restriction.

I might add this. In the course of argument it was suggested that the justices should have embarked on some kind of inquisitorial examination of the material placed before them. I think this goes much too far. All that a reasonable bench of justices has to do in my view is satisfy themselves that such material justifies a particular restriction and that they are not being asked to make a wider restriction than is necessary.

This case is one that has attracted some publicity and I should not leave it without adding this. We have been shown some of this publicity in the shape of a leader in the West Sussex County Times, the newspaper published by the second applicant. This is couched in somewhat extreme terms and suggests that s 4(2) of the Contempt of Court Act 1981 is but one step on the road which will soon see us all being marched off to the salt mines or the concentration camp.

The language of hyperbole is seldom necessary where the argument is logically convincing. It is worth looking for a moment at what is the true position. Since the 1967 Act the overwhelming majority of committals have taken place under s 1, a procedure which involves no publicity at all. Of the minority of cases which proceed as 'old style' committals, few involve applications under s 3(2). It is only, therefore, in a very small proportion of committals that details can be published at all. I have not noticed the looming shadow of the jackboot in consequence.

Further, it should be said that it should not be supposed that Parliament, in enacting s 3(2), did so in the expectation that defendants would apply to have reporting restrictions lifted in a disinterested pursuit of the freedom of the press or the increase in circulation of a particular newspaper. The application could and should only be made if it is thought that publicity may assist the defendant in this defence.

I would allow this application to this extent, that the justices' order should be quashed and the matter should be remitted to the justices for them to give proper consideration to the question whether, in order to prevent prejudice in the administration of justice, it is necessary to postpone publication of all reports of the proceedings or whether for that purpose postponement of publication of only part of the proceedings would suffice.

GLIDEWELL J. I agree with the conclusions arrived at by Forbes J and the order he proposes. I agree also with all the reasons he has given for those conclusions save on one point which does not affect the eventual decision.

The point on which I have the temerity to disagree with him relates to the argument of counsel for West Sussex County Times Ltd that the phrase 'such proceedings' in s 4(2) of the Contempt of Court Act 1981 refers in the circumstances of this case to the committal proceedings, that no other proceedings are pending or imminent and that the only relevant risk of prejudice which should be considered is the risk of prejudice to the committal proceedings themselves, not to any subsequent trial.

I agree with counsel, for the reasons he advances, that the phrase 'such proceedings' in s 4(2) is limited to the proceedings which are being heard at the relevant time: that is to say, in this case, to the committal proceedings. If that were not right the magistrates would, as Forbes J has said, in theory at least, have the power to make an order under s 4(2) covering not only the hearing before them but also a later trial in the Crown Court. I cannot accept that Parliament intended such a result.

But I part company with counsel for West Sussex County Times Ltd and rejoin Forbes J when I come to counsel's submission that no other proceedings are pending or imminent. In my judgment the decision of this court in *R v Clarke, ex p Crippen* (1910) 103 LT 636 is clear authority binding on us for the proposition that in relation to committal proceedings the proceedings in the Crown Court which will follow if the defendant is committed for trial, are pending.

Thus in my view the magistrates' court was entitled and indeed obliged to take into account the risk of prejudicing a fair trial in the Crown Court. So I reach, by an alternative route, while not following his preferred route, the same conclusion that Forbes J has done on this issue.

There is only one other point on which I think it right, or indeed necessary, to say a word. The effect of s 4(1) of the Contempt of Court Act 1981 is that a person is not guilty of contempt of court under the strict liability rule in respect of a fair and accurate report of legal proceedings.

'The strict liability rule' is defined in s 1 of the Act as '. . . the rule of law whereby conduct may be treated as a contempt of court as tending to interfere with the course of justice in particular legal proceedings regardless of intent to do so'.

Theoretically, therefore, it seems to me, a publication which is proved to be intended to prejudice a fair trial would not be protected by s 4(1). But such a publication in a report of proceedings where there had been no order under s 4(2), or where if there had been such an order it did not order postponement of the publication of the matter under consideration, seems to me to be virtually inconceivable. In other words, in practice, in my view, a journalist who publishes a fair and accurate report of legal proceedings of a matter not ordered to be postponed under s 4(2) is protected by s 4(1).

In every other respect, as I have said, I agree with Forbes J and with the order he proposes.

Application allowed. Magistrates' order quashed and case remitted to magistrates for further consideration.

Solicitors: *Harriet Harman* (for Mr Farquharson and the National Union of Journalists); *Oswald Hickson, Collier & Co* (for West Sussex County Times Ltd); *Levene, Phillips & Swycher* (for Mr Howson and Mr Amos); *Maxwell & Gouldman* (for Mr Bukhari); *Solicitor for the Customs and Excise.*

Appeal

Mr Farquharson and the National Union of Journalists appealed against the decision of the Divisional Court on the grounds that the court should have held that the magistrates had no jurisdiction to make any order under s 4(2) of the Contempt of Court Act 1981 or that on the evidence before the magistrates no reasonable bench could have made any order under s 4(2).

Michael Beloff QC and *Andrew Nicol* for the appellants.
Simon D Brown and *E Cole* for the Customs and Excise Commissioners.
Brian Leary QC and *Sibghatullah Kadri* for Mr Bukhari.
Mordecai Levene for Mr Howson and Mr Amos.

Cur adv vult

21 December. The following judgments were read.

LORD DENNING MR. Four men are up on charges of gun-running. They were trying, it is said, to export revolvers, pistols and ammunition from Dover by ship and from Heathrow by air. The customs officers were vigilant. They detained the men and charged them with the offence of exporting, or attempting to export, prohibited goods, with intent to evade the prohibition, contrary to s 56(2) of the Customs and Excise Act 1952. Under it they are liable to a penalty in money or to imprisonment not exceeding two years.

The four men were brought before the magistrates at Horsham. They thought that the offence was more suitable to be tried by a jury. So they proceeded to inquire into it as examining justices. The accused were represented by their lawyers. One of them asked for the committal to be in the 'old style', that is, with the witnesses being examined and cross-examined so as to see if the evidence was sufficient to commit them for trial by jury.

When the men first appeared before the magistrates, the local newspaper published, as they were entitled to do, the names and addresses of the accused and the charges against them: see s 8(4) of the Magistrates' Courts Act 1980. The newspapers were, however, restricted from publishing anything more (such as the opening speech or the evidence) unless any one of the men asked for restrictions to be lifted. On 23 June 1981 one of the four did so ask. The others objected. But their objections were useless. Under the statute any one of the accused can ask for restrictions to be lifted: see s 8(2) of the Magistrates' Courts Act 1980. If he asks, the magistrates have no option. They have to make an order permitting all the committal proceedings to be reported as against all the accused: see *R v Russell, ex p Beaverbrook Newspapers Ltd* [1968] 3 All ER 695, [1969] 1 QB 342.

As a matter of interest, I may say that it is different now. When proceedings are commenced after 2 October 1981 the other accused can object to restrictions being lifted: and the magistrates will only lift them if it is in the interests of justice to do so: see s 1 of the Criminal Justice (Amendment) Act 1981. But as the proceedings were started earlier, that provision does not apply.

On appearances in June and July 1981 the case was adjourned and the men were remanded on bail. No speeches were made and no evidence was given. Arrangements were made for a full hearing to be started on 16 October 1981. It was expected to last for four days. But then on 27 August 1981 there came into force the Contempt of Court Act 1981. The lawyers for the accused read this Act. They saw in it an opportunity of preventing any report in any of the newspapers about the case. But one of the accused (who had previously asked for restrictions to be lifted) changed his mind and asked for there to be no reporting.

Accordingly when the case started on 16 October 1981 the lawyer for the accused made an application that there should be no reporting of the case on this ground as stated in his affidavit:

> 'The basis of the application . . . was that the details of the case that were going to be aired in the committal were of a highly prejudicial nature and likely to inflame people's feelings because of the political and social implications . . . of the case, namely, the political assassination side, which was the aspect of the case likely to attract widespread publicity notwithstanding the fact that such matters were not relevant to the actual charges.'

The bench acceded to the application and made an order 'prohibiting reporting of any part of the proceedings until the commencement of any trial hearing'.

This order is in such wide terms that it prohibits the reporting of anything, not only of the speeches or evidence, but also of the things which are permitted by the Magistrates' Courts Act 1980, such as the names and addresses of parties or witnesses or the charges or the decision of the magistrates. It put a blanket over everything in the case.

This order upset the newspaper reporters greatly. The very respectable and staid West Sussex County Times said on its first page:

'Towards secret courts

... Last week Horsham magistrates used sweeping new powers available under
the Contempt of Court Act to prevent the West Sussex County Times publishing all
information concerning charges faced by four defendants ... The public may still
sit through and listen to the committal proceedings, although the Press remains
gagged ... The day of the secret court is barely a step away. It could be just a
matter of time before we are plunged into a frightening world of justice
administered behind a lock and key.'

Being so upset, the newspaper reporters sought the help of the National Union of
Journalists. Together they applied to the High Court for judicial review so as to quash
the order of the Horsham magistrates. The High Court did so and remitted the matter
to the magistrates for reconsideration: but meanwhile prohibited any further reporting
of the case. The journalists appeal to this court.

Locus standi

No doubt Mr Farquharson, the reporter for the West Sussex County Times, has
sufficient standing to apply for judicial review: see *R v Russell, ex p Beaverbrook Newspapers
Ltd* [1968] 3 All ER 695, [1969] 1 QB 342. But a question was raised as to the National
Union of Journalists. I think they have locus standi, on the principle I endeavoured to
state in *R v Greater London Council, ex p Blackburn* [1976] 3 All ER 184 at 192, [1976] 1
WLR 550 at 559 and in *R v IRC, ex p National Federation of Self-Employed and Small
Businesses* [1980] 2 All ER 378 at 390, [1980] 1 QB 407 at 422 which was indorsed by Lord
Diplock in the House of Lords when he said ([1981] 2 All ER 93 at 107, [1981] 2 WLR
722 at 737–740):

'It would, in my view, be a grave lacuna in our system of public law if a pressure
group, like the federation, or even a single public spirited taxpayer, were prevented
by outdated technical rules of locus standi from bringing the matter to the attention
of the court to vindicate the rule of law and get the unlawful conduct stopped.'

As there with the federation, so here with the National Union of Journalists. They are,
in my view, entitled to come to the High Court to see if the magistrates were entitled to
make this order.

Section 4(2) of the Contempt of Court Act 1981

The Horsham magistrates made this order in reliance on s 4(2) of the Contempt of
Court Act 1981 which says:

'In any such proceedings [that is legal proceedings held in public] the court may,
where it appears to be necessary for avoiding a substantial risk of prejudice to the
administration of justice in those proceedings, or in any proceedings pending or
imminent, order that the publication of any report of the proceedings, or any part
of the proceedings, be postponed for such period as the court thinks necessary for
that purpose.'

Does it apply to committal proceedings?

Counsel for the appellants contended that Parliament has considered committal
proceedings as a special kind of proceedings and has made special provision for them in
s 3 of the Criminal Justice Act 1967, now replaced by s 8 of the Magistrates' Courts Act
1980 as amended by s 1 of the Criminal Justice (Amendment) Act 1981. He urged that
those special provisions should take priority over the general provision in s 4(2) and
render that general provision unnecessary and inapplicable on the accepted principle of
statute law that generalia specialibus non derogant: general provisions will not abrogate
special provisions. That principle has been repeatedly affirmed in the House of Lords:
see *Seward v The Vera Cruz* (1884) 10 App Cas 59 at 68, [1881–5] All ER Rep 216 at 220
per Lord Selborne and *Blackpool Corp v Starr Estate Co Ltd* [1922] 1 AC 27 at 34, [1921] All
ER Rep 79 at 82 per Viscount Haldane.

To see if this principle applies I would first describe the origin of the special provisions. In 1957 there was much concern because when Dr John Bodkin Adams was charged with murder, evidence was given at the committal proceedings of earlier deaths which was not given at this subsequent trial. This concern led to Lord Tucker's Committee in 1958 (see *Report of the Departmental Committee on Proceedings before Examining Magistrates* Cmnd 479 (1958)). Their report was implemented by s 3 of the Criminal Justice Act 1967. Then in 1980 there was much concern because, when Mr Jeremy Thorpe and others were charged, one of the accused asked for reporting restrictions to be be lifted. The others did not. This concern led to an amendment in the Criminal Justice (Amendment) Act 1981 by which the others could be heard to ask that the reporting restrictions remain.

In those special provisions, now contained in the Magistrates' Courts Act 1980 as amended, Parliament has given clear and definite directions to everybody concerned with committal proceedings. Everyone knows from the very beginning what can be reported and what not. The matters which can be reported are specified in s 8(4)(a) to (i). Everything else is restricted by sub-s (1), unless the restrictions are lifted in accordance with sub-ss (2) and (2A). As a result of those special provisions, nobody has to consider whether the reporting of the proceedings will cause any risk of prejudice to anyone. No one has to consider what parts should be allowed to be reported and what parts not. No one has to consider whether the administration of justice will be prejudiced or not. No problem is entrusted to the magistrates, save when one accused wants restrictions lifted and others do not. Then they have to decide between them, according to the interests of justice, a simple operation well within their capacity.

I will next describe the impact of the new s 4(2) of the Contempt of Court Act 1981. Counsel for the accused Bukhari suggested that under it, at the very outset of the committal proceedings, the magistrates could make an order postponing any report of the proceedings in the newspapers. I do not agree. It would be an impossible task to put on the magistrates. Somehow or other, someone or other, before any evidence was called would have to tell the magistrates enough about the case for them to embark on the task. They would have to consider, on such information as they could glean, whether, if the case were reported in the press, there would be 'a substantial risk of prejudice to the administration of justice'. They would have to consider whether it is 'necessary' to make an order. They would have to consider whether it is to be for the 'whole' or for 'part'. Then they would have to exercise a discretion. The section only says 'may . . . order'. So I think no order can be made at the outset.

But if s 4(2) is applied to committal proceedings, not at the outset, but later on in the hearing, then I see no conflict between the general provision and the special provisions. It used to occur in previous times that on committal proceedings or applications for bail, the police would give evidence of previous convictions, the magistrates would not make an order forbidding publication, and the newspapers would report them. This was most undesirable because it might prejudice the man at his trial. It was so said by two of the strongest courts of criminal appeal you could find: in 1915 in *R v Sanderson* 31 TLR 447 per Lord Reading CJ, Avory and Low JJ and in *R v Armstrong* [1951] 2 All ER 219 per Lord Goddard CJ, Lynskey and Devlin JJ.

This new s 4(2) provides a solution. It enables magistrates in such a case to make an order postponing publication of the evidence of previous convictions. Likewise, in a case like that of Dr Bodkin Adams, they could make an order postponing publication of the evidence of the earlier deaths, or, in a blackmail case, the name of the person blackmailed. In all these cases the trial would be 'other proceedings pending or imminent'. I agree with the interpretation put on those words by Glidewell J.

From those illustrations it appears to me that the Magistrates' Courts Act 1980 does not contain a complete code for committal proceedings. There is still a place for s 4(2) of the Contempt of Court Act 1981. I would, therefore, reject the contention of counsel for appellants.

Counsel for the accused Bukhari was quite frank as to what he wanted. He would be content if the restrictions imposed by the Magistrates' Courts Act 1980 were retained:

just as if his client had never asked for them to be lifted. That would have been possible if the committal proceedings had been after 2 October 1981. But that does not apply here, because they were commenced beforehand. So this is an entirely exceptional case, of a transitional nature which will never occur again.

The effect of section 4(2) of the Contempt of Court Act 1981

Now I turn to the next and more important point. What is the effect of an order under s 4(2)?

Counsel for the Customs and Excise Commissioners suggested that once an order is made by a court under s 4(2), and a newspaper publishes in breach of it, then the newspaper is automatically guilty of a contempt of court without any inquiry as to whether the order was rightly made or not. I cannot accept this suggestion for one moment. It would mean that every court in the land would be given a new power, by its own order, to postpone indefinitely publication in the newspapers of the whole or any part of the proceedings before it or in another court. Such an order could be made, and would be made, *against* the newspaper without their having any notice of it or any opportunity of being heard on it. They have no right of appeal against it. It could be done on the application of one party, and the acquiescence of the other, without the court itself giving much, if any, thought to the public interest. It would be nothing more nor less than a power, by consent of the parties, to muzzle the press. I hope that every High Court judge would be slow to make any such order. I trust that he would consider the public interest in the proceedings being reported as proclaimed by the House of Lords in *Scott v Scott* [1913] AC 417, [1911–13] All ER Rep 1. But can we be sure that all other bodies and tribunals would do so? The power is given to any tribunal or body exercising the judicial power of the state: see s 19 of the Contempt of Court Act 1981. Can we be sure that all the chairmen of all these will be able to withstand the persuasiveness of the advocate who is anxious to save his client from damaging publicity, or a witness from embarrassing revelations, when the other side do not object? Such disclosures may be prejudicial to their name or fame, but not in the least prejudicial to the administration of justice. Take it to the extreme. An order might be made by someone or other, in some tribunal or other, out of lack of knowledge or dislike of the press or even a sense of power. Is there not a danger that one of them will be like the 'man, proud man' of whom Shakespeare wrote in *Measure for Measure* ii.ii.117—

'Drest in a little brief authority,
Most ignorant of what he 's most assur'd . . .
Plays such fantastic tricks before high heaven
As make the angels weep . . .'

Section 6(b) of the Contempt of Court Act 1981

Parliament has, I think, guarded against this danger. It has done so by s 6(b) which says that:

'Nothing in the foregoing provisions of this Act [ie ss 1 to 5] . . . (b) implies that any publication is punishable as contempt of court under that rule [ie the strict liability rule] which would not be so punishable [ie as contempt of court] apart from those provisions . . .'

That section is much the same as s 12(4) of the Administration of Justice Act 1960, which we considered in this court in *Re F (a minor) (publication of information)* [1977] 1 All ER 114 at 120, [1977] Fam 58 at 86, and which the House of Lords considered in *A-G v Leveller Magazine Ltd* [1979] 1 All ER 745, [1979] AC 440. In regard to it, I would follow the words of Scarman LJ, with which Lord Edmund-Davies agreed in the House of Lords:

'. . . I think it likely that the subsection was enacted to ensure that no one would in future be found guilty of contempt who would not also under the pre-existing law have been found guilty. Certainly such a construction is consistent with the law's basic concern to protect freedom of speech and individual liberty . . .'

(See [1977] 1 All ER 114 at 131, [1977] Fam 58 at 99, and [1979] 1 All ER 745 at 761, [1979] AC 440 at 465.)

Applying this interpretation of s 6(b), I think the right approach is to put the foregoing provisions of ss 1 to 5 on one side and ask whether the publication would be punishable as a contempt of court apart from those provisions. That is, apart even from s 1 which speaks of the strict liability rule. The question then becomes: would the publication be a contempt of court punishable at common law?

At common law

So I turn to the question: what are the circumstances in which publication of a fair and accurate report would be a contempt at common law?

(i) *Postponing publication*

It has long been settled that the courts have power to make an order *postponing* publication (but not prohibiting it) if the postponement is necessary for the furtherance of justice in proceedings which are pending or imminent. It was so held in *R v Clement* (1821) 4 B & Ald 218, 106 ER 918, which was approved by the House of Lords in *Scott v Scott* [1913] AC 417 at 438, 453, [1911–13] All ER Rep 1 at 10, 17–18. It concerned the Cato Street conspiracy. Several men were charged in one indictment with high treason. They were to be tried successively one after the other. Before the trial of the first man, Lord Abbott CJ in open court prohibited the publication of the proceedings of that or any other day until the whole trial was brought to a conclusion. The editor of the Observer on the next Sunday, in breach of the order, published a fair and accurate account of the first three days. He was held guilty of contempt and fined £500. On a rule being obtained to set it aside, the Court of King's Bench held that the order of the Chief Justice was perfectly good, because all the trials could be regarded as one proceeding and it was only an order *postponing* publication until the end of the trial, and not prohibiting it altogether.

(ii) *Trial within a trial*

In addition, at common law whenever the judge sends the jury out, he expressly or impliedly directs that there should be no publication of what is said in their absence: such as when a question arises at a trial whether a confession is admissible or not; or whether evidence of similar facts can be given or not; or whether a man has put his character in issue so as to let in his previous convictions. In such a case the judge sends the jury out and conducts a 'trial within a trial' so as to decide the question. It is well understood by the press that there must be no publication of what takes place at the 'trial within a trial'. If there should be premature publication, it would constitute contempt of court: see per Lord Diplock in *A-G v Leveller Magazine Ltd* [1979] 1 All ER 745 at 750, [1979] AC 440 at 450.

(iii) *Use of pseudonym*

At other times, at common law the judge may permit the use of a pseudonym. Such as 'Mr Y' for the person blackmailed. The judge expressly or impliedly directs that the true name should not be published. In such a case both the magistrate who conducts the committal proceedings and the trial judge can direct that the true name should not be published: else people would be afraid to prosecute for blackmail. Thus, when a newspaper did publish the true name, it was guilty of contempt. The newspaper and the editor were each fined £250: see *R v Socialist Worker Printers and Publishers Ltd, ex p A-G* [1975] 1 All ER 142, [1975] QB 637.

(iv) *The Poulson warning*

Yet another instance at common law may arise when two men are jointly indicted but tried separately. Then it may be necessary to make an order postponing publication, as in *R v Clement* (1821) 4 B & Ald, 218, 106 ER 918. Similarly, when there is another case going on at the same time, such as happened in *R v Poulson* (1974) Times, 2 January.

Waller J gave a warning in open court that certain items of evidence given at the trial should not be published because of the risk of causing prejudice to other criminal proceedings which had already begun. He cited *R v Clement* and *Scott v Scott* (see the *Report of the Committee on Contempt of Court* Cmnd 5794 (1974) para 134).

There may be other instances at common law too, but none at the moment occurs to me.

Section 4(1) of the Contempt of Court Act 1981

Before reading s 4(2) it is very desirable to read s 4(1) to understand the impact of it. It gives protection to every fair and accurate report of legal proceedings in open court published contemporaneously in good faith. In so providing, Parliament was carrying out the recommendation contained in the report of Lord Justice Phillimore's Committee (see *Report of the Committee on Contempt of Court* Cmnd 5794 (1974) para 141). It is significant that the report contained no recommendation corresponding to s 4(2). But, in view of the width of s 4(1) (which contained no exceptions) it was obviously desirable to preserve the common law exceptions to it. (The committee had recognised their existence in paras 134 to 140.) These exceptions are preserved by s 4(2).

Section 4(2)

Section 4(2) retains the common law about the occasions when a report (otherwise fair and accurate) may be a contempt of court, but with this improvement: nothing is to be left to implication. It is for the court to make an order telling the newspapers what things they are not to publish. Thus, giving the newspaper that warning which the Lords felt was desirable in the *Leveller* case [1979] 1 All ER 745 esp at 753, 761–762, [1979] AC 440 esp at 453, 465 per Lord Diplock and Lord Edmund-Davies.

In short, s 4(2) only applies to cases where the courts themselves would at common law have jurisdiction to make an order postponing publication: but now it needs an order, not an implication. Thus, when the jury is sent out, the judge should tell the newspaper reporters, 'You are not to publish anything of what takes place whilst the jury are out', or, when a pseudonym is used, 'You are not to publish his true name or anything which may disclose his identity'.

Such an order operates now so as to bind not only persons within the courtroom but also those outside, thus clearing up the doubts expressed by some of the Lords in the *Leveller* case [1979] 1 All ER 745 at 761, 766, [1979] AC 440 at 464, 471 per Lord Edmund-Davies and Lord Scarman. This is done by s 11 of the Contempt of Court Act 1981.

The intention of the legislature

On this reading of the statute it will be seen that s 4(2) is to be very strictly confined. It applies only to a very limited type of case. So read, the statute is not a measure for restricting the freedom of the press. It is a measure for liberating it. It is intended to remove the uncertainties which previously troubled editors. It is intended that the court should be able to make an order telling the editors whether the publication would be a contempt or not. Such as the report of a 'trial within a trial', or publishing a name which the court for good reason orders should be kept secret, or if magistrates in committal proceedings order that the person blackmailed should not be named. Unless the court makes such an order then the newspaper is given complete protection by s 4(1) from being subjected to proceedings for contempt of court.

The freedom of the press

This interpretation is, in my mind, necessary so as to ensure two of our most fundamental principles. One is open justice. The other is freedom of the press. It is of the first importance that justice should be done openly in public: that anyone who wishes should be entitled to come into court and hear and see what takes place; and that any newspaper should be entitled to publish a fair and accurate report of the proceedings, without fear of a libel action or proceedings for contempt of court. Even though the report may be most damaging to the reputation of individuals, even though it may be embarrassing to the most powerful in the land, even though it may be political dynamite, nevertheless it can be published freely, so long as it is part of a fair and accurate report. The only case in which it will be punishable as a contempt of a court is when the court makes an order postponing publication in the legitimate exercise of its powers in that behalf.

The most illuminating case is that of *R v Evening News, ex p Hobbs* [1925] 2 KB 158. It was in 1925 when we still had grand juries. It was for them to decide whether or not there was a true bill. If they found a true bill, the man would be tried by a petty jury during those very sittings. On 3 February 1925 the Recorder of London in his charge to the grand jury said:

'... there can be no doubt, I should say—it is for you to judge—that Hobbs was a party to a gigantic fraud, as monumental and perhaps as impudent a fraud as has ever been perpetrated in the course of our law.'

The newspapers that very evening and the next day made big headlines: 'HOBBS'S PART. "NO DOUBT PARTY TO A MONUMENTAL FRAUD."', omitting the words 'it is for you to judge'.

On 6 February 1925 William Cooper Hobbs applied to attach the Evening News and the editor for contempt of court. He put it on the ground that it was a serious prejudice to his trial which would be held in a few days. On 10 February 1925 the application was heard by Lord Hewart CJ together with Salter J, one of the best common law judges, and Fraser J, who was of the highest authority on the law of libel and of publication in newspapers. They held that the article was a fair and accurate report of judicial proceedings and that it was not a contempt of court. If the recorder had directed the press that they should not publish his charge to the grand jury it would no doubt have been a contempt of court for them to do so. It would come within *R v Clement* (1821) 4 B & Ald 218, 106 ER 918.

I cannot think that Parliament in s 4(2) ever intended to cut down or abridge the freedom of the press as hitherto established by law. All it does is to make clear to editors what is permissible and what is not. In considering whether to make an order under s 4(2), the sole consideration is the risk of prejudice to the administration of justice. Whoever has to consider it should remember that at a trial judges are not influenced by what they may have read in the newspapers. Nor are the ordinary folk who sit on juries. They are good, sensible people. They go by the evidence that is adduced before them and not by what they may have read in the newspapers. The risk of their being influenced is so slight that it can usually be disregarded as insubstantial, and therefore not the subject of an order under s 4(2).

Our present case

Returning to our present case, I cannot see any risk of prejudice to the administration of justice. Let me assume that in the course of the evidence, there will be talk about political assassination of one kind or another. It is probably irrelevant to the charges. It may be damaging to the reputation of some person or other. It may be embarrassing to some group or other. But it is most unlikely to influence the administration of justice. I do not think it would influence any judge or juror who might read it and who might, weeks or months later, sit on the trial. So I think the magistrates were wrong to make the blanket order as they did at the outset of the hearing. The Divisional Court was quite right to set their order aside.

But I do not exclude the possibility that there may, in the course of the proceedings, arise circumstances which would justify the making of an order in regard to some name or other, or to some point or other in which it would be *necessary* to make an order in the interests of the administration of justice. But whenever an application is made by one party for an order under s 4(2) the magistrates must remember that there is a third party to be considered who is neither seen nor heard. The third party is the public at large. Ever since *Scott v Scott* [1913] AC 417, [1911–13] All ER Rep 1 the court has attached great importance to the public interest in having justice done in open court with the press able to publish a fair and accurate report of all that takes place. The magistrates should remember this and give proper weight to it in coming to their decision.

With this consideration in mind, I agree with the Divisional Court that the case should be remitted to the magistrates so that they can consider any particular point that may arise in the course of the case.

I would dismiss the appeal accordingly and also the cross-appeal.

SHAW LJ. In the course of his elaborate argument counsel for the appellants put forward a number of interesting propositions. His basic contention was that publication of committal proceedings is governed in the present case by, and only by, the provisions of s 3 of the Criminal Justice Act 1967. They have now been replaced with amendments by the Criminal Justice (Amendment) Act 1981. Those provisions constituted, so he argued, a compendious and complete code governing the topic of publication of committal proceedings; they defined the general principle as to publication, the rights of the defendants in those proceedings and the powers of the examining magistrates. Nothing more was necessary or relevant to the question of publication. On this assumption the provisions of s 4(2) of the Contempt of Court Act 1981 have no application to committal proceedings; in that regard they are irrelevant and inapt. It would follow that if examining magistrates in committal proceedings purported to make an order postponing any report of the proceedings that order would be ultra vires and ineffectual. Its making could be ignored and contemporaneous publication would not be a contempt of court so long as it was a fair and accurate report published in good faith.

The exposition was attractive, but it stumbles at the first hurdle. There is no philosophical connection between the subject matter of s 3 of the Criminal Justice Act 1967 and that of s 4(2) of the Contempt of Court Act 1981. To describe the former section as providing a complete and exhaustive code governing the question of publication of committal proceedings is, with all respect to forensic prowess of counsel for the appellants, talking in the air.

Before the 1967 Act, committal proceedings were freely reported subject only to the general principle that reports had to be fair and accurate and so on. After a notorious case which attracted much public attention it became more and more apparent that the propagation of the evidence which was almost invariably only the prosecution side of a grave accusation might prejudice the subsequent trial of that accusation by a jury. The media disseminate such matters widely and impressively. Accordingly, the 1967 Act adopted a simple expedient. By s 3 it prohibited, subject to the exception of some innocuous or essential details, all publication of reports of committal proceedings. This prohibition was solely in the interests of justice to the defendant. It had nothing whatever to do with the possible effect of publication on third parties who might be referred to in the proceedings in sinister or discreditable contexts. If ever the press and other media had considered that they had a vested right to publish what passed in court in the course of committal proceedings, they had to reconcile themselves to the surrender or, at least, the constriction of that right after the enactment of s 3. Parliament recognised, however, that in exceptional situations a defendant (who might be one of a number of accused) might have an interest in the dissemination of news of his predicament. He might have grounds to believe that amongst those who read the published accounts there would be some who could provide evidence favourable to him. Section 3 of the 1967 Act provided, therefore, what proved to be a crude response to such a situation. It enacted that if a defendant (possibly one of a number) asked that the prohibition on publication should be lifted, then, ipso facto, whatever others charged might say or the justices might think, the statutory ban on publication went. Personal and individual considerations affecting other defendants could not avail them at all. As for the impact on, and possible prejudice to, the processes of justice so far as third parties were concerned, they mattered not at all. The 'code' created by s 3 had no reference to or concern with any such external procedures or their subject matter.

It was designed to protect the position only of the defendant or defendants whom the prosecution were asking to be committed for trial. In particular scandalous or horrific cases the minds of the jury who later had to try those committed might be prejudiced and their impartiality warped by the impressions they recalled from their reading of reports of what was given in evidence before the committing justices. It might be that some of that evidence would not be tendered or might be held inadmissible at the trial. It would be unfortunate indeed if some lingering recollection affected a juror's judgment.

What the 1967 Act was *not* concerned with was the position of persons who were not defendants in the committal proceedings but who were referred to in some discreditable and possibly criminal context in regard to which proceedings were or could be in contemplation. It might be that such proceedings were already in train; at any rate, there might be a substantial prospect of the institution of proceedings. Section 3 had no bearing on such situations. It was not concerned with possible prejudice to the interests of justice save in relation to the actual defendants. Even so far as their interests were concerned, it provided an ineffectual and inadequate scheme. The deficiencies apparent in s 3 have been ameliorated by s 1 of the Criminal Justice (Amendment) Act 1981. Although that section introduces 'the interests of justice' as a factor which must be considered by the justices in determining whether to lift the prohibition on publication, it would seem that it is the interests of justice as affecting the defendants that the court must consider, for only they are entitled to make representations to the court in this regard.

This aspect of the argument in support of the appeal may be finally disposed of by noting first that in the vast majority of committal proceedings no oral testimony is proffered. The statements of prospective witnesses are merely handed in to the court; and, second, that even where there is oral testimony, the underlying principle is that nothing can be published unless a defendant applies that it should be. The deprivation to the press and other organs of publicity is, in regard to committal proceedings, all but universal. Section 4(2) of the Contempt of Court Act 1981 may in practice have little to do with committal proceedings, but that is a far cry from the proposition that it can have no application to such proceedings and to what may transpire from them. If those proceedings end in the committal of any defendant for trial at a Crown Court it may, in general, be unlikely that a jury sitting on that trial will be adversely influenced by the recollection of advance publication of the committal proceedings, but it is not outside the bounds of possibility. Counsel for the appellants contended that while the committal proceedings are in progress a trial at the Crown Court is neither pending nor imminent. It would follow that s 4(2) had no operation in relation to the committal proceedings. This seems to me fallacious. The words 'pending of imminent' have been held to include the possible (not necessarily the inevitable) outcome of legal process. This has nothing to do with proceedings being 'active'. That expression is used as a term of art in the 1981 Act for the purpose of defining the scope and application of the strict liability rule as defined by s 1. The purpose and intent of s 4(2) is wider and different. It is designed to prevent injustice to individuals whose interests might be unduly and unjustifiably threatened or prejudiced by premature publication of matters which could adversely affect their rights or status. It is, of course, of high importance that the freedom of the press should be preserved. It reflects the right of society to know what goes on within it. At the same time individual rights, and in particular the right to good repute, must not be exposed to unwarranted assault. While a person whose character has been unjustifiably impugned may have in general a right of redress, none is available to him if the publication which injures him is protected by privilege. The appellants complain that the order of the justices militates against their interests as purveyors of news to the public; but private interests matter also and in some situations a balance has to be struck. It is to be borne in mind that s 3 of the 1967 Act virtually deprived the press of the right to publish any but the most meagre report of committal proceedings. In the present case it may be that if the justices have an opportunity of further considering the position they may come to the view that blanket postponement of publication is not necessary; this must be a matter for their discretion when they are in possession of all relevant material.

Yet another proposition advanced on behalf of the appellants was that when s 4(2) is considered in relation to s 6(b) of the 1981 Act, the logical outcome is that even though the examining justices make an order postponing publication, an intentional disregard of that order would not amount to a contempt unless what was published prematurely did not come within the protection afforded by s 4(1). Thus, if in defiance of an order for postponement there was a published a contemporaneous report which was fair and accurate and published in good faith, there would be no contempt. I was puzzled while this argument progressed and confess that I remain so still. The effect of the proposition thus put forward is that an order made under s 4(2) in relation to committal proceedings would be quite futile. A short answer is that a premature publication in contravention of an order of which the publisher is aware could not be said to be made in good faith. In this regard I find myself at variance with the view expressed by Lord Denning MR in the course of his judgment.

The wider proposition which was also hinted at, namely that s 4(2) has no operation whatever in relation to committal proceedings, is refuted by the language of s 4 itself. Subsection (1) refers to 'legal proceedings held in public'; sub-s (2) opens with the phrase 'in any such proceedings'; and, moreover, sub-s 3(b) makes specific reference to 'a report of committal proceedings'.

Accordingly, I agree with the judgment of the Divisional Court with the reservation that where Glidewell J differs from Forbes J, I agree with the view of the former.

I would dismiss the appeal.

ACKNER LJ. The press are, of course, wise to be alert to any new restrictions on their freedom to report cases coming before the courts. The freedom to report trials is one of the essential freedoms. As Lord Diplock observed in his speech in *A-G v Leveller Magazine Ltd* [1979] 1 All ER 745 at 749–750, [1979] AC 440 at 449–450:

> 'As a general rule the English system of administering justice does require that it be done in public: *Scott v Scott* [1913] AC 417, [1911–13] All ER Rep 1. If the way that courts behave cannot be hidden from the public ear and eye this provides a safeguard against judicial arbitrariness or idiosyncrasy and maintains the public confidence in the administration of justice. The application of this principle of open justice has two aspects: as respects proceedings in the court itself it requires that they should be held in open court to which the Press and public are admitted and that, in criminal cases at any rate, all evidence communicated to the court is communicated publicly. As respects the publication to a wider public of fair and accurate reports of proceedings that have taken place in court the principle requires that nothing should be done to discourage this. However, since the purpose of the general rule is to serve the ends of justice it may be necessary to depart from it where the nature or circumstances of the particular proceeding are such that the application of the general rule in its entirety would frustrate or render impracticable the administration of justice or would damage some other public interest for whose protection Parliament has made some statutory derogation from the rule.'

In an emotionally charged situation it is also wise to keep a sense of proportion. This appeal concerns committal proceedings, and a clear distinction can be drawn between reporting the trial itself and preliminary proceedings. Further, since the 1967 Act the overwhelming majority of committals have taken place under s 1, a procedure which involves no publicity at all. As to those relatively few committals which proceed as 'old style' committals, only a small proportion of them involve applications under s 3(2) of that Act. It is thus only in respect of this small residue of committals that any detailed evidence can be published at all. Moreover, in my judgment, the irony of this application when properly analysed is that, despite its clarion call for greater freedom of press reporting, were it to succeed, the practical result would be even less freedom to report committal proceedings since defendants, properly advised, would make even fewer applications to lift reporting restrictions which, since the 1967 Act, except for those few matters referred to in s 3(4), are automatic.

My reasons for this conclusion are simple. Counsel for the appellants submits that s 3 of the 1967 Act and its successor, s 8 of the 1980 Act, in effect makes a fair and accurate report of committal proceedings held in public, published contemporaneously and in good faith, immune from contempt proceedings, however prejudicial that publication may be to the accused. He submits that the magistrates have no jurisdiction under s 4(2) of the Contempt of Court Act 1981 to make an order postponing publication of any part of the committal proceedings until the trial, in order to avoid prejudice to the accused, however great that prejudice may be. Thus, for example, evidence at the magistrates' court of previous convictions, of confessions which are alleged by the defendant never to have been made, or, if made, to have been made involuntarily, or facts relating to other alleged offences said by the defence to be inadmissible, could all be reported with impunity. As I have said, if such were the state of the law, it would indeed be a very rare case where a defendant, properly advised, would ever seek to raise the automatic restrictions on the report of committal proceedings. How could he be sure, as this appeal so clearly demonstrates, that in the course of the proceedings evidence of which he had no notice, or proper appreciation, might not appear which provided good grounds for apprehending that there was a substantial risk of prejudice to the administration of justice which adversely affected him if published prior to his trial.

I am therefore content to find that this is not the law and accordingly the failure of this application, so far from further restricting the freedom of the press to publish committal proceedings, should in practice have the reverse effect. An accused knowing that he has at any time the right to apply to the magistrates for an order for the postponement of the reporting of any part of the committal proceedings prior to his trial, providing that he can establish that such an order is necessary for avoiding a substantial risk of prejudice to the administration of justice, will be giving fewer hostages to fortune by applying at the outset for the reporting restrictions on his committal proceedings to be lifted. It may not be without significance that the West Sussex County Times, who were one of the applicants in the Divisional Court, are not appealing against its decision.

The stages in counsel's clear, concise and admirably presented submissions on behalf of the appellants were as follows:

1. *At common law no contempt could be committed by the publication of a fair and accurate report of committal proceedings notwithstanding that such publication might seriously prejudice the accused at his subsequent trial*

In making this submission, counsel accepted that at common law contempt could be committed where there was an interference, with knowledge of the court's proceedings, with the due administration of justice as a continuing process. At common law a court has an inherent power to sit in camera for the due administration of justice and a fair and accurate report of what had taken place in private would be no defence to contempt proceedings, nor would the publication of the names of witnesses whose anonymity had been ordered to protect the due administration of justice, as in blackmail cases: see *A-G v Leveller Magazine Ltd* [1979] 1 All ER 745, [1979] AC 440 and *R v Socialist Worker Printers and Publishers Ltd, ex p A-G* [1975] 1 All ER 142, [1975] QB 637.

He, however, submitted that a substantial part of the Divisional Court's premise for concluding that the magistrates had jurisdiction to make an order under s 4(2) of the Contempt of Court Act 1981 was erroneous. Counsel who appeared for the prosecutor, HM Customs and Excise, and who properly asserted that the prosecution had no interest in the extent of the reporting in this case, accepted the validity of this part of counsel's submission on behalf of the appellants as did counsel for the respondents, the accused in the committal proceedings. Our attention was drawn to the cases of *Kimber v Press Association* [1893] 1 QB 65 and *R v Evening News, ex p Hobbs* [1925] 2 KB 158. Whereas the former case related to privilege in libel proceedings, the latter case related specifically to contempt proceedings. The Evening News had published a report of the charge delivered by the Recorder of London to the grand jury, which report it was alleged was calculated to prejudice the fair trial of Hobbs. Lord Hewart CJ, with whose judgment Salter and Fraser JJ agreed, said (at 167–168):

> 'It is now, I think, much too late in the day to argue that newspapers are not entitled to print reports of a charge to the grand jury. It is within the knowledge of all of us that for a long time past such reports have been printed. The principle which applies has been laid down in several cases. Thus in *Lewis* v. *Levy* ((1858) E B & E 537 at 557, 120 ER 610 at 617) Lord Campbell C.J., in delivering the judgment of the Court, said: "In *Curry* v. *Walter* ((1796) 1 Bos & P 525, 126 ER 1046) it was decided, above sixty years ago, that an action cannot be maintained for publishing a true account of the proceedings of a Court of justice, however injurious such publication may be to the character of an individual." And later in the course of the same judgment he said (E B & E 537 at 558, 120 ER 610 at 617–618): ". . . although a magistrate upon any preliminary inquiry respecting an indictable offence may, if he thinks fit, carry on the inquiry in private, and the publication of any such proceedings before him would undoubtedly be unlawful, we conceive that, while he continues to sit foribus apertis, admitting into the room where he sits as many of the public as can be conveniently accommodated, and thinking that this course is best calculated for the investigation of truth and the satisfactory administration of justice (as in most cases it certainly will be), we think the Court in which he sits is to be considered a public Court of justice. The case of *Curry* v. *Walter* has been often criticised, but never overturned and often acted upon. And in *Rex* v. *Wright* ((1799) 8 TR 293 at 298, 101 ER 1396 at 1399) it received the unqualified approbation of that great judge, Mr Justice Lawrence, who observed that, though the publication of such proceedings may be to the disadvantage of the particular individual concerned, yet it is of vast importance to the public that the proceedings of Courts of justice should be universally known." In the same sense in *Reg.* v. *Gray* ((1865) 10 Cox CC 184 at 193) Fitzgerald J. said: "It appears to me that the security obtained by publicity for the due administration of justice is this, that it brings to bear on that administration at once the pressure and the support of public opinion—its pressure to prevent intemperance on the part of the judge—to prevent corrupt or improper proceedings, and, on the contrary, its support where justice is administered in a pure, fair and legitimate manner. It has been said, and said truly, that possibly in particular cases there may be inconvenience to individuals from the early publication of evidence or of statements with respect to matters that are subsequently to be tried more solemnly; but it has been well observed, too, that this inconvenience to individuals is infinitesimal in comparison to the great public advantage given by that publicity." In my opinion, these remarks apply a fortiori to a report of a charge to a grand jury; and if the report published is a fair and accurate report of the charge, it comes within the privilege which belongs to fair and accurate reports of public proceedings in a Court of justice.'

Our attention was also drawn to *R v Sanderson* (1915) 31 TLR 447, where Low J described as 'an extremely undesirable practice' the publication by the press of references to an accused's previous convictions given at the magistrates' court in cases which were committed for trial. He did not suggest that it was unlawful so to report. In *R v Armstrong* [1951] 2 All ER 219 Lynskey J, in giving the judgment of the court in an application for leave to appeal against conviction on the grounds that his previous convictions, referred to at the magistrates' court when he was applying for bail, had been reported in the local newspapers, observed (at 219):

'So far as the publication of that information is concerned, this court has no power to compel the press, but this court agrees that it is very undesirable that such information should be given.'

Counsel for the Commissioners of Customs and Excise adopted the view expressed in Miller *Contempt of Court* (1976) p 113 that:

'Cases appear to have established that a fair and substantially accurate report of committal proceedings was lawful notwithstanding any resultant prejudice to an accused.'

I accept the accuracy of this statement. As Mr Miller points out, the immunity produced indefensible anomalies and matters finally came to a head in the trial for murder of Dr John Bodkins Adams in 1957, where the prosecution led evidence at the committal proceedings of earlier deaths which they claimed were attributable to Dr Adams but did not offer the evidence at the trial itself. This led to the setting up of the Tucker Committee, which in its report in 1958 recommended, inter alia, that until the trial has ended, any report of committal proceedings should be restricted to particulars of the name of the accused, the charge, the decision of the court and the like. They did not recommend that the defence should be entitled to say whether the restrictions should operate or not.

2. *The Criminal Justice Act 1967 provides a complete code in so far as it relates to an embargo in the interests of the accused on publication of reports of committal proceedings*

Section 3(1) of the Criminal Justice Act 1967 provided the general restriction on reports of committal proceedings. Section 3(2) provided for the lifting of these restrictions on the application by the defendant or any one of the defendants. Section 3(4) specified those matters that may be contained in a report of committal proceedings without any order having been made under s 3(2) to lift the restrictions. They included the identity of the court and the names of the examining justices, the names, addresses and occupation of the parties and witnesses, etc. It is clearly established that, once any defendant applied, the 1967 Act gave the justices no discretion to refuse and no reasons had to be given by the defendant who so applied. The interest which any co-accused might have in maintaining restrictions on reporting was not a matter which justices could take into account. Further, once the application and the inevitable order had been made, there was no possibility of recalling that order. The Criminal Justice (Amendment) Act 1981 has modified the inflexibility of that situation. It provides for the insertion of a new sub-s (2A) after sub-s (2) of s 8 of the Magistrates' Courts Act 1980 (which re-enacts s 3 of the 1967 Act) in the following terms:

'Where in the case of two or more accused one of them objects to the making of an order under subsection (2) above, the court shall make the order if, and only if, it is satisfied, after hearing the representations of the accused, that it is in the interests of justice to do so.'

This Act received the royal assent on 2 July 1981 and came into force on 2 October 1981. It thus came into force after these proceedings had started and after the Contempt of Court Act 1981 which came into force on 26 August 1981.

The proposition of counsel for the appellants is that in s 3 of the 1967 Act and s 8(2) of the Criminal Justice (Amendment) Act 1981, Parliament was dealing with a specific area, that of committal proceedings and the rules to be followed in reporting them and that those rules included the irrevocable nature to be attributed to a decision to lift reporting restrictions. He accepts that although on the face of it s 4(2) of the Contempt of Court Act 1981 provides a discretion on all courts to impose reporting restrictions, it cannot be construed so as to upset the rules specifically laid down in the 1967 Act for committal proceedings. He bases his argument on the principle generalia specialibus non derogant. He relies on the words of Lord Selborne LC in *Seward v The Vera Cruz* (1884) 10 App Cas 59 at 68, [1881–5] All ER Rep 216 at 220:

'Now if anything be certain it is this, that where there are general words in a later Act capable of reasonable and sensible application without extending them to subjects specially dealt with by earlier legislation, you are not to hold that earlier and special legislation indirectly repealed, altered, or derogated from merely by force of such general words, without any indication of a particular intention to do so.'

He further relies on the later case of *Blackpool Corp v Starr Estate Co Ltd* [1922] AC 27 at 34, [1921] All ER Rep 79 at 82 where Viscount Haldane said:

'... we are bound ... to apply a rule of construction which has been repeatedly laid down and is firmly established. It is that wherever Parliament in an earlier statute has directed its attention to an individual case and has made provision for it unambiguously, there arises a presumption that if in a subsequent statute the Legislature lays down a general principle, that general principle is not to be taken as meant to rip up what the Legislature had before provided for individually, unless an intention to do so is specifically declared.'

I do not take the view that the legislature in the 1967 Act, as subsequently re-enacted and amended, did provide a complete code in relation to all publications in respect of committal proceedings and counsel for the appellants does not so submit. He is careful to limit his submission to embargoes on publications in the interests of the accused. This he must do because under s 3(4) of the 1967 Act, as I have previously pointed out, provision is made specifically for the publication, despite the general embargo imposed by s 3(1) of, inter alia, the names of witnesses. This right to publish is, he accepts, subject to the general law of contempt and indeed to any relevant statutory exceptions, such as the Children and Young Persons Acts. The 1967 Act was clearly designed to provide protection to an accused against the wide publication previously permitted of committal proceedings. It was not, however, concerned with the law of contempt which, although a related is nevertheless a different subject. The effect of recognising that the justices have power under s 4(2) of the Contempt of Court Act 1981 does not involve 'ripping up' what is provided by the Criminal Justice (Amendment) Act 1981. On the contrary, it enables the court in operating the new subsection and thereunder considering the interests of justice to have regard to its ability to order the postponement of the reporting of a part of the proceedings, a power which is not provided for in the Criminal Justice (Amendment) Act.

3. *The effect of s 6(b) of the Contempt of Court Act 1981 prevents the justices from making an order the breach of which would render a journalist liable to contempt proceedings in circumstances in which they could not have been so liable at common law. Thus, since at common law a journalist is entitled to publish a fair and accurate report of the committal proceedings irrespective of possible prejudice to an accused, s 4(2) of the Contempt of Court Act 1981 cannot apply to magistrates' courts*

Section 6(b) reads as follows:

'Nothing in the foregoing provisions of this Act ... implies that any publication is punishable as contempt of court under that rule which would not be so punishable apart from those provisions ...'

This section is not dissimilar from that of s 12(4) of the Administration of Justice Act 1960 which deals with the publication of information relating to proceedings before any court sitting in private. That subsection provides:

'Nothing in this section shall be construed as implying that any publication is punishable as contempt of court which would not be so punishable apart from this section.'

The obscurity of that section was commented on by Scarman LJ in *Re F (a minor) (publication of information)* [1977] 1 All ER 114 at 131, [1977] Fam 58 at 99. He decided that it was enacted to ensure that no one would in future be found guilty of contempt who would not also under the pre-existing law have been found guilty. This construction was accepted by Lord Edmund-Davies in *A-G v Leveller Magazine Ltd* [1979] 1 All ER 745 at 761, [1979] AC 440 at 460.

However, s 6(*b*) contains the words 'under that rule'. The only rule to which it is referring is the 'strict liability rule' referred to in s 1 of the Act, namely 'the rule of law whereby conduct may be treated as a contempt of court as tending to interfere with the course of justice in particular legal proceedings regardless of intent to do so'.

Counsel's submission on behalf of the appellants raises a point of fundamental importance in relation to the Contempt of Court Act 1981. He submits that (a) by virtue of s 4(1) of the Act, so long as it is a fair and accurate report of legal proceedings held in public published contemporaneously and in good faith, it is not contempt to publish that which might be clearly prejudicial to a fair trial, (b) the onus is now put on the court to make an order postponing publication in whole or in part of the proceedings where it considers this to be necessary for avoiding a substantial risk of prejudice to the administration of justice, (c) thus the making of an order under s 4(2) is a necessary pre-condition for the bringing of contempt proceedings in respect of contemporary reports of legal proceedings.

The rationale is, he submits, to remove the previous uncertainty and make the position clear so that journalists are able to know where they stand.

Thus far I would be inclined to accept counsel's submission, although they involve the inconvenient consequence of the court having to be alert to the necessity of making the necessary orders and not to rely on what hitherto has been looked on as self-evident; for example, that when evidence is given in the absence of the jury then it follows that unless repeated in their presence it is obviously material that should be kept from them: see *R v Border Television Ltd, ex p A-G* (1978) 68 Cr App R 375. But, submits counsel, and this is a point which was neither taken before the Divisional Court nor even mentioned in the notice of appeal, a breach of an order made under s 4(2) does not per se amount to a contempt. The breach of such an order merely removes a possible defence to a charge of contempt under the strict liability rule. He submits that, in addition to establishing the breach of a s 4(2) order, the following must also be established. (a) The breach of the strict liability rule, which under s 2(2) involves establishing that the publication created 'a substantial risk that the course of justice in the proceedings in question will be seriously impeded or prejudiced'. Counsel for the appellants, while conceding that the test laid down in s 2(2) does not follow word for word that which has to be applied by a court exercising its powers under s 4(2), maintains that the test is essentially the same. He therefore contends that, in essence, the question which has been decided by the court making the order under s 4(2) has to be decided all over again by another court. (b) The conduct complained of would have amounted to contempt prior to the passing of the Contempt of Court Act 1981.

I find this submission quite unacceptable. It would be an odd situation indeed if the contravention of an order of a court that the publication of a report of its proceedings should be postponed for a specified period, made because the court thought that such a postponement was necessary for avoiding a substantial risk of prejudice to the administration of justice, could carry with it no sanction other than the removal of a defence to a charge of contempt under the strict liability rule. To my mind, and in this respect I with diffidence dissent from the view expressed by Lord Denning MR, it is clear that as a corollary of the onus now being put on the court to specify whether a report of its proceedings or any part thereof should be postponed, instead of leaving the journalist to publish at his peril, a new head of contempt of court has been created, separate and distinct from the strict liability rule ('that rule' referred to in para 6(*b*)). If a journalist reports proceedings that are the subject matter of a postponement order under s 4(2), then he is guilty of a contempt of court.

Understandably counsel for the appellants refers to the definition of 'court' in s 19 and stresses that since this includes any tribunal or body exercising the judicial power of the state, then a very widespread power has been given not only to make orders, but orders which are not appealable, although as this appeal illustrates they are nevertheless reviewable by the courts. I do not think this is as powerful a point as may seem at first sight. First of all, the power is a power to *postpone*, not to prohibit totally, publication. Second, the power may be exercised in relation to only a *part* of the proceedings. Third, that in order for the jurisdiction to be exercised the court must be satisfied that an order is necessary for avoiding a substantial risk of prejudice to the administration of justice. The obvious case for the postponement of a report of proceedings is where the substantive trial or a retrial has yet to take place, or where a fair and accurate report of one trial might still prejudice another trial still to be heard. The prejudice to the administration of justice which is envisaged is the reduction in the power of the court to do that which is the end for which it exists, namely to administer justice duly, impartially, and with reference solely to the facts judicially brought before it (per Wills J in *R v Parke* [1903] 2 KB 432, [1900–3] All ER Rep 721). What the court is generally concerned with is the position of a juryman who, unlike the judge, has neither the training nor the experience to assist him in putting out of his mind matters which are not evidence in the case. I find it difficult to conceive of a case in which *a tribunal*, properly directing itself in the terms of s 4(2), could find it necessary to order the postponement of the report of its proceedings. In so far as its proceedings might be the subject matter of an appeal, in most cases the appeal will be restricted to a point of law and heard by an appellate tribunal who in the majority, if not all, cases will comprise a lawyer. To contemplate a case where there would be a real risk, as opposed to a remote possibility, that a report would so influence such a tribunal as to affect their impartiality, either consciously or even unconsciously, is to impose an unreasonable strain on one's imagination.

If counsel for the appellants is right in his submissions, it would be necessary to look behind every order made under s 4(2) and not only to reconsider the very basis of the order, but to revive all the old uncertainties recognised to exist at common law as to whether the conduct complained of could have amounted to contempt. This cannot have been Parliament's intention. It would involve a s 4(2) order having *no effect* at all in regard to committal proceedings and little effect in regard to other proceedings. Moreover, I believe that some assistance can be obtained from the terms of s 11 of the Contempt of Court Act 1981. This provides that:

> 'In any case where a court (having power to do so) allows a name or other matter to be withheld from the public in proceedings before the court, the court may give such directions prohibiting the publication of that name or matter in connection with the proceedings as appear to the court to be necessary for the purpose for which it was so withheld.'

By expressly incorporating the words 'having power to do so', attention is specifically invited to the pre-existing state of the law. Moreover, s 11 clearly itself contemplates contempt, other than contempt under the strict liability rule. I further accept the submission of counsel for the Commissioners of Customs and Excise that within the language of s 4(2) there are pointers to the conclusion that there is a liability for a breach of an order under s 4(2) which is different from liability under the strict liability rule. The substantial risk of prejudice may relate to 'any other proceedings pending or imminent'. This goes wider than proceedings which are 'active' within the meaning of s 2(3) and Sch 1 to the Contempt of Court Act 1981. Moreover, I consider that Parliament by use of additional words was contemplating a more stringent test in s 2(2) than that provided in s 4(2).

4. The proceedings in the Crown Court were not 'those proceedings' or 'any other proceedings pending or imminent'

It was accepted on all sides that the decision of Forbes J as to the meaning of 'those proceedings' could not be sustained. 'Those proceedings' must, as indeed was the view of Glidewell J, be limited to proceedings being heard at the relevant time. Counsel's

contention on behalf of the appellants, however, was that the Crown Court proceedings
could not be pending, because the accused had not yet been committed. A committal
may or may not take place and so long as the situation was a contingent one the
proceedings could not be said to be 'pending'. Again I accept the submission of counsel
for the Commissioners of Customs and Excise that, in the context of the law of contempt,
'pending' is a term of legal art. It has long been established that from the time a person
is charged, even though he has not been committed for trial, his trial is 'pending' (see *R
v Parke* [1903] 2 KB 432, [1900–3] All ER Rep 721 followed in *R v Duffy, ex p Nash* [1960]
2 All ER 891 at 893, [1960] 2 QB 188 at 195). Proceedings are 'imminent' even before
that event.

*5. On the facts of this case there was no material which could justify the magistrates in postponing
the reporting of any part of the proceedings*

To my mind the Divisional Court was entirely correct in deciding that the blanket
order imposed by the magistrates was too wide. It therefore ordered that the case be
remitted to the magistrates for them to consider whether any order should be made
postponing publication of reports and, if so, whether it should relate to only part of the
committal proceedings. Before the Divisional Court the submission that there was not
sufficient material before the magistrates to enable them to make *any* postponement
order was abandoned. However, before us counsel for the appellants sought to argue
that a decision by the magistrates, even to order the postponement of the reporting of
what has been called 'the sensitive material', the mosque shooting aspect of the case,
would be a perverse decision. In my judgment, the appellants' first thoughts, namely
those before the Divisional Court, when they abandoned this point, were correct. There
was material before the magistrates to support the submission that, not only was the
prosecution proposing to tender evidence which was irrelevant and therefore inadmissible
to the charges which they were hearing, but that such evidence was likely to be the
subject of sensational reporting. Therefore, there was a real risk of prejudice to the
administration of justice. Potential jurors who would be trying the case at the Crown
Court, if the magistrates committed, might well start the trial with a bias against the
accused, having inferred from the press reports that the accused were involved in far
more serious offences than those charged. Whether or not the magistrates are satisfied
that the material placed before them makes it necessary for them to make an order
postponing the reporting of this particular aspect of the case is a matter for their
discretion. In my judgment, it would be quite wrong to say that, if they made such an
order, it would be perverse because there was no material to suggest a substantial risk of
prejudice to the administration of justice.

I would therefore dismiss this appeal.

*Appeal dismissed. Reporting restrictions to continue until matter reconsidered by magistrates.
Leave to appeal to the House of Lords granted.*

Solicitors: *Harriet Harman* (for the appellants); *Solicitor for the Customs and Excise ; Maxwell
& Gouldman* (for Mr Bukhari); *Levene, Phillips & Swycher* (for Mr Howson and Mr Amos).

Frances Rustin   Barrister.

McLoughlin v O'Brian and others   *a*

HOUSE OF LORDS

LORD WILBERFORCE, LORD EDMUND-DAVIES, LORD RUSSELL OF KILLOWEN, LORD SCARMAN AND LORD BRIDGE OF HARWICH

15, 16 FEBRUARY, 6 MAY 1982

Negligence – Duty to take care – Foreseeable harm – Duty to take care to avoid injury to persons *b*
who might foreseeably suffer injury from want of care – Driver of motor vehicle – Duty to other
road users and owners of property – Nervous shock – Plaintiff suffering nervous shock on hearing
that family involved in road accident – Plaintiff at home at time of accident – Whether duty of
care owed to plaintiff by driver causing accident.

Damages – Personal injury – Nervous shock – Plaintiff's family killed or badly injured in road *c*
accident caused by defendant's negligence – Plaintiff at home at time of accident – Plaintiff
informed of accident and going to hospital – Plaintiff suffering nervous shock as a result –
Whether defendant owing duty of care to plaintiff – Whether plaintiff's injury reasonably
foreseeable – Whether as matter of policy court would not impose duty of care on defendant to
plaintiff.

 d

Damages – Personal injury – Nervous shock – Public policy – Whether public policy requiring
legal limitations on recovery of damages for nervous shock.

The plaintiff's husband and three children were involved in a road accident caused by the
negligence of the defendants. One of the plaintiff's children was killed and her husband
and other two children were severely injured. At the time of the accident the plaintiff *e*
was at home two miles away. She was told of the accident by a motorist who had been
at the scene of the accident and was taken to hospital where she saw the injured members
of her family and the extent of their injuries and shock and heard that her daughter had
been killed. As a results of hearing, and seeing the results of, the accident the plaintiff
suffered severe and persisting nervous shock. The plaintiff claimed damages against the
defendants for the nervous shock, distress and injury to her health caused by the *f*
defendants' negligence. The judge dismissed her claim on the ground that her injury
was not reasonably foreseeable. On appeal, the Court of Appeal held that the plaintiff
was not entitled to claim against the defendants either because as a matter of policy a
duty of care was not to be imposed on a negligent defendant beyond that owed to persons
in close proximity, both in time and place, to an accident, even though the injuries
received by the plaintiff might be reasonably foreseeable as being a consequence of the *g*
defendants' negligence, or because the duty of care owed by a driver of a motor vehicle
was limited to persons on or near the road. The plaintiff appealed to the House of Lords.

Held – The test of liability for damages for nervous shock was reasonable foreseeability
of the plaintiff being injured by nervous shock as a result of the defendant's negligence.
Applying that test, the plaintiff was entitled to recover damages from the defendants *h*
because even though the plaintiff was not at or near the scene of the accident at the time
or shortly afterwards the nervous shock suffered by her was a reasonably foreseeable
consequence of the defendant's negligence. The appeal would accordingly be allowed
(see p 301 *j*, p 302 *a b* and *h* to p 303 *a*, p 305 *e* to *g*, p 306 *f g*, p 309 *g*, p 310 *a d e*,
p 311 *f g*, p 313 *b c* and p 320 *h j*, post).

    Dictum of Denning LJ in *King v Phillips* [1953] 1 All ER at 623 approved. *j*
    Dictum of Bankes LJ in *Hambrook v Stokes Bros* [1924] All ER Rep at 113 and of Lord
Wright in *Hay (or Bourhill) v Young* [1942] 2 All ER at 405–406 applied.
    Dillon v Legg (1968) 68 C 2d 728 considered.
    Chester v Waverley Municipal Council (1939) 62 CLR 1 not followed.
    Per Lord Russell, Lord Scarman and Lord Bridge (Lord Edmund-Davies not con-

curring). In the area of nervous shock caused by negligence on the highway, the sole test of liability is reasonable foreseeability without any legal limitation in terms of space, time, distance, the nature of the injuries sustained or the relationship of the plaintiff to the victim (although those are factors to be considered), since (per Lord Bridge) there are no policy considerations sufficient to justify limiting the liability of negligent tortfeasors by some narrower criterion than that of reasonable foreseeability. If (per Lord Scarman) public policy requires such a limitation, the policy issue where to draw the line is not justiciable but a matter for legislation (see p 310 b to h, p 311 c to g, p 317 h j, p 319 f to j and p 320 e to g, post).

Per Lord Wilberforce. The application of the reasonable foreseeability test in nervous shock claims ought to be limited, in terms of proximity, so that what is foreseeable is circumscribed by the proximity of the tie or relationship between the plaintiff and the injured person, the proximity of the plaintiff to the accident both in time and place, and the proximity of communication of the accident to the plaintiff through sight or hearing of the event or its immediate aftermath (see p 303 d to f and p 304 f to p 305 e, post).

Decision of the Court of Appeal [1981] 1 All ER 809 reversed.

Notes

For liability for nervous shock, see 34 Halsbury's Laws (4th edn) para 8, and for cases on the subject, see 17 Digest (Reissue) 145–147, 377–391.

For remoteness of damage, see 12 Halsbury's Laws (4th edn) para 1127, and for cases on the subject, see 36(1) Digest (Reissue) 63–65, 306–307, 227–236, 1232–1236.

Cases referred to in opinions

Abramzik v Brenner (1967) 65 DLR (2d) 651, 17 Digest (Reissue) 152, *283.

Anns v Merton London Borough [1977] 2 All ER 492, [1978] AC 728, [1977] 2 WLR 1024, HL, 1(1) Digest (Reissue) 128, 721.

Bell v Great Northern Rly Co of Ireland (1890) 26 LR Ir 428, 36(1) Digest (Reissue) 310, *2558.

Benson v Lee [1972] VR 879, 17 Digest (Reissue) 151, *277.

Boardman v Sanderson [1964] 1 WLR 1317, CA, 17 Digest (Reissue) 145, 378.

British Rlys Board v Herrington [1972] 1 All ER 749, [1972] AC 877, [1972] 2 WLR 537, HL, 36(1) Digest (Reissue) 121, 466.

Byrne v Great Southern and Western Rly Co of Ireland (1884) unreported, cited in 26 LR Ir at 428, 36(1) Digest (Reissue) 310, *2557.

Chadwick v British Transport Commission [1967] 2 All ER 945, [1967] 1 WLR 912, 17 Digest (Reissue) 147, 390.

Chester v Waverley Municipal Council (1939) 62 CLR 1, 36(1) Digest (Reissue) 33, *103.

Dillon v Legg (1968) 68 C 2d 728, Cal SC.

Donoghue (or M'Alister) v Stevenson [1932] AC 562, [1932] All ER Rep 1, HL, 36(1) Digest (Reissue) 144, 562.

Dulieu v White & Sons [1901] 2 KB 669, [1900–3] All ER Rep 353, DC, 17 Digest (Reissue) 146, 385.

Fender v Mildmay [1937] 3 All ER 402, [1938] AC 1, HL, 12 Digest (Reissue) 325, 2352.

Hambrook v Stokes Bros [1925] 1 KB 141, [1924] All ER Rep 110, CA, 17 Digest (Reissue) 145, 377.

Hay (or Bourhill) v Young [1942] 2 All ER 396, [1943] AC 92, HL; *affg* 1941 SC 395, 17 Digest (Reissue) 146, 388.

Haynes v Harwood [1935] 1 KB 146, [1934] All ER Rep 103, CA, 36(1) Digest (Reissue) 245, 953.

Hedley Byrne & Co Ltd v Heller & Partners Ltd [1963] 2 All ER 575, [1964] AC 465, [1963] 3 WLR 101, HL, 36(1) Digest (Reissue) 24, 84.

Hinz v Berry [1970] 1 All ER 1074, [1970] 2 QB 40, [1970] 2 WLR 684, CA, 17 Digest (Reissue) 147, 391.

Home Office v Dorset Yacht Co Ltd [1970] 2 All ER 294, [1970] AC 1004, [1970] 2 WLR 1140, HL, 36(1) Digest (Reissue) 27, 93.

Janson v Driefontein Consolidated Mines Ltd [1902] AC 484, [1900–3] All ER Rep 426, HL,
    12 Digest (Reissue) 296, *2132*.
King v Phillips [1953] 1 All ER 617, [1953] 1 QB 429, [1953] 2 WLR 526, CA, 17 Digest
    (Reissue) 147, *389*.
Lambert v Lewis [1980] 1 All ER 978, [1980] 2 WLR 299, CA; *rvsd in part* [1981] 1 All ER
    1185, [1981] 2 WLR 713, HL.
Marshall v Lionel Enterprises Inc (1971) 25 DLR (3d) 141, 17 Digest (Reissue) 152, *284*.
McKew v Holland & Hannen & Cubitts (Scotland) Ltd [1969] 3 All ER 1621, HL, 17 Digest
    (Reissue) 115, *187*.
Morgans v Launchbury [1972] 2 All ER 606, [1973] AC 127, [1972] 2 WLR 1217, HL,
    36(1) Digest (Reissue) 173, *643*.
Nova Mink Ltd v Trans-Canada Airlines [1951] 2 DLR 241, 36(1) Digest (Reissue) 47, *208*.
Overseas Tankship (UK) Ltd v Morts Dock and Engineering Co Ltd, The Wagon Mound (No 1)
    [1961] 1 All ER 404, [1961] AC 388, [1961] 2 WLR 126, DC, 36(1) Digest (Reissue) 63,
    227.
Rondel v Worsley [1967] 3 All ER 993, [1969] 1 AC 191, [1967] 3 WLR 1666, HL, 3 Digest
    (Reissue) 786, *4877*.
Smith v Johnson & Co (1897) unreported, cited in [1897] 2 QB at 61, DC, 36(1) Digest
    (Reissue) 308, *1241*.
Victorian Rlys Comrs v Coultas (1888) 13 App Cas 222, PC, 36(1) Digest (Reissue) 308,
    1239.
Wagner v International Rlys Co (1921) 232 NY Rep 176.

Appeal
The plaintiff, Rosina McLoughlin, appealed against the judgment of the Court of Appeal
(Stephenson, Cumming-Bruce and Griffiths LJJ) ([1981] 1 All ER 809, [1981] QB 599)
given on 16 December 1980 dismissing her appeal against the judgment of Boreham J
on 11 December 1978 whereby the judge dismissed her claim against the defendants,
Thomas Alan O'Brian, A E Docker & Sons Ltd, Raymond Sygrove and Ernest Doe & Sons
Ltd, the respondents to the appeal, for damages for shock, distress and injury to her
health. The facts are set out in the opinion of Lord Wilberforce.

Michael Ogden QC and *Jonathan Haworth* for the appellant.
Michael Turner QC and *John Leighton Williams* for the respondents.

Their Lordships took time for consideration.

6 May. The following opinions were delivered.

LORD WILBERFORCE. My Lords, this appeal arises from a very serious and tragic
road accident which occurred on 19 October 1973 near Withersfield, Suffolk. The
appellant's husband, Thomas McLoughlin, and three of her children, George, aged 17,
Kathleen, aged 7, and Gillian, nearly 3, were in a Ford motor car; George was driving.
A fourth child, Michael, then aged 11, was a passenger in a following motor car driven
by Mr Pilgrim; this car did not become involved in the accident. The Ford car was in
collision with a lorry driven by the first respondent and owned by the second
respondent. That lorry had been in collision with another lorry driven by the third
respondent and owned by the fourth respondent. It is admitted that the accident to the
Ford car was caused by the respondents' negligence. It is necessary to state what followed
in full detail.
    As a result of the accident, the appellant's husband suffered bruising and shock; George
suffered injuries to his head and face, cerebral concussion, fractures of both scapulae and
bruising and abrasions; Kathleen suffered concussion, fracture of the right clavicle,
bruising, abrasions and shock; Gillian was so seriously injured that she died almost
immediately.
    At the time, the appellant was at her home about two miles away; an hour or so
afterwards the accident was reported to her by Mr Pilgrim, who told her that he thought

George was dying, and that he did not know the whereabouts of her husband or the condition of her daughter. He then drove her to Addenbrooke's hospital, Cambridge. There she saw Michael, who told her that Gillian was dead. She was taken down a corridor and through a window she saw Kathleen, crying, with her face cut and begrimed with dirt and oil. She could hear George shouting and screaming. She was taken to her husband who was sitting with his head in his hands. His shirt was hanging off him and he was covered in mud and oil. He saw the appellant and started sobbing. The appellant was then taken to see George. The whole of his left face and left side was covered. He appeared to recognise the appellant and then lapsed into unconsciousness. Finally, the appellant was taken to Kathleen who by now had been cleaned up. The child was too upset to speak and simply clung to her mother. There can be no doubt that these circumstances, witnessed by the appellant, were distressing in the extreme and were capable of producing an effect going well beyond that of grief and sorrow.

The appellant subsequently brought proceedings against the respondents. At the trial, the judge assumed, for the purpose of enabling him to decide the issue of legal liability, that the appellant subsequently suffered the condition of which she complained. This was described as severe shock, organic depression and a change of personality. Numerous symptoms of a physiological character are said to have been manifested. The details were not investigated at the trial, the court being asked to assume that the appellant's condition had been caused or contributed to by shock, as distinct from grief or sorrow, and that the appellant was a person of reasonable fortitude.

On these facts, or assumed facts, the trial judge, Boreham J, gave judgment for the respondents holding, in a most careful judgment reviewing the authorities, that the respondents owed no duty of care to the appellant because the possibility of her suffering injury by nervous shock, in the circumstances, was not reasonably foreseeable.

On appeal by the appellant, the judgment of Boreham J was upheld, but not on the same ground (see [1981] 1 All ER 809, [1981] QB 599). Stephenson LJ took the view that the possibility of injury to the appellant by nervous shock *was* reasonably foreseeable and that the respondents owed the appellant a duty of care. However, he held that considerations of policy prevented the appellant from recovering. Griffiths LJ held that injury by nervous shock to the appellant was 'readily foreseeable' but that the respondents owed no duty of care to the appellant. The duty was limited to those on the road nearby. Cumming-Bruce LJ agreed with both judgments. The appellant now appeals to this House. The critical question to be decided is whether a person in the position of the appellant, ie one who was not present at the scene of grievous injuries to her family but who comes on those injuries at an interval of time and space, can recover damages for nervous shock.

Although we continue to use the hallowed expression 'nervous shock', English law, and common understanding, have moved some distance since recognition was given to this symptom as a basis for liability. Whatever is unknown about the mind-body relationship (and the area of ignorance seems to expand with that of knowledge), it is now accepted by medical science that recognisable and severe physical damage to the human body and system may be caused by the impact, through the senses, of external events on the mind. There may thus be produced what is as identifiable an illness as any that may be caused by direct physical impact. It is safe to say that this, in general terms, is understood by the ordinary man or woman who is hypothesised by the courts in situations where claims for negligence are made. Although in the only case which has reached this House (*Hay (or Bourhill) v Young* [1942] 2 All ER 396, [1943] AC 92) a claim for damages in respect of 'nervous shock' was rejected on its facts, the House gave clear recognition to the legitimacy, in principle, of claims of that character. As the result of that and other cases, assuming that they are accepted as correct, the following position has been reached:

1. While damages cannot, at common law, be awarded for grief and sorrow, a claim for damages for 'nervous shock' caused by negligence can be made without the necessity of showing direct impact or fear of immediate personal injuries for oneself. The reservation made by Kennedy J in *Dulieu v White & Sons* [1901] 2 KB 669, [1900–3] All ER Rep 353, though taken up by Sargant LJ in *Hambrook v Stokes Bros* [1925] 1 KB 141,

[1924] All ER Rep 110, has not gained acceptance, and although the respondents, in the courts below, reserved their right to revive it, they did not do so in argument. I think that it is now too late to do so. The arguments on this issue were fully and admirably stated by the Supreme Court of California in *Dillon v Legg* (1968) 29 ALR 3d 1316.

2. A plaintiff may recover damages for 'nervous shock' brought on by injury caused not to him or herself but to a near relative, or by the fear of such injury. So far (subject to 5 below), the cases do not extend beyond the spouse or children of the plaintiff (*Hambrook v Stokes Bros* [1925] 1 KB 141, [1924] All ER Rep 110, *Boardman v Sanderson* [1964] 1 WLR 1317, *Hinz v Berry* [1970] 1 All ER 1074, [1970] 2 QB 40, including foster children (where liability was assumed), and see *King v Phillips* [1953] 1 All ER 617, [1953] 1 QB 429).

3. Subject to the next paragraph, there is no English case in which a plaintiff has been able to recover nervous shock damages where the injury to the near relative occurred out of sight and earshot of the plaintiff. In *Hambrook v Stokes Bros* an express distinction was made between shock caused by what the mother saw with her own eyes and what she might have been told by bystanders, liability being excluded in the latter case.

4. An exception from, or I would prefer to call it an extension of, the latter case has been made where the plaintiff does not see or hear the incident but comes on its immediate aftermath. In *Boardman v Sanderson* the father was within earshot of the accident to his child and likely to come on the scene; he did so and suffered damage from what he then saw. In *Marshall v Lionel Enterprises* (1971) 25 DLR (3d) 141 the wife came immediately on the badly injured body of her husband. And in *Benson v Lee* [1972] VR 879 a situation existed with some similarity to the present case. The mother was in her home 100 yards away, and, on communication by a third party, ran out to the scene of the accident and there suffered shock. Your Lordships have to decide whether or not to validate these extensions.

5. A remedy on account of nervous shock has been given to a man who came on a serious accident involving people immediately thereafter and acted as a rescuer of those involved (*Chadwick v British Transport Commission* [1967] 2 All ER 945, [1967] 1 WLR 912). 'Shock' was caused neither by fear for himself nor by fear or horror on account of a near relative. The principle of 'rescuer' cases was not challenged by the respondents and ought, in my opinion, to be accepted. But we have to consider whether, and how far, it can be applied to such cases as the present.

Throughout these developments, as can be seen, the courts have proceeded in the traditional manner of the common law from case to case, on a basis of logical necessity. If a mother, with or without accompanying children, could recover on account of fear for herself, how can she be denied recovery on account of fear for her accompanying children? If a father could recover had he seen his child run over by a backing car, how can he be denied recovery if he is in the immediate vicinity and runs to the child's assistance? If a wife and mother could recover if she had witnessed a serious accident to her husband and children, does she fail because she was a short distance away and immediately rushes to the scene? (cf *Benson v Lee*). I think that, unless the law is to draw an arbitrary line at the point of direct sight and sound, these arguments require acceptance of the extension mentioned above under principle 4 in the interests of justice.

If one continues to follow the process of logical progression, it is hard to see why the present plaintiff also should not succeed. She was not present at the accident, but she came very soon after on its aftermath. If, from a distance of some 100 yards (cf *Benson v Lee*), she had found her family by the roadside, she would have come within principle 4 above. Can it make any difference that she comes on them in an ambulance, or, as here, in a nearby hospital, when, as the evidence shows, they were in the same condition, covered with oil and mud, and distraught with pain? If Mr Chadwick can recover when, acting in accordance with normal and irresistible human instinct, and indeed moral compulsion, he goes to the scene of an accident, may not a mother recover if, acting under the same motives, she goes to where her family can be found?

I could agree that a line can be drawn above her case with less hardship than would have been apparent in *Boardman's* and *Hinz's* cases, but so to draw it would not appeal to most people's sense of justice. To allow her claim may be, I think it is, on the margin of what the process of logical progression would allow. But where the facts are strong and exceptional, and, as I think, fairly analogous, her case ought, prima facie, to be assimilated to those which have passed the test.

To argue from one factual situation to another and to decide by analogy is a natural tendency of the human and legal mind. But the lawyer still has to inquire whether, in so doing, he has crossed some critical line behind which he ought to stop. That is said to be the present case. The reasoning by which the Lords Justices decided not to grant relief to the plaintiff is instructive. Both Stephenson and Griffiths LJJ accepted that the 'shock' to the plaintiff was foreseeable; but from this, at least in presentation, they diverge. Stephenson LJ considered that the defendants owed a duty of care to the plaintiff, but that for reasons of policy the law should stop short of giving her damages: it should limit relief to those on or near the highway at or near the time of the accident caused by the defendants' negligence. He was influenced by the fact that the courts of this country, and of other common law jurisdictions, had stopped at this point: it was indicated by the barrier of commercial sense and practical convenience. Griffiths LJ took the view that, although the injury to the plaintiff was foreseeable, there was no duty of care. The duty of care of drivers of motor vehicles was, according to decided cases, limited to persons and owners of property on the road or near to it who might be directly affected. The line should be drawn at this point. It was not even in the interest of those suffering from shock as a class to extend the scope of the defendants' liability: to do so would quite likely delay their recovery by immersing them in the anxiety of litigation.

I am deeply impressed by both of these arguments, which I have only briefly summarised. Though differing in expression, in the end, in my opinion, the two presentations rest on a common principle, namely that, at the margin, the boundaries of a man's responsibility for acts of negligence have to be fixed as a matter of policy. Whatever is the correct jurisprudential analysis, it does not make any essential difference whether one says, with Stephenson LJ, that there is a duty but, as a matter of policy, the consequences of breach of it ought to be limited at a certain point, or whether, with Griffiths LJ, one says that the fact that consequences may be foreseeable does not automatically impose a duty of care, does not do so in fact where policy indicates the contrary. This is an approach which one can see very clearly from the way in which Lord Atkin stated the neighbour principle in *Donoghue v Stevenson* [1932] AC 462 at 580, [1932] All ER Rep 1 at 11: '. . . persons who are so closely and directly affected by my act that I ought reasonably to have them in contemplation as being so affected . . .'

This is saying that foreseeability must be accompanied and limited by the law's judgment as to persons who ought, according to its standards of value or justice, to have been in contemplation. Foreseeability, which involves a hypothetical person, looking with hindsight at an event which has occurred, is a formula adopted by English law, not merely for defining, but also for limiting the persons to whom duty may be owed, and the consequences for which an actor may be held responsible. It is not merely an issue of fact to be left to be found as such. When it is said to result in a duty of care being owed to a person or a class, the statement that there is a 'duty of care' denotes a conclusion into the forming of which considerations of policy have entered. That foreseeability does not of itself, and automatically, lead to a duty of care is, I think, clear. I gave some examples in *Anns v Merton London Borough* [1977] 2 All ER 492 at 498, [1978] AC 728 at 752, *Anns* itself being one. I may add what Lord Reid said in *McKew v Holland & Hannen & Cubitts (Scotland) Ltd* [1969] 3 All ER 1621 at 1623: 'A defender is not liable for a consequence of a kind which is not foreseeable. But it does not follow that he is liable for every consequence which a reasonable man could foresee.'

We must then consider the policy arguments. In doing so we must bear in mind that cases of 'nervous shock' and the possibility of claiming damages for it are not necessarily confined to those arising out of accidents in public roads. To state, therefore, a rule that recoverable damages must be confined to persons on or near the highway is to state not a principle in itself but only an example of a more general rule that recoverable damages must be confined to those within sight and sound of an event caused by negligence or, at least, to those in close, or very close, proximity to such a situation.

The policy arguments against a wider extension can be stated under four heads. First, it may be said that such extension may lead to a proliferation of claims, and possibly fraudulent claims, to the establishment of an industry of lawyers and psychiatrists who will formulate a claim for nervous shock damages, including what in America is called the customary miscarriage, for all, or many, road accidents and industrial accidents. Second, it may be claimed that an extension of liability would be unfair to defendants, as imposing damages out of proportion to the negligent conduct complained of. In so far as such defendants are insured, a large additional burden will be placed on insurers, and ultimately on the class of persons insured: road users or employers. Third, to extend liability beyond the most direct and plain cases would greatly increase evidentiary difficulties and tend to lengthen litigation. Fourth, it may be said (and the Court of Appeal agreed with this) that an extension of the scope of liability ought only to be made by the legislature, after careful research. This is the course which has been taken in New South Wales and the Australian Capital Territory.

The whole argument has been well summed up by Dean Prosser in *The Law of Torts* (4th edn, 1971) p 256:

> 'The reluctance of courts to enter this zone even where the mental injury is clearly foreseeable, and the frequent mention of the difficulties of proof, the facility of fraud and the problem of finding a place to stop and draw the line, suggest that here it is the nature of the interest invaded and the type of damages which is the real obstacle.'

Since he wrote, the type of damage has, in this country at least, become more familiar and less deterrent to recovery. And some of the arguments are susceptible of answer. Fraudulent claims can be contained by the courts, which, also, can cope with evidentiary difficulties. The scarcity of cases which have occurred in the past, and the modest sums recovered, give some indication that fears of a flood of litigation may be exaggerated: experience in other fields suggests that such fears usually are. If some increase does occur, that may only reveal the existence of a genuine social need; that legislation has been found necessary in Australia may indicate the same thing.

But, these discounts accepted, there remains, in my opinion, just because 'shock' in its nature is capable of affecting so wide a range of people, a real need for the law to place some limitation on the extent of admissible claims. It is necessary to consider three elements inherent in any claim: the class of persons whose claims should be recognised; the proximity of such persons to the accident; and the means by which the shock is caused. As regards the class of persons, the possible range is between the closest of family ties, of parent and child, or husband and wife, and the ordinary bystander. Existing law recognises the claims of the first; it denies that of the second, either on the basis that such persons must be assumed to be possessed of fortitude sufficient to enable them to endure the calamities of modern life or that defendants cannot be expected to compensate the world at large. In my opinion, these positions are justifiable, and since the present case falls within the first class it is strictly unnecessary to say more. I think, however, that it should follow that other cases involving less close relationships must be very carefully scrutinised. I cannot say that they should never be admitted. The closer the tie (not merely in relationship, but in care) the greater the claim for consideration. The claim, in any case, has to be judged in the light of the other factors, such as proximity to the scene in time and place, and the nature of the accident.

As regards proximity to the accident, it is obvious that this must be close in both time and space. It is after all, the fact and consequence of the defendant's negligence that must be proved to have caused the 'nervous shock'. Experience has shown that to insist on direct and immediate sight or hearing would be impractical and unjust and that under what may be called the 'aftermath' doctrine, one who, from close proximity comes very soon on the scene, should not be excluded. In my opinion, the result in *Benson v Lee* [1972] VR 879 was correct and indeed inescapable. It was based, soundly, on 'direct perception of some of the events which go to make up the accident as an entire event, and this includes ... the immediate aftermath'. The High Court of Australia's majority decision in *Chester v Waverley Municipal Council* (1939) 62 CLR 1, where a child's body was found floating in a trench after a prolonged search, may perhaps be placed on the other side of a recognisable line (Evatt J in a powerful dissent placed it on the same side), but in addition, I find the conclusion of Lush J in *Benson v Lee* to reflect developments in the law.

Finally, and by way of reinforcement of 'aftermath' cases, I would accept, by analogy with 'rescue' situations, that a person of whom it could be said that one could expect nothing else than that he or she would come immediately to the scene (normally a parent or a spouse) could be regarded as being within the scope of foresight and duty. Where there is not immediate presence, account must be taken of the possibility of alterations in the circumstances, for which the defendant should not be responsible.

Subject only to these qualifications, I think that a strict test of proximity by sight or hearing should be applied by the courts.

Lastly, as regards communication, there is no case in which the law has compensated shock brought about by communication by a third party. In *Hambrook v Stokes Bros* [1925] 1 KB 141, [1924] All ER Rep 110, indeed, it was said that liability would not arise in such a case, and this is surely right. It was so decided in *Abramzik v Brenner* (1967) 65 DLR (2d) 651. The shock must come through sight or hearing of the event or of its immediate aftermath. Whether some equivalent of sight or hearing, eg through simultaneous television, would suffice may have to be considered.

My Lords, I believe that these indications, imperfectly sketched, and certainly to be applied with common sense to individual situations in their entirety, represent either the existing law, or the existing law with only such circumstantial extension as the common law process may legitimately make. They do not introduce a new principle. Nor do I see any reason why the law should retreat behind the lines already drawn. I find on this appeal that the appellant's case falls within the boundaries of the law so drawn. I would allow her appeal.

LORD EDMUND-DAVIES. My Lords, I am for allowing this appeal. The facts giving rise to it have been related in detail by my noble and learned friend, Lord Wilberforce, and both he and my noble and learned friend Lord Bridge have spaciously reviewed the case law relating to the recovery of damages for personal injury resulting from nervous shock. My own observations can, in the circumstances, be substantially briefer than I had originally planned.

It is common ground in the appeal that, the appellant's claim being based on shock, '. . . there can be no doubt since *Hay* (or *Bourhill*) v. *Young* ([1942] 2 All ER 396, [1943] AC 92 that the test of liability . . . is foreseeability of injury by shock' (per Denning LJ in *King v Phillips* [1953] 1 All ER 617 at 623, [1953] 1 QB 429 at 441). But this was not always the law, and great confusion arose in the cases from applying to claims based on shock restrictions hedging negligence actions based on the infliction of *physical* injuries. In the same year as that in which *King v Phillips* was decided, Goodhart perceptively asked why it was considered that the area of possible physical injury should be relevant to a case based on the unlawful infliction of shock, and continued (16 MLR, p 22):

> 'A woman standing at the window of a second-floor room is just as likely to receive a shock when witnessing an accident as she would be if she were standing on the pavement. To say that the careless driver of a motor-car could not reasonably foresee such a self-evident fact is to hide the truth behind a fiction which must disappear as soon as we examine it. The driver obviously cannot foresee that the woman at the window will receive a physical injury, but it does not follow from this that he cannot foresee that she will receive a shock. As the cause of action is based on shock it is only foresight of shock which is relevant.'

Indeed, in *King v Phillips* itself Denning LJ expressly held that the fact that the plaintiff was in an upstairs room 80 yards away from the scene of the accident was immaterial.

It is true that, as Goodhart observed, in most cases the foresight concerning emotional injury and that concerning physical injury are identical, the shock following the physical injury, and the result was that, in the early development of this branch of the law, the courts tended to assume that this must be so in all cases. But in fact, as Goodhart laconically put it, 'The area of risk of physical injury may extend to only X yards, while the area of risk of emotional injury may extend to Y yards'. That error still persists is indicated by the holding of Stephenson LJ in the instant case that the ambit of duty of care owed by a motorist is restricted to persons 'on or near the highway at or near the time of the accident' (see [1981] 1 All ER 809 at 820, [1981] QB 599 at 614), and by Griffiths LJ to those 'on the road or near to it who may be directly affected by the bad driving. It is not owed to those who are nowhere near the scene' (see [1981] 1 All ER 809 at 827, [1981] QB 599 at 623). The most striking feature in the present case is that such limits on the duty of care were imposed notwithstanding the unanimous conclusion of the Court of Appeal that it was reasonably foreseeable (and even 'readily' so in the judgment of Griffiths LJ) that injury by shock could be caused to a person in the position of the appellant.

Similar restrictions were unsuccessfully sought to be imposed in *Haynes v Harwood* [1935] 1 KB 146, [1934] All ER Rep 103, the plaintiff having been inside a police station when he first saw the bolting horses and therefore out of sight and seemingly out of danger. And they were again rejected in *Chadwick v British Transport Commission* [1967] 2 All ER 945, [1967] 1 WLR 912, where the plaintiff was in his home 200 yards away when the Lewisham railway accident occurred. Griffiths LJ expressed himself as 'quite unable to include in the category of rescuers to whom a duty [of care] is owed a relative visiting victims in hospital' (see [1981] 1 All ER 809 at 827, [1981] QB 599 at 623). I do not share the difficulty, and in my respectful judgment none exists. I am here content to repeat once more the noble words of Cardozo J in *Wagner v International Rlys Co* (1921) 232 NY Rep 176 at 180:

> 'Danger invites rescue. The cry of distress is the summons to relief. The law does not ignore these reactions of the mind in tracing conduct to its consequences. It recognises them as normal. It places their effect within the range of the natural and probable. The wrong that imperils life is a wrong to the imperilled victim; it is wrong also to his rescuer.'

Was not the action of the appellant in visiting her family in hospital immediately she heard of the accident basically indistinguishable from that of a 'rescuer', being intent on comforting the injured? And was not her action 'natural and probable' in the circumstances? I regard the questions as capable only of affirmative answers, and, indeed, Stephenson LJ so answered them.

I turn to consider the sole basis on which the Court of Appeal dismissed the claim, that of public policy. They did so on the ground of what, for short, may be called the 'floodgates' argument. Griffiths LJ presented it in the following way ([1981] 1 All ER 809 at 823, [1981] QB 599 at 617):

> 'If the [appellant's] argument is right it will certainly have far-reaching consequences, for it will not only apply to road traffic accidents. Whenever anybody is injured it is foreseeable that the relatives will be told and will visit them in hospital, and it is further foreseeable that in cases of grave injury and death some of those relatives are likely to have a severe reaction causing illness. Of course, the closer the relationship the more readily it is foreseeable that they may be so affected, but if we just confine our consideration to parents and children and husbands and wives, it is clear that the potential liability of the tortfeasor is vastly increased if he has to compensate the relatives as well as the immediate victims of his carelessness.'

He continued ([1981] 1 All ER 809 at 827, [1981] QB 599 at 623):

> 'Every system of law must set some bounds to the consequences for which a wrongdoer must make reparation. If the burden is too great it cannot and will not be met, the law will fall into disrepute, and it will be a disservice to those victims who might reasonably have expected compensation. In any state of society it is ultimately a question of policy to decide the limits of liability.'

Stephenson LJ expressed the same view by citing his own observation when giving the judgment of the Court of Appeal in *Lambert v Lewis* [1980] 1 All ER 978 at 1006, [1980] 2 WLR 299 at 331 that 'There comes a point where the logical extension of the boundaries of duty and damage is halted by the barrier of commercial sense and practical convenience'.

My Lords, the experiences of a long life in the law have made me very familiar with this 'floodgates' argument. I do not, of course, suggest that it can invariably be dismissed as lacking cogency; on the contrary, it has to be weighed carefully, but I have often seen it disproved by later events. It was urged when abolition of the doctrine of common employment was being canvassed, and it raised its head again when the abolition of contributory negligence as a total bar to a claim in negligence was being urged. And, even before my time, on the basis of conjecture later shown to be ill-founded it provided a fatal stumbling-block to the plaintiff's claim in the 'shock' case of *Victorian Rlys Comrs v Coultas* (1888) 13 App Cas 222, where Sir Richard Couch sounded the 'floodgates' alarm in stirring words which are quoted in the speech of my noble and learned friend Lord Bridge.

My Lords, for such reasons as those developed in the speech of my noble and learned friend Lord Wilberforce and which it would serve no purpose for me to repeat in less felicitous words of my own, I remain unconvinced that the number and area of claims in 'shock' cases would be substantially increased or enlarged were the respondents here held liable. It is a question which Kennedy J answered in *Dulieu v White & Sons* [1901] 2 KB 669 at 681, [1900–3] All ER Rep 353 at 360 in the following terms, which commend themselves strongly to me:

'I should be sorry to adopt a rule which would bar all such claims on grounds of policy alone, and in order to prevent the possible success of unrighteous or groundless actions. Such a course involves the denial of redress in meritorious cases, and it necessarily implies a certain amount of distrust, which I do not share, in the capacity of legal tribunals to get at the truth in this class of claim.'

My Lords, in the present case two totally different points arising from the speeches of two of your Lordships call for further attention. Both relate to the Court of Appeal's invoking public policy. Unless I have completely misunderstood my noble and learned friend Lord Bridge, he doubts that any regard should have been had to such a consideration, and seemingly considered the Court of Appeal went wrong in paying any attention to it. The sole test of liability, I read him as saying, is the reasonable foreseeability of injury to the plaintiff through nervous shock resulting from the defendant's conceded default. And, such foreseeability having been established to their unanimous satisfaction, it followed that in law no other course was open to the Court of Appeal than to allow this appeal. I have respectfully to say that I cannot accept this approach. It is true that no decision was cited to your Lordships in which the contrary has been held, but that is not to say that reasonable foreseeability is the *only* test of the validity of a claim brought in negligence. If it is surmounted, the defendant would probably be hard put to escape liability.

Lord Wright found it difficult to conceive that any new head of public policy could be discovered (see *Fender v Mildmay* [1937] 3 All ER 402 at 427, [1938] AC 1 at 41), and, were Lord Halsbury LC sound in denying that any court could invent a new head of policy (see *Janson v Driefontein Consolidated Mines* [1902] AC 484 at 491, [1900–3] All ER Rep 426 at 429), I should have been in the happy position of accepting the standpoint adopted by my noble and learned friend Lord Bridge. But, as I shall later indicate, the more recent view which has found favour in your Lordships' House is that public policy is not immutable. Accordingly, whilst I would have strongly preferred indicating with clarity where the limit of liability should be drawn in such cases as the present, in my judgment the possibility of a wholly new type of policy being raised renders the attainment of such finality unfortunately unattainable.

As I think, all we can say is that any invocation of public policy calls for the closest scrutiny, and the defendant might well fail to discharge the burden of making it good, as indeed, happened in *Rondel v Worsley* [1967] 3 All ER 993, [1969] 1 AC 191. But that is not to say that success for the defendant would be unthinkable, for, in the words of MacDonald J in *Nova Mink Ltd v Trans-Canada Airlines* [1951] 2 DLR 241 at 254:

> '... there is always a large element of judicial policy and social expediency involved in the determination of the duty-problem, however it may be obscured by the use of traditional formulae.'

I accordingly hold, as Griffiths LJ did, that 'The test of foreseeability is not a universal touchstone to determine the extent of liability for the consequences of wrongdoing' (see [1981] 1 All ER 809 at 823 [1981] QB 599 at 618). Authority for that proposition is both ample in quantity and exalted in status. My noble and learned friend Lord Wilberforce has already quoted in this context the observation of Lord Reid in *McKew v Holland & Hannen & Cubitts (Scotland) Ltd* [1969] 3 All ER 1621 at 1623, and referred to his own treatment of the topic in *Anns v Merton London Borough* [1977] 2 All ER 492 at 498, [1978] AC 728 at 752, where further citations are furnished. To add yet another, let me conclude by recalling that in *Hedley Byrne & Co Ltd v Heller & Partners Ltd* [1963] 2 All ER 575 at 615, [1964] AC 465 at 536 Lord Pearce observed:

> 'How wide the sphere of the duty of care in negligence is to be laid depends *ultimately* on the courts' assessment of the demands of society for protection from the carelessness of others.' (My emphasis.)

I finally turn to consider the following passage in the speech of my noble and learned friend Lord Scarman:

> 'Policy considerations will have to be weighed; but the objective of the judges is the formulation of principle. And, if principle inexorably requires a decision which entails a degree of policy risk, the court's function is to adjudicate according to principle, leaving policy curtailment to the judgment of Parliament ... If principle leads to results which are thought to be socially unacceptable, Parliament can legislate to draw a line or map out a new path.'

And at a later stage my noble and learned friend adds:

> 'Why then should not the courts draw the line, as the Court of Appeal manfully tried to do in this case? Simply, because the policy issue where to draw the line is not justiciable.'

My understanding of these words is that my noble and learned friend shares (though for a different reason) the conclusion of my noble and learned friend Lord Bridge that, in adverting to public policy, the Court of Appeal here embarked on a sleeveless errand, for public policy has no relevance to liability at law. In my judgment, the proposition that '... the policy issue ... is not justiciable' is as novel as it is startling. So novel is it in relation to this appeal that it was never mentioned during the hearing before your Lordships. And it is startling because in my respectful judgment it runs counter to well-established and wholly acceptable law.

I restrict myself to recent decisions of your Lordships' House. In *Rondel v Worsley* [1967] 3 All ER 993, [1969] 1 AC 191 their Lordships unanimously held that public policy required that a barrister should be immune from an action for negligence in respect of his conduct and management of a case in court and the work preliminary thereto, Lord Reid saying ([1967] 3 All ER 993 at 998, [1969] 1 AC 191 at 228):

> 'Is it in the public interest that barristers and advocates should be protected against such actions? Like so many questions which raise the public interest, a decision one way will cause hardships to individuals while a decision the other way will involve disadvantage to the public interest ... So the issue appears to me to be whether the abolition of the rule would probably be attended by such disadvantage to the public interest as to make its retention clearly justifiable.'

In *Home Office v Dorset Yacht Co* [1970] 2 All ER 294, [1970] AC 1004 your Lordships'

House was called on to decide whether the English law of civil wrongs should be extended to impose legal liability for loss caused by conduct of a kind which had not hitherto been recognised by the courts as entailing liability. In expressing the view that it did, Lord Diplock said ([1970] 2 All ER 294 at 324, [1970] AC 1004 at 1058):

> '... I agree with Lord Denning MR that what we are concerned with in this appeal "is ... at bottom a matter of public policy which we, as judges, must resolve".'

And in *British Rlys Board v Herrington* [1972] 1 All ER 749 at 756–757, [1972] AC 877 at 897, dealing with an occupier's duty to trespassing children, Lord Reid said:

> 'Legal principles cannot solve the problem. How far occupiers are to be required by law to take steps to safeguard such children must be a matter of public policy.'

My Lords, in accordance with such a line of authorities, I hold that public policy issues *are* 'justiciable'. Their invocation calls for close scrutiny, and the conclusion may be that its nature and existence have not been established with the clarity and cogency required before recognition can be granted to any legal doctrine and before any litigant can properly be deprived of what would otherwise be his manifest legal rights. Or the conclusion may be that adoption of the public policy relied on would involve the introduction of new legal principles so fundamental that they are best left to the legislature: see, for example, *Morgans v Launchbury* [1972] 2 All ER 606 esp at 615, [1973] AC 127 esp at 142, per Lord Pearson. And 'Public policy is not immutable' (per Lord Reid in *Rondel v Worsley* [1967] 3 All ER 993 at 998, [1969] 1 AC 199 at 227). Indeed, Winfield described it as '*necessarily* variable', and wisely added ((1928) 42 Harv LR at 93):

> 'This variability ... is a stone in the edifice of the doctrine, and not a missile to be flung at it. Public policy would be almost useless without it. The march of civilization and the difficulty of ascertaining public policy at any given time make it essential ... How is public policy evidenced? If it is so variable, if it depends on the welfare of the community at any given time, how are the courts to ascertain it? Some judges have thought this difficulty so great that they have urged that it would be solved much better by the legislature and have considered it to be the main reason why the courts should leave public policy alone ... This admonition is a wise one and judges are not likely to forget it. But the better view seems to be that the difficulty of discovering what public policy is at any given moment certainly does not absolve the bench from the duty of doing so. The judges are bound to take notice of it and of the changes which it undergoes, and it is immaterial that the question may be one of ethics rather than of law.'

In the present case the Court of Appeal did just that, and in my judgment they were right in doing so. But they concluded that public policy required them to dismiss what they clearly regarded as an otherwise irrefragable claim. In so concluding, I respectfully hold that they were wrong, and I would accordingly allow the appeal.

LORD RUSSELL OF KILLOWEN. My Lords, I make two comments at the outset. First, we are not concerned with any problem that might have been posed had the accident been not wholly attributable to the negligence of the defendants, but partly attributable to negligent driving by the injured son of the plaintiff. Second, the plaintiff is to be regarded as of normal disposition or phlegm; we are therefore not concerned to investigate the applicability of the 'thin skull' cases to this type of case.

The facts in this case, and the physical illness suffered by the plaintiff as a result of mental trauma caused to her by what she learned, heard and saw at the hospital have been set out in the speech of my noble and learned friend Lord Wilberforce and I do not repeat them.

All members of the Court of Appeal concluded that that which happened to the plaintiff was reasonably foreseeable by the defendants as a consequence of their negligence on the road. (In some cases, and at all levels, a reasonable *bystander* seems to be introduced as a relevant mind; I do not understand why: reasonable foreseeability must surely be something to be attributed to the person guilty of negligence.)

But, if the effect on this wife and mother of the results of the negligence is considered to have been reasonably foreseeable, I do not see the justification for not finding the defendants liable in damages therefor. I would not shrink from regarding in an appropriate case policy as something which may feature in a judicial decision. But in this case what policy should inhibit a decision in favour of liability to the plaintiff? Negligent driving on the highway is only one form of negligence which may cause wounding or death and thus induce a relevant mental trauma in a person such as the plaintiff. There seems to be no policy requirement that the damage to the plaintiff should be on or adjacent to the highway. In the last analysis any policy consideration seems to be rooted in a fear of floodgates opening, the tacit question: what next? I am not impressed by that fear, certainly not sufficiently to deprive this plaintiff of just compensation for the reasonably foreseeable damage done to her. I do not consider that such deprivation is justified by trying to answer in advance the question posed, What next? by a consideration of relationships of plaintiff to the sufferers or deceased, or other circumstances; to attempt in advance solutions, or even guidelines, in hypothetical cases may well, it seems to me, in this field, do more harm than good.

I also would allow this appeal.

LORD SCARMAN. My Lords, I have had the advantage of reading in draft the speech of my noble and learned friend Lord Bridge. It cannot be strengthened or improved by any words of mine. I accept his approach to the law and the conclusion he reaches. But I also share the anxieties of the Court of Appeal. I differ, however, from the Court of Appeal in that I am persuaded that in this branch of the law it is not for the courts but for the legislature to set limits, if any be needed, to the law's development.

The appeal raises directly a question as to the balance in our law between the functions of judge and legislature. The common law, which in a constitutional context includes judicially developed equity, covers everything which is not covered by statute. It knows no gaps: there can be no casus omissus. The function of the court is to decide the case before it, even though the decision may require the extension or adaptation of a principle or in some cases the creation of new law to meet the justice of the case. But, whatever the court decides to do, it starts from a baseline of existing principle and seeks a solution consistent with or analogous to a principle or principles already recognised.

The distinguishing feature of the common law is this judicial development and formulation of principle. Policy considerations will have to be weighed; but the objective of the judges is the formulation of principle. And, if principle inexorably requires a decision which entails a degree of policy risk, the court's function is to adjudicate according to principle, leaving policy curtailment to the judgment of Parliament. Here lies the true role of the two law-making institutions in our constitution. By concentrating on principle the judges can keep the common law alive, flexible and consistent, and can keep the legal system clear of policy problems which neither they, nor the forensic process which it is their duty to operate, are equipped to resolve. If principle leads to results which are thought to be socially unacceptable, Parliament can legislate to draw a line or map out a new path.

The real risk to the common law is not its movement to cover new situations and new knowledge but lest it should stand still, halted by a conservative judicial approach. If that should happen, and since the 1966 practice direction of the House (see *Note* [1966] 3 All ER 77, [1966] 1 WLR 1234) it has become less likely, there would be a danger of the law becoming irrelevant to the consideration, and inept in its treatment, of modern social problems. Justice would be defeated. The common law has, however, avoided this catastrophe by the flexibility given it by generations of judges. Flexibility carries with it, of course, certain risks, notably a degree of uncertainty in the law and the 'floodgates' risk which so impressed the Court of Appeal in the present case.

The importance to be attached to certainty and the size of the 'floodgates' risk vary from one branch of the law to another. What is required of the law in its approach to a commercial transaction will be very different from the approach appropriate to problems of tortious liability for personal injuries. In some branches of the law, notably that now under consideration, the search for certainty can obstruct the law's pursuit of justice, and can become the enemy of the good.

The present case is a good illustration. Certainty could have been achieved by leaving the law as it was left by *Victorian Rlys Comrs v Coultas* (1888) 13 App Cas 222 or, again, by holding the line drawn in 1901 by *Dulieu v White & Sons* [1901] 1 KB 669, [1900–3] All ER Rep 353 or today by confining the law to what was regarded by Lord Denning MR in *Hinz v Berry* [1970] 1 All ER 1074 at 1075, [1970] 2 QB 40 at 42 as 'settled law', namely that 'damages can be given for nervous shock caused by the sight of an accident, at any rate to a close relative'.

But at each landmark stage common law principle, when considered in the context of developing medical science, has beckoned the judges on. And now, as has been made clear by Evatt J, dissenting in *Chester v Waverley Municipal Council* (1939) 62 CLR 1 in the High Court of Australia, by Tobriner J, giving the majority judgment in the Californian case of *Dillon v Legg* (1968) 68 C 2d 728, and by my noble and learned friend in this case, common law principle requires the judges to follow the logic of the 'reasonably foreseeable test' so as, in circumstances where it is appropriate, to apply it untrammelled by spatial, physical or temporal limits. Space, time, distance, the nature of the injuries sustained and the relationship of the plaintiff to the immediate victim of the accident are factors to be weighed, but not legal limitations, when the test of reasonable foreseeability is to be applied.

But I am by no means sure that the result is socially desirable. The 'floodgates' argument may be exaggerated. Time alone will tell; but I foresee social and financial problems if damages for 'nervous shock' should be made available to persons other than parents and children who without seeing or hearing the accident, or being present in the immediate aftermath, suffer nervous shock in consequence of it. There is, I think, a powerful case for legislation such as has been enacted in New South Wales and the Australian Capital Territory.

Why then should not the courts draw the line, as the Court of Appeal manfully tried to do in this case? Simply, because the policy issue where to draw the line is not justiciable. The problem is one of social, economic, and financial policy. The considerations relevant to a decision are not such as to be capable of being handled within the limits of the forensic process.

My Lords, I would allow the appeal for the reasons developed by my noble and learned friend Lord Bridge, while putting on record my view that there is here a case for legislation.

LORD BRIDGE OF HARWICH. My Lords, I gratefully adopt the account given by my noble and learned friend Lord Wilberforce of the facts giving rise to this appeal.

This is only the second case ever to reach your Lordships' House concerning the liability of a tortfeasor who has negligently killed or physically injured A to pay damages to B for a psychiatric illness resulting from A's death or injury. The previous case was *Hay (or Bourhill) v Young* [1942] 2 All ER 396, [1943] AC 92. The impression with which I am left, after being taken in argument through all the relevant English authorities, a number of Commonwealth authorities and one important decision of the Supreme Court of California, is that this whole area of English law stands in urgent need of review.

The basic difficulty of the subject arises from the fact that the crucial answers to the questions which it raises lie in the difficult field of psychiatric medicine. The common law gives no damages for the emotional distress which any normal person experiences when someone he loves is killed or injured. Anxiety and depression are normal human emotions. Yet an anxiety neurosis or a reactive depression may be recognisable psychiatric illnesses, with or without psychosomatic symptoms. So, the first hurdle which a plaintiff claiming damages of the kind in question must surmount is to establish that he is suffering, not merely grief, distress or any other normal emotion, but a positive psychiatric illness. That is here not in issue. A plaintiff must then establish the necessary chain of causation in fact between his psychiatric illness and the death or injury of one or more third parties negligently caused by the defendant. Here again, this is not in dispute in the instant case. But, when causation in fact is in issue, it must no doubt be determined by the judge on the basis of the evidence of psychiatrists. Then, here comes the all important question. Given the fact of the plaintiff's psychiatric illness cased by the defendant's negligence in killing or physically injuring another, was the chain of causation from the one event to the other, considered ex post facto in the light of all that has happened, 'reasonably foreseeable' by the 'reasonable man'? A moment's thought will show that the answer to that question depends on what knowledge is to be attributed to the hypothetical reasonable man of the operation of cause and effect in medicine. There are at least two theoretically possible approaches. The first is that the judge should receive the evidence of psychiatrists as to the degree of probability that the particular cause would produce the particular effect, and apply to that the appropriate legal test of reasonable foreseeability as the criterion of the defendant's duty of care. The second is that the judge, relying on his own opinion of the operation of cause and effect in psychiatric medicine, as fairly representative of that of the educated layman, should treat himself as the reasonable man and form his own view from the primary facts whether the proven chain of cause and effect was reasonably foreseeable. In principle, I think there is much to be said for the first approach. Foreseeability, in any given set of circumstances, is ultimately a question of fact. If a claim in negligence depends on whether some defect in a complicated piece of machinery was foreseeably a cause of injury, I apprehend that the judge will decide that question on the basis of the expert evidence of engineers. But the authorities give no support to this approach in relation to the foreseeability of psychiatric illness. The judges, in all the decisions we have been referred to, have assumed that it lay within their own competence to determine whether the plaintiff's 'nervous shock' (as lawyers quaintly persist in calling it) was in any given circumstances a sufficiently foreseeable consequence of the defendant's act or omission relied on as negligent to bring the plaintiff within the scope of those to whom the defendant owed a duty of care. To depart from this practice and treat the question of foreseeable causation in this field, and hence the scope of the defendant's duty, as a question of fact to be determined in the light of the expert evidence adduced in each case would, no doubt, be too large an innovation in the law to be regarded as properly within the com., etence, even since the liberating 1966 practice direction (see *Note* [1966] 3 All ER 77, [1966] 1 WLR 1234), of your Lordships' House. Moreover, psychiatric medicine is far from being an exact science. The opinions of its practitioners may differ widely. Clearly it is desirable in this, as in any other, field that the law should achieve such a measure of certainty as is consistent with the demands of justice. It would seem that the consensus of informed judicial opinion is probably the best yardstick available to determine whether, in any given circumstances, the emotional trauma resulting from the death or injury of third parties, or indeed the threat of such death or injury, ex hypothesi attributable to the defendant's negligence, was a foreseeable cause in law, as well as the actual cause in fact, of the plaintiff's psychiatric or psychosomatic illness. But the word I would emphasise in the foregoing sentence is 'informed'. For too long earlier generations of judges have regarded psychiatry and psychiatrists with suspicion, if not hostility. Now, I venture to hope, that attitude has quite disappeared. No judge who has spent any length of time trying personal injury claims in recent years would doubt that physical injuries can give rise not only to organic but also to psychiatric disorders. The sufferings of the patient from the latter are no less real and frequently no less painful and disabling than from the former. Likewise, I would suppose that the legal profession well understands that an acute emotional trauma, like a physical trauma, can well cause a psychiatric illness in a wide range of circumstances and in a wide range of individuals whom it would be wrong to regard as having any abnormal psychological make-up. It is in comparatively recent times that these insights have come to be generally accepted by the judiciary. It is only by giving effect to these insights in the developing law of negligence that we can do justice to an important, though no doubt small, class of plaintiffs whose genuine psychiatric illnesses are caused by negligent defendants.

My Lords, in the instant case I cannot help thinking that the learned trial judge's conclusion that the appellant's illness was not the foreseeable consequence of the respondents' negligence was one to which, understandably, he felt himself driven by the authorities. Free of authority, and applying the ordinary criterion of reasonable foreseeability to the facts, with an eye 'enlightened by progressive awareness of mental illness' (the language of Stephenson LJ (see [1981] 1 All ER 809 at 819, [1981] QB 599 at 612)), any judge must, I would think, share the view of all three members of the Court of Appeal, with which I understand all your Lordships agree, that, in the words of Griffiths LJ, it was 'readily foreseeable that a significant number of mothers exposed to such an experience might break down under the shock of the event and suffer illness' (see [1981] 1 All ER 809 at 822, [1981] QB 599 at 617).

The question, then, for your Lordships' decision is whether the law, as a matter of policy, draws a line which exempts from liability a defendant whose negligent act or omission was actually and foreseeably the cause of the plaintiff's psychiatric illness and, if so, where that line is to be drawn. In thus formulating the question, I do not, of course, use the word 'negligent' as prejudging the question whether the defendant owes the plaintiff a duty, but I do use the word 'foreseeably' as connoting the normally accepted criterion of such a duty.

Before attempting to answer the question, it is instructive to consider the historical development of the subject as illustrated by the authorities, and to note, in particular, three features of that development. First, it will be seen that successive attempts have been made to draw a line beyond which liability should not extend, each of which has in due course had to be abandoned. Second, the ostensible justification for drawing the line has been related to the current criterion of a defendant's duty of care, which, however expressed in earlier judgments, we should now describe as that of reasonable foreseeability. But, third, in so far as policy considerations can be seen to have influenced any of the decisions, they appear to have sprung from the fear that to cross the chosen line would be to open the floodgates to claims without limit and largely without merit.

Perhaps the most vivid illustration of all three features is in the very first case in the series, the decision of the Privy Council in *Victorian Rlys Comrs v Coultas* (1888) 13 App Cas 222. The plaintiff, a pregnant lady, was a passenger in a buggy which was negligently allowed by the defendants' gatekeeper to cross the railway line when a train was approaching. The buggy crossed just in time, ahead of the train, but only narrowly escaped collision. The plaintiff was so alarmed that she suffered what was described as 'a severe nervous shock'. She fainted, and subsequently miscarried. She succeeded in her claim for damages in the courts below. Delivering the judgment of the Privy Council, allowing the appeal, Sir Richard Couch said (at 225–226):

> 'According to the evidence of the female plaintiff her fright was caused by seeing the train approaching, and thinking they were going to be killed. Damages arising from mere sudden terror unaccompanied by an actual physical injury, but occasioning a nervous or mental shock, cannot under such circumstances, their Lordships think, be considered a consequence which, in the ordinary course of things, would flow from the negligence of the gate-keeper. If it were held that they can, it appears to their Lordships that it would be extending the liability for negligence much beyond what that liability has hitherto been held to be. Not only in such a case as the present, but in every case where an accident caused by negligence had given a person a serious nervous shock, there might be a claim for damages on account of mental injury. The difficulty which now often exists in case of alleged physical injuries of determining whether they were caused by the negligent act would be greatly increased, and a wide field opened for imaginary claims.'

Two Irish courts declined to follow this decision: *Bell v Great Northern Rly Co of Ireland* (1890) 26 LR Ir 428, following *Byrne v Great Southern and Western Rly Co of Ireland* (1884) unreported. The next English case followed the Irish courts' lead. This was *Dulieu v White & Sons* [1901] 2 KB 669, [1900–3] All ER Rep 353. The case was argued on a preliminary point of law. The plaintiff, again a pregnant lady, pleaded that she had suffered nervous shock when the defendants' horse-drawn van was negligently driven into the public house where she was behind the bar. Kennedy J gave the leading judgment of the Divisional Court in the plaintiff's favour. It is worth quoting the passage which is central to his decision, if only to show how far we have travelled in the last eighty years in the judicial approach to the kind of medical question presently under consideration. He said ([1901] 2 KB 669 at 677, [1900–3] All ER Rep 353 at 358):

'For my own part, I should not like to assume it to be scientifically true that a nervous shock which causes serious bodily illness is not actually accompanied by physical injury, although it may be impossible, or at least difficult, to detect the injury at the time in the living subject. I should not be surprised if the surgeon or the physiologist told us that nervous shock is or may be in itself an injurious affection of the physical organism. Let it be assumed, however, that the physical injury follows the shock, but that the jury are satisfied upon proper and sufficient medical evidence that it follows the shock as its direct and natural effect, is there any legal reason for saying that the damage is less proximate in the legal sense than damage which arises contemporaneously?'

But earlier in his judgment Kennedy J had drawn a new line of limitation when he said ([1901] 2 KB 669 at 675; cf [1900–3] All ER Rep 353 at 357): 'The shock, where it operates through the mind, must be a shock which arises from a reasonable fear of immediate personal injury to oneself.' He supported this by reference to an earlier case (*Smith v Johnson & Co* (1898) unreported), where the unsuccessful plaintiff suffered from the shock of seeing another person killed and said of such a case:

'I should myself . . . have been inclined to go a step further, and to hold . . . that, as the defendant neither intended to affect the plaintiff injuriously nor did anything which could reasonably or naturally be expected to affect him injuriously, there was no evidence of any breach of legal duty towards the plaintiff . . .'

The next landmark is *Hambrook v Stokes Bros* [1925] 1 KB 141, [1924] All ER Rep 110. This was the case which turned on whether 'nervous shock' caused to a mother by fear for her children, who had just disappeared round a corner going up a hill when a runaway lorry appeared round the corner going downhill, and when, as it turned out, one of her children was injured, gave a cause of action against the driver whose negligence allowed the lorry to run down the hill. The court by a majority held that it did. The leading judgment of Bankes LJ sought to demonstrate the absurdity of maintaining the boundary of a defendant's liability for 'nervous shock' on the line drawn by Kennedy J, saying ([1925] 1 KB 141 at 151, [1924] All ER Rep 110 at 113):

'Assume two mothers crossing the street at the same time when this lorry comes thundering down, each holding a small child by the hand. One mother is courageous and devoted to her child. She is terrified, but thinks only of the damage to the child, and not at all about herself. The other woman is timid and lacking in the motherly instinct. She also is terrified, but thinks only of the damage to herself and not at all about her child. The health of both mothers is seriously affected by the mental shock occasioned by the fright. Can any real distinction be drawn between the two cases? Will the law recognise a cause of action in the case of the less deserving mother, and none in the case of the more deserving one? Does the law say that the defendant ought reasonably to have anticipated the non-natural feeling of the timid mother, and not the natural feeling of the courageous mother? I think not.'

Sargant LJ, in his dissenting judgment, nevertheless sought to uphold the distinction essentially on the basis that 'nervous shock' caused to a plaintiff by fear of injury to himself occasioned by a 'near miss' is indistinguishable, so far as the defendant's duty is concerned, from injury by direct impact, whereas 'nervous shock' caused by the fear or sight of injury to another is beyond the defendant's anticipation and hence beyond the range of his duty.

When one comes to the decision of your Lordships' House in *Hay (or Bourhill) v Young* [1942] 2 All ER 396, [1943] AC 92 it is important to bear in mind, as the speeches delivered show, that the difference of judicial opinion in *Hambrook v Stokes Bros* remained unresolved, and indeed that their Lordships did not purport to resolve it. Furthermore, on the facts of that case, the result was surely a foregone conclusion. The pursuer was alighting from a tram when she heard, but did not see, the impact of a collision between a motor cyclist (on whose negligence in driving too fast her claim was based) and a car. The motor cyclist, a stranger to the pursuer, was killed. There is nothing in the report to indicate that she ever saw the body, but after the body had been removed she saw the blood left on the road. In these circumstances I cannot suppose that any judge today would dissent from the view that 'nervous shock' to the pursuer was not reasonably foreseeable. Nor would anyone, I think, quarrel with the following passage from the speech of Lord Porter as expressing a view of the law as acceptable in 1982 as it was in 1942 ([1942] 2 All ER 396 at 409, [1943] AC 92 at 117):

> 'The question whether emotional disturbance or shock, which a defender ought reasonably to have anticipated as likely to follow from his reckless driving, can ever form the basis of a claim is not in issue. It is not every emotional disturbance or every shock which should have been foreseen. The driver of a car or vehicle even though careless is entitled to assume that the ordinary frequenter of the streets has sufficient fortitude to endure such incidents as may from time to time be expected to occur in them, including the noise of a collision and the sight of injury to others, and is not to be considered negligent towards one who does not possess the customary phlegm.'

On the difference of opinion in *Hambrook v Stokes Bros* Lord Russell in terms expressed a preference for the dissenting view of Sargant LJ. Lord Thankerton and Lord Macmillan, although not saying so in terms, appear by necessary implication to support the same view by confining a driver's duty of care to those in the area of potential physical danger which may arise from the manner of his driving. Lord Porter's speech is neutral. Lord Wright expressed provisional agreement with the majority decision in *Hambrook v Stokes Bros*. His speech also contained the following and, as I think, far-sighted passage ([1942] 2 All ER 396 at 405–406, [1943] AC 92 at 110):

> 'What is now being considered is the question of liability, and this, I think, in a question whether there is a duty owing to members of the public who come within the ambit of the act, must generally depend on a normal standard of susceptibility. This, it may be said, is somewhat vague. That is true; but definition involves limitation, which it is desirable to avoid further than is necessary in a principle of law like negligence, which is widely ranging and is still in the stage of development. It is here, as elsewhere, a question of what the hypothetical reasonable man, viewing the position, I suppose *ex post facto*, would say it was proper to foresee. What danger of particular infirmity that would include must depend on all the circumstances; but generally, I think, a reasonably normal condition, if medical evidence is capable of defining it, would be the standard. The test of the plaintiff's extraordinary susceptibility, if unknown to the defendant, would in effect make the defendant an insurer. The lawyer likes to draw fixed and definite lines and is apt to ask where the thing is to stop. I should reply it should stop where in the particular case the good sense of the jury, or of the judge, decides ... I cannot, however, forbear referring to a most important case in the High Court of Australia, *Chester* v.

Waverley Municipal Council ((1939) 62 CLR 1), where the court by a majority held that no duty was made out. The dissenting judgment of EVATT, J., will demand the consideration of any judge who is called upon to consider these questions.'

I shall return later to the judgment of Evatt J to which Lord Wright there refers.

I need not consider in detail the subsequent English Court of Appeal decisions in *King v Phillips* [1953] 1 All ER 617, [1953] 1 QB 429, *Boardman v Sanderson* [1964] 1 WLR 1317 and *Hinz v Berry* [1970] 1 All ER 1074, [1970] 2 QB 40. In *King v Phillips* [1953] 1 All ER 617 at 623, [1953] 1 QB 429 at 441, Denning LJ said: '. . . there can be no doubt since *Hay (or Bourhill)* v. *Young* that the test of liability for shock is foreseeability of injury by shock.'

This observation was cited with approval in *Overseas Tankship (UK) Ltd v Morts Dock and Engineering Co Ltd The Wagon Mound (No 1)* [1961] 1 All ER 404 at 415, [1961] AC 388 at 426. I would add, however, that *King v Phillips*, a case in which the plaintiff failed, would, as I think, clearly be decided differently today. By 1970 it was clear that no one could any longer contend for the limitation of liability for 'nervous shock' to those who were themselves put in danger by the defendant's negligence, so much so that in *Hinz v Berry* a mother who witnessed from one side of the road a terrible accident to her family picnicking on the other side of the road recovered damages for her resulting psychiatric illness without dispute on the issue of liability, and the case reached the Court of Appeal on the issue of quantum of damages only. Lord Denning MR said ([1970] 1 All ER 1074 at 1075, [1970] 2 QB 40 at 42):

> 'The law at one time said that there could not be damages for nervous shock; but for these last 25 years, it has been settled that damages can be given for nervous shock caused by the sight of an accident, at any rate to a close relative.'

The only other important English decision is *Chadwick v British Transport Commission* [1967] 2 All ER 945, [1967] 1 WLR 912. The plaintiff's husband lived 200 yards from the scene of the terrible Lewisham railway accident in 1957 in which 90 people were killed. On hearing of the accident in the evening he went at once to the scene and assisted in the rescue work through the night until early next morning. As a result of his experiences of the night he developed an acute anxiety neurosis for which he required hospital treatment as an in-patient for over six months. After his death from unrelated causes his wife, as administratrix of his estate, recovered damages for his psychiatric illness. This was a decision of Waller J. It was not challenged on appeal and no one, I believe, has ever doubted that it was rightly decided.

I should mention two Commonwealth decisions of first instance. In *Benson v Lee* [1972] VR 879 Lush J, in the Supreme Court of Victoria, held that a mother who did not witness, but was told of, an accident to her son 100 yards from her home, went to the scene and accompanied the child in an ambulance to hospital where he died, was entitled to damages for 'nervous shock' notwithstanding evidence that she was prone to mental illness from stress. In *Marshal v Lionel Enterprises Inc* (1971) 25 DLR (3d) 141 Haines J, in the Ontario High Court, held that a wife who found her husband seriously injured shortly after an accident caused by defective machinery was not, as a matter of law, disentitled to damages for the 'nervous shock' which she claimed to have suffered as a result. On the other hand in *Abramzik v Brenner* (1967) 65 DLR (2d) 651 the Saskatchewan Court of Appeal held that a mother who suffered 'nervous shock' on being informed by her husband that two of her children had been killed in a road accident was not entitled to recover.

Chester v Waverley Municipal Council (1939) 62 CLR 1, referred to by Lord Wright in the passage quoted above, was a decision of the High Court of Australia. The plaintiff's seven-year-old son having been out to play, failed to return home when expected. A search was mounted which continued for some hours. Eventually, in the presence of the plaintiff, his mother, the child's dead body was recovered from a flooded trench which the defendant authority had left inadequately fenced. The plaintiff claimed damages for 'nervous shock'. The majority of the court (Latham CJ, Rich and Starke JJ) rejected the claim. The decision was based squarely on the ground that, the plaintiff's injury not being a foreseeable consequence of the defendant's omission to fence the trench, they owed her no duty. But the judgment of Latham CJ contains an interesting example of the 'floodgates' argument. He said (at 7–8):

> 'But in this case the plaintiff must establish a duty owed by the defendant to herself and a breach of that duty. The duty which it is suggested the defendant owed to the plaintiff was a duty not to injure her child so as to cause her a nervous shock when she saw, not the happening of the injury, but the result of the injury, namely, the dead body of the child. It is rather difficult to state the limit of the alleged duty. If a duty of the character suggested exists at all it is not really said that it should be confined to mothers of children who are injured. It must extend to some wider class—but to what class? There appears to be no reason why it should not extend to other relatives or to all other persons, whether they are relatives or not. If this is the true principle of law, then a person who is guilty of negligence with the result that A is injured will be liable in damages to B, C, D and any other persons who receive a nervous shock (as distinguished from passing fright or distress) at any time upon perceiving the results of the negligence, whether in disfigurement of person, physical injury, or death.'

In a powerful dissenting judgment, which I find wholly convincing, Evatt J drew a vivid picture of the mother's agony of mind as the search continued, culminating in the gruesome discovery in her presence of the child's drowned body. I cannot for a moment doubt the correctness of his conclusion that the mother's mental illness was the reasonably foreseeable consequence of the defendant's negligence. This was a case from New South Wales and I cannot help wondering whether it was not the manifest injustice of the result which led, a few years later, to the intervention of the New South Wales legislature, to enable the parent, husband or wife of a person 'killed, injured or put in peril' by another's negligence to recover damages for 'mental or nervous shock' irrespective of any spatial or temporal relationship to the accident in which the death, injury or peril occurred.

My Lords, looking back I think it is possible to discern that there only ever were two clear lines of limitation of a defendant's liability for 'nervous shock' for which any rational justification could be advanced, in the light both of the state of the law of negligence and the state of medical science as judicially understood, at the time when those limitations were propounded. In 1888 it was, no doubt, perfectly sensible to say:

> 'Damages arising from mere sudden terror unaccompanied by any actual physical injury, but occasioning a nervous or mental shock, cannot ... be considered a consequence which, in the ordinary course of things, would flow from ... negligence.'

(See *Victorian Rlys Comrs v Coultas* 13 App Cas 222 at 225.) Here the test, whether of duty or of remoteness, can be recognised as a relatively distant ancestor of the modern criterion of reasonable foreseeability. Again, in 1901 it was, I would suppose, equally sensible to limit a defendant's liability for 'nervous shock' which could 'reasonably or naturally be expected' to be such as was suffered by a plaintiff who was himself physically endangered by the defendant's negligence (see *Dulieu v White & Sons* [1901] 2 KB 669 at 675; cf [1900–3] All ER Rep 353 at 357). But once that line of limitation has been crossed, as it was by the majority in *Hambrook v Stokes Bros*, there can be no logical reason whatever for limiting the defendant's duty to persons in physical proximity to the place where the accident, caused by the defendant's negligence, occurred. Much of the confusion in the authorities since *Hay (or Bourhill) v Young*, including, if I may say so, the judgments of the courts below in the instant case, has arisen, as it seems to me, from the deference still accorded, notwithstanding the acceptance of the *Hambrook* principle, to dicta of their Lordships in *Hay (or Bourhill) v Young* which only make sense if understood as based on the limited principle of liability propounded by Kennedy J in *Dulieu v White*

& *Sons*, and adopted in the dissenting judgment of Sargant LJ in *Hambrook v Stokes Bros*.

My Lords, before returning to the policy question, it is, I think, highly instructive to consider the decision of the Supreme Court of California in *Dillon v Legg* (1968) 68 C 2d 728. Before this decision the law of California, and evidently of other states of the Union, had adhered to the English position before *Hambrook v Stokes Bros* that damages for nervous shock could only be recovered if resulting from the plaintiff's apprehension of danger to himself, and, indeed, this view had been affirmed by the Californian Supreme Court only five years earlier. The majority in *Dillon v Legg* adopted a contrary view in refusing a motion to dismiss a mother's claim for damages for emotional trauma caused by seeing her infant daughter killed by a car as she crossed the road.

In delivering the majority judgment of the court, Tobriner J said (at 740–741):

'Since the chief element in determining whether defendant owes a duty or an obligation to plaintiff is the foreseeability of the risk, that factor will be of prime concern in every case. Because it is inherently intertwined with foreseeability such duty or obligation must necessarily be adjudicated only upon a case-by-case basis. We cannot now predetermine defendant's obligation in every situation by a fixed category; no immutable rule can establish the extent of that obligation for every circumstance of the future. We can, however, define guidelines which will aid in the resolution of such an issue as the instant one. We note, first, that we deal here with a case in which plaintiff suffered a shock which resulted in physical injury and we confine our ruling to that case. In determining, in such a case, whether defendant should reasonably foresee the injury to plaintiff, or, in other terminology, whether defendant owes plaintiff a duty of due care, the courts will take into account such factors as the following: (1) Whether plaintiff was located near the scene of the accident as contrasted with one who was a distance away from it. (2) Whether the shock resulted from a direct emotional impact upon plaintiff from the sensory and contemporaneous observance of the accident, as contrasted with learning of the accident from others after its occurrence. (3) Whether plaintiff and the victim were closely related, as contrasted with an absence of any relationship or the presence of only a distant relationship. The evaluation of these factors will indicate the *degree* of the defendant's foreseeability: obviously defendant is more likely to foresee that a mother who observes an accident affecting her child will suffer harm than to foretell that a stranger witness will do so. Similarly, the degree of foreseeability of the third person's injury is far greater in the case of his contemporaneous observance of the accident than that in which he subsequently learns of it. The defendant is more likely to foresee that shock to the nearby, witnessing mother will cause physical harm than to anticipate that someone distant from the accident will suffer more than a temporary emotional reaction. All these elements, of course, shade into each other; the fixing of obligation, intimately tied into the facts, depends upon each case. In light of these factors the court will determine whether the accident and harm was *reasonably* foreseeable. Such reasonable foreseeability does not turn on whether the particular plaintiff as an individual would have in actuality foreseen the exact accident and loss; it contemplates that courts, on a case-to-case basis, analyzing all the circumstances, will decide what the ordinary man under such circumstances should reasonably have foreseen. The courts thus mark out the areas of liability, excluding the remote and unexpected. In the instant case, the presence of all the above factors indicates that plaintiff has alleged a sufficient prima facie case. Surely the negligent driver who causes the death of a young child may reasonably expect that the mother will not be far distant and will upon witnessing the accident suffer emotional trauma. As Dean Prosser has stated: "when a child is endangered, it is not beyond contemplation that its mother will be somewhere in the vicinity, and will suffer serious shock." (Prosser, The Law of Torts (3rd edn, 1964) p 353. See also 2 Harper & James, The Law of Torts (1956) p 1039.) We are not now called upon to decide whether, in the absence or reduced weight of some of the above factors, we would conclude that the accident and injury were not reasonably foreseeable and that therefore defendant owed no duty of due care to plaintiff. In future cases the courts will draw lines of demarcation upon facts more subtle than the compelling one alleged in the complaint before us.'

The leading minority judgment castigated the majority for embarking on a first excursion into the 'fantastic realm of infinite liability', a colourful variant of the familiar 'floodgates' argument.

In approaching the question whether the law should, as a matter of policy, define the criterion of liability in negligence for causing psychiatric illness by reference to some test other than that of reasonable foreseeability it is well to remember that we are concerned only with the question of liability of a defendant who is, ex hypothesi, guilty of fault in causing the death, injury or danger which has in turn triggered the psychiatric illness. A policy which is to be relied on to narrow the scope of the negligent tortfeasor's duty must be justified by cogent and readily intelligible considerations, and must be capable of defining the appropriate limits of liability by reference to factors which are not purely arbitrary. A number of policy considerations which have been suggested as satisfying these requirements appear to me, with respect, to be wholly insufficient. I can see no ground whatever for suggesting that to make the defendant liable for reasonably foreseeable psychiatric illness caused by his negligence would be to impose a crushing burden on him out of proportion to his moral responsibility. However liberally the criterion of reasonable foreseeability is interpreted, both the number of successful claims in this field and the quantum of damages they will attract are likely to be moderate. I cannot accept as relevant the well-known phenomenon that litigation may delay recovery from a psychiatric illness. If this were a valid policy consideration, it would lead to the conclusion that psychiatric illness should be excluded altogether from the heads of damage which the law will recognise. It cannot justify limiting the cases in which damages will be awarded for psychiatric illness by reference to the circumstances of its causation. To attempt to draw a line at the furthest point which any of the decided cases happen to have reached, and to say that it is for the legislature, not the courts, to extend the limits of liability any further, would be, to my mind, an unwarranted abdication of the court's function of developing and adapting principles of the common law to changing conditions, in a particular corner of the common law which exemplifies, par excellence, the important and indeed necessary part which that function has to play. In the end I believe that the policy question depends on weighing against each other two conflicting considerations. On the one hand, if the criterion of liability is to be reasonable foreseeability simpliciter, this must, precisely because questions of causation in psychiatric medicine give rise to difficulty and uncertainty, introduce an element of uncertainty into the law and open the way to a number of arguable claims which a more precisely fixed criterion of liability would exclude. I accept that the element of uncertainty is an important factor. I believe that the 'floodgates' argument, however, is, as it always has been, greatly exaggerated. On the other hand, it seems to me inescapable that any attempt to define the limit of liability by requiring, in addition to reasonable foreseeability, that the plaintiff claiming damages for psychiatric illness should have witnessed the relevant accident, should have been present at or near the place where it happened, should have come on its aftermath and thus have some direct perception of it, as opposed to merely learning of it after the event, should be related in some particular degree to the accident victim—to draw a line by reference to any of these criteria must impose a largely arbitrary limit of liability. I accept, of course, the importance of the factors indicated in the guidelines suggested by Tobriner J in *Dillon v Legg* as bearing on the *degree* of foreseeability of the plaintiff's psychiatric illness. But let me give two examples to illustrate what injustice would be wrought by any such hard and fast lines of policy as have been suggested. First, consider the plaintiff who learned after the event of the relevant accident. Take the case of a mother who knows that her husband and children are staying in a certain hotel. She reads in her morning newspaper that it has been the scene of a disastrous fire. She sees in the paper a photograph of unidentifiable victims trapped on the top floor waving for help from the windows. She learns shortly afterwards that all her family have perished. She suffers an acute psychiatric illness. That her illness in these circumstances was a reasonably foreseeable consequence of the events resulting from the fire is undeniable. Yet, is the law to deny her damages as against a defendant whose negligence was responsible for the fire simply on the ground that an important link in the chain of causation of her psychiatric illness was supplied by her imagination of the agonies of mind and body in which her family died, rather than by direct perception of the event? Second, consider the plaintiff who is unrelated to the victims of the relevant accident. If rigidly applied, an exclusion of liability to him would have defeated the plaintiff's claim in *Chadwick v British Transport Commission*. The Court of Appeal treated that case as in a special category because Mr Chadwick was a rescuer. Now, the special duty owed to a rescuer who voluntarily places himself in physical danger to save others is well understood, and is illustrated by *Haynes v Harwood* [1935] 1 KB 146, [1934] All ER Rep 103, the case of the constable injured in stopping a runaway horse in a crowded street. But, in relation to the psychiatric consequences of witnessing such terrible carnage as must have resulted from the Lewisham train disaster, I would find it difficult to distinguish in principle the position of a rescuer, like Mr Chadwick, from a mere spectator, as, for example, an uninjured or only slightly injured passenger in the train, who took no part in the rescue operations but was present at the scene after the accident for some time, perforce observing the rescue operations while he waited for transport to take him home.

My Lords, I have no doubt that this is an area of the law of negligence where we should resist the temptation to try yet once more to freeze the law in a rigid posture which would deny justice to some who, in the application of the classic principles of negligence derived from *Donoghue v Stevenson* [1932] AC 562, [1932] All ER Rep 1, ought to succeed, in the interests of certainty, where the very subject matter is uncertain and continuously developing, or in the interests of saving defendants and their insurers from the burden of having sometimes to resist doubtful claims. I find myself in complete agreement with Tobriner J that the defendant's duty must depend on reasonable foreseeability and—

> 'must necessarily be adjudicated only upon a case-by-case basis. We cannot now predetermine defendant's obligation in every situation by a fixed category; no immutable rule can establish the extent of that obligation for every circumstance of the future.'

To put the matter in another way, if asked where the thing is to stop, I should answer, in an adaptation of the language of Lord Wright and Stephenson LJ, 'Where in the particular case the good sense of the judge, enlightened by progressive awareness of mental illness, decides'.

I regret that my noble and learned friend Lord Edmund-Davies, who criticises my conclusion that in this area of the law there are no policy considerations sufficient to justify limiting the liability of negligent tortfeasors by reference to some narrower criterion than that of reasonable foreseeability, stops short of indicating his view where the limit of liability should be drawn or the nature of the policy considerations (other than the 'floodgates' argument, which I understand he rejects) which he would invoke to justify such a limit.

My Lords, I would accordingly allow the appeal.

Appeal allowed.

Solicitors: *Vinters*, Cambridge (for the appellant); *Hextall, Erskine & Co* (for the respondents).

Mary Rose Plummer   Barrister.

R v Tottenham Juvenile Court, ex parte A R C
(an infant)
and other appeals

QUEEN'S BENCH DIVISION
LORD LANE CJ, WOOLF AND STUART-SMITH JJ
18 JANUARY, 8 FEBRUARY 1982

Magistrates – Summary trial – Offence triable summarily or on indictment – Determination of mode of trial of person attaining age of 17 after pleading to charge – Trial by juvenile court or in magistrates' court with right to elect trial by jury – Defendant attaining 17 before commencement of trial but after pleading to charge – Whether defendant entitled to elect trial by jury on attaining 17 – Whether defendant attaining 17 before he first 'appears or is brought before' magistrates' court – What constitutes appearance before court – Whether juvenile court having discretion as to mode of trial after defendant attaining 17 – Children and Young Persons Act 1963, s 29 – Magistrates' Courts Act 1980, ss 18, 23, 24, 122.

For the purposes of ss 18(1)^a and 24(1)^b of the Magistrates' Courts Act 1980 (which make provision for determining the mode of trial for an offence triable summarily or on indictment of a person who has attained the age of 17 or for the summary trial of a person under the age of 17 charged with an indictable offence) a person's age is to be determined at the time he first appears or is brought before a magistrates' court in connection with the offence charged. Where he is under arrest and has been in custody since arrest he first appears or is brought before the court when he is physically brought before the court to be remanded in custody or on bail, and where he is on police bail he first appears or is brought before the court when he actually surrenders to bail; however, mere attendance at court on an occasion when he is not required to attend (eg on the date originally fixed for surrendering to his bail when that date has been postponed) does not qualify as the moment when he first appears or is brought before the court. A person summoned to appear in court first appears or is brought before the court when he appears in answer to the summons (see p 326 b to d h j, post); *R v Amersham Juvenile Court, ex p Wilson* [1981] 2 All ER 315 applied; *R v St Albans Juvenile Court, ex p Godman* [1981] 2 All ER 311 not followed.

The appearance in court of a person under the age of 17 by his counsel or solicitor in his absence, pursuant to s 122^c of the 1980 Act, is a sufficient appearance of the accused for the purpose of s 24 if the appearance of counsel or the solicitor is a formal appearance on behalf of the accused and not merely a courtesy appearance to agree a date of hearing when there is no requirement to attend. Similarly, appearance by counsel or a solicitor under s 23^d of the 1980 Act when the accused consents to the procedure for trial being determined in his absence constitutes a sufficient appearance for the purpose of s 18 (see p 327 d e, post).

---

a Section 18(1) provides: 'Sections 19 to 23 below shall have effect where a person who has attained the age of 17 appears or is brought before a magistrates' court on an information charging him with an offence triable either way.'

b Section 24(1), so far as material, provides: 'Where a person under the age of 17 appears or is brought before a magistrates' court on an information charging him with an indictable offence other than homicide, he shall be tried summarily unless—(a) he has attained the age of 14 and the offence is such as is mentioned in subsection (2) of section 53 of the Children and Young Persons Act 1933 . . . and the court considers that if he is found guilty of the offence it ought to be possible to sentence him in pursuance of that subsection; or (b) he is charged jointly with a person who had attained the age of 17 and the court considers it necessary in the interests of justice to commit them both for trial . . .'

c Section 122 is set out at p 327 a b, post

d Section 23 is set out at p 327 b c, post

Section 29^e of the Children and Young Persons Act 1963, which provides, inter alia, that where proceedings for an offence are begun in respect of a person under the age of 17 and he attains the age of 17 before the conclusion of the proceedings the juvenile court may deal with the case and make any order which it could have made if he had not attained that age, deals with both the trial and disposal of a case; it does not confer a discretion on magistrates to override the mandatory provisions in ss 18 and 24 of the 1980 Act and permit the accused to elect trial by jury if he was under the age of 17 when he first appeared or was brought before the court and attains 17 before the conclusion of the juvenile court proceedings (see p 326 f g, post); *R v Amersham Juvenile Court, ex p Wilson* [1981] 2 All ER 315 approved.

Notes

For summary trial of a young person and the power to change from summary trial to committal proceedings, see 24 Halsbury's Laws (4th edn) paras 898: 9–10.

For presumption and determination of age of a person charged with an offence, see ibid para 898:6.

For the mode of trial for offences triable either way, see 29 ibid para 303.

For the Children and Young Persons Act 1963, s 29, see 17 Halsbury's Statutes (3rd edn) 719.

For the Magistrates' Courts Act 1980, ss 18, 23, 24, 122, see 50(2) ibid 1459, 1464, 1465, 1549.

Cases referred to in judgment

R v Amersham Juvenile Court, ex p Wilson [1981] 2 All ER 315, [1981] QB 969, [1981] 2 WLR 887, DC.

R v St Albans Juvenile Court, ex p Godman [1981] 2 All ER 311, [1981] QB 964, [1981] 2 WLR 882, DC.

Case also cited

R v Leeds Justices, ex p Hanson, [1981] 3 All ER 72, [1981] QB 892, DC.

Applications for judicial review

R v Tottenham Juvenile Court, ex p ARC (an infant)

ARC (an infant) applied, with the leave of Woolf J granted on 15 September 1981, for (i) an order of certiorari to quash a decision of the Tottenham Juvenile Court made on 17 June 1981 that it had jurisdiction to determine summarily a charge of assault with intent to rob against the applicant's co-defendant, Desmond Fitzroy Dobson, and was therefore precluded from inquiring, under s 6(1)(b) of the Children and Young Persons Act 1969, whether the interests of justice required the applicant to be committed for trial with Dobson, and (ii) an order of prohibition to prohibit the juvenile court from proceeding to try Dobson summarily. The ground on which the relief was sought was that the juvenile court had no jurisdiction to hear and determine the charge against Dobson other than as examining justices because by the time he and the applicant first appeared before the court, on 18 March 1981, Dobson had attained the age of 17 and s 6 of the 1969 Act no longer applied to him so as to require summary trial of the charge against him. The facts are set out in the judgment of the court.

R v Islington North Juvenile Court, ex p CD (an infant)

CD (an infant) applied, with the leave of Hodgson J granted on 29 October 1981, for (i) an order of certiorari to quash a decision of the Islington North Juvenile Court made on 7 August 1981 refusing to permit the applicant to elect for trial by jury and (ii) an order of mandamus directing the court to permit the applicant to elect for trial by jury. The grounds on which the relief was sought were (1) that the juvenile court wrongly applied dicta in *R v Amersham Juvenile Court, ex p Wilson* [1981] 2 All ER 315, [1981] QB 969 in preference to the decision in *R v St Albans Crown Court, ex p Godman* [1981] 2 All ER 311, [1981] QB 964, (2) that the court erred in holding that s 29 of the Children and Young

---

e   Section 29 is set out at p 326 e f, post

Persons Act 1963 qualified s 19 of the Criminal Law Act 1977 by providing that a juvenile who attained 17 before his plea had been taken had no right to elect jury trial and (3) alternatively, that the court erred in the exercise of its discretion under s 29 of the 1963 Act by refusing to permit the applicant to elect trial by jury because in any event he would not have been tried before he became 17. The facts are set out in the judgment of the court.

R v Feltham Justices, ex p NC (an infant)

NC, through his father and next friend, applied, with the leave of Hodgson J granted on 29 October 1981, for (i) an order of certiorari to quash a decision of the Feltham Juvenile Court on 31 July 1981 refusing to allow the applicant to elect trial by jury, (ii) an order of prohibition to forbid the juvenile court from further hearing and adjudicating on the information against the applicant and (iii) an order of mandamus directing the juvenile court to permit the applicant to exercise his right to choose trial by jury. The ground on which the relief was sought was that the applicant had a statutory right to elect trial by jury since he had reached the age of 17 prior to any plea being taken in the case or the mode of trial being suggested. The facts are set out in the judgment of the court.

Gordon Hodgson for ARC.
Martin Russell for CD.
Ian Bourne for NC.
Simon D Brown as amicus curiae.
The prosecutors and the justices did not appear.

Cur adv vult

8 February. **LORD LANE CJ** read the following judgment of the court: These three applications for judicial review raise the question at what point in criminal proceedings the defendant must achieve the age of 17 in order to qualify as an adult in those proceedings.

The matter is governed by two statutory provisions: the first deals with offences which in the case of an adult would be tried on indictment. Section 6(1) of the Children and Young Persons Act 1969 provides: •

> 'Where a person under the age of seventeen appears or is brought before a magistrates' court on an information charging him with an offence, other than homicide, which is an indictable offence within the meaning of the Magistrates' Courts Act 1952, he shall be tried summarily unless—(a) he is a young person and the offence is such as is mentioned in subsection (2) of section 53 of the Act of 1933 ... and the court considers that if he is found guilty of the offence it ought to be possible to sentence him in pursuance of that subsection; or (b) he is charged jointly with a person who has attained the age of seventeen and the court considers it necessary in the interests of justice to commit them both for trial ...'

The second deals with cases which in the case of an adult are triable either way, either summarily or on indictment. Section 19(1) of the Criminal Law Act 1977 provides:

> 'Sections 20 to 24 ... shall have effect where a person who has attained the age of seventeen appears or is brought before a magistrates' court on an information charging him with an offence triable either way.'

These provisions are now contained in the Magistrates' Courts Act 1980, ss 24 and 18. The question that falls to be determined in these applications concerns the proper construction of the words 'appears or is brought before a magistrates' court' and the time when that event occurs. It is a question that has given rise to a conflict of judicial view. In *R v St Albans Juvenile Court, ex p Godman* [1981] 2 All ER 311, [1981] QB 964 the Divisional Court, consisting of Ackner LJ and Skinner J, held that the applicant was entitled to elect trial by jury pursuant to s 19(1) of the Criminal Law Act 1977 at any time before the magistrates' court had started to hear evidence, notwithstanding that he might have appeared or been brought before the court on previous occasions. In *R v Amersham*

Juvenile Court, ex p Wilson [1981] 2 All ER 315, [1981] QB 969 the Divisional Court, consisting of Donaldson LJ and Bingham J, expressed the view obiter that the operative words in this context must mean when the alleged offender first appears or is brought before such a court in connection with the offence charged.

The facts of the present applications are as follows.

The case of ARC

On 12 November 1980 the applicant and two other youths, Dobson and Davis, were charged at Tottenham Magistrates' Court with an offence of assault occasioning actual bodily harm contrary to s 47 of the Offences against the Person Act 1861, and assault with intent to rob contrary to s 8 of the Theft Act 1968. They were bailed to appear at Tottenham Juvenile Court on 7 January 1981. All three youths were then under 17. Dobson, the eldest, attained the age of 17 on 22 February 1981; the applicant on 31 March 1981.

In accordance with their usual practice the Tottenham Juvenile Court sent a letter to all three youths inviting them to let the court know if they intended to plead not guilty, in which event the hearing would be adjourned to a later date. Provided the court was notified in writing before 7 January 1981 of the intention to contest the case, it was not necessary for the defendant to attend court on that date; he would be notified of a fresh date of hearing when he would be required to attend.

Both ARC and Davis completed the form indicating their intention to contest the case and accordingly did not attend court on 7 January. Dobson attended the court building and was represented by counsel. He too indicated he intended to contest the charge, whereupon he was told by the deputy clerk that he might leave the court building and that he would be notified of a new hearing date. He then left without surrendering to his bail or appearing in person before the magistrates. His counsel remained in court and was present when the case was called on before the magistrates. The circumstances were outlined to them and they adjourned the hearing until 18 March 1981. The applicant's counsel remained solely as a matter of courtesy and to discuss the proposed date of the adjourned hearing.

On 18 March all three accused attended with their parents and legal representatives but the case was further adjourned for lack of time. Eventually on 17 June 1981, when the court was ready to hear the case, it was contended on behalf of the applicant that Dobson, having attained the age of 17 on 22 February 1981, was entitled, and indeed bound, to be tried on indictment on the charge of assault with intent to rob and that that being so the magistrates should consider, pursuant to s 6(1)(b) of the Children and Young Persons Act 1969, whether the applicant was a person who was charged jointly with a person who had attained the age of 17 (namely Dobson) and whether it was necessary in the interests of justice to commit them both for trial.

The justices, following the reasoning of the court in the *Amersham* case in preference to that in the *St Albans* case, were of the opinion that the relevant time at which to consider whether Dobson was 17 was when he first appeared before the court; and that he had done so on 7 January, when he was still 16. Accordingly they did not consider the question under s 6(1)(b) whether ARC should be committed for trial; they proposed to hear the cases against all three accused summarily.

The applicant now seeks judicial review in the form of an order of certiorari to quash that decision and an order of prohibition to prevent the justices from proceeding with the trial of Dobson other than as examining magistrates and against the applicant without considering whether the interests of justice require him to be committed for trial. Counsel on his behalf submits that even accepting that the correct test was that laid down by Donaldson LJ in the *Amersham* case, what occurred on 7 January did not amount to appearing or being brought before the court.

The case of CD

On 24 June 1981 this applicant was charged with handling stolen goods contrary to s 22 of the Theft Act 1968. This is an offence triable in the case of an adult either way at the election of the accused. He was bailed to appear at Islington North Juvenile Court on 26 June 1981 and he did so. He surrendered to his bail and was remanded on bail to appear on 24 July; he did so, and was further remanded to appear on 7 August. On 3 August he was 17. On 7 August, he being anxious to be tried by a jury, it was submitted on his behalf that the facts were similar to those in the *St Albans* case and that he had a right to elect trial by jury pursuant to s 19(1) of the Criminal Law Act 1977; alternatively, if he had no right to elect trial by jury, the magistrates could, in the exercise of their discretion under s 29 of the Children and Young Persons Act 1963 as amended, permit him to do so and should so permit him.

The magistrates rejected the submission. They preferred the reasoning in the *Amersham* case and held that the applicant had no right to elect trial by jury, and that if they had a discretion in the matter they would exercise it against the applicant's contention.

The applicant now seeks judicial review in the form of an order of certiorari to quash the refusal of the magistrates to permit the application to elect trial by jury and an order for mandamus directing them to permit such an election. Counsel on behalf of the applicant submits that neither of the alternative occasions suggested by the court in the *St Albans* case or the *Amersham* case were correct. He submits that the relevant moment so far as s 19 of the Criminal Law Act 1977 is concerned is when the court comes to decide the place and mode of trial. If at this moment the accused is over 17, he has a right to elect trial by jury. He contends that s 19 stands on its own, independent of s 6(1)(*b*) of the 1969 Act and that whatever the appropriate moment may be under s 6(1)(*b*) of the 1969 Act, it is, or may be, different under s 19(1). He further submits that in so far as the justices purported to exercise their discretion, they exercised it wrongly and should have permitted the applicant to elect trial by jury.

The case of NC

On 26 May 1981 the applicant was arrested and subsequently charged together with two adults and two juveniles with burglary, contrary to s 9(1)(*b*) of the Theft Act 1968 (an offence triable either way). All the accused were bailed to appear at Feltham Magistrates' Court on 23 June 1981. On that date he duly surrendered to his bail and was further remanded to 30 June 1981. He was 17 on 25 June 1981. On 30 June 1981 he was again remanded to 31 July. On that day the two adult co-accused elected summary trial. The applicant claimed he had a right to elect trial by jury pursuant to s 19(1) of the 1977 Act. The magistrates rejected this contention and held that he had no right to elect jury trial. The facts are essentially similar to those in CD's case save that his appearances were in the adult rather than the juvenile court. The applicant in this case seeks judicial review on similar grounds to those in CD's case.

Meaning of the words 'appears or is brought before a magistrates' court'

In the *St Albans* case [1981] 2 All ER 311 at 313–314, [1981] QB 964 at 967, after setting out the statutory provisions, Ackner LJ stated:

> 'It is clear from the facts set out above that the applicant has not as yet begun to be tried for the offence alleged against him. All he has done is to enter a plea of not guilty. Accordingly the question that had to be decided on 13th November, was: how was this young man of 17 to be tried? To this question the short answer would appear to be: in accordance with the procedure laid down by ss 20 to 24 of the Criminal Law Act 1977, having regard to the provisions of s 19(1) as set out above. To this counsel for the justices makes but one short submission. Under s 21(2) it is clear that the mode of trial is decided before the plea is entered. Here, the plea having been entered, it is too late to seek to alter the mode of trial.'

But it is difficult to reconcile this with the provisions of s 6(1)(*b*) of the 1969 Act. When one looks at the provisions of that section, if the applicant has already appeared, or been brought before the magistrates' court while still under 17, the mode of his trial has been determined, namely summary trial, unless one of the two exceptions apply. If

Parliament had intended that a further exception should apply in the case of a person who had not yet attained 17 but did so before evidence was given, then the appropriate *a* way of doing so was to add a further para (*c*) in s 6(1) to that effect. Moreover there seems no justification for substituting for the words that do appear in the section some such words as '. . . if at the time the magistrates begin to hear evidence (or the plea is taken or the magistrates decide on the mode of trial) a person is under the age of 17'.

There can be little doubt therefore that the words as they appear in s 6(1) of the 1969 Act must in the context mean when the accused first appears or is brought before the *b* court. Counsel in the present cases do not submit the contrary; any other interpretation would be unworkable and lead to uncertainty; this accords with the view of the court in the *Amersham* case. What justification is there for applying any other interpretation to those words when they appear in s 19(1) of the 1977 Act, especially now that these two provisions are incorporated in the same Act? The court in the *St Albans* case thought that clearer words were required to achieve such a result, particularly since the common law *c* right to trial by jury was being removed. But that right appears to be removed by clear words in s 6(1) of the 1969 Act. We consider it would be more surprising, if Parliament intended a different point in time to apply in relation to the two sections, that it did not say so. Accordingly we agree with the view expressed by Donaldson LJ in the *Amersham* case [1981] 2 All ER 315 at 317, [1981] QB 969 at 973, that in the context of the statutes the words must mean when he first appears or is brought before the court. *d*

Is there any discretion in the magistrates to override these provisions?

It was submitted to us in CD's case that s 29 of the Children and Young Persons Act 1963, as amended by the Children and Young Persons Act 1969, affords the magistrates a discretion to override the provisions of s 19(1) of the Criminal Law Act 1977 and presumably also of s 6(1) of the 1969 Act. *e*

Section 29, as amended, provides:

> 'Provisions as to persons between the ages of 17 and 18. (1) Where proceedings in respect of a young person are begun under section 1 of the Children and Young Persons Act 1969 or for an offence and he attains the age of seventeen before the conclusion of the proceedings, the court may deal with the case and make any order which it could have made if he had not attained that age.' *f*

We agree with what Donaldson LJ said about this provision in the *Amersham* case [1981] 2 All ER 315 at 317–318, [1981] QB 969 at 973–974. This section deals with an entirely different matter, namely what is to happen in the case of a young person who attains the age of 17 years and so becomes an adult and the concern of the adult magistrates' court before the end of proceedings against him or concerning him in the *g* juvenile court. It enables the juvenile court to deal or continue to deal with him. It is also clear that the section deals with questions of disposal and trial. In our judgment it affords no discretion to the magistrates sitting in the juvenile court to override the mandatory provisions of s 6(1) of the 1969 Act or s 19(1) of the 1977 Act.

What amounts to appearing or being brought before the court? *h*

Where a person has been kept in custody by the police since his arrest, he must be physically brought before the magistrates either to be remanded in custody or on bail. That is the moment when he appears or is brought before the court. In the case of a person who has been bailed by the police, the moment is when he surrenders to his bail. If he is told by the court that he need not attend on the date originally fixed to surrender to his bail, but should appear on a later date, the later date is the relevant one, when he *j* in fact surrenders. The mere attendance at the court building when he is not required to do so will not suffice. In the case of those summoned to appear, the relevant date is when they appear in answer to the summons.

In certain circumstances a defendant need not appear in person, he may do so by his legal representative, either solicitor or counsel. Section 122 of the Magistrates' Court Act 1980 (which re-enacts s 99 of the Magistrates' Courts Act 1952) provides:

'(1) A party to any proceedings before a magistrates' court may be represented by counsel or solicitor.

(2) Subject to subsection (3) below, an absent party so represented shall be deemed not to be absent.

(3) Appearance of a party by counsel or solicitor shall not satisfy any provision of any enactment or any condition of a recognizance expressly requiring his presence.'

Section 23 of the Magistrates' Courts Act 1980 (which re-enacts s 24 of the Criminal Law Act 1977) provides:

'(1) Where—(a) the accused is represented by counsel or a solicitor who in his absence signifies to the court the accused's consent to the proceedings for determining how he is to be tried for the offence being conducted in his absence; and (b) the court is satisfied that there is good reason for proceeding in the absence of the accused, the following provisions of this section shall apply.

(2) Subject to the following provisions of this section, the court may proceed in the absence of the accused in accordance with such of the provisions of sections 19 to 22 above as are applicable in the circumstances . . .'

The remaining subsections deal with the procedure to be adopted. Thus where a case falls within s 23, the appearance by counsel or solicitor will constitute a sufficient appearance for the purpose of s 19(1) of the Criminal Law Act 1977 (now s 18(1) of the Magistrates' Courts Act 1980).

Section 23 does not apply to those under 17. However, if counsel or solicitor appear before justices in the absence of a client who has not attained 17, pursuant to s 122 of the Magistrates' Courts Act 1980, that will be a sufficient appearance for the purposes of s 6(1) of the Children and Young Persons Act 1969 (now s 24(1) of the Magistrates' Courts Act 1980). The appearance by counsel or solicitor needs to be a formal appearance on behalf of the client. For example, it is not sufficient if counsel merely attends out of courtesy to agree a date for hearing when the accused or his legal representative are not required to attend.

Result

The case of ARC. Neither the attendance at the court building of Dobson or that of his counsel before the magistrates to agree a date for hearing on 7 January 1981 amount to appearance or being brought before the court. The first appearance was on 18 March by which time Dobson was 17 and had to be tried on indictment. The magistrates then had to consider, pursuant to s 6(1) of the 1969 Act, the proper mode of trial for ARC and Davis. By their decision they precluded themselves from this consideration. Their decision will be quashed; they will be prohibited from further proceeding with the trial of Dobson other than as examining magistrates, and against the applicant without considering whether the interests of justice require him to be committed for trial.

The case of CD. The relevant appearance was on 26 June 1981, when he surrendered to his bail. He was then 16 and was triable summarily in the juvenile court. He had no right of election pursuant to s 19(1) of the 1977 Act. The magistrates had no discretion in this matter. They came to the correct decision and no order will be made.

The case of NC. The relevant appearance was on 23 June 1981, when he surrendered to his bail. He was then 16 and triable summarily. He had no right of election to trial by jury. The adult co-accused elected summary trial. The magistrates reached the correct conclusion and no order will be made.

Application of ARC granted. No order on the applications of CD and NC. In the case of CD the court refused leave to appeal to the House of Lords but certified, under s 1(2) of the Administration of Justice Act 1960, that the following point of law of general public importance was involved in the decision: whether a defendant in criminal proceedings who was charged with an offence triable either way in the case of an adult had to have attained the age of 17 on his first court appearance in order to be entitled to elect trial by jury pursuant to s 19(1) of the Criminal Law Act 1977.

29 *March. The Appeal Committee of the House of Lords granted CD leave to appeal.*

a

Solicitors: *Montague Gardner & Co* (for ARC); *Clifford Watts, Compton & Co* (for CD); *Mylles & Co*, Windsor (for NC); *Treasury Solicitor.*

N P Metcalfe Esq   Barrister.

b

Holden v White

COURT OF APPEAL, CIVIL DIVISION
ORMROD, OLIVER LJJ AND WOOD J
2, 17 MARCH 1982

c

Occupier's liability – Visitor – Permission to be on premises – Right of way – Defendant owning and occupying land over which right of way granted – Milkman using right of way to deliver milk to third party who had right of access over right of way – Milkman injured when falling through defective manhole in right of way – Whether milkman an invitee or licensee or would be treated as such at common law – Whether milkman a visitor of owner of land over which right of way granted – Whether owner of land over which right of way granted owing duty of care to milkman – Occupiers' Liability Act 1957, s 1(2).

d

The plaintiff was a milkman who was injured when he stepped on a defective manhole cover in a pathway while delivering milk to a house. The house was owned by a third party and had 'a right of way at all times and for all purposes' over and along the pathway. The defendant was the owner of the land over which the pathway giving access to the house was laid. The plaintiff claimed damages against the defendant for breach of the duty of care she as an occupier owed to the plaintiff as a visitor pursuant to s 1(2)[a] of the Occupiers' Liability Act 1957. The trial judge held that the defendant, as owner of the pathway in which the manhole was situated, was an occupier and owed a duty of care to the plaintiff as a lawful visitor. The defendant appealed, contending that the plaintiff was not her visitor and therefore she owed him no duty of care under the 1957 Act.

e

f

Held – In order to determine whether a person was a 'visitor' under s 1(2) of the 1957 Act, that person had to be regarded at common law as an invitee or licensee or to be treated as such, and, because at common law a person who crossed land in pursuance of a public or private right of way was not an invitee or licensee or treated as such, such a person was not a 'visitor' under s 1(2). Accordingly, since the plaintiff was using the pathway pursuant to a right of way granted to a third party and since the defendant had no control over persons lawfully using the pathway pursuant to the rights of the third party, the plaintiff was there pursuant to an implied licence or invitation of the third party and not by the permission or invitation of the defendant. It followed that the plaintiff was not the defendant's visitor and had no cause of action against the defendant under the 1957 Act. Accordingly the appeal would be allowed (see p 332 b to p 333 c and g to p 334 f, post).

g

h

Dictum of Lord Denning MR in *Greenhalgh v British Rlys Board* [1969] 2 All ER at 117 applied.

j

Notes

For the duty of occupiers, see 34 Halsbury's Laws (4th edn) paras 18–30, and for cases on the subject, see 36(1) Digest (Reissue) 104–126, 402–486.

For the Occupiers' Liability Act 1957, s 1, see 23 Halsbury's Statutes (3rd edn) 792.

a Section 1(2) is set out at p 330 h, post

Cases referred to in judgments

Fairman v Perpetual Investment Building Society [1923] AC 74, HL, 36(1) Digest (Reissue) 109, 416.

Gautret v Egerton, Jones v Egerton (1867) LR 2 CP 371, 36(1) Digest (Reissue) 108, 412.

Greenhalgh v British Rlys Board [1969] 2 All ER 114, [1969] 2 QB 286, [1969] 2 WLR 892, CA, 36(1) Digest (Reissue) 104, 403.

Jacobs v London CC [1950] 1 All ER 737, [1950] AC 361, HL, 36(1) Digest (Reissue) 110, 424.

Wheat v E Lacon & Co Ltd [1966] 1 All ER 582, [1966] AC 552, [1966] 2 WLR 581, HL, 36(1) Digest (Reissue) 76, 300.

Appeal

The plaintiff, Michael George Holden, claimed damages for breach of statutory duty under the Occupiers' Liability Act 1957, or alternatively for negligence, against the first and second defendants, Edna White and William Frederick White, for injuries sustained by him on the defendants' land. On 16 January 1981 Stocker J held that the first defendant as owner and occupier of the land was in breach of her statutory duty under the 1957 Act to the plaintiff and ordered that she pay the plaintiff damages to the sum of £2,250. The first defendant appealed, contending that the judge had misdirected himself in law in holding that the plaintiff was a visitor of the first defendant and that she owed a duty of care to the plaintiff. By a respondent's notice dated 3 March 1981 the plaintiff contended that the judgment should be upheld. The facts are set out in the judgment of Oliver LJ.

John Cherry for the first defendant.
Cyril Newman for the plaintiff.

Cur adv vult

17 March. The following judgments were read.

OLIVER LJ (delivering the first judgment at the invitation of Ormrod LJ). This is an appeal from an order of Stocker J made on 16 January 1981 awarding a sum of £2,250 agreed damages and costs in respect of personal injuries sustained by the plaintiff against the first defendant to the action, Mrs Edna White. The appeal is one which raises an interesting and unusual point with regard to liability under the Occupiers' Liability Act 1957 and since the point is one which may have repercussions which go much wider than the instant case we thought it right to take time to consider our judgments.

The facts are simple and can be stated quite shortly. At Lion Lane, Haslemere, Surrey there is a row of five terraced houses lying more or less at right angles to the main road. These are numbered 4 to 12 (even numbers) and they are approached by a broad way which narrows to a three-foot wide footway where it reaches the north-western corner of number 4 and which then runs in an almost easterly direction along the front of nos 4, 6 and 8, terminating at the entrance to no 10 and providing pedestrian access (and it is the only access) to these four houses. In front of the houses it is concreted and in front of each house there is a manhole or inspection cover giving access to what is no doubt a combined drainage system.

So much for the physical layout. I must state a little of the conveyancing history of nos 4 to 10. These properties belonged originally to two ladies, the Misses Rogers. On 15 July 1968 they sold and conveyed nos 6 and 8 to the second defendant, William Frederick White, and the conveyance contained a grant of 'a right of way at all times and for all purposes (but on foot only) over and along the pathways shown coloured yellow on the plan' (the yellow land including the path which I have already described). On 20 July 1968 they sold and conveyed no 10 to a Mr Hooper with a similar grant, and on 28 August 1968 they sold and conveyed no 4, and all the land coloured

yellow in the two prior conveyances, to a Mr Roe, but subject to 'right of way at all times
and for all purposes (but on foot only) over and along the pathways shown yellow on the *a*
said plan for the benefit of Nos 6, 8, 10 and 12 Lion Lane aforesaid'.

On 10 August 1970 Mr Roe died, having by his will devised no 4 and the yellow land
to Mrs White, the first defendant, and she was registered as proprietor under the Land
Registration Acts on 13 November 1970.

Each conveyance included a right to use the drains, watercourses, pipes etc on the
adjoining properties.   *b*

As regards the actual occupation of the properties the first defendant and her husband
live in nos 6 and 8; nos 10 and 12 are occupied by another family, and no 4 is occupied
by a tenant of Mrs White.

The plaintiff in the action was at the material time a servery manager employed by
Unigate, but he had from time to time acted as a relief milk roundsman and was so acting
at the time of the accident on 17 April 1975. At about 10 am on that day he was walking *c*
along the concrete path in front of nos 4, 6 and 8 for the purpose of delivering milk to
no 10. He trod on the manhole cover in the pathway in front of no 10 and it disintegrated
into four or five pieces so that his leg went through and he suffered the injuries in respect
of which the agreed damages were awarded. His evidence was that the cover was made
of metal and was cracked across. His opinion was that the crack was probably due to the
impact of some heavy object. He had visited the premises on one or two previous *d*
occasions, his last previous visit being some two or three weeks before the accident.

There was no evidence before the judge with regard to the function of the manholes
or to their age or the age of the covers. He inferred however (as was no doubt the case)
that they were for the purpose of giving access to drains or services.

Although the claim was framed as a claim against both Mr and Mrs White, it was in
fact pursued only against the latter, she being the owner of no 4 and, accordingly, of the *e*
soil of the pathway: and the foundation of the claim was the Occupiers' Liability Act
1957 although there was an alternative claim for negligence at common law.

Before referring to the Act it is well to remember its purpose which was to eradicate
some of the unsatisfactory features of the way in which the common law had developed
as regards the liability of occupiers of premises for injuries sustained by third parties
lawfully resorting there, the extent of the duty owed varying according to whether the *f*
person injured was vis-à-vis the occupier an invitee or a licensee. The 1957 Act removed
this distinction and substituted a single common duty to all visitors, whether licensees or
invitees, but it was not its purpose to enlarge the overall class of persons to whom the
duty was owed. Section 1(1) and (2) provides as follows:

> '(1) The rules enacted by the two next following sections shall have effect, in *g*
> place of the rules of the common law, to regulate the duty which an occupier of
> premises owes to his visitors in respect of dangers due to the state of the premises or
> to things done or omitted to be done on them.
> (2) The rules so enacted shall regulate the nature of the duty imposed by law in
> consequence of a person's occupation or control of premises and of any invitation or
> permission he gives (or is to be treated as giving) to another to enter or use the *h*
> premises, but they shall not alter the rules of the common law as to the persons on
> whom a duty is so imposed or to whom it is owed; and accordingly for the purpose
> of the rules so enacted the persons who are to be treated as an occupier and as his
> visitors are the same (subject to subsection (4) of this section) as the persons who
> would at common law be treated as an occupier and as his invitees or licensees.'
>   *j*

Subsection (4), which relates to persons exercising rights under the National Parks and
Access to the Countryside Act 1949, does not matter for present purposes.

The duty of care is regulated by s 2(1) and (2), which, so far as material, is in the
following terms:

'(1) An occupier of premises owes the same duty, the "common duty of care", to all his visitors, except in so far as he is free to and does extend, restrict, modify or exclude his duty to any visitor or visitors by agreement or otherwise.

(2) The common duty of care is a duty to take such care as in all the circumstances of the case is reasonable to see that the visitor will be reasonably safe in using the premises for the purposes for which he is invited or permitted by the occupier to be there.'

I ought perhaps to refer to s 2(6) because it is referred to in one of the authorities to which we have been referred:

'For the purposes of this section, persons who enter premises for any purpose in the exercise of a right conferred by law are to be treated as permitted by the occupier to be there for that purpose, whether they in fact have his permission or not.'

These are the only two sections which are material to the present case. The judge held that Mrs White, as the owner of the pathway in which the manhole cover was situated, owed a common duty of care to the plaintiff who was a lawful visitor on it. He did so on the basis that she was the owner of the pathway, there being no evidence of any arrangements made between the owners of the various cottages inter se. It seems therefore that the judge was treating ownership as equivalent to occupation. Whether or not that is strictly correct need not be further considered, although it does open up some rather startling possibilities having regard to the not uncommon situation where a non-resident vendor of land for development retains the soil of paths and passageways over which the purchasers enjoy rights in common, because counsel for the first defendant has conceded in this court that Mrs White is the occupier. What he contests is the judge's conclusion that the plaintiff ever was *her* visitor for it is only in relation to *her* visitors that the Act imposes any duty on her.

Having regard to the specific provisions of s 1(2) the question may be postulated in this way: prior to the Act was a person making use of a private right of way for the purpose of obtaining access to the dominant tenement either an invitee or a licensee of the occupier of the servient tenement?

Certainly it was well established that, in the absence of contract, the servient owner had no duty at all to the dominant owner himself to keep the way in repair, and it is difficult to see any logical reason why he should have been burdened with a duty to the licensee or invitees of the dominant owner. The owner of the servient tenement is simply a person who takes his land subject to an incumbrance which he can do nothing to avoid. No doubt he owes the ordinary duty of an occupier to persons whom, either expressly or impliedly, he invites onto his land or to whom *he* can be said to have granted permissive entry. But it is entirely unreal to regard him as having in any sense issued any invitation or permission to persons who enter the land in exercise of the dominant owner's rights. That would, I think, be so even in the case of the original grantor, but it is a fortiori the case where, as here, the owner of the servient tenement acquired the land already burdened with the easement, for at no time does he have any choice about whether to admit the invitees or licensees of the dominant owner nor does he have any control over the activities of such persons so long as they do no more than exercise the right conferred on their invitor or licensor by virtue of his estate in the land.

Counsel for the plaintiff argues that the instant case is no different in principle from that of the owner of a block of flats who retains control of the common staircase or lifts. The only difference, he submits, is that the instant case is concerned with an easement over something lying in a horizontal plane instead of vertical plane. He submits that the effect of *Fairman v Perpetual Investment Building Society* [1923] AC 74 and *Jacobs v London CC* [1950] 1 All ER 737, [1950] AC 361 is to establish the position of one using a means of access as the licensee of the owner of the land or through which the access runs.

I find myself quite unable to deduce any such general principle from those cases which

were concerned only with the question of whether the person injured was an invitee, her
position as licensee being, in effect, assumed for the purpose of the argument. But in any *a*
event the position of the landlord of a building is, in my judgment, entirely different and
it is significant that in this case the legislature has found it necessary to legislate expressly
(see s 4 of the Act) in terms which would, I think, have been otiose if counsel's submission
were correct.

Quite apart from the difficulty of spelling out a permission from the landowner over
whose land the easement is exercisable, counsel for the plaintiff has to face the difficulty *b*
created by the decision of this court in *Greenhalgh v British Rlys Board* [1969] 2 All ER 114,
[1969] 2 QB 286, a case in which the plaintiff was injured by the defective surface of the
defendant's bridge over which she was passing in the exercise of a public right of way.
This court unanimously rejected the submission that she was a 'visitor' of the defendants
and the judgment on which counsel for the defendant relies particularly is that of Lord
Denning MR. The Master of the Rolls said ([1969] 2 All ER 114 at 117, [1969] 2 QB 286 *c*
at 292):

> 'In the second place, it was said that the [board] owed a duty to [Mrs Greenhalgh]
> under the Occupiers' Liability Act 1957. It was said that she was a "visitor". But I
> do not think she was. Section 1(2) shows that, in order to determine whether a
> person is a "visitor", we must go back to the common law. A person is a "visitor" if
> at common law he would be regarded as an invitee or licensee; or be treated as such, *d*
> as for instance, a person lawfully using premises provided for the use of the public
> (e.g., a public park) or a person entering by lawful authority (e.g., a policeman with
> a search warrant). But a "visitor" does not include a person who crosses land in
> pursuance of a public or private right of way. Such a person was never regarded as
> an invitee or licensee, or treated as such. [Lord Denning MR then referred to the
> judgment of Willes J in *Gautret v Egerton* (1867) LR 2 CP 371 at 373 and *e*
> continued:] Some mention was also made of s. 2(6) of the Act of 1957 [and he read
> that subsection]. The important words to notice are the opening words: "For the
> purposes of this section", i.e., for the purpose of s. 2, which defines only the *extent*
> of the occupier's duty to acknowledged visitors. It does not expand the range of
> persons who are to be treated as visitors. Section 2(6) applies, for instance, to persons
> who enter a public park, or a policeman who enters on a search warrant, for they *f*
> enter in the exercise of a right conferred by law and are treated as if they were
> invitees or licensees. They are acknowledged "visitors". Section 2(6) shows that the
> occupier owes to such persons a duty of care when they are using the place for the
> authorised purpose, but not when they are abusing it. But s. 2(6) does not apply to
> persons crossing land by virtue of a public or private way; because they are never
> "visitors" at all.' *g*

Then Lord Denning MR referred to various text books, including *Clerk and Lindsell on
Tort* (12th edn, 1961), *Salmond on Law of Torts* (14th edn, 1965), *Winfield and Jolowicz on
the Law of Tort* (8th edn, 1967).

I add only that the Act not only requires the person to be a 'visitor' but to be *'his* visitor',
ie the visitor (by definition an invitee or licensee) of the occupier. *h*

Davies LJ agreed entirely with everything that fell from Lord Denning MR.

Widgery LJ expressed himself as 'in entire agreement' but added some observations
which were entirely directed to the question of whether there was any duty owed at
common law by the occupier of land to the user of a highway across the land.

Counsel for the plaintiff seeks to avoid the impact of this decision by submitting that
Lord Denning MR's reference to private rights of way was obiter and was nothing more *j*
than a collective Homeric nod on the part of the court. Obiter it may have been, but it
was very powerful obiter nevertheless. In point of fact, I am not, for myself, convinced
that it should be treated strictly obiter. Whilst it is true that the case was directly
concerned with a public right of way, the ratio of the decision is the absence of duty to
a person using the way, a consideration which, at common law, applied equally I think

to a person using a private way. At any rate no authority has been cited to us establishing any such duty, apart from the very special landlord and tenant cases where very different considerations apply.

The judge distinguished *Greenhalgh's* case on the footing that it did not support the broad proposition that a person such as a milkman, lawfully using the only pathway to the door of one of a terrace of houses, is owed no duty by anyone in respect of dangers which cause him injury. That may be so, but the question was not whether anyone owed the plaintiff a duty but whether Mrs White, as owner of the land on which the manhole was situate, owed him a duty, and in order to substantiate the existence of such a duty under the statute, he had to bring himself within the four corners of the statute by establishing his status as *her* visitor, ie her invitee or licensee. For my part, I am unable to conclude that he ever did do that, for it does not seem to me that any analysis of the position enables one to arrive at a conclusion that Mrs White had issued any invitation or permission to him to be at the place where he was injured. He was there because the owners of no 10 had a legal easement which enabled them to insist, as against Mrs White, on his being there.

The judge was clearly much influenced by the thought that if there was no duty owed by Mrs White, there was no duty owed by anybody.

It is unnecessary for the purposes of the present appeal to decide the point, but I am not, speaking entirely for myself, convinced that this assumption is right. There is no statutory definition of an 'occupier' and in *Wheat v E Lacon & Co Ltd* [1966] 1 All ER 582 at 594, [1966] AC 552 at 579 Lord Denning favoured a definition which would include having any degree of control over the state of the premises. In the instant case, for example, the manhole cover set in the path prima facie would appear to have been put there for the benefit of, and was presumably maintained by, the owner of no 10 and, without expressing any concluded view on the point, it may well be that those owners, whose visitor the plaintiff was, had a sufficient degree of control to render them occupiers for the purposes of the 1957 Act. The point is, however, an academic one in relation to the claim against Mrs White.

Counsel for the plaintiff further sought to distinguish *Greenhalgh's* case on another ground, namely that that case excluded from the category of visitors only a person 'crossing' land in exercise of a right of way. This is a variant of the judge's view that the principle of the case could not apply to an access way to a row of terraced houses. But 'crossing' means, I think, only 'passing over or along' and the nature or proximity of the two termini cannot, in my judgment, affect the principle which rests, as I read the decision, simply on the fact that one who exercises the right vested in the dominant owner with *his* permission, does not become the visitor of the servient owner.

I therefore, take a different view from that taken by the judge. In my judgment, the plaintiff failed, vis-à-vis Mrs White to bring himself within the terms of the statute, and counsel for the plaintiff was not able to suggest any convincing means by which he could establish any liability in Mrs White apart from the statute.

Counsel for the first defendent also submits, as an alternative ground of appeal, that the judge was wrong in applying the maxim res ipsa loquitur to the liability of Mrs White and in holding that the burden of proving reasonable care had shifted to her.

I find myself unpersuaded by this part of his argument, but on the view which I take of the effect of the statutory provisions, it is not necessary to decide the point. I would allow the appeal.

ORMROD LJ. I entirely agree with the judgment which has just been delivered by Oliver LJ, but, as we are differing from Stocker J, I would like to state as briefly as possible, the reasons for my conclusion.

The Occupiers' Liability Act 1957 did not extend the scope of the common law duty of care in relation to users of land (see s 1(2)): it altered the nature of the duty owed to such persons by abolishing the distinction between invitees and licensees, and substituting a duty of care common to both classes, which is defined by s 2(2).

To establish a cause of action against the defendant the plaintiff must show, therefore, that she owed a duty of care to him at common law. The common law imposed no duty *a* on the owner of land towards a person exercising a right of way over his land to maintain the way in reasonable condition; his only duty was not to obstruct it. This is clearly established where public rights of way are concerned: see *Gautret v Egerton* (1867) LR CP 371 and *Greenhalgh v British Rlys Board* [1969] 2 All ER 114, [1969] 2 QB 286; and no authority has been cited to us to show that the user of a private right of way is in any better position. In fact, this must be so because, although at first sight the grant of a right *b* of way may seem to be equivalent to a licence, in fact it is quite different, as the language, which is universally used, demonstrates. It is a legal 'right' to pass over another person's land which is 'subject to' the right, so that on transfer of the land the grantee takes an encumbered title. The customary words 'dominant' and 'servient' express the position accurately. It would be quite illogical, therefore, to impose on the servient owner any obligation other than not to obstruct, ie diminish, the right of way. *c*

In this case the defendant took the land which she owns 'subject to' the right of way described in the conveyance. The plaintiff was using the pathway pursuant to the right of way owned by the owner of no 10. He was, of course, not a trespasser: he was on the path pursuant to an implied licence or invitation by the owner of no 10 in the exercise of the right of way attached to no 10, and not by the permission or invitation of the defendant, who has no control over persons lawfully using the path pursuant to the *d* rights of the owner of no 10.

Consequently, assuming that the defendant is to be regarded for this purpose as the 'occupier', which is a point which may have to be decided in a later case, the plaintiff was not *her* visitor. He had no cause of action at common law and, therefore, none under the Occupiers' Liability Act 1957. I would, therefore, allow the defendant's appeal on this ground. *e*

In these circumstances it is not necessary to consider the res ipsa loquitur point.

WOOD J. I have had the advantage of being able to read the judgments of Oliver and Ormrod LJJ before each was delivered, and agree with the result and the reasons given.

I would only seek to add that despite the concession by counsel for the defendant, on the facts of the present case I am far from satisfied that for the purposes of s 1 of the *f* Occupiers' Liability Act 1957 Mrs White was the occupier vis-à-vis the plaintiff.

I agree that the appeal should be allowed.

Appeal allowed.

Solicitors: *W R Kirk* (for the first defendant); *Derek Holden & Co*, Staines (for the plaintiff).

Bebe Chua   Barrister.

Hehir v Commissioner of Police of the Metropolis

COURT OF APPEAL, CIVIL DIVISION
LAWTON AND BRIGHTMAN LJJ
3, 4, 19 MARCH 1982

Discovery – Privilege – Production contrary to public interest – Class of documents – Statements taken by police in statutory investigation into complaints by member of the public – Waiver of privilege – Complainant arrested and charged with offence but later acquitted – Complainant making statement to police during investigation into his complaint about police treatment – Complainant later bringing civil action against police – Police claiming privilege from production of documents concerning investigation into complaint – Police later seeking to cross-examine plaintiff on statement made by him during investigation into complaint – Whether police entitled to waive privilege previously claimed by them on grounds of public interest immunity.

The plaintiff was arrested by two police officers for, and charged with, a minor offence under the Vagrancy Act 1824. The charge was later dismissed. The plaintiff brought an action against the Commissioner of Police of the Metropolis, who was liable by virtue of s 48 of the Police Act 1964 for any wrongful acts done by constables under his direction and control, claiming in effect damages for false imprisonment and malicious prosecution. In the course of mutual discovery of documents the commissioner claimed privilege in respect of police reports, statements, documents and correspondence made for the purpose of an inquiry pursuant to s 49 of the 1964 Act on the ground of public interest immunity. One of those statements had been made by the plaintiff, as a complainant, concerning the way he had been treated by the police officers after his arrest. At the trial counsel for the commissioner sought to cross-examine the plaintiff on that statement. The plaintiff's counsel objected on the ground that the commissioner, having claimed public interest immunity for all the statements, could not properly use the plaintiff's statement for the purpose of cross-examination. The commissioner's counsel then claimed that the commissioner was entitled to waive his claim to public interest immunity in respect of the statement. The trial judge ruled that the commissioner's counsel was entitled to cross-examine the plaintiff on the statement. The plaintiff appealed.

Held – Public interest immunity attached to all statements made in the course of an investigation carried out pursuant to s 49 of the 1964 Act and the complainant's statements could not be excluded from the protection of that immunity, since the object of the immunity was to free those who made such statements from the fear that at some future time their statements might be used against them in civil proceedings. Furthermore, since the reason for the immunity was the need to protect the public interest, the recipient of a statement which was protected from production on the ground of public interest immunity could not waive that immunity. It followed that the plaintiff's statement was protected from production and it was not open to the commissioner to waive that immunity in order to cross-examine him on it. The appeal would therefore be allowed (see p 336 *j*, p 340 *d e* and p 341 *d* to *f*, post).

Neilson v Laugharne [1981] 1 All ER 829 applied.

Quaere. Whether public interest immunity can ever be waived (see p 341 *f* to *j*, post).

Notes

For withholding documents from production on the ground that disclosure would be injurious to the public interest, see 13 Halsbury's Laws (4th edn) paras 86–91, and for cases on the subject, see 18 Digest (Reissue) 154–160, *1265–1301*.

For the Police Act 1964, s 49, see 25 Halsbury's Statutes (3rd edn) 363.

Cases referred to in judgments

Auten v Rayner [1958] 3 All ER 566, [1958] 1 WLR 1300, CA, 18 Digest (Reissue) 158, *a*
    1283.
Conway v Rimmer [1968] 1 All ER 874, [1968] AC 910, [1968] 2 WLR 998, HL, 18 Digest
    (Reissue) 155, 1273.
Crompton (Alfred) Amusement Machines Ltd v Customs and Excise Comrs (No 2) [1973] 2 All
    ER 1169, [1974] AC 405, [1973] 3 WLR 268, HL, 18 Digest (Reissue) 102, 756.
Farrell v Alexander [1976] 2 All ER 721, [1977] AC 59, [1976] 3 WLR 145, HL, Digest *b*
    (Cont Vol E) 382, 8375b.
Marks v Beyfus (1890) 25 QBD 494, CA, 22 Digest (Reissue) 432, 4297.
Neilson v Laugharne [1981] 1 All ER 829, [1981] QB 736, [1981] 2 WLR 537, CA.
R v Hardy (1794) 24 State Tr 199, 1 East PC 60, 14(1) Digest (Reissue) 400, 3371.
Rogers v Secretary of State for the Home Dept, Gaming Board of Great Britain v Rogers [1972]
    2 All ER 1057, [1973] AC 388, [1972] 3 WLR 279, HL, Digest (Cont Vol D) 267, *c*
    2835c.
Young v Bristol Aeroplane Co Ltd [1944] 2 All ER 293, [1944] KB 718, CA; *affd* [1946] 1 All
    ER 98, [1946] AC 163, HL, 30 Digest (Reissue) 269, 765.

Cases also cited

Burnell v British Transport Commission [1955] 3 All ER 822, [1956] 1 QB 187, CA.   *d*
*Buttes Gas and Oil Co v Hammer (No 3), Occidental Petroleum Corp v Buttes Gas and Oil Co
    (No 2)* [1980] 3 All ER 475, [1981] QB 223, CA.
D v National Society for the Prevention of Cruelty to Children [1977] 1 All ER 589, [1978] AC
    171, HL.
Science Research Council v Nassé, BL Cars Ltd (formerly Leyland Cars) v Vyas [1979] 3 All ER
    673, [1980] AC 1028, HL.   *e*

Interlocutory appeal

The plaintiff, Gerard Anthony Hehir, appealed against the judgment of Russell J given
on 3 March 1982 in favour of the defendant, the Commissioner of Police of the
Metropolis, whereby the judge ruled that the defendant should be permitted to cross-
examine the plaintiff, during the course of a civil trial, on a statement he had made as a *f*
complainant in the course of an inquiry pursuant to s 49 of the Police Act 1964. The
facts are set out in the judgment of Lawton LJ.

Colin Ross-Munro QC and *Alan Bayliss* for the plaintiff
Laurence Marshall for the defendant.

At the conclusion of the argument Lawton LJ said that having regard to the decision of *g*
the Court of Appeal in *Neilson v Laugharne* [1981] 1 All ER 829, [1981] QB 736 the
defendant should not be allowed to cross-examine the plaintiff on the statement which
he had made in the course of an investigation carried out pursuant to s 49 of the Police
Act 1964 and that the court would give its reasons at a later date. The court refused the
defendant leave to appeal to the House of Lords.   *h*

19 March. The following judgments were read.

LAWTON LJ. On 4 March 1982 we adjudged that the decision of this court in *Neilson
v Laugharne* [1981] 1 All ER 829, [1981] QB 736, which is binding on us, applies to this
case and that in consequence the defendant, the Commissioner of Police of the
Metropolis, through counsel, could not during the course of a civil trial cross-examine *j*
the plaintiff on a statement which he had made as a complainant in the course of an
investigation carried out pursuant to s 49 of the Police Act 1964. That section imposes
a statutory duty on chief officers of police to investigate complaints against a member of
a police force. We stated that we would amplify this decision later.

On 27 January 1977 two detective constables arrested for and charged the plaintiff with a minor offence under the Vagrancy Act 1824. The charge was later dismissed. By a writ issued on 17 January 1980 and a reamended statement of claim he sought damages against the commissioner for what seems to be false imprisonment and malicious prosecution. Pursuant to s 48 of the Police Act 1964 the commissioner is liable in damages for any wrongful acts done by constables under his direction and control.

In the course of the preparations for trial the parties exchanged lists of documents. The defendant, in Part 2 of the first schedule to his list, enumerated the documents in his possession, custody or power which he objected to produce. Item 2 was in these terms: 'Police reports, statements, documents and correspondence made for the purpose of an enquiry pursuant to Section 49 of the Police Act 1964.' One of these statements had been made in April 1978 by the plaintiff, as a complainant, about the way he had been treated by the police after his arrest. It is likely that statements were also made at this time by the two detective constables about whose conduct the plaintiff was complaining in the action. Such statements as were made came into existence in the course of an investigation held pursuant to s 49 of the Police Act 1964. The plaintiff's statement was on a form with a printed heading 'Statement of Witness'. After particulars identifying the witness came these words:

'This statement consisting of 10 pages each signed by me, is true to the best of my knowledge and belief and I make it knowing that, if it is tendered in evidence, I shall be liable to prosecution if I have wilfully stated in it anything which I know to be false or do not believe to be true.'

The plaintiff's objection to production by the defendant was based on the decision in *Neilson v Laugharne.*

Before the decision of the House of Lords in *Conway v Rimmer* [1968] 1 All ER 874, [1968] AC 910 it had been the practice of the solicitor to the Metropolitan Police to advise police officer defendants in civil proceedings to disclose all relevant documents save those which were clearly subject to public interest immunity such as statements made by informers and police documents revealing what had happened in the course of police investigations. If necessary, any claim for immunity from discovery was supported by a certificate by a high officer of state, such as the Home Secretary or the Attorney General; for an example of the old practice, see *Auten v Rayner* [1958] 3 All ER 566, [1958] 1 WLR 1300. After the decision in *Conway v Rimmer* the solicitor advised that statements made in the course of investigations undertaken pursuant to s 49 should be disclosed. This meant that the plaintiff in any civil proceedings which he brought because of alleged misconduct by Metropolitan Police officers would be able to see and take copies not only of any statement he had made as a complainant but also copies of any statements which had been made by the police officers about whose conduct he was complaining, and that the defendant could cross-examine the complainant on any statement made by him. In my opinion, this was a fair way of dealing with this kind of litigation. It matters not to the court of trial who is the plaintiff and who is the defendant. The court wants to get at the truth; and one of the best ways of getting at the truth is for witnesses to be cross-examined on previous inconsistent statements. Long ago such cross-examination was regulated by Parliament: see the Criminal Procedure Act 1865 (commonly known as Denman's Act), ss 4 and 5.

After the decision of this court in *Neilson v Laugharne* the solicitor concluded that statements taken in the course of a s 49 investigation should not be disclosed, the reason being that the public interest made them immune from discovery; and if they were so immune, they could not be produced at the trial, nor could secondary evidence be given of their contents.

At the trial, this claim for immunity put the defendant's counsel in a difficulty. The plaintiff gave evidence in chief. Counsel for the defendant, in the exercise of his forensic judgment, was of the opinion that the plaintiff had deposed to matters which he had not mentioned during the s 49 investigation and had given evidence which was inconsistent with the statement he had then made. He wanted to cross-examine the plaintiff on his s 49 statement. The plaintiff's counsel objected on the ground that the defendant, having claimed public interest immunity for all the statements, could not properly use the plaintiff's statement for the purposes of cross-examining him on it. The defendant's counsel then claimed that the defendant was entitled to waive his claim for public interest immunity in respect of this document. The trial judge ruled that the defendant's counsel was entitled to cross-examine the plaintiff on the statement he had made as a complainant in the course of the s 49 investigation. The consequences of this ruling reveal the difficulty with which judges trying civil claims against police officers have to deal as a result of the decision in *Neilson v Laugharne*. The plaintiff had put himself forward as a truthful man who had been the victim of improper and unlawful conduct on the part of two detective constables. The defendant is of the opinion that he is not what he holds himself out to be and that this may be shown by his being cross-examined on his s 49 statement. Forensic experience goes to show that cross-examination on previous statements may reveal this. But, if the plaintiff is cross-examined, what is going to happen if and when the two detective constables give evidence? The defendant's counsel has had the plaintiff's statement in his brief because it is in the possession of the defendant. The plaintiff's counsel has not got, and will not get because of the defendant's claim to public interest immunity, copies of any statements made by the two detective constables. If *Neilson v Laugharne* applies to this case and the trial judge's ruling is right, police officers are put into a privileged position in this class of litigation.

In the course of counsel's submissions a number of other consequences of the application of the decision in *Neilson v Laugharne* were discussed. Its application may prevent prosecutions for offences under s 5(2) of the Criminal Law Act 1967 of persons who cause any wasteful employment of the police by knowingly making false reports about police officers. Further, in the past, when such reports have been made by persons worth suing for defamation, some of their police officer victims, who may have suffered much worry, have claimed damages for libel. Such claims will now be barred because the defamatory statements cannot be put in evidence. The other side to the same forensic coin is the difficulty in which a victim of police misbehaviour may find himself. Those who have injured him may have lied themselves out of trouble during the course of a s 49 investigation. If this has happened, in subsequent civil proceedings the lying police statements would not be available to support the victim's case.

Counsel for the plaintiff accepted that *Neilson v Laugharne* could cause difficulties for both parties in civil litigation of this kind. He went on to submit, however, that this was the price which had to be paid for the greater benefit to the public which arose from covering all statements made in s 49 investigations with the mantle of public interest immunity. Some may doubt whether what results from such immunity is worth the price which has to be paid; but if *Neilson v Laugharne* does apply to this case any opinion I may have about its merits as an authority are irrelevant: see *Farrell v Alexander* [1976] 2 All ER 721, [1977] AC 59.

Since it was not suggested that *Neilson v Laugharne* came within the rare exceptions set out in *Young v Bristol Aeroplane Co Ltd* [1944] 2 All ER 293, [1944] KB 718, that decision is binding on us if it applies. The first question is whether it does; and, if it does, the second question is whether the defendant could waive such rights, if any, as he had arising out of public interest immunity.

The plaintiff in that case brought a civil action for damages against a chief constable for alleged misconduct by two detective constables. He had complained to the chief constable about what they had done to him. The chief constable had ordered a s 49 investigation. Statements were taken from several persons, including the plaintiff. In the end it was decided that no proceedings, either criminal or disciplinary, should be taken against the two detective constables. The plaintiff was not satisfied and started civil proceedings. When the time came for lists of documents to be exchanged the chief constable objected to producing any of the statements, other than that of the plaintiff, taken during the statutory investigation. He did so on two grounds: first, legal professional privilege (which has not been claimed in this case), and second, the production would be contrary to the public interest. The court, which had as members Lord Denning MR, Oliver and O'Connor LJJ, rejected the claim based on legal professional privilege but upheld that based on public interest immunity. Lord Denning MR said ([1981] 1 All ER 829 at 835–836, [1981] QB 736 at 748):

'Statements were taken on the basis that they were to be used for a private investigation, to see if the police had acted improperly in any way . . . Yet now the plaintiff wants to see the statements for another purpose altogether. . . . I cannot think it incumbent on the police, or the court, to go through all these statements, or to consider the contents of them, so as to assert a "contents" privilege. It is in the public interest that the whole "class" should be privileged from disclosure to the plaintiff.'

Oliver LJ examined the problem of public interest immunity in depth. He asked himself these questions (see [1981] 1 All ER 829 at 838, [1981] QB 736 at 751):

'What, as it seems to me, one has to look at is the likely consequences of a general right to disclosure in civil litigation in the context of the statutory purpose sought to be achieved by the section, and to ask, first, whether these likely consequences support the contention that such disclosure would be contrary to the public interest, and, second, if so, whether that interest is a consideration of such importance as to outweigh the public interest in disclosure.'

When answering them he considered the position of the complainant in a statutory investigation. He said ([1981] 1 All ER 829 at 839, [1981] QB 736 at 753):

'Finally, there is the position of the complainant himself. Counsel for the plaintiff, in the course of his argument, stressed the unfairness of a position in which, in effect, the defendant got a proof of the plaintiff's evidence in advance whilst he was deprived of the opportunity of seeing the defendant's evidence. But this seems to me to be an argument in favour of, rather than against, the protection which is sought. There is no compulsion on the complainant to co-operate in the inquiry. Having made his complaint, he may refuse to give a statement to the investigating officer, and he is, I should have thought, very much more likely to do so if he thinks that any statement which he makes may be quoted against him in any civil proceedings which he has in contemplation. If, however, these statements are protected from disclosure in any proceedings, that consequence will be avoided. If public policy prevents disclosure, it prevents it, in my judgment, in all circumstances except to establish innocence in criminal proceedings. It is not like legal professional privilege, which is the personal right of the party entitled to it and can be waived (see *Rogers v Secretary of State for the Home Department* [1972] 2 All ER 1057 at 1066, 1070, [1973] AC 388 at 407, 412 per Lord Simon and Lord Salmon respectively). As a consequence, therefore, although no doubt the complainant's statement may be included in counsel's brief and may form the basis of a cross-examination, it cannot be used as evidence to controvert anything which the complainant's witnesses may say (see *Alfred Crompton Amusement Machines Ltd v Customs and Excise Comrs (No 2)* [1973] 2 All ER 1169 at 1184, [1974] AC 405 at 434 per Lord Cross). Thus, it seems to me, that here again the protection sought in this case would assist the proper carrying out of the statutory purpose if it is allowed, and impede it if it is refused.'

He summed up his answers to his questions as follows ([1981] 1 All ER 829 at 840, [1981] QB 736 at 754):

'Taking all these considerations into account, I think that there is a very real danger that the prospect of disclosure on discovery of material gathered in the course of such an inquiry will inhibit the proper conduct of the inquiry and thus frustrate the purpose of the legislature in making statutory provision for it. In my judgment, therefore, the public interest requires that these documents should be protected as a class, and I accordingly concur in the conclusion of Lord Denning MR.'

O'Connor LJ said ([1981] 1 All ER 829 at 842, [1981] QB 736 at 757):

'In the alternative the defendant claims public interest privilege for the statements. The basis for this claim is found in the affidavit of Mr Moody, the deputy chief constable; in effect he says that the s 49 inquiry would be prejudiced if persons approached to make statements thought that such statements might at some future time be used in civil litigation and revealed to parties thereto. For my part I am sure that this is right. We were told that there are a great many complaints every year which have to be investigated under the s 49 procedure ranging from trivial complaints to very serious allegations. The complaints may come from honest citizens; on the other hand they also come from criminals. The reasons for protecting such statements have been set out by Lord Denning MR and Oliver LJ and I do not wish to add to them. I agree with what each of them has said.'

The inference which I draw from all three judgments is that the court was throwing the mantle of public interest immunity over *all* statements made in the course of a s 49 investigation.

At the invitation of the Bench counsel considered whether the complainant could be excluded from the protection of the mantle. Oliver LJ clearly thought he could not. This opinion must be right if the object of the immunity is to free those who make statements from the fear that at some future time what they have said may be used against them in civil proceedings. I find it impossible to distinguish *Neilson v Laugharne* from this case on the ground that in the earlier case the court did not have to consider specifically whether public interest immunity attached to the complainant's statement.

There remains the question whether it was competent in this case for the defendant to waive public interest immunity. That bare statement of the issue at once poses another question. If the immunity exists in law for the protection of the public interest what right has the defendant to say whether it should be waived in his own interest?

The issue of waiver was not raised in *Neilson v Laugharne*; but Lord Denning MR in the course of his judgment said that public interest immunity could be waived (see [1981] 1 All ER 829 at 834, [1981] QB 736 at 747). He did not cite any authority in support of his opinion. He may have overlooked what was said in the speech of Lord Simon in *Rogers v Secretary of State for the Home Dept, Gaming Board of Great Britain v Rogers* [1972] 2 All ER 1057 at 1066, [1973] AC 388 at 407. His Lordship said:

'It is true that the public interest which demands that the evidence be withheld has to be weighed against the public interest in the administration of justice that courts should have the fullest possible access to all relevant material (*R v Hardy* (1794) 24 State Tr 199; *Marks v Beyfus* (1890) 25 QBD 494; *Conway v Rimmer* [1968] 1 All ER 874, [1968] AC 910); but once the former public interest is held to outweigh the latter, the evidence cannot in any circumstances be admitted. It is not a privilege which may be waived—by the Crown (see *Marks v Beyfus* at 500) or by any one else.'

In *Alfred Crompton Amusement Machines Ltd v Customs and Excise Comrs (No 2)* [1973] 2 All ER 1169, [1974] AC 405 Lord Cross made an obiter comment which suggests that in some circumstances public interest immunity may be waived. That case concerned an assessment for purchase tax. The commissioners claimed 'Crown privilege' for a class of routine documents the disclosure of which the head of the department swore would be injurious in the public interest since they would reveal the commissioners' methods and contained confidential information from third parties supplied both voluntarily and pursuant to the exercise of the commissioners' powers under s 24(6) of the Purchase Tax Act 1963. The House of Lords upheld this claim. In the course of commenting on a critical comment which the judge at first instance had made about the chairman of the commissioners Lord Cross said ([1973] 2 All ER 1169 at 1185, [1974] AC 405 at 434):

> 'His [that is the chairman's] objections to disclosure were taken in the interests of the third parties concerned as much as in the interests of the commissioners and if any of them is in fact willing to give evidence, privilege in respect of any documents or information obtained from him will be waived.'

I find this statement impossible to reconcile with what Lord Simon said. If the reason for the immunity is the need to protect the public interest individuals should be unable to waive it for their own purposes. Lord Cross seems to have thought that the chairman could waive immunity in respect of any documents or information obtained from third parties who were interested in maintaining non-disclosure if they were willing to give evidence. As I understand his Lordship, waiver would depend on what the provider of the document or information was willing to do, not on what the chairman wanted. In this case it was the plaintiff who had given the statement. It was the defendant, not the plaintiff, who wanted waiver of the immunity. If there can be waiver of public interest immunity, then the waiver should be by whoever provides the statement, not by him who receives it. This seems to have been Lord Simon's opinion in *Rogers v Secretary of State for the Home Dept* [1972] 2 All ER 1057 at 1067, [1973] AC 388 at 408.

It was for these reasons that I adjudged that the defendant by his counsel could not cross-examine the plaintiff on the statement which he had made in the course of the s 49 investigation.

BRIGHTMAN LJ. I agree with the reasons given by Lawton LJ for allowing the appeal from the trial judge. I also agree that if the plaintiff's statement is protected from production on the ground of public interest immunity, it is not open to the defendant commissioner to waive that immunity.

I also wish to reserve for further consideration the proposition that public interest immunity can never be waived. In *Neilson v Laugharne* [1981] 1 All ER 829, [1981] QB 736, where waiver did not arise but seems to have been discussed, the defendant chief constable claimed protection from production for statements made for the purposes of the inquiry, except the statement of the complainant. In that case the complainant was seeking production of statements made by other persons. In the instant case, the defendant commissioner seeks to make use of the complainant's statement against his wishes. So in each case production was sought by persons other than the maker of the statement. In such a case, if public interest immunity exists, it would seem clear that the recipient of the statement cannot waive protection from production. The question of waiver by the maker of the statement, however, seems to raise different considerations. Suppose that the complainant compiles his statement at home, and keeps a carbon copy for his own use. He would be bound to disclose the copy in his list of documents. He would not be obliged in his list of documents to claim for it protection from production. Nor does it seem to me that there would be any public interest entitling other parties, or obliging the court, to assert immunity unless the statement was said to contain matter affecting the security of the state or the like. It seems to me at least arguable that the public interest would not in all circumstances continue to attach immunity to a statement given for the purposes of s 49 of the Police Act 1964 if the maker of the statement wished disclosure to be made. Perhaps this is not strictly a question of waiver, but of public interest immunity ceasing to attach to a statement if particular circumstances exist. In this sense only I respectfully question the view that there cannot be waiver of public interest immunity.

Appeal allowed. Order in accordance with ruling given on 4 March 1982. Trial to proceed in accordance with the law of evidence and the practice of the court. Leave to appeal to the House of Lords refused.

Solicitors: *Davis Hanson* (for the plaintiff); *R E T Birch* (for the defendant).

Mary Rose Plummer   Barrister.

Emanuel v Emanuel

FAMILY DIVISION
WOOD J
10 NOVEMBER, 2 DECEMBER 1981

Divorce – Practice – Ancillary relief – Application for monetary provision – Discovery – Anton Piller order – Inspection of property – Document not subject matter of action – Jurisdiction of Family Division to make order.

The parties were divorced in 1976 and shortly thereafter the wife made an application for ancillary relief. Between 1976 and 1979 the husband ignored various orders for discovery and further information made by the registrar in the proceedings for ancillary relief. In September 1979 the wife's solicitor learnt that the husband had disposed of certain property included in the matrimonial assets and obtained an order freezing all the husband's assets. In October 1979, in the course of a hearing regarding the husband's alleged disposal of property contrary to the order, the husband gave an undertaking not to dispose of a certain cottage. In December the judge made orders in favour of the wife in the ancillary proceedings for the transfer of two properties, including the cottage, a lump sum payment and periodical payments. The husband failed to make any payment in respect of the lump sum and made only a partial payment in respect of the periodical payments. Unknown to the wife the husband had disposed of the cottage prior to the transfer order being made. In April 1980 the wife learnt that the husband had sold the cottage and the wife applied for the orders of December 1979 to be set aside on the grounds of fraud and for her application for ancillary relief to be reheard. She also applied ex parte for an Anton Piller order permitting her, inter alia, to enter the husband's premises to locate evidence relating to the husband's financial position and assets disposed of by him and to remove such evidence into the custody of her solicitor.

Held – Where the petitioner or respondent sought by an Anton Piller order documents which were not themselves the subject matter of the proceedings, the Family Division had jurisdiction to grant the order if the applicant had a strong prima facie case that the relevant documents were essential for his case and were at serious risk of being removed or destroyed. Accordingly, since the husband was clearly ready to flaunt the authority of the court and to mislead it if it was to his advantage so to do, and since there was a grave danger that the documents sought by the wife would be removed and destroyed, the wife would be granted the order sought (see p 348 *f* to *j*, post).

Anton Piller KG v Manufacturing Processes Ltd [1976] 1 All ER 779 and *Yousif v Salama* [1980] 3 All ER 405 applied.

Notes

For restraining disposition of property, see 24 Halsbury's Laws (4th edn) para 1018, and for cases on the subject, see 28(2) Digest (Reissue) 1125, 1234–1242.

Cases referred to in judgment

Anton Piller KG v Manufacturing Processes Ltd [1976] 1 All ER 779, [1976] Ch 55, [1976] 2 WLR 162, CA, Digest (Cont Vol E) 338, *1238b*.

East India Co v Kynaston (1821) 3 Bli 153, 4 ER 561, HL.

EMI Ltd v Pandit [1975] 1 All ER 418, [1975] 1 WLR 302, Digest (Cont Vol D) 543, *1238a*.

Hennessey v Bohman, Osborne & Co (1877) 36 LT 51, 28(2) Digest (Reissue) 1125, *1238*.

Morris v Howell (1888) 22 LR Ir 77, 28(2) Digest (Reissue) 1125, *694*.

Paxton v Douglas (1809) 16 Ves 239, 33 ER 975; *subsequent proceedings* (1812) 19 Ves 225, 34 ER 502, 18 Digest (Reissue) 245, *1934*.

Rank Film Distributors Ltd v Video Information Centre [1981] 2 All ER 76, [1981] 2 WLR 668, HL; *affg* [1980] 2 All ER 273, [1980] 3 WLR 487, CA.

Rice v Gordon (1843) 13 Sim 580, 60 ER 225, 18 Digest (Reissue) 150, *1227*.

Yousif v Salama [1980] 3 All ER 405, [1980] 1 WLR 1540, CA.

Application

The wife, Minnie Rosemary Emanuel, applied ex parte for an order (1) to set aside orders for financial provision made by Wood J on 7 December 1979 and (2) for an order permitting her to enter the premises of the husband, Dan Emanuel, and the second respondent, Adele Vale, for the purpose of searching for and inspecting all documents relating to the husband's earnings and capital and the disposal of assets, and removing them to the custody of her solicitors. The facts are set out in the judgment.

Daniel Serota for the wife.
Lionel Levine (who appeared only for the giving of judgment) for the husband.
David Friedman (who appeared only for the giving of judgment) for the second respondent.

At the conclusion of argument Wood J made the orders sought and said that he would give his reasons at a later date.

2 December. **WOOD J** read the following judgment: This is an application made ex parte for an Anton Piller order. It is said to be the first such application in the Family Division. I should perhaps refer to it as a *Yousif v Salama* order, because as in that case it is referable only to documentation which is not itself the subject matter of the proceedings. The form of order sought is set out at the end of this judgment. I granted the order. I now set out my reasons and look first at jurisdiction.

The line of authority starts with *EMI Ltd v Pandit* [1975] 1 All ER 418, [1975] 1 WLR 302. That was an action in which the plaintiffs had been granted an interlocutory injunction to restrain infringement of copyright and certain sound recordings together with an order requiring the defendants to supply certain information concerning the alleged infringement on affidavit. The affidavit when produced was shown by the plaintiffs to be false and there were very probably more documents in existence than those disclosed in that affidavit. The matter came before Templeman J on an ex parte application for an order under RSC Ord 29 authorising the plaintiffs within specified hours to enter certain premises occupied by the defendant and to inspect, photograph and remove allegedly infringing articles and to photograph certain documents and inspect and photograph and test typewriters. The order was granted ex parte. The judge said ([1975] 1 All ER 418 at 422, [1975] 1 WLR 302 at 305–306):

> 'In the normal course of events, a defendant will have notice of the relief which is sought against him in the exercise of the powers given by this rule and will be able to come along to the court and to give reasons why the order should not be made or why, if it is made, particular safeguards should be included. Nevertheless, in my judgment, if it appears that the object of the plaintiffs' litigation will be unfairly and improperly frustrated by the very giving of the notice which is normally required

to protect the defendant, there must be exceptional and emergency cases in which the court can dispense with the notice and, either under power in the rules to dispense with notice or by the exercise of its inherent jurisdiction, make such a limited order, albeit ex parte, as will give the plaintiffs the relief which they would otherwise be unable to obtain. In the present case I am satisfied that, if notice were given to the defendant, that would almost certainly result in the immediate destruction of the articles and information to which the plaintiffs are entitled and which they now seek.'

Later in his judgment he said ([1975] 1 All ER 418 at 424, [1975] 1 WLR 302 at 307–308):

'In essence, the plaintiffs are seeking discovery, but this form of discovery will only be granted where it is vital either to the success of the plaintiffs in the action or vital to the plaintiffs in proving damages; in other words, it must be shown that irreparable harm will accrue, or there is a high probability that irreparable harm may accrue to the plaintiffs, unless the particular form of relief now sought is granted to them.'

The decision in that case was approved in the leading authority of *Anton Piller KG v Manufacturing Processes Ltd* [1976] 1 All ER 779, [1976] Ch 55. In that case the plaintiffs, German manufacturers of equipment, alleged that the defendants, who were their agents in the United Kingdom, were in secret communication with other German manufacturers and giving them confidential information about the plaintiffs' equipment. The plaintiffs sought and obtained ex parte an interim injunction to restrain the defendants from infringing their copyrights and disclosing confidential information. On this ex parte application they also sought permission to enter the defendants' premises to remove documents into the plaintiffs' solicitors' custody. This part of the application was refused by Brightman J. The plaintiffs' appeal was allowed and an order made. In the leading judgment Lord Denning MR said ([1976] 1 All ER 779 at 783, [1976] Ch 55 at 60–61):

'Accepting such to be the case, the question is in what circumstances ought such an order be made. If the defendant is given notice beforehand and is able to argue the pros and cons, it is warranted by that case in the House of Lords [*East India Co v Kynaston* (1821) 3 Bli 153, 4 ER 561] and by RSC Ord 29, r 2(1) and (5). But it is a far stronger thing to make such an order ex parte without giving him notice. This is not covered by the rules of court and must be based on the inherent jurisdiction of the court. There are one or two old precedents which give some colour for it, *Hennessy v Bohmann Osborne & Co* (1877) 36 LT 51 and *Morris v Howell* (1888) 22 LR Ir 77, an Irish case. But they do not go very far. So it falls to us to consider it on principle. It seems to me that such an order can be made by a judge ex parte, but it should only be made where it is essential that the plaintiff should have inspection so that justice can be done between the parties; and when, if the defendant were forewarned, there is a grave danger that vital evidence will be destroyed, that papers will be burnt or lost or hidden, or taken beyond the jurisdiction, and so the ends of justice be defeated; and when the inspection would do no real harm to the defendant or his case.'

Ormrod LJ agreed with the judgment of Lord Denning MR and added this ([1976] 1 All ER 779 at 784, [1976] Ch 55 at 61–62):

'The proposed order is at the extremity of this court's powers. Such orders, therefore, will rarely be made, and only when there is no alternative way of ensuring that justice is done to the plaintiff. There are three essential pre-conditions for the making of such an order, in my judgment. First, there must be an extremely strong prima facie case. Secondly, the damage, potential or actual, must be very serious for the plaintiff. Thirdly, there must be clear evidence that the defendants have in their possession incriminating documents or things, and that there is a real possibility that they may destroy such material before any application inter partes can be made.'

Shaw LJ put the question in this way ([1976] 1 All ER 779 at 784, [1976] Ch 55 at 62):

'The overriding consideration in the exercise of this salutary jurisdiction is that it is to be resorted to only in circumstances where the normal processes of the law would be rendered nugatory if some immediate and effective measure was not available. And, when such an order is made, the party who had procured the court to make it must act with prudence and caution in pursuance of it.'

The principles set out in that case have been followed in a number of other cases, to which I need not refer, and I therefore turn to *Yousif v Salama* [1980] 3 All ER 405, [1980] 1 WLR 1540. This was the first authority to which I was referred in which the ex parte application only concerned documents which were to be used as evidence. The facts are conveniently set out in the leading judgment of Lord Denning MR ([1980] 3 All ER 405 at 406, [1980] 1 WLR 1540 at 1541–1542):

'This application raises an interesting new point. The plaintiff says that he made an agreement with the defendant, who was resident in the Middle East. Certain goods were to be purchased in England and dispatched to the Middle East. They were then to be resold there. In respect of those transactions, the plaintiff was to divide the profits between himself and the first defendant: 30% in some cases and 50% in others. That was the agreement. Several transactions took place for a year or two. A statement of account was rendered by the defendant's limited company (giving the letter of credit references) showing a sum due. Business continued thereafter. Extra commission was accruing. The result was that in March 1980 the plaintiff went with the first defendant to the second defendant company's office to go throught the accounts. Two files were produced containing the various accounts. They showed sums due to the plaintiff. Also a desk diary. The plaintiff, being very anxious about the matter, brought proceedings in the court for the sum due to him. On 16th April 1980 he issued a writ for that purpose. The total sum claimed was £14,000 odd. The writ was served. The solicitors for the defendant wrote to the plaintiff's solicitors saying that they were going to defend the claim strenuously. The plaintiff then became very anxious about the file and the desk diary he had seen which contained details of the transactions. He became fearful that the defendant would destroy those documents before the actual hearing of the case. On 2nd May 1980 the plaintiff applied for an Anton Piller order. He did not notify the defendant that he was making that application: because he was afraid the defendant would destroy the documents if he were notified. The plaintiff asked that he should be granted an Anton Piller order to enable him to go to the defendant company's offices and inspect the documents before the defendant has an opportunity to destroy them. In many cases such an order would not be granted. But in this case there is evidence (if it is accepted) which shows the defendant to be untrustworthy. The plaintiff has a legitimate fear that the documents will be destroyed. In the circumstances, it seems to me that it would be proper to make an Anton Piller order to the effect that the plaintiff's solicitor would be able to go and get the documents, take them into his personal custody for a while, make copies of them, and then return the originals to the defendant. He would have to keep them personally himself, and not let them out of his possession. It seems to me that that would be an aid to justice. It would be preserving the evidence in the case. Under RSC Ord 29, r 2, there is a far-reaching power for preserving documents which are the subject matter of the action. These files here are not the subject matter of the action. But they are the best possible evidence to prove the plaintiff's case. There is a genuine fear that, if the plaintiff waits till after the application is heard, the defendant may destroy the documents before the date of the hearing. That is the sort of danger which the Anton Piller order is designed to prevent.'

A little later in his judgment Lord Denning MR says this about the principle ([1980] 3 All ER 405 at 406–407, [1980] 1 WLR 1540 at 1542):

'It is an aid to justice as far as the plaintiff is concerned. Instead of having to speculate or try and get evidence from elsewhere, it should all be available in the files. It can do no harm to the defendant at all. If he is honest, he will produce the documents in any case. If he is dishonest, that is all the more reason why the order should be made. Meanwhile, once the documents are handed to the plaintiff's solicitor, copies can be made of them and the originals returned to the defendants.'

Brightman LJ agreed with the judgment of Lord Denning MR and said ([1980] 3 All ER 405 at 408, [1980] 1 WLR 1540 at 1544):

'In my view the order sought in this case is justified if, but only if, there is prima facie evidence that essential documents are at risk. If essential documents are at risk, then it seems to me that this court ought to permit the plaintiff to take such steps as are necessary to preserve them. So there are two questions to be asked. First, are the documents sought to be seized essential to the plaintiff's case? If so, are such documents at serious risk? Might they be dishonestly destroyed?'

In that case, although the third member of the court, Donaldson LJ, dissented on the facts, he stated the principle in very much the same way as the other two members of the court, and said ([1980] 3 All ER 405 at 407, [1980] 1 WLR 1540 at 1543):

'The essential feature of those cases, as I understand them, is that there is a very clear prima facie case leading the court to fear that the defendant will conceal or destroy essential evidence in the grossest possible contempt of the court and (this is an important second limb) that should he do so the whole processes of justice will be frustrated because the plaintiff will be left without any evidence to enable him to put forward his claim. In that limited class of case I, for my part, think that the Anton Piller order is absolutely right. No court can stand by and see the processes of justice totally frustrated by a defendant in contempt of its order. But I cannot find anything in this case which brings it within that category. I regard the evidence of an intention to destroy the documentation as flimsy in the extreme. It is based on an allegation of forgery in the indorsement of a cheque. This has nothing whatever to do with the destruction of documents which the plaintiff says that he fears.'

In one of the most recent cases on this topic, *Rank Film Distributors Ltd v Video Information Centre* [1980] 2 All ER 273 at 283, [1980] 3 WLR 487 at 508, Bridge LJ referred to this type of order as 'a form of order for what may be called instant discovery granted on ex parte application'.

In the same case, when dealing with the general principle, Templeman LJ said ([1980] 2 All ER 273 at 287, [1980] 3 WLR 487 at 513–514):

'We were not referred to any statutory or procedural or authoritative limitation on the power of a court of equity to devise injunctions of different kinds to meet different circumstances. In my judgment a court of equity has jurisdiction to make mandatory and other peremptory and penal orders at any stage of any proceedings or in contemplation of proceedings where damages will not be an adequate remedy and where rights or properties or remedies claimed by the plaintiff are in jeopardy. Of course an injunction is a discretionary remedy which will only be exercised in such a manner as is necessary to safeguard the plaintiff and after balancing the potential harm to the plaintiff if an effective injunction is withheld against the potential harm to the defendant if the injunction is granted. The court must decide in the light of the evidence whether the plaintiff has established that the injunction sought is necessary and is no more onerous than is necessary to protect the plaintiff. The court must decide whether the interference with the defendant as a result of the injunction and the consequences of such interference are justifiable in the circumstances. The more severe and peremptory the order which is sought, the greater will be the reluctance of the court to exercise its discretion by granting the order. If the defendant is not given notice of the application for an injunction the court will require to be satisfied that secrecy is essential and will require much persuasion that the interference with the defendant is justifiable. Finally, the court must be satisfied that a penal order is essential to secure compliance and to achieve the legitimate purposes of the injunction.'

Those being the principles which are applicable, and this Division being merely one of the Divisions of the Supreme Court, I turn to the facts. The present proceedings before the court are applications by the plaintiff for me to set aside my order of 7 December 1979 on the ground, amongst others, of fraud, and for a rehearing of her claim for financial relief. I am also asked to set aside a conveyance by the respondent husband to his sister of the premises at 12 Redcliff Gardens, Ilford, Essex. As it will be necessary for me to rehear this whole case I consider it undesirable that I should say more about the history of this case than is absolutely necessary to indicate my reasons for making the present order. A full history is to be found in the affidavit of the wife's solicitor, Miss Scannell, sworn in support of this application.

On 6 October 1976, the wife obtained a decree nisi of divorce and on 17 November an application was made for financial ancillary relief. On 2 December an order for directions was made. This was in effect ignored and a further order in substantially similar terms was made on 15 July 1977. This order was also substantially ignored by the husband despite correspondence about discovery; as also was a questionnaire served pursuant to the Matrimonial Causes Rules 1977, SI 1977/344, on the 14 June 1978. The whole matter was returned once more to the registrar on 15 February 1979. The husband's attitude to this order was wholly unsatisfactory and a peremptory order was made on 10 May. The husband has showed scant respect for this order also, and on 11 July he and his accountant were ordered by the registrar to appear before him. The petitioner's advisers had difficulty in serving this order and on 18 September an order for substituted service was made.

On 26 September 1979 the wife's advisers heard that the husband had disposed of 12 Redcliff Gardens, Ilford, and on 27 September Mr Registrar Garland made an order 'freezing' all the husband's assets. On 9 October 1979, it was discovered that the husband was disposing of some shares in a company of which he was the main shareholder. Thus, on 22 October the matter came before Sheldon J, to whom the husband gave an undertaking not to dispose of a property known as 'Neupers Cottage', Stapleford Abbots, Romford, Essex.

The case was fixed for hearing before me on 5 December, 1979. On that day the husband failed to appear and discovery was still most unsatisfactory. I made an order that he attend the following day and gave leave to issue a number of subpoenas.

When the matter came before me the husband appeared in person, having very recently decided so to do. I heard some evidence from him and based on his admissions I decided that without further expensive delays and widespread additional discovery and financial investigation, I could do justice between the parties on the basis of the admitted assets and the figures of income and capital. I made the following order:

'1. The respondent do within 28 days of today transfer to the petitioner the following properties: The Moorings, 56 Point Clear, St. Osyth, Essex, free of encumbrance, and Neupers Cottage, Neupers Lane, Stapleford Abbots, Romford, Essex, subject to the rights of the present occupants.
2. In default of the respondent executing the deeds of conveyance in respect of the said properties within the time so specified, a registrar of the Principal Registry do execute the same pursuant to section 47 of the Supreme Court of Judicature (Consolidation) Act 1925.'

I need not read para 3; it dealt with the costs of the conveyance.

'4. The respondent to make to the petitioner a lump sum payment of £10,000 payable in instalments as follows: £5,000 on or before 1st April, 1980, and £5,000 on or before 31st December, 1980.

5. The respondent do pay or cause to be paid to the petitioner as from the 1st November, 1979, maintenance pending suit and periodical payments at the rate of £8,000 per annum, less tax, payable monthly in arrears, the first payment to be on 1st January, 1980, until the date that the second instalment of £5,000 referred to in paragraph 5 hereof is paid and thereafter do pay or cause to be paid to the petitioner during their joint lives or until her remarriage or further order periodical payments at the rate of £7,500 per annum less tax payable monthly in arrears.'

Paragraph 6 is not relevant.

'7. There be no order on the said application for an order to set aside the sale, with no order as to costs.

8. That the respondent pay taxed costs of the petitioner, including costs reserved.'

I am told that no payment has been made in respect of the lump sum and a much reduced figure has been paid in respect of periodical payments. After considerable delay and after ignoring correspondence the husband, on 17 April 1980, attended the petitioner's solicitors' office to sign documents for the transfer of title in the two properties mentioned in para 1 of my order. He told the wife's solicitor that he had sold Neupers Cottage.

A judgment summons was issued and on 27 February 1980, his Honour Judge Willis ordered substituted service if the husband could not be found. On 26 March his Honour Judge Tumin ordered the attendance of the husband. On 7 May the husband appeared before his Honour Judge Willis. He was committed to prison for six weeks. In October 1980 the matter came back before me and I adjourned it for a day to be fixed. In the interim investigations have been continuing.

At the hearing on 7 May 1980, before Judge Willis, the husband admitted that he had signed contracts for the sale of Neupers Cottage on 5 November 1979. The price was £11,500. This sum had been paid to him prior to the hearing before me on 6 December 1979. It had almost all been spent by him. He also disclosed that, contrary to the evidence given before me, he had for some three years been living at an address at 250 Cranbrook Road, Ilford. I am satisfied that there is at least prima facie evidence that the husband lied to me on these two issues.

What inferences is it right for me to draw from this history, bearing in mind the order now sought is one 'at the extremity of this court's powers' and one which will be made only very rarely?

The husband is clearly ready to flaunt the authority of this court and to mislead it if he thinks that it is to his advantage so to do. The normal process of law is liable to be rendered nugatory. I have no doubt that justice in the present matter cannot be achieved without making the present order, and that there is a grave danger that evidence will be removed or destroyed. I cannot think that real harm will be caused to the husband by making the order, as the only documents sought are those which he ought properly to produce and, indeed, ought to have produced in the past. I am quite satisfied that the wife has a strong prima facie case to the effect that relevant documentation has not been produced in the past and is most unlikely to be produced in the future without the present order. Such essential documents are at risk.

I would respectfully refer back to the words of Lord Denning MR in *Yousif v Salama*, and put it in my own way as follows: that this order is an aid to justice as far as the wife is concerned. Instead of having to speculate or try to get evidence from elsewhere this evidence should be available. It can do no harm to the husband at all. If he is honest, he will produce the documents in any case. If he is dishonest, that is all the more reason why my present order should be made. Meanwhile, once the documents are handed to the wife's solicitors, copies can be made of them and the originals returned to the husband.

This, in my judgment, is an exceptional case.

There was, however, one further matter of law to which I must refer. The *Rank Film Distributors* case was argued in the House of Lords in March 1981: see [1981] 2 All ER 76, [1981] 2 WLR 668. The issue was the existence of the privilege against self-incrimination where the Anton Piller type of order has been made. The Court of Appeal had decided that the court should abstain from making an order ex parte requiring immediate answers to interrogatories or disclosure of documents when it can see that the defendant would be in danger of self-incrimination, and all requirements to answer those interrogatories or to disclose documents were deleted from the order originally made at first instance. The appeal was dismissed and the House of Lords held that the privilege against self-incrimination was capable of being invoked.

In the present case there was prima facie evidence before me that it might be alleged that the respondent husband had committed perjury. I, therefore, had to consider whether some provision should be made in the order to protect him against self-incrimination. I was referred to *Rice v Gordon* (1843) 13 Sim 580, 60 ER 225. The report of this case, which was decided in November 1843, is very short and I set it out in full:

> 'In this case an indictment was pending, against the Defendant for perjury committed *in the cause*; and on Mr. Cole, for the Plaintiff, moving for the production of documents which the Defendant had admitted in his answer to be in his custody, Mr. Chandless contended that he was not bound to produce them, because they tended to support the indictment; and cited *Paxton* v. *Douglas* ((1809) 16 Ves 239, 33 ER 975). The VICE-CHANCELLOR [Sir L. Shadwell] said that in the case cited the offence was committed *prior to the institution of the suit*; but, in the present case, it was committed in the very cause in which the motion was made; and that, if he were to refuse the motion, he should be holding out an inducement to a Defendant to commit perjury in an early stage of the cause, in order to prevent the Court from administering justice in the suit. Motion granted.'

That case was cited by Templeman LJ in the *Rank Film Distributors* case without criticism (see [1980] 2 All ER 273 at 290, [1980] 3 WLR 487 at 518). In the present case the only possible criminal offence that is disclosed is the prima facie evidence of perjury, and in the circumstances I did not require any special clause to be inserted in the order to encourage the respondent husband to invoke the principle of privilege against self-incrimination.

The order which I made in chambers ex parte was made in the following form. I direct that the whole order should be inserted for the assistance of those reading the report:

> 'ON MOTION this day made into this court by counsel for the petitioner
> AND ON READING the affidavit of Elizabeth Anne Scannell filed this day and the exhibits therein referred to
> AND THE PETITIONER BY HER COUNSEL UNDERTAKING (1) to serve this order together with a copy of the affidavit of Elizabeth Scannell by a solicitor of the Supreme Court, (2) to abide by any order this court may make as to damage in case this court shall hereafter be of the opinion that the first or second respondent shall have suffered any by reason of this order which the petitioner ought to pay, (3) to notify the first and second respondents or the person on whom this order is served by the solicitor of the Supreme Court who serves this order on them that they may seek legal advice and to explain fairly and in everyday language the meaning or effect thereof, (4) to issue a summons to set aside such order as may have been made by the Honourable Mr Justice Wood on 7 December 1979 in relation to the disposition of 12 Redcliffe Gardens, Ilford, Essex, (5) to issue a summons to set aside the order made by the Honourable Mr Justice Wood on 7 December 1979 on the grounds, inter alia, of the first respondent's fraud and non-disclosure and to make such order for ancillary relief as may be just
> AND the solicitors for the petitioner by counsel for the petitioner being their

counsel for this purpose undertaking that all documents obtained as a result of this order will be retained in their safe custody until further order

IT IS ORDERED that the first respondent or such person as shall appear to be in charge of the premises at 250 Cranbrook Road, Ilford do forthwith permit the person who shall serve this order on him, together with such person not exceeding two as may be duly authorised by the petitioner to enter the premises at 250 Cranbrook Road, Ilford at any hour between 8 o'clock in the forenoon and 8 o'clock in the evening for the purpose of (a) looking for and inspecting any of the following: (1) all documents relating to the first respondent's earnings, income and capital from 1 January 1976 to date; (2) all documents relating to the sale by the first respondent and the proceeds of sale of shares in any company and of any capital asset including Neupers Cottage, and 12 Redcliffe Gardens, Ilford; (3) all bank statements and building society passbooks and documents related thereto including passbooks, cheque stubs, paid cheques, and paying-in books; (4) all documents relating to the purchase by the second respondent of 12 Redcliffe Gardens, Ilford, including documents relating to the provision of the purchase price; (b) taking into the petitioner's solicitors' custody all and any of the above-mentioned documents and of making copies of the same

AND IT IS ORDERED that the second respondent or such person as shall appear to be in charge of the premises at 12 Redcliffe Gardens, Ilford do forthwith permit the person who shall serve this order on him, together with such persons not exceeding two as may be duly authorised by the petitioner to enter the premises at 12 Redcliffe Gardens, Ilford at any hour between 8 o'clock in the forenoon and 8 o'clock in the evening for the purpose of (a) looking for and inspecting any of the following: (1) all documents relating to the first respondent's earnings, income and capital from 1 January 1976 to date; (2) all documents relating to the sale by the first respondent and the proceeds of sale of shares in any company and of any capital asset including Neupers Cottage or 12 Redcliffe Gardens, Ilford; (3) all bank statements and building society passbooks, cheque stubs, paid cheques and paying-in books, (4) all documents relating to the purchase by the second respondent of 12 Redcliffe Gardens, Ilford, including all documents relating to provision of the purchase price; (b) taking into the petitioner's solicitors' custody all and any of the above-mentioned documents and of making copies of the same

AND IT IS ORDERED that the first and second respondent and each of them and/or the person or persons appearing for the time being to be in charge of the premises aforesaid do produce forthwith to the person serving this order all of the documents referred to in the last two preceding orders

Liberty to apply.'

Solicitors: *Scannell & Co*, Brentwood (for the wife); *S S Bookatz & Co*, Ilford (for the husband); *Edward Oliver & Bellis*, Ilford (for the second respondent).

Bebe Chua   Barrister.

Re St Nicholas's, Baddesley Ensor

BIRMINGHAM CONSISTORY COURT
CHANCELLOR HIS HONOUR JUDGE AGLIONBY
21 DECEMBER 1981

Ecclesiastical law – Consistory Court – Jurisdiction – Faculty for burial of non-parishioner in parish churchyard or burial ground – Circumstances where court can entertain petition for such a faculty – Whether court can entertain petition where incumbent has refused consent for burial – Church of England (Miscellaneous Provisions) Measure 1976, s 6(2).

A consistory court does not have power to entertain a faculty for the burial of a non-parishioner in a parish churchyard or burial ground if the incumbent opposes the burial, and s 6(2)[a] of the Church of England (Miscellaneous Provisions) Measure 1976, which provides that a non-parishioner shall not be buried in the churchyard or other burial ground of a parish without the incumbent's consent, does not provide for review by a consistory court of the incumbent's refusal to give consent. Accordingly, a petition for a faculty for burial of a non-parishioner in a parish churchyard or burial ground can only be entertained by a court where there is evidence that the incumbent in fact gave his consent to the burial of the non-parishioner and the non-parishioner has acted on the consent and would be prejudiced by its withdrawal, so that the incumbent is estopped in equity from refusing his consent to the burial (see p 352 *h j* and p 353 *a* to *c*, post).

Hendon Churchyard Case (1910) 27 TLR 1 applied.

Notes

For the burial of non-parishioners in the parish churchyard, see 10 Halsbury's Laws (4th edn) para 1120, and for cases on the subject, see 7 Digest (Reissue) 546–547, 3091–3094, 3103–3106.

For faculties relating to churchyards, see 14 Halsbury's Laws (4th edn) para 1315.

For the Church of England (Miscellaneous Provisions) Measure 1976, s 6, see 46 Halsbury's Statutes (3rd edn) 488.

Cases referred to in judgment

Hendon Churchyard Case (1910) 27 TLR 1, 7 Digest (Reissue) 547, 3106.
Kellet v St John's, Burscough Bridge (1916) 32 TLR 571, 7 Digest (Reissue) 548, 3114.
Perivale Faculty, The, De Romana v Roberts [1906] P 332, 7 Digest (Reissue) 547, 3105.
Sargent, Re (1890) 15 PD 168, 7 Digest (Reissue) 547, 3104.

Petition for faculty

By a petition dated 11 July 1981 Keith Samuel Lunn Daffern prayed for a faculty authorising (1) the erection of a memorial stone on the grave of his daughter, Amanda Jane, in Baddesley Ensor churchyard in accordance with an attached drawing, (2) the reservation of two grave spaces within her grave for the petitioner and his wife and (3) the reservation in the churchyard of a grave space for the petitioner's mother-in-law, Ida Lucy Meer. The facts are set out in the judgment.

Andrew Jordan for the petitioner.
The incumbent appeared in person.

Cur adv vult

21 December. **THE CHANCELLOR** delivered the following judgment: On 11 July 1981 Keith Samuel Lunn Daffern presented a petition for a faculty for (1) the erection of

---

a   Section 6(2) is set out at p 352 *e*, post

a memorial on a grave of his daughter Amanda in accordance with a drawing attached
to the petition, (2) the reservation of two grave spaces within her grave for himself and
his wife, and (3) the reservation of a grave space in the churchyard for his mother-in-law
Ida Lucy Meer. All three matters are opposed by the incumbent and the parochial
church council of the parish.

The petitioner is not and never has been a parishioner or on the electoral roll of the
parish. His wife was a parishioner until her marriage to the petitioner. They were
married in Baddesley Ensor church and, as they were living only a few miles away, two
of their children were baptised in the church. Their daughter Amanda died in tragic
circumstances in 1974 at the age of 22. At that time she was not a parishioner or on the
electoral roll but permission was given by the incumbent for her burial in the
churchyard. Mrs Ida Lucy Meer died on 9 September 1981. It is agreed by the
incumbent that Mrs Meer was a parishioner and at the date of her death had the right of
burial in the churchyard. She has not yet been buried because there is a dispute as to
where her coffin should be interred. Her personal representatives are Mrs Rosemary
Daffern, her daughter and the wife of the petitioner, and Brian Joseph Meer who is the
son of Mrs Meer and so the brother of Mrs Daffern. He gave evidence for the parties
opponent. Mrs Meer's husband Edgar Meer died in March 1981. He was a parishioner
at the date of his death, but he was cremated and his ashes interred in the grave of Mrs
Meer's parents in the churchyard.

The Church of England (Miscellaneous Provisions) Measure 1976 came into force on
15 December 1976. Section 6(2) of the Measure provides:

> 'No person, other than a person having a right of burial in the churchyard or
> other burial ground of a parish, shall be buried therein without the consent of the
> minister of the parish, but in deciding whether to give such consent the minister
> shall have regard to any general guidance given by the parochial church council of
> the parish with respect to the matter.'

Counsel on behalf of the petitioner submitted that this subsection did not effect any
fundamental change in the law, but that it was merely intended to clarify the law which
obtained before the Measure came into effect. He submitted that, despite the wording
of the subsection, the court retained jurisdiction and could grant faculties in the same
manner as it had done prior to the Measure. Before the Measure came into force he
contended that the court had the power to grant a faculty after considering the merits of
the case to a non-parishioner who thereby can acquire the right of burial. Counsel for the
petitioner relied principally on four cases to support his submissions: *Re Sargent* (1890)
15 PD 168, *The Perivale Faculty, De Romana v Roberts* [1906] P 332, *Hendon Churchyard
Case* (1910) 27 TLR 1 and *Kellet v St John's, Burscough Bridge* (1916) 32 TLR 571.

In *Hendon Churchyard Case* the petition for reservation of two grave spaces was opposed
by the incumbent but granted on the grounds that the previous incumbent had lawfully
sold the two grave spaces to the petitioner's husband and that the incumbent was bound
by his predecessor's agreement. In the other three cases the petitions were all unopposed
and supported by the respective incumbents. These cases do not in my judgment lend
any support to the proposition·that the court has had the power to grant a faculty
reserving a grave space where the incumbent has refused the request for burial of a non-
parishioner, but they do demonstrate that once the incumbent's consent has been
obtained those having the right of burial may object to the petition for reservation of a
grave space and the matter will be considered on its merits.

Indeed it has long been regarded as settled law that a non-parishioner cannot be buried
in a churchyard without the consent of the incumbent in whom the freehold is vested
and of the churchwardens, but now the parochial church council, on behalf of the
parishioners who have the right of burial: Phillimore *Ecclesiastical Law* (2nd edn, 1895)
pp 654–655. Difficulties arose in obtaining the consent of the parochial church council
on any particular request because under the Church Representation Rules 10 clear days'
notice of a meeting is required except in cases of sudden emergency when three clear

days' notice in writing is required and a quorum of members might not be available. Hence s 6(2) of the Measure altered the law only to the extent of reducing the role of the parochial church council. The section makes no reference to any review by the court of a refusal by the incumbent to give consent and in my judgment there was no power to review a refusal before the Measure. If it had been and is otherwise, some parishes with attractive churchyards would have faced and be facing intolerable burdens in opposing petitions by strangers taking a liking to the thought of interment in such churchyards.

Counsel for the petitioner pointed out that *Hendon Churchyard Case* is an example of the operation of the doctrine of equitable estoppel. In my view that case is authority for the proposition that if an incumbent gives consent to the burial of a non-parishioner he is estopped from withdrawing it if the non-parishioner has in some way acted on it and would be prejudiced if it were to be withdrawn.

Therefore in my judgment the petition can only be entertained by the court if the evidence accepted brings the matter within the ambit of equitable estoppel. I turn therefore to consider the evidence.

The petitioner said in evidence that when his daughter died he and his wife considered where her body should be buried. At that time Baddesley Ensor had no particular significance for him or for his wife except that her relations lived there. His mother-in-law Mrs Meer spoke to him about the matter and in consequence he telephoned Canon Williams to ask if Amanda could be buried in the churchyard in a grave in which he and his wife would subsequently be buried. Canon Williams replied that he needed time to think about it as she was not a parishioner. Later he spoke again on the telephone to Canon Williams who said that Amanda could be buried there. It was against the general rule but that if there were any complaints they would call it 'grandma's grave' and hope that grandma would live another five years so that people would forget. The petitioner said that relying on that assurance Amanda was buried in Baddesley Ensor and that, if it had not been given, she would have been buried in Atherstone where he lived.

Canon Williams gave evidence that in consequence of a telephone call from the local undertakers he went to see the petitioner and Mrs Daffern at their home. He said that he told them that as they were not parishioners Amanda could not be buried at Baddesley Ensor but that he would discuss it with the churchwardens. He did so and then spoke to the Dafferns again telling them that Amanda could be buried in his churchyard but that she would have to be in a triple grave into which Mr and Mrs Meer could be put when they passed away. He said that the Dafferns accepted that arrangement.

The next contact between the petitioner and Canon Williams took place in 1979 when the petitioner said that he approached Canon Williams with a sketch plan prepared by Mr John Skelton of a memorial stone for the grave. He told me that the wording for the gravestone on the sketch plan was identical to that on the plan annexed to the petition. That plan shows the wording to include the names of Amanda and her parents but not the names of the Meers. The petitioner said that Canon Williams said that they would allow black upright memorial stones only. He left the sketch plan with Canon Williams who said that he knew a man in the diocesan hierarchy who might be able to help. The petitioner also told Canon Williams that 'grandma' had lived for more than five years and got the reply 'Ah, they have not forgotten'. He said that he informed Canon Williams that Mr Meer, his father-in-law, was quite ill and likely to die before Mrs Meer in which case he could have a new grave and that Mrs Meer would be able to be buried with her husband. A statement to which Canon Williams made no comment.

Canon Williams remembered being approached by the petitioner but said that although there was a discussion about a flat gravestone, to which he objected, no sketch for a memorial was produced, otherwise he would have put it into his file, and he could not remember any conversation about Mr and Mrs Meer.

The petitioner also gave evidence of conversations with Canon Williams following the death of Mr Meer in March 1981 when he was horrified, he said, by Canon Williams' insistence that Mr Meer should be buried in Amanda's grave and that in consequence Mr Meer's remains were cremated so that they could be deposited in the grave of Mrs Meer's parents, Mr and Mrs Joseph Wood, close to the church. Canon Williams conducted the service following which the petitioner said he again raised the question and was told by Canon Williams that if Mrs Meer was cremated when she died her ashes could be put into the Wood grave and then the two spaces would be available for the petitioner and his wife in due course. The petitioner queried the honouring of that arrangement by any subsequent incumbent and said that Canon Williams shook him by the hand and said 'Man, I guarantee it'.

Canon Williams agreed that he first stipulated that Mrs Meer should be buried in Amanda's grave but that when told she would be cremated agreed to her ashes being placed in the Wood grave. He denied that any conversation of the kind spoken of by the petitioner took place after the service and said that he did not say 'Man, I guarantee it'. He went further and said that he does not use the word 'Man' in the way attributed to him.

The petitioner called two witnesses on his behalf. First, his mother Mrs Clara Daffern said that Mrs Meer never wanted to be buried in Amanda's grave and that she said so twice just after her husband had been cremated in March 1981 and secondly just before her own death. On both occasions Mrs Meer said 'I hope we beat him' referring to Canon Williams. Second, his son Nicholas Daffern spoke of a conversation he had with Canon Williams in September 1981 when he referred to the plan to call the triple grave 'grandma's grave' for only about five years until people forgot and got the reply 'People don't forget'.

Canon Williams called one supporting witness Mr Brian Joseph Meer who said that both his parents had said to him that where Amanda was buried would be their grave. He did not go to the interment of his father's ashes as he did not want him cremated.

Although no other witnesses were called to give evidence it was clear to me from the demeanour of others in court that this dispute has stirred up strong feelings on both sides and the evidence was given in an atmosphere charged with emotion.

I prefer the evidence of Canon Williams and Mr Meer to that of the petitioner and his witnesses. The petitioner said that in 1974 following Amanda's death he was distraught and that he had the added worry of his wife who then had a nervous breakdown. Having heard Canon Williams give evidence I am sure that he is not the kind of man who would enter into a scheme to deceive his parishioners and church council by pretending that the two empty spaces in the triple grave were for Mr and Mrs Meer whereas they were for the Dafferns. He has been incumbent of the parish since 1956. He fully supported the parochial church council's rule that only parishioners and those on the electoral roll could be buried in the churchyard and he gave evidence that the ground available for burials would be filled in about 20 years at the current rate of burials. He was able to agree to Amanda's burial only because the triple grave would also accommodate the Meers and so no extra burial plot would be used. Amanda was the only person who did not have the right of burial to be interred in the churchyard during his incumbency. I accept his evidence on these matters.

As to the 1979 conversation I do not accept the petitioner's evidence that he produced a sketch drawing to Canon Williams, who in my view is to be believed when he said that if it had been he would have put it in his file. Moreover after that conversation Mr Skelton, the sculptor, wrote to Canon Williams on 15 December 1980 a letter which was put in evidence and which makes no reference to an earlier sketch which one would have expected if it had existed.

My views on these earlier conversations lead me to prefer Canon Williams' evidence about events following the interment of Mr Meer's ashes in March 1981. There may well have been a handshake but I do not accept that Canon Williams expressed himself in the dramatic manner stated by the petitioner.

Mrs Daffern's evidence as to Mrs Meer's remarks in the last few weeks of her life have little probative value except to demonstrate how high feelings were running in the Meer/Daffern family. I prefer Mr Meer's evidence of his mother's views given earlier in her life. The son's evidence also had very limited evidential value as to what was agreed in 1974.

For these reasons I reject the request for the reservation of two spaces in Amanda's grave for the petitioner and his wife.

The petitioner, not being the personal representative of Mrs Meer, cannot pursue the matter of the reservation of a grave space for her. Her two personal representatives are in dispute whether she should be cremated. Clearly her remains ought to be disposed of quickly. If there is room in the Wood grave for another coffin and she is buried there or if she is cremated and her ashes deposited in that grave then I hope the parish would agree to the reservation of two spaces in Amanda's grave for the Dafferns as no prejudice would then arise to adversely affect the rights of the parishioners. It is a natural, common and decent wish to be buried with members of one's family. I have no doubt that the Dafferns now ardently wish to be buried in Amanda's grave in due course. Despite the feelings which have been aroused in the parish I hope that following this judgment charitable compassion would ease the way to satisfying this wish. Even if Mrs Meer cannot be placed in the Wood grave the Dafferns' wish can in my judgment be regarded as now set in wholly exceptional circumstances and not regarded as a dangerous precedent. Mrs Daffern's family have over three generations rendered loyal service to the parish within their capabilities. If the parish do accede to the request then they should certainly not feel inhibited in refusing any other request. However the decision is a matter for the incumbent in accordance with s 6 of the 1976 Measure.

There remains the issue of the design of the gravestone. The parish have loyally followed the churchyard regulations which I issued in 1972 but those regulations are in fact guidelines within which incumbents may grant permission for the erection of gravestones. The regulations make it clear that a person wishing to erect a gravestone outside those guidelines may apply to do so under a faculty. Such applications will be treated on their own merits.

Baddesley Ensor church council has a long tradition of caring for its churchyard. I was shown the parochial regulations of December 1935. It is of importance that churchyards are maintained as easily and as inexpensively as possible. The burden of such maintenance falls on the parish and not usually on those who erect gravestones. Photographs of the churchyard were produced in evidence and it is apparent that close to Amanda's grave there are headstones with kerbs such monuments being in black or white stone. The proposed gravestone is horizontal but its edges are to be at grass level with only the central portion raised. The materials suggested are Hornton and York stone. The diocesan advisory council has commended the design materials and lettering in a full report. In my view, although it falls outside the scope of the diocesan regulations, this is one of those instances where an exception can be made. I do not think that an occasional distinguished stone of this type will materially increase the maintenance of the churchyard nor will it look unpleasant in it. Indeed having seen a sample of stone the gravestone would be an attractive addition to the churchyard. The wording will require alteration following my decision on the other matters and I hope such alterations as are necessary can be agreed between the parties.

There will therefore be a faculty granted only for a gravestone of the design and material proposed by the petitioner but with liberty to apply to the court in the absence of agreement.

The petitioner must pay the costs of these proceedings including the costs of the parties opponent.

Faculty granted only for erection of the memorial.

Solicitors: *Lee, Bolton & Lee* (for the petitioner).

Evelyn M C Budd   Barrister.

R v City of Birmingham District Council, ex parte O

COURT OF APPEAL, CIVIL DIVISION

LORD DENNING MR, DONALDSON LJ AND SIR SEBAG SHAW

1, 2, 19 FEBRUARY 1982

Local government – Documents – Inspection – Inspection by councillor – Application for adoption order – Social services committee report on suitability of prospective adoptive parents – Councillor of housing sub-committee requesting disclosure of social services report – Councillor claiming disclosure necessary to enable her to perform duties as councillor – Social services committee withholding report – Whether councillor entitled to see report.

The applicants were the foster parents of a child who was in the care of a city council. The applicants wished to adopt the child and applied for approval to do so to the council which was a recognised adoption agency and which had, as required by s 2(1)[a] of the Local Authority Social Services Act 1970, delegated its social services functions to a social services committee. That committee had in turn set up a sub-committee to deal with adoption matters and the applicants' request for approval was referred to the sub-committee. While the application was being considered, the applicants fell into arrears with the rent of their council house and were called before a councillor acting as a housing committee. As a result of an interview with the foster mother, during which the foster mother mentioned that her husband had served a prison sentence, the councillor began to doubt the suitability of the applicants as foster parents. She referred the matter to the social services department and both the department and the social services committee reviewed the case and eventually gave unqualified and unanimous approval to the foster parents as prospective adoptive parents. However, the councillor was not satisfied with the result and asked to see the files of the social services department. The department refused to produce them to her on the ground that it would be a breach of confidence. The council's solicitor advised that she should be allowed to see the files in order that she could properly carry out her duties as a councillor. The applicants applied for an order prohibiting the council from disclosing to the councillor any information about the foster parents which had been obtained in confidence by the social services department. The Divisional Court refused the application on the grounds that the function of the council in adoption matters could not be delegated so as to divest the council of all power in the matter, and that the councillor had a right to see the information, whether or not she was a member of the social services committee, because her right to do so rested on her membership of the council itself which had primary responsibility for exercising the functions relating to adoption. The applicants appealed.

Held (Donaldson LJ dissenting) – Where a council formally delegated its duties under the 1970 Act to a social services committee, that committee, although not displacing the council, exercised the powers and discharged the functions of the council in respect of social services unless and until some further effective resolution of the council altered that situation. Accordingly, it was for the committee to decide how to use the information which came to it in the exercise of its responsibilities and whether that information was to be treated as confidential. Furthermore, on balance, the public interest in maintaining the confidentiality of the files, so as to ensure that the contents were not communicated more widely than necessary, overrode the public interest in the members of the council being sufficiently informed to carry out their duties properly, and therefore the files should be available only to the members of the social services

---

a   Section 2(1), so far as material, is set out at p 367 *a b*, post

committee and officers of the social services department. It followed that the appeal
would be allowed and an order of prohibition made preventing disclosure of the files to
the councillor (see p 360 *a* and *e* to p 361 *b*, p 367 *g* to *j* and p 368 *j*, post).

Notes

For a local councillor's right to inspect documents in the council's possession, see 28
Halsbury's Laws (4th edn) para 1349, and for cases on inspection of a corporation's books
and documents, see 13 Digest (Reissue) 234–236, 2044–2062, and 33 Digest (Repl) 117,
123–124, 756–759, 798–799.

For the Local Authority Social Services Act 1970, s 2, see 40 Halsbury's Statutes (3rd
edn) 992.

Cases referred to in judgments

D v National Society for the Prevention of Cruelty to Children [1977] 1 All ER 589, [1978] AC
171, [1977] 2 WLR 201, HL, Digest (Cont Vol E) 185, *1301b*.
D (infants), Re [1970] 1 All ER 1088, [1970] 1 WLR 599, CA, 18 Digest (Reissue) 18, *95*.
Gaskin v Liverpool City Council [1980] 1 WLR 1549, CA.
M (an infant) (adoption: parental consent), Re [1972] 3 All ER 321, [1973] QB 108, [1972]
3 WLR 531, CA, Digest (Cont Vol D) 522, *1371a*.
Manton v Brighton Corp [1951] 2 All ER 101, [1951] 2 KB 393, 33 Digest (Repl) 19, *84*.
Official Solicitor v K [1963] 3 All ER 191, [1965] AC 201, [1963] 2 WLR 408, HL, 28(2)
Digest (Reissue) 912, *2233*.
P A (an infant), Re [1971] 3 All ER 522, [1971] 1 WLR 1530, CA, Digest (Cont Vol D) 524,
1398a.
R v Barnes BC, ex p Conlan [1938] 3 All ER 226, 16 Digest (Reissue) 362, *3839*.
R v Clerk to Lancashire Police Committee, ex p Hook [1980] 2 All ER 353, [1980] QB 603,
[1980] 3 WLR 70, CA.
R v Greater London Council, ex p Blackburn [1976] 3 All ER 184, [1976] 1 WLR 550, CA,
Digest (Cont Vol E) 587, *183a*.
*R v Local Comr for Administration for the North and East Area of England, ex p Bradford
Metropolitan City Council* [1979] 2 All ER 881, [1979] QB 287, [1979] 2 WLR 1, QBD
and CA, Digest (Cont Vol E) 394, *902*.
R v Southwold Corp, ex p Wrightson (1907) 97 LT 431, DC, 16 Digest (Reissue) 362, *3838*.
Science Research Council v Nassé, BL Cars Ltd (formerly Leyland Cars) v Vyas [1979] 3 All ER
673, [1980] AC 1028, [1979] 3 WLR 762, HL, Digest (Cont Vol E) 186, *1301d*.

Cases also cited

Battelley v Finsbury BC (1958) 122 JP 169.
Blackpool Corp v Locker [1948] 1 All ER 85, [1948] 1 KB 349, CA.
Liverpool City Council, Re a complaint against [1977] 2 All ER 650, [1977] 1 WLR 995, DC.

Appeal

The applicants appealed against the decision of the Divisional Court of the Queen's Bench
Division (Eveleigh LJ and Watkins J) on 25 March 1980 whereby the court refused an
application for judicial review by way of an order of prohibition to prevent the City of
Birmingham District Council, by its officers, servants or agents, from disclosing to
Councillor Mrs Willetts any information about the applicants or either of them obtained
or recorded about them in confidence by the social services department of the council.
The facts are set out in the judgment of Lord Denning MR.

Stephen Sedley and *Elizabeth Lawson* for the applicants.
Raymond Sears QC, David Lamming and *Ian Croxford* for the council.

Cur adv vult

19 February. The following judgments were read.

LORD DENNING MR. Emma was born in 1974. She is now seven years old. When she was a baby of only five months her father and mother placed her out with foster parents. The foster parents were a married couple, who already had four children of their own. Later, in 1976, Emma's father and mother were at variance in matrimonial proceedings in the magistrates' court. The magistrates thought it was undesirable for either of them to have the care of Emma, so they made an order under s 2(1)(e) of the Matrimonial Proceedings (Magistrates' Courts) Act 1960. They committed the care of Emma to the local authority, which was the City of Birmingham District Council. The magistrates had evidence from the probation officer who had looked into the case most carefully. The magistrates made a care order and made a specific request that the local authority should allow Emma to remain in the care of the foster parents.

Ever since that time Emma has been with the foster parents and brought up as one of the family. So much so that in 1977, when Emma was three years old, the foster parents desired to adopt her as one of their own children. They made their application to the Birmingham council. The council is itself an adoption agency authorised under the Adoption Agencies Regulations 1976, SI 1976/1796. It fulfils its duties in this regard by means of a central adoption panel. That is composed of qualified members of the staff of the social services department. No councillors sat on the panel at that time. In March 1978 the panel gave approval in principle to the foster parents as prospective adoptives of Emma. There was every prospect of the adoption going through without difficulty. It would have to go, of course, before the county court judge. But there should have been no difficulty about it. But now everything has been held up because of an incident which has brought about this case before us. Emma is now seven. She has been with the foster parents as a member of the family of five children ever since she was three months old. Yet the adoption is still held up by this incident.

The incident was this. The foster parents were the tenants of a council house. They fell into arrears with their rent. The amount unpaid was £183·59. They were called before a housing committee of the Birmingham council on 26 July 1978. The housing committee was a committee of one. That one was Mrs Alice Willetts, a councillor. She was accompanied by Mr D Wright, who was an officer of the housing department. The foster mother attended accompanied by the five children. They were well behaved and well looked after. Mrs Willetts sought to investigate the question of the rent arrears and how they could be paid off. The rent arrears have since been paid off. But the effects of the interview have remained.

The foster mother talked a good deal. In the course of it she blurted out that her husband (the foster father) had served a prison sentence, and said other things which made Mrs Willetts doubt their suitability as foster parents. Mrs Willetts then asked for the file of the housing department about them. She discovered from it that in 1976 the housing department had advised against the child being placed with the foster parents; but the social services department had ignored that advice. She discovered other things from the housing department's file which led her to doubt the suitability of the foster parents.

Mrs Willetts became so concerned that she took the matter up with the social services department. The department made careful inquiries and reviewed the whole case again. The chairman of the relevant sub-committee, Mrs Cooke, called for all information from the officers and looked into it herself, with the other members of the committee. Eventually the central adoption panel gave unqualified and unanimous approval to the foster parents as prospective adoptive parents to Emma.

Nevertheless, Mrs Willetts was not satisfied. She wanted to see all the files of the social services department. They declined to produce them to her because 'it would itself be a serious breach of confidence' on the part of the department. Their case is put in an affidavit in these words:

'12. (iii) In so far as Mrs Willetts has been in possession of information or of grounds for suspicion concerning matters relevant to the Applicants' suitability to be foster parents or adoptive parents, she has always been at liberty to convey that information to my Department, which has conscientiously investigated it on every occasion; and a scrutiny by Mrs Willetts of our files would not advance that object for her but would make the local authority's work as an adoption agency, which my Department carries out, impossible by destroying the guarantee of confidentiality which we are at present able to give to applicants and to all other sources of information upon which we rely in trying to ensure that children are safely and happily placed for fostering and adoption.'

Mrs Willetts did not accept that view. She sought the advice of Mr Wilson, the solicitor to the City of Birmingham District Council. He advised that she should be allowed to see the files. This is what he said in his affidavit:

'In the circumstances of the matter I advised [the deputy director of social services] that it had been, and was reasonably necessary, for the Councillor to see the files in order that she could properly carry out her duties as a City Councillor. It appeared to me that the request had arisen out of the discharge by Councillor Mrs. Willetts of her duties as a member of the Housing Committee, and seemed to be a natural progression from problems thereby disclosed. Of course I further advised that the Councillor be reminded of the confidential nature of the contents of the files.'

Then the foster parents applied for judicial review, asking that the council be prohibited 'from disclosing to Councillor Mrs. Willetts any information about [the foster parents] or either of them obtained or recorded in confidence by the Social Services Department of the said Council'.

We are told that the local authority ombudsman has been asked to consider the case, but his inquiry is held up pending this case.

Confidential files

There is no doubt that all the files relating to Emma in the possession of the social services department are confidential. So confidential, indeed, that in general the courts will not allow or require them to be disclosed: not in wardship proceedings or custody proceedings (see *Official Solicitor v K* [1963] 3 All ER 191, [1965] AC 201, *Re D (infants)* [1970] 1 All ER 1088, [1970] 1 WLR 599); nor in actions by the parents or foster parents (see *D v National Society for the Prevention of Cruelty to Children* [1977] 1 All ER 589, [1978] AC 171); nor in an action by the child himself (see *Gaskin v Liverpool City Council* [1980] 1 WLR 1549); nor in adoptive proceedings (see reg 10 of the Adoption Agencies Regulations 1976); but it might do so if the interests of justice were so great as to outweigh the interest in preserving confidentiality (see *Re P A (an infant)* [1971] 3 All ER 522, [1971] 1 WLR 1530, *Re M (an infant)* [1972] 3 All ER 321, [1973] QB 108).

The social services committee

Every local authority is bound by statute to set up a special committee to deal with its social services functions. These functions include, inter alia, the functions of the local authority under the Children Act 1948 and the Adoption Act 1958: see s 2 of the Local Authority Social Services Act 1970. It is to that committee alone that the local authority can delegate its functions under those Acts: see s 101(10) of the Local Government Act 1972. But the local authority can arrange for the discharge of its functions by an officer of that committee or by one of the committee: see s 101(10) of the 1972 Act.

In this case the City of Birmingham District Council duly set up its social services committee. It consisted of about twenty councillors. That committee in turn set up a 'case committee' to consider questions relating to adoption: see regs 2(1) and 6 of the 1976 regulations. It is called in Birmingham the adoptive panel.

The duty of the local authority

Although those provisions authorise the local authority to delegate its social services functions to the social services committee, nevertheless the duties of the local authority remain the duties of the local authority itself. Section 12 of the Children Act 1948 places this duty on the 'local authority'. That was the foundation of the argument put forward by counsel for Mrs Willetts and the Birmingham council. He said that the duties of the council were placed on the council itself, and that the delegation to the social services committee did not detract from the fact that it was the duty of the council itself. Seeing that it was the duty of the council itself, it was reasonable for any one of the councillors to make due inquiry to see that the social services committee was properly carrying out that duty, and, for that purpose, to see the files.

The advice of the city solicitor

In support of his argument counsel for the council placed much reliance on the advice of the city solicitor. The city solicitor advised the deputy director of social services that it was reasonably necessary for Councillor Mrs Willetts to see the files in order that she could properly carry out her duties as a city councillor. Thereupon the deputy director of social services had arranged to show them to her. But it was stopped by these proceedings for judicial review. The council resists these proceedings, and has authorised the city solicitor to swear an affidavit in opposition. By so doing counsel submitted that the council has affirmed and ratified the advice which he gave and that there is no room for judicial review.

On principle

We considered many of the cases on this subject in the recent case of *R v Clerk to Lancashire Police Committee, ex p Hook* [1980] 2 All ER 353, [1980] QB 603. But I think this case stands on its own. It is because of the confidentiality of the documents and because they concerned the welfare of a child. This brings into play the consideration of the public interests involved. It requires us to hold the balance between them, such as was done by this court and the House of Lords in *Science Research Council v Nassé* [1979] 3 All ER 673, [1980] AC 1028. On the one hand there is the public interest in maintaining the confidence in the files, so as to ensure that the contents are not communicated any more widely than is necessary. On the other hand, there is the public interest in the members of the council being sufficiently well informed to carry out their duties. Holding the balance between these two public interests, I am quite clear that the files should be available only to the members of the social services committee and the officers of the social services department. The duties and the responsibilities of the council have been specially delegated to them. There is no need whatever for the files to be shown to other members, like Mrs Willetts, who are not members of the committee and have no particular duty or responsibility in the matter. I think that Mrs Willetts did all that was required of her when she communicated her discoveries to the social services department. It took them all into account and, nevertheless, thought that the foster parents should be recommended as suitable to be adoptive parents. If Mrs Willetts still felt uneasy, she could raise the matter at a full meeting of the council. If they thought it right, they could appoint her to be a member of the social services committee. Then she would be able to see all the files. I should not think they would do this, however, because the matter is now under review by the local authority ombudsman, and he will be able to see if anything has gone wrong: see ss 23 to 34 of the Local Government Act 1974 and *R v Local Comr for Administration for the North and East Area of England, ex p Bradford Metropolitan City Council* [1979] 2 All ER 881, [1979] QB 787. That is the proper way to get it all cleared up.

It would, I think, be quite improper for Mrs Willetts to conduct an investigation all on her own, by getting access to the confidential files and so forth. In my opinion the advice of the city solicitor was erroneous. It would be quite wrong to allow Mrs Willetts to see

these confidential files. She should not be allowed to appoint herself a one-woman
a committee to investigate the conduct of the social services department. This court can
and should issue an order of prohibition to prevent their disclosure to her, even though
it is a prohibition to an administrative authority: see *R v Greater London Council, ex p
Blackburn* [1976] 3 All ER 184, [1976] 1 WLR 550.

I would, therefore, allow the appeal and issue an order of prohibition accordingly.

b **DONALDSON LJ.** This appeal raises issues of some general importance. The care,
welfare and adoption of children are extremely sensitive subjects. So, too, is the
professional status of social workers employed by local authorities and their relationship
both to those whom they regard as their 'clients' and to the elected members of the
employing authorities.

The applicants, Mr and Mrs O, have taken proceedings designed to prevent the
c disclosure of confidential files to Councillor Mrs Willetts, an elected member of the City
of Birmingham District Council. The confidential files have been compiled by the social
services department of the council and relate to the suitability of the applicants as foster
parents and as prospective adoptive parents of the child Emma. At least one of the social
workers who have been involved, a Mrs Dolan, supported the applicants.

In 1975 the applicants began to look after Emma, the child principally concerned,
d when her natural parents abandoned her at the age of five months. A year later the
Birmingham city magistrates made a care order in favour of the city council on the
understanding that the council would maintain and regularise the existing situation by
placing Emma with the applicants as foster parents. This was done. The applicants have
four older children of their own and Emma was brought up as a member of the family.
In 1977 the applicants applied to adopt Emma.

e It was at the end of July 1978 that Councillor Mrs Willetts became involved, but in a
quite different context. She was the councillor member of a housing sub-committee of
two which had to inquire into arrears of rent said to be owed by the applicants. There
was an interview and the second applicant, Mrs O, explained her circumstances at some
length and, as Mrs Willetts would no doubt say, at some irrelevance. However, Mrs O
revealed that her husband had served a prison sentence in 1973, although she did not
f explain for what offence. Mrs O also mentioned that all four of her children occupied a
single bedroom whilst Emma occupied another. The context of this revelation was,
according to Mrs Willetts, an expressed wish by Mrs O to have larger accommodation.

At the end of the interview Mrs Willetts became concerned at the suitability of the
applicants as foster parents because of the prison sentence, because of the inadequate
amount of accommodation available and because of an unauthorised exchange of council
g properties in 1975 which Mrs O had also mentioned. The justification for this exchange
was said to be that the neighbours had been causing difficulties about Mr O's prison
sentence. Mrs Willetts was not directly concerned with the fostering arrangement,
because whilst she was a member of the housing committee she was not a member of the
social services committee. However, she thought that it was her duty to investigate a
little further to the extent of reading the housing department's file on the applicants. As
h she was a member of the housing committee, she had no difficulty in obtaining access to
that file.

In this file Mrs Willetts came across correspondence between the housing and social
services department in 1976 in which the housing department had been asked to provide
any information about the applicants which might be relevant in deciding whether to
board Emma with the applicants or, more accurately, to leave her with them. The
j housing department had not recommended the placement. The file also revealed a long
history of rent arrears, eviction from their house at the end of 1975 and placement in a
hostel. There was then an unexplained gap between about 1 and 12 January 1976, when
the applicants moved into their current home. Mrs Willetts inferred, wrongly as it
happened, that the whole family must have been homeless during this period.

At this stage Councillor Mrs Willetts decided that it was her duty as a councillor to get in touch with the social services department to find out why Mr O had been in prison and *a* where the children had been during the period of apparent homelessness in January 1976. She spoke on the telephone to Mrs Dolan of the social services. Her inquiries of Mrs Dolan led to the deputy director of social services calling for a full report on the case, which was prepared by Mrs Dolan on the basis not only of the material in the files but further inquiries with the police. The report went to Mr Bellshaw, Mrs Dolan's group leader, and with or without amendment he forwarded it to the chairman of the social *b* services committee, who passed it to Councillor Mrs Willetts. Councillor Mrs Willetts was not satisfied and telephoned to the deputy director of social services.

This telephone call led to further activity by the social services department. Further inquiries were made, a special case conference was held presided over by Councillor Mrs Cooke, the chairman of the social services committee, and in January 1979 Mrs Cooke wrote to Mrs Willetts saying that she was satisfied that the applicants were offering *c* satisfactory care to Emma. Although this was a long and careful letter, Mrs Willetts felt that it did not adequately deal with the position. She expressed her dissatisfaction in another letter to Mrs Cooke and received a long reply giving further information. Unfortunately Mrs Willetts was still not satisfied.

At about this stage two things appear to have happened. First, the adoption panel of the council decided to support the adoption application. This panel was a sub-committee *d* of the social services committee and is the 'case committee' referred to in the Adoption Agencies Regulations 1976, SI 1976/1796, made under the Adoption Act 1958. Contrary to the provisions of s 5(4) of the Local Authority Social Services Act 1970 it included no elected members of the council. That error is admitted and has now been remedied. The second thing to happen was that Councillor Mrs Willetts sought personally to inspect the confidential files of the social services department relating to the applicants. *e*

This application caused consternation to Mrs Dolan and, it may be, to other social workers. It also became known to the applicants, who were very aggrieved. Mrs Dolan's objection was that social workers could only obtain the information which they needed for their work on terms, express or implied, that the information would be treated on a basis of strict confidentiality. If the raw material, as opposed to reports based on that material, were to be available to members of the council regardless of whether or not *f* they were members of the social services committee, their sources of information would dry up. She was also concerned at the effect which continued inquiries were having on the applicants and their family. The applicants, for their part, no doubt felt that they were the victims of a campaign to prevent them adopting Emma.

Councillor Mrs Willetts's attitude was that as a member of the council she had an indirect responsibility for the activities of the social services committee and, having been *g* put on inquiry that all might not be well, she was entitled to make a full personal investigation, provided only that she undertook to treat the material as confidential, and this she was fully prepared to do.

This conflict of view led to Mr Williamson, the deputy director of social services, taking the advice of Mr Wilson, the city solicitor. Mr Wilson has sworn an affidavit a passage of which has already been quoted by Lord Denning MR. *h*

In the light of this advice the director of social services agreed to let Councillor Mrs Willetts see the files, but before she could do so the applicants applied to the Divisional Court for judicial review and prohibition. That was in June 1979. The Divisional Court refused to make such an order when the matter was heard in March 1980. The applicants appealed, and now, nearly two years later, we have to decide whether the Divisional Court was right. A most unhappy result of what, on any view, has been a most *j* unfortunate affair is that the applicants have not felt it right to press ahead with their application to adopt Emma whilst these proceedings were on foot and her future still remains uncertain. The delays in disposing of this application are wholly lamentable and largely unexplained, but the present is not the moment at which to inquire why and how they occurred.

The Local Authority Social Services Act 1970, and in particular s 3(3), provides some gems of obscure Parliamentary draftsmanship. However, there was some measure of agreement between the parties as to the purpose and meaning of the Act. It requires local authorities to set up social services committees, either alone or jointly with other authorities. It provides, by s 2(1), that—

'there shall stand referred to that committee all matters relating to the discharge by the authority of—(a) their functions under the enactments specified in the first column of Schedule 1 to this Act (being the functions which are described in general terms in the second column of that Schedule); and (b) such other of their functions as, by virtue of the following subsection, fall within the responsibility of the committee.'

That schedule lists a very large range of functions, including, under the Children Act 1948, children in care; and, under the Adoption Act 1958:

'Making, etc. arrangements for the adoption of children . . . care, possession and supervision of children awaiting adoption . . .'

It is reasonably clear from the context in which similar wording is used in Sch 1 to the Education Act 1944 and in Sch 4 to the National Health Service Act 1946 that the statutory reference to the social services committee is not intended to produce a delegation, still less a transfer, of functions. It simply requires, subject to immaterial exceptions, that all these matters shall be considered and reported on by the committee before the local authority takes any action. However, the 1970 Act also enables a local authority to delegate executive powers to the committee in respect of these matters, and this has been done by this council.

The work done by 'social workers' is not new, but until modern times was undertaken by voluntary organisations, family doctors, the clergy and neighbours. The change to paid and trained workers and the growth of their professionalism are of recent origin. In many ways this is all to the good, particularly the professionalism. Every profession has to develop its own ethics and those ethics must take full account of the circumstances in which the member is working and his or her relationship with those with whom they are working. In the case of the social work professions, this development is taking place, but in some respects it is going astray. Their work necessarily involves acquiring highly confidential and sensitive information from and about those whom they seek to help. Indeed, it would be impossible to obtain such information without an express or implied promise of confidentiality. The social workers' recognition of their own professionalism has led them to speak and think of those whom they seek to help as their 'clients'. This in turn has led some of them to equate their relationship with their 'clients' to that of a doctor, lawyer or accountant with their patients or clients. From this it has been a short step to the belief that professional ethics should and do prevent them revealing the full details of confidential information to anyone other than professional colleagues under seal of professional secrecy and further prevents them passing on even the substance of this information to anyone other than one who has the immediate responsibility for decision making.

I do not criticise this. Indeed, I applaud the professional instinct which engenders it. But I think that it is to some extent misguided. The fundamental fallacy is to regard a local authority social worker as being in the same position as a general practitioner operating under the national health service. One is not more professional than the other. It is just that they are different. It is no part of the duties of the national health service to treat patients. Its function is to provide doctors who will do so. The resulting relationships are (a) employer and employed doctor and (b) doctor and patient. By contrast, it is the duty of a local authority to care for children and to play a part in the process of their adoption. For this purpose local authorities employ social workers. The resulting relationships are (a) local authority and employed social workers and (b) local authority, social workers and the 'clients/patients' of both. Once this is understood, it disposes of the professional objection to revealing confidential information to members of the local authority, on the basis that to do so would be a breach of a professional relationship. In fact, such a dissemination of confidential information still keeps it within the bounds of the professional relationship, since this exists not only between the social worker and the 'client' but also embraces the local authority itself.

Nevertheless, having said this, I recognise that there are practical problems involved because of the large number of members of some local authorities and the fact that where there is a joint social services committee more than one local authority may be involved. Similar, and indeed far more acute, practical problems arise in the police force in the context of confidential information from informers. The more widely that that confidential information is disseminated, albeit quite properly in terms of professionalism and professional ethics, the greater will be the risk of leakage of that information. This in turn will make it more difficult to obtain the information, yet its acquisition is essential if the service is to be provided. Accordingly, it is often necessary to impose a 'need to know' limitation on the dissemination of confidential information. But this limitation is based on practical rather than professional or ethical considerations.

Bearing in mind that it is the local authority and not the individual social worker which is performing the statutory duty (the social worker is, as it were, the instrument used by the authority) confidential information given to the social worker is given to the authority. However, those who give it are entitled to expect, and social workers can reasonably assure them, that, save as may be necessary for the performance of the authority's statutory duties, the information will never be divulged to anyone outside the authority or to anyone within the authority who has no need to know.

Thus far I have been considering the problem from the points of view of the person being helped, 'the client', the social worker and the social worker's sources of information. It is now necessary to look at it from the point of view of the local authority, its officers and elected members, and Councillor Mrs Willetts.

As I have already said, all relevant information acquired by a local authority's social workers in the course of their duties, whether or not it be confidential, is acquired on behalf of the local authority. It becomes the authority's information. This creates no problem, because the authority itself is not a natural person. It is a body corporate which neither reads, hears nor understands. Even more important, it does not speak or write. Problems only arise when the information is disseminated amongst its officials or elected members.

Take first the officials. I do not believe that this creates any problem. No official has any right to acquire any part of the authority's stock of information, whether or not confidential, save in so far as it is needed by him in order that he should be able to do his job. In a word, he has to have a 'need to know'. In practice I have no doubt that this 'need to know' principle will be applied. For example, the parks superintendent of the city council, if there is such an officer, would not ask to see confidential files of the social services department because he has no 'need to know', and, if he did ask, he would most certainly be refused.

Now let me turn to the members of the authority. Here again the 'need to know' principle applies, and it is established, albeit not in that phrase, by decided cases. In *R v Barnes BC, ex p Conlan* [1938] 3 All ER 226 Humphreys J delivered the judgment of a Divisional Court consisting of himself, Lord Hewitt CJ and Branson J. He said (at 230):

> 'As to the right of a councillor to inspect all documents in possession of the council, there was no dispute at the bar that such a right exists, so far as his access to the documents is reasonably necessary to enable the councillor properly to perform his duties as a member of the council. The common law right of a councillor to inspect documents in the possession of the council arises from his common law duty to keep himself informed of all matters necessary to enable him properly to discharge his duty as a councillor. There must be some limit to this duty. To hold that each councillor of such a body as, for instance, the London County Council, is charged with the duty of making himself familiar with every document in the possession of that body would be to impose an impossible burden upon individual

councillors. The duties are therefore divided amongst various committees and sub-committees. In our judgment, it is plain that, as was decided in *R. v. Southwold Corpn., Ex p. Wrightson* ((1907) 97 LT 431 at 431–432): "a councillor has no right to a roving commission to go and examine books or documents of a corporation because he is a councillor. Mere curiosity or desire to see and inspect documents is not sufficient".'

Counsel for the applicants points out that the quotation, from Lord Alverstone CJ's judgment, in the *Southwold* case could have been lengthened to include the next succeeding words, which were:

'... but I consider this court has the power to order the production of any public documents where the person who applies to see them has a right to see, and a *bonâ fide* ground for wishing to see.'

Counsel then submits that the court was only concerned with *public* as contrasted with confidential documents. I do not so read Lord Alverstone CJ's judgment. By 'public' I think that he meant a document which was the property of a public body or authority. But however that may be, Humphreys J was adopting the shorter quotation as an accurate statement of the law. This view of the law was affirmed by this court in *R v Clerk to Lancashire Police Committee, ex p Hook* [1980] 2 All ER 353, [1980] QB 603.

This brings me to the last problem raised by the appeal: who decides whether an elected member of a local authority can see particular documents? At one time I thought that the *Lancashire Police Committee* case was authority for the proposition that it was the relevant committee. However, counsel for the council pointed out that the committee in that case was not a committee of the county council. It was the police committee, which is the independent police authority composed of councillors and magistrates. No doubt it used the services of the county council, but it was a quite separate body. The answer is that in the case of dispute as to the 'need to know' and consequent right to see local authority documents the decision is that of the authority.

In the instant case the decision to allow Councillor Mrs Willetts to see the files was that of an officer, the director of social services, acting on the advice of the city solicitor. His decision has been supported to the extent at least that the council has resisted the applicants' claim for an order of prohibition. But, until his decision was challenged in the courts, it was a decision taken by officers. Is this right? I yield to no one in my belief that control of local authorities must not pass into the hands of the officers, but must be retained by the elected representatives. However, in any local authority there are hundreds of day-to-day decisions which have to be taken. They cannot be taken by councillors and are rightly taken by officers on the basis of standing orders and established policies and practices.

As a matter of law, Councillor Mrs Willetts, as a member of the council, was entitled to access to any council information if, prima facie, she had a 'need to know'. True it is that the council had given delegated powers to the social services committee to deal with problems such as had arisen in the case of the O family. However, as was pointed out by Slade J in *Manton v Brighton Corp* [1951] 2 All ER 101, [1951] 2 KB 393, delegation leaves the principal (the local authority and its members) with a residual responsibility for the activities of the delegate and an obligation, in appropriate circumstances, to exercise some degree of control.

If, despite reassurances from the chairman of the social services committee, Councillor Mrs Willetts remained genuinely anxious lest something was going wrong, it was both her right and duty to consider all the local authority's papers, whether confidential or not, with a view to deciding what further action, if any, she should take. For example, after fully informing herself, she might have decided to take no further action, she might have wished to object to a report by the social services committee, or she might have wished to place a substantive motion on the agenda for the next meeting of the authority. Assuming that Councillor Mrs Willetts's anxieties were genuine and not inspired by pique induced either by Mrs O's conduct at the housing sub-committee meeting or by the failure of the social services committee to take the same view as the housing committee nearly three years before in 1976, Councillor Mrs Willetts had indeed a 'need to know'. Mrs Willetts's request appeared to the city solicitor to be of a more or less routine nature. Certainly it did not strike him that she had any improper motive or extraneous purpose and, of course, it has never been suggested that she had. Had he thought that the position was or might be otherwise, there would have been grounds for refusing Mrs Willetts access to the files, and that is not a decision which can properly be taken by officers. In such circumstances he should, and I doubt not would, have referred the matter to an appropriate elected member, such as the chairman of the social services committee. If she had instructed the social services department to refuse Councillor Mrs Willetts access to the confidential files, Mrs Willetts, if she still wished to pursue the matter, could have referred the problem to the full council.

This brings me to the nature of the court's jurisdiction. It is a review jurisdiction. It is not for us to substitute our judgment for that of the local authority or its officers. The court can only intervene if the decision is such that no reasonable local authority could have taken and, accordingly, the inference can be drawn that there was a failure to take account of a relevant factor or that some irrelevant factor was taken into account, in other words, the local authority erred in law rather than merely in judgment.

Did it so err? As a practical matter there must be several alternatives to either refusing all access to confidential files or allowing complete access. For instance, a personal interview between Councillor Mrs Willetts, the director of social services and Mrs Dolan might have resolved Mrs Willetts's anxieties. However, this does not seem to have been considered once the letters from Councillor Mrs Cooke, the chairman of the social services committee, failed to pacify Councillor Mrs Willetts. Again, the authority could have pressed Mrs Willetts to define more clearly what precisely was her 'need to know'. Indeed, I should not have been in the least surprised if the director of social services and the chairman of the social services committee had hesitated rather longer before agreeing to give Mrs Willetts the opportunity for a roving commission through the confidential files. But, that said, the applicants have to satisfy me that the local authority's decision was necessarily wrong in the sense that I have already explained. I have little doubt that a different decision might well have been taken, but I am not convinced that the decision in fact taken was necessarily wrong.

No one who has studied the amount of time and effort devoted to answering Councillor Mrs Willetts's questions and seeking to allay her anxieties can fail to appreciate that there are substantial practical difficulties in getting through the work which falls on local authorities if elected members are not prepared to have confidence in the skill and judgment of other councillors serving on committees of which they are not themselves members. To this extent it is surprising that Councillor Mrs Willetts should have shown such tenacity in seeking this confidential information. Probably she saw any reluctance to reveal the information as confirmation of her suspicions that all was not well. In fact, it was probably nothing of the sort, but merely an understandable, but mistaken, view by the social workers of their undoubted professional duty to preserve confidences. Bearing in mind the time which has now elapsed and the success of the authority before the Divisional Court in establishing the right of elected members to access to confidential informations in the hands of that authority if and to the extent that they have a 'need to know', Councillor Mrs Willetts might have felt that it would have been a generous gesture to the members of the social services committee and their chairman, to the authority's social workers and to the applicants if she had said that she would now let the matter drop, thus allowing the adoption application to be placed before the county court for decision. But that was a matter for her.

For my part I would dismiss the appeal.

SIR SEBAG SHAW. I have had the advantage of reading in draft the respective judgments of Lord Denning MR and Donaldson LJ. I do not, therefore, recapitulate the history of the events which have led to this appeal and I need not examine at large the statutory provisions which govern the administration by local authorities of their function as adoption agencies. I cite only the basic relevant provisions. The first is contained in s 2(1)(*a*) of the Local Authority Social Services Act 1970, which enacts:

'Every local authority shall establish a social services committee and . . . there shall stand referred to that committee all matters relating to the discharge by the authority of—(*a*) their functions under the enactments specified in the first column of Schedule 1 to this Act (being the functions which are described in general terms in the second column of that Schedule) . . .'

The relevant item in Sch 1 reads:

| 'Adoption Act 1958 . . . | Making, etc. arrangements for the adoption of children; regulation of adoption societies; care, possession and supervision of children awaiting adoption; prosecution of offences.' |

Section 2(2) has also to be referred to. It provides:

'The Secretary of State may by order designate functions of local authorities under any other enactment for the time being in force as being appropriate for discharge through a local authority's social services committee other than functions which by virtue of that or any other enactment are required to be discharged through some other committee of a local authority . . . '

Section 3 of the Act further identifies the business of the social services committee by providing:

'(1) Except with the consent of the Secretary of State . . . or as provided by this section, no matter, other than a matter which by virtue of section 2 of this Act stands referred to a local authority's social services committee, shall be referred to, or dealt with by, the committee . . .'

Thus the intensely personal functions of the social services committee as set out in Sch 1 are isolated from other functions of the local authority. Whether dealing with the sick or the dying or the mentally afflicted or with disabled persons or orphans or adoption, the committee is concerned with matters which are individual, intimate and private. Information which is gleaned and gathered for the purpose of discharging the duties of the committee must generally be of a kind which demands that it be regarded as confidential and that it be used in no other way than for the due discharge of the obligations and responsibilities of the social services committee. That committee does not displace the powers and duties in these regards of the local authority concerned; but it operates those powers and discharges those functions. In the present case the City of Birmingham District Council has since 1975 formally delegated to the social services committee the functions, powers and duties of the council under the Local Authority Social Services Act 1970. The council can no doubt by appropriate resolution retract that delegation, but no individual councillor, however insistent, can do so by himself or herself. The functions to which s 2(1) relates do not (since 1975) simply stand referred to the social services committee, but are actually to be discharged by that committee unless and until some further effective resolution of the council alters that situation. It must accordingly fall to the committee to decide how to use information which comes to it in the exercise of its responsibilities. It must form its judgment as to what may properly be disseminated and what must be treated as confidential. I sympathise with the view expressed by Donaldson LJ that members of a social services committee, and perhaps even more so of the adoption panel, tend to regard themselves as professional advisers and, as such, as protectors of those who come to them on what are in a real sense matters of life and death. There does develop a synthetic relationship of adviser and client carrying with it the duty of the adviser not to betray any confidences which the 'client' may repose in him or her. But the obligation of confidence in truth rests on a more fundamental, more significant and more real foundation. In the exercise of public duties which impinge on sensitive aspects of the lives of individuals, it is not only that moral principle and ethical standards support the maintenance of confidentiality but public interest and policy demand it. The administration of public functions in this sensitive area would become disreputable if confidences were betrayed, and the very exercise of those functions would be inevitably impaired. Confidences would be withheld when candour was imperative. Those who came to the social services committee would be reticent when they should be open and frank. Counsel for the council does not dispute the obligation to maintain confidence in relation to matters dealt with the the social services committee, but he submits that no breach of confidence is involved in letting Mrs Willetts look at the confidential files of the social services committee in relation to the applicants. He founded this contention on two propositions: first, that the files were the property of the council, as was the information they contained; and, second, that a confidence given to the social services committee was ipso facto a confidence reposed in the council. It followed, so the argument went, that no breach of confidence could be involved in showing the contents of the files of that committee to a member of the council.

As to the first proposition, the physical property in the files was no doubt vested in the council; but whether it was entitled to regard the information they contained as its to use in any context or connection is a different matter. It might involve an informant in an action for defamation or some other adverse proceedings. As to the second proposition, even if it is to be accepted in its widest sense it does not follow that the confidence given to the social services committee can be said to be given to individual councillors. If the council as a body called for the production of certain files no doubt they would have to be produced, but one supposes that such a step would be taken in regard to the operation of a professional committee like the social services committee only after responsible discussion and consideration by the council. It seems to me intolerable that any individual councillor should presume to assert a personal authority over a committee of the council of which she is not a member. Mrs Willetts as a member of the housing committee rota sub-committee would, I strongly suspect, be up in arms if a member of some other committee, albeit a councillor, demanded that Mrs Willetts should produce her sub-committee's files for inspection. The functioning of a local authority would be reduced to chaotic intermeddling if this sort of activity by individual councillors were to be recognised as legitimate or in any way encouraged. If, as doubtless is the case, Mrs Willetts had her misgivings about the applicants despite the assurances given by Mrs Dolan of the social services and by Councillor Mrs Cooke, chairman of the social services committee, her proper course was to raise the matter before the council. In my judgment the advice given by the city solicitor to Mr Williamson, the deputy director of social services, was the wrong advice. It was not the fact that (I quote from the city solicitor's affidavit) 'it had been, and was reasonably necessary, for [Mrs Willetts] to see the files in order that she could properly carry out her duties as a City Councillor'. As an individual councillor she was concerned with housing and not with adoption. As a member of the council she could raise in council whatever matters appeared to her to call for inquiry or investigation; it is quite a different matter to make peremptory inroads into the functioning of committees with which she had no direct concern.

We were told by counsel for the council that the city council have by resolution approved the advice given by the city solicitor. That unfortunately gives it no better validity. When the council resolve in due form that they wish the files in question to be produced to them, no doubt Mrs Willetts will be accorded her rights, as a member of the council, to inspect those files for her satisfaction. I would, however, expect that no local authority would call for the production of confidential material without due caution and only after being satisfied that there exist strong and good reasons for taking such a course. This must be the more so in the case of a committee which is given by statute a delicate function to discharge and to which the statutory responsibilities in that regard have been delegated by the authority which that committee serves.

I would allow this appeal and order that prohibition should go.

Appeal allowed. No order of prohibition on undertaking by council that files would not be disclosed. Leave to appeal to the House of Lords granted on conditions (1) that the present case will not be affected, (2) that Mrs Willett will not seek to see the files, (3) that adoption of the child will proceed forthwith, and (4) that costs of both sides will be paid by the council.

Solicitors: *Patrick Skemp*, Birmingham (for the applicants); *Sharpe, Pritchard & Co*, agents for *F H Wilson*, Birmingham (for the council).

Frances Rustin   Barrister.

Whitter v Peters
Peart v Stewart

COURT OF APPEAL, CIVIL DIVISION
ORMROD LJ AND BOOTH J
13 NOVEMBER, 21 DECEMBER 1981

Contempt of court – Committal – Breach of injunction – Jurisdiction – County court – Period of committal – County court committing persons to prison for four and six months for breaches of injunctions – Whether county court having power to commit persons to prison for more than one month for breaches of its orders – Whether county court a 'superior court' when exercising its power to commit persons to prison for breaching its orders – County Courts Act 1959, s 74 – Contempt of Court Act 1981, ss 14(1), 19.

The appellants in two separate cases were committed to prison for four and six months respectively by the county court for breaches of orders made by the court under the Domestic Violence and Matrimonial Proceedings Act 1976. Under s 14(1)[a] of the Contempt of Court Act 1981, the period of committal was required to be for a fixed term not exceeding two years in the case of committal by a 'superior court' or one month in the case of committal by an 'inferior court'. Under s 19[b] of the 1981 Act, a superior court included 'any ... court exercising ... powers equivalent to those of the High Court'. The appellants appealed against the committal orders, contending that the county court was an inferior court for the purposes of s 14(1) of the 1981 Act and that accordingly the term of imprisonment should not have exceeded one month in each case.

Held – The county court was entitled to impose periods of committal in excess of one month by virtue of the jurisdiction conferred on it by s 74[c] of the County Courts Act 1959 to grant the same relief and remedies as the High Court in similar cases, because (per Ormrod LJ) in granting injunctions and, where necessary, enforcing them by committal the county court was exercising powers 'equivalent to those of the High Court' and was accordingly a 'superior court' within the meaning of s 19 of the 1981 Act, and (per Booth J) there was nothing in s 14(1) of the 1981 Act which derogated from the power bestowed on the county court by s 74 of the 1959 Act to grant such relief or remedy as ought to be granted in the like case by the High Court. It followed that the committal orders were within the county court's jurisdiction and the appeals would accordingly be dismissed (see p 372 j to p 373 b and j, p 374 a b and p 375 e to j, post).

Martin v Bannister (1879) 4 QBD 491 and *Jennison v Baker* [1972] 1 All ER 997 applied.

---

a   Section 14(1) is set out at p 371 c, post
b   Section 19, so far as material, is set out at p 371 e f, post
c   Section 74 is set out at p 372 g h, post

Quaere. Whether the 1981 Act applies to 'civil contempt' arising out of disobedience to an order of the court as well as to contempt committed in or within the vicinity of the court (see p 372 *c* to *e* and p 375 *d e*, post).

Notes

For the breach of an injunction as contempt of court, see 9 Halsbury's Laws (4th edn) paras 52, 66, and for cases on the subject, see 28(2) Digest (Reissue) 1142–1143, *1441–1448*.

For the power of a county court to order committal for breaches of its orders, see 10 Halsbury's Laws (4th edn) paras 59, 561, and for cases on the subject, see 13 Digest (Reissue) 408–409, *3404–3411*.

For the distinction between superior and inferior courts, see 10 Halsbury's Laws (4th edn) paras 710–714, and for cases on the subject, see 16 Digest (Reissue) 140, *1414–1422*.

For the County Courts Act 1959, s 74, see 7 Halsbury's Statutes (3rd edn) 349.

For the Domestic Violence and Matrimonial Proceedings Act 1976, see 46 ibid 713.

Cases referred to in judgments

Jennison v Baker [1972] 1 All ER 997, [1972] 2 QB 52, [1972] 2 WLR 429, CA, 13 Digest (Reissue) 408, *3404.*

Martin v Bannister (1879) 4 QBD 491, CA: *affg* sub nom *Ex p Martin* 4 QBD 212, DC, 13 Digest (Reissue) 407, *3397.*

Pryor v City Offices Co (1883) 10 QBD 504, CA, 13 Digest (Reissue) 396, *3322.*

Case also cited

Hymas v Ogden [1905] 1 KB 246, CA.

Interlocutory appeals

Whitter v Peters

Patrick Peters appealed from the order of his Honour Judge McDonnell sitting in the Lambeth County Court committing him to prison on 14 October 1981 for a period of four months for breach of an undertaking given by him to the court on 18 August 1981 to vacate 32 Lorne Road, London SW9 by 6 pm on 19 August 1981 and not to molest the respondent, Ann Marie Whitter. The facts are set out in the judgment of Ormrod LJ.

Peart v Stewart

Desmond Anthony Stewart appealed from the order of his Honour Judge McDonnell sitting in the Lambeth County Court committing him to prison on 19 October 1981 for a period of six months for breach of an injunction dated 2 July 1981 restraining him from assaulting the respondent, Marcia Patricia Peart, and requiring him to leave 26 Cossall Walk, Gordon Road, Peckham, London SE15 within three days of the service of the order. The facts are set out in the judgment of Ormrod LJ.

Nasreen Pearce for both appellants.
Diane Redgrave for the respondent in the first case.
Jacqueline Comyns for the respondent in the second case.

Cur adv vult

21 December. The following judgments were read.

ORMROD LJ. These two appeals from committal orders made by his Honour Judge McDonnell at Lambeth County Court raise the same point of law and were heard together. In neither case is there any reference in the grounds of appeal to the merits, so this judgment is confined to the point of law.

In *Whitter v Peters* the appellant Peters was committed to prison on 14 October 1981 for a period of four months for breaches of an undertaking given by him to the court on

18 August 1981 to vacate 32 Lorne Road, London SW9 by 6pm on 19 August 1981 and not to molest the respondent. In *Peart v Stewart* the appellant Stewart was committed to prison on 19 October 1981 for a period of six months for breaches of an order dated 2 July 1981 restraining him from assaulting the respondent and requiring him to leave 26 Cossall Walk, Gordon Road, Peckham, London SE15 within three days of the service of the order on him and not to return thereto. In both cases the orders were made under s 1 of the Domestic Violence and Matrimonial Proceedings Act 1976.

The question of law which arises is whether the judge had power to make a committal order for a period longer than one month having regard to the terms of s 14(1) of the Contempt of Court Act 1981, which came into force one month after 27 July 1981, the date on which it was passed. Section 14(1) is in these terms:

> 'In any case where a court has power to commit a person to prison for contempt of court and (apart from this provision) no limitation applies to the period of committal, the committal shall (without prejudice to the power of the court to order his earlier discharge) be for a fixed term, and that term shall not on any occasion exceed two years in the case of committal by a superior court, or one month in the case of committal by an inferior court.'

The appellants contend that the Lambeth County Court is an inferior court within the meaning of this subsection, and that, accordingly, the term of imprisonment should not have exceeded one month.

The respondents submit that the 1981 Act does not apply to this species of contempt of court (sometimes referred to for convenience as 'civil contempt') which arises out of disobedience to an order of the court. Alternatively, they say that in so far as the proceedings in each case are concerned the county court judge, on the true construction of s 19 of the 1981 Act, had the power of a superior court, and that his orders were accordingly valid. Section 19, so far as it is relevant, reads thus:

> '... "superior court" means the Court of Appeal, the High Court, the Crown Court, the Courts-Martial Appeal Court, the Restrictive Practices Court, the Employment Appeal Tribunal and any other court exercising in relation to its proceedings powers equivalent to those of the High Court, and includes the House of Lords in the exercise of its appellate jurisdiction.'

The first point depends on the meaning to be given to the words 'contempt of court' in s 14(1). As is well known, this phrase, though very widely used, has always been a source of confusion. In its original meaning, it no doubt meant what it said, namely conduct which was contemptuous of the court, but it has come to be used to describe any conduct which might give rise to committal to prison by order of a civil court. So, it has come to comprise widely different kinds of conduct, ranging from insulting behaviour in the face of the court, or conduct which interferes with the due administration of justice to disobedience of orders made by the court. To distinguish these different categories it has become customary to speak of 'criminal contempts' and 'civil contempts'; the distinction was of considerable importance in the past when different rules applied to each category. There is a useful classification of the different types of contempt in the notes to RSC Ord 52, r 1: see *The Supreme Court Practice 1979*, vol 1, p 808, para 52/1/4 ff.

The respondents argue that consideration of the Contempt of Court Act 1981, as a whole, shows that it is concerned only with what used to be called 'criminal contempts'. It is undoubtedly true that ss 1 to 13 inclusive relate to this category of contempt, and that there is no express reference anywhere in the Act to the power of the court to make what are now called committal orders, but formerly were called orders of attachment, in respect of disobedience of an order of a court requiring a person to do or to refrain from doing some specified act or acts. The same comment may be made on the remaining sections, other than s 14, which they submit is ambiguous.

This argument gains some support from the cross-heading in the Act under which s 14 comes. This reads 'Penalties for contempt and kindred offences'. There is authority for the proposition that the power to commit for breach of an order of a court is not a penalty, strictly so-called, and that failure to obey such an order is not properly described as an offence. In *Martin v Bannister* (1879) 4 QBD 491 a very strong Court of Appeal (Bramwell, Brett and Cotton LJJ) affirmed the opinion of an equally strong Divisional Court (Kelly CB and Pollock B) (4 QBD 212) that attachment for disobedience to an order of a county court in the nature of an injunction was a 'remedy' and not a 'penalty'. Bramwell LJ said (at 492):

> 'It is said an attachment is not part of the remedy given by the Court, but a punishment inflicted for disobedience to an injunction, but that is not really so; it is part of the remedy, which consists of an injunction and consequent attachment. The remedy is, in fact, an injunction enforceable by attachment.'

Brett LJ said (at 493) that attachment was 'part of the redress'. (The distinction between attachment and committal, as a matter of nomenclature, has now been dropped in favour of committal.) As recently as 1972, this court, in *Jennison v Baker* [1972] 1 All ER 997, [1972] 2 QB 52, indorsed the views expressed in *Martin v Bannister*.

On the other hand, s 14 of the 1981 Act refers to 'contempt of court' without any qualification, except with reference to the former extent of the power to commit. The section expressly refers to cases where no limitation previously applied to the period of committal.

The only cases in which the county court formerly had the power to commit for an unlimited period were cases of disobedience to its orders. All its other powers to commit are limited by express statutory provision.

There is considerable force in the submissions of both sides on this point, and they raise important issues which go far beyond the question of the jurisdiction of the county court. Since it is possible, in my judgment, to dispose of these appeals on the respondents' alternative and much narrower submission, I prefer to reserve my opinion on the wider question until it is necessary to decide it.

This narrower submission turns on the construction of s 14 in the light of s 19. The first question is whether the county court is an 'inferior court'. In view of s 19, the answer must be in the affirmative unless the county court, for the purposes of cases such as these, is a 'superior court' within the definition of that phrase in the section. It is not necessary to consider any of the other characteristics of inferior courts for present purposes.

The definition of a superior court has been set out at the beginning of this judgment. The question then resolves itself into whether the county court in these cases is 'any other court exercising in relation to its proceedings powers equivalent to those of the High Court'. This language, whatever it means, contains an unmistakable echo of the provisions now contained in s 74 of the County Courts Act 1959, as amended. Section 74 reads:

> '(1) Every county court, as regards any cause of action for the time being within its jurisdiction, shall—(a) grant such relief, redress or remedy or combination of remedies, either absolute or conditional; and (b) give such and the like effect to every ground of defence or counterclaim equitable or legal (subject to the provisions of section sixty-five of this Act); as ought to be granted or given in the like case by the High Court and in as full and ample a manner.
>
> (2) For the purposes of this section it shall be assumed (notwithstanding any enactment to the contrary) that any proceedings which can be commenced in a county court could be commenced in the High Court.'

This section is the lineal descendant of s 202 of the Supreme Court of Judicature (Consolidation) Act 1925, and s 89 of the Supreme Court of Judicature Act 1873. It was from s 89 that this court in *Martin v Bannister* derived the power of the county court to grant injunctions and enforce them by attachment (now committal) (see 4 QBD 212 at 213, 216). In other words, in relation to its proceedings the county court exercises powers equivalent to those of the High Court with regard to granting and enforcing injunctions. It is to be regretted that the 1981 Act does not deal in explicit terms with the jurisdiction of the county court, the court by which most of the committal orders for contempt are made.

In my judgment, it is unnecessary to consider the precise terms of the Domestic Violence and Matrimonial Proceedings Act 1976, which does give the county court in one respect (where the parties are not married) possibly wider powers than the High Court, because s 74(2) of the County Courts Act 1959, which was added by the Administration of Justice Act 1969, covers the point.

Accordingly I agree with the reasoning of Judge McDonnell, and hold that these appeals should be dismissed.

BOOTH J. In these two cases each appellant appeals against a committal order made in the Lambeth County Court in respect of his breach of an order made under the Domestic Violence and Matrimonial Proceedings Act 1976. In *Whitter v Peters* his Honour Judge McDonnell committed the appellant to a term of four months' imprisonment for breach of an undertaking by him not to assault or molest the respondent and to leave the house in which they had lived together and not thereafter return. In *Peart v Stewart* the appellant was committed to prison for six months for breach of an injunction made against him in similar terms, that is not to assault the respondent or return to her home. On behalf of each appellant it is argued that, since the Contempt of Court Act 1981 came into force on 27 August 1981, the county court, being an inferior court, does not have the power to commit for contempt of court for a term exceeding one month. So each appeal raises the same point of law as to the construction of s 14 of the 1981 Act and it is to that point of law only that this hearing has been confined.

Before considering the provisions of the 1981 Act I think it is helpful to consider the power of the county court to commit for what is now generally termed contempt of court. The phrase 'contempt of court' has come to be used in two quite separate contexts. On the one hand it can mean behaviour which tends to obstruct the administration of justice, and on the other it means a refusal to obey an order of the court. But Parliament has always drawn a distinction between the power of the county court to enforce obedience to its orders and its power to commit for contempt in the face of the court or what was frequently called 'criminal contempt'.

From the statutory inception of the county courts by the Small Debts Act 1846 (better known as the County Courts Act 1846), the county court has been empowered to commit or to fine a person for contempt of court, although limits have been imposed as to the length of the sentence or the amount of the fine. The power originally contained in s 113 of the 1846 Act has been re-enacted in each succeeding County Courts Act and is now contained in s 157 of the County Courts Act 1959. This power to commit for contempt is exercisable if any person (a) wilfully insults the judge of a county court, or any juror or witness, or any officer of the court during his sitting or attendance in court, or in going to or returning from the court, or (b) wilfully interrupts the proceedings of a county court or otherwise misbehaves in court. Thus the jurisdiction under this section is confined to contempt committed in court or in its immediate vicinity and it has no application to the power of the court to commit for breaches of injunction or other orders. The section further provides that following on such an offence the judge may, if he thinks fit, (i) make an order committing the offender for a specified period not exceeding one month or (ii) impose on the offender a fine not exceeding £20 for every offence.

The power of the county court to enforce obedience to its orders comes from a quite different statutory source. It was originally contained in the Supreme Court of Judicature Act 1873, s 89, which was subsequently re-enacted in the Supreme Court of Judicature (Consolidation) Act 1925, s 202 and is now contained in s 74 of the County Courts Act 1959. Section 74(1), as amended, provides:

'Every county court, as regards any cause of action for the time being within its jurisdiction, shall—(a) grant such relief, redress or remedy or combination of remedies, either absolute or conditional; and (b) give such and the like effect to every ground of defence or counterclaim equitable or legal (subject to the provision of section sixty-five of this Act); as ought to be granted or given in the like case by the High Court and in as full and ample a manner.'

The power of the county court to commit under this section and its predecessors has long been seen as a remedy or redress given in order to enforce its orders, in contrast to the punishment or penalty that could be imposed under what is now s 157 of the 1959 Act. This was the view of the Court of Appeal, upholding the Divisional Court, in *Martin v Bannister* (1879) 4 QBD 491. Bramwell LJ said (at 492):

'As to attachment, it is only necessary to shew that an injunction may be granted, to prove that an attachment may also be granted. It is said an attachment is not part of the remedy given by the Court, but a punishment inflicted for disobedience to an injunction, but that is not really so; it is part of the remedy, which consists of an injunction and consequent attachment. The remedy is, in fact, an injunction enforceable by attachment.'

That view of the purpose and nature of the order for committal under this section was again applied by the Court of Appeal as recently as 1972 in *Jennison v Baker* [1972] 1 All ER 997, [1972] 2 QB 52. In *Pryor v City Offices Co* (1883) 10 QBD 504 at 509 Bowen LJ expressed the view that the object of the power was to clothe the inferior courts with the same power of doing effectual justice by their judgments and orders as the High Court and that it was intended that these judgments or orders should not be limited and ineffectual, but there should be a complete power of affording relief by them. In *Jennison v Baker* the Court of Appeal held that a county court judge, having jurisdiction to grant a remedy as 'full and ample' as a remedy granted by the High Court, had power to order committal under s 74 of the 1959 Act not only when an injunction was still capable of being obeyed but also when there had been past disobedience to an injunction which no longer subsisted.

Not only is a statutory distinction drawn between the power of the county court to commit for contempt and its power to enforce obedience to its orders, but the necessary procedures are also distinguished under the County Court Rules. The procedure for enforcement of orders by committal is presently governed by CCR 1936 Ord 25, r 67. Until as recently as March 1979 the process was by way of a warrant of attachment, but since that time, and in line with proceedings in the High Court, attachment has been abolished as a remedy and enforcement is now by way of a warrant of committal. The form of the order prescribed for use in such circumstances is one specifically designed for 'committal for breach or neglect to obey an order'. The procedure which governs committal for contempt of court is contained in CCR 1936 Ord 34, r 7, and that rule specifically relates to offences committed under s 157 of the 1959 Act. The form of the order which is required to be used is headed 'An order of commitment for insult or misbehaviour'.

I turn now to the Contempt of Court Act 1981. Section 14(1), which is the linchpin of the appellants' argument, provides:

'In any case where a court has power to commit a person to prison for contempt of court and (apart from this provision) no limitation applies to the period of committal, the committal shall (without prejudice to the power of the court to order his earlier discharge) be for a fixed term, and that term shall not on any occasion exceed two years in the case of committal by a superior court, or one month in the case of committal by an inferior court.'

It is argued that the county court is an inferior court within the meaning of the section and that since the Act draws no distinction between the power to commit for contempt in the face of the court and the power to commit for disobedience of its orders, the limitation on the period of committal must apply in each case.

A superior court for the purposes of the 1981 Act is defined in s 19 as meaning—

'the Court of Appeal, the High Court, the Crown Court, the Courts-Martial Appeal Court, the Restrictive Practices Court, the Employment Appeal Tribunal and any other court exercising in relation to its proceedings powers equivalent to those of the High Court, and includes the House of Lords in the exercise of its appellate jurisdiction.'

The county court is not included among those courts designated as being superior courts and I have no doubt that for the purposes of this statute it is an 'inferior court'. If there were any doubt about it regard need only be had to s 14(2) which restricts the power of an inferior court to fine a person for contempt of court to a limit of £500 thus necessitating the amendment, by Part III of Sch 2 to the 1981 Act, of a number of sections of the County Courts Act 1959, including s 157.

The term 'contempt of court' is not defined in the 1981 Act. But it is contended on behalf of the respondents that s 14 of the Act was never intended by Parliament to have any application to the power of the county court to commit for disobedience to its orders. A number of facts support that argument. Sections 1 to 13 contain provisions which relate to conduct which might tend to interfere with the course of justice, such conduct including, by way of example, publication of material which may impede or prejudice the course of justice, breaches of the confidentiality of a jury's deliberations and the use in court of tape recorders. All these matters fall within the category of contempt formerly described as 'criminal contempt'. Further force is given to this contention by the sub-heading which precedes s 14 and which reads, 'Penalties for contempt and kindred offences', and by s 14(2) to which I have already referred and which necessitated a consequential amendment to s 157 of the County Courts Act 1959.

These are powerful factors to support the respondents' arguments that s 14(1) of the 1981 Act does not apply to limit the power of the county court to enforce its orders by way of committal but is confined in its effect to committals under s 157 of the County Courts Act 1959, despite the fact that the term 'contempt of court' is not limited by definition in the 1981 Act. But for the purposes of these appeals I do not think it is necessary to determine that matter since, in my judgment, these are cases which fall fairly and squarely within s 74 of the 1959 Act.

There is nothing in s 14 of the 1981 Act, nor indeed in the whole statute, which derogates in any way from the power bestowed on the county court by s 74 of the 1959 Act to grant such relief, redress or remedy as ought to be granted or given in the like case by the High Court. In both the cases before us the committal orders were made under s 74 by way of enforcement of county court orders. Thus the county court was exercising its power to grant to the respondents the same redress or remedy as the High Court could grant them. If s 14 of the 1981 Act applies to such committal orders it follows from the provisions of that section itself that the terms of imprisonment imposed in these cases were within the jurisdiction of the High Court and, therefore, under the provisions of s 74 of the 1959 Act, were within the jurisdiction of the county court. In my judgment that is sufficient to determine that in law these committal orders were valid and that these appeals should be dismissed.

Like Ormrod LJ, I do not think it is necessary to consider the further arguments submitted on behalf of the respondents that the county court in exercising its jurisdiction under the Domestic Violence and Matrimonial Proceedings Act 1976 is exercising powers equivalent to those of the High Court so that it may be considered to be a superior court within the meaning of s 19 of the 1981 Act.

For these reasons, therefore, I agree that these appeals should be dismissed.

Appeals dismissed. Leave to appeal to the House of Lords refused.

9 March. The Appeal Committee of the House of Lords granted the appellant Stewart leave to appeal.

Solicitors: *Ronald Fletcher, Baker & Co* (for both appellants); *Michael Cohen, Adams & Co* (for the respondent in the first case); *Harveys*, Lewisham (for the respondent in the second case).

Patricia Hargrove   Barrister.

Re Sutton Common, Wimborne

CHANCERY DIVISION
WALTON J
10, 19 NOVEMBER 1981

Commons – Registration – Disputed claims – Confirmation of registration by commissioner – No objection by owner of land to registration – Evidence before commissioner that land not common land – Owner seeking to adduce further evidence that land not common land – Commissioner refusing to hear evidence from owner and confirming registration without calling on person making registration to prove case despite evidence before him – Whether commissioner entitled to confirm registration – Whether commissioner ought to have required person making registration to prove his case – Whether commissioner ought to have taken into account evidence before him and to have heard evidence from owner before confirming registration – Commons Registration Act 1965, ss 5(6), 6(1).

In January 1969, following an application by the respondent on behalf of the Ramblers' Association, some 74 acres of land were provisionally registered, pursuant to s 4[a] of the Commons Registration Act 1965, as common land in the register of common land maintained by a local authority. The land was not in unitary ownership and different parts were owned by different landowners, T Ltd being one such owner. In July 1969 certain rights claimed by B over T Ltd's land were also registered. Two other landowners lodged objections to the registration of their part of the land as common land but T Ltd did not make any such objection and merely objected to the registration of B's rights over its land. The objections were not withdrawn and 'the matter', ie the validity of the registrations made by the respondent and B, was referred to a commons commissioner, under s 5(6)[b] of the 1965 Act. In the course of the hearing before the commissioner B's alleged rights over T Ltd's land were found to be non-existent. That left for the commissioner's consideration the question of the validity of the registration of the 74 acres as common land on the only basis available, namely that it was waste land of a manor. Having heard evidence relating to the objections by the two landowners to the registration of their land, the commissioner refused to confirm that registration. T Ltd then applied to the commissioner for the registration of its land as common land not to be confirmed, but the commissioner refused to entertain the application on the ground that, because the only formal objection made by T Ltd had been to the registration of B's rights, T Ltd was not a party entitled to be heard under the Commons Commissioners Regulations 1971 on the question of the validity of the registration of the 74 acres as common land. The commissioner, pursuant to s 6(1)[c] of the 1965 Act, confirmed the registration but without calling on the respondent to prove her case in relation to T Ltd's land, and without taking into account evidence that was before him which cast grave doubts on whether T Ltd's land was waste land of a manor and without allowing T Ltd to adduce evidence to support that doubt. T Ltd appealed, contending that the commissioner ought to have required the respondent to prove her case before making the confirmation and ought to have taken into account the evidence before him and to have allowed T Ltd to adduce relevant evidence. The respondent submitted that where the provisional registration was not challenged by a specific objection the commissioner could properly exercise his discretion to confirm a registration without calling on the person making the registration to prove his case even though there was evidence before him against confirmation.

Held – Where the validity of a provisional registration of land as common land was

---

a   Section 4, so far as material, is set out at p 378 *g* to p 379 *b*, post
b   Section 5(6) is set out at p 379 *h*, post
c   Section 6(1) is set out at p 380 *b c*, post

referred to a commons commissioner under s 5(6) of the 1965 Act, the person who made the registration had to prove to the satisfaction of the commissioner that the registration was valid. Therefore, even if no objection was made under the 1965 Act to the registration of a part of the land provisionally registered, the person making the registration nevertheless had to establish that registration of that part was valid and should be confirmed, and in deciding whether the person making the registration had discharged that burden of proof the commissioner was required to take into account any relevant evidence which was already before him or which was sought to be adduced, even if that involved hearing a person who had no right under the 1971 regulations to be heard. Since there was evidence before the commissioner that T Ltd's land might not be waste land of a manor, the commissioner ought, as a matter of law, to have required the respondent to prove her case in regard to the registration of T Ltd's land and ought to have heard and taken into account any relevant evidence, and in failing to do so he had erred in law. In all the circumstances the case would be remitted to the commissioner with a direction to hear and determine the validity of the registration so far as it affected T Ltd's land (see p 383 *f* and *j* to p 384 *d* and *g* to p 385 *b* and *d* to *f*, post).

Notes
For referral of the registration of common land to a commons commissioner, see 6 Halsbury's Laws (4th edn) para 673, and for the hearing before the commissioner, see ibid paras 695–696.

For the Commons Registration Act 1965, ss 4, 5, 6, see 3 Halsbury's Statutes (3rd edn) 922, 923, 924.

Cases referred to in judgment
Box Parish Council v Lacey [1979] 1 All ER 113, [1980] Ch 109, [1979] 2 WLR 177, CA, Digest (Cont Vol E) 81, 366a.
Central Electricity Generating Board v Clwyd CC [1976] 1 All ER 251, [1976] 1 WLR 151, Digest (Cont Vol E) 83, 1101a.
Cock Moor, Brompton by Sawdon, North Yorkshire (No 2), Re (21 June 1977, unreported), Chief Commons Commissioner.
Incleborough Mill and other Commons at Runton, Norfolk, Re (23 February 1977, unreported) Commons Commissioner.
Walton Heath, Surrey, Re (11 November 1977, unreported) Commons Commissioner.

Case also cited
Beck v Value Capital Ltd [1976] 2 All ER 102, [1976] 1 WLR 572, CA.

Case stated
By a case stated, at the request of Robert Thorne Ltd (Thorne), on 27 July 1981 by L J Morris Smith Esq, a commons commissioner, as amended by agreement between the parties, the point of law for the court's decision was whether the commissioner (i) was right in law in confirming the registration of land belonging to Thorne forming part of a unit of land (unit CL 141) registered as common land by the respondents, Ruth Colyer and the Ramblers' Association, without requiring the respondents to prove their case, and (ii) was right in law in refusing to admit evidence from Thorne in relation to the status of unit CL 141 as waste land of a manor in the circumstance that there was sufficient material evidence before the commissioner to cast grave doubts on the validity of the registration of Thorne's land. By notice of motion dated 13 August 1981 Thorne sought the following relief: (i) determination of the question of law raised in the case stated; (ii) an order refusing to confirm the registration in the land section of the register of common land under register unit CL 141 of that part of the land owned by Thorne; (iii) an order directing Dorset County Council as registration authority to delete from the land section of the register that part of the land which was owned by Thorne; and (iv) alternatively, an order that there should be a rehearing by the commissioner of the

respondents' claim that the provisional registration of Thorne's land as common land be confirmed. The facts are set out in the judgment.

Sheila Cameron for Thorne
Vivian Chapman for the respondents.

Cur adv vult

19 November. **WALTON J** read the following judgment: In this matter it will be convenient if I first of all call attention to some of the provisions of the Commons Registration Act 1965. The purpose of this Act was, as expressed in its long title, basically to provide for the registration of common land and of town or village greens. It first of all provided for such registration in s 1:

'(1) There shall be registered, in accordance with the provisions of this Act and subject to the exceptions mentioned therein—(a) land in England or Wales which is common land or a town or village green; (b) rights of common over such land; and (c) persons claiming to be or found to be owners of such land or becoming the owners thereof by virtue of this Act; and no rights of common over land which is capable of being registered under this Act shall be registered under the Land Registration Acts 1925 and 1936.
(2) After the end of such period, not being less than three years from the commencement of this Act, as the Minister may by order determine—(a) no land capable of being registered under this Act shall be deemed to be common land or a town or village green unless it is so registered; and (b) no rights of common shall be exercisable over any such land unless they are registered either under this Act or under the Land Registration Acts 1925 and 1936.'

Section 2 deals with registration authorities and is of no present moment. Section 3 deals with the registers:

'(1) For the purpose of registering such land as is mentioned in section 1(1) of this Act and rights of common over and ownership of such land every registration authority shall maintain—(a) a register of common land; and (b) a register of town or village greens; and regulations under this Act may require or authorise a registration authority to note on those registers such other information as may be prescribed.'

Section 4 deals with initial, and hence provisional, registrations:

'(1) Subject to the provisions of this section, a registration authority shall register any land as common land or a town or village green or, as the case may be, any rights of common over or ownership of such land, on application duly made to it and accompanied by such declaration and such other documents (if any) as may be prescribed for the purpose of verification or of proving compliance with any prescribed conditions.'

Pausing at the end of this subsection, it is quite clear that the onus of establishing the validity of the registration is thus fairly placed, as obviously it would have to be placed, on the person making the registration. It would have been a gross departure from all civilised law if the onus had, either at that or at any other stage, been a negative one placed on the owner of the land to establish that the rights claimed were not in fact properly claimed. The section continues:

'(2) An application for the registration of any land as common land or as a town or village green may be made by any person, and a registration authority—(a) may so register any land notwithstanding that no application for that registration has been made, and (b) shall so register any land in any case where it registers any rights over it under this section . . .

(5) A registration under this section shall be provisional only until it has become final under the following provisions of this Act.

(6) An application for registration under this section shall not be entertained if made after such date, not less than three years from the commencement of this Act, as the Minister may by order specify; and different dates may be so specified for different classes of applications.

(7) Every local authority shall take such steps as may be prescribed for informing the public of the period within which and the manner in which applications for registration under this section may be made.'

I have no doubt but that this obligation on local authorities was duly complied with, and, in the nature of things, such publicity has brought forth a crop of claims which are entirely without merit, and some of these, as is well known and recognised, because of the subsequent provisions of the Act have by now become final and therefore indisputable. It was never, I am persuaded, the intention of Parliament to facilitate the establishment of entirely bogus claims in this way, Parliament having doubtless counted on the fact of landowners' self interest being sufficient to ensure that all such claims were in due time objected to, but it is notorious that, whatever the intentions of Parliament, the matter has not worked out in that way.

Section 5 deals with notification of, and objections to, registration:

'(1) A registration authority shall give such notices and take such other steps as may be prescribed for informing the public of any registration made by it under section 4 of this Act, of the times and places where copies of the relevant entries in the register may be inspected and of the period during which and the manner in which objections to the registration may be made to the authority.'

Once again, I am sure that these obligations were duly complied with, but, for whatever reason, they do not in the event appear to have been as successful in alerting landowners to the registrations made against their land as they were in alerting would-be busybodies that they were able at their hearts' content to register anything they pleased against any portion of land they pleased. The section continues:

'(2) The period during which objections to any registration under section 4 of this Act may be made shall be such period, ending not less than two years after the date of the registration, as may be prescribed.'

Again, I am certain that Parliament, in granting such a long period of time, was anxious that all proper objections should be taken, and for that reason did not proscribe, nor did the regulations proscribe, any extension of the period. Then, sub-ss (4) and (6) provide:

'(4) Where an objection to a registration under section 4 of this Act is made, the registration authority shall note the objection on the register and shall give such notice as may be prescribed to the person (if any) on whose application the registration was made and to any person whose application is noted under section 4(4) of this Act . . .

(6) Where such an objection is made, then, unless the objection is withdrawn or the registration cancelled before the end of such period as may be prescribed, the registration authority shall refer the matter to a Commons Commissioner.'

This subsection is in many ways the crux of the system of referrals to the Commons Commissioners; for present purposes it is sufficient to note that what is referred to a commissioner is not the dispute arising from the making of any objection but 'the matter', that is to say the validity of the registration which has been put into question by the objection.

Thus the commissioner is inquiring, de novo, into whether the registration as a whole should or should not be confirmed, and there can be no presumption of any description that the registration has been proper, or that any part thereof has been proper: it is this into which the commissioner is inquiring: see per Goff J in *Central Electricity Generating Board v Clwyd CC* [1976] 1 All ER 251 at 256, [1976] 1 WLR 151 at 157.

'(7) An objection to the registration of any land as common land or as a town or village green shall be treated for the purpose of this Act as being also an objection to any registration (whenever made) under section 4 of this Act of any rights over the land.'

This, of course, is obvious; objection to the registration of the land must ipso facto question the existence of any rights over it.

Section 6 deals with the disposal of disputed claims:

'(1) The Commons Commissioner to whom any matter has been referred under section 5 of this Act shall inquire into it and shall either confirm the registration, with or without modification, or refuse to confirm it; and the registration shall, if it is confirmed, become final, and, if the confirmation is refused, become void—(a) if no appeal is brought against the confirmation or refusal, at the end of the period during which such an appeal could have been brought; (b) if such an appeal is brought, when it is finally disposed of.
(2) On being informed in the prescribed manner that a registration has become final (with or without modifications) or has become void a registration authority shall indicate that fact in the prescribed manner in the register and, if it has become void, cancel the registration.'

Section 7 then provides for the finality of undisputed registration, and it is as the result of this section, wholly unintended, I am persuaded, by Parliament, that numerous bogus registrations have attained a legitimacy which they do not in the slightest deserve:

'(1) If no objection is made to a registration under section 4 of this Act or if all objections made to such a registration are withdrawn the registration shall become final at the end of the period during which such objections could have been made under section 5 of this Act or, if an objection made during that period is withdrawn after the end thereof, at the date of the withdrawal.
(2) Where by virtue of this section a registration has become final the registration authority shall indicate that fact in the prescribed manner in the register.'

I can now pass to s 10:

'The registration under this Act of any land as common land or as a town or village green, or of any rights of common over any such land, shall be conclusive evidence of the matters registered, as at the date of registration, except where the registration is provisional only.'

Section 18(1) deals with an appeal from a decision of a commissioner: this is, as is usual, restricted to an appeal on a question of law. Section 19 deals with the power of the minister to make regulations. Finally, for present purposes, s 22(1) defines 'common land' as follows:

'In this Act, unless the context otherwise requires,—"common land" means—(a) land subject to rights of common (as defined in this Act) whether those rights are exercisable at all times or only during limited periods; (b) waste land of a manor not subject to rights of common; but does not include a town or village green or any land which forms part of a highway.'

Now what happened in the present case is that the tract of land called Enclosure 225 Sutton Common, Wimborne, Dorset, was registered as entry 1/1 in the lands section of register unit CL 141 in the register of common land maintained by the Dorset County Council on 1 January 1969 pursuant to an application made on 1 November 1968 by Mrs Ruth Colyer, the first respondent to the motion herein, on behalf of the Ramblers' Association, Wessex area. It is convenient to notice here that a small part of the area was in any event included by mistake: it formed part of the garden of a house belonging to the Misses Jackson. And, as the result of an objection made by them, and accepted by

Mrs Colyer, an amendment was made to the registration of CL 141 by excluding such land therefrom. This reduced the area from 74·5 acres to 74·3 acres.

In point of fact, however, even after excluding the land of the Misses Jackson, it appears now that the remaining 74·3 acres of land was not in unitary ownership. The crucial importance of this fact will become clear later.

On 22 July 1969 a Mr T H Butler made an application to be registered in the rights section of the register applicable to CL 141 in respect of various rights of grazing, turbary, and estovers over part of the land therein comprised. The provisional entry in the register was duly made on 13 August 1969.

I now turn to the objections made. Two were made in respect of entry 1 in the land section, by the Medlycott Trust and the tenth Earl of Shaftesbury respectively. And there was a further objection made by the appellants in this matter, Robert Thorne Ltd, in respect of Mr Butler's entry in the rights section. This objection was dated 11 September 1970; it was noted on the register on 24 August 1972. The grounds of objection were simply that as freehold owners of part of the property they said that no such rights existed, and that none of them had been exercised during their ownership and occupation of the land.

Of course, from their own point of view, it was highly unfortunate that Robert Thorne Ltd did not also object to the registration in the land section. But it is quite clear that their notice of objection was compiled without the benefit of legal advice, and they may well have thought that by objecting to the only adverse right over the land which appeared to be being claimed they would have, if successful, put paid to all forms of registration.

The objections not being withdrawn, the matter was in due course referred to Mr L J Morris Smith, one of the Commons Commissioners. The claim of Mr Butler disappeared in the course of the hearing in a puff of smoke. There were left for considering the remaining 'matter', which was, of course, whether the registration of CL 141 should be confirmed in the land section, on the basis, there was obviously none other available once Mr Butler's rights disappeared, that the land was waste land of a manor. So at this stage it would have appeared that the correct course for the commissioner to take would have been to have called on Mrs Colyer, who appeared on behalf of the Ramblers' Association, to demonstrate (i) what was the manor in question and (ii) what lands comprised waste of that manor. I need not enter into the question, which may be a difficult one to answer, whether the correct date for ascertainment was at the date of registration or the date of the hearing. For present purposes it matters not which. But the course that the commissioner took was to deal with the matter piecemeal, just as if what was before him was not 'the matter', ie the registration of CL 141 as a whole, but simply two quite separate disputes, namely one between the Medlycott Trust and the Ramblers' Association, and one between the Earl of Shaftesbury and the Ramblers' Association. This appears to me to have been altogether a wrong approach.

Counsel who appeared for the respondents in this matter before me, accepted that, pursuant to s 5(6) of the Act, what was referred to the commissioner was indeed 'the matter', that is to say the validity or invalidity of the registration as a whole, but sought to urge on me that the commissioner had a discretion whether or not to proceed to consider the validity of the registration in so far as it was not directly challenged by the objections specifically made. And in the present case, he submitted, the commissioner had considered the matter, and in the exercise of his discretion come to the conclusion that he should not look further into the status of those other portions of the unit CL 141.

What the commissioner said in his decision on this particular point is as follows:

'Mr Harrington sought on behalf of Thorne to attack the entry in the Land Section. It appears that in 1951 Thorne purchased from the Shaftesbury Estates Company that part of the Register Unit which is not the subject of Lord Shaftesbury's (provisionally) registered ownership ie. the part not edged red on the Register Map, which I will refer to as "the Thorne part". Thorne's Objection No. 324 was an objection only to the Rights, and did not take effect as an objection to the entry in the Land Section and accordingly Thorne was not a party entitled under Reg. 19(1) of the Commons Commissioners Regulations 1971 (S.I. 1971 No. 1727) to be heard on the disputes as to the registration of the land. What were referred to me in relation to the Land Section were the three disputes occasioned by Objections Nos. 18. 366 and 1069, which were not disputes in relation to the Thorne part. Mr Harrington submitted that there was jurisdiction to deal with the Entry in the land section because by virtue of the three objections, the matter before me comprised the Entry as a whole. This may be right, but having regard to the form of the references (which are as prescribed by the Regulations) I am not convinced that it is so: if it is, it still remains the fact that Thorne is not entitled to be heard. Quite apart from these considerations, and assuming I have jurisdiction, it would in my view be wrong to consider an objection of which parties entitled to be heard would have had no notice. For these reasons I reject the application by Thorne that I should consider an application to deal with a contention that the Thorne part is not common land.'

In the case stated which is before me the commissioner again said:

'6. At the hearing the Solicitor appearing for Thorne sought to attack the registration in the Land Section in regard to a part of the land ("the Thorne part") which was not the subject of the disputes occasioned by the Land Objections. Thorne had not made an Objection to the registration in the Land Section and, for the reasons given in the penultimate paragraph on page 3 of my decision, I refused the application to deal with the registration of the Thorne part.

7. The written request of Thorne's Solicitors dated 15 June 1981 for a case to be stated refers to the point of law involved as "whether the Commissioner erred in holding that he had no jurisdiction to give a decision relating to the registration in the Land Section in the absence of an Objection to registration in the land section notwithstanding that he refused to confirm the registration in the rights section upon which the registration in the Land Section was based".

8. It should be observed that the registration in the Land Section was made on 14 January 1969 in consequence of the application dated 1 November 1968 of Mrs R Colyer and not in consequence of the registration in the Rights Section for which the application was made on 22 July 1969.'

I shall have something to say about the point of law as so formulated later. Paragraph 8 appears factually correct, but in my judgment not ad rem.

Counsel for the appellants, on the other hand, submitted that this was not really a matter of discretion in the commissioner; it was primarily a matter of the commissioner requiring Mrs Colyer to prove her case. The commissioner had correctly done so in relation to the other two portions of land to which the objections were specifically directed, and he should also have done so in relation to the third portion, since he was inquiring into 'the matter' and not merely the two objections. True it was that under the regulations Thorne had no *right* to be heard, but, the proceedings before the commissioner not being a mere lis inter partes, he would, in the circumstances of the present case, have been failing in his duty if he had failed to invite Thorne's representative to address him and adduce any relevant evidence. Alternatively, if the matter was a matter of discretion, then on the facts of the present case, where (as will appear hereafter) the commissioner had material staring him in the face which clearly showed that there was something far wrong with the registration, there was only one way in which the discretion could properly be exercised.

This case therefore raises fairly and squarely the problem, when faced with such a situation, that is to say a situation where 'the matter', being the registration of the land in the land section, or of rights in the rights section, or both, is before him, but, on the one hand, there is no specific objection which has been made to the registration of certain parts of the land or certain of the rights, and on the other there are facts, or likely facts, which have been brought to his attention, or there is somebody before him who wishes to tender relevant facts, which, if established, would invalidate the relevant registration in whole or in part, what course ought the commissioner properly to take? It is apparent from the copies of three unreported decisions of different commissioners with which I was most helpfully supplied by counsel for the appellants, *Re Incleborough Mill and other Commons at Runton, Norfolk* (Commissioner C A Settle, 23 February 1977), *Re Cock Moor, Brompton by Sawdon, North Yorkshire (No 2)* (Chief Commons Commissioner G D Squibb, 21 June 1977) and *Re Walton Heath, Surrey* (Commissioner A A Baden Fuller, 11 November 1977), that there is no uniformity of approach in this matter. Thus the Chief Commons Commissioner was led to confirm the registration of three entries in the rights section which referred to 'The right to shoot game' when he was well aware, as his decision showed, that such a right cannot be a right of common. Similarly, Commissioner Baden Fuller, whilst acknowledging that—

> 'The exercise of these discretions may sometimes benefit persons who have failed within due time to make any objection relating to the matter with which they are particularly concerned, and I can think of many cases in which such persons have by actual decisions of mine so benefited'

refused to enter into the question of the validity of the rights section entries as a matter of discretion, although he had before him persons wishing to tender evidence which if established strongly suggested that such rights did not, in fact, exist.

Commissioner Settle however took a totally different view. He said:

> 'For my part the view which I take is that Sections 5 and 6 of the Act must be read together and that the matter which is referred to a Commissioner is the provisional registration for his decision as to whether to confirm it with or without modification or alternatively refuse to confirm it'

and he also said:

> 'Whilst my experience has disclosed numerous entries in registers which have become final by reason of their being undisputed, the Act cannot have intended a Commissioner when dealing with a provisional registration to confirm a registration which ought not to have been made.'

Now it appears to me that basically the matter is a very simple one. Throughout, it appears to me that the onus of proving his case is on the person making the registration, once that registration requires confirmation by a commissioner. He must be prepared to establish his case. Of course, in many situations extremely little in the way of proof will be required. To take an example used at the hearing in this case, if there is a large area of land which is registered as a common, and an objection is taken as to a small piece on the fringes of the land, which happens to be somebody's back garden, then although the objection of that person theoretically puts in question the status of the whole of the area, provided that nothing else arises to case the slightest doubt on the status of the remainder of the land, the commissioner will, I think, be fully entitled to rely on the original statutory declarations made by the registrant pursuant to reg 8(1) of the Commons Registration (General) Regulations 1966, SI 1966/1471, as discharging the necessary burden of proof.

I do not, of course, intend to lay down any general rules as to how the burden of proof is to be satisfied in any case where the matter is not so simple. That must depend on precisely how the matter presents itself to the commissioner in any particular set of circumstances, which may, of course, vary almost infinitely. But if it is borne in on the commissioner, as the result of information which is either before him or which is sought to be placed before him and which, if correct, is relevant, that the registration is questionable, then he should, in my view, insist that the burden of proof is properly discharged to his satisfaction so as to establish (if possible) that the registration has, in fact, been properly made.

I fully appreciate that this will mean in many cases (indeed it entails in the present case) that a person who has no entitlement to be heard under the provisions of the Commons Commissioners Regulations 1971, SI 1971/1727, will have to be heard. This does not seem to me objectionable in the slightest. In matters of this nature, if a general right to be heard had been conferred on the whole world, then I doubt if a single case would ever yet have come to an end. There being no general right to be heard, the commissioner has the fullest power to ensure that only relevant evidence is placed before him; but that he should not exclude any relevant evidence appears to me to be quite plain, no matter from what quarter that evidence may come.

Thus, in my judgment, the correct course for the Chief Commons Commissioner to have followed in the case already cited would have been to have caused notices to be sent to the persons who had entered unsustainable rights of common in their claims, and to have informed them that he was *not* prepared to confirm them as they stood, but (doubtless) was prepared to confirm them with the appropriate deletions, and that if they did not accept this ruling he would appoint a time and place for them to try to convince him that the rights claimed were capable of being rights of common. Or he might well, on the special facts of that case, have taken the bolder but fully justified course of confirming them as so modified without more ado. Of course, the registration authority should never have effected the registration in that form in the first place.

Now in the present case, once the rights of Mr Butler were out of the way, the only manner in which the registration in the land section would possibly be good was if the land was waste land of a manor: see s 22(1)(b) of the 1965 Act. And, having regard to the decision of the Court of Appeal in *Box Parish Council v Lacey* [1974] 1 All ER 113, [1980] Ch 109, this requires that all the land should, at the date of the registration, be in the ownership of the lord of the manor, that is to say, in unitary ownership. If not in unitary ownership, then the land cannot, as a matter of law, all be waste land of the manor.

Here, the commissioner was faced with the fact that, quite apart from the Misses Jackson, whose land was probably included in error in the first place anyway, and who therefore for present purposes can be left out of the reckoning, there were, or appeared to be, no less than three owners of the land comprised in CL 141: the Earl of Shaftesbury, the Medleycott Trust and Robert Thorne Ltd. Now of course I have not before me in any shape or form that I can take judicial cognisance of the conveyance of 30 July 1951 from the Shaftesbury Estates Co to Robert Thorne Ltd. However, the commissioner himself acknowledged that 'it appeared that in 1951 Thorne purchased from the Shaftesbury Estates Company' so that on the face of matters they themselves did not even purchase from the lord of the manor.

So the commissioner was faced with the fact that, if he would only open his eyes and not deliberately close them to matters which had been forcibly brought home to him already, the registration in question was, as regards a certain portion of the land, that claimed by Thorne, at the least highly questionable. I take the view that, having reached this position, then as a matter of law it was his clear duty to require proper proof from Mrs Colyer, and that he failed as a matter of law in not requiring her to prove her case against Thorne in the same manner that she had been required to prove it against those who had actually objected.

Counsel for the respondent urged on me that the commissioner had two discretions. The first, to confirm the registration without requiring Mrs Colyer to prove her case, and the second, whether or not to admit evidence from Thorne, and that in exercising his discretion under these heads the commissioner had not erred in point of law. I cannot accept that any judicial tribunal, of whatever nature, unless expressly constrained thereto by statute, has any discretion to shut out from its consideration evidence which it is aware is available to be given, and which, if established, would be directly material to the issue in hand, and I think that this situation is underlined by the fact that even where all the persons entitled to be heard at the hearing of a dispute have agreed on the terms of the decision to be given by the commissioner, he is not bound to decide in those terms. He can, of course, do so; he is not bound: see the Commons Commissioners Regulations

1971, reg 31. And the reason is that he may know, or have good grounds to suspect, that the proposed terms are not in accordance with law.

Accordingly, it appears to me that the only course which I can properly adopt is to remit the matter back to the commissioner with a direction to hear and determine the validity of the registration in CL 141 in so far as it affects the land claimed by Robert Thorne Ltd, and to hear evidence and submissions on their behalf as to the ownership of such land, the lordship of the manor in which the same is situate, and the consequential effects thereof on the proposed registration.

Now it will be observed that this conclusion hardly squares with what is, in the case stated, set out as the point of law at issue. Counsel for the respondent did not raise any objection to the real point at issue being debated between the parties, so that it seems to me that I ought to accede to the request of counsel for the appellants to amend the case stated by substituting for the point of law therein set out the following, which are in substance taken from the contentions set out in the appellant's notice of motion herein: whether (i) the commissioner was right in law in confirming the registration of the remainder of unit CL 141 without requiring the respondents to prove their case in relation thereto? (ii) the commissioner was right in law in refusing to admit evidence from the appellants in relation to the status of the unit CL 141 as waste of the manor, in the circumstances that there was sufficient evidence before the commissioner to cast grave doubts on the validity of the registration, and that such evidence was material to the resolution of those doubts? Both of which questions, of course, I would answer in the negative.

The relief sought by the notice of motion herein is as follows. (1) The determination of the question of law; and I have just dealt with that aspect of the matter. (2) An order refusing to confirm the registration in the land section of the register of common land under register unit CL 141 of that part of the land which is owned by the appellant. This I cannot do; there is just not sufficient evidence before me, although it is obvious that unless the appellants are persons who are prepared to put forward a wholly bogus claim, there can be no conceivable doubt as to the answer. (3) An order directing the Dorset County Council as registration authority to delete from the said land section of the register that part of the land which is owned by the appellant. For the same reasons as under (2) above, I cannot give effect to this. (4) Alternatively an order that there shall be a rehearing by the Commons Commissioner of the respondent's claim that the provisional registration of the appellant's land as common land should be confirmed. It is to this part of the relief sought that I have, in substance, acceded.

Order accordingly.

Solicitors: *Withers* (for Thorne); *Paul Clayden*, Henley-on-Thames (for the respondents).

Hazel Hartman   Barrister.

R v Miller

COURT OF APPEAL, CRIMINAL DIVISION
ACKNER, MAY LJJ AND STOCKER J
4 FEBRUARY, 3 MARCH 1982

Criminal law – Damage to property – Arson – Actus reus – Coincidence of actus reus and mens rea – Accused accidentally starting fire – Accused later having opportunity to put out fire – Accused failing to do so – Property damaged as a result – Whether omission of accused to act a sufficient actus reus – Whether coincidence of actus reus and mens rea – Criminal Damage Act 1971, s 1(1)(3).

One night, while squatting in someone else's house, the appellant lit a cigarette and then lay down on a mattress in one of the rooms. He fell asleep before he had finished smoking the cigarette and it dropped onto the mattress. Later he woke up and saw that the mattress was smouldering. He did nothing about it; he merely moved to another room and went to sleep again. The house caught fire. The appellant was rescued and subsequently charged with arson, contrary to s 1(1) and (3)[a] of the Criminal Damage Act 1971. At his trial, he submitted that there was no case to go to the jury because his omission to put out the fire, which he had started accidentally, could not in the circumstances amount to a sufficient actus reus. The judge ruled that once he had discovered the mattress was smouldering the appellant had been under a duty to act. He directed the jury that they must find the appellant guilty if they concluded that by failing to act the appellant had given no thought to the possibility of there being an obvious risk that property would be damaged or that, if he had recognised that there was such a risk, he had still done nothing about it. The appellant was convicted. On appeal,

Held – (1) A mere omission to act did not, by itself, give rise to criminal liability unless a statute specifically so provided or the case was one in which in a criminal context the common law imposed a duty on a person to act in a particular way towards another, such as a parent to his child (see p 392 *d e*, post).

(2) Furthermore, the actus reus and the mens rea normally had to coincide. The conduct of the accused person had, however, to be looked at as a whole, and if as a whole it contained both the actus reus and the mens rea they were sufficiently coincident (see p 392 *d* to *f h*, post).

(3) An unintentional act followed by an intentional or reckless omission to rectify it or its consequences could in certain circumstances amount to an intentional or reckless act, ie where there was on the part of the accused person an element of adoption of what he had unintentionally done earlier by what he deliberately or recklessly failed to do later (see p 392 *j* to p 393 *a*, post); *Commonwealth v Cali* (1923) 247 Mass 20, *Green v Cross* (1910) 103 LT 279 and *Fagan v Metropolitan Police Comr* [1968] 3 All ER 442 considered.

(4) In the circumstances the whole of the appellant's conduct, from the moment he lay down with the lighted cigarette until the time he left the mattress smouldering and moved to another room, had to be regarded as one act, and his failure to extinguish the incipient fire, once he had discovered it, had a substantial element of adoption on his part of what he had unintentionally done earlier. It followed that the judge had been correct to leave the case to the jury. The appeal would accordingly be dismissed (see p 393 *a* to *c*, post).

---

a   Section 1, so far as material, provides:

'(1) A person who without lawful excuse destroys or damages any property belonging to another intending to destroy or damage any such property or being reckless as to whether any such property would be destroyed or damaged shall be guilty of an offence . . .

(3) An offence committed under this section by destroying or damaging property by fire shall be charged as arson.'

Notes

For the offence of destroying or damaging property, see 11 Halsbury's Laws (4th edn) para 1306, and for cases on the subject, see 15 Digest (Reissue) 1439–1440, 12,690–12,693.

For the the Criminal Damage Act 1971, s 1, see 41 Halsbury's Statutes (3rd edn) 409.

Cases referred to in judgment

Commonwealth v Cali (1923) 247 Mass 20.
Fagan v Metropolitan Police Comr [1968] 3 All ER 442, [1969] 1 QB 439, [1968] 3 WLR 1120, DC, 15 Digest (Reissue) 1175, 9992.
Green v Cross (1910) 103 LT 279, 2 Digest (Reissue) 434, 2411.
Powell v Knight (1878) 38 LT 607, 2 Digest (Reissue) 433, 2407.
R v Caldwell [1981] 1 All ER 961, [1981] 2 WLR 509, HL.
R v St George (1840) 9 C & P 483, 173 ER 921, 15 Digest (Reissue) 1180, 10,063.

Application for leave to appeal

On 26 June 1981 in the Crown Court at Leicester before Mr Recorder Matthewman QC and a jury James Miller was convicted of arson, contrary to s 1(1) and (3) of the Criminal Damage Act 1971, and sentenced to six months' imprisonment. He applied to a single judge for leave to appeal against conviction. The judge referred the application to the full court, which granted leave and went on to consider the appeal. The facts are set out in the judgment of the court.

Patrick Thomas (assigned by the Registrar of Criminal Appeals) for the appellant.
David McCarthy (who did not appear below) for the Crown.

Cur adv vult

3 March. **MAY LJ** read the following judgment of the court: On 26 June 1981 in the Crown Court at Leicester the appellant was convicted of arson and sentenced to six months' imprisonment. His application for leave to appeal against conviction was referred to the full court by the single judge. At the outset of the hearing of this case we granted leave to appeal as it seemed to the court that a pure question of law was involved.

The facts of this case were not in dispute. The appellant is a man in his late thirties and a vagrant by nature. Early in August 1980 he began squatting, or 'skipping' as he described it, in an unoccupied house owned by a housing association in Grantham Road, Sparkbrook, in Birmingham. On the evening of 14 August 1980, having certainly taken drink, though not to any extent to be relevant to this case, the appellant returned to his squat, went to one of the first floor rear bedrooms which he was using, lit a cigarette and then lay down on a mattress in that room preparatory to going to sleep. Unfortunately he fell asleep before he had finished smoking the cigarette and, either because he had had it in his hand or it was in his mouth when he fell asleep, it dropped onto the mattress on which he was sleeping and set it alight. Some time later the appellant awoke, saw and realised that the mattress was smouldering but did nothing about it. Indeed, he moved into an adjoining room, leaving the mattress smouldering, and went to sleep in the company of a friend of his who was also occupying the same house. At about 4.15 am on 15 August 1980 a police constable saw that the house was on fire. Damage to the extent of some £800 was caused to it. Both the appellant and his friend had to be woken and rescued from the burning house by the fire brigade. The appellant was taken to the police station and questioned. To begin with he disclaimed any knowledge of the fire or how it started, but after burns had been discovered on his clothing and on his arm, he accepted that the fire had been his fault. He ultimately made a written statement to the police in these terms:

'Last night I went out for a few drinks and at closing time I went back to the house where I have been skipping for a couple of weeks. I went upstairs into the back bedroom where I've been sleeping. I lay on my mattress and lit a cigarette. I must have fell asleep because I woke up to find the mattress on fire. I just got up and went into the next room and went back to sleep. Then the next thing I remember was the police and fire people arriving. I hadn't got anything to put the fire out and so I just left it.'

The indictment charged the appellant with arson contrary to s 1(1) of the Criminal Damage Act 1971. The particulars of the offence alleged that without lawful excuse he had damaged by fire the relevant property, intending to damage it or being reckless whether it would be damaged. Following the decision of the House of Lords on the meaning of 'reckless' in R v Caldwell [1981] 1 All ER 961, [1981] 2 WLR 509, there could be no question that the appellant had been reckless when, with realisation of what the situation was, he failed to put out the fire in the smouldering mattress and merely moved next door to another room. The mens rea for the alleged offence was therefore present and no question has been raised on this either below or before us.

The issue in this case is whether the actual omission of the appellant to act to put out the fire in the mattress was in law a sufficient actus reus to constitute the offence alleged. This appeal therefore raises the question to what extent, if at all, except as specifically provided by statute, an omission to act can sufficiently found criminal liability.

At the close of the case for the Crown, counsel for the appellant submitted that there was no case to go to the jury. He argued that no sufficient actus reus had been proved as, on the admitted facts, the mattress had been set on fire accidentally. A mere omission thereafter to put that fire out could not give rise to criminal liability.

This submission was overruled. In his ruling the learned recorder referred to what he described as the old established doctrine that no one is held criminally responsible in criminal law for the harmful consequences of his omission to act, whether the omission was careless or intentional, unless the prosecution is able to prove that he was under a legal obligation to take action in the particular circumstances in which he was placed. As it is put in Smith and Hogan *Criminal Law* (4th edn, 1978) p 45: 'The question is to determine when the criminal law imposes a duty to act.' Be that as it may, the learned recorder then went on to express the view that the law would and must draw a distinction between the case of persons coming across what is an already existing dangerous situation and doing nothing, when the law would not impose on them a duty to act, and the very different situation of somebody who either accidentally or deliberately was responsible for the dangerous situation and failed to act. He took the view that in the latter case the criminal law would impose on the person involved a duty to take action. He then quoted and relied on the passage to which he had been referred in Professor Glanville Williams's *Textbook of Criminal Law* (1978) pp 143–144.

Having so ruled, the learned recorder summed up by directing the jury that as the defendant had himself originally set fire to the mattress, and when he woke up realised that it was on fire, there was consequently then a duty on him to act to put that fire out. As the summing up then proceeded, it was perhaps not necessary for him to go that far. He directed the jury on the question of recklessness precisely in the words from the speech of Lord Diplock in R v Caldwell [1981] 1 All ER 961 at 967, [1981] 2 WLR 509 at 516, and then left the issue to the jury in this way:

'If you come to the conclusion that by failing to act, his conscious failure to act, he gave no thought to the possibility of there being an obvious risk of damage, or recognising that his failure to act would involve some risk, but still failing to act to put out the mattress fire, then he is guilty. If you are not so sure of these matters, then he is not guilty.'

On this summing up the jury convicted and the appellant was sentenced to six months' imprisonment. He now appeals against his conviction on the grounds that the direction given by the learned recorder to the jury was erroneous in law.

Counsel for the appellant repeated his submission before us that a mere omission to act cannot be a sufficient actus reus for the offence of arson. He continued that one who innocently creates danger to another person or to another person's property is on principle in the same situation as that of a mere bystander who happens by when a situation of danger has developed. Counsel submitted that there must be a criminal act: one cannot adopt an accidental act by doing nothing about it and thus be guilty of crime. In addition he contended that, save in exceptional cases of which this is not one, there must be a coincidence of the appropriate mens rea and the actus reus.

In support of these submissions he referred us to the passages in *Russell on Crime* (12th edn, 1964) vol 1, pp 20, 402, to the relevant passage in Kenny *Outlines of Criminal Law* (19th edn, 1966), which substantially follows the view of Russell, and to *Smith and Hogan* p 45, to which we have already referred.

The only case in any way directly in point in so far as arson is concerned is that of *Commonwealth v Cali* (1923) 247 Mass 20. That was a case in which the defendant, Cali, was convicted of burning a building in Leominster in Massachusetts with intent to injure the insurers of it. At the defendant's trial there was apparently evidence which tended to show that the defendant either started the fire or, after it had got under way, purposely refrained from any attempt to extinguish it. He was duly convicted and appealed. The judgment of the Court of Appeal, delivered by Braley J, ended in this way (at 24–25):

> 'The instructions to the jury that, "If a man does start an accidental fire what is his conduct in respect to it? A question might arise—as if after the fire has started accidentally, and he then has it within his power and ability to extinguish the fire and he realizes and knows that he can, and then he forms and entertains an intent to injure an insurance company he can be guilty of this offence. It is not necessary that the intent be formed before the fire is started," also show no error of law. It is true as the defendant contends, that, if he merely neglected in the emergency of the moment to act, his negligence was not proof of a purpose to commit the crime charged. The intention, however, to injure could be formed after as well as before the fire started. On his own admissions the jury were to say whether, when considered in connection with all the circumstances, his immediate departure from the premises for his home in Fitchburg, without giving any alarm, warranted the inference of a criminal intent or state of mind, that the building should be consumed.'

Counsel for the appellant before us of course argued that this decision was of persuasive value only. In any event, when one reads the report the two principal issues in the case were, first, how far the jury were entitled to have regard to the manner in which the defendant gave his evidence and what he said, to decide whether he had actually lit the fire, and, second, that having regard to the terms of the statute under which Cali was indicted, even if the fire had originally been started by accident, if he then stood back and let the building burn with the intent of damaging the insurers, then he still was guilty of the offence charged.

Counsel then drew our attention to *Fagan v Metropolitan Police Comr* [1968] 3 All ER 442, [1969] 1 QB 439, which is the authority referred to by Professor Glanville Williams in the passage from his book which we have already quoted. In *Fagan's* case the defendant accidentally drove his motor car so that one tyre went onto and remained on a police constable's foot. It was only after the latter had told him several times to get off his foot that the defendant reversed his car. He was subsequently convicted by justices of assaulting a police constable in the execution of his duty. On his appeal to quarter sessions, the latter found that although they were left in doubt whether the initial mounting of the wheel was intentional or accidental, they were satisfied beyond all reasonable doubt that the defendant knowingly, provocatively and unnecessarily allowed the wheel to remain on the foot after he had been told to drive off. On those facts they found an assault proved. The defendant appealed to the Divisional Court, which dismissed the appeal by a majority, Bridge J dissenting. Counsel argued, we think correctly, that the majority in the Divisional Court decided the case on its own particular facts. In their judgment, the appellant's act of which complaint could be made had not been completed at the moment when the car wheel came to rest on the constable's foot, but had to be regarded as a continuing act operating until the wheel was removed. Looking at the facts in this way, although the original mounting of the foot may have been accidental, there was thereafter a sufficient actus reus together with a coincident mens rea. It was on this basis that they dismissed the appeal. Nevertheless, in the course of delivering the reserved judgment of the majority, James J said ([1968] 3 All ER 442 at 445, [1969] 1 QB 439 at 444): 'To constitute this offence, some intentional act must have been performed; a *mere* omission to act cannot amount to an assault.' A little later in the judgment there is this passage ([1968] 3 All ER 442 at 445, [1969] 1 QB 439 at 445):

> 'If the assault involves a battery and that battery continues there is a continuing act of assault. For an assault to be committed both the elements of actus reus and mens rea must be present at the same time. The "actus reus" is the action causing the effect on the victim's mind: see the observations of PARKE, B., in *R. v. St. George* ((1840) 9 C & P 483 at 490, 493, 173 ER 921 at 925, 926). The "mens rea" is the intention to cause that effect. It is not necessary that mens rea should be present at the inception of the actus reus; it can be superimposed on an existing act. On the other hand the subsequent inception of mens rea cannot convert an act which has been completed without mens rea into an assault.'

Bridge J dissented on the basis that, after the wheel of the appellant's car had accidentally come to rest on the constable's foot, there was nothing that he then did which constituted the act of assault. He would therefore have allowed the appeal on that question of fact. In so far as the principles to be applied were concerned, however, he started his judgment in this way ([1968] 3 All ER 442 at 446, [1969] 1 QB 439 at 446):

> 'I fully agree with my lords as to the relevant principles to be applied. No mere omission to act can amount to an assault. Both the elements of actus reus and mens rea must be present at the same time, but the one may be superimposed on the other. It is in the application of these principles to the highly unusual facts of this case that I have, with regret, reached a different conclusion from the majority of the court.'

Counsel then referred us to the earlier case of *Green v Cross* (1910) 103 LT 279. That was another appeal by way of case stated from justices to the Divisional Court. The respondent had been acquitted by the justices of cruelty to a dog under the Cruelty to Animals Act 1849, which was the statute then in force. The prosecutor appealed. In brief the facts of the case were that a dog had been caught in a trap innocently set by the respondent. Instead of immediately releasing the animal, for reasons which it was for the justices to consider whether they were sufficient or not, the respondent did not attempt immediately to release the animal, but went about his own business leaving the dog to be let free two hours later by police officers. One of the arguments advanced on the respondent's behalf was that he could not be convicted of cruelly treating an animal by omission and it was on this point that the magistrates had acquitted him. The Divisional Court, again by a majority only, remitted the case to the magistrates with the direction, in effect, that for the purposes of the statute then under consideration a mere omission could render a person guilty, dependent on the view which the magistrates took of the facts as a matter of degree. As Lord Coleridge J said (at 282):

> 'It seems to me that as soon as he was made aware of the dog being in that trap he from that moment, by permitting it to remain in the trap, caused it, within the meaning of the Act, to be ill-treated, abused, or tortured. Whether or not he took sufficient steps to remedy that pain is a question of degree, and I cannot agree that the proposition of law is sound which is suggested to us—namely, that in these

circumstances he has only to look on, to do nothing, and then to rely on the words of Cockburn, C.J. in *Powell* v. *Knight* ((1878) 38 LT 607), and say, "I was only passive; I did nothing myself actively; I was guilty therefore of no act of commission, and the provisions of the Act do not apply."'

Lord Alverstone CJ, agreeing, said at one point in his judgment (at 283): 'It seems to me that a point might arise when omission becomes commission . . .' A little later he said: 'It all comes back to this, that there are acts of omission which in some circumstances may be said to be acts which the person has caused to be committed.'

In his dissenting judgment, Channell J refers specifically to the words of the relevant statute and said at one point in his judgment (at 282):

'One does not wish unduly to restrict the operation of a beneficial statute, and I do not wish to lay down a positive definite rule that there could be no possible case of omission which would come within "cruelly ill-treating." I think it would be mischievous to lay down such a rule as an abstract proposition; but I think that it is extremely difficult to define the cases in which one can say that a mere omission amounts to cruelly ill-treating. Where there is a definite duty to do a thing and there is an omission to do it, then I think we might say, although even then it would be rather straining words, that the not doing that which there was a positive duty to do was cruelly ill-treating an animal.'

The learned judge then went on to hold, contrary to the views of his brethren, that there was no evidence in the circumstances of that case on which the justices could have convicted the respondent and that consequently it would not be right to remit the case to them.

Green v Cross was, therefore, a case which really turned on its own facts; but in addition to the passages from the judgments to which I have already referred one may quote a further short statement from the judgment of Lord Coleridge J (at 281–282):

'Argument has been adduced to show that an act of omission is not in the contemplation of the statute, and that there must be some act of commission, and the case of *Powell* v. *Knight* has been cited to prove that proposition. It is true that in *Powell* v. *Knight* Cockburn, C.J. uses the expression "passive act," applying it to the facts of that case, and holding that, as there was only a passive act on the part of the accused, he had not infringed the law by any act of commission or any neglect of any duty it was incumbent upon him to fulfil. I do not think that case can be cited for the general proposition that no act of omission is sufficient to bring the accused within the statute.'

In addition to his first submission that a mere omission cannot give rise to criminal liability, unless there be a duty to act, counsel also submitted that, save in certain exceptional cases of which this was not one, there must be a coincidence of the actus reus and the mens rea, as was suggested in the judgments in *Fagan*'s case to which we have already referred. He submitted that it was plain that the two did not coincide on the agreed facts of the present case.

Finally, counsel drew our attention to the words of the relevant statute itself, namely s 1(1) of the Criminal Damage Act 1971 in these terms:

'A person who without lawful excuse destroys or damages any property belonging to another intending to destroy or damage any such property or being reckless as to whether any such property would be destroyed or damaged shall be guilty of an offence.'

He contended, very much on the lines of the submissions on behalf of the respondent in *Green v Cross*, that 'destroying or damaging' are words of action and are not apt to comprise omissions.

In reply, counsel for the Crown submitted that, although the learned recorder's summing up could be criticised in minor respects, once the jury took the view that they quite clearly did about the mental state, that is to say the recklessness of the appellant, and then convicted, their verdict cannot be disturbed on the basis of the way in which the case was left to the jury.

He further submitted that the authorities to which we have referred were each decided on their own facts, and that as a matter of law the field is wide open. In *Fagan's* case the question whether, if there was a duty to act, an omission would amount to an assault was specifically left open. In *Green v Cross* he suggested, we think rightly, that the ratio of the decision was that it was open to the justices to convict on the evidence of omission, it was a matter for them on the facts as they decided them.

Counsel for the Crown invited us to find the law as suggested by Professor Glanville Williams in his *Textbook of Criminal Law* pp 143–144. As an alternative to the way in which the rule is there stated, counsel submitted that the law is or should be that where a person has created a state of affairs himself, the consequences of which the criminal law would punish given the relevant mens rea, then if that person subsequently and with the appropriate mens rea omits to do something which he could do to prevent the mischief against which the law is directed he is guilty of the relevant criminal offence.

On such limited authority as there is, we do not dissent from the proposition that unless a statute specifically so provides, or the case is one in which in the criminal context the common law imposes a duty on one person to act in a particular way towards another, such as a parent to his or her child, then a *mere* omission to act, with nothing more, cannot make the person who so fails to do something guilty of a criminal offence. Further, save in exceptional cases and subject to what follows, we think that normally the actus reus and the mens rea must coincide. Nevertheless, we also think that the answer to the problem which arises in the instant case depends on what is really meant by that last proposition. Some criminal offences are committed and complete in a second, others occupy a much longer period in time. We feel that it may well be artificial to consider merely the parts of what is alleged to be criminal conduct and to conclude that just because they are separate in point of time an actus reus cannot be conjoined to either a previous or subsequent mens rea to complete the commission of a crime.

Further, in both *Fagan's* case and the present, justice and good sense required that the defendant should not escape liability merely because the last thing that happened in the relevant story was an omission on his part. With respect to the Divisional Court in *Fagan's* case, we agree with Professor Glanville Williams's criticism of the reasoning of the majority of the court. In reality, driving the car wheel onto the policeman's foot was an act, was something which the driver did: the latter's failure thereafter to drive it off, despite the officer's request, was something which the driver did not do, it was an omission, and we think that it is unreal to describe it as any more than that.

On the other hand, in the driver's failure to release the officer's foot in the knowledge that he had just driven onto it, we think that there was clearly a substantial element of adoption by the driver, at the later stage, of what he had done a little earlier. We think that the conduct of the driver in that case can and should have been looked at as a whole and as the whole contained both the actus reus and the mens rea they were sufficiently coincident to render the driver guilty of an assault, without having to resort to the somewhat artificial reasoning of the majority of the Divisional Court. In our opinion, an unintentional act followed by an intentional omission to rectify that act or its consequences can be regarded in toto as an intentional act. We do not seek to define the rule, if rule it be, any more precisely because each case must depend on its own facts and we prefer to leave it to the trial judge to give the jury what he considers to be the appropriate direction in any given case. We would only say that an unintentional act followed by an intentional omission to rectify it or its consequences, or a reckless omission to do so when recklessness is a sufficient mens rea for the particular case, should only be regarded in toto as an intentional or reckless act when reality and common sense so require; this may well be a matter to be left to the jury. Further, in the relevant

analysis we think that whether or no there is on the facts an element of adoption on the
a part of the alleged offender of what he has done earlier by what he deliberately or
recklessly fails to do later is an important consideration.

In these circumstances, although we doubt whether the learned recorder was correct
in holding that when the appellant in the present case woke up there was any duty on
him at criminal law to extinguish the smouldering mattress, nevertheless we do think
that the whole of the appellant's conduct in relation to the mattress from the moment he
b lay on it with a lighted cigarette until the time he left it smouldering and moved to the
adjoining room can and should be regarded as one act. Clearly his failure with
knowledge to extinguish the incipient fire had in it a substantial element of adoption on
his part of what he had unintentionally done earlier, namely set it on fire. In these
circumstances, we think that on the admitted facts the learned recorder was nevertheless
correct in leaving the case to the jury, as he did, on the basis that the question was
c whether the appellant's failure to act was reckless, as defined by their Lordships' House
in *R v Caldwell* [1981] 1 All ER 961, [1981] 2 WLR 509.

For these reasons, this appeal is dismissed.

Appeal dismissed. Leave to appeal to the House of Lords granted.

Solicitors: *Ian S Manson*, Birmingham (for the Crown).

Raina Levy   Barrister.

Lambert v Ealing London Borough Council *a*

COURT OF APPEAL, CIVIL DIVISION
LORD DENNING MR, KERR AND MAY LJJ
27, 28, 29 JANUARY 1982

Housing – Homeless person – Person becoming homeless intentionally – Act or omission causing *b*
applicant to cease occupying accommodation available for him – Applicant voluntarily leaving
accommodation in France to settle in England – Applicant taking short-term holiday lettings –
Applicant required to vacate holiday letting – Whether local authority entitled to consider
circumstances of accommodation other than that last occupied by applicant – Whether applicant's
voluntary homelessness in France relevant – Whether applicant became homeless intentionally –
Housing (Homeless Persons) Act 1977, s 17.

c

In 1978 the plaintiff sold his business and left a flat which he had been occupying in
France and moved to England with his family with a view to settling permanently in
England. He took successive short-term holiday lettings from September 1978 until
February 1980, when the landlord of his accommodation obtained an order for
possession. The plaintiff then applied to the local authority for accommodation for *d*
himself and his family under the provisions of the Housing (Homeless Persons) Act
1977. The authority, after making inquiries as required by that Act, decided that,
although the plaintiff and his family were homeless and in priority need, he had become
'homeless intentionally' within the meaning of s 17(1)[a] of the 1977 Act as a result of his
voluntary removal from France and his subsequent failure to secure settled accommodation in England. The authority accordingly concluded that it was not under a duty to
provide permanent accommodation for the plaintiff and his family under the 1977 *e*
Act. The plaintiff brought an action in the county court seeking, inter alia, a declaration
that the local authority had not properly determined his application for accommodation. He contended that the period of holiday accommodation was sufficient to displace
the original voluntary homelessness which had occurred when he left France in 1978, so
that when the order for possession was made against him in 1980 he then became
unintentionally homeless. The judge accepted that contention and held that, because the *f*
plaintiff had not become homeless intentionally when the possession order was made
against him in 1980, the local authority was under a duty under the 1977 Act to provide
him with accommodation. The local authority appealed.

Held – On the true construction of the 1977 Act, the accommodation which a person
left 'intentionally' within the meaning of s 17 of that Act did not necessarily have to be *g*
the same accommodation the leaving of which gave rise to his ultimate homelessness.
It was a question of fact for the relevant local authority whether that which the applicant
did or failed to do which caused him to leave secure accommodation remained a cause of
the homelessness which resulted from his leaving subsequent accommodation.
Accordingly, the local authority was entitled to conclude that the applicant's homelessness
had resulted from his having intentionally ceased to occupy his secure home in France in *h*
1978 and having failed to obtain secure accommodation in England. Accordingly the
appeal would be allowed (see p 398 *e f* and *j* to p 399 *c e f*, p 400 *a* to *d f* to *j* and p 401 *e*,
post).

Dyson v Kerrier DC [1980] 3 All ER 313 followed.
Youngs v Thanet DC (1980) 78 LGR 474 and *Din v Wandsworth London Borough* [1981] *j*
3 All ER 881 considered.

---

a   Section 17(1), so far as material, provides: '. . . for the purposes of this Act a person becomes
      homeless intentionally if he deliberately does or fails to do anything in consequence of which he
      ceases to occupy accommodation which is available for his occupation and which it would have
      been reasonable for him to continue to occupy.'

Per Lord Denning MR and May LJ. Questions concerning decisions by local authorities
a under the 1977 Act should be brought before the High Court by way of applications for
judicial review rather than by actions for damages or injunctions in the county court (see
p 399 *c* to *f* and p 401 *a* to *c*, post).

Notes

For a housing authority's duties as to a homeless person, see 22 Halsbury's Laws (4th edn)
b para 513.
For the Housing (Homeless Persons) Act 1977, s 17, see 47 Halsbury's Statutes (3rd
edn) 330.

Cases referred to in judgments

Associated Provincial Picture Houses Ltd v Wednesbury Corp [1947] 2 All ER 680, [1948] 1
c   KB 223, CA, 45 Digest (Repl) 215, 189.
De Falco v Crawley BC [1980] 1 All ER 913, [1980] QB 460, [1980] 2 WLR 664, CA.
Din v Wandsworth London Borough [1981] 3 All ER 881, [1981] 3 WLR 918, HL.
Dyson v Kerrier DC [1980] 3 All ER 313, [1980] 1 WLR 1205, CA.
Islam v Hillingdon London Borough [1981] 3 All ER 901, [1981] 3 WLR 942, HL; *rvsg*
   [1981] 2 All ER 1089, [1981] 3 WLR 109, CA.
d *Secretary of State for Education and Science v Tameside Metropolitan Borough* [1976] 3 All ER
   665, [1977] AC 1014, [1976] 3 WLR 641, HL, 19 Digest (Reissue) 494, 3873.
*Secretary of State for Employment v Associated Society of Locomotive Engineers and Firemen
   (No 2)* [1972] 2 All ER 949, [1972] 2 QB 455, [1972] 2 WLR 1370, CA, Digest (Cont
   Vol D) 974, 1514.
Youngs v Thanet DC (1980) 78 LGR 474.

Cases also cited

Delahaye v Oswestry BC (1980) Times, 29 July.
Preston v Norfolk CC [1947] 2 All ER 124, [1947] KB 775, CA.
R v Hillingdon BC, ex p Streeting [1980] 3 All ER 413, [1980] 1 WLR 1425, CA.

Appeal

By amended particulars of claim dated 25 July 1980 the plaintiff, René Gaston Lambert,
brought an action against the defendant, Ealing London Borough Council, seeking (i) a
declaration that the council had not validly determined the plaintiff's application under
the Housing (Homeless Persons) Act 1977 for accommodation, (ii) an order that the
council consider the application in accordance with the law, (iii) an injunction restraining
f the council from withdrawing the accommodation made available to the plaintiff
pending a determination under any such order made and (iv) damages limited to
£2,000. By a counterclaim dated 27 March 1981 the council sought to recover from the
plaintiff the reasonable charges for accommodation provided pursuant to s 10 of the
1977 Act. On 29 May 1981 his Honour Judge Hayman sitting in Brentford County
Court granted the plaintiff the declaration sought and adjourned the claim for damages
g and the counterclaim. The council appealed. The facts are set out in the judgment of
Lord Denning MR.

Patrick Clarkson for the council.
Andrew Bano for the plaintiff.

LORD DENNING MR. This is another housing case which shows the impact of our
joining the European Community. In *De Falco v Crawley BC* [1980] 1 All ER 913, [1980]
QB 460 two families came from Italy, and claimed afterwards to be housed here. In this
case a French family has come from France and claims the benefit of the Housing
(Homeless Persons) Act 1977. They have the benefit of our legal aid. They are a very
nice family, who deserve to be well housed. They will, I am sure, contribute much to

our society. But still we have to see what the legal position is in regard to the housing of
them.   *a*

René Lambert is a real Frenchman. He cannot speak English. At the age of 51 he
came over from France to settle in England. He previously had a good business as a
bookseller in Grenoble. His wife had died, but he had three charming daughters:
Veronique, aged 19, at the university, Pascalle, aged 16, and Mirielle, aged 13, both at
school. Yet in the summer of 1978 he sold his business and all his possessions in
France. He had £6,000 left, and he came over to England.   *b*

Previously, with his savings, he had bought a motor caravan in which he and his three
daughters came to England and were on holiday here from July to August or
September. Then he decided to stay. He made that decision, he says, because of his
daughters: they would be better educated here than in France. This has proved true.
Veronique, the eldest, is at Queen Mary College, London E1, studying for a degree in
French and Spanish. The younger two are at the Lycée Française, London SW7.   *c*

Once he had decided to stay, he had to find accommodation here for himself, his
daughters and apparently their dog. He had some savings out of the money he received
from selling his business in France. So he could pay a good rent for a time. He obtained
a 'holiday let' at 7 St Helen's Road, Ealing. That was for six months from 12 September
1978 until 11 March 1979. The rent was £42 a week. When that expired, he took
another 'holiday let' at 9 Southfield Road, London W4. The rent was £56 a week for six   *d*
months from 10 March 1979 until 10 September 1979.

During this period M Lambert got a job here as a van driver for a French concern with
an attractive name, Maison Bouquillon Patisserie. He has worked well for them, and
they have every confidence in him.

When the second 'holiday let' came to an end in September 1979 he could not find
other accommodation. So a few days later, on 9 October 1979, he went to the Ealing   *e*
council and asked them to house him. Veronique went with him because her English
was getting very good. He was still struggling along with his bad English. They told the
housing department of their difficulties. The housing department said: 'Go back and
await a possession order.' (Housing authorities do not house people until they are
actually turned out of their accommodation.)

The landlord of the 'holiday let' took proceedings for possession. On 4 February 1980   *f*
the Brentford County Court made an order for M Lambert to give up possession of 9
Southfield Road on 17 March 1980. So M Lambert and his family had to leave.

They went to the Ealing council, who made inquiries. They provided the family with
temporary accommodation ('bed and breakfast' accommodation) at a motel at 82 Gordon
Road, Ealing. The council said that they were under no obligation to house them
permanently because they took the view that M Lambert was 'intentionally homeless'.   *g*
They wrote him a letter giving their reasons, which they have to do under the statute.
The director of housing wrote:

> 'Dear Mr Lambert,
>   In response to your application to this housing authority for accommodation,
> appropriate enquiries have been carried out and the following decisions arrived   *h*
> at:—
>   1. The authority are satisfied that you are homeless or threatened with
>   homelessness.
>   2. The authority are satisfied that you have a priority need.
>   3. The authority are satisfied that you became homeless, or were threatened with
>   homelessness intentionally.
>   For the purposes of Section 8 of the Housing (Homeless Persons) Act 1977, you   *j*
> are hereby notified that this decision has been determined for the following
> reasons:—
>   That you failed to secure for yourself and your family permanent accommodation
> when you came to this country.'

We do not analyse the housing department's reasons too closely in this court. As we
a said in *De Falco*, we look at the substance of the matter. The substance here is that the
local authority were saying, 'When you left France, you made yourself intentionally
homeless. We know that you have had those two "holiday lets" since, but your original
"intentional homelessness" is still the cause of your being homeless now. We are not
bound to house you permanently. All we are bound to do is to give you temporary
accommodation until you find something for yourself.'
b   M Lambert then went to a solicitor. The solicitor found a case which helped him. It
was *Youngs v Thanet DC* (1980) 78 LGR 474. It had been decided by his Honour Judge
Mervyn Davies QC sitting as a High Court judge in the Chancery Division. The solicitor
had seen it in The Times newspaper. On the basis of that case, M Lambert, through his
solicitor, claimed that he was unintentionally homeless. If he was right, it would mean
that he would go to the top of the housing list. He would take priority over all the young
c married couples and others in the council's area who were waiting for accommodation.
The council disputed M Lambert's claim. As the matter was in dispute, they allowed
him to remain in the 'bed and breakfast' accommodation pending its resolution. M
Lambert, with his solicitor, went to the county court. The matter was argued before his
Honour Judge Hayman. He gave judgment on 29 May 1981 in which he held in favour
of M Lambert. He thought that the case was covered by *Youngs v Thanet DC*. He gave
d judgment for M Lambert. Now Ealing council come to this court.
Since our previous decision, there have been two cases in the House of Lords. They
were decided in November 1981. They are *Din v Wandsworth London Borough* [1981] 3
All ER 881, [1981] 3 WLR 918 and *Islam v Hillingdon London Borough* [1981] 2 All ER
1089, [1981] 3 WLR 942.
Counsel for M Lambert said that the House of Lords had put a strict construction on
e the Housing (Homeless Persons) Act 1977. He urged us to do the same. He said that on
the simple words of ss 1(1) and 17(1) of the Act, M Lambert was homeless
unintentionally. He had not done anything deliberately to make himself homeless. He
had been living in England for 18 months before the possession order was obtained. He
had his home here. He was then turned out by the landlord. So he became
'unintentionally homeless', and the council ought to have provided permanent
f accommodation for him.
That simple approach, however, cannot stand. It is contrary to the decision in *De Falco
v Crawley BC*. In that case an Italian family gave up their accommodation in Naples.
They were EEC nationals who came to England to work. They stayed with relatives here
for a few weeks, and got jobs here. Then, when the relatives would not let them stay any
longer, they went to the local authority and said: 'We want to be housed by you. We are
g unintentionally homeless. Our relatives have turned us out.' But this court held, as a
matter of good sense, that you have to look at the position when they left Italy. They left
their home in Italy, packed up and came over here, and so became intentionally homeless
in Italy. That intentional homelessness carried on when they were in England. Therefore
the local authority were entitled to find that they were intentionally homeless.
The authority of that case was not shaken in the least by anything said in the House of
h Lords. On the contrary, it was commended. Lord Wilberforce said in *Islam v Hillingdon
London Borough* [1981] 3 All ER 901 at 905, [1981] 3 WLR 942 at 945:

> 'The difficulties of the [1977] Act are certainly diminished to some extent by the
> decision of the Court of Appeal in *De Falco v Crawley Borough Council* . . . But many
> foreseeable difficulties remain.'

Lord Lowry, after pointing out the difficulties, said ([1981] 3 All ER 901 at 911, [1981]
3 WLR 942 at 953): 'The principle of *De Falco*'s case is the safeguard . . .' So, although
De Falco put a liberal interpretation on the statute, it was upheld by the House of Lords.
The next case is *Dyson v Kerrier DC* [1980] 3 All ER 313, [1980] 1 WLR 1205. A lady
had a flat in Huntingdon. She left that flat and went to stay at Helston in Cornwall on
a 'winter let' for six months. She was turned out of the 'winter let' at the end of that

period. She then went to the local authority, the Kerrier District Council, and said:
'Please house me. I am unintentionally homeless. I have been turned out of the "winter a
let".' The Court of Appeal were faced with the literal construction of the statute; they
were faced with the difficulties of interpretation; and they were faced with the fact that
she had been staying at a 'winter let' in Cornwall for six months. They said that
nevertheless she was intentionally homeless because she had left her accommodation in
Huntingdon to take on the 'winter let'.

Dyson v Kerrier DC was on the same lines as De Falco, but it extended it a little. The b
lady had been living in a settled 'winter let' of six months; and yet she was held to be
intentionally homeless.

Now we have the case of M Lambert. He did not have just one 'holiday let' in
England: he had two. He started living here in September 1978; and he was not turned
out of the second 'holiday let' until 18 months later. After living here for 18 months, he
said: 'I am now homeless. I had a good home here which satisfied s 1 of the Housing c
(Homeless Persons) Act 1977. Now, after all that time, I am unintentionally homeless.
So I ought to be housed permanently.'

It seems to me that our present case is covered full square by Dyson v Kerrier DC. But
counsel for M Lambert has urged us to distinguish Dyson v Kerrier DC. He points out
that in the House of Lords in Din v Wandsworth London Borough [1981] 3 All ER 881 at
895, [1981] 3 WLR 918 at 934 Lord Lowry threw a great deal of doubt on it, saying: 'I d
am far from satisfied that it was correctly decided.' But the other Law Lords took a
different view. Lord Wilberforce said that he agreed with Dyson v Kerrier DC, and so did
Lord Fraser. As for Lord Russell and Lord Bridge, they did not comment on Dyson, nor
did they throw any doubt on it.

On the state of the authorities, it seems to me that Dyson v Kerrier DC is good law and
should be followed. It comes to this. When M Lambert sold up and left France, he e
became homeless. He was intentionally homeless here because he had given up his
home in France. That intentional homelessness was the effective cause of his becoming
homeless in England. The intervening 18 months do not alter the fact that he was
intentionally homeless.

In those circumstances, it seems to me that the local authority was quite right. In
other cases the facts may be different. Sometimes a person will have been settled here for f
so long that his accommodation will be of a permanent nature. Ackner LJ envisaged this
in the Din case. His words were approved by Lord Wilberforce (see [1981] 3 All ER 881
at 887, [1981] 3 WLR 918 at 924). Ackner LJ's words are not reported. So I will read
them from the transcript.

> 'For the sake of completeness I should perhaps add that the manner in which I
> have construed s 17(1) in no way accepts the proposition: once an intentionally g
> homeless person, always an intentionally homeless person, dramatically described
> by counsel as "the mark of Cain". Having become homeless intentionally a would-
> be applicant for local authority housing is of course at a disadvantage. So he should
> be, otherwise the opportunity for unfair "queue jumping" would be increased.'

Stopping there, one can well see, as May LJ pointed out in the course of the argument, h
that it would be easy for a person who has secure accommodation here to think to
himself, 'I would like to get a council house, so I will give up that secure accommodation.
I will take up a "holiday let" for a few months. Then, when I am turned out, I will ask
for a council house', and get priority over all the young married couples waiting on the
housing list. That is what Ackner LJ had in mind. If this argument were allowed to
prevail, and you only looked at the last place from which the applicant was turned out, j
the opportunity for unfair 'queue jumping' would be increased. Ackner LJ went on to
say:

> 'To remove his self-imposed disqualification, he must therefore have achieved
> what can be loosely described as "a settled residence", as opposed to what from the
> outset is known (as in Dyson's case) to be only temporary accommodation. What

amounts to "a settled residence" is a question of fact and degree depending on the
circumstances of each individual case. I can see no reason why the good sense of the
local authority cannot be relied on for making the right decision. There is always
the court's supervisory jurisdiction on which an unsuccessful applicant can, in a
proper case, rely.'

It seems to me that, in our present case, M Lambert and his daughters had in no sense
acquired a settled residence here. It was unsettled because they were only in 'holiday
lets'. They had nothing whatever in the sense of permanent accommodation here. They
were in no way settled so as to entitle them to ignore the original cause of their
homelessness. The original cause was the intentional homelessness which prevailed so as
to prevent their qualifying for permanent housing under the Housing (Homeless
Persons) Act 1977.

In parting from this case I would like to say, as I think the House of Lords have rather
indicated, that these cases should be reviewed, if at all, by the process of judicial review
in the High Court here, not by actions for damages, or injunctions, in the county
court. The only way in which a local authority's decision in these cases can properly be
interfered with is by way of judicial review, applying the well-known principles of
judicial review to ascertain whether the decision is so unreasonable that it cannot stand.
That is the right and proper way of considering these matters. It is important to
remember that the decision is entrusted by Parliament to the local authority. They have
a difficult job to do. They have to try to maintain a balance between incomers, who may
be unintentionally homeless, and the people on the housing list, who have been waiting
for houses for years. They have to try to keep a balance between competing claims on the
housing stock. It seems to me that their decision in these matters should be looked on
benevolently, because of the difficulties with which they are faced. Their decision
should not be interfered with except when they have clearly gone wrong in point of law
or of fact.

I can understand the judge being influenced by *Youngs v Thanet DC*, but it seems to me,
in the light of all that has happened since, that *Youngs* was incorrectly decided. I would
allow the appeal accordingly.

KERR LJ. I agree that this appeal should be allowed. I would only add a few words on
the recent authorities and the construction of ss 1 and 17 of the Housing (Homeless
Persons) Act 1977 in the context of facts such as those in the present case.

In *Dyson v Kerrier DC* [1980] 3 All ER 313, [1980] 1 WLR 1205 and in *Youngs v Thanet
DC* (1980) 78 LGR 474, as in this case, the common feature was that the applicants had
left secure accommodation in circumstances in which the local authority was in each case
entitled to come to the conclusion that they had left that accommodation intentionally.
The applicants then went into intervening temporary or precarious accommodation
from which they were ultimately turned out involuntarily. That was the situation with
which this court was faced in *Dyson's* case and, as has been mentioned by Lord Denning
MR, it was there submitted that under s 17 the local authority must only look to the last
accommodation which the application had left involuntarily.

The formidable character of that argument was fully recognised in the judgment of
this court delivered by Brightman LJ (see [1980] 3 All ER 313 at 319–320, [1980] 1 WLR
1205 at 1214–1215). This court came to the conclusion that, for the purpose of defining
a condition of homelessness or threatened homelessness under s 1 of the 1977 Act, the
accommodation referred to in s 17, while it must fall within the definition in s 1, need
not be that same accommodation, but can be accommodation which the applicant had
intentionally left earlier. That, as it seems to me, is the ratio of the decision in *Dyson*.

However, it was submitted to us that that ratio can no longer apply because of what
the House of Lords said in relation to *Dyson* in *Din v Wandsworth London Borough* [1981]
3 All ER 881, [1981] 3 WLR 918. Other than Lord Lowry, I can see nothing in the
speeches of their Lordships which doubted either the ratio or the result in *Dyson*; and
even Lord Lowry found a way whereby he was able to rationalise the result of that

decision. Lord Wilberforce, Lord Fraser and Lord Russell clearly approved *Dyson*; and as
I read Lord Wilberforce and particularly Lord Fraser, they also approved its ratio (see ***a***
[1981] 3 All ER 881 at 887, 890, [1981] 3 WLR 918 at 924, 928). For my part, I see no
reason why this court should not follow both the decision and the ratio of *Dyson's* case,
and indeed I think that we are bound to do so. This leads to a sensible construction of the
Act. A contrary construction would make it possible to drive a coach and horses through
it, in the way in which Lord Denning MR has explained.

However, both in *Youngs's* case and in the present case, which followed that decision, ***b***
the local authority's decision was set aside because s 17 of the 1977 Act was construed as
though it could only apply to the last accommodation occupied by the applicant. I see
no need for this construction, and therefore see no misdirection of law on the part of the
local authority in either *Youngs's* case or the present case.

For these reasons and those given by Lord Denning MR, I consider that the respondent
authority in the present case was entitled to conclude that the applicant's homelessness ***c***
in 1980 was due to his having intentionally ceased to occupy his secure home in France
in 1978 and having failed to obtain secure accommodation here. I also consider, in
relation to the cross-notice of appeal, that the local authority made wholly adequate
inquiries in order to satisfy itself that this was the appropriate decision. Accordingly I
would allow this appeal.

d

MAY LJ. The facts of this case have already been stated by Lord Denning MR and Kerr
LJ, and I need not repeat them. This, as has been indicated, is another case under the
Housing (Homeless Persons) Act 1977. The general intent of that Act is, I think, clear.
However, its drafting is poor, and the result has been that it is very difficult for local
authorities precisely to work out in any given case the general intent that lies behind the
statute. That is particularly so in circumstances such as those referred to by Kerr LJ in the ***e***
judgment which he has just delivered, where there is occupation of intermediate
accommodation between what might be said to be intentional homelessness under s 17
of the 1977 Act and the ultimate homelessness under s 1 which leads the applicant to go
to the relevant local authority.

It is quite clear that the two recent decisions in the House of Lords have shown that
this Act is one which must be construed strictly. There is no warrant to read anything ***f***
into it which is not there on its face. In those circumstances, although the word
'accommodation' in ss 1 and 17 must of course as a matter of strict construction be given
the same meaning, to me, as to Kerr LJ, there is nothing in the Act to lead to the
conclusion that the accommodation which a person leaves intentionally under s 17 need
necessarily be the same, and frequently is not the same, accommodation as gives rise to
the ultimate homelessness under s 1. Once that lack of connection between ss 1 and 17 ***g***
is appreciated, in my view a lot of the difficulties disappear and the various cases can be
understood principally as decisions on their own facts.

When a person becomes homeless under s 1 of the 1977 Act, the council has to make
appropriate inquiries under s 3. They are, in making those inquiries, to look into what
I may by way of shorthand describe as the accommodation history of the particular
applicant who has come to them. In that history they may find, as they did in this ***h***
particular case and as indeed the relevant local authorities did in the other cases, an
instance where the applicant left secure accommodation intentionally. It is then, in my
judgment, purely a question of causation, purely a jury question of fact for the local
authority, having made the appropriate inquiries, to answer, namely: did the act which
the person did, or that which he failed to do, which rendered him homeless in relation
to the secure accommodation under s 17 remain a cause of the homelessness which ***j***
resulted from his leaving the subsequent accommodation referred to in s 1?

Each case must depend on its own facts. Some local authorities may take one view of
certain facts and other local authorities may take the opposite view. It is frequently the
case that no one can say that either of them is being unreasonable. That is important in
this type of case because, as Lord Denning MR has pointed out, even though this and

other cases have been county court proceedings rather than applications for judicial review, the nature of the proceedings in the county court, or indeed in the High Court, should be precisely the same as proceedings for judicial review. I respectfully echo what Lord Denning MR has said about the undesirability of going to the county court or the High Court rather than for judicial review. I would much prefer applicants to go by way of applications for judicial review for this reason, that, where one does have an action in the county court or the High Court and the facts are gone into, it is very tempting for the judge trying the case to reach his own conclusion on the facts, and decide then whether, or those facts so found, the applicant was intentionally homeless, rather than ask the correct question: were the local authority justified on appropriate inquiries in coming to the conclusion to which they came, applying the usual tests from the well-known case of *Associated Provincial Picture Houses Ltd v Wednesbury Corp* [1947] 2 All ER 680, [1948] 1 KB 223, Lord Denning MR's judgment in *Secretary of State for Employment v Associated Society of Locomotive Engineers and Firemen (No 2)* [1972] 2 All ER 949, [1972] 2 QB 445 and the recent decision in their Lordships' House in *Secretary of State for Education and Science v Tameside Metropolitan Borough* [1976] 3 All ER 665, [1977] AC 1014? That that is a risk is I think apparent from the circumstances of the present case.

With all respect to the judge, although on the face of his judgment he directed himself in accordance with the *Wednesbury* principles, in my view he thereafter proceeded not to consider what the local authority thought or found but what he himself found. I think that it is on the basis of his own findings that he came to the conclusion at the end of his judgment that no reasonable local authority would properly have been satisfied that this plaintiff was intentionally homeless in April 1980.

Having regard to all the circumstances of this case and for the reasons which I have sought to give, I cannot come to the conclusion that, on the material which the local authority had and putting oneself in their shoes, the decision to which they came was one to which no reasonable local authority could have come in all the circumstances of the case.

For those reasons, therefore, I agree that this appeal should be allowed.

Appeal allowed. Application for leave to appeal to the House of Lords refused. Counterclaim remitted to county court judge.

Solicitors: *Sharpe, Pritchard & Co*, agents for *Norman L Green*, Ealing (for the council); *Douglas-Mann & Co* (for the plaintiff).

Diana Procter　Barrister.

Garland v British Rail Engineering Ltd

(Case 12/81)

COURT OF JUSTICE OF THE EUROPEAN COMMUNITIES

JUDGES BOSCO (ACTING PRESIDENT), TOUFFAIT, DUE (PRESIDENTS OF CHAMBERS), PESCATORE, LORD MACKENZIE STUART, O'KEEFFE, KOOPMANS, CHLOROS AND GRÉVISSE

ADVOCATE-GENERAL VERLOREN VAN THEMAAT

7 OCTOBER, 8 DECEMBER 1981, 9 FEBRUARY 1982

HOUSE OF LORDS

LORD DIPLOCK, LORD EDMUND-DAVIES, LORD FRASER OF TULLYBELTON, LORD RUSSELL OF KILLOWEN AND LORD SCARMAN

26 NOVEMBER 1980, 22 APRIL 1982

Employment – Discrimination against a woman – Provision in relation to retirement – Continuation after retirement of benefit enjoyed during employment – Male employees provided with non-contractual concessionary travel facilities for their families before and after retirement – Female employees enjoying same facilities before retirement but for themselves alone after retirement – Whether facilities to be treated as 'pay' – Whether arrangement 'a provision in relation to ... retirement' – Whether arrangement exempt from statutory provisions making discrimination unlawful – Sex Discrimination Act 1975, s 6(2)(4) – EEC Treaty, art 119.

The appellant, a married woman, complained to an industrial tribunal that her employer was discriminating against her because of sex contrary to s 6(2)[a] of the Sex Discrimination Act 1975 by continuing to provide male employees after they retired with non-contractual concessionary travel facilities for themselves and for their wives and dependent children whereas when female employees retired the provision of such facilities for their families was withdrawn. The industrial tribunal dismissed the complaint on the ground that the concessionary travel rights afforded to ex-employees was 'a provision in relation to ... retirement' within s 6(4) of the 1975 Act and accordingly that the discrimination was not unlawful. The appellant appealed to the Employment Appeal Tribunal, which upheld her complaint and reversed the industrial tribunal's decision on the ground that the continuation after retirement of a privilege which existed during employment and which was not part of the employer's system for catering for an employee's retirement was not 'a provision in relation to ... retirement'. The Court of Appeal restored the decision of the industrial tribunal on the ground that 'provision in relation to ... retirement' was a wide expression and included any provision about retirement. The appellant appealed to the House of Lords, which referred to the Court of Justice of the European Communities for a preliminary ruling the questions, inter alia, whether the discrimination was contrary to art 119[b] of the EEC Treaty and if so whether the article was directly applicable so as to confer enforceable Community rights on individuals.

Held (by the Court of Justice of the European Communities) – Where an employer (although not contractually bound to do so) granted special travel facilities to former male employees to enjoy after their retirement which were an extension of the facilities granted during the period of employment, thereby enabling them to be treated as pay within the meaning of art 119 of the EEC Treaty, that constituted discrimination within art 119 against female employees who did not receive the same facilities on their retirement. Furthermore, the provisions of art 119 applied directly where a national court was able, using the criteria of equal work and equal pay, without the operation of Community or national measures, to establish that the grant of special travel facilities

---

a   Section 6, so far as material, is set out at p 414 *f g*, post

b   Article 119, so far as material, is set out at p 415 *a b*, post

solely to retired male employees represented discrimination based on difference of sex (see p 412 *a* to p 413 *a*, post).

    Defrenne v Belgian State [1971] ECR 445 and *Jenkins v Kingsgate (Clothing Productions) Ltd* [1981] 1 WLR 972 applied.

Accordingly, **Held** (by the House of Lords) – The words 'provision in relation to … retirement' in s 6(4) of the 1975 Act were to be construed, if they were reasonably capable of bearing such a meaning, as being intended to carry out the obligation to observe the provisions of art 119 of the EEC Treaty and not to be inconsistent with it. Accordingly although the words in s 6(4), without undue straining of the ordinary language used, were capable of bearing either the narrow meaning accepted by the Employment Appeal Tribunal or the wider meaning preferred by the Court of Appeal, since the construction adopted by the Employment Appeal Tribunal was the only one consistent with art 119 of the EEC Treaty that construction was to be preferred. It followed, therefore, that the appellant was being unlawfully discriminated against by her employer, and the appeal would accordingly be allowed (see p 415 *b* to *g* and p 416 *c* to *e*, post).

    Decision of the Court of Appeal [1979] 2 All ER 1163 reversed.

Notes

For discrimination against employees, see 16 Halsbury's Laws (4th edn) paras 771:2, 771:5.

    For the Sex Discrimination Act 1975, s 6, see 45 Halsbury's Statutes (3rd edn) 229.

    For the EEC Treaty, art 119, see 42A ibid 779.

Cases cited

Burton v British Rlys Board Case 19/81 (16 February 1982, unreported), CJEC.
Defrenne v Belgian State Case 80/70 [1971] ECR 445, CJEC.
Defrenne v Sabena Case 43/75 (1976) [1981] 1 All ER 122, [1976] ECR 455, CJEC, 20 Digest (Reissue) 587, *4488*.
Defrenne v Sabena Case 149/77 [1978] ECR 1365, CJEC, 20 Digest (Reissue) 592, *4510*.
Jenkins v Kingsgate (Clothing Productions) Ltd Case 96/80 [1981] 1 WLR 972, [1981] ECR 911, CJEC.
Worringham v Lloyds Bank Ltd Case 69/80 [1981] 2 All ER 434, [1981] 1 WLR 950, [1981] ECR 767, CJEC.

Appeal

The applicant, Eileen Mary Garland (the employee), appealed against the decision of the Court of Appeal (Lord Denning MR, Lawton and Geoffrey Lane LJJ) ([1979] 2 All ER 1163, [1979] 1 WLR 754) on 4 April 1979 allowing an appeal by British Rail Engineering Ltd (BREL) (the employer) against the decision of the Employment Appeal Tribunal (Phillips J, Mr L D Cowan and Miss P Smith) ([1978] 2 All ER 789) dated 11 November 1977 allowing the appeal of Mrs Garland against the decision of an industrial tribunal (chairman Mr D B Williams) sitting in London North on 23 February 1977 dismissing a complaint by her that BREL had committed an act of discrimination against her in that BREL provided for male employees when they retired concessionary travel facilities for themselves, their wives and dependent children, whereas female employees when they retired were provided with such facilities for themselves alone and not for their husbands or dependent children.

Thomas Morison QC and *Nicholas Underhill* for Mrs Garland.
Anthony Scrivener QC and *Frederick Marr-Johnson* for BREL.

After hearing preliminary argument their Lordships referred, by order dated 19 January 1981, certain questions (set out at p 411 *h j*, post) concerning the interpretation of art 119 of the EEC Treaty and of two directives made by the Council of Ministers for a preliminary ruling under art 177 of the treaty.

Reference

The following summary of the order for reference and the written observations submitted pursuant to art 20 of the Protocol on the Statute of the Court of Justice is taken from the judgment of the court. The language of the case was English.

I—FACTS AND WRITTEN PROCEDURE

The appellant in the main action, Mrs Garland, is a married woman employed by British Rail Engineering Ltd (BREL), the whole of the shareholding in which is held by the British Railways Board, a public authority charged by statute with the duty of providing railway services in Great Britain.

During the period of their employment all employees of BREL enjoy certain valuable travel facilities which are also extended to their spouses and dependent children. On retirement former employees, men and women, continue to enjoy travel facilities but they are reduced in comparison with those which they enjoyed during the period of their employment. However, although male employees continue to be granted facilities for themselves and for their wives and dependent children as well, female employees no longer have such facilities granted in respect of their families. According to the House of Lords 'these facilities are not enjoyed by former employees as a matter of contractual right, but employees have a legitimate expectation that they will enjoy them after retirement and it would be difficult in practice for BREL to withdraw them unilaterally' without the agreement of the trade unions of which its employees are members.

On 25 November 1976 Mrs Garland complained to an industrial tribunal that BREL was discriminating against her contrary to the provisions of the Sex Discrimination Act 1975. The tribunal rejected Mrs Garland's application and she then appealed to the Employment Appeal Tribunal which, by a judgment of 11 November 1977, reversed the first decision (see [1978] 2 All ER 789). Following a new appeal, by a judgment of 4 April 1979 the Court of Appeal annulled the second decision (see [1979] 2 All ER 1163, [1979] 1 WLR 754).

Only the provisions of the Sex Discrimination Act 1975 were invoked on each occasion and the argument centred in particular on the interpretation of s 6(4) which excludes 'provision in relation to death or retirement' from certain provisions of the Act.

The issues of Community law were not raised until the case reached the House of Lords. In view of those issues the House of Lords made an order dated 19 January 1981 in which it puts the following two questions to the court:

'1. Where an employer provides (although not bound to do so by contract) special travel facilities for former employees to enjoy after retirement which discriminate against former female employees in the manner described above, is this contrary to: (a) Article 119 of the EEC Treaty? (b) Article 1 of Council Directive 75/117/EEC? (c) Article 1 of Council Directive 76/207/EEC?

2. If the answer to Questions 1(a), 1(b) or 1(c) is affirmative, is Article 119 or either of the said directives directly applicable in Member States so as to confer enforceable Community rights upon individuals in the above circumstances?'

That order making the reference for a preliminary ruling was registered at the court on 22 January 1981. In accordance with art 20 of the Protocol on the Statute of the Court of Justice of the European Communities, written observations were submitted on 23 March 1981 by the Commission of the European Communities represented by John Forman, a member of its legal department, acting as agent, on 14 April 1981 by BREL, represented by Anthony Scrivener QC and Frederick Marr-Johnson, on 15 April 1981 by Mrs Garland, represented by Thomas Morison QC and Nicholas Underhill, and on 21 April 1981 by the government of the United Kingdom, represented by R D Munrow of the Treasury Solicitor's Department, assisted by Peter Scott QC.

On hearing the report of the Judge-Rapporteur and the views of the Advocate-General the court decided to open the oral procedure without any preparatory inquiry. It did however ask the representative of BREL to send it before 30 September 1981 the notices by which employees are informed, before or after their retirement, about the travel facilities in question.

II—WRITTEN OBSERVATIONS SUBMITTED UNDER ART 20 OF THE PROTOCOL ON THE STATUTE OF THE COURT
A. *Observations of Mrs Garland the appellant in the main action*
Mrs Garland deals with the questions put to the court mainly in relation to art 119 of the EEC Treaty and EEC Council Directive 75/117 on equal pay and, in the alternative (in the event of the court's rejecting the submissions on art 119 and the directive on equal pay) in relation to EEC Council Directive 76/207 on equal treatment.

(a) *Article 119 and EEC Council Directive 75/117 on equal pay*   Mrs Garland first of all considers whether 'pay' includes special travel facilities and submits that the case law of the court and above all the opinions of Advocates-General have conferred a wide ambit on that definition. The benefits in question are of considerable value, they are featured prominently in recruitment advertising, they form a significant part of an employee's remuneration and are granted as a result of the employment relationship; consequently those benefits fall squarely within the definition of art 119 of the EEC Treaty.

Mrs Garland then sets out to demonstrate that the grant of those benefits to former employees comes within the ambit of art 119 or the directive on equal pay. She relies on the judgment in *Defrenne v Belgian State* Case 80/70 [1971] ECR 445 and submits that, since the only essential question is whether the benefit in issue is provided as a result of the employment relationship, it is immaterial whether its actual receipt is deferred until after the termination of the employment.

Lastly Mrs Garland submits that the grant of the benefits in question to the employee's family rather than to the employee alone is also immaterial since, in human and economic terms, the interests of the employee and those of his family are the same; Mr Advocate-General Warner came to the same conclusion in his opinion in *Worringham v Lloyds Bank Ltd* Case 69/80 [1981] 2 All ER 434 at 437 when he stated:

'The conferment of the right to those benefits on his dependants can, however, in my opinion, properly be regarded as an advantage to the member arising from his employment.'

Mrs Garland submits that the benefit in question is pay within the meaning of art 119 of the treaty and that art 119 is directly applicable. She believes that the principles formulated by the court in the *Worringham* case should apply in this case since BREL has admitted both direct and overt discrimination, and has not sought to argue that the discrimination is objectively justifiable on any grounds other than sex; its case has been based simply on the argument that such discrimination is not unlawful by reason of the exception contained in s 6(4) of the Sex Discrimination Act 1975.

(b) *EEC Council Directive 76/207 on equal treatment*   Mrs Garland takes the same line of argument as that which she took in regard to art 119 and the directive on equal pay. She therefore sets out to demonstrate first of all that if the special facilities in question do not come within the definition of pay they must come within the definition of 'working conditions' provided for in that directive on equal treatment since the two directives referred to in the order making the reference for a preliminary ruling as well as the social security directive together form a comprehensive code prohibiting discrimination in all aspects of employment.

She further repeats her submission that the fact that the benefits in question are granted to former employees does not prevent their forming part of 'working conditions' referred to in art 5 of the directive on equal treatment. In any event they are a present right vested in the employee during his period of employment, although only to be enjoyed after retirement.

Finally, Mrs Garland considers that her previous submissions on the grant of the benefits in question to families apply a fortiori when the relevant concept is 'working conditions' rather than 'pay'.

Therefore, should those travel benefits not be 'pay' within the meaning of art 119 of the EEC Treaty and the directive on equal pay, they are in any event 'working conditions' within the meaning of the directive on equal treatment.

That directive also has 'direct effect'. The provisions of the directive are sufficiently clear and precise and leave the member states no relevant margin of discretion in the performance of the obligations which it imposes. If the obligations are not complied with, then, as Mr Advocate-General Capotorti said, 'the way would be open for the enforcement, in the Community system, of personal rights of individuals on the basis of the directive itself' (see *Defrenne v Sabena* Case 149/77 [1978] ECR 1365 at 1388).

Although in the cases decided by the court there has been no decision clearly establishing that a directive may have direct effect to confer rights on an individual against another individual rather than against the government of a member state, Mrs Garland submits that there is no good reason who a directive should impose obligations only on the governments of member states especially since the purpose of the directive was to ensure that the obligations as to equal treatment were imposed on both member states and individuals. Furthermore, since BREL is a wholly-owned subsidiary of a corporation created by statute for the purpose of operating the national railway service, it is to be regarded as an emanation of the national government.

Mrs Garland appreciates that the period within which member states were obliged to comply with the directive in question by adopting the provisions necessary for its implementation did not expire until August 1978, that is to say after the making of the application in this case. However, the discrimination complained of by Mrs Garland is not merely a single act occurring before that date but a continuous act which will not 'bite' until the date in the future when she retires. Therefore, the court should be prepared to consider the legal position at the material time rather than at the time of the application, if they are different.

B. *Observations of the commission*

After quoting the definition of 'pay' set out in the second paragraph of art 119 of the EEC Treaty the Commission states that special travel facilities granted to employees represent benefits in kind paid to workers directly by the employer.

The Commission takes the view, first, that such benefits granted by an employer to his employees should properly be treated as being 'in respect of' an employment. Second, special travel facilities, which also benefit an employee's spouse and children, nevertheless represent consideration in kind which a worker receives directly from the employer in respect of his employment. Third, the fact that the benefits continue to be enjoyed beyond the active working life of an employee and into retirement does not prevent him from receiving them in respect of his employment because they would hardly be 'in respect of retirement'. Consequently the Commission accepts that the concept of equal pay extends to special travel facilities granted to spouses and dependent children of employees which continue into retirement.

Relying on the judgment in *Defrenne v Sabena* Case 43/75 (1976) [1981] 1 All ER 122 the Commission submits that the concept of equal pay may be taken advantage of before the national courts by employees vis-à-vis their employers on the basis of the direct effect of art 119.

Finally, the Commission considers that if its arguments are correct it would follow that neither Council Directive 75/117 nor Council Directive 76/207 would find application in the case at hand.

The Commission accordingly suggests the following reply to the questions raised by the House of Lords: 'Special travel facilities enjoyed by the spouses and dependent children of employees which continue on the retirement of the employee constitute "pay" within the meaning of the second paragraph of art 119 of the EEC Treaty. In this connection art 119 may be relied on before the national courts.'

C. *Observations of BREL, the respondent in the main action*

BREL first of all submits that the special travel facilities in question do not constitute 'pay' within the meaning of that expression as used in art 119 of the EEC Treaty and art 1 of Council Directive 75/117; consequently the alleged discrimination is not a contravention of either of those provisions. BREL argues that such facilities are not 'consideration in cash' or 'other consideration in kind, which the worker receives in respect of his employment from his employer', first because they are provided as a matter of concession by BREL and not pursuant to any agreement between employer and worker and, second, because they are incapable of assessment in financial terms. A fortiori the receipt of such facilities by a retired employee shows that the provision of such facilities after retirement forms part of the provision which an employer makes voluntarily for the retirement of that employee; it forms no part of the 'pay' which that employee earned during his working years.

BREL also submits that the facilities in question do not constitute 'working conditions' either, within the meaning of art 1 of Council Directive 76/207.

According to the BREL it is not arguable that the provision of special travel facilities relates to matters of access to employment, promotion or vocational training. The argument must be that those facilities are part of the 'working conditions' of an employee; that expression must be construed as indicating that the conditions in question must relate to the work being carried out by the employee at the material time. Viewed in this light the provision of free travel between an employee's place of work and his home is a 'working condition'. However, discrimination in relation to the provision of other travel facilities would not be discrimination in regard to an employee's 'working conditions'; it would only be discrimination in regard to the facilities which the employer afforded to an employee outside his work. In any event, there cannot possibly be discrimination in regard to an employee's 'working conditions' after that employee retires from work since there can be no 'working conditions' if the employee is no longer working.

In view of the answers proposed to questions 1 (a), (b) and (c), question 2 does not arise, but even if those questions were answered in the affirmative, BREL submits in the alternative that neither art 119 nor either of the directives is directly applicable in member states so as to confer enforceable Community rights on individuals in the circumstances outlined in the order making the reference for a preliminary ruling.

In conclusion BREL submits that the questions referred to the court should be answered as follows: '(1) Where an employer provides (although not bound to do so by contract) special travel facilities for former employees to enjoy after retirement which discriminate against former female employees, such provision is not contrary to art 119 of the EEC Treaty or Council Directives 75/117 or 76/207; (2) in the circumstances, question 2 does not arise.'

D. *Observations of the United Kingdom*

As far as the nature of the facility in question is concerned, the United Kingdom states that it could be varied or stopped by BREL at any time but emphasises that in practice that would be difficult and would need to be discussed first with the trade unions concerned. It also points out that the facility is to the greater benefit of women than men since women retire five years before men. The United Kingdom then goes on to examine successively the three provisions referred to in the questions of the House of Lords.

Article 119 That article signifies that men and women should receive equal pay for equal work. According to the United Kingdom the test of whether there is unlawful discrimination based on sex is whether the relationship between pay on the one hand and work or work's value on the other is different because of the worker's sex. The nature of the facility in question is such that neither its cost nor its value can be compared with the amount or value of the work done to earn it by male and female employees. It is true that the facility may be described as arising out of the worker's employment and that without that employment it would not have been granted, but once the benefit cannot be related to the work, the principle of art 119 cannot be invoked. Furthermore, and in any event, such a facility provided after a worker has retired is not within art 119 at all. That article is meant to affect legal relationships only and is not intended to cover gratuitous gestures by the employer.

As regards the direct applicability of art 119, the United Kingdom submits with reference to the judgment in *Jenkins v Kingsgate (Clothing Productions) Ltd* Case 96/80 [1981] 1 WLR 972 that even if free travel facilities after retirement are pay for the purpose of art 119, the provisions of that article cannot be applied directly without the aid of national or Community measures which resolve the questions of how to approach the differing retiring ages and life expectations which directly affect the cost of the benefit to the employer and its value to the employee.

Article 1 of Council Directive 75/117   Again with reference to the *Jenkins* judgment, the United Kingdom states that if the benefit in question is not pay for the purposes of art 119, which it had tried to demonstrate, Council Directive 75/117 is irrelevant.

If on the other hand the benefit is pay for the purposes of art 119 of the EEC Treaty a question might in theory arise as to the effect of the directive. The United Kingdom here reminds the court that it does not consider that directives can have the effect of imposing obligations on individuals. Directives are addressed only to member states and purport to impose obligations only on those states. Furthermore art 1 of Council Directive 75/117 contains no provisions which are capable of conferring rights or imposing obligations on individuals as the terms of the directive do not even refer to retirement benefits and afford no guidance as to how they should apply to such matters. It is plain that individuals may not rely on directives as having horizontal effect so as to create rights inter se which may be enforced as a matter of law.

Article 1 of Council Directive 76/207   In the submission of the government of the United Kingdom this directive does not touch the lawfulness of the provision of free travel facilities after retirement since, of the items referred to in art 1 of the directive, the only one which could conceivably be relevant is social security but as matters of social security are excluded from the directive, the benefits in question do not come within the scope of that directive.

For the same reasons as those advanced in relation to Council Directive 75/117 the government of the United Kingdom submits that Council Directive 76/207 does not have direct effect either, especially as art 5 plainly shows that detailed legislation is contemplated to give effect to the general principle with which the directive is concerned. What is more, since the time limit in art 9(1) of that directive expired on 12 August 1978, that is to say after the proceedings in the present case were commenced, no question of the application of this directive can in any event arise in the present proceedings.

Accordingly, in the view of the government of the United Kingdom, the court should answer the questions referred to it by the House of Lords as follows: '(1) Travel facilities voluntarily granted by an employer to employees after their retirement are not pay within the meaning of art 119 of the EEC Treaty and, if they were, discrimination on the grounds of sex in the granting of such facilities would not give rise to rights enforceable by an individual against his employer or former employer; (2) such facilities are not within the provisions of art 1 of Council Directive 75/117 or art 1 of Council Directive 76/207 and, if they were, those articles would not give rise to rights enforceable by an individual against his employer or former employer.'

Christopher Carr for Mrs Garland.
Anthony Scrivener QC for BREL.
Peter Scott QC for the United Kingdom.
John Forman, agent for the EC Commission, for the Commission.

8 December. **The Advocate-General (P VerLoren van Themaat)** delivered the following opinion[1]: Mr President, Members of the Court, the background to Case 12/81, now before the court, is the understandable desire of Mrs Garland to be able to continue to enjoy the same travel facilities as retired male employees of her employer, British Rail Engineering Ltd (BREL), after she attains pensionable age. The travel facilities for retired male employees are also available to their wives and dependent children. It appears from a letter of 4 December 1975 which was sent by the British Railways Board to the trade unions and is contained in the file on the case that since 1976 female employees have in this respect been treated in the same way as men during their employment. However, it appears from the same letter that after female employees retire facilities for the members of their families are withdrawn. Mrs Garland's dispute with her employer eventually reached the House of Lords. The House of Lords has put the following questions on the case to the court:

'1. Where an employer provides (although not bound to do so by contract) special travel facilities for former employees to enjoy after retirement which discriminate against former female employees in the manner described above, is this contrary to: (a) Article 119 of the EEC Treaty? (b) Article 1 of Council Directive 75/117/EEC? (c) Article 1 of Council Directive 76/207/EEC?

2. If the answer to Questions 1(a), 1(b) or 1(c) is affirmative, is Article 119 or either of the said directives directly applicable in Member States so as to confer enforceable Community rights upon individuals in the above circumstances?'

Question 1

For a summary of the arguments put forward by Mrs Garland, the Commission, BREL and the government of the United Kingdom in this case I refer as usual to the report for the hearing (see pp 405–408, ante).

Like the applicant and the Commission I am of the opinion that the questions raised may be answered on the basis of the court's previous decisions wholly in the context of art 119 of the EEC Treaty.

I shall consider question 1 first. To begin I would remind the court that besides applying to the ordinary basic or minimum wage or salary the principle of equal pay enunciated in art 119 also applies to any other consideration, whether in cash or in kind, provided that two conditions are fulfilled: (1) it must be paid directly or indirectly by the employer to the employee; (2) the payment must be in respect of his employment.

In his opinion in *Defrenne v Belgian State* Case 80/70 [1971] ECR 445 at 453ff Mr Advocate-General Dutheillet de Lamothe explained in detail why in his opinion pensions, inter alia, paid directly by an employer to a former employee fall within the ambit of art 119. I find his arguments convincing and believe that they also apply mutatis mutandis to facilities like those at issue here. I shall however return to that point later on in my opinion. The judgment in *Defrenne v Belgian State* [1971] ECR 445 at 451 itself states at para 6:

'The provision in the second paragraph of the article extends the concept of pay to any other consideration, whether in cash or in kind, whether immediate or future, provided that the worker receives it, albeit indirectly, in respect of his employment from his employer.'

Therefore the assumption in that judgment too is that art 119 also encompasses future consideration fulfilling the other conditions of art 119 to which I have referred. Mr Advocate-General Warner in his opinion in *Worringham v Lloyds Bank Ltd* Case 69/80 [1981] 2 All ER 434 at 437, so far as here material, came to similar conclusions to those of Mr Advocate-General Dutheillet de Lamothe.

It is therefore clear in any event from the court's previous decisions that art 119 also covers future consideration. It is also clear from Form BR 7103/6, 'Concessions For Retired Staff', which has been produced, that the consideration in question is given to

---

1 Translated from the Dutch

employees by the employer directly in the United Kingdom and indirectly outside it. Third, it follows from the wording of art 119 that the principle of equal pay which it lays down is not restricted to contractually agreed consideration within the meaning of that article. During the oral procedure BREL also admitted that during the course of an employment contract the travel facilities in question must be regarded as pay within the meaning of art 119. The only difference of opinion remaining is therefore on the question whether the continuance of the travel facilities for an employee after his retirement may also be regarded as consideration 'in respect of his employment', in which case, the connection with employment cannot be deduced from a contract otherwise than by virtue of company pension rules. Nevertheless in my opinion Mr Advocate-General Dutheillet de Lamothe's observation in *Defrenne v Belgian State* [1971] ECR 445 at 458 also applies to those travel facilities. He said: 'It is moreover because of the post, which it is true he no longer occupies but which he had necessarily to occupy, that he may receive this benefit.' There is nothing in the file on the case to indicate that the travel facilities are granted in any respect other than employment. On the contrary the relevant notice to staff expressly bears the title '*Information for railway staff* at the time of their retirement' (my emphasis). The connection with the employment is therefore expressly recognised. It is still more clear from the letter of 4 December 1975 to the trade unions, to which I referred earlier and which was produced at the court's request, that after retirement the facilities must be regarded as a continuation of the travel facilities granted at the time of employment. Otherwise it would not have been possible for the letter to refer to partial withdrawal of those facilities. As I have said, BREL has already admitted during the oral procedure that at the time of employment the facilities fall under art 119. That must also be so in the case of the subsequent continuation of the facilities.

Therefore in my view the first question put to the court by the House of Lords must be answered in the affirmative: the discrimination in question is contrary to art 119 of the EEC Treaty.

Question 2

In its written observations the government of the United Kingdom refers to para 17 of the court's judgment in *Jenkins v Kingsgate (Clothing Productions) Ltd* Case 96/80 [1981] 1 WLR 972 at 983, and denies that if question 1(a) is answered in the affirmative art 119 would in addition be directly applicable in this case. In para 17, after referring to its previous decisions on art 119 of the EEC Treaty, the court held that it—

'applies directly to all forms of discrimination which may be identified solely with the aid of criteria of equal work and equal pay referred to by the article in question, without national or Community measures being required to define them with greater precision in order to permit of their application.'

In the opinion of the government of the United Kingdom such national or Community measures would be necessary in this case in order to resolve the questions regarding the differing retiring age and life expectancy which directly affect the cost of the benefit to the employer and its value to the employee.

With regard to that argument I should first like to concur with the Commission's observation made during the oral procedure that, in contrast to *Burton v British Rlys Board* Case 19/81 (16 February 1982, unreported), differing retiring ages are not in point here. The question raised concerns the travel facilities granted after retirement for the benefit of members of a former employee's family, irrespective of whether or not the retiring age of the employee himself is different. In my analysis those facilities fall within the ambit of art 119. There is no indication in the wording of art 119 that the application of the article in this case should depend on the answer to questions such as those mentioned by the government of the United Kingdom. The form of discrimination in question can on the contrary be identified as such merely with the aid of the criteria set forth in that article. Moreover I would add that in my view if the questions raised by the United Kingdom are in fact relevant further elaboration of its argument tends precisely to refute it. If it is true that the life expectancy of women is higher than that of men and it is possible to take that into account, then the grant of travel facilities to the husband of a female employee would entail not more, but less, cost than travel facilities granted to the wife of a male employee. So in that respect too the retiring age of the employee has no relevance at all in this case.

On the basis of the court's dicta in para 17 of its judgment in *Jenkins v Kingsgate (Clothing Productions) Ltd* I therefore come to the conclusion that the second question raised by the House of Lords should also be answered in the affirmative.

Summing up

In my view the questions raised should accordingly be answered as follows: (1) if an employer continues to grant former employees and members of their family special travel facilities after they attain their retirement age those facilities constitute 'pay' within the meaning of the second paragraph of art 119 of the EEC Treaty and should comply with the principle of equal pay for equal work within the meaning of that article; (2) if discrimination in that respect is identifiable as such with the aid of the criteria of 'equal work' and 'equal pay' set forth in art 119 of the EEC Treaty that article is directly applicable in the member states so as to confer enforceable Community rights on the former employees discriminated against.

9 February. **THE COURT OF JUSTICE** delivered its judgment which having summarised the facts, procedure and submissions of the parties, dealt with the law as follows:

1. By order dated 19 January 1981 which was received at the court on 22 January 1981 the House of Lords referred to the court for a preliminary ruling under art 177 of the EEC Treaty two questions as to the interpretation of art 119 of the treaty, art 1 of EEC Council Directive 75/117 of 10 February 1975 on the approximation of the laws of the member states relating to the application of the principle of equal pay for men and women and of art 1 of EEC Council Directive 76/207 of 9 February 1976 on the implementation of the principle of equal treatment for men and women as regards access to employment, vocational training and promotion, and working conditions.

2. Those questions were raised in the context of a dispute between an employee of British Rail Engineering Ltd (BREL), a subsidiary of the British Railways Board, which is a body created by the Transport Act 1962 charged with the duty of managing the railways in the United Kingdom, concerning discrimination alleged to be suffered by female employees who on retirement no longer continue to enjoy travel facilities for their spouses and dependent children although male employees continue to do so.

3. It was submitted before the House of Lords that that situation was contrary to art 119 and the directives implementing it and the House of Lords therefore referred the following two questions to the court:

'1. Where an employer provides (although not bound to do so by contract) special travel facilities for former employees to enjoy after retirement which discriminate against former female employees in the manner described above, is this contrary to: (a) Article 119 of the EEC Treaty? (b) Article 1 of Council Directive 75/117/EEC? (c) Article 1 of Council Directive 76/207/EEC?

2. If the answer to Questions 1(a), 1(b) or 1(c) is affirmative, is Article 119 or either of the said directives directly applicable in Member States so as to confer enforceable Community rights upon individuals in the above circumstances?'

Question 1

4. To assist in answering the first question it is first of all necessary to investigate the legal nature of the special travel facilities at issue in this case which the employer grants although not contractually bound to do so.

5. It is important to note in this regard that in para 6 of its judgment in *Defrenne v*

Belgian State Case 80/70 [1971] ECR 445 at 451 the court stated that the concept of pay contained in the second paragraph of art 119 comprises any other consideration, whether in cash or in kind, whether immediate or future, provided that the worker receives it, albeit indirectly, in respect of his employment from his employer.

6. According to the order making the reference for a preliminary ruling, when male employees of the BREL undertaking retire from their employment on reaching retirement age they continue to be granted special travel facilities for themselves, their wives and their dependent children.

7. A feature of those facilities is that they are granted in kind by the employer to the retired male employee or his dependants directly or indirectly in respect of his employment.

8. Moreover, it appears from a letter sent by BREL to the trade unions on 4 December 1975 that the special travel facilities granted after retirement must be considered to be an extension of the facilities granted during the period of employment.

9. It follows from those considerations that rail travel facilities such as those referred to by the House of Lords fulfil the criteria enabling them to be treated as pay within the meaning of art 119 of the EEC Treaty.

10. The argument that the facilities are not related to a contractual obligation is immaterial. The legal nature of the facilities is not important for the purposes of the application of art 119 provided that they are granted in respect of the employment.

11. It follows that where an employer (although not bound to do so by contract) provides special travel facilities for former male employees to enjoy after their retirement this constitutes discrimination within the meaning of art 119 against former female employees who do not receive the same facilities.

12. In view of the interpretation given to art 119 of the EEC Treaty, which by itself answers the question posed by the House of Lords, there is no need to consider points (b) and (c) of question 1 which raise the same question with reference to art 1 of EEC Council Directive 75/117 and of EEC Council Directive 76/207.

Question 2

13. Since question 1(a) has been answered in the affirmative the question arises of the direct applicability of art 119 in the member states and of the rights which individuals may invoke on that basis before national courts.

14. In para 17 of its judgment *Jenkins v Kingsgate (Clothing Productions) Ltd* Case 96/80 [1981] 1 WLR 972 at 983 the court stated that art 119 of the treaty applies directly to all forms of discrimination which may be identified solely with the aid of the criteria of equal work and equal pay referred to by the article in question, without national or Community measures being required to define them with greater precision in order to permit of their application.

15. Where a national court is able, using the criteria of equal work and equal pay, without the operation of Community or national measures, to establish that the grant of special transport facilities solely to retired male employees represents discrimination based on difference of sex, the provisions of art 119 of the treaty apply directly to such a situation.

Costs

16. The costs incurred by the Commission of the European Communities and the government of the United Kingdom of Great Britain and Northern Ireland, which have submitted observations to the court, are not recoverable. As this case is, in so far as the parties to the main action are concerned, in the nature of a step in the proceedings before the national court, the decision as to costs is a matter for that court.

On those grounds, the court hereby rules: (1) where an employer (although not bound to do so by contract) provides special travel facilities for former male employees to enjoy after their retirement this constitutes discrimination within the meaning of art 119 against former female employees who do not receive the same facilities; (2) where a national court is able, using the criteria of equal work and equal pay, without the operation of Community or national measures, to establish that the grant of special travel facilities solely to retired male employees represents discrimination based on difference of sex, the provisions of art 119 of the treaty apply directly to such a situation.

Agents: *A F Whitehead* (for Mrs Garland); *E J Doble* (for BREL); *R D Munrow*, Treasury Solicitor's Department (for the United Kingdom); *John Forman*, Legal Service of the EC Commission (for the Commission).

Appeal

Following the receipt by the House of Lords of the answers to the questions returned to it by the Court of Justice of the European Communities the respondent, British Rail Engineering Ltd (BREL), conceded that the construction put on s 6(4) of the Sex Discrimination Act 1975 by the Employment Appeal Tribunal ([1978] 2 All ER 789) was correct and accordingly that the appeal had to be allowed. The matter was reconsidered by the House of Lords without further argument by counsel.

22 April. The following opinions were delivered.

LORD DIPLOCK. My Lords, the facts which give rise to this appeal are sufficiently stated in the four explanatory paragraphs incorporated in a reference to the Court of Justice of the European Communities, made by this House under art 177 of the EEC Treaty, of questions concerning the interpretation of art 119 of that treaty and of two directives made by the Council of Ministers. The reference was in the following terms:
    1. Mrs Eileen Mary Garland is a married woman employed by the respondent, British Rail Engineering Ltd (BREL). The whole of the shareholding in BREL is held by the British Railways Board which is a public authority charged by statute with the duty of providing railway services in Great Britain.
    2. All employees of BREL enjoy certain valuable concessionary travel facilities during the period of their employment. These facilities entitle each employee, regardless of sex to travel free or at a reduced rate on British Rail and certain foreign railways. Such facilities are extended not only to the employee, but to his or her spouse and dependent children.
    3. After employees of BREL retire from their employment on reaching retiring age (which is earlier for women than for men) there is a difference in their treatment depending on their sex. In the case of former male employees, they continue to be granted (though on a reduced scale) travel facilities for themselves, their wives and dependent children. In the case of former female employees, they receive (on a similarly reduced scale) travel facilities for themselves, but no such facilities are granted in respect of their husbands or dependent children. These facilities are not enjoyed by former employees as a matter of contractual right, but employees have a legitimate expectation that they will enjoy them after retirement and it would be difficult in practice for BREL to withdraw them unilaterally without the agreement of the trade unions of which its employees are members.
    4. On 25 November 1976 Mrs Garland complained to an industrial tribunal that BREL was discriminating against her contrary to the provisions of a United Kingdom Act of Parliament, the Sex Discrimination Act 1975. Her complaint after consideration also by two intermediate appellate courts (Employment Appeal Tribunal, [1978] 2 All ER 789; Court of Appeal, [1979] 2 All ER 1163, [1979] 1 WLR 754) has now reached the House of Lords which is a court against whose decision there is no judicial remedy under United Kingdom law.
    5. In order to enable it to give judgment on the appeal, this House considers that a decision is necessary on the following questions:
        '1. Where an employer provides (although not bound to do so by contract) special travel facilities for former employees to enjoy after retirement which discriminate

against former female employees in the manner described above, is this contrary to: (a) Article 119 of the EEC Treaty? (b) Article 1 of Council Directive 75/117/EEC? (c) Article 1 of Council Directive 76/207/EEC?

2. If the answer to Questions 1(a), 1(b) or 1(c) is affirmative, is Article 119 or either of the directives directly applicable in Member States so as to confer enforceable Community rights upon individuals in the above circumstances?'

Before it reached this House, Mrs Garland's claim had been dealt with in an industrial court, the Employment Appeal Tribunal and the Court of Appeal on the footing that it turned on the true construction of s 6(4) of the Sex Discrimination Act 1975, but without any consideration being given to the fact that equal pay without discrimination on the grounds of sex is required by art 119 of the EEC Treaty and that the application of this article had also been the subject of directives made by the Council of the EEC under art 189 of the treaty. Furthermore, after the passing of the Sex Discrimination Act 1975, the European Court had held in *Defrenne v Sabena* Case 43/75 (1976) [1981] 1 All ER 122 that art 119 was directly applicable in member states, without the necessity of any further act by any institution of the Community or legislative action by a member state, to make unlawful any discrimination between men and women in the amount of compensation receivable by them for equal work performed in the same establishment whether private or public.

Section 6 of the Sex Discrimination Act 1975 appears in Part II of the Act which bears the general heading 'Discrimination in the Employment Field' and is the first of a fasciculus of five sections under the sub-heading 'Discrimination by employers'. For present purposes it is sufficient to set out the following provisions of s 6:

'(1) It is unlawful for a person, in relation to employment by him at an establishment in Great Britain, to discriminate against a woman—(a) in the arrangements he makes for the purpose of determining who should be offered that employment, or (b) in the terms on which he offers her that employment, or (c) by refusing or deliberately omitting to offer her that employment.

(2) It is unlawful for a person, in the case of a woman employed by him at an establishment in Great Britain, to discriminate against her—(a) in the way he affords her access to opportunities for promotion, transfer or training, or to any other benefits, facilities or services, or by refusing or deliberately omitting to afford her access to them, or (b) by dismissing her, or subjecting her to any other detriment
. . .

(4) Subsections 1(b) and (2) do not apply to provisions in relation to death or retirement . . .'

The industrial tribunal was of opinion that concessionary travel facilities afforded to ex-employees after their retirement fell within sub-s (4): they were 'provision in relation to . . . retirement' and so were not subject to the prohibition on discrimination imposed by sub-s (1)(b) or sub-s (2)(a). The Employment Appeal Tribunal took the contrary view. They considered that the words of the exception created by sub-s (4) ought not to be construed so widely as to include 'a privilege [that] has existed during employment' and is allowed by the employer 'to continue after retirement'. The Court of Appeal (Lord Denning MR, Lawton and Geoffrey Lane LJJ) restored the decision of the industrial tribunal. Lawton LJ described the question of construction of sub-s (4) as being 'largely a matter of first impression'. His own first impression, which was shared and adopted by Lord Denning MR, was that 'provision in relation to . . . retirement' was a wide expression and included any provision *about* retirement.

In neither the Employment Appeal Tribunal nor the Court of Appeal was attention drawn by counsel, as it should have been, to art 119 of the EEC Treaty or to either of the two directives dealing with sex discrimination, EEC Council Directive 75/117 of 10 February 1975 and EEC Council Directive 76/207 of 9 February 1976, although in the light of the answers given by the European Court to the questions referred by this House, reference to art 119 is sufficient to dispose of the matter and reliance on neither of these directives has turned out to be necessary.

The relevant provisions of art 119 are:

> 'Each Member State shall during the first stage ensure and subsequently maintain the application of the principle that men and women should receive equal pay for equal work.
>
> For the purpose of this Article, "pay" means the ordinary basic or minimum wage or salary and any other consideration, whether in cash or in kind, which the worker receives, directly, or indirectly, in respect of his employment from his employer . . .'

My Lords, even if the obligation to observe the provisions of art 119 were an obligation assumed by the United Kingdom under an ordinary international treaty or convention and there were no question of the treaty obligation being directly applicable as part of the law to be applied by the courts in this country without need for any further enactment, it is a principle of construction of United Kingdom statutes, now too well established to call for citation of authority, that the words of a statute passed after the treaty has been signed and dealing with the subject matter of the international obligation of the United Kingdom, are to be construed, if they are reasonably capable of bearing such a meaning, as intended to carry out the obligation and not to be inconsistent with it. A fortiori is this the case where the treaty obligation arises under one of the Community treaties to which s 2 of the European Communities Act 1972 applies.

The instant appeal does not present an appropriate occasion to consider whether, having regard to the express direction as to the construction of enactments 'to be passed' which is contained in s 2(4), anything short of an express positive statement in an Act of Parliament passed after 1 January 1973 that a particular provision is intended to be made in breach of an obligation assumed by the United Kingdom under a Community treaty would justify an English court in construing that provision in a manner inconsistent with a Community treaty obligation of the United Kingdom however wide a departure from the prima facie meaning of the language of the provision might be needed in order to achieve consistency. For, in the instant case the words of s 6(4) of the Sex Discrimination Act 1975 that fall to be construed, 'provision in relation to . . . retirement', without any undue straining of the ordinary meaning of the language used, are capable of bearing either the narrow meaning accepted by the Employment Appeal Tribunal or the wider meaning preferred by the Court of Appeal but acknowledged by that court to be largely a matter of first impression. Had the attention of the court been drawn to art 119 of the EEC Treaty and the judgment of the European Court in *Defrenne v Sabena* Case 43/75 (1976) [1981] 1 All ER 122, I have no doubt that, consistently with statements made by Lord Denning MR in previous cases, they would have construed s 6(4) so as not to make it inconsistent with art 119.

In order to decide whether the construction of s 6(4) in fact adopted by the Court of Appeal was inconsistent with art 119, and whether that alternative construction adopted by the Employment Appeal Tribunal was consistent with it, it was desirable to obtain a ruling of the European Court that would be binding on all courts in England, including this House, on the question of the effect of art 119 on the kind of discrimination as respects concessionary travel facilities after retirement to which Mrs Garland was subjected by her employer simply because she was a woman and not a man.

Although I do not believe that any of your Lordships had any serious doubt what answer would be given to that question by the European Court, there was not in existence at 19 January 1981, the date when the order of reference under art 177 was made, so considerable and consistent a line of case law of the European Court on the interpretation and direct applicability of art 119 as would make the answer too obvious and inevitable to be capable of giving rise to what could properly be regarded as 'a question' within the meaning of art 177. It thus became mandatory on this House, as a court from whose decisions there is no possibility of appeal under internal law, to refer to the European Court the questions that were in fact referred by the order that I have quoted at the beginning of this speech, so as to provide the House with material necessary to aid it in construing s 6(4) of the Sex Discrimination Act 1975.

To those questions the answers by the European Court are:

> '... the court hereby rules: (1) where an employer (although not bound to do so by contract) provides special travel facilities for former male employees to enjoy after their retirement this constitutes discrimination within the meaning of art 119 against former female employees who do not receive the same facilities; (2) where a national court is able, using the criteria of equal work and equal pay, without the operation of Community or national measures, to establish that the grant of special travel facilities solely to retired male employees represents discrimination based on difference of sex, the provisions of art 119 of the treaty apply directly to such a situation.'

As is rightly conceded by the respondent employer, BREL, these answers make it clear that the construction put on s 6(4) of the Sex Discrimination Act 1975 by the Employment Appeal Tribunal was correct, with the result that the appeal must be allowed.

LORD EDMUND-DAVIES. My Lords, I have had the privilege of reading in draft the speech of my noble and learned friend Lord Diplock, with which I concur.

LORD FRASER OF TULLYBELTON. My Lords, I concur with Lord Diplock.

LORD RUSSELL OF KILLOWEN. My Lords, I concur with Lord Diplock.

LORD SCARMAN. My Lords, I concur with Lord Diplock.

Appeal allowed.

Solicitors: *Russell, Jones & Walker* (for Mrs Garland); *Evan Harding* (for BREL).

Mary Rose Plummer   Barrister.

Attorney General's Reference (No 1 of 1981)

COURT OF APPEAL, CRIMINAL DIVISION

LORD LANE CJ, TALBOT AND MCCOWAN JJ

19 FEBRUARY, 11 MARCH 1982

Customs and excise – Importation of prohibited goods – Knowingly concerned in fraudulent evasion of prohibition or restriction – Fraudulent – Whether necessary to prove that acts of deceit practised in presence of customs officer – Whether sufficient to prove dishonest conduct which was deliberately intended to evade prohibition or duty – Customs and Excise Management Act 1979, s 170(2).

In the early hours of the morning when there were normally no customs officials on duty the defendants unloaded a quantity of smuggled cannabis from a cargo vessel docked at a quayside. Unknown to the defendants, they were observed by customs officials keeping a special watch on the defendants and when the defendants drove off with the cannabis they were pursued and stopped. They were subsequently charged, under s 170(2)[a] of the Customs and Excise Management Act 1979, with being knowingly concerned in a fraudulent evasion of the prohibition on the importation of cannabis. At their trial they submitted that the evidence did not establish that they had 'fraudulently' evaded the prohibition within the meaning of s 170(2). The judge ruled that for the evasion to be 'fraudulent' it had to be shown that the accused had actually deceived or attempted to deceive the customs officials and that, since the evidence did not prove that, the defendants should be acquitted. On a reference by the Attorney General to the court for its opinion on the true effect of the word 'fraudulent' on a prosecution under s 170(2),

Held – In order to prove an offence under s 170(2) of the 1979 Act, it was not necessary to prove that acts of deceit had been practised in the presence of a customs officer but merely that there had been fraudulent conduct, in the sense of dishonest conduct deliberately intended to evade the prohibition or restriction with respect to goods or the duty chargeable thereon (see p 422 *b c*, post).

Dictum of Viscount Dilhorne in *Scott v Comr of Police for the Metropolis* [1974] 3 All ER at 1038 applied.

R v Williams [1953] 1 All ER 1068 and *R v Smith (Donald)* [1973] 2 All ER 1161 considered.

R v Borro and Abdullah [1973] Crim LR 513 not followed.

Notes

For fraudulent evasion of duty or prohibition or restriction on importation of goods, see 12 Halsbury's Laws (4th edn) para 642.

For the Customs and Excise Management Act 1979, s 170, see 49 Halsbury's Statutes (3rd edn) 443.

Cases referred to in judgment

R v Borro and Abdullah [1973] Crim LR 513, CA.

R v Holloway (1849) 2 Car & Kir 942, 175 ER 395, CCR, 15 Digest (Reissue) 1289, 11,097.

---

[a]   Section 170(2), so far as material, provides: '. . . if any person is, in relation to any goods, in any way knowingly concerned in any fraudulent evasion or attempt at evasion—(*a*) of any duty chargeable on the goods; (*b*) of any prohibition or restriction . . . with respects to the goods . . . or (*c*) of any provision of the Customs and Excise Acts 1979 applicable to the goods, he shall be guilty of an offence under this section . . .'

R v Smith (Donald) [1973] 2 All ER 1161, [1973] QB 924, [1973] 3 WLR 88, CA, 17 Digest
(Reissue) 535, *311.*

R v Williams [1953] 1 All ER 1068, [1953] 1 QB 660, [1953] 2 WLR 1308, CCA, 15 Digest
(Reissue) 1286, *11,071.*

Scott v Comr of Police for the Metropolis [1974] 3 All ER 1032, [1975] AC 819, [1974] 3
WLR 741, HL, 15 Digest (Reissue) 1401, *12,272.*

Reference

This was a reference by the Attorney General, under s 36 of the Criminal Justice Act
1972, for the opinion of the Court of Appeal on a point of law arising in a case where the
accused had been acquitted on the direction of the trial judge on an indictment charging
them with being knowingly concerned in the fraudulent evasion of the prohibition on
the importation of cannabis, contrary to s 170(2) of the Customs and Excise Management
Act 1979. The terms of the reference and the facts are set out in the judgment of the
court.

Robin Auld QC and *D A Evans* for the Attorney General.
Simon D Brown as amicus curiae.
The respondents did not appear.

Cur adv vult

11 March. **LORD LANE CJ** read the following judgment of the court: The question
for the consideration of the court is this: whether the presence of the word 'fraudulent'
in s 170(2) of the Customs and Excise Management Act 1979 has the effect, that in
prosecutions under that provision for fraudulent evasion or attempted evasion of a
prohibition or restriction with respect to goods or of duty chargeable thereon, the
prosecution must prove fraudulent conduct in the sense of (1) acts of deceit practised on
a customs officer in this presence or merely (2) conduct deliberately intended to evade the
prohibition of restriction with respect to, or the duty chargeable on, goods as the case
may be.

The facts on which this reference is based are as follows. On 6 August 1980 some
32·64 kg of cannabis were smuggled into the United Kingdom on a banana boat from
Jamaica. The drugs were unloaded from the ship by the defendants in the early hours of
the morning at a time when there was no customs officer on regular duty at the port.
However, unknown to the defendants, they were being watched by officers of the
Customs and Excise, specially assigned for the purpose.

The defendants with the drugs in the car drove it towards the dock gates where they
were signalled to stop by a police officer. They did not stop. A car chase ensued and they
were eventually arrested and the drugs were found in the car. When interviewed by the
officers of the Customs and Excise, one of the defendants admitted his complicity in the
importation of the drugs, the other made no admission of guilt but told a number of lies.

Events at the trial took the following course: at the close of the prosecution's case,
submissions were made on behalf of both defendants that the evidence did not establish
that the evasion of the prohibition on importation of drugs was 'fraudulent' within the
meaning of s 170(2) of the Customs and Excise Management Act 1979.

The learned judge in a careful ruling on this submission first of all reviewed such
authorities as exist on the subject. He came to the conclusion, with which this court
respectfully agrees, that, apart from one case, to which reference must be made in a
moment, the courts which have had the task of examining convictions under this section
of the Act, or under its predecessors which contain similar words, have not felt themselves
obliged to devote attention to the precise meaning of the word 'fraudulent' in the
section. The judge felt himself bound however by the decision in *R v Borro and Abdullah*
[1973] Crim LR 513 (a decision of this court delivered on 22 May 1973) to come to the
conclusion that the prosecution, in order to satisfy the word 'fraudulent', had to prove

that there was something done by the defendant which amounted to acting or telling lies or deceiving ot attempting to deceive customs officers. He took the view that the evidence in the instant case amounted only to bringing goods on shore and then making off with them and seeking to evade capture. That did not seem to him to amount to deceit in the traditional sense or to come within the definition of 'fraudulent' which he found in *R v Borro and Abdullah*. The defendants were accordingly acquitted.

The judge's decision is challenged by counsel appearing on behalf of the Attorney General. His arguments are supported by those of counsel who appeared before us as amicus curiae.

Their submission is that the word 'fraudulent' in this particular section means no more than a deliberate intention to break the prohibition contained in the Act, and that in preventing a customs officer from doing his duty in relation to the importation of prohibited goods, there can be no difference in principle between a defendant who avoids the customs control by choosing a time or place or route to conceal his smuggling activity and a defendant who conceals the goods or tries to lie when passing through customs control. In short, their submission is that it is enough for the prosecution to prove dishonesty to satisfy the word 'fraudulent' in the section.

We turn first to consider the decision of this court in *R v Borro and Abdullah* [1973] Crim LR 513. That was a charge of conspiracy; the allegation being that the defendants had conspired together fraudulently to evade the restriction on the importation of cannabis into the United Kingdom. The direction given to the jury by the judge of trial was as follows:

> '"Fraudulently" is a word which sometimes gives trouble in court. In many cases it is obvious to courts where somebody is swindling somebody else out of money. But in the courts, "fraudulently" has a much wider usage than that. It involves, first, acting or telling lies, deceit; that is the first essential. Something you know to be untrue; I underline the word "know"; know to be untrue; and if you do that with intent in this case to cause the customs officers to act contrary to otherwise what would be their duty, then you have a fraudulent intent: first you commit or carry out a deceit; secondly, it is done with an intention to make the customs officers not carry out what would otherwise be their duty. Their duty is not to allow the importation of cannabis and to seize it if it comes into this country. If that was the intention in the conspirators' minds when they entered into the conspiracy then it is fraudulent.'

That was held to be a correct direction. Much of the argument in that case was taken up with a discussion as to whether there were sufficient acts within the jurisdiction to render the defendants liable to prosecution for conspiracy in the courts of this country.

The acts which were said to amount to deceit practised on the customs officers were somewhat tenuous. The defendants were en route from Beirut to Antigua. Their journey took them through Heathrow Airport where they had to change aircraft. They stayed overnight at the Skyways Hotel, and on the following morning went to the airport to resume their journey. They had a number of suitcases. These were not released to the passengers but remained in the custody of the airline on their behalf pending the continuance of their journey. Some of the suitcases contained cannabis.

There was no evidence that anything had been done directly by the defendants in an endeavour to deceive the customs officer. The evidence relied on as amounting to deceit was what was described as the 'charade' performed by the defendants of being passengers in charge of 'passengers' baggage' within the meaning of s 28 of the Customs and Excise Act 1952. This relieved an importer of goods from the duty to deliver in proper form what is described as an entry of the goods imported, provided the goods were 'passengers' baggage'.

The way the argument went was that 'passengers' baggage' only relates to that which can properly be called part of the baggage of passengers and does not apply to what which accompanies the passenger but which is in fact merchandise imported, not as part of his baggage, but for purposes other than his personal use. Since the cannabis was not for the passenger's personal use, therefore it was not 'passengers' baggage', therefore the defendants were within the jurisdiction living the lie 'that the suitcases were passengers' baggage'. That, in the view of the court in that case, was a sufficient deceit on the customs officers to amount to fraudulent conduct and so to satisfy the definition of 'fraudulent' which was approved by the court in that case.

We think that if the court in that case had been able to consider the authorities which have been placed before us they would have come to a different conclusion as to the meaning of 'fraudulent'. Not only was *R v Borro and Abdullah* an ex tempore judgment of the court, but since the decision in that case there have been helpful speeches in the House of Lords defining the ambit of the word 'fraudulent'. Consequently we feel that we are in a position to reassess the meaning of the word.

The wording adopted in the 1979 Act can be traced back certainly as far as the Customs Consolidation Act 1853. If one reads s 232 of that Act, one finds the equivalent of four subsections of the 1979 Act contained in the one section. Those are (in order) ss 50(3) and (2) and 170(1) and (2). The wording in that section equivalent to s 170(2) is as follows: 'or who shall be in any way knowingly concerned in any fraudulent evasion or attempt at evasion of such duties or any part thereof'.

It is to be noted that neither in that forerunner of the modern Act nor in the 1979 Act itself is there any suggestion that customs officers need be deceived or defrauded in order to establish guilt. Indeed, what has to be 'fraudulent' is not behaviour towards a customs officer but the evasion or attempt at evasion of the prohibition. Consequently, it seems to us to be inappropriate to import narrow definitions of the word 'fraudulent' from branches of the law dealing with fraud practised on other persons.

The wider meaning of the word is well illustrated by the decision in *R v Williams* [1953] 1 All ER 1068 at 1069–1070, [1953] 1 QB 660 at 665–666. Lord Goddard CJ, having set out the definition of larceny found in s 1(1) of the Larceny Act 1916, went on as follows:

> 'It is well known that the Larceny Act, 1916, which was a codifying Act, was never intended to alter the law. The question is: What is the meaning of the word "fraudulently", and does it add anything to the words "without claim of right"? It was apparently, the opinion of PARKE, B., in *R. v. Holloway* ((1849) 2 Car & Kir 942), that the words "wrongful" and "fraudulent" meant without claim of right ... The court thinks that the word "fraudulently" does add, and is intended to add, something to the words "without a claim of right", and it means (though I am not saying that the words I am about to use will fit every case, but they certainly will fit this particular case) that the taking must be intentional and deliberate, that is to say, without mistake. You must know, when you take the property, that it is the property of another person and that you are taking it deliberately, not by mistake, and with an intention to deprive the person of the property in it.'

This use of the word 'fraudulent' is to be found in the very first comprehensive definition of theft in English law by Bracton, who borrowed it with some modification from Roman law, that is to say 'the fraudulent handling of another man's goods without his agreement and with the intention of stealing them'. Accordingly, this use of the word 'fraudulent' as explained by Lord Goddard CJ was well known to those who drafted the Act of 1853.

Stephen's *History of the Criminal Law of England* (1883) vol 2, p 121 reads as follows:

> 'Fraud—There has always been a great reluctance amongst lawyers to attempt to define fraud, and this is not unnatural when we consider the number of different kinds of conduct to which the word is applied in connection with different branches of law, and especially in connection with the equitable branch of it. I shall not attempt to construct a definition which will meet every case which might be suggested, but there is little danger in saying that whenever the words "fraud" or

"intent to defraud" or "fraudulently" occur in the definition of a crime, two elements at least are essential to the commission of the crime: namely, first, deceit or an intention to deceive or in some cases mere secrecy; and, secondly, either actual injury or possible injury or an intent to expose some person either to actual injury or to a risk of possible injury by means of that deceit or secrecy.'

This passage from Stephen was cited by Viscount Dilhorne in *Scott v Comr of Police for the Metropolis* [1974] 3 All ER 1032 at 1035–1036, [1975] AC 819 at 836–837. He went on to say:

'In the course of the argument many cases were cited. It is not necessary to refer to all of them. Many were cases in which the conspiracy alleged was to defraud by deceit. Those cases do not establish that there can only be a conspiracy to defraud if deceit is involved and there are a number of cases where that was not the case.'

He then went on to cite some six cases as examples.

The following passage appears again from the speech of Viscount Dilhorne ([1974] 3 All ER 1032 at 1038, [1975] AC 819 at 839):

'One must not confuse the object of a conspiracy with the means by which it is intended to be carried out ... I have not the temerity to attempt an exhaustive definition of the meaning of "defraud". As I have said, words take colour from the context in which they are used, but the words "fraudulently" and "defraud" must ordinarily have a very similar meaning. If, as I think, and as the Criminal Law Revision Committee appears to have thought, "fraudulently" means "dishonestly", then to "defraud" ordinarily means, in my opinion, to deprive a person dishonestly of something which is his or of something to which he is or would or might but for the perpetration of the fraud be entitled.'

In our view this exhaustive consideration of the meaning of the words 'fraud' and 'fraudulent' has a direct bearing on the issue which we have to determine in the instant case.

If the view of the judge in the present case on the meaning of the word 'fraudulent' is correct, it produces some quite remarkable results. Evasion may, and often does, commence before the customs control point is reached. Indeed, if goods are in transit, that point may never be reached. *R v Borro and Abdullah* is an example of that. Another example is to be found in *R v Smith (Donald)* [1973] 2 All ER 1161 at 1167, [1973] QB 924 at 935. Willis J, delivering the judgment of the court, said:

'It seems quite clear that the Act contemplates that goods can be imported before they are either landed from a ship or unloaded from an aircraft ... it is plain that goods entering the country by air are imported before they are unloaded, as are goods brought by sea before they are landed ... It is sufficient to say that in this case we have no doubt that the cannabis in question was imported when the aircraft bringing it landed at Heathrow, and was exported when it was placed on board the BOAC aircraft and that it is quite irrelevant to the question of importation that it remained between unloading and reloading in a customs area.'

The court in that case was concerned with the Customs and Excise Act 1952, but the wording was similar to that of the 1979 Act.

What had happened in *Smith's* case was that packets containing cannabis addressed to a person in Bermuda were put on board an aircraft in Kenya which was bound for Heathrow Airport. At Heathrow the packets were unloaded and, without leaving the customs area, were put on board a second aircraft bound for Bermuda. The cannabis was discovered when the packets arrived in Bermuda. The defendant was charged with being knowingly concerned in the fraudulent evasion of the prohibition against the importation of cannabis. There was no possibility of deceit being practised on any customs officer. If deceit is a requirement, then in this sort of case there can never be a conviction under this subsection of the Act. This seems contrary to good sense. Moreover, if actual deceit of a customs officer is required, then no one involved in the importation after the customs point has been passed could normally be convicted. But importation is a continuing offence, and consequently this interpretation might mean that the eventual recipients and others who may have been primarily responsible for the evasion might escape justice.

It seems to us to be a misinterpretation of Parliament's intention, and a path to absurdity, to make guilt depend on whether a customs officer is met and deceived on the one hand, or simply intentionally avoided on the other.

In the result we have come to the conclusion that the presence of the word 'fraudulent' in s 170(2) of the Customs and Excise Management Act 1979 has the effect that, in prosecutions under that provision for fraudulent evasion or attempted evasion of a prohibition or restriction with respect to goods or duty chargeable thereon, the prosecution must prove fraudulent conduct in the sense of dishonest conduct deliberately intended to evade the prohibition or restriction with respect to, or the duty chargeable on, goods as the case may be. There is no necessity for the prosecution to prove acts of deceit practised on a customs officer in his presence.

Determination accordingly.

Solicitors: *Solicitor for the Customs and Excise; Treasury Solicitor.*

Sepala Munasinghe Esq   Barrister.

Re Creehouse Ltd

CHANCERY DIVISION
VINELOTT J
8 FEBRUARY 1982

Solicitor – Withdrawal – Application for order declaring that solicitor has ceased to act for party to litigation – Service of application – Whether application must be served on every party to the litigation or merely on party for whom solicitor was acting – Whether if removal of solicitor from record making conduct of litigation more time-consuming and expensive declaration should be refused – RSC Ord 32, r 3, Ord 67, r 6(2).

Since RSC Ord 67, r 6(2)[a] contemplates that an application by a solicitor for an order declaring that he has ceased to act for a party to litigation need only be served on that party, the general rule contained in Ord 32, r 3[b] that a summons must be served on 'every other party' does not apply to an application made under Ord 67, r 6(2). It follows that an application under Ord 67, r 6(2) need not be served on the other parties to litigation and that such other parties have no right to apply to set aside an order made under r 6(1) on the ground that the application for the order was not served on them. Furthermore,

---

a   Rule 6, so far as material, provides: '(1) Where a solicitor who has acted for a party in a cause or matter has ceased so to act and the party has not given notice of change . . . the solicitor may apply to the Court for an order declaring that the solicitor has ceased to be the solicitor acting for the party in the cause or matter, and the Court . . . may make an order accordingly . . .
(2) An application for an order under this rule must be made by summons . . . and the summons . . . must, unless the Court . . . otherwise directs, be served on the party for whom the solicitor acted. The application must be supported by an affidavit stating the grounds of the application . . .'
b   Rule 3, so far as material, provides: '. . . unless the Court otherwise orders or any of these rules otherwise provides, a summons must be served on every other party not less than two clear days before the day so specified.'

the fact that an order for a declaration under r 6(1) and the consequent removal of the solicitor's name from the record will make the conduct of the litigation more time-consuming and expensive for the other parties is not a ground for refusing to make an order under r 6 (see p 424 *g h* and p 425 *b* and *f*, post).

De Mora v Concha [1887] WN 194 considered.

Notes

For application by a solicitor for an order terminating his position as solicitor on the record, see 36 Halsbury's Laws (3rd edn) 72, para 102 and supplement to 36 Halsbury's Laws (3rd edn) para 102.

Case referred to in judgment

De Mora v Concha, Re Ward, Mills, Witham & Lambert [1887] WN 194, 43 Digest (Repl) 55, 433.

Motion

By a notice of motion dated 4 February 1982 the applicants, Rochem Group SA (formerly Taulay SA), Chalvey Ltd and Techem Laboratories LP, the plaintiffs by counterclaim to a petition presented by Rochem Group SA (the Swiss Rochem) a Swiss company, for the compulsory winding up of an English company, Creehouse Ltd, applied, inter alia, for an order setting aside orders made by Mr Registrar Bradburn on 3 February 1982, on summonses issued pursuant to RSC Ord 67, r 6(1) by solicitors, Messrs Payne, Hicks Beach & Co, declaring that the solicitors had ceased to be the solicitors acting for the Swiss Rochem. The orders were served on the applicants on 4 February and on the same day the solicitors were taken off the record. The facts are set out in the judgment.

C A Brodie QC, David Oliver and *Ian Geering* for the applicants.
Robin Potts for the solicitors.

VINELOTT J. The applications which are now before me arise out of a petition presented by a Swiss company, Rochem Group SA (the Swiss Rochem), seeking the compulsory winding up of a United Kingdom company, Creehouse Ltd, and an application, made a few days before the winding-up petition was presented, by a Panamanian company also called Rochem Group SA but which was originally called Taulay SA under s 135 of the Companies Act 1948, which asks the court to call a meeting of Creehouse Ltd. The petition is opposed by the Panamanian company (Taulay) and by two other bodies, a Cayman Island company, Chalvey Ltd (Chalvey), and a limited partnership established under the law of Delaware, USA, called Techem Laboratories LP (Techem).

On 10 June 1981 I ordered that the winding-up petition and the application under s 135 be heard together, and that Taulay, Chalvey and Techem (the last two of whom claimed to appear on the petition as creditors of Creehouse) should be at liberty to file points of defence and counterclaim to the petition. The Swiss Rochem appealed from that decision. The appeal was dismissed on 3 December 1981 and the Court of Appeal refused leave to appeal. A petition to the House of Lords for leave to appeal was dismissed on 21 January 1982.

On 28 January 1982 Messrs Payne, Hicks Beach & Co, who have acted on behalf of the Swiss Rochem throughout these proceedings, issued a summons pursuant to RSC Ord 67, r 6(1), seeking a declaration that they had ceased to be the solicitors acting for the Swiss Rochem in both sets of proceedings. That summons came before Mr Registrar Bradburn on 3 February. It was supported by an affidavit by a partner in the firm of Messrs Payne, Hicks Beach & Co, which exhibited a bundle of copy telexes. In the first telex dated 26 January addressed to Messrs Payne, Hicks Beach & Co by Dr Hans Rohrer he terminated 'your mandate in the matter of Creehouse Ltd with immediate effect'. On 28 January Messrs Payne, Hicks Beach & Co telexed the Swiss Rochem and, having stated that they proposed to apply in both sets of proceedings for orders declaring that they had

ceased to be the solicitors acting for the Swiss Rochem, that the Swiss Rochem pay the
costs of the application and that service on the Swiss Rochem be dispensed with, asked *a*
the Swiss Rochem to telex their consent to an order being made in those terms. That
consent was given by telex on the same day.

The summons came before Mr Registrar Bradburn on 3 February. He made an order
in each set of proceedings whereby he dispensed with service of the summons, ordered
that Messrs Payne, Hicks Beach & Co 'cease to be the solicitors acting for' the Swiss
Rochem, and ordered that the Swiss Rochem pay the costs of the application. That order *b*
was served on Taulay, Chalvey and Techem on 4 February, and on that day a certificate
of service was filed in the Companies Court and Payne, Hicks Beach & Co were taken off
the record. On the same day (or the day following, I am not sure which) Taulay, Chalvey
and Techem applied to me for leave which I gave to serve notice of motion for an order
setting aside the order of Mr Registrar Bradburn in each set of proceedings on the Swiss
Rochem by serving it at the offices of Messrs Payne, Hicks Beach & Co as if they had *c*
continued to be the solicitors acting for the Swiss Rochem on the record. The notices of
motion are in fact expressed to be given both to Messrs Payne, Hicks Beach & Co and to
the Swiss Rochem.

Two questions arise. The first is whether Taulay, Chalvey and Techem have any right
to apply to set aside Mr Registrar Bradburn's orders now that they have been drawn up
and served and acted on by the removal of Messrs Payne, Hicks Beach & Co from the *d*
record. The second is whether, if I am entitled to review the decision of Mr Registrar
Bradburn on the application of Taulay, Chalvey and Techem, I should set the orders
aside.

On the first question, counsel for the applicants submitted that Taulay, Chalvey and
Techem ought to have been served with the summonses issued by Messrs Payne, Hicks
Beach & Co on 28 January, and that as they were not served with those summonses the *e*
orders were not properly made and should be set aside. He submitted first that the
reason why Ord 67, r 6(2) provides specifically that an application for an order under that
rule must, unless the court otherwise directs, 'be served on the party for whom the
solicitor acted' is that there is nothing in the Rules of the Supreme Court which requires
an application by the solicitor for a party to litigation to serve his own client so that, in
the absence of this provision, an application might be made by a solicitor without his *f*
client knowing anything about it. He submitted second that there is nothing in Ord 67,
r 6(2), which excludes the application of the general rule in Ord 32, r 3, that unless the
court otherwise orders, or any of the Rules of the Supreme Court otherwise provide, a
summons by any party must be served on 'every other party not less than two clear days
before the day' specified for the hearing thereof.

I am not persuaded that this argument is well founded. Ord 32, r 3 deals with the *g*
extension or abridgment of the period of notice which must be given for the hearing of
an application in chambers made inter partes. In this context the words 'must be served
on every other party' do not direct service on every person who is a party to litigation in
the course of which an application in chambers is made, whether that person is affected
by the application or not. They provide for two clear days' notice to be given to persons
who ought properly to be served with a notice. It is, to my mind, clear that Ord 67, r 6(2) *h*
contemplates that an application by a solicitor under that rule will, at least in the
ordinary course, be served only on the party for whom the solicitor acted.

Counsel for the applicants referred me to a decision of Stirling J in *De Mora v Concha*
[1887] WN 194, which is very briefly reported. There an application was made ex parte
by a firm of solicitors to have their name taken off the record as solicitors for the
defendants to an action. An order was made on that application by Charles J during the *j*
Long Vacation in 1887. Later, on 31 October 1887, solicitors for other parties apparently
obtained liberty to attend the proceedings and served notice on one of the defendants,
JJC, addressed to him and his solicitors or agents of their intention to move to discharge
or vary another order made in the action in July 1879. The former solicitors for JJC
returned the notice of motion saying that they were not the solicitors on the record for

either defendant. A search of the cause book showed that an entry had been made on 13 October 1887 taking the solicitors off the record as solicitors for the defendants. Stirling J none the less held that service of the notice of motion on JJC's former solicitors was sufficient. The explanation of this decision may lie in the fact that it appears from the report that there was evidence that 'no notice of any change of solicitors had been served upon or received by the solicitors of the party moving'. It may be that in the absence of notice of the order of Charles J the party moving was entitled to treat JJC's former solicitors as still on the record for the purposes of service. So under Ord 67, r 6(1)(a) of the current Rules of the Supreme Court an order made under r 6 is not to take effect until served 'on every party to the cause or matter'. But be that as it may, I do not find anything in that decision which supports the argument that an application for an order under Ord 67, r 6 must be served on every party to the litigation, and the decision throws no light on the circumstances in which the court can entertain an application to discharge an order made under Ord 67, r 6 otherwise than by the party for whom the solicitor who made the application acted.

However, I do not propose to consider further whether there are circumstances in which the court can entertain such an application. In my judgment, Taulay, Chalvey and Techem have not shown that they have any legitimate ground for seeking to set aside the orders made by Mr Registrar Bradburn.

Counsel for the applicants stressed that the removal of Messrs Payne, Hicks Beach & Co from the record will make it far more difficult for his clients to pursue the litigation, and in particular to enforce an order made by Sir Robert Megarry V-C appointing a receiver and vesting certain assets in the receiver. It is clear from evidence filed in support of this application that it would be difficult, expensive and time-consuming to serve orders or notices of applications in Switzerland, and that while orders for substituted service can be made it would be expensive and time-consuming to obtain such an order every time an order is made or notice of an application is given. But that is not, I think, a ground that can be relied on in support of an application to set aside the orders made under Ord 67, r 6. What the court is authorised to do by that rule is to declare that a solicitor who has ceased to be the solicitor acting for a party in a cause or matter has ceased so to act. If the solicitor applying can show, as in this case he undoubtedly can, that he has ceased so to act, the fact that the declaration and the consequent removal of the solicitor's name from the record will make the conduct of the litigation more time-consuming and expensive for other parties is not, as I see it, a ground for refusing to make the declaration. Counsel for the applicants stressed that Ord 67, r 6 is permissive and that the court is not bound to make a declaration once it is shown that a solicitor has ceased to act for a party. The reason why the court has a discretion is, as the notes in *The Supreme Court Practice 1982* vol 1, p 1157, para 67/6/2 indicate, that a party for whom a solicitor has acted in a cause may be entitled to object to his withdrawal from the cause. It would, in my judgment, be contrary to principle and good sense to allow a party to a cause to object to an order being made under Ord 67, r 6 on the application of the solicitor to the other party, notwithstanding that the solicitor has ceased to act for the other party with his consent or at his request, with a view to compelling the solicitor to act after his instructions have been terminated as no more than a post box for his former client in the same manner as if his instructions had never been terminated.

In these circumstances, though with regret, I must dismiss these applications, with the usual consequences as to costs.

Applications dismissed.

Solicitors: *Herbert Smith & Co* (for the applicants); *Payne, Hicks Beach & Co.*

Jacqueline Metcalfe   Barrister.

Roche v Sherrington and others

CHANCERY DIVISION
SLADE J
6, 7, 8, 13 OCTOBER 1981

Equity – Undue influence – Presumption of undue influence – Unincorporated association – Religious organisation – Former member of religious order suing present member as representative of all members of order – Plaintiff claiming repayment of sums paid by him to order during his membership – Claim based on presumption of undue influence – Defendant applying to dismiss action as disclosing no reasonable cause of action – Whether claim based on presumption of undue influence can be raised against unincorporated association – Whether fiduciary relationship between parties – Whether action properly constituted as representative action – RSC Ord 15, r 12.

For some years the plaintiff had been a member of Opus Dei, an international unincorporated association of certain members of the Roman Catholic Church. After he ceased to be a member, he brought a representative action under RSC Ord 15, r 12[a] against the defendant (an English member of Opus Dei) as a representative of all the members of Opus Dei, claiming that Opus Dei was liable to repay him certain sums which he had paid to the association during his period of membership. He alleged that during that period he had been bound to Opus Dei by vows of poverty, chastity and obedience, that he had relied on it for spiritual advice and instruction and had trusted it to provide for him materially, which raised the presumption that he had been under the domination of Opus Dei during the whole of the period and the payments made by him had been procured by undue influence. The defendant applied to the court for the action to be dismissed on the grounds (i) that the writ and statement of claim disclosed no reasonable cause of action against him or against Opus Dei on behalf of whom he was sued, because a claim based on presumed undue influence could not be made against an unincorporated association where there was no special fiduciary relationship between the plaintiff and any one or more members of it, and (ii) that the action was not properly constituted as a representative action under Ord 15, r 12.

Held – (1) It was arguable that a transaction between an individual and an unincorporated association might give rise to the presumption of undue influence on the part of the members of the association. It was also arguable that there was a relevant fiduciary relationship between the plaintiff and the persons who were members of Opus Dei at the dates of the alleged transactions (see p 432 g to p 433 c, post).

(2) However, the action would be dismissed for the following reasons—

(a) The plaintiff was suing the defendant as a representative of all the present members who included many persons who were not members at the dates of the alleged transactions and who could not be personally liable in equity for the repayment of the plaintiff, and therefore it was impossible to argue that the plaintiff had a reasonable cause of action against the defendant as their representative (see p 433 c to h and p 435 d e, post).

(b) The action was not properly constituted as a representative action under RSC Ord 15, r 12, because, on the evidence, not all the persons represented by the named defendant had a common interest in defending the proceedings in question, as was required by Ord 15, r 12 (see p 434 e to p 435 e, post).

Notes

For representative parties and representative proceedings, see 30 Halsbury's Laws (3rd edn) 315–317, paras 575–576, and for cases on the subject of representative proceedings, see 50 Digest (Repl) 465–472, 1603–1658.

---

a Rule 12, so far as material, is set out at p 428 c, post

For striking out pleadings, see 36 Halsbury's Laws (4th edn) paras 73, 74, and for cases on the subject, see 50 Digest (Repl) 60–65, 491–520.

Cases referred to in judgment

Allcard v Skinner (1887) 36 Ch D 145, [1886–90] All ER Rep 90, CA, 12 Digest (Reissue) 126, 689.

Brocklehurst (decd), Re, Hall v Roberts [1978] 1 All ER 767, [1978] Ch 14, [1977] 3 WLR 696, Digest (Cont Vol E) 105, 691a.

Hardie & Lane Ltd v Chiltern [1928] 1 KB 663, CA, 50 Digest (Repl) 467, 1612.

London Association for Protection of Trade v Greenlands Ltd [1916] 2 AC 15, [1916–17] All ER Rep 452, HL, 50 Digest (Repl) 471, 1639.

Tufton v Sperni [1952] 2 TLR 516, CA, 25 Digest (Reissue) 189, 1550.

Wenlock v Moloney [1965] 2 All ER 871, [1965] 1 WLR 1238, CA, 50 Digest (Repl) 63, 502.

Cases also cited

Bollinger (J) SA v Goldwell Ltd [1971] RPC 412.

Campbell v Thompson [1953] 1 All ER 831, [1953] 1 QB 445.

Craig, Re, Meneces v Middleton [1970] 2 All ER 390, [1971] Ch 95.

Hunt v Worsfold [1896] 2 Ch 224.

Lloyds Bank Ltd v Bundy [1974] 3 All ER 757, [1975] QB 326, CA.

Markt & Co Ltd v Knight Steamship Co Ltd [1910] 2 KB 1021, CA.

Mercantile Marine Service Association v Toms [1916] 2 KB 243, [1914–15] All ER Rep 1147, CA.

Morley v Loughnan [1893] 1 Ch 736.

Taff Vale Rly Co v Amalgamated Society of Rly Servants [1901] AC 426, HL.

Walker v Sur [1914] 2 KB 930, CA.

Wilkinson v Barking Corp [1948] 1 All ER 564, [1948] 1 KB 721, CA.

Wood v McCarthy [1893] 1 QB 775, DC.

Motions

By a writ issued on 26 June 1979 the plaintiff, John James Roche, brought an action against the first defendant, Philip Sherrington, the second defendant, R C Farrell, both of whom were sued on behalf of themselves and on behalf of all other members of the sect called 'Opus Dei', and the third defendant, Netherhall Educational Association, seeking, inter alia, (i) a declaration that certain payments made by him to Opus Dei or the third defendant had been or were deemed to have been procured by undue influence and ought to be set aside and (ii) the repayment of certain sums. By notice of motion, dated 23 July 1980, the first defendant applied to the court for an order (i) that the indorsement on the writ and the statement of claim, in so far as they referred to him, be struck out, and (ii) that the action as against him be dismissed. By notice of motion, also dated 23 July 1980, the third defendant applied for an order that the action against it be stayed until the plaintiff joined Martyn Drakard and Silvano Borruso as plaintiffs or until further order. Both motions were heard together. The facts are set out in the judgment.

Mark Blackett-Ord for the plaintiff.
Michael Brooke for the first and third defendants.
The second defendant did not appear.

Cur adv vult

13 October. **SLADE J** read the following judgment: There are before me two motions in an action in which the plaintiff is Mr John James Roche and the three defendants are respectively Mr Philip Sherrington, Mr R C Farrell and Netherhall Educational Association. The first motion is moved on behalf of the first defendant, and the second

is moved on behalf of the third defendant. The second defendant is not represented before me.

In the title to the proceedings, as shown on the indorsement on the writ and on the statement of claim in the action, Mr Sherrington and Mr Farrell are described as 'Each sued on behalf of themselves and on behalf of all other members of the sect called "Opus Dei".' The third defendant is an English registered charity which is described in the statement of claim as 'controlled by Opus Dei', though such control is denied by the third defendant in its evidence.

Opus Dei is an international unincorporated association of certain members of the Roman Catholic Church. The statement of claim does not assert, and it has not been asserted in argument, that it has any legal existence apart from the members of which it is composed. It is not alleged to be a partnership or a registered society.

The plaintiff, in raising his claims against Opus Dei, is attempting to avail himself of RSC Ord 15, r 12, of which para (1) reads as follows:

'Where numerous persons have the same interest in any proceedings, not being such proceedings as are mentioned in Rule 13, the proceedings may be begun, and, unless the Court otherwise orders, continued, by or against any one or more of them as representing all or as representing all except one or more of them.'

Neither side has suggested that r 13 has any relevance in the present case. As appears from Lord Atkinson's speech in *London Association for Protection of Trade v Greenlands Ltd* [1916] 2 AC 15, [1916–17] All ER Rep 452, one of the objects of r 12, and its predecessors, has been 'to facilitate the bringing of actions against unincorporated aggregates of persons' (see [1916] 2 AC 15 at 30).

In a case where numerous persons have the same interest in any proceedings, not being such proceedings as are mentioned in RSC Ord 15, r 13, the plaintiff in the first instance requires no leave either to bring the action against representative defendants, or in selecting the persons whom he will sue as representing the others of the class. Order 15, r 12(2), however, enables him at any time after the proceedings have begun to apply for a representation order. In the event of such application, the court will only make such a representation order if it is satisfied that the suggested defendants are proper persons to defend the proceedings on behalf of all the other members of the class. If in any particular case the court were to take the view that the purported representative defendants selected by the plaintiff, without its leave, were not proper persons to represent the relevant class, then, on the application of the persons, so joined as defendants, it would no doubt exercise its powers under RSC Ord 15, r 12(1) by refusing to permit the continuation of the proceedings.

In the present case, Mr Sherrington and Mr Farrell have been selected by the plaintiff as defendants solely in a representative capacity. The body of the statement of claim in the action makes no allegation whatever against either of them personally and indeed does not even mention them by name or refer to them individually.

The plaintiff was a member of Opus Dei from about 1959 until about 1973. Substantially, the claims made by him in the action, which was instituted by writ issued on 26 June 1979, are for the repayment of certain moneys alleged to have been paid by him to Opus Dei during the years in which he was a member of Opus Dei, and for the repayment of loans of £4,940·44 alleged to have been made to the third defendant by the plaintiff during the years 1968 to 1974. The grounds on which the claims are based are substantially that the payments or loans must be deemed to have been made under the presumed undue influence of Opus Dei on the mind of the plaintiff.

By the first motion, the first defendant, Mr Sherrington, applies for orders that the indorsements on the writ and the statement of claim, in so far as they refer to him, be struck out and that the action as against him be dismissed with costs on the grounds:

'(a) that this action is not properly constituted as a representative action under Order 15, rule 12 of the Rules of the Supreme Court. (b) That the Writ of Summons and Statement of Claim disclose no reasonable cause of action against the first named defendant or against the association on behalf of whom he is sued. (c) That

insofar as they concern the first named Defendant, the Writ of Summons and
Statement of Claim are frivolous, vexatious and an abuse of the process of the Court.'

By the second motion the third defendant, Netherhall Educational Association, applies
for an order that the action be stayed against the third defendant until the plaintiff joins
one Martyn Drakard and one Silvano Borruso as plaintiffs or until further order.

The first defendant's motion

Turning to the first defendant's motion, I will begin by considering the second of the
grounds relied on by him. Do the writ and statement of claim disclose no reasonable
cause of action against him or the members of Opus Dei, on whose behalf the plaintiff
seeks to sue him? RSC Ord 18, r 19(2) precludes the admission of any evidence on the
first defendant's application, in so far as it is based on this particular ground. For the
purpose of considering this limb of his application, it is therefore necessary to analyse the
statement of claim as a bare pleading, on the assumption that the plaintiff will be able,
in due course, to prove any fact alleged therein by suitable evidence.

The statement of claim, as amended at the hearing by my leave and without opposition
from the first and third defendants' counsel, reads as follows:

'1. Opus Dei is an international proselytising sect or organisation within the
Roman Catholic Church but whose members hold certain doctrines which are not
orthodox, and of which the constitution is secret. Its members are in the main laity
and lead secular lives but all are privately bound by vows of poverty, chastity and
obedience to Opus Dei.

2. The Third Defendant (hereinafter called 'Netherhall') is an English registered
charity controlled by Opus Dei.

3. During the year 1959 the Plaintiff, whilst in his first term teaching at
University College Galway, part of the University of Ireland, became a probationary
member of Opus Dei and after one year one of the Numerarii. Thereafter he
considered himself to be, and was considered by Opus Dei to be, a full member of
Opus Dei and subject to its rule of obedience. At such time the Plaintiff was earning
£660 per annum from the University.

4. During 1961 in pursuance of a request by Opus Dei, the Plaintiff travelled to
Kenya to start a physics department at a Kenya Government school controlled by
members of Opus Dei called Strathmore College. The Plaintiff remained teaching
at the said school (which is of high academic standards) until 1972, and during the
years 1965–1971 he was warden of the residence at the school and at all material
times discharged his duties to the entire satisfaction of the Kenya Government and
of Opus Dei.

5. When during 1962 the Plaintiff consulted Opus Dei and a life assurance
adviser as to the desirability of taking out an insurance policy on his own life to
provide for his retirement he was assured by Opus Dei that to do so would be
unnecessary because Opus Dei would provide for him in his old age.

6. The Plaintiff's salary was paid as to one-third by the U.K. Department of
Overseas Development and as to two-thirds by the Kenya Government. The whole
was paid to the Plaintiff in Kenya save that in 1965 or thereabouts the U.K.
contribution began to be paid to the Plaintiff in the U.K. and so continued until the
Plaintiff left Kenya.

7. During June 1972 the Plaintiff left Kenya to spend two months in the
University of Pamplona in Spain studying Spanish which is the official language of
Opus Dei. In Spain the Plaintiff became dissatisfied with the aims and methods of
Opus Dei.

8. In October 1972 (with the permission of Opus Dei) the Plaintiff commenced
study at Linacre College, Oxford, and there (without the permission of Opus Dei) he
prepared a respectful report critical of Opus Dei. During 1973 he was asked to
retract the opinions he expressed therein, but refused and was asked to resign from
Opus Dei.

9. On 14th November 1973, in pursuance of the said request and under *a* considerable pressure from Opus Dei, the Plaintiff resigned.

10. Throught [sic] the period of the Plaintiff's membership of Opus Dei the Plaintiff paid the whole of his salary (after tax) to Opus Dei subject as is mentioned in the next paragraph, and the total of the money thus paid as gifts to Opus Dei was £16,465. The salary was paid to Opus Dei initially through Opus Dei Registered Trustees and latterly to a three-signature account with the Standard Bank Ltd. Nairobi in the joint names of the Plaintiff and two fellow members of Opus Dei, any *b* two of whom had drawing rights on the said account. The said account was used exclusively for the purposes of Opus Dei.

11. The part of the Plaintiff's salary paid in the U.K. as mentioned above was not given to Opus Dei but was lent to Netherhall. At the request of Fr. Paul Cummings, the head of Opus Dei in Kenya, made in or about the year 1965, the Plaintiff caused the same to be paid into a bank account in the names of himself, Martyn Drakard *c* and Silvano Baruso [sic] (who were fellow members of Opus Dei) at the Standard Bank, 117 Park Lane, London W.1.

12. All moneys paid into the said bank account were paid by standing order as loans to Netherhall by the Plaintiff and his co-signatories at the request of the said Fr. Paul Cummings for the alleged purpose of reducing Netherhall's overdraft. The total sum so lent to Netherhall by the Plaintiff was £4,940·44. The plaintiff has *d* demanded return of the said loan but no part thereof has been repaid.

13. Throughout the period of the Plaintiff's membership of Opus Dei the Plaintiff's mind must be presumed to have been under the domination of Opus Dei by reason of   a) the reliance of the Plaintiff on Opus Dei for spiritual advice and instruction   b) the nature of the vows to Opus Dei made by the Plaintiff and mentioned in paragraph 1 hereof   c) the trust that the Plaintiff placed in Opus Dei *e* that Opus Dei would provide materially for the Plaintiff.

In the premises the gifts and loan above-mentioned must be presumed to have been procured by the undue influence of Opus Dei on the mind of the Plaintiff who at no time had independent advice.

AND THE PLAINTIFF CLAIMS: *f*
1. A declaration that all payments made by the Plaintiff to Opus Dei or Netherhall during the years in which the Plaintiff was a member of Opus Dei were or are deemed to have been procured by undue influence and ought to be set aside.

2. Repayment of the sum of £16,465 or such other sum as may on enquiry be found to have been paid to Opus Dei by the Plaintiff by instalments during the years 1961–1972 inclusive.   *g*

3. In so far as may be necessary an enquiry as to the amount of the said sum.

4. Repayment of the loan of £4,940·44 made to Netherhall by the Plaintiff during the years 1968 to 1974 inclusive.

5. Alternatively, an enquiry what sums are due to the Plaintiff in respect of the said loan and an order for the repayment of such sums.

6. In so far as may be necessary, an account of what is due to the Plaintiffs from *h* Opus Dei and Netherhall and an order that the same to be paid to the Plaintiff.

7. All proper accounts, directions and enquiries.

8. Further or other relief.

9. Costs.'

Stripped to its essentials, the statement of claim, as I read it, thus formulates the *j* plaintiff's claim in the following manner. (a) The plaintiff became a full member of Opus Dei in 1960 and ceased to be a member in 1973. (b) From 1961 until June 1972 he was working as a schoolmaster in Kenya. His salary was paid as to one-third by the UK Department of Overseas Development and as to two-thirds by the Kenya government. The whole of it was paid to him in Kenya, save that in about 1965 the UK contribution began to be paid to him in the United Kingdom and so continued until he left Kenya.

(c) At the request of the head of Opus Dei in Kenya, Father Paul Cummings, the plaintiff caused the part of his salary paid in the United Kingdom to be paid into a bank account at the Standard Bank, Park Lane, London, in the joint names of himself and two fellow members of Opus Dei, Mr Martyn Drakard and Mr Silvano Borruso, referred to in the statement of claim as 'Baruso'. All moneys in this account were then paid out of it by standing order, signed by the plaintiff, Mr Drakard and Mr Borruso, by way of loans to the third defendant. (d) Save as aforesaid, the plaintiff paid the whole of the net salary, after tax received by him for his work in Kenya initially to 'Opus Dei Registered Trustees' and latterly to a bank account at the Standard Bank, Nairobi, in the joint names of the plaintiff and two unidentified fellow members of Opus Dei, any two of whom had drawing rights on the account. Paragraph 10 of the statement of claim describes these payments as being payments 'to Opus Dei'. It further states that the last-mentioned bank account was 'used exclusively for the purposes of Opus Dei.' These allegations, like certain other allegations in the statement of claim, are somewhat underparticularised. Counsel, however, on behalf of the plaintiff, invited me to construe them as alleging that the payments to 'Opus Dei Registered Trustees', whoever they may be, and to the three persons who held the account at Standard Bank, Nairobi, constituted payments to the recipients as agents for the whole unincorporated association, Opus Dei. While I do not think this paragraph of the statement of claim is very clearly drafted, I will for present purposes treat it as bearing the meaning which counsel for the plaintiff invites me to attribute to it. (e) During his membership of Opus Dei, the plaintiff, so he alleges, was bound to it by vows of poverty, chastity and obedience, relied on it for spiritual advice and instruction and trusted it to provide for him materially. In the premises, so it is alleged, during the whole period of his membership, his mind must be presumed to have been under the domination of Opus Dei and the gifts and loans must be presumed to have been procured by the undue influence of that association on the mind of the plaintiff, who had no independent advice. (f) For these reasons the plaintiff claims that all the gifts and loans in question should be set aside, that Opus Dei is liable to repay to him the relevant gifts and that Netherhall, the third defendant, is liable to repay to him the relevant loans.

Cotton LJ in *Allcard v Skinner* (1887) 36 Ch D 145 at 171, [1886–90] All ER Rep 90 at 93 divided the cases relating to undue influence into two classes:

'(i) Where the court has been satisfied that the gift was the result of influence expressly used by the donee for the purpose; (ii) where the relations between the donor and the donee have at or shortly before the execution of the gift been such as to raise a presumption that the donee had influence over the donor. In such a case the court sets aside the voluntary gift, unless it is proved that in fact the gift was the spontaneous act of the donor acting under circumstances which enabled him to exercise an independent will and which justifies the court in holding that the gift was the result of a free exercise of the donor's will. The first class of cases may be considered as depending on the principle that no one shall be allowed to retain any benefit arising from his own fraud or wrongful act. In the second class of cases the court interferes, not on the ground that any wrongful act has in fact been committed by the donee, but on the ground of public policy, and to prevent the relations which existed between the parties and the influence arising therefrom being abused.'

The accuracy of this statement of the law, so far as I know, has not been questioned. In a case of the second class referred to by Cotton LJ, where the relevant relationship exists at the time of the transaction in question, the onus falls on the recipient to rebut the relevant presumption and justify the transaction, by affirmatively proving that it was in fact the spontaneous act of the donor, resulting from a free exercise of his independent will: see *Snell's Principles of Equity* (27th edn, 1973) pp 546–548 and the cases there cited.

In the present case the form of the amended statement of claim makes it clear that only the second class of undue influence referred to by Cotton LJ, that is to say presumed undue influence, is relied on by the plaintiff; and indeed the amendments were designed for this purpose. No actual undue influence on the part of Father Paul Cummings or of any other individual is alleged. The statement of claim does not suggest that there are any facts which operate to place Mr Sherrington, who is not even mentioned in the body of the pleading, under a personal liability different from that which it suggests falls on each and every present member of Opus Dei, whomsoever and wheresoever, in any part of the world.

In relation to the claim against Opus Dei, the first substantive question that arises is whether or not a claim for rescission of a transaction on the grounds of undue influence, and the consequential repayment of moneys paid under that transaction, is in law capable of being raised against the members of an unincorporated associated, when that claim is based only on a presumption of undue influence, as opposed to actual undue influence on the part of particular members or agents of that association. This appears to be a novel point of law on which neither side could point to any directly apposite authority.

Counsel on behalf of the first defendant, submitted that as a matter of law the plaintiff's claim based on presumed undue influence can have no hope of success unless he can point to the existence of a *personal* relationship between himself of the one part and one or more individuals of the other part, out of which relationships the gifts and loans sprang. It is nonsense, he submitted in effect, to speak of a special relationship of the relevant nature as existing between an individual and an amorphous corporate or unincorporated body, unless this is linked to particular individuals representing such body. A personal relationship of some kind is an essential ingredient. He referred me to what was said by Jenkins LJ in *Tufton v Sperni* [1952] 2 TLR 516 at 530:

'It must be shown that the transaction in question did in fact arise out of some special relationship between the parties and that the relationship was a fiduciary one. Moreover, it must be shown not merely that there was a fiduciary relationship of some sort, but that the fiduciary relationship was of such a character as to warrant the interference of the court.'

The recent decision of the Court of Appeal in *Re Brocklehurst (decd)* [1978] 1 All ER 767, [1978] Ch 14 again emphasises the importance of the existence of a relationship of the relevant kind.

Counsel for the plaintiff in answer submitted that in principle there was no reason why, in appropriate circumstances, a claim based on presumed undue influence should not be raised against a corporate or unincorporated body, even though the plaintiff could point to no human agency of such body with whom a special relationship of the relevant nature could be said to have existed.

I bear in mind, as counsel for the plaintiff reminded me, that the first defendant's application is a striking-out application and that the jurisdiction to strike out a statement of claim is one that is sparingly exercised and only in what the court regards as a plain and obvious case: see, for example, *Wenlock v Moloney* [1965] 2 All ER 871, [1965] 1 WLR 1238.

I have come to the conclusion that, on the basis of the facts pleaded by him, the plaintiff has an arguable case in so far as he asserts that there existed the relevant fiduciary relationship between himself and the persons who were for the time being members of Opus Dei *at the several dates of the relevant transactions.* In considering whether, as a matter of principle, a transaction between an individual and an unincorporated association may give rise to a presumption of undue influence on the part of the members of such association, I think it may be helpful to give a hypothetical example. A man might entrust the management of his assets to a corporate merchant bank, in circumstances which made it plain that he was looking to the bank as a whole to safeguard his interests. He might do so without entering into a special personal relationship with any individual representatives of it. Subsequently, during the continuance of this arrangement he might enter into a particular transaction with that bank dealing with one of those assets but without receiving independent advice. It could be that this transaction conferred substantial benefits on the bank but had not, on the facts, been induced by any particular representative of it. On such hypothetical facts, I see no reason in principle why the court should not hold that there existed a special fiduciary relationship between bank and customer, which placed on the bank the onus to justify the transaction. If this be right, I think it must at least be arguable that the relevant relationship could have existed, even if the bank were an unincorporated association. Accordingly, the first defendant has not satisfied me that the plaintiff's case must inevitably fail on this particular point.

There is, however, another formidable hurdle which the plaintiff must surmount, if he is to have any hope of success in the action as at present constituted against the first defendant. Let it be assumed in his favour that between 1961 and 1972 he paid moneys either to Opus Dei Registered Trustees or to the three holders of the account at Standard Bank Ltd, Nairobi, in each case as agents for the unincorporated association, Opus Dei, and that, on each occasion when he made these payments, there must be deemed to have existed a relationship of the relevant nature between himself and the members for the time being of the association. On this assumption, though I would still see many other hurdles in his path, he might perhaps have an arguable claim for recovery of each respective payment against all those persons who were for the time being members at the date of each such payment.

In the present action, however, his claim is not formulated in this manner. It is a claim against all the *present* members of Opus Dei. The statement of claim does not allege, and it has not been suggested, that the present membership of Opus Dei is by any means the same as it was at the respective dates when the relevant payments were made. It is common ground that the present membership must include many persons who were not members at those dates. In these circumstances it has to be asked on what grounds a person who became a member of Opus Dei after the date of a relevant payment by the plaintiff could possibly be personally liable in equity to make repayment to the plaintiff. Counsel for the plaintiff suggested that he could, because (I quote from my note of his argument) 'members worldwide hold my client's money today'. The statement of claim, however, does not allege that any common fund of the association exists into which the moneys are now traceable in equity. While it alleges that the account at Standard Bank, Nairobi, was 'used exclusively for the purposes of Opus Dei' it does not allege that the present members of Opus Dei either have benefited or are capable of benefiting by one penny from the relevant payments. It is conceivable that the plaintiff might have some arguable case against Opus Dei Registered Trustees or the other two parties to the joint account in Nairobi, or against the actual recipients of moneys paid out of his joint account, or paid out by Opus Dei Registered Trustees. I have not the material to express any opinion on this point and it is not the issue before me. In the present circumstances, however, I am unable to see how the claim, as at present formulated against all the present members of Opus Dei, whomsoever and wheresoever, has any hope of success at all.

Mr Sherrington has been joined as a party to the action solely to represent all such members. It has not been suggested that he personally has done anything wrong or that he personally has benefited or is capable of benefiting from the relevant payments in any special manner different from the rest of the membership.

For these reasons I conclude that the first defendant must succeed on the second of the grounds set out in his notice of motion, namely that the writ discloses no reasonable cause of action against him, or against all the members of Opus Dei, on behalf of whom he is sued.

The first of the grounds relied on in the first defendant's notice of motion is that the action is not properly constituted as a representative action under RSC Ord 15, r 12. I think I should deal with this submission also, because it is closely linked with the ground already considered. Evidence is admissible under this head and has indeed been sworn on both sides in the motion. From this evidence it emerges that the unincorporated international organisation of members of the Roman Catholic Church, known as Opus Dei, has branches in many countries and its headquarters in Rome, where the head of the organisation, the President General, is also based. In paras 3 to 8 (inclusive) of an affidavit sworn on 24 July 1980, Mr Sherrington gave a description of the constitution and activities of Opus Dei. In an affidavit in answer, sworn on 24 November 1980, the plaintiff stated in general terms that the picture of Opus Dei given by Mr Sherrington in that affidavit is a false one and specifically challenged a number of assertions made in it. He did not, however, specifically challenge the facts deposed to by Mr Sherrington in paras 5 and 6 of his affidavit, which had been stated as follows:

'5. Opus Dei is made up of two sections, one of men and the other of women. These two sections are absolutely independent, each with its own government, to the point of forming two distinct associations united only in the person of the President General.
6. Government in Opus Dei is based on two principles, decentralisation and collegiality. In the men's section the President General is assisted by a General Council which has its seat in Rome and at present comprises people from 14 countries. In each country where Opus Dei works there exists a collegiate government presided over by a counsellor. In the women's section there is an analogous system of government.'

For the purpose of this part of the first defendant's motion I think I am entitled to assume the correctness of at least the facts stated in these two paragraphs in Mr Sherrington's affidavit. The evidence further shows that he is the counsellor presiding over the collegiate government of Opus Dei in England, Wales and Scotland, an office which he has held since 1976. Though I do not think that this had been explicitly stated in the plaintiff's evidence, this is no doubt the reason why he or his legal advisers have selected Mr Sherrington as one of the representative defendants. It would no doubt be hoped that if the action were to succeed the plaintiff's claims could in practice be enforced against the membership or assets of Opus Dei situated in this country.

If a plaintiff wishes to invoke RSC Ord 15, r 12 for the purpose of bringing an action against named defendants as representatives of a wider class, one essential condition is that the persons represented should have the same common interest in defending the proceedings in question. This is made clear by the opening words of the rule. In a case where separate defences may be opened to some members of the class in question, there can be no common interest within the rule: see *London Association for Protection of Trade v Greenlands Ltd* [1916] 2 AC 15 at 39 per Lord Parker. The first and second defendants are sued on behalf of themselves and all other present members of Opus Dei, male and female, whomsoever and wheresoever. The following points seem to me to be manifest:

(a) There might be separate defences open to members of Opus Dei who were not such members at the respective dates of the relevant payments which would not be open to persons who were members at such dates.

(b) In view of what is said in paras 5 and 6 of Mr Sherrington's affidavit, there might be separate defences open to female members of Opus Dei which would not be open to male members. According to this evidence, the women's branch of Opus Dei is independent of the men's branch, to the extent of forming a distinct association united only in the person of the President General.

(c) There might be separate defences open to members of Opus Dei resident in certain countries of the world, which would not be open to persons resident in other countries. Mr Roche asserts that he was 'under the undue influence of Opus Dei in the United Kingdom as well as in Ireland, Kenya and Spain' (see para 10(b) of his affidavit sworn on 24 November 1980). It is therefore the activities of Opus Dei in those four countries which give rise to his complaint. It is, however, quite possible that defences would be open to members of the association resident in other countries which would not be open to members resident in the United Kingdom, Ireland, Kenya or Spain. This action is not to enforce a right against a fund in which all the members of Opus Dei have a common interest. It is to enforce an alleged, strictly personal, liability against the named first and second defendants and all other members of the association: cf *Hardie & Lane Ltd v Chiltern* [1928] 1 KB 663 at 699 per Sargant LJ.

Further examples could, I think, be given showing why the totality of the present membership of Opus Dei cannot be said to have a *common* interest in defending these proceedings, even if Mr Sherrington were a suitable person to represent all of them, which in his evidence he strongly denies. In this context it may be observed that the plaintiff in para 8(e) of his first affidavit expressly accepted that the first defendant's authority extends to England only, though he did go on to assert that he is a senior officer of a thoroughly united international whole.

I therefore conclude that this action is not properly constituted as a representative action under RSC Ord 15, r 12. Counsel for the plaintiff submitted that even if it was not properly constituted, the first defendant has waived the defect by entering an unconditional appearance to the writ, as sued in a representative capacity. RSC Ord 2, r 2(1) provides:

> 'An application to set aside for irregularity any proceedings, any step taken in any proceedings or any document, judgment or order therein shall not be allowed unless it is made within a reasonable time and before the party applying has taken any fresh step after becoming aware of the irregularity.'

In my judgment, however, the objection of the first defendant to the constitution of these proceedings is not an objection as to a mere irregularity; it is an objection as to substance, which cannot have been waived by the mere entry of an unconditional appearance. For these reasons, I think that the first of the three grounds on which the first defendant's motion is based is no less well founded than the second. I do not have to consider the third of these grounds.

On the first defendant's motion, I therefore dismiss the action against him and direct that all references to him in the title to the writ and the statement of claim be struck out. Subject to further submissions, I think that the plaintiff must be ordered to pay the first defendant's costs of the first defendant's motion.

The third defendant's motion

I now turn to the third defendant's motion, which can be dealt with quite briefly. RSC Ord 15, r 4(2) provides:

> 'Where the plaintiff in any action claims any relief to which any other person is entitled jointly with him, all persons so entitled must, subject to the provisions of any Act and unless the Court gives leave to the contrary, be parties to the action, and any of them who does not consent to being joined as a plaintiff must, subject to any order made by the Court on an application for leave under this paragraph, be made a defendant.'

Paragraphs 11 and 12 of the amended statement of claim allege that the loans to the third defendant were made out of moneys standing in a joint account in the names of the plaintiff, Mr Drakard and Mr Borruso. In these circumstances, counsel submitted on behalf of the third defendant that if, as alleged, the plaintiff is entitled to repayment of the loans by the third defendant, then Mr Drakard and Mr Borruso must be jointly entitled to this relief with him. He submitted that, if the plaintiff wished to bring the action against the third defendant in his own sole name, he should have applied to the court for leave to do so. Such leave would, in his submission, have been refused, because the plaintiff, Mr Drakard and Mr Borruso all had the legal title to the moneys in the joint account. He contended that the action should be stayed against the third defendant until the plaintiff joins Mr Drakard and Mr Borruso as plaintiffs.

The plaintiff, in his affidavit of 24 November 1980, asserted that Mr Drakard and Mr Borruso had no interest whatever in the moneys lent to the third defendant and that the money in the account at Standard Bank Ltd, 117 Park Lane, referred to in para 11 in the statement of claim, was wholly his own. He stated that they became signatories of the joint account simply because they were fellow members of the Kenya Local Council of Opus Dei, which, as he stated, sought to control its officers' private bank accounts, by insisting on two members of the local council becoming signatories of it. In his affidavit sworn on 5 October 1981, he stated that all the money in this account represented his salary from the British government and that it was he who instructed the bank to transfer money from his account to the third defendant.

It may well be that, if and when the action comes to trial, the plaintiff would be able to show that at the date when the loans were made he alone was beneficially entitled to the moneys standing to the credit of the relevant joint account, though four exhibits to an affidavit sworn on behalf of the third defendant by Mr I L X MaCarenhas suggest that the situation is, to say the least, somewhat confused. There is however no clear evidence whatever before me that Mr Borruso and Mr Drakard do *not* claim any beneficial interest in the moneys. There are in evidence, what purport to be copies of letters, respectively dated 10 and 11 December 1978, written respectively by Mr Drakard and Mr Borruso to the third defendant's solicitors from addresses in Nairobi. But these do no more than state that Mr Drakard and Mr Borruso are not aware of any agreement between the joint parties to the account and the third defendant. There is also in evidence what purports to be a copy of a document signed by the plaintiff, Mr Drakard and Mr Borruso, by which the signatories declared that, inter alia, the moneys in the joint bank account at Park Lane were held by them in trust for Opus Dei Registered Trustees. However, the authenticity of this document is disputed by the plaintiff in his evidence and there is no evidence that Mr Drakard and Mr Borruso admit its authenticity. Nor is there any evidence as to whether Mr Drakard and Mr Borruso have ever been asked whether or not they claim any interest in the moneys which the plaintiff seeks to recover from the third defendant in this action.

In all the circumstances, Mr Drakard and Mr Borruso are, in my judgment, at least prima facie, jointly entitled with the plaintiff to any relief to which the plaintiff may be entitled in respect of the loans to the third defendant. Though counsel for the plaintiff submitted to the contrary, there is at present no sufficient evidence on which the court can properly give 'leave to the contrary' within RSC Ord 15, r 4(2) by directing that Mr Drakard and Mr Borruso need not be joined as parties to the action. In my judgment it would be quite unsatisfactory for this action to come on for trial before their position had been clarified, because an order made in the plaintiff's favour, in proceedings to which these two gentlemen were not parties, might leave the third defendant still exposed to future claims at their suit.

Nevertheless, it seems to me possible that an immediate order obliging the joinder of Mr Drakard and Mr Borruso as parties to the proceedings would do no one any good. Though there is no up-to-date evidence as to their addresses, it appears that they may well be resident abroad, so that their joinder would in any event be likely considerably to delay the proceedings. Furthermore, it appears by no means impossible that, when asked to define their attitude, they might state that they neither claimed any interest in the moneys lent to the third defendant, nor wished to be joined as parties to the proceedings.

In the circumstances, the order which I propose to make today is one simply staying the action against the third defendant until either the plaintiff joins Mr Drakard and Mr Borruso as parties to the proceedings or further order. I propose to give the plaintiff liberty to apply on suitable evidence for an order under RSC Ord 15, r 4(2) dispensing with the need for the joinder of either or both of Mr Drakard and Mr Borruso. I contemplate that very shortly after this hearing has been concluded the plaintiff's solicitors will write, or procure the writing, of a letter to Mr Drakard and Mr Borruso, specifically asking them whether they wish to claim any interest in the moneys in question and whether or not they wish to be joined as parties to the proceedings, either as co-plaintiffs or as defendants. Counsel for the defendants, on instructions, has told me that his instructing solicitors, if so requested by the plaintiff's solicitors, would be willing themselves to write such letters to Mr Drakard and Mr Borruso, if the plaintiff's advisers thought that letters emanating from the third defendant's solicitors would be more likely to produce a response. I will, in any event, direct the third defendant to disclose to the plaintiff's solicitors the present postal addresses of Mr Drakard and Mr Borruso, if known to the third defendant.

I have heard submissions in relation to the question of costs of the third defendant's motion. I think that I must order the plaintiff to pay the costs of the third defendant's motion up to and including today's hearing, in any event. Prima facie, Mr Drakard and Mr Borruso are plainly necessary parties to these proceedings and, despite the persuasive submissions to the contrary of counsel for the plaintiff, it seems to me that the responsibility has rested, and still rests, with the plaintiff to show why it is not necessary to join them as parties to these proceedings, if indeed their joinder is not required.

Order accordingly.

Solicitors: *Bower & Bowerman*, Oxford (for the plaintiff); *Titmuss, Sainer & Webb* (for the defendants).

Jacqueline Metcalfe   Barrister.

International Sea Tankers Inc v Hemisphere Shipping Co Ltd
The Wenjiang

COURT OF APPEAL, CIVIL DIVISION
LORD DENNING MR, DUNN AND FOX LJJ
23, 24 NOVEMBER, 1 DECEMBER 1981

Arbitration – Award – Leave to appeal against award – Catastrophic event affecting many similar transactions – Need for uniformity of decisions by arbitrators – Vessels trapped in Shatt al-Arab river by war between Iran and Iraq – Charterparties frustrated – Arbitrators in identical arbitrations deciding on different dates of frustration – Whether leave to appeal against award should be granted to enable court to give guidance to arbitrators – Arbitration Act 1979, s 1.

The shipowners chartered a tanker to the charterers on a 12-month time charter commencing on 28 April 1980. In September 1980 the charterers ordered the vessel to proceed to Basrah on the Shatt al-Arab river in Iraq near the border with Iran in order to load a cargo of oil. While loading, the vessel became one of some sixty ships trapped on the Shatt al-Arab river when war broke out between Iran and Iraq. The vessel completed loading on 22 September, but when she was unable to leave her berth on the river because of the hostilities the shipowners advised the master, on 7 October, that the crew should be evacuated. A Swedish peace envoy attempted to arrange a limited ceasefire to enable foreign ships trapped at Shatt al-Arab to leave the war zone but by 24 November his efforts to arrange a ceasefire had foundered and he turned his attention to getting the vessels out of the river. That was also unsuccessful and the vessels remained trapped. The parties were agreed that in those circumstances the charterparty was frustrated but a dispute arose as to the date of frustration, the charterers contending that the charterparty was frustrated either when war broke out on 23 September or at the latest by 7 October when it became clear, as the arbitrator found, that the hostilities were likely to be lengthy, while the owners contended that frustration did not occur until the end of November or early December at the earliest. The arbitrator held in a reasoned award that the charterparty was frustrated on 24 November when it became apparent that the peace envoy's efforts to arrange a ceasefire had failed. In so holding the arbitrator differed from arbitrators in other arbitrations concerning vessels trapped on the Shatt al-Arab river who had decided on 4 October and 9 December respectively as the date of frustration, while yet another arbitrator had agreed with the date of 24 November. The charterers applied under s 1 of the Arbitration Act 1979 for leave to appeal against the award. The judge granted leave because of the conflicting decision of arbitrators on the date of frustration when the circumstances were virtually identical. The owners appealed against the grant of leave, contending that having found that the arbitrator had not misdirected himself or reached an unreasonable decision the judge ought not to have granted leave.

Held – The appeal would be dismissed for the following reasons—

(1) Having regard to the large number of vessels in the same situation as the chartered tanker the arbitrator's award could not be considered in isolation as if it concerned a 'one-off' case. Instead, applying the principle that it was in the interests of legal certainty that there should be uniformity in the decisions of arbitrators as to the effect of a single catastrophic event on similar transactions, it was appropriate to grant leave to appeal against the arbitrator's award so that the court could give guidance binding on arbitrators in other arbitrations concerning vessels trapped on the Shatt al-Arab river (see p 440 j to p 441 d and g, p 443 g to j, p 444 f and p 445 b to d and h j, post); dictum of Lord Diplock in *Pioneer Shipping Ltd v BTP Tioxide Ltd, The Nema* [1981] 2 All ER at 1041 applied.

(2) In any event, since the arbitrator's findings of fact suggested that the charterparty was frustrated on 7 October 1980, the court was entitled to form the provisional view that he was not right in deciding that it was not frustrated until 24 November, and that was a further reason for granting leave to appeal against his award (see p 441 e to g, p 443 e, p 444 a b f and p 445 g to j, post); dictum of Lord Diplock in *Pioneer Shipping Ltd v BTP Tioxide Ltd, The Nema* [1981] 2 All ER at 1041 applied.

Notes

For appeal to the High Court from an arbitrator's award, see 2 Halsbury's Laws (4th edn) para 627.

For the Arbitration Act 1979, s 1, see 49 Halsbury's Statutes (3rd edn) 58.

Cases cited in judgments

British Launderers Research Association v Central Middlesex Assessment Committee and Hendon Rating Authority [1949] 1 All ER 21, [1949] 1 KB 434, CA, 38 Digest (Repl) 583, 627.

BVS SA v Kerman Shipping Co SA, The Kerman [1982] 1 All ER 616, [1982] 1 WLR 166.

Davis Contractors Ltd v Fareham UDC [1956] 2 All ER 145, [1956] AC 696, [1956] 3 WLR 37, 7 Digest (Reissue) 368, 2356.

Italmare Shipping Co v Ocean Tanker Co Inc, The Rio Sun [1982] 1 All ER 517, [1982] 1 WLR 158, CA.

Kodros Shipping Corp v Empresa Cubana de Fletes, The Evia (No 2) [1981] 2 Lloyd's Rep 613.

National Carriers Ltd v Panalpina (Northern) Ltd [1981] 1 All ER 161, [1981] AC 675, [1981] 2 WLR 45, HL.

Pioneer Shipping Ltd v BTP Tioxide Ltd, The Nema [1981] 2 All ER 1030, [1981] 3 WLR 292, HL; *affg* [1980] 3 All ER 117, [1980] QB 547, [1980] 3 WLR 426, CA.

Schiffahrtsagentur Hamburg Middle East Line GmbH v Virtue Shipping Corp, The Oinoussian Virtue [1981] 2 All ER 887.

Tsakiroglou & Co Ltd v Noblee Thorl GmbH [1961] 2 All ER 179, [1962] AC 93, [1961] 2 WLR 633, HL, 12 Digest (Reissue) 497, 3488.

Cases also cited

Actis Co Ltd v Sanko Steamship Co Ltd, The Aquacharm, CA, [1982] 1 All ER 390, [1982] 1 WLR 119.

Bank Line Ltd v A Capel & Co [1919] AC 435, [1918–19] All ER Rep 504.

Court Line Ltd v Dant and Russell Inc (1939) 44 Com Cas 345.

Interlocutory appeal

Hemisphere Shipping Co Ltd of Hong Kong (the shipowners) appealed against the order of Robert Goff J made on 21 May 1981 granting International Sea Tankers Inc of Liberia (the charterers) leave to appeal to the High Court pursuant to s 1 of the Arbitration Act 1979 against an interim award of the arbitrator, Mr Donald Davies, made on 2 March 1981 in respect of an arbitration concerning a charterparty of the vessel Wenjiang. The facts are set out in the judgment of Lord Denning MR.

R J Thomas for the shipowners.
Michael Dean QC for the charterers.

Cur adv vult

1 December. The following judgments were read.

LORD DENNING MR. In September 1980 war broke out between Iran and Iraq. The fighting became intense, especially along the waterway which divides the two countries. It is the Shatt al-Arab river, running into the Arabian Gulf. On it there are the important ports of Abadan, Khorramshahr and Basrah. Big ships go there to discharge goods and load with oil. Owing to the fighting, 60 vessels were trapped there. They were flying flags of many nations and sailing under different charterparties. In the early days it was hoped that the vessels would be allowed out. But this hope vanished in the first few weeks. The crews left. The vessels remained there. They are still there. All the charterparties became frustrated. That is agreed on all sides. But at what date? That is the question. It is vital because from that date onwards no hire will be payable by the charterers. The owners will have to suffer the loss. Four cases have been heard by arbitrators. In each case different arbitrators have given different dates as the date of frustration. In *The Evia* Mr Eckersley held 4 October 1980. In *The Wenjiang* Mr Donald Davies held 24 November 1980. In another Mr Clifford Clark, Mr Donald Davies and Mr Selwyn held 9 December 1980. In yet another Mr MacCrindle QC held 24 November 1980. We are told that in all the cases the arbitrators have been supplied with much the same evidence. It consists of newpaper cuttings giving the contemporaneous view of the probable length of the war and also of the opinions of experts in international affairs and so forth. These differences between arbitrators show how difficult it is to fix the date of frustration. Something should be done so as to get uniformity of treatment. How is this to be done?

Our particular case today concerns the Wenjiang. She is a tanker vessel flying the British flag and owned in Hong Kong. She was let on time charter for 12 months to a Liberian company. It was on a Shelltime 3 form. The charter started on 28 April 1980 and was to expire on 28 April 1981. In September 1980 the charterers ordered her to proceed to Basrah to load a cargo of oil. She arrived at Basrah on 21 September 1980 at 1130 hours. She was loaded with oil, the loading being completed the next day, 22 September at 0800 hours. Fighting was already taking place about the town and port. She was not allowed to leave her berth for some days. She was then moved to a berth three miles down the river from Basrah. On 9 October 1980 the last of the crew left her. She has since remained at that berth, looked after by watchmen.

Compare her case with that of the Evia. She was let on time charter by her Monrovian owners to Cuban charterers. It was for 18 months from 20 November 1979. It would expire on 20 May 1981. In March 1980 the Cuban charterers ordered her to load a cargo in Cuba and carry it to Basrah. She berthed at Basrah on 20 August 1980. Discharge was completed on 22 September 1980 at 1000 hours. Fighting was already taking place about the town and port. She was not allowed to leave. Most of the crew left on 1 October 1980. The master and a skeleton crew remained on board. She has since remained at Basrah.

On those facts the two cases are indistinguishable. Yet the arbitrators came to different conclusions about dates. The first to be decided was *The Wenjiang*. The parties agreed on a sole arbitrator, Mr Donald Davies. On 2 March 1981 he fixed the date of frustration as 24 November 1980. The next to be heard was *The Evia*. The two arbitrators disagreed.

The umpire was Mr Basil Eckersley, a member of the Bar, well-versed in commercial matters. On 20 March 1981 he fixed the date of frustration as 4 October 1980. In each case the awards were reasoned awards under the 1979 Act. In each case there was application to the commercial judge for leave to appeal. In each case he gave leave to appeal.

But then the two ships went off in different directions. In *The Wenjiang* the owners appealed to this court saying that the judge ought not to have given leave to appeal. In *The Evia* the appeal itself came before the judge (see *Kodros Shipping Corp v Empresa Cubana de Fletes, The Evia (No 2)* [1981] 2 Lloyd's Rep 613).

In *The Evia (No 2)*, on 6 August 1981, Robert Goff J gave judgment. He said (at 619):

'Speaking for myself, I can find no fault in the reasoning and conclusion of the umpire. Indeed, it seems to me plain beyond argument that, on the facts found by him . . . the charter-party was frustrated; and I also agree with him that, judging the situation on the basis of reasonable commercial probabilities, the contract was frustrated on Oct. 4, 1980, for the reasons stated by him . . .'

The Wenjiang was held up awaiting the decision of the House of Lords in *Pioneer Shipping Ltd v BTP Tioxide Ltd, The Nema* [1982] 2 All ER 1030, [1981] 3 WLR 292. They gave judgment on 16 July 1981. Now it has come before us on this point: The owners say that the commercial judge should not have given leave to appeal to him; and that the arbitrator's decision should remain undisturbed by any appeal to the judge.

So in *The Wenjiang* the question is this: was the judge right to give leave to appeal from the arbitrator to the judge? This brings us once again to consider the guidelines under the new Act. We tried our hand in *The Nema* [1980] 3 All ER 117, [1980] QB 547. The House of Lords have given authoritative guidance in *The Nema* [1981] 2 All ER 1030, [1981] 3 WLR 292. We said a word or two in *Italmare Shipping Co v Ocean Tanker Co Inc, The Rio Sun* [1982] 1 All ER 517, [1982] 1 WLR 158. Parker J has added to the literature in *BVS SA v Kerman Shipping Co SA, The Kerman* [1982] 1 All ER 616, [1982] 1 WLR 166. I am afraid we have got our guidelines a little twisted up. So I will try and disentangle them.

One thing is quite clear. The guidelines should be such that the commercial judge can decide, quite quickly, whether or not to grant leave to appeal from the arbitrator to the judge. You do not want to have the whole case argued out at that stage, except in those cases where the matter is so urgent or so short that the judge can give leave to appeal and hear it at once at that very first stage without more ado.

In the ordinary way, on the application the judge will have the award before him and counsel to argue it. The judge should look at once to see if it is a one-off case. It may be one-off because the facts are so exceptional that they are singular to this case and not likely to occur again; or because it is a point of construction of a clause singular to this case which is not likely to be repeated. In such a case the judge should not give leave to appeal from the arbitrator if he thinks the arbitrator was right or probably right or may have been right. He should only give leave to appeal if he forms the provisional view that the arbitrator was wrong on a point of law which could substantially affect the rights of one or other of the parties.

When the case is not one-off as so described, but it gives rise to a question of construction of a standard form with facts which may occur repeatedly or from time to time, then the judge should give leave if he thinks that the arbitrator may have gone wrong on the construction of the standard form: but not if he thinks the arbitrator was right.

Our present case is different. It is not a singular case. It is one of 60 ships trapped in the Shatt. If each award by each arbitrator, as to the date of frustration, were considered *in isolation*, with no knowledge of the others, there would seem to be no good ground for interfering with it. On analysing each award separately, the judge could not say that the arbitrator had misdirected himself in point of law or that the decision was such that no reasonable arbitrator could reach. But when 60 ships are all trapped, it is a mistake to consider each award in isolation. It is of great importance to the trade that there should be uniformity of decision. When the question of frustration arises on 60 ships in a like situation, on like evidence, each decision should be the same as the other. In such a case if the judge in the first case thinks the decision of the arbitrator was 'not right', to use Lord Diplock's words, or may not have been right, he should give leave to appeal from the arbitrator and then, on the hearing of the appeal, himself consider what should be the correct decision on the facts. His decision on it will be a question of law: just as it was in the Suez Canal case (*Tsakiroglou & Co Ltd v Noblee Thorl GmbH* [1961] 2 All ER 179, [1962] AC 93). It will be as to the proper inference to be drawn from the facts: see the *British Launderers* case [1949] 1 All ER 21 at 25–26, [1949] 1 KB 434 at 471–472. If the judge finds that the arbitrator's decision is right, it will, in Lord Diplock's words, 'afford guidance binding on the arbitrators in other arbitrations arising out of the same event': see *The Nema* [1981] 2 All ER 1030 at 1041, [1981] 3 WLR 292 at 305. If he thinks that the decision is 'not right', it will not afford any guidance. The judge will himself decide on the facts what is the correct decision in point of law: and it is his decision which will afford guidance binding on the arbitrators. So also if the first case does not stop at the Commercial Court but is carried to the Court of Appeal. Then the Court of Appeal will give guidance which should be regarded as binding in future cases. In short, the first authoritative decision should be treated as governing all others.

Applying these principles to the present case, where the umpire in *The Evia* fixed 4 October, and the arbitrator in *The Wenjiang* fixed 24 November, on like evidence as the date of frustration, I am quite clear that the judge was right to give leave to appeal in both cases, so that he, or the Court of Appeal, could consider and decide, what is the correct date to take as the date of frustration.

Apart from this point about uniformity, there is ground for thinking that in *The Wenjiang* the arbitrator may have applied the wrong test of frustration. He was, he says, much attracted by the 7 October date because by then 'there had been sufficient time, since the outbreak of the war, to see the pattern of events and to conclude that the conflict might be of a prolonged nature'. He seems only to have departed from that date because he had regard to the principle which he describes as the 'deprivation/unexpiration principle' and that may have led him into error. On the further ground that he may have been 'not right', I think it would be proper for the judge to give leave to appeal.

There are two other points.

One is the off-hire point. This is a point on a standard form and is applicable to all the 60 ships trapped. But I think the arbitrator was right on it. So right that I do not think that leave should be given.

Then there is the point on war risk insurance. On this point, again I think the arbitrator was clearly right, and I do not think leave should be given.

DUNN LJ. I agree. By his award the arbitrator made three declarations as follows: (1) the charterparty of 29 February 1980 was frustrated by 24 November 1980; (2) no time has been lost to the charterers within the context of the off-hire clause; (3) the charterers are liable for additional war risk insurance premiums on the vessel in excess of the levels in effect at the date of the charterparty.

Robert Goff J granted leave to appeal to the High Court on each of these three issues pursuant to s 1 of the Arbitration Act 1979. The question in this appeal is whether the judge correctly exercised his discretion in granting leave to appeal from the decision of the arbitrator.

The first and most important question relates to the issue of frustration. This was not a one-off case. The frustrating event was the war between Iraq and Iran which broke out towards the end of September 1980 and still continues. As a result of that war, the Shatt al-Arab was closed to shipping. Some 60 vessels were caught in the river and are still there, together with a further 15 vessels in the north-west passage. There have been four arbitration awards in London arising out of these events.

The first award related to the Evia. She was under a time charter in the Baltime form dated 20 November 1979 for eighteen months, two months more or less. The arbitrator was Mr Eckersley. He decided that the charterparty was frustrated on 4 October 1980, and his decision was upheld by Robert Goff J on appeal.

The second arbitration is this present arbitration, relating to the Wenjiang. She was under time charter on the Shelltime form dated 28 April 1980 for twelve months one month more or less. The arbitrator, as I have said, held that the charterparty was frustrated on 24 November 1980.

A third arbitration was held before three arbitrators, Mr Clifford Clark, Mr Donald Davies, and Mr Selwyn. The vessel was under a time/trip charter on the New York produce form dated 14 July 1980. The trip was Sudan/Black Sea/Basrah/redelivery Red Sea. The arbitrators unanimously held that the charterparty was frustrated on 9 December 1980.

Finally, Mr MacCrindle QC as sole arbitrator, where the vessel was under time/trip charter dated 19 March 1980. The trip was United States/Gulf/redelivery Muscat. Mr MacCrindle held that the charterparty was frustrated on 24 November 1980.

In this present case it is not now disputed that the charterparty was frustrated. The only issue is as to the date. The charterers maintain that the charterparty was frustrated during the first week in October, when it became clear that Iraqi forces were not going to achieve a quick victory, and on the contrary that the war was likely to be prolonged and of indefinite duration. The charterers suggest 7 October as the date of frustration, being the date when the owners advised the master that the crew should evacuate the vessel. The owners pressed for a later date, and this was accepted by the arbitrator on the basis that until the end of November international efforts were being made to release foreign vessels from the Shatt, and that those efforts could not be said to have failed until 24 November.

The judge granted leave to appeal on policy considerations. He held that in a situation where a single catastrophic event had occurred which had affected or might affect a number of contracts in the same way, and in which arbitrators in this country had reached or might reach inconsistent conclusions as to the date of frustration, judicial review of those inconsistent awards should not be excluded where the parties had not taken advantage of the opportunity open to them under the 1979 Act to agree to exclude judicial review.

That judgment was given before the decision of the House of Lords in *Pioneer Shipping Ltd v BTP Tioxide Ltd, The Nema* [1981] 2 All ER 1030, [1981] 3 WLR 292. *The Nema* was a one-off case, but the House had the judgment of Robert Goff J in this case before them, and Lord Diplock dealt expressly with the situation which arises in cases such as this, where an event or events of a general character occur which affect similar transactions between many other persons engaged in the same kind of commercial activity. Indeed Lord Diplock referred in terms to the war between Iraq and Iran as one example of such an event. What he said about such cases was technically obiter but I agree with the view expressed by Griffiths LJ in *Italmare Shipping Co v Ocean Tanker Co Inc, The Rio Sun* [1982] 1 All ER 517 at 523, [1982] 1 WLR 158 at 165, where he said:

'Whatever may be the technicalities of the matter, it would make a mockery of our system of judicial precedent if we were not to follow and apply that decision [in *The Nema*]. Lord Diplock, at the outset of his speech, stressed that the only reason why the Appeal Committee of the House of Lords gave leave for the appeal to be heard was to give the House of Lords the opportunity to give guidance to the commercial judges as to the manner in which they should exercise the discretion vested in them by the Arbitration Act 1979 . . . That guidance has now been given by the unanimous decision of the House of Lords, and it would be an act of judicial anarchy for this court to refuse to accept and follow that guidance. I consider myself bound to do so.'

In *The Nema* [1981] 2 All ER 1030 at 1041, [1981] 3 WLR 292 at 305 Lord Diplock said:

'Where such is the case [that is to say, where there are events of a general character affecting similar transactions] it is in the interests of legal certainty that there should be some uniformity in the decisions of arbitrators as to the effect, frustrating or otherwise, of such an event on similar transactions, in order that other traders may be sufficiently certain where they stand as to be able to close their own transactions without recourse to arbitration. In such a case, unless there were prospects of an appeal being brought by consent of all the parties as a test case under s 1(3)(a) [of the Arbitration Act 1979], it might be a proper exercise of the judge's discretion to give leave to appeal in order to express a conclusion as to the frustrating effect of the event that would afford guidance binding on the arbitrators in other arbitrations arising out of the same event, if the judge thought that in the particular case in which leave to appeal was sought the conclusion reached by the arbitrator, although not deserving to be stigmatised as one which no reasonable person could have reached, was, in the judge's view, not right.'

Three of their Lordships expressly agreed with those remarks and Lord Roskill did not disagree.

So the question is whether on a provisional view the judge should have come to the conclusion that the arbitrator was not right in his conclusion. Robert Goff J was not disposed to hold that the arbitrator either misdirected himself in point of law or reached a conclusion as to the date of frustration which no reasonable arbitrator could reach. But in the circumstances of this case, and following Lord Diplock's guidelines in *The Nema*, that is not now the test.

The arbitrator drew certain important inferences from his findings of fact. He found that by 7 October there was 'a high probability' that the duration of the conflict might be lengthy, and was in any event incapable of being defined. He then went on to hold that the contract was not frustrated until 24 November because of the possibility (as he put it) that the vessel might be released before that date. My provisional view is that that conclusion cannot be right, although when the matter is fully argued it may turn out to be so. Moreover, although the arbitrator referred to the classic statement of frustration by Lord Radcliffe in *Davis Contractors Ltd v Fareham UDC* [1956] 2 All ER 145, [1956] AC 696, recently accepted unanimously by the House of Lords in *National Carriers Ltd v Panalpina (Northern) Ltd* [1981] 1 All ER 161, [1981] AC 675, as being the true basis of the doctrine of frustration, when he reached his conclusion he appears to have based himself on what he called the 'deprivation/unexpiration principle'. This principle was first stated by Lord Loreburn in 1916, when the doctrine of frustration was in its infancy, and has occasionally been referred to in subsequent cases. Whether it now forms any and if so what part of the developed doctrine of frustration is I think a matter on which the courts should have an opportunity of pronouncing.

But there is another ground on which the judge's decision to grant leave to appeal on the issue of frustration should be upheld. In *Kodros Shipping Corp v Empresa Cubana de Fletes, The Evia (No 2)* [1981] 2 Lloyd's Rep 613 Robert Goff J upheld Mr Eckersley's conclusion that the charterparty in that case was frustrated on 4 October. This it seems to me, to paraphrase Lord Diplock, is a decision which will afford guidance binding on arbitrators in other arbitrations arising out of the Iraq/Iran war, save to the extent that it can be distinguished on its facts, and subject of course to any review in this court. This view seems to me to be consistent with the underlying policy laid down by Lord Diplock that it is, in circumstances such as this, in the interest of legal certainty that there should be some uniformity in the decision of arbitrators as to the effect of a single catastrophic event on similar transactions.

The primary facts found by the arbitrator in *The Evia* arbitration·are strikingly similar to the primary facts found by the arbitrator in this present case. The only question is as to the proper inference to be drawn from those facts by commercial men. In one-off cases, the court will only interfere with decision of arbitrators on issues of frustration if the arbitrator had misdirected himself in law, or his decision was such that no reasonable arbitrator could reach it. But where as here two arbitrators have drawn different inferences from substantially the same primary facts, then the court should intervene in the interest of certainty.

After all, as was held in *Tsakiroglou & Co Ltd v Noblee Thorl GmbH* [1961] 2 All ER 179,

[1962] AC 93, frustration is in the final analysis a question of law, and if the courts do not intervene, as Lord Hodson said 'the same set of facts could be decided by arbitrators either way in successive cases' (see [1961] 2 All ER 179 at 193, [1962] AC 93 at 130). This would certainly not redound to the credit of London arbitration. Where arbitrators cannot agree on the inferences which commercial men would draw from substantially the same primary facts, then the disagreement must be resolved by the court and the question of law decided. On those grounds I would uphold the decision of the judge in relation to the frustration issue.

The other two issues on which the judge granted leave to appeal were both concerned with the construction of standard clauses in the charterparty. The judge followed his own decision in *Schiffahrtsagentur Hamburg Middle East Line GmbH v Virtue Shipping Corp, The Oinoussian Virtue* [1981] 2 All ER 887 and granted leave to appeal on the ground that a question of construction and therefore of law arose in each case, and the charterers' argument could not in either case be regarded as flimsy.

Once again his judgment has been overtaken by the decision of the House of Lords in *The Nema*. Lord Diplock said ([1981] 2 All ER 1030 at 1040, [1981] 3 WLR 292 at 304):

'For reasons already sufficiently discussed, rather less strict criteria are in my view appropriate where questions of construction of contracts in standard terms are concerned. That there should be as high a degree of legal certainty as it is practicable to obtain as to how such terms apply on the occurrence of events of a kind that it is not unlikely may reproduce themselves in similar transactions between other parties engaged in the same trade is a public interest that is recognised by the 1979 Act, particularly in s 4. So, if the decision of the question of construction in the circumstances of a particular case would add significantly to the clarity and certainty of English commercial law it would be proper to give leave in a case sufficiently substantial to escape the ban imposed by the first part of s 1(4), bearing in mind always that a superabundance of citeable judicial decisions arising out of slightly different facts is calculated to hinder rather than to promote clarity in settled principles of commercial law. But leave should not be given, even in such a case, unless the judge considered that a strong prima facie case had been made out that the arbitrator had been wrong in his construction . . .'

Having read the award of the arbitrator in relation to those two issues of construction, I am not persuaded by the able argument of counsel for the shipowners that a strong prima facie case has been made out that the arbitrator was wrong in his construction, and I would refuse leave to appeal in respect of those two issues. To that extent only I would allow the appeal.

FOX LJ. The principal issue in this case is whether the judge should have given leave to appeal on the question of the date of frustration.

It was recognised by the House of Lords in *Pioneer Shipping Ltd v BTP Tioxide Ltd, The Nema* [1981] 2 All ER 1030, [1981] 3 WLR 292 that a catastrophic event, such as war which may affect a number of contracts in the same way, may require a different approach on the question of leave to appeal from an arbitrator from that which is appropriate in the one-off cases. Lord Diplock said ([1981] 2 All ER 1030 at 1041, [1981] 3 WLR 292 at 305):

'. . . it is in the interests of legal certainty that there should be some uniformity in the decisions of arbitrators as to the effect, frustrating or otherwise, of such an event on similar transactions in order that other traders can be sufficiently certain where they stand as to be able to close their own transactions without recourse to arbitration . . . [And a little later he said, in relation to such cases] unless there were prospects of an appeal being brought by consent . . . it might be a proper exercise of the judge's discretion to give leave to appeal in order to express a conclusion as to the frustrating effect of the event that would afford guidance binding on the arbitrators in other arbitrations arising out of the same event, if the judge thought that in the particular case in which leave to appeal was sought the conclusion reached by the arbitrator, although not deserving to be stigmatised as one which no reasonable person could have reached, was, in the judge's view, not right.'

That approach gives rise, in the present case, to two questions.

First, would an appeal enable the judge to give guidance to arbitrators in other arbitrations?

It is true that, although a considerable number of ships were affected by the war situation in or near the Shatt al-Arab, the circumstances of individual ships may vary either because of the terms of their charterparties or because of the particular conditions in which they found themselves on the material dates. Accordingly, it might be said that the ambit of any general guidance that the court could give would be limited. I do not think that there is substance in that. It seems to me that the general conditions, namely the hostilities between Iraq and Iran, in which the ships found themselves, were the same and that there are sufficient similarities of substance on important matters relevant to frustration to make it probable that the courts could offer general advice of value. The similarity between the primary facts in the arbitration in *Kodros Shipping Corp v Empresa Cubana de Fletes, The Evia (No 2)* [1981] 2 Lloyd's Rep 613 and those in the present case suggest at first sight a similarity in terms of consequence which has not, in fact, been achieved by the decisions. If the cases are indeed substantially the same, the disparity in the results should be remedied.

Thus far, therefore, it seems to me that the case comes within the principle outlined by Lord Diplock in *The Nema*.

The second question is whether one can reach the view in the present case that the arbitrator's decision was 'not right'.

The arbitrator found that by 7 October there had been sufficient time since the outbreak of the war to see the pattern of events and to conclude that the conflict might be of prolonged duration. The arbitrator stated:

'I agree with the charterers' contention that the outlook of those who governed Iran was very germane to what was likely to happen during the ensuing weeks/months, thus resulting in a high probability that the duration of the conflict might be lengthy and, in any event incapable of being defined.'

Those findings point to a conclusion that, events by early October, suggested a conflict of prolonged duration. As against that, there are the efforts of Mr Olaf Palme in November to secure a ceasefire. And the arbitrator found that it was always foreseeable that efforts would be made to secure agreement for permission for foreign vessels to clear the Shatt. The arbitrator, however, did not, it seems, regard it as more than a possibility that the vessels would have been released before 24 November.

In deciding that an arbitrator was 'not right' for the purposes of *The Nema* guidelines, the court will, normally, be expressing a provisional conclusion only; that follows from the nature of the application itself: it is merely an application for leave to appeal. The provisional conclusion may, on the substantive hearing, turn out to be wrong.

Within those limits the provisional conclusion which I reach is that the arbitrator was not right in deciding on 24 November as the date of frustration. His findings of fact, in my view, suggest that the proper date was early October by which time there was a 'high probability' that the duration of the war might be lengthy.

In the circumstances, I think that the judge was right to give leave to appeal on the question of the date of frustration.

I agree that no case has been made out in favour of giving leave to appeal on the two questions of construction, and on those I would allow the appeal.

Appeal allowed in part only; leave to appeal against arbitrator's award granted below to stand.

Solicitors: *Holman, Fenwick & Willan* (for the shipowners); *Sinclair, Roche & Temperley* (for the charterers).

Frances Rustin   Barrister.

Chakki v United Yeast Co Ltd

EMPLOYMENT APPEAL TRIBUNAL

NEILL J, MRS D EWING AND MR R THOMAS

12 OCTOBER, 9 DECEMBER 1981

Master and servant – Contract of service – Frustration – Imprisonment – Employee sentenced to 11 months' imprisonment – Sentence passed at beginning of employee's annual holiday – Employee released on bail pending appeal after one night in prison – Employer engaging permanent replacement for employee – On employee's appeal probation substituted for imprisonment – Whether sentence frustrating contract of employment – Whether employee unfairly dismissed.

The appellant was employed by the respondent company as a heavy goods vehicle driver. In August 1980, at the start of his two weeks' annual holiday, the appellant was sentenced to 11 months' imprisonment for unlawful wounding. On the same day his wife informed the respondents of what had occurred and the respondents arranged for a replacement for the appellant because they felt there was no prospect of his returning to work in the near future. The appellant spent one night in prison but was released on bail the next day pending an appeal against sentence. The appeal was heard in September, when the sentence was varied to probation. In the meantime, the respondents had engaged another driver on a permanent basis to replace the appellant. The appellant complained to an industrial tribunal that he had been unfairly dismissed but the tribunal dismissed his claim on the ground that his contract of employment had been frustrated immediately on the imposition of the prison sentence in August 1980. The appellant appealed, contending, inter alia, that where an employee was imprisoned for a substantial period the frustrating event was not the sentence of imprisonment itself but the disruption of the contractual relationship which made it impossible for the imprisoned employee to carry out his work, and accordingly, since the appellant had remained in prison for less than 24 hours and the period of his imprisonment was in any event during his annual holiday and therefore at a time when he was not required to work, his contract of employment had not been frustrated in August 1980.

Held – Whether a sentence of imprisonment was a cause of instantaneous frustration of a contract of employment or merely a potentially frustrating event depended on the time at which frustration occurred, being the time at which the parties became aware of the cause and the likely outcome of the interruption and had to decide on a future course of action. Accordingly, the question whether a sentence of imprisonment amounted to frustration of an employee's contract of employment was to be determined by considering (a) when it was commercially necessary for the employer to make a decision about the employee's future, (b) what a reasonable employer would consider to be the likely length of the employee's absence over the next few months, and (c) whether, in the light of the employee's likely absence, it was reasonable to engage a permanent rather than a temporary replacement. It followed that, although the respondents were not obliged to wait until the end of the appellant's holiday before deciding what to do, the appellant's contract could not be regarded as being frustrated immediately on the imposition of the sentence of imprisonment. The case would therefore be remitted to another tribunal to reconsider the application (see p 449 *h* to p 450 *d*, post).

Dicta of Branson J in *Court Line Ltd v Dant & Russell Inc* [1939] 3 All ER at 317 and of Evershed MR in *Atlantic Maritime Co Inc v Gibbon* [1953] 2 All ER at 1095–1096 applied.

Hare v Murphy Bros Ltd [1974] 3 All ER 940 considered.

Notes

For the dismissal of an employee on the ground of misconduct, see 16 Halsbury's Laws

(4th edn) paras 616, 628, 630, and for cases on the subject, see 20 Digest (Reissue) 434–442, *3530–3623*.

For the doctrine of frustration of contracts generally, see 9 Halsbury's Laws (4th edn) para 450–459, and for cases on frustration of contracts of employment, see 12 Digest (Reissue) 508–509, *3519–3528*.

Cases referred to in judgment

Atlantic Maritime Co Inc v Gibbon [1953] 2 All ER 1086, [1954] 1 QB 88, [1953] 3 WLR 714, 29 Digest (Reissue) 280, *2439*.

Court Line Ltd v Dant & Russell Inc [1939] 3 All ER 314, 12 Digest (Reissue) 490, *3464.*

Egg Stores (Stamford Hill) Ltd v Leibovici [1977] ICR 260, EAT, 20 Digest (Reissue) 459, *3719.*

Hare v Murphy Bros Ltd [1974] 3 All ER 940, CA, 20 Digest (Reissue) 376, *3245.*

Harman v Flexible Lamps Ltd [1980] IRLR 418.

Harrington v Kent CC [1980] IRLR 353.

Tarnesby v Kensington and Chelsea Hospital Authority [1981] ICR 615.

Case also cited

Morgan v Manser [1947] 2 All ER 666, [1948] 1 KB 184.

Appeal

Naurang Gordon Chakki appealed against the decision of an industrial tribunal (Chairman Mr P T Gray) sitting at Birmingham on 16 February 1981 dismissing his application for compensation for unfair dismissal against the respondents, United Yeast Co Ltd. The facts are set out in the judgment of the appeal tribunal.

J Hand for the appellant.
Mr D Grindall, solicitor, for the respondents.

Cur adv vult

9 December.   **NEILL J** delivered the following judgment of the tribunal: This is an appeal from a decision of an industrial tribunal held at Birmingham on 16 February 1981. By their decision the tribunal unanimously dismissed an application by the appellant for a finding that he had been unfairly dismissed by the respondents. The question raised by this appeal is whether the industrial tribunal erred in law in finding that the appellant's contract of employment was frustrated on 19 August 1980 when he was sentenced to a term of 11 months' imprisonment.

The relevant facts are set out in the decision and the reasons and can be shortly stated. The appellant was employed by the respondents as a heavy goods vehicle driver. His employment began in about 1973. He was entitled to two weeks' annual holiday. In January 1980 his holiday for the year was arranged to be for the two weeks beginning on Monday 18 August.

On Friday 11 July 1980 the appellant committed a wounding offence on his eldest son. On the next day he appeared in court, but the matter was adjourned and he was released on bail. He reported for work on 13 July, when he informed his employers of what had happened. The adjourned hearing took place on Tuesday 19 August, the day after the appellant's holiday had begun. At the time of the hearing the appellant was subject to a suspended sentence of imprisonment for a similar offence. The magistrates decided that an immediate sentence of imprisonment should be imposed and the appellant was sentenced to 11 months. In their reasons the industrial tribunal set out their findings as to what happened later on 19 August in these terms:

'His wife telephoned the respondents on the afternoon of 19 August and spoke to Mr Harris [the warehouse supervisor] and told him what had happened. She did not remember having mentioned the sentence of 11 months, but Mr Harris said she was very upset, and he did remember quite clearly that she told him that her husband had been sentenced to 11 months' imprisonment. We accept Mr Harris's evidence of that conversation and we are satisfied that . . . on 19 August 1980 the respondents were fully aware that the applicant had been sentenced to 11 months' imprisonment.'

The appellant spent the night of 19–20 August in custody at Winson Green prison, but at 1 pm on Wednesday 20 August he was released on bail pending an appeal against sentence. He went immediately to see Mr Harris and Mr Brierley (the respondents' manager) to say he was appealing.

The industrial tribunal found, however, that when they heard of the sentence, Mr Harris and Mr Brierley decided that interviews should be arranged to find a replacement for the appellant because they saw no prospect of his returning to work in the near future. The tribunal also found that the appellant himself did not consider that he stood any chance of avoiding going to prison for some length of time.

In the event, however, when the appeal was heard on 11 September the appellant was placed on probation.

At the hearing on 16 February the industrial tribunal were referred by the respondents to the decision of this tribunal in *Harrington v Kent CC* [1980] IRLR 353. In para 5 of their reasons the industrial tribunal referred to part of the judgment in that case and continued:

'The tribunal is directed to consider the fact at the date of the conviction and sentence. We are not to look at what happened afterwards. In particular we are directed to ignore the fact that an appeal is being launched.'

In para 6 the tribunal continued:

'On 19 August 1980 the applicant was convicted under sentence of 11 months' imprisonment. It was not anticipated that he would be back at work for a considerable length of time regardless of any question of appeal. It is therefore our unanimous decision that the respondents are correct in their submission in this case and that the applicant's contract of employment was in fact frustrated and terminated on 19 August 1980.'

The appellant has appealed to this tribunal against the decision that his contract of employment was frustrated on 19 August 1980. In his submissions to us, counsel on behalf of the appellant said that he wished to reserve for argument in a higher court the question whether a sentence of imprisonment can frustrate a contract of employment or can be treated as a frustrating event. He made reference to the speeches in *Tarnesby v Kensington and Chelsea Hospital Authority* [1981] ICR 615 and to a dictum in *Harman v Flexible Lamps Ltd* [1980] IRLR 418 at 419.

We see force in the argument that the doctrine of frustration should not be invoked in cases where the contract of employment can be determined by a short period of notice. In the light of the decision of the Court of Appeal in *Hare v Murphy Bros Ltd* [1974] 3 All ER 940 and of other authorities, however, it is not open to us to decide, even if we wished to do so, that the doctrine of frustration can have no application in the present case.

We turn therefore to the main submission of counsel for the appellant, which was that where an employee is imprisoned for a substantial period the frustrating event is not the sentence of imprisonment itself but the disruption of the contractual relationship which makes it impossible for the imprisoned employee to carry out his work. Counsel emphasised that in the present case the appellant remained in prison for less than 24 hours and that the period of his imprisonment was during his annual holiday and therefore at a time when he was not required to work. Cases such as *Harrington v Kent CC* and *Hare v Murphy Bros Ltd*, said counsel, could therefore be distinguished.

In order to examine this argument it is necessary for us to say something about the doctrine of frustration in the context of a contract of employment. As, however, we understand that this case is likely to be taken to the Court of Appeal we do not propose to set out the law at length.

The doctrine of frustration has long been applied to contracts of employment in cases where an employee has died. The death of the employee is treated as discharging the contract. The contract is also discharged where, though the employee is still alive, he becomes incapable in a business sense of performing the contract. A common reason for this incapacity is illness or an accident, but in that event it is not always possible to say at once whether the contract has been frustrated. As was pointed out by the Employment Appeal Tribunal in *Egg Stores (Stamford Hill) Ltd v Leibovici* [1977] ICR 260 at 265:

> 'There may be an event (eg a crippling accident) so dramatic and shattering that everyone concerned will realise immediately that to all intents and purposes the contract must be regarded as at an end. Or there may be an event, such as illness or accident, the course and outcome of which is uncertain. It may be a long process before one is able to say whether the event is such as to bring about the frustration of the contract. But there *will* have been frustration of the contract, even though at the time of the event the outcome was uncertain, if the time arrives when, looking back, one can say that at some point (even if it is not possible to say precisely when) matters had gone on so long, and the prospects for the future were so poor, that it was no longer practical to regard the contract as still subsisting.'

How then is a sentence of imprisonment to be regarded? It can certainly be argued, on the basis of the decision in *Hare v Murphy Bros Ltd*, that a substantial sentence of imprisonment, as was imposed in the present case, has the effect of frustrating a contract of employment from the moment of its imposition. But we find the argument that the contract is frustrated immediately unconvincing. Suppose in the present case the appellant had had four weeks' holiday and had not told the respondents about his imprisonment. Or suppose that the appellant's wife had not telephoned Mr Harris until 20 August and had then, on rather different facts, been able to say that the prospects of a successful appeal were excellent.

It seems to us that in some cases a sentence of imprisonment will be similar to an accident or an illness and thus a potentially frustrating event rather than a cause of instantaneous frustration. It has to be recognised, however, that a sentence of imprisonment differs from an accident or an illness in that, unless and until it is varied on appeal, the length of the employee's absence and the effect on the contract of employment is immediately predictable. One has therefore to try to find the moment at which the question of frustration or not has to be determined.

Counsel for the appellant argued that the appellant's contract of employment could not have been frustrated before the end of his holiday at the earliest because there could not have been any actual disruption of the appellant's performance of his contract until that date. Furthermore, said counsel, by the end of his holiday the appellant was on bail awaiting the hearing of his appeal and he could have continued working. Accordingly, he submitted, as the appeal was successful there was in the event no sufficient disruption of the contract as to amount to frustration.

We have given careful consideration to this argument, but in our view it would not necessarily be right to impose on the respondents an obligation to wait until the end of the appellant's holiday before deciding what to do. We would use the words used by Branson J in *Court Line Ltd v Dant & Russell Inc* [1939] 3 All ER 314 at 317 where, in considering whether a time charter of a ship had been frustrated by delay, he said:

> '... the time as at which the question must be decided is the time when the parties came to know of the cause, and the probabilities of the delay, and had to decide what to do.'

We find further support for this approach in the test which was approved by Evershed MR in *Atlantic Maritime Co Inc v Gibbon* [1953] 2 All ER 1086 at 1095–1096, [1954] 1 QB 88 at 113:

'Would a reasonable man in the position of the party alleging frustration, after taking all reasonable steps to ascertain the facts then available, and without snapping at the opportunity of extricating himself from the contract, come to the conclusion that the interruption was of such a character and was likely to last so long that the subsequent performance or further performance of the contract would really amount to the performance of a new contract?'

We have therefore come to the conclusion that in this case the question of frustration has to be decided by finding the answers to the following questions. (1) Looking at the matter from a practical commercial point of view, when was it necessary for the respondents to decide as to the appellant's future and as to whether a replacement driver would have to be engaged? (2) At the time when the decision had to be taken, what would a reasonable employer have considered to be the likely length of the appellant's absence over the next few months? (3) If in the light of the appellant's likely absence it appeared necessary to engage a replacement, was it reasonable to engage a permanent replacement rather than a temporary one?

It follows from what we have said that we consider that the industrial tribunal erred in law in deciding that the contract of employment was frustrated immediately on the imposition of the sentence of imprisonment on 19 August. The matter should therefore be remitted to another industrial tribunal to consider the matter of frustration afresh and to deal with the questions which we have sought to formulate.

It may well be that when these questions are answered the industrial tribunal will come to the same conclusion as the earlier tribunal, but we see no alternative other than to remit the case so that the facts can be looked at as at the moment when the decision to treat the contract as discharged was taken.

Both sides asked for leave to appeal in the event of our decision being adverse to them. The case raises a question of some general importance. We therefore give leave to the respondents to appeal to the Court of Appeal, if they are so advised.

Appeal allowed. Matter to be remitted to be reheard. Leave to the respondent to appeal to the Court of Appeal

Solicitors: *J Thornley*, Ashton-under-Lyne (for the appellant); *D Grindall* (for the respondents).

Diana Procter   Barrister.

Devlin v F (a juvenile)

QUEEN'S BENCH DIVISION (CROWN OFFICE LIST)
WOOLF J
4 FEBRUARY 1982

Case stated – Limitation of time – Application for extension of time – Criminal cause or matter – Jurisdiction of single judge to extend time – Factors to be considered in deciding whether to grant extension of time – RSC Ord 56.

A case stated by a magistrates' court in a criminal case was not lodged within the time prescribed by RSC Ord 56, r 6(1), due to an oversight on the part of the prosecuting authority. Six weeks after the expiry of the time limit the prosecuting authority applied to a single judge for leave to extend the period on the ground that the case stated raised a point of law which needed to be resolved in the interests of the administration of justice. The respondent submitted that only a Divisional Court could deal with the application since the case was a criminal one which could be heard only by a Divisional Court consisting of at least two judges.

Held – (1) A single judge could deal with an application to extend the time within which
a to lodge a case stated by a magistrates' court in a criminal case (see p 453 *b* to *d*, post);
Whittingham v Nattrass [1958] 3 All ER 145 explained.

(2) Leave to extend the time limit should be granted where a case stated raised a
genuine point of law which needed to be resolved in the interests of the administration
of justice, and any prejudice which a respondent might suffer if the matter were allowed
to proceed could be dealt with by the Divisional Court when hearing the appeal itself.
b Accordingly, in the circumstances leave to extend the time limit for filing the case stated
would be granted (see p 454 *a* to *c*, post); *Parsons v F W Woolworth & Co Ltd* [1980] 3 All
ER 456 considered.

Notes

For time limit for stating a case, see 29 Halsbury's Laws (4th edn) para 478, and for cases
c on the subject, see 33 Digest (Repl) 319, *1426–1430*.

Cases referred to in judgment

Parsons v F W Woolworth & Co Ltd [1980] 3 All ER 456, [1980] 1 WLR 1472, DC.
Whittingham v Nattrass [1958] 3 All ER 145, [1958] 1 WLR 1016, 33 Digest (Repl) 319,
1430.

Interlocutory appeal

F (a juvenile) appealed against the order of Master Thompson QC dated 20 January 1982
whereby, on an application by the respondent, Peter Devlin, it was directed that the time
limit imposed by RSC Ord 56, r 6(1) should be extended to allow a case stated by a
magistrates' court to be lodged in the Crown Office of the Queen's Bench Division. The
e appeal was heard in chambers but judgment was given by Woolf J in open court.

Anthony Higgins for the appellant.
Mr *Clive Winston*, solicitor, for the respondent.

WOOLF J. I have adjourned into open court this application for extending time in
which to lodge a case stated under RSC Ord 56.

Order 56, r 1(4), dealing with appeals from the Crown Court, says:

> 'No such appeal shall be entered after the expiration of 6 months from the date
> of the judgment, order or decision in respect of which the case was stated unless the
> delay is accounted for to the satisfaction of the Divisional Court. Notice of intention
> to apply for an extension of time for entry of the appeal must be served on the
> *f* respondent at least 2 clear days before the day named in the notice for the hearing
> of the application.'

There is no provision made in Ord 56, r 6, which deals with cases stated by a
magistrates' court, which is equivalent to Ord 56, r 1(4). There is only the requirement
that the case must be lodged within ten days of its receipt. The explanation for that
distinction may well be because in the normal way a case stated from the magistrates will
g be lodged well within the six-month period referred to in Ord 56, r 1.

The appellant in this appeal submits that where a case stated by a magistrates' court is
not lodged within the required period then, while the Divisional Court can extend time
(and when I use the term 'Divisional Court' I mean a full Divisional Court of at least two
judges), a single judge of the Queen's Bench Division has no jurisdiction to do so. It is
therefore contended that in relation to the present application, which is an application to
lodge a case outside the time prescribed by Ord 56, r 6(1), I have no jurisdiction to extend
the period so as to allow the case now to be lodged.

The matter has in fact come before me by an indirect route. It originally came before
the Master of the Crown Office. It was argued before him and he decided to extend
time. It was argued before him on the merits and on the basis that as these were criminal

proceedings he had no jurisdiction to determine the matter. He rejected that contention as to jurisdiction and there was an appeal to this court.

When the matter came before me today counsel for the appellant (who has put his arguments, if I may say so, very clearly) recognised that to canvass the argument as to the master's jurisdiction would be an academic exercise and that the practical manner in which to deal with the question of jurisdiction was to challenge my jurisdiction to give leave for the period to be extended. He took that view because he recognised that, if he were to succeed on the jurisdiction point, having heard the merits I would then be in a position to accede to an application made direct to me if I had jurisdiction. I therefore intend to approach this matter on the same basis as the matter was approached by counsel and deal with it as being an application which is being made to me.

In support of his argument that I have no jurisdiction, the way the matter is put by counsel is that, as this is a criminal cause which would be heard by the Divisional Court consisting of two judges, it would be wrong for a single judge as a matter of discretion to seek to exercise the power of the court to extend time.

I drew counsel's attention to the provisions of Ord 3, r 5, of which of course he was already fully aware, and he did not seek to advance any argument before me on the specific terms of that order. It provides:

'The Court may, on such terms as it thinks just, by order extend or abridge the period within which a person is required or authorised by these rules, or by any judgment, order or direction, to do any act in any proceedings.'

I emphasise the words 'any act in any proceedings'.

The term 'the Court' is defined in Ord 1, r 4(2) in these terms: 'In these rules, unless the context otherwise requires, "the Court" means the High Court or any one or more judges thereof . . .'

Although this did not figure as part of the argument of counsel, I think it is right to draw attention to the terms of Ord 56, r 5, which provides:

'(1) Except as provided by paragraph (2), all appeals from a magistrates' court shall be heard and determined—(a) in any criminal cause or matter, by a Divisional Court of the Queen's Bench Division; (b) in any other matter, by a single judge sitting in court or, if the Court so directs, by a Divisional Court of the Queen's Bench Division . . .'

I draw attention to that provision because, first of all, it draws a distinction between the hearing of criminal appeals by way of case stated and other appeals, so that anything I have to say is limited to the situation with regard to criminal cases because, in my view, there could be no suggestion of lack of jurisdiction of a single judge in matters which are not criminal causes or matters.

I also draw attention to that provision because it refers to the hearing and determination of appeals. I am not engaged today on the hearing or determination of the cause. I am merely concerned with an interlocutory matter of deciding whether or not time to lodge the case should be extended.

With regard to that, I was referred to the case of *Whittingham v Nattrass* [1958] 3 All ER 145, [1958] 1 WLR 1016. According to the headnote, that was a case where the court had decided ([1958] 1 WLR 1016):

'Where it is desired to have a case stated by magistrates or a case lodged in the Crown Office out of time, application to extend the time must be made to the Divisional Court. There is no power to extend the time by consent. Statement to the contrary effect in the Annual Practice . . . disapproved.'

When one looks at the judgment of Lord Goddard CJ, however, one finds that he did not use the words 'Divisional Court' but the words 'court', and so that judgment is of no assistance to me with regard to the position of my jurisdiction. The distinction between

the headnote in that case and the judgment of Lord Goddard CJ is readily explainable
a because at that time the Divisional Court as a matter of practice dealt with these
applications and they were made in open court. Now, however, a substantial part of the
Divisional Court's jurisdiction is exercised in chambers and a considerable part of the
jurisdiction is exercised by a single judge. The question, therefore, arises whether this
interlocutory application has to be made to a court consisting of two judges.

So far as appeals to the Court of Appeal, Criminal Division are concerned, the initial
b application for leave in those cases is made to a single judge, who also deals with
questions of time. It is true that a single judge's decision can in effect be reviewed by the
full court because the applicant has the right to renew his application to the full court if
leave is refused. However, that the single judge has there a discretion is clear.

The position can therefore be summarised in this way. On the argument that has
been advanced before me it is not said that the court consisting of a single judge does not
c have jurisdiction. It is only put that the single judge should not deal with it as a matter
of discretion. It seems to me that, looking at the matter as one of discretion and bearing
in mind the position with regard to appeals to the Court of Appeal, Criminal Division,
the proper approach is to regard the single judge as having jurisdiction to deal with
questions of time. If he is in any particular case of opinion that for some reason which
is hard to imagine it would be more appropriate for the application to be dealt with by
d a full court, he can always adjourn the matter to enable that to happen. If that safeguard
is borne in mind, it seems to me that there is no disadvantage in a single judge dealing
with the ordinary case.

The present case is very much an ordinary case. The short point raised by the case
stated is whether or not the fact that the appellant spat at a police officer causing the
spittle to land on the police officer's trousers is sufficient to amount to an assault in law.
e On any showing the matter is not a serious one. However, it has to be borne in mind
that the appellant is 16 years of age and any criminal matter is particularly important for
a youth of that age.

Considering the position from the appellant's point of view, other than the fact that if
he is convicted the matter would appear on his record, it is difficult to see how any real
prejudice would be caused to him if the matter were now to come before the Divisional
f Court.

Mr Winston, who appears on behalf of the respondent, at my pressing indicated that
it would not be a case where, if the appellant succeeded, he would ask for the matter to
be remitted to the justices so that the justices could pass an appropriate sentence having
entered a conviction at the direction of the court. It would be one of those cases where
the court having considered the legal position in its discretion could make no further
g order. He certainly indicates that it is not a case where the appellant would seek an order
for costs against the respondent.

It is of course for the Divisional Court before whom the matter would come to decide
what should be the ultimate outcome if the appeal succeeds. However, bearing in mind
the attitude indicated by Mr Winston, I consider that it is extremely unlikely that the
Divisional Court, once it has decided the short point of law, would come to any
h conclusion which could lead to adverse results to the appellant.

It is against that background that I consider the question of delay. There is absolutely
no excuse for the delay, which amounts to approximately six weeks. Time expired on
3 October 1981. The situation is one where there was clearly no more than an oversight
by the respondent, and, if it had not been for that oversight, the case could have been
lodged in time.

This court, and here I am using that term in relation to the court exercising jurisdiction
in relation to criminal appeals of this sort, is always very concerned about any delay in
criminal matters and will take a rigid and robust attitude if it is appropriate to do so.

Counsel for the appellant properly referred me to *Parsons v F W Woolworth & Co Ltd*
[1980] 3 All ER 456, [1980] 1 WLR 1472. In that case Donaldson LJ in respect of a lesser
period of delay than we are involved with here refused leave to extend time. However,

I regard the remarks of the learned Lord Justice in that case as applying to the facts of that case and certainly not laying down a rule that in no circumstances where there is delay *a* which is not delay which can be satisfactorily explained the court will extend time.

In exercising its discretion, I follow the general approach indicated by Donaldson LJ. But, notwithstanding that general approach, it seems to me that, where there is a genuine point of law which, quite apart from this case, the prosecuting authority submit needs to be resolved in the general interests of the administration of justice, and when little or no prejudice will be caused to a respondent if the matter is to proceed and that *b* little injustice which could possibly arise can be avoided by the court acting in the way I anticipate it will act when it hears the appeal, it would be wrong not to extend time.

Accordingly I am prepared to do so for the reasons that I have indicated, and I direct that the time should be extended so as to allow the case to be lodged today.

Order accordingly.   *c*

Solicitors: *Powell, Magrath & Co,* Kilburn (for the appellant); *R E T Birch* (for the respondent).

N P Metcalfe Esq   Barrister.

d

Practice Direction

e

Practice – Companies Court – Applications in Long Vacation – Applications for schemes of arrangement or reconstruction, for reduction of share capital or in respect of capital redemption reserve funds or share premium accounts – Modification of existing arrangements.

1. The Practice Direction of 3 March 1977 ([1977] 1 All ER 688, [1977] 1 WLR 317) set out arrangements for hearing in the Long Vacation 1977 certain applications *f* concerning schemes of arrangement and reductions of capital, capital redemption reserve funds and share premium accounts. The Practice Direction of 23 February 1978 ([1978] 1 All ER 820, [1978] 1 WLR 429) extended those arrangements until further notice and provided that a judge of the Companies Court would be available for sitting on an early Wednesday in August and each Wednesday in September.

2. Experience has shown that it is unnecessary for a judge of the Companies Court to *g* be available each Wednesday in September. It has been decided that in the Long Vacation 1982 and until further notice a judge of the Companies Court will be available on two Wednesdays in September on dates to be notified in the Long Vacation Notice which is printed in the Daily Cause List. The judge may also sit on some other day by special arrangement if he considers that there is sufficient need for this. Prior to the publication of the Long Vacation Notice parties who wish to prepare a timetable which *h* includes a date for hearing by the judge in September should inquire of the Chief Clerk, Companies Court, Room 307, Thomas More Building, Royal Courts of Justice as to the dates in September when the judge will be available.

3. It is again emphasised that parties wishing to have proceedings heard during the Long Vacation should give the earliest possible warning of the fact to the office of the Companies Court Registrar before the Long Vacation begins and should attend on the *j* Chief Clerk in order to have any proposed timetable approved by him.

By direction of the Vice-Chancellor.

11 May 1982

Warner Bros Records Inc v Parr

a

CHANCERY DIVISION
JULIAN JEFFS QC SITTING AS A DEPUTY JUDGE OF THE HIGH COURT
10, 18 DECEMBER 1981

b
Copyright – Infringement – Right of action – Bootlegging – Persons entitled to bring action to prevent bootlegging – Action by record manufacturer and distributor – Record company having exclusive contract to sell performer's records – Whether performer having civil right of action against bootlegger under performers' protection legislation – Whether record company having similar right of action against bootlegger under legislation – Dramatic and Musical Performers' Protection Act 1958, s 1 – Performers' Protection Act 1963, s 1(1).

c
A group of record companies which had exclusive contracts with musical performers to record their performances and to distribute the performers' records brought an action against the defendant, alleging in their statement of claim that he was a 'bootlegger', ie a person who knowingly, and without the performers' consent, made unauthorised recordings of their performances and dealt in them for trade, in contravention of the Performers' Protection Acts 1958 to 1972[a], and seeking, inter alia, (i) an injunction *d* restraining the defendant from making such illegal recordings and from selling, hiring or distributing them for trade or using them for public performances and (ii) an inquiry as to damages. The defendant failed to serve a defence and the plaintiffs moved for judgment in default of defence. The motion was heard on the basis that the facts pleaded were true. The plaintiffs submitted that, although s 1[b] of the 1958 Act made any breach thereof a criminal offence only, they were nevertheless entitled to bring a civil action *e* against the defendant for breach of s 1 because (i) the damage caused by the defendant's unlawful acts was of the kind which the Acts were designed to prevent, (ii) s 1 of the 1958 Act conferred on record companies a cause of action for breach of s 1 and (iii) s 1 gave the performers a cause of action against the defendant and, because of the plaintiffs' contractual relationship with the performers, the plaintiffs also could maintain a civil *f* action against the defendant for breach of s 1.

Held – (1) Although, having regard to art 10[c] of the Rome Convention and s 1(1)[d] of the 1963 Act which amended the 1958 Act to give effect to that convention, s 1 of the 1958 Act was to be regarded as having been passed for the protection of record companies as well as performers, nevertheless s 1 of the 1958 Act did not confer on either performers or record companies any private right of action for breach of s 1 and accordingly neither *g* the performers nor the record companies had a private civil right of action against the defendant in respect of his contravention of s 1 (see p 466 *g* to *j* and p 467 *f g*, post); *Ex p Island Records Ltd* [1978] 3 All ER 824 followed; dictum of Lord Diplock in *Lonrho Ltd v Shell Petroleum Co Ltd* [1981] 2 All ER at 462 considered.

(2) However, even though s 1 of the 1958 Act only provided criminal penalties for breach thereof, the plaintiffs were entitled, under the established exceptions to the *h* general rule that performance of a statutory obligation could only be enforced in the manner provided by the statute, to bring a civil action for damages and an injunction against the defendant, either on the ground that the damage they had suffered was of the kind which the Performers' Protection Acts were designed to prevent and that they were members of the class which the Acts were designed to protect or on the ground that s 1 *j* of the 1958 Act created a public right and the plaintiffs had suffered particular damage

---

a   Ie the Dramatic and Musical Performers' Protection Act 1958, the Performers' Protection Act 1963 and the Performers' Protection Act 1972
b   Section 1, so far as material, is set out at p 459 *d e*, post
c   Article 10 is set out at p 460 *d*, post
d   Section 1(1) is set out at p 459 *j* to p 460 *a*, post

peculiar to themselves in respect of that public right.   Accordingly, the plaintiffs were
entitled to the relief sought (see p 465 *j*, p 466 *g h* and p 467 *h*, post); dictum of Lord *a*
Diplock in *Lonrho Ltd v Shell Petroleum Co Ltd* [1981] 2 All ER at 461–462 applied.

Notes

For protection of performers of, inter alia, musical works, see 9 Halsbury's Laws (4th edn)
para 962, and for a case on the subject, see 13 Digest (Reissue) 158, *1332.*

    For civil actions in respect of a breach of a duty imposed by statute, see 36 Halsbury's *b*
Laws (3rd edn) 449–454, paras 684–690, and for cases on the subject, see 44 Digest (Repl)
320, *1510–1512.*

    For the tort of interference with contractual relations, see 37 Halsbury's Laws (3rd edn)
124, para 216, and for cases on the subject, see 45 Digest (Repl) 303–310, *194–228.*

    For threatened invasion of a legal right, see 24 Halsbury's Laws (4th edn) para 932, and
for cases on the subject, see 28(2) Digest (Reissue) 1010–1011, *378–383.* *c*

    For the Dramatic and Musical Performers' Protection Act 1958, s 1, see 7 Halsbury's
Statutes (3rd edn) 226.

    For the Performers' Protection Act 1963, s 1, see ibid 231.

Cases referred to in judgment

Acrow (Automation) Ltd v Rex Chainbelt Inc [1971] 3 All ER 1175, [1971] 1 WLR 1676, CA, *d*
    Digest (Cont Vol D) 909, *221a.*
Anton Piller KG v Manufacturing Processes Ltd [1976] 1 All ER 779, [1976] Ch 55, [1976]
    2 WLR 162, CA, Digest (Cont Vol E) 338, *1238b.*
Apple Corps Ltd v Lingasong Ltd [1977] FSR 345.
Argyll (Margaret, Duchess of) v Duke of Argyll [1965] 1 All ER 611, [1967] Ch 302, [1965]
    2 WLR 790, 28(2) Digest (Reissue) 1089, *916.* *e*
Austria (Emperor) v Day and Kossuth (1861) 3 De GF & J 217, 45 ER 861, LC and LJJ, 28(2)
    Digest (Reissue) 1095, *962.*
Beaudesert Shire Council v Smith (1966) 120 CLR 145, Aust HC.
Benjamin v Storr (1874) LR 9 CP 400, 26 Digest (Reissue) 627, *4348.*
Boyce v Paddington BC [1903] 1 Ch 109; *on appeal* [1903] 2 Ch 556, CA: *rvsd sub nom*
    Paddington Corp v A-G [1906] AC 1, HL, 28(2) Digest (Reissue) 1110, *1069.* *f*
Butler (or Black) v Fife Coal Co Ltd [1912] AC 149, HL, 33 Digest (Repl) 892, *1287.*
Chamberlaine v Chester and Birkenhead Rly Co (1848) 1 Exch 870, 154 ER 371, 28(2) Digest
    (Reissue) 1112, *1085.*
Cutler v Wandsworth Stadium Ltd [1949] 1 All ER 544, [1949] AC 398, HL, 25 Digest
    (Reissue) 504, *4396.*
Doe d Bishop of Rochester v Bridges (1831) 1 B & Ad 847, [1824–34] All ER Rep 167, 109 *g*
    ER 1001, 44 Digest (Repl) 346, *1813.*
Gouriet v Union of Post Office Workers [1977] 3 All ER 70, [1978] AC 435, [1977] 3 WLR
    300, HL, 16 Digest (Reissue) 265, *2528.*
Greig v Insole, World Series Cricket Pty Ltd v Insole [1978] 3 All ER 449, [1978] 1 WLR 302,
    Digest (Cont Vol E) 604, *288d.*
Groves v Lord Wimborne [1898] 2 QB 402, [1895–9] All ER Rep 147, CA, 44 Digest (Repl) *h*
    357, *1938.*
Island Records Ltd, Ex p [1978] 3 All ER 824, [1978] Ch 122, [1978] 3 WLR 23, CA, Digest
    (Cont Vol E) 339, *1238e.*
Iveson v Moore (1699) 1 Ld Raym 486, 91 ER 1224, 36(1) Digest (Reissue) 481, *594.*
Levy v Walker (1879) 10 Ch D 436, [1874–80] All ER Rep 1173, CA, 36(2) Digest
    (Reissue) 777, *1551.* *j*
Lonrho Ltd v Shell Petroleum Co Ltd [1981] 2 All ER 456, [1982] AC 173, [1981] 3 WLR 33,
    HL.
McCall v Abelesz [1976] 1 All ER 727, [1976] QB 585, [1976] 2 WLR 151, CA, Digest
    (Cont Vol E) 372, *7633a.*
Ministry of Housing and Local Government v Sharp [1970] 1 All ER 1009, [1970] 2 QB 223,
    [1970] 2 WLR 802, CA, Digest (Cont Vol C) 830, *926f.*

Musical Performers' Protection Association Ltd v British International Pictures Ltd (1930) 46
TLR 485, 13 Digest (Reissue) 158, *1332.*

National Phonograph Co Ltd v Edison-Bell Consolidated Phonograph Co Ltd [1908] 1 Ch 335,
[1904–7] All ER Rep 116, CA, 17 Digest (Reissue) 91, *51.*

Patent Agents Institute v Lockwood [1894] AC 347, HL, 36(2) Digest (Reissue) 1348, *4320.*

Simmonds v Newport Abercarn Black Vein Steam Coal Co Ltd [1921] 1 KB 616, 33 Digest
(Repl) 879, *1209.*

Springhead Spinning Co v Riley (1868) LR 6 Eq 551, 45 Digest (Reissue) 569, *1413.*

Torquay Hotel Co Ltd v Cousins [1969] 1 All ER 522, [1969] 2 Ch 106, [1969] 2 WLR 289,
CA, 28(2) Digest (Reissue) 1009, *369.*

Action

By writ dated 22 July 1981 the plaintiffs, Warner Bros Records Inc, Phonogram Ltd,
United Artists Ltd, EMI Records Ltd, Charisma Records Ltd, CBS Inc, CBS United
Kingdom Ltd, Polydor Ltd and WEA Records Ltd, brought an action against the
defendant, Henry Vincent Parr, alleging in the statement of claim that prior to the issue
of the writ the defendant had been 'bootlegging', ie acting in contravention of the
Performers' Protection Acts 1958 to 1972, in regard to, and dealing in bootleg records of
performances of, performers who had exclusive recording contracts with one or other of
the plaintiffs, by reason of which the plaintiffs and each of them had suffered loss and
damage, and that the defendant threatened and intended to continued the acts
complained of unless he was restrained by the court. The plaintiffs sought (1) an
injunction to restrain the defendant (whether acting by himself, his servants or agents)
from doing or authorising (i) the making, directly or indirectly, from or by means of a
performance of any performer who had granted the exclusive manufacturing and
distributing rights in the United Kingdom in relation to records of his performances to
one of the plaintiffs, or to an organisation which had granted those rights to one of the
plaintiffs, any record, tape or like contrivance for reproducing sound without the consent
in writing of the performer or in the case of a group of each and every performer, (ii) the
selling or letting for hire or distributing for the purposes of trade or exposing or offering
for sale or hire any such records and (iii) the using for a public performance any such
record, (2) an order for delivery up forthwith to the plaintiffs' solicitors of every record
made in contravention of the Performers' Protection Acts of a performance in which one
of the plaintiffs had an interest, (3) special damages of £360·50, and (4) an inquiry into
the general damages sustained by the plaintiffs by reason of acts carried out by the
defendant in contravention of the Performers' Protection Acts. The facts are set out in
the judgment.

John Baldwin for the plaintiffs.
The defendant did not appear.

Cur adv vult

18 December. **JULIAN JEFFS QC** read the following judgment: This is an action
brought by a number of record companies against a defendant who is alleged to be a
bootlegger, bootleggers being those who act in contravention of the Performers'
Protection Acts 1958 to 1972 by making records of performances which they are not
licensed to record. This is a kind of action which is becoming increasingly common.

Counsel for the plaintiffs moves for judgment in default of defence. The service of the
writ was acknowledged, and, although an intention to defend was indicated at the time,
no defence has been forthcoming. I am satisfied that proper attempts have been made
to serve the defendant with notice of this motion and that in the circumstances it was
correct that I should proceed to a hearing.

In view of the fact that I intend to grant to the plaintiffs the relief that they seek, I shall
delay the drawing up of the order for seven days in order to give the defendant the
opportunity to move the court if he wishes to do so and I shall request the plaintiffs to

give an undertaking to serve notice of the nature of the order I have made on the defendant immediately.

I shall proceed on the basis that all the facts pleaded in the statement of claim are proved. I do not propose to set the statement of claim out in detail but I can summarise briefly what it says.

The plaintiffs are record manufacturers who make and distribute copyright recordings, being the owners of or the exclusive licensees of the copyrights. In respect of the vast majority of popular records so made, the performer has an exclusive recording contract with one of the plaintiffs or with some other organisation that has licensed the plaintiffs. Full particulars are provided in respect of eight records in which the performers are a number of groups of individual artists. The plaintiffs claim the right, to the exclusion of all others, to exploit for profit records of these performances. The plaintiffs' businesses depend on their receiving money from the sale of their records and the major part of their individual businesses arises out of the fact that they have in being exclusive recording contracts with successful musical performers. Bootlegging causes them damage. There is a large trade in this country in bootleg records and records made in infringement of copyright which, by reason of its size and clandestine nature, constitutes a continuing threat to the plaintiffs' interests.

Tracking down the bootleggers is difficult and expensive. The plaintiffs have accordingly combined with each other and employ a full-time investigation and legal staff for this purpose, this being one of the functions of the British Phonographic Industry Ltd. All members of this company, which include the second, fourth, fifth, sixth, seventh and ninth plaintiffs, contribute to its running expenses. This action has been brought as a result of inquiries made by and with the assistance of that company. The defendant has been bootlegging and dealing in bootleg records of performances of performers who have exclusive recording contracts with one or other of the plaintiffs. Certain records are particularised but I need not, for the purpose of the judgment, go into those details. Particulars are also given of the fact that the defendant acted 'knowingly' within the meaning of s 1 of the Dramatic and Musical Performers' Protection Act 1958.

These particulars are as follows: (i) the particulars previously set out in the pleading and which I have summarised; (ii) the fact that it is well-known to the public at large, and in particular to persons interested in pop music, that popular musicians record through exclusive recording contracts with major record companies such as the plaintiffs herein; (iii) the fact that it is well-known to the public at large, and in particular to the public interested in pop music, that illicit recordings of the performances of popular musicians are sometimes made and offered for sale and are called bootleg records; (iv) the fact that it is well-known, as aforesaid, that bootleg records are made without the permission either in writing or at all of the relevant performers, not least because their exclusive recording contracts preclude them from giving such permissions; (v) the fact that none of the relevant performers have consented to the defendant's activities which are complained of herein; in the premises the defendant must have known that he did not have the written consent of each and every such performer; (vi) the fact that each of the records complained of looks like a bootleg record.

On this latter point I was informed by counsel for the plaintiffs that bootleg records are generally inferior in the printed matter and get-up generally which distinguishes them. None of the records complained of was made with the consent in writing, or any other form of consent, of the performers involved. The defendant is aware of the source from which the bootleg records complained of can be obtained, the names and addresses of the persons who have supplied them or who have offered to supply them, and those to whom he has supplied or offered to supply the same. Solicitors acting for the plaintiffs requested that he should disclose this information but he has not done so. Unless restrained he will continue the acts complained of.

Apart from any question of general damages, in respect of which an inquiry is sought, the plaintiffs have suffered special damage of £360·50, being the cost of tracking down the bootlegger.

That is the factual background on the basis of which I must proceed.

What, then, is the law? Counsel for the plaintiffs has arranged his argument under three heads. First, this is a case which is within the narrow principle first expressed in *Gouriet v Union of Post Office Workers* [1977] 3 All ER 70, [1978] AC 435, and amplified in a case called *Ex p Island Records Ltd* [1978] 3 All ER 824, [1978] Ch 122, which I shall shortly come to, that principle being that where there is an unlawful act causing special damage to property rights it is actionable if the damage is of the kind contemplated by the statute and is of the type it was designed to prevent.

Second, there is a cause of action for breach of statutory duty based on the Performers' Protection Acts.

Third, at minimum this is a case where there is a cause of action for breach of statutory duty maintainable on behalf of the performers and the record companies can sue on the principle enunciated by the Court of Appeal in *Ministry of Housing and Local Government v Sharp* [1970] 1 All ER 1009, [1970] 2 QB 223.

The first two submissions, to a large extent, overlap and I shall initially consider them together. I shall consider the third separately. But before I do so it will be convenient to refer to the statutory provisions on which the action is founded.

The Dramatic and Musical Performers' Protection Act 1958, s 1 reads:

> 'Subject to the provisions of this Act, if a person knowingly—(*a*) makes a record, directly or indirectly from or by means of the performance of a dramatic or musical work without the consent in writing of the performers, or (*b*) sells or lets for hire, or distributes for the purposes of trade, or by way of trade exposes or offers for sale or hire, a record made in contravention of this Act, or (*c*) uses for the purposes of a public performance a record so made, he shall be guilty of an offence under this Act, and shall be liable, on summary conviction, to a fine not exceeding [£20] for each record in respect of which an offence is proved, but not exceeding [£400] in respect of any one transaction or, on conviction on indictment, to imprisonment for a term not exceeding two years, or to a fine, or to both . . .'

There is then a proviso, which I need not read.

Section 5 reads:

> 'The court before which any proceedings are taken under this Act may, on conviction of the offender, order that all records, cinematograph films, plates or similar contrivances in the possession of the offender which appear to the court to have been made in contravention of this Act, or to be adapted for the making of records in contravention of this Act, and in respect of which the offender has been convicted, be destroyed, or otherwise dealt with as the court may think fit.'

I come now to the Performers' Protection Act 1963. This is stated to be 'An Act to amend the law relating to the protection of performers so as to enable effect to be given to a Convention entered into at Rome on 26th October 1961'. The Act commences with the words:

> 'Whereas, with a view to the ratification by Her Majesty of the International Convention for the Protection of Performers, Producers of Phonograms and Broadcasting Organisations entered into at Rome on 26th October 1961, it is expedient to amend and supplement the Dramatic and Musical Performers' Protection Act 1958 (in this Act referred to as "the principal Act").'

It then goes on to s 1. I think, for the purposes of this judgment, I need only read s 1(1) which reads thus:

> 'The principal Act shall have effect as if for references therein to the performance of a dramatic or musical work there were substituted references to the performance of any actors, singers, musicians, dancers or other persons who act, sing, deliver, declaim, play in or otherwise perform literary, dramatic, musical or artistic works, and the definition contained in section 8(1) of that Act [I pause here to say that s 8(1) is the interpretation section] of the expression "performance of a dramatic or musical work" (by which that expression is made to include a performance rendered or

intended to be rendered audible by mechanical or electrical means) shall be construed accordingly.'

This, then, takes me to the International Convention for the Protection of Performers, Producers of Phonograms and Broadcasting Organisation (Rome, 26 October 1961; Cmnd 1635). I would refer first to art 7(1):

'The protection provided for performers by this Convention shall include the possibility of preventing: (a) the broadcasting and the communication to the public, without their consent, of their performance, except where the performance used in the broadcasting or the public communication is itself already a broadcast performance or is made from a fixation; (b) the fixation, without their consent, of their unfixed performance; (c) the reproduction, without their consent, of a fixation of their performance: (i) if the original fixation itself was made without their consent; (ii) if the reproduction is made for purposes different from those for which the performers gave their consent; (iii) if the original fixation was made in accordance with the provisions of Article 15, and the reproduction is made for purposes different from those referred to in those provisions.'

Article 15 is not an article that I need consider for the purposes of this judgment, but I will go to art 10 which is short and reads thus: 'Producers of phonograms shall enjoy the right to authorise or prohibit the direct or indirect reproduction of their phonograms.'

That, in turn, takes me back to art 3, which is an article concerned with definitions. By art 3(b), '"Phonogram" means any exclusively aural fixation of sounds of a performance or of other sounds'. A phonogram being an aural fixation of the sounds of a performance, it is an indirect reproduction of that performance to make another record of it.

The express intention of the 1963 Act was to give effect to the Rome Convention and, in my judgment, it has done so. The Performers' Protection Acts were clearly passed for the protection of a class of persons. I have already read out s 1 of the 1958 Act. Section 1(a) and (c) is intended to protect performers but the clear intention of s 1(b) is to extend the protection to another class, namely the record companies with whom the performers are in the habit of contracting.

This is supported by the 1963 Act, bringing into our law the provisions of the Rome Convention, one object of which (I have read art 10) is to protect phonogram producers.

Thus the statutes confer on performers the right not to have their performances recorded and on recording companies not to have their records reproduced unless, of course, consent is given in writing.

The question of bootlegging came before the Court of Appeal in *Ex p Island Records Ltd* [1978] 3 All ER 824, [1978] Ch 122. After quoting s 1 of the 1958 Act, which I have already read, the headnote says ([1978] Ch 122):

'Thirty plaintiffs, performers and recording companies with which the performers had exclusive contracts to record their performances in the best possible conditions, who complained that they were suffering serious damage by reason of the activities of unauthorised recorders ("bootleggers") of live performances and subsequent trading in reproductions of those recordings, applied ex parte in the Chancery Division for, inter alia, an injunction to restrain a named defendant from committing any acts in contravention of section 1 of the Act of 1958 or interfering with contractual relations or otherwise interfering with their business by unlawful means, and an order that the defendant deliver up all recordings in his possession. Walton J. held, without looking at the evidence on affidavit or exhibits thereto, that the court had no jurisdiction to grant relief to persons who, although they could show damage by the unlawful acts, had no right of property infringed by those activities.
On appeal ex parte by the plaintiffs on the preliminary question of jurisdiction: Held, (1) (per Shaw and Waller L.JJ.) that section 1 of the Act of 1958 provided only for penalties in criminal proceedings against a person found guilty of the statutory

offences and did not impose any defined duty to any particular class of persons so that no civil action could be brought for a simple breach of the statutory provisions.

Per Lord Denning M.R. The determination of the question whether a criminal statute also created a civil cause of action has left the courts with a guess-work puzzle. The dividing line between the pro-cases and the contra-cases is so blurred and so ill-defined that you might as well toss a coin to decide it. The court should seek for other ways to do "therein what to justice shall appertain" . . .

But (2), allowing the appeal (Shaw L.J. dissenting), that where a private or corporate person could show a private right which was being interfered with by a criminal act, thus causing or threatening to cause him special damage over and above damage to the public in general, there was jurisdiction in equity for the court to grant an injunction ex parte to restrain the defendant from damaging that private interest; and that where the recording companies and the performers could show a strong case that the companies were losing sales of records and the performers were losing royalties on those lost sales, that was interference with a private right which would entitle them to the relief sought.'

I will now turn to part of the judgment of Lord Denning MR ([1978] 3 All ER 824 at 829–831, [1978] Ch 122 at 135–137):

> '*The protection of private rights*   The way was pointed out by Mr Gibson acting as amicus curiae, who was engaged in the recent case of *Gouriet v Union of Post Office Workers* [1977] 3 All ER 70, [1978] AC 435. He drew attention to the rule of the court of equity in these matters. It intervened to protect a private individual in his rights of property, and in aid of this would grant an injunction to restrain a defendant from committing an unlawful act, even though it was a crime punishable by the criminal court; and would supplement its jurisdiction in this regard by its power under Lord Cairns's Act to award damages in lieu of or in addition to an injunction. The result of *Gouriet's* case may be summarised thus: when a statute creates a criminal offence, prescribing a penalty for the breach of it but not giving any civil remedy, the general rule is that no private individual can bring an action to enforce the criminal law, neither by way of an injunction nor by damages. It must be left to the Attorney-General to bring an action, either of his own motion or at the instance of a member of the public who "relates" the facts to him. But there is an exception to this rule in any case where the criminal act is not only an offence against the public at large, but also causes or threatens to cause special damage to a private individual. If a private individual can show that he has a private right which is being interfered with by the criminal act, thus causing or threatening to cause him special damage over and above the generality of the public, then he can come to the court as a private individual and ask that his private right be protected: see *Gouriet's* case [1970] 3 All ER 70 at 92, 98, 104, 110, 114, [1978] AC 435 at 492, 499, 506, 513, 518 by Viscount Dilhorne, Lord Diplock, Lord Edmund-Davies and Lord Fraser. The court can, in those circumstances, grant an injunction to restrain the offender from continuing or repeating his criminal act. It is no answer then for the defendant to say: "It is a crime which I am about to commit. If an injunction is granted, I shall be in double jeopardy if I break it, on the one hand for contempt of court in the civil jurisdiction, and on the other hand for a penalty in the criminal jurisdiction." The reply to him is simple: "All the more reason why you should not break the law. You will then be in no jeopardy. If you do break it, you will not be punished twice over. Whichever court deals with you, it will take into consideration the punishment which has been, or can be, inflicted by the other." The exception depends, however on the private individual having a private right which he is entitled to have protected. That was made clear long ago by Holt C J in the leading case of *Iveson v Moore* (1699) 1 Ld Raym 486, 91 ER 1224, when he was considering a public nuisance by stopping up a highway leading to a colliery. It was a criminal act, but it was held that the colliery owner could bring an action against the offender

if he could show special damage. Holt CJ said (1 Ld Raym 486 at 492–493, 91 ER 1224 at 1228): ". . . actions upon the case for nuisances are founded upon particular rights; but where there is not any particular right, the plaintiff shall not have an action." The question, therefore, becomes this: has the plaintiff a particular right which he is entitled to have protected? To this the answer which runs through all the cases is this: a man who is carrying on a lawful trade or calling has a right to be protected from any unlawful interference with it: see *Acrow (Automation) Ltd v Rex Chainbelt Inc* [1971] 3 All ER 1175, [1971] 1 WLR 1676. It is a right which is in the nature of a right of property. Such as a right to have the access to your premises kept clear without being obstructed by nuisance or smells (see *Benjamin v Storr* (1874) LR 9 CP 400), or a right to run a ferry for profit across the river Mersey without being injured by rail traffic contrary to the penal statute (see *Chamberlaine v Chester and Birkenhead Rly Co* (1848) 1 Exch 870), or a right to prevent spurious notes being circulated to the damage of the plaintiff's interests (see *Emperor of Austria v Day and Kossuth* (1861) 3 De GF & J 217 at 251–255, 45 ER 861 at 874–876), or a right to prevent passing-off (see *Levy v Walker* (1879) 10 Ch D 436 at 448, [1874–80] All ER Rep 1173 at 1175 by James LJ), or a right to have your servants come unhindered to work, even though it is only made unlawful by a penal statute (see *Springhead Spinning Co v Riley* (1868) LR 6 Eq 551), or a right to have your contractual relations maintained inviolate without interference by others, unless there is just cause or excuse (see *National Phonograph Co Ltd v Edison-Bell Consolidated Phonograph Co Ltd* [1908] 1 Ch 335, [1904–7] All ER Rep 116, *Torquay Hotel Co Ltd v Cousins* [1969] 1 All ER 522, [1969] 2 Ch 106 and the recent cricketers case of *Greig v Insole* [1978] 3 All ER 449 at 484–490, [1978] 1 WLR 302 at 332–338), or a right in a workman to have his pay slip properly vouched, even though it is only made unlawful by a penal statute (see *Simmonds v Newport Abercarn Black Vein Steam Coal Co Ltd* [1921] 1 KB 616, where a declaration was granted). In all these cases the unlawful interference may be a tort, such as fraud or passing-off; or it may be a crime, such as a public nuisance or a breach of a statute which imposes only criminal penalties; but whatever be the nature of the unlawful interference, the party concerned is entitled to come himself to the courts of law and ask to be protected from the unlawful interference. It is no answer for the defendant to say: "It is a crime and so you cannot sue me." It would be a sorry state of the law if a man could excuse himself by such a plea, and thus cause special damage with impunity. For the fact must be faced: the criminal law is a broken reed in some of these cases; at any rate in this particular case. The police have not the men or the means to investigate the offence or to track down the offenders or to prosecute them. Nor have they the will. Nor has the Attorney-General. He has, we are told, refused his consent to a relator action, presumably because no public rights are involved. So perforce, if the law is to be obeyed, and justice be done, the courts must allow a private individual himself to bring an action against the offender in those cases where his private rights and interests are specially affected by the breach. This principle is capable of extension so as to apply not only to rights of property or rights in the nature of it, but to other rights or interests, such as the right of a man to his good name and reputation (see *Margaret, Duchess of Argyll v Duke of Argyll* [1965] 1 All ER 611 at 633, [1967] Ch 302 at 344) and his right to the lawful transmission of his mail (see my illustration in *Gouriet's* case [1977] 1 All ER 696 at 714–715, [1977] QB 729 at 756–757).

The present case In the present case both the performers and the recording companies have, to my mind, private rights and interests which they are entitled to have protected from unlawful interference. The recording companies have the right to exploit the records made by them of the performances. The performers have the right to the royalty payable to them out of those records. Those rights are buttressed by the contracts between the recording companies and the performers. They are rights in the nature of rights of property. Both the recording companies and the performers suffer severe damage if those rights are unlawfully interfered with. Suppose that the bootlegger in the audience had in his hand or his pocket, instead of a recording device, a distorting device, and by it he could introduce a squeak or a screech into the musical performance and thus ruin its commercial value. No one could doubt that the recording company and the performers could bring an action to stop him and claim damages. That illustration shows that they have a private right which they are entitled to have protected; and this is so, no matter whether the interference be by means of a tortious act or a criminal act. The wrongdoer cannot take advantage of his own crime so as to damage a private individual with impunity. All the cases suggested to the contrary can be distinguished. Thus in *Patent Agents Institute v Lockwood* [1894] AC 347 the plaintiffs had nothing in the nature of a right of property and had suffered no special damages. In the cases before McCardie J (*Musical Performers' Protection Association Ltd v British International Pictures Ltd* (1930) 46 TLR 485) and Megarry V-C (*Apple Corps Ltd v Lingasong Ltd* [1977] FSR 345) it was thought that the courts can only give relief in the case of rights of property, strictly so called, whereas the cases I have cited show that the courts give relief whenever there is unlawful interference with the plaintiff's trade or calling. So my conclusion is that the courts have jurisdiction to grant an Anton Piller injunction in regard to bootleggers, just as they have in regard to pirates. I am confirmed in this view by the fact that it carries out to the full the recommendations of the committee presided over by Whitford J (see Report of the Committee to consider the Law on Copyright and Designs (1977) Cmnd 6732, paras 412(iii), 414(iv), 419(iv)). The granting of the Anton Piller injunction is subject to the safeguards mentioned in the report of that case (*Anton Piller KG v Manufacturing Processes Ltd* [1976] 1 All ER 779, [1976] Ch 55). I would, therefore, allow this appeal and remit the case to the judge for him to deal with bootleggers just as is done in the case of pirates.'

I turn now to the judgment of Waller LJ. I shall not read the sections of the judgment in which he considers the authorities but shall go to two short passages. The first is ([1978] 3 All ER 824 at 836, [1978] Ch 122 at 144):

'In the present case, therefore, assuming that there has been a breach of s 1 of the 1958 Act, can it be said that there is a right of property which is being damaged? The record company has contracted with performers to have their exclusive services. If therefore somebody makes a record of a performance by one of the performers to whose services one of the record companies has the exclusive right, the record company will suffer an injury to a right of property. That exclusive contractual right would be interfered with by actions which would be a breach of the law and would in fact be criminal offences. Similarly the performer who is entitled to a royalty for each copy of a recording of his performance would also suffer injury because a recording of his performance would be being sold without his drawing the royalty to which he is entitled.'

The next passage I will quote is ([1978] 3 All ER 824 at 837, [1978] Ch 122 at 144–145):

'Accordingly I am satisfied that in equity there is jurisdiction for a court to grant an injunction to a person who claims that he suffered special damage to a property interest of his by a crime and that in the circumstances of this case both the record company and the performer would be entitled to such injunction.'

So far, so good. On the basis of that case, if it stood alone, I should have no hesitation in giving the plaintiffs the relief they seek. However, counsel for the plaintiffs, very fairly in his duty to the court, pointed out to me that it does not stand alone and directed my attention to a recent decision of the House of Lords in *Lonrho Ltd v Shell Petroleum Co*

Ltd [1981] 2 All ER 456, [1981] 3 WLR 33. The headnote reads as follows ([1982] AC 173–174):

'The appellants' claim arose out of the construction and operation of an oil refinery in Southern Rhodesia by the respondents and other participating companies and the construction and operation of a pipeline from a port in Mozambique by the appellants, the enterprise being governed by complex interconnected contracts entered into in 1962. The commercial expectation of all the parties was that all the oil for the refinery would be shipped to Mozambique and pass through the pipeline in accordance with a shippers' agreement made between the appellants and the participating companies. The refinery and pipeline were completed in January 1965. In November 1965 the government of Southern Rhodesia declared unilateral independence (U.D.I.). Immediately the United Kingdom passed the Southern Rhodesia Act 1965, pursuant to which the Southern Rhodesia (Petroleum) Order 1965 made it a criminal offence to supply oil to Southern Rhodesia, prescribing punishment for infringement. No further oil was supplied to Southern Rhodesia through the pipeline with consequent loss of revenue to the appellants, but it was alleged by the appellants that before the Order the participating companies had assured Southern Rhodesia of a continual supply of oil and that, after it, through associated companies which they controlled, they did maintain the supply. The appellants claimed that their actions had influenced the inception of U.D.I. and had prolonged the period of disuse of the pipeline. In an arbitration they sought damages against the respondents, the principal participating companies. Parker J. and the Court of Appeal held that the appellants had no cause of action for breach of contract or in tort.

On appeal:—*Held*, dismissing the appeal, that the alleged breaches of the Order gave the appellants no cause of action in tort, since breach of a mere prohibition upon members of the public from doing what would otherwise be lawful was not enough to found such a right, and, further, there was no such right based on the civil tort of conspiracy, which was not to be extended to cover acts done in execution of an agreement by persons to protect their own interests and not for the purpose of injuring the appellants, even when the acts agreed to be done amounted to criminal offences under a penal statute . . . *Ex parte Island Records Ltd.* distinguished.'

I would emphasise that *Ex p Island Records Ltd* was distinguished, as was pointed out in the headnote, and not overruled, the facts of the case being, as I have indicated from the facts set forth in the headnote (which I believe to be adequate for the purpose), very different from those in the one I am now considering.

I shall now go to the speech of Lord Diplock. I would add that the opinion of Lord Diplock met with the approval of all the other Law Lords who were sitting on that case. He said ([1981] 2 All ER 456 at 460, [1982] AC 173 at 183):

'My Lords, it is well settled by authority of this House in *Cutler v Wandsworth Stadium Ltd* [1949] 1 All ER 544, [1949] AC 398 that the question whether legislation which makes the doing or omitting to do a particular act a criminal offence renders the person guilty of such offence liable also in a civil action for damages at the suit of any person who thereby suffers loss or damage is a question of construction of the legislation. So first it is necessary to set out the relevant provisions of the Southern Rhodesia Act 1965 and of the 1965 sanctions order'

which he then did. I can take the matter up again ([1981] 2 All ER 456 at 461, [1982] AC 173 at 185):

'The sanctions order thus creates a statutory prohibition on the doing of certain classes of acts and provides the means of enforcing the prohibition by prosecution for a criminal offence which is subject to heavy penalties including imprisonment. So one starts with the presumption laid down originally by Lord Tenterden CJ in *Doe d Bishop of Rochester v Bridges* (1831) 1 B & Ad 847 at 859, [1824–34] All ER Rep

167 at 170, where he spoke of the "general rule" that "where an act creates an obligation, and enforces the performance in a specified manner . . . that performance cannot be enforced in any other manner", a statement that has frequently been cited with approval ever since, including on several occasions in speeches in this House. Where the only manner of enforcing performance for which the Act provides is prosecution for the criminal offence of failure to perform the statutory obligation or for contravening the statutory prohibition which the Act creates, there are two classes of exception to this general rule. The first is where on the true construction of the Act it is apparent that the obligation or prohibition was imposed for the benefit or protection of a particular class of individuals, as in the case of the Factories Acts and similar legislation.'

I would emphasise that passage. I have already given my construction of the Acts on which this instant case is based. His Lordship then went on to say ([1981] 2 All ER 456 at 461–462, [1982] AC 173 at 185–186):

'As Lord Kinnear put it in *Black v Fife Coal Co Ltd* [1912] AC 149 at 165, in the case of such a statute: "There is no reasonable ground for maintaining that a proceeding by way of penalty is the only remedy allowed by the statute . . . We are to consider the scope and purpose of the statute and in particular for whose benefit it is intended. Now the object of the present statute is plain. It was intended to compel mine owners to make due provision for the safety of the men working in their mines, and the persons for whose benefit all these rules are to be enforced are the persons exposed to danger. But when a duty of this kind is imposed for the benefit of particular persons there arises at common law a correlative right in those persons who may be injured by its contravention." The second exception is where the statute creates a public right (ie a right to be enjoyed by all those of Her Majesty's subjects who wish to avail themselves of it) and a particular member of the public suffers what Brett J in *Benjamin v Storr* (1874) LR 9 CP 400 at 407 described as "particular, direct, and substantial" damage "other and different from that which was common to all the rest of the public." Most of the authorities about this second exception deal not with public rights created by statute but with public rights existing at common law, particularly in respect of use of highways. *Boyce v Paddington Borough Council* [1903] 1 Ch 109 is one of the comparatively few cases about a right conferred on the general public by statute. [I would emphasise these next words:] It is in relation to that class of statute only that Buckley J's oft-cited statement (at 114) as to the two cases in which a plaintiff, without joining the Attorney General, could himself sue in private law for interference with that public right must be understood. The two cases he said were: "... first, where the interference with the public right is such as that some private right of his is at the same time interfered with ... and, secondly, where no private right is interfered with, but the plaintiff, in respect of his public right, suffers special damage peculiar to himself from the interference with the public right." The first case does not appear to depend on the existence of a public right in addition to the private one; while to come within the second case at all it has first to be shown that the statute, having regard to its scope and language, does fall within that class of statutes which creates a legal right to be enjoyed by all of Her Majesty's subjects who wish to avail themselves of it. A mere prohibition on members of the public generally from doing what it would otherwise be lawful for them to do is not enough.'

I think I can pause there. It seems to me to be clear that the acts complained of by the plaintiffs in the instant case fall within both the two exceptions in the passages that I have read out and in particular the second limb of the second exception. However, *Ex p Island Records Ltd* was specifically considered in the speech of Lord Diplock and I must go to the place where he considered it ([1981] 2 All ER 456 at 462–463, [1982] AC 173 at 186–187):

'Before parting from this part of the case, however, I should mention briefly two
cases, one in the Court of Appeal of England, *Ex parte Island Records Ltd* [1978] 3 All
ER 824, [1978] Ch 122, and one in the High Court of Australia, *Beaudesert Shire
Council v Smith* (1966) 120 CLR 145, which counsel for Lonrho, as a last resort, relied
on as showing that some broader principle has of recent years replaced those long-
established principles that I have just stated for determining whether a contravention
of a particular statutory prohibition by one private individual makes him liable in
tort to another private individual who can prove that he has suffered damage as a
result of the contravention. *Ex parte Island Records Ltd* was an unopposed application
for an Anton Piller order against a defendant who, without the consent of the
performers, had made records of musical performances for the purposes of trade.
This was an offence, punishable by a relatively small penalty under the Dramatic
and Musical Performers' Protection Act 1958. The application for the Anton Piller
order was made by performers whose performances had been "bootlegged" by the
defendant without their consent and also by record companies with whom the
performers had entered into exclusive contracts. So far as the application by
performers was concerned, it could have been granted for entirely orthodox
reasons. The Act was passed for the protection of a particular class of individuals,
dramatic and musical performers; even the short title said so. Whether the record
companies would have been entitled to obtain the order in a civil action to which
the performers whose performances had been bootlegged were not parties is a
matter which for present purposes it is not necessary to decide. Lord Denning MR,
however, with whom Waller LJ agreed (Shaw LJ dissenting) appears to enunciate a
wider general rule, which does not depend on the scope and language of the statute
by which a criminal offence is committed, that whenever a lawful business carried
on by one individual in fact suffers damage as the consequence of a contravention
by another individual of any statutory prohibition the former has a civil right of
action against the latter for such damage. My Lords, with respect, I am unable to
accept that this is the law; and I observe that in his judgment rejecting a similar
argument by the appellants in the instant appeal Lord Denning MR accepts that the
question whether a breach of sanctions orders give rise to a civil action depends on
the object and intent of those orders, and refers to *Ex parte Island Records Ltd* as an
example of a statute passed for the protection of private rights and interests, viz
those of the performers.'

From this passage I do not understand Lord Diplock as disapproving the decision in
Ex p Island Records Ltd but only the obiter dicta in which Lord Denning MR formulated
the law in extremely wide terms, as he did in a passage which I read earlier in my
judgment. The House of Lords held that a narrower approach was appropriate but not
that the Court of Appeal was wrong in applying the law that it did apply to the specific
provisions of the Performers' Protection Acts.

That covers the first of the submissions of counsel for the plaintiffs which I have set out
above and on which I am satisfied he is entitled to succeed.

On his second submission, the decision of the Court of Appeal in *Ex p Island Records
Ltd* is against him and I am bound by it, even though there are dicta in the House of
Lords in the *Lonrho* case (which I shall come to in considering the third submission)
which counsel for the plaintiffs argues favour the minority judgments in the Court of
Appeal. It would serve no useful purpose for me to give my own views and if the matter
is to be elucidated it must be for the House of Lords to do it.

I come, finally, to counsel for the plaintiffs' ingenious third submission. I have already
construed the statute and have come to the view that it is intended, inter alia, to protect
performers. Counsel for the plaintiffs argues that there is a statutory duty maintainable
by the performers and that this extends to the record companies following the principle
enunciated by the Court of Appeal in *Ministry of Housing and Local Government v Sharp*
[1970] 1 All ER 1009, [1970] 2 QB 223.

I have already read parts of the judgments in *Ex p Island Records Ltd* and I must now go back to it again and to part of the judgment of Shaw LJ with which Waller LJ concurred ([1978] 3 All ER 824 at 832–833, [1978] Ch 122 at 139):

> 'Counsel for the plaintiffs' submission was that this language in its proper construction had the result of creating a statutory duty to performers which invested them with a cause of action and gave them a right of action for appropriate relief against any person who was in breach of that duty by reason of committing an offence under the section. The essential issue, therefore, is whether the terms of the section are to be so construed as to bring contraventions of it within the class of case exemplified by *Groves v Lord Wimborne* [1898] 2 QB 402, [1895–9] All ER Rep 147, or whether they give rise to the interpretation and effect demonstrated by *Cutler v Wandsworth Stadium Ltd* [1949] 1 All ER 544, [1949] AC 398. It seems to me to be beyond contention that the section falls within the scope of the latter decision. A similar problem fell to be considered in *McCall v Abelesz* [1976] 1 All ER 727, [1976] QB 585 in regard to harassment by a landlord in contravention of s 30 of the Rent Act 1965. I ventured there in the course of my judgment ([1976] 1 All ER 727 at 735, [1976] QB 585 at 600) to emphasise that the essential requirement for the conferring of a civil remedy by a penal provision was that the offence created must consist of a failure to perform a defined duty which the statute imposes on the potential offender for the benefit of a particular class of person. In a general sense no doubt every penal statute imposes a duty owed to the public not to offend against its provisions. This is very far from a situation in which a duty is defined for the benefit of a particular class. One looks in vain at s 1 of the 1958 Act for any definition in terms of such a duty. It does no more than provide for the punishment of certain conduct in relation to dramatic or musical works. To distil from the language of the section a specific duty to performers would involve an illicit process of interpretation. That the product might be potable cannot justify the method or the result. The decision in *Musical Performers' Protection Association Ltd v British International Pictures Ltd* (1930) 46 TLR 485 was right; and it was affirmed in *Apple Corps Ltd v Lingasong Ltd* [1977] FSR 345. The first proposition advanced on behalf of the appellants is accordingly, in my view, untenable and should be rejected.'

It was accepted obiter by Lord Diplock in the *Lonrho* case (in a passage I have already read out) that 'So far as the application by performers [are] concerned, it [the *Anton Piller* order] could have been granted for entirely orthodox reasons.' However, this does not appear to have been the view taken by the Court of Appeal on this aspect of the matter (I have read out the relevant part of the headnote) and I am bound by their judgment. Even if this were not so, I would not willingly have applied *Ministry of Housing and Local Government v Sharp* [1970] 1 All ER 1009, [1970] 2 QB 223 to the very different facts of the case before me. I do not read that case as enunciating a principle of broad application to extend relief to third parties falling outside the contemplation of a statute, but rather to providing relief in respect of negligent acts for those to whom a duty of care is owed and who suffer damage of a kind that could reasonably have been foreseen when the act was done.

Accordingly, I find in favour of the plaintiffs in this action on the first of the submissions put forward by counsel for the plaintiffs and he is entitled to the relief that he seeks subject to the protection which I have indicated I think it proper should be given in the circumstances of this case where the position of the defendant was not wholly clear.

Order accordingly.

Solicitors: *A E Hamlin & Co* (for the plaintiffs).

Hazel Hartman   Barrister.

RCA Corp and another v Pollard

CHANCERY DIVISION
VINELOTT J
15, 19 JANUARY, 26 FEBRUARY 1982

Copyright – Infringement – Right of action – Bootlegging – Persons entitled to bring action to prevent bootlegging – Action by record manufacturer and distributor – Record company having exclusive contract to sell performer's records – Whether performer having civil right of action against bootlegger under performers' protection legislation – Whether record company having similar right of action against bootlegger under legislation – Dramatic and Musical Performers' Protection Act 1958, s 1 – Performers' Protection Act 1963, s 1(1).

The plaintiffs were record companies engaged in making and distributing records. They brought an action against the defendant alleging in the statement of claim that the first plaintiff had had an exclusive recording contract with a well-known musical performer, that the second plaintiff had been licensed by the first plaintiff to manufacture, sell and distribute the performer's records in the United Kingdom, and that the defendant had knowingly traded in 'bootleg' records by the performer, ie records made without the performer's consent, in contravention of the Performers' Protection Acts 1958 to 1972[a]. However, it was not alleged that the defendant had taken part in making the bootleg records. The plaintiffs sought as against the defendant a declaration that his acts were an unlawful interference with the plaintiffs' proprietary rights and injunctions restraining him from dealing in or using for public performance bootleg records by the performer. The defendant applied to strike out the statement of claim and for the action to be dismissed, on the ground that the statement of claim disclosed no reasonable cause of action.

Held – (1) Having regard to the fact that the Performers' Protection Acts were passed for the protection of performers, on their true construction the Acts conferred a private civil right of action against a bootlegger or dealer in bootleg records for breach of s 1[b] of the 1958 Act only on performers, and did not, despite the terms of art 10[c] of the Rome Convention to which s 1(1)[d] of the 1963 Act gave effect, confer a similar right of action on recording companies, independently of performers, against a bootlegger or dealer in bootleg records for breach of s 1 of the 1958 Act which had caused them damage, since at the date when each of the Acts was passed recording companies enjoyed sufficient

---

a   Ie the Dramatic and Musical Performers' Protection Act 1958, the Performers' Protection Act 1963 and the Performers' Protection Act 1972

b   Section 1, so far as material, provides: 'Subject to the provisions of this Act, if a person knowingly—(a) makes a record, directly or indirectly from or by means of the performance of a dramatic or musical work without the consent in writing of the performers, or (b) sells or lets for hire, or distributes for the purposes of trade, or by way or trade exposes or offers for sale or hire, a record made in contravention of this Act, or (c) uses for the purposes of a public performance a record so made, he shall be guilty of an offence under this Act, and shall be liable, on summary conviction, to a fine not exceeding [£20] for each record in respect of which an offence is proved, but not exceeding [£400] in respect of any one transaction or, on conviction on indictment, to imprisonment for a term not exceeding two years, or to a fine, or to both . . .'

c   Article 10 is set out at p 476 f, post

d   Section 1(1) provides: 'The principal Act [ie the 1958 Act] shall have effect as if for references therein to the performance of a dramatic or musical work there were substituted references to the performance of any actors, singers, musicians, dancers or other persons who act, sing, deliver, declaim, play in or otherwise perform literary, dramatic, musical or artistic works, and the definition contained in section 8(1) of that Act of the expression "performance of a dramatic or musical work" (by which that expression is made to include a performance rendered or intended to be rendered audible by mechanical or electrical means) shall be construed accordingly.'

protection under copyright legislation so that it could not be said that the Acts had been passed for their protection. It followed that the plaintiffs did not have a private civil right of action against the defendant under the Acts for breach of s 1 of the 1958 Act (see p 475 d to p 476 d, post); *Lonrho Ltd v Shell Petroleum Co Ltd* [1981] 2 All ER 456 applied; dictum of Lord Diplock in *Lonrho Ltd v Shell Petroleum Co Ltd* [1981] 2 All ER at 462–463 considered; *Ex p Island Records Ltd* [1978] 3 All ER 824 and *Warner Bros Records Inc v Parr* [1982] 2 All ER 455 not followed.

(2) Furthermore, applying the established principle that a statute which created a criminal offence and in addition conferred a public but not a private right of action could not confer a civil right of action on a potential plaintiff unless he suffered special damage beyond that suffered by the public at large, the plaintiffs had no cause of action against the defendant under the Acts because (a) on its true construction s 1 of the 1958 Act merely prohibited the doing of certain acts and did not create a public right of enforcement and (b) there was no private right of enforcement in the plaintiffs as recording companies and the mere fact that the damage suffered by the plaintiffs was of the kind which the statute was designed to prevent and was suffered only by them, and not by the public at large, did not give them a cause of action (see p 476 h to p 477 c, post); *Lonrho Ltd v Shell Petroleum Co Ltd* [1981] 2 All ER 456 applied; *Warner Bros Records Inc v Parr* [1982] 2 All ER 455 not followed.

(3) However, on the facts as pleaded, the plaintiffs might succeed at the trial on the narrower ground that the defendant's acts in dealing with bootleg records constituted the tort of unlawful interference with the plaintiffs' rights of property under their contracts, and it could not, therefore, be said that the statement of claim disclosed no reasonable cause of action. Accordingly, in the exercise of its discretion, the court would refuse the defendant's application to strike out the statement of claim (see p 478 g to p 479 g, post); dictum of Bowen LJ in *Mogul Steamship Co Ltd v McGregor, Gow & Co* (1889) 23 QBD at 614, *National Phonograph Co Ltd v Edison-Bell Consolidated Phonograph Co Ltd* [1904–7] All ER Rep 116, *GWK Ltd v Dunlop Rubber Co Ltd* (1926) 42 TLR 376 and dictum of Jenkins LJ in *D C Thomson & Co Ltd v Deakin* [1952] 2 All ER at 378 applied; *Ex p Island Records Ltd* [1978] 3 All ER 824 and dictum of Lord Diplock in *Lonrho Ltd v Shell Petroleum Co Ltd* [1981] 2 All ER at 463 considered.

Notes

For protection of performers of, inter alia, musical works, see 9 Halsbury's Laws (4th edn) para 962, and for a case on the subject, see 13 Digest (Reissue) 158, *1332*.

For civil actions in respect of a breach of a duty imposed by statute, see 36 Halsbury's Laws (3rd edn) 449–454, paras 684–690, and for cases on the subject, see 44 Digest (Repl) 320, *1510–1512*.

For the tort of interference with contractual relations, see 37 Halsbury's Laws (3rd edn) 124, para 216, and for cases on the subject, see 45 Digest (Repl) 303–310, *194–228*.

For threatened invasion of a legal right, see 24 Halsbury's Laws (4th edn) para 932, and for cases on the subject, see 28(2) Digest (Reissue) 1010–1011, *378–383*.

For the Dramatic and Musical Performers' Protection Act 1958, s 1, see 7 Halsbury's Statutes (3rd edn) 226.

For the Performers' Protection Act 1963, s 1, see ibid 231.

Cases referred to in judgment

Anton Piller KG v Manufacturing Processes Ltd [1976] 1 All ER 779, [1976] Ch 55, [1976] 2 WLR 162, CA, Digest (Cont Vol E) 338, *1238b*.

Apple Corps Ltd v Lingasong Ltd [1977] FSR 345.

Argyll (Margaret, Duchess of) v Duke of Argyll [1965] 1 All ER 611, [1967] Ch 302, [1965] 2 WLR 790, 28(2) Digest (Reissue) 1089, *916*.

Beaudesert Shire Council v Smith (1966) 120 CLR 145, Aust HC.

Benjamin v Storr (1874) LR 9 CP 400, 26 Digest (Reissue) 627, *4348*.

Boyce v Paddington BC [1903] 1 Ch 109; *on appeal* [1903] 2 Ch 556, CA; *rvsd sub nom Paddington Corp v A-G* [1906] AC 1, HL, 28(2) Digest (Reissue) 1110, *1069.*

British Industrial Plastics Ltd v Ferguson [1940] 1 All ER 479, HL, 45 Digest (Repl) 303, *197.*

British Motor Trade Association v Salvadori [1949] 1 All ER 208, [1949] Ch 556, 45 Digest (Repl) 305, *207.*

Butler (or Black) v Fife Coal Co Ltd [1912] AC 149, HL, 33 Digest (Repl) 892, *1287.*

Cutler v Wandsworth Stadium Ltd [1949] 1 All ER 544, [1949] AC 398, HL, 25 Digest (Reissue) 504, *4396.*

De Francesco v Barnum (1890) 45 Ch D 430, 34 Digest (Repl) 319, *2372.*

Doe d Bishop of Rochester v Bridges (1831) 1 B & Ad 847, [1824–34] All ER Rep 167, 109 ER 1001, 44 Digest (Repl) 346, *1813.*

Exchange Telegraph Co Ltd v Gregory & Co [1896] 1 QB 147, [1895–9] All ER Rep 1116, 45 Digest (Repl) 305, *208.*

Gouriet v Union of Post Office Workers [1977] 3 All ER 70, [1978] AC 435, [1977] 3 WLR 300, HL, 16 Digest (Reissue) 265, *2528.*

GWK Ltd v Dunlop Rubber Co Ltd (1926) 42 TLR 376; *on appeal* 42 TLR 593, CA, 45 Digest (Repl) 307, *213.*

Island Records Ltd, Ex p [1978] 3 All ER 824, [1978] Ch 122, [1978] 3 WLR 23, CA, Digest (Cont Vol E) 339, *1238e.*

Lonrho Ltd v Shell Petroleum Co Ltd [1981] 2 All ER 456, [1982] AC 173, [1981] 3 WLR 33, HL.

Mogul Steamship Co Ltd v McGregor, Gow & Co (1889) 23 QBD 598, CA; *affd* [1892] AC 25, [1891–4] All ER Rep 263, 45 Digest (Repl) 275, *6.*

Musical Performers' Protection Association Ltd v British International Pictures Ltd (1930) 46 TLR 485, 13 Digest (Reissue) 158, *1332.*

National Phonograph Co Ltd v Edison-Bell Consolidated Phonograph Co Ltd [1908] 1 Ch 335, [1904–7] All ER Rep 116, CA, 17 Digest (Reissue) 91, *51.*

Prudential Assurance Co v Knott (1875) LR 10 Ch App 142, LC and LJJ, 28(2) Digest (Reissue) 1080, *863.*

Thomson (D C) & Co Ltd v Deakin [1952] 2 All ER 361, [1952] Ch 646, CA, 45 Digest (Repl) 562, *1379.*

Warner Bros Records Inc v Parr [1982] 2 All ER 455.

Cases also cited

Austria (Emperor) v Day and Kossuth (1861) 3 De GF & J 217, 45 ER 861, LC and LJJ.

Dixon v Holden (1869) LR 7 Eq 488.

Dyson v A-G [1911] 1 KB 410, CA.

Jade, The, The Eschersheim [1976] 1 All ER 920, [1976] 1 WLR 430, HL.

Springhead Spinning Co v Riley (1868) LR 6 Eq 551.

Motion

By a notice of motion dated 22 December 1981 the defendant, Geoffrey Pollard, applied for an order that the statement of claim in an action brought against him by the plaintiffs, RCA Corp and RCA Ltd, be struck out and the action dismissed on the ground that the statement of claim disclosed no reasonable cause of action. The facts are set out in the judgment.

Nicholas Pumfrey for the defendant.
Mary Vitoria for the plaintiffs.

Cur adv vult

26 February. **VINELOTT J** read the following judgment: This is an application by one Geoffrey Pollard, the defendant to an action brought by a United States company, RCA Corp, and its wholly-owned United Kingdom subsidiary, RCA Ltd. In this application

the defendant seeks an order striking out the statement of claim and dismissing the action on the ground that the statement of claim discloses no reasonable cause of action. The application raises an issue of considerable importance, namely whether a recording company which has a contract with a performer under which it has the exclusive right to record and exploit for profit records of performances by that performer and under which the performer expressly or by necessary implication agrees not to give his consent under the Performers' Protection Acts 1958 to 1972 to the making of records of his performances by any other person can obtain an injunction restraining a defendant from copying or dealing by way of trade with or using for public performance a record of a performance by that performer made by a person other than the recording company with whom the performer had that exclusive contract.

For the purpose of deciding this issue I must assume that the facts alleged in the statement of claim will be established at the trial. The statement of claim is a lengthy document and is in a form which is becoming familiar to the judges of this division. The relevant allegations can be briefly summarised. Paragraph 1 defines a 'bootleg record' as one made in contravention of the Performers' Protection Acts 1958 to 1972 and defines an 'exclusive recording contract' in the terms I have already outlined.

Paragraphs 2 and 3 allege that each of the plaintiff companies had at all material times been engaged in the business of making and distributing records, that the first plaintiff had an exclusive recording contract with the late Elvis Presley and that the second plaintiff has been licensed by the first plaintiff to manufacture, sell and distribute in the United Kingdom records of performances of Elvis Presley.

Paragraphs 4, 5 and 6 allege that the plaintiffs' business depends largely on their receipts from sales of the records of performances by performers with whom they have exclusive recording contracts, that they and each of them make and distribute records of performances by Elvis Presley and that in consequence they have 'private or proprietary rights and interests which they are entitled to have protected from unlawful interference which causes them damage'.

Paragraphs 7 and 8 allege that bootlegging is unlawful and causes damage to the plaintiffs' proprietary rights and interests, that the practice of bootlegging is widespread and poses a threat to the plaintiffs and to other recording companies and that recording companies have combined together to form, to finance and to staff a company called British Phonographic Industry Ltd, of which the second plaintiff is a member, to track down and to suppress the trade in bootleg records.

Paragraph 9 alleges that the defendant has been bootlegging and dealing in bootleg records of performances of Elvis Presley. I do not need to refer in detail to the lengthy particulars of this allegation, which incorporate facts alleged in an affidavit in other proceedings against a defendant who was found in possession of bootleg records. It is sufficient to say that the plaintiffs rely on dealings by the defendant with records said to be bootleg records of such performances and particularise facts which found the prima facie inference that the defendant acted 'knowingly' in those transactions within s 1 of the Dramatic and Musical Performers' Protection Act 1958. The particulars of the allegation that the defendant acted knowingly include an allegation that it is public knowledge that popular musicians record through exclusive recording contracts with the major record companies, that bootleg records are sometimes made without the consent of the performers and are offered for sale and that Elvis Presley did not consent and that the defendant must have known that he did not consent to the making of the recording from which was made the records dealt with by the defendant. It is not alleged that the defendant himself took any part in the making of the original bootleg recording.

Paragraph 12 alleges that the defendant is aware of the source from which bootleg records can be obtained and the whereabouts of the persons who supplied him and of the persons to whom he has supplied bootleg records himself.

Paragraph 14 alleges that the second plaintiff has suffered special damage, being its contribution to the expenses of a bureau establish by British Phonographic Industry Ltd for the purposes I have indicated.

In the prayer to the statement of claim the plaintiffs seek first a declaration that the defendant is not entitled to make, deal in by way of trade or use for public performance any bootleg record and that any such act would be an unlawful interference with the proprietary rights of the plaintiffs, second, injunctions in the terms I have indicated, third, an order compelling the defendant to deliver to the plaintiffs' solicitors any bootleg records in his possession; and, lastly, damages.

The facts pleaded in the statement of claim bear a close resemblance to the facts relied on by the plaintiffs in *Ex p Island Records Ltd* [1978] 3 All ER 824, [1978] Ch 122, but they differ in at least one and possibly in two respects. First, it is clear from the report of that case that the plaintiffs included both recording companies and performers with whom those companies had exclusive recording contracts. The personal representatives of Elvis Presley have not been joined as plaintiffs in these proceedings. Second, although it is not explicitly so stated in the summary of facts at the beginning of the report, it is, I think, implicit in the judgment of Waller LJ that the defendant in that case had been directly concerned in making the original unlawful recording from which the bootleg records said to have been in his possession were derived. I shall return to analyse the judgment of Waller LJ later in this judgment. It is not alleged in the particulars of the allegations in para 9 of the statement of claim in the instant case that the defendant has done more than deal by way of trade in bootleg records.

In *Ex p Island Records Ltd* the plaintiffs sought an interlocutory injunction in the terms of the injunction granted in *Anton Piller KG v Manufacturing Processes Ltd* [1976] 1 All ER 779, [1976] Ch 55 and founded their claim to that relief on two main grounds. The first was that the Performers' Protection Acts were passed for the protection of performers and of recording companies and created a right of action in the civil courts, which founded a claim to damages and for an injunction to restrain a bootlegger from doing any act that would be an offence under those Acts and for an interlocutory order in Anton Piller form. The second was that, if a plaintiff could show that he had a private right or proprietary interest which was being interfered with by a criminal act by the defendant in a way which caused or threatened to cause him damage over and above that caused to the public at large, the court could at his suit grant the same relief.

As to the first of these two grounds, Shaw and Waller LJJ approved the decisions of McCardie J in *Musical Performers' Protection Association Ltd v British International Pictures Ltd* (1930) 46 TLR 485 and of Sir Robert Megarry V-C in *Apple Corps Ltd v Lingasong Ltd* [1977] FSR 345, who had held that the Performers' Protection Acts did not create a right of action in the civil courts enforceable either by performers or by recording companies. Lord Denning MR, although he expressed the opinion that 'A pirate is guilty of a civil wrong. He is infringing the copyright of the recording companies in their tapes and records. But a bootlegger is not guilty of a civil wrong. He is only guilty of a crime' (see [1978] 3 All ER 824 at 828, [1978] Ch 122 at 133), later in his judgment, after referring to a number of cases in which the question whether a penal statute created a civil action for damages has been considered, said ([1978] 3 All ER 824 at 829, [1978] Ch 122 at 134–135):

> 'The truth is that in many of these statutes the legislature has left the point open. It has ignored the plea of Lord du Parcq in *Cutler's* case [1949] 1 All ER 544 at 549, [1949] AC 398 at 410. So it has left the courts with a guesswork puzzle. The dividing line between the pro-cases and the contra-cases is so blurred and so ill-defined that you might as well toss a coin to decide it. I decline to indulge in such a game of chance. To my mind, we should seek for other ways to do "therein what to justice shall appertain".'

However, Lord Denning MR and Waller LJ held that the plaintiffs were entitled to the relief sought on the second ground. Lord Denning MR stated the principle in very wide terms. He said ([1978] 3 All ER 824 at 830, [1978] Ch 122 at 136):

> 'The question, therefore, becomes this: has the plaintiff a particular right which he is entitled to have protected? To this the answer which runs through all the cases

is this: a man who is carrying on a lawful trade or calling has a right to be protected from any unlawful interference with it . . .'

Then, having referred to a number of cases as illustrating this principle, he said ([1978] 3 All ER 824 at 830, [1978] Ch 122 at 136–137):

'In all these cases the unlawful interference may be a tort, such as fraud or passing-off; or it may be a crime, such as a public nuisance; or a breach of a statute which imposes only criminal penalties; but whatever be the nature of the unlawful interference, the party concerned is entitled to come himself to the courts of law and ask to be protected from the unlawful interference. It is no answer for the defendant to say: "It is a crime and so you cannot sue me." It would be a sorry state of the law if a man could excuse himself by such a plea, and thus cause special damage with impunity. For the fact must be faced: the criminal law is a broken reed in some of these cases; at any rate in this particular case. The police have not the men or the means to investigate the offence or to track down the offenders or to prosecute them. Nor have they the will. Nor has the Attorney-General. He has, we are told, refused his consent to a relator action, presumably because no public rights are involved. So perforce if the law is to be obeyed, and justice be done, the courts must allow a private individual himself to bring an action against the offender in those cases where his private rights and interests are specially affected by the breach.'

Waller LJ reached the same conclusion but on a narrower ground. He said ([1978] 3 All ER 824 at 836, [1978] Ch 122 at 144):

'In the present case, therefore, assuming that there has been a breach of s 1 of the 1958 Act, can it be said that there is a right of property which is being damaged? The record company has contracted with performers to have their exclusive services. If, therefore, somebody makes a record of a performance by one of the performers to whose services one of the record companies has the exclusive right, the record company will suffer an injury to a right of property. That exclusive contractual right would be interfered with by actions which would be a breach of the law and would in fact be criminal offences. Similarly the performer who is entitled to a royalty for each copy of a recording of his performance would also suffer injury because a recording of his performance would be being sold without his drawing the royalty to which he is entitled.'

The decision of the Court of Appeal on the second of these two grounds was relied on by the appellants in the appeal to the House of Lords in the recent case of *Lonrho Ltd v Shell Petroleum Co Ltd* [1981] 2 All ER 456, [1982] AC 173. The question in that case very briefly stated was whether the appellant, Lonrho Ltd, had a right of action in tort for damages said to have been suffered as a consequence of a breach by the defendant company and others of a sanctions order which made the supply of oil to Rhodesia a criminal offence. Lord Diplock (with whose speech all the others of their Lordships who heard the appeal agreed), having held that the alleged contravention by Shell of the sanctions order did not constitute a tort for which Lonrho could recover damages, said ([1981] 2 All ER 456 at 462–463, [1982] AC 173 at 186–187):

'Before parting from this part of the case, however, I should mention briefly two cases, one in the Court of Appeal of England, *Ex parte Island Records Ltd* [1978] 3 All ER 824, [1978] Ch 122, and one in the High Court of Australia, *Beaudesert Shire Council v Smith* (1966) 120 CLR 145, which counsel for Lonrho, as a last resort, relied on as showing that some broader principle has of recent years replaced those long-established principles that I have just stated for determining whether the contravention of a particular statutory prohibition by one private individual makes him liable in tort to another private individual who can prove that he has suffered damage as a result of the contravention. *Ex parte Island Records Ltd* was an unopposed application for an Anton Piller order against a defendant who, without the consent of the performers, had made records of musical performances for the purposes of trade. This was an offence, punishable by a relatively small penalty under the Dramatic and Musical Performers' Protection Act 1958. The application for the Anton Piller order was made by performers whose performances had been "bootlegged" by the defendant without their consent and also by record companies with whom the performers had entered into exclusive contracts. So far as the application by performers was concerned, it could have been granted for entirely orthodox reasons. The Act was passed for the protection of a particular class of individuals, dramatic and musical performers; even the short title said so. Whether the record companies would have been entitled to obtain the order in a civil action to which the performers whose performances had been bootlegged were not parties is a matter which for present purposes it is not necessary to decide. Lord Denning MR, however, with whom Waller LJ agreed (Shaw LJ dissenting) appears to enunciate a wider general rule, which does not depend on the scope and language of the statute by which a criminal offence is committed, that whenever a lawful business carried on by one individual in fact suffers damage as the consequence of a contravention by another individual of any statutory prohibition the former has a civil right of action against the latter for such damage. My Lords, with respect, I am unable to accept that this is the law; and I observe that in his judgment rejecting a similar argument by the appellants in the instant appeal Lord Denning MR accepts that the question whether a breach of the sanctions orders gives rise to a civil action depends on the object and intent of those orders, and refers to *Ex parte Island Records Ltd* as an example of a statute passed for the protection of private rights and interests, viz those of the performers.'

What were the 'orthodox reasons' which justified the making of an Anton Piller order on the application of the performers? To answer that question it is necessary to go back to an earlier passage in the speech of Lord Diplock ([1981] 2 All ER 456 at 461, [1982] AC 173 at 185). Having referred to the general rule or presumption laid down by Lord Tenterden CJ in *Doe d Bishop of Rochester v Bridges* (1831) 1 B & Ad 847 at 859, [1824–34] All ER Rep 167 at 170 that 'where an Act creates an obligation, and enforces the performance in a specified manner . . . that performance cannot be enforced in any other manner', Lord Diplock explained the scope of two familiar exceptions to it. The first he stated in these terms:

> 'The first is where on the true construction of the Act it is apparent that the obligation or prohibition was imposed for the benefit or protection of a particular class of individuals, as in the case of the Factories Acts and similar legislation.'

He then referred to the decision in *Butler (or Black) v Fife Coal Co Ltd* [1912] AC 149 as exemplifying that rule.

The second he stated in these terms:

> 'The second exception is where the statute creates a public right (ie a right to be enjoyed by all those of Her Majesty's subjects who wish to avail themselves of it) and a particular member of the public suffers what Brett J in *Benjamin v Storr* (1874) LR 9 CP 400 at 407 described as "particular, direct and substantial" damage "other and different from that which was common to all the rest of the public".'

He then made some observations on the extent of the two categories of cases explained by Buckley J in *Boyce v Paddington BC* [1903] 1 Ch 109, where a plaintiff without joining the Attorney General can sue for intereference with a public right. The first is where the plaintiff relies on some private right which is co-extensive with or overlaps a public right. Lord Diplock pointed out that in those cases the plaintiff's right of action 'would not appear to depend on the existence of a public right in addition to the private one'. The second is where the plaintiff relies on a public right and claims that interference with it inflicts on him 'particular, direct and substantial' damage 'other and different from that which was common to all the rest of the public'. Lord Diplock stressed that in those cases the plaintiff must be able to show that as a member of the public he can assert a right and, if a statute is relied on as creating the right, that—

> 'the statute, having regard to its scope and language, does fall within that class of statutes which create a legal right to be enjoyed by all of Her Majesty's subjects who wish to avail themselves of it. A mere prohibition on members of the public generally from doing what it would otherwise be lawful for them to do is not enough'.

(See [1981] 2 All ER 456 at 462, [1982] AC 173 at 186.)

In making that last observation Lord Diplock clearly had in mind the decision of the House of Lords in *Gouriet v Union of Post Office Workers* [1977] 3 All ER 70, [1978] AC 435, where it was held that, although a member of the public may have an interest in ensuring that the law is obeyed by others, he cannot found an action in the civil courts merely on the ground that the defendant has done or threatens to do an act which was or, if done, would be a breach of a prohibition to which sanctions are attached by the criminal law. That is so even though he himself may have suffered or fears damage beyond that affecting other members of the public. He must go further and show that as a members of the public he has a right the exercise of which has been interfered with by the defendant.

It is, I think, clear, if the observations of Lord Diplock concerning the decision of the Court of Appeal in *Ex p Island Records Ltd* [1978] 3 All ER 824, [1978] Ch 122 are read in the light of the earlier passages in his speech to which I have referred, that Lord Diplock was of the opinion that the Performers' Protection Acts fell within the first of the two exceptions to the rule stated in *Doe d Bishop of Rochester v Bridges* (1831) 1 B & Ad 847, [1824–34] All ER Rep 167, that is that they created a right of action in the civil courts enforceable by performers and that to that extent the decision of the Court of Appeal in *Ex p Island Records Ltd* was wrong.

In *Warner Bros Records Inc v Parr* [1982] 2 All ER 455 at 460, 467, in which Warner Bros Records Inc and other recording companies were the plaintiffs and one Henry Vincent Parr was the defendant, Mr Julian Jeffs QC sitting as a deputy judge of the High Court held, first, that the Performers' Protection Acts 'confer on performers the right not to have their performances recorded and on recording companies not to have their records reproduced unless, of course, consent is given in writing'. He also held that, notwithstanding the decision in *Lonrho Ltd v Shell Petroleum Co Ltd*, he was bound by the decision of the Court of Appeal in *Ex p Island Records Ltd* to conclude that the Performers' Protection Acts did not confer on performers or recording companies a right of action in the civil courts. Although I differ from Mr Julian Jeffs with reluctance, I think that, as regards performers, the decision of the Court of Appeal that the Performers' Protection Acts did not create a right of action in the civil courts must be taken to have been overruled by the House of Lord in *Lonrho Ltd v Shell Petroleum Co Ltd*.

Counsel for the plaintiffs invited me to follow the decision of Mr Julian Jeffs in so far as he held that the Performers' Protection Acts must be regarded as having been passed for the protection of recording companies as well as performers, and, in the light of the decision of the House of Lords in the *Lonrho* case, to treat those Acts as conferring a right of action in the civil courts on recording companies at least in a case where a recording company has entered into an exclusive contract with a performer. I can see nothing in the Performers' Protection Acts which indicates that those Acts were passed for the protection of recording companies, and for reasons which I shall later explain I do not think that Lord Diplock, in leaving open the question 'whether the record companies would have been entitled to obtain the order in a civil action to which the performers whose performances had been bootlegged were not parties', had in mind the possibility that the Performers' Protection Acts could be construed as having been passed for the protection of recording companies. Lord Diplock pointed out that the short title to each of the successive Acts shows that it was passed for the protection of dramatic and musical performers. There is nothing in the short title or elsewhere in the Acts which affords any indication that the legislature intended to extend that protection to recording companies, whether they had exclusive contracts or not. Performers need the protection afforded by the Act because a performer cannot claim copyright in an ephemeral live performance. The primary protection is afforded by para (a) of s 1 of the Dramatic and Musical Performers' Protection Act 1958, which makes it an offence to make a record of a live performance without the written consent of the performer; paras (b) and (c) are ancillary and extend that protection by making it an offence to deal by way of trade or to use for the purposes of public performance any record so made. I see no ground for inferring from paras (b) and (c) an intention to afford protection to recording companies. At the date of each of the Performers' Protection Acts recording companies enjoyed a considerable measure of protection under copyright legislation, in particular at the date of the 1958 Act under the Copyright Act 1956, including (at least under the 1956 Act) a right of action in the civil courts against persons infringing their copyright. The Performers' Protection Acts of course gave them a further measure of indirect protection, because it is open to a recording company on entering into an exclusive contract with a performer to require the performer at its request and on being given a proper indemnity as to costs to institute proceedings in the civil courts to restrain a threatened breach of the Performers' Protection Acts. I can see nothing in the Acts which gives any support at all to the view that the legislature intended that the recording companies should themselves have the right to bring such proceedings independently of the performer.

Mr Julian Jeffs, in reaching the contrary conclusion, relied on the provisions of the International Convention for the Protection of Performers, Producers of Phonograms and Broadcasting Organisations (Rome, 26 October 1961; Cmnd 1635). As the recital to the Performers' Protection Act 1963 indicates, that Act was passed with a view to the ratification of that convention. Article 7 requires each contracting state to afford a degree of protection to performers which is not materially different from the protection already afforded to performers by the 1958 Act, though the required protection is defined in art 7 by reference to the performance of actors etc instead of by reference to the performance of a dramatic or musical work. Section 1 of the 1963 Act gave effect to this difference in the form of the protection required to be afforded to performers and made other ancillary provisions to make the Performers' Protection Acts accord with the convention. Article 10 provided that: 'Producers of phonograms shall enjoy the right to authorise or prohibit the direct or indirect reproduction of their phonograms.' The words 'phonogram' and 'reproduction' are defined in art 3 as meaning 'any exclusively aural fixation of sounds of a performance or of other sounds' and 'the making of a copy or copies of a fixation' respectively. I do not see how art 10 can be read as requiring the law of a contracting state to afford any protection to producers of phonograms more extensive than that already afforded under English law by s 12 of the Copyright Act 1956. Moreover, it seems to me impossible to read the 1963 Act by reference to the convention as conferring on recording companies a right of action in the civil courts which was not conferred by the 1958 Act.

I turn therefore to the second ground. In *Lonrho Ltd v Shell Petroleum Co Ltd* [1981] 2 All ER 456 at 463, [1982] AC 173 at 187 Lord Diplock specifically rejected the proposition 'that whenever a lawful business carried on by one individual in fact suffers damage as a consequence of a contravention by another individual of any statutory prohibition the former has a civil right of action against the latter for such damage'.

Counsel for the plaintiffs submitted that a person who suffers damage in the circumstances envisaged by Lord Diplock has a right of action in the civil courts if the damage is of the kind which the statute was designed to prevent and is suffered by a person who is a member of the class which the statute was designed to protect, albeit that it did not confer any private right on the members of that class. As I understand it that was the ground on which Mr Julian Jeffs QC held that the plaintiff was entitled to interlocutory relief in the *Warner Bros* case. After reading the observations of Lord Diplock on the decision of the Court of Appeal in *Ex p Island Records Ltd*, Mr Julian Jeffs said ([1982] 2 All ER 455 at 466): 'The House of Lords held that a narrower approach was appropriate but not that the Court of Appeal was wrong in applying the law that it did apply to the specific provisions of the Performers' Protection Acts.' In my judgment this submission is inconsistent with the principles enunciated by Lord Diplock. As I have pointed out, Lord Diplock stressed earlier in his speech that, absent any private right, a person who relies on the fact that the acts of the defendant have caused him special damage beyond that suffered by the public at large cannot found a civil action unless he can show that the statute relied on created 'a legal right to be enjoyed by all of Her Majesty's subjects who wish to avail themselves of it'. A statute which merely prohibits the doing of the act complained of cannot be relied on as creating any public right and (again absent any private right created by the statute) the fact that the damage is of the kind which the statute was designed to prevent and is also of a kind suffered only by the plaintiff or a class which he represents and not by the public at large must be irrelevant.

However, there is, I think, another narrower ground on which at the trial the plaintiffs may succeed. It is, I think, the ground which Lord Diplock had in mind when he left open the question whether in *Ex p Island Records Ltd* the recording companies, if they had sued alone, would have been entitled to an Anton Piller order. In *D C Thomson & Co Ltd v Deakin* [1952] 2 All ER 361 at 378, [1952] Ch 646 at 694 Jenkins LJ, having first stated that it is a necessary ingredient of the tort of actionable interference with contractual rights that the breach of contract must be brought about by some act of a third party which is itself unlawful, went on to give instances where the interference would be unlawful in a passage which I think I should read in full:

> 'Direct persuasion or procurement or inducement applied by the third party to the contract breaker, with knowledge of the contract and with the intention of bringing about its breach, is clearly to be regarded as a wrongful act in itself, and where this is shown a case of actionable interference in its primary form is made out ... But the contract breaker may himself be a willing party to the breach, without any persuasion by the third party, and there seems to be no doubt that if a third party, with knowledge of a contract between the contract breaker and another, has dealings with the contract breaker which the third party knows to be inconsistent with the contract, he has committed an actionable interference: see, for example, *British Industrial Plastics, Ltd. v. Ferguson* ([1940] 1 All ER 479), where the necessary knowledge was held not to have been brought home to the third party; and *British Motor Trade Assocn. v. Salvadori* ([1949] 1 All ER 208, [1949] Ch 556). The inconsistent dealing between the third party and the contract breaker may, indeed, be commenced without knowledge by the third party of the contract thus broken, but, if it is continued after the third party has notice of the contract, an actionable interference has been committed by him: see, for example, *De Francesco v. Barnum* ((1890) 45 Ch D 430). Again, so far from persuading or inducing or procuring one of the parties to the contract to break it, the third party may commit an actionable interference with the contract, against the will of both and without the knowledge of either, if, with knowledge of the contract, he does an act which, if done by one of the parties to it, would have been a breach. Of this type of interference the case of *G.W.K., Ltd. v. Dunlop Rubber Co., Ltd.* ((1926) 42 TLR 376) affords a striking example.'

In *GWK Ltd v Dunlop Rubber Co Ltd* the first plaintiffs, who manufactured motor cars, had an agreement with the second plaintiffs, manufacturers of motor car tyres, under which certain cars manufactured by the first plaintiffs were to be fitted with tyres manufactured by the second plaintiffs whenever they were exhibited. The defendants, who knew of the agreement, secretly substituted their own tyres immediately before the first plaintiffs' cars were to be exhibited at an exhibition. Their acts were a trespass and unlawful, and also an interference with the contractual rights of the tyre manufacturing company on which it was held entitled to sue. Another example will be found in the decision of the Court of Appeal in *National Phonograph Co Ltd v Edison-Bell Consolidated Phonograph Co Ltd* [1908] 1 Ch 335, [1904–7] All ER Rep 116. In that case the plaintiffs sold goods which they manufactured to factors or wholesalers on terms that they would only sell to retailers who had signed a retailer's agreement which in turn imposed on the retailers an obligation not to sell at less than a specified price and not to sell to dealers on the plaintiffs' proscribed list. The defendant company, which was on the proscribed list, employed agents to obtain the plaintiffs' goods by deceitfully pretending to be independent dealers and by using fictitious names. It was held by the Court of Appeal that the defendants had interfered with the contractual relationship between the plaintiffs and the factors and had done so by unlawful means, that is by deliberate deceit.

It must be I think at least strongly arguable that a person who obtains admission to a performance by a pop star, knowing that the performer has entered into an exclusive recording contract with a recording company, and who makes a secret recording with a view to distributing it by way of trade equally commits an unlawful act (indeed one which might be unlawful apart from the Performers' Protection Acts inasmuch as it might be possible to infer that persons admitted to the concert impliedly agreed not to make any recording of it) and one which interferes directly with the recording company's contractual rights. That Lord Diplock had this possibility in mind is I think supported by the fact that he described *Ex p Island Records Ltd* as a case brought against a defendant 'who, without the consent of the performers, *had made* records of musical performances for the purposes of trade' (see [1981] 2 All ER 456 at 462, [1982] AC 173 at 187; my emphasis). That was, as I can see it, also the ground on which Waller LJ held that the plaintiffs were entitled to interlocutory relief in that case. He said in a passage I have already cited: 'If . . . somebody *makes a record* of a performance by one of the performers to whose services one of the record companies has the exclusive right, the record company will suffer an injury to a right of property' (see [1978] 3 All ER 824 at 836, [1978] Ch 122 at 144; my emphasis).

In the instant case it is not alleged that the defendant had any part in the making of any bootleg record. What is alleged is that he has dealt with bootleg records for the purposes of trade. Counsel for the defendant submitted that in dealing with bootleg records copied directly or indirectly from a record made by another of a performance by Elvis Presley the defendant did not himself interfere directly or indirectly with the first plaintiff's exclusive recording contract with Elvis Presley and did not interfere directly or indirectly with the first plaintiff's exclusive right to exploit recordings made by it. He submitted that there is nothing in the speech of Lord Diplock or in the judgment of Waller LJ that supports the proposition that one who, like the defendant, deals with bootleg records derived from a recording made by another in breach of an exclusive recording contract commits a wrong for which damages can be recovered in the civil court at the suit of the recording company. However, there are dicta in cases cited by the Court of Appeal in *Ex p Island Records Ltd* which suggest that an unlawful act which infringes a right of property is an actionable wrong founding a claim for damages and, in an appropriate case, a right to an injunction. Statements in cases before the Judicature Acts that the Court of Chancery would grant an injunction to restrain interference with the rights of property must be read with some caution. Before the Judicature Acts the Court of Chancery did not have jurisdiction to issue an injunction to restrain any act which was an actionable wrong and for which damages could be obtained in the common law courts; the Court of Chancery only had jurisdiction to issue an injunction if it was required for 'the protection of infants . . . or of civil rights, which it was bound to protect': see *Margaret, Duchess of Argyll v Duke of Argyll* [1965] 1 All ER 611 at 633, [1967] Ch 302 at 344, and see *Prudential Assurance Co v Knott* (1875) LR 10 Ch App 142, where the principles on which the Court of Chancery acted are explained by Lord Cairns LC. However, there are cases decided since the Judicature Acts which support the proposition that the High Court can issue an injunction to restrain an act unlawful in itself which interferes with a right of property. That was the alternative ground on which Buckley LJ founded his decision in the *National Phonograph* case [1908] 1 Ch 335 at 361, [1904–7] All ER Rep 116 at 120 (see the passage cited by Waller LJ in *Ex p Island Records Ltd* [1978] 3 All ER 824 at 835, [1978] Ch 122 at 143). Buckley LJ went on to cite the well-known passage from the judgment of Bowen LJ in *Mogul Steamship Co Ltd v McGregor, Gow & Co* (1889) 23 QBD 598 at 614:

'No man, whether trader or not, can, however, justify damaging another in his commercial business by fraud or misrepresentation. Intimidation, obstruction, and molestation are forbidden; so is the intentional procurement of a violation of individual rights, contractual or other, assuming always that there is no just cause for it.'

Buckley LJ continued ([1908] 1 Ch 355 at 361, [1904–7] All ER Rep 116 at 120):

'In *Exchange Telegraph Co.* v. *Gregory & Co.* ([1896] 1 QB 147 at 156; cf [1895–9] All ER Rep 1116 at 1119) an action was held to be maintainable which thus affected property. It is the third case put in Rigby L.J.'s judgment—that is to say, "an attack made upon the right or interest of persons in the business which they carry on." In such case, he says, the fact of damage is the thing which brings the defendant into relation with the plaintiff.'

In the instant case it is possible that the first plaintiff may be able to establish that it has a right of property in performances by Elvis Presley which it had the exclusive right to record and that the acts complained of were unlawful interferences with that right of property, giving rise to a cause of action on the part of the first plaintiff. I am not persuaded that the disapproval by Lord Diplock of the wider proposition that a plaintiff has a civil right of action for damage whenever a lawful business carried on by him is damaged as a result of an act by a defendant which is in breach of a statutory prohibition is necessarily inconsistent with the existence of such a cause of action. I do not of course decide that on the facts pleaded in the statement of claim that the plaintiffs are entitled to succeed. The existence and if it exists the extent of the tort of interference, by means unlawful in themselves, with a right of property of the kind relied on are questions which will have to be decided at the trial. I do not think it would be right in the exercise of my discretion to dismiss the action now on the ground that the facts pleaded in the statement of claim give rise to no reasonable cause of action.

There is one other matter which I should mention. The first plaintiff is a company incorporated in one of the states of the United States of America and I am I think entitled to take judicial notice of the fact that the late Elvis Presley was resident in and performed largely if not wholly within that jurisdiction. The application of the Performers' Protection Acts to bootleg records of performances which took place abroad and in particular whether it is necessary under s 2 of the 1963 Act to show that written consent was obtained under the 1958 Act gives rise to difficult questions. However, counsel for the defendant conceded, and I think rightly, that these are matters which will have to be decided at the trial and do not afford a ground on which he can rely in an application to strike out the statement of claim.

For the reasons which I have given, I think this application fails.

Application dismissed. Leave to appeal.

Solicitors: *George W Mills & Son*, Washington (for the defendant); *A E Hamlin & Co* (for the plaintiffs).

Jacqueline Metcalfe   Barrister.

Practice Direction

ADMIRALTY COURT

Admiralty – Practice – Directions – Summons for directions – Copies of summons and documents to be lodged – Counter-notice – Copies of counter-notice and documents to be lodged.

Admiralty – Investment of funds in court – Funds paid into court – Proceeds of sale – Sterling and foreign currency – Applications to place funds on deposit or transfer them to short term investment account – Procedure for applications.

The following amendments to the Admiralty Practice Directions ([1973] 3 All ER 446, [1973] 1 WLR 1146, as amended; *The Supreme Court Practice 1982*, vol 2, para 1056, p 290) have been announced:

4. *Summons for directions* (see RSC Ord 75, r 25)
   The following paragraphs shall be substituted for the existing para (2):

   '(2) When the summons for directions is issued an additional copy of it and two copies of the following documents must be lodged in the registry: (a) writ, (b) pleadings (if any pleading has been amended copies of the amended pleading only should be lodged), (c) any further and better particulars of any pleading which have been served, (d) any other document to which the applicant intends to refer on the hearing of the summons.

   (3) A party lodging a counter-notice must lodge with it two copies of any further document to which he intends to refer on the hearing of the summons.'

8. *Investment of funds in court*
   The following practice direction shall be substituted for the existing directions numbered 8 and 8B (direction 8B was inserted by the Practice Direction of 24 January 1977 ([1977] 1 All ER 544, [1977] 1 WLR 184)):

   '(1) An application to invest sterling paid into court (including proceeds of sale paid into court by the marshal) by placing it on deposit or transferring it to a short term investment account may be made at any time by any party to the action by letter to the Chief Clerk of the Admiralty Registry.

   (2) When the proceeds of sale in a foreign currency are paid into court by the marshal they will normally be retained in that currency; they will not however be placed on deposit or otherwise invested for the benefit of claimants against them without an order being made by the court.

   (3) An application to place on deposit or otherwise invest the proceeds of sale in a foreign currency, unless made at the same time as the application for an order for sale, must be made by summons in the action in which the order for sale was made. Several types of deposit are usually available and an application to place on deposit should specify the type of deposit required. Advice as to these matters cannot be given by the registry staff.

   (4) An application to invest foreign currency paid into court (other than proceeds of sale) must be made by summons.'

JAMES ROCHFORD
Admiralty Registrar.

26 April 1982

Haron bin Mohd Zaid v Central Securities (Holdings) Bhd

PRIVY COUNCIL

LORD WILBERFORCE, LORD SIMON OF GLAISDALE, LORD KEITH OF KINKEL, LORD BRIDGE OF HARWICH AND SIR WILLIAM DOUGLAS

24, 25 FEBRUARY, I MARCH, 26 APRIL 1982

Judgment – Final or interlocutory order – Test to be applied – Leave granted to enter final judgment – Appeal – Malaysia – Judge not certifying that he required further argument – No leave obtained from Federal Court of Malaya or judge of High Court to bring appeal – Whether appeal competently brought – Courts of Judicature Act 1964 (Malaysia), s 68(2).

By an agreement in writing dated 7 December 1974 the respondents, a Malaysian company, agreed to sell to the appellant, a businessman, 1,400,000 fully paid up shares in a public company (UH) for $11,200,000. On payment of the purchase price the respondents delivered to the appellant certain share certificates, including share certificate 0227 for 523,278 shares, together with a document which purported to be a registrable memorandum of transfer signed by the registered owner. On 12 March 1975 the appellant sold on to a company (SSP) 560,000 of the shares in UH which he had acquired from the respondents and delivered to SSP the share certificates, including share certificate 0227 and the memorandum of transfer relating to it. Thereafter the transfer of the shares was registered in favour of SSP by UH. However, a dispute arose concerning the ownership of the shares comprised in certificate 0227 and in October 1976 the appellant commenced proceedings (the first action) against the respondents for rescission of the agreement of 7 December 1974, the return of the purchase price and damages for fraud and misrepresentation. In May 1977 SSP brought an action (the second action) against the appellant claiming the sum of $4,186,224, being the purchase price of 523,278 shares alleged not to have been delivered. The appellant issued a third party notice in those proceedings against the respondents, which the respondents applied to have set aside on the grounds that (i) there was no proper question to be tried between the appellant and the respondents and (ii) the issue between them formed the subject of a separate action (viz the first action) pending before the court. In October 1977 the appellant applied for leave to enter final judgment in the first action against the respondents or alternatively for third party directions, and SSP applied for leave to enter final judgment in the second action against the appellant. All three applications were heard together. The High Court of Malaya dismissed the respondents' application to set aside the appellant's third party notice, gave leave to SSP to enter final judgment against the appellant and gave leave to the appellant to enter final judgment against the respondents. The respondents applied for the three applications to be adjourned into open court for further argument in accordance with RSC (Malaysia) Ord 54, r 22A, but the judge certified that he required no further argument. The respondents appealed to the Federal Court of Malaysia. Before the appeal came on for hearing, the appellant applied for an order that the appeal be dismissed, contending that it had been brought incompetently because the three orders appealed against were interlocutory and no leave had been obtained from a judge of the High Court or from the Federal Court as required by s 68(2)[a] of the Courts of Judicature Act 1964. On 27 February 1979 the Federal Court dismissed the application and on 16 May 1979 it allowed the respondents' appeal from the order giving the appellant judgment against the respondents in the first action, gave directions in the third party proceedings brought by the appellant against the respondents, gave the respondents unconditional leave to defend in the third party

---

a   Section 68(2) is set out at p 484 *j* to p 485 *a*, post proceedings and ordered the consolidation of the third party proceedings with the proceedings in the first action. The appellant appealed to the Privy Council.   *a*

Held – The appeal would be dismissed for the following reasons—

(1) The appropriate test for determining whether an order was final or interlocutory was whether the judgment or order, as made, finally disposed of the rights of the parties. If it did, it was a final order, but if it did not, it was an interlocutory order. Since the Federal Court had applied that test and since it had not been shown that the court had   *b* misconstrued the law of Malaysia, the Federal Court had been entitled to hold that the orders made by the High Court of Malaya were final orders and that leave was not required to bring an appeal against them (see p 486 *c* to *j* and p 487 *e*, post); dictum of Lord Alverstone CJ in *Bozson v Altrincham UDC* [1903] 1 KB at 548–549 approved.

(2) Furthermore, the Federal Court had been justified in granting the respondents unconditional leave to defend the claim brought against them since the material it had   *c* before it showed among other things that a number of important issues were in contention between the parties, including the precise circumstances in which the appellant had accepted certificate 0227 and the memorandum of transfer relating to it. Moreover, there was material to show that it might be impossible to restore the parties to their original position (see p 487 *b* to *e*, post).

                                                                               d

Notes
For final and interlocutory judgments and orders, see 26 Halsbury's Laws (4th edn) paras 504–507, and for cases on the subject, see 30 Digest (Reissue) 173–175, 66–90.

Cases referred to in judgment   *e*
Arumugam Pillai v Government of Malaysia [1980] 2 MLJ 283.
Becker v City of Marion Corp [1977] AC 271, [1976] 2 WLR 728, PC, Digest (Cont Vol E) 51, 905*a*.
Boston v Lelièvre (1870) LR 3 PC 157, PC, 16 Digest (Reissue) 207, 2056.
Bozson v Altrincham UDC [1903] 1 KB 547, CA, 30 Digest (Reissue) 182, 152.
Hong Kim Sui v Malayan Banking Bhd [1971] 1 MLJ 289.   *f*
Malayan Banking Bhd v Yap Seng Hock (11 October 1980), unreported.
Nagappa Rengasamy Pillai v Lim Lee Chong [1968] 2 MLJ 91.
Ng Cheng Yoon v Mah Binti Mat Isa [1981] 1 MLJ 218.
Peninsular Land Development Sdn Bhd v K Ahmad (No 2) [1970] 1 MLJ 253.
Ratnam v Cumarasamy (1962) 28 MLJ 330.
Salaman v Warner [1891] 1 QB 734, CA, 30 Digest (Reissue) 182, 151.   *g*
Smith v Leech Brain & Co Ltd [1961] 3 All ER 1159, [1962] 2 QB 405.
Sri Jaya Transport Co Ltd v Fernandez [1970] 1 MLJ 87.
Standard Discount Co v Otard de la Grange (1877) 3 CPD 67, CA, 30 Digest (Reissue) 178, 108.
Tampion v Anderson (1973) 48 ALJR 11, PC.
Thomas v Reddy [1974] 2 MLJ 87.

Appeal
Haron bin Mohd Zaid appealed by special leave to appeal granted by the Judicial Committee of the Privy Council on 8 May 1980 against two orders made by the Federal Court of Malaysia (Suffian LP, Raja Azlan Shah ACJ Malaya and Wan Suleiman FJ) on 27 February and 16 May 1979 in favour of the respondents, Central Securities (Holdings) Bhd. The facts are set out in the judgment of the Board.

Lord Rawlinson QC, Keith Hornby, Nicholas Stewart and *K S Narayanan* (of the Malaysian Bar) for the appellant.
Samuel Stamler QC and *Nicolas Bratza* for the respondents.

SIR WILLIAM DOUGLAS. This is an appeal by the appellant from two orders made in the Federal Court of Malaysia (Suffian LP, Raja Azlan Shah ACJ Malaya and Wan Suleiman FJ) namely: (i) an order dated 27 February 1979 wherein the Federal Court dismissed the appellant's notice of motion dated 13 October 1978 in which the appellant had moved to dismiss the respondents' appeal from two orders of Harun J, both dated 28 June 1978, on the ground that the respondents had not obtained leave from a judge of the High Court or from the Federal Court in compliance with s 68(2) of the Courts of Judicature Act 1964; (ii) an order dated 16 May 1979 which (a) allowed the respondents' appeal from the order of Harun J dated 28 June 1978 giving the appellant judgment against the respondents in the sum of $4,186,224 together with interest thereon and costs, (b) gave directions in the third party proceedings brought by the appellant against the respondents, (c) gave the respondents unconditional leave to defend in the said third party proceedings, and (d) ordered the consolidation of the said third party proceedings with proceedings brought by the appellant against the respondents in the Kuala Lumpur High Court in suit no 2323 of 1976.

By an agreement in writing dated 7 December 1974 the respondents, a public limited company incorporated in Malaysia, agreed to sell to the appellant, a businessman and a company director, 1,400,000 fully paid up $1 shares in a public company known as United Holdings Bhd (hereinafter referred to as 'UH') at $8 per share and at a total purchase price of $11,200,000. The purchase price was paid on or about 22 January 1975 and the respondents delivered to the appellant share certificates for the 1,400,000 shares in UH including a share certificate numbered 0227 for 523,278 shares, in relation to which the appellant received from the respondents a memorandum of transfer signed by a certain Dr Chong Kim Choy.

On 12 March 1975 the appellant sold on to a company called Syarikat Seri Padu Sdn Bhd (hereinafter referred to as 'SSP') 560,000 of the shares in UH which he had acquired from the respondents for the sum of $4,480,000. The appellant delivered the share certificates for these shares to SSP and included among them share certificate 0227 and the memorandum of transfer relating to it. The transfer of shares was registered by UH in favour of SSP but, that notwithstanding, on 17 March 1975 the secretary of UH, Mr Yap Ping Kon, wrote to Dr Chong Kim Choy in these terms:

> 'I refer to the transfer form signed by you to cover certificate No. 0227 for 523,278 shares of United Holdings Bhd. and return herewith the said form for your cancellation. As you are aware these shares were sold to Central Securities and subsequently to Mr Koh Kim Chai, the transfer form executed by you is invalid as the transferee, International Holdings Pte Ltd has been inserted in the transfer form. As such I enclose herewith a new transfer form for your execution. Kindly sign on both sides of the transfer form marked by a pencil cross. On completion I shall be glad if you will return this to me immediately. Your kind attention to this matter is greatly appreciated.'

On 22 April 1975 Mr Yap addressed another letter to Dr Chong enclosing a copy of a transfer form for Dr Chong's signature. Dr Chong's reply is dated 25 April 1975, and is as follows:

> 'I acknowledge with thanks your registered letter dated 22nd instant. This share certificate was held by us in trust for International Holdings (Pte.) Ltd., and I had already transferred the same shares back to them without any monetary consideration. I am therefore returning the original transfer form signed by me (transferee being I.H.P.L.) to you. It is only proper that you transfer the shares to I.H.P.L. and get them to transfer the shares to whoever are the present legal owners. I regret that I cannot in good faith declare that I have received a sum of $1,486,109·52 from Sharikat Seri Padu Sdn. Bhd. when this is not true, as it will give rise to further problems for me.'

On 8 October 1976 the appellant commenced proceedings in the High Court at Kuala Lumpur in suit no 2323 claiming against the respondents rescission of the agreement for the sale of 1,400,000 shares in UH, the return of the purchase price and damages for fraudulent misrepresentation on the part of the respondents. The appellant pleaded, inter alia, that verbally and by letter of 23 December 1974, he had given the respondents notice of rescission of the agreement for the sale of the shares and had demanded the return of the purchase price. The respondents, in their defence, admitted the agreement to sell the shares but denied the representations alleged by the appellant. They stated that they had no knowledge of the letter dated 23 December 1974 giving notice of rescission and went on to plead that the agreement for the sale of the shares was affirmed by a supplemental agreement made between the parties on 22 January 1975. The respondents further pleaded that the appellant and his nominees had taken over control of UH and in consequence the appellant was not entitled to rescission.

According to the appellant's case it was only in December 1976 that Mr Koh Kim Chai, an associate of the appellant and a director of UH discovered that the memorandum of transfer in respect of the shares comprised in certificate 0227 did not support the transfer of the shares to anybody other than International Holdings (Pte) Ltd. However this may be, on a date prior to 15 December 1977 SSP was deregistered in respect of the shares comprised in certificate 0227 and Dr Chong reregistered as the holder of those shares.

On 21 May 1977 SSP commenced proceedings against the appellant claiming the sum of $4,186,224, the purchase price of 523,278 shares alleged not to have been delivered. On 16 August 1977 the appellant issued a third party notice against the respondents. The respondents entered a conditional appearance and on 30 September 1977 took out a summons to set aside the third party notice on the grounds, inter alia, (a) that there was no proper question to be tried between the appellant and the respondents, and (b) that the issue between the appellant and the respondents formed the subject of a separate action already pending before the court, namely civil suit no 2323 of 1976. On 3 October 1977 the appellant applied by summons for leave to enter final judgment against the respondents or alternatively for third party directions. On 28 October 1977 SSP applied for leave to enter final judgment against the appellant.

All three of these applications came on for hearing on 28 June 1978 before Harun J in chambers whence they were adjourned by consent into court. The judge dismissed the summons to set aside the third party notice. He gave leave to SSP to enter final judgment against the appellant and after argument gave leave to enter judgment against the respondents. Those judgments were entered in due course.

On 29 June 1978 the respondents applied in writing for the summonses to be adjourned into open court for further argument in accordance with RSC (Malaysia) Ord 54, r 22A. Harun J certified that he required no further argument and the respondents appealed to the Federal Court.

Before the appeal came on for hearing before the Federal Court, the appellant applied by notice of motion for an order that the appeal be dismissed on the ground that no leave had been obtained from a judge of the High Court or from the Federal Court in accordance with the provisions of s 68(2) of the Courts of Judicature Act 1964. That motion was dismissed on 27 February 1979.

On 16 May 1979 the Federal Court allowed the respondents' appeal and made orders in the terms set out above. Thereafter, on 22 August 1979 the appellant applied to the Federal Court for leave to appeal to His Majesty the Yang di-Pertuan Agong against the orders of the Federal Court but leave was refused. On 8 May 1980 the appellant, on petition to their Lordships, obtained special leave to appeal to His Majesty the Yang di-Pertuan Agong from the orders of the Federal Court dated 27 February and 16 May 1979.

The first issue which arises in this appeal is whether the orders made in these proceedings by Harun J are final or interlocutory. It is contended on behalf of the appellant that they are interlocutory and thus fall within the scope of s 68(2) of the Courts of Judicature Act 1964, which provides:

'No appeal shall lie from an interlocutory order made by a Judge of the High Court in Chambers unless the Judge has certified, after application, within four days after the making of the order by any party for further argument in court, that he requires no further argument, or unless leave is obtained from the Federal Court or from a Judge of the High Court.'

It is further argued that, as the orders were made in open court and not in chambers, the question of obtaining a certificate that no further argument was required did not arise, and, as no leave had been obtained, the appeal was not properly before the Federal Court.

The Malaysian courts have considered the question of whether orders are final or interlocutory in a number of cases extending over a period of twenty years and commencing with *Ratnam v Cumarasamy* (1962) 28 MLJ 330. In that case the Malayan Court of Appeal examined several English cases including *Salaman v Warner* [1891] 1 QB 734 at 736 where Fry LJ formulated the test in these terms:

'I think that the true definition is this. I conceive that an order is "final" only where it is made upon an application or other proceeding which must, whether such application or other proceeding fail or succeed, determine the action. Conversely I think that an order is "interlocutory" where it cannot be affirmed that in either event the action will be determined.'

The court compared this with the test advanced by Lord Alverstone CJ in *Bozson v Altrincham UDC* [1903] 1 KB 547 at 548–549, namely:

'Does the judgment or order, as made, finally dispose of the rights of the parties? If it does, then I think it ought to be treated as a final order; but if it does not, it is then, in my opinion, an interlocutory order.'

The Malayan Court of Appeal unanimously adopted the test in the *Bozson* case in preference to that in the *Salaman* case. In delivering the judgment of the court, Good JA stated (28 MLJ 330 at 333):

'In the present case our order refusing an extension of time for the applicant to file the record of appeal put an end to the proceedings and applying Lord Alverstone's test finally disposed of the rights of the parties by barring the unsuccessful plaintiff from appealing against the order of the High Court. Our order . . . is therefore for the purposes of appeal a final order . . .'

In his short concurring judgment Hill ACJ observed:

'Out of a number of conflicting opinions and decisions that of Lord Alverstone in *Bozson's* case stands out as the one judgment that provides a real and practical test for determining whether an order is final or interlocutory and I too would apply it here.'

Ratnam v Cumarasamy was followed by the Federal Court in *Peninsular Land Development Sdn Bhd v K Ahmad (No 2)* [1970] 1 MLJ 253. Again there was a careful review of the leading English cases on the subject starting with *Standard Discount Co v Otard de la Grange* (1877) 3 CPD 67 where it was held that an order empowering a plaintiff to sign judgment on a specially indorsed writ is interlocutory. Again the court decided that the appropriate test for determining whether an order is final or interlocutory is that stated by Lord Alverstone CJ in the *Bozson* case. And thus the Malaysian courts treat an order of court giving leave to a plaintiff to sign final judgment as a final order, thus entitling a defendant to appeal to the Federal Court without the necessity of obtaining leave.

It must be recalled that in England and Wales s 68(2) of the Supreme Court of Judicature (Consolidation) Act 1925 (now repealed and substantially re-enacted by s 60(2) of the Supreme Court Act 1981), provided:

'Any doubt which may arise as to what orders or judgments are final, and what are interlocutory, shall be determined by the Court of Appeal.'

Thus, the Court of Appeal's decision whether the order is final or not is not subject to appeal and, as Lord Edmund-Davies pointed out in *Becker v City of Marion Corp* [1977] AC 271 at 282, some of its decisions on the point are difficult to reconcile.

In *Tampion v Anderson* (1973) 48 ALJR 11 the question before the Board on a petition for special leave to appeal against an order made in the Supreme Court of Victoria staying an action on the ground that it was frivolous, vexatious and an abuse of the process of the court was whether that order was final or interlocutory. It appears from the judgment of Lord Kilbrandon that the Australian courts accept as authoritative the English decisions on this topic. Lord Kilbrandon continued (at 12):

> 'It was submitted, and their Lordships would be inclined to agree, that the authorities are not in an altogether satisfactory state. There is a continuing controversy whether the broad test of finality in a judgment depends on the effect of the order made, as decided in *Bozson v. Altrincham U.D.C.* ([1903] 1 KB 547 at 548) *per* Lord Alverstone C.J. or on the application being of such a character that whatever order had been made thereon must finally have disposed of the matter in dispute—*Salaman v. Warner* ([1891] 1 QB 734). But the difficulty seems to arise out of attempts to frame a definition of "final" (or of "interlocutory") which will enable a judgment to be recognized for what it is by appealing to some formula universally applicable in any contingency in which the classification falls to be made.'

Their Lordships are mindful of the great reliance placed by the Federal Court on English precedents and of the observation made by Lord Parker CJ in *Smith v Leech Brain & Co Ltd* [1961] 3 All ER 1159 at 1162, [1962] 2 QB 405 at 415 that 'it is important that the common law, and the development of the common law, should be homogeneous in the various sections of the Commonwealth'. But it must be remembered that in England the practice with respect to appeals from orders in summary proceedings refusing the defendant unconditional leave to defend an action has since 1925 been governed by statute. The Supreme Court of Judicature (Consolidation) Act 1925 provided in s 31(2) (now repealed and substantially re-enacted in s 18(2)(a) of the Supreme Court Act 1981):

> 'An order refusing unconditional leave to defend an action shall not be deemed to be an interlocutory order within the meaning of this section.'

The effect of this is to give a defendant an appeal as of right against an order giving leave to a plaintiff to sign final judgment against him in summary proceedings. Moreover it would seem to their Lordships that it would be wrong to overrule the Federal Court on a matter of procedure as distinct from substantive law, unless it can be clearly shown that the court has misconstrued the statute law of Malaysia. As Lord Westbury observed in *Boston v Lelièvre* (1870) LR 3 PC 157 at 163:

> 'Their Lordships would hesitate very much to interfere with the unanimous judgment of the Court below upon a matter of this kind, which is to be regarded as a matter of procedure only, unless they were clearly satisfied that the Court had made a great mistake in the construction put upon these Statutes.'

It appears to their Lordships that the Federal Court in *Ratnam v Cumarasamy* and *Peninsular Land Development Sdn Bhd v K Ahmad (No 2)* and subsequently in *Hong Kim Sui v Malayan Banking Bhd* [1971] 1 MLJ 289, *Arumugam Pillai v Government of Malaysia* [1980] 2 MLJ 283 and *Ng Cheng Yoon v Mah Binti Mat Isa* [1981] 1 MLJ 218, all of which are unanimous, reserved judgments, has established over the years a settled practice of applying Lord Alverstone CJ's test in the *Bozson* case in order to determine whether an order is final or interlocutory. Their Lordships are unable to find any error in this reasoning; on the contrary their Lordships feel entitled to say that the test is both sound and convenient. In three of the five cases cited above the appeal was against leave to sign judgment in summary proceedings. Thus the effect of the practice adopted by the Federal Court in such cases is in line with the English practice as established by statute since 1925. In any event, this being a matter of practice and procedure, their Lordships, in accordance with their practice, will uphold the decision of the Federal Court.

Counsel for the appellant drew attention to the cases of *Nagappa Rengasamy Pillai v Lim Lee Chong* [1968] 2 MLJ 91, *Sri Jaya Transport Co Ltd v Fernandez* [1970] 1 MLJ 87 and *Thomas v Reddy* [1974] 2 MLJ 87 as well as the unreported case of *Malayan Banking Bhd v*

Yap Seng Hock (11 October 1980) and invited the Board to express a view on what were said to be inconsistencies in the application of RSC (Malaysia) Ord 54, rr 22 and 22A. Their Lordships consider that they must decline from so doing first, because any views they express would be purely obiter in the light of the conclusion they have reached on the main issue in this appeal, and second, because the points raised are purely procedural and ought to be resolved by the Federal Court.

The second main issue in this appeal is whether the Federal Court was wrong in granting to the respondents unconditional leave to defend the claim brought by the appellant against them. It is also contended that the respondents were allowed on appeal to the Federal Court to put forward new and different grounds from that relied on by them before Harun J. As to the putting forward of new and different grounds, this involves the discretion of the court and since it has not been shown that the court proceeded on some wrong principle the Board will not intervene. As to the granting of unconditional leave the Federal Court had before it material which, among other things, showed that a number of important issues of fact are in contention between the appellant and the respondents including the precise circumstances in which the appellant accepted certificate 0227 and the memorandum of transfer signed by Dr Chong. It would be inappropriate for their Lordships to say more, at this stage, than that these issues require to be tried. There was in addition material showing that it may be impossible to restore the parties to their original positions, some 2½ years having elapsed before the matter came before the courts during which time the appellant and his associates had control of UH and made substantial changes in the company's affairs. These considerations commend themselves to their Lordships as justifying the conclusion reached by the Federal Court that the respondents should have unconditional leave to defend.

Their Lordships will advise His Majesty the Yang di-Pertuan Agong that the appeal should be dismissed, with costs.

Appeal dismissed.

Solicitors: *Kingsford Dorman* (for the appellant); *Macfarlanes* (for the respondents).

Mary Rose Plummer   Barrister.

Raymond v Attorney General

COURT OF APPEAL, CIVIL DIVISION
CUMMING-BRUCE LJ AND SIR SEBAG SHAW
12 JANUARY, 9 MARCH 1982

Criminal law – Proceedings – Duties of Director of Public Prosecutions – Undertaking conduct of proceedings – Scope of 'conduct' of proceedings – Whether undertaking conduct of proceedings including power to abort private prosecution – Prosecution of Offences Act 1979, s 4.

At committal proceedings before justices C gave evidence for the prosecution. The proceedings resulted in the committal of the appellant to the Crown Court for trial on various charges including conspiring to pervert the course of justice. C was to be a Crown witness at the trial. While the trial was pending the appellant laid informations against C alleging perjury and other criminal offences in regard to the committal proceedings. The justices issued summonses against C on the information but because C was a Crown witness at the pending trial the clerk to the justices notified the Director of Public Prosecutions of the issue of the summonses. The director took the view that the appellant might have instituted the proceedings to inhibit, or at least discredit, C as a Crown witness at the trial and that he ought to 'undertake ... the conduct' of the

appellant's proceedings against C pursuant to the power conferred on him by s 4[a] of the
Prosecution of Offences Act 1979. Accordingly, a member of the director's office   *a*
attended the magistrates' court and submitted that, because the director was satisfied that
the appellant's proceedings were vexatious and designed to discredit C as a witness at the
appellant's trial, it was in the public interest that the proceedings should not be continued,
and he informed the court that no evidence would be offered against C. The justices
therefore dismissed the information and discharged C. The appellant, having failed in
the Divisional Court to obtain an order of mandamus requiring the director to pursue his   *b*
charges against C, brought an action against the director and others, seeking declarations,
an injunction and damages on the basis that the director had acted unlawfully in
deciding not to proceed with the appellant's charges against C. The director applied for,
and was granted by a master in chambers, an order striking out the claim as disclosing no
reasonable cause of action. The master's order was upheld on appeal by the judge. The
appellant appealed.   *c*

Held – Because s 4 of the 1979 Act enabled the Director of Public Prosecutions to
'conduct' any criminal proceedings, if he thought fit, and not merely to 'carry on' the
proceedings, the director had power under s 4 to intervene in a private prosecution for
the purpose of aborting it if it appeared expedient in the public interest to do so, and he
was not limited to intervening for the purpose of pursuing or carrying on the   *d*
proceedings. Accordingly, if it appeared to the director that there were substantial
reasons in the public interest for not pursuing a private prosecution because, for example,
matters might emerge from it adverse to a pending public prosecution which involved
more serious issues, the director was entitled to intervene in the private prosecution for
the purpose of aborting it, and unless his decision to do so was manifestly unreasonable
it could not be impugned. It followed that the appellant's statement of claim disclosed   *e*
no reasonable cause of action and that his action was vexatious and an abuse of the court's
process. The appeal would therefore be dismissed (see p 491 *g* to *j* and p 492 *b*, post).
    Turner v DPP (1978) 68 Cr App R 70 and dictum of Viscount Dilhorne in *Gouriet v
Union of Post Office Workers* [1977] 3 All ER at 88 applied.
    Per curiam. The safeguard against the Director of Public Prosecutions exercising his
power under s 4 of the 1979 Act to abort private prosecutions unnecessarily or   *f*
gratuitously is that under s 2 the director is answerable to the Attorney General for any
abuse of his powers (see p 491 *j*, post).

Notes
For the duties of the Director of Public Prosecutions, see 11 Halsbury's Laws (4th edn)
para 96.   *g*
    For the Prosecution of Offences Act 1979, s 4, see 49 Halsbury's Statutes (3rd edn) 284.

Cases referred to in judgment
Dyson v A-G [1911] 1 KB 410, CA; *subsequent proceedings* [1912] 1 Ch 158, CA, 11 Digest
    (Reissue) 693, 308.
Gouriet v Union of Post Office Workers [1977] 3 All ER 70, [1978] AC 435, [1977] 3 WLR   *h*
    300, HL, 16 Digest (Reissue) 265, 2528.
Turner v DPP (1978) 68 Cr App R 70.

Interlocutory appeal
Steven Patrick Raymond appealed against the decision of Glidewell J on 7 May 1981
dismissing his appeal from an order of Master Creightmore dated 28 February 1980   *j*
striking out Mr Raymond's statement of claim, seeking declarations, an injunction and
damages against the Director of Public Prosecutions and others, as showing no reasonable
cause of action, pursuant to RSC Ord 18, r 19 and as being vexatious and an abuse of the

---

a   Section 4 is set out at p 489 *g*, post

process of the court. The respondent was the Attorney General who was treated as the defendant to Mr Raymond's action. The facts are set out in the judgment of the court.

Louis Blom-Cooper QC and *Justin Philips* for Mr Raymond.
Andrew Collins for the Attorney General.

Cur adv vult

9 March. **SIR SEBAG SHAW** delivered the following judgment of the court: The appellant, referred to in this judgment as 'Mr Raymond', was, together with others, convicted in February 1980 in the Crown Court at St Albans of conspiring to pervert the course of justice. The trial in which he was involved had begun on 3 October 1979. At the outset Mr Raymond pleaded not guilty, but on 4 February 1980 he changed his plea in respect of a number of counts and was sentenced to terms of imprisonment.

Amongst those implicated in the offences of which the defendants at the trial were accused was one Desmond Roy Carne (referred to as 'Mr Carne'). His role was not, however, that of a defendant but of a witness for the Crown. He had given evidence on behalf of the prosecution in the committal proceedings before the examining justices at the St Albans Magistrates' Court which led to the trial at the Crown Court.

Those proceedings began on 5 September 1978, and continued until 11 March 1979, when the defendants (with one exception) were all sent for trial. On 11 May 1979, when that trial was still pending, Mr Raymond laid informations before the St Albans justices alleging that Mr Carne had committed perjury and other criminal offences in relation to the matters which had been the subject of the committal proceedings in which Mr Carne had given evidence for the prosecution.

The clerk to the justices took the step (very properly, in our view) of writing on 14 May 1979 to the Director of Public Prosecutions calling attention to the fact that the justices had issued summonses on the informations laid by Mr Raymond against a witness for the Crown who would in the ordinary course be called to give evidence at the trial then in prospect. The director's response at that stage was that he would take no action in relation to those summonses. However, he had second thoughts in the matter. One view of Mr Raymond's initiative in instituting criminal proceedings against Mr Carne at that time was that it was intended to inhibit, or at least to discredit, Mr Carne in his role as a witness for the prosecution. On 10 July 1979 the director intimated that he proposed, as he was satisfied it was appropriate in the circumstances, to exercise the powers conferred on him by s 4 of the Prosecution of Offences Act 1979. That section provides:

'Nothing in this Act shall preclude any person from instituting or carrying on any criminal proceedings; but the Director may undertake, at any stage, the conduct of those proceedings, if he thinks fit.'

Notice was accordingly given to the court and to Mr Raymond of the director's intended intervention. On 16 July 1979 Mr John Wooler, a senior member of the office of the Director of Public Prosecutions attended the St Albans Magistrates' Court. He outlined the history of the matter to the bench and explained that it had become apparent from what Mr Raymond had said when applying for the summonses that the allegations he intended to make against Mr Carne had already been canvassed in the earlier committal proceedings. He went on to inform the court that the director was satisfied in regard to a number of factors which, in his view, showed that the proceedings instituted by Mr Raymond were vexatious and were designed to discredit Mr Carne as a witness and not to bring him to justice in regard to the allegations on which the summonses were founded. Overall, the general public interest, and in particular the ends of justice, would be disserved if the summonses were proceeded with.

Accordingly, so Mr Wooler informed the court, he offered no evidence against Mr

Carne. The major offences alleged by Mr Raymond were triable only on indictment. The bench accordingly discharged Mr Carne.

Mr Raymond's first reaction was to seek judicial review by way of an order of mandamus requiring the director to pursue the charges laid against Mr Carne. Having obtained leave Mr Raymond moved the Queen's Bench Divisional Court accordingly. Lord Widgery CJ dealt with the matter very concisely. He said that—

> 'the Director's conduct cannot be attacked except on the footing of *proving* bad faith, not just talking about it; or, alternatively, showing he worked on a wrong principle. We are all of the opinion that no progress has been made by the applicant on any of these matters, and that being the case the motion must be refused.'

Mr Raymond sought to appeal to the Court of Appeal but this proved abortive on the ground of jurisdiction, that court being of the view that the subject of the application to it was a criminal cause or matter within the meaning of s 31 of the Supreme Court of Judicature (Consolidation) Act 1925. In the course of his judgment Lord Denning MR said (see *R v DPP, ex p Raymond* (1979) 70 Cr App R 233 at 235):

> 'Mr. Raymond did put before us a suggestion that he might bring civil proceedings in order to obtain a declaration as to the powers . . . of the Director of Public Prosecutions. I would simply say that this is not the sort of case in which the Court in its discretion would grant a declaration.'

Undeterred by this intimation, which was given to him on 29 October 1979, Mr Raymond caused to be issued on 18 December 1979 the writ in the proceedings which give rise to this appeal.

By his statement of claim, which was indorsed on the writ, he sought a series of declarations as well as an injunction and damages. The defendants were the Director of Public Prosecutions, Mr Wooler, Mr Dowling (also in the office of the director) and Mr Carne. The real target of the action was, however, the director, whose conduct Mr Raymond seeks to call in question. As that officer of justice acts on behalf of the Attorney General that officer of the Crown is treated as the defendant in place of the first three defendants named in the writ.

In support of his prayer for the various forms of relief sought, Mr Raymond pleaded that the director had first declined to become involved in the proceedings instituted against Mr Carne but had, some two months later, reversed that attitude and that Mr Wooler had told the St Albans justices that the reason he was offering no evidence was that the prosecution of Mr Carne would complicate the proceedings in which that person was a witness. A further allegation was that Mr Carne had made it known that he would not be prepared to give evidence for the prosecution at the Crown Court if he was faced with further private proceedings.

There follows the allegation in para 10 of the pleadings:

> 'On the facts as they are known to me it appears that [the director of Public Prosecutions] has acted unlawfully by deciding as a matter of policy not to prosecute, or allow to be prosecuted for any offence [Mr Carne] for many different offences.'

Then in para 11 it is alleged that:

> 'In all the circumstances it is clear that [the Director of Public Prosecutions] . . . has improperly agreed with [Mr Carne] that he will not be prosecuted. . . In return for this [Mr Carne] is going to give evidence against me and my co-defendants. Such course of action is a breach of the rules of natural justice and/or unlawful and/or ultra vires the provisions of the Prosecution of Offences Act 1979.'

The Director of Public Prosecutions applied to have the statement of claim struck out under RSC Ord 18, r 19 as disclosing no reasonable cause of action. The order sought was made by Master Creightmore on 28 February 1980. The plaintiff (Mr Raymond) appealed, and on 7 May 1981 Glidewell J gave judgment dismissing the appeal and upholding the striking out of the statement of claim as disclosing no reasonable cause of action and under the inherent jurisdiction of the court as being frivolous or vexatious or an abuse of the process of the court.

In the course of his judgment the judge cited the well-known passage from the judgment of Fletcher Moulton LJ in *Dyson v A-G* [1911] 1 KB 410 at 418, where it was emphasised that the—

> 'power of arresting an action and deciding it without trial is one to be very sparingly used and rarely, if ever, excepting in cases where the action is an abuse of legal procedure.'

Glidewell J went on to state that, as counsel for Mr Raymond acknowledged in this court:

> 'The major question is one of law, namely, what are the limits of the discretion of the Director of Public Prosecutions under s 4 of the Prosecution of Offences Act 1979 to "undertake the conduct of a prosecution commenced privately"?'

This question was considered by Mars-Jones J in *Turner v DPP* (1978) 68 Cr App R 70 at 76. He there stated that—

> 'having regard to the wide powers conferred by the statutes and regulations to which I have referred, it is impossible to argue that it was unlawful or *ultra vires* for the Director of Public Prosecutions to intervene in this private prosecution only for the purpose of offering no evidence. As [counsel for the Director of Public Prosecutions] has pointed out there is nothing novel about such a procedure. The Attorney-General could always enter a *nolle prosequi* in criminal proceedings before Courts of record, and the Courts have never sought to interfere with the exercise of that power.'

In *Gouriet v Union of Post Office Workers* [1977] 3 All ER 70 at 88, [1978] AC 435 at 487 Viscount Dilhorne observed:

> 'The Attorney-General has many powers and duties. He may stop any prosecution on indictment by entering a nolle prosequi. . . He need not give any reasons. he can direct the institution of a prosecution and direct the Director of Public Prosecutions to take over the conduct of any criminal proceedings and he may tell him to offer no evidence.'

Section 4 of the 1979 Act has already been cited. It may be observed that while any person may institute or 'carry on' any criminal proceedings the director may undertake, at any stage, the 'conduct' of those proceedings. The word 'conduct' appears to us to be wider than the phrase 'carry on' and suggests to our minds that when the director intervenes in a prosecution which has been privately instituted he may do so not exclusively for the purpose of pursuing it by carrying it on, but also with the object of aborting it, that is to say he may 'conduct' the proceedings in whatever manner may appear expedient in the public interest. The director will thus intervene in a private prosecution where the issues in the public interest are so grave that the expertise and the resources of the director's office should be brought to bear in order to ensure that the proceedings are properly conducted from the point of view of the prosecution.

On the other hand there may be what appear to the director substantial reasons in the public interest for not pursuing a prosecution privately commenced. What may emerge from those proceedings might have an adverse effect on a pending prosecution involving far more serious issues. The director, in such a case, is called on to make a value judgment. Unless his decision is manifestly such that it could not be honestly and reasonably arrived at it cannot, in our opinion, be impugned. The safeguard against an unnecessary or gratuitous exercise of this power is that by s 2 of the 1979 Act the director's duties are exercised 'under the superintendence of the Attorney General'. That officer of the Crown is, in his turn, answerable to Parliament if it should appear that his or the director's powers under the statute have in any case been abused.

Mr Raymond, if he is still concerned to bring Mr Carne to trial, can seek to start again at the St Albans Magistrates' Court. The major reasons which prompted the intervention of the Director of Public Prosecutions in 1979 may no longer exist. Mr Raymond's insistence on justice being done might be better served by such a course than by the fruitless pursuit of those engaged in the important and sensitive duties attaching to prosecutions. We are by no means encouraging Mr Raymond to lay fresh informations. The justices might take the view that such a course would be oppressive, or in any case that the evidence was inadequate, or even, possibly, that the intended prosecution by Mr Raymond was itself tainted by mala fides or spite or some other oblique motive.

In our opinion the careful judgment of Glidewell J was entirely right in its reasons and its conclusions and we accordingly dismiss this appeal.

Appeal dismissed. Leave to appeal to the House of Lords refused.

Solicitors: *Hallinan, Blackburn Gittings & Co* (for Mr Raymond); *Treasury Solicitor.*

Henrietta Steinberg   Barrister.

R v Governor of Blundeston Prison, ex parte Gaffney

QUEEN'S BENCH DIVISION
LORD LANE CJ, LLOYD AND EASTHAM JJ
23 MARCH 1982

Sentence – Reduction – Period spent in custody – Concurrent sentences – Defendant spending separate periods in custody pending sentence for separate offences – Defendant sentenced to concurrent periods of imprisonment – Whether defendant's sentence should be reduced by both periods spent in custody pending sentence – Criminal Justice Act 1967, s 67(1).

In May 1979 the applicant was convicted by a magistrates' court of a series of offences and was committed to the Crown Court for sentence. He was detained in custody from 6 June to 2 July (the first custody period) pending sentence in the Crown Court. On 2 July the Crown Court deferred sentence and the applicant was released from custody. On 4 October during the deferment period the applicant was convicted by another magistrates' court of a second series of offences and was again detained in custody from 4 October to 7 December (the second custody period) pending sentence in the Crown Court. On 7 December the Crown Court sentenced him to 37 months' imprisonment for the first series of offences and three years concurrent therewith for the second series of offences, which effectively meant that the applicant was required to serve the longer sentence of 37 months reduced, under s 67(1)[a] of the Criminal Justice Act 1967, 'by any period during which he was in custody . . . in connection with [the] sentence or the offence'. The Home Office maintained that under s 67(1) the applicant's sentence could only be reduced by the time spent in custody during the first custody period, since he was not in custody during the second custody period in connection with proceedings relating to the sentence for the first offences. When his term of imprisonment, less the periods of custody, expired the applicant applied for a writ of habeas corpus addressed to the

---

a   Section 67(1), so far as material, provides: 'The length of any sentence of imprisonment imposed on an offender by a court shall be treated as reduced by any period during which he was in custody by reason only of having been committed to custody by an order of a court made in connection with any proceedings relating to that sentence or the offence for which it was passed or any proceedings from which those proceedings arose . . .'

governor of the prison where he was detained to show cause why he should not be released immediately.

Held – On the true construction of s 67(1) of the 1967 Act the applicant was only entitled to have the time spent in custody during the first custody period credited against his sentence because that was the only period in which he had been in custody 'in connection with' proceedings relating to his sentence of 37 months for the first series of offences; the second custody period could only be credited against the sentence of three years imposed in respect of the second series of offences, and that sentence had been incorporated into the longer sentence for the first series of offences. Accordingly, the application would be refused (see p 494 e to h, post).

Notes

For the duration of a sentence, see 11 Halsbury's Laws (4th edn) para 497.

For the Criminal Justice Act 1967, s 67, see 25 Halsbury's Statutes (3rd edn) 894.

Application for habeas corpus

The applicant, Kevin Patrick Gaffney, was convicted in the Ipswich Magistrates' Court, on 14 May 1979, of receiving stolen property, theft, obtaining property by deception and forgery, and, on 24 May 1979, of handling stolen goods and failing to surrender to bail when he also admitted ten further offences. In respect of all those offences the Ipswich magistrates committed the applicant to the Crown Court for sentence and from 6 June to 2 July 1979 he was in custody pending his appearance in the Crown Court at Ipswich for sentence. On 2 July the Crown Court deferred sentence. On 4 October 1979, during the period of deferment, the applicant was convicted in the Middlesborough Magistrates' Court of a further series of offences involving dishonesty and in relation to those offences the Middlesborough magistrates committed him in custody to the Crown Court for sentence. He remained in custody until 7 December 1979 when the Crown Court at Ipswich sentenced him to 37 months in respect of the convictions in the Ipswich Magistrates' Court and to three years, concurrent therewith, in respect of the convictions in the Middlesborough court. In accordance with Home office practice in the case of concurrent sentences the department adopted the longer sentence of 37 months (for the convictions in the Ipswich court) as the one which determined the date of the applicant's release from prison, and, pursuant to s 67(1) of the Criminal Justice Act 1967, reduced the 37 months' sentence by the period spent in custody in connection with the Ipswich convictions between 6 June and 2 July 1979, but did not reduce the 37 months by the later period spent in custody from 4 October to 7 December 1979, on the ground that it was time spent in custody in connection with the convictions in the Middlesborough court and did not, under s 67(1), fall to be deducted from the sentence for the Ipswich convictions. Accordingly the Home Office maintained that the applicant was not due to be released from Blundeston Prison, where he was detained, until 23 May 1982. The applicant applied for a writ of habeas corpus ad subjiciendum addressed to the governor of Blundeston Prison to show cause why he should not be released from prison immediately, on the ground that the Home Office was erroneous in failing to deduct both the periods he had spent in custody from the 37 months' sentence and, on the basis that both periods were deducted, he was entitled to be released on 19 March 1982.

Graham Parkins for the applicant.
Simon D Brown for the governor.

EASTHAM J delivered the first judgment at the invitation of Lord Lane CJ. This matter came before McNeill J yesterday on an ex parte application, and by direction of the judge the matter was adjourned so that notice could be given to the governor of the prison involved and to the Treasury Solicitor. It is a short but difficult point for the decision of the court.

It is the submission of the applicant that his proper release date from prison was last

Saturday, 20 March, whereas the Home Office, for reasons which at first blush were difficult to follow, in a letter which it wrote to the applicant's solicitors maintain that the   *a* earliest release date has not yet arrived and will not arrive until 23 May 1982. The difference between these dates depends on the particular construction which the court takes to be the proper construction of s 67(1) of the Criminal Justice Act 1967.

The facts of this matter can be shortly stated. Attached to the letter from the Home Office there is a diagram. The position is that this applicant first appeared on 14 May 1979 before the Ipswich magistrates. He appeared again on 24 May for further offences   *b* of dishonesty, including some offences which were taken into consideration and an offence of failing to surrender to his bail. Between 24 May and 6 June 1979, although the applicant was in custody (that was for non-payment of fines), it is common ground that that period does not count. However after 6 June until 2 July 1979 he remained in custody pending his appearance in the Crown Court at Ipswich for offences which he committed and had been dealt with in the Ipswich Magistrates' Court. It is conceded by   *c* the Home Office that credit must be given for the period 6 June to 2 July 1979, which is marked 'A' on the diagram, when sentence was ultimately passed.

When he appeared on 2 July 1979, the Crown Court deferred sentence. Unfortunately the applicant committed further offences in the north of England. He was arrested and appeared on 4 October 1979 at the Middlesborough Magistrates' Court on three charges of theft and asked for six further offences to be taken into consideration. The   *d* Middlesborough magistrates, in relation to those offences, and those offences only, committed the applicant in custody to the Crown Court at Ipswich. The Crown Court at Ipswich dealt with him not only for the Ipswich offences but also for the Middlesborough offences. The applicant remained in custody in relation to the Middlesborough magistrates' order from 4 October until 7 December 1979 when he was dealt with.

On behalf of the applicant it is urged that, as he received three years for the Middlesborough offences and 37 months for the Ipswich offences, the two periods 'A' and 'B' shown on the diagram attached to the Home office letter should be added together, and that he should receive a total credit for the periods involved in 'A' and 'B'.

The Home Office on the other hand maintains that, having regard to the wording of s 67(1) of the Criminal Justice Act 1967, and in particular to the words 'by reason only of   *f* having been committed to custody by an order of a court made in connection with any proceedings relating to that sentence', in relation to any sentence for the Ipswich offences the applicant is entitled to credit in respect of period 'A' only, and that, as he was committed in custody by the Middlesborough justices, in relation to period 'B' he is only entitled to credit in respect of that period as against any sentence imposed in respect of the Middlesborough offences.

For my part I think the construction placed on this very difficult section by the Home Office is the right one. In those circumstances in relation to the 37 months, which was the total of the Ipswich sentences, in my judgment the applicant is only entitled to the period 'A' and not 'B'. If I am wrong about that, in any event, as this is a discretionary matter, it would not be a matter for habeas corpus.

LLOYD J. I agree.

LORD LANE CJ. I also agree. It may be that the result appears to be unjust, but it is a result which we are forced to achieve by reason of the wording of s 67(1) of the Criminal Justice Act 1967.

Application refused.

Solicitors: *Prettys*, Ipswich (for the applicant); *Treasury Solicitor*.

N P Metcalfe Esq   Barrister.

Horner v Horner

COURT OF APPEAL, CIVIL DIVISION
ORMROD, DUNN LJJ AND SIR SEBAG SHAW
18 FEBRUARY 1982

Injunction – Husband and wife – Molestation – Meaning – Harassment by husband – Jurisdiction of county court – Wife obtaining order in magistrates' court restraining husband from using violence – Husband refraining from violence but continuing to harass wife – Whether magistrates' court order extending to husband's harassment – Whether wife entitled to obtain county court order restraining husband from molesting her – Domestic Violence and Matrimonial Proceedings Act 1976, s 1(1)(a) – Domestic Proceedings and Magistrates' Courts Act 1978, s 16.

Injunction – Molestation – Domestic violence – County court – Jurisdiction – Wife obtaining order in magistrates' court restraining husband from using violence – Jurisdiction of county court to restrain husband from molesting wife – Domestic Violence and Matrimonial Proceedings Act 1976, s 1(1)(a) – Domestic Proceedings and Magistrates' Courts Act 1978, s 16.

Injunction – Husband and wife – Domestic violence – Attachment of power of arrest to injunction – Husband not violent for nine months but continuing to harass wife – Wife entitled to injunction in county court restraining husband from assaulting, molesting or interfering with her – Whether power of arrest should be attached to injunction – Domestic Violence and Matrimonial Proceedings Act 1976, s 2(1).

The wife, who had separated from the husband, obtained an order in a magistrates' court under s 16[a] of the Domestic Proceedings and Magistrates' Courts Act 1978 that the husband not use or threaten violence against her. A power of arrest was attached to the order. Thereafter the husband stopped being violent to the wife and instead harassed in ways which did not involve or threaten violence. On the basis that the s 16 order was not wide enough to protect her from the husband's harassment, the wife applied to the county court for an injunction under s 1(1)(a)[b] of the Domestic Violence and Matrimonial Proceedings Act 1976 restraining the husband from molesting her. The wife also applied for a power of arrest to be attached to the injunction, under s 2(1)[c] of the 1976 Act. The judge refused to grant the injunction sought, on the ground that his jurisdiction under the 1976 Act was no wider than that of the magistrates' court under s 16 of the

---

a   Section 16, so far as material, provides:
    '(1) Either party to a marriage may, whether or not an application is made by that party for an order under section 2 of this Act, apply to a magistrates' court for an order under this section.
    (2) Where on an application for an order under this section the court is satisfied that the respondent has used, or threatened to use, violence against the person of the applicant . . . and that it is necessary for the protection of the applicant . . . that an order should be made under this subsection, the court may make . . . (a) an order that the respondent shall not use, or threaten to use, violence against the person of the applicant . . .'

b   Section 1(1), so far as material, provides: 'Without prejudice to the jurisdiction of the High Court, on an application by a party to a marriage a county court shall have jurisdiction to grant an injunction containing one or more of the following provisions, namely,—(a) a provision restraining the other party to the marriage from molesting the applicant . . . whether or not any other relief is sought in the proceedings.'

c   Section 2(1), so far as material, provides: 'Where, on an application by a party to a marriage, a judge grants an injunction containing a provision (in whatever terms)—(a) restraining the other party to the marriage from using violence against the applicant . . . the judge may, if he is satisfied that the other party has caused actual bodily harm to the applicant . . . and considers that he is likely to do so again, attach a power of arrest to the injunction.'

1978 Act and that therefore her proper course was to go back to the magistrates' court. The wife appealed.

Held – (1) A county court's power under s 1(1)(a) of the 1976 Act to grant an injunction restraining a party to a marriage from 'molesting' the other party was wider than the power of a magistrates' court under s 16 of the 1978 Act to make an order restraining a party from using 'violence', because the term 'molesting' in s 1(1)(a) of the 1976 Act covered harassment falling short of violence or threatened violence which nevertheless called for the court's intervention, whereas the jurisdiction to make an order under s 16 of the 1978 Act was restricted to situations where there was violence or threatened violence. Since the husband's harassment was such that the court should intervene, the county court judge had had jurisdiction to grant the wife an injunction under s 1(1)(a) of the 1976 Act restraining the husband from assaulting, molesting or interfering with her. The wife would therefore be granted such an injunction forthwith, on terms that she undertook to obtain discharge of the existing order made in the magistrates' court under s 16 of the 1978 Act, since it was desirable that the case should be dealt with by only one court (see p 497 f to j and p 498 b to g, post).

(2) The jurisdiction under s 2(1) of the 1976 to attach a power of arrest to an injunction arose only if the court was satisfied that the respondent had caused actual bodily harm to the applicant and was likely to do so again. Since some nine months had elapsed since the husband had been violent towards the wife, and since a power of arrest attached to the injunction would expose the husband to immediate arrest on breach of the injunction and would cause problems of police enforcement, the court would not, in all the circumstances, attach a power of arrest to the injunction (see p 497 j to p 498 c and f g, post).

Per curiam. Cases of personal idiosyncratic behaviour by a party to a marriage require careful handling by the court, in the sense of being both sensitive and firm, and in general the attachment to an injunction of a power of arrest, which operates automatically on breach of the injunction, is to be deprecated (see p 498 a to c and f g, post).

Notes
For matrimonial injunctions in the county court, see 22 Halsbury's Statutes (4th edn) para 1118.

For the grant of relief by a magistrates' court, see ibid para 1175 and 13 ibid para 1261.

For the Domestic Violence and Matrimonial Proceedings Act 1976, ss 1, 2, see 46 Halsbury's Statutes (3rd edn) 714.

For the Domestic Proceedings and Magistrates' Courts Act 1978, s 16, see 48 ibid 761.

Appeal
The wife, Caroline Mary Horner, appealed from the order of his Honour Judge MacManus QC made in the Horsham County Court on 13 November 1981 dismissing her application for an injunction under s 1(1)(a) of the Domestic Violence and Matrimonial Proceedings Act 1976 restraining the husband, Bryan Edward Lorenzo Horner, from molesting her. The facts are set out in the judgment of Ormrod LJ.

Philip Newman for the wife.
The husband did not appear.

ORMROD LJ. This is an appeal from an order made by his Honour Judge MacManus QC on 13 November 1981 at Horsham County Court, when he refused the wife's application for an injunction restraining the husband from molesting her pursuant to s 1 of the Domestic Violence and Matrimonial Proceedings Act 1976.

With great respect to the judge, he seems to have misappreciated the situation fundamentally.

The short facts are that these parties, who are by no means young, were married on 11 August 1979 and parted on 24 May 1981. The husband had been behaving in a very peculiar manner prior to the separation, and had indeed on occasion been physically violent to the wife; but since then he has been harassing her in all kinds of ways: handing her threatening letters, intercepting her on the way to the station, and so on: the kind of conduct which makes life extremely difficult.

On 24 July 1981 the wife, on the advice of her solicitors, which cannot be criticised, applied to the magistrates' court for an order under s 16 of the Domestic Proceedings and Magistrates' Courts Act 1978 for an order that the husband should not use, or threaten to use, violence against the applicant. An order was made by the court and a power of arrest was attached to it. Since that order was made, the husband has adopted a different tactic. He has been harassing the wife in various ways which probably fall outside the limited powers of s 16 of the 1978 Act, ie the wife probably cannot satisfy the magistrates that the husband has used violence or threatened to use violence against her person. Consequently the wife's solicitors were reasonably doubtful whether the order which had been obtained in the magistrates' court was going to be an effective protection for her in the future, having regard to the change of tactics adopted by the husband. They applied to the county court judge for an order under s 1 of the Domestic Violence and Matrimonial Proceedings Act 1976, which is appreciably wider than the magistrates' powers. It is perhaps a pity that there should be two courts sitting in the same area, dealing with very similar problems, but with significantly different powers.

The judge took the view (for reasons which are not clear) that the application to him was simply a way of duplicating proceedings and building up the costs, whereas the proper course for the wife was to go back to the magistrates' court. He does not appear to have appreciated, from reading his notes, the crucial point, which is that the wife was suffering a form of harassment which it was doubtful that the magistrates could control by reason of the more limited powers given to them by the 1978 Act, and so he was critical of the wife's solicitors for starting the proceedings in the county court. The result is that the wife has had to appeal to this court.

It seems to me quite plain that under s 1 of the 1976 Act the county court has power to grant injunctions containing one or more of the provisions there set out. Paragraph (a) of sub-s (1) is a provision 'restraining the other party to the marriage from molesting the applicant'; para (b) refers to molesting a child; para (c) refers to excluding a party from the matrimonial home (which does not apply here); and para (d) also refers to the use of the matrimonial home.

In divorce proceedings the court, in its inherent jurisdiction, has for years been granting injunctions restraining molestation and/or interference of one party to the marriage by the other. For my part I have no doubt that the word 'molesting' in s 1(1)(a) of the 1976 Act does not imply necessarily either violence or threats of violence. It applies to any conduct which can properly be regarded as such a degree of harassment as to call for the intervention of the court.

Consequently the judge was wrong in thinking that his jurisdiction was not wider and much more effective in this particular case than that of the magistrates. He ought to have granted an injunction and he ought to have granted it in the usual form restraining the husband in this case from assaulting, molesting or interfering with the wife. I would be in favour, in this court, of granting that injunction forthwith; but it should be on the undertaking by the wife to obtain the discharge of the existing order in the magistrates' court because, if we have two courts with jurisdiction in a matter like this, there is bound to be confusion and waste of money. This case clearly must be dealt with by one tribunal and not by two.

There only remains to consider the submission of counsel for the wife that we should attach a power of arrest to the order. Section 2 of the 1976 Act is quite specific. The jurisdiction to attach a power of arrest arises only if the judge is satisfied that the other party has caused actual bodily harm to the applicant, or to the child, and considers that he is likely to do it again.

It is true that there is evidence in the past, now some nine months ago, of actual violence, so it could perhaps be said that the wife may just be able to bring herself within the limits of s 2(1), although I would be cautious about that, having regard to the lapse of time. But it has been said many times that to attach a power of arrest to an injunction is very serious because it exposes the husband to immediate arrest; it causes great problems for police officers who have to enforce it; it leads to the husband being kept in custody for a period up to 24 hours before being produced before a judge and it often involves a committal order to prison. Anything in this sphere which operates more or less automatically is to be deprecated. These cases of personal idiosyncratic behaviour require careful handling by the tribunal, careful in the sense of being both sensitive and firm. I would be against running any risk of an automatic enforcement of an order such as this on the facts of this case, so I would not attach a power of arrest. I would allow the appeal.

DUNN LJ. I entirely agree. The judge did not appear to appreciate that his powers under s 1 of the Domestic Violence and Matrimonial Proceedings Act 1976 were considerably wider than the powers of the magistrates under s 16 of the Domestic Proceedings and Magistrates' Courts Act 1978 and, in my view, that was the reason that he fell into error, as I think he did. He appeared to be suspicious of the bona fides of the wife's application, but I see no reason whatever for that suspicion. Her affidavits disclosed a strong case of harassment by the husband and she plainly needed the protection of the court. In my view, the judge should have given it to her.

I agree with Ormrod LJ that, although on the face of it, s 1 of the 1976 Act appears to be confined simply to molestation, it is quite plain from s 2 that the court has the power to order an injunction in the wide terms in which injunctions are ordered in divorce proceedings. By implication s 2 shows that the judge is to have power to make an order restraining the other party to the marriage from using violence.

I therefore agree that the appropriate order under this section is the form of order which has been used for years in the divorce courts, namely restraining the husband from assaulting, molesting or otherwise interfering with the wife. That is the order which, in my view, the judge should have made for the protection of this wife and, for the reasons given by Ormrod LJ, I would allow this appeal.

I also agree with everything that Ormrod LJ has said about the circumstances in which a power of arrest should be exercised and I agree that this is not a case in which a power of arrest is appropriate.

SIR SEBAG SHAW. I agree with the order proposed by Ormrod LJ and I particularly wish to associate myself as to the caution which should be exercised before attaching a power of arrest under the Domestic Violence and Matrimonial Proceedings Act 1976. I would allow the appeal accordingly.

Appeal allowed.

Solicitors: *Hextall, Erskine & Co,* Horsham (for the wife).

Patricia Hargrove   Barrister.

Commission for Racial Equality v Amari Plastics Ltd

COURT OF APPEAL, CIVIL DIVISION

LORD DENNING MR, GRIFFITHS LJ AND SIR SEBAG SHAW

22, 23 FEBRUARY 1982

Race relations – Non-discrimination notice – Requirements of notice – Appeal – Scope of appeal – Whether appeal limited to appeal against reasonableness of requirements of the notice – Whether appellant entitled to challenge all findings of fact on which notice was based – Race Relations Act 1976, s 59.

Race relations – Non-discrimination notice – Requirements of notice – Appeal – Procedure – Race Relations Act 1976, s 59.

In 1978 the Commission for Racial Equality notified the respondent company that they intended to investigate, under s 48 of the Race Relations Act 1976, certain allegations of unlawful discriminatory conduct which had been made against it, and informed the company of its right under s 49(4)(*b*) of the 1976 Act to submit representations to the commission. The company did so, and ten months later the commission informed it, pursuant to s 58[a] of the 1976 Act, that they were minded to conclude that it had contravened specified sections of that Act and that, subject to any representations which the company might make, they were minded to issue a non-discrimination notice under s 58. The company submitted detailed representations. The commission nevertheless decided in February 1980 to issue a non-discrimination notice against the company. The notice stated that the commission were satisfied that the company had committed acts to which s 58 applied and required it not to commit such unlawful acts and to make certain changes in its practices to prevent further breaches of the 1976 Act occurring. The company lodged an appeal, under s 59[b] of the 1976 Act, against the notice and applied to an industrial tribunal for an order that the commission should give particulars of the allegations which had been made. The tribunal directed that particulars should be given of every fact found by the commission in the course of their investigation. The commission appealed against the order to the Employment Appeal Tribunal, contending that the right of appeal conferred by s 59(2) was limited to challenging findings of fact relevant to the reasonableness of the requirements imposed in a non-discrimination notice and that the whole of a lengthy administrative inquiry by the commission should not be reopened on appeal, particularly in view of the fact that a person who was subject to an investigation under the 1976 Act was given a statutory right to make representations to the commission both before the investigation began and before a non-discrimination notice was served. The Employment Appeal Tribunal dismissed the appeal. The commission appealed to the Court of Appeal.

Held – The appeal would be dismissed because it was clear that s 59 of the 1976 Act did not confine the company to appealing against the reasonableness of the requirements of a non-discrimination notice but also entitled it to challenge all and any of the findings of fact on which the requirements of the notice were based (see p 502 *c* to *g*, p 503 *b c*, p 504 *f g*, p 505 *g h* and p 506 *b* to *e*, post).

Observations on the procedure to be adopted on an appeal under s 59 of the 1976 Act (see p 502 *h j* and p 506 *c* to *e*, post).

Per Griffiths LJ and Sir Sebag Shaw. If the commission find that the procedures laid down in the 1976 Act are unworkable they should make representations for changes in

---

a   Section 58, so far as material, is set out at p 504 *h* to p 505 *a*, post

b   Section 59 is set out at p 505 *c* to *e*, post

the legislation to the Secretary of State pursuant to s 43(1)(c)^c of that Act (see p 503 e f and p 506 d e, post).

a

Notes

For the Commission for Racial Equality's powers to conduct investigations and issue non-discrimination notices, see Supplement to 4 Halsbury's Laws (4th edn) paras 1042B.3, 1042C.4.

For the Race Relations Act 1976, ss 43, 48, 49, 58, 59, see 46 Halsbury's Statutes (3rd edn) 425, 429, 437, 438.

b

Cases referred to in judgments

Jones v A-G [1973] 3 All ER 518, [1974] Ch 148, [1973] 3 WLR 608, CA, 8(1) Digest (Reissue) 461, 2149.

R v Commission for Racial Equality, ex p Cottrell & Rothon (a firm) [1980] 3 All ER 265, [1980] 1 WLR 1580, DC.

c

R v Commission for Racial Equality, ex p Hillingdon London Borough Council [1982] QB 276, [1981] 3 WLR 520, CA.

Case also cited

Selvarajan v Race Relations Board [1976] 1 All ER 12, [1975] 1 WLR 1686, CA.

d

Appeal

The Commission for Racial Equality appealed, with leave, against an order of the Employment Appeal Tribunal (Browne-Wilkinson J, Mr W P Blair and Mr A J Nicol ([1982] QB 265)), made on 25 June 1981 (following an appeal by the commission against a written interim decision, dated 25 June 1980, of Mr D J Walker, chairman of an industrial tribunal held at London South on 13 June 1980), whereby it was ordered (i) that within 28 days the commission should serve on the respondent company, Amari Plastics Ltd, a single document containing all the facts relied on by the commission in serving a non-discrimination notice dated 13 February 1980, and (ii) that thereafter the respondent company should serve an amended notice of appeal specifying each finding of fact challenged. The facts are set out in the judgment of Lord Denning MR.

e

f

Desmond Browne for the commission.
Eldred Tabachnik for the respondent company.

LORD DENNING MR. Racial discrimination is one of the problems of our time. Parliament in 1976 drew up a statute, the Race Relations Act 1976, in order to deal with it. It set up machinery to be operated by the Commission for Racial Equality. It was designed to reduce or eliminate discrimination, but it had to be done fairly. On the one hand there would be people who were complaining of being victimised on account of their colour; on the other hand those complaints might well be unjustified, and it was necessary to protect those against whom discrimination was alleged. In R v Commission for Racial Equality, ex p Hillingdon London Borough Council [1982] QB 276, there was said to be discrimination in housing matters against coloured people by the Hillingdon Borough Council. In this case there is said to be discrimination in the employment field by Amari Plastics Ltd. It is said that they, through their managing director and through their chairman, refused to employ coloured people and gave preference to the white. Further, when they were employing hands through agencies, they gave the employment agencies instructions not to employ coloured people, but only white. Those complaints are vigorously resisted by the company.

g

h

j

The machinery set up under the Act is exceedingly complicated. So complicated that I will not attempt to explain it. I will only tell what happened in this case. In July 1978 the Commission for Racial Equality decided to embark on a formal investigation. They gave the company, Amari Plastics Ltd, an opportunity to submit oral or written representations in accordance with s 49(4)(b) of the Act. The company made their representations with regard to it. It covered 11 pages. That was 'the first investigation'. That was in November 1978. After about ten months the commission were 'minded' to issue a non-discrimination notice. They sent a 'minded' letter in accordance with s 58(5). It is dated 21 September 1979. It covers nine closely-typed pages. In it the commission say they 'are minded to conclude that the company have contravened the Race Relations Act 1976 in the following ways'. They then set out many pages of these complaints about unlawful discrimination against certain people in the employment field. After all those pages of complaints the letter ends:

> 'In the light of the above evidence, the Commission is minded, subject to any representations which may be made, to issue a non-discrimination notice in pursuant of Section 58 of the Act.'

Two months later, in answer to that 'minded' letter, the company put in their representations. These came to nearly 40 pages. They answer all the complaints in detail. That was in November 1979. The commission, having received all those representations, decided nevertheless to issue a non-discrimination notice. On 13 February 1980 the commission issued a non-discrimination notice under s 58 of the Act. That is what we have to consider today.

The non-discrimination notice is in a prescribed form. It covers four pages. It starts off: 'Whereas in the course of a formal investigation the Commission for Racial Equality . . . have become satisfied that you had committed acts to which Section 58(2) of . . . the Act . . . applies, namely . . .' and then they set out there a whole series of acts in 1977 and 1978 by reason of which they say that the company were guilty of unlawful discrimination. They go on to say: 'and we are of the opinion that further such acts are likely to be committed unless changes are made in your practices . . . now, therefore . . . you are required . . . not to commit any such act as aforesaid' and to make such changes. I will not go further into details. That is the non-discrimination notice which was given in February 1980. Under s 59 of the Act the company were entitled to appeal to an industrial tribunal. On 25 March 1980 in accordance with the Act, the company lodged an appeal with the industrial tribunal. Annexed to it were ten pages of particulars. At the same time they made an application for further particulars, covering ten pages, applying for particulars of the allegations against them.

The chairman heard the application for directions. It was whether particulars should be ordered of this or that. The chairman gave his decision covering over many pages. He directed that particulars should be given of every fact found by the commission in the course of the formal investigation. That direction was given on 13 June 1980. There was an appeal to the Employment Appeal Tribunal. It came before Browne-Wilkinson J and his two colleagues. They gave their decision in June 1981 (see [1982] QB 265). Now there is an appeal to this court.

Such is the long procedure which has taken place already. Even so we have only got to this preliminary question: should particulars be ordered or not by the industrial tribunal? The appeal itself to the tribunal is a long way off.

The point is this: when the appeal does come before the industrial tribunal, is there to be a full-dress hearing with witnesses on every dispute of fact? or is the appeal to be limited in some way? Section 59 is important. Subsection (1) says:

> '(1) Not later than six weeks after a non-discrimination notice is served on any person he may appeal against any requirement of the notice—(a) to an industrial tribunal, so far as the requirement relates to acts which are within the jurisdiction of the tribunal . . .'

That is simple enough; but sub-s (2) goes on:

> '(2) Where the tribunal or court considers a requirement in respect of which an appeal is brought under subsection (1) to be unreasonable because it is based on an incorrect finding of fact or for any other reason, the tribunal or court shall quash the requirement.'

So there it is. Counsel for the Commission says the appeal is against a 'requirement'. That is perfectly true. He says, therefore, the appeal should be limited to the 'requirement' in the notice and to matters which are relevant to the 'requirements'. He submitted that there should not be an inquiry into all the various findings of fact which the commission have made, and as to which they were satisfied, before they gave the notice. That argument was well put by counsel on behalf of the commission.

I can understand the difficulty in which the commission are placed. They have had to go through all these long procedures, all these pages and pages of documents, all these representations being considered by them, and so forth. Yet, here they are, faced with a full-dress hearing on whether the findings of fact were right or not, with evidence to be given by witnesses, cross-examined, and the like. They say: 'This is an intolerable burden to put on the commission in the course of an appeal to the industrial tribunal.'

I can see that all this must hinder the commission greatly in getting on with their work. But, nevertheless, on the wording of this statute, it seems to me that it is only on the appeal that the company get a proper hearing. The appeal to the industrial tribunal is the first time that the company are able to put their case. It is the first time they are able to say that the findings of fact are wrong. It is the first time that they can be heard by an impartial tribunal. You have got to remember that the non-discrimination notice is founded on 'findings of fact'; findings of fact on which the commission say they are 'satisfied'. They are 'satisfied' that there have been such acts, and the 'requirement' is that the company are not to commit any such acts in the future. It seems to me the whole structure of s 58(2), about the non-discrimination notice, is that it is founded on findings of fact already made by the commission. It says that the company have committed or are committing those acts. It requires the company not to commit them. The foundation of the whole non-discrimination notice is those findings of fact already made by the commission themselves.

Section 59(2) says that if the requirement is unreasonable 'because it is based on an incorrect finding of fact or for any other reason' it must be quashed. On that provision, it must be open to the company to say those findings of fact (on which the commission based their decision) are incorrect. There must be a proper judicial inquiry whether those findings of fact are right. That means evidence of witnesses, with opportunity of cross-examination, and the like. It is to be remembered that at the earlier stages when these complainants give their information, and the like, to the commission or other people, there is no opportunity for cross-examination. That is shown by *R v Commission for Racial Equality, ex p Cottrell & Rothon (a firm)* [1980] 3 All ER 265, [1980] 1 WLR 1580. So, in fairness to the company and in justice to them, it seems to me that on the appeal the company should be also able to challenge the findings of fact which the commission have already made; and to challenge them before the industrial tribunal which is the first impartial judicial tribunal to hear it.

This accords entirely with the decision of Browne-Wilkinson J and his colleagues in the Employment Appeal Tribunal. They had, further (which we have not had discussed before us), the proper procedure to be undertaken on such an appeal. They based themselves on the decision of this court in *Jones v A-G* [1973] 3 All ER 518, [1974] Ch 148. They did do something to simplify the procedure. They said it ought to be divided into these two stages: the commission ought to state the facts on which they relied as the basis of their requirements. Then the company, in answer, ought to say which of those findings of fact they challenge. These exchanges would be in the nature of pleadings. So the industrial tribunal will have before them the findings of fact on which the commission rely, and, on the other hand, they will have the company's challenge to them. It will be a simplified procedure, but a very appropriate procedure for the purposes of the appeal.

Another question was raised before us. It was whether the report of the findings of the formal investigation ought to be published or made available as soon as the investigation is concluded. Under s 51(2) of the Act, 'The Commission shall prepare a report of their findings in any formal investigation conducted by them'. Subsections (4) and (5) provide for the publication of the report or making of it available. In the present case the commission have not concluded the preparation of their report. So they have not published it or made it available. It might be undesirable because it might contain a defamatory or other statements. So the commission hesitated to conclude their report or to make it available. The statute does not give any timetable about it. I do not think the commission were wrong in holding back that report, as they have done.

This case shows that the machinery of the Act is extremely cumbersome. This case has taken four years already, from 1978 until now. It is still only at a stage in which further particulars have been ordered to be given by both sides. That will take some time. Then there is to be a hearing. Goodness knows when it will take place. The machinery is so elaborate and so cumbersome that it is in danger of grinding to a halt.

I am very sorry for the commission, but they have been caught up in a spider's web spun by Parliament, from which there is little hope of their escaping.

I would dismiss the appeal.

GRIFFITHS LJ. For the first time, the Employment Appeal Tribunal and now this court are required to consider the scope of an appeal against a non-discrimination notice served on a person or company by the Commission for Racial Equality.

Before coming to this point, it is necessary to say a word or two about the nature of the duties of the commissioners known as the Commission for Racial Equality. They have been charged by Parliament with a demanding, delicate and difficult task. Their duties are to be found under s 43(1) of the Race Relations Act 1976, and they are:

> '(a) to work towards the elimination of discrimination; (b) to promote equality of opportunity, and good relations, between persons of different racial groups generally; and (c) to keep under review the working of this Act and, when they are so required by the Secretary of State or otherwise think it necessary, draw up and submit to the Secretary of State proposals for amending it.'

In view of what has just fallen from Lord Denning MR, and in view of what I shall have to say in the course of this judgment, it may well be that the commissioners will think it time to consider putting forward certain amendments to the machinery of the Act.

Among the powers given to the commissioners to enable them to perform their duties is the power to hold a formal investigation into the activities of a person that they suspect is guilty of unlawful racial discrimination. Before the commission embark on the investigation, they must give the person the chance to make representations, which may show that the commission's suspicions are ill-founded and that there is no need for the investigation; but if, despite anything the person may say, the commission decide to hold the formal investigation, the Act gives the commission wide powers to obtain information for the purposes of their investigation. At the end of the investigation the commission are required to prepare a report of their findings and either to publish it or to make it available to anyone who wishes to inspect it. The experience of this and other cases satisfies me that the commissioners approach these formal investigations in a painstaking and conscientious manner. I have no doubt that they carry out a most thorough investigation. If, as a result of the investigation, the commission are satisfied that the person has been guilty of racial discrimination, the only step open to the commission to prevent him continuing that conduct is to serve a non-discrimination notice on him; but it is to be observed that, before taking this step, the commission must warn the person that they are minded to do so and must specify the grounds on which they contemplate doing so, and must offer him another chance to make yet more representations, both oral and in writing, to dissuade them from this course. A non-dis-crimination notice does not of itself impose any punishment for past unlawful discrimination, but it does provide the foundation to prevent further unlawful acts. The notice will require the person not to commit any such acts in the future and, if the notice is not obeyed, the commission can take him before a county court judge to obtain an injunction to restrain him from committing these unlawful acts.

There is no doubt that before a non-discrimination notice is served, the commission have carried out a searching inquisitorial inquiry to satisfy themselves of the truth of the facts on which the notice is based and have given at least two and probably three opportunities to the person to put his case, either orally or in writing, either by himself, through solicitors, counsel or any person of his choice. This is necessarily an expensive and a time-consuming process. In the present case it has already been going on over four years, and I can understand the frustration that the commissioners must feel if the Act requires that their findings of fact are liable to be reopened and reversed on appeal. It also results in a most unsatisfactory and confused state of affairs surrounding the report of their findings which they are obliged to publish or make available at the end of a formal investigation. Whenever the commission serve a non-discrimination notice it must follow that their report will condemn the person they have been investigating of unlawful discrimination. Otherwise, they would have no grounds for issuing a non-discrimination notice. If a report is published, and perhaps given wide publicity, containing the commission's finding of unlawful discrimination against an employer, it is bound to cause damage to that employer. If subsequently the findings of unlawful discrimination are reversed by an industrial tribunal, it will tend to undermine confidence in the commission and is unlikely to undo all the damage to the employer caused by the publication of the report. But what is the commission to do? If they hold up the report until after the appeal is heard, the whole affair is likely to be years old and stale·and to have ceased to be of any interest to anyone. Furthermore, it does not necessarily follow that the commission will modify their views even if the appeal is successful. They may not agree with the views of the industrial tribunal, and the Act requires the commission to publish a report of their findings, not those of the industrial tribunal. This is no phantom problem, for we have been told that every single non-discrimination notice that has been issued against an employer has been appealed, but as yet not one of them has·been heard.

Against this background the commission submit that it cannot have been the intention of Parliament that the findings of fact at which they have so painstakingly arrived in the course of a formal investigation should be reopened on appeal. The commission submit that Parliament has constituted them as the fact-finding body for the purpose of a non-discrimination notice, subject only to the safeguard that if they do not conduct the investigation properly and fairly, it can be challenged by the process of judicial review in the Divisional Court. If it were not for the plain wording of s 59(2), I should be most sympathetic to the commission's argument. If Parliament empowers a body to carry out a formal investigation and hedges the procedure with safeguards to ensure that the person investigated shall have every opportunity to state his case and then requires that body to publish its findings, one might be forgiven for thinking that Parliament intended that that would be the end of the matter. But it is to my mind clear from the language of this statute that such is not the case.

The issue of non-discrimination notices is dealt with in s 58, the relevant subsections of which are sub-ss (1), (2) and (3):

'(1) This section applies to—(a) an unlawful discriminatory act; and (b) an act contravening section 28; and (c) an act contravening section 29, 30 or 31, and so applies whether or not proceedings have been brought in respect of the act.

(2) If in the course of a formal investigation the Commission become satisfied that a person is committing, or has committed, any such acts, the Commission may in the prescribed manner serve on him a notice in the prescribed form ("a non-discrimination notice") requiring him—(a) not to commit any such acts; and (b) where compliance with paragraph (a) involves changes in any of his practices or other arrangements—(i) to inform the Commission that he has effected those changes and what those changes are; and (ii) to take such steps as may be reasonably required by the notice for the purpose of affording that information to other persons concerned.

(3) A non-discrimination notice may also require the person on whom it is served

to furnish the Commission with such other information as may be reasonably required by the notice in order to verify that the notice has been complied with.'

It is to be observed that a non-discrimination notice can only be issued if the commission are satisfied that the person is committing or has committed acts of unlawful racial discrimination. In other words, it has to be based on the commission finding as a fact that the person has been guilty of acts of racial discrimination. The notice has to be in a prescribed form, and the primary requirement is that the person does not commit such unlawful acts. Every notice must contain this primary requirement. Ancillary to the primary requirement, the notice may set out the subsidiary requirements referred to in s 58(2)(b) and sub-s (3), the purpose of which is to ensure that the primary requirement is observed. Section 59 gives the right of appeal:

'(1) Not later than six weeks after a non-discrimination notice is served on any person he may appeal against any requirement of the notice—(a) to an industrial tribunal, so far as the requirement relates to acts which are within the jurisdiction of the tribunal; (b) to a designated county court or a sheriff court, so far as the requirement relates to acts which are within the jurisdiction of the court and are not within the jurisdiction of an industrial tribunal.

(2) Where the tribunal or court considers a requirement in respect of which an appeal is brought under subsection (1) to be unreasonable because it is based on an incorrect finding of fact or for any other reason, the tribunal or court shall quash the requirement.

(3) On quashing a requirement under subsection (2) the tribunal or court may direct that the non-discrimination notice shall be treated as if, in place of the requirement quashed, it had contained a requirement in terms specified in the direction.

(4) Subsection (1) does not apply to a requirement treated as included in a non-discrimination notice by virtue of a direction under subsection (3).'

The commission submit that on the true construction of s 59 an appeal against the requirements of a non-discrimination notice is limited to an appeal as to the reasonableness of the requirements as they relate to the implementation of the notice in the future and that it gives no right to challenge the findings of fact made by the commission in the course of their formal inquiry in so far as they relate to past or present acts of discrimination. As Sir Sebag Shaw succinctly put it in the course of the argument, the commission effectively submits that the appeal is against sentence and not conviction. If this is right, it very seriously limits the value of an appeal, which is of great importance to the employer because it is only by a successful appeal that he can remove the slur cast on him by the non-discrimination notice.

In support of their argument, the commission submitted that it was significant that the right of appeal is expressed to be only against the requirements of the notice and not against the notice as a whole. I find, for myself, no substance in this point. The whole purpose of the notice is to set out requirements, and it makes no difference to the meaning of the introductory words in s 59(1) if one substitutes for the words 'he may appeal against any requirement of the notice' the words 'he may appeal against the notice'; and it is to be observed that in s 78(4) one finds the alternative form of wording is used, for s 78(4) provides: 'For the purposes of this Act a non-discrimination notice or a finding by a court or tribunal becomes final when an appeal against the notice or finding is dismissed.'

The real thrust of the commission's argument in support of their construction is that it is the policy of Parliament to entrust them with the duty of finding facts relating to past discrimination; but, to my mind, that approach was demolished by counsel for the respondent company, who points out that a notice may only contain the primary requirement under s 58(2)(a) not to commit an unlawful act; that is, not to commit an unlawful act of the kind which the commission is satisfied has been committed in the past. This requirement is based on the commission's finding of fact as to the past conduct of the appellant. If the commission are right there could be no appeal from such a requirement. But, not only does the section give an appeal against any requirement of the notice; it specifically provides that the tribunal or court is to quash the requirement if it considers it to be unreasonable because it is based on an incorrect finding of fact. It is, I think, beyond argument that it is unreasonable to require someone to stop doing something that he has never done. This is particularly so in the case of a non-discrimination notice which is based on discreditable conduct and which, if not quashed on appeal, is entered on a register open for all to inspect and copy. It must therefore follow that it is open to the appellant to challenge the commission's finding of fact relating to past unlawful discrimination, because it was on those findings of fact that the commission must have based the primary requirement set out in the notice.

Accordingly, I agree that the decision of the Employment Appeal Tribunal was correct and that an appeal lies against the commission's finding of past misconduct in so far as it is that misconduct on which they based their determination to issue the non-discrimination notice; and, for the reasons given by Lord Denning MR, I agree that the Employment Appeal Tribunal has set out a satisfactory procedure for conducting such appeals.

I return to where I began. If the commission find that these procedures are in fact proving to be unworkable, then the remedy may lie in their own hands. They should make such representations as they consider necessary to the Secretary of State, pursuant to s 43(1)(c).

I agree that this appeal must be dismissed.

SIR SEBAG SHAW. I agree with both judgments. I would only add that it seems to me that the language of s 59 incontrovertibly entitles an appellant to put in issue all and any of the facts on which the requirements of the non-discrimination notice which is challenged was founded. Counsel for the commission's attempted dichotomy between facts which relate to the reasonableness of the requirements and facts which, on the other hand, relate to the justification for the requirements seems to me, having regard to the plain language of the section, to be quite untenable.

I too would dismiss this appeal.

Appeal dismissed. Leave to appeal to the House of Lords granted on terms.

Solicitors: *Bindman & Partners* (for the commission); *Richards, Butler & Co* (for the respondent company).

Frances Rustin   Barrister.

R v Tottenham Justices, ex parte Joshi

QUEEN'S BENCH DIVISION
LORD LANE CJ AND WOOLF J
20 JANUARY 1982

Criminal law – Costs – Magistrates' court – Just and reasonable costs – Magistrates imposing costs of £575 on 37 undefended charges under food hygiene regulations – Magistrates using scale of legal aid costs as yardstick and multiplying costs in respect of one offence by number of charges – Whether magistrates' order as to costs 'just and reasonable' – Costs in Criminal Cases Act 1973, s 2(2).

The applicant pleaded guilty to 37 breaches of the Food Hygiene (General) Regulations 1970. The applicant entered his plea by post and neither he nor the prosecuting local authority were legally represented in the magistrates' court. The magistrates imposed fines of £25, with £15 costs, for each of 35 of the offences and of £50, with £25 costs, for the remaining two offences, ie a total of £975 in fines and £575 in costs. The fines were reduced to a total of £450 on appeal to the Crown Court. The applicant then applied to the Divisional Court for an order of certiorari in respect of the order for costs, on the grounds that (i) the justices had approached the question of costs with rigid criteria in mind which they had applied without regard to the merits of the case, and (ii) the totality of the order as to costs was harsh and oppressive or so far outside the normal sum imposed as to involve an error of law and was therefore not a 'just and reasonable' order as to costs as required by s 2(2)ᵃ of the Costs in Criminal Cases Act 1973. The magistrates' reasons for making that order were that they had used as their yardstick the scale of costs applicable in legal aid cases in magistrates' courts and had multiplied the costs in respect of one offence by the number of charges involved because each offence was the subject of a separate charge under the 1970 regulations.

Held – (1) Where magistrates made an order as to costs in the exercise of their discretion under s 2(2) of the 1973 Act the Divisional Court could properly review such an order if it was so far outside the normal discretionary limits as to show that the magistrates had misdirected themselves in law (see p 510 *f* to *j* and p 512 *g h*, post); *R v Crown Court at St Albans, ex p Cinnamond* [1981] 1 All ER 802 applied.

(2) The magistrates had misdirected themselves in using the yardstick of legal aid costs in magistrates' courts, since the legal aid scale of costs was inappropriate where no legal representation was involved. Furthermore, the magistrates had been wrong to multiply the costs incurred in respect of one offence by the number of summonses issued, since what they were required to consider was the total sum of money which would reimburse the local authority for the time and trouble it had expended in connection with all of the offences. Since the appropriate sum was, in the circumstances, so small the magistrates' order as to costs would be quashed (see p 512 *a* to *h*, post).

Notes

For the award of costs by a magistrates' court in a criminal case, see 29 Halsbury's Laws (4th edn) para 392, and for cases on the subject, see 14(2) Digest (Reissue) 858–859, 7419–7422.

For the Costs in Criminal Cases Act 1973, s 2, see 43 Halsbury's Statutes (3rd edn) 716.

Cases referred to in judgment

Associated Provincial Picture Houses Ltd v Wednesbury Corp [1947] 2 All ER 680, [1948] 1 KB 223, CA, 45 Digest (Repl) 215, *189*.

---

a Section 2(2), so far as material, is set out at p 509 *j*, post

R v Crown Court at St Albans, ex p Cinnamond [1981] 1 All ER 802, [1981] QB 480, [1981] 2 WLR 681, DC.
R v Highgate Justices, ex p Petrou [1954] 1 All ER 406, [1954] 1 WLR 485, DC, 8(2) Digest (Reissue) 640, *161*.

Application for judicial review

Dwarkados H Joshi applied, with the leave of Phillips J granted on 15 September 1981, for an order of certiorari to bring up and quash an order for costs made against him by the Tottenham justices when convicting him on 11 September 1980 of 37 offences under the Food Hygiene (General) Regulations 1970, SI 1970/1172, in respect of charges brought by the respondent, Enfield London Borough Council. The facts are set out in the judgment of Lord Lane CJ.

Stephen Rich for the applicant.
The respondent and the justices did not appear.

LORD LANE CJ. In this appeal Dwarkados Joshi applies for judicial review directed to the Tottenham justices, leave having been given by the single judge to prosecute this application. The remedy which is sought is an order of certiorari directed to the justices in respect of an order for costs which they made against the applicant.

The background to the case is somewhat unusual and it is necessary, in order to understand what happened, to explain it in some little detail. The applicant at the material time was the proprietor of an Indian take-away food business. It seems from the affidavit which he has filed that he had fallen on hard times and his son, Kirit Joshi, put up the money in order to enable the applicant to buy these premises as a going concern.

In May 1980 the premises were visited by a gentleman called Mr Curtis, who was the senior environmental health officer of the borough of Enfield. He inspected these premises, it took him about an hour to do it, and it is plain that he was not impressed by what he saw, to put it mildly. There was a further visit which took place a week or two later, at which the son was also present.

To cut a long story short, the officer, Mr Curtis, found that the premises on which the food was prepared and the various appurtenances connected therewith, the cooking utensils, the shelves, refrigerators and so on, were almost without exception filthy and constituted a danger to health. There was no doubt that there were a large number of items of equipment with which fault could properly be found and was found.

The result of that was that in July 1980 both the applicant and his son received a large number of summonses. There were 35 allegations of breaches of the Food Hygiene (General) Regulations 1970, SI 1970/1172, and those were identical allegations made against each of the two defendants, this applicant and his son. There were, in addition, two further allegations against the applicant alone; one of them involved smoking whilst he was handling food, and the other failing to wear the proper overalls whilst he was engaged on the business.

The applicant and his son both pleaded guilty by post. A letter was sent by the son accompanying his plea of guilty which purported to explain the circumstances under which the offences had taken place. The hearing was on 11 September 1980. Neither of the defendants appeared at that hearing, nor were they represented. The local authority appeared through their servant, Mr Curtis. They were not legally represented.

The result of the hearing was this. The justices fined each of the defendants £25 in respect of each of the 35 breaches which were alleged against them, that is the breaches common to the both, and the applicant £50 in respect of the two breaches which were peculiar to him alone. The result in terms of cash was that the son was fined £875, and the applicant £975. The justices further imposed an order for costs against each of these two defendants, and that order was in the sum of £15 in respect of each of the 35 breaches, and a further £25 against the applicant in respect of each of the two breaches which he faced on his own. So far as costs were concerned, the son had the sum of £525 ordered against him, and the applicant £575, the total of the costs being no less than £1,100.

The story then takes a somewhat unusual turn. This is what happened. The son appealed to the Crown Court against both conviction and sentence. That appeal was heard on 12 November 1980, at the Crown Court at Wood Green before his Honour Judge McLean. The appeal against conviction was not persisted in. That was abandoned on counsel's advice. The appeal against sentence, however, stood, and the appeal against sentence was allowed by the judge. It was allowed to this extent: that the fines on the 35 charges which had been £25 in respect of each were reduced to 50p per count. That reduced the total fines on the son from £875 to £17·50.

It seems that the judge took the view, which would be the reason for that very drastic reduction, that the order for costs, over which he had no jurisdiction because there is no appeal to the Crown Court on the question of costs under these circumstances, was in the nature of a disguised penalty imposed by the magistrates which was improper, and he sought to remedy that situation by adjusting the fines. It is said, and one cannot put it higher than that, and we are informed (it is probably reliable information) that on that occasion the prosecution agreed not to ask for the costs of the appeal against conviction, which had been abandoned as I have just said, on the understanding that the son would not, in the Divisional Court (this court), challenge the justices' order for costs against him. It is also said, and once again I cannot put it higher than that, that during the hearing of that case before Judge McLean a figure of £200 to £300 was mentioned as being the likely actual amount of costs incurred by the prosecution.

The applicant (the father with whom we are concerned today) then in his turn appealed to the Crown Court against sentence. His appeal was also heard at the Crown Court at Wood Green but before a different judge, not Judge McLean but his Honour Judge Salmon QC. The fines of £25 on the 35 charges were reduced to £10 each, but the fines of £50 on the two charges which he faced alone were left standing as they were. The total, accordingly, was reduced from £975 to £450.

That being the background, the applicant now, as I have said, challenges by way of asking for an order of certiorari the order for costs made against him in the Tottenham Magistrates' Court on four bases. They are as follows, as set out in the grounds of the present case: (1) the justices, in the purported exercise of the power given them by the statute to order costs as they think just and reasonable to be paid by the accused to the prosecutor, made the 72 orders that they did 'blindly' without appreciating the arithmetic thereof; (2) the justices approached the question of costs with rigid criteria in mind which they then proceeded to apply without regard to the merits of the whole case before them; (3) the totality of the orders was 'harsh and oppressive or . . . so far outside the normal [sum imposed]' that it must have involved an error of law, as explained in *R v Crown Court at St Albans, ex p Cinnamond* [1981] 1 All ER 802 at 805, [1981] QB 480 at 484; (4) the orders were made contrary to natural justice; in particular, no opportunity to be heard was afforded to the applicant, and the justices must have known that they were proposing to take a course that the applicant could not have reasonably anticipated and which they could not be certain he had the means to discharge; (5) the orders for costs were not true orders at all but in the nature of disguised additional penalties of the type condemned in *R v Highgate Justices, ex p Petrou* [1954] 1 All ER 406, [1954] 1 WLR 485. It is really grounds (2) and (3) on which the arguments in this case, presented to the court by counsel for the applicant, have depended.

The relevant statutory enactment, as already indicated, is the Costs in Criminal Cases Act 1973, s 2, which reads as follows:

> '(1) On the summary trial of an information a magistrates' court shall, on dismissal of the information, have power to make such order as to costs to be paid by the prosecutor to the accused as it thinks just and reasonable.
> (2) On the summary trial of an information a magistrates' court shall, on conviction, have power to make such order as to costs to be paid by the accused to the prosecutor as it thinks just and reasonable . . .'

and then there are certain provisos to that. Those are the words which must govern the justices' determination: 'such order as to costs to be paid by the accused to the prosecutor as it thinks just and reasonable.'

As already indicated, there is no direct appeal to the Crown Court against a magistrates' determination as to costs. The only basis on which an appeal to this court can be made is if it can be shown that the magistrates, in purporting to exercise their discretion under that section, have acted on some improper principle, have taken into consideration something they ought not to have taken into consideration or have failed to take into consideration something which they should. It is not enough that the fines imposed were more than this court would have imposed, or even if they were very much more than this court would have imposed. We have to ask ourselves this question: has there been an error of law? Has there been a purported exercise of discretion based on some wrong principle or assumption? Could any reasonable bench of magistrates have reached this decision without having misdirected themselves?

It follows from what I have just said that a successful appeal to this court, in the circumstances such as the present, is likely to be a rare event. It so happens that there has recently been a decision of this court, not in precisely similar circumstances but in a way which is certainly comparable with the present case, namely *R v Crown Court at St Albans, ex p Cinnamond* [1981] 1 All ER 802, [1981] QB 480. It was a decision of this court, with Donaldson LJ delivering the judgment of the court. That was a case where the applicant had been convicted by the justices of driving with excess alcohol contrary to s 6(1) of the Road Traffic Act 1972 and, amongst other things, the justices ordered him to be disqualified for a period of two years altogether. The 1972 Act permitted them to order him 'to be disqualified for such period as the court thinks fit'. The submission to the court there by the applicant was that the justices had acted so far outside the normal way in which justices would act in a case of this sort that it was open to the Divisional Court to order certiorari to bring up and quash that order for disqualification.

The material part of the judgment of Donaldson LJ reads as follows ([1981] 1 All ER 802 at 804–805, [1981] QB 480 at 484):

'For my part, I think that this court is empowered to exercise a similar jurisdiction, probably subject to rather similar restrictions, namely that it is not sufficient to decide that the sentence is severe, perhaps even unduly severe or surprisingly severe. It is necessary to decide that it is either harsh and oppressive or, if those adjectives are thought to be unfortunate or in any way offensive, that it is so far outside the normal discretionary limits as to enable this court to say that its imposition must involve an error of law of some description, even if it may not be apparent at once what is the precise nature of that error. It seems to me that the jurisdiction which this court is empowered to exercise in this field can be considered analogous to the jurisdiction which it exercises in relation to the Crown and government departments where, on the tests in *Associated Provincial Picture Houses Ltd v Wednesbury Corpn* [1947] 2 All ER 680, [1948] 1 KB 223, it examines a decision and says that no reasonable authority could have reached this decision without a self-misdirection of some sort and therefore is satisfied that there has been some such misdirection.'

I would respectfully agree with what Donaldson LJ said there and, mutatis mutandis, it seems to me that those principles can properly be invoked in the present case which is, of course, dealing with costs, and not with a penalty strictly so called.

It seems to me that if there had been no explanation by the justices in the present case of the reason for imposing the orders for costs which they did, then it would be an inevitable conclusion that they must have, in some way, misdirected themselves to have imposed an order for no less than £1,100 in total in respect of the two defendants when there had been pleas of guilty and there had been no legal representation on either side. But in the present case the justices, very helpfully and properly if we may say so, have filed an affidavit in which the process of thought which led them to the conclusions on costs which they reached are set out. We are grateful to them for having done that because it lightens the burden on this court and avoids, to a great extent, the necessity for us to speculate. I read now para 6 of the affidavit from Mr John Barrett Turner, who was chairman of the justices for the division of Edmonton on the occasion in question:

> 'Having determined the question of penalties we directed our attention to the prosecutor's application for costs. In deciding costs we had regard to the following factors: (i) the prosecuting authority, by and large, looked to the general rate as its source of revenue.'

That is perfectly true but the relevance to the question of costs is not to me, at any rate, immediately apparent.

> '(ii) the general duty to prosecute offences of the kind in question rested with the local authority.'

That, again, is perfectly true but of doubtful relevance.

> '(iii) it appeared to us that, where public money had been used to launch 37 prosecutions which were demonstrably justifiable, it was our duty to ensure the public purse did not suffer as a result of the Applicant's misdeeds.'

With that I would respectfully agree. It is perfectly correct, and it means that the local authority are entitled to be reimbursed for the cost which they have properly incurred in prosecuting this case.

> '(iv) it is a general practice within the Edmonton Division, when assessments of costs to be awarded under the provisions of the Costs in Criminal Cases [Act] 1973, are made, to use as a yardstick the scale of rates applicable in legal aid cases in magistrates courts. At the relevant time these were: Hearing time—£22 per hour; Preparation and interview time—£18 per hour; Travelling and waiting time—£17 per hour; Letter irrespective of length—£1·50 per hour; Telephone call irrespective of length—£1·50 per hour; Photocopying—10p per copy; Travel allowance—18p per mile.'

The affidavit continues as follows:

> '(v) whilst it was open to us to invite the prosecutor to submit a detailed account of the local authority's costs incurred in bringing the proceedings against the Applicant (and against Kirit D. Joshi) we did not expect the prosecutor to be able to do so on the occasion of the hearing of 11th September, 1980 since it was the practice for prosecutors in summary proceedings to make applications for costs in general terms leaving it as a matter for the justices' discretion as to the amount to be awarded, subject to such enquiries as the Bench should wish to make. And it did not appear to us appropriate for the proceedings to be adjourned for the purpose of being provided with a detailed account of costs incurred.'

With those sentiments, speaking for myself, I would entirely agree.

Paragraph 7 of the affidavit reads as follows:

> 'Bearing in mind all the foregoing factors we looked at the number of charges brought by the prosecutor. We took into account that there was not one global offence created by the Food Hygiene (General) Regulations or by the Food and Drugs Act, 1953 to which resort might be had by the prosecutor in properly presenting to the Court a true picture of the conditions prevailing at the Applicant's food premises. We considered that the investigations leading to the issue of the summonses must have taken up much time, and many hours must have been expended on the part of the Environmental Health Inspectorate, legal staff and clerical staff of the London Borough of Enfield in the preparation and bringing of the proceedings. In all the circumstances we determined [and then it goes on to deal with the amounts which they imposed by way of costs].'

So far as those matters are concerned, first of all, with regard to the yardstick which is said was used, namely the scale of rates applicable in legal aid cases, it seems to me that those considerations were inappropriate. The legal aid rates are, of course, rates which are to be applied when legal representation exists for the parties, when, for example, the solicitor presents the case on one side or the other and it is that type of time and that type of activity which is referred to in the list of charges to which reference has been made. It is not appropriate to apply that sort of scale when, as here, there was a plea of guilty beforehand and the case is being presented before the justices by the local authority officer, in this case Mr Curtis, who was not a lawyer but who was in charge of the division in question.

Second, it seems to me that what was overlooked with the expression 'many hours must have been expended on the part of the Environmental Health Inspectorate' and so on, is this. The environmental health inspectorate staff is, of course, properly doing its duty when it inspects these premises (the restaurant premises) as it did in the present case. We are told the inspection took an hour to do. There is no contradiction of that and it does not seem an unreasonable figure. There was a shorter visit a few days later, but to suggest that in a case like this, when there are a number of items of filth, each of which appear in a different summons, as they have to, the cost should be multiplied by each of those items, as was done here, seems to me to be introducing a principle which, in the circumstances of this case, was wrong.

In the upshot, what had to be dealt with so far as the clerical staff were concerned were ten pages of summary of the charges, three pages of statements of the facts and then there were two more pages, one of which contained five lines only of typing and the other three lines of typing in respect of the two offences which this applicant faced on his own. Added to that was the time spent in court, which cannot have been very long in the circumstances, by Mr Curtis, who was not a legally qualified person.

The matter which the justices had to consider then was: what sum of money would reimburse the local authority for those items of time and trouble which the offences committed by these two men had made necessary? The case is to some extent complicated by the fact that the applicant's son, the other defendant, has since died and by the fact that the order for costs against him not only stood but has, in fact, been paid by him. In the particular rather peculiar circumstances which surrounded his conviction and appeal, it seems to me that we ought really to disregard his case and ask ourselves what would be in these circumstances a proper sum to reimburse the local authority for the trouble which they had taken with regard to this applicant, the father. It must, of course, be a matter of guesswork to some extent, but speaking for myself I should have thought the sum of 37 multiplied by 2, that is £2 in respect of each of the offences alleged against this man, would be an adequate sum by way of costs. That would make the sum of £74 in all. [After the court heard further submissions, his Lordship continued:] In view of the small amount at issue, rather than take any further action I would in the circumstances simply quash the order for costs.

WOOLF J. I agree.

Order for costs quashed.

Solicitors: *Ronald Fletcher, Dervish & Co*, Tottenham (for the applicant).

Sepala Munasinghe Esq   Barrister.

Zezza v Government of Italy and another

HOUSE OF LORDS
LORD RUSSELL OF KILLOWEN, LORD KEITH OF KINKEL, LORD LOWRY, LORD ROSKILL AND LORD
BRANDON OF OAKBROOK
28 APRIL, 20 MAY 1982

Extradition – Surrender – Persons accused or convicted of extradition crime – Conviction not including conviction which under foreign law conviction for contumacy – Conviction and sentence in contumacy – Nature and effect of procedure under which fugitive convicted – Fugitive convicted and sentenced in his absence by Italian court for crime in Italy – Procedure in Italian court described as 'in contumacia' – No right of review or to fresh trial in event of subsequent surrender and appearance once trial had finished – Whether fugitive to be treated as a 'convicted' person or an 'accused' person – Extradition Act 1870, ss 10, 26.

In September 1975 the appellant was convicted by a criminal court in Italy of an extraditable offence for which he was sentenced to eight years' imprisonment, a fine of 600,000 lire and a loss of civil rights for five years. He was tried and convicted in his absence in accordance with the provisions of the Italian Code of Criminal Procedure introduced in 1931 but was represented at the trial as required by that procedure. In June 1976 the appellant appealed to the appropriate court, being again represented, and the court reduced his sentence. In March 1979 the same court by way of amnesty further reduced the appellant's sentence, leaving the appellant liable to serve a sentence of six years and pay a fine of 300,000 lire. The form of the proceedings authorised by the code was described therein as 'in contumacia'. Meanwhile the appellant had come to the United Kingdom and in due course the Italian government sought his extradition under the extradition treaty between the United Kingdom and Italy of 1873 on the ground that the appellant was a convicted person. The appellant was duly brought before a magistrate who ordered his committal to prison under s 10[a] of the Extradition Act 1870. The appellant applied for a writ of habeas corpus, contending that the demand for his extradition was founded on a sentence 'in contumacia' and that by virtue of s 26[b] of the 1870 Act and art IX[c] of the extradition treaty he was not to be treated as a convicted person but was to be included in the category of an accused person. He accordingly contended that the conviction was not one in respect of which extradition proceedings could be founded. The Divisional Court rejected those contentions and dismissed his application on the ground that, although at the time when the extradition treaty was concluded in 1873 there was in force in Italy a form of conviction and sentence known as 'in contumacia' which was of a provisional nature, the 1931 code had changed the nature and effect of those proceedings, despite the fact that the nomenclature remained the same, and an accused person sentenced 'in contumacia' no longer had a right to a review or to a fresh trial in the event of subsequent surrender and appearance once the trial had been finished. The appellant appealed to the House of Lords.

Held – Whether a person whose extradition was sought could properly be treated as a convicted person and not simply a suspected and accused person depended on the true nature and effect of the procedure under which he had been convicted and sentenced. Accordingly, notwithstanding the label attached to the Italian proceedings under which the appellant had been convicted and sentenced in his absence, since the conviction did not bear the characteristics of a conviction or sentence in contumacy within s 26 of the 1870 Act and art IX of the 1873 extradition treaty, the appellant was to be treated as a convicted person and not as an accused person. It followed that the appeal would be dismissed (see p 514 f to h and p 518 d to h, post).
Re Caborn-Waterfield [1960] 2 All ER 178 approved.

---

a   Section 10, so far as material, is set out at p 516 c d, post
b   Section 26, so far as material, is set out at p 516 e f, post
c   Article IX, so far as material, is set out at p 516 h, post

Notes

For the meaning of 'conviction for contumacy' in relation to extradition crimes, see 18
Halsbury's Laws (4th edn) para 210, and for cases on the subject, see 24 Digest (Reissue)
1120–1121, 11922–11925.

For the Extradition Act 1870, ss 10, 26, see 13 Halsbury's Statutes (3rd edn) 257, 265.

Cases referred to in opinions

Athanassiadis v Government of Greece (1967) [1969] 3 All ER 293, [1971] AC 282, [1969] 3
  WLR 544, HL, 24 Digest (Reissue) 1120, 11922.
Caborn-Waterfield, Re [1960] 2 All ER 178, [1960] 2 QB 498, [1960] 2 WLR 792, DC, 24
  Digest (Reissue) 1121, 11925.
Coppin, Re (1866) LR 2 Ch App 47, LC, 24 Digest (Reissue) 1141, 12136.

Appeal

Nicola Zezza appealed by leave of the House of Lords granted on 12 November 1981
against the decision of the Divisional Court of the Queen's Bench Division (Donaldson LJ
and Forbes J) on 20 October 1981 dismissing his application for a writ of habeas corpus
ad subjiciendum directed to the governor of Pentonville Prison following his committal
in custody on 5 March 1981 by order of a metropolitan stipendiary magistrate sitting at
Bow Street Magistrates' Court in extradition proceedings brought against him by the
government of Italy. The facts are set out in the opinion of Lord Roskill.

Stephen Sedley and *Owen Davies* for the appellant.
Laurence Giovene and *Jeremy Russell* for the government of Italy.
Michael Neligan for the governor of Pentonville Prison.

Their Lordships took time for consideration.

20 May. The following opinions were delivered.

LORD RUSSELL OF KILLOWEN. My Lords, I have had the advantage of reading
in draft the speech to be delivered by my noble and learned friend Lord Roskill. I agree
with it and with his conclusion that this appeal must be dismissed.

LORD KEITH OF KINKEL. My Lords, I have had the benefit of reading in draft the
speech to be delivered by my noble and learned friend Lord Roskill. I agree with it, and
for the reasons he gives I too would dimiss the appeal.

LORD LOWRY. My Lords, I have had the advantage of reading in draft the speech
prepared by my noble and learned friend Lord Roskill, with which I agree. I too would
dismiss the appeal.

LORD ROSKILL. My Lords, on 19 September 1975 the appellant Nicola Zezza was
one of three men convicted by the Tribunale di Bologna in Italy of armed robbery, that
robbery having taken place at a bank in Bologna on 24 July 1975. He was tried and
convicted in his absence in accordance with the relevant Italian legal procedure for the
trial of those who are absent at the time their trials take place. He was however
represented at the trial as that procedure requires. The Tribunale di Bologna at the
conclusion of the trial sentenced the appellant to eight years' imprisonment and a fine of
600,000 lire. One of his co-accused who stood trial received a sentence of six years'
imprisonment and a fine of 300,000 lire. The other co-accused was acquitted 'due to
insufficient evidence'. The appellant was also sentenced to loss of civil rights for five
years. The co-accused who was convicted suffered the like further penalty. Subsequently
on 24 June 1976 the Court of Appeal in Bologna heard an appeal by the appellant and
that co-accused, the appellant again being represented. The appellant's prison sentence

was reduced to one of seven years and a fine of 500,000 lire. On 24 March 1979 that court by way of amnesty remitted one year of that seven year sentence and 200,000 lire of the already reduced fine, leaving the appellant if extradited to serve a sentence of six years and pay a fine of 300,000 lire.

My Lords, the appellant had meanwhile come to this country, and in due course the Italian government, the first respondent to this appeal, sought the appellant's extradition pursuant to the provisions of the extradition treaty between the United Kingdom and Italy which was first concluded in 1873. The Italian government contended that the appellant was a convicted person, having been duly tried, convicted and sentenced in accordance with arts 497 to 501 of the Italian Code of Criminal Procedure.

My Lords, your Lordships were provided with copies of those articles, both in Italian and in translation in English. It is clear that those articles provide for trials to proceed in the absence of an accused in cases where it is not proved that their absence is 'due to absolute impossibility to appear by reason of a legitimate impediment'. Provision is also made for the representation of an absent accused and to enable him to appeal. It is not necessary to cite the text of those articles in full. It is to be observed that the English translation uses the Italian phrase 'in contumacia', itself derived directly from the Latin, to describe the form of proceedings which are authorised by these articles.

My Lords, following the arrest of the appellant as a result of these extradition proceedings he was, on 5 March 1981, duly brought before Mr W Robins, one of the metropolitan stipendiary magistrates, sitting at Bow Street Magistrates' Court. The magistrate duly heard the evidence, including evidence called by both sides as to the relevant Italian law. He also heard the arguments advanced on either side, and on the same day at the conclusion of those arguments he ordered the appellant's committal to prison 'to await the directions of the Secretary of State'. That order as appears from its face was made on the ground that the appellant had been convicted and sentenced on 19 September 1975 for the robbery committed on 24 July 1975, the appellant having been 'finally sentenced at the Court of Appeal of Bologna' on 24 March 1979. Your Lordships were supplied with a note of the magistrate's reason for his decision. It should be mentioned that there was a difference of opinion as to the relevant Italian law between the experts who gave evidence before the magistrate and he stated that he preferred the evidence called for the first respondent where there was such a difference of opinion.

My Lords, the appellant, as was his right, thereafter moved the Divisional Court for a writ of habeas corpus. On 20 October 1981 the Divisional Court (Donaldson LJ and Forbes J) refused the motion and also refused the appellant leave to appeal to your Lordships' House. Your Lordships' House, however, subsequently granted leave to appeal.

My Lords, in giving the judgment of the Divisional Court, Donaldson LJ summarised the relevant facts which were not in dispute and for brevity I adopt that summary. By Italian law the appellant's conviction, he having been tried and sentenced 'in contumacia', is valid and final. It follows that if the appellant be extradited no further proceedings can thereafter be taken by him in Italy to secure the review of his conviction and sentence. On any return to that country the appellant must serve that sentence. This has been the position in Italian law since 1931 when the then new Rocco Criminal Code was introduced. Before 1931 and indeed at the time of the Anglo-Italian extradition treaty concluded in 1873 there was in force in Italy a form of conviction and sentence known as 'in contumacia'. Under this procedure the conviction and sentence could be re-opened on the subsequent appearance of the accused and a new trial could be held. Thus the conviction and sentence 'in contumacia' might be described as condition or provisional. But since 1931 the position in Italian law is as I have just stated and as the magistrate and the Divisional Court held. Although an accused since 1931 is given the right to take part in the 'in contumacia' trial if he appears before that trial is concluded, he has no right whatever to a review or to a fresh trial once that trial has been finished.

My Lords, the sole question for your Lordships to determine is whether the appellant, having been convicted and sentenced 'in contumacia' pursuant to the 1931 legislation, is liable to extradition under the Extradition Act 1870 and the Anglo-Italian extradition treaty of 1873. In connection with the treaty, I should mention that on the outbreak of war between the United Kingdom and Italy in 1940 that treaty was abrogated. But, following the conclusion of the Treaty of Peace between the United Kingdom and Italy in 1947, this and other treaties were revived by an exchange of notes dated 13 March 1948, of which your Lordships were provided with copies.

My Lords, the Extradition Act 1870 authorised Her Majesty by Order in Council to direct that, where an arrangement was made with any foreign state with respect to the surrender to that state of any fugitive criminals, the Act should apply in the case of that state. Section 10 of the 1870 Act distinguishes clearly between a fugitive criminal accused of an extradition crime, as defined, and a fugitive criminal alleged to have been convicted of such a crime. The relevant part of s 10 of the 1870 Act reads thus:

'In the case of a fugitive criminal accused of an extradition crime, if the foreign warrant authorising the arrest of such criminal is duly authenticated, and such evidence is produced as (subject to the provisions of this Act) would, according to the law of England, justify the committal for trial of the prisoner if the crime of which he is accused had been committed in England, the police magistrate shall commit him to prison, but otherwise shall order him to be discharged. In the case of a fugitive criminal alleged to have been convicted of an extradition crime, if such evidence is produced as (subject to the provisions of this Act) would, according to the law of England, prove that the prisoner was convicted of such crime, the police magistrate shall commit him to prison, but otherwise shall order him to be discharged . . .'

It was not disputed that the crime in respect of which the appellant had been convicted and sentenced in Bologna was an extradition crime.

But my Lords, s 26 of the 1870 Act, the definition section, includes the following definitions:

'The terms "conviction" and "convicted" do not include or refer to a conviction which under foreign law is a conviction for contumacy, but the term "accused person" includes a person so convicted for contumacy.'

It will be observed that the phrase 'conviction for contumacy' is not defined but the definition of 'conviction' and 'convicted' clearly envisages that there may be what can properly be called a 'conviction for contumacy' under a number of different systems of foreign law.

As already stated, in 1873 the extradition treaty was concluded between the then newly incorporated Kingdom of Italy and the United Kingdom. I need only draw your Lordships' attention to parts of art IX of that treaty.

'. . . The demand for the extradition of an accused person must be accompanied by a warrant of arrest issued by the competent authority of the State applying for the extradition, and by such proof as, according to the law of the place where the fugitive is found, would justify his arrest if the crime had been committed there.

If the requisition relates to a person convicted, it must be accompanied by the sentence of condemnation of the competent Court of the State applying for the extradition.

The demand for extradition must not be founded upon a sentence *in contumacia*.'

My Lords, here again the contrast between extradition of 'an accused person' and of 'a person convicted' is emphasised as in the 1870 Act. The last paragraph of art IX seems to me clearly to be referring to and only to the immediately preceding paragraph, that is to say to persons who have been convicted. It will be observed that the English version of the last paragraph speaks of 'a sentence *in contumacia*' and not of 'a conviction for contumacy'. But I think it is clear that the phrase 'a sentence *in contumacia*' refers to the whole process of trial culminating in conviction and sentence and not just to the final stage of the passing of sentence.

My Lords, following the conclusion of the treaty and in furtherance of the powers conferred on Her Majesty by s 2 of the 1870 Act, an Order in Council was made on 17 March 1874 which, after reciting the entirety of the treaty, ordered that the 1870 Act should apply to the Kingdom of Italy.

My Lords, the principal submission for the appellant which was rejected both by the magistrate and by the Divisional Court was that the present case fell within the exception in s 26 and in art IX as being 'a conviction for contumacy' or 'a sentence *in contumacia*'. Counsel for the appellant accepted on his behalf that there was no relevant difference between the two phrases. It was contended that since 1931 the fact that the proceedings were described as 'in contumacia' was enough to bring this case within s 26 and the last paragraph of art IX, and that it was illegitimate to look behind the phrase in order to determine whether the proceedings fell within or without those provisions. It was accepted, as I have already stated, that there was in 1931 a complete change in the nature and effect of these proceedings 'in contumacia' but it was said that the nomenclature had remained the same and that was enough.

My Lords, shortly before the passing of the 1870 Act, *Re Coppin* (1866) LR 2 Ch App 47 had been decided by Lord Chelmsford LC sitting at first instance. The proceedings arose under earlier Extradition Acts. Extradition was sought by the French government on the ground that Coppin was an accused person. Coppin applied to the Lord Chancellor for a writ of habeas corpus. He had been convicted by a Paris court of competent jurisdiction in his absence of forgery and fraud. The judgment by which he was convicted was a judgment 'par contumace'. It was urged on his behalf that he had already been convicted in France and that the English court was bound to accept the fact of that conviction without looking at the nature of the proceedings on which the conviction was founded (see LR 2 Ch App 47 at 53). Lord Chelmsford LC emphatically rejected this argument. Expert evidence was called as to the nature of those proceedings. This evidence made it plain that if following the conviction 'par contumace' Coppin had surrendered the conviction was annulled and he would be tried as if no proceedings had already been taken against him. Lord Chelmsford LC took the view, after reciting the relevant provisions of the French Criminal Code and setting out the effect of the expert evidence to which he had listened as to its effect, that it was impossible to treat Coppin otherwise than as an accused person. Accordingly Coppin was ordered to be detained with a view to extradition.

My Lords, two comments should be made on this decision which has stood unchallenged for over a century. First, it negatives the contention that an English court must look only at the name of the process and not receive expert evidence as to its true nature. Second, it was accepted on the appellant's behalf that the purpose of the provision in s 26 of the 1870 Act, to which I have already referred, was to give statutory effect to the decision in *Re Coppin* so as to ensure that a person convicted 'in contumacy' was not to be treated as a convicted person but was to be included in the category of 'an accused person'.

The language of this provision to my mind clearly contemplates that the English court will receive evidence of the relevant foreign law, and having done so will then decide in the light of its findings on that foreign law, which is of course a question of fact, whether or not the conviction in question could properly be described as a 'conviction in contumacy' within the meaning of the statute, that phrase being, as I have already pointed out, left undefined in the statute.

My Lords, in my view precisely the same reasoning must apply to the construction of the relevant part of art IX of the treaty. The English court must inform itself by expert evidence, where the application for extradition asserts that the person whose extradition is sought is a convicted person, whether the demand is founded on a sentence 'in contumacia'. That evidence will show whether or not the conviction on which the demand is founded bears the characteristics of a conviction or sentence 'in contumacy', so that the whole matter can be reopened in the event of subsequent surrender and appearance. If it can, then the person concerned must not be treated as a convicted person but as an accused person.

My Lords, I think this is the reasoning underlying the decision of the Divisional Court in *Re Caborn-Waterfield* [1960] 2 All ER 178, [1960] 2 QB 498, which in some respects is the obverse of the present case. Caborn-Waterfield had been convicted in France in his absence by virtue of a 'jugement itératif défaut', a procedure which the evidence showed was not included in the concept of a conviction 'par contumace' since persons in the latter category were able to be retried on their surrender while people in the former category would on surrender begin serving their sentence without more ado. Extradition had been sought by the French government on the grounds that Caborn-Waterfield was a suspected and an accused person. In support of the application it was argued that the English courts were bound by the fact of the conviction in France. But it was argued for Caborn-Waterfield that he was a convicted person and not simply a suspected and accused person and therefore could not be extradited as such. The judgment of the Divisional Court (Lord Parker CJ, Ashworth and Salmon J) was delivered by Salmon J. The Divisional Court reluctantly accepted the argument for Caborn-Waterfield. It did so after a close examination of the different procedures available in France. The court distinguished between a conviction 'par contumace' and 'par défaut' on the one hand and a conviction by 'jugement itératif défaut' on the other and concluded that the procedure in question prevented the reopening of the case on any surrender by Caborn-Waterfield. Accordingly, Caborn-Waterfield had not been convicted 'par contumace' and could not be extradited as an accused person.

Re Caborn-Waterfield was in my view clearly correctly decided and is plain authority against the view that the English court will not look at the nature or substance of the conviction on the basis of which extradition is sought. *Re Caborn-Waterfield* was considered by your Lordships' House in *Athanassiadis v Government of Greece* [1969] 3 All ER 293, [1971] AC 282, a case decided in 1967 but only reported some years later. There is no suggestion in the latter case that *Re Caborn-Waterfield* was wrongly decided. My Lords, I do not however think that the *Athanassiadis* case assists the determination of the present appeal because, as the evidence ultimately placed before your Lordships' House showed, there was no Greek criminal procedure akin to 'par contumace' or 'in contumacia' and accordingly the person whose extradition was sought was properly treated as a convicted and not as an accused person.

My Lords, in my opinion, notwithstanding the name given to, or one might say the label attaching to, the Italian procedure pursuant to which the appellant was convicted and sentenced in his absence, your Lordships should look at the true nature and effect of that procedure as it has operated in Italy since 1931. This I have already explained. When this has been done, it seems to me apparent that the decision of the magistrates and of the Divisional Court were correct and I would dismiss this appeal.

LORD BRANDON OF OAKBROOK. My Lords, I have had the advantage of reading in draft the speech prepared by my noble and learned friend Lord Roskill. I agree with it and would dismiss the appeal accordingly.

Appeal dismissed.

Solicitors: *Winstanley-Burgess* (for the appellant); *Colombotti & Partners* (for the government of Italy); *Director of Public Prosecutions.*

Mary Rose Plummer   Barrister.

R v Varley

COURT OF APPEAL, CRIMINAL DIVISION
GRIFFITHS LJ, KILNER BROWN AND HIRST JJ
I, 18 FEBRUARY 1982

Criminal evidence – Character of accused – Evidence against co-accused – Evidence against – Meaning – Guidelines for determining whether accused has given evidence against co-accused – Right of co-accused to cross-examine where evidence has been given against him – Criminal Evidence Act 1898, s 1(f)(iii).

The appellant and D were jointly charged with robbery. At their trial D admitted that they had both participated in the robbery but stated that he had been forced to do so by threats on his life by the appellant. The appellant denied that he had taken any part in the robbery and asserted that D's evidence was untrue. On the basis that the appellant's evidence was evidence 'against' D for the purposes of s 1(f)(iii)[a] of the Criminal Evidence Act 1898, D's counsel applied for and was granted leave to cross-examine the appellant as to his previous convictions. D and the appellant were both convicted. The appellant appealed, contending that his evidence was not evidence 'against' D and that leave to cross-examine him about his previous convictions should not have been granted.

Held – (1) In deciding for the purposes of s 1(f)(iii) of the 1898 Act whether evidence given by an accused was 'evidence against' his co-accused the principles to be applied were (a) that the term 'evidence against' a co-accused in s 1(f)(iii) meant evidence which supported the prosecution case in a material respect or which undermined the defence of the co-accused, (b) that, where it was established that a person jointly charged had given evidence against a co-defendant, that defendant had the right to cross-examine the other as to previous convictions, and the trial judge had no discretion to refuse an application to do so, (c) that evidence against a co-accused might be given either in chief or during cross-examination, (d) that it was to be objectively decided whether the evidence supported the prosecution case in a material respect or undermined the defence of the co-defendant, hostile intent being irrelevant, (e) that, where consideration had to be given to the question whether the co-accused's defence was undermined, care had be taken to see that the evidence was clearly to that effect; inconvenience to or inconsistency with the co-accused's defence was not of itself sufficient, (f) that a mere denial of participation in a joint venture was not of itself enough to rank as evidence against a co-defendant; for s 1(f)(iii) to apply the denial had to lead to the conclusion that if the witness did not participate then it must have been the other defendant who did, and (g) that, where one defendant asserted a view of the joint venture which was directly contradicted by the other, that contradiction might be evidence against the co-defendant (see p 522 b to f, post); *R v Ellis* [1961] 2 All ER 928, *R v Stannard* [1964] 1 All ER 34, *Murdoch v Taylor* [1965] 1 All ER 406, *R v Davis (Alan Douglas)* [1975] 1 All ER 233, *R v Bruce* [1975] 3 All ER 277 and *R v Hatton* (1976) 64 Cr App R 88 applied.

(2) The appellant's evidence was 'evidence against' his co-accused for the purposes of s 1(f)(iii) because it not only contradicted the evidence of D and amounted to an assertion that D was lying but also led to the conclusion that he had participated in the crime on his own and had not acted under duress. It followed that the judge had been right to rule that cross-examination as to the appellant's previous convictions was permissible. The appeal would therefore be dismissed (see p 522 f g, post).

Notes

For admissibility of evidence of bad character and cross-examination of the defendant as

---

a   Section 1, so far as material, is set out at p 521 *f*, post

to character, see 11 Halsbury's Laws (4th edn) paras 388–389, and for cases on the subject, see 14(2) Digest (Reissue) 644–645, 5206–5215.

For the Criminal Evidence Act 1898, s 1, see 12 Halsbury's Statutes (3rd edn) 865.

Cases referred to in judgment

Murdoch v Taylor [1965] 1 All ER 406, [1965] AC 574, [1965] 2 WLR 425, HL, 14(2) Digest (Reissue) 634, 5135.

R v Bruce [1975] 3 All ER 277, [1975] 1 WLR 1252, CA, 14(2) Digest (Reissue) 644, 5209.

R v Davis (Alan Douglas) [1975] 1 All ER 233, [1975] 1 WLR 345, CA, 14(2) Digest (Reissue) 634, 5136.

R v Ellis, R v Ellis [1961] 2 All ER 928, [1961] 1 WLR 1064, CCA, 14(2) Digest (Reissue) 644, 5208.

R v Hatton (1976) 64 Cr App R 88, CA.

R v Stannard [1964] 1 All ER 34, [1965] 2 QB 1, [1964] 2 WLR 461, CCA, 14(2) Digest (Reissue) 645, 5211.

Appeal

On 15 September 1980 in the Crown Court at Bristol before his Honour Judge Hutton and a jury the appellant, Raymond John Varley, was convicted of robbery (count 1) and of possessing a firearm at the time of the commission of an offence of theft (count 2), and was sentenced to 12 years' imprisonment on count 1 and to a concurrent term of five years' imprisonment on count 2. He appealed against conviction by leave of the full court (O'Connor LJ, Kilner Brown and McCowan JJ) and applied for leave to appeal against sentence. The facts are set out in the judgment of the court.

Lionel Read QC and *Stewart Patterson* (assigned by the Registrar of Criminal Appeals) for the appellant.

James W Black QC and *Charles Barton* for the Crown.

Cur adv vult

18 February.   **KILNER BROWN J** read the following judgment of the court: The appellant was convicted on 15 September 1980 in the Crown Court at Bristol of an offence of robbery and an offence of possession of a firearm at the time of committing an offence of theft. He was sentenced to concurrent terms of 12 years' imprisonment on the first count and five years' imprisonment on the second. He now appeals against conviction by leave of the full court and applies for leave to appeal against sentence.

The appellant was jointly charged on the indictment with a young man named Dibble, who was aged 19, but who was already a sophisticated young criminal with convictions for theft, burglary, dishonest handling and assault occasioning actual bodily harm. He had already served three months in a detention centre and a period of borstal training. The appellant was aged 29 and had many convictions to his discredit, including two for robbery, the first of which, in April 1975, earned for him a three-year sentence of imprisonment and the second of which was in March 1977, when he was sentenced to six years' imprisonment.

He was on weekend leave from prison when the offence of robbery occurred on 17 April 1980. On that day, a man armed with a sawn-off shotgun raided a sub-post office in the Bridlington area of Bristol and made off with some £1,672 odd. This man was identified by a woman who said it was the appellant. Other witnesses saw a man running away with something which looked like an iron bar wrapped in a jumper but were unable to say that it was the appellant. As it happened, the appellant overstayed his leave and went to stay with a man named Clarke and his wife. Clarke shared the use of a van with Dibble, who was known to have been driving it about, and the prosecution case was that this was the getaway vehicle. At one stage Clarke was arrested as well as the

appellant and Dibble and the appellant was at pains, during the time he was being
a questioned, to exonerate Clarke. He admitted his part in the robbery and Clarke was
released without being charged.

Now Dibble had made a statement implicating the appellant. Evidence was given
that whilst they were all three in custody, the appellant had said to Dibble: 'It's all right
Tony, I'm not going to get you. Look, tomorrow, when we get to Court, I'll even say I
forced you to take me down there. I did it, not you.' The appellant stoutly denied saying
b this. However, whether he did or did not and whether or not this inspired the manner
of Dibble's defence in court, or whether the idea came to Dibble spontaneously, the fact
remains that, at the trial, Dibble's defence was that he did take part but was forced to do
so by threats made by the appellant against his life and only acted under duress. The
appellant, at the trial, resiled from his oral admissions saying that they had been falsely
made in order to protect and exonerate his friend Clarke. So, at the trial, there was
c Dibble saying that both of them took part, but that he should be acquitted because he
acted under duress imposed on him by the appellant and there was the appellant saying
that he was not there at all and that Dibble's evidence was untrue.

Now was Dibble's evidence 'against' the appellant? Clearly it was. Was the appellant's
testimony evidence 'against' Dibble? That is what this appeal is all about. Fortunately,
in the interests of justice, the jury learned about Dibble's criminal history because he was
d cross-examined about his convictions. The jury rejected his defence of duress and
convicted him of participation in the robbery but acquitted him of possession of the
firearm. He was sentenced to a term of 18 months' imprisonment.

The trial reached the stage of cross-examination of Varley by counsel on behalf of
Dibble when, knowing the nature of Dibble's case, he applied for leave to put questions
as to Varley's previous convictions on the basis that his evidence was evidence against
e Dibble. He made the application relying on the words of s 1(f)(iii) of the Criminal
Evidence Act 1898, citing the case of *Murdoch v Taylor* [1965] 1 All ER 406, [1965] AC
574, in which the House of Lords applied and followed the reasoning of the Court of
Criminal Appeal in *R v Stannard* [1964] 1 All ER 34, [1965] 2 QB 1. The relevant parts
of the section read as follows:

f '(f) A person charged and called as a witness in pursuance of this Act shall not be
asked, and if asked shall not be required to answer, any question tending to show
that he has committed or been convicted of or been charged with any offence other
than that wherewith he is then charged, or is of bad character, unless . . . (iii) he has
given evidence against any other person charged with the same offence.'

The operation of this particular part of the proviso seems to have given rise to no
g difficulty and no detailed analysis for well over 60 years. No doubt, as Lord Pearce
indicated in his speech in *Murdoch v Taylor* [1965] 1 All ER 406 at 411, [1965] AC 574
at 586, 'the practice and the general view of bench and bar alike was that a judge had a
discretion whether to give leave to cross-examine under s. 1(f)(iii)' and, in difficult cases
where it was not easy to determine whether the evidence could be categorised as 'against'
or where such questioning could well be unduly prejudicial, a judge would decline to
h rule that the proposed questions could be put. But this discretionary power was removed
from trial judges by the Court of Criminal Appeal in *R v Ellis, R v Ellis* [1961] 2 All ER
928, [1961] 1 WLR 1064, when it was decided that cross-examination of a co-defendant
who had given evidence against a person jointly charged with him was a matter of right
and not of discretion.

The decision was approved by four of the Lords of Appeal (Lord Pearce dissenting) in
j *Murdoch's* case [1965] 1 All ER 406, [1965] AC 574. This decision created difficult
problems in practice because either to establish or to destroy this right involved, in many
cases, an acute analysis of whether or not the evidence which had been given was 'against'
the other party charged. It sparked off a whole series of cases which have come before
this court and at least the one (*Murdoch's* case) in the House of Lords. The instant case is
a very good example of the additional burden placed on the trial judge. The application

and the resistance to it occupied many hours of judicial time and took up no less than 57
pages of recorded transcript.

Although the judgment of the Court of Criminal Appeal in *R v Stannard* [1964] 1 All
ER 34, [1965] 2 QB 1 was undoubtedly meant to have been of assistance to trial judges
in their consideration of whether evidence was 'against' or not, in practice, it has in fact
added to their burden and it has caused considerable anxiety to other divisions of this
court as it did to Lord Reid and was tacitly ignored by Lord Morris in *Murdoch's* case.
What was the nature of the guidance in *R v Stannard* [1964] 1 All ER 34, [1965] 2 QB 1?
It was this, approved as amended by Lord Donovan in *Murdoch's* case [1965] 1 All ER 406
at 416, [1965] AC 574 at 592: '. . ."evidence against" means evidence which supports the
prosecution's case in a material respect or which undermines the defence of the co-
accused.' There are three reported cases in the Court of Appeal, Criminal Division, in
which this interpretation has been considered and to which we were referred. They are
R v Davis (Alan Douglas) [1975] 1 All ER 233, [1975] 1 WLR 345, *R v Bruce* [1975] 3 All
ER 277, [1975] 1 WLR 1252 and *R v Hatton* (1976) 64 Cr App R 88. Now, putting all the
reported cases together, are there established principles which might serve as guidance to
trial judges when called on to give rulings in this very difficult area of the law? We
venture to think that they are these and, if they are borne in mind, it may not be
necessary to investigate all the relevant authorities. (1) If it is established that a person
jointly charged has given evidence against the co-defendant that defendant has a right to
cross-examine the other as to previous convictions and the trial judge has no discretion
to refuse an application. (2) Such evidence may be given either in chief or during cross-
examination. (3) It has to be objectively decided whether the evidence either supports
the prosecution case in a material respect or undermines the defence of the co-accused.
A hostile intent is irrelevant. (4) If consideration has to be given to the undermining of
the other's defence care must be taken to see that the evidence clearly undermines the
defence. Inconvenience to or inconsistency with the other's defence is not of itself
sufficient. (5) Mere denial of participation in a joint venture is not of itself sufficient to
rank as evidence against the co-defendant. For the proviso to apply, such denial must
lead to the conclusion that if the witness did not participate then it must have been the
other who did. (6) Where the one defendant asserts or in due course would assert one
view of the joint venture which is directly contradicted by the other such contradiction
may be evidence against the co-defendant.

We apply these principles to the facts of this case and particularly the latter two. Here
was Dibble going to say, as he did, that he took part in the joint venture because he was
forced to do so by Varley. The appellant, Varley, was saying that he was not a participant
and had not gone with Dibble and had not forced Dibble to go. His evidence therefore
was against Dibble because it amounted to saying that not only was Dibble telling lies
but that Dibble would be left as a participant on his own and not acting under duress.
In our view, the judge was right to rule that cross-examination as to previous convictions
was permissible. This ground of appeal is rejected.

The other ground put forward was that the judge wrongly exercised his discretion by
refusing to order separate trials. We recognise that there may well be occasions where
there has been a successful application to cross-examine a co-defendant on his convictions
and the trial judge, in his duty to ensure a fair trial, may properly exercise a discretion to
order separate trials. We have in mind the situation where the effect of such cross-
examination is such as to create such undue prejudice that a fair trial is impossible. But
that is not this case. The truth of the matter is that this was a case where two experienced
criminals metaphorically cut each other's throats in the course of their respective
defences. If separate trials had been ordered, one or other or both might have succeeded
in preventing a just result. This ground of appeal is also rejected and the appeal against
conviction is dismissed.

Turning now to sentence, there is an application for leave to appeal. As has already
been observed, he was sentenced to 12 years' imprisonment for the robbery and five
years' concurrent imprisonment for possession of a firearm. This was a typically bad case

of armed robbery when a sawn-off shotgun was used to threaten, but not fired. The applicant was aged 29 at the time and was actually an overstayer on leave from prison, where he was serving a six-year sentence for robbery imposed in March 1977. He had previously been sentenced in April 1975 to three years' imprisonment also for robbery. He had begun his catalogue of convictions in June 1969, when he was sent to borstal training for malicious wounding. Thereafter, leniency had been tried by way of probation and conditional discharge. He is plainly a determined and dangerous man. The sentence was entirely appropriate and the application for leave to appeal against sentence is refused.

Appeal against conviction dismissed. Leave to appeal against sentence refused.

Solicitors: *R O M Lovibond,* Bristol.

Sepala Munasinghe Esq   Barrister.

R v Secretary of State for the Home Department, ex parte Khawaja

COURT OF APPEAL, CIVIL DIVISION
LORD DENNING MR, EVELEIGH AND DONALDSON LJJ
17, 18, 26 FEBRUARY 1982

Immigration – Leave to enter – Non-patrial – Right of entry – Duty to disclose facts – Vitiation of leave to enter by non-disclosure – Immigrant seeking entry required to disclose material facts decisively affecting grant of leave to enter – Failure to disclose material facts vitiating leave to enter.

The applicant, who was a Pakistani national living in Belgium, paid a sum of money to a woman, B, living in England to facilitate the applicant's entry into the United Kingdom. In March 1980 he arrived at Manchester airport and told the immigration officer that he had come for a visit of one week. Consequently the immigration officer granted him limited leave to enter for one month. In April he married B in England. The applicant then applied to the Home Office for an extension of his leave to enter, stating that he desired to visit members of his family in the United Kingdom but not mentioning his marriage. Subsequently he informed the Home Office that he had married B and applied for indefinite leave to remain. The Home Office rejected his application and decided that his leave to enter had been vitiated by deception and that he was to be treated as an illegal entrant who had no right of appeal while in the United Kingdom and who could only appeal against the refusal of leave to enter after he had been deported. The Home Office accordingly authorised the detention of the applicant pending deportation. The applicant applied for an order to quash the detention on the ground that he was not an illegal entrant but merely a person who had overstayed his leave and was consequently entitled to remain in the United Kingdom until his appeal was finally decided. The judge dismissed the application, holding that, although in exceptional circumstances a false representation would not vitiate leave to enter, the applicant's deception was sufficiently material to the grant of leave to enter to vitiate that leave and render him an illegal entrant with no right of appeal in the United Kingdom. The applicant appealed.

Held – Where an immigrant who sought leave to enter the United Kingdom had, by fraud and non-disclosure, concealed facts material to the grant of leave to enter, which if disclosed would in all probability have induced the immigration authorities to refuse leave altogether, the deception rendered the leave to enter voidable and entitled the Secretary of State to treat such a person as an illegal entrant. Since the applicant had *a* obtained leave to enter by a false and fraudulent representation and the Secretary of State had elected to treat the leave granted as being void, the applicant was an illegal entrant liable to be detained and deported with no right of appeal while in the United Kingdom (see p 525 *j*, p 526 *c* to *h* and p 527 *g* to *j*, post).

Mackender v Feldia AG [1966] 3 All ER 847, *Zamir v Secretary of State for the Home Dept* [1980] 2 All ER 768 and *R v Secretary of State for the Home Dept, ex p Jayakody* [1982] 1 All *b* ER 461 applied.

Notes
For illegal entry into the United Kingdom, see 4 Halsbury's Laws (4th edn) paras 976, 1027.

Cases referred to in judgments   *c*
Mackender v Feldia AG [1966] 3 All ER 847, [1967] 2 QB 590, [1967] 2 WLR 119, CA, 50 Digest (Repl) 341, 689.
R v Secretary of State for the Home Dept, ex p Jayakody [1982] 1 All ER 461, [1982] 1 WLR 405, CA.
Zamir v Secretary of State for the Home Dept [1980] 2 All ER 768, [1980] AC 930, [1980] 3 *d* WLR 249, HL.

Case also cited
Goordin v Secretary of State for the Home Dept [1981] CA Bound Transcript 368.

Appeal   *e*
Salamatullah Khawaja appealed against the decision of Forbes J, hearing the Crown office list, on 11 November 1981 dismissing an application for judicial review by way of (i) an order of certiorari to quash the decision of the Secretary of State that the applicant was an illegal entrant under the Immigration Act 1971 and authorising the detention of the applicant under para 16(2) of Sch 2 of the 1971 Act and (ii) an order of mandamus directing the Secretary of State to redetermine the application for variation of leave made *f* by the applicant on 11 April 1980. The facts are set out in the judgment of Lord Denning MR.

Sibghatullah Kadri for the applicant.
Andrew Collins for the Secretary of State.

Cur adv vult   *g*

26 February. The following judgments were read.

LORD DENNING MR. This case is about Salamatullah Khawaja. I will call him SK. He was born in Pakistan in 1940. He did well and became the manager of a silk mill at Lahore. In October 1978 he enrolled at the University of Brussels as a student for an industrial course for two years. Whilst there in August 1979 he applied to the British *h* Embassy for a visa to come to the United Kingdom as a visitor for two weeks. This application took some time to process. Meanwhile the immigration authorities were told by an informant that he had paid £10,000 to a Pakistani woman in England, by name Mrs Butt, so as to facilitate his entry into the United Kingdom. So the British Embassy in Brussels were instructed to refuse his application to come here.

But SK did not wait for the refusal. He jumped the gun. Whilst his application was *j* being processed, and before the result of it was known, he came to England on 17 March 1980. He arrived at Manchester airport and told the immigration officer that he had come for one week to visit his cousin here. He was in possession of a return ticket for 23 March 1980. It appeared genuine. So the immigration officer granted him limited leave to stay for one month.

It so happened that on the same aircraft there was this Mrs Butt. She went to a
a different desk at Manchester airport. She produced a passport. It described her as Mrs
Butt going back to 1973, and containing in 1977 an entry of 'indefinite leave to enter'.
She told the immigration officer that she had divorced her husband, Mr Butt, and had
remarried SK. There was an entry to this effect in her passport. So she was allowed to
enter. The immigration officer did not know that SK had got in at a different desk.

SK went to solicitors in Rochdale. On 11 April 1980 the solicitors applied for an
b extension of his visa. They said:

'Our client has come to this country to visit the several members of his family
here, whom he has not seen for many years, having been studying for some time at
Brussels University. Our client wishes to obtain an extension of his visa and we
enclose herewith his passport for consideration by your Department of his request,
and endorsement of the passport if granted.'

c
The Home Office by this time were on their guard. They looked into the matter
closely. It then appeared that Mrs Butt had a chequered history. She had married a Mr
Butt in Rochdale in 1975. She had got a decree nisi of divorce on 24 January 1980. It was
made absolute on 3 April 1980. Meanwhile, in December 1979 she had gone through
a Moslem marriage with SK in Brussels. On 10 April 1980 she married SK in Rochdale.
d Then on 29 April 1980 SK's solicitors applied for indefinite leave to remain. His
solicitors made great play with his marriage to Mrs Butt. They said:

'Mr. Khawaja has since visited our office and informs us that he was actually
married on 10th April, 1980 to Mrs. Nusrat Butt, who was formerly known prior
to her previous marriage to Mohammed Aslam Butt, as Nusrat Dar (certificate
enclosed herewith). Mrs. Butt was actually divorced from Mohammed Aslam Butt
e during 1979, having been given leave to enter the United Kingdom for an indefinite
period, two years prior to that. Mr. Khawaja has asked to inform you that he now
wishes to obtain indefinite leave to remain here himself and also that his wife is
expecting a child by him in approximately one month's time. We are, therefore,
asked to request you to consider his application for indefinite leave to remain here
and we await to hear from you in reply.'

The Home Office rejected his application. They made many inquiries and came to the
conclusion that his leave to enter was vitiated by deception. They decided to treat him
as an illegal entrant. They made a detention order in these terms:

'To Salamatullah Khawaja
     Having considered all the information available to me I am satisfied that there are
f reasonable grounds to conclude that you are an illegal entrant in accordance with
the provisions of the Immigration Act 1971. I have therefore authorised your
detention in Manchester Airport under the provisions of paragraph 16(2) of
Schedule 2 of the Act pending the completion of arrangements for dealing with you
under the Act.'

g SK applied at once for judicial review. He asked for the detention order to be quashed
on the ground that he was not an illegal entrant but an overstayer. The difference is of
the first importance. If he is treated as an illegal entrant, he has no appeal whilst in this
country. He must go back to Pakistan and appeal from there. But, if he is treated as an
overstayer, he can appeal here to an adjudicator and can remain here until his appeal is
finally determined, which may be a long time.

Now when an immigrant obtains 'indefinite leave to enter' and that leave is vitiated by
fraud or non-disclosure, it is clear that he is an 'illegal entrant' and can be deported. If he
wishes to appeal, he must do it from overseas: see *Zamir v Secretary of State for the Home
Dept* [1980] 2 All ER 768, [1980] AC 930.

Counsel for SK says that the present case is different because SK obtained a *limited* leave
to enter. It was for one month. He then applied for a variation so as to have it

extended. Such a case, says counsel, is governed by r 88 of the Statement of Changes in
Immigration Rules (HC Paper (1979–80) no 394) which makes him an overstayer. It   *a*
says:

> '. . . refusal will be the normal course if the applicant has made false representations
> in obtaining leave to enter (including the giving of undertakings, express or implied,
> which he has not honoured, as to the duration and purpose of his stay); if he has not
> observed the time limit or conditions subject to which he was admitted, or given
> leave to remain . . .'   *b*

So counsel for SK says that refusal to vary only makes him an overstayer. It does not
make him an illegal entrant. Whereas counsel for the Secretary of State says that his
deception may sometimes make him an illegal entrant. In order to decide the point,
much help is to be obtained from the cases on the effect of fraud on a simple contract or
of non-disclosure on a contract of insurance. Such fraud or non-disclosure does not   *c*
automatically vitiate the contract. It only makes it voidable. It gives the other party a
right to elect. When he discovers the deception, he can either avoid the contract or
affirm it: see *Mackender v Feldia AG* [1966] 3 All ER 847 at 849–850, [1967] 2 QB 590 at
598.

Likewise when a man obtains a limited leave to enter by fraud or non-disclosure. As
soon as it is discovered, it is open to the Home Secretary either to avoid the leave or to   *d*
affirm it. If he elects to avoid the leave, the effect is that the man is to be treated as an
illegal entrant and liable, as such, to be detained and deported. But, if the Home
Secretary elects to affirm the leave, the effect is that he is to be treated as an overstayer,
who is at liberty to apply for a variation. If it is refused, he can appeal to an adjudicator
and stay here until his appeal is disposed of.

We were told by counsel for the Secretary of State that in most of these cases the Home   *e*
Secretary treats the man as an overstayer. But that in cases of gross deception (by fraud
or non-disclosure) he treats the man as an illegal entrant. I regard that as an entirely
proper way of exercising his election. The Home Secretary looks into the case. If he
thinks that the fraud or non-disclosure was of most material facts, such that the
immigration officer would in all probability have refused the leave altogether had he
known the truth, then the Home Secretary may treat the man as an illegal entrant. But   *f*
if it was not of that character, he may treat him as an overstayer: see *R v Secretary of State
for the Home Dept, ex p Jayakody* [1982] 1 All ER 461, [1982] 1 WLR 405.

In our present case SK made a false and fraudulent representation that he intended to
stay only one month; whereas, in fact, he had conspired with Mrs Butt to stay indefinitely
and to give credence to it by going through a form of marriage with her. It was a piece
of gross deception. The Home Secretary was quite entitled to treat him as an illegal   *g*
entrant. I would dismiss the appeal accordingly.

EVELEIGH LJ. I have had the advantage of reading the judgments of Lord Denning
MR and of Donaldson LJ, and I respectfully agree with them.

DONALDSON LJ. By s 14 of the Immigration Act 1971 a person who has limited   *h*
leave to enter and remain in the United Kingdom has a right of appeal to an adjudicator
against any variation of the leave or against any refusal to vary it. A person who has
unlimited leave has no need for any right of appeal and accordingly none is given.

In *Zamir v Secretary of State for the Home Dept* [1980] 2 All ER 768, [1980] AC 930 the
House of Lords held that deception, whether active or passive, vitiates the permission to
enter.

In *R v Secretary of State for the Home Dept, ex p Jayakody* [1982] 1 All ER 461, [1982] 1   *j*
WLR 405 this court held that not every deception vitiated the permission to enter, but
only deception of a decisive character.

Paragraph 88 of the Statement of Changes in Immigration Rules (HC Paper (1979–80)
no 394) states that where application is made to vary leave to enter or to remain, refusal

will be the normal course if the applicant has made 'false representations in obtaining
a leave to enter' and this phrase is amplified in parenthesis. The necessary implication is
that in the abnormal course an application to vary may be granted in these circumstances.

Counsel for the applicant submits that since deception vitiates leave to enter and a
valid and subsisting leave to enter is the necessary prerequisite of an effective application
to vary, there is prima facie a contradiction between *Zamir* and para 88 of the
immigration rules. He submits that this is resolved if *Zamir's* decision is confined to cases
b in which unlimited leave has been obtained and there is, in consequence, no question of
any application to vary and no scope for the application of para 88. I should be more
attracted to this submission if I could see any logical basis for this distinction or if there
was the slightest indication in *Zamir's* case that this was intended.

Counsel for the Secretary of State submits, and Forbes J held, that para 88 contemplates,
as was held in *Jayakody*, that not every false representation will vitiate the leave to
c enter. Accordingly provision was made for how account should be taken of false, but
non-vitiatory, representations. Normally they will be fatal to the application, but
exceptionally they may not be.

I have no doubt that the submission of counsel for the Secretary of State is correct. It
leaves a right of appeal to the adjudicator in the case of minor, that is to say non-decisive,
deceptions, but withholds it in the case of major deception. This is a logical way of
d resolving any superficial contradiction between *Zamir's* case and para 88, whereas a
resolution based on the nature of the leave originally given to the immigrant is not.

This leaves the question of whether any particular deception is vitiatory and how this
is decided. Initially the decision must be that of the Secretary of State or of authorised
officers of the Home Department. But is there any appeal to the adjudicator? Section 14
of the 1971 Act gives a right of appeal only where the applicant has a valid leave under
e the Act and accordingly this issue goes to the adjudicator's jurisdiction. Prima facie no
court or tribunal of limited jurisdiction has power to reach a binding decision on
whether it has jurisdiction, but it can, and no doubt should, decline to act if satisfied in
its own mind that it lacks jurisdiction.

This situation has created difficulties. This can happen where the Secretary of State
does not regard a particular deception as being sufficiently decisive to vitiate a leave to
enter, but refuses an application to vary. If the applicant then appeals to the adjudicator,
who declines to adjudicate because he considers that the deception vitiated the leave
which forms the basis of his jurisdiction, the applicant is deprived of his right of appeal
notwithstanding that the Home Secretary was quite content that he should have it.

This problem does not arise on the facts of the present appeal, but it may be helpful if
I say a word about it. In my judgment material deception vitiates leave to enter in the
f sense that it renders that leave voidable. It is for the Secretary of State to decide whether
to avoid it. If he does so, his decision is reviewable by the courts on ordinary principles
of administrative law. If he does not, the applicant will have no cause to complain and
the leave to enter will remain effective to form a basis for a decision to vary it and to give
the adjudicator jurisdiction if the Secretary of State declines to vary it.

In the present case the Secretary of State has treated the applicant's leave to enter as
voidable and he has avoided it. It is conceded that this decision cannot be attacked on
ordinary principles of administrative law. It follows that there is no extant leave to enter
and no jurisdiction in the Secretary of State or, on appeal, in any adjudicator to make any
variation.

I would dismiss the appeal.

Appeal dismissed.

Solicitors: *Charnley & Afzal*, Manchester (for the applicant); *Treasury Solicitor.*

Diana Procter   Barrister.

R v Kanwar

COURT OF APPEAL, CRIMINAL DIVISION
DUNN LJ, CANTLEY AND SHELDON JJ
2, 8 MARCH 1982

Criminal law – Handling stolen goods – Assisting in their retention – Wife using stolen goods brought home by husband – Wife making verbal representations to police searching house that goods not stolen in order to protect husband – Whether mere use of stolen goods constituting assisting in their retention – Whether verbal representations amounting to 'assisting' in retention of goods – Theft Act 1968, s 22(1).

The appellant's husband brought home some stolen goods which the appellant, who knew they were stolen, used to furnish the house. When the police searched the house the appellant told them there were no stolen goods in the house and, in answer to questions regarding specific articles in the house, lied to the police by saying that she had purchased the articles. The appellant was charged with handling stolen goods by dishonestly assisting in their retention for the benefit of another (her husband), contrary to s 22(1)[a] of the Theft Act 1968. She did not give evidence at her trial and the police evidence of what she had said during the search was uncontradicted. The judge directed the jury that if they were satisfied that the appellant had actively assisted her husband to keep the goods by using them herself in the house she was guilty of the offence charged. The jury found the appellant guilty and she was convicted. The appellant appealed.

Held – On the true construction of s 22(1) of the 1968 Act, merely using stolen goods in the possession of another could not constitute the offence of assisting in their retention, because to constitute that offence the offender had to do something intentionally and dishonestly in order to enable the stolen goods to be retained, such as concealing them. Accordingly, the judge had misdirected the jury. However, to constitute the offence the requisite assistance did not have to be physical assistance: verbal representations dishonestly made for the benefit of another to conceal that goods were stolen, even if unsuccessful, could constitute 'assisting' in the retention of the stolen goods. It followed that, since there was uncontradicted evidence that the appellant had dishonestly represented to the police that the goods were not stolen goods in order to protect her husband, the offence charged had been established and therefore, despite the judge's misdirection, there had been no miscarriage of justice. The appeal would therefore be dismissed (see p 529 g to p 530 b and f g, post).

Notes

For handling stolen goods, see 11 Halsbury's Laws (4th edn) para 1289, and for cases on the subject, see 15 Digest (Reissue) 1362–1363, 11,900–11,904.

For the Theft Act 1968, s 22, see 8 Halsbury's Statutes (3rd edn) 796.

Cases referred to in judgment

R v Sanders (25 February 1982, unreported), CA.
R v Thornhill (15 May 1981, unreported), CA.

Appeal

On 20 November 1980 in the Crown Court at Kingston before his Honour Judge Bax QC and a jury the appellant, Rena Louise Kanwar, was convicted of handling stolen goods by

---

[a] Section 22(1), so far as material, provides: 'A person handles stolen goods if (otherwise than in the course of the stealing) knowing or believing them to be stolen goods he dishonestly . . . assists in their retention . . . by or for the benefit of another person, or if he arranges to do so.'

dishonestly assisting in their retention, for the benefit of another, contrary to s 22 of the Theft Act 1968. She was given a conditional discharge. She appealed against her conviction with leave of the single judge. The facts are set out in the judgment of the court.

Andrew Sharpe (assigned by the Registrar of Criminal Appeals) for the appellant.
John Crocker for the Crown.

Cur adv vult

8 March. **CANTLEY J** read the following judgment of the court: In counts 7 and 9 of an indictment on which she was tried with others, the appellant was charged with dishonestly assisting in the retention of stolen goods for the benefit of Maninder Singh Kanwar, who was her husband. She was convicted and by way of sentence was given a conditional discharge. She now appeals against her conviction.

Her husband had brought the stolen goods to their house where the goods were used in the home. It was conceded that the appellant was not present when the goods were brought to the house. She was in hospital at the time.

On 2 November 1978 police officers, armed with a search warrant, came to the house to look for and take away any goods which they found there which corresponded with a list of stolen goods in their possession. The appellant arrived during the search and was told of the object of the search. She replied: 'There's no stolen property here.'

She was subsequently asked a number of questions with regard to specific articles which were in the house and in reply to those questions, she gave answers which were lies. It is sufficient for present purposes to take two examples. She was asked about a painting which was in the living room and she replied: 'I bought it from a shop. I have a receipt.' The officer said: 'That's not true.' She said: 'Yes, I have.' He said: 'If you can find a receipt, please have a look.' She made some pretence of looking for the receipt but none was produced and ultimately she at least tacitly admitted there was none. The painting is one of the articles in the particulars to count 9.

She was also asked about a mirror which was in the kitchen. This is one of the articles in the particulars to count 7. The officer said: 'What about the mirror?' She said: 'I bought it from the market.' The officer asked: 'When?' She said: 'Sometime last year.' There is no dispute that that answer was a lie as was the answer about the painting. Later on, she was warned that she was telling lies and that the property was stolen. She said: 'No, it isn't. We're trying to build up a nice home.' Ultimately, although the officer had had no intention of arresting her when he came to the house, he did arrest her and she was subsequently charged.

The appellant did not give evidence and the evidence of the police officer stood uncontradicted.

In *R v Thornhill*, decided in this court on 15 May 1981, and in *R v Sanders*, decided in this court on 25 February 1982, both unreported, it was held that merely using stolen goods in the possession of another does not constitute the offence of assisting in their retention. To constitute the offence, something must be done by the offender, and done intentionally and dishonestly, for the purpose of enabling the goods to be retained. Examples of such conduct are concealing or helping to conceal the goods, or doing something to make them more difficult to find or to identify. Such conduct must be done knowing or believing the goods to be stolen and done dishonestly and for the benefit of another.

We see no reason why the requisite assistance should be restricted to physical acts. Verbal representations, whether oral or in writing, for the purpose of concealing the identity of stolen goods may, if made dishonestly and for the benefit of another, amount to handling stolen goods by assisting in their retention within the meaning of s 22 of the Theft Act 1968.

The requisite assistance need not be successful in its object. It would be absurd if a person dishonestly concealing stolen goods for the benefit of a receiver could establish a defence by showing that he was caught in the act. In the present case, if, while the police were in one part of the house, the appellant, in order to conceal the painting had put it under a mattress in the bedroom, it would not alter the nature of her conduct that the police subsequently looked under the mattress and found the picture because they expected to find it there or that they caught her in the act of putting it there.

The appellant told these lies to the police to persuade them that the picture and the mirror were not the stolen property which they had come to take away but were her lawful property which she had bought. If that was true, the articles should be left in the house. She was, of course, telling these lies to protect her husband, who had dishonestly brought the articles there but, in our view, she was nonetheless, at the time, dishonestly assisting in the retention of the stolen articles.

In his summing up, the judge directed the jury as follows:

'It would be quite wrong for you to convict this lady if all she did was to watch her husband bring goods into the house, even if she knew or believed that they were stolen goods because, no doubt, you would say to yourselves, "What would she be expected to do about it?" Well, what the Crown say is that she knew or believed them to be stolen and that she was a knowing and willing party to their being kept in that house in those circumstances. The reason the Crown say that, and we shall be coming to the evidence, is that when questioned about a certain number of items, [the appellant] gave answers which the Crown say were not true and that she could not possibly have believed to be true and that she knew perfectly well were untruthful. So, say the prosecution, she was not just an acquiescent wife who could not do much about it, she was, by her conduct in trying to put the police officers as best she could off the scent, demonstrating that she was a willing and knowing part to those things being there and that she was trying to account for them. Well, it will be for you to say, but you must be satisfied before you can convict her on either of these counts, not only that she knew or believed the goods to be stolen, but that she actively assisted her husband in keeping them there; not by just passive acquiescence in the sense of saying, "What can I do about it?" but in the sense of saying, "How nice to have these things in our home, although they are stolen goods".'

In so far as this direction suggests that the appellant would be guilty of the offence if she was merely willing for the goods to be kept and used in the house and was thinking that it was nice to have them there, although they were stolen goods, it is a misdirection. We have considered whether on that account the conviction ought to be quashed. However, the offence was established by the uncontradicted evidence of the police officer which, looked at in full, clearly shows that in order to mislead the officer who had come to take away stolen goods, she misrepresented the identity of the goods which she knew or believed to be stolen. We are satisfied that no miscarriage of justice has occurred and the appeal is accordingly dismissed.

Appeal dismissed.

Solicitors: *R E T Birch.*

Sepala Munasinghe Esq   Barrister.

Court v Court

FAMILY DIVISION
ARNOLD P
16 DECEMBER 1981

Divorce – Decree absolute – Application for leave to apply for decree to be made absolute – Application made out of time – Cohabitation after decree nisi – Wife's cohabitation after decree nisi reasonable in all the circumstances – Whether court should exercise discretion to make decree absolute out of time notwithstanding cohabitation after decree nisi – Matrimonial Causes Rules 1977, r 65(2) proviso.

In 1979 the wife filed a petition for divorce on the ground that the husband had behaved in such a way that she could not reasonably be expected to live with him. The petition alleged substantial acts of violence and threatened violence by the husband. The petition was undefended and in July 1979 the wife was granted a decree nisi. She was then in a vulnerable position because her family had rejected her, she had no friends and she had three children by a previous marriage and a young child by the husband to look after. She therefore succumbed to the husband's insistent persuasion that they attempt a reconciliation and in about October 1979 she resumed cohabitation with him. Soon afterwards, the husband began to ill-treat her again. Nevertheless, in June 1980, being too afraid to tell anyone about the husband's violence, she moved with him and the children into new accommodation offered to them by the local authority. After the move she ceased to perform any services for the husband and they lived separate lives in the accommodation. After six months, in December 1980, the husband left the accommodation. Within days of his departure the wife consulted solicitors about having the decree nisi made absolute but the solicitors made no progress in the matter and it was not until June 1981, after the wife had consulted different solicitors, that an application was made to the registrar for the decree nisi to be made absolute more than 12 months after the grant of the decree nisi. The registrar referred the application to a judge. The judge had before him both affidavit and oral evidence by the wife regarding the circumstances of the attempted reconciliation and the period of cohabitation after the decree nisi. The question arose whether the court could, if the parties had cohabited after the decree nisi, exercise its discretion under the proviso to r 65(2)[a] of the Matrimonial Causes Rules 1977 to make the decree absolute notwithstanding that more than 12 months had elapsed since the decree nisi.

Held – By analogy with the court's discretion to grant a decree nisi on a petition filed on the ground of the respondent's behaviour notwithstanding that the parties had cohabited for more than six months since the last act of behaviour complained of in the petition if the cohabitation had in all the circumstances been reasonable, the court could, if it considered that it had been reasonable for the petitioner to cohabit with the respondent after the decree nisi, exercise its discretion under the proviso to r 65(2) of the 1977 rules to make the decree absolute out of time notwithstanding the cohabitation after the decree nisi. Since it had been reasonable in all the circumstances for the wife to cohabit with the husband after the decree nisi and since the wife's delay did not, in the circumstances, preclude the court from exercising its discretion under the proviso to

---

a   Rule 65(2), so far as material, provides: 'On the lodging of . . . a notice [of an application by a spouse to make absolute a decree nisi], the registrar shall search the court minutes and if he is satisfied [with respect to specified matters] the registrar shall make the decree absolute: Provided that if the notice is lodged more than 12 months after the decree nisi, the registrar may require the applicant to file an affidavit accounting for the delay and may make such order on the application as he thinks fit or refer the application to a judge.'

r 65(2) in her favour, the court would grant her application and make the decree absolute (see p 534 g to j and p 536 b, post).

Per curiam. (1) Applications under the proviso to r 65(2) to make a decree absolute should be tried with the same solemnity as a suit for divorce, namely in open court (see p 535 d, post).

(2) The provision in the proviso to r 65(2) that the registrar 'may require the applicant to file an affidavit accounting for the delay' in applying to make the decree absolute is discretionary and not mandatory and accordingly oral evidence accounting for the delay may be sufficient (see p 535 b to d, post).

(3) In exercising the discretion conferred by the proviso to r 65(2) the court should take into account those matters affecting any children of the family which are relevant to the exercise of its jurisdiction to make a decree absolute under s 41 of the Matrimonial Causes Act 1973 (see p 535 e f, post).

Quaere. Whether, by analogy with the rule under s 1(5) of the 1973 Act that six weeks must elapse between the making of a decree nisi and the making of the decree absolute, the decision to grant a decree absolute under the proviso to r 65(2) should not take effect until six weeks after the date of the court's decision (see p 535 h to p 536 b, post).

Notes

For decree absolute on lodging notice, see 13 Halsbury's Laws (4th edn) para 977.

For the Matrimonial Causes Act 1973, s 41, see 43 Halsbury's Statutes (3rd edn) 588.

For the Matrimonial Causes Rules 1977, r 65, see 10 Halsbury's Statutory Instruments (4th reissue) 261.

Application

The wife, Jill Sonia Court, applied to make absolute out of time a decree nisi of divorce granted to her on 11 July 1979. The application was transferred by the registrar to the judge. The facts are set out in the judgment.

Andrew Barnett for the wife.
E James Holman, as amicus curiae, for the Queen's Proctor.

ARNOLD P. This is an unusual application which arises strictly under the proviso to r 65(2) of the Matrimonial Causes Rules 1977, SI 1977/344, although the particular circumstances of the case carry it far beyond the considerations which are usual when considering that matter.

The history is a simple one. In 1979 a petition was filed by Mrs Jill Sonia Court for the dissolution of her marriage to Peter Court on the ground that that marriage had irretrievably broken down and that there had been such behaviour on the part of the respondent as made it unreasonable to require the petitioner to continue to live with him (see s 1(2)(b) of the Matrimonial Causes Act 1973), and in due course, on 11 July 1979, in an undefended suit, a decree nisi was pronounced. But in the following October an attempted reconciliation took place between Mr and Mrs Court, and they lived under the same roof thereafter until 22 December 1980. In June 1981 this application was made to the court for the making absolute of the decree nisi pronounced in July 1979, notwithstanding the lapse of 12 months and more.

The matter comes before me because, as is foreshadowed by the terms of the proviso to r 65(2), it can be, and in this case has been, referred by the registrar to a judge.

The matters which have been canvassed in the evidence by affidavit and orally relate to the circumstances in which the attempted reconciliation came about and the period during which the cohabitation endured, which was plainly a very relevant matter because it could be that a history of cohabitation after a decree nisi which had been pronounced on the ground that a marriage had irretrievably broken down and that the behaviour of the respondent had been such as to make it unreasonable to require the petitioner to live with him might be seen, in the light of what happened afterwards, to have been obtained on the basis of a factual presentation which would be impossible to support when one examines and draws inferences from the subsequent history; and therefore it became necessary to look at the circumstances which brought the reconciliation and the cohabitation about. But, moreover, one has this, that it is relevant in all cases in which the proviso to r 65(2) has to be operated to observe the promptitude with which appeal to that jurisdiction has been made, and in this case, at the conclusion of the period of living under the same roof on 22 December 1980, something like seven months went by before recourse was had to the discretionary jurisdiction. So that, too, was a matter which had to be dealt with inevitably. In fact it was not dealt with in affidavit evidence, but it was dealt with by evidence in the witness box. I say at the outset that I regard Mrs Court as a wholly truthful witness and accept everything that she said.

Now the allegations in the petition were allegations of very substantial violence and threats of violence, allegations which might well, if established, as they were established to the satisfaction of the registrar (I suppose this was a special procedure divorce) make it unlikely that a wife complaining of those matters would willingly go back to her husband and, as was said in one of the cases, take her chance on a repetition of those violent acts. Therefore, it was a case in which the closest examination was necessary to see whether in fact the posterior resumption of cohabitation did cast a substantial doubt on the accuracy of the allegations on which the decree nisi was founded, and for that reason, no doubt, I have been given the assistance of the Queen's Proctor as amicus curiae to assist in the examination of these important matters.

I have seen Mrs Court in the witness box, and it is plain to me that she is not a person of great competence in relation to the ordering of her life. She has been for a long time, I think, a victim of events, perhaps for that reason, and, although it may very well be that in many cases the doubt which I have indicated would arise in a very acute form through a succession of events similar to those in the present case, I do not think that, having regard to the personality of Mrs Court, any such conclusion would be justified here. Her circumstances were dismal. She had been rejected by her family. She had recently returned from residence in the United States of America and was therefore short of friends. She had three children by her previous marriage, two of whom were with her, and a small daughter by her marriage to Mr Court, and her case was a sad one. That is a background which makes it at least likely that, in considering the blandishments of Mr Court and his invitation to a trial reconciliation, she would perhaps not be likely to think as clearly or logically or even sensibly about the matter as might otherwise have been the case. For these blandishments were substantial. The decree nisi having been pronounced on 11 July 1979, by the end of August Mr Court started writing a series of letters to her which continued for about a month before she decided to yield to his invitation to give the marriage another trial.

She is by trade or profession a qualified child care officer, and she was in Essex, I think, and he in Portsmouth or Southsea at a time when this correspondence took place. Having made the decision to accept his suggestion, she then applied for a child care job in Portsmouth. This application was successful by the end of September and was deferred in its operation for some weeks because of establishment problems. Nevertheless, she moved down to Portsmouth to some accommodation which she obtained in the form of a holiday flat, where she lived for three weeks or so before obtaining with Mr Court, with whom up to that point she had not been living, some council accommodation of a 'homeless' character, as it is said, substandard accommodation as she tells me.

Her hopes were dashed within a very short period of time. It was made clear to her that Mr Court's invitation, so far from being genuine, was really based partly on a desire for revenge against Mrs Court for what she had done in connection with her divorce proceeding, which included an ouster application against Mr Court, and partly because he had missed his little daughter. The bad treatment started again, and she was cowed, miserable and maltreated.

Then perhaps the most extraordinary incident of all in this case took place. After a period of six months or rather more in this emergency accommodation, the council, as was its duty under the relevant statute, resolved to move Mr and Mrs Court and the children to better, more permanent accommodation; and in the following June they did so. Mrs Court was under no illusion at all at that stage that there was any serious prospect of a success of the reconciliation attempt. Experience had caused that hope to die long since. And yet she moved with Mr Court and the children to the new accommodation. She says, and I have no reason to disbelieve her, that the arrangements between the family and the council were made by Mr Court. That does not seem at all surprising. But she acquiesced; and if I had not seen Mrs Court in the witness box I should quite simply have disbelieved her account. But I did see her. I am satisfied that she speaks the truth about the arrangements being out of her hands, but, more relevantly, of the brutal threats which were made by Mr Court as to the consequences of her enlisting any outside help in her predicament, and plainly there would come within the general ambit of that any explanation given by her to the council why she might be unwilling to resume cohabitation with Mr Court in the new premises. I believe that she was so cowed, helpless, at that stage that, however improbable it may seem, her explanation how she came to acquiesce in the move ought to be accepted.

The residence under the same roof continued for six months and then finally Mr Court left the scene.

During the period when Mrs Court was in the holiday accommodation in Portsmouth or Southsea before the first council accommodation was obtained by Mr and Mrs Court there was an intermittent history of sexual intercourse. Mrs Court says that that did not take place in fact after they moved in together, but it is quite plain, I think, that up to the move in June 1980 to the second council accommodation Mrs Court was rendering wifely services to Mr Court in the general domestic field. After the move she says that she was not and that they really were living quite separate lives in the new accommodation, and I accept that.

It is pointed out in the course of the very helpful submissions on behalf of the Queen's Proctor that there is a contrast in the way in which adultery and behaviour are respectively dealt with in s 2 of the Matrimonial Causes Act 1973. While the residence of a petitioner with an adulterous respondent is fatal to a petition based on s 1(2)(a) of the 1973 Act if it has endured for six months continuous or discontinuous after the knowledge of the last act of adultery and a shorter time is to be disregarded under s 2(1) and (2) in relation to the question whether the petitioner finds it intolerable to live with the respondent, which is one of the integers of s 1(2)(a), the way in which behaviour is dealt with is rather different. In s 2(3) any cohabitation after the last complained of act of behaviour which does not amount to more than six months is to be disregarded when considering the reasonableness of expecting the petitioner to live with the respondent. That is all that is provided.

It therefore follows, and this is the point, that where a longer period has elapsed it is nevertheless open to the court, although bound to take that into account, to conclude that it does not operate against a general conclusion as to the reasonableness of the matter; and that is highly relevant to the present case, if one applies, as I think one should apply, to the exercise of the discretion under the proviso in r 65(2) in a case like this the same considerations as would have moved one to conclude on the reasonableness of expecting the spouses to live together had one been dealing with the case at a decree nisi stage under s 1(2)(b) of the 1973 Act. In this particular case I should have had no hesitation in the light of the circumstances, had they occurred prior to decree nisi, in concluding that Mrs Court had demonstrated that it was unreasonable to expect her to live with Mr Court on the basis of a history similar to what has transpired since the decree nisi was in fact pronounced in this case.

So that does not stand in the way of exercising the discretion under the proviso favourably to Mrs Court.

As to the matter of delay, the history as explained in the witness box is a simple one. Within days rather than weeks after Mr Court's departure from the scene on 22

December 1980, up to which time I do believe that she was very frightened indeed, she went to a solicitor and initially made progress; but from about February to about May the solicitor's enthusiasm apparently waned, and it was not until she switched to her present solicitors in May that progress was made, and from then on everything went promptly. The delay, therefore, does not stand in Mrs Court's way, and I have no hesitation in this particular case in exercising the discretion favourably to her.

In the course of the hearing a number of matters have come up. It is pointed out that in the proviso to r 65(2) there is a stipulation for an affidavit. It is a discretionary matter: 'the registrar may require the applicant to file an affidavit accounting for the delay' in any case in which a notice is lodged more than 12 months after the decree nisi asking for the decree to be made absolute; and it is suggested that that should really be not so much a discretionary matter as a positive requirement where there has been cohabitation after the making of the decree nisi.

I agree to this extent, that there should certainly be evidence accounting for the matter in such a way, if the application is to succeed, as to enable the court to conclude that the cohabitation should not be regarded as raising substantial doubts about the validity of the evidence on which the decree nisi was based. But for my part I see no reason why that evidence cannot be given as well in the witness box as by affidavit. The important requirement is that there should be evidence.

It is also pointed out, and in my judgment rightly pointed out, that these cases should be tried with the same solemnity as a suit resulting in a decree nisi, namely in open court.

It is further pointed out that there is an anomalous situation as regards the requirements of s 41 of the Matrimonial Causes Act 1973, in that the court will not permit a decree to be made absolute unless there has been a certificate and an approbation under s 41 and that where, as in a case like this, the matter comes to be at large again where a discretion has to be exercised as to the making absolute out of time of a decree nisi, there cannot be a further direct requirement for such certificate and approbation, for the force of s 41 will by then by definition be spent.

That is right, but it does not seem to me that that is really a serious obstacle, because, as it seems to me, in exercising the discretion conferred by the proviso, the court ought in every case to take into account the matters relevant to the exercise of the jurisdiction under s 41 for the purpose of exercising the discretion under the proviso.

There are two other matters which arose, interestingly, and I do not propose to come to any final conclusion on them because it is not necessary for the purposes of this case. The first is this, that it is within the jurisdiction of the registrar or the judge when an appeal is made to the discretion under the proviso to adjourn the court's process; and one of the reasons why that course might well be taken in most imaginable cases is that the registrar or the judge would wish to know what the respondent had to say about the matter, and in such a case a term of the adjournment might well be (plainly it is within the jurisdiction of the court) that notice should be given to the respondent of the application. I am not entirely satisfied that notice should always and in all circumstances be given to the respondent. One can imagine cases in which that would not be necessary. That is a matter I think for consideration as regards policy in the future.

The other matter is this, that the statute requires an interval of six weeks, which can, however, be abridged by the court in its discretion, and in certain circumstances often is, between the making of the decree nisi and the making absolute of that decree. It is suggested that the analogy is so strong between the occasion of the exercise of the discretion under the proviso and the occasion of the making of a decree nisi that the same rule ought in discretion to be imported into the giving of leave to make absolute a decree nisi out of time, so that in effect it could not be made absolute, notwithstanding a favourable reception of the application, for six weeks after the decision.

I am not persuaded that this is right, precisely because, as on the one hand the making of a decree nisi, the analogy to which I wholly accept, can be the occasion for abridging the period of six weeks, so it seems to me that the same sort of discretion can inform what is plainly within the jurisdiction, namely the extent of the desirable deferment in a particular case of the making absolute of the decree. The only difference is that instead of it being an 'exclusion' discretion it would be an 'inclusion' discretion; and I am not persuaded that the difference between those two things makes it necessary or desirable to lay down any rule of practice as to what should be the interval after the granting of discretionary leave to make the decree absolute after the lapse of 12 months such as to impose a particular requirement as to time.

Accordingly, in this case I grant the application, and I do not think it necessary in this particular case to impose any period of delay.

Application for decree absolute granted.

Solicitors: *Saulet & Co*, Portsmouth (for the wife); *Queen's Proctor.*

Bebe Chua   Barrister.

R v Rose and others

COURT OF APPEAL, CRIMINAL DIVISION
LORD LANE CJ, WATKINS LJ AND STEPHEN BROWN J
8 MARCH 1982

Criminal law – Trial – Retirement of jury – Communication with jury – Judge communicating with jury through court clerk without consulting counsel – Whether material irregularity – Whether conviction should be quashed.

Jury – Intimidating or threatening jury – What constitutes intimidation or threat – Judge giving jury time limit in which to reach verdict – Whether conviction should be quashed.

Criminal law – Trial – Retrial – Jury's verdict vitiated by material irregularity – Trial not retrospectively invalidated by irregularity – Whether Court of Appeal having power to order retrial.

The appellants were variously charged with murder and attempting to pervert the course of public justice. At the end of a trial lasting four weeks, the jury retired to consider their verdicts and 2 hours and 40 minutes later the judge directed them that they could bring in a majority verdict. Later the same day, on the instructions of the judge, who did not consult counsel in the case, the court clerk entered the jury room and told the jury that they would be discharged if they did not reach a verdict by a certain time. A matter of minutes later, the jury, who said that they had wrongly calculated their ballot, convicted the appellants by majority verdicts of ten to two. The appellants appealed, contending that the judge had applied improper pressure on the jury to reach a verdict by the imposition of a time limit.

Held – Where it appeared from the length of their retirement and the circumstances of the case that a jury might be unable to agree on a verdict, even after a majority direction had been given, the appropriate course was for the judge to reassemble the court and ask the jury whether there was any chance of their reaching an agreement and then, depending on their answer, to decide whether to discharge the jury. The trial judge was wrong both to communicate with the jury through the court staff behind the scenes without consulting counsel and also to pass a private message which imposed, or might have been interpreted by the jury as imposing, a time limit on their deliberations. Accordingly, there had been a grave and material irregularity in the proceedings which required that the verdict be quashed. Furthermore, since the irregularity was not one

which retrospectively invalidated the trial, the court could not order a retrial (see p 541
f to p 542 *d*, p 543 *b h* and p 544 *d e*, post).

    R v Neal [1949] 2 All ER 438, *R v Middlesex Justices, ex p DPP* [1952] 2 All ER 312 and
R v McKenna [1960] 1 All ER 326 applied.

Notes

For communications between judge and jury, see 11 Halsbury's Laws (4th edn) para 309,
and for cases on the subject, see 14(1) Digest (Reissue) 427–428, *3631–3637*.

    For retrial, see 11 Halsbury's Laws (4th edn) para 667.

Cases referred to in judgment

Crane v DPP [1921] 2 AC 299, [1921] All ER Rep 19, HL, 14(1) Digest (Reissue) 315,
    2428.
R v Gee, R v Bibby, R v Dunscombe [1936] 2 All ER 89, [1936] 2 KB 442, CCA, 14(1) Digest
    (Reissue) 226, *1618.*
R v Hancock (1931) 100 LJKB 419, CCA, 14(1) Digest (Reissue) 409, *3475.*
R v McKenna, R v McKenna, R v Busby [1960] 1 All ER 326, [1960] 1 QB 411, [1960] 2
    WLR 306, 44 Cr App R 63, CCA, 14(2) Digest (Reissue) 829, *7115.*
R v Middlesex Justices, ex p DPP [1952] 2 All ER 312, [1952] 2 QB 758, 16 Digest (Reissue)
    427, *4697.*
R v Neal [1949] 2 All ER 438, [1949] 2 KB 590, 33 Cr App R 189, CCA, 14(2) Digest
    (Reissue) 826, *7088.*
R v Townsend [1982] 1 All ER 509, CA.
R v Wakefield [1918] 1 KB 216, [1918–19] All ER Rep 842, CCA, 14(2) Digest (Reissue)
    826, *7082.*
R v Williams (1925) 19 Cr App R 67, CCA, 14(2) Digest (Reissue) 850, *7362.*

Cases also cited

R v Davis (No 2) (1960) 44 Cr App R 235, CCA.
R v Dubarry (1976) 64 Cr App R 7, CA.
R v Furlong [1950] 1 All ER 636, CCA.
R v Green [1950] 1 All ER 38, CCA.
R v Lamb (Stephen John) (1974) 59 Cr App R 196, CA.
R v Willmont (1914) 10 Cr App R 173, CCA.
R v Yeadon and Birch (1861) Le & Ca 81, 169 ER 1312, CCR.
Stirland v DPP [1944] 2 All ER 13, [1944] AC 315, HL.

Appeal

Newton Samuel Rose appealed against his conviction on 4 December 1981 on count 1 of
an indictment charging him with murder and Ian Henry, Michael Carson Clarke and
Orville Alexander Johnson appealed against their convictions, together with the appellant
Rose, on the same date on count 2 of the indictment charging them with attempting to
pervert the course of public justice following their trial at the Central Criminal Court
before his Honour Judge Clarke QC and a jury. The appellant Rose was sentenced to life
imprisonment in respect of count 1, but no separate sentence was passed on him in
respect of count 2, and the appellants Henry, Clarke and Johnson were each sentenced to
six months' imprisonment in respect of count 2. The facts are set out in the judgment
of the court.

Ian Macdonald and *Michael House* for the appellant Rose.
Peter Thornton for the appellants Henry and Clarke.
Diana Ellis for the appellant Johnson.
Ann Curnow and *Barbara Mills* for the Crown.

LORD LANE CJ delivered the following judgment of the court: On 4 December 1981
at the Central Criminal Court before Judge Clarke QC and a jury, the appellants were

convicted, Rose of murder (count 1), for which he was sentenced to life imprisonment, and all four appellants of attempting to pervert the course of public justice. The three other appellants apart from Rose were each sentenced to six months' imprisonment on the second count, and no separate sentence was imposed on Rose in respect of that count. All these verdicts were majority verdicts of ten to two.

Each of them now appeals against conviction by leave of the single judge.

In the light of the arguments which have been presented to this court, the facts, which were far from simple at the trial, can be dealt with with comparative brevity. At 6 o'clock in the morning of 8 May 1981, the dead body of a young man called Donnelly was found in Glynn Road, which is a street in Hackney, London E8. He had died of serious stab wounds to his chest and back which had punctured vital organs of the body.

Of course the police immediately instituted inquiries. It seemed from those inquiries that Donnelly had been at a party in a discotheque in Hackney up to a time round about 1 o'clock in the morning of 8 May. The party left the discotheque then, and it seems that there was a conversation about a taxi. Eventually most of the party dispersed, leaving Donnelly alone together with a girl called Sandra Alexander. To cut a long story short, he saw her home. She went inside her house, it seems, at about 1.55 in the early hours of that morning, leaving Donnelly alone on the pavement outside. Very soon after that he must have been murdered. Inquiries were made in the locality and a number of witnesses were discovered who heard noises and screams in the area at a time between 1.30 and 2 o'clock.

The police inquiries extended thereafter to Rose, and the reason seems to have been that Rose had been very friendly with Sandra Alexander, and for a time had been her boyfriend. Consequently they questioned Rose.

He made a witness statement which in effect said that he had been to a party that evening. He had left the party at about 3.30 in the morning in a taxi. At Lea Bridge roundabout the taxi had stopped and he and his three colleagues had got out of the taxi and run away without paying. They ran down the road to another taxi firm, Jimacs. There they hired another taxi which took them to their various addresses and he arrived home at about 4 o'clock in the morning and went straight to bed. It was not until Sandra Alexander came round the next morning and gave him the news that he knew of the death of Donnelly. If that story were true, then of course he would have an alibi covering the whole of the period during which it was possible for the murder to have been committed. The other three appellants were in due course interviewed, and they each made statements supporting what Rose himself had said.

The next line of inquiry for the police was the taxi driver who had first picked them up. He said that he had picked the appellants up at about 2 o'clock in the morning and that they had decamped without paying the fare of £1·80 in Lea Bridge Road.

It was the second taxi driver, a man called Simpson, who really was the foundation at this stage of the prosecution's case against the appellants, because he confirmed that on the night in question, he had picked up four West Indian youths and had taken them to addresses which precisely matched the addresses where these four young men lived. So far so good. But it was the timing of that journey which caused the difficulty, because on an examination of the records it was clearly indicated that that journey started at 5.30 in the morning. Consequently there was a gap of two hours or more in what had appeared at first blush an alibi covering the whole of the material time.

What happened after that was that the appellants were arrested and interviewed. An interview took place first of all with Clarke. According to the prosecution he made a statement in effect admitting that he was at the scene, he had seen Donnelly talking to Sandra Alexander, Rose had an argument and a fight with Donnelly in which he, Henry and Johnson had taken no part; he actually saw the blade go in, Donnelly fell down and they ran away.

Henry was seen again and he was reported by the police to have made similar admissions. The same thing happened with Johnson, who in due course came back from Germany where he had been, let it be said, on perfectly legitimate business. It was said by the police that Rose was confronted with the statements made by the first two of the other two appellants and that he had made oral admissions indicating his guilt. The charge of attempting to pervert the course of justice was based on the alleged falsity of the original statements.

At the trial Henry, Johnson and Clarke said that the statements they had made to the police containing apparent admissions had been obtained by illicit means and that they were not true. Rose himself denied having made any material admissions.

There were features about the timing, both of the disappearance of Sandra into the house and of the hearing of the noises by the neighbours, compared with the time of the first taxi, which presented difficulties to the prosecution. But the main contest quite plainly was the issue for the jury: 'Are we convinced that these young men made the admissions which they were reported to have made of their free will or not?'

The trial started on 9 November. The evidence started on 12 November. On 3 December the learned judge started to give his directions to the jury and on 4 December, which was a Friday, that summing up finished at about 10.05 in the morning, leaving the rest of the day for the jury to consider their verdict in a case which, to say the least, had its difficulties and required very close attention, not only in the light of the grave nature of the charge against Rose, but also in the light of the various complications which we have endeavoured to explain.

At 12.08 pm the jury returned with two questions directed to a statement which Johnson had made to the police. Very properly the court reassembled and the questions were answered in open court in the presence of the defendants.

At about 12.45 pm, that is to say some 2 hours and 40 minutes after the jury had retired to consider their verdicts, they were given a majority direction. That of course was perfectly correct according to the statute, the necessary time of two hours having elapsed. But perhaps in a case of this nature it was, if one may say so, a little soon to have the jury back to give a majority direction. We do not criticise, but merely pass comment on it.

They were out of court until 6.10 pm when they returned with majority verdicts, as already indicated, of ten to two. They had been out for 5 hours and 25 minutes after the majority direction had been given. So stood matters.

But things were not as simple as they seemed, because a report was made on this matter by Mr Philip Spencer, who was the court clerk at the Central Criminal Court, and it is necessary for me to read the statement that he made:

'On the 4th December 1981 I was the Clerk in Judge Edward Clarke's Court, when the Jury in The Queen against NEWTON ROSE and others were sent out to deliberate upon their verdicts. They retired at 10.05 a.m. and were called back by the Judge at 12.45 p.m. and given a direction on majority verdicts in respect of each of the four defendants; the Jury retired again. At approximately 3.00 p.m. having received from the Jury a request for coffee, I entered the Jury Room on the Judge's instructions to ask whether they were near to reaching a verdict and was told that the Jury were unable to say but that they were making progress. At approximately 4.30 p.m. again on the Judge's instructions, I entered the Jury Room to ask if they had reached a verdict and was told that they had not but that they were still making progress. Some added that they were tired and unable to think further and one said she had a headache. At approximately 5.35 p.m. a note was sent from the Jury Room requesting a London A–Z Directory. The Judge informed me that he did not intend to assemble the Court and I was asked to go to the Jury and tell them that the answer to their request was "No". This I did. At approximately 5.45 p.m. Judge Clarke instructed me to enter the Jury Room and inform the Jury that he wanted them to try to reach verdicts by 6.05 p.m. but that if they could not, he would then discharge them. I left the Judge's room and hesitated for some minutes as to whether I should convey the message. I decided that in view of the Judge's instructions I should do so but I took the view that I should add when conveying the

Judge's message that the Judge in no way wanted them to feel that they were under pressure but that as they had complained of tiredness he did not want them to think that there would be no end to their deliberation, and I added that to the Judge's message. At 6.05 p.m. again on instructions from the Judge, I re-entered the Jury Room to ask if they had reached verdicts and was told they had not. I left the room and the Court was re-assembled. As the Jury was about to return to Court at 6.10 p.m. I received a message from the Jury Bailiff that the Jury had wrongly calculated their ballot and that they had in fact reached acceptable verdicts. Those verdicts were taken and were returned as guilty by a majority of 10–2 in relation to each count and defendant. The defendant ROSE was sentenced to life imprisonment on Count 1 and the Judge passed no sentence on Count 2. HENRY, CLARKE and JOHNSON were each sentenced to six months imprisonment in respect of the Count of attempting to pervert the course of public justice. This Statement has been made by me with the aid of a note which I wrote for the Courts Administrator on Monday the 7th December 1981, a copy of which remains in my possession; the original was handed to Judge Clarke and retained by him.'

On 15 December 1981 a letter was written by the judge himself and sent to all counsel who had been concerned in the defence. It read as follows:

'On 4th December 1981 the jury retired to consider their verdicts in the above case in which you were defending. The case had lasted four weeks and there was a strong conflict of evidence between each side. The final question for the jury was whether Rose was the person who had stabbed the victim. The defence was an alibi but there was no dispute that the victim was murdered. The jury retired at 10.05 a.m. At 12.45 they were given the majority directive. At 4.30 p.m. the jury said that they were making progress but some were getting tired and one said he had a headache. By then I had decided that in no circumstances would the jury be sent away for the night and that if they had not reached a verdict by 6 p.m. I would discharge them. At 5.45 on my instructions the Clerk told the jury: 1. That if they could not reach a verdict by 6 p.m. they would be discharged. 2. That they were to feel under no pressure to reach a verdict.'

We pause there to say that that is slightly different from the version of events given by the clerk himself. The letter went on:

'At 6.10 p.m. the jury had found a verdict of guilty of murder by 10–2 and said that they had miscalculated their ballot taken some time earlier. After talking to the Recorder who had been told of these facts, I have decided to inform you of these facts so that you make make what use of them that you wish. You have my permission to use this letter as counsel for the defence in the interests of Rose. I have sent this letter to the counsel for the other three defendants.'

Counsel now, in respect of each of the four appellants, submits that there was a material irregularity in the proceedings and that accordingly the convictions should be quashed and the appeals allowed. Counsel for the appellant Rose, to whom we are indebted for a succinct and lucid argument, has acted as protagonist and the other two counsel really adopted the arguments put forward to this court by him.

The basis on which he puts his appeal is this. First of all the actions of the judge infringed the principle that all communication between judge and jury relevant to the issues, other than inquiries whether they have reached a verdict, should take place in open court, and that, he points out, is simply putting into effect the terms of the oath which the jury bailiff takes, not to suffer any person to speak to the jury nor to speak to them himself, save to inquire whether they are agreed on their verdict, without the leave of the court. Secondly he submits that what the judge did infringes the principle that a jury should be free to take as much time as they require, subject to the inherent jurisdiction of the court to discharge the jury in the event of it becoming apparent that no agreement is likely. Furthermore, no jury, as he put it, should be pressurised into reaching a verdict either by the imposition of a time limit or by a threat of being locked up if they fail to reach a verdict by a particular point in time.

He directs his arguments to two separate facets of the judge's conduct of the matter. The first facet is the application of the jury that they should be allowed to see a London A to Z street directory. Counsel for the appellant Rose submits that that was a typical occasion when the court should have been reassembled, that counsel for the defence should have been invited to submit to him their views on whether the jury should be allowed to see that street directory, and, he submits, the failure to make any mention of that request by the learned judge was a material irregularity, which can only result in this verdict being quashed.

On the other hand counsel for the Crown suggests that there was really only one answer to the jury's request, namely: 'No, you may not see a London street directory.' She points out that the map which the jury had before them was a photostat copy of two pages of a full spread of the A to Z directory, and it would have been quite improper for the learned judge to allow the jury, so to speak, to roam through the whole of the A to Z directory at their will when only those two pages were in issue.

Counsel for the appellant Rose submits that it may very well have been that the photostat copy with which the jury were equipped was illegible for some reason, which could have been cured quite simply if they had been allowed to see the full two pages, if necessary the rest of the volume being sellotaped so that it could not be used.

So far as this court is concerned, we are quite clear in our mind that the correct course for the judge to have adopted was to inform counsel what had happened, of the request that had been made and, if necessary, as it would have been in these circumstances, to re-assemble the court to hear what counsel had to say about this request. On the other hand, if this particular irregularity had stood on its own, we do not think that this court would have interfered. We doubt that it was of sufficient materiality. If it was material, then it probably would, on its own, have been a case for the application of the proviso to s 2(1) of the Criminal Appeal Act 1968.

It is the second matter which has caused this court grave worry, and that is the time limit which the learned judge, without informing counsel until after the case was over, imposed on the jury. It is axiomatic that where it appears from the length of their retirement and the circumstances of the case, even after a majority direction has been given to them, the jury may be unable to agree on a verdict and therefore further deliberation by them may be simply a waste of time, the judge should reassemble the court, send for the jury and in open court ask the jury, through their foreman, whether there is any chance of their reaching an agreement, emphasising, needless to say, that he is not inquiring how they are divided. According to the answer which the judge gets from the jury, he will then decide whether to discharge the jury there and then, or whether he should asked the jury to retire once again to make a further effort to reach agreement between them. What he must under no circumstances do is to have any material communication through the court staff with the jury behind the scenes without consulting counsel. It is doubly wrong for the judge to pass a private message to the jury imposing some sort of time limit, or something which might be interpreted as a time limit, on the deliberations of the jury, and that is so however well-intentioned such a message may be. No one can know precisely what was said. No one can know precisely how it was said by the messenger to the jury, and no one can know what the effect of the message may have been on the members of the jury in their room.

In the present case it is clear, in the way the message was delivered to the jury, that there was no threat contained in it. Indeed on one view of the words said to have been used, it might be said that the judge was relieving the jurors of the burden of arguing further amongst themselves if, before the time limit was reached, they had not reached an agreement. But one does not know how in these circumstances each juror might have reacted to what was said, nor indeed may one inquire as to the effect it had on individual jurors.

The fact remains that the whole incident was, in our judgment, a grave material irregularity which we deplore. The very way in which matters went after that, the statement by the jury at one moment that they were unable to agree and then within a matter of minutes later saying that they had miscounted the ballot, and then unexpectedly coming back into court not to announce disagreement but to announce agreement by a majority, inevitably leads this court to fear that justice may not have been done.

Two questions have exercised us greatly. The first question is whether this is a case where we would be entitled to apply the proviso to s 2(1) of the Criminal Appeal Act 1968 despite the material irregularity, and the second question is whether this irregularity was so fundamental that it vitiated the trial, thereby constituting this case a proper one in which to order a venire de novo, namely a retrial.

So far as the proviso is concerned, we feel it impossible to say that had the message not been passed as it was to the jury the result would necessarily have been the same. Waller LJ in *R v Townsend* [1982] 1 All ER 509 at 511 said this as to the standard test to be applied by the court in deciding whether to apply the proviso: 'The test to be applied in deciding that question is whether "a reasonable jury, after being properly directed, would, on the evidence properly admissible, without doubt convict" . . .' Changing the scene to the circumstances of this case, would a reasonable jury which had not received the message which this jury received have, without doubt, come to the same conclusion as this jury reached? We are bound to say that we are not so satisfied. Accordingly this is not a proper case for the application of the proviso.

What is much more difficult, in our judgment, is the question whether it is a proper case to order a venire de novo.

We have taken the opportunity of examining a number of cases in the past which have concerned themselves with this difficult problem. We have also had the advantage of reading an article by Sir Robin Cooke in the Law Quarterly Review ((1955) 71 LQR 100), an article of great scholarship dealing with this very subject. A reading of this article will show that he has examined the history of this subject going back over the years, and he points out that there are a number of categories in which retrials have been ordered. He then names seven of them: (1) error as to the true plea of the defendant, when there has been some doubt about the nature of his plea, guilty or not guilty; (2) misjoinder of defendants (*Crane v DPP* [1921] 2 AC 299, [1921] All ER Rep 19); (3) failure to take the verdict of the jury when there is a change of plea from not guilty to guilty (*R v Hancock* (1931) 100 LJKB 419); (4) irregularity in the committal proceedings (*R v Gee, R v Bibby, R v Dunscombe* [1936] 2 All ER 89, [1936] 2 KB 442); (5) personation of a juror (*R v Wakefield* [1918] 1 KB 216, [1918–19] All ER Rep 842); (6) denial of right of challenge of juror (*R v Williams* (1925) 19 Cr App R 67); (7) judge unqualified to act as such. If we may add respectfully what appears to be the eighth, at common law, where the verdict is so ambiguous or ill-expressed that no judgment could be given on it.

It will be noted that all these examples are matters of procedure, and it has never been held, nor indeed suggested, that a venire de novo is appropriate where, for instance, there has been some mistake in the direction to the jury, or some other issue left to the jury which ought not to have been left and so on. The first requirement is irregularity in procedure. Secondly, it seems from this analysis that the irregular incident may happen at any stage of the proceedings. Thirdly, the defect must be fundamental. The trial must be marred by an irregularity so serious as to entitle the defendant to a retrial at the least, so serious that it can be properly termed a 'mistrial' or, as some authorities put it, a 'nullity'.

It seems to us, we are bound to say, that if a case arises in which it can be shown quite clearly that the jury may have been pressurised, may have given their verdict under a feeling of duress, then that can be described as a jury failing to carry out the terms of the oath which they took at the outset of the trial, because they have been sworn to give a true verdict according to the evidence. If they have been pressurised, or may have been pressurised, then they have failed to carry out the terms of their oath. In those circumstances, it seems to us, it would be a proper case in which to order a retrial.

Take an extreme example. If the jury, as was suggested in argument in this case, had been forced to come to their verdict at gun point, it is plain that that would be nothing other than a mistrial, and would be a case where the matter should be tried again.

In this case things are not so easy as that. First of all counsel, to whom we are indebted for her argument on behalf of the Crown, concedes that the way in which she argued the question of the application of the proviso really inhibits her, as a matter of logic, from suggesting that the irregularity is so fundamental here as to amount to a proper occasion for us to order a venire de novo. More important perhaps are the three authorities to which we have been referred, authorities which are binding on us, which seem to indicate that in cases such as this a venire de novo is not possible.

The first and most striking is R v McKenna [1960] 1 All ER 326 at 328, [1960] 1 QB 411 at 413. That was a well-known case, where the judge said to the jury:

> 'I have disorganised my travel arrangements out of consideration for you pretty considerably already. I am not going to disorganise them any further. In ten minutes I shall leave this building and if by that time you have not arrived at a conclusion in this case you will have to be kept all night and we will resume this matter at 11.45 a.m. tomorrow.'

The jury thereupon retired once again, coming back into court six minutes later with verdicts of guilty in respect of all the defendants. It was held (see 44 Cr App R 63)—

> 'that it was a fundamental principle that a jury should deliberate in complete freedom, uninfluenced by any promise and unintimidated by any threat, and should be free to take such time to consider their verdict as they felt they needed, subject always to the right of the judge to discharge them if protracted consideration still produced disagreement . . .'

In due course the conviction was quashed. It seems that that is the basis of the submission to this court of counsel for the appellant Rose to which reference has already been made.

In that case the Crown was represented by Mr Fitzwalter Butler. At that time he was the editor of *Archbold's Criminal Pleading Evidence and Practice* and one of the most erudite members of the Bar so far as criminal matters were concerned. He argued the question of venire de novo at length (see [1960] 1 QB 411 at 417–418). He cited the House of Lords decision in *Crane v DPP* [1921] 2 AC 299, [1921] All ER Rep 19, to which we have already referred, and he cited R v Neal [1949] 2 All ER 438, [1949] 2 KB 590, another case to which we shall have to refer. He submitted to the court that R v McKenna was a typical example of a situation in which venire de novo would be appropriate.

Cassels J, reading the judgment of the Court of Criminal Appeal, said ([1960] 1 All ER 326 at 330, [1960] 1 QB 411 at 423):

> 'This being so, the court does not think it right to resort to the proviso to section 4(1). The prosecution also submits, as an alternative, that a venire de novo should be ordered, but this trial was not, in the true sense of the word, a nullity.'

There the court deals very briefly with the arguments which were put before them, but on the facts, which were stronger than the facts in the present case, they came to the conclusion that that was not a proper case for ordering a retrial. By that we are bound. But it is necessary for us to say, with respect, that had the court there perhaps been referred to the authorities which appear in the Law Quarterly Review and the article by Sir Robin Cooke it may very well have been that they would have given closer consideration to the problem.

The next case to which it is necessary to refer is R v Neal [1949] 2 All ER 438, [1949] 2 KB 590. The headnote in the Criminal Appeal Reports reads (see 33 Cr App R 189):

> 'After a jury had retired to consider their verdict and had been given into the charge of the bailiff, they sent a message to the Recorder asking if they might be allowed to leave the Court for the purpose of getting luncheon during the midday adjournment. The Recorder gave them permission to do so, and they afterwards

returned and gave their verdict. *Held*, that the irregularity was one which constituted a departure from the established rules of criminal procedure and which rendered the trial abortive ... *Held*, further, that the Court was obliged to quash the conviction and could not order a *venire de novo*, as the trial had been regular up to the moment when the jury were allowed to disperse and could not be treated as having been a nullity.'

There is no need for this court to read any passage from the judgment of Lord Goddard CJ, who read the judgment of the court. We venture to doubt whether that part of the judgment dealing with venire de novo was properly founded. If a fundamental error in procedure takes place even at the close of a trial, it seems to us that that would retrospectively invalidate the whole of the trial, even if the trial had been regular up to the moment when the irregularity occurred, as in this case it was up to the moment when the message was passed to the jury.

The final case is that of *R v Middlesex Justices, ex p DPP* [1952] 2 All ER 312, [1952] 2 QB 758. There, following *R v Neal*, it was held that to constitute a mistrial the proceedings must have been abortive from beginning to end so that had the record been drawn up the error would have been apparent.

Although we hope that in the not too distant future it will be possible for their Lordships in the House of Lords to reconsider the whole of this matter, we feel that we are bound by those decisions, and particularly *R v McKenna* [1960] 1 All ER 326, [1960] 1 QB 411.

.The result is accordingly that we do not apply the proviso, we do not order a retrial and, for the reasons which I hope have emerged from this judgment, we consider that the material irregularity was such that we are bound to allow the appeal and quash the conviction.

Appeals allowed. Convictions quashed.

9 March. The court refused leave to appeal to the House of Lords but certified, under s 33(2) of the Criminal Appeal Act 1968, that the following point of law of general public importance was involved in the decision: whether the Court of Appeal, Criminal Division, may in its discretion order a venire de novo when it is satisfied that a verdict of guilty must be set aside by reason of a material irregularity consisting of improper pressure imposed on the jury at any time before verdict.

29 March. The Appeal Committee of the House of Lords granted leave to appeal.

Solicitors: *Bindman & Partners* (for the appellant Rose); *Seifert, Sedley & Co* (for the appellants Henry, Clarke and Johnson); *Director of Public Prosecutions*.

N P Metcalfe Esq   Barrister.

R v Surrey Coroner, ex parte Campbell

QUEEN'S BENCH DIVISION
WATKINS LJ AND GLIDEWELL J
17, 18, 19 JUNE, 9 DECEMBER 1981

Coroner – Inquest – Judicial review – Jurisdiction of High Court – Application for judicial review not made or authorised by Attorney General – Extent of jurisdiction to review inquest proceedings – Coroners Act 1887, s 6.

Coroner – Inquest – Verdict – Lack of care – Rule against verdict determining civil liability on the part of named person – Inquest on death in remand centre – Coroner advising jury to return verdict of self-neglect – Whether lack of care a possible verdict – Whether such a verdict contravening requirements of rule against determining civil liability – Whether rule valid – Coroners (Amendment) Act 1926, ss 26, 27 – Coroners Rules 1953, r 33.

Coroner – Inquest – Jury – Selection of jurors – Practice of selecting only men as jurors – Validity.

The deceased died at a remand centre after having persistently refused to take food or drink. The inquest into his death was initially held before a coroner alone, who heard from medical experts that the cause of death was dehydration due to schizophrenia. The inquest was adjourned so that a jury could be summoned. The coroner's officer called at houses in the area asking, as was his custom, only men to be jurors, although when a woman protested at not being asked he immediately agreed to include her. Before the inquest was resumed, the form of inquisition for use at the conclusion of the inquest was prepared giving as the cause of death 'dehydration due to schizophrenia' but leaving the name of the coroner and the verdict blank. When the inquest resumed the coroner recalled for the benefit of the jury the evidence which he had heard and allowed the witnesses to be questioned. In his summing up the coroner advised the jury against returning an open verdict or a verdict of suicide and suggested that they might return a verdict of self-neglect. The jury asked if they could return a verdict of 'neglect by the authorities' but the coroner, apparently bearing in mind that r 33[a] of the Coroners Rules 1953 required that a verdict should not appear to determine civil liability on the part of a named person, informed them that they could not. The jury later asked for a further explanation of a verdict of self-neglect. The coroner again summarised the possible verdicts but this time included 'lack of care' while pointing out that such a verdict might reflect on the staff at the remand centre. The jury returned a verdict of self-neglect but added a rider expressing concern at the lack of specialist care facilities available to the deceased. The coroner asked them if they wished to add the words 'suffering from schizophrenia' to the verdict. The jury informed him that they were not happy about that. When the coroner entered the verdict on the form of inquisition he did not delete the words 'due to schizophrenia' from the entry regarding the cause of death, and in the rider, which was attached to the inquisition, the cause of death was given as 'dehydration due to schizophrenia'. The deceased's mother applied to the Attorney General for authority to bring proceedings under s 6[b] of the Coroners Act 1887 to have the verdict set aside. When the Attorney General refused to give authority the mother applied for judicial review by way of certiorari to bring up and quash the verdict, inquisition and rider, on the grounds (i) that the coroner had withdrawn from the jury a possible verdict of neglect or lack of care and had put improper pressure on them to return a verdict of self-neglect, (ii) that r 33 of the 1953 rules, on which he had apparently relied, was ultra vires ss 26 and 27 of the Coroners (Amendment) Act 1926 and void, (iii) that the jury had

---

a   Rule 33 is set out at p 554 g, post
b   Section 6, so far as material, is set out at p 552 d, post

been summoned with partiality and therefore unlawfully, and (iv) that the inquisition and rider misrepresented the findings and verdict of the jury.

Held – (1) Because the court was not entitled to use the wide powers to quash a coroner's verdict contained in s 6 of the 1887 Act if the Attorney General refused to make or authorise the application, and because a coroner's inquest was a court and not a tribunal and therefore the wide supervisory powers over statutory tribunals were not available, the court could only order judicial review of an inquest on the grounds of error on the face of the record, fraud or an excess or refusal of jurisdiction when a private application to quash an inquest was made (see p 552 *e f* and p 554 *b* to *f*, post); *Garnett v Ferrand* [1824–34] All ER Rep 244, *A-G v BBC* [1980] 3 All ER 161 and *Re Racal Communications Ltd* [1980] 2 All ER 634 considered; *Anisminic Ltd v Foreign Compensation Commission* [1969] 1 All ER 208 distinguished.

(2) A verdict of 'lack of care by another or others' did not contravene the requirement of r 33 of the 1953 rules that no verdict should appear to determine civil liability on the part of a named person (see p 555 *a* to *c*, post).

(3) There had been no failure by the coroner to exercise his jurisdiction because he had in the end not withdrawn from the jury the verdict of lack of care, so that they were not improperly restricted when deciding, as they were required to by s 4(3)[c] of the 1887 Act, how the deceased died. Putting pressure on a jury to return a particular verdict was not a matter which affected jurisdiction, but, even if it was, the jury had withstood any such pressure and there had therefore been no irregularity (see p 554 *f* and p 555 *a* to *c*, post).

(4) The practice of excluding women from a coroner's jury by prior decision or custom was wrong but it could not be said that the particular jury had been summoned with partiality because there was one woman on it and there was nothing to indicate that it was not composed of a random selection of local people (see p 556 *b* to *d*, post).

(5) Although s 13(4)[d] of the 1926 Act provided that where any part of an inquest was held without a jury anything done at that part of the inquest by or before a coroner alone was as valid as if it had been done by or before the jury, the court could none the less set aside the coroner's original decision that the cause of death was 'dehydration due to schizophrenia' because that decision ceased to be effective once he recalled the medical evidence at the adjourned hearing and thereby left the decision as to the cause of death to the jury. The court would also give effect to the verdict of the jury by deleting the words 'due to schizophrenia' from both the inquisition and the rider (see p 556 *g h*, post).

Per curiam. Such conflict as may in any given circumstances appear to arise between r 33 of the 1953 rules and the duty under s 4 of the 1887 Act to inquire into how the death of the deceased was caused must be resolved in favour of the statutory duty under s 4 to inquire into the cause of death, whatever the consequences of that might be (see p 555 *c*, post).

Notes
For the power of the High Court to quash a coroner's inquisition and the grounds for doing so, see 9 Halsbury's Laws (4th edn) paras 1144–1146, and for a case on the subject, see 13 Digest (Reissue) 184, 1607.

For the Coroners Act 1887, ss 4, 6, see 7 Halsbury's Statutes (3rd edn) 243, 245.

For the Coroners (Amendment) Act 1926, ss 13, 26, 27, see ibid 269, 277, 278.

For the Coroners Rules 1953, r 33, see 5 Halsbury's Statutory Instruments (4th reissue) 150.

Cases referred to in judgment
A-G v BBC [1980] 3 All ER 161, [1981] AC 303, [1980] 3 WLR 109, HL.

---

c Section 4(3), so far as material, is set out at p 554 *f*, post
d Section 13(4), so far as material, is set out at p 556 *e*, post

Anisminic Ltd v Foreign Compensation Commission [1969] 1 All ER 208, [1969] 2 AC 147, [1969] 2 WLR 163, HL, Digest (Cont Vol C) 281, 2557b.
Dutton, Re [1892] 1 QB 486, 13 Digest (Reissue) 173, 1468.
Garnett v Ferrand (1827) 6 B & C 611, [1824–34] All ER Rep 244, 108 ER 576, 13 Digest (Reissue) 162, 1342.
R v Divine, ex p Walton [1930] 2 KB 29, [1930] All ER Rep 302, DC, 13 Digest (Reissue) 174, 1473.
R v Ingham (1864) 5 B & S 257, 122 ER 827, 13 Digest (Reissue) 181, 1559.
R v McIntosh (1858) 7 WR 52, 13 Digest (Reissue) 186, 1624.
R v Nat Bell Liquors Ltd [1922] AC 128, [1922] All ER Rep 335, 16 Digest (Reissue) 415, 4572.
Racal Communications Ltd, Re [1980] 2 All ER 634, [1981] AC 374, [1980] 3 WLR 181, HL.

Cases also cited
Anon (1680) 1 Vent 352.
Barty-King v Ministry of Defence [1979] 2 All ER 80.
Bird v Keep [1918] 2 KB 692, CA.
Davis (decd), Re [1967] 1 All ER 688, [1968] 1 QB 72, CA.
Devis (W) & Sons Ltd v Atkins [1977] 3 All ER 40, [1977] AC 931, HL.
Guilfoyle v Home Office [1981] 1 All ER 943, [1981] QB 309, CA.
Jewison v Dyson (1842) 9 M & W 540.
R v Bunney (1689) 1 Salk 190.
R v Directors of Great Western Rly Co (1888) 20 QBD 410, DC.

Application for judicial review
Paulette Campbell, the mother of Richard Campbell who died in Ashford Remand Centre on 31 March 1980, applied, with the leave of Donaldson LJ and Hodgson J granted on 24 November 1980, for an order of certiorari to bring up and quash the verdict, inquisition and rider on his death, returned at Chertsey Coroner's Court on 10 July 1980, by the respondent coroner, George Murdoch McEwen, and a jury. The facts are set out in the judgment of the court.

Stephen Sedley for the applicant.
Robert Webb for the respondent.

Cur adv vult

9 December. **WATKINS LJ** read the following judgment of the court: This is an application for an order of certiorari to quash the verdict and inquisition and rider upon the death of Richard Campbell, returned at Chertsey Coroner's Court on 10 July 1980 by the respondent, who is Her Majesty's Coroner for Surrey, and a jury. The deceased Richard Campbell was the son of the applicant.

The statement originally filed with the notice of motion under RSC Ord 53, r 3(2) set out three grounds on which relief was sought, namely: (i) the coroner withdrew from the jury its power and duty to return a true verdict according to the evidence, and instead sought (a) to persuade the jury to return a verdict of self-neglect and (b) to withdraw a possible verdict of negligence or of lack of care on the part of the authorities; (ii) in so far as the direction of the coroner to the jury was derived from the provisions of r 33 of the Coroners Rules 1953, SI 1953/205, as amended by the Coroners' (Amendment) Rules 1977, SI 1977/1881, the provisions of that rule purporting to forbid the framing of a verdict in such a way as to appear to determine any questions of civil liability is beyond the rule-making power contained in ss 26 and 27 of the Coroners (Amendment) Act 1926, and so void; (iii) the forms of verdict open to a coroner's jury are not subject to any limitation save those laid down by statute. At the commencement of the hearing, counsel for the applicant, sought to add three further grounds, of which we allowed two,

namely; (iv) the jury was summoned with partiality and therefore unlawfully, rendering
the constitution of the court void; (v) the inquisitions and rider misrepresent the findings   *a*
and verdict of the jury.

The relevant facts are as follows: on 1 March 1980 Richard Campbell, aged 19, was
arrested for attempted burglary, and was charged with that offence the following day.
He said his name was Anthony Benjamin Brown, but otherwise refused to give any
particulars of himself. On 2 March 1980 he made a statement under caution in which
he said that he intended to steal clothing and sell it to give money to the poor. He was   *b*
remanded in custody on 3 March by a magistrate, who ordered that his fingerprints be
taken. This established his true identity. On 10 March at Camberwell Green Magistrates'
Court he pleaded guilty to the charge of attempted burglary. He was again remanded in
custody for social inquiry and medical reports, and was taken to Ashford Remand
Centre. He was at this time the subject of both supervision and probation orders in
relation to the commission by him of criminal offences. His criminal record includes the   *c*
offence of possessing cannabis.

From the time that he arrived at the remand centre, where he was visited by the
probation officer who had supervised him, Richard Campbell refused both food and
drink. On 21 March Dr Chauhan, one of the medical officers at the remand centre,
diagnosed that he was suffering from schizophrenia. Dr Chauhan and Dr Booth signed
orders made under s 60 of the Mental Health Act 1959. On 23 March he was found to   *d*
be in a collapsed state, suffering from circulatory failure. Immediate arrangements were
made for his admission to a general hospital. While there he was unco-operative, and
after an episode of violence the medical staff decided that he was unsuitable for a general
hospital and arranged to transfer him to a psychiatric hospital. On arrival there, he was
seen by a doctor who considered that he was not showing signs of mental illness and that
there was no need for him to be admitted to that hospital. Richard Campbell was
therefore returned to the remand centre. The staff there were so concerned about his
condition that they took the only course open to them, which was to feed him forcibly
by tube. This resulted in a considerable increase in his weight, and the doctors expected
him to recover, but he died suddenly on the morning of 31 March.

The inquest was opened on 8 May 1980 before the coroner sitting alone. Evidence of
identification and as to the medical cause of death was given. The coroner then adjourned
the hearing until 10 July 1980, and issued a certificate for burial. The medical evidence
was that the cause of death was dehydration due to schizophrenia.

On 10 July the coroner sat with a jury of 10 persons. The way in which the members
of that jury were selected is a separate issue, the subject of counsel for the applicant's
ground (iv), and we will relate the relevant facts when we come to deal with that issue.

At some time before 10 July, a form of inquisition for use at the conclusion of the
inquest was prepared. The document as finally completed was put in evidence before
us. It consists of a printed pro forma, with spaces in which the following information
can be inserted: (a) the place at which and dates upon which the inquest was held; (b) the
name of the coroner; (c) the name of the deceased; (d) the place, time and date of death;
(e) the cause of death; (f) the verdict; and (g) the age and occupation of the deceased. At
the foot are spaces for the signatures of the coroner and the members of the jury.

Before the resumed hearing on 10 July, the information under all the headings except
the name of the coroner (which never was recorded) and the verdict was typed on the
form. In accordance with the evidence which the coroner had already received on 8
May, the cause of death was recorded as 'Dehydration due to Schizophrenia, which
developed while he was a Prisoner on Remand at that establishment, H.M. Remand
Centre'. Thus all that remained was for the verdict to be inserted and the document to
be signed.

On 10 July the coroner, having informed the jury of their functions, the nature of a
coroner's court and the kinds of verdicts they were entitled to consider, recalled all the
evidence which he had heard on 8 May, including all the evidence of the medical
witnesses as to the cause of death, together with other evidence, mainly that of officers

at the remand centre. The coroner allowed the witnesses to be questioned by Sir Lionel Thompson, on behalf of the family of the deceased, and Mr Robert Griffiths, on behalf of the Treasury Solicitor.

At the conclusion of the evidence, the coroner summed up to the jury. Having summarised the evidence he turned to explain the verdicts which were open to them. He dealt first with verdicts which were not relevant, in effect directing the jury that it would not be proper to bring in a verdict of homicide, death by natural causes or accidental death. He then proceeded to deal with verdicts which were open to the jury. He explained what he called the two common verdicts of suicide and an open verdict. Justifiably, in our view, he strongly advised the jury against a verdict of suicide and in some detail invited them to refrain, because of the unsatisfactory nature of it, from returning an open verdict. He then went on to say:

> 'That leaves the one rare verdict I spoke of and that is self-neglect. That explains itself in the case of a person found dead in a house with plenty of food available and heating to enable him to survive. Dr Lee and Dr Chauhan said that he [sic] had dealt with several cases which to my surprise were death from dehydration. He went on to speak of an instance of an elderly recluse neglecting themselves [sic]. There may be no psychiatric diagnosis for an elderly person being found dead in such circumstances apart from eccentricity, and eccentricity is not of course a psychiatric diagnosis. You may consider on the evidence you have heard that a verdict of self-neglect would be appropriate on this evidence you have heard in this case, but in this case (you have got clear psychiatric evidence to account for eccentricity and that psychiatric diagnosis is schizophrenia. If you think that this applies you enter the cause of death as dehydration due to schizophrenia. You must give that as the cause, the cause that was given by the expert witness, Dr Lee. You must accept his opinion. So the cause is as given by him and your verdict if you think that appropriate would be self-neglect. It would only be right to add "whilst suffering from schizophrenia". It may be that you would wish to retire to consider your verdict or deliberate your verdict. Your verdict need not be unanimous provided you have not more than two dissenters. Is there any more you wish me to explain about verdicts?'

In response to this question, the jury asked: 'Could there be a fourth verdict, negligence by the authorities?' The coroner replied: 'If you remember at the beginning I said that your duty does not include apportioning blame to anybody. There is no such verdict as the one you are suggesting.' The jury then retired to consider their verdict. After 25 minutes they returned and asked for further assistance, which they were given as follows:

> *Jury.* The question is we are hazy on the interpretation of a couple of the verdicts we can bring in. Perhaps you might go through them again. Certainly we hold that suicide did not apply in this case out of the three but the other two options, open verdict or self-neglect, we are a little bit hazy on the interpretation.
>
> *Coroner.* Let us look firstly at what I said on the open verdict. We can miss out the one I suggested about the person known to have suicidal tendencies, otherwise an open verdict is appropriate when, on the evidence you have heard, you are unable to make up your mind that any verdict applies. I said it was a verdict that should be avoided if at all possible.
>
> *Jury.* Can you elaborate more please?
>
> *Coroner.* It is when you are forced into a corner and there is no other verdict you think is available to you. In other words, you do not know, you cannot decide. To enlarge perhaps as to neglect, there is also a form of neglect, not necessarily self-neglect but perhaps by other people, that is appropriate. Listen carefully to that. That is appropriate either in cases when a person who is legally responsible for the care of another has shown lack of care which, whilst not amounting to negligence

sufficient to justify a charge of manslaughter—you cannot charge anyone because this is not a criminal court. So where a person who is legally responsible for the care of another and shows a lack of care which whilst not amounting to negligence sufficient to justify a trial of manslaughter is thought worthy of censure. You may look at it in that way, that it is lack of care of somebody else rather than his neglect. The difficulty you get into on that is that if you bring such a verdict as lack of care, you have heard or at least it appears to me that you have heard that the Ashford Remand Centre were looking after him to the best of their ability when the circumstances were against them. In other words, they would like to have put him into physical care or into psychiatric care but neither hospital would accept him. The reason for that as you heard from Dr Booth is that there is no room apart from these very specialised hospitals and even then they have to have a bed to put the patient into. The deficiency is not in the staff of the Ashford Remand Centre not doing their best, the problem for them is that they are stuffed with patients they are wanting to get into other physical hospitals or mental hospitals, physical hospitals come first. It is the more desirable place for the patient to go. But he is not accepted there because he has shown violence. Of course, the general hospital, as a mental hospital, has to think of all the patients. One cannot be cared for to the complete exclusion of all the others. If this man had been repeatedly violent there would not be any doubt about this. There is only this one instance of violence. So I feel on the evidence you have heard that certainly Ashford Remand Centre was responsible for the care of this man. They were stuck from doing what they wanted to do, not that that they did not do what they wanted to do or could do, but they were stuck because of the deficiency of the lack of facilities to receive him. In addition to there not being a place that would take him, of course even then there is this lack of co-operation and Dr Booth in particular said that probably, had he gone into psychiatric unit, they could not have done any more for him than they did at the Remand Centre. Equally, while he does not co-operate there is nothing much more that the general hospital can do for him. It is this lack of co-operation and this, as I suggested to you, is not like an elderly recluse who fails to look after himself, he does not have a psychiatric diagnosis to account for his not trying to survive or survive when the facilities are there. As far as this man is concerned the facilities for survival were there had he co-operated. It was lack of co-operation because as Dr Booth said it was this psychiatric condition that he suffered from.

Jury. We are not sure about that. In discussion we felt obviously that the chap in question because of his mental condition which we have heard contributed to his death, about not eating and drinking; the question in our mind is how we should interpret this in the verdict inasmuch as was everything done to keep the man alive.

Coroner. Would you like to hear again from Dr Booth, who is the best person to try to help you on this answer. I think he is the best person.

Jury. I do not think he could be much help.

Coroner. Can I help you any more?

Jury. No.

Coroner. I can see the difficulty you are in with your duty to come to a satisfactory verdict. Dr Booth I am suggesting might be able to enlarge on what could have been done for him elsewhere than in the Remand Centre.

One of the spectators at the inquest. We beg you to have the witnesses please.

Jury. Another question: it was suggested he was a likeable sort of chap and he was not suffering from schizophrenia and then the evidence suggested in a very short time, three or four weeks . . .

Coroner (interrupting). That is a question the doctor could help you on. Let us have Dr Booth again.'

Dr Booth who is a psychiatrist and who signed the s 60 order was then recalled. He gave further evidence which included an explanation of his diagnosis of schizophrenia, a mental illness which he told the jury can suddenly affect someone who previously had always been regarded as a normal person. The jury then asked a further question, and the coroner advised them as follows. The jury asked: 'There were three verdicts you directed to us, is that correct?' The coroner again referred to all the verdicts he had left to the jury including lack of care, of which he said:

> 'I said at the beginning there is no duty on this court to apportion blame and the people who are responsible who might come under this head of lack of care are the staff and the medical staff of the Ashford Remand Centre. On the evidence you heard they apparently did what they could. The difficulty as I said was not that there was lack of care, it was that they got landed with a patient who was extremely difficult for them and they were making every effort to get him to a place that might perhaps look after him to a greater degree. But nevertheless, one of the major factors was probably told to you within the evidence and that was this man's lack of co-operation. I have suggested that Dr Booth might enlarge on whether, had he got into either a psychiatric room or a general hospital, they might have done any better than the remand centre did remembering always that there is this lack of co-operation. Do you think Dr Booth can help you on that.
>
> *Jury.* No.
>
> *Coroner.* I do not think anyone else can. I started this inquest on 8 May so that the new Coroners Rules apply which did not allow riders from 1 June [sic]. So we can add a rider which points out, I think it probably would point that we draw attention to this lack of facilities to receive such a patient.
>
> *Jury.* We are not being asked about the cause?
>
> *Coroner.* You have been given the cause of death and nobody would argue with Dr Lee. It is not only Dr Lee, it has been accepted by counsel on Dr Lee's evidence; everything he did was confirmed by their Dr Pullar.'

The jury then retired again, and in due course returned a verdict of self-neglect, with a rider relating to the lack of specialist facilities, both medical staff and premises, to deal with such cases. The coroner asked then whether they wished to add: 'suffering from schizophrenia' to their verdict, but the jury replied: 'We are not very happy with that particular aspect.'

The coroner then filled in the blank space on the form of inquisition that the deceased 'Died from self neglect (accompanying rider)'. He did not delete the words 'due to schizophrenia' as the cause of death. The rider, which was prepared in manuscript was in the following terms:

> 'At an inquest held at Chertsey to enquire into the death of Richard Campbell the jury added a rider expressing its concern at the lack of specialist care facilities both in staff and accommodation available to the deceased who died in the medical block of A.R.C. from dehydration due to schizophrenia.'

After seeing the rider, all the members of the jury signed the inquisition as did the coroner. The rider was signed by the coroner only.

We now turn to consider the submissions made to us.

The first three grounds on which relief is sought can be summarised in two sentences, namely: (a) the coroner withdrew from the jury a verdict which was properly open to them, namely neglect by another person or persons; (b) the coroner put improper pressure on the jury to return a verdict of self-neglect. We will deal with these two points together.

It is necessary to start by considering how far a coroner is amenable to judicial reivew, ie what is the extent of the High Court's powers to control a coroner's inquest?

Until the Coroners Act 1887 came into force, the only such power was at common law. We were referred to a decision of the Court of Queen's Bench, namely *R v McIntosh* (1858) 7 WR 52, a motion for a rule nisi for certiorari to bring up and quash a coroner's inquisition on the ground that the coroner misdirected the jury as to the law. Lord Campbell CJ is briefly reported as saying:

> 'I think the law gives us no such power. If the inquisition is bad on the face of it, or fraud is alleged, we might interfere, but this court cannot interpose on account of alleged misdirection of the coroner which does not appear on the record. We all think that you have shown no ground for our interference.'

A similar decision was reached in *R v Ingham* (1864) 5 B & S 257, 122 ER 827.

Counsel for the applicant submitted that, in addition to the grounds for intervention referred to by Lord Campbell CJ, the High Court both before 1887 and now had power to intervene if it were shown that the coroner had exceeded his jurisdiction, eg if he brought in a verdict not permitted by law, or if he refused jurisdiction. In this part of his submission, counsel for the applicant was using the word 'jurisdiction' in its narrow, technical sense. So limited, we agree with this submission.

Apart from this limited right to challenge the result of a coroner's inquest, it is clear that there was no other before 1887. Section 6 of the Coroners Act 1887 introduced a wide power for the High Court to quash a coroner's inquisition and order a new inquest to be held. The power is granted—

> 'Where Her Majesty's High Court . . . is satisfied either—(*a*) that a coroner refuses or neglects to hold an inquest which ought to be held; or (*b*) where an inquest has been held by a coroner that by reason of fraud, rejection of evidence, irregularity of proceedings, insufficiency of inquiry, or otherwise, it is necessary or desirable in the interests of justice that another inquest should be held . . .'

There is, however, a restriction on this power: an application under the section may only be made 'by or under the authority of the Attorney-General'. It seems to us that the grounds on which an application may be made under s 6 comprehend the grounds on which, before 1887, the court had power to intervene. Nevertheless, s 35 of the 1887 Act specifically preserved 'the jurisdiction of the High Court or of any judge thereof in relation to or over a coroner of his duties'. Thus it follows in our judgment that, in such a case as the present in which the Attorney General declines to make or authorise the making of an application under s 6, the court retains the power to order judicial review where there has been an error on the face of the inquisition, fraud, or an excess or refusal of jurisdiction by the coroner.

Counsel for the applicant then submits that since the judgment of the House of Lords in *Anisminic Ltd v Foreign Compensation Commission* [1969] 1 All ER 208, [1969] 2 AC 147 a misdirection by the coroner can be understood as a matter going to his jurisdiction, and thus is within the control of the High Court at common law. In *Anisminic* the plaintiffs, an English company, owned property in Egypt which was sequestrated by the Egyptian government at the time of the Suez incident in 1956. The plaintiffs claimed compensation under an order made under the Foreign Compensation Act 1950. The Foreign Compensation Commission decided that the plaintiffs were not persons entitled to claim compensation under the order. Section 4(4) of the 1950 Act provided: 'The determination by the Commission of any application made to them under this Act shall not be called in question in any court of law.' The plaintiffs sought a declaration that the commission's decision was based on a misinterpretation of the order and was a nullity.

The commission argued that, by virtue of s 4, their decision was a determination which could not be challenged in a court of law. The House of Lords, by a majority, held that the commission had misdirected themselves, that their decision was thus a nullity which went to their jurisdiction, and that s 4 did not operate to prevent the courts from granting the declaration sought.

In his speech Lord Reid said ([1969] 1 All ER 208 at 213–214, [1969] 2 AC 147 at 171):

> 'I have come without hesitation to the conclusion that in this case we are not prevented from enquiring whether the order of the Commission was a nullity. It has sometimes been said that it is only where a tribunal acts without jurisdiction

that its decision is a nullity. But in such cases the word "jurisdiction" has been used in a very wide sense, and I have come to the conclusion that it is better not to use the term except in the narrow and original sense of the tribunal being entitled to enter on the enquiry in question. But there are many cases where, although the tribunal had jurisdiction to enter on the enquiry, it has done or failed to do something in the course of the enquiry which is of such a nature that its decision is a nullity. It may have given its decision in bad faith. It may have made a decision which it had no power to make. It may have failed in the course of the enquiry to comply with the requirements of natural justice. It may in perfect good faith have misconstrued the provisions giving it the power to act so that it failed to deal with the question remitted to it and decided some question which was not remitted to it. It may have refused to take into account something which it was required to take into account. Or it may have based its decision on some matter which, under the provisions setting it up, it had no right to take into account. I do not intend this list to be exhaustive. But if it decides a question remitted to it for decision without committing any of these errors it is as much entitled to decide that question wrongly as it is to decide it rightly.'

Lord Pearce said ([1969] 1 All ER 208 at 233–234, [1969] 2 AC 147 at 195):

'The courts have, however, always been careful to distinguish their intervention whether on excess of jurisdiction or error of law from an appellate function. Their jurisdiction over inferior tribunals is supervision, not review. "That supervision goes to two points: one is the area of the inferior jurisdiction and the qualifications and conditions of its exercise; the other is the observance of the law in the course of its exercise" (R. v. Nat Bell Liquors, Ltd. [1922] 2 AC 128 at 156, [1922] All ER Rep 335 at 351). It is simply an enforcement of Parliament's mandate to the tribunal. If the tribunal is intended, on a true construction of the Act, to enquire into and finally decide questions within a certain area, the courts' supervisory duty is to see that it makes the authorised enquiry according to natural justice and arrives at a decision whether right or wrong. They will intervene if the tribunal asks itself the wrong questions (i.e., questions other than those which Parliament directed it to ask itself). But if it directs itself to the right enquiry, asking the right questions, they will not intervene merely because it has or may have come to the wrong answer, provided that this is an answer that lies within its jurisdiction.'

For convenience, we shall refer to this definition of the ambit of the court's supervisory powers as 'the Anisminic principle'. The question we have to decide is whether this principle applies, as counsel for the applicant contends, to a coroner's inquest, so as to give the High Court at common law a power of control over a much wider field than the limited categories to which we have referred above.

Counsel for the coroner argues that a coroner's inquest is a court and that the Anisminic principle in terms relates to, and is restricted to, statutory tribunals, and that thus it has no application to any inferior court. In support of the contention that a coroner's inquest is a court he relies not merely on the common usage of referring to 'the coroner's court', but to passages in some of the speeches in the recent decision of the House of Lords in A-G v BBC [1980] 3 All ER 161, [1981] AC 303, in which several of their Lordships specifically said that the coroner's court is a court (see [1980] 3 All ER 161 at 166, 169, 179, [1981] AC 303 at 338, 342, 356 per Viscount Dilhorne, Lord Salmon and Lord Scarman). Counsel for the coroner also refers to Garnett v Ferrand (1827) 6 B & C 611 at 625, [1824–34] All ER Rep 244 at 245, in which Lord Tenterden CJ said:

'The Court of the coroner is a Court of Record of which the coroner is the Judge; and it is a general rule of very great antiquity, that no action will lie against a Judge of Record for any matter done by him in the exercise of his judicial functions.'

For his proposition that the Anisminic principle relates only to statutory tribunals, counsel for the coroner relies not only on the passages from the speeches in that case to which we have referred, but also on the speech of Lord Diplock in *Re Racal Communications Ltd* [1980] 2 All ER 634 at 638, [1981] AC 374 at 382, in which he said: 'In *Anisminic*, this House was concerned only with decisions of administrative tribunals.'

Counsel for the applicant in reply submits that the issue is not whether a coroner's inquest is a court, but whether it is a body to which the *Anisminic* principle applies.

In 3 Co Inst (1817 edn) p 271, Coke refers to the court of the coroner and states: 'the court which he holdeth is a court of record'. In his day it was a court with very considerable powers, some of which it does not now possess. However that may be, we have no doubt that a coroner's inquest is still a court, though one having characteristics which are unique in the English legal system, in that its function is to investigate but not to reach a final decision such as a judgment order or verdict of guilt. In our judgment the *Anisminic* principle was not intended to be applied to a court. The passages from that decision and from *Re Racal Communications Ltd* which we have cited make it clear, in our view, that the principle is limited to tribunals established by statute, and probably to those tribunals from whose decisions, under the relevant statute, there is no right of appeal. Thus in our view the principle does not apply to coroners' inquests.

There is, however, a second, more general, reason which leads us to the same conclusion. From most inferior courts, the county court, the Crown Court and magistrates' courts, there is a statutory right of appeal. The High Court, in addition, exercises a supervisory role over these courts, but within a strictly limited sphere. The effect of *Anisminic* is that the High Court has powers to control the decisions of statutory tribunals, which extend over a wider field than the powers relating to courts because there is no, or only a limited, right to appeal from the decisions of such tribunals. It is for this reason that in principle a wider power of intervention in relation to tribunals exists. They resemble in most respects the wide powers given by s 6 of the 1887 Act to challenge decisions of coroners' inquests, subject only to the application being made by or under the authority of the Attorney General. These powers were a considerable addition to those which existed previously and which were expressly saved by s 35.

We must now decide whether, on the facts, the coroner has exceeded or failed to exercise his proper jurisdiction. Section 4(3) of the 1887 Act requires a coroner and his jury to inquire 'who the deceased was, and how, when, and where he came by his death'. If a coroner withdraws from the jury a verdict which should be open to them, he is improperly restricting their answer to the question 'how?' This would, in our view, be failure to exercise his jurisdiction. Counsel for the applicant submits, and we agree, that in this case the coroner was apparently concerned not to transgress r 33 of the Coroners Rules 1953, as amended in 1977. That rule now reads:

'No verdict shall be framed in such a way as to appear to determine any question of—(*a*) criminal liability on the part of a named person, or (*b*) civil liability.'

It is immediately apparent that there may, in some cases, be a possibility of conflict between r 33(*b*) and the duty under s 4 to inquire 'how' the deceased came by his death. Counsel for the applicant therefore submits that r 33(*b*) is ultra vires. This apparent conflict is discussed in a passage in *Jervis on Coroners* (9th edn, 1957) p 179, in a section dealing with the verdicts of 'self-neglect and lack of care'. The passage reads:

'The verdict of lack of care is recommended where a person who, owing to his inability to look after himself, is being cared for by others, dies and his death is due to starvation or exposure or similar causes brought about by the failure of such other persons to look after him properly. There is an obvious danger that such a verdict will conflict or appear to conflict with rule 33 of the Coroners Rules 1953, which forbids the verdict to appear to determine any question of civil liability. To avoid such conflict the verdict is careful to refrain from stating that the death was aggravated by the lack of care of any particular person or persons and merely states it was aggravated by lack of care. There is, therefore, no suggestion that any person owed a duty of care towards the deceased, breach of which would render that person liable for civil or criminal negligence.'

We agree with this comment. A verdict of 'lack of care by another or others' without more is clearly one which a jury is competent to find if the evidence warrants it without transgressing r 33.

On this issue it seems to us that there may have been a misunderstanding between the coroner and the jury. It appears to have been the coroner's view that a verdict of lack of care would inevitably be understood to mean lack of care by the staff of the Ashford Remand Centre. The jury, on the other hand, seem to have been concerned about the lack of facilities and staff at the two hospitals which declined to keep, or admit, the deceased. Be that as it may, it is our view that on the facts of this case a verdict of 'lack of care' would not have contravened r 33. It is therefore not necessary for us to decide whether the rule is ultra vires. But, we think we ought nevertheless to express our conclusion on this point, which is that counsel for the applicant's submission on it is ill-founded. Such conflict as may in any given circumstance appear to arise between r 33 and the duty to inquire 'how' must be resolved in favour of the statutory duty to inquire whatever the consequences of this may be. Thus the question is: did the coroner withdraw from the jury the verdict of 'lack of care'? It seems that at first he did intend to do so, but when the jury returned for further directions he revised his view and directed them that they could return such a verdict. This was the direction they received immediately before bringing in their verdict, and thus was the effective direction. It follows that the first point of counsel for the applicant fails on the facts.

His second point, that the coroner put improper pressure on the jury to bring in a verdict of self-neglect, is not in our view a point which goes to jurisdiction. It is a point which could be taken on an application under s 6, but it cannot form the basis of an application for judicial review.

We are not called on, therefore, to consider what comments a coroner is properly entitled to make to his jury which reflect his own feelings about whether or not the evidence justifies the bringing in of one of the permissible verdicts. It is only right to say, however, that it seems to us that if there was any pressure (we do not think the coroner's expressions of his views could be so described) the jury resolutely withstood it. From the extracts we have quoted of the questions asked, and comments made, by the jury, we think it beyond doubt that the verdict of self-neglect with the rider expressing concern about lack of facilities was the result they wished to achieve. Their difficulty lay, until they were made aware of what a rider could achieve, in finding a suitable way of expressing it.

Ground (iv) of the amended notice of motion is that the decision should be quashed because the jury was summoned with partiality. The relevant facts are contained in the affidavits sworn by Mrs Newsome, by the coroner on 5 May 1981, and by the coroner's officer, Mr Scott, on 7 May 1981. A week before the inquest on Richard Campbell the coroner's officer visited the village of Ottershaw, near Chertsey, in order to select 10 persons to serve on the jury. He deposed: 'I do not generally ask women to serve as it has always been my practice and habit to call at a house and ask for the husband.' He called at 88 Brox Road, where Mrs Newsome was cleaning a car. He asked for her husband and told her the purpose of his request. She said that her husband was not in, whereupon Mr Scott walked away to the house next door. While he was there, Mrs Newsome approached him and protested that he had not asked her to serve on the jury. After some discussion Mr Scott agreed that she could do so, and she did. In the event she was the only woman on the jury of 10, presumably because Mr Scott had continued to ask only men to serve.

We are prepared to assume that this is an issue which falls within the control of this court at common law. The statutory requirement for membership of a coroner's jury is in s 3 of the Coroners Act 1887: it shall be not less than 7 nor more than 11 'good and lawful men'. The word 'men' clearly includes 'women' under the Interpretation Act 1889 and as a result of the Sex Disqualification (Removal) Act 1919. The Juries Act 1974 does not apply to coroners' juries.

There are very few authorities as to the criteria to be used in the choice of such a jury.
R v Divine, ex p Walton [1930] 2 KB 29, [1930] All ER Rep 302 established that the
practice of summoning juries from a small panel of regular jurymen is improper. A
coroner's jury is not, however, to be equated with a jury in the Crown Court, and the
procedure for selection of such a jury does not apply to a coroner's inquest. Hawkins J
said in *Re Dutton* [1892] 1 QB 486 at 488: 'Coroners' juries have to be called together in
haste, and for this reason the ordinary rules for summoning juries do not apply to them.'

But the practice of excluding women, by prior decision or custom, from a coroner's
jury is nowadays wrong. Thus we have no doubt that Mr Scott's custom of not asking
women to serve on the jury, no matter what his motives for this were, was misguided
and incorrect in law. If such a practice is adopted elsewhere, it should cease.

Does that invalidate the decision of this jury? In our judgment it does not. When Mrs
Newsome asked that she should serve, Mr Scott agreed immediately. While no other
women were selected, there is nothing to suggest that this particular jury was otherwise
not composed of a random selection of local people. All the indications are that they
possessed independence of mind, intelligence and judgment. Thus there is no ground
here for quashing the decision.

Ground (vi) relates to the inclusion both in the inquisition and the rider of the words
'due to schizophrenia'. This is, in our view, a point within the control of this court. We
have already referred to the relevant facts. We have the distinct impression that the jury
did not wish a reference to schizophrenia to be included either in the cause of death, or
in the rider. The words are in the inquisition because they had already been typed in and
were not deleted. Counsel for the coroner makes two submissions on this issue: (a) the
members of the jury all signed the inquisition and approved the wording of the rider;
and (b) s 13(4) of the Coroners (Amendment) Act 1926 provides, in so far as it is relevant:

'Where . . . any part of an inquest is held without a jury, anything done . . . at that
part of the inquest, by or before the coroner alone shall be as validly done as if it had
been done by or before the coroner and a jury.'

Thus the conclusion as to the cause of death reached by the coroner alone was valid and
should not be set aside.

As to the first point, the signatures of the jurors do not of themselves make a verdict
which was not theirs into one which was, though they are of course strong evidence.
Since we have concluded that the jury did not intend to include schizophrenia as a cause
of death, this argument fails. The insertion of the word 'schizophrenia' in the rider was
made by the coroner because we suspect he thought that for the sake of uniformity the
cause of death in the rider should coincide with that already recorded in the
inquisition. This was a mistake in the circumstances of this case. The second point we
think might prevail if the coroner had not, quite properly, recalled the medical
evidence. But he did recall that evidence, and thereby left the decision as to the cause of
death to the jury. Thus his own prior decision ceased to be effective.

It follows that on this issue the applicant succeeds. How should this decision take
effect? The relief claimed, according to the amended statement, is the quashing of the
inquisition and rider. We will hear any further representations on this matter which
counsel wish to address to us, but our present view is that we can and should direct to
issue: (a) an amended inquisition from which the words 'due to schizophrenia' are
deleted; and (b) an amended rider from which the words 'due to schizophrenia'
are deleted.

*Order under s 20 of the Coroners Act 1887 directing officer of the court to amend inquisition and
rider accordingly.*

Solicitors: *Harazi*, Brixton (for the applicant); *Le Brasseur & Bury* (for the coroner).

Jacqueline Charles   Barrister.

Inland Revenue Commissioners v Metrolands (Property Finance) Ltd

HOUSE OF LORDS

LORD WILBERFORCE, LORD SIMON OF GLAISDALE, LORD RUSSELL OF KILLOWEN, LORD SCARMAN AND LORD BRIDGE OF HARWICH

10, 11 FEBRUARY, 4 MARCH 1982

Development land tax – Disposal of interest in land – Time of disposal – Compulsory acquisition of interest in land – Taxpayer serving purchase notice on planning authority – Acceptance of purchase notice by planning authority – Parties subsequently agreeing amount of compensation – Deemed compulsory acquisition of interest in land – When interest in land disposed of for purposes of liability to tax – Town and Country Planning Act 1971, s 181(1)(2) – Development Land Tax Act 1976, s 45(2)(4).

On 9 May 1974 a local authority (the council) refused planning permission for houses to be built on the taxpayer's land and on 8 October the taxpayer served a purchase notice on the council under s 180[a] of the Town and Country Planning Act 1971 requiring the council to purchase the land. On 20 December, pursuant to s 181(1)[b] of the 1971 Act, the council served a notice on the taxpayer that it was willing to comply with the purchase notice. On 11 August 1976 the taxpayer and the council agreed the compensation payable for the acquisition of the interest in land, with the benefit of a certificate of alternative development which had meanwhile been granted, in the sum of £64,650. The taxpayer was assessed to development land tax in the sum of £29,085 under s 1 of the Development Land Tax Act 1976, on the ground that the disposal of the land to the council had taken place on 11 August 1976. The taxpayer appealed to the Special Commissioners against the assessment, contending that the service of the purchase notice and its acceptance, or the notification of its acceptance, by the council on 20 December 1974 constituted an enforceable contract for sale between the parties within s 45(2)[c] of the 1976 Act and accordingly that the land had been disposed of before 1 August 1976, the date when development land tax first became chargeable. The Crown contended that once the council had accepted the purchase notice it was deemed by s 181(2) to be authorised to acquire the land compulsorily and to have served a notice to treat in respect of such acquisition, that there was no enforceable contract between the parties until the amount of the compensation had been agreed between them, that no agreement was reached until 11 August 1976 when the council approved the compensation terms and that, consequently, s 45(4) of the 1976 Act applied, with the result that 11 August 1976 was the date on which the interest in the land had been disposed of. The commissioners allowed the appeal, holding that there was a contract between the parties when the council informed the taxpayer that it had accepted the purchase notice on 20 December 1974 and that accordingly the disposal by the taxpayer of its land occurred on that date so that no tax was chargeable. The judge allowed an appeal by the Crown holding that the deeming provision in s 181(2) was applicable to s 45(4) of the 1976 Act, with the result that the council's acquisition of the taxpayer's interest in the land following the purchase notice fell to be treated as a compulsory acquisition of that interest within s 45(4) of the 1976 Act and that the disposal of the taxpayer's interest in the land did not take place until 11 August 1976 when the amount of the compensation was approved by the council. The taxpayer appealed direct to the House of Lords.

Held – Land acquired pursuant to a purchase notice under s 180 of the 1971 Act by way of a compliance notice under s 181(1)(a) or (b) of that Act and the deeming provisions

---

a   Section 180, so far as material, is set out at p 560 *c* to *f*, post

b   Section 181, so far as material, is set out at p 560 *f* to *h*, post

c   Section 45, so far as material, is set out at p 559 *f* to *j*, post

under s 181(2) could just as aptly be described as having been 'acquired compulsorily' within s 45(4) of the 1976 Act as if it had been acquired by way of confirmation of the purchase notice under s 183(1)^d of the 1971 Act and the deeming provisions under s 186(1)^e thereof. It followed that the taxpayer was to be taken to have disposed of its interest in land only on 11 August 1976 when the amount of the compensation was approved by the council and accordingly was chargeable to development land tax on the disposal. The appeal would therefore be dismissed (see p 558 *g* to p 559 *a* and *j* to p 560 *a*, p 562 *b c* and *j* to p 563 *a* and *j* to p 564 *a*, post).

Decision of Nourse J [1981] 2 All ER 166 affirmed.

Notes

For the charge to development land tax, see Supplement to 5 Halsbury's Laws (4th edn) para 300A.1.

For deemed notice to treat on notice of compliance and the effect of a notice to treat, see 8 ibid paras 94, 136.

For the Town and Country Planning Act 1971, ss 180, 181, 183, 186, see 41 Halsbury's Statutes (3rd edn) 1788, 1790, 1792, 1796.

For the Development Land Tax Act 1976, ss 1, 45, see 46 ibid 1427, 1501.

Case referred to in opinions

Cary-Elwes's Contract, Re [1906] 2 Ch 143, 17 Digest (Reissue) 281, 482.

Appeal

Metrolands (Property Finance) Ltd (the taxpayer company) appealed direct to the House of Lords pursuant to a certificate granted by Nourse J under s 12 of the Administration of Justice Act 1969 and with leave of the House granted on 18 February 1981 against the order of Nourse J ([1981] 2 All ER 166, [1981] 1 WLR 637) dated 11 December 1980 whereby he allowed an appeal by way of case stated (the case is set out at [1981] 2 All ER 168–174) by the Crown from a determination of the Commissioners for the Special Purposes of the Income Tax Acts discharging an assessment to development land tax in the sum of £29,085 made on the taxpayer company. The facts are set out in the opinion of Lord Bridge.

D C Potter QC, R M K Gray and *N G A King* for the taxpayer company.
D R Woolley QC, Robert Carnwath and *Viscount Dilhorne* for the Crown.

Their Lordships took time for consideration.

4 March. The following opinions were delivered.

LORD WILBERFORCE. My Lords, I have had the advantage of reading in draft the speech prepared by my noble and learned friend Lord Bridge, with which I agree. For the reasons he has given I, too, would dismiss the appeal.

LORD SIMON OF GLAISDALE. My Lords, I have been privileged to read in draft the speech about to be delivered by my noble and learned friend Lord Bridge. I agree with it and I would therefore dismiss the appeal.

LORD RUSSELL OF KILLOWEN. My Lords, I have had the advantage of reading in advance the speech to be delivered by my noble and learned friend Lord Bridge. I agree that for the reasons given by him this appeal fails.

---

d Section 183(1), so far as material, is set out at p 560 *j*, post
e Section 186(1) is set out at p 561 *c*, post

LORD SCARMAN. My Lords, I have had the advantage of reading in draft the speech
a to be delivered by my noble and learned friend Lord Bridge. I agree with it and would
therefore dismiss the appeal.

LORD BRIDGE OF HARWICH. My Lords, the taxpayer company formerly owned
a piece of land (the subject land), some 4·31 acres in extent, in the metropolitan borough
of Bolton. On 24 August 1973 they applied for planning permission for residential
b development of the subject land. Permission was refused on 9 May 1974. On 8 October
1974 the taxpayer company served on the Bolton Metropolitan Borough Council a
purchase notice pursuant to s 180(1) of the Town and Country Planning Act 1971
requiring the council to purchase their interest in the subject land. On 20 December
1974 the council served a notice on the taxpayer company, pursuant to s 181(1)(a) of the
1971 Act, stating that they were willing to comply with the purchase notice (the
c compliance notice). On 11 August 1976 the taxpayer company and the council agreed
the compensation payable for the acquisition of the subject land, with the benefit of a
certificate of alternative development which had meanwhile been granted by the local
planning authority, in the sum of £64,650.

The Development Land Tax Act 1976 imposed a new tax, originally at the rate of 80%,
on the realised development value accruing to a landowner on the disposal of his interest
d in land on or after the appointed day, which was 1 August 1976. The sole issue in this
appeal is whether the taxpayer company are chargeable to development land tax on the
disposal of the subject land. If, as the taxpayer company contend, they disposed of the
subject land on 20 December 1974, the date of the compliance notice, they are not so
chargeable. If, as the Crown contends, they disposed of the subject land on 11 August
1976, the date when the compensation was agreed, they are chargeable to tax in the sum
e of £29,085.

The resolution of the issue depends on the true construction of s 45 of the 1976 Act as
applied to the circumstances of the acquisition in question under the statutory machinery
of the 1971 Act set in motion by the service of a purchase notice under s 180. Section 45
of the 1976 Act provides, so far as relevant:

'(1) The provisions of this section shall have effect for determining the time at
which, for the purposes of liability to development land tax, an interest in land is to
be taken to be disposed of . . .
(2) Subject to . . . the following provisions of this section, where under a contract
f an interest in land is disposed of . . . then . . . (b) . . . the time at which the disposal
. . . is made is the time the contract is made and not, if it is different, the time at
which the interest is conveyed or transferred . . .
(4) Subject to subsections (5) and (8) below, where an interest in land is acquired
compulsorily by an authority possessing compulsory powers, the time at which the
disposal . . . is made is the time at which the compensation for the acquisition is
agreed or otherwise determined (variations on appeal being disregarded for this
purpose) or, if earlier, the time when the authority enter on the land in pursuance
of their powers . . .
g (8) . . . where an interest in land is disposed of on or after the appointed day to an
authority possessing compulsory powers then, if notice to treat in respect of that
interest was (or is by virtue of any enactment deemed to have been) served before
13th September 1974 on the person making the disposal, the disposal shall be
treated for the purposes of this Act as having been made before the appointed day
. . .'

The question is whether sub-s (2)(b) or sub-s (4) is the governing provision. It is not
disputed that the council were 'an authority possessing compulsory powers' within sub-
s (4). Since sub-s (2) is subject to sub-s (4), it follows that the first question is whether the
subject land was 'acquired compulsorily'. If so, sub-s (4) applies, the disposal was on 11
August 1976, and the Crown succeeds. If not, and if as the taxpayer company contend,

a binding contract was concluded on service of the compliance notice, the disposal was
on 20 December 1974, and the taxpayer company succeed. There are other theoretical
possibilities, but it will be unnecessary to consider them.

The taxpayer company, having been assessed to development land tax in the sum
mentioned, appealed against the assessment to the Special Commissioners. The Special
Commissioners decided that the subject land had not been acquired compulsorily but
that by service of the compliance notice the council had concluded a binding contract to
purchase it. They accordingly allowed the appeal. On appeal to the Chancery Division
by case stated, Nourse J ([1981] 2 All ER 166, [1981] 1 WLR 637) took the opposite view
and allowed the appeal of the Crown. From that decision the taxpayer company appeal
under the 'leap-frog' procedure of s 12 of the Administration of Justice Act 1969 pursuant
to a certificate granted by the learned judge and by leave of your Lordships' House.

Before proceeding further it will be convenient to set out the provisions of the 1971
Act necessary to an understanding of the purchase notice procedure, so far as relevant to
the issue arising in this case. They are as follows:

'180.—(1) Where, on an application for planning permission to develop any
land, permission is refused . . . then if any owner of the land claims—(a) that the
land has become incapable of reasonably beneficial use in its existing state; and . . .
(c) . . . that the land cannot be rendered capable of reasonably beneficial use by the
carrying out of any other development for which planning permission has been
granted or for which the local planning authority or the Secretary of State has
undertaken to grant planning permission, he may, within the time and in the
manner prescribed by regulations under this Act, serve on the council of the
London borough or county district in which the land is situated a notice requiring
that council to purchase his interest in the land in accordance with the following
provisions of this Part of this Act . . .

(7) A notice under this section, or under any other provision of this Part of this
Act to which this subsection is applied, is in this Act referred to as a "purchase
notice".

181.—(1) The council on whom a purchase notice is served under section 180 of
this Act shall, before the end of the period of three months beginning with the date
of service of that notice, serve on the owner by whom the purchase notice was
served a notice stating either—(a) that the council are willing to comply with the
purchase notice; or (b) that another local authority or statutory undertakers specified
in the notice under this subsection have agreed to comply with it in their place; or
(c) that, for reasons specified in the notice under this subsection, the council are not
willing to comply with the purchase notice and have not found any other local
authority or statutory undertakers who will agree to comply with it in their place,
and that they have transmitted a copy of the purchase notice to the Secretary of
State, on a date specified in the notice under this subsection, together with a
statement of the reasons so specified.

(2) Where the council on whom a purchase notice is served by an owner have
served on him a notice in accordance with subsection (1)(a) or (b) of this section, the
council, or the other local authority or statutory undertakers specified in the notice,
as the case may be, shall be deemed to be authorised to acquire the interest of the
owner compulsorily in accordance with the relevant provisions, and to have served
a notice to treat in respect thereof on the date of service of the notice under that
subsection . . .

183.—(1) Subject to the following provisions of this section . . . if the Secretary
of State is satisfied that the conditions specified in section 180(1)(a) to (c) of this Act
are fulfilled in relation to a purchase notice, he shall confirm the notice.

(2) If it appears to the Secretary of State to be expedient to do so, he may, in lieu
of confirming the purchase notice, grant planning permission for the development
in respect of which the application was made . . .

(3) If it appears to the Secretary of State that the land . . . could be rendered capable of reasonably beneficial use within a reasonable time by the carrying out of any other development for which planning permission ought to be granted, he may, in lieu of confirming the purchase notice . . . direct that planning permission for that development shall be granted in the event of an application being made in that behalf.

(4) If it appears to the Secretary of State, having regard to the probable ultimate use of the land, that it is expedient to do so, he may, if he confirms the notice, modify it, either in relation to the whole or in relation to any part of the land to which it relates, by substituting another local authority or statutory undertakers for the council on whom the notice was served . . .

186.—(1) Where the Secretary of State confirms a purchase notice, the council on whom the purchase notice was served (or, if under section 183(4) of this Act the Secretary of State modified the purchase notice by substituting another local authority or statutory undertakers for that council, that other local authority or those statutory undertakers) shall be deemed to be authorised to acquire the interest of the owner compulsorily in accordance with the relevant provisions and to have served a notice to treat in respect thereof on such date as the Secretary of State may direct . . .

208 . . . the power conferred by section 31 of the Land Compensation Act 1961 to withdraw a notice to treat shall not be exercisable in the case of a notice to treat which is deemed to have been served by virtue of any of the provisions of this Part of this Act.' ·

It is common ground that certain features of the ordinary compulsory purchase procedure flow from the deeming provisions of ss 181(2) and 186(1) in the same way as they would flow from an actual authorisation of compulsory acquisition and the actual service of a notice to treat, subject only to the exclusion by s 208 of the acquiring authority's statutory power to withdraw the notice to treat. Thus, the acquiring authority can at any time enter and take possession of the land on 14 days' notice: see the Compulsory Purchase Act 1965, s 11(1). If the compensation is not agreed either party may refer the question of disputed compensation to the Lands Tribunal: see the 1965 Act, s 6. Once the compensation has been agreed or determined, either party can, if necessary, enforce completion of the acquisition, the acquiring authority by payment of the compensation into court and execution of a deed poll vesting the land in itself (see the 1965 Act, s 9), the landowners by an action for specific performance (see *Re Cary-Elwes's Contract* [1906] 2 Ch 143).

The essence of the argument for the taxpayer company is that the service of the purchase notice was an unconditional offer by the taxpayer company to sell the subject land at a price to be determined in accordance with the statutory provisions which would be applicable to the assessment of compensation on a compulsory purchase and that the council's service of the compliance notice was a voluntary and unconditional acceptance of that offer. Thus, on the principle id certum est quod certum reddi potest, it is submitted that the offer and acceptance concluded a binding contract for the sale of the subject land on 20 December 1974. Counsel for the taxpayer company supported this argument by reference to a number of nineteenth century decisions in which the situation arising from service of notice to treat in the course of a compulsory acquisition, followed by a determination of the compensation due by the appropriate statutory procedure, has been referred to as a 'statutory contract', or even as an 'agreement'. I do not refer to these cases, since they are of no relevance unless the taxpayer company can surmount their first hurdle by showing that the transaction is not caught by s 45(4) of the 1976 Act because the subject land was not 'acquired compulsorily'.

Before Nourse J the question whether s 45(4) applied was argued on the footing that it depended on the scope of the purpose of the provisions of s 181(2) of the 1971 Act, whereby the council were 'deemed to be authorised to acquire' the subject land and 'to

have served a notice to treat in respect thereof'. The learned judge examined a number
of authorities bearing on the question of the scope to be attributed to deeming provisions
and based his decision in favour of the Crown largely, but by no means exclusively, on
the principles which he derived from those authorities. The same authorities were fully
canvassed again in the argument for the taxpayer company before your Lordships'
House. With respect, I do not find it necessary, in order to reach a conclusion in this
matter, to consider those authorities. That is because I do not think the question
whether the subject land was 'acquired compulsorily' within the meaning of s 45(4) of
the 1976 Act depends in any way on the scope of the deeming provisions of s 181(2) of
the 1971 Act. It depends, in my view, on the much broader and, as I think, much
simpler question, whether the whole process of acquisition, ie purchase notice,
compliance notice, deemed authorisation to acquire, deemed service of notice to treat,
determination of compensation (whether by agreement, as in this case, or by the Lands
Tribunal) and completion, is or is not properly described as compulsory for the purposes
of s 45(4) of the 1976 Act.

The starting point in the quest for the true interpretation of s 45(4) of the 1976 Act is
found in sub-s (8). Subsection (4) is expressly made subject to sub-s (8) which expressly
provides that a disposal pursuant to a notice to treat deemed to have been served before
13 September 1974 (the date of publication of the White Paper (Cmnd 5730) adumbrating
proposals for the legislation which, in the event, reached the statute book as the 1976 Act)
'shall be treated . . . as having been made before the appointed day', in other words shall
be exempt from liability to development land tax to which, if the compensation was not
agreed or determined until on or after the appointed day, the disposal would otherwise
be subject by the operation of sub-s (4). This collocation clearly indicates to my mind
that the two subsections were drafted on the hypothesis that the class of statutory
acquisitions involving the deemed service of a notice to treat fell within the ambit of sub-
s (4) and hence required the exemption provided by sub-s (8). The draftsman cannot
have intended that any of the class should be left in limbo, with the all-important date
of disposal not determinable under the provisions of s 45. If all acquisitions under
statutory machinery pursuant to notices to treat deemed to have been served could fairly
be described as compulsory, there was no need, such as there clearly was in sub-s (8), to
add any express amplifying words in sub-s (4) to cover the case of such acquisitions.

These considerations cannot, of course, be decisive. The instant case may turn out to
have been a casus omissus. But at least the matters to which I have drawn attention in
the foregoing paragraph make it legitimate, in my view, to approach the application of
s 45(4) of the 1976 Act to an acquisition under the purchase notice procedure of the 1971
Act, and in particular to the circumstances of the acquisition in issue in this appeal, with
a strong disinclination to give any narrow or restrictive interpretation to the words
'acquired compulsorily' in s 45(4).

I do not think there can be any dispute that an acquisition can fairly be described as
compulsory, whether the compulsion to acquire is exercised by the acquiring authority
against the landowner (commonly called a 'compulsory purchase') or vice versa
(sometimes called a 'reverse compulsory purchase'). Take, first, a simple and common
case under the purchase notice procedure of the 1971 Act. The landowner serves a
purchase notice on the appropriate council; the council opposes the notice on the ground
that the land has not become incapable of reasonably beneficial use in its existing state;
the Secretary of State, being satisfied that the land has become incapable of beneficial use
in its existing state, confirms the notice. Thereupon the deeming provisions of s 186(1)
take effect and the acquisition proceeds pursuant to the deemed authorisation to acquire
and deemed service of a notice to treat in just the same way as in the case of an ordinary
compulsory purchase: I do not understand how anyone could sensibly deny (pace
counsel for the taxpayer company, who strove to avoid conceding the point) that in this
case there was a compulsory acquisition. The council were compelled to acquire by the
operation of the statutory machinery, whether they liked it or not.

Finding then that an acquisition pursuant to a purchase notice under s 180 which takes effect by way of the deeming provisions under s 186(1) is plainly a compulsory acquisition, it would seem to me a surprising anomaly if a different conclusion results when the acquisition takes effect by way of the parallel deeming provision under s 181(2). But this again is not decisive.

It is necessary to consider the nature and operation of the purchase notice procedure as a whole. First, a purchase notice under s 180, while in one sense it may loosely be described as an unconditional offer to sell the land to which it relates, is in truth much more than that: it is a claim to enforce a statutory right to dispose of the land and to receive the appropriate compensation. Second, providing the landowner can make good his claim that the land satisfies the conditions of s 180(1)(a) and (c), the purchase notice must lead (subject to the special provisions of ss 184 and 185, which are not presently relevant) to one or other of the following results: (1) acquisition of the land by the council on whom the notice was served, either pursuant to a compliance notice under s 181(1)(a) or pursuant to confirmation of the purchase notice by the Secretary of State under s 183(1); (2) acquisition of the land by another local authority or statutory undertakers, either pursuant to a compliance notice under s 181(1)(b) or pursuant to confirmation of the purchase notice with an appropriate modification by the Secretary of State under s 183(4); or (3) the opportunity to render the land capable of beneficial use by the grant of permission for the development originally refused or for some other development by or by direction of the Secretary of State under s 183(2) or (3).

Thus it will be seen that the landowner's claim to compel the acquisition of his land by serving a purchase notice can only be defeated by showing that it is not incapable of reasonably beneficial use or by the removal of that incapacity by a decision of the Secretary of State that permission for some appropriate development should be granted.

It is against this background that I approach the detailed consideration of s 181. A council receiving a purchase notice *must*, within the time limited, take action ('shall . . . serve . . . a notice stating either . . .') under para (a), (b) or (c) of sub-s (1). A notice under para (c) is, in effect, a notice opposing confirmation of the purchase notice and the reasons required to be specified in the notice under para (c) must be intended to state the grounds of that opposition. These can only be that the land is not incapable of beneficial use, that permission for some beneficial development ought to be granted or that the purchase notice should be modified to require acquisition by another local authority or statutory undertakers. If the council are not in a position to advance any such grounds, and no other local authority or statutory undertakers will agree to comply with the purchase notice, the council have no option but to serve a compliance notice under para (a). Likewise, another local authority or statutory undertakers cannot be expected to agree to comply with the purchase notice, to enable the council to serve a notice under para (b), unless the purchase notice cannot be opposed on other grounds, and they recognise that, in the words of s 183(4), 'having regard to the probable ultimate use of the land', it is expedient that they, rather than the council on whom the purchase notice was served, should accept the responsibility for complying with it.

I recognise that there may be cases when either the council receiving a purchase notice or another local authority or statutory undertakers will welcome the opportunity to acquire the land the subject of the notice. But, in the ordinary case, service of a compliance notice under s 181(1)(a) or (b) is likely to result rather from the constraints indicated in the foregoing paragraph than from a free act of volition, and in any event the constraints are inherent in the statutory machinery and deprive the element of consensus implied by the language of paras (a) and (b), if read out of context, of any significance in relation to the application of s 45(4) of the 1976 Act. I have no hesitation in concluding that land acquired pursuant to a purchase notice by way of a compliance notice under s 181(1)(a) or (b) and the deeming provisions under s 181(2) is just as aptly described as 'acquired compulsorily' under s 45(4) of the 1976 Act as if it has been acquired by way of confirmation of the purchase notice under s 183(1) and the deeming provisions under s 186(1). It follows that the taxpayer company must be taken to have disposed of the subject land on 11 August 1976 and to be chargeable to development land tax on that *a* disposal.

Appeal dismissed.

Solicitors: *Whitehouse, Gibson & Alton*, agents for *Henry Fallows & Co*, Darwen (for the taxpayer company); *Solicitor of Inland Revenue.*   *b*

Rengan Krishnan Esq   Barrister.

Williams v Home Office (No 2)   *c*

COURT OF APPEAL, CIVIL DIVISION

CUMMING-BRUCE, BRIGHTMAN AND ACKNER LJJ

23, 24 NOVEMBER 1981

Pleading – Amendment – Leave to amend after trial of action – Statement of claim – Issue which *d* *trial judge bound to find against plaintiff or on which no evidence given at trial – Whether Court of Appeal should refuse leave to amend statement of claim – Whether Court of Appeal should give leave to appeal to House of Lords against refusal of leave to amend.*

Where a plaintiff wishes to plead a case which, as a result of a prior decision of the Court of Appeal, the trial judge would be bound to find against him, his correct course is to *e* plead that case before the trial of the action or, at the latest, by applying to the trial judge to amend his pleadings to include that case. If the trial judge refuses leave to amend, the Court of Appeal will hear the matter as an interlocutory appeal and as a matter of great urgency, and if it refuses leave to amend it will consider whether it is right to give leave for an interlocutory appeal to the House of Lords. If the plaintiff does not plead the case and fails at the trial, the Court of Appeal will not give leave to amend the pleadings to *f* include that case nor will it give leave to appeal to the House of Lords against the refusal of leave to amend, since if the House of Lords were to allow the appeal and give leave to amend the result would be that the action would then have to be remitted by the House of Lords to a court of first instance for it to determine, perhaps several years after the original trial, matters which should have been canvassed, if at all, at the original trial. Similar considerations apply where a plaintiff, who has failed at the trial, seeks on appeal *g* to amend his statement of claim to include an issue on which evidence was not given at the trial (see p 568 *e* to p 569 *a* and *d e*, post).
    Appeal against decision of Tudor Evans J [1981] 1 All ER 1211 dismissed on procedural grounds.

Notes
For the amendment of pleadings with the leave of the court, see 36 Halsbury's Laws (4th *h* edn) paras 68–72, and for cases on the subject, see 50 Digest (Repl) 99–132, 816–1163.

Cases referred to in judgments
Arbon v Anderson [1943] 1 All ER 154, [1943] KB 252, 37 Digest (Repl) 446, 52.
Becker v Home Office [1972] 2 All ER 676, [1972] 2 QB 407, [1972] 2 WLR 1193, CA, *j* Digest (Cont Vol D) 729, 33*b*.

Appeal
The plaintiff, Michael Sidney Williams, appealed against the decision of Tudor Evans J ([1981] 1 All ER 1211) on 9 May 1980 whereby the judge (i) dismissed an action brought

by the plaintiff against the defendant, the Home Office, for damages for false imprisonment in respect of the period from 23 August 1974 to 18 February 1975 which he spent in the part of Wakefield Prison known as the control unit and (ii) refused to grant the plaintiff a declaration that in setting up and operating the control unit pursuant to circular instructions CI 35/1974 the defendant acted ultra vires and unlawfully. On the appeal, it being conceded for the plaintiff that the appeal would fail, the plaintiff sought leave to amend his statement of claim by adding a claim for breach of statutory duty resulting in loss of opportunity not to be removed from the control unit and by including in the prayer for damages a prayer for damages for breach of statutory duty. The plaintiff also sought leave to appeal to the House of Lords on a point of law of general public importance. The facts are set out in the judgment of Cumming-Bruce LJ.

Michael Beloff QC and *Stephen Sedley* for the plaintiff.
Hugh Carlisle QC for the defendant.

CUMMING-BRUCE LJ. By an amended notice of appeal, first served in June 1980 and amended and re-served in May 1981, an appeal is brought before this court, seeking an order that the judgment of Tudor Evans J given at the trial of the action on 9 May 1980 should be set aside and asking for an order that judgment be entered for the plaintiff for damages to be assessed, if not agreed. The grounds of appeal, as amended, set out five grounds, being the grounds on which the order is sought from this court.

The proceedings were instituted by originating summons dated 30 January 1975 and then sought the determination of the court on three questions, namely whether the defendant's circular instruction (CI 35/1974) was a lawful exercise of the powers contained in the Prison Act 1952 or a lawful implementation of the Prison Rules 1964, SI 1964/388, as amended, second, a similar question in relation to modifications of that instruction, and, third, a question whether in the premises the plaintiff's detention in a control unit at Wakefield prison since September 1974 had at any time been lawful. There was a claim for a declaration that since September 1974 the plaintiff had been falsely imprisoned by or with the authority of the defendant. At the date of that originating summons the plaintiff was still serving a sentence of imprisonment and was serving part of that sentence under the regime described in CI 35/1974 as a control unit.

Pursuant to an order of the master, in June 1976 a statement of claim was served. That pleaded that the plaintiff had been serving a sentence of 14 years' imprisonment since April 1971 and that from a date in August 1974 he was detained for a period of 180 days by the defendant in a part of Wakefield prison designated as a control unit. It pleaded that for the first 90 days the plaintiff was kept in solitary confinement and thereafter allowed limited association with two other prisoners likewise held in the control unit. The pleader then pleads that that detention in the control unit was unlawful, in that he was placed in confinement otherwise than was permitted by the Prison Rules 1964 without having been accused of any specified disciplinary offence, without being given a hearing, and that he had been held for a longer period than that permitted under the 1964 rules. It was pleaded in sub-para (iii) of the particulars that, in breach of r 43 of the 1964 Rules the plaintiff was deprived of association with other prisoners, which was later amended in February 1980 to read 'was removed from association with other prisoners . . . (a) otherwise than by the Governor of the prison and/or (b) for more than 24 hours and/or for more than one month without the authority of an authorised visitor or of the Secretary of State for Home Affairs'. There was a pleading that the treatment of the plaintiff by the defendant constituted a cruel or unusual punishment inflicted on the plaintiff in breach of the provisions of the Bill of Rights (1688); and there was reliance on the European Convention for the Protection of Human Rights and Fundamental Freedoms (TS 71 (1953); Cmd 8969). Finally, there was a contention that the control unit and its regime were instituted without power to do so and in breach of the Bill of Rights, of the Prison Act 1952 and the Prison Rules 1964. Then there is a plea that the detention was unlawful and that the plaintiff was subjected thereto in breach of natural justice. By para 6 of the statement of claim it is pleaded: 'In consequence of the matters aforesaid and each of them the Plaintiff has suffered mental stress, anxiety, fear, unhappiness, damage and loss.' The claim for damages read: 'Damages, including exemplary damages, for false imprisonment and/or trespass to the person.' And there was a claim for a declaration.

To that statement of claim the defendant pleaded and put in issue the allegation that the detention and regime in the control unit were unlawful, and pleaded that they were in accordance with the Prison Act 1952 and the Prison Rules 1964, as amended. No admissions were made as to the damage pleaded in para 6 of the statement of claim.

After a prolonged interlocutory period, the case came on for trial. The judge, in a detailed judgment transcribed into 149 pages gave his reasons for dismissing the claim for damages and for a declaration. In the course of that judgment the judge held that there had been a breach of the Prison Rules, namely r 43 of the 1964 rules. He held that, on the authorities, r 43 did not, on a proper construction, confer a right of action on the subject for breach of the rule. The judge explained that he arrived at that decision on a consideration of the authorities, including the familiar authority of *Arbon v Anderson* [1943] 1 All ER 154, [1943] KB 252 and a case in this court, *Becker v Home Office* [1972] 2 All ER 676, [1972] 2 QB 407. The judge refused to exercise his discretion to grant any declaration, and dismissed the action.

In this court counsel for the plaintiff, opening the appeal accepted that it was not open to the plaintiff in this court to invite the court to depart from the law as stated in *Becker v Home Office*, which indorsed the judgment of Goddard LJ, sitting at first instance, in *Arbon v Anderson*. The question, said counsel, whether a breach of r 43 of the 1964 rules gave rise to an action for breach of statutory duty at the instance of a prisoner was a matter which had not been decided in their Lordships' House and that it was his intention, after explaining why he was not asking this court to allow the appeal, to seek from this court leave to appeal to their Lordships' House in order that the House might consider the correctness or otherwise of the law as stated in the Court of Appeal in *Becker's* case. In those circumstances, the plaintiff not seeking from this court an order that the appeal should be allowed, the appeal will be dismissed.

So the court comes to the application made by the plaintiff for leave to appeal to the House of Lords, in order that their Lordships' House should consider whether, on a proper understanding of the law, the plaintiff has established his case. I should explain that in the course of his opening counsel for the plaintiff stated that he was not proceeding in this court, and did not intend to proceed in their Lordships' House, to argue any ground of appeal other than that the plaintiff was entitled to damages for a breach of the 1964 rules. Therefore, all the other grounds of appeal, it is conceded, are not open to the plaintiff on consideration of his application for leave to appeal to the House of Lords. That application is founded solely on an application for leave so that their Lordships might consider the plaintiff's claim for damages for a breach of r 43 of the 1964 rules. The particular breach which it is alleged, on the judge's findings, arises for consideration is a failure by the statutory authorities specified in r 43 to consider whether the confinement of the plaintiff in the control unit and under the regime described in CI 35/1974 was unlawful because the Secretary of State or the committee to whom he delegated consideration of the question of renewal of the confinement or its continuance never, as a committee, entertained the question that it was their statutory duty as a committee to decide.

Opening his application for leave to appeal to the House of Lords, counsel defined three questions for the consideration of this court. First, he submitted that he had to show that, as a matter of principle, there was an arguable question of construction whether r 43 of the 1964 rules conferred on the subject a right of action for breach of statutory duty in the event that the rules had not been complied with. In my view, counsel established that there was an arguable case for such a construction of the rules; and, having said that, I think it is unnecessary for me, and inappropriate, to express my opinion on the validity of the argument.

The second matter on which counsel stated that he should satisfy the court was that the case gave rise to a question of such importance that it was appropriate that their Lordships should consider the matter. The way in which he then put it, if I understood it, was that the question of construction, namely whether r 43 gave rise to a right of action for breach of statutory duty, was the question of real importance which should appropriately be considered by their Lordships' House. For reasons that I shall explain, I doubt if that is the correct formulation of the matter for consideration here.

The third matter on which counsel said he had to satisfy us was this: if he succeeds in satisfying their Lordships that a breach of r 43 confers on the subject a right of action for breach of statutory duty, he has then to establish that the plaintiff has suffered damage by reason of the breach. In the context of fact found by the judge, that would give rise to this question: if r 43 of the 1964 rules had been observed in the matter in respect of which it is submitted it was not observed, namely a failure by the appropriate statutory authority to consider properly whether the confinement of the plaintiff in the control unit under the regime described in CI 35/1974 should be continued, did he suffer damage because he was deprived of what his counsel described as a 'live chance' to be removed from the regime and the control unit to some other less unattractive condition of confinement?

At that point in this court the statement of claim was considered and it was observed that in the proceedings so far conducted there has been no prayer for damages for breach of statutory duty and that in para 6 of the statement of claim, in which the pleader pleads the matters relied on as giving rise to damages and loss, there has been no claim in respect of the loss of opporunity not to be removed into or detained in the control unit. So, in order to plead a case for damages for the breach of statutory duty now relied on, it became necessary for the plaintiff to seek leave from this court to reamend the statement of claim in order that there might on the pleadings be a case for the consideration of their Lordships' House, because the present pleadings disclose no such case. A draft reamendment of the statement of claim was handed in, in order that this court might consider whether, in the exercise of discretion, it should give the plaintiff leave to amend the pleadings by adding in para 6 of the statement of claim the words 'including loss of the opportunity not to be removed to or detained in the control unit', and to amend the prayer in the statement of claim by adding to the first prayer, which is the prayer for damages, a prayer for damages in the words 'and/or breach of statutory duty'.

The principles on which this court gives leave to amend are briefly set out in a note under RSC Ord 59, r 10, set out in *The Supreme Court Practice 1982*, vol 1, para 59/10/5, p 942. The principle on which this court gives leave to amend is that it will do so provided that it can do so without injustice and, in particular, will not usually give leave to amend if the amendment sought gives rise to an issue on which the relevant evidence was not given, or comprehensively given, in the court below. It is accepted that in the proceedings before the judge there was no submission by the plaintiff of the existence of facts specifically founding a claim for damages for loss of the chance of ending the period of his confinement by reason of a decision by the relevant committee to that effect and, as that matter was not canvassed in opening or throughout, the defendant had no occasion at trial for calling evidence to meet the allegation that the loss of chance alleged held out any chance to the plaintiff of termination of confinement under CI 35/1974. Counsel for the defendant indicated that if amendment was granted he would wish at some appropriate stage to call evidence in order to rebut the allegation that consideration by the relevant committee held out any prospect at all of termination of the confinement under CI 35/1974 a day earlier than it was in fact terminated.

Counsel for the plaintiff accepted before us that if leave to amend was granted and if leave to appeal was granted and if their Lordships held that the plaintiff had established a breach of statutory duty and a right to claim damages for that breach, the question whether the plaintiff had suffered any damage and, if so, the amount of that damage would have to be remitted by their Lordships' House to a court of first instance in order to hear evidence and decide whether any damage was proved and, if so, the quantum of that damage. In elaboration of the situation envisaged, counsel for the plaintiff (or counsel who conducted the case for the plaintiff below) indicated that it was probable that on remission the plaintiff would rely on documentary evidence, which I understood to mean documents exhibited in the court below at the trial. Therein I may be wrong. But counsel for the defendant made it quite clear in this court that on such remission the defendant would call evidence of witnesses with a view to rebutting the allegation that the plaintiff had sustained any damage at all by reason of the failure of the committee as a committee to consider the question of continued confinement or renewal.

On behalf of the plaintiff it was submitted that in reality it has always been impracticable for the plaintiff to plead the case that he now seeks to plead by amendment. The reason given is that, as the court below was bound, as is this court, by authority to hold that a breach of the 1964 rules does not give rise to a cause of action for damages for breach of statutory authority vested in the subject, it would have been impossible for the plaintiff to obtain from the judge at first instance, or in interlocutory proceedings before the trial, an order giving leave to amend; and, had he sought so to do, he would have been faced with an application to strike out the amendment of the pleadings which would have imposed on the plaintiff the obligation, if he wished to sustain the amendment, to come to this court for an interlocutory decision on the application for leave to amend and, if this court refused it, to seek leave to go to their Lordships' House in order that the interlocutory question of amendment might be considered. That, it was submitted on behalf of the plaintiff, was in reality a quite impractical exercise involving time and expense that a litigant who is proceeding with the support of public funds could not and should not advise or encourage.

For myself, I disagree entirely with the validity of the explanation given. It seems to me quite wrong that the plaintiff by his pleading should embark on a case which in practice took I think something like three weeks or a month to try, to fail below and then come to this court and seek an amendment which, if successful, can only mean, after a successful hearing in their Lordships' House, a remission to a court of first instance of matters which in my view should have been canvassed, if at all, at the trial. There is, in my view, a measure of oppression in subjecting the defendant to the prospect of a second hearing at first instance in which he will seek to call evidence as to the probable outcome of a consideration by a statutory committee or a Home Office committee, acting as delegate of the Secretary of State, in 1974 pursuant to leave to amend granted in this court, if it was granted, in 1981. If the plaintiff or the plaintiff's advisers ever envisaged a claim for damages for the loss of the chance that the relevant committee would have ended his confinement under CI 35/1974 earlier than they did, that claim should have been pleaded before the trial at first instance or, at latest, an application to plead that case should have been made at the trial before the judge. If the judge had refused leave to amend, the practice of this court would come into play. This court is always ready to hear interlocutory applications which affect, or are expected to affect, the course of the trial with as little delay as possible. If the application had been made in the interlocutory stage, I can see no reason to think that this court would not have entertained an appeal before the hearing ever began. If the application had been made during the trial, the probability is that, if the judge refused leave and there was an appeal, the trial being suspended pending the appeal, this court would have heard the appeal without any delay at all as a matter of the greatest urgency. If this court had refused leave to amend, the court would then have considered whether it was appropriate to give leave in the circumstances for an interlocutory appeal to their Lordships' House. In spite of the state of business before their Lordships, such an appeal to the House of Lords is given a very great priority, as it is appreciated that a part-heard trial is suspended pending the decision of the House. That is the procedure that should have been followed, in my view, and the only procedure that would enable the evidence for the issues now sought to be raised to be complete at the trial. In my view, it would be quite wrong for this court to give leave to amend knowing that the consequence of such leave must be that if the plaintiff's appeal was successful before their Lordship's House if leave to appeal was given, the only

practical consequence could be that their Lordships would be invited to remit the
question whether there was a claim for damages and, if so, what that claim was, to a court
of first instance in order that evidence that could have been called below should be called,
perhaps some years later.

   For those reasons, I would refuse the plaintiff's application for leave to amend the
statement of claim at this stage. To do so, to my mind, would be unreasonably to
prejudice the defendant.

   That being so, what is there for this court to consider on the application for leave to
appeal to the House of Lords? There is no pleaded claim which raises a claim for
damages for the one breach of statutory duty which it is sought now to bring before their
Lordships' House. This brings me to the question: what is the kind of matter for which
this court, on ordinary principles, gives leave for an appeal to the House of Lords? It is
perfectly well established that leave to appeal is not granted in order to enable their
Lordships to give a decision on hypothetical questions, however interesting. This court
is only entitled to give leave to appeal to the House of Lords if it is satisfied that by so
doing their Lordships will decide the real rights of the parties in a real action, which in
this case would be a claim for damages for a specific breach of r 43 of the Prison Rules
1964. As without leave to amend there is no such claim, there is in my view no practical
claim for their Lordships' House to consider.

   For those reasons, I would refuse the plaintiff's application for leave to appeal to the
House of Lords.

BRIGHTMAN LJ. I entirely agree. I only wish to add one further brief point, which
does not go to the arguability of the case or to the merits of the application for leave to
amend the pleadings. There is, I think, an additional reason why we ought not ourselves
to grant leave to appeal in this case, but should leave it to the House of Lords to decide
for itself. I accept that the question whether r 43 of the Prison Rules 1964, SI 1964/388,
gives rise to a right of action would be an arguable point in the House of Lords. There
is, however, this consideration, that in *Arbon v Anderson* [1943] 1 All ER 154, [1943] KB
252 the High Court decided that the Prison Rules 1933, SR & O 1933/809, which had
been made under the Prison Act 1898, did not give any rights to a prisoner the breach of
which would found a cause of action. That was the unchallenged interpretation of the
law at the time when Parliament passed, ten years later, the Prison Act 1952, under
which the current Prison Rules were made. The Bill must therefore have passed through
the House of Commons and through their Lordships' House on the understanding that
the Prison Rules which were to be made under s 47(1) of the Prison Act 1952, as it
became, would not confer any rights which, if breached, would give rise to a claim in
damages. It would not, in those circumstances, in my view, be appropriate for us to give
leave to appeal to the House of Lords. In the light of the legislative history of the Act, I
think that the granting of leave to appeal should be left to the House itself.

ACKNER LJ. I also agree, for the reasons given by Cumming-Bruce and Brightman
LJJ, that the application for leave to appeal to the House of Lords should be rejected. I
would only wish to add my appreciation of the realistic approach adopted by counsel for
the plaintiff in relation to this appeal and of the clarity and conciseness of his submission.

*Appeal dismissed. Application for leave to amend statement of claim refused. Leave to appeal to
the House of Lords refused.*

Solicitors: *Harriet Harman* (for the plaintiff); *Treasury Solicitor.*

                                        Henrietta Steinberg   Barrister.

Cullen v Rogers

HOUSE OF LORDS

LORD DIPLOCK, LORD FRASER OF TULLYBELTON, LORD KEITH OF KINKEL, LORD BRIDGE OF HARWICH AND LORD BRANDON OF OAKBROOK

30 MARCH, 6 MAY 1982

Sentence – Probation order – Terms of order – Additional requirements – Attendance at day training centre – Non-statutory day centre – Whether conditions for attendance at statutory centres also applicable to non-statutory centres – Powers of Criminal Courts Act 1973, ss 2(3), 4.

Sentence – Probation order – Willingness of offender to comply with order – Jurisdiction of court – Willingness of offender to comply with order not giving court jurisdiction to impose conditions not authorised by legislation – Powers of Criminal Courts Act 1973, s 2(6).

Sentence – Probation order – Terms of order – Additional requirements – Limitations on additional requirements – Custodial or other element amounting to a sentence not to be imposed – Discretion conferred on probation officer to be properly defined – Powers of Criminal Courts Act 1973, s 2(3).

The respondent was the subject of a probation order imposed by the court with her consent. The order, which was for two years and had an additional requirement that she attend a day centre, was made under s 2(3)[a] of the Powers of Criminal Courts Act 1973, which provided that a probation order could require the offender to comply with such requirements as the court 'considers necessary for securing the good conduct of the offender'. Section 4[b] of the 1973 Act provided that a probation order could include a requirement to attend a day training centre (of which four had been established) or at 'other establishments for use in connection with the rehabilitation of offenders'. A large number of non-statutory day centres had been established by individual probation services, including the centre which the respondent was required to attend. Those centres had no statutory authority save that they had been approved by the Secretary of State under s 4 as 'other establishments for use in connection with the rehabilitation of offenders'. The respondent failed to comply with the day centre requirements. In proceedings brought against her for breach of the probation order, the magistrates upheld the legality of the day centre requirement and ordered that the probation order be continued. On appeal, the Divisional Court held that the day centre requirement was invalid and set aside the order of the magistrates' court. The probation officer appealed to the House of Lords.

Held – Since s 2(3) of the 1973 Act was expressed to be 'Subject to the provisions of' s 4 of that Act, it followed that the provisions of s 4(2) regulating the requirements to attend at day training centres generally were not intended to apply only to such day training centres as the Secretary of State chose to notify to a court under s 4(2), leaving other equivalent establishments to be operated independently of any statutory regulation, but were intended to be comprehensive and to permit a requirement to attend at a day training centre, however called, to be made by a court only if the statutory conditions applicable to attendance at a 'day training centre' as defined by s 57(1)[c] of the 1973 Act were satisfied. Since the terms of the day centre attendance requirement imposed on the respondent by the magistrates were so wide as not to impose any practical limit on her required attendance, it followed that the magistrates had no power under s 2(3) to make

---

a   Section 2(3) is set out at p 572 *h*, post
b   Section 4, so far as material, is set out at p 573 *b* to *e*, post
c   Section 57(1), so far as material, is set out at p 573 *e f*, post

such an order. The appeal would accordingly be dismissed (see p 571 *j* to p 572 *b*, p 573 *j*, p 574 *e* to *h* and p 575 *e* to *h*, post).

Per curiam. (1) The provisions of s 2(6) of the 1973 Act which prohibit the court from making a probation order unless the offender 'expresses his willingness to comply with its requirements' cannot be considered as in any way giving jurisdiction to include requirements in a probation order which are not otherwise authorised by the terms of the 1973 Act (see p 571 *j* to p 572 *b*, p 574 *j* and p 575 *h*, post).

(2) The power of the court under s 2(3) of the 1973 Act to impose such requirements on a probation order as it 'considers necessary for securing the good conduct of the offender or for preventing a repetition by him of the same offence or the commission of other offences' is subject to at least two limitations: (a) the court must not impose a requirement which introduces such a custodial or other element as will amount in substance to the imposition of a sentence, since the making of a probation order is a course taken by the court to avoid passing a sentence, and (b) any discretion conferred on the probation officer pursuant to the terms of the order to regulate a probationer's activities must be confined within well-defined limits, since it is the court alone which can define the requirements of the order (see p 571 *j* to p 572 *b* and p 574 *j* to p 575 *b* and *h*, post).

Notes

For probation orders and requirements attached thereto, see 11 Halsbury's Laws (4th edn) paras 526–532.

For the Powers of Criminal Courts Act 1973, ss 2, 4, 57, see 43 Halsbury's Statutes (3rd edn) 291, 295, 346.

Case referred to in opinions

Farrell v Alexander [1976] 2 All ER 721, [1977] AC 59, [1976] 3 WLR 145, HL, Digest (Cont Vol E) 382, 8375*b*.

Appeal

The respondent, Deborah Rogers, was convicted, on her own admission, on 23 February 1981 in the Crown Court at Newcastle upon Tyne before Mr Recorder H A Richardson of assault and theft for which, with her consent, she was placed on probation for two years with a day centre attendance requirement. The respondent failed to comply with the day centre attendance requirement and, on remission of the matter by the Crown Court to the North Tyneside Magistrates' Court, the respondent was, on 25 June 1981 on the hearing of an information laid by the appellant, Peter Francis Cullen of the Northumbria Probation and After Care Service, fined £25 and the probation order was ordered to continue. On appeal by way of case stated, the Divisional Court of the Queen's Bench Division (Thompson and Cantley JJ, Waller LJ dissenting) on 9 October 1981 held the attendance requirement to be invalid and accordingly set aside the order of the magistrates' court. The Divisional Court granted the appellant leave to appeal to the House of Lords and certified that the following point of law of general public importance was involved in its decision: in what way was the power contained in s 2(3) of the Powers of Criminal Courts Act 1973 limited by s 4 of that Act if at all?

R M Stewart QC and *Michael Hodson* for the appellant.
James Chadwin QC and *Michael Cartlidge* for the respondent.

Their Lordships took time for consideration.

6 May. The following opinions were delivered.

LORD DIPLOCK. My Lords, I have had the advantage of reading in draft the speech to be delivered by my noble and learned friend Lord Bridge, with which I agree. I too would therefore dismiss the appeal.

LORD FRASER OF TULLYBELTON. My Lords, I have had the advantage of reading in draft the speech of my noble and learned friend Lord Bridge, and I agree with it. For the reasons given by him I would dismiss this appeal. I agree that the appellant's costs should be paid out of central funds.

LORD KEITH OF KINKEL. My Lords, I have had the benefit of reading in draft the speech to be delivered by my noble and learned friend Lord Bridge. I agree with it, and for the reasons which he gives I too would dismiss the appeal.

LORD BRIDGE OF HARWICH. My Lords, this appeal raises questions of importance as to the nature and extent of the 'requirements' which can be imposed on a probationer in exercise of the courts' general power under s 2(3) of the Powers of Criminal Courts Act 1973.

The respondent was the subject of a probation order imposed by the Crown Court at Newcastle upon Tyne on 23 February 1981 with her consent. The order was expressed to be for two years and under the heading 'Additional requirements' there was embodied in the order the following:

'Shall attend the Northumbria Probation and After Care Day Centre in North Shields as instructed by the Probation Officer. During such attendance, shall undertake and participate in such activities as the Probation Officer directs.'

I shall refer to this as 'the day centre attendance requirement'.

The respondent failed to comply with the day centre attendance requirement and in due course proceedings against her for breach of the probation order were instituted, then remitted by the Crown Court to the North Tyneside Magistrates' Court and heard on 25 June 1981. The legality of the day centre attendance requirement was challenged on behalf of the respondent but upheld by the justices. The respondent was fined £25 and the probation order ordered to continue. On appeal by case stated the Divisional Court by a majority (Thompson and Cantley JJ, Waller LJ dissenting) held the day centre attendance requirement to be invalid and accordingly set aside the order of the magistrates' court. The court certified that the following point of law of general public importance was involved in its decision: 'In what way is the power contained in s 2(3) of the Powers of Criminal Courts Act 1973 limited by s 4 of the Powers of Criminal Courts Act if at all?'

The 1973 Act is a consolidating Act. Probation orders are made under s 2. The essence of a probation order is that it is an order which the court considers it is 'expedient [to make] instead of sentencing' the offender and which requires him 'to be under the supervision of a probation officer for a period to be specified in the order of not less than six months nor more than three years': see s 2(1) (as amended by the Probation Orders (Variation of Statutory Limits) Order 1978, SI 1978/474). Section 2(3) provides:

'Subject to the provisions of subsection (4) below and sections 3 and 4 of this Act a probation order may in addition require the offender to comply during the whole or any part of the probation period with such requirements as the court, having regard to the circumstances of the case, considers necessary for securing the good conduct of the offender or for preventing a repetition by him of the same offence or the commission of other offences.'

Subsection (4) prohibits the inclusion in a probation order of a requirement to pay damages or compensation. Section 2(5) provides:

'Without prejudice to the generality of subsection (3) above, a probation order may include requirements relating to the residence of the offender, but—(a) before making an order containing any such requirements, the court shall consider the home surroundings of the offender; and (b) where the order requires the offender to reside in an approved probation hostel, an approved probation home or any other institution, the name of the institution and the period for which he is so required to reside shall be specified in the order, and that period shall not extend beyond twelve months from the date of the order.'

This subsection has subsequently been amended, but the amendments are immaterial to the question of construction which concerns your Lordships' House. Section 2(6) includes a requirement that the court shall not make a probation order unless the offender 'expresses his willingness to comply with its requirements'.

Section 3 contains detailed provisions for including in a probation order requirements to submit to medical treatment.

The main section with which your Lordships are concerned is s 4, of which I set out the first three subsections in full:

'(1) Where a court makes a probation order in the case of an offender it may, subject to the provisions of this section, include in the order a requirement that he shall during the probation period attend at a day training centre specified in the order.

(2) A court shall not include such a requirement in a probation order unless— (a) it has been notified by the Secretary of State that a day training centre exists for persons of the offender's class or description who reside in the petty sessions area in which he resides or will reside; and (b) it is satisfied that arrangements can be made for his attendance at that centre; and no such requirement shall be included in a probation order which includes a requirement under section 3 of this Act with respect to treatment of the probationer for his mental condition.

(3) A requirement included in a probation order by virtue of this section shall operate to require the probationer—(a) in accordance with instructions given by the probation officer responsible for his supervision, to attend on not more than sixty days at the centre specified in the order; (b) while attending there to comply with instructions given by, or under the authority of, the person in charge of the centre.'

By s 57(1) 'day training centre' is defined to mean 'premises at which persons may be required to attend by a probation order containing a requirement under section 4 of this Act'. Section 48(3) gives to the Secretary of State an extensive power to make rules regulating the conduct of day training centres. Schedule 3, para 11 provides:

'A probation and after-care committee may, with the approval of the Secretary of State, provide and carry on day training centres . . . and other establishments for use in connection with the rehabilitation of offenders.'

The statutory day training centres to which s 4 of the 1973 Act applies were first introduced by the Criminal Justice Act 1972. Four such centres were established on an experimental basis. It appears that they were designed with a particular view to the needs of the inadequate recidivist, though there is nothing whatever in the statutory language to indicate that statutory day training centres need be limited to provide for persons of that class or description. However that may be, the experiment was apparently not regarded as a success and no further statutory day training centres have been established. Instead a large number of non-statutory 'day centres' (the Divisional Court was told as many as 70) have been established by individual probation services, of which the centre at North Shields, the subject of the day centre attendance requirement presently in question, is one. The North Shields centre enjoys no statutory authority save that it has been approved by the Secretary of State as an 'other establishment for use in connection with the rehabilitation of offenders' pursuant to para 11 of Sch 3 to the 1973 Act. The Divisional Court was not informed of this approval, but since it is of significance only to the funding, not to the operation, of the establishment, it is of no relevance to the question under appeal.

It is to be observed that under the terms of the day centre attendance requirement in question the respondent could, in theory, have been required to attend the centre for, say, 12 hours a day on every day of the two years of her probation and throughout her attendance to spend her time scrubbing floors or sewing mail bags.

Waller LJ, in his dissenting judgment, examined the legislative history lying behind the 1973 Act and considered that the language of s 3(3) of the Criminal Justice Act 1948, corresponding to the language of s 2(3) of the 1973 Act, would have been wide enough to authorise the imposition in a probation order of such a requirement as the day centre attendance requirement imposed in the instant case. He then asked whether either the introduction in 1972 of statutory day training centres, which he treated as being limited to such as were in fact provided for inadequate recidivists, or the introduction of the words 'Subject to . . . section . . . 4' in s 2(3) of the 1973 Act, operated to cut down the power originally conferred by s 3(3) of the 1948 Act. He found himself able to answer that question in the negative on the simple ground that the North Shields day centre was not a day training centre to which s 4 of the 1973 Act applies.

With all respect, this is not a legitimate approach. It is now well established that in construing a consolidating Act recourse to legislative history is only permissible 'when there is a real and substantial difficulty or ambiguity which classical methods of construction cannot resolve': see *Farrell v Alexander* [1976] 2 All ER 721 at 726, [1977] AC 59 at 73 per Lord Wilberforce. The starting point here, then, must be to construe the 1973 Act as it stands. The opening words of s 2(3), 'Subject to the provisions of subsection (4) below and sections 3 and 4 of this Act', must be intended to limit, restrict or qualify the general power to impose requirements in a probation order under s 2(3). Subsection (4) imposes an express prohibition and presents no problem. Section 3 embodies a self-contained code governing the conditions which must be satisfied before a requirement to submit to medical treatment may be imposed and the nature of such requirements as may be imposed. The words 'Subject to the provisions of . . . section 3' in s 2(3) put it beyond doubt that s 3 ousts any power there might otherwise be under s 2(3) to impose a requirement to submit to medical treatment. It seems to me that the words 'Subject to the provisions of . . . section . . . 4' must have a similar effect. Although s 4 cannot perhaps be said to embody so elaborate a self-contained code as s 3, it nevertheless incorporates (when read with s 48) important provisions which must have been intended to regulate the character of requirements to attend at day training centres generally. The attendance that can be required is to be limited to 60 days. The nature of the training, the hours of attendance and the reckoning of the days of attendance are to be the subject of rules made by the Secretary of State under s 48, and the person in charge of the centre, with whose instructions the probationer attending the centre will be bound to comply, is to be a person to whose appointment the Secretary of State has consented pursuant to rules made under s 48. I find it impossible to read these important regulatory provisions as intended to operate only in relation to such day training centres as the Secretary of State chooses to 'notify' to a court under s 4(2), leaving other equivalent establishments to be operated independently of any statutory regulation. Section 4(2) is prohibitory: 'A court shall not include such a requirement' (sc to attend at a day training centre) unless the existence of the centre has been notified by the Secretary of State. To seek escape from this prohibition by reference to the definition of 'day training centre' (which necessarily applies only to centres which have been duly notified) is, to my mind, to argue in a circle. On its true construction, I have no doubt, s 4 is intended to be comprehensive and to permit a requirement to attend at a day training centre, however called, only if the statutory conditions applicable to attendance at a 'day training centre', as defined, are satisfied.

This conclusion would be sufficient to dispose of the appeal, but since wider issues were canvassed in argument and since the decision of your Lordships' House in this case may expose the necessity for amending legislation, it may be appropriate to add some general observations.

I would first mention that the provisions of s 2(6) of the 1973 Act which prohibit the court from making a probation order unless the probationer 'expresses his willingness to comply with its requirements' cannot be considered as in any way giving jurisdiction to include requirements in a probation order which are not otherwise authorised by the terms of the statute.

It has been said that the language of s 2(3) of the 1973 Act which authorises the court

to impose such requirements as it 'considers necessary for securing the good conduct of
the offender or for preventing a repetition by him of the same offence or the commission
of other offences' is very wide. So indeed it is. But the power to impose requirements
under this provision must be subject to some limitation in at least two respects. First,
since the making of a probation order is a course taken by the court to avoid passing a
sentence, a requirement imposed under s 2(3) must not introduce such a custodial or
other element as will amount in substance to the imposition of a sentence. Second, since
it is the court alone which can define the requirements of the order, any discretion
conferred on the probation officer pursuant to the terms of the order to regulate a
probationer's activities, must itself be confined within well-defined limits. Your
Lordships have not heard full argument on this subject, and I shall not, therefore,
undertake the difficult task of attempting precisely to delineate the limits inherent in the
court's power under s 2(3) in either of these respects. However, the issue was sufficiently
explored in argument to justify the statement of certain broad conclusions. First, it was
rightly conceded by counsel for the appellant that a court could not, under the guise of
a requirement imposed pursuant to s 2(3), require a probationer to perform such unpaid
work as would appropriately be the subject of a community service order under s 14 of
the 1973 Act. Second, it is appropriate to consider how far the court could, acting under
s 2(3), impose requirements as to residence, if not specifically authorised so to do, under
s 2(5). Curiously, sub-s (5) opens with the words 'Without prejudice to the generality of
subsection (3)'. Yet it is clear that para (b) of sub-s (5) (as originally enacted) was
restrictive: a requirement to reside at any of the institutions referred to in that paragraph
could only be made for twelve months. This indicates that no requirement to reside in
any sort of institution could properly be imposed under s 2(3). There can be no other
reason why the power should be expressly provided, and expressly limited, by sub-s
(5)(b). Similarly, it seems to me, quite independently of the presence in s 2(3) of the
words 'Subject to . . . section . . . 4', that a requirement to attend for a given number of
hours on a given number of days at an institutional establishment and there to comply
with instructions of a wholly unspecified character given by the probation officer would
go far beyond the range of such requirements as could properly be imposed under s 2(3),
on the ground both that it would involve a substantial element of custodial punishment
and that it would subject the probationer to the unfettered discretionary control of the
probation officer. It follows that, in my view, there never was any power to require a
probationer to attend at a day training centre or any similar institution, however called,
until Parliament expressly conferred that power, subject to appropriate regulation and
restriction, first by s 20 of the Criminal Justice Act 1972, now by s 4 of the 1973 Act.

My Lords, for these reasons I would dismiss the appeal. The certified question is so
narrowly framed that a direct answer to it would be misleading. The substance of the
answer to the wider questions inherent in the issues raised by the appeal will, I hope, be
found in the foregoing paragraphs of this speech. The questions being of importance to
probation services throughout the country and, no doubt, also to the Home Office, I
would think it appropriate to order that the appellant's costs be paid out of central funds.

LORD BRANDON OF OAKBROOK. My Lords, I have had the advantage of
reading in draft the speech prepared by my noble and learned friend Lord Bridge. I
agree with it and would dismiss the appeal accordingly. I agree also that the appellant's
costs should be paid out of central funds.

Appeal dismissed.

Solicitors: *Radcliffes & Co*, agents for *R & R F Kidd & Spoor*, Whitley Bay (for the
appellant); *Gregory Rowcliffe & Co*, agents for *Hadaway & Hadaway*, North Shields (for
the respondent).

Mary Rose Plummer   Barrister.

Gilbert v Spoor

a

COURT OF APPEAL, CIVIL DIVISION
WALLER, EVELEIGH AND KERR LJJ
14, 15 DECEMBER 1981, 5 FEBRUARY 1982

Restrictive covenant affecting land – Discharge or modification – Conditions to be satisfied –
Restriction not securing to persons entitled to benefit of it any practical benefits of substantial value b
or advantage – Benefits – Whether landscape view not visible from land itself but visible from land
close by capable of being a 'practical benefit' – Whether evidence required that persons entitled to
benefit actually taking advantage of it – Law of Property Act 1925, s 84(1)(1A).

The appellant bought a plot of land which was subject to a restrictive covenant not to
erect more than one house on the land. Subsequently he obtained planning permission c
to erect three houses on it and applied to the Lands Tribunal for an order under s 84(1)[a]
of the Law of Property Act 1925 that the restrictive covenant be discharged or modified
so as to permit the erection of the additional houses. The owners of neighbouring plots,
who derived their title from the same vendor as the appellant and who therefore had the
benefit of the covenant objected to the application. Their plots were close to, but not
adjoining, a road which ran along the northern boundary of the appellant's plot. The d
tribunal, after visiting the area, found that the extra houses on the appellant's plot would
interfere with a fine view of the surrounding countryside, which could be enjoyed from
the road but which was not visible from the objectors' plots. The tribunal held that the
power to preserve the view was a 'practical benefit of substantial value or advantage' to
the objectors, within s 84(1A) of the 1925 Act, and that, accordingly, it had no jurisdiction
to discharge or modify the covenant. The tribunal indicated, however, that even if it had e
jurisdiction it would, in any event, have exercised its discretion by dismissing the
application. The appellant appealed against the decision contending, inter alia, (i) that a
view which was not obtainable from the objectors' land could not constitute a practical
'benefit' within s 84(1A), (ii) that there was no evidence to support the finding that the
enjoyment of the view was in fact a practical benefit to the objectors, and (iii) that since
planning permission had already been granted and the implementation of it depended f
on the successful outcome of his application, the tribunal should not, when deciding how
to exercise its discretion, have taken the view into account.

Held – The appeal would be dismissed for the following reasons—
  (1) The tribunal was entitled to hold that the view was a 'benefit' irrespective of
whether it touched and concerned the land of the objectors because s 84(1A) of the 1925
Act applied to 'any' practical benefits and was not confined to benefits which ran with the g
land (see p 579 e to j, p 581 d e and p 582 a b d e and h, post).
  (2) In any event, the land of each of the objectors was touched and concerned by the
covenant because it was intended to preserve the amenities or standard of the
neighbourhood generally and the loss of a view close to the land having the benefit of the
covenant might have an adverse effect on the land itself (see p 579 j to p 580 b, p 581 d e
and p 582 a b and h, post).
  (3) Evidence that objectors did in fact take advantage of the benefits was not always
essential and, in the particular circumstances, the tribunal was entitled to conclude that
the existence of a view easily accessible to an occupier was a benefit of substantial value
(see p 580 c d, p 581 d e and p 582 e and h j, post).
  Per curiam. The grant of planning permission is not decisive of whether a covenant
restricting development should be lifted and does not prevent the Lands Tribunal from
exercising its discretion under s 84(1) of the 1925 Act to refuse to lift a restrictive
covenant on the grounds that to do so would impede a landscape view (see p 581 b e and
p 582 h j, post).

---

a   Section 84, so far as material, is set out at p 577 j to p 578 d, post

Notes

For restrictive covenants and the right to have them discharged or modified, see 16 Halsbury's Laws (4th edn) para 1360, and for cases on the subject, see 40 Digest (Repl) 364–367, 2925–2936.

For the Law of Property Act 1925, s 84, see 27 Halsbury's Statutes (3rd edn) 467.

Cases referred to in judgments

Ridley v Taylor [1965] 2 All ER 51, [1965] 1 WLR 611, CA, Digest (Cont Vol B) 644, 2927a.

Saviker's Application (No 2), Re (1973) 26 P & CR 441, Lands Tribunal.

Tulk v Moxhay (1848) 2 Ph 774, 41 ER 1143, LC, 40 Digest (Repl) 342, 2774.

Union of London and Smith's Bank Ltd's Conveyance, Re, Miles v Easter [1933] Ch 611, CA, 40 Digest (Repl) 329, 2702.

Appeal

Donald David Gilbert (the applicant) appealed by way of case stated against a decision of the Lands Tribunal whereby, following objections by the respondent, Winifred Mary Spoor, and others, it dismissed his application for an order under s 84(1) of the Law of Property Act 1925 that a restriction affecting land at Heddon Banks, Heddon-on-the-Wall, Northumberland be discharged in part or modified. The facts are set out in the judgment of Eveleigh LJ.

John H Fryer-Spedding for the applicant.
The respondent appeared in person.

Cur adv vult

5 February. The following judgments were read.

EVELEIGH LJ (delivering the first judgment at the invitation of Waller LJ). The applicant applied to the Lands Tribunal under s 84(1) of the Law of Property Act 1925 for the discharge in part or modification of restrictive covenants affecting land at Heddon Banks, Heddon-on-the-Wall, Northumberland. There were a number of objectors who, like the applicant, derived title under a common vendor in circumstances in which it is agreed the land was subject to a scheme of reciprocal rights and obligations amounting to a local law. We are only concerned with one restriction and the ground for the application based on s 84(1)(*aa*) although the original application covered a wider field.

The restriction is contained in the first schedule to a conveyance dated 3 November 1954. So far as is material it reads:

'Not to erect on the piece of land hereby conveyed any building whatsoever other than one private dwellinghouse with proper offices and outbuildings (including at the Purchaser's option a private garage) . . .'

The application was for an order that the restriction be discharged wholly or modified by—

'Permitting the erection and maintenance on the said land of three dwelling houses with proper offices, outbuildings and garages, of design and specification approved by the Castle Morpeth Borough Council by and or pursuant to the said Council's grant of planning permission to the Applicant dated the 11th day of October one thousand nine hundred and seventy six . . .'

Section 84 of the Law of Property Act 1925, as amended by the Law of Property Act 1969, reads, so far as is material for this case, as follows:

'(1) The Lands Tribunal shall (without prejudice to any concurrent jurisdiction of the court) have power from time to time, on the application of any person interested

in any freehold land affected by any restriction arising under covenant or otherwise
as to the user thereof or the building thereon, by order wholly or partially to *a*
discharge or modify any such restriction on being satisfied . . . (*aa*) that (in a case
falling within subsection (1A) below) the continued existence thereof would impede
some reasonable user of the land for public or private purposes or, as the case may
be, would unless modified so impede such user . . .

(1A) Subsection (1)(*aa*) above authorises the discharge or modification of a
restriction by reference to its impeding some reasonable user of land in any case in *b*
which the Lands Tribunal is satisfied that the restriction, in impeding that user,
either—(*a*) does not secure to persons entitled to the benefit of it any practical
benefits of substantial value or advantage to them; or (*b*) is contrary to the public
interest; and that money will be an adequate compensation for the loss or
disadvantage (if any) which any such person will suffer from the discharge or
modification.

(1B) In determining whether a case is one falling within subsection (1A) above, *c*
and in determining whether (in any such case or otherwise) a restriction ought to be
discharged or modified, the Lands Tribunal shall take into account the development
plan and any declared or ascertainable pattern for the grant or refusal of planning
permissions in the relevant areas, as well as the period at which and context in which
the restriction was created or imposed and any other material circumstances . . .' *d*

Before the tribunal the argument centred on the question whether or not the applicant
had brought his case within sub-s (1A). The member of the tribunal visited the land and
came to the conclusion that—

'the power which the relevant restrictions gave to the persons entitled to the
benefit of them to prevent interference, by the erection of dwelling-houses, with the *e*
landscape view from a certain part of Centurion Way, Heddon-on-the-Wall, or from
the public seats situate thereon or from the road itself or the vicinity of the said seats
was a practical benefit to the persons aforesaid.'

The applicant's land measures approximately 111 yards from west to east and 20 yards
from north to south. A road called Centurion Way runs along the northern boundary *f*
for two-thirds of the distance from east to west and then turns sharply north for
approximately 50 yards when it turns sharply east for another 50 yards to form the stem
of a T-junction with Heddon Banks.

The objectors are the owners of nos 18, 19, 21, 23, and 25 Heddon Banks. Number 18
is situated on the east side of the road right opposite its junction with Centurion Way.
The remaining properties lie within the area bordered by Centurion Way from where it *g*
turns north and then east to the T-junction, by Heddon Banks running north and south,
and by approximately 50 yards of the northern boundary of the applicant's land from
Heddon Banks to where Centurion Way turns north. Very roughly it forms a
quadrilateral with sides approximately 50 yards long.

The land to the south of the applicant's land is approved Green Belt which falls rapidly
away and becomes the valley of the River Tyne. In the decision attached to the stated *h*
case it is said to be a resplendent landscape view which is almost entirely rural. In
Centurion Way, about 50 yards from the beginning of the area in which four of the
objectors' houses are situated, two seats commanding the view have been fixed for public
use. The tribunal found that the construction of the two extra houses would obscure that
view and interfere with the view at present enjoyed from the road when walking along
it.

The decision has been attacked on the following grounds: (1) that the enjoyment of *j*
the landscape view could not in law be a practical benefit to the objectors for the purposes
of s 84(1A) of the 1925 Act because it was not a benefit annexed to the land owned by the
objectors for the view was not one obtainable from their land; (2) that there was no
evidence to support the finding that the enjoyment of the view was in fact a practical

benefit to the objectors or, alternatively, that it was of substantial advantage; (3) that the
a applicant could not reasonably have been expected to know that he was going to meet a
case based on the landscape view and the tribunal failed to afford justice to the applicant
by not giving his counsel an opportunity to make submissions or call evidence in relation
thereto; (4) that since detailed planning permission had been given for a development,
the implementation of which depended on the successful outcome of the applicant's
application, the tribunal should not have taken into account the landscape view in
b exercising its discretion against the applicant.

While the tribunal specifically held that the power to preserve the view was a benefit,
it is to be inferred that the tribunal was referring to the power of the objectors to preserve
the view for the occupiers of the objectors' land. No distinction was made in argument
between the view itself as a benefit and the power to preserve it.

It is submitted that as the view is not enjoyed from the land of the objectors it cannot
c constitute a practical benefit within the meaning of the subsection. It was argued that
we are concerned with covenants which are said to run with the land. Such covenants
must directly affect the land of the covenantor by controlling its user and they must
directly benefit the land of the covenantee. From this it is argued that the 'practical
benefits' referred to in the subsection are restricted to benefits the observance of which
directly benefit the land of the covenantee. The view, it is submitted, does not do this
d because it is not a view from the covenantee's land.

We are concerned to construe the words of a statute. The limited construction for
which the applicant contends might be more firmly based if s 84 were concerned only
with the situation where it is necessary to rely on the rule in *Tulk v Moxhay* (1848) 2 Ph
774, 41 ER 1143 or in *Re Union of London and Smith's Bank Ltd's Conveyance, Miles v Easter*
[1933] Ch 611, in other words cases which can only arise when the covenant was in its
e inception capable of benefiting the land of the covenantee.

It is clear from the introductory sentence of sub-s (1) of s 84 of the 1925 Act that its
provisions apply as between the original parties and to restrictions of any kind: see the
observations in *Ridley v Taylor* [1965] 2 All ER 51, [1965] 1 WLR 611. I therefore do not
think that it is permissible to construe sub-s (1A) only in the context of restrictive
covenants which run with the land. The first task is to construe the section in isolation
and then to relate it to the facts of the present case.

The words of the subsection, in my opinion, are used quite generally. The phrase 'any
practical benefits of substantial value or advantage to them' is wide. The subsection does
not speak of a restriction for the benefit or protection of land, which is a reasonably
common phrase, but rather to a restriction which secures any practical benefits. The
expression 'any practical benefits' is so wide that I would require very compelling
g considerations before I felt able to limit them in the manner contended for. When one
remembers that Parliament is authorising the Lands Tribunal to take away from a person
a vested right either in law or in equity, it is not surprising that the tribunal is required
to consider the adverse effects on a broad basis.

Had this application been one where all the original parties were concerned, I do not
understand counsel for the applicant to argue that the preservation of the view could not
be said to be a practical benefit secured by the restriction. If this is correct, and I think
that it is, I see no reason to give the words a different meaning because successors in title
are involved. The successor in title may well have to establish certain conditions before
the covenant is enforceable by him, but that fact will not alter the nature of the benefits
or advantage in fact secured to him by the existence of the restriction.

In my judgment the tribunal was entitled to hold that the view was a benefit whether
or not that benefit could be said to touch and concern the land. However, I am also of the
view that the land of the objectors is, in each case, touched and concerned by the
covenant. The covenant is intended to preserve the amenity or standard of the
neighbourhood generally. The covenant is specifically aimed at density of housing.
Extensive building can effect the amenity of a district in many ways. An estate can easily
lose its character when buildings obstruct the views. It seems to me to be perfectly

reasonable to say that the loss of a view 'at a point just a short distance from the land' may have an adverse effect on the land itself for the loss of the view could prove detrimental *a* to the estate as a whole. In my opinion therefore the tribunal was entitled to find as it did.

As to the second ground, in so far as the decision was based on the power to preserve the view there was clearly evidence to support it. There was a visit to the area. The magnificence of the view was there to be observed and to my mind it is easy to see that the power to preserve it could be regarded as a practical benefit to the person possessing *b* such power and a benefit of substantial value or advantage.

However, counsel for the applicant took the point that no evidence was given by any of the objectors to the effect that he or she had ever personally admired the view. Thus, it is said, there was no evidence to support the finding that the enjoyment of the view was a practical benefit to any of the objectors. This argument seems to me to be based on the mistaken interpretation that the expression 'practical benefits of substantial value or *c* advantage' means benefits which the objectors are in the habit of enjoying. Evidence that the objectors do in fact take advantage of the benefits may well be relevant but cannot always be essential. As a result of the visit to the area the tribunal was entitled to conclude that the existence of a view easily accessible to an occupier was a benefit of substantial value.

The third ground advanced by the applicant was that he could not reasonably have *d* been expected to know that he was going to meet a case based on the landscape view and the tribunal failed to afford justice to him by not giving his counsel an opportunity to make submissions or call evidence in relation thereto. I cannot accept this. The objection by Mrs Spoor, the owner of Heddon Banks, stated:

'The proposed change will injure persons entitled to the benefit of the restriction and also all the neighbouring house owners and tenants. The amenities of view, *e* space and openness will be diminished. There is already much adverse comment on the unsightliness of the present one house allowed.'

Mr Edmonds, an experienced chartered surveyor called by the applicant, was cross-examined as to the view on behalf of the objectors. He agreed that there was what he called a 'pleasant view' where Centurion Way borders the northern boundary of the *f* applicant's land, and he accepted that the roofs of the two extra buildings would obscure it. In those circumstances I cannot accept that the applicant was taken by surprise. Furthermore, counsel has been quite unable to tell us that there would have been or that there is available to him evidence which he would have wished to call.

I can see no obligation on the tribunal to reflect on the case and then inform counsel as to the way it may possibly find so that counsel can then argue that particular matter. *g* It is for counsel to make such submissions as he thinks fit in each particular case. It is not the task of the judge to direct his thoughts, although it sometimes happens that the court invites submissions on certain specific points. This is not a case where the tribunal took a point of its own.

In this case, as I have said, there was no evidence which counsel thinks he might have called and I consequently cannot see that he was prevented from submitting any *h* argument on the facts.

As to the law, again it was counsel's duty to make such submissions as he thought proper. The tribunal did nothing to prevent him. In any event, however, there were no submissions on the law which counsel could have made to the tribunal that have not been made to us. As I reject those submissions on the law, it follows that in my opinion the applicant has lost nothing by the fact that counsel did not address the tribunal to the *j* same effect.

The final ground set forth in the applicant's notice reads:

'Since detailed planning permission had been given for a development the implementation of which depended on the successful outcome of the Applicant's

application the Tribunal should not have taken into account the said landscape view
in exercising its discretion against the Applicant.'

The reference to the discretion arises because, having said that none of the grounds in
s 84(1) of the 1925 Act had been made out, the tribunal went on to say that alternatively
it would exercise its discretion in favour of the objectors. As in my opinion the tribunal
was entitled to hold that the conditions in sub-s (1A) had not been established there was
no jurisdiction to discharge or modify the restrictions. Consequently it is unnecessary to
deal with this final ground. However, if the tribunal had been satisfied that the
conditions of sub-s (1A) had been made out, I do not think that the fact that detailed
planning permission had been given must prevent the tribunal from taking the landscape
view into account in exercising its discretion.

Subsection (1B) does not lead to such a conclusion. It does not in fact refer to detailed
planning permission. It refers to 'the development plan and any declared or ascertainable
pattern for the grant or refusal of planning permissions in the relevant areas'. In other
words any anticipated change generally in the neighbourhood is specifically stated to be
a relevant consideration which must be taken into account. The subsection does not
make planning decisions decisive.

In *Re Saviker's Application (No 2)* (1973) 26 P & CR 441 the tribunal held that its
jurisdiction did not arise, but went on to say that if it had arisen the discretion would
have been exercised against the applicant in spite of his having obtained planning
permission. The tribunal made the same pronouncement in this case, and I see nothing
wrong with it.

I would answer all of the questions in the stated case in a manner favourable to the
objectors, and I would dismiss this appeal.

WALLER LJ. I agree. The restriction with which this case is concerned was contained
in a conveyance dated 3 November 1954, and it was agreed at the bar that the restriction
has to be treated as a covenant within a building scheme or, as is sometimes said, as local
law. The effect therefore was that the covenant to build only one house on the land
edged red on the plan and belonging to the applicant was a covenant for the benefit of all
other purchasers of land within the building scheme or their successors in title. As
between each of these owners, including the applicant, there were mutual rights and
mutual obligations. These rights and obligations were for the benefit of the whole
estate. Each owner would be aware of the restrictions imposed on the other owners
including the restriction imposed on the applicant. These restrictions would influence
and control the development of the whole estate. Accordingly, if the restriction remains
in force, the objectors or other owners of land within the building scheme could enforce
the restriction.

The facts concerning the location of the appellant's property and the view southwards
over the Tyne valley have already been set out in the judgment of Eveleigh LJ. I would
only add that it does appear that the erection of two additional houses on the applicant's
land would be visible from the property of the objector, Mrs Spoor, although it would
not interfere with the view southwards which has been blocked by the house already
completed.

The member of the Lands Tribunal in considering the case has come to the conclusion
that there is no detrimental effect from the proposed development on no 25, ie the house
of Mr Spoor. He comes to a similar conclusion in relation to the other objectors save for
no 23, where he is of opinion that the value of the house would be reduced and that that
could be compensated by a sum of money. However, from Centurion Way where it
borders the northern boundary of the red land there is a view southwards over the Tyne
valley described by Mr Edmunds, a witness, as a pleasant view and by the member as a
resplendent view. All the objectors' houses are within a short distance of this part of
Centurion Way and the member finds that there are marks showing that, from no 21 for
example, there is a well-worn path leading through the hedge to Centurion Way. Mr

Spoor submits that the fact that he can walk out of his house and within a minute walk along the edge of the land and enjoy the magnificent view to the south is a benefit of substantial value or advantage to him.

The applicant's case is that in order to bring this within s 84(1A) of the Law of Property Act 1925 the benefit of substantial value must be one enjoyed actually from the land, in other words that the fact that the owner of the land has to walk off his own plot in order to enjoy this view does not bring the case within sub-s (1A). I do not accept the applicant's argument that because the view is the most important thing it must be a view from the objector's land that is being interrupted. In my judgment the question is one of degree. If on a building estate a restrictive covenant is broken by any plot-holder it is potentially an interference with the rights of all the other plot owners. It may be such that it is a momentary irritation to the owner of land some distance away. The nearer it is the greater the possibility of it being an interference with the amenities of owners. If a building estate contains a pleasant approach with restrictions on it and some building is done contrary to those restrictions which spoils the approach, if then the owner of a plot complains about that breach, the fact that he does not see it until he drives along the road in my opinion does not affect the matter. He is entitled to the estate being administered in accordance with the mutual covenants, or local law; so in this case.

The objectors on this estate have the advantage of the view over the Tyne valley for many miles, a wholly rural view in what is an industrial neighbourhood. A view is not something which can be valued in money terms; indeed it may be, and perhaps I would say in this case is, priceless. It is in my opinion a matter for the tribunal to decide whether or not it can properly be said to be of substantial value or advantage to the objectors and, for my part, he has come to that conclusion and it is one which is abundantly justified. Even if I am wrong about this I have no doubt that he is fully entitled to exercise his discretion in the way in which he did.

The member, in his judgment, finds:

'In my judgment the power which the restrictions give to the persons entitled to the benefit of them to prevent interference with the view at present enjoyed from this road, Centurion Way, from the seats and indeed when walking along the road or in the vicinity of the seats is a practical benefit of substantial advantage to them.'

It does not seem to me to be necessary to go so far as to say that it is the power which is a practical benefit because in my judgment it is the restriction securing the view which is of practical benefit of substantial value or advantage. Subject to this point, in my judgment there was evidence to support the finding of the member and there was evidence to support the finding that none of the grounds in s 84(1) were made out. I do not find that the applicant was not afforded justice in relation to the question affecting the view because it was quite clearly raised and I agree with what has already been said about that. Finally, in my judgment, the landscape view is not an irrelevant circumstance.

KERR LJ. I also agree. The member of the tribunal was in my view clearly entitled to conclude that the open view across the Tyne valley, which could be enjoyed from the immediate vicinity of the objectors' land, secured to them a practical benefit of special value or advantage, and that the discharge or modification of the restriction binding the applicant's land should therefore not be authorised.

I also agree that the special case is not open to any of the other criticisms raised on behalf of the applicant, and that this appeal should accordingly be dismissed.

Appeal dismissed.

Solicitors: *Marshall Hall & Levy*, South Shields (for the applicant).

Diana Brahams   Barrister.

a

Parkin v Norman
Valentine v Lilley

QUEEN'S BENCH DIVISION
DONALDSON LJ AND MCCULLOUGH J
23 FEBRUARY, 10 MARCH 1982

b

Public order – Offensive conduct conducive to breaches of peace – Threatening, abusive or insulting words or behaviour – Insulting – Nature of insulting behaviour – Homosexual activity in public lavatory – Accused making homosexual advances to plain clothes police officer – Accused's behaviour not observed by anyone else – Whether accused using 'insulting behaviour ... likely' to occasion breach of peace – Whether likelihood of disturbance short of violence
c *sufficient to constitute breach of peace – Public Order Act 1936, s 5.*

In two separate cases the appellant entered a public lavatory and while there made homosexual advances to a plain clothes police officer (who was there to investigate any homosexual conduct) by making indecent gestures and masturbating while looking at the officer. In the first case the appellant desisted from his behaviour when a third
d person entered the lavatory; in the second case no one else was present in the lavatory. In each case the appellant was convicted of insulting behaviour whereby a breach of the peace was likely to be occasioned, contrary to s 5[a] of the Public Order Act 1936. In the second case the justices concluded that a breach of the peace could occur by way of a disturbance or by violence. In each case the appellant appealed against his conviction on the grounds (i) that his conduct was not capable of amounting to 'insulting behaviour'
e within s 5 because the officers concerned were not insulted, and in any event s 5 required an intent to insult and neither appellant had intended to insult the police officer or anyone else, and (ii) that a breach of the peace was not 'likely' to be occasioned by the appellant's behaviour because it was not likely that the police officer or the appellant would break the peace by violence, and the mere possibility that a third person might have entered the lavatory and become so incensed by the appellant's behaviour as to use
f or threaten violence did not amount to a likelihood that there would be a breach of the peace. In addition the appellant in the second case appealed on the further ground that a mere disturbance could not constitute a breach of the peace, since a breach of the peace required threatened or actual violence.

Held – (1) Since the purpose of the 1936 Act was to promote good order in places to
g which the public had access, conduct of an insulting character which was likely to occasion a breach of the peace came within s 5 of that Act whether or not it was intended to be insulting conduct, and therefore an intention to insult was not a necessary ingredient of the offence under s 5. Furthermore, insulting conduct did not lose its insulting character merely because the persons who had witnessed it had not been insulted. To constitute insulting conduct it was necessary that one person should have
h directed an insult at another who could perceive it to be such. Thus, although neither appellant had been trying to insult the police officer, but on the contrary had thought he was another homosexual, and although the police officers would not have been insulted by the appellants' behaviour, nevertheless, as the person importuned by each appellant might have been an ordinary heterosexual person using the lavatory for normal purposes and might have been insulted by the appellants' behaviour because it was tantamount to a statement by the appellant that he believed the other to be a homosexual, the behaviour of each appellant could fairly be regarded as being potentially insulting, and therefore constituting insulting behaviour within s 5 (see p 586 h j, p 587 a b j, p 588 d e and g to

---

a   Section 5, so far as material, is set out at p 585 *d*, post

p 589 *b* and p 590 *a b*, post); dictum of Viscount Dilhorne in *Brutus v Cozens* [1972] 2 All
ER at 1302 considered.

 (2) However, although it was proper when determining whether a breach of the peace
was 'likely' to result from insulting behaviour to take into account the reactions of others
who might have observed the behaviour apart from the person to whom the behaviour
was addressed, since neither the appellants nor the police officers to whom their
behaviour was addressed would have been likely to break the peace and there was only
a possibility, as opposed to a probability, that any other person who might have entered
the lavatories and observed the appellants' behaviour towards the police officers would
have been so incensed as to use or threaten violence, the evidence in both cases did not
establish that the appellants' insulting behaviour was likely to (as distinct from liable to)
occasion breaches of the peace within s 5. Furthermore, in the second case the justices
had been wrong to hold that a breach of the peace could occur by way of a disturbance
not involving violence or a threat of violence, because to constitute a breach of the peace
there had to be threatened or actual violence. It followed that breaches of the peace were
not likely to have been occasioned by the appellants' insulting behaviour and their
convictions would accordingly be quashed (see p 589 *b* to *d* and p 590 *b c* and *j*, post);
dictum of Watkins LJ in *R v Howell* [1981] 3 All ER at 389 applied.

 Per curiam. If proper attention is paid to the word 'likely' in the phrase 'whereby a
breach of the peace is likely to be occasioned' in s 5 of the 1936 Act, a charge under s 5 will
more often than not be inappropriate in the case of homosexual activity in public
lavatories (see p 591 *a b*, post).

Notes

For the offence of using insulting words or behaviour likely to cause a breach of the
peace, see 11 Halsbury's Laws (4th edn) para 850, and for cases on the subject, see 15
Digest (Reissue) 908–910, 7797–7807.

 For the Public Order Act 1936, s 5, see 8 Halsbury's Statutes (3rd edn) 332.

Cases referred to in judgment

Ballard v Blythe (3 November 1980, unreported), QBD.
Brutus v Cozens [1972] 2 All ER 1297, [1973] AC 854, [1972] 3 WLR 521, HL; rvsg [1972]
 2 All ER 1, [1972] 1 WLR 484, DC, 15 Digest (Reissue) 910, 7807.
Cawley v Frost [1976] 3 All ER 743, [1976] 1 WLR 1207, DC, 15 Digest (Reissue) 910,
 7805.
R v Chief Constable of Devon and Cornwall, ex p Central Electricity Generating Board [1981]
 3 All ER 826, [1981] 3 WLR 967, CA.
R v Howell [1981] 3 All ER 383, [1981] 3 WLR 501, CA.

Cases also cited

Jordan v Burgoyne [1963] 2 All ER 225, [1963] 2 QB 744, DC.
R v Ambrose (1973) 57 Cr App R 538, CA.
R v Preece, R v Howells [1976] 2 All ER 690, [1977] QB 370, CA.
R v Venna [1975] 3 All ER 788, [1976] QB 421, CA.

Cases stated

Parkin v Norman

Thomas Henry Parkin appealed by way of case stated by the Crown Court at Nottingham
(his Honour Judge Ellis sitting with justices) in respect of its adjudication on 30
September 1981 whereby it dismissed his appeal against his conviction in the Mansfield
Magistrates' Court on 4 August 1981 on a charge laid by the respondent, Leslie James
Norman, a police constable, of using threatening, abusive or insulting words or behaviour
in a public place with intent to provoke a breach of the peace whereby a breach of the
peace was likely to be occasioned, contrary to s 5 of the Public Order Act 1936. The facts
are set out in the judgment of the court.

Valentine v Lilley

a James Valentine appealed by way of case stated by the justices for the County of Nottingham sitting as a magistrates' court at Mansfield in respect of their adjudication on 12 August 1981 whereby they convicted the appellant on a charge laid by the respondent, John Lilley, a superintendent of police, of using insulting behaviour whereby a breach of the peace was likely to be occasioned, contrary to s 5 of the Public Order Act 1936. The facts are set out in the judgment of the court.

b

Adrian Fulford for the appellant Parkin.
Richard Payne for the appellant Valentine.
Richard S A Benson for both respondents.

Cur adv vult

c

10 March. **McCULLOUGH J** read the following judgment of the court: These two cases raise questions involving the application of s 5 of the Public Order Act 1936, where accusations are made of indecent behaviour of a homosexual nature in public lavatories. With the consent of all the parties they were heard together.

The material words of the section are:

d

'Any person who in any public place . . . (*a*) uses threatening, abusive or insulting words or behaviour . . . with intent to provoke a breach of the peace or whereby a breach of the peace is likely to be occasioned, shall be guilty of an offence . . .'

Immaterial amendments were made by later Acts.

Each appellant was found to have been handling his penis in a way which clearly indicated that he wanted his behaviour to be seen by the only other person present at the **e** urinals in a public lavatory. In each case, unknown to the appellant, the other person was a police officer in plain clothes who, after a suitable interval, arrested him. Each was convicted. Each appeals to this court by way of case stated. Each argues that his behaviour was not insulting and that no breach of the peace was likely to be occasioned by it.

f

Parkin v Norman

On 4 August 1981, at the Mansfield Magistrates' Court, the appellant was convicted of an offence under s 5 of the Public Order Act 1936, the particulars being that he—

'on 17th February, 1981 . . . at a public place, namely New Street Public Toilets, Sutton in Ashfield, did use threatening, abusive or insulting words or behaviour **g** with intent to provoke a breach of the peace or whereby a breach of the peace was likely to be occasioned.'

On 21 August 1981 his appeal against conviction was dismissed by the Crown Court at Nottingham.

The following facts were found. At 4.52 pm the appellant entered a gentlemen's **h** public lavatory in New Street, Sutton in Ashfield, where the respondent, a plain clothes police officer, was already standing at a urinal. The appellant went to a urinal two clear spaces away; he stood back about a foot from it, holding his penis and looked several times at the respondent.

At 4.53 pm a third man came in, used a urinal between the other two and left. While he was present the appellant stood forward and did not look towards the respondent. **i** After the man left he stepped back, partly turned towards the respondent and began masturbating. The appellant appeared nervous and was continually looking at the respondent and at the entrance to the lavatories. At 5.00 pm he turned to face the respondent still holding his penis. He had stopped masturbating. The respondent then identified himself and arrested him. When questioned at the police station he denied that he had been masturbating.

A submission that there was no case to answer was made at the close of the respondent's case. This was rejected. The appellant gave evidence and, although this does not appear from the case, we understand that he denied that he had been masturbating.

The Crown Court rejected submissions made on his behalf that, even if the police evidence was accepted, his conduct was not capable of amounting to 'insulting behaviour' and that there was no likelihood of any breach of the peace. The court's reasoning is not given in the case, which merely records that they were of the opinion that the behaviour was insulting and that a breach of the peace was likely to be occasioned thereby. The question posed is 'whether upon the facts which we found there was sufficient evidence to support our decision'.

The evidence has not been set out; so its sufficiency cannot be assessed. Counsel for the appellant accepts that there was evidence on which the court could properly find the facts as it did, but, he submits, on a correct interpretation of the law, those facts could not sustain a conviction.

There was, he submits, no insulting behaviour. The officer was not insulted. Only one other person entered the lavatory while the appellant was doing what he did and, while this third person was present, he desisted. Had anyone else entered there is no reason to suppose that he would not have done so again. Thus no one was insulted, nor was anyone likely to have been.

He further submits that in any event an insult requires an intention to insult. The appellant never intended to insult any third person and, whatever his intention may have been in doing what he did in sight of the respondent, it was not to insult him.

Counsel for the appellant next submits that no breach of the peace was likely to be occasioned. Likely means 'probable'. There was no likelihood that the respondent would break the peace, nor the appellant himself, nor any other visitor to the lavatory, since the likelihood was that the appellant would desist and no newcomer would see him behaving indecently. While there was a chance that someone might come in, catch the appellant unawares and be so incensed by what he saw that he would either use or threaten violence, this was no more than an outside possibility.

Counsel for the appellant bolsters these submissions by references to various other criminal offences of which the appellant might have been convicted. That being so, he submits it is wholly wrong to strain the language of s 5 of the Public Order Act 1936 to embrace circumstances which Parliament can never have intended they should cover. He draws our attention to the long title to the Act and to the scheme of its provisions as a whole which, he says, were intended to deal with political and quasi-military activities.

Our task is to construe the words of s 5 in the light of the Act as a whole, including its long title, to which reference can properly be made if the words of the section are ambiguous. If, having construed it, we are led to the conclusion that those who behave as the appellant is found to have done may also be guilty of offences against other provisions (e g s 28 of the Town Police Clauses Act 1847 or s 32 of the Sexual Offences Act 1956) this cannot alter the construction arrived at. In such an event it is for others, not us, to decide which provision to use.

Equally, if the words of the section, properly construed, are apt to fit behaviour of the kind in question (ie homosexual activity in public lavatories) it is immaterial that, when Parliament enacted the section, it did not contemplate that it would be so used.

The purpose of the 1936 Act was to promote good order in places to which the public have access: see *Cawley v Frost* [1976] 3 All ER 743 at 748, [1976] 1 WLR 1207 at 1212 per Lord Widgery CJ. It is clear, both from the long title and from ss 1, 2 and 4, that Parliament intended to prevent activities liable to lead to public disorder, regardless of whether or not those engaging in them intended that disorder should result. The use of the phrase 'whereby a breach of the peace is likely to be occasioned' in s 5 reflects this thinking. The phrase is absent from the earlier sections, no doubt because Parliament regarded the wearing of any political uniform (s 1), the training of any quasi-military body (s 2) and the taking of offensive weapons to public meetings or on public processions (s 4) as threats to public order per se. But not all threats, abuse or insults necessarily have this result. Qualifying words were therefore required, and conduct of this kind was only

prohibited if it was likely to lead to a breach of the peace or, as was added, if it was so
intended.

It was the likely effect of the conduct on those who witnessed it with which Parliament
was chiefly concerned. What is likely to cause someone to break the peace is his feeling
that he has been threatened or abused or insulted, and this will be so whether or not the
words or behaviour were intended to threaten or to abuse or to insult.

In our judgment, threats, abuse and insults are within the section whether or not they
were intended to be threats, abuse or insults. 'Threatening, abusive or insulting words
or behaviour' are simply words or behaviour that are threatening, abusive or insulting in
character. We have reached this conclusion despite some words of Viscount Dilhorne to
be found in *Brutus v Cozens* [1972] 2 All ER 1297, [1973] AC 854. In that case B had
interrupted play on the no 2 court at Wimbledon during the annual open tennis
tournament of the All England Lawn Tennis Club. A match was in progress; one of the
players was a South African. B went onto the court, blew a whistle and threw leaflets
about. Nine or ten others joined him with placards or banners, on which anti-apartheid
slogans were written, and more leaflets were distributed. The spectators were upset;
some shouted; some shook their fists. B was removed from the court bodily by C, a
police constable, with whom he went quietly. As he was being led away some of the
crowd showed hostility to him and attempted to strike him. He was charged with
having used insulting behaviour whereby a breach of the peace was likely to be
occasioned. The magistrates upheld a submission that the behaviour, although annoying,
was not insulting, and dismissed the charge. C successfully appealed to the Divisional
Court ([1972] 2 All ER 1, [1972] 1 WLR 484), but the House of Lords overturned their
decision and restored that of the magistrates.

Four of their Lordships said that 'insulting' was a straightforward word in ordinary
usage. They deprecated the attempt which the Divisional Court had made to define it.
They found it impossible to say that the magistrates had made a decision which could not
properly have been reached on the evidence: see Lord Reid, Lord Morris and Lord
Kilbrandon ([1972] 2 All ER 1297 at 1299–1301, 1303, [1973] AC 854 at 861–863,
867). Lord Diplock gave no reasons. Only Viscount Dilhorne touched on the question
of intent. He said ([1972] 2 All ER 1297 at 1302, [1973] AC 854 at 865–866):

> 'Unless the context otherwise requires, words in a statute have to be given their
> ordinary natural meaning and there is in this Act, in my opinion, nothing to
> indicate or suggest that the word "insulting" should be given any other than its
> ordinary natural meaning. The justices had two questions to decide; first, was the
> appellant's behaviour insulting and, secondly, if so, was it likely to occasion a breach
> of the peace. Both were questions of fact for them to decide. In considering the
> first, it was relevant for them to consider whether the behaviour was such as to
> indicate an intention to insult anyone, and if so whom; and if the justices in this case
> did so, they may well have concluded that the appellant's behaviour did not evince
> any intention to insult either players or spectators, and so could not properly be
> regarded as insulting.'

The question of intent was not material to the decision in *Brutus v Cozens*. The decision
was simply that, whatever annoyance, resentment and anger had been occasioned by B's
behaviour, no one, on any ordinary use of the word, had been insulted; nor was anyone
likely to have been insulted. So there had been no 'insulting behaviour'. There was
therefore no need to consider whether an intention to insult was required.

Having regard to the tenor of the 1936 Act as a whole, we believe that no such intent
need be proved. What is required is conduct of a threatening, abusive or insulting
character which is likely in the circumstances to occasion a breach of the peace. If the
conduct in question is of this character it does not, in our judgment, matter whether
anyone feels himself to have been threatened, abused or insulted. Insulting behaviour
does not lose its insulting character simply because no one who witnessed it was insulted,
any more than it would lose its liability to provoke a breach of the peace merely because
no one who witnessed it broke the peace. In *Ballard v Blythe* (3 November 1980,

unreported) the appellant insulted, abused, threatened and spat at a man who, unknown to him, was a headmaster, and who reacted with an unusual degree of self-restraint. In dismissing his appeal against conviction Donaldson LJ said:

'... the court has to find the circumstances in which the conduct takes place and to consider the question posed by the statute: is this conduct such as is inherently likely to occasion a breach of the peace? ... the general test is: what is the natural and probable result of the conduct?'

Where the defendant is addressing an audience which he knows has special susceptibilities, a breach of the peace may be the natural and probable result of behaviour which would not provoke an audience not having this susceptibility in such a way.

It is to be noted that the words of the statute are 'whereby a breach of the peace is likely to be occasioned' and not 'whereby a breach of the peace is liable to be occasioned'. This is a penal measure and the courts must take care to see that the former expression is not treated as if it were the latter.

The Act does not make it criminal to use offensive or disgusting behaviour whereby a breach of the peace is likely to be occasioned. It requires, in the circumstances material to this case, 'insulting behaviour'. What then is an insult? We do not propose to attempt any sort of definition, particularly after the speeches in *Brutus v Cozens*, but some consideration of its characteristics are necessary in the light of counsel's submissions that behaviour of the type here is not insulting.

One cannot insult nothing. The word presupposes a subject and an object and, in this day and age, a human object. An insult is perceived by someone who feels insulted. It is given by someone who is directing his words or his behaviour to another person or persons. When A is insulting B, and is clearly directing his words and behaviour to B alone, if C hears and sees is he insulted? He may be disgusted, offended, annoyed, angered and no doubt a number of other things as well; and he may be provoked by what he sees and hears into breaking the peace. But will he be insulted?

One must take care not to become too analytical or too refined about these things, and we are not beginning to attempt either to define or to lay down any sort of principle, but these considerations may help to clear the mind before one asks oneself whether homosexual behaviour of the type in question here is really properly described as 'insulting'.

At one stage, a third person did come in, but he, so far as we know, saw nothing. So he was not insulted, nor was he likely to have been. Had further people come in the position would no doubt have been the same. If, by chance, anyone had surprised the appellant and seen what was happening, we think it would be difficult to say that he would have been insulted.

The appellant's conduct was aimed at one person and only one person. He obviously hoped, and after a little while would presumably have believed, that the person to whom it was directed was another homosexual. Whatever he was trying to do, he was not trying to insult him. Whatever another homosexual would have felt, he would not, presumably, have felt insulted. In fact the second person was a police officer. Was he insulted? He had gone there in plain clothes to catch anyone whom he saw doing this sort of thing, and he caught one. It seems to us quite unrealistic to say that he would have felt insulted. Suppose, as was possible, that the person to whom the behaviour was directed had been a heterosexual using the lavatory for its proper purpose. He would almost certainly have felt disgusted and perhaps angry, but would he have felt insulted? The argument that he would is that the behaviour was tantamount to a statement, 'I believe you are another homosexual', which the average heterosexual would surely regard as insulting. We regard this as the only basis on which the behaviour could fairly be characterised as 'insulting'. However, that did not happen in this case. The only person importuned, for that is what it comes to, was the policeman, but the person importuned might very well have been an ordinary heterosexual using the lavatory for its proper purpose. On this basis we think that the behaviour can fairly be regarded as

potentially insulting, and we would regard this as sufficient to give it the description
a 'insulting behaviour'.

For this reason, and this reason alone, we are not prepared to say that the court was in
error in making a finding that there had been 'insulting behaviour'. And, as has already
been indicated, we do not think the court was prevented from making this finding by
the fact that the appellant did not intend to insult, nor by the fact that no one was
insulted, nor by his having taken steps to ensure that no third person saw what he was
b doing. This is not to hold that such a finding was inevitable. It was for the court to
decide on the whole of the evidence. We could only interfere if it had been demonstrated
that the finding must have been wrong.

But was a breach of the peace likely to result? Neither the appellant nor the police
officer was likely to break the peace. No third party was likely to have seen. One came
in and the appellant desisted. Had others come in he would no doubt have done the
c same. It is true that someone might have caught him unawares and there must have
been a possibility that such a person might have gone so far as to cause a breach of the
peace, ie to use or threaten violence, but we think counsel for the appellant is right in
saying that on the evidence, as we assume it to have been, no court could have been sure
that this was likely. In our judgment the court can only have reached the conclusion that
it did by treating 'likely' as if it had read 'liable', which it does not.
d We therefore quash this conviction.

Valentine v Lilley

On 12 August 1981 the appellant was convicted by the Mansfield magistrates of the
following offence, that he—

> 'on Monday, 6th day of April, 1981 at Titchfield Park public toilets, Nottingham
> Road, Mansfield, did use certain insulting behaviour whereby a breach of the peace
> was likely to be occasioned. Contrary to Section 5 of the Public Order Act, 1936, as
> amended . . .'

The justices found the following facts. At 1.20 pm on 6 April the appellant entered
the lavatory. About 15 minutes later Pc Beck in plain clothes entered and stood at the
urinal next to him. Almost at once the appellant turned towards him, smiled and
masturbated. He was unaware of the true identity of the police constable at the time.
No one else was present. He was then arrested.

The appellant argued that his behaviour was not insulting, because it was not insulting
to the police officer, and that, as violence was unlikely, it could not be said to have been
likely to provoke a breach of the peace. The respondent argued that the behaviour was
in itself insulting and that whether it had this character or not could not depend on the
unknown identity of the person to whom it was addressed. Further, a mere disturbance,
short of violence, amounted to a breach of the peace, and therefore the conduct was likely
to provoke a breach of the peace.

The justices found the behaviour to have been insulting. Their opinion continues:

> 'In deciding whether a breach of the peace was likely to be occasioned, we took
> the view that, as the toilets were a public place, we were entitled to take into account
> the likelihood of a member of the public either entering or being present instead of
> the police officer in the toilets and his probable response when he encountered the
> actions of the appellant. The mere chance that the actual audience consisted solely
> of a police officer did not preclude us in our opinion from considering other
> possibilities. We therefore concluded in view of all the circumstances of the case,
> there was a strong probability of a breach of the peace occurring whether by way of
> a disturbance or out of violence.'

Three questions were set out in the case. Only the second need be read. It is: 'Is a
"breach of the peace" restricted to acts of violence?' The other two questions have been
canvassed in the other case, namely whether or not, in deciding whether behaviour is

insulting, and whether a breach of the peace is likely, it is proper to take into account the reactions not only of the person to whom the behaviour is addressed but of others who might have observed it.

Counsel for the appellant was not disposed to challenge the finding of 'insulting behaviour', but, for safety's sake, he adopted the arguments of the appellant in the other case. For reasons which will already be apparent it is impossible for this court to interfere with the finding of 'insulting behaviour'.

Counsel for the appellant concentrated his argument on the justices' finding that there was a strong probability of a breach of the peace occurring whether by way of a disturbance or out of violence. As counsel for the respondents concedes, the justices were in error in thinking that a mere disturbance not involving violence or a threat of violence could amount to a breach of the peace. The matter is put beyond doubt by the remarks of Watkins LJ, reading the judgment of the court in *R v Howell* [1981] 3 All ER 383 at 389, [1981] 3 WLR 501 at 508:

> '. . . we cannot accept that there can be a breach of the peace unless there has been an act done or threatened to be done which either actually harms a person, or in his presence his property, or is likely to cause such harm, or which puts someone in fear of such harm being done.'

A little later, after reciting a passage in 11 Halsbury's Laws (4th edn) para 108, he went on ([1981] 3 All ER 383 at 389, [1981] 1 WLR 501 at 509):

> 'The statement in Halsbury's Laws of England is in parts, we think, inaccurate because of its failure to relate all the kinds of behaviour there mentioned to violence. Furthermore, we think the word "disturbance" when used in isolation cannot constitute a breach of the peace. We are emboldened to say that there is a breach of the peace whenever harm is actually done or is likely to be done to a person or in his presence to his property or a person is in fear of being so harmed through an assault, an affray, a riot, an unlawful assembly or other disturbance.'

We have also been referred to some remarks of Lord Denning MR in *R v Chief Constable of Devon and Cornwall, ex p Central Electricity Generating Board* [1981] 3 All ER 826 at 832, [1981] 3 WLR 967 at 975:

> 'There is a breach of the peace whenever a person who is lawfully carrying out his work is unlawfully and physically prevented by another from doing it. He is entitled by law peacefully to go on with his work on his lawful occasions. If anyone unlawfully and physically obstructs the worker, by lying down or chaining himself to a rig or the like, he is guilty of a breach of the peace.'

These comments were not indorsed by either Lawton LJ or Templeman LJ. As the passage cited shows, the case was concerned with facts quite unlike those here. In the present case there was of course no question of the appellant preventing anyone from carrying out his lawful work.

In fairness to the justices it is only right to say that the report of *R v Howell* would not have been available to them in either the Weekly Law Reports or the All England Law Reports at the time the matter was before them, and they may very well have relied, in part at least, on the inaccurate statement in Halsbury's Laws of England. Nor could they have known of the remarks of Lord Denning MR.

The conviction must be quashed. Had the respondent so asked we would have been obliged to remit the case to the justices with a direction to continue the hearing by determining the likelihood of a breach of the peace in accordance with the law as declared by this court, but we have not been asked to do so, the respondent recognising that this incident occurred nearly a year ago and that the appellant will already have suffered severely by the publicity surrounding his conviction.

Footnote

a   Where the words of a statutory provision aptly describe the conduct complained of there can be no objection in law to framing a charge under that provision. But these cases demonstrate the difficulties which can sometimes occur when behaviour is charged under a provision which was never designed to deal with it. Each case will depend on its own facts, but it seems to us that, if proper attention is paid, as it must be, to the word 'likely' in the phrase 'whereby a breach of the peace is likely to be occasioned', s 5 of the

b   Public Order Act 1936 will, more often than not, prove to be an inappropriate charge in the case of homosexual activity in public lavatories.

Appeals allowed. Convictions quashed.

Solicitors: *Hawley & Rodgers*, Nottingham (for the appellant Parkin); *Temple Wallis*, Nottingham (for the appellant Valentine); *D W Ritchie*, Nottingham (for both

c   respondents).

Jacqueline Charles   Barrister.

R v Pigg

COURT OF APPEAL, CRIMINAL DIVISION
LORD LANE CJ, TALBOT AND McCOWAN JJ
5 FEBRUARY 1982

Jury – Majority verdict – Statement of number of assenting and dissenting jurors – Number of dissenting jurors – Failure to comply with requirement that number of dissenting jurors be stated by foreman in open court – Validity of verdict – Whether mandatory to state number of dissenting jurors – Whether failure to comply with requirement rendering verdict nugatory – Juries Act 1974, s 17(3).

Criminal law – Rape – Consent – Recklessness whether victim consented – Recklessness – Direction to jury – Sexual Offences (Amendment) Act 1976, s 1.

At the trial of the appellant on two charges of attempted rape (as defined in s 1(1)[a] of the Sexual Offences (Amendment) Act 1976), the judge directed the jury that the appellant was 'reckless' as to whether the victim consented to sexual intercourse if he was aware of the possibility that she might not be consenting and yet went ahead regardless. The jury, consisting of 12 jurors, were unable to reach a unanimous verdict in respect of the first charge and the judge gave them a majority direction. The jury then returned a majority verdict of guilty. The clerk of the court asked the foreman of the jury how many agreed on the verdict and how many dissented. The foreman replied: 'Ten agreed.' The clerk then said: 'Ten agreed to two of you.' The judge accepted that verdict. The jury returned a unanimous verdict of guilty in respect of the second charge. The appellant was convicted of both charges and sentenced. He appealed against conviction on the grounds (i) that the verdict on the first charge was void because the foreman had failed to state in open court the number of jurors who dissented, contrary to s 17(3)[b] of the Juries Act 1974 which required that a majority verdict of guilty should not be accepted by the court unless the foreman stated in open court 'the number of jurors who respectively agreed to and dissented from the verdict', and (ii) that the judge had misdirected the jury on the meaning of 'reckless' in that he had failed to tell the jury that the appellant had to be aware of a serious and obvious risk that the victim was not consenting and not merely that there was a possibility that she was not.

---

a   Section 1 is set out at p 595 *j* to p 596 *a*, post
b   Section 17(3) is set out at p 593 *h*, post

Held – (1) Since the requirements of s 17(3) of the 1974 Act were mandatory and had
to be meticulously followed, the foreman's failure to state in open court the number of
dissenting jurors rendered the verdict on the first charge void. Accordingly the appeal
in respect of the first charge would be allowed and the conviction quashed (see p 594 d
e, p 595 c e and p 599 j, post); *R v Barry* [1975] 2 All ER 760 and *R v Reynolds* [1981] 3 All
ER 849 followed.

(2) In order to prove that a man charged with rape was 'reckless' as to whether the
woman consented, it had to be shown either (a) that he was indifferent and gave no
thought to the possibility that she might not be consenting in circumstances where, if
any thought had been given to the matter, it would have been obvious that there was a
risk that she was not consenting, or (b) that he was aware of the possibility that she might
not be consenting but persisted regardless of whether she did so. The judge's direction
to the jury was, if anything, too favourable to the appellant and the appeal in relation to
the second charge would be dismissed (see p 597 a and p 599 f to h j, post); *R v Caldwell*
[1981] 1 All ER 961 and *R v Lawrence* [1981] 1 All ER 974 applied; *DPP v Morgan* [1975]
2 All ER 347 considered.

Per curiam. While it is highly desirable and necessary that it should be mandatory for
the foreman of a jury to state in open court that ten of the jury (in a case where there is
a full complement of twelve) are agreed on the prisoner's guilt, it seems absurd to say that
it is other than discretionary that the foreman should then go on to state how many
dissented (see p 595 d, post).

Notes

For rape, see 11 Halsbury's Laws (4th edn) para 1226, and for cases on the subject, see 15
Digest (Reissue) 1209–1216, 10,373–10,431.

For recklessness, see 11 Halsbury's Laws (4th edn) para 14.

For the Juries Act 1974, s 17, see 44 Halsbury's Statutes (3rd edn) 576.

For the Sexual Offences (Amendment) Act 1976, s 1, see 46 ibid 322.

Cases referred to in judgment

DPP v Morgan [1975] 2 All ER 347, [1976] AC 182, [1975] 2 WLR 913, HL, 15 Digest
(Reissue) 1212, 10,398.

R v Barry [1975] 2 All ER 760, [1975] 1 WLR 1190, CA, Digest (Cont Vol D) 573, 524a.

R v Caldwell [1981] 1 All ER 961, [1982] AC 341, [1981] 2 WLR 509, HL.

R v Cunningham [1957] 2 All ER 412, [1957] 2 QB 396, [1957] 3 WLR 76, CA, 15 Digest
(Reissue) 1198, 10,292.

R v Lawrence [1981] 1 All ER 974, [1982] AC 510, [1981] 2 WLR 524, HL.

R v Reynolds [1981] 3 All ER 849, CA.

R v Stephenson [1979] 2 All ER 1198, [1979] QB 695, [1979] 3 WLR 193, CA, Digest (Cont
Vol E) 161, 12,692a.

R v Tolson (1889) 23 QBD 168, [1886–90] All ER Rep 26, CCR, 15 Digest (Reissue) 1028,
8922.

Appeal

The appellant, Stephen Pigg, was charged on indictment with, inter alia, attempting to
rape a girl B (count 1), attempting to rape a girl F (count 2), having unlawful sexual
intercourse with B (count 7) and indecently assaulting F (count 8). On 22 January 1981
he was convicted on count 7, and on 6 March 1981 in the Crown Court at York before his
Honour Judge Bennett QC and a jury, after a retrial, he was convicted on counts 1, 2 and
8. He was sentenced to five years' imprisonment on counts 1 and 2 and to one year's
imprisonment on counts 7 and 8. The sentences were ordered to run concurrently. He
appealed against conviction on counts 1 and 2 by leave of a single judge. The facts are set
out in the judgment of the court.

Paul Worsley (assigned by the Registrar of Criminal Appeals) for the appellant.
Peter Charlesworth for the Crown.

LORD LANE CJ delivered the following judgment of the court: On 6 March 1981 in the Crown Court at York before his Honour Judge Bennett QC and a jury, the appellant was convicted and sentenced on the following charges. On count 1, for attempted rape of a girl B, he was sentenced to five years' imprisonment. On count 2, for attempted rape of a girl F, he was sentenced to five years' imprisonment. On count 7, for unlawful sexual intercourse with B, he was sentenced to one year's imprisonment and on count 8, for indecent assault on F, he was sentenced to one year's imprisonment. All those sentences were ordered to run concurrently. It should be pointed out that this was the second occasion on which these matters had been tried. Count 7, which was unlawful sexual intercourse, was a conviction which was recorded at the earlier trial in January 1981. The appellant now appeals against conviction by leave of the single judge.

The facts of the case are, to say the least, nauseating, and this court does not propose to go into them in any detail at all. B was 15 years of age and F was 17 years of age. They had been staying at a Butlin's Holiday Camp at Filey, Yorkshire. On the evening of 16 September 1980 they determined to leave the camp and go for a drink in a public house near by. They were reluctant to go round by the gate (apparently it involved a detour) so they climbed through a hole in the fence and made their way to the public house. They came back again. It was an unpleasant evening and they could not find the hole in the fence to return to their chalet.

At that time the appellant came onto the scene and initially he offered to help them, pretending that he was some sort of official to do with the holiday camp. The first thing untoward which happened was when the appellant came up behind B and, according to her, seized her round the neck with one of his arms and said: 'I'm the Yorkshire Ripper.' This was at a time before any arrest in that notorious case had taken place.

The events that succeeded that incident were horrifying. On the appellant's own statement and according to the police later on, it is apparent that the girls were subjected to a catalogue of almost every sexual indignity of which one can think. There is no doubt that there was ample evidence, if the jury took one view of the facts, on which they could come to the conclusion that the charges laid against this man, which were much lengthier and much more detailed than those of which he was found guilty, were substantiated. In the upshot, the jury came to the conclusion which we have already indicated.

The issue in the case was, practically speaking, one of consent or no consent. That is the basis of the appeal so far as the direction to the jury is concerned. We will return to that later, but the first ground of appeal is nothing to do with the merits of the case at all. It is a technical point on which it is necessary for us to pass judgment. It arises in this way. The powers of a jury to return a majority verdict are enshrined in the Juries Act 1974. Section 17(1) of that Act reads as follows:

'Subject to subsections (3) and (4) below, the verdict of a jury in proceedings in the Crown Court or the High Court need not be unanimous if—(a) in a case where there are not less than eleven jurors, ten of them agree on the verdict; and (b) in a case where there are ten jurors, nine of them agree on the verdict.'

In this case, there was a full complement of twelve jurors. We need not read sub-s (2). Subsection (3) is the important one. It reads as follows:

'The Crown Court shall not accept a verdict of guilty by virtue of subsection (1) above unless the foreman of the jury has stated in open court the number of jurors who respectively agreed to and dissented from the verdict.'

In the present case, what happened with regard to count 1 was this. Initially, count 1 was a charge of rape, not of attempted rape, and the jury were obviously having some difficulty in coming to their conclusion. After the requisite time had elapsed, the judge gave them a majority direction in impeccable terms. The jury then retired again, and some thirteen minutes later they returned into court where the following interchange took place between the clerk and the foreman:

'*The clerk.* Would the foreman please stand? Mr Foreman, would you answer my
question either Yes or No only? Members of the jury, have at least ten of you agreed
on a verdict? *The foreman.* Yes.
The clerk. On the charge of rape do you find the accused guilty or not guilty? *The
foreman.* Not guilty.
The clerk. On the charge of attempted rape do you find him guilty or not
guilty? *The foreman.* Guilty.
The clerk. Is that the verdict of you all, or by a majority? *The foreman.* By a
majority.
The clerk. How many of you agreed to the verdict and how many dissented?'

Up to that point, everything had gone precisely as it should have done according to the
practice direction given by Lord Parker CJ ([1967] 3 All ER 137, [1967] 1 WLR 1198).
It was the following question and answer to which objection is taken: '*The foreman.* Ten
agreed. *The clerk.* Ten agreed to two of you.' That was the end of the interchange.
One would have thought, applying common sense to the matter, that it was thereby
made abundantly clear to everyone that the foreman, on behalf of the jury, had said that
ten of the members of the jury had agreed that the prosecution had made out the offence
of attempted rape and, therefore, arithmetically it followed that two of the jury were
dissenting from that view. Unfortunately, this is apparently an area where common
sense does not apply. It has been held in a number of previous cases that the wording in
s 17(3) of the Juries Act 1974 is mandatory and it requires what is set out there to be
followed precisely. If it is not followed precisely, then the verdict is null and void and,
if necessary, the trial has to start all over again.
It is necessary only to refer to two cases. The first is *R v Barry* [1975] 2 All ER 760,
[1975] 1 WLR 1190. That was a case where the clerk asked: 'Do you find this defendant
guilty or not guilty upon this indictment?' And the foreman replied: 'Guilty'. The clerk
then said: 'And that is the verdict of ten of you?' to which the shorthand writer appended
the question mark. If that statement was in the form of a question, it was not
answered. That was a much stronger case than this one because the foreman of the jury
had not expressed any view as to how many jurors had agreed and how many had
dissented. It was held in that case that the conviction must be quashed.
There is a further decision of this court, *R v Reynolds* [1981] 3 All ER 849. The facts
were indistinguishable from the facts of the present case. Everything went correctly, as
it did in this case, up to the point where the clerk asked:

'Is that the verdict of you all or by a majority? *The foreman.* By a majority.
The clerk. How many agreed and how many opposed? *The foreman.* Ten agreed.'

The judgment of the court was delivered by Shaw LJ. He said (at 851):

'The requirement that where there is a majority verdict the foreman of a jury
should state in open court how many dissented is neither more nor less imperative
than stating how many agreed. It was argued in the present case that since the
foreman had stated in open court that ten agreed, it was superfluous to go further.
The number who dissented became a matter of the simplest arithmetic. This is a
fallacious argument. As has been said already, s 17, like its precursor, is in
peremptory and mandatory terms. Its insistence on requiring a statement in open
court by the foreman of how many dissented is to preclude a verdict being accepted
where ten had agreed but one or both of the remaining jurors had not formed a
final view at all. On hearing the foreman say that two dissented, that one or those
two would have the opportunity of demurring publicly to the foreman's assertion.
Otherwise, the verdict might operate against a defendant when only ten of the jury
had made up their minds one way or the other. The statutory requirements are
plainly stated and they must be meticulously followed if a majority verdict is to be
legitimately accepted. It is the duty of the presiding judge to see that they are

followed. In the present case, counsel very properly sought to alert the judge to the irregularity but his intervention was regrettably ignored.'

Accordingly, the conviction was quashed.

It seems to us, if we may respectfully say so, that the reasoning in that case was possibly open to a certain amount of doubt. It is said that the requirement of a statement being made in open court by the foreman of how many dissented is to preclude a verdict being accepted when ten had agreed but one or both of the remaining jurors had not formed a final view at all. It seems to us that if one or two jurors have not formed a final view at all, they are of necessity dissenting from the view of the other ten who have made up their minds. Perhaps that is a carping criticism but it occurs to this court that that must be the case, otherwise a jury could never return a majority verdict if one or two of their number refused to take part in the discussion at all or refused to express a view. That seems to be a very strange result and certainly not one which is envisaged by the Juries Act 1974. However, it is plain that we are bound by that authority and it is plain, accordingly, that there was a breach of that authority which states it as a mandatory requirement.

It may be that the matter should be considered elsewhere but it does seem to us that it is highly unlikely that Parliament should intend that the validity of a verdict should depend on the following of a precise formula of words. No doubt it is highly desirable and necessary that the foreman should himself state in open court that ten of the jury, in a case where there is a full complement of twelve, are agreed on the prisoner's guilt. That should be mandatory. But to say that it is other than discretionary that he should then go on to say how many dissented seems to us to be bordering on the absurd.

In the event, we have no alternative save to quash this conviction.

The next ground of appeal advanced by counsel for the appellant is that the judge misdirected the jury on the question of recklessness as it applies to the crime of rape. The part of the direction to which he directs his attention is as follows:

'Thirdly, it must be proved, members of the jury, either that the man, he, the defendant, knew that she did not consent or was reckless as to whether she consented. There has been a great deal of public concern of recent years, members of the jury, about the offence of rape, and so Parliament took the opportunity recently of restating the offence. That third element, members of the jury, is a matter which is of the utmost importance, because it must be proved either that he knew that she did not consent or that he was reckless as to whether she so consented. The meaning of the phrase "being reckless as to whether she so consented", to prove that a man, members of the jury, is reckless as to whether she consented, it must be proved that he was aware of the possibility that she might not be consenting, but nevertheless, went ahead [and the word in the transcript is 'reckless', which should be 'regardless'] of whether she consented or not.'

'Reckless' is either a slip of the tongue or a corrupt text, because if one looks at a later stage of the summing up, where the judge repeats the direction, the word 'regardless' appears in place of the word 'reckless', when the jury came back to ask a further question. Counsel for the appellant agrees and takes no point on this.

The argument advanced on behalf of the appellant goes as follows: first of all, one turns to the statutory provisions under s 1 of the Sexual Offences (Amendment) Act 1976:

'(1) For the purposes of section 1 of the Sexual Offences Act 1956 (which relates to rape) a man commits rape if—(a) he has unlawful sexual intercourse with a woman who at the time of the intercourse does not consent to it; and (b) at that time he knows that she does not consent to the intercourse or he is reckless as to whether she consents to it; and references to rape in other enactments (including the following provisions of this Act) shall be construed accordingly.

(2) It is hereby declared that if at a trial for a rape offence the jury has to consider

whether a man believed that a woman was consenting to sexual intercourse, the
presence or absence of reasonable grounds for such a belief is a matter to which the
jury is to have regard, in conjunction with any other relevant matters, in considering
whether he so believed.'

The way in which counsel for the appellant puts it is this. He concedes that the
direction given by the judge, which I have just read, was favourable to the defendant in
the sense that it sought to inquire as to the defendant's own frame of mind. But, he
suggests it was not put strongly enough. The judge, he submits, should have made it
clear to the jury that the defendant must have been aware of a serious and obvious risk
that the girl was not consenting before they could come to the conclusion that the word
'reckless' was made out. He invited us to define rape in the following terms: where a
man has sexual intercourse with a woman who does not consent to it when he appreciates
from the situation that a real risk exists that she is not consenting and none the less carries
on with the act. That is rape, he submits, and nothing short of that will do.

He is faced at the outset by two well-known decisions of the House of Lords in R v
Caldwell [1981] 1 All ER 961, [1982] AC 341 and R v Lawrence [1981] 1 All ER 974,
[1982] AC 510. It should be pointed out in fairness to the judge at the trial that those two
decisions were not reported until about a fortnight after he had given his direction to the
jury. Consequently, the likelihood is that he was basing that direction on a decision of
this court in R v Stephenson [1979] 2 All ER 1198, [1979] QB 695. Counsel for the
appellant submits to us that those two cases do not help in the present circumstances.
First of all, because they are dealing on the one hand with criminal damage and on the
other hand with the Road Traffic Acts, he submits that the word 'reckless' must mean
something different from the word 'reckless' in the Act which we are considering.
Secondly, he invites us to distinguish the two cases on the basis that those two cases were
dealing with recklessness as to a consequence of the defendant's acts, whereas the present
case is dealing with recklessness as to existing circumstances, recklessness, if you like, as
to the state of mind of the girls. That latter distinction is, if we may say so, a correct
distinction in logic, but it is doubtful whether it has the effect, in our view, of making
the present case any different from the two cases in the House of Lords, and is not a
sufficient basis for us to distinguish those two cases from the present one.

The next point made by counsel is this. He submits that s 1(2) of the 1976 Act, which
we have already read, is a rule peculiar to the offence of rape, and indeed it is. It indicates
something which might perhaps be considered as a matter of common sense to be
determined or applied by the jury. But he points out correctly that that subsection was
inserted as a result of the recommendation in the Heilbron Committee, that being
contained in the report of the Advisory Group on the Law of Rape (Cmnd 6352 (1975)).

The submission is that that subsection is concerned with what a man believes and that
is different from what he does not think about. This, submits counsel, indicates that the
Act is concerned with belief, but not with a man who holds no belief, one way or the
other, as to what the girl is thinking. It seems to us that, so far as that is concerned, the
subsection is dealing with another situation altogether, namely the man who mistakenly
believes the woman to be consenting. Counsel submits that what must be proved must
be an intent or a serious state of mind; inattention or not thinking about it is less than
recklessness as to whether the woman is consenting or not. Those, briefly and in outline,
are the submissions which are made on behalf of the appellant.

The Sexual Offences Act 1956, by s 1(1), provided that it is an offence for a man to rape
a woman. The definition of rape was a matter for the common law, and so it remained
until 1976 when the Sexual Offences (Amendment) Act, s 1 of which I have already read,
was passed. In order to prove the offence of rape, the prosecution has to satisfy the jury
so they feel sure of the following items: (1) that an act of sexual intercourse took place;
(2) that the woman did not consent; (3)(a) that the man knew she was not consenting; or
(3)(b) that he was reckless as to whether she was consenting or not.

On any view of the word 'reckless' it seems to us that it clearly includes a case where the man appreciates the possibility that the woman may not be consenting and, nevertheless, goes on to have sexual intercourse with her. That is the direction in the present case. We take the view that the judge's directions are at least as favourable to the accused as they should be.

What is of concern, and what has exercised the court in this case, is the theoretically possible case where the man never addresses his mind at all to the possibility of the woman not consenting, even though she is not consenting in fact. Can it be said that in those circumstances he is reckless as to whether she consents? That is the problem, stated broadly, with which this court has been dealing today.

It is perhaps fair to say that the word 'reckless' is a somewhat strange word for the Act to employ in these circumstances. As already indicated, reckless as to consequences or as to the foresight of them is a common enough expression, but recklessness on the part of A as to what is going on in the mind of B is a concept which has its difficulties. However that may be, the word is in the Act, and there are certain matters which may prove of assistance in order to try to discover what it means. First of all, the law prior to 1976: the mens rea in rape was intention to have forcible intercourse with a woman without her consent. That is adverted to by their Lordships in DPP v Morgan [1975] 2 All ER 347, [1976] AC 182, and it has a respectable lineage starting off with R v Tolson (1889) 23 QBD 168, [1886–90] All ER Rep 26. Mistake was a defence, but if the defendant was or might have been labouring under the belief, albeit a mistaken belief, that the woman was consenting, the prosecution failed and he was entitled to be acquitted. If the evidence, however, was that he had no belief one way or the other, then there would have been no basis for his defence of mistake, because he had no belief mistaken or otherwise and, all other things being equal, the prosecution would have succeeded. There is no suggestion that Parliament, in the 1976 Act, meant to make things easier for people charged with rape. Accordingly, on that basis it seems the word 'reckless' was probably intended to cover the man who does not apply his mind to what the woman may be thinking.

The next point is this. The genesis of the 1976 Act was DPP v Morgan. It is perhaps helpful to read certain passages of their Lordships' opinions in that case. Lord Hailsham said ([1975] 2 All ER 347 at 357, [1976] AC 182 at 209):

> 'The prohibited act in rape is to have intercourse without the victim's consent. The minimum mens rea or guilty mind in most common law offences, including rape, is the intention to do the prohibited act, and that is correctly stated in the proposition stated "in the first place" of the judge's direction. In murder the situation is different, because the murder is only complete when the victim dies, and an intention to do really serious bodily harm has been held to be enough if such be the case. The only qualification I would make to the direction of the learned judge's "in the first place" is the refinement for which, as I shall show, there is both Australian and English authority, that if the intention of the accused is to have intercourse nolens volens, that is recklessly and not caring whether the victim be a consenting party or not, that is equivalent on ordinary principles to an intent to do the prohibited act without the consent of the victim.'

We draw assistance from that as to the possible meaning of reckless in the 1976 Act, although of course this decision of the House of Lords preceded the Act. Between the decision in Morgan and the 1976 Act came the report of the Heilbron Committee, to which we have already referred, which approved the basis of the decision in Morgan and made certain suggestions as to future legislation, suggestions which were adopted by the framers of the Act.

The next matter to which we turn, and it is the most important matter, is the decision of their Lordships in R v Caldwell and R v Lawrence. I have already endeavoured to describe the reasons which counsel for the appellant advances for suggesting to us that these decisions can be distinguished and/or are not binding on us. We do not think, however, even had we wished to do so, that we are entitled to distinguish either of these cases, or to take the view that they are not binding on us, as we have been invited to do. They are decisions on the meaning of the word 'reckless', albeit in different Acts, and they are decisions from which we cannot depart in so far as they apply to the present case.

The first passage I wish to read is from *R v Caldwell* ([1981] 1 All ER 961 at 965, [1982] AC 341 at 351–352, where Lord Diplock said:

'My Lords, the restricted meaning that the Court of Appeal in *R v Cunningham* [1957] 2 All ER 412, [1957] 2 QB 396 had placed on the adverb "maliciously" in the Malicious Damage Act 1861 in cases where the prosecution did not rely on an actual intention of the accused to cause the damage that was in fact done called for a meticulous analysis by the jury of the thoughts that passed through the mind of the accused at or before the time he did the act that caused the damage, in order to see on which side of a narrow dividing line they fell. If it had crossed his mind that there was a risk that someone's property might be damaged but, because his mind was affected by rage or excitement or confused by drink, he did not appreciate the seriousness of the risk or trusted that good luck would prevent its happening, this state of mind would amount to malice in the restricted meaning placed on that term by the Court of Appeal; whereas if, for any of these reasons, he did not even trouble to give his mind to the question whether there was any risk of damaging the property, this state of mind would not suffice to make him guilty of an offence under the Malicious Damage Act 1861. Neither state of mind seems to me to be less blameworthy than the other; but, if the difference between the two constituted the distinction between what does and what does not in legal theory amount to a guilty state of mind for the purposes of a statutory offence of damage to property, it would not be a practicable distinction for use in a trial by jury. The only person who knows what the accused's mental processes were is the accused himself, and probably not even he can recall them accurately when the rage or excitement under which he acted has passed, or he has sobered up if he were under the influence of drink at the relevant time.'

Lord Diplock continued ([1981] 1 All ER 961 at 966, [1982] AC 341 at 353–354):

'"Reckless" as used in the new statutory definition of the mens rea of these offences is an ordinary English word. It had not by 1971 become a term of legal art with some more limited esoteric meaning than that which it bore in ordinary speech, a meaning which surely includes not only deciding to ignore a risk of harmful consequences resulting from one's acts that one has recognised as existing, but also failing to give any thought to whether or not there is any such risk in circumstances where, if any thought were given to the matter, it would be obvious that there was.'

We then turn to *R v Lawrence* for two reasons. First of all, it is suggested by counsel for the appellant that that passage which I have just read in *Caldwell* was obiter. We do not take the view that it was. But even if it had been, it is quite plain from what is said in *Lawrence* that that passage is still the view of the House of Lords when dealing with something which was certainly not obiter, when dealing with the ratio decidendi of *Lawrence*. Lord Hailsham LC said ([1981] 1 All ER 974 at 978, [1982] AC 510 at 520):

'It only surprises me that there should have been any question regarding the existence of mens rea in relation to the words "reckless", "recklessly" or "recklessness". Unlike most English words it has been in the English language as a word in general use at least since the eighth century AD almost always with the same meaning, applied to a person or conduct evincing a state of mind stopping short of deliberate intention, and going beyond mere inadvertence, or, in its modern though not its etymological and original sense, mere carelessness. The Oxford English Dictionary quotes several examples from Old English, many from the Middle English period, and many more from modern English. The word was familiar to the Venerable Bede, to Langland, to Chaucer, to Sir Thomas More and to Shakespeare. In its alternative and possibly older pronunciation, and etymologically incorrect spelling (wretchless, wretchlessly, wretchlessness) it was known to the authors of the Articles of religion printed in the book of Common Prayer. Though its pronunciation has varied, so far as I know its meaning has not.'

Lord Diplock said ([1981] 1 All ER 974 at 981, [1982] AC 510 at 525):

'My Lords, this House has very recently had occasion in *R v Caldwell* to give close consideration to the concept of recklessness as constituting mens rea in criminal law. The conclusion reached by the majority was that the adjective "reckless" when used in a criminal statute, ie the Criminal Damage Act 1971, had not acquired a special meaning as a term of legal art, but bore its popular or dictionary meaning of careless, regardless, or heedless of the possible harmful consequences of one's acts. The same must be true of the adverbial derivative "recklessly".'

Then, finally, Lord Diplock said ([1981] 1 All ER 974 at 982, [1982] AC 510 at 526):

'I turn now to the mens rea. My task is greatly simplified by what has already been said about the concept of recklessness in criminal law in *R v Caldwell*. Warning was there given against adopting the simplistic approach of treating all problems of criminal liability as soluble by classifying the test of liability as being either "subjective" or "objective". Recklessness on the part of the doer of an act does presuppose that there is something in the circumstances that would have drawn the attention of an ordinary prudent individual to the possibility that his act was capable of causing the kind of serious harmful consequences that the section which creates the offence was intended to prevent, and that the risk of those harmful consequences occurring was not so slight that an ordinary prudent individual would feel justified in treating them as negligible. It is only when this is so that the doer of the act is acting "recklessly" if, before doing the act, he either fails to give any thought to the possibility of there being any such risk or, having recognised that there was such risk, he nevertheless goes on to do it.'

Of course it is plain that that opinion cannot, so to speak, be lifted bodily and applied to rape. There has to be a modification in certain of the matters which are there dealt with. But, in the end, it seems to us that in the light of that decision, so far as rape is concerned, a man is reckless if either he was indifferent and gave no thought to the possibility that the woman might not be consenting in circumstances where if any thought had been given to the matter it would have been obvious that there was a risk she was not or he was aware of the possibility that she might not be consenting but nevertheless persisted regardless of whether she consented or not.

That being the case, it is plain that the judge's direction was, if anything, too favourable to the defendant. Accordingly, this aspect of the appeal must fail. But before passing from there, it is perhaps only fair to say that the learned judge, basing himself on *R v Stephenson*, gave a direction which, not only on this aspect of the case but on every other aspect of the case, was a model of clarity, conciseness and fairness.

There is a further submission from counsel for the appellant that the judge was in error in the way that he dealt with the question of corroboration, in so far as he suggested that the distress exhibited by these girls immediately after the offence was possible corroboration. The complaint is that the judge overemphasised that particular matter. We do not think that he did. But even if he had, overemphasis is, generally speaking, a poor ground of appeal.

That being so, it only remains to say that, for the reasons already dealt with before the adjournment, this appeal must be allowed on the first point, but so far as the question of the misdirection on the rape is concerned that appeal fails.

Appeal allowed in part; conviction on count 1 quashed. The court granted the Crown leave to appeal to the House of Lords and certified, under s 33(2) of the Criminal Appeal Act 1968, that the following point of law of general public importance was involved in the decision: whether it was necessary in order to comply with the terms of s 17(3) of the Juries Act 1974 for the foreman of the jury, having stated in open court the number agreeing to the verdict, to go on to state the number of those dissenting. The court refused the appellant leave to appeal to the House of Lords but certified, under s 33(2) of the 1968 Act, that the following point of law of general public importance was involved in the decision: whether it was a proper direction on the word 'reckless' in the definition of rape to say, 'To prove that a man is reckless it must be proved either that he is indifferent and gave no thought to the possibility that the woman might not be consenting or that he was aware of the possibility that she might not be consenting but nevertheless persisted regardless of whether she consented or not.' Appellant to be detained in custody, pursuant to s 37 of the 1968 Act, pending an appeal by the Crown.

29 March. *The Appeal Committee of the House of Lords (Lord Diplock, Lord Fraser of Tullybelton and Lord Bridge of Harwich) dismissed a petition by the appellant for leave to appeal.*

Solicitors: *Thorpe & Co,* Scarborough.

N P Metcalfe Esq   Barrister.

Re Stern (a bankrupt), ex parte Keyser Ullmann Ltd and others v The bankrupt and others

COURT OF APPEAL, CIVIL DIVISION

LAWTON, TEMPLEMAN AND BRIGHTMAN LJJ

8, 9, 10, 11, 18 FEBRUARY 1982

Bankruptcy – Discharge – Application for discharge – Opposition on ground that bankrupt brought on, or contributed to, his bankruptcy by rash and hazardous speculations – Bankrupt having debts of over £118m and assets of only £20,252 – Whether bankrupt's conduct prior to bankruptcy a relevant issue when application for discharge considered – Whether opposing creditors entitled to cross-examine bankrupt and deponents of affidavits in support of his application – Bankruptcy Act 1914, s 26(3)(7).

A receiving order was made against the bankrupt on 18 April 1978 and he was adjudicated bankrupt on 30 May 1978. The trustee in bankruptcy received claims amounting to over £118m, mostly arising out of personal guarantees given by the bankrupt to creditors in respect of loans made to property companies controlled by him. The bankrupt had assets of only £20,252. In March 1981 the bankrupt applied to the court for his discharge from bankruptcy. In his application he stated that his mother and brother intended to offer £25,000 for the benefit of his creditors, subject to his being discharged immediately, and that he himself would undertake to pay £10,000 per annum for three years immediately following his discharge. Since his adjudication the bankrupt had not changed the comfortable life-style he had enjoyed prior to his bankruptcy. He attributed his ability to go on living in the same style as before partly to the generosity of his family and partly to his earnings as a business consultant. The bankrupt and his family were living in a house which had been sold in 1974 to the bankrupt's father when the bankrupt was in financial difficulties and settled in a family trust. The current value of the house could be as much as £1m. Following the bankrupt's public examination, the Official Receiver reported that the bankrupt's assets were less than 50p in the pound of the amount of his unsecured liabilities and that he had contracted debts provable in the bankruptcy without at the time having any reasonable or probable expectation of being able to pay them, those being grounds on which the court was entitled, by virtue of s 26(3)(a) and (d)[a] of the Bankruptcy Act 1914, to refuse or suspend a discharge or to impose conditions on discharge. Two of the bankrupt's creditors, whose debts amounted to over £60m, opposed his application for discharge on the ground referred to in s 26(3)(f) that the bankrupt had brought on or contributed to his bankruptcy by rash and hazardous speculations and that therefore his discharge should be refused. In support of his application the bankrupt filed affidavits by other persons to show that he had been co-operative and helpful in the liquidation of his companies and also to corroborate his explanation for giving worthless guarantees, but he did not swear an affidavit himself. At the hearing of the bankrupt's application the opposing creditors sought to cross-examine the bankrupt and two of the deponents of the affidavits in support of his application about the bankrupt's 'rash and hazardous speculations', his life-style and his business conduct and commercial morality in running his various companies. The registrar refused to allow the creditors to cross-examine either the bankrupt or the deponents, on the ground that the cross-examination was likely to be directed to the bankrupt's conduct prior to the receiving order being made and that was irrelevant to the issue the court had to decide on the application. The creditors appealed, contending that by virtue of s 26(7)[b] of the 1914 Act, which provided that the Court might 'receive such evidence as it may think fit', a creditor had a right to cross-examine a bankrupt who applied for a discharge.

Held – On its true construction s 26(7) of the 1914 Act did not entitle an opposing creditor to cross-examine the bankrupt as of right but it did confer on the court a discretion to receive evidence, including evidence elicited from the bankrupt by cross-examination on behalf of the opposing creditors, relevant to issues which the court had to consider in relation to the bankrupt's discharge, which issues included the bankrupt's conduct if the size of the indebtedness or the circumstances in which the debts were incurred called for an explanation by the bankrupt, since the purpose of the court's right to question the bankrupt was to ensure that his discharge would not prejudice the public generally. In the circumstances, the opposing creditors ought to have been allowed to discharge the onus of proving that the bankrupt had made rash and hazardous speculations, having regard to the fact that the amassing of such colossal debts by the bankrupt called for some less specious explanation than that provided. It followed therefore that the appeal would be allowed and the bankrupt's application for discharge transferred to a judge of the Chancery Division to be heard de novo (see p 604 j to p 605 b and j to p 606 f and p 608 a to h, post).

Notes

For procedure at hearing of application for discharge, see 3 Halsbury's Laws (4th edn) para 845.

For the Bankruptcy Act 1914, s 26, see 3 Halsbury's Statutes (3rd edn) 69.

Cases referred to in judgments

Barker, Re, ex p Constable, Re Jones, ex p Jones (1890) 25 QBD 285, CA, 4 Digest (Reissue) 619, 5481.

Payne, Re, ex p Castle Mail Packets Co (1886) 18 QBD 154, CA, 4 Digest (Reissue) 614, 5450.

Sharp, Re, ex p Sharp (1893) 10 Morr 114, DC, 4 Digest (Reissue) 602, 5348.

Cases also cited

Child, Ex p, re Ottaway (1882) 20 Ch D 126, CA.

Debtor (No 37 of 1976, Liverpool), Re a, ex p Taylor v The debtor [1980] 1 All ER 129, [1980] Ch 565, [1980] 3 WLR 345, DC.

Godfrey (a bankrupt), Re (21 June 1977), The Banker, August 1977, p 139.

Hooley, Re, ex p the debtor (1899) 80 LT 495.

---

a   Section 26(3), so far as material, is set out at p 603 h and p 607 h, post

b   Section 26(7) is set out at p 605 g, post

Quartz Hill &c Co, Re, ex p Young (1882) 21 Ch D 642, CA.
Reed (a debtor), Re [1979] 2 All ER 22, [1980] Ch 212, DC.
Shields, Re, ex p the bankrupt (1912) 106 LT 345, DC.
Wood and Tarrant, Re, ex p Turner (1858) 3 De G & J 46, 44 ER 1186, LJJ.

Interlocutory appeal

Keyser Ullmann Ltd, Four Millbank Nominees Ltd and First National Bank of Chicago, who were creditors opposing the application of a bankrupt, William George Stern, for his discharge from bankruptcy, appealed against the decision of Mr Registrar Dewhurst sitting in bankruptcy on 25 August 1981 refusing the appellants leave to question the bankrupt by way of cross-examination or at all, and refusing their application for an order that Sir Kenneth Cork and Mr Norman Hewins should attend before the court to be cross-examined on affidavits sworn by them in support of the bankrupt's application for discharge. Pursuant to leave granted at the commencement of the hearing of the appeal the Official Receiver and the trustee in bankruptcy were joined as respondents to the appeal. The facts are set out in the judgment of Lawton LJ.

Stanley Brodie QC, Presiley Baxendale and *Rupert Anderson* for the opposing creditors.
E C Evans-Lombe QC and *John Vallat* for the bankrupt.
Michael Crystal for the Official Receiver.
Alan Steinfeld for the trustee in bankruptcy.

At the conclusion of argument Lawton LJ announced that, for reasons to be given later, the case would be transferred to the Chancery Division to be heard de novo by the appropriate judge of that division.

18 February. The following judgments were read.

LAWTON LJ. The issue in this interlocutory appeal is this: was Mr Registrar Dewhurst right to refuse to allow counsel acting on behalf of three of a bankrupt's creditors to cross-examine him and two deponents of affidavits when he applied for his discharge from bankruptcy?

The amounts involved in this case are startling. The bankrupt is William George Stern, now aged about 46. A receiving order was made against him on 18 April 1978 on the petition of a merchant bank creditor, Keyser Ullmann Ltd, who were owed £20,509,899 on guarantees which he had given in respect of loans to property companies which he controlled. He was adjudicated bankrupt on 30 May 1978. At the first meeting of creditors an experienced trustee of the bankrupt's estate was appointed with a committee of inspection. The trustee received claims amounting to £118,690,524 of which sum no less than £103,510,207 represented liabilities on guarantees which the bankrupt had given to 31 creditors in respect of loans made to his companies. One of these creditors was Four Millbank Nominees Ltd, who were owed £38,642,329 on four guarantees; another was the First National Bank of Chicago, who were owed £675,977. Against these huge debts the bankrupt had assets which produced no more than £20,252.

The bankrupt in a few years before 1974 had constructed a pyramid of companies, mainly in the United Kingdom, with interests primarily in property but also in other activities. The base was borrowed money, unsupported by any assets belonging to the bankrupt. When the property market began to collapse in the latter part of 1973, the pyramid started to crumble. The principal holding company, Wilstar Securities Ltd, went into liquidation on 6 June 1974.

When before June 1974 the bankrupt was holding himself out to banks and finance houses as a man able to give personal guarantees for huge loans he lived at 3 West Heath Avenue, London NW11, which he and his wife had bought in 1965 for £52,500. Large sums were spent on rebuilding and refurnishing it; but all the contents were said by the bankrupt to belong to his wife. He has lived in this house ever since. In December 1974, when he knew that he was in grave financial difficulties, his father bought the house for

£110,000, taking over a mortgage of £57,000 and making a cash payment of £53,000. The father settled the house in a trust set up in the United States of America and allowed the bankrupt to live in it in return for a rent equivalent to the mortgage repayments. The trustee was not satisfied about the circumstances in which the house had been sold to the bankrupt's father. He started proceedings. His claim was settled for £202,346.

Since being adjudicated bankrupt, Mr Stern's life-style does not seem to have changed much. He attributes his ability to go on living in the same style as before partly to the generosity of his family and partly to what he has earned as a business consultant since being made bankrupt. Some idea of his style of living at the present time is shown by the answers he gave to the questions he had to answer when making his application for discharge from bankruptcy. His net income after payment of tax in 1980 was £14,728. He estimated his current household expenses for 1981 as likely to be £23,400 which included £4,000 for electricity, gas and telephone.

The bankrupt's public examination started on 20 October 1978. At the end of that day it was adjourned and concluded with another day's hearing on 14 February 1979. As is the usual practice, the Official Receiver questioned the bankrupt. The trustee was represented by leading counsel who asked some questions. Mr Registrar Parbury, as far as I can judge from the shorthand note, seems to have discouraged counsel from asking questions about conduct generally. The Official Receiver who was conducting the public examination then made this comment: 'This is a story which is so familiar in the Bankruptcy Court. This is the story of a company director who has given guarantees and can't meet them. It is, in fact, a very ordinary bankruptcy but with noughts on the end, so it seems to me.' In my opinion, this was not an ordinary bankruptcy and I am surprised that any member of the Official Receivers' department should have thought it was. A bankruptcy of this kind and size must have been disturbing to the banking world and may have shaken the confidence of the French, Swiss and American creditor banks in the worth of personal guarantees given by British businessmen.

On 2 March 1981 the bankrupt applied to the Bankruptcy Court for his discharge. In his application he said that his mother and brother intended to offer £25,000 for the benefit of his creditors, subject to his being discharged from bankruptcy immediately and he himself would for three years immediately following his discharge pay £10,000 per annum. The court fixed 10 June 1981 for the hearing of the application and on 20 May 1981 the Official Receiver informed the creditors of the date of hearing. Two of them, Four Millbank Nominees Ltd and Keyser Ullmann Ltd, gave written notice of opposition on the grounds set out in the Official Receiver's report and also on other grounds, namely 'that the bankrupt has brought on or contributed to his bankruptcy by rash and hazardous speculations or by unjustifiable extravagance in living or by gambling or by culpable neglect of his business affairs'. The only part of this allegation which was in fact relied on was that relating to rash and hazardous speculations.

The Official Receiver's report was factual. Pursuant to s 26(3) of the Bankruptcy Act 1914, as amended by the Bankruptcy (Amendment) Act 1926, he submitted that the facts prove that 'the bankrupt's assets [were] not of a value equal to 50p in the pound on the amount of his unsecured liabilities' (sub-s (3)(a)) and that he had 'contracted [debts] provable in the bankruptcy without having at the time of contracting [them] any reasonable or probable ground of expectation . . . of being able to pay [them]' (sub-s (3)(d)). If the court accepted that these facts had been proved, an unconditional discharge could not be given forthwith. The opposing creditors, by their notice of opposition, alleged that the facts proved brought sub-s (3)(f) into operation, that is rash and hazardous speculations. The application for discharge came on for hearing before Mr Registrar Dewhurst on 10 June 1981. The Official Receiver, Mr O'Reilly, was present. He had not conducted the public examination. The bankrupt was represented by leading counsel, as were the opposing creditors. Junior counsel represented the trustee. Before the hearing began three affidavits were handed to the opposing creditors' lawyers. One had been sworn by Sir Kenneth Cork, who had acted as the liquidator of the Wilstar group of companies, a second had been sworn by a Mr Adelson and a third by a Mr Hewins. All three seem to have been intended to support the bankrupt's application for discharge, Sir Kenneth's by showing that he had been co-operative and helpful in the liquidation of his group of companies and Mr Hewins's to corroborate his explanation for giving worthless guarantees, namely that 'the lenders did not imagine for a moment that he had independent assets to meet the guarantees and that they were in fact sought as a means of ensuring his commitment to the future of the borrowing companies'.

The hearing began, as is the practice, by the Official Receiver reading his report. Mr S Brodie QC, acting for the creditors, asked for an adjournment and stated that his clients wished to rely on s 26(3)(*f*). Mr Evans-Lombe QC, for the bankrupt, opposed the application and for some reason which is not clear to me he read the three affidavits which had been served on the creditors' lawyers that morning. As far as I can judge from the registrar's note, Mr Evans-Lombe's argument was that when opposing the bankrupt's application for discharge the creditors would have to rely on what had been said by the bankrupt in the course of his public examination and what was in the Official Receiver's report. As the creditors had had all this information for some time there was no need for an adjournment. The learned registrar granted one until 22 July 1981.

On that occasion Mr Brodie was unable to be present. His junior, Miss Baxendale, asked for another adjournment. This was refused. She then read three affidavits in opposition. One had been sworn by a Mr Chilvers, a senior partner in the well-known firm of Coopers & Lybrand; the second was by a Mr White, who is the corporate secretary to the Crown Agents and the company secretary of Four Millbank Nominees Ltd; and the third was by a Mr Wilde, who is the present chairman of Keyser Ullmann Ltd and has had a lifetime's experience of banking, including five years as the vice-chairman of Barclays Bank. All three affidavits were directed to showing that the bankrupt brought on, or contributed to, his bankruptcy by rash and hazardous speculations. Even if the facts set out in the Official Receiver's report had not already alerted the registrar to call on the bankrupt for some explanation for what had happened, these affidavits should have done so.

After Miss Baxendale had read these affidavits, Mr Evans-Lombe seems to have told the registrar that the opposing creditors had given notice that they wished through counsel to cross-examine Sir Kenneth Cork and Mr Hewins. He said that he withdrew Mr Hewins's affidavit and pointed out that the facts in Sir Kenneth's affidavit were not contested. The registrar said that he would give his ruling about cross-examination of the deponents later although his prima facie view was that there was no need for cross-examination. The Official Receiver then explained why he had not submitted that para (*f*) applied.

By this time someone, probably the usher, had guided the bankrupt into the witness box. This is what usually happens after the Official Receiver's report has been read. He was questioned by the Official Receiver about his post-adjudication earnings and his living expenses. Mr Steinfeld, counsel for the trustee, asked some questions about some property dealings. Mr Evans-Lombe then invited the registrar's attention to s 26(7) of the Bankruptcy Act 1914, as amended, and stated that he would submit that no questions should be put to the bankrupt on behalf of the creditors. The registrar then adjourned the hearing until 24 July 1981.

On the adjourned hearing Mr Brodie was able to be present. He submitted that the creditors were entitled to cross-examine the bankrupt and the deponents of the affidavits which had been read in support of his application for discharge and that Mr Evans-Lombe could not stop Mr Hewins's cross-examination by the tactical device of withdrawing his affidavit since it had already been read. Mr Evans-Lombe made submissions to the contrary effect. The submissions went on for three days. The registrar reserved his judgment and delivered it on 25 August 1981. He adjudged that the creditors would not be allowed to cross-examine the bankrupt or the two deponents of affidavits. From that ruling the creditors have appealed to this court. The reasons which the registrar gave for deciding as he did reveal, in my judgment, a fundamental misunderstanding of what discharge from bankruptcy is all about. He seems to have been of the opinion that the creditors had no financial interest to protect when the bankrupt made his application for discharge save to the extent of any further contribution which he proposed to make. He also seems to have thought that on the hearing of an application for discharge it was not right to allow evidence to be called in support of new allegations about the bankrupt's conduct. So far as the creditors were concerned they could make submissions on the evidence provided by the public examination. If there were any new evidence the proper course was for the application for discharge to be adjourned so that the Official Receiver could make further investigations and, if necessary, apply to reinstate the public examination. As to Mr Hewins and Sir Kenneth Cork, he considered that their cross-examination was unnecessary, in Mr Hewins's case because his affidavit did not deal with rash and hazardous speculations and in Sir Kenneth's case because the facts to which he deposed were not in dispute and the opinion which he expressed in the last paragraph of his affidavit was an inference from undisputed facts.

I turn now to the law. The modern law of bankruptcy has its origins in a number of Victorian statutes which were intended to relieve those in financial difficulties from the burden of debt and the possibilities of loss of liberty in a debtors' prison and to enable them to make a fresh start free from debt. The price they had to pay for these benefits was the surrender to their creditors of all their property save the tools, if any, of their trade and the wearing apparel and bedding of themselves and their families. It was recognised, however, that not all debtors were the victims of misfortune. Some were rogues, some were fools and some were willing to risk other people's money when trying to make their own fortunes. For over a hundred years the law has required the Bankruptcy Court to consider whether the conduct of the bankrupt has been such that the public ought to be protected against his further operations for a period of time or even permanently.

Section 26 of the 1914 Act, as amended, now governs the discharge of bankrupts. Subsection (2) gives the court a general discretion, subject to some limitations, whether to grant or refuse an absolute order of discharge, or suspend the operation of the order for a specified time or grant an order of discharge subject to conditions. When exercising this discretion the court may take into consideration 'such conduct or affairs as may or can have had some effect upon the bankruptcy itself': see *Re Barker, ex p Constable* (1890) 25 QBD 285 at 293 per Lord Esher MR. How is the court to get evidence of relevant conduct? It may come from the public examination or the Official Receiver's report. The registrar seems to have thought that they were the only sources. I do not agree that they are. Subsection (7) provides as follows:

> 'Notice of the appointment by the court of the day for hearing the application for discharge shall be published in the prescribed manner, and sent fourteen days at least before the day so appointed to each creditor who has proved, and the court may hear the official receiver, and the trustee, and may also hear any creditor. At the hearing the court may put such questions to the debtor and receive such evidence as it may think fit.'

On this subsection the following questions call for an answer: first, for what purpose should the court hear any creditor; second, for what purpose should the court put questions to the bankrupt; and, third, for what purpose should the court receive such evidence as it may think fit?

Creditors are entitled to make submissions to the court to protect their own financial interests and to ensure that they and others are never again, or for some time, exposed to the kind of financial operations which the bankrupt used to their discomfort. They may never deal with him again, but in the word of high finance and commerce one reckless operator can cause havoc amongst many besides his immediate victims. The registrar was wrong to state that the creditors had no financial interest save to the extent of any contribution which the bankrupt might make. As Lindley LJ pointed out in *Re Payne, ex p Castle Mail Packets Co* (1886) 18 QBD 154 at 158: 'The operation of the order, if granted, is to preclude [the creditor] from all remedy against the debtor, and to limit his rights to a right of payment of a dividend out of the debtor's estate.'

The court's right to question the bankrupt is for the purpose of ensuring that the grant of discharge will not prejudice the public generally. In most cases the facts set out in the Official Receiver's report will indicate that a discharge, with or without conditions, should be granted. In others, and this is such a case, the size of the indebtedness or the circumstances in which the debts were incurred may call for some explanation from the bankrupt. In such circumstances the registrar himself can put questions or may ask, or allow, some other person to do the questioning. In most cases the appropriate person will probably be the Official Receiver or the trustee; but it may be a creditor. A creditor has no right to cross-examine the bankrupt, as Mr Brodie contended both before the registrar and this court; but the registrar in the exercise of his discretion may allow a creditor to cross-examine. As counsel for the opposing creditors in this case had been briefed by experienced solicitors about the allegation of rash and hazardous speculations which had been made, in my opinion there was, and still is, a strong case for allowing him to cross-examine the bankrupt; but whether the judge who rehears this application will take the same view is for him, not me.

As to the court receiving evidence, it can do so if satisfied that it is relevant to any issue which the court has to consider in relation to discharge. This includes the bankrupt's conduct provided it is relevant conduct. No doubt in most cases all the facts will have been elicited during the public examination and the Official Receiver's preliminary investigations. In this case, however, highly complex transactions were reviewed in a public examination which only took two days. There is now available the evidence of two exceptionally qualified witnesses who have sworn that the accounts of the Wilstar Group of companies show rash and hazardous speculations. Whether it does prove rash and hazardous speculations is not for this court to decide. It suffices to say that the burden of proving that it does will rest on the creditors: see *Re Sharp, ex p Sharp* (1890) 10 Morr 114.

As to the problems raised about cross-examining Mr Hewins and Sir Kenneth Cork as deponents, I will say little because of what I consider to be the best way of dealing with this case having regard to my finding that the registrar misdirected himself in law as to what was relevant on the hearing of an application for discharge from bankruptcy. It will be enough for me to say that in my judgment the registrar misdirected himself in law that the cross-examination of Mr Hewins would be irrelevant to any issue which the court had to decide. It would be relevant to the issue of the bankrupt's conduct.

In my judgment, the best way of dealing with this application for discharge is to adjourn it to be heard by a judge of the Chancery Division and for the hearing to start again.

TEMPLEMAN LJ. A receiving order in bankruptcy was made against the bankrupt, William George Stern, on 18 April 1978 and he was adjudicated bankrupt on 30 May 1978. Claims against the bankrupt amount to £118m. The assets of the estate produced £20,252. On 2 March 1981 the bankrupt applied for his discharge and offered to pay £55,000 by instalments over three years. His answers to a common form questionnaire supplied by the Official Receiver disclosed, inter alia, that in 1980 the bankrupt earned £22,000, received a gift of £12,000 from a family trust and occupied rent free a mansion owned by the trustees of the family trust, who also paid out £5,000 in mortgage payments. During 1980 the bankrupt paid £1,500 to his trustee in bankruptcy. We were informed and it was not denied that ever since the date of the receiving order the bankrupt has continued a Rolls-Royce existence and that it is not necessary for him to obtained his discharge in bankruptcy in order that he may be able to maintain himself and his family in style. The bankrupt filed three affidavits in support of his application for discharge but did not swear an affidavit himself.

In a report dated 19 May 1981 the Official Receiver gave a history of the bankrupt outlining the circumstances in which the bankrupt's debts had arisen through personal guarantees of the liabilities of a group of companies controlled by the bankrupt, recorded the bankrupt's assertion that the lenders did not rely on the bankrupt's guarantees, and stated that the group in 1974 suffered from liquidity problems and went into voluntary liquidation.

On 20 May 1981 the Official Receiver gave notice to the bankrupt's creditors that the bankrupt had applied to the court for his discharge and that the application was due to be heard on 10 June 1981. By r 229(2) of the Bankruptcy Rules 1952, SI 1952/2113:

> 'Any creditor who intends to oppose the discharge of a bankrupt on grounds other than those mentioned in the Official Receiver's report shall . . . file . . . a notice . . . stating his intended opposition and the grounds thereof . . .'

Two of the opposing creditors, Keyser Ullmann Ltd and Four Millbank Nominees Ltd, whose debts amount to £60m out of the bankrupt's total liabilities of £118m, gave notice of opposition to the discharge of the bankrupt on the grounds that his bankruptcy was brought on or contributed to by rash and hazardous speculation.

On 10 June 1981 the bankrupt's application was adjourned at the request of the opposing creditors who then filed evidence. Mr Chilvers, a senior partner in Coopers & Lybrand, exhibited the accounts of the parent company of the bankrupt's group and concluded in his affidavit—

> 'that Mr. Stern's business activities which consisted of creating and expanding the Stern companies with the aid of substantial loan finance supported by his own personal guarantees amounted to rash and hazardous speculation which contributed to the downfall of his companies and to the destruction of his personal assets, which were mainly his shareholdings in the Stern companies, and to his own bankruptcy.'

Mr White, the corporate secretary to the Crown Agents, swore an affidavit accepting the conclusions of Mr Chilvers and asking on behalf of the opposing creditors 'to examine Mr Stern on his life style and his business conduct and commercial morality in connection with' his companies.

The hearing of the bankrupt's application for discharge was first heard on 22 June 1981 by Mr Registrar Dewhurst. The bankrupt, who was represented by leading counsel, announced that he would not seek to cross-examine the opposing creditors' witnesses on their affidavits. The opposing creditors stated that they wished to cross-examine the bankrupt and two of the deponents who had sworn affidavits supporting the bankrupt's application.

The bankrupt was examined by the Official Receiver. The examination was largely confined to events which happened after the date of the receiving order and was not directed to the opposing creditors' allegations of rash and hazardous speculation. The bankrupt stated that he hoped 'to expand when free of the stigma of bankruptcy' and that it would be 'very valuable to him to get discharged'.

The bankrupt was then cross-examined by counsel for the trustee in bankruptcy, again merely on the events which happened after the date of the receiving order.

On 24, 30 and 31 July there was argument concerning the application by the opposing creditors to cross-examine the bankrupt and his witnesses. On 25 August 1981 the registrar gave judgment refusing to allow any cross-examination by the opposing creditors. The opposing creditors appeal to this court.

Section 26(2) of the Bankruptcy Act 1914 provides that on the hearing of an application by a bankrupt for his discharge 'the court shall take into consideration a report of the official receiver . . . and may either grant or refuse an absolute order of discharge . . .'. The court is, however, precluded from granting an immediate unconditional discharge where, inter alia, it is proved that 'the bankrupt has brought on, or contributed to, his bankruptcy by rash and hazardous speculations . . .' (see s 26(3)(f)).

In the present case the court must, therefore, decide whether the opposing creditors discharge the onus of proving rash and hazardous speculations by the bankrupt. If the opposing creditors do not discharge that onus the court must then proceed to consider whether in the exercise of the court's discretion the bankrupt should be discharged and, if so, on what terms.

By s 26(7):

> '. . . the court may hear the official receiver, and the trustee, and may also hear any creditor. At the hearing the court may put such questions to the debtor and receive such evidence as it may think fit.'

In my judgment, s 26(7) does not entitle an opposing creditor to cross-examine the bankrupt as of right but confers on the court a discretion to receive evidence, including evidence from the bankrupt elicited by cross-examination on behalf of the opposing creditors.

A discretion lies with the court because of the waste of money and time and unfairness which might result if an opposing creditor, possibly unaffected by the outcome and possibly activated by malice, was entitled to cross-examine as of right. In many, if not most, cases the court may conclude that examination of the bankrupt by the court itself, by the Official Receiver and possibly by the trustee in bankruptcy is sufficient and that the court would not be assisted by further cross-examination on behalf of the creditors.

In other cases the court may be assisted by cross-examination on behalf of the opposing creditors or may feel that under the circumstances it would be unfair to an opposing creditor to refuse him an opportunity of asking questions to establish the grounds of his opposition. The subject matter and extent of any such cross-examination are always under the control of the court by virtue of the discretion conferred on the court by s 26(7).

In the present case the registrar was persuaded that on the true construction of the Bankruptcy Acts 1914 opposing creditors ought not to be allowed to cross-examine on the hearing of an application for discharge from bankruptcy. I cannot spell this inhibition out of the Act. In my judgment, the registrar erred in law. He had a discretion to allow cross-examination by the opposing creditors and should have proceeded to consider whether it was right in the circumstances of the present case to allow them to do so.

I have no doubt that the opposing creditors should have been allowed to cross-examine. In the first place, the opposing creditors should have been allowed to develop their allegations of rash and hazardous speculation. The bankrupt owed £118m. Res ipsa loquitur. The amassing of these colossal debts calls for some less specious explanation than that so far provided. It was positively unjust that the opposing creditors who have suffered losses of £60m should not have been allowed at their own risk as to costs to put to the bankrupt allegations of rash and hazardous speculation which the Official Receiver had not been able to deal with adequately or at all and may not be in as good a position as the opposing creditors to deal with. In the second place, if the opposing creditors had been allowed to question the bankrupt about the current value of the house in which he is now living, a value which may exceed £1m, and about the origins and present value, and trusts and trustees of the family trusts from which he has benefited, the court might conclude that the offer of £55,000 was derisory and that rejection of the present application might at some future date produce a more substantial offer of a sum about half of which would accrue to the opposing creditors. In the third place, cross-examination by responsible leading counsel on the part of the opposing creditors might have confirmed or dispelled a submission that this was an impudent application at the present stage by a bankrupt who ought to be left languishing in a state of bankruptcy which is only irksome to his pride and an obstacle to his ambitions.

For these reasons, and for the reasons given by Lawton LJ, I agree that the appeal should be allowed and that the application should take the course proposed by Lawton LJ.

BRIGHTMAN LJ. I agree with both judgments.

Appeal allowed. Bankrupt's application for discharge to be transferred to a judge of the Chancery Division and the hearing to start de novo. Leave to appeal to House of Lords refused. Sum of £75 in court as security to be repaid to opposing creditors.

Solicitors: *Norton Rose, Botterell & Roche* (for the opposing creditors); *Nicholson, Graham & Jones* (for the bankrupt); *Treasury Solicitor; Harold Stern & Co* (for the trustee in bankruptcy).

Mary Rose Plummer   Barrister.

Note
Re Signland Ltd

CHANCERY DIVISION
SLADE J
15 FEBRUARY 1982

Company – Compulsory winding up – Advertisement of petition – Time – Seven clear days after service – Premature advertisement – Advertisement before service – Whether petition should be struck out – Companies (Winding-up) Rules 1949, r 28(3).

Notes
For the advertisement of a petition to wind up a company, see 7 Halsbury's Laws (4th edn) para 1017, and for cases on the subject, see 10 Digest (Reissue) 955–957, 5604–5636.

For the Companies (Winding-up) Rules 1949, r 28, see 4 Halsbury's Statutory Instruments (3rd reissue) 147.

Petition
By a petition presented on 5 January 1982 by Billing & Sons Ltd the petitioner sought the winding up by the court of a company, Signland Ltd. The petition, which was opposed, was supported by the Inland Revenue Commissioners. The facts are set out in the judgment.

Grant Crawford for the petitioner.
John Brisby for the company.
J E Rayner James for the Inland Revenue Commissioners.
Robin Hollington for the opposing creditor.

SLADE J. This is a petition seeking the usual compulsory winding-up order in respect of a company, Signland Ltd. It was presented by Billing & Sons Ltd, the petitioner, on 5 January 1982. Rule 28 of the Companies (Winding-up) Rules 1949, SI 1949/330 (amended by SI 1979/209; SI 1981/1309), provides that, unless the court otherwise directs, every petition shall be advertised once in the London Gazette not less than seven clear days after it has been served on the company and not less than seven clear days before the day fixed for the hearing.

As I understand it, the principal reasons why the rules have directed that advertisement shall take place not less than seven clear days after service on the company are (1) to give a company served with a winding-up petition the opportunity to discharge the debt in question, if it is undisputed, before advertisement takes place, with all the necessarily potentially damaging consequences to the company, and (2) to enable the company, if it wishes to dispute the debt, to apply to the court to restrain advertisement. As a matter of indulgence, however, it has been my practice during this term to accept premature advertisement where it has taken place less than seven clear days after service on the company and the company has not appeared to take the point.

In the present case, I understand, not only was there a failure to allow the company seven clear days after service of the petition before advertisement took place, but the advertisement in fact took place two days before the petition was served. Furthermore the company has appeared to take the point. While I am quite content to accept the assurance of counsel appearing on behalf of the petitioner to the effect that this breach of the rules was not deliberate, it seems to me to have been a flagrant and serious breach and one of a type which the court must take every step to discourage.

Rule 28(3) of the 1949 rules, which was recently added by the Companies (Winding-Up) (Amendment) (No 2) Rules 1981, SI 1981/1309, now expressly empowers the court to order the removal from the file of a petition if it is not duly advertised in accordance with r 28.

    In the past, as I have indicated, I have not ordinarily exercised this power in cases where advertisement has been premature but the company has taken no objection. However, in none of the earlier cases before me, so far as I can remember, has advertisement actually preceded the service of the petition. To advertise before service of the petition appears to me not only an infringement of the rules but a serious abuse of the whole process of advertisement.

    In the circumstances, I would ordinarily strike out this petition. But counsel for the Inland Revenue Commissioners has indicated that his clients, whose names appear on the list as supporting creditors, wish to be substituted as petitioners. Subject to further submissions, I propose to give them leave to be substituted and make the usual directions.

Order accordingly. Petitioner to pay company's and opposing creditor's costs.

11 March. The court dismissed the petition prior to the return date on being informed that the company had paid the Inland Revenue Commissioners and the original petitioning creditor.

Solicitors: *Church, Adams, Tatham & Co*, agents for *Letcher & Son*, Verwood (for the petitioner); *Howard A Rivers*, Hounslow (for the company); *Solicitor of Inland Revenue; Amhurst, Brown, Martin & Nicholson* (for the opposing creditor).

Jacqueline Metcalfe   Barrister.

Marshall v Osmond and another

QUEEN'S BENCH DIVISION AT WINCHESTER
MILMO J
27, 28 OCTOBER 1981, 1 FEBRUARY 1982

Negligence – Duty to take care – Driver of motor vehicle – Police officer – Police officer pursuing person attempting to avoid arrest for arrestable offence – Extent of policeman's duty of care to that person.

The plaintiff was travelling as a passenger in a car which he knew to be stolen and which was being pursued by a police vehicle driven by a police officer. The car stopped and the plaintiff tried to escape in order to avoid arrest. As he attempted to do so, he was struck and injured either by the police vehicle itself or by some part of the stolen car after it had been hit by the police vehicle. He brought an action for damages against the police officer, claiming that his injuries had been caused by the officer's negligent driving.

Held – (1) A police officer driving a motor vehicle in hot pursuit of a person whom he rightly suspected of having committed an arrestable offence did not owe that person the same duty of care which he owed to innocent and law-abiding users of the highway. Although a police officer was not entitled deliberately to injure such a person unless it was reasonably necessary to do so in order to arrest him, the officer's actions were not to be judged by the same standards as those which would apply if he had time to consider all the possible alternative courses of action which he could take to enable him to discharge his duty successfully (see p 613 c d and p 614 d, post); *Gaynor v Allen* [1959] 2 All ER 644, *Wooldridge v Sumner* [1962] 2 All ER 978, *Woods v Richards* (1977) 65 Cr App R 300 and *Ashton v Turner* [1980] 3 All ER 870 considered.

    (2) Since the evidence showed that the police officer had not intended to injure the plaintiff and had not in all the circumstances been guilty of any want of reasonable care, the plaintiff's claim failed and would be dismissed (see p 614 e to h, post).

Notes

For the duty to take care and the standard of care, see 34 Halsbury's Laws (4th edn) paras 5–11, and for cases on the subject, see 36(1) Digest (Reissue) 17–46, 34–148.

For negligence in relation to the performance of statutory functions, see 34 Halsbury's Laws (4th edn) para 4.

Cases referred to in judgment

Ashton v Turner [1980] 3 All ER 870, [1981] QB 137, [1980] 3 WLR 736.
Gaynor v Allen [1959] 2 All ER 644, [1959] 2 QB 403, [1959] 3 WLR 221, 45 Digest (Repl) 33, 115.
Woods v Richards (1977) 65 Cr App R 300, DC, Digest (Cont Vol E) 579, 302h.
Wooldridge v Sumner [1962] 2 All ER 978, [1963] 2 QB 43, [1962] 3 WLR 616, CA, 36(1) Digest (Reissue) 32, 102.

Action

By a writ issued on 24 March 1977 the plaintiff, Victor Marshall, brought an action against the first defendant, Sir Douglas Osmond, the Chief Constable of Hampshire, and the second defendant, Maximilian Anthony Needham, a police constable of the Hampshire Police Force, claiming damages for personal injuries arising from the negligent driving of the second defendant on the C11 road in the vicinity of Wilverley Plain on 2 May 1976. The action was heard in Winchester, but judgment was given in London. The facts are set out in the judgment.

C H E Gabb for the plaintiff.
Richard Dening for the defendants.

Cur adv vult

1 February. **MILMO J** read the following judgment: At about 1.10 on the morning of 2 May 1976 Pc Needham, the second defendant, and Pc Ford of the Hampshire constabulary were on special observation duty in an unmarked red police Mini saloon in the Brockenhurst area. Pc Needham, who was the driver, was in civilian dress and the other officer was wearing uniform. In the course of the immediately preceding weeks a number of private motor cars had been stolen in the vicinity or illegally taken without the consent of the owners. The suspicions of the officers were aroused by a Mk II Cortina car, full of youths, being driven towards Brockenhurst village. Being in an unmarked vehicle, the officers decided to follow it and set off after it, but when it came to a forest road they radioed to a uniform police car to stop the Cortina.

At about 2½ to 3 miles from Brockenhurst the Cortina pulled up in a lay-by on its near side and Pc Needham drew up in the Mini in front of it. Pc Ford, who, as I have already stated, was in uniform, got out of the Mini and walked back to speak to the occupants of the Cortina. As he did so, the Cortina suddenly reversed, apparently in order to get past the Mini. It then swung back to the roadway, causing Pc Ford to jump out of the way. It set off at speed in its original direction towards Wilverley. In doing so, it went from one side of the road to the other somewhat out of control, its offside wheels going into a shallow ditch, which resulted in high revolutions of the engine and wheel spin. It managed, however, to get back on the road.

When Pc Ford regained his seat in the Mini, the officers commenced to chase the Cortina, which was by then well ahead of them. Suddenly the Cortina's brake lights came on and it was pulled up sharply in a lay-by on its offside. Both doors opened, it was a two-door saloon, and a number of people started to get out in a hurry and disperse into the bushes. At this point the Cortina had travelled some 300 to 400 yards from its earlier stopping place. The officers intending to give chase to the occupants, whom they suspected, and rightly suspected, of being in unlawful possession of the Cortina, Pc Needham drove the police car alongside the Cortina and stopped parallel with it and about 4 feet from it, with the bonnet of the Mini virtually level with that of the

Cortina. In the course of this operation, the plaintiff, who had left the Cortina in which he had been a passenger, came by the injuries in respect of which he now seeks to recover damages from the Hampshire police authority.

It was the plaintiff's case that on the evening of 2 May 1976 he and a friend of his, Stephen Nolan, fell in with four other youths who had been celebrating the victory that afternoon of Southampton in the final of the Football Association Cup. The suggestion of 'stealing' a motor car was made. I use the word 'stealing' because this was the word used by the plaintiff in evidence, but it would probably be more correct to say that the car, to the knowledge of all its occupants at the material time, was being taken and driven away without the consent of the owner by one of their number. The occupants became aware of a car behind them and suspected that it might be following them. It was for this reason that the Cortina pulled up and stopped at the first lay-by. When a uniformed police officer was seen to get out of the Mini, the driver of the Cortina, one Williams, decided to get away quickly. He reversed and went forward, causing the police officer to jump out of the way. When the Cortina stopped at the second lay-by, all the occupants got out hurriedly and all except the plaintiff disappeared into the thick bushes shown in the photographs of the locus in quo.

The plaintiff claims damages on the ground that his injuries were caused by the negligent driving of Pc Needham, the second defendant. The claim against the first defendant is made on the ground that at the material time the first defendant was the Chief Officer of Police for the Hampshire police area and the second defendant was a police constable under the direction and control of the first defendant and was acting in the course of his duty driving a police car when it collided with the plaintiff. It was not disputed that the first defendant was vicariously liable for the second defendant, if it were established that the second defendant's negligence was the cause of the plaintiff's injuries.

It is not necessary for me to recite the details of the negligence pleaded against the second defendant. Suffice it to say that the particulars are the standard allegations of negligence to be found in the ordinary road accident case, founded on the ordinary duty of care owed by a road user to fellow users of the highway engaged on their lawful pursuits.

The defence admits that at the time of the occurrence the second defendant was driving the police car in the course of his duty but denies that the car was in collision with the plaintiff. Negligence on the part of the second defendant is denied, as also is the allegation that negligence on the part of the second defendant was causative of the plaintiff's injuries, which the defence alleges were caused by the plaintiff's own negligence. The particulars given of such alleged negligence are (a) that at the material time the plaintiff was travelling with four other youths in a motor vehicle which had been taken without the owner's consent, and (b) that his injuries were sustained whilst endeavouring to escape in order to avoid arrest by the second defendant and other police officers acting in the course of their duty.

At the outset of the trial an unopposed application was made by the defence to amend the defence by adding a plea in the following terms: 'In the alternative, in the premises, the plaintiff impliedly consented to running the risk of injury.'

This case involved the consideration of the duty of care owed to a person endeavouring to avoid arrest for the commission of an arrestable offence by a police constable in hot pursuit in the execution of his duty to effect such arrest. A number of authorities have been brought to my attention, but none of them is directly in point. I will deal chronologically with these cases.

The earliest of these authorities is *Gaynor v Allen* [1959] 2 All ER 644, [1959] 2 QB 403. This was the case of a pedestrian crossing a road subject to a 40 miles per hour speed limit who was knocked down by a police motor cyclist driving at 60 miles per hour in the course of his duty. The argument was advanced that, by reason of s 3 of the Road Traffic Act 1934, the fact that the policeman was driving at 60 miles per hour on a restricted road did not prima facie show negligence on his part. It does not appear from the report what duty the constable was performing at the time, though it was held that the section did not affect his civil liability and that on the occasion in question he owed the same duty to a member of the public as would any other user of the highway. In the course of his judgment McNair J said ([1959] 2 QB 403 at 407; cf [1959] 2 All ER 644 at 646):

> 'In my judgment, the driver of this police motor-cycle on this occasion must be judged, as regards civil liability, in exactly the same way as any other driver of a motor-cycle in similar circumstances. He, like any other driver, owed a duty to the public to drive with due care and attention and without exposing the members of the public to unnecessary danger . . . The question, as I see it, is this: First, is it clear that the police motor-cyclist, judged by the standard of an ordinary driver of a motor-vehicle on his private occasions, is to be held guilty of negligence causing the accident? I think the answer to that clearly must be "Yes." To drive at that speed on a restricted road, in the half-light at a time of the evening when it must be known that there may be pedestrians making their way home, is itself, in my judgment, to drive at an improper and unsafe speed.'

The present case in my judgment is materially different. The plaintiff in *Gaynor's* case was an innocent citizen using the highway lawfully. It would be a sorry state of affairs if the police in this country involved in the pursuit of criminals were to be held to owe the same duty of care to the criminals whom they are endeavouring to arrest as they owe to ordinary law-abiding users of the highway.

The next case is *Wooldridge v Sumner* [1962] 2 All ER 978, [1963] 1 QB 43, which was decided in the Court of Appeal. This is a case where an equestrian taking part in a horse show rode so fast round a corner in the arena that the horse took the wide sweep at the side of the course and became temporarily out of control, with the result that it plunged into a row of shrubs bordering on the arena where the plaintiff, a photographer, was standing on a bench. The judge at first instance found that the defendant rider was guilty of negligence, but this finding was reversed on appeal. The importance of the case, so far as the present case is concerned, is that it recognised that in a case of negligence a special relationship can exist between the plaintiff and the defendant which can be a determining factor in defining the duty of care owed by the defendant to the plaintiff. Sellers LJ said ([1962] 2 All ER 978 at 983, [1963] 2 QB 43 at 56–57):

> 'In my opinion a competitor or player cannot, at least, in the normal case of competition or game, rely on the maxim volenti non fit injuria in answer to a spectator's claim, for there is no liability unless there is negligence, and the spectator comes to witness skill and with the expectation that it will be exercised. But, provided the competition or game is being performed within the rules and the requirement of the sport and by a person of adequate skill and competence, the spectator does not expect his safety to be regarded by the participant. If the conduct is deliberately intended to injure someone whose presence is known, or is reckless and in disregard of all safety of others so that it is a departure from the standards which might reasonably be expected in anyone pursuing the competition or game, then the performer might well be held liable for any injury his act caused. There would, I think, be a difference, for instance, in assessing blame which is actionable between an injury caused by a tennis ball or a racket accidentally thrown in the course of play into the spectators at Wimbledon and a ball hit or a racket thrown into the stands in temper or annoyance when play was not in progress. The relationship of spectator and competitor or player is a special one, as I see it, as the standard of conduct of the participant, as accepted and expected by the spectator, is that which the sport permits or involves. The different relationship involves its own standard of care.'

I now come to *Woods v Richards* (1977) 65 Cr App R 300, a case decided in the Queen's Bench Division, in which a police driver on duty on a motorway was involved in an accident when proceeding to an emergency call and, as a result of the accident, was charged with careless driving contrary to s 3 of the Road Traffic Act 1972 and was convicted. It was held on appeal against conviction that no special standard was applicable to a police driver and that the test had to be what was due care and attention in all the circumstances of the case.

Finally, there is *Ashton v Turner* [1980] 3 All ER 870, [1981] QB 137, which has some similarity with the notorious highwayman's case. Three men spent the evening drinking and two of them committed a burglary, making their getaway in a car belonging to the third. There was an accident, in which the plaintiff, one of the three, was injured. He claimed damages, alleging negligence against the driver, the first defendant, who pleaded guilty to driving in a dangerous manner and driving with blood alcohol above the prescribed levels, and against the car owner, the second defendant, who was alleged to have permitted the first defendant to use the car without insurance. It was held that in certain circumstances as a matter of public policy the law might not recognise that a duty of care was owed by one participant in a crime to another in relation to an act done in the course of the commission of the crime and that on the facts the defendants did not owe a duty of care to the plaintiff during the burglary or the subsequent flight from the scene of the crime. If the present plaintiff had brought his action against Williams, the driver of the car, *Ashton v Turner* might have been relevant, but I do not think that it is much assistance in the present case.

In my judgment a police officer driving a motor car in hot pursuit of a person or persons whom he rightly suspects of having committed an arrestable offence does not owe that person the same duty of care which he owes to a lawful and innocent user of the highway going about his lawful occasions. He must not deliberately injure such a person unless it is reasonably necessary to do so in order to arrest him, and his actions must not be judged by standards which would be applicable if the situation were such that the officer had time to consider all possible alternative courses of action that he could have taken to discharge his duty successfully.

I make the following findings of fact: (1) at all material times the plaintiff was willingly being carried in the Cortina motor car knowing that it had been taken and driven away without the consent of the owner; (2) at the time when he sustained his injury the plaintiff was fully aware of the fact that the police were in hot pursuit of the Cortina and were seeking to stop, question and inevitably arrest its occupants; (3) the other occupants of the Cortina had already made their getaway into the bushes and it was the plaintiff's intention to do so himself as quickly as possible; (4) the whole incident between the high-speed chase from the first lay-by until the Cortina stopped by the second lay-by took a very short time and the events thereafter occurred in a matter of seconds; (5) when he was endeavouring to make his escape and avoid arrest, the plaintiff sustained the injuries in respect of which he now claims damages by reason of being struck by some part of the police vehicle or by some part of the Cortina after it had been struck by the police vehicle; and (6) the defendant did not intend to injure the plaintiff or any of the occupants of the car and was not guilty of any want of reasonable care in all the circumstances of the case.

I therefore find that the claim in negligence fails and that in consequence the defendants' plea of volenti non fit injuria does not have to be considered. There will be judgment for the defendants against the plaintiff, with an order for costs against the plaintiff not to be enforced without leave of the court.

Judgment for the defendants.

Solicitors: *Blatch & Co*, Southampton (for the plaintiff); *R A Leyland*, Winchester (for the defendants).

K Mydeen Esq   Barrister.

Re Tillmire Common, Heslington

CHANCERY DIVISION
DILLON J
17, 18, 19, 22 FEBRUARY, 3 MARCH 1982

Commons – Registration – Common land and rights of common – Amendment of register – Procedure – Whether applicant for amendment can apply to Chancery Division for declaration entitling him to have land removed from register – Whether applicant required to apply to Queen's Bench Division for judicial review.

Judicial review – Declaration – Circumvention of procedure for judicial review – Landowner applying to Chancery Division for declaration entitling him to have land removed from commons register – Whether landowner required to apply to Queen's Bench Division for judicial review.

The defendant council provisionally registered, under s 4 of the Commons Registration Act 1965, certain land as common land. The registration became final in accordance with ss 4 to 7 of the 1965 Act, but no rights of common over the land were registered within the period prescribed by that Act. The plaintiffs, who claimed to be the owners of the land, applied to the council to have the land removed from the register under s 13(*a*)[a] of the 1965 Act and reg 27 of the Commons Registration (General) Regulations 1966, on the ground that it had ceased to be 'common land' within the meaning of s 22(1)(*a*)[b] of the 1965 Act because no rights of common had been, or could any longer be, registered in respect of it. The council rejected the application because they considered that the land was still 'common land'. The plaintiffs issued an originating summons in the Chancery Division (to which proceedings under the 1965 Act were assigned) seeking a declaration that the council's decision was erroneous in law and that they were entitled, under s 13(*a*) of the 1965 Act, to have the land removed from the register. The council applied for an order under RSC Ord 18, r 19 that the summons be struck out and that all further proceedings be stayed on the grounds that, even if the court had jurisdiction to grant the declaration sought, the matter could be more appropriately dealt with on an application to the Queen's Bench Division for judicial review under RSC Ord 53.

Held – (1) Even if the court had jurisdiction to grant the declaration, it nevertheless had a discretion to strike out a summons or stay proceedings if it considered that the issue of law which the plaintiff wished to raise should be decided by the Queen's Bench Division on an application for judicial review. Furthermore, proceedings in which the High Court was asked to exercise its supervisory jurisdiction by quashing a decision of an inferior tribunal for an error of law on the face of the record should be brought in the Chancery Division only in very exceptional circumstances (see p 621 *c* to *e* and p 622 *d*, post); *Anisminic Ltd v Foreign Compensation Commission* [1969] 1 All ER 208 and *Heywood v Hull Prison Board of Visitors* [1980] 3 All ER 594 considered.

(2) Since the question of law which the plaintiffs sought to raise did not involve matters which were peculiarly within the purview of the Chancery Division but related solely to the true construction and effect of the 1965 Act, there was no reason why those matters should not be determined by the Queen's Bench Division on an application for judicial review under RSC Ord 53. It followed that the summons was an abuse of the process of the court and accordingly all further proceedings in the action would be stayed (see p 622 *f* to *j*, post).

---

a   Section 13, so far as material, is set out at p 617 *j*, post
b   Section 22(1), so far as material, is set out at p 618 *b c*, post

Notes

For the availability of a declaration as a remedy, see 1 Halsbury's Laws (4th edn) paras 82, 185, and for cases on the subject, see 30 Digest (Reissue) 189–194, 202–234.

For judicial review, see 1 Halsbury's Laws (4th edn) para 50, and for cases on the subject, see 1(1) Digest (Reissue) 75–82, 494–540, and 16 Digest (Reissue) 321–431, 3362-4738.

For the supervisory jurisdiction of the Queen's Bench Division, see 10 Halsbury's Laws (4th edn) para 852.

For the Commons Registration Act 1965, ss 4–7, 13, 22, see 3 Halsbury's Statutes (3rd edn) 922–925, 928, 933.

Cases referred to in judgment

Anisminic Ltd v Foreign Compensation Commission [1969] 1 All ER 208, [1969] 2 AC 147, [1969] 2 WLR 163, HL, 30 Digest (Reissue) 209, 313.

Barraclough v Brown [1897] AC 615, [1895–9] All ER Rep 239, HL, 30 Digest (Reissue) 200, 265.

Gilmore's Application, Re [1957] 1 All ER 796, sub nom *R v Medical Appeal Tribunal, ex p Gilmore* [1957] 1 QB 574, [1957] 2 WLR 498, CA, 16 Digest (Reissue) 427, 4700.

Heywood v Hull Prison Board of Visitors [1980] 3 All ER 594, [1980] 1 WLR 1386.

Punton v Ministry of Pensions and National Insurance (No 2) [1964] 1 All ER 448, [1964] 1 WLR 226, CA, Digest (Cont Vol B) 552, 3a.

Pyx Granite Co Ltd v Ministry of Housing and Local Government [1959] 3 All ER 1, [1960] AC 260, [1959] 3 WLR 346, HL, 30 Digest (Reissue) 202, 277.

Uppal v Home Office [1978] CA Transcript 719.

Cases also cited

Al-Fin Corpn's Patent, Re [1969] 3 All ER 396, [1970] Ch 160.

Barnard v National Dock Labour Board [1953] 1 All ER 1113, [1953] 2 QB 18, CA.

Barrs v Bethel [1982] 1 All ER 106, [1981] 3 WLR 874.

Barty-King v Ministry of Defence [1979] 2 All ER 80.

East Midlands Gas Board v Doncaster Corp [1953] 1 All ER 54, [1953] 1 WLR 54.

Healey v Minister of Health [1954] 3 All ER 449, [1955] 1 QB 221, CA.

Irlam Brick Co Ltd v Warrington BC (1982) Times, 5 February.

Lambert v Ealing London Borough Council [1982] 2 All ER 394, [1982] 1 WLR 550, CA.

Pearlman v Keepers and Governors of Harrow School [1979] 1 All ER 365, [1979] QB 56, CA.

Racal Communications Ltd, Re [1980] 2 All ER 634, [1981] AC 374, HL.

R v Northumberland Compensation Appeal Tribunal, ex p Shaw [1952] 1 All ER 122, [1952] 1 KB 338, CA.

Reitzes de Marienwert (Baron) v Administrator of Austrian Property [1924] 2 Ch 282, CA.

Smith v East Sussex CC (1977) 76 LGR 332.

South East Asia Fire Bricks Sdn Bhd v Non-Metallic Mineral Products Manufacturing Employees Union [1980] 2 All ER 689, [1981] AC 363, PC.

Taylor (formerly Kräupl) v National Assistance Board and Law Society [1956] 2 All ER 455, [1956] P 470.

Thorne RDC v Bunting [1972] 1 All ER 439, [1972] Ch 470.

Wilkes v Gee [1973] 2 All ER 1214, [1973] 1 WLR 742, CA.

Motion

By an originating summons dated 14 August 1981, the plaintiffs, Eric Charles Bousfield, Jeremy David Spofforth and Ian Hamish Leslie Melville, acting as trustees of a settlement created by the second Earl of Halifax, claimed a declaration that, on a lawful application under s 13 of the Commons Registration Act 1965, they were entitled to have that part of Tillmire Common, Heslington, North Yorkshire, in their freehold ownership, forming part of unit number CL84, removed from the register of common land held by the defendants, the North Yorkshire County Council. By notice of motion dated 24

November 1981, the defendant council applied for an order under RSC Ord 18, r 19 that
a the originating summons be struck out or that all further proceedings in the action be
stayed on the grounds (i) that the court had no jurisdiction to grant the declaration
sought by the originating summons, and (ii) if the court did have jurisdiction, that the
action was nevertheless an abuse of the process of the court and that the appropriate
procedure for raising the matters complained of in the action was by an application for
judicial review under RSC Ord 53. The facts are set out in the judgment.

b

Robin Auld QC and *W R Griffiths* for the trustees.
F M Ferris QC and *Nicholas Asprey* for the council.

Cur adv vult

c 3 March. **DILLON J** read the following judgment: These proceedings relate to certain
land known as Tillmire Common at Heslington, North Yorkshire, which has been
registered as common land under the Commons Registration Act 1965. The plaintiffs,
who are the trustees of a settlement created by the Earl of Halifax, are or claim to be the
fee simple owners of the land. The defendants are the registration authority who
maintain the relevant register under the Act. The relevant provisions of the Act,
d omitting references to town and village greens, are as follows.
Section 1(1) provides:

'There shall be registered . . . (*a*) land in England or Wales which is common land
. . . (*b*) rights of common over such land; and (*c*) persons claiming to be or found to
be the owners of such land . . .'

e Section 1(2) provides that after a date determined by the minister, which is now long
past—

'(*a*) no land capable of being registered under this Act shall be deemed to be
common land . . . unless it is so registered; and (*b*) no rights of common shall be
exercisable over any such land unless they are registered . . .'

f Section 4(1) provides that 'a registration authority shall register any land as common
land . . . on application duly made . . . for the purpose . . .' and may register land as
common land without any such application. Any registration under s 4 was only
provisional in the first place, but the time for making further provisional registrations
has expired.
Section 5 provides for the notification of provisional registrations and for objections
g thereto. Any objection to a provisional registration is referred to a commons
commissioner.
By ss 6 and 7 any provisional registration which is confirmed by a commons
commissioner on a reference under s 5, or to which no objection in due time is ever
made, becomes final and is to be recorded accordingly in the register.
In s 18 there is provision for an appeal by way of case stated to the High Court against
h any decision of a commons commissioner. Such appeals are assigned by rules of court to
the Chancery Division. These proceedings are not, however, such an appeal. What
happened in this case, and I apprehend it is a not infrequent situation, is that the
registration of Tillmire Common has become final in accordance with the provisions of
ss 4 to 7 of the Act, but no rights of common at all have been registered in respect of the
land.
i Section 13 provides:

'Regulations under this Act shall provide for the amendment of the registers
maintained under this Act where [and the relevant instance is] (*a*) any land registered
under this Act ceases to be common land . . .'

The relevant regulation is reg 27 of the Commons Registration (General) Regulations
1966, SI 1966/1471.

Section 14 of the 1965 Act provides:

'The High Court may order a register maintained under this Act to be amended *a* if . . . (*b*) the register has been amended in pursuance of section 13 of this Act and it appears to the court that no amendment or a different amendment ought to have been made and that the error cannot be corrected in pursuance of regulations made under this Act; and . . . the court deems it just to rectify the register.'

Proceedings under s 14 are assigned by rules of court to the Chancery Division.   *b*
Section 22(1) defines 'common land' as meaning—

'(*a*) land subject to rights of common (as defined in this Act) whether those rights are exercisable at all times or only during limited periods; (*b*) waste land of a manor not subject to rights of common; but does not include a town or village green or any land which forms part of a highway.'

The trustees take the view that the registration of Tillmire Common as common land *c* carried the seeds of its own destruction, and they say that, as no rights of common over it have been or can be registered, it is outside the statutory definition of 'common land' and so has ceased to be common land.

Accordingly, on 18 December 1980 they applied to the council to amend the register under s 13(*a*) and reg 27. The basis of the application is formulated as follows:

d

'The Council having provisionally registered Tillmire Common under Section 4 of the Commons Registration Act, 1965, no rights of common over Tillmire Common have been registered. By virtue of Section 1(2)(*b*) of the 1965 Act, no rights of common are now exercisable. The land is not waste land of a manor. Tillmire Common accordingly no longer has the status of common land and application is now made under Part V of the Commons Registration (General) *e* Regulations, 1966, S.I. 1966, No. 1471 as amended, made under Section 13(*a*) of the 1965 Act for the amendment of the register so as to delete the registration of Tillmire Common as common land.'

That application was rejected by the council and notice of the rejection was given to the trustees by a letter of 7 April 1981. This gives as the reason for rejection that the land *f* 'has not ceased to be common land'. The trustees say that in essence the council was thereby rejecting the construction of s 13(*a*) of the 1965 Act put forward by the trustees, that is to say that by virtue of the Act itself land ceases to be common land if no rights of common over it are or can be registered.

The council, it seems, at that stage, assumed without inquiry that the trustees were right in saying that the land was not waste land of a manor. In the course of the present hearing, however, counsel for the council has stated, and this is the first time this point *g* has been adumbrated against the trustees, that information has reached the council from a third party to the effect that Tillmire Common may once have been, and if so, still is, waste land of a manor. The council having given the decision which I have mentioned, the trustees on 14 August 1981 issued the originating summons in these proceedings in the Chancery Division. On 24 November 1981 the council issued the notice of motion which is now before me. By this notice of motion the council asks that the originating *h* summons should be struck out or that all further proceedings on it should be stayed. The council puts its case on the grounds either (1) as a matter of jurisdiction that this court has no jurisdiction to entertain such an originating summons or (2) as a matter of discretion even if there is jurisdiction, because the appropriate procedure for raising the matters complained of by the trustees, in so far as they can be the subject of complaint at all, is by an application to a Divisional Court of the Queen's Bench Division for judicial *j* review under RSC Ord 53.

The originating summons as issued seeks a declaration in the following terms:

'That the Plaintiffs upon lawful application under Section 13 of the Commons Registration Act 1965 are entitled to have that part of Tillmire Common, *a*　　Heslington, North Yorkshire in their freehold ownership forming part of unit number CL84 removed from the register of common land held by the Defendants . . .'

I read those words, as counsel for the council did, as referring to some future application contemplated by the trustees. The court is asked to decide the issue of law on which the trustees and the council are in disagreement, and if it decides in favour of the trustees then the court is asked to declare that they are entitled on making a further application under reg 27 of the 1966 regulations to have the register amended by the removal of this land from the register. That is clearly, in my judgment, relief which the court has no power to give. Jurisdiction to amend the register has been conferred by Parliament on the council and not on the court, and the court has no jurisdiction to anticipate the decision of the council on a future application: see the speeches of Lord Herschell and Lord Watson in *Barraclough v Brown* [1897] AC 615, [1895–9] All ER Rep 239, especially the speech of Lord Herschell, where he says ([1897] AC 615 at 620, [1895–9] All ER Rep 239 at 241–242):

d　　'. . . I think it would be very mischievous to hold that when a party is compelled by statute to resort to an inferior court he can come first to the High Court to have his right to recover—the very matter relegated to the inferior court—determined. Such a proposition was not supported by authority, and is, I think unsound in principle.'

This is a fortiori the case in that, if a further application were to be made by the trustees under reg 27, the council would be bound to publicise that application and to give notice of it to the district council and to consider any written representations received.

Counsel for the trustees tells me, however, that the originating summons was not intended to refer to any future application yet to be made by the trustees. The lawful application referred to in the originating summons is the application which the trustees made in December 1980 and the council rejected in April 1981. The trustees' case is that the council erred in law in rejecting that application and so the trustees should be declared entitled to have the land removed from the register. Inasmuch as it is not the normal practice for proceedings to be struck out if they are capable of being cured by amendment, the argument has proceeded in the alternative on the basis that the trustees are, by these proceedings, challenging the decision which the council has already made on the trustees' application of December 1980. In the course of his argument, counsel for the trustees expressed what he was seeking in several different ways. What it seems to come down to is, broadly, a declaration that the council's refusal to amend the register by removing the land from the register is invalid because it is erroneous in law as no rights of common have been or can be registered in respect of the land and the land is thus no longer within the statutory definition of common land.

Several points are clear. The first is that this division of the High Court has no appellate jurisdiction to hear an appeal from the council's decision refusing to amend the register. The second is that, although if the council had amended the register this division would have had original jurisdiction under s 14 of the 1965 Act to consider the amendment, this division has, on the plain wording of s 14, no such jurisdiction where the defendant has refused to make any amendment. The High Court has no inherent power to try afresh a matter decided by an inferior tribunal where the decision of that matter has been committed by Parliament to that tribunal. Beyond that, counsel for the council concedes that the council's refusal to amend the register could have been challenged by the trustees by an application to a Divisional Court of the Queen's Bench Division for judicial review under RSC Ord 53 if made in due time, and could be so challenged now if the Divisional Court gives leave for the application to be made. An application for judicial review does not, however, involve a rehearing of the application which was rejected by the council, nor does it involve an appeal against the council's decision. It is merely the way in which the courts act in a supervisory capacity on well-recognised principles in relation to inferior tribunals: see the observations of Lord Pearce *a* in *Anisminic Ltd v Foreign Compensation Commission* [1969] 1 All ER 208 at 233, [1969] 2 AC 147 at 195:

> 'It is, therefore, for the courts to decide the true construction of the statute which defines the area of a tribunal's jurisdiction. This is the only logical way of dealing with the situation and it is the way in which the courts have acted in a supervisory capacity. Lack of jurisdiction may arise in various ways. There may be an absence *b* of those formalities or things which are conditions precedent to the tribunal having any jurisdiction to embark on an enquiry. Or the tribunal may at the end make an order that it has no jurisdiction to make. Or in the intervening stage, while engaged on a proper enquiry, the tribunal may depart from the rules òf natural justice; or it may ask itself the wrong questions; or it may take into account matters which it was not directed to take into account. Thereby it would step outside its *c* jurisdiction. It would turn its enquiry into something not directed by Parliament and fail to make the enquiry which Parliament did direct. Any of these things would cause its purported decision to be a nullity. Further it is assumed, unless special provisions provide otherwise, that the tribunal will make its enquiry and decision according to the law of the land. For that reason the courts will intervene when it is manifest from the record that the tribunal, though keeping within its *d* mandated area of jurisdiction, comes to an erroneous decision through an error of law. In such a case the courts have intervened to correct the error. The courts have, however, always been careful to distinguish their intervention whether on excess of jurisdictiòn or error of law from an appellate function. Their jurisdiction over inferior tribunals is supervision, not review.'
>   *e*

Counsel for the council also concedes, in the light of the *Anisminic* decision, that if the error of the inferior tribunal goes to jurisdiction in the very broad sense in which that term was used by Lord Reid in the *Anisminic* case (see [1969] 1 All ER 208 at 213, [1969] 2 AC 147 at 171) and by Lord Pearce in the passage I have just read, the High Court has jurisdiction to entertain an action by an aggrieved party for a declaration that the decision of the inferior tribunal is a nullity and for appropriate other declaratory relief as *f* was done in *Anisminic*. He submits, even so, that as a matter of discretion the court ought to refuse to entertain proceedings for a declaration and ought instead to leave the aggrieved party to apply to a Divisional Court for judicial review.

The question of jurisdiction, as opposed to discretion, therefore, comes down to this: counsel for the council submits that an error of law by an inferior tribunal within its jurisdiction as opposed to an excess of jurisdiction can only be corrected by an application *g* for judicial review and not by an action for a declaration even if the error of law appears on the face of the record. Counsel adopts the statement in Professor Wade's *Administrative Law* (4th edn, 1977) p 508 that 'declaration is not an available remedy for error on the face of the record: only certiorari will do'.

In the present case, the trustees say that the council asked the right question but gave the wrong answer. If an inferior tribunal gives a decision in excess of its jurisdiction, as *h* that term is used by Lord Reid and Lord Pearce, the decision is a nullity from the outset. The aggrieved party ought not to be burdened by it, and it is not difficult to conclude that the High Court has jurisdiction to entertain an action for a declaration that the decision is a nullity. That is in line with the views as to the subject's rights of recourse to Her Majesty's courts trenchantly expressed by Viscount Simonds in *Pyx Granite Co Ltd v Ministry of Housing and Local Government* [1959] 3 All ER 1 at 6, [1960] AC 260 at 286. *j* Where however the complaint is that the inferior tribunal has erred in law on the face of its decision, the decision is not a nullity. It is a wrong exercise of a jurisdiction which the tribunal has, as opposed to a usurpation of a jurisdiction which it does not have: see the observations of Parker LJ in *Re Gilmore's Application* [1957] 1 All ER 796 at 804, [1957] 1 QB 574 at 588.

As I see it, the questions that arise under the issue of jurisdiction are (1) whether the logic which has led the High Court to entertain as an alternative to proceedings for judicial review actions for declarations that decisions of inferior tribunals are nullities for errors of law which go to jurisdiction leads to the conclusion that the High Court also has jurisdiction to entertain an action for a declaration that a decision of an inferior tribunal is invalid for error of law on the face of the record even though such a decision is not a nullity, and (2) whether, so far, at any rate, as a judge at first instance is concerned, the decision of the Court of Appeal in *Punton v Ministry of Pensions and National Insurance (No 2)* [1964] 1 All ER 448, [1964] 1 WLR 226 precludes the court from entertaining the present originating summons, even amended as I have indicated to include a claim for a declaration that the decision of the council is invalid, or whether the decision in *Punton* depended entirely on the form of relief sought in that case which merely raised a question of law for decision and would, whatever the answer given by the court to that question, have left the decision of the inferior tribunal, the national insurance commissioner, standing.

Even if, however, the court has jurisdiction to entertain proceedings for a declaration that the decision of an inferior tribunal is invalid for error of law on the face of the record, the remedy of a declaration is discretionary and the court clearly has full power to strike out or stay the proceedings if, as a matter of discretion, the court considers that the plaintiffs in any proceedings should apply to a Divisional Court for judicial review. These proceedings in this division can, therefore, only continue if the plaintiff trustees satisfy me that the court has jurisdiction to entertain this originating summons in suitably amended form, and if I take the view as a matter of discretion that the issue of law which the trustees wish to raise ought to be decided in this division and not by a Divisional Court of the Queen's Bench Division on an application for judicial review.

As I have formed a clear view that even if there is jurisdiction the trustees' claim ought to be heard by a Divisional Court on an application for judicial review and not in this division, I do not propose to say any more on the question of jurisdiction; anything I did say would be obiter and of no assistance.

RSC Ord 53 provides a code of procedure carefully designed to secure the expeditious disposal of applications for judicial review of decisions of inferior tribunals. There is a specially important requirement that the would-be applicant for judicial review must obtain preliminary leave to make the application from a Divisional Court ex parte. There are guarantees from the outset under the present practice that any application for which preliminary leave is granted will come on quickly. In *Heywood v Hull Prison Board of Visitors* [1980] 3 All ER 594 at 598, [1980] 1 WLR 1386 at 1390–1391 Goulding J stated that it was obviously undesirable that the plaintiff in that case should seek relief by action rather than by application for judicial review. He went on, and I quote:

'There are a number of considerations which to my mind justify that opinion. First of all, the Rules of the Supreme Court as they stand must be construed as a whole. Where, in a code of procedural rules, carefully designed machinery is provided for determining a special class of issues or questions, it is in general inconvenient to use some broader form of process designed to cover not only that, but much larger categories of question. Secondly, Ord 53, r 5(1) requires a would-be applicant for judicial review to obtain preliminary leave ex parte from a Divisional Court of the Queen's Bench Division or in vacation from a judge in chambers. There are very good reasons (among them an economy of public time and the avoidance of injustice to persons whom it is desired to make respondents) for that requirement of preliminary leave. If an action commenced by writ or originating summons is used instead of the machinery of Ord 53, that requirement of leave is circumvented. Thirdly, under Ord 53, r 4, certain requirements of expedition are laid down to be observed by an applicant for judicial review, though they are not inflexible and within limits the court has a discretion as to their application. Once again, there are very good reasons for such a requirement. Once again, the provisions of the rule are obviated if the relief is sought by action instead of by application for judicial review.'

Goulding J ([1980] 3 All ER 594 at 601, [1980] 1 WLR 1386 at 1395) quoted from the judgment of Roskill LJ in *Uppal v Home Office* [1978] CA Transcript 719 as follows:

'... it would be wrong that this procedure [that is, procedure by action in Chancery] should be adopted in order to bypass the need for getting leave from the Divisional Court to move for the relevant order where what in truth is sought is judicial review ...'

I am not saying that the trustees' claim in this case is one on which a Divisional Court would, on the ex parte application, necessarily refuse to give leave to apply for judicial review, nor am I saying that the trustees' object in coming to the Chancery Division in this case is particularly to avoid the necessity of an ex parte application to the Divisional Court. I am well aware that, for a plaintiff who is eager to get his case on, the procedure by originating summons in the Chancery Division for the determination of a point of law on affidavit evidence can be extremely expeditious and, as litigation goes, cheap. Moreover, the trustees are the only persons in this case who would suffer from delay.

Chancery judges are not, however, versed in the refinements of certiorari, and in all but the most exceptional cases it must, in my judgment, be the wrong procedure to come to the Chancery Division to exercise the supervisory jurisdiction of the court by quashing a decision of an inferior tribunal for error of law on the face of the record.

The matters with which the proceedings were concerned in *Uppal v Home Office* and in *Heywood v Hull Prison Board of Visitors*, immigration law and the duties of prison visitors, were matters peculiarly within the territory of the Queen's Bench Division and the knowledge of judges of that division. By contrast, the Commons Registration Act 1965 is concerned with common land and rights of common, which are matters peculiarly within the territory of the Chancery Division. In addition, as counsel for the trustees has stressed, the proceedings expressly provided for by that Act under ss 14 and 18 are specifically assigned to the Chancery Division and all cases which have come before the courts in relation to the Act, whether under s 14 or s 18 or otherwise, have, so far as I am aware, been brought in the Chancery Division. The judges of the Chancery Division are probably more aware, though I say it with deference, of some of the difficulties which have emerged from the introduction by the 1965 Act of the system of registration of common land and of the rights of common to which I have referred. None the less, the question of law which the trustees seek to raise is not a question of ancient law or ancient right; it does not involve any investigation of the title of Tillmire Common or any problem as to manorial waste. It is merely a question of the true construction and effect of an Act of Parliament which is less than 20 years old. Such a question, be it easy or difficult, can just as well be decided by judges of the Queen's Bench Division as by judges of the Chancery Division.

Therefore, there is nothing in my judgment in the nature of the question sought to be raised to override, assuming there is jurisdiction, the general practice that proceedings under the supervisory jurisdiction of the court where it is claimed that a decision of an inferior tribunal ought to be quashed for error of law on the face of the record, ought to be brought before a Divisional Court of the Queen's Bench Division and not in the Chancery Division. Therefore, this originating summons, both in its original form and as it is suggested it might be amended, is in my judgment misconceived and an abuse of the process of the court.

The appropriate course is, therefore, that I should stay all further proceedings on it.

Order accordingly.

Solicitors: *Dibb Lupton & Co*, Leeds (for the trustees); *Lee, Bolton & Lee* (for the council).

Evelyn M C Budd   Barrister.

Percy Bilton Ltd v Greater London Council

HOUSE OF LORDS

LORD DIPLOCK, LORD FRASER OF TULLYBELTON, LORD KEITH OF KINKEL, LORD BRIDGE OF HARWICH AND LORD BRANDON OF OAKBROOK

31 MARCH, 1 APRIL, 20 MAY 1982

Building contract – Time for completion – Delay – Withdrawal of sub-contractor – Delay caused by withdrawal of sub-contractor and failure of employer to nominate replacement – Extension of time granted for failure to nominate replacement sub-contractor – Failure to complete within extended time – Whether risk of delay arising from withdrawal of sub-contractor falling on employer or main contractor – Whether failure of employer to nominate replacement sub-contractor disentitling employer to deduct liquidated damages – RIBA form of contract (1963 edn), cll 22, 23(f)(g).

Under the terms of a building contract dated October 1976 between the employer and the main contractor based on the RIBA form of contract (1963 edn as revised), the completion date for the work was agreed to be January 1979. By cl 22 of the contract the employer was entitled to liquidated damages for any period during which the work remained uncompleted after the date for completion as stated in the contract or as extended under the terms of cl 23 of the contract, if the architect certified that they ought reasonably to have been so completed. Clause 23 provided for an extension of the date for completion where, inter alia, under para (f), the contractor had not received in due time necessary instructions for which he had specifically applied, or where, under para (g), there was delay on the part of a nominated sub-contractor which the contractor had taken all reasonable steps to avoid or reduce. The employer nominated L as sub-contractor for mechanical services. In July 1978 L, which was in financial difficulties, withdrew its labour. By that date, the time for completion had already been extended to March 1979. Several extensions were subsequently granted and the completion date was finally fixed for February 1980. The architect issued a certificate under cl 22 that the work ought to be completed by February 1980. The day before L's actual withdrawal, the main contractor called on the employer to nominate another sub-contractor. There was considerable delay in making an effective nomination, and eventually H was nominated in November 1978. In December H entered into a sub-contract with the main contractor to complete its work by January 1980. In March 1980 the employer deducted from moneys certified as due to the main contractor £24,661 as liquidated and ascertained damages under cl 22. The main contractor brought an action seeking declarations (i) that, on the true construction of the contract, time was at large and the certificate issued under cl 22 was invalid and (ii) that the employer was required to honour the architect's certificate by paying to the main contractor the sum wrongfully deducted by way of liquidated damages. It was common ground between the parties that the delay which followed the withdrawal of L should be divided into two parts, viz (i) the period of delay arising directly from the withdrawal and (ii) the period of delay arising from the failure of the employer to nominate a replacement within a reasonable time. Since it was clear that the employer had been responsible for the second part of the delay, for which the main contractor would have been entitled to a reasonable extension of time under cl 23(f), the dispute centred on the consequence of the first period of delay which, it was agreed, did not fall within the provisions of cl 23. The main contractor contended that the loss directly caused by the withdrawal of L fell on the employer, because it had a responsibility not only to nominate the original sub-contractor and any necessary replacement but also to maintain a sub-contractor in the field so long as work of the kind allotted to him needed to be done. The main contractor further contended that cl 23(f) did not apply even to the second period of delay, since it could only apply where the main contractor made his application for instructions at a time when the employer, through its architect, could by timeous nomination have avoided the delay

altogether. The judge held that the certificate issued under cl 22 of the contract was
invalid and made the declarations sought. On appeal by the employer, the Court of *a*
Appeal set aside the judge's order and gave judgment for the employer. The main
contractor appealed to the House of Lords.

Held – The appeal would be dismissed for the following reasons—

(1) The general rule in relation to a building contract was, subject to any amendment
by the express terms of the particular contract, that the main contractor was bound to *b*
complete the work by the date for completion stated in the contract and if he failed to do
so he was liable for liquidated damages to the employer. The employer was, however,
not entitled to liquidated damages if by his acts or omissions he had prevented the main
contractor from completing his work by the completion date (see p 625 *d*, p 628 *d* to *f*
and p 629 *e* to *g*, post); *Holme v Guppy* (1838) 2 M & W 387 and *Wells v Army and Navy
Co-operative Society Ltd*, (1902) 86 LT 764 followed.

(2) Although cl 23(g) of the contract between the parties expressly applied to 'delay' *c*
on the part of a nominated sub-contractor, such delay did not include complete
withdrawal by the sub-contractor. Accordingly, withdrawal by the sub-contractor fell
within the general rule and the main contractor took the risk of any delay directly caused
thereby. There was nothing in the terms of contract which turned the employer's duty
of nominating a sub-contractor and if necessary a replacement into a duty on the *d*
employer to ensure that the main contractor was not impeded by want of a nominated
sub-contractor. Such a warranty would place an unreasonable burden on the employer,
particularly as he had no direct contractual relationship with a nominated sub-contractor
and no control over him. Accordingly, the main contractor was not entitled to any
extension of time in respect of the delay caused by the withdrawal of L, with the result
that the date for completion remained unaltered by that period of delay (see p 625 *d*, *e*
p 627 *f g*, p 628 *a b g h* and p 629 *e* to *g*, post); *North West Metropolitan Regional Hospital
Board v T A Bickerton & Son Ltd* [1970] 1 All ER 1039 considered.

(3) When L withdrew, the duty of the employer, acting through its architect, was
limited to giving instructions for the nomination of a replacement within a reasonable
time after receiving a specific application in writing from the main contractor under cl
23(f). Delay by the employer in making the timeous nomination was within the express *f*
terms of cl 23(f), and accordingly, since the employer had failed to give instructions
within a reasonable time which resulted in the second part of the delay, the main
contractor became entitled to an extension of the time for completion to cover the second
part of the delay, but such an extension had in fact been given. Accordingly, the
certificate had been validly issued under cl 22, and the employer had been entitled to
deduct the £24,661 liquidated damages when the work was not completed within the *g*
extended time for completion (see p 625 *d*, p 627 *g h*, p 628 *b* to *d h* and p 629 *e* to *g*, post);
North West Metropolitan Regional Hospital Board v T A Bickerton & Son Ltd [1970] 1 All ER
1039 considered.

Cases referred to in opinions
Holme v Guppy (1838) 3 M & W 387, 150 ER 1195, 7 Digest (Reissue) 327, 2214.
North West Metropolitan Regional Hospital Board v T A Bickerton & Son Ltd [1970] 1 All ER *h*
1039, [1970] 1 WLR 607, HL, 7 Digest (Reissue) 325, 2213.
Wells v Army and Navy Co-operative Society Ltd (1902) 86 LT 764, 7 Digest (Reissue) 447,
2604.

Notes
For extension of time and liquidated damages for delay under a building contract, see 4 *j*
Halsbury's Laws (4th edn) paras 1182–1186, and for cases on the subject, see 7 Digest
(Reissue) 338–339, 403–404, 2252–2257, 2446–2449.

Appeal and cross-appeal
The appellant, Percy Bilton Ltd, appealed and the respondent, the Greater London

Council, cross-appealed against the order of the Court of Appeal (Stephenson, Dunn LJJ and Sir David Cairns) dated 27 February 1981 setting aside the order of his Honour Judge Stabb QC sitting as official referee dated 15 August 1980 granting the appellant declarations (1) that on the true construction of a contract between the appellant and the respondent under which the respondent agreed to employ the appellant to carry out building works at an estate at Swains Road, Merton time was at large and that a certificate purported to have been issued under cl 22 of the contract was invalid, and (2) that the respondent was required to honour the architect's certificate by paying to the appellant the sum of £24,661 wrongfully deducted on 17 March 1980 by way of liquidated damages. The facts are set out in the judgment of Lord Fraser.

Patrick Garland QC and *Richard Guy* for the appellants.
Oliver Popplewell QC and *Peter Lewis* for the respondents.

Their Lordships took time for consideration.

20 May. The following opinions were delivered.

LORD DIPLOCK. My Lords, for the reasons given in the speech prepared by my noble and learned friend Lord Fraser with which I agree, I would dismiss this appeal and the cross-appeal.

LORD FRASER OF TULLYBELTON. My Lords, this appeal is concerned with the legal consequences of failure by the main contractor to complete work under a building contract by the due date, where the delay has been partly caused by the withdrawal of a nominated sub-contractor at a time when withdrawal inevitably delays completion of the works. In particular, the question is whether such a withdrawal, which causes delay in completion of the works by the main contractor, prevents the employer from relying on a clause in his contract with the main contractor giving the employer the right to deduct liquidated damages for delay in completion.

The contract between the respondent (as employer) and the appellant (as main contractor) was for building a large number of houses in the London borough of Merton. The conditions of contract were based on the RIBA (now the JCT) conditions (1963 edn, as revised). They included a condition, in cl 22, whereby the employer was entitled to liquidated damages for any period during which the works remained uncompleted after the time for completion stated in the contract, or as extended in terms of cl 23, if the architect certified that in his opinion they ought reasonably to have been so completed. The works were not completed by the (extended) time for completion and the architect certified that they ought to have been so completed. The respondent deducted from payments due under the contract sums representing liquidated damages, and the appellant raised these proceedings in which it seeks a declaration to the effect that the deductions were wrongly made, and claims payment of the amounts deducted. The action first came before his Honour Judge Stabb QC, who decided in favour of the appellant. The Court of Appeal (Stephenson, Dunn LJJ and Sir David Cairns) allowed the appeal and gave judgment for the respondent.

The relevant facts have been conveniently set out in an agreed statement of facts, and I shall only mention the bare minimum which is essential to make this speech intelligible. The contract was dated 25 October 1976 and the original completion date was 24 January 1979, giving a construction period of 27 months. The respondent nominated as sub-contractor for mechanical services a firm called W S Lowdell (Nuthurst) Ltd (Lowdells). On 28 July 1978 Lowdells, who were in financial difficulty, withdrew their labour from the site and shortly afterwards they went into liquidation. Their withdrawal has been referred to in the course of the proceedings for convenience as 'dropping out', and I shall consider later what is the correct legal analysis of the episode. For the moment it is enough to note that by 28 July 1978 the time for completion had already been extended to 9 March 1979, that the work was considerably in arrears and that negotiations for further extension of time were likely. Several extensions were subsequently granted, and the completion date finally fixed was 1 February 1980. The architect issued a certificate under cl 22 that the works ought to have been completed by 1 February 1980. On 27 July 1978, the day before Lowdells actually withdrew, the appellant called on the respondent to nominate another sub-contractor to replace Lowdells. It was then the duty of the respondent to make a fresh nomination: see *North West Metropolitan Regional Hospital Board v T A Bickerton & Son Ltd* [1970] 1 All ER 1039, [1970] 1 WLR 607. There was considerable delay in making an effective fresh nomination. The first firm nominated by the respondent (in September 1978) withdrew without ever starting work, and eventually a firm named Home Counties Heating and Plumbing Ltd (Home Counties) was nominated but that was not until November 1978, about four months after the appellant had applied for a fresh nomination. On 22 December 1978 the appellant agreed to enter into a sub-contract with Home Counties on the basis that Home Counties would start work on 22 January 1979 and would need 53 weeks for their work. Their estimated completion date was, therefore, about 25 January 1980.

The provisions of the contract which are directly relevant to the dispute are contained in cll 21, 22, 23 and 27. The portions of those clauses most directly in point are as follows:

'21   (1) On the Date for Possession stated in the appendix to these Conditions possession of the site shall be given to the Contractor who shall thereupon begin the Works and regularly and diligently proceed with the same, and who shall complete the same on or before the Date for Completion stated in the said appendix subject nevertheless to the provisions for extension of time contained in clauses 23 and 33(1)(c) of these Conditions . . .

22   If the Contractor fails to complete the Works by the Date for Completion stated in the appendix to these Conditions or within any extended time fixed under clause 23 or clause 33(1)(c) of these Conditions and the Architect/Supervising Officer certifies in writing that in his opinion the same ought reasonably so to have been completed, then the Contractor shall pay or allow to the Employer a sum calculated at the rate stated in the said appendix as Liquidated and Ascertained Damages for the period during which the works shall so remain or have remained incomplete, and the Employer may deduct such sum from any monies due or to become due to the Contractor under this Contract. [Clause 33(1)(c) has no application to the events that happened in this case.]

23   Upon it becoming reasonably apparent that the progress of the Works is delayed, the Contractor shall forthwith give written notice of the cause of the delay to the Architect/Supervising Officer, and if in the opinion of the Architect/Supervising Officer the completion of the Works is likely to be or has been delayed beyond the Date for Completion stated in the appendix to these Conditions or beyond any extended time previously fixed under either this clause or clause 33(1)(c) of these Conditions . . . (f) by reason of the Contractor not having received in due time necessary instructions, drawings, details or levels from the Architect/Supervising Officer for which he specifically applied in writing on a date which having regard to the Date for Completion stated in the appendix to these Conditions or to any extension of time then fixed under this clause or clause 33(1)(c) of these Conditions was neither unreasonably distant from nor unreasonably close to the date on which it was necessary for him to receive the same, or (g) by delay on the part of nominated sub-contractors or nominated suppliers which the Contractor has taken all practicable steps to avoid or reduce . . . then the Architect/Supervising Officer shall so soon as he is able to estimate the length of the delay beyond the date or time aforesaid make in writing a fair and reasonable extension of time for completion of the Works. Provided always that the Contractor shall use constantly

his best endeavours to prevent delay and shall do all that may reasonably be required to the satisfaction of the Architect/Supervising Officer to proceed with the Works.'

Clause 27 provides, inter alia, that the employer's architect 'shall not nominate any person as a sub-contractor against whom the [main] Contractor shall make reasonable objection'.

It is common ground between the parties that the delay which followed the dropping out of Lowdells should be divided into two parts: first, the part arising directly from the withdrawal and, second, that arising from the failure of the respondent to nominate a replacement with reasonable promptness. The respondent was clearly responsible for the second part, and there is no doubt that, if that had been the only delay, the appellant would have been entitled to a reasonable extension of time to allow for it in accordance with cl 23(f). The dispute centres on the consequence of the first period of the delay which, as parties are agreed, does not fall within any of the provisions of cl 23. The appellant contends that the loss directly caused by the withdrawal of the nominated sub-contractor must fall on the respondent, on the ground that it has a responsibility not only to nominate the original sub-contractor and any necessary replacement, but to maintain a sub-contractor in the field so long as work of the kind allotted to him needs to be done. This is said to flow from the decision of your Lordships' House in *Bickerton's* case. What was actually decided in that case was that, where the original nominated sub-contractor had gone into liquidation and dropped out, the main contractor had neither the right nor the duty to do any of the sub-contractor's work himself, and that it was the duty of the employer to make a new nomination. Consequently (so it was argued for the appellant), if the nominated sub-contractor withdraws at a time when his withdrawal must inevitably cause delay, the main contractor is disabled from performing his obligations for want of a sub-contractor whom only the employer can provide, and the main contractor is thus 'impeded' from working: see *Bickerton's* case [1970] 1 All ER 1039 at 1044, [1970] 1 WLR 607 at 613 per Lord Reid. In these circumstances, it was said that the contractual time limit ceases to apply, the time for completion becomes at large and the employer cannot rely on the provisions for liquidated damages in cl 22.

If that argument is correct, its effect would be to turn the employer's duty of nominating a sub-contractor, and if necessary a replacement, into a duty to ensure that the main contractor is not impeded by want of a nominal sub-contractor. That would be virtually a warranty that a nominated sub-contractor would carry on work continuously, or at least that he would be available to do so. But I see nothing in cl 22 or cl 23, or elsewhere in the conditions of contract, to impose such a high duty on the employer. Such a warranty would, in my opinion, place an unreasonable burden on the employer, particularly as he has no direct contractual relationship with a nominated sub-contractor, and no control over him. When the nominated sub-contractor withdrew, the duty of the employer, acting through its architect, was in my opinion limited to giving instructions for nomination of a replacement within a reasonable time after receiving a specific application in writing from the main contractor under cl 23(f). In this case, the employer failed to perform that duty. It did not give instructions within a reasonable time, and the second part of the delay occurred, with the result that the appellant became entitled to an extension of the time for completion to cover the second part. But it never became entitled to any extension to cover the first part of the delay.

In fact, an extension of 14 weeks was allowed (by certificate dated 9 May 1979, which mistakenly refers to 13 weeks) under cl 23(f) and was treated by both parties as being for 'delays arising from the nominated subcontractor . . . going into liquidation' without distinguishing the two elements of delay: that is clear from a letter dated 20 November 1979 from the appellant to the architect. In so far as the extension took account of the first element of delay, it gave the appellant more than it was strictly entitled to. But the appellant's argument that the first period of delay had put the time at large drove it logically into the strange position of arguing that no extension at all of the time limit ought to have been allowed and that the architect's certificate, which purported to have been granted under cl 22, was invalid. That would mean that any delay, however short, directly caused by withdrawal of a nominated sub-contractor has the immediate effect of cancelling any time limit and destroying any right by the employer to recover liquidated damages. I cannot accept the argument. I respectfully agree with the passage in the judgment of the Court of Appeal to the effect that—

> 'in so far as delay was caused by the departure of Lowdells . . . it was a delay which is not within any of the provisions of cl 23 and therefore the plaintiff was not entitled to any extension in respect of it, with the result not that time became at large but that, at that stage, the date for completion remained unaffected by that period of delay. The delay that followed, a delay caused by the failure of the employer for several months to renominate, [was] quite separate and clearly within the provisions of cl 23(f).'

The appellant submitted further that cl 23(f) did not apply even to the second part of the delay, because it can only apply where the main contractor makes his application for instructions at a time when the employer, through the architect, could by timeous nomination have avoided the delay altogether. Clause 23(f) applies to delay caused by the contractor not having received instructions 'in due time', and the argument was that those words meant 'in time to avoid delay'. I do not agree. In my opinion, the words mean 'in a reasonable time' and they are therefore applicable in a case such as the present where some delay is inevitable but it has been increased by the employer's fault. Accordingly, I agree with the Court of Appeal that the second part of the delay does fall within cl 23(f).

The true position is, I think, correctly stated in the following propositions which I take with only minor amendment from the submissions of counsel for the respondent. (1) The general rule is that the main contractor is bound to complete the work by the date for completion stated in the contract. If he fails to do so, he will be liable for liquidated damages to the employer. (2) That is subject to the exception that the employer is not entitled to liquidated damages if by his acts or omissions he has prevented the main contractor from completing his work by completion date: see, for example, *Holme v Guppy* (1838) 2 M & W 387, 150 ER 1195 and *Wells v Army and Navy Co-operative Society* (1902) 86 LT 764. (3) These general rules may be amended by the express terms of the contract. (4) In this case, the express terms of cl 23 of the contract do affect the general rule. For example, where completion is delayed '(a) by *force majeure*, or (b) by reason of any exceptionally inclement weather', the architect is bound to make a fair and reasonable extension of time for completion of the work. Without that express provision, the main contractor would be left to take the risk of delay caused by force majeure or exceptionally inclement weather under the general rule. (5) Withdrawal of a nominated sub-contractor is not caused by the fault of the employer, nor is it covered by any of the express provisions of cl 23. Clause 23(g) expressly applies to 'delay' on the part of a nominated sub-contractor but such 'delay' does not include complete withdrawal (this was accepted in argument by counsel for the appellant, rightly in my opinion). (6) Accordingly, withdrawal falls under the general rule and the main contractor takes the risk of any delay directly caused thereby. (7) Delay by the employer in making the timeous nomination of a new sub-contractor is within the express terms of cl 23(f), and the main contractor, the appellant, was entitled to an extension of time to cover that delay. Such an extension has been given.

These principles do not, in my opinion, operate in any way harshly or unfairly against the appellant. The so-called 'dropping out' of the nominated sub-contractor was not merely unilateral action by him. The mechanics of the matter were that on 26 July 1978 a firm of building and quantity surveyors, acting on the instructions of the receiver and manager of Lowdells, wrote to the appellant intimating that their labour would be withdrawn by 28 July 1978. That was a notice of intention to repudiate the sub-contract. It was in effect, accepted by the appellant in a reply dated 31 July, in which it purported to 'determine' the sub-contract under cl 20(a)(i) which entitled it to determine the sub-contract if the sub-contractor 'wholly suspends the carrying out of the Sub-Contract Works' and continues in such default for ten days. But the clause was not applicable because the appellant's letter of 31 July was sent before the default had lasted for ten days. It must, in my opinion, be read simply as an acceptance of the repudiatory breach by the receiver on behalf of the sub-contractors. Accordingly, the sub-contract was terminated by the appellant's acceptance of repudiation, which it was under no obligation to give. If it had withheld acceptance of the repudiation, the sub-contract would have remained alive; it is possible that the appellant might then have been entitled to claim an extension of time under cl 23(g) on account of the sub-contractor's 'delay'. But this point was not fully argued and I express no concluded view on it. There was also another course open to the appellant. It could have exercised its right of 'reasonable objection' under cl 27(a) to prevent the nomination of any new sub-contractor who did not offer to complete his part of the work within the overall completion period for the contract as a whole. In fact, the appellant accepted the nomination, and relied on the probability that it would be allowed an extension of time. Its reliance was not misplaced, for, as already mentioned, it was allowed 14 weeks for the delay arising from the withdrawal of the sub-contractor.

The appellant submitted an alternative argument to the effect that, even if the time for completion did not become at large on the dropping out of Lowdells, it must have done so when it agreed to the nomination of a new sub-contractor who could not complete the sub-contract work until after the extended time for completion of the works. But the factual basis for this argument is lacking. As I have mentioned, the substituted sub-contractor undertook to complete his part of the work by 25 January 1980, the completion date for the whole work was extended to 1 February 1980 and the architect certified that they ought to have been completed by the latter date. Accordingly there is no substance in this submission.

In these circumstances it is unnecessary to consider the cross-appeal, based on the correspondence between the parties.

For these reasons I would dismiss the appeal and the cross-appeal, with costs to the respondent.

LORD KEITH OF KINKEL. My Lords, I have had the advantage of reading in draft the speech delivered by my noble and learned friend Lord Fraser. I agree with it, and for the reasons he gives I too would dismiss the appeal and the cross-appeal.

LORD BRIDGE OF HARWICH. My Lords, I have had the advantage of reading in draft the speech of my noble and learned friend Lord Fraser. I agree with it and for the reasons he gives I also would dismiss the appeal and the cross-appeal.

LORD BRANDON OF OAKBROOK. My Lords, I have had the advantage of reading in draft the speech of my noble and learned friend Lord Fraser. I agree with it and would dismiss the appeal and the cross-appeal accordingly.

Appeal and cross-appeal dismissed.

Solicitors: *P G Myers*, Ealing (for the appellants); *R A Lanham* (for the respondents).

Mary Rose Plummer   Barrister.

Berry v Warnett (Inspector of Taxes)

HOUSE OF LORDS

LORD WILBERFORCE, LORD FRASER OF TULLYBELTON, LORD SCARMAN, LORD ROSKILL AND LORD BRIDGE OF HARWICH

8, 9 MARCH, 6 MAY 1982

Capital gains tax – Settlement – Settled property – Gift in settlement – Transfer of fund to trustees – Settlement whereby beneficial interest in fund assigned to trustees on trust for settlor for life with remainder to company – Consideration paid by company to settlor equal to market value of interest in remainder – Whether fund acquired by trustees by way of gift – Whether transfer of 'gift in settlement' – Whether settlement effected only part disposal of fund – Finance Act 1965, ss 22(2)(4), 25(2).

In March 1972 the taxpayer transferred a fund consisting of his holding of stock and shares in R Ltd to a Guernsey company. On 4 April the taxpayer executed a deed of settlement between himself as vendor, a Jersey company as purchaser and the Guernsey company as trustees, whereby, in consideration of the full market value of £14,500 paid to him by the Jersey company, he assigned his beneficial interest in the fund to the Guernsey company on trust to pay the income of the fund to himself for life with remainder to the Jersey company absolutely. The taxpayer was assessed to capital gains tax for the year 1971–72 in the sum of £150,483 on the basis that the assignment of the fund to the Guernsey company on 4 April was a disposal of the entirety of the fund for the purposes of s 19(1)[a] of the Finance Act 1965 or, alternatively, that it was a 'gift in settlement' within s 25(2)[b] of the 1965 Act and that under s 22(4)[c] of that Act it was deemed to have been disposed of for a consideration equal to its full market value. The taxpayer appealed, contending (i) that, since on the making of the settlement his life interest in the fund remained undisposed of, there was only a part disposal of his beneficial interest in the fund within s 22(2)(b)[d] of the 1965 Act and (ii) that, since the creation of the interest in remainder in favour of the Jersey company had been for full consideration, there was no 'gift in settlement' of the fund within s 25(2) and accordingly the assessment should be reduced to the sum of £14,839. The Special Commissioners held that the assignment of the fund to the Guernsey company was a disposal of the whole fund and confirmed the assessment. The judge allowed an appeal by the taxpayer, holding that the assignment of the fund did not amount to a 'gift in settlement' of the whole fund within s 25(2), that the taxpayer and the trustees were not connected persons within para 21 of Sch 7 to the 1965 Act, that there was no consideration on which any gain could be computed other than the price paid by the Jersey company and that the assessment should be reduced to £14,839 on the basis that the taxpayer had made only a part disposal of the fund within s 22(2). The Court of Appeal upheld the judge's decision. The Crown appealed to the House of Lords.

Held – (1) Since s 25, in particular sub-s (1), of the 1965 Act proceeded on the assumption that tax was chargeable on disposals to trustees, it followed that, when the disposal of the legal title to the fund to the Guernsey company became effective on the creation of the settlement on 4 April 1972, the taxpayer as settlor was liable to capital

---

a Section 19(1), so far as material, provides: 'Tax shall be charged . . . in respect of capital gains . . . accruing to a person on the disposal of assets.'

b Section 25(2) is set out at p 633 *e f*, post

c Section 22(4), so far as material, provides: '. . . a person's acquisition of an asset and the disposal of it to him shall for the purposes of this Part of this Act be deemed to be for a consideration equal to the market value of the asset—(a) where he acquires the asset otherwise than by way of a bargain made at arm's length and in particular where he acquires it by way of gift or by way of distribution from a company in respect of shares in the company . . .'

d Section 22(2) is set out at p 634 *c*, post

gains tax on the basis that the entire fund had been disposed of. Furthermore, the life interest of the taxpayer in the fund on the creation of the settlement could not be said to be 'any description of property derived from the asset [remaining] undisposed of' within s 22(2)(b) of the 1965 Act since the wording and intention of the settlement was such that the whole interest in the fund passed to the Guernsey company and the taxpayer became entitled to a new interest, namely an interest in the trust fund (see p 633 *j* to p 634 *a d* to *g j* to p 635 *a e* to *g* and p 636 *a*, post).

(2) The asset (viz the fund) acquired by the Guernsey company was not the subject matter of a bargain between the taxpayer and the Guernsey company and accordingly the Guernsey company was to be deemed under s 22(4) of the 1965 Act to have acquired the fund otherwise than by way of a bargain made at arm's length (see p 634 *b j* to p 635 *a j* and p 636 *a*, post).

(3) It followed therefore that the taxpayer was liable to capital gains tax on the basis that on the making of the settlement the whole of the fund had been disposed of. The appeal would accordingly be allowed (see p 634 *a g* to p 635 *b g* and p 636 *a*, post).

Per Lord Wilberforce, Lord Scarman and Lord Bridge. The natural meaning of 'gift in settlement' in s 25(2) is related to the beneficial interests created, not to the legal transfer of title (see p 633 *h*, p 634 *j* to p 635 *a* and p 636 *a*, post).

Per Lord Roskill and Lord Fraser. The expression 'gift in settlement' in s 25(2) is used to distinguish a disposal of an asset to trustees of a settlement by a settlor for which the trustees give no consideration on the one hand from a disposal of an asset to trustees of a settlement by a vendor on a purchase by the trustees out of their trust fund on the other (see p 634 *h j* and p 635 *h j*, post).

Decision of the Court of Appeal [1980] 3 All ER 798 reversed.

Notes

For gifts in settlement, see 5 Halsbury's Laws (4th edn) para 50, and for the distinction between disposal and part disposal for the purposes of capital gains taxation, see ibid para 36.

For the Finance Act 1965, ss 19, 22, 25, Sch 7, para 21, see 34 Halsbury's Statutes (3rd edn) 870, 877, 884, 962.

With effect from 6 April 1979, ss 19(1), 22(2) and (4) and 25(2) of and para 21 of Sch 7 to the 1965 Act were replaced by ss 1(1), 19(2) and (3), 53 and 63 of the Capital Gains Tax Act 1979.

Appeal

The Crown appealed against an order of the Court of Appeal (Oliver and Ackner LJJ, Buckley LJ dissenting) ([1980] 3 All ER 798, [1981] 1 WLR 1) made on 15 July 1980 dismissing the Crown's appeal against an order of Goulding J ([1978] 3 All ER 267, [1978] 1 WLR 957) made on 22 March 1978 reversing a decision of the Commissioners for the Special Purposes of the Income Tax Acts on an appeal by way of case stated (set out at [1978] 3 All ER 268–273) by Norman Charles Berry (the taxpayer) reducing an assessment to capital gains tax in the sum of £150,483 for the year 1971–72 to £14,839. The facts are set out in the opinion of Lord Wilberforce.

Andrew Morritt QC and *C H McCall* for the Crown.
D C Potter QC, David Braham QC and *Thomas Ivory* for the taxpayer.

Their Lordships took time for consideration.

6 May. The following opinions were delivered.

LORD WILBERFORCE. My Lords, this is an appeal by the Crown from a majority decision of the Court of Appeal ([1980] 3 All ER 798, [1981] 1 WLR 1) in a matter of capital gains tax.

The taxpayer was the beneficial owner, in 1972, of certain shares and stock in

Rothschild Investment Trust Ltd registered partly in his name, partly in the name of nominees. His wife was also the beneficial owner of other shares and stock in the same company. It is accepted that the same result as to the incidence of capital gains tax follows as regards the taxpayer's holdings and those of his wife, and irrespective of the details of registration. I shall, therefore, deal with the case as if all relevant holdings were those of the taxpayer and registered in his name.

In March 1972 the taxpayer and his nominees executed transfers of the shares and stock in favour of a trustee in Guernsey and forwarded the transfers and certificates to the trustee or its agent.

On 4 April 1972 the taxpayer entered into a deed expressed to be a settlement made between himself, described as 'the vendor', and a Jersey company, described as 'the purchaser'. It is necessary to set out the relevant part verbatim. After reciting that the taxpayer was the beneficial owner of the stocks and shares specified in the schedule, the deed continued:

> 'AND WHEREAS the Vendor and the Purchaser have bargained and agreed for the consideration hereinafter mentioned that the same shall be settled in manner hereinafter appearing NOW THIS DEED WITNESSETH as follows:—1. "THE Trust Fund" means the said property specified in the Schedule hereto and the property for the time being representing the same. 2. IN pursuance of the said agreement and in consideration of the sum of £14,500 now paid by the Purchaser to the Vendor (the receipt whereof the Vendor hereby acknowledges) the Vendor as Beneficial Owner HEREBY ASSIGNS unto the Trustees ALL THAT the Trust Fund and the income thereof TO HOLD the same unto the Trustees absolutely and the Vendor hereby directs and declares that the Trust Fund and the income thereof shall henceforth be held after the death of the Vendor and subject in the meantime to the life interest of the Vendor and the powers and provisions hereinafter reserved and contained UPON TRUST for the Purchaser absolutely. 3. PROVIDED ALWAYS that during the life of the Vendor the Trustees shall pay the income of the Trust Fund to the Vendor for his own use and benefit absolutely.'

The deed then set out various administrative powers, including a trust for sale or retention, an investment clause and a trustees' charging clause. The schedule specified shares and loan stock in Rothschild Investment Trust Ltd.

The essence of this document was that the taxpayer assigned the specified shares and stocks, and the income thereof, to the trustees to hold on declared trusts, which included a power of sale and reinvestment, and which, beneficially, gave the income of the 'trust fund' to the taxpayer and the reversion to the purchaser.

On 6 April 1972 (ie in the next financial year 1972–73) the taxpayer executed an assignment on sale of his life interest under the settlement of 4 April 1972 to a Bahamas company for £130,753·72. This was expressed as assigning all the dividends interest and income to become payable or to accrue during the remainder of the life of the taxpayer from or in respect of 'the Trust Fund and the investments and property from time to time . . . representing the same'.

On these documents the taxpayer admits liability for capital gains tax in respect of the disposal of his reversionary interest for £14,500. He is in a position to claim (this is not before us) that no capital gains tax is payable in respect of the assignment of his life interest; this is by virtue of Sch 7, para 13 to the Finance Act 1965. But the Crown claims capital gains tax in respect of the total value of the shares and stock on the basis that they were disposed of on 4 April 1972. The taxpayer contends that on that date there was a partial disposal only, viz of his reversionary interest. The Crown's contention results in a claim for capital gains tax on the taxpayer and his wife of £150,483, the taxpayer's of £14,839.

The capital gains tax, introduced in 1965, is by now reasonably familiar and understood. (I refer throughout to the 1965 Act which applied to the transactions in question rather than to the consolidation of 1979.) But it is desirable to outline its main provisions. The tax is levied on chargeable gains accruing on the disposal of assets (see s 19). All forms of property, unless specifically exempted, rank as assets (see s 22). There is no limitation on the generality of the word 'disposal', which must be taken to bear its normal meaning. On the other hand, there are cases where certain transactions, which would not normally qualify as disposals, are deemed to be disposals. The 1965 Act dealt specifically with trusts and settlements, settled property being defined (with exceptions) as any property held in trust. In general, the scheme of the 1965 Act was to deal separately with property placed in or coming out of trust, on the one hand, and with beneficial interests under trusts on the other. There was no charge on disposals of the latter, unless by persons who have themselves acquired the interest for consideration (see Sch 7, para 13). But tax was charged when property was placed in trust (unless the trustee held it merely as nominee for the transferor) on the basis of a disposal, or when property came out of trust, more accurately, when a person became absolutely entitled as against the trustees (recent changes in the law do not apply to this case). In that case there was a deemed disposal (see s 25(3)). There was also a deemed disposal, when a life interest terminated, on the basis of a deemed disposal of all the trust assets (see s 25(4)). An acquisition and disposal was deemed to be for a consideration equal to the market value of the asset if acquired otherwise than by way of a bargain at arm's length or by way of gift. The 1965 Act also introduced the, by now familiar, concept of the trustees of a settlement as a body of persons distinct from the persons who are actually trustees.

On the basis of this scheme, which is clear and logical, one would expect that the settlement of 4 April 1972 would constitute a disposal of the assets comprised in it, and that no charge would be leviable on the immediate assignments of the life interest or the reversionary interest arising after it, though a charge might arise on a subsequent assignment. I must now, however, consider certain specific provisions on which reliance is placed.

1. Much argument revolved round s 25(2), which I quote:

> 'A gift in settlement, whether revocable or irrevocable, is a disposal of the entire property thereby becoming settled property notwithstanding that the donor has some interest as a beneficiary under the settlement and notwithstanding that he is a trustee, or the sole trustee, of the settlement.'

The taxpayer's argument is that there was no gift in settlement: a 'gift in settlement' is what it says, a gift. But there was no element of gift in the settlement of 4 April 1972, since the settlor took full value for all that he parted with, viz the reversionary interest. Against this, the Crown says that when the subsection refers to 'gift' it is fastening on the transaction as between the settlor and the trustees, so that the subsection applies so long as there is no consideration passing between these parties. The word 'gift', they contend, is used so as to exclude the case where the trustees purchase property for consideration.

Although Buckley LJ, with whose judgment I generally agree, felt able to accept this argument, I have difficulty with it. The natural meaning of gift in settlement seems to me to be related to beneficial interests created, not to the legal transfer of title. I find the same words used in s 31(3) together with 'gift' where the latter is clearly directed towards the donee, suggesting that the former are similarly directed. So, however much I may suspect (as I do) that 'gift' is a draftsman's error for 'transfer', I am reluctant, in a taxing Act, to depart from the natural meaning of the words. However, I do not regard s 25(2) as decisive of the issue for another reason. It does not appear to me that this is the basic provision on which settlements are taxed. Rather I read it as a special provision dealing with the cases where a donor, ie a person who gives some interest beneficially under a settlement, has himself a beneficial interest and where the donor is himself a trustee. Neither is this case, and the Crown does not need to rely on the subsection. There is here simply a disposal, a disposal in March 1972 of the legal title to the shares and loan stock, itself liable to be disregarded, under s 22(5), as conferring only a nominee interest, but becoming an effective disposal when, on 4 April 1972, trusts were declared other than in favour of the settlor, thus making the shares and loan stock settled property. I think that the whole of s 25, particularly s 25(1), proceeds on the assumption that the tax attaches to disposals in favour of trustees, and that sub-ss (2), (3) and (4) are special cases. In my opinion there was a disposal on 4 April 1972 of the shares and stock by the taxpayer which attracts a charge for capital gains tax.

2. There is no difficulty that I can see in fixing the amount on which tax is charged. This is dealt with by s 22(4). I agree with Oliver and Buckley LJJ (who though differing in the ultimate conclusion agreed on this) that the asset (ie the shares and stock) were acquired (sc by the trustee) otherwise than by way of a bargain made at arm's length. The existence of a bargain between the taxpayer and a third party, the purchaser of the reversion, is, in my opinion, irrelevant in this context.

3. The final provision relied on, this time by the taxpayer, is s 22(2)(b). Section 22(2) is as follows:

> 'For the purposes of this Part of this Act—(a) references to a disposal of an asset include, except where the context otherwise requires, references to a part disposal of an asset, and (b) there is a part disposal of an asset where an interest or right in or over the asset is created by the disposal, as well as where it subsists before the disposal, and generally, there is a part disposal of an asset where, on a person making a disposal, any description of property derived from the asset remains undisposed of.'

The technical argument revolves round the latter words of para (b), 'any description of property derived from the asset remains undisposed of'. The taxpayer argues that the life interest satisfied these words: it was an interest in the asset and so an interest derived from the asset. The Crown, on the other hand, contends that there was nothing undisposed of: the wording and intention of the settlement was such that the whole interest in the shares and stock passed to the trustees, and the settlor became entitled to a new interest, namely an interest in the trust fund.

It is to be noticed first, that s 22(2) is not, on its face, a relieving section; it is not a section directed at cutting down what might otherwise be a total disposal to a partial disposal. It seems rather, as para (a) makes clear, to be a provision of extension, enabling something which might not be regarded as a disposal to be taxed as a part disposal. Where there is a clear total disposal, the subsection does not attach. However, if the taxpayer can bring himself within its wording, he is entitled to do so, even if the result may seem unexpected. But I have no doubt that the Crown's argument is correct. The whole tenor and purpose of the document of 4 April 1972 was to put the shares and stock into settlement or trust; to do so was essential in order to enable the taxpayer to obtain exemption on the sale of his life interest. This was only obtainable if he could be shown to have 'an interest created by or arising under a settlement' (see Sch 7, para 13). He cannot (though counsel bravely so contended) at one and the same time assert this and also maintain that he retained or reserved something undisposed of. I cannot, therefore, on any view accept that here there was only a part disposal.

Since, on these grounds, I am of opinion that the Crown's appeal must succeed, it is not necessary to consider a further argument based on the existence of 'connected persons'.

I would uphold the judgment of Buckley LJ, allow the appeal and restore the decision of the Special Commissioners.

LORD FRASER OF TULLYBELTON. My Lords, I have had the advantage of reading in draft the speeches prepared by my noble and learned friends Lord Wilberforce and Lord Roskill. I agree with Lord Roskill that the appeal should be allowed for both the reasons mentioned by him. I agree with Lord Wilberforce except on the question of a 'gift in settlement'. I would allow the appeal.

LORD SCARMAN. My Lords, for the reasons given by my noble and learned friend Lord Wilberforce, a draft of whose speech I have had the opportunity of studying, I would allow the appeal. Like Lord Wilberforce, I do not accept the Crown's submission as to the meaning of 'a gift in settlement' in s 25(2) of the Finance Act 1965, but the point is no longer of importance in view of the recent amendment of the subsections.

LORD ROSKILL. My Lords, in common with all your Lordships I agree that this appeal should be allowed and the determination by the Special Commissioners restored. But there has been a wide difference of opinion in this case and therefore in deference to the judgments of Goulding J ([1978] 3 All ER 267, [1978] 1 WLR 957) and of Oliver and Ackner LJJ in the Court of Appeal ([1980] 3 All ER 798, [1981] 1 WLR 1) I add some observations of my own. My noble and learned friend Lord Wilberforce has recited the relevant facts and set out the relevant statutory provisions and I do not repeat them.

The first question is whether the settlement of 4 April 1972 was a disposal for the purposes of s 19 or whether the taxpayer can claim that there was no more than a part disposal within s 22(2)(b). The majority in the Court of Appeal took the latter view, holding that the settlement reserved 'from the beneficial interest the absolute right to payment of income during the vendor's life' (see [1980] 3 All ER 798 at 806, [1981] 1 WLR 1 at 11 per Oliver LJ). Therefore, so the reasoning ran, the life interest remained undisposed of. The absolute right to receive the income was, again to quote Oliver LJ, 'cut . . . down to a life interest only'. Ackner LJ spoke of the taxpayer 'retaining a life interest in the same property' (see [1980] 3 All ER 798 at 809, [1981] 1 WLR 1 at 15).

My Lords, the correctness or otherwise of this conclusion must, I think, depend on the true construction of the settlement. The settlement recited that the vendor, that is the taxpayer, was the beneficial owner of the securities listed in the schedule and that he had agreed that those securities should be settled on the terms of the settlement as thereinafter provided. Then in cl 1 the trust fund is defined as representing the securities listed in the schedule and property from time to time representing those securities. It is cll 2 and 3 and only those clauses which, to my mind, created the taxpayer's life interest in the income of the trust fund and from 4 April 1972 onwards the taxpayer had no right of disposal of those securities or of any securities substituted for them. His only other right was to appoint a trustee: see cl 6. For my part I cannot construe this settlement as bringing about the retention of a life interest by the taxpayer. I think he parted with everything for the stated consideration and independently acquired the life interest created by cll 2 and 3. I am unable to regard the life interest as falling within the phrase in s 22(2)(b) 'any description of property derived from the asset [remaining] undisposed of'.

My Lords, on this question I find the reasoning of Buckley LJ ([1980] 3 All ER 798 at 813–814, [1981] 1 WLR 1 at 20–21) compelling. I agree with him and with my noble and learned friend Lord Wilberforce that there was on 4 April 1972 an entire disposal of the scheduled securities to the trustees of the settlement.

My Lords, I think the Crown is also entitled to succeed on the other principal question which was argued: whether or not there was a 'gift in settlement' within s 25(2). My noble and learned friend Lord Wilberforce has rehearsed the rival arguments and I do not repeat them. The phrase is indeed a strange one and the draftsman has refrained from giving it a definition. It is, of course, irrelevant that, as counsel informed your Lordships, this subsection has recently been amended so that at least for the future its obscurities have been removed. At first sight the word 'gift' would seem to be used in its ordinary meaning and it is forcibly argued that there was no element of gift in the settlement of 4 April 1972. But to my mind the reasoning of Buckley LJ ([1980] 3 All ER 798 at 811–814, [1981] 1 WLR 1 at 18–22) is once again compelling; I do not repeat it. I would respectfully adopt it as my own.

My Lords, it is for both these reasons that I would allow this appeal by the Crown. On the only remaining point, I respectfully agree with my noble and learned friend Lord Wilberforce as well as with both Buckley and Oliver LJJ in the Court of Appeal, that the scheduled securities were acquired by the trustees otherwise than by way of a bargain made at arm's length.

LORD BRIDGE OF HARWICH. My Lords, I have had the advantage of reading in advance the speech of my noble and learned friend Lord Wilberforce. I agree with it and *a* for the reasons he gives I too would allow the appeal.

Appeal allowed.

Solicitors: *Solicitor of Inland Revenue; Norton Rose, Botterell & Roche* (for the taxpayer).

b

Rengan Krishnan Esq   Barrister.

Southwark London Borough Council v C (a minor) and another
C (minors) v Martin and another

c

FAMILY DIVISION
ARNOLD P AND EWBANK J
8 FEBRUARY 1982

d

Children and young persons – Care proceedings in juvenile court – Care order – Appeal – Who may appeal – Child represented in juvenile court by solicitor instructed independently of parents – Whether parents can nevertheless appeal to Crown Court on behalf of child – Children and Young Persons Act 1969, s 2(12) – Magistrates' Courts (Children and Young Persons) Rules 1970, r 17(1)(a).

e

In proceedings in a juvenile court in which a care order was made under s 1 of the Children and Young Persons Act 1969, the child concerned was represented by a solicitor instructed independently of his parents. The parents wished to appeal, under s 2(12) of the 1969 Act, to the Crown Court on the child's behalf against the order. The question arose whether they were prevented from doing so by r 17(1)(a)[a] of the Magistrates' *f* Courts (Children and Young Persons) Rules 1970, which provided that, except where the relevant infant was legally represented, the court was to allow his parent or guardian to conduct the case on his behalf.

Held – On its true construction, r 17 of the 1970 rules only applied to proceedings in the juvenile court, so that the fact that the child had been separately represented in proceedings in that court did not affect the parents' right, under s 2(12) of the 1969 Act, *g* to appeal to the Crown Court on his behalf against a care order made by the juvenile court (see p 639 *f* and p 640 *b c f g*, post).
    B v Gloucestershire CC [1980] 2 All ER 746 considered.

Notes
For appeal against a care order, see 24 Halsbury's Laws (4th edn) para 773.

h

    For the Children and Young Persons Act 1969, ss 1, 2, see 40 Halsbury's Statutes (3rd edn) 849, 852.
    For the Magistrates' Courts (Children and Young Persons) Rules 1970, r 17, see 11 Halsbury's Statutory Instruments (3rd reissue) 356.

Case referred to in judgment
B v Gloucestershire CC [1980] 2 All ER 746, DC.

j

---

a   Rule 17(1), so far as material, is set out at p 639 *d*, post

Cases also cited

R v Northampton Justices, ex p McElkennon (1976) 120 SJ 677, DC.
R v Worthing Justices, ex p Stevenson [1976] 2 All ER 194, DC.
W (a minor), Re (1981) Times, 16 June, CA.

Cases stated

These were two appeals by case stated: (i) by the Crown Court at Inner London Sessions (his Honour Judge MacLean sitting with justices) in respect of its adjudication on an appeal from a decision of a juvenile court for the petty sessional division of West Central, Inner London, making a care order under s 1 of the Children and Young Persons Act 1969 in favour of the present appellants, Southwark London Borough Council, in respect of the first respondent, the child of the second respondent; (ii) by the Crown Court at Doncaster (his Honour Judge Barker sitting with justices) in respect of its adjudication on an appeal to the court from a decision of a juvenile court sitting at Doncaster, making a care order under s 1 of the 1969 Act in favour of the second respondent, the Doncaster Metropolitan Borough Council, in respect of the present appellants, the children of the first respondents, Mr and Mrs Martin. Both cases raised the same point of law. The facts are set out in the judgment of Arnold P.

Gayle Hallon for Southwark London Borough Council.
Graham Lodge for the minor in the first appeal.
Robert Good for the mother of the minor in the first appeal.
Timothy Clayson for the minors in the second appeal.
Trevor Barber for the parents of the minors in the second appeal.
James Goss for Doncaster Metropolitan Borough Council.
Paul Collins as amicus curiae.

ARNOLD P. We have before us two appeals by way of case stated. One is an appeal from the Crown Court at Inner London Sessions in the case of *Southwark London Borough Council v C (a minor) and C*. The other comes from the Crown Court at Doncaster, and is, or at any rate I think should be, entitled *C (minors) v Martin and the Doncaster Metropolitan Borough Council*.

Both appeals raise the same point, which is, shortly put, this: whether a parent, who is generally entitled to exercise, on behalf of an infant minor child, that child's right under s 2(12) of the Children and Young Persons Act 1969 to appeal to the Crown Court against a care order made under s 1, is nevertheless still entitled to do so notwithstanding that in the proceedings before the juvenile court in which the care order was made the child was represented by solicitors instructed independently of the parent.

The basic proposition built into that formulation of the question is of course that the parent in the ordinary way does have such a right, and that was decided quite specifically in *B v Gloucestershire CC* [1980] 2 All ER 746 by a Divisional Court of the Queen's Bench Division. But that was not a case in which the infant had been represented in the juvenile court independently of the parent. It is plain that the appeal is the child's appeal, by whomsoever it may be conducted on behalf of the child; and, if there is, as perhaps there might be, in the headnote in the report of the *Gloucestershire* case a suggestion that somehow what was being said in that case was that the appeal was not the child's appeal being conducted on its behalf by the parent, then that suggestion would be misleading.

The facts in the present cases which give rise to the question are these.

In the Southwark case, the local authority brought the child before the Southwark North Juvenile Court under s 1(1) of the Children and Young Persons Act 1969 against the background that there was a place of safety order in existence, although I think that cannot alter the situation; and on the same day, 19 December 1980, on an application by the local authority to the justices' clerk, legal aid was granted to the child, and for legal aid purposes a certain firm of solicitors was nominated to represent the child. Then in

February 1981 the effective hearing before the juvenile court took place, and the solicitors who had been thus nominated instructed counsel to appear for the child, as they were, at any rate for legal aid purposes, fully entitled to do. The local authority were of course represented, and the child's mother was also represented, by a different firm of solicitors of course, also instructing counsel; and there is no question or doubt that at that stage the mother's representation was for herself, and not for the child.

The relevant finding that the proper development of the infant was being avoidably prevented or neglected, or his health was being avoidably impaired or neglected, or he was being ill-treated and that he was in need of care and control which he was unlikely to receive unless an order under the section was made, was duly found by the justices who made a care order. Now, it is that finding which it is sought to attack in the appeal.

The representing counsel instructed by the solicitor of the child at the hearing before the juvenile court did not oppose the making of the order and by inference therefore did not oppose the finding because the solicitor, no doubt with the advice of the counsel, or the two together, came to the conclusion that it was not in the interests of the child to oppose the application. Not surprisingly, therefore, no appeal on behalf of the child against the care order was launched by that solicitor. The mother, however, objected to the finding and in due time she filed notice of intention to appeal, but she filed notice of intention to appeal on her own behalf. And thus the matter stood when on 6 July 1981 the appeal came before the Crown Court. The child was represented by the solicitor or on behalf of the solicitor and by counsel instructed by the solicitor who had originally been nominated in the juvenile court as the legal aid solicitor. The local authority were also represented and so was the mother. She at that point saw the danger that she might be in of appealing on her own behalf, and applied for leave to amend her notice of appeal to recite, as it is said in the case stated, that she on behalf of the infant intended to appeal against the care order. And that brought up the preliminary point which comes to this court on the case stated, which was decided by the Crown Court in favour of the view that the mother had the right to appeal notwithstanding the history of the representation of the child in the juvenile court.

Well, that may have perhaps been a little complicated, but its complications shade into insignificance in comparison with the facts in the other appeal. In that appeal, there are concerned altogether six children. The three eldest are the appellants before us, or at any rate that is what the appeal purports to show. And those are the three eldest children of the family of the respondents, Mr and Mrs Martin. They also have three younger children. In this case, the Doncaster Metropolitan Borough Council having commenced care proceedings on 9 April 1981 in respect of all the children, the magistrates in the juvenile court, when the matter came before them, took the view that there was a potential conflict of interest between the children and the parents, and therefore made a legal aid order which nominated as the legal aid solicitor Mr Kitson to act on behalf of all six children. He considered the matter and came to the conclusion that, acting as he was bound to do in the best interests of the children, his duty was not to oppose the making of a care order on behalf of the three eldest children but, equally regarding his duty, he submitted that the case was not made out as regards the three youngest children. He said that no care order should be made in respect of them and that they should be sent home. But his representations on behalf of the three youngest were not successful and all six children were made the subject of care orders.

On 16 June 1981, which was in due time, the parents issued a notice of appeal in relation to each of the six children, or perhaps a collective notice in relation to all of them. We have not seen that document. This raised the same problem of course as that to which I have referred in relation to the Southwark case; and this problem having occurred to the chief clerk of the Crown Court at Doncaster he communicated with the solicitor who had appeared for the children in the juvenile court and suggested to him that he too should lodge a notice of appeal on behalf of all six children, which he did. And so on 7 August 1981 when the matter came before the Crown Court there were two notices of appeal, each of them covering all six cases. The matter was argued on behalf of the children by the solicitor who had been instructed for them in the juvenile court;

and on behalf of the parents in support of their notice of appeal against the six care orders. So it was that two legal aid orders were made in the Crown Court. One legal aid order was made, according to the notice of appeal, in favour of the solicitor who had been involved in the juvenile court proceedings for the children and that related to the three youngest children. Another legal aid order was made in relation to solicitors instructed by the parents as regards the appeals on behalf of the three eldest children. The difficulty which arose of course was that, as in the Southwark case, there was as regards the three eldest children in the Doncaster case a purported appeal by the parents against the care orders made in the juvenile court in respect of the children on whose behalf they were purporting to appeal at a time when those children were represented before the juvenile court by a solicitor who was not instructed by the parents and who did not oppose the making of the orders.

The same question is therefore raised in that case.

It is necessary to refer very briefly, and only very briefly, to the statutory provisions and the rules. Under s 1 of the Children and Young Persons Act 1969 the jurisdiction to make a care order is conferred on the juvenile court if certain findings are made; the findings are listed in sub-s (2) and they are of course alternatives. If a care order is made, then under section 2(12) the child may appeal to the Crown Court in every case (except one irrelevant one which it is not necessary to refer to) and the appeal is plainly, therefore, the appeal of the child. Now, there is nothing in the rules which specifically relates to appeals, but r 17(1) of the Magistrates' Courts (Children and Young Persons) Rules 1970, SI 1970/1792, provides:

> 'Except where—(a) the relevant infant or his parent or guardian is legally represented [or certain other events which are not material] the court shall, unless the relevant infant otherwise requests, allow his parent or guardian to conduct the case on his behalf . . .'

That suggests that if the child is legally represented that instruction to the court does not apply. Now, the court, there is no doubt, is the juvenile court because that is so provided in r 2(1) of the rules, and it does seem therefore that, where a provision is made that the juvenile court should allow the parent to conduct the case on a child's behalf, what must be being referred to is the case being conducted before the juvenile court; and I can find nothing in any provision in these rules to suggest that that is not what r 17 is dealing with.

Whatever r 17 does therefore, what it does not do, in my judgment, is to make any provision in terms for the conduct of a case on appeal from the juvenile court, or for the persons who should be permitted to have the conduct of that case, that is to say the conduct of that case on behalf of the infant whose appeal it is under s 2(12) of the 1969 Act.

It is suggested that the provisions of s 30(5) of the Legal Aid Act 1974 militate against that conclusion because they extend the ambit of a legal aid order granted for the purpose of proceedings before a magistrates' court to include the giving of advice on the merits of an appeal and assistance by the solicitor in giving notice of appeal or making an application for a case stated. Therefore, it is suggested that because this is so the ambit of r 17 of the 1970 rules extends at least so far as the relevant section or subsection of the 1974 Act, that it extends therefore to giving the conduct of the appeal up to and including the notice of appeal and that therefore, as a matter, I suppose, of necessary extension, it applies to the appeal throughout, or, if as a matter of implication the parents are excluded from giving a notice of appeal, so it must follow that they have no hand in the appeal of the infant at all.

It is relevant to refer to the legal aid provisions, as I think, for the reason that somewhat surprisingly there is no power presently exercisable in the juvenile court to direct the choice of representation of the child as between solicitors instructed without benefit of legal aid nominated by the court and solicitors similarly instructed by the parents. That will all change one day when, or perhaps I should say if, the provisions of the new s 32A(1) of the Children and Young Persons Act 1969 imported by s 64 of the Children Act 1975 are brought into operation; then there will be, where there is a conflict, or allegedly a conflict, between parent and child, provision for the appointment of a guardian ad litem and that appointment will extend not only to the conduct of the proceedings before the juvenile court but also to any appeal consequent thereon, and the new r 14A of the 1970 rules has been helpfully devised to deal with that contingency of the section being brought into operation.

It was remarked in *B v Gloucestershire CC*, [1980] 2 All ER 746 at 748 that the section had not been brought into operation, and the court noted that there was no known reason for that. Their inability to discern the reason is one that I share. But as it stands, it is only by implication from the fact that legal aid is given to an independent solicitor so-called that one is to infer that that is how the juvenile court thinks the case should be conducted. No such clear indication is available how such a matter might be regulated if the parents are prepared to pay for legal representation for their child. Perhaps that is the untypical case.

But, although the ambit of the legal aid order extends to advising on and giving notice of appeal, it does not seem to me to follow from that that the right clearly recognised, and in my judgment rightly recognised by the Queen's Bench Divisional Court in the *Gloucestershire* case, of parents to operate the child's right of appeal on the child's behalf is abrogated merely because the child has been represented by solicitors in the juvenile court instructed separately from and independently of the parents. It is not suggested that the exclusion operates only in a case in which the independent solicitor did not oppose the making of a care order; and presumably therefore where the solicitor opposed, and unsuccessfully opposed, the making of a care order, and for one reason or another did not or was not in a position to appeal, if this exclusion operates the parents would be equally helpless to pursue the appeal on behalf of the child. And there could be no logic for that. Nor does it seem possible to evolve a theory of law which would justify the parents' right to forward the child's appeal being excluded if, but only if, a particular line was taken on behalf of the child by the independent solicitor before the juvenile court. There does not seem to be any jurisprudential basis for that sort of distinction.

How far in the course of presenting the appeal it might or might not be regarded as legitimate by the Crown Court that there should be put forward on behalf of the child arguments which were not put forward on behalf of the child in the tribunal appealed from is a matter which the Crown Court will no doubt regulate according to the ordinary principles. But, although it may be that objection could be taken to that course of conduct, I know of no principle which says that an objection of that sort would necessarily and in all circumstances be upheld. But that cannot have anything to do with the question of the right of audience of the parents acting on behalf of the child.

It seems to me that, at the end of it all, this matter falls to be resolved on a perfectly simple basis, namely that there is the right of the parents to prosecute the appeal on behalf of the child recognised by the *Gloucestershire* case, and that on the true construction of r 17 there is nothing to make that right inapplicable in the circumstance with which this case is concerned, namely that of a separate representation in the juvenile court; what is in question concerns only the appeal. I would therefore dismiss both appeals.

EWBANK J. I agree with Arnold P and I too would dismiss these appeals.

Appeals dismissed.

Solicitors: *J B Parker*, Camberwell (for Southwark London Borough Council); *Sabine Read & Co*, Catford (for the minor in the first appeal); *Gaiso & Co* (for the mother of the minor in the first appeal); *Ward Bracewell & Co*, Doncaster (for the minors in the second appeal); *Frank Allen & Co*, Doncaster (for the parents of the minors in the second appeal); *William Bugler*, Doncaster (for Doncaster Metropolitan Borough Council); *Official Solicitor*.

Bebe Chua   Barrister.

Nottinghamshire County Council v Q

a

FAMILY DIVISION
ARNOLD P AND EASTHAM J
22 FEBRUARY 1982

Children and young persons – Detention – Place of safety order – Appeal – Parents not having
b *right of appeal against place of safety order – Parents applying to justices for interim care order*
as device to obtain child's release from detention – Whether application abuse of court's process
– Children and Young Persons Act 1969, s 28(1)(6).

A local authority obtained a place of safety order under s 28(1)[a] of the Children and
Young Persons Act 1969 in respect of a young child, on the ground that he was being ill-
treated at home, and detained him under the order. Before the authority had reached a
c decision on the child's future the parents, who had no right of appeal against the place of
safety order, applied to the magistrates for an interim care order in respect of the child,
purporting to do so under s 28(6) of the 1969 Act. They admitted to the magistrates that
the application was an attempt to appeal against the place of safety order and that the
purpose of the application was not to obtain an interim care order but to persuade the
court to refuse to make such an order and direct the child's immediate release from
d detention. The magistrates treated the application as being duly made under s 28(6) and,
having heard evidence from the parents, the social worker and a doctor who had
examined the child, concluded that the child would not be at risk if it was returned to its
parents and therefore, pursuant to s 28(6), refused to make an interim care order and
directed that the child be released by the local authority forthwith. The local authority
appealed.

e

Held – The deliberate use of s 28(6) of the 1969 Act as a device for appealing against a
place of safety order made under s 28(1) when Parliament did not intend that s 28(6)
should be so used would frustrate the will of Parliament and therefore amounted to an
abuse of the court's process. The magistrates should therefore have declined to entertain
the application. The appeal would accordingly be allowed (see p 643 *d e g* to p 644 *a*,
post).

Dictum of Lord Widgery CJ in *R v Justice for Lincoln (Kesteven), ex p M (a minor)* [1976]
1 All ER at 494 applied.

Notes
For a place of safety order, see 24 Halsbury's Laws (4th edn) para 776, and for persons who
may apply to a juvenile court for a care order, see ibid para 729.

For the Children and Young Persons Act 1969, s 28, see 40 Halsbury's Statutes (3rd
edn) 887.

Case referred to in judgments
R v Justice for Lincoln (Kesteven), ex p M (a minor) [1976] 1 All ER 490, [1976] QB 957,
[1976] 2 WLR 143, DC, Digest (Cont Vol E) 330, 2451a.

---

a   Section 28, so far as material, provides:
    '(1) If, upon an application to a justice by a person for authority to detain a child or young
    person and take him to a place of safety, the justice is satisfied that the applicant has reasonable
    cause to believe that—(a) any of the conditions set out in section 1(2)(a) to (e) of this Act is satisfied
    in respect of the child or young person . . . the justice may grant the application; and the child or
    young person in respect of whom an authorisation is issued under this subsection may be detained
    in a place of safety by virtue of the authorisation for twenty-eight days beginning with the date of
    authorisation, or for such shorter period beginning with that date as may be specified in the
    authorisation . . .
    (6) If while a person is detained in pursuance of this section an application for an interim order
    in respect of him is made to a magistrates' court or a justice, the court or justice shall either make
    or refuse to make the order and, in the case of a refusal, may direct that he be released forthwith.'

Case stated

This was a case stated by justices sitting at Nottingham. On 22 June 1981 the justices *a* heard an application by the parents of a boy, born on 2 July 1978, in respect of whom a place of safety order under s 28(1) of the Children and Young Persons Act 1969 had been made by a single justice on the application of Nottinghamshire County Council (the local authority), for an interim care order in respect of the child. The application purported to be made under s 28(6) of the 1969 Act.

The justices found the following material facts on the hearing of the parents' *b* application. Although in form the application was for an interim care order, in fact the parents wished to secure the child's release from detention by the local authority under the place of safety order and it was stated on their behalf that their application was a legal fiction. The boy was the only child of the parents. He had been diagnosed as deaf and as a result suffered from behavioural difficulties, in particular from temper tantrums. The parents were able to communicate with him by sign language, the mother having *c* attended sign language classes. From time to time the boy suffered bruising as a result of his difficulties. On 13 June 1981 he fell off a swing made by his father. On the same day his parents took him swimming. After the swim his father took him into the changing room where he had a temper tantrum. The father did not tell the wife of the incident but that evening she noticed bruising on the child's face. On 15 June a social worker saw bruising on the child and interviewed the mother about it. The social *d* worker was not satisfied with the mother's explanation of the bruising and, the child having been taken to a doctor, the local authority applied for a place of safety order in respect of the child, which was granted. A doctor who examined the child on 17 June found four bruises on the child's cheek and a bruise at the bottom of his back. He thought it unlikely the cheek bruises were caused by slapping or a fall and that the bruise on the back had not been caused by shaking but was more likely to have been caused by *e* a temper tantrum. Prior to the incident in the changing room there had been no suggestion of any non-accidental injuries caused to the child.

The justices were of the opinion that s 28(6) of the 1969 Act did not prohibit an application for an interim care order being made by the parent of a child detained under a place of safety order, and that as there was no right of appeal against a place of safety order a parent's only means of challenging such an order was by applying for an interim *f* care order under s 28(6) and then asking the court to release the child from detention. Once such an application was made it was for the court to decide on the evidence what was the appropriate order to make. That view was supported by Feldman *Care Proceedings* (1978) p 12. The justices further took the view that it was not in the child's interests to delay hearing the parents' application, and that, as the justices were in a position to hear evidence from the parents, the doctor who had examined the child and *g* the social worker, they could reach a reasonable and judicial decision on the application. Having heard all the evidence and submissions the justices concluded that the child would not be at risk if he were returned to his parents and accordingly declined to make an interim care order and directed that the child should be released from detention by the local authority forthwith.

The questions for the opinion of the court were: (1) whether on the proper construction *h* of s 28(6) of the 1969 Act the justices were correct in law in holding that an application thereunder could be made by a parent of a child detained under s 28(1); (2) whether they were correct in law in holding that an application for an interim order had been duly made by the parents; (3) whether in the absence of representation on behalf of the child their decision to hear and determine the application was one which a reasonable bench of justices could have reached; and (4) whether on the evidence the exercise of the court's *j* discretion by directing the child's release from detention was one which a reasonable bench of justices could have reached.

John Mitchell for the local authority.
The parents did not appear.

EASTHAM J delivered the first judgment at the invitation of Arnold P. In this case, the appellant local authority, the Nottinghamshire County Council, obtained a place of safety order in respect of a young child. During the subsistence of that place of safety order and before a case conference had taken place with a view to deciding, inter alia, whether or not to pursue an application for a care order under s 1 of the Children and Young Persons Act 1969, the parents, purporting to act under s 28(6) of the 1969 Act, applied to the justices for the petty sessional division of Nottingham sitting in Nottingham for an interim care order. Section 28(6) reads:

> 'If while a person is detained in pursuance of this section an application for an interim order in respect of him is made to a magistrates' court or a justice, the court or justice shall either make or refuse to make the order and, in the case of a refusal, may direct that he be released forthwith.'

There is in fact no right of appeal whatsoever vested in a parent against a place of safety order, and what was done in this case, as the solicitor who was appearing on behalf of the parents frankly admitted to the bench, was to make an application under this section for an interim order, not because the parents wanted an interim order but because they wanted exactly the opposite; and, if the opposite result was achieved and no such order was made, then of course there was power for the direction by the justices that the child should be released forthwith. In other words, the solicitor was attempting to devise a method of providing an appeal against a place of safety order which Parliament had not conferred in the 1969 Act. In my judgment, in spite of the frankness which one would expect from an officer of the court, this was simply an abuse of the process of the court and the justices should have declined to entertain the so-called application for an interim order on any basis. And in those circumstances, on that ground alone, I for my part would allow this appeal.

There is a further point of importance in that counsel for the local authority has submitted that, notwithstanding the decision of a Divisional Court of the Queen's Bench Division in *R v Justice for Lincoln (Kesteven), ex p M (a minor)* [1976] 1 All ER 490, [1976] QB 957, when one analyses the provisions of the 1969 Act, only certain specified people can invoke the interim order procedure and those are the local authority, the National Society for the Prevention of Cruelty to Children and a constable. For my part, I would be reluctant to go into the matter as the decision of the Queen's Bench Divisional Court deserves the utmost respect from this court, and I for my part would think it more appropriate for the Court of Appeal to come to the conclusion that *Lincoln* was wrongly decided on that point.

ARNOLD P. I agree. In the case stated, it is said that the application was 'duly made' by the parents for an interim care order, and the justices find as a fact that the application was brought under s 28(6) of the Children and Young Persons Act 1969 in the form that an interim order be made in respect of the child, whereas in fact the parents wished to secure the release of the child and it was stated on their behalf that the application was a legal fiction. It seems to me impossible to say that the application was duly made if indeed the making of it was an abuse of the process of the court; and, if it was an abuse of the process of the court, then in my judgment the application was not made in the sense that its result could be regarded as satisfactory.

In *R v Justice for Lincoln (Kesteven), ex p M (a minor)* [1976] 1 All ER 490, [1976] QB 957, to which Eastham J has referred, Lord Widgery CJ refers to what is within the relevant area an abuse of the process of the court (see [1976] 1 All ER 490 at 494, [1976] QB 957 at 963), and later on he defines as an abuse something done which was quite inconsistent with the intention of Parliament, using a section of an Act of Parliament for a purpose which Parliament had never intended it to be used for, and deliberately so using it with a view to frustrating the true will of Parliament as expressed in the Act (see [1976] 1 All ER 490 at 494–495, [1976] QB 957 at 964). This is not a very good Act, as I suppose everybody now recognises. Indeed, it is a pity, as I think is now universally thought, that

there is no right of appeal from a place of safety order under s 28(1), but two wrongs do
not make a right and, if s 28(6) was provided for the purpose there stated of applying for
an interim order, its use for a different purpose altogether seems to me to come within
the definition of Lord Widgery CJ.

For my part, I would agree that the appeal should be allowed.

Appeal allowed.

Solicitors: *A Sandford*, Nottingham (for the local authority).

Bebe Chua   Barrister.

Leedale (Inspector of Taxes) v Lewis
Toovey v Pepper (Inspector of Taxes)
and related appeals

COURT OF APPEAL, CIVIL DIVISION
LAWTON, BRIGHTMAN AND FOX LJJ
28, 29, 30 OCTOBER, 2 NOVEMBER, 16 DECEMBER 1981

*Capital gains tax – Settlement – Interest in settled property – Gains accruing to non-resident
trustee – Apportionment of gains to beneficiaries – Beneficiaries resident in United Kingdom –
Trustee having power to pay income and appoint capital to beneficiaries – Beneficiaries equally
entitled to capital contingently on being alive at end of perpetuity period specified in settlement
– Whether beneficiaries having 'interests in the settled property' – Whether apportionment of
gains to beneficiaries 'just and reasonable' – Finance Act 1965, s 42(2).*

In the first case the settlor, who was domiciled and resident in the United Kingdom,
directed the non-resident trustees of the settlement to hold the capital and income of the
trust fund on such trusts for such members of a specified class as the trustees might
appoint. The class included, among others, all the settlor's grandchildren and remoter
issue born within a defined perpetuity period. The settlement gave the trustees the
power to apply income for the benefit of any members of the class or to accumulate it.
Any fund undistributed at the close of the perpetuity period was to go to such of the
grandchildren and remoter issue of the settlor then living per stirpes and, subject thereto,
to the settlor's son and daughter equally. Immediately after the creation of the settlement
the settlor delivered a letter of intent to the trustees indicating that she wished her
grandchildren to be regarded as the primary beneficiaries under the settlement and to
receive income at the age of 21 and capital at 30. At all material times the only potential
beneficiaries of the settlement in existence were the settlor's five minor grandchildren
and their respective parents and guardians who were the settlor's son and daughter. No
distribution of capital or income had been made by the trustees. The taxpayers, as
parents and guardians of the grandchildren, were assessed to capital gains tax in respect
of gains realised by the trustees on the basis that under s 42(2)[a] of the Finance Act 1965
those gains were apportionable among the settlor's grandchildren equally. The taxpayers
appealed to the Special Commissioners, contending, inter alia, that the grandchildren, as
objects of a discretionary trust or power, did not have 'interests in the settled property'
within s 42(2). The commissioners allowed the appeal, holding that, even if the
grandchildren each had an 'interest', their interests were negligible, and, therefore the

---

a   Section 42(2) is set out at p 647 *f* to *h*, post

just and reasonable course was not to apportion any part of the gain to them. The Crown
appealed, contending that under s 42(2) apportionment of chargeable gains realised by a
non-resident trustee between persons having 'interests in the settled property' in the
United Kingdom was mandatory, that the possible defeasance of a defeasible interest was
to be disregarded, that 'defeasible interest' within s 42(2) included all contingent interests,
however remote the contingencies, that the five grandchildren had, therefore, 'interests
in the settled property' within s 42(2) and that since those interests were of broadly equal
value the chargeable gains of the trustees fell to be apportioned equally between the five
grandchildren.

In the second case, the settlor, who was domiciled and resident in the United Kingdom,
settled property on discretionary trusts for the benefit of the settlor's children or remoter
issue then living or born during the trust period. The same beneficiaries were also to
take as remaindermen if no appointment of capital or income was made before the end
of the trust period. The only living potential beneficiaries were the settlor's five adult
children, who were assessed to capital gains tax under s 42(2) of the 1965 Act on gains
made by the non-resident trustees. The gains were apportioned among them equally.
The General Commissioners dismissed an appeal by the beneficiaries. The beneficiaries
appealed.

The judge held that the assessments in both cases had been properly made, that the
interests of the beneficiaries did not include their respective rights or expectations as
possible objects of the trustees' discretionary power over income or of their overriding
powers of appointment, that the only interests of the beneficiaries to which s 42(2)
applied were their interests contingent on their being alive at the end of the trust period
and that the words 'just and reasonable' governed the selection of persons among whom
the apportionment was to be made. The taxpayers in the first case and the beneficiaries
in the second case appealed.

Held – (1) The words 'any beneficiary' in s 42(2) of the 1965 Act were wide enough to
include the object of a discretionary power under a settlement, and 'any beneficiary' and
'interests' were so closely connected in s 42(2) that the rights under the settlement which
qualified the holder to be described as a 'beneficiary' also qualified to be described as
'interests' for the purpose of the subsection (see p 648 j to p 649 a, post); *Gartside v IRC*
[1968] 1 All ER 121 distinguished.

(2) On the true construction of s 42(2), the amount to be apportioned was the whole
of the amount of the gain to which the trustees would have been chargeable, the words
'just and reasonable' relating solely to the mode of apportionment between the persons
having interests and not to the amount to be apportioned; and, since s 42(2) required that
the 'just and reasonable' apportionment was to be made as near as might be according to
the value of the beneficiaries' interests, to that extent the circumstances of individual
beneficiaries were irrelevant. It followed that the whole amount of the chargeable gain
was to be apportioned between the persons having interests in the trust property at the
date the chargeable gain accrued, and that only living persons were capable of having
interests for that purpose (see p 650 j to p 651 f, post).

(3) Accordingly, the whole of the capital gain in each case fell to be apportioned,
equally among the settlor's grandchildren in the first case and equally among the
beneficiaries in the second case. The appeals would therefore be dismissed (see p 653 b
to e, post).

Notes
For the liability of beneficiaries resident in the United Kingdom to capital gains tax on
gains accruing to non-resident trustees, see 5 Halsbury's Laws (4th edn) para 113.

For the Finance Act 1965, s 42, see 34 Halsbury's Statutes (3rd edn) 912.

With effect from 6 April 1979, s 42 of the 1965 Act was replaced by s 17 of the Capital
Gains Tax Act 1979, which in turn was replaced by s 80 of the Finance Act 1981.

Cases referred to in judgment

A-G v Heywood (1887) 19 QBD 326, DC.   *a*

Gartside v IRC [1968] 1 All ER 121, [1968] AC 553, [1968] 2 WLR 277, HL, 26 Digest (Reissue) 17, 66.

Cases also cited

A-G v Farrell [1931] 1 KB 81, CA.

Bristol's Settled Estates, Re, Bristol v Jermyn [1964] 3 All ER 939, [1965] 1 WLR 469.   *b*

Customs and Excise Comrs v Top Ten Promotions Ltd [1969] 3 All ER 39, [1969] 1 WLR 1163, QBD, CA and HL.

Edwards (Inspector of Taxes) v Bairstow [1955] 3 All ER 48, [1956] AC 14, HL.

FPH Finance Trust Ltd v IRC [1944] 1 All ER 653, [1944] AC 285.

Gulbenkian's Settlement Trusts, Re, Whishaw v Stephens [1968] 3 All ER 785, [1970] AC 508, HL.   *c*

India (Government of), Ministry of Finance (Revenue Division) v Taylor [1955] 1 All ER 292, [1955] AC 491, HL.

IRC v Ayrshire Employers Mutual Insurance Assurance Ltd [1946] 1 All ER 637, HL.

IRC v Berrill [1982] 1 All ER 867, [1981] 1 WLR 1449.

IRC v Wesleyan and General Assurance Society [1948] 1 All ER 555, HL.

Latham (decd), Re, IRC v Barclays Bank Ltd [1961] 3 All ER 903, [1962] Ch 616.   *d*

Latilla v IRC [1943] 1 All ER 265, [1943] AC 377, HL.

Luke v IRC [1963] 1 All ER 655, [1963] AC 557, HL.

Mangin v IRC [1971] 1 All ER 179, [1971] AC 739, PC.

McPhail v Doulton [1970] 2 All ER 228, [1971] AC 424, HL.

Ramsay (WT) Ltd v IRC, Eilbeck (Inspector of Taxes) v Rawling [1981] 1 All ER 865, [1982] AC 300, HL.   *e*

Rank Xerox v Lane (Inspector of Taxes) [1979] 3 All ER 657, [1981] AC 629, HL.

Roome v Edwards (Inspector of Taxes) [1981] 1 All ER 736, [1982] AC 279, HL.

Vestey v IRC (Nos 1 & 2) [1979] 3 All ER 976, [1980] AC 1148, HL.

Yuill v Wilson (Inspector of Taxes) [1980] 3 All ER 7, [1980] 1 WLR 910, HL.

                                                                                                                                  f

Appeals

Leedale (Inspector of Taxes) v Lewis
Pearson (Inspector of Taxes) v Page

The taxpayers, Thomas Rosling Haselden Lewis (Mr Lewis) and Rodney Colin Page (Mr Page), appealed against an order of Dillon J ([1980] STC 679) made on 18 July 1980   *g* reversing a decision of the Commissioners for the Special Purposes of the Income Tax Acts on appeals by Mr Lewis and Mr Page by way of case stated (set out at [1980] STC 681–690) against assessments to capital gains tax made on behalf of Mr Lewis's three minor children and Mr Page's two minor children for the years 1968–69 and 1969–70 on the footing that gains realised by the trustee of a settlement resident in Bermuda should be apportioned equally among the five children under the provisions of s 42(2) of the Finance Act 1965.   *h* The facts are set out in the judgment of the court.

Toovey v Pepper (Inspector of Taxes)
Southall v Pepper (Inspector of Taxes)

The taxpayers, Mrs S M Toovey, Simon Jonathan Southall, Michael Thomas Southall,   *j* Richard Anthony Southall and Peter Timothy Southall (the beneficiaries) appealed against an order of Dillon J ([1980] STC 679) made on 18 July 1980 affirming a decision of the Commissioners for the General Purposes of the Income Tax dismissing appeals by way of case stated (set out at [1980] STC 690) against assessments to capital gains tax for the year 1970–71 made on the footing that a gain of £34,000 realised by the trustees of a settlement .

(the Southall settlement) resident in the Channel Islands should be apportioned among
a them under the provisions of s 42(2) of the Finance Act 1965. The facts are set out in the
judgment of the court.

D C Potter QC, Philip Lawton QC and *Robert Walker* for Mr Lewis and Mr Page.
David Goldberg for the beneficiaries under the Southall settlement.
Edward Nugee QC and *C H McCall* for the Crown.

b

Cur adv vult

16 December. Lawton LJ read the following judgment of the court prepared by
FOX LJ. There are before us appeals by adult beneficiaries under a settlement made by Mr
A A P Southall and further appeals by the parents of minor beneficiaries under a settlement
c made by Mrs H E Lewis. The appeals relate to assessments to capital gains tax on or in
respect of those beneficiaries. The cases were heard before Dillon J, who dealt with them,
in effect, in one judgment.

We heard argument in the two groups of cases separately but since substantially the
same questions of law arise in all the cases it is again convenient to deal with them in the
same judgment.
d The cases are concerned with the mode of apportionment between beneficiaries resident
in the United Kingdom of capital gains realised by non-resident trustees of discretionary
trusts.

We will deal first with the law and then with its application to the two groups of cases.

The law is contained in the Finance Act 1965, which imposed the long-term capital gains
tax. The crucial enactment is s 42.
e By s 42(1) the section applies to capital gains accruing to trustees of a settlement if the
trustees are not resident and not ordinarily resident in the United Kingdom and if the
settlor when the settlement was made was domiciled and either resident or ordinarily
resident in the United Kingdom. These conditions are satisfied as regards both the Southall
and the Lewis settlements.

Section 42(2), (3) and (4) are in the following terms:

> '(2) Any beneficiary under the settlement who is domiciled and either resident
> or ordinarily resident in the United Kingdom during any year of assessment shall be
> treated for the purposes of this Part of this Act as if an apportioned part of the
> amount, if any, on which the trustees would have been chargeable to capital gains
> tax under section 20(4) of this Act, if domiciled and either resident or ordinarily
> *g* resident in the United Kingdom in that year of assessment, had been chargeable
> gains accruing to the beneficiary in that year of assessment; and for the purposes of
> this section any such amount shall be apportioned in such manner as is just and
> reasonable between persons having interests in the settled property, whether the
> interest be a life interest or an interest in reversion, and so that the chargeable gain
> is apportioned, as near as may be, according to the respective values of those
> *h* interests, disregarding in the case of a defeasible interest the possibility of defeasance.
> (3) For the purposes of this section—(*a*) if in any of the three years ending with
> that in which the chargeable gain accrues a person has received a payment or
> payments out of the income of the settled property made in exercise of a discretion
> he shall be regarded, in relation to that chargeable gain, as having an interest in the
> settled property of a value equal to that of an annuity of a yearly amount equal to
> one-third of the total of the payments so received by him in the said three years, and
> (*b*) if a person receives at any time after the chargeable gain accrues a capital
> payment made out of the settled property in exercise of a discretion, being a
> payment which represents the chargeable gain in whole or part then, except so far
> as any part of the gain has been attributed under this section to some other person
> who is domiciled and resident or ordinarily resident in the United Kingdom, that

person shall, if domiciled and resident or ordinarily resident in the United Kingdom, be treated as if the chargeable gain, or as the case may be the part of the chargeable *a* gain represented by the capital payment, had accrued to him at the time when he received the capital payment.

(4) In the case of a settlement made before 6th April 1965—(*a*) subsection (2) of this section shall not apply to a beneficiary whose interest is solely in the income of the settled property, and who cannot, by means of the exercise of any power of appointment or power of revocation or otherwise, obtain for himself, whether with *b* . or without the consent of any other person, any part of the capital represented by the settled property, and (*b*) payment of capital gains tax chargeable on a gain apportioned to a beneficiary in respect of an interest in reversion in any part of the capital represented by the settled property may be postponed until that person becomes absolutely entitled to that part of the settled property, or disposes of the whole or any part of his interest, unless he can, by any means described in paragraph *c* (*a*) above, obtain for himself any of it at any earlier time, and for the purposes of this subsection, property added to a settlement after the settlement is made shall be regarded as property under a separate settlement made at the time when the property is so added.'

The section gives rise, for present purposes, to two questions. The first is the meaning *d* of the word 'interest' in s 42(2): does it include the rights of an object of a discretionary power of trustees? The second question concerns the manner in which the apportionment required by the section is to be carried out. We will deal with those questions in turn.

The word 'interest', as Lord Reid observed in *Gartside v IRC* [1968] 1 All ER 121 at 125, [1968] AC 553 at 603, is an ordinary English word which is capable of having many meanings. As a matter of language it is certainly wide enough to cover the rights of *e* discretionary objects. These rights are 'a right to be considered as a potential recipient of benefit by the trustees and a right to have his interest protected by a court of equity' (see per Lord Wilberforce in *Gartside v IRC* [1968] 1 All ER 121 at 134, [1968] AC 553 at 617).

These rights could quite accurately be called an interest in the trust property. Indeed in *A-G v Heywood* (1887) 19 QBD 326 it was held that the rights of a discretionary object did constitute an interest for the purposes of a taxing statute (the Customs and Inland *f* Revenue Act 1881). In *Gartside v IRC* the House of Lords held that such rights did not constitute an interest for the purposes of s 43 of the Finance Act 1940.

In the present case counsel for the beneficiaries in the Southall cases accepted that such rights do constitute interests for the purposes of s 42 of the Finance Act 1965. Counsel for the appellants in the Lewis cases (Mr Lewis and Mr Page) asserted that they did not. Dillon J held that they did not. *g*

The matter must be one of construction of the section considered in the light of the purposes of the statute. Section 42(2) opens with the words:

'Any beneficiary under a settlement who is domiciled and either resident or ordinarily resident in the United Kingdom during any year of assessment shall be treated ... as if an apportioned part of the amount, if any, on which the trustees would have been chargeable to capital gains tax ... if domiciled and either resident *h* or ordinarily resident in the United Kingdom ... had been chargeable gains accruing to the beneficiary ...'

The judge regarded those words as introductory and so, in a sense, they are. But, in our view, they are of value in determining the ambit of the section. The words 'Any beneficiary' are wide. They must, we think, include the object of a discretionary *j* power. Such a person must be a beneficiary under the settlement. He is entitled to the benefit of being considered by the trustees as a potential recipient of the settlor's bounty.

The section then continues, 'and for the purposes of this section any such amount shall be apportioned in such manner as is just and reasonable between persons having interests in the settled property, whether the interest be a life interest or an interest in reversion'. This is the first reference to 'interests' in the subsection. It is so closely connected with the reference to 'Any beneficiary' in the earlier part of the subsection as to suggest that the rights which qualify the holder to the description 'beneficiary' would also qualify for the description 'interest' for the purpose of the subsection.

Our attention is drawn to the words 'whether ... a life interest or an interest in reversion'. We do not think that those words give guidance on the ambit of s 42(2). They are not comprehensive and cannot have been intended to be so. There are rights which are clearly 'interests' and which are neither life interests nor interests in reversion, for example an absolute interest which is subject to defeasance by the exercise of a power or on a specified event, an immediate contingent interest and a right to income for a term of years certain.

The main argument which was pressed on us in support of the contention that discretionary objects do not have interests for the purposes of s 42(2) is to be found in s 42(3). That provision, it is said, establishes a full code in respect of discretionary trusts which are thus removed from the scope of s 42(2) altogether.

We do not feel able to accept that. The principal provision is s 42(3)(b). In our opinion that provision is not dealing with all capital payments in exercise of powers. It is, in our view, dealing only with the case where, in the year of assessment in which the gain arose, either there were no beneficiaries who were domiciled and resident or ordinarily resident in the United Kingdom (so that no apportionment could be made under sub-s (2)) or only some of the beneficiaries were so domiciled and resident or ordinarily resident (so that only part of the gain could be apportioned under sub-s (2)). We think that the important words in the provision are 'except so far as any part of the gain has been attributed under this section to some other person who is domiciled and resident or ordinarily resident in the United Kingdom'.

Those words are necessary to give protection against double charging. But if sub-s (3)(b) is intended to deal comprehensively with all appointments of capital it fails altogether to give protection to an appointee to whom part of the gain had already been apportioned under sub-s (2) (on account, for example, of a reversionary interest to which he was entitled in the settled property). The language of sub-s (3)(b) does not cover that. We do not think that is an oversight by the draftsman. It is the consequence of the fact that the draftsman intended the paragraph to apply only to persons to whom no apportionment could have been made under sub-s (2) when the gain arose either because they were not in existence or were not then United Kingdom residents.

The present case, in our view, is not like *Gartside v IRC* where, if the rights of a discretionary object were treated as an 'interest', it was not possible to operate the mechanism of the statute because of the need to identify with precision the property on which the interest subsisted; the precise extent of the interest was important.

In the present case we are concerned with much more imprecise tests. The apportionment has to be in such manner as is just and reasonable; and the valuation merely 'as near as may be'. The section, it seems to us, is not contemplating a market value (it merely uses the word 'value').

We should add that it is said that it is not possible at all to give a value to the rights of a discretionary object. In the sense of market value that is true. But within the very broad approach of the section it seems to us that, in practice, the respective values of the discretionary interests inter se and of discretionary interests as opposed to fixed interests can be adequately judged.

The provisions of s 42(3)(a) do not, we think, take the matter much further. They merely quantify the extent of an interest in certain, fairly common, circumstances. If they are consistent with the view that s 42(3) is a code in relation to discretionary trusts they are equally consistent with the contrary view. There is no difficulty, on the assumption that the rights of discretionary objects are 'interests' within s 42(2), in applying s 42(3)(a). Suppose that a fund is held on discretionary trusts for 20 years and subject thereto for B absolutely. And suppose that, in consequence of the provisions of s 42(3)(a), Y is to be treated at the relevant date as being entitled to an annuity of £1,000 per annum (being less than the whole income of the fund). The result for the purposes of s 42(2) is that the fund is to be treated as being held on trust to pay Y's annuity and subject thereto on the discretionary trusts for 20 years and subject thereto for B absolutely.

Accordingly, we see nothing in the language of s 42 which compels the conclusion that sub-s (3) is a code in relation to discretionary trusts, which should therefore be regarded as outside the ambit of s 42(2).

And looking at the matter more widely, we think it is unlikely that Parliament can have intended such a limitation on the scope of s 42(2). The statute is imposing a tax on capital gains. The obvious time for collecting such a tax is in the year of assessment after the gain arose. But under s 42(3)(b) the Revenue could be kept out of its tax for many years after the gain arose.

Moreover, it is necessary to keep in mind the reality behind the structure of discretionary trusts. A discretionary trust is intended for the benefit of the discretionary objects. If property is settled on discretionary trusts for the benefit of the children and remoter issue of the settlor and subject thereto for X, it is unlikely that X will ever take anything under the ultimate trust. If a capital gain arises during the subsistence of the discretionary trust, it is reasonable that it should be apportioned in the main, if not wholly, to the living discretionary objects. We deal at a later stage with the question of hardship on beneficiaries of meeting assessments out of their own resources.

Our conclusion is that s 42(3) is merely auxiliary to the wider provision of s 42(2) and is not setting up an independent system in respect of discretionary trusts.

We come to the second question. That concerns the mode of apportionment directed by s 42(2). An example of the problem in its most acute form is the following.

Suppose a fund is held on discretionary trusts during a period of 50 years with a trust to accumulate income during 21 years so long as no discretionary object is living, and subject thereto for X (who is not a discretionary object) absolutely. Suppose that a year after the settlement was made and while no discretionary object is living, but there is every likelihood that one or more would be born, a capital gain is realised. Does s 42(2) require that the whole gain be apportioned to X who is the only living person with an interest in the fund? The value of X's interest, by any test, is small; the possibility is that X will receive nothing from the fund at all. Counsel for the beneficiaries in the Southall cases contended that, to avoid unfairness, a beneficiary with an interest which is subject to an overriding power of appointment should not be required to bear a greater percentage of the gain than the percentage value of his interest in the fund. Thus, if, in the example, the value of X's interest is only 2% of the value of the fund, there should be apportioned to him not more than 2% of the gain. The remainder of the gain would not be apportioned to anybody unless and until an appointment was made which attracted the provisions of s 42(3)(b).

Section 42(2) requires that 'an apportioned' part of the amount if any to which the trustees would have been chargeable to capital gains tax under s 20(4) if domiciled and either resident or ordinarily resident in the United Kingdom in that year of assessment 'be treated . . . [as] chargeable gains accruing to the beneficiary in that year'.

The word 'amount' must mean the whole amount of the gain to which the trustees would have been chargeable.

The section then continues:

> 'and for the purposes of this section any such amount shall be apportioned in such manner as is just and reasonable between persons having interests in the settled property . . . and so that the chargeable gain is apportioned, as near as may be, according to the respective values of those interests . . .'

The word 'amount' in this passage clearly has the same meaning as in the earlier part of the subsection.

In our opinion, therefore, what has to be apportioned is the whole of the amount to which the trustees would have been chargeable. It is that amount which has to be

apportioned. That is mandatory; there is no discretion given to any person to alter
_a_ that. The amount is to be apportioned in such manner as is just and reasonable between
persons having interests in the settled property. The words 'just and reasonable' relate
solely to the mode of apportionment between the persons having interests. Thus the
words enable account to be taken of the circumstance of the case, for example, the
existence of a letter of intent by the settlor as to the manner in which the trustees should
exercise their discretionary powers. The words do not, however, alter the total burden
_b_ to be borne. In short, the section requires that the amount shall be apportioned in such
a manner as is just and reasonable; it does not require that such an amount as is just and
reasonable shall be apportioned.

In our opinion, therefore, the whole of the gain, in the example which we have given,
would be assessed on X (assuming him to be domiciled and resident or ordinarily resident
in the United Kingdom at the relevant time). In reaching that conclusion we differ from
_c_ the view of Dillon J, who said ([1980] STC 679 at 695):

> 'It must in my judgment follow that there could be cases in which justice and
> reason would require that there be no apportionment at all because the interests of
> those with interests, within the meaning of sub-s (2), in the settled property are too
> remote.'

_d_ For the reasons which we have indicated, we do not think that is correct.

Section 42(2) concludes with the words 'and so that the chargeable gain is apportioned,
as near as may be, according to the respective values of those interests . . .' We do not
think that the introduction, in this passage, of the words 'chargeable gain' is of any
significance. In our view it is merely a stylistic change; the draftsman, it seems to us, is
still referring to the 'amount' previously mentioned in the subsection.

_e_ As to the general effect of the direction for apportionment as near as may be according
to value, we think that it is a limitation on the 'just and reasonable' principle. There is
to be a just and reasonable apportionment as near as may be according to value. Thus the
fact that one beneficiary is poor and another is rich might, purely on a just and reasonable
test, result in the apportionment of a larger amount to the rich beneficiary. The
reference to value prevents that. On the other hand, the requirement that the
apportionment shall be just and reasonable permits account being taken of, for example,
the likely effect of a letter of intent.

Our conclusion is that the whole amount of the chargeable gain must be apportioned
between the persons having interests in the trust property at the relevant date. The word
'persons' in the section must mean living persons; an unborn person cannot, we think,
have an 'interest' for this purpose.

_f_ We come to the question of hardship. On the construction of s 42 which we have
adopted it is possible that a person having a remote interest in the trust property would
be required to pay the whole of the tax on a gain realised by the trustees, or that a
discretionary object who has received no payment out of the fund will have to bear tax.

So far as settlements which were subsisting before the passing of the Finance Act 1965
are concerned, a wide protection is given by the provisions of s 42(4). In so far as that
_g_ protection does not extend to certain discretionary beneficiaries (there may be a question
whether an object of an immediate discretionary trust of capital could be said to fall
within either para (_a_) or para (_b_) of s 42(4)) the trustees can always give protection to the
beneficiary by making an appointment of capital to them with which to pay the tax.

As regards settlements executed after the passing of the Finance Act 1965, the settlor
himself can always provide protection by directing the trustees to pay any capital gains
tax out of the trust property. And if he does not do so, the trustees of a discretionary trust
_h_ can, so far as a discretionary object is concerned, put him in funds to discharge any tax
payable in consequence of an appointment to him.

In general it seems to us that the construction which we have adopted imposes no
strain on the language of the section and is likely to secure, so far as possible, that the tax
burden falls on the persons who, in truth, are likely to be the main beneficiaries of the

settlement. We see no reason to put a restrictive construction on s 42. Settlements created by persons domiciled and resident in the United Kingdom but with trustees *a* abroad are potential instruments of tax avoidance. Section 42 is the recognition of that. It is contended on behalf of Mr Lewis and Mr Page that the section has simply failed in its purpose. The discretionary objects, it is said, do not have 'interests' and are therefore outside s 42(2). So far as persons having fixed interests are concerned, it is said that the effects of the section may be so burdensome that Parliament cannot have intended them. We do not accept that. As we have indicated, we think that the language of the *b* section is sufficiently clear. And, so far as burdens are concerned, they will result from the deliberate choice of the settlor or of the trustees or both.

We come to the facts of the two sets of appeals.

The Southall cases

The settlement was made in March 1966 by Mr Southall. The trusts so far as material *c* were as follows:

(1) On such trusts for the benefit of any one or more of the beneficiaries as the trustees should before the expiry of the trust period appoint. The beneficiaries were defined, in effect, as the children or remoter issue of the settlor then living or born during the trust period. The latter was the earlier of a period of 80 years from the execution of the settlement or such date as the trustees should declare. *d*

(2) Subject as aforesaid, on trust during the trust period to pay or apply the income of the trust fund to or for the benefit of any of the beneficiaries for the time being living; there was also a power to accumulate during a 21 year period.

(3) Subject to the foregoing, on trust as to both capital and income in equal shares for the children of the settlor living at the end of the trust period with substitutionary provisions for the issue then living of any child then dead. *e*

(4) Subject to the foregoing trusts, on trust for the children of the settlor living at the date of the settlement.

The settlor had had five children, who are the present taxpayers. At no time material to any of the issues in this case did he have any remoter issue. No appointment has been made by the trustees in exercise of the powers conferred by the settlement. The taxpayers were at all material times resident or ordinarily resident in the United Kingdom. The *f* trustees were at all material times resident and ordinarily resident outside the United Kingdom. In the year of assessment 1970–71 the trustees realised certain capital gains.

The Lewis cases

The settlement was made on 19 March 1968 by Mrs Lewis. The settlement defined a 'Specified Class' consisting of the grandchildren and remoter issue of the settlor, their *g* spouses, widows and widowers whether then living or born before a perpetuity day (defined by reference to a Royal lives period plus 21 years). The settled property was directed to be held on such trusts and in such shares for members of the specified class as the trustees should appoint before the perpetuity day. The settlement conferred power on the trustees until the perpetuity day to apply income for the benefit of any of the specified class. Subject as aforesaid, the trustees were to accumulate the income until the *h* perpetuity day. Subject to the foregoing trusts and provisions, the settled property was to be held on trust as to both capital and income for the grandchildren and remoter issue of the settlor living on the perpetuity day equally per stirpes; and subject thereto for the children of the settlor living at the date of the settlement.

There were two children of the settlor living at the date of the settlement. There were five grandchildren living in the relevant year of assessment; they were all at the relevant *j* time domiciled and resident or ordinarily resident in the United Kingdom.

The settlor delivered a letter of intent to the trustees indicating that she wished the grandchildren to be regarded as the primary beneficiaries and to receive income at the age of 21 and capital at 30. All income has been accumulated. There has been no material exercise of the power of appointment.

The trustees realised capital gains of modest amount in the relevant tax year. The
a trustees were at all material times resident and ordinarily resident outside the United
Kingdom. The five grandchildren were at all material times domiciled and resident in
the United Kingdom.

Dillon J held: (i) in relation to the Southall settlement, that the gain should be
apportioned to the five children equally; (ii) in relation to the Lewis settlement, that the
b gain should be apportioned to the five grandchildren equally.

Having regard to our conclusions as to the effect of s 42 it seems to us that the judge
reached the correct decision in each case.

In our judgment, the whole capital gain fell to be apportioned in each case. And in
each case the five beneficiaries were the persons to whom the apportionment properly
fell to be made. In the Southall cases they were the only living beneficiaries (whether one
c treats discretionary objects as having interests or not). There is no reason for
distinguishing between them in point of value; the apportionment should be in equal
shares.

The Lewis cases are not, in substance, any different. There are two matters to which
we should refer. First, the letter of intent: that reinforces the case in favour of
apportionment to the five grandchildren in equal shares. Second, the interests of the
d children. We think, as did the judge, that these should be disregarded. They are remote
in the extreme, and, particularly having regard to the letter of intent, it is just and
reasonable that they should be disregarded. The only living persons who, in the year
of assessment, were substantially interested in the trust property were the five grandchildren. There is no reason for distinguishing between them; the apportionment
should be in equal shares.

Accordingly, we would dismiss the appeals.

Appeals dismissed. Leave to appeal to House of Lords refused.

Solicitors: *Norton Rose, Botterell & Roche* (for Mr Lewis and Mr Page); *Southall & Knight*
(for the beneficiaries under the Southall settlement); *Solicitor of Inland Revenue.*

Edwina Epstein   Barrister.

Wills v Bowley

HOUSE OF LORDS

LORD WILBERFORCE, LORD ELWYN-JONES, LORD RUSSELL OF KILLOWEN, LORD LOWRY AND LORD BRIDGE OF HARWICH

25, 26, 27 JANUARY, 26 MAY 1982

Arrest – Arrest without warrant – Constable – Arrest for using obscene language in street to annoyance of passers-by – Grounds for arrest – Belief of constable – Constable honestly and on reasonable grounds believing that offence had been committed in his sight – Person arrested assaulting constable in course of being arrested – Person arrested later acquitted of obscene language offence but convicted of assaulting constable in execution of his duty – Validity of arrest – Whether arrested person liable for assault on constable in execution of his duty – Town Police Clauses Act 1847, s 28.

The appellant was arrested without a warrant by the respondent, a police constable, for using obscene language in the street to the annoyance of passengers, ie passers-by, contrary to s 28[a] of the Town Police Clauses Act 1847. In the course of being arrested she assaulted the respondent and two other constables who came to his assistance. Although the appellant was later acquitted of the obscene language offence on the ground that although obscene language had been used there had been no passers-by who had been annoyed by it, she was, however, convicted on informations alleging that she had assaulted the three constables acting in the execution of their duty. The appellant appealed against her conviction, contending that since she had been acquitted of the primary offence there had been no power of arrest in the respondent and any interference by way of assault was therefore not an assault on the constables in the execution of their duty. The Divisional Court dismissed her appeal on the ground that since the respondent had honestly and reasonably believed that an offence under s 28 was being committed in his sight the appellant's arrest was lawful. The appellant appealed to the House of Lords.

Held (Lord Elwyn-Jones and Lord Lowry dissenting) – The extent of a constable's power of arrest under s 28 of the 1847 Act was not confined to cases where the offence had in fact been committed but extended to cases where a constable honestly believed, on reasonable grounds derived wholly from his own observation, that an offence had been committed within his sight. It followed therefore that the appeal would be dismissed (see p 655 *h*, p 659 *e*, p 672 *e h j*, p 680 *f g*, p 681 *f* and p 682 *f g*, post).

Parrington v Moore (1848) 2 Exch 223 overruled.

Observations on the principles for determining the extent of a power of arrest in flagrante delicto (see p 673 *f* to p 681 *e*, post).

Notes

For specific statutory powers of arrest without warrant conferred on constables, see 11 Halsbury's Laws (4th edn) para 113.

For the Town Police Clauses Act 1847, s 28, see 28 Halsbury's Statutes (3rd edn) 72.

Cases referred to in opinions

Barnard v Gorman [1941] 3 All ER 45, [1941] AC 378, HL, 39 Digest (Repl) 254, 88.

Barry v Midland Rly Co (1867) IR 1 CL 130, 8(1) Digest (Reissue) 128, *574.

Bowditch v Balchin (1850) 5 Exch 378, [1843–60] All ER Rep 674, 155 ER 165, 14(1) Digest (Reissue) 204, *1481*.

Christie v Leachinsky [1947] 1 All ER 567, [1947] AC 573, HL, 14(1) Digest (Reissue) 206, *1491*.

Downing v Capel (1867) LR 2 CP 461, 14(1) Digest (Reissue) 209, *1511*.

Fitch v Murray (1876) Temp Wood 74, 22 Digest (Reissue) 535, *2926*.

---

a   Section 28, so far as material, is set out at p 671 *g* to *j*, post.

Griffith v Taylor (1876) 2 CPD 194, 14(1) Digest (Reissue) 209, *1512*.

Isaacs v Keech [1925] 2 KB 354, DC, 14(1) Digest (Reissue) 205, *1487*.

Ledwith v Roberts [1936] 3 All ER 570, [1937] 1 KB 232, CA, 14(1) Digest (Reissue) 205, *1488*.

Leighton v Lines [1942] 1 DLR 568, 14(1) Digest (Reissue) 200, *960.

Marks v Frogley [1898] 1 QB 888, CA, 39 Digest (Repl) 389, *128*.

Murugiah v Jainudeen [1955] AC 145, [1954] 3 WLR 682, PC, 8(2) Digest (Reissue) 786, *503*.

National Assistance Board v Wilkinson [1952] 2 All ER 255, [1952] 2 QB 648, DC, 27(1) Digest (Reissue) 86, *661*.

Parrington v Moore (1848) 2 Exch 223, 154 ER 473, 14(1) Digest (Reissue) 207, *1500*.

R v Bottley [1929] 3 DLR 766, 14(1) Digest (Reissue) 208, *977.

R v Hughes (1879) 4 QBD 614, CCR, 14(1) Digest (Reissue) 183, *1311*.

Thompson v Goold & Co [1910] AC 409, HL, 34 Digest (Repl) 652, *4494*.

Timothy v Simpson (1835) 1 Cr M & R 757, 149 ER 1285, 14(1) Digest (Reissue) 199, *1437*.

Trebeck v Croudace [1918] 1 KB 158, [1916–17] All ER Rep 441, CA, 14(1) Digest (Reissue) 205, *1486*.

Vickers Sons & Maxim Ltd v Evans [1910] AC 444, HL.

Walker v Lovell [1975] 3 All ER 107, [1975] 1 WLR 1141, HL, Digest (Cont Vol D) 883, *322llq*.

Wiltshire v Barrett [1965] 2 All ER 271, [1966] 1 QB 312, [1965] 2 WLR 1195, CA, 14(1) Digest (Reissue) 206, *1492*.

Wimpey (George) & Co Ltd v British Overseas Airways Corp [1954] 3 All ER 661, [1955] AC 169, HL, 45 Digest (Repl) 292, *128*.

Appeal

Susan Ann Wills appealed with leave of the Appeal Committee of the House of Lords granted on 9 April 1981 against the dismissal by the Divisional Court of the Queen's Bench Division (Donaldson LJ and Bingham J) on 3 February 1981 of her appeal by way of case stated against her conviction on 8 July 1980 in the Cardiff Magistrates' Court for three offences of assaulting police constables, including the respondent, Pc Anthony Bowley, in the execution of their duty contrary to s 51(1) of the Police Act 1964. The facts are set out in the opinion of Lord Bridge.

Martin Thomas QC and *Nicholas Cooke* for the appellant.
John Roch QC and *Gerard Elias* for the respondent.

Their Lordships took time for consideration.

26 May. The following opinions were delivered.

LORD WILBERFORCE. My Lords, I have had the benefit of reading in advance a draft of the speech to be delivered by my noble and learned friend Lord Bridge. I agree with it and would dismiss the appeal.

LORD ELWYN-JONES. My Lords, the appellant was charged at Cardiff Magistrates' Court with the offence of using obscene language in a street to the annoyance of passengers. She had resisted arrest and the justices found that two police constables were kicked and another was bitten by her in the course of the struggle to get her into a police van. The justices were of opinion that the contention of the appellant that no obscene language was used by her could not be upheld but that her contention that 'there were no passengers annoyed by the language used' could be upheld and they accordingly dismissed that information. However they convicted her on those informations alleging that she had assaulted the three police constables acting in the execution of their duty. They found that the respondent constable had an honest and reasonable belief that the appellant 'was a person who within his view' was committing the obscene language offence.

It was common ground that the three police constables were only acting in due execution of their duty if the arrest of the appellant was lawful. The justification for the arrest relied on by the respondent was s 28 of the Town Police Clauses Act 1847. Section 28 provides:

> 'Every person who in any street, to the obstruction, annoyance or danger of the residents or passengers, commits any of the following offences, shall be liable to a penalty not exceeding forty shilling for each offence, or . . . may be committed to prison . . . for a period not exceeding fourteen days; and . . . any constable shall take into custody, without warrant, and forthwith convey before a justice, any person who within his view commits any such offence; (that is to say,) . . .'

It is common ground that 'within his view' means 'in his sight' and not 'in his opinion'.

There follow in s 28 thirty paragraphs setting out the various acts which constituted offences if done in the circumstances set out in the opening paragraph. They are a remarkable assortment of street offences relevant to the conditions in towns in 1847. Some are serious, e g 'Every person who rides or drives furiously any horse or carriage or drives furiously any cattle', 'Every person who wantonly discharges any firearm . . .' Some are trivial nuisances, e g 'Every person who flies any kite . . .', 'Every person who places any line . . . across any street, or hangs or places any clothes thereon', 'Every person who beats or shakes any carpet, rug or mat (except door mats, beaten or shaken before the hour of eight in the morning)'. They range from causing annoyance to causing danger. Some are obsolete. It is a measure calling for early attention by Parliament if it is still considered necessary to use it despite the many changes in the law relating to public order which have been made since 1847.

The relevant part of the paragraph relied on in the obscene language information reads: 'Every person who in any street . . . uses any profane or obscene language.'

The question at issue in the appeal is the extent of a constable's power of arrest without warrant under s 28. It is an important question, for the arrest of a person without warrant and taking him into custody for however short a time is a serious interference with the liberty of the subject. The appellant's submission is that the power is confined to cases where the relevant offence has actually been committed 'within his view' and that it does not, save where prompt action is called for in the interests of public safety or because of threatened danger to life, limb or property, extend to mere nuisance and annoyance cases.

The first case directly in point is *Parrington v Moore* (1848) 2 Exch 223, 154 ER 473, a decision of the Court of Exchequer in 1848, the year following the passing of the Town Police Clauses Act. Pollock CB observed (2 Exch 223 at 225, 154 ER 473 at 474):

> 'The defendant's counsel asks us to read the act [the Malicious Trespass Act 1827], as protecting persons who apprehend not only offenders against the act, but those whom they reasonably suppose to be so.'

The powerful court refused to do so.

The same court two years later in *Bowditch v Balchin* (1850) 5 Exch 378, [1843–60] All ER Rep 674 held that a police constable in the City of London had no power under a local Act of 1839 for regulating the police in the City of London to take a person into custody without a warrant merely on suspicion that he had committed a misdemeanour. Pollock CB observed in the course of argument (5 Exch 378 at 381, [1843–60] All ER Rep 674 at 675): 'In a case in which the liberty of the subject is concerned, we cannot go beyond the natural construction of the statute.'

Trebeck v Croudace [1918] 1 KB 158, [1916–17] All ER Rep 441 is in my view distinguishable from the present case. In that case the police officer was held entitled to make the arrest of a taxicab driver on his honest and reasonable belief that the offence there charged was being committed, because of the imminent danger to the public

which was involved in the commission of that offence. Bankes LJ said ([1918] 1 KB 158
at 167):

> 'It was in aid of the common law on this point, and to supplement the powers of
> constables and others, that the Legislature has from time to time given authority for
> arrest without warrant in a number of cases of misdemeanour. Though the
> language in which the authority has been conferred varies greatly in different
> statutes, and in different sections of the same statute, the object of the Legislature
> must have been the same, namely, to provide for cases where, in the interests of
> public safety, or where danger to life or limb or property is threatened, prompt
> action is called for, and action which must of necessity be founded on the
> circumstances of the moment, and mainly probably on such information as the
> senses of a police constable, his sight and hearing, convey to him.'

No such circumstances arose in the present case. Public safety was not endangered, nor
was danger to life or limb or property threatened.

In *Ledwith v Roberts* [1936] 3 All ER 570 at 583–584, [1937] 1 KB 232 at 257 Greene
LJ, in examining the judgment of Bankes LJ in *Trebeck v Croudace*, quotes the above
passage as the real basis of the decision in that case. He adds:

> 'It is true that later on in his judgment ([see [1918] 1 KB 158 at 168) he uses
> language which appears to deal with all cases where power to arrest without warrant
> is given by statute, but I think that this language must be construed as dealing only
> with the class of statutes where the nature of the offence is of the kind described in
> the passage above ... I cannot myself read this decision as extending to cases other
> than those where the nature of the suspected offence requires prompt action.'

Scott LJ said ([1936] 3 All ER 570 at 593, [1937] 1 KB 232 at 270):

> '... powers of arrest without warrant should be expressed in quite unambiguous
> and simple language which anyone can understand, and also that the occasions for
> reliance on the constable's discretion should be defined with care in any statutory
> provision conferring such a power.'

In *Isaacs v Keech* [1925] 2 KB 354 an earlier Divisional Court authority by which the
court in this case felt bound (while holding that independently of authority they would
have reached the same conclusion on the construction of the section), the plaintiff was
arrested as a common prostitute and taken into custody without a warrant, the defendant
constable purporting to act under s 28 of the Town Police Clauses Act 1847. The medical
evidence showed that she was not a prostitute and there was no evidence to show she was
importuning passengers to their annoyance. The magistrate dismissed the charge and
the plaintiff brought an action against Pc Keech in the county court for alleged wrongful
arrest and false imprisonment.

The county court judge ruled that the plaintiff's arrest was not justified under s 28 but,
believing that the defendant had acted bona fide in the honest discharge of his duty, he
assessed the damages at seven guineas only. The defendant appealed.

On appeal Bankes LJ said that in enacting a provision like s 28 of the Town Police
Clauses Act 1947—

> 'empowering a constable to take into custody without a warrant a person who
> commits an offence, the Legislature has two conflicting interests to consider. There
> is on the one side the interest of the individual, who should be protected against
> illegal arrest, and there is on the other side the interest of the public, which requires
> that for the maintenance of order and safety there should be an immediate
> interference with persons committing certain offences, and the Legislature no doubt
> always intends that the former of these interests as well as the latter should receive
> due attention.'

(See [1925] 2 KB 354 at 360.)

Bankes LJ added:

> 'I think, however, that the whole trend of authority has been to put a uniform *a* construction upon enactments giving power to arrest without a warrant a person found committing an offence, and to hold that what the Legislature has in mind is not a mere power to arrest the person ultimately found guilty of the offence, but is a power to be exercised by the proper authority of acting at once on an honest and reasonable belief that the person is committing the particular offence.'

In my view this goes too wide. In his judgment Scrutton LJ said ([1925] 2 KB 354 at 362): *b*

> 'I endeavour to appreciate the argument that the Courts should be slow to construe an enactment of this kind as giving the constable power to arrest a person on a mere honest and reasonable belief that that person has committed an offence, and if the question were free of authority I should take time to consider whether we *c* ought to read into this section the words "in his honest and reasonable belief". I find myself bound, however, by the decision of the Court of Appeal in the case of *Trebeck v. Croudace*. I am unable to distinguish between the present case and that case, except in so far as they arose under different Acts.'

In my view *Isaacs v Keech* was, with respect, distinguishable. It had none of the *d* elements which, as Bankes LJ indicated in *Trebeck v Croudace*, it was the object of the legislature to deal with and was, in my opinion, wrongly decided.

In *Barnard v Gorman* [1941] 3 All ER 45, [1941] AC 378, a decision of your Lordships' House, it was held that the word 'offender' in s 186 of the Customs Consolidation Act 1876 included a person who was suspected on reasonable ground to have committed the offence and that a person so suspected might be detained. The Court of Appeal had held *e* that 'offender' was confined in its application to a person who had in fact committed an offence. Viscount Simon LC said ([1941] 3 All ER 45 at 48, [1941] AC 378 at 383):

> 'The question is a very serious one, for, on the one hand, it is rightly stressed that the liberty of the subject is involved, and, if an innocent man is detained under official authority, his personal freedom is for the time being interfered with . . .'

In a later passage Viscount Simon LC said ([1941] 3 All ER 45 at 50–51, [1941] AC 378 *f* at 387):

> '. . . when the question arises whether a statute which authorises arrest for a crime should be construed as authorising arrest on reasonable suspicion, that question has to be answered by examining the contents of the particular statute concerned rather than by reference to any supposed general rule of construction.' *g*

I respectfully agree. Where the liberty of the subject is concerned, the court should not go beyond the natural construction of the statute and the strict terms of the grant of the power to arrest without warrant.

In *Wiltshire v Barrett* [1965] 2 All ER 271 at 274, [1966] 1 QB 312 at 321, a civil action for assault arising from the plaintiff's arrest for allegedly driving when he was unfit to *h* drive through drink, Lord Denning MR emphasised that the statute under the provisions of which the appellant was arrested without warrant was 'concerned with the safety of all of Her Majesty's subjects who use the roads in this country'. It was a case within the *Trebeck v Croudace* principle and one calling for police action at once in the interests of public safety. However, I think, with respect, that Lord Denning MR generalised too far in stating that 'in all the many cases where a statute gives power to arrest when a man is *j* "committing" or "found committing", that is, "apparently committing" an offence' (see [1965] 2 All ER 271 at 275, [1966] 1 QB 312 at 323). In my view this depends on the particular provisions of the statutory power relied on and the mischief against which it is directed.

In construing s 28 and the paragraph describing the offence, 'Every person who . . . uses any profane or obscene language', it is necessary to balance the position of the

arresting constable acting in honest and reasonable belief that an offence has been
committed, against the person arrested without warrant who has not in fact committed
the offence.   In striking that balance in this case it is at least in the appellant's favour that
prior to the arrest without warrant there was no element of danger to life or limb or
property in her use of obscene language, which the justices found did not even annoy
those in the street.   The use of obscene language in a public street is no doubt deplorable,
particularly when directed at a police constable, but in my view it could not be said in
this case that the interests of public safety were threatened.

To extend in the circumstances of this case a constable's power of arrest without
warrant by a construction which adds to the words in s 28 'any person who within his
view commits . . . [the offence]' the words 'or where the constable honestly believes an
offence to have been committed' is in my view unwarranted.   Is this construction to
apply also to the case of the housewife who is honestly believed by a constable to have
beaten a carpet in a street after the hour of eight in the morning, another provision of
s 28?

My Lords, for the reason I have given I would answer the certified question in the
amended form suggested by my noble and learned friend Lord Bridge as follows: a
constable's power of arrest without warrant under s 28 is confined to cases where the
offence has in fact been committed within his view, save for cases where a constable
honestly believes that, in the interests of public safety or where danger to life or limb or
property is threatened, prompt action is called for.

This case in my opinion does not come within the latter category and I would allow
the appeal.

LORD RUSSELL OF KILLOWEN.   My Lords, I have had the advantage of reading
in draft the speech to be delivered by my noble and learned friend Lord Bridge.   I agree
with it and would dismiss the appeal.

LORD LOWRY.   My Lords, with a view to considering this case I gratefully adopt the
statements of the facts which are contained in the speeches of my noble and learned
friends Lord Elwyn-Jones and Lord Bridge.   Noting also that the magistrates' court found
that the respondent 'had an honest and reasonable belief that the appellant was a person
who within his view was committing an offence under section 28', I respectfully accept
Lord Bridge's proposed notional rephrasing of the certified question and also the view
about to be expressed by him that it is of paramount importance that the law should be
clear and certain, especially in so far as it relates to the power of constables to arrest
without warrant.   It may, however, be convenient to set out here the material portion of
s 28 of the Town Police Clauses Act 1947:

> 'Every person who in any street, to the obstruction, annoyance or danger of the
> residents or passengers, commits any of the following offences, shall be liable to a
> penalty not exceeding forty shillings for each offence, or, in the discretion of the
> justice before whom he is convicted, may be committed to prison, there to remain
> for a period not exceeding fourteen days, and any officer appointed by virtue of this
> or the special Act or any constable shall take into custody, without warrant, and
> forthwith convey before a justice, any person who within his view commits any
> such offence; (that is to say,) . . . Every person who publicly offers for sale or
> distribution, or exhibits to public view, any profane, indecent, or obscene book,
> paper, print, drawing, painting, or representation, or sings any profane or obscene
> song or ballad, or uses any profane or obscene language . . .'

My Lords, the conflict, or possible conflict, in this case is between two important
aspects of public policy: one consists of respect for the liberty of the subject in the sense
of protecting his common law right of freedom from arrest without a warrant except in
cases where a power of arrest without a warrant is clearly given by statute, while the
other aspect has as its object the promotion and maintenance of public order.

Respect for the liberty of the subject is promoted here by construing literally the words of s 28, whereas, as the respondent frankly conceded in argument, the policy of promoting public order requires us to read into the section words importing reasonable belief on the part of the constable or other officer in order to justify an arrest where ultimately no offence is shown to have been committed by the alleged offender. I shall call this 'the wide interpretation'.

Those, my Lords, are the alternatives baldly stated, and in such a contest I would require the arguments to be clear and compelling before I could reject the literal meaning, which conduces to the liberty of the subject, in favour of reading into the statute words which it does not contain, with a view to promoting public order. So far from the arguments for the wide interpretation being persuasive, my opinion, for the reasons which I shall adduce, is that those which lead to the literal interpretation must be accepted and that the principle of the liberty of the subject should prevail.

I shall have to examine presently the arguments for and against the wide interpretation of s 28 and of similar provisions in other statutes, but first let me attempt to identify the fallacy (if I may venture so to describe it) on which that interpretation is based. Its supporters in this and earlier cases have said that, where there may be danger to life and limb or where the nature of the offence calls for prompt action, a constable, provided always that he acts on reasonable grounds, ought to feel able to make an arrest, without fear of the consequences to himself if he should turn out (or be found by a court) to have been mistaken: hence the demand for the wide interpretation 'in the public interest'.

But, if a constable *believes* (and not merely *suspects*) that a person has committed *within his view* an offence for which he has the power or duty to arrest that person without a warrant, then, because his eyes and ears tell him that the circumstances justifying or requiring an arrest exist, he *will*, if he is trying to do his duty, almost certainly arrest, or try to arrest, that person. Therefore the wide interpretation is not needed in order to ensure or encourage an arrest; the constable arrests on the basis of what he *believes* he has seen and heard.

A constable who, believing the offence to have been committed within his view, is sufficiently cautious or self-regarding to refrain from arresting the supposed offender on the ground that the court may hold that his belief was not *correct* is almost as likely to refrain (if the wide interpretation holds sway) on the ground that the same court may hold that his belief was not *reasonable*. Thus, whichever interpretation is adopted, if the constable decides to make the arrest, it is still possible that he will end up in the wrong.

Therefore, my Lords, the main effect of the wide interpretation is probably not to protect the community by ensuring and encouraging the arrest of guilty persons who might otherwise avoid being arrested through a constable's reluctance to take action. Rather it is to protect a constable who wrongly but reasonably arrests an 'innocent' person (that is a person who turns out to be innocent or is not found to be guilty) against being successfully sued by that person in tort. If one views the conflict of policy in this light, the wide interpretation becomes, in my submission, even less attractive. Furthermore, if we are to approach the question on the basis that policy considerations are an important guide to the meaning, I have found little evidence to show that, in considering whether to make an arrest in a s 28 situation, police officers have been either deterred by the literal interpretation or encouraged by the wide interpretation or that the bringing of actions for wrongful arrest in the given circumstances has been a common enough experience to amount to a problem.

But quite apart from all this, I come back, my Lords, to the point that the question at issue is one of statutory construction. What, then, is the justification for departing in the manner suggested from the ordinary meaning of the words '*any person who within his view commits any such offence*'?

The case for the wide interpretation is best and most persuasively set forth in the speech of my noble and learned friend Lord Bridge. I have read it in draft with close attention and great appreciation, even though I find myself unable to concur in the conclusion reached. My noble and learned friend poses the question whether provisions like s 28 should be treated as separate problems or be construed 'not necessarily according to a simple rule of universal application, but at least in the light of some common guiding principle'. The attraction of the second course (which he prefers) is the prospect of bringing some order into a confused area of the law; and that is the goal towards which my noble and learned friend has tenaciously steered.

After referring to *Parrington v Moore* (1848) 2 Exch 223, 154 ER 473 and *Bowditch v Balchin* (1850) 5 Exch 378, [1843–60] All ER Rep 674, two decisions of the Court of Exchequer (Pollock CB, Alderson, Rolfe and Platt BB) which support the literal construction, and to obiter dicta in *Downing v Capel* (1867) LR 2 CP 461 and *Griffith v Taylor* (1877) 2 CPD 194, which adopt the wide interpretation, he comes to the first important wide interpretation case, *Trebeck v Croudace* [1918] 1 KB 158, [1916–17] All ER Rep 441, in which the Court of Appeal decided, in an action for false imprisonment, that a police sergeant was justified in arresting the plaintiff by an honest belief on reasonable grounds that he was drunk in charge of a taxi cab on the highway.

My noble and learned friend has quoted at length from the judgments. Therefore I shall be content to say that Swinfen Eady LJ points out that the cases mentioned in s 12 of the Licensing Act 1872 are 'all matters where it is reasonable to apprehend danger to life or limb of innocent persons unless the man who appears to be drunk be immediately apprehended' (see [1918] 1 KB 158 at 165). Bankes LJ observed (at 167) that, in supplementing common law powers of arrest by statute from time to time, the legislature must have had the object of providing for 'cases where, in the interests of public safety, or where danger to life or limb or property is threatened, prompt action is called for', and concluded that in such cases it is enough for an arresting constable to show that he acted without malice and with reasonable and probable cause. Warrington LJ reached the same conclusion on similar grounds.

Isaacs v Keech [1925] 2 KB 354 was a decision on s 28 itself. Bankes LJ, who presided, derived support for the wide interpretation from *Trebeck v Croudace*, but his approach was much wider in that (perforce, by reason of the subject matter) he did not rely specifically on danger to life and limb, and favoured a uniform construction of enactments giving power to arrest without a warrant a person found committing an offence so as to authorise an arrest on an honest and reasonable belief. Scrutton LJ, the other member of the court, considered himself bound by the decision in *Trebeck v Croudace*, to which he was not a party.

My noble and learned friend also notices *Ledwith v Roberts* [1936] 3 All ER 570, [1937] 1 KB 232 in a spirit of impartial inquiry, but I pass over this Court of Appeal decision for the moment, since it is, so far as relevant, an authority for the literal construction.

The next case is *Barnard v Gorman* [1941] 3 All ER 45, [1941] AC 378. Although the result was to construe the word 'offender' as 'alleged offender' in s 186 of the Customs Consolidation Act 1876, I consider that this decision of your Lordship's House is an important authority in favour of the appellant and I shall come back to it.

Wiltshire v Barrett [1965] 2 All ER 271, [1966] 1 QB 312, like the other cases, has been felicitously summarised by my noble and learned friend. It may be regarded, by reason of its subject matter, as a near relation of *Trebeck v Croudace*, though it should be recorded that Lord Denning MR appears to adopt the general approach of Bankes LJ in *Isaacs v Keech*, saying ([1965] 2 All ER 271 at 275, [1966] 1 QB 312 at 323): 'Likewise, in all the many cases where a statute gives power to arrest when a man is "committing" or "found committing", that is, apparently committing, an offence.'

After this instructive and illuminating review of the cases (some of which I should be reluctant to call authorities) my noble and learned friend comes down to principles. Starting from the principle that one must ascertain the intention of Parliament as expressed in the statutory language and suggesting that this must be done with due regard to social conditions at the date of the enactment and also taking account of the prevailing style and standard of draftmanship, he found it clear from the authorities, while recognising 'a strong presumption in favour of the innocent subject' (my emphasis), that a statute may be held to have rebutted the presumption by something falling short of clear express language.

My noble and learned friend observed that no judge has questioned the reasoning in *Trebeck v Croudace* that a threat to public safety permits an arrest on reasonable belief but, accepting Greene LJ's 'all or nothing' test in *Ledwith v Roberts*, concedes that the *Trebeck* reasoning does not help the respondent in regard to the Vagrancy Act 1824, the Act 7 & 8 Geo 4 c 30 (Malicious Injury to Property 1827), the 1847 Act itself or the Larceny Act 1861. Yet he points out that the relevant provisions of these Acts require the person arrested to be taken forthwith before a justice. He is convinced by the wider approach of Bankes LJ (also in *Trebeck v Croudace*) to the effect (1) that the arrest is the first step to a judicial or quasi-judicial proceeding, (2) that the person intended to judge whether the arrest is justified is the person called on to act, that is the constable, and (3) that it must follow that an arrest is justified by reasonable belief.

My noble and learned friend considers it nonsensical (by reference to *Barnard v Gorman*) to say that the legality of an arrest can only be established by a verdict of guilty, because the person making the arrest cannot *know* that guilt will be proved, and therefore he can only be protected by his honest belief of guilt on reasonable grounds. Without such protection, it is argued, the power of arrest is ineffective; therefore Parliament must have intended to grant the protection.

My noble and learned friend considers that this approach has particular force if (as in the 1847 Act) there is a duty to arrest and a criminal sanction for neglect of that duty, but he would also adopt the same construction where the statute confers a mere power of arrest coupled with a duty to take the person arrested forthwith before a justice.

My Lords, I respectfully cannot agree that these conclusions follow from the cases cited or from any criteria which can be deduced therefrom or set up independently. I take as my starting point the following principles:

(1) *Words should, where possible, be construed in their ordinary natural meaning* and (2) *additional words ought not to be read into a statute unless they are required in order to make the provision intelligible* In *Thompson v Goold & Co* [1910] AC 409 at 420 Lord Mersey said:

'It is a strong thing to read into an Act of Parliament words which are not there, and in the absence of clear necessity it is a wrong thing to do.'

Lord Loreburn LC put it thus in *Vickers Sons & Maxim Ltd v Evans* [1910] AC 444 at 445:

'My Lords, this appeal may serve to remind us of a truth sometimes forgotten, that this House sitting judicially does not sit for the purpose of hearing appeals against Acts of Parliament, or of providing by judicial construction what ought to be in an Act, but simply of construing what the Act says ... we are not entitled to read words into an Act of Parliament unless clear reason for it is to be found within the four corners of the Act itself.'

(3) *A provision creating a power or duty of arrest, particularly without a warrant, should be construed in favour of the liberty of the subject* See *Bowditch v Balchin* (1850) 5 Exch 378 at 381, [1843–60] All ER Rep 674 at 675 per Pollock CB, *Barry v Midland Rly Co* (1867) IR 1 CL 130 at 141, per George J, *Ledwith v Roberts* [1936] 3 All ER 570 at 582, 584, 593, [1937] 1 KB 232 at 255, 258, 269–270 per Greene and Scott LJJ, and *Barnard v Gorman* [1941] 3 All ER 45 at 48, [1941] AC 378 at 383 per Viscount Simon LC.

(4) *A statute should be interpreted as making the least change in the law which is consistent with its meaning* It is presumed that the legislature does not intend to make any change in the existing law beyond that which is expressly stated in, or follows by necessary implication from, the language of the statute in question: see *Maxwell on the Interpretation of Statutes* (12 edn, 1969) p 116 and cases there cited; see also *Craies on Statute Law* (7th edn, 1971) pp 121–122. The statement in *Maxwell* was approved in *Murugiah v Jainudeen* [1955] AC 145 at 152–153. To alter any clearly established principle of law, a distinct and positive legislative enactment is necessary and statutes are not presumed to alter the common law further or otherwise than the Act expressly declares.

Devlin J put it thus in *National Assistance Board v Wilkinson* [1952] 2 All ER 255 at 260, [1952] 2 QB 648 at 661:

'It is a well-established principle of construction that a statute is not to be taken as effecting a fundamental alteration in the general law unless it uses words that point unmistakably to that conclusion.'

And in *George Wimpey & Co Ltd v British Overseas Airways Corp* [1954] 3 All ER 661 at 672–673, [1955] AC 169 at 191 Lord Reid said:

'... if the arguments are fairly evenly balanced, that interpretation should be chosen which involves the least alteration of the existing law.'

My purpose in mentioning principle (4) is to relate it to the development of the law of England with regard to the power of arrest at common law as modified by statute and thereby to emphasise the difficulty (in the light of this and the other principles) of attributing either to constables or to ordinary citizens a power or a duty of arrest without warrant on reasonable belief.

Stephen's statement of the common law power of arrest without warrant is as follows (see *A History of the Criminal Law of England* (1883) vol 1, p 193):

'1. Any person may arrest any person who is actually committing or has actually committed any felony. 2. Any person may arrest any person whom he suspects on reasonable grounds to have committed any felony, if a felony has actually been committed. 3. Any constable may arrest any person whom he suspects on reasonable grounds of having committed any felony, whether in fact any such felony has been committed or not. The common law did not authorise the arrest of persons guilty or suspected of misdemeanours, except in cases of an actual breach of the peace either by an affray or by violence to an individual. In such cases the arrest had to be made not so much for the purpose of bringing the offender to justice as in order to preserve the peace, and the right to arrest was accordingly limited to cases in which the person to be arrested was taken in the fact or immediately after its commission.'

It was, and is, also lawful to arrest for an apprehended breach of the peace.

As your Lordships have been reminded during this appeal, statutes have conferred powers and imposed duties of arrest for different offences on both constables and ordinary citizens. Many refer to persons 'found committing' offences and some give power to arrest on reasonable suspicion.

On the other hand, neither at common law nor, expressly at least, under statute is the concept of arrest on 'reasonable belief' introduced except, so far as I can see, by art 30 of the Canadian Criminal Code; and, even where felony was concerned, the ordinary citizen had no power of arrest on reasonable suspicion, unless a felony had actually been committed by someone. Nor has anyone ever tried to suggest that an ordinary citizen had a power of arrest for felony on *reasonable belief* where no felony had been committed.

My Lords, before I comment further on the nineteenth century statutes, I would just bring this review up to date by reference to the Criminal Law Act 1967, which by s 1(1) abolished the distinction between felony and misdemeanour and by s 2 made statutory provision for arrest without warrant based on the new concept of an 'arrestable offence'. Section 2 provides:

'... (2) Any person may arrest without warrant anyone who is, or whom he, with reasonable cause, suspects to be, in the act of committing an arrestable offence.

(3) Where an arrestable offence has been committed, any person may arrest without warrant anyone who is, or whom he, with reasonable cause, suspects to be, guilty of the offence.

(4) Where a constable, with reasonable cause, suspects that an arrestable offence has been committed, he may arrest without warrant anyone whom he, with reasonable cause, suspects to be guilty of the offence.

(5) A constable may arrest without warrant any person who is, or whom he, with reasonable cause, suspects to be, about to commit an arrestable offence...

(7) This section shall not . . . prejudice any power of arrest conferred by law apart from this section.'

Thus the ordinary citizen under sub-s (2) has acquired a power of arrest if he reasonably suspects that he has caught someone in the act. Subsection (3) renews a power of arrest corresponding to the ordinary citizen's power of arrest for felony. Subsection (4) performs the same service for a constable, while sub-s (5) gives him a power which is new in some cases.

But, my Lords, I submit that it is impossible to find any ground for holding that the statutes which have conferred on ordinary citizens in plain, unadorned language a power of arresting without warrant persons who commit offences 'within their view' or are 'found committing' offences have at the same time *as a general principle* so altered the common law that an ordinary citizen can arrest such a person *where no offence has actually been committed*, no matter how reasonably the ordinary citizen may believe that it has. So to hold would be to give the ordinary citizen a power which he never had at common law in the case of either felony or misdemeanour, only acquired (expressly) in 1967 in the case of an arrestable offence and still does not have in general (because the law formerly relevant to misdemeanour will apply).

And now, my Lords, I must look at the cases which, it has been suggested, are powerful enough authorities to overcome, not by express language but by implication, the principles of construction which I have set out above.

Trebeck v Croudance [1918] 1 KB 158, [1916–17] All ER Rep 441 arose out of s 12 of the Licensing Act 1872. The nature of the offences there listed calls, to a greater or lesser degree, for prompt action and Swinfen Eady LJ's loaded firearm illustration is certainly persuasive. I have already noted that every member of the court placed reliance on the nature of the offences in s 12 and on the danger to life and limb when giving the wide interpretation, and I respectfully agree with my noble and learned friend Lord Elwyn-Jones that that case is distinguishable from the present case where, in my opinion, the nature of the offence we are dealing with, and indeed of most of the offences in s 28, is such that the respondent cannot hope to succeed except by reliance on some general principle, as applying to the 'within view' and 'found committing' cases. This, indeed, seems to be implicit in the opinion of my noble and learned friend Lord Bridge, to which I have already made such frequent reference.

Frankly, it is difficult to be entirely satisfied that *Trebeck v Croudace* was rightly decided, but the case has been, on the whole, unquestioningly accepted on the narrow point which grounded its decision: see *Wiltshire v Barrett* [1965] 2 All ER 271, [1966] 1 QB 312 and *Walker v Lovell* [1975] 3 All ER 107 at 115, [1975] 1 WLR 1141 at 1149–1150, which show that 'drink and drive' cases have acquired a special place in the 'found committing' category by reason of the potential danger to members of the public and to the driver himself. *Trebeck v Croudace* should be regarded as an exception to the general rule, and not an example of it.

Isaacs v Keech [1925] 2 KB 354 is the case directly in point. My Lords, I respectfully consider it to be wrongly decided and I believe that the court there relied on *Trebeck v Croudace* for a much wider proposition than the decision and dicta in that case could support. The decision in *Isaacs v Keech* was, in my view, doubly wrong in that (1) honest belief on reasonable grounds was held to justify arrest for importuning and (2) the person arrested was not in fact a common prostitute or nightwalker. By disregarding the second point the court failed to follow the decision of the Court of Exchequer in *Bowditch v Balchin* (1850) 5 Exch 378, [1843–60] All ER Rep 674 (which was mentioned in argument but not in the extempore judgments) and was in conflict with *Ledwith v Roberts* [1936] 3 All ER 570, [1937] 1 KB 232, a later decision of the Court of Appeal.

Bankes LJ expressed the opinion that 'the whole trend of authority has been to put a uniform construction upon enactments giving power to arrest without a warrant a person found committing an offence' (see [1925] 2 KB 354 at 360). I have found no reported case before *Isaacs v Keech* which could support that statement except by obiter dicta. Scrutton LJ observed (at 362): '. . . if the question were free of authority I should take time to consider whether we ought to read into this section the words "in his honest and reasonable belief",' and, rather surprisingly to me, considered himself bound by *Trebeck v Croudace*. It seems likely, and again is well brought out in the opinion of my noble and learned friend Lord Bridge, that Bankes LJ was much influenced by his own dicta in *Trebeck v Croudace* which went much farther than the decision of that case required. To say that the arrest is the initial step to some form of judicial or quasi-judicial proceedings does not prove that innocent persons may lawfully be arrested without warrant on reasonable belief; the court before which the arrested person is brought has jurisdiction whether the arrested person is guilty or innocent and whether the arrest is lawful or not: see *R v Hughes* (1879) 4 QBD 614. And to hold that 'the person intended to judge whether what he observes justifies the arrest is the person called upon to act' appears to make the constable or other arresting party judge in his own cause; why should he not also be the judge (if this becomes the relevant question) of whether he made his arrest on reasonable grounds or on reasonable belief or suspicion, as the case may be? With respect, my Lords, it does not at all follow from the foregoing propositions that the arresting officer's action is 'justified by an honest belief on reasonable grounds that he has observed the person he arrests committing a relevant offence'.

What Bankes LJ said in *Isaacs v Keech* attracted adverse notice in *Ledwith v Roberts* [1936] 3 All ER 570 at 584, 593, [1937] 1 KB 232 at 258, 269 from Greene and Scott LJJ. It was also criticised in *Barnard v Gorman* [1941] 3 All ER 45 at 50, 56, [1941] AC 378 at 387, 395, impliedly by Viscount Simon LC and expressly by Lord Wright.

My Lords, I have already noticed *Wiltshire v Barrett*, another 'drink and drive' case where, given the binding precedent of *Trebeck v Croudace*, the decision is easily understood. Only Lord Denning MR ([1965] 2 All ER 271 at 275, [1966] 1 QB 312 at 323) (obiter) supports the wide interpretation of *Isaacs v Keech*. Davies LJ and Salmon LJ (who described the point as 'one of importance and some difficulty') regretted the statute's ambiguous language and favoured a clarifying amendment (see [1965] 2 All ER 271 at 277, 279, 281, [1966] 1 QB 312 at 326, 329, 332). The words of the latter, when concurring in the opinions already expressed, are important with a view to considering how far he would have allowed the wide interpretation to go. Having adverted to *Bowditch v Balchin* and *Ledwith v Roberts*, he continued ([1965] 2 All ER 271 at 281, [1966] 1 QB 312 at 332–333):

> 'It is our duty to apply those principles and to give the language of this subsection its natural meaning if possible, but none the less in the end to give it its appropriate construction according to its context and the subject-matter with which it deals: see *Barnard* v. *Gorman*; *Trebeck* v. *Croudace*. I entirely agree with my lords that these considerations lead irresistibly to our construing the word "committing" as "apparently committing". This must have been the intention of Parliament . . . Parliament could not have intended to obstruct the police in discharging such an important duty . . . It is a pity that the draftsman of s 6(4) of the Act of 1960 did not state expressly the intention of Parliament in plain and unambiguous language. It may be that he had *Trebeck* v. *Croudace* well in mind, and thought that that decision was so obviously applicable that any further clarification of this subsection was not only unnecessary but undesirable. If so, he was wrong. I can only respectfully express the hope that in any further statute in which a power of arrest on reasonable suspicion without warrant may be given, the intention of Parliament will be expressed in plain terms.'

My Lords, I suggest that this language, by clear implication, rejects the wide interpretation as a general principle.

The combined weight of these three cases, two of which were 'drink and drive' authorities, is in my opinion quite inadequate to overcome the general principles of construction to which I have referred, especially when I recall that those principles are exemplified by such decisions of the Court of Exchequer as *Parrington v Moore* (1848) 2 Exch 223, 154 ER 473 and *Bowditch v Balchin*. And I now turn to two other cases which are dealt with in detail by my noble and learned friends Lord Elwyn-Jones and Lord

Bridge, and which, although they bear indirectly on the question at issue, seem to me to provide very powerful support for the appellant's case.

Ledwith v Roberts was a decision of the Court of Appeal on the Vagrancy Act 1824. Speaking of the power to arrest on reasonable suspicion, Greene LJ said ([1936] 3 All ER 570 at 582, [1937] 1 KB 232 at 255):

> 'This is not what the section says; and if the legislature had intended so to extend the very limited power of arrest without a warrant which exists at common law, I should have expected it to say so in clear language, having regard to the importance of the subject matter in relation to the liberty of the subject . . .'

He did not read the ground of decision in Trebeck v Croudace as extending beyond those cases where the nature of the suspected offence requires prompt action.

Then, noting what Bankes LJ had said in Isaacs v Keech [1925] 2 KB 354 at 360, he said, using words which I have already seen reproduced in Lord Bridge's speech, but which are important to my argument ([1936] 3 All ER 570 at 584, [1937] 1 KB 232 at 258):

> 'This appears to me to go a great deal farther than what was said in Trebeck v. Croudace, and lays down a principle of construction applicable to all cases where a statute gives power to arrest without warrant. SCRUTTON, L.J., thought that the case was governed by Trebeck v. Croudace—a decision with regard to which he apparently felt some doubts, which I respectfully share [my emphasis], particularly if, contrary to my own view, it is to be construed as extending beyond cases where in the nature of things prompt action is required. I am not myself prepared to write words into a section dealing with a subject matter so important unless on a fair construction of the section and its context or by reason of clear authority I am compelled to do so and in the present case I do not find either of these reasons. In the words of POLLOCK, C.B. in Bowditch v. Balchin ((1850) 5 Exch 378 at 381, [1843–60] All ER Rep 674 at 675): "In a case in which the liberty of the subject is concerned, we cannot go beyond the natural construction of the statute."'

In the same case, having agreed with Greene LJ about Trebeck v Croudace and Isaacs v Keech, Scott LJ went on ([1936] 3 All ER 570 at 593, [1937] 1 KB 232 at 269–270):

> 'But I feel bound to add a caveat. If the view of the Court of Appeal in the former case actually was that where the offence, for which a constable has it in mind to arrest a person, is one of immediate importance to public order, he is empowered to act on a reasonable belief that the crime has been committed or that the intent to commit it is in fact present, even although the statute does not contain any express words to that effect—if that is the law of this country (and until revised by the House of Lords it is), a very difficult discretion is entrusted to the police, and one as I think fraught with considerable danger to the liberty of the subject. I should like respectfully, but earnestly, to express the opinion that powers of arrest without warrant should be expressed in quite unambiguous and simple language which anyone can understand, and also that the occasions when the constable's discretion should be defined with care in any statutory provision conferring such a power.'

In Ledwith v Roberts [1936] 3 All ER 570 at 583, [1937] 1 KB 232 at 256–257 Greene LJ expressed the view (the 'all or none' rule) that, among a list of offences contemplated by a single provision, one cannot make a selection of those which, by reason of their nature, permit arrest without warrant on reasonable belief. For example, if Trebeck v Croudace is right, the wide interpretation must apply to all offences in s 12 of the Intoxicating Liquor Act 1872, which, given the wide interpretation in the first place, is not unreasonable. I think that Greene LJ's view must be right on both grammatical and policy grounds. Otherwise the constable could never be sure; and judges, including appellate judges, would be likely to differ hopelessly on where to draw the line. My noble and learned friend Lord Bridge would resolve the question by applying the wide interpretation to every provision of the kind we are discussing and to every offence covered thereby, following the example of Bankes LJ, whereas (consistently, I suggest, with respecting the liberty of the subject) I would apply it to none, with the possible exception of s 12 of the 1872 Act and the road traffic provisions which have stemmed from it.

I have already tried to show why in reality the literal and natural construction is unlikely to do the harm which its enemies foresee, and it must also not be overlooked that there is always power to arrest without warrant for an actual or apprehended breach of the peace.

Where the merits are strongly against an alleged offender, as they will usually, though not always, turn out to be if the arresting constable has acted reasonably but mistakenly (and as, with respect to the appellant, they certainly seem to be in the case now before your Lordships) there are procedures for ensuring that the subsequent proceedings, if any, for false imprisonment will not be too painful for the constable and his superior authorities.

My Lords, I come now to *Barnard v Gorman* [1941] 3 All ER 45, [1941] AC 378, which decided that the word 'offender' in s 186 of the Customs Consolidation Act 1876 included a person suspected on reasonable grounds to have committed the offence. This meant that customs officials could justify having detained without warrant a ship's steward whom they reasonably believed to be guilty of an offence against the section. I need not go over the arguments. It is enough to say that the decision followed from the construction given to the words 'and the offender may either be detained or proceeded against by summons' in s 186. The preferred interpretation was assisted by the extended meaning of 'offender' found in other sections of the Act. What was done was to construe in its context a word in the Act, not (as in this case) to read in additional words which are not in the Act (and, in my opinion, are not needed there).

Viscount Simon LC said ([1941] 3 All ER 45 at 48, [1941] AC 378 at 383–384):

> 'The question is a very serious one, for, on the one hand, it is rightly stressed that the liberty of the subject is involved, and, if an innocent man is detained under official authority, his personal freedom is for the time being interfered with, even though he may be treated with all consideration, and may, in fact, have suffered little from being in temporary custody. On the other hand, if officers of Customs cannot detain a man who is coming off a ship and whom they suspect on reasonable grounds of endeavouring to defraud the Customs, but must either let him go and rely upon a subsequent summons being effectually served on him, or, if not, must arrest him at their own risk, the working of our Customs law is likely to be seriously impeded, and the question would arise whether it did not require to be amended. *Our duty in the matter is plain* [my emphasis]. We must not give the statutory words a wider meaning merely because, on a narrower construction, the words might leave a loophole for frauds against the Revenue. If, on the proper construction of the section, that is the result, it is not for judges to attempt to cure it. That is the business of Parliament. Our duty is to take the words as they stand and to give them their true construction, having regard to the language of the whole section, and, as far as relevant, of the whole Act, always preferring the natural meaning of the word involved, but none the less always giving the word its appropriate construction according to the context.'

Later he said ([1941] 3 All ER 45 at 49, [1941] AC 378 at 385): 'I arrive at this conclusion, and, indeed, see no possible way of avoiding it, on the construction of sect. 186 itself.' Viscount Simon LC then pointed out that the word 'offender' has both a narrower and a wider meaning and finally makes the important observation (see [1941] 3 All ER 45 at 50–51, [1941] AC 378 and 387) which my noble and learned friends have noted:

> 'My own view, however, is that, when the question arises whether a statute which authorises arrest for a crime should be construed as authorising arrest on reasonable suspicion, that question has to be answered by examining the contents of the

particular statute concerned rather than by reference to any supposed general rule of construction.'

My Lords, I maintain that the court in *Isaacs v Keech* wrongly applied a supposed general rule of construction and that, by adopting the wide interpretation here, your Lordships would fall into the same error.

Lord Thankerton completely agreed with Viscount Simon LC's opinion and expressly agreed with his reasons.

Lord Wright's approach to the task is most instructive, if we take the trouble to follow it in detail. First he said ([1941] 3 All ER 45 at 53, [1941] AC 378 at 390):

'Arrest for a misdemeanour without a warrant, whether by a private person or by a police officer or by any public functionary, may be either under a power conferred by common law or by statute, but, if it is not made under such a power, it is wrongful. In the case of a misdemeanour there is at common law no power to arrest without a warrant, unless for a breach of the peace being committed in the presence of a person arresting, or the renewal of which is reasonably apprehended, or where there is escape and fresh pursuit after the breach is committed. There is, apart from this common law power, no right to arrest without a warrant in the case of a misdemeanour unless that power is expressly given by statute. The offence in question here is a misdemeanour. For the purposes of the present case, if the power is given at all, it is given by the last twelve words of section 186.'

Then, having analysed s 186 and other provisions, and having held against the plaintiff, he commented ([1941] 3 All ER 45 at 54, [1941] AC 378 at 393):

'I thus here define the ambit of the power to detain from the actual language of the statute and not from any implication. I am not prepared to construe the power to detain by holding that "offender" in the relevant section means actual offender and then reading in by implication as a further definition or extension of the power to detain words such as: "the offender [the actual offender] or such person as the officer reasonably and honestly believes to be an offender." There are statutes where power to arrest without warrant on reasonable cause to suspect is given in express terms, but in general I think such an extension of the express power merely by implication would be unjustified.'

Lord Wright then cited Pollock CB's famous dictum in *Bowditch v Blachin* and devoted the next four pages to that case, *Trebeck v Croudace, Isaacs v Keech* and *Ledwith v Roberts*, as if to demonstrate that the decision in *Barnard v Gorman* was reached on the particular language of the Act. He concluded ([1941] 3 All ER 45 at 56, [1941] AC 378 at 396):

'I think that this appeal should be decided simply on the language of sect. 186. As I construe the language of the section, the detention was, in my opinion, justified.'

Regarding *Trebeck v Croudace* he said ([1941] 3 All ER 45 at 55, [1941] AC 378 at 394):

'While I do not wish to express any final opinion on a case not now before me, I am not prepared to dissent from the actual decision of the Court of Appeal that the arrest was justified if the constable reasonably believed from the man's appearance and behaviour that the man was drunk, even though eventually the magistrates dismissed the charge. As at present advised, I think that "drunk" in that context means "apparently drunk."'

He continued ([1941] 3 All ER 45 at 56, [1941] AC 378 at 395):

'However, I must not be taken to be assenting to the proposition of Bankes, L.J., in *Isaacs v. Keech* ([1925] 2 KB 354 at 360), that a power to arrest without warrant a person found committing an offence is in general or *prima facie* a power to be exercised by the proper authority of acting at once on an honest and reasonable belief that the person is committing the particular offence. In every case, the power to arrest without warrant must be justified either by the common law or by statute. In the latter case, the power must be found in the words of the particular statute relied upon, construed according to ordinary principles. Thus a decision on one statute may afford no real guidance deciding what is the effect of another statute. This general rule was emphasised by the Court of Appeal in *Ledwith* v. *Roberts*, where it was said that it was essential to scrutinise the particular statute and see what precisely are the powers to arrest given and what are the conditions of their exercise.'

It is, my Lords, not too much to suggest that these observations amount to a complete rejection of any 'supposed general rule of construction' and also demonstrate a clear preference for the reasoning in *Ledwith v Roberts* over that of *Isaacs v Keech*.

Lord Romer crisply introduced the subject ([1941] 3 All ER 45 at 56–57, [1941] AC 378 at 396):

'My Lords, the question to be decided upon this appeal is undoubtedly one of considerable importance, for it is concerned with the liberty of the subject. It is nevertheless, as I see it, a very short and a very simple one, for it is concerned with the meaning to be attributed to merely one word in one section of the Customs Consolidation Act, 1876.'

My Lords, it seems to me that *Barnard v Gorman* is a very strong authority against the general approach which prevailed in *Isaacs v Keech*, both on the question of a general rule of construction and in relation to any attempt to rely on a general policy in favour of wide powers of arrest. In *Trebeck v Croudace* [1918] 1 KB 158 at 169, Bankes LJ had already observed that 'individual interests have often to give way to the public good'. I suggest, however, that this is a potentially dangerous doctrine and that, in a free society, individual liberty is itself an important aspect of the public good.

I would just mention, as a kind of footnote to *Barnard v Gorman*, the case of *Marks v Frogley* [1898] 1 QB 888, where a member of a volunteer corps was arrested for larceny. He was tried and acquitted but, in an action against three soldiers for false imprisonment, he failed because the phrase 'where an offence under the Act has been committed' was construed to mean where an 'offence . . . is alleged to have been committed'. The reason for the decision was that, as in *Barnard v Gorman*, the words had to be construed as they were, having regard to the entire scheme of the Act in which they appeared.

Both in *Barnard v Gorman* (per Lord Romer) and in *Marks v Frogley*, your Lordships will have noticed what I may call the 'cart before the horse' argument, to the effect that, since it does not make sense to have the verdict before the trial, it therefore follows that it does not make sense to arrest only guilty parties and then hold a trial to see whether they really are guilty. I would just make the following points: (1) if a constable is allowed by law to arrest *guilty parties* without a warrant, and he arrests someone who is innocent, the court has jurisdiction, but the constable may be penalised (if there is statutory provision for this) and also sued; (2) the cart before the horse argument in *Barnard v Gorman* and *Marks v Frogley* was used to illustrate the special meaning of 'offender' and 'offence' in context; (3) if the cart before the horse argument had any independent validity, it would be the complete answer in every case where the lawfulness of arresting an innocent person without a warrant on reasonable belief or suspicion has had to be debated. The proposition, I suggest, is manifestly absurd.

I have carefully read the Canadian cases produced to your Lordships both for their instructive value and because they refer to some of the English cases we have had to study, but they exhibit the same divergency of opinion that we have seen already, and in the end they do not really help me to answer the question.

Section 648(1) of the Criminal Code empowers a peace officer to arrest without a warrant anyone whom he finds committing any criminal offence. It was interpreted by Fisher J in *Leighton v Lines* [1942] 1 DLR 568 as authorising the arrest of a person whom the peace officer honestly and reasonably believes to have committed an offence which is of such a nature as to call for prompt action. On the other hand, the decision in *R v*

Bottley [1929] 3 DLR 766 went the opposite way. Section 30 of the Criminal Code provides:

> 'Every peace officer who, on reasonable and probable grounds, believes that an offence for which the offender may be arrested without warrant has been committed, whether it has been committed or not, and who, on reasonable and probable grounds, believes that any person has committed that offence, is justified in arresting such person without warrant, whether such person is guilty or not.'

If Parliament wishes to establish a clear statutory rule consistent with *Isaacs v Keech*, it is only necessary to enact a provision like s 30.

My Lords, I might venture, before leaving Canada, to redress the balance of opinion in favour of protecting the police by citing a passage from the judgment of Wood CJ in *Fitch v Murray* (1876) *Temp* Wood 74 at 91:

> 'The law has always been jealous of personal liberty. The great charter declared that "no-one shall be deprived of his liberty without due process of law." The Common Law has always guarded with sleepless vigilance the individual liberty of the subject, and surrounded his house with its broad shield, and declared it, however lowly, however humble, to be his castle. The Statute Law has from time to time made inroads upon the Common Law, as in the case of police regulations for the apprehension of persons without previous information on the issue of a warrant. But the Courts have always construed all such statutes strictly; and it must be understood that police officers must know the law relating to their powers, authorities and duties, or be prepared to take the consequences of ignorance.'

This passage was directed to a different situation from the present, but I quote it for its uncompromising championship of the liberty of the subject.

The principle that 'ambiguous' statutory provisions, not least those dealing with the power of arrest, should be construed in favour of the liberty of the subject is not a mere incantation to be recited only where its observance can do no possible harm to the cause of public order. It is a real and compelling guide which has been hallowed by authority and usage and we must recognise that its application can have inconvenient consequences.

It is, in my opinion, not for the judges but for Parliament, which represents the subjects whose liberty has been accorded priority by the common law and by the rules for interpreting statutes, to say in a particular case whether those consequences are not only inconvenient but insupportable. If they are indeed insupportable, Parliament can decide, after an informed debate, whether a statute should be amended and, if so, in what way.

My Lords, it is not, in my respectful submission, our function to anticipate the will of Parliament and to forestall debate by deciding that it would produce a better result if we inserted into a statute at the expense of the liberty of innocent subjects words which are not there, and which are not needed in order to make the Act intelligible and workable. I stress the word 'needed', in contrast to a phrase like 'desirable, in the opinion of the court', believing that the role of the judge is to construe and apply the legislation, and not to frame policy by rewriting it.

It is quite reasonable to argue that a constable *ought* to be regarded as acting in the execution of his duty if he arrests without a warrant a person whom he reasonably but wrongly believes to be committing an offence against s 28, but the proposition that he *is* so acting is not self-evident. The conflict, which everyone has recognised in this case, between public order and the liberty of the subject is for Parliament to resolve and not for the court.

Finally, my Lords, as counsel for the appellant aptly reminded us in his printed case, Lord Simonds in *Christie v Leachinsky* [1947] 1 All ER 567 at 576, [1947] AC 573 at 595 said, in a different context but, as your Lordships may agree, appropriately to any situation in which personal liberty is at stake:

'My Lords, the liberty of the subject and the convenience of the police or any other executive authority are not to be weighed in the scales against each other. This case will have served a useful purpose if it enables your Lordships once more to proclaim that a man is not to be deprived of his liberty except in due course and process of law.'

My Lords, for the reasons I have given, and also for the reasons contained in the speech of my noble and learned friend Lord Elwyn-Jones, I would allow the appeal. I would also answer the certified question by holding that a constable's power of arrest without warrant under s 28 is confined to cases where the offence has been committed within his view.

LORD BRIDGE OF HARWICH. My Lords, on 8 July 1980 the appellant was convicted at Cardiff Magistrates' Court of the offences of assaulting three named constables in the execution of their duty. She was acquitted of the offence of using obscene language in a street to the annoyance of passengers (the obscene language offence). She appealed by case stated against her convictions to the Divisional Court (Donaldson LJ and Bingham J) who, on 3 February 1981, dismissed her appeal. The present appeal is brought by leave of your Lordships' House.

The incident out of which the prosecution arose occurred in St Mary Street, Cardiff in the early hours of 8 December 1979. The surrounding circumstances do not matter for the purposes of any question your Lordships have to decide. According to the facts found by the justices, the appellant addressed to the respondent, a police constable, abusive remarks couched in language which any ordinary person would regard as obscene. He thereupon arrested her for the obscene language offence. She resisted violently, so much so that the respondent required the assistance of two other constables before she was eventually subdued and placed in the police van. It was in the course of the appellant's fight to resist arrest that the assaults on the constables occurred which are the subject of the convictions under appeal. The justices further found that the respondent honestly and reasonably believed that the appellant 'was a person who within his view was committing' the obscene language offence. Presumably, they acquitted her of the offence because they were not satisfied that the language used was 'to the annoyance of passengers'.

It is common ground that the convictions can only be upheld if the appellant's arrest was lawful. This depends on the true construction of s 28 of the Town Police Clauses Act 1847, under which the information charging the obscene language offence was laid. The section opens with the following words:

'Every person who in any street, to the obstruction, annoyance, or danger of the residents or passengers, commits any of the following offences, shall be liable to a penalty not exceeding forty shillings for each offence, or, in the discretion of the justice before whom he is convicted, may be committed to prison, there to remain for a period not exceeding fourteen days, and any officer appointed by virtue of this or the special Act or any constable shall take into custody, without warrant, and forthwith convey before a justice, any person who within his view commits any such offence; (that is to say,) . . .'

There then follow no less then 30 paragraphs describing the various acts which will constitute offences if done in the circumstances indicated in the opening paragraph. The paragraph immediately in point reads:

'Every person who publicly offers for sale or distribution, or exhibits to public view, any profane, indecent, or obscene book, paper, print, drawing, painting, or representation, or sings any profane or obscene song or ballad, or uses any profane or obscene language.'

It is impossible to suggest any narrower or more precise classification of the numerous different offences which the 30 paragraphs of s 28 create than that implied by the opening words of the section, sc that they are street offences of a kind that may annoy, obstruct or endanger residents and others using urban streets. They cover a remarkable miscellany of activities and range in gravity through a wide spectrum from, at one end, such relatively serious matters as wantonly discharging a firearm, setting on a dog to attack a person, and riding or driving furiously, to such trivia, at the other end, as beating carpets or causing a vehicle to stand longer than is necessary for loading or unloading goods. It is also to be noted that when an offence under the section is committed in the constable's view he is not merely empowered but under a duty to take the offender into custody and forthwith convey him before a justice. Neglect of his duty as a constable was subject under s 16 of the 1847 Act (now repealed by the Police Act 1964) to the not inconsiderable criminal sanction of a penalty not exceeding £10 or imprisonment not exceeding one month, with or without hard labour.

It had been contended at all stages for the appellant that a constable only has a power of arrest under this section if the person to be arrested in fact commits an offence under the section. The justices rejected this contention and held that an honest and reasonable belief on the part of the constable that an offence is committed within his view is sufficient. The Divisional Court upheld the justices' decision on the grounds both that they were bound so to do by an earlier Divisional Court authority, *Isaacs v Keech* [1925] 2 KB 354 and that, independently of authority, they would have reached the same conclusion on the construction of the section. The court certified the following point of law of general public importance:

'Is the extent of a constable's power of arrest under section 28 of the Town Police Clauses Act 1847 confined to cases where the offence has been committed or does it extend to cases where a constable reasonably believes an offence to have been committed contrary to the section?'

It is common ground that 'within his view' in the section means 'in his sight' not 'in his opinion'. It is implicit in this that the honest belief of the constable, on which the respondent relies as justifying the arrest, can in any event only do so if the reasonable grounds on which it is based are derived entirely from his own observation of what happens in his presence, not from anything he is told by someone else. The contrary has never been argued for the respondent, nor has it been argued for the appellant that in this case the respondent's own belief that she committed the obscene language offence was based on anything other than his own observation.

In the light of these considerations I suggest, with respect and without, I hope, being too pedantic, that the certified question would more precisely formulate the point of law which falls for decision if it were slightly amended to read as follows: 'Is the extent of a constable's power of arrest under s 28 of the Town Police Clauses Act 1847 confined to cases where the offence has in fact been committed or does it extend to cases where a constable honestly believes an offence to have been committed within his view on reasonable grounds derived wholly from his own observation?'

My Lords, it is trite law that every issue arising on the construction of a particular statutory provision must, in the last analysis, be decided in its own statutory context and, accordingly, it is by no means to be assumed that particular words, phrases or expressions which are either the same or to the like effect, necessarily bear the same meaning in one statute as in another. Your Lordships' decision in the instant case will be binding authority for nothing but the extent of a constable's power of arrest under s 28 of the 1847 Act. Nevertheless, it is apparent that the particular provision in question is one of a very large 'family', if I may so describe them, of provisions to be found in criminal statutes which have this in common, that by the use of various expressions (the most frequent is, I think, 'found committing') they all provide for the immediate arrest without warrant of an offender caught in flagrante delicto sometimes by a constable, sometimes by a member of some other defined class, sometimes by any person, but without the addition of any express language to indicate that the power, or as it is in some cases, the duty, to arrest is exercisable not only if the supposed offender is actually committing the offence, but also if the arrester honestly and on reasonable grounds

believes that he is. Most, but not all, members of the family are to be found in
nineteenth century statutes. It may be that the family is dying out. In modern statutes
one may confidently expect the extent of any new power of arrest to be expressly spelt
out in precise and unambiguous terms, as for instance, in s 2 of the Criminal Law Act
1967 to which I shall refer later. But some members of the family, which I will call, for
short, 'powers of arrest in flagrante delicto', remain of practical importance. None has
previously been directly in point in your Lordships' House. This is an area of law in
which, in my view, it is of paramount importance that the law should be clear and
certain, especially in so far as it relates to the power of constables to arrest without
warrant. Police officers charged with the difficult task of maintaining law and order
should be able to receive in their training clear and confident instructions as to the
circumstances in which they may, and those in which they may not, lawfully arrest
without warrant persons whom they find, to all appearances, engaged in the commission
of a criminal offence. Unhappily, the authorities reveal a sharp conflict of opinion on
this subject between judges of great eminence, at least as expressed in their obiter dicta.
Whether any of the decisions, as such, should be regarded as conflicting depends on
whether one may regard every statute conferring a power of arrest in flagrante delicto as
giving rise to a wholly different question of construction, or whether the members of the
family should be construed, not necessarily according to a single rule of universal
application, but at least in the light of some common guiding principle.

As I recall, having been party to the grant of leave to appeal in this case, it was not only
the involvement of the liberty of the subject but also awareness of the conflict in the
authorities to which I have referred and the hope that it might be resolved that influenced
the decision to grant leave. Still more unhappily, the same conflict is in the event
reflected in a division of opinion between your Lordships as to the result of this appeal.
The persisting conflict may disappoint but need surprise no one, since it does no more
than reflect on a small scale a wider conflict which touches many social, political and legal
problems, between two equally important aims of public policy, respect for the liberty
of the subject on the one hand and the maintenance of law and order on the other.

Against this background it is perhaps presumptuous to search for some common
guiding principle by which the extent of a power of arrest in flagrante delicto may
reasonably be determined. But if even a majority of your Lordships' House were able to
concur in an opinion which clarified the law on the subject, this would at least bring
some order into an area of law which is presently subject to much confusion. It is this
which encourages me to make the endeavour.

The first case directly in point is the decision of the Court of Exchequer in 1848 in
Parrington v Moore 2 Exch 233, 154 ER 473. The plaintiff in an action for assault and
false imprisonment was an employee of a railway company authorised by their special
Act to enter the first defendant's land on giving the requisite notice. At a time when no
such notice had been given, the plaintiff went on the land and began digging holes. He
was arrested by the first defendant and his gamekeeper, the second defendant, and taken
before a justice who imposed a fine. The offence alleged under s 24 of the Act 7 & 8 Geo
4 c 30 (Malicious Injury to Property 1827) ('. . . if any person shall wilfully or maliciously
commit any damage, injury, or spoil to or upon any real or personal property whatsoever
. . . for which no remedy or punishment is herein before provided') was subject to the
proviso: . . . nothing herein contained shall extend to any case where the party trespassing
acted under a fair and reasonable supposition that he had a right to do the act complained
of'. Section 28 of the Act provided:

> 'for the more effectual apprehension of all offenders against this act, that any
> person found committing any offence against this act . . . may be immediately
> apprehended, without a warrant, by . . . the owner of the property injured, or his
> servant . . .'

At the civil trial, the jury found that the plaintiff fairly and reasonably believed himself
justified in entering on and digging in the first defendant's land. They also found that
the defendants reasonably and bona fide believed they were justified in apprehending the

plaintiff. A verdict was entered for the plaintiff. On motion for a rule to enter a verdict for the defendant, it was argued that the finding of the defendants' reasonable and bona fide belief justified the arrest under s 28. The court (Pollock CB, Alderson, Rolfe and Platt BB) rejected the argument. The reported observations of the learned judges in the course of the argument seem to show that they thought it plain that the power to arrest 'any person found committing any offence against this act' must be construed literally and narrowly as applying only to actual offenders.

In 1850 the same court, similarly constituted, decided *Bowditch v Balchin* 5 Exch 378, [1843–60] All ER Rep 674. This again was a civil action by a plaintiff alleging false arrest. The defendant, a London constable, relied in his defence on s 18 of the City of London Police Act 1839 (2 & 3 Vict c xciv), which empowered 'any man belonging to the said police force to take into custody without warrant all loose, idle, and disorderly persons . . . whom he shall have good cause to suspect of having committed . . . any . . . misdemeanour' but omitted to include in his plea any allegation that the plaintiff was a loose, idle, or disorderly person. The case was argued on demurrer. The court held it to be essential to the power of arrest on suspicion of misdemeanour that the person arrested be a 'loose, idle, or disorderly person'. The case is not directly relevant to the issue before your Lordships, but is important for the much quoted observation of Pollock CB in the course of the argument (5 Exch 378 at 381, [1843–60] All ER Rep 674 at 675): 'In a case in which the liberty of the subject is concerned, we cannot go beyond the natural construction of the statute.'

The next two cases both relate to certain provisions of the Larceny Act 1861. To appreciate their significance, it is necessary to set out the critical section at slightly greater length than the words quoted in either of the reported decisions. Section 103 of that Act provided:

> 'Any person found committing any offence punishable, either upon indictment or upon summary conviction, by virtue of this Act . . . may be immediately apprehended with a warrant by any person, and forthwith taken, together with such property, if any, before some neighbouring justice of the peace, to be dealt with according to law; . . . and any person to whom any property shall be offered to be sold, pawned, or delivered, if he shall have reasonable cause to suspect that any such offence has been committed on or with respect to such property, is hereby authorised, and, if in his power, is required to apprehend and forthwith to take before a justice of the peace the party offering the same, together with such property, to be dealt with according to law.'

Now it might be argued that the use of the words 'if he shall have reasonable cause to suspect' in the second quoted part of the section, contrasted with the absence of any comparable words in the first part, point in favour of a narrow and literal construction of the words 'found committing any offence'. Conversely, it would seem absurd that if reasonable cause to suspect authorises and, if practicable, requires immediate arrest in the second case, honest belief on reasonable grounds should not suffice in the first. If the latter view is right, the inference must be that Parliament in 1861, notwithstanding the decision in *Parrington v Moore*, did not hesitate to use the common form 'found committing' in conferring a power of arrest in flagrante delicto when they intended that the arrest should be justified by honest belief on reasonable grounds.

In *Downing v Capel* (1867) LR 2 CP 461 at 464 Keating J said:

> 'The intention of the statute evidently is, that the criminal should be apprehended immediately on the commission of the offence. It is sufficient, if the person apprehended has been seen in a position which justified the belief that he had committed the offence . . .'

In *Griffith v Taylor* (1877) 2 CPD 194 at 201 Cockburn CJ said:

> 'The decision in the present case turns on two separate and distinct parts of s. 103. The first relates to the person arrested having been "found committing" an

offence against the statute; and as to that part of the case the question of the bona
fide belief of the defendant is essential. The second part relates to the
"immediateness" of the apprehension, and there the question turns, not on what
was in the mind of the defendant, but on what was actually done by him. On the
one question, bona fide belief in a certain state of facts is enough, although no felony
was actually committed; on the other, it is necessary, in order to obtain the statutory
protection, to shew that the defendant acted in conformity with the Act. While in
the one case misapprehension of fact, if bona fide entertained, will not disentitle
him to the protection, in the other misapprehension of the law, that is, of what the
statute enables him to do, will disentitle him. If the defendant acted under a bona
fide, though mistaken, belief that the person arrested had been found committing
the offence, he would be so far within the protection of the statute; but if he acted
under a mistake of the meaning of the words "may be immediately apprehended",
and caused the plaintiffs to be arrested under circumstances which would make the
apprehension not immediate, he would not be protected.'

It is right to point out that these expressions of opinon as to the sufficiency of bona fide
belief to justify arrest under s 103 of the Larceny Act 1861 of 'any person found
committing any offence' were strictly obiter.

In *Trebeck v Croudace* [1918] 1 KB 158, [1916–17] All ER Rep 441, the Court of Appeal
decided, in an action for false imprisonment, that a police sergeant was justified in
arresting the plaintiff by an honest belief on reasonable grounds that he was drunk in
charge of a taxicab on the highway. Here again, it is convenient to set out the relevant
statutory provision before turning to the judgments. It is part of s 12 of the Licensing
Act 1872, which provides:

'. . . every person who in any highway or other public place, whether a building
or not, is guilty while drunk of riotous or disorderly behaviour, or who is drunk
while in charge on any highway or other public place of any carriage, horse, cattle,
or steam engine, or who is drunk when in possession of any loaded firearms, may
be apprehended . . .'

The essential ground on which Swinfen Eady LJ based his decision sufficiently appears
from the following passage ([1918] 1 KB at 164–165):

'The statute confers a power of immediate arrest, and obviously intends that it
should be acted upon at once, and without waiting to obtain a warrant. In the case
of the offence of being drunk in a highway and in possession of a loaded firearm
usually a police officer would be unable to say whether the firearm was loaded or not
without taking it into his possession and examining it. Is it to be said that if he sees
a drunken man in a street in possession of a gun and brandishing it about he must
abstain from intervening unless he is sure that the gun is loaded, or otherwise risk
an action being brought against him? Is he to wait until the drunken man shows
that the gun was loaded by discharging it? And then perhaps it may no longer be
a loaded firearm. The nature of the offence mentioned in s.12 shows, in my
opinion, that the Legislature intended the authority to apprehend to apply where
the circumstances are such as to enable an honest belief upon reasonable grounds to
exist that the offence is being committed by the person being apprehended. The
cases mentioned in the section are all matters where it is reasonable to apprehend
danger to life or limb of innocent persons unless the man who appears to be drunk
be immediately apprehended.'

I make no apology for quoting at greater length from the judgment of Bankes LJ, who
said (at 166–168):

'That the defendant would have had no defence to the action at common law is
quite clear. Not only has a constable no power at common law of arresting a person
without warrant on suspicion of having committed a misdemeanour, but he has no
power of arresting without warrant in any case of misdemeanour except when a

breach of the peace had been committed in his presence, or when there was
reasonable ground for supposing that a breach of the peace was about to be   *a*
committed or renewed in his presence. It was in aid of the common law on this
point, and to supplement the powers of constables and others, that the Legislature
has from time to time given authority for arrest without warrant in a number of
cases of misdemeanour. Though the language in which this authority has been
conferred varies greatly in different statutes, and in different sections of the same
statute, the object of the Legislature must have been the same, namely, to provide   *b*
for cases where, in the interests of public safety, or where danger to life or limb or
property is threatened, prompt action is called for, and action which must of
necessity be founded on the circumstances of the moment, and mainly probably on
such information as the senses of a police constable, his sight and hearing, convey to
him. This authority to arrest without warrant which is conferred by statute is in all
cases practically the initial step to some form of judicial or quasi-judicial   *c*
proceeding. Section 38 of the Summary Jurisdiction Act, 1879 (42 & 43 Vict. c.49),
and s.69 of the Metropolitan Police Act, 1839 (2 & 3 Vict. c.47), both provide that
the person taken into custody must be forthwith dealt with so as to enable him to
be brought at once before a magistrate, or have an opportunity of being discharged
or of giving bail for his appearance. These provisions reproduce, with such
alterations as are necessary, the provisions of the common law applicable to arrests   *d*
for breach of the peace, and which Parke B. in *Timothy* v. *Simpson* ([1835] 1 Cr M
& R 757 at 763, 149 ER 1285 at 1288) describes as arrests "not absolutely, but only
until a magistrate could inquire into all the circumstances on oath, and bind over
one party to prosecute, or the other to keep the peace, as upon a review of all the
circumstances, he might think fit". Under these circumstances the question which
has to be decided is whether a constable who arrests a person without warrant must   *e*
prove in order to justify his action that the person arrested was actually guilty of the
offence, or whether it is sufficient, as in a case of an action for malicious prosecution,
to show that he acted without malice and with reasonable and probable cause. Who
is it that the Legislature intends to be the judge of whether the circumstances are
such as to justify or to call for an arrest? Surely it must be the person who is called
upon to act upon such information as is available to him at the moment, and not   *f*
some judge or jury at some later time upon materials of which the person making
the arrest had not only no knowledge but no means of knowledge. In many
instances in which the power of arrest is given to constables by statute the language
used gives an indication as to the intention of the legislature. In many cases the
expression used in relation to the offender is "found offending" or "who shall
commit in view of the constable". Language such as this appears to indicate pretty   *g*
plainly that the person intended by the Legislature to be the judge of whether the
occasion warrants the arrest is the constable. If that is so, the honest belief of a
constable on reasonable grounds is a sufficient justification for his action.'

Finally, Warrington LJ, after reading the section said (at 169–170):

'It is to observed that in each of the three cases mentioned in the second part of the   *h*
section the apprehension of the person in question must be immediate if it is to
serve the purpose for which it is obviously intended, namely, to prevent disorder or
injury to the person in question himself or to others. It would in my opinion
reduce the section to an absurdity if a constable under such circumstances were to
be liable to an action for false imprisonment if, though he honestly believed the
man he apprehends to be drunk, the tribunal afterwards on evidence which could   *j*
not be before the constable at the time comes to the conclusion that he was not.'

Isaacs v Keech is, as earlier stated, the decision of the Divisional Court by which that
court, in the instant case, held itself bound. It was another civil action for false
imprisonment following the plaintiff's arrest without warrant under s 28 of the 1847
Act, for an offence under the paragraph which reads: 'Every common prostitute or

nightwalker loitering and importuning passengers for the purpose of prostitution.' She was acquitted of the offence by the magistrate. She succeeded in her action in the county court, but the Divisional Court allowed the defendant constable's appeal on the ground that his honest belief on reasonable grounds that she was committing the offence within his view (as found by the county court judge) made the arrest lawful. I quote again from Bankes LJ, a passage which immediately follows his reading of the relevant parts of s 28 (at 360):

'In enacting a provision of that kind empowering a constable to take into custody without a warrant a person who commits an offence, the legislature has two conflicting interests to consider. There is on the one side the interest of the individual, who should be protected against illegal arrest, and there is on the other side the interest of the public, which requires that for the maintenance of order and safety there should be an immediate interference with persons committing certain offences, and the legislature no doubt always intends that the former of these interests as well as the latter should receive due attention. I think, however, that the whole trend of authority has been to put a uniform construction upon enactments giving power to arrest without a warrant a person found committing an offence, and to hold that what the legislature has in mind is not a mere power to arrest the person ultimately found guilty of the offence, but is a power to be exercised by the proper authority of acting at once on an honest and reasonable belief that the person is committing the particular offence.'

He then referred to *Trebeck v Croudace*.

Scrutton LJ concurred in the decision, if not with reluctance, at least without enthusiasm, as the following passage from his judgment shows (at 362):

'I endeavour to appreciate the argument that the Courts should be slow to construe an enactment of this kind as giving the constable power to arrest a person on a mere honest and reasonable belief that that person has committed an offence, and if the question were free of authority I should take time to consider whether we ought to read into this section the words "in his honest and reasonable belief." I find myself bound, however, by the decision of the Court of Appeal in the case of *Trebeck v. Croudace*.'

Ledwith v Roberts [1936] 3 All ER 570, [1937] 1 KB 232 is another decision of the Court of Appeal, this time dismissing an appeal by the two defendant constables against an award of damages for false imprisonment to the two plaintiffs by the Liverpool Court of Passage. The plaintiffs had been arrested by the defendants but later released and, in the event, no criminal proceedings, were brought against them. The defendants sought to justify the arrest, inter alia, in reliance on the provision in s 6 of the Vagrancy Act 1824 that 'it shall be lawful for any person whatsoever to apprehend any person who shall be found offending against this Act . . .' and on s 4 of the same Act (as amended by the Prevention of Crimes Act 1871, s 15 and construed in accordance with the Penal Servitude Act 1891, s 7), which provided:

'. . . every suspected person or reputed thief, frequenting . . . any street or any highway or any place adjacent to a street or highway, with intent to commit felony; [and every suspected person or reputed thief loitering about or in any of the said places and with the said intent] . . . shall be deemed a rogue and vagabond.'

At the trial, no evidence was called, but a preliminary question of liability was argued on the basis of the defence as pleaded, defending counsel having indicated that he could prove no facts going beyond those pleaded, a procedure equivalent to the old demurrer. The pleaded defence alleged, in effect, that the defendants reasonably suspected that the plaintiffs were loitering in a street with intent to commit felony. There was no allegation that either plaintiff was a reputed thief, nor that either came within the words 'suspected person' independently of the suspicion aroused by the circumstances of the particular incident which led to their arrest.

Greer LJ rejected the Vagrancy Act defence on the single ground that in order to justify an arrest under s 6 for an offence under s 4, the person arrested must in fact be proved to belong, by reason of his antecedent conduct, to the class of persons denoted by the words 'suspected person or reputed thief' and that the immediate circumstances giving rise to the suspicion that he is loitering with intent will not suffice. This ground is also relied on by both the other members of the court.

Greene LJ construed the power of arrest given by s 6 of the Vagrancy Act 1824 as available only when an offence against the Act has in fact been committed. He examined the judgments in *Trebeck v Croudace* at some length and concluded in effect that the true ground of the decision was confined, in the language of Bankes LJ ([1918] 1 KB 158 at 167), to 'cases where, in the interests of public safety, or where danger to life or limb or property, is threatened, prompt action is called for'. He said ([1936] 3 All ER 570 at 583–584, [1937] 1 KB 232 at 257):

'It is true that later on in his judgment (see [1918] 1 KB 158 at 168) he uses language which appears to deal with all cases where power to arrest without warrant is given by statute, but I think that this language must be construed as dealing only with the case of statutes where the nature of the offence is of the kind described in the passage above quoted from his judgment.'

He then quoted the concluding sentence of the passage I have set out above from the judgment of Bankes LJ in *Isaacs v Keech* and said ([1936] 3 All ER 570 at 584, [1937] 1 KB 232 at 258):

'This appears to me to go a great deal farther than what was said in *Trebeck v. Croudace*, and lays down a principle of construction applicable to all cases where a statute gives power to arrest without warrant. SCRUTTON, L.J., thought that the case was governed by *Trebeck v. Croudace*—a decision with regard to which he apparently felt some doubts which I respectfully share, particularly if, contrary to my own view, it is to be construed as extending beyond cases where in the nature of things prompt action is required. I am not myself prepared to write words into a section dealing with a subject matter so important unless, on a fair construction of the section and its context or by reason of clear authority I am compelled to do so and in the present case I do not find either of these reasons.'

Scott LJ also concluded 'that to constitute an offence under sect. 4 and confer the right of arrest under sect. 6 an actual intent to commit a felony was essential' ([1936] 3 All ER 570 at 590, [1937] 1 KB 232 at 266). He agreed with all that Greene LJ had said about *Trebeck v Croudace* and *Isaacs v Keech*.

The only relevant decision of your Lordships' House is *Barnard v Gorman* [1941] 3 All ER 45, [1941] AC 378. The short point to be decided turned on the construction of the concluding words of s 186 of the Customs Consolidation Act 1876. The section creates a variety of offences in relation to uncustomed goods; it concludes with the words 'and the offender may either be detained or proceeded against by summons.' Their Lordships unanimously decided that the word 'offender' could bear only one meaning in the single sentence, that in relation to the words 'may be proceeded against by summons' it must mean a person suspected on reasonable grounds to have offended and that, accordingly, it must bear the same meaning in relation to the phrase 'may be detained'. As Lord Romer put it ([1941] 3 All ER 45 at 57, [1941] AC 378 at 396–397):

'. . . the section provides that the offender may be proceeded against by summons, and to give the word "offender" in this connection its ordinary meaning would be to render the provision nonsensical. It would mean that, before issuing the summons, the magistrate would have to decide that the offence had in fact been committed. The principle of "Verdict first and trial afterwards" might, as on one occasion did that of "Sentence first and verdict afterwards," find some support in the Court of Wonderland, but it is not one that is regarded with favour in this country.'

a   *Trebeck v Croudace, Isaacs v Keech*, and *Ledwith v Roberts* were discussed shortly by
Viscount Simon LC and Lord Wright. Viscount Simon said ([1941] 3 All ER 45 at 50–
51, [1941] AC 378 at 387):

> '. . . I do not find it necessary, for the purpose of reaching my conclusion in the
> present appeal, to pronounce upon these earlier decisions. My own view, however,
> is that, when the question arises whether a statute which authorises arrest for a
> crime should be construed as authorising arrest on reasonable suspicion, that
b   > question has to be answered by examining the contents of the particular statute
> concerned rather than by reference to any supposed general rule of construction.'

Lord Wright expressed provisional approval of the decision in *Trebeck v Croudace*, saying
([1941] 3 All ER 45 at 55, [1941] AC 378 at 394): 'As at present advised, I think that
"drunk" in that context means "apparently drunk."' Later he added ([1941] 3 All ER 45
c   at 56, [1941] AC 378 at 395):

> 'However, I must not be taken to be assenting to the proposition of Bankes, L.J.,
> in *Isaacs v. Keech* ([1925] 2 KB 354 at 360), that a power to arrest without warrant a
> person found committing an offence is in general or *prima facie* a power to be
> exercised by the proper authority of acting at once on an honest and reasonable
> belief that the person is committing the particular offence. In every case, the power
d   > to arrest without warrant must be justified by the common law or by statute. In the
> latter case, the power must be found in the words of the particular statute relied
> upon, construed according to ordinary principles.'

The last authority to which I need refer is *Wiltshire v Barrett* [1965] 2 All ER 271,
[1966] 1 QB 312. This was another civil action for assault arising from the arrest of the
e   plaintiff allegedly driving when he was unfit to drive through drink. This was at the
material time an offence under s 6(1) of the Road Traffic Act 1960, s 6(4) of which
provided: 'A police constable may arrest without warrant a person committing an
offence under this section.' The Court of Appeal (Lord Denning MR, Davies and Salmon
LJJ) unanimously rejected the contention advanced for the plaintiff that the arrest was
unlawful if he was not proved to have been in fact committing the offence when
f   arrested. They were, indeed, virtually bound so to decide by *Trebeck v Croudace*. The
court further unanimously construed 'committing' in the relevant provision as meaning
'apparently committing', following Lord Wright's dictum in *Barnard v Gorman*. Lord
Denning MR explained why he preferred this test to the test of honest belief on
reasonable grounds. He said ([1965] 2 All ER 271 at 275, [1966] 1 QB 312 at 322–323):

> 'I prefer to approach the case in this way: The constable is justified if the facts, as
g   > they appeared to him at the time, were such as to warrant him bringing the man
> before the court on the ground that the man was unfit to drive through drink. In
> other words, such as to warrant him thinking that the man was probably guilty.
> . . . Likewise, in all the many cases where a statute gives power to arrest when a man
> is "committing" or "found committing", that is, apparently committing, an offence.'

h   Davies LJ put it rather differently. He said ([1965] 2 All ER 271 at 279, [1966] 1 QB 312
at 328–329):

> 'I am of the opinion, adapting the language of Lord Wright in *Barnard v. Gorman*
> ([1941] 3 All ER 45 at 55, [1941] AC 378 at 394) quoted above, that the word
> "committing" in s. 6(4) must in the context and for the reasons stated be read as
> "apparently committing", so that, if a police officer by reason of the conduct of the
i   > suspected person presently before him, whether evidenced by speech, actions, smell,
> general bearing or condition, comes reasonably to the conclusion that there is an
> offence, he may arrest. But he may not arrest, however, for an offence antecedent
> by any substantial period of time to the moment of the arrest or on information or
> belief not based on facts directly observed by himself.'

My Lords, I regret to have had to tread so long and tortuous a path through the authorities. I thought it necessary to do so, not only to see what light, if any, they may *a* throw on the issue arising for your Lordships' decision, but also to make good my proposition, expressed earlier, that the law on the subject of statutory powers of arrest in flagrante delicto stands in urgent need of clarification, if such should be possible.

In this situation it is necessary to go back to first principles, and ask what are the factors which may legitimately influence the construction of a statute conferring a power or imposing a duty of arrest in flagrante delicto. The aim is to ascertain the intention of *b* Parliament as expressed in the statutory language, but always with due regard to social conditions at the date of the enactment in question. I think it is also legitimate to take account, when construing old statutes, of the prevailing style and standards of draftmanship. No one doubts that a prime factor in the process of construction is a strong presumption in favour of the liberty of the innocent subject. But it is clear from the authorities at least that a statute may be held to have rebutted the presumption by *c* something falling short of clear express language.

If one next asks what is the mischief which Parliament, by conferring the power of arrest in flagrante delicto, intended to cure, the question admits of an easy answer where the power is applied to a single offence, as in the case of the drunken driver. No judge has questioned the soundness of the reasoning in *Trebeck v Croudace* that when an offence is apparently being committed of a kind involving a threat to public safety, a power of *d* immediate arrest must be intended to be exercisable on the basis of an honest belief on reasonable grounds, even though the statute has not said so.

But this line of reasoning is not available in those cases where the power applies to a wide range of offences of differing nature and gravity, such as s 6 of the Vagrancy Act 1824, s 28 of the Act 7 & 8 Geo 4 c 30 (Malicious Injury to Property 1827), s 28 of the 1847 Act and s 103 of the Larceny Act 1861. I understand that your Lordships are all *e* agreed, and I think it clear beyond argument, that the extent in each such case of the power of arrest must be the same whatever the particular offence to which it is applied. But all these sections have this in common, and no doubt many other examples could be found of provisions to the like effect, that the power of arrest in flagrante delicto is coupled with an obligation to take the person arrested before a justice 'forthwith'. In relation to such provisions I find totally convincing the passage I have cited above from *f* the judgment of Bankes LJ in *Trebeck v Croudace* as justifying his conclusions: (1) that the arrest is the initial step to some form of judicial or quasi-judicial proceeding; (2) that the person intended to judge whether what he observes justifies the arrest is the person called on to act; (3) that it must follow that he is justified by an honest belief on reasonable grounds that he has observed the person he arrests committing a relevant offence.

It seems to me scarcely less nonsensical than the construction of 'offender' in s 186 of *g* the Customs Consolidation Act 1876, which your Lordships' House rejected in *Barnard v Gorman*, to construe such provisions as these in the sense that the legality of the arrest can only be established by an ex post facto verdict of guilty against the person arrested. Parliament, in enacting any such provision, must have intended that any person who *was* committing any of the specified offences, whether serious or trivial, should be arrested and brought to justice, very often, no doubt, because this might be the only way he could *h* be brought to justice at all. But the person making the arrest cannot determine guilt in advance; he cannot *know* that guilt will in due course be established; his only protection, if he is to have any, at the time of making the arrest must be found in his honest belief on reasonable grounds that he has observed the commission of a relevant offence by the person he arrests. If a power of arrest in flagrante delicto is to be effective at all, the person who exercises it needs protection; protection not only against liability to pay *j* damages in tort, but, perhaps more important, as the instant case shows, protection, so far as the law can give it, against violent resistance to the reasonable force which a person exercising a lawful power of arrest is entitled to use in order to effect and maintain his arrest. If the protection the law affords is contingent and unpredictable, how can Parliament reasonably have expected anyone to rely on it? Yet, surely Parliament must

have intended the protection to be relied on in order that the power of arrest should be
a effective. Making an arrest can never be an agreeable task and may often be very
disagreeable; how much more so if the law gives no assurance of protection.

The considerations to which I have directed attention in the foregoing paragraph
apply with particular force to a provision, such as s 28 of 1847 Act, where the constable
is put under a duty to arrest, and neglect of that duty may be visited with criminal
sanctions. The same applies to s 6 of the Vagrancy Act 1824 which, besides the general
b powers of arrest given to any person referred to in *Ledwith v Roberts*, provided:

> '. . . and in case any constable . . . shall not use his best endeavours to apprehend
> and to convey before some justice of the peace any person that he shall find
> offending against this Act, it shall be deemed a neglect of duty in such constable
> . . . and he shall on conviction be punished in such manner as is herein-after
> directed.'

c
It would seem to me quite ridiculous to construe these provisions in such a way as to
force on the constable a choice between the risk of making an unlawful arrest and the
risk of committing a criminal neglect of duty. This would be to impale him on the
horns of an impossible dilemma. A conclusion to that effect is sufficient to dispose of the
present appeal. But the whole subject, in so far as provisions of the kind under discussion
d are still in operation, is so important that I would not confine my opinion to provisions
imposing a duty to arrest in flagrante delicto but would extend it to all cases where a
power of arrest in flagrante delicto is coupled with a duty to convey the person arrested
'forthwith' (or some equivalent expression) before a justice. Arrest by a private citizen
of a person found to all appearances committing an offence may be a moral, if not a legal
duty, and is likely to be a more dangerous, difficult and unpleasant one than arrest by a
trained police officer. The citizen, too, in my opinion, must have been intended by
e Parliament to be protected when exercising a power of arrest in flagrante delicto, by an
honest belief on reasonable grounds that an offence is being or has been committed in his
presence.

My Lords, I need hardly say that I have not reached this conclusion without due regard
to the eminence of the judges who decided *Parrington v Moore* (1848) 2 Exch 223, 154 ER
f 473 (which, as will be apparent from what I have already said, I would overrule), to the
celebrated dictum of Pollock CB in *Bowditch v Blachin*, to the construction put on s 6 of the
Vagrancy Act 1824 by Greene and Scott LJJ in *Ledwith v Roberts* and to their criticisms of
the dicta of Bankes LJ in *Trebeck v Croudace* and *Isaacs v Keech*, and to the dicta in *Barnard
v Gorman* of Viscount Simon LC and Lord Wright, which I have quoted above. The
respect due to judicial pronouncements, whether obiter or by way of decision, from such
g sources naturally carries great weight. But for me it is outweighed in relation to the
question under discussion by the considerations of principle and reason which I have
sought to expound as justifying a construction of a very common form of nineteenth
century enactment giving effect to what I believe must clearly have been Parliament's
common intention in using that form.

I do not question the correctness of the decisions in *Bowditch v Balchin* or *Ledwith v
h Roberts*. Each was decided on the pleadings and on the ground that the pleaded defence
failed to allege that the plaintiff belonged to the class of persons ('loose, idle, and
disorderly persons' in one case, 'suspected person or reputed thief' in the other) who were
alone liable to arrest under the power relied on by the defendants. With reference to
Wiltshire v Barrett, while the word 'apparently' is convenient enough to indicate what is
to be implied in such phrases as 'found committing' or 'who in his view commits' I
cannot accept that this imports any watering down of the test of honest belief on
reasonable grounds. In particular, I must respectfully dissent from the view expressed by
Lord Denning MR that 'the constable is justified if the facts, as they appeared to him at
the time, were such as to warrant him . . . thinking that the man was *probably* guilty' (my
emphasis). This is, in effect, to substitute suspicion for belief. The distinction may be a
fine one, but when it is necessary to extend the ambit of an express statutory power of

arrest without warrant by the process of necessary implication I do not believe the
implication should go any further than is strictly necessary to make the statutory power *a*
workable.

The common law power of arrest on suspicion of felony drew a distinction between
constables and others. The constable could, if he reasonably suspected that a felony had
been committed, arrest any person whom he reasonably suspected of having committed
it. The citizen, if a felony had in fact been committed, could arrest any person whom he
reasonably suspected of having committed it. The Criminal Law Act 1967 abolished all *b*
distinction between felony and misdemeanour (see s 1(1)). It substituted for the
common law power of arrest in relation to felony the new general statutory power of
arrest without warrant in relation to 'arrestable offences', sc any offence punishable on
first conviction by imprisonment for five years or more and any attempt to commit such
an offence. The new power, in general, preserves the old common law distinction
between the powers of constables and others in that, to justify the citizens arrest, an *c*
arrestable offence must in fact have been committed, whereas the constable can rely on
reasonable suspicion both as to the commission of an offence and as to the person who
committed it (see s 2(3) and (4)).

But a new provision is found in s 2(2) which provides:

'Any person may arrest without warrant anyone who is, or whom he, with
reasonable cause, suspects to be, in the act of committing an arrestable offence.' *d*

I recognise that this relates to serious offences far removed from the odd collection of
offences in s 28 of the 1847 Act. But I thought it right to draw attention to it as it affords
a good example of a modern statute, using language with the precision one expects,
expressly recognising the futility of giving to anybody the power to arrest a person
caught in the act of committing an offence, or appearing to do so, if the legality of the *e*
arrest depends on whether the person arrested turns out later to have been in fact
committing an offence or not. That, at all events, seems to me to be the rationale which
underlies s 2(2) of the Criminal Law Act 1967, just as it is the rationale which underlies
the construction I have felt obliged to put on the category of statutes, in an age when
Parliament was less articulate than it is now, which conferred a power of arrest in
flagrante delicto to be followed by a prompt appearance before a justice. *f*

My Lords, for these reasons, expressed, I fear, at inordinate length, I would answer the
certified question, in the slightly amended form I have earlier suggested, as follows: 'The
extent of a constable's power of arrest under s 28 of the Town Police Clauses Act 1847 is
not confined to cases where the offence has in fact been committed but extends to cases
where a constable honestly believes an offence to have been committed within his view
on reasonable grounds derived wholly from his own observation.' *g*

I would accordingly dismiss the appeal.

Appeal dismissed.

Solicitors: *Turner Peacock*, agents for *Loveluck-Edwards & Green*, Cardiff (for the appellant);
Darley Cumberland & Co, agents for *J M Timmons*, Cardiff (for the respondent).

Mary Rose Plummer   Barrister.

a

Re Solicitors, Re Taxation of Costs

CHANCERY DIVISION

SIR ROBERT MEGARRY V-C SITTING WITH ASSESSORS

8, 21 DECEMBER 1981

b *Legal aid – Taxation of costs – Counsel's fees – Leading counsel – Duty of solicitor acting for legally-aided client – Duty not to brief leading counsel or take unusual or unusually expensive step without client's authority – Duty to explain to client effect of cost of briefing leading counsel – When leading counsel should not be briefed for legally-aided client – Whether court entitled under inherent jurisdiction to inquire into propriety of briefing leading counsel – Solicitors Act 1974, s 50(2) – Legal Aid (General) Regulations 1980, regs 60(1), 64(2).*

c Although the effect of regs 60(1)[a] and 64(2)[b] of the Legal Aid (General) Regulations 1980 is that if the legal aid authority has authorised the instruction of leading counsel the propriety of doing so cannot be raised on a taxation, those regulations do not prevent the court, under its inherent jurisdiction over solicitors preserved by s 50(2)[c] of the Solicitors Act 1974, from inquiring into the propriety of briefing leading counsel if it becomes apprised of the case (see p 687 g h, post).

d   As a general rule solicitors in legally-aided cases are under a duty not to instruct leading counsel, even though authorised to do so by the legal aid authority, unless they have first obtained their client's specific agreement and authority to do so after fully advising the client of the probable cost of briefing leading counsel and the effect of that cost on the client's assets, having regard to the legal aid fund's charge on property recovered or preserved in the proceedings. The same considerations apply where solicitors in such e cases propose taking some unusual or unusually expensive step (see p 686 d to f and p 688 d e, post).

    Although the fact that legal aid has been granted to one party to proceedings may be some justification for the other assisted party employing leading counsel, the mere fact that the decision in the case is likely to be of interest to the legal profession generally and to provide a definitive judgment on the point in issue is slender justification for f increasing the costs of an assisted person by taking in a leader. Moreover, where relatively small sums are at stake in the proceedings the legal aid authorities should be cautious in authorising the briefing of leading counsel (see p 687 b to f, post).

    The rule-making authority ought to prescribe a procedure whereby a taxing master who perceives a breach of a solicitor's duty not to brief leading counsel or take some unusual or unusually expensive step without his client's specific instruction can refer the matter to a judge or master for investigation, and ought also to prescribe the procedure g for dealing with such an investigation (see p 688 c e f, post).

Notes

For the Supreme Court's inherent disciplinary jurisdiction over solicitors, see 36 Halsbury's Laws (3rd edn) 192, para 263.

    For the Solicitors Act 1974, s 50, see 44 Halsbury's Statutes (3rd edn) 1522.

h

---

a   Regulation 60(1), so far as material, provides: 'Where it appears to an assisted person's solicitor that the proper conduct of the proceedings so requires, counsel may be instructed; but, unless authority has been given in the certificate or by the general committee . . . (b) a Queen's Counsel or more than one counsel shall not be instructed.'

j b   Regulation 64(2), so far as material, provides: '. . . no question as to the propriety of any step or act in relation to which prior authority has been obtained under regulations 60 . . . shall be raised on any taxation.'

c   Section 50(2), so far as material, provides: '. . . the High Court, the Crown Court and the Court of Appeal respectively, or any division or judge of those courts, may exercise the same jurisdiction in respect of solicitors as any one of the superior courts of law or equity from which the Supreme Court was constituted might have exercised immediately before the passing of the Supreme Court of Judicature Act 1873 in respect of any solicitor, attorney or proctor admitted to practise there.'

Case referred to in judgment
Thew (R & T) Ltd v Reeves [1981] 2 All ER 964, [1982] QB 172, [1981] 3 WLR 190, CA.   *a*

Inquiry
In consequence of the issue of a summons to review the taxation of the fees of counsel appearing for a legally-aided defendant in the Court of Appeal, which was subsequently withdrawn, the court became apprised of the circumstances in which leading counsel for the defendant had been briefed by the defendant's solicitors. Accordingly, Sir Robert   *b*
Megarry V-C acting under the court's inherent jurisdiction over solicitors under s 50(2) of the Solicitors Act 1974 directed the defendant's solicitors to attend before him so that he could consider whether there was a case for further investigation into the briefing of leading counsel and if so to give appropriate directions for the investigation. Sir Robert Megarry V-C, who sat with assessors, heard the proceedings and gave judgment in chambers but gave leave for the judgment to be reported. The facts are set out in the   *c*
judgment.

Cur adv vult

21 December. **SIR ROBERT MEGARRY V-C** read the following judgment: These proceedings raise a short but important point on legal aid; and although I am giving   *d*
judgment in chambers, I am also giving leave for the judgment to be reported.

The question arises out of a review of a taxation of the costs of Chancery proceedings which were carried to the Court of Appeal. At first instance, the case was argued by juniors on each side, but in the Court of Appeal both sides briefed leaders. The claim was made under the Inheritance (Provision for Family and Dependants) Act 1975, and the plaintiff and the defendant were each legally aided throughout. The plaintiff's claim to   *e*
have provision made for him out of the estate of the deceased was successfully resisted by the defendant, who was entitled to the whole estate; and on appeal this decision was affirmed. The trial judge said that, after allowing for the costs of the proceedings before him, the disposable balance was some £7,000. I am concerned with the defendant's costs. It was clear from the outset that the plaintiff, being legally aided, would be unlikely to pay any of the costs awarded against him, and that the legal aid fund would   *f*
have the usual charge for the defendant's costs on the fund which had been preserved in the litigation.

On the taxation of the defendant's costs in the Court of Appeal on a common fund basis under the Legal Aid Act 1974, the claim for the leader was for a brief fee of £750 and a refresher of £250: the hearing took some 6¾ hours. For the junior, the claim was for a brief fee of £500 and a refresher of £165. The taxing master reduced the leader's fees to £350 and £150 respectively, and the junior's to £175 and £100 respectively. In   *g*
the court below, the brief fee asked for the junior had been £175, and this was allowed in full. In each case, of course, VAT had to be paid on these fees as well. In due course the defendant's solicitors brought in objections to the taxation on this and other points; and when the taxing master disallowed all the objections, they issued a summons to review the taxation. Some three weeks before the date on which the summons was to be   *h*
heard, the defendant's solicitors wrote to say that they would pursue the review in relation to counsel's fees alone, and not in relation to their own costs. Six days before the date for hearing the summons, the defendant's solicitors wrote again; and this time they wholly withdrew their summons. On the face of it, that appeared to be the end of the proceedings; but a feature had emerged from the taxation which prevented this from being the case. It concerns the briefing of the leader.   *j*

In the taxing master's written reasons for disallowing the objections to the taxation, he recorded that 'the leader was briefed, so I am told, without specific instructions of the client'. He also stated that 'the defendant, as I was told by her and her solicitors, would have preferred not to have had two counsel'. The defendant had, it seems, attended the taxation. As the disposable fund was some £7,000, the act of briefing a leader who claimed fees of £1,000, and was allowed a fee of £500, was plainly an act which would

materially diminish the fund left in the hands of the defendant after satisfying the charge
a on that fund which the Legal Aid Act 1974 gives to the legal aid fund. I leave on one side
the effect which briefing a leader appeared to have on the brief fee claimed by the junior;
in place of conducting the case himself at a brief fee of £175, he sought a brief fee of
£500 for being led. Looking at the leader's fee alone, was it right that the defendant's
fund should be diminished by the fees of a leader who had not been briefed on her
instructions and whom she would have preferred not to have had? And was it right that
b the withdrawal of the summons for a review should prevent this matter from being
considered by the court unless, as in fact occurred, the court had read the papers and
decided to act of its own motion?

In those circumstances I thought it right to apply and adapt a course taken by the
Court of Appeal in *R & T Thew Ltd v Reeves* [1982] QB 172 at 207. A copy of the order
dated 19 June 1981 is before me. The court was composed of Lord Denning MR, Dunn
c and O'Connor LJJ. Acting under the inherent jurisdiction over solicitors, which the
Solicitors Act 1974, s 50(2) preserves, the Court of Appeal, on its own direction and
notice, ordered solicitors to attend for the purpose of considering whether or not they
should be ordered to pay certain costs personally, on the ground that these had been
incurred by the mistake of their clerk or articled clerk and were not recoverable under
the Legal Aid Act 1974. It was also ordered that the Attorney General should be asked
d to consider the appointment of an amicus curiae to assist the court.

In the present case, it seemed to me desirable that the defendant's solicitors should be
asked to attend before me so that I could consider initially whether there was a sufficient
case to require further investigation, and so that if there were such a case, I could give
appropriate directions for that investigation. I accordingly gave certain directions to this
end; and at the same time I nominated to sit with me as assessors the chief taxing master
e and Mr G R Church, who had previously been nominated to sit with me as assessors
under the summons for review which had been withdrawn. I have also had the assistance
of Mr M E Mead of the Treasury Solicitor's Department. The Law Society had previously
written to the Lord Chancellor's Department to ascertain whether, under reg 115 of the
Legal Aid (General) Regulations 1980, SI 1980/1894, the Lord Chancellor would appoint
a solicitor to intervene in the review of taxation that was then sought; but Mr Mead
f made it clear that he was present before me not under any appointment by the Lord
Chancellor but purely as amicus curiae. The hearing took a morning, and most of that
time was occupied by explanations and submissions which were put forward by the
representative of the defendant's solicitors. By the end of the hearing it had become
plain both to the assessors and myself that there was no sufficient case for requiring any
further investigation. At the same time it had also become plain that it was highly
g desirable that the profession should be informed of the problems that had arisen in this
case so that further instances could be avoided. It further seemed desirable that
consideration should be given to the method by which cases such as the present could be
dealt with in future. For these reasons, I stated that I would give judgment in chambers
at a later date, with leave to report the judgment, so that I could set out the reasons for
the decision and the other matters that I have mentioned.

h First, then, there are the reasons for the decision. The information put before us by
the defendant's solicitors makes it reasonably plain how and why events took the course
that they did. After the decision at first instance, the defendant's solicitors learned that
the plaintiff had been given a legal aid certificate for the appeal which included authority
for a leader to be instructed. On the oral advice of junior counsel, the defendant's
solicitors applied for a similar authority to instruct a leader; and nearly four months
before the appeal came on, that authority was given. The defendant's solicitors promptly
wrote to the defendant to inform her of this; and there is nothing to suggest that she
made any objection to it then. No steps were taken at that stage to brief a leader; but
ultimately, some ten days before the hearing before the Court of Appeal began, a leader
was briefed. He had to return his brief four days before the hearing began, and the
leader who conducted the appeal was then briefed. The representative of the defendant's
solicitors who appeared before us only came into the case some five or six weeks before

the appeal was heard, in place of a person who has now retired from practice. It is accepted, however, that neither person ever obtained any specific instructions or authority from the defendant to employ a leader. Further, while the defendant's solicitors say that from time to time the defendant was told that costs would be a charge on the fund in issue, they accept that nothing specific was said to her about the cost of briefing a leader being a charge on that fund. Nor is there anything to suggest that the probable amount of a leader's fees was discussed with her. The present representative of the defendant's solicitors said frankly that he had assumed that his predecessor had explored with the defendant the question of the leader's fees being a charge on the fund at the time when legal aid authority for a leader was given.

In view of the matters that were to be argued on the appeal, I do not think that it can be said to have been wrong to employ a leader. Certainly it was not culpable. The case, I think, was marginal for the employment of a leader; and in view of the facts that the plaintiff was having a leader and that the legal aid authorities had authorised a leader for the defendant, I can readily understand why it was that the defendant's solicitors resolved to employ a leader. What, however, is disturbing is that this should have been done without the authority of the defendant, and without explaining to her the probable cost of a leader, and the effect on her assets, in the fund and apart from it, of employing a leader. If the defendant had had means enough to make her ineligible for legal aid, the defendant's solicitors accept that the briefing of a leader, and the cost of doing so, was something that they should have discussed with her, and that they would have done this. I cannot see that she is any the less entitled to have this discussed with her just because she is legally aided. In such matters there ought not to be two different standards, one for ordinary litigants and another for legally-aided litigants: see, for instance, the Legal Aid Act 1974, s 7(6).

If, then, there is a proposal to employ a leader, this is a matter on which in all normal circumstances the litigant's solicitor should obtain specific instructions from the litigant, after explaining the probable cost, and the consequences in relation to the litigant's assets and the assets in dispute. No doubt the authorisation by the legal aid authorities for the briefing of a leader is an encouragement to take in a leader; but that authority does not have to be acted on. The client, on being informed of the probable increase in costs which would result from briefing a leader, and the financial impact of this on the litigant's means and the assets in dispute, may choose to avoid that increase in costs, and rely on the case being conducted by junior counsel. At least the litigant must be given the opportunity of making this choice, no matter how firmly the litigant's solicitors and junior counsel advise that a leader ought to be briefed. There may, of course, be cases where the employment of a leader can have no possible financial effect on the litigant, as where he has a nil contribution and there is no asset or monetary claim in dispute to which the statutory charge could attach. Even there, I would have thought that the solicitors should consult the litigant, though the decision will be easier and the consequences of a failure to consult far less grave; but I decide nothing on that, for of course this is not that sort of case.

In the present case, I am satisfied that at all material times the defendant's solicitors acted in good faith in what they believed to be the best interests of the defendant. Legal aid authority to brief a leader was sought on the oral advice of junior counsel, and they believed that the defendant, if asked, would have agreed to the employment of a leader. This belief was based on their knowledge of the defendant's character, they said. At the same time, the representative of the defendant's solicitors, who throughout spoke with transparent frankness and openness, made no attempt to contend that such a belief was any substitute for asking the defendant directly, and giving her proper advice about the consequences. As I have indicated, he had assumed (wrongly, as it emerged) that at the time when legal aid authority to employ a leader had been given the person previously conducting the case had explained to the defendant the financial consequences of a charge on the fund in dispute. He had therefore not gone into this with the defendant before the brief was actually delivered, shortly before the appeal came on.

In all these cases one has to hold firmly in mind the difference between what appears on an examination of the facts made with hindsight, after segregating the relevant facts, and what must have appeared when all lay in prospect and what was relevant stood embedded in the whole mass of facts. In my judgment (with which each of the assessors fully concurs) the course taken by the defendant's solicitors was wrong, but it falls far short of any conduct by them which would justify the court in invoking, of its own motion, either RSC Ord 62, r 8, or any other jurisdiction over them. The matter will therefore proceed no further. I say nothing, of course, about any rights that the defendant may have, for she has not been a party to these proceedings.

Before leaving this part of the case, I should add something about the reason for junior counsel advising that authority to brief a leader should be sought. According to the written statement put before me by the representative of the defendant's solicitors, the reasons were, at any rate in part, that the legal aid authorities had authorised a leader for the plaintiff; that there was a good deal of interest in the case on both sides of the profession; and that the decision of the Court of Appeal would be likely to be one which would be carefully read by both branches of the profession as providing a definitive judgment. On at any rate one view, these reasons, and certainly the second and third, provide slender justification for increasing the costs of an assisted person by taking in a leader. Neither assisted persons nor the legal aid fund exist for the purpose of satisfying the interest of either branch of the profession, or in order to improve the clarity of the law. Such advice should be given in the best interests of the client, rather than of others. It may be that these expressions were intended to do little more than to indicate the difficulty and weight of the case, and so the need for a leader; and in that sense they are unobjectionable. But they are at least capable of being read in the other sense, and I wish to make it plain that I give no countenance to them in that sense.

I should also add that I hope that in cases where relatively small sums are at stake the legal aid authorities will be more chary of authorising the briefing of leaders than this case suggests; and similarly for unusual acts or unusually large expenditure, eg within reg 62 of the Legal Aid (General) Regulations 1980, SI 1980/1894. Once a leader for the plaintiff in this case had been authorised, I can well understand that the defendant's legal aid committee may have felt it only just to follow suit; but so far as the facts are known to me, and with the advantage of hindsight, I feel considerable reservations about the suitability of authorising a leader for the plaintiff when the fund in dispute was so modest. I would not for a moment accept that there is any shortage of juniors practising in the Chancery Division who are fully capable of conducting complex cases and arguing difficult points of law without being led.

That brings me to the second point. This matter has come to light only by reason of the summons to review the taxation which the defendant's solicitors took out. If they had not done this, the questions considered in this judgment would not have come before the court. The combined effect of regs 60(1) and 64(2) of the Legal Aid (General) Regulations 1980 is that no question as to the propriety of instructing a Queen's Counsel can be raised on any taxation if the legal aid authorities have authorised that instruction. I think that it is plain that these regulations in no way tie the hands of the court when acting under its inherent jurisdiction, and that the court can accordingly inquire into the propriety of briefing a leader and the propriety of the circumstances in which he was briefed. Yet the court can make no inquiry unless apprised of the case. It appears that there may be a not insubstantial number of cases in which it is questionable whether the briefing of a leader, even though authorised by the legal aid authorities, has been effected with the full and informed consent or instructions of the litigant, or is otherwise for the benefit of the litigant; and the same applies to the taking of some step that is unusual or unusually expensive. If such a case comes before a taxing master, I do not know what is the proper course for him to take. I do not think that he has any power to deal with the matter himself otherwise than by taxing the costs in the usual way, as the taxing master has done in the present case. He cannot make the solicitor personally liable for costs under Ord 62, r 8 (apart from his limited power under r 8(6)), because although this power is given to 'the Court', and by Ord 1, r 4(2) 'the Court' includes a master, Ord 1, r 4(1) excludes a taxing master from the definition of 'master'. I suppose that the taxing master could refer the case to the judge who made the order, so that he could consider the point; but it would be better if rules were to prescribe what should be done.

I turn to the third point, the process of investigation itself. In the present case both I and the assessors found it necessary to ask the representative of the defendant's solicitors a great many questions to ascertain the facts as well as to test his contentions. (Most of the questions, I should say, were asked by me.) At times this process made me doubtful how far it was proper or desirable for the court to be asking questions about the facts which might lead the defendant's solicitors to make admissions injurious to their interests. English courts are not accustomed to conducting inquiries of an inquisitorial nature. No doubt if a prima facie case for further and more detailed investigation had been disclosed it would have been possible, perhaps with the aid of the Official Solicitor or the Attorney General, to make arrangements for some form of adversary process; and it would have been necessary to determine what part the defendant, or someone on her behalf, was to play. However, that stage was never reached, and so I need say no more than that it seems to me that it is highly desirable that a suitable procedure for dealing with cases of this type should be laid down in whatever are the appropriate rules, rather than leaving it to be evolved ad hoc in each case.

In the result, I may summarise my conclusions on the general questions as follows. First, in my judgment solicitors in legal aid cases are in all ordinary circumstances under a duty not to instruct leading counsel, even though authorised by the legal aid authorities, unless they have obtained the agreement of their client to this course being taken; and similarly as to taking some unusual or unusually expensive step. Further, before this agreement is given, the client must have been fully informed of the probable additional cost involved, and the effect of this additional cost in relation to the client's own assets and the statutory charge on any property recovered or preserved in the proceedings; and the client must have been properly advised on this. Second, there ought to be some convenient procedure whereby any taxing master who perceives some apparent infraction of this duty, or some other matter which ought to be investigated and cannot at present be dealt with on a taxation of costs, can refer the matter to a judge or master so that it can be investigated. Third, some procedure for dealing with such investigations ought to be laid down. I commend these last two matters to the appropriate rule-making authority for due consideration. I do not presume to suggest what that procedure should be, or whether any powers to deal with the matters should be conferred on the taxing masters, or should be exercised by other masters, or only by the judges. That is all for mature consideration by the proper authorities, and there are many factors to be borne in mind. All I say is that this case has shown that something ought to be done. I need only add that if any satisfactory procedure for dealing with these matters does in fact already exist, it has not emerged in these proceedings, and obviously it ought to be made better known.

Decision accordingly.

Azza M Abdallah   Barrister.

R v Ghosh

COURT OF APPEAL, CRIMINAL DIVISION
LORD LANE CJ, LLOYD AND EASTHAM JJ
15 MARCH, 5 APRIL 1982

Criminal law – Theft – Obtaining property by deception – Dishonesty – Test to be applied in determining whether accused was dishonest – Whether test of dishonesty subjective or objective – Theft Act 1968, ss 1(1), 15(1).

The defendant, a consultant who had been acting as a locum tenens at a hospital, was charged on indictment with attempting to obtain, and obtaining, money by deception, contrary to s 15(1)[a] of the Theft Act 1968, by falsely pretending that money was due to him in respect of an operation which had in fact been carried out by someone else and/or under the national health service. His defence was that he had not acted dishonestly because the sums in question were legitimately payable to him as consultation fees. The judge directed the jury that it was for them to decide, by applying their own standards of honesty, whether the defendant had acted 'dishonestly' within the meaning of the 1968 Act. The defendant was convicted. He appealed against conviction, contending that the judge had misdirected the jury. The question arose whether the test of 'dishonesty' for the purposes of s 1(1)[b] of the 1968 Act was a subjective test descriptive of the accused's state of mind (ie whether the accused had known he was acting dishonestly) or an objective test intended to characterise a course of conduct (ie whether the accused had in fact acted dishonestly).

Held – (1) The question whether an accused person had acted dishonestly could not be determined completely objectively by the jury applying their own standards of honesty, because for the purposes of s 1(1) of the 1968 Act acting dishonestly described not a course of conduct but a state of mind which could not be established independently of the knowledge and belief of the accused. In determining whether the accused had acted dishonestly, the test was first whether the accused's actions had been dishonest according to the ordinary standards of reasonable and honest people and if so, whether the accused himself had realised that his actions were, according to those standards, dishonest. Thus a genuine belief by the accused that he was morally justified in acting as he did was no defence if he knew that ordinary people would consider such conduct to be dishonest (see p 696 *a b e g* to *j*, post); *R v Waterfall* [1969] 3 All ER 1048, *R v Royle* [1971] 3 All ER 1359, *R v Gilks* [1972] 3 All ER 280, *R v Feely* [1973] 1 All ER 341, *Scott v Comr of Police for the Metropolis* [1974] 3 All ER 1032, *R v Greenstein* [1976] 1 All ER 1 and *R v Landy* [1981] 1 All ER 1172 considered; *R v McIvor* [1982] 1 All ER 491 disapproved.

(2) In so far as the judge had misdirected the jury, there had been no miscarriage of justice because once the jury had rejected the defendant's explanation of what had happened (which they clearly had), the finding of dishonesty was inevitable whichever of the tests of dishonesty was applied. The appeal would accordingly be dismissed (see p 697 *a b*, post).

Notes

For the meaning of 'dishonesty', see 11 Halsbury's Laws (4th edn) para 1263, and for cases on the subject, see 15 Digest (Reissue) 1263–1264, 10,829–10,832.

For the Theft Act 1968, ss 1, 15, see 8 Halsbury's Statutes (3rd edn) 783, 792.

---

a   Section 15(1) provides: 'A person who by any deception dishonestly obtains property belonging to another, with the intention of permanently depriving the other of it, shall on conviction on indictment be liable to imprisonment for a term not exceeding ten years.'

b   Section 1(1), so far as material, provides: 'A person is guilty of theft if he dishonestly appropriates property belonging to another with the intention of permanently depriving the other of it; and "thief" and "steal" shall be construed accordingly.'

Cases referred to in judgment

Boggeln v Williams [1978] 2 All ER 1061, [1978] 1 WLR 873, DC, Digest (Cont Vol E) 158,
 10,728a.

R v Feely [1973] 1 All ER 341, [1973] QB 530, [1973] 2 WLR 201, CA, 15 Digest (Reissue)
 1263, *10,830*.

R v Gilks [1972] 3 All ER 280, [1972] 1 WLR 1341, CA, 15 Digest (Reissue) 1255, *10,735*.

R v Greenstein, R v Green [1976] 1 All ER 1, [1975] 1 WLR 1353, CA, 15 Digest (Reissue)
 1386, *12,133*.

R v Landy [1981] 1 All ER 1172, [1981] 1 WLR 355, CA.

R v McIvor [1982] 1 All ER 491, [1982] 1 WLR 409, CA.

R v Royle [1971] 3 All ER 1359, [1971] 1 WLR 1764, CA, 15 Digest (Reissue) 1389,
 12,146.

R v Waterfall [1969] 3 All ER 1048, [1970] 1 QB 148, [1969] 3 WLR 947, CA, 15 Digest
 (Reissue) 1387, *12,139*.

Scott v Comr of Police for the Metropolis [1974] 3 All ER 1032, [1975] AC 819, [1974] 3
 WLR 741, HL, 15 Digest (Reissue) 1400, *12,271*.

Appeal

On 29 April 1981 at the Crown Court at St Albans, before his Honour Judge Anwyl-Davies QC and a jury, the appellant, Deb Baran Ghosh, was convicted, on count 1 of an indictment, of attempting to procure the execution of a cheque by deception, contrary to s 20(2) of the Theft Act 1968, on count 2, of attempting to obtain money by deception, contrary to s 15(1) of the Act, and, on counts 3 and 4, of obtaining money by deception, contrary to s 15(1) of the Act. He was fined £250 on each count with a term of imprisonment to be served in default of payment. He appealed against conviction. The facts are set out in the judgment of the court.

Robert Francis (assigned by the Registrar of Criminal Appeals) for the appellant.
John Drinkwater QC and *Anthony Glass* for the Crown.

Cur adv vult

5 April. **LORD LANE CJ** read the following judgment of the court: On 29 April 1981 before the Crown Court at St Albans, the appellant was convicted on four counts of an indictment laid under the Theft Act 1968: on count 1, attempting to procure the execution of a cheque by deception; on count 2, attempting to obtain money by deception; on counts 3 and 4, obtaining money by deception. Count 1 was laid under s 20(2) and the remainder under s 15(1). He was fined the sum of £250 on each count with a term of imprisonment to be served in default of payment.

At all material times the appellant was a surgeon acting as a locum tenens consultant at a hospital. The charges alleged that he had falsely represented that he had himself carried out a surgical operation to terminate pregnancy or that money was due to himself or an anaesthetist for such an operation, when in fact the operation had been carried out by someone else, and/or under the national health service provisions.

His defence was that there was no deception; that the sums paid to him were due for consultation fees which were legitimately payable under the regulations, or else were the balance of fees properly payable; in other words that there was nothing dishonest about his behaviour on any of the counts.

The effect of the jury's verdict was as follows: as to count 1, that the appellant had falsely represented that he had carried out a surgical operation and had intended dishonestly to obtain money thereby; that as to count 2 he had falsely pretended that an operation had been carried out under the national health service; that as to count 3 he had falsely pretended that money was due to an anaesthetist; and as to count 4 that he had obtained money by falsely pretending that an operation had been carried out on a fee-paying basis when in fact it had been conducted under the terms of the national health service.

The grounds of appeal are simply that the judge misdirected the jury as to the meaning of dishonesty.

What the judge had to say on that topic was as follows:

'Now, finally dishonesty. There are, sad to say, infinite categories of dishonesty. It is for you. Jurors in the past and, whilst we have criminal law in the future, jurors in the future have to set the standards of honesty. Now it is your turn today, having heard what you have, to consider contemporary standards of honesty and dishonesty in the context of all that you have heard. I cannot really expand on this too much, but probably it is something rather like getting something for nothing, sharp practice, manipulating systems and many other matters which come to your mind.'

The law on this branch of the Theft Act 1968 is in a complicated state and we embark on an examination of the authorities with great diffidence.

When *R v McIvor* [1982] 1 All ER 491, [1982] 1 WLR 409 came before the Court of Appeal, there were two conflicting lines of authority. On the one hand there were cases which decided that the test of dishonesty for the purposes of the Theft Act 1968 is, what we venture to call, subjective, that is to say, the jury should be directed to look into the mind of the defendant and determine whether he knew he was acting dishonestly: see *R v Landy* [1981] 1 All ER 1172 at 1181, [1981] 1 WLR 355 at 365 where Lawton LJ, giving the reserved judgment of the Court of Appeal said:

'An assertion by a defendant that throughout a transaction he acted honestly does not have to be accepted but has to be weighed like any other piece of evidence. If that was the defendant's state of mind, or may have been, he is entitled to be acquitted. But if the jury, applying their own motions of what is honest and what is not, conclude that he could not have believed he was acting honestly, then the element of dishonesty will have been established. What a jury must not do is to say to themselves: "If we had been in his place we would have known we were acting dishonestly, so he must have known he was."'

On the other hand there were cases which decided that the test of dishonesty is objective. Thus in *R v Greenstein, R v Green* [1976] 1 All ER 1 at 6, [1975] 1 WLR 1353 at 1359 the judge in the court below had directed the jury:

'. . . there is nothing illegal in stagging. The question you have to decide and what this case is all about is whether these defendants, or either of them, carried out their stagging operations in a dishonest way. To that question you apply your own standards of dishonesty. It is no good, you see, applying the standards of anyone accused of dishonesty otherwise everybody accused of dishonesty, if he were to be tested by his own standards, would be acquitted automatically, you may think. The question is essentially one for a jury to decide and it is essentially one which the jury must decide by applying its own standards.'

The Court of Appeal, in a reserved judgment, approved that direction.

In *R v McIvor* [1982] 1 All ER 491 at 497, [1982] 1 WLR 409 at 417 the Court of Appeal sought to reconcile these conflicting lines of authority. They did so on the basis that the subjective test is appropriate where the charge is conspiracy to defraud, but in the case of theft the test should be objective. We quote the relevant passage in full:

'It seems elementary, first, that where the charge is conspiracy to defraud the prosecution must prove actual dishonesty in the minds of the defendants in relation to the agreement concerned, and, second, that where the charge is an offence contrary to s 15 of the Theft Act 1968 the prosecution must prove that the defendant knew or was reckless regarding the representation concerned. The passage in my judgment in *R v Landy* [1981] 1 All ER 1172 at 1181, [1981] 1 WLR 355 at 365 per Lawton LJ to which we have referred should be read in relation to charges of conspiracy to defraud, and not in relation to charges of theft contrary to s 1 of the 1968 Act. Theft is in a different category from conspiracy to defraud, so that dishonesty can be established independently of the knowledge or belief of the defendant, subject to the special cases provided for in s 2 of the Act. Nevertheless, where a defendant has given evidence of his state of mind at the time of the alleged offence, the jury should be told to give that evidence such weight as they consider right, and they may also be directed that they should apply their own standards to the meaning of dishonesty.'

The question we have to decide in the present case is, first, whether the distinction suggested in *R v McIvor* is justifiable in theory and, second, whether it is workable in practice.

In *Scott v Comr of Police for the Metropolis* [1974] 3 All ER 1032, [1975] AC 819 the House of Lords had to consider whether deceit is a necessary element in the common law crime of conspiracy to defraud. They held that it is not. It is sufficient for the Crown to prove dishonesty. In the course of his speech Viscount Dilhorne traced the meaning of the words 'fraud', 'fraudulently' and 'defraud' in relation to simple larceny, as well as the common law offence of conspiracy to defraud. After referring to *Stephen's History of the Criminal Law of England* ((1883) vol 2, pp 121–122) and *East's Pleas of the Crown* ((1803) vol 2, p 553) he continued as follows ([1974] 3 All ER 1032 at 1036, [1975] AC 819 at 836–837):

> 'The Criminal Law Revision Committee in their eighth report on "Theft and Related Offences" (Cmnd 2977 (1966)) in para 33 expressed the view that the important element of larceny, embezzlement and fraudulent conversion was "undoubtedly the dishonest appropriation of another person's property"; in para 35 that the words "dishonestly appropriates" meant the same as "fraudulently converts to his own use or benefit, or the use or benefit of any other person", and in para 39 that "dishonestly" seemed to them a better word than "fraudulently". Parliament endorsed these views in the Theft Act 1968, which by s 1(1) defined theft as the dishonest appropriation of property belonging to another with the intention of permanently depriving the other of it. Section 17 of that Act replaces ss 82 and 83 of the Larceny Act 1861 and the Falsification of Accounts Act 1875. The offences created by those sections and by that Act made it necessary to prove that there had been an "intent to defraud". Section 17 of the Theft Act 1968 substitutes the words "dishonestly with a view to gain for himself or another or with intent to cause loss to another" for the words "intent to defraud". If "fraudulently" in relation to larceny meant "dishonestly" and "intent to defraud" in relation to falsification of accounts is equivalent to the words now contained in s 17 of the Theft Act 1968 which I have quoted, it would indeed be odd if "defraud" in the phrase "conspiracy to defraud" has a different meaning and means only a conspiracy which is to be carried out by deceit.'

Later on in the same speech Viscount Dilhorne continued as follows ([1974] 3 All ER 1032 at 1038, [1975] AC 819 at 839):

> 'As I have said, words take colour from the context in which they are used, but the words "fraudulently" and "defraud" must ordinarily have a very similar meaning. If, as I think, and as the Criminal Law Revision Committee appears to have thought, "fraudulently" means "dishonestly", then "to defraud" ordinarily means, in my opinion, to deprive a person dishonestly of something which is his or of something to which he is or would or might but for the perpetration of the fraud be entitled.'

In *Scott* the House of Lords were only concerned with the question whether deceit is an essential ingredient in cases of conspiracy to defraud; and they held not. As Lord Diplock said ([1974] 3 All ER 1032 at 1040, [1975] AC 819 at 841), 'dishonesty of any kind is enough'. But there is nothing in *Scott* which supports the view that, so far as the element of dishonesty is concerned, 'theft is in a different category from conspiracy to defraud'. On the contrary the analogy drawn by Viscount Dilhorne between the two offences, and indeed the whole tenor of his speech, suggests the precise opposite.

Nor is there anything in *R v Landy* itself which justifies putting theft and conspiracy to defraud into different categories. Indeed the court went out of its way to stress that the test for dishonesty, whatever it might be, should be the same whether the offence charged be theft or conspiracy to defraud. This is clear from the reference to *R v Feely* [1973] 1 All ER 341, [1973] QB 530, which was a case under s 1 of the Theft Act 1968. Having set out what we have for convenience called the subjective test, the court in *R v Landy* [1981] 1 All ER 1172 at 1181, [1981] 1 WLR 355 at 365 continued:

> 'In our judgment this is the way *R v Feely* should be applied in cases where the issue of dishonesty arises. It is also the way in which the jury should have been directed in this case . . .'

In support of the distinction it is said that in conspiracy to defraud the question arises in relation to an agreement. But we cannot see that this makes any difference. If A and B agree to deprive a person dishonestly of his goods, they are guilty of conspiracy to defraud: see *Scott's* case. If they dishonestly and with the necessary intent deprive him of his goods, they are presumably guilty of theft. Why, one asks respectfully, should the test be objective in the case of simple theft, but subjective where they have agreed to commit a theft?

The difficulties do not stop there. The court in *McIvor* evidently regarded cases under s 15 of the Theft Act 1968 as being on the subjective side of the line, at any rate so far as proof of deception is concerned. This was the way they sought to explain *R v Greenstein*. In that case, after directing the jury in the passage which we have already quoted, the judge in the court below continued as follows ([1976] 1 All ER 1 at 7, [1975] 1 WLR 1353 at 1360):

> 'Now in considering whether Mr Green or Mr Greenstein had or may have had an honest belief in the truth of their representations . . . the test is a subjective one. That is to say, it is not what you would have believed in similar circumstances. It is what you think they believed and if you think that they, or either of them, had an honest belief to that effect, well then, of course, there would not be any dishonesty. On the other hand, if there is an absence of reasonable grounds for so believing, you might think that that points to the conclusion that they or either of them, as the case may be, had no genuine belief in the truth of their representations. In which case, applying your own standards, you may think that they acted dishonestly and it would be for you to say whether it has been established by the prosecution that they had no such honest belief . . .'

The Court of Appeal in *R v Greenstein* appear to have approved that passage. At any rate they expressed no disapproval.

In *R v McIvor* [1982] 1 All ER 491 at 496, [1982] 1 WLR 409 at 415 the court reconciled the two passages quoted from the judge's summing up as follows:

> 'It seems that those two passages are concerned with different points. The first, which follows and adopts the standards laid down in *R v Feely*, is concerned with the element of dishonesty in s 15 offences, whilst the second is specifically concerned with the mental element in relation to the false representation the subject matter of the charge. Clearly, if a defendant honestly believes that the representation made was true the prosecution cannot prove that he knew of, or was reckless as to, its falsity.'

The difficulty with s 15 of the Theft Act 1968 is that dishonesty comes in twice. If a person knows that he is not telling the truth he is guilty of dishonesty. Indeed deliberate deception is one of the two most obvious forms of dishonesty. One wonders therefore whether 'dishonestly' in s 15(1) adds anything, except in the case of reckless deception. But assuming it does, there are two consequences of the distinction drawn in *McIvor*. In the first place it would mean that the legislation has gone further than its framers intended. For it is clear from paras 87–88 of the Criminal Law Revision Committee's eighth report that 'deception' was to replace 'false pretence' in the old s 32(1) of the

Larceny Act 1916, and 'dishonestly' was to replace 'with intent to defraud'. If the test of dishonesty in conspiracy to defraud cases is subjective, it is difficult to see how it could have been anything other than subjective in considering 'intent to defraud'. It follows that, if the distinction drawn in *McIvor* is correct, the Criminal Law Revision Committee were recommending an important change in the law by substituting 'dishonestly' for 'with intent to defraud'; for they were implicitly substituting an objective for a subjective test.

The second consequence is that in cases of deliberate deception the jury will have to be given two different tests of dishonesty to apply: the subjective tests in relation to deception and the objective test in relation to obtaining. This is indeed what seems to have happened in *R v Greenstein*. We cannot regard this as satisfactory from a practical point of view. If it be sought to obviate the difficulty by making the test subjective in relation to both aspects of s 15, but objective in relation to s 1, then that would certainly be contrary to what was intended by the Criminal Law Revision Committee. For in para 88 they say:

'The provision in clause 12(1) making a person guilty of criminal deception if he "dishonestly obtains" the property replaces the provision in the 1916 Act, section 32 (1) making a person guilty of obtaining by false pretences if he "with intent to defraud, obtains" the things there mentioned. The change will correspond to the change from "fraudulently" to "dishonestly" in the definition of stealing (contained in section 1).'

We feel, with the greatest respect, that in seeking to reconcile the two lines of authority in the way we have mentioned, the Court of Appeal in *McIvor* was seeking to reconcile the irreconcilable. It therefore falls to us now either to choose between the two lines of authority or to propose some other solution.

In the current supplement to *Archbold's, Pleading, Evidence and Practice in Criminal Cases* (40th edn, 1979) para 1460, the editors suggest that the observations on dishonesty by the Court of Appeal in *R v Landy* can be disregarded 'in view of the wealth of authority to the contrary'. The matter, we feel is not as simple as that.

In *R v Waterfall* [1969] 3 All ER 1048, [1970] 1 QB 148 the defendant was charged under s 16 of the 1968 Act with dishonestly obtaining a pecuniary advantage from a taxi driver. Lord Parker CJ, giving the judgment of the Court of Appeal, said ([1969] 3 All ER 1048 at 1049–1050, [1970] 1 QB 148 at 150–151):

'The sole question as it seems to me in this case revolves round the third ingredient, namely, whether that what was done was done dishonestly. In regard to that the deputy recorder directed the jury in this way: ". . . if on reflection and deliberation you came to the conclusion that [the appellant] never did have any genuine belief that [the appellant's accountant] would pay the taxi fare, then you would be entitled to convict him . . ." In other words, in that passage the deputy recorder is telling the jury they had to consider what was in this particular appellant's mind; had he a genuine belief that the accountant would provide the money? That, as it seems to this court, is a perfectly proper direction subject to this, that it would be right to tell the jury that they can use as a test, although not a conclusive test, whether there were any reasonable grounds for that belief. Unfortunately, however, just before the jury retired, in two passages of the transcript the deputy recorder, as it seems to this court, was saying that one cannot hold that the appellant had a genuine belief unless he had reasonable grounds for that belief.'

Lord Parker CJ then sets out the passages in question and continues:

'. . . the court is quite satisfied that those directions cannot be justified. The test here is a subjective test, whether the appellant had an honest belief, and of course whereas the absence of reasonable ground may point strongly to the fact that that belief is not genuine, it is at the end of the day for the jury to say whether or not in the case of this particular man he did have that genuine belief.'

That decision was criticised by academic writers. But it was followed shortly afterwards in *R v Royle* [1971] 3 All ER 1359, [1971] 1 WLR 1764, another case under s 16 of the 1968 Act. Edmund Davies LJ, giving the judgment of the court, said ([1971] 3 All ER 1359 at 1365, [1971] 1 WLR 1764 at 1769–1770):

> 'The charges being that debts had been dishonestly "evaded" by deception, contrary to s 16(2)(a), it was incumbent on the commissioner to direct the jury on the fundamental ingredient of dishonesty. In accordance with *R v Waterfall* they should have been told that the test is whether the accused had an honest belief and that, whereas the absence of reasonable ground might point strongly to the conclusion that he entertained no genuine belief in the truth of his representation, it was for them to say whether or not it had been established that the appellant had no such genuine belief.'

It is to be noted that the court in that case treated the 'fundamental ingredient of dishonesty' as being the same as whether the defendant had a genuine belief in the truth of the representation.

In *R v Gilks* [1972] 3 All ER 280, [1972] 1 WLR 1341, which was decided by the Court of Appeal the following year, the appellant had been convicted of theft contrary to s 1 of the 1968 Act. The facts were that he had been overpaid by a bookmaker. He knew that the bookmaker had made a mistake, and that he was not entitled to the money. But he kept it. The case for the defence was that 'bookmakers are a race apart'. It would be dishonest if your grocer gave you too much change and you kept it, knowing that he had made a mistake. But it was not dishonest in the case of a bookmaker.

The deputy chairman of the court below directed the jury as follows:

> 'Well, it is a matter for you to consider, members of the jury, but try and place yourselves in [the appellant's] position at that time and answer the question whether in your view he thought he was acting honestly or dishonestly.'

(See [1972] 3 All ER 280 at 283, [1972] 1 WLR 1341 at 1345)

Cairns LJ, giving the judgment of the court of appeal held that that was, in the circumstances of the case, a proper and sufficient direction on the matter of dishonesty. He continued ([1972] 3 All ER 280 at 283, [1972] 1 WLR 1341 at 1345):

> 'On the face of it the appellant's conduct was dishonest; the only possible basis on which the jury could find that the prosecution had not established dishonesty would be if they thought it possible that the appellant did have the belief which he claimed to have.'

A little later *R v Feely* came before a court of five judges. The case is often treated as having laid down an objective test of dishonesty for the purpose of s 1 of the 1968 Act. But what it actually decided was (i) that it is for the jury to determine whether the defendant acted dishonestly and not for the judge, (ii) that the word 'dishonestly' can only relate to the defendant's own state of mind, and (iii) that it is unnecessary and undesirable for judges to define what is meant by 'dishonestly'.

It is true that the court said ([1973] 3 All ER 341 at 345, [1973] QB 530 at 537–538):

> 'Jurors, when deciding whether an appropriation was dishonest can be reasonably expected to, and should, apply the current standards of ordinary decent people.'

It is that sentence which is usually taken as laying down the objective test. But the passage goes on:

> 'In their own lives they have to decide what is and what is not dishonest. We can see no reason why, when in a jury box, they should require the help of a judge to tell them what amounts to dishonesty.'

The sentence requiring the jury to apply current standards leads up to the prohibition on judges from applying *their* standards. That is the context in which the sentence appears. It seems to be reading too much into that sentence to treat it as authority for the view that 'dishonesty can be established independently of the knowledge or belief of the defendant'. If it could, then any reference to the state of mind of the defendant would be beside the point.

This brings us to the heart of the problem. Is 'dishonestly' in s 1 of the 1968 Act intended to characterise a course of conduct? Or is it intended to describe a state of mind? If the former, then we can well understand that it could be established independently of the knowledge or belief of the accused. But if, as we think, it is the latter, then the knowledge and belief of the accused are at the root of the problem.

Take for example a man who comes from a country where public transport is free. On his first day here he travels on a bus. He gets off without paying. He never had any intention of paying. His mind is clearly honest; but his conduct, judged objectively by what he has done, is dishonest. It seems to us that, in using the word 'dishonestly' in the 1968 Act, Parliament cannot have intended to catch dishonest conduct in that sense, that is to say conduct to which no moral obloquy could possibly attach. This is sufficiently established by the partial definition in s 2 of the Theft Act 1968 itself. All the matters covered by s 2(1) relate to the belief of the accused. Section 2(2) relates to his willingness to pay. A man's belief and his willingness to pay are things which can only be established subjectively. It is difficult to see how a partially subjective definition can be made to work in harness with the test which in all other respects is wholly objective.

If we are right that dishonesty is something in the mind of the accused (what Professor Glanville Williams calls 'a special mental state'), then if the mind of the accused is honest, it cannot be deemed dishonest merely because members of the jury would have regarded it as dishonest to embark on that course of conduct.

So we would reject the simple uncomplicated approach that the test is purely objective, however attractive from the practical point of view that solution may be.

There remains the objection that to adopt a subjective test is to abandon all standards but that of the accused himself, and to bring about a state of affairs in which 'Robin Hood would be no robber' (see *R v Greenstein*). This objection misunderstands the nature of the subjective test. It is no defence for a man to say, 'I knew that what I was doing is generally regarded as dishonest; but I do not regard it as dishonest myself. Therefore I am not guilty.' What he is, however, entitled to say is, 'I did not know that anybody would regard what I was doing as dishonest.' He may not be believed; just as he may not be believed if he sets up 'a claim of right' under s 2(1) of the 1968 Act, or asserts that he believed in the truth of a misrepresentation under s 15 of the 1968 Act. But if he *is* believed, or raises a real doubt about the matter, the jury cannot be sure that he was dishonest.

In determining whether the prosecution has proved that the defendant was acting dishonestly, a jury must first of all decide whether according to the ordinary standards of reasonable and honest people what was done was dishonest. If it was not dishonest by those standards, that is the end of the matter and the prosecution fails. If it was dishonest by those standards, then the jury must consider whether the defendant himself must have realised that what he was doing was by those standards dishonest. In most cases, where the actions are obviously dishonest by ordinary standards, there will be no doubt about it. It will be obvious that the defendant himself knew that he was acting dishonestly. It is dishonest for a defendant to act in a way which he knows ordinary people consider to be dishonest, even if he asserts or genuinely believes that he is morally justified in acting as he did. For example, Robin Hood or those ardent anti-vivisectionists who remove animals from vivisection laboratories are acting dishonestly, even though they may consider themselves to be morally justified in doing what they do, because they know that ordinary people would consider these actions to be dishonest.

Cases which might be described as borderline, such as *Boggeln v Williams* [1978] 2 All ER 1061, [1978] 1 WLR 873, will depend on the view taken by the jury whether the defendant may have believed what he was doing was in accordance with the ordinary man's idea of honesty. A jury might have come to the conclusion that the defendant in that case was disobedient or impudent, but not dishonest in what he did.

So far as the present case is concerned, it seems to us that once the jury had rejected the defendant's account in respect of each count in the indictment (as they plainly did), the finding of dishonesty was inevitable, whichever of the tests of dishonesty was applied. If the judge had asked the jury to determine whether the defendant might have believed that what he did was in accordance with the ordinary man's idea of honesty, there could have only been one answer, and that is No, once the jury had rejected the defendant's explanation of what happened.

In so far as there was a misdirection on the meaning of dishonesty, it is plainly a case for the application of the proviso to s 2(1) of the Criminal Appeal Act 1968.

This appeal is accordingly dismissed.

Appeal dismissed.

Solicitors: *Director of Public Prosecutions.*

April Weiss   Barrister.

Bunston v Rawlings

QUEEN'S BENCH DIVISION
LORD LANE CJ AND WOOLF J
21 JANUARY, 15 FEBRUARY 1982

Criminal law – Costs – Magistrates' court – Just and reasonable costs – Magistrates not having sufficient material to enable just determination on costs – Magistrates ordering costs to be taxed by justices' clerk – Whether magistrates having jurisdiction to do so – Costs in Criminal Cases Act 1973, s 2(1).

After an information which had been laid against him had been dismissed the defendant applied to the magistrates for his costs to be paid by the prosecutor. The magistrates considered that they could not, on the material before them, reach a just determination of what the costs should be and so they made an order, purportedly under s 2(1)[a] of the Costs in Criminal Cases Act 1973, that the defendant's costs be taxed by their clerk and paid by the prosecutor. On the question whether the magistrates had jurisdiction to make such an order under s 2(1),

Held – Magistrates had no power to delegate their duties in respect of costs to their clerk, and where they considered that it was impossible to reach a just determination without further information the appropriate course was to adjourn the matter in order to enable the clerk to make inquiries from the parties as to the costs incurred. The information obtained by the clerk should then be communicated to the magistrates and the parties, who should then be given an opportunity to make representations to the Bench before the magistrates made a final decision (see p 698 *j* to p 699 *a*, post).

Notes
For costs between parties in magistrates' courts, see 29 Halsbury's Laws (4th edn) para 392.

For the Costs in Criminal Cases Act 1973, s 2 see 43 Halsbury's Statutes (3rd edn) 716.

---

a   Section 2(1) is set out at p 698 *f*, post

Case stated

On 28 February 1981 Alan Richard Bunston, an officer of the Trading Standards Department of Gloucestershire County Council, laid certain informations against the defendant, Peter Rawlings, relating to offences under the Trade Descriptions Act 1968. On 16 April 1981 the defendant appeared before the justices sitting at Whitminster Magistrates' Court. He elected summary trial and pleaded not guilty. After hearing the evidence, the justices dismissed the informations, whereupon the defendant applied for an order for costs against the prosecutor. Finding it impossible to reach a just determination of what the costs should be on the material before them, the justices made an order that the defendant's costs be taxed by their clerk and paid by the prosecutor. At the request of the prosecutor, the justices stated a case for the opinion of the High Court. The questions of law for the opinion of the court related mainly to the Trade Descriptions Act 1968, but the final question was whether the justices had any jurisdiction or power under the Costs in Criminal Cases Act 1973, s 2(1), to make the order that the defendant's costs should be taxed by their clerk and paid by the prosecutor.

Malcolm Bishop for the prosecutor.
Gavin Chalmers for the defendant.
The justices did not appear.

Cur adv vult

15 February. **LORD LANE CJ** read the following judgment of the court: On 21 January 1982 we gave judgment on the main issues raised in this appeal by way of case stated. We made no order as to costs.

Nothing turns on those matters now, but we took time to consider the final question posed by the justices for answer by this court. The question was:

'Whether the Justices had any jurisdiction or power under the Costs in Criminal Cases Act 1973, section 2(1), to make an order that the said Defendant's costs be taxed by the Clerk to the Justices and paid by the Prosecutor.'

Section 2(1) provides as follows:

'On the summary trial of an information a magistrates' court shall, on dismissal of the information, have power to make such order as to costs to be paid by the prosecutor to the accused as it thinks just and reasonable.'

Section 2(2) makes similar provision (subject to certain safeguards) as to costs to be paid by the accused to the prosecutor.

There is no such provision as is to be found in s 1(6) of the Act in the case of orders for costs out of central funds. That subsection provides:

'The amount of costs ordered to be paid under this section shall be ascertained as soon as practicable by the proper officer of the court.'

In the vast majority of cases, the magistrates will have no difficulty, with the help of the parties or their advisers, at the end of the hearing in arriving quickly at a just figure to compensate a successful defendant for the money which he has properly expended in carrying on his defence. It is in the rare case where the necessary information is lacking or not readily available on which to base a decision that difficulties may arise. It is on these occasions that magistrates may wish to use the services of their clerk as the question in the present case indicates.

Where the magistrates consider that it is not possible to reach a just determination without further information, it is open to them to adjourn the matter in order to enable their clerk to make inquiries from the parties as to the costs incurred. When that information has been obtained, it should be communicated to the prosecutor and to the defendant and also of course laid before the magistrates. The parties should be given the opportunity of making any representations to the Bench they may wish before the magistrates finally decide the matter.

There is no power in the magistrates simply to delegate their duties in regard to costs
a to their clerk or to anyone else. They must retain control. That does not prevent them
from obtaining assistance as we have indicated.

Determination accordingly.

Solicitors: *D A Dean*, Gloucester (for the prosecutor); *Wellington & Clifford*, Gloucester,
b agents for *Anthony Courtney & Co*, Dartmouth (for the defendant).

Dilys Tausz   Barrister.

Note
Robinson v Robinson

d COURT OF APPEAL, CIVIL DIVISION
ORMROD, TEMPLEMAN LJJ AND WOOD J
10, 11, 12 MARCH 1982

*Divorce – Financial provision – Setting aside order – Final order – Fraud, mistake or material
non-disclosure – Practice – Appeal against order or action to set order aside – Advantages of*
e *bringing action to set order aside.*

Divorce – Financial provision – Consent order – Disclosure – Full and frank disclosure of
respondent's financial position – Setting aside consent order where disclosure not full and frank.

Notes
f For the court's power to vary consent orders for ancillary relief, see 13 Halsbury's Laws
(4th edn) para 1170, and for cases on the subject, see 27(2) Digest (Reissue) 842, 6700–
6701.
For setting aside a consent judgment or order obtained by fraud, mistake or material
non-disclosure, see 26 Halsbury's Laws (4th edn) para 562, and for cases on setting aside
judgments and orders so obtained, see 51 Digest (Repl) 842, 3280–3296.

g
Cases referred to
de Lasala v de Lasala [1979] 2 All ER 1146, [1980] AC 546, [1979] 3 WLR 390, PC, Digest
(Cont Vol E) 354, 708a.
Minton v Minton [1979] 1 All ER 79, [1979] AC 593, [1979] 2 WLR 31, Digest (Cont Vol
E) 268, 6702a.

h
Appeal
By amended notice of motion dated 18 December 1981 and pursuant to the leave of the
Court of Appeal granted on 14 January 1982 the petitioner, Moira Rosalind Robinson,
appealed against (i) an order of Cumming-Bruce J dated 16 July 1973 that the respondent,
Donald Edgar Robinson, pay the petitioner £1,200 per annum less tax by way of
periodical payments for the support of herself and the four children of the family, (ii) an
order of the Court of Appeal dated 19 December 1973 that, inter alia, the respondent pay
the petitioner £2,500 by way of periodical payments and (iii) an order made by
Cumming-Bruce J by consent of the parties and dated 12 April 1976 that in full and final
satisfaction of all the petitioner's claims for ancillary relief the respondent pay the
petitioner £5,000 within three months and £5,000 on 12 April 1981. The grounds of
the appeal were that the respondent continually and repeatedly misrepresented to the

court in 1973, 1975–1976 and 1981 the true positions as to his capital and income entitlements.

Mathew Thorpe QC and *Clare Tritton* for the appellant.
Robert Johnson QC and *Paul Coleridge* for the respondent.

ORMROD LJ, after saying that he agreed with the judgments given by Templeman LJ and Wood J, continued: ... I would like to say one or two things on the procedural question which both counsel have helpfully raised.

There is no doubt that both the Court of Appeal and the judge at first instance have jurisdiction in the situation with which we are faced in this case, where the application is to set aside a final order. Lord Diplock said so in *de Lasala v de Lasala* [1979] 2 All ER 1146 at 1155, [1980] AC 546 at 561:

> 'Where a party to an action who seeks to challenge, on the ground that it was obtained by fraud or mistake, a judgment or order that finally disposes of the issues raised between the parties, the only ways of doing it that are open to him are by appeal from the judgment or order to a higher court or by bringing a fresh action to set it aside.'

There are many references in the books to separate actions to set aside a judgment on the ground of fraud. In the Family Division, as has been said many times, this power to set aside final orders is not limited to cases where fraud or mistake can be alleged. It extends, and has always extended, to cases of material non-disclosure. If one looks for a basis for that, one can find it in the Matrimonial Causes Rules 1977, SI 1977/344. There are many authorities to the same effect.

A distinction has to be drawn between the restrictions imposed by the Matrimonial Causes Act 1973 on varying lump sum orders or property adjustment orders which cannot be varied, and the power to set aside an order which has been obtained by fraud or mistake, or by material non-disclosure. The essence of the distinction is that the power to vary usually reflects changes of circumstances subsequent to the date of the order, whereas the power to set aside arises when there has been fraud, mistake or material non-disclosure as to the facts at the time the order was made. From the point of view of convenience, there is a lot to be said for proceedings of this kind taking place before a judge at first instance, because there will usually be serious and often difficult issues of fact to be determined before the power to set aside can be exercised. These can be determined more easily, as a rule, by a judge at first instance. Moreover he can go on to make the appropriate order which we cannot do in this court. I think that these proceedings should normally be started before a judge at first instance, although there may be special circumstances which make it better to proceed by way of appeal.

If it is objected, and indeed counsel for the respondent has indicated this point, that this power to set aside threatens the principle of the so-called 'clean break', the answer is, and it should be appreciated, that a wife whose claim for periodical payments is dismissed with her consent, surrenders (and 'surrenders' is the right word) a very important and valuable statutory right to apply for periodical payments, in the words of the Act 'at any time after decree'. If she is to be asked, or encouraged, to surrender rights of that kind, she is, in my judgment, entitled to have full and frank disclosure of the husband's financial position. He is required to provide it by the rules and it is essential in her interests that he does so. Manoeuvring with accounts prepared for other purposes is not complying with this rule. All too much time is wasted in these cases in exchanging uninformative accounts of private companies and more effort must be made to give a true picture of the husband's financial position. If the husband wants to avoid the risk of a consent order being set aside, he should make a frank disclosure to the wife before she agrees to it and the court makes the order. I do not think that is an unreasonable requirement.

It is essential in these cases that the court retains its power to protect both parties against injustice which may arise from failure to comply with their obligations to disclose. In other words there is a lot to be said for the principle of the clean break but I have no doubt that Lord Scarman, when he used the phrase in *Minton v Minton* [1979] 1 All ER 79 at 87, [1979] AC 593 at 608, had in mind the break should be clean in more senses than one. I would also agree with the order proposed by Templeman LJ.

Appeal allowed.

Solicitors: *Kenwright & Cox* (for the appellant); *Gordon Dadds & Co* (for the respondent).

Patricia Hargrove   Barrister.

Harakas and others v Baltic Mercantile and Shipping Exchange Ltd and another

COURT OF APPEAL, CIVIL DIVISION
LORD DENNING MR, GRIFFITHS AND KERR LJJ
8 MARCH 1982

Libel and slander – Injunction – Interlocutory – Justification – Defendant pleading justification – Whether injunction restraining further publication should be granted.

The International Chamber of Commerce established a maritime bureau to combat maritime fraud by obtaining information and giving warning of fraud to interested persons. In the course of its investigations the bureau obtained information about a particular shipping company and issued a notice published in the Baltic Exchange stating that it had certain information concerning the company which would be made available to persons contemplating business with the company. The company and its owners applied for an injunction restraining the bureau and the exchange from further publishing information alleging that the company and the owners had been engaged in fraudulent dealings. The bureau submitted that an injunction should not be granted because it had reasonable grounds for honestly believing the information to be true. The judge rejected that submission and granted the injunction sought. The bureau appealed.

Held – Where there was a defence of justification or qualified privilege in respect of a libel, an injunction restraining further publication would not be granted unless it could be shown that the defendant dishonestly and maliciously proposed to say or publish information which he knew to be untrue. Since the bureau had acted honestly and in good faith and should not be prevented from carrying out its investigations, the injunction would be discharged (see p 703 *a* to *e g h*, post).

Quartz Hill Consolidated Gold Mining Co v Beall (1882) 20 Ch D 501 applied.

Notes

For the granting of an interlocutory injunction in defamation cases, see 28 Halsbury's Laws (4th edn) paras 166–167, and for cases on the subject, see 32 Digest (Reissue) 323–327, 2682–2719.

Case referred to in judgments

Quartz Hill Consolidated Gold Mining Co v Beall (1882) 20 Ch D 501, CA, 32 Digest (Reissue) 324, 2701.

Interlocutory appeal

The second defendants, ICC International Maritime Bureau, appealed against the order of Peter Pain J made on 28 February 1982 granting an interlocutory injunction, which was continued by order of Boreham J made on 5 March 1982, restraining the bureau from further publishing words alleging, inter alia, that the plaintiffs, Harilaos Kleomenis Harakas, Seal Holdings SA, trading as Grecian Lines, and Maritime Tradition SA, had been engaged in fraudulent, dishonest and/or improper dealings. The facts are set out in judgment of Lord Denning MR.

Geoffrey Shaw for the bureau.
Roger Buckley QC and *Richard Rampton* for the plaintiffs.

LORD DENNING MR. Maritime fraud has increased, is increasing, and ought to be stopped. In 1980 the International Chamber of Commerce set up a bureau to combat maritime fraud. It was called the International Maritime Bureau. One of the tasks of the bureau was to give warning of dangers ahead. In February 1982, having received certain information, the International Maritime Bureau told the secretary of the Baltic Exchange about it. On 22 February 1982 this notice was published in the Baltic Exchange:

> 'Grecian Lines
> Members contemplating business with above named company whose agents are, it is understood, called "Maritime Tradition" may be interested in information available from the Secretary.'

The intention was that interested members of the Baltic Exchange should communicate with the secretary who would put them in touch with the International Maritime Bureau. If the member had a legitimate interest in dealing with Grecian Lines, the International Maritime Bureau would give him information.

The owner of Grecian Lines takes strong objection to this being done. Mr Harakas is the president of two Panamanian companies: Maritime Tradition SA and Seal Holdings SA, trading as Grecian Lines. Mr Harakas owns all the shares in those companies. He has brought these proceedings to try and stop the bureau giving information about Grecian Lines.

At the hearing before the judge the Baltic Exchange said that they were ready to take down the notice; and they did. So there was no further problem with regard to them. But the International Maritime Bureau said, 'No. We are not going to say anything which we know to be untrue. We only give such information as we think may be urgently needed by people who may be doing business with Grecian Lines.' They said that an injunction ought not to be granted against them. The judge granted an injunction on Friday evening. Now there is an appeal to this court.

I need not go into the details of the matter. I would simply say this. There is a man called Costas Kamateros who is notorious as a maritime fraudster. The International Maritime Bureau received some evidence suggesting that Costas Kamateros was behind some of the operations of Grecian Lines. Mr Harakas has sworn an affidavit that that suggestion is entirely untrue. He says that he did have a man working for him called Andreou. But he is not the same man as Costas Kamateros. he says that the International Maritime Bureau are 'barking up the wrong tree'. They are making suggestions against Grecian Lines which ought never to have been made. So he asks the court to make an injunction against the Baltic Exchange and the International Maritime Bureau.

I will read a sentence from the affidavit of Mr Eric Ellen, a director of the International Maritime Bureau. He says:

> 'The ICC International Maritime Bureau does not at present contend that it is true that Costas Kamateros is behind the Plaintiffs' operation: such evidence of that as is set out herein is included in an attempt to demonstrate that there are reasonable grounds for an honest belief that he may be.'

In addition we have been shown today a photograph which it is said goes some way towards proving that Andreou and Costas Kamateros are one and the same man.

This case raises a matter of principle which must be observed. This court never grants an injunction in respect of libel when it is said by the defendant that the words are true and that he is going to justify them. So also, when an occasion is protected by qualified privilege, this court never grants an injunction to restrain a slander or libel, to prevent a person from exercising that privilege, unless it is shown that what the defendant proposes to say is known by him to be untrue so that it is clearly malicious. So long as he proposes to say what he honestly believes to be true, no injunction should be granted against him. That was made clear in *Quartz Hill Consolidated Gold Mining Co v Beall* (1882) 20 Ch D 501.

When there is a bureau of this kind, which is specially charged with the responsibility of obtaining information and giving it to those interested, to warn them of possible dangers, it is very important that they should be able to give information to people who are properly interested, so long as it is done honestly and in good faith. That is all the bureau wish to do in this case. They should not be prevented from so doing by an injunction unless it is clearly shown that they are dishonestly and maliciously saying what they know to be untrue. There is not a shred of evidence to support a suggestion of that kind. In my opinion this injunction should never have been granted, and should be discharged here and now.

I would allow the appeal accordingly.

GRIFFITHS LJ. I agree. I would also allow the appeal for the reasons give by Lord Denning MR, and there is nothing I wish to add.

KERR LJ. I also agree. In deference to Boreham J, I should perhaps say that we have had a good deal more evidence before us than he had.

There is one other matter which I think should be added. One ground which was urged before us for maintaining this injunction is that a hearing in this case is due to take place in a few days, the day after tomorrow I think, and that the dispute as to the identification or otherwise of the man employed by Grecian Lines with Costas Kamateros will then be cleared up one way or the other. Indeed, we were told that the employee is at this moment on a flight from Athens and that he is expected later today. On this basis it is said that we should in any event let the injunction stand until the hearing.

I cannot accept this submission. If the injunction is wrong in principle, as I think it is for the reasons given by Lord Denning MR, then it must be lifted at once. Moreover, I am sceptical about the suggestion that the issue about identification will necessarily be cleared up in a few days. As one knows from experience, it is often hoped or expected that certain evidence will dispose of some disputed issue of fact, but it then turns out that the question mark is not removed by the evidence, or that it merely leads to the substitution of one or more other question marks.. The only safe and correct approach is not to allow an injunction to remain, even for a single day, if it was clearly wrong for it to have been granted.

I accordingly agree that this appeal must be allowed.

Appeal allowed. Injunction discharged   .

Solicitors: *Lovell White & King* (for the bureau); *Peter Carter-Ruck & Partners* (for the plaintiffs).

Frances Rustin   Barrister.

Practice Direction

QUEEN'S BENCH DIVISION
LORD LANE CJ AND WOOLF J
11 JUNE 1982

Practice – Uncontested proceedings – Crown Office list – Civil proceedings – Judicial review, cases stated, statutory appeals etc – Disposal – Disposal without attendance.

LORD LANE CJ gave the following direction at the sitting of court: Where the parties are agreed as to the terms on which civil proceedings entered in the Crown Office list, including applications for judicial review, appeals by way of case stated and statutory appeals, can be disposed of and require an order of the court to put these terms into effect, they should hand into the Crown Office a document (together with two copies thereof) signed by the parties setting out the terms of the proposed agreed order and a short statement of the matters relied on as justifying the making of the order, authorities and statutory provisions relied on being quoted. Where practicable, copies of statutory instruments which are relevant should be annexed to the document.

The Crown Office will then submit the document to a judge and, if he is satisfied that an order can be made, he will cause the proceedings to be listed for hearing and the order will be announced in open court without the parties or their representatives having to attend.

If, on the information originally provided and any information subsequently provided at the judge's request, the judge is not satisfied that it is proper for the order to be made, he will cause the proceedings to be listed for hearing in the normal way.

It is hoped that wherever possible parties and their advisers will take advantage of this direction and provide sufficient information to enable the judge to be satisfied as to the propriety of making an order without hearing the parties, since the direction is designed to save the expense to the parties and the time of the court.

N P Metcalfe Esq   Barrister.

R v Tottenham Magistrates' Court, ex parte Williams

QUEEN'S BENCH DIVISION

DONALDSON LJ AND WOOLF J

4, 12 JUNE 1980

Consitutional law – Foreign sovereign state – Armed forces of foreign state – Deserter or absentee without leave from forces of designated country – Proceedings before civil court in respect of person suspected of desertion – Evidence – Burden of proof – Evidential value of certificate from foreign commanding officer that person is a deserter – Visiting Forces Act 1952, ss 13, 14(b) – Army Act 1955, s 187(3).

In 1975 the applicant, a Nigerian citizen, entered the United Kingdom lawfully and settled there. In August 1979 he was arrested under a warrant issued under the Visiting Forces Act 1952 alleging that he was a deserter from the Nigerian Air Force and brought before a magistrate. The police constable who had arrested him gave evidence and exhibited a certificate under s 14*ᵃ* of the 1952 Act, dated 26 July 1979, purporting to be signed by an officer commanding a unit of the Nigerian forces stating that the person named and described in it was at the date of the certificate a deserter. The applicant denied that he was a deserter or that he was the person named in the certificate and told the magistrate that his term of service with the Nigerian Air Force had expired before he came to the United Kingdom. The magistrate was advised by her clerk that the only matter in issue was whether the applicant was the person named in the certificate, since s 14 of the 1952 Act provided that in proceedings under that Act in relation to a deserter such a certificate was 'sufficient evidence . . . of the facts appearing from the document to be certified'. The magistrate accordingly made an order under s 187(3)*ᵇ* of the Army Act 1955 (which applied to proceedings in respect of a deserter from a foreign armed force by virtue of s 13 of the 1952 Act) that the applicant be remanded in custody for the purpose of being handed over to the Nigerian authorities. The applicant applied for an order of certiorari to quash the magistrate's order on the ground that the magistrate had failed to consider the evidence and statement of the applicant in accordance with s 187(3) of the 1955 Act.

Held – (1) When a person accused of being a deserter from the armed forces of a foreign country denied the charge, the magistrate hearing the case was not entitled to make an order under s 187(3) of the 1955 Act delivering the accused into military custody unless he first considered all the evidence adduced and not merely that put forward by the prosecution and then only if he was satisfied (a) beyond all reasonable doubt that the accused was subject to foreign military law and (b) that there was sufficient evidence to justify the trial of the accused by the foreign military authorities (see p 707 *h j* and p 709 *f g* and *j*, post).

(2) Although a certificate under s 14 of the 1952 Act that the accused was a deserter might be 'sufficient evidence', in the absence of proof to the contrary, to justify the trial of the accused by the foreign military authorities, it could not, having regard to the strict standard of proof required, by itself establish beyond reasonable doubt that the accused was subject to foreign military law. Since the magistrate had apparently acted on a mistaken view as to the burden of proof when deciding that the applicant was a member of the Nigerian armed forces, the order directing that he be handed over to the Nigerian authorities would be quashed (see p 708 *d e* and p 709 *c d g* to *j*, post).

---

a   Section 14 is set out at p 708 *b c*, post

b   Section 187(3) is set out at p 707 *e f*, post

Notes
For procedure following arrest of suspected deserters, see 33 Halsbury's Laws (3rd edn) a
855, para 1443.
　For the Visiting Forces Act 1952, ss 13, 14, see 29 Halsbury's Statutes (3rd edn) 935.
　For the Army Act 1955, s 187, see ibid 295.

Case referred to in judgments
Amand v Secretary of State for Home Affairs [1942] 2 All ER 381, [1943] AC 147, HL, 39 b
　Digest (Repl) 430, 402.

Application for judicial review
Pursuant to leave given by McNeill J on 5 September 1979, the applicant, James Williams,
applied for an order of certiorari to remove into the High Court for the purpose of its
being quashed an order made by the Tottenham Magistrates' Court on 1 September c
1979, whereby it was directed that the applicant be detained in police custody for the
purpose of being handed over to the Nigerian authorities.　The grounds of the application
were that the court (i) had failed to consider the evidence and the statement of the
applicant, contrary to s 187(3) of the Army Act 1955, (ii) had failed to exercise its powers
of remand and (iii) had acted contrary to natural justice and/or in excess of its
jurisdiction.　The respondent to the application was the chief officer of police for d
Tottenham.　The facts are set out in the judgment of Donaldson LJ.

Lord Gifford for Mr Williams.
John L Reide for the respondent.

At the conclusion of the argument Donaldson LJ announced that the order would be set e
aside for reasons to be given later.

12 June.　The following judgments were read.

DONALDSON LJ. James Williams is a Nigerian citizen.　He entered this country
lawfully in December 1975.　He has settled here and in April 1979 he married.　He has f
Home Office permission to take employment and in fact works on the night shift for the
Ford Motor Co.　In addition, during the day he studies hotel management at Westminster
College.　So, whatever else may be said about Mr Williams, his industry is not in
question.
　Disaster struck when, on 31 August 1979, he was arrested under a warrant issued
under the Visiting Forces Act 1952.　The allegation was that he was a deserter from the g
Nigerian Air Force.　Within 24 hours he had been brought before a justice of the peace
sitting at the Tottenham Magistrates' Court.　After a hearing, the magistrate made an
order that Mr Williams be remanded in police custody for the purpose of being handed
over to such Nigerian authority as might be designated by the Nigerian High
Commissioner.
　Mr Williams has been on bail since 5 September 1979, pending a hearing of his h
application for judicial review.　At the end of that hearing we held that this order should
be set aside and I now give my reasons for that decision.
　It is of some importance to remember, as was pointed out by Lord Wright in Amand
v Secretary of State for Home Affairs [1942] 2 All ER 381 at 386, [1943] AC 147 at 157, that
both the burden and the benefit of the law of this country extend not only to its citizens,
but to all who live within the Queen's Peace.　Mr Williams, as a lawful resident, is in this j
category.　He is entitled to personal freedom under the law.　Accordingly, he is not to be
imprisoned or delivered into the custody of any authority, whether British or Nigerian,
save in strict compliance with the law.
　The relevant law is contained in the Visiting Forces Act 1952, as amended, and in the
Army Act 1955.　The 1952 Act deals, as its name implies, with the position of members

of the armed forces of other countries who are visiting the United Kingdom. But it also
makes provision 'for the apprehension and disposal of deserters or absentees without
leave in the United Kingdom . . . of such countries'. It is with the latter provision that
we have been concerned in this application. The 1952 Act applies to the countries
specified in s 1 including Nigeria.

Section 13 of the Visiting Forces Act 1952 applies ss 186 to 188 and s 190 of the Army
Act 1955 'to deserters and absentees without leave from the forces of any country to
which this section applies as they apply in relation to deserters and absentees without
leave from the regular forces'. Section 186 of the Army Act 1955 deals with powers of
arrest and s 187 with 'proceedings before a civil court where persons suspected of illegal
absence'. In this context the words 'civil court' are used in contradistinction to a military
court and refer to a court of summary jurisdiction. Section 187 prescribes how the
proceedings shall be conducted in the following subsections:

'(2) If he admits that he is illegally absent from the regular forces and the court
is satisfied of the truth of the admission, then—(a) unless he is in custody for some
other cause the court shall, and (b) notwithstanding that he is in custody for some
other cause, the court may, forthwith either cause him to be delivered into military
custody in such manner as the court may think fit or commit him to some prison,
police station or other place provided for the confinement of persons in custody, to
be kept there for such reasonable time as the court may specify (not exceeding such
time as appears to the court reasonably necessary for the purpose of enabling him to
be delivered into military custody) or until sooner delivered into such custody. Any
time specified by the court may be extended by the court from time to time if it
appears to the court reasonably necessary so to do for the purpose aforesaid.
(3) If he does not admit that he is illegally absent as aforesaid, or the court is not
satisfied of the truth of the admission, the court shall consider the evidence and any
statement of the accused, and if satisfied that he is subject to military law and if of
opinion that there is sufficient evidence to justify his being tried under this Act for
an offence of desertion or absence without leave then, unless he is in custody for
some other cause, the court shall cause him to be delivered into military custody or
commit him as aforesaid, but otherwise shall discharge him: Provided that if he is
in custody for some other cause the court shall have power, but shall not be
required, to act in accordance with this subsection.
(4) The following provisions of the Magistrates' Courts Act, 1952, or any
corresponding enactment in force as respects the court in question, that is to say the
provisions relating to the constitution and procedure of courts of summary
jurisdiction acting as examining justices and conferring powers of adjournment and
remand on such courts so acting, and the provisions as to evidence and the issue and
enforcement of summonses or warrants to secure the attendance of witnesses, shall
apply to any proceedings under this section.'

When Mr Williams appeared before the magistrate, he did not admit that he was
illegally absent from the Nigerian Air Force and accordingly sub-s (3) applied. It followed
that the magistrate had to consider the evidence and any statement of the accused and
then to ask herself the following two questions: (a) 'Am I satisfied that Mr Williams is
subject to Nigerian military law? "Satisfaction" in this context means "satisfied so that
I am sure" or "satisfied beyond reasonable doubt": the criminal standard of proof.' (b) 'If
so, is there sufficient evidence to justify Mr Williams being tried by the Nigerian
authorities for the offence of desertion?' This is the same test as has to be applied by a
magistrate conducting committal proceedings with a view to the accused being tried
before a judge and jury in the Crown Court. It involves considering all the evidence
tendered and not just that tendered by the prosecution.

The differences in approach in answering the two question are of vital importance.
Before a citizen is put in peril of British or other military law, it must be established

beyond reasonable doubt that he is subject to that law. If, but only if, this is established, does the second question with its less onerous test arise.   **a**

It is against this background that I turn to s 14 of the Visiting Forces Act 1952, which provides special rules of evidence applicable in proceedings under the Act in relation to deserters and absentees without leave. It is in the following terms:

> 'For the purposes of any proceedings under or arising out of any provision of the Army Act, 1955 as applied by the last foregoing section—(a) a document purporting **b** to be a certificate under the hand of the Secretary of the Admiralty, the Secretary of the Army Council or the Secretary of the Air Council, stating that a request has been made for the exercise of the powers mentioned in subsection (2) of the last foregoing section, and indicating the effect of the request, shall be sufficient evidence, unless the contrary is proved, that the request has been made and of its effect; and (b) a document purporting to be a certificate under the hand of the officer commanding **c** a unit or detachment of any of the forces of a country to which this section applies, stating that a person named and described therein was at the date of the certificate a deserter, or absentee without leave, from those forces shall be sufficient evidence, unless the contrary is proved, of the facts appearing from the document to be so certified.'

In Mr Williams's case it was not disputed that the Nigerian authorities had duly **d** invoked the 1952 Act and it is therefore only necessary to consider para (b). The words 'sufficient evidence' clearly reflect the same words in s 187(3) of the Army Act 1955. The provision therefore relates, primarily at least, to the second question which had to be considered by the magistrate, namely whether there was a sufficient case to justify committal for trial by the Nigerian Army authorities.

Let me now return to Mr Williams and his appearance before the magistrate. A police **e** constable gave evidence that she had approached Mr Williams on 31 August 1979, and told him that she believed he was a deserter from the Nigerian Air Force. He had replied: 'Yes, I suppose so. I was in the Air Force of my own country, but I left.' When asked if he had been discharged, Mr Williams said: 'No, I just left. I was not discharged.' When asked why he had just left, he replied: 'Because there was so much trouble in my country and I could not get on in my work.' The police constable had then **f** arrested Mr Williams. In addition to giving this evidence, the police constable produced a certificate purporting to be signed by the officer commanding the Defence Section of the Nigerian High Commission. This certified that Aircraftsman James Williams of the Nigerian Air Force was a deserter from the force on 26 July 1979. It also contained a description of Aircraftsman Williams.

Before Mr Williams gave evidence, his counsel submitted that the prosecution should **g** call the signatory to the certificate in order that he might be cross-examined. This submission was ill-founded, but what is important is that the clerk to the magistrates intervened to say that the only question was whether Mr Williams was the Aircraftsman Williams named in the certificate.

Mr Williams then gave evidence. In substance he said that he had enlisted in the Nigerian Air Force in 1968 on a six-year agreement. In 1974 he had visited England on **h** an air force course and reported back to his unit on its conclusion in October 1975. He had refused to sign on for a further term. He added that he had been to the Nigerian High Commission on many occasions and was known to the Nigerian military attaché, but no one had ever suggested that he was a deserter. He then gave evidence about visiting the Home Office to get his wife's passport extended. At this point the clerk to the magistrates intervened to say that the court might think these questions irrelevant **j** since the issue was whether the person named in the certificate was the one in court.

The magistrate has filed an affidavit which contains the following paragraphs:

> '2. The Applicant was represented by counsel and denied the charge. Evidence in the form of depositions was given by Wpc Steadman and by the Applicant. In the course of her evidence Wpc Steadman exhibited a certificate purporting to be signed

by an officer commanding a unit or detachment of the Nigerian Forces. A copy of the said depositions is now produced and shown to me marked "DKME.1".

3. Counsel for the Applicant argued that there was no evidence that the Applicant was a deserter from the Nigerian Air Force or that the certificate exhibited to the evidence of Wpc Steadman referred to the Applicant.

4. I was satisfied from the evidence I had heard that the Applicant was subject to the military law applicable to the Nigerian Air Force and it was a matter for the appropriate authority of Nigeria to determine whether or not he was a deserter. Accordingly I ordered that the Applicant be delivered into police custody for the purpose of being handed over to such authority of Nigeria as designated by the Nigerian High Commissioner.'

Bearing in mind that the magistrate had been advised by her clerk that the only issue was whether Mr Williams was the man named in the certificate, there is a real problem in deciding exactly what she means when she says: 'I was satisfied from the evidence I had heard that the Applicant was subject to the military law applicable to the Nigerian Air Force.' Was she treating the certificate as 'sufficient evidence' of this fact as invited by her clerk? Or was she sure of this fact on all the evidence. For my part I am most reluctant to assume that she disregarded the advice of her clerk, particularly as I quite fail to see how, on the evidence tendered, she could possibly have been sure that Mr Williams was subject to Nigerian military law.

There will sometimes be cases in which the person before the courts admits that he is subject to military law, but contends that he had leave of absence or had no intention of deserting. In such cases the magistrate will have to consider whether the evidence given by the arrested person is sufficiently credible to disprove the fact of illegal absence which has been certified or whether, taking the evidence as a whole, there is a case fit for trial by a military tribunal of the forces concerned. If that had been the position in Mr Williams's case, I could have understood the magistrate's order.

But Mr Williams's case was different. True it is that he was saying that he had no intention to desert and accordingly was denying any illegal absence. This went to the second question: was there a case for committal? But his reason for saying this was that his term of service with the Nigerian Air Force had expired before he came to England in December 1975. If this was right, it not only cast doubt on the alleged desertion, the subject matter of the certificate, but also involved the proposition that neither in December 1975 nor now was he subject to Nigerian military law.

It is here that it becomes of vital importance to distinguish between the two questions: (i) 'Was Mr Williams subject to Nigerian military law?', which must be proved to the strict standard required by criminal law, and (ii) 'If so, is there sufficient evidence to justify his being tried by the Nigerian military authorities?', which necessarily involves a less onerous test. Even if the certificate by implication asserts that Mr Williams is subject to Nigerian military law and even if, in the absence of proof to the contrary, it would be sufficient evidence for the purposes of question (ii), it is of comparatively little weight in relation to question (i) once that has become a live issue. As it is likely, if not certain, that the magistrate, having been mistakenly advised by her clerk, misdirected herself as to the burden of proof in relation to the issue of whether Mr Williams was subject to Nigerian military law at all, her order must be quashed.

Whether the Nigerian authorities wish to take further proceedings against Mr Williams is a matter for them. But, if they do so, they will no doubt bear in mind that they will have to produce more than a certificate by way of evidence that Mr Williams is subject to Nigerian military law. There is a very heavy onus on them and, for the reasons which I have sought to explain, it is right that it should be so.

WOOLF J. I agree.

Application allowed.

Solicitors: *Osbornes* (for Mr Williams); *R E T Birch* (for the respondent).

Dilys Tausz   Barrister.

Birkett v Hayes and another   *a*

COURT OF APPEAL, CIVIL DIVISION
LORD DENNING MR, EVELEIGH AND WATKINS LJJ
8, 9, 10 FEBRUARY, 18 MARCH 1982

Interest – Damages – Personal injury – Pain, suffering and loss of amenities – Rate of interest **b**
– Interest to be awarded at rate of 2% from date of writ to date of trial – Interest to be awarded
for lesser period if plaintiff unjustifiably delays trial.

When awarding general damages for pain and suffering and loss of amenities the court
should normally exercise its discretion under s 3*a* of the Law Reform (Miscellaneous
Provisions) Act 1934 to award interest by ordering that the damages bear interest at the
rate of 2% from the date of service of the writ to the date of trial. However, where the   **c**
trial has been unjustifiably delayed by the plaintiff, the court may award interest for such
lesser period as it thinks fit (see p 713 *j* to p 714 *a* and p 717 *a b* and *e f*, post).
  Pickett v British Rail Engineering Ltd [1979] 1 All ER 774 applied.
  Jefford v Gee [1970] 1 All ER 1202 and *Cookson v Knowles* [1978] 2 All ER 604
considered.
                                                                                                  d

Notes
For interest payable on damages, see 12 Halsbury's Laws (4th edn) para 1204.
  For the Law Reform (Miscellaneous Provisions) Act 1934, s 3, see 25 Halsbury's
Statutes (3rd edn) 752.

Cases referred to in judgments   **e**
British Transport Commission v Gourley [1955] 3 All ER 796, [1956] AC 185, [1956] 2 WLR
  41, HL, 17 Digest (Reissue) 88, 35.
Cookson v Knowles [1977] 2 All ER 820, [1977] QB 913, [1977] 3 WLR 279, CA; *affd*
  [1978] 2 All ER 604, [1979] AC 556, [1978] 2 WLR 978, HL, Digest (Cont Vol E) 462,
  1473*a*.
Jefford v Gee [1970] 1 All ER 1202, [1970] 2 QB 130, [1970] 2 WLR 702, CA, Digest (Cont **f**
  Vol C) 709, 182*a*.
London Chatham and Dover Rly Co v South Eastern Rly Co [1893] AC 429, HL, 17 Digest
  (Reissue) 290, 571.
Pickett v British Rail Engineering Ltd [1979] 1 All ER 774, [1980] AC 136, [1978] 3 WLR
  955, HL, Digest (Cont Vol E) 459, 1314*b*.
                                                                                                  g

Cases also cited
Cremer v General Carriers SA [1974] 1 All ER 1, [1974] 1 WLR 341.
Funabashi, The, Sycamore Steamship Co Ltd v Owners of the Steamship White Mountain [1972]
  2 All ER 181, [1972] 1 WLR 666.
Lim Poh Choo v Camden and Islington Area Health Authority [1979] 2 All ER 910, [1980] AC **h**
  174, HL.
Miliangos v George Frank (Textiles) Ltd (No 2) [1976] 3 All ER 599, [1977] QB 489.
Roberts, Re, Goodchap v Roberts (1880) 14 Ch D 49, CA.
Walker v John McLean & Sons Ltd [1979] 2 All ER 965, [1979] 1 WLR 760, CA.

Appeal   **j**
By a writ dated 10 May 1976 the plaintiff, Sandra Elizabeth Birkett, claimed damages
against her husband, Peter Philip Birkett, and the first defendant, Brian Hayes, for
injuries sustained when a car driven by her husband and in which she was a passenger
collided with a car driven by the first defendant. Following litigation between the two

_____

a   Section 3, so far as material, is set out at p 714 *b* to *d*, post defendants it was agreed that the plaintiff was entitled to judgment against the first defendant. By a judgment dated 19 January 1981 in the plaintiff's action Michael Davies J, after taking into account that the plaintiff had been 25% contributorily negligent, awarded the plaintiff damages of £299,663 (reduced to £224,747) which included general damages of £30,000 (reduced to £22,500) for pain and suffering and loss of amenity. The judge adjourned for further argument the question of the amount of interest to be awarded on the general damages. By a supplemental judgment dated 21 July 1981 the judge awarded interest at the rate for short-term investment accounts for the period from the date of service of the writ to the date of trial, amounting to £12,028. The first defendant appealed against the award of interest. The facts are set out in the judgment of Lord Denning MR.

Mark Potter QC and *Michael Baker* for the plaintiff.
Piers Ashworth QC and *Peter Ripman* for the defendant.

Cur adv vult

18 March. The following judgments were read.

LORD DENNING MR. It was a tragic accident. It happened on 23 February 1975. Mrs Birkett was in the passenger seat. Her husband was driving. She was not wearing her seat belt. There was a collision with another car. She was thrown forward and upward. She received a devastating head injury. Her brain suffered a grave and profound shock. She has ever since been in hospitals or in homes. It has left her with a 'behaviour disorder'. Whereas before the accident she was exceptionally able, intelligent and attractive, now she behaves so strangely that she needs constant attention. She tires out everyone who tries to look after her.

On 10 May 1976 Mrs Birkett by her next friend issued a writ claiming damages for negligence. The action did not come on for trial for 4½ years. The judge was Michael Davies J. He gave judgment on 19 January 1981. He assessed the total damages as £299,663, but he reduced them by 25% because she was not wearing her seat belt, thus giving judgment for £224,747. No question has arisen on that award except as to one item. That is as to the damages for pain and suffering and loss of amenities. The judge said of it:

'. . . the plaintiff's life has been virtually ruined; and she knows it. Apart from her disability, including the loss of the enjoyment of her work and most of the pleasurable activities of life, she has lost her happy marriage, and I repeat, she knows it. At my invitation counsel suggested what the bracket should be. Counsel for the plaintiff submits £25,000 to £30,000; counsel for the defendant submits £20,000 to £30,000. In my judgment this is clearly a case for an award at the top of the bracket, and I award the sum of £30,000.'

In addition, the judge awarded interest on that sum of £30,000. He awarded it from the date of the service of the writ (10 May 1976) to the date of trial (19 January 1981). That is, for 4⅔ years. He took the rate of interest allowed by the court on short-term investment account: that may be 9% or 10% or even more. It came to over £16,000. That is, in all, £30,000 plus £16,000. Reduced, of course, by 25% to £12,000, as she was not wearing a seat belt.

The guidelines in Jefford v Gee
The question in this case is as to that award of interest of £16,000. In *Jefford v Gee* [1970] 1 All ER 1202 at 1209, [1970] 2 QB 130 at 147 we gave a guideline as to the interest on the item for pain and suffering and loss of amenities. We said that it should be awarded from the date of the service of the writ until the date of trial. This is what I said, speaking for the court:

'In the words of Lord Herschell LC [in *London Chatham and Dover Rly Co v South Eastern Rly Co* [1893] AC 429 at 437], interest should be awarded "from the time of

action brought at all events". From that time onwards it can properly be said that
the plaintiff has been out of the whole sum and a defendant has had the benefit of   *a*
it. Speaking generally, therefore, we think that interest on this item (pain and
suffering and loss of amenities) should run from the date of service of the writ to the
date of trial.'

Looking back at it now, I feel that guideline was an error. It treats the item (for pain,
suffering and loss of amenities) as accruing due at the date of service of the writ, whereas
it does not. It is more like the item for cost of future care or for loss of future earnings   *b*
in which interest only runs from the date of trial. But still the guideline has stood since
1971, and, as I will show, it is now too late to alter it.

Meanwhile, however, we made an attempt to alter it. It was in *Cookson v Knowles*
[1977] 2 All ER 820, [1977] QB 913.

The alteration in Cookson v Knowles

In the succeeding years we met with racing inflation. So in *Cookson v Knowles* [1977]
2 All ER 820 at 823, [1977] QB 913 at 921 in one single judgment we altered the
guideline. I said:

'The plaintiff thus stands to gain by the delay in bringing the case to trial. He
ought not to gain still more by having interest from the date of service of the   *e*
writ. We would alter the guideline, therefore, by suggesting that no interest should
be awarded on the lump sum awarded at the trial for pain and suffering and loss of
amenities.'

That judgment was given on 25 May 1977. Our view was given immense support by
the Report of the Royal Commission (Cmnd 7054) eight months later, in March 1978.   *f*
The reasoning is so compelling that I venture to set it out in full (see ch 16, paras 747–
748):

'Nevertheless, we agree with the Law Commission's conclusion, and with the rule
in *Cookson v. Knowles*, that no interest should be awarded on non-pecuniary
damages. As we have pointed out elsewhere, in present economic conditions an
investor may well be unable to do more than maintain the real value of his
investment, once tax and inflation are taken into account, if indeed he can manage
to do this. To award no interest on non-pecuniary damages may, therefore, be at
least as favourable as the award of interest at a market rate on damages for past
pecuniary loss. A more important justification, however, lies in the conventional
nature of non-pecuniary damages. We do not think that it would be appropriate to
subject essentially arbitrary figures to detailed financial calculations. If an attempt
were to be made, allowance would have to be made for inflation in selecting the
appropriate interest rate. It would also, strictly speaking, be necessary to apply
interest at the half rate only to that part of the damages relating to non-pecuniary
loss before trial, assessed on the scale current at the date of injury. This would all be
highly artificial. We recommend that the rule in *Cookson v. Knowles* that no interest
should be awarded on damages for non-pecuniary loss should stand; and that it
should be applied in Scotland and Northern Ireland.'

Cookson v Knowles was taken to the House of Lords, but no view was expressed on this
point: see Lord Diplock's judgment ([1978] 2 All ER 604 at 612, [1979] AC 556 at 573):

'The question of damages for non-economic loss which bulks large in personal
injury actions, however, does not arise in the instant case. It has not been argued
before your Lordships and I refrain from expressing any view about it.'

The overruling of Cookson v Knowles

In *Pickett v British Rail Engineering Ltd* [1979] 1 All ER 774, [1980] AC 136 the House
of Lords did consider the point. They overruled *Cookson v Knowles*. In doing so they

made no mention of the Report of the Royal Commission or the reasoning in it. In
a deference to the decision of the House in *Pickett*, counsel for the defendant felt bound to
concede that we were bound to give some interest on the award of damages for pain and
suffering and loss of amenities. But he contended that we were free to determine what
should be the *rate* of interest. He pointed to one or two indications that this might be
varied according to the circumstances of the case. In *Cookson v Knowles* [1978] 2 All ER
604 at 617, [1979] AC 556 at 579 Lord Scarman said it might depend on 'currently
b prevailing financial conditions'. And the Royal Commission said that 'allowance would
have to be made for inflation in selecting the appropriate interest rate'. I turn, therefore,
to consider the relevant considerations on this point.

The method of assessment

The important thing to notice is that the judge assessed the figure of £30,000 (for pain
c and suffering and loss of amenities) on the value of money at the date of the trial on 19
January 1981, and on the plaintiff's condition at that date. Everyone accepted that this
was the right way of doing it. The figure for pain, suffering and loss of amenities is
always assessed at the date of the trial. The judge then has before him the full story up
to that date, and the outlook for the future. This plaintiff's condition may have
deteriorated more than expected, or it may have improved. The judge has to award
d compensation *for the past*, and also *for the future* pain, suffering and loss of amenities. The
future that lies ahead, beyond the date of trial, is often of more consequence than the
past. The judge awards a lump sum at the date of trial to cover all.

Apart from inflation

If the currency had remained stable from 1976 to 1981, and the plaintiff's condition
e had remained unchanged, neither improved nor deteriorated, I should have thought that
the award in 1976 would have been not £30,000, but only £20,000 or thereabouts. I can
see no reason why that £20,000 should be any different from a contract debt. Suppose
that this plaintiff was owed a debt of £20,000 due in May 1976, but judgment was only
given in January 1981. The plaintiff would get interest only on £20,000 for those 4¾
years. The interest would have been about £8,000. She would only have got £28,000
f at the trial. She would not get £30,000.

The effect of inflation

But the currency did not remain stable from 1976 to 1981. There was racing
inflation. So that the plaintiff in 1981 received £30,000. I can see no possible
justification for giving her interest on that inflated figure for the 4¾ years, when she
g would not be given it on an admitted debt of £20,000 due at the date of the service of the
writ. Taking Lord Herschell LC's words, she was not kept out of £30,000 for those 4¾
years. She was only kept out of £20,000. Nor did the defendants get the benefit of the
use of £20,000.

The effect of tax

Even if she is to be regarded as having been kept out of £30,000 from the date of the
service of the writ (10 May 1976) the plaintiff may, or may not, have invested it on short-
term investment account. If she had invested it, she would have had to pay tax on the
interest she received from it. But now, if interest is awarded her on £30,000 from the
date of the service of the writ, for 4¾ years, she gets the interest without deduction of tax
and without having to pay tax on it. Alternatively, she might not have invested it, but
spent it in other ways. In that case she would have got no interest at all.

Conclusion

All these considerations convince me that, if interest is to be awarded from the date of
the service of the writ (as *Pickett's* case compels), then that interest should be very low
indeed. There is nothing to guide us but the feeling of what is fair. You must remember

that the plaintiff is getting the £30,000 assessed at the date of trial, and also she is getting
interest on it over the preceding 4¾ years. Having discussed it with Eveleigh and *a*
Watkins LJJ, I would put the interest at 2% and recommend it as a guideline for future
cases.

EVELEIGH LJ. Section 3 of the Law Reform (Miscellaneous Provisions) Act 1934, as *b*
amended by s 22 of the Administration of Justice Act 1969, reads:

'(1) In any proceedings tried in any court of record for the recovery of any debt
or damages, the court may, if it thinks fit, order that there shall be included in the
sum for which judgment is given interest at such rate as it thinks fit on the whole
or any part of the debt or damages for the whole or any part of the period between
the date when the cause of action arose and the date of the judgment ... *c*
(1A) ... the court shall exercise that power so as to include in that sum [ie the
judgment for damages] interest on those damages or on such part of them as the
court considers appropriate, unless the court is satisfied that there are special reasons
why no interest should be given in respect of those damages ...'

In *Jefford v Gee* [1970] 1 All ER 1202, [1970] 2 QB 130 the Court of Appeal laid down *d*
guidelines as to the appropriate rate of interest and in so far as damages for pain and
suffering and loss of amenities was concerned, that rate was said to be the rate allowed by
the court on the short-term investment account, taken as an average over the period for
which interest is awarded. That period in relation to such general damages was held to
be from the date of service of the writ to the date of trial.

In *Cookson v Knowles* [1977] 2 All ER 820 at 823, [1977] QB 913 at 921, in relation to *e*
Jefford v Gee, Lord Denning MR said: 'At that time inflation did not stare us in the face.
We had not in mind continuing inflation and its effects on awards.' He went on to say
that as awards were assessed on the current value of money as at the date of judgment the
plaintiff would receive a larger sum than he would have done at the date of the writ and
said:

'We would alter the guideline, therefore, by suggesting that no interest should be *f*
awarded on the lump sum awarded at the trial for pain and suffering and loss of
amenities.'

However, in *Pickett v British Rail Engineering Ltd* [1979] 1 All ER 774, [1980] AC 136
the House of Lords held that as interest on general damages was awarded for the purpose
of compensating a plaintiff for being kept out of the capital sum between the date of the *g*
service of the writ and judgment, the Court of Appeal erred in not awarding such
interest and the order of the trial judge should be restored. It is therefore clear in the
present case that the plaintiff was entitled to interest, for there were no special reasons
why it should not be given. The change in the value of money was not a special reason,
for it affected everyone alike.

In *Pickett*'s case the argument was concerned only with the question whether interest *h*
was recoverable. Concentrating as they did on this vital issue, counsel had agreed the rate
of interest between themselves. The House of Lords did not consider it. Consequently,
while in the present case there is an entitlement to interest, that rate is such 'as the court
considers appropriate'. What is appropriate must be determined in the light of all the
relevant circumstances at the date of the trial.

While inflation does not amount to a special reason for the court to refuse to award *j*
interest, it does not follow that the inflationary element which exists in the relevant
current interest rates is not a factor to consider when determining the appropriate rate of
interest.

In *Pickett*'s case [1979] 1 All ER 774 at 782, [1980] AC 136 at 151 Lord Wilberforce
said:

'Increase for inflation is designed to preserve the "real" value of money, interest to compensate for being kept out of that "real" value. The one has no relation to the other. If the damages claimed remained, nominally, the same, because there was no inflation, interest would normally be given. The same should follow if the damages remain in real terms the same.'

Lord Wilberforce is saying that the two objectives are separate, but he does not say that current rates of interest have no relation to inflation. Moreover, he does not say what the compensatory rate of interest shall be.

It cannot be disputed that current rates of interest today have a large inflationary element. This element was adverted to in *Cookson v Knowles* [1978] 2 All ER 604 at 611, [1979] AC 556 at 571 where Lord Diplock said: 'Inflation is taken care of in a rough and ready way by the higher rates of interest obtainable as one of the consequences of it . . .' If damages were assessed on the basis of the value of the pound at the date of the writ, then there would be an overwhelming case for the award of interest at rates which carry an inflationary element. Such rates would seek, albeit imperfectly, to achieve two objects, namely to preserve the value of the award and to compensate for the late receipt of the money. In my opinion, however, it cannot be right to apply such interest rates to an award which already takes into account the need for preserving the value of money. We must look for some other rate of interest.

There have been various statements giving reasons for the award of interest. In many we find a reference to the defendant wrongfully withholding the money from the plaintiff. Thus in *London Chatham and Dover Rly Co v South Eastern Rly Co* [1893] AC 429 at 437 Lord Herschel LC said:

'. . . I think that when money is owing from one party to another and that other is driven to have recourse to legal proceedings in order to recover the amount due to him, the party who is wrongfully withholding the money from the other ought not in justice to benefit by having that money in his possession and enjoying the use of it, when the money ought to be in the possession of the other party who is entitled to its use.'

However, I do not think it is right in determining the rate of interest to proceed on the basis that a defendant should be penalised. Indeed, I do not understand Lord Herschel LC to be suggesting this. There are many cases where the plaintiff does not wish to have his damages assessed as quickly as possible. The medical reports may be uncertain. His prospect of employment may be difficult to determine. There are a number of reasons where neither side is anxious to proceed expeditiously. On the other hand, it is fair to say that the plaintiff has not had the money, while the defendant has had the advantage of not having been compelled to pay. It seems to me that we should seek to discover a rate of interest which will compensate the plaintiff in recognition of the fact that a sum of money in respect of general damages should be considered, over the relevant period, as existing for his benefit.

That sum of money might have been thought to be the value of the award at the date of the writ with interest rates which counter inflation or the value at the date of the judgment with interest rates less the counter-inflationary element. However, *Pickett's* case tells us that it is on the award at the date of the judgment that interest must be based and therefore the lower rate of interest is appropriate.

In *Cookson v Knowles* [1978] 2 All ER 604 at 611, [1979] AC 556 at 571 Lord Diplock in relation to the calculation of fatal accident damages said:

'In times of stable currency the multipliers that were used by judges were appropriate to interest rates of four per cent to five per cent whether the judges using them were conscious of this or not.'

The Judgments Act 1838, now repealed, provided for interest at 4%. At the time of *Jefford v Gee* the court regarded 6½% as appropriate. In retrospect one can discern the early signs of inflation. I therefore think that we should start by assuming a true earnings rate of interest of 4%.   a

At the time that *Jefford v Gee* was decided, an award of interest was taxable in the hands of the plaintiff. The Finance Act 1971 removed the liability for tax. In *British Transport Commission v Gourley* [1955] 3 All ER 796, [1956] AC 185 it was held that in assessing damages for loss of earnings the plaintiff's liability for tax on those earnings should be taken into account. In awarding interest on general damages at a true earnings rate, we are seeking to compensate the plaintiff for the loss of the money which his award could b have earned. This would indicate that the principle in *Gourley's* case should apply. On the other hand, the sums payable as interest will be relatively small and it will generally be undesirable to add to the expense of litigation by seeking to achieve a precise determination of the plaintiff's actual loss. Most plaintiffs will be paying tax at the basic rate. Some would not have invested the money at all. Others might have skilfully used it in interest free stock.   c

In awarding interest the judge is exercising a discretion. In the great majority of cases the plaintiff could have proceeded with greater dispatch; and yet it may well be wrong to deprive him of interest particularly as the defendant will have had the use of the money. I therefore think that we should approach this matter on the basis that the court should arrive at a final figure which will be fair, generally speaking, to both parties.

It is not a fair basis on which to award interest to assume that the defendant should d have paid the proper sum (and this means the exact sum) at the moment of service of the writ. It is true that the plaintiff must be paid some interest from that date because a sum of money was due to him. Unlike the case of a claim for a fixed money debt, no one can say exactly how much. The plaintiff does not have to quantify his demand and yet in most cases he is in the best position to evaluate his claim. The defendant may not have the material on which to do so. He may not have had the necessary opportunity for e medical examination. The plaintiff may not have given sufficient details of his injuries for anything like an estimate, as opposed to a guess, to be made of the value of the claim.

Moreover, in many cases the plaintiff's condition will not have stabilised. We all know that the picture at the date of trial can be very different from that which was given at the date of writ. It is nobody's fault as a rule, but simply a reflection of the difficulty in forming an accurate medical opinion. There may be an unexpected change for the f worse. In this case the interval after service of the writ will help to ensure a proper figure for damages which will be greater than that which the plaintiff would have obtained at the time of the writ. On the other hand, if his condition has improved and his award is less in consequence, this will mean that the defendant has been saved from the possibility of paying more than he should have done. These considerations show that, while it is right to regard the plaintiff as having been kept out of an award, we should not regard g it as necessarily resulting in a loss to him of 4% of the judgment sum. I appreciate that against this argument it may be said that the judgment sum is the true figure to work on and that any lower figure, inflation apart, which might have been awarded at an earlier trial, would have been unfair to the plaintiff because, as we now know, the claim was really worth the sum now awarded. However, to award interest on this sum as though it were a debt is to call on a defendant to pay interest on a figure that was never demanded h and which at the date of the writ is usually sheer guesswork. These considerations lead me to the conclusion that what I call the true earnings rate of interest, namely 4%, if appropriate to a debt, is too high when applied to general damages.

Moreover, the recipient of interest at 4% will generally pay tax of at least 30% and therefore, after tax, the net interest is only 2·8%.

As the plaintiff does not pay tax on the interest on general damages and as I regard 4% j gross as too high, we must look for a net figure below 2·8%. There was evidence in this case that to very select bodies, such as pension funds, two recent government stock issues which are index linked had all been taken up. The actual interest rate which these produced of course fluctuates according to the figure at which the stock stands after issue but the evidence was that around 2% was enough to attract investors. 'Granny bonds' also produce only a very low rate of interest.

These considerations lead me to regard the figure of 2% as appropriate for interest on an award of general damages. I would further say that I respectfully agree with the comments which Watkins LJ has told me he proposes to add.

WATKINS LJ. For the reasons provided by Lord Denning MR and for those just given by Eveleigh LJ, I agree that (1) the appeal should be allowed so that the rate of interest awarded to the plaintiff on general damages will be 2%, and (2) in future all awards of general damages should bear the like rate of interest.

I would add a reference to s 22 of the Administration of Justice Act 1969 which, in amending s 3 of the Law Reform (Miscellaneous Provisions) Act 1934, provides that the court shall exercise its power to award interest on damages or on such part of the damages as the court considers appropriate, unless the court is satisfied that there are special reasons why no interest should be given in respect of those damages.

Clearly these provisions confer a discretion on the court to decide what part of an award of damages shall carry interest, the rate of that interest and the period for which it should be given. That discretion has now to be exercised so as, following the decision in *Pickett v British Rail Engineering Ltd* [1979] 1 All ER 774, [1980] AC 136, to award interest on general damages in personal injury cases at, following the guidelines now laid down by this court, the rate of 2% and, having regard to the circumstances of the case, for the period deemed to be appropriate.

Usually this period will run from the date of the writ to the date of trial, but the court may in its discretion abridge this period when it thinks it is just so to do. Far too often there is unjustifiable delay in bringing an action to trial. It is, in my view, wrong that interest should run during a time which can properly be called unjustifiable delay after the date of the writ. During that time the plaintiff will have been kept out of the sum awarded to him by his own fault. The fact that the defendants have had the use of the sum during that time is no good reason for excusing that fault and allowing interest to run during that time.

LORD DENNING MR. I would like to add one word after hearing Watkins LJ's judgment. It means that there can be an addition to the guideline. The interest, even at 2%, should not necessarily be awarded for the whole period from the date of the service of the writ. The period may be reduced considerably: and only awarded for a lesser time according to the circumstances of the case.

Appeal allowed.

Solicitors: *Mowll & Mowll*, Canterbury (for the plaintiff); *Hextall Erskine & Co* (for the defendant).

Frances Rustin   Barrister.

Shaw v Hamilton   a

QUEEN'S BENCH DIVISION
DONALDSON LJ AND MCCULLOUGH J
22 FEBRUARY 1982

Crown Court – Appeal to Crown Court – Procedure at appeal – Appeal against binding-over
order made by magistrates – Appeal by way of rehearing – Evidence – Facts justifying making b
of binding-over order to be proved afresh in Crown Court – Magistrates' Courts (Appeals from
Binding Over Orders) Act 1956, s 1(1).

An appeal under s 1(1)[a] of the Magistrates' Courts (Appeals from Binding Over Orders)
Act 1956 to the Crown Court against a binding-over order made by a magistrates' court
is by way of a rehearing, and, unless the appellant is prepared to admit the evidence   c
which was before the magistrates, the facts justifying the making of the binding-over
order must be strictly proved in the Crown Court by sworn evidence which may be cross-
examined (see p 719 *e* to *j*, post).

Notes
For appeals to the Crown Court against binding-over orders, see 29 Halsbury's Laws (4th   d
edn) para 472.
    For the Magistrates' Courts (Appeals from Binding Over Orders) Act 1956, see 21
Halsbury's Statutes (3rd edn) 315.

Case stated
Trevor Francis Shaw, a police constable in the Lincolnshire Police, appealed by way of   e
case stated by the Crown Court at Lincoln (his Honour Judge Geoffrey Jones sitting with
justices) in respect of its adjudication on 30 April 1981 whereby it allowed an appeal by
the respondent, James Hamilton, against an order by the Grantham Justices binding him
over in the sum of £100 to be of good behaviour for one year following the dismissal by
the justices of an information charging the respondent with using threatening, abusive
or insulting words or behaviour whereby a breach of the peace was likely to be occasioned,   f
contrary to s 5 of the Public Order Act 1936. The facts are set out in the judgment of
Donaldson LJ.

Collingwood Thompson for the appellant.
The respondent did not appear.
                                                                            g

DONALDSON LJ. This is an appeal by a policeman against a procedural decision of
his Honour Judge Geoffrey Jones sitting in the Crown Court at Lincoln.
    Before I come to the decision under appeal I ought to mention the background facts.
At Grantham Magistrates' Court on 19 February 1981 the respondent had pleaded not
guilty to a charge instituted by the appellant alleging that the respondent, at Grantham   h
on 28 December 1980 in a public place, namely the Earlsfield Hotel, had used abusive or
threatening or insulting words or behaviour whereby a breach of the peace was likely to
be occasioned, contrary to s 5 of the Public Order Act 1936, as amended.
    The justices had considered the evidence and found the respondent not guilty, and
accordingly dismissed the charge. However, they had gone on to exercise their powers
under the Justices of the Peace Act 1361 and had bound over the respondent in the sum
of £100 to be of good behaviour for one year.

___

a   Section 1(1) provides: 'Where, under the Justices of the Peace Act, 1361, or otherwise, a person is
    ordered by a magistrates' court (as defined in the Magistrates' Courts Act 1980) to enter into a
    recognisance with or without sureties to keep the peace or to be of good behaviour, he may appeal
    to the Crown Court.'

The respondent was not very pleased at the outcome of the proceedings. He exercised
a his right under s 1(1) of the Magistrates' Courts (Appeals from Binding Over Orders) Act
1956 to appeal to the Crown Court, that being the court which has been substituted for
quarter sessions referred to in the Act.

At the hearing the police in the form of the appellant, who was represented, wanted
to call three witnesses who had given evidence below for the prosecution. The
respondent apparently objected and sought a preliminary ruling from the judge on how
b the proceedings were to be conducted. The judge, after hearing argument, was of the
opinion which he expressed in the case stated:

> '(i) An order of bind over was analogous to a sentence and not a conviction. The
> appropriate procedure to be followed was as in an appeal against sentence. (ii)
> Accordingly it was for the appellant [the police] to open the evidence given to the
c > Magistrates from a note of evidence taken by the clerk to the justices or in default
> of such a note an agreed summary of the evidence by the parties to the Appeal. (iii)
> The Crown Court should then examine these facts in the light that the magistrates
> had acquitted the Respondent and that initially he had consented to the magistrates
> binding him over. (iv) The alternative procedure of allowing the appellant to call
> evidence, although at first sight attractive, was undesirable since it might appear
d > that the issue of guilt or innocence was being re-opened.'

With the greatest respect to the circuit judge, I think that he was wrong. I think that
he fell into the error of trying to equate an appeal against a bind over with either an
appeal against conviction or an appeal against sentence. It is, in truth, sui generis. In
order to justify making the bind-over order in the first instance the magistrates had to
satisfy themselves on admissible material before them that unless steps were taken to
e prevent it there might be a breach of the peace in the future. A bind-over order is a
preventive order, but it has to be justified by existing evidence.

Having reached a decision that that situation existed and having made the order, if the
appellant wanted to appeal it was to be by way of rehearing, and the same or perhaps
improved material had to be before the Crown Court. If the person bound over was
prepared to admit the material before the court below and was arguing simply that it was
f insufficient to justify the binding-over order, one could by agreement between the
parties use the evidence of the notes given below. But if the matter was contested, the
facts which justified the magistrates and, as the police would say, which justified the
Crown Court, had to be strictly proved, just as strictly proved as they had to be in front
of the magistrates. The judge's order prevented this happening and accordingly that
order must be quashed.

There does appear to be an implication in the judge's opinion that where there is an
g appeal against sentence, which this was not, it is impossible to have sworn evidence. For
my part, I would not accept that proposition. It is rare of course that the underlying facts
are disputed on a sentence appeal. That rarity arises usually because the prosecution put
only admitted or found facts in front of the appellate court. But, if there was a challenge
which did not go to conviction and went solely to sentence, I have no doubt that it would
h be possible for the court to hear evidence, and in some circumstances they ought to do
so. When I say 'hear evidence' I mean of course sworn evidence which is cross-examined
to.

For those reasons I would quash the decision and send it back to the Crown Court for
rehearing.

McCULLOUGH J. I agree with what Donaldson LJ has said.

Appeal allowed.

Solicitors: *Sharpe, Pritchard & Co*, agents for *B G Coase*, Lincoln (for the appellant).

Dilys Tausz   Barrister.

United City Merchants (Investments) Ltd and others v Royal Bank of Canada and others

HOUSE OF LORDS

LORD DIPLOCK, LORD FRASER OF TULLYBELTON, LORD RUSSELL OF KILLOWEN, LORD SCARMAN AND LORD BRIDGE OF HARWICH

16, 17, 18, 22 MARCH, 20 MAY 1982

Currency control – Exchange control – Bretton Woods Agreements – Exchange contracts – Enforceability – Exchange contract involving currency of member of International Monetary Fund and contrary to exchange control regulations of that member – Meaning of 'exchange contract' – Contract for sale of goods – Peruvian resident buying goods from English company at inflated US dollar price and requesting excess to be deposited in bank in United States of America – Peruvian exchange control regulations prohibiting Peruvian residents from maintaining foreign currency accounts in Peru or abroad – Whether 'exchange contract' and therefore unenforceable in England – Whether contract only partly an 'exchange contract' – Whether contract enforceable as to part relating to genuine price of goods and freight – Bretton Woods Agreements Order in Council 1946, Sch, Part I, art VIII, s 2(b).

Bank – Documentary credit – Irrevocable credit – Duty of bank on presentation of documents – Non-conforming documents – Bill of lading falsely and fraudulently completed by shipping agent – Seller presenting documents in good faith – Bank aware of fraud – Whether bank obliged to refuse payment – Whether seller's good faith relevant.

In 1975 the seller, an English company, contracted to sell fibreglass making machinery to the buyer, a Peruvian company concerned in the glass fibre industry. The terms of the contract, although having all the appearances of a genuine sale fob United Kingdom port, involved (i) the buyer (at its suggestion) paying the seller double the price originally quoted, (ii) the seller agreeing to remit the excess price to the credit of an associate company of the buyer at a bank in the United States of America, and (iii) the price being paid by an irrevocable letter of credit issued by a Peruvian bank. Payment was to be made as to 20% with the order, as to 70% (plus 100% of the freight) against shipping documents and as to 10% on completion of erection of the machinery. The buyer arranged the transaction in that way so that not only could it acquire the machinery but also its associate company could acquire in the United States of America a large quantity of United States dollars for which the buyer, through the Peruvian bank, would pay in Peruvian currency. The excess price was to be held beneficially for the buyer by its associated company. Such a scheme was not illegal in the United Kingdom, but it was illegal under Peruvian law which made it an offence for Peruvian residents to maintain or establish foreign currency accounts in Peru or abroad or to overvalue imports and obligations payable in foreign currency in violation of Peruvian exchange control regulations. In accordance with the scheme the buyer, using the inflated invoice, obtained permission to buy the United States dollars; it then opened a letter of credit with the Peruvian bank, which in turn arranged with the defendant, a bank in England, to open a confirmed irrevocable letter of credit in favour of the seller, payable in London. The seller collected the first 20% of the inflated price under the terms of the letter of credit and duly remitted half the dollars to the buyer's associate company at its bank in the United States of America. The machinery was shipped on 16 December 1976, but the shipping agent, who was aware that the letter of credit required shipment no later than 15 December 1976, falsely and fraudulently, but not as agent of the seller or of a merchant bank to which it had assigned the letter of credit, entered the date of shipment on the bill of lading as 15 December 1976. When the merchant bank presented

the shipping documents to the defendant's London branch it refused to pay because it
a had discovered that the date on the bill of lading was false and that the machinery had
been shipped after the contract date. At that stage the defendant was unaware that the
transaction infringed Peruvian exchange control regulations. The seller and the assignee
of the letter of credit brought an action against the defendant seeking payment of the
70% of the purchase price plus the freight which was to be paid against the shipping
documents. The trial judge rejected the defendant's defence that it was entitled to reject
b the documents for non-conformity with the terms of the credit and fraud, but he refused
to give judgment for the plaintiffs, on the ground that the letter of credit was
unenforceable under the Bretton Woods Agreements Order in Council 1946, which was
made under the Bretton Woods Agreements Act 1945 and which gave force to art VIII,
s 2(b)[a] of the Bretton Woods Agreement establishing the International Monetary Fund.
The plaintiffs appealed to the Court of Appeal, which held that the letter of credit was
c unenforceable under the Bretton Woods Agreement to the extent that it infringed the
exchange control regulations and accordingly would have given judgment for the
plaintiffs for the amount of the letter of credit which did not constitute a monetary
transaction in disguise. However, the Court of Appeal dismissed the appeal on the
ground that the issuing or confirming bank was entitled to refuse to pay under a letter
of credit against fraudulent documents even when the person presenting the documents
d was not a party to the fraud. The plaintiffs appealed to the House of Lords.

Held – (1) The whole commercial purpose for which the system of confirmed irrevocable
documentary credits had been developed in international trade was to give the seller of
goods an assured right to be paid before he parted with control of the goods without risk
of the payment being refused, reduced or deferred because of a dispute with the buyer.
e It followed that the contractual duty owed by an issuing or confirming bank to the buyer
to honour the credit notified by him on presentation of apparently conforming
documents by the seller was matched by a corresponding contractual liability on the part
of the bank to the seller to pay him the amount of the credit on presentation of the
documents. The bank's duty to the seller was only vitiated if there was fraud on the part
of the seller, and the bank remained under a duty to pay the amount of the credit to the
seller even if the documents presented, although conforming on their face with the
terms of the credit, nevertheless contained a statement of material fact that was not
accurate. Nor was the bank relieved from liability to the seller even if the documents
presented by the seller contained a material misrepresentation of fact which the person
issuing the documents knew to be false and which was intended by him to deceive
persons, including the seller himself, who might thereafter deal in the documents.
f Accordingly, since the shipping documents had been fraudulently completed by the
shipping agent but not by the seller, the defendant remained under a duty, as the
confirming bank, to pay to the seller and its assignee the amount due under the letter of
credit (see p 725 *f g j*, p 726 *b e f* and *j* to p 727 *a*, p 728 *b* to *f* and *j* to p 729 *a* and p 730
j to p 731 *c*, post).
   (2) The substance of the contract between the buyer and the seller, which the
enforcement of the contract between the seller and the confirming bank under the
documentary credit would give effect to, was a monetary transaction which was
unenforceable under the Bretton Woods Agreement to the extent of that half of the
invoice price which the seller had agreed to hold as trustee for the buyer and transmit to
the buyer's American company in Florida. The seller was entitled to recover the other
half of the invoice price representing the true price of the goods and the whole of the
freight, since those amounts were not a monetary transaction in disguise (see p 729 *d* to
f and p 730 *a* to p 731 *c*, post); *Wilson, Smithett & Cope Ltd v Terruzzi* [1976] 1 All ER 817
approved.
   (3) It followed that, although the Court of Appeal had been right to hold that the

---

a   Section 2(*b*), so far as material, is set out at p 729 *c d*, post

letter of credit was unenforceable under the Bretton Woods Agreement to the extent that
it infringed the exchange control regulations, it had been wrong to hold that the *a*
defendant was entitled to refuse to pay under the letter of credit against the fraudulently
completed shipping documents. The appeal would accordingly be allowed (see p 729 *a*
b and p 730 *a b* and *j* to p 731 *c*, post).
    Decision of the Court of Appeal [1981] 3 All ER 142 reversed.

Notes   *b*
For the unenforceability of contracts contravening exchange control regulations of
countries which are members of the International Monetary Fund, see 32 Halsbury's
Laws (4th edn) para 267.
    For the tender of documents under a letter of credit, see 3 ibid para 141, and for cases
on letters of credit, see 3 Digest (Reissue) 665–670, 4121–4136.
    For the Bretton Woods Agreements Act 1945, see 22 Halsbury's Statutes (3rd edn) 886. *c*

Cases referred to in opinions
Batra v Ebrahim [1977] CA Transcript 197B.
Gian Singh & Co Ltd v Banque de l'Indochine [1974] 2 All ER 754, [1974] 1 WLR 1234, PC,
    3 Digest (Reissue) 670, *3138.
Owen (Edward) Engineering Ltd v Barclays Bank International Ltd [1978] 1 All ER 976, *d*
    [1978] QB 159, [1977] 3 WLR 764, CA, Digest (Cont Vol E) 18, 4136a.
Sztejn v J Henry Schroder Banking Corp (1941) 31 NYS 2d 631.
Wilson, Smithett & Cope Ltd v Terruzzi [1976] 1 All ER 817, [1976] QB 683, [1976] 2 WLR
    418, CA, Digest (Cont Vol E) 178, 213a.

Appeal   *e*
The plaintiffs, United City Merchants (Investments) Ltd and Glass Fibres and Equipment
Ltd, appealed against the decision of the Court of Appeal (Stephenson, Ackner and
Griffiths LJJ) ([1981] 3 All ER 142, [1982] AC 208) on 13 March 1981 dismissing their
appeal from the judgment of Mocatta J dated 12 March 1979 whereby he dismissed the
plaintiffs' action against the defendants, the Royal Bank of Canada, for payment under an *f*
irrevocable letter of credit issued by the second third party, Banco Continental SA of
Lima, Peru (Banco) on instructions of the first third party, Vitrorefuerzos SA of Lima,
Peru (Vitro). By agreement between the defendants and Banco and with the leave of the
court, Banco was the respondent before the Court of Appeal and the House of Lords and
the defendants were not represented thereat, although they remained nominally the
respondent. The facts are set out in the opinion of Lord Diplock.   *g*

Alexander Irvine QC and *Andrew Longmore* for the appellants.
David Johnson QC and *Richard Wood* for Banco.

Their Lordships took time for consideration.

20 May. The following opinions were delivered.   *h*

LORD DIPLOCK. My Lords, this appeal, which is the culmination of protracted
litigation, raises two distinct questions of law which it is convenient to deal with
separately. The first, which I will call the documentary credit point, relates to the
mutual rights and obligations of the confirming bank and the beneficiary under a *j*
documentary credit. It is of general importance to all those engaged in the conduct and
financing of international trade for it challenges the basic principle of documentary
credit operations that banks that are parties to them deal in documents only, not in the
goods to which those documents purport to relate. The second question, which I will call
the Bretton Woods point, is of less general importance. It turns on the construction of

the Bretton Woods Agreements Order in Council 1946, SR & O 1946/36 and its
a application to the particular facts of the instant case.

All parties to the transaction of sale of goods and its financing which have given rise
to the appeal were represented at the original hearings before Mocatta J. The sellers and
their own merchant bankers to whom they had transferred the credit as security for
advances were the plaintiffs, the confirming bank was the defendant, the buyers and the
issuing bank were joined as first and second third parties respectively. The issuing bank
b admitted its liability to indemnify the confirming bank for any sums for which the latter
as defendant should be held liable to the plaintiffs, and in the later stages of the
proceedings, although the confirming bank has remained nominally the respondent, the
conduct of the appeals both in the Court of Appeal and in your Lordships' House has
been undertaken by counsel for the issuing bank. Your Lordships are, however, only
indirectly concerned with the contractual relationship between the buyers and the
c issuing bank or between the issuing bank and the confirming bank. The documentary
credit point depends on the contractual relationship between the sellers (or their
transferee) and the confirming bank. The Bretton Woods point is about the effect on
that relationship of certain special provisions in an agreement between the sellers and the
buyers that was collateral to their contract of sale.

Mocatta J delivered his judgment in two parts with an interval between them. The
d facts that are relevant to the documentary credit point are set out in detail in the first part
(reported in [1979] 1 Lloyd's Rep 267); the additional facts that are relevant to the
Bretton Woods point are set out in the second part (reported in [1979] 2 Lloyd's Rep
498). For the purpose of identifying the questions of law that are dispositive of this
appeal it is sufficient to state those facts in summarised form, starting with those that
raise the documentary credit point.

e A Peruvian company, Vitrorefuerzos SA (the buyer), agreed to buy from the second
appellant (the seller) plant for the manufacture of glass fibres (the goods) at a price of
$662,086 fob London for shipment to Callao. Payment was to be in London by
confirmed irrevocable transferable letter of credit for the invoice price plus freight,
payable as to 20% of the invoice price on the opening of the credit, as to 70% of the
invoice price and 100% of the freight on presentation of shipping documents and as to
f the balance of 10% of the invoice price on completion of erection of the plant in Peru.

The buyer arranged with its Peruvian bank, Banco Continental SA (the issuing bank),
to issue the necessary credit and the issuing bank appointed the respondent, Royal Bank
of Canada (the confirming bank), to advise and confirm on its own behalf the credit to
the seller. The confirming bank duly notified the seller on 30 March 1976 of the
opening of the confirmed irrevocable transferable letter of credit. So far as concerned the
g 70% of the invoice price and 100% freight there was nothing that was unusual in its
terms. It was expressed to be subject to the Uniform Customs and Practice for
Documentary Credits (1974 revision) of the International Chamber of Commerce (the
Uniform Customs) and to be available by sight drafts on the issuing bank against
delivery, inter alia, of a full set 'on board' bills of lading evidencing receipt for shipment
of the goods from London to Callao on or before a date in October 1976, which was
h subsequently extended to 15 December 1976.

The initial payment of 20% of the invoice price was duly made by the confirming
bank to the seller. Thereafter, in July 1976, the seller transferred to its own merchant
bankers, the first appellant, its interest under the credit as security for advances; but
nothing turns on this so far as either the documentary credit point or the Bretton Woods
point is concerned. In dealing with the relevant law on each of these points I shall
j accordingly treat the seller as having continued throughout to be the beneficiary of the
confirmed credit.

The goods, which had to be manufactured by the seller, were ready for shipment by
the beginning of December 1976. It was intended by the loading brokers acting on
behalf of Prudential Lines Inc (the carriers) that they should be shipped on a vessel
belonging to the carriers (the American Legend) due to arrive at Felixstowe on 10

December 1976. (The substitution of Felixstowe for London as the loading port is
immaterial. It was acquiesced in by all parties to the transaction.) The arrival of the   *a*
American Legend at Felixstowe was cancelled and another vessel, the American Accord,
was substituted by the loading brokers; but its date of arrival was scheduled for 16
December 1976, one day after the latest date of shipment required by the documentary
credit. The goods were in fact loaded on the American Accord on 16 December 1976;
but the loading brokers, who also acted as agents for the carriers in issuing bills of lading,
issued in the first instance a set of 'received for shipment' bills of lading dated 15   *b*
December 1976 and handed them over to the sellers in return for payment of the
freight. On presentation of the shipping documents to the confirming bank on 17
December that bank raised various objections to their form, of which the only one that
is relevant to the documentary credit point was that the bills of lading did not bear any
dated 'on board' notation. The bills of lading were returned to the carriers' freight
brokers who issued a fresh set bearing the notation, which was untrue: 'These goods are   *c*
actually on board 15th December 1976. E. H. Mundy and Co. (Freight Agents) Ltd. as
Agents.' The amended bills of lading together with the other documents were represented to the confirming bank on 22 December 1976, but the confirming bank again
refused to pay on the ground that they 'had information in their possession which
suggested that shipment was not effected as it appears in the bill of lading'.

Mocatta J, after a careful hearing lasting for no less than 30 days, held that Mr Baker,   *d*
the employee of the loading brokers to the carriers who was in charge of the transaction
on their behalf, had acted fraudulently in issuing the bills of lading bearing what was to
his knowledge a false statement as to the date on which the plant was actually on board
the American Accord. The judge held, however, that neither the seller (nor its transferee)
were parties or privies to any fraud by Mr Baker; at the time of both presentations of the
shipping documents to the confirming bank on 17 and 22 December 1976 they bona   *e*
fide believed that the plant had in fact been loaded on the American Accord on or before
15 December 1976, and that the annotation on the reissued bill of lading, stating the
goods to be actually on board at that date, was true.

The additional facts that give rise to the Bretton Woods point may be stated even more
concisely. The seller's original quotation for the sale price of the glass fibre making plant
was half the figure that ultimately became the invoice price for the purposes of the   *f*
documentary credit. The buyer who was desirous of converting Peruvian currency into
United States dollars available to it in the United States, a transaction which was contrary
to Peruvian exchange control regulations, persuaded the seller to invoice the plant to it
at double the real sale price in United States dollars and to agree that it would within ten
days after drawing on the documentary credit for each of the three instalments of the
invoice price remit one-half of the amount so drawn to the dollar account in Miami,   *g*
Florida, of an American corporation controlled by the buyer. This the seller agreed to
do; and of the first instalment of 20% of the now doubled invoice price of $662,086,
which was the only drawing that it succeeded in making under the credit, it transmitted
one-half, viz $66,208, to the American corporation in Florida. It would have done the
same with one-half of the next drawing of 70% of the invoice price payable against
shipping documents, if the confirming bank had paid this instalment.   *h*

The documentary credit point

My Lords, for the proposition on the documentary credit point, both in the broad
form for which counsel for the confirming bank have strenuously argued at all stages of
this appeal and in the narrower form or 'halfway house' that commended itself to the
Court of Appeal, there is no direct authority to be found either in English or Privy   *j*
Council cases or among the numerous decisions of courts in the United States of America
to which reference was made in the judgments of the Court of Appeal in the instant
case. So the point falls to be decided by reference to first principles as to the legal nature
of the contractual obligations assumed by the various parties to a transaction consisting
of an international sale of goods to be financed by means of a confirmed irrevocable

documentary credit. It is trite law that there are four autonomous though interconnected
a contractual relationships involved: (1) the underlying contract for the sale of goods, to
which the only parties are the buyer and the seller; (2) the contract between the buyer
and the issuing bank under which the latter agrees to issue the credit and either itself or
through a confirming bank to notify the credit to the seller and to make payments to or
to the order of the seller (or to pay, accept or negotiate bills of exchange drawn by the
seller) against presentation of stipulated documents; and the buyer agrees to reimburse
b the issuing bank for payments made under the credit. For such reimbursement the
stipulated documents, if they include a document of title such as a bill of lading,
constitute a security available to the issuing bank; (3) if payment is to be made through
a confirming bank, the contract between the issuing bank and the confirming bank
authorising and requiring the latter to make such payments and to remit the stipulated
documents to the issuing bank when they are received, the issuing bank in turn agreeing
c to reimburse the confirming bank for payments made under the credit; (4) the contract
between the confirming bank and the seller under which the confirming bank undertakes
to pay to the seller (or to accept or negotiate without recourse to drawer bills of exchange
drawn by him) up to the amount of the credit against presentation of the stipulated
documents.

Again, it is trite law that in contract (4), with which alone the instant appeal is directly
d concerned, the parties to it, the seller and the confirming bank, 'deal in documents and
not in goods', as art 8 of the Uniform Customs puts it. If, on their face, the documents
presented to the confirming bank by the seller conform with the requirements of the
credit as notified to him by the confirming bank, that bank is under a contractual
obligation to the seller to honour the credit, notwithstanding that the bank has
knowledge that the seller at the time of presentation of the conforming documents is
e alleged by the buyer to have, and in fact has already, committed a breach of his contract
with the buyer for the sale of the goods to which the documents appear on their face to
relate that would have entitled the buyer to treat the contract of sale as rescinded and to
reject the goods and refuse to pay the seller the purchase price. The whole commercial
purpose for which the system of confirmed irrevocable documentary credits has been
developed in international trade is to give to the seller an assured right to be paid before
f he parts with control of the goods and that does not permit of any dispute with the buyer
as to the performance of the contract of sale being used as a ground for non-payment or
reduction or deferment of payment.

To this general statement of principle as to the contractual obligations of the
confirming bank to the seller, there is one established exception: that is, where the seller,
for the purpose of drawing on the credit, fraudulently presents to the confirming bank
g documents that contain, expressly or by implication, material representations of fact that
to his knowledge are untrue. Although there does not appear among the English
authorities any case in which this exception has been applied, it is well established in the
American cases, of which the leading or 'landmark' case is *Sztejn v J Henry Schroder
Banking Corp* (1941) 31 NYS 2d 631. This judgment of the New York Court of Appeals
was referred to with approval by the English Court of Appeal in *Edward Owen Engineering
h Ltd v Barclays Bank International Ltd* [1978] 1 All ER 979, [1978] QB 159, though this was
actually a case about a performance bond under which a bank assumes obligations to a
buyer analogous to those assumed by a confirming bank to the seller under a
documentary credit. The exception for fraud on the part of the beneficiary seeking to
avail himself of the credit is a clear application of the maxim ex turpi causa non oritur
actio or, if plain English is to be preferred, 'fraud unravels all'. The courts will not allow
their process to be used by a dishonest person to carry out a fraud.

The instant case, however, does not fall within the fraud exception. Mocatta J found
the seller to have been unaware of the inaccuracy of Mr Baker's notation of the date at
which the goods were actually on board the American Accord. It believed that it was
true and that the goods had actually been loaded on or before 15 December 1976, as
required by the documentary credit.

Faced by this finding, the argument for the confirming bank before Mocatta J was directed to supporting the broad proposition that a confirming bank is not under any *a* obligation, legally enforceable against it by the seller/beneficiary of a documentary credit, to pay to him the sum stipulated in the credit against presentation of documents, if the documents presented, although conforming on their face with the terms of the credit, nevertheless contain some statement of material fact that is not accurate. This proposition which does not call for knowledge on the part of the seller/beneficiary of the existence of any inaccuracy would embrace the fraud exception and render it superfluous. *b*

My Lords, the more closely this bold proposition is subjected to legal analysis, the more implausible it becomes; to assent to it would, in my view, undermine the whole system of financing international trade by means of documentary credits.

It has, so far as I know, never been disputed that as between confirming bank and issuing bank and as between issuing bank and the buyer the contractual duty of each bank under a confirmed irrevocable credit is to examine with reasonable care all *c* documents presented in order to ascertain that they appear *on their face* to be in accordance with the terms and conditions of the credit, and, if they do so appear, to pay to the seller/beneficiary by whom the documents have been presented the sum stipulated by the credit, or to accept or negotiate without recourse to drawer drafts drawn by the seller/beneficiary if the credit so provides. It is so stated in the latest edition of the Uniform Customs. It is equally clear law, and is so provided by art 9 of the Uniform *d* Customs, that confirming banks and issuing banks assume no liability or responsibility to one another or to the buyer 'for the form, sufficiency, accuracy, genuineness, falsification or legal effect of any documents'. This is well illustrated by the Privy Council case of *Gian Singh & Co Ltd v Banque de l'Indochine* [1974] 2 All ER 754, [1974] 1 WLR 1234, where the customer was held liable to reimburse the issuing bank for honouring a documentary credit on presentation of an apparently conforming document *e* which was an ingenious forgery, a fact that the bank had not been negligent in failing to detect on examination of the document.

It would be strange from the commercial point of view, although not theoretically impossible in law, if the contractual duty owed by confirming and issuing banks to the buyer to honour the credit on presentation of apparently conforming documents despite the fact that they contain inaccuracies or even are forged were not matched by a *f* corresponding contractual liability of the confirming bank to the seller/beneficiary (in the absence, of course, of any fraud on his part) to pay the sum stipulated in the credit on presentation of apparently confirming documents. Yet, as is conceded by counsel for the confirming bank in the instant case, if the broad proposition for which he argues is correct, the contractual duties do not match. As respects the confirming bank's contractual duty to the seller to honour the credit, the bank, it is submitted, is only *g* bound to pay on presentation of documents which not only appear on their face to be in accordance with the terms and conditions of the credit but also do not in fact contain any material statement that is inaccurate. If this submission be correct, the bank's contractual right to refuse to honour the documentary credit cannot, as a matter of legal analysis, depend on whether *at the time of the refusal* the bank was virtually certain from information obtained by means other than reasonably careful examination of the *h* documents themselves that they contained some material statement that was inaccurate or whether the bank merely suspected this or even had no suspicion that apparently conforming documents contained any inaccuracies at all. If there be any such right of refusal it must depend on whether the bank, when sued by the seller/beneficiary for breach of its contract to honour the credit, is able to prove that one of the documents did in fact contain what was a material misstatement. *j*

It is conceded that to justify refusal the misstatement must be 'material' but this invites the query: material to what? The suggested answer to this query was: a misstatement of a fact which if the true fact had been disclosed would have entitled the buyer to reject the goods; date of shipment (as in the instant case) or misdescription of the goods are examples. But this is to destroy the autonomy of the documentary credit which is its raison d'être; it is to make the seller's right to payment by the confirming bank dependent on the buyer's rights against the seller under the terms of the contract for the sale of goods, of which the confirming bank will have no knowledge.

Counsel sought to evade the difficulties disclosed by an analysis of the legal consequences of his broad proposition by praying in aid the practical consideration that a bank, desirous as it would be of protecting its reputation in the competitive business of providing documentary credits, would never exercise its right against a seller/beneficiary to refuse to honour the credit except in cases where at the time of the refusal it already was in possession of irrefutable evidence of the inaccuracy in the documents presented. I must confess that the argument that a seller should be content to rely on the exercise by banks of business expediency, unbacked by any legal liability, to ensure prompt payment by a foreign buyer does not impress me; but the assumption that underlies reliance on expediency does not, in my view, itself stand up to legal analysis. Business expediency would not induce the bank to pay the seller/beneficiary against presentation of documents which it was not legally liable to accept as complying with the documentary credit unless, in doing so, it acquired a right legally enforceable against the buyer to require him to take up the documents himself and reimburse the bank for the amount paid. So any reliance on business expediency to make the system work if the broad proposition contended for by counsel is correct must involve that, as against the buyer, the bank, when presented with apparently conforming documents by the seller, is legally entitled to the option, *exercisable at its own discretion and regardless of any instructions to the contrary from the buyer*, either (1) to take up the documents and pay the credit and claim reimbursement from the buyer, notwithstanding that the bank has been provided with information that makes it virtually certain that the existence of such inaccuracies can be proved, or (2) to reject the documents and to refuse to pay the credit.

The legal justification for the existence of such an independently exercisable option, it is suggested, lies in the bank's own interest in the goods to which the documents relate, as security for the advance made by the bank to the buyer, when it pays the seller under the documentary credit. But, if this were so, the answer to the question, 'To what must the misstatement in the documents be material?' should be, 'Material to the price which the goods to which the documents relate would fetch on sale if, failing reimbursement by the buyer, the bank should be driven to realise its security.' But this would not justify the confirming bank's refusal to honour the credit in the instant case; the realisable value on arrival at Callao of a glass fibre manufacturing plant made to the specification of the buyers could not be in any way affected by its having been loaded on board a ship at Felixstowe on 16 December instead of 15 December 1976.

My Lords, in rejecting this broad proposition I have dealt with it at greater length than otherwise I would have done, because it formed the main plank of the confirming bank's argument on the documentary credit point before Mocatta J, who, however, had no hesitation in rejecting it, but found for the confirming bank on the Bretton Woods point. It formed the main ground also in the confirming bank's notice of cross-appeal to the Court of Appeal on which the confirming bank would seek to uphold the judgment in its favour if the seller's appeal should succeed on the Bretton Woods point. It was not until halfway through the actual hearing in the Court of Appeal that the notice of cross-appeal was amended to include a narrower proposition referred to as a 'halfway house' which the Court of Appeal accepted as being decisive in the confirming bank's favour. This rendered it unnecessary for that court to rule on the broad proposition that I have so far been discussing, although Stephenson LJ indicated obiter that for this part he would have rejected it. In the confirming bank's argument before this House a marked lack of enthusiasm has been shown for reliance on the 'halfway house' and the broad proposition has again formed the main ground on which the confirming bank has sought to uphold the actual decision of the Court of Appeal in its favour on the documentary credit point.

The proposition accepted by the Court of Appeal as constituting a complete defence available to the confirming bank on the documentary credit point has been referred to as a 'halfway house' because it lies not only halfway between the unqualified liability of the confirming bank to honour a documentary credit on presentation of documents which on reasonably careful examination appear to conform to the terms and conditions of the credit and what I have referred to as the fraud exception to this unqualified liability which is available to the confirming bank where the seller/beneficiary presents to the confirming bank documents that contain, expressly or by implication, material representations of fact that to his own knowledge are untrue; but it also lies halfway between the fraud exception and the broad proposition favoured by the confirming bank with which I have hitherto been dealing. The halfway house is erected on the narrower proposition that, if any of the documents presented under the credit by the seller/beneficiary contain a material misrepresentation of fact that was *false to the knowledge of the person who issued the document* and intended by him to deceive persons into whose hands the document might come, the confirming bank is under no liability to honour the credit, even though, as in the instant case, the persons whom the issuer of the document intended to, and did, deceive included the seller/beneficiary himself.

My Lords, if the broad proposition for which the confirming bank has argued is unacceptable for the reasons that I have already discussed, what rational ground can there be for drawing any distinction between apparently conforming documents that, unknown to the seller, in fact contain a statement of fact that is inaccurate where the inaccuracy was due to inadvertence by the maker of the document, and the like documents where the same inaccuracy had been inserted by the maker of the document with intent to deceive, among others, the seller/beneficiary himself? Ex hypothesi we are dealing only with a case in which the seller/beneficiary claiming under the credit *has* been deceived, for, if he presented documents to the confirming bank with knowledge that this apparent conformity with the terms and conditions of the credit was due to the fact that the documents told a lie, the seller/beneficiary would himself be a party to the misrepresentation made to the confirming bank by the lie in the documents and the case would come within the fraud exception, as did all the American cases referred to as persuasive authority in the judgments of the Court of Appeal in the instant case.

The American cases refer indifferently to documents that are 'forged or fraudulent', as does the Uniform Commercial Code that has been adopted in nearly all states of the United States of America. The Court of Appeal reached their halfway house in the instant case by starting from the premise that a confirming bank could refuse to pay against a document that it knew to be forged, even though the seller/beneficiary had no knowledge of that fact. From this premise they reasoned that, if forgery by a third party relieves the confirming bank of liability to pay the seller/beneficiary, fraud by a third party ought to have the same consequence.

I would not wish to be taken as accepting that the premise as to forged documents is correct, even where the fact that the document is forged deprives it of all legal effect and makes it a nullity, and so worthless to the confirming bank as security for its advances to the buyer. This is certainly not so under the Uniform Commercial Code as against a person who has taken a draft drawn under the credit in circumstances that would make him a holder in due course, and I see no reason why, and there is nothing in the Uniform Commercial Code to suggest that, a seller/beneficiary who is ignorant of the forgery should be in any worse position because he has not negotiated the draft before presentation. I would prefer to leave open the question of the rights of an innocent seller/beneficiary against the confirming bank when a document presented by him is a nullity because unknown to him it was forged by some third party, for that question does not arise in the instant case. The bill of lading with the wrong date of loading placed on it by the carrier's agents was far from being a nullity. It was a valid transferable receipt for the goods giving the holder a right to claim them at their destination, Callao, and was evidence of the terms of the contract under which they were being carried.

But, even assuming the correctness of the Court of Appeal's premise as respects forgery by a third party of a kind that makes a document a nullity for which at least a rational case can be made out, to say that this lead to the conclusion that fraud by a third party which does not render the document a nullity has the same consequence appears to me, with respect, to be a non sequitur, and I am not persuaded by the reasoning in any of the judgments of the Court of Appeal that it is not.

On the documentary credit point I think that Mocatta J was right in deciding it in favour of the sellers and that the Court of Appeal was wrong in reversing him on this point.

The Bretton Woods point

The Bretton Woods point arises out of the agreement between the buyers and the seller collateral to the contract of sale of the goods between the same parties that out of the payments in United States dollars received by the sellers under the documentary credit in respect of each instalment of the invoice price of the goods they would transmit to the account of the buyers in America one-half of the United States dollars received.

The Bretton Woods Agreements Order in Council 1946, made under the Bretton Woods Agreements Act 1945, gives the force of law in England to art VIII, s 2(*b*) of the Bretton Woods Agreements, which is in the following terms:

'Exchange contracts which involve the currency of any Member and which are contrary to the exchange control regulations of that member maintained or imposed consistently with this Agreement shall be unenforceable in the territories of any member . . .'

My Lords, I accept as correct the narrow interpretation that was placed on the expression 'exchange contracts' in this provision of the Bretton Woods Agreements by the Court of Appeal in *Wilson, Smithett & Cope Ltd v Teruzzi* [1976] 1 All ER 817, [1976] QB 683. It is confined to contracts to exchange the currency of one country for the currency of another; it does not include contracts entered into in connection with sales of goods which require the conversion by the buyer of one currency into another in order to enable him to pay the purchase price. As was said by Lord Denning MR in his judgment in the *Teruzzi* case, the court in considering the application of the provision should look at the substance of the contracts and not at the form. It should not enforce a contract that is a mere 'monetary transaction in disguise'.

I also accept as accurate what was said by Lord Denning MR in a subsequent case as to the effect that should be given by English courts to the word 'unenforceable'. The case, *Batra v Ebrahim* [1977] CA Transcript 197B, is unreported, but the relevant passage from Lord Denning's judgment is helpfully cited by Ackner LJ in his own judgment in the instant case (see [1981] 3 All ER 142 at 166, [1982] AC 208 at 241–242). If in the course of the hearing of an action the court becomes aware that the contract on which a party is suing is one that this country has accepted an international obligation to treat as unenforceable, the court must take the point itself, even though the defendant has not pleaded it, and must refuse to lend its aid to enforce the contract. But this does not have the effect of making an exchange contract that is contrary to the exchange control regulations of a member state other than the United Kingdom into a contract that is 'illegal' under English law or render acts undertaken in this country in performance of such a contract unlawful. Like a contract of guarantee of which there is no note or memorandum in writing it is unenforceable by the courts and nothing more.

Mocatta J, professing to follow the guidance given in the *Teruzzi* case, took the view that the contract of sale between the buyer and the seller at the inflated invoice price was a monetary transaction in disguise and that, despite the autonomous character of the contract between the seller and the confirming bank under the documentary credit, this too was tarred with the same brush and was a monetary transaction in disguise and therefore one which the court should not enforce. He rejected out of hand what he described as a 'rather remarkable submission' that the seller could recover that half of the invoice price which represented the true sale price of the goods, even if they could not recover that other half of the invoice price which they would receive as trustees for the buyers on trust to transmit it to the buyer's American company in Florida. He held that it was impossible to sever the contract constituted by the documentary credit: it was either enforceable in full or not at all.

In refusing to treat the seller's claim under the documentary credit for that part of the invoice price that it was to retain for itself as the sale price of the goods in a different way from that in which he treated its claim to that part of the invoice price which they would receive as trustees for the buyer, I agree with all three members of the Court of Appeal the judge fell into error.

I avoid speaking of 'severability', for this expression is appropriate where the task on which the court is engaged is construing the language that the parties have used in a written contract. The question whether and to what extent a contract is unenforceable under the Bretton Woods Agreements Order in Council 1946 because it is a monetary transaction in disguise is *not* a question of construction of the contract but a question of the substance of the transaction to which enforcement of the contract will give effect. If the matter were to be determined simply as a question of construction, the contract between the sellers and the confirming bank constituted by the documentary credit fell altogether outside the Bretton Woods Agreements: it was not a contract to exchange one currency for another currency but a contract to pay currency for documents which included documents of title to goods. On the contrary, the task on which the court is engaged is to penetrate any disguise presented by the actual words the parties have used, to identify any monetary transaction (in the narrow sense of that expression as used in the *Teruzzi* case) which those words were intended to conceal and to refuse to enforce the contract to the extent that to do so would give effect to the monetary transaction.

In the instant case there is no difficulty in identifying the monetary transaction that was sought to be concealed by the actual words used in the documentary credit and in the underlying contract of sale. It was to exchange Peruvian currency provided by the buyer in Peru for $US331,043 to be made available to it in Florida; and to do this was contrary to the exchange control regulations of Peru. Payment under the documentary credit by the confirming bank to the seller of that half of the invoice price (viz $331,043) that the seller would receive as trustee for the buyer on trust to remit it to the account of the buyer's American company in Florida was an essential part of that monetary transaction and therefore unenforceable; but payment of the other half of the invoice price and of the freight was not: the seller would receive that part of the payment under the documentary credit on its own behalf and retain it as the genuine purchase price of goods sold by it to the buyer. I agree with the Court of Appeal that there is nothing in the Bretton Woods Agreements Order in Council 1946 that prevents the payment under the documentary credit being enforceable to this extent.

As regards the first instalment of 20% of the invoice price, this was paid by the confirming bank in full. No enforcement by the court of this payment is needed by the buyers. The confirming bank, if it had known at the time of the monetary transaction by the buyer that was involved, could have successfully resisted payment of one-half of that instalment; but even if it was in possession of such knowledge there was nothing in English law to prevent it from voluntarily paying that half too. As regards the third instalment of 10% of the invoice price, that never fell due within the period of the credit. What is in issue in this appeal is the second instalment of 70% of the invoice price and 100% of the freight which, as I have held under the documentary credit point, fell due on the re-presentation of the documents on 22 December 1976. In my opinion the seller is entitled to judgment for that part of the second instalment which was not a monetary transaction in disguise, that is to say 35% of the invoice price and 100% of the freight, amounting in all to $US262,807·49, with interest thereon from 22 December 1976.

LORD FRASER OF TULLYBELTON. My Lords, I have had the advantage of reading in draft the speech of my noble and learned friend Lord Diplock. I agree with it and with the order he proposes.

LORD RUSSELL OF KILLOWEN. My Lords, I have had the advantage of reading in draft the opinion of my noble and learned friend Lord Diplock. I agree with it and the order proposed by him.

LORD SCARMAN. My Lords, I have had the advantage of reading in draft the speech of my noble and learned friend Lord Diplock. I agree with it and with the order proposed.

LORD BRIDGE OF HARWICH. My Lords, I have had the advantage of reading in draft the speech of my noble and learned friend Lord Diplock. I agree with it and with the order he proposed.

Appeal allowed.

Solicitors: *Nicholson, Graham & Jones* (for the appellants); *Thomas Cooper & Stibbard* (for Banco).

Mary Rose Plummer   Barrister.

R v Rose and others

HOUSE OF LORDS
LORD DIPLOCK, LORD SCARMAN, LORD ROSKILL, LORD BRIDGE OF HARWICH AND LORD BRANDON OF OAKBROOK
14 JUNE, 1 JULY 1982

Criminal law – Trial – Retrial – Jury's verdict vitiated by material irregularity – Whether Court of Appeal having power to order retrial.

The respondents were variously charged with murder and attempting to pervert the course of public justice. At the end of the trial and after the jury had retired the judge privately sent messages to the jury through the clerk of the court imposing a time limit within which he required them to reach a majority verdict failing which he threatened to discharge them. The jury convicted the respondents by a majority of ten to two. The respondents appealed against their convictions, contending that the judge had applied improper pressure on the jury to reach a verdict by the imposition of a time limit. The Court of Appeal allowed their appeals on the ground that there had been a material irregularity in the proceedings which required that the verdict be quashed but it refused to order a venire de novo for which the prosecution applied. The Crown appealed, contending that a new trial ought to have been ordered.

Held – Where in the course of a trial that had been validly commenced there was a material irregularity between the time the trial commenced and its conclusion with a judgment of conviction following an unequivocal verdict of guilty by the jury, the Court of Appeal had no jurisdiction to order a new trial by the issue of a writ of venire de novo but was required to quash the conviction. It followed therefore that the appeal would be dismissed (see p 736 e to j, post).

Decision of the Court of Appeal [1982] 2 All ER 536 affirmed.

Notes
For venire de novo, see 11 Halsbury's Laws (4th edn) para 667, and for cases on the subject, see 14(2) Digest (Reissue) 850, 7359–7380.

Cases referred to in opinions

Crane v DPP [1921] 2 AC 299, [1921] All ER Rep 19, HL, 14(1) Digest (Reissue) 315, *a*
2428.

R v Cronin [1940] 2 All ER 242, CCA, 14(2) Digest (Reissue) 825, 7070.

R v Hancock (1931) 100 LJKB 419, CCA, 14(1) Digest (Reissue) 409, 3475.

R v McKenna, R v McKenna, R v Busby [1960] 1 All ER 326, [1960] 1 QB 411, [1960] 2
WLR 306, CCA, 14(2) Digest (Reissue) 829, 7115.

R v Neal [1949] 2 All ER 438, [1949] 2 KB 590, CCA, 14(2) Digest (Reissue) 826, 7088. *b*

R v Yeadon and Birch (1861) Le & Ca 81, 169 ER 1312, CCA, 14(1) Digest (Reissue) 418,
3557.

Appeal

The Director of Public Prosecutions appealed with leave of the Appeal Committee of the
House of Lords granted on 29 March 1982 against the judgment and order of the Court *c*
of Appeal, Criminal Division (Lord Lane CJ, Watkins LJ and Stephen Brown J) ([1982] 2
All ER 536, [1982] 1 WLR 614) dated 8 March 1982 whereby the court allowed appeals
by Newton Samuel Rose, Ian Henry, Michael Carson Clarke and Orville Alexander
Johnson (the respondents to this appeal) against their convictions at the Central Criminal
Court on 4 December 1981 before his Honour Judge Clarke QC and a jury, the
respondent Rose for murder and the other three respondents for attempting to pervert *d*
the course of public justice. The facts are set out in the opinion of Lord Diplock.

Ann Curnow and *Barbara Mills* for the Crown.
Ian Macdonald and *Nicholas Blake* for the respondents.

Their Lordships took time for consideration.   *e*

1 July. The following opinions were delivered.

LORD DIPLOCK. My Lords, these consolidated appeals are brought by the Director
of Public Prosecutions from orders of the Court of Appeal, Criminal Division, quashing
the convictions of the first respondent, Rose, for murder, and of the other three *f*
respondents for attempting to pervert the course of justice, instead of ordering a venire
de novo for which the prosecution had applied.

The respondents were tried together and the point of law involved in each of the four
cases was certified by the Court of Appeal as follows:

> 'Whether the Court of Appeal Criminal Division may in their discretion order a
> venire de novo when they are satisfied that a verdict of guilty must be set aside by *g*
> reason of a material irregularity consisting of improper pressure imposed upon the
> jury at any time before verdict.'

Although their historical origins are different the issue of a writ of venire de novo has
the same effect as an order for retrial, such as may be made under s 7 of the Criminal
Appeal Act 1968 but only if the conditions stated in that section are fulfilled. *h*

There is no need to say any more about the facts in the instant case than that after the
jury had retired the judge had privately sent messages to them through the clerk of the
court imposing a time limit within which he required them to reach a majority verdict,
failing which he threatened that he would discharge them. The case presented close
similarities to that of *R v McKenna* [1960] 1 All ER 326, [1960] 1 QB 411, and the Court
of Appeal, regarding itself as bound by that case and the earlier case of *R v Neal* [1949] 2
All ER 438, [1949] 2 KB 590, considered that it had no jurisdiction to order a venire de *i*
novo. Since it felt unable to apply the provisos to s 2(1) of the 1968 Act, it allowed the
respondents' appeals on the ground specified in para (c) of that subsection, viz 'that there
was a material irregularity in the course of the trial'. Accordingly it quashed the
conviction as it was required to do by s 2(2).

In giving judgment and certifying the above-quoted question, Lord Lane CJ expressed
the hope that this House would take the opportunity to reconsider the circumstances in
which the jurisdiction of the Criminal Division of the Court of Appeal to issue a writ of
venire de novo could be exercised.

My Lords, the Criminal Division of the Court of Appeal was created by the Criminal
Appeal Act 1966, which abolished the former Court of Criminal Appeal that had itself
been created by the Criminal Appeal Act 1907. Its jurisdiction is entirely statutory, and
was conferred on it by s 1(1) and (2)(b) of the 1966 Act. Subsection (1) of s 1 of the 1966
Act provided:

'The jurisdiction exercisable before the commencement of this Act by the Court
of Criminal Appeal shall, subject to the provisions of this section be exercisable by
the Court of Appeal and the Court of Criminal Appeal shall cease to exist.'

That subsection was repealed by Sch 7 to the 1968 Act, which also repealed sub-s (8) of s 1
of the 1966 Act. The 1968 Act by Sch 5 substituted a new para (b) in s 1(2) of the 1966
Act. Section 1(8) of the 1966 Act had read:

'The Crown Cases Act 1848 is hereby repealed, but the repeal shall not affect the
jurisdiction to order the issue of writs of venire de novo vested by virtue of section
2 of that Act and section 20(4) of the 1907 Act in the Court of Criminal Appeal, and
that jurisdiction is transferred with the other jurisdiction of the court to the Court
of Appeal by subsection (1) of this section.'

This subsection contains clear parliamentary recognition that immediately before its
abolition the Court of Criminal Appeal by s 20(4) of the 1907 Act had been vested with
jurisdiction to order the issue of writs of venire de novo. Such recognition was continued
by the amendment by the 1968 Act of s 1(2) of the 1966 Act. In the result, the
jurisdiction now vested in the Court of Appeal, Criminal Division, is conferred on it in
the following terms by s 1(2) as amended by the 1968 Act:

'The Court of Appeal shall consist of two divisions, namely—(a) the civil division
which shall, subject to rules of court under subsection (5) of this section, exercise the
jurisdiction exercisable immediately before the commencement of this Act by the
court, and (b) the criminal division which shall, subject to any such rules, exercise—
(i) all jurisdiction of the Court of Appeal under Parts I and II of the Criminal Appeal
Act 1968; and (ii) all other jurisdiction which was that of the Court of Criminal
Appeal immediately before it ceased to exist (including the jurisdiction to order the
issue of writs of venire de novo).'

The 1966 Act has since been wholly repealed by the Supreme Court Act 1981, s 53(2)
of which re-enacts the provisions relating to the criminal jurisdiction of the Court of
Appeal which were in s 1(2)(b) of the 1966 Act.

The Criminal Division of the Court of Appeal thus has a twofold jurisdiction, viz (i) its
principal jurisdiction under Part I of the 1968 Act (Part II deals only with its functions in
relation to appeals to the House of Lords), and (ii) such supplemental jurisdiction as was
conferred on the Court of Criminal Appeal by s 20(4) of the 1907 Act. Section 20,
notwithstanding that, by sub-s (1), it had abolished 'Writs of error and the powers and
practice' which prior to the passing of the Act in 1907 then existed 'in the High Court in
respect of motions for new trials or the granting thereof in criminal cases' had, by sub-s
(4), preserved and vested in the Court of Criminal Appeal certain jurisdiction which had
originally been vested in the Court for Crown Cases Reserved by the Crown Cases Act
1848. Subsection (4), so far as is relevant to the instant appeals, was in the following
terms:

'All jurisdiction and authority under the Crown Cases Act 1848, in relation to
questions of law arising in criminal trials which is transferred to the judges of the

High Court by section forty-seven of the Supreme Court of Judicature Act, 1873, shall be vested in the Court of Criminal Appeal under this Act . . .'

So it is in this provision of the 1907 Act that any limits on the current jurisdiction of the Criminal Division of the Court of Appeal to issue writs of venire de novo must be found.

My Lords, the question whether, despite the abolition of the power to grant new trials by s 20(1) of the 1907 Act, the jurisdiction vested in the Court of Criminal Appeal by s 20(4) did include a power to issue writs of venire de novo, and, if so, in what circumstances such power could be exercised, came before this House in 1921 in *Crane v DPP* [1921] 2 AC 299, [1921] All ER Rep 19. This was a case in which Crane and another defendant, who had been charged on separate indictments, had been tried together at Leicester City Sessions at one and the same hearing by one and the same jury. After close consideration of the old authorities, which are far from clear and difficult to reconcile with one another, this House, by a majority of three to one, with Viscount Finlay dissenting, reached the conclusion that s 20(4) did vest in the Court of Criminal Appeal some jurisdiction to issue writs of venire de novo. The majority also held that the jurisdiction to do so was exercisable in the case before them. The reason why it was exercisable was because on the only indictment on which Crane could be lawfully tried there had not been any trial at all. This, in my view, fairly represents the ground of the decision of all three members of the majority of this House although each expressed it in slightly different language. As Lord Atkinson put it, what had occurred at Leicester City Sessions had been 'a mis-trial and a nullity' and he made it clear that by 'mis-trial' he meant a purported trial 'which is actually no trial at all' (see [1921] 2 AC 299 at 321, 330, [1921] All ER Rep 19 at 27, 31). Lord Sumner used similar language ([1921] 2 AC 299 at 331, [1921] All ER Rep 19 at 31): '. . . it is clear that the appellant purported to have been tried and convicted on an indictment which did not exist. It was a mis-trial, and in truth no trial at all.' Lord Parmoor expressed the view that the indictment so far as Crane was concerned was 'non-existent' and that 'the trial was void ab initio' (see [1921] 2 AC 299 at 336, 338, [1921] All ER Rep 19 at 33, 35). In Crane's case the reason why there had been no trial at all was because he had never been arraigned on the only indictment on which he could lawfully be tried. Another reason for a purported trial being no trial at all is when it is brought before a tribunal which lacks the qualification necessary in law to give it jurisdiction to try the offence with which the accused is charged. Of this an example is to be found in *R v Cronin* [1940] 2 All ER 242.

These are cases, and others are to be found cited in an article by Sir Robin Cooke (see (1955) 71 LQR 100 at 102ff), where no trial has been validly begun at all. This erudite article was written before the 1966 Act and the 1968 Act had been passed and the jurisdiction of the Court of Appeal, Criminal Division, had been defined in terms that differed from and were more specific as respects its powers in cases where there had been a material irregularity in the course of the trial than the terms in which jurisdiction was conferred on the Court of Criminal Appeal by the 1907 Act. The question whether venire de novo would lie in consequence of some irregularity in the course of the proceedings after a trial has been validly commenced first came before the Court of Appeal in *R v Neal* [1949] 2 All ER 438, [1949] 2 KB 590. In that case the irregularity occurred after the jury had retired to consider their verdict. They were permitted by the recorder to leave the court to lunch together in the town, and after their return brought in a verdict of guilty against the defendant. Lord Goddard CJ, giving the judgment of the Court of Criminal Appeal quashing the conviction and refusing to order a venire de novo, said ([1949] 2 All ER 438 at 441, [1949] 2 KB 590 at 597):

'In our opinion, if it transpires that there has been a mis-trial, then . . . the court can order the case to be re-tried, but in order that it may be said that it is a mis-trial the circumstances must be such as render the trial a nullity from the outset.'

Dealing with the case before the court in *R v Neal* [1949] 2 All ER 438 at 442, [1949] 2 KB 590 at 598–599, he said:

'This trial cannot in any sense be said to have been a nullity because of an
irregularity on the part of either judge or jury down to the time when all the
evidence had been heard and the summing-up had taken place. Down to that point
everything was regular and in order.'

I do not, with respect, find helpful his subsequent suggestion that one test of what would
amount to a mistrial sufficient to render the trial abortive and void would be whether the
irregularity would be patent on the record if it were drawn up. What in modern times
would be regarded as 'the record if it were drawn up' that Lord Goddard CJ had in mind
is far from clear.

R v Neal, as already mentioned, was followed by the Court of Criminal Appeal in R v
McKenna [1960] 1 All ER 326, [1960] 1 QB 411, in which, although the conviction was
quashed because of improper pressure by the judge on the jury, jurisdiction to order a
venire de novo was disclaimed on the ground that the trial had not been a nullity from
the outset.

Cases where venire de novo lies because of some irregularity in procedure which
prevents the trial from ever having been validly commenced are to be distinguished
from those cases of trials which, although validly commenced, have not been validly
concluded by a properly constituted jury bringing an unequivocal verdict of guilty or
not guilty followed by sentence or discharge of the defendant by the court. That the
Court of Criminal Appeal had jurisdiction to grant a venire de novo where a purported
conviction had been recorded despite there having been no valid verdict by the jury was
recognised by that court in R v Hancock (1931) 100 LJKB 419, where the accused who had
been put in charge of the jury changed his original pleas of not guilty to one of guilty
during the course of the hearing and the judge discharged the jury without obtaining a
verdict of guilty from them. Other examples would be where the verdict of the jury was
ambiguous or, as in the old case of R v Yeadon and Birch (1861) Le & Ca 81, 169 ER 1312,
the jury brought in two successive verdicts inconsistent with one another as a result of
the chairman of quarter sessions unlawfully refusing to accept the first. These, and other
examples cited in Sir Robin Cooke's article above-mentioned, in effect, are cases in which
the jury has been discharged without having arrived at a lawful verdict, and in
consequence of this there has been neither a conviction nor an acquittal of the defendant.

Such then was the state of judicial authority as to the extent of the jurisdiction of the
Court of Criminal Appeal to issue writs of venire de novo at the date of its abolition in
1966. That court could do so if there had been an irregularity of procedure which had
resulted in there having been no trial that had been validly commenced. It could do so
if the trial had come to an end without a properly constituted jury ever having returned
a valid verdict. It could not do so because of an irregularity in the course of the trial
occurring between the time that it had been validly commenced and the discharge of the
jury after returning a verdict.

Parliament, or, more realistically, the parliamentary draftsmen of the 1966 Act and
the 1968 Act, must be taken to have known the limits of the jurisdiction of the Court of
Criminal Appeal to issue writs of venire de novo as they had been laid down by judicial
authority at the time the 1966 Act was passed. It was a jurisdiction subject to these limits
that was expressly preserved by s 1(8) of the 1966 Act and transferred to the Court of
Appeal, Criminal Division, notwithstanding the repeal of the Crown Cases Act 1848; and
it is a jurisdiction subject to the same limits that is vested in the Court of Appeal,
Criminal Division, by s 1(2)(b)(ii) of the 1966 Act as amended by Sch 5 to the 1968 Act.

Strong confirmation of this is, in my view, to be found in Part I of the 1968 Act which
now regulates the exercise by the Court of Appeal, Criminal Division, of its principal
jurisdiction. Section 2(1) specifies the circumstances in which the court must allow an
appeal against conviction, unless it feels able to apply the proviso. These differ from and
are more specific than those stated in the corresponding provisions of s 4(1) of the 1907
Act. They are:

'(a) That the conviction should be set aside on the ground that under all the circumstances of the case it is unsafe or unsatisfactory; or (b) that the judgment of the court of trial should be set aside on the ground of a wrong decision of any question of law; or (c) that there was a material irregularity in the course of the trial.' **a**

Paragraph (c) refers to material irregularities 'in the course of the trial'. This presupposes that there has been a 'trial', ie one that has been validly commenced. If there has and there has been a material irregularity of procedure in the course of it, then, subject to the proviso, sub-s (2) leaves only one course open to the court, viz to quash the conviction; and sub-s (3) makes the consequence of such quashing operate as a judgment and verdict **b** of acquittal so as to enable the successful appellant if retried for the same offence to plead autrefois acquit, a plea that would not be open to him if he were retried on a venire de novo.

Section 2(1) is subject to such exceptions as are provided by the 1968 Act. The exception that is relevant for present purposes is to be found in s 7 which gives to the court jurisdiction, instead of quashing a conviction, to order a retrial; but this may be **c** done only when the conviction is allowed by reason of fresh evidence received by the court on the appeal. This strictly limited power to order a retrial is, in my view, inconsistent with the coexistence of any *general* power to order a new trial by issuing a writ of venire de novo, where there has been a material irregularity in the course of the trial.

In those cases where the Court of Criminal Appeal, immediately before its abolition, **d** would have had jurisdiction to issue a writ of venire de novo because there had been no valid verdict of guilty or not guilty by the jury, Part I of the 1968 Act would have no application, since there would have been no conviction within the meaning of that Act, which (with the exception of appeals against verdicts of not guilty by reason of insanity) deals only with appeals against conviction. The court's jurisdiction to deal with this class of case, where there has not been any conviction, is derived exclusively from **e** s 1(2)(b)(ii) of the 1966 Act as amended by the 1968 Act and enables the Court of Appeal, Criminal Division, to issue a writ of venire de novo.

My Lords, the certified question postulates a material irregularity occurring in the course of a trial that has been validly commenced between the time that it was so commenced and its conclusion with a judgment of conviction following an unequivocal verdict of guilty by the jury, as happened in the instant case. In my opinion, for the **f** reasons I have given, the answer to this question must be No. I would therefore dimiss this appeal.

LORD SCARMAN. My Lords, I have had the advantage of reading in draft the speech of my noble and learned friend Lord Diplock. I agree with him and would therefore dismiss this appeal. **g**

LORD ROSKILL. My Lords, I have had the advantage of reading in draft the speech by my noble and learned friend Lord Diplock. I agree with it, and for the reasons he gives I, too, would dismiss this appeal.

LORD BRIDGE OF HARWICH. My Lords, for the reasons given by my noble and **h** learned friend Lord Diplock, whose speech I have had the advantage of reading in advance, I would dismiss this appeal.

LORD BRANDON OF OAKBROOK. My Lords, I have had the advantage of reading in advance the speech prepared by my noble and learned friend Lord Diplock. I agree with it and for the reasons which he gives I too would dismiss the appeal. **j**

Appeal dismissed. Certified question answered in the negative.

Solicitors: *Director of Public Prosecutions; Bindman & Partners* (for the respondents).

Mary Rose Plummer   Barrister.

a Ellerine Bros (Pty) Ltd and another v Klinger

COURT OF APPEAL, CIVIL DIVISION
TEMPLEMAN, WATKINS AND FOX LJJ
22, 23 MARCH 1982

b *Arbitration – Stay of court proceedings – Matter agreed to be referred to arbitration – Defendant under obligation to account to plaintiffs for net receipts under distribution agreement – Defendant ignoring requests for account – Plaintiffs issuing writ claiming an account and payment of moneys found due on taking of such account – Whether 'any dispute between the parties with regard to the matter agreed to be referred' – Whether court should stay court proceedings – Arbitration Act 1975, s 1(1).*

c In October 1978 an agreement was made between, inter alios, the plaintiffs (two South African companies) and the defendant which provided that the defendant should be the principal distributor of a film, the making of which had been financed by the plaintiffs, and that the plaintiffs should each receive 20% of the net receipts of the film. The defendant undertook in the exercise of his appointment to distribute the film to account to the plaintiffs for the net receipts of the film and to keep proper books of account which d should be opened to the inspection of the plaintiffs. The agreement provided that all disputes or differences should be referred to an arbitrator. The defendant ignored repeated requests by the plaintiffs to account until May 1981, when the plaintiffs issued a specially indorsed writ against him alleging breach of the agreement and seeking an account of moneys due and payment of the amount found due on the taking of such account. On that date the defendant produced an account which showed that after deduction of distribution expenses and general overhead costs nothing was due to the e plaintiffs. Shortly after the rendering of that account the plaintiffs issued a summons for an account under RSC Ord 43, r 1 asking that an account be taken as claimed in the writ. The defendant applied under s 1(1)[a] of the Arbitration Act 1975 for an order that all proceedings be stayed pending arbitration. The plaintiffs opposed the application on the ground that their writ did not constitute legal proceedings 'in respect of any matter f agreed to be referred' within s 1(1) because all that they were doing was seeking an order to which they were entitled under the terms of the agreement and that accordingly, since 'there [was] not in fact any dispute between the parties with regard to the matter agreed to be referred' within s 1(1), the court had no power to stay the proceedings. The judge rejected the plaintiffs' submission and granted the stay sought. The plaintiffs appealed.

g **Held** – Section 1(1) of the 1975 Act was not limited either in content or in subject matter and accordingly if the plaintiff made some request or demand and the defendant did not reply a dispute arose between the parties. It followed therefore that, at the time when the writ was issued, there was a dispute between the parties because the defendant had never agreed that he was under an obligation to account or to vouch or to pay anything. Thus s 1(1) applied and the judge had been bound to refer the dispute to h arbitration. The appeal would therefore be dismissed (see p 741 e f, p 742 d to g, p 743 f to h and p 744 b to d, post).

Tradax Internacional SA v Cerrahogullari TAS, The M Eregli [1981] 3 All ER 344 applied.
London and North Western and Great Western Joint Rly Cos v J H Billington Ltd [1899] AC 79 distinguished.

Notes
For the nature of a dispute for the purpose of a reference to arbitration, see 2 Halsbury's Laws (4th edn) para 503.
For staying court proceedings by a party to arbitration, see ibid para 555.
For the Arbitration Act 1975, s 1, see 45 Halsbury's Statutes (3rd edn) 33.

---

a   Section 1(1), so far as material, is set out at p 740 h, post

Cases referred to in judgments

London and North Western and Great Western Joint Rly Cos v J H Billington Ltd [1899] AC 79, **a**
HL.
S L Sethia Liners Ltd v Naviagro Maritime Corp, The Kostas Melas [1981] 1 Lloyd's Rep 18.
Tradax Internacional SA v Cerrahogullari TAS, The M Eregli [1981] 3 All ER 344.

Cases also cited

Associated Bulk Carriers Ltd v Koch Shipping Inc, The Fuohsan Maru [1978] 2 All ER 254, CA. **b**
Cannan v Fowler (1853) 14 CB 181, 139 ER 75.
London and North Western Rly Co v Jones [1915] 2 KB 35, DC.

Interlocutory appeal

The plaintiffs, Ellerine Bros (Pty) Ltd and Soco Properties (Pty) Ltd, appealed against the
order made by his Honour Judge Newey QC dealing with official referees' business, dated **c**
27 August 1981, whereby, pursuant to s 1(1) of the Arbitration Act 1971, he ordered a
stay of an action brought by the plaintiffs against the defendant, Michael Klinger,
claiming an account of net receipts accruing from the distribution of a film called 'Gold'
and order for payment of sums due. The facts are set out in the judgment of Templeman
LJ.

Martin Harty for the plaintiffs. **d**
Trevor Philipson for the defendant.

TEMPLEMAN LJ. This is an appeal against an order of his Honour Judge Newey QC
dealing with official referees' business, dated 27 August 1981, whereby he stayed all
proceedings in the present action pursuant to s 1 of the Arbitration Act 1975. **e**
    By an agreement dated 13 October 1978 it was recited, inter alia, that the plaintiffs,
who were parties to the agreement, had provided finance for making a film entitled
'Gold'. The plaintiffs' registered addresses were given as Johannesburg and Germiston in
the Republic of South Africa. That is of some importance having regard to the provisions
of the Arbitration Act 1975.
    The agreement recited that the film had been distributed and had recovered its **f**
certified costs of production and was in profit. Certain disputes had arisen between all
parties to the agreement, a squabble over how much was due to each and one or two
other squabbles. In the event the defendant was appointed, and accepted appointment
as, principal distributor of the film. By the agreement each plaintiff became entitled to
20% of the net receipts of the film.
    The expression 'the net receipts' was defined as meaning— **g**

    'the gross monies in the hands of [the defendant] of the Film from all sources and
    hereafter arising from the exploitation of the Film after deduction of all fees
    deductible from such gross monies in accordance with any contractual obligation
    (provided that no such deduction of fees shall be made to . . . [the defendant] or any
    company with which [the defendant] is associated) and after deduction also of all
    expenses of distribution and exploitation of the Film actually incurred by [the **h**
    defendant] or by any sub-distributor of the Film.'

    The defendant undertook in the exercise of his appointment to distribute the film 'and
to account to the parties entitled thereto for the Net Receipts of the Film' in accordance
with certain instructions which had been given and which are not material.
    There was also a provision that the defendant— **j**

    'shall keep all usual and proper books of Account showing the Net Receipts
    accruing from the distribution and exploitation of the Film throughout the world
    . . . which books of account and all contracts relating to the distribution of the Film
    shall be opened to the inspection of those authorised by [the plaintiffs] jointly and
    severally at reasonable times and they may take extracts therefrom or copies thereof.'

There was a provision that—

a   'Within thirty days of receiving reports or statements of account rendered by distributors under distribution or sub-distribution agreements [the defendant] shall render a copy of each such report to each of [the plaintiffs] or as they may direct and shall at the time of delivering each such report deal with all monies received by [the defendant] and accounted for such report in the manner provided herein.'

b   The agreement was dated 13 October 1978 but, so far as the present evidence goes, nothing was done by the defendant in fulfilment of his obligations to account until May 1981.

Clause 12 of the agreement said it was to be read and construed in all respects in accordance with the laws of England.   Clause 13 was an arbitration clause in this form:

c   'All disputes or differences whatsoever which shall at any time hereafter arise between the parties hereto or any of them touching or concerning this Deed or its construction or effect or as to the rights duties or liabilities of the parties hereto or any of them under or by virtue of this Deed shall be referred to a single Arbitrator to be agreed upon by the parties hereto or in default of Agreement to be nominated by the President for the time being of the Institute of Chartered Accountants in accordance with and subject to the provisions of the Arbitration Act 1950 or any

d   statutory modification or re-enactment thereof.'

So far as the evidence goes, all was silent for nearly a year and then the plaintiffs woke up and they wrote to the defendant on 4 September 1980 saying: 'We have not received any statement of accounts or payments in respect of "Gold". Could we have a report from you please.'   The silence continued and they wrote a reminder on 11 December

e   1980.   There was then an oral request by one of the representatives of the plaintiffs who happened to see the defendant.   Another reminder was sent on 8 January 1981 drawing attention to the clause of the agreement which cast on him the duties of keeping accounts and making reports and asking for an urgent reply.   The plaintiffs received back on 19 January 1981 a perfectly polite but useless letter from the defendant's secretary saying that unfortunately the defendant was in the United States and would not be returning to

f   London until the end of the month and that the plaintiffs might rest assured that their letters would be brought to his attention as soon as possible.   Nothing of course happened.   A reminder was sent on 11 February 1981 and a further apology was received from the secretary on 2 March 1981.

Finally, the plaintiffs lost patience and on 24 March 1981 they wrote to the defendant's solicitors giving an ultimatum saying:

g   '. . . unless we receive a full and proper account together with payment of all sums due, within the course of the next seven days, proceedings will be instituted without further notice or delay.'

The reply to that, of course, was that the defendant's solicitors would take instructions. On 3 April the plaintiffs issued a writ, served by post on 7 April.   That writ, after reciting

h   the agreement, alleged that the defendant had duly distributed and exploited the film, though the plaintiffs could not give particulars until after discovery.   The plaintiffs complained that—

'In breach of the said agreement and of the terms thereof although requested to do so by letter dated 24th March 1981 the Defendant has wrongfully failed and is failing: (i) To render any or any true or full or accurate accounts showing the net receipts accruing from the distribution and the exploitation of the film. (ii) To pay to the Plaintiffs and each of them a sum equal to 20% of the net receipts or any sums. AND THE PLAINTIFFS AND EACH OF THEM CLAIM: 1. An account of the net receipts accruing on the distribution and the exploitation of the film. 2. An order for the payment by the Defendant to the Plaintiffs and to each of them of all monies found due to them on the taking of such accounts . . .'

This produced some results, though unsatisfactory, because on 6 May the defendant
sent to the plaintiffs' solicitors what he called Report no 22 for the period 1 April 1979   *a*
to 31 January 1981. The account showed that he had received £12,921·14 and that, after
deduction of distribution expenses and costs, he was £8,440·22 out of pocket and
nothing was due to the plaintiffs. But the details given of the expenses which absorbed
£12,921 of income, and more, included not only £6,895·22 of expenses paid to other
persons, which appear to have been estimated, but also a charge for general overhead
costs at the rate of £7,500 per annum. The plaintiffs are far from accepting the figures   *b*
shown in the account. They wish the expenses which have been incurred to be vouched
and they wish to dispute the entitlement of the defendant, on the true construction of
the agreement, to claim general overhead costs and possibly some of the other items
which he claims to deduct.

The day after the rendering of that account, that is to say on 7 May 1971, the plaintiffs
took out a summons for an account under RSC Ord 43, r 1. That asked 'that an account   *c*
may be taken as claimed in the writ of summons and that payment be made by the
defendant to the plaintiffs on the amount found to be due on the taking of such account',
and they asked for costs. They were sent some additional documentation, some of the
vouchers, but not enough to satisfy them or make them accept that the defendant had
discharged all his obligations under the agreement.

The defendant, in a letter of 1 June 1981, said: 'As you have questioned the precis of   *d*
expenses incurred, we will prepare supporting evidence in respect of the expenses in
question which are quite clearly allowed under the terms of our contract.' Nothing has
been received to date.

In support of their application for an account, the plaintiffs put in an affidavit which
was sworn by their solicitor on 17 June, complaining that the account which had been
produced purported to make deductions which were not authorised under the agreement   *e*
and were not supported by vouchers. On 18 June the summons for an account was
transferred to an official referee.

On 2 July the defendant took out a summons asking for the proceedings to be stayed
pending arbitration. He relied on s 4 of the Arbitration Act 1975. When the matter
came before his Honour Judge Newey on 27 August the defendant obtained leave to
amend and to ask for relief under s 1 of the 1975 Act.   *f*

At that hearing the judge had before him the summons by the plaintiffs for an
account, the application by the defendant to stay the proceedings on the ground that the
matter ought to go to arbitration and also an application by the plaintiffs for summary
judgment under RSC Ord 14 for an amount which would be due to them if the overhead
expenses claimed by the defendant were wholly disallowed. In the event, the battle took
place round the defendant's application to stay and that application, as amended, was   *g*
made under s 1(1) of the 1975 Act, which, if it applies, gives the court no choice in the
matter.

Section 1(1) says:

'If any party to an arbitration agreement to which this section applies . . .
commences any legal proceedings in any court against any other party . . . in respect
of any matter agreed to be referred, any party to the proceedings may at any time   *h*
after appearance, and before delivering any pleadings or taking any other steps in
the proceedings, apply to the court to stay the proceedings; and the court, unless
satisfied that the arbitration agreement is null and void . . . or that there is not in fact
any dispute between the parties with regard to the matter agreed to be referred,
shall make an order staying the proceedings.'

Subsection (2) says that sub-s (1), which ties the hand of the court, is not to apply to a   *j*
domestic arbitration agreement. Subsection (4)(b) makes it clear that 'domestic
arbitration agreement' does not include an agreement if one of the parties to the
agreement is 'a body corporate which is incorporated in, or whose central management
and control is exercised in, any State other than the United Kingdom'. The plaintiffs

being incorporated in, or carrying on business with central management and control in
South Africa, the agreement which I have recited was not a domestic arbitration
agreement and, therefore, if the conditions provided by s 1(1) are satisfied, the court
must stay the proceedings. The judge so held and stayed the action accordingly.

Section 1(1) of the 1975 Act only applies, as indeed it expressly says it only applies, if
an action is brought claiming in respect of any matter agreed to be referred to
arbitration. What is said is that all the plaintiffs were doing was seeking an order to
which they were entitled under the terms of the agreement (they were entitled to an
account, there can be no dispute about that) and therefore the writ which they issued did
not constitute legal proceedings 'in respect of any matter agreed to be referred' at the date
when the writ was issued and the last phrase of the subsection, which enables the court
to continue the action if 'there is not in fact any dispute between the parties with regard
to the matter agreed to be referred', does not avail the defendant, because it must again
be supported by 'a matter agreed to be referred' and which was the proper subject of
arbitration at the date of the writ. If a dispute arose between the date of the writ and the
date of the hearing by the court, nevertheless there was no relevant dispute, because the
relevant time is the date when the writ was issued.

That submission, by the light of nature and without reference to authority, would
produce an awkward result. It would mean that if, in the present case, for example, there
was no dispute and all the plaintiffs were asking for was for the defendant to do what he
is admittedly bound to do, namely to furnish an account, then, notwithstanding that
there were hidden behind the application for an account all kinds of embryonic questions
which were bound to arise and which were the proper subject of arbitration, the
arbitration clause would fail to have effect and the court would be entitled to continue to
hear the action, notwithstanding that the real grievances between the parties fell fairly
and squarely within the mischief of the arbitration clause. This would put a premium
on plaintiffs issuing proceedings without waiting to hear from a defendant or without
drawing reference to matters which were almost bound to be in dispute. Again by the
light of nature, it seems to me that s 1(1) is not limited either in content or in subject
matter; that if letters are written by the plaintiff making some request or some demand
and the defendant does not reply, then there is a dispute. It is not necessary, for a dispute
to arise, that the defendant should write back and say, 'I don't agree.' If, on analysis, what
the plaintiff is asking or demanding involves a matter on which agreement has not been
reached and which falls fairly and squarely within the terms of the arbitration agreement,
then the applicant is entitled to insist on arbitration instead of litigation.

Counsel for the plaintiffs rested his submissions on two matters. First, on what I
would refer to as the literal wording of the section, which refers to an action 'in respect
of any matter agreed to be referred'. He also relied on the House of Lords case of *London
and North Western and Great Western Joint Rly Cos v J H Billington Ltd* [1899] AC 79. In that
case there was statutory provision for arbitration as to sums which a railway company
was entitled to charge for services rendered to traders. The railway company was
empowered to make a reasonable charge and it was provided that 'any difference arising
under this section shall be determined by an arbitrator to be appointed by the Board of
Trade at the instance of either party'.

The facts of that case were that the railway company had fixed what they said was a
reasonable sum and the sum was 6d a day siding rent 'for every wagon not released and
remaining on the company's premises after four days allowed to the respondents for
unloading'. The defendants were held by the trial judge to know that was what the
railway company was charging and, with that knowledge, apparently, they did allow
their wagons to remain on the company's premises for more than the initial four days
allowed to them; they were then sent a bill for the amount of the charge and it was then
that they demanded that the question of the reasonableness of the charge should be
referred to arbitration. As I read the speeches in the House of Lords, they are simply
saying that the judge found that there was a contract between the railway company and
the trader, accepted by this trader, that he would pay the charge, namely 6d a day levied

by the railway company if he took advantage of the company's facilities and services; and, that being the contract between the parties, there was no room for arbitration: what he had agreed to pay he had to pay. If he did not like the charges he should either not have made use of the services or at any rate he should have gone to arbitration beforehand or made his acceptance of the contract conditional, if the railway company would allow him to do so, on the amount of the charge being settled by arbitration.

Counsel for the plaintiffs relies in particular on a passage from the Earl of Halsbury LC, where he said (at 81):

'The question which has been argued apparently before the Court of Appeal is a question no doubt of very great and serious importance both to the traders and to the railway companies; but, my Lords, so far as I am concerned, I propose to give no opinion upon the true construction of the statute, except this: that a condition precedent to the invocation of the arbitrator on whatever grounds is that a difference between the parties should have arisen; and I think that must mean a difference of opinion before the action is launched either by formal plaint in the county court or by writ in the superior Courts. Any contention that the parties could, when they are sued for the price of the services, raise then for the first time the question whether or not the charges were reasonable and that therefore they have a right to go to an arbitrator, seems to me to be absolutely untenable.'

That speech was made against the background of the finding by the trial judge that there was no difference existing between the parties at the time the action was brought, because of the contract which had been made between them in the terms I have mentioned. That case seems to me to be a far cry from the present when the parties had in fact agreed nothing. It is quite clear that the rights claimed are an account and payment of the sum found due on the account and to have the account vouched. It is also quite clear that the defendant never accepted, never agreed that he was under an obligation to send an account or to vouch or to pay anything: he simply did nothing. In those circumstances, it seems to me that, even when the writ was issued, there was a dispute between the parties and that is illustrated by the relief sought in the writ, which claims not only an account but payment of the amount found due on the taking of the account. It appears from those words that there had been no agreement, that there was a dispute at the time when the writ was issued, namely the three issues whether there was a duty to account, whether that account should be proved by vouching and finally whether there was any money due to the plaintiffs or not. Although the defendant did not write back and say so, he was disputing the plaintiffs' claims by refusing to comply with the requests which were made on him by the plaintiffs. I do not excuse the conduct of the defendant. So far as the present evidence goes, it seems clear that he was prevaricating and playing for time. It may well be, and probably is, that his new-found enthusiasm for arbitration is another method of avoiding the evil day when he will have either to pay or to reveal the fact that he cannot pay. But these considerations cannot affect the question of cold law, namely whether there was a dispute at the date when the writ was issued which entitles the defendant to arbitration as against litigation.

Although in a different context, the conclusion which Kerr J reached in *Tradax Internacional SA v Cerrahogullari TAS, The M Eregli* [1981] 3 All ER 344 is in point. In that case there was a voyage charterparty which provided that all disputes from time to time arising out of the contract were to be referred to arbitration, but there was a time limit in that it was provided that—

'Any claim must be made in writing and Claimant's Arbitrator appointed within nine months of final discharge and where this provision is not complied with the claim shall be deemed to be waived and absolutely barred . . .'

Under the terms of the charterparty the plaintiffs became entitled to dispatch money and they sent invoices for the money which was due to them to the defendants. The defendants admitted that the invoices were correct and did not dispute the claim for dispatch money, but they did not expressly admit liability for the claim and simply

ignored it and all communications relating to it. The plaintiffs allowed the nine months
to run out. They then purported to appoint an arbitrator. The defendants contested the
appointment on the grounds that the time had run out. The plaintiffs in turn said that
time had not run out, because there was no dispute. There was no dispute because the
defendants had simply ignored the demand which had been made but had never got
round to saying, either then or subsequently, that the plaintiffs were or were not entitled
to the sums claimed in the invoices.

Kerr J said (at 349) that the plaintiffs' claim was for a liquidated sum in relation to
which there had never been any arguable defence but which was not expressly
admitted. He continued (at 350):

> 'Where an arbitration clause contains a time limit barring all claims unless an
> arbitrator is appointed within the limited time, it seems to me that the time limit
> can only be ignored on the ground that there is no dispute between the parties if the
> claim has been admitted to be due and payable. Such an admission would, in effect,
> amount to an agreement to pay the claim, and there would then clearly be no
> further basis for referring it to arbitration or treating it as time-barred if no arbitrator
> is appointed. But if, as here, a claim is made and is neither admitted nor disputed,
> but simply ignored, then I think that the time limit clearly applies and that the
> claimant is obliged (subject to any possible extension of time) to appoint an
> arbitrator within the limited time. The fallacy in the plaintiffs' argument can be
> seen at once if one considers what would have been the position if the plaintiffs had
> in fact purported to appoint ... their arbitrator within the time limit of nine
> months. They could clearly have done so, and indeed any commercial lawyer or
> business man would say that this is what they should have done under the clause to
> enforce their claim. Arbitrators are appointed every day by claimants who believe,
> rightly or wrongly, that their claim is indisputable. However, on the plaintiffs' own
> argument, [the arbitrator] would have had no jurisdiction, since there was then, as
> they now say, no "dispute" to which the arbitration clause could have applied. In
> my view this argument is obviously unsustainable.'

As I understand it, the judge is saying (and I agree) that silence does not mean
consent. If you can point, as was the case in *London and North Western and Great Western
Joint Rly Cos v J H Billington Ltd* [1899] AC 79, to an express or implied agreement to pay
a particular sum, then there is no dispute and the action can proceed. But the fact that
the plaintiffs make certain claims which, if disputed, would be referable to arbitration
and the fact that the defendant then does nothing (he does not admit the claim, he
merely continues a policy of masterly inactivity) does not mean that there is no
dispute. There is a dispute until the defendant admits that a sum is due and payable, as
Kerr J said in the *Tradax* case. There was in the instant case a dispute when the writ was
issued and there remained a dispute and there still is a dispute and the judge had no
choice but to refer the dispute to arbitration.

In my judgment, the judge came to the right conclusion for the right reasons and I
would dismiss the appeal.

WATKINS LJ. For some while I was persuaded by counsel for the plaintiffs in the
course of his very able argument into thinking that this appeal ought to be allowed for
the reason that the plaintiffs had properly claimed what was indisputably (so it could be
said to be) a claim for an account under the arbitration agreement. That, an arbitration
agreement notwithstanding, there can be such a remedy available either in the courts or
in arbitration proceedings is, on the authority of Kerr J in *Tradax Internacional SA v
Cerrahogullari TAS, The M Eregli* [1981] 3 All ER 344, without doubt.

In the *Tradax* case he stated (at 351):

> 'Claims which are covered by an arbitration clause, but which are said to be
> indisputable, are nowadays frequently put forward in an aribtration, but then also
> pursued concurrently by an attempt to obtain summary judgment in the courts. In

effect, a claimant can, and in my view should be able to, obtain an order for payment
in such cases by either means, and the coexistence of both avenues towards a speedy *a*
payment of an amount which is indisputably due was recently referred to in this
court by Robert Goff J in *The Kostas Melas* [1981] 1 Lloyd's Rep 18 at 27. It was there
held that, as an alternative to an application for summary judgment under Ord 14
in an action, there was jurisdiction to make an interim award for an indisputable
part of the claim in an arbitration; which also shows, incidentally, the misconception
of the plaintiffs' first submission in the present case with which I have already dealt.' *b*

If the various claims contained in the plaintiffs' statement of claim could properly be
said to be severable, then I should have been tempted to hold that the claim for an
account was allowable in the proceedings which were commenced by writ on 3 April
1981. But, for the reasons explained by Templeman LJ, I have not the slightest doubt
now that these claims, which include a claim not only for a true or full or accurate
account but also for a distribution of moneys found due as a result of that account to the *c*
plaintiffs, cannot be severed. This must mean that there was at all material times a
running dispute between the parties which had under the agreement to be referred to
arbitration.

Accordingly, I too agree that this appeal must be dismissed.

FOX LJ. I agree with the judgment that Templeman LJ has delivered and I too would *d*
dismiss the appeal.

*Appeal dismissed, the court making it clear that the stay imposed in the order below not to bar an
order for the sum claimed under Ord 14 if the judge or master so decides.*

Solicitors: *Wright & Webb, Syrett & Sons* (for the plaintiffs); *Bartletts, de Reya* (for the
defendant).

Mary Rose Plummer   Barrister.

a
Crewe and others v Social Security Commissioner

COURT OF APPEAL, CIVIL DIVISION

LORD DENNING MR, DONALDSON AND SLADE LJJ

22 APRIL, 5 MAY 1982

b

National insurance – Unemployment benefit – Disqualification for benefit – Voluntarily leaving employment without just cause – Just cause – Teacher voluntarily leaving employment pursuant to scheme for premature retirement of older teachers – Scheme containing financial inducements for voluntary early retirement – Whether teacher voluntarily retiring early under scheme having 'just cause' for leaving employment – Whether teacher entitled to receive benefit for first six weeks c *after retirement – Social Security Act 1975, s 20(1)(a).*

A local education authority wished to decrease the number of its teachers because the number of school children was decreasing, and also wished to employ younger teachers for social, educational and financial reasons. The authority therefore, with the support of the Department of Education and Science, introduced a scheme for early retirement d of teachers over 50. The scheme offered teachers to which it applied considerable financial inducement to retire early, including a pension almost equivalent to that payable on retirement after full-time service. The claimant, a teacher aged 61, voluntarily retired early under the scheme. He did not, nor did he intend to, seek alternative employment but instead claimed unemployment benefit. The insurance officer and, on appeal, the local appeal tribunal decided that he had voluntarily left his employment e 'without just cause', within s 20(1)(a)ᵈ of the Social Security Act 1975 and was therefore disqualified for receiving unemployment benefit for the first six weeks of his retirement under s 20(1)(a), although he would be entitled to receive benefit thereafter. The claimant appealed to a social security commissioner, who upheld the tribunal's decision. On appeal to the Court of Appeal on the construction of s 20(1)(a), the claimant submitted that, since his voluntary retirement under the education authority's scheme f was in the interests of his employer and was also in the interests of the community as a whole, he had 'just cause' within s 20(1)(a) to voluntarily leave his employment and was therefore entitled to receive unemployment benefit for the first six weeks of his retirement.

Held – Since the purpose of the national insurance scheme was to insure against g unemployment incurred involuntarily and since it was implicit in the scheme that each insured person owed a duty to the general body of persons underwriting the scheme not to incur unemployment voluntarily, a person seeking to show that he had voluntarily left his employment with 'just cause' within s 20(1)(a) of the 1975 Act had to show that he had left voluntarily in circumstances which made it right and reasonable for the burden of paying him unemployment benefit to be borne by the national insurance h fund. Thus it was not sufficient for an employee to prove that his voluntary leaving was reasonable as between himself and his employer or that it was in the interests of the community, since that did not necessarily indicate that as between the employee and the general body of persons underwriting the insurance fund he had left with 'just cause' within s 20(1)(a). Since the claimant had received a substantial financial benefit by leaving his employment and did not intend to seek other employment, it would not be i right and reasonable for the insurance fund to bear the cost of unemployment benefit for the first six weeks of his retirement. The claimant's appeal would therefore be dismissed (see p 749 a to d, p 750 e to p 751 h and p 752 c to g, post).

---

d   Section 20(1), so far as material, is set out at p 749 e, post

Case referred to in judgments
R v National Insurance Comr, ex p Stratton [1979] 2 All ER 278, [1979] QB 361, [1979] 2 **a**
WLR 389, CA, Digest (Cont Vol E) 445, 12(1).

Notes
For disqualification for unemployment benefit, see 27 Halsbury's Laws (3rd edn) 731,
para 1326.
For the Social Security Act 1975, s 20, see 45 Halsbury's Statutes (3rd edn) 1100.   **b**

Appeal
The first appellant, Ernest Graham Crewe, voluntarily left his employment as a teacher
pursuant to a scheme introduced by the local education authority for premature
retirement for teachers over 50. His retirement took effect from 1 September 1979 and   **c**
thereupon he applied for unemployment benefit, his case being taken up by the second
appellants, the Assistant Masters and Mistresses Association. The insurance officer and
the local appeal tribunal decided that Mr Crewe was disqualified for receiving
unemployment benefit for the first six weeks of his unemployment, from 18 September
to 27 October 1979, on the ground, in s 20(1)(*a*) of the Social Security Act 1975, that he
had voluntarily left his employment 'without just cause'. The appellants appealed to a   **d**
social security commissioner, Mr E Roderic Bowen QC, who dismissed the appeal for the
reasons, set out in para 10 of his decision dated 15 January 1981, that Mr Crewe did not
have 'just cause' for voluntarily leaving his employment, because the aim of s 20(1)(*a*) was
to protect the national insurance fund and therefore in deciding whether a claimant had
just cause to leave his employment the question was not whether it had been reasonable
for him to leave his employment but whether it was reasonable that he should be   **e**
allowed to derive benefit from the national insurance fund, and therefore the fact that
Mr Crewe believed he was acting reasonably and in the public interest in leaving his
employment pursuant to the education authority's retirement scheme did not provide
him with 'just cause' for leaving when, because of his age, he had no reasonable prospects
of obtaining alternative employment. The social security commissioner gave leave to
appeal from his decision and the appellants appealed seeking reversal of the decision that   **f**
Mr Crewe was disqualified for receiving unemployment benefit from 18 September to
27 October 1979 and for an order that he was entitled to receive unemployment benefit
in respect of that period. The ground of the appeal was that the commissioner erred in
his construction of s 20(1)(*a*) that in retiring pursuant to the premature retirement
scheme Mr Crewe did not have 'just cause' for leaving his employment. The facts are set
out in the judgment of Lord Denning MR.   **g**

Rupert Jackson for the appellants.
Simon D Brown for the commissioner.

Cur adv vult
     h

5 May. The following judgments were read.

LORD DENNING MR. Ernest Crewe was a schoolteacher. He was aged 61. He had
taught in schools for 39 years. But then the education authority wanted the older
teachers to retire voluntarily. This was because the number of children was decreasing   **j**
and they did not want so many teachers. It was also because the education authority
wanted to get young teachers into work instead of being on the dole. Also they did not
want too many old teachers for young children. There was a financial advantage too.
Young teachers would be paid less than the older ones. So the education authority, with
the active support of the Department of Education and Science, introduced a scheme for

early retirement for teachers over 50. They offered considerable inducements. Whereas
previously a schoolteacher was not at liberty to retire early, now he was to be at liberty
to retire early: and to get nearly as high a pension as if he had served his full time. He
got so many 'added years' added notionally to his credit although he had not served
them. There were other inducements too. These proved sufficiently attractive to induce
Ernest Crewe to apply for early retirement. He did so. His retirement took effect from
1 September 1979. Thereupon he applied for unemployment benefit. His case was
taken up by his association, the Assistant Masters and Mistresses Association. The
insurance officer said that he was disqualified from obtaining it for the first six weeks,
but thereafter he would receive it. He did not agree with this six weeks' ban. He
appealed to the local tribunal. They refused by a majority to allow him the six weeks'
benefit. He applied to a social security commissioner (Mr E Roderic Bowen QC). He
refused it too, but gave leave to appeal to this court. It is the first appeal under the Social
Security Act 1980. It comes only as a point of law.

The law

The difference arises on a provision about unemployment benefit which goes back for
70 years. In 1911 there was introduced into England a scheme for unemployment
benefit for those out of work. In the very first Act, the National Insurance Act 1911,
there was a clause which disqualified a man for unemployment benefit. It was s 87(2).
The clause was repeated in the same words in s 8(2) of the Unemployment Insurance Act
1920 and in the National Insurance Act 1946. It has been repeated in every Act since that
time. It is now contained in s 20(1)(a) of the Social Security Act 1975. It says that a man
is disqualified for a period not exceeding six weeks if 'he has lost his employment as an
employed earner through his own misconduct or has voluntarily left such employment
without just cause'.

Mr Crewe is, of course, not guilty of any misconduct; but he did voluntarily leave his
employment. The question is whether he left it 'without just cause'. At first sight it
would look as if Ernest Crewe had 'just cause' for leaving his employment. His employers
wanted him to go, not for his own sake, but for their own sake. That is shown by the
regulations about premature retirement. They apply only when his employer is satisfied
that his services have been terminated 'in the interests of the efficient discharge of his
employer's function'. The education authority here were so satisfied because the
educational system would be more efficient if he retired and was replaced by a younger
man.

But this simple approach is contrary to a long line of decisions by the commissioners.
These I will summarise.

(1) In 1930 (Case 11760/30) an employee of a local authority left his employment to
obtain a pension which would bring him in an income of about £2 a week. The
commissioner said:

'... This does not afford "just cause" for leaving any more than it would have
done had the claimant left his employment because somebody had left him a legacy
which brought him in a similar or larger income.'

(2) In 1951 (Case R(U) 26/51) an employee voluntarily left his employment at 60
when he could have stayed on to 65. He got the pension applicable to his period of
service. It was held that he had left 'without just cause'. The commissioner said:

'The question is not whether it was reasonable and proper for the claimant to
retire on pension but whether, when he elects to do so and thereby "abandons
employment", it is reasonable that he should be allowed to derive benefit from the
Unemployment Fund.'

(3) In 1952 (Case R(U) 14/52) an employee aged 61 was employed at a place 70 miles
from his home. He gave it up so as to be with his wife and to try to get work nearer
home. It was held that he had 'just cause' for leaving. The commissioner said:

'... I do not think that he should incur disqualification for unemployment benefit because in the circumstances he made up his mind to bring his employment *a* to an end and go home.'

(4) In 1959 (Case R(U) 23/59) a police officer retired at 52 when he could have continued until 55. As he had done 30 years' service, he got the maximum pension. There was some suggestion that the Home Secretary thought that police officers should retire when they had qualified for maximum pension. The commissioner held that he left 'without just cause'. He felt that the case was indistinguishable from the 1951 case *b* (No 2 above). He explained that the previous decisions should be followed. He said:

'Other insured persons similarly situated have failed to establish just cause for leaving when they did and have been disqualified for receiving unemployment benefit . . .'

(5) In 1964 (Decision R(U) 20/64) a police officer retired at 47 after doing 25 years' *c* service and earned a pension. He could have stayed on for several more years. He had bought a house two miles away, but was then transferred to a station 11 miles away from his house. He retired in the hope of getting work near his home. The case was decided by a tribunal of commissioners presided over by the Chief Commissioner, Sir Robert Micklethwait QC. He gave a closely reasoned decision, holding that the police sergeant was disqualified from receiving unemployment benefit. He said: *d*

'It is not sufficient for him to prove that he acted reasonably, in the sense of acting reasonably in his own interests. The interests of the National Insurance Fund and other contributors have to be taken into account as well . . . if he wishes to claim unemployment benefit, he must not leave his employment without due regard to the interests of the rest of the community . . .' *e*

(6) In 1970 (Decision R(U) 4/70) a police inspector retired at 51 after he had completed 30 years' service. Although he could have stayed on longer, the terms of his service would become less favourable. The commissioner (Mr Lazarus QC) held that he left 'without just cause':

'The primary purpose of the unemployment insurance scheme is to insure against *f* unemployment involuntarily incurred, and it is implicit in it that each insured person owes a duty to all the other contributors to the unemployment insurance fund not to incur unemployment by his own conduct . . . I find it hard to conceive of a case in which the pursuit of a personal financial advantage could by itself be held to constitute a "just cause".'

I have cited those decisions because they are of much persuasive force. As I said in *R v* *g* *National Insurance Comr, ex p Stratton* [1979] 2 All ER 278 at 282, [1979] 1 QB 361 at 369:

'. . . if a decision of the commissioners has remained undisturbed for a long time, not amended by regulation, nor challenged by certiorari, and has been acted on by all concerned, it should normally be regarded as binding. The High Court should not interfere with it save in exceptional circumstances . . .' *h*

I think those decisions are best understood by remembering that most of them were given at a time when a man had no proprietary right in his job. There was no provision for redundancy payment and no compensation for unfair dismissal. Even though a man was an excellent workman, he could be dismissed at a week's notice and put on the street with no payment from anyone. Such a man ought to be entitled to unemployment *j* benefit straight away as soon as he lost his job, which was his source of income. But, if he voluntarily retired from his work, with no other job to go to, his loss of income was his own choice. He had no 'just cause' for retiring. He would not be entitled to unemployment benefit. But, suppose his retirement was due to illness or old age, or having to look after a sick wife. He would have lost his income for a 'just cause'. He

should be entitled to unemployment benefit. But, if he voluntarily retired because he
a had been left a legacy or was entitled to a retirement pension, then there was no 'just
cause' for giving him unemployment benefit straight away. He should be disqualified
for six weeks anyway.

That line of approach explains, I think, all the previous decisions. They warrant the
following propositions. (1) When a man voluntarily leaves his employment, he is
disqualified from receiving unemployment benefit for six weeks, unless he proves (and
b the burden is on him to prove) that he had 'just cause' for leaving his employment. (2) It
is not sufficient for him to prove that he was quite reasonable in leaving his
employment. Reasonableness may be 'good cause', but it is not necessarily 'just cause'.
(3) 'Without just cause' means without any just cause for throwing on to the
unemployment fund the payment of unemployment benefit. If he voluntarily retires
on pension, he is getting a substantial financial benefit for himself, and it is not fair or
c just to the unemployment fund that he should also get unemployment benefit for the six
weeks.

To which I would add this. Even though the employer wants him to retire, and offers
him inducements to do so, for the employer's benefit, nevertheless he is still getting a
substantial financial benefit for himself and is disqualified from obtaining unemployment
benefit.

d   I would, therefore, dismiss this appeal.

DONALDSON LJ. This is the first occasion on which the courts have been asked to
consider the true construction and effect of a statutory provision which appears to have
existed since the enactment of s 87 of the National Insurance Act 1911. It is now
contained in s 20(1) of the Social Security Act 1975, and is in the following terms:
e
'A person shall be disqualified for receiving unemployment benefit for such
period not exceeding 6 weeks as may be determined [by an insurance officer, a local
appeal tribunal or a social security commissioner] if—(a) he has lost his employment
as an employed earner through his misconduct, or has voluntarily left such
employment without just cause . . .'

f   Mr Crewe, in the circumstances stated in the judgment of Lord Denning MR,
voluntarily left his employment as a teacher pursuant to a scheme for premature
retirement. This scheme was designed to ensure that the teaching staff of the local
education authority was appropriate in terms of age, qualifications and numbers to the
needs of its school age population. All concerned have held that in so doing Mr Crewe
left his employment 'without just cause'. This decision is now appealed.

g   The meaning of 'without just cause' has been debated by those concerned with the
administration of the employment insurance schemes since at least 1930, but the most
authoritative exposition, and that which is now accepted by insurance officers, local
appeal tribunals and the social security commissioners, is contained in the decision of a
tribunal of three commissioners under the chairmanship of Sir Robert Micklethwait QC
in 1964 in decision R(U) 20/64. The provision then in force, which was expressed in
h identical language, was s 13(2)(a) of the National Insurance Act 1946.

The essence of the decision is contained in para 8, which is expressed in the following
terms:

'The basic purpose of unemployment benefit is to provide against the misfortune
of unemployment happening against a person's will. Section 13(2) however clearly
i recognises that it may be payable in certain cases where the claimant leaves
voluntarily, if he does not do so without just cause. It is not sufficient for him to
prove that he acted reasonably, in the sense of acting reasonably in his own
interests. The interests of the National Insurance Fund and other contributors have
to be taken into account as well. "The notion of 'just cause' involves a compromise
between the rights of the individual and the interests of the rest of the community.

So long as he does not break his contract with his employer, the individual is free to
leave his employment when he likes. But if he wishes to claim unemployment *a*
benefit he must not leave his employment without due regard to the interests of the
rest of the community ..." (Decision C.U. 164/50 (not reported)). This has been
expressed in different ways in many decisions: see Decisions R(U) 14/55, paragraph
5 and R(U) 23/59, paragraph 12. The difficulty however lies in making a comparison
between such very different elements.'

This concept is re-expressed in more succinct form in para 13 where the commissioners *b*
said:

'... the claimant ought to take such steps as are reasonably open to him to avoid
voluntarily becoming unemployed and dependent on the National Insurance Fund.'

Counsel for the appellants submits to this court, as he submitted below, that the *c*
fundamental justification for a premature retirement scheme of this type is that is it
necessary in the interests of the community as a whole and that accordingly there can be
no argument but that, in accepting premature retirement, Mr Crewe had just cause. Mr
E Roderic Bowen QC, the social security commissioner, rejected this argument on the
basis that it was not for him to consider whether or not the premature retirement scheme
was in the public interest, and that the essential facts were quite simply that Mr Crewe *d*
wanted to retire, that he was entitled to retire, that he had no intention of seeking
alternative employment following his retirement and that he took no steps to do so. In
such circumstances, in the context of an unemployment insurance scheme, he had no
just cause for leaving his secure employment.

In my judgment it is crucial to reaching a decision on this appeal to remember that
this is an insurance scheme, however it may be funded, and that it is an insurance against *e*
unemployment. It is of the essence of insurance that the assured shall not deliberately
create or increase the risk. Prima facie an employee has not done so if he loses his
employment involuntarily, that is to say by the action of the employer in terminating
the contract of employment. But this is subject to one obvious exception, namely that
the employer was moved to take this action through the misconduct of the employee.
This is reflected in the first part of s 20(1)(a). *f*

The converse is true where the employee voluntarily leaves his employment. The risk
that he will be unemployed is prima facie that of the employee's own creation. But this
presumption is rebuttable. There may be circumstances which leave him no reasonable
alternative to leaving his employment. Thus his wife or family may have an overriding
need for his attendance and the place of his employment may be such that he cannot
provide it. Again, although the risk of unemployment may arise from his voluntary act *g*
in terminating his employment, he may have taken such steps to minimise that risk, by
obtaining a promise of immediate fresh employment or by taking steps which may
reasonably be expected to lead to such employment, as to make it right and reasonable
to leave his employment. 'Just cause' means no more than 'right' or 'right and reasonable'
in the context of the risk of unemployment. Any change of employment is likely to
involve *some* risk of temporary or interim unemployment and the question is whether *h*
the voluntary conduct of the claimant has been such as to create an unreasonable risk of
such unemployment. If it has, the claimant has acted without just cause.

Whilst I understand the triumvirate of commissioners seeking to define 'just cause' by
reference to the rights of the rest of the community (and in the sense in which I think
they meant it I do not disagree) I think that it is a definition which can lead to
misunderstanding and has in fact been misunderstood by the appellants in this case. For *j*
my part, I am quite prepared to assume that Mr Crewe's acceptance of premature
retirement was in the interests of the rest of the community or, at least, that part of the
community which lived in the area of the local education authority. But I do not think
that this was the issue. The compromise which was involved, or the balance which had
to be struck, was between Mr Crewe's personal wishes and interests on the one hand and

the interests of his unemployment underwriters on the other. In so far as the interests
a of the rest of the community were involved, it was only in its capacity as such
underwriters.

On the facts, Mr Crewe voluntarily created a very high risk of unemployment
amounting virtually to a certainty and accordingly left his employment without just
cause. I too would dismiss the appeal.

b **SLADE LJ.** I agree with both judgments that have been delivered.

The phrase 'without just cause' which appears in para (*a*) of s 20(1) of the Social
Security Act 1975 is in striking contrast with the phrase 'without good cause' which
appears in paras (*b*), (*d*) and (*e*). One can only assume that this different use of language
by the legislature was deliberate. Though this point does not fall now to be decided, the
phrase 'without good cause' may perhaps mean no more than 'without reasonable
c cause'. However, I think it plain that the phrase 'without just cause' casts a heavier
burden than that on a person who seeks to show that the disqualification imposed by s 20
does not apply to him, even though he voluntarily left his employment. The phrase
'without just cause' necessarily imports the notion of balancing competing interests of
the employee on the one hand and certain other persons on the other hand. It may be
said to raise the query: 'Justice to whom?'

d The first limb of para (*a*) of the subsection reads 'he has lost his employment as an
employed earner through his misconduct'. These words clearly refer to the case where
the employer has terminated the employee's employment on account of his
misconduct. My first impression was that the second limb of para (*a*), which reads 'or has
voluntarily left such employment without just cause', might likewise be looking solely
to the position between employer and employee and might be intended merely to refer
e to the case where the employee has voluntarily terminated his own employment without
grounds that made it just for him to do so as between himself and his employer. On this
footing the concept of 'just cause' would be looking to the position simply as between
employer and employee.

However, having been reminded of the purpose of the unemployment insurance
scheme, I am now satisfied that this construction of the phrase is too narrow. The
f primary purpose is to ensure against unemployment involuntarily incurred. It is
implicit in the scheme that, in broad terms, each insured person owes a responsibility to
all the other persons who underwrite the national insurance fund not to incur
unemployment by his own voluntary act. One statutory exception to this general
responsibility arises in a case where the insured person had 'just cause' for voluntarily
leaving his employment. Thus, even in the absence of authority, I would have concluded
g that the justice which the legislature had in mind was justice as between the employee
and the general body of persons underwriting the fund. A measure of support for this
conclusion is to be derived from s 20(3) of the 1975 Act, which enables regulations to be
made in regard to certain matters where it appears to the Secretary of State necessary to
do so 'for the purpose of preventing inequalities, or injustice to the general body of
employed earners, or of earners generally, as the case may be'.

h More solid support for this conclusion, however, is to be derived from the long line of
decisions of the commissioners to which Lord Denning MR has referred. In Decision
11760/30 the commissioner described the purpose of s 8(2) of the Unemployment
Insurance Act 1920 (a predecessor of s 20(1)(*a*) of the Act of 1975) in the following terms:

> 'Section 8(2) disqualifies for benefit a person who has voluntarily left his
> employment without just cause and in my view it was intended that a person who
> could not show reasonable grounds for abandoning his employment and thereby
> casting himself on the Unemployment Fund should not be allowed to derive benefit
> from the Fund.'

The commissioner thereby indicated his opinion that the fact that the voluntarily
departing employee would be thereby casting himself on the fund would itself be an

important factor in considering whether or not he had left his employment 'without just cause'.

A similar opinion was reflected in Decision R(U) 26/51, para 9, and in Decision R(U) 23/59 (see in particular paras 12 to 16).

It was also reflected in the important decision of the tribunal R(U) 20/64, para 8 of which Donaldson LJ has quoted in his judgment.

Counsel on behalf of the appellants seized on the words 'without due regard to the interests of the rest of the community', which appear at the end of the passage quoted in the middle of this para 8, to found an argument that it was justice to *the whole of the public* which the tribunal had in mind. But I do not think that this is a correct reading of the paragraph as a whole. The quotation was immediately prefaced by the words 'the interests of the National Insurance Fund and other contributors have to be taken into account as well'. This, I think, is what the tribunal had in mind. A person seeking to show that he has voluntarily left his employment with just cause must show not only that in leaving he acted reasonably in his own interests, but in circumstances which made it just that he should be cast on the national insurance fund. The same concept is reflected in para 13 of the tribunal's decision from which Donaldson LJ has quoted. It follows the thinking of the three earlier decisions to which I have referred.

Finally, as to the authorities on this point, the same concept is to be reflected in para 15 of Decision R(U) 4/70.

Even if I felt doubts as to the correctness of this approach, I would be slow to differ from this long and undisturbed line of decisions of experienced commissioners, in view of the warning given by this court in R v National Insurance Comr, ex p Stratton [1979] 2 All ER 278 at 282, [1979] 1 QB 361 at 369, to which Lord Denning MR has referred. But I feel no such doubt.

So far as I can see, the commissioner, in para 10 of his decision in the present case, applied entirely the correct legal principles in accordance with this line of authority, in approaching the question whether or not Mr Crewe left his employment 'without just cause'. In particular he was justified in rejecting the arguments submitted to him on behalf of the appellants based on the public interest. It may well be, as he himself recognised, that the arrangements made between the appellant, Mr Crewe, and his employers were in the public interest; they certainly believed them to be so. But these, I think, are not the relevant considerations. Though he did not state explicitly that he was applying this test, I think the commissioner made it clear by necessary implication that he was in effect treating 'just cause' as meaning right and reasonable in the context of the risk of unemployment, which seems to me the correct test in law. For reasons set out in para 10 of his careful decision, the commissioner concluded that on the evidence no 'just cause' had been shown. This was in my view a conclusion to which he was perfectly entitled to come on the facts found by him. I find myself unable to say that it was wrong.

I would therefore concur in dismissing this appeal.

Appeal dismissed. Leave to appeal to the House of Lords refused.

Solicitors: *Reynolds, Porter, Chamberlain* (for the appellants); *Solicitor to the Department of Health and Social Security.*

Frances Rustin   Barrister.

a

Forster v Outred & Co (a firm)

COURT OF APPEAL, CIVIL DIVISION
STEPHENSON, DUNN LJJ AND SIR DAVID CAIRNS
9, 10, 11 MARCH 1981

b *Limitation of action – Accrual of cause of action – Negligence – Solicitor – Economic loss suffered in consequence of solicitor's negligent advice – Plaintiff executing mortgage as guarantor following solicitor's negligent advice – Date from which limitation period running – Whether cause of action against solicitor complete when plaintiff incurred contingent liability on executing mortgage – Whether cause of action not complete until mortgagee demanding payment under mortgage.*

c *Solicitor – Negligence – Cause of action – Negligent advice – Accrual of action – Whether cause of action against solicitor complete when client acts on solicitor's negligent advice or when loss or damage occurs.*

The plaintiff was the freehold owner of property. On 8 February 1973 at the office of the defendants, her solicitors, she executed a mortgage deed in the presence of a member of the defendants' firm, who witnessed the deed, which charged her property by way of legal mortgage in favour of a company as continuing security for payment, on demand by the company, of all present or future, actual or contingent, liabilities owed by her son to the company. The mortgage stated that it was deemed to be the primary security for the son's liabilities. The son went bankrupt owing money to the company. On 23 April 1974 the company threatened to foreclose on the plaintiff's property unless she paid the amount of the son's liabilities and on 21 January 1975 made a formal demand to the plaintiff under the terms of the mortgage for payment of the son's liabilities. In consequence, on 29 August 1975 the plaintiff paid almost £70,000 to the company. On 7 January 1977 the plaintiff issued a writ claiming damages for negligence against the defendants and alleging that the defendants were in breach of their duty to explain the contents of the mortgage to the plaintiff before she signed it. The plaintiff claimed that in particular the defendants should have explained that the mortgage was security for all the son's present and future liabilities to the company and not merely, as the plaintiff believed, temporary security for a bridging loan from the company to her son. On 9 March 1977 the defendants served a defence. Thereafter the plaintiff took no further steps in the action until 14 December 1979, when she gave notice of intention to proceed. On 27 February 1980 the defendants applied to strike out the action for want of prosecution. On 27 March the plaintiff issued a second writ against the defendants claiming damages for negligent advice in regard to the mortgage. The master refused to strike out the first action. The defendants appealed to a judge, who on 30 July allowed the appeal and struck out the first action for want of prosecution because he found that there had been inordinate and inexcusable delay by the plaintiff to the defendants' prejudice in prosecuting the first action and he thought it was only arguable, and not clear, that the second writ had been issued within the limitation period. The judge decided that, since the defendants would not be able to raise the limitation defence if the plaintiff was allowed to proceed with the first action, justice required him to strike out the first action and let the plaintiff proceed with the second action when the defendants could raise the limitation defence. The plaintiff appealed, submitting that the judge ought not to have struck out the first action, since the second action had been commenced within the six years' limitation period applicable to the plaintiff's cause of action for negligence because the cause of action was not complete until she had suffered actual damage in consequence of the defendants' alleged negligence, and that had occurred at the earliest on 23 April 1975 when the company threatened foreclosure, or possibly on 21 January 1975 when the company made its demand or on 29 August 1975 when she made the payment to the company under the mortgage. On the hearing of the appeal, the Court of Appeal upheld the judge's decision that there had been inordinate and inexcusable delay, causing prejudice to the defendants, in prosecuting the first action. *a* On the question whether the judge was right to strike out the first action so that the defendants could raise the limitation defence in the second action,

Held – Where a plaintiff alleged that he had suffered economic loss in consequence of a solicitor's negligent advice, actual damage occurred and the plaintiff's cause of action was complete when in reliance on the solicitor's negligent advice the plaintiff acted to his *b* detriment by incurring a contingent liability which was capable of monetary assessment. Accordingly, the plaintiff had suffered actual damage through the defendants' negligence, and her cause of action was therefore complete, when she entered into the mortgage on 8 February 1973, because the effect of her entering into the mortgage was to encumber her freehold property with a legal charge and to subject her to a contingent liability to discharge her son's liabilities to the company, which might *c* (as it in fact did) mature into financial loss and in consequence diminish her equity of redemption. It followed that, although the plaintiff had not become liable to pay under the mortgage until 21 January 1975, when the company made its demand for payment, her cause of action against the defendants was complete on 8 February 1973 and therefore the second writ had been issued outside the six years' limitation period. It followed that the issue of the second writ was not a reason for refusing to dismiss the first action, which *d* had therefore rightly been dismissed for want of prosecution. The appeal would accordingly be dismissed (see p 759 *d e*, p 760 *g h*, p 764 *b* to *e* and p 765 *b c* and *f* to *j*, post).

Howell v Young [1824–34] All ER Rep 377, *Nocton v Lord Ashburton* [1914–15] All ER Rep 45, *Sykes v Midland Bank Exor and Trustee Co Ltd* [1970] 2 All ER 471 and *Birkett v James* [1977] 2 All ER 801 considered.

e

Notes

For limitation of action in respect of negligence and for the accrual of a cause of action, see 34 Halsbury's Laws (4th edn) para 66; and for cases on the subject, see 32 Digest (Reissue) 505–508, 3856–3869.

For dismissal of actions for want of prosecution, see 30 Halsbury's Laws (3rd edn) 410, *f* 411, para 771.

Cases referred to in judgments

Anns v Merton London Borough Council [1977] 2 All ER 492, [1978] AC 728, [1977] 2 WLR 1024, HL, 1(1) Digest (Reissue) 128, 721.

Birkett v James [1977] 2 All ER 801, [1978] AC 297, [1977] 3 WLR 38, HL, Digest (Cont *g* Vol E) 666, 2698b.

Donoghue (or McAlister) v Stevenson [1932] AC 562, [1932] All ER Rep 1, HL, 36(1) Digest (Reissue) 144, 562.

Ford v White & Co [1964] 2 All ER 755, [1964] 1 WLR 885, Digest (Cont Vol B) 659, 1083a.

Hedley Byrne & Co Ltd v Heller & Partners Ltd [1963] 2 All ER 575, [1964] AC 465, [1963] *h* 3 WLR 101, HL, 36(1) Digest (Reissue) 24, 84.

Howell v Young (1826) 5 B & C 259, [1824–34] All ER Rep 377, 108 ER 97, 32 Digest (Reissue) 506, 3857.

Lloyds Bank Ltd v Margolis [1954] 1 All ER 734, [1954] 1 WLR 644, 32 Digest (Reissue) 582, 4383.

Midland Bank Trust Co Ltd v Hett, Stubbs & Kemp (a firm) [1978] 3 All ER 571, [1979] Ch *j* 384, [1978] 3 WLR 167, Digest (Cont Vol E) 565, 978a.

Ministry of Housing and Local Government v Sharp [1970] 1 All ER 1009, [1970] 2 QB 223, [1970] 2 WLR 802, CA, 36(1) Digest (Reissue) 49, 157.

Nocton v Lord Ashburton [1914] AC 932, [1914–15] All ER Rep 45, HL, 32 Digest (Reissue) 729, 5281.

Philips v Ward [1956] 1 All ER 874, [1956] 1 WLR 471, CA, 47 Digest (Repl) 564, 35.
a   *Simple Simon Catering Ltd v Binstock Miller & Co* (1973) 228 EG 527, CA.
Sparham-Souter v Town and Country Developments (Essex) Ltd [1976] 2 All ER 65, [1976] QB
     858, [1976] 2 WLR 493, CA, 32 Digest (Reissue) 507, 3864.
Sykes v Midland Bank Exor and Trustee Co Ltd [1969] 2 All ER 1238, [1969] 2 QB 518,
     [1969] 2 WLR 1173; *on appeal* [1970] 2 All ER 471, [1971] 1 QB 113, [1970] 3 WLR
     273, CA, Digest (Cont Vol C) 897, 862a.
b

Cases also cited
Battley v Faulkner (1820) 3 B & Ald 288, [1814–23] All ER Rep 409, 106 ER 668.
Batty v Metropolitan Property Realizations Ltd [1978] 2 All ER 445, [1978] QB 554, CA.
Bean v Wade (1885) 2 TLR 157, CA.
Bradford Old Bank Ltd v Sutcliffe [1918] 2 KB 833, CA.
c   *Brown v Howard* (1820) 2 Brod & Bing 73, 129 ER 885.
Cartledge v E Jopling & Sons Ltd [1963] 1 All ER 341, [1963] AC 758, HL.
Clark v Kirby-Smith [1964] 2 All ER 835, [1964] Ch 506.
Darley Main Colliery Co v Mitchell (1886) 11 App Cas 127, [1886–90] All ER Rep 449, HL.
Esso Petroleum Co Ltd v Mardon [1976] 2 All ER 5, [1976] QB 801, CA.
Groom v Crocker [1938] 2 All ER 394, [1939] 1 KB 194, CA.
d   *Jarvis v Moy, Davies, Smith, Vandervell & Co* [1936] 1 KB 399, CA.
Kelly v Metropolitan Rly Co [1895] 1 QB 944, CA.
Letang v Cooper [1964] 2 All ER 929, [1965] 1 QB 232, CA.
Nicholls v Ely Beet Sugar Factory Ltd [1936] Ch 343, CA.
Ross v Caunters [1979] 3 All ER 580, [1980] Ch 297.
Short v M'Carthy (1820) 3 B & Ald 626, 106 ER 789.
e   *Turner v Stallibrass* [1898] 1 QB 56, CA.

Appeal
The plaintiff, Eileen Betty Forster, appealed from the order of Peter Pain J made on 30
July 1980 dismissing for want of prosecution an action brought by her, by writ dated 7
January 1977, against the defendants, Messrs Outred & Co, a firm of solicitors, claiming
f   damages for negligence, and allowing the defendants' appeal from the order of Master
Waldman made on 14 July 1980 by which he refused to strike out the action for want of
prosecution. The grounds of the appeal were that (1) the judge misdirected himself in
refusing to determine the issue whether or not the limitation period in relation to the
plaintiff's cause of action in negligence had expired by the date of the defendants'
summons (27 February 1980) to dismiss the action for want of prosecution and/or by the
g   date of a second writ for the same cause of action issued by the plaintiff against the
defendants on 25 March 1980, and ought to have determined that issue and to have held
that the plaintiff's cause of action did not accrue before 29 August 1975 or, at the earliest,
on 23 April 1974, (2) in the premises the judge ought to have found that the limitation
period in respect of the plaintiff's cause of action had not expired by the date of the
defendants' summons to strike out the first action or by the date of issue of the second
h   writ and should accordingly have allowed the action to proceed, (3) the judge ought not
to have found that the plaintiff's delay was inexcusable, and (4) the judge ought not to
have found that the defendants had established that they would be prejudiced as a result
of the plaintiff's delay. The facts are set out in the judgment of Stephenson LJ.

Anthony Scrivener QC and *Julien Hooper* for the plaintiff.
j   *Murray Stuart-Smith QC* and *Alexander Layton* for the defendants.

STEPHENSON LJ. On 7 January 1977 the plaintiff, Mrs Forster, issued a writ
indorsed with a statement of claim against the defendants, Messrs Outred & Co, a firm
of solicitors, claiming damages for their negligence as her solicitors. Her present

solicitors served that writ and statement of claim on 24 January 1977. On 9 March 1977 the defendants' solicitors served a defence and a request for particulars of the statement of claim. No step was taken in the action for two years and nine months. On 14 December 1979 the plaintiff's present solicitors gave notice of intention to proceed. On 27 February 1980 the defendants' solicitors applied to strike out the action for want of prosecution. The master refused to do so, but on appeal Peter Pain J dismissed the action with costs on 30 July 1980 and gave the plaintiff leave to appeal to this court. It is the plaintiff's appeal that has occupied us over the last two days.

We have a note of the judge's judgment which begins in this way: 'In deference to the arguments of counsel, I should say that this matter is a good deal more difficult than the usual cases of striking out.' The note has been prepared by the plaintiff's solicitors but has not been submitted to the judge for approval, though it had been sent to the defendants' solicitors for agreement in September 1980 and they had suggested minor amendments to it. I am unable to understand why the correct procedure has not been followed, or why the judge has been deprived of the opportunity of correcting or approving this note. However, it has been agreed in this court by counsel, we have admitted it and it appears to be a good note which gives us a reliable idea of what the judge said in coming to the conclusion to which he did.

The judge had no difficulty in finding the plaintiff's (or her solicitors') delay inordinate because that was very properly conceded on behalf of the plaintiff: and the judge had no difficulty in finding it inexcusable, since the only excuse put forward was that, since the plaintiff's present solicitors were first instructed in November 1975, they had been so busy principally with four other actions which she was bringing, two of them against other firms of solicitors, that they had not had time to get on with this one.

The judge had more difficulty, but not much more, about the question of prejudice. There would seem to be little difficulty in accepting that there was real prejudice to the defendants here, additional to the prejudice that might have resulted from the lapse of over three years between the vital interview in February 1973 and the letter before action in March 1976, because the claim is based on what the defendants said or did not say to the plaintiff at a meeting in their office on 8 February 1973. The judge said that he would have struck out the action were it not for the fact that a second writ was issued on 25 March 1980. That is what has caused the unusual difficulty presented by this case, both for the judge and for this court. If the March 1980 writ was effectively issued within the limitation period, it would be an almost conclusive ground for refusing to dismiss the action: see *Birkett v James* [1977] 2 All ER 801, [1978] AC 297. For where there is, or could be, a second action begun in time, it is a waste of time and money not to let the first action go on, and to dismiss it merely causes further delay and expense and increases any prejudice to the defendant and reduces the chances of a fair trial still further. The judge had real doubt whether the second writ was issued in time. He said:

> 'The real point of this is that if Mr. Phillips [counsel then appearing for the defendants] is right, then he has a defence under the Limitation Act. If I strike out this action, the plaintiff can proceed on her new writ and the defendants can argue a defence under the Limitation Act. If I dismiss the appeal, the defendant is shut out from taking the Limitation Act defence. There is therefore no need to decide whether Mr. Phillips is right or wrong. If I were to decide which argument is correct, I would want to go into the matter a lot further. It is very much an arguable point as a matter of law. In those circumstances, justice requires that I should strike out the existing writ and let the plaintiff proceed if she is so advised with her new writ.'

The plaintiff is a divorced lady in her sixties, with a mother and children to house and one unfortunately improvident son. The sad story of her woes and why she holds the defendants responsible for them is set out in her statement of claim. That alleges:

> '1. At all material times the Plaintiff was the freehold owner of a property known

as Home Farm, Fox Warren Park, Surrey, and the Defendants practised as Solicitors in Guildford and Weybridge.

2. On or about the 8th day of February, 1973 the Plaintiff signed a mortgage deed in respect of the said property in favour of the Hume Corporation Limited. The purpose of the said mortgage was to enable the Plaintiff's son, John Forster to borrow money from the Hume Corporation Limited to complete the purchase of an hotel known as "The Sheffield Arms".

3. The Plaintiff signed the said deed at the Defendants' office in Weybridge and one Simon Outred, a servant or agent of the Defendants, signed the deed as a witness in his capacity of the Plaintiff's Solicitor. At all material times the said Simon Outred knew that the Hume Corporation Limited required that the mortgage deed should be executed by the Plaintiff in the presence of her Solicitor and his signature followed the words "after the contents had been explained to her". The said John Forster was present when the deed was signed and the said Simon Outred had, for some time, acted as his Solicitor.

4. In the premises, the said Simon Outred was under a duty to explain fully the contents of the mortgage deed including the full implications of signing the same and should, in particular, have pointed out in such a way that the Plaintiff could understand, the fact that; (a) No other long-term mortgage had been arranged by the said John Forster to replace the monies lent or to be lent by the Hume Corporation Limited in consideration of the mortgage on Home Farm. (b) The mortgage covered all present and future liabilities of the said John Forster and there was a real danger that she would be liable in respect of any liability already or subsequently incurred by the said John Forster. (c) No arrangements or no adequate arrangements had been made to discharge the liability of the said John Forster to the Hume Corporation Limited and/or to relieve the Plaintiff of liability under the mortgage. (d) There was no safeguard to prevent the subsequent release of the charge on the "Sheffield Arms" so that Home Farm remained the only security in respect of John Forster's indebtedness to the Hume Corporation Limited. (e) The Defendant was acting not only for John Forster, but also for one Benavidos, who was a joint purchaser of the "Sheffield Arms". (f) The Hume Corporation Limited had agreed with the said John Forster that if he obtained a mortgage of £50,000 so that his indebtedness to them would be reduced, they were prepared to make further loans up to a total indebtedness of £40,000.

5. Alternatively, on account of the fact that the said Simon Outred had for some time acted as the Solicitor for John Forster and that there was a clear conflict of interest between him and the Plaintiff, the said Simon Outred was under a duty to send the Plaintiff to another Solicitor and/or to advise her to seek completely independent advice before signing the mortgage. The said Simon Outred knew that another firm of Solicitors, L. Dawson & Company, acted for the Plaintiff in respect of other transactions relating to Home Farm.

6. The said Simon Outred failed to explain to the Plaintiff fully or at all the matters set out in Paragraph 4 including the real dangers of signing the mortgage and/or failed to advise her to seek independent legal advice as a result of which the Plaintiff signed the mortgage deed in the belief that the mortgage was going to provide only temporary security for a bridging loan from the Hume Corporation Limited and that as soon as the permanent mortgage had been obtained the whole indebtedness of John Forster to the Hume Corporation Limited would be paid off and she would be released from any further liability under the mortgage.

7. Had the Plaintiff been advised by the said Simon Outred or by an independent Solicitor of the true position, she would never have granted the mortgage over "Home Farm" but by reason of the Defendants' said negligence and/or breach of contract the Plaintiff became liable to and did pay to the Hume Corporation Limited the total sum of £69,281·52.'

There is then a further reference to what she might have been told by a careful solicitor.
From what I have read it is plain that she did become liable to pay, and did pay, nearly   *a*
£70,000 to Hume Corp Ltd and that came about because the hotel venture was a failure
and because her son John went bankrupt.

On 23 April 1974 Hume Corp Ltd wrote to her threatening to foreclose on Home
Farm unless she paid up. On 21 January 1975 they made a formal demand under the
terms of the mortgage deed, to which I will refer in a moment, and on 29 August 1975
she did actually pay up all that was due under the mortgage deed.   *b*

Finding herself in that position she attempted to sell her property, Home Farm, to a
company called Silvermere Golf and Equestrian Centre Ltd, the principal person
concerned on behalf of that company being a Mr Gabbert. She went to her solicitors,
Messrs L Dawson & Co, in connection with that transaction and she also went to a fourth
firm of solicitors, Messrs Herbert Smith & Co, who gave her specialist advice as to the
circumstances in which she found herself. As I have said, in November 1975 she   *c*
instructed her present solicitors and they then busied themselves with bringing a number
of actions against other persons. The actions against the present defendants were not
brought until 1977; an action was brought against Messrs L Dawson & Co about the
same time; another one at the same time against Messrs Herbert Smith & Co; another
one against the Silvermere company and another one against Mr Gabbert (or it may have
been that he was joined in the action against Silvermere) because the agreement that was *d*
entered into with the Silvermere company was that they should buy Home Farm but
should build a house for her to inhabit and everything went wrong with that agreement
too. I need not go into further details but that is how she comes to be suing Messrs
Outred & Co because she says all the loss that she has suffered arises from their fault,
whether it be called breach of contract or negligence or breach of duty.

I have come to the clear conclusion that the judge was fully justified in saying what he *e*
did about the prejudice to a fair trial of the action and the defendants' defence if this very
stale action is allowed to go on, and in spite of the arguments of counsel for the plaintiff
to the contrary I would agree with the judge that, were it not for this second writ, the
court would have no option but to affirm his judgment and strike out this first action.

The master refused to strike it out and although we have no note of what he said it
appears that the main reason why he refused to strike it out was that he thought the   *f*
plaintiff would have a strong chance of succeeding against the defendants on the failure
of Mr Simon Outred to advise her that she should seek independent advice and he
regarded that as a matter on which the passage of time and almost inevitable dimming
of recollection would not have any appreciable effect.

I have considered that point, and it clearly is a point which requires consideration, but
I have come to the conclusion that the allegation of failure to advise her that independent *g*
advice was desirable or necessary is really all bound up with the question of explaining
the matter to her and it is difficult to separate one part of a witness's recollection as to
what happened at this interview from another. It seems to me, although I appreciate the
reason that the master gave in coming to the contrary conclusion, that it is not a
sufficient ground for disturbing the view which I have formed that there is real additional
prejudice here arising from the further 2¾ years' delay in the way in which this first   *h*
action was pursued by the plaintiff and her solicitors.

I find difficulty in accepting the judge's view of the allegation of failure to advise that
an independent solicitor or other adviser should be consulted by the plaintiff as being
merely an afterthought. From what I have read in the statement of claim it appears to
me that it was a perfectly properly pleaded alternative. I do not regard it as a make-
weight, although if the matter went to trial no doubt the principal issue might turn out   *j*
to be whether or not the matter was explained fully to the plaintiff as, of course, is more
incumbent on the defendants if they had not warned her that she should have
independent advice, than if they had.

It therefore becomes necessary to consider whether the judge was right in the view
that he took of the limitation point, and whether he was right in deciding to adhere to

his decision to strike out the action on the ground that there was an arguable point, which he was not going to decide, on the question whether the March 1980 writ had been issued in time and whether the second action would or would not be defeated by a plea of the Limitation Act.

In this court counsel for both parties want us to decide the question whether the plaintiff's second writ is effective, that is to say whether the action begun by it will be statute-barred if the action begun by the first writ is struck out and judge's order stands. Counsel for the plaintiff submits that the second action is not statute-barred because the plaintiff's claim is for damages for negligence, actual damage is accordingly the gist of the action, the cause of action is not complete until actual damage is suffered by the plaintiff and the plaintiff suffered no actual damage as a consequence of the defendants' negligence until, at the earliest, 23 or 24 April 1974, when Hume Corp Ltd's (the mortgagees) first demand was made by letter, or perhaps the two other dates I have given, 21 January 1975 (the date of the demand pleaded by the mortgagees in their action against her) or 29 August 1975 when she paid them £69,281·52 under the mortgage deed.

Counsel for the defendants concedes for the purpose of this appeal (though he wishes to reserve the point for a higher court) that the plaintiff's claim is for damages for negligence and not simply for damages for breach of contract, that actual damage is necessary to constitute her cause of action, and that, if she suffered no actual damage until 23 April 1974 or later, her second action would not be statute-barred. But he submits first that she suffered actual damage on 8 February 1973 when she signed the mortgage deed, by incumbering her freehold interest in the mortgaged property, and subjecting herself to liability to discharge her son's debts under the mortgage deed. He asks us to affirm the judge's order on this ground, and counsel for the plaintiff takes no objection to the point not having been taken by a cross-notice because he also wants the point decided. But counsel for the defendants submits in the alternative that we should affirm the judge's order on the ground on which he made it, namely that, the success of the defence of the Limitation Act to the second action being arguable, it should be left to the trial judge to decide, on facts which may not be fully before the court at this stage, whether to uphold or reject it.

Accordingly the first point which we have to decide is when the plaintiff's cause of action accrued. No such decision was involved in *Birkett v James* [1977] 2 All ER 801, [1978] AC 297, where the second action could be commenced within the limitation period.

Counsel for the plaintiff has called our attention to a number of cases where the courts have had to consider the date when a cause of action in negligence was completed by damage in order to see whether it was statute-barred, and in particular the date when time began to run in favour of solicitors sued by clients. They are most, if not all, to be found helpfully reviewed in the judgment of Oliver J in *Midland Bank Trust Co Ltd v Hett, Stubbs & Kemp (a firm)* [1978] 3 All ER 571, [1979] Ch 384. On their authority counsel for the plaintiff submits that in the tort of negligence (whether or not the parties are in a contractual relationship does not matter, as the plaintiff's claim is conceded to be a claim in negligence) the plaintiff must prove actual damage before the cause of action accrues; notional damage or damage arising on a contingency will not do, nor will damage be presumed; purely financial loss will do provided it is reasonably foreseeable. Such earlier cases as *Howell v Young* (1826) 5 B & C 259, [1824–34] All ER Rep 377 proceeded on the basis of a breach of duty which arose from a common calling and considered the terms of the contract between the parties in order to determine whether and when damage was suffered and so do not apply to modern cases of negligence. Before the period of limitation began to run the plaintiff had not advanced any money or become liable to pay any interest or lost any expected benefit; she had only agreed to provide collateral security without necessarily incurring any liability to pay anything; she was free to treat the mortgaged property as her own and sell it, its market value unaffected; and as it was a farm the prohibition in the clause of the deed which prohibits leasing was invalid by reason of para 2 of Sch 7 to the Agricultural Holdings Act 1948. She was merely subject to the detriment of a contingent liability and a purely academic temporary diminution in the equity of the mortgaged property.

Counsel for the defendants contends that when she signed the mortgage deed she suffered actual damage. By entering into a burdensome bond or contract or mortgage she sustained immediate economic loss; her valuable freehold became incumbered with a charge and its value to her was diminished because she had merely the equity of redemption, varying in value at the whim of her son's creditors; she could not sell the land without discharging the mortgage; she could not prevent her son from borrowing on the security of her mortgage to the extent of the full value of the land; she could have sued the defendants in February 1973 for an indemnity or for damages on the basis of the diminished value of the land or the amount of the outstanding debt to the mortgagor.

I should refer to the terms of the mortgage deed (it is in common form) to see to what it was to which the plaintiff had subjected herself and what was the incumbrance with which the land had been charged. It is a legal mortgage and states:

'1. (a) The Mortgagor as beneficial owner charges by way of legal mortgage and as a continuing security the property referred to in the Schedule hereto . . . with the payment to the Bank on demand by the Bank on the Mortgagor of all present or future actual or contingent liabilities of John Francis Foote Forster (the Debtor) to the Bank whether on account of monies advanced . . . 2. The Morgagor will keep the Morgaged Property in a good state of repair and condition and will keep it insured against such risks and in such office and for such amounts as the Bank may from time to time approve . . . 5. The statutory powers of leasing or of accepting surrenders of leases conferred on mortgagors shall not be exercised by the Mortgagor without the consent in writing of the Bank but the Bank may grant or accept surrenders of leases without restriction . . . 10. . . . this Mortgage is to be deemed to be a primary security and the Mortgaged Property is to be deemed to stand charged with the moneys or liabilities hereby secured as if they were primarily due from the Mortgagor.'

As I have quoted from the statement of claim the deed is signed, sealed and delivered by the plaintiff in the presence of what appears to be the signature of Mr Simon Outred, after the typewritten words 'after the contents had been explained to her'.

I should also refer to the fact that in their defence to the action the defendants positively averred that 'Simon Outred explained to the Plaintiff the nature and extent of the said mortgage deed before the Plaintiff signed it'. They also admitted that they acted for John Forster in the transaction alleged and that they knew the firm of Messrs L Dawson & Co had also acted for the plaintiff. The allegation that they failed to give her independent advice is simply met by a general traverse to be found in their defence.

What is meant by actual damage? Counsel for the defendants says that it is any detriment, liability or loss capable of assessment in money terms and it includes liabilities which may arise on a contingency, particularly a contingency over which the plaintiff has no control; things like loss of earning capacity, loss of a chance or bargain, loss of profit, losses incurred from onerous provisions or covenants in leases. They are all illustrations of a kind of loss which is meant by 'actual' damage. It was also suggested in argument, and I would accept it, that 'actual' is really used in contrast to 'presumed' or 'assumed'. Whereas damage is presumed in trespass and libel, it is not presumed in negligence and has to be proved. There has to be some actual damage.

A question which has led to much argument, and which I have not found altogether easy to answer, is whether what happened to the plaintiff, to use a neutral phrase, when she signed the deed constituted actual damage. Counsel for the defendants says that it did because there was an immediate reduction in the value of her equity and a contingent liability, contingent, it is true, but nevertheless a liability, to repay the principle and interest on demand and that that was capable of assessment in money terms. He also relied, with less success in my judgment, on the restriction on leasing, which he suggested

might not apply (although there is no evidence about it) to the whole of the mortgaged
a property, and on the covenant to repair and insure the mortgaged property which may
or may not (again there is no evidence) have added to what the plaintiff was doing already
or was indeed contractually bound to do.

'No,' says counsel for the plaintiff, 'that is to strain the meaning of the words "actual
damage".' And we were, of course, referred to a number of cases, of which perhaps *Anns
v Merton London Borough Council* [1977] 2 All ER 492, [1978] AC 728 is the most notable,
b where questions have arisen and been decided as to when damage to constitute a cause of
action in negligence against architects or builders of houses arises, and when statutes of
limitation begin to run; questions of physical damage such as cracks appearing in
inadequately built or designed foundations, and their not only appearing but becoming
known to a particular person against whom it is sought to invoke the statute of
limitation. Here, there is no question of knowledge by the plaintiff of damage coming
c later than actual damage being caused; the question is: when was actual damage first
caused?

It is perfectly true that she was under no matured or actual liability to pay the sums
that she ultimately did pay to Hume Corp Ltd until they made a demand, and if there
was no actual damage before that date then it is agreed that counsel for the plaintiff is
right and that the second writ was issued within the period of limitation running from
d no date earlier than that. Counsel for the plaintiff has also submitted that there is no
single case in which either a solicitor or anybody else has been deprived of the power of
relying on the Limitation Act by the occurrence of what might be called a 'worsening'
of a plaintiff's financial position such as is to be found on the facts of this case.

Of all the authorities which have been cited to us the only ones which have been of
assistance to me in making my choice between the submissions of counsel for the
e defendants and counsel for the plaintiff are *Howell v Young* (1826) 5 B & C 259, [1824–34]
All ER Rep 377, *Nocton v Lord Ashburton* [1914] AC 932, [1914–15] All ER Rep 45 and
Simple Simon Catering Ltd v Binstock Miller & Co (1973) 228 EG 527.

Howell v Young has had a long career since it was decided in 1826 by Bayley and
Holroyd JJ. It was an action, either in assumpsit or in case (it was treated by Oliver J in
Midland Bank Trust Co Ltd v Hett, Stubbs & Kemp [1978] 3 All ER 571, [1979] Ch 384 as an
f action on the case), in which an attorney was sued for taking an insufficient security on
behalf of his client. The interest of the case, and it has been very fully expounded by
Oliver J in his judgment in the *Midland Bank Trust Co* case [1978] 3 All ER 571 at 586–
587, [1979] Ch 384 at 406–407, is that there was, subsequent to the taking of inadequate
security, a loss of interest which was regarded as special damage. In that case the statute
was held to defeat the claim and what was said, first of all by Bayley J (5 B & C 259 at 266,
g [1824–34] All ER Rep 377 at 380), was this: ·

> 'Whatever be the form of action, the breach of duty is substantially the cause of
> action. That being so, the cause of action accrued at the time when the defendant
> in this case took the bad and insufficient security, that was more than six years
> before the commencement of the action, which is consequently barred by the
> Statute of Limitations.'

h Holroyd J said (5 B & C 259 at 266, [1824–34] All ER Rep 377 at 380): 'The breach of
promise or of duty took place as soon as the defendant took the insufficient security' and
later he said (5 B & C 259 at 268, [1824–34] All ER Rep 377 at 381):

> 'So here, if the action had been brought immediately after the insufficient security
> had been taken, the jury would have been bound to give damages for the probable
> loss which the plaintiff was likely to sustain from the invalidity of the security. It
> appears to me, therefore, that the subsequent special damage alleged in this
> declaration did not constitute any fresh cause of action.'

As I read that case and those judgments, the court was saying that the taking of
insufficient security, although at the time it was taken it caused no actual damage in the

sense of financial loss causing the plaintiff/client to lose the chance of getting any money
or to pay out any money, was nevertheless the cause of probable loss and that constituted   *a*
the cause of action. The cause of action arose because the damage occurred at that time,
which was more than six years before the action was brought, and the fact that there was
an actual loss at a later period within the six years did not help the plaintiff to overcome
the defence of the Limitation Act, and his claim was statute-barred. That was the taking
of inadequate security negligently, and perhaps in breach of contract, by a solicitor.

In *Nocton v Lord Ashburton* [1914] AC 932, [1914–15] All ER Rep 45 the solicitor, Mr   *b*
Nocton, advised Lord Ashburton to release part of a security. That well-known authority
covers in its many pages a complicated history of facts and some well-known
pronouncements in the House of Lords on the fiduciary duty of solicitors; and the case
has won renewed recognition from its treatment in *Hedley Byrne & Co v Heller & Partners
Ltd* [1963] 2 All ER 575, [1964] AC 465.

Counsel for the defendants submits that the relevance of that case to the present case   *c*
lies in the facts. Without disentangling them in detail it appears that Lord Ashburton
advanced a sum of £65,000 on the security of a mortgage, but he did not take the
£65,000 out of his own account or his own pocket, he borrowed it from an insurance
company. That was in September 1904. He brought an action of deceit against Mr
Nocton when things went wrong. He was advancing the money to further a building
development being carried out by or on behalf of his brother and Mr Nocton and he later   *d*
lost interest which was payable to him, as a result, he alleged, of Mr Nocton's fraud. The
judge refused to find fraud and the Court of Appeal, as the House of Lords said, 'rashly',
reversed his decision on that point. What the Court of Appeal also did appears in the
Law Reports ([1914] AC 932 at 939):

> 'The Court of Appeal, while agreeing with Neville J. that it would be wrong to
> allow a charge of fraud to be converted into a charge of negligence, differed from   *e*
> him on the facts. So far as regards the claim in respect of the £65,000 they held
> that, in view of the warnings given to the plaintiff by the defendant Nocton's
> partners, the plaintiff had failed to establish any case of concealed fraud against the
> defendant Nocton, and that the Statute of Limitations was therefore a complete
> answer to the claim. But with regard to the release they found that the defendant
> Nocton had been guilty of fraud, and granted relief on that footing.'   *f*

They then made orders as to payment.

The 'release' was the release of part of the security and that was done on the advice of
Mr Nocton in December 1905 within the period of six years before action was brought
in March 1911. The 'borrowed advance' of £65,000 in 1904 was well before the six years
before the action was brought. As I read what is said of the judgment of the Court of   *g*
Appeal they held that the statute was a complete answer to the principal claim, the claim
for the £65,000 and interest thereon; and they must have held that that was statute-
barred because they regarded actual damage as having been suffered by Lord Ashburton
at the time when he was negligently advised by Mr Nocton to make the advance.

The House of Lords had only to deal with the question of the subsequent release, as to
which no statutory defence of limitation could, on the facts, arise, and they did feel able   *h*
to do what the Court of Appeal and Neville J had felt unable to do, namely, to give the
plaintiff some damages for breach of fiduciary duty although they upheld the trial judge,
reversing the Court of Appeal, in saying that there was no fraud proved. Consequently
in their Lordships' House there was no discussion of the Statute of Limitations, or of
when the original action accrued, and there is just a statement in the judgment of Lord
Parmoor (see [1914] AC 932 at 977, [1914–15] All ER Rep 45 at 62) confirming what I   *j*
have said about the Court of Appeal's decision, that it would have been impossible to
amend the original claim for fraud by adding a claim for negligence because that would
have been to deprive the defendant of his otherwise successful defence under the Statute
of Limitations.

The comment of counsel for the plaintiff on that case is that it would be very rash to

base any conclusion as to what was actual damage and when the cause of action originally
a accrued on what is known of the Court of Appeal's apparently unreported decision in
that case as it is summarised in the statement of the facts in the report of the case in the
House of Lords, and he has pointed to passages in their Lordships' speeches which treat
the £65,000 as being an advance, without saying that it was an advance from borrowed
money, and he says that makes no difference. If the money was advanced then there was
quite clearly actual damage to Lord Ashburton at the time when it was advanced,
b notwithstanding that it may not have come from his pocket at that stage, and therefore
it does not help counsel for the defendants' argument.

Accepting those reservations I nevertheless think that it does help counsel for the
defendants' argument because it does seem to me that, whether the point was taken or
not, the Court of Appeal must have decided that there might be actual damage even
though there was no actual financial expenditure by the plaintiff.

c The last case on which counsel for the defendants relied is a case which also deals with
solicitors but it is a rather different case from a case of taking an inadequate security, or
wrongly advising the taking of a security or the release of a security. It is *Simple Simon
Catering Ltd v Binstock Miller & Co* (1973) 228 EG 527. That was a claim for negligence
against a firm of solicitors by two plaintiffs who had employed a solicitor to take an
underlease of some premises in London for use as a restaurant at a rent of £30 a week, in
d addition to which they were prepared to pay the landlords £20 a week over 4½ years for
the hire purchase of certain equipment. The solicitors failed to carry out their
instructions, negligently as it was found, first of all in that they got for the plaintiffs a
lease at a rent not of £30 a week but of £50 a week and, secondly, that they got a lease
containing the unusual provision that the landlords should have the right to use the
kitchen of the restaurant when they so required, a most unusual and, one would think,
e damaging addition to the ordinary terms of the lease.

This court decided, Megaw and Scarman LJJ agreeing with Lord Denning MR, that
the plaintiffs had suffered a loss, and as I read it a loss of actual damage by entering into
this lease at a rent of £50 a week instead of £30 a week, with a clause giving the landlords
a right to use the kitchen which diminished the value of the lease to them. In giving
judgment Lord Denning MR said:

f   'Applying the principle in those cases [he referred to *Ford v White & Co* [1964] 2
All ER 755, [1964] 1 WLR 885 and *Philips v Ward* [1956] 1 All ER 874, [1956] 1
WLR 471], I think the measure of damage is to be found by ascertaining what
would be the value of a lease which the landlords would have presented to the
tenants (if the tenants had been properly advised) and the value of this lease as it is
(the tenants having been negligently advised). If the solicitors had given proper
g   advice to the tenants, they would have got the *exclusive* right to the kitchen. As it
is, they have only the right to a *shared* use. The difference is substantial and not
nominal. It is not capable of precise assessment but must be done as a matter of
estimate. I think the case should be remitted for reassessment on the issue of
damages in respect of that one item. I would allow the appeal accordingly.'

h Damages had been assessed for the previous item.

From what appears from the facts the plaintiffs in that case had not actually lost
anything in expenditure. It is true that they were paying £20 a week more rent as a
result of the negligence of the solicitors than the rent which they had instructed the
solicitors to get the underleases for but they were still liable to pay the £50 which the
solicitor had made them liable to pay as rent, partly as rent of £30 and partly as hire
i purchase charges of £20, because it seems difficult to believe that the 4½ years during
which they were hiring the equipment could have expired at the time when they
entered into the lease. Equally there was no evidence that the landlord exercised his
right to use the kitchen; indeed there were great difficulties in his exercising his right.
He needed perhaps the creation of a right of way and there were various physical
obstacles to the landlord making use of this kitchen on the ground floor which had been

underlet to the plaintiffs. Nevertheless the judge, upheld by the Court of Appeal, gave the plaintiffs judgment for damages being, as it were, stuck with a lease at a rent of £50 *a* a week instead of a lease at £30 at week, and one which contained this damaging provision.

There again, the case is not exactly parallel to this, but it seems to me that it does support counsel for the defendants' submission because there is a decision assessing damages or requiring damages to be assessed against a solicitor for his negligence at a date when no actual loss of the kind which counsel for the plaintiff submits is necessary had *b* occurred.

Although there is no more direct authority than those cases among those which have been cited to us, I would accept counsel for the defendants' statement of the law and would conclude that, on the facts of this case, the plaintiff has suffered actual damage through the negligence of her solicitors by entering into the mortgage deed, the effect of which has been to incumber her interest in her freehold estate with this legal charge and *c* subject her to a liability which may, according to matters completely outside her control, mature into financial loss, as indeed it did. It seems to me that the plaintiff did suffer actual damage in those ways, and subject to that liability and with that incumbrance on the mortgage property was then entitled to claim damages (not, I would think, an indemnity and probably not a declaration) for the alleged negligence of the solicitor which she alleges caused her that damage. In those circumstances her cause of action was *d* complete on 8 February 1973 and the writ which she issued on 25 March 1980 was issued too late to come within the six years' period of limitation.

For these reasons, differing from those of the judge, I would do what the judge did and dismiss the action. I would therefore dismiss the appeal.

DUNN LJ. I agree. The judge held that the delay in this action was inordinate and *e* inexcusable, causing prejudice to the defendants, and in my view he was right to strike out the action unless the limitation period was still running. The judge thought that this was an arguable point and he struck out the action so that the question could be decided in a second action which had been commenced by writ, without himself deciding whether the limitation period had run or not.

As the point is wholly one of law, which the judge was in as good a position to decide *f* on an application to strike out, as would have been the judge in the second action, I think that Peter Pain J should have decided it. It would have been different if contested questions of fact had arisen as to the limitation period.

Although counsel for the defendants wishes to keep the point open, the argument proceeded in this court on the basis that an action against a solicitor for negligent advice lies in tort as well as in contract, and I accept that such a claim does also lie in tort. I find *g* the reasoning of Oliver J in *Midland Bank Trust Co Ltd v Hett, Stubbs & Kemp (a firm)* [1978] 3 All ER 571, [1979] Ch 384 wholly convincing.

The cause of action in negligence requires not only carelessness by the defendant but also for damage to have been suffered by the plaintiff. So the question in this case is: when did the plaintiff suffer damage?

Under the express terms of the mortgage the plaintiff was under no liability to the *h* mortgagees for repayment of her son's overdraft and the mortgagees could not exercise their power of sale of the mortgaged property until demand had been made under the mortgage: see *Lloyds Bank Ltd v Margolis* [1954] 1 All ER 734, [1954] 1 WLR 644. But does that mean that no damage was suffered by the plaintiff until there had been a demand (as was submitted by counsel for the plaintiff)?

Speaking for myself I do not find the cases on physical and material damage very *j* helpful. This is a case of economic loss. In *Ministry of Housing and Local Government v Sharp* [1970] 1 All ER 1009 at 1026–1027, [1970] 2 QB 223 at 278 Salmon LJ said:

'It is true that in *Donoghue v Stevenson* [1932] AC 562, [1932] All ER Rep 1 it was physical injury that was to be foreseen as a result of the failure to take reasonable a care whereas in the present case it is financial loss. But this no longer matters, and it is now well established that quite apart from any contractual or fiduciary relationship, a man may owe a duty of care in what he writes or says just as much as in what he does: see *Hedley Bryne & Co Ltd v Heller & Partners Ltd* [1963] 2 All ER 575, [1964] AC 465. No doubt in our criminal law, injury to the person is or should be regarded as more serious than damage to property and punished accordingly. So far, however, as the law of negligence relating to civil actions is concerned, the existence of a duty to take reasonable care no longer depends upon whether it is

b physical injury or financial loss which can reasonably be foreseen as a result of a failure to take such care.'

I approach this case on the basis that it is sufficient that it is financial loss that should be foreseen, and I would hold that in cases of financial or economic loss the damage crystallises and the cause of action is complete at the date when the plaintiff, in reliance

c on negligent advice, acts to his detriment.

In *Sykes v Midland Bank Exor and Trustee Co Ltd* [1969] 2 All ER 1238, [1969] 2 QB 518; *on appeal* [1970] 2 All ER 471, [1971] 1 QB 113 the damage crystallised when the plaintiff, in reliance on the negligent advice, executed the lease. It may be that at that time the plaintiff had not paid any money, but it is sufficient if he has suffered some loss capable of quantification in terms of money: see *Simple Simon Catering Ltd v Binstock Miller*

d *& Co* (1973) 228 EG 527.

The principle which emerges from those cases seems to me to be in line with *Howell v Young* (1826) 5 B & C 259, [1824–34] All ER Rep 377. In that case, both Bayley and Holroyd JJ held that it made no difference 'whether the plaintiff elects to bring an action of assumpsit founded upon a breach of promise, or a special action on the case founded upon a breach of duty. The breach of promise or of duty took place as soon as the

e defendant took the insufficient security' (see 5 B & C 259 at 266, [1824–34] All ER Rep 377 at 380), and that, as Holroyd J made plain at the end of his judgment, without any proof of 'special damage'. I believe that when counsel for the plaintiff used the expression 'actual damage', he really meant 'special damage'. Similarly, when the facts of *Nocton v Lord Ashburton* [1914] AC 932, [1914–15] All ER Rep 45 are properly understood, I believe that the same principle emerges.

f In this case, as soon as she executed the mortgage the plaintiff not only became liable under its express terms but also, and more importantly, the value of the equity of redemption of her property was reduced. Before she executed the mortgage deed she owned the property free from incumbrance; thereafter she became the owner of a property subject to a mortgage. That, in my view, was a quantifiable loss and as from that date her cause of action against her solicitor was complete, because at that date she

g had suffered damage. The actual quantum of damages would, of course, depend on events between that date and the date when the damages had finally to be assessed, but the cause of action was complete when she executed the mortgage, without proof of special damage.

I would therefore hold that the cause of action accrued on 8 February 1973 and the time had expired by the date of the issue of the second writ. For these reasons and for the

h reasons given by Stephenson LJ I, too, would dismiss the appeal.

SIR DAVID CAIRNS. I agree that this appeal should be dismissed for the reasons that have been given in both the judgments that have already been delivered.

I was at one time impressed with the argument by counsel for the plaintiff founded on *Sparham-Souter v Town and Country Developments (Essex) Ltd* [1976] 2 All ER 65, [1976] 1 QB 858 and particularly on the observations of Lord Denning MR in the course of his judgment in that case (see [1976] 2 All ER 65 at 68, [1976] 1 QB 858 at 866), but on further reflection I am satisfied that the considerations which apply in the case of economic loss, as in the present proceedings, are different from those which fall to be taken into account where the negligence relied on is negligence in relation to the building of a house and the damage which is concerned is damage arising because of defects in the house.   **a**

Appeal dismissed. Leave to appeal to the House of Lords refused.

12 May. *The Appeal Committee of the House of Lords (Lord Fraser of Tullybelton, Lord Scarman and Lord Roskill) dismissed the plaintiff's petition for leave to appeal.*

     b

Solicitors: *Randall, Rose & Phillips* (for the plaintiff); *Barlow, Lyde & Gilbert* (for the defendants).

John Greenslade Esq   Barrister.

     c

Alexander v Immigration Appeal Tribunal

HOUSE OF LORDS

LORD DIPLOCK, LORD KEITH OF KINKEL, LORD ROSKILL, LORD BRANDON OF OAKBROOK AND LORD   **d**
BRIGHTMAN

17 JUNE, 8 JULY 1982

Immigration – Leave to enter – Non-patrial – Student – Requirements for entry – Applicant producing evidence of genuine intention to study in United Kingdom – Applicant unable to satisfy immigration officer of intention to leave United Kingdom on completion of course – Immigration   **e**
officer refusing leave to enter – Whether necessity to satisfy immigration officer of intention to leave country on completion of course a 'requirement' for entry – Whether applicant not satisfying 'requirements' for entry – Whether immigration officer having discretion to admit student for short period despite failure to show intention to leave country on completion of course – Statement of Immigration Rules for Control on Entry: Commonwealth Citizens (HC Paper (1972–73) no 79), paras 19, 21.   **f**

The applicant obtained an entry certificate in Sri Lanka to enter the United Kingdom as a student but on her arrival in England the certificate was found to be invalid. The applicant therefore applied to the immigration officer for leave to enter the country as a student, in order to take a three-year course in marketing. Although she satisfied the immigration officer that she had a genuine and realistic intention of studying in the   **g**
United Kingdom he refused her leave to enter, on the ground that she had not satisfied the requirements of either para 18[a] of the Statement of Immigration Rules for Control on Entry: Commonwealth Citizens, namely that she was able to meet the full cost of the course and her own maintenance during the course, or para 19[b] of those rules, namely that she was able to satisfy the immigration officer that she intended to leave the country on completion of the course. The applicant appealed to an adjudicator, who allowed the   **h**
appeal and directed that she should be admitted as a student for a short period, within the limit of her means, under para 21[c] of the immigration rules. The immigration officer appealed to the Immigration Appeal Tribunal, which held that the officer had properly refused the applicant leave to enter. The applicant applied to the Divisional Court for an order of certiorari to quash the tribunal's determination on the ground that the tribunal had erred in law in failing to take into consideration the discretion under para 21 to   **j**
admit for a short period a student who satisfied the immigration officer that he or she had a genuine and realistic intention of studying but who was unable to satisfy the

---

a   Paragraph 18 is set out at p 769 *c*, post.
b   Paragraph 19 is set out at p 769 *d* to *f*, post.
c   Paragraph 21 is set out at p 769 *g h*, post.

'requirements' for the issue of an entry certificate, including the requirement in para 19 of satisfying the immigration officer that he or she intended to leave at the end of his of her course. The Divisional Court held that, even though a student could not satisfy the immigration officer that he or she intended to leave the country on completion of a course of study, the immigration officer nevertheless had a general discretion under para 21 to admit the student for a short period within the limit of his or her means. The appeal tribunal appealed to the Court of Appeal, which reversed the decision, holding that an immigration officer had no discretion under para 21 to override the prohibition on entry of a person who did not fulfil the conditions contained in para 19. The applicant appealed to the House of Lords.

Held – The immigration rules were to be construed sensibly according to the natural meaning of the language which was employed and not with the strictness applicable to a statute or statutory instrument. Accordingly, the 'requirements of the preceding paragraphs' referred to in para 21 of the rules were not restricted to the requirements of para 18 alone but covered all the requirements in paras 18 and 19. The discretion of an immigration officer to admit a person under para 21 therefore extended to a person who did not fulfil the requirements of para 19. It followed that the appeal would be allowed (see p 767 j, p 770 d to h and p 771 a to e, post).

Decision of the Court of Appeal sub nom *R v Immigration Appeal Tribunal, ex p Alexander* [1982] 1 All ER 763 reversed.

Notes
For the entry of non-patrial students, see 4 Halsbury's Laws (4th edn) para 984.

Appeal
On 25 September 1978 the appellant, Miss Kamalawathie Alexander, was refused leave by the immigration officer to enter the United Kingdom as a student for a short period within the limit of her means, under para 21 of the Statement of Immigration Rules for Control on Entry: Commonwealth Citizens (HC Paper (1972–73) no 79). She appealed to the adjudicator who on 9 October 1978 allowed her appeal. The Secretary of State for the Home Department appealed against the decision to the respondent the Immigration Appeal Tribunal, and on 16 November 1978 the appeal was allowed. The appellant applied, with leave of the Divisional Court granted on 12 July 1979, for judicial review by way of an order of certiorari to quash the determination of the respondent. On 7 December 1980 the Divisional Court (Donaldson LJ and Forbes J) quashed the respondent's determination and remitted the matter to the respondent for reconsideration. The respondent appealed and on 28 October 1981 the Court of Appeal (Lord Denning MR and Watkins LJ, Oliver LJ dissenting) ([1982] 1 All ER 763, [1982] 1 WLR 430) allowed the appeal. The appellant appealed to the House of Lords with leave of the Appeal Committee granted on 21 January 1982. The facts are set out in the opinion of Lord Roskill.

Michael Beloff QC and *David Pannick* for the appellant.
Simon D Brown and *Stephen Aitchison* for the respondent.

Their Lordships took time for consideration.

8 July. The following opinions were delivered.

LORD DIPLOCK. My Lords, for the reasons given in the speech prepared by my noble and learned friend Lord Roskill, with which I agree, I too would allow the appeal.

LORD KEITH OF KINKEL. My Lords, I have had the benefit of reading in draft the speech to be delivered by my noble and learned friend Lord Roskill. I agree with it, and for the reasons he gives I too would allow the appeal.

LORD ROSKILL. My Lords, nearly four years ago, on 19 September 1978, the
appellant arrived at Heathrow Airport. She was, and is, a citizen of Sri Lanka, and thus
subject to immigration control under the Immigration Act 1971 and the then current
immigration rules made pursuant to s 3(2) of the 1971 Act (Statement of Immigration
Rules for Control on Entry: Commonwealth Citizens (HC Paper (1972–73) no 79). At
the time of her arrival the appellant had an entry clearance. The immigration officer
took the view that this entry clearance had been obtained by a material deception. This
conclusion has at no time been challenged in any of the subsequent proceedings. This
entry clearance was, therefore, of no avail to her at the time of her arrival, and is of no
further relevance to this appeal. The appellant then applied for leave to enter as a student
to begin a three-years' course in marketing studies. The immigration officer at Heathrow
was satisfied that the appellant had at the material time a genuine and realistic intention
of studying in this country, and that fact has never been in issue. But he was not satisfied
either that she had sufficient means available to her to meet the whole cost of her
intended course or to maintain herself, or, which is presently the important conclusion,
that she intended to leave the United Kingdom after completing her studies. The
immigration officer, being of that opinion, took the view that in those circumstances he
possessed no discretion to admit her, and accordingly he did not purport to exercise any
discretion. He, therefore, on 21 September 1978, refused the appellant leave to enter the
United Kingdom as a student.

My Lords, the question of the appellant's means is no longer relevant. The sole issue
for determination by your Lordships' House is whether, notwithstanding the
immigration officer's conclusion that he was not satisfied that she intended to leave the
United Kingdom after completing her studies, the rules accorded to him a discretion
under para 21 to admit her for 'a short period'.

My Lords, the immigration officer's decision has led to a remarkable succession of
legal proceedings during the currency of which the appellant has, your Lordships were
told by counsel, remained in this country albeit without pursuing her intended studies.
That remarkable succession of legal proceedings has resulted in a remarkable difference
of opinion on what was agreed by counsel during the hearing of this appeal to be a very
short, and your Lordships may think, simple point of construction of the last sentence of
para 21 of the rules which must, of course, be interpreted in the context of the antecedent
paras, 18, 19 and 20, and in particular, paras 18 and 19.

The succession of proceedings began with an appeal by the appellant to an
adjudicator. On 9 October 1978 the adjudicator allowed her appeal. It is not necessary
to refer to his reasons. They occupy some four closely printed pages. The immigration
officer then appealed to the Immigration Appeal Tribunal. That tribunal, on 16
November 1978, reversed the decision of the adjudicator, and allowed the immigration
officer's appeal. Their reasons for so doing also occupy some four closely printed pages.
The appellant then obtained leave, substantially out of time, to move the Divisional
Court for an order of judicial review to quash the determination of the Immigration
Appeal Tribunal. On 7 November 1980, some two years after the date of that
determination, the Divisional Court (Donaldson LJ and Forbes J) quashed that
determination and sent the matter back to the Immigration Appeal Tribunal for
reconsideration in the light of their decision that, on the facts which I have outlined, the
immigration officer on the true construction of para 21 possessed the discretion to decide
whether or not to admit the appellant 'for a short period'. They directed that the
Immigration Appeal Tribunal must consider, as they had not previously done, whether
or not that discretion should be exercised in the appellant's favour. An appeal to the
Court of Appeal was then brought against that decision. On 28 October 1981 the Court
of Appeal (Lord Denning MR, Oliver and Watkins LJJ) ([1982] 1 All ER 763, [1982] 1
WLR 430) by a majority allowed that appeal, holding that there was no such discretion
vested in the immigration officer. Oliver LJ delivered a powerful and closely reasoned
dissenting judgment, agreeing with the conclusion of the Divisional Court. On 21
January 1982 your Lordships' House gave the appellant leave to appeal against that
decision of the Court of Appeal.

My Lords, since the date on which the appellant was originally refused leave to enter,
a the rules have been changed with effect from 1 March 1980 (Statement of Changes in
Immigration Rules (HC Paper (1979–80) no 394). What were paras 18 to 21 inclusive of
the rules have become paras 21–25 inclusive of the new rules. In para 25 of the new
rules, formerly para 21 of the rules, there is a slight change in phraseology. Your
Lordships are not concerned with the new rules but it is right to record that counsel for
the respondent did not suggest that whatever was the correct answer to the true
b construction of para 21 of the rules, a different result could be arrived at on the true
construction of the new para 25.

My Lords, for ease of reference I set out paras 18, 19, 20 and 21 of the rules in their
entirety:

'*Students*

c 18. A passenger seeking entry to study in the United Kingdom should be
admitted (subject to *paragraph 12*) if he presents a current entry clearance granted
for that purpose. An entry clearance will be granted if the applicant produces
evidence which satisfies the officer to whom he applies that he has been accepted for
a course of study at a university, a college of education or further education, an
independent school or any *bona fide* private educational institution; that the course
d will occupy the whole or a substantial part of his time; and that he can meet the cost
of the course and of his own maintenance and that of any dependants during the
course.

19. An applicant is to be refused an entry clearance as a student if the officer is
not satisfied that the applicant is able, and intends, to follow a full-time course of
study and to leave the country on completion of it. In assessing the case the officer
should consider such points as whether the applicant's qualifications are adequate
e for the course he proposes to follow, and whether there is any evidence of
sponsorship by his home government or any other official body. As a general rule
an entry clearance is not to be granted unless the applicant proposes to spend not less
than 15 hours a week in organised day-time study of a single subject or of related
subjects, and is not to be granted for the taking of a correspondence course.

20. An applicant accepted for training as a nurse or midwife at a hospital should
be granted an entry clearance as a student unless there is evidence that he or she has
obtained acceptance by misrepresentation or does not intend to follow the course.
Doctors and dentists are admissible for full-time post-graduate study even though
they also intend during their stay to seek employment in training posts related to
their studies.

f 21. A passenger who holds a current entry clearance, or who can satisfy the
Immigration Officer that he fulfils all the requirements of the preceding paragraphs,
may be admitted for a period of up to 12 months, depending on the length of the
course of study and on his means, with a condition restricting his freedom to take
employment; he should be advised that he may apply to the Home Office in due
course for an extension of stay. A passenger who satisfies the Immigration Officer
that he has genuine and realistic intentions of studying in the United Kingdom but
cannot satisfy the requirements of the preceding paragraphs may be admitted for a
short period, within the limit of his means, with a prohibition on the taking of
employment, and should be advised to apply to the Home Office for further
consideration of his case.'

My Lords, reading paras 18 and 19 together it seems clear that there are five requirements
which a student seeking entry clearance must satisfy. The 'officer' (let it be noted that he
is different from the 'Immigration Officer' in para 21) will grant entry clearance if the
applicant produces evidence which satisfies him that (1) the applicant has been accepted
for a course of study at a university etc, (2) the course will occupy the whole or substantial
part of the applicant's time, (3) the applicant can meet the cost of the course and of his
own maintenance and of the maintenance of any dependants during the course, (4) the
applicant is able and intends to follow a full-time course of study, and (5) the applicant

intends to leave the country on completion of that course. Under para 21, if the
applicant holds a current entry clearance, which means that he has already satisfied the
relevant officer of the five requirements, or if he can satisfy 'the Immigration Officer'
that he fulfils all the requirements of the 'preceding paragraphs', he may be admitted for
a period of up to twelve months. It seems to me clear that the phrase 'the requirements
of the preceding paragraphs' are those five requirements specified in paras 18 and 19
which I have just enumerated. If, however, he can only satisfy the immigration officer
that—

> 'he has genuine and realistic intentions of studying in the United Kingdom [that
> plainly refers to requirement (4) above] but cannot satisfy the requirements of the
> preceding paragraphs [he] may be admitted for a short period, within the limit of
> his means, with a prohibition on the taking of employment, and should be advised
> to apply to the Home Office for further consideration of his case.'

Plainly the word 'may' in that context is permissive. But does the last phrase permit the
exercise of the discretion in favour of the applicant, if he fails to satisfy the immigration
officer that he intends to leave the country at the end of the course in question?

My Lords, Lord Denning MR thought that the crucial words in para 19 were
imperative. They required the immigration officer to refuse entry if requirement (5)
was not satisfied. Those words, he said, 'took priority' over the last words in para 21.
Watkins LJ, in agreeing with Lord Denning MR, drew a distinction between what the
learned Lord Justice called 'the requirements' of para 18 and 'the prohibitions' of para
19. But though the two paragraphs are differently worded, para 18 does not use the
word 'requirements' and para 19 does not use the word 'prohibitions'. The word
'requirements' is used in para 21 in two places, and with reference to the 'preceding
paragraphs' which as a matter of construction must, I think, include both paras 18 and
19. With all respect to the learned Lord Justice I see no justification for distinguishing
between the provision of these two paragraphs as he suggests.

My Lords, the construction which found favour with both Lord Denning MR and
Watkins LJ demands the restriction of the phrase 'all the requirements of the preceding
paragraphs' in para 21, to the requirements of para 18 only. With respect I am unable so
to read the relevant part of para 21. These rules are not to be construed with all the
strictness applicable to the construction of a statute or a statutory instrument. They must
be construed sensibly according to the natural meaning of the language which is
employed. The rules gives guidance to the various officers concerned and contain
statements of general policy regarding the operation of the relevant immigration
legislation.

My Lords, I have found the reasoning of Donaldson LJ in the Divisional Court and of
Oliver LJ in the Court of Appeal convincing, for like them I can see no justification for
cutting down what I would regard as the natural meaning of the last sentence of para
21. A student who has not got a prior entry clearance can properly, in an appropriate
case, if the immigration officer thinks fit, be admitted for a short period to get his affairs
in order and then satisfy those of the requirements which in the opinion of the
immigration officer he has not previously satisfied on arrival, leaving it to him in due
course, when he is in a position to do so, to apply to the Home Office. Counsel for the
respondent argued that because para 21 required that the student must satisfy the
immigration officer of his genuine and realistic intention of studying in the United
Kingdom before any question of the exercise of any discretion could arise, there should
as it were be treated as 'built in' to that mandatory requirement a further mandatory
requirement that the student should also be able to satisfy the immigration officer of his
intention to leave the United Kingdom on completion of the course. My Lords, I can
only say, with respect, that I cannot extract that meaning from the language of para 21.
He also prayed in aid what he called the complementary requirement regarding students
in the rules for control after their entry (Statement of Immigration Rules for Control
after Entry: Commonwealth Citizens, HC Paper (1972–73) no 80) and in particular para

12 of those rules. My Lords, I am afraid that I cannot find anything in para 12 of those
a rules which would assist in the construction of the rules with which your Lordships are
concerned.

My Lords, the word 'requirements' must clearly be given the same meaning in both
places where that word is used in para 21. Giving it the same meaning in both places it
seems to me clear that the word refers to all the requirements of both paras 18 and 19
once the immigration officer is satisfied of the student's genuine and realistic intention
b of studying in the United Kingdom. My Lords, I might have contented myself with
adopting as my own the judgment of Oliver LJ, but in deference to those who have
expressed a contrary view I have endeavoured to state my own views in my own words.
I would, therefore, allow this appeal. I would restore the order of the Divisional Court
dated 7 November 1980, quashing the determination of the Immigration Appeal
Tribunal dated 16 November 1978, and remitting the matter to that tribunal for
c reconsideration in the light of the decision of your Lordships' House that the discretion
in question exists and must now be exercised by them. How the discretion is to be
exercised is entirely a matter for them.

LORD BRANDON OF OAKBROOK. My Lords, I have had the advantage of
reading in draft the speech prepared by my noble and learned friend Lord Roskill. I
d agree with it and would allow the appeal accordingly.

LORD BRIGHTMAN. My Lords, I agree with the speech prepared by my noble and
learned friend Lord Roskill, and would allow the appeal.

Appeal allowed.

Solicitors: *Seifert, Sedley & Co* (for the appellant); *Treasury Solicitor.*

Mary Rose Plummer   Barrister.

McKay and another v Essex Area Health Authority and another

COURT OF APPEAL, CIVIL DIVISION
STEPHENSON, ACKNER AND GRIFFITHS LJJ
20, 21, 25 JANUARY, 19 FEBRUARY 1982

*Negligence – Duty to take care – Persons to whom duty owed – Fetus – Wrongful entry into life
– Mother contracting infection during pregnancy – Doctor failing to diagnose and treat infection
– Child born severely disabled – Child claiming damages against doctor for wrongful entry into
life – Whether doctor owing duty to fetus to terminate pregnancy in order to prevent existence
in disabled state – Whether child's claim disclosing reasonable cause of action – Whether claim
should be struck out – RSC Ord 18, r 19(1).*

*Medical practitioner – Negligence – Duty owed to fetus – Extent of duty – Mother contracting
infection during pregnancy – Infection involving risk of damage to fetus – Whether doctor having
legal obligation to fetus to terminate its life to prevent existence in disabled state.*

A pregnant mother contracted rubella (German measles) in the early months of her
pregnancy. Her doctor took blood samples from her which were tested by the local
health authority, but the infection was not diagnosed and the child was born severely
disabled. In an action for negligence by the mother and child against the doctor and the
health authority, it was alleged on behalf of the child that the doctor had been negligent

in failing to treat the infection and in not advising the mother of the desirability of an abortion. The child claimed damages for, inter alia, her 'entry into a life in which her injuries [were] highly debilitating'. On the application of the defendants, the master struck out that part of the child's claim for damages for 'wrongful life' (ie being allowed to enter life damaged) under RSC Ord 18, r 19(1)ª as disclosing no reasonable cause of action. On appeal, the judge set aside the order of the master, holding that the defendants owed a duty of care to the child and that since the child's real claim was not that she had suffered damage by reason of 'wrongful entry into life' but that she had been born with deformities there was a reasonable and arguable cause of action. The defendants appealed.

Held – (1) The duty owed to an unborn child was a duty not to injure it and, on the facts, the child had not been injured by either the doctor or the health authority but by the infection contracted by the mother without any fault on their part. If the child's action were to succeed, it could only do so on the basis of a right not to be born deformed or disabled, which in the case of a child deformed or disabled before birth by nature or disease meant a right to be aborted; and, although the doctor owed a duty to the mother to advise her of the infection and its potential and serious effects and on the desirability of an abortion in those circumstances, it did not follow that the doctor was under a legal obligation to the fetus to terminate its life or that a fetus had a legal right to die. Such a claim for 'wrongful life' would be contrary to public policy as a violation of the sanctity of human life. Furthermore, it would be impossible for the court to evaluate damages by comparing the value of non-existence and the value of existence in a disabled state. Accordingly, the claim showed no reasonable cause of action (see p 774 b c, p 779 c and g to j, p 781 d to f and j to p 782 h, p 784 d e, p 787 a and f to p 788 a c d and p 790 b to h, post); Re B (a minor) (wardship: medical treatment) [1981] 1 WLR 1421 considered.

(2) (Griffiths LJ dissenting) Although the power to strike out a claim under RSC Ord 18, r 19(1) was discretionary, a defendant had a prima facie right to be relieved of having to meet a claim which disclosed no reasonable cause of action, and, if he could succeed in showing that the claim was bound to fail, he ought not to be denied that relief merely because he still had to meet other claims by the plaintiff, unless there were strong reasons for allowing the bad claim to go to trial. Since the child's claim showed no reasonable cause of action it should be struck out, and the appeal would accordingly be allowed (see p 778 j, p 779 a to c, p 784 d e, p 786 f and p 787 j to p 788 a, post); Drummond-Jackson v British Medical Association [1970] 1 All ER 1094 applied; Dyson v A-G [1911] 1 KB 410 distinguished.

Notes

For striking out a pleading showing no reasonable cause of action, see 36 Halsbury's Laws (4th edn) paras 73–74, and for cases on the subject, see 50 Digest (Repl) 61–65, 491–520.

For duty of care generally, see 34 Halsbury's Laws (4th edn) paras 5, 7, and for cases on the subject, see 36(1) Digest (Reissue) 17–55, 34–177.

For civil liability of medical practitioners and health authorities, see 30 Halsbury's Laws (4th edn) paras 34–40, and for cases on the subject, see 33 Digest (Repl) 525–535, 53–112.

Cases referred to in judgments

A-G of Duchy of Lancaster v London and North Western Rly Co [1892] 3 Ch 274, CA, 50 Digest (Repl) 61, 492.

B (a minor) (wardship: medical treatment), Re [1981] 1 WLR 1421, CA.

Becker v Schwartz, Park v Chessin (1978) 46 NY 2d 401, 413 NYS 2d 895.

---

a   Rule 19(1), so far as material, provides: 'The Court may at any stage of the proceedings order to be struck out or amended any pleading or the indorsement of any writ in the action, or anything in any pleading or in the indorsement, on the ground that—(a) it discloses no reasonable cause of action or defence, as the case may be ... and may order the action to be stayed or dismissed or judgment to be entered accordingly, as the case may be.'

Benham v Gambling [1941] 1 All ER 7, [1941] AC 157, HL, 36(1) Digest (Reissue) 383, 1544.
Berman v Allen (1979) 80 NJ 421, 404 A 2d 8.
Croke v Wiseman [1981] 3 All ER 852, [1982] 1 WLR 71, CA.
Curlender v Bio-Science Laboratories (1980) 106 CA 3d 811, 165 Cal 477.
Distillers Co (Biochemicals) Ltd v Thompson [1971] 1 All ER 694, [1971] AC 458, [1971] 2 WLR 441, PC.
Drummond-Jackson v British Medical Association [1970] 1 All ER 1094, [1970] 1 WLR 688, CA, 32 Digest (Reissue) 139, 969.
Dyson v A-G [1911] 1 KB 410, CA, 50 Digest (Repl) 65, 515.
Gleitman v Cosgrove (1967) 44 NJ 22, 227 A 2d 689.
Hubbuck & Sons Ltd v Wilkinson, Heywood & Clark Ltd [1899] 1 QB 86, [1895–9] All ER Rep 244, CA, 50 Digest (Reissue) 49, 381.
Metropolitan Bank Ltd v Pooley (1885) 10 App Cas 210, [1881–5] All ER Rep 949, HL, 51 Digest (Repl) 1000, 5357.
Nagle v Fielden [1966] 1 All ER 689, [1966] 2 QB 633, [1966] 2 WLR 1027, CA, 25 Digest (Reissue), 503, 4388.
Phillips v USA (1980) 508 F Supp 537.
Riches v DPP [1973] 2 All ER 935, [1973] 1 WLR 1019, CA, Digest (Cont Vol D) 1038, 520a.
Rose v Ford [1937] 3 All ER 359, [1937] AC 826, HL; rvsg [1936] 1 KB 90, CA, 36(1) Digest (Reissue) 382, 1530.
Schmidt v Secretary of State for Home Affairs [1969] 1 All ER 904, [1969] 2 Ch 149, [1969] 2 WLR 337, CA, 2 Digest (Reissue) 203, 1160.
Speck v Finegold (1979) 268 Pa Super 342, 408 A 2d 496.
Turpin v Sortini (1981) 119 CA 3d 690, 174 Cal 128.

Cases also cited

Chaplin v Hicks [1911] 2 KB 786, [1911–13] All ER Rep 224, CA.
Donoghue (or McAlister) v Stevenson [1932] AC 562, [1932] All ER Rep 1, HL.
Mediana (owners) v Comet (owners), The Mediana [1900] AC 113, [1900–3] All ER Rep 126, HL.
Rondel v Worsley [1967] 3 All ER 993, [1969] 1 AC 191, HL.
Scuriaga v Powell (1979) 123 SJ 406.
Wiseman v Borneman [1969] 3 All ER 275, [1971] AC 297, HL.

Interlocutory appeal

The first defendants, Essex Area Health Authority, appealed against the order of Lawson J made on 18 June 1981 setting aside an order of Master Bickford Smith made on 17 February 1981 granting the first defendant's application to strike out a claim against them and the second defendant, Dr Gower-Davies, for damages for 'wrongful entry into life' brought by the first plaintiff, Mary McKay, a minor suing by her uncle and next friend, Michael William Davies, on the ground that the statement of claim disclosed no reasonable cause of action. The second plaintiff, Jacinta McKay, the mother, also claimed damages for negligence against the defendants. By a respondent's notice dated 20 January 1982 the plaintiffs contended that Lawson J's decision should be affirmed on the additional grounds that the matter was not proper to be decided under RSC Ord 19, r 18 because (a) it was not a plain and obvious case, (b) the rule was not intended to take the place of demurrers, and (c) serious and prolonged investigation into areas of law were involved. The facts are set out in the judgment of Stephenson LJ.

Michael Hutchison QC and *Terence Coghlan* for the first defendants.
Roderick Adams for the second defendant.
John Willmer QC and *James Harris* for the plaintiffs.

Cur adv vult

19 February. The following judgments were read.

STEPHENSON LJ. There is before the court a claim by an infant daughter (suing by her uncle and next friend) and by her mother against a health authority and against a doctor. On 17 February 1981 Master Bickford Smith struck out part of the infant plaintiff's claim, but on 18 June 1981 Lawson J allowed her appeal and allowed all her claim to proceed, but gave leave to appeal. This court is asked by both defendants to restore the master's order.

In this case we are unanimously of the opinion that the infant plaintiff's claim for what has been called 'wrongful life' discloses no reasonable cause of action. We were all clearly of that opinion at the conclusion of the argument, and we reserved judgment in order to put into writing our reasons for allowing the appeal. In the course of doing so Griffiths LJ has come to the conclusion that, though the claims disclosed no reasonable cause of action, the judge was nevertheless right in exercising his discretion not to strike them out and that on that ground the appeal should be dismissed. I have not felt able to agree with him on that point and shall give my reasons for disagreeing with him and for allowing the appeal.

The claims arise from the fact that the child was born disabled by rubella (German measles), which infected the mother in the early months of her pregnancy. That misfortune is alleged to have been the fault of the defendants, of the authority in one respect and of the doctor in two respects.

The statement of claim has been slightly amended at the suggestion of the judge. For the purpose of these interlocutory proceedings its allegations must be assumed to be true. It reads as follows:

'1. The First Plaintiff is a little girl born in 1975 and the Second Plaintiff is her mother.

2. The First Defendant operated a laboratory which inter alia tested samples of body fluids in order to discover whether the donor of the fluid sample was suffering from Rubella ("German Measles"). At all material times the Second Plaintiff was the patient of the Second Defendant.

2A. The First Defendant and the Second Defendant owed to the First Plaintiff and to the Second Plaintiff a duty of care.

3. The First and Second Plaintiffs will contend that Rubella is an infection which is capable of giving rise to severe and irreversible damage to unborn children in the womb if it infects the mother of such an unborn child in the first four months of pregnancy. The risk of such damage is very substantial if the infection occurs in the first month and while the risk declines thereafter it is significant even in the fourth month. The progress of Rubella in the mother and unborn child may be arrested by the injection of globulins into the mother but this cannot reverse or ameliorate damage already done by Rubella to the unborn child. Once damage has actually occurred to the unborn child it is irreversible and the only method of preventing that child and its family or guardian from being burdened with those injuries in life is to abort the unborn child as provided by the Abortion Act 1967.

4. The Plaintiffs will contend that the First and Second Defendants knew or should have known of the matters set out in the preceding paragraph.

5. On or about February 1975 the Second Plaintiff by her husband conceived the First Plaintiff.

6. On or about April 1975 the Second Plaintiff attended the surgery of the Second Defendant and told him that she was pregnant and that she thought she had been in contact with Rubella. The Second Defendant took a blood sample from her with a view to its being tested for infection with Rubella.

7. That blood sample or the results of any tests which may have been performed upon it were mislaid by the First and Second Defendants. The Second Plaintiff again provided a blood sample for tests.

8. In due course the Second Plaintiff was informed by the Second Defendant that she and her unborn child had not been infected with Rubella during the pregnancy and that she need not consider an abortion of it.

9. The Second Plaintiff would at all times have been willing to undergo an abortion of the unborn child within her if she had been informed that it had been infected with Rubella and that there was a significant risk that it had suffered damage.

10. In reliance upon the advice of the Second Defendant the Second Plaintiff did not request an abortion but continued with her pregnancy. On or about 15th August the First Plaintiff was born (prematurely, for a reason unconnected with the matters complained of herein).

11. The First Plaintiff had been infected with Rubella whilst still in her mother's womb and as a result of such infection she suffered injuries while still in the womb.

PARTICULARS OF INJURIES OF THE FIRST PLAINTIFF

The First Plaintiff has suffered serious damage to her neural tissues and full particulars of the First Plaintiff's current medical condition will be served in due course upon the Defendants when it has been possible to make a reasonably full assessment.

12. The above injuries, or the extent of them, were a result of the negligence of the Second Defendant.

PARTICULARS OF NEGLIGENCE OF THE SECOND DEFENDANT UNDER THIS PARAGRAPH

The Second Defendant was negligent in that he failed to guard against or to treat the suspected infection with Rubella by an injection of globulins into the Second Plaintiff which he knew or ought to have known would combat the disease and reduce the likelihood of further damage. The Plaintiffs will aver that this should have been done when the Second Plaintiff first complained of contact with Rubella but without resiling in any way from that contention the Plaintiffs aver that the opportunity should not have been missed to administer such an injection at any later stage.

13. As a result of the negligence of the Second Defendant the First and Second Plaintiffs have been burdened with the injuries of the First Plaintiff in that the Second Defendant failed to advise the Second Plaintiff of the desirability of an abortion of the First Plaintiff.

PARTICULARS OF NEGLIGENCE OF THE SECOND DEFENDANT UNDER THIS PARAGRAPH

The Second Defendant was negligent in that he:—

(a) failed to appreciate or to pass on to the First Defendant some or all of the information provided by the Second Plaintiff;

(b) failed to elicit all relevant information from the Second Plaintiff;

(c) failed to require all appropriate tests to be performed upon the test sample provided by the Second Plaintiff;

(d) caused or permitted a test sample or the results of any tests that may have been performed thereon to become mislaid;

(e) took only two blood samples from the Second Plaintiff (one of those having been mislaid);

(f) confused the blood sample provided by the Second Plaintiff or the results of any testing that may have been done thereon with some other blood sample, sample, test results or piece of paper;

(g) failed to interpret such results of tests that may have been passed to him correctly, or at all;

(h) failed to advise the Second Plaintiff of the infection with Rubella and of the

risk that if the First Plaintiff were born into the world she would suffer from serious
and irreversible injuries;   *a*
   (i) failed to inform the Second Plaintiff of the advisability of an abortion.

14. As a result of the negligence of the First Defendant the First and Second
Plaintiffs have been burdened with the injuries of the First Plaintiff in that the First
Defendant acted negligently in respect of the testing of blood samples for Rubella
whereby the Second Plaintiff was misled as to the advisability of an abortion.   *b*

PARTICULARS OF NEGLIGENCE OF THE FIRST DEFENDANT UNDER THIS PARAGRAPH
The First Defendant was negligent in that it:—

   (i) failed to perform all the tests that may have been required by the Second
Defendant upon the blood sample of the Second Plaintiff, or to perform any of those
tests;   *c*
   (ii) failed to appreciate properly or at all any instructions or additional
information that the Second Defendant may have provided in connection with the
proposed testing;
   (iii) in so far as there was a duty upon them so to do, failed to perform all
appropriate tests or to require all relevant information whether requested or
supplied by the Second Defendant or not;   *d*
   (iv) failed to conduct any testing that may have been performed with due care;
   (v) in so far as there was a duty upon them so to do, failed to interpret the results
of any testing that may have been performed, correctly or at all;
   (vi) failed to inform the Second Defendant properly or at all of the results of any
testing that may have been performed;
   (vii) lost one of the blood samples provided by the Second Plaintiff or the results *e*
of any tests that may have been performed upon it;
   (viii) confused the blood sample provided by the Second Plaintiff with another
sample or confused the results of any testing that may have been performed on that
blood sample with the results of other tests or other pieces of information.

15. In the circumstances, the Defendants are in breach of the duties referred to *f*
in paragraph 2A hereof.
16. By reason of the foregoing, the First Plaintiff has suffered (a) under paragraph
12 hereof, personal injuries, distress, loss and damage; (b) under paragraphs 13 and
14 hereof, entry into a life in which her injuries are highly debilitating, and distress
loss and damage.
17. By reason of the foregoing, the Second Plaintiff has been burdened with a *g*
child with serious congenital disabilities and has suffered distress loss and damage.

PARTICULARS OF EXPENDITURE OF THE SECOND PLAINTIFF UPON THE FIRST PLAINTIFF
Cost of feeding and clothing the First Plaintiff—£10 each week, and continuing.
Cost of medical treatment and care, and any other expenses which would not have
been required had the First Plaintiff been born without deformities. (Full particulars *h*
of these will be delivered as and when known).

18. AND the Plaintiffs claim damages, and interest pursuant to statute.'

So each plaintiff alleges that the authority's laboratory was negligent in respect of
testing the mother's blood samples, with the result that she was misled as to the
advisability of an abortion and the child has entered life handicapped by highly *j*
debilitating injuries and the mother has been burdened with a child with serious
congenital disabilities (paras 14 and 16(b)); and each plaintiff alleges that the doctor was
negligent (1) in failing to treat the mother and notice the likelihood of further damage
to the child in her womb and (2) in failing to advise the mother of the desirability of an
abortion, with the same results to mother and child (paras 13 and 16(b)). But the child

also alleges that the doctor's negligence in failing to treat her caused her injuries (paras 12
a   and 16(a)).

What the master did, and we are asked to do, is to strike out the whole of the child's
claim (under paras 14 and 16(b)) against the authority, and the second part of her claim
(under paras 13 and 16(b)) against the doctor, leaving only the first part of her claim
(under paras 12 and 16(a)) against the doctor and the whole of the mother's claim against
both. So paras 14 and 16(b) would be struck out, and para 13 would be amended to read:

b   'As a result of the negligence of the second defendant the second plaintiff has been
        burdened with the injuries of the first plaintiff . . .'

The mother then has a cause of action against both defendants for in effect being
deprived of the opportunity of choosing to abort the damaged child. The child has a
cause of action for injury to her in her mother's womb before birth. What we have to
c   decide is whether the child has also a cause of action for being allowed to enter life
damaged, what has been called 'wrongful life', or whether that is not 'a reasonable cause
of action' and should therefore be struck out now.

It is trite law that the court can only exercise its discretion to strike out a claim under
RSC Ord 18, r 19 and its inherent jurisdiction in plain and obvious cases, and this court
will not interfere with the judge's exercise of the court's discretion in a matter in which
d   he has a discretion unless it is plainly wrong.

Lawson J, in the approved note that we have of his judgment, thought that the child's
cause of action against the authority and her second cause of action against the doctor was
'a highly reasonable and arguable cause of action'. He rejected the two basic points made
by the defendants in support of the master's order and held (1) that they owed a duty to
the child and (2) that the child's real complaint was not that 'she was born at all, wrongful
e   entry into life', but that she was 'born with deformities'. As to (1), neither counsel for the
health authority nor counsel for the doctor has disputed in this court that it is at least
arguable that a fetus has rights which the courts will recognise by imposing a duty on
others not to injure it before birth; the child's remaining claim against the doctor is a
reasonable cause of action. But, as to (2), they submit that the judge went wrong, and,
though the child would have brought no claim if she had been born without deformities,
f   the claims which the judge has allowed are, on examination, claims that the defendants
caused or allowed her to be born at all in breach of their duty to prevent her being born
and, properly understood, are claims for wrongful entry into life and therefore disclose
no arguable or reasonable cause of action.

Counsel for the plaintiffs has submitted on behalf of the child, with the aid of a
respondent's notice, that this is not a plain and obvious case, but the case which the child
g   is to be prevented from making, if her claims are struck out, is a substantial case
involving serious and prolonged investigation into areas of law; as such it cannot be
termed frivolous or vexatious, and, if it cannot, it cannot be struck out as disclosing no
reasonable cause of action; the rule is not intended to take the place of demurrer.

He supports that submission by citation from some of the well-known authorities
collected in the notes to Ord 18, r 19 in *The Supreme Court Practice 1982*, vol 1, beginning
h   with *A-G of Duchy of Lancaster v London and North Western Rly Co* [1892] 3 Ch 274, and
ending with *Drummond-Jackson v British Medical Association* [1970] 1 All ER 1094, [1970]
1 WLR 688. When I extend his line of authorities by beginning a little earlier with the
judgments in the House of Lords in *Metropolitan Bank Ltd v Pooley* (1885) 10 App Cas 210,
[1881–5] All ER Rep 949 and ending a little later with the judgments in this court in
Riches v DPP [1973] 2 All ER 935, [1973] 1 WLR 1019, I cannot accept his submission in
j   its entirety. Though the two sets of grounds now distinguished in sub-paras (a) and (b)
of r 19(1) of Ord 18, overlap and throw light on, and perhaps give colour to, each other,
they are not the same now any more than they were the same under the old 1883 rule,
Ord 25, r 4. Paragraph (1)(a), reproducing the first part of the old rule, does indeed retain
the character of demurrer, subject to one qualification, as r 19(2) demonstrates by making
evidence inadmissible, and it is the later paragraphs, sub-para (b) included, expanding the

latter part of the old rule by incorporating the old Ord 19, r 27, which go beyond
demurrer and allow affidavit evidence in support. I am content to follow the judge and   *a*
decide this appeal on the basis, favourable to counsel for the plaintiffs, that it is sub-para
(*a*) and the question whether the statement of claim discloses a reasonable cause of action
in the two disputed respects with which alone the defendants' summons to strike out is
concerned.

The defendants have to show that the case is 'obviously unsustainable': see *A-G of Duchy
of Lancaster v London and North Western Rly Co* [1892] 3 Ch 274 at 277 per Lindley LJ;   *b*
'obviously and almost incontestably bad': see *Dyson v A-G* [1911] 1 KB 410 at 419 per
Fletcher-Moulton LJ; 'one which cannot succeed', 'unarguable': see *Nagle v Feilden* [1966]
1 All ER 689 at 695, 697, [1966] 2 QB 633 at 648, 651 per Danckwerts and Salmon LJJ;
'quite unsustainable': see *Schmidt v Secretary of State for Home Affairs* [1969] 1 All ER 904
at 910, [1969] 2 Ch 149 at 171 per Lord Denning MR; 'hopeless': see *Riches v DPP* [1973]
2 All ER 935 at 942, [1973] 1 WLR 1019 at 1027 per Lawton LJ. This is all summed up   *c*
in a sentence from the judgment of Lord Pearson in *Drummond-Jackson v British Medical
Association* [1970] 1 All ER 1094 at 1101, [1970] 1 WLR 688 at 696, which Lawson J
followed in this case: '. . . the order for striking out should only be made if it becomes
plain and obvious that the claim or defence cannot succeed'. But it need not become
plain 'so that any master or judge can say *at once* that the statement of claim as it stands
is insufficient': see *Hubbuck & Sons Ltd v Wilkinson, Heywood & Clark Ltd* [1899] 1 QB 86   *d*
at 91, [1895-9] All ER Rep 244 at 247 per Lindley MR (my italics). Though this court
held in *Dyson v A-G* that the court's power to strike out a statement of claim disclosing no
reasonable cause of action was never intended to apply to an action involving a serious
investigation of ancient law and questions of general importance, and in that respect to
take the place of the old demurrer on which such questions could be fully argued and
decided (see [1911] 1 KB 410 at 414, 418 per Cozens-Hardy MR and Fletcher-Moulton   *e*
LJ), it can become plain and obvious to a master or a judge that a claim cannot succeed
after a relatively long and elaborate hearing: see *Drummond-Jackson v British Medical
Association* [1970] 1 All ER 1094 at 1101, [1970] 1 WLR 688 at 696 per Lord Pearson.
'The question whether a point is plain and obvious does not depend upon the length of
time it takes to argue. Rather the question is whether, when the point has been argued,
it has become plain and obvious that there can be but one result' (see [1970] 1 All ER   *f*
1094 at 1105, [1970] 1 WLR 688 at 700 per Sir Gordon Willmer).

Here the court is considering not 'ancient law' but a novel cause of action, for or against
which there is no authority in any reported case in the courts of the United Kingdom or
the Commonwealth. It is tempting to say that the question whether it exists is so
difficult and so important that it should be argued out at a trial and on appeal up to the
House of Lords. But it may become just as plain and obvious, after argument on the   *g*
defendants' application to strike it out, that the novel cause of action is unarguable or
unsustainable or has no chance of succeeding. I think that the judge recognised this
when he said it was not wrong of the defendants to try to strike out these claims.

Counsel for the health authority (and counsel for the doctor adopts all his submissions)
has suggested that the power of the judge (and the master) to strike out a claim as
disclosing no reasonable cause of action may not be a discretionary power and that this   *h*
court's power to set aside the judge's order does not therefore depend on its being
satisfied that he was plainly wrong. But I understood him to be content that we should
deal with the judge's order on the assumption that he made it in the exercise of a
discretionary power.

In my judgment the power is a discretionary power. The word 'may' in Ord 18,
r 19(1) does not mean 'must'. But a defendant has a prima facie right to be relieved of   *j*
having to meet a claim which discloses no reasonable cause of action, and, if he can
succeed in showing that a claim must fail, he ought not to be denied that relief simply
because he still has to meet other claims by the plaintiff or unless there are strong reasons
for allowing the bad claim to go to trial.

On this point I have anxiously considered the divergent opinions expressed by Ackner a and Griffiths LJJ in the judgments which they are about to deliver and which I have had the advantage of reading in draft. I think that the right decision must be in favour of the course which on balance does the better justice. I would accept Lord Pearson's opinion in *Drummond-Jackson v British Medical Association* that a relatively long and elaborate hearing is an unusual procedural method only to be adopted 'in special cases when it is seen to be advantageous'. And I feel the force of the considerations which lead Griffiths LJ to his conclusion that the use of this procedure gives the defendant no significant

b advantage and inflicts disadvantages on the plaintiffs. But I conclude that this is such a special case, for the reasons given by Ackner LJ, and that the weighty matters to which he refers tip the balance in favour of this procedure, although it has not been as short and summary as I hope most such cases will continue to be.

Thus the only remaining question is: has the child a reasonable cause of action in the claims the master struck out or was the judge right in regarding them as arguable?

c I have come, at the end of two days' argument, to the same answer as I felt inclined to give the question before I heard argument, namely that plainly and obviously the claims disclose no reasonable cause of action. The general importance of that decision is much restricted by the Congenital Disabilities (Civil Liability) Act 1976, and in particular s 4(5) to which counsel for the doctor called our attention. That enactment has the effect explained by Ackner LJ of depriving any child born after its passing on 22 July 1976 of

d this cause of action. Section 1(2)(b) repeats the same clause of the draft Bill annexed as an appendix to the Law Commission's Report on Injuries to Unborn Children (Law Com no 60, August 1974; Cmnd 5709), and was intended to give the child no right of action for 'wrongful life' and to import the assumption that, but for the occurrence giving rise to a disabled birth, the child would have been born normal and healthy (not that it would not have been born at all) (see pp 46–47 of the report). I reject counsel for the plaintiffs'

e submission that it did not carry out that intention, which, in my judgment, the language of the paragraph plainly expresses. But the Act went further than the draft Bill in replacing, by s 4(5), 'any law in force before its passing, whereby a person could be liable to a child in respect of disabilities with which it might be born'.

The importance of this cause of action to this child is somewhat reduced by the existence of her other claim and the mother's claims, which, if successful, will give her

f some compensation in money or in care.

However, this is the first occasion on which the courts of this country or the Commonwealth have had to consider this cause of action, and I shall give my reasons for holding that it should be struck out.

If, as is conceded, any duty is owed to an unborn child, the authority's hospital laboratory and the doctor looking after the mother during her pregnancy undoubtedly

g owed the child a duty not to injure it, and, if she had been injured as a result of lack of reasonable care and skill on their part after birth, she could have sued them (as she is suing the doctor) for damages to compensate her for the injury they had caused her in the womb. (Cf the thalidomide cases, where it was assumed that such an action might lie: eg *Distillers Co (Biochemicals) Ltd v Thompson* [1971] 1 All ER 694, [1971] AC 458.) But this child has not been injured by either defendant, but by the rubella which has infected

h the mother without fault on anybody's part. Her right not to be injured before birth by the carelessness of others has not been infringed by either defendant, any more than it would have been if she had been disabled by disease after birth. Neither defendant has broken any duty to take reasonable care not to injure her. The only right on which she can rely as having been infringed is a right not to be born deformed or disabled, which means, for a child deformed or disabled before birth by nature or disease, a right to be

j aborted or killed; or, if that last plain word is thought dangerously emotive, deprived of the opportunity to live after being delivered from the body of her mother. The only duty which either defendant can owe to the unborn child infected with disabling rubella is a duty to abort or kill her or deprive her of that opportunity.

It is said that the duty does not go as far as that, but only as far as a duty to give the mother an opportunity to choose her abortion and death. That is true as far as it goes.

The doctor's alleged negligence is in misleading the mother as to the advisability of an
abortion, failing to inform or advise her of its advisability or desirability; the laboratory's   *a*
alleged negligence is not so pleaded in terms but the negligence pleaded against them in
failing to make or interpret the tests of the mother's blood samples or to inform the
doctor of their results must, like the doctor's negligence, be a breach of their duty to give
the doctor an opportunity to advise the mother of the risks in continuing to let the fetus
live in the womb and be born alive. But the complaint of the child, as of the mother,
against the health authority, as against the doctor, is that their negligence burdened her   *b*
(and her mother) with her injuries. That is another way of saying that the defendants'
breaches of their duties resulted not just in the child's being born but in her being born
injured or, as the judge put it, with deformities. But, as the injuries or deformities were
not the result of any act or omission of the defendants, the only result for which they
were responsible was her being born. For that they were responsible because if they had
exercised due care the mother would have known that the child might be born injured   *c*
or deformed, and the plaintiffs' pleaded case is that, if the mother had known that, she
would have been willing to undergo an abortion, which must mean she would have
undergone one or she could not claim that the defendants were responsible for burdening
her with an injured child. If she would not have undergone an abortion had she known
the risk of the child being born injured, any negligence on the defendants' part could not
give either plaintiff a cause of action in respect of the child being born injured.   *d*
    I am accordingly of opinion that, though the judge was right in saying that the child's
complaint is that she was born with deformities without which she would have suffered
no damage and have no complaint, her claim against the defendants is a claim that they
were negligent in allowing her, injured as she was in the womb, to be born at all, a claim
for 'wrongful entry into life' or 'wrongful life'.
    This analysis leads inexorably on to the question: how can there be a duty to take away   *e*
life? How indeed can it be lawful? It is still the law that it is unlawful to take away the
life of a born child or of any living person after birth. But the Abortion Act 1967 has
given mothers a right to terminate the lives of their unborn children and made it lawful
for doctors to help to abort them.
    That statute (on which counsel for the plaintiffs relies) permits abortion in specified
cases of risks to the mother and the child. I need not read those provisions which are   *f*
enacted in the mother's interests, but there is one provision relevant to the interests of the
child. Section 1(1) provides:

> 'Subject to the provisions of this section, a person shall not be guilty of an offence
> under the law relating to abortion when a pregnancy is terminated by a registered
> medical practitioner if two registered medical practitioners are of the opinion,
> formed in good faith . . . (b) that there is a substantial risk that if the child were born   *g*
> it would suffer from such physical or mental abnormalities as to be seriously
> handicapped.'

    That paragraph may have been passed in the interests of the mother, the family and
the general public, but I would prefer to believe that its main purpose, if not its sole
purpose, was to benefit the unborn child; and, if and in so far as that was the intention   *h*
of the legislature, the legislature did make a notable inroad on the sanctity of human life
by recognising that it would be better for a child, born to suffer from such abnormalities
as to be seriously handicapped, not to have been born at all. That inroad, however, seems
to stop short of a child capable of being born alive, because the sanctity of the life of a
viable fetus is preserved by the enactment of s 5(1) that 'Nothing in this Act shall affect
the provisions of the Infant Life (Preservation) Act 1929 (protecting the life of the viable   *j*
foetus).'
    Another notable feature of the 1967 Act is that it does not directly impose any duty on
a medical practitioner or anyone else to terminate a pregnancy, though it relieves
conscientious objectors of a duty to participate in any treatment authorised by the Act in
all cases with one exception: see s 4 of the Act. It is, however, conceded in this case that

a a medical practitioner is under a duty to the mother to advise her of her right under the Act to have her pregnancy terminated in cases such as the present. There was, on the pleaded facts of this case, a substantial risk that if the child were born it would suffer from such physical or mental abnormalities as to be seriously handicapped. And, from what we have been told without objection of her present mental and physical condition, that risk has become tragically actual.

b There is no doubt that this child could legally have been deprived of life by the mother's undergoing an abortion with the doctor's advice and help. So the law recognises a difference between the life of a fetus and the life of those who have been born. But, because a doctor can lawfully by statute do to a fetus what he cannot lawfully do to a person who has been born, it does not follow that he is under a legal obligation to a fetus to do it and terminate its life, or that the fetus has a legal right to die.

c Like this court when it had to consider the interests of a child born with Down's syndrome in *Re B (a minor) (wardship: medical treatment)* [1981] 1 WLR 1421, I would not answer until it is necessary to do so the question whether the life of a child could be so certainly 'awful' and 'intolerable' that it would be in its best interests to end it and it might be considered that it had a right to be put to death. But that is not this case. We have no exact information about the extent of this child's serious and highly debilitating congenital injuries; the judge was told that she is partly blind and deaf, but it is not and

d could not be suggested that the quality of her life is such that she is certainly better dead, or would herself wish that she had not been born or should now die.

I am therefore compelled to hold that neither defendant was under any duty to the child to give the child's mother an opportunity to terminate the child's life. That duty may be owed to the mother, but it cannot be owed to the child.

To impose such a duty towards the child would, in my opinion, make a further inroad

e on the sanctity of human life which would be contrary to public policy. It would mean regarding the life of a handicapped child as not only less valuable than the life of a normal child, but so much less valuable that it was not worth preserving, and it would even mean that a doctor would be obliged to pay damages to a child infected with rubella before birth who was in fact born with some mercifully trivial abnormality. These are the consequences of the necessary basic assumption that a child has a right to be born

f whole or not at all, not to be born unless it can be born perfect or 'normal', whatever that may mean.

Added to that objection must be the opening of the courts to claims by children born handicapped against their mothers for not having an abortion. For the reasons given by the Royal Commission on Civil Liability and Compensation for Personal Injury (report, vol 1; Cmnd 7054–I), cited by Ackner LJ, that is, to my mind, a graver objection than the

g extra burden on doctors already open to actions for negligent treatment of a fetus, which weighed with the Law Commission.

Finally, there is the nature of the injury and damage which the court is being asked to ascertain and evaluate.

The only duty of care which courts of law can recognise and enforce are duties owed to those who can be compensated for loss by those who owe the duties, in most cases,

h including cases of personal injury, by money damages which will as far as possible put the injured party in the condition in which he or she was before being injured. The only way in which a child injured in the womb can be compensated in damages is by measuring what it has lost, which is the difference between the value of its life as a whole and healthy normal child and the value of its life as an injured child. But to make those who have not injured the child pay for that difference is to treat them as if they injured

j the child, when all they have done is not taken steps to prevent its being born injured by another cause.

The only loss for which those who have not injured the child can be held liable to compensate the child is the difference between its condition as a result of their allowing it to be born alive and injured and its condition if its embryonic life had been ended before its life in the world had begun. But how can a court of law evaluate that second

condition and so measure the loss to the child? Even if a court were competent to decide
between the conflicting views of theologians and philosophers and to assume an 'afterlife'   *a*
or non-existence as the basis for the comparison, how can a judge put a value on the one
or the other, compare either alternative with the injured child's life in this world and
determine that the child has lost anything, without the means of knowing what, if
anything, it has gained?

Judges have to pluck figures from the air in putting many imponderables into pounds
and pence. Loss of expectation of life, for instance, has been held so difficult that the   *b*
courts have been driven to fix for it a constant and arbitrary figure. Counsel for the
plaintiffs referred us to what judges have said on that topic in *Rose v Ford* [1937] 3 All ER
359, [1937] AC 826 and *Benham v Gambling* [1941] 1 All ER 7, [1941] AC 157. But, in
measuring the loss caused by shortened life, courts are dealing with a thing, human life,
of which they have some experience; here the court is being asked to deal with the
consequences of death for the dead, a thing of which it has none. And the statements of   *c*
judges on the necessity for juries to assess damages and their ability to do so in cases of
extreme difficulty do not touch the problem presented by the assessment of the claims
we are considering. To measure loss of expectation of death would require a value
judgment where a crucial factor lies altogether outside the range of human knowledge
and could only be achieved, if at all, by resorting to the personal beliefs of the judge who
has the misfortune to attempt the task. If difficulty in assessing damages is a bad reason   *d*
for refusing the task, impossibility of assessing them is a good one. A court must have
a starting point for giving damages for a breach of duty. The only means of giving a
starting point to a court asked to hold that there is the duty on a doctor or a hospital
which this child alleges is to require the court to measure injured life against uninjured
life, and that is to treat the doctor and the hospital as responsible not for the child's birth
but for its injuries. That is what in effect counsel for the plaintiffs suggests that the court   *e*
should do, tempering the injustice to the defendants by some unspecified discount. This
seems almost as desperate an expedient as an American judge's suggestion that the
measure of damages should be the 'diminished childhood' resulting from the substantial
diminution of the parents' capacity to give the child special care: see the dissenting
judgment of Handler J in *Berman v Allan* (1979) 404 A 2d 8 at 15, 19, 21. If there is no
measure of damage which is not unjustified and indeed unjust, courts of law cannot   *f*
entertain claims by a child affected with prenatal damage against those who fail to
provide its mother with the opportunity to end its damaged life, however careless and
unskilful they may have been and however liable they may be to the mother for that
negligent failure.

If a court had to decide whether it were better to enter into life maimed or halt than
not to enter it at all, it would, I think, be bound to say it was better in all cases of mental   *g*
and physical disability, except possibly those extreme cases already mentioned, of which
perhaps the recent case of *Croke v Wiseman* [1981] 3 All ER 852, [1982] 1 WLR 71 is an
example, but certainly not excepting such a case as the present. However that may be,
it is not for the courts to take such a decision by weighing life against death or to take
cognisance of a claim like this child's. I would regard it on principle as disclosing no
reasonable cause of action and would accordingly prefer the master's decision to the   *h*
judge's.

I am happy to find support for this view of the matter in the Law Commission's
Report and the Congenital Disabilities (Civil Liability) Act 1976, to which I have already
referred, and in the strong current of American authority, to which we have been
referred. Direct decisions of courts in the United States of America on the same topic are
of no more than persuasive authority but contain valuable material and with one   *j*
exception would rule out the infant plaintiff's claims in our case.

The first of the American cases is a decision of the Supreme Court of New Jersey in
1967: *Gleitman v Cosgrove* 227 A 2d 689. It was preceded by an article by G Tedeschi, 'On
Tort Liability for Wrongful Life' (1966) Israel LR 513. That article treated of earlier cases
mainly concerned with illegitimate children and of the acts of parents in producing a

child likely to be diseased, but concentrated on the impossibility of comparing the two
a alternatives of non-existence and existence with the disease. Gleitman's case has been
followed in New Jersey and in other jurisdictions of the United States of America, all but
one finally approving the decision on this point that the child has no claim for wrongful
life against medical advisers for incompetent advice about the riks of being born severely
disabled.

The facts in Gleitman's case are very like the facts of this case. The infant plaintiff was
b born handicapped as a result of the mother's 'German measles' during pregnancy. Dr
Cosgrove and another doctor, who was also a defendant, had advised the mother (though
they denied it) that the disease would have no effect on her unborn child. The doctor
agreed that, if the mother had told him of the disease, his duty as a physician required
him to inform her of the possibility of birth defects. The boy sued the doctors for his
birth defects, the mother for the effects on her emotional state caused by her son's
c condition, the father for the costs incurred in caring for him. The trial judge dismissed
the boy's complaint at the close of the plaintiff's case and the parents' complaint after all
the evidence was heard. The Supreme Court, by a majority, affirmed the judge's
decision. Proctor J, delivering the judgment of the court, held that the boy's complaint
was not actionable because the conduct complained of, even if true, did not give rise to
damages cognisable at law (see 227 A 2d 689 at 692). Both Proctor J and Weintraub CJ,
d assenting on this point, stated that the boy's complaint involved saying that he would
have been better off not to have been born at all. 'Man, who knows nothing of death or
nothingness, cannot possibly know whether that is so.' (See 227 A 2d 689 at 711.)

Between 1977 and 1981 are to be found other reported decisions on claims by
handicapped children and their parents against medical men and hospital authorities. In
the earliest of them the Appeals Court of New York upheld motions to dismiss complaints
e by children suffering from Down's syndrome (mongolism) and polycystic kidney disease:
see Becker v Schwartz, Park v Chessin (1978) 413 NYS 2d 895. Judge Jasen regarded the
complaints as failing to state 'legally cognizable causes of action' (at 901), Judge Fuchsberg
as 'not justiciable' (at 903).

These and later cases are helpfully reviewed by District Judge Blatt in dismissing
another mongol child's claim for wrongful life in a South Carolina District Court: see
f Phillips v USA (1980) 508 F Supp 537, where he points out that the decision of the Court
of Appeal in California in Curlender v Bio-Science Laboratories (1980) 165 Cal 477 is the
only case recognising such a cause of action.

I have not found in the judgment of Presiding Justice Jefferson in the Curlender case
any answer to the reasoned objections to this cause of action which are to be found in
Gleitman's case and those cases which have followed it. Indeed, counsel for the plaintiffs
g said he could not rely on the Presiding Justice's reasoning and it seems that the courts of
California may now be coming into line with the rest: see Turpin v Sortini (1981) 174 Cal
128, of which we have only a summary in West's General Digest for 1981, 5th series, vol
32.

Judicial opinion expressed in the American decisions can, I think, be summarised in
the following propositions: (1) though what gives rise to the cause of action is not just life
h but life with defects, the real cause of action is negligence in causing life; (2) negligent
advice or failure to advise is the proximate cause of the child's life (though not of its
defects); (3) a child has no right to be born as a whole, functional being (without defects);
(4) it is contrary to public policy, which is to preserve human life, to give a child a right
not to be born except as a whole, functional being, and to impose on another a
corresponding duty to prevent a child being born except without defects, that is, a duty
j to cause the death of an unborn child with defects; (5) it is impossible to measure the
damages for being born with defects because it is impossible to compare the life of a child
born with defects and non-existence as a human being; (6) accordingly, by being born
with defects a child has suffered no injury cognisable by law and if it is to have a claim
for being so born the law must be reformed by legislation.

The current of opinion has run in favour of the fourth consideration and against the

fifth consideration even to the point of dismissing it altogether. Authority for that, and
for the consideration which I have formulated, is to be found in particular in the   *a*
judgment of the Supreme Court of New Jersey given by Pashman J in *Berman v Allan*
(1979) 404 A 2d 8 at 11–13, in the judgments of Presiding Judge Cercone and Judge
Spaeth in *Speck v Finegold* (1979) 408 A 2d 496 at 508, 512 and in the judgment of District
Judge Blatt in *Phillips v USA* (1980) 508 F Supp 537 at 543, which I have already
mentioned.

There are indications, to which counsel for the plaintiffs called our attention, that   *b*
some of the judges' opinions on the sanctity of human life were influenced by the
illegality of abortion in some states; but those indications do not, in my opinion, play a
decisive part in their decisions or weaken their persuasive force in considering the right
answer to the same question in a jurisdiction where abortion has some statutory sanction.

I do not think it matters whether the injury is not an injury recognised by the law or
the damages are not damages which the law can award. Whichever way it is put, the   *c*
objection means that the cause of action is not cognisable or justiciable or 'reasonable',
and I can draw no distinction between the first two terms and the third as it is rather
artificially used in RSC Ord 18, r 19.

The defendants must be assumed to have been careless. The child suffers from serious
disabilities. If the defendants had not been careless, the child would not be suffering now
because it would not be alive. Why should the defendants not pay the child for its   *d*
suffering? The answer lies in the implications and consequences of holding that they
should. If public policy favoured the introduction of this novel cause of action, I would
not let the strict application of logic or the absence of precedent defeat it. But, as it would
be, in my judgment, against public policy for the courts to entertain claims like those
which are the subject of this appeal, I would for this reason, and for the other reasons
which I have given, allow the appeal, set aside the judge's order and restore the master's   *e*
order.

ACKNER LJ. Mary McKay was born on 15 August 1975 and is therefore 6½ years
old. Whilst in her mother's womb she was infected with rubella (German measles) and
as a result she is partly blind and deaf and is apparently disabled in other respects, the
details of which have not been provided to us. She alleges in her statement of claim that   *f*
Dr Gower-Davies, the second defendant, owed her a duty of care when she was in
utero. She claims that he was negligent in that he failed to treat the rubella infection,
after being told that it was suspected by her mother, the second plaintiff. She contends
that this can be arrested by the injection of globulins into the mother which, although
it cannot reverse or ameliorate damage already done to the unborn child, can reduce the
likelihood of further damage.   *g*

It has not been contested that, if the facts set out above are established, Mary has an
arguable cause of action against the doctor. In fact, without it being in terms conceded,
it was assumed that on those facts she would indeed recover damages.

Mrs McKay is also claiming against Dr Gower-Davies on a similar basis. Further, she
alleges that within two months of the conception of the child, she told the doctor she
thought she had been in contact with rubella. He therefore took a blood sample from   *h*
her with a view to its being tested for infection. He negligently mislaid this sample and
the further sample provided by her; alternatively he failed to interpret the results of such
tests that may have been carried out by the first defendants, the Essex Area Health
Authority. In the result, the doctor informed Mrs McKay that she and her unborn child
had not been affected by rubella during the pregnancy and that she need not consider an
abortion. Mrs McKay claims that if she had been properly advised by the doctor she   *j*
would have decided to undergo an abortion and thus Mary would never have been
born. She therefore claims damages on the basis that she has been 'burdened with a child
with serious congenital disabilities', and accordingly claims cost of medical treatment
and care and any other expense which would not have been required had the child been
born without deformities. She makes a similar claim against the Essex Area Health

Authority for their alleged negligence in failing to perform the appropriate tests on any
a samples provided to them by the doctor, in failing to inform the doctor properly or at all
of the results of the tests, and in losing or confusing the blood samples.

Again, there was no suggestion that if Mrs McKay established the facts referred to
above she would nevertheless fail to recover damages. However, in addition to the
claims referred to above, Mary seeks to add an additional claim against the doctor. Quite
apart from his alleged failure to arrest the progress of the rubella infection by a process
b of injections, she claims that the duty of care which the doctor owed her when she was
in utero involved advising her mother of the desirability of an abortion, which advice, as
previously stated, the mother alleges she would have accepted. She accordingly claims
that she has suffered damage by 'entry into a life in which her injuries are highly
debilitating, and distress, loss and damage'. She makes a similar claim, mutatis mutandis,
against the Essex Area Health Authority by reason of their alleged negligence in relation
c to their handling and testing of the samples and their failure to advise the doctor of the
results of any such tests as they may have performed.

On 17 February 1981 Master Bickford Smith struck out Mary's additional claim
against the doctor and the similar claim against the Essex Area Health Authority on the
basis that they disclosed no reasonable cause of action. On 18 June 1981 his decision was
reversed by Lawson J, who, while accepting that it was a proper case in which to apply
d under RSC Ord 18, r 19 to strike out these claims, held that the child had 'a highly
reasonable and arguable cause of action'.

In a respondent's notice counsel for the plaintiffs took the point that the application to
strike out was misconceived because a serious and prolonged investigation into an area
of law was involved and accordingly it could not be said that it was plain and obvious that
the case was unarguable. I think it is convenient to take this point first.

e I respectfully agree with the observation of Sir Gordon Willmer in *Drummond-Jackson
v British Medical Association* [1970] 1 All ER 1094 at 1105, [1970] 1 WLR 688 at 700,
where he said:

> 'The question whether a point is plain and obvious does not depend on the length
> of time it takes to argue. Rather the question is whether, when the point has been
> argued, it has become plain and obvious that there can be but one result.'

f Moreover, when one considers the following matters, the judge's view that this was a
proper case under the rules to make such an application appears to me to be wholly
justified. (1) The child's additional claim is in essence a claim based on the negligent
failure of the doctor and the health authority to prevent her birth. But for their
negligent conduct her mother would have obtained an abortion and this would have
g terminated her prenatal existence. This is a wholly novel claim, supported by no English
authority. (2) The only courts which have considered such a claim are American
courts. With one exception they have all denied the existence of such a cause of action.
The respondents do not seek to justify the reasoning in that one exceptional decision. No
prolonged legal argument was therefore available. (3) The Congenital Disabilities (Civil
Liability) Act 1976 received the royal assent on 22 July 1976. Section 1, which deals with
h civil liability to a child born disabled, was in the terms of cl 1 of a draft annexed to the
Law Commission's Report on Injuries to Unborn Children (Law Com no 60, August
1974; Cmnd 5709). It provides:

> '(1) If a child is born disabled as the result of such an occurrence before its birth
> as is mentioned in subsection (2) below, and a person (other than the child's own
> mother) is under this section answerable to the child in respect of the occurrence,
j > the child's disabilities are to be regarded as damage resulting from the wrongful act
> of that person and actionable accordingly at the suit of the child.
> (2) An occurrence to which this section applies is one which . . . (b) affected the
> mother during her pregnancy, or affected her or the child in the course of its birth,
> so that the child is born with disabilities which would not otherwise have been
> present . . .'

Subsection (2)(*b*) is so worded as to import the assumption that, but for the occurrence giving rise to a disabled birth, the child would have been born normal and healthy, not that it would not have been born at all. Thus, the object of the Law Commission that the child should have no right of action for 'wrongful life' is achieved. In para 89 of the report the commission stated that they were clear in their opinion that no cause of action should lie:

> 'Such a cause of action, if it existed, would place an almost intolerable burden on medical advisers in their socially and morally exacting role. The danger that doctors would be under subconscious pressures to advise abortions in doubtful cases through fear of an action of damages, is, we think, a real one.'

This view was adopted by the Royal Commission on Civil Liability and Compensation for Personal Injury (report vol 1; Cmnd 7054–I, para 1485). (4) Section 4(5) of the 1976 Act provides as follows:

> 'This Act applies in respect of births after (but not before) its passing, and in respect of any such birth it replaces any law in force before its passing, whereby a person could be liable to a child in respect of disabilities with which it might be born ...'

Thus, there can be no question of such a cause of action arising in respect of births after 22 July 1976. This case therefore raises no point of general public importance. It can, for all practical purposes, be considered as a 'one-off' case.

The complaint that the application to strike out inevitably involves delay in the trial of those claims which are accepted as being arguable is of no real moment in this case. We have been told that it is not yet possible properly to assess the child's injuries and it appears to be common ground that liability cannot conveniently be tried separately. Although the determination of the question whether the child's additional claims are plainly unarguable will, if decided in favour of the doctor and the health authority, not dispose of the action, it will clearly simplify it and probably add to the prospects of its settlement. Although the interlocutory application and appeals have involved expense, if the application is successful it will reduce the expense of the trial. Moreover, in my judgment, a defendant, and likewise a plaintiff, is prima facie entitled to have pruned out of a statement of claim, equally a defence, such dead wood as he can clearly identify, so that the parties, and indeed the court, may more readily focus on the live issues.

Reasonable cause of action

I now turn to consider whether the child's additional claim discloses any reasonable cause of action.

(1) *The duty* I can consider this in relation to the claim against the doctor, since what can be said in relation to the claim made against him applies, mutatis mutandis, to the claim against the area health authority.

The duty alleged is the duty to take care in relation to the unborn child. Hence the first claim for failing to treat the suspected rubella by injection, so as to reduce the likelihood of further damage. Thus, the selfsame duty is relied on for prenatal injuries as would be relied on postnatally, if there was a failure to give proper treatment after the child had been born. The embryo, or fetus, is in a comparable position to the child and adult which it may ultimately become. However, in stark contrast to the plea that the doctor should have advanced the prospect of a healthy birth of the child, the additional plea, which is still based on the same duty of care to the unborn child, relies on a negligent failure to prevent its birth. The basis of this additional claim is that, had the doctor properly discharged his obligation of care *towards the unborn child*, he would have advised the mother 'of the desirability of an abortion' (para 13), which advice the mother would have accepted (para 9). Accordingly, the fetus's existence in utero would have been terminated. Thus, the duty of care is said to involve a duty *to the fetus*, albeit indirectly, by advice to the mother to cause its death.

I cannot accept that the common law duty of care to a person can involve, without specific legislation to achieve this end, the legal obligation to that person, whether or not in utero, to terminate his existence. Such a proposition runs wholly contrary to the concept of the sanctity of human life.

Counsel for the plaintiffs contends that, where it can be established that a child's disabilities are so severe that it can be properly stated that she would be better off dead, the duty of care involves the duty to terminate its life. He seeks to support this proposition by reference to *Re B (a minor) (wardship: medical treatment)* [1981] 1 WLR 1421. As Griffiths LJ has pointed out, this was an urgent application made to the Court of Appeal in vacation and the two judgments were extempore. I am quite satisfied that Templeman LJ was saying no more than that, conceding for the purpose of argument that where the life of a child is so bound to be full of pain and suffering that it could be contended that the court could, in the exercise of its wardship jurisdiction, refuse to sanction an operation to prolong its life, the case before it clearly was not such a case. I do not consider that *Re B* provides any support to counsel for the plaintiffs' contention.

Counsel for the plaintiffs was constrained to concede that, if his submission was correct, then a child born with a very minor disability, such as a squint, would be entitled to sue the doctor for not advising an abortion, which advice would have been accepted, given that the risk (which fortunately did not eventuate) of serious disabilities was due to some infection which the doctor should have diagnosed. This would indeed be an odd position. Moreover, he accepted that, if the duty of care to the fetus involved a duty on the doctor, albeit indirectly, to prevent its birth, the child would have a cause of action against its mother who had unreasonably refused to have an abortion. Apart from the complicated religious and philosophical points that such an action would raise, the social implications in the potential disruption of family life and bitterness which it would cause between parent and child led the Royal Commission to conclude that such a right of action would be against public policy (see Cmnd 7054–I, para 1465).

Of course, the doctor, in accordance with his duty of care *to the mother*, owes her a duty to advise her of the rubella infection and its potential serious and irreversible effects and on the advisability of an abortion, such an operation having in such circumstances been legalised by the Abortion Act 1967. This is, however, nihil ad rem.

(2) *The injury and the damages* The disabilities were caused by the rubella and not by the doctor (I ignore whether their extent could have been reduced through injections, because that is the subject of the infant's first claim). What then are her injuries, which the doctor's negligence has caused? The answer must be that there are none in any accepted sense. Her complaint is that she was allowed to be born at all, given the existence of her prenatal injuries. How then are her damages to be assessed? Not by awarding compensation for her pain, suffering and loss of amenities attributable to the disabilities, since these were already in existence before the doctor was consulted. She cannot say that, but for his negligence, she would have been born without her disabilities. What the doctor is blamed for is causing or permitting her to be born at all. Thus, the compensation must be based on a comparison between the value of non-existence (the doctor's alleged negligence having deprived her of this) and the value of her existence in a disabled state.

But how can a court begin to evaluate non-existence, 'The undiscover'd country from whose bourn No traveller returns'? No comparison is possible and therefore no damage can be established which a court could recognise. This goes to the root of the whole cause of action.

Counsel for the plaintiffs has provided no answer to the damage problem. His suggestion that you assess the compensation on the basis that the doctor had caused the disabilities and then you make some discount on a basis which he could not particularise because the doctor did not cause the disabilities does not, in my judgment, advance the matter, except to tend to confirm the impossibility of making such an assessment.

For the above reasons, which are reflected in one or more of the American decisions to which Stephenson LJ has referred, I conclude that the child's additional claims against the doctor and the area health authority are clearly unsustainable and therefore have no chance of success.

Accordingly I would allow the appeal and restore the order of Master Bickford Smith.

GRIFFITHS LJ. In this action the plaintiffs, for the first time in our courts, seek to bring a claim for what the Americans call 'wrongful life'. The defendants say that there is no such cause of action, and seek to strike it out of the plaintiffs' pleading pursuant to RSC Ord 18, r 19. If they succeed it will not put an end to the action because the statement of claim makes other claims which it is conceded disclose at least arguable causes of action. The plaintiffs resist the defendants' application on the ground that the claim for 'wrongful life' raises at least an arguable cause of action and the discretion to strike out should only be exercised in plain and obvious cases which can be decided without serious and prolonged investigation of the law, and this, say the plaintiffs, is not such a case. Furthermore, the plaintiffs rely strongly on the fact that, even if this cause of action is struck out, it will not put an end to the action and say that this is a factor which should weigh heavily in the balance against exercising the discretion to strike out.

After two days of argument I have come to the firm conclusion that our law cannot recognise a claim for 'wrongful life'; nevertheless I should not have been prepared to interfere with the judge's discretion to refuse to strike out the claim as disclosing no reasonable cause of action. By deciding this question as a preliminary point, the trial of the action, which involves investigation of facts occurring as long ago as 1975, has inevitably been substantially delayed, which is highly undesirable, and it may be delayed further if this case goes to the House of Lords. I do not accept the argument that the plaintiffs brought that result on themselves by putting forward an unsustainable claim. Although at the end of the day this court has unanimously decided that there is no claim for 'wrongful life', Lawson J (without of course having heard the full argument) thought the matter highly arguable, and it was my view manifestly reasonable to put the claim forward on behalf of this grievously disabled child. I cannot see that deciding this issue at this stage brings any real advantage to the defendants. It was suggested that it might make settlement easier if the parties knew that the child had no claim against the hospital. This is pure speculation; we have no idea if the hospital has any thought of settlement, and if it really wanted to settle I do not believe the possibility that the child might have a claim as well as the mother would present any real obstacle to a settlement; obviously any lawyer acting for the child would make a very heavy discount against the risk that the court would refuse to allow a claim for 'wrongful life'.

The older authorities cited by counsel for the plaintiffs, *A-G of Duchy of Lancaster v London and North Western Rly Co* [1892] 3 Ch 274, *Hubbuck & Sons Ltd v Wilkinson, Heywood & Clark Ltd* [1899] 1 QB 86, [1895–9] All ER Rep 244 and *Dyson v A-G* [1911] 1 KB 410, show that, if this application to strike out had been made at the time when those authorities were decided, the court would have unhesitatingly refused it on the ground that it involved a serious investigation into a question of law quite unsuited to be decided by a judge sitting in chambers. But times change, and the pressure on the courts caused by the advent of legal aid, union support for many plaintiffs and insurers acting for many defendants is vastly greater than at the turn of the century. The courts must and do adapt their procedures to cope with these new pressures. Today many matters are decided in chambers which involve substantial legal argument, where it is of advantage to the litigants. Sometimes I think it is carried too far, particularly where applications for judgment under RSC Ord 14 lead to special appointments and hearings lasting several days and the consideration of a mass of documentary evidence. Judges should generally resist the temptation to embark on such an inquiry and let the matter proceed to trial.

Today, in an appropriate case, the mere fact that a substantial and not frivolous argument can be presented to support a novel cause of action is not of itself sufficient to require a judge to exercise his discretion in favour of refusing to strike out, and in an appropriate case if at the end of the argument the judge comes to the conclusion that it is plain and obvious that the claim cannot succeed he should strike it out: see *Drummond-Jackson v British Medical Association* [1970] 1 All ER 1094, [1970] 1 WLR 688.

It was however stressed by Lord Pearson in that case that, although there was a

discretion to hold a long and elaborate hearing to determine the point in special cases
where it could be seen to be advantageous, there should be no change in the general
practice of only striking out where the answer was so plain and obvious that it could be
determined at a short and summary hearing (see [1970] 1 All ER 1094 at 1101, [1970] 1
WLR 688 at 696).

If on an application to strike out as disclosing no cause of action a judge realises that he
cannot brush aside the argument, and can only decide the question after a prolonged and
serious legal argument, he should refuse to embark on that argument and should dismiss
the application unless there is a real benefit to the parties in determining the point at that
stage. For example, where striking out the cause of action will put an end to the
litigation a judge may well be disposed to embark on a substantial hearing because of the
possibility of finally disposing of the action. But even in such a case the judge must be
on his guard that the facts as they emerge at the trial may not make it easier to resolve the
legal question. In this case I can see no significant advantage in deciding whether the
child has a cause of action for wrongful life against the hospital or the doctor at this stage
of the litigation, and I can see positive disadvantages in doing so because it delays the trial
and increases costs. Therefore in my opinion this claim should not have been struck out
under Ord 18, r 19, and the question should have been left to be resolved at the trial of
the action.

I realise of course the temptation of saying: well, this point has now been argued
before a master, a High Court judge, and very ably before the Court of Appeal, and it
really would be ridiculous to send it back to be argued all over again before another High
Court judge and then before another division of the Court of Appeal; especially when it
is a one-off point because claims for 'wrongful life' in all cases subsequent to the
Congenital Disabilities (Civil Liability) Act 1976 are excluded by the wording of s 1(2)(b)
of that Act. Despite the force of these considerations, I would resist the temptation
because I think to allow this appeal is to fly in the face of established practice and may set
an unfortunate precedent. For these reasons I would have dismissed this appeal.

As however I am in the minority and as the point has been fully argued I must state
my opinion on whether or not our common law recognises a claim for 'wrongful life'.

The child's claim for 'wrongful life' is put against the hospital by the following steps.
(1) The hospital when analysing the mother's blood owed a duty of care to the fetus in her
womb. This point is conceded by the hospital for the purposes of this appeal. (2) The
hospital discharge that duty of care by correctly advising whether the analysis shows that
the mother has been infected. (3) In breach of that duty the hospital negligently advised
that the analysis showed that the mother was not infected. (4) That breach of duty
caused the birth of the child because, if the hospital had correctly advised that the mother
was infected, she would have decided to have an abortion. (5) As a result of being born
the child has to bear the afflictions of deafness, partial blindness and some degree of
mental retardation, which society and the law should concur in treating as something
that should not have happened to the child and for which she should be compensated by
the negligent hospital.

It can thus be seen that the child's allegation is that but for the negligence of the
hospital she would not have been born; it is a result of their wrong that she has been
born; hence the term 'wrongful life'. The claim is put in a similar manner against the
doctor.

Whether the law should give a remedy in such circumstances has been considered by
the Law Commission. They concluded that there should be no liability for wrongful life
and deliberately drafted cl 1 of the Congenital Disabilities (Civil Liability) Bill to exclude
any such liability. Parliament accepted that advice and enacted the material part of the
Congenital Disabilities (Civil Liability) Act 1976 in precisely the same language as the
Law Commission's Bill. I am unable to accept the submission of counsel for the plaintiffs
that the language of s 1 does not exclude the action for wrongful life; I have no doubt
that it achieves its objective.

We have referred to seven decisions of courts in the United States of America; all save
one of those courts have denied a remedy for wrongful life.

The remedy has been denied on a variety of different grounds. The Law Commission were of the opinion that it would impose an intolerable burden on the medical profession because of a subconscious pressure to advise abortions in doubtful cases for fear of actions *a* for damages. I do not myself find this a convincing reason for denying the action if it would otherwise lie. The decision whether or not to have an abortion must always be the mother's; the duty of the medical profession can be no more than to advise her of her right to have an abortion and of the pros and cons of doing so. If there is a risk that the child will be born deformed, that risk must be explained to the mother, but it surely cannot be asserted that the doctor owes a duty to the fetus to urge its destruction. *b* Provided the doctor gives a balanced explanation of the risks involved in continuing the pregnancy, including the risk of injury to the fetus, he cannot be expected to do more, and need have no fear of an action being brought against him.

To my mind, the most compelling reason to reject this cause of action is the intolerable and insoluble problem it would create in the assessment of damage. The basis of damages for personal injury is the comparison between the state of the plaintiff before he *c* was injured and his condition after he was injured. This is often a hard enough task in all conscience and it has an element of artificiality about it, for who can say that there is any sensible correlation between pain and money? Nevertheless, the courts have been able to produce a broad tariff that appears at the moment to be acceptable to society as doing rough justice. But the whole exercise, difficult as it is, is anchored in the first place to the condition of the plaintiff before the injury which the court can comprehend and *c* evaluate. In a claim for wrongful life how does the court begin to make an assessment? The plaintiff does not say, 'But for your negligence I would have been born uninjured'; the plaintiff says, 'But for your negligence I would never have been born.' The court then has to compare the state of the plaintiff with non-existence, of which the court can know nothing; this I regard as an impossible task. Counsel for the plaintiffs suggested that the court should assess the damages on the assumption that the plaintiff's *e* injury had been caused by the hospital, and then discount the damages because it had not been so caused. But he was quite unable, and I do not blame him, to suggest any principle on which the discount should be calculated.

Again, suppose by some happy chance the child is born with only a slight deformity, can it bring an action on the basis that it would have been killed in the womb if the mother had been told of the risk of greater deformity? Such a claim seems utterly *f* offensive; there should be rejoicing that the hospital's mistake bestowed the gift of life on the child. If such claims are rejected, on what basis could a claim be brought for a more serious injury? Only, it would seem, on the basis that the state of the child is such that it were better dead than alive. But, knowing nothing of death, who is to answer this question, and what two minds will approach the answer by the same route? I regard the question as wholly outside the competence of judicial determination. *g*

I would reject this novel cause of action because I see no way of determining which plaintiffs can claim, that is, how gravely deformed must the child be before a claim will lie? and secondly because of the impossibility of assessing the damage it has suffered.

The common law does not have the tools to fashion a remedy in these cases. If society feels that such cases are deserving of compensation, some entirely novel and arbitrary measure of damage is called for, which I agree with the American judge would be better *h* introduced by legislation than by judges striving to solve the insoluble.

Appeal allowed; order of Lawson J set aside and order of Master Bickford Smith restored. Leave to appeal to House of Lords refused.

Solicitors: *T R Dibley* (for the first defendants); *Hempsons* (for the second defendant); *Steggles, Palmer,* Benfleet (for the plaintiffs).

Sophie Craven   Barrister.

Campbell v Tameside Metropolitan Borough Council

COURT OF APPEAL, CIVIL DIVISION
LORD DENNING MR, ACKNER AND O'CONNOR LJJ
26 MARCH, 29 APRIL 1982

Discovery – Privilege – Production contrary to public interest – Confidential documents – Confidential reports by psychologists on school pupil – Teacher bringing action against education authority for personal injuries following attack by violent pupil – Teacher contending reports showed education authority had knowledge of pupil's violent disposition – Whether teacher entitled to inspect reports – Whether reports privileged on grounds of confidentiality – Whether disclosure necessary for proceedings to be fairly disposed of.

Education – Local education authority – Documents – Inspection – Reports made on pupil by education authority pursuant to statutory duties – Teacher bringing action against education authority for personal injuries following attack by violent pupil – Teacher contending reports showed education authority had knowledge of pupil's violent disposition – Whether teacher entitled to inspect reports – Whether reports privileged on grounds of confidentiality – Whether disclosure necessary for proceedings to be fairly disposed of.

The plaintiff, a schoolteacher, was attacked in school by an 11-year-old pupil. She suffered severe injuries and in consequence had to take early retirement. She sought to bring proceedings against the local education authority for personal injuries, contending that they were negligent in allowing a child of such violent disposition to attend an ordinary school. The teacher applied for preliminary discovery of certain reports by psychologists on the child made pursuant to the statutory obligations of the education authority, which, she contended, showed that they had knowledge of the violent nature of the pupil. The education authority objected to disclosure of any of the reports on the ground that such reports were highly confidential and, if they might be used in legal proceedings, the making of such reports would be inhibited. The district registrar upheld the objection, but on appeal the judge ordered discovery of the reports. The education authority appealed.

Held – (1) The proper approach of the court in cases where the disclosure of documents was resisted on the ground of public interest immunity was to weigh in the balance the public interest of the nation or the public service in non-disclosure against the public interest of justice in the production of the documents. In weighing the balance the court should consider the significance of the documents in relation to their likely effect on the decision in the case and whether their absence would result in a complete or partial denial of justice to one or other of the parties or to both, and the importance of the particular litigation to the parties and the public, and in making such an assessment it was open to the court to inspect the documents (see p 794 *e*, p 795 *h*, p 796 *a* to *c*, p 797 *e* to *h* and p 800 *a b*, post); dicta of Lord Reid, Lord Pearce and Lord Upjohn in *Conway v Rimmer* [1968] 1 All ER at 888–889, 911, 915–916, of Lord Diplock in *D v National Society for the Prevention of Cruelty to Children* [1977] 1 All ER at 594, of Lord Keith and Lord Scarman in *Burmah Oil Co Ltd v Bank of England (A-G intervening)* [1979] 3 All ER at 725, 732–733 and *Neilson v Laugharne* [1981] 1 All ER 829 applied.

(2) Although the reports were of a confidential nature it did not follow that those whose duty it was to write such reports would be inhibited by the possibility that the reports might be disclosed, nor was there any real risk that the disclosure sought would impede the carrying out of the statutory obligations of the education authority. On the other hand, it was of the greatest importance from the point of view of public policy that proceedings in court should be fairly disposed of. On inspection of the documents, it was

apparent to the court that there was a real risk of the teacher being denied justice if the documents were not disclosed. Accordingly the order for discovery would be upheld *a* and the appeal would be dismissed (see p 796 *d* to *f*, p 798 *d* to p 799 *d g* and *j* to p 800 *d*, post); dicta of Lord Salmon and Lord Fraser in *Science Research Council v Nassé* [1979] 3 All ER at 683–684, 692 applied; *Re D (infants)* [1970] 1 All ER 1088 and *D v National Society for the Prevention of Cruelty to Children* [1977] 1 All ER 589 distinguished.

Per Ackner LJ. All documents relevant to contemplated litigation, whether confidential or not, are prima facie subject to disclosure unless non-disclosure can be *b* justified on some recognised ground such as public interest. Furthermore, there is a heavy burden on the party seeking to prevent disclosure of documents to justify their non-disclosure. The fact that information has been communicated by one person to another in confidence is not, of itself, a sufficient ground for protection from disclosure in a court of law of either the nature of the information or the identity of the informant if either of those matters would assist the court to ascertain facts which are relevant to an *c* issue on which it is adjudicating; the private promise of confidentiality must yield to the general public interest that the documents ought to be disclosed in the interests of the administration of justice, unless by reason of the character of the information or the relationship of the recipient of the information to the informant a more important public interest is served by protecting the information or the identity of the informant from disclosure in court (see p 796 *g* to p 797 *a*, post); *Alfred Crompton Amusement* *d* *Machines Ltd v Customs and Excise Comrs (No 2)* [1973] 2 All ER 1169 and dictum of Lord Diplock in *D v National Society for the Prevention of Cruelty to Children* [1977] 1 All ER at 594 applied.

Notes

For withholding documents from production on the ground that disclosure would be *e* injurious to the public interest, see 13 Halsbury's Laws (4th edn) paras 86–91, and for cases on the subject, see 13 Digest (Reissue) 154–160, 1265–1301.

Cases referred to in judgments

Boys v Chaplin [1968] 1 All ER 283, [1968] 2 QB 1, [1968] 2 WLR 328, CA; *affd on other* *f* *grounds* [1969] 2 All ER 1085, [1971] AC 356, [1969] 3 WLR 322, HL, 30 Digest (Reissue) 272, 787.

Burmah Oil Co Ltd v Bank of England (A-G intervening) [1979] 3 All ER 700, [1980] AC 1090, [1979] 3 WLR 722, HL, Digest (Cont Vol E) 184, 1277a.

Burnell v British Transport Commission [1955] 3 All ER 822, [1956] 1 QB 187, [1956] 2 WLR 61, [1955] 2 Lloyd's Rep 549, CA, 22 Digest (Reissue) 513, 5215.

Conway v Rimmer [1968] 1 All ER 874, [1968] AC 910, [1968] 2 WLR 998, HL; *subsequent* *g* *proceedings* [1968] 2 All ER 304n, [1968] AC 996, [1968] 2 WLR 1535n, HL, 18 Digest (Reissue) 155, 1273.

Crompton (Alfred) Amusement Machines Ltd v Customs and Excise Comrs (No 2) [1973] 2 All ER 1169, [1974] AC 405, [1973] 3 WLR 268, HL, 18 Digest (Reissue) 102, 756.

D v National Society for the Prevention of Cruelty to Children [1977] 1 All ER 589, [1978] AC *h* 171, [1977] 2 WLR 201, HL; *rvsg* [1976] 2 All ER 993, [1978] AC 171, [1976] 3 WLR 124, CA, Digest (Cont Vol E) 185, 1301b.

D (infants), Re [1970] 1 All ER 1088, [1970] 1 WLR 599, CA, 18 Digest (Reissue) 18, 95.

Duncan v Cammell Laird & Co Ltd [1942] 1 All ER 587, [1942] AC 624, HL, 18 Digest (Reissue) 155, 1272.

Gaskin v Liverpool City Council [1980] 1 WLR 1549, CA.

Hehir v Comr of Police of the Metropolis [1982] 2 All ER 335, [1982] 1 WLR 715, CA.

Home Office v Harman [1982] 1 All ER 532, [1982] 2 WLR 338, HL.

Neilson v Laugharne [1981] 1 All ER 829, [1981] QB 736, [1981] 2 WLR 537, CA.

North Australian Territory Co Ltd v Goldsborough, Mort & Co Ltd [1893] 2 Ch 381, CA, 22 Digest (Reissue) 513, 5218.

R v City of Birmingham DC, ex p O [1982] 2 All ER 356, [1982] 1 WLR 679, CA.

a *Riddick v Thames Board Mills Ltd* [1977] 3 All 677, [1977] QB 881, [1977] 3 WLR 63, CA,
   Digest (Cont Vol E) 180, 495b.
   Rogers v Secretary of State for the Home Dept, Gaming Board for Great Britain v Rogers [1972]
   2 All ER 1057, [1973] AC 388, [1972] 3 WLR 279, 22 Digest (Reissue) 461, 4600.
   Science Research Council v Nassé, BL Cars Ltd (formerly Leyland Cars) v Vyas [1979] 3 All ER
   673, [1980] AC 1028, [1979] 3 WLR 762, HL, Digest (Cont Vol E) 186, 1301d.

b **Interlocutory appeal**
   The defendants, Tameside Metropolitan Borough Council (the education authority),
   appealed against the order of Russell J made on 28 October 1981 reversing the decision
   of Mr District Registrar Delroy made on 3 September 1981 refusing the application by
   the plaintiff, Mrs Joyce Campbell, for preliminary discovery under RSC Ord 24, r 7A(1)
   in her action against the education authority for personal injuries sustained when she was
c attacked by a schoolchild while in the employ of the education authority as a teacher.
   The plaintiff sought discovery of, inter alia, documents in the possession of the education
   authority concerning the education and psychological welfare of the child. The facts are
   set out in the judgment of Lord Denning MR.

   Richard Clegg QC and *Daniel Brennan* for the education authority.
d *Christopher Rose QC* and *L R Portnoy* for the plaintiff.

                                                                    Cur adv vult

   29 April. The following judgments were read.

   LORD DENNING MR. Joyce Campbell is a schoolteacher in her fifties. She is highly
e regarded by all. Yet whilst in the schoolroom she was violently attacked by an 11-year-
   old boy. She suffered severe injuries and has had to take early retirement in
   consequence. A solicitor has looked into her case and thinks she may have a cause of
   action against the local education authority, but he wishes to be sure of his ground before
   bringing proceedings. He wants to see the various reports about this boy, so as to know
   whether they did their duty by the teachers. So the solicitor has applied for preliminary
f discovery. That is now permitted by statute and by the rules. The solicitor's affidavit is
   in such clear terms that I quote it:

       '3. From information which has come into my possession, there seems to be
       strong grounds to believe that the said child was of violent disposition and
       propensities and that the Defendants by their servants or agents knew of such
g   disposition and propensities. The said child has been described to me as being
       known throughout the said school as a violent bully. I verily believe that a "dossier"
       on the said child was being compiled in a notebook kept specially for that purpose,
       in which a teacher or teachers kept contemporaneous notes on the behaviour of
       the said child, which notes were for the use of an educational psychologist
       or psychologist or psychiatrist. I am informed that at least one psychologist or
h   psychiatrist reported on the said child to the Defendants. I am informed that a
       special form, described as being green in colour, was completed with details of some
       of the behaviour of the said child and handed to the headmaster of the said School.
       It is further believed that a form of referral was prepared by the said headmaster for
       the use of the said psychologist or psychiatrist. In addition, I have been informed
       that a record known as the school log book will contain contemporaneous records
i   of each and every physical assault perpetuated by the said child. I am further
       instructed that it is believed that a petition was presented by parents of children
       attending the said School to the Defendants or some servant or agent of theirs,
       which said petition is said to have prayed that the said child be not permitted to
       continue to attend the said School.
       4. In addition, I am instructed that the said child is believed to have spent some

time attending a special school, at which establishment careful observations would be kept upon him, the results of which observations I verily believe will have been *a* embodied in reports presently in the possession, custody and control of the Defendants.'

The education authority object to the disclosure of any of their reports or documents relating to this boy. They have produced affidavits by the Director of Education, the acting head teacher and the deputy head teacher of a school for maladjusted children and an educational psychologist employed by the education authority. All these declare that *b* it is in the public interest that these reports and documents should not be disclosed to Mrs Campbell or her advisers. The theme running through all these affidavits is that the reports on the child are very confidential and that those who made them, if they realised that they might be used in legal proceedings, would be inhibited in making them as frankly as they should.

The district registrar in a careful and reasoned judgment upheld the education *c* authority in their objection to discovery. Russell J took a different view. He ordered discovery. Now the education authority appeal to this court.

We have many cases about children in the care of local authorities. One side or the other asks to see the reports which the children's officers have made on the children. They are always confidential. Never, I think, have we ordered them to be disclosed. They are privileged, not because of their actual contents, but because as a class they *d* should be kept confidential. We have always found that justice can be done in the individual case without compelling disclosure of these documents.

The first case was *Re D (infants)* [1970] 1 All ER 1088, [1970] 1 WLR 599, which was approved by the House of Lords in *D v National Society for the Prevention of Cruelty to Children* [1977] 1 All ER 589, [1978] AC 171. Another is *Gaskin v Liverpool City Council* [1980] 1 WLR 1549. The latest is *R v City of Birmingham DC, ex p O* [1982] 2 All ER 356, *e* [1982] 1 WLR 679. In every case our task was to hold the balance between the interests involved: on the one hand the public interest in keeping the reports confidential; on the other hand the public interest in seeing that justice is done.

Neilson v Laugharne   *f*

Counsel for the education authority relied on those cases. But in addition he relied particularly on a recent case in this court of *Neilson v Laugharne* [1981] 1 All ER 829, [1981] QB 736. That was not a child case. It was a case where a man brought an action against the Chief Constable of Lancashire alleging that some police officers had wrongfully entered his house whilst he was away. The chief constable had held an investigation under s 49 of the Police Act 1964. He claimed privilege for all the *g* statements taken for the purposes of that inquiry. This court upheld the claim. I myself said ([1981] 1 All ER 829 at 836, [1981] QB 736 at 749):

'In my opinion the statements taken in pursuance of s 49 are privileged from production in a way analogous to legal professional privilege, and child care privilege. This case bears a striking resemblance to *Gaskin's* case. It looks like a "fishing expedition".'   *h*

Hehir v Comr of Police of the Metropolis

Neilson v Laugharne was considered by the court a few weeks ago in *Hehir v Comr of Police of the Metropolis* [1982] 2 All ER 335, [1982] 1 WLR 715. The court doubted its correctness but felt it was bound by it. The plaintiff in *Hehir* was arrested for a minor *·* offence under the Vagrancy Act 1824. The charge was dismissed. He made a complaint *j* against the police officers. An inquiry was held under s 49. His complaint was disallowed. Despite its disallowance, he issued a writ against the police for false imprisonment and malicious prosecution. It was tried by judge and jury. When the plaintiff went into the box, counsel for the police wished to cross-examine him on the statement he had made to the inquiry under s 49. The trial judge ruled that he would

permit it, but adjourned the hearing for a day in order to obtain the guidance of this
a court. The appeal was heard the next day by two Lords Justices. They gave their ruling
at once, so that the trial could proceed with the jury. They held that the statement under
s 49 could not be used to cross-examine the man. They were most reluctant to come to
that decision but felt they had to do so because they were bound by *Neilson v Laugharne*
[1981] 1 All ER 829, [1981] QB 736. That ruling by two Lords Justices on an
interlocutory matter made on a single day is not binding: see *Boys v Chaplin* [1968] 1 All
b ER 283, [1968] 2 QB 1. In my opinion it should not be followed. I do not think that
Neilson v Laugharne compelled the result. This court has not referred to the line of cases
where a man has made a statement in a confidential document and then afterwards goes
into the witness box and gives evidence contrary to what he said in the confidential
document. It has always been held that he can be cross-examined on the confidential
document, in which case the whole document is to be made available: see *North Australian*
c *Territory Co Ltd v Goldsborough, Mort & Co Ltd* [1893] 2 Ch 381, *Burnell v British Transport*
Commission [1955] 3 All ER 822, [1956] 1 QB 187 (more fully in [1955] 2 Lloyd's Rep 549)
and *Alfred Crompton Amusement Machines Ltd v Customs and Excise Comrs (No 2)* [1973] 2
All ER 1169 at 1184, [1974] AC 405 at 434, in which Lord Cross said: 'No doubt it will
form part of the brief delivered to counsel for the commissioners and may help him to
probe the appellants' evidence in cross-examination.'
d   The reasoning behind it is that the maker of a confidential document can always waive
the privilege which attaches to it, or by his conduct become disentitled to it. When he
goes into the box and gives evidence which is contrary to his previous statement, then
the public interest in the administration of justice outweighs the public interest in
keeping the document confidential. He can be cross-examined to show that his evidence
in the box is not trustworthy.
e   I know that in the days of the old Crown privilege it was often said that it could not
be waived. That is still correct when the documents are in the vital category spoken of
by Lord Reid in *Conway v Rimmer* [1968] 1 All ER 874 at 880, [1968] AC 910 at 940. This
category includes all those documents which must be kept top secret because the
disclosure of them would be injurious to national defence or to diplomatic relations or
the detection of crime (as the names of informers). But not where the documents come
f within Lord Reid's lower category. This category includes those documents which are
kept confidential in order that subordinates should be frank and candid in their reports,
or for any other good reason. In those cases the privilege can be waived by the maker and
recipients of the confidential document. It was so held by Lord Cross in *Alfred Crompton*
Amusement Machines Ltd v Customs and Excise Comrs (No 2) [1973] 2 All ER 1169 at 1185,
[1974] AC 405 at 434, when he said: '. . . if any of them is in fact willing to give evidence,
g privilege in respect of any documents or information obtained from him will be waived.'
      I am still of opinion, therefore, that *Neilson v Laugharne* was correctly decided. It is
worth noticing that the House of Lords refused leave to appeal in it. I would, therefore,
stand by the principle stated therein ([1981] 1 All ER 829 at 835, [1981] QB 736 at 748):

> 'This modern development shows that, on a question of discovery, the court can
h   consider the competing public interests involved. The case is decided by the court
> holding the balance between the two sides. One of them is asserting that, in the
> interest of justice, the documents should be disclosed. The other is asserting that,
> in the public interest, they should not be disclosed. Confidentiality is often to be
> considered. So is the need for candour and frankness. So is the desirability of co-
> operation. Or any other factors which present themselves. On weighing them all
> the judge decides acccording to which side the balance comes down. Once it is
> decided that the public interest is in favour of non-disclosure, the decision is
> regarded as a precedent for later situations of the same kind. So the body of law is
> built up. As Lord Hailsham said in *D v National Society for the Prevention of Cruelty*
> *to Children* [1977] 1 All ER 589 at 605, [1978] AC 171 at 230: "The categories of
> public interest are not closed, and must alter from time to time whether by
> restriction or extension as social conditions and social legislation develop."'

Holding the balance

In holding the balance, I would add an additional factor. It applies especially to the *a* lower category spoken of by Lord Reid. In these cases the court can and should consider the *significance* of the documents in relation to the decision of the case. If they are of such significance that they may well affect the very decision of the case, then justice may require them to be disclosed. The public interest in justice being done, in the instant case, may well outweigh the public interest in keeping them confidential. But, if they are of little significance, so that they are very unlikely to affect the decision of the case, *b* then the greater public interest may be to keep them confidential. In order to assess their significance, it is open to the court itself to inspect the documents. If disclosure is necessary in the interest of justice in the instant case, the court will order their disclosure. But otherwise not. That is the basic reason why the Burmah Oil Co did not get discovery of the documents of the Bank of England. It was not necessary for fairly disposing of the matter: see *Burmah Oil Co Ltd v Bank of England (A-G intervening)* [1979] *c* 3 All ER 700 at 715–716, 721–722, 726–727, 734–735, [1980] AC 1090 at 1121–1122, 1129–1130, 1136, 1145, 1147 by Lord Salmon, Lord Edmund-Davies, Lord Keith and Lord Scarman.

Our present case

Like the judge, I have looked at the documents. I think that they may be of *d* considerable significance. They go to show whether or not the boy was of a violent disposition. They go to show whether he should have been allowed to go into this class or not. And so forth. I see no difference between this case and any other school case where a child is injured in the playground by defective equipment, or by the want of supervision by the teacher. Full discovery would be ordered there. There is no difference in principle between a child being injured and a teacher being injured. Nor indeed do *e* I see any difference between this case and the ordinary case against a hospital authority for negligence. The reports of nurses and doctors are, of course, confidential; but they must always be disclosed, subject to the safeguard that they are only for use in connection with the instant case and not for any other purpose: see *Riddick v Thames Board Mills Ltd* [1977] 3 All ER 677, [1977] QB 881 and *Home Office v Harman* [1982] 1 All ER 532, [1982] 2 WLR 338. *f*

So here, I am quite clear that these documents must be disclosed for use in this litigation. They must not, of course, be used for any other purpose.

I would, therefore, dismiss this appeal.

ACKNER LJ. Despite the apparent conflict in the able submissions addressed to us, the *g* basic principles which we must apply in the resolution of this dispute do not seem to me to be much in issue. These are:

1. The exclusion of relevant evidence always calls for clear justification. All relevant documents, whether or not confidential, are subject to disclosure unless on some recognised ground, including the public interest, their non-disclosure is permissible.

2. Since it has been accepted in this court that the documents for which the plaintiff *h* seeks discovery are relevant to the contemplated litigation, there is a heavy burden on the education authority to justify withholding them from disclosure: see in particular *Conway v Rimmer* [1968] 1 All ER 874, [1968] AC 910 and *Rogers v Secretary of State for the Home Dept, Gaming Board for Great Britain v Rogers* [1972] 2 All ER 1057 at 1060, [1973] AC 388 at 400 per Lord Reid.

3. The fact that information has been communicated by one person to another in *j* confidence is not, of itself, a sufficient ground for protection from disclosure in a court of law of either the nature of the information or the identity of the informant if either of these matters would assist the court to ascertain facts which are relevant to an issue on which it is adjudicating: see *Alfred Crompton Amusement Machines Ltd v Customs and Excise Comrs (No 2)* [1973] 2 All ER 1169 at 1184–1185, [1974] AC 405 at 433–434. The private promise of confidentiality must yield to the general public interest, that in the

administration of justice truth will out, unless by reason of the character of the
a information or the relationship of the recipient of the information to the informant a
more important public interest is served by protecting the information or identity of the
informant from disclosure in a court of law: see *D v National Society for the Prevention of
Cruelty to Children* [1977] 1 All ER 589 at 594, [1978] AC 171 at 218 per Lord Diplock.
Immunity from disclosure was permitted in that case because the House of Lords
recognised the special position of the NSPCC in the enforcement process of the provisions
b of the Children and Young Persons Act 1969, a position which the House saw as
comparable with that of a prosecuting authority in criminal proceedings. It applied the
rationale of the rule as it applies to police informers, that if their identity was liable to be
disclosed in a court of law this source of information would dry up and the police would
be hindered in their duty of detecting and preventing crime.
    4. Documents in respect of which a claim is made for immunity from disclosure
c come under a rough but accepted categorisation known as a 'class' claim or a 'contents'
claim. The distinction between them is that with a 'class' claim it is immaterial whether
the disclosure of the particular contents of particular documents would be injurious to
the public interest, the point being that it is the maintenance of the immunity of the
'class' from disclosure in litigation that is important. In the 'contents' claim, the
protection is claimed for particular 'contents' in a particular document. A claim remains
d a 'class' even though something may be known about the documents; it remains a 'class'
even if part of documents are revealed and part disclosed: see *Burmah Oil Co Ltd v Bank of
England (A-G intervening)* [1979] 3 All ER 700 at 706–707, [1980] AC 1090 at 1111 per
Lord Wilberforce.
    5. The proper approach where there is a question of public interest immunity is a
weighing, on balance, of the two public interests, that of the nation or the public service
e in non-disclosure and that of justice in the production of the documents. Both in the
'class' objection and the 'contents' objection the courts retain the residual power to
inspect and to order disclosure: see *Burmah Oil Co Ltd v Bank of England (A-G intervening)*
[1979] 3 All ER 700 at 725, 732–733, [1980] AC 1090 at 1134, 1143–1144 per Lord Keith
and Lord Scarman.
    6. A judge conducting the balancing exercise needs to know whether the documents
f in question are of much or little weight in the litigation, whether their absence will
result in a complete or partial denial of justice to one or other of the parties or perhaps to
both, and what is the importance of the particular litigation to the parties and the
public. All these are matters which should be considered if the court is to decide where
the public interest lies: see *Conway v Rimmer* [1968] 1 All ER 874 at 911, [1968] AC 910
at 987 per Lord Pearce quoted by Lord Edmund-Davies in *Burmah Oil Co Ltd v Bank of
g* *England* [1979] 3 All ER 700 at 721, [1980] AC 1090 at 1129. Lord Edmund-Davies
commented that a judge may well feel that he cannot profitably embark on such a
balancing exercise without himself seeing the disputed documents and cited in support
of that view the observations of Lord Reid and Lord Upjohn in *Conway v Rimmer* [1968]
1 All ER 874 at 888–889, 915–916, [1968] AC 910 at 953, 995.
    I now turn to the basis of the education authority's submission in this case. They
h submit that the reports by the teacher in forms SE1 and BG1 are designed to provide the
educational psychologist with all possible relevant information concerning the pupil in
order that, with the benefit of the psychologist's report, the education authority, pursuant
to their statutory obligations under the Education Acts, may make the appropriate
decision as to the education of the child. Therefore, they must contain the fullest and
frankest information and be made with the utmost candour. So must the report on form
j SE3, which is made by the educational psychologist stimulated into action by forms SE1
and BG1. Counsel for the education authority relies heavily on *Re D (infants)* [1970] 1 All
ER 1088, [1970] 1 WLR 599 and submits this is a 'class' claim. In that case the court held
that case records kept by a local authority pursuant to the Boarding-Out of Children
Regulations 1955, SI 1955/1377, were documents which the public interest required to
be withheld from disclosure in wardship proceedings. Harman LJ said ([1970] 1 All ER
1088 at 1090, [1970] 1 WLR 599 at 601):

'It is said that whether or not the county council are a party, either party or the foster parents may oblige the county council to disclose their statutory records. The *a* answer made is: first of all, that is giving discovery in a wardship case. It is quite contrary to practice. Secondly, that it is contrary to public policy, because these records must not be kept by people looking over their shoulders in case they should be attacked for some opinion which they may feel it is their duty to express. It seems to me it would be a very bad precedent, whether the county council be a party or not, that documents of this kind should be uncovered and looked through to see *b* whether in the past some opinion has not been expressed which is said to be inconsistent with the present attitude.'

I respectfully agree with the observations of Scarman LJ in his judgment in *D v National Society for the Prevention of Cruelty to Children* [1976] 2 All ER 993 at 1005–1006, [1978] AC 171 at 198. *Re D (infants)* [1970] 1 All ER 1088, [1970] 1 WLR 599 was a very *c* special case, firstly, because it was quite contrary to practice to give discovery in a wardship case, secondly, because it was thought very undesirable that in wardship proceedings even the mind of the judge should be exposed to the risk of being coloured by opinions expressed in such documents, and thirdly, because the local authority were under a statutory duty to keep the records, which could be inspected only by a person duly authorised by the Secretary of State. Accordingly, the decision turned on its special *d* facts.

Moreover, recent dicta in the House of Lords has given the candour 'doctrine' its quietus. In the words of Lord Salmon in *Science Research Council v Nassé* [1979] 3 All ER 673 at 683, [1980] AC 1028 at 1070:

'I cannot accept the proposition that those whose duty it was to write reports about a candidate and his record, suitability for promotion etc would lack in *e* candour because the reports, or some of them, might possibly sometimes see the light of day.'

The matter was put perhaps even more strongly by Lord Fraser when he said ([1979] 3 All ER 673 at 692, [1980] AC 1028 at 1081):

'The argument based on the need for candour in reporting echoes the argument *f* which was presented in *Conway v Rimmer* [1968] 1 All ER 874, [1968] AC 910 and I do not think it has any greater weight now than it had then. The objections by and on behalf of the employees other than the complainers for having their confidential reports disclosed, readily understandable as they are, do not create a public interest against disclosure. They are based on a private interest which must yield, in accordance with well-established principles, to the greater public interest that is *g* deemed to exist in ascertaining the truth in order to do justice between parties to litigation.'

There may indeed be some who might regard the occasional and rare exposure of these reports to the public gaze as a spur to greater efficiency in their production and intelligibility in their expression. I do not therefore consider that there is any real risk *h* that the disclosure sought will impede the carrying out of the statutory purpose.

I echo the words of Lord Salmon in *Science Research Council v Nassé* [1979] 3 All ER 673 at 684, [1980] AC 1028 at 1071:

'The law has always recognised that it is of the greatest importance from the point of view of public policy that proceedings in the courts or before tribunals shall be fairly disposed of. This, no doubt, is why the law has never accorded privileges *j* against discovery and inspection to confidential documents which are necessary for fairly disposing of the proceedings. What does "necessary" in this context mean? It, of course, includes the case where the party applying for an order for discovery and inspection of certain documents could not possibly succeed in the proceedings unless he obtained the order; but it is not confined to such cases. Suppose, for a example, a man had a very slim chance of success without inspection of documents, but a very strong chance of success with inspection, surely the proceedings could not be regarded as being fairly disposed of, were he to be denied inspection.'

The learned judge, who both at the Bar and on the Bench has had a very wide experience of personal injury litigation, did inspect the documents and concluded that there was a real risk of the plaintiff being the victim of a denial of justice if the documents were not disclosed. Having also inspected the documents, I agree with his

b conclusion. What the plaintiff teacher seeks to do is to establish knowledge in the education authority of the nature and propensity of the child which should have prevented them from causing him to be educated in an ordinary school. I can well imagine that in these or similar documents there may be 'sensitive' material which the education authority would not wish to have disclosed and which might have no relevance to the issues in the case, eg hearsay material concerning the behaviour or attitude of the

c parents. Such material, if it be irrelevant, can of course always be covered up. Like Oliver LJ in *Neilson v Laugharne* [1981] 1 All ER 829, [1981] QB 736, I am also unimpressed by the argument that, although this application is a meritorious one, there may be other claims where discovery could be abused and therefore it must be inhibited altogether. Such an argument could only have relevance, and in my judgment it has none in this case, if it could be shown that the production of the documents is likely to

d impede the carrying out of the public statutory purpose for which they were brought into existence.

I accordingly conclude that the learned judge in no way erred in law in ordering discovery of these documents, and I would therefore also dismiss this appeal.

O'CONNOR LJ. The plaintiff was a teacher employed by the defendant education

e authority. In December 1979 she was teaching at the Smallshaw County Junior School. On 11 December she was violently assaulted by an 11-year-old boy in the classroom and so badly injured that she was off work for seven months. She is advised that she may have a cause of action against her employers on the ground that they were negligent in permitting this boy to remain in a normal school. Her advisers knew that the boy had been referred by the head teacher to the educational psychologist for a report

f and that a report had been made. That procedure brought into existence three documents: SE1, the head teacher's request for advice; BG1, an assessment of the boy's behaviour by the teachers; and SE3, the psychologist's report and recommendations.

It is obvious that these documents are crucial to the issue whether the education authority should or should not have permitted the boy to stay in this school and whether they knew or ought to have known that he might make a violent attack on a teacher or

g pupil. The plaintiff's solicitors asked the education authority for a sight of the documents; this was refused on the grounds that they were confidential documents protected by public interest immunity. The plaintiff applied to the court under s 31 of the Administration of Justice Act 1970 and RSC Ord 24, r 7A(1) for the production of the documents. The district registrar refused the application, the judge made the order, and the education authority appeal.

h The education authority submit that the documents are of a class which the public interest requires that they be protected from discovery. The claim for immunity is supported by four affidavits from teachers and an educational psychologist, who all say that they would be inhibited from making a full and frank disclosure of their assessment as required by the three documents if there were any chance of their being seen by anyone other than those concerned with the education programme for the child for

j whose benefit the documents came into existence.

This ground for claiming immunity was founded on dicta in the Thetis case, *Duncan v Cammell Laird & Co Ltd* [1942] 1 All ER 587, [1942] AC 624, and was acted on in various cases for 30 years. Counsel for the plaintiff has submitted that what may be called the candour argument has not survived the decision of the House of Lords in *Conway v Rimmer* [1968] 1 All ER 874, [1968] AC 910: see Lord Salmon in *Science Research Council v Nassé* [1979] 3 All ER 673 at 683–684, [1980] AC 1028 at 1070. I agree with this submission.

    a

Counsel for the education authority has submitted that these are confidential documents closely analogous to those in the child care cases to which the courts have given immunity. For my part for the reasons given by Lord Denning MR and Ackner LJ I do not think that they are. It is, I think, only necessary to look at the documents in blank to come to this conclusion. Counsel for the education authority submitted that the learned judge was wrong to look at the actual documents as he was setting up a class *b* privilege rather than a contents privilege. He did not, however, object to the court seeing the blank forms. These are in printed questionnaire form, most of the information being provided by the 'tick in space' formula, even in the psychologist's report SE3. I agree that, on the authority of *Burmah Oil Co Ltd v Bank of England (A-G intervening)* [1974] 3 All ER 700, [1980] AC 1090, the judge was entitled to look at the documents, and I have done so too in order to make sure that I was not misleading myself by considering *c* the blank forms.

I am satisfied that the judge came to a correct decision. This case is quite different from the child care cases and the police informer cases.

I would dismiss this appeal.

Appeal dismissed. Leave to appeal to the House of Lords refused.

    d

Solicitors: *A W Mawer & Co*, Manchester (for the education authority); *Westbrook, Ince & Co*, Denton (for the plaintiff).

Francis Rustin   Barrister.

    e

Practice Direction

    f

FAMILY DIVISION

Practice – Family Division – Lump sum applications – Costs – Estimate of parties' costs to be made – Party and party costs and balance payable to be distinguished in non-legal aid cases.

The costs of lump sum applications are, in many cases, so high that a judge or registrar *g* needs to have an estimate of what, approximately, they will amount to on each side before he can fix the amount of the lump sum to be awarded.

In future, in cases proceeding in the Principal Registry, those representing the parties will be expected to have made an estimate of the costs on their side, distinguishing in non-legal aid cases between party and party costs and the balance payable, and to be prepared to supply it on request by the court.

    h

R L BAYNE-POWELL
13 July 1982   Senior Registrar.

a # R v West Yorkshire Coroner, ex parte Smith

QUEEN'S BENCH DIVISION
ORMROD LJ AND FORBES J
25 MARCH, 2 APRIL 1982

b *Coroner – Inquest – Jurisdiction – Death occurring abroad – Body brought to England and lying within coroner's district – Reasonable cause to suspect violent or unnatural death – Whether coroner having jurisdiction to hold inquest – Coroners Act 1877, ss 3(1), 7(1).*

Where the cause of death of a person and the death itself occur outside the jurisdiction of English courts a coroner has no jurisdiction under the Coroners Act 1887 (which consolidates earlier legislation) to hold an inquest merely because the body has been *c* brought into and is lying within the coroner's district and there is reasonable cause to suspect that the person died a violent or unnatural death, because—

(a) at common law a coroner's jurisdiction was local in character and required the cause of death and the death itself to have occurred in England and the earlier legislation was primarily concerned with adjusting the jurisdiction as between one coroner and another (see p 804 *d e* and p 805 *c*, post);

d (b) s 3(1)*a* of the 1887 Act, which requires that a coroner 'shall' hold an inquest 'whether the cause of death arose within his jurisdiction or not', although mandatory in terms, is primarily procedural and describes the circumstances in which a coroner is required to hold an inquest, and, having regard to the common law and the purpose of the earlier legislation, cannot have been intended to require a coroner to hold an inquest whenever a body is brought into the area of his jurisdiction from abroad (see p 805 *d*, *e* post); *R v Great Western Rly Co* (1842) 3 QB 333 considered.

(c) s 7(1)*b* of the 1887 Act, which deals with a coroner's jurisdiction, repeats the terms of s 1*c* of the Coroners Act 1843 (repealed) and provides that a coroner only has jurisdiction where the body of a person 'upon whose death an inquest ought to be holden' is lying within the coroner's district and there is reasonable suspicion that death *f* was caused by violence or was unnatural, and thereby makes it clear that for a coroner to have jurisdiction to hold an inquest the cause of death and the death itself must have occurred in England (see p 805 *d* to *f*, post).

Notes

For a coroner's jurisdiction, see 9 Halsbury's Laws (4th edn) paras 1011, 1013, for his duty to hold an inquest, see ibid para 1036, and for cases on the subject, see 13 Digest (Reissue) *g* 171–172, 1436–1452.

For the Coroners Act 1887, ss 3, 7, see 7 Halsbury's Statutes (3rd edn) 242, 246.

Cases referred to in judgment

Farrell v Alexander [1970] 2 All ER 721, [1977] AC 59, [1976] 3 WLR 145, HL, Digest (Cont Vol E) 382, 8375*b*.
h *Maunsell v Olins* [1975] 1 All ER 16, [1975] AC 373, [1974] 3 WLR 835, HL, Digest (Cont Vol D) 596, 8565*a*.
R v Great Western Rly Co (1842) 3 QB 333, 114 ER 533, 13 Digest (Reissue) 171, 1444.

Cases also cited

j *R v Berwick-on-Tweed Coroner* (1843) 7 JP 676.
R v Brighthelmston Guardians (1842) 3 QB 342, 114 ER 537.

---

a   Section 3(1), so far as material, is set out at p 802 *g*, post
b   Section 7(1), so far as material, provides: '. . . the coroner only within whose jurisdiction the body of a person upon whose death an inquest ought to be holden is lying shall hold the inquest.'
c   Section 1, so far as material, is set out at p 805 *b*, post

Application for judicial review

Ronald Smith applied, with the leave of Forbes J granted on 10 November 1981, for (i) *a*
an order of certiorari to bring up and quash the decision of the coroner for the Eastern
District of the Metropolitan County of West Yorkshire, Mr Philip S Gill, refusing to hold
an inquest on the body of Helen Linda Smith, the applicant's daughter, and (ii) an order
of mandamus requiring the coroner to hold an inquest on her body. The grounds on
which the relief was sought were (1) that the deceased's body lay and had lain since 18
June 1980 within the coroner's jurisdiction, (2) that evidence was and had at all material *b*
times been in the coroner's possession that the deceased died a violent death in Jeddah,
Saudi Arabia on 20 May 1979, (3) that the coroner refused to hold an inquest on the
ground that the case did not fall within his jurisdiction since the death occurred outside
the jurisdiction of the English courts and (4) that the reasons given by the coroner for
declining jurisdiction were bad in law and that the materials in his possession were such
as to require him to hold an inquest. The facts are set out in the judgment of the court. *c*

Stephen Sedley for the applicant.
Simon D Brown as amicus curiae.

Cur adv vult

d

2 April. **ORMROD LJ** read the following judgment of the court: In this case the
applicant, Mr Ronald Smith, applies for judicial review of a decision by Mr Philip S Gill,
Her Majesty's Coroner for the Eastern District of the Metropolitan County of West
Yorkshire, refusing to hold an inquest on the body of Helen Linda Smith. By way of
relief he asks for an order of certiorari to quash this decision and an order of mandamus
requiring Mr Gill to hold an inquest accordingly.   *e*

The facts which are relevant to this application are that on 20 May 1979 the applicant's
daughter, Helen Linda Smith, died a violent death in Jeddah, Saudi Arabia. On 17 June
1980 her body was brought back to England and is at present lying in the area for which
Mr Gill is, at present, the coroner. By a letter dated 3 August 1981 and sent to the
applicant, Mr Gill refused to proceed with an inquest on the ground that 'her death
occurred outside the jurisdiction of the English courts, and I am satisfied that this case *f*
does not fall within my jurisdiction for the hearing of an inquest'.

The submission of counsel on behalf of the applicant is as simple as it is succinct. He
relies on s 3(1) of the Coroners Act 1887, which is still the basic enactment governing the
jurisdiction of coroners, although it has been amended by subsequent legislation. Section
3(1), so far as material, reads:

> 'Where a coroner is informed that the dead body of a person is lying within his *g*
> jurisdiction, and there is reasonable cause to suspect that such person has died either
> a violent or an unnatural death . . . the coroner, whether the cause of death arose
> within his jurisdiction or not, shall, as soon as practicable, [hold an inquest].'

Accordingly, counsel for the applicant submits that the requirements of this subsection
are satisfied and the coroner is obliged to hold an inquest.   *h*

A little reflection suggests that this proposition is too simple. If it is right, it means
that the coroner is obliged to hold an inquest on any body which has been brought into
his area by any person, from anywhere, for any purpose, provided only that there is
reason to suspect that the death has been violent or unnatural. It follows that any person,
having no connection with this country, could bring in the body of a person having no
connection with this country, who died anywhere in the world, and demand that an *j*
inquest be held. It would also mean that, subject to any restriction on the removal of
bodies from place to place, a person might move a body from one coroner's area to
another coroner's area and demand that another inquest be held.

Such a remarkable, if not absurd, conclusion, throws doubt on the validity of the
proposition, and raises the question whether Parliament, in enacting this provision,

could have contemplated the possibility of bodies being imported into England, solely
a for the purpose of having an inquest on them. Such a possibility must have been
extremely remote in 1887, when refrigeration was in its infancy and air transport
unknown.

It goes even further for it implies that Parliament has conferred on coroners an extra-
territorial jurisdiction much wider than that of any other court or tribunal in this
country. It also raises the possibility of serious conflicts of jurisdiction between states,
b and of interference by English coroners in matters which are peculiarly the affairs of
foreign governments. Moreover, it creates the anomaly that a coroner would be required
to hold an inquest into a death where he is powerless to take any action, so that the
verdict would be a mere brutum fulmen.

These considerations show that the wide language of this section must be read subject
to some form of limitation. This has been recognised by the text writers, who have
c attempted to limit its scope by suggesting that where the death has occurred abroad the
coroner has a discretion to hold an inquest or not, depending on the circumstances of the
case. In 9 Halsbury's Laws (4th edn) para 1013, it is stated:

> '*Deaths abroad.* Where a death has occurred abroad and the body has been
> brought into England or Wales for disposal, the coroner for the district in which it
> is lying has jurisdiction. If the death appears to have been natural or to have been
> *d* properly investigated at the place where it occurred the coroner does not usually
> make further inquiry. If there seems to be good reason for inquiring into the death,
> such as suspicion of homicide, complaint by relatives or apparent failure to make
> full investigation, the coroner may assume jurisdiction.'

The learned editor of the title *Coroners* in Halsbury's Laws was the late Dr Gavin
e Thurston FRCP, and a similar view is expressed in his book *Coronership* (2nd edn, 1980)
p 39. The editor of *Jervis on Coroners* (9th edn, 1957) p 69 was of the same opinion. Both
counsel in the present case, however, are agreed that s 3(1) does not leave any room for
the exercise of discretion by the coroner. There can be no doubt that they are right; the
language of the subsection is plainly mandatory for it uses the word 'shall'. The necessary
limitation must, therefore, be sought elsewhere.

The Coroners Act 1887 is described in the short title as 'An Act to consolidate the Law
relating to Coroners'. It would, therefore, be in the highest degree unusual, though not
impossible, for Parliament, in a consolidating statute, to enlarge the jurisdiction of
coroners to the extent suggested. The rules relating to construction of consolidating
statutes were discussed in considerable detail in the speeches in the House of Lords in
Farrell v Alexander [1976] 2 All ER 721, [1977] AC 59. Lord Simon said ([1976] 2 All ER
721 at 735–736, [1977] AC 59 at 84–85):

> 'If a court of construction puts itself in the position of the draftsman, acquires his
> knowledge, recognises his statutory objectives, tunes in to his linguistic register, and
> then ascertains the primary and natural meaning in their context of the words he
> has used, that will generally be an end of the task of construction. But occasionally
> something will go wrong. It may become apparent that the primary and natural
> meaning cannot be what Parliament intended; it produces injustice, absurdity,
> anomaly or contradiction, or it stultifies or runs counter to the statutory objective.
> Or sometimes the words have no primary meaning in their context; they are fairly
> capable in all the circumstances of being taken in two senses: there is, in other
> words, an ambiguity. There are a number of secondary canons of construction
> available to resolve ambiguity; which of them is most helpful will vary from case
> to case. But in nothing of the foregoing does the construction of a consolidation Act
> differ from that of any other statute. Its only peculiarity is that if the primary
> approach to construction discloses an ambiguity in a consolidation Act, that may
> sometimes (though rarely) be resolved by examination of the superseded
> legislation. Since, as will appear, I cannot for myself see any ambiguity in s 85, I

venture merely to refer summarily to what, in a speech prepared in collaboration
with my noble and learned friend, Lord Diplock, I said in *Maunsell v Olins* [1975] 1   a
All ER 16 at 27, [1975] AC 373 at 392–393 about this exceptional use of the
superseded enactments. There is however one canon of construction relevant to the
interpretation of s 85, which is deducible from the submissions I have been making
to your Lordships. It is not peculiar to the construction of consolidation Acts,
though it is equally applicable to them. The first or "golden" rule is to ascertain the
primary and natural sense of the statutory words in their context, since it is to be   b
presumed that it is in this sense that the draftsman is using the words in order to
convey what it is that Parliament meant to say. They will only be read in some
other sense if that is necessary to obviate injustice, absurdity, anomaly or
contradiction, or to prevent impediment of the statutory objective.'

This case, for the reasons already stated, falls within the category in which it is
permissible to examine the earlier legislation and the common law rules.   c
Mr Simon Brown, who has appeared as amicus curiae, has, as always, been of the
greatest help to us. He, and those assisting him, have done considerable reasearch into
the law relating to coroners and have provided us with a valuable synopsis of the relevant
provisions from early days, and in a most convenient and time-saving form. He submits
that there is no jurisdiction in an English or Welsh coroner to hold an inquest in respect
of a death which is known to have been caused or to have occurred outside the jurisdiction   d
of our courts. There is no hint or suggestion in this material that a coroner has any form
of extra-territorial jurisdiction. On the contrary, this historical survey shows that the
coroner's jurisdiction was always exceedingly local in character and that the earlier
legislation was concerned, primarily, with adjusting the jurisdiction as between one
coroner and another. The problems seem to have arisen from two conflicting
requirements. Until quite recently a coroner could not hold an inquest without viewing   e
the body, super visum corporis, so the body had to be in his area. But in early days if the
death was caused in another area he could not take any effective action against the
assailant because of the rules governing venue in criminal cases. So Hale says (2 Hale PC
(1778 edn, p 66):

> 'And therefore in antient times, if a man were hurt in the county of A. and died   f
> in the county of B. the coroner of the county of B. could not take an inquisition of
> his death, because the stroke was not given in that county, nor could the coroner of
> the county of A. take an inquisition, because the body was in the county of B. but
> they used to remove the body into the county of A. and there the coroner of that
> county to take the inquisition.'

This problem was dealt with by a 1548 statute (2 & 3 Edw 6 c 24; criminal law), which   g
settled the matter in favour of the place of death. A 1728 Act (2 Geo 2 c 21; murder) gave
jurisdiction to the criminal courts, and by implication to the coroner, if he could view
the body, in any case of felonious killing where either the stroke, that is the cause of
death, or the death occurred in England.
The jurisdiction of the coroner was considered by the Court of Queen's Bench in *R v
Great Western Rly Co* (1842) 3 QB 333, 114 ER 533, one of the few cases in which the   h
jurisdiction of coroners has been judicially considered. The case concerned an accident
on the railway, and a deodand laid on the railway carriage by a coroner's jury for the
borough of Reading, where the body was lying (because the death had occurred in the
Royal Berkshire Hospital). The verdict of deodand was challenged for want of
jurisdiction, on the ground that the cause of death, that is the accident, had happened
outside the borough. The court upheld this contention; it was a non-criminal death, the   j
1548 Act did not apply, and so the matter was governed by common law. Lord Denman
CJ held that at common law there was no jurisdiction because the circumstances which
occasioned the death happened outside the geographical area of the Reading coroner. In
the course of his judgment he made an observation which is directly in point in the
present case. He said (3 QB 333 at 339–340, 114 ER 533 at 536):

'After these authorities, it is startling to hear it asserted broadly at the Bar that, if a mortal stroke be given in county A., and the party go to and die in county B., and the body after death be taken into county C., the coroner of county C. may hold an inquest and inquire into the whole matter, and that by the common law. No authority is cited for such assertion: and in truth there is no foundation for it.'

In consequence of this decision the Coroners Act 1843 was passed. It provided in s 1 that—

'the Coroner only within whose Jurisdiction the Body of any Person upon whose Death an Inquest ought to be holden shall be lying dead shall hold the Inquest, notwithstanding that the cause of Death did not arise within the Jurisdiction of such Coroner.'

It is clear that this Act was intended to do no more than regulate the holding of inquests as between coroners, and to enable inquests to be held where it is not known where the death occurred.

This is the only relevant statutory provision prior to the 1887 consolidating Act. Counsel for the applicant concedes that there is nothing in its provisions on which a jurisdiction to investigate deaths abroad could be founded.

Returning to s 3(1) of the Coroners Act 1887, it can now be seen that the provisions of this subsection are not related to the question of jurisdiction, but describe the circumstances in which a coroner should summon a jury and hold an inquest. In other words, it is primarily a procedural section. Jurisdiction is dealt with in s 7(1), which repeats, verbatim, the terms of s 1 of the 1843 Act, which contains the important words 'upon whose Death an Inquest ought to be holden'. These words make it clear that jurisdiction to hold an inquest requires something more than the fact that the body is lying within the geographical limits of the coroner's jurisdiction, and there is reasonable cause to suspect a violent or unnatural death. There is no warrant in any of the legislation or at common law to support the proposition that an inquest can be held where both the cause of death and the death itself occurred out of the jurisdiction of the English courts. Accordingly, Mr Gill's reason for refusing to hold an inquest in this case was right in law. The fact is that in this situation the coroner has no function in the English legal system to perform.

Counsel for the applicant referred to the provisions of s 61 of the Merchant Shipping Act 1970, as amended by the Merchant Shipping Act 1979, which refer to inquiries into the deaths in a ship registered in the United Kingdom, and to deaths abroad of seamen employed in such a ship, or of seamen who had been employed in such a ship within a year of the death, and drew attention to sub-s (4) which, as he said, appears to contemplate the possibility in such a case of an inquest by a coroner in England. It is not clear what the draftsman had in mind when he included this subsection, but it is enough to say that it cannot create jurisdiction of itself, and for reasons already given there is no provision giving the coroner jurisdiction in a case such as the present.

Some reliance was also placed on the fact that in a few cases where death occurred overseas some coroners have agreed, in their discretion, to hold inquests, largely for the benefit of relatives of the deceased. No doubt they acted on the passages in the textbooks referred to at the beginning of his judgment which state erroneously that a coroner has a discretion to hold an inquest in such circumstances. Such inquests were held without jurisdiction.

The result is that the application for judicial review must be dismissed.

Application dismissed.

Solicitors: *Bindman & Partners*, agents for *Howard Cohen & Co*, Leeds (for the applicant); *Treasury Solicitor*.

Dilys Tausz   Barrister.

Bernstein and another v Jackson and others   *a*

COURT OF APPEAL, CIVIL DIVISION
DUNN AND SLADE LJJ
19 MARCH 1982

Writ – Extension of validity – Failure to renew writ – Order for service of notice of writ – Order   *b*
made after expiry of validity of writ – Impossibility of extending validity of writ after date of
order for service of notice of writ – Whether failure to renew writ an 'irregularity' – Whether
jurisdiction to cure failure to renew writ – Whether order for service of notice of writ valid – RSC
Ord 2, r 1, Ord 6, r 8.

In May 1977 the plaintiffs, who were resident in South Africa, obtained judgment there   *c*
for R6,000 against the first defendant, who was also resident in South Africa. The
judgment remained unsatisfied but the first defendant agreed with the plaintiffs to
transfer £3,000 deposited with a building society in England to South Africa in part
satisfaction of the judgment debt. However, that money was never transferred to South
Africa. On 7 December 1977 the plaintiffs issued a writ in England against the first
defendant to enforce the agreement, and joined the building society as second
defendant. As the first defendant was still resident in South Africa the plaintiffs were   *d*
given leave to serve notice of the writ on her out of the jurisdiction, but it proved
impossible to do so. The second defendant entered an appearance to the action. Time
for service of the writ expired on 6 December 1978 but the plaintiff did not apply under
RSC Ord 6, r 8[a] to renew the writ. On 28 January 1981 a district registrar, without
renewing the writ, gave the plaintiffs leave to serve notice of the writ on the first
defendant by substituted service by means of posting a copy of the notice to the first   *e*
defendant at the second defendant's address. The first defendant or her solicitors received
notice of the writ but she failed to acknowledge service of it or to enter an appearance to
the action. On 22 May 1981 the plaintiffs signed judgment against her in default of
appearance for damages to be assessed. On 13 July the first defendant issued a summons
applying to set aside the order for substituted service and the judgment in default. The   *f*
judge held that, although the order for substituted service was irregular because the
failure to renew the writ had rendered it invalid for service, he had jurisdiction under
RSC Ord 2, r 1[b] to cure the irregularity, and in the exercise of his discretion under that
rule he made an order that in effect treated the writ as having been validly renewed and
the order for substituted service validly made. However, the judge then went on to hold
that, even though service of notice of the writ had thus been validly effected on the first
defendant, she should nevertheless be given leave to defend the action on condition that   *g*
she filed a memorandum of appearance or acknowledged service of the notice of the writ
within 14 days of judgment. The judge also set aside the judgment in default of 22
May. The first defendant appealed, contending (i) that the failure to renew the writ
meant that it was not valid for service after 6 December 1978 and that, even if there had
been an application to renew the writ, the judge could not have extended its validity
beyond 5 December 1979 under Ord 6, r 8 (ie for more than 12 months from 6   *h*
December 1978) and the writ was therefore not valid for service on 21 January 1981
when the order for substituted service was made, and (ii) that the irregularity caused by
the writ's invalidity for service could not be cured under Ord 2, r 1. The first defendant
further contended that the judge ought instead to have set aside the order for substituted
service and given the first defendant unconditional leave to defend because, by making
the leave to defend conditional on entering a memorandum of appearance, the judge was   *j*
obliging her to waive the irregularity in procedure which she could otherwise have relied

---

a   Rule 8, so far as material, is set out at p 810 *a b*, post
b   Rule 1, so far as material, is set out at p 811 *e* to *g*, post

on. The plaintiffs contended (i) that, even if, as they conceded, a writ which had not been
a renewed under Ord 6, r 8 was not valid for service, notice of the writ could still be validly
served, and (ii) alternatively that the failure to renew the writ was an irregularity that
could be cured under Ord 2, r 1.

Held – Since RSC Ord 6, r 8 provided a comprehensive code for the renewal of a writ, an
irregularity in procedure caused by failure to renew a writ was not the kind of irregularity
b which Ord 2, r 1 was intended to deal with. However, even assuming that such an
irregularity could be cured under Ord 2, r 1, the invalidity of the writ for service due to
failure to renew it was such a fundamental defect in the proceedings that the judge ought
not to have exercised his discretion under Ord 2, r 1 by making the order that he did.
Accordingly, since at the date of the order for substituted service the writ had not been
renewed and the judge could not have renewed it so as to extend its validity beyond 5
c December 1979, the writ and the order for substituted service would be set aside under
Ord 2, r 1(2). The appeal would therefore be allowed (see p 811 *j* to p 812 *a* and *d* to
p 813 *a*, post).
Dictum of Robert Goff J in *Carmel Exporters (Sales) Ltd v Sea-Land Services Inc* [1981] 1
All ER at 991 applied.
Dictum of Lord Denning MR in *Harkness v Bell's Asbestos and Engineering Ltd* [1966] 3
d All ER at 845–846 and *Dawson (Bradford) Ltd v Dove* [1971] 1 All ER 554 considered.

Notes
For renewal of writ, see 37 Halsbury's Laws (4th edn) para 124, and for cases on the
subject, see 50 Digest (Repl) 291–293, 328–346.

e **Cases referred to in judgments**
Carmel Exporters (Sales) Ltd v Sea-Land Services Inc [1981] 1 All ER 984, [1981] 1 WLR
1068.
Chittenden (decd), Re, Chittenden v Doe [1970] 3 All ER 562, [1970] 1 WLR 1618, Digest
(Cont Vol C) 1079, 80a.
Dawson (Bradford) Ltd v Dove [1971] 1 All ER 554, [1971] 1 QB 330, [1971] 2 WLR 1,
Digest (Cont Vol D) 1046, 215b.
Harkness v Bell's Asbestos and Engineering Ltd [1966] 3 All ER 843, [1967] 2 QB 729, [1967]
2 WLR 29, CA, 50 Digest (Repl) 251, 54.
Pritchard (decd), Re [1963] 1 All ER 873, [1963] Ch 502, CA, [1963] 2 WLR 685, 50
Digest (Repl) 252, 62.
Sheldon v Brown Bayley's Steelworks Ltd [1953] 2 All ER 894, [1953] 2 QB 393, [1953] 3
f WLR 542, CA, 50 Digest (Repl) 293, 345.

Cases also cited
Hewitson v Fabre (1888) 21 QBD 6, DC.
Hope v Hope (1854) 4 De GM & G 328, [1843–60] All ER Rep 41, 43 ER 328, LC.
Kerly, Son & Verden, Re [1901] 1 Ch 467, CA.
Porter v Freudenberg, Kreglinger v S Samuel and Rosenfeld, Re Merten's Patents [1915] 1 KB
857, [1914–15] All ER Rep 918, CA.
Reynolds v Coleman (1887) 36 Ch D 453, CA.
Western Suburban and Notting Hill Permanent Benefit Building Society v Rucklidge [1905] 2 Ch
472.

Interlocutory appeal
On 13 July 1981, in an action by the plaintiffs, Gillies Martin Bernstein and Stanley
Maurice Caminsky, against the first defendant, Mrs Maureen Jackson, and the second
defendants, Leeds Permanent Building Society, the first defendant issued a summons
applying, inter alia, (i) to set aside an order made by the district registrar on 28 January
1981 for substituted service of notice of the writ in the action on the first defendant by

serving a copy of the notice at the second defendants' address and (ii) to set aside the judgment in default of appearance against the first defendant obtained by the plaintiffs *a* on 22 May 1981. By a judgment given on 23 November 1981 Lawson J held, inter alia, that, although when the district registrar made his order for substituted service time for service of the writ had expired and the writ had not been renewed pursuant to RSC Ord 6, r 8, and the writ was therefore invalid for service and the order for substituted service therefore irregular, that irregularity could be cured under RSC Ord 2, r 1. Accordingly, in the exercise of his discretion under that rule, the judge held that the order for *b* substituted service was valid and that substituted service had been effected on the first defendant but that, in all the circumstances, it was proper to set aside the judgment in default of 22 May 1981 and to give the first defendant leave to defend on condition that she filed a memorandum of appearance or acknowledgment of service of the notice within 14 days. The first defendant appealed against that part of the judgment on the grounds (1) that the judge was wrong in law in failing to set aside the order for *c* substituted service and (2) that his decision to give the first defendant conditional leave to defend was unjust because (i) the validity of the writ had expired on 6 December 1978, (ii) the notice of the writ was thereby invalid, (iii) the notice of the writ had therefore not been validly served, (iv) by requiring the first defendant to file a memorandum of appearance as a condition of leave to defend she was being required to waive the irregularity caused by the plaintiffs' failure to renew the writ and (v) the judge was *d* wrong in purporting to cure the irregularity by invoking the provisions of Ord 2, r 1. The facts are set out in the judgment of Dunn LJ.

Gerald Lumley for the first defendant.
John M Collins for the plaintiffs.

                                                                 e

DUNN LJ. This is an interlocutory appeal by leave of this court from part of an order made by Lawson J in chambers on 23 November 1981 whereby he ordered that the first defendant, who is the appellant in this court, should be at liberty to defend the action on condition that she file a memorandum of appearance or acknowledgment of service within 14 days, and he dismissed an application by the first defendant that the action should be struck out for want of prosecution.   *f*

    The facts of the case are exceedingly unusual, if not unique, and I take them from the judgment of the judge. On 13 May 1977 the plaintiffs, who are a firm of attorneys resident in South Africa, obtained a judgment in South Africa in the sum of some R6,000 against the first defendant, Mrs Jackson, and her husband and son. Nothing was paid under that judgment, which was a default judgment in the sense that she did not appear and none of the defendants appeared, and in May 1977 execution was levied on the *g* judgment.

    The first defendant had a sum of some £3,000 on deposit with the Leeds Building Society and she gave the society authority to transfer that sum of money to South Africa in part satisfaction of the judgment. In fact, the money was never transferred, it is said, because she took no steps to obtain exchange control and, accordingly, the plaintiffs in South Africa proceeded with the execution, and certain goods and chattels of the first *h* defendant and her family which had been seized were put up for auction. On 7 December 1977 the writ in these present proceedings was issued in this country, relying on the agreement to transfer the £3,000 from the Leeds Building Society to the plaintiffs in South Africa. The building society had been joined as second defendants in the proceedings and an injunction was sought against them and against the first defendant restraining them from paying out any sums standing to the credit of the first defendant *j* with the building society so as to reduce the amount held below £3,000. On 20 December 1977 Bush J granted an interlocutory injunction effectively in those terms. The injunction recited an undertaking by the plaintiffs to prosecute the action with expedition.

    At that time the first defendant was still resident in South Africa and on 6 January

1978 the district registrar gave the plaintiffs leave to serve notice of the writ out of the
a jurisdiction under the provisions of RSC Ord 11. It proved impossible to serve the notice
out of the jurisdiction. We were told that early in 1978 the first defendant and her
family returned on a slow boat to this country. In March 1978 there was some
communication between the plaintiffs' solicitors and the solicitors for the building
society, and on 29 March 1978 those latter solicitors wrote to the plaintiffs' solicitors
saying that they had forwarded to the first defendant a letter from the plaintiffs' solicitors
b in effect giving her notice of the proceedings. By October 1978 the first defendant and
her family were in the Leeds area and arrangements were made for her to attend at the
offices of the solicitors for the second defendants for the purpose of accepting service of
the writ; but, due to a misunderstanding, the solicitors for the plaintiffs were unable to
attend the meeting and no service was effected.

On 6 December 1978 the time for service of the writ on the first defendant expired
c and there has never at any time been an application to renew the writ for service on the
first defendant, although the second defendants entered an appearance on 12 December
1977.

The action then appears to have gone to sleep until the end of 1980, when the plaintiffs
made an application to the district registrar, who, on 28 January 1981, made what the
judge described as 'a most unusual order'. He gave the plaintiffs leave to serve notice of
d the writ on the first defendant by substituted service by serving a copy of the notice by
first class prepaid letter post addressed to the second defendants, ie the Leeds Permanent
Building Society. When he made that order the registrar did not renew the writ, nor was
there any application to renew the writ. However, the first defendant had, by that time,
instructed solicitors. The writ or notice of the writ appears to have been served on them
because, on 27 February 1981, they wrote to the plaintiffs' solicitors:
e
'We have been instructed by Mrs. Jackson to defend the proceedings commenced
by your clients and we will file a Memorandum of Appearance in due course.'

According to the judge, it was common ground that the first defendant in fact had the
proceedings handed to her.

In spite of that, the first defendant took no step to acknowledge service or enter an
f appearance and, indeed, instructed her solicitors that she was not prepared to disclose her
whereabouts to the plaintiffs; and, having given due notice by letter during April, on 22
May 1981 the plaintiffs' solicitors signed judgment in default against the first defendant
for damages to be assessed. On 13 July 1981 the first defendant issued her summons,
applying to set aside the order for substituted service made on 28 January and also the
judgment of 22 May. She also made application that the plaintiffs' action be dismissed
g for want of prosecution and those matters were adjourned to the judge; and he made the
orders in the form that I have indicated.

The judge held that it was a 'condition precedent of obtaining an order for substituted
service, or an order for substituted service of notice of the writ, that there must be a writ
valid for service'. He also held that the writ in this action was not valid for service
because it had not been renewed in accordance with the provisions of Ord 6, r 8. But he
h went on to hold that that was an irregularity with which he had jurisdiction to deal
under Ord 2, r 1. Accordingly, as a matter of discretion, he made the order which he did,
namely that the first defendant should have liberty to defend the action on condition that
she filed a memorandum of appearance or acknowledgment of service within 14 days.
He took that course, as appears from his judgment, first, because he was of the opinion
that, to a substantial part of the claim, the first defendant had no defence and, second,
because he was quite satisfied that 'the first defendant has known about these proceedings
and exactly what they were about for quite a long time'.

Counsel for the first defendant has submitted basically that this is not a case which falls
within Ord 2, r 1 at all, or, alternatively, if it is, that the judge should not have exercised
his discretion under the rule. The power in the court to renew writs is contained in Ord
6, r 8. Rule 8 provides:

'(1) For the purpose of service, a writ (other than a concurrent writ) is valid in the first instance for twelve months beginning with the date of its issue . . . *a*
(2) Where a writ has not been served on a defendant, the Court may by order extend the validity of the writ from time to time for such period, not exceeding twelve months at any one time, beginning with the day next following that on which it would otherwise expire as may be specified in the order, if an application for extension is made to the Court before that day or such later day (if any) as the Court may allow . . .' *b*

Accordingly, counsel for the first defendant submitted that this writ was not valid for service after 6 December 1978, which was 12 months after it was issued; no application was made to renew it and, even if such an application had been made, the judge would not have had power to extend the validity of the writ for more than 12 months from 6 December 1978, that is to say until 5 December 1979. Counsel for the first defendant, *c* while conceding that the failure to extend the writ and the impossibility now of extending the writ beyond 5 December 1979 did not render the writ null and void, submitted that it rendered the writ invalid for service, although it was in all other respects valid.

He relied, in support of that proposition, on *Sheldon v Brown Bayley's Steelworks Ltd* [1953] 2 All ER 894 at 896, [1953] 2 QB 393 at 400, where Singleton LJ said: *d*

'I do not regard it as strictly accurate to describe a writ which has not been served within twelve months as a nullity. It is not as though it had never been issued. It is something which can be renewed. A nullity cannot be renewed. The court can grant an application which results in making it just as effective as it was before the twelve months' period had elapsed.' *e*

Then, a little later, he dealt with the question of waiver.

Counsel for the first defendant submitted that, by making the order which he had made, the judge had in fact obliged the first defendant to waive the irregularity which it would have been open to her to rely on if the writ had been served on her. He also referred to *Re Chittenden (decd), Chittenden v Doe* [1970] 3 All ER 562, [1970] 1 WLR 1618, *f* in which, again, it was held that an unconditional appearance to a summons waived the irregularity.

Although counsel for the first defendant conceded that the order that was made for substituted service was a mere irregularity and did not render the writ itself null and void, he submitted that it was not the kind of irregularity which was intended to be covered by the provisions of Ord 2, r 1. He submitted that, although the court is given a wide discretion under Order 2, r 1, that discretion has to be exercised with a proper *g* regard to the special provisions in the rest of the rules and, in particular, he submitted that Ord 2, r 1 had never been used, in effect, to circumvent the provisions of Ord 6, r 8.

He referred us to the statement of Lord Denning MR in *Harkness v Bell's Asbestos and Engineering Ltd* [1966] 3 All ER 843 at 845–846, [1967] 2 QB 729 at 735–736 where, with reference to the rule (Ord 2, r 1) under consideration, he said: *h*

'This new rule does away with the old distinction between nullities and irregularities. Every omission or mistake in practice or procedure is henceforward to be regarded as an irregularity which the court can and should rectify so long as it can do so without injustice. It can at last be asserted that "it is not possible . . . for an honest litigant in Her Majesty's Supreme Court to be defeated by any mere technicality, any slip, any mistaken step in his litigation." That could not be said in *j* 1963; see *Re Pritchard (decd.)* ([1963] 1 All ER 873 at 879, [1963] Ch 502 at 518); but it can be in 1966. The new rule does it.'

Counsel for the first defendant submitted that what had happened here was not a mere technicality or slip or mistaken step in the litigation because the renewal of the writ was

a fundamental step in the proceedings, which was governed exclusively by the provision
a of Ord 6, r 8.

He referred us by analogy to a decision of MacKenna J in *Dawson (Bradford) Ltd v Dove*
[1971] 1 All ER 554, [1971] 1 QB 330, where it was held that Ord 15, r 6 did not
empower the court to substitute executors of a deceased person as a party to proceedings
where the action had been commenced against that person, and Ord 2, r 1 did not enable
the plaintiffs to have the executors substituted as defendants because the action could not
b be said to be a failure to comply with the requirements of the rules. The judge said
([1971] 1 All ER 554 at 557–558, [1971] 1 QB 330 at 335):

> 'To substitute the defendants for the deceased would not be correcting a mistake
> about the deceased's name. It would be doing something quite different. Order 2,
> r 1, as I read its provisions, does not help the plaintiffs here. To commence an action
> against a dead person can hardly be described as "a failure to comply with the
> **c** provisions of these rules", which is the case dealt with by Ord 2, r 1. Even if it could
> be so described, the rule does not give any power to add new parties in substitution
> for dead men. It only provides that the powers of amending or making orders
> conferred by the other rules shall be exercisable in the cases it is dealing with. If the
> relief required is the addition of new parties, the power to give such relief must be
> sought in the provisions of Ord 15, r 6 or in those of Ord 20, r 5. If the power is not
> **d** given by these rules it is not exercisable under Ord 2, r 1.'

So counsel for the first defendant says that, as the power is not given by Ord 6, r 8 in
the circumstances of this case to renew the writ, it is not exercisable under Ord 2, r 1.
Order 2, r 1 is in the following terms:

> '(1) Where, in beginning or purporting to begin any proceedings or at any stage
> **e** in the course of or in connection with any proceedings, there has, by reason of any
> thing done or left undone, been a failure to comply with the requirements of these
> rules, whether in respect of time, place, manner, form or content or in any other
> respect, the failure shall be treated as an irregularity and shall not nullify the
> proceedings, any step taken in the proceedings, or any document, judgment or
> order therein.
> **f** (2) Subject to paragraph (3), the Court may, on the ground that there has been
> such a failure as is mentioned in paragraph (1), and on such terms as to costs or
> otherwise as it thinks just, set aside either wholly or in part the proceedings in
> which the failure occurred, any step taken in those proceedings or any document,
> judgment or order therein or exercise its powers under these rules to allow such
> amendments (if any) to be made and to make such order (if any) dealing with the
> **g** proceedings generally as it thinks fit . . .'

Counsel for the first defendant referred us finally to *Carmel Exporters (Sales) Ltd v Sea-
Land Services Inc* [1981] 1 All ER 984, [1981] 1 WLR 1068. That was a decision of Robert
Goff J where he exercised his discretion under Ord 2, r 1 to permit an application under
Ord 12, r 8 notwithstanding that the affidavit in support of that application had not been
h filed within the time limited by the rules. The judge said ([1981] 1 All ER 984 at 991,
[1981] 1 WLR 1068 at 1076):

> 'Counsel for the plaintiffs then referred me to a number of situations in which the
> defect in procedure is so fundamental that the court will, he submitted, always set
> aside the relevant proceedings or step in the proceedings: for example, where a writ
> has not been served as required by the rules, or notice of discontinuance has been
> **i** given without leave where leave was needed; or a writ has, without leave to renew,
> been served more than 12 months after its issue; or a judgment in default has been
> irregularly signed.'

Counsel for the first defendant adopted that argument and submitted that, in this case,
where an order has been made for substituted service of notice of a writ which has not

been renewed and which could not be renewed, then that is such a fundamental defect in procedure that, even if the judge had discretion, he should not have exercised it under *a* Ord 2, r 1.

Counsel for the plaintiffs has submitted basically that, although a writ which has not been renewed is not valid for service, which he accepted, the same does not apply to notice of a writ. The expression 'notice of a writ' is referred to in the rules which were at the material time in existence and there is nothing in those rules to suggest that such a notice is not valid for service after 12 months. *b*

So far as that is concerned, I entirely agree with the judge that notice of a writ must refer to a valid writ. But counsel for the plaintiffs went on to submit that, assuming that he was wrong about that, none the less the failure to renew the writ was, on the authorities, an irregularity that could, in effect, be cured in the discretion of the judge under Ord 2, r 1. He submitted that the judge was quite right to exercise his discretion in the way in which he had done, and that no prejudice would be caused to the first *c* defendant by the order that the judge had made because she was able to put forward a defence on the merits if she had one. On the other hand, considerable prejudice would be caused to the plaintiffs because they had been kept out of their money for a considerable time already and, furthermore, as the first defendant had in fact received the writ and statement of claim, it would simply be adding to the costs of the litigation to strike out the proceedings, in which case the plaintiffs would be quite entitled to issue *d* another writ because the limitation period has not expired; and the judge was right to allow the action to go ahead and be determined on its merits.

While I completely understand the reason why the judge made the order in the way in which he did and while I have a certain amount of sympathy for the plaintiffs, I have come to the clear conclusion that counsel for the first defendant was right in the submissions that he made. I do not think that the judge could have extended the writ *e* under Ord 6, r 8 and, that being the case, I think that there is great force in the submission that Ord 6, r 8 provides a compendious code for extension and renewal of writs, and that it is not the type of irregularity which it was envisaged could be dealt with by the provisions of Ord 2, r 1. But, assuming that it could, in my view this was such a fundamental defect in the proceedings that the judge should not have exercised his discretion to make an order under Ord 2, r 1. Accordingly, I would allow the appeal and *f* set aside the writ under the provisions of Ord 2, r 1(2) and also the order for substituted service on the ground of the plaintiffs' failure to comply with the requirements of Ord 6, r 8(2).

I would allow the appeal.

SLADE LJ. I agree that this appeal should be allowed for the reasons given by Dunn LJ *g* and would add only a few words of my own.

The judge, in the course of his judgment, said this with reference to the argument advanced by counsel for the plaintiffs:

'Finally he relies on the provisions of Ord 2, r 1 as his longstop, and I take the view that he is entitled to rely on the provisions of Ord 2, r 1, and that, notwithstanding *h* the irregularity caused by the non-renewal of the writ and the irregularity of the order made on 28 January 1981, I should uphold the validity of that order.'

The judge did not explicitly state what he meant by the phrase 'uphold the validity of that order'. However, it was necessarily implicit in his judgment that he thought it right, notwithstanding all the previous irregularities, to treat the writ as a writ which had *j* been validly renewed. If a specific application to renew the writ had been before him, I do not think that he could have properly extended its validity for the reasons already given by Dunn LJ. Correspondingly, I do not think that the plaintiffs can be in a better position than they would have been if such a specific application had been before the judge.

a   In all the circumstances I agree that the appeal should be allowed and with the form of order proposed by Dunn LJ.

Appeal allowed.

Solicitors: *Beachcroft, Hyman Isaacs*, agents for *Emsley, Collins & Co*, Leeds (for the first defendant); *Waterhouse & Co*, agents for *Walker, Morris & Coles*, Leeds (for the plaintiffs).

b

Henrietta Steinberg   Barrister.

c # Commissioner of Police of the Metropolis v Simeon

HOUSE OF LORDS

LORD DIPLOCK, LORD ELWYN-JONES, LORD KEITH OF KINKEL, LORD ROSKILL AND LORD BRIDGE OF
d HARWICH

28 JUNE, 15 JULY 1982

Statute – Penal statute – Abolition of offence – Repeal of enactment which created offence – Effect of repeal – Double repeal – Repealed provisions to 'cease to have effect' – Prosecution after repeal for offence committed before repeal after abolition – Frequenting or loitering with intent –
e *Whether person may be prosecuted after repeal for offence committed before repeal – Whether repealing statute showing contrary intention – Vagrancy Act 1824, s 4 – Interpretation Act 1978, s 16 – Criminal Attempts Act 1981, ss 8, 10, Sch, Part II.*

Criminal law – Vagrancy – Frequenting or loitering with intent – Abolition of offence – Date from which offence abolished – Prosecution of persons alleged to have committed offence before
f *offence abolished – Vagrancy Act 1824, s 4 – Criminal Attempts Act 1981, ss 8, 10, Sch, Part II.*

Neither the fact that ss 8[*a*] and 10[*b*] of, and Part II[*c*] of the schedule to, the Criminal Attempts Act 1981 effect a 'double repeal' of the provisions of s 4[*d*] of the Vagrancy Act 1824 which apply to suspected persons and reputed thieves frequenting or loitering with
g intent to commit an arrestable offence nor the fact that s 8 effects the repeal not by using the word 'repeal' but by providing that the repealed provisions 'shall cease to have effect' is sufficient to indicate a 'contrary intention' within s 16(1)[*e*] of the Interpretation Act 1978 for s 16 not to apply to the repeal. Accordingly, the repeal is governed by the normal rule set out in s 16 of the 1978 Act relating to the repeal of enactments, namely that the repeal does not affect, inter alia, the institution or continuation of legal
h proceedings in respect of offences alleged to have been committed before the date of the repeal (see p 814 *f* to *h*, p 816 *f g*, p 817 *j* and p 818 *h*,post).

Hough v Windus (1884) 12 QBD 224 and *R v Fisher* [1969] 1 All ER 100 applied.

Decision of the Divisional Court of the Queen's Bench Division sub nom *R v West London Stipendiary Magistrate, ex p Simeon* [1982] 1 All ER 847 reversed.

---

a   Section 8 is set out at p 815 *j*, post
b   Section 10 is set out at p 815 *j*, post
c   Part II, so far as material, is set out at p 816 *a*, post
d   Section 4, so far as material, is set out at p 815 *g h*, post
e   Section 16(1), so far as material, is set out at p 816 *c d*, post

Notes

For the effects of the repeal of an enactment, see 36 Halsbury's Laws (3rd edn) 469–473, *a*
paras 714–717, and for cases on the subject, see 44 Digest (Repl) 371–372, 2098–2117.
  For the Vagrancy Act 1824, s 4, see 8 Halsbury's Statutes (3rd edn) 73.
  For the Interpretation Act 1978, s 16, see 48 ibid 1305.
  For the Criminal Attempts Act 1981, ss 8, 10, Sch, Part II, see 51 ibid 743, 744, 745.

Cases referred to in opinions   *b*
Hough v Windus (1884) 12 QBD 224, CA, 44 Digest (Repl) 294, 1240.
R v Fisher [1969] 1 All ER 100, [1969] 1 WLR 8, CA, 14(1) Digest (Reissue) 104, 709.

Appeal
The Commissioner of Police of the Metropolis appealed with leave of the Appeal
Committee of the House of Lords granted on 29 March 1982 against the decision of the *c*
Divisional Court of the Queen's Bench Division (Ackner LJ and Woolf J) ([1982] 1 All ER
847, [1982] 1 WLR 705) on 15 February 1982 granting the respondent, Casimir Simeon,
an order of prohibition prohibiting the stipendiary magistrate sitting at West London
Magistrates' Court, Eric Crowther Esq, from further proceeding with the trial of the
respondent on a charge of being a suspected person loitering with intent to commit an
arrestable offence contrary to s 4 of the Vagrancy Act 1824 on an information laid by an *d*
officer of the Metropolitan Police and an order of mandamus requiring the magistrate to
dismiss the charge. The magistrate on 18 November 1981 had rejected a submission by
the respondent that he had no jurisdiction to hear the charge because the relevant offence
with which he had been charged had been repealed by s 8 of the Criminal Attempts Act
1981. The facts are set out in the opinion of Lord Roskill.

Andrew Collins and *Vivian Robinson* for the appellant.   *e*
Lord Gifford QC for the respondent.

Their Lordships took time for consideration.

15 July. The following opinions were delivered.   *f*

LORD DIPLOCK. My Lords, I have had the advantage of reading in draft the speech
prepared by my noble and learned friend Lord Roskill, and for the reasons he has given
I would allow this appeal.

LORD ELWYN-JONES. My Lords, for the reasons given in the speech prepared by *g*
my noble and learned friend Lord Roskill, with which I agree, I would allow the appeal.

LORD KEITH OF KINKEL. My Lords, I have had the benefit of reading in draft the
speech of my noble and learned friend Lord Roskill. I agree with it, and for the reasons
he gives I too would allow the appeal.
                                                                                          h

LORD ROSKILL. My Lords, on 30 June 1981 the respondent was arrested and was
charged with an offence against s 4 of the Vagrancy Act 1824, namely loitering with
intent. He was admitted to bail by the police to appear in court on 21 July 1981. For
various reasons into which it is not now necessary to enter, the charge was not heard until
18 November 1981. The respondent then appeared before Mr Eric Crowther, sitting as
the stipendiary magistrate at West London Magistrates' Court. On that occasion the *j*
respondent's solicitor took a preliminary objection to the hearing of the charge against
the respondent on the ground that the relevant offence with which he had been charged
had been repealed by s 8 of the Criminal Attempts Act 1981. The 1981 Act had received
the royal assent on 27 July 1981 and by virtue of s 11(1) came into force one month
later. The magistrate rejected the submission. Thereupon, the respondent applied for

judicial review. Leave was given on 13 January 1982, and on 15 February the Divisional
Court (Ackner LJ and Woolf J) ([1982] 1 All ER 847, [1982] 1 WLR 705) made an order
prohibiting the magistrate from proceeding with the trial of the respondent and
enjoining him to dismiss the charge. The judgment of the Divisional Court was
delivered by Woolf J. The Divisional Court certified the following question as raising a
point of law of general public importance:

> 'Whether after the coming into force of the Criminal Attempts Act 1981 a person
> can be prosecuted for an offence of "loitering with intent" contrary to section 4 of
> the Vagrancy Act 1824 alleged to have been committed before the coming into
> force of the 1981 Act.'

The Divisional Court refused leave to appeal to your Lordships' House but your Lordships
subsequently gave that leave.

My Lords, the short question raised by this appeal is, therefore, whether those who are
alleged to have committed offences against the relevant part of s 4 of the 1824 Act before
the 1981 Act took effect can be prosecuted after that date. My Lords, the criticisms
which have in recent times been directed against the relevant part of s 4, popularly
known as the 'sus' law, need no re-emphasis from your Lordships' House. They are well
known, as is the purpose of s 8 of the 1981 Act repealing the relevant part of s 4. Counsel
for the appellant made it absolutely plain in opening this appeal that, in inviting your
Lordships' House to reverse the decision of the Divisional Court, the appellant was in no
way seeking to restore to temporary life that much criticised piece of legislation so as to
continue prosecutions against those who were alleged to have offended against its
provisions before s 8 of the 1981 Act took effect. Indeed, your Lordships were assured
that a policy decision had already been taken by the appellant that should this appeal
succeed there would be no further prosecutions within Metropolitan Police District
against such alleged offenders.

My Lords, the reason for the appeal to your Lordships' House, as your Lordships were
informed, was that, if the reasoning by which the Divisional Court in the judgment
delivered by Woolf J reached the conclusion that s 8 of the 1981 Act operated to prevent
such further prosecutions for alleged offences committed before that section came into
effect were correct, the consequences were indeed far-reaching, and raised questions of
general importance in relation to the construction of statutes and affected matters far
removed from the subject matter with which this appeal is immediately concerned.

My Lords, s 4 of the 1824 Act forms part of a statute which prescribed severe
punishment for certain classes of persons, those deemed 'idle and disorderly' (s 3), those
deemed 'rogues and vagabonds' (s 4), and those deemed 'incorrigible rogues' (s 5). My
Lords, s 4 has been amended and construed by statute from time to time, but
immediately before the coming into force of the 1981 Act, the relevant part read:

> '... every suspected person or reputed thief, frequenting [or loitering about or in]
> any river, canal, or navigable stream, dock, or basin, or any quay, wharf, or
> warehouse near or adjoining thereto, or any street, highway, or avenue leading
> thereto, or any place of public resort, or any avenue leading thereto, or any street, or
> any highway or any place adjacent to a street or highway with intent to commit an
> arrestable offence ... shall be deemed a rogue and vagabond, within the true intent
> and meaning of this Act ...'

My Lords, s 8 in Part II of the 1981 Act provides:

> 'The provisions of section 4 of the Vagrancy Act 1824 which apply to suspected
> persons and reputed thieves frequenting or loitering about the places described in
> that section with the intent there specified shall cease to have effect.'

Section 10 provides:

> 'The enactments mentioned in the Schedule to this Act are hereby repealed to the
> extent specified in the third column of that Schedule.'

Part II of the schedule, which is headed 'Repeals consequential on Part II', in the third
column reads: *a*

'In section 4 [ie of the Vagrancy Act 1824] the words from "every suspected
person" to "arrestable offence".'

Thus, the entire passage which I have quoted above, except the concluding words, was
repealed by the 1981 Act.

My Lords, there is no doubt, as indeed the Divisional Court stated, that the normal *b*
rule governing the effect of a statute which repeals a previous statute is to be found in
s 16(1) of the Interpretation Act 1978. This was a consolidating Act and s 16(1)
substantially reproduced s 38(2) of the Interpretation Act 1889. My Lords, s 16(1) reads
thus:

'Without prejudice to section 15, where an Act repeals an enactment, the repeal
does not, unless the contrary intention appears . . . (c) affect any right, privilege, *c*
obligation or liability acquired, accrued or incurred under that enactment; (d) affect
any penalty, forfeiture or punishment incurred in respect of any offence committed
against that enactment; (e) affect any investigation, legal proceeding or remedy in
respect of any such right, privilege, obligation, liability, penalty, forfeiture or
punishment; and any such investigation, legal proceeding or remedy may be
instituted, continued or enforced, and any such penalty, forfeiture or punishment *d*
may be imposed, as if the repealing Act had not been passed.'

My Lords, is there then any contrary intention to be found in the language of the 1981
Act and in particular of ss 8 and 10 of, and Part II of the schedule to, that Act? The
Divisional Court appears to have regarded as the most important provision pointing to
the existence of such a contrary intention the fact that there are these three provisions, *e*
ss 8 and 10 and Part II of the schedule. It was argued for the respondent in that court, and
accepted by the court, that because s 10 and Part II of the schedule were differently
worded from s 8, and words there appeared which might have but did not appear in s 8,
this showed the contrary intention envisaged by s 16(1) of the Interpretation Act 1978.
Put into other words, the Divisional Court thought that, because there was what was
called in argument before your Lordships' House a 'double repeal' provision in ss 8 and *f*
10 and the schedule, it must have been the intention of s 8, worded as it was, to have the
further effect of abolishing the relevant part of s 4 of the 1824 Act so as to prevent future
prosecutions for offences against that part of s 4 which had already been allegedly
committed.

My Lords, with profound respect to the Divisional Court in my view they fell into
error in so construing s 8. This form of drafting statutes is in no way novel. It is almost *g*
a century old, if not older. Counsel for the appellant drew your Lordships' attention to
a decision of the full Court of Appeal in *Hough v Windus* (1884) 12 QBD 224, where a very
similar question arose under the Bankruptcy Act 1883. The relevant facts can be briefly
stated. A judgment creditor issued a writ of elegit against the defendant's goods on 20
December 1883 pursuant to a statute of Edward I (13 Edw 1 c 18 (1285)). Two days later
the sheriff took possession of those goods. But, before the necessary valuation had been *h*
completed, the Bankruptcy Act 1883 took effect on 1 January 1884. The question was
whether the plaintiff should be restrained from further proceedings pursuant to that
writ of elegit.

My Lords, the relevant statutory provisions were as follows:

'**146.**—(1.) The sheriff shall not under a writ of elegit deliver the goods of a debtor *j*
nor shall a writ of elegit extend to goods . . .'

Section 169(1) repealed the enactments described in Sch 5 'as from the commencement
of this Act to the extent mentioned in that Schedule' and that schedule included the
relevant part of the statute of Edward I.

Section 169(2) enacted that:

'The repeal effected by this Act shall not affect—(a.) anything done or suffered before the commencement of this Act under any enactment repealed by this Act; nor (b.) any right or privilege acquired, or duty imposed, or liability or disqualification incurred, under any enactment so repealed . . .'

I need only refer to a passage in the judgment of Bowen LJ. After referring to the two relevant sections of the Bankruptcy Act 1883, he said (12 QBD 224 at 234–236):

'The first observation to be made upon this section is that the writ of elegit is not abolished altogether like the writ of levari facias; but is only restricted in future to lands as distinct from goods and chattels of the debtor. It is to be remarked in the second place that the words of the section as regards writs of elegit are couched in the very widest form, and in their ordinary signification would comprehend the case not merely of writs issued after the 1st of January, 1884, but also of writs issued before that date, whether seizure had or had not been effected by the sheriff. In spite of this generality of expression, we should be still bound to search for such a construction to be put upon them as would neither prejudicially affect vested rights nor render abortive the legal effect of things already done; and even if the words stood alone it would be more in conformity with known canons of interpretation to assume that they were not meant to apply to cases where the sheriff had already seized before the Act came into operation . . . It was forcibly argued before us that the effect of this latter section taken alone being of itself to prevent goods and chattels being taken in execution under any writ of elegit issued after the 1st of January, 1884, it followed as a matter of reasoning that the enactment contained in s. 146 would have nothing at all upon which to operate unless it was intended expressly to apply to cases where the execution had begun, but had not been perfected by delivery, before that date. And the counsel for the respondents urged upon us that it was our duty so to construe the Act as to give effect to the language of s. 146, and not to adopt an interpretation which would render s. 146 superfluous. It appears to me that the answer to this somewhat formidable argument is to be found in a study of the framework of the Bankruptcy Act, 1883, so far as it works a repeal of previous legislation. It does not seem to me to be possible, without misunderstanding the scheme of drafting which the legislature had adopted, to treat the repealing s. 169 as an independent section, or one intended to do more than for sake of symmetry to repeal expressly in a group those portions of previous statutes which had already been repealed by implication in the body of the Act. I have examined Schedule 5 in detail, which contains the list of previous Acts of Parliament, all or part of which is to be repealed by s. 169, and I have come to the conclusion that the idea upon which the Bankruptcy Act, 1883, has been framed was to enact in the first place specifically a complete code of provisions which, so far as they are inconsistent with any previous legislation, would repeal it by implication, and then over again, at the very last, to clear the statute book, so to speak, by s. 169, and to sweep into one compendious repeal section all the statutes, and sections of statutes, which in the earlier part of the Act had been impliedly done away with already, the Bankruptcy Act, 1869, being itself among the number.'

My Lords, I venture to quote this passage as some length (I should mention that this decision of the Court of Appeal was not drawn to the attention of the Divisional Court) to show that the argument there rejected by the Court of Appeal was in substance the same argument as that which the Divisional Court accepted in the present case.

My Lords, just as in Hough v Windus, the structure of the relevant provisions of the 1981 Act is, in my view, first to enact the relevant new law, and then to clear the statute book of the old law which had become irrelevant because of the new law. This is a well-recognised system of drafting legislation and with all respect I am unable to deduce from its adoption in the 1981 Act, and from the absence of an express reference to the word 'repeal' in s 8, and the presence of such words in s 10 and Part II of the schedule, any contrary intention such as is required by s 16(1) of the Interpretation Act 1978.

My Lords, I have dealt with this matter at some length because of the consequences which would follow were the reasoning of the Divisional Court to be correct. But it is *a* only right that I should say that counsel for the respondent found himself unable to support that reasoning based on the so-called 'double repeal' submission.

Counsel for the respondent founded his submission on behalf of the respondent on other grounds. First he said that s 8 of the 1981 Act must be read in conjunction with the other sections of the statute, notably ss 3(6), 5(2) and 6(1). He pointed out, correctly, that s 3(6) expressly provides that sub-ss (2) to (5) of that section are not to have effect in *b* relation to an act done before the commencement of the 1981 Act. Section 5(2), following s 5(1) which enlarges the definition of conspiracy in s 1 of the Criminal Law Act 1977, provides that s 5 should not apply to a conspiracy entered into before the commencement of the Act unless it continued after that date. The abolition in s 6(1) is expressly stated not to relate to acts done before the commencement of the 1981 Act. Yet, said counsel for the respondent, s 8 contained no similar provisions. *c*

My Lords, as regards s 3(6), the Interpretation Act 1978 only applies to repeals, and does not deal with the retrospective effect of legislation which is not achieving a repeal. On any view s 3(6) may well have been included ex abundanti cautela. Section 5(2) is clearly necessary because conspiracy is a continuing offence. Section 6(1) is necessary because the Interpretation Act 1978, so far as relevant, is not concerned with common law offences but only with statutory offences. My Lords, I can find nothing in these *d* other sections to which counsel for the respondent referred which leads me to deduce the relevant contrary intention from the omission of any similar words in s 8, especially when s 8 is construed together with s 10 and Part II of the schedule.

My Lords, I think the relevant principles were correctly stated by the Court of Appeal in *R v Fisher* [1969] 1 All ER 100, [1969] 1 WLR 8, a case arising from the abolition of the distinction between felony and misdemeanour by the Criminal Law Act 1967. The *e* Court of Appeal correctly applied s 38(2) of the Interpretation Act 1889, which, as I have already stated, was the statutory precursor of s 16(1) of the Interpretation Act 1978. It is worth noting that your Lordships refused leave to appeal in that case (see [1969] 1 WLR 102).

Finally, counsel for the respondent submitted that, having regard to the criticisms of the old 'sus' law, Parliament should be taken to have intended no one to remain in what *f* he called further penal jeopardy under that law. My Lords, if that had been the intention of Parliament, I should have expected to have found it expressly stated in s 8. But it was not. But happily the respondent and others similarly placed in the Metropolitan Police District, as a result of what your Lordships were told, will not in fact remain in penal jeopardy as a result of this decision of your Lordships' House.

My Lords, for the reasons I have given I would allow this appeal and set aside the order *g* of the Divisional Court. But as no further proceedings are contemplated I suggest that it is not necessary for your Lordships to make any further substantive order regarding the future course of proceedings against the respondent.

LORD BRIDGE OF HARWICH. My Lords, I have had the advantage of reading in advance the speech of my noble and learned friend Lord Roskill. I agree with it and *h* would allow the appeal.

Appeal allowed.

Solicitors: *R E T Birch* (for the appellant); *Marcus-Barnett* (for the respondent).

Mary Rose Plummer   Barrister.

a

Lincoln v Hayman and another

COURT OF APPEAL, CIVIL DIVISION

WALLER, DUNN LJJ AND SIR DAVID CAIRNS

27, 28 JANUARY, 12 FEBRUARY 1982

b
Damages – Personal injury – Special damage – Deductions – Supplementary benefit – Plaintiff in need as direct consequence of injuries and receiving supplementary benefit – Whether supplementary benefit deductible from special damages.

Since special damages are awarded in actions for personal injuries to compensate a plaintiff for loss actually incurred by him between the date of the accident and the date of the trial by reason of his injuries, and since any payments of supplementary benefit under the Supplementary Benefits Act 1976 to such a plaintiff who is in need as a direct *c* consequence of the injuries suffered by him in the accident are made as of right and if not deducted from the award of special damages would have the effect that the plaintiff would pro tanto achieve double recovery for his loss, it follows that the amount of any such payments of supplementary benefit should be deducted from any special damages awarded to the plaintiff. Moreover, if supplementary benefit were not deductible it *d* would be in the interests of plaintiffs not to proceed expeditiously with their claims in order to increase the element of double recovery (see p 821 *a b e* to *g* and p 822 *d* to p 823 *a* and *f* to p 824 *b*, post).

Plummer v P W Wilkins & Son Ltd [1981] 1 All ER 91 and *Gaskill v Preston* [1981] 3 All ER 427 followed.

Parsons v BNM Laboratories Ltd [1963] 2 All ER 658 applied.

e   *Foxley v Olton* [1964] 3 All ER 248, *Daish v Wauton* [1972] 1 All ER 25 and *Bowker v Rose* (1978) 122 SJ 147 distinguished.

Notes

For deduction for benefits received or receivable in assessing damages in tort, see 12 Halsbury's Laws (4th edn) para 1152, and for cases on the subject, see 17 Digest (Reissue) *f* 87–90, 32–46.

Cases referred to in judgments

Bowker v Rose (1978) 122 SJ 147, CA.

British Transport Commission v Gourley [1955] 3 All ER 796, [1956] AC 185, [1956] 2 WLR 41, HL, 17 Digest (Reissue) 88, 35.

g *Daish (an infant by his next friend Daish) v Wauton* [1972] 1 All ER 25, [1972] 2 QB 262, [1972] 2 WLR 29, CA, 36(1) Digest (Reissue) 322, 1314.

Foxley v Olton [1964] 3 All ER 248, [1965] 2 QB 306, [1964] 3 WLR 1155, 36(1) Digest (Reissue) 325, 1323.

Gaskill v Preston [1981] 3 All ER 427.

Nabi v British Leyland (UK) Ltd [1980] 1 All ER 667, [1980] 1 WLR 529, CA.

h *National Insurance Co of New Zealand Ltd v Espagne* (1961) 105 CLR 569.

Parry v Cleaver [1969] 1 All ER 555, [1970] AC 1, [1969] 2 WLR 821, HL, 36(1) Digest (Reissue) 320, 1295.

Parsons v BNM Laboratories Ltd [1963] 2 All ER 658, [1964] 1 QB 95, [1963] 2 WLR 1273, CA, 17 Digest (Reissue) 90, 45.

Plummer v P W Wilkins & Son Ltd [1981] 1 All ER 91, [1981] 1 WLR 831.

i

Appeal

The defendants, Hubert Reginald Hayman and Bridge Haulage Ltd, appealed against the decision of his Honour Judge Tibber sitting as a judge of the High Court on 21 July 1980 whereby, in an action for damages for personal injury and loss suffered by the plaintiff in a collision between a lorry owned by the second defendant and driven by the first defendant and a lorry driven by the plaintiff in Chequers Road, Noak Hill, Romford, Essex on or about 7 April 1976, it was ordered that there should be judgment for the *a* plaintiff, Richard Thomas Lincoln, for £60,138·75, being £15,000·00 with £5,658·00 interest for pain, suffering and loss of amenity, £18,082·27 with £4,238·48 interest as special damages and £17,160·00 for loss of future earnings. The case is reported only with respect to the defendants' contention that the trial judge was wrong in law in refusing to deduct from the special damages awarded £6,887·93 being the amount of supplementary benefit received by the plaintiff pending trial of the action. *b*

William Crowther QC and Roger Hetherington for the defendants.
Raymond Croxon for the plaintiff.

Cur adv vult

c

12 February. The following judgments were read.

DUNN LJ (delivering the first judgment at the invitation of Waller LJ). This is an appeal by the second defendants from a judgment of his Honour Judge Tibber sitting as a judge of the High Court, whereby on 21 July 1980 he found the first defendant, who at the material time was employed by the second defendant, wholly to blame for the *d* serious injuries sustained by the plaintiff in a collision between two lorries which occurred on 7 April 1976 in a country road called Chequers Road near Romford in Essex.

[His Lordship, having outlined the facts and considered the evidence, stated that, since the trial judge's reasoning was based on inferences from plans and photographs rather than on the demeanour of witnesses, the Court of Appeal was in as good a position as the judge to draw its own inferences from the undisputed primary material. His Lordship *e* went on to find that on the evidence the plaintiff was more blameworthy than the first defendant and held him two-thirds to blame and the first defendant one-third to blame for the damage caused by the collision. His Lordship then considered the question of damages and held that there were no grounds for interfering with the trial judge's assessment of damages for pain and suffering and loss of amenity, for loss of earnings between the accident and the trial and for loss of future earnings, although his Lordship *f* decreased the allowance for inflation made by the judge. His Lordship continued:] Finally it was said on behalf of the appellants that the judge was wrong not to deduct from the special damage the amount of supplementary benefit paid to the plaintiff pending trial, which amounted to £6,887·93. This raises a question of principle as to which there is no decision binding on this court. In *Parsons v BNM Laboratories Ltd* [1963] 2 All ER 658, [1964] 1 QB 95, a case of wrongful dismissal, this court held that *g* unemployment benefit was deductible from the plaintiff's damages, and this decision was followed by John Stephenson J in *Foxley v Olton* [1964] 3 All ER 248, [1965] 2 QB 306, a personal injuries case. Despite the obiter dictum of Lord Reid in *Parry v Cleaver* [1969] 1 All ER 555 at 558, [1970] AC 1 at 14, *Parsons v BNM Laboratories Ltd* is binding on this court. Can supplementary benefit be distinguished from unemployment benefit so that it should not be deducted from damages payable to a plaintiff? In *Foxley v Olton* *h* John Stephenson J held that national assistance received by the plaintiff during a period of unemployment resulting from injuries caused by the defendant's tort was not to be taken into account in assessing damages. But he decided the point on the basis that the payment of national assistance was discretionary, which the payment of supplementary benefit is not. Payments of supplementary benefit are made as of right to every person in Great Britain of or over the age of 16 whose resources are insufficient to meet his *j* needs: see s 1 of the Supplementary Benefits Act 1976. Similarly a person who satisfies any of the three conditions laid down in the relevant section is entitled as of right to unemployment benefit: see s 14 of the Social Security Act 1975.

It is said by counsel for the plaintiff that the ratio decidendi of *Parsons v BNM Laboratories Ltd* was that the defendant employers had contributed to the unemployment benefit, and that it was therefore inequitable that they should in effect have to pay twice over, whereas there is no contributory element in supplementary benefit except through the general incidence of taxation. But, inasmuch as unemployment benefit contains a contributory element making it more akin to insurance than supplementary benefit, it seems to me to provide a distinction in favour of deducting supplementary benefit rather than unemployment benefit, and counsel for the plaintiff was unable to point to any distinction the other way.

He referred us to *Daish (an infant by his next friend Daish) v Wauton* [1972] 1 All ER 25, [1972] 2 QB 262 and *Bowker v Rose* (1978) 122 SJ 147, when this court held respectively that free support in an institution under national health service legislation and sums paid to a plaintiff by way of attendance allowances and mobility allowances under ss 35 and 37A of the Social Security Act 1975 were not deductible from a plaintiff's damages for prospective loss. Free support in an institution is however a benefit in kind to which a plaintiff is entitled even after he has received his damages, whereas supplementary benefit is a payment in cash which is the subject of a means test and so would not normally be payable to a plaintiff who had received damages to compensate him for loss of earning capacity. In any event I venture to think that a plaintiff could not claim as special damage the cost of his free support in an institution, since it is not an expense that he had incurred. And in *Bowker v Rose* Megaw LJ said that attendance and mobility allowances were more akin to benefits in kind under the national health service legislation than to unemployment benefit.

There are conflicting decisions at first instance whether or not supplementary benefit is deductible from damages. I prefer the reasoning of Latey J in *Plummer v P W Wilkins & Son Ltd* [1981] 1 All ER 91, [1981] 1 WLR 831 and Stocker J in *Gaskill v Preston* [1981] 3 All ER 427 to that of those judges who have held that supplementary benefit is not deductible. In particular I agree with Latey J that there is no difference in principle between unemployment benefit and supplementary benefit and with Stocker J that in practice each form of benefit, together with family income supplement with which he was concerned, achieves the same effect, ie the replacement of all or part of the earnings lost by the plaintiff, and should be dealt with by courts on the same basis. Since therefore *Parsons v BNM Laboratories Ltd* is binding on us I would hold that the supplementary benefit received is deductible from the plaintiff's damages.

However, the decision in *Parsons v BNM Laboratories Ltd* has been questioned by Lord Reid in *Parry v Cleaver* [1969] 1 All ER 555, [1970] AC 1, and by inference by this court in *Nabi v British Leyland (UK) Ltd* [1980] 1 All ER 667, [1980] 1 WLR 529, and by some textbook writers, and I go on to consider the question on principle.

We are not here considering prospective loss. We are considering special damage, that is to say compensation to the plaintiff for loss actually incurred by him between the date of the accident and the date of the trial by reason of his injuries. In *National Insurance Co of New Zealand Ltd v Espagne* (1961) 105 CLR 569 at 573, which was cited with approval in *Parry v Cleaver* Dixon CJ said:

'. . . I think that it is wiser as well as better in the general interest to say simply what is the reasoning which leads to the conclusion that the pension under the Social Services Act 1947–1957 should not be taken into account in reduction of damages. The reasoning begins with a distinction which I think is clear enough in general conception. There are certain special services, aids, benefits, subventions and the like which in most communities are available to injured people. Simple examples are hospital and pharmaceutical benefits which lighten the monetary burden of illness. If the injured plaintiff has availed himself of these, he cannot establish or calculate his damages on the footing that he did not do so. On the other hand there may be advantages which accrue to the injured plaintiff, whether as a result of legislation or of contract or of benevolence, which have an additional characteristic. It may be true that they are conferred because he is intended to enjoy them in the events which have happened. Yet they have this distinguishing characteristic, namely they are conferred on him not only independently of the existence in him of a right of redress against others but so that they may be enjoyed *a* by him although he may enforce that right: they are the product of a disposition in his favour intended for his enjoyment and not provided in relief of any liability in others fully to compensate him.'

The question is therefore: when the right to supplementary benefit was conferred, did Parliament intend that a plaintiff should enjoy it in addition to payment of his damages? In some statutes Parliament has expressly provided that certain benefits or a *b* proportion thereof shall be disregarded in assessing damages. So s 2 of the Law Reform (Personal Injuries) Act 1948 provides that one-half of any sickness benefit, invalidity benefit, non-contributory invalidity pension, injury benefit or disablement benefit for five years after the accident shall be taken into account. Section 4 of the Fatal Accidents Act 1976 (re-enacting s 2 of the Fatal Accidents Act 1959) provides that in assessing damages in respect of a person's death, there shall not be taken into account any *c* insurance money, benefit, pension, or gratuity, which has been or will or may be paid as a result of the death. But there is no statutory provision in respect of supplementary benefit paid to a person who has been injured in an accident, and Parliament must therefore be assumed to have left the question to the judges to be decided on principle.

The principle is clear. A plaintiff is entitled to compensation for the loss he has suffered by reason of a tort. No more and no less. A plaintiff cannot recover more than *d* he has lost. ' On the other hand completely collateral benefits are to be left out of account. Whether benefits are or are not collateral depends on whether or not they are too remote, and in considering that question the court will always look at the realities: see *British Transport Commission v Gourley* [1955] 3 All ER 796, [1956] AC 185. Two types of benefit have generally been excluded: sums received under insurance policies since they are payable by reason of the plaintiff's contractual rights against the insurance *e* company, and sums coming to him by benevolence. The latter have not been deducted because it is presumed that the benefactor intended that they should not be deducted.

Where as here there is no indication in the statute as to the intention of Parliament I ask myself whether the payment of supplementary benefit is so remote from the damage caused in the accident that it should not be taken into account? The payments were made to the plaintiff because he was in need as a direct consequence of the injuries he *f* suffered in the accident. They were made as of right, and if they are not deductible from his damages the plaintiff will pro tanto achieve double recovery, which is contrary to the basic principle of damages as compensation for loss actually suffered.

To say that it is wrong that the tortfeasor should benefit from payment of supplementary benefit seems to me to ignore the realities of personal injuries litigation. In the great majority of the cases the damages will be paid by an insurance company, and *g* the effect of not deducting supplementary benefit will be to increase premiums to employers and motorists, who together form a large section of the public. Moreover, if supplementary benefit is not deductible it will be in the interests of plaintiffs not to proceed expeditiously with their claims, so as to increase the element of double recovery.

For all those reasons I think the judge was wrong not to deduct the amount of supplementary benefit received by the plaintiff from his special damage, and I would *h* allow the appeal against damages accordingly.

It follows that in my judgment the plaintiff should recover one-third of the revised figure of damages. To that extent I would allow the appeal.

SIR DAVID CAIRNS. I agree that the appeal should be allowed and responsibility for the plaintiff's injuries should be attributed as to two-thirds to himself and one-third to *j* the defendant driver. [His Lordship then gave his reasons for attributing liability for the collision as he had and went on to consider the award of damages. His Lordship continued:] By far the most important and most interesting problem in this appeal is whether supplementary benefit received by the plaintiff falls to be deducted from his damages. While it appears to me that there is no authority either way binding on us, I

am satisfied that the better view is that the deduction ought to be made. I entirely agree
with Dunn LJ's analysis of the cases and his reasoning on the matter, and I have nothing
of my own to add thereto.

Indeed, having had the opportunity of reading, in draft, the judgment which Dunn LJ
has delivered, and the judgment which Waller LJ is about to deliver, I am in full
agreement with both of them on all the points arising in this appeal.

WALLER LJ. I agree that this appeal on liability should be allowed. [His Lordship
expressed his reasons for allowing the appeal on liability and agreed that the division of
responsibility for the collision should be as to two-thirds to the plaintiff and as to one-
third to the defendant. His Lordship continued:] The only other matter on which I wish
to express an opinion is the deductibility or not of the supplementary benefit received by
the plaintiff. We have been referred to a number of cases relating to the question of
deductibility and I do not propose to refer to them all. They have all been cited in the
judgment of Dunn LJ. The effect of the various reported cases is fully set out in the
judgment of Brightman LJ in *Nabi v British Leyland (UK) Ltd* [1980] 1 All ER 667, [1980]
1 WLR 529, where this court was considering the deductibility of unemployment
benefit, and in the judgments of Latey J in *Plummer v P W Wilkins & Sons Ltd* [1981] 1 All
ER 91, [1981] 1 WLR 831 and of Stocker J in *Gaskill v Preston* [1981] 3 All ER 427, both
dealing with supplementary benefit. I content myself with expressing my respectful
agreement with Pearson LJ's observations in *Parsons v BNM Laboratories Ltd* [1963] 2 All
ER 658 at 684, [1964] 1 QB 95 at 143–144 where he said:

> 'Is the plaintiff's receipt of unemployment benefit a matter too remote to be
> taken into consideration in ascertaining his net loss resulting from the wrongful
> dismissal? The common-sense answer is that of course it is not too remote. It is not
> "completely collateral". The dismissal caused the plaintiff to become unemployed,
> and therefore entitled, as a matter of general right under the system of state
> insurance and not by virtue of any private insurance policy of his own, to receive
> unemployment benefit. The effect of the dismissal was not to deprive him of all
> income but to reduce his income by substituting unemployment benefit for his
> salary. It would be unrealistic to disregard the unemployment benefit, because to
> do so would confer on the plaintiff, to the extent of £59 2s. 6d., a fortuitous
> windfall in addition to compensation.'

The words of Pearson LJ are wholly appropriate to this case. The plaintiff is suing to
recover damages and to replace that which he has actually lost. When he became
unemployed he did not lose the total of his wages because part of that loss was replaced
by supplementary benefit. If the supplementary benefit is not taken into account and
deducted the plaintiff will recover more damages than he has suffered. It will be a
fortuitous windfall. The fact that the defendant has to pay less damages as a result does
not lead me to change this view. There are so many considerations in an award of
damages for personal injuries which may make a difference to the award that I do not see
anything intrinsically wrong in taking this into account. Nor does calling the defendant
a wrongdoer affect this view, especially where the wrongfulness of the negligence may
be minimal. Furthermore, although in a trial the question of insurance or not is
irrelevant when considering broader principles, it is a matter to be considered. In cases
of personal injury arising out of road traffic accidents the defendant will almost always
be insured. The ideal answer might be that the insurers should get credit for the
supplementary benefit but should be obliged to reimburse the Supplementary Benefit
Commission for the benefit paid. This, however, cannot be done without legislation.

However, the case for taking supplementary benefit into account is even stronger in
a case such as the present. It is in the public interest that litigation should be disposed of
with such expedition as is possible. If, however, supplementary benefit were not
deductible it would be in the interests of the claimant to delay as long as possible and so
increase the amount of supplementary benefit which he would receive. I agree with

both Latey and Stocker JJ that the case is indistinguishable in principle from
unemployment benefit. I would go further and respectfully adopt the words which I
have quoted from Pearson LJ and apply them to supplementary benefit.

I agree with Dunn LJ in the order which he proposes, namely that the plaintiff should
bear two-thirds of the blame for this accident and that credit should be given by the
plaintiff for the supplementary benefit which he has received in considering the
assessment of damage.

Appeal allowed. Leave to appeal to the House of Lords refused.

Solicitors: *Hall-Clark* (for the second defendants); *Gepp & Sons*, Chelmsford (for the
plaintiff).

Diana Brahams   Barrister.

R v Welch

COURT OF APPEAL, CRIMINAL DIVISION
LORD LANE CJ AND SKINNER J
21 MAY 1982

*Sentence – Parole – Release on licence – Conviction for further offence – Judge sentencing accused
to term of imprisonment and revoking release on licence – Whether accused having right of appeal
against revocation of licence – Whether order revoking licence a 'sentence' – Criminal Justice Act
1967, ss 60, 61, 62(7) – Criminal Appeal Act 1968, s 9.*

In March 1966 the appellant was sentenced to life imprisonment for robbery with
violence and associated offences. He served seven years of the sentence until June 1973
when he was released on licence pursuant to s 61(1)[a] of the Criminal Justice Act 1967.
In August 1981, while released on licence, he committed a further offence of robbery
with violence. He pleaded guilty in the Crown Court to that offence and was sentenced
to eight years' imprisonment. The judge also ordered that his release on licence be
revoked, pursuant to s 62(7)[b] of the 1967 Act. The appellant appealed against, inter alia,
the order revoking his release on licence, and the question arose whether the revocation
of a release on licence was a 'sentence' in respect of which there was a right of appeal
under s 9[c] of the Criminal Appeal Act 1968.

Held – Since a condition precedent to the exercise of the power under s 62(7) of the 1967
Act to revoke a licence granted under s 60[d] or s 61 of that Act was that the person whose
licence was being revoked had been 'convicted' of another indictable offence, and since
under s 62(7) revocation of the licence could be the only sentence passed on that
conviction, it followed that an order under s 62(7) revoking a licence was a 'sentence'
passed in respect of that conviction, within s 9 of the 1968 Act. Accordingly, the

---

a Section 61(1), so far as material, provides: 'The Secretary of State may, if recommended to do so by
   the Parole Board, release on licence a person serving a sentence of imprisonment for life . . . but
   shall not do so . . . except after consultation with the Lord Chief Justice of England together with
   the trial judge if available.'
b Section 62(7) is set out at p 826 c d, post
c Section 9, so far as material, provides; 'A person who has been convicted of an offence on
   indictment may appeal to the Court of Appeal against any sentence . . . passed on him for the
   offence, whether passed on his conviction or in subsequent proceedings.'
d Section 60, so far as material, provides: 'The Secretary of State may, if recommended to do so by the
   Parole Board, release on licence a person serving a sentence of imprisonment, other than
   imprisonment for life, after he has served not less than one-third of his sentence of twelve months
   thereof, whichever expires the later.'

appellant was entitled to appeal against the order revoking his release on licence (see p 826 g h, post).

R v Raeburn (1980) 74 Cr App R 21 considered.

Notes

For appeal against sentence following conviction on indictment, see 11 Halsbury's Laws (4th edn) para 615.

For the Criminal Justice Act 1967, ss 60, 61, 62, see 25 Halsbury's Statutes (3rd edn) 888, 890, 891.

For the Criminal Appeal Act 1968, s 9, see 8 ibid 695.

Case referred to in judgment

R v Raeburn (1980) 74 Cr App R 21, CA.

Appeal against sentence

On 9 December 1981 the appellant, James Hutchinson Alan Welch, pleaded guilty to robbery in the Crown Court at Newcastle upon Tyne before his Honour Judge Hall and a jury and on 10 December the judge sentenced him to eight years' imprisonment and also revoked his release on licence from a sentence of life imprisonment imposed for robbery and related offences in March 1966, under the power to do so contained in s 62(7) of the Criminal Justice Act 1967. The appellant appealed against the sentence of eight years' imprisonment and against the revocation of his release on licence. The grounds of the appeal against revocation of the licence were (1) that the life sentence was imposed for offences which at the date of the appeal would attract only a determinate sentence and not an indeterminate sentence of life imprisonment, (2) that the appellant had served seven years of the life sentence before he was released on licence which was equivalent to a long determinate sentence, and (3) that, since he was receiving a substantial determinate sentence (eight years) for the later offence of robbery, to revoke the licence and impose a further indeterminate sentence under the life sentence imposed in 1966 was a wrong exercise of the judge's discretion. On the hearing of the appeal the question arose whether there was a right of appeal against the revocation under s 62(7) of a release on licence granted under s 60 or s 61 of the 1967 Act. The facts are set out in the judgment of·the court.

Toby Hedworth (assigned by the Registrar of Criminal Appeals) for the appellant.

J T Milford for the Crown.

SKINNER J delivered the following judgment of the court: On 9 December 1981 in the Crown Court at Newcastle upon Tyne before his Honour Judge Hall the appellant was convicted of robbery after changing his plea to guilty from not guilty on the second day of his trial. He was sentenced to eight years' imprisonment for that offence. At the time the robbery was committed he was on licence from a sentence of life imprisonment imposed for robbery, and the licence was revoked.

He now appeals against those sentences by leave of the single judge.

[His Lordship stated, inter alia, that on 1 March 1966 the appellant was sentenced to life imprisonment for two offences of aggravated robbery and associated offences of burglary and wounding with intent, 20 other offences of housebreaking being taken into consideration, that he had served seven years and three months of that sentence until June 1973 when he was released on licence, that the present offence of robbery had been committed on 10 August 1981, and that, having regard both to the circumstances of that offence, which involved a terrifying attack on an elderly man in his home at night, and to the appellant's record, eight years' imprisonment was a proper sentence. His Lordship continued:] One other matter arises in this case, because some doubt has been expressed whether an order revoking a licence granted under s 60 or s 61 of the Criminal Justice Act 1967 is a 'sentence' within s 9 of the Criminal Appeal Act 1968.

Counsel for the appellant drew our attention initially to s 50(1) of the Criminal Appeal Act 1968, which defines 'sentence' for the purpose of an appeal to this court. Section 50(1) reads:

'In this Act, "sentence", in relation to an offence, includes any order made by a court when dealing with an offender (including a hospital order under Part V of the *a* Mental Health Act 1959, with or without an order restricting discharge) and also includes a recommendation for deportation.'

By s 62(1) to (5) of the Criminal Justice Act 1967, the Home Secretary is given the power to revoke a licence subject to the right of the prisoner to make representations to the parole board. Section 62(6) and (7) deals with the powers of the court to revoke a licence on reconviction and provides: *b*

'(6) If a person subject to a licence under section 60 or 61 of this Act is convicted by a magistrates' court of an offence punishable on indictment with imprisonment, the court may commit him in custody or on bail to the Crown Court for sentence in accordance with section 42 of the Powers of Criminal Courts Act 1973 (power of the Crown Court to sentence persons convicted by magistrates' courts of indictable offences). *c*

(7) If a person subject to any such licence is convicted on indictment of such an offence as aforesaid or is committed to the Crown Court for sentence as aforesaid or under section 38 of the Magistrates' Courts Act 1980 (committal of persons convicted of indictable offences for sentence), the court by which he is convicted or to which he is committed, as the case may be, may, whether or not it passes any other sentence on him, revoke the licence.' *d*

There is no decision of this court directly in point, but the decision in *R v Raeburn* (1980) 74 Cr App R 21 throws light on the question. That was an appeal against a sentence which had included a criminal bankruptcy order and an order that the appellant should pay £25,000 towards the costs of his defence under a legal aid certificate. In holding that the latter was not a sentence within s 50(1) of the Criminal Appeal Act 1968, Lord Lane CJ, in delivering the judgment of the court, said (at 26): *e*

'Prima facie then an order to pay a contribution towards legal aid costs may be an order by a Court when dealing with an offender. But that is not enough. It is not enough to invoke the jurisdiction of this Court. It must be an order made or sentence passed on him for the offence of which he was convicted. That this order plainly was not. It is made clear by the Act that a contribution order of this sort can *f* be made whether or not there has been a conviction. That is plain under the Legal Aid Act 1974, section 32(1). In short the contribution order is made not for the offence of which he is convicted, but in respect of costs incurred in the criminal proceedings against him.'

By contrast, under s 62(7) of the 1967 Act, a conviction is a sine qua non of the power to revoke. What is more, the words 'Whether or not it passes any other sentence on him' *g* make it clear not only that revocation is a sentence but also that it may be the only sentence which results from conviction.

In these circumstances the court is satisfied that an order revoking a licence, whether granted under s 60 or s 61 of the 1967 Act, is a sentence for the purpose of s 9 of the Criminal Appeal Act 1968.

On the question whether it was right in the present case to revoke the licence, counsel *h* for the appellant did not address any argument to us. It seems to this court that the only possible course that the judge could have taken in the present circumstances was to revoke the appellant's licence. It was obvious that there was a close relationship between the earlier offence and the later one. Both were for violent robbery. The only factors in the appellant's favour were his marriage and clean record from June 1973 to November 1980. Those are factors which can, if the Home Secretary thinks right, be taken into *j* account if and when the time comes to consider whether or not his licence should be renewed. In these circumstances this appeal is dismissed.

Appeal dismissed.

Solicitors: *D E Brown*, Newcastle upon Tyne (for the Crown).

N P Metcalfe Esq   Barrister.

Swain v Law Society

HOUSE OF LORDS
LORD DIPLOCK, LORD FRASER OF TULLYBELTON, LORD SCARMAN, LORD ROSKILL AND LORD BRIGHTMAN
24, 25, 26 MAY, 1 JULY 1982

Insurance – Liability insurance – Professional indemnity insurance – Solicitors – Law Society's group scheme – Law Society authorised to 'take out and maintain insurance with authorised insurer's' against loss arising from claims against solicitors and their employees etc in respect of liability for professional negligence or breach of duty – Law Society arranging master policy with specified insurers – Law Society requiring all solicitors to participate in group scheme and pay premiums set under master policy – Law Society sharing commission with brokers – Whether Law Society accountable to individual solicitors for commission received – Whether Law Society placing itself in fiduciary position to premium payers – Whether Law Society in exercising its powers performing public or private duty – Whether necessary to imply trust to secure commercial viability of scheme – Solicitors Act 1974, s 37.

Trust and trustee – Profit from trust – Account of profits – Commission – Professional indemnity insurance – Solicitors – Law Society's group scheme – Law Society arranging master policy with specified insurers through brokers – Law Society and brokers agreeing to share commission – Whether Law Society accountable to individual solicitors for commission received – Whether Law Society in fiduciary relationship with solicitors when making commission agreement with brokers.

By virtue of s 37(1)[a] of the Solicitors Act 1974 the Law Society was empowered to make rules concerning indemnity against loss arising from claims made against solicitors and former solicitors and their employees and former employees in respect of liability for professional negligence or breach of duty. Section 37(2) specified that 'For the purpose of providing such indemnity' such rules could, inter alia, '(b) . . . authorise or require the Society to take out and maintain insurance with authorised insurers'. In exercise of those powers the Law Society in 1975 established a group scheme, whereby it arranged indemnity insurance through a particular firm of brokers and then required solicitors to participate in the scheme or else risk being refused a practising certificate. The society entered into a contract with specified insurers in November 1975 and later made the Solicitors' Indemnity Rules 1975, which provided for the society to take out and maintain with authorised insurers a 'master policy' and required solicitors to pay the premiums prescribed under that policy and to produce a certificate of insurance issued under the master policy when applying each year for a practising certificate. By s 37(3)(c) of the 1974 Act the society was authorised to require solicitors to 'make payments by way of premium on any insurance policy maintained by the Society [under s 37(2)(b)]'. The master policy, which was deemed to form part of the indemnity rules, was arranged by the society with specified insurers. The policy recited that the insurers agreed 'with the Law Society on behalf of all solicitors . . . required to be insured' by the indemnity rules to provide such insurance and provided for fixed premiums according to whether a solicitor was a partner or sole practitioner and later according to whether a solicitor practised in Inner London or elsewhere. A specified firm were to act as sole brokers under the scheme and all claims were required to be submitted to them. The brokers agreed that in return for being appointed sole brokers they would share with the society commission received by them from the insurers, and in fact the society received substantial amounts of revenue from that source. That agreement (the commission arrangement) was made in May 1976 following renegotiation by the society and the brokers of an earlier commission agreement made in February 1975 in respect of a

---

a Section 37 is set out at p 830 *j* to p 831 *e*, post

voluntary insurance scheme which the society ran in conjunction with the brokers prior
to the compulsory scheme set up in November 1975. The February 1975 agreement
provided for such renegotiation at the request of either party in the event of the
introduction of a compulsory indemnity insurance scheme. As a result of the
renegotiation the society received a much greater share of the commission than before.

The respondent, who was a practising solicitor, preferred to negotiate his own
insurance cover but he took no action in the matter until 1979, when he and another
solicitor took out an originating summons seeking, inter alia, a declaration that the
society was not entitled to retain for its own purposes commission received by it from the
brokers in respect of premiums paid by individual solicitors but was instead accountable
to them for the commission. The judge refused to grant the declaration sought on the
ground that, although the society had entered into the contract with the insurers as
trustee for the solicitors concerned and therefore a fiduciary relationship came into
existence between the society and the solicitors when the contract was concluded, the
society owed no duty to solicitors when negotiating the contract from which the
arrangement relating to the commission arose, and accordingly the society was not
bound to account to the plaintiffs for any part of the commission received by it. The
respondent appealed to the Court of Appeal, which allowed the appeal, holding that in
principle the Law Society was accountable to individual solicitors who paid premiums
under the scheme for the commission received by it because the Law Society had
constituted itself a trustee of the master policy contract. However, the court held that
the respondent was debarred by acquiescence from enforcing his right to his share of the
commission received by the Law Society prior to 1979. The Law Society appealed to the
House of Lords.

Held – The power conferred on the Law Society by s 37 of the 1974 Act was a power to
be exercised not only in the interests of professional practitioners but also in the interests
of the lay public who resorted to solicitors for legal advice. The Law Society in exercising
its power under s 37 was therefore performing not merely a private duty to premium-
paying solicitors but a public duty, and accordingly there was no remedy in breach of
trust or equitable account. Furthermore, the Law Society by entering into the master
policy contract had not placed itself in a fiduciary position in relation to the premium-
payers so as to constitute itself trustee of the master policy contract by virtue of the
statement in the form of master policy that the agreement was made with the Law
Society 'on behalf of' all solicitors because those words clearly did not create an express
trust and neither did they necessarily imply a trust. Moreover, it was not necessary to
imply a trust in order to secure commercial viability of the indemnity scheme because
the scheme had the force of a statutory indemnity scheme and all persons, whether
premium-paying solicitors or others insured by the scheme, would have a direct remedy
against the insurers in the event of breach by the insurers of the obligations expressed to
be imposed on them by the scheme. It followed therefore that the Law Society was not
accountable to the respondent for the commission it received, and the appeal would
accordingly be allowed (see p 830 b to g, p 832 c to e j, p 833 c d f to j, p 834 a to c, p 837
g to p 838 b, p 840 c to h and p 841 h, post).

Skinners' Co v Irish Society (1845) 12 Cl & Fin 425 applied.

Decision of the Court of Appeal [1981] 3 All ER 797 reversed.

Notes

For professional indemnity insurance, see 25 Halsbury's Laws (4th edn) paras 719–724.

For the accountability of a trustee arising out of a fiduciary relationship, see 38
Halsbury's Laws (3rd edn) 957, para 1658, and for cases on the subject, see 47 Digest
(Repl) 364–367, 3275–3298.

For the Solicitors Act 1974, s 37, see 44 Halsbury's Statutes (3rd edn) 1508.

Cases referred to in opinions

a   *Beswick v Beswick* [1967] 2 All ER 1197, [1968] AC 58, [1967] 3 WLR 932, HL, 12 Digest (Reissue) 50, 256.

Morgan v Palmer (1824) 2 B & C 729, 107 ER 554, 12 Digest (Reissue) 688, 4965.

Skinners' Co v Irish Society (1845) 12 Cl & Fin 425, 8 ER 1474, HL, 8(1) Digest (Reissue) 447, 1948.

b   **Appeal**

By an originating summons dated 25 October 1979 as amended the first plaintiff, James Midwood Swain (the respondent), and the second plaintiff, Alan Stephen McLaren, sought as against the Law Society (1) a declaration that on the true construction of s 37 of the Solicitors Act 1974 and the Solicitors' Indemnity Rules 1975, the Solicitors' Indemnity Rules 1978 and the Solicitors' Indemnity Rules 1979 the Council of the Law

c   Society had no power to make all or any such rules, which were accordingly null and void, and (2) the determination of the question whether, on the true construction of the 1974 Act and the indemnity rules and in the events which had happened, the Law Society was entitled to retain for its own purposes the commission received by it from London Assurance Brokers Ltd in respect of premiums paid by individual solicitors pursuant to the society's Solicitors' Indemnity Insurance Scheme, or whether it was

d   accountable for such commission to individual solicitors or otherwise. On 17 March 1980 Slade J ([1980] 3 All ER 615, [1980] 1 WLR 1355) dismissed the summons holding in respect of para (2) thereof that the Law Society was not accountable for the commission it received. The respondent appealed. On 31 July 1981 the Court of Appeal (Stephenson, Oliver and Fox LJJ) ([1981] 3 All ER 797, [1982] 1 WLR 17) allowed the appeal in respect of para (2). The Law Society appealed to the House of Lords with leave of the Court of

e   Appeal. The facts are set out in the opinion of Lord Brightman.

Leonard Hoffmann QC, Patrick Phillips QC and *Robert Walker QC* for the Law Society.
John M Bowyer and *John McDonnell* for the respondent.

Their Lordships took time for consideration.

f   1 July. The following opinions were delivered.

LORD DIPLOCK. My Lords, this appeal is about the way in which the Law Society has exercised its powers under s 37 of the Solicitors Act 1974 in relation to the compulsory insurance of solicitors against liability to third parties arising out of the conduct by them

g   of their private practices. In dealing with the appeal it is, in my view, essential throughout to bear in mind that in performance of its functions the Law Society acts in two distinct capacities: a private capacity as the successor, incorporated by royal charter of 1845 as subsequently amended (the charter), to the Society of Gentlemen Practisers in the Courts of Law and Equity; and a public capacity as the authority on whom, or on whose council elected in accordance with the provisions of the charter, various statutory

h   duties are imposed and powers conferred by the Solicitors Act 1974.

When acting in its private capacity the Law Society is subject to private law alone. What may be done on behalf of the Law Society by the council in whom the management of the Law Society is vested by the charter, must fall within the wide description in the charter of the general purposes of the Law Society, viz 'promoting professional improvement and facilitating the acquisition of legal knowledge'. Subject to this

i   limitation, however, the Law Society acting in its private capacity can do anything that a natural person could lawfully do, with all the consequences that flow in private law from doing it; and in deciding how to act on behalf of the Law Society in this capacity the council's only duty is one owed to the Law Society's members to do what it believes to be in the best interest of those members; and for the way in which it performs that duty the council is answerable to those members alone. Membership of the Law Society by solicitors is voluntary; it does not comprise the whole of the profession; your *a* Lordships were informed that some 10% of practising solicitors are not members and over these the Law Society, acting in its private capacity, can exercise no coercive powers.

It is quite otherwise when the Law Society is acting in its public capacity. The Solicitors Act 1974 imposes on the Law Society a number of statutory duties in relation to solicitors whether they are members of the Law Society or not. It also confers on the council of the Law Society, acting either alone or with the concurrence of the Lord Chief *b* Justice and the Master of the Rolls or of the latter only, power to make rules and regulations having the effect of subordinate legislation under the Act. Such rules and regulations may themselves confer on the Law Society further statutory powers or impose on it further statutory duties. The purpose for which these statutory functions are vested in the Law Society and the council is the protection of the public or, more specifically, that section of the public that may be in need of legal advice, assistance or *c* representation. In exercising its statutory functions the duty of the council is to act in what it believes to be the best interests of that section of the public, even in the event (unlikely though this may be on any long-term view) that those public interests should conflict with the special interests of members of the Law Society or of members of the solicitors' profession as a whole. The council, in exercising its powers under the Act to make rules and regulations and the Law Society in discharging functions vested in it by *d* the Act or by such rules or regulations, is acting in a public capacity and what it does in that capacity is governed by public law; and, although the legal consequences of doing it may result in creating rights enforceable in private law, those rights are not necessarily the same as those that would flow in private law from doing a similar act otherwise than in the exercise of statutory powers.

My Lords, it is beyond question that the acts done by the Law Society that resulted in *e* its receiving a share of the brokerage allowed by insurers in respect of the premium paid by the respondent, Mr Swain, for insurance cover against liability to third parties arising out of the conduct of his private practice as a solicitor, for which share Mr Swain seeks to make it accountable to him, were done by the Law Society in its public capacity. It was exercising statutory powers, conferred on it by s 37 of the Solicitors Act 1974 and rules made by its council under that section. That what the Law Society did in exercise of *f* those powers was intra vires, though vigorously contested in the courts below, was conceded by the respondent in this House. The relevant facts are set out in considerable detail in the judgment of Slade J at first instance (see [1980] 3 All ER 615, [1980] 1 WLR 1335). In the speech to be delivered by my noble and learned friend Lord Brightman they are reproduced in summarised form sufficient to make plain his reasons for allowing the appeal. Since I agree with his reasoning, no useful purpose would be served by my *g* providing a paraphrase of what he says in language of my own. I will limit my own comments to what I regard as the initial error, resulting from the way in which the cases of both parties had been presented in the courts below and uncorrected until the hearing in this House, of failing to distinguish between public law and private law and because of that failure seeking to discover the legal relationsips between the Law Society, the insurers, the brokers and the individual premium-paying solicitors by applying to these *h* relationships concepts of private law alone.

Section 37 under which the Law Society was acting in its public capacity provides:

'(1) The Council, with the concurrence of the Master of the Rolls, may make rules (in this Act referred to as "indemnity rules") concerning indemnity against loss arising from claims in respect of any description of civil liability incurred—(*a*) by *j* a solicitor or former solicitor in connection with his practice or with any trust of which he is or formerly was a trustee; (*b*) by an employee or former employee of a solicitor or former solicitor in connection with that solicitor's practice or with any trust of which that solicitor or the employee is or formerly was a trustee.

(2) For the purpose of providing such indemnity, indemnity rules—(*a*) may authorise or require the Society to establish and maintain a fund or funds; (*b*) may authorise or require the Society to take out and maintain insurance with authorised insurers; (*c*) may require solicitors or any specified class of solicitors to take out and maintain insurance with authorised insurers.

(3) Without prejudice to the generality of subsections (1) and (2), indemnity rules—(*a*) may specify the terms and conditions on which indemnity is to be available, and any circumstances in which the right to it is to be excluded or modified; (*b*) may provide for the management, administration and protection of any fund maintained by virtue of subsection (2)(*a*) and require solicitors or any class of solicitors to make payments to any such fund; (*c*) may require solicitors or any class of solicitors to make payments by way of premium on any insurance policy maintained by the Society by virtue of subsection (2)(*b*); (*d*) may prescribe the conditions which an insurance policy must satisfy for the purposes of subsection (2)(*c*); (*e*) may authorise the Society to determine the amount of any payments required by the rules, subject to such limits, or in accordance with such provisions, as may be prescribed by the rules; (*f*) may specify circumstances in which, where a solicitor for whom indemnity is provided has failed to comply with the rules, the Society or insurers may take proceedings against him in respect of sums paid by way of indemnity in connection with a matter in relation to which he has failed to comply; (*g*) may specify circumstances in which solicitors are exempt from the rules; (*h*) may empower the Council to take such steps as they consider necessary or expedient to ascertain whether or not the rules are being complied with; and (*i*) may contain incidental, procedural or supplementary provisions.

(4) If any solicitor fails to comply with indemnity rules, any person may make a complaint in respect of that failure to the Tribunal.

(5) The Society shall have power, without prejudice to any of its other powers, to carry into effect any arrangements which it considers necessary or expedient for the purpose of indemnity under this section.'

Subsection (1) defines the class of persons who may be required by indemnity rules to be insured, and the risk, which I shall refer to as 'professional liability', that persons falling within that class may be required to be insured against. Crucial to a true and purposive construction of the later subsections is the fact that the Law Society itself neither falls within that class nor is it subject to that risk. The class is wider than solicitors who are or have been engaged in private practice as principals, for it includes employees and former employees whether qualified solicitors or not; but, since the only sanctions for non-compliance with indemnity rules (viz refusal of a practising certificate under s 10 and complaint to the Solicitors Disciplinary Tribunal under s 37(4)) are available against solicitors alone, any obligation to obtain insurance cover for employees who are not themselves solicitors can only be imposed by the rules on the solicitor who employs them.

Subsection (2) specifies in paras (*a*), (*b*) and (*c*) three methods and three methods only by any one or any combination of which solicitors may be required by indemnity rules to obtain insurance cover against professional liability referred to in sub-s (1). These are: (a) mutual insurance financed by contributions by solicitors to a fund established and maintained by the Law Society, a method for which para (*a*) and sub-s (3)(*a*), (*b*) and (*f*) provide; (b) a form of group insurance, a method for which para (*b*) and sub-s (3)(*c*) and (*f*) provide; and (c) policies of insurance with insurers of their own choice taken out directly by individual solicitors, a method for which para (*c*) and sub-s (3)(*d*) provide.

In the event the council adopted method (b). It thus becomes necessary to consider what form of group insurance Parliament intended should be authorised by the subsection, of which the paramount purpose was the protection of that section of the public that makes use of the services of solicitors. The insurance is to be taken out and maintained by the Law Society itself who ex hypothesi will have no insurable interest in

the risk insured against. The only person with any insurable interest in the policy of
insurance to be taken out and maintained by the Law Society are those solicitors (and   *a*
their employees) whose professional liability is required by the indemnity rules to be
insured. If the public was to be adequately protected by method (b) it must have been
intended that as against the insurers each such solicitor should have the rights and be
subject to the duties of an assured under the policy. This is borne out not only by sub-s
(3)(*f*) which contemplates the possibility of direct proceedings by insurers against
solicitors but also by the description in sub-s (3)(*c*) of the payments to be made by   *b*
solicitors if method (b) is adopted; they are to be made 'by way of premium on [the]
insurance policy maintained by the Society'. 'Premium' in the context of insurance law
is a term of art. It means a sum of money paid by an assured to an insurer in consideration
of his indemnifying the assured for loss sustained in consequence of the risk insured
against. Having regard to the many thousands of solicitors in private practice each one
of whom might be required by the indemnity rules to be personally insured against   *c*
professional liability if adequate protection were to be afforded to the public, it cannot,
in my view, be sensibly supposed that Parliament intended otherwise than that any
policy of insurance taken out and maintained by the Law Society under s 37(2)(*b*) should
be one capable of creating legal rights and obligation between the insurers and each
individual solicitor whose professional liability was insured by it, and that such rights
should be directly enforceable against one another by the insurers and each assured,   *d*
without any need for the Law Society's intervention as intermediary.

If this be right the policy of insurance which the Law Society is empowered to take out
and maintain by s 37(2)(*b*) is a contract which creates a jus quaesitio tertio. It does so
by virtue of public law, not the ordinary English private law of contract. This makes it
unnecessary in the instant case to have recourse to any of those juristic subterfuges to
which courts have, from time to time, felt driven to resort in cases in which English   *e*
private law is applicable, to mitigate the effect of the lacuna resulting from the non-
recognition of a jus quaesitium tertio, an anachronistic shortcoming that has for many
years been regarded as a reproach to English private law: see the Law Revision
Committee's Report of 1937 (Cmd 5449) referred to in the speeches in this House in
Beswick v Beswick [1967] 2 All ER 1197, [1968] AC 58. The principal means by which the
courts have tried to mitigate this reproach are by extensions of the concepts of agency   *f*
and of constructive trusteeship of the benefit of promises, and by the recognition of an
innominate equitable right, although not coupled with a duty, to enforce specific
performance of contracts which benefit third parties. The existence of such a right
received the unanalytical approval of this House in *Beswick v Beswick*.

My Lords, the master policy taken out and maintained by the Law Society under these
statutory powers incorporated the provisions of the certificate of insurance attached to it,   *g*
and set out the terms on which individual solicitors and their employees were to be
entitled to recover from the insurers indemnity against professional liability. Those
provisions were made part of the indemnity rules themselves; they gave to each solicitor
to whom the rules applied, viz principals in private practice and also to solicitors
formerly in private practice, a statutory right against the insurers to be granted insurance
cover on the terms of the provisions of the master policy and certificate of insurance, and
imposed (a) on solicitors currently engaged in private practice a statutory obligation to   *h*
pay the annual premium at the rate agreed between the insurers and the Law Society,
and (b) on them and also on solicitors formerly in private practice, other statutory duties
of a positive nature owed to the insurers in relation to notice and settlement of claims,
conduct of litigation and the reimbursement to the insurers of sums paid by them in
certain events. The source of these rights and duties is not contract; it is statute. But for
the statutory powers conferred on the council and the Law Society and the way that they   *j*
chose to exercise those statutory powers, the master policy could not confer on solicitors
and former solicitors any rights in private law to demand insurance cover against
professional liability from the insurers who underwrote the master policy.

By confining its attention to the question in what capacity might the Law Society, if

it were able to rely on private law, have entered into the master policy so as to confer on
a individual solicitors a right, enforceable against the insurers, either directly or through
the Law Society as intermediary, to obtain insurance cover against professional liability,
the Court of Appeal was driven to consider whether the Law Society had acted as agent
for each such solicitor, or as trustee of a promise for his benefit. If it were in either of
these capacities that the Law Society entered into the master policy, it could be
persuasively argued that the Law Society's ability to bargain with the brokers for a share
b of the customary 15% commission paid by the insurers to the brokers out of the
premiums received from individual solicitors in current practice, arose out the Law
Society's position as agent or constructive trustee for the individual solicitors, and for that
reason constituted a profit for which the Law Society was accountable to each of them for
an aliquot part attributable to the premium which each had paid.

The Court of Appeal in agreement with Slade J held that the concept of agency in
c private law could not be extended to cover the legal relationship in which the Law
Society stood to individual solicitors required by the indemnity rules to be insured. For
the reasons given by them and mentioned by my noble and learned friend Lord
Brightman I agree that they were right to do so. This left constructive trusteeship, and
the Court of Appeal held that, although the Law Society did not act in the capacity of
agent in entering into and maintaining the master policy, it nevertheless did so as trustee
d for the individual solicitors of the benefit of the promises by the insurers made in the
master policy to insure those individual solicitors against professional liability. In this,
for the reasons given by Lord Brightman, I think they erred. There is one of those
reasons which for my part I find conclusive in itself. The obligations imposed by the
master policy and certificate of insurance on the insurers and each assured are mutual;
they are not limited to promises by the insurers to indemnify the assured against
e professional liability conditional on the assured's acting in a particular way, as in a
unilateral or 'if' contract. To an 'if' contract, since it involves no promise by the promisee
to act in that way, it may be that the concept of constructive trusteeship of the benefit of
a promise may properly be applied. But the master policy imposes on the assured as well
positive obligations to the insurers, as in synallagmatic contracts. The concept of
constructive trusteeship of promises which confer a benefit on a cestui qui trust is not, in
f my view, capable in private law of extension to promises which impose a burden on a
cestui qui trust; an agent acting within his authority can create burdensome obligations
on the part of his principal, a constructive trustee cannot.

So one is left with mutual rights and obligations of insurers and individual solicitors
entitled to insurance cover by the master policy whose source is statutory only; they do
not depend on private law concepts either of agency or of constructive trusteeship of
g promises and so do not attract the principles of accountability of agent to his principal or
trustee to his cestui qui trust for any profit made by virtue of his position as agent or
trustee that follow in private law from the existence of such relationships.

In adopting method (b), ie group insurance effected under a master policy taken out
and maintained by the Law Society, it chose a method which, having regard to the
magnitude of the total risk, could only be placed by brokers in the London market in
h which brokerage of 15% was customarily payable by insurers to the brokers. The Law
Society would have been lacking in business acumen had it not taken advantage of its
ability to choose the brokers by whom that brokerage would be earned, by obtaining for
itself a share of the net brokerage (after deduction of expenses) paid by the insurers to the
brokers. For what particular purposes the Law Society should use the moneys
representing that share of brokerage after it had been received is a matter within the
j discretion of the council to determine as it thinks fit. That it should use it for the
purposes of the Law Society (as it is expressly authorised by s 11(3) to do with fees paid
to it for practising certificates) or for the benefit of the solicitors' profession as a whole
does not seem to me to be unconscionable in any way. It is a perfectly lawful and proper
way of using those moneys.

I would allow the appeal.

LORD FRASER OF TULLYBELTON. My Lords, I have had the advantage of reading in draft the speeches prepared by my noble and learned friends Lord Diplock and *a* Lord Brightman. I agree with them; and for the reasons stated therein I would allow this appeal.

LORD SCARMAN. My Lords, I have had the advantage of reading in draft the speech delivered by my noble and learned friend Lord Diplock, and also the speech to be delivered by my noble and learned friend Lord Brightman. I agree with both speeches *b* and would allow the appeal.

LORD ROSKILL. My Lords, I have had the advantage of reading in draft the speeches of my noble and learned friends Lord Diplock and Lord Brightman. I agree with them both, and for the reasons therein contained I too would allow this appeal.

c

LORD BRIGHTMAN. My Lords, the question raised by this appeal is whether the Law Society is accountable to solicitors for the money it receives under a commission-sharing arrangement. Premiums are paid by solicitors when effecting insurances under the Law Society's professional indemnity scheme. This is a compulsory scheme established by the Law Society under statute. The brokers employed by the Law Society in connection with the scheme receive a commission from the insurers on the premiums *d* so paid. The brokers share this commission with the Law Society, which uses the money for the benefit of the profession as a whole. The respondent claims that the Law Society should, instead, return the money to the solicitors paying the premiums that gave rise to the commission.

The proceedings were begun in the Chancery Division by the respondent, Mr Swain, a London solicitor, and his co-plaintiff, Mr McLaren, who practices in Somerset, with the *e* primary object of obtaining a declaration that the indemnity scheme did not conform to the requirements of the statute and was void. The scheme was not popular with all solicitors, some of whom would have preferred to negotiate their own separate insurance cover with insurers of their own choice. The originating summons additonally sought an answer to the question whether on the true construction of the statutory power and the rules made thereunder, and in the events which had happened, the Law Society was *f* accountable for the commission it received. The ultra vires aspect of the dispute was the predominant feature of the proceedings in both courts below. That aspect was decided against the plaintiffs, both at first instance and in the Court of Appeal. The Court of Appeal, differing from the trial judge, found against the Law Society on the issue of accountability, and in consequence the Law Society has launched this appeal to your Lordships' House. It was not originally the intention of the respondent plaintiff to be *g* represented before your Lordships; he no doubt considered, as did his co-plaintiff, that the ultra vires attack was unlikely to succeed in your Lordships' House and that the issue of accountability was of secondary, if not minor, importance. The Law Society, however, took the view that it would be of assistance to your Lordships' House to hear argument on both sides, and arranged with the respondent, Mr Swain, that he should be represented before your Lordships at the expense of the Law Society. Your Lordships may feel that *h* we are greatly indebted to the Law Society for the helpful attitude it has adopted in arranging for Mr Swain to be represented.

My Lords, the Law Society was incorporated by royal charter in 1831, and was granted its present charter in 1845. Its purposes are defined in the preamble to the 1845 charter as the promotion of professional improvement and the facilitating of the acquisition of legal knowledge. The Law Society has a number of important statutory functions under *j* the Solicitors Act 1974, which affect not merely the solicitors' profession but also the public well-being; for example, power to make regulations, with the concurrence of the Lord Chancellor, the Lord Chief Justice and the Master of the Rolls, for educating and training persons seeking to become solicitors (s 2); power, with the concurrence of the Master of the Rolls, to make rules for regulating the professional practice, conduct and

discipline of solicitors (s 31); the duty under s 32, with the concurrence of the Master of
a the Rolls, to make rules for the maintenance by solicitors of separate accounts for clients'
money.

Part II of the Solicitors Act 1974 is headed 'Professional Practice, Conduct and
Discipline of Solicitors and Clerks'. Sections 35, 36 and 37 are contained in this part, and
are set out under the sub-heading 'Intervention in solicitor's practice, Compensation
Fund and professional indemnity'. Section 35 is the intervention section, and enables the
b Council of the Law Society to step in where a solicitor's practice has, or is thought to have,
ceased to be under satisfactory control. Section 36 requires the Law Society to maintain,
by means of contributions and levies, a compensation fund to make good losses to clients
occasioned by dishonesty on the part of a solicitor or his employee. Section 37 empowers
the Law Society to establish a scheme of professional indemnity to cover solicitors
directly, and therefore their clients indirectly, against loss resulting from negligence and
c the like on the part of solicitors and their employees.

Under the latter section the council, with the concurrence of the Master of the Rolls,
was authorised to make rules concerning indemnity against loss arising from claims in
respect of any description of civil liability incurred by a solicitor, or former solicitor, in
connection with his practice, or with any trust of which he is, or formerly was, a trustee;
or by any employee or former employee of such solicitor.

d Indemnity rules so made might provide for indemnity in one of three ways: by the
establishment of an indemnity fund by the Law Society; by the taking out by the Law
Society of insurance with any persons authorised by the Insurance Companies Act 1974
to carry on such insurance business; or by the taking out by solicitors of their own
insurance without the intervention of the Law Society.

Compliance with rules so established is enforced by a provision in s 1 of the Act that
e a person is not qualified to act as a solicitor unless he has a practising certificate in force;
and by a provision in s 10, that it is a condition precedent to the issue by the Law Society
of a practising certificate that the Law Society shall be satisfied that the applicant is
complying with any indemnity rules or is exempt from them.

Section 37 came into force on 1 May 1975. On 12 December 1975 the Council of the
Law Society, with the concurrence of the Master of the Rolls, made the Solicitors'
Indemnity Rules 1975 under sub-s (1). Under r 2, the Law Society was authorised to take
out and maintain a master policy in the form set out in the schedule, and to arrange for
the issue 'to solicitors to whom these rules apply' of certificates of insurance in the form
there set out. It is important to observe that, under r 2, the provisions of the master
policy and of the certificate of insurance were expressed to form part of the rules. By r 3
such a solicitor was required to pay the premiums payable by him under the master
f policy and certificate of insurance as they fell due. Under r 4, the rules were expressed
to apply to every solicitor who was a principal in private practice in England and Wales;
that is to say, excluding a solicitor commonly described as a consultant (who is usually a
solicitor retired from his former firm); and an associate or assistant solicitor who is an
employee and not a partner.

These rules came into operation on the day they were made, except the element of
g compulsion contained in r 3, which was deferred to 1 September 1976, no doubt to allow
latitude for solicitors who were already covered for negligence by their own private
insurance arrangements.

My Lords, I turn now to examine the form of master policy scheduled to the rules.
Clause 1 of the master policy provides as follows:

> 'The Insurers agree with the Law Society on behalf of all solicitors from time to
> time required to be insured by Indemnity Rules made under s. 37 of the Solicitors'
> Act 1974, and on behalf of former solicitors, to provide such insurance in accordance
> with the terms of the Certificate attached hereto . . .'

Reading the prescribed form of master policy with the rules, I find that cl 1 is expressed
as an agreement by the insurers with the Law Society 'on behalf of all solicitors who are,

or are held out to the public as, principals in private practice . . . and on behalf of former solicitors'. Under cl 2 the master policy was to run for a period ending on 31 August **a** 1978, unless extended. Clause 5 provided that in respect of former solicitors certificates of insurance did not require to be issued, and no premium was payable.

By cl 6 of the master policy the insurers gave authority to the brokers (defined in cl 4 as London Insurance Brokers Ltd) to issue on behalf of the insurers to solicitors seeking insurance in accordance with cl 1, certificates in the form attached to the master policy. The form of certificate of insurance began as follows: **b**

'This is to certify that in accordance with the authorisation granted to [London Insurance Brokers Ltd] under the Master Policy referred to in the Schedule by the Insurers subscribing such Master Policy (hereinafter called "The Insurers") insurance is granted by the Insurers in accordance with the terms and conditions following, and in consideration of the payment of the premium stated in the Schedule.'

c

Clause 1 contains definitions. 'The Solicitor' is the person named as such in the schedule. The definition of 'The Assured' is:

'the Solicitor, any person employed in connection with the Practice (including any articled clerk, and any solicitor who is a Consultant or Associate in the Firm), and the estate and/or the legal representatives of any of the foregoing, to the intent that each of the foregoing shall be severally insured hereunder.' **d**

'The Practice' and 'the Firm' were defined but the expressions are self-explanatory.

The certificate contains a number of special and general conditions, some of which are expressed to impose obligations on the assured, notably special condition 3(b). This provides that where a breach by the assured of a condition of insurance has prejudiced the handling or settlement of a claim against the assured or the firm, the assured shall **e** reimburse to the insurers the difference between the sum actually paid by the insurers in respect of the claim, and the lesser sum that would have been payable in the absence of prejudice, but it is a condition precedent to the right of the insurers to such reimbursement that they shall have first met the claim in full.

My Lords, it appears to me that once the master policy is in force and certificates of insurance are issued, the legal position can be analysed as follows. (1) The master policy **f** is a contract between the insurers and the Law Society under which the insurers bind themselves to provide solicitors with insurance on the terms of the certificate of insurance on payment of the appropriate premium, and to provide insurance for former solicitors without payment of premium. (2) The certificate of insurance evidences a contract between the insurers and the named solicitor under which the insurers bind themselves to indemnify the solicitor and all others who come within the definition of the assured. **g**

No master policy was, in fact, issued, but the judge found that on 18 November 1975 a contract was concluded between the Law Society and the insurers, conditional on the 1975 indemnity rules being made in the form of the final draft already in existence, which gave the Law Society the same contractual rights against the insurers as it would have had if the master policy had been actually issued. I will refer to this as 'the master policy contract'. **h**

As one would expect, the imposition of this indemnity scheme was preceded by discussion within the profession. In May 1975, which was the time when the Solicitors Act 1974 came into force, the Law Society circulated a summary of the main features of the scheme. In October 1975 the Law Society circulated a further paper and sought the views of the profession by means of a vote, which in the result favoured the scheme. The fact that the Law Society intended to secure a share of the brokerage commission was disclosed in both the original summary and the further paper. It is sufficient to quote **j** from the former:

'The brokers to the Scheme . . . will be remunerated on the usual commission basis from which they will meet the major cost of operating the Scheme and

handling claims. Hitherto the Society, through the Insurance Advisory Service, has
received a share of the brokers' commission and as regards solicitors' professional
indemnity business this amounted to approximately £46,000 gross in 1974 (the
equivalent of nearly £2 on a practising certificate fee) . . . Under the Scheme it is
likely that if the existing arrangments are continued the commission income to the
Society will be of the order of £250,000 per annum gross. The benefit of the net
excess receipts will inure for the profession as a whole, but, subject to taxation and
other important considerations, the Council will consider whether the surplus can
be appropriately earmarked for possible future improvements in the Scheme. The
surplus, however it is generally applied, will correspondingly reduce future calls
upon the practising members of the profession.'

The commission-sharing arrangement was set out in an agreement executed on 11
May 1976 by the Law Society, the Law Society Services Ltd, London Insurance Brokers
Ltd and certain companies associated with the brokers. The Law Society Services Ltd is
the Law Society's trading subsidiary. It is wholly identified with the Law Society and it
need not be distinguished from it.

By cl 3 the Law Society appointed the brokers with effect from 1 October 1975 as
insurance brokers to the Law Society for the purposes of the master policy, and in respect
of all 'solicitors' business'. Solicitors' business was defined as including not only the
indemnity scheme, but also various other insurance schemes operated by the Law Society
for solicitors. Under the agreement, the brokers were to pay the expenses of operating
the insurance service covered by the agreement. The Law Society does not receive a
share of brokerage as such under the agreement, but a percentage of the profits of the
brokers calculated in accordance with the formula in the agreement. The Law Society
receives a sum equal to 40% of the net brokerage up to £700,000 and 30% of the net
brokerage above that figure. For the year 1978 the sum received by the Law Society
referable to the indemnity insurance scheme was £648,000 and in respect of other
business of the brokers, £22,000. The sums received each year in respect of the
indemnity scheme are utilised by the Law Society for the benefit of the whole profession,
and not merely for the benefit of those solicitors who are members of the Law Society.

The claim of the respondent is that the Law Society is legally obliged to account to all
solicitor-insurers, the premium payers, for all money received by the Law Society from
the brokers under the 1976 agreement, and to hand over to each such solicitor a due
proportion of such money, calculated no doubt pro rata according to the premium paid
by the solicitor-insurer.

My Lords, the insurance scheme is statutory. It flows from s 37 and the rules made
thereunder, of which the form of master policy and the form of insurance certificate are
an integral part. In exercising its power under s 37 the Law Society is performing a
public duty, a duty which is designed to benefit, not only solicitor-principals and their
staff, but also solicitors' clients. The scheme is not only for the protection of the
premium-paying solicitor against the financial consequences of his own mistakes, the
mistakes of his partners and of his staff, but also, and far more importantly, to secure that
the solicitor is financially able to compensate his client. Indeed, I think it is clear that the
principal purpose of s 37 was to confer on the Law Society the power to safeguard the lay
public and not professional practitioners, since the latter can look after themselves. This
is underlined by the position of s 37, which is one of a group of three sections, the other
two of which are plainly enacted in the interests of the lay public. So, there is no doubt
at all in my mind that the power given to the Law Society by s 37 is a power to be
exercised not only in the interests of the solicitors' profession but also, and more
importantly, in the interests of those members of the public who resort to solicitors for
legal advice. So, as I have said, in exercising the power conferred on it, the Law Society
was performing a public duty, and not a private duty to premium-paying solicitors. This
approach, which in my opinion is fundamental, has important consequences, because the
nature of a public duty and the remedies of those who seek to challenge the manner in

which it is performed differ markedly from the nature of a private duty and the remedies of those who say that the private duty has been breached. If a public duty is breached, *a* there are the remedies of judicial review, declaration, injunction and recovery of money if wrongly demanded and paid. There is no remedy in breach of trust or equitable account. The latter remedies are available, and available only, where a private trust has been created: see the decision of your Lordships' House in *Skinners' Co v Irish Society* (1845) 12 Cl & Fin 425, 8 ER 1474. The duty imposed on the possessor of a statutory power for public purposes is not accurately described as fiduciary because there is no *b* beneficiary in the equitable sense.

The 1975 indemnity scheme ended on 31 August 1978. New rules were made, incorporating a new form of master policy and certificate of insurance, in 1979 and again in 1980, which slightly amended the original scheme. The later schemes give rise to no new points of any significance and I need not weary your Lordships with the details.

My Lords, I turn, as briefly as I can, to the decisions at first instance and on appeal. As *c* I have already mentioned, the thrust of the argument on those occasions was against the validity of the scheme. In your Lordships' House no such challenge is made. Nor is it asserted, nor could it be asserted, that the 1976 agreement was a breach of the statutory powers of the Law Society or a breach of the private rights of premium-paying solicitors.

The argument of the plaintiffs that the Law Society was accountable to them and other premium-paying solicitors was based on the assertion that the Law Society entered into *d* the master policy contract in such manner as to place it in a fiduciary position in relation to the premium payers. As a matter of law, that fiduciary relationship could arise either under the law of agency or under the law of trusts. The agency argument foundered at an early stage, because inevitably some of the supposed principals would be unascertained at the date when the master policy contract was made. But trusteeship was advocated and found favour with the judge. He said ([1980] 3 All ER 615 at 624, [1980] 1 WLR *e* 1335 at 1344):

> 'In my judgment it is reasonably clear that the effect of the phrase which I have quoted from cl 1 of the draft master policy ["on behalf of all solicitors . . . and on behalf of former solicitors"] is this: on its true construction it indicates the intention of the makers of the rules that the Law Society should enter into the agreement of *f* insurance as *trustees* for the persons, ascertained and unascertained, referred to in that clause, the purpose of the provision being to entitle such persons, as beneficiaries under the trust, to require the insurers to provide them with insurance in accordance with the terms of the proposed certificate, on paying the specified premium.'

He formed the view, however, that the Law Society was not accountable for its share of brokerage for reasons which I need not elaborate, beyond saying that they were based *g* principally on the absence of any fiduciary relationship in the run-up to the master policy contract.

On appeal, a similar conclusion was reached on the existence of the trusteeship, but a different conclusion on accountability. I respectfully adopt Oliver LJ's analysis of the problem ([1981] 3 All ER 797 at 814, [1982] 1 WLR 17 at 37):

> '. . . what one has to do is to ascertain first of all whether there was a fiduciary relationship and, if there was, from what it arose and what, if there was any, the trust property was; and then to inquire whether that of which an account is claimed either arose, directly or indirectly, from the trust property itself or was acquired not only in the course of but by reason of, the fiduciary relationship.'

The Court of Appeal was unanimous in its conclusion that the Law Society constituted *j* itself a trustee of the benefit of the master policy contract. All three judgments proceed on the same basis, and I find it sufficient to turn to the judgment of Oliver LJ ([1981] 3 All ER 797 at 817, [1982] 1 WLR 17 at 41) for a summary of the reasoning. First, the existence of trusteeship,

'. . . is what is suggested by the words "on behalf of" etc. Those words cannot just be treated as a descriptive declaration that the Law Society was representing the profession generally and indeed the agreement defines the class of persons on whose behalf the agreement is made by reference to the requirements of the rules. They define, and must, I think, have been intended to define, the particular class of individuals for whom the benefit of the agreement was to be held and for whom anything to be performed by the Law Society was to be performed. The agreement was, after all, one in which, by its very nature, the Law Society was not itself to have any beneficial interest or right to insurance. Secondly, the whole way in which the scheme was constructed suggests that the intention was that every solicitor required to be insured should have an enforceable right, on paying the requisite premium, to have the insurance cover offered by the scheme without the risk of the insurers declining cover, for instance, on the ground of a multiplicity of previous claims. It should perhaps be said, however, that such a concept, whilst it was in fact the preferred machinery adopted, was not perhaps the only or an essential mechanism for producing the result which the statute envisaged, although it was a natural one. It might, for instance, have been equally effective from the Law Society's point of view if there had been no right of enforcement conferred on individual solicitors by the creation of an equitable interest in them, reliance being placed simply on the Law Society's own right of enforcement against the insurers (see, for instance, *Beswick v Beswick* [1967] 2 All ER 1197, [1968] AC 58). But the express declaration of trust was the method in fact adopted and I take as the starting point that, as a matter of machinery, the scheme itself involved the consequences that the Law Society held the benefit of the master policy on trust for those solicitors designated by the rules as persons required to be insured.'

Having reached that conclusion, all three Lords Justices decided that the existence of the trusteeship led to the result that the Law Society was accountable for the commission it received under the 1976 agreement. That conclusion was based on the existence of a sufficient causal connection between the trusteeship and the right to the commission. In so holding the Court of Appeal did, however, draw a line in the year 1978. As Oliver LJ said ([1981] 3 All ER 797 at 820, [1982] 1 WLR 17 at 45):

'It would, I think, clearly be inequitable for the court to order the Law Society to account to the plaintiffs for commission received prior to 1979 in respect of which no challenge was made until the Law Society had irrevocably altered its position on the footing that no objection was being taken to the validity of the scheme or anything done under it.'

If it be correct that the Law Society constituted itself a trustee of the master policy contract, I would not, for my part, dispute the conclusion that the Law Society must account to the premium payers for its share of commission. The all important question is, did the Law Society constitute itself a trustee of the master policy contract?

My Lords, it is clear that there is nothing in the wording of s 37 which makes it obligatory on the Law Society, if it establishes an indemnity scheme on the lines of that adopted, to assume the role of trustee for the benefit of premium-paying solicitors or anyone else. This was rightly recognised by the Court of Appeal: see, for example, Oliver LJ ([1981] 3 All ER 797 at 816, [1982] 1 WLR 17 at 39–40). The question is one of intention, the relevant intention being that of the Law Society. The intention of the Law Society is to be ascertained from the words which are used in the form of master policy and from such of the surrounding circumstances as are admissible in evidence.

The argument advanced before your Lordships in favour of a trust can be summarised as follows. (1) The respondent relies on the statement in the form of master policy that the agreement was made with the Law Society 'on behalf of all solicitors from time to time required to be insured and on behalf of former solicitors'. It is said that the words 'on behalf of' are prima facie words of agency or trust. They are more appropriate to the creation of agency, but as agency cannot exist on the facts of the instant case, they must, it is said, be read as words of trust. (2) There is no other meaning, except the creation of a trust, that can sensibly be attributed to the words 'on behalf of' etc. If no trust, the words are devoid of any effect. (3) The implication of a trust may not be necessary for 'solicitors . . . required to be insured' since they are parties to the contract evidenced by the certificate of insurance. But no premium is paid by, and no certificate of insurance is issued to, former solicitors so that the implication of a trust is needed to secure their intended rights. (4) The form of the scheme deprives solicitors of the opportunity which they would otherwise have had to negotiate their own insurance, and thus their own commission-sharing arrangement. It is, therefore, appropriate to find the existence of a trust of the commission recovered by the Law Society which, in the absence of a compulsory insurance scheme, would have been available for the premium payers. (5) The manner in which the scheme was constructed suggests that it was intended that every solicitor required to be insured should have a legally enforceable right, on paying his premium, to have the insurance cover offered by the scheme.

My Lords, I find myself unable to accept the proposition that the Law Society should have imputed to it the intention to constitute itself a trustee of the master policy contract. The words 'on behalf' clearly do not *express* a trust, and they do not necessarily *imply* a trust. There are numerous authorities to that effect, to which it is unnecessary to refer. It would, indeed, be surprising if a society of lawyers, who above all might be expected to make their intention clear in a document they compose, should have failed to express the existence of a trust if that was what they intended to create.

Nor, if one examines the practicalities of the case, was it necessary to imply a trust in order to secure the commercial viability of the indemnity scheme. It was urged before us that in the absence of a trust, a solicitor who was intended under the terms of the master policy to have the right to be insured would have no legal remedy against the insurers for refusing to insure him; and that, for example, a person coming within the description of former solicitor, who was refused the indemnity against loss which was purported to be secured for him, would find himself without remedy against insurers who refused to pay up. My Lords, I find this reasoning unconvincing. This is a statutory indemnity scheme. The rules have the force of a statute, and the form of master policy and the form of certificate of insurance have statutory authority, just as much as if the rules, master policy and certificate were set out in a schedule to the Act. In those circumstances, I am of the opinion that all persons insured by the scheme, former solicitors, salaried solicitors, legal executives and others as well as premium-paying solicitors, would have a direct remedy against the insurers in the unlikely event of the insurers declining to perform an obligation imposed on them; and such persons, likewise, are legally bound by the obligations expressed to be imposed on them by the scheme. Unless one gives a statutory vitality to the terms of the master policy and certificate of insurance, outside the remedies of contract law based on narrow propositions of privity of contract, how, I ask myself, is effect to be given to the right of the insurers to reimbursement from an assured (not being a contracting party) under special condition 3(*b*) of the master policy to which I have already referred? Yet that is part of the statutory scheme.

My Lords, I do not think that the words 'on behalf of' etc are devoid of content in the absence of agency and trusteeship. It may well be that the words were inserted to comply with the requirements of s 2 of the Life Assurance Act 1774, as amended by the Insurance Companies Amendment Act 1973, s 50. The 1774 Act, despite its title, is not confined to life policies. The amending Act, with retrospective effect, validates—

'a policy for the benefit of unnamed persons from time to time falling within a specified class or description if the class or description is stated in the policy with sufficient particularity to make it possible to establish the identity of all persons who at any given time are entitled to benefit under the policy.'

Attention to these statutory provisions, to which we were referred by the Law Society's

counsel, may well have led the draftsman of the master policy to introduce into cl 1 a
a statement in broad terms of those entitled to benefit.

The respondent raised two further submissions. First, it was said that the commission
received was an exaction which was unlawful in the context of the compulsory nature of
the insurance scheme established by the Law Society and that reported authority
recognised the right of a person, from whom an unlawful exaction had been made under
colour of statute, to require reimbursement. Reliance was placed on *Morgan v Palmer*
b (1824) 2 B & C 729, 107 ER 554. That argument quickly came to grief when it was
appreciated that the unlawful exaction, if any were made, was at the expense of the
brokers and they were not seeking recovery.

Second, it was submitted that, in the absence of an *implied* trusteeship of the master
policy contract, there was a *constructive* trusteeship of the commission received by the
Law Society. The basis of this proposition was that it would be unconscionable conduct
c on the part of the Law Society to take advantage of its statutory position so as to make a
profit from premiums which it compelled solicitors to pay.

If the Law Society failed to negotiate insurance at the most advantageous rate in order
to enhance the commission received by the brokers, and thus entitle itself to a larger sum
under the formula in the 1976 agreement, I would see the force of the grievance, and I
have no doubt whatever that the law would provide a remedy in some form. But there
d is no suggestion in the present case of any such impropriety. Nor, impropriety apart, is
there any evidence that the Law Society could have persuaded the insurers to charge
solicitors lower premiums on the basis that the brokers would be content to accept a
lower rate of commission which they could keep wholly for themselves instead of
sharing with the Law Society. The premiums negotiated must be assumed to be fair
premiums properly negotiated, in the absence of evidence to the contrary. The 1976
e agreement is no more than an example of a commission-sharing arrangement between
brokers and those introducing insurance business. Unless the 1976 agreement can be
shown to be illegal, which is not suggested, and unless the Law Society can be shown to
be a trustee, which is asserted but not established, I fail to see any legal basis for the claim
that the Law Society has been acting contrary to the requirements of justice and good
conscience. It would, in my view, be extravagant to claim that the Law Society is acting
f in an unconscionable manner because it has turned its unique bargaining position to
account and obtained a sum of money (which would otherwise have enhanced the profits
of the brokers) and applied such money for the benefit of the profession as a whole.

My Lords, I venture to emphasise once more that the respondent, Mr Swain, is not
arguing this case before your Lordships' House at his own volition. I doubt whether he
is remotely interested in recovering for himself a few pounds of premium. His challenge
g was to the validity of the scheme as a whole, because he would rather fend for himself in
the insurance market than have the work done for him. With that I sympathise. Mr
Swain has only been represented before your Lordships because the Law Society desired
the decision of your Lordships' House. I venture these observations only because the
arguments of unconscionable conduct on the part of the Law Society ought not, I think,
to be interpreted as a reflection of Mr Swain's sentiments towards his professional body.
h   I would allow this appeal.

Appeal allowed.

Solicitors: *Slaughter & May* (for the Law Society); *Lovell, Son & Pitfield*, agents for
Pethybridges & Best, Torrington (for the respondent).

Mary Rose Plummer   Barrister.

Kelly v London Transport Executive   *a*

COURT OF APPEAL, CIVIL DIVISION
LORD DENNING MR, ACKNER AND O'CONNOR LJJ
18, 19, 22 MARCH 1982

Legal aid – Unassisted person's costs out of legal aid fund – Proceedings finally decided in favour **b**
of unassisted party – Sufficient if unassisted party substantially successful – Legally-aided
plaintiff given judgment for considerably less than amount paid into court by unassisted defendant
– Whether proceedings determined in favour of plaintiff because judgment given for him –
Whether proceedings determined in favour of defendant because award less than amount paid
into court – Legal Aid Act 1974, s 13(1)

Legal aid – Unassisted person's costs out of legal aid fund – Just and equitable – Action for **c**
personal injuries – Assisted plaintiff's claim without foundation – Plaintiff refusing £750 paid
into court and offer of £4,000 before trial – Plaintiff awarded damages of £75 – Defendant put
to trouble and expense to expose plaintiff's groundless claim – Whether 'just and equitable' to
order payment of defendant's costs out of legal aid fund – Legal Aid Act 1974, s 13(2).

Legal aid – Unassisted person's costs out of legal aid fund – Severe financial hardship – **d**
Corporation – Large public transport undertaking – Corporation having £100,000 overdraft on
its operations after receiving local government grant of £179m – Whether corporation would
suffer severe financial hardship if its costs of £8,000 in successfully defending action not paid out
of legal aid fund – Legal Aid Act 1974, s 13(3)(b).

Legal aid – Unassisted person's costs out of legal aid fund – Appeal against refusal of order for **e**
payment – Judge finding that unassisted party would not suffer severe financial hardship if order
not made – Whether appeal lying from judge's decision – Legal Aid Act 1974, s 13(5).

Legal aid – Solicitor – Duty of solicitior and counsel for legally-aided client – Duty owed to
unassisted party and to legal aid fund – Guidelines. **f**

Counsel – Duty – Legally-aided client – Duty owed to unassisted party and to legal aid fund –
Breach of duty – Immunity from suit for work done in course of litigation – Immunity only
applying in relation to counsel's own client.

Evidence – Expert – Experts' reports – Alteration of reports – Reports not to be 'settled' by **g**
counsel – Reports to be independent product of expert.

In October 1974 in the course of his employment with the defendants, who were a large
public transport undertaking, the plaintiff, a chronic alcoholic, was injured when he
bumped his head and received a slight cut. He was given first aid and returned to
work. In March 1975 he ceased to work. In July he complained of depression, eye **h**
trouble and bad hearing, all of which he attributed to his injury in October 1974. In
March 1977 he saw a firm of solicitors, who, on the advice of counsel, applied for legal
aid on his behalf to bring an action against the defendants. In April the plaintiff was
granted legal aid limited to obtaining counsel's further opinion. On the basis of that
opinion a further certificate was granted to enable the action to go on to the close of
pleadings. The solicitors obtained 19 medical reports on the plaintiff's condition. In **j**
January 1980 the matter was put before counsel, who advised that the action should be
proceeded with. In February the plaintiff was given unlimited leave to go on with the
action, and for leading counsel to be instructed. A further five medical examinations
were made of the plaintiff at which specialists engaged by the defendants were present.
The defendants' specialists reported that the plaintiff's condition was caused not by the

accident but by chronic alcoholism. The defendants sent copies of their reports to the

a plaintiff's solicitors as soon as they were received, but the plaintiff's solicitors did not send copies of their experts' reports to the defendants, other than one report which had been altered to remove an unfavourable reference. The defendants frequently sought copies of the reports and on the summons for directions an order was made for their production, but they were only produced a fortnight before the trial. In July 1980 the defendants paid £750 into court in satisfaction of the plaintiff's claim, but on counsel's

b advice it was not accepted. The trial was fixed for October 1980. In September 1980 and without having seen the plaintiff's medical reports, the defendants wrote to the plaintiff's solicitors, saying that, in view of the costs they would incur at the trial which, even if they were successful, they would be unable to recover from the legally-aided plaintiff, they were prepared to pay £4,000 in settlement of the plaintiff's damages and costs. On legal advice that offer was rejected. On 13 October the plaintiff's medical reports were

c sent to the defendants. At the hearing, which lasted three days, the defendants did not deny liability for such injury as resulted from the accident. On 30 October judgment was given and the plaintiff was awarded £75. The judge found the plaintiff to be an unreliable witness and rejected his medical evidence.

The defendants applied under s 13ᵃ of the Legal Aid Act 1974 for an order for the payment to them out of the legal aid fund of costs of £8,000 incurred by them from the

d date of their payment of £750 into court in July 1980 to the date of judgment, on the ground that they would 'suffer severe financial hardship', within s 13(3)(b), if such an order was not made. There was evidence that, after a local government grant of £179m, the defendants financial deficit for 1980 would be about £100,000. The judge held that the proceedings had been decided in favour of the defendants but that on the facts the defendants would not suffer severe financial hardship if the order was not made. The

e defendants appealed to the Court of Appeal. The Law Society contended that, because the plaintiff had obtained judgment for £75, the proceedings had been decided in his favour and not in favour of the unassisted party, ie the defendants. Alternatively, the Law Society contended that a body corporate could not in law 'suffer hardship', since that connoted some form of human suffering, and accordingly the defendants could not 'suffer severe financial hardship'.

f

Held – (1) For proceedings to be 'finally decided in favour of the unassisted party' within s 13(1) of the 1974 Act, it was not necessary for those proceedings to be decided wholly in favour of the unassisted party but merely that they be substantially so decided (see p 849 b to e, p 851 g, p 852 d to h and p 854 c, post); dictum of Lord Denning MR in *General Accident, Fire and Life Assurance Corp Ltd v Foster* [1972] 3 All ER at 880 applied.

g

---

a   Section 13, so far as material, provides:

'(1) Where a party receives legal aid in connection with any proceedings between him and a party not receiving legal aid (in this . . . section . . . referred to as "the unassisted party") and those proceedings are finally decided in favour of the unassisted party, the court by which the proceedings are so decided may, subject to the provisions of this section, make an order for the

h   payment to the unassisted party out of the legal aid fund of the whole or any part of the costs incurred by him in those proceedings.

(2) An order may be made under this section in respect of any costs if (and only if) the court is satisfied that it is just and equitable in all the circumstances that provision for those costs should be made out of public funds . . .

(3) Without prejudice to subsection (2) above, no order shall be made under this section in respect of costs incurred in a court of first instance, whether by that court or by any appellate court,

j   unless—(a) the proceedings in the court of first instance were instituted by the party receiving legal aid; and (b) the court is satisfied that the unassisted party will suffer severe financial hardship unless the order is made . . .

(5) Without prejudice to any other provision restricting appeals from any court, no appeal shall lie against an order under this section, or a refusal to make such an order, except on a point of law . . .'

(2) (Per Lord Denning MR and Ackner LJ) In view of the lack of foundation of the plaintiff's claim and the nuisance that had been caused to the defendants, it was clearly *a* 'just and equitable in all the circumstances', within s 13(2) of the 1974 Act, that provision for the defendants' costs be made out of the legal aid fund (see p 849 *g*, p 851 *g* and p 852 *h*, post).

(3) However, although a limited company or a body corporate could suffer 'severe financial hardship' within s 13(3)(b) of the 1974 Act since 'suffering hardship' in that context was not limited to human suffering, it could not, in view of the defendants' *b* overall financial position, be said that payment by them of £8,000 in costs would make any appreciable difference to their affairs, and accordingly it could not be said that the defendants would suffer 'severe financial hardship' if an order for the payment of their costs out of the legal aid fund was not made. The appeal would therefore be dismissed (see p 850 *a d e*, p 851 *g* and p 852 *j* to p 853 *a e* and *g* to p 854 *a*, post); dictum of Salmon LJ in *Hanning v Maitland (No 2)* [1970] 1 All ER at 818 applied; *R & T Thew Ltd v Reeves* *c* [1981] 2 All ER 964 considered.

(4) Moreover (per Ackner and O'Connor LJJ) the judge's finding that the defendants would not suffer severe financial hardship if the order was not made was a finding of fact and accordingly, by virtue of s 13(5) of the 1974 Act, no appeal lay from his decision (see p 853 *j* to p 854 *a*, post).

Guidelines on the duties of solicitors and counsel who act for legally-aided clients (see *d* p 851 *a* to *f*, post).

Per Lord Denning MR. (1) A solicitor is under a duty not only to his client who is legally aided but also to the unassisted party who is not legally aided, and if he fails in that duty the unassisted party is entitled to call him before the court for an order that he is to make good any loss or expense caused to the unassisted party by any breach of that duty (see p 850 *g h*, post); *Blundell v Blundell* (1822) 5 B & Ald 533, dicta of Lord Hatherley LC *e* in *Re Jones* (1870) LR 6 Ch App at 499 and of Viscount Maugham in *Myers v Elman* [1939] 4 All ER at 489 applied.

(2) Counsel who represents a legally-aided client and who fails in the duty he owes to the other side cannot claim immunity from suit on the ground that the work was done in the course of litigation since that immunity only applies in relation to his own client (see p 851 *f*, post); *Rondel v Worsley* [1967] 3 All ER 993 distinguished.   *f*

(3) Counsel must not 'settle' the evidence of a medical expert by asking the expert to change his report so as to favour counsel's client or conceal things that may be against him; such evidence should be, and should be seen to be, the independent product of the expert, uninfluenced as to form or content by the exigencies of litigation (see p 851 *c* to *e*, post); dictum of Lord Wilberforce in *Whitehouse v Jordan* [1981] 1 All ER at 276 applied.

(4) Where an unassisted defendant has made a payment into court, the proceedings *g* are 'finally decided in favour of the unassisted party' whenever that payment exceeds the sum eventually recovered by the legally-aided plaintiff (see p 849 *e*, post).

Per O'Connor LJ. Where an unassisted defendant has made a payment into court, the proceedings are 'finally decided in favour of the unassisted party' only where the effect of what happens is that the plaintiff recovers nothing or that, had he not been legally aided he would have had to pay more in costs to his own legal advisers and to the defendant *h* than has been recovered (see p 854 *b c*, post).

Notes
For the award of costs to an unassisted person out of the legal aid fund, see supplement *j* to 30 Halsbury's Laws (3rd edn) para 933A.

For the Legal Aid Act 1974, ss 13, 14(5), see 44 Halsbury's Statutes (3rd edn) 1053, 1058.

As from 1 January 1981, reg 12 of the 1971 regulations has been replaced by reg 78 of the Legal Aid (General) Regulations 1980, SI 1980/1894.

Cases referred to in judgments

a *Blundell v Blundell* (1822) 5 B & Ald 533, 106 ER 1286, 43 Digest (Repl) 377, 4005.

General Accident, Fire and Life Assurance Corp Ltd v Foster [1972] 3 All ER 877, [1973] QB 50, [1972] 3 WLR 657, Digest (Cont Vol D) 1053, *1733d*.

Hanning v Maitland (No 2) [1970] 1 All ER 812, [1970] 1 QB 580, [1970] 2 WLR 151, Digest (Cont Vol C) 1087, *1736a*.

Jones, Re (1870) LR 6 Ch App 497, LC, 43 Digest (Repl) 386, *4118*.

b *Kenny v Taylor* (8 July 1981, unreported), Ch D.

Kyle v Mason (1963) Times, 3 July, CA.

Miller v Littner (1979) 123 SJ 473.

Myers v Elman [1939] 4 All ER 484, [1940] AC 282, HL, 43 Digest (Repl) 375, *3981*.

Nowotnik v Nowotnik (Hyatt intervening) [1965] 3 All ER 167, [1967] P 83, [1965] 3 WLR 920, CA, 27(2) Digest (Reissue) 769, *6144*.

c *Rondel v Worsley* [1967] 3 All ER 993, [1969] 1 AC 191, [1967] 3 WLR 1666, HL, 3 Digest (Reissue) 786, *4877*.

Saunders (Exrx of estate of Gallie (decd)) v Anglia Building Society (formerly Northampton Town and County Building Society) (No 2) [1971] 1 All ER 243, [1971] AC 1039, [1971] 2 WLR 349, HL, Digest (Cont Vol D) 1052, *1733b*.

Thew (R & T) Ltd v Reeves [1981] 2 All ER 964, [1982] QB 172, [1981] 3 WLR 190, CA.

d *Whitehouse v Jordan* [1980] 1 All ER 650, CA: *affd* [1981] 1 All ER 267, [1981] 1 WLR 246, HL, 33 Digest (Reissue) 265, *2182*.

Cases also cited

Clifford v Walker [1972] 2 All ER 806, [1972] 1 WLR 724, CA.

e *Megarity v D J Ryan & Sons Ltd (No 2)* [1981] 1 All ER 641, [1982] AC 81, HL.

Appeal

The defendants, the London Transport Executive, appealed against the decision of Caulfield J on 16 January 1981 dismissing their application for an order under s 13 of the Legal Aid Act 1974 for the payment to them out of the legal aid fund of their costs from f 29 July 1980, when they paid £750 into court, to 30 October 1980, when judgment for the sum of £75 was entered for the plaintiff, Michael Kelly, who was legally aided, in an action for damages for personal injuries and consequential loss caused by the negligence and breach of statutory duty of the defendants, their servants or agents on or about 22 October 1974 at Northfields Railway Depot, Northfields, West Ealing, London W13. Caulfield J had held that, although the substantive proceedings had been finally decided g in favour of the defendants, the defendants would not in the circumstances suffer severe financial hardship if the order was not made. By a respondent's notice amended on 18 March 1982 the area secretary for the legal aid fund contended that Caulfield J's order should be affirmed on the additional grounds that the proceedings had not been 'finally decided in favour of the unassisted party' (viz the defendants) within s 13(1) of the 1974 Act and that, as a public corporation, body or undertaking, the defendants were not h capable in law of suffering 'severe financial hardship' within s 13(3)(b) of the 1974 Act. The facts are set out in the judgment of Lord Denning MR.

Anthony Scrivener QC and *Christopher Carling* for the London Transport Executive.
Duncan Matheson and *Nigel Pitt* for the Law Society.

j **LORD DENNING MR.** Michael Kelly is a plausible Irishman and a chronic alcoholic. He put forward a claim for £100,000 for personal injury against London Transport. It was completely bogus. He got legal aid and brought an action against them. He put them to a great deal of trouble and expense. So much so that London Transport now ask that their costs should be paid out of the legal aid fund.

This is the story. Michael Kelly is 60. He was born in Southern Ireland and came over to England when he was 23. He worked here, off and on, until he was 53. On 21 October 1974 he got a job with London Transport. Next day he bumped his head and got a slight cut. It was a trivial injury. It was patched up and he went back to work. Six months later, in March 1975, he stopped work and has never worked since. He has lived on social security benefits and spent much of it on drink.

Starting in July 1975 he has made complaints of all sorts of ills, depression, eye trouble, bad hearing, all of which he attributes to the trivial injury on 22 October 1974.

In March 1977, or thereabouts, a firm of solicitors interviewed him. They got the opinion of two counsel. As a result, they applied for legal aid on his behalf to promote an action against the London Transport Executive. He was granted legal aid in April 1977, but it was limited to obtaining counsel's further opinion. They obtained counsel's further opinion. That seems to have been favourable. So much so that in July 1977 a further certificate was granted to enable the action to go on until the close of pleadings. The proceedings commenced. Many medical reports were obtained. The judge said: 'There are more documents on the medical issue in this case than I have ever seen in the whole of my career at the Bar and on the Bench.' Leave was given to obtain the evidence of a machinery expert. Then in January 1980 (this is an important date) the matter was put before counsel. We are told that counsel wrote an 18-page opinion, advising that the action should be proceeded with. As a result, on 12 February 1980, the legal aid committee gave Mr Kelly unlimited leave to go on with the action, and for leading counsel to be instructed.

Armed with that legal aid certificate, the solicitors pursued his claim most diligently. They spared no expense. Taking his various complaints:

(1) *Eye trouble.* They instructed two specialists, who reported on him four times. It was eventually discovered that in 1971, three years before the accident, he had been in a drunken fight and got a black eye. That was the cause of his eye trouble. One of the specialists reported to the man's solicitors on 19 June 1980:

'If I appeared in court I feel that I would have to say that I fully accept that the injury to his right eye was most likely caused by the injury which he received in 1971. I regret that we have all rather been led "up the garden path" in this matter.'

(2) *Deafness.* His solicitors instructed a specialist, who reported on him eight times. All sorts of tests were done. Eventually, on 19 June 1980, the specialist reported to the man's solicitors:

'... I am unable to establish that Mr. Kelly has any measurable hearing loss resulting from his claim ... I must agree that when I refer to "all his hearing problems" these mainly appear to be in a psychological realm rather than having any difficulty actually hearing people speak to him.'

(3) *Depression.* The solicitors instructed three specialists, who made seven reports on him. Two of them were not at all helpful. The other was a specialist, Dr Denham, who made a report on 4 December 1979 but changed it at the request of the solicitors and dated it 3 March 1980. Later, the judge rejected Dr Denham's evidence completely. This specialist, Dr Denham, said positively:

'Mr. Michael Kelly is a man of fifty-eight, disabled by subsequent depression. His depression is typical in every respect. His illness is caused by and consequent to the accident on the 22nd October 1974 and the ensuing injury.'

As against all those doctors for Mr Kelly, London Transport engaged five specialists who attended at the various examinations by Mr Kelly's doctors. They were able conclusively to demonstrate the falsity of Mr Kelly's claims. The most illuminating of them is the report of Dr Denis Leigh of the Bethlem Royal and the Maudsley Hospitals of 28 June 1980:

a   '. . . I consider that the accident of 22.10.74 in which Mr Kelly seems to have lacerated his scalp has no relationship to Mr Kelly's present mental, or indeed physical, condition. He is a chronic alcoholic and was a chronic alcoholic in 1974. In July 1975 he showed evidence of an early dementia and of a delusional state characteristic of chronic alcoholism. He has continued to drink heavily over the years, has had an attack of delirium tremens in 1979, but still continues to drink heavily, and to do little else . . . Finally, I consider that Mr Kelly is unfit to continue

b   to be responsible for his affairs. He should be placed under the care of the Court of Protection—but that is a matter for his solicitors to arrange.'

His solicitors did consider it and refused to put him under the care of the Court of Protection. On leading counsel's opinion they refused to consent to the appointment of a guardian and said that they would contest any application that might be made in that respect.

c

Medical reports

The solicitors for London Transport sent copies of their medical reports to the solicitors for Mr Kelly. One in February 1980, and the others as soon as they were received in July 1980. But Mr Kelly's solicitors did not reciprocate. They only sent at one stage the 'doctored' report of Dr Denham. Otherwise, they did not send any of their medical

d   reports to London Transport. Time after time London Transport asked for these reports. They were not produced until a fortnight before the trial, although, months before, on a summons for directions, an order had been made for their production.

In addition to the medical experts, Mr Kelly's solicitors asked for and obtained leave to call a machinery expert, a Colonel Hands. The judge dismissed his evidence as of no consequence because he 'attempted to prove the obvious'.

e

Payment into court

On 29 July 1980 London Transport Executive paid into court £750 in satisfaction of the plaintiff's claim. It was not accepted. We are told that, informally, the solicitors took the advice of counsel on the matter. On his advice, it was not accepted. The trial was fixed for 28 October 1980. On 24 September 1980 (still not having received the

f   plaintiff's medical reports) London Transport wrote a letter offering £4,000, saying:

'. . . The Executive have given further consideration to this matter, especially in the light of the costs which they will incur on the trial and which, even if they are successful in resisting the claim, they will be unable to recover from your Legally Aided client. I am now instructed that the Executive are prepared to pay a global sum of £4000·00 (inclusive of the amount of £750·00 already in Court) in

g   settlement of the Plaintiff's damages and costs . . .'

The plaintiff's advisers did not accept that offer. We are told that they again informally took the advice of counsel on the matter. As we know from the specialist's opinion, the man himself was unable to conduct his affairs. It was his advisers, solicitors or counsel or both, who must have advised him not to accept the £4,000.

h   Then on 13 October 1980 (a fortnight before the trial) Mr Kelly's solicitors at last forwarded the medical reports. Although on their own reports there was no conceivable claim in respect of the eye trouble and the hearing, they went on with those claims. The specialists on those points were required to attend the court, but only one was called. The others were not necessary.

j   *The judge's ruling*

The hearing lasted three days. On 30 October 1980 Caulfield J gave judgment. In picturesque language, he exposed the bogus claim. He found the plaintiff a wholly unacceptable witness. He rejected completely the evidence of Dr Denham. He said that he was 'over-obliging in his quest for the plaintiff'. He condemned him for changing his report at the request of the plaintiff. He said:

'I do not think the solicitor should have asked him anyway to have changed his
report and, secondly, if a consultant was asked, knowing that he is delivering a   a
forensic report, one that is going to be used in the courts, he should not have obliged
and therefore he falls down in my estimation.'

Counsel for the Law Society has told us today that it was not really the solicitor who
was responsible for changing the report. The matter had been put to counsel. Counsel
had advised the obliteration of references to previous medical reports. But, whoever it
was, it is quite plain to my mind that the specialist's report should not have been changed   b
at the request either of the solicitor or counsel.

The judgment

I must add that London Transport at an early stage in the trial did not contest
liability. They admitted that Mr Kelly had a slight cut on the head in 1974. For this the   c
judge awarded him £75. The legal aid fund took all that. So Mr Kelly went away with
nothing. His solicitors were expecting, no doubt, to be paid for all their work out of the
legal aid fund, including all the costs of the medical experts, and so forth, leaving London
Transport to bear all their own costs of fighting this bogus claim.

The claim against the legal aid fund   d

London Transport felt, quite rightly, that they had had a 'raw deal' over this claim. It
was a bogus claim which had been maintained and supported by the legal aid fund. If
the legal aid fund had not supported it, it would never have got going at all. Yet here are
London Transport. They had been put to great trouble and expense. In addition the
medical men and the lawyers on both sides, and, I would add, now the courts, have been
engaged for hours and hours and days and days on it. It is a disgrace to the administration   e
of the law that this should be allowed to happen.

Counsel for the Law Society, quite rightly, told us all that the legal aid committee had
done, all the inquiries they had made and received. The Legal Aid Regulations contain
many provisions seeking to ensure that the legal aid system is not abused. Counsel for
the Law Society drew our attention to various regulations. Regulation 68 of the Legal
Aid (General Regulations) 1980, SI 1980/1894, puts on the legally-aided person's solicitor   f
or counsel the duty to report any abuse of legal aid. If the man is being unreasonable in
any way, they have a duty to report it to the area committee. In addition, under reg 78,
if there is an abuse of legal aid, anyone can bring the information before the committee,
and the certificate will be discharged. It was said that the London Transport Executive
might have done that. But it is a difficult matter to try and get a certificate discharged.
It would mean a new contest, because it would be fought out. It might mean virtually   g
trying the whole case.

Counsel for the Law Society told us what the area committees had done. From their
point of view they dealt with the matter most conscientiously. They relied to a great
extent on what they were told by the solicitor, and on counsel's advice. So I do not think
any blame can be put on the legal aid fund itself. The blame must be put on the solicitors
and counsel who were advising Mr Kelly.   h

The Legal Aid Act 1974

We have again to consider s 13 of the Legal Aid Act 1974. It was much considered by
us in *Nowotnik v Nowotnik (Hyatt intervening)* [1965] 3 All ER 167, [1967] P 83, and in
Hanning v Maitland (No 2) [1970] 1 All ER 812, [1970] 1 QB 580, and by the House of   j
Lords in *Saunders (Exrx of estate of Gallie (decd)) v Anglia Building Society (No 2)* [1971] 1 All
ER 243, [1971] AC 1039. Further discussion today convinces me that the facts bring this
case within the scope of that section, save on one point which I will consider later.

Taking the six conditions as outlined in *Nowotnik v Nowotnik* [1965] 3 All ER 167 at
170–173, [1967] P 83 at 99–103:

a First: the proceedings were instituted by Mr Kelly who was the person receiving legal aid.

Second (and this raises a point of law): the proceedings must have been finally decided in favour of the unassisted party. Counsel for the Law Society submitted to us today that they were decided, not in favour of the unassisted party, but of the legally-aided person Mr Kelly: because Mr Kelly got judgment for £75, although it did him no good.

I must say that that argument does not appeal to me in the least. Counsel for the Law
b Society referred us to s 14(5) as to the meaning of the word 'finally', and so forth. He said that, as there was a judgment in Mr Kelly's favour for £75, the action had not been decided in favour of the unassisted person. He said that payment into court does not matter. Even though £750 was paid into court in July 1980, that does not alter the position at all. For my part, I think it makes all the difference in the world. It is quite absurd to suggest that a party who has been sued by an assisted person, and has made a
c payment into court in order to get rid of the case, should have to pay all his own costs without any recourse to the legal aid fund at all. As I said in *General Accident, Fire and Life Assurance Corp Ltd v Foster* [1972] 3 All ER 877 at 880, [1973] QB 50 at 55:

> 'I would prefer to ask: was the unassisted party substantially successful? The proceedings need not have been decided wholly in favour of the unassisted party, but they must have been substantially in his favour.'

d
In this case I have no doubt, as the judge had no doubt, that substantially the proceedings were finally decided in favour of the unassisted party. The London Transport Executive paid £750 into court long before the hearing commenced. That sum should have been accepted. They afterwards offered £4,000. But that too was rejected. I take the same view as the judge. Substantially the proceedings were finally
e decided in favour of the London Transport Executive.

I would go on to say that whenever a defendant makes a payment into court in sufficient time, which exceeds the sum eventually recovered by the plaintiff, the proceedings are finally decided in favour of the unassisted party.

Third: the court must consider what order for costs should be made against the party receiving legal aid. The judge did so consider. He made no order against Mr Kelly
f because it would be useless to do so.

Fourth: apart from legal aid, an order would have been made for the payment of the costs of the unassisted party. Clearly it would have been.

Fifth condition: to this I will return.

Sixth: the court must be satisfied 'that it is just and equitable in all the circumstances that provision for those costs should be made out of public funds'. The judge so found
g and I wholeheartedly agree. If ever there was a case where it would be just and equitable for the costs of London Transport Executive to be paid out of public funds, this is that case.

Severe financial hardship
I come back to the fifth condition. It is that the unassisted party will suffer *severe*
h *financial hardship* unless the order is made for payment out of the costs of the legal aid fund.

Counsel for the Law Society submitted that companies or bodies corporate do not qualify. They are not eligible to claim against the legal aid fund because they have 'no body to be kicked nor soul to be damned'. Therefore they can suffer no hardship.

But he came up against a number of cases where the court had held that a company can
j suffer severe financial hardship. There was *R & T Thew Ltd v Reeves* [1981] 2 All ER 964, [1982] QB 172. That was a case involving a small private company. This court said that it could suffer severe financial hardship because of the impact on a man and his wife (who were the sole shareholders in the company) if the company had to pay its own costs. There was also *Miller v Littner* (1979) 123 SJ 473, in which Oliver J held that an estate being administered could suffer severe financial hardship. Also in *Kenny v Taylor* (8 July

1981, unreported) Dillon J held that a company could suffer severe financial hardship.
So I will not pause long on that point. I hold that a limited company or a body corporate   *a*
can suffer severe financial hardship.

But here is the rub. Can the London Transport Executive suffer 'severe financial
hardship'? They are a huge corporation. They are under a statutory duty to charge fares
to the public so as to meet their expenditure if they can. But they simply cannot do so.
They are in deficit, hopelessly and continuously, to the tune of nearly £175m. They
have to be supported by a grant from the Greater London Council. The deficit is so large   *b*
that it is said that it is no severe financial hardship for them to meet a bill of £8,000,
which are their costs in this case. Nor, I suppose, for £50,000 or £100,000. So it is said
that the London Transport Executive can never recover any costs from the legal aid fund;
not even if it is shown conclusively that it would be just and equitable for them to do so.

I can well see the difficulty. I confess that I would like to overcome it. I am tempted
to accept the ingenious suggestion made by O'Connor LJ. It was a 'hardship' on London   *c*
Transport Executive to have to go to all the trouble and expense of instructing doctors
and counsel to fight this bogus claim. It was a 'severe' hardship because it took up so
much of their time when they could have been better employed on other things. It was
a 'financial' hardship because it put them to the expense of £8,000.

But I feel that I must go with my brethren. They feel that this ingenious suggestion
is too ingenious. The phrase 'severe financial hardship' is to be read as a whole. No one   *d*
could ever say that this sum of £8,000 for costs would make any appreciable difference
to London Transport's affairs. That was the view of the judge, and I feel we must affirm
it. So the London Transport Executive cannot recover against the legal aid fund.

Another remedy is open

Nevertheless, I cannot leave this case without pointing out to London Transport   *e*
Executive that there may be another remedy open to them. They can proceed against
the solicitors and counsel personally and require them to pay the costs. That was done
in *Kyle v Mason* (1963) Times, 3 July, which was decided by this court. The solicitor for
the appellant submitted to an order for costs because he had not properly carried out his
duties with regard to legal aid: see the Legal Aid Handbook for 1981, p 184. In *R & T
Thew Ltd v Reeves* [1982] QB 172 at 207 this court ordered that the defendant's solicitors   *f*
should attend before the court on a date and time to be arranged for the purpose of
considering whether or not they should be ordered to pay the costs personally on the
ground that such costs were incurred and occasioned as a result of a mistake of their clerk.

Over the weekend I have looked at the authorities in this matter. As a result, the
principle is clear that a solicitor is under a duty, not only to his own client who is legally
aided, but also to the unassisted party who is not legally aided. If the solicitor fails in that
duty, the unassisted party is at liberty to call him before the court, whereupon the court   *g*
can make an order that he is to make good any loss or expense caused to the unassisted
party by any breach of it. This is well established. It is not confined to legally-aided
cases, but to all cases, an order to make the solicitor pay the costs of the other side. As
Abbott CJ said as long ago as 1822 in *Blundell v Blundell* 5 B & Ald 533 at 534, 106 ER
1286: '. . . it will be a wholesome lesson to others . . .' Lord Hatherley LC said in *Re Jones*   *h*
(1870) LR 6 Ch App 497 at 499 that solicitors must—

> 'not only perform their duty towards their own clients, but also towards all those
> *against* whom they are concerned, and that care should be taken to see that the
> litigation is the *bonâ fide* litigation of the client who instructs the solicitor, and not
> a litigation carried on altogether on the solicitor's account.' (My emphasis.)

This principle was emphatically affirmed by the House of Lords in *Myers v Elman*   *j*
[1939] 4 All ER 484 at 489, [1940] AC 282 at 290, where Viscount Maughan said:

> 'These cases did not depend on disgraceful or dishonourable conduct by the
> solicitor, but on mere negligence of a serious character, the result of which was to
> occasion *useless costs to the other parties*.' (My emphasis).

These then are the duties of solicitors who act for legally-aided clients. They must
a inquire carefully into the claim made by their own legally-aided client so as to see that
it is well founded and justified, so much so that they would have advised him to bring
it on his own if he had enough means to do so, with all the risks that failure would
entail. They must consider also the position of the other side. They must not take any
advantage of the fact that their own client is legally aided and so not able to pay any
costs. They must not use legal aid as a means to extort a settlement from the other
b side. They must remember the position of the defendant and that he is bound to incur
a lot of costs to fight the case. If a reasonable payment is made into court, or a reasonable
offer is made, they must advise its acceptance. They must not proceed with the case on
the chance of getting more. They must put out of their minds altogether the fact that,
by going on with the case, they will get more costs for themselves. They must not run
up costs by instructing endless medical experts for endless reports or by any unnecessary
c expenditure. They must not ask a medical expert to change his report, at their own
instance, so as to favour their own legally-aided client or conceal things that may be
against him. They must not 'settle' the evidence of the medical experts as they did in
Whitehouse v Jordan, which received the condemnation of this court (see [1980] 1 All ER
650 at 655) and the House of Lords. As Lord Wilberforce said ([1981] 1 All ER 267 at
276, [1981] 1 WLR 246 at 256–257):
d
'Expert evidence presented to the court should be, and should be seen to be, the
independent product of the expert, uninfluenced as to form or content by the
exigencies of litigation.'

All this is not only in regard to solicitors but also to counsel as well. We all know that
the area committees depend largely on the opinion of counsel, whether legal aid should
e be given for the purpose or not, and whether the case should proceed further or not. So
much so that counsel have a special responsibility in these cases. They owe a duty to the
area committees who rely on their opinions. They owe a duty to the court which has to
try the case. They owe a duty to the other side who have to fight it and pay all the costs
of doing so. If they fail in their duty, I have no doubt that the court can call them to
account and make them pay the costs of the other side. They will not be able to escape
f on the ground that it was work done by them in the course of litigation. They cannot
claim the immunity given to them by *Rondel v Worsley* [1967] 3 All ER 993, [1969] 1 AC
191. That only avails them in regard to their own client. They have no immunity if
they fail to have regard to their duty to the court and to the other side.
If these precepts are observed, I hope we shall in future have no more disgraces such
as have attended this case. But for the reasons I have given, I would dismiss this appeal.
g

ACKNER LJ. I agree. The facts as recounted by Lord Denning MR demonstrate, with
depressing clarity, the extent to which legal aid granted to the respondent Mr Kelly was
abused by him and/or his legal advisers. By 29 July 1980, when payment into court of
£750 was made by London Transport Executive, the appellants, a sum which turned out
to be ten times more than the claim was worth, it would have been easy to have
h established a strong prima facie case that Mr Kelly and/or his advisers were conducting
the proceedings so unreasonably as to incur substantial and unjustifiable expenses to the
fund, and that it was unreasonable that he should continue to receive legal aid. It was a
great pity that the London Transport Executive did not write to the area committee,
with a copy of course to Mr Kelly's solicitors, referring to the fact and amount of the
payment into court, the order made on directions with regard to the exchange of medical
j reports, the failure by Mr Kelly's solicitors to comply with that order, the necessity to
vacate the date for trial the previous June and the continued failure to date by Mr Kelly's
solicitors to comply with that order. If this information had been provided to the area
committee, together with the medical reports and hospital notes obtained by the London
Transport Executive and indeed provided to Mr Kelly's solicitors, the area committee
would have been under an obligation to call for a report from Mr Kelly's solicitors asking

them to show cause why the certificate should not be discharged (see reg 12 of the Legal
Aid (General) Regulations 1971, SI 1971/62, now reg 78 of the Legal Aid (General) *a*
Regulations 1980, SI 1980/1894). Had this action been taken, I have little doubt that
these proceedings, either by reason of the money in court being taken out or by the
discharge of the certificate, would never have come to trial and a great deal of public
money would thereby have been saved. One has only to consider the disarray in which
Mr Kelly's medical experts stood, as described by Lord Denning MR, as at July 1980 to
reach this conclusion. *b*

London Transport Executive now seek, by virtue of s 13(1) of the Legal Aid Act 1974,
to recover their costs which they limit, after the payment into court, to £8,000.

Three questions arise out of this appeal. I will deal shortly with each separately.

1. *Were the proceedings finally decided in favour of London Transport Executive (the
unassisted party)?* *c*

The order made by the learned judge was that judgment should be entered for Mr
Kelly for the sum of £75. It was further adjudged that judgment should be entered for
the defendants for their costs in the action from the date of payment in. By reason of Mr
Kelly being legally assisted with a nil contribution, his liability for such costs was
determined in the sum of £75, being of course the amount for which he had been given
judgment. The learned judge ordered that the sum of £750 standing to the credit of this *d*
action in the short term investment account should be dealt with as follows: 'The sum of
£75 shall be held in court pending taxation in this action and the balance of £675, with
accrued interest, be paid out to the defendants' solicitors.' To assert that the proceedings
were finally decided in favour of Mr Kelly, that is to say that Mr Kelly was the successful
party, is to ignore reality. It is not difficult to imagine what at least in substance Mr Kelly
would have said if, as he had just finished hearing the judgment, some grossly insensitive *e*
friend of his had come up to him and warmly congratulated him on the 'success' he had
achieved in his case. I have no doubt that he would have regarded himself, not merely
as having substantially failed in his claim, but having totally failed. An accident which
he had represented as having disastrous consequences justifying a claim for tens of
thousands of pounds had been dismissed as trivial with an award of damages which
would not have carried costs if it had been brought in the only proper venue, the county *f*
court. He had no residual disabilities from the accident. Such disabilities from which he
did suffer were attributable to his chronic alcoholism. By persisting in his claim he had
lost the £750 paid into court. I have no doubt that the proceedings were 'finally decided
in favour' of London Transport Executive. The proceedings do not have to be decided
wholly in favour of the unassisted person; but they must have been 'substantially' so
found: see *General Accident, Fire and Life Assurance Corp Ltd v Foster* [1972] 3 All ER 877 *g*
at 880, [1973] QB 50 at 55.

2. *Was it just and equitable in all the circumstances to make the order for costs in favour of the
London Transport Executive?*

Although the contrary was apparently contended before Caulfield J, the point is no
longer a live one in this appeal. This concession was clearly right. The judge correctly *h*
held that it was just and equitable for London Transport Executive to seek to obtain costs
against the legal aid fund in a claim that had no foundation, which was riddled with
defects and which they had sought to buy off because of its nuisance value.

3. *Had London Transport Executive established that they would suffer severe financial
hardship unless the order was made?* *j*

It is contended on behalf of the Law Society that the defendants are not capable in law
of 'suffering hardship', since the words connote some form of human suffering.

There is clear authority of this court (see *R & T Thew Ltd v Reeves* [1981] 2 All ER 964,
[1982] QB 172) that a private company can suffer 'financial hardship' within the meaning
of the section. I can see no basis for differentiating a private company from a public

company. In July 1981 in *Kenny v Taylor* (8 July 1981, unreported) Dillon J rejected the
a selfsame submission made by counsel for the Law Society, and earlier in *Miller v Littner*
(1979) 123 SJ 473 Oliver J decided that financial hardship could be suffered by an
inanimate estate. The matter must, in my judgment, be a question of fact and degree in
each case. A small public company might well be obliged to sell off some of its vital
assets in order to pay a substantial bill of costs. In such a case there would clearly be
material for contending that the public company would suffer hardship if the order was
b not made.

The real question in this case is whether London Transport Executive can establish
that they would suffer not only financial hardship but severe financial hardship if the
legal aid fund did not pay the £8,000 which they estimate to be a modest assessment of
their costs since the payment into court. The basis of the submissions of counsel for the
London Transport Executive is that, as the London Transport Executive are already
c overdrawn to the extent of £100,000, despite subsidies totalling £179m, any further
significant expense must involve them in not only financial hardship, but severe financial
hardship.

To my mind it is essential, when considering a potential claim of financial hardship,
to ascertain what are the likely consequences to the unassisted person of the legal aid fund
not bearing his costs. If they bear heavily on the unassisted person, be he an individual
d or a company, then a possible claim for hardship may be made out. Whether or not such
financial hardship is severe must be essentially a question of fact and degree in the
particular circumstances of the case. To take a clear case, if the obligation to pay its own
costs might force a company into liquidation, then a prima facie case would have been
made out of severe financial hardship. However, if the consequences of paying a
substantial bill of costs results merely in the company having to increase its overdraft and
e thus reduce to some minor extent its profitability, I would not view such a situation as
being one of severe financial hardship or probably even of hardship at all. As Salmon LJ
pointed out in *Hanning v Maitland (No 2)* [1970] 1 All ER 812 at 818, [1970] 1 QB 580 at
590 when dealing with the Legal Aid Act 1964:

> 'The Act was passed because it had been generally recognised for years that there
> was a small number of cases in which a defendant of modest means, but outside the
> ambit of legal aid, was sued unsuccessfully by a legally aided plaintiff and that in
> such a case it was only fair that the defendant should be paid his taxed costs out of
> public funds. Clearly the Act was not intended to operate for the benefit of
> insurance companies or other persons of very substantial means.'

What are or will be the consequences of the London Transport Executive having to
f pay a bill of £8,000 costs? They will have to, or may have to, apply to the Greater
London Council for further funds. This is hardly likely to result, of itself, in an increase
in the rates raised by the GLC, but if it does this figure spread around the ratepayers
would be minimal. In a sentence, the London Transport Executive cannot establish that
if the legal aid fund does not pay the £8,000 costs they will suffer severe financial
hardship.

g I fully accept that it is very hard to bear the payment out of large sums in order to
defeat a legally-assisted claim which should never have been brought. That is not the
same as saying it is *financially* very hard to bear such a situation. What has to be evaluated
is not the degree of legitimate indignation or sense of grievance but the extent of
financial hardship, if any, which such a situation causes.

I therefore would also dismiss this appeal, but I should add that by virtue of s 13(5) 'no
appeal shall lie against an order under this section, or a refusal to make such an order
except on a point of law'. The only points of law which have arisen in this appeal seem
to me to have arisen solely on the respondent's notice.

O'CONNOR LJ. I too would dismiss this appeal on the two grounds that London
Transport Executive have failed to satisfy me that they would suffer severe financial

hardship if the order is not made and, secondly, on the ground that the finding to that effect by the judge was a finding of fact and no appeal lies from it to this court.

I would only wish to add a few words of my own on the question whether these proceedings were finally decided in favour of the unassisted party. I do not think that it is possible to say that in every case where a plaintiff gets judgment for less than the sum of money which the defendant has paid into court those proceedings are finally decided in favour of the defendant. In the great majority of such cases that would not be the position. The facts in the present case were exceptional. It is, I think, only in a case where the effect of what has happened is that the plaintiff recovers nothing, or, indeed, in this case had he not been assisted would have come out with a very substantial minus quantity, considering the sum of money that he would have had to pay in costs both to his own legal advisers and to the successful defendants. It is in that class of case that it seems to me that it is proper to say, as Lord Denning MR and Ackner LJ have said in the present case and I agree, that this case has been finally decided in favour of the unassisted party.

Appeal dismissed. Plaintiff's solicitors to be ordered to attend before court for consideration of whether they should pay defendants' costs.

Solicitors: *V J Moorfoot* (for the London Transport Executive); *David Edwards*, Secretary, Legal Aid (for the Law Society).

Francis Rustin   Barrister.

Note
Tate & Lyle Food and Distribution Ltd and another v Greater London Council and another

COURT OF APPEAL, CIVIL DIVISION
CUMMING-BRUCE, DUNN AND OLIVER LJJ
21–23, 26–30 APRIL, 4–6, 10, 11, 28 MAY 1982

An appeal by the defendants, the Greater London Council and the Port of London Authority, against the decision of Forbes J on 15 May 1980 (unreported) on the issue of liability in an action for damages for negligence and nuisance brought against them by the plaintiffs, Tate & Lyle Food and Distribution Ltd and Silvertown Services Lighterage Ltd, was allowed. Since the defendants did not appeal on the issue of damages, the Court of Appeal did not refer to the decision of Forbes J on 22 May 1981 ([1981] 3 All ER 716, [1982] 1 WLR 149) on the quantum of damages. The decision of the Court of Appeal accordingly does not call for a fuller report.

Henrietta Steinberg   Barrister.

Re GKN Bolts and Nuts Ltd Sports and Social Club
Leek and others v Donkersley and others

CHANCERY DIVISION

SIR ROBERT MEGARRY V-C

8, 9, 10 JUNE, 21 DECEMBER 1981

Club – Members' club – Property of club – Dissolution of club – Distribution of assets on dissolution – Club becoming inactive – Club rules not indicating that assets to be distributed otherwise than equally among members on dissolution – Resolution passed at meeting that club's remaining asset be sold and proceeds distributed according to length of service – Whether club's inactivity amounting to spontaneous dissolution – Whether other events pointing to dissolution of club – Whether rules of club governing distribution of assets can be altered at meeting dissolving club without prior notice.

In 1946 a club was formed for the benefit of the employees of a company with the object of promoting sport and recreational facilities for the employees. Shortly after, the trustees of the club purchased a sports ground for the club for about £2,200. The club prospered for a while but by 1969 was in financial difficulties. No further membership cards were issued after January 1975 and during that year the club ceased to be active or registered for value added tax, dismissed its steward and sold its stock of drinks to pay debts. The last club accounts covered the year ending December 1974. At the end of 1975 the club's membership stood at 650. Sale of the sports ground, the club's remaining asset, had been under discussion for some time and attempts had been made to get planning permission to develop the ground. On 18 December 1975 a special meeting of the club was held to discuss the sale of the ground. Resolutions were passed at the meeting that the ground be sold for £19,000 (the current offer for it), and that the proceeds be divided among those who were paying members of the club at 18 December 1975 on the basis of each member receiving one unit for every year of service with the company up to a maximum of 30 units. In August 1978 the ground was in fact sold to another purchaser for £253,000. The trustees of the club issued an originating summons to determine (i) whether the club had ceased to exist and if so the date at which it had ceased to exist, and (ii) if the club had ceased to exist, the basis on which the proceeds of sale should be distributed, namely either according to the resolution passed on 18 December 1975 or by distribution to the members, inter alia, as at that date on a per capita basis.

Held – (1) Although as a matter of principle there could be spontaneous dissolution of a club, the mere inactivity of a club, being an equivocal act, was insufficient to constitute spontaneous dissolution unless the inactivity was so prolonged that the only reasonable inference, having regard to such inactivity and the surrounding circumstances, was that the club had been dissolved. If that was the case, the court would select as the date when the club ceased to exist a reasonable date between the time when the club could still be said to exist and the time when its existence had clearly ended. Applying that test, the club had, in all the circumstances, ceased to exist on 18 December 1975 because by then not only had the club been inactive for several months but positive acts towards winding it up had been taken, including the passing on that date of a valid resolution (despite possible irregularities in convening the meeting) to sell its remaining asset, the sports ground. Even if the resolution to sell the sports ground was invalid, the club had still ceased to exist on 18 December 1975 because by then its activities had ceased and it had become incapable of carrying out its objects (see p 860 *a* to *c* and h *j* and p 861 *b* to *d* and h to p 862 *b*, post); *Abbatt v Treasury Solicitor* [1969] 1 All ER 52, *Re St Andrew's Allotment*

Association's Trusts [1969] 1 All ER 147 and *Re William Denby & Sons Ltd Sick and Benevolent Fund* [1971] 2 All ER 1196 considered.

    (2) The rules of a club regarding property rights of members on dissolution could not be altered at a meeting dissolving the club unless proper notice of the proposed change in the rules had been given. Furthermore, where the rules did not indicate to the contrary, it was to be presumed that the distribution of a club's assets on dissolution was to be on the basis of equality regardless of length of membership or the amount of the subscriptions paid. Since there was nothing in the club's rules to indicate that the club's assets were to be distributed otherwise than equally among the members, the scheme to distribute the club's assets on the basis of length of service with the company amounted to a change in the rules regarding distribution on dissolution, and since no notice of any proposal to alter the rules had been given, the resolution passed at the meeting of 18 December 1975 requiring the proceeds of sale of the sports ground to be distributed according to length of service was invalid. The proceeds of the sale were therefore required to be distributed equally among those who were members of the club on 18 December 1975 (see p 863 *b* to *f*, post); *Re Sick and Funeral Society of St John's Sunday School, Golcar* [1972] 2 All ER 439 applied; *Allen v Gold Reefs of West Africa Ltd* [1900–3] All ER Rep 746 considered.

Notes

For dissolution of a members' club, and where club may have ceased to exist, see 6 Halsbury's Laws (4th edn) paras 201, 267.

Cases referred to in judgment

Abbatt v Treasury Solicitor [1969] 3 All ER 1175, [1969] 1 WLR 1575, CA; *rvsg* [1969] 1 All ER 52, [1969] 1 WLR 561, 8(2) Digest (Reissue) 646, 189.

Allen v Gold Reefs of West Africa Ltd [1900] 1 Ch 656, [1900–3] All ER Rep 746, 9 Digest (Reissue) 624, 3716.

Blue Albion Cattle Society, Re [1966] CLY 1274.

Bucks Constabulary Widows' and Orphans' Fund Friendly Society, Re, Thompson v Holdsworth (No 2) [1979] 1 All ER 623, [1979] 1 WLR 936.

Denby (William) & Sons Ltd Sick and Benevolent Fund, Re, Rowling v Wilks [1971] 2 All ER 1196, [1971] 1 WLR 973, 25 Digest (Reissue) 381, 3460.

St Andrew's Allotment Association's Trusts, Re, Sargeant v Probert [1969] 1 All ER 147, [1969] 1 WLR 229, Digest (Cont Vol C) 896, 20a.

Sick and Funeral Society of St John's Sunday School, Golcar, Re, Dyson v Davies [1972] 2 All ER 439, [1973] Ch 51, [1972] 2 WLR 962, 8(2) Digest (Reissue) 618, 32.

Cases also cited

Blake v Smither (1906) 22 TLR 698.

Customs and Excise Officers' Mutual Guarantee Fund, Re, Robson v A-G [1917] 2 Ch 18.

Feeney and Shannon v MacManus [1937] IR 23.

Grand Canal Boatmen and Workmen's Benefit Society Funds, Re [1914] 1 IR 142.

Greenhalgh v Arderne Cinemas Ltd [1950] 2 All ER 1120, [1951] Ch 286, CA.

Labouchere v Earl of Wharncliffe (1879) 13 Ch D 346.

Lead Co's Workmen's Fund Society, Re [1904] 2 Ch 196, [1904–7] All ER Rep 933.

Originating summons

By an originating summons dated 6 July 1979 the plaintiffs, Peter William Leek, Richard William Edward Spencer and Henry James Humpston, the trustees of a fund representing the net proceeds of sale of a sports ground at Bills Lane, Solihull, West Midlands, belonging to a club, the GKN Bolts and Nuts Ltd (Automotive Division) Birmingham Works, Sports and Social Club, sought determination of, inter alia, the following questions: (1) whether on the true construction of the rules of the club and in the events which had happened, the fund fell to be distributed; (2) If the answer to question (1) was in the negative, how else the fund ought to be dealt with; (3) if the answer to question

(1) was in the affirmative, whether the fund should be distributed (a) between the
members of the club on 18 December 1975 per capita, (b) between the club members on
18 December 1975 on the basis that each member took one share of the fund for each
year of service he had completed up to 18 December 1975, no member being entitled to
more than 30 shares, (c) between the club members on 21 July 1978 per capita, (d)
between the club members for the time being per capita or (e) to some other and if so
what persons and in what manner. The proceedings were brought against five
defendants, representing those who were members at various dates but were discontinued
against the fifth defendant. The four remaining defendants were John Francis
Donkersley, Arthur Briggs, Diana Mary Keates and Rene Frear. The facts are set out in
the judgment.

Gabriel Hughes for the trustees.
Stephen Lloyd for the first defendant.
Jules Sher QC for the second defendant.
W A Blackburne for the third defendant.
J H G Sunnucks for the fourth defendant.

Cur adv vult

21 December. **SIR ROBERT MEGARRY V-C** read the following judgment: This
is a case of a sports and social club which became defunct. Shortly after the last war a
sports ground for the club at Solihull was purchased by trustees for the club for a little
under £2,200. The result of a small addition and an exchange made in the 1950s
resulted in the net cost of the ground being a little under £1,000. In 1978, after the club
had become inactive, the ground was sold for £253,000; and the question is how the net
assets of the club are to be distributed. As is common in club cases, there are many
obscurities and uncertainties, and some difficulty in the law. In such cases, the court
usually has to take a broad sword to the problems, and eschew an unduly meticulous
examination of the rules and resolutions. I am not, of course, saying that these should be
ignored; but usually there is a considerable degree of informality in the conduct of the
affairs of such clubs, and I think that the courts have to be ready to allow general concepts
of reasonableness, fairness and common sense to be given more than their usual weight
when confronted by claims to the contrary which appear to be based on any strict
interpretation and rigid application of the letter of the rules. In other words, allowance
must be made for some play in the joints.

The starting point is to summarise the history of the club; and in doing this I
supplement the evidence in the affidavits with certain facts agreed during argument. In
considering the rival contentions, I shall add any further relevant details, but at this stage
I shall merely state the facts in outline. The club was formed just after the 1939–45 war,
probably in 1946, under the name 'The L H Newton Sports and Social Club'. The name
was derived from L H Newton & Co Ltd, and the club was formed for the benefit of
employees of that company and any subsidiary or associated companies. For some time
the club was open to employees of another company, but they all withdrew from
membership some years before the matters in dispute arose. As a result of company
mergers, the club became the 'GKN Bolts and Nuts Ltd (Automotive Division)
Birmingham Works Sports and Social Club'. I need not go into the complexities of
mergers and nomenclature since there is no relevant dispute about those who were
entitled to become members. I need only say that the membership was based on
employment by a particular company at particular premises.

There is some obscurity about the rules. There are in evidence two sets of rules for the
club under its old name, and three sets for the club under its new name. I think it is
reasonably clear that under its old name the club had one set of rules which probably
dates from the 1950s, and another set in 1962. For the club under its new name, a set of
rules was adopted by the club in general meeting in 1972, though it is not clear whether
the rules were the second draft or the third draft: a set of each is in evidence. There is also
a set of rules for 1974 which the club committee approved, though it is doubtful whether

this set of rules was ever approved by the club in general meeting. Fortunately, although there are certain differences between the sets of rules for the club under its old name and *a* those for the club under its new name, the variations between the differing versions of the rules for each name do not appear to have any great materiality. By the end of the argument, all concerned had put their cases on the 1974 version, and I shall deal with the case on that footing.

For a while the club prospered; but then it began to decline. From 1947 to 1967 the club had a football team which used the sports ground. But then in 1967 the team ceased *b* to exist, and members of the club, as such, ceased to use the ground. Thereafter, the secretary of the club, who held the keys of the ground, allowed individual employees of the company to use the ground on various occasions; and at times the ground was hired out to other clubs, though by March 1975 all such hiring had ceased. The ground was also used occasionally for charity matches; and for a while a horse was allowed to graze the ground.

c
Other activities of the club were carried on in certain rooms on the company premises, and latterly in a pair of rooms known as the 'club room' and the 'sports room'. These rooms were provided by the company free of charge. In the club room food and drink could be bought and consumed, while in the sports room there was a billards table, a table tennis table, a darts board and so on. A paid steward was in charge. The committee minutes also disclose various other activities. Yet although for a while many activities *d* flourished, by 1969 the club was in financial difficulties. On 11 April 1975 the club ceased to be registered for value added tax, at about that time the steward was dismissed, and on 11 September 1975, the club's stocks of drinks were sold and the proceeds were used towards meeting the club's debts. By the middle of 1975 the club had ceased to organise any activities for its members; and the last annual general meeting of the club was held on 11 February 1975. The last accounts for the club were those for the period *e* ended on 31 December 1974. No membership cards were issued after January 1975. Since December 1975 the secretary, who holds the keys, has allowed individual employees of the company to use the club room during the lunch hour if it was not being used for company purposes. The club subscription, which since March 1975 had been 2p per week, is still deducted from the wages of the members, though since December 1975 the company has retained the money instead of paying it to the club. This *f* apparently preserves the right of the members to associate membership of other sports clubs. The uniform picture is one of a club that during 1975 ceased to be active in any way as a club; and one of the contentions has been that the club ceased to exist at some time during that year. If it did, the question is when that was; and that question depends to a considerable extent on a special general meeting of the club which was held on 18 December 1975. That meeting was called to discuss a proposal to sell the sports ground. *g*

The possible sale of the sports ground had been a subject for discussion since the middle of 1970. At that time the club no longer used the ground, and had financial problems. In 1973 an application for planning permission to carry out residential development on the land was made and refused, and in 1974 a possible sale was discussed both at the annual general meeting and subsequently at a committee meeting. Towards the end of 1974 a further planning application was made, and this was discussed at the *h* annual general meeting held in February 1975; but again permission was refused, some 2½ months after the meeting. Then an offer to buy the sports ground for £19,000 was made; and by a notice dated 15 December 1975, a special general meeting of the club on 18 December 1975 was convened 'in order to discuss sale of sports ground', to quote the words in the notice convening the meeting. The minutes record nine named persons as being present; but as they also record motions as being proposed and seconded by persons *j* not included in the nine, even from the minutes it seems probable that the record of those 'present' is merely a record of members of the committee, and that the meeting was much better attended than that. In fact, there is evidence that some 70 or 80 members were there.

The minutes record the offer of £19,000, and a unanimous decision that 'we should sell the property now'. There were then further proposals about the disposition of the

a proceeds of sale. These were that 'one unit should be allocated for each year's service. . . A maximum number of units was established at 30; eligible participants to be those employees who were paying members as at the 18th December 1975'. The minutes do not say anything about these resolutions having been passed; but the inference is that they were, and there is evidence to this effect, though there is also evidence that there was one dissentient who wanted the money to go to charity. The sale for £19,000 did not in

b fact take place as the purchaser was unable to proceed. Various efforts to sell the ground came to nothing, and in 1977 a further application for planning permission was rejected. This time there was an appeal, and after a local inquiry in May 1978, the appeal was allowed and planning permission was granted. On 21 July 1978 the trustees of the club entered into a conditional contract to sell the sports ground for £253,000, and on 4 August 1978 this contract became unconditional. On 18 August 1978 completion took

c place. After deducting the costs of the appeal, and the conveyancing and other costs, the gross proceeds of sale yielded some £240,000 net; and this is the sum in dispute.

    I now indicate the rival contentions. The membership of the club, which was a little under 650 at the end of 1975 (I speak of full members only), has of course been changing, and so the starting point is to determine whether the club has ceased to exist, and, if so, at what date this occurred, and so when the assets of the club became distributable

d among its members. In order to resolve this, the proceedings were constituted with five defendants to represent those who were members at various dates. The proceedings against the fifth defendant were discontinued by order on 25 July 1980, but the other four put forward four different contentions. Counsel on behalf of the first defendant contended for a per capita distribution for members as at 18 December 1975, the date of the resolution to sell. Counsel on behalf of the second defendant sought a distribution

e as at the same date, but on a proportionate basis in accordance with the resolution, so that the share of each member would vary with his years of service, subject to a maximum of 30 years. Counsel for the fourth defendant sought a per capita distribution among the members on 21 July 1978, the date of the conditional contract for sale. On it appearing that one member had left the club on 28 July 1978, counsel who appeared for the trustees advanced a similar contention on behalf of those who were members on 4 August 1978,

f the date when the contract became unconditional; and she also said what little could be said on behalf of honorary members.

    Finally, counsel on behalf of the third defendant rejected all these dates, and contended that the club had remained in existence to this day, and so it was those who were still members who, if the club were now to cease to exist, would be entitled to the proceeds of sale. It was common ground that, apart from questions about who was entitled and

g in what shares, there were likely to be certain consequential fiscal results which depended on the date to be taken. Under the Development Land Tax Act 1976 (and I put it in broad terms) there would be one exemption not exceeding £10,000 for the entire club if it still existed when completion took place on 18 August 1978, but one such exemption for every member of the club who was entitled to a share if the club had ceased to exist before that date: see ss 12(1), 28(1), 45(2)(*a*) and 47(1) of the Act. (The amount of the

h exemption was subsequently increased from £10,000 to £50,000, I was told). Accordingly, if counsel for the third defendant is right, the fund will be subject to a heavy burden of tax which it will escape if any of the other arguments are right. The Inland Revenue authorities have been notified of these proceedings, I may say, but have indicated that they do not wish to take part in them. I should also mention that advertisements inserted in local newspapers, giving notice of these proceedings, have

j evoked a healthy response from those claiming to be entitled.

    The starting point is to consider whether there was a dissolution of the club on 18 December 1975, the date of the resolution to sell. The rules of the club do not help, for they are all directed to the operation of the club as a going concern. It is plain that there never was an agreement by the entire membership that the club should be dissolved, and of course there has been no exercise by the court of its inherent jurisdiction to order a dissolution. The question therefore is whether there has been what was called in argument a spontaneous dissolution of the club.

As a matter of principle I would hold that it is perfectly possible for a club to be dissolved spontaneously. I do not think that mere inactivity is enough: a club may do little or nothing for a long period, and yet continue in existence. A cataleptic trance may look like death without being death. But inactivity may be so prolonged or so circumstanced that the only reasonable inference is that the club has become dissolved. In such cases there may be difficulty in determining the punctum temporis of dissolution: the less activity there is, the greater the difficulty of fastening on one date rather than another as the moment of dissolution. In such cases the court must do the best it can by picking a reasonable date somewhere between the time when the club could still be said to exist, and the time when its existence had clearly come to an end.

I think that some such doctrine is supported by authority. In *Abbatt v Treasury Solicitor* [1969] 1 All ER 52, [1969] 1 WLR 561, a British Legion Club ceased to function, and in 1954 a meeting of the members of the club resolved to change the club into a working men's club, though without specifying any details. Some five months later the change-over took place; and Pennycuick J held that at the date of the changeover the former club ceased to exist and its property became distributable among those who were then members. The members of a club, he said, were, by an implied term in the contract of membership, precluded from obtaining the realisation and distribution of the property of the club so long as the club functioned; but 'once the club ceases to function the reason for this disappears and the right of the existing members must, I think, crystallise once and for all' (see [1969] 1 All ER 52 at 58, [1969] 1 WLR 561 at 567). He made it clear that no resolution or order of the court was needed to bring about this result (see [1969] 1 All ER 52 at 58–59, [1969] 1 WLR 561 at 568–569). This decision was reversed on appeal (see [1969] 3 All ER 1175, [1969] 1 WLR 1575), but on different grounds which did not affect this point; and I think counsel were right to concede that the decision on spontaneous dissolution was of the ratio and was not affected by the appeal.

In *Re William Denby & Sons Ltd Sick and Benevolent Fund* [1971] 2 All ER 1196, [1971] 1 WLR 973, Brightman J classified four categories of case in which an unregistered friendly society or benevolent fund should be regarded as having been dissolved or terminated so that its assets became distributable. The first three categories of dissolution or termination were (1) in accordance with the rules, (2) by agreement of all persons interested, and (3) by order of the court in the exercise of its inherent jurisdiction. The fourth category was when the substratum on which the society or fund was founded had gone, so that the society or fund no longer had any effective purpose, and the assets became distributable without any order of the court. On the facts of the case it was held that the substratum had not gone, so that the fund was not distributable; but the judgment considered a number of the authorities, and plainly supports the view that there may be a spontaneous dissolution of a society. The judgment does not mention the *Abbatt case* [1969] 1 All ER 52, [1969] 1 WLR 561, though it was cited in argument; but I think the two cases have much in common as supporting a doctrine of spontaneous dissolution. Brightman J expressed grave doubts whether mere inactivity of the officers of the society or the fund would suffice (see [1971] 2 All ER 1196 at 1204–1205, [1971] 1 WLR 973 at 981–982), and in this I would respectfully concur. Mere inactivity is equivocal: suspended animation may be continued life, not death; and the mere cessation of function that was mentioned in the *Abbatt* case would not, I think, suffice per se. But inactivity coupled with other circumstances may demonstrate that all concerned regard the society as having ceased to have any purpose or function, and so as no longer existing. I think that short inactivity coupled with strong circumstances, or long inactivity coupled with weaker circumstances may equally suffice. The question is whether, put together, the facts carry sufficient conviction that the society is at an end and not merely dormant.

For myself, I would hesitate a little about the use of the phrase 'substratum has gone' in this context. It has a beguiling sound; but it has strong overtones of the Companies

Court. There, it may form the basis of a winding-up order, but it does not by itself
a initiate or complete the termination of the existence of the company. It therefore seems
not altogether appropriate for establishing that there has been a spontaneous dissolution.
I also hesitate to use the term 'frustration', with all its contractual overtones. However,
this is a mere matter of nomenclature, and does not affect the principle. The question is
whether on the facts of the present case the society ceased to exist on 18 December 1975.

On that date, the position was that the club had ceased to operate as a club for several
b months. The picture was not one of mere inactivity alone; there were positive acts
towards the winding up of the club. The sale of the club's stock of drinks was one
instance, and others were the ending of the registration for value added tax, and the
dismissal of the steward. The cessation of any club activities, the ending of the use of the
sports ground and the abandonment of preparing accounts or issuing membership cards
were all in one sense examples of inactivity; but I think that there was in all probability
c some element of deliberation in these matters, and not a mere inertia. In the phrase of
counsel for the second defendant, there was a systematic dismantling of the club and its
activities.

However that may be, the resolution to sell the sports ground seems to me to conclude
the matter. Having taken all steps, active or passive, required to terminate the activities
of the club, short of passing a formal resolution to wind it up or dissolve it, the general
d meeting of the club resolved to sell the club's last asset. There are some questions about
the validity or effectiveness of the resolutions passed at the meeting, and I shall consider
these in a moment; but even if the resolutions were invalid, I would reach the same
conclusion. I must first, however, consider the resolutions.

It has been contended on various grounds that the resolutions at the meeting on 18
December 1975 were invalid. As I have mentioned, this meeting was convened by a
e notice dated 15 December 1975; and this was exhibited on the company's notice board,
which stood opposite the canteen used by all the company's employees. One objection
is that under the rules of the club 14 days' notice of any extraordinary general meeting
was required, and three days fall far short of that. Counsel for the third defendant also
objected that notices should have been inserted in all the pay packets instead of being
merely put on a notice board. It was also said that the resolution was merely to accept the
f offer of £19,000 then being made, and that this did not embrace the offer of £253,000
ultimately accepted.

As the evidence stands, it appears that in practice the requirement of 14 days' notice
was never observed. Seven days' notice was normal, and three days' notice was not
unusual, though there were instances of ten days, and once 13. There is no evidence that
anyone ever objected to notice being shorter than 14 days. One must remember that this
g was a club composed of employees of a particular company, and that all were entitled to
use the one canteen, no matter in what part of the company's premises they worked.
With a total membership of some 650, all employed in this way, with the history of
attempts to get planning permission with a view to sale, and with the prospect that a sale
would bring some money to each member of the club, it seems obvious that news of the
meeting would speedily reach all, if not quite all, of the members of the club. Even
h more obviously, those who wished to sell for £19,000 would not shrink from the
prospect of selling for £253,000. In my judgment, the resolution to sell was valid, it was
fortified by acquiescence, it authorised the sale that in fact took place, and it brought the
existence of the club to an end.

If I am wrong in this, then as I have indicated I still think the club ceased to exist on
18 December 1975. The cessation of all club activities, the general knowledge of
j attempts to get planning permission in order to sell the sports ground, and then the
holding of a general meeting to discuss a sale, even with (on this assumption) inadequate
notice, seem to me to mark an acceptance by all concerned that the club was a club no
more but merely a collection of individuals with expectations of dividing the proceeds
of sale of the one remaining asset of the club. Whether it is put in terms of the club
ceasing to function, or whether it is expressed as being a case where the substratum has

gone or whether it is said that the club had become inactive and the surrounding circumstances sufficiently indicated that those concerned regarded the club as having ceased to have any purpose or function, and so as no longer existing, the answer in each case is the same. The rules of 1974 stated that the objects of the club were 'to promote the different games of sport, to provide facilities for recreation and to encourage good fellowship among all members'; and all must have recognised that the club had become incapable of carrying out any of its objects. If the resolution to sell the sports ground is valid, as I think it is, that merely reinforces my conclusion that the club ceased to exist as such on 18 December 1975.

On this footing it is unnecessary to consider whether the club continued in existence until the conditional contract for sale was made on 21 July 1978 (as counsel for the fourth defendant contends), or until that contract became unconditional on 4 August 1978 (as counsel for the plaintiffs, the trustees, contends), or whether the club still continues in existence, as counsel for the third defendant submits. I do not read cases such as Re Blue Albion Cattle Society [1966] CLY 1274 (which is only recorded in a brief summary of a newspaper report) or Re St Andrew's Allotment Association's Trusts [1969] 1 All ER 147, [1969] 1 WLR 229, as negating the doctrine of spontaneous dissolution. The Blue Albion case was a case of long inactivity in which the court was asked to decree the society's dissolution, and there is no trace of any contention that there had been a spontaneous dissolution. The court merely did what was sought, and decreed a dissolution, holding that the date of the dissolution was the date of the court's order and that the society's assets were divisible amongst those who were then members. There may be many cases where there is doubt or uncertainty whether the facts are strong enough to justify the conclusion that there has been a spontaneous dissolution, and in such cases the court, if not satisfied that the club has already ceased to exist, may well decree a dissolution. Neither the existence of the power to do this, nor the doing of it, in any way demonstrates that a club cannot previously have come to an automatic end. The passage in the St Andrew's case [1969] 1 All ER 147 at 155–156, [1969] 1 WLR 229 at 240 which was mainly relied on also falls far short of impugning the contention that the club ceased to exist at the date of the meeting.

I turn to the question of the shares in which those who were members on 18 December 1975 are to divide the assets of the club. First, there is the resolution passed on that date for one unit for each year of service, with a maximum of 30 units. Is this valid and effective? Counsel for the second defendant said Yes and counsel for the first defendant said No; and I think counsel for the first defendant is right. As counsel for the second defendant realistically recognised at the opening of his address, many hurdles stood in his path; and despite his gallant attempts to leap them, more than one brought him to grief. The rules provide that they may be altered, added to or varied by a simple majority at a general meeting, but that no such alteration, addition or variation is to take effect until confirmed by the company. It is accepted that no such confirmation has been given, or even sought, and I do not think that a consent given now, when the club is no more, would have any effect.

Furthermore, the notice convening the meeting gave no indication whatever that any such proposal would be considered; it stated no more than that the meeting would 'discuss sale' of the sports ground. A drastic proposal to change the rules, to be made at the moment when the club ceases to exist, which will give some members 30 times as much as other members, is the sort of proposal that in my judgment must be spelled out in the notice convening the meeting. (The rules, I may say, are silent on the content of any such notice.) I do not know the length of service of those members who attended the meeting, but it would be lamentable if a meeting attended by 10 or 15% of the membership of a club could, without any notice to the rest of the members, alter the rules so as to give a far greater share of the club's assets to one group of members (including, perhaps, most of themselves) than to other groups. I do not for a moment suggest that in this case those who voted for the motion were in fact selfishly preferring themselves, but the possibility that this could be done is enough to make the point.

Yet again, I look with considerable suspicion on any resolution to alter the rules of a club at the moment of its dissolution where the alteration is not, and cannot be, regarded

as being for the benefit of the club as a whole but is for the benefit of certain categories
a of members. If the majority of the members are long-serving members who will benefit
by the resolution, why should they have power to bind the short-serving members who
constitute the minority? There appears to be no authority on this point on clubs; but
consider *Allen v Gold Reefs of West Africa Ltd* [1900] 1 Ch 656 at 671, [1900–3] All ER Rep
746 at 749. Whatever may be the position about a change in the rules made while the
club is a going concern, I think that an alteration of the rules so as to change the property
b rights of members on a dissolution cannot be made at the meeting which brings about
that dissolution unless at the very least there has been a scrupulous observance of the
rules, and in any case proper notice of the proposal has been given to all members. This
is plainly not the case here, and accordingly I hold that the resolution has no effect on the
shares to be taken on the dissolution.

That being so, the question is what the basis of distribution should be. For the reasons
c that I gave in *Re Sick and Funeral Society of St John's Sunday School, Golcar* [1972] 2 All ER
439, [1973] Ch 51 (a case which was applied by Walton J in *Re Bucks Constabulary Widows'
and Orphans' Fund Friendly Society (No 2)* [1979] 1 All ER 623, [1979] 1 WLR 936), I think
that where, as here, there is nothing in the rules or anything else to indicate a different
basis, the distribution should be on a basis of equality, irrespective of the length of
membership or the amount of the subscriptions paid. That seems to me to be particularly
d appropriate where, as here, the amount of the subscription is so small and the acquisition
of the last remaining asset of the club occurred so long ago. The provenance of the sports
ground is a matter of some obscurity. Whether the ground was purchased with money
given to the club, or whether it was bought with the aid of a loan which was long ago
either repaid or released, is not at all clear. (There is, I may say, no problem about the
existence of a possible resulting trust to the donor (if the land was acquired by means of
e a gift), for I was told that the personal representatives of the only donor suggested have
disclaimed any interest in the fund.) Some of the original members of the club are still
living, and it has quite rightly not been suggested that they, or those who were still
members while the possible loan was possibly being paid off, should take to the exclusion
of other members. I would reject any concept of even a modified form of tontine for
members of a social and sports club. Nor do I think that in this case there is any possible
f nexus between the length of membership or the number of subscriptions paid and the
property rights of members on a dissolution. Each member on 18 December 1975 is
entitled to one equal share in the proceeds of sale, whether his membership has lasted 30
years or a single day.

I have not so far differentiated between the different classes of members. Rule 2 of the
1974 rules begins by providing that the club should consist of 'ordinary and honorary
g members and, in special cases, of temporary members as hereinafter provided'. The rule
then turns to deal with 'full members', 'honorary members', 'associates', 'temporary
members' and the spouses of members and their children up to 18 years old who are
'entitled to membership without voting rights'. There is nothing to explain any
difference between 'ordinary members' and 'full members', and I think that they are
merely different names for the same thing: see, e g, rr 2.6, 2.7, 7.4. Only full members
h or ordinary members had voting rights at general meetings, but I must consider whether
any other categories of membership are entitled to share in the assets of the club. I do not
think that they are.

'Associates' are 'employees who are members of a Group Company Club having
similar objects' (r 2.4). They have to write their names in a book, with the names of their
clubs, and that gives them 'the same rights and privileges' as ordinary members, and
j makes them 'subject to the same rules', save that they may not vote at a meeting of the
club or take away intoxicating liquor for consumption off the premises. 'Temporary
members' (r 2.5) are those invited by the committee to participate in the sporting and
other amenities of the club; and this is limited to the day of the sporting or social
event. The spouses and minor children of members, who are merely 'entitled to
membership without voting rights' (r 2.2) seem to me to fall within much the same
category as associates and temporary members. The object in each case seems to me to
confer the right to use the club premises and facilities without imposing the powers and

responsibilities of full members, for whom alone do the rules provide for the payment
of subscriptions.

The position of honorary members is more complex; and I am not at all sure that there
are in fact any. By r 8 of the 1962 rules, each employee was able to nominate one person
for free honorary membership until the following 31 December. Honorary membership
was also open to those whom the club wished to honour, to persons temporarily engaged
in the company's organisation to whom the club wished to extend its activities, and to
'other persons sponsored by Employee Members who shall pay a subscription at the rate
of ten shillings per annum'. Rule 9 provided that honorary members should 'have no
voting powers or interest in the Club's assets', so that even those who paid their ten
shillings a year had no property rights.

During the last three years of the club's life, there were certain difficulties about
honorary members. Their position was much discussed, as described in the second
affidavit of Mr Newley, the club secretary, and the 1974 rules contain no counterpart to
r 9 of the 1962 rules. Nevertheless, r 7.4 of the 1974 rules makes it plain, by confining
the right to vote to ordinary members, that honorary members were to have no vote;
and I cannot think that the silence in the 1974 rules about property rights was intended
to confer such rights on those who, under the 1962 rules, had none, or on subsequent
honorary members, as distinguished from those who had become honorary members
while the 1962 rules were in force.

Furthermore, the whole atmosphere in these last years of the club's existence was to
restrict the numbers of honorary members. Formerly the honorary members would
apply annually for membership for each club year, which commenced on 1 October.
However, late in 1974 the committee changed the procedure, and issued invitations to
become honorary members rather than considering applications. The secretary said that
after the end of 1974 only 11 people were invited to be honorary members for the year
1974–75, and thereafter no invitations for any subsequent years were issued to anyone.
From this it looks as if there were no honorary members on 18 December 1975, though
on instructions I was told that there was one at that date who paid an annual £1, and five
honorary life members who paid nothing. The whole matter is obscure.

If there were no honorary members left, whether life members or subscribing, there
is nothing to decide on this point. If there were any such members, I would hold that,
as matters stand, they are not entitled to share in the club's assets. I say that partly
because of r 9 of the 1962 rules, partly because of what is generally understood by the
term 'honorary member', and partly because of the general background for honorary
membership of this club. I therefore hold that no members except those who are
properly called 'full members' or 'ordinary members' are entitled to any interest in the
assets of the club.

That, I think, disposes of the matter. I answer Yes to question 1 in the originating
summons, and so question 2 does not arise. I answer question 3 in sense (a), and I make
the representation orders sought under questions 4 to 7 inclusive. As the proceedings
against the fifth defendant have been discontinued, question 7a does not appear now to
arise. I would only add a word of gratitude to the members of the Bar who argued the
case, and especially to Mr Blackburne, counsel for the third defendant, for his careful and
thorough submissions, made in what at times must have seemed to him to be
discouraging circumstances.

Order accordingly.

Solicitors: *Waltons & Morse*, agents for *Pinsent & Co*, Birmingham (for the trustees);
Rooks, Rider & Co, agents for *Eyre & Co*, Birmingham (for the first defendant); *Church,
Adams Tatham & Co*, agents for *Rowleys & Blewitts*, Birmingham (for the second
defendant); *Blair Allison & Co*, Birmingham (for the third defendant); *Edge & Ellison,
Hatwell, Pritchett & Co*, Birmingham (for the fourth defendant).

Azza M Abdallah   Barrister.

Mears v Safecar Security Ltd

COURT OF APPEAL, CIVIL DIVISION
STEPHENSON, O'CONNOR LJJ AND SIR STANLEY REES
16, 17 FEBRUARY, 5 APRIL 1982

Master and servant – Contract of service – Written particulars of terms of employment – Particulars which ought to have been included – Sick pay – Employee's contract not including any provision for sick pay – Employer's practice not to pay sick pay – Test for determining what terms ought to have been included in contract of employment – Proper approach for resolving doubts about particulars which ought to have been included – Whether any presumption in favour of payment of sick pay – Whether employee entitled to sick pay – Employment Protection (Consolidation) Act 1978, ss 1, 11.

The appellant was employed by a company as a security guard from 9 July 1978. Shortly after he began to work for the company he was given a written form of agreement entitled 'Terms of Reference' which set out the title of the job he was employed to do, the date the employment began, the rate of remuneration, his hours of work, his entitlement to holidays, the conditions for payment of an annual bonus and the notice required to terminate the agreement. There was no provision in the agreement relating to sick pay. At no time before or during the appellant's employment with the company was any mention made by either party of what would happen financially if the appellant was absent sick. From December 1978 to January 1979 and from March to September 1979 the appellant was off work sick. During his absence fellow employees told him that he would not get any sick pay from the company. In September 1979 he gave the company written notice that he was unable to carry out his duties, which the company accepted. The appellant made an application requiring a reference to be made to an industrial tribunal under s 11*ᵃ* of the Employment Protection (Consolidation) Act 1978 to determine what particulars, particularly with respect to the payment of wages during any period of absence through sickness, ought to have been included or referred to in the written statement of the particulars of the terms of his employment to which he was entitled under s 1*ᵇ* of the 1978 Act. The industrial tribunal held that there was a presumption that an employee's wages were payable during absence due to sickness and that the company had not displaced that presumption in the case of the appellant. Accordingly the tribunal determined that the written 'Terms of Reference' the appellant had been given shortly after commencing work for the company should have included a term that the company would continue to pay the appellant's wages during any period of absence through sickness, but subject to deduction of any state sickness benefit received. The appellant appealed to the Employment Appeal Tribunal against the decision that the payment of wages was subject to any deductions, and the company cross-appealed against the decision that any term for the payment of the appellant's wages during periods of absence through sickness should be implied into the particulars of his terms of employment. The Employment Appeal Tribunal held that, on a consideration of all the facts and circumstances, it was the practice of the company not to pay wages to employees absent sick, and that the company would not have made an exception in the appellant's favour. Accordingly it dismissed the appellant's appeal and allowed the company's cross-appeal. The appellant appealed to the Court of Appeal.

Held – (1) In exercising its duty under s 11 of the 1978 Act to determine what particulars ought to have been included or referred to in an employee's written statement of the terms of his employment, an industrial tribunal was not bound by the test appropriate for commercial contracts. It should first determine whether the term had been agreed

---

a Section 11, so far as material, is set out at p 870 *j* to p 871 *a*, post
b Section 1, so far as material, is set out at p 869 *j* to p 870 *d*, post

expressly either orally or by necessary implication. If it had, the tribunal should then
determine that particulars of it ought to be included in the employee's statement of *a*
terms; but, if it had not, the tribunal should, with an open mind unprejudiced by any
preconception, presumption or assumption, consider all the facts and circumstances of
the relationship between the employer and employee concerned, including the way in
which they had worked the particular contract of employment since it was made, in
order to imply and determine the missing term which ought to have been particularised
by the employer and so to complete the contract (see p 876 *f*, p 877 *d e*, p 880 *b* to *e* and *b*
p 881 *g*, post); dicta of Viscount Simonds and Lord Tucker in *Lister v Romford Ice and Cold
Storage Co Ltd* [1957] 1 All ER at 133–135, 143–144, of Lord Wilberforce, Lord Cross,
Lord Edmund-Davies and Lord Fraser in *Liverpool City Council v Irwin* [1976] 2 All ER at
43–44, 46–47, 53, 57, of Megaw and Browne LJJ in *Ferguson v John Dawson & Partners
(Contractors) Ltd* [1976] 3 All ER at 824, 831, of Megaw LJ in *Wilson v Maynard
Shipbuilding Consultants AB* [1978] 2 All ER at 83–84 and of Lord Denning MR in *Todd v* *c*
British Midland Airways Ltd [1978] ICR at 964 applied; *Marrison v Bell* [1939] 1 All ER 745
considered; *The Moorcock* [1886–90] All ER 530, dicta of Scrutton LJ in *Reigate v Union
Manufacturing Co (Ramsbottom) Ltd* [1918–19] All ER Rep at 149, of MacKinnon LJ in
O'Grady v M Saper Ltd [1940] 3 All ER at 529, *James Miller & Partners Ltd v Whitworth
Street Estates (Manchester) Ltd* [1970] 1 All ER 796 and *L Schuler AG v Wickman Machine
Tool Sales Ltd* [1973] 2 All ER 39 distinguished; *Orman v Saville Sportswear Ltd* [1960] 3 *d*
All ER 105 disapproved.
   (2) It followed that the industrial tribunal had been wrong to treat the term which it
included in the appellant's contract as being agreed because of a presumption in favour
of payment of wages during absence through sickness unless rebutted by a term expressed
or implied on common law principles and because of the company's failure to rebut that
presumption by evidence from which such a term could be so implied. The evidence *e*
that it was the practice of the company not to pay wages to employees absent sick, that
that practice was well known to the company's employees, and that the appellant had
taken leave without sick pay for nearly 7 out of the 14 months his employment lasted,
had not asked for sick pay and had accepted what his colleagues told him was the practice,
pointed conclusively to a contract in which work was the consideration for wages and
under which there was to be no sick pay. Accordingly, the Employment Appeal Tribunal *f*
had been right to reject the conclusion of the industrial tribunal which would have
compelled the company to pay the employee sick pay when it would never have agreed
to pay any employee wages when absent sick and when the appellant had never expected
to receive sick pay. The appeal would therefore be dismissed (see p 877 *a* to *c*
and *j* to p 878 *a*, p 879 *h* to p 880 *a* and p 881 *d* and *g*, post); *O'Grady v M Saper Ltd*
[1940] 3 All ER 527 followed; *Marrison v Bell* [1939] 1 All ER 745 and *Orman v Saville* *g*
Sportswear Ltd [1960] 3 All ER 105 not followed.

Per curiam. Section 11 of the 1978 Act seems to impose on an industrial tribunal the
statutory duty to find the terms specified in ss 1, 4(1), 8 and 9(1) of that Act which have
not been included in the written particulars of an employee's terms of employment, and
in the last resort to invent them for the purpose of writing them into the contract. If the *h*
tribunal does not have enough material in the facts and circumstances to determine what
would have been agreed, it has then to determine what should have been agreed, bearing
in mind that it was the employer's breach of his statutory duty which had made the
employee's application for a reference necessary and that in consequence the tribunal
would generally be right to resolve any doubt about what particulars ought to be
included in favour of the employee (see p 880 *j* to p 881 *b* and *g*, post). *j*
   Observations on the appropriate provisions of s 11 of the 1978 Act under which
references to industrial tribunals for the enforcement of employees' rights to written
particulars of the terms of their employment should be made (see p 871 *g*, p 872 *f* and
p 873 *c d*, post).

Notes

a For payment of wages to an employee while on sick leave, see 16 Halsbury's Laws (4th edn) para 556, and for cases on the subject, see 20 Digest (Reissue) 296–299, 2676–2692.
For the Employment Protection (Consolidation) Act 1978 ss 1, 11, see 48 Halsbury's Statutes (3rd edn) 457, 465.

Cases referred to in judgments

b *Barrington v Lee* [1971] 3 All ER 1231, [1972] 1 QB 326, [1971] 3 WLR 962, CA, 1(1) Digest (Reissue) 535, 3736.
Brown v Stuart Scott & Co Ltd [1981] ICR 166, EAT, 20 Digest (Reissue) 375, 3243.
Comptoir Commercial Anversois and Power, Son & Co Arbitration, Re [1920] 1 KB 868, [1918–19] All ER Rep 661, CA, 12 Digest (Reissue) 747, 5375.
Construction Industry Training Board v Leighton [1978] 2 All ER 723, EAT, 20 Digest
c (Reissue) 276, 2579.
Ferguson v John Dawson & Partners (Contractors) Ltd [1976] 3 All ER 817, [1976] 1 WLR 1213, CA, Digest (Cont Vol E) 445, 6f.
Hancock v BSA Tools Ltd [1939] 4 All ER 538, 20 Digest (Reissue) 298, 2689.
Lister v Romford Ice and Cold Storage Co Ltd [1957] 1 All ER 125, [1957] AC 555, [1957] 2 WLR 158, HL, 20 Digest (Reissue) 276, 2583.
d *Liverpool City Council v Irwin* [1976] 2 All ER 39, [1977] AC 239, [1976] 2 WLR 562, HL, Digest (Cont Vol E) 366, 4870a.
Marrison v Bell [1939] 1 All ER 745, [1939] 2 KB 187, CA, 20 Digest (Reissue) 299, 2691.
Miller (James) & Partners Ltd v Whitworth Street Estates (Manchester) Ltd [1970] 1 All ER 796, [1970] AC 583, [1970] 2 WLR 728, HL, 11 Digest (Reissue) 462, 776.
Moorcock, The (1889) 14 PD 64, [1886–90] All ER Rep 530, CA, 12 Digest (Reissue) 751,
e 5395.
O'Grady v M Saper Ltd [1940] 3 All ER 527, [1940] 2 KB 469, CA, 20 Digest (Reissue) 297, 2682.
Orman v Saville Sportswear Ltd [1960] 3 All ER 105, [1960] 1 WLR 1055, 20 Digest (Reissue) 297, 2683.
Petrie v MacFisheries Ltd [1939] 4 All ER 281, [1940] 1 KB 258, CA, 20 Digest (Reissue)
f 297, 2681.
Reigate v Union Manufacturing Co (Ramsbottom) Ltd [1918] 1 KB 592, [1918–19] All ER Rep 143, CA, 20 Digest (Reissue) 321, 2851.
Schuler (L) AG v Wickman Machine Tool Sales Ltd [1973] 2 All ER 39, [1974] AC 235, [1973] 2 WLR 683, HL, Digest (Cont Vol D) 123, 3613a.
Shirlaw v Southern Foundries (1926) Ltd and Federated Foundries Ltd [1939] 2 All ER 113,
g [1939] 2 KB 206, CA; *affd* [1940] 2 All ER 445, [1940] AC 701, HL, 9 Digest (Reissue) 569, 3406.
Todd v British Midland Airways Ltd [1978] ICR 959, CA, 20 Digest (Reissue) 384, 3280.
Wilson v Maynard Shipbuilding Consultants AB [1978] 2 All ER 78, [1978] QB 665, [1978] 2 WLR 466, CA, 20 Digest (Reissue) 384, 3279.

h **Cases also cited**

Cutter v Powell (1795) 6 Term Rep 320, 101 ER 573.
Davis v Johnson [1978] 1 All ER 1132, [1979] AC 264, HL.
Massey v Crown Life Insurance Co [1978] 2 All ER 576, [1978] 1 WLR 676, CA.
Niblett v Midland Rly Co (1907) 96 LT 462, [1904–7] All ER Rep 248, DC.
Young v Bristol Aeroplane Co Ltd [1944] 2 All ER 293, [1944] KB 718, CA; *affd* [1946] 1 All ER 98, [1946] AC 163, HL.

j **Appeal**

Royston John Mears appealed against the decision of the Employment Appeal Tribunal (Slynn J, Mrs D Lancaster and Mr J G C Milligan) on 14 November 1980 whereby it

dismissed the appeal of Mr Mears and allowed the cross-appeal of Safecar Security Ltd
(the company) against the decision of an industrial tribunal (chairman Mr Mark Nesbitt)   *a*
held at Exeter on 21 January 1980 whereby it decided that the written statement dated
12 July 1978 of terms of Mr Mears's employment by the company ought to have
included a term that the company would continue to pay Mr Mears's wages during any
period of absence through sickness, but subject to deduction of all sickness benefits
received by Mr Mears under the Social Security Act 1975 in respect of such period. The
facts are set out in the judgment of Stephenson LJ.   *b*

Peter Clark for Mr Mears.
Eldred Tabachnik for the company.

At the conclusion of the arguments the court announced that the appeal would be
dismissed for reasons to be given later.
                                                                                       c
5 April. The following judgments were read.

STEPHENSON LJ. We dismissed this appeal at the end of the hearing and now give
our reasons for that decision.

On 21 January 1980 the industrial tribunal decided on a reference by the appellant
employee, Mr R J Mears, under s 11 of the Employment Protection (Consolidation) Act   *d*
1978 that—

> 'the written statement dated 12 July 1978 of the terms of Mr Mears' employment
> by the respondents ought to have included the following term:—"The Company
> will continue to pay your wages during any period of absence through sickness, but
> subject to deduction of all sickness benefits received by you under the Social Security
> Act 1975 in respect of such period."'   *e*

The industrial tribunal had to decide two issues; those they state at para 9 of their
decision:

> '(i) Whether a term is to be implied in Mr Mears' contract of employment that
> the respondents will pay him his wages whilst he is absent through sickness. (ii) If
> the answer to that is yes, whether a term is to be so implied that such wages will be   *f*
> paid without deduction of sickness benefit received by Mr Mears from the State in
> respect of such absence.'

On the first issue one member would have included a term that the respondent
company would *not* continue to pay the appellant's wages during any period of absence
through sickness. But the majority disagreed with him. On the second issue the   *g*
decision was unanimous, the minority member agreeing that if wages were payable
during absence through sickness they were subject to deduction of sickness benefits
received by the appellant under the Social Security Act 1975.

From the industrial tribunal's decision both Mr Mears and the company appealed. On
14 November 1980 the Employment Appeal Tribunal dismissed Mr Mears's appeal,
allowed the company's cross-appeal and gave Mr Mears leave to appeal. The effect of the   *h*
Employment Appeal Tribunal's decision, which agrees with the opinion of the minority
member of the industrial tribunal, is that Mr Mears is not entitled to be paid wages
during the periods when he was absent from work through sickness.

We have to decide which of the answers of these two tribunals to these two questions
is wrong in law and so to answer the question what, if any, payment of wages is due to
Mr Mears under his contract of employment with the company during the periods of his   *j*
absence through sickness.

Mr Mears started working for the company on 9 July 1978 as a security guard. Soon
after he was given a signed 'Personnel Contract Form', on which nothing turns, and
'Terms of Reference', on which this appeal turns. They are as follows:

'TERMS OF REFERENCE

It is hereby confirmed that R. J. MEARS, be engaged as a full time Patrolman/Static Guard as from 9th July 1978 at a weekly wage of £53.80 based on a 50 hour week, subject to three months satisfactory service.

The Company agrees to pay fifteen days holiday per annum after twelve months service, providing one month's notice be given in writing of the employee's holiday dates.

The Company also agrees that an annual bonus payable before Christmas will be awarded on the following basis:—(After twelve months service). Care of Company vehicles, equipment etc. Duties carried out satisfactory in accordance with instructions laid down by the Company. Personal appearance on reporting for duty. It must be remembered that points will be lost for any disregard of the above requirements.

Two weeks notice must be given in writing either by the employee or the Company to terminate this agreement.'

And it is signed by Mr Mears, witnessed and dated 12 July 1978.

Thereafter Mr Mears was off work sick for two periods amounting to nearly 7 months out of the 14 months for which he was employed: 20 December 1978 to 15 January 1979, and 26 March 1979 to 18 September 1979. On 17 September 1979 he gave the company written notice that he was unable to carry out his duties, which they accepted on 19 September 1979. During the short time he worked for the company his take-home pay was £48 a week. During his periods of absence he was paid sickness benefit under the 1975 Act amounting to £43 a week initially, and £33 a week subsequently, but he was not paid any wages. It is common ground that he never asked for them and that, according to para 5 of the reasons of the tribunal—

'at no time, whether at the initial interview with Mr Johns senior, or when Mr Mears started work, or when he was given his written terms of employment, or on any other occasion, did anyone on either side ask or mention what would happen financially if or when Mr Mears was off work because of sickness. At no point was the question of his wages or sick pay entitlement during any such period raised by anyone.'

The company was a small family business run by a father and son named Johns with only 12 or 13 employees. In para 8 of their reasons the tribunal said:

'Mr Mears, like Mr Johns junior, was a patently honest witness holding nothing back and we accept his evidence that when his colleagues visited him whilst he was ill they talked about sick pay and told him that he would not get sick pay from the company. He frankly accepted Mr Radway's suggestion in cross-examination that because he, Mr Mears, never asked for sick pay it could be said this was because he thought he was not entitled to it. When asked by the Chairman he said he would not mind if he had to bring his sickness benefit into account; that it was not fair to any company to get full wages and the sickness benefit on top but that most firms paid the difference. We equally have no difficulty in accepting Mr Johns' evidence that it is not the policy of the company to pay sick pay and that had any employee or applicant for a job enquired about the position he would have been so informed.' [Tribunal's emphasis]

Part I of the 1978 Act treats of 'Particulars of Terms of Employment', and s 1 provides for written particulars of terms of employment in these terms:

'(1) Not later than thirteen weeks after the beginning of an employee's period of employment with an employer, the employer shall give to the employee a written statement in accordance with the following provisions of this section.

(2) An employer shall in a statement under this section—(a) identify the parties;

(b) specify the date when the employment began; (c) state whether any employment with a previous employer counts as part of the employee's continuous period of *a* employment, and, if so, specify the date when the continuous period of employment began.

(3) A statement under this section shall contain the following particulars of the terms of employment as at a specified date not more than one week before the statement is given, that is to say—(a) the scale or rate of remuneration, or the method of calculating remuneration, (b) the intervals at which remuneration is paid *b* (that is, whether weekly or monthly or by some other period), (c) any terms and conditions relating to hours of work (including any terms and conditions relating to normal working hours), (d) any terms and conditions relating to—(i) entitlement to holidays, including public holidays, and holiday pay (the particulars given being sufficient to enable the employee's entitlement, including any entitlement to accrued holiday pay on the termination of employment, to be precisely calculated), *c* (ii) incapacity for work due to sickness or injury, including any provision for sick pay, (iii) pensions and pension schemes, (e) the length of notice which the employee is obliged to give and entitled to receive to determine his contract of employment, and (f) the title of the job which the employee is employed to do . . .'

I do not think I need read the proviso or any of the rest of the section. Section 2(1) provides: *d*

'If there are no particulars to be entered under any of the heads of paragraph (d) of subsection (3) of section 1, or under any of the other provisions of section 1(2) and (3), that fact shall be stated.'

Section 4(1) provides: *e*

'If after the date to which a statement given under section 1 relates there is a change in the terms of employment to be included, or referred to, in that statement the employer shall, not more than one month after the change, inform the employee of the nature of the change by a written statement and, if he does not leave a copy of the statement with the employee, shall preserve the statement and ensure that the employee has reasonable opportunities of reading it in the course of his employment, *f* or that it is made reasonably accessible to him in some other way.'

Then s 8 gives the employee the right to an itemised pay statement, and s 9 gives him the right to a standing statement of fixed deductions.

Mr Johns junior appeared to be unaware of these provisions and the written particulars of Mr Mears's terms of employment were rightly branded by the industrial tribunal as 'lamentably deficient as regards the requirements of Section 1'. Had Mr Johns read the *g* section and complied with it, there would have been no reference to the industrial tribunal, for I have little doubt that the company would have incorporated their policy of not paying sick pay in those terms and either Mr Mears would have accepted the terms or, less likely, he would have rejected the employment. However, he accepted the employment without considering whether he would be paid any wages if he went sick, *h* and has now made an application requiring a reference to an industrial tribunal under s 11 of the 1978 Act, which I must now read. That section is headed 'Enforcement of rights under Part I', and provides:

'(1) Where an employer does not give an employee a statement as required by section 1 or 4(1) or 8, the employee may require a reference to be made to an industrial tribunal to determine what particulars ought to have been included or *j* referred to in a statement so as to comply with the requirements of the relevant section.

(2) Where— (a) a statement purporting to be a statement under section 1 or 4(1), or (b) a pay statement, or a standing statement of fixed deductions, purporting to comply with section 8 or 9(1), has been given to an employee, and a question arises

a as to the particulars which ought to have been included or referred to in the statement so as to comply with the requirements of this Part, either the employer or the employee may require that question to be referred to and determined by an industrial tribunal . . .'

It is not at first sight plain whether the terms of reference given to Mr Mears were a statement as required by s 1 or a statement purporting to be a statement under s 1, or *b* whether his application, which was in form an application for a copy of his contract of employment, was a reference under s 11(1) to determine what particulars ought to have been included or referred to in a statement not given, or a reference under s 11(2)(a) of a question as to the particulars which ought to have been included or referred to in the statement which was given. So I read both sub-ss (5) and (6) of s 11:

c '(5) Where, on a reference under subsection (1), an industrial tribunal determines particulars as being those which ought to have been included or referred to in a statement given under section 1 or 4(1) the employer shall be deemed to have given to the employee a statement in which those particulars were included, or referred to, as specified in the decision of the tribunal.
(6) On determining a reference under subsection (2)(a), an industrial tribunal may either confirm the particulars as included or referred to in the statement given *d* by the employer, or may amend those particulars, or may substitute other particulars for them, as the tribunal may determine to be appropriate; and the statement shall be deemed to have been given by the employer to the employee in accordance with the decision of the tribunal.'

Subsection (9), requiring the application to be made before the end of three months *e* beginning with the date on which employment ceased, has been complied with.

Counsel, opening this appeal on behalf of Mr Mears, treated his application as requiring a reference under s 11(1); but in response to a suggestion from the Bench he accepted, with the assent of counsel for the company, that his application required a reference under s 11(2)(a). At a late stage in the appeal it was suggested, again from the Bench, that the reference was indeed under s 11(1) and it was then accepted by both counsel that it *f* appeared to be so. I put their acceptance no higher than that because (1) if the second suggestion was right it seemed contrary to the decision of the Employment Appeal Tribunal expressed in the judgment of Kilner Brown J in *Construction Industry Training Board v Leighton* [1978] 2 All ER 723 at 725–726, which was approved in the judgment of Waterhouse J in *Brown v Stuart Scott & Co Ltd* [1981] ICR 166 at 168–169, and (2) counsel had little time to reconsider this return to first thoughts. Having reconsidered *g* it, I am clearly of opinion that first thoughts were right, although contrary to the views of the Employment Appeal Tribunal which we are told have been accepted without challenge; and, as the correct interpretation of s 11 is of importance to the decision of this appeal as well as generally, I shall state my reasons.

Part I of the 1978 Act gives every employee a right to be informed by his employer as a matter of written record, either by a written statement (see s 1) or by a contract reduced *h* to writing (see s 5), what are the agreed terms of his employment, including any changes in them and including his pay and any fixed deductions from it. The record of his terms of employment must contain the three matters specified in s 1(2), the particulars under six heads, one subdivided into three, specified in s 1(3) and the note required by s 1(4). It is the particulars required by sub-s (2) as well as by sub-s (3) (see s 2(1)) which can be made the subject of a reference by an employee to an industrial tribunal under s 11. Particulars required by sub-s (3)(a) and (b), the scale or rate or remuneration and the intervals at which it is paid, (e) and (f), the length of notice and the title of the job, are plain enough. Particulars (c) and (d) are 'any terms and conditions relating to' different things: (c) hours of work and (d)(i) entitlement to holidays and holiday pay, (ii) 'incapacity for work due to sickness or injury, including any provision for sick pay' (with which this appeal is concerned), (iii) pensions and pension schemes. The introductory words suggest

that there need not be any terms or conditions relating to these four things and that
suggestion is confirmed by s 2(1) providing that if there are no particulars to be entered *a*
under any of the heads of s 1(3)(*d*) but going on to provide 'or under any of the other
provisions of section 1(2) and (3)', that fact shall be stated; and s 5(1)(*a*) shows similar
concern for the needs of s 1(3)(*d*). I am baffled by the reference to the other provisions
because under many of them there must be particulars to be entered, eg of the identity
of the parties required by s 1(2)(*a*) or of the scale of remuneration and the length of notice
required by s 1(3)(*a*) and (*e*). But there might be no particulars of employment with a *b*
previous employer to be entered under sub-s (2)(*c*) or of hours of work under sub-s (3)(*c*),
and the reference to the other provisions of s 1(2) and (3) than s 1(3)(*d*) may be a reference
to those provisions. However that may be, the requirement of s 2 that the fact that there
are no particulars to be entered of any terms or conditions relating to holiday pay, sick
pay and pensions shall be stated must, I think, mean that where the fact is stated the
employee is by agreement not entitled to any. An employment with no entitlement to *c*
any holiday must be rare; but, if an employee were to accept employment on those
terms, the employer would have to give him a written statement of that fact.

I start to consider s 11 with the assumption that it is intended to enable every
employee to enforce his rights to a written statement in accordance with the provisions
of ss 1, 4(1) and 8. There are three possible situations in which he may need the help of
the industrial tribunal with regard to a written statement in accordance with the *d*
provisions of s 1. (I leave out of account his right to a written statement informing him
of a change in the terms of employment in accordance with s 4(1) and his right to an
itemised pay statement under s 8 or to a standing statement of fixed deductions in
accordance with s 9(1).) Section 11 must cover all those three situations. The first is
when the employer gives the employee no written statement or particulars of his terms
of employment. The second is when he gives him an incomplete statement, which *e*
contains some, but not all, of the particulars required by s 1. The third is where he gives
him a complete but incorrect statement, which contains all the required particulars but
some of the particulars given are wrong in that they do not reproduce what was agreed
between employer and employee.

At first sight s 11(1) seems to cover the first case (of no written statement at all) and
s 11(2) the other two cases (of an incomplete statement and an incorrect statement). But *f*
on reflection I conclude that s 11(1) covers the first two cases, where the employer gives
no written statement at all or a statement which is incomplete, and s 11(2) the third case,
where the employer gives a statement which is complete but incorrect. Before giving
my reasons for this conclusion I point out that the second case, of an incomplete
statement, covers two classes where there is a shortage of particulars: (a) where there has
been no agreement on one of the terms of employment required to be recorded by s 1 *g*
and therefore no particulars have been given of it, and (b) where there has been agreement
on such a term but for some reason no particulars have been given of it. In considering
all these classes of case, and in particular class 2(a) above, industrial tribunals have to
notice that in exercising their powers on a reference under s 11 they are dealing with
particulars, not terms except in so far as they ought to have been recorded in written
statements of terms required by the statute to be given by employers to employees, and *h*
their function is to determine what particulars ought to have been included or referred
to in such statements (the alternative 'or referred to' is required by s 2(3)).

Section 11(1) is, in my judgment, ambiguous and the ambiguity is not resolved by
sub-s (5). Subsection (1) might mean 'Where an employer does not give an employee any
statement purporting to be a statement as required by s 1 or 4(1) or 8 . . .' or 'Where an
employer has failed to give an employee any statement in accordance with s 1 or 4(1) or *j*
8. . .' But the latter is the language of sub-s (8), and sub-s (1) does not use the latter or the
former phrase. It uses a phrase which may mean 'Where an employer does not give an
employee a statement *completely* in accordance with s 1 or 4(1) of 8 . . .', and that is what,
in my opinion, it does mean. Section 11(2) covers statements (a) purporting to be
statements under those sections and (b) purporting to comply with s 8 or s 9(1). Here

there is no ambiguity apparent; sub-s (2) appears to cover attempts to comply with s 1(2)
a which fail, eg for incompleteness. But sub-s (6) is, I think, repugnant to such an
interpretation of sub-s (2)(*a*). Subsection (6) refers only to 'the particulars as included or
referred to in the statement given by the employer'; it is those already given particulars
which may be confirmed if they comply with sub-s (2) or be amended or replaced by
substituted particulars if they do not; and, though amendment of the *statement* might
extend to inserting omitted particulars to complete the statement in accordance with
b sub-s (2), the tribunal are given no power to amend any *particulars* not already included
or referred to in the statement. Subsection (7) gives the tribunal the same powers in
determining a reference under sub-s (3), where the employer's statement already contains
particulars of an indication of future changes in terms of employment as mentioned in
s 4(3). Subsection (8) gives the tribunal power on a reference under s 11 (apparently
under sub-s (2)(*b*)) to declare either that an employer has failed to give an employee any
c pay statement or that a pay statement or standing statement of fixed deductions does not
contain the particulars required to be included in that statement by s 8 or s 9(1); but sub-
s (6) gives no such power.

Hence the tribunal's power under s 11(6) seems to me to be limited to applications
where the employer has given the employee something by way of particulars under
every provision of s 1(2) and (3) including each head of particulars under s 1(3)(*d*). Where
d he has not, the statement would not be 'as required by section 1'. The tribunal can only
correct those particulars by amendment or substitution if what is given is not what the
language of s 1(2) and (3) requires it to be, or if it does not represent the term agreed
between the parties. Included in the last category would, I think, be a statement under
s 2(1) that there were no particulars to be entered of a term in fact agreed. Where there
is a complete or partial lack of particulars, no statement or a statement which omits one
e or more of the particulars required by s 1(2) and (3), the tribunal has power to remedy the
employer's omission by determining what the missing particulars are. That division
between sub-ss (1) and (5) on the one hand and sub-ss (2)(*a*) and (6) on the other may leave
few cases to be referred under the latter provisions, and may not be of much practical
importance, since an employee can always require a reference under both sets of
provisions in the alternative. But it is nevertheless a division which is required by the
f statute, as I read the relevant provisions of Part I.

If that is right, Mr Mears's application has been rightly treated as requiring a reference
under s 11(1) and the industrial tribunal had to determine what particulars ought to have
been included in a statement so as to comply with s 1(3)(*d*)(ii). The tribunal must
determine some particulars under this head. Did they determine the right particulars?
Were the missing particulars omitted because no term as to sick pay had been agreed or
g for some other reason, though a term had been agreed? Before answering these questions
I should refer to the two cases which may be difficult to reconcile with my construction
of ss 1 and 11.

In *Construction Industry Training Board v Leighton* [1978] 2 All ER 723 there was a
written offer of employment by letter, accepted by the employee subject to confirmation
on two points, with a schedule attached which contained every particular required by the
h corresponding statute of 1972 (the Contracts of Employment Act 1972). The
Employment Appeal Tribunal held that, on a reference under what is now s 1(2)(*a*) of the
1978 Act, the industrial tribunal had arrogated to themselves a jurisdiction which they
did not have by amending the employee's particulars of employment so as to include in
them a term which interpreted them as the employee had asked the employer to confirm
them. In allowing the employer's appeal, Kilner Brown J said (at 725):
j
'An industrial tribunal can only embark on an exercise of amendment or
substitution of particulars where there is an omission to include or refer to a
statutory requirement when setting out the terms of a contract of employment.'

In *Brown v Stuart Scott & Co Ltd* [1981] ICR 166 a written statement had been given to
the employee at his request after he had left his employment. That statement apparently

included all the particulars required by the statute, but the employee disputed that the particulars relating to holiday entitlement with pay were accurate. The industrial *a* tribunal dismissed his complaint that the employer had unreasonably refused to provide a written statement under s 53(4) of the 1978 Act giving particulars of the reasons for his dismissal, but the report nowhere states what happened to his complaint under s 11. Waterhouse J stated that the Employment Appeal Tribunal could not detect any error of law in the industrial tribunal's conclusion in relation to that application by the employee. However, Waterhouse J, after saying that the employee could have asked for *b* a determination under s 11(1), added that it was unnecessary to comment on the strict interpretation of that provision because the employee had sensibly accepted the position that, as a purported statement had been supplied to him between his application and the hearing, the matter should be considered under s 11(2). He then proceeded to approve the reasoning in *Leighton*'s case and to apply it 'if it were necessary to do so'; but it was not necessary, as the employee did not pursue the matter (see [1981] ICR 166 at 168–169). *c*

I do not question either of these decisions. In each case there was a complete statement giving all the required particulars, and the employee disputed one of the particulars given because it was not correctly interpreted by the employer or it did not correctly reproduce the term agreed. Section 11 gives the industrial tribunal no power to interpret particulars which have been given, under either sub-s (5) or sub-s (6). It does give the tribunal power to amend or substitute particulars under sub-s (6) and a power also to *d* include an omitted statutory requirement, but that is under sub-s (5) and not, as Kilner Brown J said or implied in *Leighton*'s case, under sub-s (6). Where the tribunal fill in an omission, they determine the missing particulars under sub-s (5); they do not amend or substitute under sub-s (6). In *Brown*'s case it did not matter under which subsection the employee applied; but, in so far as Waterhouse J was saying or implying that there is a power to refer a complaint about a complete statement under sub-s (2), he was correct; *e* and, in so far as he was indicating that it was possible to refer such a complaint under sub-s (1), he was in error.

I now return to the decision of the industrial tribunal to see why they decided that the company's incomplete statement dated 12 July 1978 ought to have included (particulars of) the term set out in their decision. Was it, in the majority's view, an agreed term of the parties' contract or was it a term imposed on them and inserted into their contract by *f* the tribunal?

The industrial tribunal, in a conspicuously careful, lucid and well-reasoned decision, following *Leighton*'s case first stated (in para 9) their function to be not 'to construe or rectify a provision which was in fact agreed or to insert some new provision simply because it would be sensible if the parties had in fact agreed it', but to record 'the terms we consider ought to be implied just as we are bound to record a term which we are *g* satisfied was expressly orally agreed'. Next they followed (in para 13) a judgment of Pilcher J in *Orman v Saville Sportswear Ltd* [1960] 3 All ER 105 at 111, [1960] 1 WLR 1055 at 1065 in holding that first an employee had a right to be paid whilst absent from work through sickness—

'unless the court is prepared to infer a contrary condition from all the facts and *h* the evidence and, secondly, in deciding whether or not to imply such a condition the court will apply the test required for an implied term.'

And that test was the test laid down by Scrutton LJ in *Reigate v Union Manufacturing Co (Ramsbottom) Ltd* [1918] 1 KB 592 at 605, [1918–19] All ER Rep 143 at 149, which they cited with MacKinnon LJ's test of the officious bystander in *Shirlaw v Southern Foundries* *j* (1926) Ltd and Federated Foundries Ltd [1939] 2 All ER 113 at 124, [1939] 2 KB 206 at 227.

Though the tribunal regarded Pilcher J's decision as reversing what might have been thought the expected burden, they rightly considered that it was binding on them and compelled them to ask (in para 14)—

a   'not whether we are prepared to imply a term that Mr Mears should be paid
during sickness but whether we are prepared to imply a term he should *not* be so
paid.'

As the experience of the tribunal was that the practice as regards sick pay varied so
widely, and as the majority were unable to regard Mr Mears's subsequent conduct as
establishing that he would have regarded no sick pay as going without saying at the time
b   of entering into his contract, they held (in para 19) that the company had—

'failed to establish a contrary condition and accordingly that Mr Mears'
contract of employment included a term or condition that during its continuance Mr Mears
would be entitled to be paid whilst he was absent from work during sickness.'

One member of the industrial tribunal held that both Mr Mears and Mr Johns for the
company would have answered the question, 'Will your wages continue to be paid
c   during sickness?' with a confident, 'No, of course not; that is so obvious we need not say
it'. (See para 16 of their reasons for decision.) But the majority did not agree. They
thought (para 18) that Mr Johns would have said, 'No', and Mr Mears might then have
made the best of it and accepted the job; but he would not have agreed that it was
obvious he would not be paid wages during absence through sickness.

There was accordingly, in the opinion of the majority, no obvious unexpressed term
d   relating to sick pay; but they were able to treat the term which they included in Mr
Mears's contract of employment as agreed because of the presumption, which they
derived from the authorities, in favour of payment of wages during absence through
sickness unless rebutted by a term expressed or implied on common law principles and
because of the company's failure to rebut the presumption by evidence from which the
term could be so implied. That conclusion correctly followed from their loyal application
e   of what was said and decided in *Orman's* case.

In *Orman's* case [1960] 3 All ER 105 at 111, [1960] 1 WLR 1055 at 1064–1065 Pilcher
J said that the authorities which had been cited to him—

'establish the following proposition. Where the written terms of the contract of
service are silent as to what is to happen in regard to the employee's right to be paid
f   whilst he is absent from work due to sickness, the employer remains liable to
continue paying so long as the contract is not determined by proper notice, except
where a condition to the contrary can properly be inferred from all the facts and the
evidence in the case. If the employer seeks to establish an implied condition that no
wages are payable, it is for him to make it out, and the court, in construing the
written contract, will not accept any implied term which will not pass the test laid
g   down by SCRUTTON, L.J., in *Reigate* v. *Union Manufacturing Co (Ramsbottom)* ([1918] 1
KB 592 at 605, [1918–19] All ER Rep 143 at 149).'

Counsel for Mr Mears has submitted that that proposition correctly stated the law and
the effect of the earlier authorities. Alternatively he preferred to adopt the somewhat
narrower submission made by counsel for the plaintiff in *Orman's* case [1960] 3 All ER
h   105 at 107, [1960] 1 WLR 1055 at 1060 that:

'Where the contract contains no express term, and no unexpressed terms can
properly be implied as to the remuneration during periods of illness, the
presumption is that the contractual remuneration remains payable until the contract
of service is determined.'

j   As, however, that presumption must prevail unless rebutted and the employer is the
party who will want to rebut it, it appears in fact to place the onus of rebutting it on the
employer, as Pilcher J said.

In the Employment Appeal Tribunal's judgment (see [1981] 1 WLR 1214), Slynn J
reviewed those authorities, which were the decisions of this court in *Marrison v Bell*

[1939] 1 All ER 745, [1939] 2 KB 187, *Petrie v MacFisheries Ltd* [1939] 4 All ER 281, [1940] 1 KB 265 and *O'Grady v M Saper Ltd* [1940] 3 All ER 527, [1940] 2 KB 469, to a which he added *Hancock v BSA Tools Ltd* [1939] 4 All ER 538, a decision of Atkinson J given between the decision of the Court of Appeal, of which he had been a member, in *Petrie's* case and the decision in *O'Grady's* case. Slynn J ended his review of those cases (at 1221–1222) with the following citation from the judgment of MacKinnon LJ in *O'Grady v M Saper Ltd* [1940] 3 All ER 527 at 529; cf [1940] 2 KB 469 at 473–474:

> 'The whole question in such a case as this is what the terms of the contract b between the employer and the servant were and what those terms provided in regard to payment of wages to him during his absence from the service by reason of illness . . . Was it agreed that the man should be paid when he was ready and willing to work, or that he should be paid only when he was actually working? . . . In this case, as it seems to me, there was abundant evidence that the terms, not expressed, but no doubt implied, upon which this man was employed were that he c should not be paid wages whilst he was sick. Conclusive evidence of that is furnished by the fact that on at least three occasions during the time he had been employed he was not paid wages when he was away sick, and he acquiesced in that position.'

Slynn J proceeded (at 1222–1223) to give the Employment Appeal Tribunal's d conclusions in five paragraphs, which I adopt without repeating them, because at the end of both counsel's discussion of those and other authorities, I agree with that passage as a correct statement of the law relating to payment of wages during absence through sickness as it emerged, not without some judicial stretching and straining in 1940, and I could not improve it if I were to embark on any detailed commentary on those cases in deference to Mr Mears's counsel's carefully considered criticism of the Employment e Appeal Tribunal's judgment. It gives the industrial tribunal the authoritative guidance which they said they would welcome.

There are three things on which I should like to comment.

(1) Their decision disapproves the conclusion of Pilcher J as expressed in the proposition cited from *Orman's* case and substitutes an approach to the facts and evidence in each case with an open mind unprejudiced by any preconception, presumption or f assumption. With this I respectfully agree.

(2) For this court to affirm the Employment Appeal Tribunal's decision involves preferring, or as I think being bound by, the latest of conflicting decisions of this court, at least when that decision has considered earlier conflicting decisions and resolved the conflict: *Barrington v Lee* [1971] 3 All ER 1231, [1972] 1 QB 326. If *Marrison v Bell* had stood alone, I think I would have felt bound by it to follow *Orman's* case; in justice to the g reporter of *Marrison's* case [1939] 2 KB 187 I have to say that I regard his headnote as correctly stating the main point there argued and decided, in spite of the criticism diverted in *Petrie's* case from the decision to the report of it. But we are bound to follow *O'Grady's* case.

(3) Their decision involves *either* that the Employment Appeal Tribunal accepted the opinion of the minority member of the industrial tribunal and held that the subsequent h conduct of the parties proved that Mr Mears would have agreed on no sick pay without question when the contract was made *or* that the Employment Appeal Tribunal decided that the industrial tribunal had statutory power to determine that an employee ought to give particulars of a term which the employee is not proved to have regarded as too obvious to need expressing when the contract was made but which is nevertheless indicated by all the circumstances and in particular the subsequent conduct of the j parties.

I cannot find anything in the otherwise admirable judgment of Slynn J clearly indicating which alternative led the Employment Appeal Tribunal to their conclusion. But there is no hint of their rejecting the majority view or preferring the minority view. Indeed, the judgment refers to the majority finding of what the employer would

have said if asked but is silent as to what Mr Mears would have said. I would myself be
a prepared to adopt the minority member's view on the facts and evidence before the
industrial tribunal and infer from it proof of the necessary answer to the bystander by Mr
Mears, in chorus with Mr Johns, as MacKinnon LJ apparently inferred it in *O'Grady's*
case. It was the practice of the company not to pay wages to employees absent sick, and
the practice was well known to the company's employees. The company would not have
made an exception in Mr Mears's favour. He did not ask about sick pay before taking on
b the job, though the practice varies with different employers. If he had asked and been
told what the practice was, he would most probably have taken the job. He took leave
without sick pay for nearly 7 months out of the 14 months his employment lasted, and
never asked for sick pay but accepted what his colleagues told him was the practice, and
he probably (though he disputed this) submitted no sick certificate. Even after the end
of his employment he asked for holiday pay, for which the terms of reference expressly
c provided, and it was some time before he thought of asking for sick pay. He plainly
never expected to get sick pay and he never got it. It may well be that, as Sir Stanley Rees
suggested in argument, the nature of the job, guarding property, explains both the
company's practice and his acquiescence in it.

But without departing from the majority view of the facts and the inferences to be
drawn from them, I am of opinion that when, in exercising their statutory jurisdiction
d under s 11 of the 1978 Act, an industrial tribunal have to imply and insert missing terms,
they are not tied to the requirements of the test propounded by Scrutton and MacKinnon
LJJ, a test for commercial contracts which goes back to *The Moorcock* (1889) 14 PD 64,
[1886–90] All ER Rep 530, but can and should consider all the facts and circumstances
of the relationship between the employer and employee concerned, including the way in
which they had worked the particular contract of employment since it was made, in
e order to imply and determine the missing term which ought to have been particularised
by the employer and so to complete the contract.

And that was, I think, the view of the Employment Appeal Tribunal. In rejecting the
term included by the industrial tribunal and preferring a different term they were, in my
judgment, looking at the problem confronting them in that way and acting within their
statutory powers and on evidence which justified their preference. The industrial
f tribunal have stated (para 1) that they would welcome authoritative guidance on
'problems over implied terms which are, on the authorities, of considerable difficulty in
the modern employment context', and in the hope of giving it I shall amplify that given
by the Employment Appeal Tribunal in the judgment Slynn J and what I have already
said about s 11 of the 1978 Act and its application to this case.

The section enables the employee who has not received any statement, or a complete
g statement, of the terms of his employment to require the industrial tribunal to state
them for him. When all the specified terms have been agreed, either expressly or by
necessary implication, there is no problem for the industrial tribunal in stating any that
have not been stated by the employer. But when one or more of the specified terms have
not been agreed, even by necessary implication, the industrial tribunal may nevertheless
have to state it for them. That is a possibility which I shall discuss later. But in a case
h where as here there are two alternatives, sick pay or no sick pay (I leave out the
subdivision of the second alternative into sick pay gross and sick pay reduced by benefits
received), it is in the highest degree unlikely that neither has been agreed and the
industrial tribunal's task is the simpler task of deciding which of the two terms has been
agreed.

In this case every one of the factors which I have already set out points one way, in the
j direction of 'no work, no wages' having been agreed.

Counsel for Mr Mears submitted that the express term as to holiday pay pointed the
other way, to a contract to pay wages as long as the employee was ready and willing to
work, not only when he was actually working. Even if it does, it is overwhelmed by
every other factor, and unless the law was correctly stated in *Orman's* case or those factors
are excluded by law from consideration, the evidence points conclusively to a contract in

which work was the consideration for wages. Freed from the *Marrison* presumption or approach, and from the *Reigate* or *Shirlaw* test as combined in *Orman*, the industrial *a* tribunal would, I think, have decided the reference as the Employment Appeal Tribunal have said it should have been decided.

Counsel for Mr Mears made a more important submission, that the tribunals were not entitled to look at the subsequent actings of the parties in interpreting this written contract: to do so would be to disregard the law laid down by the House of Lords in *James Miller & Partners Ltd v Whitworth Street Estates (Manchester) Ltd* [1970] 1 All ER 796, *b* [1970] AC 583 and *L Schuler AG v Wickman Machine Tool Sales Ltd* [1973] 2 All ER 39, [1974] AC 235. I have already expressed my view that this agreement was oral, but, even if it was partly in writing, we are concerned with the search for a term that was not written down, and there is nothing in those authorities which prevents the court from looking at the way the parties acted for the purpose of ascertaining what that term was. Common sense suggests that their subsequent conduct is the best evidence of what they *c* had agreed orally but not reduced to writing, though it is not evidence of what any written terms mean; and counsel for the company has put before us binding authority for that commonsense view.

I have no doubt that the manner in which this contract of employment was in fact carried out or interpreted by both parties was properly considered to see whether it led to the implication of the term to be determined. *d*

Counsel for the company, whose helpful submissions are to a large extent adopted in this judgment, submitted that the decision of the Employment Appeal Tribunal could be supported on the ground that the parties had agreed to Mr Mears's employment on a 'no work, no pay' basis by a subsequent variation of their original agreement. But he had given no respondent's notice of this point, nor had it been argued before either tribunal, and we thought it right to exclude this alternative way of looking at the subsequent *e* actings of the parties from our consideration.

Counsel for the company legitimately sought support for consideration of the subsequent conduct of the parties in *Liverpool City Council v Irwin* [1976] 2 All ER 39, [1977] AC 239, *Ferguson v John Dawson & Partners (Contractors) Ltd* [1976] 3 All ER 817, [1976] 1 WLR 1213 and *Wilson v Maynard Shipbuilding Consultants AB* [1978] 2 All ER 78, [1978] QB 665. What was there said and decided is, I think, helpful to a court *f* approaching the task of determining from all the circumstances what the parties to an incompletely expressed contract must have agreed in fact or be taken to have agreed.

In *Wilson v Maynard Shipbuilding Consultants AB* this court held that, where one cannot ascertain from the terms of the contract itself what was agreed about a relevant term (in that case the place where under his contract an employee ordinarily works), one may look at what has happened and what the parties have done under the contract during the *g* whole contemplated period of the contract for the limited purpose of ascertaining what that term is (see [1978] 2 All ER 78 at 83–84, [1978] QB 665 at 675, 677 per Megaw LJ, applied in *Todd v British Midland Airways Ltd* [1978] ICR 959 at 964, where Lord Denning MR said that, in considering the particular question where the parties have agreed that an employee should ordinarily work, the court gets less help from the terms of the contract than from the conduct of the parties and the way they have been *h* operating the contract; see also what Sir David Cairns said (at 967)).

But in *Wilson's* case the court was applying a more general principle stated by Lord Wilberforce in *Liverpool City Council v Irwin* [1976] 2 All ER 39 at 43, [1977] AC 239 at 253 that in order to complete a contract which is partly but not wholly stated in writing 'it is necessary to take account of the actions of the parties and the circumstances'. That case was cited not only to the Court of Appeal in *Wilson's* case and in *Ferguson v John* *j* *Dawson & Partners (Contractors) Ltd* but to the Employment Appeal Tribunal in the instant case. As was pointed out in *Ferguson's* case [1976] 3 All ER 817 at 824, 831, [1976] 1 WLR 1213 at 1221, 1229 by Megaw and Browne LJJ in deciding whether an oral and only partially expressed agreement was a contract of service or a contract for services, the court was not merely entitled but bound to take into account what was done under the

a contract, not to construe the contract but to infer what its terms were, either originally
   or by subsequent variation. As I have said, we are not considering subsequent variation
   in this case.

       On examination *Liverpool City Council v Irwin* is not, in any opinion, as helpful to Mr
   Mears's case as was *Lister v Romford Ice and Cold Storage Co Ltd* [1957] 1 All ER 125, [1957]
   AC 555 to the tenants Mr and Mrs Irwin. As I read the speeches of their Lordships in
   Lister's case, particularly those of Viscount Simonds and Lord Tucker ([1957] 1 All ER
b 125 at 133–135, 143–144, [1957] AC 555 at 576–579, 594), and in *Irwin*'s case,
   particularly those of Lord Wilberforce, Lord Cross, Lord Edmund-Davies and Lord
   Fraser ([1976] 2 All ER 39 at 44, 46–47, 53, 57, [1977] AC 239 at 254–255, 257–258,
   265–266, 270), the House of Lords has laid down that there are contracts which establish
   a relationship, eg of master and servant, landlord and tenant; those contracts demand by
   their nature and subject matter certain obligations, and those obligations the general law
c will impose and imply, not as satisfying the business efficacy of officious bystander tests
   applicable to commercial contracts where there is no such relationship, but as legal
   incidents of those other kinds of contractual relationship. In considering what obligations
   to imply into contracts of these kinds which are not complete, the actions of the parties
   may property be considered. But the obligation must be a *necessary* term, that is,
   required by their relationship. It is not enough that it would be a reasonable term.

d   In *Irwin*'s case the House implied an obligation on the landlord, Liverpool City
   Council, to repair the means of access to the tenants' flat, although the obligation would
   not have been agreed to by the landlord and although the contract would have worked
   (though unsatisfactorily for the tenants) without it.

       Now it cannot be said that as a general rule a legal incident of a contract of employment
   is that there should be no sick pay; indeed, if there is a legal incident, it is that there
e should be sick pay. But it can be said that if an employee is off work sick he must either
   be paid or not be paid; there must be some term as to his remuneration when off sick and
   the best indication of what that term is is the fact that he was paid or not paid. When the
   facts of Mr Mears's absences sick are considered the right term to imply is obvious, even
   if the majority view of the industrial tribunal is preferred to the minority view and the
   strict common law test is therefore not satisfied: see *Re Comptoir Commercial Anversois and
f Power, Son & Co Arbitration* [1920] 1 KB 868 at 899, [1918–19] All ER Rep 661 at 674 per
   Scrutton LJ.

       Accordingly we are, in my judgment, entitled to rely on *Liverpool City Council v Irwin*
   applied in *Ferguson*'s case, where the parties must have worked either under a contract of
   service or under a contract for services, as supporting the decision of the Employment
   Appeal Tribunal, although Slynn J did not refer to it. We can treat as an agreed term a
g term which would not have been at once assented to by both parties at the time when
   they made the contract, eg where one party would at once have assented to it and the
   other would have done so after it had been made clear to him that unless he did so there
   would be no contract, which is, I think, this case.

       Here, the facts and circumstances all pointed, as I have said, against the term of which
   Mr Mears wanted the tribunal to include particulars and in favour of a term that there
h was to be no sick pay. If there had been no factors pointing either way, nothing for or
   against sick pay, then the statutory duty to determine particulars of a term or condition
   to comply with s 1(3)(d)(ii) of the 1978 Act could have been discharged only by resorting
   to the presumption that the wage is to be paid till the employment is ended, whether the
   employee works or is absent from work. That was, I think, rightly recognised by the
   Employment Appeal Tribunal in the conclusion of the passage which I have already
j referred to in the judgment of Slynn J ([1981] 1 WLR 1214 at 1223). Those sentences
   reflect and follow what du Parcq LJ (who had been a party to the decision in *Marrison v
   Bell* [1939] 1 All ER 745, [1939] 2 KB 187) said in *Petrie*'s case [1939] 4 All ER 281 at 287,
   291, [1940] 1 KB 258 at 265, 270 and echoed by Atkinson J in the same case.

       That is what is left of the presumption attributed to *Marrison v Bell*, and it does not
   apply to this case. To apply it, as if there were 'nothing more', would be manifestly

unjust, for it would require the industrial tribunal to compel an employer, who, though
in breach of his statutory duty to give the required particulars, would never have agreed   *a*
to pay an employee wages when absent sick, to pay them to an employee who never
expected to get them. The Employment Appeal Tribunal were right in holding that
they were not driven by law to uphold a conclusion so repugnant to common sense and
the justice of the case.

To sum up the guidance which I would give to industrial tribunals, in every reference
under s 11 of the 1978 Act in which an employee asks the industrial tribunal to   *b*
determine the particulars required by s 1 of a term (or terms) of which no written
particulars have been given by his employer, the tribunal must act under sub-s (5), and
their first duty is to determine whether that term has been agreed expressly by word of
mouth or by necessary implication. If it has, the tribunal determine that particulars of
it ought to be included in the employee's statement of terms; if it has not, the tribunal
have to find and imply the term which all the facts and circumstances, including the   *c*
subsequent actions of the employer and employee, show were agreed or must have been
agreed and to determine that particulars of that term ought to be included. Where, as
here, the tribunal are searching for the right term to imply relating to the payment of
wages during absence through sickness and are left by lack of material in doubt about
that particular term, the doubt will be resolved in favour of the employee by *Marrison v
Bell* as interpreted in the authorities ending with this case. When the missing term   *d*
relates to payment of wages during periods of absence through sickness, the tribunal
must approach the search for the missing term by considering all the facts and
circumstances, including the subsequent conduct of the parties, and only if they do not
indicate what that term is or must be, should the tribunal assume that it is a term that
wages should be paid during those periods and determine that that is the term of which
particulars ought to be included.   *e*

In most cases the tribunal will have enough material, as had this tribunal, to determine
what has, or would have been, agreed between employer and employee, and so ought to
have been particularised by the employer. By the end of the 13 weeks allowed by s 1 of
the 1978 Act, or by the time the employee's complaint is heard by the tribunal, the
problem of what was agreed generally solvitur ambulando, and the way in which the
employment has worked in practice will supply the missing term on one or other of the   *f*
common law principles of necessary implication. But there may be cases in which the
tribunal are left in doubt as to what has been agreed and what particulars ought to have
been included. What then? Are the tribunal to decide what term should have been
agreed? Is the statutory duty to determine particulars as being those which ought to
have been given in a statement a duty to decide what the tribunal think the parties ought
to have agreed? Can the employer shelter behind s 2(1) of the 1978 Act by stating that   *g*
there are no particulars to be entered under the statutory head on which the employee
relies?

If the employer has stated that there are no particulars to be entered thereunder, but
the tribunal find that there are because the term has been agreed, then they can act,
probably by amendment or substitution under s 11(6) of the 1978 Act, rather than under
s 11(5). But what if no particulars have been entered because the relevant term has not   *h*
been agreed? Are the tribunal stopped by s 2(1) from going behind the employer's
negative statement and inserting particulars which he shall be deemed to have given?

It may be that we are here considering cases which Parliament never considered and
questions to which only Parliament can supply answers. But I am inclined to think that,
when any of the terms specified in the statute has not been agreed, the tribunal have
nevertheless to state it for them. This they can only do by deciding which term fits in   *j*
best with all the circumstances of the case, which may be getting near to deciding what
is a reasonable term, or a term which, to quote the industrial tribunal's decision, 'would
be sensible if the parties had in fact agreed it'.

Section 11 would seem to impose on the tribunal the statutory duty to find the
specified terms, and in the last resort invent them for the purpose of literally writing

them into the contract. In discharging that duty, the tribunal can and must go into all
a the facts and circumstances of the case and, when those fail to provide a basis for
implying a specified term, to justice, and the implication of a reasonable term. If the
tribunal have not enough material in the facts and circumstances to determine what
would have been agreed, they must determine what *should* have been agreed, bearing in
mind that it is the employer's breach of *his* statutory duty which has made the employee's
application for a reference necessary and that in consequence they would generally be
b right to resolve any doubt about what particulars ought to be included in favour of the
employee.

But this is not a case of that kind, and we have not been asked to consider it on the basis
that there was insufficient material for the implication of the relevant term without
resorting to considering what would be reasonable or just. Not having heard argument
on that aspect of the statutory duty, I express no concluded opinion on it. No
c authoritative guidance can be given on it until tribunals are faced with a decision which
requires it. But I have ventured to raise questions which the sections of the 1978 Act
which we have had to consider, including in particular s 2(1), inevitably raise, in the hope
that Parliament may find time to consider whether some amendment of those sections
might not clarify the statutory duty thereby intended to be imposed on industrial
tribunals.

d For the reasons I have given I would decide the first issue in the company's favour and
dismiss the appeal.

As the decision is under s 11(1) and (5), the form of the industrial tribunal's order was
almost correct, but incorrect in referring to 'the written statement dated 12 July 1978 of
the terms of Mr Mears' employment'. The order which, subject to what counsel may
have to say, I would make, and the Employment Appeal Tribunal should have made,
e is: 'The following particulars ought to have been included or referred to in a statement
given under s 1 of the Employment Protection (Consolidation) Act 1978; the company
will not pay your wages during any period of absence through sickness.'

If there had been a reference under s 11(2)(a), and particulars of a term relating to sick
pay had already been given by the employer, the order would substitute the same
particulars or amend the existing particulars to the same effect.

f If the first issue is decided in the company's favour, it is unnecessary to consider the
second issue. I would only comment that on the facts of this case two tribunals, widely
experienced in such matters, have unanimously concluded that if Mr Mears was entitled
to sick pay it would be paid net after deduction of social security benefits, and it would
have taken cogent argument, possibly exceeding even counsel for Mr Mears's powers of
persuasion, to convince me that there was any error of law in the decision of either
g tribunal on the point.

I have spoken to O'Connor LJ; he agrees with the judgment I have just delivered.

SIR STANLEY REES. Having had the advantage of reading it in advance, I also agree
with the judgment that has just been delivered by Stephenson LJ.

Appeal dismissed; order of Employment Appeal Tribunal varied as indicated in judgment.

Solicitors: *Robbins Olivery & Blake Lapthorn*, agents for *Cartridge & Co*, Exeter (for the
appellant); *Gilbert H Stephens & Sons*, Exeter (for the company).

Sophie Craven   Barrister.

Re J Burrows (Leeds) Ltd   a

CHANCERY DIVISION
SLADE J
11, 17 FEBRUARY 1982

Company – Winding-up – Stay or restraint of proceedings against company – Meaning of b
'proceedings' – Government department bringing criminal proceedings against company to
recover statutory debt – Whether proceedings should be stayed – Companies Act 1948, ss 226,
307 – Social Security Act 1975, ss 150(1), 152(4).

On 19 April 1980 a company's contributions, amounting to £21,381, became due under
the Social Security Act 1975 to the Department of Health and Social Security. The
contributions had not been paid by 29 April 1980 when the company went into   c
voluntary liquidation and therefore, under s 153 of the 1975 Act, they fell to be treated
as a preferential debt in the winding up. The department submitted a proof of the debt
to the liquidator of the company, who admitted it as a preferential debt in the
liquidation. Subsequently the department instituted proceedings against the company
in the magistrates' court alleging that the company had committed an offence under
s 146^a of the 1975 Act by failing to pay the contributions when they became due. The   d
company was hopelessly insolvent and the department made it clear to the liquidator
that it had no intention of enforcing against the company any order for payment which
it might obtain under s 150(1)^b of the 1975 Act. The department's sole purpose in
bringing the proceedings was to enable it to proceed under s 152(4)^c of the 1975 Act
against the directors of the company if it obtained an order under s 150(1) which
required the company to pay the £21,381 and the company failed to do so. The   e
liquidator applied by summons to the court for an order under ss 226^d and 307^e of the
Companies Act 1948 that the proceedings be stayed on the grounds (i) that if the
department were allowed to continue with the proceedings, it would obtain an unfair
preference over the other preferential creditors, contrary to the principles of pari passu
distribution, and (ii) that since the department had submitted a proof for the full amount
of the debt and the proof had been admitted in full, its claim had been notionally   f
satisfied in full and it should not be allowed to bring proceedings of any kind outside the
winding up designed to enable it to recover the debt. At the hearing of the summons,
the department offered to give the court an undertaking that it would not, without the
leave of the court, enforce against the company any order which it might obtain against
the company in the magistrates' court.

g

Held – (1) The proceedings in the magistrates' court were a 'proceeding' within the
meaning of s 226(b) of the 1948 Act, and so the court could grant a stay (see p 885 *e f*,
post); *Re Briton Medical and General Life Assurance Association* (1886) 32 Ch D 503 applied.
   (2) However, in view of the undertaking offered by the department, the court would
not grant a stay, for the following reasons—
   (a) the other preferential creditors would not, in the circumstances, be prejudiced by   h
the proceedings in the magistrates' court (see p 886 *j* to p 887 *c*, post).
   (b) by bringing the proceedings the department was not seeking another method of
having its claim adjudicated on but was seeking to enforce a statutory right, which had
been conferred on it by the 1975 Act quite apart from the Companies Acts, to proceed

j

---

a   Section 146, so far as material, is set out at p 884 *e*, post.
b   Section 150(1) is set out at p 884 *f*, post
c   Section 152(4) is set out at p 884 *j*, post
d   Section 226, so far as material, is set out at p 885 *d*, post
e   Section 307, so far as material, is set out at p 885 *g h*, post

against the company in the magistrates' court, and it was for the magistrates to decide
a whether the department was to be deemed to have been paid all its contributions in
full. That was an arguable issue and since the proceedings would not therefore necessarily
be futile, the court would not exercise its discretion to make an order for a stay which
would otherwise prevent the department recovering in criminal proceedings a penalty
imposed by statute (see p 888 g to p 889 b, post); *Food Controller v Cork* [1923] All ER Rep
463 and *Craven v Blackpool Greyhound Stadium and Racecourse Ltd* [1936] 3 All ER 513
b distinguished.

(c) in any event, the court could not order a stay of proceedings under s 307(2) of the
1948 Act because, although such an order would clearly be beneficial to the directors of
the company, it would not be 'just and beneficial' to the department or to the other
creditors of the company, and their interests prevailed over the interests of the directors
who were prima facie responsible for the inability of the company to pay its debts (see
c p 886 a and p 889 b to d, post).

Notes

For restraint of proceedings, see 7 Halsbury's Laws (4th edn) para 1502, and for cases on
the subject, see 10 Digest (Reissue) 1167–1169, 7254–7280.

For the Companies Act 1948, ss 226, 307, see 5 Halsbury's Statutes (3rd edn) 296, 340.
d   For the Social Security Act 1975, ss 146, 150, 152, 153, see 45 ibid 1244, 1249, 1250,
1252.

Cases referred to in judgment

Anglo-Baltic and Mediterranean Bank v Barber and Co [1924] 2 KB 410, [1924] All ER Rep
226, CA, 10 Digest (Reissue) 1170, 7284.
e *Aro Co Ltd, Re*, [1980] 1 All ER 1067, [1980] Ch 196, [1980] 2 WLR 453, CA.
Briton Medical and General Life Assurance Association, Re (1886) 32 Ch D 503, 10 Digest
(Reissue) 1098, 6745.
Craven v Blackpool Greyhound Stadium and Racecourse Ltd [1936] 3 All ER 513, CA, 10
Digest (Repl) 1168, 7269.
Food Controller v Cork [1923] AC 647, [1923] All ER Rep 463, HL, 10 Digest (Reissue)
f   1074, 6594.
Keynsham Co, Re, (1863) 33 Beav 123, 55 ER 313, 10 Digest (Reissue) 1168, 7263.
Langley Constructions (Brixham) Ltd v Wells [1969] 2 All ER 46, [1969] 1 WLR 503, CA, 10
Digest (Reissue) 1097, 6743.
Morgan v Quality Tools & Engineering (Stourbridge) Ltd [1972] 1 All ER 744, [1972] 1 WLR
196, DC, Digest (Cont Vol D) 708, 10c.

g ### Cases also cited

Dept of Health and Social Security v Wayte [1972] 1 All ER 255, [1972] 1 WLR 19, CA.
McEwen v London Bombay and Mediterranean Bank Ltd (1866) 15 LT 495.
Westbury v Twigg & Co Ltd [1892] 1 QB 77.

h ### Adjourned summons

By a summons dated 6 July 1981 and subsequently reamended, the liquidator of J
Burrows (Leeds) Ltd (the company) applied to the court (i) for an order that the date of
the dissolution of the company be deferred, and (ii) for an order that all further
proceedings on an information laid, on 31 March 1981 in Leeds Magistrates' Court,
against the company by an officer of the Department of Health and Social Security be
i stayed. The facts are set out in the judgment.

Matthew Caswell for the liquidator.
John Mummery for the Department of Health and Social Security.

Cur adv vult

17 February. **SLADE J** read the following judgement: This is an application of which
the principal purpose is to restrain, under ss 226 and 307 of the Companies Act 1948, *a*
certain criminal proceedings which have been initiated against a company, J Burrows
(Leeds) Ltd, in the Leeds Magistrates' Court. The relevant facts are not in dispute.

By a notice dated 2 April 1980, pursuant to s 293 of the Companies Act 1948, the
company called a meeting of creditors for 29 April 1980. On that date the company
passed an extraordinary resolution placing itself into creditors' voluntary winding up.
At a meeting of creditors held on the same day, Mr Stanley Sefton was appointed *b*
liquidator of the company. Shortly afterwards the liquidator produced a report to
creditors and a statement of affairs, which showed that the company was hopelessly
insolvent. It disclosed secured creditors of £30,000, preferential creditors with debts of
about £55,000 and unsecured creditors with debts of about £77,000. It disclosed assets
available for the unsecured creditors worth in the aggregate only about £25,000.

On 19 April 1980, ten days before it had gone into voluntary liquidation, the company *c*
became liable to pay to the Department of Health and Social Security (which I will call
the department) the sum of £21,381·16 in respect of Class 1 contributions under the
Social Security Act 1975. This sum was still unpaid at the commencement of the
winding up, and, by virtue of s 153 of the Act of 1975, fell to be treated as a preferential
debt in the winding up. The department in fact submitted a proof of debt in a rather
larger sum. Subsequently the claim was amended to £21,381·16, and that sum was *d*
admitted by the liquidator to proof as a preferential debt in the liquidation.

On 31 March 1981, after the claim had been admitted, the department instituted
proceedings against the company by way of information laid before the Leeds
Magistrates' court, alleging an offence under s 146 of the 1975 Act constituted by the
failure of the company to pay its liability to the department when the sum fell due.
Section 146(1) of the Act of 1975 provides: *e*

> 'If a person fails to pay, at or within the time prescribed for the purpose, any
> contribution which he is liable under Part I of this Act to pay, he shall be liable on
> summary conviction to a fine not more than £50.'

Section 150(1) of the Act of 1975 provides:

> 'Where a person has been convicted of the offence under section 146(1) of this Act *f*
> of failing to pay a contribution at or within the time prescribed for the purpose and
> the contribution remains unpaid at the date of the conviction, he shall be liable to
> pay to the Secretary of State a sum equal to the amount which he failed to pay.'

On the present application, it has been common ground that, if the proceedings before
the Leeds magistrates are permitted to continue, the company will have no defence to *g*
them, because, on any footing, there has been a failure to pay at or within the time
prescribed for the purpose. Furthermore, although s 150(1) makes no express reference
to any order for payment being made by the court which enters the conviction, the
words 'shall be liable to pay' appear to impose a mandatory duty on the justices to make
an order for the payment of the contributions, so far as those contributions remain
'unpaid' at the date of the conviction: see *Morgan v Quality Tools & Engineering* *h*
(Stourbridge) Ltd [1972] 1 All ER 744, [1972] 1 WLR 196.

Section 152(4) of the Act of 1975 provides:

> 'Where a body corporate fails to pay any sum which it is liable to pay under
> sections 150 and 151 and subsection (1) of this section, that sum (or such part of it
> as remains unpaid) shall be a debt due to the Secretary of State jointly and severally *.*
> from any directors of the body corporate who knew, or could reasonably be expected *j*
> to have known, of the failure to pay the contributions or premiums in question.'

By April 1981 the affairs of the company had been fully wound up. On or about 30
April 1981 the liquidator submitted an account of the winding up of the company to the
Registrar of Companies. Section 300(4) of the Companies Act 1948 provides that on the

expiration of three months from the registration of such an account the company shall
be deemed to be dissolved, but it contains a proviso empowering the court to make an
order deferring the date at which the dissolution of the company is to take effect.

On 26 June 1981, on the liquidator's application by originating summons, Mr
Registrar Bradburn made an order giving the liquidator or any creditor or contributory
of the company liberty to apply to the court in those proceedings to determine any
question arising on the voluntary winding up of the company.

On 6 July 1981 the liquidator caused to be issued the summons which is now before
the court. As reamended, the summons seeks on behalf of the liquidator, first an order
that the date of the dissolution of the company be deferred, and second an order that all
further proceedings on the summons of 31 March 1981 issued against the company in
the Leeds Magistrates' Court be stayed. Subsequently, successive orders have been made
deferring the date at which the dissolution of the company is to take effect.

The principal question on this application is whether or not the court should make the
desired order staying the proceedings in the Leeds Magistrates' Court. I will hear further
submissions in relation to the further deferment of the date of dissolution of the
company after I have delivered this present judgment.

Section 226 of the Companies Act 1948, so far as material, provides;

> 'At any time after the presentation of a winding-up petition and before a winding-
> up order has been made, the company, or any creditor or contributory, may . . . (b)
> where any other action or proceeding is pending against the company, apply to the
> court having jurisdiction to wind up the company to restrain further proceedings
> in the action or proceeding; and the court to which application is so made may, as
> the case may be, stay or restrain the proceedings accordingly on such terms as it
> thinks fit.'

Section 231 of that Act similarly provides inter alia that when a winding-up order has
been made, no 'action or proceeding' shall be proceeded with or commenced against the
company except by leave of the court.

Counsel on behalf of the department, has conceded that the proceedings in the Leeds
Magistrates' Court would be a 'proceeding' within the meaning of s 226(b). This
concession would appear plainly correct, in view of the decision of Kay J in *Re Briton
Medical and General Life Assurance Association* (1886) 32 Ch D 503. Widgery LJ in *Langley
Constructions (Brixham) Ltd v Wells* [1969] 2 All ER 46 at 48, [1969] 1 WLR 503 at 509,
referred to authorities which he said suggested that the word 'proceeding' in s 231 of the
Act of 1948 should be given a wide meaning.

Section 307 of that Act provides:

> '(1) The liquidator or any contributory or creditor may apply to the court to
> determine any question arising in the winding up of a company, or to exercise, as
> respects the enforcing of calls or any other matter, all or any of the powers which the
> court might exercise if the company were being wound up by the court.
> (2) The court, if satisfied that the determination of the question or the required
> exercise of power will be just and beneficial, may accede wholly or partially to the
> application on such terms and conditions as it thinks fit or may make such other
> order on the application as it thinks just.'

In *Re Aro Co Ltd* [1980] 1 All ER 1067 at 1071, [1980] Ch 196 at 204, Brightman LJ
pointed out that while in terms ss 228 and 231 apply only to a compulsory liquidation,
the principle of the sections is applicable to a voluntary winding up, in the sense that in
it the court will exercise its power to stay under s 307 in circumstances in which it would
not exercise its dispensing power if the liquidation were compulsory. He explained:

> 'Thus if a winding-up order has been made, proceedings are automatically stayed
> but the court may, on application by the creditor allow them to be continued; while
> in a voluntary winding up, or where a petition has been presented but not

adjudicated on, there is no automatic stay but the court may on application by an interested party restrain proceedings.'

However, in view of the wording of s 307(2) of the Act of 1948, the court, if it is to exercise the power to stay proceedings in a voluntary winding up, must first be satisfied that the required exercise of the power would be 'just and beneficial'. Subject to this point, which I think must go to jurisdiction, it is not disputed that the court would have jurisdiction to stay the proceedings which are in the Leeds Magistrates' Court, and that, in deciding whether or not it should do so in the exercise of its discretion, it should apply mutatis mutandis the same principles as it would apply if this were a compulsory winding up.

A long line of authorities in my judgment establish that the predominant purpose of the provisions of the 1948 Act and its predecessors empowering the court to stay actions against companies in liquidation is to ensure the ultimate distribution of the assets of an insolvent company pari passu among its creditors (see for example *Re Keynsham Co* (1833) 33 Beav 123, 55 ER 313; *Anglo-Baltic and Mediterranean Bank v Barber and Co* [1924] 2 KB 410 at 417–418, [1924] All ER Rep 226 at 228 per Scrutton LJ; *Langley Constructions (Brixham) Ltd v Wells* [1969] 2 All ER 46 at 47, [1969] 1 WLR 503 at 508).

In his affidavit sworn on 17 June 1981 in support of the present summons the liquidator in effect put forward as his first submission the proposition that, if the department were allowed to continue with the proceedings in the Leeds Magistrates' Court, it would obtain an unfair preference over the other preferential creditors of the company, contrary to the principles of pari passu distribution. In paras 7 and 8 of his affidavit he said:

'7. I respectfully submit that the criminal proceedings, if allowed to continue, and if the same should result in a conviction of the company, such a result would place the Department in a position in which it would, as a preferential creditor, have preference over other preferential creditors.
8. I would further respectfully submit that the Department having been admitted to proof in the liquidation, it may not proceed at the same time with proceedings calculated to secure to the Department a recovery outside the liquidation of that which, under the rules of bankruptcy, was satisfied by the admitted proof in bankruptcy.'

It is not in dispute that the sole purpose of the department in instituting the proceedings in the Leeds Magistrates' Court was to enable it to proceed personally against the directors of the company under s 152(4) of the Act of 1975, as soon as an order had been made pursuant to s 150(1) requiring the company to pay the sum in question and the company had failed to pay it. The effect of s 152(4) is to give the department a special statutory remedy against directors of a limited company which would not exist under the ordinary civil law: cf *Morgan v Quality Tools & Engineering (Stourbridge) Ltd* [1972] 1 All ER 744 at 749, [1972] 1 WLR 196 at 202. This is the statutory remedy which the department seeks to invoke.

It is also common ground that, before instituting proceedings in the Leeds Magistrates' Court, the department (which had already submitted a proof for the relevant debt that had been accepted) made it clear to the liquidator that, if the company was convicted, the court would be asked to make an order for payment of the relevant sum, but that the department would not seek actually to enforce payment against the company. And indeed the department has offered me an undertaking that 'it will not, without the leave of the Court, enforce against the company or seek to procure the enforcement against the company of any order which may be obtained against the company on the hearing of the summons of 31st March, 1981'.

I am bound to say that, in all the circumstances, I think that para 7 of the liquidator's affidavit, in expressing concern for the position of preferential creditors of the company

other than the department, was somewhat disingenuous. The department, as I have said,
a has from the outset made it plain that it has no intention of enforcing against the
company any order for payment which it may obtain from the magistrates, and that it
is only interested in proceeding against the directors after the obtaining of such an
order. Even so, counsel for the liquidator submitted, the company and its creditors
might still be exposed to additional risks as a result of the proceedings in the magistrates'
court, for these reasons: if the department proceeded successfully against the directors
b and the directors accordingly paid sums to the department, the directors, so it was
submitted, would be entitled to be subrogated to the rights of the department pro tanto
as creditors of the company.

I am not convinced that in this contingency the directors would necessarily have any
such right. It seems to me that there are at least grounds for arguing that the personal
liability imposed on directors by s 152(4) is a special liability independent from that of
c the company and not akin to that of a security or guarantor and that no such right of
subrogation would exist. However, even assuming that it did exist, I cannot see that the
preferential creditors other than the department would be prejudiced in any way, on the
particular facts of this case. As the final statement of account submitted by the liquidator
in April 1981 showed, this company remained to the end hopelessly insolvent. Its assets
realised, in the event, a total gross sum of about £61,000, of which about £40,000 has
d been paid to the debenture holder, and the remaining £21,000 or so has already been
disbursed in paying a number of costs and charges. To mention a few, about £10,000
has been paid for the liquidator's remuneration, about £1,400 in legal costs and about
£3,500 in auctioneers' and valuers' charges. Counsel for the liquidator, as an afterthought
in his speech in reply, submitted that some or all of these disbursements might fall to be
challenged and upset by the introduction of a new claim against the company by the
e directors by way of subrogation. I do not think there is any substance in this point.

The truth of the matter, as I see it, is that this application is being pursued by the
liquidator solely for the benefit of the directors of the company who may otherwise be
exposed to a possible claim under s 152(4) of the Act of 1975 if the proceedings before the
magistrates are allowed to continue and result in conviction. And, indeed, in the course
of the hearing of the present proceedings it emerged that the directors of the company
f have offered the liquidator an indemnity against his costs of the application.

I leave open the question whether it is generally proper for the liquidator of an
insolvent company to make an application of the present nature solely for the personal
benefit of the directors of the company, as opposed to its creditors. I merely say that if
a liquidator does take this course, it is in my opinion at least incumbent on him to
volunteer a more frank and explicit explanation for his reasons for applying to the court
g than he has volunteered in his evidence in the present case.

I revert to the main question at issue. The principal submission made by counsel for
the liquidator in support of the application, beyond those submissions already mentioned,
was as follows, if I understood it correctly. Since the department has submitted a proof
for the full amount of its debt and that proof has been admitted in full, this claim, he
contended, has been notionally satisfied in full under the ordinary principles of
h bankruptcy. It ought not, as a matter of principle, so it is submitted, to bring proceedings
of any kind outside the bankruptcy, designed to enable it to recover its debt. The
department, so he contended, has already got everything that it can possibly be entitled
to get on this liquidation: that is to say nothing.

In this context he relied particularly on two cases by way of supposed analogy. In Food
Controller v Cork [1923] AC 647, [1923] All ER Rep 463, the House of Lords held in effect
that the Crown, by assenting to the statutory claim for the administration of assets
embodied in the Companies (Consolidation) Act 1908, had surrendered any prerogative
right to require repayment of Crown debts due from the company which was insolvent
and in voluntary liquidation.

In Craven v Blackpool Greyhound Stadium & Racecourse Ltd [1936] 3 All ER 513, a
director of a limited company in voluntary liquidation put in a proof in the liquidation,

which was allowed by the liquidator. The director was dissatisfied with the amount
awarded to him and brought an action for damages against the company in the King's
Bench Division. The Court of Appeal, on the company's application, stayed the action.
Greer LJ, having pointed out (see 515) that the creditor would have been entitled to
question the decision of the liquidator, by an appeal to a judge in the Chancery Division,
said (at 515–516):

'It seems to me, on general principles, that a person who selects one method of
having his claim adjudicated upon, if he is dissatisfied with the way in which that
adjudication has been decided, should not be allowed to select another method of
having it adjudicated. It is common knowledge in these matters that the court does
not allow two sets of proceedings to go on at the same time in the same matter; it
will stay either one or the other in order that there may not be a waste of costs in
asking two tribunals to decide the same question.'

Eve J said (at 517):

'He might treat himself as outside the administration of the affairs of the debtor
company, in which case, subject to any attempt that might be made to get an order
to stop him doing so, he might have presented a writ and endeavoured to have his
true position ascertained by trial before a judge or judge and jury, or he might prove
in the winding up, but he cannot have both at the same time . . .'

In the like manner, counsel for the liquidator submitted, the department, having
proved in the winding up, cannot now treat itself as outside the administration of the
affairs of the company by proceeding under the 1975 Act.

There are a number of distinctions between the facts of the *Cork* case and the *Craven*
case on the one hand and the present case on the other hand, but I think I need only
mention these points. In the *Cork* case, the Crown was attempting to assert an alleged
prerogative right, which the Court of Appeal found was quite inconsistent with the
statutory scheme for administration of the company's assets embodied in the Companies
(Consolidation) Act 1908. In the *Craven* case, the creditor was seeking the decision of a
second forum for his claim, when another forum, from which he had a right of appeal,
had already adjudicated on it. In the present case, if the department's construction of the
1975 Act is correct, it is seeking to enforce a statutory right to proceed against the
company before the Leeds magistrates, which has been conferred on it by that Act quite
outside the Companies legislation. Of course, it will be open to the company to argue
before Leeds magistrates as best it can that, simply because of the submission and
subsequent admission of the department's proof, there has been a notional payment to
the department of the full amount of the debt and that correspondingly no part of the
contribution can now be deemed to remain unpaid, for the purpose of applying ss 150(1)
and 152(4) of the 1975 Act. I do not intend by this judgment to preclude the company
from submitting this legal argument, so far as it properly can, in the magistrates' court,
in resisting the making of an order to pay under s 150(1).

However, my provisional view is that there is no substance in it. If the department
had actually received any part of the debt owing to it by way of a dividend in the
liquidation, the company would, I conceive, be entitled to be credited with this amount
in deciding to what extent, if any, any part of the relevant contributions remained
unpaid for the purpose of s 150 of the 1975 Act. However, my provisional view is that,
having regard not only to the wording but the legislative purpose of that section,
particularly when read in conjunction with s 152(4), the payment referred to therein is
actual payment and not some notional payment which may be deemed to have taken
place by virtue of the provisions of the Companies Acts relating to winding up.

In these circumstances I am not able to accept counsel for the liquidator's submission
that a prosecution will necessarily be futile because the department must now be deemed

to have been paid all its contributions in full. This will be a matter for the magistrates
a to decide, though I have thought it right to indicate my own provisional views on the
matter of principle.

In all the circumstances, I can see no sufficient grounds for ordering the stay sought.
In any event I conceive that the court should be slow to exercise its discretion by making
an order that would prevent the recovery in criminal proceedings of a penalty imposed
by Act of Parliament.

b   Apart from this point, however, I revert to the requirement contained in s 307(2) of
the Companies Act 1948, namely that, before ordering any stay, the court has to be
satisfied that this is just and beneficial. In the present case, as counsel pointed out on
.   behalf of the department, while such a course would clearly be beneficial to the directors,
it would equally clearly not be beneficial to the department, because it would, for
practical purposes, deprive it of any possible right to proceed against the directors. It
c would not, in my judgment, confer any benefit on the other creditors of the company.

In these circumstances, in my judgment it clearly would not be just to make the
order. As between the interests of the department as creditor and the interests of the
directors, who must prima facie be held responsible for the inability of this company to
pay its debts, including those of the department, the former must, in my judgment,
prevail.

d   For all these reasons, on the undertaking offered by the department, I must decline to
make the order to stay sought.

Order accordingly. Liquidator to pay costs of application personally.

Solicitors: *Ward Bowie*, agents for *David Yablon & Co*, Bradford (for the liquidator);
Solicitor, Department of Health and Social Security.

Jacqueline Metcalfe   Barrister.

Bromley Park Garden Estates Ltd v Moss

COURT OF APPEAL, CIVIL DIVISION

CUMMING-BRUCE, DUNN AND SLADE LJJ

23, 24, 25 MARCH 1982

Landlord and tenant – Assignment of lease – Consent of landlord not to be unreasonably withheld – Consent withheld in interests of good estate management – Whether withholding of consent reasonable – Landlord and Tenant Act 1927, s 19(1).

In 1980 the plaintiffs purchased an estate consisting of some 50 properties and thereby became the landlords of a two storey building, the ground floor of which was let to X and used as a restaurant and the first floor of which was let to Y and used as a residential flat. The lease of the flat contained a provision that the lease was not to be assigned without the landlords' consent. Later in 1980 Y wished to assign the lease to the defendant and applied to the plaintiffs for their consent to the assignment. The plaintiffs refused their consent stating that it was not their policy to permit assignments of residential tenancies and that if Y wished to vacate the flat she would be required to surrender the lease. Y nevertheless assigned the lease to the defendant. The plaintiffs, when notified of the assignment, informed the defendant that there had been a breach of the covenant in the lease restricting assignment and called on him to remedy the breach. When he failed to do so, the plaintiffs issued a plaint against the defendant claiming possession. At the hearing of the plaint the defendant contended that the covenant restricting assignment was subject, by virtue of s 19(1)[a] of the Landlord and Tenant Act 1927, to a proviso that the landlords' consent was 'not to be unreasonably withheld' and that the plaintiffs had withheld their consent unreasonably. The plaintiffs' agent stated in evidence that in the interests of the proper management of their estate the plaintiffs' policy was where possible not to permit multiple lettings in the same premises because it lowered their investment value. The agent further stated that X, the ground floor tenant, had in the past expressed an interest in taking a lease of the whole building. The judge adjourned the hearing so that evidence could be obtained as to X's intentions. At the resumed hearing the plaintiffs produced evidence that during the period of the adjournment they had come to an arrangement with X whereby he agreed to surrender his existing lease of the ground floor in return for the grant of a new lease of the whole building. The judge held that the relevant date for determining whether a landlord had withheld his consent unreasonably was the date of the hearing and not the date on which consent to the assignment was refused. The judge accordingly held that he was entitled to take into account the reasons for withholding consent advanced by the plaintiffs at the hearing and further held that proper estate management was a valid reason for withholding consent. The judge therefore made the possession order sought by the plaintiffs. The defendant appealed.

Held – Whether consent to the assignment of a lease was unreasonably withheld, within s 19(1) of the 1927 Act, depended on the construction of the covenant against assignment in the context of the lease and the purpose of the covenant in that context. If the landlord's refusal of consent was designed to achieve the purpose of the covenant the refusal was reasonable, but if the refusal was designed to achieve a collateral purpose or benefit wholly unconnected with the terms of the lease and the bargain made between the lessor and the lessee it was unreasonable, even if made for the purposes of good estate management. Thus (per Dunn LJ) it was not reasonable for a landlord to refuse his consent to an assignment for the purpose of destroying the lease or merging it with another lease in the same building, even though that might be good estate management

---

a   Section 19(1), so far as material, is set out at p 892 e, post

and advantageous to the landlord. Since the plaintiffs' reason for refusing to consent to
a the assignment to the defendant (namely that a single lease of the whole building would
enhance its investment value) was wholly extraneous to, and unconnected with, the
bargain made by the parties to the lease when the covenant was granted and accepted,
their refusal of consent was unreasonable. The defendant's appeal would accordingly be
allowed (see p 899 *f* to *h*, p 900 *d e j* to p 901 *c* and p 902 *c* to *h*, post).

Dictum of Sargant LJ in *Houlder Bros & Co Ltd v Gibbs* [1925] All ER Rep at 135, and
b *West Layton Ltd v Ford* [1979] 2 All ER 657 applied; *Governors of Bridewell Hospital v
Fawkner and Rogers* (1892) 8 TLR 637 distinguished.

Per curiam. The relevant date for the purpose of considering whether the landlord's
refusal of consent to an assignment of a tenancy is reasonable or unreasonable would
appear, logically, to be the date of the assignment and withholding of consent rather than
the date of hearing, since the tenant's right to proceed with the assignment if the
c landlord's reason for refusing consent is demonstrably bad would be rendered nugatory
if the landlord was later allowed to advance different reasons for his refusal. If, however,
the court is entitled to consider reasons other than those expressly put forward to the
tenant by the landlord when refusing consent, it is nevertheless clear that the landlord
can only rely on reasons which actually influenced him at the time of refusing consent
and cannot rely, for instance, on subsequent changes of circumstances (see p 901 *c* to *f j*
d to p 902 *b* and *j* to p 903 *a*, post); *Sonnenthal v Newton* (1965) 109 SJ 333 and *Welch v
Birrane* (1974) 29 P & CR 102 considered.

Notes

For grounds for refusal of consent to the assignment of a lease, see 27 Halsbury's Laws
(4th edn) para 371, and for cases on the subject, see 31(2) Digest (Reissue) 693–698, 5673–
e 5702.

For the Landlord and Tenant Act 1927, s 19, see 18 Halsbury's Statutes (3rd edn) 464.

Cases referred to in judgments

Bates v Donaldson [1896] 2 QB 241, [1895–9] All ER Rep 170, CA, 31(2) Digest (Reissue)
693, 5680.
f *Bickel v Duke of Westminster* [1976] 3 All ER 801, [1977] QB 517, [1976] 3 WLR 805, CA,
Digest (Cont Vol E) 370, 5692c.
Bridewell Hospital (Governors) v Fawkner and Rogers (1892) 8 TLR 637, 31(2) Digest
(Reissue) 692, 5668.
Gibbs and Houlder Bros & Co Ltd's Lease, Re, Houlder Bros & Co Ltd v Gibbs [1925] Ch 198;
affd [1925] Ch 575, [1925] All ER Rep 128, CA, 31(2) Digest (Reissue) 694, 5682.
g *Lehmann v McArthur* (1867) LR 3 Eq 746; *rvsd* (1868) LR 3 Ch App 496, LJJ, 31(2) Digest
(Reissue) 693, 5679.
Lovelock v Margo [1963] 2 All ER 13, [1963] 2 QB 786, [1963] 2 WLR 794, CA, 31(2)
Digest (Reissue) 698, 5701.
Premier Confectionery (London) Co Ltd v London Commercial Sale Rooms Ltd [1933] Ch 904,
[1933] All ER Rep 579, 31(2) Digest (Reissue) 694, 5684.
h *Sonnenthal v Newton* (1965) 109 SJ 333.
Town Investments Ltd Underlease, Re, McLaughlin v Town Investments Ltd [1954] 1 All ER
585, [1954] Ch 301, [1954] 2 WLR 355, 31(2) Digest (Reissue) 697, 5699.
Tredegar (Viscount) v Harwood [1929] AC 72, [1928] All ER Rep 11, HL, 31(2) Digest
(Reissue) 665, 5446.
Welch v Birrane (1974) 29 P & CR 102.
j *West Layton Ltd v Ford* [1979] 2 All ER 657, [1979] QB 593, [1979] 3 WLR 14, CA, Digest
(Cont Vol E) 370, 5688a.
Young v Ashley Gardens Properties Ltd [1903] Ch 112, CA, 31(2) Digest (Reissue) 702, 5742.

Appeal

The defendant, Peter Moss, appealed from a judgment of his Honour Judge John Warde,

given on 8 June 1981 in the Bloomsbury and Marylebone County Court, whereby it was
adjudged that the plaintiffs, Bromley Park Garden Estates Ltd, had not unreasonably   *a*
withheld their consent to a proposed assignment of a lease of premises to the defendant
and that the plaintiffs were accordingly entitled to an order for possession of the premises
known as 169A Fortess Road, Tufnell Park, London NW5. The facts are set out in the
judgment of Cumming-Bruce LJ.

Stephen Sedley for the defendant.   *b*
Robin W Belben for the plaintiffs.

CUMMING-BRUCE LJ. This appeal raises an issue of some general importance,
because the submission of counsel on behalf of the defendant (the appellant), raises the
point that the judge was misled when he followed a passage in *Woodfall on Landlord and
Tenant* (28th edn, 1978) Vol 1, para 1181. Counsel for the defendant submits that that   *c*
passage is expressed too widely and requires qualification, and that the judge fell into
error because he did not appreciate that the authorities did not support the proposition
as stated in *Woodfall.*

For the reasons that I shall explain, I accept that criticism by counsel for the defendant
of the way in which the proposition is concisely expressed by the editors of *Woodfall* and
was expressed by the judge.   *d*

On 11 May 1978 St John's College, Cambridge, granted to one Brown a lease for a term
of three years from 25 March 1978 of a flat and maisonette at 169 Fortess Road, Tufnell
Park, London NW5, at a rent of £400. In the lease there was a tenant's covenant not to
assign without the consent in writing of the landlord. There was no full repairing
covenant, but a tenant's covenant to keep the interior of the demised premises in
complete repair.   *e*

By s 19(1) of the Landlord and Tenant Act 1927 the covenant in the lease was 'deemed
to be subject—(a) to a proviso to the effect that such licence or consent is not to be
unreasonably withheld . . .'

By an indorsement dated 25 March 1978 Brown assigned the tenancy agreement to
Madeliene Wynn-Higgins. She was the daughter of an employee of Cluttons, who
managed this estate business for St John's College. No 169 Fortess Road was a building   *f*
which, at the date of the grant, consisted of a restaurant on the ground floor let by St
John's College to three persons called Mutti for a term of 15 years from 29 September
1975. On 6 October 1978 St John's College conveyed to Bromley Park Garden Estates
Ltd, the plaintiffs in these proceedings, no 169, subject to the tenancy of Miss Wynn-
Higgins, then described as 169A, and subject to the tenancy of the ground floor restaurant
held by those tenants. No 169 was one of 50 properties conveyed, five of which had   *g*
lettings of the upper parts separate from the ground floor.

At a date not in evidence, the lease of the restaurant was assigned by Mutti to two
gentlemen called Vincenzo and Di-Palma, who traded there thereafter, in the restaurant,
under the name of 'Spaghetti House'.

When her term had some eight months before expiry, Miss Wynn-Higgins wanted to
leave the premises, that is her flat and maisonette, and to assign it. The correspondence   *h*
shows that, before she approached the defendant in these proceedings, she had offered an
assignment to Di-Palma, one of the tenants of the restaurant, but he then refused the
offer because they could not agree terms. So one comes to correspondence beginning on
30 August 1980.

I read a letter dated 30 August 1980:

> 'Dear John   *j*
>
> *Re: 169A Fortess Road*
> As discussed between us some while ago, I have on behalf of Madeliene agreed to
> assign the Tenancy to Mr. Peter Moss who is a barrister. A Bankers' reference is
> enclosed but please feel free to obtain one through proper channels of your own. I

a   am obtaining two more references which I will send on to you. I shall be glad to have your consent and am definitely certain Mr. Moss will make a good tenant. I have previously explained the reason to you as to why Madeliene wants to make a move.

Yours Very Truly
Brian Wynn-Higgins.'

b   I also read the answer dated 4 September 1980:

'Dear Brian,

Tufnell Park (NW 5): 169a Fortess Road
Thank you for your letter of 30th August and for enclosing a Bank Reference in respect of a Mr. Peter Moss. Despite your first paragraph, I must tell you that this

c   is the first intimation I have of a wish on your part to have your daughter assign her Lease to Mr. Moss. My clients are not in the habit of permitting assignments in respect of residential tenancies, and you and I have discussed this aspect on previous occasions. If your daughter wishes to vacate then she must surrender her Lease to the freeholder. Mr. Moss can by all means communicate directly with me and I will see whether it might be possible for a new Lease to be granted to him. In this event

d   your daughter might perhaps be able to obtain a consideration from him for her chattels. Please let me know the intentions of your daughter, by return.

Yours sincerely,
JOHN B. BROOMFIELD.'

e   I then read the letter from the defendant to Mr John Broomfield:

'Dear Sir,
As I believe you have already been informed by Brian Wynn Higgins, I am interested in taking the assignment of the remainder of the lease of this flat. It has not been made clear to me exactly what the situation is, and has been suggested that

f   I should accordingly get in touch with you. Therefore, pursuant to clause 2(5) of the lease I ask the landlord's consent to the proposed assignment. If it is felt that such consent cannot be given I would greatly appreciate it if you could give me the reasons for this. If it will help at all I would be happy to furnish you with any character references you may need. I look forward to hearing your reply and remain

g
Yours Sincerely,
Peter Moss.'

I read Mr Broomfield's answer to the defendant dated 12 September 1980:

'Dear Sir,

h   *Tufnell Park (NW 5): 169A Fortess Road*
Thank you for your undated letter posted on 10th September last. We act on behalf of the freeholder of the above property. Whenever our clients create an unfurnished regulated tenancy letting, they do so to the specific individual named within the tenancy. Should that tenant decide at any time that the accommodation

j   is no longer required, then our clients expect the premises to be returned to them in reasonable condition. Thereafter, they will consider any application for a new letting which might be received. The position as explained above applies to the accommodation leased by our client here to Miss Wynne Higgins.

Yours faithfully,
JOHN BROOMFIELD & COMPANY.'

I also read Mr Brian Wynn-Higgins's letter to Mr Broomfield dated 12 September
1980:   a

'Dear John,
    Thank you for your letter. I am asking Peter Moss to ring you direct. It has been
intended to assign the lease for some time since I spoke to you when Mr. Di Palma
wanted it. I do not see that your clients can have any objection to it, nor have you
given me any reason for objecting to it. However, no doubt you will let me know
what transpires between you and Peter Moss.   b
                                                                            Sincerely
                                                                   Bryan Wynn-Higgins.'

    Finally, I read the letter of Mr Broomfield to Mr Wynn-Higgins dated 16 September
1980, wherein he refused to assign to any other party, but required surrender of Miss
Wynn-Higgins's tenancy: c

'Dear Brian,
                       Tufnell Park (NW 5): 169a Fortess Road
    Thank you for your letter dated 12th September last. I have received a
communication recently from Mr. Moss, and have replied to him. I do not wish
you to be under any misapprehension as to my clients' intentions, or to find that the   d
correspondence becomes prolonged. It must be clearly understood, therefore, that
under Clause 2(5) of the Lease which your daughter now holds by way of an
Assignment, my clients will not agree to the assignment of the tenancy of the flat
to any other party. Should your daughter now wish to vacate the accommodation,
therefore, I call upon you to hereby surrender the tenancy of same, which in any
event is due to expire on the 25th March next year.   e
                                                                  Yours sincerely,
                                                               JOHN B. BROOMFIELD.'

    The reason given throughout the correspondence by Mr Broomfield on behalf of the
plaintiffs was that it was the plaintiffs' policy not to permit assignments of residential
tenancies. They required surrender instead. Taking the view that this was an   f
unreasonable refusal, Miss Wynn-Higgins on 17 September 1980 assigned her interest to
the defendant, as she was entitled to do having regard to the view that she took of the
unreasonable quality of the refusal. On the same day the defendant gave notice of the
assignment to the plaintiffs. This was followed on 3 October 1980 with the plaintiffs'
formal notice to the assignee of breach of covenant, requiring him to remedy the breach.
    On 17 November 1980 the plaintiffs issued a plaint, being a plaint for possession of the   g
demised premises, with the particulars of claim founding the claim for possession on the
assignor's breach of covenant which was also a breach by the assignee who, by the
assignment, had assumed the obligations of the assignor owed to the landlord.
    On 1 October 1980 the defendant moved in. On 21 March 1981, on his behalf, his
solicitors filed a defence and counterclaim. In those pleadings the defendant pleaded
that—   h

    'By a letter dated 30th August 1980 the Plaintiffs' consent to the said assignment
    was sought by the previous assignees and on 4th September 1980 the plaintiffs,
    through their agents refused to give consent stating, inter alia, "My clients are not
    in the habit of permitting assignments in respect of residential tenancies".'

The defendant pleaded that the withholding of the consent by the plaintiffs was   j
unreasonable.
    The hearing took place on 14 April 1981 in the Bloomsbury and Marylebone County
Court before his Honour Judge John Warde. Evidence was given on behalf of the
plaintiffs by Mr John Broomfield who was managing the property on behalf of the
plaintiffs. Evidence was also given by Mr Moss, the defendant, and the judge had the
correspondence before him.

The evidence of Mr Broomfield at the hearing was to the effect that the covenant
a against assignment without the consent of the landlord was a covenant which had not
been in the interests of the then landlords, St John's College, Cambridge. He said that his
clients were not in favour of multiple occupation lettings as the investment value of that
type of letting was not such as to enhance their financial interests. He said it was much
against the landlords' interests to grant assignment of the lease. In cross-examination he
said that he accepted on behalf of the plaintiffs the bankers' reference of Mr Moss in
b relation to a rent of £400, but he was concerned that in the proceedings the defendant
was legally aided and he had doubts whether the defendant could meet a rent of £1,000
which might be the registered rent if a tribunal was asked to make decision about it. He
said that he had no knowledge of Mr Moss and nothing against him. He said that the
proposed assignment, which the plaintiffs might have contemplated, to Di-Palma, the
restaurateur on the ground floor, would have been on condition that Di-Palma
c surrendered both tenancies. He said that he recollected discussing figures with Di-Palma
in the previous year, 1980, and he said that in the new lease which the landlords
contemplated granting there would be new covenants imposing on the tenant a full
repairing obligation. He said that he last saw Mr Di-Palma in January 1981, when Mr
Di-Palma said that he was interested in the lease of the whole property.

The evidence of the defendant before the judge was to the effect that he had seen the
d correspondence between Mr Wynn-Higgins and Mr John Broomfield, but he had moved
in as no reasons which could be valid reasons had been given for refusing assignment.
He had the impression that Mr Di-Palma was not interested in the offer suggested by the
landlords, because the landlords were, he thought, asking too much and he frankly gave
evidence of his financial position. The judge adjourned the proceedings till 8 June 1981
in order to enable Mr Di-Palma to come and give evidence of his intentions. In the event
e Mr Broomfield gave further evidence of an agreement that he had very recently made
with the tenants of the restaurant for a new lease of the whole building with a full
repairing covenant. He produced the agreement and a draft lease and a vital term was
that the restaurateur on an assignment agreed to surrender both leases in consideration
of obtaining a new lease of the whole building. He said that when consent was refused
in September 1980 he was not negotiating with Di-Palma to take over the whole
f building, but he now objected because of Di-Palma's interest. After the application for
assignment had been made he intended to see if the ground floor tenants were interested
in the lease of the whole building, and before the last hearing he had had an indication
that that would be the case.

In his judgment the learned judge began by referring to and quoting two passages
from *Woodfall on Landlord and Tenant*. One was to the effect that the court was not
g confined to reasons put forward at or before the commencement of proceedings but
could take account of new reasons different from any reasons formerly given right up to
the time of judgment. If between their initial refusal and the hearing, the landlords had
pursued the matter and decided that they had new reasons, it was open to them to prefer
those reasons in evidence for the consideration of the court.

The judge then held that he was satisfied on the evidence of Mr Broomfield, whom he
h found genuine and frank, that when the application had first been made he had stalled,
his purpose being to get a new tenancy by achieving surrender of the lease of the
residential part at the top of the building and of the lease of the restaurant on the ground
floor. He held, following the statement in *Woodfall* to which I have referred, that he was
satisfied that the landlords were genuinely of the view, and reasonably of the view, that
the course that they were pursuing and their reasons for withholding the consent to the
j assignment proposed by Miss Wynn-Higgins was in the interests of the proper
management of their estate. He held that at the date of the hearing, which was the
effective date for determining whether the refusal was reasonable, the landlords had been
reasonable as they had a positive opportunity to let the whole premises as a single
building so that they would get an increased rent, a full repairing covenant and thereby
enhance the capital value which they might obtain in the market if and when they came
to sell the whole of their interest.

Counsel for the defendant submitted that the learned judge was wrong on two issues: first, accepting all the judge's findings of fact, he submitted that those facts as found by the judge still constituted an unreasonable withholding of consent; the second issue, counsel for the defendant submitted, was whether in an action for breach of covenant, as compared to an action by the plaintiffs for a declaration, the landlord, having given some reasons, could at the hearing rely on other reasons which existed on 17 September 1980, but which had not been disclosed to the opposite party, or in the pleadings, or in the action or at all until the hearing, and even then, on some material facts which were not proved until after the adjournment to 8 June 1981.

On the first of these issues counsel for the defendant submits that the statement in *Woodfall*, vol 1 at para 1181 is too wide. The statement which he criticised was this:

'A refusal of consent or licence will generally be considered unreasonable if it is on a ground having no reference either to the personality of the proposed assignee or to the effect of the proposed assignment (or under-letting) on the user and occupation of the demised premises or kindred matters arising either during or after the tenancy. This statement of principle should be regarded however rather as a guide than as a rigid doctrine; it is considered that a landlord may reasonably be influenced in his decision by considerations of the proper management of the estate of which the demised property forms part.'

Counsel for the defendant accepts that the landlord has only to consider his own interests and in pursuing those interests he may withhold consent if, by giving his consent, he apprehends that he will cause detriment to the interests granted or reserved to him by the lease, whether by reference to the personal or financial characteristics of the intended assignee, or by reference to the anticipated adverse effect on the landlord's interests of the user of the premises by the intended assignee. It is submitted that the landlord is unreasonable if he withholds consent in order to obtain a new advantage which he does not enjoy under the lease. The judge, counsel for the defendant says, was wrong because the advantage that he found to have been proved was quite outside the interest granted or reserved by the lease.

Counsel for the plaintiffs contested this proposition. He relied on a passage in the judgment of Pollock MR in *Re Gibbs and Houlder Bros & Co Ltd's Lease, Houlder Bros & Co Ltd v Gibbs* [1925] Ch 575 at 583–584, [1925] All ER Rep 128 at 132. He points to the decision and judgments in *Governors of Bridewell Hospital v Fawkner and Rogers* (1892) 8 TLR 637 and *Premier Confectionery (London) Co Ltd v London Commercial Sale Rooms Ltd* [1933] Ch 904, [1933] All ER Rep 579. He relies on *Re Town Investments Ltd Underlease, McLaughlin v Town Investments Ltd* [1954] 1 All ER 585, [1954] Ch 301, a decision of Danckwerts J, and *West Layton Ltd v Ford* [1979] 2 All ER 657, [1979] QB 593.

A convenient starting point from which to consider the issue is *Lehmann v McArthur* (1867) LR 3 Eq 746. The landlord there withheld a licence to assign to a person wholly unobjectionable, his object being to get a surrender of the lease for the purpose of rebuilding. Stuart V-C said (at 751):

'... this is a purpose not contemplated by the lease. The lease by *Shakerley* is a demise unto *McArthur*, his executors, administrators, and assigns, and this entitled him to assign to another person, if there should be no reasonable ground, within the terms of the covenant, on the part of *Shakerley* for refusing his license. The question now is, whether or not there was any power in the lessor, who has contracted to allow his lessee to assign where he might reasonably assign, to refuse to allow the lessee to assign at all, because he wishes him to give up the lease, and himself make a new bargain with the lessee. In my opinion, no lessor has a right to use a stipulation in a covenant of this kind, so as to defeat the right of the lessee to assign, where the assignment or agreement for an assignment has been honestly made.'

Then in 1896 in *Bates v Donaldson* [1896] 2 QB 241 at 247, [1895–9] All ER Rep 170

at 174, A L Smith LJ in his judgment expressed his view in a passage which in this court
a was later preferred to the judgment of Kay LJ. A L Smith LJ said:

> 'Now, when the lessor granted the lease he parted with his interest in the premises
> for the entire term. The tenant during that term can assign to any respectable and
> responsible assignee in which case the lessor is bound not to unreasonably withhold
> his permission. It is not, in my opinion, the true reading of this clause that the
> permission can be withheld in order to enable the lessor to regain possession of the
b > premises before the termination of the term. It was in my judgment inserted alio
> intuitu altogether, and in order to protect the lessor from having his premises used
> or occupied in an undesirable way or by an undesirable tenant or assignee, and not
> in order to enable the lessor to, if possible, coerce a tenant to surrender the lease so
> that the lessor might obtain possession of the premises, which was the reason why
> in the present case the assent was withheld.'

c
I come to 1925, when in *Re Gibbs and Houlder Bros & Co Ltd's Lease, Houlder Bros & Co
Ltd v Gibbs* [1925] Ch 575, [1925] All ER Rep 128 the question was whether it was
reasonable to withhold consent because the proposed assignee would leave the adjoining
premises leased by the same landlord to take possession of the assigned premises, in
circumstances in which the landlord would have difficulty in letting the premises left by
d the proposed assignee. Pollock MR expressed his view, and I quote the passage in his
judgment, as follows ([1925] Ch 575 at 583–584, [1925] All ER Rep 128 at 132):

> 'For my part, I agree with A. L. Smith L.J., and I think that one must look at these
> words in their relation to the premises, and to the contract made in reference to the
> premises between the lessor and lessee; in other words, one must have regard to the
> relation of the lessor and lessee inter se, or, perhaps one may add, to the due and
e > proper management of the property, as in *Governors of Bridewell Hospital* v. *Fawkner*
> ((1892) 8 TLR 637). The latter case is an illustration of a withholding of consent on
> broad grounds bearing upon the estate of the lessor, or it may be on grounds which
> are important between the lessor and other lessees of that property, or that estate, of
> which the lessee had cognizance. But I do not think the words of the covenant can
> be so interpreted as to entitle the lessor to exercise the right of refusal when his
f > reason given is one which is independent of the relation between the lessor and
> lessee, and is on grounds which are entirely personal to the lessor, and wholly
> extraneous to the lessee. As an illustration of what I mean I refer to *Young* v. *Ashley
> Gardens Properties, Ld.* ([1903] Ch 112), where a condition was imposed, or attempted
> to be imposed, by the lessor, not in reference to the relation between himself and the
> lessee, nor in relation to the property which was the subject of the lease, but one
g > which was wholly personal to the lessor himself, whereby he attempted to obtain
> immunity from possible increase in the rates. In the present case the lessor has
> frankly avowed that there is no objection to Roneo, Ld., as a respectable and
> responsible person or corporation, and that the sole reason operating upon his mind
> is something extraneous to the relation of landlord and tenant, something extrinsic
> from the lessee, and something which is wholly personal to the lessor. To hold that
h > such a reason absolved the lessor from the duty of giving his licence to an assignment
> under the terms of the covenant would, in my opinion, be to give far too wide an
> interpretation to the word "unreasonably," and to be going beyond the cases. While
> I think it is impossible to give an exact definition which will fit all cases, I prefer the
> reasoning which is stated by A.L. Smith L.J. in *Bates* v. *Donaldson* ([1896] 2 QB 241,
> [1895–9] All ER Rep 170), which I think has been followed by Tomlin J. I agree,
i > therefore, with the decision which Tomlin J. has reached. For these reasons I think
> the appeal must be dismissed with costs.'

I refer also to the judgment of Warrington LJ ([1925] Ch 575 at 585–586, [1925] All
ER Rep 128 at 133):

> 'The first question that arises is: What is the inference to be drawn as to the

intention of the parties in inserting in the lease a provision of this kind? What was
the danger which the lessor contemplated, and against which the lessee was content   *a*
to allow the lessor to protect himself? It must, of course, be borne in mind that
without this covenant the lessee would have had a free right to assign to whom he
pleased the premises comprised in the lease, and the covenant, therefore, was
inserted first as a protection of the lessor, and, secondly, the proviso was attached to
it in order to prevent the lessor making an unreasonable use of that protection.
Now, what is to be inferred from what may be treated as having been in the   *b*
contemplation of the parties when the contract was made? I think it must be, as I
have said, that it was intended to protect the lessor as against a lessee, who, although
respectable and responsible, might well be reasonably objectionable in other ways,
and, secondly, from the point of view of the property, to prevent the lessor from
having to accept a lessee whose user of the property might again be reasonably
objectionable. The user of the property to be reasonably objectionable need not   *c*
necessarily be objectionable to the lessor as lessor of that particular property. The
user of the property might damage the lessor in other ways, and if it did, then an
objection to that user would be reasonable; but whichever way it is looked at, I
think you must find in the objection something which connects it either with the
personality of the intended assignee suggested as the new tenant of the property, or
with the user which he is likely to make of the property to be assigned to him.   *d*
When you look at the authorities—I do not propose to go through them—this, at
any rate, is plain, that in the cases in which an objection to an assignment has been
upheld as reasonable it has always had some reference either to the personality of the
tenant, or to his proposed user of the property. The case which was, perhaps, most
relied upon by appellant was that of *Governors of Bridewell Hospital* v. *Fawkner*
((1892) 8 TLR 637), because what was there apprehended was damage to the lessor   *e*
in respect of other property of his; but the damage which was apprehended would
have resulted, if it resulted at all, either from the personality of the proposed
assignee, who was the General of the Salvation Army, or from the user to which he
was likely to put the property, so that it fell within the limitation which I have
suggested.'

I quote also from the judgment of Sargant LJ ([1925] Ch 575 at 587–588, [1925] All   *f*
ER Rep 128 at 134):

'In the present case Mr. Stamp has shown in his able argument that it is not
necessary for the success of the respondent that the operation of the covenant should
be limited even to the extent laid down by A. L. Smith L.J.; because Mr. Stamp
points out that not only is the reason given here something that is not in relation to   *g*
the use or occupation of the premises, or to the personality of the tenant, but that
the reason has nothing whatever to do with the subject matter of the demise. I was
very much impressed by his argument that in a case of this kind the reason must be
something affecting the subject matter of the contract which forms the relationship
between the landlord and the tenant, and that it must not be something wholly
extraneous and completely dissociated from the subject matter of the contract. It is   *h*
to be noticed that under the statute 32 Hen. 8, c. 34, on an assignment or conveyance
of a reversion on a lease, the relationship between landlord and tenant is completely
transferred to the new parties. The result of the appellant's view would be that, as
the personality of the lessor varied, so the reasons for refusing or withholding the
consent to the assignment of the lease might vary, if those reasons might include
any circumstance that happened for the time being to affect the pecuniary interest   *j*
of the lessor.'

This brings me to 1979 when, in *West Layton Ltd v Ford* [1979] 2 All ER 657 at 663,
[1979] QB 593 at 605, Roskill LJ repeated what Stuart V-C had said in 1867, and added:

'I think that the right approach, as Lord Denning MR suggested in the *Bickel* case a [1976] 3 All ER 801, [1977] QB 517, is to look first of all at the covenant and construe that covenant in order to see what its purpose was when the parties entered into it; what each party, one the holder of the reversion, the other the assignee of the benefit of the relevant term, must be taken to have understood when they acquired the relevant interest on either side.'

The cases on which counsel on behalf of the plaintiffs relied were, with one exception,
b cases which prove on analysis to be cases in which the reason of the landlord for withholding his consent was because he apprehended that the prospective user of the parcels after assignment would have the effect of injuring his interests, albeit they might be consequences suffered by him in neighbouring property. The landlord reasonably apprehended that the consequence of the assignment would damage his interest in neighbouring property; an example is *Governors of Bridewell Hospital v Fawkner and*
c *Rogers* (1892) 8 TLR 637. The effect of the anticipated activities of the assignee on the neighbouring property of the landlord caused reasonable apprehension to the landlord: so, too, in the case in which the expected activities of the assignee would produce adverse consequences on the trade and rental of a shop which was also held from the same landlord.

One can distinguish the uncovenanted advantage sought to be gained by the landlord
d in this case by refusing to honour the right of the tenant to assign. The only case that does not have this characteristic is *Viscount Tredegar v Harwood* [1929] AC 72, [1928] All ER Rep 11 in the House of Lords. That case was quite different. Their Lordships distinguished the covenant in that case from a covenant to assign as between landlord and tenant. They distinguished *Houlder v Gibbs* [1925] Ch 575, [1925] All ER Rep 128 without, as I see it, expressing dissent, and, even if that is not a correct reading of the
e speeches, those observations would in the circumstances (they are entitled to great respect) be obiter.

Counsel for the plaintiffs submitted that the withholding of consent had as its object and consequence a return of the premises to unified possession which he described as the status quo, but he could not bring his suggested status quo within the contemplation of the parties to the grant to Miss Wynn-Higgins or Brown, as the shop was then used as a
f restaurant by the Muttis and there was no evidence of the date when the whole house had last been in single occupation. I would therefore hold that the statement in *Woodfall* is misleading, and its reference to good estate management as a valid reason for withholding consent is altogether too wide; it does not represent the true effect of the judgments in the cases to which I have referred.

The reason described by Mr Broomfield in evidence, and accepted by the judge as his
g ground for decision, was wholly extraneous to the intention of the parties to the contract when the covenant was granted and accepted. That reason cannot be relied on merely because it would suit the plaintiffs' investment plans, or their purpose in obtaining from Miss Wynn-Higgins the surrender of her lease. It may well enhance the financial interests of the plaintiffs to obtain a single tenant holding the whole building on a full repairing covenant with long-term capital advantage when they put the building on the
h market, but that intention and policy is entirely outside the intention to be imputed to the parties at the time of the granting of the lease to Brown or the assignment to Miss Wynn-Higgins. That being my view, I find it unnecessary to decide the second issue raised on behalf of the defendant which is: how far, in the light of the reasons given in the correspondence for the refusal, it was open to the plaintiffs at the hearing of their claim, founded on a breach of covenant committed on 17 September 1981, to give
j evidence of other unpleaded grounds for withholding consent. The authorities on this issue are not altogether easy to reconcile. It is a problem of some difficulty which is best left for decision in a case in which it is necessary to decide it.

There are two subsidiary points referred to by the learned judge. The lease to Brown and the assignment to Miss Wynn-Higgins had curious features. The rent was so low as to be described by Mr Broomfield in evidence as a gift and the lady was the daughter of the man in Cluttons who was handling on behalf of St John's College, Cambridge, the business of the sale of their Tufnell Park estate to the plaintiffs. The original lease seems to have many of the characteristics of the introduction of the fictitious John Doe, but the plaintiffs did not seek to set the whole transaction aside. The grantors, St John's College, agreed to grant the first tenant, or Miss Wynn-Higgins if they knew of her existence, a covenant in the form it took in the lease. Even if the lease had the special personal character which counsel for the plaintiffs attributes to it and the grantors contemplated Miss Wynn-Higgins alone as their tenant, none the less the grantors agreed to include in the lease a covenant giving her a right to assign which, by operation of law, was an assignment as to which the landlords were not entitled to withhold their consent unless their reasons were reasonable. The judge rightly regarded this as a peripheral matter which did not assist. He took the same view of the plaintiffs' attempt to fall back on the assignee's financial position, first disclosed by the defendant when he gave evidence candidly of his financial position and prospects when he was in the witness box. As the judge said, there is no hard evidence. The judge said it did not really influence him and there is certainly no reason to take a different view. I would allow the appeal.

DUNN LJ. I agree and I only add a few words of my own because we are differing from the view expressed by the judge.

I agree with Cumming-Bruce LJ that the passage in *Woodfall on Landlord and Tenant*, vol 1, para 1181, on which the judge relied, states the law too widely. The cases cited in support of the proposition as stated by *Woodfall* show that, although the question of unreasonableness depends on all the circumstances of the case, including considerations of proper management of the estate of which the demised premises form a part, in no case has it been held reasonable for a landlord to refuse his consent for the purposes of destroying the lease in question or merging it on terms with another lease in the same building, even though that would probably be good estate management and would be a pecuniary advantage to the landlord.

In *West Layton Ltd v Ford* [1979] 2 All ER 657, [1979] QB 593, the proposal of the tenant had the effect of altering the nature of the letting from a single letting of commercial property with residential property over to two separate tenancies: the commercial tenancy downstairs and a separate residential letting upstairs. This would have been detrimental to the landlord because the residential tenancy would, as a result of the Rent Act 1974, attract Rent Act protection.

Similarly, in *Premier Confectionery (London) Co Ltd v London Commercial Sale Rooms Ltd* [1933] Ch 904, [1933] All ER Rep 579, although there were separate tenancies of a shop and a kiosk, the lease of the kiosk had been granted to the same tenant who was the lessee of the shop. The proposal of the tenant was to assign the tenancy of the kiosk so as to create two tenants instead of one. That would have been detrimental to the landlords because competition from the kiosk would have been likely to affect the rent they would be able to charge for the shop.

In both cases the withholding of consent to the assignments by the landlords were held not to have been unreasonable. In both cases the landlords were seeking to uphold the status quo and to preserve the existing contractual arrangements provided by the leases. In both cases the landlords reasonably believed that they would suffer detriment if the assignments were made. It is true that in deciding the question of unreasonableness the courts did not confine themselves to narrow considerations as to the personality of the proposed assignee or the subject matter of the lease, as had been done in some of the older cases, and it may be that the passage in *Woodfall* was intended to draw attention to that, but there is nothing in the cases to indicate that a landlord is entitled to refuse his consent in order to acquire a commercial benefit for himself by putting into effect proposals outside the contemplation of the lease under consideration, and to replace the contractual relations created by the lease by some alternative arrangements more advantageous to the landlord, even though this would be in accordance with good estate management.

West Layton Ltd v Ford [1979] 2 All ER 657, [1979] QB 593 shows that in considering whether the landlord's refusal of consent is unreasonable, the court should look first at the covenant in the context of the lease and ascertain the purpose of the covenant in that context. If the refusal of the landlord was designed to achieve that purpose then it may not be unreasonable, even in the case of a respectable and responsible assignee; but if the refusal is designed to achieve some collateral purpose wholly unconnected with the terms of the lease, as in *Houlder Bros & Co Ltd v Gibbs* [1925] Ch 575, [1925] All ER Rep 128, and as in this case, then that would be unreasonable, even though the purpose was in accordance with good estate management.

For those reasons and for the reasons given by Cumming-Bruce LJ, I agree that this appeal should be allowed on that ground.

SLADE LJ. I agree with both judgments that have been delivered.

The learned judge took the view that the date of the hearing was the relevant date for the purpose of considering whether or not the landlords' refusal of consent to the assignment of the tenancy was reasonable or unreasonable. However, in the course of argument before this court, it was conceded on behalf of the respondents (the plaintiffs) that the relevant date for this purpose is not the date of the hearing, but the date of the assignment, 17 September 1980, which puts a rather different complexion on the case.

The logic of this concession appears to me inescapable. The fetter on the tenant's right to assign which was imposed by cl 2(5) of the tenancy agreement of 11 May 1978 operated subject to a statutory proviso that the landlords' consent to an assignment was not to be unreasonably withheld. It is well settled that a tenant holding under a lease which contains a clause of this nature is released from such a fetter, and has the right to proceed with an assignment of his lease, if the landlord has unreasonably refused his consent. It is of course open to the landlord thereafter to challenge the validity of an assignment effected in such circumstances, on the grounds that his refusal of consent was not in fact unreasonable. However, the tenant's right to proceed with such an assignment would be rendered more or less nugatory, if, in subsequently advancing such a challenge, the landlord were entitled to rely on facts or considerations which had not in any way influenced his mind at the date of the assignment, but were mere afterthoughts. A tenant who decides to proceed with an assignment following an unqualified refusal of consent on the part of the landlord, must be entitled to take this course in the light of the facts as they exist at the date of the assignment. Even on this footing, he must still accept a degree of risk in adopting this course inasmuch as he may not be aware of all the factors which have in truth influenced the landlord in his refusal.

In the present case, as at 17 September 1980, the tenant found herself faced with an unqualified refusal of consent, contained in Mr Broomfield's letter of the previous day. The only reason for such refusal which had been given by the landlords or their agent to the intending assignor and assignee was that it was not the landlords' practice to permit assignments of residential tenancies. As has been conceded before the judge and before this court, this was a reason which itself constituted no valid ground for the withholding of consent. It is hardly surprising that the tenant, when she was given one reason only why consent had been withheld and that reason was demonstrably a bad one, decided to proceed with the assignment.

I find it rather more surprising that, when the landlords came subsequently to question the validity of the assignment in such circumstances, they should be free to rely on reasons for their refusal which had not been mentioned to the tenant, or even hinted at, either before or in the letter of 16 September 1980 which contained the outright refusal. In the absence of authority, I would have thought there was much to be said for the view that a landlord who, by stating to the tenant one reason only for refusing his consent to an assignment, that reason being a demonstrably bad one, provokes a tenant into assigning without consent, should not thereafter be allowed to rely on unstated reasons for the purpose of attacking the validity of the assignment. However, authorities such as *Sonnenthal v Newton* (1965) 109 SJ 333, and *Welch v Birrane* (1974) 29 P & CR 102, appear to establish that the court, in considering questions of reasonableness or otherwise in this context, is not confined to the reasons expressly put forward by the landlord prior to the date of the refusal.   *a*

For present purposes I am content to assume, without deciding, that this is the legal position, subject only to one proviso. It seems to me clear that, in so far as a landlord is allowed to rely on reasons which were not stated to the tenant, he can only be permitted to rely on reasons which did actually influence his mind at the relevant date, which in the present case is 17 September 1980. The decision of this court in *Lovelock v Margo* [1963]   *b* 2 All ER 13, [1963] 2 QB 786 clearly establishes that in cases such as the present the court has to have regard to the landlord's actual state of mind at the relevant time. The test is not a purely objective one, though no doubt inferences may be drawn as to his state of mind from his words and actions and all the other circumstances of the case. It is therefore necessary to consider what were the factors which actually influenced the plaintiff landlords in the present case, as at 17 September 1980.   *c*

The judge's findings of fact on this point, in relation to this particular date, are to be found in the following sentences from his judgment:

> 'The matters which clearly influenced the plaintiffs were these. When the consent was applied for, Mr Broomfield, who made a very good impression on me, as did Mr Moss, took the view that it was not proper for him in his position to grant consent because he felt that it was a probability, although it had not been canvassed in depth,   *d* that the restaurateurs on the ground floor might be interested and therefore it was improper for him to consent.'

In referring to the possible interest of the restaurateurs on the ground floor, the judge was referring to the possibility that these persons might take a tenancy of the whole of the premises. In my judgment, for the reasons given by Cumming-Bruce and Dunn LJJ,   *e* these considerations which influenced the landlords' minds constituted no good grounds for the refusal of consent to the desired assignment. They have not ever claimed that the assignment would actually prejudice them in any way. All the cases relied on by counsel for the plaintiffs in this context, such as *Governors of Bridewell Hospital v Fawkner and Rogers* (1892) 8 TLR 637 and *Premier Confectionery (London) Co Ltd v London Commercial Sale Rooms Ltd* [1933] Ch 904, [1933] All ER Rep 579 were, I think, cases where the   *f* successful landlords could reasonably have anticipated that they would suffer detriment if the assignment were allowed to proceed. They are therefore in my judgment distinguishable on this ground, if no other. I agree with Cumming-Bruce and Dunn LJJ that the statement in *Woodfall*, vol 1 at para 1181, to the effect that a landlord may properly be influenced in his decision by considerations of the proper management of the estate of which the demised property forms a part is too wide.   *g*

A landlord is not in my judgment entitled to rely on a clause, such as cl 2(5) of the tenancy agreement in the present case, for the purpose of securing a collateral benefit such as the landlords have sought to secure for themselves in the present case. The reason which influenced the landlords in the present case is in my judgment in the words of Sargant LJ in *Houlder Bros & Co Ltd v Gibbs* [1925] Ch 575 at 588, [1925] All ER Rep 128 at 135—   *h*

> 'a reason wholly dissociated from, and unconnected with, the bargain made between the lessor and the lessees under the lease that we have to consider, and is, from that point of view, a purely arbitrary and irrelevant reason.'

For these reasons and the further reasons given by Cumming-Bruce and Dunn LJJ, I agree that this appeal should be allowed.   *j*

CUMMING-BRUCE LJ. I did not in my judgment found any part of my decision on any consideration of the relevant date for the purpose of the judge's decision as to the facts relevant to unreasonableness. Having heard the judgment delivered by Slade LJ, I say that I entirely agree with it.

DUNN LJ. I also agree.

Appeal allowed. Possession order rescinded.

Solicitors: *Seifert, Sedley & Co* (for the defendant); *Slowes* (for the plaintiffs).

Henrietta Steinberg   Barrister.

Attorney General v English and another

QUEEN'S BENCH DIVISION
WATKINS LJ, BOREHAM AND GLIDEWELL JJ
15, 18, 21 DECEMBER 1981, 19 FEBRUARY 1982

HOUSE OF LORDS
LORD DIPLOCK, LORD ELWYN-JONES, LORD KEITH OF KINKEL, LORD SCARMAN AND LORD BRANDON
OF OAKBROOK
21, 22 JUNE, 15 JULY 1982

Contempt of court – Publications concerning legal proceedings – Pending proceedings – Publication of matter calculated to prejudice fair trial – Defence – Newspaper article on matter of public interest – Whether words complained of part of discussion of general public interest – Whether risk of prejudice to trial merely incidental to discussion – Contempt of Court Act 1981, ss 1, 2(2), 5.

In October 1981 a national newspaper published an article under the heading 'The vision of life that wins my vote' written by a well-known journalist in support of a parliamentary candidate who was seeking election as a pro-life candidate. The article was concerned with preserving the sanctity of human life, but also asserted that handicapped babies were unlikely to be allowed to survive and had either been or were likely to be allowed to die of starvation and by other means. The article was published in the same week that the trial began of a doctor for murder of a handicapped baby by starvation. The Attorney General applied to the Divisional Court for an order for committal against the editor and owners of the paper for contempt of court under the Contempt of Court Act 1981, contending that the publication of the article at the same time as the trial of the doctor had seriously prejudiced the trial. The Attorney General did not suggest that the article was intended to influence the doctor's trial but relied on the 'strict liability rule' contained in s 1[a] of the Act whereby conduct could be treated as contempt of court if it tended to interfere with the course of justice in particular proceedings, regardless of lack of intent to do so, and contended that because the article had created a substantial risk that the course of justice in the doctor's trial would be seriously impeded or prejudiced, by virtue of s 2(2)[b] the strict liability rule applied to the article. The editor and owners contended that by virtue of s 5[c] of the 1981 Act the publication of the article did not amount to contempt of court since it had been made 'as part of a discussion in good faith of public affairs or other matters of general public interest' and 'the risk of prejudice to [the] particular legal proceedings [was] merely incidental to the discussion'. The Divisional Court held that the publication of the article had created a serious risk of prejudice to the trial of the doctor and that there was no defence under s 5 for words or expressions which

---

a   Section 1 is set out at p 917 c, post
b   Section 2(2) is set out at p 917 d e, post
c   Section 5 is set out at p 918 a b, post

fell outside the ambit of a discussion of general public interest and that accordingly, on the facts, the publication of the article amounted to contempt of court. The editor and owners appealed.   *a*

Held – (1) Section 5 of the 1981 Act was not to be treated as an exception to the strict liability rule and therefore was not a matter to be raised by way of defence. Instead, both s 2(2) and s 5 stated criteria by which a publication was to be held not to amount to contempt of court despite its tendency to interfere with the course of justice in particular *b* legal proceedings. Accordingly, it was for the prosecution to prove, first that the publication created a substantial risk that the course of justice in the proceedings in question would be impeded or prejudiced within s 2(2), and then, if the publication was part of a wider discussion on a matter of general public interest, that the risk of prejudice to the particular proceedings was not merely incidental to the discussion, within s 5 (see p 918 *f g*, p 919 *g h* and p 921 *a* to *c*, post).   *c*

(2) Section 5 of the 1981 Act was intended to prevent bona fide public discussion in the press of controversial matters of general public interest being stifled merely because there were contemporaneous legal proceedings in which some particular instance of those controversial matters might have been in issue. The test of whether the risk of prejudice was 'merely incidental' to the discussion was not whether an article could have been written as effectively without those passages or whether some other phraseology *d* might have been substituted for them that could have reduced the risk of prejudicing the trial, but whether the risk created by the words actually chosen by the author was no more than an incidental consequence of expounding its main theme. Furthermore, 'discussion' was not confined to the airing of views and the propounding of principles and arguments but could include accusations made in good faith which were part of the basis of the discussion (see p 920 *a* to *c j* and p 921 *a* to *c*, post).   *e*

(3) The publication of the article suggesting that it was common practice among some doctors to do that which the doctor was charged with, created the risk of serious prejudice to the trial of the doctor within the provisions of s 2(2) of the 1981 Act. However, the absence of the accusation (which was believed to be true by the pro-life candidate and the journalist) in the passages complained of that it was common practice among some doctors to do what they were accused of doing would have meant that the *f* article had no purpose, whether as support for the pro-life views of the candidate's election policy or as a contribution to the wider controversy as to the justifiability of mercy killing. There was no mention in the article of the doctor's trial and the risk of the jury reading the article and allowing it to prejudice their minds in favour of finding the doctor guilty on evidence that did not justify such a finding was 'merely incidental' to the views sought to be portrayed in the article. Accordingly, the publication of the article *g* came within s 5 and did not amount to contempt of court. The appeal would therefore be allowed (see p 919 *d* to *g*, p 920 *c d f* to *h* and p 921 *a* to *c*, post).

Notes

For conduct amounting to contempt generally, see 9 Halsbury's Laws (4th edn) para 7, and for cases on matters likely to prejudice the fair trial or conduct of criminal *h* proceedings, see 16 Digest (Reissue) 27–33, 253–342.

Cases referred to in judgments and opinions

A-G v Times Newspapers Ltd [1973] 3 All ER 54, [1974] AC 273, [1973] 3 WLR 298, HL, 16 Digest (Reissue) 23, 221.   *j*
B (a minor) (wardship: medical treatment), Re [1981] 1 WLR 1421, CA.
Palser v Grinling, Property Holding Co Ltd v Mischeff [1948] 1 All ER 1, [1948] AC 291, HL, 31(2) Digest (Reissue) 1017, 8072.
R v Evening Standard Co Ltd, ex p A-G [1954] 1 All ER 1026, [1954] 1 QB 578, [1954] 2 WLR 861, DC, 16 Digest (Reissue) 37, 384.

Cases also cited

a   *R v Duffy, ex p Nash* [1960] 2 All ER 891, [1960] 2 QB 188, DC.
Robson v Dodds (1869) 20 LT 941.

Application
The Attorney General applied with leave of the court for an order of committal in respect
of a contempt of court allegedly committed by the editor, David English, and the
b   owners, Associated Newspapers Group Ltd, of the Daily Mail newspaper (the respondents)
in respect of an article published in the Daily Mail on 15 October 1981 under the heading
'The vision of life that wins my vote'.

Simon D Brown and *Andrew Collins* for the Attorney General.
Lord Rawlinson QC and *Richard Rampton* for the respondents.

c
On 21 December 1981 the court stated that it found the respondents to be in contempt
of court, for reasons to be given later.

19 February. **WATKINS LJ** read the following judgment of the court: This is an
application by leave of the court by Her Majesty's Attorney General for an order of
d   committal in respect of an alleged contempt of court. The respondents are, respectively,
the editor and the owners of the Daily Mail newspaper.
The application relates to an article which appeared in the issue of 15 October 1981
under the heading 'The vision of life that wins my vote'. The article was written by Mr
Malcolm Muggeridge, a well-known commentator, journalist and broadcaster. It will be
necessary to consider it in some detail later. It is sufficient to say at this stage that it
e   propounds in the author's characteristically trenchant style an approach to the question
whether or not severely disabled babies should be allowed or encouraged to survive.
It was published on the third day of the trial of Dr Arthur, a very experienced
consultant paediatrician, for the murder of John Pearson, a baby suffering from Down's
syndrome: he was mongoloid. The Attorney General submits that its publication was in
contempt of court in that it created a substantial risk that the court of justice in Dr
f   Arthur's trial would be seriously prejudiced. This submission is founded on the recently
introduced strict liability rule, which by s 1 of the Contempt of Court Act 1981 is defined
as 'the rule of law, whereby conduct may be treated as a contempt of court as tending to
interfere with the course of justice in particular legal proceedings regardless of intent to
do so'. To understand why it is said that Mr English and the owners are strictly liable for
contempt of court, a recital of the history of relevant events is indispensable.
g   On 28 June 1980 John Pearson was born in Derby City Hospital. He was almost
immediately afterwards diagnosed as suffering from Down's syndrome. He died on 1
July 1980. During his short life he had been under the care of Dr Arthur.
On 5 February 1981 Dr Arthur appeared at the Derby City Magistrates' Court charged
with the child's murder. It was alleged that he, in accordance with the child's parents'
wishes, had caused, or intended to cause, the child's death by starvation. In March he was
h   committed for trial. Because of the standing of the defendant, the circumstances of
death and the nature of the allegation, the case aroused very great public interest, but the
restrictions on reporting imposed by s 3 of the Criminal Justice Act 1967 were not lifted.
On 15 January and 6 February material had been published in the Daily Mail which
caused the Attorney General to warn the respondents by letter dated 31 March 1981 that
'the constraints placed upon the press by the law of contempt should be respected'. That
j   warning was acknowledged by the respondents in the editor's letter of 8 April 1981 as
follows:

'Thank you for your letter of March 31st. I have, of course, taken careful note of
what you say in your letter and I am grateful to you for writing to me about this
matter.'

Early in August 1981 widespread publicity was given to the decision of the Court of
Appeal in *Re B (a minor) (wardship: medical treatment)* [1981] 1 WLR 1421. That case a
concerned a Down's syndrome baby whose survival was said to depend on speedy
surgical intervention to remove an intestinal blockage. The child's parents had decided
not to sanction the operation. The decision was upheld by a judge in chambers. It was
reversed by the Court of Appeal on 7 August 1981. The problems involved and the
conflict of medical, parental and judicial opinion attracted widespread publicity and
invoked much public interest. The editor was away in America at this time but his b
deputy gave the case extensive coverage on 8 August 1981.

On 6 October nominations for a parliamentary by-election for the constituency of
Croydon North West closed. One of those nominated was Mrs Marilyn Carr, who had
been born without arms and who was seeking election as an independent pro-life
candidate. As such she was campaigning for the sanctity of life and the right of every
person, of whatever age and however severely handicapped, to be cherished and c
encouraged to live. An election address by her agent refers to thalidomide, but makes no
reference to mongoloid children.

One week later, on 13 October, the trial of Dr Arthur opened at the Crown Court at
Leicester before Farquharson J and a jury. Dr Arthur pleaded not guilty.

On the following day, 14 October, the first day's proceedings were prominently
reported under large banner headlines on p 3 of the Daily Mail. In descending order of d
prominence these headlines were 'Baby "given a hunger drug to kill him"'; 'Doctor: I
alone was responsible for treatment of mongol'; and 'Consultant accused of murdering
child that parents did not want'.

It is extremely unlikely, we think, that anyone of this national newspaper's extensive
readership failed to see these unusual headlines and to read the fairly detailed report
beneath them, which contained this passage: 'Before the jurors were sworn in, Mr e
Justice Farquharson said that if any were connected with handicapped children, they
should not serve.' In saying this the judge was obviously anxious to ensure that no one
should be a juror whose strongly-held views about handicapped children might prevent
that person from considering the grave issues involved impartially.

On the same day a press release issued by Mr Malcolm Muggeridge in support of Mrs
Carr's candidature and of the principles for which she stood was discussed at the daily f
editorial conference at the Daily Mail. It announced his intention of making an election
address on her behalf. This was considered newsworthy and so the associate editor, who
in the absence of the editor and his deputy presided over the conference, persuaded Mr
Muggeridge to present his proposed election address in the form of an article in the Daily
Mail. Thus the article was composed by Mr Muggeridge for publication by the
respondents on the following day, 15 October 1981.

The author asserts by affidavit that his purpose in writing the article was to further the g
cause of Mrs Carr. In para 8 of his affidavit he states:

'I have now retired from active journalism. I read the newspapers only
superficially and I do not have a television in my house. Accordingly although I was
aware that some sort of "mercy-killing" trial was in the offing, I knew nothing of its
detail and I certainly did not appreciate that it was in its second day when I was h
telephoned by the Daily Mail. I wrote my article without any thought of Dr.
Arthur's case in my head and without the least idea that it might be taken to reflect
upon that case. As I have said, the article was written solely in order to draw
attention to Mrs. Carr's candidature and to the importance of the cause for which
she stood.'

This court has seen a copy of the original article which was in some respects altered j
before publication by the associate editor, who in his affidavit states he altered the part
sentence 'Some doctor would surely recommend letting her die of starvation' to 'Someone
would surely. . .'. He did this because he thought the original text might suggest that Mr
Muggeridge was intending to refer to Dr Arthur's case, when in fact he was not.

Furthermore, he thinks it was he who on the grounds of taste and clarity changed the
a passage 'On the one hand the image of the broiler house or factory farm in which
concern is solely for the physical well being of the livestock and the financial well being
of the enterprise . . .' into that which reads 'Are human beings to be culled like livestock?'
   On Thursday, 15 October, the third day of Dr Arthur's trial, the article appeared on p 6
of the Daily Mail, which on p 19 contained a report of the second day of the trial
referring therein to it as 'the mongol murder baby trial'. The article was brought to the
b attention of Farquharson J, who expressed his serious disquiet at its content in these
terms:

> 'The difficulty now, of course, is that under the new Act I am only really
> concerned with contempts in the face of the court in dealing with them myself. For
> my part I nonetheless instruct that the copy of this particular article should be sent
> to the Attorney General and that could be done through the medium of the court.
c > Beyond that all I shall say at the present time is that I think that it is highly
> unfortunate that any editor, whether he had had the previous warnings or not,
> should publish an article of this kind in the middle of a trial which is very sensitive
> and very emotionally charged in the terms that appear in this article. I think it is
> quite deplorable.'

d On 3 November Dr Arthur was acquitted, by direction of the trial judge of murder
and by the jury of attempted murder.
   We now turn to Mr Muggeridge's article so as to examine it in some detail. It is
unnecessary to read all of it, though of course the allegedly contemptuous parts must be
considered in their proper context in the light of the article as a whole and to the
publicity given to the trial of Dr Arthur. It begins by referring to Mrs Carr's candidature
e as an independent pro-life candidate and extols her undoubted courage in overcoming
the handicap of her serious disabilities. Then follow the words of which complaint is
made:

> 'In fact she was born armless, with little buds where the arms should have
> come. As the doctor who delivered her put it—and he must have had a gift for
> poetic imagery somewhat rare in his profession—her arms had budded but never
f > bloomed. *Today the chances of such a baby surviving would be very small indeed. Someone
> would surely recommend letting her die of starvation, or otherwise disposing of her.* Thus
> Marilyn is a living witness to the pro-life cause: in herself an embodiment of life
> triumphant, challenging the right of any one human being to decide that another,
> whether an unborn or born child, whether a fatally ill or senile old person, has no
> right to go on living in view of circumstances—economic or physical or mental—
g > not conducive to a worthwhile life. It is the difference between the quality of life
> and the sanctity of life. The former being seen in how far the individual concerned
> may be assumed to be capable of enjoying life or contributing to life, of exercising
> the responsibilities of a parent, wage-earner, a husband or wife. The latter being
> seen in terms of the potentialities existing in every single human being, young or
> old, well or sick, intelligent or stupid, from the moment of conception to the
h > moment of death. Are human beings to be culled like livestock? No more sick or
> misshapen bodies, no more disturbed or twisted minds, no more hereditary idiots
> or mongoloid children. Babies not up to scratch to be destroyed, before or after
> birth, as would also the old beyond repair. *With the developing skills of modern
> medicine, the human race could be pruned and carefully tended until only the perfect
> blooms—the beauty queens, the Mensa IQs, the athletes—remained.*' [Mr Muggeridge's
j > emphasis.]

Having thus identified and commented on what may be called the scientific or
qualitative or selective approach, the article continues with the strongly contrasted
Christian view of the sanctity of life. No complaint is made of this latter part.
   The law of contempt relating to legal proceedings is contained in s 1 (already referred

to) and ss 2 to 5 of the Contempt of Court Act 1981, which came into force as recently as 27 August 1981. By way of preface to our reference to it, it is important to observe *a* that the Attorney General has not alleged that the respondents intended to influence the course of justice in Dr Arthur's trial. His application is founded on the rule of strict liability as defined in s 1.

By s 2 that rule is applied to an article such as that now under consideration, which is published when, as here, relevant proceedings are active. Section 2(2) is of particular importance, for it defines contempt for the purposes of the rule of strict liability. It *b* provides:

'The strict liability rule applies only to a publication which creates a substantial risk that the course of justice in the proceedings in question will be seriously impeded or prejudiced.'

The three following sections give protection to publications which might otherwise be *c* in contempt. Of these the defence under s 5 only is relied on by the respondents. It provides:

'A publication made as or as part of a discussion in good faith of public affairs or other matters of general public interest is not to be treated as a contempt of court under the strict liability rule if the risk of impediment or prejudice to particular legal proceedings is merely incidental to the discussion.' *d*

The parties accept that for present purposes the provisions of ss 2(2) and 5 pose two questions, either one or both of which we must answer.

The first question is, did the article create a substantial risk that the course of justice in Dr Arthur's trial would be seriously prejudiced? If the Attorney General, on whom lies the burden of satisfying this court so that it is sure it did create such a risk, fails to do so, *e* his application must be dismissed, in which event the second question will not have to be considered.

Are we then sure that this risk was created? From the observations previously quoted by Farquharson J, he appears to have been in no doubt that it had been. It should be made clear however that if that really was his conclusion, whilst it may be of some persuasive force, it is in no sense binding on us, and we are entitled to disregard it *f* altogether if we feel so inclined. We are called on to answer the question having regard to the totality of the material before us, of which the observations of the trial judge form only a part. This counsel for the respondents invites us to ignore altogether.

Now we take it to be self-evident that the material risk could not possibly have been created unless the article expressly, or by implication, referred or related to Dr Arthur's trial. There was no express reference to it; no mention of Dr Arthur nor of John *g* Pearson. On the other hand the allegations made, and the issues raised in the trial, were unusual. Dr Arthur was accused of murder. The particulars were that as the consultant paediatrician in charge of the baby John Pearson, he had embarked on or decreed a course of treatment which he intended should cause, and did cause, the child's death by starvation. By his plea of not guilty Dr Arthur had put all those allegations in issue.

Not only were the circumstances unusual: they had received very great publicity. *h* True there had been comparable publicity of *Re B (a minor)* [1981] 1 WLR 1421, but there the circumstances were different. There there had been a withholding of surgical intervention. In Dr Arthur's case was an allegation of withholding the basic essential to life: food. In *Re B (a minor)* the powers of the civil jurisdiction of the court had been successfully invoked, the issue of life or death had been resolved, the child lived. In the case of John Pearson it was alleged that someone had succeeded in starving him to *j* death. Moreover, some two months had passed since the public interest in baby B was at its height. John Pearson was now in all the headlines.

In these circumstances it seems to us inevitable that all sensible people, including the jurors at the Crown Court at Leicester, would conclude that such assertions as 'Someone would surely recommend letting her die of starvation', 'Babies not up to scratch to be

destroyed', and the question 'Are human beings to be culled like livestock?' followed by
a   'No more . . . mongoloid children' referred to the matters currently being investigated at
the Crown Court at Leicester.   Who would come to mind when such passages were
read? With all the publicity attending his trial, surely Dr Arthur.   But did all this create
a substantial risk that his trial would be seriously prejudiced?

The first point taken on behalf of the respondents is that in this context the word
'substantial' means something like large or great.   For this proposition reliance is placed
b   on the decision of *Palser v Grinling, Property Holding Co Ltd v Mischeff* [1948] 1 All ER 1,
[1948] AC 291, a case decided under the then current Rent Restriction Act, and concerned
with the assessment of a substantial proportion of rent.   We gain no assistance for an
interpretation or definition of the meaning of the word 'substantial' in such a very
different statutory context.   We are faced with a word of common usage, which
Parliament, we think, intended to bear its common understanding when used, as here,
c   as a qualifying adjective.   Apart, therefore, from saying that it means a risk which is real,
we think that any further definition is unnecessary and undesirable and would probably
introduce confusion where we think there is none.

Secondly, it is argued that the article restricts itself to moral argument, that it deals
with the law of God and not with the law of the land.   Thus it is said that there was no
substantial risk that a juror, bound by his oath to judge according to the evidence and
d   constrained to apply the law of the land as directed by the judge, would be influenced by
anything in the article.

We accept, of course, that the main theme of the argument deployed in the article is
founded on the Christian morality of preserving the sanctity as well as the quality of
life.   But moral argument published during, touching on and taken to refer to the issues
in an active criminal trial may be as seriously prejudicial to the course of justice in that
e   trial as any other published matter which refers to it.   And in Dr Arthur's trial one of the
most difficult tasks of the judge was successfully to strive to ensure that the jury allowed
itself to be governed not by any moral law but strictly by the law of the land.

However, as has already been demonstrated by quotations from the article, it is not
confined to argument.   It contains undisguised assertions or insinuations that babies who
are born with certain kinds of handicaps are caused or allowed by those in charge of them
f   to die within days of birth of starvation among other means.

Such statements as that may wrongly prejudice jurors, no matter how strongly a
judge, whose experience keeps him on the alert for this hazard, specifically warns them
against paying any attention to them.   At the same time he would doubtless warn them
against allowing their own privately formed prejudices, if any, to influence them in any
way.

g   One of the reasons why this branch of the law exists is in recognition of the judge's
difficulty always successfully to sweep away prejudice, regardless where it has come
from, and to assist him to do so by preventing the contents of publications bearing
prejudicial matter from going into the jury room.   Everyone surely agrees that the well
of justice must remain clear.   Thus by one means or another the poison of prejudice must
be kept away from it.   If it is not, then the possibility of a miscarriage of justice inevitably
h   accompanies prejudice.   No one will know what harm is then done except the jury
whose verdict, whatever it be, will not inform others as to whether or not it is tainted by
prejudice.   Moreover, the verdict be it guilty or not guilty, is irrelevant to the
considerations which enable us to answer this question.   These considerations have
satisfied us beyond any reasonable doubt that the words complained of created a
substantial risk of serious prejudice in the trial of Dr Arthur.   This must mean that the
j   respondents were in contempt of court unless the second question, to which we now
turn, is answered in their favour.

This question is, have the respondents, on whom, in our view and as counsel for the
respondents concedes, the burden lies of establishing a defence under s 5, proved on the
balance of probability the essential requirements of that defence, which are (1) that the
publication of the article was made as part of a discussion of a matter of general public

interest, (2) that the publication was made in good faith, and (3) that the substantial risk
of prejudice (that is undoubtedly the risk referred to in s 5), which thereby arose to the   a
trial of Dr Arthur was merely incidental to the discussion of the matter of general public
interest. A failure by the respondents to establish any one of these essential requirements
will disable them from the benefit of the defence under s 5.

It is not disputed, and it cannot be gainsaid, that the article could justifiably be claimed
to form part of a discussion of a matter of public interest. Accordingly the first
requirement is fulfilled. Counsel on behalf of the Attorney General has expressly told us   b
that he does not dispute that Mr Muggeridge and the respondents acted in good faith.
Accordingly we regarded ourselves as relieved of the necessity to inquire into facts
relevant to an issue which undoubtedly in some circumstances could be of vital
importance. So the respondents' sole task on the second question is to persuade us that
the substantial risk of prejudice was merely incidental to the discussion.

It is, we think, first of all necessary to identify the matter of public interest which,   c
according to the respondents, was the subject of the discussion of which the contents of
the article formed a part. It is expressly and succinctly stated in paras 5 and 6 of the
affidavit of the editor, Mr English, as follows:

'5. Another matter which was of considerable public interest during the late
summer and early autumn of 1981 was the forthcoming by-election at Croydon
North West, which was due to be held on the 22nd October 1981. The candidates   d
were formally nominated on the 6th October. One of the candidates was a Mrs.
Marilyn Carr, who was born without arms and who was standing as an independent
pro-life candidate.
6. The expression "pro-life" originated in the United States of America and its
currency is fast increasing in this country. It is used to describe those who believe
that all human life is sacred and who are in consequence opposed to abortion and to   e
all kinds of mercy-killing, whether of the young or the old. Mrs. Carr was the first
"pro-life" candidate to stand at a Parliamentary election, which was itself a matter of
some interest.'

Put in even shorter form, the discussion was about Mrs Carr's candidature and the pro-
life cause for which she stood.   f

It was of course a coincidence that the trial of Dr Arthur and the electioneering at
Croydon North West were going on at the same time. No one could reasonably have
expected either one to be postponed so as to avoid this clash of events, despite the
extremely unusual features involved in both of them. Dr Arthur's trial, as has been said,
received widespread publicity throughout this country and abroad. How much publicity
Mrs Carr and what she stood for received outside Croydon we do not know. It would   g
have probably been markedly less if Mr Muggeridge had not announced his intention of
going to her support, and consequently been invited to write the article in the Daily Mail
by the associate editor. When the latter issued the invitation at the time when he was
presiding at the daily editorial conference, he had observed the following entry on the
agenda:

'Marilyn Carr, a woman born without arms, who is standing in Croydon by-   h
election as independent pro-life candidate opposed to killing of handicapped new
born babies. Malcolm Muggeridge is going to Croydon to lend support.'

Immediately above this, and solely by chance, another item appeared, which reads: 'The
nurses from Derby hospital will today give evidence in trial of Dr. Leonard Arthur
accused of murdering 3 day old mongol baby. They will reveal they were instructed by   j
doctor to give death inducing drug'.

This item assisted the associate editor, who was well aware that Dr Arthur's trial had
already commenced, to give some thought, when he reviewed the article, to the
possibility of the contents of it being taken to refer to that trial. In the course of his
consideration of this he decided, among other things, against deleting the reference to
mongoloid children.

a It lay within his power to delete this reference and to eliminate all other terms such as 'Someone would surely recommend letting her die of starvation', of which complaint is made. Had these parts of the article been omitted, the point of it would still have been clear and it would, in our opinion, have remained a powerfully expressed form of support for Mrs Carr's cause.

b The respondents may nevertheless have been accused of contempt, but a defence founded on the provisions of s 5 would have been irresistible, since in our view no one could successfully argue that any remaining material claimed to be contemptuous would give rise to a risk of prejudice which was other than merely incidental to the discussion.

Thus a subsidiary question arises, could the matter complained of reasonably be said to be a necessary part of the general theme of the discussion?

c Counsel for the Attorney General submits that the use of this matter, which gave rise to the substantial risk, added nothing of value to the discussion, it was easily avoidable, and consequently wholly unnecessary. Counsel for the respondents contends that the article would have been in precisely the form it was, or almost so, if the trial of Dr Arthur had never taken place. The matter complained of was a necessary part of it, illustrating as it did attitudes and conduct towards handicapped newly born babies to which the pro-life movement was resolutely opposed. That is a view which we feel unable, as our earlier observations indicate, to share. The detailed assertions of how handicapped babies

d either have been or are likely to be destroyed were, we think, wholly expendable by the respondents without damaging the vigour and clarity of the vision of life sought to be portrayed.

However, that conclusion, it could be said, does not answer the third main question conclusively, for although the matter complained of was an unnecessary part of the article, it may be that it could still reasonably be regarded as merely incidental to the discussion.

e What do these all important words, namely 'merely incidental to the discussion', in relation to the risk of prejudice imply? What the provisions of s 5 exist for is important in this respect. They aim to strike a sensible balance between two important and often competing principles; on the one hand the maintenance of unimpeded and unprejudiced justice to every litigant and defendant, and on the other hand the preservation of the freedom of discussion of matters of general public interest. Thus s 5 provides in effect

f that bona fide discussion of matters of public interest need not be silenced if, as a mere incident of such discussion, a substantial risk of serious prejudice to a particular litigant or defendant may arise.

Counsel for the respondents submits, and we agree, that a risk of prejudice is merely incidental to a discussion when it is in subordinate conjunction to the real subject of an

g article. We should not be astute, he says, to take such an article outside the protection of s 5 merely because it contains expressions and statements which, serving no other purpose than to inflame an article, could therefore have been dispensed with. The journalist's traditional freedom of expression must not be artificially restricted, especially when, as here, the publication of the article was made in good faith and solely to support a Parliamentary candidate without intending to prejudice the fair trial of Dr Arthur.

h Furthermore, editors are placed in a genuine intellectual difficulty in trying to construe, amongst other provisions in the Act, what material may or may not be 'merely incidental'.

These submissions arouse to some extent our sympathy for editors and editorial staff who have to take decisions quickly about the contents of articles immediately prior to publication and to have regard to new legislation which may affect it. But we doubt that

j the task of avoiding being in contempt of active criminal proceedings is so difficult a task as is suggested.

In this respect we have not found, as counsel for the Attorney General submitted we might, reference to the Phillimore report (Report of the Committee on Contempt of Court (1974) (Cmnd 5794)) helpful, and we feel unable to agree with him that it is relevant to discover what activated the publication. This is particularly so where the good faith of the editor and publishers is not in question.

It seems to us that the protection of s 5 is not available once the matter complained of has been identified as extraneous to the main intendment of the article which is a *a* contribution to a discussion of a matter of general public interest and the proper inference to be drawn from the extraneous matter is that it refers to vital issues in active criminal proceedings affecting a man on trial such as Dr Arthur. Should that inference be drawn here?

We would accept that the matter may be put in this slightly different way. To qualify for the protection of s 5 the words or expressions, which by the application of s 2(2) are *b* held to create the risk of serious prejudice, must form part of a discussion of a matter of general public interest. From this it follows that protection is not provided for words or expressions which fall outside the ambit of such a discussion either because they are not, on a fair reading, part of the discussion or because they deal with matters which are not of general public interest.

In this sort of context recognition and identification are easier than definition. If *c* definition is to be attempted, discussion suggests the airing of views and the propounding and debating of principles and arguments: not the making of accusations. Matters of general public interest are to be distinguished from matters of particular personal interest. Thus to say in an article on the rights of married women, 'no man should ever beat his wife', would be acceptable as part of a discussion of general public interest. But is the position the same if there is added 'as Mr X frequently did'? We think not. Now *d* discussion has given way to accusation, and to the matter of general public interest there has been added a matter which is of particular personal interest. We think that, whichever approach is adopted, the extraneous matter or the excess is not difficult to identify.

To return to the matters complained of in the present case, suppose that in the first paragraph in italics there had been interposed after the word 'Someone' the words 'like *e* Dr Arthur', could it then be said that there was no more in the article than a discussion of a matter of general public interest and no reference to the trial? Surely not. Of course such an addition would be strong evidence of a deliberate intent to prejudice Dr Arthur's trial, whereas such an intention is not alleged here. But the absence of intention cannot avail the respondents, for this whole application is founded on the strict liability rule. Then does it make any difference that there is no express reference in the article to Dr *f* Arthur or his trial or to John Pearson? In our view it does not, since the reference to that particular trial appears, we have no doubt, by clear implication from the matter complained of as published.

For these reasons we have reached the clear conclusion that the risk of serious prejudice we have, without the assistance of the trial judge's comments, found to have been created was not incidental to a discussion of general public interest; it was created by assertions *g* of fact, which clearly implied (albeit unwittingly) that that which was alleged against Dr Arthur had in fact been done, and done by whom, if not Dr Arthur? It follows therefore that the respondents are not entitled to claim the protection afforded by s 5.

[The court heard submissions in relation to punishment]

WATKINS LJ. Mr David English and the Associated Newspaper Group Ltd having *h* been found guilty of contempt, now face judgment. In forming that judgment we have been considerably assisted by the extremely valuable address made to us by counsel for the respondents this morning.

It should be emphasised that the powers of the court to imprison and to fine in dealing with contempt under the 1981 Act are extensive. It is in the public interest and otherwise of supreme importance that juries unaffected by prejudice should do justice to *j* defendants who come to trial in criminal courts. It is of almost equal importance that litigants in civil matters have their disputes resolved by courts unaffected by prejudice. Newspapers and televisions and broadcasting authorities have a unique role to play in this respect. They have also, as must be acknowledged and never be forgotten, an essential role to play in maintaining dissemination of news and other information to the public without being unlawfully inhibited from doing so.

So having highlighted the two interests which have to be safeguarded, namely on the
one hand a fair trial and on the other a free press, we turn to see what damage may have
a been done in the instant case by the press to the trial of Dr Arthur, that is to say the
potential harm which could have come to the trial, but which, by reason of the acquittal,
obviously did not.

All litigation, in this context I refer to both criminal and civil matters, which involves
emotionally charged issues, specially of a moral kind, inevitably attracts publicity at the
b instant of those issues being raised, from no matter what quarter. In that event the care
of the press to avoid damaging the vital interests of the parties involved must be an
unceasing one.

It is well known that the Daily Mail had a warning at the beginning of 1981 about
their role in respect of publication of matters ventilated in privacy in committal
proceedings. They acknowledged that they were transgressing the rules laid down by
c Parliament at that time. But we wish to say at once that we have not allowed that failure
by the newspaper to conform to an Act of Parliament to influence us in any way in the
matter of punishment, which must exclusively, in our judgment, now relate to what was
done in October last year in very different circumstances.

We turn first of all to the activities of Mr English. He is a very experienced editor. He
knows well what great responsibilities he carries, when day by day he is surveying and
d controlling the contents of what should and what should not go into the widely circulated
newspaper, which is, generally speaking, under his direction. It so happens that on the
relevant occasions he was absent from the office, and so for most of what went on leading
up to the eventual publication of the article by Mr Muggeridge, he could not be said to
be in any way personally responsible. Moreover, as he states in his affidavit and we
accept, when he did see the article immediately before publication, it having occurred to
e him that it might be taken by some to refer to the trial by Dr Arthur, he took the
precaution of advising the associate editor to ensure that it received the approval of the
legal adviser who at night examines material of this kind for the possibility of
contemptuous material.

We have an affidavit from the gentleman who looked at the article at the invitation of
the associate editor for this purpose. He gave then as his opinion, and he has repeated in
f an affidavit to this court, that he did not regard the article as being capable of being read
by anyone as referable to the trial of Dr Arthur. We think that that was a mistaken view
and that if he read the Act more carefully, he would not have formed it.

In those circumstances we think it right to exculpate the editor altogether. We do not
therefore pass any penalty of any kind on him.

I now turn to the newspaper itself. There is no doubt, as counsel for the respondents
g has pointed out, that this was in many ways a complex matter, and the decision as to
whether or not material falls to be considered as contemptuous involves an intellectual
exercise which sometimes is not easily resolved. We are asked to say that on this occasion
what occurred was an excusable error of judgment. Parliament sought to tilt the balance
by enacting s 5 in favour of the press. No bad faith is alleged against the newspaper, nor
anyone concerned with it. That must of course weigh very heavily in favour of a
h newspaper on an occasion such as this. If bad faith is averred and is established, there can
be no doubt whatsoever that the penalty imposed by a court can in certain circumstances
be condign.

Nevertheless, whilst we acknowledge the difficulties and accept the care which was
taken by those who looked at this article before it was printed and who to some extent
altered it, we feel that discretion demanded a sharper cutting edge to the editorial knife.
j If a knife as sharp as that had been used, we have no doubt that this act of contempt
would not have been committed.

However in the light of the problems which the press at that time were exposed to by
this new legislation, which we have taken some time to consider, as is evident from the
length of the adjournment from the hearing of this case and giving of this judgment, we
believe that justice demands that we should do no more than pass on the Daily Mail a
nominal fine. In this context nominal means, we think, a fine of £500. This is a great

newspaper which has a very large circulation. No more-need to be said in furtherance of our judgment nor about the punishment, than this, the absence of bad faith has weighed *a* very heavily in favour of both the editor and the owners of the Daily Mail.

Application granted. Leave to appeal to the House of Lords.

Solicitors: *Director of Public Prosecutions; Swepstone, Walsh & Son* (for the respondents).

Jacqueline Charles   Barrister. *b*

Appeal
The respondents appealed to the House of Lords with leave of the House granted on 19 February 1982.

Lord Rawlinson QC and *Richard Rampton* for the respondents.
Simon D Brown and *Andrew Collins* for the Attorney General. *c*

Their Lordships took time for consideration.

15 July. The following opinions were delivered.

d
LORD DIPLOCK. My Lords, this is an appeal brought by the editor and publishers of the Daily Mail newspaper against a decision of the Divisional Court on 16 December 1981, holding them to be guilty of contempt of court by publishing an article entitled 'The vision of life that wins my vote' on 15 October 1980, which was the morning of the third day of the trial in the Crown Court at Leicester of a well-known paediatrician, Dr Arthur, on a charge of murdering a three-day-old mongoloid baby boy by giving *e* instructions that it should be treated with a drug which had caused it to die from starvation. The question of the punishment to be imposed for these contempts was adjourned until 19 February 1982, when the court decided that no penalty should be imposed on the editor, but fined the publishers the sum of £500 and ordered them to pay the Attorney General's costs.

The case provided the first opportunity for judicial consideration of the changes in the *f* law of contempt of court that have been effected by the Contempt of Court Act 1981; and since it raises, in particular, questions as to the extent to which discussion in the media of a matter of general public interest is to be curbed because of the effect that it may have on contemporaneous legal proceedings, it is necessary to start by stating in summary form the circumstances in which the article was published and the events that had preceded its publication. They can be found in greater detail in the judgment of the *g* Divisional Court. The matter of public interest with which the article dealt was whether it can ever be morally justifiable to allow newly-born babies, however direly handicapped physically and mentally they may be, to die as a result of withholding from them medical treatment by which they could have been kept alive longer.

Your Lordships can, I think, take judicial notice of the fact that with the recent advances made in medical science which now enables doctors to keep alive severely *h* handicapped children and the incurable and painfully sick and the senile old who would otherwise have died a natural death, there has in the past few years been a lively controversy whether it is morally justified deliberately to refrain from using every resource available to medical science to keep alive persons in these categories whose disabilities will preclude them from living what would be regarded by an ordinary human being as a worthwhile sentient life at all. Indeed, the controversy is hardly as *j* recent as all that. Arthur Hugh Clough's couplet written in the mid-nineteenth century:

'Thou shall not kill; but needst not strive
Officiously to keep alive'

shows that the issue is of long standing.

In December 1977 the Society for the Protection of Unborn Children, which was
formed in 1967 as a pressure group opposed to the liberalisation of the abortion laws and
now has over 30,000 members, decided to take up the cause of severely handicapped
babies whose lives they believed it had become a developing practice among doctors to
terminate within a few days of birth by the use of drugs or the deliberate deprivation of
nourishment.

A special effort to publicise this new aspect of the society's objects was made in 1981
which had been designated the International Year of the Disabled.

In February 1981 Dr Arthur had been charged at Derby City Magistrates' Court with
murdering a mongoloid baby, who had been born three days before. It was alleged
against him that he had administered to the new-born child a drug which prevented it
from taking nourishment, as a result of which it had died of starvation three days after
birth. These allegations, however, were not made public at the time of the committal
proceedings, as reporting restrictions were not removed. Those proceedings ended in
March 1981 with his committal for trial at the Crown Court at Leicester.

On 6 June 1981 the member of Parliament for North-West Croydon died and it
became necessary to hold a by-election, for which the polling day, by a coincidence, was
eventually fixed for 22 October 1981, a date which turned out to be in the middle of Dr
Arthur's trial. On 28 June an announcement was made to the press by the Society for the
Protection of Unborn Children that Mrs Marilyn Carr, a woman who had been born
without arms, intended to run as an independent 'pro-life' candidate in the by-election,
taking as a main plank in her election campaign the stopping of the practice that she
asserted was developing in some British hospitals of killing new-born handicapped
babies.

During the following month, Mrs Carr continued to seek by various means to obtain
publicity for this aspect of her election campaign, with what degree of success does not
appear in the material before your Lordships. But public interest in the controversy
about the morality of allowing babies born with severe incurable mental and physical
handicaps to die as a result of depriving them of medical treatment whereby their lives
could have been prolonged was fired, during August 1981, by the wide publicity given
to a decision of the Court of Appeal allowing an appeal in a case in which the parents of
a mongoloid child had refused their consent to an operation which would prolong its life
and the surgeon, respecting the parents' wishes, had refused to undertake the operation
and had expressed his belief that the great majority of surgeons would have reached the
same decision if faced with a similar situation. The Court of Appeal, reversing the
decision of the judge, made an order that the operation should be performed.

The controversy, though it may have temporarily died down, was not allowed to lapse
and on 3 October there appeared in a Sunday newspaper with a wide circulation, an
article by a well-known disc jockey, Tony Blackburn, defending the opposite point of
view to that of Mrs Carr, viz that the termination of life of unborn babies who are
hopelessly handicapped is morally justified.

On 1 October notice was given that the poll in the by-election would be held on 22
October and on 6 October Mrs Marilyn Carr became a candidate, and published her
election address. The well-known journalist and broadcaster, Mr Malcolm Muggeridge,
had agreed to speak for her at a public meeting to be held on Tuesday, 20 October, two
days before the poll.

On 13 October the trial of Dr Arthur started at the Crown Court at Leicester. It
attracted great public interest and was prominently reported in the Daily Mail and in the
national press generally on the following day. On that day, the editorial staff of the Daily
Mail learnt through a press release issued by Mr Malcolm Muggeridge that he was going
to speak at an election meeting in support of Mrs Carr's pro-life candidature in the
Croydon by-election. It was decided to invite him to put what he intended to say into
the form of an article for publication in the Daily Mail. This he did. It was published on
the following day, 15 October. This is the publication that the Divisional Court held was
a contempt of court. It was drawn to the attention of the trial judge who instructed that

a copy of the article should be sent to the Attorney General whose consent is now required for proceedings for a contempt of court. The judge commented:

'I think that it is highly unfortunate that any [paper]. . . . should publish an article of this kind in the middle of a trial which is very sensitive and very emotionally charged in the terms that appear in this article. I think it is quite deplorable.'

Dr Arthur's trial continued until 3 November. At the close of the prosecution's case, the judge had directed a verdict of 'Not Guilty' on the charge of murder, but left to the jury a charge of attempted murder, of which Dr Arthur was acquitted on 3 November 1981.

The article complained of was directed exclusively to Mr Muggeridge's support of Mrs Carr's candidature in the by-election because of her support of the pro-life cause and in particular her opposition to deliberate failure to keep alive newly-born babies suffering from what are presently regarded as incurable physical or mental disabilities so severe as to deprive them of all possibility of their enjoying what a normal person would regard as a life that was worth living. For any human being to arrogate to himself the right to decide whether a human being was fit to be born or to go on living was regarded by Mr Muggeridge as contrary to Christian morality which regarded all human life as sacred. There was no mention in the article of Dr Arthur's trial.

The first part of the article described Mrs Carr herself and how she had succeeded in overcoming the terrible physical handicap with which she had been born and in carving out a useful career for herself. He wrote, in a passage principally relied on by the Attorney General as amounting to contempt of court:

'To-day, the chances of such a baby surviving would be very small indeed. Someone would surely recommend letting her die of starvation or otherwise disposing of her.'

The article then continued with a skilful piece of polemical journalism which concluded with the following passages derisive of those whose views he was condemning:

'Are human beings to be culled like livestock? No more sick or misshapen bodies, no more disturbed or twisted minds, no more hereditary idiots or mongoloid children. Babies not up to scratch to be destroyed, before or after birth, as would also the old beyond repair. *With the developing skills of modern medicine, the human race could be pruned and carefully tended until only the perfect blooms—the beauty queens, the Mensa IQs, the athletes—remained.*' [Mr Muggeridge's emphasis.]

The article then went on to contrast this with what the writer claimed to be the Christian view of the equal sanctity of all human life, whatever may be the individual human being's physical or mental qualities or deficiencies. As an exemple of a devotion to this view of Christian morality, he cited Mother Teresa of Calcutta, to whose work and outlook the last third of the article was devoted.

My lords, that part of the Contempt of Court Act 1981 which is relevant to this appeal is to be found in the first seven sections. These appear under the crossheading 'Strict liability'. They deal with the publication to the public or a section of the public of matter which tends to interfere with the course of justice in particular legal proceedings, and they seek to hold the balance between the competing public interest of what American lawyers pithily described as 'fair trial and free press'. Apart from the provisions of ss 11 and 12 of the Administration of Justice Act 1960, of which the former is now repealed and replaced by s 3 of the Contempt of Court Act 1981, the law as to contempt of court before the passing of the 1981 Act was entirely 'judge-made' law, and the remedies for it lay within a virtually unfettered discretion of the individual judge or Divisional Court which remained unappealable until by the Administration of Justice Act 1960 a right of appeal to the Court of Appeal, and ultimately to this House, was granted in matters of contempt of court. The distinction was blurred between publications that did *not*

amount to a contempt of court and those which, although 'technically' they did, were
a regarded by the court before which the matter came as being so venial as not to merit any
punishment or even an order to pay the costs; and the criteria for determining where in
a particular case the balance lay between fair trial and free press can hardly be said to have
been rendered clear-cut by obiter dicta to be found in the five separate speeches in this
House in *A-G v Times Newspapers Ltd* [1973] 3 All ER 54, [1974] AC 273. These were
two-fold mischiefs which, as it seems to me, the first seven sections of the 1981 Act were
b intended to remedy.

In the instant appeal your Lordships will be primarily concerned with the construction
of s 2(2) and s 5 of the 1981 Act; but for this purpose it is helpful to read them in the
context of the remaining sections appearing under the cross-heading 'Strict liability', and
since the text of the Act, being recent, may not yet be readily available it is convenient
to reproduce all seven sections here:

c
'Strict liability

1. In this Act "the strict liability rule" means the rule of law whereby conduct
may be treated as a contempt of court as tending to interfere with the course of
justice in particular legal proceedings regardless of intent to do so.

2.—(1) The strict liability rule applies only in relation to publications, and for
d this purpose "publication" includes any speech, writing, broadcast or other
communication in whatever form, which is addressed to the public at large or any
section of the public.

(2) The strict liability rule applies only to a publication which creates a substantial
risk that the course of justice in the proceedings in question will be seriously
impeded or prejudiced.

(3) The strict liability rule applies to a publication only if the proceedings in
e question are active within the meaning of this section at the time of the publication.

(4) Schedule 1 applies for determining the times at which proceedings are to be
treated as active within the meaning of this section.

3.—(1) A person is not guilty of contempt of court under the strict liability rule
as the publisher of any matter to which that rule applies if at the time of publication
(having taken all reasonable care) he does not know and has no reason to suspect that
f relevant proceedings are active.

(2) A person is not guilty of contempt of court under the strict liability rule as the
distributor of a publication containing any such matter if at the time of distribution
(having taken all reasonable care) he does not know that it contains such matter and
has no reason to suspect that it is likely to do so.

(3) The burden of proof of any fact tending to establish a defence afforded by this
g section to any person lies upon that person.

(4) Section 11 of the Administration of Justice Act 1960 is repealed.

4.—(1) Subject to this section a person is not guilty of contempt of court under
the strict liability rule in respect of a fair and accurate report of legal proceedings
held in public, published contemporaneously and in good faith.

(2) In any such proceedings the court may, where it appears to be necessary for
h avoiding a substantial risk of prejudice to the administration of justice in those
proceedings, or in any other proceedings pending or imminent, order that the
publication of any report of the proceedings, or any part of the proceedings, be
postponed for such period as the court thinks necessary for that purpose.

(3) For the purposes of subsection (1) of this section and of section 3 of the Law
i of Libel Amendment Act 1888 (privilege) a report of proceedings shall be treated as
published contemporaneously—(a) in the case of a report of which publication is
postponed pursuant to an order under subsection (2) of this section, if published as
soon as practicable after that order expires; (b) in the case of a report of committal
proceedings of which publication is permitted by virtue only of subsection (3) of

section 8 of the Magistrates' Court Act 1980, if published as soon as practicable after publication is so permitted.

(4) Subsection (9) of the said section 8 is repealed.

5. A publication made as or as part of a discussion in good faith of public affairs or other matters of general public interest is not to be treated as a contempt of court under the strict liability rule if the risk of impediment or prejudice to particular legal proceedings is merely incidental to the discussion.

6. Nothing in the foregoing provisions of this Act—(a) prejudices any defence available at common law to a charge of contempt of court under the strict liability rule; (b) implies that any publication is punishable as contempt of court under that rule which would not be so punishable apart from those provisions; (c) restricts liability for contempt of court in respect of conduct intended to impede or prejudice the administration of justice.

7. Proceedings for a contempt of court under the strict liability rule (other than Scottish proceedings) shall not be instituted except by or with the consent of the Attorney General or on the motion of a court having jurisdiction to deal with it.'

The long title of the 1981 Act is 'An Act to amend the law relating to contempt of court and related matters', and it is apparent from s 6(a) and (b) that such changes as ss 1 to 5 make in the existing law are intended to effect some reduction in its severity in its application to those responsible for publications which may have a tendency to interfere with the course of justice in particular legal proceedings. So far as the reported cases go, the 'strict liability rule', as defined in s 1, had only been applied to conduct which involved some publication of offending material; and it can reasonably be inferred from the provision in s 2(1) which confines the ambit of the fasciculus of sections to publications addressed to the public at large or a section of the public, that the principal intended beneficiaries of any reduction in severity were the media, viz the press, television and radio. It is true that public speakers also are included; but unless their speeches are reported by the media these are likely to be exonerated by s 2(2).

There is, of course, no question that the article in the Daily Mail of which complaint is made by the Attorney General was a 'publication' within the meaning of s 2(1). That being so, it appears to have been accepted in the Divisional Court by both parties that the onus of proving that the article satisfied the conditions stated on s 2(2) lay on the Attorney General and that, if he satisfied that onus, the onus lay on the defendants to prove that it satisfied the conditions stated in s 5. For my part, I am unable to accept that this represents the effect of the relationship of s 5 to s 2(2). Section 5 does not take the form of a proviso or an exception to s 2(2). It stands on an equal footing with it. It does not set out exculpatory matter. Like s 2(2) it states what publications shall *not* amount to contempt of court despite their tendency to interfere with the course of justice in particular legal proceedings.

For the publication to constitute a contempt of court under the strict liability rule, it must be shown that the publication satisfies the criterion for which s 2(2) provides, viz that it 'creates a substantial risk that the course of justice in the proceedings in question will be seriously impeded or prejudiced'. It is only if it falls within s 5 that anything more need be shown. So logically the first question always is: has the publication satisfied the criterion laid down by s 2(2).

My Lords, the first thing to be observed about this criterion is that the risk that has to be assessed is that which was created by the publication of the allegedly offending matter at the time when it was published. The public policy that underlies the strict liability rule in contempt of court is deterrence. Trial by newspaper or, as it should be more compendiously expressed today, trial by the media, is not to be permitted in this country. That the risk that was created by the publication when it was actually published does not ultimately affect the outcome of the proceedings is, as Lord Goddard CJ said in *R v Evening Standard Co Ltd, ex p A-G* [1954] 1 All ER 1026 at 1028, [1954] 1 QB 578 at

582, neither here nor there. If there was a reasonable possibility that it might have done
so if in the period subsequent to the publication the proceedings had not taken the course
that in fact they did and Dr Arthur was acquitted, the offence was complete. The true
course of justice must not at any stage be put at risk.

Next for consideration is the concatenation in the subsection of the adjective
'substantial' and the adverb 'seriously', the former to describe the degree of risk, the latter
to describe the degree of impediment or prejudice to the course of justice. 'Substantial'
is hardly the most apt word to apply to 'risk' which is a noumenon. In combination I
take the two words to be intended to exclude a risk that is only remote. With regard to
the adverb 'seriously' a perusal of the cases cited in *A-G v Times Newspapers Ltd* [1973] 3
All ER 54, [1974] AC 273 discloses that the adjective 'serious' has from time to time been
used as an alternative to 'real' to describe the degree of risk of interfering with the course
of justice, but not the degree of interference itself. It is, however, an ordinary English
word that is not intrinsically inapt when used to describe the extent of an impediment
or prejudice to the cause of justice in particular legal proceedings, and I do not think that
for the purposes of the instant appeal any attempt to paraphrase it is necessary or would
be helpful. The subsection applies to all kinds of legal proceedings, not only criminal
prosecutions before a jury. If, as in the instant case and probably in most other criminal
trials on indictment, it is the outcome of the trial or the need to discharge the jury
without proceeding to a verdict that is put at risk, there can be no question that that
which in the course of justice is put at risk is as serious as anything could be.

My Lords, that Mr Malcolm Muggeridge's article was capable of prejudicing the jury
against Dr Arthur at the early stage of his trial when it was published, seems to me to be
clear. It suggested that it was a common practice among paediatricians to do that which
Dr Arthur was charged with having done, because they thought that it was justifiable in
the interests of humanity even though it was against the law. At this stage of the trial the
jury did not know what Dr Arthur's defence was going to be; and whether at that time
the risk of the jury's being influenced by their recollection of the article when they came
eventually to consider their verdict appeared to be more than a remote one, was a matter
which the judge before whom the trial was being conducted was in the best position to
evaluate; even though his evaluation, although it should carry weight, would not be
binding on the Divisional Court or on your Lordships. The judge thought at that stage
of the trial that the risk was substantial, not remote. So, too, looking at the matter in
retrospect, did the Divisional Court despite the fact that the risk had not turned into an
actuality since Dr Arthur had by then been acquitted. For my part I am not prepared to
dissent from this evaluation. I consider that the publication of the article on the third
day of what was to prove a lengthy trial satisfied the criterion for which s 2(2) of the 1981
Act provides.

The article, however, fell also within the category dealt with in s 5. It was made, in
undisputed good faith, as a discussion in itself of public affairs, viz Mrs Carr's candidature
as an independent 'pro-life' candidate in the North-West Croydon by-election for which
the polling day was in one week's time. It was also part of a wider discussion on a matter
of general public interest that had been proceeding intermittently over the last three
months, on the moral justification of mercy killing and in particular of allowing newly-
born hopelessly handicapped babies to die. So it was for the Attorney General to show
that the risk of prejudice to the fair trial of Dr Arthur, which I agree was created by the
publication of the article at the stage the trial had reached when it was published, was not
'merely incidental' to the discussion of the matter with which the article dealt.

My Lords, any article published at the time when Dr Arthur was being tried which
asserted that it was a common practice among paediatricians to let severely physically or
mentally handicapped new-born babies die of starvation or otherwise dispose of them
would (as, in common with the trial judge and the Divisional Court, I have already
accepted), involve a substantial risk of prejudicing his fair trial. But an article supporting
Mrs Carr's candidature in the by-election as a pro-life candidate that contained no such
assertion would depict her as tilting at 'imaginary windmills. One of the main planks of

the policy for which she sought the suffrage of the electors was that these things did happen and ought to be stopped.

I have drawn attention to the passages principally relied on by the Divisional Court as causing a risk of prejudice that was not 'merely incidental to the discussion'. The court described them as 'unnecessary' to the discussion and as 'accusations'. The test, however, is not whether an article could have been written as effectively without these passages or whether some other phraseology might have been substituted for them that could have reduced the risk of prejudicing Dr Arthur's fair trial; but it is whether the risk created by the words actually chosen by the author was 'merely incidental to the discussion', which I take to mean, no more than an incidental consequence of expounding its main theme. The Divisional Court also apparently regarded the passages complained of as disqualified from the immunity conferred by s 5 because they consisted of 'accusations' whereas the court considered that 'discussion' was confined to 'the airing of views and the propounding and debating of principles and arguments'. I cannot accept this limited meaning of 'discussion' in the section. As already pointed out, in the absence of any accusation, believed to be true by Mrs Carr and Mr Muggeridge, that it was a common practice among some doctors to do what they are accused of doing in the passages complained of the article would lose all its point whether as support for Mrs Carr's parliamentary candidature or as a contribution to the wider controversy as to the justifiability of mercy killing. The article would be emasculated into a mere contribution to a purely hypothetical problem appropriate, it may be, for debate between academic successors of the mediaeval schoolmen, remote from all public affairs and devoid of any general public interest to readers of the Daily Mail.

My Lords, the article that is the subject of the instant case appears to me to be in nearly all respects the antithesis of the article which this House (pace a majority of the judges of the European Court of Human Rights) held to be a contempt of court in A-G v Times Newspapers Ltd [1973] 3 All ER 54, [1974] AC 273. There the whole subject of the article was the pending civil actions against the Distillers Co arising out of their having placed on the market the new drug Thalidomide, and the whole purpose of it was to put pressure on that company in the lawful conduct of their defence in those actions. In the instant case, in contrast, there is in the article no mention at all of Dr Arthur's trial. It may well be that many readers of the Daily Mail who saw the article and had read also the previous day's report of Dr Arthur's trial, and certainly if they were members of the jury at that trial, would think 'That is the sort of thing that Dr Arthur is being tried for; it appears to be something that quite a lot of doctors do'. But the risk of their thinking that and allowing it to prejudice their minds in favour of finding him guilty on evidence that did not justify such a finding seems to me to be properly described in ordinary English language as 'merely incidental' to any meaningful discussion of Mrs Carr's election policy as a pro-life candidate in the by-election due to be held before Dr Arthur's trial was likely to be concluded, or to any meaningful discussion of the wider matters of general public interest involved in the current controversy as to the justification of mercy killing. To hold otherwise would have prevented Mrs Carr from putting forward and obtaining publicity for what was a main plank in her election programme and would have stifled all discussion in the press on the wider controversy about mercy killing from the time that Dr Arthur was charged in the magistrates' court in February 1981 until the date of his acquittal at the beginning of November of that year; for those are the dates between which under s 2(3) and Sch 1, the legal proceedings against Dr Arthur would be 'active' and so attract the strict liability rule.

Such gagging of bona fide public discussion in the press of controversial matters of general public interest, merely because there are in existence contemporaneous legal proceedings in which some particular instance of those controversial matters may be in issue, is what s 5 of the Contempt of Court Act 1981 was in my view intended to prevent. I would allow this appeal.

LORD ELWYN-JONES. My Lords, I have had the advantage of reading in draft the *a* speech of my noble and learned friend Lord Diplock. I agree with his reasons and would therefore allow the appeal.

LORD KEITH OF KINKEL. My Lords, I have had the benefit of reading in draft the speech delivered by my noble and learned friend Lord Diplock. I agree with it, and for the reasons he gives I too would allow the appeal.

b

LORD SCARMAN. My Lords, I have the advantage of reading in draft the speech delivered by my noble and learned friend Lord Diplock. I agree with him, and would allow the appeal.

LORD BRANDON OF OAKBROOK. My Lords, I have had the advantage of *c* reading in advance the speech prepared by my noble and learned friend Lord Diplock. I agree with it and for the reasons which he gives I would allow the appeal.

Appeal allowed.

Solicitors: *Swepstone, Walsh & Son* (for the respondents); *Director of Public Prosecutions.*

Mary Rose Plummer   Barrister.

Fay v Fay   a

HOUSE OF LORDS
LORD DIPLOCK, LORD SCARMAN, LORD ROSKILL, LORD BRIDGE OF HARWICH AND LORD BRANDON
OF OAKBROOK
10 JUNE, 1 JULY 1982

Divorce – Petition – Petition within three years of marriage – Discretion to allow – Exceptional   **b**
hardship or exceptional depravity – Criteria for leave – Evidence required – Matrimonial Causes
Act 1973, s 3(2) – Matrimonial Causes Rules 1977, r 5(2)(a).

Divorce – Petition within three years of marriage – Exceptional hardship – Hardship including
future hardship – Matrimonial Causes Act 1973, s 3(2).
  c

It is to be presumed that in choosing the imprecise concepts of 'exceptional hardship' or
'exceptional depravity' as the criteria which a petitioner has to meet in order to obtain
leave under s 3(2)*[a]* of the Matrimonial Causes Act 1973 to petition for divorce within
three years of the date of marriage, Parliament deliberately intended that the decision on
what is or is not exceptional hardship or depravity in a particular case should be a matter   **d**
for the judge at first instance to decide by making his own subjective value judgment as
to whether the hardship or depravity was out of the ordinary, when judged by prevailing
standards of acceptable behaviour between spouses and after taking account of all relevant
circumstances. It would be wrong therefore for an appellate court to attempt to define
the concepts of 'exceptional hardship' or 'exceptional depravity' with any precision or to
lay down guidelines as to how those concepts are to be applied. Furthermore, the   **e**
decision of the judge at first instance should be treated as final unless it can be shown to
have been clearly wrong (see p 923 g, p 926 d to g and p 928 a b d and g to j, post); *Hillier
v Hillier and Latham* [1958] 2 All ER 261 and *C v C* [1979] 1 All ER 556 approved.

'Exceptional hardship' is not limited to past hardship but includes present and future
hardship and therefore the court may properly take into account the hardship suffered
by a young wife in having to wait for the elapse of three years from the date of marriage   **f**
before petitioning for divorce (see p 923 g, p 926 a b and p 928 c and g to j, post); dicta of
Romer LJ in *Hillier v Hillier and Latham* [1958] 2 All ER at 263, of Pearson LJ in *Brewer
v Brewer* [1964] 1 All ER at 543, and of Ormrod LJ in *C v C* [1979] 1 All ER at 560
considered.

Where 'exceptional hardship' is pleaded the facts and matters relied on to show that
the applicant has suffered or is suffering exceptional hardship as a result of the
respondent's conduct must be included in the evidence and it is not sufficient merely to   **g**
comply with the evidential requirements set out in r 5(2)(a)*[b]* of the Matrimonial Causes
Rules 1977. Thus there must be evidence of the extent of the applicant's suffering, e g
evidence of ill-health or of nervous sensitivity or tension resulting in severe emotional or
mental stress or breakdown. In particular, there should be evidence of the circumstances
relied on as constituting the exceptional character of the hardship suffered (see p 923 g,   **h**
p 926 h and p 928 e and g to j, post).

Notes

For leave to petition for divorce within three years of marriage, see 13 Halsbury's Laws
(4th edn) paras 557–559, and for cases on the subject, see 27(1) Digest (Reissue) 355–357,
2614–2628.

For the Matrimonial Causes Act 1973, see 43 Halsbury's Statutes (3rd edn) 539.   *j*

For the Matrimonial Causes Rules 1977, see 10 Halsbury's Statutory Instruments (4th
reissue) 233.

---

a   Section 3 is set out at p 923 j to p 924 c, post
b   Rule 5 is set out at p 924 f to h, post

Cases referred to in opinions

a   *Brewer v Brewer* [1964] 1 All ER 539, [1964] 1 WLR 403, CA, 27(1) Digest (Reissue) 356, 2621.

C v C [1979] 1 All ER 556, [1980] Fam 23, [1979] 2 WLR 95, CA, Digest (Cont Vol E) 260, 2628b.

Fisher v Fisher [1948] P 263, CA, 27(1) Digest (Reissue) 355, 2617.

Hillier v Hillier and Latham [1958] 2 All ER 261, [1958] P 186, [1958] 2 WLR 937, CA,

b   27(1) Digest (Reissue) 356, 2622.

Winter v Winter [1944] P 72, CA, 27(1) Digest (Reissue) 355, 2614.

Cases also cited

Blackwell v Blackwell (1973) 117 SJ 939, CA.

Bowman v Bowman [1949] 2 All ER 127, [1949] P 353, CA.

c   *Charlesby v Charlesby* (1947) 176 LT 532, CA.

Fletcher v Titt (1979) 10 Fam Law 151, CA.

Larkins v Larkins (1979) 10 Fam Law 147, CA.

PMK, Re (1981) unreported, Northern Ireland.

Simpson v Simpson [1954] 2 All ER 546, [1954] 1 WLR 994, CA.

Woolf v Woolf (1978) 9 Fam Law 216, CA.

d

Appeal

Tracy Elizabeth Fay appealed with leave of the Court of Appeal, granted on 20 November 1981, against the decision of the Court of Appeal (Arnold P, O'Connor LJ, Kilner Brown J) dated 20 November 1981 dismissing her appeal from the order of his Honour Judge Watts made on 29 September 1981 refusing the application of the appellant for leave to

e   present a petition for dissolution of marriage to the respondent, James Peter Fay, within three years of the date of the marriage. The facts are set out in the judgment of Lord Scarman.

R Spon-Smith for the appellant.
The respondent was not represented.

f

Their Lordship took time for consideration.

1 July. The following opinions were delivered.

LORD DIPLOCK. My Lords, I have had the advantage of reading in draft the speech

g   of my noble and learned friend Lord Scarman. I agree with it and for the reasons he gives I would dismiss this appeal.

LORD SCARMAN. My Lords, this appeal brought to the House by leave of the Court of Appeal is concerned with the interpretation of s 3 of the Matrimonial Causes Act 1973 and the practice of the courts, appellate as well as at first instance, in dealing with cases

h   under the section.

The section has proved to be difficult to apply with any consistency as between one case and another. The difficulty arises not from the lack of judicial attempts to do so but from the imprecision of the concepts which it embodies and from the history of the law.

The section imposes a restriction on petitions for divorce before the expiration of three years from the date of the marriage and is in these terms:

j

> '(1) Subject to subsection (2) below, no petition for divorce shall be presented to the court before the expiration of the period of three years from the date of the marriage (hereafter in this section referred to as "the specified period").
>
> (2) A judge of the court may, on an application made to him, allow the presentation of a petition for divorce within the specified period on the ground that the case is one of exceptional hardship suffered by the petitioner or of exceptional

depravity on the part of the respondent; but in determining the application the judge shall have regard to the interests of any child of the family and to the question *a* whether there is reasonable probability of a reconciliation between the parties during the specified period.

(3) If it appears to the court, at the hearing of a petition for divorce presented in pursuance of leave granted under subsection (2) above, that the leave was obtained by the petitioner by any misrepresentation or concealment of the nature of the case, the court may—(*a*) dismiss the petition, without prejudice to any petition which *b* may be brought after the expiration of the specified period upon the same facts, or substantially the same facts, as those proved in support of the dismissed petition; or (*b*) if it grants a decree, direct that no application to make the decree absolute shall be made during the specified period.

(4) Nothing in this section shall be deemed to prohibit the presentation of a petition based upon matters which occurred before the expiration of the specified *c* period.'

It is the re-enactment of a provision introduced into the divorce law as s 1 of the Matrimonial Causes Act 1937. It has survived until the present day, unaltered save for some drafting amendments and some rearrangement. But, while it has survived, very little else in the divorce law has. The Divorce Reform Act 1969 introduced the major reform, namely the substitution of irretrievable breakdown of marriage for the *d* matrimonial offence as the sole ground for divorce. Inevitably this reform, which was effective from 1 January 1971 has influenced the courts in their approach to the section. When matrimonial offence was the ground for divorce, the judges naturally and properly required by way of evidence from the applicant something more than the bare recital of a matrimonial offence if they were to find 'exceptional' hardship or depravity. Since 1971 even this low level of guidance has disappeared.   *e*

And the difficulties have not been eased by the rule of court with which an applicant for leave has to comply. It is now r 5 of the Matrimonial Causes Rules 1977, SI 1977/344, and is in these terms:

'(1) An application under section 3 of the Act of 1973 for leave to present a petition for divorce before the expiration of three years from the date of the *f* marriage shall be made by originating application.

(2) The application shall be filed in the divorce county court to which it is proposed to present the petition, together with—(*a*) an affidavit by the applicant exhibiting a copy of the proposed petition and stating—(i) the grounds of the application, (ii) particulars of the hardship or depravity alleged, (iii) whether there has been any previous application for leave, (iv) whether any, and if so what, *g* attempts at reconciliation have been made, (v) particulars of any circumstances which may assist the court in determining whether there is a reasonable probability of reconciliation between the parties, (vi) the date of birth of each of the parties or, if it be the case, that he or she has attained 18; (*b*) a copy of the application and of the supporting affidavit for service on the respondent; and (*c*) unless otherwise directed on an application made *ex parte*, a certificate of the marriage.   *h*

(3) C.C.R. Order 6, rule 4(2)(*c*)(ii) and (*d*) (which deal with the service of an originating application), shall not apply but the registrar shall annex to the copy of the application for service a copy of the supporting affidavit and a notice in Form 1 with Form 6 attached.'

The rule has been all too often treated as a guide to the evidence required by the *j* section. But it is not: it does no more than state a minimum in the absence of which an application will not be entertained. It is neither the 'desideratum' nor the 'optimum': to find what the statute requires for the exercise of judgment in favour of the applicant one must look not to the rule but to the section.

In the face of these difficulties it is not surprising that the Court of Appeal has indicated that in its view the House should take a look at the section and attempt some

guidance as to the practice which should be followed in dealing with applications for the
a relief it offers. There are three fundamental questions to be considered: (1) the evidential
requirement to be satisfied by an applicant; (2) the approach to be followed by the judge
at first instance in dealing with applications under the section; and (3) the approach to be
followed by an appellate tribunal in reviewing a judge's decision under the section.

Mrs Fay, the applicant and the appellant in the Court of Appeal and this House, seeks
to be allowed to petition for divorce within the three year period on the ground that her
b case is one of exceptional hardship suffered by her. She was married on 19 July 1980,
when she was 17 years old. She applied for leave one year later, on 31 July 1981. She
sought to rely on her affidavit filed with the application. The affidavit complied with the
rule of court: but its bare recital of the matters required to be included by the rule gave
no clue as to the degree of the hardship which she asserted was exceptional. Indeed, her
affidavit did no more than incorporate as an exhibit the particulars of unreasonable
c behaviour alleged in her proposed petition. These particulars, if true, certainly revealed
a history of unreasonable behaviour on the part of the respondent: but there was no
material other than the particulars themselves to assist the judge in determining whether
the behaviour itself caused her to suffer exceptional hardship or whether there were any
other circumstances which could support an assessment of her hardship as exceptional.

The effective end of her marriage was on 28 July 1981, when she left home after an
d incident described in her written case as 'a particularly unpleasant assault'. There are no
children: and there is no prospect of reconciliation.

Her application under the section came before his Honour Judge Watts on 29
September 1981. The respondent did not appear, nor was he represented. The
application was refused. The judge delivered no judgment when dismissing the
application but in the course of the hearing he made a number of observations, from
e which it is clear, as the President pointed out in the Court of Appeal, that he concluded
that she had not made out a case of exceptional hardship. The President deduced from
the judge's observations that his reason for dismissing the application was that, in the
absence of exceptional hardship, the law did not permit him to exercise any discretion to
grant leave within the three-year period.

On appeal to the Court of Appeal, counsel for the applicant submitted that the proper
f conclusion was that this was a case of exceptional hardship, and that the judge was clearly
wrong in coming to the opposite conclusion. A second point was taken that the judge
had failed, in the exercise of his discretion, to take into account the impossibility of
reconciliation. The President, who delivered the leading judgment in the Court of
Appeal, formulated as the question in the case:

g '. . . whether it can be said by this court that the learned judge was clearly wrong
in the conclusion to which he came that there was not in this case exceptional
hardship. For my part, I cannot think that the matter is as clear as that. I do not
think, therefore, that this court would be justified in overruling the learned judge
on that point. If it is the fact that in 1981 a degree of hardship substantially less than
that which has in the past been regarded as other than exceptional, is to be regarded
h as so clearly constituting exceptional hardship that the court is justified in overruling
the decision to the opposite effect of the judge below, it seems to me that it is not for
this court to come to that conclusion. But it may very well be that this is a matter
which should have the attention of their Lordships in the House of Lords.'

Had he felt justified in holding the judge wrong on the question of exceptional hardship,
he would have been prepared to exercise the discretion conferred on the court by the
j section in favour of the applicant. O'Connor LJ agreed, adding that it must be clear, if
leave under the section is to be given, 'that there is something out of the ordinary in what
has happened'. Kilner-Brown J also agreed, and adverted to the danger 'of trying to
minimise the effect of the word "exceptional" that still remains in the wording of the
Act'.

In this House counsel for the appellant reviewed the case law, to which he had already
made reference in his admirably drafted written case, and made the following

submissions: (1) that whether or not the primary facts amount to exceptional hardship
or depravity is a matter of inference; (2) that, where there is no dispute as to the primary *a*
facts, the Court of Appeal is in as good a position as the judge at first instance to
determine whether the hardship (or depravity) is exceptional; (3) that, judged by
prevailing standards of acceptable behaviour between spouses, the hardship revealed by
the applicant's affidavit was exceptional; (4) that the hardship to which the section refers
is not limited to past hardship but includes present and future hardship; (5) that the court
may properly, therefore, take into account the hardship suffered by a young wife in *b*
having to wait until the period specified in the section has elapsed.

His criticism of the judgments in the Court of Appeal was that they had applied the
wrong test in reviewing the decision at first instance. They were not limited by any rule
against intervention unless satisfied the judge was clearly wrong, but were entitled to
substitute, and in this case should have substituted, their own 'inferential findings of fact'
for his. *c*

The fallacy in counsel's argument is that it confuses assessment with inference.
Undoubtedly, the section requires the judge to ask himself whether he is satisfied that,
on a provisional determination (for there is no trial) of the facts as disclosed in the
affidavit evidence, the would-be petitioner has suffered exceptional hardship. But he
does not proceed by inference, which is a process of reaching a finding of one fact from
primary evidence of the existence of another fact (or set of facts), but by assessment. For *d*
what is or is not exceptional is a matter of degree. The present case illustrates the
difference. There was plainly hardship suffered by the applicant as a result of her
husband's conduct and the breakdown of her marriage. But was it exceptional?
Applying prevailing standards and taking account of all relevant circumstances, the
judge had to make his assessment. He had to make a 'value' judgment, the values with
which he was concerned being not numerate as in the assessment of damages for personal *e*
injury but moral and social. Questions of degree, involving as they do a strong subjective
element, are best left to judges of first instance: and the particular statutory provision
now under review clearly places the responsibility not only of determining what is
exceptional but also for the exercise of discretion, if the hardship be assessed as exceptional, on the judge. The Court of Appeal were right, in my view, to hold that they
ought not to intervene unless it could be shown that the judge was clearly wrong. *f*

Can it be said, therefore, that the judge's decision was clearly wrong? The evidence is
totally inadequate to enable any such conclusion to be reached. It is not possible to define
with any precision what is meant by 'exceptional' hardship or depravity. The imprecision
of these concepts with the resultant impossibility of definition must have been
deliberately accepted as appropriate by the legislature and is itself an indication that the
determination of what is exceptional is essentially a matter for the judge. All that can be *g*
said with certainty is, to borrow the words of O'Connor LJ, that the hardship suffered by
the applicant (or the respondent's depravity) must be shown to be something out of the
ordinary.

There must, therefore, be evidence in a hardship case of the extent of the applicant's
suffering, eg evidence of ill-health, of nervous sensitivity or tension resulting in severe
emotional or mental stress or breakdown. In particular, evidence should be given of the *h*
circumstances relied on as constituting the exceptional character of the hardship suffered.

The two reported cases most helpful to an understanding of the way in which
applications under the section should be handled are decisions of the Court of Appeal:
Hillier v Hillier and Latham [1958] 2 All ER 261, [1958] P 186, decided under the old law,
and *C v C* [1979] 1 All ER 556, [1980] Fam 23, decided under the modern law.

In *Hillier's* case it was a husband's application. The wife had left him within a few *j*
months after the marriage. She never returned to him, but her vacillations whether to
come home or not caused him great distress, leading ultimately to something like a
nervous breakdown on his part. Some eleven months after the marriage the wife met a
man with whom she committed adultery. The judge dismissed the application. The
Court of Appeal, however, allowed further evidence to be given as to the husband's

a   suffering and were able to conclude on the basis of the new evidence that his worry and
strain were exceptional, resulting as they did in a nervous breakdown.
The case makes clear the need for full evidence as to the nature and extent of the
applicant's suffering. The court stressed (per Hodson and Romer LJJ [1958] 2 All ER 261
at 263, 264, [1958] P 186 at 190, 192) the need to approach each case 'subjectively', by
which they meant the need to look to the effect on the applicant of the situation which
had developed. The court should not merely 'confine itself to an objective view as to how
b   the ordinary man might be expected to react in given circumstances' (per Hodson LJ
[1958] 2 All ER 261 at 263, [1958] P 186 at 190). Romer LJ went on to say of the section
(then, s 2, Matrimonial Causes Act 1950) that in his view it included not only hardship
in the past but also 'the possibility or probability of exceptional hardship being suffered
in the future' if the applicant had to wait the full specified period before presenting his
petition (see [1958] 2 All ER 261 at 263, [1958] P 186 at 191). In a later case, *Brewer v*
c   *Brewer* [1964] 1 All ER 539 at 543, [1964] 1 WLR 403 at 412, Pearson LJ doubted
whether the view of Romer LJ could be correct on the wording of the section but
accepted that regard could be had to present suffering. If, as is obvious, present suffering
may include the prospect of future hardship, their difference of opinion is of little
importance. And in *C v C* [1979] 1 All ER 556 at 560, [1980] Fam 23 at 28 per Ormrod
LJ, Romer LJ's view was said to be 'now accepted'.
d   The case of *C v C* is most frequently cited for what the court said about exceptional
depravity. There have been very few cases since, in which reliance has been placed on
exceptional depravity: and, as Ormrod LJ, who delivered the judgment of the court
remarked, it seems to be unnecessary as most of such cases prove on analysis to be cases
of exceptional hardship (see [1979] 1 All ER 556 at 560, [1980] Fam 23 at 28). The
importance of *C v C* is, however, the court's treatment of exceptional hardship. As in
e   *Hillier's* case, the evidence before the judge at first instance was insufficient to make out
a case of exceptional hardship. The court allowed further evidence to be given, 'which
contained a considerable amount of new and relevant material'. In the result, the court
allowed the appeal and gave the wife leave to present a petition on the ground of
exceptional hardship. Two passages in the judgment of the court are of particular
importance. First ([1979] 1 All ER 556 at 558–559, [1980] Fam 23 at 26):
f   'Section 3 of the 1973 Act, and its predecessors, have troubled judges who have to
apply their provisions ever since these were first introduced by s 1 of the
Matrimonial Causes Act 1937. The principal difficulty lies in knowing what
standards to use in assessing exceptional hardship and what is meant by the phrase
"exceptional depravity". Both involve value judgments of an unusually subjective
character, so much so that in the earlier cases in this court these appeals were treated
g   as appeals from the exercise of a purely discretionary jurisdiction: *Winter v Winter*
[1944] P 72 and *Fisher v Fisher* [1948] P 263. Later, in *Brewer v Brewer* [1964] 1 All
ER 539, [1964] 1 WLR 403, it was held that exceptional hardship or exceptional
depravity involved provisional findings of fact. The difficulty arises, partly, because
all decisions at first instance are made in chambers and therefore cannot be reported
and, partly, because the reported cases in this court do not give much, if any,
h   guidance on the standards to be applied. Moreover, standards in society in these
matters are not stable and are subject to considerable changes over comparatively
short periods of time.'
        And, second, after referring to the difference of opinion between Romer LJ in *Hiller's*
case and Pearson LJ in *Brewer's* case, Ormrod LJ said ([1979] 1 All ER 556 at 560, [1980]
j   Fam 23 at 28):
            'Be that as it may, it is now accepted that in dealing with these applications the
judge may properly take into account hardship arising from the conduct of the
other spouse, present hardship, and hardship arising from having to wait until the
specified period has elapsed.'
        My Lords, I consider the approach of the Court of Appeal in the two cases cited and in

the present case to be correct. Applications under the section cannot have been conceived by the legislature as a mere first step in a long legal process, at each appellate stage of *a* which the court would be obliged to review all the facts so as to determine whether to substitute its view of what is exceptional for that of the judge. The law here is operating against a time scale of three years, and the language of the section supports the view that the judge's decision is final unless it can be shown to have been plainly wrong. Accordingly, I reject counsel's first two submissions and would uphold the decision and reasoning of the Court of Appeal.   *b*

As for counsel's third submission, I agree, of course, that what is exceptional must be judged by prevailing standards of acceptable behaviour between spouses. The true question is whether the evidence was sufficient: a point on which I have already expressed my opinion. I would accept his fourth and fifth submissions, subject to the comment that in the face of the language of the section (the past tense 'suffered') the strict view may well be, as Pearson LJ thought, that future hardship may be taken into account as a *c* present prospect rather than as a future event. But counsel's submissions on these points avail him nought. In the state of the evidence it was not possible for the Court of Appeal, nor is it possible for your Lordships, to say that the judge's conclusion was plainly wrong.

For these reasons I would dismiss the appeal. It was pressed on the House by counsel and suggested by the Court of Appeal that guidance might be offered as to the meaning of 'exceptional' in the context of the section. I hope that I have made clear that any *d* attempt to define a meaning would be a betrayal of the deliberate imprecision favoured by Parliament in entrusting the court with the power to grant leave to present an early petition. But guidance can be given as to the way in which professional advisers and judges should approach the section. The practice of confining the evidence to the bare minima required by r 5 of the 1977 rules is not satisfactory. The facts and matters relied on as showing that the applicant has suffered, or is suffering, exceptional hardship as a *e* result of the respondent's conduct must be included in the evidence. The *suffering* of exceptional hardship is an essential feature to the exercise of the court's power to allow the petition within the otherwise prohibited period. Secondly, the judges must be careful to avoid a superficial or perfunctory approach to the exercise of the power conferred on them. If a judge is in doubt, he would be wise to offer the applicant an opportunity of supplementing the evidence (as the Court of Appeal did in *Hillier* and *C* *f* *v C*). Finally, a judge should always state his reasons for his decision. In the exercise of a power operating on such 'subjective' material as the degree of hardship suffered by an applicant, review of his decision by an appellate court is unlikely to be effective unless the court is told the reasons which led the judge to the conclusion which in fact he reached.

I would, therefore, dismiss the appeal.

g

LORD ROSKILL. My Lords, I have had the advantage of reading in draft the speech of my noble and learned friend Lord Scarman. I agree with it and for the reasons he gives I would dismiss this appeal.

LORD BRIDGE OF HARWICH. My Lords, I agree entirely with the speech of my noble and learned friend Lord Scarman which I have had the advantage of reading in *h* draft. I would dismiss the appeal.

LORD BRANDON OF OAKBROOK. My Lords, I have had the advantage of reading in advance the speech prepared by my noble and learned friend Lord Scarman. I find myself wholly in agreement with it, and, for the reasons which he gives, I too would dismiss the appeal.   *j*

Appeal dismissed.

Solicitor: *Daniel Davies & Co* (for the appellant).

Mary Rose Plummer   Barrister.

Inland Revenue Commissioners v Trustees of Sir John Aird's Settlement

CHANCERY DIVISION

NOURSE J

17, 18 NOVEMBER, 16 DECEMBER 1981

Settlement – Contingent interest – Contingent interest distinguished from interest dependent on event bound to happen – Newspaper-Franco scheme – Interest subject to condition that beneficiary survive designated person – Designated person described by reference to newspaper announcement of his death – Possibility that no person would satisfy description of designated person remote – Whether interest dependent on real contingency.

By a deed of appointment dated 28 November 1975 the trustees of a settlement comprising a fund held on discretionary trust for, inter alios, the settlor's son, irrevocably appointed capital and income of part of the fund in favour of the settlor's son absolutely free from the trusts and from all further exercise of the powers contained in the settlement, contingently on his surviving a designated person for one day. The designated person was described in the deed of appointment as the person whose death occurred on Saturday, 29 November 1975 and who was the first in alphabetical order of the persons dying on that date to be named in the 'deaths' column of the earliest edition of The Times newspaper published in London on Monday, 1 December 1975 (or if there was no edition published on that date then of the earliest edition published after that date) and if no person answered that description the designated person was to be the person who would satisfy that description if references to the Daily Telegraph were substituted for references to The Times. The death of a Major B who died on 29 November 1975 was announced in The Times on 1 December 1975 and the settlor's son survived beyond midnight on 30 November 1975. In proceedings in respect of an assessment to capital transfer tax the question arose whether the interest conferred was in reality and in substance contingent on the settlor's son surviving another person (who might or might not materialise) for a period of one day or whether it was only contingent on his surviving until a specified time and date. There was evidence before the court that on at least one Monday over an unspecified period no death occurring on the preceding Saturday was reported in the 'deaths' column of The Times.

Held – A contingency was an event which might or might not happen, and if there was no real possibility that it would not happen, so that it was as good as certain that it would, it was a contingency without reality and substance and hence no contingency at all. But a real possibility was not the same as a probability; and, although it might be highly improbable that an event would happen, so long as there was a real possibility, however remote, that it would, the contingency was one of reality and substance. In the circumstances it was unnecessary to have more than one instance of a Monday edition of The Times during the following five months or so containing no report of a death on the previous Saturday in order to establish that on 28 November 1975 there was a real possibility that there would be no such report either in The Times or in the Daily Telegraph for the following Monday, and since there was evidence that there was at least one such instance it followed that the settlor's son's interest was dependent on a real contingency of his surviving another person for a period of one day (see p 940 *c g h* and p 941 *a* to *c g*, post).

Notes

For survivorship clauses for the purpose of gift and estate taxation, see 19 Halsbury's Laws (4th edn) para 634.

Case referred to in judgment
Pearson v IRC [1980] 2 All ER 479, [1981] AC 753, [1980] 2 WLR 872, HL, 26 Digest   *a*
(Reissue) 18, 68.

Cases also cited
Cartwright v MacCormack [1963] 1 All ER 11, [1963] 1 WLR 18, CA.
Cornfoot v Royal Exchange Assurance Corp [1904] 1 KB 40, CA.
Deloitte, Re, Griffiths v Deloitte [1926] Ch 56, [1925] All ER Rep 118.   *b*
Figgis (decd), Re, Roberts v MacLaren [1968] 1 All ER 999, [1969] 1 Ch 123.
Godson v Sanctuary (1832) 4 B & Ad 255, 110 ER 451.
Hickman v Peacey [1945] 2 All ER 215, [1945] AC 304, HL.
Hocking, Re, Michell v Loe [1898] 2 Ch 567, CA.
IRC v Bernstein [1961] 1 All ER 320, [1961] Ch 399, CA.
IRC v Duke of Westminster [1936] AC 1, [1935] All ER Rep 259, HL.   *c*
Lester v Garland (1808) 15 Ves 248, 33 ER 748.
Public Trustee v IRC [1966] 1 All ER 76, [1966] AC 520, HL.
Ramsay (W T) Ltd v IRC, Eilbeck (Inspector of Taxes) v Rawling [1981] 1 All ER 865, [1981]
   2 WLR 449, HL.

Case stated   *d*
1. At a meeting of the Commissioners for the Special Purposes of the Income Tax Acts
held on 22 and 23 June 1978 Baring Bros & Co Ltd and Lady Priscilla Aird, as trustees
(the trustees) of a voluntary settlement (the settlement) made on 31 March 1947 in
discretionary form by the late Sir John Renton Aird Bt (the settlor) appealed against a
notice of determination issued on 4 August 1977 under para 6 of Sch 4 to the Finance Act
1975 by the Board of Inland Revenue in relation to capital transfer tax. During the   *e*
course of the hearing that notice was replaced by two notices issued on 23 June 1978
under the same provisions and fresh appeals were made and heard. The case set out
below relates to the first of those notices.
2. Shortly stated the question for the commissioners' decision was whether by virtue
of para 6(7) of Sch 5 to the 1975 Act capital distributions were to be treated as having
been made on the occasion of two appointments dated 28 November 1975 whereunder   *f*
part of funds held on discretionary trusts were appointed in favour of named beneficiaries
conditionally on their surviving—

    'the person whose death shall occur on . . . the 29th day of November 1975 and
    who shall be the first (in alphabetical order) of the persons dying on that date to be
    named in the "Deaths" Column on the back page of the earliest edition of . . . "The
    Times" published in London on . . . the 1st day of December 1975 . . .'   *g*

there having been a person who answered that description.
[Paragraph 3 listed the documents admitted before the commissioners.]
4. The facts admitted between the parties and the contentions of the parties were set
out in the commissioners' decision. It was also the commissioners' understanding that
if the trustees' appeal failed in principle the amounts of the capital distributions to be   *h*
treated as having been made under the appointments made in 1975 to the settlor's son,
Sir George John Aird and daughter, Susan Priscilla Aird, were agreed between the parties
as £140,964 and £21,736 respectively.
5. The commissioners who heard the appeal took time to consider their decision and
gave it in writing on 31 July 1978. The decision dealt with both the notices of
determination referred to in para 1 above. In so far as it related to the first notice   *j*
of determination the decision is set out below.
6. On 23 August 1978 the Crown gave notice of its intention to question the decision
and requested the commissioners' to state and sign a case for the opinion of the High
Court thereon pursuant to para 10 of Sch 4 to the Finance Act 1975
7. The question of law for the opinion of the court was whether the commissioners'
decision on the appeal against the first notice of determination was correct.

DECISION

a   1. When Parliament imposed the capital transfer tax in 1975 it clearly intended that one of the events on which the tax was to be payable should be when capital was taken out of a discretionary trust and transferred to a beneficiary absolutely. The relevant provisions are contained in Sch 5 to the Finance Act 1975. Paragraph 6(7) of that schedule exempted from the charge to tax which would otherwise arise in those circumstances the case of the beneficiary 'who, on surviving another person for a specified

b   period, becomes entitled to an interest in possession as from the other person's death'. This was seen as opening a loophole for avoidance, so that, where it was desired to transfer capital out of a discretionary trust, it could be done by drafting the appointment in such a way as to postpone the entitlement of the intended absolute beneficiary until the expiry of a short specified period after the death of a person known to be dying. The device had obvious risks and inconveniences, e g of the person's being 'an unconscionable

c   time a-dying' or even of his unexpected recovery. In 1976 Parliament, by s 105 of and Part V of Sch 15 to the Finance Act 1976, plugged the loophole for the future by repealing para 6(7) and enacting new provisions to deal with survivorship clauses.

2. In November 1975, between the dates of the passing of the Finance Act 1975 and the Finance Act 1976, the taxpayers, who were trustees of a settlement made in 1947, made two appointments thereunder and in doing so tried (so we infer), by using a variant

d   of the device that we have described, to secure for the beneficiaries freedom from capital transfer tax that would otherwise have been exigible. The question before us is whether they succeeded.

[Paragraph 3 of the decision related to the second notice of determination referred to in para 1 of the case stated.]

4. The following facts are admitted. (1) On 31 March 1947 Sir John Renton Aird (the

e   settlor) made a voluntary settlement (the settlement) in discretionary form on trusts primarily in favour of his children and remoter descendants. At all material times Lady Priscilla Aird (wife of the settlor) and Baring Bros & Co Ltd (the bank) were the trustees of the settlement and are together referred to as 'the trustees'. The only provisions of the settlement directly material to the appeals are the following: (a) cll 5 and 6, which in effect, and in the events which have happened, define 'the appointed period' as the period

f   terminating on 31 March 1997 or such earlier date as the trustees should select; (b) cl 11, by which the settlor reserved to himself a special power of revocation and reappointment in favour of his children and remoter issue; and (c) cll 12 and 13, by which it was provided that the last-mentioned power could be delegated by the settlor to the trustees, and that the power could be used to create discretionary trusts and powers exercisable by the trustees or any other person or persons. (2) The settlor, who died on 20 November

g   1973, had four children, all of whom are of full age, and two of whom are married with children. (3) By a deed of delegation and release (the deed of delegation) dated 19 February 1965 made between the settlor of the one part, Lady Priscilla Aird of the second part and the trustees of the third part, the settlor delegated to the trustees the power of revocation and new appointment conferred by cl 11 of the settlement, so as to be exercisable by the trustees at any time during the appointed period. The deed of

h   delegation had the effect of releasing the power except so far as delegated to the trustees in this way. (4) By a deed of revocation and new appointment (the 1965 appointment) dated 22 February 1965 and made by the trustees, the trustees, inter alia, conferred on themselves an overriding special power of appointment in favour of the settlor's children and remoter descendants. (5) By an appointment (the 1967 appointment) dated 11 July 1967 and made by the trustees, the trustees revocably appointed the trust fund subject

j   to the settlement (other than certain excluded investments specified in a schedule) in trust for the settlor's grandson Rupert Verney contingently on his attaining the age of 21 years. (6) By an appointment (the 1970 appointment) dated 10 July 1970 and made by the trustees, the trustees (apart from making other appointments which are not material) appointed that the balance of the trust fund remaining subject to the settlement, and not comprised in the 1967 appointment, should be held on the trusts of that appointment (including the power of revocation contained in it). (7) By a deed of revocation and new

appointment (the 1972 appointment) dated 4 May 1972 and made by the trustees, the
trustees revoked the 1967 appointment (as supplemented by the 1970 appointment) in *a*
regard to a fund of investments specified in the schedule to the 1972 appointment, and
appointed those investments on trusts in discretionary form in favour of the settlor's son
George John Aird (Sir John) and his children and remoter descendants. (8) The fund
which was after the 1972 appointment left subject to the trusts of the 1967 appointment
(as supplemented by the 1970 appointment) has been administered by the trustees
separately from that comprised in and appointed by the 1972 appointment. Those funds *b*
have been designated by the bank for administrative purposes as '304A' and '304B'
respectively and are hereinafter referred to as 'fund A' and 'fund B' respectively. It is
common ground that fund A and fund B are to be regarded as comprised in separate
settlements for the purposes of the Finance Act 1975, Sch 5, para 8. (9) By an
appointment (the 1974 appointment) dated 9 May 1974 and made by the trustees, the
trustees irrevocably appointed that the sum of £38,000 should be raised out of fund B *c*
and held in trust for Sir John absolutely. (10) By a deed of appointment (Sir John's 1975
appointment) dated 28 November 1975 and made by the trustees, the trustees made an
appointment out of fund B on trust primarily in favour of Sir John. The terms hereof
(omitting the schedule and the signatures) are as follows:

'THIS APPOINTMENT is made the twenty-eighth day of November 1975 BY BARING
BROTHERS & CO LIMITED whose Registered Office is at 8 Bishopsgate in the City of *d*
London and LADY PRISCILLA AIRD of Forest Lodge the Great Park Windsor in the
County of Berks Widow (hereinafter called "the Appointors") SUPPLEMENTAL to the
following instruments (hereinafter together called "the Principal Instruments")
namely: (a) a Settlement (hereinafter called "the Settlement") dated the 31st day of
March 1947 and made between Sir John Renton Aird Baronet of the one part and
the Appointors of the other part. (b) A Deed of Revocation and New Appointment *e*
(hereinafter called "the Principal Appointment") dated the 4th day of May 1972 and
made by the Appointors and (c) the several Deeds and Appointments to which (in
addition to the Settlement) the Principal Appointment was expressed to be
supplemental.
    WHEREAS (A) In this Deed: (i) "the Appointed Property" means the investments
referred to in the Schedule hereto and the assets from time to time representing the *f*
same (ii) "Sir John" means Sir George John Aird (otherwise known as Sir John
George Aird) Baronet referred to as "John" in the Principal Appointment (iii) "the
Designated Person" means the person whose death shall occur on Saturday the 29th
day of November 1975 and who shall be the first (in alphabetical order) of the
persons dying on that date to be named in the "Deaths" Column on the back page
of the earliest edition of the newspaper called "The Times" published in London on *g*
Monday the 1st day of December 1975 (or if there shall be no edition of "The Times"
published on that date then of the earliest edition of that newspaper which is next
published in London after that date) and if there shall be no person who shall answer
the foregoing description then "the Designated Person" shall mean the person who
would satisfy that description if the words "The Daily Telegraph" were substituted
for the words "The Times" wherever the same appear. (iv) "the Specified Period" *h*
means the period of one day. (B) The Appointors (who are the present trustees both
of the Settlement and of the Principal Appointment) are desirous of making such
appointment as hereinafter appears. NOW THIS DEED WITNESSETH that in exercise of
the power for this purpose given to them by the Principal Appointment or by the
combined effect of the Settlement and the Principal Appointment and of every or
any other power then hereunto enabling the Appointors HEREBY IRREVOCABLY *j*
APPOINT AND DIRECT that subject to any capital gains tax which may be incurred as
the result of the execution of this Deed but free of all liability for capital transfer tax
(if any) which may be so incurred and free of all costs and expenses incurred by the
Appointors in the preparation and execution of this Deed and in giving effect
thereto the Appointed Property and the income thereof shall henceforth be held

upon the trusts and with and subject to the powers and provisions hereinafter mentioned (that is to say):

1. IF Sir John shall survive the Designated Person for the Specified Period the Appointed Property and the income thereof as from the death of the Designated Person shall be held upon trust for Sir John absolutely freed and discharged from the trusts and from all further exercise of the powers declared and contained in the Principal Instruments.

2. SUBJECT as aforesaid the Appointed Property and the income thereof shall be held upon the trusts and with and subject to the powers and provisions which would be applicable thereto by virtue of the Principal Instruments if this Deed had not been executed.

3. SECTION 31 of the Trustee Act 1925 shall not apply to the interest hereinbefore appointed to Sir John unless and until such interest shall become vested in possession IN WITNESS whereof Baring Brothers & Co Limited have caused their Common Seal to be hereunto affixed and Lady Priscilla Aird has set her hand and seal the day and year first before written.'

(11) By another appointment (Susan's 1975 appointment) dated 28 November 1975 and made by the trustees, the trustees revoked the 1967 appointment to the extent necessary to give effect to the appointment which they then made, out of fund A, on trust primarily in favour of the settlor's eldest daughter Susan Priscilla Aird (Susan). So far as is material to the question before us (ie the application to this appointment of para 6(7) of Sch 5 to the Finance Act 1975), Susan's 1975 appointment was in terms similar, mutatis mutandis, to those of Sir John's 1975 appointment and the two appointments are together referred to as 'the 1975 appointments'. (12) The Times newspaper was published in London on Monday, 1 December 1975, and it contained on the back page of its earliest edition a 'deaths' column which included the names of four persons who died on Saturday, 29 November 1975. The first of these four persons, in alphabetical order, was Peter Edward Bisgood (Major, retired) and his death on that date was duly registered pursuant to the Births and Deaths Registration Act 1953. Researches by the Inland Revenue Department indicate, and the trustees accept, that on every day during the year ended 29 November 1975 at least one person died whose death was subsequently reported in the 'deaths' column on the back page of the earliest London edition of The Times. It has however occurred that the earliest London edition of The Times published on a Monday has had in its 'deaths' column no report of a death of a person who died on the preceding Saturday, an instance of this being The Times for Monday, 3 May 1976. There was, however, a report in the Daily Telegraph for 3 May 1976 of a death on 1 May 1976. (13) Sir John and Susan both survived Major Bisgood by the period of one day and, at the time of the proceedings before us, were still living.

5. Following correspondence between the Capital Taxes Office and the bank, the Board of Inland Revenue notified the bank on 4 August 1977 of a determination which they had made under para 6 of Sch 4 to the Finance Act 1975. The trustees appealed on 8 September 1977 and their appeal was apparently accepted by the board as a valid appeal out of time under the provisions of para 8 of Sch 4. During the proceedings before us (on 22 and 23 June 1978) it was agreed between the parties that two new determinations should be made and appealed against and that the proceedings before us should be based on the latter appeals. Accordingly the board gave notices of two determinations dated 23 June 1978 (which we refer to as the first and second notices of determination) as follows:

(1) *First notice of determination.* In relation to the settlement and the various appointments listed earlier in our decision—

'THAT

1. Until the making of Sir George's 1975 appointment and the 304A Fund appointment (referred to below as "the Appointments"), no interest in possession subsisted in the property comprised in the 304B Fund and the 304A Fund.

2. By virtue of the Appointments, Sir George John Aird and Susan Priscilla Aird

(hereinafter called "the beneficiaries") respectively became absolutely entitled to specified property comprised in the 304B Fund and the 304A Fund.

3. Paragraph 6(7) of Schedule 5 to the Finance Act 1975 had no application to the Appointments because, although expressed to be dependent upon the beneficiary in each case surviving a "designated person", their effect was that the beneficiaries became so entitled upon surviving until a predetermined date which was not contingent on the death of any particular person or persons.

4. By virtue of paragraphs 6(2) of Schedule 5 to the Finance Act 1975, capital distributions are therefore to be treated as having been made out of the property comprised in the 304B Fund and the 304A Fund on the occasion of the beneficiaries becoming so entitled.

5. The amount of the capital distribution which is to be treated as having been made out of the 304B Fund is £140,964.

6. The amount of the capital distribution which is to be treated as having been made out of the 304A Fund is £21,736.

[Sub-paragraph (2) set out the terms of the second notice of determination.]

The trustees appealed on 23 June 1978 against both these notices of determination.

[Paragraph 6 of the decision dealt with the second notice of determination.]

7. As regards the first notice of determination it was common ground that the statements in paras 1 and 2 thereof are correct and that, unless para 6(7) Sch 5 applies, capital distributions are to be treated as having been made out of fund B and fund A on the occasion of Sir John's and Susan's becoming entitled respectively to the property comprised in those funds, with the effect that charges to capital transfer tax arose thereon under para 6(2) and (4) of Sch 5. As regards paras 5 and 6 of the notice of determination, counsel for the Crown said that in the circumstances he would not deal with the question whether the amounts of any capital distributions should be grossed up for determining the amount of capital transfer tax payable; but he expressly reserved the point of principle as one to be argued on behalf of the Crown either as a sequel to this case or in some other case.

[Paragraph 8 of the decision dealt with the second notice of determination.]

9. The contentions of counsel for trustees may be summarised as follows:

(A) *First notice of determination.* (1) Paragraph 6(7) must be construed strictly by reference to its actual words without regard to what might be expected to be found in it or to any unfairness to individuals on the one hand or to the Crown on the other that might arise from such strict construction. (2) In construing para 6(7) no weight is to be attached to the argument that the construction provides an easy means of tax avoidance. (3) If the legislature has plainly 'missed fire' the courts are not at liberty to insert words or phrases where the draftsman might have failed. It was clear from s 105 of and Sch 15 to the Finance Act 1976 that the legislature quickly recognised that para 6(7) had 'missed fire' and they quickly rectified it. (4) The legal rights of the parties must be ascertained on ordinary legal principles according to the true legal effects of the documents. (5) Where the parties have adopted a particular method of giving effect to their intention, liability to tax must be determined having regard to the method which they adopted. It is not permissible to argue that they might have adopted a different method which would have produced the same or very nearly the same effect and that tax should be levied as if they had adopted that different method. (6) Paragraph 6(7) requires three conditions to be fulfilled for the exclusion of the application of para 6(2) to the case of an appointment under a discretionary trust: (a) the appointment should designate another person living at the date of the appointment whom the beneficiary must survive in order to take; (b) the appointment should specify a period however short or long for which the beneficiary must survive that other person; (c) the appointment should provide that, if he does survive, the beneficiary should become entitled to the income of the settled property as from the death of the other person. (7) Each of those three conditions was fulfilled in the case of the 1975 appointments. As to (a), Major

Bisgood was clearly such a person. There was (as counsel conceded on behalf of the
a Crown) no requirement that he should be identifiable in his lifetime. Also there was no
requirement in 1975 on which could be based a distinction between the case of a high
probability that someone will fulfil the description and the case where the probability is
low. As to (b), the period of one day was specified. In the present case where the period
specified was as short as one day it should be measured by the clock (as 24 hours) rather
than by the calendar but either way the condition was satisfied. There were two
b uncertain events on which the effect of the 1975 appointments turned. First, neither
The Times nor the Daily Telegraph might have named in its 'deaths' column on 1
December 1975 a person who had died on 29 November 1975 and, second, the
newspapers might cease publication. If the specified period was 24 hours, that increased
the element of uncertainty. But whether the period was 24 hours or one day the
uncertainties could not be taken as de minimis. The authorities showed that where the
c destination of property depended on whether or not an event (however remote) had
occurred account must be taken of it. It was unsafe to construe the 1975 appointments
as requiring the beneficiaries to survive to a predetermined date rather than to survive
another person. As to (c) the effect of the 1975 appointments was to give the income to
Sir John and Susan, as the case might be, as from the death of 'the designated person'. It
was irrelevant that there might be an interval before it could be ascertained when and if
d the designated person had died. (8) Accordingly para 6(7) applies and the trustees' appeal
against the notice of determination should be allowed.
    [Sub-paragraph (B) related to the second notice of determination.]
    10. The contentions of counsel for the Crown may be summarised as follows:
    (A) *First notice of determination.* (1) The wording of para 6(7) of Sch 5 imports that the
person becoming entitled to an interest in possession must do so as the result of the
e fulfilment of a genuine contingency, ie on outliving another human person for a
specified period. (2) Clause 1 of Sir John's 1975 appointment should be read as if it
contained two commas, viz after the words 'Property' in the second line and 'Person' in
the third. If the provisions were that Sir John should take the appointed property and its
income as from the date of death this would have been in conflict with the idea implicit
in the opening words of cl 1 that he took a contingent interest. In order to satisfy para
f 6(7) it is necessary to ensure that a contingent interest vested in possession giving the
beneficiary the entitlement that he would have had if his interest had vested in possession
at the date of death. Clause 1 of the appointment should not be construed as if the period
of survival was to be measured by the 24-hour period from the death of 'the designated
person'. The exact time of death might be unascertainable. It was most probable that
the draftsman of the appointment contemplated that if it could be established that the
g death took place on 29 November it might still be necessary to make elaborate inquiries
as to the exact time of death as the starting point for ascertaining the destination of
income. On a proper construction of the appointment the specified period of one day
commenced at midnight on 29 November and expired at midnight on 30 November.
(3) In the circumstances of the case and on the terms of cl 1 of the appointment, there was
no genuine contingency that Sir John should survive another person. Judicial notice
h could be taken that some deaths occur every Saturday. In the normal course The Times
and the Daily Telegraph are published and report some such deaths in their 'deaths'
columns. The possibility that the death of a person on 29 November 1975 might not
appear in the 'deaths' column of either of those newspapers in its next published edition
was so remote as to be de minimis and should be disregarded as such. On a proper
construction of the appointment, survival until midnight on 30 November was the only
j condition which Sir John had to satisfy. If he did so, that was the time when he became
entitled. (4) Accordingly para 6(7) had no application either to Sir John's 1975
appointment or to Susan's 1975 appointment (as to which the material facts were
indistinguishable) and the trustees' appeal against the notice of determination should be
dismissed.
    [Sub-paragraph (B) related to the second notice of determination.]

11. Having carefully considered the rival contentions we reach the following conclusions:

(1) *First notice of determination.* The survival clauses in the 1975 appointments are geared to circumstances that make it highly probable that if the beneficiaries survived until midnight on 30 November 1975 they would have outlived (as in fact they did) a person who could be identified from the 'deaths' columns of the next published edition of The Times or the Daily Telegraph. But it was not, for the reasons expounded by counsel for the trustees, a certainty and we agree with him that there was at least an outside chance that there would never be a person meeting the full requirements of the clauses. We also agree with counsel for the trustees that such a possibility cannot, in the context of survivorship clauses, be taken to be de minimis. On this footing we accept the survivorship clauses in the appointments as contemplating a genuine contingency of the beneficiaries outliving some person who may be subsequently identified. We also accept that in the context the specified period of 'one day' should be taken as 24 hours rather than a calendar day, the circumstances being distinguishable from those in *Re Figgis (decd)* [1968] 1 All ER 999, [1969] 1 Ch 123, where the survivorship period was three months. Thus if Sir John or Susan were unfortunately to have died on 30 November 1975 it would have raised the question (to be resolved by evidence in the ordinary way) whether he or she had survived Major Bisgood by 24 hours. We think that the effect of the clauses in the events that have occurred was to confer on the beneficiaries as from the moment of Major Bisgood's death the right to the capital and income of the relevant settled property and therefore to interests in possession. We, therefore, hold that para 6(7) of Sch 5 to the Finance Act 1975 is applicable and, acting under para 9(5) of Sch 4 to that Act, we quash the determination.

[Sub-paragraph (2) related to the second notice of determination.]

John Knox QC, Michael Hart and *Launcelot Henderson* for the Crown.
Edward Nugee QC and *Robert Walker* for the trustees.

Cur adv vult

16 December. **NOURSE J** read the following judgment: In this case the Crown claims that a device used in 1975–76 in relation to settled property held on discretionary trusts and sometimes known as 'the newspaper-Franco scheme' did not succeed in avoiding a charge for capital transfer tax.

The Finance Act 1975, which abolished estate duty and replaced it with capital transfer tax, makes important distinctions in the application of the tax to settled property depending on whether there is or is not a subsisting interest in possession in the property. The 1975 Act contains no definition of 'interest in possession', and the question which most perplexed Lincoln's Inn in the early years of the new tax was to which category should be assigned settled property in which there was an absolute or lesser interest in present enjoyment subject to a mere power to divert income from the holder of the interest by accumulation or payment to others. That question was finally resolved in favour of there being no interest in possession by the decision of the House of Lords in *Pearson v IRC* [1980] 2 All ER 479, [1981] AC 753. One of the less important but more convenient results of that decision is that it is now possible, with a fair degree of accuracy, to refer to the two kinds of settled property as property held on fixed interest and discretionary trusts respectively.

Paragraph 6(2) of Sch 5 to the 1975 Act provides, shortly stated, that, where a person becomes entitled to an interest in possession in property comprised in a settlement at a time when no such interest subsists in the property, a capital distribution shall be treated as being made out of the property. Sub-paragraph (4) is the provision which imposes a

charge on capital distributions. Sub-paragraph (7), which is the provision on which this
a case depends, was in the following terms:

'Sub-paragraph (2) above shall not be taken to apply in the case of a person who,
on surviving another person for a specified period, becomes entitled to an interest
in possession as from the other person's death.'

The introduction of capital transfer tax was announced by the Chancellor of the
b Exchequer, the Rt Hon Denis Healey MP, in his budget statement on 26 March 1974.
With certain exceptions it applies to all transfers of value made after that date. The new
proposals were not published in the form of a Bill until 10 December 1974. It was then
realised that not only did the provisions of Sch 5 treat property held on discretionary
trusts far less favourably than property held on fixed interest trusts, but that the
provisions of para 6 made it impossible for the former type of trust to be converted into
c the latter except at the full rate of charge applicable to a capital distribution. That led to
representations from many quarters. In the result, the 1975 Act contained provisions for
transitional relief for settlements made before 27 March 1974.

The effect of these provisions, so far as material, was that if a capital distribution was
made before 1 April 1976 the rate at which tax was chargeable was only 10% of the
normal rate. That represented a very considerable concession. But it soon became clear
d to those who advise on these matters that advantage might be taken of para 6(7) so as to
avoid payment of tax altogether. All that appeared to be necessary in the normal case of
property held on discretionary trusts with an overriding power of appointment vested in
the trustees was for an interest in possession to be appointed to a beneficiary under the
settlement contingently on his surviving for a specified period some other person who
was on the point of death. There appeared to be no requirement that the other person
e should have any connection with the settlement or that the specified period should be of
any minimum length. It seemed clear that para 6(7) had been drawn in wider terms
than was necessary to serve the purpose which Parliament could be supposed to have
intended.

Accordingly, by the autumn of 1975 many trustees who had good reasons for making
outright distributions to adult beneficiaries or for converting from discretionary to fixed
f interest trusts during the period of maximum transitional relief had been advised that
they would have a good chance of avoiding tax altogether if they took advantage of para
6(7). The attractions were obvious. It was a form of tax avoidance where the taxpayer
could not lose. If the device did not work, the only consequence was that tax would be
paid at 10% of the normal rate. The crucial requirement was to find someone who was
on the point of death. In the autumn of 1975 it was known that General Franco was
g dying. Many appointments were made in favour of beneficiaries under discretionary
settlements contingently on their surviving General Franco for short specified periods.
That simple kind of appointment, with or without General Franco as the counter-life,
soon became known as 'the General Franco scheme'. Other individuals who were
thought to be on the point of death were often chosen, but sometimes they lived for
longer than had been expected. General Franco himself, who did not die until 20
h November 1975, was an example of that. It was therefore deemed necessary in some
quarters to devise a form of appointment which could be virtually certain of taking effect
within a short time. That led to the invention of the newspaper-Franco scheme of the
kind with which this case is concerned.

I was told by counsel for the Crown that there are a significant number of other cases
which will or may depend on the result of this. I was also told that the Revenue have
j accepted that the simple General Franco scheme was within para 6(7); also an
intermediate type of scheme where the appointed interest was made contingent on
surviving the first to die of a medium-sized and readily identifiable class, e g the members
of either or both Houses of Parliament. It is not perhaps surprising that this and other
loopholes were discovered on the introduction of what Lord Russell described in the
Pearson case [1980] 2 All ER 479 at 489, [1981] AC 753 at 778 as such a radical an

complicated experiment in fiscal novelty. And it was soon closed to all the types of
scheme to which I have referred (see s 105 of the Finance Act 1976).   a
    The present case is concerned with a settlement dated 31 March 1947 and made by the
late Sir John Renton Aird Bt, who died in 1973. The earlier history of the appointments
made and revoked under that settlement is long and complicated. It is set out in some
detail in the stated case, and I need not deal with it at all. It is enough for me to state
briefly the trusts on which the settled property was held immediately before 28
November 1975. At that stage it was divided into two funds designated for the   b
administrative purposes of the trustee bank as '304A' and '304B' respectively. Like the
Special Commissioners I will refer to those funds as 'fund A' and 'fund B' respectively.
Also like them I will state at this stage that it is common ground that fund A and fund
B are to be regarded as comprised in separate settlements for the purposes of capital
transfer tax.
    It is convenient to refer first to fund B. Immediately before 28 November 1975 the   c
capital and income of that fund were held in trust for the settlor's son, the present
baronet, Sir George John Aird (who is also known as Sir John Aird), and his children and
remoter issue as the trustees should during a period expiring in 1997 by deed appoint;
and in default of and subject to and until any such appointment with power for the
trustees during the like period to pay or apply income to or for the benefit of the like
beneficiaries; and in default of and subject to and until any exercise of either of those   d
powers or the powers by law given to the trustees the capital and the income were held
in trust for Sir John absolutely. Those powers and that trust are a classic example of a
structure whose status was doubtful before the decision of the House of Lords in the
Pearson case. It can now be seen that no interest in possession subsisted in fund B.
    Immediately before 28 November 1975 the capital and income of fund A were subject
to a revocable appointment in favour of one of the settlor's grandsons contingently on his   e
attaining the age of 21. Subject thereto, or in the event of a revocation, the trustees had
power during the like period by deed to appoint capital or income in favour of the
children and remoter issue of the settlor. It was always clear that the effect of the
contingent appointment in favour of the grandchild was that no interest in possession
subsisted in fund A.
    On Friday, 28 November 1975 the trustees of the settlement made two irrevocable   f
appointments. The first was an appointment of part of fund B in favour of Sir John. The
second was an appointment of part of fund A in favour of the settlor's eldest daughter,
Miss Susan Aird, for which purpose there was a commensurate revocation of the existing
appointment in favour of the settlor's grandson.
    So far as material for present purposes the two appointments were in identical terms,
mutatis mutandis, and it is only necessary for me to refer to that in favour of Sir John.   g
Paragraphs (i) and (ii) of recital (A) contained definitions of the appointed property and
Sir John. Paragraphs (iii) and (iv) were in the following terms:

    '(iii) "*the Designated Person*" means the person whose death shall occur on Saturday
    the 29th day of November 1975 and who shall be the first (in alphabetical order) of
    the persons dying on that date to be named in the "Deaths" Column on the back
    page of the earliest edition of the newspaper called "The Times" published in   h
    London on Monday the 1st day of December 1975 (or if there shall be no edition of
    "The Times" published on that date then of the earliest edition of that newspaper
    which is next published in London after that date) and if there shall be no person
    who shall answer the foregoing description then "the Designated Person" shall
    mean the person who would satisfy that description if the words "The Daily
    Telegraph" were substituted for the words "The Times" wherever the same   j
    appear. (iv) "*the Specified Period*" means the period of one day.'

    The operative part of the deed contained an irrevocable appointment by the trustees
expressed, inter alia, to be 'free of all liability for capital transfer tax (if any)' of the capital

and income of the appointed property on the trusts thereinafter mentioned. The first of
a those trusts was set out in cl 1. It reads as follows:

> 'IF Sir John shall survive the Designated Person for the Specified Period the
> Appointed Property and the income thereof as from the death of the Designated
> Person shall be held upon trust for Sir John absolutely freed and discharged from the
> trusts and from all further exercise of the powers declared and contained in the
> Principal Instruments.'

b
I need not refer to cl 2. Clause 3 provided that s 31 of the Trustee Act 1925 should not
apply to the interest thereinbefore appointed to Sir John unless and until such interest
should become vested in possession. That, no doubt, was intended to make doubly sure
that Sir John should become entitled to his absolute interest 'as from the other person's
death' for the purposes of para 6(7).

c   The 'deaths' column on the back page of the earliest edition of The Times newspaper
published in London on Monday, 1 December 1975 contained the names of four persons
whose deaths had occurred on Saturday, 29 November 1975. The first (in alphabetical
order) of those persons was a Major Peter Edward Bisgood. The commissioners found
that his death on that date was duly registered pursuant to the Births and Deaths
Registration Act 1953. They also found, first, that on every day during the year ended
d 29 November 1975 at least one person died whose death was subsequently reported in
the 'deaths' column on the back page of the earliest London edition of The Times, second,
that on at least one Monday over an unspecified period (namely on Monday, 3 May 1976)
the earliest London edition of The Times did not have in its 'deaths' column a report of
the death of a person who had died on the preceding Saturday, and, third, that there was
a report in the Daily Telegraph on 3 May 1976 of a death on the preceding Saturday.
e Copies of The Times for both Monday, 1 December 1975 and Monday, 3 May 1976 were
in court. No objection was made to my looking at them. In the 'deaths' column in the
1 December issue there were the names of 22 persons, of whom one was reported to have
died on 26 November, three on 27, one on 27–28, 11 on 28, four (as I have said) on 29 and
one on Sunday, 30 November. In the remaining case no date of death was given. The
death on the Sunday may be of some marginal significance, because the directions at the
f top of the back page might suggest that any classified advertisement for Monday's
edition has to be in by noon on Saturday. That cannot, however, be taken to be an
invariable rule.

    The only other material fact which needs to be stated is that both Sir John and Miss
Aird duly survived until midnight on Sunday, 30 November 1975, which is agreed to
have been the latest point of time at which they became absolutely entitled to their
g respective appointed interests. I should say at this stage that the Crown accepts that both
appointments were genuinely made in a bona fide exercise of the trustees' discretion and
that they were effective to confer on Sir John and Miss Aird the interests which were
respectively appointed to them. The argument proceeded throughout on the footing
that the interest to which Sir John and Miss Aird became entitled fell within para 6(2) of
Sch 5.

h   I will now set out in extenso what appear to me to be the requirements of para 6(7).
First, there must be a person, A, who becomes entitled to an interest in possession.
Second, A's entitlement must be contingent on his (i) being alive at the death of another
person, B, and (ii) thereafter living for a specified period. Third, A must thereafter fulfil
contingencies (i) and (ii). Fourth, A's interest must take effect as from B's death. The
third of those requirements is really an addition to, or an elaboration of, the first. The
j Crown accepts that the first, third and fourth requirements were satisfied in the present
case. It is the second requirement which is in issue. The Special Commissioners held
that it was satisfied, but the Crown submits that it was not.

    Both before the commissioners and in this court the Crown conceded that there was
no requirement that B should be identifiable in his lifetime. In other words, the fact that

B may or may not materialise does not take an interest which would otherwise be within para 6(7) outside it. The arguments of counsel for the Crown were directed not so much *a* to the construction of para 6(7), which is tolerably clear, as to the question whether the interests conferred on Sir John and Miss Aird were in reality and substance contingent on their surviving another person (who might or might not materialise) for a period of one day or whether they were only contingent on their surviving until a specified time and date, namely midnight on Sunday, 30 November 1975. Counsel for the Crown submitted, and counsel for the trustees agreed, that if the interests were in reality and *b* substance contingent on survivorship until a specified time and date and no more the case was not within the exemption conferred by para 6(7).

That makes it necessary to determine when a contingency has reality and substance and when it does not. A contingency is an event which may or may not happen. If there is no real possibility that it will not happen, so that it is as good as certain that it will, it is a contingency without reality and substance and no contingency at all. But a real *c* possibility is not the same thing as a probability. It may be highly improbable that an event will happen, but there can still be a real possibility that it will. If there is that possibility, however remote it may be, the contingency is one of reality and substance.

Counsel for the Crown started by submitting that a gift to A contingent on his (i) being alive at the death of an inhabitant of the United Kingdom who dies tomorrow and (ii) thereafter living for one day is in reality and substance a gift to A contingent only on *d* his living until midnight the day after tomorrow. That is because it is as certain as night follows day that at least one inhabitant of the United Kingdom will die tomorrow. Conversely, there is no real possibility that there will not be an inhabitant of the United Kingdom who dies tomorrow. I accept that submission. Then counsel for the Crown turned to the present case and submitted that a gift to A contingent on his (i) being alive at the death of someone who dies tomorrow, being a Saturday, and who shall be the first *e* (in alphabetical order) of the persons dying on that date to be named in the 'deaths' column of The Times for the following Monday and (ii) thereafter living for one day is equally in reality and substance a gift to A contingent only on his living until midnight on Sunday. That submission is evidently one of a different order from the first, since the class of possible decedents has been narrowed from all the inhabitants of the United Kingdom to those whose deaths are reported in the Monday editions of The Times or the *f* Daily Telegraph.

The second submission requires me to look with very great care at the definition of the designated person in order to see whether it incorporates any contingency which can fairly be said to have reality and substance. First and foremost, there must be a person who dies on 29 November 1975 whose name appears in one or other of the 'deaths' columns on the following Monday. With hindsight I might have preferred that the *g* fruits of a more extensive research had been put before the commissioners on this point. But I must deal with the matter on the evidence as it stands. On that evidence it seems to me that it is unnecessary to have more than one instance of a Monday edition of The Times during the next five months or so which contains no report of a death on the previous Saturday to establish that on 28 November 1975 there was a real possibility that there would be no such report either in The Times or in the Daily Telegraph for the *h* following Monday. The Times column for that day confirms what I might otherwise have inferred, namely that the reports of one day's deaths are usually spread over a number of different subsequent days. Therefore there could well be Mondays when no death on the previous Saturday was reported. There is no further evidence about the Daily Telegraph, but I must assume that what was a real possibility in the one case was a real possibility in the other and, further, taking account of some habitual degree of *j* overlapping between them, that there was a less substantial but nevertheless real possibility that there would be no report in either publication. You may say that that was a remote event and in the highest degree improbable, but there was still a real possibility that it would happen.

Then it is to be noted that it was necessary for The Times to be published on 1

a
December. If it was not, it had to be next published at a date not so far removed in time as to make it impracticable or inappropriate to announce the death on that date. It may well be that in November 1975 the average reader of The Times would have been shocked at the suggestion that that newspaper might cease publication for a long period or even altogether, but subsequent events have demonstrated that it was a real possibility at the time. It was altogether less likely that The Times and the Daily Telegraph would go out of publication together, but, once you accept the possibility of one of them doing

b
so as real, all the more real becomes the possibility that the other will not on a Monday report a death which occurred on the previous Saturday.

I therefore conclude that on 28 November 1975 there was a real possibility that there would be no person who would satisfy the description of the designated person. That means that the interests conferred on Sir John and Miss Aird were in reality and substance contingent on their surviving another person (who might or might not

c
materialise) for a period of one day and, unless there is any other objection, were within the exemption conferred by para 6(7).

Counsel for the Crown advanced an alternative argument which on analysis appeared to me, and I think to counsel for the trustees, to do no more than put his first argument in a slightly different way. I did not understand counsel for the Crown to submit that on 28 November 1975, when the appointments took effect, it was necessary, before para 6(7)

d
could apply, for the point of time to which the beneficiaries were to survive to be uncertain. In my view that submission could not be correct, partly because the language of para 6(7) does not admit it and partly because it would have excluded from the exemption a case which was most obviously intended to be included, namely that of a gift by will to A contingently on his being alive at the expiration of a specified period (say one month) after the testator's death. In that kind of case, and if it be assumed that the testator died on the first of the month, it can be seen when the will takes effect that A

e
must survive until midnight on the second of the following month. It would have been very strange if that kind of case was excluded from the exemption. Provided that there is in terms a gift to a person contingent on surviving another person for a specified period, it does not in my judgment cease to fall within para 6(7) merely because it can be seen, at the date on which the instrument creating it takes effect and not before, that the

f
gift will vest if the donee survives until a specified time and date.

On that footing I cannot see, and I do not think that counsel for the trustees could see, that it matters whether the period of one day which was specified in the two appointments with which this case is concerned meant a period of 24 hours starting from midnight on Saturday, 29 November 1975 or a like period from the exact point of time on that day at which Major Bisgood died. That is an interesting and difficult question

g
which both sides argued at some length, but on which my inability to see that it arises relieves me from expressing a view.

In the result I have arrived at the same conclusion as the Special Commissioners, substantially for the like reasons as those expressed in para 11 of the stated case. The appeal must be dismissed.

Appeal dismissed.

Solicitors: *Solicitor of Inland Revenue*; *Travers, Smith, Braithwaite & Co* (for the trustees).

Edwina Epstein   Barrister.

Stanton (Inspector of Taxes) v Drayton Commercial Investment Co Ltd

HOUSE OF LORDS

LORD FRASER OF TULLYBELTON, LORD RUSSELL OF KILLOWEN, LORD KEITH OF KINKEL, LORD ROSKILL AND LORD BRANDON OF OAKBROOK

4, 5, 6 MAY, 8 JULY 1982

Capital gains tax – Computation of chargeable gains – Cost of acquisition of asset – Consideration given for acquisition of asset – Value of consideration – Company purchasing securities under conditional contract – Company allotting shares to vendor at agreed price in consideration for purchase – Whether value of consideration to be ascertained by reference to agreed value or to market value of shares when contract became unconditional – Finance Act 1965, Sch 6, para 4(1)(a).

By an agreement dated 21 September 1972 the taxpayer company agreed to purchase a portfolio of investments from an insurance company at the price of £3·9m, the price to be satisfied by the allotment of 2,461,226 new ordinary shares of 25p each in the taxpayer company issued as fully paid up at 160p per share. The agreement was conditional on the passing of a resolution by the members of the taxpayer company creating the new shares and the Stock Exchange granting both permission to deal in and a quotation for the new shares before 31 October 1972. The necessary resolution was passed on 9 October 1972 and permission to deal in and a quotation for the shares was given by the Stock Exchange on 11 October. On the same day the shares were allotted to the insurance company and the agreement was completed. The shares were first quoted on the Stock Exchange on 12 October. Their market price then was 125p per share. During the accounting periods ending 31 December 1972 and 31 December 1973 the taxpayer company disposed of certain investments comprised in the portfolio. The taxpayer company was assessed to corporation tax on the footing that, in ascertaining the chargeable gains arising on the disposal, the consideration given for the investments, allowable as a deduction under para 4(1)(a)[a] of Sch 6 to the Finance Act 1965, should be the value of the shares according to their first quotation in the Stock Exchange official list on 12 October 1972. The Special Commissioners allowed an appeal by the taxpayer company against the assessments on the ground that the value of the shares allotted in satisfaction of the price of the investments should be ascertained by reference to the agreed issue price of the shares. The Crown appealed, contending that under the agreement the consideration given for the portfolio by the taxpayer company consisted of the shares themselves and that the value of the consideration was the price at which the shares were first quoted on the Stock Exchange on 12 October when the conditions to which the agreement was subject were satisfied. The judge allowed the appeal, holding that 'value' in Sch 6, para 4(1)(a) meant market value and that the market value of the shares on the date when the agreement became unconditional represented the value of the consideration given for the acquisition of the investments. The Court of Appeal allowed an appeal by the taxpayer company, holding that the consideration given by the taxpayer company was the benefit of the agreement between the taxpayer company and the insurance company and that the amount of the consideration given for the portfolio was the agreed price of £3,937,962. The Crown appealed to the House of Lords, contending, inter alia, that the value of the consideration was to be ascertained by the best evidence, and that although the market value on the day the shares were first quoted was some evidence, it was not conclusive.

Held – On the true construction of para 4(1)(a) of Sch 6 to the 1975 Act the deduction allowable in the computation of the gain accruing on the disposal of an asset was

---

Paragraph 4(1), so far as material, is set out at p 945 b, post *a* restricted to the amount of the consideration if it was in money, or the value in money's worth if it was not in money; and in the case of an honest and straightforward transaction the Revenue was not entitled to go behind the price paid, whatever the means by which the obligation to pay that price had been discharged by agreement between the parties, nor to consider whether it was commercially prudent or whether a more advantageous bargain might have been made. Where a company allotted fully-paid shares in itself as the consideration for the acquisition of property the value of the consideration was not,

b in the case of an unimpeachable transaction, the value of shares allotted but, prima facie, the cost to the taxpayer of the shares issued, and where that was different from the market value of the shares the market value was irrelevant. Since there was no evidence that the agreed value had not been honestly reached nor that the transaction was other than a bargain made at arm's length, there was no basis on which the Revenue could legitimately go behind the price of 160p per share. The appeal would accordingly be

c dismissed (see p 945 *d g*, p 946 *j* to p 947 *a* and *d* to *j*, p 948 *a* to *e*, p 950 *c d*, p 951 *e f* and p 952 *a* to *d* and *j* to p 953 *b*, post).

Dicta of Lord Greene MR in *Craddock (Inspector of Taxes) v Zevo Finance Ltd* [1944] 1 All ER at 569 and of Lord Simonds in *Craddock (Inspector of Taxes) v Zevo Finance Ltd* (1946) 27 TC at 295 applied.

Decision of the Court of Appeal [1982] 1 All ER 121 affirmed.

d **Notes**

For deductions in computing chargeable gains, see 5 Halsbury's Laws (4th edn) para 147.

For the Finance Act 1965, Sch 6, para 4, see 34 Halsbury's Statutes (3rd edn) 931.

With effect from 6th April 1979, Sch 6, para 4, to the 1965 Act was replaced by s 32 of the Capital Gains Tax Act 1979.

e **Cases referred to in opinions**

Craddock (Inspector of Taxes) v Zevo Finance Co Ltd [1944] 1 All ER 566, CA; *affd* [1946] 1 All ER 523n, 27 TC 267, HL, 28(1) Digest (Reissue) 124, 367.

Ooregum Gold Mining Co of India Ltd v Roper [1892] AC 125, HL, 9 Digest (Reissue) 321, 1901.

f *Osborne (Inspector of Taxes) v Steel Barrel Co Ltd* [1942] 1 All ER 634, CA, 28(1) Digest (Reissue) 121, 357.

Wragg Ltd, Re [1897] 1 Ch 796, [1895–9] All ER Rep 398, CA, 9 Digest (Reissue) 302, 1784.

Appeal

The Crown appealed against the decision of the Court of Appeal (Waller, Oliver and Fox

g LJJ) ([1982] 1 All ER 121, [1981] 1 WLR 1425) on 25 June 1981 allowing an appeal from the decision of Vinelott J ([1980] 3 All ER 221, [1980] 1 WLR 1162) on 24 March 1980 whereby an appeal by the Crown from a determination of the Commissioners for the Special Purposes of the Income Tax Acts reducing assessments to corporation tax for the accounting periods ending 31 December 1972 and 31 December 1973 in respect of gains realised on the sale of investments comprised in a portfolio of securities acquired by

h Drayton Commercial Investment Co Ltd (the taxpayer company) from Eagle Star Insurance Co Ltd (Eagle Star) on the basis that the value of the consideration given by the taxpayer company for the acquisition of the portfolio was the sum of £3,937,962 agreed between the taxpayer company and Eagle Star. The facts are set out in the opinion of Lord Fraser.

j *S A Stamler QC* and *C H McCall* for the Crown.

Michael Nolan QC and *Robert Venables* for the taxpayer company.

Their Lordships took time for consideration.

8 July. The following opinions were delivered.

LORD FRASER OF TULLYBELTON. My Lords, this appeal concerns the computation of chargeable gains for the purpose of corporation tax. They have to be *a* computed in accordance with the rules for capital gains tax, although they are actually assessed to corporation tax, because the taxpayer is a company: see Income and Corporation Taxes Act 1970, ss 238 and 265.

The respondent is Drayton Commercial Investment Co Ltd (the taxpayer company). In 1972 the taxpayer company (then called Union Commercial Investment Co Ltd) acquired from the Eagle Star Insurance Co Ltd (Eagle Star) a portfolio of investments at *b* the price of £3,937,962 (which I shall refer to as £3·9m). The price was satisfied, in accordance with the agreement between the companies, by the allotment by the taxpayer company to Eagle Star of 2,461,226 ordinary shares of 25p each in the taxpayer company, the issue price of each share being 160p. I shall refer to the number of shares allotted as 2·4m. The taxpayer company subsequently disposed of some of the investments, so that it became material, in order to ascertain the amount of its capital gains, to determine the *c* amount or value of the consideration which it had given for the investments. The taxpayer company contends that the value of the consideration was the issue price of the shares allotted to Eagle Star (160p) multiplied by the number of shares allotted (2·4m). The Crown originally contended that the consideration was the market price of the taxpayer company's shares allotted on the day when they were first quoted, which was the day after their allotment, multiplied by 2·4m. That price was 125p. During the *d* hearing in your Lordships' House the Crown departed from that contention to some extent and submitted that the value of the consideration fell to be ascertained by the best evidence, and that, although the market value on the day the shares were first quoted would be some evidence, it was not conclusive. The market value was probably the price paid for comparatively small parcels of shares, and evidence might well show that the price that could have been obtained for 2·4m shares, if they had all been offered for sale *e* on the day they were first quoted, would have been substantially lower. It was common ground between counsel that the only question for decision at this stage was whether the taxpayer company's contention was sound in principle, and that, if not (ie if the appeal succeeds on the question of principle), the matter must be remitted to the Special Commissioners to ascertain the true value of the consideration and to make any necessary amendment in the assessment consequent thereon. *f*

The Special Commissioners upheld the taxpayer company's contention. Vinelott J ([1980] 3 All ER 221, [1980] 1 WLR 1162) reversed their decision and remitted the case to them to value the consideration. The Court of Appeal (Waller, Oliver and Fox LJJ) ([1982] 1 All ER 121, [1981] 1 WLR 1425) allowed the appeal and restored the decision of the Special Commissioners.

The agreement under which the portfolio was acquired by the taxpayer company was *g* dated 21 September 1972. By cl 1 it provided, inter alia, as follows:

'THE Vendor [Eagle Star] will sell and the Purchaser [the taxpayer company] will purchase all the securities in the said portfolio at the price of . . . £3,937,962 . . . to be satisfied by the allotment by [the taxpayer company] to [Eagle Star] of . . . 2,461,226 . . . Ordinary Shares of twenty-five pence each in [the taxpayer company] *h* the issue price of each such Share for the purpose of satisfying the consideration being . . . 160p . . . The said Ordinary Shares in [the taxpayer company] when issued will be credited as fully paid up . . .'

The agreement was subject to two conditions set out in cl 2, which provides as follows:

'THIS Agreement is conditional upon:—(i) the Members of [the taxpayer company] *j* passing the necessary Resolution of the Company in General Meeting creating the New Shares in [the taxpayer company] required to satisfy the consideration above mentioned (ii) the Stock Exchange London granting permission to deal in and quotation for such New Shares (subject to allotment) before the thirty first day of October one thousand nine hundred and seventy-two.'

The necessary resolution was passed at a general meeting of the taxpayer company's
a shareholders on 9 October 1972, and Stock Exchange permission was granted on 11
October. The new shares were allotted on 11 October, and were first quoted on the Stock
Exchange on 12 October. I should mention that the portfolio had been valued at middle
market quotation on 31 August 1972, and that is stated in cl 4 of the agreement.

The statutory provision which is directly applicable is the Finance Act 1965, Sch 6,
para 4(1)(a), which provides as follows:

b
> 'Subject to the following provisions of this Schedule, the sums allowable as a
> deduction from the consideration in the computation under this Schedule of the
> gain accruing to a person on the disposal of an asset shall be restricted to—(a) the
> amount or value of the consideration, in money or money's worth, given by him or
> on his behalf wholly and exclusively for the acquisition of the asset, together with
> the incidental costs to him of the acquisition . . .'

c
The Crown also relied on the Finance Act 1971, Sch 10, para 10 on the question of the
date on which the consideration should be valued. I shall refer to that matter separately
later.

In my opinion, para 4(1)(a) means that the allowable deduction is to be restricted to
'the amount of the consideration if it is in money or the value in money's worth if it is
d not in money'. In the present case the consideration was in money's worth and it is
therefore necessary to ascertain its value. The first stage is to ascertain exactly what was
the consideration given by the taxpayer company. This has been the subject of acute
controversy at all stages of the appeal. Vinelott J held that the consideration was the
shares in the taxpayer company allotted to Eagle Star. The Court of Appeal held that it
was not the shares but 'the benefit of an agreement by [the taxpayer company] (i) to issue
e and allot the shares at 160p per share and (ii) to credit them as fully paid' (see [1982] 1 All
ER 121 at 126, [1981] 1 WLR 1425 at 1432). They added: 'We should mention here that,
as we understand it, the new shares did not exist at the time when the agreement became
unconditional (and when, therefore, the acquisition took place). They were issued later
on the same day.' When the appeal reached this House counsel for the taxpayer company,
while still vigorously rejecting the view that the consideration was the taxpayer
f company's shares, did not fully accept the Court of Appeal's view but submitted that the
consideration was 'the credit of £3,937,962 allowed to Eagle Star by [the taxpayer
company], which was offset against and extinguished Eagle Star's liability to pay [the
taxpayer company] £3,937,962 in consideration of the issue of the new shares in [the
taxpayer company] at 160p each'.

In my opinion, the consideration was the taxpayer company's shares. That is, I think,
g how any businessman would have seen the transaction, and it is the commercial
reality. Counsel for the taxpayer company argued that the correct legal analysis was not
for businessmen but for lawyers, and I agree, subject to this, that the lawyer must have
regard to the businessman's view. From the lawyer's point of view, it seems plain
beyond argument that what Eagle Star received as consideration for its portfolio was the
taxpayer company's shares. It may be possible for the taxpayer company to have *given*
h something different from that which Eagle Star *received*, although that seems prima facie
unlikely. I would only accept such a comparatively complicated analysis if it was the
only satisfactory way of explaining what had occurred. But in this case I do not think it
is. It is stated in the agreement that the price of £3·9m will be satisfied by the allotment
of 2·4m shares and that seems entirely consistent with the view that the shares were the
consideration. The view contended for by the taxpayer company, and substantially
j accepted by the Court of Appeal, was based mainly on two decisions on questions of
company law, namely *Osborne v Steel Barrel Co Ltd* [1942] 1 All ER 634, and *Craddock v
Zevo Finance Co Ltd* [1946] 1 All ER 523n, 27 TC 267. Neither of these cases was
concerned with the question which arises here.

In *Osborne* a new company had acquired stock in trade for a consideration consisting
partly of cash and partly of shares which it issued as fully paid. The Crown's contenti

was that the shares had cost the company nothing and that the stock should be entered
in its books simply at the amount of cash paid for it. It is perhaps not surprising that that   *a*
contention failed. In the Court of Appeal Lord Greene MR said (at 638) that 'on the facts
of [that] case' the issue of the fully paid shares represented a payment in cash equal to the
par value of the shares, mainly because the only alternative would have been that the
shares had been issued at a discount, which would have been illegal, and no illegality was
alleged. In the present appeal no question of issuing shares at a discount arises and
neither party contends that the taxpayer company's shares should be value at par. The   *b*
only part of Lord Greene MR's opinion which seems to bear on the present appeal is
where he said (at 638):

> 'A company cannot issue £1,000 nominal worth of shares for stock of the market
> value of £500, since shares cannot be issued at a discount. Accordingly, when fully-
> paid shares are properly issued for a consideration other than cash, the consideration
> moving from the company must be at the least equal in value to the par value of the   *c*
> shares *and must be based on an honest estimate by the directors of the value of the assets
> acquired.*' (Emphasis added.)

As regards the nature of the consideration moving from the company, the decision was
that the price paid for the stock was cash plus shares and it is thus entirely consistent with
the contention of the Crown in the present case that the consideration moving from   *d*
(which is the same as given by) the taxpayer company was the shares themselves. But,
on the question of value, it supports the contention of the taxpayer company that the
value must be based on an honest estimate by the directors of the value of the assets
acquired, which in this case was £3·9m, and not on the market value of the shares
allotted.

The other case, much canvassed in argument, was *Craddock*, where there had been a   *e*
reconstruction of a family company which dealt in investments. A new company had
been formed to take over and hold some of the investments of the former company, and
the question was as to the basis on which these investments should be valued for income
tax purposes in the books of the new company. The decision of the Court of Appeal,
which was upheld by this House, was that the value of the investments was their
purchase price, which was the price that the new company had agreed to pay, and that   *f*
the amount paid in shares of the new company should be taken to be the par value of the
shares. The following passage in the judgment of Lord Greene MR ([1944] 1 All ER 566
at 569) was relied on by counsel for the taxpayer company:

> 'The fallacy, if I may respectfully so call it, which underlies the argument [for the
> Crown in that case], is to be found in the assertion that where a company issues its
> own shares as consideration for the acquisition of property, those shares are to be   *g*
> treated as money's worth as though they were shares in another company altogether,
> transferred by way of consideration for the acquisition. This proposition amounts
> to saying that consideration in the form of fully-paid shares allotted by a company
> must be treated as being of the value of the shares, no more and no less. Such a
> contention will not bear a moment's examination where the transaction is a
> straightforward one and not a mere device for issuing shares at a discount.'   *h*

In this House Lord Simonds said (27 TC 267 at 295):

> 'I cannot distinguish between consideration and purchase price, and . . . I find
> that, acquiring the investments "under a bona fide and unchallengeable contract",
> they paid the price which that contract required, a price which, whether too high   *j*
> or low according to the views of third parties, was the price upon which these parties
> agreed.'

rom these judgments I extract the following propositions relevant to the present
peal. (1) A company can issue its own shares 'as consideration for the acquisition of
perty', as Lord Greene MR said. (2) The value of consideration given in the form of

a fully paid shares allotted by a company is not the value of the shares allotted but, in the case of an honest and straightforward transaction, is the price on which the parties agreed, as Lord Simonds said. The latter point was expressed even more forcibly in the House of Lords by Lord Wright where he said (27 TC 267 at 290): 'No authority was cited for the claim of the Revenue in a case like this to go behind the *agreed consideration* and substitute a different figure' (emphasis added).

b The Court of Appeal in the passage I have quoted from its decision seems to have thought that the fact that the new shares issued by the taxpayer company were not in existence at the time when the agreement with Eagle Star became unconditional was a further reason why they were not the consideration given by the taxpayer company. I confess that I do not follow the reasoning on this point. At the time when the agreement became unconditional the taxpayer company came under an unconditional obligation to hand over the consideration (whatever it might be) to Eagle Star and it did so later the *c* same day. The fact that the consideration in the form of shares did not come into existence until some hours after the obligation had become unconditional seems to me irrelevant. Indeed, if the view of the Court of Appeal is right, it might lead to the consequence that the 'benefit' or the 'credit' given by the taxpayer company must either have been transmuted into the new shares before it was received by Eagle Star, or must have been received by Eagle Star and subsequently disposed of by Eagle Star in exchange *d* for the new shares. Such a double disposal seems quite unrealistic and I see no reason for importing it.

Accordingly, I am of opinion that the consideration given by the taxpayer company was the same as that received by Eagle Star and was the new shares. The next step is to ascertain the value of that consideration. The argument for the Crown, which was accepted by Vinelott J, was that 'value' in para 4(1)(*a*) of Sch 6 to the Finance Act 1965 *e* meant 'market value' and might be different from the price agreed between the parties. It was said that the value of consideration was something to be determined by reference to an objective standard, and not by reference to the cost to a particular party. I was at first attracted by this argument. But further reflection has convinced me that it is erroneous for two reasons. First, as a pure matter of construction of para 4(1)(*a*), I see no indication that value is used as meaning market value. The paragraph is part of the *f* general provisions for computing the amount of gain accruing on the disposal of an asset in the ordinary case: see s 22(9) of the 1965 Act. It is to be contrasted with s 22(4) of the 1965 Act, which makes provision for some special cases, including the case where a person acquires an asset 'otherwise than by way of a bargain made at arm's length and in particular where he acquires it by way of gift'. Section 22(4) provides that acquisition of such an asset shall be deemed to be for a consideration equal to the 'market value' of the *g* asset, and the obvious reason is that no agreed value, arrived at by an arm's length transaction, is available. But in the ordinary case under para 4(1)(*a*) such a value is available, namely the price agreed between the parties. Consequently there is no need to look to the market value, and no need to read in the word 'market' before 'value' where Parliament has not seen fit to use it. Further, the deduction permitted by para 4(1)(*a*) includes 'the incidental costs *to him* [the taxpayer] of the acquisition' (emphasis added). *h* The words that I have emphasised show that, at least so far as the costs of acquisition are concerned, it is the costs to the particular taxpayer that are relevant and they are some indication that the value of the consideration given by him is to be calculated on the same basis.

Second, *Osborne* and *Craddock* are ample authority for saying, in the words of Lord Wright in the latter case, that the Revenue is not entitled to go behind the agreed *j* consideration in a case where, as in the present case, the transaction is not alleged to be dishonest or otherwise not straightforward.

If I am right in thinking that the agreed value of the newly allotted shares, in a bargain at arm's length, is conclusive, no question arises about the date at which the value of the shares should be ascertained. It is therefore unnecessary to refer to the contentions of the parties on that matter, or to the provisions of para 10 of Sch 10 to the Finance Act 1971, which was relied on by the Crown.

One consequence of taking the agreed value of the shares as conclusive is that cases may occur in which that value may seem surprising, because the market value of the *a* newly allotted shares on the day when they are first quoted proves to be much higher or much lower than their value agreed between the parties. That might happen, for example, because of some unexpected political event occurring between the date of the agreement and the date of the first quotation. But, provided the agreed value has been honestly reached by a bargain at arm's length, it must, in my opinion, be final and it is not open to attack by the Revenue. Not only is that right in principle, but it is very *b* much in accordance with practical convenience. Once it is accepted, as it was (rightly in my opinion) by counsel appearing for the Crown, that market value could not necessarily be ascertained almost instantly by reference to the Stock Exchange price list, but might have to be proved by the evidence of accountants and other financial experts, the practical inconvenience of leaving agreements liable to be reopened to such inquiry becomes clear. I do not believe that Parliament can have intended to permit that *c* inconvenience in cases where bargains have been made at arm's length.

For these reasons, which are somewhat different from those of the Court of Appeal, I would dismiss this appeal.

LORD RUSSELL OF KILLOWEN. My Lords, I have had the advantage of reading in draft the speeches prepared by my noble and learned friends Lord Fraser and Lord *d* Roskill. I concur with their opinions that this appeal be dismissed.

LORD KEITH OF KINKEL. My Lords, I have had the benefit of reading in draft the speech prepared by my noble and learned friend Lord Fraser. I agree with it, and for the reasons which he gives I, too, would dismiss the appeal.

e

LORD ROSKILL. My Lords, this appeal from a decision of the Court of Appeal (Waller, Oliver and Fox LJJ) ([1982] 1 All ER 121, [1981] 1 WLR 1425) dated 25 June 1981 raises a short, but to my mind difficult, question under para 4(1) of Sch 6 to the Finance Act 1971. The essential facts are simple and have been fully set out in the judgments in the courts below. I need only restate them in outline. On 21 September 1972 the taxpayer company concluded a conditional agreement with Eagle Star Insurance *f* Co Ltd (Eagle Star) for the purchase by the taxpayer company of a large portfolio of securities belonging to Eagle Star. The price was £3,937,962. That price was to be satisfied by the allotment by the taxpayer company to Eagle Star of 2,461,226 ordinary shares of 25p each. Those shares were to be issued by the taxpayer company and credited as fully paid, the issue price of each share being 160p. The agreement was subject to two conditions, first, the passing of the necessary resolution by the taxpayer company creating *g* those shares and, second, the grant by the Stock Exchange of permission to deal in them and of a quotation for them before 31 October 1972. The necessary resolution was passed by the taxpayer company on 9 October 1972. The requisite Stock Exchange permissions were granted on 11 October 1972. On that date the agreement became unconditional. It was common ground that the agreement was an arm's length transaction. Later, the taxpayer company sold some of the securities so purchased, and *h* became liable to corporation tax on the resultant gains. That corporation tax is chargeable in accordance with the law relating to capital gains tax by virtue of ss 238 and 265 of the Income and Corporation Taxes Act 1970. The question which arises is how those capital gains are to be calculated.

My Lords, the Revenue made an assessment to tax on the taxpayer company on the basis that the value of the consideration given by the taxpayer company was to be taken *j* as a sum equal to the market value of the new shares, determined by reference to Stock Exchange quoted prices on the day after those shares were first quoted after their allotment. The taxpayer company appealed to the Special Commissioners, contending that the relevant figure was the price at which those shares were issued, namely their par value plus the premium, amounting in all to £3,937,962. Since that figure was based on the issue price of 160p per share, and the first quoted price was said to be only 125p per

share, the difference was considerable, and was stated in the courts below to involve some
£800,000.

a

My Lords, the Special Commissioners upheld the taxpayer company's contentions.
Before them it was argued, on the taxpayer company's behalf, that as a matter of law they
must hold that the value of the consideration given by the taxpayer company was 160p
per share, and the Special Commissioners were invited, first, to determine whether or not
that contention was correct, it apparently being agreed that, if it were held thereafter to

b

be incorrect, the matter should be remitted to the Special Commissioners for
determination of the value of the consideration in accordance with whatever might be
held to be the correct principles.

My Lords, the Special Commissioners stated a case at the request of the Crown.
Vinelott J reversed their decision (see [1980] 3 All ER 221, [1980] 1 WLR 1162). The
taxpayer company appealed to the Court of Appeal, who restored the decision of the

c

Special Commissioners (see [1982] 1 All ER 121, [1981] 1 WLR 1425). The Court of
Appeal gave leave to appeal to your Lordships' House on condition that the Crown did
not seek to disturb the order as to costs which that court had made.

My Lords, the relevant statutory provision is to be found in para 4(1) of Sch 6 to the
Finance Act 1965. It reads, so far as relevant, as follows:

d

'Subject to the following provisions of this Schedule, the sums allowable as a
deduction from the consideration in the computation under this Schedule of the
gain accruing to a person on the disposal of an asset shall be restricted to—(a) the
amount or value of the consideration, in money or money's worth, given by him or
on his behalf wholly and exclusively for the acquisition of the asset, together with
the incidental costs to him of the acquisition . . .'

e

'Incidental costs' are defined in sub-para (2) which it is not necessary to quote. My Lords,
I think the opening words of sub-para (1)(a) must be read as meaning 'the amount in
money or the value in money's worth of the consideration'. On this view the question
is what is 'the value in money's worth of the consideration given' by the taxpayer
company for the acquisition of the new shares issued to Eagle Star and credited as fully
paid.

f

The Crown strenuously contended that the price specified in the agreement was not
the value in money's worth of the consideration but was the cost. Value, it was said, was
different from cost and was to be determined, at one time it was faintly suggested to be
determined objectively, but at any rate not exclusively by reference to the cost, even
though the transaction was an arm's length transaction.

My Lords, the argument for the taxpayer company which found favour both with the

g

Special Commissioners and the Court of Appeal for, as I read their respective reasoning,
substantially the same reasons was that the consideration which was given by the
taxpayer company was not the new shares themselves, but the taxpayer company's
agreement to issue and allot them and, most important, to credit them as fully paid. The
taxpayer company, it was said, had the right to require payment of the price of 160p per
share but forewent that right, giving credit for that amount instead. It was the value of

h

that credit which the taxpayer company so provided to Eagle Star which was the
consideration, and the value of that credit was 160p per share. The Revenue was not
entitled to go behind that figure in the case of an arm's length transaction unless it
'impeached' the agreement of 21 September 1972, which the Crown accepted it could
not do in the instant case.

My Lords, the submission was that it was the value of the credit given by the taxpayer

j

company which was in truth the consideration the value of which had to be determined
and was founded on authority. In his speech in your Lordships' House in *Ooregum Gold
Mining Co of India Ltd v Roper* [1892] AC 125 at 136–137 Lord Watson in a well-known
passage said:

'A company is free to contract with an applicant for its shares; and when he
in cash the nominal amount of the shares allotted to him, the company may a

return the money in satisfaction of its legal indebtedness for goods supplied or services rendered by him. That circuitous process is not essential. It has been decided that, under the [Companies] Act of 1862, shares may be lawfully issued as fully paid up, for considerations which the company has agreed to accept as representing in money's worth the nominal value of the shares. I do not think any other decision could have been given in the case of a genuine transaction of that nature where the consideration was the substantial equivalent of full payment of the shares in cash. The possible objection to such an arrangement is that the company may over-estimate the value of the consideration, and, therefore, receive less than nominal value for its shares. The Court would doubtless refuse effect to a colourable transaction, entered into for the purpose or with the obvious result of enabling the company to issue its shares at a discount; but it has been ruled that, so long as the company honestly regards the consideration given as fairly representing the nominal value of the shares in cash, its estimate ought not to be critically examined.'

This statement of the law was subsequently applied both by Vaughan Williams J and the Court of Appeal in *Re Wragg Ltd* [1897] 1 Ch 796 at 813–814, 831, 835 respectively. Those decisions are also clear authority for the proposition that, unless the agreement in furtherance of which the shares were issued for a consideration other than cash can be successfully impeached as, for example, colourable, the courts will not go behind it and consider whether or not it was commercially prudent, or whether a more advantageous bargain might have been made, since to do so would be to question the honest commercial judgment of the directors of the company concerned in the ordinary management of that company's business.

My Lords, a similar question arose in two later cases in the Court of Appeal, *Osborne v Steel Barrel Co Ltd* [1942] 1 All ER 634 and *Craddock v Zevo Finance Co Ltd* [1944] 1 All ER 566, the latter decision having been affirmed by your Lordships' House (see [1946] 1 All ER 523n, 27 TC 267 at 284).

Both those cases involved the determination of the cost to the taxpayer of 'stock', (in the second case the 'stock' was a number of investments) for the purpose of calculating the taxpayer's trading profit in connection with his liability to income tax. In both cases the 'stock' had been acquired in whole or in part in return for the allotment of shares credited as fully paid, the shares being issued for a consideration other than cash. In both cases the taxpayer contended that the cost was what the taxpayer had paid. In both cases the Crown sought to go behind the agreement pursuant to which those shares were so issued, and to contend that the issue of the shares credited as fully paid had cost the taxpayer either nothing, or at any rate less than the price for which the taxpayer contended. In both cases the Crown failed. It failed for substantially the same reason, namely that its contention ignored the true nature of the issue of shares credited as fully paid for a consideration other than cash. In the former case Lord Greene MR said ([1942] 1 All ER 634 at 637–638):

'The argument really rests on a misconception as to what happens when a company issues shares credited as fully paid for a consideration other than cash. The primary liability of an allottee of shares is to pay for them in cash; but, when shares are allotted credited as fully paid, this primary liability is satisfied by a consideration other than cash passing from the allottee. A company, therefore, when, in pursuance of such a transaction, it agrees to credit the shares as fully paid, is giving up what it would otherwise have had—namely, the right to call on the allottee for payment of the par value in cash. A company cannot issue £1,000 nominal worth of shares for stock of the market value of £500, since shares cannot be issued at a discount. Accordingly, when fully-paid shares are properly issued for a consideration other than cash, the consideration moving from the company must be at the least equal in value to the par value of the shares and must be based on an honest estimate by the directors of the value of the assets acquired.'

latter case Lord Greene MR said of the Crown's argument ([1944] 1 All ER 566 at 70):

'This proposition amounts to saying that consideration in the form of fully-paid
shares allotted by a company must be treated as being of the value of the shares, no
more and no less. Such a contention will not bear a moment's examination where
the transaction is a straightforward one and not a mere device for issuing shares at
a discount. In the everyday case of reconstruction, the shares in the new company
allotted to the shareholders of the old company as fully-paid will often, if not in
most cases, fetch substantially less than their nominal value if sold in the market.
But this does not mean that they are to be treated as having been issued at a
discount; or that the price paid by the new company for the assets which it acquires
from the old company ought to be treated as something less than the nominal value
of the fully-paid shares. The Crown in this case is in fact attempting to depart from
the rule (the correctness of which it itself admits) that the figure at which stock in
trade is to be brought in is its cost to the trader and to substitute the alleged market
value of the stock for its cost. Of course, in a case where stock which a company
proposes to acquire for shares is deliberately over-valued for the purpose of issuing
an inflated amount of share capital, very different considerations apply. But nothing
of the kind is present in this case which, as I have already pointed out, is a perfectly
proper and normal reconstruction. The propriety of the course adopted is manifest
when the uncertainty as to the value of the investments, which is pointed out by the
commissioners, is borne in mind. It is, I think, true as a general proposition that,
where a company acquires property for fully-paid shares of its own, the price paid
by the company is, *prima facie*, the nominal value of the shares. It is for those who
assert the contrary to establish it, as could be done, for example, in the suggested case
of a deliberately inflated valuation.'

This passage was expressly approved in your Lordships' House (see 27 TC 267 at 287, 294
per Viscount Simon LC and Lord Simonds.

My Lords, it is thus established beyond question that, in ascertaining the cost of
acquiring 'stock' for the purpose of arriving at the taxpayer's trading profit when that
stock has been acquired in return for shares credited as fully paid, being issued for a
consideration other than cash, it is the cost to the taxpayer of that stock which is, at least
prima facie, the relevant figure, and that, unless the agreement can for some reason be
'impeached', the Revenue is not entitled to go behind the price which the taxpayer has
paid whatever the means by which that obligation to pay that price has by agreement
between the parties been discharged.

My Lords, in those circumstances, the crucial question is how far these well-established
principles are to be applied to the ascertainment of 'the value of the consideration, in
. . . money's worth, given by [the taxpayer] . . . wholly and exclusively for the acquisition
of the asset' for the purposes of para 4(1)(a) of Sch 6 to the 1965 Act. For the taxpayer
company it is forcibly argued that there is no logical reason why its liability for
corporation tax on its gains should be determined in some different way from its liability
to corporation tax on its trading profits. For the Crown it is forcibly argued that the
decisions to which I have referred are decisions concerning the ascertainment of the cost
of 'stock' for the purpose of arriving at the taxpayer's trading profit for income tax
purposes, that that cost has been held in the circumstances in question to be the price
which the taxpayer paid, that cost is different from value, and that value has to be
determined by reference to matters other than cost, though ultimately it was conceded
by counsel for the Crown before your Lordships, though not, I think, in the courts
below, that cost might be relevant to the determination of value.

But, my Lords, if it be correct, as both the Special Commissioners and the Court of
Appeal thought, to say that in the present case the consideration given by the taxpayer
company was the taxpayer company's agreement to issue and allot the shares and to
credit them as fully paid, the taxpayer company must unquestionably succeed, for it is
obvious, since the agreement between Eagle Star and the taxpayer company cannot be
impeached, that the value of that credit was 160p per share. But, in the passages the
judgments of Lord Greene MR to which I have referred, he was explaining the nature of
an agreement to issue shares credited as fully paid and otherwise than for cash in orde

to lay the foundation for the rejection of the Crown's argument that the 'stock' in question had cost the taxpayer nothing. I do not think that Lord Greene MR was *a* intending to lay down a rule that in every case where there is an arm's length transaction, such as that now in question, the consideration must always be taken to be the value of the credit given by the company whose shares are being issued and credited as fully paid, and not the shares themselves. What the consideration is in any particular case must be determined by reference to the contract which the parties concerned have concluded. If one looks at para 1 of the agreement of 21 September 1972, it seems to me plain that the *b* consideration was the shares themselves. I do not think that any business man if asked would say that the consideration was the giving of the credit by the taxpayer company of 160p per share, and, if it be permissible to see how the parties themselves regarded the matter, the taxpayer company in its next annual report informed its shareholders that the authorised share capital of the taxpayer company had been increased and that the new shares had been allotted to Eagle Star at '160p per share in exchange for a portfolio *c* of investments . . .'

My Lords, I think that this statement reflects both the commercial reality of this arm's length transaction and the true nature of the consideration given by the taxpayer company. Accordingly, I think, in respectful disagreement with the Court of Appeal and the Special Commissioners, that the consideration in money's worth which has to be valued is the value of the shares and not the value of the credit of which I have spoken. *d* This was, I think, the view of Vinelott J (see [1980] 3 All ER 221 at 231, [1980] 1 WLR 1162 at 1170). ·But, my Lords, to reach that conclusion is not, with respect, to accept the rest of the learned judge's judgment. What then is the value of the shares? The Crown contended that it must be determined by reference to Stock Exchange prices on the day after the shares were first dealt in. I ask: why? Lord Greene MR himself in *Craddock's* case [1944] 1 All ER 566 at 569 said: *e*

> 'Published market quotations, which often relate to quite small and isolated transactions, are notoriously no guide to the value of investments of this character, particularly when the amounts involved are large.'

Lord Greene MR's warning is particularly apposite in the present case, and is as much applicable today as forty years ago when it was uttered. *f*

My Lords, as I have already said, the agreement was concluded on 21 September 1972. It became unconditional on 11 October 1972. My Lords, by virtue of para 10(2) of Sch 10 to the Finance Act 1971, I think it was on the latter date that the acquisition by the taxpayer company is to be treated as having been made. But I am quite unable to regard the evidence of some Stock Exchange dealings at or about the time as sufficient evidence to displace what I would regard as the almost overwhelming evidence of the *g* value of the consideration in money's worth on 11 October 1972 afforded by the agreement of 21 September 1972. For myself I would not go as far as to say that in every case of this kind the value of the consideration in money's worth must always be determined by reference to the price at which the shares credited as fully paid were issued, for it is possible that there might be a very long delay between the conclusion of the conditional agreement and the agreement becoming unconditional, during which *h* period some catastrophic event might occur gravely affecting the value on the latter date. I would wish to reserve for future consideration whether in such a case it might not be legitimate to adduce evidence, if the evidence were available, pointing to the conclusion that the value of the consideration in money's worth was less than the price previously agreed between the parties. But, on the facts of the instant case, I can see no basis on which it would be legitimate to go behind the figure of 160p per share. I think *j* this conclusion is strongly reinforced by the finding of the Special Commissioners in para 10 of the case stated ([1980] 3 All ER 221 at 224):

> 'It is not disputed by the Crown that there were bona fide commercial reasons for the figure of 160p being somewhat in excess of the price at which [the taxpayer company's] shares were currently being dealt in on the Stock Exchange.'

a My Lords, for the reasons which I have endeavoured to give I agree that this appeal fails and should be dismissed.

LORD BRANDON OF OAKBROOK. My Lords, I have had the advantage of reading in draft the speech prepared by my noble and learned friend Lord Fraser. I agree with his conclusion that the appeal should be dismissed and with the reasons which he gives for arriving at that conclusion.

b
Appeal dismissed.

Solicitors: *Solicitor of Inland Revenue; Ashurst, Morris, Crisp & Co* (for the taxpayer company)

c Rengan Krishnan Esq   Barrister.

d

Lyus & another v Prowsa Developments Ltd & others

CHANCERY DIVISION

e DILLON J

18, 19 NOVEMBER, 21 DECEMBER 1981

Trust and trustee – Constructive trust – Sale of registered land – Vendor agreeing to sell land to plaintiffs and erect house on it – Vendor going into liquidation – Vendor's bank selling land to defendant in exercise of mortgagee's power of sale – Contract between bank and defendant
f *stipulating that sale subject to plaintiffs' contract with vendor – Whether stipulation imposing constructive trust on defendant to give effect to plaintiffs' contract – Whether registration giving defendant absolute title free from plaintiffs' unregistered interest – Land Registration Act 1925, ss 20(1), 34(4).*

A company borrowed money from a bank to develop an estate. A mortgage executed by
g the company in favour of the bank to secure the borrowings was registered as a legal charge against the registered title to the estate. Subsequently, on 30 January 1978 the company, with the bank's consent, entered into a contract with the plaintiffs to sell them a plot on the estate and to build on it a house to specifications already agreed by the plaintiffs, for the sum of £14,250. The plaintiffs paid a deposit of £1,425 to the company, contracted to sell their existing house and arranged for a mortgage to cover the excess required to complete the purchase from the company. At all times the plaintiffs
h wished to complete the purchase and were in a financial position to do so. Before the house was completed the company became insolvent and was compulsorily wound up in May 1978. Thereafter it became impossible for the company to perform its contract with the plaintiffs. The bank, which was under no obligation to the plaintiffs to complete their contract with the company, exercised its power of sale as mortgagee by
j selling part of the estate, including the plaintiffs' plot, to the first defendant by a contract dated 18 October 1979. That contract contained a clause (cl 11) that the sale to the fir defendant was subject to and with the benefit of the plaintiffs' contract of 30 Janu 1978. The first defendant was fully aware of the plaintiffs' contract when entering its own contract, and moreover, gave the bank an assurance that the intere contractual purchasers of plots in the land would be dealt with quickly and

purchasers' satisfaction. The sale to the first defendant was completed by a transfer dated 16 November 1979 which contained no reference to the plaintiffs' contract of 30 January 1978. Later, by a contract dated 13 December 1979 the first defendant sold the plot and other parts of the estate to the second defendants. The contract of 13 December contained a special condition that the sale to the second defendants was subject to the plaintiffs' contract of 30 January 1978 in so far as it was enforceable against the first defendant. The sale to the second defendants was completed by a transfer dated 2 January 1980, which also did not refer to the plaintiffs' contract. The respective transfers to the first and second defendants were both registered against the title to the estate. However, at the time of registration there was apparently no reference on the register to the plaintiffs' contract of 30 January 1978. The plaintiffs brought an action against the first and second defendants seeking, inter alia, specific performance of their contract of 30 January 1978 on the ground that the first defendant, by virtue of cl 11 of its contract of 18 October 1979 with the bank, was bound by a constructive trust to complete the contract of 30 January 1978. The second defendants conceded that if cl 11 did impose such a trust on the first defendant the effect of the special condition in the second defendants' contract was to impose a similar trust on the second defendants. The defendants contended (i) that lack of mutuality between them and the plaintiffs prevented the plaintiffs from setting up a constructive trust against them, and (ii) that they were protected from any unregistered interest which the plaintiffs might have in the land by ss 20(1)^a and 34(4)^b of the Land Registration Act 1923 since under s 20 the effect of the registration of a disposition of a freehold title to a transferee was to confer on him an absolute title subject to entries on the register and overriding interests but 'free from all other estates and interests whatsoever' and under s 34(4) the same protection was extended to the purchaser from a mortgagee acting under a power of sale.

Held – The plaintiffs were entitled to an order of specific performance of their contract of 30 January 1978 against the second defendants, for the following reasons—

(1) Having regard to the fact that cl 11 of the contract of 18 October 1979 between the bank and the first defendant had not been inserted solely for the protection of the bank as vendor, since the bank was under no legal obligation to the plaintiffs, cl 11 amounted to a stipulation that the first defendant would on acquiring the land give effect to the plaintiffs' contract and as such was a stipulation in the bargain between the bank and the first defendant that a defined beneficial interest in the property would be taken by the plaintiffs, thereby giving rise to a constructive trust in favour of the plaintiffs that the first defendant would give effect to the plaintiffs' contract. A constructive trust was similarly imposed on the second defendants by virtue of the special condition in their contract with the first defendant. The fact that there was lack of mutuality between the plaintiffs and the defendants did not prevent a constructive trust arising but was only material to the question whether specific performance of the plaintiffs' contract ought to be granted (see p 959 g to j, p 960 h j and p 961 d to h, post); *Bannister v Bannister* [1948] 2 All ER 133, dictum of Lord Denning MR in *Binions v Evans* [1972] 2 All ER at 76, and *Price v Strange* [1977] 3 All ER 371 applied; *Re Schebsman* [1943] 2 All ER 768 considered and explained.

(2) Although it was not fraud for a person to rely on the legal rights conferred by

a   Section 20, so far as material, provides: 'In the case of a freehold estate registered with an absolute title, a disposition of the registered land ... for valuable consideration shall, when registered, confer on the transferee ... an estate in fee simple ... subject—(a) to the incumbrances and other entries, if any, appearing on the register; and (b) unless the contrary is expressed on the register, to the overriding interests, if any, affecting the estate transferred or created, but free from all other estates and interests whatsoever, and the disposition shall operate in like manner as if the registered transferor ... were (subject to any entry to the contrary in the register) entitled to the registered land ... in fee simple in possession for his own benefit.'

     ction 34(4), so far as material, provides: 'A sale by [the proprietor of a charge] under the power   sale shall operate and be completed by registration in the same manner, as nearly as may be   as a transfer for valuable consideration by the proprietor of the land at the time of the   ration of the charge would have operated or been completed, and, as respects the land   rred, the charge and all incumbrances and entries inferior thereto shall be cancelled.'

a ss 20(1) and 34(4) of the 1925 Act in order to obtain an absolute title 'free from all other estates and interests whatsoever', nevertheless the Act could not be used as an instrument of fraud, and for the first defendant to refuse to give effect to the plaintiffs' contract in reliance on ss 20(1) and 34(4) would be to use the Act as an instrument of fraud in order to resile from a positive stipulation in the bargain under which it had obtained the land. Accordingly, notwithstanding the provisions of the 1925 Act, the first defendant (and therefore the second defendants) was required by reason of there being a constructive

b trust in favour of the plaintiffs to give effect to the plaintiffs' contract (see p 962 a b and e to h, post); *Rochefoucauld v Boustead* [1897] 1 Ch 196 applied; *Miles v Bull (No 2)* [1969] 3 All ER 1585 distinguished.

Notes

For constructive trusts, see 38 Halsbury's Laws (3rd edn) 855, paras 1440, 1441, and for
c cases on the subject, see 47 Digest (Repl) 101–113, 727–814.

For the Land Registration Act 1925, ss 20, 34, see 27 Halsbury's Statutes (3rd edn) 801, 813.

Cases referred to in judgment

Bannister v Bannister [1948] 2 All ER 133, CA, 47 Digest (Repl) 101, *733*.
d *Beatty v Guggenheim Exploration Co* (1919) 225 NY 380.
Beswick v Beswick [1967] 2 All ER 1197, [1968] AC 58, [1967] 3 WLR 932, HL, 12 Digest (Reissue) 49, *256*.
Binions v Evans [1972] 2 All ER 70, [1972] Ch 359, [1972] 2 WLR 729, CA, Digest (Cont Vol D) 814, *2771a*.
Clore v Theatrical Properties Ltd and Westby & Co Ltd [1936] 3 All ER 483, CA, 31(1) Digest
e (Reissue) 213, *1755*.
Debtor, Re a, ex p Trustee v Solomon [1966] 3 All ER 255; sub nom *Re Solomon, a bankrupt, ex p Trustee of the Property of the Bankrupt v Solomon* [1967] Ch 573, [1967] 2 WLR 172, 27(1) Digest (Reissue) 95, *686*.
Gissing v Gissing [1970] 2 All ER 780, [1971] AC 886, [1970] 3 WLR 255, HL, 27(1) Digest (Reissue) 311, *2303*.
f *Halsall v Brizell* [1957] 1 All ER 371, [1957] Ch 169, [1957] 2 WLR 123, Digest (Cont Vol B) 641, *2719a*.
King v Allen (David) & Sons, Billposting, Ltd [1916] 2 AC 54, [1916–17] All ER Rep 268, HL, 12 Digest (Reissue) 428, *3098*.
Midland Bank Trust Co Ltd v Green [1981] 1 All ER 153, [1981] AC 513, [1981] 2 WLR 28, HL.
g *Miles v Bull (No 2)* [1969] 3 All ER 1585, 27(1) Digest (Reissue) 98, *699*.
Pallant v Morgan [1952] 2 All ER 951, [1953] Ch 43, 44 Digest (Repl) 35, *247*.
Price v Strange [1977] 3 All ER 371, [1978] Ch 337, [1977] 3 WLR 943, CA, Digest (Cont Vol E) 572, *110a*.
Rochefoucauld v Boustead [1897] 1 Ch 196, CA, 12 Digest (Reissue) 211, *1352*.
Schebsman, Re, ex p Official Receiver, Trustee v Cargo Superintendents (London) Ltd [1943] 2
h All ER 768, [1944] Ch 83, CA, 5 Digest (Reissue) 694, *6042*.
Stirling v Maitland (1864) 5 B & S 841, [1861–73] All ER Rep 358, 122 ER 1043, 12 Digest (Reissue) 761, *5448*.
White v Bijou Mansions Ltd [1938] 1 All ER 546, [1938] Ch 351, CA; affg [1937] 3 All ER 269, [1937] Ch 610, 38 Digest (Repl) 881, *921*.

j ### Action

By a writ issued on 17 June 1980 and a statement of claim dated 21 October 1980 the plaintiffs, Edward Alfred Lyus and Margaret Rose Lyus, claimed against the first defendants, Prowsa Developments Ltd, and the second defendants, Derek Arthur Enefer and Dennis Peter Enefer, (1) a declaration that an agreement dated 30 January 1978 between the plaintiffs and Pennock, Haste and Howarth Ltd (the vendor) to sell to the plaintiffs for £14,250 freehold property known as plot 29, St Martin's Green Estate, Trimley St Martin, Suffolk, was binding on the defendants; (2) specific performance that agreement; (3) damages in addition to or in lieu of specific performance and (4) alternatively, damages for breach of contract. The facts are set out in the judgment.

Charles Purle for the plaintiffs.
Hedley Marten for the first defendants.
Paul Hampton for the second defendants.

Cur adv vult

21 December. **DILLON J** read the following judgment: This action raises a question of law which I have found of considerable difficulty. The basic facts lie, however, in a small compass and are not in dispute. Around the beginning of 1978, the plaintiffs, Mr and Mrs Lyus, had occasion to move from Essex to Suffolk. They had to find a house in Suffolk, and they found an estate called the St Martin's Green Estate at Trimley St Martin which was being developed by a company called Pennock, Haste and Howarth Ltd. I shall call that company the vendor company.

By a contract in writing dated 30 January 1978, and made between the vendor company of the one part and the plaintiffs of the other part, the vendor company agreed to sell and the plaintiffs agreed to purchase plot 29 of the St Martin's Green Estate for the sum of £14,250. The plot was to be transferred together with a house built by the vendor company thereon, and completion was to take place not later than ten days after written notification had been given to the plaintiffs or their solicitors that the building of the property had been substantially completed. The contract does not itself indicate what type of house was to be built on the plot, but there is no doubt that working drawings, with a specification on them, were produced to the plaintiffs and were approved by them, and they were shown a completed version on another plot of the type of house they wanted. There is no doubt, therefore, what type of house was to be built, or what work is required to build it.

On entering into the contract, the plaintiffs paid a deposit of £1,425 to the vendor company's solicitors as agents for the vendor company. In addition, in order to put themselves in a position in which they would be able to complete the contract as soon as the house was substantially completed, they contracted to sell the house that they then owned at Benfleet, and they arranged for a building society mortgage for the small balance they would require over and above the net proceeds of the Benfleet house to complete their purchase under the contract of 30 January 1978.

It is formally asserted on the pleadings that the plaintiffs at some stage impliedly abandoned the contract of 30 January 1978, or are barred by laches from enforcing it. Those allegations were, however, rightly abandoned at the trial. The plaintiffs have at all times been extremely keen to complete their purchase, and been in a financial position to do so, provided that the house is first substantially completed fit for occupation. The formidable difficulties they encountered have not been of their making.

At the time of the contract, plot 29 was an empty plot, and the building of the house had not begun. It was then begun by the vendor company, but there were delays. The vendor company became, if it was not already, insolvent, and on 15 May 1978 it was ordered to be compulsorily wound up. The plaintiffs' solicitors endeavoured to persuade firstly the Official Receiver, and then the private liquidator who replaced him as liquidator of the vendor company, to complete the building of the plaintiffs' house, but the answer was that the vendor company was in no position to do so. I have no doubt that there was no possibility at any time after the winding-up order was made of the vendor company performing its obligations to the plaintiffs.

As is commonly the case with building development, the development by the vendor company of the St Martin's Green Estate was financed by bank borrowing. The bank concerned, National Westminster, held, initially through its associate County Bank from which it in due course took a transfer, charges by way of legal mortgage on the estate, including plot 29. These charges were prior in date to the plaintiffs' contract. The obvious and inevitable course after the vendor company had gone into liquidation was for the bank to exercise its power of sale as mortgagee over the estate. The plaintiffs' contract with the vendor company of 30 January 1978 had been entered into by the vendor company with the consent of the bank as mortgagee, but the bank had not had any negotiations with the plaintiffs and the bank was not a party to, or bound by, the

a contract. In particular, the bank was under no liability to the plaintiffs or anyone else to complete the building of the plaintiffs' house. There is no doubt at all that the bank could have sold the estate, and plot 29 in particular, free from the plaintiffs' contract. If the bank had done that, it is indisputable that the plaintiffs would have had no claim whatsoever against the purchaser.

The title to the estate was registered at HM Land Registry. The plaintiffs' solicitors

b had very properly registered a caution against the title to protect the contract, but the bank by virtue of its prior charge was in a position to override the caution and transfer plot 29 to a purchaser free from all interest of the plaintiffs. In that event, the plaintiffs' only rights would have been to prove for damages in the liquidation of the vendor company, and, it would seem, to be repaid their deposit by the National House Building Council under collateral arrangements, the details of which I do not need to set out. In

c fact, however, the bank chose to sell plot 29 subject to, and with the benefit of, the plaintiffs' contract.

The purchaser was the first defendant in these proceedings, and the contract is dated 18 October 1979. The contract comprised other land besides plot 29, and the total price payable by the first defendants was £92,500. The clause relevant to the plaintiffs' contract, and the only clause to which I need refer at the moment, is cl 11 which

d provided, so far as material, that the property contracted to be sold to the first defendant was sold subject to, but with the benefit of, the agreement dated 30 January 1978, made between the vendor company and the plaintiffs in respect of plot 29.

The question I have to decide is whether cl 11 gave the plaintiffs the right to enforce their contract of 30 January 1978 against the first defendant. There is no doubt that the first defendant entered into its agreement with the bank of 18 October 1979 with full

e knowledge of the plaintiffs' contract. Indeed, in a letter to the bank's agents, Messrs Strutt and Parker, of 27 June 1979, the first defendant's solicitors had given an assurance that their client would take all reasonable steps in its power to make sure that the interests of contractual purchasers were dealt with quickly and to their satisfaction.

The primary case for the plaintiffs is founded on the judgment of Lord Denning MR in *Binions v Evans* [1972] 2 All ER 70, [1972] Ch 359. It is submitted that it follows from

f that judgment, and from the general principles of which it is an illustration, that on accepting the land comprised in the agreement of 18 October 1979, the first defendant became bound by a constructive trust for the benefit of the plaintiffs by virtue of cl 11 to complete and carry into effect the plaintiffs' contract of 30 January 1978 in respect of plot 29. It is alternatively submitted, albeit faintly and with the hesitation inevitable whenever s 56 is invoked, that s 56 of the Law of Property Act 1925 entitles the plaintiffs

g to enforce cl 11 against the first defendant by way of a decree for specific performance of the contract of 30 January 1978.

Before examining these contentions, I should complete the history of the facts. The first defendant completed its purchase from the bank under the agreement of 18 October 1979 by a transfer which is dated 16 November 1979. That transfer contains no reference at all to the plaintiffs or their contract, but it has not been suggested that the absence of

h any such references in the transfer deprives the plaintiffs of rights if cl 11 has given them rights. The first defendant thereupon resold plot 29 and certain other parts of the land to Derek Arthur Enefer and Dennis Peter Enefer, who are described as the second defendants and who are themselves builders. The first defendant's contract with the second defendants is dated 13 December 1979. The total price under it is £57,400. Special condition (b) provided that the property was sold subject to the plaintiffs' contract

j of 30 January 1978 in respect of plot 29, so far, if at all, as it may have been enforceabl against the first defendant. It has been common ground that if the effect of cl 11 was impose a constructive trust on the first defendant, then the effect of special condition was to impose a similar trust on the second defendants. I have, therefore, to concen on cl 11, and the sale by the bank to the first defendant.

The sale by the first defendant to the second defendants was completed by a t dated 2 January 1980, which again contains no reference to the plaintiffs contract. The second defendants are now the registered proprietors of, inter ali

and I do not doubt that the register of the title is clear of all reference to the plaintiffs or their contract. The second defendants have in their own interests carried on work on the house on plot 29, and roofed it in, but work still remains to be done to complete it, and it is estimated that the current cost of the outstanding work will be £9,600. The value of plot 29 with the house completed satisfactorily would now be £27,500.

Turning from the facts to the issues of law, I deal first with s 56 of the Law of Property Act 1925. Great doubt has been felt by the court in many cases as to the true scope of that section, but the judgment of Simonds J in *White v Bijou Mansions Ltd* [1937] 3 All ER 269, [1937] Ch 610 has always been regarded as laying down correctly certain of the limitations on the apparently wide language of the section. Simonds J concluded ([1937] 3 All ER 269 at 277, [1937] Ch 610 at 625) that the only person who could sue on a deed or document in reliance on s 56 was the person who under the document can point to any grant or any covenant purported to be made to or with him. The plaintiffs cannot find any such grant or covenant purported to be made to or with them in cl 11 of the agreement of 18 December 1979 between the bank and the first defendant, or in special condition (b) of the agreement of 13 December 1979 between the first defendant and the second defendants. Therefore, s 56 does not assist the plaintiffs at all in this case.

I pass to the plaintiffs' main argument founded on *Binions v Evans* [1972] 2 All ER 70, [1972] Ch 359. The facts of that case were simple. Estate owners (the vendors) had by a somewhat ambiguously worded document granted the defendant the right to occupy a cottage rent free for her life, or until she should give notice to determine her rights. The vendors then sold the cottage to the plaintiffs, the purchasers, subject to the defendant's rights. The purchasers then claimed possession of the cottage on the ground either that on the construction of the ambiguously worded document the defendant was merely a tenant at will, or that the purchasers, as purchasers for value, albeit with notice, were not bound by the contractual licence the vendors had granted to the defendant. The purchasers failed.

The majority of the Court of Appeal, Megaw and Stephenson LJJ, decided the case on the basis that the licence agreement between the vendors and the defendant had constituted the defendant tenant for life of the cottage for the purposes of the Settled Land Act 1925. If she was tenant for life, then plainly her life interest was not overreached by the conveyance of the cottage to the purchasers, subject to her interest. That ground of decision is not relevant here. Megaw LJ also considered that the purchasers could be restrained by injunction from interfering with existing contractual rights between the vendors and the defendant. That also has no application here as there is here no question of the vendor company performing its contract with the plaintiffs.

Lord Denning MR reached the same conclusion, that the purchasers were bound by the defendant's rights and could not evict her, by a different route. He did not agree that the Settled Land Act 1925 applied. He regarded the defendant as a contractual licensee with a right to reside in the cottage for the rest of her life, and not as tenant for life for the purposes of the Settled Land Act 1925. He concluded ([1972] 2 All ER 70 at 75, [1972] Ch 359 at 367) that the effect of the making of the agreement between the vendors and the defendant was to give her an equitable interest in land, namely in the cottage, which a court of equity would protect and would enforce against a purchaser with notice. However, he proceeded to consider the position in the alternative ([1972] 2 All ER 70 at 76, [1972] Ch 359 at 368–369):

'Suppose, however, that [the defendant] did not have an equitable interest at the outset; nevertheless it is quite plain that she obtained one afterwards when the [the vendors] sold the cottage. They stipulated with the purchaser that he was to take the house 'subject to' [the defendant's] rights under the agreement. They supplied the purchaser with a copy of the contract, and the purchaser paid less because of her right to stay there. In these circumstances, this court will impose on the purchaser a constructive trust for her benefit, for the simple reason that it would be utterly inequitable for the purchaser to turn the widow out contrary to the stipulation subject to which he took the premises. That seems to me clear from the important decision of *Bannister v Bannister* [1948] 2 All ER 133, which was applied by the ... e, and which I gladly follow. This imposing of a constructive trust is entirely

in accord with the precepts of equity.   As Cardozo J once put it: "A constructive
trust is the formula through which the conscience of equity finds expression"; see
Beatty v Guggenheim Exploration Co (1919) 225 NY 380 at 385, or, as Lord Diplock put
it quite recently in *Gissing v Gissing* [1970] 2 All ER 780 at 790, [1971] AC 886 at 905,
a constructive trust is created "whenever the trustee has so conducted himself that
it would be inequitable to allow him to deny to the cestui que trust a beneficial
interest in the land acquired".   I know that there are some who have doubted
whether a contractual licensee has any protection against a purchaser, even one who
takes with full notice.   We were referred in this connection to Professor Wade's
article in the Law Quarterly Review (1952) 68 LQR 337, and to the judgment of
Goff J in *Re A Debtor, ex p The Trustee v Solomon* [1966] 3 All ER 225, [1967] Ch
573.   None of these doubts can prevail, however, when the situation gives rise to a
constructive trust.   Whenever the owner sells the land to a purchaser, and at the
same time stipulates that he shall take it "subject to" a contractual licence, I think it
plain that a court of equity will impose on the purchaser a constructive trust in
favour of the beneficiary.   It is true that the stipulation (that the purchaser shall take
it subject to the rights of the licensee) is a stipulation for the benefit of one who is
not a party to the contract of sale; but, as Lord Upjohn said in *Beswick v Beswick*
[1967] 2 All ER 1197 at 1219, [1968] AC 58 at 98, that is just the very case in which
equity will come to the aid of the common law.   It does so by imposing a
constructive trust on the purchaser.   It would be utterly inequitable that the
purchaser should be able to turn out the beneficiary.   It is to be noticed that in the
two cases which are said to give rise to difficulty, *King v David Allen & Sons,
Billposting Ltd* [1916] 2 AC 54, [1916–17] All ER Rep 268 and *Clore v Theatrical
Properties Ltd and Westby & Co Ltd* [1936] 3 All ER 483, there was no trace of a
stipulation, express or implied, that the purchaser should take the property subject
to the right of the contractual licensee.   In the first case, if Mr King had protected
himself by stipulating that the company should take the lease "subject to the rights
of David Allen", I cannot think that he would have been held liable in damages.   In
the second case the documents were exceedingly complicated, but if Mr Clore had
acquired the theatre "subject to the rights of the licensees", I cannot suppose that this
court would have allowed him to disregard those rights.   In many of these cases the
purchaser takes *expressly* "subject to" the rights of the licensee.   Obviously the
purchaser then holds the land on an imputed trust for the licensee.' [Lord Denning's
emphasis]

It has been pointed out that there are differences on the facts beteen *Binions v Evans* and
the present case.   One difference is that the defendant in *Binions v Evans* was in occupation
of the cottage before and at the time of the sale to the purchasers.   It is suggested that
equity is particularly tender to persons in occupation of land.   It seems to me, however,
that the protection equity accords to persons in occupation is accorded, so far as
unregistered land is concerned, where there is no special statutory provision, because any
purchaser has, or is treated as having, knowledge of the rights of the persons in
occupation.

In the present case, the first defendant had the fullest actual knowledge of the plaintiffs'
contract with the vendor company.   It is thus not significant, apart from any question
which may arise from the fact that this is registered land, that the plaintiffs were not in
actual occupation or physical possession of plot 29.

A more important difference is that in *Binions v Evans,* the defendant had continuing
rights as licensee against the vendors before the sale of the cottage to the purchasers.   If,
therefore, the defendant's rights as licensee did not bind the purchasers, the defendant
would seemingly have had a valid claim for damages against the vendors on the basis of
the rule in *Stirling v Maitland* (1864) 5 B & S 841, [1861–73] All ER Rep 358.   It would
be a strange result of a conveyance of the cottage by the vendors to the purchasers
expressly subject to the defendant's rights, that the purchasers could override the
defendant's rights and leave the vendors liable in damages to the defendant.   The
provision that the cottage was sold subject to the defendant's rights was thus imposed i
some part for the protection of the vendors, as Lord Denning MR seems to have had

mind in his comments on *King v David Allen & Sons*. In the factual matrix it was
necessary for the protection of the vendors to interpret the agreement between the   *a*
vendors and the purchasers as conferring rights on the defendant as against the
purchasers, and this was done through the medium, as Lord Denning MR put it, 'of
imposing a constructive trust on the purchasers for the defendant's benefit'.

By contrast, there are many cases in which land is expressly conveyed subject to
possible incumbrances when there is no thought at all of conferring any fresh rights on
third parties who may be entitled to the benefit of the incumbrances. The land is   *b*
expressed to be sold subject to incumbrances to satisfy the vendor's duty to disclose all
possible incumbrances known to him, and to protect the vendor against any possible
claim by the purchaser if a third party establishes an overriding right to the benefit of the
incumbrance against the purchaser. So, for instance, land may be contracted to be sold
and may be expressed to be conveyed subject to the restrictive covenants contained in a
conveyance some sixty or ninety years old. No one would suggest that by accepting such   *c*
a form of contract or conveyance a purchaser is assuming a new liability in favour of
third parties to observe the covenants if there was for any reason before the contract or
conveyance no one who could make out a title as against the purchaser to the benefit of
the covenants.

Counsel for the second defendants has drawn my attention to the well-known passage
in the judgment of Lord Greene MR in *Re Schebsman, ex p Official Receiver* [1943] 2 All ER   *d*
768 at 770, [1944] Ch 83 at 89 where he said:

> 'The first question which arises is whether or not [the debtor] was a trustee for his
> wife and daughter of the benefit of the undertaking given by the English company
> in their favour. An examination of the decided cases does, it is true, show that the
> courts have on occasions adopted what may be called a liberal view on questions of
> this character. But in the present case, I cannot find in the contract anything to   *e*
> justify the conclusion that a trust was intended. It is not legitimate to import into
> the contract the idea of a trust when the parties have given no indication that such
> was their intention. To interpret this contract as creating a trust would, in my
> judgment, be to disregard the dividing line between the case of a trust and the
> simple case of a contract made between two persons for the benefit of a third. That
> dividing line exists, although it may not always be easy to determine where it is to   *f*
> be drawn.'

Counsel for the second defendants has also referred to the equally well-known sentence
in the judgment of du Parcq LJ where he said ([1943] 2 All ER 768 at 779, [1944] Ch 83
at 104):

> 'It is true that, by the use possibly of unguarded language, a person may create a   *g*
> trust, as Monsieur Jourdain talked prose, without knowing it [see Molière, *Le
> Bourgeois Gentilhomme*, II iv], but unless an intention to create a trust is clearly to be
> collected from the language used and the circumstances of the case, I think that the
> court ought not to be astute to discover indications of such an intention.'

As against that, however, in *Bannister v Bannister* [1948] 2 All ER 133 Scott LJ in giving   *h*
the judgment of a Court of Appeal, which included Jenkins J, said (at 136) that it was not
necessary that the bargain on which an absolute conveyance was made should include
any express stipulation that the grantee was in so many words to hold as trustee. It was
enough that the bargain should have included a stipulation under which some
sufficiently defined beneficial interest in the property was to be taken by another. If the
bargain did include such a stipulation, then the equitable principle on which a   *j*
constructive trust is raised would be applied against a person who insisted on the absolute
character of the conveyance to himself for the purpose of defeating a beneficial interest
which, according to the true bargain, was to belong to another. In as much as the
constructive trust is raised to counter unconscionable conduct or fraud in the sense in
which that term is used in a court of equity, the application of the equitable principle to
which Scott LJ refers must depend on the facts of the particular case rather than on the
mere wording of the particular document. *Re Schebsman* is, therefore, concerned with a

somewhat different problem. It comes in, if at all, in that the absence of a clear
a declaration of trust may be one of the factors to be borne in mind in considering whether
some beneficial interest was, according to the true bargain, to belong to a third party.

It may be added by way of a footnote to the judgment of Scott LJ that even if the
beneficial interest of the claimant in the property concerned has not been fully defined,
the court may yet intervene to raise a constructive trust on appropriate terms if to leave
the defendant retaining the property free from all interest of the claimant would be
b tantamount to sanctioning a fraud on the part of the defendant: see *Pallant v Morgan*
[1952] 2 All ER 951, [1953] Ch 43. That is a further indication that the *Schebsman* test is
not the criterion for the existence of a constructive trust.

The first question is, therefore, whether the bargain between the bank and the first
defendant included a stipulation to the effect that on acquiring the land the first
defendant would give effect, in relation to plot 29, to the contract which had been made
c between the vendor company and the plaintiffs. That has to be decided on the evidence,
and on this point all the evidence in this case is documentary.

The second question is then whether the provisions of the Land Registration Act 1925
make any difference, this land having at all times been registered land. There is no
evidence in this case that the first defendant paid less for the property it bought because
it was buying under an obligation to give effect to the plaintiffs' contract in relation to
d plot 29. The documents indicate that the property was never offered to the first
defendant or anyone else, except subject to the plaintiffs' contract.

Bearing in mind that there is no basis on which it could be suggested that the bank
could be under any obligation to the plaintiffs to complete the house on plot 29 for them,
and bearing in mind the first defendant's solicitors' letter to Messrs Strutt and Parker, to
which I have referred, I conclude that cl 11 was not inserted in the agreement of 18
e October 1979 solely for the protection of the bank, like cl 7 of that agreement which sets
out other matters subject to which the property was sold, and I conclude that it was a
stipulation of the bargain between the bank and the first defendant that the first
defendant would give effect, in relation to plot 29, to the contract which had been made
between the vendor company and the plaintiffs.

If that is correct, it would follow, in my judgment, from the judgment of Scott LJ in
f *Bannister v Bannister*, and from the judgment of Lord Denning MR in *Binions v Evans*,
that, unless the Land Registration Act requires a different conclusion, the first defendant,
having accepted the land under the agreement of 18 October 1979 and the consequent
transfer, holds plot 29 on a constructive trust in favour of the plaintiffs to give effect to
the plaintiffs' contract. That trust is also imposed on the second defendants by virtue of
condition (b) of their agreement with the first defendants.

g It has been submitted for the defendants that such a conclusion would involve a want
of mutuality which is offensive to the traditional approach of the courts of equity, in that
it would involve that the plaintiffs acquire rights against the first defendant by virtue of
the agreement to which they are not parties, while the first defendant, for want of privity
of contract, has no corresponding right to sue the plaintiffs for specific performance or
damages. I do not think that that submission is valid. Want of mutuality is merely a
h factor which the court of equity may have to consider in deciding whether or not to
grant a decree of specific performance. It is not an absolute bar to specific performance:
see *Price v Strange* [1977] 3 All ER 371, [1978] Ch 337. Moreover, there are well
established authorities, such as *Halsall v Brizell* [1957] 1 All ER 371, [1957] Ch 169, to the
effect that any person who takes the benefit of a contract must assume the burden. In so
far, therefore, as the plaintiffs have sought to assert the benefit of their contract with the
j vendor company of 30 January 1978, they must submit to the burden of that contract.

This does not, however, conclude the matter since I also have to consider the effect of
the provisions of the Land Registration Act 1925, plot 29 having at all material times, a
I have mentioned, been registered land. In the course of the argument, emphasis w
laid on the effect of s 34(4) of the Land Registration Act 1925, which is concerned w
the effect on subsequent interests of a transfer of registered land by a mortgagee. Sec
34 has, however, to be read with s 20, which is concerned with the effect of
registration of a transfer of registered land by the registered proprietor. The prote

conferred by s 34 on a transfer by a morgagee is thus additional to the protection which is conferred by s 20 on registration of a transfer by a registered proprietor.

It has been pointed out by Lord Wilberforce in *Midland Bank Trust Co Ltd v Green* [1981] 1 All ER 153 at 159, [1981] AC 513 at 531 that it is not fraud to rely on legal rights conferred by Act of Parliament. Under s 20, the effect of the registration of the transferee of a freehold title is to confer an absolute title subject to entries on the register and overriding interests, but 'free from all other estates and interests whatsoever including estates and interests of His Majesty'. In *Miles v Bull (No 2)* [1969] 3 All ER 1585 at 1589, Bridge J expressed the view that the words which I have quoted embraced, prima facie, not only all kinds of legal interests, but all kinds of equitable interests. He therefore held, as I read his judgment (at 1590), that actual or constructive notice on the part of a purchaser of an unregistered interest would not have the effect of imposing a constructive trust on him. The interest in *Miles v Bull (No 2)* was the interest in the matrimonial home of a deserted wife who had failed to protect her interest by registration under the Matrimonial Homes Act 1967. The contract for sale between the husband, who was the registered proprietor, and the purchaser provided that the house concerned was sold subject to such rights of occupation as might subsist in favour of the wife with a proviso that this was not to imply that the wife had, or would after completion have, any such rights as against the purchaser. Plainly, therefore, the clause was only included in the contract for the protection of the husband who was the vendor. The wife was to get no fresh rights, and in *Miles v Bull* it was not a stipulation of the bargain between the vendor and the purchaser that the purchaser should give effect to the rights of the deserted wife as against the vendor. *Miles v Bull* is thus distinguishable from the facts of the present case as I interpret those facts.

It seems to me that the fraud on the part of the defendants in the present case lies not just in relying on the legal rights conferred by an Act of Parliament, but in the first defendant reneging on a positive stipulation in favour of the plaintiffs in the bargain under which the first defendant acquired the land. That makes, as it seems to me, all the difference. It has long since been held, for instance in *Rochefoucauld v Boustead* [1897] 1 Ch 196, that the provisions of the Statute of Frauds 1677, now incorporated in certain sections of the Law of Property Act 1925, cannot be used as an instrument of fraud, and that it is fraud for a person to whom land is agreed to be conveyed as trustee for another to deny the trust and relying on the terms of the statute to claim the land for himself. *Rochefoucauld v Boustead* was one of the authorities on which the judgment in *Bannister v Bannister* was founded.

It seems to me that the same considerations are applicable in relation to the Land Registration Act 1925. If, for instance, the agreement of 18 October 1979 between the bank and the first defendant had expressly stated that the first defendant would hold plot 29 on trust to give effect for the benefit of the plaintiffs to the plaintiffs' agreement with the vendor company, it would be difficult to say that that express trust was overreached and rendered nugatory by the Land Registration Act 1925. The Land Registration Act 1925 does not, therefore, affect the conclusion which I would otherwise have reached in reliance on *Bannister v Bannister* and the judgment of Lord Denning MR in *Binions v Evans*, had plot 29 been unregistered land.

The plaintiffs are, therefore, entitled to succeed in this action. The appropriate relief in that event is that specific performance should be ordered as against the second defendants of the sale to the plaintiffs of plot 29, with the completed house thereon, on the terms of the agreement of 30 January 1978 made between the plaintiffs and the vendor company.

Order accordingly.

Solicitors: *F Barnes & Son*, Romford (for the plaintiffs); *Turner Martin & Symes*, Ipswich for the first defendants); *Notcutts*, Ipswich (for the second defendants).

Evelyn M C Budd   Barrister.

Hill v Anderton

a

HOUSE OF LORDS

LORD DIPLOCK, LORD ELWYN-JONES, LORD KEITH OF KINKEL, LORD ROSKILL AND LORD BRIDGE OF HARWICH

30 JUNE, 1, 22 JULY 1982

b

Magistrates – Jurisdiction – Trial of information – Validity of information – Laying of information – Requirements for proper laying of information – Whether information required to be personally received by magistrate or clerk to justices – Whether information properly laid within appropriate time limit if received by member of justices' clerk's staff authorised to receive it – Magistrates' Courts Act 1980, s 127.

c

All that is required for a written information to be laid or a written complaint to be made to a justice of the peace or the clerk to the justices is the delivery of the document to a person authorised to receive it on behalf of the justice of the peace or the clerk to the justices. Accordingly, for the purposes of s 127[a] of the Magistrates' Courts Act 1980 an information is 'laid ... within six months from the time when the offence was committed, or the matter of complaint arose' if it is received within that time at the office of the clerk to the justices for the relevant area by a member of the staff of the clerk who is expressly or impliedly authorised to receive it for onward transmission to a justice of the peace or to the clerk. It is not necessary for the information to be personally received by a justice of the peace or by the clerk to the justices (see p 964 *h j*, p 971 *f* to *h*, p 973 *g h* and p 974 *a b c*, post).

d

R v Hughes (1879) 4 QBD 614 applied.

R v Gateshead Justices, ex p Tesco Stores Ltd [1981] 1 All ER 1027 overruled in part.

Per curiam. (1) If a summons or warrant is required to be issued following the making of a complaint or laying of an information, the information or complaint must, after it has been received, be laid before a magistrate or the clerk to the justices, since the function of determining whether a summons or warrant should be issued is a judicial function which must be performed judicially by the magistrate or clerk and cannot be delegated to a subordinate (see p 964 *h j*, p 971 *j*, p 972 *a b e f* and p 974 *e*, post); *R v Gateshead Justices, ex p Tesco Stores Ltd* [1981] 1 All ER 1027 approved in part.

e

f

(2) An oral information or complaint should as a matter of prudence be addressed by the informant or complainant or his authorised agent to a justice of the peace or the clerk to the justices in person (see p 964 *h j* and p 974 *c e*, post).

g

Decision of the Divisional Court of the Queen's Bench Division sub nom *R v Leeds Justices, ex p Hanson* [1981] 3 All ER 72 affirmed.

Notes

For the laying of an information and the time in which it must be laid, see 29 Halsbury's Laws (4th edn) paras 242, 291, and for cases on the subject, see 33 Digest (Repl) 205, 441–445.

h

For the Magistrates' Courts Act 1980, s 127, see 50(2) Halsbury's Statutes (3rd edn) 1552.

Cases referred to in opinions

Dixon v Wells (1890) 25 QBD 249, DC, 33 Digest (Repl) 208, 460.

R v Brentford Justices, ex p Catlin [1975] 2 All ER 201, [1975] QB 455, [1975] 2 WLR 506, DC, Digest (Cont Vol D) 631, 476a.

j

R v Gateshead Justices, ex p Tesco Stores Ltd, R v Birmingham Justices, ex p D W Parkin Construction Ltd [1981] 1 All ER 1027, [1981] QB 470, [1981] 2 WLR 419, DC.

R v Hughes (1879) 4 QBD 614, 33 Digest (Repl) 219, 535.

---

a   Section 127, so far as material, is set out at p 969 *c d*, post

Appeal

Hill v Anderton

a

Leonard Hill appealed with leave of the House of Lords granted on 26 October 1981 against the decision of the Divisional Court (Griffiths LJ and Woolf J) ([1981] 3 All ER 72) dated 22 June 1981 refusing an order prohibiting the Manchester City Stipendiary Magistrate from proceeding to try the appellant on a charge of driving a motor vehicle while having more than the permitted limit of alcohol in his blood brought against him by the respondent, Cyril James Anderton, the Chief Constable of Manchester, under s 6(1) of the Road Traffic Act 1972. The facts are set out in the judgment of Lord Roskill.

b

Dhesi v Chief Constable of Kent

Gian Singh Dhesi appealed with leave of the House of Lords granted on 26 October against the decision of the Divisional Court (Griffiths LJ and Woolf J) ([1981] 3 All ER 72) dated 22 June 1981 refusing an order of certiorari to quash the determination of the Dartford Justices on 7 April 1981 when they convicted the appellant on two summonses following the laying of informations by Chief Inspector Anthony Bentley, alleging that on 17 July 1980 he failed without reasonable excuse to provide a specimen of blood or urine, contrary to s 9(3) of the Road Traffic Act 1972, and on the same day failed to give his name and address to a police constable, contrary to s 162 of that Act. The respondent to the appeal was the Chief Constable of Kent. The facts are set out in the judgment of Lord Roskill.

c

d

Hughes v Hill

Stephen Hughes appealed with leave of the House of Lords granted on 26 October 1981 against the decision of the Divisional Court (Griffiths LJ and Woolf J) ([1981] 3 All ER 72) dated 22 June 1981 refusing an order prohibiting the justices of the peace for the petty sessional division of Edmonton from further proceeding with his trial on a summons issued against him by Inspector Robert Hill of Hornsey Police Station alleging that he drove a motor vehicle without due care and attention, contrary to s 3 of the Road Traffic Act 1972. The respondent did not appear and was not represented at the hearing of the appeal. The facts are set out in the judgment of Lord Roskill.

e

f

Martin Kershaw QC and *Adrian Salter* for the appellants.
Anthony Scrivener QC and *Gregory Stone* for the respondents.

Their Lordships took time for consideration.

g

22 July. The following opinions were delivered.

LORD DIPLOCK. My Lords, I have had the benefit of reading in draft the speech to be delivered by my noble and learned friend Lord Roskill. I agree with it, and for the reasons he gives I too would dismiss these appeals and answer the certified question as he proposes.

h

LORD ELWYN-JONES. My Lords, I have had the advantage of reading in draft the speech prepared by my noble and learned friend, Lord Roskill, with which I agree. For the reasons he gives I too would dismiss these appeals.

j

LORD KEITH OF KINKEL. My Lords, I have had the benefit of reading in draft the speech to be delivered by my noble and learned friend Lord Roskill. I agree with it, and for the reasons he gives I too would dismiss these appeals and answer the certified question as he proposes.

LORD ROSKILL. My Lords, these three appeals, consolidated by order of your
a Lordships' House, raise a question of great importance to the administration of justice in
magistrates' courts in England and Wales. They are brought from decisions dated 22
June 1981 of the Divisional Court (Griffiths LJ and Woolf J) in those three and three
other cases (see [1981] 3 All ER 72, [1981] QB 892). Of that total of six cases, orders of
prohibition or of certiorari were refused in the case of the appellants and of one other
applicant for judicial review. They were granted in the case of the two other
b applicants. No further proceedings were sought to be brought in the two last-mentioned
cases, or in the case of the applicant whose application, like those of the three appellants,
failed. But in the cases of the three appellants the Divisional Court certified the following
point of law as one of general public importance. My Lords, the certificate reads thus:
'What constitutes a laying of an information for the purposes of section 104 of the
Magistrates' Courts Act 1952 (section 127 of the Magistrates' Courts Act 1980)?'
c   The Divisional Court refused leave to appeal but subsequently leave was given by your
Lordships' House.

My Lords, one matter should be mentioned at the outset. As the certificate correctly
states, your Lordships' House is theoretically concerned with s 104 of the Magistrates'
Courts Act 1952, which is now s 127 of the Magistrates' Courts Act 1980 (the 1980
Act). The 1980 Act took effect in its entirety on 6 July 1981, and was not therefore the
d relevant statute in force at the time when the events giving rise to these appeals took
place. But since the 1980 Act was a consolidating Act, and since the effect of the decision
of your Lordships' House in these appeals is likely to be applied hereafter by reference to
the 1980 Act rather than to cases arising under the antecedent legislation, your Lordships
may think it more convenient when considering the relevant problems of construction
to do so by reference to the 1980 Act and not to the previous legislation.

e   My Lords, before the decision of the Divisional Court in these three cases, a differently
constituted Divisional Court, (Donaldson LJ, Forbes and Bingham JJ) had, on 26 February
1981, decided two cases, *R v Gateshead Justices, ex p Tesco Stores Ltd, R v Birmingham Justices,
ex p D W Parkin Construction Ltd* [1981] 1 All ER 1027, [1981] QB 470. I shall hereafter
for brevity refer to these two cases by reference to the name of the town whose justices
were concerned in the former case, that is to say, as 'the *Gateshead* case', though both cases
f raised the same point of principle. It is necessary to refer to the *Gateshead* case in some
detail in order to understand how the crucial issue in the instant appeals arises. One
applicant for judicial review had been charged with an offence against the Food and
Drugs Act 1955. The other had been charged with an offence under the Social Security
Act 1975. Both alleged offences were summary offences. The relevant time limit for the
laying of the information in the former case was six months, and in the latter, twelve
g months. As the report shows, the relevant information preferred by the prosecuting
authority concerned was in the former case posted to and received by, and in the latter
case, delivered in writing to and received by the magistrates' court concerned well within
the relevant time limit. In the former case, the information was thereafter considered by
a senior and duly authorised member of the staff of the clerk to the justices who affixed
a facsimile of that clerk's signature on the resulting summons. In the latter case, a similar
h procedure was followed and a similarly signed summons issued. In so acting the clerks
to the justices concerned, and their respective staffs, were all acting in accordance with a
circular issued by the Council of the Society of Justices' Clerks in 1975. At no time did
any justice of the peace, or the clerk to either of those justices, personally apply his mind
to the informations in question or personally decide whether or not a summons should
be issued. In due course, the respondents appeared before their respective local
j magistrates' courts. Their appearance was in the one case more than six months, and in
the other, more than twelve months after the dates of the offences respectively charged.
Each of the respondents was convicted. Each sought orders of judicial review to quash
the convictions on the ground that as the informations had not been personally
considered by a justice of the peace or by the clerk to the justices, the informations had
not been properly laid within the respective time limits to which I have already referred.

I draw attention to the fact that though each of the informations had been properly sent
to and received by the magistrates' courts concerned well within the relevant time limits, **a**
there had in neither case been an appearance in court before those time limits had
expired.

My Lords, the Divisional Court, in a reserved judgment delivered by Donaldson LJ,
held that since the informations had not been personally considered by a justice of the
peace or by the clerk to the justices, after the information had been properly sent to and
received by the magistrates' court concerned, no information had been laid before the **b**
relevant time limits had expired. Accordingly, orders of certiorari were issued and the
convictions quashed.

My Lords, I should mention that until 1970, a clerk to justices had no power to issue
summonses. But in that year, following an amendment to s 15 of the Justices of the
Peace Act 1949 made by s 5 of the Justices of the Peace Act 1968, the Lord Chancellor
made the Justices' Clerks Rules 1970 (SI 1970/231) which henceforth permitted certain **c**
things specified in the schedule to those rules which hitherto were required to be done
by, to or before a single justice of the peace for an area to be done by, to or before the clerk
to the justices for that area. Those things included, in para 1 of the Schedule, 'the laying
of an information or the making of a complaint, other than an information or complaint
substantiated on oath', and 'the issue of any summons, including a witness summons'.

My Lords, at the outset of the judgment in the *Gateshead* case, Donaldson LJ observed **d**
that deficiencies in the laying of an information or the making of a complaint could
usually be remedied by the appearance of the defendant (or the respondent) before the
court. But he pointed out that this was of no relevance in the two cases then before the
Divisional Court where there had been no such appearances before the time limits in
question had expired.

Later in his judgment Donaldson LJ said ([1981] 1 All ER 1027 at 1032, [1981] QB 470 **e**
at 477–478):

> 'An information is not "laid" within the meaning of the Magistrates' Courts Act
> 1952, and is certainly not "laid before a justice of the peace" unless it is laid before
> and considered by either a justice of the peace or the clerk to the justices acting as the
> justice of the peace pursuant to the 1970 rules and, incidentally no summons can be **f**
> issued by any other person or without a prior judicial consideration by that person
> of the information on which the summons is based.'

My Lords, it is well known that the decision in the *Gateshead* case caused what can only
be described as consternation among those responsible for the administration of justice
in magistrates' courts, for the practice mentioned in the circular to which I have already
referred had been widely followed, no doubt in the interests of saving time and of easing **g**
the ever-increasing burden of work on justices of the peace and on clerks to the
justices. But, as Donaldson LJ said, if that practice were unlawful, expediency was no
answer, and he added that the Divisional Court had no doubt that the advice in the
circular was misconceived (see [1981] 1 All ER 1027 at 1034, [1981] QB 470 at 479). The
Divisional Court certified as a question of law of general importance the question:

h

> 'Whether the Justices' Clerks Rules 1970 authorise anyone other than the clerk to
> the justices himself to carry out the functions set out in the schedule to those rules
> and whether the laying of an information and/or the issue of a summons are judicial
> acts.'

ave to appeal was refused.

ly Lords, no application for leave to appeal was ever made to your Lordships' House **j**
e *Gateshead* case and there matters rested so far as the supposed power of delegation
ncerned. It was suggested in argument before your Lordships' House that this
n by the prosecuting authorities concerned to seek leave to appeal may have been
he fact that the view was widely taken that the decision so far as it rested on the
f any right to delegate a function, held to be a judicial function, cast by statute

a on a justice of the peace or on the clerk to the justices was clearly right and that no useful purpose would have been served by pursuing the matter further.

But, my Lords, however this may be and however many people may have escaped prosecution or had their convictions quashed as a result of the decision in the *Gateshead* case it is clear that it was thought by some that an escape route existed from the consequences of that decision. It was suggested that the supposed deficiencies in the initial consideration of the information and consequently in the issue of the summons b could be remedied by a defendant's or respondent's timeous appearance before the justices.

In such circumstances it was thought that where there was such an appearance by the defendant or respondent, or by his solicitor or counsel, or where on a formal application for an adjournment the nature of the charge had been known to or at least had been or should have been apparent to the justices or their clerk because it was set out in the court c register, a copy of which would have been before them when the appearance took place or the application for the adjournment had been made and granted, it could be successfully maintained that an information had then been duly laid before the justices.

My Lords, this was the question which arose in one form or another, in the three instant cases, the facts of which I will briefly outline. The appellant, Mr Hill, was charged with having committed what I will call a 'breathalyser' offence and also with d driving the wrong way along a one-way street in Manchester on 29 November 1979. Following the laying of an information which was never personally considered by a justice of the peace or by the clerk to the justices, this appellant was summoned. The summons bore only a facsimile signature of the clerk to the justices, and ordered him to appear at Manchester Magistrates' Court on 29 May 1980. On 20 May this appellant's solicitor wrote to the magistrates' court saying that this appellant would plead not e guilty. On 29 May 1980 (six months to the day from the date of the alleged offences) this appellant's case was listed in Manchester Magistrates' Court. He did not then appear. He was not then represented. The clerk to the justices informed the court of the intended plea, and asked for an adjournment. The only other material then before the court was the particulars of the alleged offence in the court register, a copy of which was before the justices. The register also contained the names of the informant and of the appellant, as f did the copy. There was an adjournment to 15 August 1980, and then another adjournment to 6 March 1981. By this time, the *Gateshead* case had been decided. On that occasion, following the *Gateshead* case, it was submitted to the stipendiary that there was no jurisdiction to try the information since no information had been laid within the relevant six-month period. The stipendiary magistrate held that the information had been duly laid on the occasion of the application for the adjournment on 29 May 1980. g This appellant then obtained leave to move for an order of prohibition against the learned stipendiary magistrate.

The appellant, Mr Dhesi, faced a similar 'breathalyser' charge and also a charge of failing to give his name when required to do so, both in Dartford in Kent on 17 July 1980. On 22 October 1980 he was summoned to appear by a summons which also bore only a facsimile signature, the relevant information not having been personally h considered either by a justice of the peace or by the clerk to the justices. Again a plea of not guilty was indicated. On 27 November 1980 Mr Dhesi's case was listed in his absence and adjourned. The factual position regarding the information before the justices was substantially the same as in Mr Hill's case. On 7 April 1981 this appellant's case was in the list for hearing. On the strength of the *Gateshead* case the same submission on time limits as had been made in Mr Hill's case was made on behalf of this appellant. The j justices overruled the submission. The summary trial proceeded. This appellant was convicted. He, in due course, moved for an order of certiorari to quash the conviction.

The third appellant, Mr Hughes, in whose case the respondent did not appear and was not represented before your Lordships' House, being content to adopt the argument for the respondents in the first two appeals, was charged with careless driving in North London on 25 April 1980. The summons in the case of this appellant was dated 6 Aug

1980, with an appearance date of 13 October 1980. Once again, the summons had borne
a facsimile signature only and the information had not at any time been personally *a*
considered by a justice of the peace or the clerk to the justices. This appellant had also
indicated an intention to plead not guilty. The case was adjourned on 13 October 1980
in the same circumstances as in the other cases save that in this case the copy register
while stating the nature of the alleged offence did not also state where that alleged
offence was said to have taken place. On 17 March 1981 Mr Hughes appeared. Once
again, on the strength of the *Gateshead* case, the same submission on time limits was *b*
made. The justices overruled the submission. This appellant later sought an order of
prohibition.

My Lords, as I have already stated, all three cases and the others were heard at the same
time in the Divisional Court. The report shows that these cases were separately and
elaborately argued by no less than twelve counsel representing all the applicants and all
the prosecuting authorities, with Mr Simon Brown appearing as amicus curiae. *c*

My Lords, in the Divisional Court, counsel for the applicants naturally relied on the
passage in the judgment of Donaldson LJ in the *Gateshead* case [1981] 1 All ER 1027 at
1032, [1981] QB 470 at 477–478 which I have already quoted. If that passage be correct,
it would have been difficult on the facts which I have outlined for judicial review to have
been refused to all the applicants. But it was strenuously contended that that passage was
obiter in that it was not necessary to the decision, and was therefore not binding on the *d*
Divisional Court in the present case: see the report of counsel's argument ([1981] QB
892 at 898), and the judgment delivered by Griffiths LJ ([1981] 3 All ER 72 at 79, [1981]
QB 892 at 903–904). If, as was argued, an information is not laid or a complaint is not
made until it is considered by a justice of the peace or by the clerk to the justices for the
purpose of issuing a summons or, in an appropriate case, by a justice of the peace for the
purposes of issuing a warrant, then clearly on the facts which I have outlined in the *e*
present three appeals, no information was ever laid since no justice of the peace and no
clerk to the justices ever personally considered the informations in question before the
several summonses were issued. Moreover, on the occasion of the various adjournments,
the justices never considered any of the matters which it would have been their judicial
duty to consider if they had been considering whether or not to issue a summons.
Indeed, on those occasions they had no need to do so for they obviously would have *f*
believed that the relevant consideration had already been given to that question. But as
Griffiths LJ pointed out, if the argument for the applicants were right, on the occasion of
the various adjournments the justices were adjourning cases in which the prosecutions
had never yet been begun, a situation which, as Griffiths LJ observed, was somewhat
strange (see [1981] 3 All ER 72 at 79, [1981] QB 892 at 903–904).

My Lords, Griffiths LJ considered the argument which counsel for the first two *g*
respondents, placed in the forefront of his submissions to your Lordships' House, namely
that the submissions for the appellants and indeed part of the reasoning on which the
decision in the *Gateshead* case was founded confused the laying of an information before
a justice of the peace, or since 1970 the clerk to the justices, with the consideration of the
information after laying by a justice of the peace or the clerk to the justices for the
purpose of the issue of the summons (see [1981] 3 All ER 72 at 81, [1981] QB 892 at 905– *h*
906). On the basis of this submission it was argued that the information was laid when
it was delivered to the magistrates' court. Griffiths LJ said: 'As a matter of practical
reality there is a good deal to be said for that view.' But he did not further consider this
view since, amongst other matters, he rightly considered that its acceptance would be
inconsistent with the decision in the *Gateshead* case. Ultimately, the Divisional Court
concluded ([1981] 3 All ER 72 at 81, [1981] QB 892 at 906): 'In our view an information *j*
is laid when its contents are brought to the attention of a magistrate or the clerk to the
justices as a part of the prosecution process.' It was for this reason that the Divisional
Court, whilst accepting the *Gateshead* decision as correct, as it was bound to do, felt none
the less that there had been the laying of the relevant informations before the justices
concerned on the occasion of the several adjournments which I have mentioned.

My Lords, in the *Gateshead* case, detailed attention does not appear to have been paid to the structure of the predecessor of the 1980 Act. The jurisdiction of magistrates'

a courts is entirely statutory, beginning in 1848 with the passing of one of the trilogy of statutes commonly known as Jervis's Acts (11 & 12 Vict, cc 42, 43 and 44). Those statutes have, of course, long since been repealed and their provisions re-enacted and in a different form, extended and ultimately consolidated at different times until magistrates' courts acquired their present wide and crucially important jurisdiction, both civil and criminal. It is of importance not to ignore the statutory provisions relating to the civil

b jurisdiction of magistrates' courts in connection with the proper construction of s 127 of the 1980 Act.

My Lords, since s 127 is the all important section, I set it out first before setting out the other most relevant sections of that Act.

'Limitation of time

c **127.**—(1) Except as otherwise expressly provided by any enactment and subject to subsection (2) below, a magistrates' court shall not try an information or hear a complaint unless the information was laid, or the complaint made, within 6 months from the time when the offence was committed, or the matter of complaint arose.

(2) Nothing in—(a) subsection (1) above ... shall apply in relation to any indictable offence.'

d I now turn to consider the other most relevant sections of the 1980 Act.

'PART I

CRIMINAL JURISDICTION AND PROCEDURE

Jurisdiction to issue process and deal with charges

e **1.**—(1) Upon an information being laid before a justice of the peace for an area to which this section applies that any person has, or is suspected of having, committed an offence, the justice may, in any of the events mentioned in subsection (2) below, but subject to subsections (3) to (5) below—(a) issue a summons directed to that person requiring him to appear before a magistrates' court for the area to answer to the information, or (b) issue a warrant to arrest that person and bring him before a

f magistrates' court for the area or such magistrates' court as is provided in subsection (5) below.

(2) A justice of the peace for an area to which this section applies may issue a summons or warrant under this section—(a) if the offence was committed or is suspected to have been committed within the area, or (b) if it appears to the justice necessary or expedient, with a view to the better administration of justice, that the

g person charged should be tried jointly with, or in the same place as, some other person who is charged with an offence, and who is in custody, or is being or is to be proceeded against, within the area, or (c) if the person charged resides or is, or is believed to reside or be, within the area, or (d) if under any enactment a magistrates' court for the area has jurisdiction to try the offence, or (e) if the offence was committed outside England and Wales and, where it is an offence exclusively

h punishable on summary conviction, if a magistrates' court for the area would have jurisdiction to try the offence if the offender were before it.

(3) No warrant shall be issued under this section unless the information is in writing and substantiated on oath ...

(7) A justice of the peace may issue a summons or warrant under this secti⁺ upon an information being laid before him notwithstanding any enactⁿ

j requiring the information to be laid before two or more justices ...

Summary trial of information

9.—(1) On the summary trial of an information, the court shall, if th appears, state to him the substance of the information and ask him w pleads guilty or not guilty.

(2) The court, after hearing the evidence and the parties, shall convict the accused or dismiss the information.

(3) If the accused pleads guilty, the court may convict him without hearing evidence . . .

10.—(1) A magistrates' court may at any time, whether before or after beginning to try an information, adjourn the trial, and may do so, notwithstanding anything in this Act, when composed of a single justice.

(2) The court may when adjourning either fix the time and place at which the trial is to be resumed, or, unless it remands the accused, leave the time and place to be determined later by the court; but the trial shall not be resumed at that time and place unless the court is satisfied that the parties have had adequate notice thereof . . .

(4) On adjourning the trial of an information the court may remand the accused and, where the accused has attained the age of 17, shall do so if the offence is triable either way . . .

11.—(1) Subject to the provisions of this Act, where at the time and place appointed for the trial or adjourned trial of an information the prosecutor appears but the accused does not, the court may proceed in his absence.

(2) Where a summons has been issued, the court shall not begin to try the information in the absence of the accused unless either it is proved to the satisfaction of the court, on oath or in such other manner as may be prescribed, that the summons was served on the accused within what appears to the court to be a reasonable time before the trial or adjourned trial or the accused has appeared on a previous occasion to answer to the information . . .

15.—(1) Where at the time and place appointed for the trial or adjourned trial of an information the accused appears or is brought before the court and the prosecutor does not appear, the court may dismiss the information or, if evidence has been received on a previous occasion, proceed in the absence of the prosecutor.

(2) Where, instead of dismissing the information or proceeding in the absence of the prosecutor, the court adjourns the trial, it shall not remand the accused in custody unless he has been brought from custody or cannot be remanded on bail by reason of his failure to find sureties.

16.—Subject to section 11(3) and (4) and to section 12 above, where at the time and place appointed for the trial or adjourned trial of an information neither the prosecutor nor the accused appears, the court may dismiss the information or, if evidence has been received on a previous occasion, proceed . . .

PART II

CIVIL JURISDICTION AND PROCEDURE

Jurisdiction to issue summons and deal with complaints

51. Subject to the provisions of this Act, where a complaint is made to a justice of the peace acting for any petty sesssions area upon which a magistrates' court acting for that area has power to make an order against any person, the justice may issue a summons directed to that person requiring him to appear before a magistrates' court acting for that area to answer to the complaint . . .

Hearing the complaint

53.—(1) On the hearing of a complaint, the court shall, if the defendant appears, state to him the substance of the complaint.

(2) The court, after hearing the evidence and the parties, shall make the order for which the complaint is made or dismiss the complaint.

(3) Where a complaint is for an order for the payment of a sum recoverable summarily as a civil debt, or for the variation of the rate of any periodical payments ordered by a magistrates' court to be made, or for such other matter as may be prescribed, the court may make the order with the consent of the defendant without hearing evidence.

> **54.**—(1) A magistrates' court may at any time, whether before or after beginning
> to hear a complaint, adjourn the hearing, and may do so, notwithstanding anything
> in this Act, when composed of a single justice . . .'

My Lords, perusal of these and other sections which I have not thought it necessary
to set out, makes two matters abundantly clear. First, in their criminal jurisdiction what
magistrates' courts have jurisdiction to try summarily is an information, and what is
required to give them that jurisdiction is that an information has been laid before
them. Second, in their civil jurisdiction, what magistrates' courts have jurisdiction to try
is a complaint, and what is required to give them that jurisdiction is that a complaint has
been made to them. Their jurisdiction in criminal cases does not depend on a summons
or a warrant being issued and their civil jurisdiction does not depend on a summons
being issued. As to the former, as was pointed out during the argument, where a
defendant is arrested at night and after having been duly charged is brought before a
magistrates' court next morning, there is neither a summons nor a warrant. He is
charged. The information is thus laid before the magistrates' court at the latest when the
charge is read in open court, and in practice, often earlier when, no doubt, the clerk to the
justices or his or her subordinate, is informed by the police of the charge which it is
proposed to bring against the defendant later that morning. A complaint under s 51 of
the 1980 Act may legitimately be made unaccompanied by the issue of a summons. It
was common ground, as it was in the Divisional Court, that a complaint need not be in
writing. It can be and sometimes still is made orally, as for example when an aggrieved
wife arrives in the office of the clerk to the justices and complains, perhaps vehemently,
that her arrears of maintenance have not been paid and that she requires action to be
taken to secure payment. This may or may not require a summons in order to secure the
attendance of the allegedly defaulting husband.

My Lords, it is of crucial importance to appreciate that the laying of an information is
a matter for the prosecution just as the making of a complaint is a matter for the
complainant. In each case it is for the prosecutor or the complainant to decide how the
information or how the complaint shall be formulated. I agree with the Divisional
Court in the present case that the commencement of criminal proceedings lies in the
hands of the prosecutor. It is, in my opinion, the prosecutor's duty if he wishes to
prosecute to prepare and lay the information before the magistrates' court, which means
a justice of the peace or the clerk to the justices. The laying of an information before, or
the making of a complaint to, a justice of the peace or the clerk to the justices to my mind
means (in reference to a written information or complaint) procuring the delivery of the
document to a person authorised to receive it on behalf of the justice of the peace and the
clerk to the justices. The acts of delivery and receipt are ministerial and I see no reason
why the justices of the peace or the clerks to the justices should not delegate to an
appropriate subordinate authority to receive the information which the prosecutor
desires to deliver. It can sensibly be inferred that any member of the staff in the office
of the clerk to the justices authorised to handle incoming post has such authority.
Accordingly, once the information has been received at the office of the clerk to the
justices, which today in most cases is likely to be at the magistrates' court house, the
information will, in my view, have been laid. No more is required of the prosecutor to
launch the intended criminal proceedings. Similarly with a complaint; once the
complaint is received at the office of the clerk to the justices no more is required of the
complainant. What happens thereafter is not within the province of the prosecutor or
of the complainant but of the court. But (subject to one argument of counsel for the
respondents which I will shortly consider) if a summons is required the information or
complaint must then be laid before a justice of the peace or before the clerk to the
justices. This function of a justice of the peace or of the clerk to the justices in
determining whether a summons should be issued is a judicial function which must,
therefore, be performed judicially. This function, in my view, cannot be lawfully
delegated to any subordinate. Section 1(1) of the 1980 Act states the circumstances i

which a justice of the peace (and now the clerk to the justices) *may* issue a summons and
I respectfully agree with what was said by the Divisional Court in *R v Brentford Justices,*　*a*
ex p Catlin [1975] 2 All ER 201, [1975] 1 QB 455 as to the duties of justices of the peace
and of clerks to justices before issuing summonses. Similarly, a justice of the peace or
clerk to the justices must act judicially in considering an application for a summons
following the making of a complaint: see s 51 of the 1980 Act. What I have just said
applies equally to a justice of the peace where an information is on oath and a warrant is
sought.　　　*b*

My Lords, I have just referred to one argument of counsel. He bravely argued that the
decision in the *Gateshead* case [1981] 1 All ER 1027, [1981] QB 470 that there was no
right to delegate the function of issuing a summons was wrong. He based this part of his
argument on passages in certain textbooks, one written shortly after the passing of the
relevant Jervis Act (11 & 12 Vict, c 42) and the other in almost identical terms some years
later, namely, *Archbold on Jervis's Acts* (2nd edn, 1849) p 7 and *Oke's Magisterial Synopsis*　*c*
(1881) vol 1, pp 7–8, both of which stated that the issue of a summons was a 'ministerial
function'. Counsel sought reinforcement of that submission by a scholarly reference to
Lampard's Eirenarcha or of the Office of the Justices of the Peace, apparently published in
'foure books' in a revised edition in 1610: your Lordships were told that this had been
extracted from the strong-room of Lincoln's Inn library.

My Lords, it must not be overlooked in this connection that when these two　*d*
nineteenth century works were written, justices of the peace in quarter sessions were the
administrative authority as well as the judicial authority for a county, and many if not
most of their functions were administrative in character, and thus could fairly be called
'ministerial'. But interesting as these references are, the crucial question must be
resolved, not by reference to such learned works but by reference to the contemporary
and more mundane question of the true construction of the 1980 Act. With all respect　*e*
to this part of counsel's argument, reference to s 1(1) and in particular to s 1(2)(*b*) in my
view makes any submission that this duty of a justice of the peace or of the clerk to the
justices in connection with the issue of a summons is not a judicial function but is one
which can be lawfully delegated, quite untenable. In this respect I think the *Gateshead*
case was clearly rightly decided.

But the gravamen of the attack on that decision was not in this respect but in that it　*f*
confused the laying of an information and by implication the making of a complaint
with the consideration of an information or of a complaint to a justice of the peace or
before the clerk to the justices for the purpose of seeking the issue of a summons. My
Lords, I think with all respect to the Divisional Court in that case, this criticism is well
founded, for as I have already said and as the language of the various sections of the 1980
Act, and in particular, of s 9 of that Act shows, it is the laying of an information or the　*g*
making of the complaint which is the foundation of the magistrates' courts' jurisdiction
to try an information summarily or to hear a complaint, and not the issue of any
summons which may or may not follow the laying of an information or the making of
a complaint.

My Lords, I reach this conclusion simply as a matter of the construction of the 1980
Act. But if authority is sought, strong confirmation of the view I have formed as to the　*h*
nature of the laying of an information is to be found in the decision of the Court of
Crown Cases Reserved in *R v Hughes* (1879) 4 QBD 614.

My Lords, some of the judgments in that case are long, and I shall not lengthen this
speech by long citations from them. But they show clearly that a magistrates' court even
at that date possessed jurisdiction to proceed to summary trial on an information
resulting from an appearance of the defendant even though the process of securing that　*j*
defendant's appearance, in that case by warrant, was illegal. I would draw attention to
two passages in the judgment of Hawkins J; the first reads (at 624):

'There is a marked distinction between the jurisdiction to take cognisance of an
offence, and the jurisdiction to issue a particular process to compel the accused to
answer it. The former may exist; the latter may be wanting.'

The judge later said (at 625):

> 'The information, which is in the nature of an indictment, of necessity precedes the process; and it is only after the information is laid, that the question as to the particular form and nature of the process can properly arise. Process is not essential to the jurisdiction of the justices to hear and adjudicate. It is but the proceeding adopted to compel the appearance of the accused to answer the information already duly laid, without which no hearing in the nature of a trial could take place (unless under special statutory enactment). If a mere summons is required, no writing or oath is necessary. A bare verbal information is sufficient ... The illegality of the warrant and of the arrest did not however affect the jurisdiction of the justices to hear the charge, whether that hearing proceeded upon a valid verbal information, followed by an illegal process, or upon an information for the first time laid in the presence of Stanley, upon which he was then and there instantly charged.'

I should explain that Stanley was the defendant tried summarily in the proceedings in which Hughes committed perjury. Huddleston B said (at 633):

> 'An information is nothing more than what the word imports, namely the statement by which the magistrate is informed of the offence for which the summons or warrant is required, and it need not be in writing unless the statute requires ... Principle and the authorities seem to shew that objections and defects in the form of procuring the appearance of a party charged will be cured by appearance ...'

My Lords, the Divisional Court in the *Gateshead* case supported its conclusion by reference to *Dixon v Wells* (1890) 25 QBD 249, a decision of the Divisional Court. Donaldson LJ said that it was there decided that a summons was invalid because the complaint was considered by two justices and the summons had been signed by a third who had not considered the complaint. The headnote undoubtedly makes it appear that this was the effect of the decision. But perusal of the judgment of Lord Coleridge CJ shows that the true foundation for the decision was that the relevant statute pursuant to which the prosecution was launched required as a 'condition precedent' (I borrow those words from the judgment of Lord Coleridge CJ) to a successful prosecution charges to be made, the summons to be served and the hearing to take place, all within certain specified time limits: see (1890) 25 QBD 249 at 256–257. *R v Hughes* was distinguished since there was a provision as to time in this particular statute which could not be ignored. My Lords, it follows that the passage in the judgment of the Divisional Court in the *Gateshead* case which I have quoted, and which the Divisional Court in the present cases treated as obiter, was, with all respect, wrong.

My Lords, if your Lordships agree with me that an information is laid when it is received at the office of the magistrates' court and is the first step to be taken towards the initiation of a prosecution irrespective of whether it is after receipt the basis of an application for a summons, it follows that in the case of the present appeals each of the informations in question was timeously laid. It further follows that it ceases to be necessary for your Lordships to consider the ground on which the Divisional Court refused the orders for judicial review in these three cases. All three informations were timeously laid and what happened on the hearings of the several adjournments becomes irrelevant. It also follows that though the Divisional Court was right in the *Gateshead* case in holding that the judicial process after an information has been laid or a complaint made of considering whether a summons should be issued cannot be delegated but must be personally performed by a justice of the peace or by the clerk to the justices, in neither case ought relief to have been granted because in both cases the information was timeously laid. A further consequence is that the Divisional Court from whom present appeals are brought and who were bound by the *Gateshead* case to act as they were wrong in granting orders of judicial review in the two cases of Mr Ives and Moody, since it seems clear from the report that the informations in both cases timeously laid.

My Lords, in the result I would dismiss all these appeals. I would answer the certified question by saying that 'an information is laid for the purpose of s 127 of the Magistrates' Courts Act 1980 when it is received at the office of the clerk to the justices for the relevant area'. I would add that it is not necessary for the information to be personally received by a justice of the peace or by the clerk to the justices. It is enough that it is received by any member of the staff of the clerk to the justices, expressly or impliedly authorised to receive it, for onward transmission to a justice of the peace or to the clerk to the justices. The same applies to the making of a complaint.

My Lords, what I have said applies only to informations or complaints which are in writing, as no doubt the vast majority are and will be. It is not necessary for your Lordships to decide whether similar reasoning applies to an information or complaint made orally; but in the ordinary course such oral information or complaint will in practice and should as a matter of prudence be addressed by the informant or complainant or his authorised agent to a justice of the peace or the clerk to the justices in person.

I would only add that if your Lordships agree with what I have said a number of people who have had their convictions quashed, or prosecutions against them dropped on the strength of the decision in the *Gateshead* case will prove to have been fortunate, perhaps beyond their deserts. But that will be their good fortune. For the future it is to be hoped that the matter has now been clarified. My Lords, though only one of the appellants was legally aided your Lordships might think it right, as was suggested by counsel at the conclusion of argument, in view of the special nature of these appeals and of the urgent desirability of clarifying the law, to order that the costs of all the appellants and of the respondents should be paid out of central funds, notwithstanding that the appellant, Mr Hills, alone was legally aided.

LORD BRIDGE OF HARWICH. My Lords, I have had the advantage of reading in advance the speech of my noble and learned friend Lord Roskill. I agree with it and for the reasons he gives I would dismiss these appeals.

Appeals dismissed.

Solicitors: *Betesh & Co,* Manchester (for the appellant, Mr Hill); *Betesh & Co,* agents for *Hatten, Wyatt & Co,* Gravesend (for the appellant, Mr Dhesi); *Shepherd, Harris & Co,* Enfield (for the appellant, Mr Hughes); *Sharpe, Pritchard & Co* (for the respondents).

Mary Rose Plummer   Barrister.

Re Daley

HOUSE OF LORDS
LORD DIPLOCK, LORD ELWYN-JONES, LORD KEITH OF KINKEL, LORD ROSKILL AND LORD BRIDGE OF HARWICH
29 JUNE, 22 JULY 1982

Magistrates – Summary trial – Offence triable summarily or on indictment – Determination of mode of trial of person attaining age of 17 after pleading of charge – Trial by juvenile court or in magistrates' court with right to elect trial by jury – Date when defendant's age relevant for determining mode of trial – Defendant attaining 17 before commencement of trial but after pleading to charge – Whether defendant entitled to elect trial by jury on attaining 17 – Magistrates' Courts Act 1980, ss 18, 22.

An accused person who attains the age of 17 at any time before he appears or is brought before the court when it decides on the mode of trial is entitled, for the purposes of ss 18[a]

_____
[a] Section 18, so far as material, is set out at p 976 h j, post

and 24^b of the Magistrates' Courts Act 1980, to elect trial by jury for offences which
a   under ss 18 or 22 of the 1980 Act are triable summarily or on indictment, notwithstanding
that the accused may have been under the age of 17 when he first appeared or was
brought before the court to answer the information (see p 978 *a*, p 979 *e g* to *j* and p 980
a, post).

    R v St Albans Juvenile Court, ex p Godman [1981] 2 All ER 311 applied.

    R v Amersham Juvenile Court, ex p Wilson [1981] 2 All ER 315 disapproved.

b   Decision of the Divisional Court of the Queen's Bench Division sub nom *R v Tottenham
Juvenile Court, ex p ARC* [1982] 2 All ER 321 reversed.

Notes

For summary trial of a young person and the power to change from summary trial to
committal proceedings, see 24 Halsbury's Laws (4th edn) paras 898: 9, 10.

c   For presumption and determination of age of a person charged with an offence, see
ibid para 898:6.

    For the mode of trial for offences triable either way, see 29 ibid para 303.

    For the Magistrates' Courts Act 1980, ss 18, 22, see 50(2) Halsbury's Statutes (3rd edn)
1459, 1463.

d   ### Cases referred to in opinions

Hill v Anderton [1982] 2 All ER 963, [1982] 3 WLR 331, HL.

R v Amersham Juvenile Court, ex p Wilson [1981] 2 All ER 315, [1981] QB 969, [1981] 2
    WLR 887, DC.

R v St Albans Juvenile Court, ex p Godman [1981] 2 All ER 311, [1981] QB 964, [1981] 2
    WLR 882, DC.

e   ### Appeal

Calvin Daley appealed with leave of the House of Lords granted on 29 March 1982
against the decision of the Divisional Court of the Queen's Bench Division ([1982] 2 All
ER 321) made on 8 February 1982 refusing orders of certiorari and mandamas to quash
the decision of the Islington North Juvenile Court to refuse to permit the applicant to
f   elect trial by jury and direct the court to permit the applicant to elect trial by jury. The
facts are set out in the judgment of Lord Diplock.

Anthony Scrivener QC and *Martin Russell* for the appellant.
Christopher Symons as amicus curiae.
The prosecutor and the justices did not appear.

g   Their Lordships took time for consideration.

22 July. The following opinions were delivered.

LORD DIPLOCK. My Lords, the question in this appeal is at what stage of the
proceedings a defendant charged with an offence listed in Sch 1 to the Magistrates' Courts
h   Act 1980 and accordingly 'triable either way' (ie summarily or on indictment by a jury)
must attain the age of 17 years in order to entitle him to elect to be tried by a jury.

    The appellant, Daley, was born on 3 August 1964; so he attained the age of 17 on 3
August 1981. On 24 June 1981 he was arrested and charged with handling stolen goods
contrary to s 22 of the Theft Act. This is an offence that is triable either way. He was
released on police bail to appear at the Islington North Juvenile Court on 26 June 1981.
j   On that date he surrendered to his bail at the juvenile court and was remanded to appear
again there on 24 July. He did so and was further remanded to appear on 7 August
1981. It was submitted on his behalf that since he had by then attained the age of 17 he
was entitled to be tried by jury, and that was what he wanted to do. The
magistrates held that he had no such right and that they were bound to try him

---

b   Section 24, so far as material, is set out at p 977 *f g*, post

summarily because at the date of his first appearance at the juvenile court on 26 June, 1981, he was still under the age of 17.

He applied to the Divisional Court by motion for judicial review of the juvenile court's refusal of his right to elect trial by jury and sought an order of mandamus directing the juvenile court to permit him to do so.

The Divisional Court ([1982] 2 All ER 321, [1982] 2 WLR 945) dismissed the motion on the ground that the date by which he must have attained the age of 17 years in order to entitle him to elect to be tried by jury was that of his first appearance before the juvenile court on 26 June 1981. The court certified the following point of law of general public importance involved in their decision:

'whether a defendant in criminal proceedings who is charged with an offence triable either way in the case of an adult must have attained the age of 17 on his first court appearance in order to be entitled to elect trial by jury pursuant to section 19(1) of the Criminal Law Act 1977.'

[The Criminal Law Act 1977 has now been replaced by the Magistrates' Courts Act 1980, a consolidation act which came into force on 6 July 1981, between Daley's first and second appearances before the juvenile court. In this speech I shall refer throughout to the relevant sections as they are numbered in the 1980 Act where s 18 has replaced s 19 of the 1977 Act.]

When the instant case came to be heard by the Divisional Court, there had been two previous expressions of views by that court on the certified question which were in conflict with one another. They were *R v St Albans Juvenile Court, ex p Godman* and *R v Amersham Juvenile Court, ex p Wilson* which are conveniently reported consecutively in [1981] 2 All ER 311 and 315, [1981] QB 964 and 969 respectively.

In the *St Albans* case it had been held as a matter of decision that the relevant stage of the proceedings at which the defendant must have attained the age of 17 in order to be entitled to elect trial by jury was when he appeared before the juvenile court on the occasion when the court made its decision which form of trial should be adopted. In the *Amersham* case the opinion was expressed that the relevant stage was when the defendant first appeared or was brought before the juvenile court to answer to the information. Strictly speaking this expression of opinion was *obiter* since the charge against the accused was of an offence which in the case of an offender who had attained the age of 17 was triable only on indictment; there was no right to elect summary trial.

In the instant case, the Divisional Court preferred the reasoning in the *Amersham* case to that of the *St Albans* case and held that since the appellant had first appeared before the juvenile court on 26 June 1981, when he was under the age of 17, he had no right on 7 August 1981 to elect to be tried by jury, although by then he had attained the age of 17.

My Lords, this appeal turns on the construction of the Magistrates' Courts Act 1980, and in particular those ss 17 to 28 which appear under the cross-heading 'Offences triable on indictment or summarily', ie offences triable either way. There are two contrasting sections, 18 and 24, each of which is mandatory dealing with what is to be done in the case of persons who have attained the age of 17 and persons under that age, respectively. Section 18(1) and (2) read as follows:

'(1) Sections 19 to 23 below [which contain provisions enabling the accused to elect between summary trial and trial by jury] shall have effect where a person who has attained the age of 17 appears or is brought before a magistrates' court on an information charging him with an offence triable either way.

(2) Without prejudice to section 11(1) above [which deals with proceedings in the absence of the accused] everything that the court is required to do under sections 19 to 22 below must be done before any evidence is called and, subject to subsection (3) below and section 23 below, with the accused present in court.'

Offences 'triable either way' are defined in s 17 as the offences listed in Sch 1 to the Act, but s 22 contains an addition to them in relation to offences under the Criminal Damage Act 1971 where the damage caused to property is below a specified value.

Of the ss 19–23 referred to in s 18(1), ss 19 and 20 are the most important. The former requires the magistrates first to have the charge read over to the accused if this has not already been done and to give to both the prosecutor and the accused an opportunity to make representations as to which mode of trial would be the more suitable. After this has been done the magistrates are required to make up their own minds whether, having regard to the seriousness of the offence, it is more suitable to be tried on indictment or summarily. If they decide that trial by jury on indictment is more suitable, s 21 requires them so to inform the accused and to proceed to inquire into the information as examining magistrates. If, on the other hand, they decide it is more suitable for summary trial, then s 20 comes into operation. They must explain to the accused that he has a right to elect between summary trial or trial by jury. Section 20(3) reads as follows:

> 'After explaining to the accused as provided by subsection (2) above the court shall ask him whether he consents to be tried summarily or wishes to be tried by a jury, and—(a) if he consents to be tried summarily, shall proceed to the summary trial of the information; (b) if he does not so consent, shall proceed to inquire into the information as examining justices.'

Sections 18 to 23 are derived from corresponding sections in the Criminal Law Act 1977 (there numbered 19–24) whereas s 24 of the Magistrates' Courts Act 1980 is derived from s 6 of the Children and Young Persons Act 1969, which it replaces. The other provisions of the 1969 Act relating to criminal proceedings against young persons under the age of 17 remain unaltered and although in the Amersham case the Divisional Court relied on one such provision as being consistent with the construction it placed on what is now s 24 of the Magistrates' Courts Act 1980, the Childrens and Young Persons Act 1969 is not the Act that your Lordships have to construe and does not, in my view, assist on its construction. The provisions of s 24 that are relevant to the instant case are as follows:

> '24. (1) Where a person under the age of 17 appears or is brought before a magistrates' court on an information charging him with an indictable offence other than homicide, he shall be tried summarily unless—(a) he has attained the age of 14 and the offence is such as is mentioned in subsection (2) of section 53 of the Children and Young Persons Act 1933 (under which young persons convicted on indictment of certain grave crimes may be sentenced to be detained for long periods) and the court considers that if he is found guilty of the offence it ought to be possible to sentence him in pursuance of that subsection; or (b) he is charged jointly with a person who has attained the age of 17 and the court consider it necessary in the interests of justice to commit them both for trial; and accordingly in a case falling within paragraph (a) or (b) of this subsection the court shall commit the accused for trial if either it is of opinion that there is sufficient evidence to put him on trial or it has power under section 6(2) above so to commit him without consideration of the evidence.'

This section does make provision in paras (a) and (b) for some offences to be triable either way, but the category of such offences is quite different from, and much narrower than, the category dealt with in ss 18 to 23.

The key phrase in ss 18(1) and 24(1) alike is 'where a person . . . appears or is brought before a magistrates' court on an information charging him with an . . . offence . . .'

This must bear the same meaning in both subsections and if, as is frequently the case, there are several occasions on which the accused appears before the court, it must be the date of one of these occasions only that is decisive in determining the age of the accused for the purpose of seeing whether it is, on the one hand, s 24 or on the other, ss 18 to 2 that apply for the purpose of deciding on his mode of trial for an offence in the catego of those that are triable either way under ss 18 to 23. The draftsman, however, does state expressly which that occasion is.

The choice would appear to lie between (1) the occasion when the accused first ap or is brought before the court (whether on that occasion a decision is reached as mode of his trial or he is merely remanded to appear before the court on a later date without any such decision having been reached), and (2) the occasion on which the *a* accused appears or is brought before the court when the court makes its decision as to the mode of trial.

The first meaning was adopted by the Divisional Court in the instant case, preferring the opinion expressed in the *Amersham* case to that expressed in the *St Albans* case.

As against the first meaning, there are indications in s 18 itself that when the draftsman means the first of several appearances and none other he says so, as he does in s 18(4), *b* which reads as follows:

'A magistrates' court proceeding under sections 19 to 23 below may adjourn the proceedings at any time, and on doing so on any occasion when the accused is present may remand the accused, and shall remand him if—(*a*) on the occasion on which he first appeared, or was brought, before the court to answer to the information he was in custody or, having been released on bail, surrendered to the *c* custody of the court; or (*b*) he has been remanded at any time in the course of proceedings on the information; and where the court remands the accused, the time fixed for the resumption of the proceedings shall be that at which he is required to appear or be brought before the court in pursuance of the remand.'

A similar instance of this distinction between first and subsequent appearances is to be *d* found in s 10(4).

But I do not regard this in itself as being decisive that the occasion referred to in the second meaning must have been intended. It is, I think, for your Lordships to decide what, having regard to the subject-matter of the fasciculus of sections under the cross-heading 'Offences triable on indictment or summarily', Parliament must have intended to be the appropriate appearance of the accused before the court at which his age is to be *e* ascertained for the purpose of determining whether he is entitled to elect trial by jury.

It is to be noted that Parliament has not selected either the date of the offence with which the accused is charged or the date of the commencement of the criminal proceedings against him by the laying of the information which, as this House has to-day determined in *Hill v Anderton* [1982] 2 All ER 963, [1982] 3 WLR 331 bears no necessary temporal relationship to the first appearance of the accused before the court. Either of *f* these dates would provide for uniformity of treatment as between one offender and another, and some rational justification for the selection of either of these dates as the decisive date could be found.

Instead of either of these dates, Parliament has selected the date of an occasion on which the accused actually appears in court in person or is represented by counsel or solicitor in the circumstances provided for by s 23. What will be the first occasion on *g* which this happens may depend on a variety of factors which would not appear to have any rational connection with the right of the accused to elect to be tried by jury. For instance, it is a common practice in magistrates' courts to incorporate in the summons to the accused to appear before the court on a particular date, an intimation that, if he intends to plead 'not guilty' he need not attend or be represented on the date stated in the summons, but that he will be notified in due course of the new date for the hearing when *h* he should attend with any witnesses he may wish to call. If, on the other hand, he has been arrested and detained in custody or released on police bail, he will be brought before the court within 48 hours of his arrest in the latter case to answer to his bail. On this first appearance nothing more is likely to occur than a remand and there may be several consecutive appearances on remand before any decision as to the mode of trial is made or the trial, if summary, begun. *j*

It seems inconceivable that Parliament can have intended to make the right of election trial by jury by a person who attained the age of 17 between the date of commission the offence and the date when the court is ready to hear the evidence in the case, ndent on the fortuitous circumstance that, having received a summons, he had med the court in writing that he intended to plead not guilty and so had not

appeared before the court until the date when the court was ready to begin to hear the
a evidence, instead of having appeared in person under arrest or to answer police bail and
having been then remanded to appear again on some later date when the court would be
ready to begin to hear the evidence.

The right of an accused to be tried by a jury of his fellow countrymen for any offence
which ordinary people would regard as involving a grave reflection on his character, such
as those that are listed in Sch I as triable either way, is a right that is deeply rooted in
b tradition. That Parliament intended that an accused person, old enough to make an
informed choice, should not be deprived of this right except by the exercise of his own
free will is apparent from the elaborate provisions to safeguard the freedom of choice of
the accused to be tried by jury that are contained in ss 19 to 23, particularly s 20. The
mere fact that a person accused of an offence triable either way expresses to the
magistrates' court, either orally on his first appearance before the court or in writing, his
c intention to plead not guilty, whichever be the mode of trial adopted, does not constitute
the beginning of a summary trial or the opening of an inquiry by the court as examining
magistrates; nor, if the decision is subsequently reached that the offence shall be tried
summarily, does that expression of what had been his intention operate as a plea of 'not
guilty' by the accused in the summary trial itself. Section 9 provides for a summary trial
of an information to begin with the court's stating to the accused the substance of the
d information and asking him whether he pleads guilty or not guilty; and, if he pleads not
guilty, the court then proceeds to hear the evidence. It is immediately before that
happens that it is contemplated by s 20(3) the decision as to mode of trial of offences
triable either way falls to be made.

My Lords, it seems to me that reason and justice combine to indicate that the only
appropriate date at which to determine whether an accused person has attained an age
e which entitles him to elect to be tried by jury for offences which under s 18 or s 22 are
triable either way is the date of his appearance before the court on the occasion when the
court makes its decision as to the mode of trial. In this connection I would draw
attention to the fact that so far as concerns the liability of persons who have attained
particular ages to severer punishment than those who have not yet attained that age (a
matter dealt with in ss 36 to 38), this depends on whether the particular age had been
f attained by the accused at the date of his conviction, ie when the decision as to the
appropriate punishment falls to be made by the court. It would be odd if when it was a
question of deciding whether the accused was subject to a disadvantageous liability if he
had attained a specified age the date on which the decision as to the punishment is made
was crucial rather than some earlier date, whereas when it was a question of deciding
whether an accused was entitled to some advantageous right if he had attained a specified
g age, some earlier date than that of the decision should be adopted.

For these reasons I am of opinion that what I have referred to as the second meaning,
which was that adopted in the *St Albans* case, is the correct one. I would therefore allow
this appeal.

h **LORD ELWYN-JONES.** My Lords, I have had the advantage of reading in draft the
speech prepared herein by my noble and learned friend Lord Diplock, with which I
agree. For the reasons he has given I would allow this appeal.

LORD KEITH OF KINKEL. My Lords, I have had the benefit of reading in draft the
speech delivered by my noble and learned friend Lord Diplock. I agree with it, and for
j the reasons which he gives I too would allow the appeal.

LORD ROSKILL. My Lords, I have had the advantage of reading in draft the speech
prepared herein by my noble and learned friend Lord Diplock, with which I agree. For
the reasons he has given I would allow this appeal.

LORD BRIDGE OF HARWICH. My Lords, for the reasons given in the speech of my noble and learned friend Lord Diplock, which I have had the advantage of reading *a* in advance, I would allow this appeal.

Appeal allowed.

Solicitors: *Clifford Watts, Compton & Co* (for the appellant); *Treasury Solicitor.*

b

Mary Rose Plummer   Barrister.

EMI Records Ltd v Ian Cameron Wallace Ltd *c* and another

CHANCERY DIVISION

SIR ROBERT MEGARRY V-C, SITTING WITH THE CHIEF TAXING MASTER AND MR HARVEY CRUSH AS ASSESSORS

d

15 DECEMBER 1981, 17 FEBRUARY, 15 MARCH 1982

Costs – Taxation – 'Indemnity' basis – Jurisdiction of court to order costs to be paid on 'indemnity' basis – Meaning of order for costs on an 'indemnity' basis – Supreme Court Act 1981, s 51(1) – RSC Ord 62, rr 28, 29.

e

Costs – Taxation – Solicitor and own client – Jurisdiction of court to make order for costs on 'solicitor and own client' basis in inter partes proceedings – Supreme Court Act 1981, s 51(1) – RSC Ord 62, rr 28, 29.

In proceedings for contempt of court the defendants were ordered to pay the plaintiffs' costs on an 'indemnity' basis. When the costs came to be taxed, the question arose how *f* the order should be interpreted, since the Rules of the Supreme Court made no express mention of such an order. The plaintiffs submitted that the order which had been made was equivalent more or less to an order that the costs be taxed on a 'solicitor and own client' basis under RSC Ord 62, r 29.[a] The defendants contended that, on the true construction of s 51(1)[b] of the Supreme Court Act 1981 and RSC Ord 62, r 28,[c] the only orders for costs which the court could make inter partes were those authorised by r 28, *g* and that since the 'trustee' basis set out in r 28(5) was clearly inapplicable, the costs should be taxed on either the 'party and party' basis under r 28(2) or the 'common fund' basis under r 28(3) and (4).

Held – (1) On the true construction of s 51(1) of the 1981 Act and RSC Ord 62, r 28, the court was not restricted in inter partes proceedings to making an order for costs on one *h* of the three bases set out in that rule but could order the costs to be paid on other bases, eg on the 'solicitor and own client' basis, on the 'solicitor and client' basis, or on the 'indemnity' basis (see p 987 *g*, p 988 *c* and p 991 *e g j*, post); *Greenhouse v Hetherington* (1977) 122 SJ 47 explained and applied.

(2) Unless otherwise expressly provided, an order for costs on an 'indemnity' basis took *j* effect as an order for costs on the 'solicitor and own client' basis set out in RSC Ord 62, r 29(1), except that the presumptions in r 29(2) and (3) did not apply, so that all costs incurred were to be allowed except those which had been unreasonably incurred or were

---

a Rule 29, so far as material, is set out at p 984 *a*, post
b Section 51(1) is set out at p 983 *a*, post
    Rule 28, so far as material, is set out at p 984 *e f*, post

of an unreasonable amount. In deciding whether any costs were unreasonable the
a receiving party was to be given the benefit of any doubt (see p 990 *f g* and p 991 *f*, post).

Observations on orders for costs on a 'solicitor and own client' basis and on a 'solicitor
and client' basis (see p 991 *g h* and p 992 *c d f g*, post).

Notes

For taxation of costs generally, see 36 Halsbury's Laws (3rd edn) 158–167, paras 209–222.

b

Cases referred to in judgment

Andrews v Barnes (1888) 39 Ch D 133, [1886–90] All ER Rep 758, CA, 50 Digest (Repl)
242, 6.
Castillejo v Castillejo (1974) Times, 12 December.
Chanel Ltd v 3 Pears Wholesale Cash & Carry Co [1979] FSR 393.
c *Dugdale v Dugdale* (1872) LR 14 Eq 234, 23 Digest (Reissue) 502, 5724.
Faith Panton Property Plan Ltd v Hodgetts [1981] 2 All ER 877, [1981] 1 WLR 927, CA.
Farquharson v Floyer (1876) 3 Ch D 109, 23 Digest (Reissue) 502, 5726.
Fisher, Re [1894] 1 Ch 450, CA, 51 Digest (Repl) 918, 4647.
Gibbs v Gibbs [1952] 1 All ER 942, [1952] P 332, 50 Digest (Repl) 495, 1755.
Giles v Randall [1915] 1 KB 290, [1914–15] All ER Rep 285, CA, 51 Digest (Repl) 933,
d   4733.
Greenhouse v Hetherington (1977) 122 SJ 47, [1977] CA Transcript 450.
Hoffman-La Roche & Co A-G v Sieczko [1968] RPC 460, CA, 16 Digest (Reissue) 83, 815.
Kingsley (decd), Re (1978) 122 SJ 457, (1978) Times, 17 June.
Morgan v Carmarthen Corp [1957] 2 All ER 232, [1957] Ch 455, [1957] 2 WLR 869, CA;
   rvsg [1957] 1 All ER 437, [1957] Ch 455, [1957] 2 WLR 396, 51 Digest (Repl) 934,
e   4736.
Reed v Gray [1952] 1 All ER 241, [1952] Ch 337, 51 Digest (Repl) 932, 4730.
Thomason v Swan, Hunter and Wigham Richardson [1954] 2 All ER 859, [1954] 1 WLR
   1220, 23 Digest (Reissue) 51, 576.
Z Ltd v A [1982] 1 All ER 556, [1982] 2 WLR 288, CA.

f **Cases also cited**

Avery v Wood [1891] 3 Ch 115, CA.
Cohen and Cohen, Re [1905] 2 Ch 137, CA.
Cope v United Dairies (London) Ltd [1963] 2 All ER 194, [1963] 2 QB 33.
Eady v Elsdon [1901] 2 KB 460, CA.
Gundry v Sainsbury [1910] 1 KB 645, CA.
Preston v Preston [1982] 1 All ER 41, CA.
g

Review of taxation

These were two applications for review of the taxation of the costs in two sets of
proceedings for contempt in which the defendants, Ian Cameron Wallace Ltd and Ian
Cameron Wallace, were ordered to pay the costs of the plaintiffs, EMI Records Ltd, on an
'indemnity' basis. The matter was heard in chambers. The facts are set out in the
h judgment which is reported by leave of Sir Robert Megarry V-C.

Mark Potter QC and *Mark Platts-Mills* for the plaintiffs.
Mr Michael Cook, solicitor, for the defendants.

Cur adv vu
j

15 March. **SIR ROBERT MEGARRY V-C** read the following judgment: Th
applications for the review of taxations of costs raise important points of princip
therefore give leave for this judgment to be reported. First, there is the que
whether the court has any power to order a defeated litigant to pay costs to the
on an indemnity basis, or on the basis of solicitor and own client. Many such ord
been made over the years, but their validity has now been vigorously attacked.

if such orders are valid, it is far from clear what statutory or other authority there is for making them, and so the question is what that authority is. Third, it is also far from clear *a* what each of these orders means, and this, too, requires examination. The law, which affects county courts as well as the Supreme Court, is in a strange tangle.

These questions arise on two orders for costs on an indemnity basis made on successive motions for contempt in the same case. The first was an order made by Mr Vivian Price QC, sitting as a deputy High Court judge, on 4 July 1980, and the second was an order made by Foster J on 28 November 1980: I shall call these the 'first order' and the 'second *b* order' respectively. I heard the applications for review with the assistance of the Chief Taxing Master and Mr Harvey Crush, sitting as assessors. Under the first order, the defendants were required to pay the plaintiffs their costs of the motion 'on the footing of an indemnity', with an immaterial exception. Under the second order, the defendants were required to pay the plaintiffs their costs of the other motion 'on an indemnity basis'. Nothing turns on the slight difference in wording. *c*

The costs of the two motions were taxed by different taxing masters. On the first order, Master Razzall rejected the defendants' objection, which had contended that the taxation ought to be on a common fund basis, saying that he knew of no authority for allowing the costs on that basis. He ruled that the taxation should be on a solicitor and own client basis so that the costs would 'provide a complete indemnity'. He did not amplify his reasoning. He issued his certificate on 23 February 1981, and on 9 March *d* 1981 the defendants issued a summons seeking to have objections allowed to virtually the whole bill of costs.

On the second order, Master Clews treated the question as a preliminary issue. The plaintiffs had contended for a solicitor and own client basis of taxation, while the defendants argued that the right basis was party and party, or alternatively common fund. In a long and careful reserved judgment which takes some 11 pages of transcript, *e* the master reached the conclusion that neither solicitor and own client, nor party and party, nor common fund, was the right basis. Having rejected these bases, he proceeded to evolve a new basis of taxation as defining what was meant by an order for costs on an indemnity basis. This was that he should apply the general principles of taxation, and in doing this he was to exclude nothing reasonable and include nothing unreasonable, whether in nature or amount. He also held that he ought to have regard to the clear *f* intention of the judge that the plaintiffs should recover as much of their expenses as might be possible without thereby oppressing the defendants. This latter comment refers to the discussion on costs before the judge, though I am not sure about what words of the judge the master had in mind. The judge had found that a gross contempt had been committed, and he had fined the second defendant £10,000; and then, on the question of costs, the defendants had submitted that there was no jurisdiction to order *g* costs on an indemnity basis, and that the most penal basis of costs that could be imposed, and the one which came nearest to an indemnity, was the common fund basis. After some five or six pages of thrust and counter-thrust, the judge had ordered costs on an indemnity basis.

Having decided the preliminary point in this way on 13 April 1981, the master then taxed the costs accordingly, and issued his certificate on 17 July 1981. On 24 July 1981 *h* the defendants issued their summons seeking to have their objections to the basis of the taxation allowed, and alternatively seeking the reduction of certain specific items. On 30 July 1981 the plaintiffs issued a summons to review the taxation and have increases made to certain items that had been taxed down. Before me, counsel for the plaintiffs and Mr Cook of Messrs Ward Bowie for the defendants agreed that no submissions should be made on the individual items until the points of principle had been settled; and in that *j* assessors and I fully concurred.

Before turning to the rival contentions, I think it is convenient to set out the main of taxation and their principal features. The starting point must be the Supreme of Judicature (Consolidation) Act 1925, s 50(1), which is now reproduced, without amendment material to this case, by the Supreme Court Act 1981, s 51(1). In the Act the subsection runs—

'Subject to the provisions of this Act and to rules of court and to the express provisions of any other Act, the costs of and incidental to all proceedings in the Supreme Court, including the administration of estates and trusts, shall be in the discretion of the court or judge, and the court or judge shall have full power to determine by whom and to what extent the costs are to be paid.'

I shall have to return to this subsection, but for the present I need do no more than observe, first, that the power is very wide, particularly having regard to the words 'full power' and 'to what extent'; second, that the width is nevertheless confined by the words 'costs of and incidental to all proceedings in the Supreme Court', so that nothing outside this phrase can be included; and third, that the power is made 'Subject . . . to rules of court'.

With that, I turn to the RSC Ord 62, which deals with costs. The process of reading through the main body of the order, even without the appendices, is one that brings to mind Oliver Cromwell's phrase, 'an ungodly jumble'. Matters of principle and substance lie cheek by jowl with details of procedure; and if one day there is to be a rewritten order, there will be little difficulty in achieving an improvement on the present drafting. In the case before me, r 28 is at the centre of the dispute; but I must also refer to rr 29 and 31 before turning to the indemnity basis that is in issue.

On that footing, there are five main bases of taxation to be considered. I shall take them in turn.

(1) *The party and party basis.* By r 28 (2), where costs are taxed on the party and party basis, there are to be allowed 'all such costs as were necessary or proper for the attainment of justice or for enforcing or defending the rights of the party whose costs are being taxed'. The essence of this head is thus what is 'necessary or proper'; and this, of course, is the strictest of the normal heads of taxation.

(2) *The common fund basis.* Under r 28 (3), (4), the court may direct a taxation on the common fund basis; and this is stated to be 'a more generous basis' than the party and party basis. In place of 'necessary or proper', what is to be allowed is 'a reasonable amount in respect of all costs reasonably incurred'. On such a taxation 'the ordinary rules applicable on a taxation as between solicitor and client where the costs are to be paid out of a common fund' are to be applied, even if in fact the costs will not be paid out of any common fund. The common fund basis seems to have been intended to replace the old 'solicitor and client' basis (in one of the four meanings of the phrase 'solicitor and client': see *Gibbs v Gibbs* [1952] 1 All ER 942 at 949, [1952] P 332 at 347), though in doing so it not very happily uses the very phrase itself. In the end, the practical result seems to be that taxation on the common fund basis is little more than a party and party taxation conducted 'on a more generous scale': see *Giles v Randall* [1915] 1 KB 290 at 295, [1914–15] All ER Rep 285 at 286, per Buckley LJ. It is sometimes said that on average a common fund taxation produces a figure some 5 to 10% higher than a party and party taxation; and that may be so.

(3) *The trustee basis.* Under rr 28(5) and 31(2), costs may be given on a trustee basis if the costs are to be paid out of a fund, or the person to whom the costs are to be paid was a party to the proceedings qua trustee or personal representative; and in such cases 'no costs shall be disallowed, except in so far as those costs or any part of their amount should not, in accordance with the duty of the trustee or personal representative as such, have been incurred or paid, and should for that reason be borne by him personally'. No question of any such order arises in the present case, and I need not discuss it; but it will be observed that here the thrust of the taxation has been shifted from what is to be included to what is to be excluded; it is no longer a question of allowing only those items which are necessary or proper, whether on a more generous scale or not, but instead has become a matter of prohibiting the disallowance of any item unless it falls within the words of exception.

(4) *The solicitor and own client basis.* By r 29, provision is made for the taxation of solicitor's bill to his own client for contentious work, apart from legal aid cases. Un

r 29(1), on such a taxation, 'all costs shall be allowed except in so far as they are of an unreasonable amount or have been unreasonably incurred'. This resembles the trustee basis in that it allows everything except any items which fall within the words of disallowance; but it differs from all the other three heads in that it is dealing with what a litigant must pay his own solicitor, and not what he must pay the other side. The essence of the rule lies in the two phrases 'unreasonable amount' and 'unreasonably incurred'; and these phrases are qualified by two presumptions made by other paragraphs. First, by para (2), all costs incurred with the client's express or implied approval are 'conclusively presumed' to have been reasonably incurred; and similarly as to amount, if the client has expressly or impliedly approved it. These conclusive presumptions, however, take effect subject to para (3). Second, by para (3), there is a rebuttable presumption that any costs which in the circumstances are of an 'unusual nature', and would not be allowed on a party and party taxation, have been unreasonably incurred, unless the solicitor expressly informed his client before they were incurred that they might not be allowed. In due course I shall have to return to these presumptions.

(5) *The indemnity basis.* The Rules of the Supreme Court contain no express mention of any such basis, and there seems to be no clear statement of what such a basis means. Yet for many years the courts have been making such orders, particularly against contemnors, and the taxing masters have been having to do their best to tax costs under such orders. I bear in mind, of course, that the present version of Ord 62 (apart from subsequent amendments) was brought into force at the beginning of 1960 (see RSC Amendment (No 3) 1959, SI 1959/1958), and so what was said under the former rules does not necessarily apply today. Yet the practice of making such orders, long a commonplace before 1960, has continued to this day; and often such orders have been more or less equated with orders for costs as between solicitor and own client. I may refer to *Giles v Randall* [1915] 1 KB 290 at 295, 298, [1914–15] All ER Rep 285 at 286, 288; *Reed v Gray* [1952] 1 All ER 241 at 245, [1952] Ch 337 at 347 ('a solicitor and own client taxation; or, in other words, an indemnity'; and see [1952] Ch 337 at 348); and *Gibbs v Gibbs* [1952] 1 All ER 942 at 949, ([1952] P 332 at 347 quoting a note stating 'The expression "Solicitor and own client costs" has been disapproved by judges. It is more accurate to direct taxation on the footing of an indemnity'). As examples of the practice since 1959 there are not only the orders in the present case, but also cases such as *Hoffman-La Roche & Co AG v Sieczko* [1968] RPC 460 at 472. There, Harman LJ, speaking for himself and Danckwerts and Sachs LJJ, reversed the court below and held that a contempt had been committed. He then ordered the defendant to pay the costs in that court and below 'on an indemnity basis'. Again, in *Chanel Ltd v 3 Pears Wholesale Cash & Carry Co* [1979] FSR 393 at 394–395, Walton J ordered a contemnor to pay costs on an indemnity basis, emphasising that this was different from the common fund basis, and higher. There can be no doubt that orders to pay costs on an indemnity basis, *eo nomine*, were and are common, at any rate in contempt cases in the Chancery Division. I may say that despite the headnote in *Faith Panton Property Plan Ltd v Hodgetts* [1981] 1 WLR 927, I do not think that that case establishes any separate basis of 'a full indemnity', for the order seems to have been made on an ordinary 'indemnity basis': see [1981] 2 All ER 877 at 880, 882, [1981] 1 WLR 927 at 929–930, 933.

These five heads do not, of course, exhaust the possibilities, for there are other orders that can be made in special cases: see eg rr 28A, 30. I think, however, that they cover the general orders for costs that are to be found in litigious practice. I can therefore turn to the contention that the court has no power to order costs to be paid on an indemnity basis; and I must also consider the further contention that the court cannot, in inter partes proceedings, make any order for costs on a solicitor and own client basis. Mr Cook's basic contention is that the court is restricted to the orders to be found in r 28, so that with the trustee basis being obviously inapplicable the only possible orders in a case like this are either common fund or party and party.

As I have mentioned, the starting point is the Supreme Court of Judicature (Consolidation) Act 1925, s 50(1); and this is in very wide terms. Not only are the costs the discretion of the court, but the court is to have 'full power' to determine 'to what

extent the costs are to be paid'. As Willmer J once said: 'Reading these words in their
natural and ordinary sense, it appears to me that standing by themselves they are prima
facie sufficient to empower me, in a proper case, to order the payment of costs to be taxed
as between solicitor and client, and even as between solicitor and own client': *Thomason
v Swan, Hunter and Wigham Richardson Ltd* [1954] 2 All ER 859 at 863, [1954] 1 WLR
1220 at 1225. However, as the judge then pointed out, this power is 'subject . . . to rules
of court', and so it must be seen how far the rules have qualified this wide statutory
discretion.

The argument is as follows. By para (1), r 28 'applies to costs which by or under these
rules or any order or direction of the Court are to be paid to a party to any proceedings
. . . by another party to those proceedings . . .' This applies to the costs in these
motions. Paragraph (2) then provides that subject to the following provisions of the rule,
'costs to which this rule applies shall be taxed on the party and party basis . . .' Again that
applies to the costs in these motions. However, para (3) provides that in awarding costs
under the rule the court 'may in any case in which it thinks fit to do so order or direct that
the costs shall be taxed on the common fund basis'. In the present case, the court has not
done this, and so this does not apply. Then para (5) empowers the court, in a limited class
of case which admittedly does not apply here, to order costs on a trustee basis. That is all;
no other basis for costs is comprised in r 28, and so all costs are confined to the three bases
there set out. Solicitor and own client costs appear nowhere in r 28, but are dealt with
in r 29; and by contrast with the trustee basis in r 31, there is nothing in r 28 which
incorporates r 29 by reference. Apart from the limited category of cases in which the
trustee basis can be ordered, the only two bases open to the court are party and party and
common fund. Solicitor and own client is a recognised basis as between a solicitor and
his own client, but the terms of r 28, as well as the inherent unsuitability, preclude the
court from ordering an unsuccessful litigant to pay costs on that basis to the winner. The
indemnity basis is not even a recognised basis; but even if it were, the court would have
no power to make such an order, for similar reasons.

At first sight this is indeed a cogent argument. Nevertheless, it is to be observed that
there are no positive words of prohibition against adopting any basis except those in r
28. The argument really depends on the word 'shall' in para (2) as excluding any other
basis of taxation, and negativing the wide discretion given by the statute. If one leaves
on one side the limited class of case in which costs may be ordered on the trustee basis,
the contention is that the 'shall' in para (2) has cut down the apparent width of the statute
to giving the court a choice between party and party and common fund, and excluding
everything else.

There is some support for this view in the authorities. *Re Kingsley (decd)* (1978) 122 SJ
457 is a decision of Payne J which is only shortly reported; but Mr Cook kindly supplied
us with a copy of the transcript of the relevant part of the judgment. The passages on
which Mr Cook relied are plainly obiter, since the dispute arose under an agreement that
the costs of one of the parties should be taxed on a solicitor and own client basis; it was
not a case in which the court, in the exercise of its discretion, had ordered costs to be paid
on that basis. If the registrar had made such an order, the judge said, this 'would have
exceeded the limits of the discretion afforded to him by RSC Ord 62, r 28, and would
have been ultra vires'. He then referred to there being 'ample authority for this view'.
and cited certain cases.

The first case cited was *Re Fisher* [1894] 1 Ch 450. However, the passage in
judgment of Kay LJ which is cited does no more than state that the statutory pow
subject to any limitation in the rules or other Acts; and with due respect I cannot se
this advances the matter. The next case cited was *Thomason's case* [1954] 2 All F
[1954] 1 WLR 1220, which I have already mentioned. What arose there was the
of costs in a case under the Fatal Accidents Acts in which the plaintiff was ·
recover costs from the defendants 'to be taxed as between solicitor and own cl'
a full indemnity basis' (see [1954] 2 All ER 859 at 860, [1954] 1 WLR 1220 ·
the defendants contended that there was no power to make such an orde·
the Fatal Accidents Acts were then subject to a special code of rules as to

rules, in an expanded form, now appear as part of Ord 62, r 30. These included a mandatory provision that 'no costs other than those so certified shall be payable to the *a* solicitor for any plaintiff in the cause or matter'; and see now r 30(2). This and other provisions led Willmer J to say that he was 'driven to the conclusion that, so far at any rate as actions under the Fatal Accidents Acts are concerned, the discretion of the court under s 50(1) of the Supreme Court of Judicature (Consolidation) Act, 1925, is limited by the rules of Court . . .' (see [1954] 2 All ER 859 at 864, [1954] WLR 1220 at 1227). A little earlier the judge had also referred to the predecessor of the present r 28(2), and to a *b* provision in it that does not appear in the present rule. This provided that 'no costs' should be allowed which appeared to have been 'incurred or increased through over-caution, negligence or mistake . . .' In this, too, there was an express prohibition which the judge considered had precluded him from directing a taxation as between solicitor and own client. The judge was thus concerned with a special class of case subject to special rules, and with express prohibitions in the rules. With all due respect I do not see *c* how this supports any general proposition that an order for solicitor and own client costs would be ultra vires.

Finally, Payne J cited *Giles v Randall* [1915] 1 KB 290, [1914–15] All ER Rep 285, and *Morgan v Carmarthen Corp* [1957] 2 All ER 232, [1957] Ch 455. These cases both reach the not very surprising conclusion that if an order is made for solicitor and client costs, it will not be treated as if it were an order for solicitor and own client costs. However, *d* in the latter case Lord Evershed MR doubted whether the court could order a taxation inter partes as between solicitor and own client, even in a contempt case; but he expressly refrained from stating a final view on the point: (see [1957] 2 All ER 232 at 237, [1957] Ch 455 at 469. Apart from that doubt, I find it difficult to see how these cases provide authority for the view that to order solicitor and own client costs inter partes would be ultra vires. I think, however, that Payne J was citing these last two cases only for the *e* much more limited proposition that the rules of court provide certain fetters on the wide statutory discretion; and this is beyond doubt.

One case which does not seem to have been cited to Payne J is his own decision in *Castillejo v Castillejo* (1974) *Times*, 12 December, some 3½ years earlier. That was a divorce case in which certain orders of the court were varied in accordance with revised terms agreed between the parties, and the husband was ordered to pay the wife's costs on a *f* solicitor and own client basis. On a review of taxation, Payne J said that in the High Court there was no reason why the parties should not agree, or why the judge should not order, as between party and party, that the costs should be taxed as between solicitor and own client although they were to be paid by the other party. The taxing officer had taxed the costs on an indemnity basis, subject to the restraint imposed on him by the Solicitors' Act 1957, s 73(4); and it was held that the application for review failed. *g*

Since then, the Court of Appeal has decided *Greenhouse v Hetherington* (1977) 122 SJ 47, [1977] CA transcript 450. That concerned a county court order inter partes for costs to be paid by the defendants on a solicitor and own client basis; and on appeal the defendants contended that there was no power to make such an order. In the County Court Rules, Ord 47, r 1 provided that subject to the provisions of any Act or rule, 'the costs of proceedings in a county court shall be in the discretion of the court'. That corresponds *h* to the Supreme Court of Judicature (Consolidation) Act 1925, s 50(1). Then CCR Ord 47, 49 applies RSC Ord 62, rr 28, 29 and 31 to the taxation of county court costs as they ~~ply~~ to High Courts costs, with the necessary modifications. The defendants argued, as ~~Cook~~ has argued here, that there was no power to order costs to be paid on any basis ~~~one~~ or other of the bases set out in r 28. Roskill LJ, who delivered the leading ~~~ent~~, did not find it necessary to go through that rule in any detail because, as he *j* ~~~out~~, solicitor and own client costs were dealt with by r 29. He said that counsel ~~~~efendants~~ had accepted, albeit a trifle reluctantly, that if his argument were ~~~~igh~~ Court judge could order the unsuccessful party in High Court litigation ~~~~o~~ the successful party on a solicitor and own client basis. He then said:

    ~~ibmission~~ seems to me quite untenable. The position is absolutely plain.

In the county court, all costs are in the discretion of the trial judge: it is for him to determine upon what basis, whether party and party, common fund, solicitor and own client, or whatever he may think best, the assessment will take place in accordance with the relevant rule applicable to that class of order.'

Accordingly, he said that he would dismiss the appeal; and Browne and Megaw LJJ agreed, saying nothing further on this point.

Now as Mr Cook emphasised, no authorities were cited in the judgment, although both sides were represented by counsel. Whether any authorities on costs were cited in argument is not known; it is at least possible that the case was argued without their aid. Mr Cook says that had there been a proper citation of authority, the result would have been different, whereas counsel for the plaintiff says that it would have been the same. Nor is much known about the arguments which were advanced. However, there it is. I certainly cannot see that the decision was contrary to any authority binding on the Court of Appeal. If cited, Lord Evershed MR's doubts in *Morgan v Carmarthen Corp* [1957] 2 All ER 232, [1957] Ch 455, would obviously have been considered with care; yet doubts on a point expressly left unresolved are very far from being a binding authority. The decision that the county court judge had power to order the defendants to pay costs on a solicitor and own client basis plainly has, as part of its ratio, the conclusion that this can be done under the Rules of the Supreme Court. If, then, such an order can be made, the submission that, the trustee basis apart, the only orders that can be made are party and party and common fund cannot be right.

It seems to me that the decision of the Court of Appeal can be rested on reasoning on the following lines. The wide general discretion given by the Supreme Court of Judicature (Consolidation) Act 1925, s 50(1), can be curtailed by rules of court, because the subsection is expressed to be subject to them. Where there are rules which express a plain prohibition, as in *Thomason's case* [1954] 2 All ER 859, [1954] 1 WLR 1220, then the discretion cannot be exercised so as to disregard that prohibition. On the other hand, where there is no express prohibition, but merely an affirmative provision in the rules, then even if that affirmative is expressed in imperative terms, as by the word 'shall', the court is not deprived of its statutory discretion to order costs on some basis other than that set out in the affirmative provision. On this footing, the provision that all taxations 'shall' be on a party and party basis operates as a provision that all taxations shall be on that basis unless the court either exercises the express powers given by the rules to direct some other basis of taxation, or else exercises its statutory discretion to go outside r 28. In my judgment, the wording of the rules is not strong enough to confine the courts to making orders within r 28 and exclude their discretionary power to make orders on other bases.

Now I can well see that such a process of reasoning is open to attack, just as I accept that this might not be the process which the Court of Appeal itself would have expressed. I also accept that, sitting at first instance, it is a delicate matter to provide reasons for decisions or orders of the Court of Appeal which that court has not given. But I have to consider the alternative, which is to say that the decision of the Court of Appeal on solicitor and own client costs in *Greenhouse v Hetherington* (1977) 122 SJ 47, [1977] CA Transcript 450, and the Court of Appeal order for costs on an indemnity basis made in *Hoffman-La Roche & Co AG v Sieczko* [1968] RPC 460 were wrong, quite apart from many other decisions or orders made at first instance. Indeed, within the last three months the Court of Appeal has made an order for 'costs on solicitor and client basis': see *Z Ltd v A* [1982] 2 WLR 288 at 314, cf [1982] 1 All ER 556 at 578. Yet if the defendants' submissions are right, and the only orders that can be made inter partes are those authorised by r 28, an order for solicitor and client costs goes to join the orders for solicitor and own client costs and for costs on an indemnity basis as orders which cannot be made inter partes. No doubt it may not be very difficult to construe an order for solicitor and client costs as being an order for costs on a common fund basis: but orders, and not least orders of the Court of Appeal, ought not to need translation into other terms before they can be said to be within the powers of the court. I think that it is m

duty to carry out and apply what the Court of Appeal has done. I know that there was
a time when Vice-Chancellors enjoyed the luxury of refusing to follow a decision of the
Court of Appeal that they considered to be 'clearly erroneous': *Dugdale v Dugdale* (1872)
LR 14 Eq 234 at 235 (Sir John Stuart V-C); and see *Farquharson v Floyer* (1876) 3 Ch D
109. Yet I would be most reluctant to consider applying this precedent unless I were very
sure of myself; and I am not. On the contrary, I would respectfully agree with the
decisions and orders of the Court of Appeal, and give them full faith and credit. My only
hesitation is about the process of reasoning that is required to support them. Whatever
the Court of Appeal may say hereafter, I do not think that it is for me to suggest that
these orders, made in the Court of Appeal per curiam, were nevertheless made per
incuriam.

In the result, therefore, I reject Mr Cook's clear and forceful contentions on this point,
and hold that the court has power in contentious proceedings to order the unsuccessful
party to pay the successful party's costs on bases other than those contained in r 28; and
these include orders for costs on the solicitor and own client basis, on the solicitor and
client basis, or on an indemnity basis. I do this, first, on the footing of the Court of Appeal
decisions that I have mentioned. Second, the circumstances of litigation are so various
that it is a matter of high importance that the judge should have a wide discretion as to
the basis of costs, and not be subjected to the Procrustean bed of r 28. Even in party and
party taxations or in common fund taxations it is important for the judge to be able to
order that particular items which otherwise would be included should be excluded, and
vice versa, so that the taxing master will not be confined to a rigid application of the
formulae set out in the rule.

I also bear in mind that, as appears from *Andrews v Barnes* (1888) 39 Ch D 133, [1886–
90] All ER Rep 758, the High Court succeeded to the inherent discretionary jurisdiction
of the old Court of Chancery in equity matters to order costs as between solicitor and
client; and the judgment of Fry LJ sets out a selection of the phrases used in the past, such
as 'full costs', 'very good costs' and 'utmost costs' (see (1888) 39 Ch D 133 at 138, [1886–90]
All ER Rep 758 at 760)'. It may be that the wide and flexible inherent jurisdiction may
provide some aid in holding that r 28 has not confined the court to making party and
party and common fund orders (in addition, of course, to the trustee basis). At the same
time, I think that the court should be chary of departing from the settled types of orders
for costs, and should lay down new bases only if there is a real need which cannot
otherwise be met. I may add as a footnote that since the conclusion of the argument I
have become aware of the Patents Act 1977, s 65(2). This at least demonstrates that there
are some circumstances in which costs on a solicitor and own client basis may be payable
inter partes; for in cases within the subsection the litigant is entitled to his costs or
expenses 'as between solicitor and own client' unless it is otherwise ordered. In
bankruptcy, too, an order for solicitor and own client costs may be made inter partes: see
Bankruptcy Rules 1952, r 92(1).

With that, I turn to the meaning of an order for costs on the basis of an indemnity.
No such basis appears to have been laid down in the rules, or, for that matter,
elsewhere. On the footing that there is jurisdiction to make such an order, what does it
mean?

One possible meaning is that the successful party is to have every penny of his costs
reimbursed to him, however absurd, extravagant or unreasonable they were. On this
footing, the only limiting factor would be the words 'of and incidental' in the Supreme
Court of Judicature (Consolidation) Act 1925, s 50(1): costs that were neither 'of' the
proceedings nor 'incidental' to them would be excluded, but everything else would be let
in. I should be very slow to reach this conclusion, simply on the score of
unreasonableness. I do not see why the loser should have to pay for absurd extravagances
of the winner, however stringent the order.

Another possible meaning is that put forward by Master Clews. This is a new formula,
which is not to be found in the rules, and is of uncertain ambit; and as I have indicated,
I would deprecate laying down a new basis of taxation by judicial fiat unless there was no
reasonable alternative. The question, then, is whether there is such an alternative.

I think that there is. Subject to any provision in the order, I do not see why the basic

a rule for solicitor and own client costs which is set out in r 29(1) should not be applied, thereby giving to the successful party the indemnity that the court is seeking to give him. To say that on a taxation 'all costs shall be allowed except in so far as they are of an unreasonable amount or have been unreasonably incurred' seems to me to be giving the litigant a complete indemnity, shorn only of anything that is seen to be unreasonable. The litigant does not have to establish that the costs were necessary or proper, or that the

b costs were of a reasonable amount and reasonably incurred. Provided they are costs of and incidental to the proceedings, he is entitled to recover them, subject only to the qualification that they are liable to be reduced in respect of anything that the taxing master considers to fall within the headings 'unreasonable amount' or 'unreasonably incurred'. In a word, the difference is between including only the reasonable and including everything except the unreasonable. In any taxation there must be many

c items or amounts that are plainly allowable, and many others which are plainly not allowable. In between, there must also be many items or amounts which do not fall clearly within either extreme. On a party and party taxation, or on a taxation on the common fund basis, many such items may fail to be allowed; on a taxation on an indemnity basis, they will all be included.

I do not think that it would be right to express this difference in terms of the burden

d of proof being shifted from the winner to the loser, though no doubt in many matters much of the argument during the taxation will proceed on these lines. But during a taxation the taxing master sees many things which are not revealed to the party against whom the order for costs has been made, and so that party will lack some of the relevant material. Instead, it is more a question of who gets the benefit of any doubt in the mind of the taxing master. On a party and party taxation, nothing will be included unless the

e taxing master reaches the conclusion that it satisfies the requirement of 'necessary or proper'. Similarly, where the taxation is on the common fund basis, the taxing master will include nothing unless he considers that it satisfies the requirement of 'a reasonable amount in respect of all costs reasonably incurred'. On neither basis do the rules give the benefit of any doubt to the party in whose favour the order has been made. Nothing is included unless it satisfies the words of inclusion. The indemnity basis, as I would

f construe it, is the other way round. Everything is included unless it is driven out by the words of exclusion, namely, 'except in so far as they are of an unreasonable amount or have been unreasonably incurred'. I should add that in applying to an opposing party a rule intended for taxations as between a solicitor and his own client, I think that it is open to the paying party to take any point and make any objection which the client could have raised, had he been taxing the bill.

g That seems to me to be a workable basis of taxation. However, it may be asked why it is right to resort to r 29 at all, and if r 29(1) is to be applied, why r 29(2), (3), should be excluded. My answer would be that such a view accords, at least in part, with various dicta in the cases (I have already mentioned a few) which equate an indemnity basis with solicitor and own client. Further, it avoids a proliferation of bases of taxation: a known formula is adopted in place of fabricating a new and untried formula. It thus avoids

h having to draft and make workable some new definition of what 'indemnity basis' means as a separate head. On this, I would observe that, valiant though Master Clews's definition is, a rule that excludes nothing reasonable and includes nothing unreasonable makes no provision for items or amounts which stand on the borderline between reason and unreason, so that it fails to indicate who is to have the benefit of any doubt. Under a order for costs on an indemnity basis I feel no doubt that it is the successful party w

j should get this.

What, then, of r 29(2) and (3)? By para (2), all costs and all amounts which the has expressly or impliedly approved are 'conclusively presumed' to have been reas incurred. Under para (3) there is a rebuttable presumption that costs which 'a unusual nature' and would not be allowed on a party and party taxation k unreasonably incurred, unless the solicitor expressly informed his client befor incurred that they might not be allowed. Such provisions, if I may say so entirely just and proper as between a solicitor and his own client. The client ought not to be allowed to complain about what he has authorised his solicitor to do, and the solicitor ought not to be allowed to claim payment for unusual items unless he has first given his client due warning of risk. Where, on the other hand, the costs are to be paid not by the client to his own solicitor but by another party to the litigation, these provisions seem entirely inappropriate. It would be monstrous if the loser could complain of nothing that the winner had authorised. Confident of success (as many are, when moving for contempt), the winner may have authorised half a dozen conferences with three expert witnesses, when two conferences with a single expert would plainly have been ample. He may have needlessly employed the most expensive experts, two of the most fashionable silks and a pair of juniors. He may throughout have insisted on his case being conducted by two of the senior partners in his solicitors' firm, instead of one. He may have done dozens of other things which to a greater or lesser extent were costs unreasonably incurred to an unreasonable amount. Some of these matters (such as the array of counsel) may be visible to the judge when he makes his order, so that he could insert some appropriate provision in his order; but much may lie concealed until disclosed on taxation. Yet if para (2) is applied, all that the victor authorised will be conclusively presumed to be reasonable, and the vanquished must pay for it all. It does not matter whether the reason for the excesses was a superabundance of caution or a desire to run up a punitive bill of costs for the loser to meet; in either case para (2) would make the loser pay. Nor can I see the relevance, in cases inter partes, of any authorisation by the client: if an item is utterly unreasonable, why should the loser's liability to pay for it depend on whether or not the winner authorised it?

If, then, a judge makes an order for costs on an indemnity basis, is the order to be taken as bringing para (2), or anything like it, into play? I do not think that any answer save No is possible; and the same applies to para (3). If the judge were to be asked to amplify his order, I would expect him to say that it meant that the loser must indemnify the winner against the whole of his costs except those that were beyond reason, or words to that effect; but I would be dumbfounded if he were to add any words which expressed anything like the thoughts to be found in paras (2) or (3). It seems to me that para (1) clearly expresses, in well-known language, the intention that any judge would be likely to have when ordering costs on an indemnity basis; and certainly that would be my intention in making any such order. For that reason, coupled with the others that I have given, I hold that an order for costs on an indemnity basis takes effect as an order for costs on the basis set out in Ord 62, r 29(1). If it is to mean anything more than that, possibly in some wholly exceptional case, the order should make this explicit.

As for an order inter partes for costs on a solicitor and own client basis, I do not have to decide anything. I say nothing about taxation on that basis as between a solicitor and his own client, where the client is the paying party. Nor need I say much about cases in which there is some agreement for one party to pay the costs of another party on a solicitor and own client basis. In such cases the meaning and effect of such an agreement depends on the terms of the agreement; and if on its true construction the agreement applies the whole of r 29, including paras (2) and (3), then the whole of r 29 applies. All that I need do is to draw attention to the width of the rule, and the need for the person liable or potentially liable to pay such costs to realise that he may have to pay for any needless extravagance authorised by the other party. There remains, however, the effect of the decision of Master Razzall in the present case that taxation should be on a solicitor and own client basis; and I think that I should also mention the order for costs on a solicitor and own client basis that was upheld in *Greenhouse v Hetherington* (1977) 122 SJ [1977] CA Transcript 450.

Master Razzall meant that the taxation should be on the whole of the solicitor and client basis as set out in r 29, then for the reasons that I have given I think it was Only if the basis set out in r 29(1) alone is taken do I think that it was right. I do to construe the order made in *Greenhouse v Hetherington*, and I shall not presume to say whether it applied the whole of r 29, as it might on the face of it be do, or whether it applied only r 29(1). For the future, however, if an

application for solicitor and own client costs against the other side in litigation is being
a made or resisted, I hope that counsel will bear in mind not only that there may well be
some uncertainty about the meaning and effect of such an order, but also that such an
order, in its wider meaning, may have drastic and far-reaching consequences. There are
grounds for thinking that some members of the profession assume that the solicitor and
own client basis is merely the old solicitor and client basis, but a bit better; the operation
and effect of r 29(2) and (3), are not appreciated. In fact, an order for solicitor and own
b client costs seems to be not only the most stringent order that can be made but also an
order which, by virtue of r 29(2), is capable of being severely penal in its effect. Those
who seek such an order should realise that they are asking that the other side should pay
not only all their costs which are not unreasonable, but also all their other costs, however
unreasonable or extravagant they are, so long as their clients approved them; and well
might they hesitate if they were required to seek such an order in terms. In most cases
c of contempt I would have thought that an order for costs on an indemnity basis would
be both adequate and also more appropriate than an order for solicitor and own client
costs, with the uncertain and unforeseeable operation of r 29(2) and (3). Indeed, I cannot
see that it would be any great loss if orders for solicitor and own client costs disappeared
altogether inter partes, and were confined to their own proper sphere as between solicitors
and their own clients. Nor, I may add, would I mourn the return to desuetude of orders
d for solicitor and client costs, assuming that I am right in my tentative assumption that
they operate as orders on the common fund basis.

It may be convenient if I summarise my conclusions. In doing this I confine myself
to orders for costs in litigation; and for the sake of simplicity I leave on one side the orders
for costs on the trustee basis which can be made in appropriate circumstances. My views
are as follows.

e (1)The Supreme Court Act 1981, s 51(1) (replacing the Supreme Court of Judicature
(Consolidation) Act 1925, s 50(1)) gives the court a wide discretionary power over costs,
and this has not been cut down by Ord 62, r 28, so as to confine the court to making
orders only on the party and party basis or the common fund basis, and on no other basis.

(2) The court has power to order costs to be paid on an indemnity basis.

(3) The effect of an order on an indemnity basis is, unless otherwise provided, that the
f rule laid down in Ord 62, r 29(1) applies, but not the presumptions set out in r 29(2) and
(3). In brief, the result is that all the costs incurred will be allowed except any which have
been unreasonably incurred or are of an unreasonable amount; and in applying these
exceptions the receiving party will be given the benefit of any doubt.

(4) The court has power to order costs to be paid on the solicitor and own client basis
as between litigating parties; but as the meaning and effect of such an order does not arise
g for decision in the present case, I decide nothing on it.

(5) If in litigation an order for solicitor and own client costs is to be sought, those
concerned to apply for or resist the order should consider carefully the uncertain meaning
and effect of the order, and in particular whether the presumptions set out in r 29(2) and
(3) will apply, and, if so, what their effect will be. It would be no great loss if such orders
ceased to be made inter partes.

h (6) The court appears still to have power to make an order for solicitor and client costs;
and although the effect of such an order is not clear, it may well be the same as that of an
order on the common fund basis. If this is so, there is much to be said for expressing the
order as being made on the common fund basis instead.

(7) The court has power to make other forms of order, though it should be slow to
evolve a new basis of taxation unless there is a real need which cannot otherwise be
j met. In most cases one of the recognised forms of order will suffice; but if some new
basis is to be laid down, it is desirable to make explicit what the meaning and effect of
that basis is.

I return to the orders made in this case. My conclusion is that under both the first
order and the second order the costs should have been taxed on the footing set out in
r 29(1), without the rest of the rule, that being the basis on which costs on an indemnity
basis should, in my judgment, be taxed. Under the first order, Master Razzall's ruling

that the taxation should be on a solicitor and own client basis was right only if r 29(1) alone was to be applied, without the rest of the rule. Under the second order, Master *a* Clews put forward a basis of his own with which I cannot agree, though I am indebted to him for his long and detailed examination of the problem. In this case, too, I hold that the right basis of taxation is that provided by r 29(1). Any decision on what order I should make, and how the detailed items should be dealt with will, as arranged, be deferred until the parties have been able to consider this judgment and put forward their submissions as to the disposition of these cases: I decide only the question of principle. *b* This I do by holding that an order for costs on an indemnity basis should be carried out by taxing the costs on the basis of Ord 62, r 29(1), without any of the other paragraphs of r 29.

I would add two points. First, there is a valuable note to r 29 in *The Supreme Court Practice 1982*, vol 1, p 1064. This points out the difficulty in applying *Greenhouse v Hetherington*, assuming, as I think the note does, that the order in that case made not only *c* r 29(1) applicable, but also r 29(2) and (3). The note states the result as being that the paying party will be liable for costs which were beyond his knowledge and contemplation, which may have been unreasonably incurred, and which may be unreasonable in amount or unusual in their nature. On that footing, the note suggests that such an order should be made or consented to only in wholly exceptional circumstances. With that suggestion I entirely agree. Indeed, I would go further, and express the hope that such orders, *d* mystifying in their language and effect, will be replaced inter partes by orders for costs on an indemnity basis. The note then suggests an alternative form of order for such cases. This is to make a common fund order and to combine with it a direction to the taxing master to exercise his discretion under r 32(2), thereby providing for the payment of a reasonable amount for all costs reasonably incurred, and also removing any restriction on amount imposed by the scale in Appendix 2 to Ord 62, and any limitation to items *e* included in the scale. In view of what I have decided I do not think that I need pursue this point. Certainly I do not think that an order for costs on an indemnity basis could be construed as being that sort of order, and so it does not arise in this case. But the suggestion should not be overlooked should there be difficulty about costs on an indemnity basis.

That leads me to the second point. I understand that revisions to RSC Ord 62, perhaps *f* on a substantial scale, have for some while been under active consideration. Costs are complicated, and these things take time. It seems to me that without waiting for any general revision of Ord 62, some amendment should be made to the present Ord 62 which would put the position of inter partes orders for costs on an indemnity basis and on a solicitor and own client basis beyond doubt. As I have indicated, I would welcome the disappearance of the solicitor and own client basis as between opposing litigants, *g* keeping it only for what it is designed for, namely, taxation between a solicitor and his own client. But I say this on the footing that the rules will properly define the indemnity basis and confirm it as being available inter partes. In particular, it is needed in cases of contempt. In such cases, nothing should be done to deter a person from bringing a contempt to the notice of the court; and the risk of having to bear any of the costs will often be a real deterrent: see *Morgan v Carmarthen Corp* [1957] 2 All ER 232, particularly *h* at 240, [1957] Ch 455, particularly at 474. Accordingly, I would express the hope that Ord 62 will soon be amended on this point, in advance of any general revision; for orders for costs in cases of contempt are being made all the time, and they ought not to be left in any state of doubt.

Costs of each motion to be taxed on basis of RSC Ord 62, r 29(1).

Solicitors: *A E Hamlin & Co* (for the plaintiffs); *Ward Bowie* (for the defendants).

Azza M Abdallah　Barrister.

End of Volume 2